Voices of the American South

General Editor
Suzanne Disheroon-Green
Northwestern State University

Associate Editors
Lisa Abney
Northwestern State University
Philip Dubuisson Castille
Eastern Washington University
Barbara C. Ewell
Loyola University–New Orleans
Sarah E. Gardner
Mercer University
Joe Marshall Hardin
Western Kentucky University
Julie Kane
Northwestern State University
Pamela Glenn Menke
Regis College

D1254953

PEARSON
Longman

New York San Francisco Boston
London Toronto Sydney Tokyo Singapore Madrid
Mexico City Munich Paris Cape Town Hong Kong Montreal

Vice President and Editor-in-Chief: *Joseph Terry*
Managing Editor: *Erika Berg*
Development Editor: *Barbara Santoro*
Development Manager: *Janet Lanphier*
Executive Marketing Manager: *Ann Stypuloski*
Production Manager: *Charles Annis*
Project Coordination, Text Design, and Page Makeup: *Shepherd Incorporated*
Cover Design Manager: *Wendy Ann Fredericks*
Cover Designer: *Nancy Sacks*
Cover Art: *Keith Rasmussen/Superstock Royalty Free*
Manufacturing Buyer: *Lucy Hebard*
Printer and Binder: *Quebecor-World Taunton*
Cover Printer: *Coral Graphic Services, Inc.*

For permission to use copyrighted material, grateful acknowledgment is made to the copyright holders on pages 1394–1399, which are hereby made part of this copyright page.

Library of Congress Cataloging-in-Publication Data

Voices of the American South / Suzanne Disheroon-Green, general editor.
p. cm.
Includes bibliographical references and index.
ISBN 0-321-09416-6—ISBN 0-321-19870-0
1. American literature—Southern States. 2. Southern States—Literary collections. I. Green, Suzanne Disheroon, 1963–

PS551.V65 2004
810.8'0975—dc22

2004046419

Copyright © 2005 by Pearson Education, Inc.

All rights reserved. No part of this publication may be reproduced, stored in a retrieval system, or transmitted, in any form or by any means, electronic, mechanical, photocopying, recording, or otherwise, without the prior written permission of the publisher. Printed in the United States.

Please visit us at http://www.ablongman.com.

ISBN 0-321-09416-6

1 2 3 4 5 6 7 8 9 0—QWT—07 06 05 04

CONTENTS

Part V The Era of Civil Rights: The Second Generation, 1956–1974 809

LIST OF FIGURES

PREFACE

Arguably the home of one of the most sustained and productive literary traditions in American cultural history, the South's literary artists have created a body of work that embodies the region's voices. Southern writers have romanticized the "Lost Cause" of the Confederacy, observed and recorded the often harsh and generally tense race relations that have stigmatized the region since the Antebellum era, and celebrated the region's many subcultures. The literature of the American South traditionally holds sacrosanct topics such as family, honor, religion, and home, yet with an incisive stroke of the pen, Southern writers explode depictions of the region that merely repeat stereotypes.

Southern writing often leads readers to question the configurations of the region itself and the literary expressions that figuratively define it: What is this complex and diverse entity called the South? Why are the origins of literary texts important? What cultural realities are embodied in Southern writing? *Voices of the American South* seeks to place the major works of the Southern literary tradition in historical and cultural contexts that invite discussion of these questions.

Approach

The prolific literary heritage of the American South invites a comprehensive anthology because of its unique position with respect to other regions of the United States and because the region has produced some of the most enduring works in American literature. A selective list of major Southern writers demonstrates the significance of their place in American letters: Edgar Allan Poe, Mark Twain, Kate Chopin, Robert Penn Warren, Flannery O'Connor, Richard Wright, Eudora Welty, William Faulkner, and Katherine Anne Porter. Voices from historically marginalized populations, such as Zora Neale Hurston, Charles W. Chesnutt, Dorothy Allison, and Alice Walker, also play important roles in the development of the Southern literary tradition.

A serviceable anthology must be adaptable to a variety of courses and teaching styles, yet must provide enough context to stand on its own for the casual reader. Inevitably, the task of deciding which writers and works to include and omit is full of challenge and compromise. Unfortunately, selections too frequently must be made on the basis of availability or cost, and the number of exemplary works that might effectively be part of a volume like this one far exceeds the much smaller selection of works that we are finally able to present. In spite of these realities, the texts included in *Voices of the American South* sample the very best that the region has to offer, providing a systematic survey of the Southern literary tradition with enough variety to serve any number of more selective undergraduate and graduate courses.

Texts have been selected based on their literary merit, and some for their cultural importance. Both criteria have occasionally meant the inclusion of works of a gritty nature. Dirty realism—realism of a harsh, unflinching variety may extend to subject matter, language use, or personal relationships—has been an undercurrent in Southern letters for generations, but this "grit lit" has broken the surface in the contemporary era. Issues of race, gender, and class, and the repression that stems from these factors frequently arise in the works of Southern authors who represent the dark, violent, and disturbing implications of these long-standing social issues with the same honesty that may be found in descriptions of a lush Southern landscape or in depictions of complex family relationships. In presenting some of these edgy and potentially offensive texts, the editors have sought to provide a more inclusive, if not always flattering, representation of Southern writers and writing

Organization

Several goals have driven the compilation of the texts included in *Voices of the American South.* The primary goal has been to survey the development of the Southern literary tradition comprehensively, beginning with the colonial era and working up to the present. Accordingly, the selections draw from varied genres, positing Southern history and culture as the backbone of the region's literary creativity. *Voices of the American South* provides substantial coverage of the early periods of Southern history, and in choosing the texts for these eras, the editors have made every effort to present texts that are as close to the original versions of the works as possible. The Antebellum and Civil War eras have been covered lightly in many contemporary anthologies, despite the fact that the events of these eras shaped, and, to some extent, continue to shape, the Southern worldview, and hence the writing of the region. *Voices of the American South* offers readers the opportunity to see for themselves where the ideologies and struggles represented in later Southern writing originated.

The editors have sought the advice of instructors, who consistently and emphatically agreed that a "teachable" anthology should not only survey Southern writing from its inception, but place that writing in relevant historical, social, and cultural contexts. Toward that end, *Voices of the American South* does not attempt to fit Southern literature into the conventional categories that define the American literary tradition. While movements such as modernism, naturalism, and postmodernism are productive frameworks for the discussion of the American literary tradition, the development of Southern letters is more closely connected to the region's major historical events: the Civil War, Reconstruction, industrialization, urbanization, and the Civil Rights movement. Accordingly, *Voices of the American South* is structured around the most significant events of Southern history:

Antebellum Period: Beginnings Through 1860

Focusing upon the initial growth and development of the South, the first segment of the anthology positions the South not only as a part of the United States, but as a region with a unique identity and shared political ideology. Many of the selections fall into the genres of personal narrative and history, and address the roots of such issues as the slavery question, states' rights, women's roles, and day-to-day life in the Southern region. Writers from this era include Thomas Jefferson, William Gilmore Simms, George Moses Horton, Caroline Lee Hentz, and Edgar Allan Poe.

Civil War and Reconstruction Eras: 1861–1866 and 1866–1880

The selections from this tumultuous period in Southern history include discussions of battle strategies, personal and public writings of famous military figures on both sides of the battle lines, diaries of women and slaves who maintained the Southern home front while landowners were away at war, and poetry inspired by the catastrophic events of the war and its aftermath. Writers of the period include Robert E. Lee and

John C. Calhoun, as well as traditionally marginalized voices, such as Harriet Jacobs and Mary Boykin Chesnut. Reconstruction era writing, with a particular focus on the rhetoric and war-time reminiscences of its writers, is also included in this section.

Rebuilding and Repression: 1880–1910

The era following the official end of Reconstruction saw much of the ostensible progress in Southern racial relations dissipate as the Southern White male establishment regained control of both the economy and the government. At the same time, romantic concepts of the "Lost Cause" and the exotic characters and landscapes of the South captivated Northern readers. The immensely popular literary tradition that came to be known as local color disguised the political agendas of its writers. Despite these setbacks, the voices of women and people of color began to gain attention during this period. Significant authors of this era include George W. Cable, Joel Chandler Harris, Kate Chopin, Thomas Nelson Page, Alice Dunbar-Nelson, and Charles W. Chesnutt.

The Southern Renascence: 1910–1956

With the fall of the slave economy, and by extension, of plantation culture, the South was faced with rebuilding if economic prosperity were to replace poverty. The beginnings of industry, supported by a rapidly expanding rail system throughout the United States, offered new opportunities to residents of the South. Coupled with these opportunities, however, was the systematic oppression of people of color, in part because of the unarticulated fear that African Americans might develop the means to lessen their dependence on and deference to the White community. The African-American community grew increasingly dissatisfied with the discrimination and abuse that they suffered in nearly every aspect of their day-to-day lives. Racial tensions continued to be a significant influence on the culture of the South during this era, as demonstrated by authors such as Anna Julia Cooper, Lillian Smith, and Richard Wright.

The Southern Renascence heralded an unprecedented flood of literary creativity, the influence of which is still felt by contemporary writers. Ironically spawned by the publication of the little magazine *The Fugitive* and the agrarian ideals articulated by the Twelve Southerners of *I'll Take My Stand*—which responded to charges leveled by H. L. Mencken that the South was a cultural wasteland—this era is typified by the writing of such literary giants as William Faulkner, Katherine Anne Porter, and Zora Neale Hurston. These writers focused on communities and family relationships in addition to the traditional Southern issues of place, racial politics, and rural living.

The Era of Civil Rights: 1956–1974

The burgeoning Civil Rights movement, under the leadership of Southerners such as Martin Luther King, Jr., came to full flower during this era, with its proponents demanding equal recognition in society as well as under the law. Other social issues were forced to the forefront of the Southern consciousness as well. Writers offered frank consideration of alternate sexualities, explored newly redefined gender roles as they affected both the home and society, and demonstrated the further development of a unique African-American voice. The Southerner's acute sense of place, as demonstrated by the large variety of subcommunities in the region, and the (often dysfunctional) Southern family continued to be at issue in the works of writers such as Flannery O'Connor, Eudora Welty, Alice Walker, and Walker Percy.

Writers of the Contemporary South: 1974–Present

Contemporary Southern writers are perhaps more prolific than any generation before them, making their presence felt in both the literary and popular communities. Southern writers consider the plight of the Southerner in the "New South," while grappling with what, exactly, constitutes it. Issues including homosexuality, familial and marital relationships, alienation and neglect, abuse in varied forms, and poverty provide the basis for much of the best Southern writing of the last half of the twentieth century and the early twenty-first century. Major figures of the contemporary era include Dorothy Allison, Lee Smith, A. R. Ammons, Fred Chappell, and Ernest Gaines.

Prolific and profound, the Southern literary tradition can be simultaneously amusing and moving, grotesque and beautifully wrought. *Voices of the American South* assembles a smorgasbord of the best that the South has to offer in a format that will make this rich body of literature appealing and accessible to a new generation of readers.

FEATURES

Voices of the American South includes a variety of instructional features to assist both the instructor and the student:

- **Introductions** to each major section of the anthology that place the works in context, historically, culturally, and economically.
- **Headnotes** for all literary selections that place the works presented in the context of the author's life and career.
- **Questions to Consider** appear at the end of each selection. These questions encourage students to think critically about the major thematic elements in the pieces presented.
- **Voices in Context sections** group authors and their works so their common themes and interests may be explored. Recurrent themes and critical cultural and historical events are highlighted in these groupings to emphasize the importance of their influence on the region's literature.
- **Chronologies** appearing in each major section visually integrate history, literature, and culture and place these important influences upon literature alongside of the literary works themselves in a manner that will appeal to the "sound byte" generation of students who prefer to receive information quickly.
- **Maps** illustrate many significant geographic, sociological, and economic phenomena related to the development of the region.

ACKNOWLEDGMENTS

A project of this size could never be completed without assistance from many dedicated individuals. The editorial team wishes to acknowledge the assistance of the many people who helped to make this project a reality.

Shelly M. Lewis, who served as graduate research assistant to Suzanne Disheroon-Green, and by extension, to the entire editorial team, tracked and secured reprint permission. J. Alexander Green provided tireless editorial assistance during the final phases of manuscript preparation, spending hours proofreading, preparing tearsheets, and making endless copies. Interns Benita Frederick, Laurie Carroll, John Keeling, Shelly M. Lewis, and Heidi Manery Norwood assisted with research; Susie Scifres Kuilan of Louisiana State University also provided research assistance. Sharon Sweeters of the Louisiana Folklife Center and Heather Salter of Northwestern State University aided with manuscript production. In the spring of 2003, the graduate students in "Southern Literature Before 1920" read headnotes and section introductions for clarity of content and reviewed many literary selections to identify material in need of footnotes.

As the manuscript evolved into a real book, graduate research assistants Michael Quann Boyd, Kurt Jones, Maria Kimberly, Clarence Nero, and Kendell St. Brigid devoted weekends and many late nights to reading copy edits and page proofs with their tired, grouchy professor, often with only a grilled cheese sandwich and a cold drink as their thanks. Graduate assistants Autumn Campbell, Linda Freeman, and Vanessa Garcia-Rodriguez also checked facts, ran errands, and/or assisted in proofing copy edits. Bobbie Jackson and Peggy Cedars, the long-suffering administrative assistants in the Department of Language and Communication at Northwestern State University, ran countless copies and were always willing to oversee errands for us. Mary Stevenson of Regis College kindly arranged for the marathon conference calls that saved us from missing deadlines. The cheerful and flexible attitudes that each of these individuals brought to this project have been greatly appreciated.

Numerous individuals drafted or conducted research for individual author headnotes. Although not members of the editorial team, they provided a great service: Laurie M. Carroll, Ken Fontenot, Benita Frederick, Joan Wylie Hall, Susie Scifres Kuilan, David Kunian, Shelly M. Lewis, Tim Murphy, and Dale Sauter. A number of faculty members and graduate students at Northwestern State University assisted with research and initial drafts of footnotes: Linda Freeman, Alisha Hewlett, Gail Kwak, Shelly M. Lewis, Stephanie Masson, Heidi Manery Norwood, Elizabeth Robinson, Lisa Rougeou, Mariann Noonan Wilson, Jean D'Amato, and Melissa E. Roberts. We would also like to express our gratitude to the library staff at Loyola University–New Orleans, Louisiana State University, Regis College, Tulane University, and Northwestern State University of Louisiana. The reference staff of the Watson Library, as well as the Interlibrary Loan Librarian, Lisa Bond, provided countless hours of assistance, especially in locating impossible-to-find, out-of-print texts, and obscure bits of seeming trivia, without which this book would be greatly diminished.

We owe the greatest debts of gratitude to our families: Charles L. Green, Kathryn A. Green, J. Alexander Green, Douglas Hollingsworth, Sheila Geha, Susan R. Hardin, Todd Leopold, and Jerry Speir for their patience and tolerance at all times, but especially during those times when deadlines loomed, and the paper strewn about their houses resembled nothing less than a New England blizzard. We thank you for your support, your kindness, and your willingness to go out for chocolate at 2 a.m.

PART I

Antebellum Period

BEGINNINGS THROUGH 1860

VIRGINIA BEGINNINGS

In 1607, at the direction of the London Company of Virginia, a band of 105 English settlers crossed the Atlantic and landed on the southern coast of America at the Chesapeake Bay. The settlers brought rich literary traditions of poetry, prose, narrative, drama, and essays from England, but themes and styles that would make American literature unique quickly developed in the writing produced in the New World. Even the earliest letters, journals, and diaries of the colonists spoke of individuality, free will, the ability to make a new start, freedom of movement, and self-determination—the ideals that would later be called "the American Dream."

From the beginning, the profit motive was fundamental to the founding of the Virginia colony, as was the need to establish a stronghold for England in a land that had, thus far, been most successfully explored and settled by the Spanish and the French. The English settlers assumed great risks, and the mysterious disappearance of the members of an earlier English colony, established at Roanoke, Virginia, in 1586, must have weighed heavily on their minds. The London Company had organized this new venture to spread the cost of colonization among the investors in England, and the colonists agreed to accept the risks of traveling to the New World in exchange for the right to participate in any profits that might result from colonization.

The English settlers did not find a land empty of people, of course, and they always faced the danger of attack from the Native Americans. Stories of settlers being killed or abducted became a genre of early American and Southern literature, and John Smith, a member of the original Jamestown colony, wrote the earliest and perhaps most enduring of these Indian captivity narratives. American school children still learn the story of the Native American warrior called Powhatan who captured Smith and the maiden named Pocahontas who saved him.

During its first few decades, the Virginia colony faced major obstacles, the most immediate of which were starvation and disease. After the first winter, the number of colonists had dwindled to 38, and although later ships brought new colonists, nearly half of those who followed the original company died of various illnesses such as typhus. Those who survived did so only because the indigenous people agreed to share their food and their knowledge of how to live in the wilderness. After ten years of mostly peaceful relations, however, full-scale war broke out when Powhatan died, and in the resulting skirmishes, many settlers and natives were killed. The colonists finally defeated the Powhatan Confederacy, as the tribes were known, in the mid-1640s. All these problems were compounded by lack of support from the London Company, which was plagued by financial troubles in England and failed to send sufficient supplies and reinforcements. As a result, King James I revoked the company's charter, and Virginia became a royal colony.

In spite of the hardships, the letters and journals of early settlers like John Smith, William Byrd, John Hammond, William Strachey, and Thomas Hariot are filled with exciting exploits and idyllic descriptions of the New World. These documents were widely read in England, and soon more colonists traveled to the Virginia colony in search of adventure and financial gain. In fact, many were willing to come as indentured servants, agreeing to trade their services for a number of years in exchange for passage. At first, few colonists realized the dream of financial success, but in time, some began to make money planting and exporting tobacco. When grown in the rich Virginia soil, tobacco was easier to smoke than the bitter native variety that came from the Caribbean, and as more and more Europeans took up smoking, land in the South became increasingly valuable and the colonies began to be profitable.

Before the American Revolution, much of the writing produced in the Southern colonies consisted of histories, diaries, political tracts, and works that examined and described the flora and fauna of the New World. Early American authors were adventurers, businessmen, farmers, and politicians first; they were writers almost coincidentally. However, much of their work does possess literary merit. The experiences recorded in the histories produced by John Smith, William Byrd, and others were certainly dramatic, and they served as both means to record the remarkable experiences of the colonists and to encourage further colonization. Much of the earliest Southern literature takes the form of nonfiction works such as John Smith's *General Historie of Virginia, New England, and the Summer Isles*, William Byrd's *History of the Dividing Line betwixt Virginia and North Carolina*, and Caroline Howard Gilman's *Recollections of a Southern Matron*, yet these works contain exciting drama, complex characters, and fabulous description; many also demonstrate remarkable satire, wit, and perceptive observation. The themes developed in these works became central threads of Southern literature that have lasted to the present day: importance of the land, primacy of the individual, promotion of regional values, and individual freedom and self-determination. English traditions of the pastoral and satire continued to influence Southern colonial poetry, as in the work of poets such as Maryland's Ebenezer Cook, whose poem *The Sotweed Factor* describes an English gentleman's experiences in the colonies.

Enticed by exciting reports from the colonies, ambitious young sons of the middle-class gentry began to arrive from England, certain that they could attain a higher social position in the open society of Virginia than they might in England. Their arrival resulted in some social conflict, however. These entrepreneurs were anxious to build their fortunes, but much of the best land was already held by the early settlers and their families. An increasing number of indentured servants were now being released from servitude and were also ready to find their own land. Most of the area around Jamestown had been claimed, and in order to obtain acreage, more colonists began to move east and south. The problem came to a head when Nathaniel Bacon, a new arrival, sought permission from the governing council to renew the wars against the Native Americans in order to capture more land, but the colonists were split between those who supported Bacon and those who opposed him. Bacon's Rebellion, as it has come to be called, was unsuccessful in gaining widespread support for a new war against the Native Americans, but Bacon did manage to polarize the colonial population and started a riot in which Jamestown was burned nearly to the ground. In the end, the inevitable expansion of the growing colonial settlement forced the Native Americans to move deeper into the interior without the war that Bacon and others wanted.

The English Colonies Expand

In 1632, King Charles I gave George Calvert, Lord Baltimore, a charter to begin a colony north of Jamestown on the Chesapeake Bay. Calvert died before the completion of the charter, which was passed to his son, Cecelius. Cecelius was a Roman Catholic who envisioned the new Southern colony as a place where Catholics could practice their religion in a more tolerant atmosphere than they found in England, where the Anglican Church dominated. He also hoped the Maryland colony would be a place where lords of manors would control vast amounts of land in a neo-feudal society. For a while, the Roman Catholics who settled in the Chesapeake region did enjoy religious security among their Protestant neighbors, but the system of manor lords that Calvert hoped for never developed. In fact, the economic system of the new colony, called Maryland, closely resembled that of Virginia, with many of the dominating families arising from the entrepreneurial class. Eventually, the growing Protestant majority of Maryland petitioned the king for status as a royal colony and the Calvert proprietorship was dissolved for almost 30 years. During that time, Catholics were denied the right to vote, to hold office, or to perform public religious services.

After 1632, colonization of the American South slowed, as the population of England turned its attention to problems at home. England was consumed by civil war, which eventually lead to the execution of Charles I in 1649 and the overthrow of the monarchy. After the restoration of the monarchy and the crowning of Charles II in 1660, colonization of America was renewed with vigor. Charles II rewarded eight of his supporters with a charter for the Carolinas, an area that extended southward from Virginia to the Spanish territory of Florida. Once again, the Lords Proprietors of Carolina, as the charter-holders were called, saw the American South as a place to forge a new vision of social order, and their vision was a mixture of religious tolerance and neo-feudal social structure. The dream of a colony in which a hereditary nobility would control vast acreage never materialized in the Carolinas, just as it had failed to materialize in Maryland; nevertheless, this vision laid the groundwork for a Southern romanticism that emphasized the ideal of a hereditary and landed Southern aristocracy and social codes that were, at times, almost chivalric.

Tobacco had given Virginia the key to profitability, and in Carolina, rice provided the financial base. However, the commitment of the Carolinian proprietors to promote Carolina to the inhabitants of Barbados, an English-owned colony in the West Indies, finally allowed the colony to flourish. Slavery was common in Barbados, and as the connection with the West Indies grew, the colonists imported slaves from the Caribbean to supply the labor needed to produce rice.

While the original charter of Carolina included the entire region from Virginia to Florida, the English crown approved a new charter in 1732 to create the colony of

Georgia. This step served a two-fold purpose. The first was to provide a buffer between the Spanish territory of Florida and the Carolinas, and the second was to create an alternative to the English debtor's prison. Instead of going to jail, debtors could elect to help colonize Georgia. The charter limited land-holders to 500 acres and outlawed slavery, and the settlers were encouraged to grow crops that would benefit England, such as grapes and spices. The colony floundered at first, but finally it began to prosper when land restrictions were relaxed. Elite land-holders bought large tracts of land and dominated the economy and the social structure as they had in Virginia, Maryland, and the Carolinas. Finally, the trustees' lease ran out, and Georgia, too, became a royal colony.

Landowners, Servants, and Slaves

In the agrarian colonies of Virginia, Maryland, North and South Carolina, and Georgia, labor was a highly valued commodity, and for a while the institution of indentured servitude provided much of the labor needed to work the large farms of the land-holding elite. Indentured servants could expect to be free one day to acquire their own land, however, and they fulfilled the terms of their contracts and then joined the general population to become farmers or tradesmen. As the number of these workers naturally dwindled, some land-holders attempted to enslave members of the indigenous population in order to secure a permanent free labor source, but this project was mostly unsuccessful, due at least in part to the Native Americans' susceptibility to the diseases of the European settlers.

While there were Black slaves in Virginia and Maryland as early as 1619, not all Blacks were slaves. Still, even free Blacks were treated badly. For instance, a Black man or woman could be sentenced to a life of servitude for various crimes—in effect, a life of permanent slavery. Further South, indentured servitude had never been as common as it had in Virginia and Maryland, and the use of Black slaves in the Carolinas grew quickly as farms spread across the land. By the middle of the seventeenth century, Black slaves had become the answer to the labor problem in Maryland, Virginia, and the Carolinas, and by 1700, the institution of Black slavery had been codified by most colonies. In both the popular press and the literature of the time, colonial writers could justify slavery because the general population believed that Blacks were inferior to Whites and represented a class of humanity destined for poverty and servitude. Most colonists felt Blacks were largely uneducable, that they were best controlled with firm discipline, and that slavery was a necessary and even a benevolent system. William Grayson's popular poem, *The Hireling and the Slave*, for example, argues that the life of the Colonial slave is much easier than the life of the European "wage slave." By the time the American Revolution began, nearly four of every ten Southerners were Black slaves. In Virginia, Black slaves outnumbered Whites of all classes. Although slavery was legal in all the colonies, it became important to the Southern economy in a way it never did in the North.

By 1700, the basic patterns of life in the Southern colonies had become relatively stable. Land ownership was the key to social and political power, and land was generally cheap and available. The great family lines of the South—the Byrds, the Lees, the Calhouns, the Masons, the Randolphs, the Carters, the Carrolls—were established early, but even the unconnected young man could move west and become a member of the land- and slave-holding class. Women in the Southern colonies tended to marry earlier and have more children than their counterparts in England, and while there were certainly women who pursued professional activities in the South, most notably in midwifery, most women were occupied primarily in the field and in the home. Descriptions of life during these times can be found in the work of Caroline Howard Gilman, William Gilmore Simms, and John Pendleton Kennedy.

The need to express religious differences did not figure as importantly in the founding of the Southern colonies as it did in New England, and most of the Southern aristocracy were Episcopalian. Protestant dissenters were few until the Great Awakening in the 1700s, when a religious revivalism that originated in New England swept through the colonies and helped establish the Methodist, Baptist, and Presbyterian churches. Educational opportunities were few in the South, even for the elite class, and many of the richest families sent their children to school in England. A few major cities, such as Charleston and Annapolis, had free public schools, but most education occurred in the home.

Most of the population of the Southern colonies lived simply; not everyone attained vast wealth and lived in a great plantation house. Still, social and political power became tied to land ownership in a way that would influence the social order of the South far into the twentieth century. The plantation system became institutionalized, tying the economy, politics, and the social order to the land and to the production of tobacco, rice, indigo, grain, cattle and pigs, lumber, and, by the nineteenth century, cotton. Because plantations were so labor-intensive, slavery and its attendant justifications also became part of the culture. The South developed a largely agrarian economy, and many of the sons of the original settlers established grand Georgian plantations and elegant townhouses served by growing numbers of Black slaves. The South remained a rural environment, with social activity primarily centered in its clusters of plantations and small, scattered towns and villages.

The ideas of liberty and self-government came easily to the people of the Southern colonies, as the agencies of the British government were too far removed to function in any stable regulatory capacity. The colonies began to seek the power to govern themselves in their various assemblies, which led almost immediately to conflicts with the royal governors. The colonial assemblies were generally made up of members of the land-holding aristocracy and so primarily represented its interests, although power in many places was shared with lawyers and merchants. These aristocrats certainly thought of themselves as superior to the smaller, independent landholders and merchants; still, the elected assemblymen generally felt connected to their constituency by common interests and a common local culture. While the system was not exactly democratic, the assemblies did generally protect and guard the rights of all land-holding colonists.

The South During the Revolution

By 1763, England had solidified its control of eastern North America by defeating the French, and the British government began to reassert its presence in the colonies. To support its renewed interest, the British government sent 6,000 new troops to

America. To help pay for its increased presence and for the defeat of the French, the British government began to impose new taxes on the colonies, beginning with the Stamp Act of 1765. Negative reaction in the colonies was immediate, and a combination of assembly action and grass-roots rebellion, which was fueled by antitaxation tracts that appeared in the popular press and in pamphlets, forced the repeal of the Stamp Act. However, the taxes soon returned under a new set of provisions, known as the Townshend Act and the Intolerable Acts, and the movement against British interference in the colonies intensified.

In the South, the rhetoric of the struggle against taxation was particularly poignant, since much of the discourse was presented as a struggle between taxation, which was equated with slavery, and self-government, which was equated with the general right of a man to liberty. Not every White Southerner held slaves, but Southerners knew what slavery meant, and no White Southerner wanted to be a slave to English taxation. The emphasis on liberty and slavery created a great deal of tension in the South, where the plantation economy depended on actual slavery, and some revolutionary thinkers, such as Thomas Jefferson, George Mason, and Richard Henry Lee, all of Virginia, began to speak and write about the connection between the colonists' demand for liberty from British taxation and the general right of all humans to live free. For a time, it seemed that this revolutionary zeal might extend the ideal of liberty even to Blacks and women. Unfortunately, the right of a man to hold property was equally important in the rhetoric of the American Revolution, and the need to assert property rights and the persistence of traditional domestic, economic, and social structures undermined any chance that the Revolution would extend full liberty to all. At the time, the belief in White superiority proved insurmountable. Even Jefferson, who condemned slavery in the abstract, could not find the courage to rid his own plantation of it. The economy of the South had grown too dependent on slave labor.

As the colonies moved closer to war with England, many Southerners, galvanized by great orators such as Patrick Henry of Virginia and Samuel Chase of Maryland, argued that true liberty for the colonies could only exist outside British control. The events of the next few years are generally well-known: the first shots of the war; the meeting of the Continental Congress; the drafting of the Declaration of Independence (which was largely drafted by Southerner Thomas Jefferson); and the selection of another Southerner, George Washington, as commanding general of the Continental Army. The war did not spread quickly, however, and it was not until 1780 that the South became a major battleground. At first, the British moved against Charleston, and, led by Major General Cornwallis, they routed the Army of the Southern Department, under the leadership of Major General Horatio Gates, at Camden, South Carolina. But the Southerners were not finished, and a band of 1,000 Southern militia bested Cornwallis at Kings Mountain. Independent militias were common, and often, Southern militiamen loyal to opposing sides fought each other in guerilla warfare.

After the defeat at Camden, Congress moved to strengthen the Southern armies, and Washington picked Nathaniel Greene to lead the Southern contingent of the Continental Army. Cornwallis left Charleston to pursue Greene's forces, but patriot bands, led by such commanders as Francis Marion, known as the Swamp Fox, and Andrew Pickens constantly harassed the British troops and cut them to pieces. After many battles, the British were confined mostly to Savannah and Charleston. Finally, Cornwallis moved his troops into Yorktown, just up the Chesapeake Bay, where he could rely on the British navy to evacuate him if needed. Upon hearing that the French, who had by now joined in the war against the British, were sailing into American waters, Washington moved against Cornwallis and effectively ended the war, although skirmishes continued until the Treaty of Paris was signed in 1783. Southern generals such as Greene and Marion would later serve as the major characters in various histories and romances written about the war, such as those by William Gilmore Simms.

A Separate Southern Identity Emerges

While thousands had been killed in the war, the damage to the Southern countryside was minimal, and the South recovered quickly. During the war, the British promised emancipation to any slave who abandoned his or her owner, and a few did find freedom in Canada. More, unfortunately, were merely taken by the British and sold again in Florida or in the Caribbean. Thomas Jefferson, who had seen his antislavery passages deleted from the Declaration, typified the ambivalence enlightened Southerners felt over the issue of slavery. In 1780, he wrote in *Manners . . . Effects of Slavery*, that he believed the slave "to be rising from the dust" in anticipation of "total emancipation." Still, Southern planters, including Jefferson, were loath to give up the economic benefits of slavery, and most of the Southern assemblies renewed or strengthened their proslavery positions. Ironically, Southerners became more committed to slavery even as they became convinced of their own right to liberty and self-government.

Congress struggled to bring the colonies together under the Articles of Confederation, but the Southern assemblies were determined that each would retain the right to decide for itself issues such as slavery and taxes. Along these lines, Southerners began to define themselves as Southerners—and their culture as distinct from the culture of the North. Jefferson was among the first to describe the differences in regional attitudes: Northerners were "cool, sober, laborious," and Southerners were "fiery, voluptuary, indolent." Southerners also began to define their economic interests as different from those of the North. Southern planters pressed for free trade and pushed for expansion that would allow them to use the Mississippi River as a trade route to foreign markets. However, Spain attempted to solidify its presence in the West by promising to open its markets in exchange for a renunciation of all American claims to the Mississippi River. Southerners in Congress blocked the agreement, which was known as the Jay-Gardoqui Treaty of 1786. Increasingly, issues in Congress began to be decided along regional lines, with the Southern members finally coalescing into such a strong voting presence that they often dominated. If the new nation was to survive, it would have to find a way to collect taxes from the states, and this necessitated a stronger connection between states than the original Articles of Confederation provided. Once again, Southern members argued strongly for states' rights, especially regarding the issues of slavery, taxation, and trade. After a new federal constitution was offered, the state legislatures fought bitterly over ratification. In the South, many worried about the proposed strength of the federal government under the new constitution (see Map I–1), although some supporters of ratification were notable Southerners such as James Madison and Thomas Jefferson.

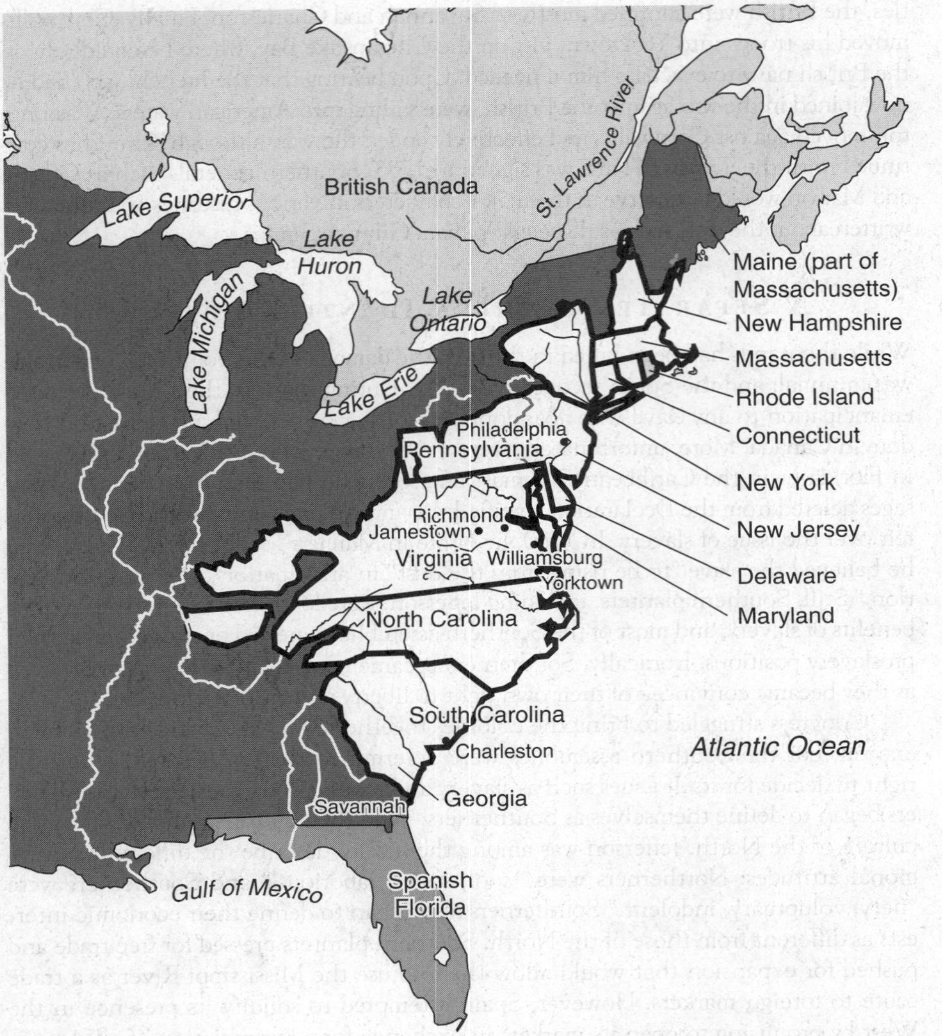

Map I–1 United States areas settled, 1780s

Madison believed that the federal government would never move to abolish slavery and succeeded in convincing many others that slavery was safe under the new Constitution. In the end, the Constitution was ratified, but not before Southerner George Mason, assisted by fellow Virginians James Madison and Thomas Jefferson, persuaded Congress to adopt the Bill of Rights.

To the dismay of many in the South, the issue of slavery came up almost immediately, as did a move to solidify the federal government's primacy through federal control of trade and through the management of the war debt. Alexander Hamilton proposed that the federal government take over the war debt, grant subsidies to manufacturers, and impose trade tariffs. Southern leaders, led by the always-vocal

Madison, had little interest in manufacturing or restricted trade and objected. Many in the South still harbored great resentment toward the British and opposed Hamilton's vision, which linked the American economy to trade with Great Britain. George Washington, a Federalist, led the pro-Hamilton movement in the South, but a decidedly anti-Federalist group began to solidify under Jefferson and Madison. The contest came to a head in the presidential election of 1796, with John Adams, the Federalist, on one side, and Thomas Jefferson, the Republican, on the other. In spite of strong Southern support for Jefferson, Adams won the election and Hamilton's proposals were accepted.

The struggle between the mostly Northern Federalists and the mostly Southern Republicans continued to contribute to the split between the South and the North. As more Western territories were added, the question of slavery arose again and again, with Congress fighting over who had the right to decide whether new states would prohibit or allow slavery. After Jefferson was elected president in 1800, the Republicans gained strength in the federal government, and Jefferson became very popular for his completion of the Louisiana Purchase (see Map I–2) in 1803, which finally gave the new nation control of the Mississippi River and of vast Western territories.

Jefferson's presidency was in trouble, though. Britain demanded that America shut down all trade with its enemy, France, and Jefferson closed all American ports to foreign trade. The result was devastating for the South, where the value of export goods fell by as much as 90 percent. Led by forceful new Southern politicians such as John C. Calhoun of South Carolina and Henry Clay of Kentucky, America moved once again toward war with Britain. In the South, many were sure that the Spanish, with the help of the Creek Indians, would try to retake Southern territory. Andrew Jackson led the Tennessee militia in violent battles against the Creeks, killing more than 8,000 in one battle, ending the Spanish threat, and opening all the Creek lands to White settlement.

Meanwhile, the British navy had sailed up the Chesapeake Bay, and the disembarked armies marched on Washington, burning the Capitol, the White House, and

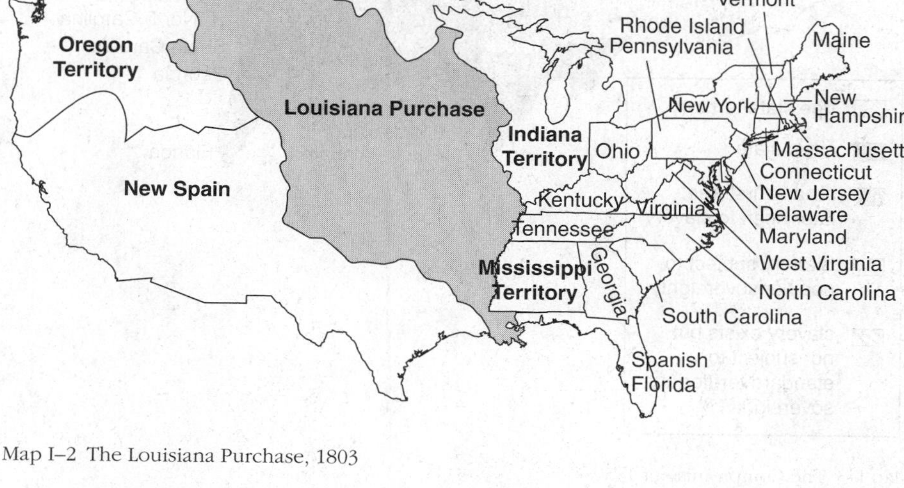

Map I–2 The Louisiana Purchase, 1803

other public buildings. Further attacks on Baltimore and Fort McHenry failed, however. Defeated in the Chesapeake, the British retreated to Jamaica and joined another force that planned to take New Orleans. Jackson, who was now in charge of federal troops, was ready for the British, however, and with the help of the militias of Kentucky, Tennessee, and Louisiana, a battalion of Black soldiers, and even a band of pirates, he defeated the British in an amazing display of military strategy.

After the War of 1812 ended, nationalist fervor brought about by the conflict dwindled, and the interests of the South and North continued to diverge. The tension came to a head in 1819, when Missouri applied for statehood. Concerned about the balance of slavery and non-slavery states, Congressman James Tallmadge proposed that Missouri be admitted as a slave state but that no more slaves be brought into the state. He also proposed that all slave children born after statehood in Missouri be freed at the age of 25. Opposition in the South was vocal, and a split between Northern Republicans and Southern Republicans allowed the amendment to pass, even though the Senate later rejected it. A final split between the North and the South was averted by the Missouri Compromise, which admitted Maine as a free state, admitted Missouri as a slave state, and drew a line across the Louisiana Purchase dividing it into slave and free territories. In spite of the Missouri Compromise, contention over the right of the federal government to impose tariffs and control banking laws, an increasing abolitionist movement in the North, and recurring eco-

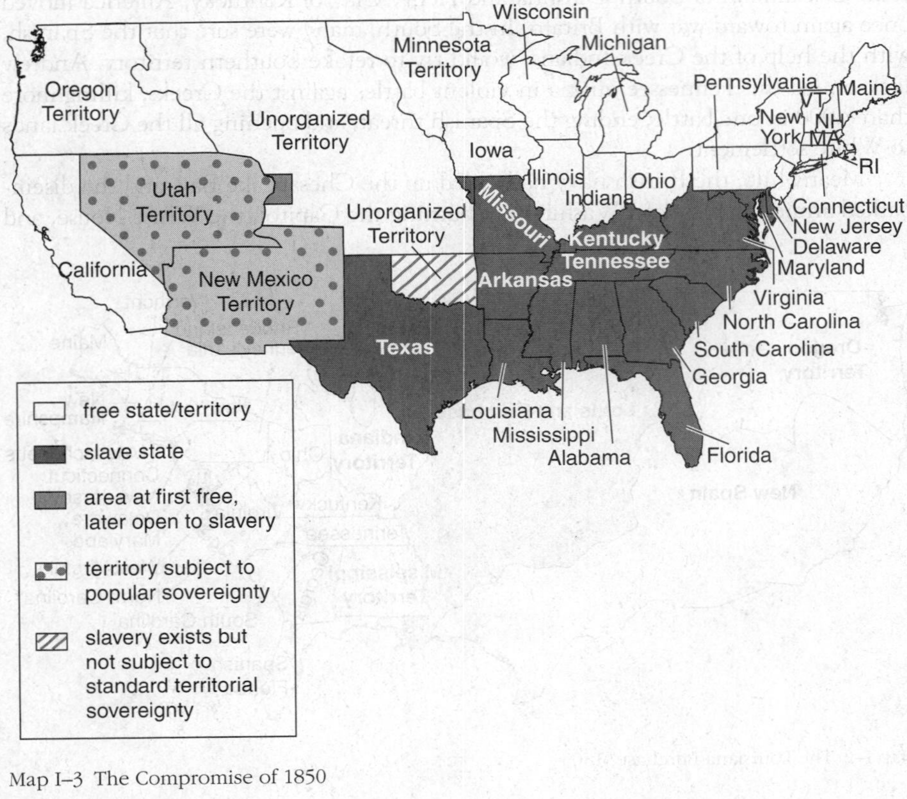

Map I–3 The Compromise of 1850

nomic problems continued to drive a wedge between Northern and Southern states. One final effort, the Compromise of 1850, failed to hold the country together (see Map I–3). The result was a final and bloody disagreement: the Civil War.

Since the founding of the Jamestown colony, early Southern writers had focused on nonfiction accounts of life in the colonies, and Thomas Jefferson, David Ramsay, William Wirt, and Mason Locke Weems carried forward the tradition of examining various regions of the South through their history and culture. Fictional depictions of colonial plantation life emerged in the work of authors such as Caroline Howard Gilman and John Pendleton Kennedy. Soon, these descriptions of a mythic, genteel South would become a staple of Southern literature and influence future generations of American gothic and romance novelists. Writers such as Nathaniel Beverly Tucker and William Alexander Caruthers, heavily influence by the work of Walter Scot, wrote highly romanticized and popular novels of Southern life. Arguably, Southern fiction reached its first high point in the literary works of William Gilmore Simms and Edgar Allan Poe. While Simms never matched the artistry of Poe, he was, at least during his time, the preeminent Southern writer and published more than thirty novels. Poe, who was born in Boston but lived primarily in the South, is not popularly thought of as a Southern writer; nevertheless, his gothic romanticism and interest in the criminal mind can be linked specifically to the traditions of Southern writing, and his influence on Southern writing is immense.

Although Blacks were generally forbidden to read and write, narratives and poetry produced by slaves and former slaves began to appear shortly before the war. William Wells Brown, a Black Southerner, produced a novel in 1853 based on the rumor that Thomas Jefferson had fathered a daughter by one of his slaves. Among the best-known slave narratives is *Narrative of the Life of Frederick Douglass, an American Slave* first published in 1845. Douglass's book established him as the leading Black political figure of his time. The first book published by a slave in the South was *The Hope of Liberty* by George Moses Horton, which was published in 1829 and contained Horton's antislavery poems.

Regional humor, which gained its greatest popularity after the Civil War, had its roots in Antebellum times, and the South boasted Augustus Baldwin Longstreet, Johnson J. Hooper, Joseph G. Baldwin, George Washington Harris, and other regional humorists and satirists. All these writers focused on the peculiarities of the region then known as the Old Southwest—the Southern borderlands of Georgia, Alabama, Tennessee, Mississippi, and Louisiana. Their influence is obvious in the work of later writers including Mark Twain, Robert Penn Warren, and even William Faulkner.

While many consider that the true Southern literary flowering occurred only after the Civil War, the roots of that flower can be seen in the literary output of the Colonial and Antebellum periods. From the fruits of these periods, the narrative traditions of a unique Southern literature emerged.

Antebellum Chronology
1492–1860

1492 • Christopher Columbus discovers the New World.
1513 • Ponce de Leon discovers Florida.
1588 • Thomas Hariot publishes a book on the exploration of Roanoke called *A Brief and True Report of the New-Found Land of Virginia.*
1604 • Acadia (Nova Scotia and New Brunswick) established for the French by Champlain.
1607 • Settlement of Jamestown.
1619 • Twenty free indentured servants, the first Blacks to settle in the colonies, arrive.
1620 • The Mayflower lands at Plymouth Rock.
1630 • Emigration to Massachusettes. Founding of Boston.
1650 • Anne Bradstreet publishes the first American book to be published by a woman, *The Tenth Muse Lately Sprung Up in America.*
1651 • William Bradford publishes a history of the Massachusetts Bay Colony, *Of Plymouth Plantation*.
1661 • Slavery legally recognized in Virginia Colony.
1673 • Marquette explores the Mississippi.
1676 • Bacon's Rebellion in Virginia.
1690 • Importation of slaves from Africa begins.
1693 • Founding of the College of William and Mary in Virginia.
1700 • Iberville plants French colony in Louisiana.
1732 • Benjamin Franklin publishes *Poor Richard's Almanack.*
1741 • Johnathon Edwards publishes his sermon "Sinners in the Hands of an Angry God."
1756 • French and Indian War begins.
1766 • Mason-Dixon Line is drawn.
1773 • The Tea Act of 1773 is passed, giving Britain's East India Company the right to export merchandise.
1776 • American Revolution begins.
• Thomas Paine publishes a pamphlet called *Common Sense*. It sells 100,000 copies in three months.
• Thomas Jefferson drafts the Declaration of Independence.
1787 • Northwest Ordinance. The Northwest includes Ohio, Indiana, Illinois, Michigan, and Wisconsin.
1789–1825 • Four of the nation's six presidents are from Virginia, serving two terms each: George Washington, Thomas Jefferson, James Madison, and James Monroe.
1790 • 1,000 tons of cotton were being produced every year in the South.
• Copyright Act of 1790.
1791 • Phillip Freneau publishes the Federalist *National Gazette*. He became the first powerful, crusading newspaper editor in America.
• Susanna Rowson publishes *Charlotte Temple*, a best-selling seduction story.
1793 • Eli Whitney invents the cotton gin.
1797 • Hannah Foster publishes *The Coquette*.

1803 • Thomas Jefferson purchases the Louisiana Territory from Napoleon.
1807 • Federal Law bans foreign slave trade.
1808 • Slave importation becomes illegal.
1819 • Founding of the University of Virginia by Thomas Jefferson.
1820 • Missouri Compromise.
1822 • Monroe Doctrine.
1829 • David Walker, the son of a slave who was born free in North Carolina, moves to Boston where he sells old clothes.
1830 • David Walker found dead near the doorway of his shop in Boston.
1831 • Nat Turner insurrection; William Lloyd Garrison begins publishing *The Liberator*.
1838 • Fredrick Douglass, a slave, escapes to the North where he becomes the most famous Black man of his time as lecturer, newspaper editor, and writer. He writes *Narrative of the Life of Fredrick Douglass*, an autobiography.
1840 • Cyrus McCormick develops the reaper, a machine that increases agricultural productivity by magnitudes.
1844 • Samuel F. B. Morse perfects electrical telegraphy.
1846 • Wilmot Proviso, banning slavery in any Mexican territory, dies in Congress.
1848 • Gold found in California.
1849 • Henry David Thoreau publishes his essay, "Civil Disobedience."
1850 • Compromise of 1850; Fugitive Slave Law.
1852 • Harriet Beecher Stowe publishes *Uncle Tom's Cabin*.
1854 • Kansas-Nebraska Act ("Bleeding Kansas" repeals Missouri Compromise; creates popular sovereignty).
1857 • Dred Scott Decision (Scott cannot sue; upholds Fugitive Slave Law; strikes Missouri Compromise).
1859 • John Brown's Raid on Harper's Ferry.
• John Brown hanged for attempting to end slavery.
1860 • Lincoln is elected.
• South Carolina secedes from the Union in December.

John Smith

1580–1631

By the time twenty-six-year-old Captain John Smith landed with a small band of colonists on the shore of Virginia in 1607, his life had already been a great adventure. According to his own accounts, he had been a soldier of fortune in the Netherlands and Eastern Europe, where he had been captured in the Austrian war against the Turks and taken to Constantinople to become the slave of the pasha's wife. According to Smith, the pasha's wife fell in love with him and helped him escape, after which he journeyed to Morocco and engaged in other daring exploits before returning to England. Historians have not always agreed on the complete veracity of Smith's reported exploits, and the story of the pasha's wife sounds similar to the tale most often told by and about Smith, in which he is saved from execution at the hands of Powhatan by the Native American woman, Pocahontas. Still, there is little doubt that Smith led an adventurous life. That he has become a legend in the story of the founding of America is due both to the actual events and to their treatment in his own writings and to those of other writers who have employed his name to create a mythic character.

At the Virginia colony, Smith was listed as an original member of the governing council, but was excluded from serving on it because he was charged with mutiny on the voyage from the Old World. He was instrumental in exploring the surrounding area and in procuring the help of the local Native Americans, although he was charged with losing two of his men after he was captured by Powhatan. At the last minute, Smith was saved from hanging for the offense when a supply ship arriving from England distracted his accusers. Although he fell in and out of favor with the ruling council, he was, eventually, made president of the colony and later governor, largely because he was able to bargain with the Native Americans for corn, which likely saved the colony from starvation. His leadership was always controversial, though, and reports of his activities led to charges being filed back in England that accused him of misusing his power. After he was injured in an explosion at Jamestown, he left the settlement and traveled throughout the Chesapeake region and back to England, where he was cleared of the charges. Smith was next employed by English merchants to explore New England, but instead of returning with gold as they had hoped, he returned with fish and furs. His contempt for their desire to exploit the New World for gold was obvious, and although they gave him the title of Admiral of New England, he was forced to seek sponsorship for further explorations elsewhere. He made two more attempts to explore New England, but both were largely unsuccessful; one expedition was forced to turn back because of bad weather, and on another Smith was briefly captured by pirates. Back in England, he offered his services as a guide to the Puritans on their voyage to the New World, but they regarded him as an undesirable person and turned him down, although they made good use of his maps. Eventually, Smith abandoned the life of an adventurer and settled in London to concentrate on his writing.

From his earliest voyages, Smith had recorded the details of his travels in numerous pamphlets, histories, and memoirs, and his writing now served both to promote his personal reputation and to argue for his particular vision of American colonization. His writings include two works on the Virginia colony and two on New England. He later reworked all four of these and published them as the *General Historie of Virginia, New England, and the Summer Isles*. Smith also published an autobiography, a book on seamanship, and a book on colonization. Each of these works employs the excitement of his daring exploits to lead the reader into a careful rationale for the further exploration and colonization of the New World.

Throughout his career, the legend of Smith's rescue by Pocahontas grew, especially after Pocahontas went to England, converted to Christianity, and became the wife of an Englishman. Smith certainly met and knew Pocahontas and had been captured by the chief Powhatan, but he constantly reworked the story of his rescue by the young woman, especially after her death, until it became the first real legend of America and a glamorized metaphor for the possibilities of the New World.

Influenced by the work of Sir Walter Raleigh and the travel literature of Richard Hakluyt and Samuel Purchas, Smith turned his personal experiences into a blueprint for success in the colonies. He believed that the colonies needed planters, craftsmen, and fishermen, and he worried that the search for easy riches and the tendency of English colonists to attempt to recreate the manors of England on American soil were both mistakes. All of these themes are clearly evident in the following selection from *General Historie of Virginia*. While his vision for the American colonies was largely disregarded, his description of America's incredible bounty and of the possibilities it held for adventurous men and women helped spur thousands to sail for its shores. He became the most active promoter of the New World, the symbol of its adventurous spirit, and its first mythic character.

from General Historie of Virginia, New England, and the Summer Isles

Chapter 5: The Accidents that hapned in the Discovery of the Bay of Chisapeack

The prodigalitie of the Presidents [*Ratcliffe*] state went so deepe into our small store, that *Smith* and *Scrivener* tyed him and his Parasites to the rules of proportion. But now *Smith* being to depart, the Presidents authoritie so overswayed the discretion of Master *Scrivener*, that our store, our time, our strength and labours were idely consumed to fulfill his phantasies.

The second of June 1608. *Smith* left the Fort to performe his Discovery with this Company. . . .[1]

These being in an open Barge neare three tuns burthen.

Leaving the *Phœnix* at Cape *Henry*, they crossed the Bay to the Easterne shore, and fell with the Isles called *Smiths Isles*, after our Captaines name.

The first people we saw were two grim and stout Salvages upon Cape *Charles*, with long poles like javelins, headed with bone, they boldly demanded what we were, and what we would; but after many circumstances they seemed very kinde, and directed us to *Accomack*, the habitation of their *Werowance*,[2] where we were kindly intreated.

This King was the comliest, proper, civill Salvage we incountred. His Country is a pleasant fertile clay soyle, some small creekes; good Harbours for small Barks, but not for Ships. He told us of a strange accident lately happened him, and it was, two children being dead; some extreame passions, or dreaming visions, phantasies, or affection moved their parents againe to revisit their dead carkases, whose benummed bodies reflected to the eyes of the beholders such delightfull countenances, as though they had regained their vitall spirits. This as a miracle drew many to behold them, all which, being a great part of his people, not long after dyed, and but few escaped.

They spake the language of *Powhatan*, wherein they made such descriptions of the Bay, Isles, and rivers, that often did us exceeding pleasure.

Passing along the coast, searching every inlet, and Bay, fit for harbours and habitations. Seeing many Isles in the midst of the Bay we bore up for them, but ere we could obtaine them, such an extreame gust of wind, rayne, thunder, and lightening

1. Six men, seven soldiers, and a doctor.

2. Tribal chief.

happened, that with great danger we escaped the unmercifull raging of that Ocean-like water. The highest land on the mayne, yet it was but low, we called *Keales* hill, and these uninhabited Isles, *Russels* Isles.

The next day searching them for fresh water, we could find none, the defect whereof forced us to follow the next Easterne Channell, which brought us to the river of *Wighcocomoco*.[3]

The people at first with great fury seemed to assault us, yet at last with songs and daunces and much mirth became very tractable; but searching their habitations for water, we could fill but three barricoes,[4] and that such puddle[5] that never till then we ever knew the want of good water. We digged and searched in many places, but before two daies were expired, we would have refused two barricoes of gold for one of that puddle water of *Wighcocomoco*.

Being past these Isles which are many in number, but all naught for habitation, falling with a high land upon the mayne, we found a great Pond of fresh water, but so exceeding hot wee supposed it some bath; that place we called poynt *Ployer*, in honor of that most honourable House of *Mousay* in *Britaine*, that in an extreame extremitie once relieved our Captaine.

From *Wighcocomoco* to this place, all the coast is low broken Isles of Morap,[6] growne a myle or two in breadth, and ten or twelve in length, good to cut for hay in Summer, and to catch fish and foule in Winter; but the Land beyond them is all covered over with wood, as is the rest of the Country.

Being thus refreshed, in crossing over from the maine to other Isles we discovered, the winde and waters so much increased, with thunder, lightning, and raine, that our mast and sayle blew overbord and such mighty waves overracked us in that small barge, that with great labour we kept her from sinking by freeing[7] out the water.

Two dayes we were inforced to inhabite these uninhabited Isles; which for the extremitie of gusts, thunder, raine, stormes, and ill wether we called *Limbo*.

Repairing our saile with our shirts, we set sayle for the maine and fell with a pretty convenient river on the East called *Cuskarawaok*;[8] the people ran as amazed in troups from place to place, and divers got into the tops of trees. They were not sparing of their arrowes, nor [of] the greatest passion they could expresse of their anger. Long they shot, we still ryding at an Anchor without the[i]re reatch making all the signes of friendship we could.

The next day they came unarmed, with every one a basket, dancing in a ring, to draw us on shore; but seeing there was nothing in them but villany, we discharged a volly of muskets charged with pistoll shot; whereat they all lay tumbling on the grownd, creeping some one way, some another into a great cluster of reedes hard by; where the[i]re companies lay in Ambuscado.[9] Towards the evening we wayed, and approaching the shoare, discharging five or six shot among the reedes. We landed where there lay a many of baskets and much bloud, but saw not a Salvage. A smoake appearing on the other side the river, we rowed thither, where we found two or three little houses, in each a fire; there we left some peeces of copper, beads, bells, and looking glasses, and then went into the bay; but when it was darke we came backe againe.

3. Now the Pocomoke River.
4. Kegs.
5. Water.
6. A marsh.
7. Bailing.
8. Now Nanticoke.
9. Ambush.

Early in the morning foure Salvages came to us in their Canow, whom we used with such courtesie, not knowing what we were, nor had done, [they] having beene in the bay a fishing; [who] bade us stay and ere long they would returne, which they did and some twentie more with them; with whom after a little conference, two or three thousand men women and children came clustring about us, every one presenting us with something, which a little bead would so well requite, that we became such friends they would contend who should fetch us water, stay with us for hostage, conduct our men any whither, and give us the best content.

Here doth inhabite the people of *Sarapinagh*, *Nause*, *Arseek*, and *Nantaquak* the best Marchants of all other Salvages.

They much extolled a great nation called *Massawomekes*, in search of whom we returned by *Limbo:* this river but onely at the entrance is very narrow, and the people of small stature as them of *Wightcocomoco*, the Land but low, yet it may prove very commodious, because it is but a ridge of land betwixt the Bay and the maine Ocean. Finding this Easterne shore, [to be] shallow broken Isles, and for most part without fresh water; we passed by the straites of *Limbo* for the Westerne shore; so broad is the bay here, we could scarce perceive the great high clifts on the other side: by them we Anchored that night and called them *Riccards Cliftes*.

Thirty leagues we sayled more Northwards not finding any inhabitants, leaving all the Easterne shore, lowe Islandes, but overgrowne with wood, as all the Coast beyond them so farre as wee could see: the Westerne shore by which we sayled we found all along well watered, but very mountanous and barren, the vallies very fertill, but extreame thicke of small wood so well as trees, and much frequented with Wolves, Beares, Deere and other wild beasts.

We passed many shallow creekes, but the first we found Navigable for a ship, we called *Bolus*,[10] for that the clay in many places under the clifts by the high water marke, did grow up in red and white knots as gum out of trees; and in some places so participated together as though they were all of one nature, excepting the coulour, the rest of the earth on both sides being hard sandy gravell, which made us thinke it *Bole-Armoniak*[11] and *Terra sigillata*.[12]

When we first set sayle some of our Gallants doubted nothing but that our Captaine would make too much hast[e] home, but having lien in this small barge not above 12 or 14 dayes, oft tyred at the Oares, our bread spoyled with wet so much that it was rotten (yet so good were their stomacks that they could disgest it) they did with continuall complaints so importune him now to returne, as caused him bespeake them in this manner [*about 14, June 1608*].

Gentlemen if you would remember the memorable history of Sir Ralph Layne, *how his company importuned him to proceed in the discovery of* Moratico,[13] *alleadging they had yet a dog, that being boyled with Saxafras leaves, would richly feede them in their returnes; then what a shame would it be for you (that have bin so suspitious of my tendernesse) to force me returne, with so much provision as we have, and scarce able to say where we have beene, nor yet heard of that we were sent to seeke? You cannot say but I have shared with you in the worst which is past: and for what is to come, of lodging, dyet, or whatsoever, I am contented you allot the worst part to my selfe. As for your feares that I will lose my selfe in these*

10. Now Patapsco.
11. Astringent clay-like earth used as an antidote.
12. Clay found on the Aegean island of Lemnos and used in making pottery.
13. A river.

unknowne large waters, or be swallowed up in some stormie gust; abandon these childish feares, for worse then is past is not likely to happen; and there is as much danger to returne as to proceede. Regaine therefore your old spirits, for returne I will not (if God please) till I have seene the Massawomeks, *found* Patawomek, *or the head of this water you conceit to be endlesse.*

Two or 3 dayes we expected [*experienced*] winde and wether, whose adverse extremities added such discouragement, that three or foure fell sicke, whose pittifull complaints caused us to to returne, leaving the bay some nine miles broad, at nine and ten fadome water.

The 16 of *June* [1608], we fell with the river *Patowomek*; feare being gone, and our men recovered, we were all content to take some paines, to know the name of that seven mile broad river. For thirtie myles sayle, we could see no inhabitants: then we were conducted by two Savages up a little bayed creeke, towards *Onawmanient*,[14] where all the woods were layd with ambuscado's to the number of three or foure thousand Salvages, so strangely paynted, grimed and disguised, shouting, yelling and crying as so many spirits from hell could not have shewed more terrible.

Many bravado's they made, but to appease their fury, our Captaine prepared with as seeming a willingnesse (as they) to incounter them. But the grazing of our bullets upon the water (many being shot on purpose they might see them) with the Ecc[h]o of the woods so amazed them, as downe went their bowes and arrowes; (and exchanging hostage) *James Watkins* was sent six myles up the woods to their Kings habitation. We were kindly used of those Salvages, of whom we understood, they were commanded to betray us, by the direction of *Powhatan*; and he so directed from the discontents [*discontented*] at *James* towne, because our Captaine did cause them stay in their country against their wills.

The like incounters we found at *Patowomek*, *Cecocawonee* and divers other places: but at *Moyaones*, *Nacotchtant* and *Toags* the people did their best to content us.

Having gone so high as we could with the bo[a]te, we met divers Salvages in Canowes, well loaden with the flesh of Beares, Deere and other beasts; whereof we had part. Here we found mighty Rocks, growing in some places above the grownd as high as the shrubby trees, and divers other solid quarries of divers tinctures: and divers places where the waters had falne from the high mountaines they had left a tinctured spangled skurfe, that made many bare places seeme as guilded. Digging the grown[d]e above in the highest clifts of rocks, we saw it was a claie sand so mingled with yeallow spangles as if it had beene halfe pindust.

In our returne inquiring still for this *Matchqueon*, the king of *Patawomeke* gave us guides to conduct us up a little river called *Quiyough*,[15] up which we rowed so high as we could. Leaving the bo[a]te; with six shot and divers Salvages, he marched seven or eight myle before they came to the mine: leading his hostages in a small chaine they were to have for their paines, being proud so richly to be adorned.

The mine is a great Rocky mountaine like *Antimony*; wherein they digged a great hole with shells and hatchets: and hard by it, runneth a fayre brooke of *Christal*-like water, where they wash away the drosse and keepe the remainder, which they put in little baggs and sell it all over the country to paint the[i]re bodyes, faces, or Idols; which makes them looke like Blackmores dusted over with silver. With so much as we could carry we returned to our bo[a]te, kindly requiting this kinde king and all his kinde people.

14. Now Nomini Bay.

15. Now Aquia Creek.

The cause of this discovery was to search [for] this mine, of which *Newport* did assure us that those small baggs (we had given him), in *England* he had tryed to hold halfe silver; but all we got proved of no value: also to search what furrs, the best whereof is at *Cuscarawaoke*, where is made so much *Rawranoke*[16] or white beads that occasion as much dissention among the Salvages, as gold and silver amongst Christians; and what other mineralls, rivers, rocks, nations, woods, fishings, fruites, victuall, and what other commodities the land afforded: and whether the bay were endlesse or how farre it extended.

Of mines we were all ignorant, but a few Bevers, Otters, Beares, Martins and minkes [skins] we found, and in divers places that aboundance of fish, lying so thicke with their heads above the water, as for want of nets (our barge driving amongst them) we attempted to catch them with a frying pan: but we found it a bad instrument to catch fish with: neither better fish, more plenty, nor more variety for smal fish, had any of us ever seene in any place so swimming in the water, but they are not to be caught with frying pans. Some small codd, also we did see swim close by the shore by *Smiths* Iles, and some as high as *Riccards* Clifts. And some we have found dead upon the shore.

To express all our quarrels, trecheries and incounters amongst those Salvages I should be too tedious: but in breefe, at all times we so incountred them, and curbed their insolencies, that they concluded with presents to purchase peace; yet we lost not a man: at our first meeting our Captaine ever observed this order, to demand their bowes and arrowes, swordes, mantells and furrs, with some childe or two for hostage, whereby we could quickly perceive, when they intended any villany.

Having finished this discovery (though our victuall was neere spent) he intended to see his imprisonment-acquaintances upon the river of *Rapahanock*, by many called *Toppahanock*, but our bo[a]te by reason of the ebbe, chansing to grownd upon a many shoules lying in the entrances, we spyed many fishes lurking in the reedes: our Captaine sporting himselfe by nayling them to the grownd with his sword, set us all a fishing in that manner: thus we tooke more in one houre then we could eate in a day.

But it chansed our Captaine taking a fish from his sword (not knowing her condition) being much of the fashion of a Thornback, but a long tayle like a ryding rodde, whereon the middest is a most poysoned sting, of two or three inches long, bearded like a saw on each side, which she strucke into the wrest of his arme neere an inch and a halfe: no bloud nor wound was seene, but a little blew spot, but the torment was instantly so extreame, that in foure houres had so swolen his hand, arme and shoulder, we all with much sorrow concluded [*anticipated*] his funerall, and prepared his grave in an Island by, as himselfe directed: yet it pleased God by a precious oyle Docter *Russell* at the first applyed to it when he sounded it with probe, (ere night) his tormenting paine was so well asswaged that he eate of the fish to his supper, which gave no lesse joy and content to us then ease to himselfe. For which we called the Island *Stingray* Isle after the name of the fish.

Having neither Chirurgian nor Chirurgery but that preservative oyle, we presently set sayles for *James* towne, passing the mouthes of the rivers of *Payankatank*, and *Pamaunkee*, the next day we safely arrived at *Kecougtan*.

16. Shells.

The simple Salvages seeing our Captaine hurt, and an other bloudy by breaking his shinne, our numbers of bowes, arrowes, swords, mantles, and furrs, would needes imagine we had beene at warres (the truth of these accidents would not satisfie them) but impatiently importuned us to know with whom. Finding their aptnesse to beleeve, we fayled not (as a great secret) to tell them any thing that might affright them, what spoyle we had got and made of the *Massawomeks*. This rumor went faster up the river then our Barge, that arrived at *Waraskoyack* the 20 of July; where trimming her with painted streamers, and such devises as we could, we made them at *James* towne jealous[17] of a Spanish Frigot, where we all, God be thanked, safely arrived the 21 of July.

There we found the last Supply[18] were all sicke; the rest some lame, some bruised: all unable to doe any thing but complaine of the pride and unreasonable needlesse crueltie of the silly President, that had riotously consumed the store: and to fulfill his follies about building him an unnecessary building for his pleasure in the woods, had brought them all to that misery; that had we not arrived, they had as strangely tormented him with revenge.

But the good newes of our Discovery, and the good hope we had by the Salvages relation, that our Bay had stretched into the South Sea, or somewhat neare it, appeased their fury; but conditionally that *Rat[c]liffe* should be deposed, and that Captaine *Smith* would take upon him the government, as by course it did belong.

Their request being effected, he substituted Master *Scrivener* his deare friend in the Presidency, equally distributing those private provisions the other [*Ratcliffe*] had ingrossed, appointing more honest officers to assist master *Scrivener* (who then lay exceeding sicke of a Callenture[19]): and in regard of the weaknesse of the company, and heate of the yeare, they being unable to worke, he left them to live at ease, to recover their healths; but imbarked himselfe to finish his Discovery.

Questions to Consider

1. Smith's writings are designed both as exciting adventure stories and as enticements for other colonists to follow. What passages can you point to that demonstrate how the selection furthers both these designs?
2. Why do you think Smith became an icon of the colonial person? What is it about his adventures and his attitude toward the New World that make him an interesting figure?

17. Suspicious of being.
18. The new settlers.
19. A mild fever.

Ebenezer Cook(e)

c. 1670–??

Not much is known for sure about Ebenezer Cook's life. He was probably born in London but traveled to the colonies when he inherited land in Maryland, which he sold in 1717. While in America, Cook practiced law in Prince George's County, Maryland, and worked as a land agent, but records show that he continued to spend a great deal of time in Europe. Although Cook is the author of several pieces, he is known almost exclusively as the author of the poetic satire, *The Sotweed Factor*, and as the protagonist of John Barth's 1960 novel of the same name, which is a ribald, fictional account of Cook's life.

If the opinions of colonial life contained in *The Sotweed Factor* are Cook's, then he was less than impressed with his experiences in the colonies. The narrator of the poem is an Englishman of high breeding who comes to the colonies to seek his fortune. There he expects to find the Eden he has been promised; instead, people he believes must be the "descendants of Cain" confront him. The Americans drink too much, fight too much, eat outlandish foods, and spend their time engaging in outrageous practical jokes and dreaming up scams and confidence schemes. In the end, the narrator, the sotweed factor, which is the name given to a tobacco agent, is tricked out of his goods in exchange for a cargo of tobacco that never appears. When he looks to the Colonial courts for settlement, he is rewarded with "country pay . . . in pipe-staves, corn, or flesh of boar," which is worthless to him. In a rage, he returns to England, cursing Maryland as he goes.

The Sotweed Factor is a satire, and generally, satire is categorized as Juvenalian or Horatian. Juvenalian satire may be quite pointed and mean-spirited; Horatian satire generally is a gentle way of poking fun at the satire's subject. *The Sotweed Factor* is without question a satire in the Juvenalian tradition, and the poem's satire is more complex than it first appears. While the poem is certainly critical of colonial life, the criticism is also aimed at the close-minded, inept, inflexible narrator and his elite English ways.

Critics have pointed to Cook as the forerunner of a strain of literary humor that would produce Benjamin Franklin and, eventually, Mark Twain, and some have argued that *The Sotweed Factor* stands as the first of the great American satires. Cook also published *The Maryland Muse*, a burlesque on Bacon's Rebellion; a serious essay on the over-reliance of the colonies on tobacco, entitled *Sotweed Redivivus;* and several elegies honoring various dignitaries. However, it is *The Sotweed Factor* that survives as Cook's literary legacy.

The Sotweed Factor,[1] &c.

CONDEMN'D by Fate, to wayward Curse,
Of Friends unkind, and empty Purse,
Plagues worse than fill'd *Pandora*'s Box,
I took my Leave of *Albion*'s[2] Rocks,
With heavy Heart, concern'd that I
Was forc'd my native Soil to fly,
And the old World must bid Good-b'ye:
But Heav'n ordain'd it shou'd be so,
And to repine is vain, we know.

1. Sotweed factor: a tobacco broker.

2. Great Britian.

FREIGHTED with Fools, from *Plimouth* Sound,
To *MARYLAND* our Ship was bound;
Where we arriv'd, in dreadfal Pain,
Shock'd by the Terrors of the Main;
For full Three Months our wav'ring Boat
Did thro' the surly Ocean float,
And furious Storms and threatning Blasts,
Both split our Sails, and sprung our Masts:
Weary'd, yet pleas'd we did escape
Such Ills, we achor'd at the *Cape;*[3]
But weighing soon, we plow'd the *Bay*,
To cove[4] it in *Piscataway*.[5]

INTENDING there to open Store,
I put myself and Goods on Shore,
Where soon repair'd a numerous Crew,
In Shirts and Draw'rs, of *Scotch*-cloth[6] blew,
With neither Stocking, Hat, nor Shoe:
These *Sotweed* Planters crowd the Shore,
In Hew as tawny as a *Moor;*
Figures, so strange, no G O D design'd
To be a Part of Human-kind:
But wanton Nature, void of Rest,
Moulded the brittle Clay in Jest.

AT last, a Fancy very odd,
Took me, This was *The Land of* Nod,[7]
Planted at first when Vagrant *Cain*
His Brother had unjustly slain;
Then, conscious of the Crime he'd done,
From Vengeance dire hither run,
And in a Hut[8] supinely dwelt,
The first in *Furrs* and *Sotweed* dealt:
And ever since that Time, this Place
Has harbour'd a detested Race,
Who, when they could not thrive at Home,
For Refuge to these Worlds did roam,
In Hopes by Flight they might prevent.
The Devil, and his fell Intent,
Obtain from Tripple-Tree[9] Reprieve,
And Heav'n and Hell alike deceive:
But e're their Manners I display,
I think it fit I open lay
My Entertainment by the Way,

3. Cape Cod.
4. To be at anchor.
5. A bay in Maryland.
6. Blue linen.
7. Biblical place described as "east of Eden" where Cain was exiled.
8. Small clump of trees at the top of a hill.
9. The gallows tree.

That Strangers well may be aware on
What homely Diet they must fare on;
To see that Shore where no good sense is found,
But Conversation's lost, and Manners drown'd.
  I cross'd unto the other Side
A River, whose impetuous Tide,
Those *Salvage* Borders do divide,
In such a swimming odd Invension,
I scarce can give it's due Dimension,
The *Indians* call this watry Waggon,
Canoe, a Vessel none can brag on,
Cut from a Poplar Tree, or Pine,
And fashion'd like a Trough for Swine:
In this most noble Fishing-boat,
I boldly put my self afloat,
Standing erect, with Legs stretch'd wide,
We paddled to the other Side;
Where being landed safe by Hap,
(As *Sol* fell into *Thetis*' Lap)[10]
A ravenous Gang, bent on the Strowl,
Of Wolves for Prey, began to howl:
This put me in a pannick Fright,
Lest I shou'd be devour'd quite:
But as I there a Musing stood,
And quite benighted in the Wood,
A Female Voice pierc'd thro' my Ears,
Crying, You Rogue drive home the Steers:
I listen'd that attractive Sound,
And streight a Herd of Cattle sound,
Drove by a Youth, and homeward bound.
Cheer'd with the Sight, I streight thought fit
To ask, Where I a Bed might get?
The surly Peasant bid me stay,
And ask'd, From whom I'd run away?[11]
Surpris'd at such a sawcy Word,
I instantly lugg'd out my Sword,
Swearing I was no Fugitive,
But from *Great Britain* did arrive,
In hopes I here might better thrive.
To which he mildly made Reply,
I beg your Pardon, Sir, that I
Shou'd talk to you unmannerly:
But if you please to go with me,
To yonder House you'll welcome be.

10. As the sun set—Sol is the sea personified; Thetis is one of the Nereids, the sea personified.

11. Peasant supposes he is a runaway servant.

ENCOUNTRING soon the smoaky Seat,
The Planter old did thus me greet,
Whether You're come from Goal,[12] *or College,*
You're Welcome, to my certain Knowledge,
And if You'll please all Night to stay,
My Son shall put You in the Way:
Which Offer I most kindly took,
And for a Seat did round me look,
When presently among the rest
He plac'd his unknown *English* Guest,
Who found 'em drinking, for a Whet,[13]
A Cask of Sider on the Fret:[14]
'Till Supper came upon the Table,
On which I fed whilst I was able;
So after hearty Entertainment,
Of Drink and Victuals, without Payment,
For Planters Tables, you must know
Are free for all that come and go,
Whilst Pone,[15] with Milk and Mush well stor'd,
In wooden Dishes grac'd the Board,
With Hominy and Sider-Pap,[16]
Which scarce an *English* Dog would lap,
Well stuff'd with Fat from Bacon fry'd,
And with Melasses dulcify'd.[17]
Then out our Landlord pulls his Pouch,
As greasy as the Leather Couch
On which he sat, and streight begun
To load with Weed his *Indian* Gun,[18]
In Length scarce longer than one's Finger,
Or that for which the Ladies linger.
His Pipe smoak'd out, with awful Grace,
With Aspect grave and solemn Pace,
The Reverend Sir, walks to a Chest,
Of all his Furniture the best,
Closely confin'd within a Room,
Which seldom felt the Weight of Broom:
From thence he lugs a Cagg of Rum,
And nodding to me, thus begun:
I find, says he, *you don't much care*
For this our Indian Country *Fare;*
But let me tell you, Friend of mine,
You may be glad of it in Time,
Tho' now you're Stomach is so fine;
And if within this Land you stay,
You'll find it true what I do say:

12. Jail.
13. A small drink as an appetizer.
14. Fermenting.
15. Corn bread.
16. Cereal made with cider.
17. Sweetened.
18. To fill his pipe with tobacco.

This said, the Rundlet up he threw,
And bending backwards strongly drew;
I pluck'd as stoutly, for my Part,
Altho' it made me sick at Heart,
And got so soon into my Head,
I scarce could find my Way to Bed;
Where I was instantly convey'd,
By one that pass'd for Chamber-Maid,
Tho' by her loose and sluttish Dress,
She rather seem'd a *Bedlam-Bess*.[19]
Curious to know from whence she came,
I press'd her to declare her Name?
She blushing, seem'd to hide her Eyes,
And thus in civil Terms replies:
In better Times, o'er to this Land
I was unhappily trepann'd,[20]
Perchance as well I did appear,
As any Gentlewoman here,
Not then a Slave for Twice Two Year;[21]
My Cloaths were fashionably new,
Nor were my Shifts of Scotch *Cloth blew:*
But Things are chang'd: Now at the Hoe
I daily work, and barefoot go,
In weeding Corn, and feeding Swine,
I spend my melancholly Time;
Kidnapp'd and fool'd, I hither fled,
To shun a hated Nuptial Bed;
And, to my Grief, already find
Worse Plagues than those I left behind.

WHATE'ER the Wand'rer did profess,
Good faith I cou'd not chuse but guess
The Cause which brought her to this Place,
Was Supping e're the Priest said Grace:
Quick as my Thoughts the Slave was fled,
Her Candle left to shew my Bed,
Which, made of Feathers soft and good,
Close in the Chimney-corner stood:
I laid me down, expecting Rest,
To be in Golden Slumbers blest;
But soon a Noise disturb'd my Quiet,
And plagu'd me with Nocturnal Riot:
A Puss, which in the Ashes lay,
With grunting Pig, began a Fray,
And prudent Dog, that Feuds might cease,
Most sharply bark'd, to keep the Peace:

19. A lunatic.
20. Trapped.
21. Indentured servants generally served for four years, then they were freed.

This Quarrel scarcely was decided
By Stick, that ready lay provided,
But *Reynard,* arch and cunning Loon,
Crept into my Apartment soon,
In hot Pursuit of Ducks and Geese,
With full Intent the same to seize;
Their cackling Plaints with strange Surprise
Chac'd Sleep's thick Vapours from my Eyes;
Raging, I jump'd upon the Floor,
And like a drunken sailor swore,
With Sword I fiercely laid about,
And soon dispers'd the feather'd Rout,
The Poultry out of Window flew,
And *Reynard* cautiously withdrew;
The Dogs who this Encounter heard,
Fiercely themselves to aid me rear'd,
And to the Place of Combat run,
Exactly as the Field was won,
Fretting and hot as roasted Capon,
And greasy as a Flitch of Bacon,[22]

I to the Orchard did repair,
To breathe the cool and open Air,
Impatient waiting for bright Day,
Extended on a Bank I lay;
But Fortune here, that sawcy Whore,
Disturb'd me worse, and plagu'd me more
Than she had done the Night before;
Hoarse croaking Frogs did round me ring,
Such Peals the Dead to Life wou'd bring,
A Noise might move their Wooden King:
I stuff'd my Ears with Cotton white,
And curs'd the melancholly Night,
For fear of being deaf outright:
But soon my Vows did recant,
And *Hearing* as a Blessing grant,
When a confounded *Rattle-Snake*
With Hissing made my Heart to ach,
Not knowing how to fly the Foe,
Or whither in the dark to go,
By strange good Luck I took a Tree,
Prepar'd by Fate to set me free,
Where, riding on a Limb astride,
Night and the Branches did me hide,
And I the De'el and Snake defy'd.
Not yet from Plagues exempted quite,
The curs'd *Muschetoes* did me bite;
'Til rising Morn, and blushing Day,
Drove both my Fears and Ills away,

22. Side of bacon.

And from Night's Terrors set me free,
Discharg'd from hospitable Tree.

I did to Planter's Booth repair,
And there at Breakfast nobly fare,
On Rasher broil'd, of infant Bear:
I thought the Cubb delicious Meat,
Which ne'er did ought but Chesnuts eat,
Nor was young *Orson's* Flesh the worse,
Because he suck'd a *Pagan* Nurse:
Our Breakfast done, the Planter stout,
Handed a Glass of Rum about.

PLEAS'D with the Treatment I did find,
I took my Leave of Host so kind.
Who, to oblige me, did provide
His eldest Son to be my Guide;
And lent me Horses of his own,
A skittish Colt and aged Roan,
The four legg'd Prop of his Wife *Joan*.
Steering our Course in Trott or Pace,
We sail'd directly for a Place,
In *MARYLAND* of high Renown;
Known by the Name of *Battle-Town:*
To view the Crowds did there resort,
Which Justice made, and Law, their Sport,
In their Sagacious County Court:
Scarce had we enter'd on the Way,
Which thro' the Woods and Marshes lay;
But *Indian* strange did soon appear
In hot Pursuit of wounded Deer;
No mortal Creature can express
His wild fantastick Air and Dress;
His painted Skin, in Colours dy'd,
His sable Hair, in Satchel ty'd,
Show'd *Salvages* not free from Pride:
His tawny Thighs and Bosom bare,
Disdain'd an useless Coat to wear,
Scorn'd Summers Heat and Winters Air;
His manly Shoulders, such as please
Widows and Wives, were bath'd with Grease,
Of Cub and Bear, whose supple Oil,
Prepar'd his Limbs in Heat and Toil.

THUS naked *Pict*[23] in Battle fought,
Or undisguis'd his Mistress sought;
And knowing well his Ware was good,
Refus'd to skreen it with a Hood:
His Visage Dun, and Chin that near
Did Razor feel, nor Scissors bear,
Or know the Ornament of Hair,

23. The Picts were an ancient race of people who once populated parts of Great Britain.

Look'd sternly grim; supriz'd with Fear,
I spurr'd my Horse as he drew near;
But Roan, who better knew than I,
The little Cause I had to fly,
Seem'd by his solemn Step and Pace,
Resolv'd I shou'd the Spector face,
Nor faster mov'd, tho' spurr'd and prick'd,
Than *Balam's* Ass by Prophet kick'd;[24]
Kekicuatop, the *Heathen* cry'd,[25]
How is it *Tom*, my Friend reply'd;
Judging from thence, the Brute was civil,
I boldly fac'd the courteous Devil,
And lugging out a Dram of Rum,
I gave his tawny Worship some;
Who in his Language as I guess,
My Guide informing me no less,
Implor'd the Devil me to bless:
I thank'd him for his good Intent,
And forward on my Journey went;
Discoursing as along I rode,
Whether this Race was fram'd of GOD,
Or whether some malignant Power,
Had fram'd them in an evil Hour,
And from his own infernal Look,
Their dusky Form and Image took.

FROM hence we fell to Argument
Whence peopl'd was this Continent?
My Friend suppos'd *Tartarians* wild,
Or *Chinese*, from their home exil'd,
Wandring thro' Mountains hid with Snow,
And Rills that in the Valleys flow,
Far to the *South of Mexico*,
Broke thro' the Bars which Nature cast,
And wide unbeaten Regions past;
'Till near those Streams the human Deluge roll'd,
Which sparkling shin'd with glittering Sands of Gold;
And fetch'd *Pisarro*[26] from th' *Iberian* Shore
To rob the *Indians* of their native Store.

I smil'd to hear my young Logician,
Thus reason like a Polititian;
Who ne'r by Father's Pains and Earning,
Had got, at Mother, *Cambridge* Learning;
Where lubber Youth just free from Birch,
Most stoutly drink to prop the Church;

24. Balaam was a Biblical soothsayer who rode an ass.
25. Translates to "How do you do."
26. Francisco Pizarro (1475–1541) Spanish Conquistador.

Nor with grey Coat had taken Pains
To purge his Head, and cleanse his Reins;
And in Obedience to the College,
Had pleas'd himself with carnal Knowledge;
And tho' I lik'd the Younster's Wit,
I judg'd the Truth he had not hit;
And could not chuse but smile to think,
What they cou'd do for Meat and Drink,
Who o'er so many Desarts ran,
With Brats and Wives in Carravan;
Unless perchance they'd got a Trick,
To eat no more than Porker sick,
Or could with well-contented Maws,
Quarter like Bears upon their Paws:[27]
Thinking his Reason to confute,
I gravely thus commenc'd Dispute;
And urg'd, that tho' a *Chinese* Host
Might penetrate this *Indian* Coast,
Yet this was certainly most true,
They never could the Isles subdue;
For knowing not to steer a Boat,
They could not on the Ocean float,
Or plant their Sun-burnt Colonies,
In Regions parted by the Seas:
I thence inferr'd, *Phoenicians* old
Discover'd first, with Vessels bold,
These *Western* Shores, and planted here,
Returning once or twice a Year,
With Naval Stores, and Lasses kind,
To comfort those were left behind;
'Till by the Winds and Tempests tore,
From their intended golden Shore,
They suffer'd Shipwreck, or were drown'd,
And lost the World so newly found:
But after long and learn'd Contention,
We could not finish our Dissention;
And when that both had talk'd their Fill,
We had the self same Notion still.

THUS Parson Grave well read, and Sage,
Does in Dispute with Priest engage,
The one protests they are not wise,
Who judge by Sense, and trust their Eyes,
And vows he'd burn for it at Stake,
That Man may GOD his Maker make;

27. Bears were mistakenly thought to suck their paws for nourishment.

The other smiles at his Religion,
And vows he's but a learned Widgeon,[28]
And when they've emptied all their Store,
From Books and Fathers, are not more
Convinc'd, or wiser than before.

SCARCE had we finish'd serious Story,
But I espy'd the Town before me;
And roaring Planters on the Ground,
Drinking of Healths, in Circle round:
Dismounting Steed with friendly Guide,
Our Horses to a Tree we ty'd,
And forward pass'd amongst the Rout,
To chuse convenient Quarters out;
But being none were to be found,
We sat like others on the Ground,
Carousing Punch in open Air,
'Till Cryer did the Court declare:
The planting Rabble being met,
Their drunken Worships likewise sat,
Cryer proclaims the Noise shou'd cease,
And streight the Lawyers broke the Peace,
Wrangling for Plantiff and Defendant,
I thought they ne'r wou'd make an End on't,
With Nonsence, Stuff, and false Quotations,
With brazen Lies, and Allegations;
And in the Splitting of the Cause,
Us'd such strange Motions with their Paws,
As shew'd their Zeal was rather bent
In Blows to end the Argument.
A Reverend Judge, who to the Shame,
Of all the Bench, cou'd write his Name,
At Petty-Fogger took Offence,
And wonder'd at his Impudence:
My Neighbour *Dash,* with Scorn replies,
And in the Face of Justice flies;
The Bench in Fury streight divide,
And Scribles take on Judge's Side;
The Jury, Lawyers, and their Clients,
Contending, fight, like Earth-born Giants,
'Till Sh'riff that slily lay perdue,[29]
Hoping Indictments would ensue;
And when———
A Hat or Wig fell in the Way,
He seiz'd 'em for the Queen, as Stray;
The Court adjourn'd in usual Manner,

28. A duck.

29. Hidden or concealed.

In Battle, Blood, and fractious Clamour.
   I thought it proper to provide,
A Lodging for my self and Guide,
So to our Inn we march'd away,
Which at a little Distance lay;
Where all Things were in such Confusion,
I thought the World at it's Conclusion;
A Heard of Planters on the Ground,
O'rewhelm'd with Punch, dead Drunk we found;
Others were fighting and contending,
Some burn'd their Cloaths, to save the mending;
A few whose Heads, by frequent Use,
Could better bear the potent Juice,
Gravely debated State Affairs,
Whilst I most nimbly tripp'd up Stairs,
Leaving my Friend discoursing oddly,
And mixing Things Prophane and Godly;
Just then beginning to be drunk,
As from the Company I slunk:
To every Room and Nook I crept,
In hopes I might have somewhere slept;
But all the Beding was possest,
By one or other drunken Guest;
But after looking long about,
I found an antient Corn-loft out;
Glad that I might in Quiet sleep,
And there my Bones unfractur'd keep:
I laid me down secur'd from Fray,
And soundly snor'd 'till break o'Day;
When waking fresh, I sat upright,
And found my Shoes were vanish'd quite,
Hat, Wig, and Stockings, all were fled,
From this extended *Indian* Bed:
Vex'd at the Loss of Goods and Chattle,
I swore I'd give the Rascal Battle,
Who had abus'd me in this Sort,
And Merchant-Stranger made his Sport:
I furiously descended Ladder,
No Hare in *March* was ever madder,
And did with Host and Servants quarrel,
But all in vain, for my Apparel;
For one whose Mind did much aspire
To Mischief, threw them in the Fire.
Equipp'd with neither Hat nor Shoe,
I did my coming hither rue,
And doubtful thoughts what I should do:
When looking round I saw my Friend,
Lye naked on a Table's End,
A Sight so dismal to behold,

One would have thought him dead and cold,
There ready laid, to be next Day
On Shoulders Four convey'd away:
'Till wringing of his bloody Nose,
By fighting got, we may suppose,
I found him not so fast asleep,
Might give his Friends some cause to weep:
Rise *Oronoko*,[30] rise, said I,
And from this *Hell* and *Bedlam* fly:
My Guide starts up, and in a Maze,
With Bloodshot Eyes did round him gaze,
At Lenth with many Sigh and Groan,
He went in search of aged Roan;
But Roan who seldom us'd to falter,
Had fairly this Time slipt his Halter,
And not content all Night to stay,
Ty'd up from Fodder, run away;
After my Guide to catch him ran,
And so I lost both Horse and Man;
Which Disappointment tho' so great,
Did only Jest and Mirth create:
'Till one more civil than the rest,
In Conversation far the best,
Observing that for want of Roan,
I should be left to walk alone,
Most readily did me intreat,
To take a Bottle at his Seat,
A Favour at that Time so great,
I blest my kind propitious Fate;
And finding soon a fresh Supply
Of Cloaths, from Store-House kept hard by,
I mounted streight on such a Steed,
Did rather Curb than Whipping need;
And straining at the usual Rate,
With Spur of Punch which lies in Pate,
E'r long we lighted at the Gate;
Where in an antient Cedar-House,
Dwelt my new Friend, a *Cockerouse*,[31]
Whose Fabrick, tho' 'twas built of Wood,
Had many Springs and Winters stood:
When sturdy Oaks and lofty Pines,
Were levell'd with Musk-Melon-Vines,
And Plants eradicated were,
By Hurricans drove in the Air;
There with good Punch and Apple Juice,
We spent our Time without Abuse,
'Till Midnight in her fable Vest,
Persuaded Gods and Men to rest;

30. Another name for tobacco planter.

31. A man of quality.

And with a pleasing kind Surprize,
Indulg'd soft Slumber to my Eyes.

FIERCE *Æthon*,[32] Courser of the Sun,
Had half his Race exactly Run,
And breath'd on me a furious Ray,
Darting hot Beams the following Day,
When Rug in Blanket white, I lay;
But Heat and Chinces[33] rais'd the Sinner,
Most opportunely to his Dinner;
Wild Fowl and Fish delicious Meats,
As good as *Neptune*'s Doxy[34] eats,
Began our hospitable Chear,
Fat Venison follow'd in the Rear,
And Turkeys-wild, luxurious Fare:
But what the Feast did most commend,
Was hearty Welcome from my Friend.

THUS having made a noble Feast,
I eat as well as pamper'd Priest;
Madera strong in flowing Bowles,
Fill'd with extreme Delight our Souls;
'Till wearied with a purple Flood,
Of gen'rous Wine, the Giants Blood,
As Poets feign, away I made
For some refreshing verdant Shade;
Where musing on my Rambles strange,
And Fortune; which so oft did change,
In midst of various Comtemplations,
Of Fancies odd and Meditations,
I slumber'd long,———
'Till airy Night and noxious Dews,
Did Sleep's unwholsome Fetters loose,
With Vapours cold and misty Air,
To Fire-side I did repair;
Near which a jolly Female Crew,
Were deep engag'd at *Lanterloo*,[34]
In Nightrails[35] white, with dirty Mien,
I thought them first some Witches, bent
On black Designs, in dire Convent;
'Till one who with affected Air,
Had nicely learn'd to Curse and Swear,
Cry'd, *Dealing's lost, 'tis but a Flam*,
And vow'd by G-- *she'd have her Pam:*[36]
When Dealing thro' the Board had run,
They ask'd me kindly, *to make one:*
Not staying often to be bid,
I sate me down as others did;
We scarce had play'd a Round about,

32. A mythical horse.
33. Bedbugs.
34. A card game.
35. Nightshirts.
36. The high card.

But that those *Indian* Frows[37] fell out:
D--m you, says one, *tho' now so Brave,*
I knew you late a Four Years Slave,
What, if for Planter's Wife you go,
Nature design'd you for the Hoe:
Rot you, replies the other streight,
The Captain kiss'd you for his Freight;
And if the Truth was known aright,
And how you walk'd the Streets by Night,
You'd blush, if one could blush for Shame,
Who from Bridewell *and* Newgate *came.*[38]
From Words they fairly fell to Blows,
And being loth to interpose,
Or meddle in the Wars of Punk,[39]
Away to Bed in Haste I slunk:
Waking next Day with aking Head,
And Thirst that made me quit the Bed,
I rigg'd my self and soon got up,
To cool my Liver with a Cup
Of *Succahanah*[40] fresh and clear,
Not half so good as *English* Beer,
Which ready stood in Kitchin Pail,
And was, in Fact, but *Adam's* Ale.

FOR Planters Cellars, you must know,
Seldom with good *October* flow,
But Perry, Quince, and Apple Juice,
Spout from the Tap, like any Sluice,
Until the Cask grows low and stale,
They're forc'd again to Goard[41] and Pail,
The soothing Draught scarce down my Throat,
Enough to set a Ship on float,
With *Cockerouse* as I was sitting
I felt a Fever intermitting,
A fiery Pulse beat in my Veins,
From cold I felt resembling Pains;
This cursed Seasoning I remember,
Lasted from *March* 'till cold *December;*
Nor could it then it's Quarter shift
Until by Cardus[42] turn'd adrift:
And had my Doct'ress wanted Skill,
Or Kitchin-Phisick at her Will,
My Father's Son had left his Lands,
And never seen the *Goodwin Sands:*[43]
But Thanks to *Fortune,* and a Nurse,
Whose Care depended on my Purse,
I saw my self in good Condition,
Without the Help of a Phisician:

37. Obsolete form of "frau," usually a Dutch or German woman.
38. Two English prisons.
39. Punk is slang for prostitute.
40. Native word for water.
41. Gourd.
42. A medicine.
43. Famous sandbars in the English Channel.

At length the shivering Ill reliev'd
My Heart and Head, which long had griev'd.

I then began to think with Care,
How I might sell my *British* Ware;
That with my Freight I might comply,
Did on my Charter-Party lye:
To this Intent, with Guide before,
I tript it to the *Eastern* Shore;
Where riding near a Sandy Bay,
I met a Planter in my Way,
A pious, consciencious Rogue,
As e're wore Bonnet, Hat, or Brogue,
Who neither swore, nor kept his Word,
But cheated in the Fear o' th' Lord;
And when his Debts he could not pay,
From trusting Fools he'd run away.

WITH this sly Zealot, soon I struck
A Bargain, for my *English* Truck,
Agreeing for Ten Thousand Weight
Of *Sotweed* good, and fit for Freight:
Broad *Oronoko*, bright and sound,
The Growth and Product of his Ground;
In Cask, that shou'd contain compleat
Five Hundred of Tobacco neat.

THE Contract thus betwixt us made,
Not well acquainted with the Trade,
My Goods I trusted to the Cheat,
Whose Crop was then o'board the Fleet;
And going to receive my own,
I found the Bird was newly flown.
Cursing this excerable Slave,
This damn'd pretended Godly Knave,
On due Revenge and Justice bent,
I instantly to Council went;
Unto an ambodexter[44] Quack,
Who learnedly had got the Knack
Of giving Clysters,[45] making Pills,
Of filling Bonds, and forging Wills;
And with a Stock of Impudence,
Supply'd his want of Wit and Sence,
With Looks demure, amazing People,
No wiser than a Daw[46] on Steeple:
My Anger flushing in my Face,
I stated the preceedng Case,
And of my Money was so free
That he'd have poison'd you or me,
And hang'd his Father on a Tree,
For such another tempting Fee.

44. Pharmacist.
45. Medicines.
46. A simpleton.

SMILING, said he, the Cause is clear,
I'll manage him, you need not fear,
The Case is judg'd, good Sir, but look
In *Galen*, no, in my Lord *Cook*,[47]
I vow to G-d, I was mistook:
I'll take out a Provincial Writ,
And trownce him for his knavish Wit,
Upon my Life, I'll win the Cause,
With as much Ease I cure the Yaws:[48]
Resolv'd to plague the Holy Brother,
I set one Rogue to catch another.

TO try the Cause then fully bent,
Up to *Annapolis* I went,
A City situate on a Plain,
Where scarce a House will keep out Rain;
The Buildings fram'd with Cypress rare,
Resembles much our *Southwark-Fair;*
But Strangers there will scarcely meet,
With Market Place, Exchange, or Street;
And if the Truth I may report,
It's not so large as *Tottenham-Court*.
St. *Mary's* once was in Repute,
Now Here the Judges try the Suit,
And Lawyers twice a Year dispute.
As oft the Bench most gravely meet,
Some to get drink, and some to eat
A swinging Share of Country Treat:
But as for Justice write or wrong,
Not one amongst the numerous Throng
Knows what it means, or has the Heart,
To vindicate a Stranger's Part.

NOW, Court being call'd by beat of Drum,
The Judges left their Punch and Rum;
When Pettifogging Doctor draws
His Papers forth, and opens Cause;
And lest I should the Better get,
Brib'd Quack suppress'd his knavish Wit:
So Maid upon the downy Field,
Pretends a Rape, and fights to yield:
The byass'd Court without Delay,
Adjudg'd my Debt in Country Pay,
In Pipe Staves, Corn, or Flesh of Boar,
Rare Cargo for the *English* Shore.
Raging with Grief, full Speed I ran,
To join the Fleet at *Kickatan:*

47. Galen was a famous physician in ancient Greece. Sir Edward Cook wrote commentary on law.

48. A skin disease.

And while I waited for a Wind,
This Wish proceeded from my Mind,
IF any Youngster cross the Ocean,
To sell his Wares—may be with Caution
Before he pays, receive each Hogshead,
Lest he be cheated by some Dogshead,
Both of his Goods and his Tobacco;
And then like me, he shall not lack-woe.
AND may that Land where Hospitalit
Is every Planter's darling Quality,
Be by each Trader kindly us'd,
And may no Trader be abus'd;
Then each of them shall deal with Pleasure,
And each encrease the other's Treasure.

Question to Consider

1. Do you believe that *The Sotweed Factor* is designed to satirize both the Colonists and the elitism of the tobacco agent? What passages can you point to in order to support that claim?

William Byrd

1674–1744

William Byrd was born in Virginia on a plantation that had been originally acquired by his great grandfather in 1630. When Byrd reached the age of seven, his father, himself a wealthy planter, trader, and merchant who had added extensively to the family holdings, sent the young boy to be educated in England. He became a lawyer, an amateur scientist, and an urbane and sophisticated English gentleman and man-about-town. Diaries from Byrd's days in England reveal the cool detachment of a classic English wit, and Byrd counted other English sophisticates and writers such as William Congreve and William Wycherley among his friends.

Upon the death of his father in 1705, Byrd returned to Virginia to take over the family businesses and his father's public offices, which included the receiver-generalship of the colony and a seat in the House of Burgesses. In Virginia, he seemed as comfortable in the dirt streets and country pubs as he had in the sophisticated circles of London society. In 1715, he returned to England to serve as agent for the Virginia House of Burgesses for nine years, where he worked to promote the interests of the Burgesses in England. After the death of his wife, Byrd renewed his acquaintance with the high life of London until he remarried in 1724. When he returned to Virginia two years later, he rebuilt his father's estate at Westover on the James River to house what was probably the largest library in colonial America and one of the country's best collections of fine portraiture. He also worked to expand the family holdings to include large tracts of land in the west and helped to found the cities of Richmond and Petersburg. On one expedition he was commissioned to help survey the Southern boundaries of Virginia, which he chronicled in *History of the Dividing Line betwixt Virginia and North Carolina*, his major work.

Byrd never considered himself an author except by avocation, and most of his writings are letters, diaries, journals, a few poems, and various personal musings, some of which are erotic in nature and almost none of which were written for publication. Still, Byrd was a highly literate and careful writer, with a keen sense of irony and satire polished by his days in London. After he settled permanently in Virginia, many of his writings were addressed to correspondents in England and demonstrate an unusual perception of the contrasts between life in America and England at the time. In these letters, he expresses a longing for the sophisticated life of London, even as he remembers it as a place overpopulated by cynics and thieves. He also demonstrates an appreciation of the warmth and natural bounty of the American South, but laments the American tendency to idleness and sloth. In the *History of the Dividing Line*, Byrd turns his ability to develop contrastive satire to such subjects as the differences between the North and the South, the religious and the agnostic, Whites and Native Americans, women and men, men and bears. Like the best English wits of his day, Byrd created an engaging and ironic style that marks him as one of the great men of letters of the colonial South and perhaps its first accomplished humorist. As one who had been privy to the loftiest circles in two very different worlds, he maintained an unusual sense of balance and humor, and one of the enduring themes in all his work is the need for an industrious character, a quality he certainly possessed.

from History of the Dividing Line Betwixt Virginia and North Carolina Run in the Year of Our Lord 1728

October 26th. We found our way grow still more mountainous, after extending the line three hundred poles farther. We came then to a rivulet that ran with a swift current towards the south. This we fancied to be another branch of the Irvin, though some of these men, who had been Indian traders, judged it rather to be the head of Deep River, that discharges its stream into that of Pee Dee, but this seemed a wild conjecture. The hills beyond that river were exceedingly lofty and not to be attempted by our jaded palfreys,1 which could now hardly drag their legs after them upon level ground. Besides, the bread began to grow scanty and the winter season to advance apace upon us. We had likewise reason to apprehend the consequences of being intercepted by deep snows and the swelling of the many waters between us and home. The first of these misfortunes would starve all our horses and the other ourselves, by cutting off our retreat and obliging us to winter in those desolate woods. These considerations determined us to stop short here and push our adventures no farther. The last tree we marked was a red oak growing on the bank of the river; and to make the place more remarkable, we blazed all the trees around it.

We found the whole distance from Currituck Inlet to the rivulet where we left off to be, in a straight line, 240 miles and 230 poles. And from the place where the Carolina commissioners deserted us, 72 miles and 302 poles. This last part of the journey was generally very hilly, or else grown up with troublesome thickets and underwoods, all which our Carolina friends had the discretion to avoid. We encamped in a dirty valley near the rivulet above-mentioned for the advantage of the canes, and so sacrificed our own convenience to that of our horses. There was a small mountain half a mile to the northward of us, which we had the curiosity to climb up in the afternoon in order to enlarge our prospect. From thence we were able to discover where the two ledges of mountains closed, as near as we could guess about thirty miles to the west of us, and lamented that our present circumstances would not permit us to advance the line to that place, which the hand of Nature had made so very remarkable.

1. Riding horses.

Not far from our quarters one of the men picked up a pair of elk's horns, not very large, and discovered the track of the elk that had shed them. It was rare to find any tokens of those animals so far to the south, because they keep commonly to the northward of thirty-seven degrees, as the buffaloes, for the most part, confine themselves to the southward of that latitude. The elk is full as big as a horse and of the deer kind. The stags only have horns and those exceedingly large and spreading. Their color is something lighter than that of the red deer and their flesh tougher. Their swiftest speed is a large trot, and in that motion they turn their horns back upon their necks and cock their noses aloft in the air. Nature has taught them this attitude to save their antlers from being entangled in the thickets, which they always retire to. They are very shy and have the sense of smelling so exquisite that they wind a man at a great distance. For this reason they are seldom seen but when the air is moist, in which case their smell is not so nice. They commonly herd together, and the Indians say if one of the drove happen by some wound to be disabled from making his escape, the rest will forsake their fears to defend their friend, which they will do with great obstinacy till they are killed upon the spot. Though, otherwise, they are so alarmed at the sight of a man that to avoid him they will sometimes throw themselves down very high precipices into the river.

A misadventure happened here which gave us no small perplexity. One of the commissioners was so unlucky as to bruise his foot against a stump, which brought on a formal fit of the gout. It must be owned there could not be a more unseasonable time, nor a more improper situation for any one to be attacked by that cruel distemper. The joint was so inflamed that he could neither draw shoe or boot upon it, and to ride without either would have exposed him to so many rude knocks and bruises in those rough woods as to be intolerable even to a stoic. It was happy indeed that we were to rest here the next day, being Sunday, that there might be leisure for trying some speedy remedy. Accordingly he was persuaded to bathe his foot in cold water in order to repel the humor and assuage the inflammation. This made it less painful and gave us hopes, too, of reducing the swelling in a short time.

Our men had the fortune to kill a brace of bears, a fat buck, and a wild turkey, all which paid them with interest for yesterday's abstinence. This constant and seasonable supply of our daily wants made us reflect thankfully on the bounty of Providence. And that we might not be unmindful of being all along fed by Heaven in this great and solitary wilderness, we agreed to wear in our hats the maosti, which is in Indian the beard of a wild turkey-cock, and on our breasts the figure of that fowl with its wings extended and holding in its claws a scroll with this motto '*Vice coturnicum*,'[2] meaning that we had been supported by them in the wilderness in the room of quails.

27th. This being Sunday we were not wanting in our thanks to Heaven for the constant support and protection we had been favored with. Nor did our chaplain fail to put us in mind of our duty by a sermon proper for the occasion. We ordered a strict inquiry to be made into the quantity of bread we had left and found no more than would subsist us a fortnight at short allowance. We made a fair distribution of our whole stock and at the same time recommended to the men to manage this, their last stake, to the best advantage, not knowing how long they would be obliged to live upon it. We likewise directed them to keep a watchful eye upon their horses, that none of them might be missing the next morning to hinder our return.

There fell some rain before noon, which made our camp more a bog than it was before. This moist situation began to infect some of the men with fevers and

2. Literally "repayed in quails."

some with fluxes, which however we soon removed with Peruvian bark and ipecacuanha.[3]

In the afternoon we marched up again to the top of the hill to entertain our eyes a second time with the view of the mountains, but a perverse fog arose that hid them from our sight. In the evening we deliberated which way it might be most proper to return. We had at first intended to cross over at the foot of the mountains to the head of James River, that we might be able to describe that natural boundary so far. But, on second thoughts, we found many good reasons against that laudable design, such as the weakness of our horses, the scantiness of our bread, and the near approach of winter. We had cause to believe the way might be full of hills, and the farther we went toward the north, the more danger there would be of snow. Such considerations as these determined us at last to make the best of our way back upon the line, which was the straightest, and consequently the shortest way to the inhabitants. We knew the worst of that course and were sure of a beaten path all the way, while we were totally ignorant what difficulties and dangers the other course might be attended with. So prudence got the better for once of curiosity, and the itch for new discoveries gave place to self-preservation.

Our inclination was the stronger to cross over according to the course of the mountains, that we might find out whether James River and Appomattox River head there, or run quite through them. 'Tis certain that Potomac passes in a large stream through the main ledge and then divides itself into two considerable rivers. That which stretches away to the northward is called Cohungaroota,[4] and that which flows to the southwest hath the name of Sharantow. The course of this last stream is near parallel to the Blue Ridge of mountains, at the distance only of about three or four miles. Though how far it may continue that course has not yet been sufficiently discovered, but some woodsmen pretend to say it runs as far as the source of Roanoke; nay, they are so very particular as to tell us that Roanoke, Sharantow, and another wide branch of Mississippi all head in one and the same mountain. What dependence there may be upon this conjectural geography, I won't pretend to say, though 'tis certain that Sharantow keeps close to the mountains, as far as we are acquainted with its tendency. We are likewise assured that the south branch of James River, within less than twenty miles east of the main ledge, makes an elbow and runs due southwest, which is parallel with the mountains on this side. But how far it stretches that way before it returns is not yet certainly known, no more than where it takes its rise.

In the meantime it is strange that our woodsmen have not had curiosity enough to inform themselves more exactly of these particulars, and it is stranger still that the government has never thought it worth the expense of making an accurate survey of the mountains, that we might be masters of that natural fortification before the French, who in some places have settlements not very distant from it. It therefore concerns His Majesty's service very nearly and the safety of his subjects in this part of the world, to take possession of so important a barrier in time, lest our good friends, the French, and the Indians through their means, prove a perpetual annoyance to these colonies. Another reason to invite us to secure this great ledge of mountains is the probability that very valuable mines may be discovered there. Nor would it be at all extravagant to hope for silver mines among the rest, because part of these mountains lie exactly in the same parallel, as well as upon the same continent with New Mexico and the mines of St. Barb.

3. An herb that produces vomiting.

4. Which by a late survey has been found to extend above two hundred miles before it reaches its source, in a mountain, from whence Allegany, one of the branches of the Mississippi, takes it rise, and runs south west, as this river does south east (author's note).

28th. We had given orders for the horses to be brought up early, but the likelihood of more rain prevented our being overhasty in decamping. Nor were we out in our conjectures, for about ten o'clock it began to fall very plentifully. Our commissioner's pain began now to abate as the swelling increased. He made an excellent figure for a mountaineer, with one boot of leather and the other of flannel. Thus accoutered he intended to mount, if the rain had not happened opportunely to prevent him. Though, in truth, it was hardly possible for him to ride with so slender a defence without exposing his foot to be bruised and tormented by the saplings that stood thick on either side of the path. It was therefore a most seasonable rain for him, as it gave more time for his distemper to abate.

Though it may be very difficult to find a certain cure for the gout, yet it is not improbable but some things may ease the pain and shorten the fits of it. And those medicines are most likely to do this that supple the parts and clear the passage through the narrow vessels that are the seat of this cruel disease. Nothing will do this more suddenly than rattlesnake's oil, which will even penetrate the pores of glass when warmed in the sun. It was unfortunate, therefore, that we had not taken out the fat of those snakes we had killed some time before for the benefit of so useful an experiment as well as for the relief of our fellow traveller. But lately the Seneca rattlesnake root has been discovered in this country, which, being infused in wine, and drank morning and evening, has in several instances had a very happy effect upon the gout, and enabled cripples to throw away their crutches and walk several miles, and, what is stranger still, it takes away the pain in half an hour.

Nor was the gout the only disease amongst us that was hard to cure. We had a man in our company who had too voracious a stomach for a woodsman. He ate as much as any other two, but all he swallowed stuck by him till it was carried off by a strong purge. Without this assistance, often repeated, his belly and bowels would swell to so enormous a bulk that he could hardly breathe, especially when he lay down, just as if he had had an asthma; though, notwithstanding this oddness of constitution, he was a very strong, lively fellow and used abundance of violent exercise, by which 'twas wonderful the peristaltic motion was not more vigorously promoted. We gave this poor man several purges, which only eased him for the present, and the next day he would grow as burly as ever. At last we gave him a moderate dose of ipecacuanha, in broth made very salt, which turned all its operation downwards. This had so happy an effect that from that day forward to the end of our journey all his complaints ceased and the passages continued unobstructed.

The rain continued most of the day and some part of the night, which incommoded us much in our dirty camp and made the men think of nothing but eating, even at the time when nobody could stir out to make provision for it.

29th. Though we were flattered in the morning with the usual tokens of a fair day, yet they all blew over, and it rained hard before we could make ready for our departure. This was still in favor of our podagrous friend, whose lameness was now grown better and the inflammation fallen. Nor did it seem to need above one day more to reduce it to its natural proportion and make it fit for the boot; and effectually the rain procured this benefit for him and gave him particular reason to believe his stars propitious.

Notwithstanding the falling weather, our hunters sallied out in the afternoon and drove the woods in a ring, which was thus performed: from the circumference of a large circle they all marched inward and drove the game toward the center. By this means they shot a brace of fat bears, which came very seasonably, because we had made clean work in the morning and were in danger of dining with St. Anthony, or

His Grace Duke Humphry.[5] But in this expedition the unhappy man who had lost himself once before straggled again so far in pursuit of a deer that he was hurried a second time quite out of his knowledge; and, night coming on before he could recover the camp, he was obliged to lie down without any of the comforts of fire, food, or covering; nor would his fears suffer him to sleep very sound, because, to his great disturbance, the wolves howled all that night, and the panthers screamed most frightfully.

In the evening a brisk northwester swept all the clouds from the sky and exposed the mountains as well as the stars to our prospect. That which was the most lofty to the southward and which we called the Lover's Leap, some of our Indian traders fondly fancied was the Kiawan Mountain, which they had formerly seen from the country of the Cherokees. They were the more positive by reason of the prodigious precipice that remarkably distinguished the west end of it. We seemed however not to be far enough south for that, though 'tis not improbable but a few miles farther the course of our line might carry us to the most northerly towns of the Cherokees. What makes this the more credible is the northwest course that our traders take from the Catawbas for some hundred miles together, when they carry goods that round-about way to the Cherokees.

It was a great pity that the want of bread and the weakness of our horses hindered us from making the discovery. Though the great service such an excursion might have been to the country would certainly have made the attempt not only pardonable but much to be commended. Our traders are now at the vast charge and fatigue of traveling above five hundred miles for the benefit of that traffic which hardly quits cost. Would it not then be worth the Assembly's while to be at some charge to find a shorter cut to carry on so profitable a trade, with more advantage and less hazard and trouble than they do at present? For I am persuaded it will not then be half the distance that our traders make it now nor half so far as Georgia lies from the northern clans of that nation. Such a discovery would certainly prove an unspeakable advantage to this colony by facilitating a trade with so considerable a nation of Indians, which have sixty-two towns and more than four thousand fighting men. Our traders at that rate would be able to undersell those sent from the other colonies so much that the Indians must have reason to deal with them preferably to all others. Of late the new colony of Georgia has made an act obliging us to go four hundred miles to take out a license to traffic with these Cherokees, though many of their towns lie out of their bounds and we had carried on this trade eighty years before that colony was thought of.

30th. In the morning early the man who had gone astray the day before found his way to the camp by the sound of the bells that were upon the horses' necks.

At nine o'clock we began our march back toward the rising sun, for though we had finished the line yet we had not yet near finished our fatigue. We had, after all, two hundred good miles at least to our several habitations, and the horses were brought so low that we were obliged to travel on foot great part of the way, and that in our boots, too, to save our legs from being torn to pieces by the bushes and briers. Had we not done this, we must have left all our horses behind, which could now hardly drag their legs after them; and with all the favor we could show the poor animals we were forced to set seven of them free not far from the foot of the mountains.

Four men were dispatched early to clear the road, that our lame commissioner's leg might be in less danger of being bruised and that the baggage horses might travel with less difficulty and more expedition. As we passed along, by favor of a serene sky

5. They were in danger of dying.

we had still from every eminence a perfect view of the mountains, as well to the north as to the south. We could not forbear now and then facing about to survey them, as if unwilling to part with a prospect which at the same time, like some rakes, was very wild and very agreeable. We encouraged the horses to exert the little strength they had and, being light, they made a shift to jog on about eleven miles.

We encamped on Crooked Creek near a thicket of canes. In the front of our camp rose a very beautiful hill that bounded our view at about a mile's distance, and all the intermediate space was covered with green canes. Though to our sorrow, firewood was scarce, which was now the harder upon us because a northwester blew very cold from the mountains.

The Indian killed a stately, fat buck, and we picked his bones as clean as a score of turkey buzzards could have done. By the advantage of a clear night, we made trial once more of the variation and found it much the same as formerly. This being His Majesty's birthday, we drank all the loyal healths in excellent water, not for the sake of the drink (like many of our fellow subjects) but purely for the sake of the toast. And because all public mirth should be a little noisy, we fired several volleys of canes, instead of guns, which gave a loud report. We threw them into the fire, where the air enclosed betwixt the joints of the canes, being expanded by the violent heat, burst its narrow bounds with a considerable explosion.

In the evening one of the men knocked down an opossum, which is a harmless little beast that will seldom go out of your way, and if you take hold of it will only grin and hardly ever bite. The flesh was well tasted and tender, approaching nearest to pig, which it also resembled in bigness. The color of its fur was a goose gray, with a swine's snout and a tail like a rat, but at least a foot long. By twisting this tail about the arm of a tree, it will hang with all its weight and swing to anything it wants to take hold of. It has five claws on the fore feet of equal length, but the hinder feet have only four claws and a sort of thumb standing off at a proper distance. Their feet being thus formed, qualify them for climbing up trees to catch little birds, which they are very fond of. But the greatest particularity of this creature, and which distinguishes it from most others that we are acquainted with, is the false belly of the female, into which her young retreat in time of danger. She can draw the slit, which is the inlet into this pouch, so close that you must look narrowly to find it, especially if she happen to be a virgin. Within the false belly may be seen seven or eight teats, on which the young ones grow from their first formation till they are big enough to fall off like ripe fruit from a tree. This is so odd a method of generation that I should not have believed it without the testimony of mine own eyes. Besides, a knowing and credible person has assured me he has more than once observed the embryo opossums growing to the teat before they were completely shaped, and afterwards watched their daily growth till they were big enough for birth. And all this he could the more easily pry into because the dam was so perfectly gentle and harmless that he could handle her just as he pleased.

I could hardly persuade myself to publish a thing so contrary to the course that nature takes in the production of other animals unless it were a matter commonly believed in all countries where that creature is produced and has been often observed by persons of undoubted credit and understanding. They say that the leather-winged bats produce their young in the same uncommon manner; and that young sharks at sea and young vipers ashore run down the throats of their dams when they are closely pursued.

The frequent crossing of Crooked Creek and mounting the steep banks of it gave the finishing stroke to the foundering our horses, and no less than two of them made a full stop here and would not advance a foot farther, either by fair means or foul. We had a dreamer of dreams amongst us who warned me in the morning to take care of myself or I should infallibly fall into the creek; I thanked him kindly and used what caution I could but was not able, it seems, to avoid my destiny, for my horse made a false step and laid me down at my full length in the water. This was enough to bring dreaming into credit, and I think it much for the honor of our expedition that it was graced not only with a priest but also with a prophet. We were so perplexed with this serpentine creek, as well as in passing the branches of the Irvin, which were swelled since we saw them before, that we could reach but five miles this whole day.

In the evening we pitched our tent near Miry Creek, though an uncomfortable place to lodge in, purely for the advantage of the canes. Our hunters killed a large doe and two bears, which made all other misfortunes easy. Certainly no Tartar ever loved horseflesh nor Hottentot guts and garbage better than woodsmen do bear. The truth of it is, it may be proper food perhaps for such as work or ride it off, but, with our chaplain's leave, who loved it much, I think it not a very proper diet for saints, because 'tis apt to make them a little too rampant. And, now, for the good of mankind and for the better peopling an infant colony, which has no want but that of inhabitants, I will venture to publish a secret of importance which our Indian disclosed to me. I asked him the reason why few or none of his countrywomen were barren. To which curious question he answered, with a broad grin upon his face, they had an infallible secret for that. Upon my being importunate to know what the secret might be, he informed me that if any Indian woman did not prove with child at a decent time after marriage, the husband, to save his reputation with the women, forthwith entered into a bear diet for six weeks, which in that time makes him so vigorous that he grows exceedingly impertinent to his poor wife, and 'tis great odds but he makes her a mother in nine months. And thus much I am able to say besides for the reputation of the bear diet, that all the married men of our company were joyful fathers within forty weeks after they got home, and most of the single men had children sworn to them within the same time, our chaplain always excepted, who, with much ado, made a shift to cast out that importunate kind of devil by dint of fasting and prayer.

Questions to Consider

1. What can you tell about William Byrd's views on religion from reading his work?
2. Byrd was well-known for his wit, which may seem remarkably absent from the selection until you look a bit closer. Where do you see signs of Byrd's sense of irony and humor?

Thomas Jefferson

1743–1826

In his epitaph, which he composed himself, Thomas Jefferson wrote that he wished to be remembered as "Author of the Declaration of American Independence, of the Statute of Virginia for Religious Freedom, and Father of the University of Virginia." The list is indicative of Jefferson's life filled with accomplishments and his lifelong concern for the future of the nation, for the place of the state within that future, and for the future of the men and women who would become Americans.

Jefferson is justified in listing his authorship of the Declaration of Independence as his greatest achievement. When the Continental Congress conceived of the Declaration, its members naturally called upon Jefferson to be its writer, as Jefferson's eloquent voice had already addressed the subject in *A Summary View of the Rights of British America*, a document he wrote as a member of the Virginia House of Burgesses in 1775. As the author of the original draft of the Declaration, Jefferson was able to give a larger voice to the ideas that he had first offered in *A Summary View:* a belief in the natural rights of humans, an assertion of self-determination for the nation, and an insistence that government reflect the will of the governed.

In the *Virginia Statute for Religious Freedom*, which he ranked as his second greatest accomplishment, Jefferson sought both to support the individual's quest for personal truth and, more importantly, to limit the state's power to direct that quest. As he asserted the right of America to be free of the tyranny of British rule in the Declaration, so Jefferson asserted the right of the individual to be free of state-sponsored religion in the *Virginia Statute*. In the last item of Jefferson's epitaph, "founder of the University of Virginia," we see the breadth of both his thought and his activity. He was, quite literally, the architect of the University, designing its curricular plan and many of its major buildings, just as he had designed his home in Monticello, the Virginia Capital, and part of the city of Washington, D.C. Appropriately, the University became his primary interest after he left the presidency, for throughout his life, he had been a student of philosophy, law, science, religion, agriculture, education, architecture, art, and government, and his vision of a modern, comprehensive university became the standard for early American education.

Jefferson was born in Virginia in 1743, and although his words and ideas have become part of the national makeup, he was also a loyal Virginian and a Southerner, and many of the ideas he brought to the nation have their roots in his Southern upbringing. His vision for an America that was largely agrarian was a distinctly Southern vision, and his belief in radical self-determination for the nation, for the state, and for the individual can be traced to the first English settlers at Jamestown, who had come ashore close to where Jefferson himself was born.

As a young man, Jefferson studied law at the College of William and Mary and practiced at the bar for a few years until he entered the Virginia House of Burgesses in 1769. He identified immediately with the strong anti-British forces in the House and distinguished himself by authoring *A Summary View*. Jefferson was selected as a delegate to the Continental Congress of 1776, and was asked, with Benjamin Franklin and John Adams, to produce the first draft of the Declaration of Independence. Adams and Franklin allowed Jefferson to write the first draft alone, which he based in part on John Locke's philosophy of human rights and which he presented to the Congress with just a few changes by Franklin and Adams. Jefferson originally included language in the Declaration that would have extended liberty to slaves, but the Congress decided against addressing the question of slavery in the document. Jefferson himself held slaves, but opposed slavery in the abstract. This inability to reconcile ideals and actions has been judged as hypocritical by today's standards; still, Jefferson believed that Black slaves would, and should, eventually be emancipated.

Back in the Virginia House, Jefferson worked to loosen the hold of the land-holding aristocracy by promoting legislation to abolish unfair inheritance laws. He also introduced a bill to establish religious freedom and worked to broaden education in the state. He was elected governor of Virginia during the Revolutionary War but resigned when he was criticized for not adequately preparing the state for the British invasion. Jefferson determined to withdraw from public life and retired to Monticello, where he finished work on *Notes on the State of Virginia* (1784).

Jefferson's retirement came to an end in 1783, when he was elected to Congress. He worked tirelessly in his six months as a legislator, introducing over thirty opinion papers and plans. In 1784, he replaced Franklin as Minister to France, where he witnessed the beginnings of the French Revolution. When he returned to America, Jefferson helped to facilitate the adoption of the Bill of Rights and was appointed the first Secretary of State during the presidency of George Washington. With the rise of the Federalists under the leadership of Alexander Hamilton, who saw America's future in industry and increased federal control of trade and money, Jefferson was again stirred politically. He became the *de facto* head of the Republican Party (later the Democratic Party), which opposed Hamilton's policies. Jefferson resigned his position as Secretary of State in 1793 and was determined to retire from public life again. The Republican Party asked Jefferson to run for president, however, and he did not object. He lost the race to John Adams, but under election rules of the time, he became vice president. Jefferson ran for president again in 1800, and when he tied with Aaron Burr he was selected by the House of Representatives to take the office.

One of Jefferson's greatest achievements as the third president was the negotiation of the Louisiana Purchase in 1803, which increased American territory by 800,000 acres and gave America final control of the Mississippi River. Jefferson was re-elected in 1804, but his second term was troubled when his attempts to keep America out of the war between Britain and France led to a very unpopular trade embargo.

Forty years after he entered government service, Jefferson finally retired from public office at the end of his presidency. He returned to Monticello, where he experimented with new farming techniques and worked on the design for the University of Virginia, which was opened shortly before his death on 4 July 1826—just hours before his long-time colleague and sometime adversary, John Adams, passed away. Each lived to see the fiftieth anniversary of the signing of the Declaration, their mutual final goal. Throughout his life, Jefferson amassed an amazing body of writing, consisting primarily of his political papers and pamphlets, over 25,000 letters, and *Notes on the State of Virginia*.

from Autobiography

Congress proceeded the same day to consider the declaration of Independance which had been reported & lain on the table the Friday preceding, and on Monday referred to a committee of the whole. The pusillanimous idea that we had friends in England worth keeping terms with, still haunted the minds of many. For this reason those passages which conveyed censures on the people of England were struck out, lest they should give them offence. The clause too, reprobating the enslaving the inhabitants of Africa, was struck out in complaisance to South Carolina and Georgia, who had never attempted to restrain the importation of slaves, and who on the contrary still wished to continue it. Our Northern brethren also I believe felt a little tender under those censures; for tho' their people have very few slaves themselves yet they had been pretty considerable carriers of them to others. The debates having taken up the greater parts of the 2d 3d & 4th days of July were, in the evening of the last, closed the declaration was reported by the commee, agreed to by the house and signed by every member present except Mr. Dickinson. As the sentiments of men are known not only by what they receive, but what they reject also, I will state the form of the declaration as originally reported. The parts struck out by Congress shall be distinguished by a Black line drawn under them; & those inserted by them shall be placed in the margin or in a concurrent column.

A Declaration by the Representatives of the United States of America, in General Congress Assembled

When in the course of human events it becomes necessary for one people to dissolve the political bands which have connected them with another, and to assume among the powers of the earth the separate & equal station to which the laws of nature and of nature's God entitle them, a decent respect to the opinions of mankind requires that they should declare the causes which impel them to the separation.

We hold these truths to be self-evident: that all men are created equal; that they are endowed by their creator with inherent and inalienable rights; that certain among these are life, liberty, & the pursuit of happiness: that to secure these rights, governments are instituted among men, deriving their just powers from the consent of the governed; that whenever any form of government becomes destructive of these ends, it is the right of the people to alter or abolish it, & to institute new government, laying its foundation on such principles, & organizing its powers in such form, as to them shall seem most likely to effect their safety & happiness. Prudence indeed will dictate that governments long established should not be changed for light & transient causes; and accordingly all experience hath shown that mankind are more disposed to suffer while evils are sufferable, than to right themselves by abolishing the forms to which they are accustomed. But when a long train of abuses & usurpations begun at a distinguished period and pursuing invariably the same object, evinces a design to reduce them under absolute despotism, it is their right, it is their duty to throw off such government, & to provide new guards for their future security. Such has been the patient sufferance of these colonies; & such is now the necessity which constrains them to expunge their former systems of government. The alter history of the present king of Great Britain[1] is a history of unremitting in- repeated juries & usurpations, among which appears no solitary fact to contradict the uniform tenor of the rest but all have in direct object the establishment of an absolute all having tyranny over these states. To prove this let facts be submitted to a candid world for the truth of which we pledge a faith yet unsullied by falsehood.

He has refused his assent to laws the most wholesome & necessary for the public good.

He has forbidden his governors to pass laws of immediate & pressing importance, unless suspended in their operation till his assent should be obtained; & when so suspended, he has utterly neglected to attend to them.

He has refused to pass other laws for the accommodation of large districts of people, unless those people would relinquish the right of representation in the legislature, a right inestimable to them, & formidable to tyrants only.

He has called together legislative bodies at places unusual, uncomfortable, and distant from the depository of their public records, for the sole purpose of fatiguing them into compliance with his measures.

He has dissolved representative houses repeatedly & continually for opposing with manly firmness his invasions on the rights of the people.

He has refused for a long time after such dissolutions to cause others to be elected, whereby the legislative powers, incapable of annihilation, have returned to the people at large for their exercise, the state remaining in the meantime exposed to all the dangers of invasion from without & convulsions within.

He has endeavored to prevent the population of these states; for that purpose obstructing the laws for naturalization of foreigners, refusing to pass others to encourage their migrations hither, & raising the conditions of new appropriations of lands.

He has suffered the administration of justice totally to cease in some obstructed by of these states refusing his assent to laws for establishing judiciary powers.

1. King George III.

He has made our judges dependant on his will alone, for the tenure of their offices, & the amount & paiment of their salaries.

He has erected a multitude of new offices by a self assumed power and sent hither swarms of new officers to harass our people and eat out their substance.

He has kept among us in times of peace standing armies and ships of war without the consent of our legislatures.

He has affected to render the military independant of, & superior to the civil power.

He has combined with others to subject us to a jurisdiction foreign to our constitutions & unacknowledged by our laws, giving his assent to their acts of pretended legislation for quartering large bodies of armed troops among us; for protecting them by a mock-trial from punishment for any murders which they should commit on the inhabitants of these states; for cutting off our trade with all parts of

in many cases

the world; for imposing taxes on us without our consent; for depriving us [ ] of the benefits of trial by jury; for transporting us beyond seas to be tried for pretended offences; for abolishing the free system of English laws in a neighboring province, establishing therein an arbitrary government, and enlarging its boundaries, so as to render it at once an example and fit instrument for introducing the

colonies

same absolute rule into these states; for taking away our charters, abolishing our most valuable laws, and altering fundamentally the forms of our governments; for suspending our own legislatures, & declaring themselves invested with power to legislate for us in all cases whatsoever.

by declaring us out of his protection, and waging war against us.

He has abdicated government here withdrawing his governors, and declaring us out of his allegiance & protection.

He has plundered our seas, ravaged our coasts, burnt our towns, & destroyed the lives of our people.

scarcely paralleled in the most barbarous ages, & totally

He is at this time transporting large armies of foreign mercenaries to compleat the works of death, desolation & tyranny already begun with circumstances of cruelty and perfidy [ ] unworthy the head of a civilized nation.

He has constrained our fellow citizens taken captive on the high seas to bear arms against their country, to become the executioners of their friends & brethren, or to fall themselves by their hands.

excited domestic insurrection among us, & has

He has [ ] endeavored to bring on the inhabitants of our frontiers the merciless Indian savages, whose known rule of warfare is an undistinguished destruction of all ages, sexes, & conditions of existence.

He has incited treasonable insurrections of our fellow-citizens, with the allurements of forfeiture & confiscation of our property.

He has waged cruel war against human nature itself, violating its most sacred rights of life and liberty in the persons of a distant people who never offended him, captivating & carrying them into slavery in another hemisphere, or to incur miserable death in their transportation thither. This piratical warfare, the opprobium of INFIDEL powers, is the warfare of the CHRISTIAN king of Great Britain. Determined to keep open a market where MEN should be bought & sold, he has prostituted his negative for suppressing every legislative attempt to prohibit or to restrain this execrable commerce. And that this assemblage of horrors might want no fact of distinguished die, he is now exciting those very people to rise in arms among us, and to purchase that liberty of which he has deprived them, by murdering the people on whom he also obtruded them: thus paying off former crimes committed against the LIBERTIES of one people, with crimes which he urges them to commit against the LIVES of another.

In every stage of these oppressions we have petitioned for redress in the most humble terms: our repeated petitions have been answered only by repeated injuries.

A prince whose character is thus marked by every act which may define a tyrant is unfit to be the ruler of a [ ] people who mean to be free. Future ages will scarcely believe that the hardiness of one man adventured, within the short compass of twelve years only, to lay a foundation so broad & so undisguised for tyranny over a people fostered & fixed in principles of freedom.

free

Nor have we been wanting in attentions to our British brethren. We have warned them from time to time of attempts by their legislature to extend a jurisdiction over these our states. We have reminded them of the circumstances of our emigration & settlement here, no one of which could warrant so strange a pretension: that these were effected at the expense of our own blood & treasure, unassisted by the wealth or the strength of Great Britain: that in constituting indeed our several forms of government, we had adopted one common king, thereby laying a foundation for perpetual league & amity with them: but that submission to their parliament was no part of our constitution, nor ever in idea, if history may be credited: and, we [ ] appealed to their native justice and magnanimity as well as to the ties of our common kindred to disavow these usurpations which were likely to interrupt our connection and correspondence. They too have been deaf to the voice of justice & of consanguinity, and when occasions have been given them, by the regular course of their laws, of removing from their councils the disturbers of our harmony, they have, by their free election, re-established them in power. At this very time too they are permitting their chief magistrate to send over not only soldiers of our common blood, but Scotch & foreign mercenaries to invade & destroy us. These facts have given the last stab to agonizing affection, and manly spirit bids us to renounce forever these unfeeling brethren. We must endeavor to forget our former love for them, and hold them as we hold the rest of mankind, enemies in war, in peace friends. We might have been a free and a great people together; but a communication of grandeur & of freedom it seems is below their dignity. Be it so, since they will have it. The road to happiness & to glory is open to us too. We will tread it apart from them, and acquiesce in the necessity which denounces our eternal separation [ ]!

an unwarrantable

us

have

and we have conjured them by

would inevitably

We must therefore

and hold them as we hold the rest of mankind, enemies in war, in peace, friends.

We therefore the representatives of the United States of America in General Congress assembled do in the name & by authority of the good people of these states reject & renounce all allegiance & subjection to the kings of Great Britain & all others who may hereafter claim by, through or under them: we utterly dissolve all political connection which may heretofore have subsisted between us & the people or parliament of Great Britain: & finally we do assert & declare these colonies to be free & independent states, & that as free & independent states, they have full power to levy war, conclude peace, contract alliances,

We therefore the representatives of the United States of America in General Congress assembled, appealing to the supreme judge of the world for the rectitude of our intentions, do in the name, & by the authority of the good people of these colonies, solemnly publish & declare that these united colonies are & of right ought to be free & independent states; that they are absolved from all allegiance to the British crown, and that all political connection between them & the state of Great Britain is, & ought to be, totally dissolved; & that as free & independent states they have full power to levy war, conclude peace, contract

establish commerce, & to do all other acts & things which independent states may of right do.	alliances, establish commerce & to do all other acts & things which independant states may of right do.
And for the support of this declaration we mutually pledge to each other our lives, our fortunes, & our sacred honor.	And for the support of this declaration, with a firm reliance on the protection of divine providence we mutually pledge to each other our lives, our fortunes, & our sacred honor.

The Declaration thus signed on the 4th, on paper was engrossed on parchment, & signed again on the 2d. of August.

from Notes on the State of Virginia

Query XIV: Laws

Many of the laws which were in force during the monarchy being relative merely to that form of government, or inculcating principles inconsistent with republicanism, the first assembly which met after the establishment of the commonwealth appointed a committee to revise the whole code, to reduce it into proper form and volume, and report it to the assembly. This work has been executed by three gentlemen, and reported; but probably will not be taken up till a restoration of peace shall leave to the legislature leisure to go through such a work.

The plan of the revisal was this. The common law of England, by which is meant, that part of the English law which was anterior to the date of the oldest statutes extant, is made the basis of the work. It was thought dangerous to attempt to reduce it to a text: it was therefore left to be collected from the usual monuments of it. Necessary alterations in that, and so much of the whole body of the British statutes, and of acts of assembly, as were thought proper to be retained, were digested into 126 new acts, in which simplicity of stile was aimed at, as far as was safe. The following are the most remarkable alterations proposed:

To change the rules of descent, so as that the lands of any person dying intestate shall be divisible equally among all his children, or other representatives, in equal degree.

To make slaves distributable among the next of kin, as other moveables.

To have all public expences, whether of the general treasury, or of a parish or county, (as for the maintenance of the poor, building bridges, court-houses, &c.) supplied by assessments on the citizens, in proportion to their property.

To hire undertakers for keeping the public roads in repair, and indemnify individuals through whose lands new roads shall be opened.

To define with precision the rules whereby aliens should become citizens, and citizens make themselves aliens.

To establish religious freedom on the broadest bottom.

To emancipate all slaves born after passing the act. The bill reported by the revisors does not itself contain this proposition; but an amendment containing it was prepared, to be offered to the legislature whenever the bill should be taken up, and further directing, that they should continue with their parents to a certain age, then be brought up, at the public expence, to tillage, arts or sciences, according to their geniusses, till the females should be eighteen, and the males twenty-one years of age, when they should be colonized to such place as the circumstances of the time should render most proper, sending them out with arms, implements of household and of the handicraft arts, feeds, pairs of the useful domestic animals, &c. to declare them a free and independant people, and extend to them our alliance and protection, till they shall have acquired strength; and to send vessels at the same time to other parts of the world for an equal number of White inhabitants; to induce whom to migrate hither, proper encouragements were to be proposed. It will probably be asked, Why not retain and incorporate the Blacks into the state, and thus save the expence of supplying, by importation of White settlers, the vacancies they will leave? Deep rooted prejudices entertained by the Whites; ten thousand recollections, by the Blacks, of the injuries they have sustained; new provocations; the real distinctions which nature has made; and many other circumstances, will divide us into parties, and produce convulsions which will probably never end but in the extermination of the one or the other race.—To these objections, which are political, may be added others, which are physical and moral. The first difference which strikes us is that of colour. Whether the black of the negro resides in the reticular membrane between the skin and scarf-skin,[1] or in the scarf-skin itself; whether it proceeds from the colour of the blood, the colour of the bile, or from that of some other secretion, the difference is fixed in nature, and is as real as if its seat and cause were better known to us. And is this difference of no importance? Is it not the foundation of a greater or less share of beauty in the two races? Are not the fine mixtures of red and white, the expressions of every passion by greater or less suffusions of colour in the one, preferable to that eternal monotony, which reigns in the countenances, that immoveable veil of black which covers all the emotions of the other race? Add to these, flowing hair, a more elegant symmetry of form, their own judgment in favour of the Whites, declared by their preference of them, as uniformly as is the preference of the Oranootan[2] for the Black women over those of his own species. The circumstance of superior beauty, is thought worthy attention in the propagation of our horses, dogs, and other domestic animals; why not in that of man? Besides those of colour, figure, and hair, there are other physical distinctions proving a difference of race. They have less hair on the face and body. They secrete less by the kidnies, and more by the glands of the skin, which gives them a very strong and disagreeable odour. This greater degree of transpiration renders them more tolerant of heat, and less so of cold, than the Whites. Perhaps too a difference of structure in the pulmonary apparatus, which a late ingenious experimentalist[3] has discovered to be the principal regulator of animal heat, may have disabled them from extricating, in the act of inspiration, so much of that fluid from the outer air, or obliged them in expiration, to part with more of it. They seem to require less sleep. A Black, after hard labour through the day, will be induced by the slightest amusements to sit up till midnight, or later, though knowing he must be out with the first dawn of the morning. They are at least as brave, and more adventuresome. But this may perhaps proceed from a want of forethought, which prevents their seeing a danger till it be present. When present, they do not go through it with more coolness or steadiness than the Whites. They are

1. The outer-most layer of skin.
2. Orangutan.
3. Crawford (author's note).

more ardent after their female: but love seems with them to be more an eager desire, than a tender delicate mixture of sentiment and sensation. Their griefs are transient. Those numberless afflictions, which render it doubtful whether heaven has given life to us in mercy or in wrath, are less felt, and sooner forgotten with them. In general, their existence appears to participate more of sensation than reflection. To this must be ascribed their disposition to sleep when abstracted from their diversions, and unemployed in labour. An animal whose body is at rest, and who does not reflect, must be disposed to sleep of course. Comparing them by their faculties of memory, reason, and imagination, it appears to me, that in memory they are equal to the Whites; in reason much inferior, as I think one could scarcely be found capable of tracing and comprehending the investigations of Euclid;[4] and that in imagination they are dull, tasteless, and anomalous. It would be unfair to follow them to Africa for this investigation. We will consider them here, on the same stage with the Whites, and where the facts are not apocryphal on which a judgment is to be formed. It will be right to make great allowances for the difference of condition, of education, of conversation, of the sphere in which they move. Many millions of them have been brought to, and born in America. Most of them indeed have been confined to tillage, to their own homes, and their own society: yet many have been so situated, that they might have availed themselves of the conversation of their masters; many have been brought up to the handicraft arts, and from that circumstance have always been associated with the Whites. Some have been liberally educated, and all have lived in countries where the arts and sciences are cultivated to a considerable degree, and have had before their eyes samples of the best works from abroad. The Indians, with no advantages of this kind, will often carve figures on their pipes not destitute of design and merit. They will crayon out an animal, a plant, or a country, so as to prove the existence of a germ in their minds which only wants cultivation. They astonish you with strokes of the most sublime oratory; such as prove their reason and sentiment strong, their imagination glowing and elevated. But never yet could I find that a Black had uttered a thought above the level of plain narration; never see even an elementary trait of painting or sculpture. In music they are more generally gifted than the Whites with accurate ears for tune and time, and they have been found capable of imagining a small catch.[5] Whether they will be equal to the composition of a more extensive run of melody, or of complicated harmony, is yet to be proved. Misery is often the parent of the most affecting touches in poetry.—Among the Blacks is misery enough, God knows, but no poetry. Love is the peculiar œstrum[6] of the poet. Their love is ardent, but it kindles the senses only, not the imagination. Religion indeed has produced a Phyllis Whately;[7] but it could not produce a poet. The compositions published under her name are below the dignity of criticism. The heroes of the Dunciad[8] are to her, as Hercules to the author of that poem. Ignatius Sancho[9] has approached nearer to merit in composition; yet his letters do more honour to

4. Euclid of Alexandria (circa 325–265 B.C.) was a mathematician who wrote *The Elements*, and developed what is today known as Euclidean geometry.
5. The instrument proper to them is the Banjar, which they brought hither from Africa, and which is the original of the guitar, its chords being precisely the four lower chords of the guitar (author's note).
6. State of being where a female of any species is in heat.
7. Phyllis Wheatley (1753–1784) was an African-American poet who is most notably responsible for helping to start the Black American and Black woman's literary tradition.
8. A collection of four books that Alexander Pope wrote during the last fifteen years of his life.
9. Ignatius Sancho was an African slave who grew up around London and composed music and wrote many letters.

the heart than the head. They breathe the purest effusions of friendship and general philanthropy, and shew how great a degree of the latter may be compounded with strong religious zeal. He is often happy in the turn of his compliments, and his stile is easy and familiar, except when he affects a Shandean[10] fabrication of words. But his imagination is wild and extravagant, escapes incessantly from every restraint of reason and taste, and, in the course of its vagaries, leaves a tract of thought as incoherent and eccentric, as is the course of a meteor through the sky. His subjects should often have led him to a process of sober reasoning: yet we find him always substituting sentiment for demonstration. Upon the whole, though we admit him to the first place among those of his own colour who have presented themselves to the public judgment, yet when we compare him with the writers of the race among whom he lived, and particularly with the epistolary class, in which he has taken his own stand, we are compelled to enroll him at the bottom of the column. This criticism supposes the letters published under his name to be genuine, and to have received amendment from no other hand; points which would not be of easy investigation. The improvement of the Blacks in body and mind, in the first instance of their mixture with the Whites, has been observed by every one, and proves that their inferiority is not the effect merely of their condition of life. We know that among the Romans, about the Augustan age especially, the condition of their slaves was much more deplorable than that of the Blacks on the continent of America. The two sexes were confined in separate apartments, because to raise a child cost the master more than to buy one. Cato,[11] for a very restricted indulgence to his slaves in this particular, took from them a certain price. But in this country the slaves multiply as fast as the free inhabitants. Their situation and manners place the commerce between the two sexes almost without restraint.—The same Cato, on a principle of œconomy, always sold his sick and superannuated slaves. He gives it as a standing precept to a master visiting his farm, to sell his old oxen, old waggons, old tools, old and diseased servants, and every thing else become useless. . . . The American slaves cannot enumerate this among the injuries and insults they receive. It was the common practice to expose in the island of Æsculapius[12] in the Tyber, diseased slaves, whose cure was like to become tedious. The Emperor Claudius, by an edict, gave freedom to such of them as should recover, and first declared, that if any person chose to kill rather than to expose them, it should be deemed homicide. The exposing them is a crime of which no instance has existed with us; and were it to be followed by death, it would be punished capitally. We are told of a certain Vedius Pollio, who, in the presence of Augustus, would have given a slave as food to his fish, for having broken a glass. With the Romans, the regular method of taking the evidence of their slaves was under torture. Here it has been thought better never to resort to their evidence. When a master was murdered, all his slaves, in the same house, or within hearing, were condemned to death. Here punishment falls on the guilty only, and as precise proof is required against him as against a freeman. Yet notwithstanding these and other discouraging circumstances among the Romans, their slaves were often their rarest artists. They excelled too in science, insomuch as to be usually employed as tutors to their master's children. Epictetus, Terence, and Phædrus, were slaves. But they

10. A reference to Tristram Shandy, the title character of a novel by Laurence Sterne (1713–1768).

11. A Greek philospher.

12. Roman god of healing.

were of the race of Whites. It is not their condition then, but nature, which has produced the distinction.—Whether further observation will or will not verify the conjecture, that nature has been less bountiful to them in the endowments of the head, I believe that in those of the heart she will be found to have done them justice. That disposition to theft with which they have been branded, must be ascribed to their situation, and not to any depravity of the moral sense. The man, in whose favour no laws of property exist, probably feels himself less bound to respect those made in favour of others. When arguing for ourselves, we lay it down as a fundamental, that laws, to be just, must give a reciprocation of right: that, without this, they are mere arbitrary rules of conduct, founded in force, and not in conscience: and it is a problem which I give to the master to solve, whether the religious precepts against the violation of property were not framed for him as well as his slave? And whether the slave may not as justifiably take a little from one, who has taken all from him, as he may slay one who would slay him? That a change in the relations in which a man is placed should change his ideas of moral right and wrong, is neither new, nor peculiar to the colour of the Blacks. Homer tells us it was so 2600 years ago.

> Jove fix'd it certain, that whatever day
> Makes man a slave, takes half his worth away.

But the slaves of which Homer speaks were Whites. Notwithstanding these considerations which must weaken their respect for the laws of property, we find among them numerous instances of the most rigid integrity, and as many as among their better instructed masters, of benevolence, gratitude, and unshaken fidelity.—The opinion, that they are inferior in the faculties of reason and imagination, must be hazarded with great diffidence. To justify a general conclusion, requires many observations, even where the subject may be submitted to the Anatomical knife, to Optical glasses, to analysis by fire, or by solvents. How much more then where it is a faculty, not a substance, we are examining; where it eludes the research of all the senses; where the conditions of its existence are various and variously combined; where the effects of those which are present or absent bid defiance to calculation; let me add too, as a circumstance of great tenderness, where our conclusion would degrade a whole race of men from the rank in the scale of beings which their Creator may perhaps have given them. To our reproach it must be said, that though for a century and a half we have had under our eyes the races of Black and of red men, they have never yet been viewed by us as subjects of natural history. I advance it therefore as a suspicion only, that the Blacks, whether originally a distinct race, or made distinct by time and circumstances, are inferior to the Whites in the endowments both of body and mind. It is not against experience to suppose, that different species of the same genus, or varieties of the same species, may possess different qualifications. Will not a lover of natural history then, one who views the gradations in all the races of animals with the eye of philosophy, excuse an effort to keep those in the department of man as distinct as nature has formed them? This unfortunate difference of colour, and perhaps of faculty, is a powerful obstacle to the emancipation of these people. Many of their advocates, while they wish to vindicate the liberty of human nature, are anxious also to preserve its dignity and beauty. Some of these, embarrassed by the question 'What further is to be done with them?' join themselves in opposition with those who are actuated by sordid avarice only. Among the Romans emancipation required but one effort. The slave, when made free, might mix with, without staining the blood of his master. But with us a second is necessary, unknown to history. When freed, he is to be removed beyond the reach of mixture.

Query XVIII: Manners

The particular customs and manners that may happen to be received in that state?

It is difficult to determine on the standard by which the manners of a nation may be tried, whether *catholic*, or *particular*. It is more difficult for a native to bring to that standard the manners of his own nation, familiarized to him by habit. There must doubtless be an unhappy influence on the manners of our people produced by the existence of slavery among us. The whole commerce between master and slave is a perpetual exercise of the most boisterous passions, the most unremitting despotism on the one part, and degrading submissions on the other. Our children see this, and learn to imitate it; for man is an imitative animal. This quality is the germ of all education in him. From his cradle to his grave he is learning to do what he sees others do. If a parent could find no motive either in his philanthropy or his self-love, for restraining the intemperance of passion towards his slave, it should always be a sufficient one that his child is present. But generally it is not sufficient. The parent storms, the child looks on, catches the lineaments of wrath, puts on the same airs in the circle of smaller slaves, gives a loose to his worst of passions, and thus nursed, educated, and daily exercised in tyranny, cannot but be stamped by it with odious peculiarities. The man must be a prodigy who can retain his manners and morals undepraved by such circumstances. And with what execration should the statesman be loaded, who permitting one half the citizens thus to trample on the rights of the other, transforms those into despots, and these into enemies, destroys the morals of the one part, and the amor patriæ[1] of the other. For if a slave can have a country in this world, it must be any other in preference to that in which he is born to live and labour for another: in which he must lock up the faculties of his nature, contribute as far as depends on his individual endeavours to the evanishment of the human race, or entail his own miserable condition on the endless generations proceeding from him. With the morals of the people, their industry also is destroyed. For in a warm climate, no man will labour for himself who can make another labour for him. This is so true, that of the proprietors of slaves a very small proportion indeed are ever seen to labour. And can the liberties of a nation be thought secure when we have removed their only firm basis, a conviction in the minds of the people that these liberties are of the gift of God? That they are not to be violated but with his wrath? Indeed I tremble for my country when I reflect that God is just: that his justice cannot sleep for ever: that considering numbers, nature and natural means only, a revolution of the wheel of fortune, an exchange of situation, is among possible events: that it may become probable by supernatural interference! The Almighty has no attribute which can take side with us in such a contest.—But it is impossible to be temperate and to pursue this subject through the various considerations of policy, of morals, of history natural and civil. We must be contented to hope they will force their way into every one's mind. I think a change already perceptible, since the origin of the present revolution. The spirit of the master is abating, that of the slave rising from the dust, his condition mollifying, the way I hope preparing, under the auspices of heaven, for a total emancipation, and that this is disposed, in the order of events, to be with the consent of the masters, rather than by their extirpation.

1. Latin for patriotism.

from Climate and American Character

To Chastellux, Paris, Sep. 2, 1785

Dear Sir, —You were so kind as to allow me a fortnight to read your journey through Virginia, but you should have thought of this indulgence while you were writing it, and have rendered it less interesting if you meant that your readers should have been longer engaged with it. In fact I devoured it at a single meal, and a second reading scarce allowed me sang-froid[1] enough to mark a few errors in the names of persons and places which I note on a paper herein inclosed, with an inconsiderable error or two in facts which I have also noted because I supposed you wished to state them correctly. From this general approbation however you must allow me to except about a dozen pages in the earlier part of the book which I read with a continued blush from beginning to end, as it presented me a lively picture of what I wish to be, but am not. No, my dear Sir, the thousand millionth part of what you there say, is more than I deserve. It might perhaps have passed in Europe at the time you wrote it, and the exaggeration might not have been detected. But consider that the animal is now brought there, and that every one will take his dimensions for himself? The friendly complexion of your mind has betrayed you into a partiality of which the European spectator will be divested. Respect to yourself therefore will require indispensably that you expunge the whole of those pages except your own judicious observations interspersed among them on animal and physical subjects. With respect to my countrymen there is surely nothing which can render them uneasy, in the observations made on them. They know that they are not perfect, and will be sensible that you have viewed them with a philanthropic eye. You say much good of them, and less ill than they are conscious may be said with truth. I have studied their character with attention. I have thought them, as you found them, aristocratical, pompous, clannish, indolent, hospitable, and I should have added disinterested, but you say attached to their interest. This is the only trait in their character wherein our observations differ. I have always thought them so careless of their interests, so thoughtless in their expences and in all their transactions of business that I had placed it among the vices of their character, as indeed most virtues when carried beyond certain bounds degenerate into vices. I had even ascribed this to its cause, to that warmth of their climate which unnerves and unmans both body and mind. While on this subject I will give you my idea of the characters of the several states.

In the North they are	In the South they are
cool	fiery
sober	voluptuary
laborious	indolent
persevering	unsteady
independant	independant
jealous of their own liberties, and just to those of others	zealous for their own liberties, but trampling on those of others
interested	generous
chicaning[2]	candid
superstitious and hypocritical in their religion	without attachment or pretensions to any religion but that of the heart

These characteristics grow weaker and weaker by gradation from North to South and South to North, insomuch that an observing traveller, without the aid of the quad-

1. Coolness and composure.

2. Given to trickery.

rant may always know his latitude by the character of the people among whom he finds himself. It is in Pennsylvania that the two characters seem to meet and blend, and form a people free from the extremes both of vice and virtue. Peculiar circumstances have given to New York the character which climate would have given had she been placed on the South instead of the north side of Pennsylvania. Perhaps too other circumstances may have occasioned in Virginia a transplantation of a particular vice foreign to its climate. You could judge of this with more impartiality than I could, and the probability is that your estimate of them is the most just. I think it for their good that the vices of their character should be pointed out to them that they may amend them; for a malady of either body or mind once known is half cured. I wish you would add to this piece your letter to Mr. Madison on the expediency of introducing the arts into America. I found in that a great deal of matter, very many observations, which would be useful to the legislators of America, and to the general mass of citizens. I read it with great pleasure and analysed its contents that I might fix them in my own mind.

I have the honor to be with very sincere esteem, dear Sir, your most obedient and most humble servt.

from African Colonization

To the Governor of Virginia (JAMES MONROE), Washington, Nov. 24, 1801

Dear Sir,—I had not been unmindful of your letter of June 15, covering a resolution of the House of Representatives of Virginia, and referred to in yours of the 17th inst. The importance of the subject, and the belief that it gave us time for consideration till the next meeting of the Legislature, have induced me to defer the answer to this date. You will perceive that some circumstances connected with the subject, & necessarily presenting themselves to view, would be improper but for yours & the legislative ear. Their publication might have an ill effect in more than one quarter. In confidence of attention to this, I shall indulge greater freedom in writing.

Common malefactors, I presume, make no part of the object of that resolution. Neither their numbers, nor the nature of their offences, seem to require any provisions beyond those practised heretofore, & found adequate to the repression of ordinary crimes. Conspiracy, insurgency, treason, rebellion, among that description of persons who brought on us the alarm, and on themselves the tragedy, of 1800, were doubtless within the view of every one; but many perhaps contemplated, and one expression of the resolution might comprehend, a much larger scope. Respect to both opinions makes it my duty to understand the resolution in all the extent of which it is susceptible.

The idea seems to be to provide for these people by a purchase of lands; and it is asked whether such a purchase can be made of the U.S. in their western territory? A very great extent of country, north of the Ohio, has been laid off into townships, and is now at market, according to the provisions of the acts of Congress, with which you are acquainted. There is nothing which would restrain the State of Virginia either in the purchase or the application of these lands; but a purchase, by the acre, might perhaps be a more expensive provision than the H of Representatives contemplated. Questions would also arise whether the establishment of such a colony within our limits, and to become a part of our union, would be desirable to the State of Virginia itself, or to the other States—especially those who would be in its vicinity?

Could we procure lands beyond the limits of the U.S. to form a receptacle for these people? On our northern boundary, the country not occupied by British subjects, is the property of Indian nations, whose title would be to be extinguished, with the consent of Great Britain; & the new settlers would be British subjects. It is hardly to be believed that either Great Britain or the Indian proprietors have so disinterested a regard for us, as to be willing to relieve us, by receiving such a colony themselves; and as much to be doubted whether that race of men could long exist in so rigorous a climate. On our western & Southern frontiers, Spain holds an immense country, the occupancy of which, however, is in the Indian natives, except a few insulated spots possessed by Spanish subjects. It is very questionable, indeed, whether the Indians would sell? Whether Spain would be willing to receive these people? And nearly certain that she would not alienate the sovereignty. The same question to ourselves would recur here also, as did in the first case: should we be willing to have such a colony in contact with us? However our present interests may restrain us within our own limits, it is impossible not to look forward to distant times, when our rapid multiplication will expand itself beyond those limits, & cover the whole Northern, if not the Southern continent, with a people speaking the same language, governed in similar forms, & by similar laws; nor can we contemplate with satisfaction either blot or mixture on that surface. Spain, France, and Portugal hold possessions on the Southern continent, as to which I am not well enough informed to say how far they might meet our views. But either there or in the Northern continent, should the constituted authorities of Virginia fix their attention, of preference, I will have the dispositions of those powers sounded in the first instance.

The West Indies offer a more probable & practicable retreat for them. Inhabited already by a people of their own race & color; climates congenial with their natural constitution; insulated from the other descriptions of men; nature seems to have formed these islands to become the receptacle of the Blacks transplanted into this hemisphere. Whether we could obtain from the European sovereigns of those islands leave to send thither the persons under consideration, I cannot say; but I think it more probable than the former propositions, because of their being already inhabited more or less by the same race. The most promising portion of them is the island of St. Domingo, where the Blacks are established into a sovereignty *de factor*,[1] & have organized themselves under regular laws & government. I should conjecture that their present ruler might be willing, on many considerations, to receive even that description which would be exiled for acts deemed criminal by us, but meritorious, perhaps, by him. The possibility that these exiles might stimulate & conduct vindicative or predatory descents on our coasts, & facilitate concert with their brethren remaining here, looks to a state of things between that island & us not probable on a contemplation of our relative strength, and of the disproportion daily growing, and it is overweighed by the humanity of the measures proposed, & the advantages of disembarrassing ourselves of such dangerous characters. Africa would offer a last & undoubted resort, if all others more desirable should fail us. Whenever the Legislature of Virginia shall have brought its mind to a point, so that I may know exactly what to propose to foreign authorities, I will execute their wishes with fidelity & zeal. I hope, however, they will pardon me for suggesting a single question for their own consideration. When we contemplate the variety of countries & of sovereigns towards which we may direct our views, the vast revolutions & changes of circumstances which are now in a course of progression, the possibilities that arrangements now to be made, with a view to any particular plan, may, at no great distance of time, be totally de-

1. Standard.

ranged by a change of sovereignty, of government, or of other circumstances, it will be for the Legislature to consider whether, after they shall have made all those general provisions which may be fixed by legislative authority, it would be reposing too much confidence in their Executive to leave the place of relegation to be decided on by *them*. They could accommodate their arrangements to the actual state of things, in which countries or powers may be found to exist at the day; and may prevent the effect of the law from being defeated by intervening changes. This, however, is for them to decide. Our duty will be to respect their decision.

Questions to Consider

1. What are the main arguments about human rights in the Declaration, and what are the main arguments made about the treatment of the colonies at the hands of the British? How do those arguments support each other?
2. How do Jefferson's descriptions of America also serve to suggest an ideal future for the colonies?
3. How do Jefferson's ideas about laws and manners correspond to his ideas about the natural rights of humans?

William J. Grayson

1788–1863

Born the son of a famous Continental Army officer, William John Grayson was a well-respected author, lawyer, and politician who became a member of the South Carolina legislature. A lifelong defender of slavery, Grayson was also elected to the national Congress in 1833, where he was one of several prominent South Carolinians who worked to avert the Civil War. After leaving Congress, he was appointed collector of the port of Charleston, and he remained active in local and national politics. Throughout his life, Grayson was a man of culture and a great lover of literature who frequently contributed poetry and essays to the *Southern Quarterly Review* and to the daily press.

As a poet, Grayson appears to have been influenced by the work of Alexander Pope and is best remembered for his long poem, *The Hireling and the Slave*. The poem is a frank and vivid piece of proslavery propaganda that attempts to justify the enslavement of Blacks by comparing the Southern slave's idyllic rural life of "light daily labor, and abundant food" to the Northern "wage slave," who might crave "the homes, the food, the clothing of the Slave." In a later version of the same poem, Grayson's writing shows the influence of Sir Walter Scot's narrative poetry in the inclusion of the romanticized Native American legend "Chicora." In 1858, Grayson published "The Country," an old-fashioned neoclassic poem praising rural life. His proslavery views were also published in *Letters to Curtis*, which is a justification of slavery based on its large-scale economic usefulness.

As a politician, Grayson was an ardent supporter of state's rights, although in his later years he bitterly opposed the secession of South Carolina from the Union. His antisecessionist views were published in 1850 in the pamphlet, "A Letter to Governor Seabrook." In political and literary circles, Grayson was generally respected for his courage and his honesty, although for a time his opposition to Southern secession made him unpopular in the South. His work demonstrates facility with classical verse, although the didactic nature of a poem like *The Hireling and the Slave* may strike some as heavy-handed. Still, the poem has become a classic of Southern Antebellum poetry, despite its proslavery agenda.

from The Hireling and the Slave

Part First

Fallen from primeval innocence and ease,
When thornless fields employed him but to please,[1]
The laborer toils; and from his dripping brow
Moistens the length'ning furrows of the plow;
In vain he scorns or spurns his altered state,
Tries each poor shift, and strives to cheat his fate;
In vain new-shapes his name to shun the ill—
Slave, hireling, help—the curse pursues him still;
Changeless the doom remains, the mincing phrase
May mock high Heaven, but not reverse its ways.
How small the choice, from cradle to the grave,
Between the lot of hireling, help, or slave!
To each alike applies the stern decree
That man shall labor; whether bond or free,
For all that toil, the recompense we claim—
Food, fire, a home and clothing—is the same.
  The manumitted serfs of Europe find
Unchanged this sad estate of all mankind;
What blessing to the churl has freedom proved,
What want supplied, what task or toil removed?
Hard work and scanty wages still their lot,
In youth o'erlabored, and in age forgot,
The mocking boon of freedom they deplore,
In wants and labors never known before.[2]
  Free but in name—the slaves of endless toil,
In Britain still they turn the stubborn soil,
Spread on each sea her sails for every mart,
Ply in her cities every useful art;
But vainly may the peasant toil and groan
To speed the plow in furrows not his own;
In vain the art is plied, the sail is spread,
The day's work offered for the daily bread;
With hopeless eye, the pauper hireling sees
The homeward sail swell proudly to the breeze,
Rich fabrics wrought by his unequaled hand,
Borne by each breeze to every distant land;
For him, no boon successful commerce yields,
For him no harvest crowns the joyous fields,
The streams of wealth that foster pomp and pride,
No food nor shelter for his wants provide;
He fails to win, by toil intensely hard,
The bare subsistence—labor's least reward.
  In squalid hut—a kennel for the poor,
Or noisome cellar, stretched upon the floor,
His clothing rags, of filthy straw his bed,
With *offal*[3] from the gutter daily fed,

1. "Cursed is the ground for thy sake; * * * thorns and thistles shall it bring forth to thee; * * * in the sweat of thy brow shalt thou eat bread."—*Genesis* (author's note).

2. Pauperism began with the abolition of serfage.—*Westminster Review* (author's note).

3. Remains of an animal carcass after it is butchered.

Thrust out from Nature's board, the hireling lies:
No place for him that common board supplies,
No neighbor helps, no charity attends,
No philanthropic sympathy befriends;
None heed the needy wretch's dying groan,
He starves unsuccor'd, perishes unknown.
These are the miseries, such the wants, the cares,
The bliss that freedom for the serf prepares;
Vain is his skill in each familiar task,
Capricious Fashion shifts her Protean[4] mask,
His ancient craft gives work and bread no more,
And Want and Death sit scowling at his door.
Close by the hovel, with benignant air,
To lordly halls illustrious crowds repair[5]—
The Levite tribes of Christian love that show
No care nor pity for a neighbor's woe;
Who meet, each distant evil to deplore,
But not to clothe or feed their country's poor;
They waste no thought on common wants or pains,
On misery hid in filthy courts and lanes,
On alms that ask no witnesses but Heaven,
By pious hands to secret suffering given;
Theirs the bright sunshine of the public eye,
The pomp and circumstance of charity,
The crowded meeting, the repeated cheer,
The sweet applause of prelate, prince, or peer,
The long report of pious trophies won
Beyond the rising or the setting sun,
The mutual smile, the self-complacent air,
The labored speech and Pharisaic[6] prayer,
Thanksgivings for their purer hearts and hands,
Scorn for the publicans of other lands,
And soft addresses—*Sutherland*'s[7] delight,
That gentle dames at pious parties write—
These are the cheats that vanity prepares,
The charmed deceits of her seductive fairs,
When Exeter expands her portals wide,
And England's saintly coteries decide
The proper nostrum for each evil known
In every land on earth, except their own,
But never heed the sufferings, wants, or sins
At home, where all true charity begins.

* * *

Companions of his toil, the axe to wield,
To guide the plow, and reap the teeming field,
A sable multitude unceasing pour
From Niger's banks and Congo's deadly shore;

4. Proteus was a herdsman for Neptune who could assume different shapes at will.
5. Exeter Hall, the show-place of English philanthropy (author's note).
6. Relating to members of a Jewish sect that believed in strict, legalistic adherence to religious law and its oral traditions.
7. Harriet Elizabeth Georgiana Leveson-Gower, Duchess of Sutherland. A British abolitionist.

No willing travelers they, that widely roam,
Allured by hope to seek a happier home,
But victims to the trader's thirst for gold,
Kidnapped by brothers, and by fathers sold,
The bondsman born, by native masters reared,
The captive band in recent battle spared;
For English merchants bought; across the main,
In British ships, they go for Britain's gain;
Forced on her subjects in dependent lands,
By cruel hearts and avaricious hands,
New tasks they learn, new masters they obey,
And bow submissive to the white man's sway.
  But Providence, by his o'erruling will,
Transmutes to lasting good the transient ill,
Makes crime itself the means of mercy prove,
And avarice minister to works of love.
In this new home, whate'er the negro's fate—
More bless'd his life than in his native state!
No mummeries dupe, no Fetich charms affright,
Nor rites obscene diffuse their moral blight;
Idolatries, more hateful than the grave,
With human sacrifice, no more enslave;
No savage rule its hecatomb supplies
Of slaves for slaughter when a master dies:
In sloth and error sunk for countless years
His race has lived, but light at last appears—
Celestial light: religion undefiled
Dawns in the heart of Congo's simple child;
Her glorious truths he hears with glad surprise,
And lifts his eye with rapture to the skies;
The noblest thoughts that erring mortals know,
Waked by her influence, in his bosom glow;
His nature owns the renovating sway,
And all the old barbarian melts away.
  And now, with sturdy hand and cheerful heart,
He learns to master every useful art,
To forge the axe, to mould the rugged share,
The ship's brave keel for angry waves prepare:
The rising wall obeys his plastic will,
And the loom's fabric owns his ready skill.
  Where once the Indian's keen, unerring aim,
With shafts of reed transfixed the forest game,
Where painted warriors late in ambush stood,
And midnight war-whoops shook the trembling wood,
The Negro wins, with well-directed toil,
Its various treasures from the virgin soil;
Swept by his axe the forests pass away,
The dense swamp opens to the light of day;
The deep morass of reeds and fetid mud,
Now dry, now covered by the rising flood,
In squares arranged by lines of bank and drain,
Smiles with rich harvests of the golden grain,

That, wrought from ooze by nature's curious art
To pearly whiteness, cheers the Negro's heart,
Smokes on the master's board in goodly show,
A mimic pyramid of seeming snow,
And borne by commerce to each distant shore,
Supplies the world with one enjoyment more.

* * *

Hence is the Negro come, by God's command,
For wiser teaching to a foreign land;
If they who brought him were by Mammon[8] driven,
Still have they served, blind instruments of Heaven;
And though the way be rough, the agent stern,
No better mode can human wits discern,
No happier system wealth or virtue find,
To tame and elevate the Negro mind:
Thus mortal purposes, whate'er their mood,
Are only means with Heaven for working good;
And wisest they who labor to fulfill,
With zeal and hope, the all-directing will,
And in each change that marks the fleeting year,
Submissive see God's guiding hand appear.
Such was the lesson that the patriarch taught,
By brothers sold, a slave to Egypt brought,
When, throned in state, vicegerent of the land,
He saw around his guilty brethren stand,
On each pale, quivering lip, remorse confess'd,
And fear and shame in each repentant breast;
No flashing eye rebuked, no scathing word
Of stern reproof the trembling brothers heard;
Love only glistened in the prophet's eyes,
And cheering told the purpose of the skies;
Grieve not your hearts, he said, dismiss your fear,
It was not you, but Heaven, that sent me here;
His chosen instrument, I come to save
Pharaoh's proud hosts and people from the grave,
From Egypt's ample granaries to give
Their hoarded stores, and bid the dying live:
To Israel's race deliverance to impart,
And soothe the sorrows of the old man's heart:[9]
This Heaven's high end; to further the design,
As he commands, your humble task and mine.
So here, though hid the end from mortal view,
Heaven's gracious purpose brings the Negro too;
He comes by God's decree, not chance nor fate,
Not force, nor fraud, nor grasping scheme of state,
As Joseph came to Pharaoh's storied land,
Not by a brother's wrath, but Heaven's command;
What though humaner Carlisle[10] disapprove,

8. Wealth or possessions that have a debasing influence; often associated with Satan in the Judeo-Christian tradition.
9. "That old man, of whom ye spake, is he yet alive?"(author's note)
10. Thomas Carlisle (1795–1881) was a Scottish historian essayist who was strongly influenced by German transcendentalism. *Sartor Resartus* is his best known work.

Profounder Brougham[11] his vote of censure move,
And Clarkson's[12] friends with modest ardor show
How much more wisely they could rule below,
Prove, with meek arrogance and lowly pride,
What ills they could remove, what bliss provide,
Forestall the Savior's mercy, and devise
A scheme to wipe all tears from mortal eyes;
Yet time shall vindicate Heaven's humbler plan,
"And justify the ways of God to man."

Questions to Consider

1. How effective is Grayson's poem as a piece of proslavery propaganda?
2. What are the images of nature in the poem, and how do they serve the proslavery argument?

Caroline Howard Gilman

1794–1888

Southern transplant Caroline Gilman wrote her New England sister-in-law, Louisa Loring, in 1833: "The South is all to me now." Along with other domestic novelists of the Antebellum South, Gilman claimed to offer fiction that championed the compatibility of the North and the South. Perhaps because she maintained close ties with family and friends north of the Mason-Dixon Line, Gilman seemed unwilling to declare her Southern partisanship publicly. She intended her twin novels, *Recollections of a Housekeeper* (1834) and *Recollections of a Southern Matron* (1838), to reveal the virtues as well as the compatibility of the two regions. As literary scholar Elizabeth Moss notes, "Convinced that sectional dissension stemmed from lack of knowledge rather than the inherent incompatibility of Northerners and Southerners, Gilman designed her two major works of fiction to familiarize her audience with the dimensions of everyday life in the North and the South." Gilman's profession of affection for her newfound homeland contradicted her stated objectives as a novelist of conciliatory literature.

Gilman believed that she was well-suited to her project. Born and educated in Boston, Caroline Howard married Samuel Gilman in 1819 and the newlyweds moved to Charleston, South Carolina, where Samuel was appointed minister to the city's new Unitarian congregation. Caroline's intimate familiarity with the two regions prepared her, she believed, to write with judicious authority on both the North and the South.

Gilman could not contain her growing distrust of Northern development or her faith in the Southern social order, however. She prefaced *Southern Matron* by claiming that she wrote the novel "to present as exact a picture as possible of local habits and manners" of South Carolina. To those who might contend that Gilman's "views of human life . . . have too much sunshine about them, I can only reply, that, to have made different descriptions, I must have resorted to imagination instead of fact." Her sunny views of the South were surely apparent. *Southern Matron* told the story of the daughter of a plantation owner, Cornelia Wilton, who "grows into womanhood" over the course of the story. Cornelia narrates the novel retrospec-

11. "Pronounced Broom from Trent to Tay."—Byron (author's note).
Scottish barrister Henry Brougham (1778–1868) who was elected to the British Parliament and was active in the anti-slavery movement.

12. Thomas Clarkson (1786–1845) was an early British abolitionist.

tively so that she "can offer the moral lessons of individual scenes to her young female readers." Not only did *Southern Matron* suggest that the United States comprised two different and incompatible regions, but it also championed the South. As Elizabeth Moss has noted, *Southern Matron* "portrayed a stable, ordered world that sharply contrasted" with the world of New England Gilman had offered in *Housekeeper*. Cornelia Wilton found "order and harmony in both her landscape and her relationships." Although Gilman admitted that the South had its problems, "she remained firmly convinced that the plantation system nourished a communitarian ethic inherently more virtuous than the burgeoning individualism she identified in the North."

Gilman penned *Southern Matron* during a time of heightened tensions between the North and the South over the issue of slavery. Christine Macdonald writes that the timing of the novel is especially significant because it appeared when "open criticism of slavery in the press and public meetings was being actively discouraged in much of the country." Indeed, the United States House of Representatives censored debate on slavery in 1836 by imposing a gag on all petitions it received on the issue. Even Gilman's adopted hometown of Charleston, South Carolina, occasionally discouraged proslavery documents if they hinted at any of the points argued by abolitionists. Within this cultural climate, Gilman published *Southern Matron*, and her depiction in this later novel of the incompatibility of the regions, contributed to the mounting tensions between them.

from Recollections of a Southern Matron
Chapter 35: The Planter's Bride

She sitteth by his chair,
  And holds his feeble hand;
She watcheth ever there,
  His wants to understand.
His yet unspoken will
She hasteneth to fulfil.

Miss Browne's, *Woman's Love*

He goes from her chamber straight
  Into life's justle;
He meets at the very gate
  Business and bustle.

Miss Browne's, *Man's Love*

The planter's bride, who leaves a numerous and cheerful family in her paternal home, little imagines the change which awaits her in her own retired residence. She dreams of an independent sway over her household, devoted love and unbroken intercourse with her husband, and indeed longs to be released from the eyes of others, that she may dwell only beneath the sunbeam of his. And so it was with me. After our bustling wedding and protracted journey, I looked forward to the retirement at Bellevue as a quiet port in which I should rest with Arthur, after drifting so long on general society. The romance of our love was still in its glow, as might be inferred by the infallible sign of his springing to pick up my pocket-handkerchief whenever it fell.

On arriving at Bellevue, which Arthur had recently purchased, with its standing furniture, I perceived the most grotesque arrangement. Whatever was too old or dilapidated for the city, the former proprietor had despatched into the country. The furniture seemed like the fag-end of all housekeeping wares. If a table had lost a leg, it was banished to Bellevue, where the disabled part was supported by a bit of hickory or pine; the mirrors, which comprised all varieties, from heavy carved mahogany frames to gilt ones, with amiable shepherds and shepherdesses pictured at the top, seemed as if the queen of the earthquakes had been angered by her own reflection, and rent them in fissures. In one I had the pleasure of seeing myself multiplied almost indefinitely; in another, an eye or a nose, a forehead or a waist, was severed in two; and in another, unless I stood on tiptoe, a grinning, unnatural thing looked at me above and below the cracks. In one room was an oldfashioned secretary, towering to the ceiling, where a few wormeaten books leaned against each other, as if for companionship in their solitude; while near it was a finical table, with its defaced gilding hidden by a piece of faded green baize. The sideboard, which was covered with rich silver, was also set off with tumblers and wineglasses for all sizes and fancies; the andirons, things with long slender stands, and Lilliputian brass heads surmounting their slight bodies, looked as if they were invoking something up the large chimneys; the bellows wheezed as if far gone in the asthma; the tongs lapped over with a sudden spasm, clutching tenaciously the unoffending brands; if I attempted to sweep the hearth, I was left with the handle only in my grasp; the large glass shades, intended to protect the candles from the air, admitted, like treacherous allies, the enemy in at various breaches; small bits of carpet were laid here and there in the apartments, as a kind of hint at warmth; the bed-curtains and spreads were mostly patterns of gorgeous birds and trees, but, being imperfectly matched in the sewing, a peacock's plumage was settled on the neck of a humming-bird, a parrot seemed in the act of eating his own tail, and a fine oak came sprouting out of a bird's nest. Arthur was infinitely amused when I called his attention to the china, which varied from the finest Dresden to the common crockery of the dram-shops. The medley, in variety, would have done credit to a modern drawing-room.

The harmonious and joyous frame of our minds rendered these things a source of amusement. For several weeks all kinds of droll associations were conjured up, and we laughed at anything and nothing. What cared we for fashion and pretension? There we were together, asking for nothing but each other's presence and love. At length it was necessary for him to tear himself away to superintend his interests. I remember when his horse was brought to the door for his first absence of two hours, an observer would have thought that he was going a far journey, had he witnessed that parting; and so it continued for some days, and his return at each time was like the sun shooting through a three days' cloud.

But the period of absence was gradually protracted; then a friend sometimes came home with him, and their talk was of crops and politics, draining the fields and draining the revenue, until I (country ladies will believe me) fell off into a state as nearly approaching sleep as a straight-backed chair would allow. Arthur, however, rarely forgot me in conversation with others; he had the art in which most men are so entirely deficient, of directing a glance to a lady, while conversing with gentlemen on themes apparently uninteresting to her—a glance which seemed not only to acknowledge her presence, but to pay deference to her thoughts. He did not, as is too often the case, forget that a sentient being was without companionship but in him; but seemed to feel what is probably true, that if women are occasionally asked for their opinions, they may be induced to look into the depths of their minds to see if an opinion is there. But Arthur had few aids in this delicate mode of complimenting, after the ordinary questions were answered, I was usually left to ponder on the strip of carpet before the hearth, and wonder why it did not come up to the chairs, while my neighbour gradually hitched himself round with one shoulder towards me and his forefinger on Arthur's thigh.

Arthur was a member of a social club—but he had allowed several citations to pass unnoticed, until it occurred to him that he was slighting his friends; I thought so too, and said so, without permitting the sigh to escape that lay at the bottom of my heart, at the idea of his passing an evening away from me.

"They shall not keep me long from you, my love," he said, as we parted; "I have little joy without you."

But it *was* very long to me. I could bear to be alone in the morning, when I pursued various occupations, and was even happy. When weary with sewing and reading, I strolled to the poultry-yard, and heard Maum Nelly's stories of how twenty fine young turkeys had just tottled backward and died *so;* or how the minks and chicken-snakes had sucked half the fowl-eggs; or see her stuff pepper-corns down the young turkeys' throats and pick the pip from the old fowls. Luckily for me I as yet cared little for the pecuniary loss, while I really enjoyed the sight of the healthy flocks, as she exhibited them with a kind of maternal pride, calling the seniors by name. I loved to hear the delicate peeping of the little things, and see how unselfishly the parent bird sacrificed the choicest morsels for them; I loved too, to stand by the duck-pond, and listen to the plash as the old ones descended to the water, and watch their proud and happy look as their offspring followed with instinctive power. I noted the chaste-robed pea-fowl, with is metallic-sounding cry, and smiled as the strutting and vapouring turkey paraded in "brief authority."

Then I visited the dairy, which was charmingly situated just where a small creek entered among the trees. A clear spring ran directly across the stone floor, and a fine spreading live-oak shaded it above. I enjoyed those days in the week when the little negroes came trooping along with their piggins for milk, the largest bearing the babies on their backs, and obtaining a double portion for them.

There is unquestionably as much a school of *old manners* among the negroes as with the Whites, and Dinah, my dairy-woman, belonged to this class, specimens of which are rapidly declining. Her reception of me at the dairy was more that of a dignified hostess than a servile dependent, as, with a low courtesy and wave of the hand, she pointed to a bench for me to be seated. She belonged to the class, also waning, who blend religious expressions and benedictions with their common phraseology. Dinah, too, possessed a native humour and keenness that sometimes amused me. Being short in stature, she asked me to reach a calibash, which was set aside on a high shelf for my especial use when I wished a draught of milk.

" 'Scuse me, missis," said she; "when *tall* was give, I no dere."

Observing that she replied in the affirmative to questions of opposite bearing, I asked her meaning.

" 'Scuse me, missis," she answered; "I is gitting hard o' hearing, and yes is more politer dan no."

Sometimes I even strayed, for companionship, to the potato-fire, which, though in the open air, was rarely extinguished, and usually found some one roasting or eating. As I lingered there one day, I inquired of an old man, who was hoeing his own ground, about some work neglected by the gardener. He rested on his hoe and shook his head.

"My missis," said he, "you no been hear 'bout Dick?"

"No," I answered; "what of him?"

"He disgrace we all," said the old man, resuming his work. "He tief one sheep—he run away las week, cause de overseer gwine for flog him. He an't desarve a good maussa, like Maussa Arthur!"

My next walk was to the sick-house. Arthur had as yet superintended the duty here, but it gradually became my pleasure to assist him; and, though with some timidity, remembering mamma's example, I prescribed and weighed the simplest medicines, and soon became interested in the individuals.

I have said that the morning passed slowly, though happily, even without Arthur; but that club afternoon seemed interminable. The weather was mild, and, tired of the house and of sitting down to *one* plate, that loneliest of all positions, I again walked out to enjoy the declining day and beguile the long hours. I involuntarily paused at the frog-pond, for there seemed a kind of sociality in their voices. Everything depends on the mood of mind. It was but the evening before that Arthur and I had astonished the frogs by our excellent imitation of their melodies. Standing at opposite sides of the little pond, he took the base and I the treble, until we were hoarse with shouting and laughter; now they had a melancholy sound, and I turned homeward. At this moment a man slowly rose from the bushes near, and looked about carefully. I discerned in him Dick, the runaway. He looked haggard, and, approaching with an humble air, confessed his fault, and begged my intercession with his master to allow him to return once more to his duties. I undertook the office, and the next day he was permitted to go into the field.

The house seemed so deserted, that, though half ashamed of my own want of energy and mental control, I walked to the piazza. I was glad of the salute of the last lingering labourers on their way from the fields, I listened to the swineherd's horn, and saw his uncouth group at a distance, turning towards their pen; the shepherd came next, with his more romantic charge, and I enticed them, by throwing corn from the piazza, to bear me company a little while; but they soon followed the shepherd as he called, individually, their well-known names. Then came the ducks, whose wings were uncut, flying from a neighbouring field to seek their night's shelter, sweeping below the deep-tinged sky with flapping wings and happy screams. The sun shot up his last rays on the twilight clouds; the crows wheeled from the field to the forest; the whippoorwill's cry, which the hum of day had stifled, came clearly and solemnly on the air; the young moon rose with her slight crescent, and rapid darkness followed. I returned to the parlour, pushed together the brands on the hearth, threw on lightwood myself, though two servants stood waiting by, and at length heard a footstep. It was Arthur's, I sprang towards him, and we had as much to say as if he had been to India.

This club-engagement, however, brought on others. I was not selfish, and even urged Arthur to go to hunt and to dinner-parties, although hoping that he would resist my urging. He went frequently, and a growing discomfort began to work upon my mind. I had undefined forebodings, I mused about past days; my views of life became slowly disorganized; my physical powers enfeebled, a nervous excitement followed; I nursed a moody discontent, and ceased a while to reason clearly. Wo to me had I yielded to this irritable temperament! I began immediately, on principle, to busy myself about my household. The location of Bellevue was picturesque—the dwelling airy and commodious; I had, therefore, only to exercise taste in external and internal arrangement to make it beautiful throughout. I was careful to consult my husband in those points which interested him, without annoying him with mere trifles. If the reign of romance was really waning, I resolved not to chill his noble confidence, but to make a steadier light rise on his affections. If he was absorbed in reading, I sat quietly waiting the pause when I should be rewarded by the communication of ripe ideas; if I saw that he prized a tree which interfered with my flowers, I sacrificed my preference to a more sacred feeling; if any habit of his annoyed me, I spoke of it once or twice calmly, and then bore it quietly if unreformed; I welcomed his friends with cordiality, entered into their family interests, and stopped my yawns, which, to say the truth, was sometimes an almost desperate effort, before they reached eye or ear.

This task of self-government was not easy. To repress a harsh answer, to confess a fault, and to stop (right or wrong) in the midst of self-defence, in gentle submission, sometimes requires a struggle like life and death, but these *three* efforts are the golden threads with which domestic happiness is woven; once begin the fabric with this woof, and trials shall not break or sorrow tarnish it.

Men are not often unreasonable; their difficulties lie in not understanding the moral and physical structure of our sex. They often wound through ignorance, and are surprised at having offended. How clear is it, then, that woman loses by petulance and recrimination! Her first study must be self-control, almost to hypocrisy. A good wife must smile amid a thousand perplexities, and clear her voice to tones of cheerfulness when her frame is drooping with disease, or else languish alone. Man, on the contrary, when trials beset him, expects to find her ear and heart a ready receptacle, and, when sickness assails him, her soft hand must nurse and sustain him.

I have not meant to suggest that, in ceasing to be a mere lover, Arthur was not a tender and devoted husband. I have only described the natural progress of a sensible, independent married man, desirous of fulfilling all the relations of society. Nor in these remarks would I chill the romance of some young dreamer, who is reposing her heart on another. Let her dream on. God has given this youthful, luxurious gift of trusting love, as he has given hues to the flower and sunbeams to the sky. It is a superadded charm to his lavish blessings, but let her be careful that when her husband

Wakes from love's romantic dream,
His eyes may open on a sweet esteem.

Let him know nothing of the struggle which follows the first chill of the affections; let no scenes of tears and apologies be acted to agitate him, until he becomes accustomed to agitation; thus shall the star of domestic peace arise in fixedness and beauty above them, and shine down in gentle light on their lives, as it has on ours.

Questions to Consider

1. How does Gilman depict the institution of slavery? How does she depict the master-slave relationship? What is the political importance of her interpretation of slavery?
2. How does Gilman characterize the Southern matron? What are the implications of her characterization of Cornelia?

John Pendleton Kennedy

1795–1879

John Pendleton Kennedy was born in Baltimore, Maryland on 25 October 1795 to John Kennedy, a member of the rising merchant class, and Nancy Pendleton Kennedy, a descendant of the Virginia planter class. As literary critic Lucinda MacKethan has noted, Kennedy thus moved between the commercial, capitalist world of his father and the agrarian, communal world of his mother. Both worlds influenced Kennedy's understanding of the future direction of the young republic. Although he cast his lot with the burgeoning middle class, becoming involved in Maryland business and politics, Kennedy chose to write about the agrarian world that increasingly held sway over America's literary imagination.

Kennedy published his first novel, *Swallow Barn,* in 1832, less than a year after Nat Turner's slave revolt in Southampton, Virginia. Turner's rebellion so frightened the landed gentry of the Old Dominion that some Virginia politicians considered a resolution that would have allowed for the gradual emancipation of slaves in the state. Kennedy's novel, however, reflects none of the anxiety many Southerners felt about the institution of slavery. Rather, suggests MacKethan, it offered the story of a peaceful plantation unconcerned with the prospects of rebellion. Kennedy populated his novel with kindly planters, well-mannered mistresses, and contented slaves, all of whom understood the beneficent and civilizing influence of slavery for the African race. *Swallow Barn* unapologetically defends slavery and, significantly, Kennedy revised and reissued it in 1851, the same year that Harriet Beecher Stowe published *Uncle Tom's Cabin* serially in an antislavery Washington newspaper. Although Kennedy's novel suggested that the institution of slavery was in need of reform, it made emphatically clear that Southerners should control the destiny of the institution, free of outside influence. As Lewis Simpson has argued, the reforms advocated by Kennedy, including the legalization of slave marriages and the elevation of a privileged class of slaves to peasant (land-renting) status, did not stem from a sense of benevolence or humanitarianism. Rather, *Swallow Barn* represents Kennedy's contribution to a Southern literary tradition seeking to offer a pastoral, or rural myth that rendered slavery economically and morally viable and thus presented a counter argument to the North's insistence on the moral superiority of a free-labor ideology. As such, the novel offers useful commentary on the increased sectional tensions of the 1830s and the 1850s.

The structure of the novel reveals Kennedy's appreciation for the divergent worldviews of the free-labor North and the slaveholding South. Mark Littleton, a Northern traveler visiting his Virginia relatives, recounts the story of Frank Meriwether, master of Swallow Barn, and the plantation denizens, through a series of letters to his hometown neighbor Zachary Huddlestone. This device allowed Kennedy to explain Southern institutions and customs to his readers interested in "travel sketches" of the South. *Swallow Barn* represents the first major work of plantation fiction and reflects a Southern literary consciousness that was developing independently from the New England literary culture of Washington Irving, Nathaniel Hawthorne, and others.

from Swallow Barn, *or* A Sojourn in the Old Dominion

Introductory Epistle

TO ZACHARY HUDDLESTONE, ESQ., PRESTON RIDGE, NEW YORK

Dear Zack:

I can imagine your surprise upon the receipt of this, when you first discover that I have really reached the Old Dominion. To requite you for my stealing off so quietly, I hold myself bound to an explanation, and, in revenge for your past friendship, to inflict upon you a full, true, and particular account of all my doings, or rather my seeings and thinkings, up to this present writing. You know my cousin Ned Hazard has been often urging it upon me—so often that he began to grow sick of it—as a sort of family duty, to come and spend some little fragment of my life amongst my Virginia relations, and I have broken so many promises on that score, that, in truth, I began to grow ashamed of myself.

Upon the first of this month a letter from Ned reached me at Longsides, on the North River, where I then was with my mother and sisters. Ned's usual tone of correspondence is that of easy, confiding intimacy, mixed up, now and then, with a slashing raillery against some imputed foibles, upon which, as they were altogether imaginary, I could afford to take his sarcasm in good part. But in this epistle he assumed a new ground, giving me some home thrusts, chiding me roundly for certain waxing *bachelorisms*, as he called them, and intimating that a crust was evidently hardening upon me. A plague upon the fellow! You know, Zachary, that neither of us is so many years ahead of him. My reckoning takes in but five years, eleven months and fifteen days—and certainly, not so much by my looks. He insinuated that I had arrived at that inveteracy of opinion for which travel was the only cure; and that, in especial, I had fallen into some unseemly prejudices against the Old Dominion which were unbecoming the character of a philosopher, to which, he affirmed, I had set up pretensions; and then came a most hyperbolical innuendo—that he had good reason to know that I was revolving the revival of a stale adventure in the war of Cupid, in which I had been aforetime egregiously baffled, "at Rhodes, at Cyprus, and on other grounds." Any reasonable man would say, that was absurd on his own showing. The letter grew more provoking—it flouted my opinions, laughed at my particularity, caricatured and derided my figure for its leanness, set at nought my complexion, satirized my temper, and gave me over corporeally and spiritually to the great bear-herd, as one predestined to all kinds of ill luck with the women, and to be led for ever as an ape. His epistle, however, wound up like a sermon, in a perfect concord of sweet sounds, beseeching me to forego my idle purpose; (Cupid, forsooth!) to weed out all my prejudicate affections, as well touching the Old Dominion as the other conceits of my vain philosophy, and to hie me, with such speed as my convenience might serve withal, to Swallow Barn, where he made bold to pledge me an entertainment worthy of my labor.

It was a brave offer, and discreetly to be perponded. I balanced the matter, in my usual see-saw fashion, for several days. It does mostly fall out, my dear Zack (to speak philosophically), that this machine of man is pulled in such contrary ways, by inclinations and appetites setting diversely; that it shall go well with him if he be not altogether balanced into a pernicious equilibrium of absolute rest. I had a great account to run up against my resolution. Longsides has so many conveniences; and the servants have fallen so well into my habitudes; and my arm-chair had such an essential adaptation to my felicity; and even my razors were on such a stationary foundation—one for every day of the week—as to render it impossible to embark them on a journey; to say nothing of the letters to write, and the books to read, and all the other little cares that make up the sum of immobility in a man who does not care much about seeing the world; so that, in faith, I had a serious matter of it. And then, after all, I was, in fact, plighted to my sister Louisa to go with her up the river, you know where. This, between you and me, was the very thing that brought down the beam. That futile, nonsensical flirtation! But for this fantastic conceit crossing my mind with the bitterness of its folly, I should indubitably have staid at home.

There are some junctures in love and war both, where your lying is your only game; for as to equivocating, or putting the question upon an *if* or a *but*, it is a downright confession. If I had refused Ned's summons, not a whole legion of devils could have driven it out of his riveted belief, that I had been kept at home by that maggot of the brain which he called a love affair. And then I should never have heard the end of it!

"I'll set that matter right, at least," quoth I, as I folded up his letter. "Ned has reason, too," said I, suddenly struck with the novelty of the proposed journey, which began to show in a pleasant light upon my imagination, as things are apt to do, when a man has once relieved his mind from a state of doubt:—"One ought to travel before he makes up his opinion: there are two sides to every question, and the world is right or wrong; I'm sure I don't know which. Your traveller is a man of privileges and authoritative, and looks well in the multitude: a man of mark, and authentic as a witness. And as for the Old Dominion, I'll warrant me it's a right jolly old place, with a good many years on its head yet, or I am mistaken—By cock and pye, I'll go and see it—What ho! my tablets,"———

Behold me now in the full career of my voyage of discovery, exploring the James River in the steamboat, on a clear, hot fifteenth of June, and looking with a sagacious perspicacity upon the commonest sights of this terra incognita. I gazed upon the receding headlands far sternward, and then upon the sedgy banks where the cattle were standing leg-deep in the water to get rid of the flies: and ever and anon, as we followed the sinuosities of the river, some sweeping eminence came into view, and on the crown thereof was seen a plain, many-windowed edifice of brick, with low wings, old, ample and stately, looking over its wide and sun-burnt domain in solitary silence: and there were the piny promontories, into whose shade we sometimes glided so close that one might have almost jumped on shore, where the wave struck the beach with a sullen plash: and there were the decayed fences jutting beyond the bank into the water, as if they had come down the hill too fast to stop themselves. All these things struck my fancy as peculiar to the region.

It is wonderful to think how much more distinct are the impressions of a man who travels pen in hand, than those of a mere business voyager. Even the crows, as we sometimes scared them from their banquets with our noisy enginery, seemed to have a more voluble, and, I may say, eloquent caw here in Virginia, than in the dialectic climates of the North. You would have laughed to see into what a state of lady-like rapture I had worked myself, in my eagerness to get a peep at Jamestown, with all my effervescence of romance kindled up by the renown of the unmatchable Smith. The steward of the boat pointed it out when we had nearly passed it—and lo! there it was—the buttress of an old steeple, a barren fallow, some melancholy heifers, a blasted pine, and, on its top, a desolate hawk's nest. What a splendid field for the fancy! What a carte blanche for a painter! With how many things might this little spot be filled!

What time bright Phœbus—you see that Jamestown has made me poetical—had thrown the reins upon his horse's neck, and got down from his chafed saddle in the western country, like a tired mail-carrier, our boat was safely moored at Rocket's, and I entered Richmond between hawk and buzzard—the very best hour, I maintain, out of the twenty-four, for a picturesque tourist. At that hour nature draws her pictures *en silhouette:* every thing jet black against a bright horizon; nothing to be seen but profiles, with all the shabby fillings-up kept dark. Shockoe Hill was crested with what seemed palaces embowered in groves and gardens of richest shade; the chimneys numberless, like minarets; and the Parthenon of Virginia, on its appropriate summit, stood in another Acropolis, tracing its broad pediment upon the sky in exaggerated lines. There, too, was the rush of waters tumbling around enchanted islands, and flashing dimly on the sight. The hum of a city fell upon my ear; the streets looked long and the houses high, and every thing brought upon my mind that misty impression which, Burke says, is an ingredient of the sublime—and which, I say, every stranger feels on entering a city at twilight.

I was set down at "The Union," where, for the first hour, being intent upon my creature comforts, my time passed well enough. The abrupt transition from long-continued motion to a state of rest makes almost every man sad, exactly as sudden speed makes us joyous; and for this reason, I take it, your traveller in a strange place is, for a space after his halt, a sullen, if not a melancholy animal. The proofs of this were all around me; for here was I—not an unpractised traveller either—at my first resting place after four days of accelerated progression, for the first time in my life in Richmond, in a large hotel, without one cognizable face before me; full of excellent feelings without a power of utterance. What would I have given for thee, or Jones, or even long Dick Hardesty! In that ludicrous conflict between the social nature of the man and his outward circumstances, which every light-hearted voyager feels in such a situation as mine, I grew desponding. Talk not to me of the comfort of mine own inn! I hold it a thing altogether insufficient. A burlesque solitariness sealed up the fountains of speech, of the crowd who were seated at the supper-table; and the same uneasy sensation of pent-up sympathies was to be seen in the groups that peopled the purlieus of the hotel. A square lamp that hung midway over the hall, was just lit up, and a few insulated beings were sauntering backward and forward in its light: some loitered in pairs, in low and reserved conversation; others stalked alone in incommunicable ruminations, with shaded brows, and their hands behind their backs. One or two stood at the door humming familiar catches in unconscious medleys, as they gazed up and down the street, now clamorous with the din of carts and the gossip of serving-maids, discordant apprentice boys and over-contented Blacks. Some sat on the pavement, leaning their chairs against the wall, and puffing segars in imperturbable silence: all composing an orderly and disconsolate little republic of humorsome spirits, most pitifully out of tune.

I was glad to take refuge in an idle occupation; so I strolled about the city. The streets, by degrees, grew less frequented. Family parties were gathered about their doors, to take the evening breeze. The moon shone bright upon some bevies of active children, who played at racing games upon the pavements. On one side of the street, a contumacious clarionet screamed a harsh bravado to a thorough-going violin, which, on the opposite side, in an illuminated barber-shop, struggled in the contortions of a Virginia reel. And, at intervals, strutted past a careering, saucy negro, with marvellous lips, whistling to the top of his bent, and throwing into shade halloo of schoolboy, scream of clarionet, and screech of fiddle.

Towards midnight a thunder gust arose, accompanied with sharp lightning, and the morning broke upon me in all the luxuriance of a cool and delicious atmosphere. You must know that when I left home, my purpose was to make my way direct to Swallow Barn. Now, what think you of my skill as a traveller, when I tell you, that until I woke in Richmond on this enchanting morning, it never once occurred to me to inquire where this same Swallow Barn was! I knew that it was in Virginia, and somewhere about the James River, and therefore I instinctively wandered to Richmond; but now, while making my toilet, my thoughts being naturally bent upon my next movement, it very reasonably occurred to me that I must have passed my proper destination the day before, and, full of this thought, I found myself humming the line from an old song, which runs, "Pray what the devil brings you here!" The communicative and obliging bar-keeper of the Union soon put me right. He knew Ned Hazard as a frequent visitor of Richmond, and his advice was, that I should take the same boat in which I came, and shape my course back as far as City Point, where he assured me that I might find some conveyance to Swallow Barn, which lay still farther down the river, and that, at all events, "go where I would, I could not go wrong in Virginia." What think you of that? Now I hold that to be, upon personal experience, as true a word as ever was set down in a traveller's breviary. There is not a by-path in Virginia that will take a gentleman, who has time on his hands, in a wrong direction. This I say in honest compliment to a state which is full to the brim of right good fellows.

The boat was not to return for two days, and I therefore employed the interval in looking about the city. Don't be frightened!—for I neither visited hospitals, nor schools, nor libraries, and therefore will not play the tourist with you: but if you wish to see a beautiful little city, built up of rich and tasteful villas, and embellished with all the varieties of town and country, scattered with a refined and exquisite skill—come and look at Shockoe Hill in the month of June—You may believe, then, I did not regret my aberration.

At the appointed day I re-embarked, and in due time was put down at City Point. Here some further delay awaited me. This is not the land of hackney coaches, and I found myself somewhat embarrassed in procuring an onward conveyance. At a small house to which I was conducted, I made my wishes known, and the proprietor kindly volunteered his services to set me forward. It was a matter of some consideration. The day was well advanced, and it was as much as could be done to reach Swallow Barn that night. An equipage, however, was at last procured for me, and off I went. You would have laughed "sans intermission" a good hour if you had seen me upon the road. I was set up in an old sulky, of a dingy hue, without springs, with its body sunk between a pair of unusually high wheels. It was drawn by an asthmatic, superannuated racer with a huge Roman nose and a most sorrowful countenance. His sides were piteously scalded with the traces, and his harness, partly of rope and partly of leather thongs, corresponded with the sobriety of his character. He had fine long legs, however, and got over the ground with surprising alacrity. At a most respectful distance behind me trotted the most venerable of outriders—an old free negro, formerly a retainer in some of the feudal establishments of the low countries. His name was Scipio. His face, which was principally composed of a pair of protuberant lips, whose luxuriance seemed intended as an indemnity for a pair of crushed nostrils, was well set off with a head of silver wool that bespoke a volume of gravity. He had, from some aristocratic conceit of elegance, indued himself for my service in a ragged regimental coat, still jagged with some points of tarnished scarlet, and a pair of coarse linen trowsers, barely reaching the ankles, beneath which two bony feet occupied shoes, each of the superficies and figure of a hoe, and on one of these was whimsically buckled a rusty spur. His horse was a short, thick-set pony, with an amazingly rough trot, which kept Scipio's legs in a state of constant warfare against the animal's sides, whilst the old fellow bounced up and down in his saddle with the ambitious ostentation of a groom in the vigor of manhood, and proud of his horsemanship.

Scipio frequently succeeded, by dint of hard spurring, to get close enough to me to open a conversation, which he conducted with such a deferential courtesy and formal politeness, as greatly to enhance my opinion of his breeding. His face was lighted up with a lambent smile, and he touched his hat with an antique grace at every accost; the tone of his voice was mild and subdued, and in short, Scipio had all the unction of an old gentleman. He had a great deal to say of the "palmy days" of Virginia, and the generations which in his time had been broken up, or, what in his conception was equivalent, had gone "over the mountain." He expatiated with a wonderful relish upon the splendors of the old-fashioned style in that part of the country; and told me very pathetically, how the estates were cut up, and what old people had died off, and how much he felt himself alone in the present times—which particulars he interlarded with sundry sage remarks, importing an affectionate attachment to the old school, of which he considered himself no unworthy survivor. He concluded these disquisitions with a reflection that amused me by its profundity—and which doubtless he had picked up from some popular orator: "When they change the circumstance, they alter the case." My expression of assent to this aphorism awoke all his vanity—for after pondering a moment upon it, he shook his head archly as he added—"People think old Scipio a fool, because he's got sense,"—and, thereupon, the old fellow laughed till the tears came into his eyes.

In this kind of colloquy we made some twenty miles before the shades of evening overtook us, and Scipio now informed me that we might soon expect to reach Swallow Barn. The road was smooth and canopied with dark foliage, and, as the last blush of twilight faded away, we swept rapidly round the head of a swamp where a thousand frogs were celebrating their vespers, and soon after reached the gate of the court-yard. Lights were glimmering through different apertures, and several stacks of chimneys were visible above the horizon; the whole mass being magnified into the dimensions of a great castle. Some half-dozen dogs bounding to the gate, brought a host of servants to receive me, as I alighted at the door.

Cousins count in Virginia, and have great privileges. Here was I in the midst of a host of them. Frank Meriwether met me as cordially as if we had spent our whole lives together, and my cousin Lucretia, his wife, came up and kissed me in the genuine country fashion. Of course, I repeated the ceremony towards all the female branches that fell in my way, and, by the by, the girls are pretty enough to make the ceremony interesting, although I think they consider me somewhat oldish. As to Ned Hazard, I need not tell you he is the quintessence of good humor, and received me with that famous hearty honesty of his, which you would have predicted.

At the moment of my arrival, a part of the family were strewed over the steps of a little porch at the front door, basking in the moonlight; and before them a troop of children, White and black, trundled hoops across the court-yard, followed by a pack of companionable curs, who seemed to have a part of the game; whilst a piano within the house served as an orchestra to the players. My arrival produced a sensation that stopped all this, and I was hurried by a kind of tumultuary welcome into the parlor.

If you have the patience to read this long epistle to the end, I would like to give you a picture of the family as it appeared to me that night; but if you are already fatigued with my gossip, as I have good reason to fear, why you may e'en skip this, and go about your more important duties. But it is not often you may meet such scenes, and as they produce some kindly impressions I think it worth while to note this.

The parlor was one of those specimens of architecture of which there are not many survivors, and in another half century, they will, perhaps, be extinct. The walls were of panelled wood, of a greenish white, with small windows seated in deep embrasures, and the mantel was high, embellished with heavy mouldings that extended up to the cornice of the room, in a figure resembling a square fortified according to Vauban. In one corner stood a tall triangular cupboard, and opposite to it a clock equally tall, with a healthy, saucy-faced full moon peering above the dial-plate. A broad sofa ranged along the wall, and was kept in countenance by a legion of leather-bottomed chairs, which sprawled their bandy legs to a perilous compass, like a high Dutch skater squaring the yard. A huge table occupied the middle of the room, whereon reposed a service of stately china, and a dozen covers flanking some lodgments of sweetmeats, and divers curiously wrought pyramids of butter tottering on pedestals of ice. In the midst of this array, like a lordly fortress, was placed an immense bowl of milk, surrounded by sundry silver goblets, reflecting their images on the polished board, as so many El Dorados in a fairy Archipelago. An uncarpeted floor glistened with a dim, but spotless lustre, in token of careful housekeeping, and around the walls were hung, in grotesque frames, some time-worn portraits, protruding their pale faces through thickets of priggish curls.

The sounding of a bell was the signal for our evening repast. My cousin Lucretia had already taken the seat of worship behind a steaming urn and a strutting coffee-pot of chased silver, that had the air of a cock about to crow—it was so erect. A little rosy gentleman, the reverend Mr. Chub, (a tutor in the family,) said a hasty and half-smothered grace, and then we all arranged ourselves at the table. An aged dame in spectacles, with the mannerly silence of a dependent, placed herself in a post at the board, that enabled her to hold in check some little moppets who were perched on high chairs, with bibs under their chins, and two barefooted boys who had just burst into the room overheated with play. A vacant seat remained, which, after a few moments, was occupied by a tall spinster, with a sentimental mien, who glided into the parlor with some stir. She was another cousin, Zachary, according to the Virginia rule of consanguinity, who was introduced to me as Miss Prudence Meriwether, a sister of Frank's—and as for her age—that's neither here nor there.

The evening went off, as you might guess, with abundance of good feeling and unaffected enjoyment. The ladies soon fell into their domestic occupations, and the parson smoked his pipe in silence at the window. The young progeny teased "uncle Ned" with importunate questions, or played at bo-peep at the parlor door, casting sly looks at me, from whence they slipt off, with a laugh, whenever they caught my eye. At last, growing tired, they rushed with one accord upon Hazard, flinging themselves across his knees, pulling his skirts, or clambering over the back of his chair, until, worn out by sport, they dropped successively upon the floor, in such childish slumber, that not even their nurses woke them when they were picked up, like sacks, and carried off to bed upon the shoulders.

It was not long before the rest of us followed, and I found myself luxuriating in a comfortable bed which would have accommodated a platoon. Here, listening to the tree-frog and the owl, I dropped into a profound slumber, and knew nothing more of this under world, until the sun shining through my window, and the voluble note of the mocking-bird, recalled me to the enjoyment of nature and the morning breeze.

So, you have all my adventures up to the moment of my arrival. And as I have set out with a premeditated purpose to register what I see and hear—an inky and therefore a black intent, say you—you shall hear from me again presently; but whether in some descriptive pictures of this old dominion, or in dramatic sketches, or in a journal, or in some rambling letters, I cannot yet foretell. I shall wait upon my occasions. Perhaps I shall give you something compounded of all these. And if a book be the upshot—who's afraid? You may read or let it alone, as you please. "That's the humor of it"—as Nym says.

It may be some time before we meet; till then, I wear you in my heart.

Mark Littleton

Swallow Barn, June 20, 1829.

Chapter II: A Country Gentleman

The master of this lordly domain is Frank Meriwether. He is now in the meridian of life—somewhere about forty-five. Good cheer and an easy temper tell well upon him. The first has given him a comfortable, portly figure, and the latter a contemplative turn of mind, which inclines him to be lazy and philosophical.

He has some right to pride himself on his personal appearance, for he has a handsome face, with a dark blue eye and a fine intellectual brow. His head is growing scant of hair on the crown, which induces him to be somewhat particular in the management of his locks in that locality, and these are assuming a decided silvery hue.

It is pleasant to see him when he is going to ride to the Court House on business occasions. He is then apt to make his appearance in a coat of blue broadcloth, astonishingly glossy, and with an unusual amount of plaited ruffle strutting through the folds of a Marseilles waistcoat. A worshipful finish is given to this costume by a large straw hat, lined with green silk. There is a magisterial fulness in his garments which betokens condition in the world, and a heavy bunch of seals, suspended by a chain of gold, jingles as he moves, pronouncing him a man of superfluities.

It is considered rather extraordinary that he has never set up for Congress: but the truth is, he is an unambitious man, and has a great dislike to currying favor—as he calls it. And, besides, he is thoroughly convinced that there will always be men enough in Virginia willing to serve the people, and therefore does not see why he should trouble his head about it. Some years ago, however, there was really an impression that he meant to come out. By some sudden whim, he took it into his head to visit Washington during the session of Congress, and returned, after a fortnight, very seriously distempered with politics. He told curious anecdotes of certain secret intrigues which had been discovered in the affairs of the capital, gave a clear insight into the views of some deep-laid combinations, and became, all at once, painfully florid in his discourse, and dogmatical to a degree that made his wife stare. Fortunately, this orgasm soon subsided, and Frank relapsed into an indolent gentleman of the opposition; but it had the effect to give a much more decided cast to his studies, for he forthwith discarded the "Richmond Whig" from his newspaper subscription, and took to "The Enquirer," like a man who was not to be disturbed by doubts. And as it was morally impossible to believe all that was written on both sides, to prevent his mind from being abused, he from this time forward took a stand against the re-election of Mr. Adams to the Presidency, and resolved to give an implicit faith to all alleged facts which set against his administration. The consequence of this straight-forward and confiding deportment was an unexpected complimentary notice of him by the Executive of the State. He was put into the commission of the peace, and having thus become a public man against his will, his opinions were observed to undergo some essential changes. He now thinks that a good citizen ought neither to solicit nor decline office; that the magistracy of Virginia is the sturdiest pillar which supports the fabric of the Constitution; and that the people, "though in their opinions they may be mistaken, in their sentiments they are never wrong;"—with some such other dogmas as, a few years ago, he did not hold in very good repute. In this temper, he has of late embarked on the millpond of county affairs, and nothwithstanding his amiable character and his doctrinary republicanism,[1] I am told he keeps the peace as if he commanded a garrison, and administers justice like a Cadi.

He has some claim to supremacy in this last department; for during three years he smoked segars in a lawyer's office in Richmond, which enabled him to obtain a bird's-eye view of Blackstone and the Revised Code. Besides this, he was a member of a Law Debating Society, which ate oysters once a week in a cellar; and he wore, in accordance with the usage of the most promising law students of that day, six cravats, one over the other, and yellow-topped boots, by which he was recognized as a blood

1. Jeffersonian belief in limited government, a strict understanding of the Constitution, and an economy fueled by the independent yeoman farmers.

of the metropolis. Having in this way qualified himself to assert and maintain his rights, he came to his estate, upon his arrival at age, a very model of landed gentlemen. Since that time his avocations have had a certain literary tincture; for having settled himself down as a married man, and got rid of his superfluous foppery, he rambled with wonderful assiduity through a wilderness of romances, poems, and dissertations, which are now collected in his library, and, with their battered blue covers, present a lively type of an army of continentals at the close of the war, or a hospital of invalids. These have all, at last, given way to the newspapers—a miscellaneous study very attractive and engrossing to country gentlemen. This line of study has rendered Meriwether almost perilous antagonist in the matter of legislative proceedings.

A landed proprietor, with a good house and a host of servants, is naturally a hospitable man. A guest is one of his daily wants. A friendly face is a necessary of life, without which the heart is apt to starve, or a luxury without which it grows parsimonious. Men who are isolated from society by distance, feel these wants by an instinct, and are grateful for the opportunity to relieve them. In Meriwether, the sentiment goes beyond this. It has, besides, something dialectic in it. His house is open to every body, as freely almost as an inn. But to see him when he has had the good fortune to pick up an intelligent, educated gentleman—and particularly one who listens well!—a respectable, assentatious stranger!—All the better if he has been in the Legislature, or better still, if in Congress. Such a person caught within the purlieus of Swallow Barn, may set down one week's entertainment as certain—inevitable, and as many more as he likes—the more the merrier. He will know something of the quality of Meriwether's rhetoric before he is gone.

Then again, it is very pleasant to see Frank's kind and considerate bearing towards his servants and dependents. His slaves appreciate this, and hold him in most affectionate reverence, and, therefore, are not only contented, but happy under his dominion.

Meriwether is not much of a traveller. He has never been in New England, and very seldom beyond the confines of Virginia. He makes now and then a winter excursion to Richmond, which, I rather think, he considers as the centre of civilization; and towards autumn, it is his custom to journey over the mountain to the Springs, which he is obliged to do to avoid the unhealthy season in the tide-water region. But the upper country is not much to his taste, and would not be endured by him if it were not for the crowds that resort there for the same reason which operates upon him; and I may add—though he would not confess it—for the opportunity this concourse affords him for discussion of opinions.

He thinks lightly of the mercantile interest, and, in fact, undervalues the manners of the large cities generally. He believes that those who live in them are hollow-hearted and insincere, and wanting in that substantial intelligence and virtue, which he affirms to be characteristic of the country. He is an ardent admirer of the genius of Virginia, and is frequent in his commendation of a toast in which the state is compared to the mother of the Gracchi[2]—indeed, it is a familiar thing with him to speak of the aristocracy of talent as only inferior to that of the landed interest—the idea of a freeholder inferring to his mind a certain constitutional pre-eminence in all the virtues of citizenship, as a matter of course.

The solitary elevation of a country gentleman, well to do in the world, begets some magnificent notions. He becomes as infallible as the Pope; gradually acquires a habit of making long speeches; is apt to be impatient of contradiction, and is always

2. Tiberius (c. 163–133 BCE) and Gaius (158–122 BCE) Gracchus, Roman statesmen and social reformers. Their mother was Cornelia, daughter of Publius Cornelius Scipio Africunus, the Roman war hero who defeated Hannibal.

very touchy on the point of honor. There is nothing more conclusive than a rich man's logic any where, but in the country, amongst his dependents, it flows with the smooth and unresisted course of a full stream irrigating a meadow, and depositing its mud in fertilizing luxuriance. Meriwether's sayings, about Swallow Barn, import absolute verity. But I have discovered that they are not so current out of his jurisdiction. Indeed, every now and then, we have quite obstinate discussions when some of the neighboring potentates, who stand in the same sphere with Frank, come to the house; for these worthies have opinions of their own, and nothing can be more dogged than the conflict between them. They sometimes fire away at each other with a most amiable and unconvinceable hardihood for a whole evening, bandying interjections, and making bows, and saying shrewd things with all the courtesy imaginable. But for unextinguishable pertinacity in argument, and utter impregnability of belief, there is no disputant like your country-gentleman who reads the newspapers. When one of these discussions fairly gets under weigh, it never comes to an anchor again of its own accord—it is either blown out so far to sea as to be given up for lost, or puts into port in distress for want of documents—or is upset by a call for the boot-jack and slippers—which is something like the previous question in Congress.

If my worthy cousin be somewhat over-argumentative as a politician, he restores the equilibrium of his character by a considerate coolness in religious matters. He piques himself upon being a high-churchman, but is not the most diligent frequenter of places of worship, and very seldom permits himself to get into a dispute upon points of faith. If Mr. Chub, the Presbyterian tutor in the family, ever succeeds in drawing him into this field, as he occasionally has the address to do, Meriwether is sure to fly the course; he gets puzzled with scripture names, and makes some odd mistakes between Peter and Paul, and then generally turns the parson over to his wife, who, he says, has an astonishing memory.

He is somewhat distinguished as a breeder of blooded horses; and, ever since the celebrated race between Eclipse and Henry, has taken to this occupation with a renewed zeal, as a matter affecting the reputation of the state. It is delightful to hear him expatiate upon the value, importance, and patriotic bearing of this employment, and to listen to all his technical lore touching the mystery of horse-craft. He has some fine colts in training, which are committed to the care of a pragmatical old negro, named Carey, who, in his reverence for the occupation, is the perfect shadow of his master. He and Frank hold grave and momentous consultations upon the affairs of the stable, in such a sagacious strain of equal debate, that it would puzzle a spectator to tell which was the leading member in the council. Carey thinks he knows a great deal more upon the subject than his master, and their frequent intercourse has begot a familiarity in the old negro which is almost fatal to Meriwether's supremacy. The old man feels himself authorized to maintain his positions according to the freest parliamentary form, and sometimes with a violence of asseveration that compels his master to abandon his ground, purely out of faint-heartedness. Meriwether gets a little nettled by Carey's doggedness, but generally turns it off in a laugh. I was in the stable with him, a few mornings after my arrival, when he ventured to expostulate with the venerable groom upon a professional point, but the controversy terminated in its customary way. "Who sot you up, Master Frank, to tell me how to fodder that 'ere cretur, when I as good as nursed you on my knee?"

"Well, tie up your tongue, you old mastiff," replied Frank, as he walked out of the stable, "and cease growling, since you will have it your own way"—and then, as we left the old man's presence, he added, with an affectionate chuckle—"a faithful old cur, too, that snaps at me out of pure honesty; he has not many years left, and it does no harm to humor him!"

Chapter XLVI: The Quarter

Having despatched these important matters at the stable, we left our horses in charge of the servants, and walked towards the cabins, which were not more than a few hundred paces distant. These hovels, with their appurtenances, formed an exceedingly picturesque landscape. They were scattered, without order, over the slope of a gentle hill; and many of them were embowered under old and majestic trees. The rudeness of their construction rather enhanced the attractiveness of the scene. Some few were built after the fashion of the better sort of cottages; but age had stamped its heavy traces upon their exterior: the green moss had gathered upon the roofs, and the course weatherboarding had broken, here and there, into chinks. But the more lowly of these structures, and the most numerous, were nothing more than plain log-cabins, compacted pretty much on the model by which boys build partridge-traps; being composed of the trunks of trees, still clothed with their bark, and knit together at the corners with so little regard to neatness that the timbers, being of unequal lengths, jutted beyond each other, sometimes to the length of a foot. Perhaps, none of these latter sort were more than twelve feet square, and not above seven in height. A door swung upon wooden hinges, and a small window of two narrow panes of glass were, in general, the only openings in the front. The intervals between the logs were filled with clay; and the roof, which was constructed of smaller timbers, laid lengthwise along it and projecting two or three feet beyond the side or gable walls, heightened, in a very marked degree, the rustic effect. The chimneys communicated even a droll expression to these habitations. They were, oddly enough, built of billets of wood, having a broad foundation of stone, and growing narrower as they rose, each receding gradually from the house to which it was attached, until it reached the height of the roof. These combustible materials were saved from the access of the fire by a thick coating of mud; and the whole structure, from its tapering form, might be said to bear some resemblance to the spout of a tea kettle; indeed, this domestic implement would furnish no unapt type of the complete cabin.

From this description, which may serve to illustrate a whole species of habitations very common in Virginia, it will be seen, that on the score of accommodation, the inmates of these dwellings were furnished according to a very primitive notion of comfort. Still, however, there were little garden-patches attached to each, where cymblings, cucumbers, sweet potatoes, water-melons and cabbages flourished in unrestrained luxuriance. Add to this, that there were abundance of poultry domesticated about the premises, and it may be perceived that, whatever might be the inconveniences of shelter, there was no want of what, in all countries, would be considered a reasonable supply of luxuries.

Nothing more attracted my observation than the swarms of little negroes that basked on the sunny sides of these cabins, and congregated to gaze at us as we surveyed their haunts. They were nearly all in that costume of the golden age which I have heretofore described; and showed their slim shanks and long heels in all varieties of their grotesque natures. Their predominant love of sunshine, and their lazy, listless postures, and apparent content to be silently looking abroad, might well afford a comparison to a set of terrapins luxuriating in the genial warmth of summer, on the logs of a mill-pond.

And there, too, were the prolific mothers of this redundant brood—a number of stout negro-women who thronged the doors of the huts, full of idle curiosity to see us. And, when to these are added a few reverend, wrinkled, decrepit old men, with faces shortened as if with drawing-strings, noses that seemed to have run all to nostril, and with feet of the configuration of a mattock, my reader will have a tolerably correct idea of this negro-quarter, its population, buildings, external appearance, situation and extent.

Meriwether, I have said before, is a kind and considerate master. It is his custom frequently to visit his slaves, in order to inspect their condition, and, where it may be necessary, to add to their comforts or relieve their wants. His coming amongst them, therefore, is always hailed with pleasure. He has constituted himself into a high court of appeal, and makes it a rule to give all their petitions a patient hearing, and to do justice in the premises. This, he tells me, he considers as indispensably necessary—he says, that no overseer is entirely to be trusted: that there are few men who have the temper to administer wholesome laws to any population, however small, without some omissions or irregularities; and that this is more emphatically true of those who administer them entirely at their own will. On the present occasion, in almost every house where Frank entered, there was some boon to be asked; and I observed, that in every case, the petitioner was either gratified or refused in such a tone as left no occasion or disposition to murmur. Most of the women had some bargains to offer, of fowls or eggs or other commodities of household use, and Meriwether generally referred them to his wife, who, I found, relied almost entirely on this resource, for the supply of such commodities; the negroes being regularly paid for whatever was offered in this way.

One old fellow had a special favour to ask—a little money to get a new padding for his saddle, which, he said, "galled his cretur's back." Frank, after a few jocular passages with the veteran, gave him what he desired, and sent him off rejoicing.

"That, sir," said Meriwether, "is no less a personage than Jupiter. He is an old bachelor, and has his cabin here on the hill. He is now near seventy, and is a kind of King of the Quarter. He has a horse, which he extorted from me last Christmas; and I seldom come here without finding myself involved in some new demand, as a consequence of my donation. Now he wants a pair of spurs which, I suppose, I must give him. He is a preposterous coxcomb, and Ned has administered to his vanity by a present of a *chapeau de bras*—a relic of my military era, which he wears on Sundays with a conceit that has brought upon him as much envy as admiration—the usual condition of greatness."

The air of contentment and good humor and kind family attachment, which was apparent throughout this little community, and the familiar relations existing between them and the proprietor struck me very pleasantly. I came here a stranger, in great degree, to the negro character, knowing but little of the domestic history of these people, their duties, habits or temper, and somewhat disposed, indeed, from prepossessions, to look upon them as severely dealt with, and expecting to have my sympathies excited towards them as objects of commiseration. I have had, therefore, rather a special interest in observing them. The contrast between my preconceptions of their condition and the reality which I have witnessed, has brought me a most agreeable surprise. I will not say that, in a high state of cultivation and of such self-dependence as they might possibly attain in a separate national existence, they might not become a more respectable people; but I am quite sure they never could become a happier people than I find them here. Perhaps they are destined, ultimately, to that national existence, in the clime from which they derive their origin—that this is a transition state in which we see them in Virginia. If it be so, no tribe of people have ever passed from barbarism to civilization whose middle stage of progress has been more secure from harm, more genial to their character, or better supplied with mild and beneficent guardianship, adapted to the actual state of their intellectual feebleness, than the negroes of Swallow

Barn. And, from what I can gather, it is pretty much the same on the other estates in this region. I hear of an unpleasant exception to this remark now and then; but under such conditions as warrant the opinion that the unfavorable case is not more common than that which may be found in a survey of any other department of society. The oppression of apprentices, of seamen, of soldiers, of subordinates, indeed, in every relation, may furnish elements for a bead-roll of social grievances quite as striking, if they were diligently noted and brought to view.

What the negro is finally capable of, in the way of civilization, I am not philosopher enough to determine. In the present stage of his existence, he presents himself to my mind as essentially parasitical in his nature. I mean that he is, in his moral constitution, a dependant upon the White race; dependant for guidance and direction even to the procurement of his most indispensable necessaries. Apart from this protection he has the helplessness of a child—without foresight, without faculty of contrivance, without thrift of any kind. We have instances, in the neighborhood of this estate, of individuals of the tribe falling into the most deplorable destitution from the want of that constant supervision which the race seems to require. This helplessness may be the due and natural impression which two centuries of servitude have stamped upon the tribe. But it is not the less a present and insurmountable impediment to that most cruel of all projects—the direct, broad emancipation of these people—an act of legislation in comparison with which the revocation of the edict of Nantes[3] would be entitled to be ranked among political benefactions. Taking instruction from history, all organized slavery is inevitably but a temporary phase of human condition. Interest, necessity and instinct, all work to give progression to the relations of mankind, and finally to elevate each tribe or race to its maximum of refinement and power. We have no reason to suppose that the negro will be an exception to this law.

At present, I have said, he is parasitical. He grows upward, only as the vine to which nature has supplied the sturdy tree as a support. He is extravagantly imitative. The older negroes here have—with some spice of comic mixture in it—that formal, grave and ostentatious style of manners, which belonged to the gentlemen of former days; they are profuse of bows and compliments, and very aristocratic in their way. The younger ones are equally to be remarked for aping the style of the present time, and especially for such tags of dandyism in dress as come within their reach. Their fondness for music and dancing is a predominant passion. I never meet a negro man—unless he is quite old—that he is not whistling; and the women sing from morning-till night. And as to dancing, the hardest day's work does not restrain their desire to indulge in such pastime. During the harvest, when their toil is pushed to its utmost—the time being one of recognized privileges—they dance almost the whole night. They are great sportsmen, too. They angle and haul the seine, and hunt and tend their traps, with a zest that never grows weary. Their gayety of heart is constitutional and perennial, and when they are together they are as voluble and noisy as so many black-birds. In short, I think them the most good-natured, careless, light-hearted, and happily-constructed human beings I have ever seen. Having but few and simple wants, they seem to me to be provided with every comfort which falls within the ordinary compass of their wishes; and, I might say, that they find even more enjoyment—as that word

3. The edict, promulgated by King Henry IV of France in 1598, granted French Protestants equal rights with Catholics. Its revocation in 1658 by King Louis XIV declared Protestantism illegal in France, ushering in a period of religious intolerance, persecution, and protestant expatriation.

may be applied to express positive pleasures scattered through the course of daily occupation—than any other laboring people I am acquainted with.

I took occasion to express these opinions to Meriwether, and to tell him how much I was struck by the mild and kindly aspect of this society at the Quarter.

This, as I expected, brought him into a discourse.

"The world," said he, "has begun very seriously to discuss the evils of slavery, and the debate has sometimes, unfortunately, been levelled to the comprehension of our negroes, and pains have even been taken that it should reach them. I believe there are but few men who may not be persuaded that they suffer some wrong in the organization of society—for society has many wrongs, both accidental and contrived, in its structure. Extreme poverty is, perhaps, always a wrong done to the individual upon whom it is cast. Society can have no honest excuse for starving a human being. I dare say you can follow out that train of thought and find numerous evils to complain of. Ingenious men, some of them not very honest, have found in these topics themes for agitation and popular appeal in all ages. How likely are they to find, in this question of slavery, a theme for the highest excitement; and, especially, how easy is it to inflame the passions of these untutored and unreckoning people, our Black population, with this subject! For slavery, as an original question, is wholly without justification or defence. It is theoretically and morally wrong—and fanatical and one-sided thinkers will call its continuance, even for a day, a wrong, under any modification of it. But, surely, if these people are consigned to our care by the accident, or, what is worse, the premeditated policy which has put them upon our commonwealth, the great duty that is left to us is, to shape our conduct, in reference to them, by a wise and beneficent consideration of the case as it exists, and to administer wholesome laws for their government, making their servitude as tolerable to them as we can consistently with our own safety and their ultimate good. We should not be justified in taking the hazard of internal convulsions to get rid of them; nor have we a right, in the desire to free ourselves, to whelm them in greater evils than their present bondage. A violent removal of them, or a general emancipation, would assuredly produce one or the other of these calamities. Has any sensible man, who takes a different view of this subject, ever reflected upon the consequences of committing two or three millions of persons, born and bred in a state so completely dependent as that of slavery—so unfurnished, so unintellectual, so utterly helpless, I may say—to all the responsibilities, cares and labors of a state of freedom? Must he not acknowledge, that the utmost we could give them would be but a nominal freedom, in doing which we should be guilty of a cruel desertion of our trust—inevitably leading them to progressive debasement, penury, oppression, and finally to extermination? I would not argue with that man whose bigotry to a sentiment was so blind and so fatal as to insist on this expedient. When the time comes, as I apprehend it will come—and all the sooner, if it be not delayed by these efforts to arouse something like a vindictive feeling between the disputants on both sides—in which the roots of slavery will begin to lose their hold in our soil; and when we shall have the means for providing these people a proper asylum, I shall be glad to see the State devote her thoughts to that enterprise, and, if I am alive, will cheerfully and gratefully assist in it. In the mean time, we owe it to justice and humanity to treat these people with the most considerate kindness. As to what are ordinarily imagined to be the evils or sufferings of their condition. I do not believe in them. The evil is generally felt on the side of the master. Less work is exacted of them than voluntary laborers choose to perform: they have as many privileges as are compatible with the nature of their occupations: they are subsisted, in general, as comfortably—nay, in their estimation of comforts, more comfortably, than the rural population of other countries. And as to the severities that are alleged to be practised upon them, there is much more malice or invention than truth in the accusation. The slaveholders in this region are, in the main, men of kind and humane tempers—as pliant to the touch of compassion, and as sensible of its duties, as the best men in any community, and as little disposed to inflict injury upon their dependents. Indeed, the owner of slaves is less apt to be harsh in his requisitions of labor than those who toil much themselves. I suspect it is invariably characteristic of those who are in the habit of severely tasking themselves, that they are inclined to regulate their demands upon others by their own standard. Our slaves are punished for misdemeanors, pretty much as disorderly persons are punished in all societies; and I am quite of opinion that our statistics of crime and punishment will compare favorably with those of any other population. But the punishment, on our side, is remarked as the personal act of the master; whilst, elsewhere, it goes free of ill-natured comment, because it is set down to the course of justice. We, therefore, suffer a reproach which other politics escape, and the conclusion is made an item of complaint against slavery.

"It has not escaped the attention of our legislation to provide against the ill-treatment of our negro population. I heartily concur in all effective laws to punish cruelty in masters. Public opinion on that subject, however, is even stronger than law, and no man can hold up his head in this community who is chargeable with mal-treatment of his slaves.

"One thing I desire you specially to note: the question of emancipation is exclusively our own, and every intermeddling with it from abroad will but mar its chance of success. We cannot but regard such interference as an unwarrantable and mischievous design to do us injury, and, therefore, we resent it—sometimes, I am sorry to say, even to the point of involving the innocent negro in the rigor which it provokes. We think, and, indeed, we know, that we alone are able to deal properly with the subject; all others are misled by the feeling which the natural sentiment against slavery, in the abstract, excites. They act under imperfect knowledge and impulsive prejudices which are totally incompatible with wise action on any subject. We, on the contrary, have every motive to calm and prudent counsel. Our lives, fortunes, families—our commonwealth itself, are put at the hazard of this resolve. You gentlemen of the North greatly misapprehend us, if you suppose that we are in love with this slave institution—or that, for the most part, we even deem it profitable to us. There are amongst us, it is true, some persons who are inclined to be fanatical on this side of the question, and who bring themselves to adopt some bold dogmas tending to these extreme views—and it is not out of the course of events that the violence of the agitations against us may lead ultimately to a wide adoption of these dogmas amongst the slaveholding States. It is in the nature of men to recalcitrate against continual assault, and, through the zeal of such opposition, to run into ultraisms which cannot be defended. But at present, I am sure the Southern sentiment on this question is temporate and wise, and that we neither regard slavery as a good, nor account it, except in some favorable conditions, as profitable. The most we can say of it is that, as matters stand, it is the best auxiliary within our reach.

"Without troubling you with further reflections upon a dull subject, my conclusion is that the real friends of humanity should conspire to allay the ferments on this question, and, even at some cost, to endeavor to encourage the natural contentment of the slave himself, by arguments to reconcile him to a present destiny, which is, in fact, more free from sorrow and want than that of almost any other class of men occupying the same field of labor."

Meriwether was about to finish his discourse at this point, when a new vein of thought struck him:

"It has sometimes occurred to me," he continued, "that we might elevate our slave population, very advantageously to them and to us, by some reforms in our code. I think we are justly liable to reproach, for the neglect or omission of our laws to recognize and regulate marriages, and the relation of family amongst the negroes. We owe it to humanity and to the sacred obligation of Christian ordinances, to respect and secure the bonds of husband and wife, and parent and child. I am ashamed to acknowledge that I have no answer to make, in the way of justification of this neglect. We have no right to put man and wife asunder. The law should declare this, and forbid the separation under any contingency, except of crime. It should be equally peremptory in forbidding the coercive separation of children from the mother—at least during that period when the one requires the care of the other. A disregard of these attachments has brought more odium upon the conditions of servitude than all the rest of its imputed hardships; and a suitable provision for them would tend greatly to gratify the feelings of benevolent and conscientious slaveholders, whilst it would disarm all considerate and fair-minded men, of what they deem the strongest objection to the existing relations of master and slave.

"I have also another reform to propose," said Meriwether, smiling. "It is, to establish by law, an upper or privileged class of slaves—selecting them from the most deserving, above the age of forty-five years. These I would endue with something of a feudal character. They should be entitled to hold small tracts of land under their masters, rendering for it a certain rent, payable either in personal service or money. They should be elevated into this class through some order of court, founded on certificates of good conduct, and showing the assent of the master. And I think I would create legal jurisdictions, giving the masters or stewards civil and criminal judicial authority. I have some dream of a project of this kind in my head," he continued, "which I have not fully matured as yet. You will think, Mr. Littleton, that I am a man of schemes, if I go on much longer—but there is something in this notion which may be improved to advantage, and I should like, myself, to begin the experiment. Jupiter, here, shall be my first feudatory—my tenant in socage—my old villain!"

"I suspect," said I, "Jupiter considers that his dignity is not to be enhanced by any enlargement of privilege, as long as he is allowed to walk about in his military hat as King of the Quarter."

"Perhaps not," replied Meriwether, laughing; "then I shall be forced to make my commencement upon Carey."

"Carey," interrupted Hazard, "would think it small promotion to be allowed to hold land under you!"

"Faith! I shall be without a feudatory to begin with," said Meriwether. "But come with me; I have a visit to make to the cabin of old Lucy."

Questions to Consider

1. Why did Kennedy write an epistolary novel? How can the tension between participant and observer elucidate the manners, customs, and institutions of a particular region?
2. How does Frank Meriwether cast his defense of the institution of slavery? Why did he claim that Northerners misunderstood the South's position on the institution?

George Moses Horton

c. 1798–1883

George Moses Horton was born a few miles from the Roanoke River around 1798, although birth records generally were not kept for slaves, so the exact date is unknown. A few years later, his master, William Horton, moved his enterprise to just outside Chapel Hill, North Carolina, where Horton lived as a slave until the close of the Civil War. Horton's life as a slave was exceptional, however, due largely to unusually tolerant masters and his own abilities as an orator and a poet. Horton taught himself to read by studying what tattered pages of spelling books he could lay his hands on, and by reading the New Testament and his mother's hymnal. As might be expected, his attempt caused him to be the object of much derision, and he became an accomplished reader only because of his indefatigable resolution to learn. Through his studies, Horton developed an extraordinary vocabulary, and although he did not learn to write until much later, he began to compose sophisticated religious themes and poetry in his head when he was still a young man.

After William Horton died, his son inherited the plantation, and George Horton seems to have enjoyed a bit more freedom of movement than might be expected, owing to the more liberal attitude of the new master and to Horton's unsuitability for physical labor. Slaves were generally at liberty on Saturday afternoons and Sundays, and George began spending most of his weekends in Chapel Hill. There, he made a name for himself by reciting themes he had composed in his head, and he began to spend most of his time on the campus of the University of North Carolina. Oration was an important part of campus life for the students, and they encouraged Horton to "stand forth and display" in public oration, no doubt seeing him primarily as an entertaining diversion. The students were mostly the sons of wealthy landowners, and in his account of these years, Horton derides them for their drinking, gambling, womanizing, and "pranking," all of which interested them more than studying.

Horton writes that he soon realized his public performances were "foolish harangues," and he began to think of himself "as nothing but a public ignoramus," although he did dictate and publish his first book, *The Hope of Liberty* (1829), during this time, before he had learned to write. After its publication, he turned his attention to poetry, composing in his head during the week and dictating to students on the weekend. The students began to buy Horton's poems for 25 to 75 cents apiece—quite a sum of money in those days—and they would pass them off as original compositions. Often, Horton would create love poems for the male students using acrostics of the intended young ladies' names.

The atmosphere on the campus was open and tolerant toward Horton, and he became hugely popular with the students and won the support of the university president, Joseph Caldwell. Horton worked for Caldwell for extra money, and the students supplied Horton with clothing and a library of classic books that ranged from Milton and Shakespeare to *Murray's English Grammar* and the dictionary. Horton's poetry is filled with mythological and historical allusions garnered from his readings. With the support of Caldwell and the students, Horton began to buy his time from his master for twenty-five cents a week and to spend most of his hours on campus studying, composing, and selling his poems. He was, in some ways, North Carolina's first professional poet.

At the end of the Civil War, when he was approximately sixty-eight years old, Horton traveled with the federal troops to Raleigh, where William B. Smith published *Naked Genius*, a collection of poems composed during Horton's three-month travels with the army. The emotional toll of this time is obvious in the poems, and many of them express great longing for home, family, and friends. After that, little is known for certain about Horton's life, although it is reported that he lived in Philadelphia, where he published short stories in various newspapers. Horton lived until at least 1883, when he would have been about eighty-six, an advanced age for a slave. The details of his death are unknown.

The two poems included here reveal that Horton is deserving of respect and study for the deep, humanistic tone of his religious verse, for his antislavery poems, which draw on his personal experiences as a slave and his longing for liberty, and for his extraordinary achievements in spite of his position. He stands alone among Black writers and poets of his time for the breadth of his subject matter and for his wit and ironic good humor. He was the first Black man to publish a book in the South and the first to express the personal toll of slavery in verse.

George Moses Horton, Myself

I feel myself in need
  Of the inspiring strains of ancient lore,
My heart to lift, my empty mind to feed,
  And all the world explore.

I know that I am old
  And never can recover what is past,
But for the future may some light unfold
  And soar from ages blast.

I feel resolved to try,
  My wish to prove, my calling to pursue,
Or mount up from the earth into the sky,
  To show what Heaven can do.

My genius from a boy,
  Has fluttered like a bird within my heart;
But could not thus confined her powers employ,
  Impatient to depart.

She like a restless bird,
  Would spread her wings, her power to be unfurl'd,
And let her songs be loudly heard,
  And dart from world to world.

Division of an Estate

It well bespeaks a man beheaded, quite
Divested of the laurel robe of life,
When every member struggles for its base,
The head, the power of order, now recedes,
Unheeded efforts rise on every side,
With dull emotion rolling through the brain
Of apprehending slaves. The flocks and herds,
In sad confusion now run to and fro,
And seem to ask, distressed, the reason why
That they are thus prostrated. Howl, ye dogs!
Ye cattle, low! Ye sheep, astonish'd, bleat!
Ye bristling swine, trudge squealing through the glades,
Void of an owner to impart your food.
Sad horses, lift your heads and neigh aloud,
And caper, frantic, from the dismal scene;
Mow the last food upon your grass clad lea,
And leave a solitary home behind,
In hopeless widowhood, no longer gay.
The trav'ling sun of gain his journey ends

In unavailing pain; he sets with tears;
A king sequestered sinking from his throne,
Succeeded by a train of busy friends,
Like stars which rise with smiles, to mark the flight
Of awful Phoebus to another world.
Stars after stars in fleet succession rise
Into the wide empire of fortune clear,
Regardless of the donor of their lamps,
Like heirs forgetful of parental care,
Without a grateful smile or filial tear,
Redound in reverence to expiring age.
But soon parental benediction flies
Like vivid meteors in a moment gone,
As though they ne'er had been; but O! the state,
The dark suspense in which poor vassals stand;
Each mind upon the spire of chance hangs, fluctuant;
The day of separation is at hand;
Imagination lifts her gloomy curtain,
Like ev'ning's mantle at the flight of day,
Through which the trembling pinnacle we spy,
On which we soon must stand with hopeful smiles,
Or apprehending frowns; to tumble on
The right or left forever.

Questions to Consider

1. Horton was obviously inspired by classic stories from the Greek and Roman ages, or, as he wrote, "the inspiring strains of ancient lore." Why do you suppose that stories from Greek and Roman classics so stirred a young slave in the South?
2. Horton learned to write long after he learned to compose and recite. Do you find elements of orality in his poetry that link it to his history as a public speaker?

William Gilmore Simms

1806–1870

William Gilmore Simms was born the son of a poor shopkeeper in Charleston, South Carolina, in 1806. His mother died when he was young, and after his father's business failed, his grandfather raised Simms. At first, the young Simms tried his hand as a pharmacist's apprentice but then determined to become a lawyer. His first and most enduring love, however, was literature, and although his low social position made his admission to aristocratic and cultured circles difficult, he became a preeminent Southern writer. After his initial success as an author, Simms worked to build the prestige of Southern literature by editing several Southern literary journals and by helping to promote the reputations of other Southern writers. He remained a loyal Southerner and South Carolinian his entire life, and he wrote essays and delivered orations in defense of slavery and against Northern interference in Southern politics. He also did much to preserve a record of the state's history and traditions, and he wrote an influential history and geography of South Carolina, as well as respected biographies of Francis Marion, John Smith, and Nathanael Greene.

Simms's father was a wanderer and a soldier in Tennessee, Alabama, and Mississippi, and Simms joined him for a time on the frontier. Although Simms did not follow his father's advice to seek his fortune in the Southwest, his experiences in the frontier colonies would serve as inspiration for the romance novels he began to write after returning to South Carolina, where he also tried his hand as a lawyer, dabbled in politics, and wrote for various newspapers. Simms primarily considered himself a poet and was greatly influenced by the verse of *Lord Byron*, as were many of the Southern poets of the time. Although he was better received as a novelist, Simms published eighteen volumes of poetry through 1860.

Simms's first novel was *Martin Faber*, published in 1833. While the novel is not indicative of Simms's talent, the book was a well-received look at the criminal mind, a subject Simms would return to in several other novels. A year later, Simms published *Guy Rivers*, a chronicle of a fiendish Georgia criminal that would become the first in a series that came to be called the Border Romances, all of which were sensationalized stories of life on the Southern borders. In 1835, Simms published *Yemassee*, a story set in colonial South Carolina, and *The Partisan*, which dealt with the Revolutionary War. In the space of three years, he had published novels on three different subjects and had laid the groundwork for the major themes of all of his subsequent fiction, which, in the end, numbered more than thirty novels.

Included in the Border Romances are the novels *Guy Rivers* (1834), *Richard Hurdis* (1838), *Border Beagles* (1840), *Beauchamp*, or *The Kentucky Tragedy* (1842), and *Charlemano* (1856). All are set in the colonial and nineteenth-century South and provide a rich source for understanding the social and cultural traditions of the area. *The Partisan* begins a series of novels generally known as the Revolutionary Romances. Each of these novels centers on the activities of a Southern general such as Francis Marion or Nathaniel Greene, and the stories are generally faithful and detailed accountings of the Revolutionary War era in the South and particularly in South Carolina.

Simms's novels are often compared to those of James Fennimore Cooper, although Simms's novels never achieved the lasting popularity of Cooper's *Leatherstocking Tales*, possibly because they lack the cohesion of that series and Cooper's vivid natural descriptions. Often, the aristocratic lead characters in Simms's novels betray the author's excessive respect for the upper classes, and many critics have complained that this generally makes the characters one-dimensional. Still, his treatment of secondary characters, low-lifes, and criminals was critically acclaimed. In all the novels, Simms focuses on the importance of social class to Southern life, and his depictions of colonial, revolutionary, and frontier life are considered more realistic than those found in Cooper's works. Like Cooper, Simms makes use of romantic style, melodramatic plots, and stock characters to create an accessible and revealing look at Southern life, as the selection from *Woodcraft* that follows demonstrates.

Simms was a towering figure in Southern literature, intensely loyal to the South and to South Carolina, and even to the social system that had, at first, shut him out. Some critics have argued that his deference to local cultural standards may have damaged the realism of his books. Still, he did much to make Charleston the literary center of the South and to preserve and promote Southern literature in the nineteenth century. His work is generally thought to be among the best produced during the Antebellum period.

from Woodcraft; *or* Hawks About the Dovecote

Chapter 66: The Grapes Are Sour!

It was a remarkable proof of providential interposition—so thought in those days at least—that not one of the persons who came in contact with the squatter in his last illness, caught the small-pox from him. Yet his wife, little Dory, and the two other children, had been, for three days at least, constantly in the sick man's chamber. This was held a wonderful proof of God's gracious favor; and to those who knew the contagious character of that malignant pest, it was certainly a very remarkable circumstance.

After a proper interval, the humble family was again permitted to commune with its former patrons. Mrs. Eveleigh took Dory into her house, and the united appropriations of the widow and our captain, made ample provision for the future comfort of the mother and the other children, in a little farm of her own, where she dwelt forever after, in a condition of humble comfort which left her little to desire. Porgy gave her an old negro, and the widow Eveleigh a young one. Little Dory had a teacher provided for her, and, in a superior society, and with proper education, the native talents and graces of the child daily exhibited new blooms, and the sweetest developments. In process of time, when she grew to womanhood, her charms made themselves felt in every heart with which her own came in contact, until—but let us not anticipate. Let us return to our principal parties.

Glen-Eberley, by the events recorded in our last chapter, was made secure to its proprietor. Our captain of partisans was relieved of all his embarrassments. His debt to Mrs. Eveleigh was not of this order. The profits of the plantation were quite adequate, with a few years of indulgence, to liquidate this, and all other obligations of a pecuniary[1] nature. Porgy, at last, found shelter beneath his fig-tree, with none to make him afraid. He had his friends about him, his singing-bird and his puzzle in a bottle. George Dennison and Doctor Oakenburg, much to the disquiet of Millhouse, became portions of the establishment. The one furnished the ballads for the evening fireside; the other was content to provoke the wit of others, without possesing a spark of it himself. The sergeant still delivered the law from his self-established tripod. He was still an oracle who suffered no dog to bark. Lance Frampton was a frequent visitor, and so once more, was Arthur Eveleigh, satisfied to seek good fellowship, and piquant matter of remark, though still occasionally suspicious of the captain's inclinations to his mother. On this subject, however, he no longer ventured to exhibit his boyish petulance. The one stern rebuke of his otherwise gentle and affectionate mother, had proved quite sufficient to curb, at least for the present, the young tiger striving within him; and, to sum up in a word. Glen-Eberley presented to the eye the condition of a well-managed household, in which the parties were all at peace with themselves and one another.

The same thing might be said of the neighborhood. The genial moods prevailing in the one household radiated in all directions. Glen-Eberley became a sort of center for the parish civilization. The charm was great—a sort of salient attraction—which drew the gentry, all around, within the sphere of its genial, yet provocative influences. Free of anxiety, Porgy resumed his ancient spirit. The piquancy of his society, was everywhere acknowledged; and, with the sergeant and Doctor Oakenburg as his foils, the humor of our captain of partisans was irresistible. Fun and philosophy were strangely mingled in him, and they wrought together in unison. To rise from a practical jest into fields of fanciful speculation, was an habitual exercise with our camp philosopher. To narrate the experiences through which he had gone, delivering history and biography, anecdote and opinion, with the ease of a well bred gentleman over his wine and walnuts, was to him an art familiar as the adjustment of his neckcloth—And these things were all delivered with a spirit and a quaintness giving them wonderful relish, and which was peculiarly his own. Thus the days glided by as if all were winged with sunshine—Thus the nights escaped all efforts to delay them, too brief for the enjoyment which they brought. It may be that we shall some days

1. Relating to money.

depict these happy times, the "Humors of Glen-Eberley," even as they were well remembered by many, thirty years ago, in all that cluster of parishes which lie between the Ashley and the eastern margin of the Savannah; but, at present, we can refer to them only. Enough, that peace reigned in the household, under the strong will, and the happy temperament of its chief; that the dangers which threatened from without, were all overcome, in consequence of the events already recorded; the sheriff had been soothed by ample apologies from Porgy, to which Pinckney easily persuaded him; and Crooks, the deputy, seasonably sauced with good words and hush-money, was easily persuaded to believe that his digestion was totally unhurt by the unnatural sort of repast which he had been made to swallow by the lawless partisans. Tom, we may here mention, was bought back from the widow Eveleigh, and received a gift of himself, from Porgy, which he cunningly rejected.

"No! no! maussa," he cried, with a sly shake of the head, "I kain't t'ink ob letting you off dis way. Ef *I* doesn't b'long to *you, you* b'longs to *me!* You hab for keep dis nigger long as he lib; and him for keep you. You hab for fin' he didner, and Tom hab for cook 'em. Free nigger no hab any body for fin' 'em he bittle [victuals]; and de man wha' hab sense and good maussa, at de same time, he's a d—n pertickilar great big fool, for let he maussa off from keep 'em and fin' 'em. I no guine to be free no way you kln fix it; so maussa, don't you bodder me wid dis nonsense t'ing 'bout free paper any more. I's well off whar' I is, I tell you; and I much rudder [rather] b'long to good maussa, wha' I lub, dan be my own maussa and quarrel wid mese'f ebbery day. Da's it! You yerry now? I say de wud for all! *You* b'longs to *me* Tom, jes' as much as me Tom b'long to *you;* and you nebber guine git *you* free paper from me long as you lib."

Thus the matter was settled, and Tom continued to the end of the chapter, the cook and proprietor of his master.

It was probably three months after his emancipation from the bond of the sheriff, that Captain Porgy, one morning, made his appearance at breakfast in full dress. His toilet had been prepared—with a much nicer care than usual. His beard, which, we shame to confess, was sometimes allowed to grow wild for a week, was now carefully pruned down, leaving the smoothest possible surface of chin and cheek. He wore his buff small clothes, and his new blue coat, with great shining buttons. His neck-cloth was a sky blue silk, which had before been worn. His silk stockings were of the most irreproachable flesh color, and Pompey had done his best to polish his shoes, so as to make them emulate, in some degree, the glittering shine of the fine patent leather of the present day. The whole appearance of our captain was so fresh and so unique, that his presence caused an immediate sensation. The improvement in his toilet struck all parties. Millhouse could not forbear an exclamation, and even Oakenburg opened his eyes as he might have done at the discovery of a new and hitherto unsuspected species of rattlesnake or viper. Dennison only smiled, and said something touching the premature coming of the spring.

"We shall soon be looking for the swallows, captain."

"One would think that we had them here already," replied the captain, glancing obliquely at the enormous bowls of coffee which Pomp was pouring out at the moment. No more was said. But when, after breakfast, Porgy ordered his horse, the sergeant immediately became enlightened on the subject. The disappearance of the captain opened the fountains of his speech.

"I knowed it," quoth the overseer—"It's to happen at last. Well, its all right. It mout ha' been done, a year ago, and 'twould ha' saved some trouble. But it's never too late. I see I'll have to open new lands."

"What's to happen?" demanded Dennison.

"Don't you see. He's gone a-courting."

"A courting?"

"Yes! he' gone off now, I'm main sartin, to pop the question to the widow. Well, she's got a smart chaince of niggers, and when they gits hitched fairly, my force will be something worth counting. I'll begin to c'lar up my gum land to-morrow. I'll put in a hundred more acres this season. Lord! what we miout ha' done a year ago, ef the cappin hadn't been so mealy-mouthed."

"And you think he's gone to be married!" demanded Oakenburg—"a wife."

"To be sure! What else! I knows it—a wife it is! and sich a wife. She's got more than a hundred niggers, and I'll hev' to manage 'em all. But I'll tell you what—she'll manage you. She'll not hev' you idle fellers about the premises. A wife that has been a wife before, and's had the managing of her own affairs so long, she ain't gwine to hev' her house filled up with warmin. She'll hev' a clearing, I tell you both. Singing-birds and snake-catchers aint gwine to eat her out of house and home. She'll find out what's the wartues of work in you, or she'll make you pack. Sich a broom as she'll bring with her when she comes, will sweep away all the rubbish."

The communication caused Oakenburg to look blank. Dennison, with that rare disregard of to-morrow, which is supposed to mark the poetical nature, only laughed, and went off, humming an old English ditty about stirring housewives and fairy besoms. Meanwhile, Porgy pursued his way, as the sergeant had truly conjectured, to the dwelling of the widow Eveleigh. The sergeant had no less truly divined his object in the visit. For some time past, the captain had been meditating the obligations which he owed the widow. He reflected upon what Millhouse had repeatedly suggested to him in respect to the tender sort of interest which she was supposed to feel for himself. This might be a well-founded suggestion. Repeated examinations of the matter, in his own mind, had not persuaded him that the interest of the widow was anything more than that of a friend. Still, it was possible; and if it were really the case that she entertained any stronger sentiment in his favor, it would certainly, as the sergeant had said—"be a most cruelsome thing that she shouldn't hev' the man she wanted, pertickilarly when she had done so much for his sarcumstances." Porgy felt the ingratitude—of any such neglect, on his part. Supposing any such feeling on hers, and gratitude furnished a crutch where love might have faltered lamely and failed in his approaches. Repeated meditations had brought the captain to a definite conclusion; and he had armed himself to "come to the sticking point," in other words, to make her a formal offer, of hand and heart and household.

Fortunately for his purposes he found her at home and alone. Dory had gone on a visit to her mother—Arthur had set forth on a deer hunt with Frampton and some other young men. This was probably known to Porgy when he chose this day for his demonstrations. He found the widow as kind and frank, lively and agreeable, as ever; and after chatting on a variety of topics, he gradually brought the one subject in particular to bear. He was very nice, and as he thought, very judicious in his preliminaries. He discoursed of marriage in the abstract as a beautiful and admirably-conceived condition for human beings; he discoursed of his own wants in particular. Of course, he forbore any allusion to what might be supposed her wants also. He was pleading and humble and solicitous, and reasonable and reverential, and touching and truthful—and, in short, without throwing himself absolutely at her feet, he declared himself so, and without actually taking her in his arms, he avowed his great anxiety to do so—and this, we are bound to say, in the best possible style with proper modesty and misgiving.

The widow, with a sweet smile, laid her hand upon his own, and said as gently and tenderly, but as calmly as possible:—

"My dear captain, why is it that men and women can not maintain an intercourse, as friends, without seeking any other relation. Is it not astonishing that such a thing should seem impossible to everybody? Now, why should not you and I be true friends, loving friends, trusting each other with the utmost confidence, coming and going when we please—welcomed when we come, regretted when we have to depart—and never perilling the intimacy of friendship by the fetters of matrimony. Can't it be so with us, my dear captain—and why not? I confess I think—I feel—that we may be very dear friends, captain, for all our lives; glad in each other's society, doing each other kindly and affectionate offices—faithful always and always confiding, as friends, and—nothing more."

The captain answered confusedly. The widow proceeded.

"The fact is, captain, if you look at the matter properly, you will see that it is quite impossible that we should marry. We should risk much and gain little by such a tie. I confess to you that were I again to marry, I know no person to whom I should be more willing to trust my happiness than yourself."

The captain squeezed her hand.

"But, captain, I am willing to trust myself to nobody again. I have been too long my own mistress to submit to authority. I have a certain spice of independence in my temper, which would argue no security for the rule which seeks to restrain me; and you, if I am any judge of men, have a certain imperative mood which would make you very despotic, should you meet with resistance. There would be peace and friendship between us, my dear captain—nay love—so long as we maintain our separate independence; and, in this faith, I am unwilling to risk anything by any change in our relations. Let there be peace, and friendship, and love between us—but never a word more of marriage. There is my hand, captain, in pledge of my good faith, my friendship, my affectionate interest in yourself and fortunes—my pleasure in your society—and you must be content with that. Will you, captain? For my sake, let me entreat, and please say no more of other matters."

Porgy took her hand and carried it to his lips.

"God bless you, my dear widow, and believe me grateful for what you are willing to bestow. I must be content—will be—assured of such a friendship as your heart is capable of. You are right, perhaps, and yet—"

"No doubt I am right. We know each other, and there shall be no misunderstanding between us. You must stay to dinner with me today, that I may be sure you feel no impatience with me."

And he stayed.

* * *

But the idea of marriage had, for the time, taken particular possession of the brain of our captain. Three days after, he rode over to see the widow Griffin; but on this occasion, he did not take the same pains with his costume as when he visited the other widow. His dress was less pretending, and more somber of hue. The captain knew, before he started that the widow was alone. Lance Frampton had gone on a visit with his wife to Dorchester, the scene of some his own exploits during the war, and where he had some relatives. Porgy found the widow in good health and trim, and especially in good spirits. Her welcome was always genial, and she looked particularly charming, though in ordinary household gear. She was at her spinning-wheel when he came. A basket of carded cotton stood beside her, and as she drew off the threads from the wheel, approached it and retired, he thought her as graceful as a young damsel of sixteen. For the first time in his life, he fancied that spinning was a particularly picturesque performance, and wondered that he had not seen it more frequently delineated in pictures.

Mrs. Griffin was very lively and good-humored, and the captain gradually became more and more gallant. After awhile, he officiated somewhat in her operations. Now, he drew the basket of cotton to her side. Anon, when she desired to move the wheel, he caught up one end of it, while she took the other. It was thus borne into the piazza, the better to afford room for her proceedings. In the obscure situation of the cottage, off the public road, and surrounded by great shady evergreens, the piazza was scarcely less private than the hall. The feeling of privacy had its effect on Porgy. Soon, he became more frequent in the little helps he gave the widow, and, at length, when putting aside her spinning, she proceeded to reel off a pile of yarn, the captain forced away the reel, and gallantly thrust his own arms through the hanks. It was in vain that the good, simple Griffin, wondering in discomfiture at this self-humiliation on the part of the captain, strove against it. He gave her a fierce smack upon the lips with his own, and thus put an end to all her efforts to repossess herself of the thread.

Then he placed himself before her in a great chair, his arms extended to the uttermost, his eyes surveying her tenderly, while she, with downcast looks, proceeded, as the sultan ruled, to reel off the threads as well as she might from the digits of her awkward auxiliary. The picture was a sufficiently ludicrous one, but it may be better fancied than described. Griffin might have seen—probably did see—the grotesque absurdity of the scene; but Porgy was in his Arcadian mood, and certain feelings which he had in reserve, made him obtuse in respect to the queer figure which he cut in this novel employment.

He was startled into a full consciousness of his ridiculous situation, by the sudden appearance, in front of the house, on horseback, of the widow Eveleigh and her son Arthur. In the chat which the captain had kept up, tender and sentimental, and perhaps a little saucy, neither Griffin nor himself had heard the sound of the horses, until escape was impossible. The parties were fairly caught. The first thought of the captain, when he looked up at the sudden noise and saw who were the visitors, was to fling the yarn over Griffin's head; at all events to fling it from his arms; but the mischievous threads adhered tenaciously to the broadcloth, and caught upon the buttons at his wrist, and tangled itself about his fingers, as if each thread were a spirit of disorder, sent especially for his discomfort and defeat. When he sought to rise it fell in a mass upon his feet, and when he strove to kick it off, the feet got involved within the meshes, so that he dared not take a step forward lest he should lay himself out, at full length, along the piazza. As for the yarn, before he got out of its meshes, it was one inextricable mass of disorder, which filled the eyes of Griffin with consternation to behold.

The pair were really in most pitiable plight; an awkward consciousness of the ludicrousness of the picture they afforded to the new-comers, striking them both irresistibly for the first time. But Porgy's consciousness was particularly vexing upon other grounds. To be seen in such a relation to the one widow, after seeking *such* a relation with the other! As the poor captain meditated upon the matter, which he did in a single instant of time, his face streamed with perspiration, though the month of March, when the event happened, is considered a tolerably cool one, even in a Carolina climate.

Porgy hardly dared encounter the eye of the widow Eveleigh, who had alighted with her son, and now entered. But he strove to pluck up courage, and, in seeking to appear lively, he simply showed himself nervous. When he did catch the eyes of the widow, he saw them filled with a significantly smiling speech, which added to his confusion. She gave him her hand, however, very frankly observing, as she did so—

"What, in our times, Hercules subdued to the distaff!"

"Ah! my dear widow, it is only woman that finds the hero weak. That *you* should have seen me at this folly!"

This was said in something of a whisper.

"Do not count it folly," answered the widow. "It is through the weakness of the man that we know his proper strength. That one is able to forget his dignities, only shows that his heart has not been forgotten. But, truth to speak, my dear captain, the picture was an amusing one."

"Funny! very! It must have been." This was said with a ludicrous attempt to smile, which resulted in a grin. Porgy's plan of courtship was exploded for that day, and for a goodly week afterward. But the purpose was not abandoned.

* * *

It was about ten days after, when the captain took occasion to revisit the widow Griffin. Frampton and his wife were still absent. Millhouse Arthur Eveleigh, and George Dennison, were off on a deer hunt somewhere down the river; and Porgy having smoked his after-dinner pipe, and feeling dull, if not drowsy, having dined alone, resolved briefly the desolateness of his state, and, under a sudden call to change it, ordered his horse, determined to woo the widow Griffin after the most lion-like fashion. To confess another of our captain's weaknesses, he had but little doubt of success in his present quest. Griffin had been so docile, so gentle, so solicitous of his ease and comfort, that he really persuaded himself he had but to seek to secure. And so he rode.

A pretty smart canter soon brought him to her door, where the spectacle that confounded him was even more astonishing to his sight, than the situation could have been to the widow Eveleigh, when she caught himself. He could scarce believe his eyes. There, in the piazza, stood the fair Griffin, clasped close in the arms of the overseer, Fordham, and that audacious personage was actually engaged in tasting of her lips, as a sort of dessert after dinner. The situation was as apparent as the noonday sun. The facts were beyond all question or denial. The parties were fairly caught, and so conscious was the wicked widow of the sinfulness of suffering herself to be caught, that, not able to face the captain she broke away from the arms of Fordham, and rushed headlong into the house. Porgy was swallowed up in astonishment. He was about to wheel his horse around, and ride off, at greater speed than that which brought him, when Fordham sallied out, and asked him to alight, and with the coolest manner in the world said—

"Well, cappin, you've caught us at it; but no harm done, I hope. The widow and me hev' struck hands on a bargain, and I reckon we'll be mighty soon man and wife; and I hope, cappin to see you at the wedding."

"The d—l you do!" was the only response of the captain, as, looking fiercely indignant at such cold-blooded audacity, he wheeled his horse, clapped spurs to his sides, and sent him homeward at full gallop.

"Mighty strange!" quoth Fordham. "The cappin doesn't seem to like it!"

Simple-minded Fordham, to suppose that a man should like to see his neighbor feeding on the very fruit he had thought to gather for himself.

* * *

With the defeat of these attempts, Captain Porgy gave up all notion of marriage.

"Woman!" quoth he, "woman!" and there his soliloquy ended; but the one word, repeated, was full of significance. When at length his comrades were again assembled about the board, and the cheerful fires were blazing on the hearth, and the philosophic cloud wreaths floated about the apartment, and the tankards were filled with potent floods of sunny liquor, Porgy said suddenly to his companions—

"My good fellows, there have been moments when I thought of deserting you—that is, I sometimes meditated bringing in upon you a fearful influence, which might have lessened your happiness, and destroyed the harmony which prevails among us. I have had various notions of taking a wife—"

"A wife!" cried Dennison. "Oh! hush, captain, and don't frighten a body so! A wife! What madness prompted such a thought?"

"A wife!" cried Oakenburg,—"the Lord deliver us!"

"Ef she'd ha' come, she'd ha' delivered you mighty soon," quoth Millhouse: "I don't see what's to skear a body in a wife, pervided she's in proper sarcumstances, and is kept strict by a man usen to army rigilations."

"Maussa better widout 'em," quoth Tom; "I nebber kin 'tan for be happy in house whar woman's is de maussa."

"Well, you will all be pleased to hear, then, that I have determined to live a bachelor for your sakes. I sacrifice my happiness for your own. I renounce the temptations of the flesh. It has been a pang to me, gentlemen, to do so, for beauty is precious in my sight. There are women whom I could love. There are charms which persuade my very eyes to sin. There are sweets which make my mouth water. But, for your sakes, I renounce them all. I shall live for you only. You could not well do without me; I will not suffer myself to do without you. You shall be mine always—I shall be yours. To woman, except as friend or companion, I say depart! I renounce ye! Avoid, ye sweet tempters to mortal weakness—ye beguile me with your charms no more! For your sakes, dear comrades, there shall be no mistress, while I live, at Glen-Eberley."

"And may you live for ever!" was the cry from all but Millhouse. He only muttered in the ears of Dennison—

I sees it all! He disowns the women bekaise be kaint help himself. The grapes is sour!"

Questions to Consider

1. Simms considered himself primarily a poet, although he is best remembered for his novels. Can you point to passages in the selection that are particularly poetic?
2. Why do you suppose Simms's work has not become as popular as that of Poe or Hawthorne, the two authors with whom Simms is most often compared?

Edgar Allan Poe

1809–1849

The sensational stories about Edgar Allan Poe's life and death are almost as enduring as his greatest literary works, and although many of the stories are based in truth, much of the information about his life has been slanted to emphasize his reputation as a tortured, decadent genius. Poe himself saw the value of an interesting personal history and helped to create his mysterious public persona. For instance, he claimed to have joined an expedition to fight for Greek independence, as the English poet Lord Byron had actually done, and he claimed to have been at the University of Virginia much longer than he actually had. Poe also often gave a later date for his own birth and claimed to have published works earlier than he actually had, in order to make himself look more like a prodigy. Poe's literary executor, Rufus Griswold, contributed to the controversy by mounting a campaign to discredit Poe and to promote his reputation as a degenerate misfit. In his obituary of Poe, Griswald acknowledged that the author had become a "literary star" but wrote that he "had few or no friends," and that his death would "startle many but few will be grieved by it." Unhappily, Griswold's plan to blacken Poe's character was largely successful, in part because he had possession of Poe's correspondence and rewrote some of it to ensure that Poe's possible defenders would believe him to be two-faced. For some, the dark themes of Poe's writings are strictly the expression of a melancholic temperament. However, the loss and horror in his work are as much a product of Poe's unique literary philosophy as they are of his unusually dark psychology and exquisitely odd life.

Poe was born in Boston on 19 January 1809, to David and Elizabeth Poe, who were both itinerant actors. Shortly after Edgar's birth, David, who was a native of Baltimore, disappeared, and Elizabeth resumed her own acting career, which carried her all along the Eastern seaboard. His mother's profession and his father's absence ensured that Edgar's first years were lived in poverty and instability, but when Elizabeth died of tuberculosis, Edgar, who was not yet three, was taken in by John Allan, a successful merchant in Richmond, Virginia, and his wife, Frances. Poe was lucky to have been taken in by the Allans, for the alternative was the orphanage. Much has been made of Edgar's relationship with disciplined businessman John Allan, and some critics have argued that Allan took on the role of Poe's nemesis. Poe and Allan did fall in and out with each other over the years, and although Allan raised Poe as his legal heir, he later cut him out of his will. Still, all indications are that the Allan home was a safe and structured environment and that Poe enjoyed a close relationship with Frances. John and Frances Allan raised Poe to be an athletic and learned gentleman, taking him to be schooled for a while in England.

When Poe returned to Virginia with the Allans, his uncertain future and shame about his background began to affect both his temperament and his relationships. He attended the University of Virginia for a year, where he did well in some subjects but got into trouble with gambling and drinking, common pastimes among many of the undisciplined aristocratic students. Poe ran up gambling debts of at least $2,000 while at school, and John Allan refused to pay the debts, although he certainly could have afforded to. Poe then left the University and sailed to Boston, where he joined the army.

While in Boston, Poe began to publish his poetry. He first paid a printer to publish *Tamerlane,* and then shortened the poem and added others to make up the volume *Al Aaraaf, Tamerlane, and Minor Poems* (1827). With the support of John Allan, he enrolled in West Point, although he was past the usual age of admittance. However, Poe was not destined for a military career. When Frances died, John Allan remarried, and his new wife was not interested in John's support of Edgar. Realizing that he could not fit in at the academy without Allan's support and that his future as Allan's heir was growing dimmer, Poe caused himself to be expelled from West Point by missing classes and roll calls. Before he left, however, Poe persuaded many of the young cadets to subscribe to his next edition of verse, *Poems,* which was published in 1831.

Poems contained two verses that were to become among his most famous: "Israfel" and "To Helen." "To Helen" is a classic lyric poem, and in "Israfel," Poe begins to demonstrate his idea of what verse should accomplish. Praising the angel Israfel, who "has the sweetest voice of all God's creatures," the poet aspires to "dwell where Israfel has dwelt" and laments that his own poetry cannot attain the transcendent beauty of Israfel's song. In this mortal world of "sweets and sours," he writes, "our flowers are merely—flowers."

As Poe argues in his essay "The Poetic Principle," all verse should aspire to what he called "supernal Loveliness"—a divine and unattainable beauty that results in "an elevating excitement of the Soul." The poet should desire to express a beauty that is beyond expression: "It is the desire of the moth for the star." The voice of the poet must be sorrowful and full of longing: "this certain taint of sadness is inseparably connected with all the higher manifestations of true Beauty." The profound metaphysical sadness and longing in Poe's work is thus essential to his poetic principle, but longing is also a result, certainly, of his actual experiences, especially since Poe regarded the unattainable longing for love—often realized in the form of a lost or unattainable woman—as the ultimate poetic theme. Such love, he wrote, rises above both reason and passion and excites the soul to experience supernal beauty.

Once again, a look at the facts of Poe's life may provide an insight into his literary philosophy, for all the women who mattered in his young life were unattainable or lost to him: his mother, whom he never knew, left him with only a watercolor portrait of herself; his first love, the mother of a childhood friend, died in mental anguish when Poe was only fifteen; Frances Allan, his foster mother, died of tuberculosis as Poe's mother had; his first fiancée, Elmira Royster, married another man after her father inexplicably intercepted Poe's letters to her. This pattern of loss continued throughout Poe's life and provided a great deal of material for a writer whose ultimate theme was lost and unattainable love. Poe's popular poem, "The Raven," may be the most notable demonstration of how longing for a lost love can lead the poet to "supernal loveliness."

Now detached from the Allans, the university, and the military, Poe returned to Baltimore and the home of his aunt, Maria Clemm. Soon after, in an action often cited as one of the more sensational of Poe's life, he married Maria's daughter, his thirteen-year-old first cousin, Virginia. Some evidence suggests that the marriage was never consummated, which might simply be another sensational detail of Poe's life if not for a consideration of his poetic principles.

At the age of twenty-four, Poe began his literary career in earnest, publishing poetry and fiction and becoming the editor of literary journals such as *Graham's Magazine*, *The New York Mirror*, *Broadway Journal*, and *Godey's Lady's Book*. He was an excellent editor and helped set the standards for American poetry, fiction, and literary criticism. His life as a journal editor was one of constant travel and was marked equally by success and failure. He always increased the sales and reputations of the journals he edited, but he never made any real money as an editor and usually managed to get himself dismissed because of artistic differences with the journals' publishers or because of his chronic drinking problem. For some unknown reason, Poe's reaction to alcohol was intense; he may have suffered from an allergic reaction to alcohol, as he would generally become very drunk on a very small amount of liquor.

In the last decade of his short life he published *The Narrative of Arthur Gordon Pym* (1838), *Tales of the Grotesque and Arabesque* (1840), *The Prose Romances of Edgar A. Poe* (1843), and *Tales* (1845). He also published a collection of his poetry in 1845, entitled *The Raven and Other Poems*, and *Eureka, A Prose Poem*, his last book, in 1848. Throughout this period, his literary successes were always accompanied by personal tragedy. He became famous as an author and traveled throughout the East giving lectures and reading his poetry, but he never made any money and lived his whole life in poverty. In 1847, his young wife Virginia died of tuberculosis, as had his mother and Frances Allan. He was engaged to at least three women after Virginia died, but the relationships never lasted long enough to bring the couples to the altar.

On 27 September 1849, Poe left Virginia on a ship bound for Philadelphia, where he was to take an editing job. No record exists of his activities for the next week until he was found in a state of semiconsciousness in Baltimore and was taken to the Washington College Hospital, where he died four days later of congestion of the brain. General opinion would have it that he had broken a recent temperance pledge and damaged his brain with drinking, but others have argued for causes as various as a brain lesion or rabies. In the end, Poe's death, appropriately perhaps, is as mysterious as his life.

Poe's international fame came with the publication of *The Raven*, and grew posthumously in spite of, or perhaps even because of, the wild stories of his life that were promoted by Poe's literary executor, Rufus Griswold, and enlarged by the reading public. Some critics and writers have criticized Poe's work for its themes, which tend to progress little beyond the initial romantic Gothicism of his early work, but few can argue with Poe's ability to affect the reader. While the public may regard Poe as a genius, he believed in the hard work of writing and developed his own critical facility to a very high degree. He was a remarkable literary critic, although not always a fair one. He once accused American poet Henry Wadsworth Longfellow of plagiarism, and he often engaged in protracted literary and critical battles with other authors and critics.

Poe must, however, be credited with developing a truly American critical sensibility. His prose work influenced American authors such as Hart Crane and Ambrose Bierce, and his work had a huge effect on the French symbolists. Like other Southern writers such as William Gilmore Simms, Poe expressed a keen interest in criminal and abnormal psychology. His satire can be traced to the English traditions as they were developed by Southern writers. "A Tale of the Ragged Mountains" is a fine example of the Southern Gothic tale, as is "The Fall of the House of Usher."

American writers and critics have often been ambivalent about Poe's talents. Novelist Henry James believed that a love of Poe's work was the mark of a "primitive stage of reflection," and T. S. Eliot derided Poe's intellect as that of a "gifted young man before puberty," yet Poe's influence has been profound on both writers and on the reading public. Seldom has a writer embodied the longing of the human condition as well as Poe, nor has any writer more successfully plunged into the dark side of the human mind and come back with more universally accessible art. The absolute merits of Poe's art and the details of his life are controversial, but his place with the reading public is secure.

To Helen

Helen, thy beauty is to me
Like those Nicéan barks[1] of yore,
That gently, o'er a perfumed sea,
The weary, way-worn wanderer bore
To his own native shore.

On desperate seas long wont to roam,
Thy hyacinth[2] hair, thy classic face,
Thy Naiad[3] airs have brought me home
To the glory that was Greece,
And the grandeur that was Rome.

Lo! in yon brilliant window-niche
How statue-like I see thee stand,
The agate lamp within thy hand!
Ah, Psyche, from the regions which
Are Holy-Land!

Israfel[1]

In Heaven a spirit doth dwell
"Whose heart-strings are a lute;"
None sing so wildly well
As the angel Israfel,
And the giddy stars (so legends tell)
Ceasing their hymns, attend the spell
Of his voice, all mute.

1. Boats from the ancient city of Nicéan.
2. In Greek myth, the hyacinth is a flower that grows from the blood of the dead.
3. Fairylike.

1. And the angel Israfel, whose heart strings are a lute, and who has the sweetest voice of all God's creatures—Koran (author's note).

Tottering above
In her highest noon,
The enamoured moon
Blushes with love,
While, to listen, the red levin[2]
(With the rapid Pleiads,[3] even,
Which were seven,)
Pauses in Heaven.

And they say (the starry choir
And the other listening things)
That Israfeli's fire
Is owing to that lyre
By which he sits and sings—
The trembling living wire
Of those unusual strings.

But the skies that angel trod,
Where deep thoughts are a duty—
Where Love's a grown-up God—
Where the Houri[4] glances are
Imbued with all the beauty
Which we worship in a star.

Therefore, thou art not wrong,
Israfeli, who despisest
An unimpassioned song;
To thee the laurels belong,
Best bard, because the wisest!
Merrily live, and long!

The ecstasics above
With thy burning measures suit—
Thy grief, thy joy, thy hate, thy love,
With the fervour of thy lute—
Well may the stars be mute!

Yes, Heaven is thine; but this
Is a world of sweets and sours;
Our flowers are merely—flowers,
And the shadow of thy perfect bliss
Is the sunshine of ours.

If I could dwell
Where Israfel
Hath dwelt, and he where I,
He might not sing so wildly well
A mortal melody,
While a bolder note than this might swell
From my lyre within the sky.

2. Lightning.
3. In mythology, the seven daughters of Atlas and Pleione, who the god Jupiter has made into a constellation of stars.
4. A nymph of paradise; in the Koran, the houri are the most beautiful of virgins, whose beauty is unfading.

The Raven

Once upon a midnight dreary, while I pondered, weak and weary,
Over many a quaint and curious volume of forgotten lore—
While I nodded, nearly napping, suddenly there came a tapping,
As of some one gently rapping, rapping at my chamber door.
" 'Tis some visiter," I muttered, "tapping at my chamber door—
Only this and nothing more."

Ah, distinctly I remember it was in the bleak December;
And each separate dying ember wrought its ghost upon the floor.
Eagerly I wished the morrow;—vainly I had sought to borrow
From my books surcease of sorrow—sorrow for the lost Lenore—
For the rare and radiant maiden whom the angels name Lenore—
Nameless *here* for evermore.

And the silken, sad, uncertain rustling of each purple curtain
Thrilled me—filled me with fantastic terrors never felt before;
So that now, to still the beating of my heart, I stood repeating
" 'Tis some visiter entreating entrance at my chamber door—
Some late visiter entreating entrance at my chamber door;—
This it is and nothing more."

Presently my soul grew stronger; hesitating then no longer,
"Sir," said I, "or Madam, truly your forgiveness I implore;
But the fact is I was napping, and so gently you came rapping,
And so faintly you came tapping, tapping at my chamber door,
That I scarce was sure I heard you"—here I opened wide the door;—
Darkness there and nothing more.

Deep into that darkness peering, long I stood there wondering, fearing,
Doubting, dreaming dreams no mortal ever dared to dream before;
But the silence was unbroken, and the stillness gave no token,
And the only word there spoken was the whispered word, "Lenore?"
This I whispered, and an echo murmured back the word, "Lenore!"
Merely this and nothing more.

Back into the chamber turning, all my soul within me burning,
Soon again I heard a tapping somewhat louder than before.
"Surely," said I, "surely that is something at my window lattice;
Let me see, then, what thereat is, and this mystery explore—
Let my heart be still a moment and this mystery explore;—
'Tis the wind and nothing more!"

Open here I flung the shutter, when, with many a flirt and flutter,
In there stepped a stately Raven of the saintly days of yore;
Not the least obeisance made he; not a minute stopped or stayed he;
But, with mien of lord or lady, perched above my chamber door—
Perched upon a bust of Pallas[1] just above my chamber door—
Perched, and sat, and nothing more.

1. Greek goddess of wisdom; also known as Athena.

Then this ebony bird beguiling my sad fancy into smiling,
By the grave and stern decorum of the countenance it wore,
"Though thy crest be shorn and shaven, thou," I said, "art sure no craven,
Ghastly grim and ancient Raven wandering from the Nightly shore—
Tell me what thy lordly name is on the Night's Plutonian[2] shore!"
Quoth the Raven "Nevermore."

Much I marvelled this ungainly fowl to hear discourse so plainly,
Though its answer little meaning—little relevancy bore;
For we cannot help agreeing that no living human being
Ever yet was blessed with seeing bird above his chamber door—
Bird or beast upon the sculptured bust above his chamber door,
With such name as "Nevermore."

But the Raven, sitting lonely on the placid bust, spoke only
That one word, as if his soul in that one word he did outpour.
Nothing farther then he uttered—not a feather then he fluttered—
Till I scarcely more than muttered "Other friends have flown before—
On the morrow *he* will leave me, as my Hopes have flown before."
Then the bird said "Nevermore."

Startled at the stillness broken by reply so aptly spoken,
"Doubtless," said I, "what it utters is its only stock and store
Caught from some unhappy master whom unmerciful Disaster
Followed fast and followed faster till his songs one burden bore—
Till the dirges of his Hope that melancholy burden bore
Of 'Never—nevermore.' "

But the Raven still beguiling my sad fancy into smiling,
Straight I wheeled a cushioned seat in front of bird, and bust and door;
Then, upon the velvet sinking, I betook myself to linking
Fancy unto fancy, thinking what this ominous bird of yore—
What this grim, ungainly, ghastly, gaunt, and ominous bird of yore
Meant in croaking "Nevermore."

This I sat engaged in guessing, but no syllable expressing
To the fowl whose fiery eyes now burned into my bosom's core;
This and more I sat divining, with my head at ease reclining
On the cushion's velvet lining that the lamp-light gloated o'er,
But whose velvet-violet lining with the lamp-light gloating o'er,
She shall press, ah, nevermore!

Then, methought, the air grew denser, perfumed from an unseen censer
Swung by seraphim whose foot-falls tinkled on the tufted floor.
"Wretch," I cried, "thy God hath lent thee—by these angels he hath sent thee
Respite—respite and nepenthe[3] from thy memories of Lenore;
Quaff, oh quaff this kind nepenthe and forget this lost Lenore!"
Quoth the Raven "Nevermore."

2. Black.

3. A potion causing forgetfulness of pain or suffering.

"Prophet!" said I, "thing of evil!—prophet still, if bird or devil!—
Whether Tempter sent, or whether tempest tossed thee here ashore,
Desolate yet all undaunted, on this desert land enchanted—
On this home by Horror haunted—tell me truly, I implore—
Is there—*is* there balm in Gilead?[4]—tell me—tell me, I implore!"
Quoth the Raven "Nevermore."

"Prophet!" said I, "thing of evil!—prophet still, if bird or devil!
By that Heaven that bends above us—by that God we both adore—
Tell this soul with sorrow laden if, within the distant Aidenn,[5]
It shall clasp a sainted maiden whom the angels name Lenore—
Clasp a rare and radiant maiden whom the angels name Lenore."
Quoth the Raven "Nevermore."

"Be that word our sign of parting, bird or fiend!" I shrieked, upstarting—
"Get thee back into the tempest and the Night's Plutonian shore!
Leave no black plume as a token of that lie thy soul hath spoken!
Leave my loneliness unbroken!—quit the bust above my door!
Take thy beak from out my heart, and take thy form from off my door!"
Quoth the Raven "Nevermore."

And the Raven, never flitting, still is sitting, *still* is sitting
On the pallid bust of Pallas just above my chamber door;
And his eyes have all the seeming of a demon's that is dreaming,
And the lamp-light o'er him streaming throws his shadow on the floor;
And my soul from out that shadow that lies floating on the floor
Shall be lifted—nevermore!

Sonnet—To Science

Science! true daughter of Old Time thou art!
Who alterest all things with thy peering eyes.
Why preyest thou thus upon the poet's heart,
Vulture, whose wings are dull realities?
How should he love thee? or how deem thee wise,
Who wouldst not leave him in his wandering
To seek for treasure in the jewelled skies,
Albeit he soared with an undaunted wing?
Hast thou not dragged Diana[1] from her car?
And driven the Hamadryad[2] from the wood
To seek a shelter in some happier star?
Hast thou not torn the Naiad[3] from her flood,
The Elfin from the green grass, and from me
The summer dream beneath the tamarind tree?

Annabel Lee

It was many and many a year ago,
In a kingdom by the sea,
That a maiden there lived whom you may know
By the name of Annabel Lee;—

4. Refers to Jeremiah 8:22, in the King James Version which reads, "Is there no balm in Gilead; is there no physician there?"
5. Eden.

1. Roman goddess of the moon.
2. A wood nymph who lives only as long as the tree she inhabits.
3. A nymph who commonly lived in brooks.

And this maiden she lived with no other thought
Than to love and be loved by me.

She was a child and *I* was a child,
In this kingdom by the sea,
But we loved with a love that was more than love—
I and my Annabel Lee—
With a love that the wingéd seraphs of Heaven
Coveted her and me.

And this was the reason that, long ago,
In this kingdom by the sea,
A wind blew out of a cloud by night
Chilling my Annabel Lee;
So that her high-born kinsmen came
And bore her away from me,
To shut her up in a sepulchre
In this kingdom by the sea.

The angels, not half so happy in Heaven,
Went envying her and me;
Yes! that was the reason (as all men know,
In this kingdom by the sea)
That the wind came out of the cloud, chilling
And killing my Annabel Lee.

But our love it was stronger by far than the love
Of those who were older than we—
Of many far wiser than we—
And neither the angels in Heaven above
Nor the demons down under the sea
Can ever dissever my soul from the soul
Of the beautiful Annabel Lee:—

For the moon never beams without bringing me dreams
Of the beautiful Annabel Lee;
And the stars never rise but I see the bright eyes
Of the beautiful Annabel Lee;
And so, all the night-tide, I lie down by the side
Of my darling, my darling, my life and my bride
In her sepulchre there by the sea—
In her tomb by the side of the sea.

A Tale of the Ragged Mountains

During the fall of the year 1827, while residing near Charlottesville, Virginia, I casually made the acquaintance of Mr. Augustus Bedloe. This young gentleman was remarkable in every respect, and excited in me a profound interest and curiosity. I found it impossible to comprehend him either in his moral or his physical relations. Of his family I could obtain no satisfactory account. Whence he came, I never ascertained. Even about his age—although I call him a young gentleman—there was something which perplexed me in no little degree. He certainly *seemed* young—and he made a point of speaking about his youth—yet there were moments when I should have had little trouble in imagining him a hundred years of age. But in no regard was he more peculiar than in his personal appearance. He was singularly tall and thin. He stooped much. His limbs were exceedingly long and emaciated. His forehead was broad and low. His complexion was absolutely bloodless. His mouth was large and flexible, and his teeth were more wildly uneven, although sound, than I had ever before seen teeth in a human head. The expression of his smile, however, was by no means unpleasing, as might be supposed; but it had no variation whatever. It was one of profound melancholy—of a phaseless and unceasing gloom. His eyes were abnormally large, and round like those of a cat. The pupils, too, upon any accession or diminution of light, underwent contraction or dilation, just such as is observed in the feline tribe. In moments of excitement the orbs grew bright to a degree almost inconceivable; seeming to emit luminous rays, not of a reflected, but of an intrinsic lustre, as does a candle or the sun; yet their ordinary condition was so totally vapid, filmy and dull, as to convey the idea of the eyes of a long-interred corpse.

These peculiarities of person appeared to cause him much annoyance, and he was continually alluding to them in a sort of half explanatory, half apologetic strain, which, when I first heard it, impressed me very painfully. I soon, however, grew accustomed to it, and my uneasiness wore off. It seemed to be his design rather to insinuate than directly to assert that, physically, he had not always been what he was—that a long series of neuralgic attacks had reduced him from a condition of more than usual personal beauty, to that which I saw. For many years past he had been attended by a physician, named Templeton—an old gentleman, perhaps seventy years of age—whom he had first encountered at Saratoga, and from whose attention, while there, he either received, or fancied that he received, great benefit. The result was that Bedloe, who was wealthy, had made an arrangement with Doctor Templeton, by which the latter, in consideration of a liberal annual allowance, had consented to devote his time and medical experience exclusively to the care of the invalid.

Doctor Templeton had been a traveller in his younger days, and, at Paris, had become a convert, in great measure, to the doctrines of Mesmer.[1] It was altogether by means of magnetic remedies that he had succeeded in alleviating the acute pains of his patient; and this success had very naturally inspired the latter with a certain degree of confidence in the opinions from which the remedies had been educed. The Doctor, however, like all enthusiasts, had struggled hard to make a thorough convert of his pupil, and finally so far gained his point as to induce the sufferer to submit to numerous experiments. By a frequent repetition of these, a result had arisen, which of late days has become so common as to attract little or no attention, but which, at the period of which I write, had very rarely been known in America. I mean to say, that between Doctor Templeton and Bedloe there had grown up, little by little, a very distinct and strongly marked *rapport,* or magnetic relation. I am not prepared to assert, however, that this *rapport* extended beyond the limits of the simple sleep-producing power; but this power itself had attained great intensity. At the first attempt to induce the magnetic somnolency, the mesmerist entirely failed. In the fifth or sixth he succeeded very partially, and after long continued effort. Only at the twelfth was the triumph complete. After this the will of the patient succumbed rapidly to that of the physician, so that, when I first became acquainted with the two, sleep was brought about almost instantaneously, by the mere volition of the operator, even when the invalid was unaware of his presence. It is only now, in the year 1845, when similar miracles are witnessed daily by thousands, that I dare venture to record this apparent impossibility as a matter of serious fact.

The temperament of Bedloe was, in the highest degree, sensitive, excitable, enthusiastic. His imagination was singularly vigorous and creative; and no doubt it

1. Franz Anton Mesmer (1734–1815) was a German psychologist and founder of psychotherapy.

derived additional force from the habitual use of morphine, which he swallowed in great quantity, and without which he would have found it impossible to exist. It was his practice to take a very large dose of it immediately after breakfast, each morning—or rather immediately after a cup of strong coffee, for he ate nothing in the forenoon—and then set forth alone, or attended only by a dog, upon a long ramble among the chain of wild and dreary hills that lie westward and southward of Charlottesville, and are there dignified by the title of the Ragged Mountains.

Upon a dim, warm, misty day, towards the close of November, and during the strange *interregnum* of the seasons which in America is termed the Indian Summer, Mr. Bedloe departed, as usual, for the hills. The day passed, and still he did not return.

About eight o'clock at night, having become seriously alarmed at his protracted absence, we were about setting out in search of him, when he unexpectedly made his appearance, in health no worse than usual, and in rather more than ordinary spirits. The account which he gave of his expedition, and of the events which had detained him, was a singular one indeed.

"You will remember," said he, "that it was about nine in the morning when I left Charlottesville. I bent my steps immediately to the mountains, and, about ten, entered a gorge which was entirely new to me. I followed the windings of this pass with much interest. The scenery which presented itself on all sides, although scarcely entitled to be called grand, had about it an indescribable, and to me, a delicious aspect of dreary desolation. The solitude seemed absolutely virgin. I could not help believing that the green sods and the gray rocks upon which I trod, had been trodden never before by the foot of a human being. So entirely secluded, and in fact inaccessible, except through a series of accidents, is the entrance of the ravine, that it is by no means impossible that I was indeed the first adventurer—the very first and sole adventurer who had ever penetrated its recesses.

"The thick and peculiar mist, or smoke, which distinguishes the Indian Summer, and which now hung heavily over all objects, served, no doubt, to deepen the vague impressions which these objects created. So dense was this pleasant fog, that I could at no time see more than a dozen yards of the path before me. This path was excessively sinuous, and as the sun could not be seen, I soon lost all idea of the direction in which I journeyed. In the meantime the morphine had its customary effect—that of enduing all the external world with an intensity of interest. In the quivering of a leaf—in the hue of a blade of grass—in the shape of a trefoil—in the humming of a bee—in the gleaming of a dewdrop—in the breathing of the wind—in the faint odors that came from the forest—there came a whole universe of suggestion—a gay and motly train of rhapsodical and immethodical thought.

"Busied in this, I walked on for several hours, during which the mist deepened around me to so great an extent, that at length I was reduced to an absolute groping of the way. And now an indescribable uneasiness possessed me—a species of nervous hesitation and tremor. I feared to tread, lest I should be precipitated into some abyss. I remembered, too, strange stories told about these Ragged Hills, and of the uncouth and fierce races of men who tenanted their groves and caverns. A thousand vague fancies oppressed and disconcerted me—fancies the more distressing because vague. Very suddenly my attention was arrested by the loud beating of a drum.

"My amazement was, of course, extreme. A drum in these hills was a thing unknown. I could not have been more surprised at the sound of the trump of the Archangel. But a new and still more astounding source of interest and perplexity arose. There came a wild rattling or jingling sound, as if of a bunch of large keys—and upon the instant a dusky-visaged and half-naked man rushed past me with a shriek. He came so close to my person that I felt his hot breath upon my face. He bore in one hand an instrument composed of an assemblage of steel rings, and shook them vigorously as he ran. Scarcely had he disappeared in the mist, before, panting after him, with open mouth and glaring eyes, there darted a huge beast. I could not be mistaken in its character. It was a hyena.

"The sight of this monster rather relieved than heightened my terrors—for I now made sure that I dreamed, and endeavored to arouse myself to waking consciousness. I stepped boldly and briskly forward. I rubbed my eyes. I called aloud. I pinched my limbs. A small spring of water presented itself to my view, and here, stooping, I bathed my hands and my head and neck. This seemed to dissipate the equivocal sensations which had hitherto annoyed me. I arose, as I thought, a new man, and proceeded steadily and complacently on my unknown way.

"At length, quite overcome by exertion, and by a certain oppressive closeness of the atmosphere, I seated myself beneath a tree. Presently there came a feeble gleam of sunshine, and the shadow of the leaves of the tree fell faintly but definitely upon the grass. At this shadow I gazed wonderingly for many minutes. Its character stupified me with astonishment. I looked upward. The tree was a palm.

"I now arose hurriedly, and in a state of fearful agitation—for the fancy that I dreamed would serve me no longer. I saw—I felt that I had perfect command of my senses—and these senses now brought to my soul a world of novel and singular sensation. The heat became all at once intolerable. A strange odor loaded the breeze. A low continuous murmur, like that arising from a full, but gently-flowing river, came to my ears, intermingled with the peculiar hum of multitudinous human voices.

"While I listened in an extremity of astonishment which I need not attempt to describe, a strong and brief gust of wind bore off the incumbent fog as if by the wand of an enchanter.

"I found myself at the foot of a high mountain, and looking down into a vast plain, through which wound a majestic river. On the margin of this river stood an Eastern-looking city, such as we read of in the Arabian Tales, but of a character even more singular than any there described. From my position, which was far above the level of the town, I could perceive its every nook and corner, as if delineated on a map. The streets seemed innumerable, and crossed each other irregularly in all directions, but were rather long winding alleys than streets, and absolutely swarmed with inhabitants. The houses were wildly picturesque. On every hand was a wilderness of balconies, of verandahs, of minarets, of shrines, and fantastically carved oriels. Bazaars abounded; and in these were displayed rich wares in infinite variety and profusion—silks, muslims, the most dazzling cutlery, the most magnificent jewels and gems. Besides these things, were seen, on all sides, banners and palanquins, litters with stately dames close veiled, elephants gorgeously caparisoned, idols grotesquely hewn, drums, banners and gongs, spears, silver and gilded maces. And amid the crowd, and the clamor, and the general intricacy and confusion—amid the million of Black and yellow men, turbaned and robed, and of flowing beard, there roamed a countless multitude of holy filleted bulls, while vast legions of the filthy but sacred ape clambered, chattering and shrieking, about the cornices of the mosques, or clung to the minarets and oriels. From the swarming streets to the banks of the river, there descended innumerable flights of steps leading to bathing places, while the river itself seemed to force a passage with difficulty through the vast fleets of deeply-burthened ships that far and wide encumbered its surface. Beyond the limits of the city arose, in frequent majestic groups, the palm and the cocoa, with other gigantic and wierd trees of vast age; and here and there might be seen a field of rice, the thatched hut of a peasant, a tank, a stray temple, a gypsy camp, or a solitary graceful maiden taking her way, with a pitcher upon her head, to the banks of the magnificent river.

"You will say now, of course, that I dreamed; but not so. What I saw—what I heard—what I felt—what I thought—had about it nothing of the unmistakeable idiosyncrasy of the dream. All was rigorously self-consistent. At first, doubting that I was really awake, I entered into a series of tests, which soon convinced me that I really was. Now, when one dreams, and, in the dream, suspects that he dreams, the suspicion *never fails to confirm itself,* and the sleeper is almost immediately aroused. Thus Novalis[2] errs not in saying that 'we are near waking when we dream that we dream.' Had the vision occurred to me as I describe it, without my suspecting it as a dream, then a dream it might absolutely have been, but, occurring as it did, and suspected and tested as it was, I am forced to class it among other phenomena."

"In this I am not sure that you are wrong," observed Dr. Templeton, "but proceed. You arose and descended into the city."

"I arose," continued Bedloe, regarding the Doctor with an air of profound astonishment, "I arose, as you say, and descended into the city. On my way, I fell in with an immense populace, crowding, through every avenue, all in the same direction, and exhibiting in every action the wildest excitement. Very suddenly, and by some inconceivable impulse, I became intensely imbued with personal interest in what was going on. I seemed to feel that I had an important part to play, without exactly understanding what it was. Against the crowd which environed me, however, I experienced a deep sentiment of animosity. I shrank from amid them, and, swiftly, by a circuitous path, reached and entered the city. Here all was the wildest tumult and contention. A small party of men, clad in garments half-Indian half European, and officered by gentlemen in a uniform partly British, were engaged, at great odds, with the swarming rabble of the alleys. I joined the weaker party, arming myself with the weapons of a fallen officer, and fighting I knew not whom with the nervous ferocity of despair. We were soon overpowered by numbers, and driven to seek refuge in a species of kiosk. Here we barricaded ourselves, and, for the present, were secure. From a loop-hole near the summit of the kiosk,[3] I perceived a vast crowd, in furious agitation, surrounding and assaulting a gay palace that overhung the river. Presently, from an upper window of this palace, there descended an effeminate-looking person, by means of a string made of the turbans of his attendants. A boat was at hand, in which he escaped to the opposite bank of the river.

"And now a new object took possession of my soul. I spoke a few hurried but energetic words to my companions, and, having succeeded in gaining over a few of them to my purpose, made a frantic sally from the kiosk. We rushed amid the crowd that surrounded it. They retreated, at first, before us. They rallied, fought madly, and retreated again. In the mean time we were borne far from the kiosk, and became bewildered and entangled among the narrow streets of tall overhanging houses, into the recesses of which the sun had never been able to shine. The rabble pressed impetuously upon us, harassing us with their spears, and overwhelming us with flights of arrows. These latter were very remarkable, and resembled in some respects the writhing creese of the Malay. They were made to imitate the body of a creeping serpent, and were long and black, with a poisoned barb. One of them struck me upon the right temple. I reeled and fell. An instantaneous and deadly sickness seized me. I struggled—I gasped—I died."

"You will hardly persist *now,*" said I, smiling, "that the whole of your adventure was not a dream. You are not prepared to maintain that you are dead?"

2. Novalis (1772–1801) was a German Romantic poet.

3. An open pavilion.

When I said these words, I of course expected some lively sally from Bedloe in reply; but, to my astonishment, he hesitated, trembled, became fearfully pallid, and remained silent. I looked towards Templeton. He sat erect and rigid in his chair—his teeth chattered, and his eyes were starting from their sockets. "Proceed!" he at length said hoarsely to Bedloe.

"For many minutes," continued the latter, "my sole sentiment—my sole feeling—was that of darkness and nonentity, with the consciousness of death. At length, there seemed to pass a violent and sudden shock through my soul, as if of electricity. With it came the sense of elasticity and of light. This latter I felt—not saw. In an instant I seemed to rise from the ground. But I had no bodily, no visible, audible, or palpable presence. The crowd had departed. The tumult had ceased. The city was in comparative repose. Beneath me lay my corpse, with the arrow in my temple, the whole head greatly swollen and disfigured. But all these things I felt—not saw. I took interest in nothing. Even the corpse seemed a matter in which I had no concern. Volition I had none, but appeared to be impelled into motion, and flitted buoyantly out of the city, retracing the circuitous path by which I had entered it. When I had attained that point of the ravine in the mountains, at which I had encountered the hyena, I again experienced a shock as of a galvanic battery; the sense of weight, of volition, of substance, returned. I became my original self, and bent my steps eagerly homewards—but the past had not lost the vividness of the real—and not now, even for an instant, can I compel my understanding to regard it as a dream."

"Nor was it," said Templeton, with an air of deep solemnity, "yet it would be difficult to say how otherwise it should be termed. Let us suppose only, that the soul of the man of to-day is upon the verge of some stupendous psychal discoveries. Let us content ourselves with this supposition. For the rest I have some explanation to make. Here is a water-colour drawing, which I should have shown you before, but which an unaccountable sentiment of horror has hitherto prevented me from showing."

We looked at the picture which he presented. I saw nothing in it of an extraordinary character; but its effect upon Bedloe was prodigious. He nearly fainted as he gazed. And yet it was but a miniature portrait—a miraculously accurate one, to be sure—of his own very remarkable features. At least this was my thought as I regarded it.

"You will perceive," said Templeton, "the date of this picture—it is here, scarcely visible, in this corner—1780. In this year was the portrait taken. It is the likeness of a dead friend—a Mr. Oldeb—to whom I became much attached at Calcutta, during the administration of Warren Hastings. I was then only twenty years old. When I first saw you, Mr. Bedloe, at Saratoga, it was the miraculous similarity which existed between yourself and the painting, which induced me to accost you, to seek your friendship, and to bring about those arrangements which resulted in my becoming your constant companion. In accomplishing this point, I was urged partly, and perhaps principally, by a regretful memory of the deceased, but also, in part, by an uneasy, and not altogether horrorless curiosity respecting yourself.

"In your detail of the vision which presented itself to you amid the hills, you have described, with the minutest accuracy, the Indian city of Benares, upon the Holy River. The riots, the combats, the massacre, were the actual events of the insurrection of Cheyte Sing, which took place in 1780, when Hastings was put in imminent peril of his life. The man escaping by the string of turbans, was Cheyte Sing himself. The party in the kiosk were sepoys[4] and British officers, headed by Hastings.

4. An Indian officer in the employ of the British.

Of this party I was one, and did all I could to prevent the rash and fatal sally of the officer who fell, in the crowded alleys, by the poisoned arrow of a Bengalee. That officer was my dearest friend. It was Oldeb. You will perceive by these manuscripts," (here the speaker produced a notebook in which several pages appeared to have been freshly written) "that at the very period in which you fancied these things amid the hills, I was engaged in detailing them upon paper here at home."

In about a week after this conversation, the following paragraphs appeared in a Charlottesville paper.

"We have the painful duty of announcing the death of Mr. AUGUSTUS BEDLO, a gentleman whose amiable manners and many virtues have long endeared him to the citizens of Charlottesville.

"Mr. B., for some years past, has been subject to neuralgia, which has often threatened to terminate fatally; but this can be regarded only as the mediate cause of his decease. The proximate cause was one of especial singularity. In an excursion to the Ragged Mountains, a few days since, a slight cold and fever were contracted, attended with great determination of blood to the head. To relieve this, Dr. Templeton resorted to topical bleeding. Leeches were applied to the temples. In a fearfully brief period the patient died, when it appeared that, in the jar containing the leeches, had been introduced, by accident, one of the venomous vermicular sangsues[5] which are now and then found in the neighboring ponds. This creature fastened itself upon a small artery in the right temple. Its close resemblance to the medicinal leech caused the mistake to be overlooked until too late.

"N. B. The poisonous sangsue of Charlottesville may always be distinguished from the medicinal leech by its blackness, and especially by its writhing or vermicular motions, which very nearly resemble those of a snake."

I was speaking with the editor of the paper in question, upon the topic of this remarkable accident, when it occurred to me to ask how it happened that the name of the deceased had been given as Bedlo.

"I presume," said I, "you have authority for this spelling, but I have always supposed the name to be written with an *e* at the end."

"Authority?—no," he replied. "It is a mere typographical error. The name is Bedlo with an *e*, all the world over, and I never knew it to be spelt otherwise in my life."

"Then," said I mutteringly, as I turned upon my heel, "then indeed has it come to pass that one truth is stranger than any fiction—for Bedlo, without the *e*, what is it but Oldeb conversed? And this man tells me it is a typographical error."

Questions to Consider

1. How does Poe's description of the forest in "A Tale of the Ragged Mountains" work to construct the Southern forest as a place of fantasy and dread? How might that construction relate to traditional descriptions of the forest in Southern literature found in the work of John Smith or William Byrd?
2. What is the relationship of knowledge to loss in "The Raven," and how is that relationship portrayed in the poem's symbols and language?
3. What do you find in Poe that marks him as a Southern writer? How does his work transcend the Southern traditions?

5. Leeches indigenous to the Charlottesville, VA region.

VOICES IN CONTEXT

Southwestern Humor

In the early 1800s, the frontier of the American South began to extend into territories that would become the states of Georgia, Alabama, Tennessee, Mississippi, Missouri, Arkansas, and Louisiana. From the early 1830s to the beginning of the Civil War in 1861, sketches appeared in the newspapers of frontier towns describing the backwoods life and characters of the new Southern frontier. Written by authors who were often transplanted lawyers, judges, doctors, and newspapermen, these sketches were largely humorous depictions of life on the frontier and owed much to oral narrative traditions such as the tall tale. Many of these entertaining sketches became widely circulated in the newspapers and magazines back east. One such magazine was William Porter's *Spirit of the Times*, which published a great many of these sketches. The popularity of these sketches spawned a genre of Southern literature known as the Humor of the Old Southwest.

Generally, these sketches were the action-adventure stories of the day, and most of them featured a garrulous main character who was either a great hunter or a free-spirited con man, such as George Washington Harris's character, Sut Lovingood. Harris's character became so popular that his motto, "it is good to be shifty in a new country," became a national catchphrase. Like many of the characters of these sketches, Sut was a coarse and semi-literate man who possessed an uncanny gift for verbal expression and was prone to exaggeration, digression, and calculated understatement. Often, the primary narrator of these sketches would be the author himself, who would describe his own adventures in the frontier and his encounters with lazy backwoodsmen and shiftless mountaineers. In other sketches, the narrator would encounter a backwoods yarn-spinner, who would then regale the narrator with burlesque and supposedly improvised tales of his adventures in the frontier.

Modern readers may find these stories offensive. Often, they are full of violence, cruelty, and a basic disregard for human life, especially the lives of Native Americans, African Americans, and women. They often contain light obscenity and offensive racial epithet, and many feature euphemistically described instances of promiscuity and references to bodily and excretory functions. Nevertheless, the authors of these sketches generally wrote them to be enjoyed by a predominately male readership, and the authors justified the coarseness of the language and the featuring of questionable topics by claiming only to represent Southern dialect and frontier life honestly. Often, the tales glorified the freedom of the frontier and focused on the pleasantries of a life of hunting, fishing, and trapping, activities that remain popular throughout the region today, perhaps accounting for the appeal of these works to modern readers.

Critics have noted that this genre, which included authors such as Augustus Baldwin Longstreet of Georgia, Joseph Glover Baldwin and Johnson Jones Hooper of Alabama, George Washington Harris of Tennessee, Thomas Bangs Thorpe of Mississippi, and Henry Clay Lewis of Louisiana, was influential on the work of Mark Twain and, later, William Faulkner and Flannery O'Connor. While modern readers may find the dialect and content of these stories troublesome, they generally offer an interesting if somewhat exaggerated look at what life was like in the Southern frontier.

Augustus Baldwin Longstreet

1790–1870

Augustus Baldwin Longstreet considered himself a social and cultural historian and hoped his stories and sketches would serve as a record of nineteenth-century Southern life. They usually employ light humor and draw upon the local customs and traditions of Georgia, but their main effect is to accent the differences in values among the various classes of Southerners. The characters and situations Longstreet described allowed him to comment on the relative morality of those differences as well.

Born in Augusta, Georgia, in 1790, Longstreet consciously followed in the footsteps of his idol, John C. Calhoun, by studying at Yale and at the Litchfield Law School. A vital and energetic young man, he returned to Georgia to practice law and begin a political career, serving in the State Assembly. For several years he was judge of the Georgia Superior Court, during which time he traveled throughout Georgia and began writing realistic stories about the people and places he saw. He published these under several pseudonyms in newspapers such as the Milledgeville *Southern Recorder*. Longstreet later ran for Congress as an ardent advocate of states' rights. He abandoned his campaign and public service as well, however, when his son died in 1824. He was ordained a Methodist minister in 1838 and went on to serve as president of Emory College (now Emory University) in Georgia, Centenary College in Louisiana, the University of Mississippi, and South Carolina College (now the University of South Carolina).

In 1834, Longstreet became owner and editor of the *States' Rights Sentinel*. In this paper, he republished many of his sketches and stories and wrote articles and pamphlets opposing the increasing power of the federal government. While at the paper, he also published a collection of his stories and sketches under the unwieldy title *Georgia Scenes, Characters, Incidents, and etc., in the First Half Century of the Republic: by a Native Georgian*. The book enjoyed a wide readership and was favorably reviewed in the *Southern Literary Messenger* by Edgar Allan Poe, a notoriously harsh critic. *Harper's* reprinted the book in 1840 because it had become so popular.

Following the success of his book, Longstreet continued to publish stories in journals and newspapers such as in the *Augusta Mirror, Southern Miscellany*, and *The Magnolia*, but he never completed another collection. In 1864, he published a novel, *Master William Mitten*, which was largely autobiographical.

Longstreet is considered to be among the first of a group of authors including Joseph Glover Baldwin, George Washington Harris, Johnson Jones Hooper, and Thomas Bangs Thorpe, who are known as the Southwestern Humorists. Like Longstreet's "The Dance," the works of these authors often describe customs of the region and feature garrulous narrators and characters who speak in the local idiom.

The influence of Longstreet's writing can be found in the work of his contemporary George Washington Harris, as well as in the works of Mark Twain and, later, William Faulkner. Faulkner, in particular, took much from Longstreet, and Faulkner's story "Spotted Horses" is often compared to Longstreet's "The Horse Swap." As more attention has been given to Southern literature, the label "regionalist" has become a limiting perspective, especially for Longstreet. Despite the regional flavor of much of his work—and Longstreet demonstrated great facility for the settings, characters, customs and speech of Georgia—he is best remembered as a literary realist.

from Georgia Scenes, Characters, Incidents, and etc., in the First Half Century of the Republic: by a Native Georgian

The Dance. A Personal Adventure of the Author

Some years ago I was called by business to one of the frontier counties, then but recently settled. It became necessary for me, while there, to enlist the services of Thomas Gibson, Esq., one of the magistrates of the county, who resided about a mile and a half from my lodgings; and to this circumstance was I indebted for my introduction to him. I had made the intended disposition of my business, and was on the eve of my departure for the city of my residence, when I was induced to remain a day longer by an invitation from the squire to attend a dance at his house on the following day. Having learned from my landlord that I would probably "be expected at the frolic" about the hour of 10 in the forenoon, and being desirous of seeing all that passed upon the occasion, I went over about an hour before the time.

The squire's dwelling consisted of but one room, which answered the threefold purpose of dining-room, bed-room, and kitchen. The house was constructed of logs, and the floor was of *puncheons;* a term which, in Georgia, means split logs, with their faces a little smoothed with the axe or hatchet. To gratify his daughters, Polly and Silvy, the old gentleman and his lady had consented to *camp out* for a day, and to surrender the habitation to the girls and their young friends.

When I reached there I found all things in readiness for the promised amusement. The girls, as the old gentleman informed me, had compelled the family to breakfast under the trees, for they had completely stripped the house of its furniture before the sun rose. They were already attired for the dance, in neat but plain habiliments of their own manufacture. "What!" says some weakly, sickly, delicate, useless, affected, "charming creature" of the city, "dressed for a ball at 9 in the morning!" Even so, my delectable Miss Octavia Matilda Juliana Claudia Ipecacuanha; and what have you to say against it? If people must dance, is it not much more rational to employ the hour allotted to exercise in that amusement, than the hours sacred to repose and meditation? And which is entitled to the most credit: the young lady who rises with the dawn, and puts herself and whole house in order for a ball four hours before it begins, or the one who requires a fortnight to get herself dressed for it?

The squire and I employed the interval in conversation about the first settlement of the country, in the course of which I picked up some useful and much interesting information. We were at length interrupted, however, by the sound of a violin, which proceeded from a thick wood at my left. The performer soon after made his appearance, and proved to be no other than Billy Porter, a negro fellow of much harmless wit and humour, who was well known throughout the State. Poor Billy! "His harp is now hung upon the willow;" and I would not blush to offer a tear to his memory, for his name is associated with some of the happiest scenes of my life, and he sleeps with many a dear friend, who used to join me in provoking his wit and in laughing at his eccentricities; but I am leading my reader to the grave instead of the dance, which I promised. If, however, his memory reaches twelve years back, he will excuse this short tribute of respect to Billy Porter.

Billy, to give his own account of himself, "had been taking a turn with the brethren (the bar); and, hearing the ladies wanted to see *pretty Billy*, had come to give them a benefit." The squire had not seen him before; and it is no disrespect to his understanding or politeness to say, that he found it impossible to give me his attention for half an hour after Billy arrived. I had nothing to do, therefore, while the young people were assembling, but to improve my knowledge of Billy's character, to the squire's amusement. I had been thus engaged about thirty minutes, when I saw several fine, bouncing, ruddy-cheeked girls descending a hill about the eighth of a mile off. They, too, were attired in manufactures of their own hands. The refinements of the present day in female dress had not even reached our republican *cities* at this time; and, of course, the *country girls* were wholly ignorant of them. They carried no more cloth upon their arms or straw upon their heads than was necessary to cover them. They used no artificial means of spreading their frock tails to an interesting extent from their ankles. They had no boards laced to their breasts, nor any corsets laced to their sides; consequently, they looked, for all the world, like human beings, and could be distinctly recognised as such at the distance of two hundred paces. Their movements were as free and active as nature would permit them to be. Let me not be understood as interposing the least objection to any lady in this land of liberty dressing just as she pleases. If she choose to lay her neck and shoulders bare, what right have I to look at them? much less to find fault with them. If she choose to put three yards of muslin in a frock sleeve, what right have I to ask why a little strip of it was not put in the body? If she like the pattern of a hoisted umbrella for a frock, and the shape of a cheese-cask for her body, what is all that to me? But to return.

The girls were met by Polly and Silvy Gibson at some distance from the house, who welcomed them—"with a kiss, of course"—oh, no; but with something much less equivocal: a hearty shake of the hand and smiling countenances, which had some meaning.

[*Note.*—The custom of kissing, as practiced in these days by the *amiables,* is borrowed from the French, and by them from Judas.]

The young ladies had generally collected before any of the young men appeared. It was not long, however, before a large number of both sexes were assembled, and they adjourned to the *ballroom*.

But for the snapping of a fiddle-string, the young people would have been engaged in the amusement of the day in less than three minutes from the time they entered the house. Here were no formal introductions to be given, no drawing for places or partners, no parade of managers, no ceremonies. It was perfectly understood that all were invited *to dance,* and that none were invited who were unworthy to be danced with; consequently, no gentleman hesitated to ask any lady present to dance with him, and no lady refused to dance with a gentleman merely because she had not been made acquainted with him.

In a short time the string was repaired, and off went the party to a good old republican six reel. I had been thrown among *fashionables* so long that I had almost forgotten my native dance. But it revived rapidly as they wheeled through its mazes, and with it returned many long-forgotten, pleasing recollections. Not only did the reel return to me, but the very persons who used to figure in it with me, in the heyday of youth.

Here was my old sweetheart, Polly Jackson, identically personified in Polly Gibson; and here was Jim Johnson's, in Silvy; and Bill Martin's, in Nancy Ware. Polly Gibson had my old flame's very steps as well as her looks. "Ah!" said I, "squire, this puts me in mind of old times. I have not seen a six reel for five-and-twenty years. It recalls to my mind many a happy hour, and many a jovial friend who used to enliven it with me. Your Polly looks so much like my old sweetheart, Polly Jackson, that, were I young again, I certainly should fall in love with her."

"That was the name of her mother," said the squire.

"Where did you marry her?" inquired I.

"In Wilkes," said he; "she was the daughter of old Nathan Jackson, of that county."

"It isn't possible!" returned I. "Then it is the very girl of whom I am speaking. Where is she?"

"She's out," said the squire, "preparing dinner for the young people; but she'll be in towards the close of the day. But come along, and I'll make you acquainted with her at once, if you'll promise not to run away with her, for I tell you what it is, she's the likeliest *gal* in all these parts yet."

"Well," said I, "I'll promise not to run away with her, but you must not let her know who I am. I wish to make myself known to her; and, for fear of the worst, you shall witness the introduction. But don't get jealous, squire, if she seems a little too glad to see me; for, I assure you, we had a strong notion of each other when we were young."

"No danger," replied the squire; "she hadn't seen *me* then, or she never could have loved such a hard favoured man as you are."

In the meantime the dance went on, and I employed myself in selecting from the party the best examples of the dancers of my day and Mrs. Gibson's for her entertainment. In this I had not the least difficulty; for the dancers before me and those of my day were in all respects identical.

Jim Johnson kept up the double shuffle from the beginning to the end of the reel; and here was Jim over again in Sammy Tant. Bill Martin always set to his partner with the same step; and a very curious step it was. He brought his right foot close behind his left, and with it performed precisely the motion of the thumb in cracking that insect which Burns has immortalized; then moved his right back, threw his weight upon it, brought his left behind it, and *cracked* with that as before; and so on alternately. Just so did Bill Kemp, to a nail. Bob Simons danced for all the world like a "Suple Jack" (or, as we commonly call it, a "*Suple* Sawney"), when the string is pulled with varied force, at intervals of seconds: and so did *Jake* Slack. Davy Moore went like a suit of clothes upon a clothing line on a windy day; and here was his antitype in Ned Clark. Rhoda Nobles swam through the reel like a cork on wavy waters; always giving two or three pretty little perchbite *diddles* as she rose from a coupee: Nancy Ware was her very self. Becky Lewis made a business of dancing; she disposed of her part as quick as possible, stopped dead short as soon as she got through, and looked as sober as a judge all the time; even so did Chloe Dawson. I used to tell Polly Jackson, that Becky's countenance, when she closed a dance, always seemed to say, "Now, if you want any more dancing, you may do it yourself."

The dance grew merrier as it progressed; the young people became more easy in each other's company, and often enlivened the scene with most humorous remarks. Occasionally some sharp cuts passed between the boys, such as would have produced half a dozen duels at a city ball; but here they were taken as they were meant, in good humour. Jim Johnson being a little tardy in meeting his partner at a turn of the reel, "I *ax* pardon, Miss Chloe," said he; "Jake Slack went to make a crosshop just now, and tied his legs in a hard knot, and I stop'd to help him untie them." A little after, Jake hung his toe in a crack of the floor, and nearly fell. "Ding my buttons;" said he, "if I didn't know I should stumble over Jim Johnson's foot at last; Jim, draw your foot up to your own end of the reel." (Jim was at the other end of the reel, and had, in truth, a prodigious foot.)

Towards the middle of the day, many of the neighbouring farmers dropped in and joined the squire and myself in talking of old times. At length dinner was announced. It consisted of plain *fare*, but there was a profusion of it. Rough planks, supported by stakes driven in the ground, served for a table, at which the old and young of both sexes seated themselves at the same time. I soon recognized Mrs. Gibson from all the matrons present. Thirty years had wrought great changes in her appearance, but they had left some of her features entirely unimpaired. Her eye beamed with all its youthful fire, and, to my astonishment, her mouth was still beautified with a full set of teeth, unblemished by time. The rose on her cheek had rather freshened than faded and her smile was the very same that first subdued my heart, but her fine form was wholly lost, and, with it, all the grace of her movements. Pleasing but melancholy reflections occupied my mind as I gazed on her dispensing her cheerful hospitalities. I thought of the sad history of many of her companions and mine, who used to carry light hearts through the merry dance. I compared my after life with the cloudless days of my attachment to Polly. Then I was light hearted, gay, contented and happy. I aspired to nothing but a good name, a good wife, and an easy competence. The first and last were mine already, and Polly had given me too many little tokens of her favour to leave a doubt now that the second was at my command. But I was foolishly told that my talents were of too high an order to be employed in the drudgeries of a farm, and I more foolishly believed it. I forsook the pleasures which I had tried and proved and went in pursuit of those imaginary joys which seemed to encircle the seat of Fame. From that moment to the present, my life had been little else than one unbroken scene of disaster, disappointment, vexation, and toil. And now, when I was too old to enjoy the pleasures which I had discarded, I found that my aim was absolutely hopeless, and that my pursuits had only served to unfit me for the humbler walks of life, and to exclude me from the higher. The gloom of these reflections was, however, lightened in a measure by the promises of the coming hour, when I was to live over again with Mrs. Gibson some of the happiest moments of my life.

After a hasty repast the young people returned to their amusement, followed by myself, with several of the elders of the company. An hour had scarcely elapsed before Mrs. Gibson entered, accompanied by a goodly number of matrons of her own age. This accession to the company produced its usual effects. It raised the tone of conversation a full octave, and gave it a triple time movement; added new life to the wit and limbs of the young folk and set the old men to cracking jokes.

At length the time arrived for me to surprise and delight Mrs. Gibson. The young people insisted upon the old folks taking a reel, and this was just what I had been waiting for, for, after many plans for making the discovery, I had finally concluded upon that which I thought would make *her* joy general among the company; and that was to announce myself, just before leading her to the dance, in a voice audible to most of the assembly. I therefore readily assented to the proposition of the young folks, as did two others of my age, and we made to the ladies for our partners. I, of course, offered my hand to Mrs. Gibson.

"Come," said I, "Mrs. Gibson, let us see if we can't out dance these young people."

"Dear me, sir," said she, "I haven't danced a step these twenty years."

"Neither have I; but I've resolved to try once more, if you will join me, just for old time's sake."

"I really cannot think of dancing," said she.

"Well," continued I (raising my voice to a pretty high pitch, on purpose to be heard, while my countenance kindled with exultation at the astonishment and delight which I was about to produce), "you surely will dance with an old friend and sweetheart, who used to dance with you when a girl!"

At this disclosure her features assumed a vast variety of expressions, but none of them responded precisely to my expectation; indeed, some of them were of such an equivocal and alarming character that I deemed it advisable not to prolong her suspense. I therefore proceeded:

"Have you forgot your old sweetheart, Abram Baldwin?"

"What!" she said, looking more astonished and confused than ever. "Abram Baldwin! Abram Baldwin! I don't think I ever heard the name before."

"Do you remember Jim Johnson?" said I.

"Oh, yes," said she, "mighty well," her countenance brightening with a smile.

"And Bill Martin?"

"Yes, perfectly well; why, *who* are you?"

Here we were interrupted by one of the gentlemen, who had led his partner to the floor, with, "Come, stranger, we're getting mighty tired o' standing. It won't do for old people that's going to dance to take up much time in standing; they'll lose all their *spryness*. Don't stand begging Polly Gibson, she never dances, but take my Sal there, next to her; she'll run a reel with you, to old Nick's house and back *agin*."

No alternative was left me, and therefore I offered my hand to Mrs. Sally—I didn't know who.

"Well," thought I, as I moved to my place, "the squire is pretty secure from jealousy; but Polly will soon remember me when she sees my steps in the reel. I will dance precisely as I used to in my youth, if it tire me to death." There was one step that was almost exclusively my own, for few of the dancers of my day could perform it at all, and none with the grace and ease that I did. "She'll remember Abram Baldwin," thought I, "as soon as she sees the *double cross-hop*." It was performed by rising and crossing the legs twice or thrice before lighting, and I used to carry it to the third cross with considerable ease. It was a step solely adapted to setting or balancing, as all will perceive; but I thought the occasion would justify a little perversion of it, and therefore resolved to lead off with it, that Polly might be at once relieved from suspense. Just, however, as I reached my place, Mrs. Gibson's youngest son, a boy about eight years old, ran in and cried out, "Mammy, old Boler's jump'd upon the planks, and dragg'd off a great hunk o' meat as big as your head, and broke a dish and two plates all to darn smashes!" Away went Mrs. Gibson, and off went the music. Still I hoped that matters would be adjusted in time for Polly to return and see the double cross-hop, and I felt the mortification which my delay in getting a partner had occasioned somewhat solaced by the reflection that it had thrown me at the foot of the reel.

The first and second couples had nearly completed their performances, and Polly had not returned. I began to grow uneasy, and to interpose as many delays as I could without attracting notice.

The six reel is closed by the foot couple balancing at the head of the set, then in the middle, then at the foot, again in the middle, meeting at the head, and leading down.

My partner and I had commenced balancing at the head and Polly had not returned. I balanced until my partner forced me on. I now deemed it advisable to give myself up wholly to the double cross-hop, so that, if Polly should return in time to see any step, it should be this, though I was already nearly exhausted. Accordingly, I made the attempt to introduce it in the turns of the reel; but the first experiment convinced me of three things at once: 1st. That I could not have used the step in this way in my best days; 2d. That my strength would not more than support it in its proper place for the remainder of the reel; and 3d. If I tried it again in this way I should knock my brains out against the puncheons, for my partner, who seemed determined to confirm her husband's report of her, evinced no disposition to wait upon experiments, but, fetching me a jerk while I was up and my legs crossed, had well-nigh sent me head foremost to Old Nick's house, sure enough.

We met in the middle, my back to the door, and from the silence that prevailed in the yard, I flattered myself that Polly might be even now catching the first glimpse of the fovourite step, when I heard her voice at some distance from the house: "Get you gone! G-e-e-t you gone! G-e-e-e-e-e-t you gone!" Matters out doors were now clearly explained. There had been a struggle to get the meat from Boler; Boler had triumphed and retreated to the woods with his booty, and Mrs. Gibson was heaping indignities upon him in the last resort.

The three *"Get-you-gones"* met me precisely at the three closing balances; and the last brought my moral energies to a perfect level with my physical.

Mrs. Gibson returned, however, in a few minutes after in a good humour; for she possessed a lovely disposition, which even marriage could not spoil. As soon as I could collect breath enough for regular conversation (for, to speak in my native dialect, I was *"mortal tired"*), I took a seat by her, resolved not to quit the house without making myself known to her, if possible.

"How much," said I, "your Polly looks and dances like you used to at her age."

"I've told my old man so a hundred times," said she. "Why, who upon earth are you!"

"Did you ever see two persons dance more alike than Jim Johnson and Sammy Tant?"

"Never. Why, who can you be?"

"You remember Becky Lewis?"

"Yes!"

"Well, look at Chloe Dawson, and you'll see her over again."

"Well, law me! Now I know I must have seen you somewhere; but, to save my life, I can't tell where. Where did your father live?"

"He died when I was small."

"And where did you use to see me?"

"At your father's, and old Mr. Dawson's, and at Mrs. Barnes's, and at Squire Noble's, and many other places."

"Well, goodness me! it's mighty strange I can't call you to mind."

I now began to get petulant, and thought it best to leave her.

The dance wound up with the old merry jig, and the company dispersed.

The next day I set out for my residence. I had been at home rather more than two months, when I received the following letter from Squire Gibson:

"DEAR SIR: I send you the money collected on the notes you left with me. Since you left here, Polly has been thinking about old times, and she says, to save her life, she can't recollect you."

Baldwin

Questions to Consider

1. In "The Dance," how does Longstreet use the hour of the dance, the method of greeting, the dress of the locals, and their behavior to comment on the morals of the frontier people?
2. The use of humor in Longstreet's sketches is lighter and more removed than that of many other Southwestern Humorists. What purpose does the light humor serve in Longstreet's comments on frontier life?

George Washington Harris

1814–1869

George Washington Harris was born in western Pennsylvania in 1814. As a boy, he was apprenticed to his half-brother, who owned a metalworking shop in Knoxville, Tennessee. By the time he was nineteen, Harris had become a captain on the steamboat The Knoxville, although he left the river after a few years to try his hand at farming just outside Knoxville. After the farm failed, he moved back to the city to open a jewelry and metalworking shop of his own.

Harris received very little formal education, but he loved a good story and had an ear for regional dialect. He began publishing sketches of rural Southern life in the local newspapers and in the New York sporting journal *Spirit of the Times*, often under the pseudonym, Mr. Free. In 1845, Harris published "The Knob Dance," which featured a comic, folksy narrator named Dick Harlan who spoke in rural Southern dialect. In 1854, he expanded his use of Southern vernacular and humor in the first of a series of sketches featuring a character named Sut Lovingood, a somewhat ribald and intense backwoods Tennessee youth who called himself a "nat'ral born durn'd fool." Throughout the series, which came to be known as the Lovingood Tales, Harris carefully sought to reproduce the cadences of backwoods Tennessee dialect in humorous and satirical sketches, which are filled with interesting, self-possessed characters and uninhibited, comic scenes.

Generally, the tales told by Sut Lovingood center on his search for adventure and sexual conquest, his disrespect for authority and love of drinking, and his struggles in the battle of the sexes. Increasingly, the Lovingood Tales became more political, at first focusing on the insularity of Southern rural communities and then expanding to include satires of various prominent public figures, usually abolitionists, suffragettes, and idealists of all stripes. Harris was an outspoken secessionist and a supporter of slavery and states' rights, which are all political perspectives evident in the Lovingood Tales. Often, the character Sut Lovingood plays the role of amiable fool in the stories, but through his character, Harris points his satiric wit at various aspects of Southern and American culture, mixing humor with biting satire. In 1867, twenty-four of the Lovingood Tales were collected and published as *Sut Lovingood, Yarns Spun by a "Nat'ral Born Durn'd Fool,"* Harris's only published book. In 1869, Harris produced a new volume of Lovingood tales entitled *High Times and Hard Times*, but before he could find a publisher, he died under mysterious circumstances. The manuscript for the book has never been found, although a collection of Harris's work assembled by a modern editor appears under that title.

The Lovingood Tales were extremely popular, and Harris is considered to have influenced Mark Twain, Robert Penn Warren, Flannery O'Connor, and William Faulkner. However, some early readers found Harris's politics and Sut Lovingood's ribald humor and promiscuous ways to be offensive. Readers may chaff at the chauvinistic and intolerant attitudes evident in the following selection, but Harris was a fine humorist and satirist, and his attention to the vernacular dialect and to Southern folkways make the Lovingood Tales worthy of contemporary attention.

Sut at a Negro Night-Meeting

"Quit yer kerd playin an' ritin, an' listen tu me; I'se swell'd up wif a tale, an' I'll bust rite yere in this camp ef I don't git hit outen me. I 'sisted wunst at a nigger meetin at Log Chapil camp-groun', tu more pupus an' wif more pint than folks ginerly 'sists on sich cashuns."

"You assisted? When?"

"Yas, yu may whistil, but durn ef I didn't. Aint the word rite? Ef a feller stands up when anuther's a-gittin tied tu an 'oman, don't the noospapers say he 'sisted? Ef a wun-hoss preacher sits intu the pulpit while a two-hoss one preaches, don't they print hit that he 'sisted? An' if a big-bug's wife's dorg wer tu hold a cow's tail in his teef while she milk'd, they'd say he 'sisted. Well, ef 'sistance is what the noospapers makes hit out tu be, I 'sisted sum, durn'd ef I didn't!

"Well, wun Sat'd'y nite, all the he, an' mos' ove the she niggers fur ten miles roun, started tu hold a big meetin. They cum a-foot, on hoss's, on muels, on oxes, on bulls, on sleds, in carts, waggins an' buggys. The meetin wer wuf ni ontu five hundred thousin dullars in flush times, an' yu cud a-smelt hit a mile, *afore* I begun tu 'sist, an' fifteen mile *arter* I 'sisted. An' the nise—well, when I larns tu spell an' pernounce the flavor ove a ded hoss, play the shape ove a yeathen war-jug ontu a fiddil, ur paint the swifness ove these yere laigs ontu a clap-board, then I'll 'scribe the nise ove that meetin, purticulerly arter I 'sisted awhile. 'Sumthin mus be lef tu the 'maginashun,' ole Bullen sed, when he wer given in his lizzerd 'sperience, an' hit am es true es sayin yas, when a man axes yu ur me ef we want a ho'n ove skin-gut when hits rainin, an' sich kerryins on hesn't been seed since ole Tam Shadrick wer a-seein the witches a-dansin thru the ode chu'ch winders what yu narrated tuther nite. I b'leves intu witches, ghostez, an' all long-nebbed things mysef, an' so dus mos' folks, but they's tu cowardly tu say so.

"I wer in the setilment runnin a daily line, wif no failures, atween Wheeler's hill-hous' an' Kidd's grocery, leavin a mail at ole Missis Cruze's wif the gals, an' a-shufflin roun' ginerally twixt trips ove a nite. I hearn hit narrated that the meetin wer a-goin tu be so I sot in an' fix'd mysef fur hit, so es tu be abil tu 'sist 'em sum.

"I purvided about a dozen ho'nets' nestes, big soun' wuns, an' stopped em up full ove disapinted, bewild'red 'vengeful, savidge, oncircumsized ball ho'nets, sharpnin thar stings redy, an' jis' waitin hot an' willin fur the holes tu be open'd, tu spread pizin an' sweet hurtin an' swellin onder the skin ove everybody. They own'd tu no non-cumbitants outside them ar nestes.

"Then I got Doctur Stone, hu wer fond uv seein fun, tu fill a big passel ove beef-bladders wif sum kind ove a'r ur gas—he call'd hit ox-gin, ur steer-gin, ur sum kind ove cattil drink, an' I hes furgot plum hits cristen name."

"Perhaps it was carbureted hydrogen."[1]

"Durn my ole galluses, an' buttuns tu, ef that warn't adzackly hit. *Hu* tole yu? say George? *Did* yu smell hit?"

"Oh, often."

"Well, by golly, that counts fur that shriveled up nose ove yourn, an' yer cussed ill temper. George, I furgives yu fur every cussin yu's ever sprinkled ontu me. No man shu'd be hilt sponsibil fur his acts arter a sniff at that ar devil's own parfume; hit am the super latif ove the yeath; yu kin see, feel, an' taste hit six weeks arter hit hes et up yure power ove smellin altugether. I hilt a bladder uv hit tu a bull's nose, tu see ef he wer a jedge ove perfumery. He jis' histed his tail, like tu hev snorted his brains out at wun snort, an jis' kill'd hissef a-runnin, a-pawin at his snout wif his fore-laigs like he wer a-tryin tu scrape off a bull tarrier. Twer the bes thing he cud do, wer tu die jis' then.

"I fix't my 'sortment ove stink skins onder the long seat ove the pulpit in the chu'ch, wif slip nots ontu the necks, so that pullin wun string ontied all ove em, an' let down a big slab tu squeese em flat. I planted my ball ho'nets colonys onder the bainches amung the straw onder the big shed what jined the chu'ch, an wun peculuer an' chosen nestes I laid away onder the exhortin box, ur shed pulpit. All on em hed strings so I cud open em at wunst frum the thickets, when I thort hit time tu take sich a sponsabil step. They hed hawl'd straw untill hit cum up ni ontu levil wif he tops ove the bainches, tu git happy in, an' du thar huggin an' wallerin on; hit hid the inemy what I hed ambush'd thar fus'rate, an' arterwards wer put tu a diffrent use than gittin happy on, I'll swar tu that fac'.

"Well, nite cum, an' fotch wif hit the mos pufick 'sortment ove niggers yu ever seed outen Orleans ur Tophett, a big pine torch-lite at ni ontu every uther tree roun the shed, an' taller candils intu the chu'ch hous whar they cumenc'd thar wurk; but I'm sistimatikally durn'd if they finished hit thar; not by a sirkil ove five mile.

1. Marsh gas.

"A pimpil-face, greasy-collar'd, limber-mouf'd suckit rider drap't ofen a fat hoss, an' sot in tu sorter startin the nigger brethrin in the rite track. He warn't fur frum bein a nat'ral born durn'd fool hissef, fur I seed him peep onder the seat es he sot down in the pulpit, whar he seed the bulge ove wun ove the bladders, stickin out frum onder the slab a littil. He licked his lips, then smak't em, an' wink'd a oily sort ove wink at a Baptis' nigger preacher, what sot by him, an' *he* show'd all ove his teef arter he'd tuck a peep, an' swaller'd like he wer gittin down a ho'n. They wer bof on em showin thar instinks: the suckit rider tuck hit tu be the breast ove a fat roas hen, an' the Baptis' thot hit wer the bulge ove a jug. *Shapes*, George, can't be 'pended upon, *taste* am the thing.

"Well, the pot-gutted, ball-heded Baptis' bull nigger, what wer fool'd on the jug question, sot his specks an' tuck a tex; hit wer:

"Yu shall smell sweet-smellin yarbs, an' eat honey vittils dar, fur thars no stink, nur bitter, whar you's gwine, in Caneyan."

"He wer jis' in the middil ove the sweet-smellin yarb part, a-citin ove poseys, sinamint draps, fried bacon, an' the scent ove the cupboard, as good yeathly smells, a-gittin hot, an' a-breakin a holesum sweat, when a ole she shouted—

"'Oh, bress hebin! I smell him now.'

"As she smack's her han's, I pull'd the string. The stinkabus begun tu roll an' rise, an' spread. Oh my lordy! lordy! Pimple-face wall'd up his eyes, coff'd blow'd his nose in his hankecher, an' sorter looked behine the preacher, like he 'spected tu see a buzzard, or an' onbelever, or sich like, atween him an' the wall.

"The nigger stop't as short as ef he'd been shot, rite in the middil ove the wurd 'Caneyan,' histed the pint ove his snout up atween his eyes, turn'd his upper lip inside out, throw'd his head back, an' scented slowly all roun. I hes seed ole steers du hit adzackly the same way. He shook his hed till his years slapt like a hog's when he's a-gittin mad, an' his specks lit in the straw; then he scented roun' agin.

"By this time bout two hundred miserlanus niggers wer a-sayin *Hu-uu* thru thar snouts, wif thar moufs shot; 'bout half es meny a-coffin, a few sickly wuns tryin not tu vomit, an' wun skaley heel'd he wer a-stuffin two corn-cob pints intu his nose, an' a saft wool hat intu his mouf. Sum ten ur fifteen said 'Oh, lor a massy! what dat?' Wun ole feller wif meal on his wool, 'lowed sum fat brudder dun bust hissef, an' am leakin out the cabbage. Better 'tire tu de woods, git sow' up, an' den stay dar.' One ventered 'pole-cat;' anuther, 'twenty pole-cat;' 'an' a dorg a-stirrin em,' added anuther; 'ded hoss,' sed a big he, wif a hoarse cold; 'spild crout,' squeak't a she; 'buzzard's nes'; frum a back bainch; 'rotten aigs an' a heap on em,' grunted a ole mammy wif a belly like a dinner-pot, an' a wool mitten in her mouf; 'wus nur dat, by golly,' snorted a dandy nigger, a-holdin his snout; 'burnt leder,' frum a fool gal; 'burnt brimstone,' frum a boy; 'maggoty soap grease,' guess'd two or three; 'all dem tings mix an' a-bilin, *dat's hit*,' said a knowin-lookin bow-laiged buck; 'de cumin ob de debil,' surjisted a ole she, a-pullin her aprun over her hed. 'Redy, heah, mum?' answered her darter. 'Meetin dun busted,' said one; 'hope I neber smell nuder bust,' said anuther. 'Less git outen heah,' said ten, while swarms ove em wer aready at hit.

"The passun nigger now holler'd, 'Sea heah, brudren an' sistren; sum fool niggah cum trou de back ob de gardin, an' sile he foot, on he way heah; let 'im make hesef scase, an' take he shoe wid 'im, fur he 'noxshus tu dis chosen congregashun, he am.' 'Sh-u-u-u tree hunder git sile in dat gardin on bof foot, shuah yu born,' added a chicken stealin yung he, wif feathers then in his wool.

"Here the passun's feelins overcum him, an' he cummenced a-yerkin like he'd swaller'd a hame string, an' the knot hed stuck in his froat.

" 'Preachin frum that fool tex what done hit,' growl'd a ole daddy wif wun toof, as he hobbled apas the passon a-rubbin his sleeve onder his nose like he wer sawin wood, an' a snortin like a hoss atween every rub.

" 'Missus kill me shuah yu lib, ef I totes *dis* stink home wid me. Hu got eny sinamint draps?' said a trim-lookin cook.

" 'Sum ob de sistren am dun faint,' holler'd a bow-laiged, bladder-lipped he, a-rushin thru the crowd wif a gourd ove warter.

" 'Bress de Lord, dey'se rite tu faint, dey no smell him now,' said a knowin ole darky.

" 'This am more disagreabil than whisky an' inyuns' said Pimple-face, tu me.

" 'Yas, perticulerly the inyuns,' sez I.

"He looked at me like he wer sorry fur me, an' wud es leve pray fur me es not, an' went an' dipt his hed in the branch.

"By this time the chu'ch wer empty, 'sceptin the stink, an' hit wer everywhar, oozin thru the shingles like smoke. The candils burnt dim like thar wer a fog in the hous', an' hit wer onhelthy tu preach in till fros', an' thar aint a nigger in that settilment what kin tell the smell ove a scent bottil frum a barril ove rotten fish tu this day. They'd be pow'ful good stock tu wurk in a soap factory. Don't yu speck they wud? The soggy an' muddy heded wuns hilt a pow-wow, an' narrated hit that in spite 'ob de ole sarpint de debil an' he stink in he hous,' they ment tu tote on the meetin tu a shoutin aind, onder the shed. So they shot up the door an' winder shutters ove the chu'ch, an' as the wind hed sorter ris, the outside smells warn't much wus nor yu ginerally smell et pork-killin houses, ur camp meetins. This wur the wust 'clusion ever a mess ove niggers did cum tu, since ole Shadwick's darkys ondertuck tu make white folks outen tharsefs by paintin thar cackuses wif onslack't lime. Ole Shadwick gethered enuff *wool* tu pay thar doctur's bills.

"Well, they blow'd a ho'n, an' 'Pimple face' tuck the crank ove the 'make happy cum' mersheen, es all the preachin an' grace hed been plum stunk outen his culler'd bruther. The sistren mos on em got ni ontu the pulpit, whar the straw wer deepest wif sich ove the he's es hed a appertite tu help du the huggin an' wallerin. 'Pimpil-face,' blow'd his nose, flung his hanketcher across the pulpit, an' sed 'hit wer all fur the bes' that they wer druv frum the hous'; grace allers spread hitsef better an' smoofer, outen doors then hit did in the hous'. Tu git happy *good,* yu mus, hev elbow-room an' straw; these cundishuns wer fill'd, an' he'd be disapinted ef that wurn't a warm activ meetin.' Thinks I, wif me to "sist,' ef hit aint all yu's sed, an' more tu, I'se no jedge ove the nater ove ball ho'nets, an' the power ove stimiluses.

"He sed, arter he'd dun preachin, he ment tu pass roun' a small hat, tu git sum means tu buy flannin petticoats wif, fur the freezin sistren in Africa. Ef ever *he* 'pass'd a hat' hit warn't at Log Chappil, 'sceptin what loose wuns be pass'd a runnin outen thar; I 'sisted in spilin wun coleckshun, I'm durn'd ef I didn't.

"He tuck a tex: *Thar shall be weepin an' railin an' chompin ove teef, bad, an' then wif no teef, shall smash thar gums tugether like ontu wolf traps*. Sez I tu mysef, that's hit, that is hit, dorg on me ef yu haint draw'd the rite kerd this pop, fur I know'd I wer 'sistin' ove him.

"He sot in in yeanest, ontied his choke-string, then shucked his coat, nex his jackid. He play'd pow'ful bad, didn't he? fur me tu hole the 'sisten han,' fur shuckin hissef didn't fortify again my ho'nets much, hit didn't. About the time he drapt his jackid, an' wer a-tryin tu jump outen his trowsis wifout onbuttunin em, the niggers wer a-mixin, he an' she, hollerin an' beginin tu hug, an' rar, an' waller, rite peart, an' nat'ral like, the dus, an' the same ole stink, wif the sweat variashun a-risin agin. Wun ole she fotch her fat han's a slap like killin flies, an' she squall'd 'gloree,' an' her mouf look't like the muzzil ove a boot, wif red linin.

"Thinks I, jis' now is es good a time es eny; the pat rollers mite cum in an' spile hit wif thar durn'd foolishness; so I jis' draw'd the strings keerfully. The fust fruit ove that ac', what I notised, wer ontu Pimple-face hissef. I seed him fotch hissef a lick a-side the hed what stagger'd him, then he hit hissef wif bof han's ontu the place whar they brands Freemasons an' mustangs, an' he shot his belly forwards an' his shoulders back'ards, like ontu a 'oman shettin the nex' tu the top drawer ove a beauro; an' he cum outen that pulpit back'ards a-tarin, his hans a-flyin roun his hed like a par ove windin blades. I thort he hed eitey fingers an twenty thumbs. He embraced a bruther, back-holts, what wer a-tryin tu roll off the hurtin in the straw, an' they jis' kick'd an' roll'd on in cahoote.

"Thar wer lots ove niggers, mix'd heads an' tails in that orful straw-pile—heds, laigs, arms, feet, ainds ove bainches, bunches ove straw an' strings ove dartin ho'nets a-showin tharsefs a-top fur a moment; then sum uther things wud cum upermos'. Hit looked like forty-eight cords ove black cats a-fitin, wif tupentine a soakin in roun the roots ove all thar tails.

"Sich nises—screechin like painters, cryin, hollerin, a few a-cussin, an' more a-jinin em, beggin, prayin, groanin, gruntin, nickerin, an' wun or two fool wuns singin. Ho'nets don't keer a durn fur music, when they's a-fitin, while abuv em a-flyin in the ar, jis' like they weighed nuthin, wer a desirabil 'sortmint ove hyme books, fans, hanketchers, hats, caps, umerellers, walkin-sticks, biskits, chicken-laigs, strings ove beads, Gouber peas, year-rings, ginger-cakes, collars, garters, babies, terbacker-pipes, ridicules, littil baskits, popco'n, scent bottils, ribbons, hollyhawk bokays, pint ticklers, bits ove straw, an' wun shiff—how she got outen hit wifout takin off her frock, I be durn'd ef I ken tell; but thar hit wer a-sailin roun wif a deck-load ove ho'nets ontu hit what wer the resarve I reckon. All this wer set off tu advantige by dus', an' millions ove insex, jis' a-hoverin over the sufferers an' then divin down fur a sting.

"Now, while this wer gwine on onder the shed, niggers wer a-shootin intu the woods in all direckshuns, like ontu arrers shot frum orful bows, an' every durn'd nigger hed a brigade ove insex roun his hed, tellin him tu hurry an' makin him du hit too, fur they went crashin outen site intu the brush like canyun shots.

"Now, I thinks the ho'nets hed boun tharsefs wif a oath, while they wer shot up in thar nestes, tu fite furever every livin thing they met, frum the way they actid. Fur them what follered the niggers intu the woods foun' the hosses, muels, an' oxes, tied out thar, an' part ove em fastened ontu the beastes, an' they immejuntly sot in tu imitatin the niggers in actin dam fool; they jis' broke loose, rar'd, kick'd, fell down, roll'd over, run away, bawl'd, beller'd, nicker'd, screem'd, an' bray'd, till they farly shuck the leaves ontu the trees.

"Wun yoke ove steers wif a big sled cum tarin heds down, an' tails strait up, rite thru the shed, an' I think they mus hev swep' out ni ontu thuty niggers, big an' littil, an' a few bainches, intu the woods wif em, a-stickin ontu thar ho'ns, ontu the yoke, on thar backs, an' on the stakes ove the sled. Yere cum a big gray hoss, like a streak, draggin a buggy ontu hits side wif the top up. His eyes wer red, an' his years laid back; he scoop'd up his buggy plum full, an' jis' kep on. I obsarved Pimpil-face tangled up in the runnin gear, an' true tu the suckit rider's instink, he wer climbin powful fur a inside seat. He run a-pas' a postes what hed a ole tin pan atop ove hit full ove rich pine knots a burnin: he scoop'd that in amung his cargo ove niggers tu warm em on thar thorny way, an' then he jis' run by the lite ove hit. Thar went a big grizly muel, wif a side saddil way back ontu his rump, an' half a peach tree fas' tu his bridil; he gobbled up two ur three littil niggers in the tree-top, an' tuck em outen the trubbil.

"Wun long laiged nigger busted outen the bunch what wer down in the straw, hollerin 'whoosh! Oh goramity! hit hurts till he feel sorter good,' an' tuck a rush skull fus' agin a weatherboarded camp, busted thru hit like hit wer a aig shell, an' out at tuther side thru a winder, a-totin the sash wif him roun his neck like a collar, an' his wool full ove plank splinters, broken glass, an' tangled ball ho'nets. I likes that nigger: he's the only feller I ever seed what tuck in the rale pure Lovingood idear ove what orter be dun onder strong hurtin an' a big skeer. Jis run over ur thru everthing yure durndest, till yu gits cumfort, that's hit.

"A hames-laiged spur-heel'd wun tuck up a white oak, sayin 'whoosh!' outen his nose every yerk he made, an' findin no pease ove mine up thar, tuck down agin hed fus', squirrel fashion, an' run onder the chu'ch ontu his all fours, sum ho'nets makin the same trip on the same skedule.

"Wun big she run her hed onder a lean gal's coat-tail tu save her years, but a few activ ball ho'nets what wer a scoutin in her rar, made her git up blinefol' wif the gal 'stradil her neck, her long black snake laigs stickin strait out ahead, an' she a-holdin on tu the fat wun's wool thru the dress wif wun han, an' a fitin ho'nets wif a hat in tuther, her hed throw'd back, an' a yowlin like a scalded houn. 'Fatty' run her derndest, not seein ur keerin whar she went, down hill kerslunge intu the branch, an' like tu drownded bof ove em, an' sum ho'nets too.

"Wun slim buck nigger shot rat-like intu a littil jug closet, onder the pulpit, swell'd up in thar ontil they hed tu tar up the floor nex day tu git him out. He tuck in wif him about forty ho'nets, an' they helpt him tu be cumfortabil in thar; I knows they did frum thar nater an' what he sed in his hole.

"Jis' bout this time I foun' out how that gal got outen her shiff, fur I seed sumthin dispersin hitssef intu the woods, an' frum the glimpse I got hit look'd sorter like a black munkey shaved wif white hine laigs; hit wer that tormented gal in white stockins. The thing wer pufeckly plain, she hed jis' run outen her dress an' shiff at the same time. That's what cums ove bein a plum natral born'd durn fool; *yu'd* hev onderstood how she got outen hit, without eny studyin at all.

"Now I'se only narrated the main pints, an' hits tuck me a good spell. But in three minits an' a 'alf arter I finish'd my 'sistin ove em by pullin them ar strings, hit wer all over scept the swellin, hurtin, an' gittin home. Thar warn't even a dorg lef on that campgroun', an' yu cud hear nuffin but the humin ove the huntin ho'nets, an' the distunt nise ove scatterin niggers, ur urther beastez still gwine furder frum that place ove torment, an' general discumfort.

"People wer huntin thar niggers thru the county fur a week, an' sumtimes when they foun em, didn't know em, they'd fatten'd so. Dreadful! warn't hit? Thar haint been a nigger nite meetin hilt in the county since, an' they's mos' on em becum pius, an' morril.

"Jis' pullin a string wer my hole sheer in all that ar cumbustifikashun, hurtin, an' trubbil; yet as usual every body sez I'se tu blame fur the hole ove hit. Yu know that every time a ho'net shoots a nigger, hit makes a white spot that's the center ove the imejut hurtin, an' ove corse mos' ove em looked like ontu secon' mournin calliker, an' the durn'd fool white folks roun' thar, thot hit wer the small pox, an' that I hed gin hit tu the niggers, so they sot in tu huntin fur *me*, wif shot guns an' dorgs, but *du* yu see these yere laigs? they toted me out enthar safe an' soun.

"I can't git jestis nowhar, fur nuthin I du. I'l, turn buzzard, an' eat ded hosses fur a livin; I b'leve theyse not blam'd fur enything much, only thar stink, an' as I hes got that aready es good es the olest buzzard ontu the roos', that makes no differ."

"Well, Sut," said I, "I think I understand fully now what '*assisting*' at a meetin means."

Sut eyed me for a moment suspiciously, and said dryly—

"I speck yu dus."

QUESTIONS TO CONSIDER

1. Many readers find the dialect in the Sut Lovingood stories hard to read. What would the stories lose without the dialect?
2. Despite his vulgar and racist attitudes, the character of Sut Lovingood became quite popular with readers in the Antebellum South. With today's attitudes about racism, is there anything likeable left about Sut?

Johnson Jones Hooper

1815–1862

Johnson Jones Hooper was born in Wilmington, North Carolina, but at the age of twenty he joined his brother on the Alabama frontier and is generally identified with that area. Although he had little formal education in his early years, Hooper eventually studied law in Alabama and served as the census taker in Tallapoosa County in 1840. Western Alabama had only recently been taken from the Creek Indians, and the job of going door to door on the frontier was a dangerous business. In 1843, Hooper turned his experience as a census taker on the frontier into a humorous sketch, which he originally published in the *East Alabamian*, a newspaper that he had recently purchased. The sketch was reprinted in *Spirit of the Times*, New York's widely read sporting journal.

Inspired by the success of his first story, Hooper created the character of Simon Suggs, confidence man and ne'er-do-well and managed to have a story featuring Suggs included in a collection of humorous tales being published in Philadelphia. Later, that same publisher brought out a collection of Hooper's Simon Suggs stories as a mock campaign biography entitled *Some Adventures of Captain Simon Suggs, Late of the Tallapoosa Volunteers*, together with "Taking the Census" and other Alabama sketches. The book was quite successful, and Suggs's campaign motto, "It is good to be shifty in a new country," became a popular catch-phrase throughout the nation.

As the political rift between the unionists and the supporters of states' rights began to intensify, Hooper turned his attention to politics and journalism, publishing his views as a proponent of Southern secession and serving as founder and editor of *The Montgomery Mail*. After the Civil War began, he was appointed Secretary to the Southern Convention, which met in Montgomery in 1861. When the Provisional Congress of the Confederate States moved to Richmond, Virginia, Hooper continued to serve as the secretary, moving to Richmond and enjoying the lifestyle of the Southern aristocrat. Now a respected leader in the Confederate government, he resisted appeals to publish more of his stories and tried to distance himself from his popular creation. In 1862, Hooper died of tuberculosis at the age of forty-six.

Hooper is remembered almost exclusively for the creation of Simon Suggs, a rascally, rowdy swindler who would pass himself off as a doctor, lawyer, gambler, or horse trader in order to win the confidence of those he planned to cheat. Nevertheless, as the following Simon

Suggs tale illustrates, Hooper's stories are also interesting for the way they chronicle the folkways of Alabama and provide a glimpse into the politics of the day. Hooper is certain to have influenced Mark Twain, and many readers and critics have drawn a comparison between Hooper's Simon Suggs and Twain's confidence men in *Huckleberry Finn*.

from Adventures of Captain Simon Suggs, Late of The Tallapoosa Volunteers

The Captain Attends a Camp-Meeting

Captain Suggs found himself as poor at the conclusion of the Creek war, as he had been at its commencement. Although no "arbitrary," "despotic," "corrupt," and "unprincipled" judge had fined him a thousand dollars for his proclamation of martial law at Fort Suggs, or the enforcement of its rules in the case of Mrs. Haycock; yet somehow—the thing is alike inexplicable to him and to us—the money which he had contrived, by various shifts to obtain, melted away and was gone for ever. To a man like the Captain, of intense domestic affections, this state of destitution was most distressing. "He could stand it himself—didn't care a d--n for it, no way," he observed, "but the old woman and the children; *that* bothered him!"

As he sat one day, ruminating upon the unpleasant condition of his "financial concerns," Mrs. Suggs informed him that "the sugar and coffee was nigh about out," and that there were not "a dozen j'ints and middlins, *all put together*, in the smoke-house." Suggs bounced up on the instant, exclaiming, "D--n it! *somebody* must suffer!" But whether this remark was intended to convey the idea that he and his family were about to experience the want of the necessaries of life; or that some other, and as yet unknown individual should "suffer" to prevent that prospective exigency, must be left to the commentators, if perchance any of that ingenious class of persons should hereafter see proper to write notes for this history. It is enough for us that we give all the facts in this connection, so that ignorance of the subsequent conduct of Captain Suggs may not lead to an erroneous judgement in respect to his words.

Having uttered the exclamation we have repeated—and perhaps, hurriedly walked once or twice across the room—Captain Suggs drew on his famous old green-blanket overcoat, and ordered his horse, and within five minutes was on his way to a camp-meeting, then in full blast on Sandy creek, twenty miles distant, where he hoped to find amusement, at least. When he arrived there, he found the hollow square of the encampment filled with people, listening to the mid-day sermon and its dozen accompanying "exhortations." A half-dozen preachers were dispensing the word; the one in the pulpit, a meek-faced old man, of great simplicity and benevolence. His voice was weak and cracked, notwithstanding which, however, he contrived to make himself heard occasionally, above the din of the exhorting, the singing, and the shouting which were going on around him. The rest were walking to and fro, (engaged in the other exercises we have indicated,) among the "mourners"—a host of whom occupied the seat set apart for their especial use—or made personal appeals to the mere spectators. The excitement was intense. Men and women rolled about on the ground, or lay sobbing or shouting in promiscuous heaps. More than all, the negroes sang and screamed and prayed. Several, under the influence of what is technically called "the jerks," were plunging and pitching about with convulsive energy. The great object of all seemed to be, to see who could make the greatest noise—

"And each—for madness ruled the hour—Would try his own expressive power."[1]

"Bless my poor old soul!" screamed the preacher in the pulpit; "ef yonder aint a squad in that corner that we aint got one outen yet! It'll never do"—raising his voice—"you must come outen that! Brother Fant, fetch up that youngster in the blue coat! I see the Lord's a-workin' upon him! Fetch him along—glory—yes!—hold to him!"

"Keep the thing warm!" roared a sensual seeming man, of stout mould and florid countenance, who was exhorting among a bevy of young women, upon whom he was lavishing caresses. "Keep the thing warm, breethring!—come to the Lord, honey!" he added, as he vigorously hugged one of the damsels he sought to save.

"Oh, I've got him!" said another in exulting tones, as he led up a gawky youth among the mourners—"I've got him—he tried to git off, but—ha! Lord!"—shaking his head as much as to say, it took a smart fellow to escape him—"ha! Lord!"—and he wiped the perspiration from his face with one hand, and with the other, patted his neophyte on the shoulder—"he couldn't do it! No! Then he tried to argy wi' me—but bless the Lord!—he couldn't do that nother! Ha! Lord! I tuk him, fust in the Old Testament—bless the Lord!—and I argyed him all thro' Kings—then I throwed him into Proverbs—and from that, here we had it up and down, kleer down to the New Testament, and then I begun to see it work him!—then we got into Matthy[2] and from Matthy right straight along to Acts; and *thar* I throwed him! Y-e-s L-o-r-d!"—assuming the nasal twang and high pitch which are, in some parts, considered the perfection of rhetorical art—"Y-e-s L-o-r-d! and h-e-r-e he is! Now g-i-t down thar," addressing the subject, "and s-e-e ef the L-o-r-d won't do somethin' f-o-r you!" Having thus deposited his charge among the mourners, he started out, summarily to convert another soul!

"Gl-o-*ree!*" yelled a huge, greasy negro woman, as in a fit of the jerks, she threw herself convulsively from her feet, and fell "like a thousand of brick," across a diminutive old man in a little round hat, who was squeaking consolation to one of the mourners.

"Good Lord, have mercy!" ejaculated the little man earnestly and unaffectedly, as he strove to crawl from under the sable mass which was crushing him.

In another part of the square a dozen old women were singing. They were in a state of absolute extasy, as their shrill pipes gave forth,

"I rode on the sky,
Quite ondestified I,
And the moon it was under my feet!"[3]

Near these last, stood a delicate woman in that hysterical condition in which the nerves are incontrollable, and which is vulgarly—and almost blasphemously—termed the "holy laugh." A hideous grin distorted her mouth, and was accompanied with a maniac's chuckle; while every muscle and nerve of her face twitched and jerked in horrible spasms.[4]

Amid all this confusion and excitement Suggs stood unmoved. He viewed the whole affair as a grand deception—a sort of "opposition line" running against his

1. From William Collin's "An Ode for Music."
2. The Book of Matthew.
3. From a hymn by Charles Wesley.
4. The reader is requested to bear in mind, that the scenes described in this chapter are not *now* to be witnessed. Eight or ten years ago, all classes of population of the Creek country were very different from what they now are. Of course, no disrespect is intended to any denomination of Christians. We believe that camp-meetings are not peculiar to any church, though most usual in the Methodist—a denomination whose respectability in Alabama is attested by the fact, that *very many* of its worthy clergymen and lay members, hold honourable and profitable offices in the gift of the state legislature; of which, indeed, almost a controlling portion are themselves Methodists (author's note).

own, and looked on with a sort of professional jealousy. Sometimes he would mutter running comments upon what passed before him.

"Well now," said he, as he observed the full-faced brother who was "officiating" among the women, "that ere feller takes *my* eye!—thar he's een this half-hour, a-figurin amongst them galls, and's never said the fust word to nobody else. Wonder what's the reason these here preachers never hugs up the old, ugly women? Never seed one do it in my life—the sperrit never moves 'em that way! It's nater tho'; and the women, *they* never flocks round one o' the old dried-up breethring—bet two to one old splinter-legs thar,"—nodding at one of the ministers—"won't git a chance to say turkey to a good-lookin gall to-day! Well! who blames 'em? Nater will be nater, all the world over; and I judge ef I was a preacher, I should save the purtiest souls fust, myself!"

While the Captain was in the middle of this conversation with himself, he caught the attention of the preacher in the pulpit, who inferring from an indescribable something about his appearance that he was a person of some consequence, immediately determined to add him at once to the church if it could be done; and to that end began a vigorous, direct personal attack.

"Breethring," he exclaimed, "I see yonder a man that's a sinner; I *know* he's a sinner! Thar he stands," pointing at Simon, "a missubble old crittur, with his head a-blossomin for the grave! A few more short years, and d-o-w-n he'll go to perdition, lessen the Lord have mer-cy on him! Come up here, you old hoary-headed sinner, a-n-d git down upon your knees, a-n-d put up your cry for the Lord to snatch you from the bottomless pit! You're ripe for the devil—you're b-o-u-n-d for hell, and the Lord only knows what'll become on you!"

"D--n it," thought Suggs, "*ef* I only had you down in the krick swamp for a minit or so, *I'd* show you who's *old! I'd* alter your tune *mighty* sudden, you sassy, 'saitful old rascal!" But he judiciously held his tongue and gave no utterance to the thought.

The attention of many having been directed to the Captain by the preacher's remarks, he was soon surrounded by numerous well-meaning, and doubtless very pious persons, each one of whom seemed bent on the application of his own particular recipe for the salvation of souls. For a long time the Captain stood silent, or answered the incessant stream of exhortation only with a sneer; but at length, his countenance began to give token of inward emotion. First his eye-lids twitched—then his upper lip quivered—next a transparent drop formed on one of his eye-lashes, and a similar one on the tip of his nose—and, at last, a sudden bursting of air from nose and mouth, told that Captain Suggs was overpowered by his emotions. At the moment of the explosion, he made a feint as if to rush from the crowd, but he was in experienced hands, who well knew that the battle was more than half won.

"Hold to him!" said one—"it's a-workin in him as strong as a Dick horse!"

"Pour it into him," said another, "it'll all come right directly!"

"That's the way I love to see 'em do," observed a third; when you begin to draw the water from their eyes, taint gwine to be long afore you'll have 'em on their knees!"

And so they clung to the Captain manfully, and half dragged, half led him to the mourner's bench; by which he threw himself down, altogether unmanned, and bathed in tears. Great was the rejoicing of the brethren, as they sang, shouted, and prayed around him—for by this time it had come to be generally known that the "convicted" old man was Captain Simon Suggs, the very "chief of sinners" in all that region.

The Captain remained grovelling in the dust during the usual time, and gave vent to even more than the requisite number of sobs, and groans, and heart-piercing cries. At length, when the proper time had arrived, he bounced up, and with a face radiant with joy, commenced a series of vaultings and tumblings, which "laid in the shade" all previous performances of the sort at that camp-meeting. The brethren were in extasies at this demonstrative evidence of completion of the work; and whenever Suggs shouted "Gloree!" at the top of his lungs, every one of them shouted it back, until the woods rang with echoes.

The effervescence having partially subsided, Suggs was put upon his pins to relate his experience, which he did somewhat in this style—first brushing the tear-drops from his eyes, and giving the end of his nose a preparatory wring with his fingers, to free it of the superabundant moisture:

"Friends," he said, "it don't take long to curry a short horse, accordin' to the old sayin', and I'll give you the perticklers of the way I was 'brought to a knowledge' "—here the Captain wiped his eyes, brushed the tip of his nose and snuffled a little—"in less'n no time."

"Praise the Lord!" ejaculated a bystander.

"You see I come here full o' romancin' and devilment, and jist to make game of all the purceedins. Well, sure enough, I done so for some time, and was a-thinkin how I should play some trick—"

"Dear soul alive! *don't* he talk sweet!" cried an old lady in black silk—"Whar's John Dobbs? You Sukey!" screaming at a negro woman on the other side of the square—"ef you don't hunt up your mass John in a minute, and have him here to listen to his 'sperience, I'll tuck you up when I git home and give you a hundred and fifty lashes, madam!—see ef I don't! Blessed Lord!"—referring again to the Captain's relation—"aint it a *precious* 'scource!"

"I was jist a-thinkin' how I should play some trick to turn it all into redecule, when they began to come round me and talk. Long at fust I didn't mind it, but arter a little that brother"—pointing to the reverend gentlemen who had so successfully carried the unbeliever through the Old and New Testaments, and who Simon was convinced was the "big dog of the tanyard"—"that brother spoke a word that struck me kleen to the heart, and run all over me, like fire in dry grass—"

"*I–I–I* can bring 'em!" cried the preacher alluded to, in a tone of exultation—"Lord thou knows ef thy servant can't stir 'em up, nobody else needn't try—but the glory aint mine! I'm a poor worrum of the dust" he added, with ill-managed affectation.

"And so from that I felt somethin' a-pullin' me inside—"

"Grace! grace! nothin' but grace!" exclaimed one; meaning that "grace" had been operating in the Captain's gastric region.

"And then," continued Suggs, "I wanted to git off, but they hilt me, and bimeby I felt so missuble, I had to go yonder"—pointing to the mourners' seat—"and when I lay down thar it got wuss and wuss, and 'peared like somethin' was a-mashin' down on my back—"

"That was his load o' sin," said one of the brethren—"never mind, it'll tumble off presently, see ef it don't!" and he shook his head professionally and knowingly.

"And it kept a-gittin heavier and heavier, ontwell it looked like it might be a four year old steer, or a big pine log, or somethin' of that sort—"

"Glory to my soul," shouted Mrs. Dobbs, "it's the sweetest talk I *ever* hearn! You Sukey! aint you got John yit? never mind, my lady, *I'll* settle wi' you!" Sukey quailed before the finger which her mistress shook at her.

"And arter awhile," Suggs went on, " 'peared like I fell into a trance, like, and I seed—"

"Now we'll git the good on it!" cried one of the sanctified.

"And I seed the biggest, longest, rip-roarenest, blackest, scaliest—"Captain Suggs paused, wiped his brow, and ejaculated "Ah, L-o-r-d!" so as to give full time for curiosity to become impatience to know what he saw.

"*Sarpent!* warn't it?" asked one of the preachers.

"No, not a sarpent," replied Suggs, blowing his nose.

"Do tell us *what* it war, soul alive!—whar *is* John?" said Mrs. Dobbs.

"Allegator!" said the Captain.

"Alligator!" repeated every woman present, and screamed for very life.

Mrs. Dobb's nerves were so shaken by the announcement, that after repeating the horrible word, she screamed to Sukey, "you Sukey, I say, you Su-u-ke-e-y! ef you let John come a-nigh this way, whar the dreadful alliga—shaw! what am I thinkin 'bout? 'Twarn't nothin' but a vishin!"

"Well," said the Captain in continuation, "the allegator kept a-comin' and a-comin' to'ards me, with his great long jaws a-gapin' open like a ten-foot pair o' tailors' shears—"

"Oh! oh! oh! Lord! gracious above!" cried the women.

"SATAN!" was the laconic ejaculation of the oldest preacher present, who thus informed the congregation that it was the devil which had attacked Suggs in the shape of an alligator.

"And then I concluded the jig was up, 'thout I could block his game some way; for I seed his idee was to snap off my head—"

The women screamed again.

"So I fixed myself jist like I was purfectly willin' for him to take my head, and rather he'd do it as not"—here the women shuddered perceptibly—"and so I hilt my head straight out"—the Captain illustrated by elongating his neck—"and when he come up and was a gwine to *shet down* on it, I jist pitched in a big rock which choked him to death, and that minit I felt the weight slide off, and I had the best feelins—sorter like you'll have from *good* sperrits—any body ever had!"

"Didn't I *tell* you so? Didn't I *tell* you so?" asked the brother who had predicted the off-tumbling of the load of sin. "Ha, Lord! fool *who!* I've been *all* along thar!—yes, *all along thar!* and I know every inch of the way jist as good as I do the road home!"—and then he turned round and round, and looked at all, to receive a silent tribute to his superior penetration.

Captain Suggs was now the "lion of the day." Nobody could pray so well, or exhort so movingly, as "brother Suggs." Nor did his natural modesty prevent the proper performance of appropriate exercises. With the reverend Bela Bugg (him to whom, under providence, he ascribed his conversion,) he was a most especial favourite. They walked, sang, and prayed together for hours.

"Come, come up; thar's room for all!" cried brother Bugg, in his evening exhortation. "Come to the 'seat,' and ef you won't pray yourselves, let *me* pray for you!"

"Yes!" said Simon, by way of assisting his friend; "it's a game that all can win at! Ante up! ante up, boys—friends I mean—don't back out!"

"Thar aint a sinner here," said Bugg, "no matter ef his soul's black as a nigger, but what thar's room for him!"

"No matter what sort of a hand you've got," added Simon in the fulness of his benevolence; "take stock! Here am *I*, the wickedest and blindest of sinners—has spent my whole life in the sarvice of the devil—has now come in on *narry pair* and won a *pile!*" and the Captain's face beamed with holy pleasure.

"D-o-n-'t be afeard!" cried the preacher; "come along! the meanest won't be turned away! humble yourselves and come!"

"No!" said Simon, still indulging in his favourite style of metaphor; "the bluff game aint played here! No runnin' of a body off! Every body holds four aces, and when you bet, you win!"

And thus the Captain continued, until the services were concluded, to assist in adding to the number at the mourners' seat; and up to the hour of retiring, he exhibited such enthusiasm in the cause, that he was unanimously voted to be the most efficient addition the church had made during that meeting.

The next morning, when the preacher of the day first entered the pulpit, he announced that "brother Simon Suggs," mourning over his past iniquities, and desirous of going to work in the cause as speedily as possible, would take up a collection to found a church in his own neighbourhood, at which he hoped to make himself useful as soon as he could prepare himself for the ministry, which the preacher didn't doubt, would be in a very few weeks, as brother Suggs was "a man of mighty good judge*ment*, and of *a great discorse*." The funds were to be collected by "brother Suggs," and held in trust by brother Bela Bugg, who was the financial officer of the circuit, until some arrangement could be made to build a suitable house.

"Yes, breethring," said the Captain, rising to his feet; "I want to start a little 'sociation close to me, and I want you all to help. I'm mighty poor myself, as poor as any of you—don't leave breethring"—observing that several of the well-to-do were about to go off—"don't leave; ef you aint able to afford any thing, jist give us your blessin' and it'll be all the same!"

This insinuation did the business, and the sensitive individuals re-seated themselves.

"It's mighty little of this world's goods I've got," resumed Suggs, pulling off his hat and holding it before him; "but I'll bury *that* in the cause any how," and he deposited his last five-dollar bill in the hat.

There was a murmur of approbation at the Captain's liberality throughout the assembly.

Suggs now commenced collecting, and very prudently attacked first the gentlemen who had shown a disposition to escape. These, to exculpate themselves from any thing like poverty, contributed handsomely.

"Look here, breethring," said the Captain, displaying the bank-notes thus received, "brother Snooks has drapt a five wi' me, and brother Snodgrass a ten! In course 'taint expected that you *that aint as well off as them*, will give *as much*; let every one give *accordin'* to ther means."

This was another chain-shot that raked as it went! "Who so low" as not to be able to contribute as much as Snooks and Snodgrass?

"Here's all the *small* money I've got about me," said a burly old fellow, ostentatiously handing to Suggs, over the heads of a half dozen, a ten dollar bill.

"That's what I call maganimus!" exclaimed the Captain; "that's the way *every* rich man ought to do!"

These examples were followed, more or less closely, by almost all present, for Simon had excited the pride of purse of the congregation, and a very handsome sum was collected in a very short time.

The reverend Mr. Bugg, as soon as he observed that our hero had obtained all that was to be had at that time, went to him and inquired what amount had been collected. The Captain replied that it was still uncounted, but that it couldn't be much under a hundred.

"Well, brother Suggs, you'd better count it and turn it over to me now. I'm goin' to leave presently."

"No!" said Suggs—"can't do it!"

"Why?—what's the matter?" inquired Bugg.

"It's got to be *prayed over*, fust!" said Simon, a heavenly smile illuminating his whole face.

"Well," replied Bugg, "less go one side and do it!"

"No!" said Simon, solemnly.

Mr. Bugg gave a look of inquiry.

"You see that krick swamp?" asked Suggs—"I'm gwine down in *thar*, and I'd gwine to lay this money down *so*"—showing how he would place it on the ground—"and I'm gwine to git on these here knees"—slapping the right one—"and I'm *n-e-v-e-r* gwine to quit the grit ontwell I feel it's got the blessin'! And nobody aint got to be thar but me!"

Mr. Bugg greatly admired the Captain's fervent piety, and bidding him God-speed, turned off.

Captain Suggs "struck for" the swamp sure enough, where his horse was already hitched. "Ef them fellers aint done to a cracklin," he muttered to himself as he mounted, "I'll never bet on two pair agin! They're peart at the snap game, theyselves; but they're badly lewed this hitch! Well! Live and let live is a good old motter, and it's my sentiments adzactly!" And giving the spur to his horse, off he cantered.

Questions to Consider

1. What does it say about American culture before the Civil War that "it is good to be shifty in a new country" became such a popular catch-phrase?
2. What aspects of Alabama's folk traditions does Hooper draw upon in this selection?

Thomas Bangs Thorpe
1815–1878

Born in Westfield, Massachusetts, Thomas Bangs Thorpe was the son of a Methodist minister who died when Thomas was only four years old. Thorpe began his career as a painter and illustrator, studying under John Quidor, who had illustrated the works of Washington Irving. In 1834, Thorpe enrolled in Wesleyan University in Connecticut, but after three years his health deteriorated, causing him to withdraw from classes and move south, where he hoped to recover. Thorpe spent the next year painting portraits of plantation families in Mississippi and Louisiana and was married in 1838. A year later, he made quite a name for himself as a writer when he published a sketch of Southern life entitled "Tom Owen, the Bee Hunter," in William Porter's sporting journal, the *Spirit of the Times*.

Thorpe continued to paint and to write sketches and stories of Southern life. The stories were generally detailed accounts of rural life that emphasized interesting characters, detailed description of frontier scenery, and outdoor activities. Thorpe settled in New Orleans, where he became the editor of one of the leading newspapers. He published several collections of his own sketches and stories, *The Mysteries of the Backwoods*, in 1846, and *The Hive of the Bee Hunter*, in 1854. Among the best of these stories is "The Big Bear of Arkansas," which became the title of a collection of Southern writing that was published by William Porter in 1845.

When war broke out with Mexico, Thorpe was active in recruiting for the Army and joined General Zachary Taylor in the field. He wrote dispatches from the campaign, which were first published in New Orleans but were also widely read across the country. At the end of the war, Thorpe collected his wartime letters in two volumes, *Our Army on the Rio Grande* and *Our Army at Monterey* (1846). When Taylor ran for president, Thorpe became a popular speaker for the campaign and remained involved in politics, primarily as a Whig, his entire life. In 1854, Thorpe moved to New York, where he wrote, painted, and worked as an editor. During the Civil War, he returned to New Orleans during the Union occupation, overseeing sanitation and food distribution. He was also appointed to the pro-Union Constitutional Convention of Louisiana. After the war, Thorpe returned to New York where he worked at the New York City Custom House and wrote for the journal *Appleton's* until he died.

Thorpe's sketches of Southern life such as *The Hive of the Bee Hunter* are unique in that the roughness of frontier life is generally presented in delicate and straightforward prose. His descriptions of camp life, both in the war and on the frontier, are generally considered to be among the most accurate of this genre.

from The Hive of the Bee Hunter

The Big Bear of Arkansas

A steamboat on the Mississippi, frequently, in making her regular trips, carries between places varying from one to two thousand miles apart; and, as these boats advertise to land passengers and freight at "all intermediate landings," the heterogeneous character of the passengers of one up-country boats can scarcely be imagined by one who has never seen it with his own eyes.

Starting from New Orleans in one of these boats, you will find yourself associated with men from every State in the Union, and from every portion of the globe; and a man of observation need not lack for amusement or instruction in such a crowd, if he will take the trouble to read the great book of character so favorably opened before him.

Here may be seen, jostling together, the wealthy Southern planter and the pedler of tin-ware from New England—the Northern merchant and the Southern jockey—a venerable bishop, and a desperate gambler—the land speculator, and the honest farmer—professional men of all creeds and characters—Wolvereens, Suckers, Hoosiers, Buckeyes, and Corncrackers, beside a "plentiful sprinkling" of the half-horse and half-alligator species of men, who are peculiar to "old Mississippi," and who appear to gain a livelihood by simply going up and down the river. In the pursuit of pleasure or business, I have frequently found myself in such a crowd.

On one occasion, when in New Orleans, I had occasion to take a trip of a few miles up the Mississippi, and I hurried on board the well-known "high-pressure-and-beat-every-thing" steamboat "Invincible," just as the last note of the last bell was sounding; and when the confusion and bustle that is natural to a boat's getting under way had subsided, I discovered that I was associated in as heterogeneous a crowd as was ever got together. As my trip was to be of a few hours' duration only, I made no endeavors to become acquainted with my fellow-passengers, most of whom would be together many days. Instead of this, I took out of my pocket the "latest paper," and more critically than usual examined its contents; my fellow-passengers, at the same time, disposed of themselves in little groups.

While I was thus busily employed in reading, and my companions were more busily still employed, in discussing such subjects as suited their humors best, we were most unexpectedly startled by a loud Indian whoop, uttered in the "social hall," that part of the cabin fitted off for a bar; then was to be heard a loud crowing, which would not have continued to interest us—such sounds being quite common in that *place of spirits*—had not the hero of these windy accomplishments stuck his head into the cabin, and hallooed out, "Hurra for the Big Bear of Arkansaw!"

Then might be heard a confused hum of voices, unintelligible, save in such broken sentences as "horse," "screamer," "lightning is slow," &c.

As might have been expected, this continued interruption, attracted the attention of every one in the cabin; all conversation ceased, and in the midst of this surprise, the "Big Bear" walked into the cabin, took a chair, put his feet on the stove, and looking back over his shoulder, passed the general and familiar salute—"Strangers, how are you?"

He then expressed himself as much at home as if he had been at "the Forks of Cypress," and "prehaps a little more so."

Some of the company at this familiarity looked a little angry, and some astonished; but in a moment every face was wreathed in a smile. There was something about the intruder that won the heart on sight. He appeared to be a man enjoying perfect health and contentment; his eyes were as sparkling as diamonds, and good-natured to simplicity. Then his perfect confidence in himself was irresistibly droll.

"Prehaps," said he, "gentlemen," running on without a person interrupting, "prehaps you have been to New Orleans often; I never made the *first visit before,* and I don't intend to make another in a crow's life. I am thrown away in that ar place, and useless, that ar a fact. Some of the gentlemen thar called me *green*—well, prehaps I am, said I, *but I arn't so at home*; and if I aint off my trail much, the heads of them perlite chaps themselves wern't much the hardest; for according to my notion, they were *real know-nothings,* green as a pumpkin-vine—couldn't, in farming, I'll bet, raise a crop of turnips; and as for shooting, they'd miss a barn if the door was swinging, and that, too, with the best rifle in the country. And then they talked to me 'bout hunting, and laughed at my calling the principal game in Arkansaw poker, and high-low-jack.

" 'Prehaps,' said I, 'you prefer checkers and roulette;' at this they laughed harder than ever, and asked me if I lived in the woods, and didn't know what *game* was?

"At this, I rather think *I* laughed.

" 'Yes,' I roared, and says, I, 'Strangers, if you'd asked me *how we got our meat* in Arkansaw, I'd a told you at once, and given you a list of varmints that would make a caravan, beginning with the bar, and ending off with the cat; that's *meat* though, not game.'

"Game, indeed,—that's what city folks call it; and with them it means chippenbirds and shite-pokes; may be such trash live in my diggins, but I arn't noticed them yet: a bird anyway is too trifling. I never did shoot at but one, and I'd never forgiven myself for that, had it weighed less than forty pounds. I wouldn't draw a rifle on any thing less heavy than that; and when I meet with another wild turkey of the same size, I will drap him."

"A wild turkey weighing forty pounds!" exclaimed twenty voices in the cabin at once.

"Yes, strangers, and wasn't it a whopper? You see, the thing was so fat that it couldn't fly far; and when he fell out of the tree, after I shot him, on striking the ground he bust open behind, and the way the pound gobs of tallow rolled out of the opening was perfectly beautiful."

"Where did all that happen?" asked a cynical-looking Hoosier.

"Happen! happened in Arkansaw: where else could it have happened, but in the creation State, the finishing up country—a State where the *sile* runs down to the centre of the 'arth, and government gives you a title to every inch of it? Then its airs—just breathe them, and they will make you snort like a horse. It's a State without a fault, it is."

"Excepting mosquitoes," cried the Hoosier.

"Well, stranger, except them; for it ar a fact that they are rather *enormous* and do push themselves in somewhat troublesome. But, stranger, they never stick twice in the same place; and give them a fair chance for a few months, and you will get as much above noticing them as an alligator. They can't hurt my feelings, for they lay under the skin; and I never knew but one case of injury resulting from them, and that was to a Yankee and they take worse to foreigners, any how, than they do to natives. But the way they used that fellow up! first they punched him until he swelled up and busted; then he sup-per-a-ted, as the doctor called it, until he was as raw as beef; then, owing to the warm weather, he tuck the ager, and finally he tuck a steamboat and left the country. He was the only man that ever tuck mosquitoes at heart that I knowd of.

"But mosquitoes is natur, and I never find fault with her. If they ar large, Arkansaw is large, her varmints ar large, her trees ar large, her rivers ar large, and a small mosquito would be of no more use in Arkansaw than preaching in a cane-brake."

This knock-down argument in favor of big mosquitoes used the Hoosier up, and the logician started on a new track, to explain how numerous bear were in his "diggins," where, he represented them to be "about as plenty as blackberries, and a little plentifuller."

Upon the utterance of this assertion, a timid little man near me inquired, if the bear in Arkansaw ever attacked the settlers in numbers?

"No," said our hero, warming with the subject, "no, stranger, for you see it ain't the natur of bear to go in droves; but the way they squander about in pairs and single ones is edifying.

"And then the way I hunt them—the old black rascals know the crack of my gun as well as they know a pig's squealing. They grow thin in our parts, it frightens them so, and they do take the noise dreadfully, poor things. That gun of mine is a perfect *epidemic among bear:* if not watched closely, it will go off as quick on a warm scent as my dog Bowieknife will: and then that dog—whew! why the fellow thinks that the world is full of bear, he finds them so easy. It's lucky he don't talk as well as think; for with his natural modesty, if he should suddenly learn how much he is acknowledged to be ahead of all other dogs in the universe, he would be astonished to death in two minutes.

"Strangers, that dog knows a bear's way as well as a horse-jockey knows a woman's: he always barks at the right time, bites at the exact place, and whips without getting a scratch.

"I never could tell whether he was made expressly to hunt bear, or whether bear was made expressly for him to hunt; any way, I believe they were ordained to go together as naturally as Squire Jones says a man and woman is, when he moralizes in marrying a couple. In fact, Jones once said, said he, 'Marriage according to law is a civil contract of divine origin; it's common to all countries as well as Arkansaw, and people take to it as naturally as Jim Doggett's Bowieknife takes to bear.' "

"What season of the year do your hunts take place?" inquired a gentlemanly foreigner, who, from some peculiarities of his baggage, I suspected to be an Englishman, on some hunting expedition, probably at the foot of the Rocky Mountains.

"The season for bear hunting, stranger," said the man of Arkansaw, "is generally all the year round, and the hunts take place about as regular. I read in history that varmints have their fat season, and their lean season. That is not the case in Arkansaw, feeding as they do upon the *spontenacious* productions of the sile, they have one continued fat season the year round; though in winter things in this way is rather more greasy than in summer, I must admit. For that reason bear with us run in warm weather, but in winter they only waddle.

"Fat, fat! its an enemy to speed; it tames every thing that has plenty of it. I have seen wild turkeys, from its influence, as gentle as chickens. Run a bear in this fat condition, and the way it improves the critter for eating is amazing; it sort of mixes the ile up with the meat, until you can't tell t'other from which. I've done this often.

"I recollect one perty morning in particular, of putting an old he fellow on the stretch, and considering the weight he carried, be run well. But the dogs soon tired him down, and when I came up with him wasn't he in a beautiful sweat—I might say fever; and then to see his tongue sticking out of his mouth a feet, and his sides sinking and opening like a bellows, and his cheeks so fat that he couldn't look cross. In this fix I blazed at him, and pitch me naked into a briar patch, if the steam didn't come out of the bullet-hole ten foot in a straight line. The fellow, I reckon, was made on the high-pressure system, and the lead sort of bust his biler."

"That column of steam was rather curious, or else the bear must have been very *warm*," observed the foreigner, with a laugh.

"Stranger, as you observe, that bear was WARM, and the blowing off of the steam show'd it, and also how hard the varmint had been run. I have no doubt if he had kept on two miles farther his insides would have been stewed; and I expect to meet with a varmint yet of extra bottom, that will run himself into a skinfull of bear's grease: it is possible; much onlikelier things have happened."

"Whereabouts are these bears so abundant?" inquired the foreigner, with increasing interest.

"Why, stranger, they inhabit the neighborhood of my settlement, one of the prettiest places on old Mississippi—a perfect location, and no mistake; a place that had some defects until the river made the 'cut-off' at 'Shirt-tail bend,' and that remedied the evil, as it brought my cabin on the edge of the river—a great advantage in wet weather, I assure you, as you can now roll a barrel of whiskey into my yard in high water from a boat, as easy as falling off a log. It's a great improvement, as toting it by land in a jug, as I used to do, *evaporated* it too fast, and it became expensive.

"Just stop with me, stranger, a month or two, or a year, if you like, and you will appreciate my place. I can give you plenty to eat; for beside hog and hominy, you can have bear-ham, and bear-sausages, and a mattress of bear-skins to sleep on, and a wildcat-skin, pulled off hull, stuffed with corn-shucks, for a pillow. That bed would put you to sleep if you had the rheumatics in every joint in your body. I call that ar bed, a *quietus*.[1]

"Then look at my 'pre-emption'—the government aint got another like it to dispose of. Such timber, and such bottom land,—why you can't preserve any thing natural you plant in it unless you pick it young, things thar will grow out of shape so quick.

"I once planted in those diggins a few potatoes and beets; they took a fine start, and after that, an ox team couldn't have kept them from growing. About that time I went off to old Kaintuck on business, and did not hear from them things in three months, when I accidentally stumbled on a fellow who had drapped in at my place, with an idea of buying me out.

1. From the Latin "to quit"; implies quiet, rest, repose, and death.

" 'How did you like things?' said I.

" 'Pretty well,' said he; 'the cabin is convenient, and the timber land is good; but that bottom land aint worth the first red cent.'

" 'Why?' said I.

" 'Cause,' said he.

" 'Cause what?' said I.

" 'Cause it's full of cedar stumps and Indian mounds, and *can't be cleared*.'

" 'Lord,' said I, 'them ar "cedar stumps" is beets, and them ar "Indian mounds" tater hills.'

"As I had expected, the crop was overgrown and useless: the sile is too rich, *and planting in Arkansaw is dangerous*.

"I had a good-sized sow killed in that same bottomland. The old thief stole an ear of corn, and took it down to eat where she slept at night. Well, she left a grain or two on the ground, and lay down on them: before morning the corn shot up, and the percussion killed her dead. I don't plant any more: natur intended Arkansaw for a hunting ground, and I go according to natur."

The questioner, who had thus elicited the description of our hero's settlement, seemed to be perfectly satisfied, and said no more; but the "Big Bear of Arkansaw" rambled on from one thing to another with a volubility perfectly astonishing, occasionally disputing with those around him, particularly with a "live Sucker" from Illinois, who had the daring to say that our Arkansaw friend's stories "smelt rather tall."

The evening was nearly spent by the incidents we have detailed; and conscious that my own association with so singular a personage would probably end before morning, I asked him if he would not give me a description of some particular bear hunt; adding, that I took great interest in such things, though I was no sportsman. The desire seemed to please him, and he squared himself round towards me, saying, that he could give me an idea of a bear hunt that was never beat in this world, or in any other. His manner was so singular, that half of his story consisted in his excellent way of telling it, the great peculiarity of which was, the happy manner he had of emphasizing the prominent parts of his conversation. As near as I can recollect, I have italicized the words, and given the story in his own way.

"Stranger," said he, "in bear hunts *I am numerous*, and which particular one, as you say, I shall tell puzzles me.

"There was the old she devil I shot at the Hurricane last fall—then there was the old hog thief I popped over at the Bloody Crossing, and then—Yes, I have it! I will give you an idea of a hunt, in which the greatest bear was killed that ever lived, *none excepted;* about an old fellow that I hunted, more or less, for two or three years; and if that aint a *particular bear hunt*, I aint got one to tell.

"But in the first place, stranger, let me say, I am pleased with you because you aint ashamed to gain information by asking and listening; and that's what I say to Countess's pups every day when I'm home; and I have got great hopes of them ar pups, because they are continually *nosing* about; and though they stick it sometimes in the wrong place, they gain experience any how, and may learn something useful to boot.

"Well, as I was saying about this big bear, you see when I and some more first settled in our region we were drivin to hunting naturally; we soon liked it, and after that we found it an easy matter to make the thing our business. One old chap who had pioneered 'afore us, gave us to understand that we had settled in the right place. He dwelt upon its merits until it was affecting, and showed us, to prove his assertions, more scratches on the bark of the sassafras trees, than I ever saw chalk marks on a tavern door lection time.

" 'Who keeps that ar reckoning?' said I.

" 'The bear,' said he.

" 'What for?' said I.

" 'Can't tell,' said he; 'but so it is: the bear bite the bark and wood too, at the highest point from the ground they can reach, and you can tell, by the marks,' said he, 'the length of the bear to an inch.'

" 'Enough,' said I; 'I've learned something here a'ready, and I'll put it in practice.'

"Well, stranger, just one month from that time I killed a bar, and told its exact length before I measured it, by those very marks; and when I did that, I swelled up considerably—I've been a prouder man ever since.

"So I went on, larning something every day, until I was reckoned a buster, and allowed to be decidedly the best bear hunter in my district; and that is a reputation as much harder to earn than to be reckoned first man in Congress, as an iron ramrod is harder than a toadstool.

"Do the varmints grow over-cunning by being fooled with by greenhorn hunters, and by this means get troublesome, they send for me, as a matter of course; and thus I do my own hunting, and most of my neighbors'. I walk into the varmints though, and it has become about as much the same to me as drinking. It is told in two sentences—

"A bear is started, and he is killed.

"The thing is somewhat monotonous now—I know just how much they will run, where they will tire, how much they will growl, and what a thundering time I will have in getting their meat home. I could give you the history of the chase with all the particulars at the commencement, I know the signs so well—*Stranger, I'm certain*. Once I met with a match, though, and I will tell you about it; for a common hunt would not be worth relating.

"On a fine fall day, long time ago, I was trailing about for bear, and what should I see but fresh marks on the sassafras trees, about eight inches above any in the forests that I knew of. Says I, 'Them marks is a hoax, Or it indicates the d--t bear that was ever grown.' In fact, stranger, I couldn't believe it was real, and I went on. Again I saw the same marks, at the same height, and *I knew the thing lived*. That conviction came home to my soul like an earthquake.

"Says I, 'Here is something a-purpose for me: that bear is mine, or I give up the hunting business.' The very next morning, what should I see but a number of buzzards hovering over my corn-field. 'The rascal has been there,' said I, 'for that sign is certain:' and, sure enough, on examining, I found the bones of what had been as beautiful a hog the day before, as was ever raised by a Buckeye. Then I tracked the critter out of the field to the woods, and all the marks he left behind, showed me that he was *the bear*.

"Well, stranger, the first fair chase I ever had with that big critter, I saw him no less than three distinct times at a distance: the dogs run him over eighteen miles and broke down, my horse gave out, and I was as nearly used up as a man can be, made on *my* principle, *which is patent*.

"Before this adventure, such things were unknown to me as possible; but, strange as it was, that bear got me used to it before I was done with him; for he got so at last, that he would leave me on a long chase *quite easy*. How he did it, I never could understand.

"That a bear runs at all, is puzzling; but how this one could tire down and bust up a pack of hounds and a horse, that were used to overhauling every thing they started after in no time, was past my understanding. Well, stranger, that bear finally got so sassy, that he used to help himself to a hog off my premises whenever he wanted one; the buzzards followed after what he left, and so, between *bear and buzzard,* I rather think I got *out of pork*.

"Well, missing that bear so often took hold of my vitals, and I wasted away. The thing had been carried too far, and it reduced me in flesh faster than an ager. I would see that bear in every thing I did: *he hunted me*, and that, too, like a devil, which I began to think he was.

"While in this shaky fix, I made preparations to give him a last brush, and be done with it. Having completed every thing to my satisfaction, I started at sunrise, and to my great joy, I discovered from the way the dogs run, that they were near him. Finding his trail was nothing, for that had become as plain to the pack as a turnpike road.

"On we went, and coming to an open country, what should I see but the bear very leisurely ascending a hill, and the dogs close at his heels, either a match for him this time in speed, or else he did not care to get out of their way—I don't know which. But wasn't he a beauty, though! I loved him like a brother.

"On he went, until he came to a tree, the limbs of which formed a crotch about six feet from the ground. Into this crotch he got and seated himself, the dogs yelling all around it; and there he sat eyeing them as quiet as a pond in low water.

"A greenhorn friend of mine, in company, reached shooting distance before me, and blazed away, hitting the critter in the centre of his forehead. The bear shook his head as the ball struck it, and then walked down from that tree, as gently as a lady would from a carriage.

" 'Twas a beautiful sight to see him do that—he was in such a rage, that he seemed to be as little afraid of the dogs as if they had been sucking pigs; and the dogs warn't slow in making a ring around him at a respectful distance, I tell you; even Bowieknife himself, stood off. Then the way his eyes flashed!—why the fire of them would have singed a cat's hair; in fact, that bear was in a *wrath all over*. Only one pup came near him, and he was brushed out so totally with the bear's left paw, that he entirely disappeared; and that made the old dogs more cautious still. In the mean time, I came up, and taking deliberate aim, as a man should do, at his side, just back of his foreleg, *if my gun did not snap,*[2] call me a coward, and I won't take it personal.

"Yes, stranger, *it snapped,* and I could not find a cap[3] about my person. While in this predicament, I turned round to my fool friend—'Bill,' says I, 'you're an ass—you're a fool—you might as well have tried to kill that bear by barking the tree under his belly, as to have done it by hitting him in the head. Your shot has made a tiger of him; and blast me, if a dog gets killed or wounded when they come to blows, I will stick my knife into your liver, I will—'My wrath was up. I had lost my caps, my gun had snapped, the fellow with me had fired at the bear's head, and I expected every moment to see him close in with the dogs and kill a dozen of them at least. In this thing I was mistaken; for the bear leaped over the ring formed by the dogs, and giving a fierce growl, was off—the pack, of course, in full cry after him. The run this time was short, for coming to the edge of a lake, the varmint jumped in, and swam to a little island in the lake, which it reached, just a moment before the dogs.

" 'I'll have him now,' said I, for I had found my caps in the *lining of my coat*—so, rolling a log into the lake, I paddled myself across to the island, just as the dogs had cornered the bear in a thicket. I rushed up and fired—at the same time the critter leaped over the dogs and came within three feet of me, running like mad; he jumped

2. Misfire.

3. Firing caps.

into the lake, and tried to mount the log I had just deserted, but every time he got half his body on it, it would roll over and send him under; the dogs, too, got around him, and pulled him about, and finally Bowieknife clenched with him, and they sunk into the lake together.

"Stranger, about this time I was excited, and I stripped off my coat, drew my knife, and intended to have taken a part with Bowieknife myself, when the bear rose to the surface. But the varmint staid under—Bowieknife came up alone, more dead than alive, and with the pack came ashore.

" 'Thank God!' said I, 'the old villain has got his deserts at last.'

"Determined to have the body, I cut a grape-vine for a rope, and dove down where I could see the bear in the water, fastened my rope to his leg, and fished him, with great difficulty, ashore. Stranger, may I be chewed to death by young alligators, if the thing I looked at wasn't a *she bear, and not the old critter after all*.

"The way matters got mixed on that island was onaccountably curious, and thinking of it made me more than ever convinced that I was hunting the devil himself. I went home that night and took to my bed—the thing was killing me. The entire team of Arkansaw in bear-hunting acknowledged himself used up, and the fact sunk into my feelings as a snagged boat will in the Mississippi. I grew as cross as a bear with two cubs and a sore tail. The thing got out 'mong my neighbors, and I was asked how come on that individ-u-al that never lost a bear when once started? and if that same individ-u-al didn't wear telescopes when he turned a she-bear, of ordinary size, into an old he one, a little larger than a horse?

" 'Prehaps,' said I, 'friends'—getting wrathy—'prehaps you want to call somebody a liar?'

" 'Oh, no,' said they, 'we only heard of such things being *rather common* of late, but we don't believe one word of it; oh, no,'—and then they would ride off, and laugh like so many hyenas over a dead nigger.

It was too much, and I determined to catch that bear, go to Texas, or die,—and I made my preparations accordin.'

"I had the pack shut up and rested. I took my rifle to pieces, and iled it.

"I put caps in every pocket about my person, *for fear of the lining*.

"I then told my neighbors, that on Monday morning—naming the day—I would start THAT B(E)AR, and bring him home with me, or they might divide my settlement among them, the owner having disappeared.

"Well, stranger, on the morning previous to the great day of my hunting expedition, I went into the woods near my house, taking my gun and Bowieknife along, just *from habit*, and there sitting down, also from habit, what should I see, getting over my fence, but *the bear!* Yes, the old varmint was within a hundred yards of me, and the way he walked *over that fence*—stranger; he loomed up like a *black mist*, he seemed so large, and he walked right towards me.

"I raised myself, took deliberate aim, and fired. Instantly the varmint wheeled, gave a yell, and *walked through the fence*, as easy as a falling tree would through a cobweb.

"I started after, but was tripped up by my inexpressibles,[4] which, either from habit or the excitement of the moment, were about my heels, and before I had really gathered myself up, I heard the old varmint groaning, like a thousand sinners, in a thicket near by, and, by the time I reached him, he was a corpse.

"Stranger, it took five niggers and myself to put that carcass on a mule's back, and old long-ears waddled under his load, as if he was foundered in every leg of his

4. Undergarments.

body; and with a common whopper of a bear, he would have trotted off, and enjoyed himself.

" 'Twould astonish you to know how big he was: I made a *bed-spread of his skin*, and the way it used to cover my bear mattress, and leave several feet on each side to tuck up, would have delighted you. It was, in fact, a creation bear, and if it had lived in Samson's time, and had met him in a fair fight, he would have licked him in the twinkling of a dice-box.

"But, stranger, I never liked the way I hunted him, *and missed him*. There is something curious about it, that I never could understand—and I never was satisfied at his giving in so *easy at last*. Prehaps he had heard of my preparations to hunt him the next day, so he jist guv up, like Captain Scott's coon, to save his wind to grunt with in dying; but that ain't likely. My private opinion is, that that bear was an *unhuntable bear, and died when his time come*."

When this story was ended, our hero sat some minutes with his auditors, in a grave silence; I saw there was a mystery to him connected with the bear whose death he had just related, that had evidently made a strong impression on his mind. It was also evident that there was some superstitious awe connected with the affair—a feeling common with all "children of the wood," when they meet with any thing out of their everyday experience.

He was the first one, however, to break the silence, and, jumping up, he asked all present to "liquor" before going to bed—a thing which he did, with a number of companions, evidently to his heart's content.

Long before day, I was put ashore at my place of destination, and I can only follow with the reader, in imagination, our Arkansas friend, in his adventures at the "Forks of Cypress" on the Mississippi.

Question to Consider

1. If you were going to create a tall tale to rival that told by the "Big Bear," what would you consider the necessary elements to be? Why would the elements you selected be critical to your tale?

Henry Clay Lewis

1825–1850

In *Odd Leaves from the Life of a Louisiana Swamp Doctor* (1849), Henry Clay Lewis describes himself as "having been steamboat cook, cabin boy, gentleman of leisure, ploughboy, cotton picker, and almost a printer." To the reading public, he is better known by his pseudonym, Madison Tensas, M.D., or simply as "the Louisiana Swamp Doctor."

Most of the details of Lewis's life must be drawn from his own writings, and much of what is known about him is sketchy, at best. Lewis was born in Charleston, South Carolina, on 26 June 1825, although the family moved to Cincinnati, Ohio, shortly after his birth. Lewis's mother died when he was six, and he went to live with an older brother. According to his own story, Lewis was unhappy in his brother's home and stowed away on a steamboat bound for New Orleans. Although he was only ten, he worked for the next year as a cook's helper and cabin boy on steamboats that plowed both the Mississippi and Yazoo Rivers. While working on the Yazoo, Lewis visited another brother, Joseph, who lived in Manchester, Mississippi, which would soon be renamed Yazoo City. Joseph persuaded Henry to leave the steamboat by promising to pay for his education. Joseph was ruined, however, in the depression of the 1850s, and

Lewis was forced to work in the cotton fields. When Lewis was sixteen, his brother arranged for him to be apprenticed to a medical doctor, and he finally received an education under the tutelage of Dr. Washington Dorsey.

Meanwhile, Joseph had become a well-known businessman in Yazoo City, and Lewis, aided by his brother's influence and his own association with Dr. Dorsey, gained entry to the higher social circles in the town. He became active in local politics, and published two satiric political poems in the local newspaper, the *Whig*. Both poems appeared under the pseudonym "Ion."

In 1844, Lewis left for medical school in Louisville, Kentucky. While there, he published several poems in the *Louisville Journal* and the *Yazoo Democrat*. Returning to Yazoo City after his first term at medical school, Lewis published his first humorous sketch, "The Cupping of the Sternum," in the influential and widely read New York journal, *Spirit of the Times*. Lewis returned to medical school in the fall, and in "Being Examined for My Degree," he describes how he passed his second-year oral exams by answering in a voice too low for one deaf professor to hear and distracting another by bringing up a paper opposing the professor's pet theory. The story, which must be a humorous exaggeration, nevertheless shows Lewis's ability to turn the events of his life into burlesque narratives.

Upon graduation, Dr. Lewis returned to Yazoo City, but after six days without a single medical case, he determined to leave. In "Seeking a Location," he recounts how he moved to a remote area on the Tensas River, in Madison Parish, Louisiana, to set up his practice in a log cabin that became both his home and his office. He adopted the frontier manner of dress and began to treat patients in the remote area of Northeast Louisiana. Lewis describes his experiences as a frontier doctor in sketches such as "A Tight Race Considerin'," "The Curious Widow," "Stealing a Baby," and "A Struggle for Life." He was generally successful as the local doctor and managed to buy a sizeable piece of land. He continued to write and publish humorous sketches under the pen name "Madison Tensas, M.D." many of which appeared in the *Spirit of the Times*. Lewis also continued to publish poetry under the pseudonym "Ion."

In 1848, Lewis moved to Richmond, the Madison Parish seat, where he continued to work as a doctor and began to gather his sketches for a collection, which was published in 1849 as *Odd Leaves from the Life of a Louisiana Swamp Doctor*. The selections included here are from that collection. Returning from a visit to Vicksburg that he had taken to recuperate from fighting a cholera epidemic, Henry Clay Lewis slipped into a bayou and drowned at the young age of twenty-five.

Lewis's sketches continued to be popular after his death, and many were reprinted in various collections of humorous writing. Like other successful writers of what has come to be called Southwest Humor, a genre which influenced Southern writers such as Mark Twain and William Faulkner, Lewis employs the devices of the framework story, the garrulous narrator, authentic dialect, colorful characters, and biting satire, all told in a mock oral style.

Stealing a Baby

I never was partial to dogs (although I dined some years ago very heartily upon the haunch of one that a rascally Indian sold to the family for venison—the scoundrel's back gave proof not long after, that it, to him at least, was really deer meat). They have always been my aversion, and the antipathy of my earlier years has not been in the least diminished by the part one took—not only out of my leg—but in breaking off as pretty a love scrape as ever Cupid rejoiced at.

I was attending my last course of lectures, previous to graduation in a northern state and as a matter of course had but very little leisure to devote to amusement or love. But nevertheless, even amidst all my occupation, I found time to renew and continue a friendship bordering closely upon love even then, which I had formed the previous winter with a young lady residing in the city.

We were both young—alas! that there similarity ceased—she was beautiful—my ugliness was so apparent that I acknowledged it myself. She was wealthy—I had nothing but my profession, it not then secure. She was—but why continue the enumeration of our contrasts? Suffice it to say that we were fast approaching the condition when love in a cottage and thoughts of an annual searching for sentimental and beautiful names occupy so much of the mind, when an infernal dog (not only of a daddy—but a real caniner) jumped—like a swamp gal into a jar of pickles—into the ring of our felicity and left me to wail him first and myself afterwards.

I hated dogs, and the father of my beloved had an equal aversion to Southerners, and according to the degree that class stood in his estimation, the old man and myself disliked the same objects, and so his daughter and myself had to meet by stealth.

Twice a week the class of medical students attended clinical lectures at the hospital which was situated in a retired part of the town. Thither the young lady on the appointed evenings would repair, and awaiting the departure of the class, we, on our walk homewards, could talk over our love affairs without fear or interruption.

This pleasant arrangement had continued until nearly the close of the session, and we had agreed that when graduated, if her father's obduracy did not soften, we would elope, when some good-natured friend kindly informed her father of our intimacy and that even as he came then to apprise him he had met her going to keep her appointment.

Highly incensed, the old man started off to pursue her but unfortunately did not arrive to prevent but only witness an occurrence which attracted considerable attention at the time.

Anatomy has been ever with me a favourite branch of my profession, and when a student I never let slip an opportunity, time and material permitting, to improve myself in it by dissection. It was a passion with me. Whenever I met with persons extremely emaciated or finely developed, my anatomical eye would scan their proportions, and instead of paying them the usual courtesies of life, I would be thinking what glorious subjects they would be for museum preparations or dissection. Even when my audacious lips were stealing a kiss from the pulpy mouth of my lady-love, instead of floating into ecstasies of delight, my anatomical mind would wonder whether, even in death, electricity by some peculiar adaptation might not be able to continue their bewitching suction. When holding her soft hand in mine and gazing into the star-lit ocean of her soul, I would wonder if there was not some peculiarity in the formation of her optic nerve which gave her eyes such brilliancy. My poetical rhapsodies were mingled with scraps of anatomy, and in attempting to write her some verses after writing the first line,

> "The clouds which clothed yon beauteous shore
> with garments dark and hazy—

to save me, the nearest approximation I could make to a rhyme, was:

> "Pray use with me not the *'levator labii superioris*
> *alaque nasi*.' "[1]

To tell the truth, I was becoming clean daft upon the *subject*. Consumptive people[2] and orphan children began to look on me with suspicion, but Lucy attributed my conduct to the eccentricities of genius and love.

1. The Latin name for the facial muscle that lifts the upper lip and flares the nostril.

2. People with tuberculosis.

Connected with the hospital the class attended was a dead-house, as is usual in such establishments, where such patients whose constitutions are not strong enough to stand the treatment, are deposited after death for forty-eight hours in order that their friends may reclaim their bodies. The *morgue* in this institution was directly under the lecture room, but, as the door was kept locked it was regarded as sufficiently private.

On the day when my intended father-in-law was made acquainted with the clandestine meetings of his daughter and myself, I had as usual, accompanied the class to the hospital, and, during the delivering of the lecture, becoming suddenly very faint, I was forced to leave the crowded room and seek the fresh air.

As I passed the door of the dead-house on my return, I noticed that it was ajar, and curiosity prompting me to see what was within, I pushed it open and entered, closing it behind me. There were several bodies, male and female, cleanly arrayed upon the table, but the object that attracted my attention the most was an infant a few weeks old lying by the side of its dead mother. They were both so black in the face that I would have suspected foul play, had it not been accounted for by the fact that they were Negroes. I strove to depart, but something formed a bond of association between that dead nigger baby and myself, which held me to my place my gaze riveted upon it.

I wanted just such a subject—one I could carry up in my private room and dissect whilst I was waiting for my meals—something to wile away my tedious hours with—but how to get it was the thing. The rules of the college and hospital were imperative, and I did not wish to be expelled. I could not beg, borrow, or buy—there was but one way left and that was stealing.

The plan was simple and easily arranged. It was very cold weather, and under the ample folds of my cloak the baby would be concealed effectually.

Separating it from its dead mother's embrace, I rolled it, tenderly as if alive, into as small a space as possible, and tying it up in my handkerchief, I placed it under my cloak and left the dead-house.

Had I left immediately for home, on the baby's absence being discovered I would have been suspected immediately, and so great as was the danger, I had no other resource than to return to the lecture room, and await our regular dismissal, running the chances of detection. No one, on looking at me then, would have accused me of feigning sickness, for manfully as I strove to be composed, the danger of discovery unnerved me completely and gave me such a tremor as would have passed for a creditable ague.

I have been often enough in imminent danger of my life to know what cold sweat and minutes appearing hours are, but the longest life in the shortest space of time I ever led was when, in the midst of four hundred students, I sat on those hard old benches with the dead nigger baby under my cloak waiting for the lecture to conclude.

It had its end at last, and waiting till the class had pretty well dispersed, I sauntered slowly away towards my boarding-house, hoping that the inclemency of the weather had kept Lucy from keeping our usual appointment.

A sleety rain had fallen the preceding night, and like Mrs. Blennerhasset's tears, freezing as it fell, had covered the pavement with a thin coat of ice, making the walking for pedestrians very insecure.

Surely, I thought, as a keen gust came round the corner, piercing my marrow with its coldness, her tender frame will not be exposed on such a day as this! 'Tis a good thing, too, for she would be horrified if she found what my burden was—when her smiling face with her beautiful nose red as an inflamed eye appeared and told me I did not possess a proper appreciation of the strength of a Kentucky gal's affection.

Somewhat vexed and for the first time in my life sorry to see her, I wished her (as it was so cold) in the hottest place I knew of. But dissembling my feelings, I vowed when she came up that if I had received the appointment of surgeon-general to the angels, it could not give me more pleasure than to see her then. I appeared as unconcerned as I could and sedulously talked to her of such things as are very interesting to lovers and old maids but deuced tiresome to all other parties concerned.

We had nearly reached the street corner where we usually parted, when, horror of horrors, who should we see coming round the identical corner but the lady's father, accompanied by a man that bore a marvellous resemblance to the city marshal!

Instead of fainting, Lucy uttered a stifled shriek and gritting her teeth dragged me into a house, the door of which stood invitingly open. One step more and if Fate had not been against me, these pages would never have been written, that baby would have been anatomized, and in all probability instead of being an old rusty swamp doctor, "caring a cuss for nobody, nobody caring for me," I would have been the happy head of a family, and rolling in my carriage describing the great operation of extracting two jaw teeth I saw performed the last time I was in Paris. But the beautiful hath departed and never was.

A growl, a loud yell, bow! wow! wow! and with mouth distended like an alligator catching his dessert of flies, a huge bulldog sprang at us, placing us in rather a dilemma—it was the dog of a daddy on one hand and the daddy of a dog on the other.

Unlike Miss Ullin who preferred meeting the raging of the skies to an angry father embarked in a skiff and got drowned, I preferred an angry father to a mad bull dog. Seizing Lucy, I made a spring backwards, forgetting in my haste the slippery pavement. Our feet flew up, and down we came in the open street, cross and pile, our inferior extremities considerably intermingled, and her ankles not as well protected from the heat as they might have been.

My cloak flew open as I fell, and the force of the fall bursting its envelope, out in all its hideous realities rolled the infernal imp of darkness upon the gaze of the laughing but now horrified spectators.

The old man had witnessed the whole scene. Springing to my feet, I assisted the lady to rise and handed her over to her father. As he disappeared with her round the corner, I volunteered to whip the crowd, individually or collectively, but nobody seemed disposed to accept of my services. Picking up my baby, I explained the whole to a constable who was on the point of arresting me for child-murder.

I sent the subject back to the dead-room and came as near being expelled from college as ever a lover of knowledge did—to miss it. I have never seen Lucy since, and my haggard features and buttonless coat testify that the swamp doctor is still a bachelor.

A Struggle for Life

It was the spring of 183– [1846?]. The water from the Mississippi had commenced overflowing the low swamps and rendering travelling on horseback very disagreeable. The water had got to that troublesome height, when it was rather too high for a horse and not high enough for a canoe or skiff to pass easily over the submerged grounds.

I was sitting out under my favourite oak congratulating myself that I had no travelling to do just then—it was very healthy—when my joy was suddenly nipped in the bud by a loud hallo from the opposite side of the bayou. Looking over and answering the hail, I discerned first a mule and then something which so closely resembled an ape or an orang-outang that I was in doubt whether the voice had proceeded from it until a repetition of the hail, this time coming unmistakably from it, assured me that it was a human.

"Massa Doctor at home?" yelled the voice.

"Yes, I am the doctor. What do you want?"

"Massa sent me with a letter to you."

Jumping in the skiff, a few vigorous strokes sent me to the opposite shore where the singular being awaited my coming.

He was a Negro dwarf of the most frightful appearance. His diminutive body was garnished with legs and arms of enormously disproportionate length. His face was hideous—a pair of tushes projected from either side of a double hare-lip. Taking him altogether, he was the nearest resemblance to the orang-outang mixed with the devil that human eyes ever dwelt upon. I could not look at him without feeling disgust.

"Massa Bill sent me with a letter," was his reply to my asking him his business.

Opening it, I found a summons to see a patient, the mother of a man named Disney, living some twenty miles distant by the usual road. It was in no good humour that I told the dwarf to wait until I could swim my horse over and I would accompany him.

By the time I had concluded my preparations and put a large bottle of brandy in my pocket, my steed was awaiting me upon the opposite shore.

"Massa tole me to tell you ef you didn't mine swimming a little you had better kum de nere way."

"Do you have to swim much?"

"Oh no, Massa, onely swim Plurisy Lake and wade de backwater a few miles, you'll save haf de way at leste."

I looked at the sun. It was only about two hours high, and the roads were in such miserable condition that six miles an hour would be making fine speed. So I determined to go the near way and swim "Pleurisy slough."

"You are certain you know the road, boy?"

"Oh, yes, massa, me know um ebery inch ob de groun', hunted possum an' coon ober him many a night. Massa, you ain't got any 'baccy, is you?"

"There's a chaw—and here's a drink of brandy. I'll give you another if you pilot me safe through and a good pounding if you get lost."

"Dank you, Massa, um's good. No fere I lose you, know ebery inch of de groun'."

I had poured him out a dram, not considering his diminutive stature, sufficient to unsettle the nerves of a stout man, but he drank it off with great apparent relish. By this time, everything being ready, we commenced ploughing our way through the muddy roads.

We made but slow progress. I would dash on and then have to wait for the dwarf, who, belabouring his mule with a cudgel almost as large as himself, strove in vain to keep up.

The road was directly down the bayou for some miles. There were few settlers on it then and the extent of their clearing consisted of a corn patch. They were the pre-emptioners or squatters, men who settled upon government land before its survey and awaited the incoming of planters with several Negroes to buy their claims, themselves to be bought out by more affluent emigrants. To one of the first-mentioned class—the pre-emptioners—my visit was directed, or rather to his mother, who occupied an intermediate grade between the squatter and the small planter in as much as she possessed one Negro, the delectable morsel for whom I was waiting every few hundred yards.

It wanted but an hour to sundown when we reached the place where it was optional with me either to go the longer route by the bayou or save several miles by cutting across the bend of the stream, having, however, to swim "Pleurisy slough" if I did so.

The path across was quite obscure, and it would be dark by the time we crossed. But the Negro declared he knew every inch of the way, and as saving distance was a serious consideration, I determined to try it and "Pleurisy slough."

Taking a drink to warm me for the dew that had commenced to fall was quite chilling, I gave one to the Negro, not noticing the wild sparkle of his eye or the exhilaration of his manner.

We pressed on eagerly, I ahead as long as the path lasted, but it giving out at the edge of the backwater, it became necessary for the Negro to precede and pilot the way.

I followed him mechanically for some distance, relying on his intimate knowledge of the swamp, our steeds making but slow progress through the mud and water.

When we entered the swamp I had remarked that the sun was in our faces, and great was my astonishment when we had travelled some time, on glancing my eye upwards to see if it had left the tree tops, to perceive its last beams directly at my back, the very reverse of what it should have been. Thinking perhaps that it was some optical illusion, I consulted the moss on the trees, and its indication was that we were taking the back track. I addressed the Negro very sharply for having misled me, when, instead of excusing himself, he turned on me his hideous countenance and chuckled the low laugh of drunkenness. I saw that I had given him too much brandy for his weak brain and that he was too far gone to be of any assistance to me in finding the way.

Mine was a pleasant situation truly. To return home would be as bad as to endeavour to go on. It would be night at any rate before I could get out of the swamp, and after it fell, as there was no moon, it would be dangerous to travel as the whole country was full of lakes and sloughs and we might be precipitated suddenly into one of them, losing our animals if not being drowned ourselves.

It was evident that I would have to pass the night in the swamp, my only companion the drunken dwarf. I had nothing to eat and no weapons to protect myself if assailed by wild beasts, but the swamp was high enough to preclude the attack of anything but alligators, and their bellow was resounding in too close proximity to be agreeable.

Fortunately, being a cigar smoker, I had a box of matches in my pocket, so I would have a fire at least. My next care was to find a ridge sufficiently above the water to furnish a dry place for building a fire and camp. After considerable search, just at night fall the welcome prospect of a cane ridge above the overflow met my gaze. Hurrying up the Negro, who by this time was maudlin drunk, I reached the cane and forcing my way with considerable difficulty through it until I got out of the reach of the water, dismounted, and tying my horse took the Negro down and performed the same office for his mule.

My next care was to gather materials for a fire before impenetrable darkness closed over the swamp. Fortunately for me, a fallen oak presented itself not ten steps from where I stood. To have a cheerful blazing fire was the work of a few minutes. Breaking off sufficient cane tops to last the steeds till morning, I stripped my horse—the mule had nothing on but a bridle—and with the saddle and cane leaves made me a couch that a monarch, had he been as tired as I was, would have found no fault with. As the Negro was perfectly helpless and nearly naked, I gave him my saddle blanket and making him a bed at a respectful distance bade him go to sleep.

Replenishing the fire with sufficient fuel to last till morning, I lit a cigar, and throwing myself down upon my fragrant couch, gave myself up to reflections upon the peculiarity of my situation. Had it been a voluntary bivouac with a set of chosen companions, it would not have awakened half the interest in my mind that it did, for the attending circumstances imparted to it much of the romantic.

There, far from human habitation, my only companion a hideous dwarf, surrounded with water, and the night draperied darkly around, I lay, the cane leaves for my bed, the saddle for my pillow, the huge fire lighting up the darkness for a space around, giving natural objects a strange, distorted appearance, and bringing the two steeds into high relief against the dark background of waving cane which nodded over, discoursing a wild, peculiar melody of its own. Occasionally a loud explosion would be heard as the fire communicated with a green reed. The wild hoot of an owl was heard and directly I almost felt the sweep of his wings as he went sailing by and alighted upon an old tree just where the light sank mingling with the darkness. I followed him with my eye, and as he settled himself, he turned his gaze towards me. I moved one of the logs, and his huge eyes fairly glistened with light as the flames shot up with increased vigor. The swamp moss was flowing around him in long, tangled masses, and as a more vivid gleam uprose, I gazed and started involuntarily. Had I not known it was an owl surrounded with moss that sat upon that stricken tree, I would have sworn it was the form of an old man, clad in a sombre flowing mantle, his arm raised in an attitude of warning, that I gazed upon. A cane exploding startled the owl and with a loud tu-whit, tu whoo he went sailing away in the darkness. The unmelodious bellow of the alligator, and the jarring cry of the heron arose from a lake on the opposite side of the cane, whilst the voices of a myriad of frogs and the many undistinguishable sounds of the swamp made the night vocal with discordancy.

My cigar being by this time exhausted, I took the bottle from my pocket and taking a hearty drink to keep the night air from chilling me when asleep was about to restore it to its place and commend myself to slumber, when, glancing at the dwarf, I saw his eyes fixed upon me with a demoniac expression that I shall never forget.

"Give me a dram," he said very abruptly, not prefacing the request by those deferential words never omitted by the slave when in his proper mind.

"No, sir, you have already taken too much. I will give you no more," I replied.

"Give me a dram," he again said, more fiercely than before.

Breaking off a cane, I told him that if he spoke to me in that manner again I would give him a severe flogging.

But to my surprise he retorted, "D--n you, white man, I will kill you ef you don't give me more brandy," his eyes flashing and sparkling with electric light.

I rose to correct him but a comparison of my well developed frame with his stunted deformed proportions, and the reflection that his drunkenness was attributable to my giving him the brandy deterred me.

"I will kill you," he again screamed, his fangs clashing and the foam flying from his mouth, his long arms extended as if to clutch me and the fingers quivering nervously.

I took a hasty glance of my condition. I was lost in the midst of the swamp, an unknown watery expanse surrounding me, remote from any possible assistance. The swamps were rapidly filling with water, and if we did not get out tomorrow or next day we would in all probability be starved or drowned. The Negro was my only dependence to pilot me to the settlements, and he was threatening my life if I did not give him more brandy. Should I do it or not? Judging from the effects of the two drinks I had given him, if he got possession of the bottle it might destroy him, or at least render him incapable of travelling until starvation and exposure would destroy us. My mind was resolved upon that subject. I would give him no more. There was no alternative, I would have to stand his assault. Considering I was three times his size, a fearful adventure, truly thought I, not doubting a moment but that my greater size would give me proportionate strength, I must not hurt him, but will tie him until he recovers.

The dwarf, now aroused to maniacal fury by the persistance in my refusal, slowly approached me to carry his threat into execution. The idea of such a diminutive object destroying without weapons a man of my size presented something ludicrous, and I laughingly awaited his attack, ready to tie his hands before he could bite or scratch me. Woefully I underrated his powers!

With a yell like a wild beast's, he precipitated himself upon me. Evading my blow, he clutched with his long fingers at my throat, burying his talons in my flesh and writhing his little body around mine strove to bear me to earth.

I summoned my whole strength, and endeavoured to shake him off. But possessing the proverbial power of the dwarf increased by his drunken mania to an immense degree, I found all my efforts unavailing—and oh God! horrors of horrors—what awful anguish was mine when I found him bearing me slowly to earth and his piercing talons buried in my throat, cutting off my breath! My eyes met his with a more horrid gleam than that he glared upon me. His was the fire of brutal nature aroused by desire to intense malignancy and mine the gaze of despair and death. Closer and firmer his grip closed upon my throat, barring out the sweet life's breath. I strove to shriek for help but could not. How shall I describe the racking agony that tortured me? A mountain, heavier than any earth's bosom holds, was pressing upon my breast, slowly crushing me to fragments. All kinds of colors first floated before my eyes and then everything wore a settled, intensely fiery red. I felt my jaw slowly dropping and my tongue protruding till it rested on the hellish fangs that encircled my throat. I could hear distinctly every pulsation of even the minutest artery in my frame. Its wild singing was in my ears like the ocean wave playing over the shell-clad shore. I remember it all perfectly, for the mind through all this awful struggle still remained full of thought and clearness. Closer grew the grip of those talons around my throat, and I knew that I could live but a few moments more.

I did not pray. I did not commend my soul to God. I had not a fear of death. But oh! awful were my thoughts at dying in such a way—suffocated by a hellish Negro in the midst of the noisome swamp, my flesh to be devoured by the carrion crow, my bones to whiten where they lay for long years and then startle the settler, when civilization had strode into the wilderness and the cane that would conceal my bones would be falling before the knife of the cane cutter. I ceased to breathe. I was dead. I had suffered the last pangs of that awful hour, and either it was the soul not yet resigned to leave its human tenement or else immortal mind triumphing over death, but I still retained the sentient principle within my corpse. I remember distinctly when the demon relaxed his clutch and shaking me to see if I were really dead broke into a hellish laugh. I remember distinctly when tearing the bottle from me, he pulled my limber body off my couch and stretched himself upon it.

And what were my thoughts? I was dead—yet am living now. Ay, dead as human ever becomes. My lungs had ceased to play, my heart was still, my muscles were inactive, and even my skin had the dead clammy touch. Had men been there, they would have placed me in a coffin and buried me deep in the ground. The worm would have eaten me, and the death rats made nests in my heart, and what was lately a strong man would have become a loathsome mass. But still in that coffin amidst those writhing worms would have been the immortal mind, and still would it have thought and pondered on till the last day was come. For such is the course of soul and death, as my interpretation has it. I was dead all but my mind and that still thought on as vividly, as ramblingly as during life. My body lay dead in that murderer's swamp—my mind roamed far away in thought, reviewing my carnal life. I stood, as when a boy, by my mother's grave. The tall grass was waving over it, and the green sod smiled at my feet. "Mother," I whispered, "your child is weary—the world looks harsh upon him—coldness comes from those who should shelter the orphan. Mother, open your large black eyes and smile upon your child." Again, I stood upon the steamer a childish fugitive, giving a last look upon my fleeing home and mingling my tears with the foaming wave beneath. I dragged my exhausted frame through the cotton fields of the South.

My back was wearied with stooping—we were picking the first opening—and as dreams of future distinction would break upon my soul, the strap of the cotton sack, galling my shoulder, recalled me to myself. All the phases of my life were repeated until they ended where I lay dead—dead as mortal ever becomes. I thought what will my friends say when they hear, that on a visit to the sick, I disappeared in the swamp and was never heard of more—drowned or starved to death? Will they weep for me, for me?—Not many, I ween, will be the tears that will be shed for me. Then, after the lapse of long years, my bones will be found. I wonder who will get my skull? Perhaps an humble doctor like myself, who, meditating upon it, will not think that it holds the mind of a creature of his own ambition—his own lofty instincts. He will deem it but an empty skull and little dream that it held a sentient principle. But I know that the mind will still tenant it.

Ha, ha! how that foul ape is gurgling his blood-bought pleasure. I would move if I could, and wrench the bottle from him, but mine is thought, not action. Hark! there is a storm arising. I hear with my ear that is pressed on the earth the thunder of the hurricane. How the trees crash beneath it! Will it prostrate those above me! Hark! what awful thunder! Ah me! what fierce pang is that piercing my very vitals? There is a glimmering of light before my eyes. Can it be that I the dead am being restored to human life? Another thunder peal! 'Tis the second stroke of my heart—my blood is red hot—it comes with fire through my veins—the earth quakes—the mountain is rolling off my chest—I live!—I breathe!—I see!—I hear!—where am I? Who brought me here? I hear other sounds but cannot my own voice. Where am I? Ah! I remember the dwarf strangled me. Hark! where is he? Is that the sunbeam playing over the trees? What noisome odor like consuming flesh is that which poisons the gale? Great God! can that disfigured half-consumed mass be my evil genius?

I rose up and staggering fell again. My strength was nearly gone. I lay until I thought myself sufficiently recruited to stand and then got up and surveyed the scene. The animals were tied as I left them and were eating their cane unconcernedly, but fearfully my well-nigh murderer had paid for his crime and awful was the retribution. Maddened by the spirits, he had rushed into the flames and in the charred and loathsome mass nothing of the human remained. He had died the murderer's death and been buried in his grave—a tomb of fire.

To remain longer in the horrid place was impossible. My throat pained me excessively where the talons had penetrated the flesh, and I could not speak above a whisper. I turned the mule loose, thinking that it would return home and conduct me out of the swamp. I was not incorrect in my supposition. The creature led me to his owner's cabin. The patient had died during the night.

My account of the dwarf's attack did not surprise the family. He had once, when in a similar condition, made an attack upon his mistress and would have strangled her had assistance not been near.

His bones were left to bleach where they lay. I would not for the universe have looked again upon the place, and his mistress being dead, there were none to care for giving him the rites of sepulture.

Questions to Consider

1. Do the common folks have any common sense, or are they merely buffoons meant to serve as comic foils for the narrator? Do they possess any admirable traits?
2. How does Lewis's training as a medical doctor give him a different view of the frontier people than that of other Southwestern Humorists, who were primarily lawyers and politicians?

Part II

Civil War and Reconstruction Eras

1861–1865 and 1866–1880

Sectional Conflict

Writing in October 1856, a Southern partisan, publishing under only the initials W. R. A. declared that "If there is any wish for the accomplishment of which we could breathe forth our most earnest prayers, it is for the establishment of a *Southern* literature, standing secure and independent upon its own pedestal, lighting up the threshold of its temple with the refulgent beams of its self-illumination." Choosing the pages of the *Southern Literary Messenger* because of its dedication to the South and "to the maintenance of her literature and institutions," W. R. A. outlined the duties of Southern authors. No other obligation, according to the author, warranted greater attention. "If there is any enterprise, toward which the energy of every Southern mind ought to be bent in unrelaxing effort," the author explained, "it is such an enterprise as will give to the South a literature that will command the respect and admiration of the world."

Although W. R. A. recognized that every civilization had an obligation to develop its literature, the author maintained that "to the *Southern* writer . . . there should be other inducements and incentives to literary labors." The need to defend the South's "peculiar institution" (see Map II–1) compelled the region's authors to pick up their pens. Although White Southerners understood slavery as a "great social, moral and political blessing . . . the rest of Christendom stands united against us, and are almost unanimous in pronouncing a verdict of condemnation." Because literature had been the abolitionists' "greatest weapon" against the institution of slavery, the author advocated Southern authors using literature as a vehicle to counter the critics' attacks. "Let Southern authors, men who see and know slavery as it is, make it their duty to deluge all the realms of literature with a flood of light upon this subject," W. R. A. advised. "Let them dispel with the sun of genius the mists and clouds which ignorance and fanaticism have thrown around slavery, purposely involving it in an obscurity and darkness, through which men will not grope to find the truths upon which it reposes. This then," the writer asserted, "is the Duty of Southern Authors."

By the time W. R. A. wrote "The Duty of Southern Authors," the country had become polarized by sectional tensions. Six years earlier, Congress had passed the Compromise of 1850 in order to deal with the question of whether slavery would be

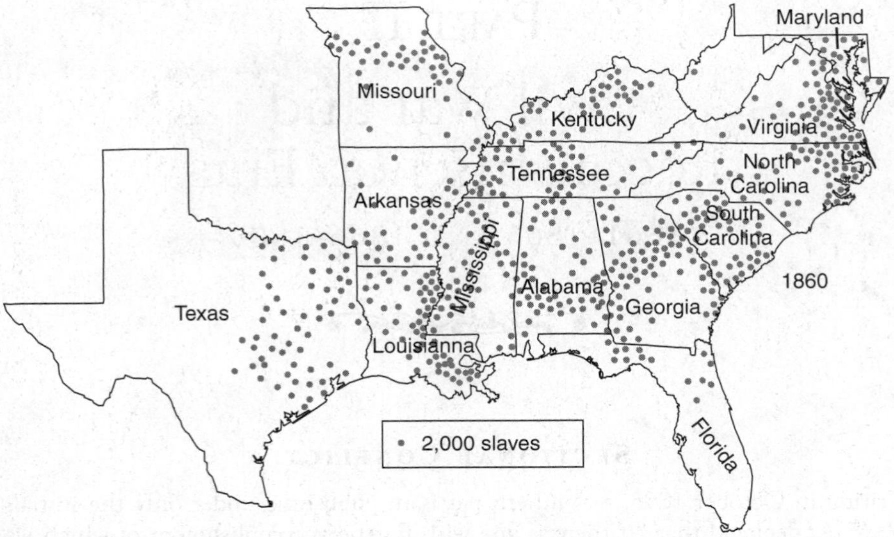

Map II–1: Distribution of slave population, 1860

extended into the territory acquired from Mexico. The Compromise of 1820, which had prevented slavery above the 36°30' latitude in territories acquired from the Louisiana Purchase, had held the country together for a generation. The decision to allow or forbid slavery in territories that were not part of the Louisiana Purchase, however, proved explosive and caused the two-party system to unravel. Factions of both major parties, the Democrats and the Whigs, began to align along sectional, rather than political lines, threatening to upset the political order. When President Zachary Taylor, a Southern Whig, advocated the admission of California as a free state, White Southerners of all political stripes protested.

In response to these protests, Congress eventually passed a series of bills known as the Compromise of 1850. The provisions of this compromise preserved the peace temporarily by allowing California to join the Union as a free state, organizing New Mexico and Utah as territories in which the question of slavery would be decided by settlers, and ending the slave trade in Washington, D.C. The Compromise also provided for a strict Fugitive Slave Act, perhaps the most controversial of its measures. This provision outraged Northerners and prompted Harriet Beecher Stowe, who had only a limited knowledge of plantation life, to render the plight of slaves real to Northern readers. Her novel, *Uncle Tom's Cabin*, serialized in a Washington, D.C. antislavery newspaper in 1851, sold more than three hundred thousand copies within a year of its publication in book form in 1852. One of the most memorable scenes in the novel describes Eliza, a fugitive slave who, carrying her infant, steals across the frozen Ohio River to freedom. As historian Julie Roy Jeffrey has noted, Stowe ably captured "the inherent drama of fleeing slaves to create propaganda highlighting the evils of Southern slaveholding." *Uncle Tom's Cabin* successfully demonstrated "the power of images connected with the fugitive." Indeed, the influence of the novel was profound. White Southerners responded to Stowe's novel by publishing rebuttals, such as Louisa McCord's review of *Uncle Tom's Cabin* and Caroline Hentz's *The Planter's Northern Bride*.

Of course, White Northern abolitionists were not the only critics of the institution of slavery to enter the literary market. Former slaves, including Frederick Douglass and Harriet Jacobs, published first-hand indictments of slavery, contributing to an important genre, the slave narrative. As literary scholar William Andrews explains, beginning with Olaudah Equiano's *Interesting Narrative of the Life of Olaudah Equiano, or Gustavus Vassa, The African* (1789), slave narratives "became virtual testaments in the hands of abolitionists proclaiming the anti-slavery gospel during the antebellum era." These works not only exposed the brutality of the South's "peculiar institution," but, perhaps more importantly, they "gave *incontestable* evidence of the humanity of the African American." Andrews suggests that during the 1850s and early 1860s, the slave narrative evolved: "it addressed the problem of slavery with unprecedented candor, unmasking as never before the moral and social complexities of the American caste and class system in the North as well as the South." Harriet Jacobs's powerful 1861 narrative *Incidents in the Life of a Slave Girl,* coupled with Frederick Douglass's 1852 speech "What to the Slave is the Fourth of July," testify to the importance of the words of former slaves.

Much of the literature produced by White Southerners during the late Antebellum period defended the institution of slavery against outside attack by White and Black abolitionists. Although compelling evidence suggests that Southern intellectuals did concern themselves with issues other than slavery, White Southerners nevertheless spent a great deal of energy defending the institution of slavery. Many scholars agree that White Southerners began a spirited defense of slavery as a "positive good" in the 1830s in response to mounting abolitionist attacks against the institution. Excerpts from John C. Calhoun's 1837 speech on abolition petition outline many of the important elements of this argument. In addition to producing political, theological, and sociological defenses of slavery, White Southerners penned fictional works that supported their worldview. Literary critics consider John Pendleton Kennedy's 1832 novel *Swallow Barn* to be the first important work in this genre of Southern plantation literature. *Swallow Barn*, according to Lucinda MacKethan,

> provided authoritative treatment of the plantation in three important ways: its image of the planter's house as the moral center of order for the culture as a whole; its portrayal of the planter himself as a generous, unmaterialistic gentleman whose paternalistic relation to his slaves constituted an honorable, inescapable obligation; and its pastoral contrast of the simple grace of rural habits to the rude bustle of the expanding America Kennedy saw emerging in the 1830s.

Following in the tradition established by Kennedy, late Antebellum authors placed the slave plantation at the center of their fiction. The pens of these authors transformed the plantation, making it the locus of Southern values and serving to reinforce the region's hierarchical order. As Elizabeth Fox-Genovese has explained in her article "The Anxiety of History: The Southern Confrontation with Modernity," White Southern authors understood their project to be a "quest for a narrative that would represent the values of legitimate authority, hierarchy, and particularism, which most proslavery intellectuals saw as the true substance of their distinct culture." Southern authors, it seems, understood their "duty," regardless of whether they had read W. R. A's article in the *Southern Literary Messenger*.

The author of "The Duty of Southern Authors" believed, in 1856, that "the power of the pen exceeds that of the sword, purse and tongue. It has been truly said," W. R. A. continued, "that the bloodiest conquests of the pen surpass in grandeur and extent, the triumphs of war." The institution of slavery provided White Southerners with "so much leisure for thought and literary activity" and assured them so confidently of "every advantage of order and security" that W. R. A. bemoaned Southerners' neglect of "their duty to the slandered South and to the fame of their fathers." The author hoped that the article would inspire a renewed effort to defend the South against outside attack.

W. R. A. was, of course, a poor predictor of future events. The power of the pen did not quell the power of the sword. White Southerners' defense of the institution of slavery did not prevent the country from unraveling. Southerners became increasingly anxious, especially after the formation of the Republican Party, which championed a free labor ideology and advocated the restriction of slavery to the Southern states. Abraham Lincoln, who had become a leading voice of the Republican Party, articulated a key position of the party in his 1858 "A House Divided" speech. Slave labor and free labor were fundamentally incompatible, Lincoln argued, and the party charged that the South's "slave power" conspired to extend slavery, subvert the Constitution, and threaten liberty.

Lincoln's political star had risen during the 1858 Illinois senatorial campaign, despite his loss to Stephen Douglas, and the Republican Party nominated him as its candidate in the 1860 presidential election. This election was like none other in American history, with four candidates vying for the top office in two contests that broke down along sectional lines. In the North, Abraham Lincoln faced Democrat Stephen Douglas. In the South, John C. Breckinridge, running as a Southern Democrat, faced John Bell of the Constitutional Union Party. White Southerners believed that Lincoln posed a real danger to their region and blocked his name from appearing on the ballot in ten of the fifteen slave states, and many White Southerners threatened to leave the Union if Lincoln emerged victorious. Lincoln won a plurality of the popular vote—39.8 percent—and soundly won in the Electoral College with 180 votes. Fire-eaters, or pro-Southern ideologues, urged immediate secession, claiming that the Republican Party advocated "Negro equality" and vowed to destroy the institution of slavery. In spite of the arguments of Southern unionists, the secessionists prevailed. Lincoln's victory signaled the departure of seven Deep South states by February 1861 and the Confederate States of America was formed (see Map II–2). The creation of the Confederacy forced Southern propagandists to redefine their roles in society. No longer championing their region, by 1861 these authors had become pen and ink warriors, defending a new nation.

The Civil War Era

Much of the Southern literature of the Civil War era centers on an effort to create a sense of Confederate nationalism. Augusta Jane Evans, for example, carefully detailed the Antebellum political climate, cataloguing perceived Northern abuses against the South and outlining the irreconcilable philosophical and cultural differences between the two regions in her Civil War novel *Macaria,* or *The Altars of Sacrifice*. Evans believed the Confederacy to be a viable, independent government. "We are now . . . a thoroughly homogeneous people," explains Irene, her novel's heroine. In a burst of patriotic enthusiasm, Irene proclaims the South: "purified from all con-

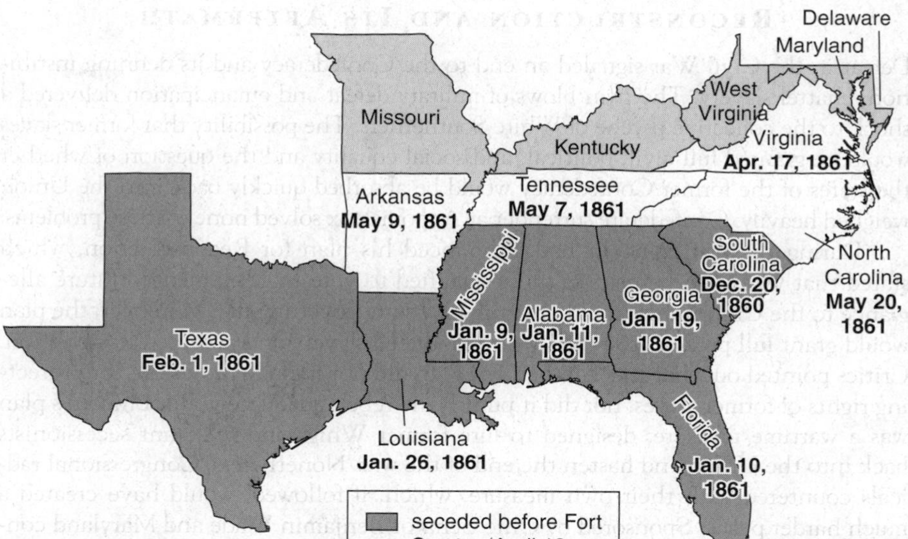

Map II–2: States that seceded from the Union with dates of secession

nection with the North and with no vestige of the mischievous element of New England Puritanism, which, like other poisonous Mycelium, springs up perniciously where even a shred is permitted, we can be a prosperous and noble people." The poetry and prose writings of White Southerners also reflect this desire to create a sense of Confederate nationalism. Whether the political speeches delivered by the Confederacy's president, Jefferson Davis, the journals penned by the women of the Confederacy, the private correspondence of one of the South's ablest generals, Robert E. Lee, or the poems of Henry Timrod, these disparate works reveal, in part, an effort to defend, justify, and promote the Confederate nation.

Fiction allowed Southern authors to imagine a Confederate victory. Diarists, military leaders, and politicians did not have that luxury. Their writings and speeches reflect the course of the Confederate war effort. Early writings exude confidence and enthusiasm. The addition of four Upper South states to the Confederacy and military victory at Manassas, Virginia, the first major battle of the Civil War, encouraged these chroniclers of the war. Wartime reversals, mounting casualty figures, and frustrations about Confederate domestic policy caused many diarists to doubt the success of their cause. Surrender at Appomattox led many White Southerners to mourn the passing of the Confederacy and to contemplate the viability of reuniting with their erstwhile foes.

Reconstruction and Its Aftermath

Defeat in the Civil War signaled an end to the Confederacy and its defining institution, chattel slavery. The twin blows of military defeat and emancipation delivered a shock to the collective psyche of White Southerners. The possibility that former slaves would be granted full civil, political, and social equality and the question of whether the states of the former Confederacy would be absorbed quickly back into the Union weighed heavily. Confederate surrender at Appomattox solved none of these problems.

During the war, Lincoln had announced his plan for Reconstruction, which stated that when ten percent of those qualified to vote in 1860 pledged future allegiance to the Union, they could organize new state governments. Moreover, the plan would grant full pardons to rebels who renounced slavery and accepted its abolition. Critics pointed out that the Ten Percent Plan did not include provisions for protecting rights of former slaves, nor did it punish the rebels adequately. But Lincoln's plan was a wartime measure, designed to lure former Whigs and reluctant secessionists back into the Union and hasten the end of the war. Nonetheless, Congressional radicals countered with their own measure, which, if followed, would have created a much harder peace. Sponsored by Ohio Senator Benjamin Wade and Maryland congressional representative Henry Winter Davis, the bill demanded that over fifty percent of qualified voters in 1860 take an iron-clad oath of allegiance before the state could be readmitted to the Union. Moreover, the bill banned ex-Confederates from participating in the formation of new state constitutions. Finally, the plan extended civil equality to the ex-slaves. Lincoln refused to sign the Wade-Davis bill, and it died. In the meantime, four states—Louisiana, Arkansas, Tennessee, and Virginia—fulfilled Lincoln's requirements, but Congress refused to seat the representatives from these states. Lincoln defended his plan but, equally important, he indicated that he was considering extending suffrage to African Americans. In his last speech, delivered four days before his assassination, Lincoln suggested that he was moving toward a more radical reconstruction policy. The events at Ford's Theater, however, prevented Lincoln's plan from being implemented.

Like Abraham Lincoln, the new president, Andrew Johnson, believed that the fate of Reconstruction rested with the president, not with Congress. Congress had adjourned in March, 1865, which left Johnson alone in Washington to implement his plan for reconstructing the Union. Johnson advocated an easy peace, pardoning and granting amnesty to most former Confederates, although high-ranking military and political officials were to appeal to the president personally. He appointed governors to seven of the former states of the Confederacy, charging them with calling conventions that would draft new constitutions. Johnson made three demands: that these new constitutions ratify the Thirteenth Amendment abolishing slavery, which became part of the Constitution in December, 1865; that they repudiate the ordinances of secession; and that they forgive all war debts. These seven states soon complied with Johnson's plan, and he was ready to accept these states, along with the four states reorganized under Lincoln, back into the Union. In his State of the Union address, Johnson declared the Union restored and made no mention of federal involvement in the lives of African Americans. Congress had other plans, however.

Congress again refused to seat representatives from the former Confederate States. Interpreting the Constitution differently than Johnson, members of Congress

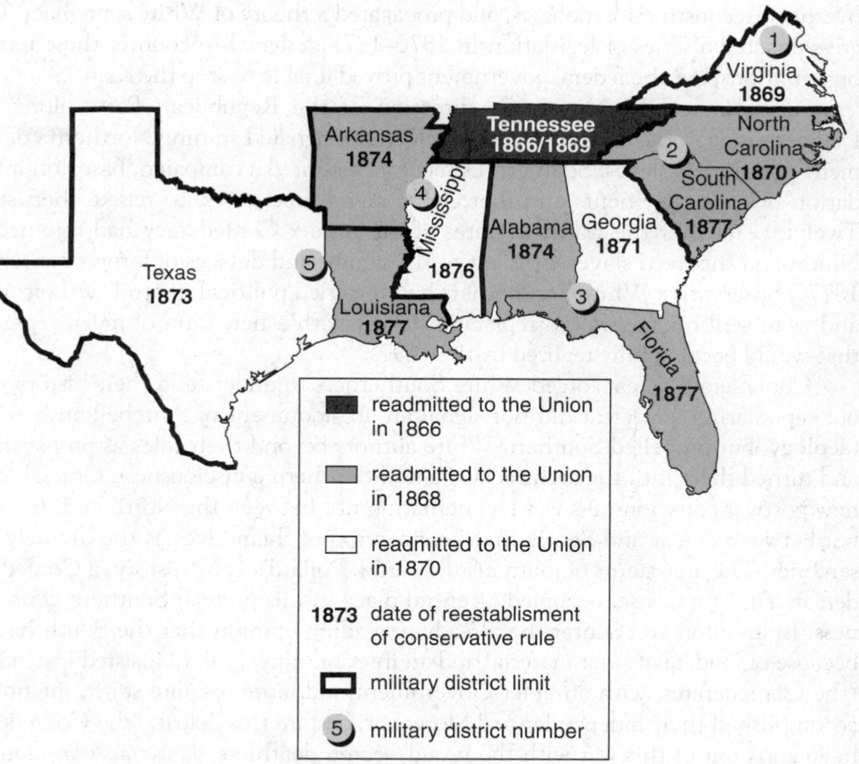

Map II–3: Reconstruction and readmission of states to the Union

believed that Reconstruction fell under their purview. Moreover, the defiance of Southern states suggested that former Confederates refused to accept the implications of the events at Appomattox. Congress was particularly incensed at the Black Codes enacted by most Southern states, which attempted to subvert the Thirteenth Amendment by severely restricting the movement and activity of former slaves. Congress responded by enacting the Civil Rights Act of 1866 and introducing the Fourteenth Amendment, which was ratified in 1868, to guarantee the rights of all citizens before the law, regardless of race, color, or previous condition of servitude. Johnson's opposition to these and other measures prompted even moderate Republicans to move toward the radical position, demanding that guarantees of Black suffrage also become part of Reconstruction (see Map II–3).

For freed slaves, abolitionists, and White Southern dissenters, Reconstruction held the promise to remake the South and grant civil and political equality to African Americans. Frederick Douglass's speech "What the Black Man Wants" examines the potential found in Reconstruction. Moreover, it demonstrates that ex-slaves had their own conceptions of freedom. Conservative White Southern recalcitrance, coupled with Northern abandonment of the South, however, combined to ensure that Reconstruction failed to fulfill its promises. Terrorist organizations, such as the Ku Klux Klan and the Knights of the White Camilla, took aim at Southern Republicans, sought to overturn Reconstruction policies, and propagated a theory of White supremacy. Congress enacted a series of legislation in 1870–1871 designed to counter these terrorist organizations, but the federal government proved unable to stop the Klan.

Furthermore, changes in the direction of the Republican Party along with Democratic victories in Congressional elections signaled waning Northern commitment to the freed slaves. Southern Democrats mounted a campaign, based on intimidation of their opponents and rhetoric of racial superiority, to retake their states. Twelve years after the war, the states of the former Confederacy had rejoined the Union and the freed slaves were left to the whims and devices of former masters. By 1877, conservative White Southerners had regained political control of their region and were well on the way to replacing slavery with a new form of racial repression that would become fully realized by the 1890s.

Confederate defeat forced White Southerners to understand their history without repudiating it. Defeat did not signal an abandonment of Antebellum Southern ideology, but propelled Southern White authors beyond their roles as propagandists and turned them into the architects of a new Southern consciousness. Crucial to this new postwar consciousness was reconciliation not between the North and the South but between defeat and Southerners' conception of themselves as the divinely chosen ones. The arguments of journalist Edward J. Pollard's 1867 history of Confederate defeat, *The Lost Cause*, occupied a central place in this postwar Southern consciousness. In an effort to counter the already prevailing opinion that the South had lost because of inadequate war material and an inferior army, Pollard insisted instead that "the Confederates, with an abler Government and more resolute spirit, might have accomplished their independence." Moreover, despite this defeat, "the Confederates have gone out of this war with the proud, secret, deathless, *dangerous* consciousness that they are THE BETTER MEN, and there was nothing wanting but a change in a set of circumstances and a firmer resolve to make them the victors." The memory of defeat, coupled with this knowledge that theirs was a nobler cause, reasoned Pollard, had left Southerners with a "deathless heritage of glory." "Under these traditions," he proclaimed, "sons will grow to manhood and lessons sink deep that are learned from the lips of widowed mothers." Pollard's version of the Confederacy's downfall became the foundation for a myth of the lost cause, which, as some historians have argued, dominated the postwar White Southern consciousness.

The business of creating a postwar Southern consciousness was still new during Reconstruction. Writers had yet to solidify elements of the lost cause myth that would later dominate the South's understanding of the war. Certain plotlines and literary conventions were becoming familiar, but they had yet to become standardized. The myth of the lost cause was most malleable during Reconstruction, as writers attempted to establish its boundaries. The ever-increasing amount of literature generated by White Southerners fascinated with the Civil War never daunted aspiring novelists, poets, historians, biographers, and autobiographers. Indeed, the late nineteenth-century surge in the publication of Civil War narratives encouraged White Southern authors to believe that the literary market would accommodate yet another story. As they continued to write, they would soon come to appreciate the expansiveness of the literary market and the Southern reading public. Recent generations of historians and literary critics have turned to Southerners' accounts of the Civil War in order to understand both the historic and the imagined past.

Civil War and Reconstruction Chronology

1861–1865 and 1866–1880

1846 • Congress declares war on Mexico.

1848 • Treaty of Guadalupe Hidalgo ends Mexican War. Mexico abandons claims to Texas north of the Rio Grande and cedes provinces of New Mexico and California to the United States.

• Free-Soil Party founded by opponents of the expansion of slavery into the territories.

1850 • Congress passes the Compromise of 1850, which provided for a strict fugitive slave law, allowed California to come into the Union as a free state, provided for the organization of the Utah and New Mexico territories in which the question of slavery would be determined by popular sovereignty, and outlawed the slave trade in Washington, D.C.

1852 • Harriet Beecher Stowe publishes *Uncle Tom's Cabin*.

1854 • Kansas-Nebraska Act opens the territories for settlement in which the question of slavery would be determined by popular sovereignty.

1856 • Violence erupts between pro- and antislavery forces in Kansas.

1857 • Supreme Court hands down its decision in *Dred Scott v. Sandford*. Court declares that African Americans, whether slave or free, are not citizens and therefore have no constitutional rights, that Congress cannot exclude slavery in the territories, and that the Missouri Compromise is unconstitutional.

1858 • Lincoln-Douglas debates.

1859 • John Brown's raid on federal arsenal in Harper's Ferry, Virginia.

1860 • Abraham Lincoln elected president.

• South Carolina secedes from the Union on 12 April.

1861 • Representatives from South Carolina, Georgia, Alabama, Mississippi, Florida, Texas, and Louisiana meet in Montgomery, Alabama and form the Confederate States of America.

• Confederate forces open fire on Fort Sumter, South Carolina in the opening clash of the Civil War.

• Virginia, Tennessee, North Carolina, and Arkansas secede from the Union and join the Confederacy.

• Confederate forces defeat Union forces at Manassas in the first major battle of the Civil War.

1862 • Union forces capture Fort Henry and Fort Donaldson in Tennessee.

• Battle of Shiloh in Tennessee results in significant casualties for both Confederate and Union forces and ends the Confederacy's bid to secure the Mississippi Valley.

• Battle of Antietam stops the Confederate advance into Maryland.

• Lincoln announces the preliminary emancipation proclamation.

1863 • Emancipation Proclamation goes into effect, freeing all slaves in areas still in rebellion.

• Vicksburg falls to Union forces.

• Confederate forces defeated in the Battle of Gettysburg, Lee's last offensive in the North.

1864 • Atlanta falls to Union forces.
• Lincoln reelected President.

1865 • Congress establishes Freedmen's Bureau.
• Lee surrenders to Grant at Appomattox Court House, Virginia.
• Lincoln assassinated by John Wilkes Booth at Ford's Theater in Washington, D.C. Vice President Andrew Johnson assumes the presidency.
• Southern legislatures enact Black codes.
• The Thirteenth Amendment, which abolishes slavery, becomes part of the Constitution.

1866 • Congress approves the Fourteenth Amendment, which grants birthright citizenship and guarantees all Americans "equal protection of the laws." Amendment becomes part of the Constitution in 1868.
• Ku Klux Klan founded in Tennessee.

1867 • Congress passes Military Reconstruction Act, imposing military rule on the South and requiring states to guarantee the vote to Black men.

1868 • President Johnson acquitted in impeachment trial in U.S. Senate.
• Ulysses S. Grant elected president.

1869 • Congress approves Fifteenth Amendment, which prohibits racial discrimination in voting rights. Amendment becomes part of the Constitution in 1870.

1871 • Congress passes Ku Klux Klan Act in an attempt to rid the South of White terrorism.

1875 • Congress passes Civil Rights Act of 1875, which outlaws racial discrimination. Act receives little federal enforcement.

1877 • Disputed election of 1876 resolved.
• Congressional committee awards contested electoral votes to Republican Rutherford B. Hayes, making him president.
• Hayes agrees to pull military forces out of the South, effectively ending Reconstruction in the South.

John C. Calhoun

1782–1850

John C. Calhoun was one of the foremost statesmen and orators in Antebellum America. He began his political career in the South Carolina legislature and quickly moved to the United States House of Representatives. He then served as secretary of war under President Monroe, and as vice president under Presidents John Quincy Adams and Andrew Jackson. After he resigned from the vice presidency in 1832, Calhoun took a seat in the U.S. Senate, where he served until 1844. He was John Tyler's secretary of state from 1844 to 1845 and then returned as a member of the Senate and served there until his death in 1850. Calhoun used his considerable rhetorical skill to argue in favor of states' rights, to defend slavery, and, in the words of Ross M. Lence, to articulate the right of "significant interests to have a veto over either the enactment or the implementation of public law." The following excerpts represent Calhoun's most famous works on these themes.

Calhoun took the lead in the nullification crisis of the early 1830s. In 1828 Congress had passed a revised tariff, known as the Tariff of Abominations, that set some rates as high as fifty percent. The tariff protected domestic manufacturing in the Northeast at the expense of the South, especially South Carolina, because the high tariff rates hurt the cotton export market. Calhoun, then the nation's vice president, penned the "Exposition and Protest" anonymously in 1828 to challenge the consolidation of federal power at the expense of the sovereign state. The United States government had exceeded its authority, Calhoun believed, by instituting the protective tariff. A strict constructionist, he pointed out in the "Exposition" that the Constitution makes provisions for tariffs to raise funds for national defense but not to protect domestic industry. The Tariff of 1828 was, therefore, unconstitutional. Calhoun used the "Exposition" to detail the theory of interposition, which argues that the state must "interpose" itself between its citizens and a tyrannical federal state by declaring unconstitutional federal laws null and void. In developing the theory of interposition, Calhoun borrowed heavily from the language of Jefferson's Kentucky Resolutions. Interposition, according to the "Exposition," is the only constitutional remedy for disputes between the federal government and individual states.

The president thought otherwise. Andrew Jackson ignored Calhoun's "Exposition" when he assumed the presidency in 1829. Yet the 1832 tariff revisions scarcely brought relief to the South. Calhoun, knowing that he wielded little power in the Jackson administration, resigned from the vice presidency in 1832 and took a seat in the U.S. Senate. His persuasive argument, according to historian Lacy K. Ford, coupled with a number of factors, including an economic slump and a sense of unity in the South Carolina upcountry, persuaded South Carolina to nullify the Tariff of Abominations in February 1833. Jackson threatened to invade South Carolina and pushed through Congress a Force Bill, which declared South Carolina's actions treasonous and authorized military personnel to collect federal tariffs. Congress, meanwhile, quickly moved to lower the tariff rate to the level that prevailed in 1816. South Carolina responded by withdrawing its nullification of the Tariff of Abominations. Federal power had prevailed over an assertion of states' rights.

Many historians point to this episode as evidence of the inevitability of the Civil War. But nullification, according to Ford, "should be viewed not so much as a harbinger of future radicalism as the logical, though not inevitable, culmination of the continuing debate over how best to defend the republican principles inherited from the Founding Fathers against the centralizing and corrupting tendencies of the age." In other words, only by looking backward "to the Revolution, the Constitution, and the age of Jefferson," and not by looking forward to secession and the Civil War, can South Carolina's decision to nullify be understood fully.

As Lence has noted, from the 1830s on, "Calhoun was increasingly called upon to defend the South's peculiar institution—slavery—which came progressively to the fore as the defining characteristic of the South and became connected to the debate over states' rights. With one notable exception, Calhoun always couched his defense of slavery in the language of history, economics, and philosophy. That one exception was his 1837 address to the Senate, in which he declares slavery to be a positive good." As historian Manisha Sinha has observed, however, Calhoun's reputation as a political theorist "is intrinsically connected with the institution he so well defended."

The South Carolina Exposition, 1828

The committee have bestowed on the subjects referred to them the deliberate attention which their importance demands; and the result, on full investigation, is a unanimous opinion that the act of Congress of the last session, with the whole system of legislation imposing duties on imports—not for revenue, but the protection of one branch of industry at the expense of others—is unconstitutional, unequal, and oppressive, and calculated to corrupt the public virtue and destroy the liberty of the country; which propositions they propose to consider in the order stated, and then to conclude their report with the consideration of the important question of the remedy. . . .

. . . The General Government is one of specific powers, and it can rightfully exercise only the powers expressly granted, and those that may be "necessary and proper" to carry them into effect; all others being reserved expressly to the States, or to the people. It results necessarily, that those who claim to exercise a power under the Constitution, are bound to shew, that it is expressly granted, or that it is necessary and proper, as a means to some of the granted powers. The advocates of the Tariff[1] have offered no such proof. It is true, that the third [*sic*] section of the first article of the Constitution of the United States authorizes Congress to lay and collect an impost duty, but it is granted as a tax power, for the sole purpose of revenue; a power in its nature essentially different from that of imposing protective or prohibitory duties. The two are incompatable [*sic*]; for the prohibitory system must end in destroying the revenue from impost. It has been said that the system is a violation of the spirit and not the letter of the Constitution. The distinction is not material. The Constitution may be as grossly violated by acting against its meaning as against its letter; but it may be proper to dwell a moment on the point, in order to understand more fully the real character of the acts, under which the interest of this, and other States similarly situated, has been sacrificed. The facts are few and simple. The Constitution grants to Congress the power of imposing a duty on imports for revenue; which power is abused by being converted into an instrument for rearing up the industry of one section of the country on the ruins of another. The violation then consists in using a power, granted for one object, to advance another, and that by the sacrifice of the original object. It is, in a word, *a violation of perversion*, the most dangerous of all, because the most insidious, and difficult to resist. Others cannot be perpetrated without the aid of the judiciary; this may be, by the executive and legislative alone. The courts by their own decisions cannot look into the motives of legislators—they are obliged to take acts by their titles and professed objects, and if *they* be constitutional they cannot interpose their power, however grossly the acts may violate the Constitution. The proceedings of the last session sufficiently prove, that the House of Representatives are aware of the distinction, and determined to avail themselves of the advantage. . . .

1. Tariff of Abominations.

If there be a political proposition universally true, one which springs directly from the nature of man, and is independent of circumstances, it is, that irresponsible power is inconsistent with liberty and must corrupt those who exercise it. On this great principle our political system rests. We consider all powers as delegated from the people and to be controlled by those who are interested in their just and proper exercise; and our governments, both State and General, are but a system of judicious contrivances to bring this fundamental principle into fair practical operation. Among the most prominent of these is, the responsibility of the representatives to their constituents, through frequent elections, in order to enforce a faithful performance of their delegated trust. Without such a check on their powers, however clearly they may be defined, and distinctly prescribed, our liberty would be but a mockery. The Government, instead of being directed to the general good, would speedily become the instrument to aggrandize those who might be intrusted with its administration . . .

. . . From diversity of interest in the several classes of the people and sections of the country, laws act differently, so that the same law, though couched in general terms and apparently fair, shall in reality transfer the power and prosperity of one class or section to another; in such case responsibility to constituents, which is but the means of enforcing the fidelity of representatives to them, must prove wholly insufficient to preserve the purity of public agents, or the liberty of the country. It would in fact be inapplicable to the evil. The disease would be in the community itself; in the constituents, not in the representatives. The opposing interest of the community would engender necessarily opposing hostile parties, organized in this very diversity of interest; the stronger of which, if the government provided no efficient check, would exercise unlimited and unrestrained power over the weaker. The relations of equality between them would thus be destroyed, and in its place there would be substituted the relation of sovereign and subject, between the stronger and the weaker interest, in its most odious and oppressive form. . . . On the great and vital point, the industry of the country, which comprehends nearly all the other interests, two great sections of the Union are opposed. *We* want free trade; they, restrictions. We want moderate taxes, frugality in the government, economy, accountability, and a rigid application of the public money, to the payment of the public debt, and the objects authorized by the Constitution; in all these particulars, if we may judge by experience, their views of their interest are the opposite. They act and feel on all questions connected with the American System,[2] as sovereigns; as those always do who impose burdens on others for their own benefit; and we, on the contrary, like those on whom such burdens are imposed. In a word, to the extent stated, the country is divided and organized into two great opposing parties, one sovereign and the other subject; marked by all the characteristics which must ever accompany that relation, under whatever form it may exist. That our industry is controlled by the many, instead of one, by a majority in Congress elected by a majority in the community having an opposing interest, instead of hereditary rulers, forms not the slightest mitigation of the evil. In fact, instead of mitigating, it aggravates. In our case one opposing branch of industry cannot prevail without associating others, and thus instead of a single act of oppression we must bear many. . . . Liberty comprehends the idea of *responsible power*, that those who make and execute the laws should be controlled by those on whom they operate; that the governed should govern. Thus to prevent rulers from abusing their trust, constituents must controul [*sic*] them through elections; and so to prevent the major from oppressing the minor interests of society, the Constitution must provide . . . a check founded on the same principle, and

2. Devised by Henry Clay, a package of protective tariffs and federal expenditures for internal improvements.

equally efficacious. In fact the abuse of delegated power, and the tyranny of the greater over the less interests of society, are the two great dangers, and the only two, to be guarded against; and if *they* be effectually guarded liberty must be *eternal*. . . . No government based on the naked principle, that the majority ought to govern, however true the maxim in its proper sense and under proper restrictions, ever preserved its liberty, even for a single generation. . . . Those governments only, which provide checks, which limit and restrain within proper bounds the power of the majority, have had a prolonged existence, and been distinguished for virtue, power and happiness. Constitutional government, and the government of a majority, are utterly incompatible, it being the sole purpose of a Constitution to impose limitations and checks upon the majority. An unchecked majority, is a despotism—and government is free, and will be permanent in proportion to the number, complexity and efficiency of the checks, by which its powers are controlled. . . .

Our system, then consists of two distinct and independent sovereignties. The general powers conferred on the General Government, are subject to its sole and separate control, and the States cannot, without violating the Constitution, interpose their authority to check, or in any manner counteract its movements, so long, as they are confined to its proper sphere; so also the peculiar and local powers, reserved to the States, are subject to their exclusive control, nor can the General Government interfere with them, without on its part, also violating the Constitution. In order to have a full and clear conception of our institutions, it will be proper to remark, that there is in our system a striking distinction between the government and the sovereign power. Whatever may be the true doctrine in regard to the sovereignty of the States individually, it is unquestionably clear that while the government of the union is vested in its legislative, executive and political departments, the actual sovereign power, resides in the several States, who created it, in their separate and distinct political character. . . .

. . . The constitutional power to protect their rights as members of the confederacy, results necessarily, by the most simple and demonstrable arguments, from the very nature of the relation subsisting between the States and General Government. If it be conceded, as it must by every one who is the least conversant with our institutions, that the sovereign power is divided between the States and General Government, and that the former holds its reserved rights, in the same high sovereign capacity, which the latter does its delegated rights; it will be impossible to deny to the States the right of deciding on the infraction of their rights, and the proper remedy to be applied for the correction. The right of judging, in such cases, is an essential attribute of sovereignty of which the States cannot be divested, without losing their sovereignty itself; and being reduced to a subordinate corporate condition. In fact, to divide power, and to give to one of the parties the exclusive right of judging of the portion allotted to each, is in reality not to divide at all; and to reserve such exclusive right to the General Government, (it matters not by what department it be exercised,) is in fact to constitute it one great consolidated government, with unlimited powers, and to reduce the States to mere corporations. It is impossible to understand the force of terms, and to deny these conclusions. The opposite opinion can be embraced only on hasty and imperfect views of the relation existing between the States and the General Government. But the existence of the right of judging of their powers, clearly established from the sovereignty of the States, as clearly implies a veto, or controul on the action of the General Government on contested points of authority; and this very controul is the remedy, which the Constitution has provided to prevent the encroachment of the General Government on the reserved right of the States;

and by the exercise of which, the distribution of power between the General and State Governments, may be preserved forever inviolate, as is established by the Constitution; and thus afford effectual protection to the great minor interest of the community, against the oppression of the majority.

The South Carolina Protest, 1828[1]

The Senate and House of Representatives of South Carolina, now met, and sitting in General Assembly, through the Hon. William Smith and the Hon. Robert Y. Hayne, their representatives in the Senate of the United States, do, in the name and on behalf of the good people of the said commonwealth, solemnly PROTEST against the system of protecting duties, lately adopted by the federal government, for the following reasons:—

1st. *Because* the good people of this commonwealth believe that the powers of Congress were delegated to it in trust for the accomplishment of certain specified objects which limit and control them, and that every exercise of them for any other purposes, is a violation of the Constitution as unwarrantable as the undisguised assumption of substantive, independent powers not granted or expressly withheld.

2d. *Because* the power to lay duties on imports is, and in its very nature can be, only a means of effecting objects specified by the Constitution; since no free government, and least of all a government of enumerated powers, can of right impose any tax, any more than a penalty, which is not at once justified by public necessity, and clearly within the scope and purview of the social compact; and since the right of confining appropriations of the public money to such legitimate and constitutional objects is as essential to the liberty of the people as their unquestionable privilege to be taxed only by their consent.

3d. *Because* they believe that the tariff law passed by Congress at its last session, and all other acts of which the principal object is the protection of manufactures, or any other branch of domestic industry, if they be considered as the exercise of a power in Congress to tax the people at its own good will and pleasure, and to apply the money raised to objects not specified in the Constitution, is a violation of these fundamental principles, a breach of a well-defined trust, and a perversion of the high powers vested in the federal government for federal purposes only.

4th. *Because* such acts, considered in the light of a regulation of commerce, are equally liable to objection; since, although the power to regulate commerce may, like all other powers, be exercised so as to protect domestic manufactures, yet it is clearly distinguishable from a power to do so *eonomine*,[2] both in the nature of the thing and in the common acception of the terms; and because the confounding of them would lead to the most extravagant results, since the encouragement of domestic industry implies an absolute control over all the interests, resources, and pursuits of a people, and is consistent with the idea of any other than a simple, consolidated government.

5th. *Because*, from the contemporaneous exposition of the Constitution in the numbers of the *Federalist*, (which is cited only because the Supreme Court has recognized its authority), it is clear that the power to regulate commerce was considered by the Convention as only incidentally connected with the encouragement of agriculture and manufactures; and because the power of laying imposts and duties on imports was not understood to justify in any case, a prohibition of foreign commodities,

1. The "Protest" followed the "Exposition," excerpted in the previous selection.

2. By that name.

except as a means of extending commerce, by coercing foreign nations to a fair reciprocity in their intercourse with us, or for some *bona fide* commercial purpose.

6th. *Because*, whilst the power to protect manufactures is nowhere expressly granted to Congress, nor can be considered as necessary and proper to carry into effect any specified power, it seems to be expressly reserved to the states, by the 10th section of the 1st article of the Constitution.

7th. *Because* even admitting Congress to have a constitutional right to protect manufactures by the imposition of duties, or by regulations of commerce, designed principally for that purpose, yet a tariff of which the operation is grossly unequal and oppressive, is such an abuse of power as is incompatible with the principles of a free government and the great ends of civil society, justice, and equality of rights and protection.

8th. *Finally*, because South Carolina, from her climate, situation, and peculiar institutions, is, and must ever continue to be, wholly dependent upon agriculture and commerce, not only for her prosperity, but for her very existence as a state; because the valuable products of her soil—the blessings by which Divine Providence seems to have designed to compensate for the great disadvantages under which she suffers in other respects—are among the very few that can be cultivated with any profit by slave labor; and if, by the loss of her foreign commerce, these products should be confined to an inadequate market, the fate of this fertile state would be poverty and utter desolation; her citizens, in despair, would emigrate to more fortunate regions, and the whole frame and constitution of her civil policy be impaired and deranged, if not dissolved entirely.

Deeply impressed with these considerations, the representatives of the good people of this commonwealth, anxiously desiring to live in peace with their fellow-citizens, and to do all that in them lies to preserve and perpetuate the union of the states, and liberties of which it is the surest pledge, but feeling it to be their bounden duty to expose and resist all encroachments upon the true spirit of the Constitution, lest an apparent acquiescence in the system of protecting duties should be drawn into precedent—do, in the name of the commonwealth of South Carolina, claim to enter upon the Journal of the Senate their *protest* against it as unconstitutional, oppressive, and unjust.

Speech on the Reception of Abolition Petitions, February 16, 1837, Revised Report

I do not belong, said Mr. C., to the school which holds that aggression is to be met by concession. Mine is the opposite creed, which teaches that encroachments must be met at the beginning, and that those who act on the opposite principle are prepared to become slaves. In this case, in particular. I hold concession or compromise to be fatal. If we concede an inch, concession would follow concession—compromise would follow compromise, until our ranks would be so broken that effectual resistance would be impossible. We must meet the enemy on the frontier, with a fixed determination of maintaining our position at every hazard. Consent to receive these insulting petitions, and the next demand will be that they be referred to a committee in order that they may be deliberated and acted upon. At the last session we were modestly asked to receive them, simply to lay them on the table, without any view to ulterior action. . . . I then said, that the next step would be to refer the petition to a committee, and I already see indications that such is now the intention. If we yield, that will be followed by another, and we will thus proceed, step by step, to the final consummation of the object of these petitions. We are now told that the most effectual mode of arresting the progress of abolition is, to reason it down; and with this view it is urged that the petitions ought to be referred to a committee. That is the very ground which was taken at the last session in the other House, but instead of arresting its progress it has since advanced more rapidly than ever. The most unquestionable right may be rendered doubtful, if once admitted to be a subject of controversy, and that would be the case in the present instance. The subject is beyond the jurisdiction of Congress—they have no right to touch it in any shape or form, or to make it the subject of deliberation or discussion. . . .

As widely as this incendiary spirit has spread, it has not yet infected this body, or the great mass of the intelligent and business portion of the North; but unless it be speedily stopped, it will spread and work upwards till it brings the two great sections of the Union into deadly conflict. This is not a new impression with me. Several years since, in a discussion with one of the Senators from Massachusetts (Mr. Webster), before this fell spirit had showed itself, I then predicted that the doctrine of the proclamation and the Force Bill—that this Government had a right, in the last resort, to determine the extent of its own powers, and enforce its decision at the point of the bayonet, which was so warmly maintained by that Senator, would at no distant day arouse the dormant spirit of abolitionism. I told him that the doctrine was tantamount to the assumption of unlimited power on the part of the Government, and that such would be the impression on the public mind in a large portion of the Union. The consequence would be inevitable. A large portion of the Northern States believed slavery to be a sin, and would consider it as an obligation of conscience to abolish it if they should feel themselves in any degree responsible for its continuance, and that this doctrine would necessarily lead to the belief of such responsibility. I then predicted that it would commence as it has with this fanatical portion of society, and that they would begin their operations on the ignorant, the weak, the young, and the thoughtless,—and gradually extend upwards till they would become strong enough to obtain political control, when he and others holding the highest stations in society, would, however reluctant, be compelled to yield to their doctrines, or be driven into obscurity. But four years have since elapsed, and all this is already in a course of regular fulfilment.

Standing at the point of time at which we have now arrived, it will not be more difficult to trace the course of future events now than it was then. They who imagine that the spirit now abroad in the North, will die away of itself without a shock or convulsion, have formed a very inadequate conception of its real character; it will continue to rise and spread, unless prompt and efficient measures to stay its progress be adopted. Already it has taken possession of the pulpit, of the schools, and, to a considerable extent, of the press; those great instruments by which the mind of the rising generation will be formed.

However sound the great body of the non-slaveholding States are at present, in the course of a few years they will be succeeded by those who will have been taught to hate the people and institutions of nearly one-half of this Union, with a hatred more deadly than one hostile nation ever entertained towards another. It is easy to see the end. By the necessary course of events, if left to themselves, we must become, finally, two people. It is impossible under the deadly hatred which must spring up between the two great nations, if the present causes are permitted to operate unchecked, that we should continue under the same political system. The conflicting elements would burst the Union asunder, powerful as are the links which hold it together. Abolition and the Union cannot coexist. As the friend of the Union I openly proclaim it—and the sooner it is known the better. The former may now be controlled, but in a short time it will be beyond the power of man to arrest the course of events. We of the South will not, cannot, surrender our institutions. To maintain the existing relations between the two races, inhabiting that section of the Union, is indispensable to the peace and happiness of both. It cannot be subverted without drenching the country or the other of the races. . . . But let me not be understood as admitting, even by implication, that the existing relations between the two races in the slaveholding States is an evil—far otherwise; I hold it to be a good, as it has thus far proved itself to be to both, and will continue to prove so if not disturbed by the fell spirit of abolition. I appeal to facts. Never before has the Black race of Central Africa, from the dawn of history to the present day, attained a condition so civilized and so improved, not only physically, but morally and intellectually.

In the meantime, the White or European race, has not degenerated. It has kept pace with its brethren in other sections of the Union where slavery does not exist. It is odious to make comparison; but I appeal to all sides whether the South is not equal in virtue, intelligence, patriotism, courage, disinterestedness, and all the high qualities which adorn our nature.

But I take higher ground. I hold that in the present state of civilization, where two races of different origin, and distinguished by color, and other physical differences, as well as intellectual, are brought together, the relation now existing in the slaveholding States between the two, is, instead of an evil, a good—a positive good. I feel myself called upon to speak freely upon the subject where the honor and interests of those I represent are involved. I hold then, that there never has yet existed a wealthy and civilized society in which one portion of the community did not, in point of fact, live on the labor of the other. Broad and general as is this assertion, it is fully borne out by history. This is not the proper occasion, but, if it were, it would not be difficult to trace the various devices by which the wealth of all civilized communities has been so unequally divided, and to show by what means so small a share has been allotted to those by whose labor it was produced, and so large a share given to the non-producing classes. The devices are almost innumerable, from the brute force and gross superstition of ancient times, to the subtle and artful fiscal contrivances of modern. I might well challenge a comparison between them and the more direct, simple, and patriarchal mode by which the labor of the African race is, among us, commanded by the European. I may say with truth, that in few countries so much is left to the share of the laborer, and so little exacted from him, or where there is more kind attention paid to him in sickness or infirmities of age. Compare his condition with the tenants of the poor houses in the more civilized portions of Europe—look at the sick, and the old and infirm slave, on one hand, in the midst of his family and friends, under the kind superintending care of his master and mistress, and compare it with the forlorn and wretched condition of the pauper in the poorhouse. But I will not dwell on this aspect of the question; I turn to the political; and here I fearlessly assert that the existing relation between the two races in the South, against which these blind fanatics are waging war, forms the most solid and durable foundation on which to rear free and stable political institutions. It is useless to disguise the fact. There is and always has been in an advanced stage of wealth and civilization, a conflict between labor and capital. The condition of society in the South exempts us from the disorders and dangers resulting from this conflict; and which explains why it is that the political condition of the slaveholding States has been so much more stable and quiet than that of the North. . . .

. . . Surrounded as the slaveholding States are with such imminent perils, I rejoice to think that our means of defense are ample, if we shall prove to have the intelligence and spirit to see and apply them before it is too late. All we want is concert, to lay aside all party differences and unite with zeal and energy in repelling approaching dangers. Let there be concert of action, and we shall find ample means of security without resorting to secession or disunion. I speak with full knowledge and a thorough examination of the subject, and for one see my way clearly. . . . I dare not hope that anything I can say will arouse the South to a due sense of danger; I fear it is beyond the power of mortal voice to awaken it in time from the fatal security into which it has fallen.

Questions to Consider

1. How convincing was Calhoun's reading of the Constitution?
2. How does Calhoun's defense of slavery compare with that of Louisa McCord? What is the importance of declaring slavery a "positive good" rather than a "necessary evil?" How central do you imagine Calhoun's works to be in the creation of a proslavery ideology in the Antebellum South?

Caroline Lee Whiting Hentz

1800–1856

The publication of Harriet Beecher Stowe's 1852 abolitionist novel *Uncle Tom's Cabin* signaled to White Southerners a heightening of sectional tensions. The novel's immediate popularity with Northern readers prompted the *Southern Literary Messenger* to declare that Stowe's work was "an evidence of the manner in which our enemies are employing literature for our overthrow. Is that effusion, in which a woman, instigated by the devil, sows the seeds of future strife between the two sections of her country, likely to be the last?" the editor asked. The answer was an emphatic "no." Many White Southerners believed that the novel demanded a response. Elizabeth Moss notes that "while the South was championed in a variety of forums by a broad cross-section of its sons and daughters, the most consistent and convincing effort came from the handful of Southern domestic novelists." Caroline Hentz issued one of the most stinging rebukes when she published *The Planter's Northern Bride* in 1854.

In many ways, Hentz seemed an unlikely pro-Southern partisan. Born into a prominent New England family, she traveled widely before settling in the South with her husband, a professor at the University of North Carolina. Her early works reflect her desire to promote national harmony. Moss explains that Hentz "portrayed Northerners with some degree of consistency" in her earlier novels, "emphasizing the common humanity of residents above and below the Mason-Dixon Line." Evidence suggests that Stowe's novel offended her personally. Hentz wrote her publisher, Abraham Hart, that "slavery as [Stowe] describes it is an entirely new institution to us." Hentz proposed to pen a response, promising that "there shall be no Cabin in it most assuredly." Of Stowe's depiction of slavery, Hentz declared, "the public have had enough for one century."

Hentz believed she needed to publish her novel in a timely fashion. Telling Hart that "everyone says that the excitement produced by the Nebraska bill will be favorable" to the novel's reception, Hentz urged her publisher to issue *The Planter's Northern Bride* ahead of publication schedule. She worried that "antislavery lectures and meetings" had already poisoned the reading public's view, predisposing it to accept Stowe's version of slavery as accurate. Hart was apparently unmoved by Hentz's pleas.

Hentz's insistence that she would not populate her novel with slave cabins may have been disingenuous, for she borrowed plotlines and characters from *Uncle Tom's Cabin*. Her tale, however, championed the moral superiority of the institution of slavery. As Moss summarized, "In Hentz's version of the story, a plantation owner articulates the true principles of the early Republic, an abolitionist's daughter champions slavery, Northern laborers envy Southern slaves, and, in perhaps the most obvious inversion of Stowe's plot, a mulatto slave crosses the Ohio in a desperate flight for freedom." Hentz wondered whether her novel could counter the tremendous influence of *Uncle Tom's Cabin*. "Should the burning lava of anarchy and servile war roll over the plans of the South, and bury, under its fiery waves, its social and domestic institutions," she wrote Hart in 1854, "it will not suffer alone." Indeed, *The Planter's Northern Bride* ended apocalyptically: "The North and the South are branches of the same parent tree," she noted, echoing sentiments she harbored earlier in the century, "and the lightening bolt that shivers the one, must scorch and wither the other."

from The Planter's Northern Bride

I saw her, and I lov'd her—I sought her and I won;
A dozen pleasant summers, and more, since then have run;
And half as many voices now prattling by her side,
Remind me of the autumn when she became my bride.

Thomas MacKellar

Nothing shall assuage
Your love but marriage: for such is
The tying of two in wedlock, as is
The tuning of two lutes in one key: for
Striking the strings of the one, straws will stir
Upon the strings of the other; and in
Two minds linked in love, one cannot be
Delighted but the other rejoiceth.

Lilly's Sappho

CHAPTER I

Mr. Moreland, a Southern planter, was travelling through the New England States in the bright season of a Northern spring. Business with some of the merchant princes of Boston had brought him to the North; but a desire to become familiar with the beautiful surroundings of the metropolis induced him to linger long after it was transacted, to gratify the taste and curiosity of an intelligent and liberal mind. He was rich and independent, had leisure as well as wealth at his command, and there was something in the deep green fields and clear blue waters of New England that gave a freshness, and brightness, and elasticity to his spirits, wanting in his milder, sunnier latitude.

He found himself one Saturday night in a sweet country village, whose boundaries were marked by the most luxuriant shubbery and trees, in the midst of which a thousand silver rills were gushing. He was pleased with the prospect of passing the ensuing Sunday in a valley so serene and quiet, that it seemed as if Nature enjoyed in its shades the repose of an eternal Sabbath. The inn where he stopped was a neat, orderly place, and though the landlord impressed him, at first, as a hard, repulsive looking man, with a dark, Indian face, and large, iron-bound frame, he found him ready to perform all the duties of a host. Requesting to be shown to a private apartment, he ordered Albert, a young mulatto who accompanied him on his journey, to follow him with his valise. Albert was a handsome, golden-skinned youth, with shining black hair and eyes, dressed very nearly as genteelly as his master, and who generally attracted more attention on their Northern tour. Accustomed to wait on his master and listen to the conversation of refined and educated gentlemen, he had very little of the dialect of the negro, and those familiar with the almost unintelligible jargon which delineators of the sable character put into their lips, could not but be astonished at the propriety of his language and pronunciation.

When Mr. Moreland started on his journey to the North, his friends endeavoured to dissuade him from taking a servant with him, as he would incur the danger of losing him among the granite hills to which he was bound:—they especially warned him of the risk of taking Albert, whose superior intelligence and cultivation would render him more accessible to the arguments which would probably be brought forward to lure him from his allegiance.

"I defy all the eloquence of the North to induce Albert to leave me," exclaimed Mr. Moreland. "Let them do it if they can. Albert," he said, calling the boy to him, who was busily employed in brushing and polishing his master's boots, with a friction quick enough to create sparkles of light. "Albert—I am going to the North—would you like to go with me?"

"To be sure I would, master, I would like to go anywhere in the world with you."

"You know the people are all free at the North, Albert."

"Yes, master."

"And when you are there, they will very likely try to persuade you that you are free too, and tell you it is your duty to run away from me, and set up for a gentleman yourself. What do you think of all this?"

Albert suspended his brush in the air, drew up his left shoulder with a significant shrug, darted an oblique glance at his master from his bright black eyes, and then renewed his friction with accelerated velocity.

"Well, my boy, you have not answered me," cried Mr. Moreland, in a careless, yet interested manner, peculiar to himself.

"Why, you see, Mars. Russell (when he addressed his master by his Christian name, he always abbreviated his title in this manner, though when the name was omitted he uttered the title in all its dignity)—"you see, Mars. Russell"—here the mulatto slipped the boot from his arm, placed it on the floor, and still retaining the brush in his right hand, folded his arms across his breast, and spoke deliberately and earnestly,—"they couldn't come round this boy with that story; I've hearn it often enough already; I ain't afraid of anything they can say and do, to get me away from you as long as you want me to stay with you. But if you are afraid to trust me, master, that's another thing. You'd better leave me, if you think I'd be mean enough to run away."

"Well said, Albert!" exclaimed Mr. Moreland, laughing at the air of injured honour and conscious self-appreciation he assumed; "I do trust you, and shall surely take you with me; you can make yourself very amusing to the people, by telling them of your home frolics, such as being chained, handcuffed, scourged, flayed, and burned alive, and all those little trifles they are so much interested in."

"Oh! master, I wish I may find everybody as well off as I am. If there's no lies told on you but what I tell, you'll be mighty safe, I know. Ever since Miss Claudia"—

"Enough," cried Mr. Moreland, hastily interrupting him. He had breathed a name which evidently awakened painful recollections, for his sunshiny countenance became suddenly dark and cold. Albert, who seemed familiar with his master's varying moods, respectfully resumed his occupation, while Mr. Moreland took up his hat and plunged into the soft, balmy atmosphere of a Southern spring morning.

It is not our intention to go back and relate the past history of Mr. Moreland. It will be gathered in the midst of unfolding events, at least all that is necessary for the interest of our story. We will therefore return to the white-walled inn of the fair New England village, where our traveller was seated, enjoying the long, dewy twilight of the new region in which he was making a temporary rest. The sun had gone down, but the glow of his parting smile lingered on the landscape and reddened the stream that gleamed and flashed through the distant shrubbery. Not far from the inn, on a gradual eminence, rose the village church, whose tall spire, surmounted by a horizontal vane, reposed on the golden clouds of sunset, resembling the crucifix of some gorgeous cathedral. This edifice was situated far back from the road, surrounded by a common of the richest green, in the centre of which rose the swelling mound, consecrated by the house of God. Some very handsome buildings were seen at regular intervals, on either side of the road, among which the court-house stood conspicuous, with its freestone-coloured wall and lofty cupola. There was something in the aspect of that church, with its heaven-ascending spire, whose glory-crown of lingering day-beams glittered with a kind of celestial splendour, reminding him of the halo which encircles the brows of saints; something in the deep tranquillity of the hour, the soft, hazy, undulating outline of the distant horizon, the swaying motion of the tall poplars that margined the street far as his eye could reach, and through whose darkening vista a solitary figure gradually lessened on the eye, that solemnized and even saddened the spirits of our traveller. The remembrances of early youth and opening manhood pressed upon him with suddenly awakened force. Hopes, on which so sad and awful a blight had fallen, raised themselves like faded flowers sprinkled with dew, and mocked him with their visionary bloom. In the excitement of travelling, the realities of business, the frequent collision of interests, the championship of oft invaded rights, he had lost much of that morbidness of feeling and restlessness of character, which, being more accidental than inherent, would naturally yield to the force of circumstances counter to those in which they were born. But at the close of any arbitrary division of time, such as the last day of the week or the year, the mind is disposed to deeper meditation, and the mental burden, whose weight has been equipoised by worldly six-day cares, rolls back upon the mind with leaden oppression.

Moreland had too great a respect for the institutions of religion, too deep an inner sense of its power, to think of continuing his journey on the Sabbath, and he was glad that the chamber which he occupied looked out upon that serene landscape, and that the morning shadow of the lofty church-spire would be thrown across his window. It seemed to him he had seen this valley before, with its beautiful green, grassy slopes, its sunset-gilded church, and dark poplar avenue. And it seemed to him also, that he had seen a fair maiden form gliding through the central aisle of that temple, in robes of virgin white, and soft, down-bending eyes of dark brown lustre, and brow of moonlight calmness. It was one of those dim reminiscences, those vague, dream-like consciousnesses of a previous existence, which every being of poetic temperament is sometimes aware of, and though they come, faint shadows of a far-off world, quick and vanishing as lightning, they nevertheless leave certain traces of their presence, "trails of glory," as a great poet has called them, proceeding from the spirit's home.

While he sat leaning in silence against the window frame, the bell of the church began to toll slowly and solemnly, and as the sounds rolled heavily and gloomily along, then reverberated and vibrated with melancholy prolongation, sending out a sad, dying echo, followed by another majestic, startling peal, he wondered to hear such a funeral knell at that twilight hour, and looked up the shadowy line of poplars for the dark procession leading to the grave. Nothing was seen, however, and nothing heard but those monotonous, heavy, mournful peals, which seemed to sweep by him with the flaps of the raven's wings. Twenty times the bell tolled, and then all was still.

"What means the tolling of the bell?" asked he of the landlord, who was walking beneath the window. "Is there a funeral at this late hour?"

"A young woman has just died," replied the landlord. "They are tolling her age. It is a custom of our village."

Moreland drew back with a shudder. Just twenty. That was *her* age. *She* had not died, and yet the death-bell might well ring a deeper knell over her than the being who had just departed. In the grave the remembrance of the bitterest wrongs are buried, and the most vindictive cease to thirst for vengeance. Moreland was glad when a summons to supper turned his thoughts into a different channel.

There might have been a dozen men seated around the table, some whose dress and manners proclaimed that they were gentlemen, others evidently of a coarser grain. They all looked up at the entrance of Moreland, who, with a bow, such as the courteous stranger is always ready to make, took his seat, while Albert placed himself behind his master's chair.

"Take a seat," said Mr. Grimby, the landlord, looking at Albert. "There's one by the gentleman. Plenty of room for us all."

"My boy will wait," cried Mr. Moreland with unconscious haughtiness, while his pale cheek visibly reddened. "I would thank you to leave the arrangement of such things to myself."

"No offence, I hope, sir," rejoined Mr. Grimby. "We look upon everybody here as free and equal. This is a free country, and when folks come among us we don't see why they can't conform to our ways of thinking. There's a proverb that says—'when you're with the Romans, it's best to do as the Romans do.' "

"Am I to understand," said Mr. Moreland, fixing his eye deliberately on his Indian-visaged host, "that you wish my servant to sit down with yourself and these gentlemen?"

"To be sure I do," replied the landlord, winking his small black eye knowingly at his left-hand neighbour. "I don't see why he isn't as good as the rest of us. I'm an enemy to all distinctions myself, and I'd like to bring everybody round to my opinion."

"Albert!" cried his master, "obey the landlord's wishes. *I* want no supper; take my seat and see that you are well attended to."

"Mars. Russell," said the mulatto, in a confused and deprecating tone.

"Do as I tell you," exclaimed Mr. Moreland, in a tone of authority, which, though tempered by kindness, Albert understood too well to resist. As Moreland passed from the room, a gentleman, with a very preposessing countenance and address, who was seated on the opposite side of the table, rose and followed him.

"I am sorry you have had so poor a specimen of Northern politeness," said the gentleman, accosting Moreland, with a slight embarrassment of manner. "I trust you do not think we all endorse such sentiments."

"I certainly must make you an exception, sir," replied Moreland, holding out his hand with involuntary frankness; "but I fear there are but very few. This is, however, the first direct attack I have received, and I hardly knew in what way to meet it. I have too much self-respect to place myself on a level with a man so infinitely my inferior. That he intended to insult me, I know by his manner. He knows our customs at home, and that nothing could be done in more positive violation of them than his unwarrantable proposition."

They had walked out in the open air while they were speaking, and continued their walk through the poplar avenue, through whose stiff and stately branches the first stars of evening were beginning to glisten.

"I should think you would fear the effect of these things on your servant," said the gentleman—"that it would make him insolent and rebellious. Pardon me, sir, but I think you were rather imprudent in bringing him with you, and exposing him to the influences which must meet him on every side. You will not be surprised, after the instance which has just occurred, when I tell you, that, in this village, you are in the very hot-bed of fanaticism; and that a Southern planter, accompanied by his slave, can meet but little sympathy, consideration, or toleration; I fear there will be strong efforts made to induce your boy to leave you."

"I fear nothing of that kind," answered Moreland. "If they can bribe him from me, let him go. I brought him far less to minister to my wants than to test his fidelity and affection. I believe them proof against any temptation or assault; if I am deceived I wish to know it, though the pang would be as severe as if my own brother should lift his hand against me."

"Indeed!—I did not imagine that the feelings were ever so deeply interested. While I respect your rights, and resent any ungentlemanlike infringement of them, as in the case of our landlord, I cannot conceive how beings, who are ranked as goods and chattels, things of bargain and traffic, can ever fill the place of a friend or brother in the heart."

"Nevertheless, I assure you, that next to our own kindred, we look upon our slaves as our best friends."

As they came out of the avenue into the open street, they perceived the figure of a woman, walking with slow steps before them, bearing a large bundle under her arm; she paused several times, as if to recover breath, and once she stopped and leaned against the fence, while a dry, hollow cough rent her frame.

"Nancy," said the gentleman, "is that you?—you should not be out in the night air."

The woman turned round, and the starlight fell on a pale and wasted face.

"I can't help it," she answered—"I can't hold out any longer,—I can't work any more;—I ain't strong enough to do a single chore now; and Mr. Grimby says he hain't got any room for me to lay by in. My wages stopped three weeks ago. He says there's no use in my hanging on any longer, for I'll never be good for anything any more."

"Where are you going now?" said the gentleman.

"Home!" was the reply, in a tone of deep and hopeless despondency,—"Home, to my poor old mother. I've supported her by my wages ever since I've been hired out; that's the reason I haven't laid up any. God knows—"

Here she stopped, for her words were evidently choked by an awful realization of the irremediable misery of her condition. Moreland listened with eager interest. His compassion was awakened, and so were other feelings. Here was a problem he earnestly desired to solve, and he determined to avail himself of the opportunity thrown in his path.

"How far is your home from here?" he asked.

"About three-quarters of a mile."

"Give me your bundle—I'll carry it for you, you are too feeble; nay, I insist upon it."

Taking the bundle from the reluctant hand of the poor woman, he swung it lightly upward and poised it on his left shoulder. His companion turned with a look of unfeigned surprise towards the elegant and evidently high-bred stranger, thus courteously relieving poverty and weakness of an oppressive burden.

"Suffer me to assist you," said he. "You must be very unaccustomed to services of this kind; I ought to have anticipated you."

"I am not accustomed to do such things for myself," answered Moreland, "because there is no occasion; but it only makes me more willing to do them for others. You look upon us as very self-indulging beings, do you not?"

"We think your institutions calculated to promote the growth of self-indulgence and selfishness. The virtues that resist their opposing influences must have more than common vitality."

"We, who know the full length and breadth of our responsibilities, have less time than any other men for self-indulgence. We feel that life is too short for the performance of our duties, made doubly arduous and irksome by the misapprehension and prejudice of those who ought to know us better and judge us more justly and kindly. My good woman, do we walk too fast?"

"Oh, no, sir. I so long to get home, but I am so ashamed to have you carry that bundle."

He had forgotten the encumbrance in studying the domestic problem, presented to him for solution. Here was a poor young woman, entirely dependent on her daily labour for the support of herself and aged mother, incapacitated by sickness from ministering to their necessities, thrown back upon her home, without the means of subsistence: in prospective, a death of lingering torture for herself, for her mother a life of destitution or a shelter in the almshouse. For every comfort, for the bare necessaries of life, they must depend upon the compassion of the public; the attendance of a physician must be the work of charity, their existence a burden on others.

She had probably been a faithful labourer in her employer's family, while health and strength lasted. He was an honest man in the common acceptation of the word, and had doled out her weekly wages as long as they were earned; but he was not rich, he had no superfluous gold, and could not afford to pay to her what was due to her stronger and more healthy successor; he could not afford to give her even the room which was required by another. What could she do but go to her desolate home and die? She could not murmur. She had no claim on the affection of the man in whose service she had been employed. She had lived with him in the capacity of a hireling, and he, satisfied that he paid her the utmost farthing which justice required, dismissed her, without incurring the censure of unkindness or injustice. We ought to add, without deserving it. There were others far more able than himself to take care of her, and a home provided by the parish for every unsheltered head.

Moreland, whose moral perceptions were rendered very acute by observation, drew a contrast in his own mind, between the Northern and Southern labourer, when reduced to a state of sickness and dependence. He brought his own experience in comparison with the lesson of the present hour, and thought that the sick and dying negro, retained under his master's roof, kindly nursed and ministered unto, with no sad, anxious lookings forward into the morrow for the supply of nature's wants, no fears of being cast into the pauper's home, or of being made a member of that unhappy family, consecrated by no head, hallowed by no domestic relationship, had in contrast a far happier lot. In the latter case there was no sickness, without its most horrible concomitant, poverty, without the harrowing circumstances connected with public charity, or the capricious influence of private compassion. It is true, the nominal bondage of the slave was wanting, but there was the bondage of poverty, whose iron chains are heard clanking in every region of God's earth, whose dark links are wrought in the forge of human suffering, eating slowly into the quivering flesh, till they reach and dry up the life-blood of the heart. It has often been said that there need be no such thing as poverty in this free and happy land; that here it is only the offspring of vice and intemperance; that the avenues of wealth and distinction are open to all; and that all who choose may arrive at the golden portals of success and honour, and enter boldly in. Whether this be true or not, let the thousand toiling operatives of the Northern manufactories tell; let the poor, starving seamstresses, whose pallid faces mingle their chill, wintry gleams with the summer glow and splendour of the Northern cities, tell; let the free negroes, congregated in the suburbs of some of our modern Babylons, lured from their homes by hopes based on sand, without forethought, experience, or employment, without sympathy, influence, or caste, let them also tell.

When Moreland reached the low, dark-walled cottage which Nancy pointed out as her home, he gave her back her bundle, and at the same time slipped a bill into her hand, of whose amount she could not be aware. But she knew by the soft, yielding paper the nature of the gift, and something whispered her that it was no niggard boon.

"Oh, sir," she cried, "you are too good. God bless you, sir, over and over again!"

She stood in the doorway of the little cabin, and the dull light within played luridly on her sharpened and emaciated features. Her large black eyes were burning with consumption's wasting fires, and a deep red, central spot in each concave cheek, like the flame of the magic cauldron, was fed with blood alone. Large tears were now sparkling in those glowing flame-spots, but they did not extinguish their wasting brightness.

"Poor creature!" thought Moreland. "Her day of toil is indeed over. There is nothing left for her but to endure and to die. She has learned to *labour*, she must now learn to *wait*."

As he turned from the door, resolving to call again before he left the village, he saw his companion step back and speak to her, extending his hand at the same time. Perceiving that he was actuated by the Christian spirit, which does not wish the left hand to know what the right hand doeth, he walked slowly on, through an atmosphere perfumed by the delicious but oppressive fragrance of the blossoming lilacs, that lent to this obscure habitation a certain poetic charm.

During their walk back to the inn, he became more and more pleased with his new acquaintance, whose name he ascertained was Brooks, by profession an architect of bridges. He was not a resident of the village, but was now engaged in erecting a central bridge over the river that divided the village from the main body of the town. As his interests were not identified with the place or the people, his opinions were received by Moreland with more faith and confidence than if they issued from the lips of a native inhabitant.

When they returned to the inn, they found Albert waiting at the door, with a countenance of mingled vexation and triumph. The landlord and several other men were standing near him, and had evidently been engaged in earnest conversation. The sudden cessation of this, on the approach of Mr. Moreland, proved that he had been the subject of it, and from the manner in which they drew back as he entered the passage, he imagined their remarks were not of the most flattering nature.

"Well, Albert, my boy," said he, when they were alone in his chamber, "I hope you relished your supper."

"Please, Mars. Russell, don't do that again. I made 'em wait on me this time, but it don't seem right. Besides, I don't feel on an equality with 'em, no way. They are no gentlemen."

Moreland laughed.

"What were they talking to you about so earnestly as I entered?" asked he.

"About how you treated me and the rest of us. Why, Mars. Russell, they don't know nothing about us. They want to know if we don't wear chains at home and manacles about our wrists. One asked if you didn't give us fodder to eat. Another wanted to strip off my coat, to see if my back wa'n't all covered with scars. I wish you'd heard what I told 'em. Master, I wish you'd heard the way I give it to 'em."

"I have no doubt you did me justice, Albert. My feelings are not in the least wounded, though my sense of justice is pained. Why, I should think the sight of your round, sleek cheeks, and sound, active limbs would be the best argument in my favour. They must believe you thrive wonderfully on fodder."

"What you think one of 'em said, Mars. Russell? They say you fatten me up, you dress me up, and carry me 'bout as a show-boy, to make folks think you treat us all well, but that the niggers at home are treated worse than dogs or cattle, a heap worse. I tell 'em it's all one big lie. I tell 'em you're the best—"

"Never mind, Albert. That will do. I want to think—"

Albert never ventured to intrude on his master's thinking moments, and, turning away in respectful silence, he soon stretched himself on the carpet and sunk in a profound sleep. In the mean time Moreland waded through a deep current of thought, that swelled as it rolled, and ofttimes it was turbid and foaming, and sometimes it seemed of icy chillness. He was a man of strong intellect and strong passions; but the latter, being under the control of principle, gave force and energy and warmth to a character which, if unrestrained, they would have defaced and laid waste. He was a searcher after truth, and felt ready and brave enough to plunge into the cold abyss, where it is said to be hidden, or to encounter the fires of persecution, the thorns of prejudice, to hazard everything, to suffer everything, rather than relinquish the hope of attaining it. He pondered much on the condition of mankind, its inequalities and wrongs. He thought of the poor and subservient in other lands, and compared them with our own. He thought of the groaning serfs of Russia; the starving sons of Ireland; the squalid operatives of England, its dark, subterranean workshops, sunless abodes of want, misery, and sin, its toiling millions, doomed to drain their hearts' best blood to add to the splendours and luxuries of royalty and rank; of the free hirelings of the North, who, as a *class*, travail in discontent and repining, anxious to throw off the yoke of servitude, sighing for an equality which exists only in name; and then he turned his thoughts homeward, to the enslaved children of Africa, and, taking them as a *class*, as a *distinct race* of beings, he came to the irresistible conclusion, that they were the happiest *subservient* race that were found on the face of the globe. He did not seek to disguise to himself the evils which were inseparably connected with their condition, or that man too oft abused the power he owned; but in view of all this, in view of the great, commanding truth, that wherever civilized man exists, there is the dividing line of the high and the low, the rich and the poor, the thinking and the labouring, in view of the God-proclaimed fact that "all Creation toileth and groaneth together," and that labour and suffering are the solemn sacraments of life, he believed that the slaves of the South were blest beyond the pallid slaves of Europe, or the anxious, care-worn labourers of the North.

With this conviction he fell asleep, and in his dreams he still tried to unravel the mystery of life, and to reconcile its inequalities with the justice and mercy of an omnipotent God.

Chapter II

Moreland breakfasted in his own room, and the peace of the Sabbath morning brooded on his heart. He took his seat at the window, and watched the shadows of the trees playing on the white walls of the church, and the golden gleam of its vane flashing on the blue of the sky. He was glad when the deep-toned bell called the worshippers together, and the people began to ascend the grassy slope that led up to the house of God. Mr. Brooks, his new friend, offered to accompany him and usher him to a seat; an offer he gratefully accepted. The pew to which he conducted him was situated at the right hand of the pulpit, in one of the wings of the church, so that he was facing the congregation, and could see them without appearing to gaze, as they glided, one by one, up the central aisle, to their accustomed places.

The interior of the church was very simple and pure. The green curtains and hangings of the pulpit, and the green screen that ran around the gallery, made a charming contrast with the unsullied whiteness of the walls, and harmonized with the green boughs that shaded the windows, and the green grass that carpeted the common.

There was no organ, with gilded pipes and sounding bellows, to give dignity to the orchestra, but Moreland caught a glimpse of white robes behind the curtain of the gallery, and he was sure some beautiful daughters of Zion were assembled there to sing praises to their God. He wanted the service to commence, so that he could see the figures of that vestal choir, as well as hear their mingling voices. His ear was gratified before his eye, for while waiting the coming of the minister, an anthem began to roll forth from the invisible band, whose notes filled the intervals of sound between the echoing peals of the bell. The commencing words of the anthem were grand. Moreland had heard them before, but they came to him with a new sense, because he was prepared to receive new impressions.

> Before Jehovah's awful throne,
> Ye nations bow with sacred joy;
> Know that the Lord is God alone,
> He can create, and He destroy.

Among the voices that gave utterance to these adoring words, was one which, though sweet and soft and feminine beyond expression, seemed to drown every other. It rose, like the imagined hymn of an angel, clear and swelling, and then died gently away, to rise again with richer, fuller harmony. Moreland, whose devotional feelings were always exalted by sacred music, listened with breathless rapture, wondering what sweet bird of song had folded its wings behind that green enclosure.

At the conclusion of the anthem, where it is affirmed that the truth of God shall stand firm as a rock,

> While rolling years shall cease to move

when again and again the sublime refrain was repeated, that single voice alone fell upon his ear. On that alone the "rolling years" seemed borne onward to eternity. Other voices sang, and their notes died away; but hers kept rolling and warbling round the arching walls of the church, till the house was filled with their melody, and Moreland kept looking up, almost expecting to see them forming into something visible, as well as audible, into silvery or crystal rings, sparkling and glittering on the eye. He held his breath so long, that the act of respiration became painful, when renewed, and so intensely had he listened that the moisture gathered on his brow.

The anthem ceased as the venerable minister walked up the aisle and ascended the pulpit. He looked congenial with the music that heralded his approach, with his silver hair, mild, benignant countenance, and deep set thoughtful eyes. He was just such a minister as one would associate in idea with that pure, simple church, and white-robed singing band. His prayer breathed the very spirit of devotion. It reminded Moreland of the "Lord, save or we perish" of drowning Peter—"God be merciful to me a sinner" of the weeping publican. After the reading of a beautiful opening hymn, the choir rose, and the eyes of Moreland rested on one fair face, which he knew, by intuition, belonged to the minstrel maiden whose voice had so charmed his ear. It rose above the green curtain like a lily from its bed of sheathing leaves, so fair, so spiritual, so serene, it was impossible not to imagine an atmosphere of fragrance surrounding its purity and bloom. He was right. The hymn commenced, and the same sweet strains gushed from the lips, on which he was now gazing. He could not see the colour of her eyes, for they were downcast, but he could see the soft shadow of long, dark, drooping lashes on her cheeks, and he could see the bright, deep hue of chestnut brown that dyed her hair. He remembered the vision that had flitted before him the preceding evening, and it seemed to him that he had met this maiden stranger in some of the dim-remembered scenes of a past eternity. He could not shake off this wild idea, born of a poetic temperament and excited imagination. What was there about this young female that so singularly attracted him;—him, who had lately abjured the very thought of woman, in a widowhood of heart, far deeper and sadder than that which death creates; who had torn from his bosom the wilted garlands of love, and cast them, in indignation and despair, at the feet of a fallen and degraded idol? She was not more beautiful than some of her companions, perhaps not as beautiful as some, and yet he gazed only on her, watching the lifting of her drooping lids, as the Persian watches the rising of the star of day. It was not till the close of the hymn, the beginning of the sermon, after the curtain was drawn on one side and the singers seated, that she raised her eyes and fixed them steadily on the evangelical countenance of the pastor. Though bent on another, Moreland felt their dark magnetism to his heart's core. This sudden, powerful attraction, exercised by the simple village maiden, would not have been so strange had he been a young, romantic boy; but he was a man of some sad experience, who, before he entered that church, believed himself cold and insensible to the most seductive charms of womankind. At length, roused to the reflection that he might attract observation by the intensity of his gaze, he turned also towards the minister and endeavoured to rivet his attention on the truths he uttered. It is not to be supposed that a distinguished-looking stranger would pass entirely unnoticed in a village church, and there was many an eye perusing his face, while his was bent on the gallery; and there were some who thought his fixed and earnest gaze the bold, free stare of conscious wealth and arrogance. They had heard that a Southern gentleman, accompanied by a mulatto slave, had stopped at the inn the preceding night, and they were not slow in identifying the individual with the handsome stranger before them. There were a few, however, who did not judge him in this harsh manner, who had heard—(strange how quickly such things are winged in a country village)—how he had carried Nancy Brown's bundle all the way home for her, and put in her hand a ten dollar bill, without saying a word about it, and they lifted up their hearts and blessed him, though he knew it not.

When the benediction was pronounced, and the congregation passed out, Moreland lingered in the vestibule waiting for the choristers to descend. SHE came at last, leading by the hand a little girl of about five years of age, whose countenance bore a strong resemblance to her own. So many people were crowded in the doorways, she was obliged to pass so close to Moreland that her white dress floated against him; and if it had been the wing of a seraph he could not have felt a thrill of deeper reverence. She did not look at him, but he felt, by the colour that glowed on the lilies of her cheek, that she was aware of his presence and his gaze.

"Eula!" said the little girl, "don't walk so fast; Papa is coming."

Eula!—blessings on that cherub mouth for pronouncing the name he so longed to know. But that large bustling gentleman, with reddish-auburn hair and florid complexion, and small, keen, restless black eyes, was that Eula's father? To be sure, it must be, for does she not take his arm with an affectionate, confiding air; and does not the little smiling five-year old thing frisk round to the other side of him, catching hold of his hand as if it were an ingot of gold she was grasping, instead of four freckled fingers and one stout thumb!

"Who is that reddish-haired gentleman?" asked Moreland of Mr. Brooks, as they walked slowly in the wake of light the sweet-voiced maiden seemed to leave behind her.

"His name is Hastings," replied his companion, "one of the most conspicuous characters in the village. He is considered a very shrewd, intelligent man, and, although not at all popular, has nevertheless a great deal of influence in the community."

"What is his profession?"

"He cannot be said to have any exclusive profession. He prepares young men for college, edits a paper called the "Emancipator," writes essays, delivers public lectures on all the leading topics of the day, and, among these, as you are doubtless prepared to hear, slavery, or rather anti-slavery, occupies a very conspicuous place."

"Indeed!" cried Moreland, with an unaccountable feeling of pain at the intelligence; "and is that young lady on his right arm his own daughter?"

"Yes! that is Miss Eulalia Hastings, or, as she is often called, the Flower of the village. She sings like an angel. You heard her voice in church. She is highly educated and accomplished, though she is so modest and retiring she makes no display. She is universally beloved and admired, and makes friends even of her father's enemies."

"Of course, she inherits all her father's prejudices against the South?" remarked Moreland, in a tone that seemed to ask a negation.

"Very probably; though they must be softened by passing through such a medium. I heard him say once, that if wife or child of his were languishing in a consumption, and he knew he could add ten years to their lives by sending them to the milder climate of the South, his conscience would not justify the act, so utterly does he abhor its institutions."

"You think, then, he would not allow his daughter to marry a Southerner?" This was said in a light, sarcastic tone, which was followed by one more serious. "Is he a man of wealth as well as influence?"

"No, not at all. His father left him considerable property, but he has wasted it in fruitless speculations and visionary schemes for the improvement of the age. He always has a hobby which he rides without mercy or judgment. The one on which he is mounted at present is the immediate emancipation of the negro race. You must not feel slighted if he invites your servant (I do not like the word *slave*) to come and break bread with him, without extending towards you the rites of hospitality."

"Is there a possibility of his doing this?" asked Moreland.

"We can only judge of the future by the past," replied the architect. "Not very long ago, while travelling in a neighbouring state, he came across, a runaway negro, one of the most repulsive objects I ever saw—gigantic in stature, black as ebony, with coarse and brutal features, and manners corresponding to his appearance. He took him at once under his protection, gave him a seat in his carriage, brought him home, introduced him to his family, gave him a seat at table between his wife and eldest daughter, put him in their best bedroom, and appeared to feel himself honoured by having such a guest."

"I like this," interrupted Moreland; "it shows that he is sincere, and is willing to put his principles to the proof. But Miss Hastings, surely this must have been very repugnant to her feelings; she could not willingly submit to such an infliction."

He said this with a shudder of inexpressible loathing, as he looked on the delicate, graceful figure walking before him, and imagined it placed in such close juxtaposition with the rough, gigantic negro.

"I suspect Miss Eulalia did not relish it very much," said Mr. Brooks; "but filial respect closed her lips. She happened to fall sick immediately after his arrival, whether as a consequence I know not, and thus escaped further personal contact. But the best part of the story is to come. Mr. Hastings, after he had gained sufficient éclat for his philanthropy and great-heartedness, was very willing to transfer his protegé to some of his neighbours, but no one was willing to accept the responsibility, and the fellow liked his quarters too well to think of leaving them. He grew very insolent and overbearing, and his host was at last compelled to turn him out of the house. Since then, he has had a double bolt fastened to his doors; and his dreams, I suspect, are haunted by black spectres, armed and equipped for murder and robbery."

The attention of Moreland was diverted by the diverging steps of the party before him. They turned aside into a path leading to a neat, modest-looking dwelling, shaded by sycamore trees, beside whose deep green, the scarlet berries of the mountain ash gleamed with coral splendour. Like most of the other houses, it wanted the graceful verandah,—the pillared piazza of Southern climes,—and gave one an impression of glare and exposure; but the smooth, beautiful green that surrounded it, and the richness of branching shade that embosomed it, compensated for the want of these artificial embellishments. As Mr. Hastings opened the gate that shut in the front yard, and held it open for his daughters to pass through, the handkerchief of Eulalia dropped from her hand, and a light breeze blew it back directly at the feet of Moreland; he caught it with eagerness, and as she turned immediately, with a consciousness of the loss, he stepped forward and presented it, with a respectful and graceful bow. He was thus brought face to face with her, and the soft, electric-beaming eyes seemed to shed into his bosom a flood of living light. With an impulse bold as irresistible, he, pressed the hand which received the handkerchief from his; and though he saw the startled crimson rush to her cheek, he could not repent of his presumption. He could not help doing it,—it was an expression of sympathy as involuntary as it was sincere. He felt as if a mighty barrier of prejudice separated him from one to whom he was irresistibly attracted, and he was forced in this, perhaps their only meeting, to give expression in some way to his suddenly awakened, but passionate emotions. It was like taking the hand of a friend through the grate of a convent, the bars of a dungeon, in token of a long farewell. He walked in silence the rest of the way; and his companion smiled to himself at the impression the Flower of the Village had evidently made on the Southern planter.

Moreland had the good sense to tell Albert to remain in the kitchen during meal-times, so that the equilibrium of the landlord might not be disturbed by an appearance of servility on one part, and aristocracy on the other. And, whether Mr. Grimby thought he had taken an ultra step the preceding evening, or whether he was influenced by Albert's warm praises of his master, and his evident attachment and devotion to him, he was much more polite in his deportment and respectful in his manners. Still, he was anxious to draw him into a political or sectional discussion, for he believed himself, in strength of argument, superior to even his oracle, Mr. Hastings. So, in imitation of the play of the fox and glove, he went round and round, ready to drop the gauntlet at the most favourable moment. But Moreland's mind was preoccupied, and he did not think the Sabbath calm should be ruffled by the contentions of party, or the warrings of self-love.

He did not attend church the after part of the day. He was resolved to struggle with the weakness which he blushed to feel. He would not place himself again within the influence of that seraph voice, or that fair, music-breathing face. He could not bridge the gulf of prejudice that yawned between them; and he would not linger on the opposite side sighing for the flowers that bloomed in vain for him. So he seated himself at the window, with book in hand, respecting himself for the dignified stand he had mentally taken; but the position he occupied was very unfavourable for the strength of his resolution. The church was so near that through its open windows he could hear distinctly the venerable accents of the minister, and the sweet and solemn notes of the choristers. He could distinguish the nightingale-voice, which, once heard, never could be forgotten,—it came flowing out into the sunshine, mingling with and melting into the blue waves of ether; rolling in the "upper deep;" it came floating across the gulf, over whose bridgeless depths he had been lamenting, on soft and downy wings, like a messenger dove, bearing promises of peace and love; it hovered over the dim retreats of memory, and its thrilling strains blended with the echoes of a voice which had in other hours enthralled his soul;—but that had breathed of the passions of earth, this of the hopes of immortality. Of course he could not read, and, suffering the book to fall from his fingers, he sunk into a long, deep revery.

Intending to recommence his journey early the following morning, he thought he would walk out before sunset, and take his last look of the charming valley in which the village was set, like a polished gem. Not seeing his agreeable and intelligent new friend, the architect, he sauntered along without any companion but his own thoughts, turning into by-paths, without knowing whither they went, assured they would lead him only to green fields and tranquil waters, or, perchance, to some garden of the dead. He was surprised to find himself close to Nancy Brown's little cottage. He recognised the pale purple of the lilac bushes through the old dark fence, and the air was heavy with their fragrance. A natural movement of humanity urged him to enter, and see if he could do anything more for the poor invalid, who had interested his feelings so much. The door was open, and he stood on its threshold without having his approach perceived. *She* was there, the white-robed singing maiden worshipper of the temple, and she had already heard the story of his kindness and liberality from the lips of the grateful Nancy. She had just been listening to it, and the glow was on her heart when he entered. A smile of welcome, involuntary as the heart-beat, which at that moment was quickened, dawned on her lips, but was instantaneously overcast by a cloud of reserve. It was probably the recollection of his presumptuous act in the morning, which drew the sudden cloud over her dawning smile. It is impossible to describe the effect of her appearance in that little, low, dark cottage, in contrast with extreme age and decrepitude on one side, and deadliness and emaciation on the other. She sat between Nancy and her mother, and each poor, pale, drooping figure caught something of life and brightness from her youthful and benignant aspect. She was pale too, but hers was the pallor of moonlight, so fair, so lustrous, it diffused around a kindred softness and repose. When Moreland first stepped upon the threshold, a very quick, slight, vanishing blush flitted over her cheek, then left it as colourless and calm as before.

Nancy, whose eyes were fixed on her face, did not perceive as quickly the entrance of her benevolent visiter.

"There is a gentleman at the door," said Eulalia, rising from her seat.

Nancy turned round, and, recognising the kind and liberal stranger, asked him to walk in, and offering him her own chair, took a seat on the side of the bed. Her surprise and embarrassment brought on a violent fit of coughing, whose hollow, wasting sound reverberated painfully in the narrow apartment.

"This is the good gentleman I was just telling you about," said she, as soon as she could recover breath. "Mother, this is the gentleman that carried my bundle for me, and gave me that money last night. Oh, sir, I don't know what to say to you. I never did know how to talk, but there are a heap of words here, if I could only get 'em out." Here Nancy pressed her wasted hand on her heart, with a great deal of expression, though with little grace.

"The Lord bless you, sir!" cried the old mother, her voice trembling and quavering with age and imbecility. "The Lord reward you for your good deeds! Well, well, I never would have believed such a fine gentleman as you would have carried Nancy's bundle for her. I never would. Well, it's a blessed thing not to be proud. Just like Miss Euly here. She ha'in't got one bit of pride. She's just as willing to wait on such a poor old creatur as me, as if I was of some account in the world."

It was pleasant to the ear of Moreland to find himself associated with Eulalia Hastings, even in the mind of this humble, indigent creature. There was another thing that pleased him. The woman was not mercenary. She appreciated more highly the simple act of condescension, the carrying of the bundle, than the money which was given to relieve their wants. He had too much ease of manner, had seen too much of the world, to suffer himself to be embarrassed by this unexpected meeting. He thought there was something peculiar in it; the accidental arrangement of circumstances which brought him in contact with the lovely chorister. The distance between them seemed wonderfully diminished. When he first saw her, in her elevated position in the gallery, singing the praise of God in words of surpassing grandeur, his imagination exalted her into one of that celestial band who stand in white robes about the throne, day and night, chanting the eternal chorus, "Hallelujah! the Lord God omnipotent reigneth." Now, she was on a level with himself, seated near him in the abode of indigence and suffering; he heard her gentle, speaking accents, fraught with human sympathy and sensibility. He began to think it possible that he might defer his journey a few days longer. There was nothing particularly to hasten his return. It was far better for him to be away, far from the remembrances that darkened his home. He could not possibly find a more quiet resting spot than in this beautiful valley, where

> The green of the earth and the blue of the sky

seemed to meet in gorgeous rivalship.

Would it not be well to seek an acquaintance with Mr. Hastings, and endeavour, with earnestness and deliberation, to remove his prejudices and give him juster views of his fellow beings? While he thus communed with himself, Mrs. Brown was not idle. In the innocence and curiosity of second childhood, she sat gazing on their elegant visiter, through the spectacles, which she wiped at least a dozen times with the corner of her checked apron, so as to assist her faded vision.

"May I make bold to ask your name, sir?" said she. "I know most everybody that lives hereabouts, but I don't think you live in these parts, do you?"

"I should ask your pardon for not introducing myself sooner, madam," was the courteous reply. "My name is Moreland. I reside in the distant South."

"The South!" repeated the octogenarian. "Well, that is far off. What part of the South?"

"I reside in Georgia."

"The South!" again repeated she, bewildered by the idea of such immense distance. "Ain't it there where they have so many black folks to wait on 'em, with great iron chains on their hands and feet? Well, well, who would have thought it? You don't look as if you come from among such a dreadful set of people—not one bit. Law me! you don't say so!"

Here she again took off her spectacles, wiped them laboriously, readjusted them, and fixed her dim, glimmering glance once more on the face of the Southern stranger. She was probably searching for those lineaments of harshness and cruelty, those lines of tiger grimness and ferocity, she had so often heard described.

"Mother!" exclaimed Nancy, whose natural delicacy of feeling and deep gratitude were greatly shocked by these remarks, "you'll offend the gentleman. She don't mean any harm, sir—no more than a child."

"Do not fear that I shall be offended," said Moreland, with an irrepressible smile at the old lady's persevering scrutiny. "I like to hear what people think of us. It may do us good. You are mistaken, madam," added he, addressing the mother; "our black people do not wear chains, unless outrageous and criminal behaviour force us to such severity."

Perhaps Moreland would not have thought it worth the effort, to refute the charges of a poor, imbecile, ignorant woman, who only repeated what she had heard from higher powers, had not the daughter of Hastings been present to listen to his words. But he could not bear that she should look upon him as one of that "dreadful set," represented as dwelling amid clanking chains and galling manacles, and banqueting on human blood. He saw, that though her eye was cast modestly downward, she was no inattentive or uninterested listener.

"Well," ejaculated the old lady, half in soliloquy and half in harangue—"I don't mean to give offence, to be sure. You've been mighty good to Nancy, and I can't take away the blessing that's gone up to heaven for you now, if I wanted to. But I'm sorry such a likely, kindhearted gentleman as you seem to be, should live where such a sinful traffic is carried on. I've hearn Squire Hastings tell such awful things about it, it e'enamost made my hair stand on end. He used to lecture and speechify in the school-house close by, and as long as I could hobble out doors I went to hear him, for it always helped me powerfully in spirit. He's a mighty knowing man, and has a way of telling things that makes one's flesh creep. He's *her* father, Squire Hastings is. She ain't ashamed to hear me tell on't."

Eulalia made a scarcely perceptible shrinking, backward motion, at this eulogium on her father. She had heard it many a time before, but it never had seemed so exaggerated or ill-timed as at the present moment.

"I am sorry you have been led to believe us so awfully wicked and cruel, my good woman," said Moreland, looking at Eulalia's evidently troubled countenance, though his words were addressed to Dame Brown. "I cannot wonder so much at yourself, who have probably lived secluded from the world, and received your opinions from those around; but that those, who have had abundant opportunities of knowing what we really are, beings of like passions with themselves, as upright in principle, as honest in opinion, as kind in action, should represent us as such monsters of iniquity, does indeed seem wonderful. We claim no exemption from the faults and failings of poor fallen humanity, but we do claim a share of its virtues. The clanking chains of which you speak are mere figures of speech. You hear instead merry voices singing in the fields of labour or filling up the pauses of toil. Sadly have I missed in my northern travels, the joyous songs and exhilarating laughter of our slaves."

"You don't say so! Well, well! One does hear such strange things. You don't say they ever sing and laugh! Why, I thought they did nothing but cry and groan and gnash their teeth, all the day long. Well, it is hard to know what to believe."

"I wish you were able to travel so far," said Moreland, looking compassionately at Nancy's hectic cheeks, "and occupy a cabin in one of my plantations, where the balmy air would restore you to health. One day passed in the midst of the negroes would be worth a thousand arguments in our favour. You would see there, age free from care or labour, sickness tenderly nursed, and helplessness amply provided for. The poor invalid is not compelled to leave the master whom she has served, when health and strength are exhausted, but, without any care or forethought of her own, is watched over as kindly as if born of a fairer race."

Nancy sighed. She thought of her days of servitude, her waning health, her anxious fears and torturing apprehensions of future want, and it seemed to her the mere exemption from such far-reaching solicitudes must be a blessing. She thought, too, of the soft, mild atmosphere that flowed around those children of toil, and wished she could breathe its balm.

"I wish it was not so far off," she exclaimed; "but," she added, with a deeper sigh, "I never could live to reach there. And if I could, mother is too old to bear the journey. And then we couldn't afford it."

Moreland was sorry he had suggested an impracticable idea. He did not intend to raise hopes which could not be realized, though so uncalculating was his benevolence he would willingly have paid the expenses of the journey, if by so doing he could have restored health to her frail and broken constitution.

"We've mighty good friends here," said the old lady, wiping away the falling tears with the corner of her apron. "Miss Euly is just like an angel to us; and there are others too, who, if they don't look as pretty, are 'most as kind as she is."

Eulalia rose to depart. She had lingered in the hope that Moreland would go, but the sun was darting his horizontal rays through the window, throwing rosy lines across her fair face, and she felt he was waiting her motion. She felt embarrassed when he also rose, doubting the propriety of being escorted by a stranger.

"I will see you again," were his parting words to Nancy and her mother. So it was evident he had made up his mind not to leave on the morrow.

"May I escort you home?" he asked, when he opened the gate for her to pass out. "Though we have had no formal introduction, I have announced my own name, and I know it is Miss Hastings whom I have the honour of addressing."

"We village maidens are quite independent," she replied, with a smile; "we are not accustomed to escorts in our rural walks, especially when leading from such lowly dwellings. Strangers seldom find out as readily as you have done, sir, the abodes of poverty."

"It was accident," he answered, gratified by her manner, which implied approbation, if not interest, "I can claim no credit for seeking. Though you must have discovered that I am disposed to arrogate to myself all the merit I can possibly lay hold of, I hope you will not think me a vain boaster."

"I think you have the power of making the worse appear the better reason," she said, with a smile that softened the sarcasm of her words.

"You have no pleasing impressions, I fear, of our beautiful South, Miss Hastings. You have had dark and forbidding pictures drawn of it. You look upon it as a moral Aceldama, and shudder at the view. Is it not so?"

"I love to think of your sunny clime," she answered, while a dawning colour mingled with the glow of sunset on her cheek, "of your magnolia bowers and flowery plains. I have heard a great deal of your chivalry and liberality, and love to listen to their praises; but I do not love to think of the dark spot in your social system, that is gradually spreading and deepening, and destroying all its beauty and happiness. I do shudder when I think of this. I did not mean to say so much, but you have forced it from me."

"I admire your candour. I did not expect to hear you speak so mildly, considering the prejudices of birth and education. Your father is, I understand, an avowed champion of what he believes to be truth, and it is perfectly natural that you should respect his opinions and adopt them as your own. Yet, if you grant me the privilege of your acquaintance, I hope to be able to convince you that those opinions are erroneous, and that though we have a dark spot in our social system, like every other cloud, 'it turns its silver lining to the light.' "

"My father does not adopt his opinions lightly," said she, with modest emphasis; "he has been a great student from his youth up, and something of a traveller, too. He does not wish to believe evil of mankind, neither does he, until the conviction is forced upon him."

"But you would not regret, if I could prove to you that he was mistaken in his estimate of Southern character,—that there is far less of cruelty, oppression, and sorrow in our midst than you now believe,—would you?"

This was said with such irresistible frankness, that had Eulalia been a more obstinate adherent than she was to her father's sentiments, she could not have uttered a cold negation. Naturally as reserved as she was modest, she was surprised at the freedom of her conversation with an utter stranger. His morning boldness, which she had at first deeply resented (though she made no commentary on it to her father), now occurred to her as accidental; he had probably merely intended to take a firm hold of the handkerchief, and grasped her hand instead. She could not help being pleased with the ease and grace of his manners; and the kindness and condescension she had witnessed in Mrs. Brown's cottage were genuine passports to her favour. It was not often, in the retirement of her village home, that her exquisite sense of refinement was so fully gratified; she had lived in a world of her own, whose visionary inhabitants were very much such beings as Moreland. He did not seem like a stranger, but rather as the incarnation of her own bright and beautiful idealities. She wanted her father to know him, to hear him talk, and listen to his eloquent self-defence. She was astonished when she reached their own gate, the walk had seemed so very short, and wondered what had become of the setting sun—she had not marked its going down.

"Sister Eula! have you come back?" exclaimed a sweet voice, through the bars of the gate, and a little sunshiny head was seen beaming behind it. She, Eula's morning companion, stood with her feet on the lower round of the gate, and, when it was opened, swung back with it, laughing merrily at having secured so brave a ride.

Moreland, who was very fond of children, caught her in his arms, promising her a better and longer ride than the limits of the gate could furnish.

"I've seen you before," said she, peeping at him through her bright hair, which fell shadingly over her brow; "I saw you this morning; you picked up sister Eula's handkerchief. Papa said—"

"Dora!" interrupted Eulalia, "here are some flowers for you. Nancy gave them to me. Don't you want them?"

"Oh, yes!" exclaimed the child, eagerly extending her hand, and forgetting what papa had said, which Moreland would have very much liked to hear.

Papa was standing in the door, looking very portly and dignified, not a little surprised at seeing the stranger whom he had so keenly observed in the morning, walking quietly up his own yard, in company with one daughter, and bearing the other, perched like a bird on his shoulder.

"Papa, don't you see me riding?" cried Dora, from her elevated seat, long before they reached the door.

Mr. Hastings descended the steps, and the child leaped into his arms.

"Little romp!" cried he, setting her down very kindly, "go to your mother." And away she flew to tell her mother of the stranger's coming, and her own marvellous adventure.

"Mr. Moreland, father," said Eulalia. "He met me at Mrs. Brown's cottage, and it being late, he accompanied me home."

Moreland felt something as if a gimlet were boring in his flesh, while enduring the piercing glance of the philanthropist; but he did not wince under the infliction, though it somewhat galled him.

"Won't you walk in, sir?" said Mr. Hastings, holding out his hand. "Glad to see you, if you have time to sit down."

This was an unexpected condescension, of which Moreland unhesitatingly availed himself. He wanted to enter the home of Eulalia, and see her in the midst of domestic associations.

"He has not seen the tiger's claws," thought Moreland; "or, perhaps, like the keeper of a menagerie, he confronts the wild beast that he may have the glory of taming him."

They entered a very neat and modestly furnished parlour, curtained with white muslin and carpeted with domestic manufacture. The furniture was of the simplest kind, though there was an air of taste and even elegance diffused over the room. There was a pretty work-box inlaid with pearl and surrounded by handsomely bound books, on the centre table. These he set down at once as the property of Eulalia. There were beautiful flowers, not in gilded vases, but set in crystals on the mantelpiece. These, he was convinced, had been arranged by the hands of Eulalia. He looked in vain for a piano or guitar, as accompaniments to her enchanting voice.

"Take a seat, sir," said Mr. Hastings, trying to draw forward a prim-looking armchair, which was known in the household by the patronymic of *old maid*, from its peculiarly precise appearance—"and make yourself at home. We don't use any ceremony here."

"Ceremony is the greatest enemy of enjoyment," said Moreland, waiving the chair of state, and seating himself in one of less ambitious appearance. "I trust I am not encroaching on your hospitality, by accepting your invitation too readily. This is a Sabbath evening, and you may be accustomed to pass it with your family alone. A stranger may intermeddle with your joys. If so, I would not, for any consideration, intrude."

"Not at all, not at all, sir," replied his host. "We commence our Sundays on Saturday night, and when the Sabbath sun goes down, we feel privileged to enjoy social intercourse with our neighbours and friends; quiet, sober intercourse of course, but we do not object to a friendly call. Stay and take tea with us. We will be happy to have you. Eula, tell your mother a gentleman will partake of our family supper."

How could Moreland refuse such a cordial invitation? Of course he did not, but accepted it with all imaginable readiness. He could not account for this unexpected hospitality, where he had looked scarcely for ordinary courtesy. He was unconsciously doing Mr. Hastings great injustice. It does not follow, because a man is narrow and one-sided in his views, and bitter and obstinate in his prejudices, that he is destitute of social graces and domestic virtues. Moreland had his prejudices too, though he did not know it. He had imagined there was very little hospitality at the North, and that strangers were looked upon with a cold and suspicious eye. He thought the hearts of people were cold in proportion as they receded from the burning sun of the tropics, and that passion, the great central fire of the human bosom, giving life and splendour to every other element, was wanting in the less genial latitude he was now crossing.

Mr. Hastings, like most men, was actuated by mixed motives. He believed in the good old scripture injunction of hospitality to strangers, and he was exceedingly fond of making *impressions*, and enlarging the bounds of his influence. He took great pride in his argumentative powers, and thought he should have a dazzling opportunity to display them. He saw in prospective a glorious field of disputation, where he would gather more laurels than he could possibly dispose of. His prophetic glance pierced still further, and he beheld one black wave rolling after another from the Southern shores, before the resistless gales of his eloquence.

He was very fond of distinction. He loved to have strangers call at his house, assured that when they left the place, they would carry the impression that Mr. Hastings was the greatest man in the village, nay more, the greatest man in the country. Then he was very fond of his children. Eulalia was the pride of his heart and the delight of his eyes. The simple attention of escorting her home pleased him. The caressing kindness to little Dora charmed him; and, though the stranger belonged to a class of men whom he denounced as devoid of humanity, principle, or religion, against whom he had commenced a deadly crusade, with all the fanaticism of Peter the Hermit, and the rashness of Richard Coeur de Lion; moved by all these blended motives, he smiled blandly upon him, giving a gentle friction to his hands, as if to warm and ignite his hospitable feelings.

It was not long before little Dora came into the room with a hop-skip-and-jump step, announcing that supper was ready; and Mr. Hastings, with a courteous bow, ushered his guest into an adjoining room, where the family board was spread; here he was introduced to "my wife,"—a very intelligent and dignified-looking lady,—and "my son Reuben," a handsome, bright-eyed, auburn-locked youth of about seventeen, who perused the stranger's lineaments with vivid curiosity,—"Eulalia, my daughter, you have already seen." Yes! he had seen Eulalia,—it was a circumstance he was not likely to forget. He had seen her in the house of God, surrounded by a halo of music and prayer;—he had seen her in the cottage of the poor, making the dark and lowly places of life beautiful by her presence;—he now saw her presiding with quiet grace and self-possession at her father's board, for she occupied her mother's seat at the head of the table, behind an old-fashioned, massy silver urn. This shining relic of antiquity reflected brilliantly the lamp-light that flowed from the centre of the table, and it also seemed to reflect the soft, virgin lustre of Eulalia's illuminated face. It was a real patriarch, this old tiger-footed silver urn, having descended through three generations, and it set off the table wonderfully.

Dora slided into a seat on the left hand of Moreland, who, in gratitude for the compliment, helped her most munificently to butter and honey, which a glance from her mother's eye admonished her not to eat too lavishly.

"We are accustomed to wait upon ourselves at table," said Mr. Hastings, as Moreland received his cup of coffee from Eulalia's hand; "I fear our independent mode of living cannot be very agreeable to you, sir, whose customs are so different."

"On the contrary, nothing can be more agreeable than a family circle like this, uninterrupted by the presence of attendants, oftentimes as useless as they are annoying."

"Indeed! I thought a table at the South was never considered properly set without a negro placed at the back of every chair."

"I do not think the number of chairs governs the number of attendants," answered Moreland, with a smile; "though there is usually a superfluity. Yielding to the force of habit, I allow myself to be waited on, without thinking of it, though I consider it by no means indispensable."

"I am glad you can conform so readily to our plain, republican habits. How do you like our Northern portion of the country, sir?"

"I see much to admire in the luxuriance of your vegetation, your rich, blooming clover fields and cultivated plains. I admire it most as a proof of the energy and industry of the sons of New England, which can convert your hard and granite soil into regions of beauty and fertility, rivalling the spontaneous richness of the South. I am charmed with your delightful summer climate, so soft, yet invigorating; and I honour your noble institutions. But," he added, "I admire, most of all, the intelligence, refinement, and loveliness of the daughters of New England, to which description has never done justice."

Surely, Moreland was trying to ingratiate himself in the favour of the family, by this fine and flattering speech; but though it sounded very much like one prepared and polished for the occasion, it was nevertheless spontaneous and sincere. By *pluralizing* the daughter of Mr. Hastings, he had ventured to express an admiration becoming too strong for repression. He forgot the barriers which a few hours before had seemed so insurmountable; he forgot that Mr. Hastings was the avowed enemy of his dearest social and domestic rights and privileges; that probably the very seat which he now occupied was lately filled by a gigantic negro; that the fair hands of Eulalia had poured coffee for him from that silver urn; and that the smile of welcome beamed as kindly on one as the other. He remembered only the loveliness of her person, the sweetness of her manners, the inexpressible charm that drew him towards her.

"Sister Eula stamped that butter," whispered Dora, as his knife severed a yellow rose from its stem. "She made that plum cake, too."

Moreland smiled at the communication, imparted with the innocent desire of elevating Sister Eula in his estimation, and thought the butter and the cake had a double relish. No one had heard Dora's whispered secret but himself, she had brought her rosy little mouth in such close proximity with his ear.

"It is not polite to whisper at table, Dora," said her mother, gently, but reprovingly, and Dora hung her head and put her finger in her mouth, with suddenly acquired awkwardness. Moreland, excessively amused by the remark and its consequences, glanced at Eulalia's hand, which happened to be raised at that moment to shade back a loosened ringlet from her cheek. The glance was suggested by the thought that the hand which had been employed in moulding and spatting the golden ball, and manufacturing that excellent cake could not possess much feminine delicacy of colour or lineament, but he was pleased to see that it was fair and symmetrical. Not so dazzlingly white as Claudia's snowy, but perjured hand, but pure from the stains of labour, and harmonizing with the delicacy of her face. The truth was, Eulalia knew nothing of the drudgery of housekeeping, and but little of its cares. She was wonderfully expert with her needle, as her father's and brother's shirts, her mother's and sister's dresses could testify, had they tongues to speak. But her mother who was very proud of Eulalia's beauty, and very careful to keep it in high preservation, had habituated her to sew in gloves, with truncated fingers, ingeniously adapted for such a purpose. She swept and garnished her own room every day till it was a miracle of neatness; but she had been taught, as a regular duty, to draw on a pair of thick woollen mittens before she wielded the broom and exercised the duster. Had it not been for her mother's watchfulness, Eulalia's hands might not have justified the admiration of the fastidiously observing Moreland.

Though no servant attended the supper table, and Mr. Hastings boasted of their independence, they had a woman of *all work* in the kitchen, whose labour would have shamed the toil of three of Moreland's stoutest slaves. She rose with the dawn of day, and continued her tread-mill course till its close. She baked and brewed and washed and ironed and scrubbed and scoured, hardly giving herself time to talk, or sitting down but to eat. It is true, Mrs. Hastings assisted her in many of these operations, but the heavy burden of toil rested on her, and they dreamed not, because she was willing to assume it for the weekly stipend she received, that they exacted too much of her health and strength. It is true, that every night, to use her own words, "she was fagged out and tired e'en a'most to death, but she had it to do, and there was no use in grumbling about it. If she didn't take care of herself, who would? If she didn't try and lay up something for a rainy day, she wondered how she was to be taken care of, if she was sick and had to be laid by." So Betsy Jones toiled on, and her one dollar and a half per week, supplied clothes for herself and orphan brother, who was incapacitated, by lameness, from earning his daily bread. The physician's fees, who attended him, were also drained from the same source. How much she had to lay up for a rainy day may be easily imagined. Betsy had none of the false pride which is often found in her class. She had no *ambition* to put herself upon a perfect equality with her employers. She did not care about sitting down with them at meal time, nor did she disdain the summons of a tinkling bell.

"I should look putty," she said, "sitting down in my dirty duds by the side of Miss Euly fixed off in all her niceties. I don't care about sitting down till I've done all my drudgery and all my little chores, and then I'm too jaded out to think of primping and furbishing up for company. If I've got to work I'll work, and done with it, let alone trying to be a lady."

But with all Betsy's humility, she had a just appreciation of herself, and could assert her dignity, when occasion required, with due emphasis. When Mr. Hastings installed his sable protegé into the honours of the household, when she saw him introduced into the guest chamber, where he swathed his huge limbs in the nice linen sheets she had so carefully bleached and ironed, and she was called upon to make up the bed and arrange the room, she stoutly rebelled, and declared "she wouldn't do no such thing. She wa'n't hired to wait upon a nasty runaway, who she knew never had to work half as hard as she had. Great, lazy, good-for-nothing fellow, that he was. *He* talk about being abused like a dog! Why he was as fat as stall-fed beef, and as strong as a lion."

"Well, Betsy, I must do it myself then," said Mrs. Hastings, "rather than waste any more words about it. I am sorry, however, to see that you have no more compassion for a poor, hunted, persecuted being, whom my husband has seen fit to receive under his sheltering roof."

"If the kitchen is good enough for me, it is good enough for such as him," exclaimed Betsy, opening all the windows energetically, and whisking the counterpane and sheets over the sill.

"I shall make it myself, Betsy," said Mrs. Hastings, with heroic determination, "I don't want to hear any more grumbling."

"Just as you please, Miss Hastings," cried Betsy, leaving the room with a resounding step. "He's no more persecuted than I am, the Lord knows."

Whatever were Mrs. Hastings's feelings, she expressed no opposition to the will of her lord and master, whom she looked up to as the great philanthropist of the age, as one of those martyr spirits who, though they may weave for themselves a crown of thorns in this world, will exchange it for a diadem of glory in the next.

After this unexpected digression, caused by little Dora's whisper, we will return to the supper table, or rather to the parlour, for there is no one at the table now but Mrs. Hastings and Betsy, who are both busy in putting away the best china, the cut glass preserve dishes, and silver urn, brought out for the occasion.

"Now, that's a real gentleman," said Betsy, peeping into the parlour through the crack of the door. "I'd as lieves wait upon him as not. He's as handsome as a pictur, and he don't look a bit proud neither, only sort of grand, as t'were. If I was Miss Euly—la sus!"

"Betsy!" said Mrs. Hastings, in a tone of grave rebuke, "you had better attend to your dishes."

Betsy flourished her napkin, but she would peep a little more.

"La me!" she exclaimed, "if they ha'n't got the singing books out, and, there, they are all sot round the middle table. Did you ever? Well! Miss Euly does sing like a martingale."

As there is no use in peeping through an aperture when we have the freedom of the house, we will enter the parlour and seat ourselves in the *old maid,* which, being too heavy to be moved with convenience to the centre table, chances to be standing vacant in the corner.

Mr. Hastings was proud of his daughter's singing, as well he might be. It was really music to his soul, as well as his ear. He had a fine voice himself, and so had Reuben. And even little Dora had been taught to sing the praises of her God and King, with childhood's cherub tones.

"It is our custom," said Mr. Hastings, rubbing his hands slowly and gently, "it is our custom, Mr. Moreland, to have some sacred music every Sunday evening. We have no instruments but those which God has given us, and which we try to tune to His glory. My daughter, here, has a tolerable voice, my son sings a pretty good bass, and I myself can get through a tune without much difficulty. Will you join us, sir? You look as if you could help us, if you pleased."

"With all my heart," replied Moreland, taking a seat at Eulalia's side, and appropriating a singing book for their mutual benefit. "If I can do nothing better, I can at least turn the leaves, as I listen."

But he could do a great deal better, and it was not long before his voice was heard mingling with the sweet hosannas of Eulalia, while bending over the same book, so near, that her warm, pure breath floated against his glowing cheek. He was carried back to the days of his childhood, when his mother taught him the songs of Zion, while cradled in her arms or pillowed on her knee. The recollection softened and moved him to such a degree that his voice choked and then ceased. Eulalia involuntarily turned and looked in his face, and, surprised at the emotion she saw depicted there, her own voice faltered. There was something so exquisitely soft and sympathetic in the expression of her dark hazel eyes, so innocent, yet so full of intelligence, that Moreland felt bewildered by the glance.

"Oh!" thought he, and it was with difficulty he refrained from expressing his thoughts aloud, "I am oppressed with a sense of beauty and sweetness unknown before. All that is pathetic and holy in the past rises up to hallow and subdue the intoxication of the present moment. Strange, that I, born amid the sunny groves of the South, should come to the cold clime of New England to find an influence as warm, as powerful and instantaneous as is ever felt under the glowing skies of the tropics."

"We do not seem to make out quite as well with that tune as the others," said Mr. Hastings, thinking Moreland was probably out of practice and could not help stumbling over some difficult notes; "perhaps we had better try another; or perhaps we had better stop altogether. This must be dull amusement to you, sir."

"On the contrary, my feelings have only been too deeply interested," replied Moreland, ashamed of the interruption he had caused. "This sweet family music, these words of adoration and praise, heard under the stranger's roof, reminded me so vividly of my own early home, that my heart is softened to almost boyish weakness. I pray you to continue."

After singing some charming anthems, in which Mrs. Hastings, whose voice was only less sweet than Eulalia's, also joined, the books were closed, the chairs moved back, and Moreland reluctantly rose to depart.

"No hurry, sir," said Mr. Hastings; "happy to have you sit longer. Happy to have you call again. How long do you think of remaining in our village?"

"I did think of leaving to-morrow," replied his guest; "but," involuntarily looking at Eulalia, "I may probably remain a few days longer."

"You stop at Mr. Grimby's?"

"Yes."

"Well, I shall call and have a few hours' chat with you. I like you, sir—excuse my frankness—and I want to do you good. I think I can. I am a man who have read and studied and reflected a great deal, and have arrived, I flatter myself, at very just views of men and things. In the mean time,"—here he opened a secretary, whose glass doors were lined with green silk, and took out a bundle of papers—"allow me to present you with these papers. Give them, if you please, a careful perusal, and if you are a candid man, as I trust you are, you cannot fail of being a convert to my opinions. Yes, sir," continued he, warming with his subject, "you will find my arguments unanswerable. They are founded on truth. 'The eternal days of God are hers,' and it is in vain to contend against her omnipotent power."

Moreland reddened; he saw the package consisted of numbers of the "Emancipator," edited by Mr. Hastings himself. The gauntlet was now thrown down; he must take it up and enter the lists of controversy, *coute qui coute*.

"I am an earnest seeker of truth, myself," replied he, "and, as you say, I trust a candid one. Should you prove to me that my preconceived opinions are erroneous, I will most ingenuously acknowledge it. But I, too, have read and studied and reflected, and if I have arrived at different conclusions, I shall call upon you to examine mine, with equal frankness and impartiality."

"Certainly, certainly," cried the philanthropist;—"there's not a more impartial man in the world than myself, or one more open to conviction. But once convinced I am *right,* you might as well attempt to move the everlasting hills from their base, as shake the groundwork of my firm and rooted opinions. I will call and see you to-morrow."

And thus, after exchanging the usual courtesies of the parting moment, terminated Moreland's first visit to the home of Eulalia Hastings.

Chapter XX

A long, winding blast of the bugle-horn summoned the labourers from the field, the carpenter and blacksmith from their shops, the spinsters from their wheels, the weaver from her loom, and emptied, as if by magic, the white-washed cabins. The negroes, one and all, had been told to attend their master's call, expressed by that sounding blast. It was just before the sunset hour—one of those mild, glowing days, that so often diffuse over the aspect of a Southern winter the blandness of summer and the haziness of autumn. Eulalia and Ildegerte stood in the portico, spectatresses of a scene which made their hearts throb high in their bosoms. Ildegerte's eyes flashed with excitement. Eulalia's cheek was the bed of its coming and vanishing roses. She saw her husband standing, as she had seen him once before, the centre of a dark ring, but she gazed with far different emotions. It could not be said that she feared for him. His superiority was so manifest, that it suggested, at once, the idea of triumph—the triumph of mind over matter. He seemed to her an angel of light surrounded by the spirits of darkness, and, knowing that he was defended by the breastplate of righteousness, she was assured of his safety as well as his power.

Moreland waited till they had all gathered, and they came with halting, lingering steps, very unlike their former cheerful alacrity; then, telling them to follow him, he led the way to the grave of the old prophetess, Dilsy, at whose burial he had made with them a solemn covenant, which *he* had kept inviolate. It was long since any of them had approached the burying-ground. In all their nightly meetings they had avoided passing it, fearing that the spirits of the dead would sweep their cold wings in their faces, or seize them with their stiff and icy fingers, or shriek in their ear some unearthly denunciation. As they walked through the place of graves, the long, dry yellow grass broke and crumpled under their steps, and the brambles twisted round their ankles. They had neglected their dead. The autumn leaves lay thick, damp, and rotting on the sods that covered them, choking the vines and plants, which, in happier hours, had been cultured there.

Moreland stopped by the headstone, which his own hand had placed at Dilsy's grave, and indicated by a commanding gesture the places they were to assume. Paul, the preacher, stood nearest to him, his arms folded on his brawny chest, and his hoary locks of wool bent so low they seemed scattering their powder on the ground. Vulcan, the blacksmith, black and sullen as a thunder-cloud, stood on his left. The women, who had most of them been excluded from the secret deliberations, hung timidly in the rear, curiosity and apprehension struggling in them for mastery. And beyond the edge of the burying-ground, the two children of Moreland—the one holding the hand, the other borne in the arms of Kizzie, shone in the innocence of infancy and beauty of childhood, on the gloom and duskiness of the scene.

"More than two years have passed," said Moreland, his eyes glancing from face to face, calmly and gravely, as he spoke, "since I stood on this spot, on which the grave-clods had just been thrown, and you all stood around me then, just as you are gathered now. At that hour, I renewed the vows of protection and kindness to you which I uttered, when a boy, in the ear of a dying mother. I told you, if I ever proved unkind, unjust, and tyrannical, if I ever forgot my duties to you as a master and a friend, to meet me here, in this solemn enclosure, and remind me of what I then said. You all promised then, to continue faithful, trustworthy, and obedient, and, judging of the future by the past, I believed you. And yet," he added, his voice deepening into sternness and his eye kindling with indignation, "you have basely deceived me; you have been listening to a traitor and a villain, and plotting against your master and your friend. Under presence of worshipping God, you have been engaged in the service of Satan, and doing the work of devils. I know all your horrible plans. I know what holiday frolics you are preparing. Which of you has a word to say in his defence? Which of you can look me in the face and say he does not deserve the severest punishment, for treachery and ingratitude to a master as kind and forbearing as I have ever been? Paul, you have taken upon you the office of a preacher of the gospel of peace, who, on all occasions, are the voice of your brethren; look up, speak, and if you have one word to say in your justification and theirs, let us hear it, and hear it quickly."

"No, massa!" cried Paul, slowly raising his head, without lifting his eyes; "got noting to say—noting—only Massa Brainard."

"Poor, deluded creatures!" said Moreland, "poor, blind tools of an artful, selfish, false, and cold-hearted hypocrite, who cares no more for you than the grass you are trampling under your feet. I pity you; for I sent the wretch in your midst, believing him to be a man of God. He has beguiled you with promises of freedom. What is the freedom he can offer you? Nothing but poverty, degradation, and sorrow. If you could compare your condition with those of the free coloured people at the North, you would shudder to think of all that you have escaped. Listen! You are slaves, and I am free; but I neither made you slaves nor myself a free man. We are all in the condition in which we were born. You are black, and I am white; but I did not give you those sable skins, nor myself this fairer complexion. You and I are as God Almighty made us, and, as I expect to give an account of the manner in which I fulfil my duties as a master, so you will be judged according to your fidelity, honesty, and uprightness as servants. The Bible says—'Can the Ethiopian change his skin?' No, he cannot! but there is no reason why he should have a black heart, because his skin is black. Free! how willingly would I make you free this moment, if, by so doing, I could make you better and happier! Free! I would to heaven you were all free—then I, too, should be free from a burden made intolerable by your treachery and ingratitude! I would rather, ten thousand times, cultivate these broad fields myself, than be served by faithless hands and false, hollow hearts. I have hands that can work. I would do it cheerfully, if labour was the portion God had assigned me in this world. Better, far better, the toiling limbs, than the aching heart!"

He paused a moment in indescribable emotion. Among those who were looking earnestly in his face, and drinking in his words with countenances expressive of shame, remorse, and returning devotion, were some who had been the playmates of his childhood and others in whose arms he had been dandled and caressed when a little boy, and others, again, mere boys now, whom he had made the playthings of his youthful years. He remembered sitting, many and many a time, in the lap of Paul, under an old tree, teaching him to read, while the negro would twist his dark fingers in his childish locks, and pray God Almighty to bless him and make him a blessing to mankind. A sable filament was twisted in every cord that bound him to the past. The associations of bygone years rose above the painful and gloomy present, and it was far more in sorrow than in anger, that he regarded the large family whom the most consummate art had alienated from him.

"Paul," said he, turning to the preacher, whose head was drooping still lower on his breast, and whose cheeks were marked by a wet, shining streak, where silent tears were travelling, "Paul, do you remember Davy, to whom my father gave his freedom many years ago, and who afterwards bought his wife and settled in the State of New York?"

"Yes, massa!"

"Here is a letter, which I received from him a few days since. I will read it. I want you all to listen to it."

Moreland took a letter from his pocket-book and read as follows—

Dear Young Master:—I hope you have not forgotten Davy, though you was a little boy when I came away. I'm very sick; the doctor says I can't live long. I'm willing to die; but there's one great care on my mind. I don't want to leave my wife and children here. I've made a considerable property, so they wouldn't be in want; but that ain't all a person wants, master. If I had life before me again, I'd come back myself, for I've never been as happy, or as respectable, as when I lived with old Master. I heard so much talk about the white people at the North being such friends to the blacks, I thought we'd be on perfect equality; but it's no such thing. They won't associate with us; and I never want my wife and children to put themselves on a level with the free negroes I see here,—they are a low, miserable set, and folks that respect themselves won't have anything to do with them. My dear young master, please come on, or, if you can't come yourself, send somebody to take back my wife and children,—I have but two daughters, if they were boys I would not care so much. I give them to you, just as if they had never been free. I bequeath you all my property too, and wish it was more. Oh! happy should I be, could I live to see the son of my dear old master before I die,—but the will of God be done. I've got somebody to write this letter for me, for I am too weak to sit up; but I'll put my name to it, that you may know it comes from

Davy.

"If you can't come or send directly, please write a line, just to ease my dying thoughts."

"This letter," said Moreland, "was dictated by one who has tasted the joys of freedom, as it exists among the black people at the North. His condition is far better than the majority, for he has acquired property, while most of them are miserably poor. Listen to me, sons and daughters of Africa! If I thought freedom would be a blessing to you, it should be yours. East, West, or North, anywhere, everywhere, you might go, and I would bid you God speed; but I would as soon send those poor sheep on the hill-side, among ravening wolves, as cast you amid such friends as this pretended minister of God represents! Which of you wants to trust him now? Which of you wants to leave your master and follow him? Tell me, for I will have no Judas in the field, ready to betray his too kind and trusting master!"

"Oh, massa!" exclaimed Paul—completely subdued and melted, and sinking down on his knees, right on the grave of Dilsy—"forgive us! Don't send us away! Trust us once more! We've ben 'ceived by Satan, and didn't know what we were doing!"

The moment Paul prostrated himself before his master, all but *one* followed his example, entreating for pardon, and imploring with tears and sobs not to be sent away from him. Vulcan, the blacksmith, stood firm and unmoved as the anvil in his forge. All his dark and angry passions had been whetted on the edge of the murderous weapons hidden beneath his shop, and made red hot by the flames of the midnight furnace. His stubborn knees refused to bend, and a sullen cloud added luridness to his raven-black face.

Moreland and he stood side by side;—all the rest were kneeling. The beams of the departing sun played in golden glory round the brow of Moreland; the negro seemed to absorb the rays—he looked of more intense inky blackness.

"Vulcan!" said his master, "if you expect my forgiveness, ask it. Dare to resist me, and you shall feel the full weight of my indignation."

"I'm my own master," cried the blacksmith, in a morose, defying tone. "I ain't a gwine to let no man set his feet on my neck. If the rest are a mind to be fools, let 'em!" and he shook his iron hand over the throng, and rolled his bloodshot eyes, like a tiger ready to spring from its lair.

The face of Moreland turned pale as marble, and lightnings kindled in his eyes. To brute force and passion he had nothing to oppose but moral courage and undaunted will; but he paused not to measure his strength with the muscles swelling out, like twisting serpents, in the negro's brandished arm. Laying his right hand commandingly on his shoulder, he exclaimed:—

"There is but one master here. Submit to his authority, or tremble for the consequences!"

Suddenly wrenching his shoulder from the hand that grasped it, the blacksmith leaped forward, and seizing his master in his gigantic arms, was about to hurl him to the ground, when a tremendous blow on the back of his head laid him prostrate and stunned at Moreland's feet. So sudden had been the attack, so instantaneous the release, that Moreland was hardly conscious how it had been effected, till the sight of Paul, standing with dilated nostrils and panting chest over the fallen giant, and brandishing with both hands a massy rail, which had been lying at the foot of the grave, made him aware who his deliverer was.

"Let me kill 'em, massa—let me kill 'em," cried Paul, swinging the rail above his head, and planting his foot on the broad breast of the rebel.

"Stop!" cried Moreland; "in the name of God, stop! He may be dead already! Let him be carried to the guard-house and there taken care of. Give him in charge to the overseer."

Four of the stoutest negroes sprang forward, eager to show their recovered zeal and loyalty, and lifted up the heavy mass of insensible flesh, which they would have beaten to jelly in their indignation, so powerful was the reaction of their feelings.

"Paul," said Moreland, holding out his hand, "true and faithful servant yet! Let the past be forgotten, or remembered only to forgive!"

"Oh! dear massa!" cried Paul, dropping the rail, and throwing his arms round Moreland's shoulders, he wept and sobbed like a child—"you're safe and alive yet! Bless a Lord Almighty! Paul's heart always was right, but he got a mighty poor head of hisn."

When Moreland seemed under the ruffian grasp of Vulcan, the women uttered the most terrible screams; but wilder and more piercing than all the rest was the shriek that issued from the portico, that commanded a full view of the scene. Eulalia and Ildegerte, who were standing with arms interlaced, gazing on what to them was an exciting pantomime, for they could not hear one syllable of what was uttered, beheld the giant leaping on his master, and believed it the signal of death. How they reached there they knew not, for the place was at some distance from the house—but they found themselves forcing their way through the ring just as Paul was weeping on his master's shoulder.

"All is safe!" cried Moreland, as they threw themselves into his arms, clinging to him in an agony of emotion—"all is well! Look up, my Eula! Sister, be not afraid; it is all over! Here is Paul, who is ready to die in my defence."

"Me too, master!" cried Albert, with glistening eyes; "Paul struck 'fore I got a chance, or I would have killed him!"

The little golden-brown head of the infant Russell was seen peeping behind the ring, like a sunbeam playing on the cloud-edge. Kizzie, nearly distracted, had pressed as close as possible to the scene of action, after the terrible rebel was secured; and the infant, excited by the tumult, clapped its cherub hands, and glanced its beautiful hazel eyes from face to face with innocent curiosity.

"Bring that child here," said Moreland; and Albert, springing forward, bore it in triumph over the woolly heads between, to his master's extended arms.

"This child," said he, raising it aloft in its smiling beauty, "is your future master. With its first lessons of obedience to his parents and love to his God, he shall be taught his duties to you, and yours to him. Born and brought up in your midst, he will learn to regard you as a part of his own life and soul. I trust, with the blessing of God, he will live to be a better, wiser, kinder master than I have ever been, and watch over your children's interests when I am laid low in the grave."

The infant, delighted with its elevated position, laughed in its glee, while the negroes gazed upon both father and child as beings of a superior world.

The admiration, love, and devotion which the negro feels for the children of a beloved master, is one of the strongest, most unselfish passions the human heart is capable of cherishing. The partition wall of colour is broken down. The sable arms are privileged to wreathe the neck of snow, the dusky lips to press soft kisses on the cheek of living roses. And, though, in after years, the child feels the barrier of distinction drawn by the Creator's hand, in infancy it clings with instinctive affection to the dark bosom that nurses it, and sees only the loving heart through the black and sooty skin. If such are the feelings which infancy usually inspires, it is not strange that the child of such a master as Moreland should be an object of idolatry, for, notwithstanding they had been tempted from their allegiance by the irresistible arts of Brainard, the principles of strong affection and undying loyalty existed in their hearts, and now throbbed with renovated vitality—with the exception of the fierce and rebellious artisan. His was one of those animal natures which, having had a scent of blood in the breeze, snuffed it with savage delight, and, being baffled of its prey, revenged itself for its unslaked thirst in roars of defiance and deeds of violence. He was now, however, incapable of inflicting farther injury. The well-aimed blow of Paul, though not mortal, had caused a terrible concussion in his system, from which he was likely long to suffer; and he was also strongly guarded.

That night the deepest tranquillity brooded over the plantation. The stormy elements were hushed; the late troubled waters subsided into a peaceful yet tremulous expanse. Eula, exhausted by the agitation of the several preceding days, slept as quietly as the babe that rested on her bosom. But no sleep visited the wakeful eyes of Moreland. He went abroad into the stillness, the solemnity and loneliness of night, and beyond the clear and illimitable moonlight, he looked into the darkening future. The clouds of the preceding night were all swept away, and the moon glided, slowly, majestically, radiantly over the blue and boundless firmament, a solitary bark of silver navigating the unfathomable ocean of ether. Moreland walked through the long rows of cabins, whose whitewashed walls reflected, with intense brightness, the light that illumined them, and envied the repose of the occupants. The signs of the times were dark, and portentous of disunion and ruin. The lightnings might be sheathed, but they were ready, at any moment, to rend the cloud and dart their fiery bolts around. Supposing, for one moment, the full triumph of fanaticism, how fearful would be the result! The emancipation of brute force; the reign of animal passion and power; the wisdom of eighteen centuries buried under waves of barbarism, rolling back upon the world; the beautiful cotton-fields of the South left neglected and overgrown with weeds; the looms of the North idle for walls of the downy fleece, and England, in all her pride and might, bleeding from the wound her own hands had inflicted. None but the native of a tropic zone, physically constructed to endure the heat of a Southern clime, can cultivate its soil and raise its staple products. That the African, *unguided by the white man's influence*, would suffer the fairest portions of God's earth to become uncultivated wildernesses, let St. Domingo, Jamaica, and the emancipated islands bear witness. Suppose the triumph of fanaticism, agriculture would inevitably languish and die; the negro, as well as the white man, would not only sink into an abyss of poverty and ruin, but the withered energies, the decaying commerce, and expiring manufactures of the North would show the interests of the two different sections of our common country to be connected by as vital a ligament as that which unites the twin-born brothers of Siam. Let the death-stroke pierce the bosom of one, the other must soon become a livid and putrifying corpse.

If it be God's will that our country, so long the boast and glory of the age, should become its byword and reproach; if the Genius of America is to be driven from her mountain heights into the dens and caves of earth, weeping over her banner insulted, its stars extinguished, its stripes rent asunder, with none left to vindicate its rights; if the beauty, order, and moral discipline of society are to be resolved into the gloom and darkness of chaos, the silver chords of brotherhood snapped asunder, and the golden bowl of union for ever broken:—if it be God's will, let man lay his hand upon his mouth, and his mouth in the dust, and say,

"It is good!"

But let him beware of mistaking the traces of human weakness and passion for the stately footprints of the Almighty, lest the Lord come in judgment and avenge his insulted majesty!

Such were the thoughts that banished sleep from the eyes of Moreland, and sent him abroad, a nocturnal wanderer, in the holy splendour of the night. His feet involuntarily turned to the blacksmith's shop. It was a lonely path that led to it, and, just before it reached the building, a dense thicket of pines made an impervious shade, black and heavy by contrast with the beams beyond. While he was passing through the shadows, and about to emerge into the light, he saw the figure of a man stealing cautiously round the shop and approaching the door. A low, distinct knock was heard, repeated at intervals. He was sure, from the outline, that it was the form of Brainard, and he could see that it was the face of a white man. His first impulse was to rush forward and seize him,—his next, to watch his farther motions. Stepping very cautiously, and looking round at every step, the figure went to the pile of brushwood we described in a former chapter, and removed it from the excavation. Stooping down and groping his way under, he disappeared, while Moreland, accelerating his steps, reached the spot before he had time to emerge again into the light. He could hear distinctly the clinking of steel under the house, and wondered if the man had engaged some subterranean knight in conflict. An old door, broken from its hinges, lay upon the ground. Moreland raised it as noiselessly as possible, and putting it up against the opening, planted his foot firmly against it—thus making the man, whoever he was, his prisoner. The sudden darkening of the moonlight, which streamed in under the building, made the intruder aware of his situation, and he came rushing against the barrier with headlong force; the planks vibrated and cracked, but Moreland stood his ground, firm as a rock.

"Vulcan, Vulcan! is it you? For God's sake, let me out! It is I! Don't you know my voice?" It was the voice of Brainard—not the sweet music he was accustomed to breathe from the pulpit, but the sharp, quick, startled accents of fear.

"Excuse me, Mr. Brainard," said Moreland; and a proud smile curled his lip at the ridiculous and humiliating position of his enemy. "I hope you do not find yourself uncomfortable! I was not aware that you had lodgings there before; but I believe you are fond of subterranean works!"

"Mr. Moreland," exclaimed Brainard, "it is not possible that it is you who are opposing my egress? Is this the treatment that one gentleman has a right to expect from another?"

"Gentleman!" repeated Moreland, in an accent of withering sarcasm; "coward! traitor! knave! too vile for indignation, too low for contempt! Come forth, and meet me face to face, if you dare! Rise, if you are not too grovelling to assume the attitude of a man!"

Removing his foot from the door, it fell forward, and the moon again shining into the aperture, revealed the prone and abject form of the pretended minister. Crawling a few steps on his hands and knees, he rose slowly, for his limbs were cramped and stiff, and shook the earth-soil from his garments. His face was now directly opposite Moreland; and from his blue, half closed eyes, the unsheathing daggers of hatred and revenge were furtively gleaming.

"What are you doing here?" asked Moreland, sternly, "stealing round my premises at the midnight hour, burrowing like a wild beast in the earth, after having fled like a coward at my approach, to avoid the consequences of detected perfidy?"

"I have been on my Master's business," he answered, looking upward. "I am not accountable to any man, being amenable to a higher law."

"Hypocrite!" exclaimed Moreland, his dark eyes flashing with indignation, "away with this vile cant! Throw aside the cloak with which you have tried in vain to cover your iniquitous plots! Everything is discovered. If you were seen now in the city whose hospitality you have so wantonly abused, you would fall a sacrifice to the vengeance of an incensed community. We are safe, thank Heaven, from your incendiary purposes; but what can save you, bare and exposed as you are, from the hands of an outraged public?"

Brainard was in such a position that it was impossible for him to escape. On one side was a jutting beam, an abutment of the building; on the other, the pile of brushwood he had thrown aside; before him, the proud, resolute form, and commanding glance of the man he had deceived and attempted to destroy. By what subterfuge could he now elude the doom he had brought upon himself?

"Mr. Moreland," said he, "I have sat at your board, slept in your bed, and broken bread at your table. Even the wild Arab will protect the stranger who has partaken of his hospitality. Will you, a Christian, do less than he?"

"Yes; you have done all this," replied his host. "I know it but too well. You have slept in my bed that you might strew it with thorns. You have broken my bread that you might infuse into it poison and death. It is my duty as a Christian to incapacitate you for the perpetration of new crimes."

"I may have been carried farther than I intended," said he, in an humble, adjuring tone; "but it was not for myself I was labouring. I have been made the agent of others, whose cause I embraced with premature ardour. I have been misled by false misrepresentations, to adopt a course which I now sincerely regret. A candid man, Mr. Moreland, would require no other apology."

"False as cowardly!" answered Moreland. "If you are the tool of a party, it only aggravates your meanness. There may be those who are degraded enough to employ a wretch like you, as an instrument to work the downfall of the South; but, if so, they must be the lowest dregs of society. There may be men, and women too, for I have heard of such,—but I do not believe there is a respectable town or village in the Northern States that would not consider itself disgraced by your conduct, and blush for the opprobrium which you have brought upon their name. I have travelled in the North,—I know the spirit of the times; but I know, too, that there is a conservative principle there, that would protect us from aggression, and itself from ignominy."

"It matters not whose agent I am," said Brainard, bitterly. "I see I am at your mercy. Yet, if you will suffer me to depart in peace, I will pledge my solemn word to leave this part of the country, immediately and for ever."

"What faith can be put in promises like yours? No, sir! The day of blind confidence is past. I arrest you by virtue of a warrant which I bear about me. Come with me, till better accommodations are provided for you at the public expense."

Even while speaking these words, Moreland was conscious of great perplexity, for he knew of no place of security but the guard-house, where Vulcan was already imprisoned, where he could put the arch-traitor. It is true, Vulcan was now in no situation to be influenced by his insidious arts, but he did not like their juxtaposition. Another thing, it was considerably distant from the blacksmith's shop, and it would be no easy task to conduct a desperate and infuriated man to that place of confinement. Still, he must not be suffered to escape, so, laying a firm hand on his shoulder, he commanded him to follow him. Quick as a flash of thought, Brainard drew a bowie knife from his bosom with his free right hand, and made a plunge at Moreland's breast. Moreland saw the steel glittering in the moonlight, and the next moment might have been his last, but, throwing his assailant back with a violent jerk, the stroke glanced in the air. This was the commencement of a life-struggle, fierce and bloodthirsty on one side, bold, firm, and unrelaxing on the other. One could hear the gritting of Brainard's grinding teeth, as he tried to release himself from the clenching grasp of his antagonist. Moreland was armed, for, at this time of threatened insurrection, every man was provided with defensive weapons, but, instead of drawing his own, his object was to get possession of Brainard's knife. Had he released his hold one second, his life might have been the sacrifice. Once or twice he felt the sharp steel gashing his left arm, but he heeded it not, and once, in warding off a deadly blow at his heart, he turned the point of the knife and it plunged in Brainard's right arm—the arm which wielded the destructive weapon. Moreland, after the first moment of exasperation and excitement, did not want to kill him, but to defend himself, and incapacitate him from further mischief. The knife dropped from Brainard's powerless hand, and the blood spouted from the wound. Moreland, well knowing it was not a mortal stroke, and that his left hand still had power, snatched the knife from the ground and sheathed it in the folds of his vest. The blood was flowing from his own wounds, but, without heeding it, he bound his handkerchief round Brainard's arm, who had reeled as if fainting, against the walls of the shop. He looked very pale, but Moreland could plainly see that it was not the death-like paleness preceding a swoon. Still, he did not like to drag him, in that situation to the guard-house, and, enfeebled as he was, he believed he could leave him in the shop with safety, while he went to rouse the overseer and some of the strongest hands, to assist in guarding him, and he himself obtained proper materials to dress his wound. The door of the shop was usually locked at this hour, but, in consequence of Vulcan's arrest, who had the charge of it, the key was left hanging in the padlock—a circumstance fortunate for Moreland's design. The wooden windows were barred inside, and Vulcan, while prosecuting his midnight labours, had added iron staples, as a greater security from intrusion. Had Brainard not been disabled by his wound, Moreland would not have dared to have enclosed him, even for a brief time, in a place where the weapons of deliverance might be found in the massy iron tools of the blacksmith; but he well knew that the arm, whose reeking blood had already dyed his handkerchief, could not wield the ponderous sledge-hammer or the iron bars.

"Come," said he, taking him by the left arm, "come into the shop, while I go for linen and balsam to dress your wound. I presume it is not the first time that you have found shelter in its walls."

"Bring none of your linen and balsam for me," he answered, "I'll none of it. Put me where you please, it makes no difference; I scorn and defy your power!"

Though he spoke in a faint voice, it was expressive of malignity and revenge. He no longer resisted, however, and Moreland, drawing rather than leading him round to the front side of the shop, opened the door, sprang upon the threshold with his prisoner, then releasing him suddenly, he sprang back, closed and locked the door, and returning to the rear of the building, examined the shutters on the outside.—It would not do to leave them without some barrier, for Brainard might remove the inner bar with his left hand, and leap from the window. There were two large posts lying on the ground, which seemed left there for his peculiar purpose, and though it required an exertion of strength to lift them, with his left arm weakened and painful as it was, he did it with astonishing celerity, and steadying the lower ends against the old fallen tree, suffered the upper ones to fall heavily upon the shutters, just below the jutting of the wood-piece nailed across them, and in this position every effort to open the windows would only make the posts more firm in their resistance.

"That will do," said Moreland, turning away, and directing his steps towards the overseer's dwelling-house. With an involuntary impulse, he drew forth the knife concealed in his bosom, and suffered the moonlight to gleam upon it. Half of it was stained with blood, the other half shone cold and blue, with deadly lustre, in the serene glory of the night. He shuddered at the temptation he had momentarily felt, to bury it in the false heart of Brainard, and blessed his guardian angel for covering the edge of the weapon with his interposing wings.

The chivalry of his nature had received a painful wound. He had discharged an imperative duty, but in a manner revolting to the magnanimity of his character. He had felt his cheek burn, while turning the key of that black sooty prison on a wounded enemy. Had he known that Brainard was familiar with even more gloomy walls, that, even when a boy, he had made his bed on the dungeon's floor, and worn the felon's badge of ignominy, he would have been less fastidious with regard to his accommodations.

Having awakened the overseer, and told him to rouse immediately several of the stoutest negroes, including Uncle Paul, and repair to the shop, which they were to guard during the remainder of the night; he began to feel the necessity of having his own wounds attended to,—though not deep, the flowing of the unstanched blood, and the straining of the muscles in barricading the shutters, made him feel weak and nerveless. He therefore commissioned the overseer to act as leech, as well as guard, and sought his own dwelling.

Fearing to awake his wife, and alarm her by the sight of his blood-stained garments, he entered with noiseless steps, and the faint, soft, regular breathing that met his ear gave him a sensation of exquisite repose. Eulalia still slept, and the babe still slumbered on her bosom. Again the image of the virgin mother and the infant Jesus rose before him, as when he had knelt by her, when reclining over the cradle of her son. And once more he knelt, but without awakening her, and commended them both to the God of the South as well as the North,—"to the Monarch, and Maker, and Saviour of all!"

"Ah, my sweet wife!" thought he, when, rising from his knees, he looked down upon her with unutterable tenderness, "you are paying a sad penalty for the love that lured you from your quiet village home. Better had it been for you had I left you near the shadow of that temple where your seraph voice first waked the slumbering music of my heart."

For a moment he had forgotten his arm, and the blood-stains on his dress; but a stiff, painful feeling reminded him of the past conflict, and, with the same noiseless steps with which he had entered, he left his own room, and, seeking the one where Albert slept, committed himself to his healing hands.

In the mean time Brainard was not idle. When left by Moreland in the grim retreat with which he had made himself so familiar, he stood at first perfectly still, in the centre of the shop, where the momentum given by Moreland's releasing arm had sent him. It was not utterly dark, for silvers of moonshine penetrated the chinks of the boards, and fell on the blackened planks. He looked round him, straightened himself up to his full height, and shook his left arm in defiance, as if facing an invisible enemy.

"Fool!" he muttered. "He did not know he was dealing with an ambidextrous man. There is as much cunning in this hand as in that. Does he think these drops of blood have weakened me so that I cannot burst these bars and free myself from his power? Ha, ha! I played the part of a fainting man to put him off his guard; but I have strength enough yet to perform a good night's work. These shutters are nothing but old boards. I'll soon shiver them. I'll hurl them into fragments. Yes, yes! if the morning find me a prisoner here, may I hang from the gibbet, and the fowls of heaven feed upon my carcass!"

Guided by the light of the silver bars on the floor, he seized the sledgehammer with his left hand, and, swinging it high in air, brought it down upon the shutter with a tremendous blow. There was a jarring and rattling of boards, and a cloud of black dust, but Moreland's strong barrier resisted the effort.

"Death and fury!" he exclaimed; "are the boards lignum vitae? I'll try the door. If I cannot break that open, I'll spill my own brains on these planks!"

Swinging the huge hammer once more, he hurled it against the door with maniac force. Ha! it does begin to yield. Bravo! strike again. They hear your blows, to be sure, but they think the horses are pounding and kicking in the stable, as they are wont to do. Strike again; a desperate man can do anything. No matter if every stroke makes the blood ooze from your wounded veins, and the sultry sweat-drops gush from your pores. There! don't you see the hinges strain, tug, crack, and at length give way with a sudden crash. Jump through! the avengers are coming. Make haste! they are in the dark path now. Remember you are in the moonlight.

Yes! Brainard did remember all this, and he leaped through the opening with supernatural agility, flew, rather than ran to the stable, mounted the fleetest horse, and cut the air like the arrow. He was seen, just as he reached the stable, by the party appointed to be his guard. Paul, who seemed to have the vigour and fire of youth miraculously restored, shouted till the thicket reverberated the sound, and rushed after him, his long limbs sweeping over the ground like forked lightning. The overseer and other negroes followed, but they could not begin to keep up with the streaking steps of Paul. As he reached the stable Brainard leaped into the road. Paul was on the back of Swiftsure, one of his master's strongest, fleetest horses, with the quickness of thought, and away he went in pursuit of the fugitive.

"Good Lord!" cried Paul, "let me only catch 'em! Just let massa know what Paul can do for him! Go it, go it, Swiftshur!—wide awake! wide awake!—keep a eye open—stretch a feet apart!—that the way to go!"

Paul lay almost horizontally on the barebacked animal, grasping his mane for a bridle, his body thrown up and down by the violence of the motion. Brainard had saddle and bridle, for he was on the same horse which had been caparisoned to bear him from the plantation, just before Moreland's arrival. The odds were in his favour, and he knew it. His scornful laugh was driven back into Paul's face, like a dash of cold water. Once he reeled in the saddle, and his speed perceptibly slackened, and the shadow of his pursuer appeared to be leaping on his back; but just as Paul stretched out his long arm, thinking him within reach, he shot ahead, with dizzying velocity, and Paul grasped a handful of moonbeams. It was all in vain. As he told his master the next day—"The devil was in him, and one might as well try to catch hold of a streak of lightning."

All the time Brainard was winging his way, thought, swifter than his flight, was darting in his mind, bringing messages from the future, that lit up his countenance with vindictive joy.

"Oh! I have a glorious career before me," said he to himself, dashing his spurs into his horse's smoking flanks,—for he had equipped himself like a knight when he started on his midnight expedition. "I have planned it all—and when did I ever plan without executing? Who says I have failed? I tell you, you lie, sir. I have made a plenty of dupes. The flames I have kindled will not be quenched. They will burst out afresh, when people think they are gazing on ashes. Yes! I will go back to the North, and deliver such lectures on the South as will curdle the blood with horror. No matter what I say—I'll find fools to believe it all. If I pour falsehoods hot as molten lead down their throats, they will believe them all, and smack their lips with delight. Take care, Master Moreland! the devil shall be an angel of light compared to the foul demon I will represent you to be—you, and all your tribe. Thank Heaven for the gift of eloquence! Oh! I'll rave of blood-marked chains, of flesh torn from the body with red-hot pincers, of children roasted alive, of women burned at the stake! They'll believe it all! The more horrors I manufacture the more ecstasy they will feel! Curses on the arm that failed to pierce *his* heart's core! Curses on *him* for every drop of blood he has drawn! But I'll have my revenge!—a glorious revenge!—ha! ha!"

Away with him! Close the shutters of that workshop of Satan—his breast. We shudder at the glimpses revealed. Let him go, and fill up the measure of his iniquity: brimming as it now seems, it is not quite full. The crowning drop must be blacker than all.

QUESTIONS TO CONSIDER

1. In what ways do the selections here belie Hentz's professed faith in the "potential of enlightened discourse to alleviate regional tensions?"

2. In what ways is Hentz's novel informed by proslavery thought of the early- to mid-nineteenth century? Did Hentz merely reiterate common themes found in proslavery ideology, or did she contribute an original defense of the institution?
3. Do these selections suggest that Hentz held any hope for the continuing viability of the Union? If so, what did Hentz believe would hold the Union together? If not, to what did Hentz ascribe the dividing forces?

Angelina Emily Grimké

1805–1879

Angelina Emily Grimké was born into a prominent slaveholding South Carolinian family at the turn of the nineteenth century. Her older sister Sarah, who had come to abhor the institution of slavery early in her life, profoundly influenced her. The daily abuses Angelina witnessed soon compelled her to question the institution of slavery. "If only I could be the means of exposing the cruelty and injustice," she wrote in her diary, "of bringing to light the hidden things of the darkness, of revealing the secrets of iniquity." This desire to expose soon became an obsession with Angelina; "it seemed that not a single day could pass without some kind of painful argument," suggests Gerda Lerner, one of Grimké's biographers. Grimké confessed in her diary her desperate desire to "escape from this land of slavery." Yet she remained, hoping that her example and influence might affect change. Her attempts to reform her family failed miserably, however. She soon found her situation unbearable. With her mother's consent, Grimké left Charleston for the North in the fall of 1829. "When she took the final step there could be no doubt as to the reasons for her action," Gerda Lerner has written; "her very departure was a public act of protest against the slavery system."

Grimké began attending antislavery meetings and soon became one of the nation's foremost abolitionists. Addressing a Boston audience in 1838, Angelina summarized her position: "I stand before you as a Southerner, exiled from the land of my birth by the sound of the lash and the piteous cry of the slave. I stand before you as a repentent [*sic*] slaveholder," she continued. "I stand before you as a moral being and as a moral being I feel that I owe it to the suffering slave and to the deluded master, to my country and to the world to do all that I can to overturn a system of complicated crimes, build upon the broken hearts and prostrate bodies of my countrymen in chains and cemented by the blood, sweat and tears of my sisters in bonds."

Two years before Angelina Grimké addressed that Boston audience, she had written one of the most powerful documents in abolitionist literature, *Appeal to the Christian Women of the South*. She believed that she was divinely inspired to write the tract. "God has shown me what I can do," she announced. "I can write an appeal to Southern women, one which, thus inspired, will touch their hearts, and lead them to use their influence with their husbands and brothers. I will speak to them in such tones that they *must* hear me, and, through me, the voice of justice and humanity." According to Stephen Howard Browne, Grimké originally planned the *Appeal* to take no more than a dozen pages. Over the next few weeks, however, the project grew, and she soon had over thirty-six manuscript pages. She sent her finished manuscript to the American Anti-Slavery Society of New York. She explained to her sister Sarah that the *Appeal*, once corrected and revised, was "to be published by them with my name attached, for I well know my name is worth more than myself and will add weight to it."

Angelina Grimké explained that in her *Appeal* she wanted to demonstrate that the institution of slavery contradicts the spirit of the Declaration of Independence and to "answer the objections that our forefathers were mistaken for the Bible sanctions slavery by showing it to be contrary to the great charter of human rights granted to Adam." Grimké dismantled the "curse pronounced upon Canaan" as a justification for slavery, for example. "I know this prophecy was uttered, and was most fearfully and wonderfully fulfilled," she wrote in her *Appeal*, "but I do know that prophecy does *not* tell us what *ought to be*, but what actually does take place, ages after it has been delivered, and if we justify America for enslaving the children of Africa, we must also justify Egypt for reducing the children of Israel to bondage, for the latter was foretold as explicitly as the former." She also challenged those who justified American slavery by noting that "God sanctioned Slavery, yea commanded Slavery under the Jewish Dispensation." Grimké distinguished Hebrew servitude from American slavery, admitting her "wonder and admiration at perceiving how carefully the [Hebrew] servant was guarded from violence, injustice and wrong." She then listed the six ways in which Hebrews could become servants legally, the nine laws that secured the rights of servants, and the four laws that further protected female Jewish servants. Finally, she cited a passage from Deuteronomy that forbade the return of an escaped servant to his master and a passage from Leviticus that prevented servitude from becoming perpetual. "Where, then," she asked, "is the warrant, the justification, or the palliation of American Slavery from Hebrew servitude? How many of the Southern slaves would now be in bondage according to the laws of Moses?" "Not one," she answered.

Gerda Lerner has noted that Angelina Grimké was hardly the first antislavery advocate to use the Bible to justify her cause. "Yet her appeal is unique in abolitionist literature," Lerner has argued, "because it is the only appeal by a Southern abolitionist woman to Southern women." Not surprisingly, Southerners greeted the appeal "with something less than enthusiasm." Charlestonians seized copies of the *Appeal* and officials warned Grimké not to return to the city at the risk of "her personal freedom." Abolitionists, however, hailed it, and when it was promoted heavily in William Lloyd Garrison's abolitionist newspaper, *The Liberator*, Grimké's reputation as a Southern heretic was secured.

from Appeal to the Christian Women of the South

> Then Mordecai commanded to answer Esther. Think not within thyself that thou shalt escape in the king's house more than all the Jews. For if thou altogether holdest thy peace at this time, then shall there enlargement and deliverance arise to the Jews from another place: but thou and thy father's house shall be destroyed: and who knoweth whether thou art come to the kingdom for such a time as this. And Esther bade them return Mordecai this answer—and so will I go unto the king, which is not according to law, and *if I perish, I perish*.
>
> Esther IV. 13–16.

Respected Friends,

It is because I feel a deep and tender interest in your present and eternal welfare that I am willing thus publicly to address you. Some of you have loved me as a relative, and some have felt bound to me in Christian sympathy, and Gospel friendship; and even when compelled by a strong sense of duty, to break those outward bonds of union which bound us together as members of the same community, and members of the same religious denomination, you were generous enough to give me credit, for sincerity as a Christian, though you believed I had been most strangely deceived. I thanked you then for your kindness, and I ask you *now*, for the sake of former confidence, and friendship, to read the following pages in the spirit of calm investigation and fervent prayer. It is because you have known me, that I write thus unto you.

But there are other Christian women scattered over the Southern States, a very large number of whom have never seen me, and never heard my name, and who feel *no* interest whatever in *me*. But I feel an interest in *you*, as branches of the same vine from whose root I daily draw the principle of spiritual vitality—Yes! Sisters in Christ I feel an interest in *you*, and often has the secret prayer arisen on your behalf. Lord "open thou their eyes that they may see wondrous things out of thy Law"—It is then, because I *do feel* and *do pray* for you, that I thus address you upon a subject about which of all others, perhaps you would rather not hear any thing; but, "would to God ye could bear with me a little in my folly, land indeed bear with me, for I am jealous over you with godly jealousy." Be not afraid then to read my appeal; it is *not* written in the heat of passion or prejudice, but in that solemn calmness which is the result of conviction and duty. It is true, I am going to tell you unwelcome truths, but I mean to speak those *truths in love*, and remember Solomon says, "faithful are the *wounds* of a friend." I do not believe the time has yet come when *Christian women* "will not endure sound doctrine," even on the subject of slavery, if it is spoken to them in tenderness and love, therefore I now address *you*. . . .

* * *

But perhaps you will be ready to query, why appeal to *women* on this subject? *We* do not make the laws which perpetuate slavery. *No* legislative power is vested in *us*; *we* can do nothing to overthrow the system, even if we wished to do so. To this I reply, I know you do not make the laws, but I also know that *you are the wives and mothers, the sisters and daughters of those who do;* and if you really suppose *you* can do nothing to overthrow slavery, you are greatly mistaken. You can do much in every way: four things I will name. 1st. You can read on this subject. 2d. You can pray over this subject. 3d. You can speak on this subject. 4th. You can *act* on this subject. I have not placed reading before praying because I regard it more important, but because, in order to pray aright, we must understand what we are praying for; it is only then we can "pray with the understanding and the spirit also."

1. Read then on the subject of slavery. Search the Scriptures daily, whether the things I have told you are true. Other books and papers might be a great help to you in this investigation, but they are not necessary, and it is hardly probable that your Committees of Vigilance[1] will allow you to have any other. The *Bible* then is the book I want you to read in the spirit of inquiry, and the spirit of prayer. Even the enemies of Abolitionists, acknowledge that their doctrines are drawn from it. In the great mob in Boston last autumn, when the books and papers of the Anti-Slavery Society were thrown out of the windows of their office, an individual laid hold of the Bible and was about tossing it out to the ground, when another reminded him that it was the Bible he had in his hand. "*O! 'tis all one*," he replied, and out went the sacred volume along with the rest. We thank him for the acknowledgment. Yes, "*it is all one*," for our books and papers are mostly commentaries on the Bible, and the Declaration. Read the *Bible* then, it contains the words of Jesus, and they are spirit and life. Judge for yourselves whether *he sanctioned* such a system of oppression and crime.

2. Pray over this subject. When you have entered into your closets, and shut to the doors, then pray to your father, who seeth in secret, that he would open your eyes to see whether slavery is *sinful*, and if it is, that he would enable you to bear a faithful, open and unshrinking testimony against it, and to do whatsoever your hands find to do, leaving the consequences entirely to him, who still says to us whenever we try to reason away duty from the fear of consequences. "*What is that to thee, follow thou me.*" Pray also for that poor slave, that he may be kept patient and submissive under his hard lot, until God is pleased to open the door of freedom to him without violence or bloodshed. Pray too for the master that his heart may be softened, and he made willing to acknowledge, as Joseph's brethren did, "Verily we are guilty concerning our

1. Self-appointed groups of Southern White men organized to confiscate abolitionist and other "incendiary" literature.

brother,"[2] before he will be compelled to add in consequence of Divine judgment, "therefore is all this evil come upon us." Pray also for all your brethren and sisters who are laboring in the righteous cause of Emancipation in the Northern States, England and the world. There is great encouragement for prayer in these words of our Lord. "Whatsoever ye shall ask the Father *in my name*, he *will give* it to you"[3]—Pray then without ceasing, in the closet and the social circle.

3. Speak on this subject. It is through the tongue, the pen, and the press, that truth is principally propagated. Speak then to your relatives, your friends, your acquaintances on the subject of slavery; be not afraid if you are conscientiously convinced it is *sinful*, to say so openly, but calmly, and to let your sentiments be known. If you are served by the slaves of others, try to ameliorate their condition as much as possible; never aggravate their faults, and thus add fuel to the fire of anger already kindled in a master and mistress's bosom; remember their extreme ignorance, and consider them as your Heavenly Father does the *less* culpable on this account, even when they do wrong things. Discountenance *all* cruelty to them, all starvation, all corporal chastisement; these may brutalize and *break* their spirits, but will never bond them to willing, cheerful obedience. If possible, see that they are comfortably and *seasonably* fed, whether in the house or the field; it is unreasonable and cruel to expect slaves to wait for their breakfast until eleven o'clock, when they rise at five or six. Do all you can, to induce their owners to clothe them well, and to allow them many little indulgences which would contribute to their comfort. Above all, try to persuade your husband, father, brothers and sons, that *slavery is a crime against God and man*, and that it is a great sin to keep *human beings* in such abject ignorance; to deny them the privilege of learning to read and write. The Catholics are universally condemned, for denying the Bible to the common people, but, *slaveholders must not* blame them, for *they* are doing the *very same thing*, and for the very same reason, neither of these systems can bear the light which bursts from the pages of that Holy Book. And lastly, endeavour to inculcate submission on the part of the slaves, but whilst doing this be faithful in pleading the cause of the oppressed.

Will *you* behold unheeding,
Life's holiest feelings crushed,
Where *woman's* heart is bleeding.
Shall *woman's* heart be hushed?

4. Act on this subject. Some of you *own* slaves yourselves. If you believe slavery is *Sinful*, set them at liberty, "undo the heavy burdens and let the oppressed go free." If they wish to remain with you, pay them wages, if not let them leave you. Should they remain teach them, and have them taught the common branches of an English education; they have minds and those minds, *ought to be improved*. So precious a talent as intellect, never was given to be wrapt in a napkin and buried in the earth. It is the *duty* of all, as far as they can, to improve their own mental faculties, because we are commanded to love God with *all our minds*, as well as with all our hearts, and we commit a great sin, if we *forbid or prevent* that cultivation of the mind in others, which would enable them to perform this duty. Teach your servants then to read etc., and encourage them to believe it is their *duty* to learn, if it were only that they might read the Bible.

But some of you will say, we can neither free our slaves nor teach them to read, for the laws of our state forbid it. Be not surprised when I say such wicked laws *ought to be no barrier* in the way of your duty, and I appeal to the Bible to prove this position.

2. Genesis 42:21.

3. John 16:23.

* * *

But some of you may say, if we do free our slaves, they will be taken up and sold, therefore there will be no use in doing it. Peter and John might just as well have said, we will not preach the gospel, for if we do, we shall be taken up and put in prison, therefore there will be no use in our preaching. *Consequences*, my friends, belong no more to *you*, than they did to these apostles. Duty is ours and events are God's. If you think slavery is sinful, all *you* have to do is to set your slaves at liberty, do all you can to protect them, and in humble faith and fervent prayer, commend them to your common Father. He can take care of them; but if for wise purposes he sees fit to allow them to be sold, this will afford you an opportunity of testifying openly, wherever you go, against the crime of *manstealing*. Such an act will be *clear robbery*, and if exposed, might, under the Divine direction, do the cause of Emancipation more good, than any thing that could happen, for "He makes even the wrath of man to praise him, and the remainder of wrath he will restrain."

I know that this doctrine of obeying *God*, rather than man, will be considered as dangerous and heretical by many, but I am not afraid openly to avow it, because it is the doctrine of the Bible; but I would not be understood to advocate resistance to any law however oppressive, if, in obeying it, I was not obliged to commit *sin*. If for instance, there was a law, which imposed imprisonment or a fine upon me if I manumitted a slave, I would on no account resist that law, I would set the slave free, and then go to prison or pay the fine. If a law commands me to *sin I will break it;* if it calls me to *suffer*, I will let it take its course *unresistingly*. The doctrine of blind obedience and unqualified submission to *any human* power, whether civil or ecclesiastical, is the doctrine of despotism, and ought to have no place among Republicans and Christians.

* * *

But you may say we are *women*, how can *our* hearts endure persecution? And why not? Have not *women* stood up in all the dignity and strength of moral courage to be the leaders of the people, and to bear a faithful testimony for the truth whenever the providence of God has called them to do so? Are there no *women* in that noble army of martyrs who are now singing the song of Moses and the Lamb? Who led out the women of Israel from the house of bondage, striking the timbrel, and singing the song of deliverance on the banks of that sea whose waters stood up like walls of crystal to open a passage for their escape? It was a *woman;* Miriam, the prophetess, the sister of Moses and Aaron. Who went up with Barak to Kadesh to fight against Jabin, King of Canaan, into whose hand Israel had been sold because of their iniquities? It was a *woman!*

* * *

The *women of the South can overthrow* this horrible system of oppression and cruelty, licentiousness and wrong. Such appeals to your legislatures would be irresistible, for there is something in the heart of man which *will bend under moral suasion*. There is a swift witness for truth in his bosom, which *will respond to truth* when it is uttered with calmness and dignity. If you could obtain but six signatures to such a petition in only one state, I would say, send up that petition, and be not in the least discouraged by the scoffs and jeers of the heartless, or the resolution of the house to lay it on the table. It will be a great thing if the subject can be introduced into your legislatures in any way, even by *women*, and *they* will be the most likely to introduce it there in the best possible manner, as a matter of *morals* and *religion*, not of expediency or politics. You may petition, too, the different ecclesiastical bodies of the slave states. Slavery must be attacked with the whole power of truth and the sword of the spirit. You must take it up on *Christian* ground, and fight against it with Christian weapons, whilst your feet are shod with the preparation of the gospel of peace. And *you are now* loudly called upon by the cries of the widow and the orphan, to arise and gird yourselves for this great moral conflict, with the whole armour of righteousness upon the right hand and on the left.

* * *

Sisters in Christ, I have done. As a Southern, I have felt it was my duty to address you. I have endeavoured to set before you the exceeding sinfulness of slavery, and to point you to the example of those noble women who have been raised up in the church to effect great revolutions, and to suffer for the truth's sake. I have appealed to your sympathies as women, to your sense of duty as *Christian* woman. I have attempted to vindicate the Abolitionists, to prove the entire safety of immediate Emancipation, and to plead the cause of the poor and oppressed, I have done—I have sowed the seeds of truth, but I well know, that even if an Apollos were to follow in my steps to water them, "*God only* can give the increase." To Him then who is able to prosper the work of his servant's hand, I commend this Appeal in fervent prayer, that as he "hath chosen the weak things of the world, I commend things which are mighty," so He may cause His blessing, to descend and carry conviction to the hearts of many Lydias through these speaking page. Farewell—Count me knot your "enemy because I have told you the truth," but believe me in unfeigned affection,

Your sympathizing Friend,

Angelina E. Grimké

Questions to Consider

1. In what ways did Angelina encourage Southern Christian women to see themselves as alienated from their own society? In what ways did she encourage them to see their lot as tied to that of their slaves?
2. Why is it important to understand a legacy of Southern dissent? What does this piece contribute to our understanding of Southern diversity?

Robert E. Lee

1807–1870

As the son of the famous Revolutionary War General Henry "Light-Horse Harry" Lee, Robert E. Lee was born into one of the most well-respected families in the American South. After receiving an early education in which he demonstrated a gift for mathematics, Lee attended West Point, where he graduated second in his class in 1829. He received his commission as an army officer and served as chief engineer for the next 17 years. Promoted for his gallantry during the Mexican-American War, Lee returned to West Point where he served as superintendent from 1852 until 1855. When abolitionist John Brown and a band of 21 men invaded Harper's Ferry, Virginia, in a plan to start a slave revolt in the South, Lee was in charge of the federal troops that crushed the insurrection.

Although Lee belonged to one of the oldest families in the South, he was an ardent Unionist and opposed Southern secession. Lee's loyalty to Virginia caused him to decline the appointment when President Lincoln asked him to take field command of the Union Army in the opening days of the Civil War. When he learned that his state had seceded from the Union, he resigned from the army and returned to Virginia, where he served as military advisor to Confederate President Jefferson Davis. After two months, Davis appointed Lee to the post of field commander of the Army of Virginia.

During the early part of the war, Lee waged a military campaign that was largely successful against the federal forces, but after the loss of "Stonewall" Jackson at the battle of Chancellorsville, the fortunes of the Southern army began to decline, due at least in part to the inexperience of the troops and the tendency of Southern generals to ignore Lee's strategy. After the Southern defeat at the battle of Gettysburg, Lee sought to resign his post, but Davis persuaded him to carry on as commander. The federal troops were too strong for the less experienced Southern army, however, and Lee, who had since been named commander in chief of the Confederate Army, finally surrendered to Union commander Ulysses Grant at Appomattox Courthouse on 9 April 1865. After the war, Lee became president of Washington College, which was later renamed Washington and Lee University in his honor.

Robert E. Lee exemplified many of the traits that were most valued in the Southern aristocracy, and more than a few military historians have called him one of the greatest military strategists who ever lived. In many ways, he personified the traditions of the chivalric Southern gentleman, and his noble bearing, courage, and adherence to principle have made him a towering figure in Southern literature such as Edgar Lee Masters's "Lee: A Dramatic Long Poem," John Rueben Thompson's "Lee to the Rear," and novels by authors such as MacKinlay Kantor and Mary Johnston.

Although Lee never wrote for publication, his addresses and letters, a sample of which are included here, are considered to be the product of a disciplined and serious mind. The general critical consensus is that while he was well-read in military strategy and excelled in mathematics, his familiarity with the classics of literature was not great. Nevertheless, his letters give the modern reader a window into the mind of an exceptional military man and an archetypal Southern aristocrat.

Selected Letters

April 20, 1861

My Dear Sister:

I am grieved at my inability to see you. I have been waiting for a more "convenient season," which has brought to many before me deep and lasting regret. We are now in a state of war which will yield to nothing. The whole South is in a state of revolution, into which Virginia, after a long struggle, has been drawn; and though I recognize no necessity for this state of things, and would have forborne and pleaded to the end for redress of grievances, real or supposed, yet in my own person I had to meet the question whether I should take part against my native State. With all my devotion to the Union, and the feeling of loyalty and duty of an American citizen, I have not been able to make up my mind to raise my hand against my relatives, my children, my home. I have, therefore, resigned my commission in the Army, and save in defense of my native State—with the sincere hope that my poor services may never be needed—I hope I may never be called upon to draw my sword.

I know you will blame me; but you must think as kindly of me as you can, and believe that I have endeavored to do what I thought right. To show you the feeling and struggle it has cost me, I send you a copy of my letter of resignation. I have no time for more.

May God guard and protect you and yours, and shower upon you everlasting blessings, is the prayer of

Your devoted brother,

R. E. Lee

GENERAL ORDERS, NO. 116

Headquarters, Army Northern Virginia
October 2, 1862

In reviewing the achievements of the army during the present campaign, the Commanding General cannot withhold the expression of his admiration of the indomitable courage it has displayed in battle, and its cheerful endurance of privation and hardship on the march.

Since your great victories around Richmond, you have defeated the enemy at Cedar Mountain, expelled him from the Rappahannock, and, after a conflict of three days, utterly repulsed him on the plains of Manassas, and forced him to take shelter within the fortifications around his Capital. Without halting for repose, you crossed the Potomac, stormed the heights of Harper's Ferry, made prisoners of more than 11,600 men, and captured upward of seventy pieces of artillery, all of their small arms, and other munitions of war. While one corps of the army was thus engaged another insured its success by arresting at Boonsboro the combined armies of the enemy, advancing under their favorite general to the relief of their beleaguered comrades.

On the field of Sharpsburg, with less than one-third his numbers, you resisted from daylight until dark the whole army of the enemy, and repulsed every attack along his entire front of more than four miles in extent.

The whole of the following day you stood prepared to resume the conflict on the same ground, and retired next morning without molestation across the Potomac.

Two attempts subsequently made by the enemy to follow you across the river have resulted in his complete discomfiture and his being driven back with loss. Achievements such as these demanded much valor and patriotism. History records few examples of greater fortitude and endurance than this army has exhibited, and I am commissioned by the President to thank you in the name of the Confederate States for the undying fame you have won for their arms.

Much as you have done, much more remains to be accomplished. The enemy again threatens us with invasion, and to your tried valor and patriotism the country looks with confidence for deliverance and safety. Your past exploits give assurance that this confidence is not misplaced.

R. E. Lee
General Commanding

Camp Fredericksburg
26th December, 1862

My precious little Agnes:[1]

I have not heard of you for a long time. I wish you were with me, for, always solitary, I am sometimes weary, and long for the reunion of my family once again. But I will not speak of myself, but of you. . . .

I have only seen the ladies in this vicinity when flying from the enemy, and it caused me acute grief to witness their exposure and suffering. But a more noble spirit was never displayed anywhere. The faces of old and young were wreathed with smiles and glowed with happiness at the sacrifices for the good of their country. Many have lost *everything*. What the fire and shells of the enemy spared, their pillagers destroyed.

1. Lee's daughter.

But God will shelter them, I know. So much heroism will not be unregarded. I can only hold oral communication with your sister, and have forbidden the scouts to bring any writing, and have taken back some that I had given them for her. If caught it would compromise them. They only convey messages. I learn in that way she is well. . . .

Your devoted father,
R. E. Lee

GENERAL ORDER, NO. 9

Headquarters, Army of Northern Virginia
April 10, 1865

After four years of arduous service, marked by unsurpassed courage and fortitude, the Army of Northern Virginia has been compelled to yield to overwhelming numbers and resources. I need not tell the survivors of so many hard-fought battles, who have remained steadfast to the last, that I have consented to this result from no distrust of them; but feeling that valor and devotion could accomplish nothing that could compensate for the loss that would have attended the continuation of the contest, I have determined to avoid the useless sacrifice of those whose past services have endeared them to their countrymen. By the terms of the agreement, officers and men can return to their homes, and remain there until exchanged.

You will take with you the *satisfaction that proceeds from the consciousness of duty faithfully performed;* and I earnestly pray that a merciful God will extend to you His blessing and protection. With an unceasing admiration of your constancy, and devotion to your country, and a grateful remembrance of your kind and generous consideration of myself, I bid you an affectionate farewell.

R. E. Lee
General

Lexington, Virginia
March 12, 1868

My Dear Rob:[1] I am sorry to learn from your letter of the 1st that the winter has been so hard on your wheat. I hope, however, the present good weather is shedding its influence upon it, and that it will turn out better than it promises. You must, however, take a lesson from the last season. What you do cultivate, do well. Improve and prepare the land in the best manner; your labour will be less, and your profits more. Your flat lands were always uncertain in wet winters. The uplands were more sure. Is it not possible that some unbidden guest may have been feasting on your corn? Six hundred bushels are a large deficit in casting up your account for the year. But you must make it up by economy and good management. A farmer's motto should be *toil and trust.* I am glad that you have got your lime and sown your oats and clover. Do you use the drill or sow broadcast? I shall try to get down to see you if I go to Richmond, for I am anxious to know how you are progressing and to see if in any way I can aid you. Whenever I can, you must let me know. You must still think about your house and make up your mind as to the site and kind, and collect the material. I can help you to any kind of plan, and with some ready money to pay the mechanics. I have recently had a visit from Dr. Oliver, of Scotland, who is examining lands for immigrants from his country. He seems to be a sensible and judicious man. From his account, I do not think the Scotch and

1. Lee's son.

English would suit your part of the country. It would require time for them to become acclimated, and they would probably get dissatisfied, especially as there is so much mountainous region where they could be accommodated. I think you will have to look to the Germans; perhaps the Hollanders, as a class, would be the most useful. When the railroad shall have been completed to West Point, I think there will be no difficulty in getting the Whites among you. I would try to get some of our own young men in your employ. I rode out the other day to Mr. Andrew Cameron's and went into the field where he was plowing. I took great pleasure in following the plows around the circuit. He had four in operation. Three of them were held by his former comrades in the army, who are regularly employed by him, and, he says, much to his satisfaction and profit. People have got to work now. It is creditable to them to do so; their bodies and their minds are benefited by it, and those who can and will work will be advanced by it. You will never prosper with the Blacks, and it is abhorrent to a reflecting mind to be supporting and cherishing those who are plotting and working for your injury, and all of whose sympathies and associations are antagonistic to yours. I wish them no evil in the world—on the contrary, will do them every good in my power, and know that they are misled by those to whom they have given their confidence; but our material, social, and political interests are naturally with the Whites. Mr. Davis's trial was fixed for the last of this month. If Judge Chase's presence is essential, I do not see how it can take place, unless that of Mr. Johnson is to be postponed. I suppose that will be decided to-day or to-morrow, and then I shall know what to expect. I shall not go to Richmond unless necessary, as it is always inconvenient for me to leave home, and I am not at all well. Your poor mother is also more ailing than she is ordinarily, in consequence of a cold she has taken. But it is passing away, I trust. I must leave you to her and Mildred for all local and domestic news. Custis and the boys are well, and 'Powhattie,' I hope, has got rid of the chills. We hear regularly from Mary and Agnes, who seem to be enjoying themselves, and I do not think from their programme that they will get back to us till summer. All unite in much love, and I am always,

Your father,
R. E. Lee

Questions to Consider

1. Lee is often considered the epitome of the Southern aristocratic gentleman. What values exhibited in his letters warrant this conclusion?
2. Where do you find examples of Lee's well-known logical mind demonstrated in his letters?

Jefferson Davis

1808–1889

On 9 January 1861, delegates of the Mississippi secession convention met and voted to leave the Union by a count of 84-15. U.S. Senator Jefferson Davis, who had advised caution during the turbulent months following Lincoln's election, sent a wire to Governor John Pettus, stating, "Judge what Mississippi requires of me and place me accordingly." On 19 January 1861, Davis received word to return home to Mississippi immediately. Two days later, he delivered his farewell address to the U.S. Senate, and on the following day, Davis and his wife Varina departed Washington.

Representatives from seceded states were scheduled to meet in Montgomery, Alabama on 4 February 1861. Many Southerners speculated on the role Jefferson Davis might play in the new Confederacy. According to Davis's biographer, William C. Davis, "some considered him for Secretary of War, others for general-in-chief. Most believed that Davis would be president." Varina sincerely hoped the prevailing sentiment would not bear out. "He did not know the arts of the politician," she said, "and would not practise [*sic*] them if understood." Jefferson Davis concurred. "The post of Presdt. of the provisional government is one of great responsibility and difficulty," he wrote to a delegate attending the Montgomery convention; "I have no confidence in my capacity to meet its requirements." The delegation apparently took no heed of Davis's misgivings. On 9 February 1861, in a unanimous vote, the delegates chose Jefferson Davis to serve as President of the Confederate States of America.

Jefferson Davis faced a number of challenges as president of the newly formed Confederacy. One central problem concerned the creation of a sense of nationalism in a people that championed state sovereignty. Historian Drew Faust explains that the creation of Confederate nationalism "was the South's effort to build a consensus at home, to secure a foundation of popular support for a new nation and what quickly became a costly war." The creation of this new ideology and identity was at once "a political and social act, incorporating both the powerful and the comparatively powerless into a negotiation of the terms under which all might work together for the Confederate cause." Historian Gary W. Gallagher has argued that many historians, including Faust, have overemphasized the degree to which creating a sense of Confederate nationalism posed a problem to the White South. These scholars have, according to Gallagher, "slighted the extent to which White Southerners identified with one another as Confederates and looked forward to living in a country untrammeled by political interference from the North." In any case, Davis, as president of the Confederacy, played an important role in shaping the rhetoric of nationalist thought, designed, as one Confederate claimed, "to excite in our citizens an ardent and enduring attachment to our Government and its institutions." Davis employed a number of rhetorical strategies designed to foster Confederate nationalism, many of which can be found in the excerpts included in this volume.

Other challenges faced Davis. As historian Emory M. Thomas explains in *The Confederacy as a Revolutionary Experience,* the Confederate government "albeit unwittingly, transformed the South from a state's rights confederation into a centralized, national state. In doing so," Thomas continues, "the government, or more usually Jefferson Davis as leader and symbol of the civilian Confederacy, incurred the displeasure of those who felt the government had gone too far and of those who thought the government had not gone far enough." Waging a war for state sovereignty clearly taxed the Confederate government's imagination and resources.

Two areas that proved especially problematic for the Confederacy are highlighted in these excerpts: raising its army and managing its economy. Davis, according to Thomas, recognized immediately the changing military realities that necessitated a large army responsible to the national government, and not those of the individual states. He therefore adopted the traditional practice of "accepting militia units from states and then mustering them into the Confederate States Army," thus binding troops to the national service instead of the state that sent them. Davis would have preferred to rely on volunteerism to staff the C.S.A., but when critical manpower shortages threatened the viability of the army in mid-1862, the Confederate Congress invoked military conscription. Both actions contradicted states' rights ideology. Thomas argues that White Southerners generally accepted these actions by claiming that a war for independence necessitated them. The question remains, according to Thomas, whether a political doctrine can suffer erosion and still remain a viable war aim.

Financing the war effort proved equally vexing to Confederate leaders. Thomas notes that the Confederacy initially relied on traditional methods of raising money: issuing loans and bonds and printing money. Runaway inflation prompted the government, however, to employ new strategies. The Confederate government enacted a graduated income tax in 1863. Moreover, the War Department also began not only to impress needed goods but also to subsidize the Southern war industry. Both moves, according to Thomas, "made a substantial contribution to the creation of a centralized Confederate state." None of these policies went unchallenged. Moreover, the lack of a party system in the Confederacy meant that opposition was unchanneled, often degenerating into petty bickering among politicians. In the estimation of many historians, Jefferson Davis lacked the charisma or the skill to handle this opposition deftly. Others have argued that the Confederacy's inability to withstand the crushing power of the Union Army, and not a failure of Confederate nationalism or the limits of the Confederate government, resulted in defeat. In either scenario, Jefferson Davis, as President of the Confederacy, looms large.

Farewell Address

SENATE CHAMBER, U.S. CAPITOL, JANUARY 21, 1861

I rise, Mr. President,[1] for the purpose of announcing to the Senate that I have satisfactory evidence that the State of Mississippi, by a solemn ordinance of her people in convention assembled, has declared her separation from the United States. Under these circumstances, of course my functions are terminated here. It has seemed to me proper, however, that I should appear in the Senate to announce that fact to my associates, and I will say but very little more. The occasion does not invite me to go into argument; and my physical condition would not permit me to do so if it were otherwise; and yet it seems to become me to say something on the part of the State I here represent, on an occasion so solemn as this.

It is known to Senators who have served with me here, that I have for many years advocated, as an essential attribute of State sovereignty, the right of a State to secede from the Union. Therefore, if I had not believed there was justifiable cause; if I had thought that Mississippi was acting without sufficient provocation, or without an existing necessity, I should still, under my theory of the Government, because of my allegiance to the State of which I am a citizen, have been bound by her action. I, however, may be permitted to say that I do think she has justifiable cause, and I approve of her act. I conferred with her people before that act was taken, counseled them then that if the state of things which they apprehended should exist when the convention met, they should take the action which they have now adopted.

I hope none who hear me will confound this expression of mine with the advocacy of the right of a State to remain in the Union, and to disregard its constitutional obligations by the nullification of the law. Such is not my theory. Nullification and secession,[2] so often confounded, are indeed antagonistic principles. Nullification is a remedy which it is sought to apply within the Union, and against the agent of the States. It is only to be justified when the agent has violated his constitutional obligation, and a State, assuming to judge for itself, denies the right of the agent thus to act, and appeals to the other States of the Union for a decision; but when the States themselves, and when the people of the States, have so acted as to convince us that

1. John C. Breckinridge, President James Buchanan's vice president and president of the Senate.
2. The Doctrine of Nullification was a theory put forth by such Southern politicians as John C. Calhoun, who argued that Acts of Congress could be accepted or rejected (nullified) by each individual state; this is contrasted with secession, which was the theory that any state had the right to secede from the Union for any cause.

they will not regard our constitutional rights, then, and then for the first time, arises the doctrine of secession in its practical application.

A great man who now reposes with his fathers, and who has been often arraigned for a want of fealty to the Union, advocated the doctrine of nullification, because it preserved the Union. It was because of his deep-seated attachment to the Union, his determination to find some remedy for existing ills short of a severance of the ties which bound South Carolina to the other States, that Mr. Calhoun advocated the doctrine of nullification, which he proclaimed to be peaceful, to be within the limits of State power, not to disturb the Union, but only to be a means of bringing the agent before the tribunal of the States for their judgment.

Secession belongs to a different class of remedies. It is to be justified upon the basis that the States are sovereign. There was a time when none denied it. I hope the time may come again, when a better comprehension of the theory of our Government, and the inalienable rights of the people of the States, will prevent any one from denying that each State is a sovereign, and thus may reclaim the grants which it has made to any agent whomsoever.

I therefore say I concur in the action of the people of Mississippi, believing it to be necessary and proper, and should have been bound by their action if my belief had been otherwise; and this brings me to the important point which I wish on this last occasion to present to the Senate. It is by this confounding of nullification and secession that the name of a great man, whose ashes now mingle with his mother earth, has been invoked to justify coercion against a seceded State. The phrase "to execute the laws," was an expression which General Jackson applied to the case of a State refusing to obey the laws while yet a member of the Union. That is not the case which is now presented. The laws are to be executed over the United States, and upon the people of the United States. They have no relation to any foreign country. It is a perversion of terms, at least it is a great misapprehension of the case, which cites that expression for application to a State which has withdrawn from the Union. You may make war on a foreign State. If it be the purpose of gentlemen, they may make war against a State which has withdrawn from the Union; but there are no laws of the United States to be executed within the limits of a seceded State. A State finding herself in the condition in which Mississippi has judged she is, in which her safety requires that she should provide for the maintenance of her rights out of the Union, surrenders all the benefits, (and they are known to be many,) deprives herself of the advantages, (they are known to be great,) severs all the ties of affection, (and they are close and enduring,) which have bound her to the Union; and thus divesting herself of every benefit, taking upon herself every burden, she claims to be exempt from any power to execute the laws of the United States within her limits.

I well remember an occasion when Massachusetts was arraigned before the bar of the Senate, and when then the doctrine of coercion was rife and to be applied against her because of the rescue of a fugitive slave in Boston. My opinion then was the same that it is now. Not in a spirit of egotism, but to show that I am not influenced in my opinion because the case is my own, I refer to that time and that occasion as containing the opinion which I then entertained, and on which my present conduct is based. I then said, if Massachusetts, following her through a stated line of conduct, chooses to take the last step which separates her from the Union, it is her right to go, and I will neither vote one dollar nor one man to coerce her back; but will say to her, God speed, in memory of the kind associations which once existed between her and the other States.

It has been a conviction of pressing necessity, it has been a belief that we are to be deprived in the Union of the rights which our fathers bequeathed to us, which has brought Mississippi into her present decision. She has heard proclaimed the theory that all men are created free and equal, and this made the basis of an attack upon her social institutions; and the sacred Declaration of Independence has been invoked to maintain the position of the equality of the races. That Declaration of Independence is to be construed by the circumstances and purposes for which it was made. The communities were declaring their independence; the people of those communities were asserting that no man was born—to use the language of Mr. Jefferson—booted and spurred to ride over the rest of mankind; that men were created equal—meaning the men of the political community; that there was no divine right to rule; that no man inherited the right to govern; that there were no classes by which power and place descended to families, but that all stations were equally within the grasp of each member of the body-politic. These were the great principles they announced; these were the purposes for which they made their declaration; these were the ends to which their enunciation was directed. They have no reference to the slave; else, how happened it that among the items of arraignment made against George III was that he endeavored to do just what the North has been endeavoring of late to do—to stir up insurrection among our slaves? Had the Declaration announced that the negroes were free and equal, how was the Prince to be arraigned for stirring up insurrection among them? And how was this to be enumerated among the high crimes which caused the colonies to sever their connection with the mother country? When our Constitution was formed, the same idea was rendered more palpable, for there we find provision made for that very class of persons as property; they were not put upon the footing of equality with white men—not even upon that of paupers and convicts; but, so far as representation was concerned, were discriminated against as a lower caste, only to be represented in the numerical proportion of three fifths.

Then, Senators, we recur to the compact which binds us together; we recur to the principles upon which our Government was founded; and when you deny them, and when you deny to us the right to withdraw from a Government which thus perverted threatens to be destructive of our rights, we but tread in the path of our fathers when we proclaim our independence, and take the hazard. This is done not in hostility to others, not to injure any section of the country, not even for our own pecuniary benefit; but from the high and solemn motive of defending and protecting the rights we inherited, and which it is our sacred duty to transmit unshorn to our children.

I find in myself, perhaps, a type of the general feeling of my constituents towards yours. I am sure I feel no hostility to you, Senators from the North. I am sure there is not one of you, whatever sharp discussion there may have been between us, to whom I cannot now say, in the presence of my God, I wish you well; and such, I am sure, is the feeling of the people whom I represent towards those whom you represent. I therefore feel that I but express their desire when I say I hope, and they hope, for peaceful relations with you, though we must part. They may be mutually beneficial to us in the future, as they have been in the past, if you so will it. The reverse may bring disaster on every portion of the country; and if you will have it thus, we will invoke the God of our fathers, who delivered them from the power of the lion, to protect us from the ravages of the bear; and thus, putting our trust in God and in our own firm hearts and strong arms, we will vindicate the right as best we may.

In the course of my service here, associated at different times with a great variety of Senators, I see now around me some with whom I have served long; there have been points of collision; but whatever of offense there has been to me, I leave here; I carry with me no hostile remembrance. Whatever offense I have given which has not been redressed, or for which satisfaction has not been demanded, I have, Senators, in this hour of our parting, to offer you my apology for any pain which, in heat of discussion, I have inflicted. I go hence unencumbered of the remembrance of any injury received, and having discharged the duty of making the only reparation in my power for any injury offered.

Mr. President, and Senators, having made the announcement which the occasion seemed to me to require, it only remains to me to bid you a final adieu.

Second Inaugural Address

VIRGINIA CAPITOL, RICHMOND, FEBRUARY 22, 1862

Fellow-Citizens: On this the birthday of the man most identified with the establishment of American independence, and beneath the monument erected to commemorate his heroic virtues and those of his compatriots, we have assembled to usher into existence the Permanent Government of the Confederate States. Through this instrumentality, under the favor of Divine Providence, we hope to perpetuate the principles of our revolutionary fathers. The day, the memory, and the purpose seem fitly associated.

It is with mingled feelings of humility and pride that I appear to take, in the presence of the people and before high Heaven, the oath prescribed as a qualification for the exalted station to which the unanimous voice of the people has called me. Deeply sensible of all that is implied by this manifestation of the people's confidence, I am yet more profoundly impressed by the vast responsibility of the office, and humbly feel my own unworthiness.

In return for their kindness I can offer assurances of the gratitude with which it is received; and can but pledge a zealous devotion of every faculty to the service of those who have chosen me as their Chief Magistrate.

When a long course of class legislation, directed not to the general welfare, but to the aggrandizement of the Northern section of the Union, culminated in a warfare on the domestic institutions of the Southern States—when the dogmas of a sectional party, substituted for the provisions of the constitutional compact, threatened to destroy the sovereign rights of the States, six of those States, withdrawing from the Union, confederated together to exercise the right and perform the duty of instituting a Government which would better secure the liberties for the preservation of which that Union was established.

Whatever of hope some may have entertained that a returning sense of justice would remove the danger with which our rights were threatened, and render it possible to preserve the Union of the Constitution, must have been dispelled by the malignity and barbarity of the Northern States in the prosecution of the existing war. The confidence of the most hopeful among us must have been destroyed by the disregard they have recently exhibited for all the time-honored bulwarks of civil and religious liberty. Bastiles[1] filled with prisoners, arrested without civil process or indictment duly found; the writ of *habeas corpus*[2] suspended by Executive mandate; a State Legislature controlled by the imprisonment of members whose avowed principles suggested to the Federal Executive that there might be another added to the list of seceded States; elections held

1. A reference to the Parisian prison, the Bastile, which was destroyed by the populace during the French Revolution.

2. A writ of *habeas corpus* requires that a prisoner be brought before a judge in a timely manner.

under threats of a military power; civil officers, peaceful citizens, and gentlewomen incarcerated for opinion's sake—proclaimed the incapacity of our late associates to administer a Government as free, liberal, and humane as that established for our common use.

For proof of the sincerity of our purpose to maintain our ancient institutions, we may point to the Constitution of the Confederacy and the laws enacted under it, as well as to the fact that through all the necessities of an unequal struggle there has been no act on our part to impair personal liberty or the freedom of speech, of thought, or of the press. The courts have been open, the judicial functions fully executed, and every right of the peaceful citizen maintained as securely as if a war of invasion had not disturbed the land.

The people of the States now confederated became convinced that the Government of the United States had fallen into the hands of a sectional majority, who would pervert that most sacred of all trusts to the destruction of the rights which it was pledged to protect. They believed that to remain longer in the Union would subject them to a continuance of a disparaging discrimination, submission to which would be inconsistent with their welfare, and intolerable to a proud people. They therefore determined to sever its bonds and establish a new Confederacy for themselves.

The experiment instituted by our revolutionary fathers, of a voluntary Union of sovereign States for purposes specified in a solemn compact, had been perverted by those who, feeling power and forgetting right, were determined to respect no law but their own will. The Government had ceased to answer the ends for which it was ordained and established. To save ourselves from a revolution which, in its silent but rapid progress, was about to place us under the despotism of numbers, and to preserve in spirit, as well as in form, a system of government we believed to be peculiarly fitted to our condition, and full of promise for mankind, we determined to make a new association, composed of States homogeneous in interest, in policy, and in feeling.

True to our traditions of peace and our love of justice, we sent commissioners to the United States to propose a fair and amicable settlement of all questions of public debt or property which might be in dispute. But the Government at Washington, denying our right to self-government, refused even to listen to any proposals for a peaceful separation. Nothing was then left to do but to prepare for war.

The first year in our history has been the most eventful in the annals of this continent. A new Government has been established, and its machinery put in operation over an area exceeding seven hundred thousand square miles. The great principles upon which we have been willing to hazard everything that is dear to man have made conquests for us which could never have been achieved by the sword. Our Confederacy has grown from six to thirteen States; and Maryland, already united to us by hallowed memories and material interests, will, I believe, when able to speak with unstifled voice, connect her destiny with the South. Our people have rallied with unexampled unanimity to the support of the great principles of constitutional government, with firm resolve to perpetuate by arms the right which they could not peacefully secure. A million of men, it is estimated, are now standing in hostile array, and waging war along a frontier of thousands of miles. Battles have been fought, sieges have been conducted, and, although the contest is not ended, and the tide for the moment is against us, the final result in our favor is not doubtful.

The period is near at hand when our foes must sink under the immense load of debt which they have incurred, a debt which in their effort to subjugate us has already attained such fearful dimensions as will subject them to burdens which must continue to oppress them for generations to come.

We too have had our trials and difficulties. That we are to escape them in future is not to be hoped. It was to be expected when we entered upon this war that it would expose our people to sacrifices and cost them much, both of money and blood. But we knew the value of the object for which we struggled, and understood the nature of the war in which we were engaged. Nothing could be so bad as failure, and any sacrifice would be cheap as the price of success in such a contest.

But the picture has its lights as well as its shadows. This great strife has awakened in the people the highest emotions and qualities of the human soul. It is cultivating feelings of patriotism, virtue, and courage. Instances of self-sacrifice and of generous devotion to the noble cause for which we are contending are rife throughout the land. Never has a people evinced a more determined spirit than that now animating men, women, and children in every part of our country. Upon the first call the men flew to arms, and wifes and mothers send their husbands and sons to battle without a murmur of regret.

It was, perhaps, in the ordination of Providence that we were to be taught the value of our liberties by the price which we pay for them.

The recollections of this great contest, with all its common traditions of glory, of sacrifice and blood, will be the bond of harmony and enduring affection amongst the people, producing unity in policy, fraternity in sentiment, and just effort in war.

Nor have the material sacrifices of the past year been made without some corresponding benefits. If the acquiescence of foreign nations in a pretended blockade has deprived us of our commerce with them, it is fast making us a self-supporting and an independent people. The blockade, if effectual and permanent, could only serve to divert our industry from the production of articles for export and employ it in supplying the commodities for domestic use.

It is a satisfaction that we have maintained the war by our unaided exertions. We have neither asked nor received assistance from any quarter. Yet the interest involved is not wholly our own. The world at large is concerned in opening our markets to its commerce. When the independence of the Confederate States is recognized by the nations of the earth, and we are free to follow our interests and inclinations by cultivating foreign trade, the Southern States will offer to manufacturing nations the most favorable markets which ever invited their commerce. Cotton, sugar, rice, tobacco, provisions, timber, and naval stores will furnish attractive exchanges. Nor would the constancy of these supplies be likely to be disturbed by war. Our confederate strength will be too great to tempt aggression; and never was there a people whose interests and principles committed them so fully to a peaceful policy as those of the Confederate States. By the character of their productions they are too deeply interested in foreign commerce wantonly to disturb it. War of conquest they cannot wage, because the Constitution of their Confederacy admits of no coerced association. Civil war there cannot be between States held together by their volition only. The rule of voluntary association, which cannot fail to be conservative, by securing just and impartial government at home, does not diminish the security of the obligations by which the Confederate States may be bound to foreign nations. In proof of this, it is to be remembered that, at the first moment of asserting their right to secession, these States proposed a settlement on the basis of the common liability for the obligations of the General Government.

Fellow-citizens, after the struggle of ages had consecrated the right of the Englishman to constitutional representative government, our colonial ancestors were forced to vindicate that birthright by an appeal to arms. Success crowned their efforts, and they provided for the posterity a peaceful remedy against future aggression.

The tyranny of an unbridled majority, the most odious and least responsible form of despotism, has denied us both the right and the remedy. Therefore we are in arms to renew such sacrifices as our fathers made to the holy cause of constitutional liberty. At the darkest hour of our struggle the Provisional gives place to the Permanent Government. After a series of successes and victories, which covered our arms with glory, we have recently met with serious disasters. But in the heart of a people resolved to be free these disasters tend but to stimulate to increased resistance.

To show ourselves worthy of the inheritance bequeathed to us by the patriots of the Revolution, we must emulate that heroic devotion which made reverse to them but the crucible in which their patriotism was refined.

With confidence in the wisdom and virtue of those who will share with me the responsibility and aid me in the conduct of public affairs; securely relying on the patriotism and courage of the people, of which the present war has furnished so many examples, I deeply feel the weight of the responsibilities I now, with unaffected diffidence, am about to assume; and, fully realizing the inequality of human power to guide and to sustain, my hope is reverently fixed on Him whose favor is ever vouchsafed to the cause which is just. With humble gratitude and adoration, acknowledging the Providence which has so visibly protected the Confederacy during its brief but eventful career, to thee, O God, I trustingly commit myself, and prayerfully invoke thy blessing on my country and its cause.

Speech at Jackson, Miss.

HOUSE CHAMBER, MISSISSIPPI CAPITOL, 26 DECEMBER 1862

Friends and Fellow-Citizens, Gentlemen of the House of Representatives and Senate of the State of Mississippi: After an absence of nearly two years I again find myself among those who, from the days of my childhood, have ever been the trusted objects of my affections, those for whose good I have ever striven, and whose interest I have sometimes hoped I may have contributed to subserve. Whatever fortunes I may have achieved in life have been gained as a representative of Mississippi, and before all, I have labored for the advancement of her glory and honor. I now, for the first time in my career, find myself the representative of a wider circle of interest; but a circle in which the interests of Mississippi are still embraced. Two years ago, nearly, I left you to assume the duties which had devolved on me as the representative of the new Confederacy. The responsibilities of this position have occupied all my time, and have left me no opportunity for mingling with my friends in Mississippi, or for sharing in the dangers which have menaced them. But, wherever duty may have called me, my heart has been with you and the success of the cause in which we are all engaged has been first in my thoughts and in my prayers. I thought when I left Mississippi that the service to which I was called would prove to be but temporary. The last time I had the honor of addressing you from this stand, I was influenced by that idea. I then imagined that it might be my fortune again to lead Mississippians in the field, and to be with them where danger was to be braved and glory won. I thought to find that place which I believed to be suited to my capacity: that of an officer in the service of the State of Mississippi. For, although in the discharge of my duties as President of the Confederate States, I had determined to make no distinction between the various parts of the country—to know no separate State—yet my heart has always beat more warmly for Mississippi, and I have looked on Mississippi soldiers with a pride and emotion such as no others inspired. But it was decided differently. I was called to another sphere of action. How, in that sphere, I have discharged the duties and obligations imposed on me, it does not become me to constitute myself the judge. It is for others to decide that question. But, speaking to you with that frankness and that confidence with which I have always spoken to you, and which partakes of the nature of thinking aloud, I can say with my hand upon my heart, that whatever I have done, has been done with the sincere purpose of promoting the noble cause in which we are engaged. The period which has elapsed since I left you is short; for the time, which may appear long in the life of man, is short in the history of a nation. And in that short period remarkable changes have been wrought in all the circumstances by which we are surrounded. At the time of which I speak, the question presented to our people was "will there be war!" This was the subject of universal speculation. We had chosen to exercise an indisputable right—the right to separate from those with whom we conceived association to be no longer possible, and to establish a government of our own. I was among those who, from the beginning, predicted war as the consequence of secession, although I must admit that the contest has assumed proportions more gigantic than I had anticipated. I predicted war not because our right to secede and to form a government of our own was not indisputable and clearly defined in the spirit of that declaration which rests the right to govern on the consent of the governed, but because I foresaw that the wickedness of the North would precipitate a war upon us. Those who supposed that the exercise of this right of separation could not produce war, have had cause to be convinced that they had credited their recent associates of the North with a moderation, a sagacity, a morality they did not possess. You have been involved in a war waged for the gratification of the lust of power and of aggrandizement, for your conquest and your subjugation, with a malignant ferocity and with a disregard and a contempt of the usages of civilization, entirely unequalled in history. Such, I have ever warned you, were the characteristics of the Northern people—of those with whom our ancestors entered into a Union of consent, and with whom they formed a constitutional compact. And yet, such was the attachment of our people for that Union, such their devotion to it, that those who desired preparation to be made for the inevitable conflict, were denounced as men who only wished to destroy the Union. After what has happened during the last two years, my only wonder is that we consented to live for so long a time in association with such miscreants, and have loved so much a government rotten to the core. Were it ever to be proposed again to enter into a Union with such a people, I could no more consent to do it than to trust myself in a den of thieves.

You in Mississippi, have but little experienced as yet the horrors of the war. You have seen but little of the savage manner in which it is waged by your barbarous enemies. It has been my fortune to witness it in all its terrors; in a part of the country where old men have been torn from their homes, carried into captivity and immured in distant dungeons, and where delicate women have been insulted by a brutal soldiery and forced to even cook for the dirty Yankee invaders; where property has been wantonly destroyed, the country ravaged, and every outrage committed. And it is with these people that our fathers formed a union and a solemn compact. There is indeed a difference between the two peoples. Let no man hug the delusion that there can be renewed association between them. Our enemies are a traditionless and a homeless race; from the time of Cromwell[1] to the present moment they have been disturbers of the peace of the world. Gathered together by Cromwell from the bogs and fens of the North of Ireland and of England, they commenced by disturbing the peace of their own country; they disturbed Holland, to which they fled, and they disturbed England on their return. They persecuted Catholics in England, and they hung Quakers and witches in America. Having been hurried into a war with a people so devoid of every mark of civilization you have no doubt wondered that I have not carried out the policy, which I had intended should be our policy, of fighting our battles on the fields of the enemy instead of suffering him to fight them on ours. This was not the result of my will, but of the power of the enemy. They had at their command all the accumulated wealth of seventy years—the military stores which had been laid up during that time. They had grown rich from the taxes wrung from you for the establishing and supporting their manufacturing institutions. We have entered upon a conflict with a nation contiguous to us in territory, and vastly superior to us in numbers. In the face of these facts the wonder is not that we have done little, but that we have done so much. In the first year of the war our forces were sent into the field poorly armed, and were far inferior in number to the enemy. We were compelled even to arm ourselves by the capture of weapons taken from the foe on the battle-field. Thus in every battle we exchanged our arms for those of the invaders. At the end of twelve months of the war, it was still necessary for us to adopt some expedient to enable us to maintain our ground. The only expedient remaining to us was to call on those brave men who had entered the service of their country at the beginning of the war, supposing that the conflict was to last but a short time, and that they would not be long absent from their homes. The only expedient, I say, was to call on these gallant men; to ask them to maintain their position in front of the enemy, and to surrender for a time their hopes of soon returning to their families and their friends. And nobly did they respond to the call. They answered that they were willing to stay, that they were willing to maintain their position and to breast the tide of invasion. But it was not just that they should stand alone. They asked that the men who had stayed at home—who had thus far been sluggards in the cause—should be forced, likewise, to meet the enemy. From this, resulted the law of Congress, which is known as the conscription act, which declared all men, from the age of eighteen to the age of thirty-five, to be liable to enrolment in the Confederate service. I regret that there has been some prejudice excited against that act, and that it has been subjected to harsher criticism than it deserves. And here I may say that an erroneous impression appears to prevail in regard to this act. It is no disgrace to be brought into the army by conscription. There is no more reason to expect from the citizen voluntary service in the army than to expect voluntary labor on the public roads or the voluntary payment of taxes. But these things we do not expect. We assess the property of the citizen, we appoint tax-gatherers; why should we not likewise distribute equally the labor, and enforce equally the obligation of defending the country from its enemies? I repeat that it is no disgrace to any one to be conscribed, but it is a glory for those who do not wait for the conscription. Thus resulted the conscription act; and thence arose the necessity for the exemption act. That necessity was met; but when it was found that under these acts enough men were not drawn into the ranks of the

1. Oliver Cromwell led the Puritan revolution in England in the 1640s that, for a time, overthrew the monarchy in a violent revolution, resulting in the Interegnum. The monarchy was ultimately restored to power in 1660.

army to fulfill the purposes intended, it became necessary to pass another exemption act, and another conscription act. It is only of this latter that I desire now to speak. Its policy was to leave at home those men needed to conduct the administration, and those who might be required to support and maintain the industry of the country—in other words, to exempt from military service those whose labor, employed in other avocations, might be more profitable to the country and to the government, than in the ranks of the army.

I am told that this act has excited some discontent and that it has provoked censure, far more severe, I believe, than it deserves. It has been said that it exempts the rich from military service, and forces the poor to fight the battles of the country. The poor do, indeed, fight the battles of the country. It is the poor who save nations and make revolutions. But is it true that in this war the men of property have shrunk from the ordeal of the battle-field? Look through the army; cast your eyes upon the maimed heroes of the war whom you meet in your streets and in the hospitals; remember the martyrs of the conflict; and I am sure you will find among them more than a fair proportion drawn from the ranks of men of property. The object of that portion of the act which exempts those having charge of twenty or more negroes, was not to draw any distinction of classes, but simply to provide a force, in the nature of a police force, sufficient to keep our negroes in control. This was the sole object of the clause. Had it been otherwise, it would never have received my signature. As I have already said, we have no cause to complain of the rich. All of our people have done well; and, while the poor have nobly discharged their duties, most of the wealthiest and most distinguished families of the South have representatives in the ranks. I take, as an example, the case of one of your own representatives in Congress, who was nominated for Congress and elected; but still did a sentinel's duty until Congress met. Nor is this a solitary instance, for men of the largest fortune in Mississippi are now serving in the ranks.

Permit me now to say that I have seen with peculiar pleasure the recommendation of your Governor in his message, to make some provision for the families of the absent soldiers of Mississippi. Let this provision be made for the objects of his affection and his solicitude, and the soldier engaged in fighting the battles of his country will no longer be disturbed in his slumber by dreams of an unprotected and neglected family at home. Let him know that his mother Mississippi has spread her protecting mantle over those he loves, and he will be ready to fight your battles, to protect your honor, and, in your cause, to die. There is another one of the governor's propositions to which I wish to allude. I mean the proposition to call upon those citizens who are not subject to the Confederate conscription law, and to form them into a reserve corps for the purpose of aiding in the defense of the State. Men who are exempted by law from the performance of any duty, do not generally feel the obligation to perform that duty unless called upon by the law. But I am confident that the men of Mississippi have only to know that their soil is invaded, their cities menaced, to rush to meet the enemy, even if they serve only for thirty days. I see no reason why the State may not, in an exigency like that which now presses on her, call on her reserved forces and organize them for service. Such troops could be of material benefit, by serving in intrenchments, and thus relieving the veteran and disciplined soldiers for the duties of the field, where discipline is so much needed. At the end of a short term of service they could return to their homes and to their ordinary avocations, resuming those duties necessary to the public prosperity.

The exemption act, passed by the last Congress, will probably be made the subject of revision and amendment. It seems to me that some provision might be made by which those who are exempt from enrollment now, might, on becoming subject to conscription, be turned over by the State to the Confederate authorities. But let it never be said that there is a conflict between the States and the Confederate government, by which a blow may be inflicted on the common cause. If such a page is to be written on the history of any State, I hope that you, my friends, will say that that State shall not be Mississippi. Let me repeat that there is much that the reserved corps can do. They can build bridges, construct fortifications, act as a sort of police to preserve order and promote the industrial interests of the State and to keep the negroes under control. Being of the people among whom they would act, those misunderstandings would thus be avoided which are apt to arise when strangers are employed in such a service. In this manner the capacity of the army for active operations against the enemy would be materially increased. I hope I shall not be considered intrusive for having entered into these details. The measures I have recommended are placed before you only in the form of suggestions, and, by you, I know I shall not be misinterpreted.

In considering the manner in which the war has been conducted by the enemy, nothing arrests the attention more than the magnitude of the preparations made for our subjugation. Immense navies have been constructed, vast armies have been accumulated, for the purpose of crushing out the rebellion. It has been impossible for us to meet them in equal numbers; nor have we required it. We have often whipped them three to one, and in the eventful battle of Antietam, Lee whipped them four to one. But do not understand me as saying that this will always be the case. When the troops of the enemy become disciplined, and accustomed to the obedience of the camp, they will necessarily approach more nearly to an equality with our own men. We have always whipped them in spite of disparity of numbers, and on any fair field, fighting as man to man, and relying only on those natural qualities with which men are endowed, we should not fear to meet them in the proportion of one to two. But troops must be disciplined in order to develop their efficiency; and in order to keep them at their posts. Above all, to assure this result, we need the support of public opinion. We want public opinion to frown down those who come from the army with sad tales of disaster, and prophecies of evil, and who skulk from the duties they owe their country. We rely on the women of the land to turn back these deserters from the ranks. I thank the Governor for asking the legislature to make the people of the State tributary to this service. In addition to this, it is necessary to fill up those regiments which have for so long a time been serving in the field. They have stood before the foe on many hard fought fields and have proven their courage and devotion on all. They have won the admiration of the army and of the country. And here I may repeat a compliment I have heard which, although it seems to partake of levity, appears an illustration of the esteem in which Mississippians are held. It happened that several persons were conversing of a certain battle, and one of them remarked that the Mississippians did not run. "Oh no!" said another "Mississippians never run." But those who have passed through thirteen pitched battles are not unscathed. Their ranks are thinned, and they look back to Mississippi for aid to augment their diminished numbers. They look back expecting their brothers to fly to their rescue; but it sometimes seems as if the long anticipated relief would never come. A brigade which may consist of only twelve hundred men is expected to do the work of four thousand. Humanity demands that these depleted regiments be filled up. A mere skeleton cannot reasonably be expected to perform the labor of a body with all its flesh and muscle on it. You have many who might assist in revivifying your reduced regiments—enough to fill up the ranks if they would only consent to throw off the shackles of private interest, and devote themselves to the noblest cause in which a man can be engaged. You have now in the field old men and gentle boys who have braved all the terrors and the dangers of war. I remember an instance of one of these, a brave and gallant youth who, I was told, was but sixteen years of age. In one of those bloody battles by which the soil of Virginia has been consecrated to liberty, he was twice wounded, and each time bound up the wound with his own hands, while refusing to leave the field. A third time he was struck, and the life-blood flowed in a crimson stream from his breast. His brother came to him to minister to his wants; but the noble boy said "brother, you cannot do me any good now; go where you can do the Yankees most harm." Even then, while lying on the ground, his young life fast ebbing away, he cocked his rifle and aimed it to take one last shot at the enemy. And so he died, a hero and a martyr. This was one of the boys whose names shed glory on Mississippi, and who, looking back from their distant camps, where they stand prepared to fight your battles, and to turn back the tide of Yankee invasion, ask you now to send them aid in the struggle—to send them men to stand by them in the day of trial, on the right hand and on the left.

When I came to Mississippi I was uncertain in which direction the enemy intended to come, or what point they intended to attack. It had been stated indeed in their public prints, that they would move down upon Mississippi from the North, with the object of taking Vicksburg in the rear, while their navy would attack that place in front. Such was the programme which had been proclaimed for the invasion and subjugation of your State. But when I went to Grenada, I found that the enemy had retired from our front, and that nothing was to be seen of them but their backs. It is probable that they have abandoned that line, with the intention of reinforcing the heavy column now descending the river. Vicksburg and Port Hudson are the real points of attack. Every effort will be made to capture those places with the object of forcing the navigation of the Mississippi, of cutting off our communications with the trans Mississippi department, and of severing the Western from the Eastern portion of the Confederacy. Let, then, all who have at heart the safety of the country, go without delay to Vicksburg and Port Hudson; let them go for such length of time as they can spare—for thirty, for sixty, or for ninety days. Let them assist in preserving the Mississippi river, that great artery of the country, and thus conduce more than in any other way to the perpetuation of the Confederacy and the success of the cause.

I may say here that I did not expect the Confederate enrolling officers to carry on the work of conscription. I relied for this upon the aid of the State authorities. I supposed that State officers would enroll the conscripts within the limits of their respective States, and that Confederate officers would then receive them in camps of instruction. This I believe to be the policy of your Governor's arguments. We cannot too strongly enforce the necessity of harmony between the Confederate Government and the State Governments. They must act together if our cause is to be brought to a successful issue. Of this you may rest assured, whatever the Confederate government can do for the defense of Mississippi will be done. I feel equal confidence that whatever Mississippi can do will likewise be done. It undoubtedly requires legislation to cause men to perform those duties which are purely legal. Men are not apt to feel an obligation to discharge duties from which they may have been exempted. Ours is a representative government, and it is only through the operation of the law that the obligations toward it can be equally distributed. When the last Congress proclaimed that a certain number of men were required to fill up the ranks of the army, that class of men who were already in the field and who were retained in service, would not have been satisfied had there been no conscription of those who had remained at home. I may state also, that I believe this to be the true theory for the military defense of the Confederacy. Cast your eyes forward to that time at the end of the war, when peace shall nominally be proclaimed—for peace between us and our hated enemy will be liable to be broken at short intervals for many years to come—cast your eyes forward to that time, and you will see the necessity for continued preparation and unceasing watchfulness. We have but few men in our country who will be willing to enlist in the army for a soldier's pay. But if every young man shall have served for two or three years in the army, he will be prepared when war comes to go into camp and take his place in the ranks an educated and disciplined soldier. Serving among his equals, his friends and his neighbors, he will find in the army no distinction of class. To such a system I am sure there can be no objection.

The issue before us is one of no ordinary character. We are not engaged in a conflict for conquest, or for aggrandizement, or for the settlement of a point of international law. The question for you to decide is, "will you be slaves or will you be independent?" Will you transmit to your children the freedom and equality which your fathers transmitted to you or will you bow down in adoration before an idol baser than ever was worshipped by Eastern idolators? Nothing more is necessary than the mere statement of this issue. Whatever may be the personal sacrifices involved, I am sure that you will not shrink from them whenever the question comes before you. Those men who now assail us, who have been associated with us in a common Union, who have inherited a government which they claim to be the best the world ever saw—these men, when left to themselves, have shown that they are incapable of preserving their own personal liberty. They have destroyed the freedom of the press; they have seized upon and imprisoned members of State Legislatures and of municipal councils, who were suspected of sympathy with the South. Men have been carried off into captivity in distant States without indictment, without a knowledge of the accusations brought against them, in utter defiance of all rights guaranteed by the institutions under which they live. These people, when separated from the South and left entirely to themselves, have, in six months, demonstrated their utter incapacity for self-government. And yet these are the people who claim to be your masters. These are the people who have determined to divide out the South among their Yankee troops. Mississippi they have devoted to the direst vengeance of all. "But vengeance is the Lord's," and beneath his banner you will meet and hurl back these worse than vandal hordes.

The great end and aim of the government is to make our struggle successful. The men who stand highest in this contest would fall the first sacrifice to the vengeance of the enemy in case we should be unsuccessful. You may rest assured then for that reason if for no other that whatever capacity they possess will be devoted to securing the independence of the country. Our government is not like the monarchies of the Old World, resting for support upon armies and navies. It sprang from the people and the confidence of the people is necessary for its success. When misrepresentations of the government have been circulated, when accusations have been brought against it of weakness and inefficiency, often have I felt in my heart the struggle between the desire for justice and the duty not to give information to the enemy—because at such times the correction of error would have been injurious to the safety of the cause. Thus, that great and good man, Gen. A. Sidney Johnston, was contented to rest beneath public contumely and to be pointed at by the finger of scorn, because he did not advance from Bowling Green with the little army under his command. But month after month he maintained his post, keeping the enemy ignorant of the paucity of his numbers, and thus holding the invaders in check. I take this case as one instance; it is not the only one by far.

The issue then being: will you be slaves; will you consent to be robbed of your property; to be reduced to provincial dependence; will you renounce the exercise of those rights with which you were born and which were transmitted to you by your fathers? I feel that in addressing Mississippians the answer will be that their interests, even life itself, should be willingly laid down on the altar of their country.

By the memories of the past; by the glories of the field of Chalmette, where the Mississippians, in a general order of the day, were addressed as the bravest of the brave; by the glorious dead of Mexico; by the still more glorious dead of the battle fields of the Confederacy; by the desolate widows and orphans, whom the martyrs of the war have left behind them; by your maimed and wounded heroes—I invoke you not to delay a moment, but to rush forward and place your services at the disposal of the State. I have been one of those who, from the beginning, looked forward to a long and bloody war; but I must frankly confess that its magnitude has exceeded my expectations. The enemy have displayed more power and energy and resources than I had attributed to them. Their finances have held out far better than I imagined would be the case. But I am also one of those who felt that our final success was certain, and that our people had only to be true to themselves to behold the Confederate flag among those of the recognized nations of the earth. The question is only one of time. It may be remote but it may be nearer than many people suppose. It is not possible that a war of the dimensions that this one has assumed, of proportions so gigantic, can be very long protracted. The combatants must be soon exhausted. But it is impossible, with a cause like ours, we can be the first to cry, "Hold, enough."

The sacrifices which have already been made, have perhaps fallen heavily upon a portion of the people, especially upon the noble little city of Vicksburg. After Memphis and New Orleans had fallen, two points which were considered to be admirably defended, two points which we had no reason to believe would fall, Vicksburg became the object of attack. A few earthworks were thrown up, a few guns were mounted, and Vicksburg received the shock of both fleets; the one which, under Commodore Foote had descended the river, and the one which, under Farragut,[2] had achieved the capture of New Orleans. Nobly did the little city receive the assault, and even the women said, "Rather than surrender let us give them the soil, but with the ashes of our dwellings upon it."

This was the heroic devotion of a people who deserve to be free. Your Governor left his chair, and went himself to the scene of danger. Nothing more profoundly touched me amid my duties in a distant land, than to hear that the chief magistrate of my own State was defending the town which the enemy had made the object of his attack, and that the defense was successful. Now we are far better prepared in that quarter. The works, then weak, have been greatly strengthened; the troops assigned for their defense are better disciplined and better instructed, and that gallant soldier who came with me, has been pouring in his forces to assist in its protection. Himself the son of a Revolutionary hero, he has emulated his father's glorious example upon other fields, and comes to Mississippi to defend, and, as I believe, to protect you.

2. Union Admiral David G. Farragut (1801–1870), best known for his infamous order, "Damn the torpedos! Full speed ahead!" In 1862, he led forces that captured New Orleans and went on to lead many other successful naval campaigns.

In the course of this war our eyes have been often turned abroad. We have expected sometimes recognition and sometimes intervention at the hands of foreign nations, and we have had a right to expect it. Never before in the history of the world had a people for so long a time maintained their ground, and showed themselves capable of maintaining their national existence, without securing the recognition of commercial nations. I know not why this has been so, but this I say, "put not your trust in princes," and rest not your hopes in foreign nations. This war is ours; we must fight it out ourselves, and I feel some pride in knowing that so far we have done it without the good will of anybody. It is true that there are now symptoms of a change in public opinion abroad. They give us their admiration—they sometimes even say to us God speed—and in the remarkable book written by Mr. Spence,[3] the question of secession has been discussed with more of ability than it ever has been even in this country. Yet England still holds back, but France, the ally of other days, seems disposed to hold out to us the hand of fellowship. And when France holds out to us her hand, right willingly will we grasp it.

During the last year, the war has been characterized by varied fortunes. New Orleans fell; a sad blow it was to the valley of the Mississippi, and as unexpected to me as to any one. Memphis also fell, and besides these we have lost various points on the Atlantic coast. The invading armies have pressed upon us at some points; at others they have been driven back; but take a view of our condition now and compare it with what it was a year ago—look at the enemy's position as it then was and as it now is; consider their immense power, vast numbers, and great resources; look at all these things and you will be convinced that our condition now will compare favorably with what it was then. Armies are not composed of numbers alone. Officers and men are both to be disciplined and instructed. When the war first began the teacher and the taught were in the condition of the blind leading the blind; now all this is changed for the better. Our troops have become disciplined and instructed. They have stripped the gunboat of its terrors; they have beaten superior numbers in the field; they have discovered that with their short range weapons they can close upon the long range of the enemy and capture them. Thus, in all respects, moral as well as physical, we are better prepared than we were a year ago.

There are now two prominent objects in the programme of the enemy. One is to get possession of the Mississippi river and to open it to navigation in order to appease the clamors of the West and to utilize the capture of New Orleans, which has thus far rendered them no service. The other is to seize upon the capital of the Confederacy, and hold this out as a proof that the Confederacy has no existence. We have recently repulsed them at Fredericksburg, and I believe that under God and by the valor of our troops the capital of the Confederacy will stand safe behind its wall of living breasts. Vicksburg and Port Hudson have been strengthened, and now we can concentrate at either of them a force sufficient for their protection. I have confidence that Vicksburg will stand as before, and I hope that Johnston[4] will find generals to support him if the enemy dare to land. Port Hudson is now strong. Vicksburg will stand, and Port Hudson will stand; but let every man that can be spared from other vocations, hasten to defend them, and thus hold the Mississippi river, that great artery of the Confederacy, preserve our communications with the trans-Mississippi department, and thwart

3. James Spence, author of *The American Union; Its Effect on National Character and Policy, with an Inquiry into Secession as a Constitutional right, and the Causes of the Disruption* (1862).

4. Joseph E. Johnston, Brigadier General, C.S.A., commanded the Department of the West, 4 December 1862–December 1863.

the enemy's scheme of forcing navigation through to New Orleans. By holding that section of the river between Port Hudson and Vicksburg, we shall secure these results, and the people of the West, cut off from New Orleans, will be driven to the East to seek a market for their products, and will be compelled to pay so much in the way of freights that those products will be rendered almost valueless. Thus, I should not be surprised if the first daybreak of peace were to dawn upon us from that quarter.

Some time since, for reasons not necessary to recapitulate, I sent to this State a general unknown to most of you,[5] and, perhaps, even by name, known but to few among you. This was the land of my affections. Here were situated the little of worldly goods I possessed. I selected a general who, in my view, was capable of defending my State and discharging the duties of this important service. I am happy to state, after an attentive examination, that I have not been mistaken in the general of my choice. I find that, during his administration here everything has been done that could be accomplished with the means at his command. I recommend him to your confidence as you may have confidence in me, who selected him. For the defense of Vicksburg, I selected one from the army of the Potomac,[6] of whom it is but faint praise to say he has no superior. He was sent to Virginia at the beginning of the war, with a little battery of three guns. With these he fought the Yankee gunboats, drove them off, and stripped them of their terrors. He was promoted for distinguished services on various fields. He was finally made a colonel of cavalry, and I have reason to believe that, at the last great conflict on the field of Manassas, he served to turn the tide of battle and consummate the victory.

On succeeding fields he has won equal distinction. Though yet young he has fought more battles than many officers who have lived to an advanced age and died in their beds. I have therefore sent Lee to take charge of the defenses of Vicksburg. I can say then that I have every confidence in the skill and energy of the officers in command. But when I received dispatches and heard rumors of alarm and trepidation and despondency among the people of Mississippi; when I heard even that people were fleeing to Texas in order to save themselves from the enemy; when I saw it stated by the enemy that they had handled other States with gloves, but Mississippi was to be handled without gloves, every impulse of my heart dragged me hither in spite of duties which might have claimed my attention elsewhere. When I heard of the sufferings of my own people, of the danger of their subjugation by a ruthless foe, I felt that if Mississippi were destined for such a fate, I would wish to sleep in her soil. On my way here I stopped at the headquarters of Gen. Johnston. I knew his capacity and his resolution. I imparted to him my own thoughts and asked him to come with me. I found that his ideas were directed in the same channel. He came in the shortest time for preparation; but whatever man can do will be done by him. I have perfect confidence that with your assistance and support he will drive the enemy from the soil of Mississippi. After having visited the army—after having mingled among the people of the State—I shall go away from among you with a lighter heart. I do not think the people of Mississippi are despondent or depressed; those who are so are those on whom the iron tread of the invader has fallen, or those who, skulking from their duty, go home with fearful tales to justify their desertion.

Nor is the army despondent; on the contrary, it is confident of victory. At Grenada I found the only regret to be that the enemy had not come on. At Vicks-

5. John C. Pemberton, General, C.S.A., surrendered Vicksburg to Union forces on 4 July 1863.

6. Stephen D. Lee, Lieutenant-General, C.S.A.

burg, even without reinforcements, the troops did not dream of defeat. I go, therefore, anxious but hopeful. My attachment to Mississippi, and my esteem for her people, have risen since the war began. I have been proud of her soldiers. I have endeavored to conceal my pride, for I wished to make no distinction between the States of the Confederacy; but I cannot deny that my heart has warmed with a livelier emotion when I have seen those letters upon the boy's cap that have marked him for a Mississippian. Man's affections are not subject to his will; mine are fixed upon Mississippi. And when I return to where I shall find Mississippians fighting for you in a distant State, ween I shall tell them that you are safe here, that you can be defended without calling upon them, and that they are necessary to guard the capital and to prevent the inroads of the enemy in Georgia and Alabama, I shall be proud to say to them for you that they are welcome to stay.

As to the States on the other side of the Mississippi, I can say that their future is bright. The army is organized and disciplined, and it is to be hoped that at no distant day it may be able to advance into that land which has been trodden under the foot of despotism, where old men have been torn from their homes and immured in dungeons, where even the women have been subjected to the insults of the brutal Yankee soldiery—that under the flag of the Confederacy Missouri will again be free.

Kentucky, too, that gallant State whose cause is our cause, the gallantry of whose sons has never been questioned, is still the object of the ardent wishes of Gen. Bragg.[7] I heard him say in an address to his troops, that he hoped again to lead them into Kentucky, and to the banks of the Ohio river.

I can then say with confidence that our condition is in every respect greatly improved over what it was last year. Our armies have been augmented, our troops have been instructed and disciplined. The articles necessary for the support of our troops, and our people, and from which the enemy's blockade has cut us off, are being produced in the Confederacy. Our manufactories have made rapid progress, so much is this the case that I learn with equal surprise and pleasure from the general commanding this department, that Mississippi alone can supply the army which is upon her soil.

Our people have learned to economize and are satisfied to wear home spun. I never see a woman dressed in home spun that I do not feel like taking off my hat to her; and although our women never lose their good looks, I cannot help thinking that they are improved by this garb. I never meet a man dressed in home spun but I feel like saluting him. I cannot avoid remarking with how much pleasure I have noticed the superior morality of our troops, and the contrast which in this respect they present to those of the invader. I can truly say that an army more pious and more moral than that defending our liberties, I do not believe to exist. On their valor and the assistance of God I confidently rely.

Questions to Consider

1. How do these excerpts reveal the ways in which Jefferson Davis contributed to the creation of Confederate nationalism? Do you find his rhetorical strategies compelling? Why or why not?
2. How does Jefferson Davis justify Confederate policies that challenge the states' rights doctrine?

7. Braxton Bragg, General, C.S.A. At the time of this speech, Bragg commanded the Army of Tennessee.

Abraham Lincoln

1809–1865

Accounts of Abraham Lincoln's rise from humble beginnings to prominent positions in legal and political circles in Illinois during the 1850s captivated the newly formed Republican Party. When he delivered his famous "A House Divided" speech during his bid for a seat in the Illinois senate in the summer of 1858, the nation was still reeling from recent events concerning the fate of slavery. The Supreme Court had handed down its infamous decision in the *Dred Scott* case the previous year, declaring that African Americans, whether slave or free, were not citizens of the United States. Chief Justice Roger Taney, who wrote the opinion, also argued that all congressional enactments that excluded slavery from the national territories, including the Missouri Compromise, were "not warranted by the constitution" and were therefore "void." Also in 1857, Kansas voters approved the Lecompton Constitution, and in early 1858, President James Buchanan recommended that Congress admit Kansas as a slave state. Illinois senator Stephen Douglas balked at Buchanan's recommendation on Kansas. The Republican Party had determined to fight the expansion of slavery into the territories, and some members considered backing Douglas in his reelection bid in Illinois because of his denunciation of Buchanan. Lincoln targeted his speech, then, at those wavering Republicans, trying to shore up support for the Republican Party.

Lincoln lost the Illinois Senate campaign of 1858, but his place as a leader in the Republican Party was secured. In 1860, he garnered the Republican Party nomination for the presidency in an election that was like no other in American history. Four candidates vied for the office in a contest that broke down along sectional lines. Although Lincoln won only a plurality of the popular vote, he won a majority of votes in the Electoral College.

Lincoln's victory had split the Union; by the winter of 1861, seven slave states had seceded from the United States and formed the Confederate States of America. Lincoln tried to reassure White Southerners in his inaugural address that he had no intention of interfering with slavery where it already existed. He did, however, maintain an unyielding position on the Union. "I hold, that in contemplation of universal law, and of the Constitution, the Union of these States is perpetual," he stated. "I therefore consider that, in view of the Constitution and the laws, the Union in unbroken," he continued, "and, to the extent of my ability, I shall take care, as the Constitution itself expressly enjoins upon me, that the laws of the Union be faithfully executed in all the States." Lincoln was not going to recognize the legitimacy of the Confederacy. Moreover, he made clear that the choice of war or peace rested with the South. "In *your* hands, my dissatisfied fellow countrymen, and not in *mine*, is the momentous issue of civil war. The government will not assail *you*," he promised. "You can have no conflict, without being yourselves the aggressors." Southerners made the decision for war when they fired upon the federal arsenal at Fort Sumter.

Lincoln had always maintained that the restoration of the Union was his foremost concern. He made this position clear to Horace Greeley, editor of the New York *Tribune*, on 22 August 1862. Greeley had published an editorial in his newspaper titled "The Prayer of Twenty Million" in which he charged that it was "preposterous and futile" to try to defeat the Confederacy without eradicating slavery. Lincoln's response to Greeley, reprinted in newspapers across the North, affirmed his overriding concern with saving the Union. Lincoln hoped his response to Greeley would appease the fears of Northerners who did not want to turn the war into an abolitionist crusade. But, Lincoln also used the opportunity to hint that he was contemplating making the eradication of slavery part of the Union war effort, promising that he would "adopt new views so fast as they shall appear to be true views." Lincoln could not announce those new views, however, until the Union had secured a military victory.

Union victory came at the Battle of Antietam in September 1862. Lincoln convened his cabinet on 22 September 1862 and informed its members of his intentions. He had promised himself and God that he would issue a proclamation of emancipation as soon as the Union drove the Confederate Army out of Maryland. "The rebel army is now driven out," he told his cabinet, "and I am going to fulfill that promise. I have got you together to hear what I have written down. I do not wish your advice about the main matter; for that I have determined for myself." The Emancipation Proclamation went into effect on 1 January 1863. It carried little official weight, for Lincoln had no authority to liberate slaves in Confederate states. Only invading Union armies could liberate slaves in the Confederacy as they advanced. As historian Michael P. Johnson has noted, without Union victories on the battlefield, the document would have been rendered useless.

The war dragged on, exacting tremendous sacrifices by the Union. In a brief address at the dedication of the military cemetery at Gettysburg, Lincoln explained why the North must not lose its resolve. Reminding the crowd that countless soldiers had died at Gettysburg to defend the Union, Lincoln claimed, "it is for us the living . . . to be dedicated here to the unfinished work which they who fought here have thus far so nobly advanced." Those soldiers had died to give the nation "a new birth of freedom." Michael P. Johnson has argued that with this address, Lincoln "enobled the Union cause by attaching the profession of human equality in the Declaration of Independence to both the Union and the war."

By the time Lincoln delivered his second inaugural address on 4 March 1865, the end of the war seemed imminent. Significantly, Lincoln attributed the protracted war to a God who wished to rid the earth of slavery. God may have determined the length of the battle, but the restoration of the Union rested with mortals. Lincoln eloquently promised a generous and lasting peace. He believed his second inaugural would "wear as well as—perhaps better than—anything I have produced."

John Wilkes Booth, a Southern partisan, assassinated Lincoln less than six weeks after the president delivered that address. Hearing of the president's death, Edwin Stanton, Lincoln's secretary of war, proclaimed, "Now, he belongs to the ages."

A House Divided

16 June 1858

Mr. President and Gentlemen of the Convention:[1]

If we could first know *where* we are, and *whither* we are tending, we could better judge *what* to do, and *how* to do it.

We are now far into the *fifth* year since a policy was initiated with the *avowed* object, and *confident* promise, of putting an end to slavery agitation.

Under the operation of that policy, that agitation has not only, *not ceased*, but has *constantly augmented*.

In *my opinion*, it *will* not cease, until a *crisis* shall have been reached, and passed.

"A house divided against itself cannot stand."

I believe this government cannot endure, permanently half *slave* and half *free*.

I do not expect the Union to be *dissolved*—I do not expect the house to *fall*—but I *do* expect it will cease to be divided.

It will become *all* one thing, or *all* the other.

Either the *opponents* of slavery, will arrest the further spread of it, and place it where the public mind shall rest in the belief that it is in the course of ultimate extinction; or

1. Lincoln delivered this address at the Republican State Convention at Springfield, Illinois, in 1858. Lincoln was chosen as the U.S. Senatorial candidate to oppose Stephen A. Douglas during this meeting.

its *advocates* will push it forward, till it shall become alike lawful in *all* the States, *old* as well as *new*—*North* as well as *South*.

Have we no *tendency* to the latter condition?

Let any one who doubts, carefully contemplate that now almost complete legal combination—piece of *machinery*, so to speak—compounded of the Nebraska doctrine, and the Dred Scott decision. Let him consider not only *what work* the machinery is adapted to do, and *how well* adapted; but also, let him study the *history* of its construction, and trace, if he can, or rather *fail*, if he can, to trace the evidences of design, and concert of action, among its chief bosses, from the beginning.

The new year of 1854 found slavery excluded from more than half the States by State Constitutions, and from most of the national territory by Congressional prohibition.

Four days later, commenced the struggle, which ended in repealing that Congressional prohibition.

This opened all the national territory to slavery, and was the first point gained.

But, so far, *Congress* only, had acted; and an *indorsement* by the people, *real* or apparent, was indispensable, to *save* the point already gained, and give chance for more.

This necessity had not been overlooked; but had been provided for, as well as might be, in the notable argument of "*squatter sovereignty*," otherwise called "*sacred right of self-government*," which latter phrase, though expressive of the only rightful basis of any government, was so perverted in this attempted use of it as to amount to just this: That if any *one* man, choose to enslave *another*, no *third* man shall be allowed to object.

That argument was incorporated into the Nebraska bill itself, in the language which follows: "*It being the true intent and meaning of this act not to legislate slavery into any Territory or state, nor to exclude it therefrom; but to leave the people thereof perfectly free to form and regulate their domestic institutions in their own way, subject only to the Constitution of the United States*."

Then opened the roar of loose declamation in favor of "Squatter Sovereignty," and "sacred right of self government."

"But," said opposition members, "let us be more *specific*—let us *amend* the bill so as to expressly declare that the people of the territory *may* exclude slavery." "Not we," said the friends of the measure; and down they voted the amendment.

While the Nebraska bill was passing through Congress, a *law case*, involving the question of a negroe's freedom, by reason of his owner having voluntarily taken him first into a free State and then a territory covered by the congressional prohibition, and held him as a slave, for a long time in each, was passing through the U.S. Circuit Court for the District of Missouri; and both Nebraska bill and law suit were brought to a decision in the same month of May, 1854. The negroe's name was "Dred Scott,"[2] which name now designates the decision finally made in the case.

Before the *then* next Presidential election, the law case came *to*, and was argued *in*, the Supreme Court of the United States; but the *decision* of it was deferred until *after* the election. Still, *before* the election, Senator Trumbull[3] on the floor of the Senate, requests the leading advocate[4] of the Nebraska bill to state *his opinion*

2. Supreme Court decision in 1857, which decreed that African Americans were ineligible for citizenship, regardless of their status as slaves or freedmen. This decision also forbade Congress from outlawing slavery in new territories or states.

3. Illinois Senator Lyman Trumball, an anti-Nebraska Democrat who became a Republican.

4. Stephen A. Douglas.

whether the people of a territory can constitutionally exclude slavery from their limits; and the latter answers: "That is a question for the Supreme Court."

The election came. Mr. Buchanan[5] was elected, and the *indorsement*, such as it was, secured. That was the *second* point gained. The indorsement, however, fell short of a clear popular majority by nearly four hundred thousand votes, and so, perhaps, was not overwhelmingly reliable and satisfactory.[6]

The *outgoing* President[7] in his last annual message, as impressively as possible *echoed back* upon the people the *weight* and *authority* of the endorsement.

The Supreme Court met again; *did not* announce their decision, but ordered a re-argument.

The Presidential inauguration came, and still no decision of the court; but the *incoming* President, in his inaugural address, fervently exhorted the people to abide by the forthcoming decision, *whatever it might be*.

Then, in a few days, came the decision.

The reputed author[8] of the Nebraska bill finds an early occasion to make a speech at this capitol indorsing the Dred Scott Decision, and vehemently denouncing all opposition to it.

The new President,[9] too, seizes the early occasion of the Silliman letter to *indorse* and strongly *construe* that decision, and to express his *astonishment* that any different view had ever been entertained.

At length a squabble springs up between the President and the author of the Nebraska bill, on the *mere* question of *fact*, whether the Lecompton constitution was or was not, in any just sense, made by the people of Kansas; and in that squabble the latter declares that all he wants is a fair vote for the people, and that he *cares* not whether slavery be voted *down* or voted *up*. I do not understand his declaration that he cares not whether slavery be voted down or voted up, to be intended by him other than as an *apt definition* of the *policy* he would impress upon the public mind—the *principle* for which he declares he has suffered much, and is ready to suffer to the end.

And well may he cling to that principle. If he has any parental feeling, well may he cling to it. That principle, is the only *shred* left of his original Nebraska doctrine. Under the Dred Scott decision "squatter sovereignty" squatted out of existence, tumbled down like temporary scaffolding—like the mould at the foundry served through one blast and fell back into loose sand—helped to carry an election, and then was kicked to the winds. His late *joint* struggle with the Republicans, against the Lecompton Constitution, involves nothing of the original Nebraska doctrine. That struggle was made on a point, the right of a people to make their own constitution, upon which he and the Republicans have never differed.

The several points of the Dred Scott decision, in connection with Senator Douglas' "care not" policy, constitute the piece of machinery, in its *present* state of advancement. This was the third point gained.

The *working* points of that machinery are:

First, that no negro slave, imported as such from Africa, and no descendant of such slave can ever be a *citizen* of any State, in the sense of that term as used in the Constitution of the United States.

5. James Buchanan, a Democrat from Pennsylvania.
6. In the election of 1856, Buchanan won a clear majority in the electoral college, with 174 votes against Republican John C. Frémont's 114 votes and American (Know-Nothing) Party candidate Millard Fillmore's 8 votes. Buchanan received only 45 percent of the popular vote, however.
7. Franklin Pierce, a Democratic from New Hampshire.
8. Stephen A. Douglas.
9. James Buchanan.

This point is made in order to deprive the negro, in every possible event, of the benefit of this provision of the United States Constitution, which declares that—

"The citizens of each State shall be entitled to all privileges and immunities of citizens in the several States."

Secondly, that "subject to the Constitution of the United States," neither *Congress* nor a *Territorial Legislature* can exclude slavery from any United States territory.

This point is made in order that individual men may *fill up* the territories with slaves, without danger of losing them as property, and thus to enhance the chances of *permanency* to the institution through all the future.

Thirdly, that whether the holding a negro in actual slavery in a free State, makes him free, as against the holder, the United States courts will not decide, but will leave to be decided by the courts of any slave State the negro may be forced into by the master.

This point is made, not to be pressed *immediately;* but, if acquiesced in for a while, and apparently *indorsed* by the people at an election, *then* to sustain the logical conclusion that what Dred Scott's master might lawfully do with Dred Scott, in the free State of Illinois, every other master may lawfully do with any other *one,* or one *thousand* slaves, in Illinois, or in any other free State.

Auxiliary to all this, and working hand in hand with it, the Nebraska doctrine, or what is left of it, is to *educate* and *mould* public opinion, at least *Northern* public opinion, to not *care* whether slavery is voted *down* or voted *up*.

This shows exactly where we now *are;* and *partially*, also, whither we are tending.

It will throw additional light on the latter, to go back, and run the mind over the string of historical facts already stated. Several things will *now* appear less *dark* and *mysterious* than they did *when* they were transpiring. The people were to be left "perfectly free," "subject only to the Constitution." What the *Constitution* had to do with it, outsiders could not *then* see. Plainly enough *now,* it was an exactly fitted *niche,* for the Dred Scott decision to afterwards come in, and declare the *perfect freedom* of the people, to be just no freedom at all. . . .

We cannot absolutely *know* that all these exact adaptations are the result of preconcert. But when we see a lot of framed timbers, different portions of which we know have been gotten out at different times and places and by different workmen—Stephen, Franklin, Roger and James,[10] for instance—and when we see these timbers joined together, and see they exactly make the frame of a house or a mill, all the tenons and mortices exactly fitting, and all the lengths and proportions of the different pieces exactly adapted to their respective places, and not a piece too many or too few—not omitting even scaffolding—or, if a single piece be lacking, we can see the place in the frame exactly fitted and prepared, to yet bring such a piece in—in *such* a case, we find it impossible to not *believe* that Stephen and Franklin and Roger and James all understood one another from the beginning, and all worked upon a common *plan* or *draft* drawn up before the first lick was struck.

It should not be overlooked that, by the Nebraska bill, the people of a *State* as well as *Territory*, were to be left "*perfectly free,*" "*subject only to the Constitution*."

Why mention a *State?* They were legislating for *territories*, and not *for* or *about* States. Certainly the people of a State *are* and *ought to be subject* to the Constitution of the United States; but why is mention of this *lugged* into this merely *territorial* law?

10. Senator Stephen A. Douglas, President Franklin Pierce, Supreme Court Chief Justice Roger B. Taney, and President James Buchanan, all of whom were Democrats.

Why are the people of a *territory* and the people of a *state* therein *lumped* together, and their relation to the Constitution therein treated as being *precisely* the same?

While the opinion of *the Court*, by Chief Justice Taney, in the Dred Scott case, and the separate opinions of all the concurring Judges, expressly declare that the Constitution of the United States neither permits Congress nor a Territorial legislature to exclude slavery from any United States territory, they all *omit* to declare whether or not the same Constitution permits a *state*, or the people of a State, to exclude it.

Possibly, this was a mere *omission;* but who can be *quite* sure. . . .

The nearest approach to the point of declaring the power of a State over slavery, is made by Judge Nelson.[11] He approaches it more than once, using the precise idea, and *almost* the language too, of the Nebraska act. On one occasion, his exact language is, "except in cases where the power is restrained by the Constitution of the United States, the law of the State is supreme over the subject of slavery within its jurisdiction."

In what *cases* the power of the *states* is so restrained by the United States Constitution, is left an *open* question, precisely as the same question, as to the restraint on the power of the *territories*, was left open in the Nebraska act. Put *that* and *that* together, and we have another nice little niche, which we may, ere long, see filled with another Supreme Court decision, declaring that the Constitution of the United States does not permit a *state* to exclude slavery from its limits.

And this may especially be expected if the doctrine of "care not whether slavery be voted *down* or voted *up*," shall gain upon the public mind sufficiently to give promise that such a decision can be maintained when made.

Such a decision is all that slavery now lacks of being alike lawful in all the States.

Welcome or unwelcome, such decision *is* probably coming, and will soon be upon us, unless the power of the present political dynasty shall be met and overthrown.

We shall *lie down* pleasantly dreaming that the people of *Missouri* are on the verge of making their State *free;* and we shall *awake* to the *reality* instead, that the *Supreme* Court has made *Illinois* a *slave* State.

To meet and overthrow the power of that dynasty, is the work now before all those who would prevent that consummation.

That is *what* we have to do.

But *how* can we best do it?

There are those who denounce us *openly* to their *own* friends, and yet whisper *us softly*, that *Senator Douglas* is the *aptest* instrument there is, with which to effect that object. *They* do *not* tell us, nor has *he* told us, that he *wishes* any such object to be effected. They wish us to *infer* all, from the facts, that he now has a little quarrel with the present head of the dynasty; and that he has regularly voted with us, on a single point, upon which, he and we, have never differed.

They remind us that *he* is a very *great man*, and that the largest of *us* are very small ones. Let this be granted. But "a *living dog* is better than a *dead lion*." Judge Douglas, if not a *dead* lion *for this work*, is at least a *caged* and *toothless* one. How can he oppose the advances of slavery? He don't [*sic*] *care* anything about it. His avowed *mission is impressing* the "public heart" to *care* nothing about it.

A leading Douglas Democratic newspaper thinks Douglas superior talent will be needed to resist the revival of the African slave trade.

11. Supreme Court Justice Samuel Nelson wrote a separate opinion in the *Dred Scott* case.

Does Douglas believe an effort to revive that trade is approaching? He has not said so. Does he *really* think so? But if it is, how can he resist it? For years he has labored to prove it a *sacred right* of white men to take negro slaves into the new territories. Can he possibly show that it is *less* a sacred right to *buy* them where they can be bought cheapest? And, unquestionably they can be bought *cheaper in Africa* than in *Virginia*.

He has done all in his power to reduce the whole question of slavery to one of a mere *right of property;* and as such, how can *he* oppose the foreign slave trade—how can he refuse that trade in that "property" shall be "perfectly free"—unless he does it as a *protection* to the home production? And as the home *producers* will probably not *ask* the protection, he will be wholly without a ground of opposition.

Senator Douglas holds, we know, that a man may rightfully be *wiser* to-day than he was *yesterday*—that he may rightfully *change* when he finds himself wrong.

But, can we for that reason, run ahead, and *infer* that he *will* make any particular change, of which he, himself, has given no intimation? Can we *safely* base *our* action upon any such *vague* inference?

Now, as ever, I wish to not *misrepresent* Judge Douglas' *position*, question his *motives*, or do ought that can be personally offensive to him.

Whenever, *if ever*, he and we can come together on *principle* so that *our great cause* may have assistance from *his great ability*, I hope to have interposed no adventitious obstacle.

But clearly, he is not *now* with us—he does not *pretend* to be—he does not *promise* to *ever* be.

Our cause, then, must be intrusted to, and conducted by its own undoubted friends—those whose hands are free, whose hearts are in the work—who *do care* for the result.

Two years ago the Republicans of the nation mustered over thirteen hundred thousand strong.

We did this under the single impulse of resistance to a common danger, with every external circumstance against us.

Of *strange, discordant*, and even *hostile* elements, we gathered from the four winds, and *formed* and fought the battle through, under the constant hot fire of a disciplined, proud and pampered enemy.

Did we brave all *then*, to *falter* now?—now—when that same enemy is *wavering*, dissevered and belligerent?

The result is not doubtful. We shall not fail—if we stand firm, we shall not fail. *Wise counsels* may *accelerate*, or *mistakes delay* it, but, sooner or later, the victory is *sure* to come.

Letter to Horace Greeley

EXECUTIVE MANSION WASHINGTON

22 August 1862

Hon. Horace Greeley:

Dear Sir:

I have just read yours of the 19th, addressed to myself through the *New-York Tribune*. If there be in it any statements, or assumptions of fact, which I may know to be erroneous, I do not, now and here, controvert them. If there be in it any inferences which I may believe to be falsely drawn, I do not now and here, argue against them. If there be perceptable [sic] in it an impatient and dictatorial tone, I waive it in deference to an old friend, whose heart I have always supposed to be right.

As to the policy I "seem to be pursuing" as you say, I have not meant to leave any one in doubt.

I would save the Union. I would save it the shortest way under the Constitution. The sooner the national authority can be restored; the nearer the Union will be "the Union as it was." If there be those who would not save the Union, unless they could at the same time *save* slavery, I do not agree with them. If there be those who would not save the Union unless they could at the same time *destroy* slavery, I do not agree with them. My paramount object in this struggle *is* to save the Union, and is *not* either to save or to destroy slavery. If I could save the Union without freeing *any* slave I would do it, and if I could save it by freeing *all* the slaves I would do it; and if I could save it by freeing some and leaving others alone I would also do that. What I do about slavery, and the colored race, I do because I believe it helps to save the Union; and what I forbear, I forbear because I do *not* believe it would help to save the Union. I shall do *less* whenever I shall believe what I am doing hurts the cause, and I shall do *more* whenever I shall believe doing more will help the cause. I shall try to correct errors when shown to be errors; and I shall adopt new views so fast as they shall appear to be true views.

I have here stated my purpose according to my view of *official* duty; and I intend no modification of my oft-expressed *personal* wish that all men everywhere could be free.

Yours,
A. Lincoln

Emancipation Proclamation

By the President of the United States of America: A Proclamation

January 1, 1863

Whereas, on the twentysecond day of September in the year of our Lord one thousand eight hundred and sixty two, a proclamation was issued by the President of the United States, containing, among other things, the following, towit:

> That on the first day of January, in the year of our Lord one thousand eight hundred and sixty-three all persons held as slaves within any State or designated part of a State, the people whereof shall then be in rebellion against the United States, shall be then, thenceforward, and forever free; and the Executive Government of the United States, including the military and naval authority thereof, will recognize and maintain the freedom of such persons, and will do no act or acts to repress such persons, or any of them, in any efforts they may make for their actual freedom.
>
> "That the Executive will, on the first day of January aforesaid, by proclamation, designate the States and parts of States, if any, in which the people thereof, respectively, shall then be in rebellion against the United States; and the fact that any State, or the people thereof, shall on that day be, in good faith, represented in the Congress of the United States by members chosen thereto at elections wherein a majority of the qualified voters of such State shall have participated, shall, in the absence of strong countervailing testimony, be deemed conclusive evidence that such State, and the people thereof, are not then in rebellion against the United States.

Now, therefore I, Abraham Lincoln, President of the United States, by virtue of the power in me vested as Commander-in-Chief, of the Army and Navy of the United States in time of actual armed rebellion against authority and government of the United States, and as a fit and necessary war measure for suppressing said rebellion, do, on this first day of January, in the year of our Lord one thousand eight hundred and sixty three, and in accordance with my purpose so to do publicly proclaimed for the full period of one hundred days, from the first day above mentioned, order and designate as the States and parts of States wherein the people thereof respectively, are this day in rebellion against the United States, the following, towit:

Arkansas, Texas, Louisiana (except the Parishes of St. Bernard, Palquemines, Jefferson, St. Johns, St. Charles, St. James, Ascension, Assumption, Terrebone, Lafourche, St. Mary, St. Martin, and Orleans, including the city of New-Orleans), Mississippi, Alabama, Florida, Georgia, South-Carolina, North-Carolina, and Virginia, (except the fortyeight counties designated as West Virginia, and also the counties of Berkeley, Accomac, Northhampton, Elizabeth-City, York, Princess Ann, and Norfolk, including the cities of Norfolk and Portsmouth); and which excepted parts are, for the present, left precisely as if this proclamation were not issued.

And by virtue of the power, and for the purpose aforesaid, I do order and declare that all persons held as slaves within said designated States, and parts of States, are, and henceforward shall be free; and that the Executive government of the United States, including the military and naval authorities thereof, will recognize and maintain the freedom of said persons.

And I hereby enjoin upon the people so declared to be free to abstain from all violence, unless in necessary self-defence; and I recommend to them that, in all cases when allowed, they labor faithfully for reasonable wages.

And I further declare and make known, that such persons of suitable condition, will be received into the armed service of the United States to garrison forts, positions, stations, and other places, and to man vessels of all sorts in said service.

And upon this act, sincerely believed to be an act of justice, warranted by the Constitution, upon military necessity, I invoke the considerate judgment of mankind, and the gracious favor of Almighty God. . . .

The Gettysburg Address

Delivered on the Battlefield at Gettysburg, PA, 19 November 1863

Four score and seven years ago our fathers brought forth on this continent, a new nation, conceived in Liberty and dedicated to the proposition that all men are created equal.

Now we are engaged in a great civil war, testing whether that nation, or any nation so conceived and so dedicated, can long endure. We are met on a great battlefield of that war. We have come to dedicate a portion of that field, as a final resting place for those who here gave their lives that that nation might live. It is altogether fitting and proper that we should do this.

But, in a larger sense, we cannot dedicate—we can not consecrate—we can not hallow—this ground. The brave men, living and dead, who struggled here, have consecrated it, far above our poor power to add or detract. The world will little note, nor long remember what we say here, but it can never forget what they did here. It is for us the living, rather, to be dedicated here to the unfinished work which they who fought here have thus far so nobly advanced. It is rather for us to be here dedicated to the great task remaining before us—that from these honored dead we take increased devotion to that cause for which they gave the last full measure of devotion—that we here highly resolve that these dead shall not have died in vain—that this nation, under God, shall have a new birth of freedom—and that government of the people, by the people, for the people, shall not perish from the earth.

Second Inaugural Address

DELIVERED 4 MARCH 1865

Fellow Countrymen:

At this second appearing to take the oath of the presidential office, there is less occasion for an extended address than there was at the first. Then a statement, somewhat in detail, of a course to be pursued, seemed fitting and proper. Now, at the expiration of four years, during which public declarations have been constantly called forth on every point and phase of the great contest which still absorbs the attention, and engrosses the energies of the nation, little that is new could be presented. The progress of our arms, upon which all else chiefly depends, is as well known to the public as to myself; and it is, I trust, reasonably satisfactory and encouraging to all. With high hope for the future, no prediction in regard to it is ventured.

On the occasion corresponding to this four years ago, all thoughts were anxiously directed to an impending civil-war. All dreaded it—all sought to avert it. While the inaugural address was being delivered from this place, devoted altogether to *saving* the Union without war, insurgent agents were in the city seeking to *destroy* it without war—seeking to dissolve the Union, and divide effects, by negotiation. Both parties deprecated war; but one of them would *make* war rather than let the nation survive; and the other would *accept* war rather than let it perish. And the war came.

One-eighth of the whole population were colored slaves, not distributed generally over the Union, but localized in the Southern part of it. These slaves constituted a peculiar and powerful interest. All knew that this interest was, somehow, the cause of the war. To strengthen, perpetuate, and extend this interest was the object for which the insurgents would rend the Union, even by war; while the government claimed no right to do more than to restrict the territorial enlargement of it. Neither party expected for the war, the magnitude, or the duration, which it has already attained. Neither anticipated that the *cause* of the conflict might cease with, or even before, the conflict itself should cease. Each looked for an easier triumph, and a result less fundamental and astounding. Both read the same Bible, and pray to the same God; and each invokes His aid against the other. It may seem strange that any men should dare to ask a just God's assistance in wringing their bread from the sweat of other men's faces; but let us judge not that we be not judged. The prayers of both could not be answered; that of neither has been answered fully. The Almighty has His own purposes. "Woe unto the world because of offenses! for it must needs be that offenses come; but woe to that man by whom the offense cometh!"[1] If we shall suppose that American Slavery is one of those offenses which, in the providence of God must needs come, but which, having continued through His appointed time, He now wills to remove, and that He gives to both North and South, this terrible war, as the woe due to those by whom the offence came, shall we discern therein any departure from those divine attributes which the believers in a Living God always ascribe to Him? Fondly do we hope—fervently do we pray—that this mighty scourge of war may speedily pass away. Yet, if God wills that it continue, until all the wealth piled by the bond-man's two hundred and fifty years of unrequited toil shall be sunk, and until every drop of blood drawn with the lash, shall be paid by another drawn with the sword, as was said three thousand years ago, so still it must be said "the judgments of the Lord are true and righteous altogether."[2]

1. Matthew 18:17.

2. Psalms 19:9.

With malice toward none; with charity for all; with firmness in the right, as God gives us to see the right, let us strive on to finish the work we are in; to bind up the nation's wounds; to care for him who shall have borne the battle, and for his widow, and his orphan—to do all which may achieve and cherish a just, and a lasting peace, among ourselves, and with all nations.

Questions to Consider

1. How did Lincoln's views about slavery evolve during the sectional crisis and ensuing Civil War? What might account for that evolution? Do you see any indication in these selections that his views about African Americans changed?
2. Do these selections suggest that the Union always remain paramount among Lincoln's concerns? Or did Lincoln elevate conceptions of freedom, equality, and democracy to the level of concern he felt for the Union?

Louisa Susanna Cheves McCord

1810–1879

The daughter of prominent South Carolina planter, statesman, and banker Langdon Cheves, and the wife of jurist David J. McCord, Louisa McCord was, by all accounts, one of the most "trenchant intellectuals" of the Old South. "No other woman," noted historian Michael O'Brien, "wrote with more force, across such a range of genres, or participated so influentially in social and political discourse." In her political and social essays, McCord defended slavery, argued for women's subordinate position, and vaunted the superiority of the White race. Historian Elizabeth Fox-Genovese has pointed out that Louisa McCord, unlike the few other women intellectuals of the era, "made no apparent effort to contribute to a fledgling female intellectual tradition, although . . . she assumed that her mind was a match for the other best minds of her time." In "The Enfranchisement of Woman," for example, McCord noted, "woman, we grant, may have a great, a longing, a hungering intellect, equal to man's." She frequently wrote anonymously or signed her essays with her initials, and "she never publicly asserted her right as a woman to claim authorship." Rather, "her claims to publication lay in her education, class position, and political views, not in her private identity." She wrote not for a specifically female audience but for an intellectual elite of the South.

McCord contributed to the *Southern Literary Gazette*, the *Southern Quarterly Review*, *DeBow's Review*, and the *Southern Literary Messenger*. By the 1850s she had earned a reputation as a keen intellect with a biting tongue. She dismissed advocates of women's rights, for example, as "petticoated despisers of their sex—these would-be-men—these things that puzzle us to name. They should be women," she continued with her customary invective, "but, like Macbeth's witches, they come to us in such a questionable shape, that we hesitate so to interpret them." She championed the superiority of the White race with the same vigor that she had denounced woman's rights advocates. "It is scarcely now a subject of dispute, that the Black man is of inferior race to the White. Five thousand years of captivity, slavery, and barbarism prove him incapable of civilization," she asserted. "Could any imaginable circumstances crush down, for that space of time, into such perfect stagnation, any people capable of improvement?" she asked. "In his natural home, Central Africa, what has existed to prevent his progress? Nothing," she answered, "but natural incapacity. He has enjoyed," McCord continued, "equally with the White races which have raised themselves to civilization, the undisturbed advantages of all the intellect which God Almighty has seen fit to bestow upon him. The White man, by his nature, has sought and found improvement. The Negro, by his nature, has crouched contented, in the lowest barbarism. Only under the guidance of the White man," she concluded, "has he with a kind of monkey imitativeness, sometimes followed, to a very limited extent, the White civilization, seizing of its follies, but never its higher points of development." As O'Brien has put it, there was little in McCord's writing to "ruffle her contemporaries in South Carolina." Her views were conventional, yet her prose was "violent, polemical, defiant."

Believing that Harriet Beecher Stowe's novel *Uncle Tom's Cabin* would best be reviewed by a woman, William Gilmore Simms, editor of the *Southern Quarterly Review*, invited McCord to write a response to it. In her assessment, "that abominable woman's abominable book . . . . is one mass of fanatical bitterness and foul misrepresentation wrapped in the garb of Christian Charity." Her review, which appeared in January 1853, offers a glimpse into the ways in which some White Southerners received Stowe's novel and suggests that some plantation mistresses had a vested interest in the institution of slavery.

from Review of *Uncle Tom's Cabin*

Truly it would seem that the labour of Sisyphus is laid upon us, the slaveholders of these Southern United States. Again and again have we, with all the power and talent of our clearest heads and strongest intellects, forced aside the foul load of slander and villainous aspersion so often hurled against us, and still, again and again, the unsightly mass rolls back, and, heavily as ever, fall the old refuted libels, vamped, remodelled, and lumbering down upon us with all the force, or at least impudent assumption, of new argument. We anticipate here the answer and application of our charitable opponents. We, too, have studied our mythology, and remember well, that the aforesaid Sisyphus was condemned to his torment for the sins of injustice, oppression, and tyranny. Like punishment to like sin will, no doubt, be their corollary. Boldly, however, before God and man, we dare hold up our hand and plead "not guilty." Clearly enough do we see through the juggle of this game. It is no hand of destiny, no fiat of Jove, which rolls back upon us the labouring bulk. There is an agent behind the curtain, vulnerable at least as ourselves; and the day may yet come when, if this unlucky game cease not, the destructive mass shall find another impetus, and crush beneath its unexpected weight the hand which now directs it, we scarce know whether in idle wantonness or diabolic malice.

Among the revelations of this passing year, stand prominent the volumes we are about to review. In the midst of political turmoil, Mrs. Harriet Beecher Stowe has determined to put *her* finger in the pot, and has, it would seem, made quite a successful dip. Wordy philanthropy—which blows the bellows for discontent, and sends poor fools wandering through the clouds upon its treacherous breezes, yet finds no crumb of bread for one hungry stomach—is at a high premium nowadays. Ten thousand dollars (the amount, it is said, of the sales of her work) was, we presume, in the lady's opinion, worth risking a little scalding for. We wish her joy of her ten thousand thus easily gained, but would be loath to take with it the foul imagination which could invent such scenes, and the malignant bitterness (we had almost said ferocity) which, under the veil of christian charity, could find the conscience to publish them. Over this, their new-laid egg, the abolitionists, of all colours—black, White, and yellow—foreign and domestic—have set up so astounding a cackle, it is very evident, that (labouring, perhaps, under some mesmeric biologic influence) they think the goose has laid its golden egg at last. They must wake up from their dream, to the sad disappointment of finding their fancied treasure an old addle thing, whose touch contaminates with its filth.

There is nothing new in these volumes. They are, as we have said, only the old Sisyphus rock, which we have so often tumbled over, tinkered up, with considerable talent and cunning, into a new shape, and rolled back upon us. One step, indeed, we do seem to have gained. One accusation at least, which, in bygone times, used to have its changes rung among the charges brought against us, is here forgotten. We see no reference to the old habit, so generally (according to some veracious travellers) indulged in these Southern States, of fattening negro babies for the use of the soup-pot. This, it would appear, is a species of black broth which cannot be swallowed any longer. If, however, Mrs. Stowe has spared us the story of this delectable soup, with the small *nigger paws* floating in it by way of garnish, truly it is all that she *has* spared us. Libels almost as shocking to humanity she not only indulges herself in detailing, but dwells upon with a gusto and a relish quite edifying to us benighted heathen, who, constantly surrounded (as according to her statements we are) by such moving scenes and crying iniquities, yet, having ears, hear not, and having eyes, see not,[1] those horrors whose stench become[s] an offence to the nostrils of our sensitive and self-constituted directors.

Most painful it is to us to comment upon a work of this kind. What though "our withers be unwrung"?[2] Does slander cease to be painful because it is gross? Is it enough for us to know that these obscene and degrading scenes are false as the spirit of mischief which dictated them? and can we, therefore, indifferently see these loathsome rakings of a foul fancy passed as current coin upon the world, which receives them as sketches of American life by an American citizen? We cannot; and loathsome as is the task; little as we hope to be heard in any community where such a work can be received and accredited, and where the very fact of such reception proves at once that our case is prejudged; yet will we speak and sift the argument of this fair lady, who so protests against vice that we might think her, like that "noble sister of Publicola," that "moon of Rome,"

> chaste as the icicle
> That's curdied by the frost from purest snow
> And hangs on Dian's temple[3]

were it not that her too vivid imagination, going so far ahead of facts, shows too clearly that not now, for the first time, does it travel the muddy road. Some hints from the unfortunately fashionable reading of the day, some flashes from the French school of romance, some inspirations from the Sues and the Dumas', have evidently suggested the tenor of her pages.

The literary taste of our day (i.e., the second-rate literary taste, the fashionable novel-reading taste) demands excitement. Nothing can be spiced too high. Incident, incident, and that of the vilest kind, crowds the pages of those novels which are now unfortunately all the vogue. *The Mysteries of Paris*, *Monte Cristo*, *The Wandering Jew*,[4] *et id genus omne*,[5] leave the diseased taste of the reader, who has long subsisted on such fare, sick, sick and palled as it is with the nauseous diet, still with a constant craving, like that of the diseased palate of the opium eater, for its accustomed drug. For such tastes, Mrs. Stowe has catered well. Her facts are remarkable facts—very. Let us see on what authority she bases them. This is a question worth examining, as she here assumes to have given us an exhibition of slavery in its "*living dramatic reality*." In her "concluding remarks," appended to the second volume of the edition (seventh thousand) which we have, she says:

1. Psalms, 115:5–6; Jeremiah, 5:21.
2. *Hamlet*, 3.2.237–238.
3. *Coriolanus*, 5.3.64–67.
4. *Les Mysteres de Paris* (1842–1843) and *Le Juif Errant* (1844–1845) by Eugene Sue; *Le Comte de Monte Cristo* (1844) by Alexander Dumas.
5. And all that sort.

> The writer has often been enquired of, by correspondents from different parts of the country, whether this narrative is a true one; and to these enquiries she will give one general answer.
>
> The separate incidents which compose her narrative are, to a very great extent, authentic, occurring, many of them, [either] under her own observation, or that of her personal friends. She or her friends have observed characters the counterpart of almost all that are here introduced; and many of the sayings are word for word as heard herself, or reported to her.

We can only say, in answer to this, that "she and her friends" are far from being, in our minds, decisive authority. If she says "it is," just as emphatically do we answer "it is not." What vender of falsehood but vouches for the truth of his own fabrications? She tells us, "Some of the most deeply tragic and romantic, some of the most terrible incidents, have also their parallel in reality." And again, of one of her most horrible inventions, she remarks: "That this scene has too many times had its parallel, there are living witnesses, all over our land, to testify." Living witnesses all over our land are such intangible antagonists that it would be a worse combat than that of Don Quixote against the windmills for us to undertake them, and therefore we must let them pass. One stray sheep, however, she does introduce; and as we cannot be cheated, by the clouds of dust she has kicked up, to mistake him for a giant, we will not need, to encounter him, the courage exhibited by the celebrated Don in his attack upon a flock of the same animals. She says, with reference to a story of brutal persecution and slow murder:

> The story of "old Prue," in the second volume, was an incident that fell under the personal observation of a brother of the writer, then collecting-clerk to a large mercantile house, in New Orleans. From the same source was derived the character of the planter Legree. Of him her brother thus wrote, speaking of visiting his plantation on a collecting tour: "He actually made me feel of his fist, which was like a blacksmith's hammer, or a nodule of iron, telling me that it was 'calloused with knocking down niggers.' When I left the plantation, I drew a long breath, and felt as if I had escaped from an ogre's den."

The testimony of this brother is the only one which she cites, except in the general "all over the land" style which we have noticed; and we think any one who has spent six months of his life in a Southern city will recognize the type of this her solitary authority. Who has not seen the green Yankee youth opening his eyes and mouth for every piece of stray intelligence; eager for horrors; gulping the wildest tales, and exaggerating even as he swallows them? Why, this fellow is to be met with in every shipload of candidates for clerkships who come out like bees to suck our honey; but so choke-full the while of all they have heard of the horrors and dangers incident to these latitudes, that they wink their eyes and dodge a fancied pistol or bowie-knife whenever a man but raises his hand to touch his hat to the stranger. Having made up their minds that Southerners are all brutes, what earthly power can cure the moral near-sight? Not reason, certainly, nor fact either. Their school-dame taught it to them with their catechism; and surely those green eyes could never be expected to see across the catechism and the school-dame's teachings far enough to learn the truth. Pity that this gentle Balaam[6] of a brother had not possessed a little of the cunning and courage of those favourite heroes of our childish days, "Puss in Boots," and "Jack the Giant

6. Numbers, 22–24.

Killer," that he might have decisively disposed of this redoubtable ogre with nodules of iron hands, instead of sneaking out of his den and leaving him there, like a great "Giant Despair," to devour all unfortunate pilgrims who fell in his way. How poor Balaam summoned courage to feel *of* that fist, "calloused with knocking down niggers," we cannot imagine. Verily, there are trials by land, and trials by water, and poor Balaam, apparently, cared not to put his delicate person in danger from any of them. Seriously, is it not easy here to perceive that a raw, suspicious Yankee youth, having "happened" (as he would say) in contact with a rough overseer, a species of the *genus homo* evidently quite new to him, has been half gulled by the talk of the fellow who has plainly intended to quiz him, and has half gulled himself with his own fears while in the vicinity of this novel character, whom he, poor gentle specimen of Yankee humanity, has absolutely mistaken for an ogre because his hand is hard. That the fellow himself made the speech quoted by Balaam, viz., that his fist was "*calloused* by knocking down niggers," we more than doubt—that elegant word "calloused" being one entirely new to our dictionary, and savouring, we think, much more of Yankee clerk origin and Noah Webster, than of Southern birth.

Upon the whole, the authorities of our authoress put us in mind of one of our earliest trials in life. Our first entrance upon school being made in one of our Northern cities, we found ourselves, before the first week of probation was over, the object of some comment among the younger members of the establishment, and were finally accused, by the leader of the little faction, of coming from the land of negrodom. To this charge, we, of course, could but plead guilty, wondering, in our little mind, what sin there could be in the association. A portion of our iniquities we soon had revealed to us. "Father's cousin's wife's sister was at the South once, and she knows all about how you treat your negroes! She knows that you feed them with cotton-seed, and put padlocks on their mouths to keep them from eating corn while they are in the field." Vainly we protested; as vainly reasoned. Authority was against us, and the padlock story vouched by "father's cousin's wife's sister, a very nice lady, that always told the truth," was swallowed by the majority, and received in our Lilliput community with as undisputed credence as Mrs. Stowe's brother's account of the fist "calloused by knocking down niggers" will be gulped down by her admirers. A lady-friend of ours, travelling northward a summer or two since, was similarly enlightened as to some of the iniquities constantly practiced round us, but which, blinded creatures that we are, we have to leave home to discover. Miss C., she was informed, had a cousin who had gone school-keeping to Georgia, and that cousin told Miss C., on her word, as a lady, that she had often and often seen baskets full of ears and noses cut and pulled from the negroes by way of punishment and torture. Miss C. couldn't say whether they were big baskets or little ones; she supposed they were not very big ones, because the supply of ears and noses would be exhausted, and she did not suppose it was a case to call for miraculous increase. She could not account for it all exactly, but she knew that it was true—she did. Her cousin was a lady, and had seen it herself. Pity it is that Mrs. Stowe had not made acquaintance with Miss C.'s cousin; the ears and noses would have made a fine picturesque point, graphically introduced among her "dramatic realities." The Balaam brother, however, seems to answer her purpose pretty well, and upon his testimony about the nodule-fisted gentleman, and some enlightenments from a speech of the freesoil Massachusetts senator, Horace Mann, she has manufactured a character which would shame the Caliban of Shakspeare. That great master of the human mind, when he imagined a being devoid of all human feeling and yet possessed of something like human form, remembered that, in the wildest flights of imagination, there must still be kept up a semblance of probability, and painted him, therefore, free also from human parentage. Shakspeare's Caliban was a monster of devilish origin, to whom Sycorax, his dam, bequeathed but little of humanity. Mrs. Harriet Beccher Stowe, however, gives to *her* Caliban a human mother; a gentle, fair-haired, loving mother, and does not shame to pass upon us as a man this beast, this brute, without conscience and without heart, devoid equally of common sense and common feeling.

The *Westminster Review*, in noticing, with high approbation, these volumes of Mrs. Stowe, takes upon itself to pronounce that she has therein exhibited the "concealed realities" of the system of slavery, "without falling either into vulgarity or exaggeration." The opportunities of the writers of the *Westminster* to judge of our habits and manners must, we should suppose, be small; and whence they may have received the capacity for so dogmatically determining the point at issue, we cannot well guess. Simple assertion is easily answered by counter-assertion. *We* assert that there is in this dramatic sample of abolitionism not only vulgarity and exaggeration, but gross vulgarity and absolute falsehood. The *Westminster* goes on to remark of this infamous libel upon our people, that the "darkest part of it is *possible within the law*," that "the slave-code *authorizes these very enormities*," and, therefore, whether these things be true or not, it is the "privilege of the artist" so to represent them. We answer, that such transactions are *not possible within the law*, that murder of the slave is equally punishable with murder of the free man; that the slave-code does *not authorize these enormities;* that our laws protect, as far as legislation can, the very beast from cruelty and barbarous treatment. How much more the slave! Cruelty cannot always be prevented. The parent may ill-treat his child, the man his wife, without giving tangible cause for prosecution. But where such cause can be found, an individual may with us, precisely as in any other well-governed country, be indicted for unjust oppression of any kind, whether of beast, of child, or of slave. The public feeling with us is, we believe, as delicate, and as much on the alert upon such points, as in any part of the world. Indeed, the existence of a system of slavery rather tends to increase than diminish this feeling, as, leaving a larger portion of society in a state of tutelage, naturally and necessarily greater attention is turned to the subject. If, therefore, the shadow of such enormities as these volumes describe may sometimes be, we deny that it is "the artist's privilege" to cull out the most horrible exceptional cases, and to represent them as forming the manners and habits of a whole people, vouching for them as *fac simile* representations of real life. What would the *Westminster* say if one should take the celebrated murderer Burke[7] (whose notorious name has given a new word to our language), with some half dozen other such desperadoes easy to imagine, and write a novel thereon, to depict English manners of the nineteenth century, only using so far "the privilege of the artist" as to represent Mr. Burke as an accomplished gentleman, circulating freely in English society, and his satellites as tolerated and everyday frequenters of the same? What would Mrs. Stowe herself say should we take the Parkman tragedy[8] (a much better foundation, by the way, than anything she has raked up in her Southern investigations), and represent such gentlemen as of daily frequency in the pure New England society, the morals of which she would contrast with our own. If the lowest vices of the lowest men, if the darkest crimes of the darkest villains—actions which the vilest of mankind, only in their moments of blackest passion, can perpetrate—are to be culled out with care, and piled upon each other, to form a

7. William Burke (1792–1829) killed at least 15 people in Edinburgh in order to sell cadavers to anatomy schools. Burke was eventually executed.

8. George Parkman, Boston physician, declared missing in November 1849; his body was found in the laboratory of John White Webster, a Harvard chemistry and mineralogy professor. Webster was convicted of murder and hanged.

monster disgusting to humanity, let the creator of so unnatural a conception give to his Frankenstein the name as well as the character of the monsters of fable. Let the creature stalk before us as some ghoul or afrite, and we shudder at the supernatural might of evil, which does not strike us as unnatural because it does not claim to be of the nature of anything with which we are acquainted. But let the same creature be represented to us as a man—above all, as one of many men, forming an integral part of a community of civilized men—and the effect becomes simply ridiculous where it is not disgusting. God made man in his own image; Mrs. Stowe has very decidedly set up a rival manufacture in the devil's image.

* * *

To conclude. We have undertaken the defence of slavery in no temporizing vein. We do *not* say it is a necessary evil. We do *not* allow that it is a temporary makeshift to choke the course of Providence for man's convenience. It is *not* "a sorrow and a wrong to be lived down." We proclaim it, on the contrary, a Godlike dispensation, a providential caring for the weak, and a refuge for the portionless. Nature's outcast, as for centuries he appeared to be, he—even from the dawning of tradition, the homeless, houseless, useless negro—suddenly assumes a place, suddenly becomes one of the great levers of civilization. At length the path marked out for him by Omniscience becomes plain. Unfit for all progress, so long as left to himself, the negro has hitherto appeared simply as a blot upon creation, and already the stronger races are, even in his own land, threatening him with extinction. Civilization must spread. Nature seems to require this, by a law as stringent as that through which water seeks its level. The poor negro, astounded by the torrent of progress which, bursting over the world, now hangs menacingly (for to the wild man is not civilization always menacing?) above him, would vainly follow with the stream, and is swept away in the current. Slavery, even in his own land, is his destiny and his refuge from extinction. Beautifully has the system begun to expand itself among us. Shorn of the barbarities with which a slavery established by conquest and maintained by brute force is always accompanied, we have begun to mingle with it the graces and amenities of the highest Christian civilization. Have begun, we say, for the work is but begun. The system is far from its perfection, and at every step of its progress is retarded by a meddling fanaticism, which has in it, to borrow a quotation from Mrs. Stowe herself, "a dread, unhallowed necromancy of evil, that turns things sweetest and holiest to phantoms of horror and affright". Our system of slavery, left to itself, would rapidly develop its higher features, softening at once to servant and to master. The satanic school of arguers are far too much inclined to make capital of man's original sin, and to build upon this foundation a perfect tower of iniquitous possibilities, frightful even to imagine. Men are by no means as hopelessly wicked as Mrs. Stowe and others of this school would argue; and these would do well to remember, that when God created man, "in the image of God created he him"; and though "sin came into the world and death by sin,"[9] yet is the glorious, though clouded, image still there, and erring man is still a man, and not a devil.

We, too, could speculate upon the possibilities of this system, and present a picture in beautiful contrast with Mrs. Stowe's, as purely bright as hers is foully dark; but, as we remarked earlier in our argument, the fairest reasoning is not from what a system might be, but from what it is. We grant that there is crime, there is sin, there is abuse of power under our laws; but let the abolitionist show us any rule where these are not. Utopias have been vainly dreamed. That system is the best which, not in

9. Genesis 1:27; Romans 5:12.

theory, but in practice, brings the greatest sum of good to the greatest number. We challenge history, present and past, to show any system of government which, judged by this test, will be found superior to the one we defend.

"Oh liberté!" exclaimed Mme. Roland, when led to the scaffold, "que de crimes a-t-on commis en ton nom!" *Theoretic* virtues are more dangerous than open vice. Cloaks for every crime, they are pushed boldly forward, stifling our natural sense of practical right, and blinding men with the appearance of a righteousness, which dazzles like the meteor, but warms not like the sun. Theoretic liberty and theoretic bread satisfy neither the hungry soul nor the hungry stomach, and many a poor fugitive to the land of freedom, sated full with both, has wept to return to the indulgent master and the well filled corncrib. The negro, left to himself, does not dream of liberty. He cannot indeed grasp a conception which belongs so naturally to the brain of the White man. In his natural condition, he is, by turns, tyrant and slave, but never the free man. You may talk to the blind man of light, until he fancies that he understands you, and begins to wish for that bright thing which you tell him he has not; but vainly he rolls his sightless orbs, unhappy that he cannot see the brightness of that beam whose warmth before sufficed to make him happy. Thus it is with the moral sunbeam of the poor negro. He cannot see nor conceive the "liberty" which you would thrust upon him, and it is a cruel task to disturb him in the enjoyment of that life to which God has destined him. He basks in his sunshine, and is happy. Christian slavery, in its full development, free from the fretting annoyance and galling bitterness of abolition interference, is the brightest sunbeam which Omniscience has destined for his existence.

Questions to Consider

1. What does McCord's review of *Uncle Tom's Cabin* suggest about the fears Southerners harbored about the novel? What kind of threat did Stowe's novel pose to the Southern institution of slavery?
2. How effectively does McCord dismantle Stowe's novel?

Harriet Jacobs

c. 1813–1897

When *Linda: Incidents in the Life of a Slave Girl, Written by Herself* appeared in 1861, most people assumed that the noted abolitionist Lydia Marie Child—who had purportedly edited the volume for former slave Harriet Jacobs, disguised as Linda Brent—had actually written the narrative. Over one hundred years later, the authorship of the work remained in doubt. Historian John Blassingame, for example, aptly summarized the position that *Incidents* was a work of fiction. "In spite of Lydia Marie Child's insistence that she had only revised the manuscript of Harriet Jacobs's [narrative] 'mainly for purposes of condensation and orderly arrangement,' the work is not credible," Blassingame wrote. The work, which chronicles her life in bondage, was too orderly, he maintained. "Too many of the major characters meet providentially after years of separation," according to Blassingame. "Then, too, the story is too melodramatic: miscegenation and cruelty, outraged virtue, unrequited love, and planter licentiousness appear on practically every page," he alleged. As Jacqueline Goldsby has noted, Blassingame's assessment influenced subsequent evaluations of *Incidents* for a number of years. Jean Fagan Yellin's meticulous research, however, has since demonstrated that Harriet Jacobs's role as author of her own narrative can no longer be questioned.

Undoubtedly, Harriet Jacobs wrote in the idiom of White middle-class domestic fiction. Jacobs framed her narrative for a White, Northern, middle-class audience and, in this respect, she "did not differentiate herself from the most celebrated male authors of slave narratives," most notably, Frederick Douglass. Jacobs cast her narrative in terms with which her readers could identify, making a claim to virtue. "But, O, ye happy women," she addressed her readers, "whose purity has been sheltered from childhood, who have been free to choose the objects of your affection, whose homes are protected by law, do not judge the poor desolate slave girl too severely." Jacobs then confessed that she bore a child out of wedlock, fathered by her lover, rather than submit to the sexual advances of her master. Jacobs hoped that she could gain her readers' sympathy by couching her confession in a familiar idiom. Her strategy, observed historian Elizabeth Fox-Genovese, demanded that her readers "take the oppression of slave women personally, to see it as a threat to their own sense of themselves as women." Jacobs, then, appealed to Northern gender conventions to suggest that her own story represented a tale of true womanhood.

Incidents in the Life of a Slave Girl does not merely mimic the strategies employed by Frederick Douglass in his narrative, however. Frances Smith Foster argues that Jacobs's slave narrative is "more complex and varied" than that of Douglass and other male narrators. Like other slave narratives, Jacobs presents slavery as a dehumanizing and oppressive institution. She also suggests slavery exacted its greatest toll on women. But, as Foster points out, "she also counters the prevalent literary construct of slave women as completely helpless victims." Jacobs tells of successful efforts to outwit her master and her refusal to allow her children to be sold away, for example. "Harriet Jacobs writes an account of slavery that does not excuse the evil inherent in that institution," Foster notes, "but does reveal it as a condition within which some are able to develop strong family ties, develop bonds of affection and loyalty among women, and unite themselves into a viable and resourceful community of resisters." Her narrative, then, suggests that slaves had some degree of autonomy in shaping their own lives.

from Incidents in the Life of a Slave Girl

Chapter 1: Childhood

I was born a slave; but I never knew it till six years of happy childhood had passed away. My father was a carpenter, and considered so intelligent and skilful in his trade, that, when buildings out of the common line were to be erected, he was sent for from long distances, to be head workman. On condition of paying his mistress two hundred dollars a year, and supporting himself, he was allowed to work at his trade, and manage his own affairs. His strongest wish was to purchase his children; but, though he several times offered his hard earnings for that purpose, he never succeeded. In complexion my parents were a light shade of brownish yellow, and were termed mulattoes. They lived together in a comfortable home; and, though we were all slaves, I was so fondly shielded that I never dreamed I was a piece of merchandise, trusted to them for safe keeping, and liable to be demanded of them at any moment. I had one brother, William, who was two years younger than myself—a bright, affectionate child. I had also a great treasure in my maternal grandmother, who was a remarkable woman in many respects. She was the daughter of a planter in South Carolina, who, at his death, left her mother and his three children free, with money to go to St. Augustine, where they had relatives. It was during the Revolutionary War; and they were captured on their passage, carried back, and sold to different purchasers. Such was the story my grandmother used to tell me; but I do not remember all the particulars. She was a little girl when she was captured and sold to the keeper of a large hotel. I have often heard her tell how hard she fared during childhood. But as she grew older she evinced so much intelligence, and was so faithful, that her master and mistress could not help seeing it was for their interest to take care of such a valuable piece of property. She became an indispensable personage in the household, officiating in all capacities, from cook and wet nurse to seamstress. She was much praised for her cooking; and her nice crackers became so famous in the neighborhood that many people were desirous of obtaining them. In consequence of numerous requests of this kind, she asked permission of her mistress to bake crackers at night, after all the household work was done; and she obtained leave to do it, provided she would clothe herself and her children from the profits. Upon these terms, after working hard all day for her mistress, she began her midnight bakings, assisted by her two oldest children. The business proved profitable; and each year she laid by a little, which was saved for a fund to purchase her children. Her master died, and the property was divided among his heirs. The widow had her dower in the hotel, which she continued to keep open. My grandmother remained in her service as a slave; but her children were divided among her master's children. As she had five, Benjamin, the youngest one, was sold, in order that each heir might have an equal portion of dollars and cents. There was so little difference in our ages that he seemed more like my brother than my uncle. He was a bright, handsome lad, nearly White; for he inherited the complexion my grandmother had derived from Anglo-Saxon ancestors. Though only ten years old, seven hundred and twenty dollars were paid for him. His sale was a terrible blow to my grandmother; but she was naturally hopeful, and she went to work with renewed energy, trusting in time to be able to purchase some of her children. She had laid up three hundred dollars, which her mistress one day begged as a loan, promising to pay her soon. The reader probably knows that no promise or writing given to a slave is legally binding; for, according to Southern laws, a slave, *being* property, can *hold* no property. When my grandmother lent her hard earnings to her mistress, she trusted solely to her honor. The honor of a slaveholder to a slave!

To this good grandmother I was indebted for many comforts. My brother Willie and I often received portions of the crackers, cakes, and preserves, she made to sell; and after we ceased to be children we were indebted to her for many more important services.

Such were the unusually fortunate circumstances of my early childhood. When I was six years old, my mother died; and then, for the first time, I learned, by the talk around me, that I was a slave. My mother's mistress was the daughter of my grandmother's mistress. She was the foster sister of my mother; they were both nourished at my grandmother's breast. In fact, my mother had been weaned at three months old, that the babe of the mistress might obtain sufficient food. They played together as children; and, when they became women, my mother was a most faithful servant to her Whiter foster sister. On her death-bed her mistress promised that her children should never suffer for any thing; and during her lifetime she kept her word. They all spoke kindly of my dead mother, who had been a slave merely in name, but in nature was noble and womanly. I grieved for her, and my young mind was troubled with the thought who would now take care of me and my little brother. I was told that my home was now to be with her mistress; and I found it a happy one. No toilsome or disagreeable duties were imposed upon me. My mistress was so kind to me that I was always glad to do her bidding, and proud to labor for her as much as my young years would permit. I would sit by her side for hours, sewing diligently, with a heart as free from care as that of any free-born White child. When she thought I was tired, she would send me out to run and jump; and away I bounded, to gather berries or flowers to decorate her room. Those were happy days—too happy to last. The slave child had no thought for the morrow; but there came that blight, which too surely waits on every human being born to be a chattel.

When I was nearly twelve years old, my kind mistress sickened and died. As I saw the check grow paler, and the eye more glassy, how earnestly I prayed in my heart that she might live! I loved her; for she had been almost like a mother to me. My prayers were not answered. She died, and they buried her in the little churchyard, where, day after day, my tears fell upon her grave.

I was sent to spend a week with my grandmother. I was now old enough to begin to think of the future; and again and again I asked myself what they would do with me. I felt sure I should never find another mistress so kind as the one who was gone. She had promised my dying mother that her children should never suffer for any thing; and when I remembered that, and recalled her many proofs of attachment to me, I could not help having some hopes that she had left me free. My friends were almost certain it would be so. They thought she would be sure to do it, on account of my mother's love and faithful service. But, alas! we all know that the memory of a faithful slave does not avail much to save her children from the auction block.

After a brief period of suspense, the will of my mistress was read, and we learned that she had bequeathed me to her sister's daughter, a child of five years old. So vanished our hopes. My mistress had taught me the precepts of God's Word: "Thou shalt love thy neighbor as thyself."[1] "Whatsoever ye would that men should do unto you, do ye even so unto them."[2] But I was her slave, and I suppose she did not recognize me as her neighbor. I would give much to blot out from my memory that one great wrong. As a child, I loved my mistress; and, looking back on the happy days I spent with her, I try to think with less bitterness of this act of injustice. While I was with her, she taught me to read and spell; and for this privilege, which so rarely falls to the lot of a slave, I bless her memory.

She possessed but few slaves; and at her death those were all distributed among her relatives. Five of them were my grandmother's children, and had shared the same milk that nourished her mother's children. Notwithstanding my grandmother's long and faithful service to her owners, not one of her children escaped the auction block. These God-breathing machines are no more, in the sight of their masters, than the cotton they plant, or the horses they tend.

Chapter 2: The New Master and Mistress

Dr. Flint, a physician in the neighborhood, had married the sister of my mistress, and I was now the property of their little daughter. It was not without murmuring that I prepared for my new home; and what added to my unhappiness, was the fact that my brother William was purchased by the same family. My father, by his nature, as well as by the habit of transacting business as a skilful mechanic, had more of the feelings of a freeman than is common among slaves. My brother was a spirited boy; and being brought up under such influences, he early detested the name of master and mistress. One day, when his father and his mistress had happened to call him at the same time, he hesitated between the two; being perplexed to know which had the strongest claim upon his obedience. He finally concluded to go to his mistress. When my father reproved him for it, he said, "You both called me, and I didn't know which I ought to go to first."

1. Mark 12:31.

2. Matthew 7:12.

"You are *my* child," replied our father, "and when I call you, you should come immediately, if you have to pass through fire and water."

Poor Willie! He was now to learn his first lesson of obedience to a master. Grandmother tried to cheer us with hopeful words, and they found an echo in the credulous hearts of youth.

When we entered our new home we encountered cold looks, cold words, and cold treatment. We were glad when the night came. On my narrow bed I moaned and wept, I felt so desolate and alone.

I had been there nearly a year, when a dear little friend of mine was buried. I heard her mother sob, as the clods fell on the coffin of her only child, and I turned away from the grave, feeling thankful that I still had something left to love. I met my grandmother, who said, "Come with me, Linda;" and from her tone I knew that something sad had happened. She led me apart from the people, and then said, "My child, your father is dead." Dead! How could I believe it? He had died so suddenly I had not even heard that he was sick. I went home with my grandmother. My heart rebelled against God, who had taken from me mother, father, mistress, and friend. The good grandmother tried to comfort me. "Who knows the ways of God?" said she. "Perhaps they have been kindly taken from the evil days to come." Years afterwards I often thought of this. She promised to be a mother to her grandchildren, so far as she might be permitted to do so; and strengthened by her love, I returned to my master's. I thought I should be allowed to go to my father's house the next morning; but I was ordered to go for flowers, that my mistress's house might be decorated for an evening party. I spent the day gathering flowers and weaving them into festoons, while the dead body of my father was lying within a mile of me. What cared my owners for that? he was merely a piece of property. Moreover, they thought he had spoiled his children, by teaching them to feel that they were human beings. This was blasphemous doctrine for a slave to teach; presumptuous in him, and dangerous to the masters.

The next day I followed his remains to a humble grave beside that of my dear mother. There were those who knew my father's worth, and respected his memory.

My home now seemed more dreary than ever. The laugh of the little slave-children sounded harsh and cruel. It was selfish to feel so about the joy of others. My brother moved about with a very grave face. I tried to comfort him, by saying, "Take courage, Willie; brighter days will come by and by."

"You don't know any thing about it, Linda," he replied. "We shall have to stay here all our days; we shall never be free."

I argued that we were growing older and stronger, and that perhaps we might, before long, be allowed to hire our own time, and then we could earn money to buy our freedom. William declared this was much easier to say than to do; moreover, he did not intend to *buy* his freedom. We held daily controversies upon this subject.

Little attention was paid to the slaves' meals in Dr. Flint's house. If they could catch a bit of food while it was going, well and good. I gave myself no trouble on that score, for on my various errands I passed my grandmother's house, where there was always something to spare for me. I was frequently threatened with punishment if I stopped there; and my grandmother, to avoid detaining me, often stood at the gate with something for my breakfast or dinner. I was indebted to *her* for all my comforts, spiritual or temporal. It was *her* labor that supplied my scanty wardrobe. I have a vivid recollection of the linsey-woolsey dress given me every winter by Mrs. Flint. How I hated it! It was one of the badges of slavery.

While my grandmother was thus helping to support me from her hard earnings, the three hundred dollars she had lent her mistress were never repaid. When her mistress died, her son-in-law, Dr. Flint, was appointed executor. When grandmother applied to him for payment, he said the estate was insolvent, and the law prohibited payment. It did not, however, prohibit him from retaining the silver candelabra, which had been purchased with that money. I presume they will be handed down in the family, from generation to generation.

My grandmother's mistress had always promised her that, at her death, she should be free; and it was said that in her will she made good the promise. But when the estate was settled, Dr. Flint told the faithful old servant that, under existing circumstances, it was necessary she should be sold.

On the appointed day, the customary advertisement was posted up, proclaiming that there would be a "public sale of negroes, horses, &c." Dr. Flint called to tell my grandmother that he was unwilling to wound her feelings by putting her up at auction, and that he would prefer to dispose of her at private sale. My grandmother saw through his hypocrisy; she understood very well that he was ashamed of the job. She was a very spirited woman, and if he was base enough to sell her, when her mistress intended she should be free, she was determined the public should know it. She had for a long time supplied many families with crackers and preserves; consequently, "Aunt Marthy," as she was called, was generally known, and every body who knew her respected her intelligence and good character. Her long and faithful service in the family was also well known, and the intention of her mistress to leave her free. When the day of sale came, she took her place among the chattels, and at the first call she sprang upon the auction-block. Many voices called out, "Shame! Shame! Who is going to sell *you*, aunt Marthy? Don't stand there! That is no place for *you*." Without saying a word, she quietly awaited her fate. No one bid for her. At last, a feeble voice said, "Fifty dollars." It came from a maiden lady, seventy years old, the sister of my grandmother's deceased mistress. She had lived forty years under the same roof with my grandmother; she knew how faithfully she had served her owners, and how cruelly she had been defrauded of her rights; and she resolved to protect her. The auctioneer waited for a higher bid; but her wishes were respected; no one bid above her. She could neither read nor write; and when the bill of sale was made out, she signed it with a cross. But what consequence was that, when she had a big heart overflowing with human kindness? She gave the old servant her freedom.

At that time, my grandmother was just fifty years old. Laborious years had passed since then; and now my brother and I were slaves to the man who had defrauded her of her money, and tried to defraud her of her freedom. One of my mother's sisters, called Aunt Nancy, was also a slave in his family. She was a kind, good aunt to me; and supplied the place of both housekeeper and waiting maid to her mistress. She was, in fact, at the beginning and end of every thing.

Mrs. Flint, like many Southern women, was totally deficient in energy. She had not strength to superintend her household affairs; but her nerves were so strong, that she could sit in her easy chair and see a woman whipped, till the blood trickled from every stroke of the lash. She was a member of the church; but partaking of the Lord's supper did not seem to put her in a Christian frame of mind. If dinner was not served at the exact time on that particular Sunday, she would station herself in the kitchen, and wait till it was dished, and then spit in all the kettles and pans that had been used for cooking. She did this to prevent the cook and her children from eking out their meagre fare with the remains of the gravy and other scrapings. The slaves could get nothing to eat except what she chose to give them. Provisions were weighed out by the pound and ounce, three times a day. I can assure you she gave them no chance to eat wheat bread from her flour barrel. She knew how many biscuits a quart of flour would make, and exactly what size they ought to be.

Dr. Flint was an epicure. The cook never sent a dinner to his table without fear and trembling; for if there happened to be a dish not to his liking, he would either order her to be whipped, or compel her to eat every mouthful of it in his presence. The poor, hungry creature might not have objected to eating it; but she did object to having her master cram it down her throat till she choked.

They had a pet dog, that was a nuisance in the house. The cook was ordered to make some Indian mush[3] for him. He refused to eat, and when his head was held over it, the froth flowed from his mouth into the basin. He died a few minutes after. When Dr. Flint came in, he said the mush had not been well cooked, and that was the reason the animal would not eat it. He sent for the cook, and compelled her to eat it. He thought that the woman's stomach was stronger than the dog's; but her sufferings afterwards proved that he was mistaken. This poor woman endured many cruelties from her master and mistress; sometimes she was locked up, away from her nursing baby, for a whole day and night.

When I had been in the family a few weeks, one of the plantation slaves was brought to town, by order of his master. It was near night when he arrived, and Dr. Flint ordered him to be taken to the work house, and tied up to the joist, so that his feet would just escape the ground. In that situation he was to wait till the doctor had taken his tea. I shall never forget that night. Never before, in my life, had I heard hundreds of blows fall, in succession, on a human being. His piteous groans, and his "O, pray don't, massa," rang in my ear for months afterwards. There were many conjectures as to the cause of this terrible punishment. Some said master accused him of stealing corn; others said the slave had quarrelled with his wife, in presence of the overseer, and had accused his master of being the father of her child. They were both black, and the child was very fair.

I went into the work house next morning, and saw the cowhide still wet with blood, and the boards all covered with gore. The poor man lived, and continued to quarrel with his wife. A few months afterwards Dr. Flint handed them both over to a slavetrader. The guilty man put their value into his pocket, and had the satisfaction of knowing that they were out of sight and hearing. When the mother was delivered into the trader's hands, she said, "You *promised* to treat me well." To which he replied, "You have let your tongue run too far; damn you!" She had forgotten that it was a crime for a slave to tell who was the father of her child.

From others than the master persecution also comes in such cases. I once saw a young slave girl dying soon after the birth of a child nearly White. In her agony she cried out, "O Lord, come and take me!" Her mistress stood by, and mocked at her like an incarnate fiend. "You suffer, do you?" she exclaimed. "I am glad of it. You deserve it all, and more too."

The girl's mother said, "The baby is dead, thank God; and I hope my poor child will soon be in heaven, too."

"Heaven!" retorted the mistress. "There is no such place for the like of her and her bastard."

The poor mother turned away, sobbing. Her dying daughter called her, feebly, and as she bent over her, I heard her say, "Don't grieve so, mother; God knows all about it; and HE will have mercy upon me."

3. A mush made from corn.

Her sufferings, afterwards, became so intense, that her mistress felt unable to stay; but when she left the room, the scornful smile was still on her lips. Seven children called her mother. The poor black woman had but the one child, whose eyes she saw closing in death, while she thanked God for taking her away from the greater bitterness of life.

Chapter 5: The Trials of Girlhood

During the first years of my service in Dr. Flint's family, I was accustomed to share some indulgences with the children of my mistress. Though this seemed to me no more than right, I was grateful for it, and tried to merit the kindness by the faithful discharge of my duties. But I now entered on my fifteenth year—a sad epoch in the life of a slave girl. My master began to whisper foul words in my ear. Young as I was, I could not remain ignorant of their import. I tried to treat them with indifference or contempt. The master's age, my extreme youth, and the fear that his conduct would be reported to my grandmother, made him bear this treatment for many months. He was a crafty man, and resorted to many means to accomplish his purposes. Sometimes he had stormy, terrific ways, that made his victims tremble; sometimes he assumed a gentleness that he thought must surely subdue. Of the two, I preferred his stormy moods, although they left me trembling. He tried his utmost to corrupt the pure principles my grandmother had instilled. He peopled my young mind with unclean images, such as only a vile monster could think of. I turned from him with disgust and hatred. But he was my master. I was compelled to live under the same roof with him—where I saw a man forty years my senior daily violating the most sacred commandments of nature. He told me I was his property; that I must be subject to his will in all things. My soul revolted against the mean tyranny. But where could I turn for protection? No matter whether the slave girl be as black as ebony or as fair as her mistress. In either case, there is no shadow of law to protect her from insult, from violence, or even from death; all these are inflicted by fiends who bear the shape of men. The mistress, who ought to protect the helpless victim, has no other feelings towards her but those of jealousy and rage. The degradation, the wrongs, the vices, that grow out of slavery, are more than I can describe. They are greater than you would willingly believe. Surely, if you credited one half the truths that are told you concerning the helpless millions suffering in this cruel bondage, you at the North would not help to tighten the yoke. You surely would refuse to do for the master, on your own soil, the mean and cruel work which trained bloodhounds and the lowest class of Whites do for him at the South.[4]

Every where the years bring to all enough of sin and sorrow; but in slavery the very dawn of life is darkened by these shadows. Even the little child, who is accustomed to wait on her mistress and her children, will learn, before she is twelve years old, why it is that her mistress hates such and such a one among the slaves. Perhaps the child's own mother is among those hated ones. She listens to violent outbreaks of jealous passion, and cannot help understanding what is the cause. She will become prematurely knowing in evil things. Soon she will learn to tremble when she hears her master's footfall. She will be compelled to realize that she is no longer a child. If God has bestowed beauty upon her, it will prove her greatest curse. That which commands admiration in the White woman only hastens the degradation of the female slave. I know that some are too much brutalized by slav-

4. A reference to the Fugitive Slave Law of 1850.

ery to feel the humiliation of their position; but many slaves feel it most acutely, and shrink from the memory of it. I cannot tell how much I suffered in the presence of these wrongs, nor how I am still pained by the retrospect. My master met me at every turn, reminding me that I belonged to him, and swearing by heaven and earth that he would compel me to submit to him. If I went out for a breath of fresh air, after a day of unwearied toil, his footsteps dogged me. If I knelt by my mother's grave, his dark shadow fell on me even there. The light heart which nature had given me became heavy with sad forebodings. The other slaves in my master's house noticed the change. Many of them pitied me; but none dared to ask the cause. They had no need to inquire. They knew too well the guilty practices under that roof; and they were aware that to speak of them was an offence that never went unpunished.

I longed for some one to confide in. I would have given the world to have laid my head on my grandmother's faithful bosom, and told her all my troubles. But Dr. Flint swore he would kill me, if I was not as silent as the grave. Then, although my grandmother was all in all to me, I feared her as well as loved her. I had been accustomed to look up to her with a respect bordering upon awe. I was very young, and felt shamefaced about telling her such impure things, especially as I knew her to be very strict on such subjects. Moreover, she was a woman of a high spirit. She was usually very quiet in her demeanor; but if her indignation was once roused, it was not very easily quelled. I had been told that she once chased a White gentleman with a loaded pistol, because he insulted one of her daughters. I dreaded the consequences of a violent outbreak; and both pride and fear kept me silent. But though I did not confide in my grandmother, and even evaded her vigilant watchfulness and inquiry, her presence in the neighborhood was some protection to me. Though she had been a slave. Dr. Flint was afraid of her. He dreaded her scorching rebukes. Moreover, she was known and patronized by many people; and he did not wish to have his villainy made public. It was lucky for me that I did not live on a distant plantation, but in a town not so large that the inhabitants were ignorant of each other's affairs. Bad as are the laws and customs in a slaveholding community, the doctor, as a professional man, deemed it prudent to keep up some outward show of decency.

O, what days and nights of fear and sorrow that man caused me! Reader, it is not to awaken sympathy for myself that I am telling you truthfully what I suffered in slavery. I do it to kindle a flame of compassion in your hearts for my sisters who are still in bondage, suffering as I once suffered.

I once saw two beautiful children playing together. One was a fair White child; the other was her slave, and also her sister. When I saw them embracing each other, and heard their joyous laughter, I turned sadly away from the lovely sight. I foresaw the inevitable blight that would fall on the little slave's heart. I knew how soon her laughter would be changed to sighs. The fair child grew up to be a still fairer woman. From childhood to womanhood her pathway was blooming with flowers, and overarched by a sunny sky. Scarcely one day of her life had been clouded when the sun rose on her happy bridal morning.

How had those years dealt with her slave sister, the little playmate of her childhood? She, also, was very beautiful; but the flowers and sunshine of love were not for her. She drank the cup of sin, and shame, and misery, whereof her persecuted race are compelled to drink.

In view of these things, why are ye silent, ye free men and women of the North? Why do your tongues falter in maintenance of the right? Would that I had more ability! But my heart is so full, and my pen is so weak! There are noble men and women who plead for us, striving to help those who cannot help themselves. God bless them! God give them strength and courage to go on! God bless those every where, who are laboring to advance the cause of humanity!

Chapter 10: A Perilous Passage in the Slave Girl's Life

After my lover went away, Dr. Flint contrived a new plan. He seemed to have an idea that my fear of my mistress was his greatest obstacle. In the blandest tones, he told me that he was going to build a small house for me, in a secluded place, four miles away from the town. I shuddered; but I was constrained to listen, while he talked of his intention to give me a home of my own, and to make a lady of me. Hitherto, I had escaped my dreaded fate, by being in the midst of people. My grandmother had already had high words with my master about me. She had told him pretty plainly what she thought of his character, and there was considerable gossip in the neighborhood about our affairs, to which the open-mouthed jealousy of Mrs. Flint contributed not a little. When my master said he was going to build a house for me, and that he could do it with little trouble and expense, I was in hopes something would happen to frustrate his scheme; but I soon heard that the house was actually begun. I vowed before my Maker that I would never enter it. I had rather toil on the plantation from dawn till dark; I had rather live and die in jail, than drag on, from day to day, through such a living death. I was determined that the master, whom I so hated and loathed, who had blighted the prospects of my youth, and made my life a desert, should not, after my long struggle with him, succeed at last in trampling his victim under his feet. I would do any thing, every thing, for the sake of defeating him. What *could* I do? I thought and thought, till I became desperate, and made a plunge into the abyss.

And now, reader, I come to a period in my unhappy life, which I would gladly forget if I could. The remembrance fills me with sorrow and shame. It pains me to tell you of it; but I have promised to tell you the truth, and I will do it honestly, let it cost me what it may. I will not try to screen myself behind the plea of compulsion from a master; for it was not so. Neither can I plead ignorance or thoughtlessness. For years, my master had done his utmost to pollute my mind with foul images, and to destroy the pure principles inculcated by my grandmother, and the good mistress of my childhood. The influences of slavery had had the same effect on me that they had on other young girls; they had made me prematurely knowing, concerning the evil ways of the world. I knew what I did, and I did it with deliberate calculation.

But, O, ye happy women, whose purity has been sheltered from childhood, who have been free to choose the objects of your affection, whose homes are protected by law, do not judge the poor desolate slave girl too severely! If slavery had been abolished, I, also, could have married the man of my choice; I could have had a home shielded by the laws; and I should have been spared the painful task of confessing what I am now about to relate; but all my prospects had been blighted by slavery. I wanted to keep myself pure; and, under the most adverse circumstances, I tried hard to preserve my self-respect; but I was struggling alone in the powerful grasp of the demon Slavery; and the monster proved too strong for me. I felt as if I was forsaken by God and man; as if all my efforts must be frustrated; and I became reckless in my despair.

I have told you that Dr. Flint's persecutions and his wife's jealousy had given rise to some gossip in the neighborhood. Among others, it chanced that a White unmarried gentleman had obtained some knowledge of the circumstances in which I was placed. He knew my grandmother, and often spoke to me in the street. He became interested for me, and asked questions about my master, which I answered in part. He expressed a great deal of sympathy, and a wish to aid me. He constantly sought opportunities to see me, and wrote to me frequently. I was a poor slave girl, only fifteen years old.

So much attention from a superior person was, of course, flattering; for human nature is the same in all. I also felt grateful for his sympathy, and encouraged by his kind words. It seemed to me a great thing to have such a friend. By degrees, a more tender feeling crept into my heart. He was an educated and eloquent gentleman; too eloquent, alas, for the poor slave girl who trusted in him. Of course I saw whither all this was tending. I knew the impassable gulf between us; but to be an object of interest to a man who is not married, and who is not her master, is agreeable to the pride and feelings of a slave, if her miserable situation has left her any pride or sentiment. It seems less degrading to give one's self, than to submit to compulsion. There is something akin to freedom in having a lover who has no control over you, except that which he gains by kindness and attachment. A master may treat you as rudely as he pleases, and you dare not speak; moreover, the wrong does not seem so great with an unmarried man, as with one who has a wife to be made unhappy. There may be sophistry in all this; but the condition of a slave confuses all principles of morality, and, in fact, renders the practice of them impossible.

When I found that my master had actually begun to build the lonely cottage, other feelings mixed with those I have described. Revenge, and calculations of interest, were added to flattered vanity and sincere gratitude for kindness. I knew nothing would enrage Dr. Flint so much as to know that I favored another; and it was something to triumph over my tyrant even in that small way. I thought he would revenge himself by selling me, and I was sure my friend, Mr. Sands, would buy me. He was a man of more generosity and feeling than my master, and I thought my freedom could be easily obtained from him. The crisis of my fate now came so near that I was desperate. I shuddered to think of being the mother of children that should be owned by my old tyrant. I knew that as soon as a new fancy took him, his victims were sold far off to get rid of them; especially if they had children. I had seen several women sold, with his babies at the breast. He never allowed his offspring by slaves to remain long in sight of himself and his wife. Of a man who was not my master I could ask to have my children well supported; and in this case, I felt confident I should obtain the boon. I also felt quite sure that they would be made free. With all these thoughts revolving in my mind, and seeing no other way of escaping the doom I so much dreaded, I made a headlong plunge. Pity me, and pardon me, O virtuous reader! You never knew what it is to be a slave; to be entirely unprotected by law or custom; to have the laws reduce you to the condition of a chattel, entirely subject to the will of another. You never exhausted your ingenuity in avoiding the snares, and eluding the power of a hated tyrant; you never shuddered at the sound of his footsteps, and trembled within hearing of his voice. I know I did wrong. No one can feel it more sensibly than I do. The painful and humiliating memory will haunt me to my dying day. Still, in looking back, calmly, on the events of my life, I feel that the slave woman ought not to be judged by the same standard as others.

The months passed on. I had many unhappy hours. I secretly mourned over the sorrow I was bringing on my grandmother, who had so tried to shield me from harm. I knew that I was the greatest comfort of her old age, and that it was a source of pride to her that I had not degraded myself, like most of the slaves. I wanted to confess to her that I was no longer worthy of her love; but I could not utter the dreaded words.

As for Dr. Flint, I had a feeling of satisfaction and triumph in the thought of telling *him*. From time to time he told me of his intended arrangements, and I was silent. At last, he came and told me the cottage was completed, and ordered me to go to it. I told him I would never enter it. He said, "I have heard enough of such talk as that. You shall go, if you are carried by force; and you shall remain there."

I replied, "I will never go there. In a few months I shall be a mother."

He stood and looked at me in dumb amazement, and left the house without a word. I thought I should be happy in my triumph over him. But now that the truth was out, and my relatives would hear of it, I felt wretched. Humble as were their circumstances, they had pride in my good character. Now, how could I look them in the face? My self-respect was gone! I had resolved that I would be virtuous, though I was a slave. I had said, "Let the storm beat! I will brave it till I die." And now, how humiliated I felt!

I went to my grandmother. My lips moved to make confession, but the words stuck in my throat. I sat down in the shade of a tree at her door and began to sew. I think she saw something unusual was the matter with me. The mother of slaves is very watchful. She knows there is no security for her children. After they have entered their teens she lives in daily expectation of trouble. This leads to many questions. If the girl is of a sensitive nature, timidity keeps her from answering truthfully, and this well-meant course has a tendency to drive her from maternal counsels. Presently, in came my mistress, like a mad woman, and accused me concerning her husband. My grandmother, whose suspicions had been previously awakened, believed what she said. She exclaimed, "O Linda! has it come to this? I had rather see you dead than to see you as you now are. You are a disgrace to your dead mother." She tore from my fingers my mother's wedding ring and her silver thimble. "Go away!" she exclaimed, "and never come to my house, again." Her reproaches fell so hot and heavy, that they left me no chance to answer. Bitter tears, such as the eyes never shed but once, were my only answer. I rose from my seat, but fell back again, sobbing. She did not speak to me; but the tears were running down her furrowed cheeks, and they scorched me like fire. She had always been so kind to me! *So* kind! How I longed to throw myself at her feet, and tell her all the truth! But she had ordered me to go, and never to come there again. After a few minutes, I mustered strength, and started to obey her. With what feelings did I now close that little gate, which I used to open with such an eager hand in my childhood! It closed upon me with a sound I never heard before.

Where could I go? I was afraid to return to my master's. I walked on recklessly, not caring where I went, or what would become of me. When I had gone four or five miles, fatigue compelled me to stop. I sat down on the stump of an old tree. The stars were shining through the boughs above me. How they mocked me, with their bright, calm light! The hours passed by, and as I sat there alone a chilliness and deadly sickness came over me. I sank on the ground. My mind was full of horrid thoughts. I prayed to die; but the prayer was not answered. At last, with great effort I roused myself, and walked some distance further, to the house of a woman who had been a friend of my mother. When I told her why I was there, she spoke soothingly to me; but I could not be comforted. I thought I could bear my shame if I could only be reconciled to my grandmother. I longed to open my heart to her. I thought if she could know the real state of the case, and all I had been bearing for years, she would perhaps judge me less harshly. My friend advised me to send for her. I did so; but days of agonizing suspense passed before she came. Had she utterly forsaken me? No. She came at last. I knelt before her, and told her the things that had poisoned my life; how long I had been persecuted; that I saw no way of escape; and in an hour of extremity I had become desperate. She listened in silence. I told her I would bear any thing and do any thing, if in time I had hopes of obtaining her forgiveness. I begged of her to pity me, for my dead mother's sake. And she did pity me. She did not say, "I forgive you"; but she looked at me lovingly, with her eyes full of tears. She laid her old hand gently on my head, and murmured, "Poor child! Poor child!"

Questions to Consider

1. Does Jacobs make a convincing case that women were the most vulnerable to slavery's depravities?
2. Does the language of Antebellum domestic fiction detract from Jacobs's narrative?
3. In what ways does Jacobs's narrative challenge the arguments made in defense of slavery?

Elizabeth Keckley

c. 1818–1907

Elizabeth Keckley was born a slave in Dinwiddie Court House, Virginia in the early nineteenth century. She became an accomplished seamstress and eventually bought her freedom as well as her son's for $1,200 in 1855. Once she was manumitted, she moved to Washington, D.C., where she became a dressmaker, working for Jefferson Davis's wife and later for Mary Todd Lincoln during Abraham Lincoln's first term as president. In 1868, Keckley published her autobiography, *Behind the Scenes: Thirty Years a Slave, and Four Years in the White House*, chronicling her years as a slave and as a free woman. The first three chapters follow the form of a conventional slave narrative. But unlike most slave narratives, which were originally published before the Civil War, *Behind the Scenes* does not end with freedom. Rather, the remaining chapters detail Keckley's efforts to maneuver her way through freedom.

Literary scholars and historians have noted that Elizabeth Keckley adopted many of the narrative strategies employed by Harriet Jacobs in *Incidents in the Life of a Slave Girl*. Like Jacobs, Keckley assumed that middle-class White women would constitute her reading audience. She therefore rendered her account in ways that invited her readers to sympathize with her plight and admire her resourcefulness. Like Jacobs, she told of sexual exploitation at the hands of a White man. She offered only the sketchiest of details. "Suffice it to say," she wrote, "that he persecuted me for four years, and I—I—became a mother." Keckley, however, refused to accept blame for bearing a child out of wedlock. Like Jacobs, she shifted responsibility to "the edicts of that society which deemed it no crime to undermine the virtue of girls in my then position."

Keckley also attempted to tell her story in a way that would discourage her readers from questioning her authority or authenticity. She understood that many of her readers would have a hard time believing that a former slave possessed the intelligence and a sufficient command of the language to render her own autobiography. After all, few believed that Harriet Jacobs had written *Incidents in the Life of a Slave Girl* when it appeared in 1861. Keckley also knew that many would doubt the veracity of her experiences. She therefore prefaced her account by assuring her readers of the truthfulness of her narrative even though, she conceded, it might read like fiction. "Much has been omitted" she confessed, "but nothing has been exaggerated." Despite her assurances, however, many doubted the authenticity of her authorship. For example, both the *New York Citizen* and the *Atlantic Monthly* questioned whether Keckley had written *Behind the Scenes*.

Sylvia D. Hoffert explains that Keckley's publisher protested the allegations that *Behind the Scenes* was penned by someone other than Keckley. Keckley herself wrote a letter that was printed in the *New York Citizen* accusing her critics of racism. "Let me trust," she wrote, "that I am not denounced for writing the truth simply because my skin is dark and that I was once a slave." Few were persuaded by Keckley's claims, however. One anonymous author parodied Keckley's memoirs, publishing *Behind the Seams; by a Nigger Woman Who Took in Work from Mrs. Lincoln and Mrs. Davis*. Hoffert notes that the parody's author "rejected Keckley's claim to assimilation and attempted to remind his readers that her race precluded any legitimate claim to respectability and to suggest that her self-presentation could only be considered fraudulent."

Behind the Scenes differed from *Incidents in the Life of a Slave Girl* in significant ways, however. Frances Smith Foster explains that Keckley "relies less on the mask of polite deference or strategic withdrawal than did Harriet Jacobs." Keckley could adopt a less deferential stance, according to Foster, in part because "in the postbellum era women could claim greater freedom for themselves and their literature." Keckley had to take care, however, not to threaten her postwar reading audience by suggesting that revenge motivated her actions. The reunion scene between Keckley and her former mistress suggests to her readers that, according to Keckley, the newly emancipated slaves bore no ill will toward their former masters. Like other Postbellum narrators, Keckley had to assure her readers that she was capable of assuming the responsibilities of freedom. Keckley therefore focused less on the dehumanizing aspects of slavery than she did on the development of her talent and work ethic. In this respect, *Behind the Scenes* has much in common with Booker T. Washington's *Up from Slavery*.

from Behind the Scenes

Chapter 2: Girlhood and Its Sorrows

I must pass rapidly over the stirring events of my early life. When I was about fourteen years old I went to live with my master's eldest son, a Presbyterian minister. His salary was small, and he was burdened with a helpless wife, a girl that he had married in the humble walks of life. She was morbidly sensitive, and imagined that I regarded her with contemptuous feelings because she was of poor parentage. I was their only servant, and a gracious loan at that. They were not able to buy me, so my old master sought to render them assistance by allowing them the benefit of my services. From the very first I did the work of three servants, and yet I was scolded and regarded with distrust. The years passed slowly, and I continued to serve them, and at the same time grew into strong, healthy womanhood. I was nearly eighteen when we removed from Virginia to Hillsboro', North Carolina, where young Mr. Burwell took charge of a church. The salary was small, and we still had to practise the closest economy. Mr. Bingham, a hard, cruel man, the village schoolmaster, was a member of my young master's church, and he was a frequent visitor to the parsonage. She whom I called mistress seemed to be desirous to wreak vengeance on me for something, and Bingham became her ready tool. During this time my master was unusually kind to me; he was naturally a good-hearted man, but was influenced by his wife. It was Saturday evening, and while I was bending over the bed, watching the baby that I had just hushed into slumber, Mr. Bingham came to the door and asked me to go with him to his study. Wondering what he meant by his strange request, I followed him, and when we had entered the study he closed the door, and in his blunt way remarked: "Lizzie, I am going to flog you." I was thunderstruck, and tried to think if I had been remiss in anything. I could not recollect of doing anything to deserve punishment, and with surprise exclaimed: "Whip me, Mr. Bingham! what for?"

"No matter," he replied, "I am going to whip you, so take down your dress this instant."

Recollect, I was eighteen years of age, was a woman fully developed, and yet this man coolly bade me take down my dress. I drew myself up proudly, firmly, and said: "No, Mr. Bingham, I shall not take down my dress before you. Moreover, you shall not whip me unless you prove the stronger. Nobody has a right to whip me but my own master, and nobody shall do so if I can prevent it."

My words seemed to exasperate him. He seized a rope, caught me roughly, and tried to tie me. I resisted with all my strength, but he was the stronger of the two, and after a hard struggle succeeded in binding my hands and tearing my dress from my back. Then he picked up a rawhide, and began to ply it freely over my shoulders. With steady hand and practised eye he would raise the instrument of torture, nerve himself for a blow, and with fearful force the rawhide descended upon the quivering flesh. It cut the skin, raised great welts, and the warm blood trickled down my back. Oh God! I can feel the torture now—the terrible, excruciating agony of those moments. I did not scream; I was too proud to let my tormentor know what I was suffering. I closed my lips firmly, that not even a groan might escape from them, and I stood like a statue while the keen lash cut deep into my flesh. As soon as I was released, stunned with pain, bruised and bleeding, I went home and rushed into the presence of the pastor and his wife, wildly exclaiming: "Master Robert, why did you let Mr. Bingham flog me? What have I done that I should be so punished?"

"Go away," he gruffly answered, "do not bother me."

I would not be put off thus. "What *have* I done? I *will* know why I have been flogged."

I saw his cheeks flush with anger, but I did not move. He rose to his feet, and on my refusing to go without an explanation, seized a chair, struck me, and felled me to the floor. I rose, bewildered, almost dead with pain, crept to my room, dressed my bruised arms and back as best I could, and then lay down, but not to sleep. No, I could not sleep, for I was suffering mental as well as bodily torture. My spirit rebelled against the unjustness that had been inflicted upon me, and though I tried to smother my anger and to forgive those who had been so cruel to me, it was impossible. The next morning I was more calm, and I believe that I could then have forgiven everything for the sake of one kind word. But the kind word was not proffered, and it may be possible that I grew somewhat wayward and sullen. Though I had faults, I know now, as I felt then, harshness was the poorest inducement for the correction of them. It seems that Mr. Bingham had pledged himself to Mrs. Burwell to subdue what he called my "stubborn pride." On Friday following the Saturday on which I was so savagely beaten, Mr. Bingham again directed me come to his study. I went, but with the determination to offer resistance should he attempt to flog me again. On entering the room I found him prepared with a new rope and a new cowhide. I told him that I was ready to die, but that he could not conquer me. In struggling with him I bit his finger severely, when he seized a heavy stick and beat me with it in a shameful manner. Again I went home sore and bleeding, but with pride as strong and defiant as ever. The following Thursday Mr. Bingham again tried to conquer me, but in vain. We struggled, and he struck me many savage blows. As I stood bleeding before him, nearly exhausted with his efforts, he burst into tears, and declared that it would be a sin to beat me any more. My suffering at last subdued his hard heart; he asked my forgiveness, and afterwards was an altered man. He was never known to strike one of his servants from that day forward. Mr. Burwell, he who preached the love of Heaven, who glorified the precepts and examples of Christ, who expounded the Holy Scriptures Sabbath after Sabbath from the pulpit, when Mr. Bingham refused to whip me any more, was urged by his wife to punish me himself. One morning he went to the wood-pile, took an oak broom, cut the handle off, and with this heavy handle attempted to conquer me. I fought him, but he proved the strongest. At the sight of my bleeding form, his wife fell upon her knees and begged him to desist. My distress even touched her cold, jealous heart. I was so badly bruised that I was unable to leave my bed for five days. I will not dwell upon the bitter anguish of these hours, for even the thought of them now makes me shudder. The Rev. Mr. Burwell was not yet satisfied. He resolved to make another attempt to subdue my proud, rebellious spirit—made the attempt and again failed, when he told me, with an air of penitence, that he should never strike me another blow; and faithfully he kept his word. These revolting scenes created a great sensation at the time, were the talk of the town and neighborhood, and I flatter myself that the actions of those who had conspired against me were not viewed in a light to reflect much credit upon them.

The savage efforts to subdue my pride were not the only things that brought me suffering and deep mortification during my residence at Hillsboro'. I was regarded as fair-looking for one of my race, and for four years a white man—I spare the world his name—had base designs upon me. I do not care to dwell upon this subject, for it is one that is fraught with pain. Suffice it to say, that he persecuted me for four years, and I–I–became a mother. The child of which he was the father was the only child that I ever brought into the world. If my poor boy ever suffered any humiliating pangs on account of birth, he could not blame his mother, for God knows that she did not wish to give him life; he must blame the edicts of that society which deemed it no crime to undermine the virtue of girls in my then position.

Among the old letters preserved by my mother I find the following, written by myself while at Hillsboro'. In this connection I desire to state that Rev. Robert Burwell is now living at Charlotte, North Carolina:—

Hillsboro', 10 April 1838

My Dear Mother:—I have been intending to write to you for a long time, but numerous things have prevented, and for that reason you must excuse me.

I thought very hard of you for not writing to me, but hope that you will answer this letter as soon as you receive it, and tell me how you like Marsfield, and if you have seen any of my old acquaintances, or if you yet know any of the brick-house people who I think so much of. I want to hear of the family at home very much, indeed. I really believe you and all the family have forgotten me, if not I certainly should have heard from some of you since you left Boyton, if it was only a line; nevertheless I love you all very dearly, and shall, although I may never see you again, nor do I ever expect to. Miss Anna is going to Petersburgh next winter, but she says that she does not intend to take me; what reason she has for leaving me I cannot tell. I have often wished that I lived where I knew I never could see you, for then I would not have my hopes raised, and to be disappointed in this manner; however, it is said that a bad beginning makes a good ending, but I hardly expect to see that happy day at this place. Give my love to all the family, both white and black. I was very much obliged to you for the presents you sent me last summer, though it is quite late in the day to be thanking for them. Tell Aunt Bella that I was very much obliged to her for her present; I have been so particular with it that I have only worn it once.

There have been six weddings since October; the most respectable one was about a fortnight ago; I was asked to be the first attendant, but, as usual with all my expectations, I was disappointed, for on the wedding-day I felt more like being locked up in a three-cornered box than attending a wedding. About a week before Christmas I was bridesmaid for Ann Nash; when the night came I was in quite a trouble; I did not know whether my frock was clean or dirty; I only had a week's notice, and the body and sleeves to make, and only one hour every night to work on it, so you can see with these troubles to overcome my chance was rather slim. I must now close, although I could fill ten pages with my griefs and misfortunes; no tongue could express them as I feel; don't forget me though; and answer my letters soon. I will write you again, and would write more now, but Miss Anna says it is time I had finished. Tell Miss Elizabeth that I wish she would make haste and get married, for mistress says that I belong to her when she gets married.

I wish you would send me a pretty frock this summer; if you will send it to Mrs. Robertson's Miss Bet will send it to me.

Farewell, darling mother.

Your affectionate daughter,
Elizabeth Hobbs

Chapter 3: How I Gained My Freedom

The years passed and brought many changes to me, but on these I will not dwell, as I wish to hasten to the most interesting part of my story. My troubles in North Carolina were brought to an end by my unexpected return to Virginia, where I lived with Mr. Garland, who had married Miss Ann Burwell, one of my old master's daughters. His life was not a prosperous one, and after struggling with the world for several years he left his native State, a disappointed man. He moved to St. Louis, hoping to improve his fortune in the West; but ill luck followed him there, and he seemed to be unable to escape from the influence of the evil star of his destiny. When his family, myself included, joined him in his new home on the banks of the Mississippi, we found him so poor that he was unable to pay the dues on a letter advertised as in the post-office for him. The necessities of the family were so great, that it was proposed to place my mother out at service. The idea was shocking to me. Every gray hair in her old head was dear to me, and I could not bear the thought of her going to work for strangers. She had been raised in the family, had watched the growth of each child from infancy to maturity; they had been the objects of her kindest care, and she was wound round about them as the vine winds itself about the rugged oak. They had been the central figures in her dream of life—a dream beautiful to her, since she had basked in the sunshine of no other. And now they proposed to destroy each tendril of affection, to cloud the sunshine of her existence when the day was drawing to a close, when the shadows of solemn night were rapidly approaching. My mother, my poor aged mother, go among strangers to toil for a living! No, a thousand times no! I would rather work my fingers to the bone, bend over my sewing till the film of blindness gathered in my eyes; nay, even beg from street to street. I told Mr. Garland so, and he gave me permission to see what I could do. I was fortunate in obtaining work, and in a short time I had acquired something of a reputation as a seamstress and dress-maker. The best ladies in St. Louis were my patrons, and when my reputation was once established I never lacked for orders. With my needle I kept bread in the mouths of seventeen persons for two years and five months. While I was working so hard that others might live in comparative comfort, and move in those circles of society to which their birth gave them entrance, the thought often occurred to me whether I was really worth my salt or not; and then perhaps the lips curled with a bitter sneer. It may seem strange that I should place so much emphasis upon words thoughtlessly, idly spoken; but then we do many strange things in life, and cannot always explain the motives that actuate us. The heavy task was too much for me, and my health began to give way. About this time Mr. Keckley, whom I had met in Virginia, and learned to regard with more than friendship, came to St. Louis. He sought my hand in marriage, and for a long time I refused to consider his proposal; for I could not bear the thought of bringing children into slavery—of adding one single recruit to the millions bound to hopeless servitude, fettered and shackled with chains stronger and heavier than manacles of iron. I made a proposition to buy myself and son; the proposition was bluntly declined, and I was commanded never to broach the subject again. I would not be put off thus, for hope pointed to a freer, brighter life in the future. Why should my son be held in slavery? I often asked myself. He came into the world through no will of mine, and yet, God only knows how I loved him. The Anglo-Saxon blood as well as the African flowed in his veins; the two currents commingled—one singing of freedom, the other silent and sullen with generations of despair. Why should not the Anglo-Saxon triumph—why should it be weighed down with the rich blood typical of the tropics? Must the life-current of one race bind the other race in chains as strong and enduring as if there had been no Anglo-Saxon taint? By the laws of God and nature, as interpreted by man, one-half of my boy was free, and why should not this fair birthright of freedom remove the curse from the other half—raise it into the bright, joyous sunshine of liberty?

I could not answer these questions of my heart that almost maddened me, and I learned to regard human philosophy with distrust. Much as I respected the authority of my master, I could not remain silent on a subject that so nearly concerned me. One day, when I insisted on knowing whether he would permit me to purchase myself, and what price I must pay for myself, he turned to me in a petulant manner, thrust his hand into his pocket, drew forth a bright silver quarter of a dollar, and proffering it to me, said:

"Lizzie, I have told you often not to trouble me with such a question. If you really wish to leave me, take this: it will pay the passage of yourself and boy on the ferry-boat, and when you are on the other side of the river you will be free. It is the cheapest way that I know of to accomplish what you desire."

I looked at him in astonishment, and earnestly replied: "No, master, I do not wish to be free in such a manner. If such had been my wish, I should never have troubled you about obtaining your consent to my purchasing myself. I can cross the river any day, as you well know, and have frequently done so, but will never leave you in such a manner. By the laws of the land I am your slave—you are my master, and I will only be free by such means as the laws of the country provide." He expected this answer, and I knew that he was pleased. Some time afterwards he told me that he had reconsidered the question; that I had served his family faithfully; that I deserved my freedom, and that he would take $1200 for myself and boy.

This was joyful intelligence for me, and the reflection of hope gave a silver lining to the dark cloud of my life—faint, it is true, but still a silver lining.

Taking a prospective glance at liberty, I consented to marry. The wedding was a great event in the family. The ceremony took place in the parlor, in the presence of the family and a number of guests. Mr. Garland gave me away, and the pastor, Bishop Hawks, performed the ceremony, who had solemnized the bridals of Mr. G.'s own children. The day was a happy one, but it faded all too soon. Mr. Keckley—let me speak kindly of his faults—proved dissipated, and a burden instead of a helpmate. More than all, I learned that he was a slave instead of a free man, as he represented himself to be. With the simple explanation that I lived with him eight years, let charity draw around him the mantle of silence.

I went to work in earnest to purchase my freedom, but the years passed, and I was still a slave. Mr. Garland's family claimed so much of my attention—in fact, I supported them—that I was not able to accumulate anything. In the mean time Mr. Garland died, and Mr. Burwell, a Mississippi planter, came to St. Louis to settle up the estate. He was a kind-hearted man, and said I should be free, and would afford me every facility to raise the necessary amount to pay the price of my liberty. Several schemes were urged upon me by my friends. At last I formed a resolution to go to New York, state my case, and appeal to the benevolence of the people. The plan seemed feasible, and I made preparations to carry it out. When I was almost ready to turn my face northward, Mrs. Garland told me that she would require the names of six gentlemen who would vouch for my return, and become responsible for the amount at which I was valued. I had many friends in St. Louis, and as I believed that they had confidence in me, I felt that I could readily obtain the names desired. I started out, stated my case, and obtained five signatures to the paper, and my heart throbbed with pleasure, for I did not believe that the sixth would refuse me. I called, he listened patiently, then remarked:

"Yes, yes, Lizzie; the scheme is a fair one, and you shall have my name. But I shall bid you good-by when you start."

"Good-by for a short time," I ventured to add.

"No, good-by for all time," and he looked at me as if he would read my very soul with his eyes.

I was startled. "What do you mean, Mr. Farrow? Surely you do not think that I do not mean to come back?"

"No."

"No, what then?"

"Simply this: you *mean* to come back, that is, you *mean* so *now*, but you never will. When you reach New York the abolitionists will tell you what savages we are, and they will prevail on you to stay there: and we shall never see you again."

"But I assure you, Mr. Farrow, you are mistaken. I not only *mean* to come back, but *will* come back, and pay every cent of the twelve hundred dollars for myself and child."

I was beginning to feel sick at heart, for I could not accept the signature of this man when he had no faith in my pledges. No; slavery, eternal slavery rather than be regarded with distrust by those whose respect I esteemed.

"But—I am not mistaken," he persisted. "Time will show. When you start for the North I shall bid you good-by."

The heart grew heavy. Every ray of sunshine was eclipsed. With humbled pride, weary step, tearful face, and a dull, aching pain, I left the house. I walked along the street mechanically. The cloud had no silver lining now. The rosebuds of hope had withered and died without lifting up their heads to receive the dew kiss of morning. There was no morning for me—all was night, dark night.

I reached my own home, and weeping threw myself upon the bed. My trunk was packed, my luncheon was prepared by mother, the cars were ready to bear me where I would not hear the clank of chains, where I would breathe the free, invigorating breezes of the glorious North. I had dreamed such a happy dream, in imagination had drunk of the water, the pure, sweet crystal water of life, but now—now—the flowers had withered before my eyes; darkness had settled down upon me like a pall, and I was left alone with cruel mocking shadows.

The first paroxysm of grief was scarcely over, when a carriage stopped in front of the house; Mrs. Le Bourgois, one of my kind patrons, got out of it and entered the door. She seemed to bring sunshine with her handsome cheery face. She came to where I was, and in her sweet way said:

"Lizzie, I hear that you are going to New York to beg for money to buy your freedom. I have been thinking over the matter, and told Ma it would be a shame to allow you to go North to *beg* for what we should *give* you. You have many friends in St. Louis, and I am going to raise the twelve hundred dollars required among them. I have two hundred dollars put away for a present; am indebted to you one hundred dollars; mother owes you fifty dollars, and will add another fifty to it; and as I do not want the present, I will make the money a present to you. Don't start for New York now until I see what I can do among your friends."

Like a ray of sunshine she came, and like a ray of sunshine she went away. The flowers no longer were withered, drooping. Again they seemed to bud and grow in fragrance and beauty. Mrs. Le Bourgois, God bless her dear good heart, was more than successful. The twelve hundred dollars were raised, and at last my son and myself were free. Free, free! what a glorious ring to the word. Free! the bitter heart-struggle was over. Free! the soul could go out to heaven and to God with no chains to clog its flight or pull it down. Free! the earth wore a brighter look, and the very stars seemed to sing with joy. Yes, free! free by the laws of man and the smile of God—and Heaven bless them who made me so!

The following, copied from the original papers, contain, in brief, the history of my emancipation:—

"I promise to give Lizzie and her son George their freedom, on the payment of $1200.

Anne P. Garland"

"27 June 1855"

"Lizzy:—I send you this note to sign for the sum of $75, and when I give you the whole amount you will then sign the other note for $100.

Ellen M. Doan"

"In the paper you will find $25; see it is all right before the girl leaves."

"I have received of Lizzy Keckley $950, which I have deposited with Darby & Barksdale for her—$600 on the 21st July, $300 on the 27th and 28th of July, and $50 on 13th August, 1855.

"I have and shall make use of said money for Lizzy's benefit, and hereby guarantee to her one per cent, per month—as much more as can be made she shall have. The one per cent, as it may be checked out, I will be responsible for myself, as well as for the whole amount, when it shall be needed by her.

Willis L. Williams"

"St. Louis, 13 August 1855"

"Know all men by these presents, that for and in consideration of the love and affection we bear towards our sister, Anne P. Garland, of St. Louis, Missouri, and for the further consideration of $5 in hand paid, we hereby sell and convey unto her, the said Anne P. Garland, a negro woman named Lizzie, and a negro boy, her son, named George; said Lizzie now resides at St. Louis, and is a seamstress, known there as Lizzie Garland, the wife of a yellow man named James, and called James Keckley; said George is a bright mulatto boy, and is known in St. Louis as Garland's George. We warrant these two slaves to be slaves for life, but make no representations as to age or health.

"Witness our hands and seals, this 10th day of August, 1855.

"Jas. R. Putnam, [L.S.]
"E. M. Putnam, [L.S.]
"A. Burwell, [L.S.]"

"The State of Mississippi, Warren County, City of Vicksburg"

"Be it remembered, that on the tenth day of August, in the year of our Lord one thousand eight hundred and fifty-five, before me, Francis N. Steele, a Commissioner, resident in the city of Vicksburg, duly commissioned and qualified by the executive authority, and under the laws of the State of Missouri, to take the acknowledgment of deeds, etc., to be used or recorded therein, personally appeared James R. Putnam and E. M. Putnam, his wife, and Armistead Burwell, to me known to be the individuals named in, and who executed the foregoing conveyance, and acknowledged that they executed the same for the purposes therein mentioned; and the E. M. Putnam being by me examined apart from her husband, and being fully acquainted with the contents of the foregoing conveyance, acknowledged that she executed the same freely, and relinquished her dower, and any other claim she might have in and to the property therein mentioned, freely, and without fear, compulsion, or undue influence of her said husband.

"In witness whereof I have hereunto set my hand and affixed my official seal, this 10th day of August, A.D. 1855.

"F. N. Steele,
"Commissioner for Missouri." [L.S.]

"Know all men that I, Anne P. Garland, of the County and City of St. Louis, State of Missouri, for and in consideration of the sum of $1200, to me in hand paid this day in cash, hereby emancipate my negro woman Lizzie, and her son George; the said Lizzie is known in St. Louis as the wife of James, who is called James Keckley; is of light complexion, about 37 years of age, by trade a dress-maker, and called by those who know her Garland's Lizzie. The said boy, George, is the only child of Lizzie, is about 16 years of age, and is almost white, and called by those who know him Garland's George.

"Witness my hand and seal, this 13th day of November, 1855.

"Anne P. Garland, [L.S.]
"Witness:—John Wickham,
"Willis L. Williams."

In St. Louis Circuit Court, October Term, 1855. November 15, 1855.
"State of Missouri, County of St. Louis"

"Be it remembered, that on this fifteenth day of November, eighteen hundred and fifty-five, in open court came John Wickham and Willis L. Williams, these two subscribing witnesses, examined under oath to that effect, proved the execution and acknowledgment of said deed by Anne P. Garland to Lizzie and her son George, which said proof of acknowledgment is entered on the record of the court of that day.

"In testimony whereof I hereto set my hand and affix the seal of said court, at office in the City of St. Louis, the day and year last aforesaid.

"WM. J. Hammond, *Clerk*." [L.S.]

"State of Missouri, County of St. Louis"

"I, Wm. J. Hammond, Clerk of the Circuit Court within and for the county aforesaid, certify the foregoing to be a true copy of a deed of emancipation from Anne P. Garland to Lizzie and her son George, as fully as the same remain in my office.

"In testimony whereof I hereto set my hand and affix the seal of said court, at office in the City of St. Louis, this fifteenth day of November, 1855.

"WM. J. Hammond, *Clerk*.

"By WM. A. Pennington, D. C."

"State of Missouri, County of St. Louis"

"I, the undersigned Recorder of said county, certify that the foregoing instrument of writing was filed for record in my office on the 14th day of November, 1855; it is truly recorded in Book No. 169, page 288.

"Witness my hand and official seal, date last aforesaid.

"C. Keemle, *Recorder*." [L.S.]

Chapter 10: The Second Inauguration

Mrs. Lincoln came to my apartments one day towards the close of the summer of 1864, to consult me in relation to a dress. And here let me remark, I never approved of ladies, attached to the Presidential household, coming to my rooms. I always thought that it would be more consistent with their dignity to send for me, and let me come to them, instead of their coming to me. I may have peculiar notions about some things, and this may be regarded as one of them. No matter, I have recorded my opinion. I cannot forget the associations of my early life. Well, Mrs. Lincoln came to my rooms, and, as usual, she had much to say about the Presidential election.

After some conversation, she asked: "Lizzie, where do you think I will be this time next summer?"

"Why, in the White House, of course."

"I cannot believe so. I have no hope of the re-election of Mr. Lincoln. The canvass is a heated one, the people begin to murmur at the war, and every vile charge is brought against my husband."

"No matter," I replied, "Mr. Lincoln will be re-elected. I am so confident of it, that I am tempted to ask a favor of you."

"A favor! Well, if we remain in the White House I shall be able to do you many favors. What is the special favor?"

"Simply this, Mrs. Lincoln—I should like for you to make me a present of the right-hand glove that the President wears at the first public reception after his second inaugural."

"You shall have it in welcome. It will be so filthy when he pulls it off, I shall be tempted to take the tongs and put it in the fire. I cannot imagine, Lizabeth, what you want with such a glove."

"I shall cherish it as a precious memento of the second inauguration of the man who has done so much for my race. He has been a Jehovah to my people—has lifted them out of bondage, and directed their footsteps from darkness into light. I shall keep the glove, and hand it down to posterity."

"You have some strange ideas, Lizabeth. Never mind, you shall have the glove; that is, if Mr. Lincoln continues President after the 4th of March next."

I held Mrs. Lincoln to her promise. That glove is now in my possession, bearing the marks of the thousands of hands that grasped the honest hand of Mr. Lincoln on that eventful night. Alas! it, has become a prouder, sadder memento than I ever dreamed—prior to making the request—it would be.

In due time the election came off, and all of my predictions were verified. The loyal States decided that Mr. Lincoln should continue at the nation's helm. Autumn faded, winter dragged slowly by, and still the country resounded with the clash of arms. The South was suffering, yet suffering was borne with heroic determination, and the army continued to present a bold, defiant front. With the first early breath of spring, thousands of people gathered in Washington to witness the second inauguration of Abraham Lincoln as President of the United States. It was a stirring day in the National Capital, and one that will never fade from the memory of those who witnessed the imposing ceremonies. The morning was dark and gloomy; clouds hung like a pall in the sky, as if portending some great disaster. But when the President stepped forward to receive the oath of office, the clouds parted, and a ray of sunshine streamed from the heavens to fall upon and gild his face. It is also said that a brilliant star was seen at noon-day. It was the noon-day of life with Mr. Lincoln, and the star, as viewed in the light of subsequent events, was emblematic of a summons from on high. This was Saturday, and on Monday evening I went to the White House to dress Mrs. Lincoln for the first grand levee. While arranging Mrs. L.'s hair, the President came in. It was the first time I had seen him since the inauguration, and I went up to him, proffering my hand with words of congratulation.

He grasped my outstretched hand warmly, and held it while he spoke: "Thank you. Well, Madam Elizabeth"—he always called me Madam Elizabeth—"I don't know whether I should feel thankful or not. The position brings with it many trials. We do not know what we are destined to pass through. But God will be with us all. I put my trust in God." He dropped my hand, and with solemn face walked across the room and took his seat on the sofa. Prior to this I had congratulated Mrs. Lincoln, and she had answered with a sigh, "Thank you, Elizabeth; but now that we have won the position, I almost wish it were otherwise. Poor Mr. Lincoln is looking so broken-hearted, so completely worn out, I fear he will not get through the next four years." Was it a presentiment that made her take a sad view of the future? News from the front was never more cheering. On every side the Confederates were losing ground, and the lines of blue were advancing in triumph. As I would look out my window almost every day, I could see the artillery going past on its way to the open space of ground, to fire a salute in honor of some new victory. From every point came glorious news of the success of the soldiers that fought for the Union. And yet, in their private chamber, away from the curious eyes of the world, the President and his wife wore sad, anxious faces.

I finished dressing Mrs. Lincoln, and she took the President's arm and went below. It was one of the largest receptions ever held in Washington. Thousands crowded the halls and rooms of the White House, eager to shake Mr. Lincoln by his hand, and receive a gracious smile from his wife. The jam was terrible, and the enthusiasm great. The President's hand was well shaken, and the next day, on visiting Mrs. Lincoln, I received the soiled glove that Mr. Lincoln had worn on his right hand that night.

Many colored people were in Washington, and large numbers had desired to attend the levee, but orders were issued not to admit them. A gentleman, a member of Congress, on his way to the White House, recognized Mr. Frederick Douglass, the eloquent colored orator, on the outskirts of the crowd.

"How do you do, Mr. Douglass? A fearful jam to-night. You are going in, of course?"

"No—that is, no to your last question."

"Not going in to shake the President by the hand! Why, pray?"

"The best reason in the world. Strict orders have been issued not to admit people of color."

"It is a shame, Mr. Douglass, that you should thus be placed under ban. Never mind; wait here, and I will see what can be done."

The gentleman entered the White House, and working his way to the President, asked permission to introduce Mr. Douglass to him.

"Certainly," said Mr. Lincoln. "Bring Mr. Douglass in, by all means. I shall be glad to meet him."

The gentleman returned, and soon Mr. Douglass stood face to face with the President. Mr. Lincoln pressed his hand warmly, saying: "Mr. Douglass, I am glad to meet you. I have long admired your course, and I value your opinions highly."

Mr. Douglass was very proud of the manner in which Mr. Lincoln received him. On leaving the White House he came to a friend's house where a reception was being held, and he related the incident with great pleasure to myself and others.

On the Monday following the reception at the White House, everybody was busy preparing for the grand inaugural ball to come off that night. I was in Mrs. Lincoln's room the greater portion of the day. While dressing her that night, the President came in, and I remarked to him how much Mr. Douglass had been pleased on the night he was presented to Mr. Lincoln. Mrs. L. at once turned to her husband with the inquiry, "Father, why was not Mr. Douglass introduced to me?"

"I do not know. I thought he was presented."

"But he was not."

"It must have been an oversight then, mother; I am sorry you did not meet him."

I finished dressing her for the ball, and accompanied her to the door. She was dressed magnificently, and entered the ball-room leaning on the arm of Senator Sumner, a gentleman that she very much admired. Mr. Lincoln walked into the ball-room accompanied by two gentlemen. This ball closed the season. It was the last time that the President and his wife ever appeared in public.

Some days after, Mrs. Lincoln, with a party of friends, went to City Point on a visit.

Mrs. Lincoln had returned to Washington prior to the 2d of April. On Monday, April 3d, Mrs. Secretary Harlan came into my room with material for a dress. While conversing with her, I saw artillery pass the window; and as it was on its way to fire a salute, I inferred that good news had been received at the War Department. My reception-room was on one side of the street, and my work-room on the other side. Inquiring the cause of the demonstration, we were told that Richmond had fallen. Mrs. Harlan took one of my hands in each of her own, and we rejoiced together. I ran across to my work-room, and on entering it, discovered that the girls in my employ also had heard the good news. They were particularly elated, as it was reported that the rebel capital had surrendered to colored troops. I had promised my employees a holiday when Richmond should fall; and now that Richmond had fallen, they reminded me of my promise.

I recrossed to my reception-room, and Mrs. Harlan told me that the good news was enough for her—she could afford to wait for her dress, and to give the girls a holiday and a treat, by all means. She returned to her house, and I joined my girls in the joy of the long-promised holiday. We wandered about the streets of the city with happy faces, and hearts overflowing with joy.

The clerks in the various departments also enjoyed a holiday, and they improved it by getting gloriously fuddled. Towards evening I saw S., and many other usually clear-headed men, in the street, in a confused, uncertain state of mind.

Mrs. Lincoln had invited me to accompany her to City Point. I went to the White House, and told her that if she intended to return, I would regard it as a privilege to go with her, as City Point was near Petersburg, my old home. Mrs. L. said she designed returning, and would be delighted to take me with her; so it was arranged that I should accompany her.

A few days after we were on board the steamer, *en route* for City Point. Mrs. Lincoln was joined by Mrs. Secretary Harlan and daughter, Senator Sumner, and several other gentlemen.

Prior to this, Mr. Lincoln had started for City Point, and before we reached our destination he had visited Richmond, Petersburg, and other points. We arrived on Friday, and Mrs. Lincoln was much disappointed when she learned that the President had visited the late Confederate capital, as she had greatly desired to be with him when he entered the conquered stronghold. It was immediately arranged that the entire party on board the River Queen should visit Richmond, and other points, with the President. The next morning, after the arrangement was perfected, we were steaming up James River—the river that so long had been impassable, even to our gunboats. The air was balmy, and the banks of the river were beautiful, and fragrant with the first sweet blossoms of spring. For hours I stood on deck, breathing the pure air, and viewing the landscape on either side of the majestically flowing river. Here stretched fair fields, emblematic of peace—and here deserted camps and frowning forts, speaking of the stern vicissitudes of war. Alas! how many changes had taken place since my eye had wandered over the classic fields of dear old Virginia! A birthplace is always dear, no matter under what circumstances you were born, since it revives in memory the golden hours of childhood, free from philosophy, and the warm kiss of a mother. I wondered if I should catch a glimpse of a familiar face; I wondered what had become of those I once knew; had they fallen in battle, been scattered by the relentless tide of war, or were they still living as they lived when last I saw them? I wondered, now that Richmond had fallen, and Virginia been restored to the clustering stars of the Union, if the people would come together in the bonds of peace; and as I gazed and wondered, the River Queen rapidly carried us to our destination.

The Presidential party were all curiosity on entering Richmond. They drove about the streets of the city, and examined every object of interest. The Capitol presented a desolate appearance—desks broken, and papers scattered promiscuously in the hurried flight of the Confederate Congress. I picked up a number of papers, and, by curious coincidence, the resolution prohibiting all free colored people from entering the State of Virginia. In the Senate chamber I sat in the chair that Jefferson Davis sometimes occupied; also in the chair of the Vice-President, Alexander H. Stephens. We paid a visit to the mansion occupied by Mr. Davis and family during the war, and the ladies who were in charge of it scowled darkly upon our party as we passed through and inspected the different rooms. After a delightful visit we returned to City Point.

That night, in the cabin of the River Queen, smiling faces gathered around the dinner-table. One of the guests was a young officer attached to the Sanitary Commission. He was seated near Mrs. Lincoln, and, by way of pleasantry, remarked:

"Mrs. Lincoln, you should have seen the President the other day, on his triumphal entry into Richmond. He was the cynosure of all eyes. The ladies kissed their hands to him, and greeted him with the waving of handkerchiefs. He is quite a hero when surrounded by pretty young ladies."

The young officer suddenly paused with a look of embarrassment. Mrs. Lincoln turned to him with flashing eyes, with the remark that his familiarity was offensive to her. Quite a scene followed, and I do not think that the Captain who incurred Mrs. Lincoln's displeasure will ever forget that memorable evening in the cabin of the River Queen, at City Point.

Saturday morning the whole party decided to visit Petersburg, and I was only too eager to accompany them.

When we arrived at the city, numbers crowded around the train, and a little ragged negro boy ventured timidly into the car occupied by Mr. Lincoln and immediate friends, and in replying to numerous questions, used the word "tote."

"Tote," remarked Mr. Lincoln; "what do you mean by tote?"

"Why, massa, to tote um on your back."

"Very definite, my son; I presume when you tote a thing, you carry it. By the way, Sumner," turning to the Senator, "what is the origin of tote?"

"Its origin is said to be African. The Latin word *totum*, from *totus*, means all—an entire body—the whole."

"But my young friend here did not mean an entire body, or anything of the kind, when he said he would tote my things for me," interrupted the President.

"Very true," continued the Senator. "He used the word tote in the African sense, to carry, to bear. Tote in this sense is defined in our standard dictionaries as a colloquial word of the Southern States, used especially by the negroes."

"Then you regard the word as a good one?"

"Not elegant, certainly. For myself, I should prefer a better word; but since it has been established by usage, I cannot refuse to recognize it."

Thus the conversation proceeded in pleasant style.

Getting out of the car, the President and those with him went to visit the forts and other scenes, while I wandered off by myself in search of those whom I had known in other days. War, grim-visaged war, I soon discovered had brought many changes to the city so well known to me in the days of my youth. I found a number of old friends, but the greater portion of the population were strange to me. The scenes suggested painful memories, and I was not sorry to turn my back again upon the city. A large, peculiarly shaped oak tree, I well remember, attracted the particular attention of the President; it grew upon the outskirts of Petersburg, and as he had discovered it on his first visit, a few days previous to the second, he insisted that the party should go with him to take a look at the isolated and magnificent specimen of the stately grandeur of the forest. Every member of the party was only too willing to accede to the President's request, and the visit to the oak was made, and much enjoyed.

On our return to City Point from Petersburg the train moved slowly, and the President, observing a terrapin basking in the warm sunshine on the wayside, had the conductor stop the train, and one of the brakemen bring the terrapin in to him. The movements of the ungainly little animal seemed to delight him, and he amused himself with it until we reached James River, where our steamer lay. Tad stood near, and joined in the happy laugh with his father.

For a week the River Queen remained in James River, anchored the greater portion of the time at City Point, and a pleasant and memorable week was it to all on board. During the whole of this time a yacht lay in the stream about a quarter of a mile distant, and its peculiar movements attracted the attention of all on board. General Grant and Mrs. Grant were on our steamer several times, and many distinguished officers of the army also were entertained by the President and his party.

Mr. Lincoln, when not off on an excursion of any kind, lounged about the boat, talking familiarly with every one that approached him.

The day before we started on our journey back to Washington, Mr. Lincoln was engaged in reviewing the troops in camp. He returned to the boat in the evening, with a tired, weary look.

"Mother," he said to his wife, "I have shaken so many hands to-day that my arms ache to-*night*. I almost wish that I could go to bed now."

As the twilight shadows deepened the lamps were lighted, and the boat was brilliantly illuminated; as it lay in the river, decked with many-colored lights, it looked like an enchanted floating palace. A military band was on board, and as the hours lengthened into night it discoursed sweet music. Many officers came on board to say good-by, and the scene was a brilliant one indeed. About 10 o'clock Mr. Lincoln was called upon to make a speech. Rising to his feet, he said:

"You must excuse me, ladies and gentlemen. I am too tired to speak to-night. On next Tuesday night I make a speech in Washington, at which time you will learn all I have to say. And now, by way of parting from the brave soldiers of our gallant army, I call upon the band to play Dixie. It has always been a favorite of mine, and since we have captured it, we have a perfect right to enjoy it." On taking his seat the band at once struck up with Dixie, that sweet, inspiring air; and when the music died away, there were clapping of hands and other manifestations of applause.

At 11 o'clock the last good-by was spoken, the lights were taken down, the River Queen rounded out into the water and we were on our way back to Washington. We arrived at the Capital at 6 o'clock on Sunday evening, where the party separated, each going to his and her own home. This was one of the most delightful trips of my life, and I always revert to it with feelings of genuine pleasure.

Questions to Consider

1. How did Elizabeth Keckley's image of a hard-working, honest, and successful entrepreneur challenge mid-nineteenth-century racist assumptions?
2. How did Keckley assure White readers that the newly emancipated slave posed no threat to White society?
3. In what ways do Keckley's memoirs accommodate her White readers? How does she challenge them?

Frederick Douglass

c. 1818–1895

As is the case with most American slaves, the exact circumstances of Frederick Douglass's birth are unclear. In the *Narrative of the Life of Frederick Douglass, an American Slave*, Douglass reports that the date on which he was born and the identity of his father are uncertain, although he was most likely born in 1818, the son of his first White master, Captain Anthony, and a field hand named Harriet Bailey. Slave families were often broken up on Southern plantations, and Frederick Augustus Washington Bailey, as he was originally named, barely knew his mother, who died when he was seven. Although he was of mixed heritage, he was born a slave; as the offspring of a White slave master and a Black slave woman, he was considered property and not family. In his *Narrative*, Douglass recounts the trials of his life as a slave. In a matter-of-fact tone, Douglass tells how he was stripped of his identity and forced to live like an animal. Although the details of slave life are presented in an unemotional way, the effect on the reader is one of profound aversion.

Fortunately, Douglass escaped many of the horrors of his early life for a while when he was sent by Captain Anthony to Baltimore to work for Hugh Auld, Captain Anthony's relative by marriage. Auld's wife, Sophia, initially treated Douglass with kindness and began to teach him to read and write. When Hugh Auld learned of the lessons, he convinced his wife that teaching a slave to read and write would render him "unfit" to be a slave, but the seeds of knowledge had already been planted in the young Douglass, and he determined to become literate. Douglass persuaded some of the White children in the area to help him learn, and he copied their papers in order to teach himself to write. He also purchased newspapers, in which he first read of the abolitionist movement in the North.

When Captain Anthony died in 1833, Douglass was returned to the plantation, but his new owner considered him too independent, and Douglass was put under the supervision of Edward Covey, a notorious slave-breaker. When Covey tried to break Douglass by beating him, the young slave stood up for himself and Covey backed down. According to the narrative, this event marked the first turning point in Douglass's life: he realized that although his captors could beat and abuse him physically, they could break his spirit only if he allowed them to. Shortly thereafter, Douglass tried to escape, but the attempt was unsuccessful, and he was returned to Baltimore where Hugh Auld rented him out to work in the shipyards.

On 3 September 1838, Douglass escaped from Baltimore with the aid of freedwoman Anna Murray, who would later become his wife. Making his way to New York City disguised as a free sailor, Douglass accepted the help of Northern abolitionists who gave him shelter and passage to New Bedford, Massachusetts, where he changed his name to Douglass to avoid capture. In New Bedford, he met noted abolitionist John A. Collins, who offered him a position as a salaried lecturer at meetings of various abolitionist societies. The speeches he gave over the next four years would provide the basis for the *Narrative*, and the descriptive force of both the book and his lectures did much to inform readers and listeners of the realities of slavery. The book became an instant best seller despite doubts by some that a slave with no formal education could write such a compelling and literate work.

Afraid that his notoriety would lead to capture, Douglass spent the next two years in England, until two of his English friends paid $711.16 to buy his freedom. He returned to America and updated the *Narrative*, which he published in 1855 as *My Bondage and My Freedom*. Living now in Rochester, New York, Douglass began to publish a weekly newspaper, which he would continue in some form for the next 13 years. Eventually, Douglass split from the American abolitionist movement because he believed that the evils of slavery necessitated stronger action than the Northern antislavery societies were willing to support. When radical abolitionist John Brown attempted to incite a slave revolt at Harper's Ferry, Virginia, Douglass, who was a friend and supporter of Brown, felt he might be accused in the conspiracy and left again for England when Brown and his co-conspirators were executed. Shortly before the Civil War, Douglass returned to America to campaign for Lincoln, and when the war broke out, he persuaded Lincoln to organize two Black regiments to fight for the Union. Two of Douglass's sons fought in these regiments.

When it appeared that the North would win the war, Douglass began to campaign for African-American suffrage, but he found that many abolitionists opposed his plans. Douglass believed he should have a place in government during Reconstruction and was somewhat disappointed when President Grant appointed him emissary to Santo Domingo. After he returned from the Caribbean, he accepted positions as U.S. Marshal and Recorder of Deeds for the District of Columbia, and he later served as the U.S. Ambassador to Haiti. He updated his book again and reissued it as *The Life and Times of Frederick Douglass*. While the first two versions of his life story are within the traditions of the slave narrative, the last update expands the story to include the remarkable events of his later life as a popular orator, social reformer, and diplomat. Douglass died of heart failure in 1895, at the approximate age of 77.

Douglass's effect on American political and literary thought has been profound. As perhaps the most widely read Black author of the nineteenth and twentieth centuries, he had unparalleled influence on Black writers and on the fight for civil rights and equality for all people. The selections included here, from three of his most famous speeches, reveal the depth of his contribution. His struggle for self-actualization transcends color, and the events of his life stand as a testament to what an individual can accomplish with determination and perseverance, even under the most overwhelming and adverse circumstances.

What to the Slave Is the Fourth of July?[1]

Mr. President, Friends and Fellow Citizens: He who could address this audience without a quailing sensation, has stronger nerves than I have. I do not remember ever to have appeared as a speaker before any assembly more shrinkingly, nor with greater distrust of my ability, than I do this day. A feeling has crept over me, quite unfavorable to the exercise of my limited powers of speech. The task before me is one which requires much previous thought and study for its proper performance. I know that apologies of this sort are generally considered flat and unmeaning. I trust, however, that mine will not be so considered. Should I seem at ease, my appearance would much misrepresent me. The little experience I have had in addressing public meetings, in country school houses, avails me nothing on the present occasion.

The papers and placards say, that I am to deliver a 4th [of] July oration. This certainly sounds large, and out of the common way, for me. It is true that I have often had the privilege to speak in this beautiful Hall, and to address many who now honor me with their presence. But neither their familiar faces, nor the perfect gage[2] I think I have of Corinthian Hall, seems to free me from embarrassment.

The fact is, ladies and gentlemen, the distance between this platform and the slave plantation, from which I escaped, is considerable—and the difficulties to be overcome in getting from the latter to the former, are by no means slight. That I am here to-day, is, to me, a matter of astonishment as well as of gratitude. You will not, therefore, be surprised, if in what I have to say, I evince no elaborate preparation, nor grace my speech with any high sounding exordium. With little experience and with less learning,

1. Delivered 4 July 1852, at Rochester Hall; Rochester, NY; to the Rochester Ladies' Antislavery Society.

2. Gauge; measure.

I have been able to throw my thoughts hastily and imperfectly together; and trusting to your patient and generous indulgence, I will proceed to lay them before you.

This, for the purpose of this celebration, is the 4th of July. It is the birthday of your National Independence, and of your political freedom. This, to you, is what the Passover was to the emancipated people of God. It carries your minds back to the day, and to the act of your great deliverance; and to the signs, and to the wonders, associated with that act, and that day. This celebration also marks the beginning of another year of your national life; and reminds you that the Republic of America is now 76 years old. I am glad, fellow-citizens, that your nation is so young. Seventy-six years, though a good old age for a man, is but a mere speck in the life of a nation. Three score years and ten is the allotted time for individual men; but nations number their years by thousands. According to this fact, you are, even now, only in the beginning of your national career, still lingering in the period of childhood. I repeat, I am glad this is so. There is hope in the thought, and hope is much needed, under the dark clouds which lower above the horizon. The eye of the reformer is met with angry flashes, portending disastrous times; but his heart may well beat lighter at the thought that America is young, and that she is still in the impressible stage of her existence. May he not hope that high lessons of wisdom, of justice and of truth, will yet give direction to her destiny? Were the nation older, the patriot's heart might be sadder, and the reformer's brow heavier. Its future might be shrouded in gloom, and the hope of its prophets go out in sorrow. There is consolation in the thought that America is young.—Great streams are not easily turned from channels, worn deep in the course of ages. They may sometimes rise in quiet and stately majesty, and inundate the land, refreshing and fertilizing the earth with their mysterious properties. They may also rise in wrath and fury, and bear away, on their angry waves, the accumulated wealth of years of toil and hardship. They, however, gradually flow back to the same old channel, and flow on as serenely as ever. But, while the river may not be turned aside, it may dry up, and leave nothing behind but the withered branch, and the unsightly rock, to howl in the abyss-sweeping wind, the sad tale of departed glory. As with rivers so with nations.

Fellow-citizens, I shall not presume to dwell at length on the associations that cluster about this day. The simple story of it is that, 76 years ago, the people of this country were British subjects. The style and title of your "sovereign people" (in which you now glory) was not then born. You were under the British Crown. Your fathers esteemed the English Government as the home government; and England as the fatherland. This home government, you know, although a considerable distance from your home, did, in the exercise of its parental prerogatives, impose upon its colonial children, such restraints, burdens and limitations, as, in its mature judgement, it deemed wise, right and proper.

But, your fathers, who had not adopted the fashionable idea of this day, of the infallibility of government, and the absolute character of its acts, presumed to differ from the home government in respect to the wisdom and the justice of some of those burdens and restraints. They went so far in their excitement as to pronounce the measures of government unjust, unreasonable, and oppressive, and altogether such as ought not to be quietly submitted to. I scarcely need say, fellow-citizens, that my opinion of those measures fully accords with that of your fathers. Such a declaration of agreement on my part would not be worth much to anybody. It would, certainly, prove nothing, as to what part I might have taken, had I lived during the great controversy of 1776. To say *now* that America was right, and England wrong, is exceedingly easy. Everybody can say it; the dastard, not less than the noble brave, can flippantly discant on the tyranny of England towards the American Colonies. It is fashionable to do so; but there was a time when to pronounce against England, and in favor of the cause of the colonies, tried men's souls. They who did so were accounted in their day, plotters of mischief, agitators and rebels, dangerous men. To side with the right, against the wrong, with the weak against the strong, and with the oppressed against the oppressor! *here* lies the merit, and the one which, of all others, seems unfashionable in our day. The cause of liberty may be stabbed by the men who glory in the deeds of your fathers. But, to proceed.

Feeling themselves harshly and unjustly treated by the home government, your fathers, like men of honesty, and men of spirit, earnestly sought redress. They petitioned and remonstrated; they did so in a decorous, respectful, and loyal manner. Their conduct was wholly unexceptionable. This, however, did not answer the purpose. They saw themselves treated with sovereign indifference, coldness and scorn. Yet they persevered. They were not the men to look back.

As the sheet anchor takes a firmer hold, when the ship is tossed by the storm, so did the cause of your fathers grow stronger, as it breasted the chilling blasts of kingly displeasure. The greatest and best of British statesmen admitted its justice, and the loftiest eloquence of the British Senate came to its support. But, with that blindness which seems to be the unvarying characteristic of tyrants, since Pharaoh and his hosts were drowned in the Red Sea, the British Government persisted in the exactions complained of.

The madness of this course, we believe, is admitted now, even by England; but we fear the lesson is wholly lost on our present rulers.

Oppression makes a wise man mad. Your fathers were wise men, and if they did not go mad, they became restive under this treatment. They felt themselves the victims of grievous wrongs, wholly incurable in their colonial capacity. With brave men there is always a remedy for oppression. Just here, the idea of a total separation of the colonies from the crown was born! It was a startling idea, much more so, than we, at this distance of time, regard it. The timid and the prudent (as has been intimated) of that day, were, of course, shocked and alarmed by it.

* * *

Fellow Citizens, I am not wanting in respect for the fathers of this republic. The signers of the Declaration of Independence were brave men. They were great men too—great enough to give fame to a great age. It does not often happen to a nation to raise, at one time, such a number of truly great men. The point from which I am compelled to view them is not, certainly, the most favorable; and yet I cannot contemplate their great deeds with less than admiration. They were statesmen, patriots and heroes, and for the good they did, and the principles they contended for, I will unite with you to honor their memory.

They loved their country better than their own private interests; and, though this is not the highest form of human excellence, all will concede that it is a rare virtue, and that when it is exhibited, it ought to command respect. He who will, intelligently, lay down his life for his country, is a man whom it is not in human nature to despise. Your fathers staked their lives, their fortunes, and their sacred honor, on the cause of their country. In their admiration of liberty, they lost sight of all other interests.

They were peace men; but they preferred revolution to peaceful submission to bondage. They were quiet men; but they did not shrink from agitating against oppression. They showed forbearance; but that they knew its limits. They believed in order; but not in the order of tyranny. With them, nothing was "*settled*" that was not right. With them, justice, liberty and humanity were "*final;*" not slavery and oppression. You may well cherish the memory of such men. They were great in their day and generation. Their solid manhood stands out the more as we contrast it with these degenerate times.

How circumspect, exact and proportionate were all their movements! How unlike the politicians of an hour! Their statesmanship looked beyond the passing moment, and stretched away in strength into the distant future. They seized upon eternal principles, and set a glorious example in their defence. Mark them!

Fully appreciating the hardship to be encountered, firmly believing in the right of their cause, honorably inviting the scrutiny of an on-looking world, reverently appealing to heaven to attest their sincerity, soundly comprehending the solemn responsibility they were about to assume, wisely measuring the terrible odds against them, your fathers, the fathers of this republic, did, most deliberately, under the inspiration of a glorious patriotism, and with a sublime faith in the great principles of justice and freedom, lay deep, the corner-stone of the national superstructure, which has risen and still rises in grandeur around you.

Of this fundamental work, this day is the anniversary. Our eyes are met with demonstrations of joyous enthusiasm. Banners and pennants wave exultingly on the breeze. The din of business, too, is hushed. Even mammon[3] seems to have quitted his grasp on this day. The ear-piercing fife and the stirring drum unite their accents with the ascending peal of a thousand church bells. Prayers are made, hymns are sung, and sermons are preached in honor of this day; while the quick martial tramp of a great and multitudinous nation, echoed back by all the hills, valleys and mountains of a vast continent, bespeak the occasion one of thrilling and universal interest— nation's jubilee.

Friends and citizens, I need not enter further into the causes which led to this anniversary. Many of you understand them better than I do. You could instruct me in regard to them. That is a branch of knowledge in which you feel, perhaps, a much deeper interest than your speaker. The causes which led to the separation of the colonies from the British crown have never lacked for a tongue. They have all been taught in your common schools, narrated at your firesides, unfolded from your pulpits, and thundered from your legislative halls, and are as familiar to you as household words. They form the staple of your national poetry and eloquence.

I remember, also, that, as a people, Americans are remarkably familiar with all facts which make in their own favor. This is esteemed by some as a national trait—perhaps a national weakness. It is a fact, that whatever makes for the wealth or for the reputation of Americans, and can be had *cheap!* will be found by Americans. I shall not be charged with slandering Americans, if I say I think the American side of any question may be safely left in American hands.

I leave, therefore, the great deeds of your fathers to other gentlemen whose claim to have been regularly descended will be less likely to be disputed than mine!

The Present

My business, if I have any here to-day, is with the present. The accepted time with God and his cause is the ever-living now.

3. The god of greed.

Trust no future, however pleasant,
  Let the dead past bury its dead;
Act, act in the living present,
  Heart within, and God overhead.

We have to do with the past only as we can make it useful to the present and to the future. To all inspiring motives, to noble deeds which can be gained from the past, we are welcome. But now is the time, the important time. Your fathers have lived, died, and have done their work, and have done much of it well. You live and must die, and you must do your work. You have no right to enjoy a child's share in the labor of your fathers, unless your children are to be blest by your labors. You have no right to wear out and waste the hard-earned fame of your fathers to cover your indolence. Sydney Smith tells us that men seldom eulogize the wisdom and virtues of their fathers, but to excuse some folly or wickedness of their own. This truth is not a doubtful one. There are illustrations of it near and remote, ancient and modern. It was fashionable, hundreds of years ago, for the children of Jacob to boast, we have "Abraham to our father," when they had long lost Abraham's faith and spirit. That people contented themselves under the shadow of Abraham's great name, while they repudiated the deeds which made his name great. Need I remind you that a similar thing is being done all over this country to-day? Need I tell you that the Jews are not the only people who built the tombs of the prophets, and garnished the sepulchres of the righteous? Washington could not die till he had broken the chains of his slaves. Yet his monument is built up by the price of human blood, and the traders in the bodies and souls of men, shout— "We have Washington to *our father*." Alas! that it should be so; yet so it is.

The evil that men do, lives after them.
The good is oft' interred with their bones.

Fellow-citizens, pardon me, allow me to ask, why am I called upon to speak here to-day? What have I, or those I represent, to do with your national independence? Are the great principles of political freedom and of natural justice, embodied in that Declaration of Independence, extended to us? and am I, therefore, called upon to bring our humble offering to the national altar, and to confess the benefits and express devout gratitude for the blessings resulting from your independence to us?

Would to God, both for your sakes and ours, that an affirmative answer could be truthfully returned to these questions! Then would my task be light, and my burden easy and delightful. For *who* is there so cold, that a nation's sympathy could not warm him? Who so obdurate and dead to the claims of gratitude, that would not thankfully acknowledge such priceless benefits? Who so stolid and selfish, that would not give his voice to swell the hallelujahs of a nation's jubilee, when the chains of servitude had been torn from his limbs? I am not that man. In a case like that, the dumb might eloquently speak, and the "lame man leap as an hart."[4]

But, such is not the state of the case. I say it with a sad sense of the disparity between us. I am not included within the pale of this glorious anniversary! Your high independence only reveals the immeasurable distance between us. The blessings in which you, this day, rejoice, are not enjoyed in common.—The rich inheritance of justice, liberty, prosperity and independence, bequeathed by your fathers, is shared by

4. A male red deer past the age of five, when the antlers first begin to form.

you, not by me. The sunlight that brought life and healing to you, has brought stripes and death to me. This Fourth [of] July is *yours*, not *mine*. *You* may rejoice, *I* must mourn. To drag a man in fetters into the grand illuminated temple of liberty, and call upon him to join you in joyous anthems, were inhuman mockery and sacrilegious irony. Do you mean, citizens, to mock me, by asking me to speak to-day? If so, there is a parallel to your conduct. And let me warn you that it is dangerous to copy the example of a nation whose crimes, towering up to heaven, were thrown down by the breath of the Almighty, burying that nation in irrecoverable ruin! I can to-day take up the plaintive lament of a peeled and woe-smitten people!

"By the rivers of Babylon, there we sat down. Yea! we wept when we remembered Zion. We hanged our harps upon the willows in the midst thereof. For there, they that carried us away captive, required of us a song; and they who wasted us required of us mirth, saying, Sing us one of the songs of Zion. How can we sing the Lord's song in a strange land? If I forget thee, O Jerusalem, let my right hand forget her cunning. If I do not remember thee, let my tongue cleave to the roof of my mouth."[5]

Fellow-citizens; above your national, tumultous joy, I hear the mournful wail of millions! whose chains, heavy and grievous yesterday, are, to-day, rendered more intolerable by the jubilee shouts that reach them. If I do forget, if I do not faithfully remember those bleeding children of sorrow this day, "may my right hand forget her cunning, and may my tongue cleave to the roof of my mouth!" To forget them, to pass lightly over their wrongs, and to chime in with the popular theme, would be treason most scandalous and shocking, and would make me a reproach before God and the world. My subject, then fellow-citizens, is AMERICAN SLAVERY. I shall see, this day, and its popular characteristics, from the slave's point of view. Standing, there, identified with the American bondman, making his wrongs mine, I do not hesitate to declare, with all my soul, that the character and conduct of this nation never looked blacker to me than on this 4th of July! Whether we turn to the declarations of the past, or to the professions of the present, the conduct of the nation seems equally hideous and revolting. America is false to the past, false to the present, and solemnly binds herself to be false to the future. Standing with God and the crushed and bleeding slave on this occasion, I will, in the name of humanity which is outraged, in the name of liberty which is fettered, in the name of the constitution and the Bible, which are disregarded and trampled upon, dare to call in question and to denounce, with all the emphasis I can command, everything that serves to perpetuate slavery—the great sin and shame of America! "I will not equivocate; I will not excuse;" I will use the severest language I can command; and yet not one word shall escape me that any man, whose judgement is not blinded by prejudice, or who is not at heart a slaveholder, shall not confess to be right and just.

But I fancy I hear some one of my audience say, it is just in this circumstance that you and your brother abolitionists fail to make a favorable impression on the public mind. Would you argue more, and denounce less, would you persuade more, and rebuke less, your cause would be much more likely to succeed. But, I submit, where all is plain there is nothing to be argued. What point in the anti-slavery creed would you have me argue? On what branch of the subject do the people of this country need light? Must I undertake to prove that the slave is a man? That point is conceded already. Nobody doubts it. The slaveholders themselves acknowledge it in the enactment of laws for their government. They acknowledge it when they punish dis-

5. Psalms 137: 1–6.

obedience on the part of the slave. There are seventy-two crimes in the State of Virginia, which, if committed by a black man, (no matter how ignorant he be), subject him to the punishment of death; while only two of the same crimes will subject a white man to the like punishment.—What is this but the acknowledgement that the slave is a moral, intellectual and responsible being? The manhood of the slave is conceded. It is admitted in the fact that Southern statute books are covered with enactments forbidding, under severe fines and penalties, the teaching of the slave to read or to write.—When you can point to any such laws, in reference to the beasts of the field, then I may consent to argue the manhood of the slave. When the dogs in your streets, when the fowls of the air, when the cattle on your hills, when the fish of the sea, and the reptiles that crawl, shall be unable to distinguish the slave from a brute, *then* will I argue with you that the slave is a man!

For the present, it is enough to affirm the equal manhood of the negro race. Is it not astonishing that, while we are ploughing, planting and reaping, using all kinds of mechanical tools, erecting houses, constructing bridges, building ships, working in metals of brass, iron, copper, silver and gold; that, while we are reading, writing and cyphering, acting as clerks, merchants and secretaries, having among us lawyers, doctors, ministers, poets, authors, editors, orators and teachers; that, while we are engaged in all manner of enterprises common to other men, digging gold in California, capturing the whale in the Pacific, feeding sheep and cattle on the hill-side, living, moving, acting, thinking, planning, living in families as husbands, wives and children, and, above all, confessing and worshipping the Christian's God, and looking hopefully for life and immortality beyond the grave, we are called upon to prove that we are men!

Would you have me argue that man is entitled to liberty? that he is the rightful owner of his own body? You have already declared it. Must I argue the wrongfulness of slavery? Is that a question for Republicans? Is it to be settled by the rules of logic and argumentation, as a matter beset with great difficulty, involving a doubtful application of the principle of justice, hard to be understood? How should I look to-day, in the presence of Americans, dividing, and subdividing a discourse, to show that men have a natural right to freedom? speaking of it relatively, and positively, negatively, and affirmatively. To do so, would be to make myself ridiculous, and to offer an insult to your understanding.—There is not a man beneath the canopy of heaven, that does not know that slavery is wrong *for him*.

What, am I to argue that it is wrong to make men brutes, to rob them of their liberty, to work them without wages, to keep them ignorant of their relations to their fellow men, to beat them with sticks, to flay their flesh with the lash, to load their limbs with irons, to hunt them with dogs, to sell them at auction, to sunder their families, to knock out their teeth, to burn their flesh, to starve them into obedience and submission to their masters? Must I argue that a system thus marked with blood, and stained with pollution, is *wrong?* No! I will not. I have better employments for my time and strength, than such arguments would imply.

What, then, remains to be argued? Is it that slavery is not divine; that God did not establish it; that our doctors of divinity are mistaken? There is blasphemy in the thought. That which is inhuman, cannot be divine! *Who* can reason on such a proposition? They that can, may; I cannot. The time for such argument is past.

At a time like this, scorching irony, not convincing argument, is needed. O! had I the ability, and could I reach the nation's ear, I would, to-day, pour out a fiery stream of biting ridicule, blasting reproach, withering sarcasm, and stern rebuke. For it is not light that is needed, but fire; it is not the gentle shower, but thunder. We need the storm, the whirlwind, and the earthquake. The feeling of the nation must be quickened; the conscience of the nation must be roused; the propriety of the nation must be startled; the hypocrisy of the nation must be exposed; and its crimes against God and man must be proclaimed and denounced.

What, to the American slave, is your 4th of July? I answer: a day that reveals to him, more than all other days in the year, the gross injustice and cruelty to which he is the constant victim. To him, your celebration is a sham; your boasted liberty, an unholy license; your national greatness, swelling vanity; your sounds of rejoicing are empty and heartless; your denunciations of tyrants, brass fronted impudence; your shouts of liberty and equality, hollow mockery; your prayers and hymns, your sermons and thanksgivings, with all your religious parade, and solemnity, are, to him, mere bombast, fraud, deception, impiety, and hypocrisy—a thin veil to cover up crimes which would disgrace a nation of savages. There is not a nation on the earth guilty of practices, more shocking and bloody, than are the people of these United States, at this very hour.

Go where you may, search where you will, roam through all the monarchies and despotisms of the old world, travel through South America, search out every abuse, and when you have found the last, lay your facts by the side of the everyday practices of this nation, and you will say with me, that, for revolting barbarity and shameless hypocrisy, America reigns without a rival.

Fighting the Rebels with One Hand

An Address Delivered in Philadelphia, Pennsylvania on 14 January 1862

Despite inclement weather, a "large and respectable" audience gathered at National Hall on the evening of 14 January 1862 to hear Douglass deliver the third lecture of a series sponsored by the Philadelphia Library Company, a black self-improvement organization. Although the reporter for the Philadelphia *Christian Recorder* had arrived wondering if Douglass had lost the "magnetism and melody of his wonderfully elastic voice," he was soon convinced that "the Frederick Douglass before us *was* the Frederick Douglass of former days—and even more: his majestic bearing and dignity were *not* gone . . . the power and influence of his voice, the cutting logic and lofty eloquence of other days, were not diminished." The speech that Douglass delivered on "The War" bears a marked similarity to the last half of his oration "Pictures and Progress," which received a mixed response when he gave it in Boston on 3 December 1861. On this occasion, the Philadelphia *Inquirer* backhandedly praised Douglass by noting that "the bitterness bordering on rudeness, of his speeches in past days, seemed last evening to have vanished, and his audience appeared gratified with both his matter and delivery." The *Christian Recorder* concluded: "The printed words of his address will give . . . a fair view of the *ideas*, but no printed sentences can convey any adequate idea of the manner, the tone of voice, the gesticulation, the action, the round, soft, swelling pronunciation with which Frederick Douglass spoke, and which no orator we have ever heard can use with such grace, eloquence and effect as he." [1]

LADIES AND GENTLEMEN:—My purpose to-night is not to win applause. I have no high-sounding professions of patriotism to make. He is the best friend of this country,

1. The description of this event is from Blassingame, John W., ed. *The Frederick Douglass Papers*. New Haven, CT: Yale UP, 1985. 473.

who, at this tremendous crisis, dares tell his countrymen the truth, however disagreeable that truth may be; and such a friend I will aim to be to-night. Many things have been said against the free colored people of the North, and a strong current is turned against them; but I believe that up to this time, no man, however malignant, has been able to cast the shadow of a doubt upon the loyalty and patriotism of the free colored people in this the hour of the nation's trial and danger. Without exulting, but with thankfulness, I may say it, while treason and rebellion have counted upon aid and comfort all over the North, among those who have every reason to be true and faithful to the State, no rebel or traitor has dared look at the free colored man of the North, but as an enemy. There are English rebels, Scotch rebels, Irish rebels, but I believe there are no black rebels. The black man at heart, even if found in the rebel camp, is a loyal man, forced out of his place by circumstances beyond his control. I really wish we had some other expressive title for the traitors and rebels who are now striking at the heart of this country which has nursed and brought them up. REBEL and TRAITOR are epithets too good for such monsters of perfidy and ingratitude. Washington, Jefferson, John Jay, John Adams, Benjamin Franklin, Alexander Hamilton, and many other brave and good men, have worn those appellations, and I hate to see them now worn by wretches who, instead of being rebels against slavery, are actually rebelling against the principles of human liberty and progress, for the hell-black purpose of establishing slavery in its most odious form.

I am to speak to you to-night of the civil war, by which this vast country—this continent is convulsed. The fate of the greatest of all modern Republics trembles in the balance. "To be, or not to be—that is the question."[2] The lesson of the hour is written down in characters of blood and fire. We are taught, as with the emphasis of an earthquake, that nations, not less than individuals, are subjects of the moral government of the universe, and that flagrant, long continued, and persistent transgression of the laws of this Divine government will certainly bring national sorrow, shame, suffering and death. Of all the nations of the world, we seem most in need of this solemn lesson. To-day we have it brought home to our hearths, our homes, and our hearts.

Hitherto, we have been content to study this lesson in the history of ancient governments and nationalities. To-day, every thoughtful American citizen is compelled to look at home. Egypt, Palestine, Greece and Rome *all* had their warnings. They disregarded them, and they perished. To-day, we have our warning, not in comets blazing through the troubled sky, but in the terrible calamity of a wide-spread rebellion enacted before our eyes. The American Republic is not yet a single century from the date of its birth. Measuring its age by that of other great nations, our *great* Republic—for such it truly is—great in commerce, great in numbers, great in mechanical skill, great in mental, moral and physical resources, great in all the elements of national greatness—fills but a speck on the dial plate of time, and stands within the inner circle of childhood. In the brief space of three quarters of a century, this young nation, full of promise and the hope of political liberty throughout the world, rose from three millions to thirty millions. Its mighty heart beats with the best blood of all nations. It was literally sown in weakness and raised in power. It began life in toil and poverty, and up to the present moment, it is conspicuous among the nations

2. *Hamlet*, Act 3, scene 1, line 67.

of the earth for opulence and ease. In the fullness of our national strength and glory, we had already begun to congratulate ourselves upon the wisdom and stability of our Government. When all Europe, a few years ago,[3] was convulsed with revolution and bloodshed, America was secure, and sat as a queen among the nations of the earth, knowing no sorrow and fearing none.

To-day, all is changed. The face of every loyal citizen is sicklied over with the pale cast of thought.[4] Every pillar in the national temple is shaken. The nation itself has fallen asunder in the centre. A million of armed men confront each other. Hostile flags wave defiance in sight of the National Capital during a period of six long and anxious months. Our riches take wings. Credit is disturbed, business is interrupted, national debt—the mill-stone on the neck of nations—and heavy taxation, which breaks the back of loyalty, loom in the distance. As the war progresses, property is wantonly destroyed, the wires are broken down, bridges demolished, railroads are pulled up and barricaded by fallen trees; still more and worse, the great writ of *habeas corpus* is suspended from necessity, liberty of speech and of the press have ceased to exist.[5] An order from Richmond or Washington—one stroke of the pen from Davis or Lincoln sends any citizen to prison, as in England, three centuries ago, British subjects were sent to the Tower of London. A hateful system of espionage is in process of formation, while war and blood mantles the whole land as with the shadow of death. We speak and write now by the forbearance of our rulers, not by the sacredness of our rights. I speak this not in complaint; I admit the necessity, while I lament it. The scene need not be further portrayed. It is dismal and terrible beyond all description. We have it burnt upon our very souls. I will not mock you by further painting that scene.

The spoilers of the Republic have dealt with the nation as burglars—stealing all they could carry away, and burning the residue. They have emptied your treasury, plundered your arsenals, scattered your navy, corrupted your army, seduced your officers, seized your forts, covered the sea with pirates, "heated your enemies, cooled your friends,"[6] insulted your flag, defied your Government, converted the national defences into instruments of national destruction, and have invited hostile armies of foreign nations to unite with them in completing the national ruin. All this, and more, has been done by the very men whom you have honored, paid and trusted, and that, too, while they were solemnly sworn to protect, support and defend your Constitution and Government against all foes at home and abroad.

To what cause may we trace our present sad and deplorable condition? A man of flighty brain and flippant tongue will tell you that the cause of all our national troubles lies solely in the election of Abraham Lincoln to the Presidency of the Republic. To the superficial this is final. Before Lincoln there was peace; after Lincoln there was rebellion. It stands to reason that Lincoln and rebellion are related as cause and effect. Such is their argument; such is their explanation. I hardly need waste your time in showing the folly and falsehood of either. Beyond all question, the facts show that this rebellion was planned and prepared long before the name of Abraham Lin-

3. Here Douglass refers to the Revolutions of 1848.

4. *Hamlet*, act 3, scene 2, line 96

5. With a presidential proclamation, on 27 April 1861, Lincoln suspended the writ of *habeas corpus*, a judicial mandate to a prison official ordering that an inmate be brought to the court so it can be determined whether that person is imprisoned lawfully and whether he or she should be released from custody.

6. Variation on the *Merchant of Venice*, act 3, scene 1, lines 61–62.

coln was mentioned in connection with the office he now holds, and that though the catastrophe might have been postponed, it could not have been prevented, nor long delayed. The worst of our condition is not to be sought in our disasters on flood or field. It is to be found rather in the character which contact with slavery has developed in every part of the country, so that at last there seems to be no truth, no candor left within us. We have faithfully copied all the cunning of the serpent, without any of the harmlessness of the dove, or the boldness of the lion.

In dealing with the causes of our present troubles, we find in quarters, high and low, the most painful evidences of dishonesty. It would seem, in the language of Isaiah, that the whole head is sick, and the whole heart is faint,[7] that there is no soundness in it. After-coming generations will remark with astonishment this feature in this dark chapter in our national history. They will find in no public document emanating from the loyal Government, anything like a frank and full statement of the real causes which have plunged us in the whirlpool of civil war. On the other hand, they will find the most studied and absurd attempts at concealment. Jefferson Davis is reticent. He seems ashamed to tell the world just what he is fighting for. Abraham Lincoln seems equally so, and is ashamed to tell the world what he is fighting against.

If we turn from the heads of the Government to the heads of the several Departments, we are equally befogged. The attempt is made to conceal the real facts of the case. Our astute Secretary of State[8] is careful to enjoin it upon our foreign ministers to remain dumb in respect to the real causes of the rebellion. They are to say nothing of the moral differences existing between the two sections of the country. There must be no calling things by their right names—no going straight to any point which can be reached by a crooked path. When slaves are referred to, they must be called persons held to service or labor. When in the hands of the Federal Government, they are called contrabands—a name that will apply better to a pistol, than to a person.[9] The preservation of slavery is called the preservation of the rights of the South under the Constitution. This concealment is one of the most contemptible features of the crisis. Every cause for the rebellion but the right one is pointed out and dwelt upon. Some make it geographical; others make it ethnographical.

> Lands intersected by a narrow firth abhor each other;
> Mountains interposed make enemies of nations,
> Which else like kindred drops had mingled into one.[10]

But even this cause does not hold here. There is no geographical reason for national division. Every stream is bridged, and every mountain is tunnelled. All our rivers and mountains point to union, not division—to oneness, not to warfare. There is no earthly reason why the corn fields of Pennsylvania should quarrel with the cotton fields of South Carolina. The physical and climatic differences bind them together, instead of putting them asunder.

A very large class of persons charge all our national calamities upon the busy tongues and pens of the Abolitionists. Thus we accord to a handful of men and

7. Isaiah 1:5–6.
8. William H. Seward.
9. Congress passed the First Confiscation Act on 8 August 1861, authorizing the seizure of all Confederate property, including slaves, used in the aid of the rebellion.
10. William Cowper, *The Task*. Book ii. "The Timepiece," lines 16–17.

women, everywhere despised, a power superior to all other classes in the country. Absurd and ridiculous as this is, its adherents are hoary-headed and bearded men.

Others still explain the whole matter, by telling us that it is the work of defeated and disappointed politicians at the South. I shall waste no time upon either. The cause of this rebellion is deeper down than either Southern politicians or Northern Abolitionists. They are but the hands of the clock. The machinery moves not because of the hands, but the hands because of the machinery. The ship may be great, but the ocean that bears it is greater. The Southern politicians and the Northern Abolitionists are the fruits, not the trees. They indicate, but are not original causes. The trouble is deeper down, and is fundamental; there is nothing strange about it. The conflict is in every way natural. "How can two walk together except they be agreed?"[11] "No man can serve two masters."[12] "A house divided against itself cannot stand."[13] It is something of a feat to ride two horses going the same way, and at the same pace, but a still greater feat when going in opposite directions.

Just here lies a true explanation of our troubles. We have made the mistake—the great and deplorable mistake of supposing that we could sow to the wind without reaping the whirlwind.[14] We have attempted to maintain our Union in utter defiance of the moral Chemistry of the universe. We have endeavored to join together things which in their nature stand eternally asunder. We have sought to bind the chains of slavery on the limbs of the black man, without thinking that at last we should find the other end of that hateful chain about our own necks.

A glance at the history of the settlement of the two sections of this country will show that the causes which produced the present rebellion, reach back to the dawn of civilization on this continent. In the same year that the *Mayflower* landed her liberty-seeking passengers on the bleak New England shore, a Dutch galliot landed a company of African slaves on the banks of James river, Virginia. The *Mayflower* planted liberty at the North, and the Dutch galliot slavery at the South. There is the fire, and there is the gunpowder. Contact has produced the explosion. What has followed might have been easily predicted. Great men saw it from the beginning, but no great men were found great enough to prevent it.

The statesmanship of the last half century has been mainly taxed to perpetuate the American Union. A system of compromise and concessions has been adopted. A double dealing policy—a facing both-ways statesmanship, naturally sprung up, and became fashionable—so that political success was often made to depend upon political cheating. One section or the other must be deceived. Before railroads and electric wires were spread over the country, this trickery and fraud had a chance of success. The lightning made deception more difficult, and the Union by compromise impossible. Our Union is killed by lightning.

In order to have union, either in the family, in the church, or in the State, there must be unity of idea and sentiment in all essential interests. Find a man's treasure, and you have found his heart. Now, in the North, freedom is the grand and all-comprehensive condition of comfort, prosperity and happiness. All our ideas and sentiments grow out of this free element. Free speech, free soil, free men, free schools, free inquiry, free suffrage, equality before the law, are the natural outgrowths of free-

11. Amos 3:3.
12. Matthew 6:24; Luke 16:13.
13. Versions of this text appear in Matthew, Mark, and Luke.
14. Hosea 8:7.

dom. Freedom is the centre of our Northern social system. It warms into life every other interest, and makes it beautiful in our eyes. Liberty is our treasure, and our hearts dwell with it, and receives its actuating motives from it.

What freedom is to the North as a generator of sentiment and ideas, *that* slavery is to the South. It is the treasure to which the Southern heart is fastened. It fashions all their ideas, and moulds all their sentiments. Politics, education, literature, morals and religion in the South, all bear the bloody image and superscription of slavery. Here, then, are two direct, point-blank and irreconcilable antagonisms under the same form of government. The marvel is not that civil war has come, but that it did not come sooner. But the evil is now upon us, and the question as to the causes which produced it, is of less consequence than the question as to how it ought to be, and can be thrown off. How shall the civil war be ended?

It can be ended for a time in one of two ways. One by recognizing the complete independence of the Southern Confederacy, and indemnifying the traitors and rebels for all the expense to which they have been put, in carrying out this tremendous slaveholding rebellion; and the second is by receiving the slaveholding States back into the Union with such guarantees for slavery as they may demand for the better security and preservation of slavery. In either of these two ways it may be put down for a time; but God forbid that any such methods of obtaining peace shall be adopted; for neither the one nor the other could bring any permanent peace.

I take it that these United States are to remain united. National honor requires national unity. To abandon that idea would be a disgraceful, scandalous and cowardly surrender of the majority to a rebellious minority—the capitulation of twenty million loyal men to six million rebels—and would draw after it a train of disasters such as would heap curses on the very graves of the present generation. As to giving the slave States new guarantees for the safety of slavery, that I take to be entirely out of the question. The South does not want them, and the North could not give them if the South could accept them. To concede anything to these slaveholding traitors and rebels in arms, after all their atrocious crimes against justice, humanity, and every sentiment of loyalty, would be tantamount to the nation's defeat, and would substitute in the future the bayonet for the ballot, and cannon balls for Congress, revolution and anarchy for government, and the pronounciamentoes of rebel chiefs for regulating enacted laws.

There is therefore no escape. The only road to national honor, and permanent peace to us, is to meet, fight, dislodge, drive back, conquer and subdue the rebels. When a man and woman are lawfully joined together for life, the only conditions upon which there can be anything like peace in the family, are that they shall either love or fear each other. Now, during the last fifty years, the North has been endeavoring, by all sorts of services and kindnesses, to win and secure the affection of the South. It has stepped sometimes a little beyond the requirements of true manly dignity to accomplish this, but all in vain.

We have bought Florida, waged war with friendly Seminoles, purchased Louisiana, annexed Texas, fought Mexico, trampled on the right of petition, abridged the freedom of debate, paid ten million to Texas upon a fraudulent claim, mobbed the Abolitionists, repealed the Missouri Compromise, winked at the accursed slave trade, helped to extend slavery, given slaveholders a larger share of all the offices and honors than we claimed for ourselves, paid their postage, supported the Government, persecuted free negroes, refused to recognize Hayti and Liberia, stained our souls by repeated compromises, borne with Southern bluster, allowed our ships to be robbed of their hardy sailors, defeated a central road to the Pacific, and have descended to the meanness and degradation of negro dogs, and hunted down the panting slave escaping from his tyrant master—all to make the South love us; and yet how stands our relations?

At this hour there is everywhere at the South, nursed and cherished, the most deadly hate towards every man and woman of Northern birth. We, here at the North, do not begin to understand the strength and bitter intensity of this slaveholding malice. Mingled with it is a supercillious sense of superiority—a scornful contempt—the strutting pride of the turkey, with the cunning and poison of the rattlesnake. I say again, we must meet them, defeat them, and conquer them. Do I hear you say that this is more easily said than done? I admit it. Nevertheless, there is a way to do it, and to do it effectually.

I have not a very exalted idea of Southern courage, notwithstanding the successes attending their arms, thus far, during the rebellion. Their domestic habits make them passionate and cruel, but not calm and brave. They will readily fight when they have every advantage. They can whip a negro with his hands tied, catch a Connecticut peddler a thousand miles from home, beat and ride him out of town on a rail—capture a hospital full of sick folks, or bombard, with ten thousand men, a starving garrison of seventy men.[15] I never got into a dispute with one of these Southern braves yet, but that he expressed the wish that he had me in the South, where, of course, he would have every advantage.

But how shall the rebellion be put down? I will tell you; but before I do so, you must allow me to say that the plan thus far pursued does not correspond with my humble notion of fitness. Thus far, it must be confessed, we have struck wide of the mark, and very feebly withal. The temper of our steel has proved much better than the temper of our minds. While I do not charge, as some have done, that the Government at Washington is conducting the war upon peace principles, it is very plain that the war is *not* being conducted on war principles.

We are fighting the rebels with only one hand, when we ought to be fighting them with both. We are recruiting our troops in the towns and villages of the North, when we ought to be recruiting them on the plantations of the South. We are striking the guilty rebels with our soft, white hand, when we should be striking with the iron hand of the black man, which we keep chained behind us. We have been catching slaves, instead of arming them. We have thus far repelled our natural friends to win the worthless and faithless friendship of our unnatural enemies. We have been endeavoring to heal over the rotten cancer of slavery, instead of cutting out its death-dealing roots and fibres. We pay more attention to the advice of the half-rebel State of Kentucky, than to any suggestion coming from the loyal North. We have shouldered all the burdens of slavery, and given the slaveholders and traitors all its benefits; and robbed our cause of half its dignity in the eyes of an on-looking world.

I say here and now, that if this nation is destroyed—if the Government shall, after all, be broken to pieces, and degraded in the eyes of the world—if the Union shall be shattered into fragments, it will neither be for the want of men, nor of money, nor even physical courage, for we have all these in abundance; but it will be solely owing

15. Here, Douglass refers to the bombardment of Fort Sumter.

to the want of moral courage and wise statesmanship in dealing with slavery, the *cause* and motive of the rebellion.

Witness the treatment of Frémont's[16] proclamation. When that memorable document was given to the public, all truly loyal men felt that the Pathfinder of the Rocky Mountains had found the true path out of our national troubles. His words were few and simple, but strong enough to vibrate the heart of a continent. The weakness and imbecility of the letter of the President condemning that proclamation, have thus far characterized the whole war. Slavery has been, and is yet the shield and helmet of this accursed rebellion; but for this, its brains would have been out long ago. President, Government, and army, stand paralyzed in the presence of slavery. They are determined only to save the Union so far as they can save slavery. The President attests that he approved of the proclamation of Frémont generally, but disapproved of one feature of it. What was the proclamation generally? Why this: the establishment of martial law in Missouri. The President approved of that. What was it specially? Why, the confiscation and emancipation of all the slaves belonging to rebels. The President was in favor of martial law, in favor of shooting rebels, but was not in favor of freeing their slaves. In this brief letter to Frémont, we have the secret of all our misfortune in connection with the rebellion.

I have been often asked since this war began, why I am not at the South battling for freedom. My answer is with the Government. The Washington Government wants men for its army, but thus far, it has not had the boldness to recognize the manhood of the race to which I belong. It only sees in the slave an article of commerce—a contraband. I do not wish to say aught against our Government, for good or bad; it is all we have to save us from anarchy and ruin; but I owe it to my race, in view of the cruel aspersions cast upon it, to affirm that, in denying them the privilege to fight for their country, they have been most deeply and grievously wronged. Neither in the Revolution, nor in the last war did any such narrow and contemptible policy obtain. It shows the deep degeneracy of our times—the height from which we have fallen—that, while Washington, in 1776, and Jackson, in 1814, could fight side by side with negroes, now, not even the best of our generals are willing so to fight. Is McClellan[17] better than Washington? Is Halleck[18] better than Jackson?

One situation only has been offered me, and that is the office of a body servant to a Colonel. I would not despise even that, if I could by accepting it be of service to my enslaved fellow-countrymen. In the temple of impartial liberty there is no seat too low for me. But one thing I have a right to ask when I am required to endure the hardships and brave the dangers of the battle field. I ask that I shall have either a country, or the hope of a country under me—a Government, or the hope of a Government around me, and a flag of impartial liberty floating over me.

We have recently had a solemn fast, and have offered up innumerable prayers for the deliverance of the nation from its manifold perils and calamities. I say nothing against these prayers. Their subjective power is indispensable; but I know also, that the work of making, and the work of answering them, must be performed by the same hands. If the loyal North shall succeed in suppressing this foul and scandalous rebellion, that achievement will be due to the amount of wisdom and force they bring against the rebels in arms.

16. John C. Frémont.
17. Union General George B. McClellan.
18. Union General Henry W. Halleck.

Thus far we have shown no lack of force. A call for men is answered by half a million. A call for money brings down a hundred million. A call for prayers brings a nation to its altars. But still the rebellion rages. Washington is menaced. The Potomac is blockaded. Jeff. Davis is still proud and defiant, and the rebels are looking forward hopefully to a recognition of their independence, the breaking of the blockade, and their final severance from the North.

Now, what is the remedy for all this? The answer is ready. Have done at once and forever with the wild and guilty phantasy that any one man can have a right of property in the body and soul of another man. Have done with the now exploded idea that the old Union, which has hobbled along through seventy years upon the crutches of compromise, is either desirable or possible, now, or in the future. Accept the incontestible truth of the "irrepressible conflict." It was spoken when temptations to compromise were less strong than now. Banish from your political dreams the last lingering adumbration that this great American nation can ever rest firmly and securely upon a mixed basis, part of iron, part of clay, part free, and part slave. The experiment has been tried, and tried, too, under more favorable circumstances than any which the future is likely to offer, and has deplorably failed. Now lay the axe at the root of the tree, and give it—root, top, body and branches—to the consuming fire. You have now the opportunity.

> There is a tide in the affairs of men
> Which, taken at the flood, leads on to fortune.
> Omitted, all the voyage of their lives
> Is bound in shallows and in miseries.
> On such a full sea are we now afloat.
> We must take the current when it serves,
> Or lose our ventures.[19]

To let this occasion pass unimproved, for getting rid of slavery, would be a sin against unborn generations. The cup of slaveholding iniquity is full and running over;[20] now let it be disposed of and finished forever. Reason, common sense, justice, and humanity alike concur with this necessary step for the national safety. But it is contended that the nation at large has no right to interfere with slavery in the States—that the Constitution gives no power to abolish slavery. This pretext is flung at us at every corner, by the same men who, a few months ago, told us we had no Constitutional right to coerce a seceded State—no right to collect revenue in the harbors of such State—no right to subjugate such States—and it is part and parcel of the same nonsense.

In the first place, slavery has no Constitutional existence in the country. There is not a provision of that instrument which would be contravened by its abolition. But if every line and syllable of the Constitution contained an explicit prohibition of the abolition of slavery, the right of the nation to abolish it would still remain in full force. In virtue of a principle underlying all government—that of national self-preservation—the nation can no more be bound to disregard this, than a man can be bound to commit suicide. This law of self preservation is the great end and object of

19. *Julius Caesar*, act 4, scene 2, lines 294–300.

20. Paraphrase of Psalms 23:5.

all Governments and Constitutions. The means can never be superior to the end. But will our Government ever arrive at this conclusion? That will depend upon two very opposite elements.

First, it will depend upon the sum of Northern virtue.

Secondly, upon the extent of Southern villainy.

Now, I have much confidence in Northern virtue, but much more in Southern villainy. Events are greater than either party to the conflict. We are fighting not only a wicked and determined foe, but a maddened and desperate foe. We are not fighting serviles, but our masters—men who have ruled over us for fifty years. If hard pushed, we may expect them to break through all the restraints of civilized warfare.

I am still hopeful that the Government will take direct and powerful abolition measures. That hope is founded on the fact that the Government has already traveled further in that direction than it promised. Neither our law-makers, nor our laws, are like those of the Medes and Persians.[21] They are but the breath of the people, and are under the control of events. No President, no Cabinet, no army can withstand the mighty current of events, or the surging billows of the popular will. The first flash of rebel gunpowder, ten months ago, pouring shot and shell upon the starving handful of men at Sumter, instantly changed the whole policy of the nation. Until then, the ever hopeful North, of all parties, was still dreaming of compromise. The heavens were black, the thunder rattled, the air was heavy, and vivid lightning flashed all around; but our sages were telling us there would be no rain. But all at once, down came the storm of hail and fire.

And now behold the change! Only one brief year ago, the great city of Boston, the Athens of America, was convulsed by a howling pro-slavery mob, madly trampling upon the great and sacred right of speech. It blocked the streets; it shut up the halls; it silenced and overawed the press, defied the Government, and clamored for the blood of WENDELL PHILLIPS, a name which will live and shine while Boston is remembered as the chief seat of American eloquence, philanthropy and learning. Where is that mob to-night? You must look for it on the sacred soil of old Virginia.

Nothing stands to-day where it stood yesterday. Humanity sweeps onward. To-night with saints and angels, surrounded with the glorious army of martyrs and confessors, of whom our guilty world was not worthy, the brave spirit of old JOHN BROWN serenely looks down from his eternal rest, beholding his guilty murderers in torments of their own kindling, and the faith for which he nobly died steadily becoming the saving faith of the nation. He was "*justly hanged*," was the word from patriotic lips two years ago; but now, every loyal heart in the nation would gladly call him back again. Our armies now march by the inspiration of his name; and his son, young JOHN BROWN, from being hunted like a felon, is raised to a captaincy in the loyal army.

We have seen great changes—everybody has changed—the North has changed—Republicans have changed—and even the Garrisonians, of whom it has been said that repentance is not among their virtues, even they have changed; and from being the stern advocates of a dissolution of the Union, they have become the uncompromising advocates of the perpetuity of the Union. I believed ten years ago that liberty was safer in the Union than out of the Union; but my Garrisonian friends

21. Daniel 5:6.

could not then so see it, and of consequence dealt me some heavy blows. My crime was in being ten years in advance of them. But whether the Government shall directly abolish slavery or not, the war is essentially an abolition war. When the storm clouds of this rebellion shall be lifted from the land, the slave power, broken and humbled, will be revealed. Slavery will be a conquered power in the land. I am, therefore, for the war, for the Government, for the Union, for the Constitution in any and every event.

What the Black Man Wants[1]

I came here, as I come always to the meetings in New England, as a listener, and not as a speaker; and one of the reasons why I have not been more frequently to the meetings of this society, has been because of the disposition on the part of some of my friends to call me out upon the platform, even when they knew that there was some difference of opinion and of feeling between those who rightfully belong to this platform and myself; and for fear of being misconstrued, as desiring to interrupt or disturb the proceedings of these meetings, I have usually kept away, and have thus been deprived of that educating influence, which I am always free to confess is of the highest order, descending from this platform. I have felt, since I have lived out West,[2] that in going there, I parted from a great deal that was valuable; and I feel, every time I come to these meetings that I have lost a great deal by making my home west of Boston, west of Massachusetts; for, if anywhere in the country there is to be found the highest sense of justice, or the truest demands for my race, I look for it in the East, I look for it here. The ablest discussions of the whole question of our rights occur here, and to be deprived of the privilege of listening to those discussions is a great deprivation.

I do not know, from what has been said, that there is any difference of opinion as to the duty of abolitionists at the present moment. How can we get up any difference at this point, or at any point, where we are so united, so agreed? I went especially, however, with that word of Mr. Phillips to which is the criticism of Gen. Banks and Gen. Banks' policy.[3] I hold that that policy is our chief danger at the present moment; that it practically enslaves the negro, and makes the Proclamation of 1863[4] a mockery and delusion. What is freedom? It is the right to choose one's own employment. Certainly, it means that, if it means anything; and when any individual or combination of individuals undertakes to decide for any man when he shall work, where he shall work, at what he shall work, and for what he shall work, he or they practically reduce him to slavery. [Applause.] He is a slave. That I understand Gen. Banks to do—to determine for the so-called freedman when, and where, and at what, and for how much he shall work, when he shall be punished, and by whom punished. It is absolute slavery. It defeats the beneficent intention of the Government, if it has beneficent intentions, in regard to the freedom of our people.

I have had but one idea for the last three years to present to the American people, and the phraseology in which I clothe it is the old abolition phraseology. I am for the "immediate, unconditional, and universal" enfranchisement of the black man, in

1. Delivered April 1865.
2. West of Boston, in Rochester, NY.
3. General Nathaniel Banks instituted a discriminatory labor policy against Blacks in Louisiana. He claimed that he was trying to prepare them for the bias they would face after emancipation. Wendell Phillips argued that Black men needed no more preparation for freedom than White men did.
4. The Emancipation Proclamation.

every State in the Union. [Loud applause.] Without this, his liberty is a mockery; without this, you might as well almost retain the old name of slavery for his condition; for, in fact, if he is not the slave of the individual master, he is the slave of society, and holds his liberty as a privilege, not as a right. He is at the mercy of the mob, and has no means of protecting himself.

It may be objected, however, that this pressing of the negroes' right to suffrage is premature. Let us have slavery abolished, it may be said, let us have labor organized, and then, in the natural course of events, the right of suffrage will be extended to the negro. I do not agree with this. The constitution of the human mind is such, that if it once disregards the conviction forced upon it by a revelation of truth, it requires the exercise of a higher power to produce the same conviction afterwards. The American people are now in tears. The Shenandoah has run blood—the best blood of the North. All around Richmond, the blood of New England and of the North has been shed—of your sons, your brothers, and your fathers. We all feel, in the existence of this rebellion, that judgments terrible, wide-spread, far-reaching, overwhelming, are abroad in the land; and we feel, in view of these judgments, just now, a disposition to learn righteousness. This is the hour. Our streets are in mourning, tears are falling at every fireside, and under the chastisement of this rebellion, we have almost come up to the point of conceding this great, this all-important right of suffrage. I fear that if we fail to do it now, if Abolitionists fail to press it now, we may not see, for centuries to come, the same disposition that exists at this moment. [Applause.] Hence, I say, now is the time to press this right.

It may be asked, "Why do you want it? Some men have got along very well without it. Women have not this right." Shall we justify one wrong by another? This is the sufficient answer. Shall we at this moment justify the deprivation of the negro of the right to vote because some one else is deprived of that privilege? I hold that women as well as men have the right to vote [applause], and my heart and my voice go with the movement to extend suffrage to woman. But that question rests upon another basis than that on which our right rests. We may be asked, I say, why we want it. I will tell you why we want it. We want it because it is our *right*, first of all. No class of men can, without insulting their own nature, be content with any deprivation of their rights. We want it, again, as a means for educating our race. Men are so constituted that they derive their conviction of their own possibilities largely by the estimate formed of them by others. If nothing is expected of a people, that people will find it difficult to contradict that expectation. By depriving us of suffrage, you affirm our incapacity to form an intelligent judgment respecting public men and public measures; you declare before the world that we are unfit to exercise the elective franchise, and by this means lead us to undervalue ourselves, to put a low estimate upon ourselves, and to feel that we have no possibilities like other men. Again, I want the elective franchise, for one, as a colored man, because ours is a peculiar government, based upon a peculiar idea, and that idea is universal suffrage. If I were in a monarchial government, or an autocratic or aristocratic Government, where the few bore rule and the many were subject, there would be no special stigma resting upon me because I did not exercise the elective franchise. It would do me no great violence. Mingling with the mass, I should partake of the strength of the mass; I should be supported by the mass, and I should have the same incentives to endeavor with the mass of my fellow-men; it would be no particular burden, no particular deprivation. But here, where universal suffrage is the rule, where that is the fundamental idea of the government, to rule us out is to make us an exception, to brand us with the stigma of inferiority, and to invite to our heads the missiles of those about us. Therefore I want the franchise for the black man.

There are, however, other reasons, not derived from any consideration merely of our rights, but arising out of the conditions of the South and of the country—considerations which have already been referred to by Mr. Phillips—considerations which must arrest the attention of statesmen. I believe that when the tall heads of this rebellion shall have been swept down, as they will be swept down, when the Davises and Toombses and Stephenses[5] and others who are leading this rebellion shall have been blotted out, there will be this rank undergrowth of treason, to which reference has been made, growing up there, and interfering with and thwarting the quiet operation of the Federal Government in those States. You will see those traitors handing down from sire to son the same malignant spirit which they have manifested and which they are now exhibiting, with malicious hearts, broad blades and bloody hands in the field, against our sons and brothers. That spirit will still remain; and whoever sees the Federal Government extended over those Southern States will see that government in a strange land and not only in a strange land but in an enemy's land. A postmaster of the United States in the South will find himself surrounded by a hostile spirit; a collector in a Southern port will find himself surrounded by a hostile spirit; a United States marshal or United States judge will be surrounded there by a hostile element. That enmity will not die out in a year, will not die out in an age. The Federal Government will be looked upon in those States precisely as the governments of Austria and France are looked upon in Italy at the present moment. They will endeavor to circumvent, they will endeavor to destroy the peaceful operation of this government. Now, where will you find the strength to counterbalance this spirit, if you do not find it in the negroes of the South! They are your friends, and have always been your friends. They were your friends even when the Government did not regard them as such. They comprehended the genius of this war before you did. It is a significant fact, it is a marvellous fact, it seems almost to imply a direct interposition of Providence, that this war, which began in the interest of slavery on both sides, bids fair to end in the interest of liberty on both sides. [Applause.] It was begun, I say, in the interest of slavery, on both sides. The South was fighting to take slavery out of the Union and the North fighting to keep it in the Union; the South fighting to get it beyond the limits of the United States Constitution, and the North fighting to retain it within those limits, the South fighting for new guarantees and the North fighting for the old guarantees;—both despising the negro, both insulting the negro. Yet the negro, apparently endowed with wisdom from on high, saw more clearly the end from the beginning than we did. When Seward[6] said the status of no man in the country would be changed by the war, the negro did not believe him. [Applause.] When our generals sent their underlings in shoulder straps to hunt the flying negro back from our lines into the jaws of slavery from which he had escaped, the negroes thought that a mistake had been made, and that the intentions of the Government had not been rightly understood by our officers in shoulder straps, and they continued to come into our lines, threading their way through bogs and fens,

5. Jefferson Davis, President of the Confederacy; Robert A. Toombs, Georgia senator, seccessionist, and Southern general; and Alexander H. Stephens, vice president of the Confederacy.

6. William Seward, New York senator and antislavery activist.

over briers and thorns, fording streams, swimming rivers, bringing us tidings as to the safe path to march, and pointing out the dangers that threatened us. They are our only friends in the South, and we should be true to them in this their trial hour, and see to it that they have the elective franchise.

I know that we are inferior to you in some things—virtually inferior. We walk about you like dwarfs among giants. Our heads are scarcely seen above the great sea of humanity. The Germans are superior to us; the Irish are superior to us; the Yankees are superior to us [laughter]; they can do what we cannot, that is, what we have not hitherto been allowed to do. But, while I make this admission, I utterly deny, that we are originally, or naturally, or practically, or in any way, or in any important sense, inferior to anybody on this globe. [Loud applause.] This charge of inferiority is an old dodge. It has been made available for oppression on many occasions. It is only about six centuries since the blue-eyed and fair-haired Anglo-Saxons were considered inferior by the haughty Normans, who once trampled upon them. If you read the history of the Norman Conquest, you will find that this proud Anglo-Saxon was once looked upon as of coarser clay than his Norman master, and might be found in the highways and byways of Old England laboring with a brass collar on his neck, and the name of his master marked upon it. *You were down then!* [Laughter and applause.] You are up now. I am glad you are up, and I want you to be glad to help us up also. [Applause.]

The story of our inferiority is an old dodge, as I have said; for wherever men oppress their fellows, wherever they enslave them, they will endeavor to find the needed apology for such enslavement and oppression in the character of the people oppressed and enslaved. When we wanted, a few years ago, a slice of Mexico, it was hinted that the Mexicans were an inferior race, that the old Castilian blood had become so weak that it would scarcely run down hill, and that Mexico needed the long, strong and beneficent arm of the Anglo-Saxon care extended over it. We said that it was necessary to its salvation, and a part of the "manifest destiny" of this Republic, to extend our arm over that dilapidated government. So, too, when Russia wanted to take possession of a part of the Ottoman Empire, the Turks were an "inferior race." So, too, when England wants to set the heel of her power more firmly in the quivering heart of old Ireland, the Celts are an "inferior race." So, too, the negro, when he is to be robbed of any right which is justly his, is an "inferior man." It is said that we are ignorant; I admit it. But if we know enough to be hung, we know enough to vote. If the negro knows enough to pay taxes to support the Government, he knows enough to vote—taxation and representation should go together. If he knows enough to shoulder a musket and fight for the flag, fight for the Government, he knows enough to vote. If he knows as much when he is sober as an Irishman knows when drunk, he knows enough to vote, on good American principles. [Laughter and applause.]

But I was saying that you needed a counterpoise in the persons of the slaves to the enmity that would exist at the South after the rebellion is put down. I hold that the American people are bound, not only in self-defence, to extend this right to the freedmen of the South, but they are bound by their love of country and by all their regard for the future safety of those Southern States to do this—to do it as a measure essential to the preservation of peace there. But I will not dwell upon this. I put it to the American sense of honor. The honor of a nation is an important thing. It is said in the Scriptures, "What doth it profit a man if he gain the whole world, and lose his own soul!" It may be said also, what doth it profit a nation if it gain the whole world, but lose its honor? I hold that the American Government has taken upon itself a solemn obligation of honor to see that this war, let it be long or let it be short, let it cost much, or let it cost little,—that this war shall not cease until every freedman at the South has the right to vote. [Applause.] It has bound itself to it. What have you asked the black men of the South, the black men of the whole country to do? Why, you have asked them to incure the deadly enmity of their masters, in order to befriend you and to befriend this government. You have asked us to call down, not only upon ourselves, but upon our children's children, the deadly hate of the entire Southern people. You have called upon us to turn our backs upon our masters, to abandon their cause and espouse yours; to turn against the South and in favor of the North; to shoot down the Confederacy and uphold the flag—the American flag. You have called upon us to expose ourselves to all the subtle machinations of their malignity for all time. And now, what do you propose to do when you come to make peace? To reward your enemies, and trample in the dust your friends? Do you intend to sacrifice the very men who have come to the rescue of your banner in the South, and incurred the lasting displeasure of their masters thereby? Do you intend to sacrifice them, and reward your enemies? Do you mean to give your enemies the right to vote, and take it away from your friends? Is that wise policy? Is that honorable? Could American honor withstand such a blow? I do not believe you will do it. I think you will see to it that we have the right to vote. There is something too mean in looking upon the negro when you are in trouble as a citizen, and when you are free from trouble as an alien. When this nation was in trouble, in its early struggles, it looked upon the negro as a citizen. In 1776, he was a citizen. At the time of the formation of the Constitution the negro had the right to vote in eleven States out of the old thirteen. In your trouble you have made us citizens. In 1812, Gen. Jackson addressed us as citizens, "fellow-citizens." He wanted us to fight. We were citizens then! And now, when you come to frame a conscription bill, the negro is a citizen again. He has been a citizen just three times in the history of this government, and it has always been in time of trouble. In time of trouble we are citizens. Shall we be citizens in war, and aliens in peace? Would that be just?

I ask my friends who are apologizing for not insisting upon this right, where can the black man look in this country for the assertion of this right if he may not look to the Massachusetts Anti-Slavery Society? Where under the whole heavens can he look for sympathy in asserting this right if he may not look to this platform? Have you lifted us up to a certain height to see that we are men, and then are any disposed to leave us there, without seeing that we are put in possession of all our rights? We look naturally to this platform for the assertion of all our rights, and for this one especially. I understand the anti-slavery societies of this country to be based on two principles—first, the freedom of the blacks of this country; and, second, the elevation of them. Let me not be misunderstood here. I am not asking for sympathy at the hands of Abolitionists, sympathy at the hands of any. I think the American people are disposed often to be generous rather than just. I look over this country at the present time, and I see Educational Societies, Sanitary Commissions, Freedmen's Associations, and the like,—all very good; but in regard to the colored people, there is always more that is benevolent, I perceive, than just, manifested towards us. What I ask for the negro is not benevolence, not pity, not sympathy, but simply *justice*. [Applause.] The American people have always been anxious to know what they shall do with us. Gen. Banks was distressed with solicitude as to what he should do with the negro. Everybody has asked the question, and they learned to ask it early of the abolitionists: "What shall we do with the negro?" I have had but one answer from the beginning. Do nothing with us! Your doing with us has already played the mischief with us. Do nothing with us! If the apples will not remain on the tree of their own strength, if they are worm-eaten at the core, if they are early ripe and disposed to fall, let them fall! I am not for tying or fastening them on the tree in any way, except by nature's plan, and if they will not stay there, let them fall. And if the negro cannot stand on his own legs, let him fall also. All I ask is, give him a chance to stand on his own legs! Let him alone! If you see him on his way to school, let him alone,—don't disturb him! If you see him going to the dinner table at a hotel, let him go! If you see him going to the ballot box, let him alone!—don't disturb him! [Applause.] If you see him going into a workshop, just let him alone,—your interference is doing him a positive injury. Gen. Banks's "preparation" is of a piece with this attempt to prop up the negro. Let him fall if he cannot stand alone! If the negro cannot live by the line of eternal justice, so beautifully pictured to you in the illustration used by Mr. Phillips, the fault will not be yours, it will be His who made the negro, and established that line for his government. [Applause.] Let him live or die by that. If you will only untie his hands, and give him a chance, I think he will live. He will work as readily for himself as the white man. A great many delusions have been swept away by this war. One was, that the negro would not work; he has proved his ability to work. Another was, that the negro would not fight; that he possessed only the most sheepish attributes of humanity; was a perfect lamb, or an "Uncle Tom;" disposed to take off his coat whenever required, fold his hands, and be whipped by any body who wanted to whip him;—but the war has proved that there is a great deal of human nature in the negro, and that he will fight, as Mr. Quincy, our President, said, in earlier days than these, "when there is reasonable probability of his whipping anybody." [Laughter and applause.]

Questions to Consider

1. In "What the Black Man Wants," Douglass links the idea of Black suffrage to women's suffrage. What does the argument gain by the link between the two?
2. Most of Douglass's addresses rely heavily on a logical working-out of the issues he addresses. Nevertheless, underlying the logic is a strong emotional appeal. Where do you find evidences of emotion in the selections?
3. In "What to the Slave Is the Fourth of July?" Douglass argues that the number of laws against Blacks is evidence that Blacks are, in fact, human beyond all argument. How effective do you find that argument?

Henry Timrod

1828–1867

In 1903, the critic F. V. N. Painter wrote regarding the life of Henry Timrod that there was "perhaps, no sadder story in the annals of literature." Plagued his entire life by ill health, poverty, and the inability to gain the effect he wanted in his poetry, Timrod nevertheless managed to produce a body of well-regarded poems, which are largely influenced by his love of the classics of Greek and Latin and which, when sparked by his experiences during the Civil War, earned him the title of Poet Laureate of the Confederacy.

Henry Timrod was born in Charleston on 8 December 1828. His father was himself a minor poet and a soldier, but he died of tuberculosis when Henry was ten. Timrod's education included training in Greek, Latin, French, and mathematics, and he began to write poetry as a schoolboy, although the practice was not encouraged by the school. In 1845, Timrod enrolled at the University of Georgia, but lack of funding and ill health forced him to resign after a year and a half. He began publishing his poetry in Southern newspapers and literary journals soon after leaving school, and these early poems, which are largely pastoral and love poems, show the unmistakable influence of the British Romantics Lord Byron, William Wordsworth, and Alfred, Lord Tennyson.

Timrod briefly toyed with the idea of becoming a lawyer, but he made his living before the war as a tutor on various plantations around the Charleston area. Timrod was respected in Charleston literary society, and he joined a group of Charleston writers that included William Gilmore Simms, William John Grayson, and the poet Paul Hamilton Hayne, who had been a friend of Timrod's since his childhood. The group, which met at Russell's bookstore in Charleston, began to publish a literary journal, *Russell's Magazine*, which often featured Timrod's poetry.

Like Wordsworth, Timrod believed in the power of nature to reveal truth, but he tried to surpass his mere subjective sensitivity. Timrod hoped to introduce a spiritual philosophy of supersensuous poetry, which would regard nature as the ultimate source of truth. Unlike Poe, who argued that beauty should be the poet's aim, Timrod, influenced by Milton and Wordsworth, declared that power and truth should be the poet's goals. The principles of his poetry were clear, but Timrod worried about his inability to attain the transcendental effect he wanted for his poetry, and this failure he attributed to his inability to free himself from what he called "morbid subjectivity."

When the Civil War began, Timrod enlisted in the Confederate Army, and he spent some time as a war correspondent in the Southwest until ill health forced him to return to Charleston. After convalescing, he returned to the army, but sickness once again forced him home. In 1862, he published his two most famous war poems, "Spring" and "Christmas," and largely on the basis of these poems, he was dubbed the Poet Laureate of the Confederacy. His war poem, "The Unknown Dead" is, perhaps, one of the most poignant lamentations on the tragedy of the unidentified war casualty.

In 1863, an English publisher planned a collection of Timrod's poetry, and although proofs of the book were printed, the book was never published. Timrod was disappointed, of course, and attempted to earn a living in the newspaper trade, but the day-to-day workings of the daily news were not to his liking. Timrod married in 1864, but the marriage was struck by tragedy when the couple's first son died, which cast a pall on his otherwise happy home life. During the same year, Charleston was sacked by Union forces, which also put an end to Timrod's newspaper career. Timrod sank further into poverty and illness until he died of tuberculosis in 1867.

Carolina

I

The despot treads thy sacred sands,
Thy pines give shelter to his bands,
Thy sons stand by with idle hands,
Carolina!
He breathes at ease thy airs of balm,
He scorns the lances of thy palm;
Oh! who shall break thy craven calm,
Carolina!
Thy ancient fame is growing dim,
A spot is on thy garment's rim;
Give to the winds thy battle hymn,
Carolina!

II

Call on thy children of the hill,
Wake swamp and river, coast and rill,[1]
Rouse all thy strength and all thy skill,
Carolina!
Cite wealth and science, trade and art,
Touch with thy fire the cautious mart,
And pour thee through the people's heart,
Carolina!
Till even the coward spurns his fears,
And all thy fields and fens[2] and meres[3]
Shall bristle like thy palm with spears,
Carolina!

III

Hold up the glories of thy dead;
Say how thy elder children bled,
And point to Eutaw's battle-bed,[4]
Carolina!
Tell how the patriot's soul was tried,
And what his dauntless breast defied;
How Rutledge ruled and Laurens died,[5]
Carolina!
Cry! till thy summons, heard at last,
Shall fall like Marion's bugle-blast[6]
Re-echoed from the haunted Past,
Carolina!

1. A small brook.
2. A swamp, bog, or marsh.
3. A small lake or pond.
4. Refers to the Revolutionary War battle of Eutaw Springs, South Carolina, 8 September 1781.
5. John Rutledge was governor, or "president" of South Carolina from 1776 to 1782; his vice president was Henry Laurens.
6. Refers to Francis Marion, renowned Revolutionary War general; also known as "The Swamp Fox."

IV

I hear a murmur as of waves
That grope their way through sunless caves,
Like bodies struggling in their graves,
Carolina!

And now it deepens; slow and grand
It swells, as, rolling to the land,
An ocean broke upon thy strand,
Carolina!
Shout! let it reach the startled Huns!
And roar with all thy festal[7] guns!
It is the answer of thy sons,
Carolina!

V

They will not wait to hear thee call;
From Sachem's Head[8] to Sumter's wall[9]
Resounds the voice of hut and hall,
Carolina!
No! thou hast not a stain, they say,
Or none save what the battle-day
Shall wash in seas of blood away,
Carolina!
Thy skirts indeed the foe may part,
Thy robe be pierced with sword and dart,
They shall not touch thy noble heart,
Carolina!

VI

Ere thou shalt own the tyrant's thrall
Ten times ten thousand men must fall;
Thy corpse may hearken to his call,
Carolina!

When, by thy bier,[10] in mournful throngs
The women chant thy mortal wrongs,
'Twill be their own funereal songs,
Carolina!
From thy dead breast by ruffians trod
No helpless child shall look to God;
All shall be safe beneath thy sod,
Carolina!

VII

Girt[11] with such wills to do and bear,
Assured in right, and mailed[12] in prayer,
Thou wilt not bow thee to despair,
Carolina!

7. Relating to a feast or festival.
8. The name of a local promontory.
9. The first battle of the Civil War occurred at Fort Sumter in 1861.
10. A stand for a coffin.
11. Encircled with a belt or band.
12. Armored.

Throw thy bold banner to the breeze!
Front with thy ranks the threatening seas
Like thine own proud armorial trees,
Carolina!
Fling down thy gauntlet to the Huns,
And roar the challenge from thy guns;
Then leave the future to thy sons,
Carolina!

Charleston

Calm as that second summer which precedes
The first fall of the snow,
In the broad sunlight of heroic deeds,
The City bides the foe.

As yet, behind their ramparts stern and proud,
Her bolted thunders sleep—
Dark Sumter, like a battlemented cloud,
Looms o'er the solemn deep.

No Calpe[1] frowns from lofty cliff or scar
To guard the holy strand;
But Moultrie[2] holds in leash her dogs of war
Above the level sand.

And down the dunes a thousand guns lie couched,
Unseen, beside the flood—
Like tigers in some Orient jungle crouched
That wait and watch for blood.

Meanwhile, through streets still echoing with trade,
Walk grave and thoughtful men,
Whose hands may one day wield the patriot's blade
As lightly as the pen.

And maidens, with such eyes as would grow dim
Over a bleeding hound,
Seem each one to have caught the strength of him
Whose sword she sadly bound.

Thus girt without and garrisoned at home,
Day patient following day,
Old Charleston looks from roof, and spire, and dome,
Across her tranquil bay.

Ships, through a hundred foes, from Saxon lands
And spicy Indian ports,
Bring Saxon steel and iron to her hands,
And Summer to her courts.

But still, along yon dim Atlantic line,
The only hostile smoke

1. Leader.

2. Union troops fired on Fort Sumter from Fort Moultrie.

Creeps like a harmless mist above the brine,
From some frail, floating oak.

Shall the Spring dawn, and she still clad in smiles,
And with an unscathed brow,
Rest in the strong arms of her palm-crowned isles,
As fair and free as now?

We know not; in the temple of the Fates[3]
God has inscribed her doom;
And, all untroubled in her faith, she waits
The triumph or the tomb.

Ethnogenesis

Written during the meeting of the first Southern Congress, at Montgomery. February 1861.

I

Hath not the morning dawned with added light?
And shall not evening call another star
Out of the infinite regions of the night,
To mark this day in Heaven? At last, we are
A nation among nations; and the world
Shall soon behold in many a distant port
Another flag unfurled!
Now, come what may, whose favor need we court?
And, under God, whose thunder need we fear?
Thank Him who placed us here
Beneath so kind a sky—the very sun
Takes part with us; and on our errands run
All breezes of the ocean; dew and rain
Do noiseless battle for us; and the Year,
And all the gentle daughters in her train,
March in our ranks, and in our service wield
Long spears of golden grain!
A yellow blossom as her fairy shield,
June flings her azure banner to the wind,
While in the order of their birth
Her sisters pass, and many an ample field
Grows white beneath their steps, till now, behold,
Its endless sheets unfold
THE SNOW OF SOUTHERN SUMMERS! Let the earth
Rejoice! beneath those fleeces soft and warm
Our happy land shall sleep
In a repose as deep
As if we lay intrenched behind
Whole leagues of Russian ice and Arctic storm!

3. In Greek mythology, the fates of all men were inscribed in the Temple of the Fates.

II

And what if, mad with wrongs themselves have wrought,
In their own treachery caught,
By their own fears made bold,
And leagued with him of old,
Who long since in the limits of the North
Set up his evil throne, and warred with God—
What if, both mad and blinded in their rage,
Our foes should fling us down their mortal gage,
And with a hostile step profane our sod!
We shall not shrink, my brothers, but go forth
To meet them, marshalled by the Lord of Hosts,
And overshadowed by the mighty ghosts
Of Moultrie and of Eutaw[1]—who shall foil
Auxiliars[2] such as these? Nor these alone,
But every stock and stone
Shall help us; but the very soil,
And all the generous wealth it gives to toil,
And all for which we love our noble land,
Shall fight beside, and through us; sea and strand,
The heart of woman, and her hand,
Tree, fruit, and flower, and every influence,
Gentle, or grave, or grand;
The winds in our defence
Shall seem to blow; to us the hills shall lend
Their firmness and their calm;
And in our stiffened sinews we shall blend
The strength of pine and palm!

III

Nor would we shun the battle-ground,
Though weak as we are strong;
Call up the clashing elements around,
And test the right and wrong!
On one side, creeds that dare to teach
What Christ and Paul refrained to preach;
Codes built upon a broken pledge,
And Charity that whets a poniard's[3] edge;
Fair schemes that leave the neighboring poor
To starve and shiver at the schemer's door,
While in the world's most liberal ranks enrolled,
He turns some vast philanthropy to gold;
Religion, taking every mortal form
But that a pure and Christian faith makes warm,
Where not to vile fanatic passion urged,
Or not in vague philosophies submerged,
Repulsive with all Pharisaic leaven,[4]

1. Sites of Revolutionary War battles.
2. Ones who give aid or help.
3. A dagger with a small triangular blade.
4. In Luke 12:1, Christ warns the disciples, "Beware of the leaven of the Pharisees, which is hypocrisy."

And making laws to stay the laws of Heaven!
And on the other, scorn of sordid gain,
Unblemished honor, truth without a stain,
Faith, justice, reverence, charitable wealth,
And, for the poor and humble, laws which give,
Not the mean right to buy the right to live,
    But life, and home, and health!
To doubt the end were want of trust in God,
    Who, if he has decreed
    That we must pass a redder sea
Than that which rang to Miriam's holy glee,[5]
    Will surely raise at need
    A Moses with his rod!

IV

But let our fears—if fears we have—be still,
And turn us to the future! Could we climb
Some mighty Alp, and view the coming time,
The rapturous sight would fill
    Our eyes with happy tears!
Not only for the glories which the years
Shall bring us; not for lands from sea to sea,
And wealth, and power, and peace, though these shall be;
But for the distant peoples we shall bless,
And the hushed murmurs of a world's distress:
For, to give labor to the poor,
    The whole sad planet o'er,
And save from want and crime the humblest door,
Is one among the many ends for which
    God makes us great and rich!
The hour perchance is not yet wholly ripe
When all shall own it, but the type
Whereby we shall be known in every land
Is that vast gulf which lips our Southern strand,
And through the cold, untempered ocean pours
Its genial streams, that far off Arctic shores
May sometimes catch upon the softened breeze
Strange tropic warmth and hints of summer seas.

Christmas

    How grace this hallowed day?
Shall happy bells, from yonder ancient spire,
Send their glad greetings to each Christmas fire
    Round which the children play?

    Alas! for many a moon,
That tongueless tower hath cleaved the Sabbath air,
Mute as an obelisk of ice, aglare
    Beneath an Arctic noon.

5. Miriam was an Old Testament prophetess, who sang a song of victory when the children of Israel crossed the Red Sea.

Shame to the foes that drown
Our psalms of worship with their impious drum,
The sweetest chimes in all the land lie dumb
In some far rustic town.

There, let us think, they keep,
Of the dead Yules which here beside the sea
They've ushered in with old-world, English glee,
Some echoes in their sleep.

How shall we grace the day?
With feast, and song, and dance, and antique sports,
And shout of happy children in the courts,
And tales of ghost and fay?[1]

Is there indeed a door,
Where the old pastimes, with their lawful noise,
And all the merry round of Christmas joys,
Could enter as of yore?

Would not some pallid face
Look in upon the banquet, calling up
Dread shapes of battles in the wassail cup,
And trouble all the place?

How could we bear the mirth,
While some loved reveller of a year ago
Keeps his mute Christmas now beneath the snow,
In cold Virginian earth?

How shall we grace the day?
Ah! let the thought that on this holy morn
The Prince of Peace—the Prince of Peace was born,
Employ us, while we pray!

Pray for the peace which long
Hath left this tortured land, and haply now
Holds its white court on some far mountain's brow,
There hardly safe from wrong!

Let every sacred fane[2]
Call its sad votaries[3] to the shrine of God,
And, with the cloister and the tented sod,
Join in one solemn strain!

With pomp of Roman form,
With the grave ritual brought from England's shore,
And with the simple faith which asks no more
Than that the heart be warm!

He, who, till time shall cease,
Will watch that earth, where once, not all in vain,
He died to give us peace, may not disdain
A prayer whose theme is—peace.

1. An enchanted person or place.
2. A temple.
3. A person bound by religious worship or service.

Perhaps ere yet the Spring
Hath died into the Summer, over all
The land, the peace of His vast love shall fall,
Like some protecting wing.

Oh, ponder what it means!
Oh, turn the rapturous thought in every way!
Oh, give the vision and the fancy play,
And shape the coming scenes!

Peace in the quiet dales,
Made rankly fertile by the blood of men,
Peace in the woodland, and the lonely glen,
Peace in the peopled vales!

Peace in the crowded town,
Peace in a thousand fields of waving grain,
Peace in the highway and the flowery lane,
Peace on the wind-swept down!

Peace on the farthest seas,
Peace in our sheltered bays and ample streams,
Peace wheresoe'er our starry garland gleams,
And peace in every breeze!

Peace on the whirring marts,
Peace where the scholar thinks, the hunter roams,
Peace, God of Peace! peace, peace, in all our homes,
And peace in all our hearts!

The Unknown Dead

The rain is plashing on my sill,
But all the winds of Heaven are still;
And so it falls with that dull sound
Which thrills us in the church-yard ground,
When the first spadeful drops like lead
Upon the coffin of the dead.
Beyond my streaming window-pane,
I cannot see the neighboring vane,
Yet from its old familiar tower
The bell comes, muffled, through the shower
What strange and unsuspected link
Of feeling touched, has made me think—
While with a vacant soul and eye
I watch that gray and stony sky—
Of nameless graves on battle-plains
Washed by a single winter's rains,
Where, some beneath Virginian hills,
And some by green Atlantic rills,
Some by the waters of the West,
A myriad unknown heroes rest.
Ah! not the chiefs, who, dying, see
Their flags in front of victory,

Or, at their life-blood's noble cost
Pay for a battle nobly lost,
Claim from their monumental beds
The bitterest tears a nation sheds.
Beneath yon lonely mound—the spot
By all save some fond[1] few forgot—
Lie the true martyrs of the fight
Which strikes for freedom and for right.
Of them, their patriot zeal and pride,
The lofty faith that with them died,
No grateful page shall farther tell
Than that so many bravely fell;
And we can only dimly guess
What worlds of all this world's distress,
What utter woe, despair, and dearth;
Their fate has brought to many a hearth.
Just such a sky as this should weep
Above them, always, where they sleep;
Yet, haply, at this very hour,
Their graves are like a lover's bower;
And Nature's self, with eyes unwet,
Oblivious of the crimson debt
To which she owes her April grace,
Laughs gayly o'er their burial-place.

Questions to Consider

1. Timrod's poetry glorifies the South, but do you find elements in the poems that transcend their Southern setting?
2. Could "The Unknown Dead" be read as an antiwar poem? How?

John Esten Cooke

1830–1886

A year after John Esten Cooke published his first novel of the Civil War, *Surry of Eagle's-Nest*, the noted Virginia author confessed in his diary, "Hope to become the writer of the South yet! Big Ambition." As literary scholar Mary Jo Bratton has observed, when Cooke penned these words in 1867 his ambition hardly seemed like wishful thinking. Cooke, a cousin of John Pendleton Kennedy and a close friend of William Gilmore Simms, had written ten novels before the outbreak of the Civil War. By the time of his death in 1886, he had published more than thirty volumes and written scores of articles and sketches for a variety of periodicals. Cooke drew much of his inspiration from his home state. In an autobiographical sketch, he wrote that he had wanted his fiction "to paint the Virginia phase of American society, to do for the Old Dominion what Cooper has done for the Indians, Simms for the Revolutionary drama in South Carolina, Irving for the Dutch Knickerbockers, and Hawthorne for the weird

1. Found.

Puritan life of New England." Mary Ann Wimsat has commented that Cooke's assessment of his writing aptly summarizes the "derivation and the dominant cast of his books."

While reading law in Richmond, Virginia, Cooke began working for the *Southern Literary Messenger*, developing a breezy style suitable for magazine fiction. According to Bratton, Cooke's early works displayed not only his decidedly liberal faith and democratic leanings but also his contempt for the aristocracy. Moreover, Cooke was largely silent on the issue of slavery. These early writings suggest to Bratton that Cooke was "at best an ambivalent apostle of the traditional Southern way of life." Cooke's ambivalence did not temper his support of the Confederate cause during the Civil War, however. Rather, Cooke became one of the Confederacy's most prominent literary proponents, drawing on his experiences in the Army of Northern Virginia and publishing his dispatches in the *Southern Literary Messenger*. Between 1863 and 1871, Cooke published eight volumes based on his wartime escapades. Privately, he declared that war was "fit for brutes and brutish men. And in modern war," he continued, "where men are organized in masses and converted into insensate machines there is nothing really heroic or romantic or in any way calculated to appeal to the imagination." His wartime writings, however, suggest none of his revulsion at mechanized, modern warfare. Instead, according to Daniel Aaron, Cooke's novels "invited the reader to relive with him the 'stormy days of a convulsed epoch,' when the cavaliers challenged the invaders." As Aaron conceded, however, Cooke recognized that he offered sentimental portraits of war. "Ah, those 'romances of the war!' The trifling specimens will come first," Cooke mocked, "in which the Southern leaders will be made to talk an incredible gibberish, and figure in tremendous adventures."

Cooke displayed this cynicism about his own writing on more than one occasion. In an 1879 letter to a friend Cooke professed, "I write for money. If ever you write my life put this in—money and my own satisfaction. I have made some money, about $20,000 since the war, and I have poisoned the rising Southern generation with 'Confederate lies' about the war—which is enough to retire on." Bratton encourages Cooke's readers to substitute "myth" for lies, noting that Cooke's Civil War writings advanced what historians and literary scholars have termed "the myth of the lost cause." Cooke consistently reinforced to his Southern readers that the Confederate cause had been just and noble, for example. As an apologist for the military, he never located the source for Southern defeat in the Confederate army, ascribing blame instead to an inept government and to war profiteers and speculators. In the novel *Mohun*, Cooke praised the "three classes [that] remained faithful to death:—the old men, the army, and the women." Heroic foot soldiers, who fought despite impossible odds, along with the dedicated men and women on the homefront who never lost their steely resolve, eventually became staples of the myth of the lost cause. Cooke's refusal to acknowledge the centrality of slavery to an understanding of the Civil War, moreover, must be counted among what Bratton has called his "Confederate lies."

Cooke's Civil War writings cast a homogenous haze over the Southern past. His first wartime book, a biography of Stonewall Jackson published in 1863, was the last to be cast with a democratic hero. The following works featured the aristocratic Jeb Stuart as the protagonist. "As Jackson was the greatest of his democratic heroes," Bratton concludes, "he was also the last, while Stuart was the first of his truly Cavalier aristocrats. With Jackson he broke the mold, henceforth in his own plantation romances and those that followed in his wake the heroes were Cavaliers. As all Virginians became Cavaliers, so all Southerners became Cavaliers—all White Southerners that is, as racial solidity became the watchword of the New South, blurring class distinctions while intensifying the dogma of White supremacy."

from Surry of Eagle's-Nest
or
The Memoirs of a Staff-Officer Serving in Virginia

Chapter 131: The Last Greeting Between Stuart and Jackson

Here my memoirs might terminate—for the present, if not forever. All the personages disappear, lost in the bloody gulf, or have reached that crisis in their lives when we can leave them.

But one scene remains to wind up the tragedy—another figure is about to fall,[1] as the mighty pine falls in the depths of the forest, making the woods resound as it crashes to the earth. The hours drew onward now when the form of him to whom all the South looked in her day of peril was to disappear—when the eagle eye was to flash no more, the voice to be hushed—when the hero of a hundred battles was to leave the great arena of his fame, and pass away amid the wailing of a nation.

Come with me, reader, and we will look upon this "last scene of all." Then the curtain falls.

At daylight, on the morning succeeding the events just narrated, Jackson put his column in motion, and directed his march over the same route which I had pursued on my way to find Stuart. At the Catherine Furnace he was observed and attacked by the advance force of the enemy, but, pushing on without stopping—his flank covered by the cavalry—he reached the Brock road, and, finally, the Orange plank-road.

Here I joined him at the moment when General Fitz Lee, who commanded the cavalry under Stuart,[2] informed him that, by ascending a neighboring eminence, he could obtain a good view of the enemy's works. Jackson immediately rode to the point thus indicated, in company with Generals Fitz Lee and Stuart; and the works of Hooker[3] were plainly descried over the tops of the trees.

The whole was seen at a glance, and, to attack to advantage, it was obviously necessary to move further still around the enemy's flank.

"Tell my column to cross that road," Jackson said to one of his aides; and the troops moved on steadily until they reached the Old Turnpike, at a point between the Wilderness Tavern and Chancellorsville.

Here instant preparations were made for attack. The force which Jackson had consisted of Rodes's, Colston's, and A. P. Hill's divisions[4]—in all, somewhat less than twenty-two thousand men—and line of battle was immediately formed for an advance upon the enemy. Rodes moved in front, Colston followed within two hundred yards, and Hill marched in column, with the artillery as a reserve.

Jackson gave the order to advance at about six in the evening, and, as the sinking sun began to throw its long shadows over the Wilderness, the long line of bayonets was seen in motion. Struggling on through the dense thickets on either side of the turnpike, the troops reached the open ground near Melzl Chancellor's—and there, before them, was the long line of the enemy's works.

1. Here, Cooke alludes to the death of General Thomas "Stonewall" Jackson at the Battle of Chancellorsville, 2–6 May 1863.
2. Confederate General James E. B. (Jeb) Stuart. At Chancellorsville, Stuart overtook command of Jackson's Corps after that general had been mortally wounded in combat.
3. Union General Joseph "Fighting Joe" Hooker.
4. Confederate Major General Robert Emmett Rodes, division commander under A. P. Hill; led Stonewall Jackson's flank attack at Chancellorsville. Confederate General R. E. Colston, senior brigadier of the Stonewall Division at Chancellorsville.

Jackson rode in front, and, as soon as his lines were formed for the attack, ordered the works to be stormed with the bayonet.

At the word, Rodes rushed forward—the men cheering wildly—and, in a few moments, they had swept over the Federal earthworks, driving the Eleventh Corps in wild confusion before them. The woods swarmed with panic-stricken infantry, in utter confusion; artillery galloped off, and was overturned in ditches, or by striking against the trees. At one blow the entire army of Hooker, as events subsequently proved, was entirely demoralized.

Jackson pressed straight on upon the track of the flying enemy; and I soon discovered that he was straining every nerve to extend his left; and so cut off their retreat to the Rappahannock. Unavoidable delays, however, ensued. The lines of Rodes and Colston had been mingled in inextricable confusion in the charge; officers could not find their commands: before advancing further, it was absolutely necessary to halt and re-form the line of battle.

Rodes and Colston were, accordingly, ordered to stop their advance, re-form their divisions, and give way to Hill, who was directed to take the front with his fresh division, not yet engaged.

Before these orders could be carried out, it was nearly nine o'clock at night, and the weird scene was only lit up by the struggling beams of a pallid moon. On all sides the scattered troops were seen gathering around their colors again, and forming a new line of battle—and soon A. P. Hill was heard steadily advancing to take his place in front, for the decisive attack on Chancellorsville, about a mile distant.

Such was the condition of things, when General Jackson, accompanied by his staff and escort, rode in advance of his line down the road toward Chancellorsville, listening, at every step, for some indications of a movement in the Federal camps.

When nearly opposite an old wooden house, in the thicket by the roadside, he checked his horse to listen; and the whole cortege, General, staff, and couriers, remained for some moments silent and motionless, gazing toward the enemy.

From the narrative of what followed I shrink with a sort of dread, and a throbbing heart. Again that sombre and lugubrious Wilderness rises up before me, lit by the pallid moon; again the sad whippoorwill's cry; again I see the great soldier, motionless upon his horse—and then I hear the fatal roar of the guns which laid him low!

Jackson had halted thus, and remained motionless in the middle of the road, listening intently, when, suddenly, for what reason has never yet been discovered, one of his brigades in rear, and on the right of the turnpike, opened a heavy fire upon the party.

Did they take us for Federal cavalry, or were they firing at random, under the excitement of the moment? I know not, and it is probable that the truth will never be known. But the fire had terrible results. Some of the staff were wounded; others threw themselves from their horses, who were running from the fire toward the Federal lines, not two hundred yards distant; and Captain Boswell, engineer upon the General's staff, was killed, and his body dragged by his maddened horse to Chancellorsville.

As the bullets whistled around him, Jackson wheeled his horse to the left, and galloped into the thicket. Then came the fatal moment. The troops behind him, on the left of the road, imagined that the Federal cavalry were charging; and, kneeling on the right knee, with bayonets fixed, poured a volley upon the General, at the distance of thirty yards.

Two balls passed through his left arm, shattering the bone, and a third through his right hand, breaking the fingers.

Mad with terror, his horse wheeled round and ran off; and, passing under a low bough, extending horizontally from a tree, Jackson was struck in the forehead, his cap torn from his head, and his form hurled back almost out of the saddle. He rose erect again, however; grasped the bridle with his bleeding fingers; and, regaining control of his horse, turned again into the high road, near the spot which he had left.

The fire had ceased as suddenly as it began, and not a human being was seen. Of the entire staff and escort, no one remained but myself and a single courier. The rest had disappeared before the terrible fire, as leaves disappear before the blasts of winter.

Jackson reeled in the saddle, but no sound had issued from his lips during the whole scene. He now declared, in faint tones, that his arm was broken; and, leaning forward, he fell into my arms.

More bitter distress than I experienced at that moment I would not wish to have inflicted upon my deadliest enemy. Nor was my anxiety less terrible. The lines of the enemy were in sight of the spot where the General lay. At any moment they might advance, when he would fall into their hands.

No time was to be lost. I sent the courier for an ambulance; and, taking off the General's military satchel and his arms, endeavored to stanch his wound. While I was thus engaged, I experienced a singular consciousness that other eyes than the General's were intently watching me. I can only thus describe the instinctive feeling which induced me to look up—and there, in the edge of the thicket, within ten paces of me, was a dark figure, motionless, on horseback, gazing at me

"Who is that?" I called out.

But no reply greeted my address.

"Is that one of the couriers? If so, ride up there, and see what troops those are that fired upon us."

At the order, the dark figure moved; went slowly in the direction which I indicated; and never again appeared. Who was that silent horseman? I know not, nor ever expect to know.

I had turned again to the General, and was trying to remove his bloody gauntlets, when the sound of hoofs was heard in the direction of our own lines, and soon General A. P. Hill appeared, with his staff. Hastily dismounting, he expressed the deepest regret at the fatal occurrence, and urged the General to permit himself to be borne to the rear, as the enemy might, at any moment, advance.

As he was speaking, an instant proof was afforded of the justice of his fears.

"Halt! surrender! Fire on them, if they do not surrender!" came from one of the staff in advance of the spot, toward the enemy; and, in a moment, the speaker appeared, with two Federal skirmishers, who expressed great astonishment at finding themselves so near the Southern lines.

It was now obvious that no time was to be lost in bearing off the General, and Lieutenant Morrison, one of the staff, exclaimed: "Let us take the General up in our arms and carry him off!"

"No; if you can help me up, I can walk!" replied Jackson, faintly.

And, as General Hill, who had drawn his pistol and mounted his horse, hastened back to throw forward his line, Jackson rose to his feet.

He had no sooner done so, than a roar like thunder came from the direction of Chancellorsville, and a hurricane of shell swept the road in which we stood. A fragment struck the horse of Captain Leigh, of Hill's staff, who had just ridden up with a litter, and his rider had only time to leap to the ground when the animal fell. This brave officer did not think of himself, however; he hastened to Jackson, who leaned his arm upon his shoulder; and, slowly dragging himself along, his arm bleeding profusely, the General approached his own lines again.

Hill was now in motion, steadily advancing to the attack, and the troops evidently suspected, from the number and rank of the wounded man's escort, that he was a superior officer.

"Who is that?" was the incessant question of the men; but the reply came as regularly, "Oh, only a friend of ours."

"When asked, just say it is a Confederate officer!" murmured Jackson.

And he continued to walk on, leaning heavily upon the shoulders of the two officers at his side. The horses were led along between him and the passing troops; but many of the soldiers peered curiously around them, to discover who the wounded officer was.

At last one of them recognized him as he walked, bareheaded, in the moonlight, and exclaimed, in the most piteous tone I ever heard:

"Great God! that is General Jackson!"

"You are mistaken, my friend," was the reply of one of the staff; and, as he heard this denial of Jackson's identity, the man looked utterly bewildered. He said nothing more, however, and moved on, shaking his head. Jackson then continued to drag his feet along—slowly and with obvious pain.

At last his strength was exhausted, and it was plain that he could go no further. The litter, brought by Captain Leigh, was put in requisition, the General laid upon it, and four of the party grasped the handles and bore it on toward the rear.

Such, up to this moment, had been the harrowing scenes of the great soldier's suffering; but the gloomiest and most tragic portion was yet to come.

No sooner had the litter begun to move, than the enemy, who had, doubtless, divined the advance of Hill, opened a frightful fire of artillery from the epaulments near Chancellorsville. The turnpike was swept by a veritable hurricane of shell and canister—men and horses fell before it, mowed down like grass—and, where a moment before had been seen the serried ranks of Hill, the eye could now discern only riderless horses, men writhing in the death agony, and others seeking the shelter of the woods.

That sudden and furious fire did not spare the small party who were bearing off the great soldier. Two of the litter-bearers were shot, and dropped the handles to the ground. Of all present, none remained but myself and another; and we were forced to lower the litter to the earth, and lie beside it, to escape the terrific storm of canister tearing over us. It struck millions of sparks from the flint of the turnpike, and every instant I expected would be our last.

The General attempted, during the hottest portion of the fire, to rise from the litter; but this he was prevented from doing; and the hurricane soon ceased. He then rose erect, and, leaning upon our shoulders, while another officer brought on the litter, made his way into the woods, where the troops were lying down in line of battle.

As we passed on in the moonlight, I recognized General Pender[5] in front of his brigade, and he also recognized me.

"Who is wounded, Colonel?" he said.

"Only a Confederate officer, General."

But, all at once, he caught a sight of General Jackson's face.

"Oh! General!" he exclaimed, "I am truly sorry to see you are wounded. The lines here are so much broken that I fear we will be obliged to fall back!"

5. Confederate General William Dorsey Pender, division commander under A. P. Hill at Chancellorsville.

The words brought a fiery flush to the pale face of Jackson. Raising his drooping head, his eyes flashed, and he replied:

"You must hold your ground, General Pender! You must hold your ground, sir!"

Pender bowed, and Jackson continued his slow progress to the rear.

He had given his last order on the field.

Fifty steps further, his head sank upon his bosom, his shoulders bent forward, and he seemed about to fall from exhaustion. In a tone so faint that it sounded like a murmur, he asked to be permitted to lie down and die.

Instead of yielding to this prayer, we placed him again upon the litter—some bearers were procured—and, amid bursting shell, which filled the moonlit sky above with their dazzling corruscations, we slowly bore the wounded General on, through the tangled thicket, toward the rear.

So dense was the undergrowth that we penetrated it with difficulty, and the vines which obstructed the way more than once made the litter-bearers stumble. From this proceeded a most distressing accident. One of the men, at last, caught his foot in a grape-vine, and fell—and, in his fall, he dropped the handle of the litter. It descended heavily, and then, as the General's shattered arm struck the ground, and the blood gushed forth, he uttered, for the first time, a low, piteous groan.

We raised him quickly, and at that moment, a ray of moon-light, glimmering through the deep foliage overhead, fell upon his pale face and his bleeding form. His eyes were closed, his bosom heaved—I thought that he was about to die.

What a death for the man of Manassas and Port Republic. What an end to a career so wonderful! Here, lost in the tangled and lugubrious depths of this weird Wilderness, with the wan moon gliding like a ghost through the clouds—the sad notes of the whippoorwill echoing from the thickets—the shell bursting in the air, like showers of falling stars—here, alone, without other witnesses than a few weeping officers, who held him in their arms, the hero of a hundred battles, the idol of the Southern people, seemed about to utter his last sigh! Never will the recollection of that scène be obliterated. Again my pulses throb, and my heart is oppressed with its bitter load of anguish, as I go back in memory to that night in the Wilderness.

I could only mutter a few words, asking the General if his fall had hurt him—and, at these words, his eyes slowly opened. A faint smile came to the pale face, and in a low murmur he said:

"No, my friend; do not trouble yourself about me!"

And again the eyes closed, his head fell back. With his grand courage and patience, he had suppressed all evidences of suffering; and, once more taking up the litter, we continued to bear him toward the rear.

As we approached Melzi Chancellor's, a staff-officer of General Hill recognized Jackson, and announced that Hill had been wounded by the artillery fire which had swept down the turnpike.

Jackson rose on his bleeding right arm, and exclaimed:

"Where is Stuart!"

As though in answer to that question, we heard the quick clatter of hoofs, and all at once the martial figure of the great cavalier was seen rapidly approaching.

"Where is General Jackson?" exclaimed Stuart, in a voice which I scarcely recognized.

And suddenly he checked his horse right in front of the group. His drawn sabre was in his hand—his horse foaming. In the moonlight I could see that his face was pale, and his eyes full of gloomy emotion.

For an instant no one moved or spoke—and again I return in memory to that scene. Stuart, clad in his "fighting jacket," with the dark plume floating from his looped-up hat, reining in his foaming horse, while the moonlight poured on his martial features; and before him, on the litter, the bleeding form of Jackson, the face pale, the eyes half-closed, the bosom rising and falling as the life of the great soldier ebbed away.

In an instant Stuart had recognized his friend, and had thrown himself from his horse.

"You are dangerously wounded!"

"Yes," came in a murmur from the pale lips of Jackson, as he faintly tried to hold out his hand. Then his cheeks suddenly filled with blood, his eyes flashed, and, half rising from the litter, he exclaimed:

"Oh! for two hours of daylight! I would then cut off the enemy from United States Ford, and they would be entirely surrounded!"

Stuart bent over him, and their eyes met.

"Take command of my corps!" murmured Jackson, falling back; "follow your own judgment—I have implicit confidence in you!"

Stuart's face flushed hot at this supreme recognition of his courage and capacity—and I saw a flash dart from the fiery blue eyes.

"But your will be near, General! You will still send me orders!" he exclaimed.

"You will not need them," murmured Jackson; "to-night or early to-morrow you will be in possession of Chancellorsville! Tell my men that I am watching them—that I am with them in spirit!"

"The watchword in the charge shall be, 'Remember Jackson!'"

And, with these fiery words, Stuart grasped the bleeding hand; uttered a few words of farewell, and leaped upon his horse. For a moment his sword gleamed, and his black plume floated in the moonlight; then he disappeared, at full speed, toward Chancellorsville.

At ten o'clock next morning he had stormed the intrenchments around Chancellorsville; swept the enemy, with the bayonet, back toward the Rappahannock; and as the troops, mad with victory, rushed through the blazing forest, a thousand voices were heard shouting:

"Remember Jackson!"

from Mohun *or* The Last Days of Lee and His Paladins: Final Memoirs of a Staff Officer Serving in Virginia

Chapter 26: The Charge of the Virginians

Lee's great blow at the enemy's left had failed.[1] He had thrown his entire right wing, under Longstreet,[2] against it. The enemy had been driven; victory seemed achieved—but suddenly the blue lines had rallied, they had returned to the struggle, their huge masses had rolled forward, thrown Longstreet back in turn, and now the

1. Here, Cooke is describing the Battle of Gettysburg, 1–3 July 1863.

2. Confederate James Longstreet, commander of the First Corps of the Army of Northern Virginia. Many blame Longstreet for disobeying General Robert E. Lee's orders and for being culpably slow during the Battle of Gettysburg.

pale moon looked down on the battle-field where some of the bravest souls of the South had poured out their blood in vain.

Lee had accomplished nothing, and one of his great corps was panting and bleeding. It was not shattered or even shaken. The iron fibre would stand any thing almost. But the sombre result remained—Longstreet had attacked and had been repulsed.

What course would Lee now pursue? Would he retire?

Retire? The army of Northern Virginia lose heart at a mere rebuff? Lee's veteran army give up the great invasion, after a mere repulse? Troops and commander alike shrunk from the very thought. One more trial of arms—something—an attack somewhere—not *a retreat!*

That was the spirit of the army on the night of the second of July.

A flanking movement to draw the enemy out of their works, or a second attack remained.

Lee determined to attack.

Longstreet and Ewell[3] had accomplished nothing by assailing the right and left of the enemy. Lee resolved now to throw a column against its centre—to split the stubborn obstacle, and pour into the gap with the whole army, when all would be over.

That was hazardous, you will say perhaps to-day, reader. And you have this immense argument to advance, that it failed. Ah! these arguments *after the event!* they are so fatal, and so very easy.

Right or wrong, Lee resolved to make the attack; and on the third of July he carried out his resolution.

If the writer of the South shrinks from describing the bloody repulse of Longstreet, much more gloomy is the task of painting that last charge at Gettysburg. It is one of those scenes which Lee's old soldiers approach with repugnance. That thunder of the guns which comes back to memory seems to issue, hollow and lugubrious, from a thousand tombs.

Let us pass over that tragedy rapidly. It must be touched on in these memoirs—but I leave it soon.

It is the third of July 1863. Lee's line of battle, stretching along the crest of Seminary Ridge, awaits the signal for a new conflict with a carelessness as great as on the preceding day. The infantry are laughing, jesting, cooking their rations, and smoking their pipes. The ragged cannoneers, with flashing eyes, smiling lips, and faces blackened with powder, are standing in groups, or lying down around the pieces of artillery. Near the centre of the line a gray-headed officer, in plain uniform, and entirely unattended, has dismounted, and is reconnoitring the Federal position through a pair of field-glasses.

It is Lee, and he is looking toward Cemetery Heights, the Mount St. Jean of the new Waterloo—on whose slopes the immense conflict is going to be decided.

Lee gazes for some moments through his glasses at the long range bristling with bayonets. Not a muscle moves; he resembles a statue. Then he lowers the glasses, closes them thoughtfully, and his calm glance passes along the lines of his army. You would say that this glance penetrates the forest; that he sees his old soldiers, gay, unshrinking, unmoved by the reverses of Longstreet, and believing in themselves and in him! The blood of the soldier responds to that thought. The face of the great commander suddenly flushes. He summons a staff officer and utters a few words in calm and measured tones. The order is given. The grand assault is about to begin.

3. Confederate General Richard S. Ewell, Corps commander of the Arm of Northern Virginia at Gettysburg.

That assault is going to be one of the most desperate in all history. Longstreet's has been fierce—this will be mad and full of headlong fury. At Round Top blood flowed—here the earth is going to be soaked with it. Gettysburg is to witness a charge recalling that of the six hundred horsemen at Balaklava. Each soldier will feel that the fate of the South depends on him, perhaps. If the wedge splits the tough grain, cracking it from end to end, the axe will enter after it—the work will be finished—the red flag of the South will float in triumph over a last and decisive field.

Pickett's division[4] of Virginia troops has been selected for the hazardous venture, and they prepare for the ordeal in the midst of a profound silence. Since the morning scarce a gunshot has been heard. Now and then only, a single cannon, like a signal-gun, sends its growl through the hills.

Those two tigers, the army of Northern Virginia and the army of the Potomac, are crouching, and about to spring.

At one o'clock the moment seems to have arrived. Along the whole front of Hill and Longstreet, the Southern artillery all at once bursts forth. One hundred and forty-five cannon send their threatening thunder across the peaceful valley. From Cemetery Heights eighty pieces reply to them; and for more than an hour these two hundred and twenty-five cannon tear the air with their harsh roar, hurled back in crash after crash from the rocky ramparts. That thunder is the most terrible yet heard in the war. It stirs the coolest veterans. General Hancock,[5] the composed and unexcitable soldier, is going to say of it, "Their artillery fire was most terrific; . . . it was the most terrific cannonade I ever witnessed, and the most prolonged. . . . It was a most terrific and appalling cannonade, one possibly hardly ever equalled."

For nearly two hours Lee continues this "terrific" fire. The Federal guns reply—shot and shell crossing each other; racing across the blue sky; battering the rocks; or bursting in showers of iron fragments.

Suddenly the Federal fire slackens, and then ceases. Their ammunition has run low, or they are silenced by the Southern fire. Lee's guns also cease firing. The hour has come.

The Virginians, under Pickett, form in double line in the edge of the woods, where Lee's centre is posted. These men are ragged and travelworn, but their bayonets and gun-barrels shine like silver. From the steel hedge, as the men move, dart lightnings.

From the Cemetery Heights the enemy watch that ominous apparition—the gray line of Virginians drawn up for the charge.

At the word, they move out, shoulder to shoulder, at common time. Descending the slope, they enter on the valley, and move steadily toward the heights.

The advance of the column, with its battle-flags floating proudly, and its ranks closed up and dressed with the precision of troops on parade, is a magnificent spectacle. Old soldiers, hardened in the fires of battle, and not given to emotion, lean forward watching the advance of the Virginians with fiery eyes. You would say, from the fierce clutch of the gaunt hands on the muskets, that they wish to follow; and many wish that.

The column is midway the valley, and beginning to move more rapidly, when suddenly the Federal artillery opens. The ranks are swept by round shot, shell, and canister. Bloody gaps appear, but the line closes up, and continues to advance. The fire of the Federal artillery redoubles. All the demons of the pit seem howling, roaring, yelling, and screaming. The assaulting column is torn by a whirlwind of canister, before which men fall in heaps mangled, streaming with blood, their bosoms torn to

4. Confederate General George E. Pickett. His division, of Longstreet's Corps, led the ill-fated attack from Seminary Ridge at Gettysburg.

5. Winfield Scott Hancock, General, U.S.A., directed Union troops on the second and third days in the Battle of Gettysburg.

pieces, their hands clutching the grass, their teeth biting the earth. The ranks, however, close up as before, and the Virginians continue to advance.

From common time, they have passed to quick time—now they march at the double-quick. That is to say, they run. They have reached the slope; the enemy's breastworks are right before them; and they dash at them with wild cheers.

They are still three hundred yards from the Federal works, when the real conflict commences, to which the cannonade was but child's play. Artillery has thundered, but something more deadly succeeds it—the sudden crash of musketry. From behind a stone wall the Federal infantry rise up and pour a galling fire into the charging column. It has been accompanied to this moment by a body of other troops, but those troops now disappear, like dry leaves swept off by the wind. The Virginians still advance.

Amid a concentrated fire of infantry and artillery, in their front and on both flanks, they pass over the ground between themselves and the enemy; ascend the slope; rush headlong at the breastworks; storm them; strike their bayonets into the enemy, who recoil before them, and a wild cheer rises, making the blood leap in the veins of a hundred thousand men.

The Federal works are carried, and the troops are wild with enthusiasm. With a thunder of cheers they press upon the flying enemy toward the crest.

Alas! as the smoke drifts, they see what is enough to dishearten the bravest. They have stormed the first line of works only! Beyond, is another and a stronger line still. Behind it swarm the heavy reserves of the enemy, ready for the death-struggle. But the column can not pause. It is "do or die." In their faces are thrust the muzzles of muskets spouting flame. Whole ranks go down in the fire. The survivors close up, utter a fierce cheer, and rush straight at the second tier of works.

Then is seen a spectacle which will long be remembered with a throb of the heart by many. The thinned ranks of the Virginians are advancing, unmoved, into the very jaws of death. They go forward—and are annihilated. At every step death meets them. The furious fire of the enemy, on both flanks and in their front, hurls them back, mangled and dying. The brave Garnett is killed while leading on his men. Kemper[6] is lying on the earth maimed for life. Armistead[7] is mortally wounded at the moment when he leaps upon the breastworks:—he waves his hat on the point of his sword, and staggers, and falls. Of fifteen field officers, fourteen have fallen. Three-fourths of the men are dead, wounded, or prisoners. The Federal infantry has closed in on the flanks and rear of the Virginians—whole corps assault the handful—the little band is enveloped, and cut off from succor—they turn and face the enemy, bayonet to bayonet, and die.

When the smoke drifts away, all is seen to be over. It is a panting, staggering, bleeding remnant only of the brave division that is coming back so slowly yonder. They are swept from the fatal hill—pursued by yells, cheers, cannon-shot, musket-balls, and canister. As they doggedly retire before the howling hurricane, the wounded are seen to stagger and fall. Over the dead and dying sweeps the canister. Amid volleys of musketry and the roar of cannon, all but a handful of Pickett's Virginians pass into eternity.

* * *

6. Confederate General James Kemper, one of Pickett's Brigadiers.

7. Confederate General Lewis Armistead, one of Pickett's Brigadiers.

CHAPTER 29: THE SURRENDER

Lee had surrendered the army of Northern Virginia.

Ask old soldiers of that army to describe their feelings at the announcement, reader. They will tell you that they can not; and I will not attempt to record my own.

It was, truly, the bitterness of death that we tasted at ten o'clock on the morning of that ninth of April, 1865, at Appomattox Court-House. Gray-haired soldiers cried like children. It was hard to say whether they would have preferred, at that moment, to return to their families or to throw themselves upon the bayonets of the enemy, and die.

In that hour of their agony they were not insulted, however. The deportment of the enemy was chivalric and courteous. No bands played; no cheers were heard; and General Grant was the first to salute profoundly his gray-haired adversary, who came, with a single officer, to arrange, in a house near the field, the terms of surrender.

They are known. On the tenth they were carried out.

The men stacked the old muskets, which they had carried in a hundred fights, surrendered the bullet-torn colors, which had waved over victorious fields, and silently returned, like mourners, to their desolate homes.

Two days after the surrender, Mohun was still alive.

Three months afterward, the welcome intelligence reached me that he was rapidly recovering.

He had made a narrow escape. Ten minutes after the death of the faithful Nighthawk, the Federal line had swept over him; and such was the agony of his wound, that he exclaimed to one of the enemy:—

"Take your pistol, and shoot me!"

The man cocked his weapon, and aimed at his heart. Then he turned the muzzle aside, and uncocking the pistol, replaced it in its holster.

"No," he said, "Johnny Reb, you might get well!"

And glancing at the paper on Mohun's breast, he passed on, muttering—:

"It's a general!"

The paper saved Mohun's life. An acquaintance in the Federal army saw it, and speedily had him cared for. An hour afterward his friends were informed of his whereabouts. I hastened to the house to which he had been borne. Bending over him, the beautiful Georgia was sobbing hopelessly, and dropping tears upon the paper, which contained the words—

"This is the body of General Mohun, C.S.A."

The army had surrendered; the flag was lowered: with a singular feeling of bewilderment, and a "lost" feeling that is indescribable, I set out, followed by my servant, for Eagle's Nest.

I was the possessor of a paper, which I still keep as a strange memorial.

"The bearer," ran this paper, "a paroled prisoner of the army of Northern Virginia, has permission to go to his home, and there remain undisturbed—with two horses!"

At the top of this document was, "Appomattox Court-House, Va., April, 10, 1865." On the left-hand side was, "Paroled Prisoner's Pass."

So, with his pass, the paroled prisoner passed slowly across Virginia to his home.

Oh! that Virginia of 1865—that desolate, dreary land! Oh! those poor, sad soldiers returning to their homes! Everywhere burned houses, unfenced fields, ruined homesteads! On all sides, the desolation of the torch and the sword! The "poor paroled prisoners," going home wearily in that dark April, felt a pang which only a very bitter foe will laugh at.

But all was not taken. Honor was left us—and the angels of home! As the sorrowful survivors of the great army came back, as they reached their old homes, dragging their weary feet after them, or urging on their jaded horses, suddenly the sunshine burst forth for them, and lit up their rags with a sort of glory. The wife, the mother, and the little child rushed to them. Hearts beat fast, as the gray uniforms were clasped in a long embrace. Those angels of home loved the poor prisoners better in their dark days than in their bright. The fond eyes melted to tears, the white arms held them close; and the old soldiers, who had only laughed at the roar of the enemy's guns, dropped tears on the faces of their wives and little children!

Epilogue

In the autumn of last year, 1867, I set out on horseback from "Eagle's Nest," and following the route west by Fredericksburg, Chancellorsville, Germanna Ford, Culpeper, and Orleans, reached "The Oaks" in Fauquier.

I needed the sunshine and bright faces of the old homestead, after that journey; for at every step had sprung up some gloomy or exciting recollection.

It was a veritable journey through the world of memory.

Fredericksburg! Chancellorsville! the Wilderness! the plains of Culpeper!—as I rode on amid these historic scenes, a thousand memories came to knock at the door of my heart. Some were gay, if many were sorrowful—laughter mingled with the sighs. But to return to the past is nearly always sad. As I rode through the waste land now, it was with drooping head. All the old days came back again, the cannon sent their long dull thunder through the forests; again the gray and blue lines closed in, and hurled together; again Jackson in his old dingy coat, Stuart with his floating plume, Pelham, Farley, all whom I had known, loved, and still mourned, rose before me—a line of august phantoms fading away into the night of the past.

Once more I looked upon Pelham, holding in his arms the bleeding form of Jean—passing "Camp-no-camp," only a desolate and dreary field now, all the laughing faces and brave forms of Stuart and his men returned—in the Wilderness I saw Jackson fight and fall; saw him borne through the moonlight; heard his sighs and his last greeting with Stuart. A step farther, I passed the lonely old house in the Wilderness, and all the strange and sombre scenes there surged up from the shadows of the past. Mordaunt, Achmed, Fenwick, Violet Grafton!—all reappeared, playing over again their fierce tragedy; and to this was added the fiercer drama of May, 1864, when General Grant invented the "Unseen Death."

Thus the journey which I made through the bare and deserted fields, or the mournful thickets, was not gay; and these were only a part of the panorama which passed before me. Looking toward the South, I saw as clearly with the eyes of the memory, the banks of the Po, the swamps of the Chickahominy, the trenches at Petersburg, the woods of Dinwiddie, Five Forks, Highbridge—Appomattox Court-House! Nearer was Yellow Tavern, where Stuart had fallen. Not a foot of this soil of Old Virginia but seemed to have been the scene of some fierce battle, some sombre tragedy!

"Well, well," I sighed, as I rode on toward the Oaks, "all that is buried in the past, and it is useless to think of it. I am only a poor paroled prisoner, wearing arms no more—let me forget the red cross flag which used to float so proudly here, and bow my head to the will of the Supreme Ruler of all worlds."

So I went on, and in due time reached the Oaks, in Fauquier.

You recall the good old homestead, do you not, my dear reader? I should be sorry to have you forget the spot where I have been so happy. It was to this honest old mansion that I was conducted in April, 1861, when struck from my horse by a falling limb in the storm-lashed wood, I saw come to my succor the dearest person in the world. She awaited me now—having a month before left Eagle's Nest, to pay a visit to her family—and again, as in the spring of '63, she came to meet me as I ascended the hill—only we met now as bridegroom and bride!

This May of my life had brought back the sunshine, even after that Black day of 1865. Two white arms had met the poor paroled prisoner, on his return to Eagle's Nest—a pair of violet eyes had filled with happy tears—and the red lips, smiling with exquisite emotion, murmured "All is well, since you have come back to me!"

It was this beautiful head which the sunshine of that autumn of 1867 revealed to me, on the lawn of the good old chateau of the mountains! And behind, came all my good friends of the Oaks—the kind lady of the manor, the old colonel, and Charley and Annie, who were there too! With his long gray hair, and eyes that still flashed, Colonel Beverly came to meet me—brave and smiling in 1867 as he had been in 1861. Then, with Annie's arm around me—that little sister had grown astonishingly!—I went in and was at home.

At home! You must be a soldier to know what that simple word means, reader! You must sleep under a tree, carry your effects behind your saddle, lie down in bivouac in strange countries, and feel the longing of the heart for the dear faces, the old scenes.

"Tell my mother that I die in a foreign land!" murmured my poor dear Tazewell Patton, at Gettysburg. I have often thought of those words; and they express much I think. Oh! for home! for a glimpse, if no more, of the fond faces, as life goes! You may be the bravest of the brave, as my dear Tazewell was; but 'tis home where the heart is, and you sigh for the dear old land!

The Oaks was like home to me, for the somebody with violet eyes, and chestnut hair, was here to greet me.

The sun is setting, and we wander in the fields touched by the dreamy autumn.

"Look," says the somebody who holds my hand, and smiles, "there is the rock where we stopped in the autumn of 1862, and where you behaved with so little propriety, you remember, sir!"

"I remember the rock but not the absence of propriety. What were a man's arms made for but to clasp the woman he loves!"

"Stop, sir! People would think we were two foolish young lovers."

"Young lovers are not foolish, madam. They are extremely intelligent," Madam laughs.

"Yonder is the primrose from which I plucked the bud," she says.

"That sent me through Stuart's head-quarters in April, 1863?" I say.

"Yes; you have not forgotten it I hope."

"Almost; Stay! I think it meant "Come"—did it not?—And you get it to me!" Madam pouts beautifully.

"You have 'almost forgotten' it! Have you, indeed, sir?"

"These trifles will escape us."

May loses all her smiles, and her head sinks.

I begin to laugh, taking an old porte-monnaie from my pocket. There very little money in it, but a number of worn papers, my parole at others. I take one and open it. It contains a faded primrose.

"Look!" I say, with a smile, "it said 'Come,' once, and it brings me back again to the dearest girl in the world!"

A tear falls from the violet eyes upon the faded flower, but through the tears burst a smile!

They are curious, these earthly angels—are they not, my dear reader. They are romantic and sentimental to the last, and this old soldier admires them!

So, conversing of a thousand things, we return to the Oaks wandering like boy and girl through the "happy autumn fields." May Surry flit through the old doorway and disappears.

As she goes the sun sinks behind the forest. But it will rise, as she will, to-morrow!

The smiling Colonel Beverly meets me on the threshold, with a note in his hand.

"A servant has just brought this," he says, "it is from your friend Mordaunt."

I opened the note and read the following words:—

"*My dear Surry:*—

"I send this note to await your appearance at the Oaks. Come and see me. Some old friends will give you a cordial greeting, in addition to

"Your comrade,

"Mordaunt."

I had intended visiting Mordaunt in a day or two after my arrival. On the very next morning I mounted my horse, and set out for the house in the mountain, anxious to ascertain who the "old friends" were, to whom he alluded.

In an hour I had come within sight of Mordaunt's mansion. Passing through the great gate, I rode on between the two rows of magnificent trees; approached the low mansion with its extensive wings, overshadowed by the huge black oaks; dismounted; raised the heavy bronze knocker, carved like the frowning mask of the old tragedians; and letting it fall sent a peal of low thunder through the mansion.

Mordaunt appeared in a few moments; and behind him came dear Violet Grafton, as I will still call her, smiling. Mordaunt's face glowed with pleasure, and the grasp of his strong hand was like a vice. He was unchanged, except that he wore a suit of plain gray cloth. His statuesque head, with the long black beard and mustache, the sparkling eyes, and cheeks tanned by exposure to the sun and wind, rose as proudly as on that morning in 1865, when he had charged and cut through the enemy at Appomattox.

Violet was Violet still! The beautiful tranquil face still smiled with its calm sweetness; the lips had still that expression of infantile innocence. The blue eyes still looked forth from the shower of golden ringlets which had struck me when I first met her in the lonely house in the Wilderness, in the gay month of April, 1861.

I had shaken hands with Mordaunt, but I advanced and "saluted" madam, and the cheek was suddenly filled with exquisite roses.

"For old times' sake, madam!"

"Which are the best of all possible times, Surry!" said Mordaunt, laughing.

And he led the way into the great apartment, hung round with portraits, where we had supped on the night of Pelham's hard fight at Barbee's, after Sharpsburg.

"You remember this room, do you not, my dear Surry?" said Mordaunt. "It escaped during the war; though you see that my poor little grandmother, the child of sixteen there, with the curls and laces, received a sabre thrust in the neck. But you are looking round for the friends I promised. They were here a moment since, and only retired to give you a surprise.

"See! here they are!"

The door opened, and I saw enter—Mohun and Landon!

In an instant I had grasped the hands of these dear friends; and they had explained their presence. Mohun had come to make a visit to Mordaunt, and had prolonged his stay in order to meet me. Then Mordaunt had written to Landon, at "Bizarre," just over the mountain, to come and complete the party—he had promptly arrived—and I found myself in presence of three old comrades, any one of whom it would have been a rare pleasure to have met.

Mohun and Landon were as unchanged as Mordaunt. I saw the same proud and loyal faces, listened to the same frank brave voices, touched the same firm hands. They no longer wore uniforms—that was the whole difference. Under the black coats beat the same hearts which had throbbed beneath the gray.

I spent the whole day with Mordaunt. After dinner he led the way into the room on the right of the entrance—that singular apartment into which I had been shown by accident on my first visit to him, and where afterward I witnessed the test of poor Achmed's love. The apartment was unchanged. The floor was still covered with the rich furs of lions, tigers, and leopards—the agate eyes still glared at me, and the grinning teeth seemed to utter growls or snarls. On the walls I saw still the large collection of books in every language—the hunting and battle pictures which I had before so greatly admired—the strange array of outlandish arms—and over the mantel-piece still hung the portrait of Violet Grafton.

Seated in front of a cheerful blaze, we smoked and talked—Mordaunt, Mohun, Landon, and myself—until the shades of evening drew on.

Landon told me of his life at "Bizarre," near the little village of Millwood, through which we had marched that night to bury his dead at the old chapel, and where he had surrendered in April, 1865. Arden and Annie lived near him, and were happy: and if I would come to "Bizarre," he would show me the young lady whom I had carried off, that night, from the chapel graveyard, on the croup of my saddle!

Landon laughed. His face was charming; it was easy to see that he was happy. To understand how that expression contrasted with his former appearance, the worthy reader must peruse my episodical memoir, *Hilt to Hilt*.

Mohun's face was no less smiling. He had lost every trace of gloom.

He gave me intelligence of all my old friends. General Davenant and Judge Conway had become close friends again. Will and Virginia were married. Charley was cultivating a mustache and speculating upon a new revolution. Tom Herbert and Katy were on a visit to "Disaways."

"Poor Nighthawk is the only one whom I miss, my dear Surry," said Mohun. "He died trying to save me, and I have had his body taken to Fonthill, where it is buried in the family graveyard."

"He was a faithful friend; and to be killed on that very last morning was hard. But many were. *You* had a narrow escape, Mohun."

"Yes, and was only preserved by a Bible."

"A Bible?"

"Do you remember that I was reading by the camp fire, when you came to visit me on the night preceding the surrender?"

"Yes—in your wife's Bible."

"Well, my dear Surry, when I had finished reading, I placed the volume in my breast, as usual. When I was shot, on the next morning, the bullet struck the book and glanced. Had the Bible not been there, that bullet would have pierced my heart. As it was, it only wounded me in the breast. Here is my old Bible—I carry it about me still."

As he spoke, Mohun drew from his breast the small leather-bound volume, in the cover of which was visible a deep gash.

He looked at it with a smile, and said:—

"This book has been the salvation of my body and soul, Surry. I was haughty and a man-hater once—now I try to be humble. I had no hope once, now I am happy. I have one other souvenir of that memorable day at Appomattox—this scrap of paper between the leaves of my old Bible."

He drew out the scrap, which was dirty and discolored with blood.

Upon it was written in pencil, the words:—

"This is the body of General Mohun, C.S.A."

As Mohun pointed to it, a ray of sunset shot athwart the forest, and fell on his serene features, lighting them up with a sort of glory. The clear eyes gave back the ray, and there was something exquisitely soft in them. Mordaunt and Landon too, were bathed in that crimson light of evening, disappearing beyond the shaggy crest of the Blue Ridge—and I thought I saw on their proud faces the same expression.

"These three men are happy," I thought. "Their lot has been strange; they have been nearly lost; but heaven has sent to each an angel, to bring back hope to them. Ellen Adair, Georgia Conway, Violet Grafton—these fond hearts have changed your lives, Landon, Mohun, and Mordaunt!"

In an hour I was at the "Oaks."

A month afterward, I had returned to "Eagle's Nest."

And in this April, 1868, when the flowers are blooming, and the sun is shining—when a pair of violet eyes make the sunshine still brighter—I end the last volume of my memoirs.

Questions to Consider

1. To what degree did Cooke blend biography, history, and fiction in these selections? To what effect?
2. In what ways do these selections advance the myth of the lost cause?

Augusta Jane Evans Wilson

1835–1909

Alabama novelist Augusta Jane Evans Wilson first earned her reputation as a popular author of the sentimental literary genre of the mid-nineteenth century known as domestic fiction. Introduced as a literary form in New England in the 1820s, domestic fiction became immensely popular with American women in the ensuing decades. "Typically chronicling the trials and tribulations of an intelligent, emotional, and exceedingly virtuous female temporarily forced to make her way alone," as explained by literary scholar Elizabeth Moss, "the domestic novel as formulated in the American North explored the problems and possibilities of domesticity, using stilted language and convoluted plots to emphasize the importance of home and community." Antebellum Southern authors, including Evans in her 1859 novel *Beulah,* put their own spin on this standardized plot, using the plantation as the center of their fiction, portraying the Old South as a well-ordered, harmonious society.

The outbreak of the Civil War forced Evans to abandon domestic plots in favor of a more explicitly political fiction. She began her 1864 war novel *Macaria*, or *Altars of Sacrifice* with a standard domesticity plot but ended it with an impassioned plea for the Confederacy. Evans was no longer writing solely for the moral uplift of Southern women. She had become a propagandist fighting for her civilization. Evans explained somewhat disingenuously to Confederate General

Pierre Gustave Toutant Beauregard, "It is not my privilege to enter the ranks, wielding a sword, in my country's cause, but all that my feeble, womanly pen could contribute to the consummation of our freedom, I have humbly, but at least, faithfully and untiringly *endeavored* to achieve." Breaking with the traditional form of domestic fiction, Evans broadened the scope of her novels, not just examining the inner lives of their heroines, but also addressing larger sociopolitical issues.

Evans discussed the Antebellum political climate, cataloguing Northern abuses against the South and outlining the irreconcilable philosophical and cultural differences between the two sections. Foreshadowing secession, Russell Aubrey, a lawyer and the political and Confederate hero of *Macaria*, proclaimed that Northern demagoguism, or "the hydra-headed foe of democracy," threatened the very existence of the United States. In a later scene, Irene Huntingdon, the novel's heroine, echoed Russell's sentiments, warning Southerners to be ever vigilant against demagoguism in their newly found Confederacy, lest it creep "along its customary sinuous path, with serpent eyes fastened on self-aggrandizement."

Furthermore, Evans asserted that the North had abrogated the Constitution, forcing the South to strike out on its own. Although the South had formerly revered the Federal government and cherished its position in it, " 'Union' became the synonyme [*sic*] of political duplicity," forever severing its link with the South. "The Confederacy realized that the hour had arrived when the historic sphinx must find an Oedipus," Evans explained, "or Democratic Republican Liberty would be devoured, swept away with the *debris* of other dead systems." For Evans, the North's abrogation of constitutionally guaranteed liberties engineered the Civil War, and not, as Northerners would argue, the South's adherence to the institution of slavery.

Although Evans strayed from the conventions of the Antebellum domestic novel, *Macaria* provided a degree of comfortable familiarity for her female reading audience. She developed love interests for her Confederate hero. She also championed the virtues of traditional Southern womanhood. She celebrated the potential contributions of Southern women to the Confederacy, and it was perhaps this point that made her work most attractive to female readers. In one of the final scenes of the novel, Irene explains to her friend, Electra, "You and I have much to do, during these days of gloom and national trial—for upon the purity, the devotion, and the patriotism of the women of our land, not less than upon the heroism of our armies, depends our national salvation." Once the Confederacy has secured the South's independence, women will be guaranteed "long-life usefulness" to the Republic. As literary scholar Jan Bakker has pointed out, Irene and Electra do not submit to domesticity. Rather, they imagine themselves as leaders of welfare and the arts. Bakker concludes, then, that *Macaria* "is a rather surprising literary work to have come out of the wartime South."

from Macaria[1] *or* Altars of Sacrifice

Dedication

To the army of the Southern confederacy, who have delivered the South from despotism, and who have won for generations yet unborn the precious guerdon of constitutional republican liberty:

To this vast legion of honor, whether limping on crutches through the land they have saved and immortalized, or surviving uninjured to share the blessings their unexampled heroism bought, or sleeping dreamlessly in nameless martyr-graves on

1. Macaria, daughter of Heracles. She and her siblings took refuge from Eurystheys. Macaria learned that Athens would be saved if a highborn maiden were offered as a sacrifice to Persephone. Macaria offered to die to save her siblings and the city.

hallowed battle-fields whose historic memory shall perish only with the remnants of our language, these pages are gratefully and reverently dedicated by one who, although debarred from the dangers and deathless glory of the "tented field," would fain offer a woman's inadequate tribute to the noble patriotism and sublime self-abnegation of her dear and devoted countrymen.[2]

CHAPTER XXX

. . . In July 1861, when the North, blinded by avarice and hate, rang with the cry of "On to Richmond," our Confederate Army of the Potomac was divided between Manassas and Winchester, watching at both points the glittering coils of the Union boa-constrictor, which writhed in its efforts to crush the last sanctuary of freedom. The stringency evinced along the Federal lines prevented the transmission of despatches by the Secessionists of Maryland, and for a time Generals Beauregard and Johnston[3] were kept in ignorance of the movements of the enemy. Patterson[4] hung dark and lowering around Winchester, threatening daily descent; while the main column of the grand army under McDowell[5] proceeded from Washington, confident in the expectation of overwhelming the small army stationed at Manassas. The friends of liberty who were compelled to remain in the desecrated old capital appreciated the urgent necessity of acquainting General Beauregard with the designs of McDowell, and the arch-apostate, Scott;[6] but all channels of egress seemed sealed; all roads leading across the Potomac were vigilantly guarded, to keep the great secret safely; and painful apprehensions were indulged for the fate of the Confederate army. But the Promethean spark of patriotic devotion burned in the hearts of Secession women; and, resolved to dare all things in a cause so holy, a young lady of Washington, strong in heroic faith, offered to encounter any perils, and pledged her life to give Gen. Beauregard the necessary information. Carefully concealing a letter in the twist of her luxuriant hair, which would escape detection even should she be searched, she disguised herself effectually, and, under the mask of a market-woman, drove a cart through Washington, across the Potomac, and deceived the guard by selling vegetables and milk as she proceeded. Once beyond Federal lines, and in friendly neighborhood, it was but a few minutes work to "off ye lendings" and secure a horse and riding-habit. With a courage and rapidity which must ever command the admiration of a brave people, she rode at hard gallop that burning July afternoon to Fairfax Court-house, and telegraphed to Gen. Beauregard, then at Manassa's Junction, the intelligence she had risked so much to convey. Availing himself promptly of the facts, he flashed them along electric wires to Richmond, and to General Johnston; and thus, through womanly devotion, a timely junction of the two armies was effected, ere McDowell's banners flouted the skies of Bull Run.

Carthagenian women gave their black locks to string their country's bows and furnish cordage for its shipping; and the glossy tresses of an American woman

2. Evans's Confederate propaganda novel was so persuasive that Union generals banned their soilders from reading it and burned copies when they were found. The dedication appeared in copies of the novel that were sent to the North through the blockade.
3. Brigadier General Pierre Gustave Toutant Beauregard and General Joseph E. Johnston, commanding generals at the Battle of Manassas (Bull Run).
4. Union General R. Patterson.
5. Union Brigadier General Irvin McDowell commanded the Federal Army at the Battle of Manassas.
6. Union General-in-Chief Winfield Scott, a Virginia Unionist.

veiled a few mystic ciphers more potent in General Beauregard's hands than Talmudish Shemhamphorash.

Her mission accomplished, the dauntless courier turned her horse's head and, doubtless, with an exulting, thankful heart returned in triumph to Washington. When our national jewels are made up, will not a grateful and admiring country set her name between those of Beauregard and Johnston in the revolutionary diadem, and let the three blaze through coming ages, baffling the mists of time—the Constellation of Manassas? The artillery duel of the 18th of July ended disastrously for the advance guard of the Federals—a temporary check was given.

All things seemed in abeyance; dun, sulphurous clouds of smoke lifted themselves from the dewy copse that fringed Bull Run, floating slowly to the distant purple crests of the Blue Ridge, which gazed solemnly down on the wooded Coliseum, where gladiatorial hosts were soon to pour out their blood in the hideous orgies held by loathsome Fanaticism—guarded by Federal bayonets, and canopied by the Stars and Stripes. During the silent watches of Saturday night—

> Slowly comes a hungry people, as a lion creeping nigher,
> Glares at one that nods and winks behind a slowly-dying fire.[7]

A pure Sabbath morning kindled on the distant hill-tops, wearing heavenly credentials of rest and sanctity on its pearly forehead—credentials which the passions of mankind could not pause to recognize; and with the golden glow of summer sunshine came the tramp of infantry, the clatter of cavalry, the sullen growl of artillery. Major Huntingdon had been temporarily assigned to a regiment of infantry after leaving Richmond, and was posted on the right of General Beauregard's lines, commanding one of the lower fords. Two miles higher up the stream, in a different brigade, Colonel Aubrey's regiment guarded another of the numerous crossings. As the day advanced, and the continual roar of cannon toward Stone-Bridge and Sudley's Ford indicated that the demonstrations on McLean's, Blackford's, and Mitchell's fords were mere feints to hold our right and centre, the truth flashed on General Beauregard that the main column was hurled against Evans' little band on the extreme left. Hour after hour passed, and the thunder deepened on the Warrenton road; then the General learned, with unutterable chagrin, that his order for an advance on Centreville had miscarried, that a brilliant plan had been frustrated, and that new combinations and dispositions must now be resorted to. The regiment to which Major Huntingdon was attached was ordered to the support of the left wing, and reached the distant position in an almost incredibly short time, while two regiments of the brigade to which Colonel Aubrey belonged were sent forward to the same point as a reserve.

Like incarnations of victory, Beauregard and Johnston swept to the front, where the conflict was most deadly; everywhere, at sight of them, our thin ranks dashed forward, and were mowed down by the fire of Rickett's and Griffin's batteries, which crowned the position they were so eager to regain. At half-past two o'clock the awful contest was at its height; the rattle of musketry, the ceaseless whistle of rifle-balls, the deafening boom of artillery, the hurtling hail of shot, and explosion of shell, dense volumes of smoke shrouding the combatants, and clouds of dust boiling up on all sides, lent unutterable horror to a scene which, to cold, dispassionate observers, might have seemed sublime. As the vastly superior numbers of the Federals forced our stubborn bands to give back slowly, an order came from General Beauregard for the right of his line, except the reserves, to advance and recover the long and

7. "Locksley Hall," by Alfred Tennyson.

desperately-disputed plateau. With a shout, the shattered lines sprang upon the foe and forced them temporarily back. Major Huntingdon's horse was shot under him; he disengaged himself and marched on foot, waving his sword and uttering words of encouragement. He had proceeded but a few yards when a grape-shot entered his side, tearing its way through his body, and he fell where the dead lay thickest. For a time the enemy retired, but heavy reinforcements pressed in, and they returned, reoccupying the old ground. Not a moment was to be lost; General Beauregard ordered forward his reserves for a second effort, and, with magnificent effect, led the charge in person. Then Russell Aubrey first came actively upon the field. At the word of command he dashed forward with his splendid regiment, and, high above all, towered his powerful form, with the long black plume of his hat drifting upon the wind, as he led his admiring men.

As he pressed on, with thin nostril dilated, and eyes that burned like those of a tiger seizing his prey, he saw, just in his path, leaning on his elbow, covered with blood and smeared with dust, the crushed, writhing form of his bitterest enemy. His horse's hoofs were almost upon him; he reined him back an instant and glared down at his old foe. It was only for an instant; and as Major Huntingdon looked on the stalwart figure and at the advancing regiment, life-long hatred and jealousy were forgotten—patriotism throttled all the past in her grasp—he feebly threw up his hand, cheered faintly, and, with his eyes on Russell's, smiled grimly, saying with evident difficulty:

"Beat them back, Aubrey! Give them the bayonet!"

The shock was awful—beggaring language. On, on they swept, while ceaseless cheers mingled with the cannonade; the ground was recovered, to be captured no more. The Federals were driven back across the turnpike, and now dark masses of reinforcements debouched on the plain, and marched toward our left. Was it Grouchy or Blucher? Some moments of painful suspense ensued, while General Beauregard strained his eyes to decipher the advancing banner. Red and white and blue, certainly; but was it the ensign of Despotism or of Liberty? Nearer and nearer came the rushing column, and lo! upon the breeze streamed, triumphant as the Labarum of Constantine,[8] the Stars and Bars. Kirby Smith and Elzey[9]—God be praised! The day was won, and Victory nestled proudly among the folds of our new-born banner. One more charge along our whole line, and the hireling hordes of oppression fled, panic-stricken. Russell had received a painful wound from a minie ball, which entered his shoulder and ranged down toward the elbow, but he maintained his position, and led his regiment a mile in the pursuit. When it became evident that the retreat was a complete rout, he resigned the command to Lieutenant-Colonel Blackwell and rode back to the battle-field. Hideous was the spectacle presented—dead and dying, friend and foe, huddled in indiscriminate ruin, weltering in blood, and shivering in the agonies of dissolution; blackened headless trunks and fragments of limbs—ghastly sights and sounds of woe, filling the scene of combat. Such were the first fruits of the bigotry and fanatical hate of New England, aided by the unprincipled demagogism of the West; such were the wages of Abolitionism, guided by Lincoln and Seward—the latter-day Sejanus; such the results of "higher-law," canting, puritanical hypocrisy.

Picking his way to avoid trampling the dead, Russell saw Major Huntingdon at a little distance, trying to drag himself toward a neighboring tree. The memory of his injuries crowded up—the memory of all that he had endured and lost through that

8. Name of the military standard adopted by Constantine the Great.

9. Confederate General Edmund Kirby Smith and Confederate Major General Arnold Elzey.

man's prejudice—the sorrow that might have been averted from his blind mother—and his vindictive spirit rebelled at the thought of rendering him aid. But as he paused, and struggled against his better nature, Irene's holy face, as he saw it last, lifted in prayer for him, rose, angel-like, above all that mass of death and horrors. The sufferer was Irene's father; she was hundreds of miles away; Russell set his lips firmly, and, riding up to the prostrate figure, dismounted. Exhausted by his efforts, Major Huntingdon had fallen back in the dust, and an expression of intolerable agony distorted his features as Russell stooped over him and asked, in a voice meant to be gentle:

"Can I do anything for you? Could you sit up if I placed you on my horse?"

The wounded man scowled as he recognized the voice and face, and turned his head partially away, muttering:

"What brought you here?"

"There has never been any love between us, Major Huntingdon; but we are fighting in the same cause for the first time in our lives. You are badly wounded, and, as a fellow-soldier, I should be glad to relieve your sufferings, if possible. Once more, for humanity's sake, I ask, can you ride my horse to the rear, if I assist you to mount?"

"No. But, for God's sake, give me some water!"

Russell knelt, raised the head, and unbuckling his canteen, put it to his lips, using his own wounded arm with some difficulty. Half of the contents was eagerly swallowed, and the remainder Russell poured slowly on the gaping ghastly wound in his side. The proud man eyed him steadily till the last cool drop was exhausted, and said sullenly:

"You owe me no kindness, Aubrey. I hate you, and you know it. But you have heaped coals of fire on my head. You are more generous than I thought you. Thank you, Aubrey; lay me under that tree yonder and let me die."

"I will try to find a surgeon. Who belongs to your regiment?"

"Somebody whom I never saw till last week. I won't have him hacking about me. Leave me in peace."

"Do you know anything of your servant? I saw him as I came on the field."

"Poor William! he followed me so closely that he was shot through the head. He is lying three hundred yards to the left, yonder. Poor fellow! he was faithful to the last."

A tear dimmed the master's eagle eye as he muttered, rather than spoke, these words.

"Then I will find Dr. Arnold at once, and send him to you."

It was no easy matter, on that crowded, confused Aceldama, and the afternoon was well nigh spent before Russell, faint and weary, descried Dr. Arnold busily using his instruments in a group of wounded. He rode up, and, having procured a drink of water and refilled his canteen, approached the surgeon.

"Doctor, where is your horse? I want you."

"Ho, Cyrus! bring him up. What is the matter, Aubrey? You are hurt."

"Nothing serious, I think. But Major Huntingdon is desperately wounded—mortally, I am afraid. See what you can do for him."

"You must be mistaken! I have asked repeatedly for Leonard, and they told me he was in hot pursuit, and unhurt. I hope to heaven you are mistaken!"

"Impossible; I tell you I lifted him out of a pool of his own blood. Come; I will show you the way."

At a hard gallop they crossed the intervening woods, and without difficulty Russell found the spot where the mangled form lay still. He had swooned, with his face turned up to the sky, and the ghastliness of death had settled on his strongly-marked, handsome features.

"God pity Irene!" said the doctor, as he bent down and examined the horrid wound, striving to press the red lips together.

The pain caused from handling him roused the brave spirit to consciousness, and opening his eyes, he looked around wonderingly.

"Well, Hiram! it is all over with me, old fellow."

"I hope not, Leonard; can't you turn a little, and let me feel for the ball?"

"It is of no use; I am torn all to pieces. Take me out of this dirt, on the fresh grass somewhere."

"I must first extract the ball. Aubrey, can you help me raise him a little?"

Administering some chloroform, he soon succeeded in taking out the ball, and, with Russell's assistance, passed a bandage round the body.

"There is no chance for me, Hiram; I know that. I have few minutes to live. Some water."

Russell put a cup to his white lips, and, calling in the assistance of Cyrus, who had followed his master, they carried him several yards farther, and made him comfortable, while orders were despatched for an ambulance.

"It will come after my corpse. Hiram, see that I am sent home at once. I don't want my bones mixed here with other people's; and it will be some comfort to Irene to know that I am buried in sight of home. I could not rest in a ditch here. I want to be laid in my own vault. Will you see to it?"

"Yes."

"Hiram, come nearer, where I can see you better. Break the news gently to Irene. Tell her I did my duty; that will be her only comfort, and best. Tell her I fell in the thickest of the battle, with my face to Washington; that I died gloriously, as a Huntingdon and a soldier should. Tell her I sent her my blessing, my love, and a last kiss."

He paused, and tears glided over his wan cheeks as the picture of his far-off home rose temptingly before him.

"She is a brave child; she will bear it, for the sake of the cause I died in. Take care of her, Arnold; tell Eric I leave her to his guardianship. Harris has my will. My poor lonely child! it is bitter to leave her. My Queen! my golden-haired, beautiful Irene!"

He raised his hand feebly, and covered his face.

"Don't let it trouble you, Leonard. You know how I love her; I promise you I will watch over her as long as I live."

"I believe you. But if I could see her once more, to ask her not to remember my harshness—long ago. You must tell her for me; she will understand. Oh! I—"

A horrible convulsion seized him at this moment, and so intense was the agony that a groan burst through his set teeth, and he struggled to rise. Russell knelt down and rested the haughty head against his shoulder, wiping off the cold drops that beaded the pallid brow. After a little while, lifting his eyes to the face bending over him, Major Huntingdon gazed into the melancholy black eyes, and said, almost in a whisper:

"I little thought I should ever owe you thanks. Aubrey, forgive me all my hate; you can afford to do so now. I am not a brute; I know magnanimity when I see it. Perhaps I was wrong to visit Amy's sins on you; but I could not forgive her. Aubrey, it was natural that I should hate Amy's son."

Again the spasm shook his lacerated frame, and, twenty minutes after his fierce, relentless spirit was released from torture; the proud, ambitious, dauntless man was with his God.

Dr. Arnold closed the eyes with trembling fingers, and covered his face with his hands to hide the tears that he could not repress.

"A braver man never died for freedom. He cheered me on, as my regiment charged over the spot where he lay," said Russell, looking down at the stiffening form.

"He had his faults, like the rest of us, and his were stern ones; but, for all that, I was attached to him. He had some princely traits. I would rather take my place there beside him, than have to break this to Irene. Poor desolate child! what an awful shock for her! She loves him with a devotion which I have rarely seen equalled. God only knows how she will bear it. If I were not so needed here, I would go to her to-morrow."

"Perhaps you can be spared."

"No; it would not be right to leave so much suffering behind."

He turned to Cyrus, and gave directions about bringing the body into camp, to his own tent; and the two mounted and rode slowly back.

For some moments silence reigned; then Dr. Arnold said, suddenly:

"I am glad you were kind to him, Aubrey. It will be some consolation to that pure soul in W____, who has mourned over and suffered for his violent animosity. It was very generous, Russell."

"Save your commendation for a better occasion; I do not merit it now. I had, and have, as little magnanimity as my old enemy, and what I did was through no generous oblivion of the past."

Glancing at him as these words were uttered gloomily, the doctor noticed his faint, wearied appearance, and led the way to his temporary hospital.

"Come in and let me see your arm. Your sleeve is full of blood."

An examination discovered a painful flesh-wound—the minie ball having glanced from the shoulder and passed out through the upper part of the arm. In removing the coat to dress the wound, the doctor exclaimed:

"Here is a bullet-hole in the breast, which must have just missed your heart! Was it a spent-ball?"

A peculiar smile disclosed Russell's faultless teeth an instant, but he merely took the coat, laid it over the uninjured arm, and answered:

"Don't trouble yourself about spent-balls—finish your job. I must look after my wounded."

As soon as the bandages were adjusted he walked away, and took from the inside pocket of the coat a heavy square morocco case containing Irene's ambrotype. When the coat was buttoned, as on that day, it rested over his heart; and during the second desperate charge of General Beauregard's lines Russell felt a sudden thump, and, above all the roar of that scene of carnage, heard the shivering of the glass which covered the likeness. The morocco was torn and indented, but the ball was turned aside harmless, and now, as he touched the spring, the fragments of glass fell at his feet. It was evident that his towering form had rendered him a conspicuous target; some accurate marksman had aimed at his heart, and the ambrotype-case had preserved his life. He looked at the uninjured, radiant face till a mist dimmed his eyes; nobler aspirations, purer aims possessed him, and, bending his knees, he bowed his forehead on the case and he reverently thanked God for his deliverance. With a countenance pale from physical suffering, but beaming with triumphant joy for the Nation's first great victory, he went out among the dead and dying, striving to relieve the wounded, and to find the members of his own command. Passing from group to group, he heard a feeble, fluttering voice pronounce his name, and saw one of his men sitting against a tree, mortally wounded by a fragment of shell.

"Well, Colonel, I followed that black feather of yours as long as I could. I am glad I had one good chance at the cowardly villains before I got hurt. We've thrashed them awfully, and I am willing to die now."

"I hope you are not so badly hurt. Cheer up, Martin; I will bring a doctor to dress your leg, and we will soon have you on crutches."

"No, Colonel; the doctor has seen it, and says there is nothing to be done for me. I knew it before; everybody feels when death strikes them. Dr. Arnold gave me something that has eased me of my pain, but he can't save me. Colonel, they say my captain is killed; and, as I may not see any of our company boys, I wish you would write to my poor wife, and tell her all about it. I haven't treated her as well as I ought; but a wife forgives everything, and she will grieve for me, though I did act like a brute when I was drinking. She will be proud to know that I fought well for my country, and died a faithful Confederate soldier; and so will my boy, Philip, who wanted to come with me. Tell Margaret to send him to take my place just as soon as he is old enough. The boy will revenge me; he has a noble spirit. And, Colonel, be sure to tell her to tell Miss Irene that I kept my promise to her—that I have not touched a drop of liquor since the day she talked to me before I went out to build Mr. Huntingdon's gin-house. God bless her sweet, pure soul! I believe she saved me from a drunkard's grave, to fill that of a brave soldier. I know she will never let my Margaret suffer, as long as she lives."

"Is there anything else I can do for you, Martin?"

"Nothing else, unless I could get a blanket, or something, to put under my head. I am getting very weak."

"Leavens, pick up one of those knapsacks scattered about, and bring a blanket. I promise you, Martin, I will write to your wife; and when I go home, if I outlive this war, I will see that she is taken care of. I am sorry to lose you, my brave fellow. You were one of the best sergeants in the regiment. But remember that you have helped to win a great battle, and your country will not forget her faithful sons who fell at Manassa."

"Good-by, Colonel: I should like to follow you to Washington. You have been kind to us all, and I hope you will be spared to our regiment. God bless you, Colonel Aubrey, wherever you go."

Russell changed him from his constrained posture to a more comfortable one, rested his head on a knapsack and blanket, placed his own canteen beside him, and, with a long, hard gripe of hands, and faltering "God bless you!" the soldiers parted. The day of horrors was shuddering to its close; glazing eyes were turned for the last time to the sun which set in the fiery West; the din and roar of the pursuit died away in the distance; lowering clouds draped the sky; the groans and wails of the wounded rose mournfully on the reeking air; and night and a drizzling rain came down on the blanched corpses on the torn, trampled, crimson plain of Manassa.

> I hate the dreadful hollow behind the little wood.
> Its lips in the field above are dabbled with blood-red heath,
> The red-ribbed ledges drip with a silent horror of blood,
> And Echo there, whatever is asked her, answers "Death!"[10]

But all of intolerable torture centred not there, awful as was the scene. Throughout the length and breadth of the Confederacy telegraphic despatches told that the battle was raging; and an army of women spent that 21st upon their knees, in agonizing prayer for husbands and sons who wrestled for their birthright on the far-off field of blood. Gray-haired pastors and curly-headed children alike besought the God of Justice to bless the Right, to deliver our gallant band of patriots from the insolent hordes

10. Tennyson, *Maud*, part 1, section1.

sent to destroy us; and to that vast trembling volume of prayer which ascended from early morning from the altars of the South, God lent his ear, and answered.

The people of W____ were subjected to painful suspense as hour after hour crept by, and a dense crowd collected in front of the telegraph office, whence floated an ominous red flag. Andrew waited on horseback to carry to Irene the latest intelligence, and during the entire afternoon she paced the colonnade, with her eyes fixed on the winding road. At half-past five o'clock the solemn stillness of the sultry day was suddenly broken by a wild, prolonged shout from the town; cheer after cheer was caught up by the hills, echoed among the purple valleys, and finally lost in the roar of the river. Andrew galloped up the avenue with an extra, yet damp from the printing-press, containing the joyful tidings that McDowell's army had been completely routed, and was being pursued toward Alexandria. Meagre was the account—our heroes, Bee and Bartow, had fallen. No other details were given, but the premonition, "Heavy loss on our side," sent a thrill of horror to every womanly heart, dreading to learn the price of victory. Irene's white face flushed as she read the despatch, and, raising her hands, exclaimed:

"Oh, thank God! thank God!"

"Shall I go back to the office?"

"Yes; I shall certainly get a despatch from Father sometime to-night. Go back, and wait for it. Tell Mr. Rogers, the operator, what you came for, and ask him I say please to let you have it as soon as it arrives. And, Andrew, bring me any other news that may come before my despatch."

Tediously time wore on; the shadows on the lawn and terrace grew longer and thinner; the birds deserted the hedges; the pigeons forsook the colonnade and steps; Paragon, tired of walking after Irene, fell asleep on the rug; and the slow, drowsy tinkle of cow-bells died away among the hills.

Far off to the east the blue was hidden by gray thunderous masses of rain-cloud, now and then veined by lightning; and as Irene watched their jagged, grotesque outlines, they took the form of battling hosts. Cavalry swept down on the flanks, huge forms heaved along the centre, and the lurid furrows ploughing the whole from time to time, seemed indeed death-dealing flashes of artillery. She recalled the phantom cloud-battle in the Netherlandish vision, and shuddered involuntarily as, in imagination, she

> Heard the heavens fill with shouting, and there rained a ghastly dew
> From the nations airy navies grappling in the central blue.[11]

Gradually the distant storm drifted southward, the retreat passed the horizon, a red sunset faded in the west; rose and amber and orange were quenched, and sober blue, with starry lights, was over all. How the serene regal beauty of that summer night mocked the tumultuous throbbing, the wild joy, and great exultation of the national heart! Mother Earth industriously weaves and hangs about the world her radiant lovely tapestries, pitiless of man's wails and requiems, deaf to his pæans. Irene had earnestly endeavored to commit her father and Russell to the merciful care and protection of God, and to rest in faith, banishing apprehension; but a horrible presentiment, which would not "down" at her bidding, kept her nerves strung to their utmost tension. As the night advanced, her face grew haggard and the wan lips fluttered ceaselessly. Russell she regarded as already dead to her in this world, but for her father she wrestled desperately in spirit. Mrs. Campbell joined her, uttering hopeful, encouraging words, and Nellie came out, with a cup of tea on a waiter.

11. "Locksley Hall," by Alfred, Lord Tennyson.

"Please drink your tea, just to please me, Queen. I can't bear to look at you. In all your life I never saw you worry so. Do sit down and rest; you have walked fifty miles since morning."

"Take it away, Nellie. I don't want it."

"But, child, it will be time enough to fret when you know Mas' Leonard is hurt. Don't run to meet trouble; it will face you soon enough. If you won't take the tea, for pity's sake let me get you a glass of wine."

"No; I tell you I can't swallow anything. If you want to help me, pray for father."

She resumed her walk, with her eyes strained in the direction of the town.

Thus passed three more miserable hours; then the clang of the iron gate at the foot of the avenue fell on her aching ear; the tramp of horses hoofs and roll of wheels came up the gravelled walk.

"Bad news! they are coming to break it to me!" said she hoarsely, and, pressing her hands together, she leaned heavily against one of the guardian statues which had stood so long before the door, like ancient Hermes at Athens. Was the image indeed prescient? It tilted from its pedestal, and fell with a crash, breaking into fragments. The omen chilled her, and she stood still, with the light from the hall-lamp streaming over her. The carriage stopped; Judge Harris and his wife came up the steps, followed slowly by Andrew, whose hat was slouched over his eyes. As they approached, Irene put out her hands wistfully.

"We have won a glorious victory, Irene, but many of our noble soldiers are wounded. I knew you would be anxious, and we came—"

"Is my father killed?"

"Your father was wounded. He led a splendid charge."

"Wounded! No! he is killed! Andrew, tell me the truth—is father dead?"

The faithful negro could no longer repress his grief, and sobbed convulsively, unable to reply.

"Oh, my God! I knew it! I knew it!" she gasped.

The gleaming arms were thrown up despairingly, and a low, dreary cry wailed through the stately old mansion as the orphan turned her eyes upon Nellie and Andrew—the devoted two who had petted her from childhood.

Judge Harris led her into the library, and his weeping wife endeavored to offer consolation, but she stood rigid and tearless, holding out her hand for the despatch. Finally they gave it to her, and she read:

"Charles T. Harris:

"Huntingdon was desperately wounded at three o'clock to-day, in making a charge. He died two hours ago. I was with him. The body leaves to-morrow for W____.

Hiram Arnold"

The paper fell from her fingers; with a dry sob she turned from them, and threw herself on the sofa, with her face of woe to the wall. So passed the night.

* * *

Chapter XXXVI

The sunlight of a warm spring day flashed through the open window, and made golden arabesque tracery on the walls and portraits of the parlor at Huntingdon Hill. The costly crimson damask curtains had long since been cut into shirts for the soldiers, and transported to the Army of Tennessee, and air and sunshine entered unimpeded. Electra sat before her canvas in this room, absorbed in the design which now engaged every thought. The witchery of her profession had woven its spell about her banishing for a time the spectral Past.

The extension of the Conscription statute had, several months before, deprived Irene of a valued and trusty overseer; and to satisfy herself concerning the character of his successor, and the condition of affairs at home, she and her uncle had returned to W____, bringing Electra with them.

Irene stood on the colonnade, leaning over the back of Eric Mitchell's arm-chair, dropping crumbs for the pigeons that cooed and scrambled at her feet, and looking dreamily down the avenue at the band of orphans who had just paid her a visit, and were returning to the asylum, convoyed by the matron.

"What contented-looking, merry little children those are," said her uncle, watching the small figures diminish as they threaded the avenue.

"Yes; they are as happy as orphans possibly can be. I love to look into their smiling, rosy faces, and feel their dimpled hands steal timidly into mine. But, uncle, Dr. Arnold has finished his nap, and is waiting for you."

She gave him her arm to the library-door, saw him seated comfortably at the table, where the doctor was examining a mass of papers, then joined Electra in the parlor.

"What progress are you making, Electra?"

"Very little. I can't work well to-day. Ruskin[12] says that no artist has fully grasped or matured his subject who can not quit one portion of it at any moment, and proceed to the completion of some other part. Doubtless he is correct; but I am so haunted by those blue eyes that I can paint nothing else this afternoon. Do you recognize them? Yours, Irene. Forgive me; but I can find no others, in imagination or in life, that so fully express serenity. My work has taken marvellous hold upon me; sleeping or waking, it follows, possesses me, I shall not hurry myself; I intend that the execution shall be equal to my ideal—and that ideal entirely worthy of the theme. I want to lay my '*Modern Macaria*,' as the first offering of Southern Art, upon my country's altar, as a nucleus around which nobler and grander pictures, from the hands of my countrymen and women, shall cluster. In sunny climes like ours, my glorious Art had its birth, its novitiate, its apotheosis; and who dare say that future ages shall not find Art-students from all nations pressing, like pilgrims, to the Perfected School of the Southern States? Ancient republics offered premiums, and saw the acme of the arts; why not our Confederate republic, when days of national prosperity dawn upon us? If the legislature of each state would annually purchase, for the embellishment of the galleries and grounds of its capital, the best picture or statue produced within its borders during the twelvemonths, a generous emulation would be encouraged. Our marble-hearted land will furnish materials, which Southern genius can mould into monuments of imperishable beauty. This war furnishes instances of heroism before which all other records pale, and our Poets, Sculptors, and Painters have only to look around them for subjects which Greek or Italian Art would glorify and immortalize.

> I do distrust the poet who discerns
> No character of glory in his times,
> And trundles back his soul five hundred years.[13]

"Our resources are inexhaustible, our capabilities as a people unlimited, and we require only the fostering influences which Cosmo De Medici and Niccolo Niccoli exerted in Florence, to call into action energies and latent talents of which we are, as yet, scarcely conscious. Such patrons of Art and Literature I hope to find in the

12. John Ruskin (1819–1900), preeminent Victorian art critic.

13. "Aurora Leigh," by Elizabeth Barrett Browning.

planters of the Confederacy. They have wealth, leisure, and every requisite adjunct, and upon them, as a class, must devolve this labor of love—the accomplishment of an American Renaissance—the development of the slumbering genius of our land. Burke has remarked: 'Nobility is a graceful ornament to the civil order; it is the Corinthian capital of polished society.' Certainly Southern planters possess all the elements of this highest order of social architecture, and upon their correct appreciation of the grave responsibility attending their wealth and influence depends, in great degree, our emancipation from the gross utilitarianism which has hitherto characterized us, and our progress in refinement and æsthetic culture. As we are distinct, socially and politically, from other nations, so let us be intellectually and artistically. The world has turned its back upon us in our grapple with tyranny; and, in the hour of our triumph, let us not forget that, as we won Independence without aid or sympathy, so we can maintain it in all departments."

"Electra, in order to effect this 'consummation devoutly to be wished,' it is necessary that the primary branches of Art should be popularized, and thrown open to the masses. Mill contends, in his Political Economy, that the remuneration of the peculiar employments of women is always far below that of employments of equal skill carried on by men, and he finds an explanation in the fact that they are overstocked. Hence, in improving the condition of women, it is advisable to give them the readiest access to independent industrial pursuits, and extend the circle of their appropriate occupations. Our Revolution has beggard thousands, and deprived many of their natural providers; numbers of women in the Confederacy will be thrown entirely upon their own resources for maintenance. All can not be mantua-makers, milliners, or school-teachers; and, in order to open for them new avenues of support, I have determined to establish in W____, a School of Design for women—similar in plan, though more extensive, than that founded some years ago by Mrs. Peter, of Philadelphia. The upper portion of the building will be arranged for drawing-classes, wood-engraving, and the various branches of Design; and the lower, corresponding in size and general appearance, I intend for a circulating library for our county. Over that School of Design I want you to preside; your talents, your education, your devotion to your Art fit you peculiarly for the position. The salary shall be such as to compensate you for your services; and, when calmer days dawn upon us, we may be able to secure some very valuable lecturers among our gentlemen-artists. I have a large lot on the corner of Pine street and Huntingdon avenue, opposite the courthouse, which will be a fine location for it, and I wish to appropriate it to this purpose. While you are adorning the interior of the building, the walls of which are to contain frescos of some of the most impressive scenes of our Revolution, I will embellish the grounds in front, and make them my special charge. I understand the cultivation of flowers, though the gift of painting them is denied me. Yesterday I sold my diamonds for a much larger amount than I supposed they would command, and this sum, added to other funds now at my disposal, will enable me to accomplish the scheme. Dr. Arnold and uncle Eric cordially approve my plan, will aid me very liberally, and as soon as tranquillity is restored I shall succeed in erecting the building without applying to any one else for assistance. When your picture is finished, I wish you to make me a copy to be hung up in our School of Design, that the students may be constantly reminded of the debt of gratitude we owe our armies. How life-like your figures grow; I can almost see the quiver of that wife's white lips and hear the dismal howling of the dead man's dog."

The canvas, which she leaned forward to inspect more closely, contained an allegorical design representing, in the foreground, two female figures. One stern, yet noble-featured, crowned with stars—triumph and exultation flashing in the luminous eyes; Independence, crimson-mantled, grasping the Confederate Banner of the Cross, who victorious folds streamed above a captured battery, where a Federal flag trailed in the dust. At her side stood white-robed, angelic Peace, with one hand over the touchhole of the cannon against which she leaned, and the other extended in benediction. Vividly the faces contrasted—one all athrob with national pride, beaming with brilliant destiny; the other wonderfully serene and holy. In the distance, gleaming in the evening light which streamed from the West, tents dotted a hill-side; and, intermediate between Peace and the glittering tents, stretched a torn, stained battle-field, over which the roar and rush of conflict had just swept, leaving mangled heaps of dead in attestation of its fury. Among the trampled, bloody sheaves of wheat, an aged, infirm Niobe-mother bent in tearless anguish, pressing her hand upon the pulseless heart of a handsome boy of sixteen summers, whose yellow locks were dabbled from his death wound. A few steps farther, a lovely young Wife, kneeling beside the stalwart, rigid form of her Husband, whose icy fingers still clutched his broken sword, lifted her woeful, ashen face to Heaven in mute despair, while the fair-browed infant on the ground beside her dipped its little snowy, dimpled feet in a pool of its father's blood, and, with tears of terror still glistening on its cheeks, laughed at the scarlet coloring. Just beyond these mourners, a girl of surpassing beauty, whose black hair floated like a sable banner on the breeze, clasped her rounded arms about her dead patriot Lover, and kept her sad vigil in voiceless agony—with all of Sparta's stern stoicism in her blanched, stony countenance. And, last of the stricken groups, a faithful dog, crouching close to the corpse of an old silver-haired man, threw back his head and howled in desolation. Neither blue shadows, nor wreathing, rosy mists, nor golden haze of sunset glory, softened the sacrificial scene, which showed its grim features strangely solemn in the weird, fading, crepuscular light.

"How many months do you suppose it will require to complete it?" asked Irene, whose interest in the picture was scarcely inferior to that of its creator.

"If I work steadily upon it, I can soon finish it; but if I go with you to a Tennessee hospital, I must, of course, leave it here until the war ends. After all, Irene, the joy of success does not equal that which attends the patient working. Perhaps it is because 'anticipation is the purest part of pleasure.' I love my work; no man or woman ever loved it better; and yet there is a painful feeling of isolation, of loneliness, which steals over me sometimes, and chills all my enthusiasm. It is so mournful to know that, when the labor is ended, and a new chaplet encircles my brow, I shall have no one but you to whom I can turn for sympathy in my triumph. If I feel this so keenly now, how shall I bear it when the glow of life fades into sober twilight shadows, and age creeps upon me?

> O my God! my God!
> O supreme Artist, who, as sole return
> For all the cosmic wonder of Thy work,
> Demandest of us just a word—a name,
> "My Father"—thou hast knowledge—only thou,
> How dreary 't is for women to sit still
> On winter nights by solitary fires,
> And hear the nations praising them far off,
> Too far![14]

14. "Aurora Leigh," by Ellizabeth Barrett Browning.

She threw down her brush and palette, and, turning toward her companion, leaned her purplish head against her.

"Electra, it is very true that single women have trials for which a thoughtless, happy world has little sympathy. But lonely lives are not necessarily joyless; they should be, of all others, most useful. The head of a household, a wife and mother, is occupied with family cares and affections—can find little time for considering the comfort or contributing to the enjoyment of any beyond the home-circle. Doubtless she is happier, far happier than the unmarried woman; but to the last belongs the privilege of carrying light and blessings to many firesides—of being the friend and helper of hundreds; and because she belongs exclusively to no one, her heart expands to all her suffering fellow-creatures. In my childhood I always thought of Old-Maids with a sensation of contempt and repulsion; now I regard those among them who preserve their natures from cynicism and querulousness, and prove themselves social evangels of mercy, as an uncrowned host of martyrs. Electra, remember other words of the same vigorous, gifted woman whom you so often quote:

> And since we needs must hunger—better, for man's love,
> Than God's truth! better, for companion sweet,
> Than great convictions! let us bear our weights,
> Preferring dreary hearths to desert souls![15]

"Remember that the woman who dares to live alone, and be sneered at, is braver, and nobler, and better than she who escapes both in a loveless marriage. It is true that you and I are very lonely, and yet our future holds much that is bright. You have the profession you love so well, and our new School of Design, to engage your thoughts; and I a thousand claims on my time and attention. I have uncle Eric to take care of and to love; and Dr. Arnold, who is growing quite infirm, has promised me that, as soon as he can be spared from the hospitals, he will make his home with us. When this storm of war has spent itself, your uncle's family will return from Europe and reside here with you. Harvey, too, will come to W_____ to live—will probably take charge of Mr. Campbell's church—and we shall have the pleasure and benefit of his constant counsel. If I could see you a member of that church I should be better satisfied—and you would be happier."

"I would join to-morrow, if thereby I could acquire your sublime faith, and strength, and resignation. Oh, Irene! my friend and comforter! I want to live differently in future. Once I was wedded to life and my Art—preeminence in my profession, fame, was all that I cared to attain; now I desire to spend my remaining years so that I may meet Russell beyond the grave. His death broke the ties that bound me to this world; I live now in hope of reunion in God's eternal kingdom. I have been selfish, and careless, and complaining; but, oh! I want to do my whole duty henceforth. Irene, my calm, sweet, patient guide, teach me to be more like you."

"Electra, take Christ for your model, instead of an erring human being like yourself, constantly falling short of her own duty. With Harvey to direct us, we ought to accomplish a world of good, here in sight of Russell's grave. Cheer up! God's great vineyard stretches before us, calling for laborers. Hand in hand, we will go in and work till evening shades close over us; then lift up, in token of our faithfulness, rich ripe clusters of purple fruitage. You and I have much to do, during these days of gloom and national trial—for upon the purity, the devotion, and the patriotism of the

15. "Aurora Leigh," by Ellizabeth Barrett Browning.

women of our land, not less than upon the heroism of our armies, depends our national salvation. To jealously guard our homes and social circles from the inroads of corruption, to keep the fires of patriotism burning upon the altars of the South, to sustain and encourage those who are wrestling along the border for our birthright of freedom, is the consecrated work to which we are called; and beyond this bloody baptism open vistas of life-long usefulness, when the reign of wrong and tyranny is ended, when the roar of battle, the blast of bugle, and beat of drum is hushed among our hills, and Peace! blessed Peace! again makes her abode in our smiling, flowery valleys. Hasten the hour, oh! my God! when her white wings shall hover over us once more!"

The eyes of the artist went back to the stainless robes and seraphic face of her pictured Peace in the loved "Modern Macaria," and, as she resumed her work, her brow cleared, the countenance kindled as in days of yore, bitter memories hushed their moans and fell asleep at the wizard touch of her profession, and the stormy, stricken soul found balm and rest in Heaven-appointed Labor.

Standing at the back of Electra's chair, with one hand resting on her shoulder, Irene raised her holy violet eyes, and looked through the window toward the cemetery, where glittered a tall marble shaft which the citizens of W____ had erected over the last quiet resting-place of Russell Aubrey. Sands of Time were drifting stealthily around the crumbling idols of the morning of life, levelling and tenderly shrouding the Past, but sorrow left its softening shadow on the orphan's countenance, and laid its chastening finger about the lips which meekly murmured, "Thy will be done." The rays of the setting sun gilded her mourning-dress, gleamed in the white roses that breathed their perfume in her rippling hair, and lingered like a benediction on the placid, pure face of the lonely woman who had survived every earthly hope; and who, calmly fronting her Altars of Sacrifice, here dedicated herself anew to the hallowed work of promoting the happiness and gladdening the paths of all who journeyed with her down the chequered aisles of Time.

Rise, woman, rise!
To thy peculiar and best altitudes
Of doing good and of enduring ill.
Of comforting for ill, and teaching good,
And reconciling all that ill and good
Unto the patience of a constant hope.

. . .

Henceforward, rise, aspire,
To all the calms and magnanimities,
The lofty uses and the noble ends,
The sanctified devotion and full work,
To which thou art elect for evermore![16]

QUESTIONS TO CONSIDER

1. How did Evans's novel contribute to the creation of a sense of Confederate nationalism?
2. In what ways did the novel reinforce Antebellum gender conventions? In what ways did it subvert them?

16. "A Drama of Exile," by Elizabeth Barrett Browning.

The Tennessee Civil War Veterans' Questionnaires

The volumes comprising *The Tennessee Civil War Veterans' Questionnaires* are the brainchild of two Tennessee State Library archivists, Gustavus W. Dyer and John Trotwood Moore. Gus Dyer began the project of sending a survey form to all known living Tennessee Civil War Veterans in 1914. Dyer hoped to obtain information about the daily life, social class, and education of Tennessee residents both before and after the Civil War. Dyer foresaw the loss of historical and cultural information that would occur, diminishing the body of available data each time a veteran passed away. His goal was to produce an historical account of all veterans from Tennessee who fought for both the South and the North during the Civil War. He set out to collect material from all veterans regardless of social class, education, or cultural status.

Dyer, however, was unable to complete the project, and Moore, after a gap of several years, resumed Dyer's work. By 1922, 1,650 responses to the questionnaires had been received. These questionnaires were published as a five-volume set of books in which the survey answers were typed and transcribed without editing. The material contained in these volumes is useful to researchers in linguistics, history, and literature, providing a vast set of data that enables researchers and general readers to better understand life in the South during and immediately following the Civil War.

While the majority of the veterans hail from Confederate forces, responses from members of Federal troops were also solicited and are included in the volumes. Because of Dyer's and Moore's minimal editing and their vigilance in maintaining the viability of the data, the responses of these former soldiers give a tangible sense of the lives of veterans who found themselves caught between the fading old South and the emerging new South. The questionnaires elicit a huge body of data, surveying not only historical facts about this turbulent period of American history but also providing examples of the range of human experiences both before and after the war.

The two surveys excerpted here illustrate the differences between social classes and the perceptions of the South by those who had lived in both the Antebellum and Postbellum periods. One of the respondents hails from a middle class family, while the other clearly comes from a wealthy background. Their experiences during the war, though different in many ways, show the difficulty of readjusting to a new, more rigorous way of life.

Civil War Questionnaires

Cheney, Hampton J.

(FORM NO. 1)

The chief purpose of the following questions is to bring out facts that will be of service in writing a true history of the Old South. Such a history has not yet been written. By answering these questions you will make a valuable contribution to the history of your State.

1. State your full name and present Post Office address:
   Hampton J. Cheney, Nashville, Tennessee
2. State your age now:
   85 years

3. In what State and county were you born?:
Cheneyville, Rapides Parish, Louisiana
4. In what State and county were you living when you enlisted in the service of the Confederacy, or of the Federal Government?:
Nashville, Davidson County, Tennessee
5. What was your occupation before the war?:
Farming
6. What was the occupation of your father?:
Sugar and cotton planter in Louisiana
7. If you owned land or other property at the opening of the war, state what kind of property you owned, and state the value of your property as near as you can:
House and lot in Nashville valued at $9000.00 and my share in my father's estate in Louisiana, consisting of 1200 acres of land cultivated in sugar and cotton; 125 negroes, stock, sugar house, costing $40,000.00, cotton gin, negro cabins and dwelling house. I also owned a farm in Davidson co., near Nashville, Tenn., which I sold after the war for $40,000.00
8. Did you or your parents own slaves? If so, how many?:
Yes, about 125
9. If your parents owned land, state about how many acres:
1200 acres in Rapides Parish, La.
10. State as near as you can the value of all the property owned by your parents, including land, when the war opened:
My father had died, and his plantation was sold, for division, just as the war opened. The purchaser became bankrupt through the conditions caused by the war and loss of negroes. Suits were instituted, but only one payment was ever made.
11. What kind of house did your parents occupy? State whether it was a log house or frame house or built of other materials, and state the number of rooms it had:
My father's home was a two-story frame building, with a veranda extending across the entire front, with wide halls between two rooms on each side above and below and double ell, making in all twelve large rooms.
12. As a boy and young man, state what kind of work you did. If you worked on a farm, state to what extent you plowed, worked with a hoe, and did other kinds of similar work:
When a boy, I was not excepted[1] *to do manual labor, as I was at school all the time, except a short vacation, in summer, which I generally spent in fishing, hunting and other recreative sports, until I entered College, and for three years, until I graduated, my entire time was occupied with my studies. It was not necessary for me to work with a plow or a hoe. Had it been, I feel sure that I would have done so without hesitation. It was not usual to see a man owning slaves do a slave's work, and in the cotton and sugar states a very small part of the White population were non-slave owners.*
13. Did your parents keep any servants? If so, how many?
The servants retained around the house, as I remember, were two cooks, two washerwomen, one dining room servant, two seamstresses, one house girl, one house boy, one carriage driver, one hostler, one gardner, one errand boy, all under the supervision of my mother. At the age of about forty-five, my father died, when I was quite young. My mother married again—Col. A. W. Johnson, whose home was in Nashville, Tenn. Thereafter, my time was spent partly in Louisiana and partly in Nashville. I attended

1. Spelling, grammar, mechanics, and other idiomatic usage have not been regularized to standard English in order to preserve the respondent's narrative voice.

Kentucky Military Institute, graduating three years later. This institute at that time, ranked next to West Point as a military training school. Among its graduates, were a number of gallant soldiers, on both sides, in the civil war, who gained distinction for courage and brilliant achievements. Amont them were Col. Hume Field and Capt. William C. Flourney of Pulaski, Gen. Hoke of South Carolina and Col. Porter of Brownsville and later of Nashville. While on the other side, were Gen. Boynton of Ohio, Gen. Eli Long and Gen. Lindsey of Kentucky and many others. Senator John Sharp Williams of Mississippi, whose record in Congress is a matter of pride to all Southerners, was also a graduate of K.M.I. a score of years later. After my graduation, I returned to my stepfather's home, then on the Gallatin Road near Nashville. In his household were about the same number of servants as in my home in Louisiana. They were slaves (several number of them had been brought by my mother from Louisiana.)

14. How was honest toil—as plowing, hauling and other sorts of honest work of this class—regarded in your community? Was such work considered respectable and honorable?
A White man who did manual labor, if he was honest and respectable, was held in good esteem. It was only those ne'er-do-wells whom the negroes aptly and contemptuously styled "poor White trash" that the planter regarded and treated as his inferiors.
15. Did the White men in your community generally engage in such work?
White men did not generally engage in farm labor in the states where cotton and sugar were grown, as the sun was too hot, rendering it dangerous to health, as in Louisiana. On my father's plantation only negro labor was used. In Tennessee, there was much more work done by White men, and where a man was honest and respected himself, he was respected by the community.
16. To what extent were there White men in your community leading lives of idleness and having others do their work for them?
A large plantation was a busy place and the scene of much activity. Planters had little time to indulge in idleness. To look after the sick, hear the complaints of the dissatisfied, think over and decide which was the best method of cultivating this field or that, kept them busy. In thinking over those days, and considering the master's burden of care, made heavy by the thought that he was responsible for lives and happiness of so many human beings, and at the same time had to provide food and raiment for them as well as his own family, and then think of the evenings I have spent in the negro quarters and witnessed the scenes of jollity with the banjo twanging and the fiddles making the little darkies cut all sorts of capers, with the parents looking on laughing and encouraging them and seemingly as happy as they, until everybody seemed lively and gay. Even the older ones sitting more quietly in groups, looked cheerful and bright, as they discussed the latest news from the adjoining plantation, and not one had the sad, distressed, dissatisfied look that our Northern brethren were wont to picture those "poor, abused, downtrodden people" as wearing. But seemed to have no care or foreboding for the future, and why should they, when they knew they would be well cared for, as well in sickness as in health, and when old age came and found them helpless, that same care that had been given them all their lives, would be still given with perhaps added tenderness. The [Louisiana] ladies were graceful and elegant with every accomplishment to enhance their beauty, yet gentle and kind to every one. The French element, fond of gaity and amusment, seemed to leave its impress on all Louisianans. The bayou during the winter season was kept brilliant by dinings and winings, balls and parties. The food, at these parties, was not only bountiful, but was prepared and cooked by the most accomplished French cooks, imported from New Orleans. Wine of rare vintage was

served in the finest cut glass and exquisitely cooked food was on tables gleaming with fine damask and silver. The wine and cigars were nearer perfection than I have ever seen elsewhere. The Pine Woods—as they were termed—was a series of hills, commencing about twenty miles from Cheneyville, the small village and postoffice, about which these several plantations were grouped. They were much more elevated than the lowlands along the bayou. Giant pines interspersed with magnolias and other trees, filled the woods and a soft, luxriant growth of grass covered the ground, furnishing fine pasturage for horse and cow. Numerous springs of cool delicious water formed numberless little rills of clear sparking water running over beds of sand as pure and white as snow, singing as they ran, of health and strength to all who drank. The air was pure and bracing, making it an ideal summer retreat. A few miles distant was a large lake called Cocodrie (crocodile) filled with the finest fish and on its margin was built a shed about 80 feet long by about twenty wide, with a floor as smooth as glass, with seats placed all around it. This was called the Lake House. Nearly every planter had secured as many acres as desired in these woods, built him a summer residence, and on the approach of hot weather moved his family out, taking with him such servants as were necessary for his comfort with his carriage and horses, best milch cows, best saddle horses and indeed everything that could render his temporary sojourn pleasant and comfortable. The horseback rides and races, the fishing parties at the lake and afterward the fish fry and the dance at the Lake House, the frequent dinings and dances, at first one house and then another all combined to make everything gay and lively, and made one almost fancy that they were at some swell watering place without the formality of dress and other impositions of a more formal place.

17. What was the first battle you engaged in?
Our first real battle in which the whole army participated was first Manassas (or Bull Run)
18. State in your own way your experience in the war from this time on until the close. State where you went after the first battle—what you did, what other battles you engaged in, how long they lasted, what the results were; state how you lived in camp, how you were clothed, how you slept, what you had to eat, how you were exposed to cold, hunger and disease. If you were in the hospital or in prison, state your experience here:
After the battle of Manassas (or Bull Run) our regiment's term of enlistment having expired, it then re-enlisted for the entire war. This being the first regiment to do this, it so delighted Mr. Benjamin (Secretary of War) on account of the example set the rest of the army that he armed our regiment with Springfield rifles, gave us a sixty-day furlough with the privilege of joining either army we preferred. Being Tennesseans, we selected the army of Tennessee. The second Tennessee Regiment being composed of companies from Middle Tennessee, (Davidson, Sumner, Rutherford, Trousdale and Shelby counties). Our homes in possission of the enemy, hence we were scattered all over the South, enjoying our furloughs by visiting friends and relatives. When our Col. (W. B. Bate) found that a battle was imminent, he at once issued an order directing that the regiment should assemble at Corinth Miss. in readiness to assist our comrades on that occasion. On account of the scattered condition of the regiment and the imperfect system of mails, the order did not reach them in time, and only about 300 assembled at Corinth the day before the battle of Shiloh. Without time for complete organization and without being brigaded, this gallant and devoted little band of patriots with their furloughs in their pockets, fought the battle of Shiloh. How well they fought and how dreadfully they suffered, the records will tell. Their Colonel (Bate) with a shattered leg, their Major killed outright, every captain killed or wounded, except Dick

Butler and myself, and more than one-third lying prone upon the ground, was the result of this desperate charge which helped drive the enemy to the river. After this battle I was appointed adjutant general to Gen. John C. Brown, who had just been released from prison, appointed to a brigidier general, and given command of a brigade. I remained in this capacity with Gen. Brown during the remainder of the war, fighting by his side in every battle fought by the army of Tennessee and surrendering with him and the army under Gen. Jos. E. Johnston in North Carolina, except in the disastrous campaign made by Gen. Hood from Atlanta, Ga. to Nashville, Tenn. Gen. Bate had been wounded and Brown was directed to take command of his division, until Bate was able to resume command. Brown took me with him to act as his adjutant and when Bate returned to his command, it was necessary on account of red tape, for me to make application in proper form to be returned to my proper command. My application was denied on account of Bate's endorsement that I be directed to remain, as his adjutant was wounded and absent, and he had no one suitable to fill the position. I was then directed to remain with Gen. Bate until further orders.

19. When and where were you discharged?
I surrendered with Gen. Joseph E. Johnston's army in North Carolina
20. Tell something of your trip home:
My old brigade (Brown's) was at this time commanded by Gen. Joseph B. Palmer, of Murfreesboro, Tenn. He was directed to march his command through the country by way of Asheville, N.C. and tap the railroad at Greenville, Tenn. where he would be given transportation by rail to move his command to Nashville, where they would find their way to their homes as best they could. The troops were permitted to retain one-fifth of their arms, with sufficient amunition to protect them on their way, with a small wagon train carrying "spun truck" with which we were to trade for provisions to sustain the troops on the march. I do not know why, but it was said that old women in the country would exchange anything they had for "spun truck" and we found it to be a fact, as we had no trouble to obtain enough good in exchange on the way. I was asked by Gen. Palmer to fill my old position as adjutant during this march, and so returned with the boys with whom I had soldiered so long. Nothing eventful occurred during this march, as we had not seen a yankee soldier on the way, until we reached a small village which seemed to be filled with federal soldiers. We halted our command here for a short rest. While sitting quietly on my horse resting like the others, a man dressed in citizen's clothes, came staggering up like he was drunk, caught hold of my boots and looking up into my face, said "I am not drunk, but pretending that I am, so that I will not be noticed talking to you. I am a Southern man and wish to tell you that these federal soldiers belong to Captain Kirk's notorious band of tories and bushwhackers, and are nothing but thieves and robbers. I heard them say that your wagon train was in the rear and as it passed through the village they intended cutting it off and running away with the mules and wagons." I saw at once that whatever was done must be done speedily, so I galloped to the head of the column, found Gen. Palmer, explained to him the situation, and asked permission to take command of our armed men and make this last fight for our rights. He promptly yielded to my request and in a few moments I had the wagon train in motion with an armed force on the flank, with a skirmish line thrown out in front to give notice of any aggressive movement from the enemy, but seeing our preparations they concluded it was wisest to let us pass in peace. Upon reaching Asheville, N.C. and while the command was at rest, I was invited by a gentleman to accompany him to his home nearby and join him in a julep, to which I readily acceded and found him so entertaining, and the julep so good, that I lingered longer with him than I intended and when I bade him goodbye I found my command

was miles ahead on the march. As I was hastening to overtake them was about to pass a lone confederate soldier limping along lookin tired and weary, I heard a number of Yankee soldiers who were sitting on the fence on both sides of the road jeering and taunting him, all of which he bore patiently for some time and seemingly without anger, retorting back at times until some insulting remark seemed to sting him beyond endurance and laying down his musket and pulling off his coat siad, "I can whip the man that made that speech and if he is afraid, you can pick the best man amont you to represent him and if you will see fair play I will undertake to give him a licking." I halted and seeing a lieutenant among the crowd, called him to me, and said "have your men promise they will see fair play and let us witness the last fight of the war which I am sure will bring lasting and permanent peace." He promised and several times he prevented interference when the yank seemed to need help most. And several times my heart sank and almost stood still to be more robust and stronger but the Confederate seemed to be much more active and had better knowledge of how to use his fists. Finally, a fortunate and I thought an accidental blow on the point of the yank's chin landed him flat on his back, where he acknowledged himself defeated. I picked the Confederate up behind me and rode him triumphantly up with his marching comrades. After arriving at Greeneville, our objective point, and where we were promised railroad transportation to Nashville, we had a fierce time. We were deprived of our arms, placed in a bull pen and guarded by the first negro troops we had seen, who taunted uw with our loss of "Southern rights, etc," and several bloody collisions were narrowly averted. After two days and nights of this hell we left Greenville for Nashville, where after our arrival we were permitted to seek our homes.

Civil War Questionnaires

England, David S.

(FORM NO. 1)

The chief purpose of the following questions is to bring out facts that will be of service in writing a true history of the Old South. Such a history has not yet been written. By answering these questions you will make a valuable contribution to the history of your State.

1. State your full name and present Post Office address:
   David S. England, Sparta, Tenn.
2. State your age now:
   was born April the 22nd 1845 and will be 70 next month (form dated: Mar. 26, 1915)
3. In what State and county were you born?
   Tenn. White Co.
4. In what State and county were you living when you enlisted in the service of the Confederacy, or of the Federal Government?
   Tenn. White Co.
5. What was your occupation before the war?
   working on the farm
6. What was the occupation of your father?
   farmer fruit nursery and gun smith
7. If you owned land or other property at the opening of the war, state what kind of property you owned, and state the value of your property as near as you can:
   nothing but a horse worth about two(?) hundred dollars and it was taken away from me by Stokes Homegards.

8. Did you or your parents own slaves? If so, how many?
   yes my father owned four
9. If your parents owned land, state about how many acres:
   four hundred acres
10. State as near as you can the value of all the property owned by your parents, including land, when the war opened:
    I have heard him say about ten thousand dollars
11. What kind of house did your parents occupy? State whether it was a log house or frame house or built of other materials, and state the number of rooms it had:
    an old fasion hewed log two rooms below and one up stairs and weather boarded on the out side.
12. As a boy and young man, state what kind of work you did. If you worked on a farm, state to what extent you plowed, worked with a hoe, and did other kinds of similar work:
    I worked on farm truck packed and with all kind of tools we had them times we all worked together and when one of was ____ a thrashing I would think of putting on another coat
13. Did your parents keep any servants? If so, how many?
    ___
14. How was honest toil—as plowing, hauling and other sorts of honest work of this class—regarded in your community? Was such work considered respectable and honorable?
    yes
15. Did the White men in your community generally engage in such work?
    yes
16. To what extent were there White men in your community leading lives of idleness and having others do their work for them?
    I don't think there is much of that now around here.
17. What was the first battle you engaged in?
    it is called the Readsville stampeed they chased our company to woodburr but met Capt. Carter ___ turned them back there with several empty saddles.
18. State in your own way your experience in the war from this time on until the close. State where you went after the first battle—what you did, what other battles you engaged in, how long they lasted, what the results were; state how you lived in camp, how you were clothed, how you slept, what you had to eat, how you were exposed to cold, hunger and disease. If you were in the hospital or in prison, state your experience here:
    Gen. Dibrell went from Woodburry around by McMinnville back to Sparta some of the boys become disharten and quit then. Gen. Wheeler heard of Gen. Dibrells disaster sent Williams and Robersons commands with 3 peaces of artilery to get out of this country which was surrounded with yankeys at that time we went out through Cumberland Gap drove us down near Richmond rifles at Abington or Bristol Virginia. about that time we heard there was a command of yankees going to Saltsville Va.
19. When and where were you discharged?
    I was in no more fights after Sherman taken and burnt Collumbus S.C. I was taken sick soon after with typhoid fever and was left at a private house in North Carolina.
20. Tell something of your trip home:
    the gentleman I stayed with name was Pressley Stanback he lived in Richmond Co. near the PD river and I stayed there 72 days long before I got well Lee had surrendered and

the Southern confederacy was a thing of the past there was another soldier with me by the name of Fry the first yankeys we saw after . . . .

Questions to Consider

1. What strikes you as the most significant difference between the two veterans' passages?
2. Do the responses to the questionnaire meet your expectations or surprise you? How do you think social class influences the society of the two narrators? How does class effect the way that each narrator represents himself in answering the questions?

Mark Twain (Samuel Langhorne Clemens)

1835–1910

The author, newspaperman, riverboat captain, lecturer, and businessman who became known as Mark Twain was born Samuel Langhorne Clemens in Florida, Missouri, on 30 November 1835. While working as a staff writer for the Virginia City *Territorial Enterprise*, Clemens adopted the name Mark Twain, a reference to his time on the Mississippi River, where navigators would shout "mark twain" when a riverboat was in water two fathoms deep (about 12 feet), which was the minimum depth considered safe for riverboat travel. His father, who died when Twain was only twelve, was a bit of a dreamer who was trained as a lawyer but spent most of his life unsuccessfully chasing easy money in land speculation. Twain's mother was a religious and soft-hearted woman, and critics have commented that the tensions between his father's passion for the get-rich-quick scheme and his mother's concern for the unfortunate were evident in the life of the adult Twain, whose renowned pessimism for the human race was tempered by a profound longing for social justice and human equality. Like his father, Twain was drawn to financial speculation throughout his life, and at the height of his fame he lost his entire fortune in bad publishing ventures and investments.

When Twain was four, the Clemens family moved to Hannibal, Missouri, and Twain's boyhood life in the small Mississippi River town greatly influenced his work, most notably his books *Life on the Mississippi*, *The Adventures of Tom Sawyer*, and *The Adventures of Huckleberry Finn*. Hannibal had once been at the edge of the Southwestern frontier, but by the 1840s, the town had become an odd mixture of clapboard houses and log cabins. Native Americans still lived in the forests around Hannibal, but the residents had no fear of attack, as the Native Americans had settled into a peaceful détente with the townsfolk.

After his father died, Twain left school to become an apprentice printer and journalist at his brother's newspaper. He traveled to New York and to the Midwest to continue his career in printing and journalism, but he soon made plans to pursue his fortune in South America. While traveling to New Orleans aboard a riverboat, Twain befriended the captain, who promised to teach him the difficult art of piloting riverboats on the Mississippi. Twain promptly abandoned his plans to go to South America and spent the next few years as a riverboat pilot. During the Civil War, Twain was part of a group of young Southerners who formed a Confederate militia but then disbanded it a week later. Some of the young men went on to join the Confederate Army, while Twain headed West. Joining his brother, who had been appointed secretary to the governor of Nevada, Twain worked a miner and a journalist.

Encouraged by his success with the *Territorial Enterprise*, Twain traveled to California, where he collaborated briefly with Western writer Bret Hart and also wrote "The Celebrated Jumping Frog of Calaveras County." The story became an immediate success, and launched

Twain's career as a writer. In "The Celebrated Jumping Frog," his first widely read story, Twain employs the tools that would become his literary stock in trade: vibrant realism, the naïve narrator, and brisk humor undercut by biting satire. He also demonstrates a style based on the stark realism of the journalist and the burlesque embellishment of the storyteller, and this style would come to dominate his work. In "How to Tell a Story," Twain writes that the humorous story, the "most difficult kind" to write, was America's literary gift to the world. The humorous story, he continues, should "bubble gently along, but be told gravely." "The teller does his best to conceal the fact that he even dimly suspects that there is anything funny about it; but the teller of the comic story tells you beforehand that it is one of the funniest things he has ever heard, then tells it with eager delight, and is the first person to laugh when he gets through." Twain's narrative style was essentially oral, episodic, and anecdotal, and "innocently unaware" narrators primarily tell his stories. Few other writers have approached his facility for translating the sound of authentic voices and the subtle complexity of American idioms into print.

After the success of "The Celebrated Jumping Frog," Twain published a collection of his stories and sketches entitled *The Celebrated Jumping Frog of Calaveras County and Other Sketches* (1867) and continued to travel. He sailed to the Sandwich Islands in the Pacific, toured the Eastern United States, and traveled to the Mediterranean and the Holy Land. With the publication of *Innocents Abroad* (1869), an account of his travels in Europe and the Middle East, Twain established himself as a leading American author and humorist and introduced the world to the irreverent and charming character who would become the American icon Mark Twain. After completing *Roughing It,* in 1872, Twain collaborated with C. D. Warner on *The Gilded Age* (1873), a satiric look at the postwar boom years that gave the era its popular name. Next came *A Tramp Abroad* (1880), a narrative based on his hiking tour of the Black Forest and the Alps. Through the next decade, Twain published a variety of works, including two satiric fantasies set in England, *The Prince and the Pauper* (1882) and *A Connecticut Yankee in King Arthur's Court* (1889). Twain also turned to material drawn from his boyhood experiences to produce his most representative Southern works, *The Adventures of Tom Sawyer* (1876), *Life on the Mississippi* (1883), and *The Adventures of Huckleberry Finn* (1884). Although Twain was finally satisfied with having Tom Sawyer and Huckleberry Finn marketed as "boys' books," he originally insisted that the novels were meant to "be read by adults." In fact, the books are much more than a realistic recounting of boyhood adventures. In each of these novels, Hannibal is transformed into a mythic stage called St. Petersburg on which the pranks and misadventures of two young boys become epic American myths. The characters that populate these novels transcend their romantic and comic stereotypes to become the archetypes of the Southwestern frontier. Through the characters of Tom and Huck, Twain translates the literal language of the frontier idiom into a symbolic language of essential Southern and American experience.

In 1879, Twain settled in Hartford, Connecticut, where he married Olivia Langdon, the genteel, conservative daughter of an aristocratic New England family. Critic Van Wyck Brooks argued that marriage to Olivia required Twain to fit in with the conservative community of Hartford and stifled Twain's development as a satirist of American culture. Other critics, such as Bernard De Voto, argued that if Twain failed to reach his potential as literary satirist, it was more likely due to his original beginnings as a frontier humorist and storyteller. While evaluation of Twain's literary genius has been a topic of some debate, most criticism has, in the end, come down to the critic's estimation of American and Southern literature in general, for all have agreed in some way with Ernest Hemingway, who is said to have remarked that all modern American literature derives from *Huckleberry Finn*.

While in Hartford, Twain became a partner in the publishing firm of Charles L. Webster and Company, which initially made a fortune for Twain, publishing his work and the memoirs of Ulysses S. Grant. Unfortunately, the company made some bad investments, most notably the investment of $200,000 of Twain's money in an unsuccessful typesetting machine, and by 1894, Twain was forced into bankruptcy. To salvage his finances, he embarked on an extensive tour, although he had grown tired of the lecture circuit, and the record of his tour chronicled in *Following the Equator* (1897) demonstrates quite a bit of bitterness over his situation. During the 1890s, Twain continued with his major themes, publishing *The Tragedy of Pudd'nhead Wilson* (1894); *Personal Recollections of Joan of Arc* (1896); *The American Claimant* (1892); *Tom Sawyer, Abroad* (1894); and *Tom Sawyer, Detective* (1896). Much of the work Twain published during this period is considered uneven in quality, which could possibly be due to his need to lecture constantly and publish quickly in order to regain financial stability.

After the turn of the century, Twain began to engage more directly his doubts about the human race. While his persistent pessimism is often undercut by continued humor, he felt that certain works of this period, such as *Letters from the Earth* (1962) and *The Mysterious Stranger* (1916), would be so controversial that he ordered that they be published only after his death. By the turn of the century Twain had stabilized his finances, but he continued to travel, lecture, and publish widely on current events and issues in such works as *The Man Who Corrupted Hadleyburg* (1900), *What is Man?* (1906), *Christian Science* (1907), and *Is Shakespeare Dead?* (1909). The deaths of both his wife and his daughter increased his bitterness, and he died in 1910 as Halley's comet streaked through the sky, just as it had on the day of his birth.

In the chapters that follow from *Life on the Mississippi*, readers will see how the roots of Mark Twain's work are firmly embedded in the traditions of Southern literature—in the adventure narratives and Edenic descriptions of the early settlers, in the Romantic traditions of narratives about Southern war heroes and wily criminals, and in the satire and rough characters of the Southwestern Humorists. Although uneven at times, Twain's art represents the first culmination of the variety of Southern literary voices. More, it has transcended the regional and the specific to become the national and the universal.

from **Life on the Mississippi**

CHAPTER XLI: THE METROPOLIS OF THE SOUTH

The approaches to New Orleans were familiar; general aspects were unchanged. When one goes flying through London along a railway propped in the air on tall arches, he may inspect miles of upper bedrooms through the open windows, but the lower half of the houses is under his level and out of sight. Similarly, in high-river stage, in the New Orleans region, the water is up to the top of the enclosing levee-rim, the flat country behind it lies low—representing the bottom of a dish—and as the boat swims along, high on the flood, one looks down upon the houses and into the upper windows. There is nothing but that frail breastwork of earth between the people and destruction.

The old brick salt-warehouses clustered at the upper end of the city looked as they had always looked; warehouses which had had a kind of Aladdin's lamp experience, however, since I had seen them; for when the war broke out the proprietor went to bed one night leaving them packed with thousands of sacks of vulgar salt, worth a couple of dollars a sack, and got up in the morning and found his mountain of salt turned into a mountain of gold, so to speak, so suddenly and to so dizzy a height had the war news sent up the price of the article.

The vast reach of plank wharves remained unchanged, and there were as many ships as ever: but the long array of steamboats had vanished; not altogether, of course, but not much of it was left.

The city itself had not changed—to the eye. It had greatly increased in spread and population, but the look of the town was not altered. The dust, waste-paper-littered, was still deep in the streets; the deep, trough-like gutters alongside the curb-stones were still half full of reposeful water with a dusty surface; the sidewalks were still—in the sugar and bacon region—incumbered by casks and barrels and hogsheads; the great blocks of austerely plain commercial houses were as dusty-looking as ever.

Canal Street was finer, and more attractive and stirring than formerly, with its drifting crowds of people, its several processions of hurrying street-cars, and—toward evening—its broad second-story verandas crowded with gentlemen and ladies clothed according to the latest mode.

Not that there is any "architecture" in Canal Street: to speak in broad, general terms, there is no architecture in New Orleans, except in the cemeteries. It seems a strange thing to say of a wealthy, far-seeing, and energetic city of a quarter of a million inhabitants, but it is true. There is a huge granite U.S. Custom-house—costly enough, genuine enough, but as a decoration it is inferior to a gasometer.[1] It looks like a state prison. But it was built before the war. Architecture in America may be said to have been born since the war. New Orleans, I believe, has had the good luck—and in a sense the bad luck—to have had no great fire in late years. It must be so. If the opposite had been the case, I think one would be able to tell the "burnt district" by the radical improvement in its architecture over the old forms. One can do this in Boston and Chicago. The "burnt district" of Boston was commonplace before the fire; but now there is no commercial district in any city in the world that can surpass it—or perhaps even rival it—in beauty, elegance, and tastefulness.

However, New Orleans has begun—just this moment, as one may say. When completed, the new Cotton Exchange will be a stately and beautiful building; massive, substantial, full of architectural graces; no shams or false pretences or uglinesses about it anywhere. To the city, it will be worth many times its cost, for it will breed its species. What has been lacking hitherto, was a model to build toward; something to educate eye and taste; a *suggester*, so to speak.

The city is well outfitted with progressive men—thinking, sagacious, long-headed men. The contrast between the spirit of the city and the city's architecture is like the contrast between waking and sleep. Apparently there is a "boom" in everything but that one dead feature. The water in the gutters used to be stagnant and slimy, and a potent disease-breeder; but the gutters are flushed now, two or three times a day, by powerful machinery; in many of the gutters the water never stands still, but has a steady current. Other sanitary improvements have been made; and with such effect that New Orleans claims to be (during the long intervals between the occasional yellow-fever assaults) one of the healthiest cities in the Union. There's plenty of ice now for everybody, manufactured in the town. It is a driving place commercially, and has a great river, ocean, and railway business. At the date of our visit, it was the best lighted city in the Union, electrically speaking. The New Orleans electric lights were more numerous than those of New York, and very much better. One had this modified noonday not only in Canal and some neighboring chief streets, but all along a stretch of five miles of river frontage. There are good clubs in the city now—several of them but recently organized—and inviting modern-style pleasure resorts at West End and Spanish Fort. The telephone is everywhere. One of the most notable advances is in journalism. The newspapers, as I remember them, were not a striking feature. Now they are. Money is spent upon them with a free hand. They get the news, let it cost what it may. The editorial work is not hack-grinding, but literature. As an example of New Orleans journalistic achievement, it may be mentioned that the "Times-Democrat" of August 26, 1882,

1. A reservoir for storing the gas used in lighting streetlamps and houses.

contained a report of the year's business of the towns of the Mississippi Valley, from New Orleans all the way to St. Paul—two thousand miles. That issue of the paper consisted of *forty* pages; seven columns to the page; two hundred and eighty columns in all; fifteen hundred words to the column; an aggregate of four hundred and twenty thousand words. That is to say, not much short of three times as many words as there are in this book. One may with sorrow contrast this with the architecture of New Orleans.

I have been speaking of public architecture only. The domestic article in New Orleans is reproachless, notwithstanding it remains as it always was. All the dwellings are of wood—in the American part of the town, I mean—and all have a comfortable look. Those in the wealthy quarter are spacious; painted snow-white usually, and generally have wide verandas, or double-verandas, supported by ornamental columns. These mansions stand in the centre of large grounds, and rise, garlanded with roses, out of the midst of swelling masses of shining green foliage and many-colored blossoms. No houses could well be in better harmony with their surroundings, or more pleasing to the eye, or more home-like and comfortable-looking.

One even becomes reconciled to the cistern presently; this is a mighty cask, painted green, and sometimes a couple of stories high, which is propped against the house-corner on stilts. There is a mansion-and-brewery suggestion about the combination which seems very incongruous at first. But the people cannot have wells, and so they take rain-water. Neither can they conveniently have cellars, or graves;[2] the town being built upon "made" ground; so they do without both, and few of the living complain, and none of the others.

Chapter XLVI: Enchantments and Enchanters

The largest annual event in New Orleans is a something which we arrived too late to sample—the Mardi-Gras festivities. I saw the procession of the Mystic Crew of Comus there, twenty-four years ago—with knights and nobles and so on, clothed in silken and golden Paris-made gorgeousnesses, planned and bought for that single night's use; and in their train all manner of giants, dwarfs, monstrosities, and other diverting grotesquerie—a startling and wonderful sort of show, as it filed solemnly and silently down the street in the light of its smoking and flickering torches; but it is said that in these latter days the spectacle is mightily augmented, as to cost, splendor, and variety. There is a chief personage—"Rex;" and if I remember rightly, neither this king nor any of his great following of subordinates is known to any outsider. All these people are gentlemen of position and consequence; and it is a proud thing to belong to the organization; so the mystery in which they hide their personality is merely for romance's sake, and not on account of the police.

Mardi-Gras is of course a relic of the French and Spanish occupation; but I judge that the religious feature has been pretty well knocked out of it now. Sir Walter has got the advantage of the gentlemen of the cowl and rosary, and he will stay. His mediæval business, supplemented by the monsters and the oddities, and the pleasant creatures from fairyland, is finer to look at than the poor fantastic inventions and performances of the revelling rabble of the priest's day, and serves quite as well, perhaps, to emphasize the day and admonish men that the grace-line between the worldly season and the holy one is reached.

2. The Israelites are buried in graves—by permission, I take it, not requirement; but none else, except the destitute, who are buried at public expense. The graves are but three or four feet deep (author's note).

This Mardi-Gras pageant was the exclusive possession of New Orleans until recently. But now it has spread to Memphis and St. Louis and Baltimore. It has probably reached its limit. It is a thing which could hardly exist in the practical North; would certainly last but a very brief time; as brief a time as it would last in London. For the soul of it is the romantic, not the funny and the grotesque. Take away the romantic mysteries, the kings and knights and big-sounding titles, and Mardi-Gras would die, down there in the South. The very feature that keeps it alive in the South—girly-girly romance—would kill it in the North or in London. Puck and Punch, and the press universal, would fall upon it and make merciless fun of it, and its first exhibition would be also its last.

Against the crimes of the French Revolution and of Bonaparte may be set two compensating benefactions: the Revolution broke the chains of the *ancien régime* and of the Church, and made of a nation of abject slaves a nation of freemen; and Bonaparte instituted the setting of merit above birth, and also so completely stripped the divinity from royalty, that whereas crowned heads in Europe were gods before, they are only men, since, and can never be gods again, but only figure-heads, and answerable for their acts like common clay. Such benefactions as these compensate the temporary harm which Bonaparte and the Revolution did, and leave the world in debt to them for these great and permanent services to liberty, humanity, and progress.

Then comes Sir Walter Scott with his enchantments, and by his single might checks this wave of progress, and even turns it back; sets the world in love with dreams and phantoms; with decayed and swinish forms of religion; with decayed and degraded systems of government; with the sillinesses and emptinesses, sham grandeurs, sham gauds, and sham chivalries of a brainless and worthless long-vanished society. He did measureless harm; more real and lasting harm, perhaps, than any other individual that ever wrote. Most of the world has now outlived a good part of these harms, though by no means all of them; but in our South they flourish pretty forcefully still. Not so forcefully as half a generation ago, perhaps, but still forcefully. There, the genuine and wholesome civilization of the nineteenth century is curiously confused and commingled with the Walter Scott Middle-Age sham civilization and so you have practical, common-sense, progressive ideas, and progressive works, mixed up with the duel, the inflated speech, and the jejune romanticism of an absurd past that is dead, and out of charity ought to be buried. But for the Sir Walter disease, the character of the Southerner—or Southron, according to Sir Walter's starchier way of phrasing it—would be wholly modern, in place of modern and mediæval mixed, and the South would be fully a generation further advanced than it is. It was Sir Walter that made every gentleman in the South a Major or a Colonel, or a General or a Judge, before the war; and it was he, also, that made these gentlemen value these bogus decorations. For it was he that created rank and caste down there, and also reverence for rank and caste, and pride and pleasure in them. Enough is laid on slavery, without fathering upon it these creations and contributions of Sir Walter.

Sir Walter had so large a hand in making Southern character, as it existed before the war, that he is in great measure responsible for the war. It seems a little harsh toward a dead man to say that we never should have had any war but for Sir Walter; and yet something of a plausible argument might, perhaps, be made in support of that wild proposition. The Southerner of the American revolution owned slaves; so did the Southerner of the Civil War: but the former resembles the latter as an Englishman resembles a Frenchman. The change of character can be traced rather more easily to Sir Walter's influence than to that of any other thing or person.

One may observe, by one or two signs, how deeply that influence penetrated, and how strongly it holds. If one take up a Northern or Southern literary periodical of forty or fifty years ago, he will find it filled with wordy, windy, flowery "eloquence," romanticism, sentimentality—all imitated from Sir Walter, and sufficiently badly done, too—innocent travesties of his style and methods, in fact. This sort of literature being the fashion in both sections of the country, there was opportunity for the fairest competition; and as a consequence, the South was able to show as many well-known literary names, proportioned to population, as the North could.

But a change has come, and there is no opportunity now for a fair competition between North and South. For the North has thrown out that old inflated style, whereas the Southern writer still clings to it—clings to it and has a restricted market for his wares, as a consequence. There is as much literary talent in the South, now, as ever there was, of course; but its work can gain but slight currency under present conditions; the authors write for the past, not the present; they use obsolete forms, and a dead language. But when a Southerner of genius writes modern English, his book goes upon crutches no longer, but upon wings; and they carry it swiftly all about America and England, and through the great English reprint publishing houses of Germany—as witness the experience of Mr. Cable and Uncle Remus, two of the very few Southern authors who do not write in the Southern style. Instead of three or four widely-known literary names, the South ought to have a dozen or two—and will have them when Sir Walter's time is out.

A curious exemplification of the power of a single book for good or harm is shown in the effects wrought by *Don Quixote* and those wrought by Ivanhoe. The first swept the world's admiration for the mediæval chivalry-silliness out of existence; and the other restored it. As far as our South is concerned, the good work done by Cervantes is pretty nearly a dead letter, so effectually has Scott's pernicious work undermined it.

The Suppressed Chapter[3]

Editor's Note: The following chapter of *Life on the Mississippi* was excised from Twain's original manuscript to shorten the book. His editors chose this particular chapter because they feared it would offend Southern readers. The chapter was published as a separate pamphlet in 1910. For more information on this suppressed chapter, see the May 1914 issue of *The Bookman*.

I missed one thing in the South—African slavery. That horror is gone, and permanently. Therefore, half the South is at last emancipated, half the South is free. But the white half is apparently as far from emancipation as ever.

The South is "solid" for a single political party. It is difficult to account for this; that is, in a region which purports to be free. Human beings are so constituted, that, given an intelligent, thinking, hundred of them, or thousand, or million, and convince them that they are free from personal danger or social excommunication for opinion's sake, it is absolutely impossible that they shall tie themselves in a body to any one sect, religious or political. Every thinking person in the South and elsewhere knows this; it is a truism.

Given a "solid" country, anywhere, and the ready conclusion is that it is a community of savages. But here are the facts—not conjectures, but facts—and I think they spoil that conclusion. The great mass of Southerners, both in town and country,

3. Originally Chapter 48 of *Life on the Mississippi*.

are neighborly, friendly, hospitable, peaceable, and have an aversion for disagreements and embroilments; they belong to the church, and they frequent it; they are Sabbath-observers; they are promise-keepers; they are honorable and upright in their dealings; where their prejudices are not at the front, they are just, and they like to see justice done; they are able to reason, and they reason.

These characteristics do not describe a community of savages, they describe the reverse, an excellent community. How such a community should all vote one way, is a perplexing problem. That such a people should be all democrats or all republicans seems against nature.

It may be that a minor fact or two may help toward a solution. It is imagined in the North that the South is one vast and gory murder-field, and that every man goes armed, and has at one time or another taken a neighbor's life. On the contrary, the great mass of Southerners carry no arms, and do not quarrel. In the city of New York, where killing seems so frightfully common, the mighty majority, the overwhelming majority of the citizens, have never seen a weapon drawn in their lives. This is the case in the South. The general people are unfamiliar with murder; they have never seen a murder done. Thousands of murders have been committed in the South; murders are much commoner there than in the North; but these killings are scattered over a vast domain; in small places, long intervals of time intervene between events of this kind; and in both small and large places it is the chance half dozen who witness the killing—the vast majority of that community are not present, and may live long lives and die without ever having seen an occurrence of the sort.

As I have said, the great mass of Southerners are not personally familiar with murder. And being peaceably disposed, and also accustomed to living in peace, they have a horror of murder and violence. There is a superstition, current everywhere, that the Southern temper is peculiarly hot; whereas, in truth the temper of the average Southerner is not hotter than that of the average Northerner. The temper of the Northerner, through training, heredity, and fear of the law, is kept under the better command, that is all. In a wild country where born instincts may venture to the surface, this fact shows up. In California, Nevada, and Montana, the most of the desperadoes and the deadliest of them, were not from the South, but from the North.

Now, in every community, North and South, there is one hot-head, or a dozen, or a hundred, according to distribution of population; the rest of the community are quiet folk. What do these hot-heads amount to, in the North? Nothing. Who fears them? Nobody. Their heads never get so hot but that they retain cold sense enough to remind them that they are among a people who will not allow themselves to be walked over by their sort; a people who, although they will not insanely hang them upon suspicion and without trial, nor try them, convict them, and then let them go, but who will give them a fair and honest chance in the courts, and if conviction follow will punish them with imprisonment or the halter.

In the South the case is very different. The one hot-head defies the hamlet; the half dozen or dozen defy the village and the town. In the South the expression is common, that such-and-such a ruffian is the "terror of the town." Could he come North and be the terror of a town? Such a thing is impossible. Northern resolution, backing Northern law, was too much for even the "Mollie Maguires,"[4] powerful,

4. A secret society of Irish miners active in Pennsylvania during the late 1800s.

numerous, and desperate as was that devilish secret organization. But it could have lived a long life in the South; for there it is not the rule for courts to hang murderers.

Why?—seeing that the bulk of the community are murder-hating people. It is hard to tell. Are they torpid, merely?—indifferent?—wanting in public spirit?

Their juries fail to convict, even in the clearest cases. That this is not agreeable to the public, is shown by the fact that very frequently such a miscarriage of justice so rouses the people that they rise, in a passion, and break into the jail, drag out their man and lynch him. This is quite sufficient proof that they do not approve of murder and murderers. But this hundred or two hundred men usually do this act of public justice with masks on. They go to their grim work with clear consciences, but with their faces disguised. They know that the law will not meddle with them—otherwise, at least, than by empty form—and they know that the community will applaud their act. Still, they disguise themselves.

The other day, in Kentucky, a witness testified against a young man in court, and got him fined for a violation of a law. The young man went home and got his shot gun and made short work of that witness. He did not invent that method of correcting witnesses; it had been used before, in the South. Perhaps this detail accounts for the reluctance of witnesses, there, to testify; and also the reluctance of juries to convict; and perhaps, also, for the disposition of lynchers to go to their grewsome labors disguised.

Personal courage is a rare quality. Everywhere in the Christian world—except, possibly, down South—the average citizen is not brave, he is timid. Perhaps he is timid down South, too. According to the *Times-Democrat*, "the favorite diversion of New Orleans hoodlums is crowding upon the late street cars, hustling the men passengers and insulting the ladies." They smoke, they use gross language, they successfully defy the conductor when he tries to collect their fare. All this happens, and they do not get hurt. Apparently the average Southern citizen is like the average Northern citizen—does not like to embroil himself with a ruffian.

The other day, in Kentucky, a single highwayman, revolver in hand, stopped a stagecoach and robbed the passengers, some of whom were armed—and he got away unharmed. The unaverage Kentuckian, being plucky, is not afraid to attack half a dozen average Kentuckians; and his bold enterprise succeeds—probably because the average Kentuckian is like the average of the human race, not plucky, but timid.

In one thing the average Northerner seems to be a step in advance of the average Southerner, in that he bands himself with his timid fellows to support the law, (at least in the matter of murder,) protect judges, juries, and witnesses, and also to secure all citizens from personal danger and from obloquy or social ostracism on account of opinion, political or religious; whereas the average Southerners do not band themselves together in these high interests, but leave them to look out for themselves unsupported; the results being unpunished murder, against the popular approval, and the decay and destruction of independent thought and action in politics.

I take the following paragraph from a recent article in the *Evening Post*, published at Louisville, Ky. The italics are mine:

> There is no use in mincing matters. The social condition of the State is worse than we have ever known it. Murders are more frequent, punishment is lighter, pardons more numerous, and abuses more flagrant than at any period within our recollection, running back fifteen years. Matters are getting worse day by day. The most alarming feature of all is the *indifference* of the public. No one seems to see the carnival of crime and social chaos to which we are rapidly drifting. No one seems to take to himself the lesson of cur-

> rent events. No one seems to realize the actual danger which hangs over the lives of all. *Appeals to the order-loving and law-abiding elements appear vain and idle. It is difficult to stir them.* Shocking tragedies at their very doors do not startle them to a realization of the evils that are cursing Kentucky, imperilling the lives of her own citizens, barring us against the current of immigration and commerce, and presenting us to the eyes of the world as a reckless, God-defying, reeking band of law-breakers and murderers.

That editor does not feel indifferent. He feels the opposite of indifferent. Does he think he is alone? He cannot be. I think that without question he is expressing the general feeling of the State. But it is not *organized*, therefore it is ineffective. Once organized, it would be abundantly strong for the occasion; the condition of things complained of by the editor would cease. But it is not going to organize itself; somebody has got to take upon himself the disagreeable office of making the first move. In the Knoxville region of Tennessee that office has been assumed, and a movement is now on foot there to organize and band together the best people for the protection of Courts, juries and witnesses. There is no reason why the experiment should not succeed; and if it succeeds, there is no reason why the reform should not spread.

As to white political liberty in New Orleans, I take four pages, at random, from the city directory for the present year—1882. It "samples" the book, and affords one a sort of bird's-eye view of the nationalities of New Orleans:

"Many men, many minds," says the proverb. What a lovely thing it is to see all these variegated nationalities exhibiting a miracle which makes all other miracles cheap in comparison—that is, voting and feeling all one way, in spite of an eternal law of nature which pronounces such a thing impossible. And how pretty it is to see all these Germans and Frenchmen, who bitterly differ in all things else, meet sweetly together on the platform of a single party in the free and unembarrassed political atmosphere of New Orleans. How odd it is to see the mixed nationalities of New York voting all sorts of tickets, and the very same mixed nationalities of New Orleans voting all one way—and letting on that that is just the thing they wish to do, and are entirely unhampered in the matter, and wouldn't vote otherwise, oh, not for anything. As the German phrases it, "it is not thick enough."

Journalism in Tennessee

> The editor of the Memphis *Avalanche* swoops thus mildly down upon a correspondent who posted him as a Radical: "While he was writing the first word, the middle, dotting his i's, crossing his t's, and punching his period, he knew he was concocting a sentence that was saturated with infamy and reeking with falsehood."
>
> *Exchange*

I was told by the physician that a Southern climate would improve my health, and so I went down to Tennessee, and got a berth on the *Morning Glory and Johnson County War-Whoop* as associate editor. When I went on duty I found the chief editor sitting tilted back in a three-legged chair with his feet on a pine table. There was another pine table in the room and another afflicted chair, and both were half buried under newspapers and scraps and sheets of manuscript. There was a wooden box of sand, sprinkled with cigar stubs and "old soldiers," and a stove with a door hanging by its upper hinge. The chief editor had a long-tailed black cloth frock-coat on, and white linen pants. His boots were small and neatly blacked. He wore a ruffled shirt, a large seal-ring, a standing collar of obsolete pattern, and a checkered neckerchief with the ends hanging down. Date of costume about 1848. He was smoking a cigar, and trying to think of a word, and in pawing his hair he had rumpled his locks a good deal. He was scowling fearfully, and I judged that he was concocting a particularly knotty editorial. He told me to take the exchanges and skim through them and write up the "Spirit of the Tennessee Press," condensing into the article all of their contents that seemed of interest.

I wrote as follows:

SPIRIT OF THE TENNESSEE PRESS

The editors of the Semi-Weekly Earthquake *evidently labor under a misapprehension with regard to the Ballyhack railroad. It is not the object of the company to leave Buzzardville off to one side. On the contrary, they consider it one of the most important points along the line, and consequently can have no desire to slight it. The gentlemen of the* Earthquake *will, of course, take pleasure in making the correction.*

John W. Blossom, Esq., the able editor of the Higginsville Thunderbolt and Battle Cry of Freedom, *arrived in the city yesterday. He is stopping at the Van Buren House.*

We observe that our contemporary of the Mud Springs Morning Howl *has fallen into the error of supposing that the election of Van Werter is not an established fact, but he will have discovered his mistake before this reminder reaches him, no doubt. He was doubtless misled by incomplete election returns.*

It is pleasant to note that the city of Blathersville is endeavoring to contract with some New York gentlemen to pave its well-nigh impassable streets with the Nicholson pavement. The Daily Hurrah *urges the measure with ability, and seems confident of ultimate success.*

I passed my manuscript over to the chief editor for acceptance, alteration, or destruction. He glanced at it and his face clouded. He ran his eye down the pages, and his countenance grew portentous. It was easy to see that something was wrong. Presently he sprang up and said:

"Thunder and lighting! Do you suppose I am going to speak of those cattle that way? Do you suppose my subscribers are going to stand such gruel as that? Give me the pen!"

I never saw a pen scrape and scratch its way so viciously, or plow through another man's verbs and adjectives so relentlessly. While he was in the midst of his work, somebody shot at him through the open window, and marred the symmetry of my ear.

"Ah," said he, "that is that scoundrel Smith, of the *Moral Volcano*—he was due yesterday." And he snatched a navy revolver from his belt and fired. Smith dropped, shot in the thigh. The shot spoiled Smith's aim, who was just taking a second chance, and he crippled a stranger. It was me. Merely a finger shot off.

Then the chief editor went on with his erasures and interlineations. Just as he finished them a hand-grenade came down the stove-pipe, and the explosion shivered the stove into a thousand fragments. However, it did no further damage, except that a vagrant piece knocked a couple of my teeth out.

"That stove is utterly ruined," said the chief editor.

I said I believed it was.

"Well, no matter—don't want it in this kind of weather. I know the man that did it. I'll get him. Now, *here* is the way this stuff ought to be written."

I took the manuscript. It was scarred with erasures and interlineations till its mother wouldn't have known it if it had had one. It now reads as follows:

SPIRIT OF THE TENNESSEE PRESS

The inveterate liars of the Semi-Weekly Earthquake *are evidently endeavoring to palm off upon a noble and chivalrous people another of their vile and brutal falsehoods with regard to that most glorious conception of the nineteenth century, the Ballyhack railroad. The idea that Buzzardville was to be left off at one side originated in their own fulsome brains—or rather in the settlings which they regard as brains. They had better swallow this lie if they want to save their abandoned reptile carcasses the cowhiding they so richly deserve.*

That ass, Blossom, of the Higginsville Thunderbolt and Battle Cry of Freedom, *is down here again sponging at the Van Buren.*

We observe that the besotted blackguard of the Mud Springs Morning Howl *is giving out, with his usual propensity for lying, that Van Werter is not elected. The heaven-born mission of journalism is to disseminate truth; to eradicate error; to educate, refine, and elevate the tone of public morals and manners, and make all men more gentle, more virtuous, more charitable, and in all ways better, and holier, and happier; and yet this black-hearted scoundrel degrades his great office persistently to the dissemination of falsehood, calumny, vituperation, and vulgarity.*

Blathersville wants a Nicholson pavement—it wants a jail and a poor-house more. The idea of a pavement in a one-horse town composed of two gin-mills, a blacksmith shop, and that mustard-plaster of a newspaper, the Daily Hurrah! *The crawling insect, Buckner, who edits the* Hurrah, *is braying about his business with his customary imbecility, and imagining that he is talking sense.*

"Now *that* is the way to write—peppery and to the point. Mush-and-milk journalism gives me the fan-tods."

About this time a brick came through the window with a splintering crash, and gave me a considerable of a jolt in the back. I moved out of range—I began to feel in the way.

The chief said, "That was the Colonel, likely. I've been expecting him for two days. He will be up now right away."

He was correct. The Colonel appeared in the door a moment afterward with a dragoon revolver in his hand.

He said, "Sir, have I the honor of addressing the poltroon who edits this mangy sheet?"

"You have. Be seated, sir. Be careful of the chair, one of its legs is gone. I believe I have the honor of addressing the putrid liar, Colonel Blatherskite Tecumseh?"

"Right, sir. I have a little account to settle with you. If you are at leisure we will begin."

"I have an article on the 'Encouraging Progress of Moral and Intellectual Development in America' to finish, but there is no hurry. Begin."

Both pistols rang out their fierce clamor at the same instant. The chief lost a lock of his hair, and the Colonel's bullet ended its career in the fleshy part of my thigh. The Colonel's left shoulder was clipped a little. They fired again. Both missed their men this time, but I got my share, a shot in the arm. At the third fire both gentlemen were wounded slightly, and I had a knuckle chipped. I then said, I believed I would go out and take a walk, as this was a private matter, and I had a delicacy about participating in it further. But both gentlemen begged me to keep my seat, and assured me that I was not in the way.

They then talked about the elections and the crops while they reloaded, and I fell to tying up my wounds. But presently they opened fire again with animation, and every shot took effect—but it is proper to remark that five out of the six fell to my share. The sixth one mortally wounded the Colonel, who remarked, with fine humor, that he would have to say good morning now, as he had business uptown. He then inquired the way to the undertaker's and left.

The chief turned to me and said, "I am expecting company to dinner, and shall have to get ready. It will be a favor to me if you will read proof and attend to the customers."

I winced a little at the idea of attending to the customers, but I was too bewildered by the fusillade that was still ringing in my ears to think of anything to say.

He continued, "Jones will be here at three—cowhide him. Gillespie will call earlier, perhaps—throw him out of the window. Ferguson will be along about four—kill him. That is all for to-day, I believe. If you have any odd time, you may write a blistering article on the police—give the chief inspector rats. The cowhides are under the table; weapons in the drawer—ammunition there in the corner—lint and bandages up there in the pigeonholes. In case of accident, go to Lancet, the surgeon, down-stairs. He advertises—we take it out in trade."

He was gone. I shuddered. At the end of the next three hours I had been through perils so awful that all peace of mind and all cheerfulness were gone from me. Gillespie had called and thrown *me* out of the window. Jones arrived promptly, and when I got ready to do the cowhiding he took the job off my hands. In an encounter with a stranger, not in the bill of fare, I had lost my scalp. Another stranger, by the name of Thompson, left me a mere wreck and ruin of chaotic rags. And at last, at bay in the corner, and beset by an infuriated mob of editors, blacklegs, politicians, and desperadoes, who raved and swore and flourished their weapons about my head till the air shimmered with glancing flashes of steel, I was in the act of resigning my berth on the paper when the chief arrived, and with him a rabble of charmed and enthusiastic friends. Then ensued a scene of riot and carnage such as no human pen, or steel one either, could describe. People were shot, probed, dismembered, blown up, thrown out of the window. There was a brief tornado of murky blasphemy, with a confused and frantic war-dance glimmering through it, and then all was over. In five minutes there was silence, and the gory chief and I sat alone and surveyed the sanguinary ruin that strewed the floor around us.

He said, "You'll like this place when you get used to it."

I said, "I'll have to get you to excuse me; I think maybe I might write to suit you after a while; as soon as I had had some practice and learned the language I am confident I could. But, to speak the plain truth, that sort of energy of expression has its inconveniences, and a man is liable to interruption. You see that yourself. Vigorous writing is calculated to elevate the public, no doubt, but then I do not like to attract so much attention as it calls forth. I can't write with comfort when I am interrupted so much as I have been to-day. I like this berth well enough, but I don't like to be left here to wait on the customers. The experiences are novel, I grant you, and entertaining, too, after a fashion, but they are not judiciously distributed. A gentleman shoots at you through the window and cripples *me;* a bombshell comes down the stove-pipe for your gratification and sends the stove door down *my* throat; a friend drops in to swap compliments with you, and freckles *me* with bullet-holes till my skin won't hold my principles; you go to dinner, and Jones comes with his cowhide, Gillespie throws me out of the window, Thompson tears all my clothes off, and an entire stranger takes my scalp with the easy freedom of an old acquaintance; and in less than five minutes all the blackguards in the country arrive in their war-paint, and proceed to scare the rest of me to death with their tomahawks. Take it altogether, I never had such a spirited time in all my life as I have had to-day. No; I like you, and I like your calm unruffled way of explaining things to the customers, but you see I am not used to it. The Southern heart is too impulsive; Southern hospitality is too lavish with the stranger. The paragraphs which I have written to-day, and into whose cold sentences your masterly hand has infused the fervent spirit of Tennesseean journalism, will wake up another nest of hornets. All that mob of editors will come—and they will come hungry, too, and want somebody for breakfast. I shall have to bid you adieu. I decline to be present at these festivities. I came South for my health, I will go back on the same errand, and suddenly. Tennesseean journalism is too stirring for me."

After which we parted with mutual regret, and I took apartments at the hospital.

Plymouth Rock and the Pilgrims

Address at the First Annual Dinner, N.E. Society, Philadelphia, Dec. 22, 1881

On calling upon Mr. Clemens to make response, President Rollins said:

"This sentiment has been assigned to one who was never *exactly* born in New England, nor, perhaps, were any of his ancestors. He is not *technically*, therefore, of New England descent. Under the painful circumstances in which he has found himself, however, he has done the best he could—he has had all his children born there,[1] and has made of *himself* a New England *ancestor*. He is a self-made man. More than this, and better even, in cheerful, hopeful, helpful literature he is of New England *ascent*. To *ascend* there in anything that's reasonable is difficult, for—confidentially, with the door shut—we all know that they are the brightest, ablest sons of that goodly land who never leave it, and it is among and above *them* that Mr. Twain has made his brilliant and permanent ascent—become a man of mark."

I rise to protest. I have kept still for years, but really I think there is no sufficient justification for this sort of thing. What do you want to celebrate those people for?—those ancestors of yours of 1620—the *Mayflower* tribe, I mean. What do you want to celebrate *them* for? Your pardon: the gentleman at my left assures me that you are not celebrating the Pilgrims themselves, but the landing of the Pilgrims at Plymouth Rock on the 22d of December. So you are celebrating their landing. Why, the other pretext was thin enough, but this is thinner than ever; the other was tissue, tinfoil, fish-bladder, but this is gold-leaf. Celebrating their landing! What was there remarkable about it, I would like to know? What can you be thinking of? Why, those Pilgrims had been at sea three or four months. It was the very middle of winter: it was as cold as death off Cape Cod there. Why shouldn't they come ashore? If they *hadn't* landed there would be some reason for celebrating the fact. It would have been a case of monumental leatherheadedness which the world would not willingly let die. If it had been *you*, gentlemen, you probably wouldn't have landed, but you have no shadow of right to be celebrating, in your ancestors, gifts which they did not exercise, but only transmitted. Why, to be celebrating the mere landing of the Pilgrims—to be trying to make out that this most natural and simple and customary procedure was an extraordinary circumstance—a circumstance to be amazed

1. Twain's children were actually born in Elmira, New York, not New England.

at, and admired, aggrandized and glorified, at orgies like this for two hundred and sixty years—hang it, a horse would have known enough to land; a horse—Pardon again; the gentleman on my right assures me that it was not merely the landing of the Pilgrims that we are celebrating, but the Pilgrims themselves. So we have struck an inconsistency here—one says it was the landing, the other says it was the Pilgrims. It is an inconsistency characteristic of you intractable and disputatious tribe, for you never agree about anything but Boston. Well, then, what do you want to celebrate those Pilgrims for? They were a mighty hard lot—you know it. I grant you, without the slightest unwillingness, that they were a deal more gentle and merciful and just than were the people of Europe of that day; I grant you that they are better than their predecessors. But what of that?—that is nothing. People always progress. You are better than your fathers and grandfathers were (this is the first time I have ever aimed a measureless slander at the departed, for I consider such things improper). Yes, those among you who have not been in the penitentiary, if such there be, are better than your fathers and grandfathers were; but is that any sufficient reason for getting up annual dinners and celebrating you? No, by no means—by no means. Well, I repeat, those Pilgrims were a hard lot. They took good care of themselves, but they abolished everybody else's ancestors. I am a border-ruffian from the State of Missouri. I am a Connecticut Yankee by adoption. In me, you have Missouri morals, Connecticut culture; this, gentlemen, is the combination which makes the perfect man. But where are my ancestors? Whom shall I celebrate? Where shall I find the raw material?

My first American ancestor, gentlemen, was an Indian—an early Indian. Your ancestors skinned him alive, and I am an orphan. Later ancestors of mine were the Quakers William Robinson, Marmaduke Stevenson, *et al.* Your tribe chased them out of the country for their religion's sake; promised them death if they came back; for your ancestors had forsaken the homes they loved, and braved the perils of the sea, the implacable climate, and the savage wilderness, to acquire that highest and most precious of boons, freedom for every man on this broad continent to worship according to the dictates of his own conscience—and they were not going to allow a lot of pestiferous Quakers to interfere with it. Your ancestors broke forever the chains of political slavery, and gave the vote to every man in this wide land, excluding none!—none except those who did not belong to the orthodox church. Your ancestors—yes, they were a hard lot; but, nevertheless, they gave us religious liberty to worship as they required us to worship, and political liberty to vote as the church required; and so I the bereft one, I the forlorn one, am here to do my best to help you celebrate them right.

The Quaker woman Elizabeth Hooton was an ancestress of mine. Your people were pretty severe with her—you will confess that. But, poor thing! I believe they changed her opinions before she died, and took her into their fold; and so we have every reason to presume that when she died she went to the same place which your ancestors went to. It is a great pity, for she was a good woman. Roger Williams was an ancestor of mine. I don't really remember what your people did with him. But they banished him to Rhode Island, anyway. And then, I believe, recognizing that this was really carrying harshness to an unjustifiable extreme, they took pity on him and burned him. They were a hard lot! All those Salem witches were ancestors of mine! Your people made it tropical for them. Yes, they did; by pressure and the gallows they made such a clean deal with them that there hasn't been a witch and hardly a halter in our family from that day to this, and that is one hundred and eighty-nine years. The first slave brought into New England out of Africa by your progenitors was an ancestor of mine—for I am of a mixed breed, an infinitely shaded and exquisite Mongrel. I'm not one of your sham meerschaums that you can color in a week. No, my complexion is the patient art of eight generations. Well, in my own time, I had acquired a lot of my kin—by purchase, and swapping around, and one way and another—and was getting along very well. Then, with the inborn perversity of your lineage, you got up a war, and took them all away from me. And so, again am I bereft, again am I forlorn; no drop of my blood flows in the veins of any living being who is marketable.

O my friends, hear me and reform! I seek your good, not mine. You have heard the speeches. Disband these New England societies—nurseries of a system of steadily augmenting laudation and hosannaing, which, if persisted in uncurbed, may some day in the remote future beguile you into prevaricating and bragging. Oh, stop, stop, while you are still temperate in your appreciation of your ancestors! Hear me, I beseech you; get up an auction and sell Plymouth Rock! The Pilgrims were a simple and ignorant race. They never had seen any good rocks before, or at least any that were not watched, and so they were excusable for hopping ashore in frantic delight and clapping an iron fence around this one. But you, gentlemen, are educated; you are enlightened; you know that in the rich land of your nativity, opulent New England, overflowing with rocks, this one isn't worth, at the outside, more than thirty-five cents. Therefore, sell it, before it is injured by exposure, or at least throw it open to the patent-medicine advertisements, and let it earn its taxes.

Yes, hear your true friend—your only true friend—list to his voice. Disband these societies, hotbeds of vice, of moral decay—perpetuators of ancestral superstition. Here on this board I see water, I see milk, I see the wild and deadly lemonade. These are but steps upon the downward path. Next we shall see tea, then chocolate, then coffee—hotel coffee. A few more years—all too few, I fear—mark my words, we shall have cider! Gentlemen, pause ere it be too late. You are on the broad road which leads to dissipation, physical ruin, moral decay, gory crime, and the gallows! I beseech you, I implore you, in the name of your anxious friends, in the name of your impending widows and orphans, stop ere it be too late. Disband these New England societies, renounce these soul-blistering saturnalia, cease from varnishing the rusty reputations of your long-vanished ancestors—the super-high-moral old iron-clads of Cape Cod, the pious buccaneers of Plymouth Rock—go home, and try to learn to behave!

However, chaff and nonsense aside, I think I honor and appreciate your Pilgrim stock as much as you do yourselves, perhaps; and I indorse and adopt a sentiment uttered by a grandfather of mine once—a man of sturdy opinions, of sincere make of mind, and not given to flattery. He said: "People may talk as they like about that Pilgrim stock, but, after all's said and done, it would be pretty hard to improve on those people; and, as for me, I don't mind coming out flat-footed and saying there ain't any way to improve on them—except having them born in Missouri!"

Questions to Consider

1. Twain's *Life on the Mississippi* is sometimes categorized as autobiography and sometimes as fiction. How does Twain blur the line between the two genres in the selections offered here?
2. While Twain's renowned pessimism about the human race is more evident in his later works, can you find passages in the sections offered here that hint at that pessimism? What effect does this pessimism have on his satire?
3. Twain is sometimes known as an author of children's literature. What parts of the selections would appeal to a younger reader and what parts are obviously written for the adult reader?

VOICES IN CONTEXT

Confederate Women's Civil War Diaries

On a February day in 1861, Emma C. Holmes of Charleston, South Carolina contemplated the future of her country and became incensed. The "Black Republicans," through their "malignity and fanaticism," had fragmented the United States. The election of Abraham Lincoln to the Presidency in 1860 had signaled a critical change in American politics to Holmes, and she remarked on the mounting tensions between the North and the South since that fateful November day. Although Holmes wished mightily that a civil war might be averted, she feared that bloody battle was inevitable. "A revolution, wonderful in the rapidity with which it has swept across the country," had captured her imagination and fired her spirit. "Doubly proud am I of my native State," she boasted, "that she should be the first to arise and shake off the hated chain which linked us with 'Black Republicans and Abolitionists.' " Holmes admitted only one regret as the country inched toward war. "How I wish I had kept a journal during the last three months of great political change," she confessed. In order to compensate for her laxity during the preceding months, she chronicled in her diary what she deemed to be "the most important events" in national affairs since the election of Lincoln, which had been "fraught with the happiness, the prosperity, nay, the very existence of our future." She recognized at once the importance of her work. She soon boasted of her journal's value "as a record of events which mark the formation and growth of our glorious Southern Confederacy."

Hundreds of White women throughout the South followed suit. Certainly the art of diary-keeping was not new to White Southern women. As historian Elizabeth Fox-Genovese has noted, journaling allowed women to reflect upon their lives and ponder their place in Antebellum Southern society. Most journals, she remarked, "function[ed] as chronicles of personal, intellectual, or spiritual progress." The Civil War marked a transition in journal-keeping, as Southern White women increasingly turned to their journals to comment on the world around them. Significantly, as Steven Stowe has suggested, the diary form allowed the writer to interpret events. "A diary by its nature," Stowe explained, "encourages an intellectually active, organizing voice, putting the diarist legitimately at the center of determining the meaning of things." The war, then, provided Confederate women the opportunity to analyze political events to a heretofore unprecedented degree. Moreover, because journal-keeping had never been entirely a private affair, Confederate women could expect, at the very least, their families to read their journals. Knowing that their journals would be read, Confederate women capitalized on the opportunity to preserve an accurate record of this revolution for future generations.

Rumors, inaccuracies, and false reports constantly befuddled most diarists who wished to maintain a "true" account of the war. George Rable has noted that Confederate women's isolation from public life fostered a high degree of susceptibility to conflicting reports of "great victories and crushing defeats." "Dreadful news has come of the defeat of Lee at Gettysburg," Sarah Morgan wrote in mid-July 1863. She did not credit the report fully, however. "Think I believe it all? He may have been defeated; but not one of these accounts of total overthrow and rout do I credit." A later entry suggests that Morgan may have believed the unfavorable reports more than she let on, however. Indeed, Morgan had to muster all her strength and faith in the Confederate cause to convince her mother that all was not lost at Gettysburg. "When my own faith and belief was almost exhausted, I seized the papers that induced her to despair, hunted up stray paragraphs of encouragement, followed up conflicting statements, proved the fallacy of all, gathered comfort, forced it on her, proved the decisive struggle had not come, that Bragg would join Lee, and that 'God would have mercy upon us.' " Contradictory and incomplete reports allowed Morgan to convince her mother that all was not lost at Gettysburg.

More frustrating to these Southern women who recorded the events of the war than the myriad of rumors that floated about the home front, however, was the absence of reports altogether. "No more news," Mary Chesnut recorded in her diary on 1 July 1862. "It has settled down into this—the great battle, the decisive battle, has to be yet." Kate Cumming noted shortly after she began her nursing duties that "the people here can tell us little or nothing about the battle, except that one has been fought. How our forces have come out of it, they have not learned." The news blackouts continually stymied these women's efforts to record the latest information. Faced with maddening silences from the front, diarists anxiously filled many a page with supposition, innuendo, and sheer fantasy.

Mary Chesnut commented on the ways in which Confederate women experienced the uncertainty of war. "A telegram comes to you," she wrote. "And you leave it on your lap. You are pale with fright. You handle it, or dread to touch it, as you would a rattlesnake—worse—worse. A snake would only strike you. How many, many, this scrap of paper may tell you, have gone to their death." The constant anxiety, the wild fluctuation in emotions, Chesnut speculated, threatened women on the homefront as combat endangered soliders on the battlefield. She recounted the story of a woman who had heard contradictory reports of her son's safety. "Does anybody wonder so many women die?" Chesnut asked. "Grief and constant anxiety kill nearly as many women as men die on the battle field. Miriam's friend is at the point of death with brain fever: the sudden changes from joy to grief were more than she could bear."

In addition to providing Southern White women with a means to record the events of the war, diary-keeping afforded them the means for personal reflection and to question the Providential hand that they believed guided the South's war efforts. Sarah Morgan confessed on 16 June 1862 that "to-day I believe I am tired of life. I am weary of every thing. . . . What a consolation it is to remember there are no 'Politics' in heaven! I reserve to myself the privilege of writing my opinions, since I trouble no one with the expression of them." Mary Chesnut questioned the purpose of war and wondered whether the possibility of a viable Confederacy justified the death and carnage. "Suppose we start up grand and free—a proud young republic. Think of all these young lives sacrificed. . . . The best and the bravest of one generation swept away. [T]hey are washed away, literally, in a tide of blood. There is nothing to show they were ever on earth." Diary-keeping provided Morgan, Chesnut, and indeed many Southern women, with a means to come to terms with their crises of faith, their dark nights of the soul.

Not surprisingly, Southern White women frequently turned to their diaries to record their ill will toward the Yankees. As George Rable has argued, "condemning the Yankees as the most hateful of God's creatures masked their own hatred." It also allowed them, Rable continues, to "rationalize, modify, or abandon long-held ideas about Christian charity." Sarah Morgan recognized that no degree of rationalization could disguise women's hatred. "This war has brought out wicked, malignant feelings that I did not believe could dwell in woman's heart," she wrote in 1862. "I see some with the holiest eyes, so holy one would think the very spirit of Charity lived in them, and all Christian meekness, go off in a mad tirade of abuse and say with the holy eyes wonderously changed 'I hope God will send down plague, yellow fever, famine, on these vile Yankees, and that not one will escape death.' " Most Southern women reserved the harshest words for those federal soldiers who raided their homes. Those raids brought the war from the frontline quite literally to the home front. This intrusion into their personal space shattered any notion Southern women may have harbored about a separate domestic sphere or the ability of Confederate men to protect their women. Confederate women believed Union soldiers deemed nothing sacred, noting that they destroyed livestock, larders, and personal possessions as they marched their way across the South. The intrusion of war into the home shocked, frightened, and frustrated women, and they turned to their diaries to record their emotions.

Diary-keeping provided Southern White women with an indisputable sense of calm in troubling times. In the second year of the war, Sarah Morgan confessed, "There is no use in trying to break off journalizing, particularly in 'these trying times.' It has become a necessity to me. I believe I would go off in a rapid decline," she continued, "if the Yankees prohibited journal-keeping." Whatever purposes diary-keeping may have served, at the very least it provided Southern women a leisurely activity that they most assuredly enjoyed.

The events at Appomattox Court House stripped these women of the luxury of writing their own endings to the war. For some, the news of the Union victory provided not only the ending to their stories, but also to their desire to write new stories. "A feeling of sadness hovers over me now, day and night," Mary Chesnut wrote in a short entry for 18 May 1865, "that no words of mine can express." The end of the war did not signal the end or prevent other women from writing. It did, however, so capture the imagination of White Southerners that no story of the war could be told without the pervading sense of Confederate defeat. From 1865 on, the end of the story looms large from the opening paragraphs.

Mary Boykin Miller Chesnut
1823–1886

Mary Boykin Miller Chesnut was born into an elite slaveholding family in Statesburg, South Carolina, on 31 March 1823. Her mother, Mary Boykin Miller, came from a venerable South Carolina family. Her father, Stephen Decatur Miller, came from less prominent stock. He nevertheless managed to secure a fine education, graduating from South Carolina College in 1808. He then read law, served a term in the United States Congress, and in 1823, the year Mary was born, he was serving as a senator in the South Carolina legislature.

In 1828, Stephen Decatur Miller was elected governor of the state. He assumed office during the height of the nullification crisis, during which time radicals in South Carolina argued that the Union was a compact of states, and as the creators of the compact, states were sovereign. States' rights advocates argued that states granted to the federal government only those powers specifically enumerated in the Constitution. If the national government enacted a law not sanctioned by the Constitution, a state could deem the law unconstitutional and nullify it. Stephen Miller was an ardent supporter of nullification and taught his daughter well. Indeed, Mary developed a passionate interest in politics.

Stephen Miller entered the U.S. Senate in 1833 but resigned his seat two years later and moved the family to Mississippi, but not before he decided to supplement the informal education his talented daughter had received at home by sending the young girl to Mme Talvande's celebrated French School for Young Ladies in Charleston. By all accounts Mary Boykin Miller excelled at Mme Talvande's, studying literature, history, rhetoric, music, natural science, French, and German. After two years of study, she had developed into an accomplished young woman.

At the age of 14, Mary captured the attention of James Chesnut, a 23-year-old lawyer from a wealthy and prestigious family. Her parents, believing Mary too young for a romantic alliance, opposed the relationship, withdrawing her from the school and bringing her to Mississippi. She re-enrolled a few months later but left permanently when her father's sudden death forced the family to move back to Mississippi. By this time, James Chesnut had made his intentions clear, and in 1840 Mary and James were married. The couple resided at James's parents' plantation, located three miles south of Camden, South Carolina, until moving into their own home in Camden in 1848.

At the time of his marriage, James Chesnut had embarked on a promising political career. In 1840, voters elected him to the state legislature, where he served for six years. He later served in the state senate and was elected president of that body in 1856. In 1858, James was elected to the United States Senate and by all accounts Mary, never enthralled with her life as a plantation mistress, looked forward to the move to Washington. She soon fell in with Washington society and she later referred to her two years in the nation's capital as her "happy days."

Although James had been a political moderate and had therefore remained skeptical of secession during the political crises of 1859–1860, he resigned his senate seat immediately following Abraham Lincoln's election and returned to South Carolina to help draft the Confederate ordinance of secession. James served in a variety of capacities for the Confederacy during the war, shuttling between Montgomery, Charleston, Richmond, and Camden. Through it all, Mary maintained the journal that became her legacy. As literary scholar Elisabeth Muhlenfeld has noted in her biography of Mary Chesnut, "it is for the work she did during the last five years of her life that Mary Boykin Miller Chesnut is remembered at all, for between late 1881 and 1884 she substantially completed an expansion and revision of her Civil War journals—twenty years after they had been written." She did so with a heavy editorial hand. She employed the techniques of dialogue, characterization, and narration, which she had honed in her failed attempts at fiction writing. In the process of revision she removed "trivialities, irrelevancies, and indiscretions," but she added more material to her journal than she omitted or condensed. As historian C. Vann Woodward noted in the introduction to his edition of the Chesnut diaries, in the end, "the integrity of the author's experience is maintained . . . but not the literal record of events expected of the diarist."

Before she died in 1886, Chesnut entrusted her journals to Isabella Martin, a schoolteacher in Columbia, South Carolina, whom she had met during the war. When Martin failed to find a publisher for the journals, she stashed them away until 1904, when she met fellow Southerner Myrta Lockett Avary, whose *A Virginia Girl in the Civil War* had sold well the previous year. Within a year, Avary and Martin published *A Diary from Dixie*, purging nearly three-quarters of the already edited and revised text. Indeed, the work that emerged in 1905 bore little resemblance to Chesnut's original journals. Appleton released *A Diary from Dixie* to considerable popular and critical success.

Chesnut's position as the wife of a prominent South Carolina politician gave her access to many of the most influential statesmen and officers of the Confederacy, lending a certain air of importance to her diary. As Muhlenfeld has noted, Chesnut believed herself to be eminently qualified, by virtue of education, position, and intelligence, to comment on the world around her. Chesnut's consummate skill as a diarist and as her own editor, then, distinguished her diary from the many others who published narratives of the war years during the time. Woodward has remarked, "the importance of Mary Chesnut's work . . . lies not in autobiography, fortuitous self-revelations, or opportunities for editorial detective work . . . [but] with the life and reality with which it endows people and events and with which it evokes the chaos and complexity of a society at war."

from Mary Chesnut's Civil War

FEBRUARY 18, 1861

. . . This Southern Confederacy must be supported now by calm determination and cool brains. We have risked all, and we must play our best, for the stake is life or death. I shall always regret that I had not kept a journal during the two past delightful and eventful years. The delights having exhausted themselves in the latter part of 1860 and the events crowding in so that it takes away one's breath to think about it all. I daresay I might have recorded with some distinctness the daily shocks . . . But now it is to me one nightmare from the time I left Charleston for Florida, where I remained two anxious weeks amid hammocks and everglades, oppressed and miserable, and heard on the cars returning to the world that Lincoln was elected and our fate sealed. Saw at Fernandina a few men running up a wan Palmetto flag and crying, South Carolina has seceded. Overjoyed at the tribute to South Carolina, I said, "So Florida sympathizes." I inquired the names of our *few* but undismayed supporters in Florida. Heard Gadsden, Holmes, Porcher, &c &c—names as inevitably South Carolina's as Moses or Lazarus are Jews'. When we arrived in Charleston, my room was immediately over a supper given by the city to a delegation from Savannah, and Colonel Bartow, the mayor of

Savannah, was speaking in the hot, fervid, after-supper Southern style. They contrived to speak all night and to cheer &c. I remember liking one speech so much—*voice*, tone, temper, sentiments, and all. I sent to ask the name of the orator, and the answer came: "Mr. Alfred Huger." He may not have been the wisest of wittiest man there—but certainly when on his legs he had the best of it that night. After such a night of impassioned Southern eloquence I traveled next day with (in the first place, a racking nervous headache and a morphine bottle, and also) Colonel Colcock, formerly member of Congress, and U.S. Judge Magrath, of whom likenesses were suspended, in the frightfullest signpost style of painting, across various thoroughfares in Charleston. The happy moment seized by the painter to depict him, while Magrath was in the act, most dramatically, of tearing off his robes of office in rage and disgust at Lincoln's election.

My father was a South Carolina nullifier, governor of the state at the time of the nullification row, and then U.S. Senator. So I was of necessity a rebel born. My husband's family being equally pledged to the Union party rather exasperated at my zeal, as I heard taunts and sneers so constantly thrown out against the faith I had imbibed before I understood anything at all about it. If I do yet.

I remember feeling a nervous dread and horror of this break with so great a power as U.S.A., but I was ready and willing. South Carolina had been so rampant for years. She was the torment of herself and everybody else. Nobody could live in this state unless he were a fire-eater. Come what would, I wanted them to fight and stop talking. South Carolina—Bluffton, Rhetts, &c. had exasperated and heated themselves into a fever that only bloodletting could ever cure—it was the inevitable remedy.

So I was a seceder, *but* I dreaded the future . . .

At Kingsville, I met my husband. He had resigned his seat in the Senate U.S. and was on his way home. Had burned the shops behind him. No hope now—he was in bitter earnest.

I thought him right—but going back to Mulberry to live was indeed offering up my life on the alter of country. Secession was delayed—was very near destroyed. The members were rushing away from Columbia. That band of invincibles certainly feared smallpox. But they adjourned to Charleston and the decree was rendered there. Camden was in unprecedented excitement. Minutemen arming, with immense blue cockades and red sashes, soon with sword and gun, marching and drilling.

One of the first things which depressed me was the kind of men put in office at this crisis, invariably some sleeping deadhead long forgotten or passed over. Young and active spirits ignored, places for worn-out politicians seemed the rule—when our only hope is to use *all* the talents God has given us. This thing continues. In every state, as each election comes on, they resolutely put aside everything but the inefficient. To go back to Pickens the 1st and South Carolina. Very few understood the consequences of that quiet move of Major Anderson. At first it was looked on as a misfortune. Then, as we saw that it induced the seizure of U.S. forts in other states—we thought it a blessing in disguise. So far we were out in the cold alone. And our wise men say if the president had left us there to fret and fume awhile with a little wholesome neglect, we would have come *back* in time. Certainly nobody would have joined us. But Fort Sumter in Anderson's hands united the cotton states—and we are here in Montgomery to make a new Confederacy—a new government, constitution, &c &c . . .

* * *

February 28, 1861

In the drawing room a literary lady began a violent attack upon this mischief-making South Carolina. She told me she was a successful writer in the magazines of the day. But when I found she used "incredible" for "incredulous," I said not a word in defense of my native land. I left her "incredible." Another person came in while she was pouring upon me home truths and asked her if she did not know I was a Carolinian. Then she gracefully reversed her engine and took the other tack—sounded our praises. But I left her incredible—and I remained incredulous, too.

Brewster says the war specs are growing in size. Nobody at the North nor in Virginia believes we are in earnest. They think we are sulking and that Jeff Davis and Stephens[1] are getting up a very pretty little comedy . . .

* * *

March 4, 1861

. . . So I have seen a negro woman sold—up on the block—at auction. I was walking. The woman on the block overtopped the crowd. I felt faint—seasick. The creature looked so like my good little Nancy. She was a bright mulatto with a pleasant face. She was magnificently gotten up in silks and satins. She seemed delighted with it all—sometimes ogling the bidders, sometimes looking quite coy and modest, but her mouth never relaxed from its expanded grin of excitement. I daresay the poor thing knew who would buy her.

I sat down on a stool in a shop. I disciplined my wild thoughts. I tried it Sterne[2] fashion.

You know how women sell themselves and are sold in marriage, from queens downward, eh?

You know what the Bible says about slavery—and marriage. Poor women. Poor slaves. Sterne with his starling. What did he know? He only thought—he did not feel.

* * *

November 27, 1861

. . . On the one side Mrs. Stowe, Greeley, Thoreau, Emerson, Sumner, in nice New England homes—clean, clear, sweet-smelling—shut up in libraries, writing books which ease their hearts of their bitterness to us, or editing newspapers—all [of] which pays better than anything else in the world. Even the politician's hobbyhorse—antislavery is the beast to carry him highest.

What self-denial do they practice? It is the cheapest philanthropy trade in the world—easy. Easy as setting John Brown to come down here and cut our throats in Christ's name.

Now, what I have seen of my mother's life, my grandmother's, my mother-in-law's:

These people were educated at Northern schools mostly—read the same books as their Northern contenders, the same daily newspapers, the same Bible—have the same ideas of right and wrong—are highbred, lovely, good, pious—doing their duty as they

1. Alexander Stephens, vice president of the C.S.A.

2. See Laurence Sterne, A *Sentimental Journey Through France and Italy*, (1768).

conceive it. They live in negro villages. They do not preach and teach hate as a gospel and the sacred duty of murder and insurrection, but they strive to ameliorate the condition of these Africans in every particular. They set them the example of a perfect life—life of utter self-abnegation. Think of these holy New Englanders, forced to have a negro village walk through their houses whenever they saw fit—dirty, slatternly, idle, ill-smelling by nature (when otherwise, it is the exception). These women are more troubled by their duty to negroes, have less chance to live their own lives in peace than if they were African missionaries. They have a swarm of Blacks about them as children under their care—not as Mrs. Stowe's fancy paints them, but the hard, unpleasant, unromantic, undeveloped savage Africans. And they hate slavery worse that Mrs. Stowe. Bookmaking which leads you to a round of visits among crowned heads is an easier way to be a saint than martyrdom down here, doing unpleasant duty among them—with no reward but John Browning drawn over your head in this world and threats of what is to come to you from blacker devils in the next. They have the plaudits of crowned heads. We take our chance, doing our duty as best we may among the wooly heads. I do not do anything whatever but get out of their way. When I come home, I see the negroes themselves. They look as comfortable as possible and I hear all they have to say. Then I see the overseer and the Methodist parson. *None* of these complain of each other. And I am satisfied. My husband supported his plantation by his law practice. Not it is running him in debt. We are bad managers. Our people have never earned their own bread. . . .

. . . I say we are no better than our judges North—and *no worse*. We are human beings of the nineteenth century—and slavery has to go, of course. All that has been gained by it goes to the North and to negroes. The slave-owners, when they are good men and women, are the martyrs. And as far as I have seen, the people here are quite as good as anywhere else. I hate slavery. I even hate the harsh authority I see parents think it their duty to exercise *toward their children*.

There now!! What good does it do to write all that? I have before me a letter I wrote to Mr. C while he was on our plantation in Mississippi in 1842. It is the most fervid abolition document I have ever read. I came across it, burning letters the other day. That letter I did not burn. I kept it—as showing how we are not as much of heathens down here as our enlightened enemies think. Their philanthropy is cheap. There are as noble, pure lives here as there—and a great deal more of self-sacrifice . . .

* * *

APRIL 30, 1862

The last day of this month of calamities. Lovell left the women and children to be shelled and took the army to a safe place. I do not understand. Why not send the women and children to the safe place and let the army stay where the fighting was to be? Armies are to save, not to be saved—at least, to be saved is not their raison d'être, exactly. If this goes on the spirit of our people will be broken.

* * *

JUNE 9, 1862

. . . When we read of the battles in India, in Italy, in the Crimea—what did we care? Only an interesting topic like any other to look for in the paper.

Now you hear of a battle with a thrill and a shudder. It has come home to us. Half the people that we know in the world are under the enemy's guns.

A telegram comes to you. And you leave it on your lap. You are pale with fright. You handle it, or dread to touch it, as you would a rattlesnake—worse—worse. A snake would only strike you. How many, many, this scrap of paper may tell you, have gone to their death.

When you meet people, sad and sorrowful is the greeting: thy press your hand, tears stand in their eyes or roll down their cheeks, as they happen to have more or less self-control. They have brothers, fathers, or sons—as the case may be—in the battle. And this thing now seems never to stop. We have no breathing time given us. It cannot be so at the North, for the papers say gentlemen do not go in the ranks there. They are officers or clerks of departments, &c&c&c. Then, we see so many foreign regiments among our prisoners. Germans—Irish—Scotch. The proportion of trouble is awfully against us. Every company on the field is filled with our nearest and dearest—rank and file, common soldiers.

Miriam's story today:

A woman she knew heard her son was killed—had hardly taken in the horror of it, when they came to say it was all a mistake—mistake of name. She fell on her knees with a shout of joy. "Praise the Lord, oh, my soul!" She cried in her wild delight. The household were totally upset. The swing back of the pendulum from the scene of weeping and wailing of a few moments before was very exciting. In the midst of this hubbub, the hearse drove up with the poor boy in his metallic coffin.

Does anybody wonder so many women die? Grief and constant anxiety kill nearly as many women as men die on the battlefield. Miriam's friend is at the point of death with brain fever: the sudden changes from joy to grief were more than she could bear . . .

* * *

JULY 1, 1862

No more news. It has settled down into this—the great battle, the decisive battle, has to be fought yet. . . .

Edward Cheves—only son of John Cheves—killed. His sister kept crying, "Oh, mother, what shall we do—Edward is killed!" But the mother sat dead still, white as a sheet, never uttering a word or shedding a tear.

Are our women losing the capacity to weep? The father came today, Mr. John Cheves. He has been making infernal machines in Charleston to blow up Yankee ships . . .

* * *

JULY 10, 1862

. . . After all, suppose we do all we hoped. Suppose we start up grand and free—a proud young republic. Think of all these young lives sacrificed! If three for one be killed, what comfort is that? What good will that do Mrs. Hayne or Mary DeSaussure? The best and the bravest of one generation swept away! Henry DeSaussure has left four sons to honor their father's memory and emulate his example. But those poor boys of between 18 and 20 years of age—Haynes, Trezevants, Taylors, Rhetts, &c&c.—they are washed away, literally, in a tide of blood. There is nothing to show they ever were on earth . . .

* * *

JULY 26, 1864

. . . When I remember all the true-hearted, the lighthearted, the gay and the gallant boys who have come laughing, singing, dancing in my way in the three years past, I have looked into their brave young eyes and helped them as I could every way and then seen them no more forever. They lie stark and cold, dead upon the battlefield or moldering away in hospitals or prisons—which is worse. I think, if I consider the long array of those bright youths and loyal men who have gone to their deaths almost before my very eyes, my heart might break, too.

Is anything worth it? This fearful sacrifice—this awful penalty we pay for war? . . .

* * *

FEBRUARY 16, 1865

. . . We thought if the negroes were ever so loyal to us, they could not protect me from an army bent upon sweeping us from the face of the earth. And if they tried to do so—so much the worse for the poor things with their Yankee friends. So I left them to shift for themselves, as they are accustomed to do—and I took the same liberty.

My husband does not care a fig for the property question. Never did. Perhaps if he had ever known poverty it would be different. He talked beautifully about it—as he always does about everything. I have told him often if at heaven's gates St. Peter will listen to him awhile—let him tell his own story—he will get in, and they may give him a crown extra.

Now he says he has only one care—that I should be safe and not so harassed with dread.

. . . Here I am brokenhearted—an exile . . .

The Fants are refugees here, too. They are Virginians, too, and have been in exile since Second Manassas. Poor things, they seem to have been everywhere and seen and suffered everything. They even tried to go back to their own house. Of that they found one chimney alone standing which had also been taken possession of by a Yankee in this wise . . .

The day I left home, I had packed a box of flour, sugar, rice, coffee, &c&c, but my husband would not let me bring it. He said I was coming to a land of plenty. Unexplored North Carolina, where the foot of Yankee Marauder was unknown—and in Columbia they would need food.

Now I have written to send me that box and many other things by Laurence, or I will starve.

* * *

MAY 16, 1865

We are scattered—stunned—the remnant of heart left alive with us, filled with brotherly hate.

We sit and wait until the drunken tailor who rules the U.S.A. issues a proclamation and defines our anomalous position.

Such a hue and cry—whose fault? Everybody blamed by somebody else. Only the dead heroes left stiff and stark on the battlefield escape.

"Blame every man who stayed home and did not fight. I will not stop to hear excuses. Not one word against those who stood out until the bitter end and stacked muskets at Appomattox." . . .

MAY 18, 1865

. . . A feeling of sadness hovers over me now, day and night, that no words of mine can express.

BLACK 4TH OF JULY 1865

. . . They talked of the negroes wherever the Yankees had been, who flocked to them and showed them where the silver and valuables were hid by the White people. Ladies' maids dressing themselves in their mistresses' gowns before their faces and walking off. Two sides to stories. Now, before this, everyone told me how kind and faithful and considerate the negroes had been. I am sure, after hearing these tales, the fidelity of my own servants shines out brilliantly. I had taken it too much as a matter of course.

Yesterday there was a mass meeting of negroes, thousands of them were in town, eating, drinking, dancing, speechifying. Preaching and prayer was also a popular amusement. They have no greater idea of amusement than wild prayers—unless it be getting married or going to a funeral.

In the afternoon I had some business on our place, the Hermitage. John drove me down. Our people were all at home—quiet, orderly, respectful, and at their usual work. In point of fact things looked unchanged. There was nothing to show that anyone of them had even seen a Yankee or knew that there was one in existence.

"We are in for a new St. Domingo[3] all the same. The Yankees have raised the devil, and now they cannot guide him."

QUESTIONS TO CONSIDER

1. In what ways does Mary Chesnut's diary illuminate the class position of the author? In what ways does it transcend the retelling of day-to-day events to reveal the tensions faced by a society at war?
2. How do you evaluate Mary Chesnut's diary as a historical document knowing that she revised it significantly during the 1880s?

Kate Cumming

1828–1909

Kate Cumming, the daughter of a wealthy merchant from Mobile, Alabama, began her nursing duties shortly after the Civil War's Battle of Shiloh, in April 1862. In one of the entries recorded early in her journal she noted that "there seems to be no order" at the hospital. "All do as they please. We have men for nurses," she continued, "and the doctors complain very much at the manner in which they are appointed; they are detailed from the different regiments, like guards. We have a new set every few hours. I can not see how it is possible for them to take proper care of the men, as nursing is a thing that has to be learned, and we should select our best men for it—the best, not physically, but morally—as I am certain that none but good, conscientious persons will ever do justice to the patients." Cumming expressed a common sentiment that linked nursing with virtue. Some historians have noted that perceptions of women's moral superiority softened the potential threat to gender hierarchy generated by wartime demands on women to work outside the home. "When women nursed sick, wounded, and dying soldiers," George C. Rable has argued, "they also nurtured conventional ideas about their own place and character."

3. St. Domingo, site of a 1791 slave revolt.

Other historians have stressed the transformative nature of female nursing during the Civil War. Drew Faust notes that although "the notion that woman's moral and emotional attributes uniquely fitted her for hospital work gained strength and currency," resistance to female nursing persisted. Much of the opposition stemmed from the fear of upsetting class and gender sensibilities. Nursing required some degree of intimacy with male bodies, "often those of the 'degraded' classes," Faust continues. Wartime exigencies, including "manpower shortages, escalating casualty rates, and patriotic ambition," however, "overrode custom and pushed Southern women toward work with the sick and the wounded." Yet, nursing remained "the focus of public debate as well as the site of overt class and gender conflict" within the Confederacy.

The disorder of which Kate spoke in that early diary entry was not uncommon. Many women labored in "make-shift facilities." Some opened their homes to care for the wounded, others set up hospitals near camps, while others still worked at wayside hospitals near railroad depots to care for the sick and wounded soldiers on their way home. Staffing shortages plagued many hospitals. "Hospitals followed no regular application or appointment procedures," according to George C. Rable. Although applications flooded the War Department, many women could not find positions. Moreover, the horror of hospital work forced many Confederate women to find other outlets for patriotic expression. If the sight of blood and severed body parts and the stench of disease did not give women pause, the "drudgery of daily work in the wards . . . soon took most of the romance out of hospital service." Those who remained confronted shortages and high prices for food and medical materials, contributing to the sense of chaos found in many hospitals.

Kate Cumming frequently commented on the medical procedures performed on wounded soldiers. Her account bears out studies that suggest the hospital staff was unable to "aid recovery in any medically significant way." Gerald F. Linderman notes that doctors, "still ignorant of the relationship between germs and infection, . . . amputated wounded limbs and then administered stimulants in a misguided effort to forestall sepsis." Nurses' primary duty, Linderman continues, "was to encourage in the wounded soldier a receptivity to nature's action, a task more moral than medical." Nurses held moral suasion over their patients; they encouraged their patients to suffer nobly and die courageously.

Historians evaluate the effectiveness of women's wartime nursing differently. Rable, for example, argues that "the accomplishments of Confederate nurses were impressive." He notes that most matrons managed their hospitals skillfully, pointing out that the mortality rate of hospitals run by women was half the rate of hospitals run by men. Drew Faust argues instead that "women's overall record was one of failure, not success." To support her assertion, she cites women's avoidance of hospital work, which, on some level, continued to threaten Antebellum notions of class and gender hierarchy. Both Faust and Rable agree, however, that women's nursing experiences during the Civil War did not engender much change in the postwar South. As Rable has observed, few Southerners, male or female, assumed that nursing had been anything more than a "temporary job in crisis times for women who would ultimately resume their places as wives and mothers." Women such as Kate Cumming, Rable and Faust suggest, wrote their memoirs and then faded from public view, as shown in the following excerpts, which detail Cumming's first two months as a Confederate nurse.

from Kate: The Journal of a Confederate Nurse

APRIL 7, 1862

I left Mobile by the Mobile and Ohio Railroad for Corinth, with Rev. Mr. Miller and a number of Mobile ladies. We are going for the purpose of taking care of the sick and wounded of the army.

As news has come that a battle is now raging,[1] there are not a few anxious hearts in the party—my own among the number, as I have a young brother, belonging to

1. The Battle of Shiloh (Pittsburg Landing), Tennessee, 6–7 April 1862, was one of the bloodiest battles of the Civil War.

Ketchum's Battery,[2] who I know will be in the midst of the fight, and I have also many dear friends there.

A gentleman, Mr. Skates, has heard that his son is among the killed, and is with us on his way to the front to bring back the remains of him who a short time since formed one of his family circle. May God give strength to the mother and sisters now mourning the loss of their loved one! May they find consolation in the thought that he died a martyr's death; was offered up a sacrifice upon the altar of his country; and that, when we have gained our independence, he, with the brave comrades who fought and fell with him, will ever live in the hearts and memories of a grateful people! I can not look at Mr. Skates without asking myself how many of us may ere long be likewise mourners! It is impossible to suppress these gloomy fore-bodings.

About midnight, at one of the stations, a dispatch was received prohibiting any one from going to Corinth without a special permit from head-quarters. Our disappointment can be better imagined than described. As military orders are peremptory, there is nothing for us to do but to submit. Mr. Miller has concluded to stop at one of the small towns, as near Corinth as he can get, and there wait until he receives permission for us to go on.

* * *

APRIL 11, 1862

Miss Booth and myself arrived at Corinth to-day. It was raining when we left Mrs. Henderson's, and as her carriage was out of repair, she sent us to the depot in an open wagon. We enjoyed the novel ride, and began to feel that we were in the *service* in reality. My heart beat high with expectation as we neared Corinth. As I had never been where there was a large army, and had never seen a wounded man, except in the cars, as they passed, I could not help feeling a little nervous at the prospect of now seeing both. When within a few miles of the place, we could realize the condition of an army immediately after a battle. As it had been raining for days, water and mud abounded. Here and there were wagons hopelessly left to their fate, and men on horseback trying to wade through it. As far as the eye could reach, in the midst of all this slop and mud, the white tents of our brave army could be seen through the trees, making a picture suggestive of any thing but comfort. My thoughts wandered back to the days of ancient Corinth, and the time it was besieged by the brave and warlike Romans, when the heroic Greeks had to succumb through the fault of their commander. I think of this only in contrast; for the Federals are as unlike the former as our fate will be unlike that of the latter. We have not a Diæus commanding, but the dauntless Beauregard and patriotic Bragg, who, knowing their rights, dare and will maintain them, though the whole North be arrayed against them. I am certain of one thing: that neither the Roman nor Greek armies, brave as history has portrayed them, were composed of more high-souled and determined men than those of ours.

Corinth is at the junction of the Memphis and Charleston and the Mobile and Ohio Railroads, about one hundred and twenty miles east from Memphis, and three hundred miles north from Mobile.

The crowd of men at the depot was so great that we found it impossible to get to our place of destination by ourselves. Mr. Miller was not there to meet us. I met Mr. George Redwood of Mobile, who kindly offered to pilot us. We found Mr. Miller and all the ladies busy in attending to the wants of those around them. They had not been assigned to any particular place, but there is plenty for them to do. We are at the

2. Part of the Army of Mississippi, First Division, Second Corps, Third Brigade that took part in the Battle of Shiloh.

Tishomingo Hotel, which, like every other large building, has been taken for a hospital. The yellow flag is flying from the top of each. Mrs. Ogden tried to prepare me for the scenes which I should witness upon entering the wards. But alas! nothing that I had ever heard or read had given me the faintest idea of the horrors witnessed here. I do not think that words are in our vocabulary expressive enough to present to the mind the realities of that sad scene. Certainly, none of the glories of the war were presented here. But I must not say that; for if uncomplaining endurance is glory, we had plenty of it. If it is that which makes the hero, here they were by scores. Gray-haired men—men in the pride of manhood—beardless boys—Federals and all, mutilated in every imaginable way, lying on the floor, just as they were taken from the battle-field; so close together that it was almost impossible to walk without stepping on them. I could not command my feelings enough to speak, but thoughts crowded upon me. O, if the authors of this cruel and unnatural war could but see what I saw there, they would try and put a stop to it! To think, that it is man who is working all this woe upon his fellow-man. What can be in the minds of our enemies, who are now arrayed against us, who have never harmed them in any way, but simply claim our own, and nothing more! May God forgive them, for surely they know not what they do.

This was no time for recrimination; there was work to do; so I went at it to do what I could. If I were to live a hundred years, I should never forget the poor sufferers' gratitude; for every little thing, done for them—a little water to drink, or the bathing of their wounds—seemed to afford them the greatest relief.

The Federal prisoners are receiving the same attention as our own men; they are lying side by side. Many are just being brought in from the battle-field. The roads are so bad that it is almost impossible to get them moved at all. A great many ladies are below stairs: so I thought that I had better assist above. The first thing which I did was to aid in giving the men their supper, consisting of bread, biscuit, and butter, and tea and coffee, without milk. There were neither waiters nor plates; they took what we gave them in their hands, and were glad to get it. I went with a lady to give some Federal officers their supper, who were in a room by themselves; only one or two of them were wounded. One, a captain from Cincinnati, had a broken arm. Before I went in, I thought that I would be polite, and say as little as possible to them; but when I saw them laughing, and apparently indifferent to the woe which they had been instrumental in bringing upon us, I could not help being indignant; and when one of them told me he was from Iowa, and that was generally called out of the world, I told him that was where I wished him, and all like him, so that they might not trouble us any more.

April 12, 1862

I sat up all night, bathing the men's wounds, and giving them water. Every one attending to them seemed completely worn out. Some of the doctors told me that they had scarcely slept since the battle. As far as I have seen, the surgeons are very kind to the wounded, and nurse as well as doctor them.

The men are lying all over the house, on their blankets, just as they were brought from the battle-field. They are in the hall, on the gallery, and crowded into very small rooms. The foul air from this mass of human beings at first made me giddy and sick, but I soon got over it. We have to walk, and when we give the men any thing kneel, in blood and water; but we think nothing of it at all. There was much suffering among the patients last night; one old man groaned all the time. He was about sixty years of age, and had lost a leg. He lived near Corinth, and had come there the morning of the battle to see his two sons, who were in the army, and he could not resist shouldering his musket and going into the fight. I comforted him as well as I could. He is a religious man, and prayed nearly all night.

Another, a very young man, was wounded in the leg and through the lungs, had a most excruciating cough, and seemed to suffer awfully. One fine-looking man had a dreadful wound in the shoulder. Every time I bathed it he thanked me, and seemed grateful. He died this morning before breakfast. Men who were in the room with him told me that he prayed all night. I trust that he is now at rest, far from this dreary world of strife and bloodshed. I could fill whole pages with descriptions of the scenes before me.

Other ladies have their special patients, whom they never leave. One of them, from Natchez, Miss., has been constantly by a young man, badly wounded, ever since she came here, and the doctors say that she has been the means of saving his life. Many of the others are doing the same. Mrs. Ogden and the Mobile ladies are below stairs. I have not even time to speak to them. Mr. Miller is doing much good; he is comforting the suffering and dying, and has already baptized some.

This morning, when passing the front door, a man asked me if I had any thing to eat, which I could give to some men at the depot awaiting transportation on the cars. He said that they had eaten nothing for some days. Some of the ladies assisting me, we took them hot coffee, bread, and meat. The poor fellows ate eagerly, and seemed so thankful. One of the men, who was taking care of them, asked me where I was from. When I replied Mobile, he said that Mobile was the best place in the Confederacy. He was a member of the Twenty-first Alabama Regiment; I have forgotten his name. I have been busy all day, and can scarcely tell what I have been doing; I have not taken time even to eat, and certainly not time to sit down. There seems to be no order. All do as they please. We have men for nurses, and the doctors complain very much at the manner in which they are appointed; they are detailed from the different regiments, like guards. We have a new set every few hours. I can not see how it is possible for them to take proper care of the men, as nursing is a thing that has to be learned, and we should select our best men for it—the best, not physically, but morally—as I am certain that none but good, conscientious persons will ever do justice to the patients.

* * *

APRIL 17, 1862

I was going round as usual this morning, washing the faces of the men, and had got half through with one before I found out that he was dead. He was lying on the gallery by himself, and had died with no one near him. These are terrible things, and, what is more heart-rending, no one seems to mind them. I thought that my patients were all doing well. Mr. Wasson felt better, and knew that he would soon go home. I asked the surgeon who was attending him about his condition, and was much shocked when I learned that neither he nor Mr. Regan would live to see another day. This was a sad trial to me. I had seen many die, but none of them whom I had attended so closely as these two. I felt toward them as I do toward all the soldiers—as if they were my brothers. I tried to control my feelings before Mr. Wasson, as he was so hopeful of getting well, but it was a hard task. He looked at me once and asked me what was the matter; was he going to die? I asked him if he was afraid. He replied no; but he was so young that he would like to live a little longer, and would like to see his father and mother once more. I did what I could to prepare him for the great change which was soon to come over him, but I could not muster courage to tell him that he was going to die. Poor Mr. Regan was wandering in his mind, and I found it useless to talk to him upon the subject of death. I managed to get him to tell me his mother's address. He belonged to the Twenty-second Alabama Regiment.

About dark a strange doctor was visiting the patients. When he came to Mr. Wasson, I was sitting by his bedside. He asked me if this was a relative. I informed him that he was not, but I had been attending to him for some days, and he now seemed like one. Mr. Wasson looked at him and said, "Doctor, I wish you to tell me if I am going to die." The doctor felt his pulse and replied, "Young man, you will never see another day in this world." A pallor passed over his countenance, and for a little while he could not speak. When he did, he looked at me and said, "Sister, I want to meet you in heaven," and then requested me to get a clergyman to visit him. There happened to be one in the hospital. I sent for him, and he prayed and talked with him for some time. Mr. Wasson then asked me if I could not let his brothers know his condition; he had two or three in Corinth. A friend who was with him did all in his power to inform them, so that they could see him before he died, but it was of no avail. They were sick, and we could not ascertain in what hospital they were confined. He was much disappointed in not seeing them. He then asked me to write to his mother, who lives in Grimes County, Texas. He desired me to inform her that he had made his peace with God, and hoped to meet her in that land where all is peace and happiness. He would have rejoiced to have seen her and the rest of his dear relatives before leaving this world, but the Lord had willed it otherwise, and he was resigned.

* * *

April 19, 1862

Had quite a number of deaths up-stairs to-day. Jesse H. Faught, Walker County, Ala., and John M. Purdy, Morgan County, Tennessee, were of the number. The latter had his brother with him, who is much grieved because he can not inform his mother of the death of her son, as his home is in possession of the enemy. Another man, by the name of Benjamin Smith, from Memphis, Tenn., and a member of the Sixth Tennessee, Volunteers, died. When I went to see him, I found him in the last agonies of death. I was informed that he was a native of Canada. He was scarcely able to speak; when he did so, he asked me to write to his sister, Mrs. H. Hartman, Arovia, Canada West. I regretted that I did not see him sooner, and felt grieved to see him die so far away from home and kindred—I will not say among strangers—none are who are fighting with us in our sacred cause. May his soul rest in peace! He has lost his life in defense of liberty—that of which his own country is so proud—and when maidens come to deck the graves of our Southern patriots, they will not forget one who sacrificed all for them. I have only written the names of those whom I can recollect; many a poor fellow dies of whom I know nothing.

Mrs. Gilmer is leaving us. I am informed that she has done much for the soldiers, having been in hospitals from the commencement of the war. She returns to her home in Memphis. It is rumored that we are going to evacuate that city, and she wishes to see her family before the enemy reaches it.

I received a letter, and a box filled with eggs, crackers, and nice fresh butter, from Miss Lucy Haughton. She also sends a lot of pickles, which the men relish very much. I hope all the ladies in the Confederacy will be as kind; if they could only witness one-half the suffering that we do, I know they would be. I have sometimes felt like making a vow to eat nothing but what was necessary to sustain life till the war is over, so that our soldiers can have the more. When the men are first brought to the hospital, they eat all they can get, but in a few days their wounds begin to tell upon their systems; their appetites leave them, and it is almost impossible to get them to eat any thing. None but those who are the most severely wounded are left here; all are carried to the rear as soon as they are able to be moved.

A young man, by the name of Farmer, of the Sixth Kentucky Regiment, died down-stairs a day or two ago. He is reported to have been very rich. His brother-in-law, Rev. Mr. Cook, was with him, and intends taking his body to his own home in Tennessee, as the young man's home is in the hands of the enemy. I have made the acquaintance of two of his friends, Mr. Chinn and Lieutenant Minor, both from Kentucky. I feel sorry for all from that state, as it has behaved so badly, and for those who are in our army, as they have given up their all for the cause.

I was shocked at what the men have told me about some dead Federals that they saw on the battle-field. They say that on the bands of their hats was written, "Hell or Corinth;" meaning, that they were determined to reach one of the places. Heaven help the poor wretches who could degrade themselves thus. I can not but pity them, and pray that God will turn the hearts of their living comrades. Can such a people expect to prosper? Are they really mad enough to think that they can conquer us—a people who shudder at such blasphemy; who, as a nation, have put our trust in the God of battles, and whose sense of the magnanimous would make us scorn to use such language?

I was much amused to-day at an answer that a Federal captain gave to one of our doctors. The doctor asked him how many men the Federals lost at the battle of Shiloh. He answered, not more than eight hundred. The doctor turned away from him without speaking. I laughed, and said that proved them greater cowards than ever; for if that was the case, why did they not take Corinth, as they had come there for that purpose. I do hope that we will let the Federals have the honor of telling all the untruths, and that we will hold to the truth, let the consequences be what they may—remembering that "where boasting ends true dignity begins." The captain is an intelligent man, and was an editor of a newspaper in Cincinnati. The rest of the officers who were in the room with him have left, except a lieutenant, who is sick.

April 22, 1862

All the patients are being sent away on account of the prospects of a battle; at least, those who are able to be moved.

We have had a good deal of cold, wet weather lately. This is the cause of much sickness. Dr. Hereford, chief surgeon of Ruggles's brigade, has just informed me, that nearly our whole army is sick, and if it were not that the Federals are nearly as bad off as ourselves, they could annihilate us with ease. The doctor related an incident to me, which I think worthy of record. Before the battle of Shiloh, as the brigades and divisions were in battle array, with their banners flaunting in the breeze, Dr. Hereford discovered that General Ruggles's brigade had none. He rode up to him and asked him the reason; just at that moment a rainbow appeared; the general, pointing to it with his sword, exclaimed, "Behold my battle-flag!"

Every one is talking of the impending battle with the greatest indifference. It is strange how soon we become accustomed to all things; and I suppose it is well, as it will do no good to worry about it. Let us do our duty, and leave the rest to God.

It is reported that Fremont is about to reinforce the Federals; I am afraid that it will go hard with us.

APRIL 23, 1862

A young man whom I have been attending is going to have his arm cut off. Poor fellow! I am doing all that I can to cheer him. He says that he knows that he will die, as all who have limbs amputated in this hospital have died. It is but too true; such is the case. It is said that the reason is that none but the very worst cases are left here, and they are too far gone to survive the shock which the operation gives the frame. The doctors seem to think that the enemy poisoned their balls, as the wounds inflame terribly; but I scarcely think that they are capable of so great an outrage. Our men do not seem to stand half so much as the Northerners. Many of the doctors are quite despondent about it, and think that our men will not be able to endure the hardships of camp-life, and that we may have to succumb on account of it; but I trust that they are mistaken. None of the prisoners have yet died; this is a fact that can not be denied; but we have had very few of them in comparison with the number of our own men.

APRIL 24, 1862

Mr. Isaac Fuquet, the young man who had his arm cut off, died to-day. He lived only a few hours after the amputation. The operation was performed by Surgeon Chaupin of New Orleans, whose professional abilities are very highly commended. Dr. Hereford was well acquainted with Mr. Fuquet and intends to inform his mother of his death.

It is reported that an engagement is going on at Monterey. A wounded man has just been brought in.

The amputating table for this ward is at the end of the hall, near the landing of the stairs. When an operation is to be performed, I keep as far away from it as possible. To-day, just as they had got through with Mr. Fuquet, I was compelled to pass the place, and the sight I there beheld made me shudder and sick at heart. A stream of blood ran from the table into a tub in which was the arm. It had been taken off at the socket, and the hand, which but a short time before grasped the musket and battled for the right, was hanging over the edge of the tub, a lifeless thing. I often wish I could become as callous as many seem to be, for there is no end to these horrors.

The passage to the kitchen leads directly past the amputating room below stairs, and many a time I have seen the blood running in streams from it.

There is a Mr. Pinkerton from Georgia shot through the head. A curtain is drawn across a corner where he is lying to hide the hideous spectacle, as his brains are oozing out.

* * *

APRIL 29, 1862

About one hundred sick men were brought in last night, on their way to another hospital. We gave them coffee, bread, and meat, with which they were much pleased. Some of them were too sick to eat this, so we gave these the few eggs we had.

General Sterling Price,[3] with a part of his army, has arrived. He is in this hospital. We were all introduced to him. He gave us his left hand, as his right was disabled from a wound received at the battle of Elkhorn.[4] I told him that I felt that we were

3. General Sterling Price, C.S.A. (1809–1867), arrived too late to participate in the Battle of Shiloh. He was part of General P. G. T. Beauregard's defense of Corinth, Mississippi, April 1862.

4. Battle of Elkhorn Tavern (Pea Ridge), Arkansas, 6–8 March 1862.

safe in Corinth now, since he and his brave followers had arrived. He gave me a very dignified bow, and, I thought, looked at me as if he *thought* that I was talking a great deal of nonsense. He was not behind his sex in complimenting the ladies for the sacrifices they are making in doing their duty. I have heard so much of that lately, that I sometimes wonder if the Southern women never did their duty before. I meant what I said to the general, and I felt quite proud of the honor I enjoyed in shaking hands with him whose name has become a household word with all admirers of true patriotism, and whose deeds of heroism in the West have endeared him to his followers, so that they look on him more as a father than any thing else.

In the afternoon he visited the patients. Many of them were men who had fought under him, and all were delighted to see him. One of them, Captain Dearing, was wounded at the battle of Shiloh. He was quarter-master in Blythe's Mississippi Regiment, and when the battle came off could not resist the temptation of engaging in it. He is badly wounded in two places, but is doing well. He is from Kentucky, but is a native of the Emerald Isle. I can not help contrasting these men with those born in the South, they seem to be able to endure physically so much more than the Southerners. We have had quite a number of them, and I do not recollect that any have died.

* * *

MAY 6, 1862

Mr. Jones is dead; he was eighteen years of age. He died the death of a Christian; was a brave soldier; true to his God and country. Miss Henderson sat up all night with him. She is endeavoring to procure a coffin for him. We have none now in which to bury the dead, as the Federals have destroyed the factory at which they were made. At one time, I thought that it was dreadful to have the dead buried without them; but there is so much suffering among the living, that I pay little heed to those things now. It matters little what becomes of the clay after the spirit has left it. Men who die as ours do, need "no useless coffin" to enshrine them. . . .

* * *

MAY 9, 1862

A great many wounded men, both Federal and Confederate, were brought in to-day. About twenty-five of ours were shot through mistake. A fine-looking Federal captain is wounded in three or four places. His head and face are tied up, and he can not speak. He has a Bible, on the back of which is printed the Union flag. Some of us were looking at it; one of the ladies remarked that it was still sacred in her eyes. This astonished me, after the suffering which we had seen it the innocent cause of. I said that it was the most hateful thing which I could look at; as every stripe in it recalled to my mind the gashes that I had witnessed upon our men. I have conversed with a number of the prisoners; they all express the same opinion as the others, that they dislike Lincoln and the abolitionists as much as we do, but they are fighting for the Union. What a delusion!

I am no politician. I must own to ignorance in regard to federal or state rights; but I think I have a faint idea of the meaning of the word "union." According to Webster[5] and other authorities, it is concord, agreement, and conjunction of mind.

5. Daniel Webster, Massachusetts senator, orator, and defender of the Union.

We all know how little of that and happiness exists in a forced union of man and wife, where there is neither love nor congeniality of feeling. Can these men really think it when they say it? Are they so blind as to think, even if they succeed, that it can ever bring happiness to them or us? Is it not exactly the same as the case of the marriage state? They must strike out the word union, and have in its stead monarchy or anarchy; one of these, perhaps, would be better. Why, the Czar of Russia lays no higher claim to the right to rule his empire than do these men the right to govern us. Again, supposing they do succeed in subjugating us, have they forgotten that such a thing is not on record, where the Anglo-Saxon race has ever been held in bondage? Why, it would be as much to their disgrace as ours. Are we not the same race? Let them ask themselves what they would do were the case reversed; were we the aggressors, and demanded of them what they now demand of us. I think we all know their answer. It would be that given by the immortal Washington to the haughty monarch of England, when he attempted to make slaves of men who had determined to be free. Grant that we had no lawful right to secede; that I know nothing about, and never was more grieved than when I knew that we had done so; not from any wrong or unlawfulness, but from the fact that, united, we were stronger than we would be when separated; and I also feared the bloodshed which might ensue. If we were sinners in that respect, what were our fore-fathers when they claimed the right to secede from the British crown? Calling it fighting for the Union, is about as false as the love of the abolitionist for the negro, and we all know what that is. No happiness can exist in union without concord; and there can be no concord where any two people are so diametrically opposed to each other. All this I have repeated to them often, but I might as well have saved myself the trouble, for they are as blind to reason as any bigoted, self-deluded people ever were.

I was introduced to General Hindman, who dined with us to-day. He is still lame from a wound received at the battle of Shiloh. He is a peculiar-looking man; his hair is light and long, floating around his shoulders. I always imagine, when I see a man with his hair so long, that there is a vacancy in his cranium. I believe that it is Shakespeare who says that what a man lacked in brains he had in his hair. As the former is an article that we have much use for, and whose workings are much needed at present among our leading men, I can not but regret that outward indications in this instance were unfavorable. But perhaps this is only my prejudice against foppishness and every thing effeminate in men. General Hindman may be an exception to this rule, and I trust he is.

MAY 10, 1862

The hospital is again filled with the badly wounded. There is scarcely an hour during which they are not coming in from skirmishes. I sat up all night to see that the nurses performed their duties properly, and assisted in bathing the wounds of the men. They all rested quite well, excepting one, who was severely wounded in the hand. He suffered a great deal. One died suddenly this morning. I gave him his toddy; he was then quite cheerful; and I went to give him his breakfast, but his bunk was empty—he was dead and gone. He was wounded in the arm. The doctor desired him to have it amputated, which he would on no account permit. The result was hemorrhage ensued, and he bled to death before assistance could be rendered. I did not learn his name, nor any thing about him.

These things are very sad. A few evenings since, Dr. Allen was conversing about the horrors with which we are surrounded. He remarked that it was hard to think that God was just in permitting them. "Shall we receive good at the hands of God, and shall we not receive evil?" We, as a nation, have been so prosperous, that we forget that it was from him that we derived our benefits. He often sends us sorrows to try our faith. He will not send us more than we are able to bear. How patiently the soldiers endure their trials! Who dare say that strength is not given them from on high? Let us do our part, and, whatever happens, not lose trust in him, "for he doeth all things well"; and, in the language of Bishop Wilmer, "May the trials through which we are passing serve to wean us from the world, and move us to set our affections on things above!" "May we bear the rod, and him who hath appointed it!" Dr. Allen was some time with General Floyd, in Western Virginia, and remarked that he had seen nothing here to compare with what the men endured there. They were in the mountains, where it was impossible to get any thing for them.

We gained quite a victory yesterday. Price's and Van Dorn's troops were engaged. We saw them as they marched out in the morning. They crossed a bridge opposite our bed-room window.

May 11, 1862

A very hot, sultry day. I am very tired, as I have all to attend, the other ladies being sick; many of the nurses are sick also. It is more unhealthy now than ever, and unless some change takes place I fear that we will all die.

As there is much noise and confusion constantly here, it is almost impossible to collect one's thoughts. I miss the calm of the holy Sabbath more than any thing. I have read and talked to the men, and it astonishes me to see how few are members of the Church. They all seem to think and know that it is their duty to belong to it, but still they remain out of it. How much more will they have to answer for than those who have never known God, and have not enjoyed the privileges of the gospel. "He that confesseth me before men, him will I confess before my Father which is in heaven."

May 12, 1862

Two men died this morning, Mr. Adams and Mr. Brennan, from Coffee County, Alabama. Mr. Brennan was wounded. As a friend, Mr. Adams came to nurse him. Both were taken sick this morning, and died after a few hours' illness.

We have the same sad scenes to witness as ever—sick and wounded men lying on the platform at the depot, night and day, and we are not allowed to take them any thing to eat. Dr. Smith is obliged to prohibit it, as it is contrary to orders, and he has not the food to spare for them.

A terrible circumstance happened a few nights since. Our druggist, Dr. Sizemore, went out about 9 o'clock to see some one. When within a short distance from the hospital he heard groans; went to the place from which they proceeded, and found a box-car, that had been switched off the track, filled with wounded men, some dead and others dying, and not a soul with them to do any thing for them. The conductor was censured, but I think whoever sent the men off are in fault for not sending proper persons to take care of them. If this kind of treatment of our brave men continues much longer, I fear that we will have none to fight for us, for such a total disregard of human life must have a demoralizing effect. If we had many more such kind-hearted officers as Dr. Smith, our men would suffer little through neglect. None leave this hospital without he is certain they can go comfortably, and have plenty of nourishment to last them on their journey. I have seen him, many a time, go to the cars himself, to see that they were properly put in. I am informed that he spends every cent of his pay for their comfort. He will reap his reward.

MAY 13, 1862

Our troops have gone out this morning to endeavor to tempt the enemy to fight, but they will not leave their intrenchments. It is reported that they have been heavily reinforced, but, with all that, I have no doubt that if they would only fight our men would whip them.

We have a member of the Twenty-first Alabama Regiment from Mobile, who was badly wounded at the battle of Shiloh. There is no hope of his recovery. Every thing has been done for him that it is possible to do. He is a sad spectacle; he is so worn and wasted. He is a German, and can not understand any thing said to him by us. He has no relatives in this country.

Conversing with one of the patients, a very intelligent gentleman, I asked him what he thought of President Davis. He thought that he was a good man, but not the one for the place. I did not ask him his reason for this opinion. He is the first man that I have heard say this, and I hope that he is mistaken, as at this time the country needs a great man at its head.

MAY 15, 1862

Heavy firing was heard to-day, and I felt certain that a battle had commenced. I was in the kitchen when I first heard it, and was compelled to stop what I was doing, as the sound makes me unfit for any thing.

MAY 16, 1862

The fast-day set apart by the President. I hope that it will be duly observed. I believe that it is well kept in the army. There has been no show of keeping it in this hospital; the old excuse is given—"too much to do."

A few evenings since we came very near being burned out. While the ladies downstairs were making pads for the wounded expected next day—we use hundreds of them daily—the cotton took fire and communicated to some of the ladies' dresses. A gentleman extinguished it before any serious damage occurred. I was attending some patients at the time, and was certain from the noise that the enemy had come to storm the hospital, for which I was laughed at considerably.

Dr. Griffin of Kentucky and Dr. Benedick of New Orleans are both sick.

* * *

MAY 21, 1862

News has just reached us that the battle has commenced in earnest. A number of our surgeons have been ordered to the battle-field. May God give us the victory! I feel confident that if we could gain one here the war would soon be over, and that we would be recognized by foreign nations. I can not see why they do not now recognize us. We certainly can and will be free. My only wish for them to do so is to stop bloodshed, as I think, if they would do it, the North would be compelled to let us alone.

I have just been informed that the Yankee gunboats have passed Fort Morgan. I hope, if true, that Mobile will be laid in ashes before the foot of the vandal foe is permitted to desecrate it. They have not the same excuse that the people of New Orleans had—a large population of women and children; and then we have an outlet which they did not have.

Miss Marks is still very low. I feel very sorry to see her die in this terrible place; but it matters little where we die, so that we are prepared.

MAY 22, 1862

No battle occurred yesterday. Every one is confident that if the enemy would only fight, we would *whip them soundly*. They are digging intrenchments closer and closer, and could shell Corinth at any hour. Some are not more than two and a half miles from us. We are beginning to feel a little nervous at the prospect of a shell waking us up some morning; certainly not a pleasant one to contemplate.

A prisoner is here, who eats at the table with us. He is a Presbyterian minister. He makes some very provoking remarks. Dr. Smith has advised us to take no notice of them, and say as little as possible. This appears hard, as nearly every one at the table has suffered some wrong at the hands of him and his people; nearly all their homes are in the hands of the enemy.

Dr. Sizemore has just received word of a young brother who has died in a Northern prison, and of the ill treatment of the chaplain of his regiment, an inoffensive old man of more than seventy years, who had gone with the regiment more as a father than any thing else. This old man was imprisoned as if he were a common felon. Dr. Sizemore, knowing all this, has to endure the presence of this man, and see him treated as if he were one of our best friends. I must say that we are carrying out the commands of our blessed Savior; and how proud I am of it! May we be enabled to do the same to the end; and, above all things, not to retaliate upon the innocent, for God has said, "Vengeance is mine, and I will repay." I was seated next to the prisoner to-day. He says that he is an Englishman. I would like to think that he is telling an untruth, as few Englishmen side with tyranny. But I expect that he has been long enough with the Yankees to imbibe some of their barbarous notions. He expressed the opinion that the Southern people were not united. I remarked that if he would go through the state of Mississippi alone, he would change his mind, as I believe that if the men did not fight, the women would. But there will be no need of the latter, as the men will not fail to do their duty.

We requested Dr. Smith to permit us to pay him back for the impertinent remarks he had made to us. He granted permission, and stated that he would reprimand us in his presence. As soon as the foe made his appearance, some of the ladies commenced on him. Dr. Smith said, "The ladies are very hard on you." He replied with a very submissive air, "If it pleases them, I have no objection." Mrs. Glassburn, who was at the head of the table, observed, "It does not please us; but I will tell you what will: when we know that every Yankee is laid low in the ground, then we will be pleased indeed." He made no reply, and must have felt the force of the remark. At any other time it would have been a barbarous one; but at the present it was charitable, and one that we all felt, if realized, would not only be a blessing to us, but to humanity. . . .

MAY 23, 1862

I think as soon as surgeons discover that ladies are really of service, that prejudice will cease to exist. The patients are delighted to have us, and say that we can cause them to think of the dearest of places to them now—home.

Miss Marks is a little better, and has been sent to Okolona. The other two ladies who were sick have returned to Mobile.

Every corner of the hospital is clean, and ready for patients. The last of my patients died this morning. He was a German, named Ernest; was wounded at Shiloh. He wandered a good deal in his mind; but just before he died he sent for Dr. Smith, and requested him to write to his wife, and send her all the money he had. She lived on Magazine Street, New Orleans.

One of the saddest sights witnessed are two Federals, who have been here since the battle of Shiloh. One has had his arm, the other his leg amputated. They are seventeen and eighteen years of age, respectively. They look very pitiful, dying among strangers, far away from their homes and relatives. They have been cared for the same as our own; but that is not all that is wanted. They need sympathy, and of that character which it is impossible for us to extend to them, as they came here with the full intention of taking all that is dear to us. They may have been conscientious, and thought that they were doing their duty, but we are of a different opinion, and it will be some time before we change. They will soon die; both are religious. I never look at them without thinking of the thousands of our poor men who are in the same condition in the North. I do sincerely trust that they are as well treated as these poor fellows have been.

Dr. Nott, with several other surgeons, has examined the hospital. He looked well. He has lost a son in the war.

* * *

MAY 27, 1862

We are all packed up, and intend leaving this morning. Mrs. Glassburn and nearly all the ladies are going to Brookhaven. I intend going to Okolona, and there remain until I learn in which direction the army will move.

We have seen many sad sights and much suffering since we came to this place; still, I shall ever look back on these two months with sincere gratification, and feel that I have lived for something.

The surgeons, one and all, have proved themselves kind and attentive to the brave men whom they have had under their care. The hospital is in perfect order, ready for the reception of patients. I visited Corinth Hospital this morning; they were not thinking of leaving, and had quite a number of wounded men. There I met Mrs. Palmer of Mobile, who had a son in the Twenty-first Alabama Regiment. She had visited the camp the day before with refreshments for the soldiers. She informed me that there were numbers of sick yet in camp, and if we left, she could not conceive how they could be moved.

QUESTIONS TO CONSIDER

1. In what ways did Kate Cumming derive a sense of purpose from her work? In what ways did she find her work frustrating or disheartening? What does this sense of ambivalence suggest about the nature of female nursing during the Civil War?
2. What does Kate Cumming's journal suggest about Antebellum Southern gender conventions? How were wounded soldiers expected to behave? What sorts of duties did Kate Cumming perform? In what ways did those duties conform with and depart from common perceptions of Southern ladies' place in the world?

Sarah Morgan
1843–1909

Nineteen-year-old Louisianian Sarah Morgan began her Civil War diary in January 1862, recounting the events of the preceding year. She told not of her home state's secession, the marshaling of troops, or of the major battles of 1861, but rather she recalled the story of her brother's death in a duel. She referenced the duel frequently in her diary. But Morgan soon began to record the events of the larger world around her, and from 1862 until July of 1865 she crammed her diary pages full of her observations of and commentary about the war.

Unlike Mary Chesnut, who had edited and revised her diary for a postwar reading audience, Sarah Morgan claimed that she left her manuscript untouched by the blue pencil. She therefore believed her diary to be an accurate narrative of the war. Houghton Mifflin first published the diary in 1913, four years after the author's death. According Morgan's son, Francis Warrington Dawson II, who had written the diary's introduction, his mother had determined to publish her diary after a chance encounter in the 1890s with a Northerner. The two had argued over the events surrounding a battle between the *Essex* and the *Arkansas*, and Morgan mentioned that she had recorded the incident, as it happened, in her diary. The Philadelphian, eager to see the account, implored Morgan to publish her diary. "We Northerners are sincerely anxious to know what Southern women did and thought at that time," he claimed, "but the difficulty is to find contemporaneous evidence. All that I, for one, have seen has been marred by improvement in light of subsequent events." Morgan assured her companion that the diaries remained in a tall, cedar-lined wardrobe, untouched, fading from age.

Encouraged by this meeting, Morgan set out to transcribe her diary, preparing to send it North. Her son claimed that once finished and mailed, the Northerner, "with cold regrets that the temptation to rearrange it had not been resisted," returned her manuscript. "No Southerner at that time," the man continued, "could possibly have had opinions so just or foresight so clear as those here attributed to a young girl." Keenly disappointed, Sarah Morgan returned the manuscript to its resting-place, never to see it again. His curiosity piqued, and his determination to vindicate his mother's reputation intense, Francis Warrington Dawson undertook the publication of his mother's Civil War diaries, pledging himself "to the assertion that I have taken no liberties, have made no alterations, but have strictly adhered to my task of transcription, merely omitting here and there passages which deal with matters too personal to merit the interest of the public."

Like his mother, Dawson wished to assure the diary's readers that it was an authentic document of the war and not created in the postwar years. Dawson believed his mother was particularly susceptible to charges of revision because her diary displayed such a rare degree of prescience and judicious temperament. In May of 1863, for example, Sarah Morgan, noted that should the North conquer the South, "it will be a barren victory over a desolate land." Indeed, the Union "will find herself burdened with an unparalleled debt, with nothing to show for it except deserted towns, burning homes, a standing army and an impoverished land." And while Sarah Morgan may have disparaged Benjamin F. Butler, she did not equate all federal officers with the "Beast" of New Orleans. Sarah Morgan was a young woman of great maturity when she began her diary of the war, and her work should be duly praised, according to her son, not besmirched by those who doubt its authenticity.

Historians and literary critics have commented on the importance of Morgan's diary to an understanding of the Confederate South. As Charles East points out, it allows readers to see into "a far corner of the Confederacy," Baton Rouge, Louisiana. Morgan tells the stories of those not often heard from in Civil War literature. Hers is an account of the officers and soldiers who maintained the Confederate stronghold at Port Hudson and the refugees who fled their homes in Baton Rouge and New Orleans after federal occupation. "But what we also see is Sarah herself," East continues, "one woman's spirit and courage, and occasional despair, as she lives through a time of turbulence and crisis." For these reasons, historians of Confederate women have relied on Morgan's diary.

from The Civil War Diary of Sarah Morgan

MAY 9, 1862

Our lawful (?) owners have at last arrived. About sunset day before yesterday, the Iroquois anchored here, and a graceful young Federal stepped ashore, carrying a Yankee flag over his shoulder, and asked the way to the Mayor's office. I like the style! If we girls of B. R. had been at the landing instead of the men, that Yankee would never have insulted us by flying his flag in our faces! *We* would have opposed his landing except under a flag of truce, but the men let him alone, and he even found a poor Dutchman willing to show him the road! He did not accomplish much; said a formal demand would be made next day, and asked if it was safe for the men to come ashore and buy a few necessaries, when he was assured the air of B. R. was very unhealthy for Federal soldiers at night. He promised very magnanimously not [to] shell us out, if we did not molest him; but I notice none of them dare set their feet on *terra firma,* except the officer who has now called three times on the Mayor, and who is said to tremble visibly as he walks the streets.

Last evening came the demand: the town must [be] surrendered immediately; the Federal flag Must be raised, they would grant us the same terms they granted to New Orleans. Jolly terms those were! The answer was worthy of a Southerner. It was, "the town was defenseless; if we had cannon, there were not men enough to resist; but if forty vessels lay at the landing,—it was intimated that we were in their power, and more ships coming up—we would not surrender; if they wanted, they might come Take us; if they wished the Federal flag hoisted over the Arsenal, they might put it up for themselves, the town had no control over Government property." Glorious! What a pity they did not shell the town! But they are taking us at our word, and this morning they are landing at the Garrison and presently the Bloody banner will be floating over our heads. "Better days are coming, we'll all go right."

"All devices, signs, and flags of the Confederacy shall be suppressed." So says Picayune Butler.[1] Good. I devote all my red, white, and blue silk to the manufacture of Confederate flags. As soon as one is confiscated, I make another, until my ribbon is exhausted, when I will sport a duster emblazoned in high colors, "Hurra! for the Bonny blue flag!" Henceforth, I wear one pinned to my bosom—not a duster, but a little flag—the man who says take it off, will have to pull it off for himself; the man who dares attempt it—well! a pistol in my pocket fills up the gap. I am capable, too.

This is a dreadful war to make even the hearts of women so bitter! I hardly know myself these last few weeks. I, who have such a horror of bloodshed, consider even killing in self defense murder, who cannot wish them the slightest evil, whose only prayer is to have them sent back in peace to their own country, *I* talk of killing them! For what else do I wear a pistol and carving knife? I am afraid I *will* try them on the first one who says an insolent word to me. Yes, and repent for it ever after in sackcloth and ashes. *O!* if I was only a man! Then I could don the breeches, and slay

1. Union General Benjamin F. Butler was placed in command of the fallen city of New Orleans, April 1862. The residents refused to comply with Butler's orders and unruly mobs threatened the safety of the general and his men. The behavior of the women of the city particularly infuriated Butler, prompting him on 15 May 1862 to issue General Order No. 28, which stated that any unruly or disrespectful women "shall be regarded and held liable to be treated as a woman of the town plying her avocation."

them with a will! If some few Southern women were in the ranks, they could set the men an example they would not blush to follow. Pshaw! there are *no* women here! We are *all* men!

* * *

JUNE 16, 1862

There is no use in trying to break off journalizing, particularly in "these trying times." It has become a necessity to me. I believe I would go off in a rapid decline if Butler took it in his head to prohibit that among other things. . . . I reserve to myself the privilege of writing my opinions, since I trouble no one with the expression of them. . . . I insist, that if the valor and chivalry of our men cannot save our country, I would rather have it conquered by a brave race, than owe its liberty to the Billingsgate oratory and demonstrations of some of these "ladies." If the women have the upper hand then, as they have now, I would not like to live in a country governed by such tongues.

Do I consider the female who could spit in a gentleman's face merely because he wore United States buttons, as a fit associate for me? Lieutenant Biddle assured me he did not pass a street in New Orleans without being most grossly insulted by *ladies*. It was a friend of his into whose face a lady *spit* as he walked quietly by without looking at her. (Wonder if she did it to attract his attention?) He had the sense to apply to her husband and give him two minutes to apologize or die, and of course he chose the former. Such things are enough to disgust any one. "Loud" women, what a contempt I have for you! How I despise your vulgarity!

Some of these Ultra Secessionists evidently very recently from "down East" who think themselves obliged to "kick up their heels over the Bonny blue flag," as Brother describes female patriotism, shriek out "What! see those vile Northerners pass patiently! No true Southerner could see it without rage! I could kill them! I hate them with all my soul, the murderers, liars, thieves, rascals! You are no Southerner if you do not hate them as much as I!" *Ah ça!* a true-blue Yankee tell me that I, born and bred here, am no Southerner! I always think "It is well for you, my friend, to save your credit, else you might be suspected by some people, though, your violence is enough for me." I always say, "*You* may do as you please; my brothers are fighting for me, and doing their duty, so that excess of patriotism is unnecessary for me as my position is too well known to make any demonstrations requisite." I flatter myself that "tells."

This war has brought out wicked, malignant feelings that I did not believe could dwell in woman's heart. I see some with the holiest eyes, so holy one would think the very spirit of Charity lived in them, and all Christian meekness, go off in a mad tirade of abuse and say with the holy eyes wondrously changed "I hope God will send down plague, yellow fever, famine, on these vile Yankees, and that not one will escape death." O what unutterable horror that remark causes me as often as I hear it! I think of the many mothers, wives and sisters who wait as anxiously, pray as fervently in their far away lonesome homes for their dear ones, as we do here; I fancy them waiting day after day for the footsteps that will never come, growing more sad, lonely, and heartbroken as the days wear on; I think of how awful it would be if one would say "your brothers are dead," how it would crush all life and happiness out of me; and I say, "God forgive these poor women! They know not what they say!" O woman! into what loathsome violence you have debased your holy mission! God will punish us for our hardheartedness.

Not a square off, in the new theatre, lie more than a hundred sick soldiers. What woman has stretched out her hand to save them, to give them a cup of cold water?

Where is the charity which should ignore nations and creeds, and administer help to the Indian or Heathen indifferently? Gone! all gone in Union versus Secession! *That* is what the American War has brought us. If I was independent, if I could work my own will without causing others to suffer for my deeds, I would not be poring over this stupid page, I would not be idly reading or sewing. I would put aside Woman's trash, take up woman's duty, and I would stand by some forsaken man and bid him God speed as he closes his dying eyes. *That* is Woman's mission! and not Preaching and Politics. I say I would, yet here I sit! O for liberty! the liberty that *dares* do what conscience dictates, and scorns all smaller rules!

If I could help these dying men! Yet it is as impossible as though I was a chained bear. I cant put out my hand. I am threatened with Coventry because I sent a custard to a sick man who is in the army, and with the anathema of society because I said if I could possibly do anything for Mr. Biddle—at a distance—(he is sick) I would like to very much. Charlie thinks we have acted shockingly in helping Colonel McMillan, and that we will suffer for it when the Federals leave. I would like to see the *man* who *dared* harm my father's daughter! But as he seems to think our conduct reflects on him, there is no alternative. Die, poor men, without a woman's hand to close your eyes! We women are too *patriotic* to help you! I look eagerly on, cry in my soul, "I wish—"; you die; God judges me. Behold the woman who dares not risk private ties for God's glory and her professed religion! Coward, helpless woman that I am! If I was free—!

* * *

JUNE 29, 1862

"Any more, Mr. Lincoln, any more?" cant you leave our racked homes in repose? We are all wild. Last night, five citizens were arrested, on no charge at all, and carried down to Picayune Butler's ship. What a thrill of terror ran through the whole community! we all feel so helpless, so powerless under the hand of our tyrant, the man who swore to uphold the Constitution and the laws, who is professedly only fighting to give us all Liberty, the birthright of every American, and who, neverless, has ground us down to a state where we would not reduce our negroes, who tortures and sneers at us, and rules us with an iron hand! Ah! Liberty! what a humbug!

I would rather belong to England or France, than to the North! Bondage, woman that I am, I can never stand! Even now, the northern papers, distributed among us, taunt us with our subjection, and tell us "how coolly Butler will grind them down, paying no regard to their writhing and torture beyond tightening the bonds still more!" Ah, truly! this is the bitterness of slavery, to be insulted and reviled by cowards who are safe at home, and enjoy the protection of the laws, while we, captive and overpowered, dare not raise our voices to throw back the insult, and are governed by the despotism of one man, whose word is our law! And that man, they tell us, "Is the right man in the right place. *He* will develope a union sentiment among the people, if the thing can be done!"

Come and see if he can! Hear the curse that arises from thousands of hearts at that man's name, and say if he will "speedily bring us to our senses." Will he accomplish it by love, tenderness, mercy, compassion? He might have done it; but did he try? When he came, he assumed his natural rôle as Tyrant, and bravely has he acted it through, never once turning aside for Justice or Mercy. . . .

This degradation is worse than the bitterness of death! I see no salvation [on] either side. No glory awaits the Southern Confederacy if it does achieve its independence; it will be a mere speck in the world, with no weight or authority. The North confesses its self lost with out us, and has paid an unheard of ransom to regain us. On the other hand, conquered, what hope is there in this world for us? Broken in health and fortune, reviled, contemned, abused by those who claim already to have subdued us, with out a prospect of future support for those few of our brothers who return; outcasts without home or honor, would not death or exile be preferable? O let us abandon our loved home to these implacable enemies, and find refuge elsewhere! Take from us property, every thing, only grant us liberty!

Is this rather frantic, considering I abhor politics, and women who meddle with them, above all? My opinion has not yet changed; I still feel the same contempt for a woman who would talk at the top of her voice for the edification of Federal officers, as though anxious to receive an invitation requesting her presence at the garrison. I have too much respect for my father's memory to adopt so pitiful a warfare. "I can suffer and be still" as far as outward signs are concerned; but as no word of this has passed my lips, I give it vent in writing, which is more lasting than words, partly to relieve my heart, partly to prove to my own satisfaction that I am no coward; for one line of this, surrounded as we are by soldiers, and liable to have our houses searched at any instant, would be a sufficient indictment for high treason.

Under General Williams's rule, I was perfectly satisfied that whatever was done, was done through necessity, and under orders from headquarters, beyond his control; we all liked him. But now, since Butler's arrival, I believe I am as frantic in secret as the others are openly. I know that war sanctions many hard things, and that both sides practice them; but now we are so completely lost in Louisiana, is it fair to gibe and taunt us with our humiliation? I could stand any thing save the cowardly ridicule and triumph of their papers. Honestly, I believe if all vile abusive papers on both sides were suppressed, and some of the fire eating editors who make a living by lying were soundly cowhided or had their ears clipped, it would do more towards establishing peace, than all the bloodshedding either side can afford. I hope to live to see it, too. Seems to me, more liberty is allowed to the press, than would be tolerated in speech. Let us speak as freely as any paper, and see if tomorrow we do not sleep at Fort Jackson!

This morning the excitement is rare; fifteen more citizens were arrested and carried off, and all the rest grew wild with expectation. So great a martyrdom is it considered, that I am sure those who are not arrested will be wofully disappointed. It is ludicrous to see how each man thinks he is the very one they are in search of! We asked a two-penny lawyer, of no more importance in the community than Dophy[2] is, if it was possible he was not arrested. "Not yet," was the modest reply; "But I am expecting to be, every instant!" So much for his modest self-assurance! Those arrested have some been quietly released (those are so smiling and mysterious that I suspect them), some been obliged to take the oath, some sent to Fort Jackson. "Ah, Liberty! What a blessing it is to enjoy thy privileges!" If some of these poor men are not taken prisoners, they will die of mortification at the slight.

Our valiant governor, the brave Moore, has by order of the real governor, Moïse, made himself visible at some far distant point, and issued a proclamation saying, whereas we of Baton Rouge were held forcibly in town, he therefore considered men, women, and children prisoners of war, and as such, the Yankees are bound to supply us with all necessaries, and consequently, anyone sending us aid or comfort, or provisions from the country will be severely punished. Only Moore is fool enough for such an order. Held down by the Federals, our paper money so much trash, with hardly any other

2. One of Morgan's slaves.

to buy food, and no way of earning it; threatened with starvation and utter ruin, our own friends by way of making our burden lighter, forbid our receiving the means of prolonging life, and after generously warning us to leave town, which they know is perfectly impossible, prepare to burn it over our heads, and let the women run the same risk as the men.

Penned in one little square mile, here we await our fate like sheep in the slaughter-pen. Our hour may be at hand now, it may be tonight; we have only to wait; the booming of the cannon will announce it to us soon enough.

Of the six sentenced to Fort Jackson, one is the Methodist minister Mr Craven. The only charge is, that he was heard to pray for the Confederate States by some officers who passed his house during his family prayers. According to that, which of us would escape unhung? I do not believe there is a woman in the land who closes her eyes before praying for God's blessing on the side on which her brothers are engaged. Are we all to cease? Show me the dungeon deep enough to keep me from praying for them! The man represented that he had a large family totally dependent on him, who must starve. "Let them get up a subscription" was General Butler's humane answer. "I will head it myself." It is useless to say the generous offer was declined.

* * *

AUGUST 13, 1862

I am in despair. Miss Jones, who has just made her escape from town, brings a most dreadful account. She, with seventy five others, took refuge at Dr Enders', more than a mile and a half below town, at Hall's. It was there we sent the two trunks containing father's papers and our clothing and silver. Hearing that guerrillas had been there, the Yankees went down, shelled the house in the night, turning all those women and children out, who barely escaped with their clothing, and let the soldiers loose on it. They destroyed everything they could lay their hands on, if it could not be carried off; broke open armoirs, trunks, sacked the house, and left it one scene of devastation and ruin. They even stole Miss Jones' braid! she got here with nothing but the clothes she wore. This is a dreadful blow to me.

Yesterday, I thought myself beggared when I heard that our house was probably burnt, remembering all the clothing, books, furniture, etc., that it contained; but I consoled myself with the recollection of a large trunk packed in the most scientific style; containing quantities of nightgowns, skirts, chemises, dresses, cloaks, in short our very best, which was in safety. Winter had no terrors when I thought of the nice warm clothes; I only wished I had a few of the organdie dresses I had packed up before wearing. And now? It is all gone, silver, father's law papers without which we are beggars, and clothing! Nothing left! I could stand that. But as each little article of Harry's came up before me (I had put many in the trunk) I lost heart. . . . They may clothe their negro women with my clothes, since they only steal for them; but to take things so sacred to me! O my God, teach me to forgive them! . . .

Poor Miss Jones! they went into her clothes bag and took out articles which were certainly of no service to them, for mere deviltry. There are so many sufferers in this case, that it makes it still worse. The plantation just below was served in the same way; whole families fired into before they knew of the intention of the Yankees; was it not fine sport?

I have always been an advocate of peace—if we could name the conditions *ourselves*—but I say War to the death! I would give my life to be able to take up arms against the vandals who are laying waste our fair land! I suppose it is because I have no longer any thing to lose that I am desperate. Before, I always opposed the burning of B. R., as a useless piece of barbarism in turning out five thousand women and children on the charity of the world. But I noticed that those who had no interest there, warmly advocated it. Lilly Nolan cried loudly for it; thought it only just; but the first shell that whistled over her father's house, made her crazy with rage. The brutes! the beasts! how cruel! wicked! etc. It was too near home for her, then. There is the greatest difference between *my* property and *yours*.

I notice that the farther I get from town, the more ardent are the people to have it burned. It recalls very forcibly Thackeray's cut in The Virginians, when speaking of the determination of the Rebels to burn the cities; he says he observed that all those who were most eager to burn N. York were inhabitants of Boston; while those who were most zealous to burn Boston, had all their property in New York. It is true all the world over. And I am afraid I am becoming indifferent about the fate of our town. Anything, so it is speedily settled! Tell me it would be of service to the Confederacy, and I would set fire to my home—if still standing—willingly! But would it?

AUGUST 17, 1862

Another Sunday. Strange that the time, which should seem so endless, flies so rapidly! Miriam complains that Sunday comes every day; but though that seems a little too much, I insist that it comes twice a week. Let time fly, though; for each day brings us so much nearer our destiny, which I long to know.

Thursday, we heard from a lady just from town, that our house was standing the day before, which somewhat consoled us for the loss of our silver and clothing; but yesterday came the tidings of new afflictions. I declare we have acted out the first chapter of Job, all except that verse about the death of his sons and daughters. God shield us from that! I do not mind the rest. "While he was yet speaking, another came in and said, 'thy brethren and kinsmen gathered together to wrest thine abode from the hand of the Philistines which pressed sore upon thee; when lo! the Philistines sallied forth with fire and sword, and laid thine habitation waste and desolate, and I only, am escaped to tell thee.' "

Yes! the Yankees, fearing the Confederates might slip in unseen, resolved to have full view of their movements, so put the torch to all eastward, from Colonel Matta's, to the Advocate. That would lay open a fine tract of country, alone; but unfortunately, it is said that once started, it was not so easy to control the flames which spread considerably beyond its appointed limits. Some say it went as far as Florida Street; if so, we are lost, as that is half a square below us. For several days the fire has been burning, but very little can be learned, of the particulars. I am sorry for Colonel Matta. Such a fine brown stone front, the finest in town. Poor Minna! poverty will hardly agree with her. As for our home, I hope against hope. I will not believe it is burnt, until somebody declares having been present on that occasion. Yet so many frame houses on that square must have readily caught fire from the sparks.

Wicked as it may seem, I would rather have all I own burned, than in the possession of the negroes. Fancy my magenta organdie on a dark beauty! Bah! I think the sight would enrage me! Miss Jones' trials are enough to drive her crazy. She had the pleasure of having four officers in her house, men who sported épaulets and red sashes, accompanied by a negro woman, at whose disposal all articles were placed. The worthy companion of these "gentlemen" walked around selecting things with the most natural airs and graces. "*This*," she would say, "we *must* have. And some of these books, you know, and all the preserves, and these chairs and tables, and all the clothes, of course; and yes! the rest of these things." So she would go on, the "gentlemen" assuring her she had only to choose what she wanted, and that they would have them removed immediately. Madame thought they really must have the wine, and those handsome cut glass goblets.

I hardly think I could have endured such a scene; to see all I owned given to negroes, without even an accusation being brought against me of disloyalty. One officer departed with a fine velvet cloak on his arm; another took such a bundle of Miss Jones' clothes, that he had to have it lifted by some one else on his horse, and rode off holding it with difficulty. This I heard from herself, yesterday, as I spent the day with Lilly and mother at Mr. Elder's, where she is now staying. Can anything more disgraceful be imagined? They all console me by saying there is no one in Baton Rouge who could possibly wear my dresses without adding a considerable piece to the belt. But that is nonsense. Another pull at the corset strings would bring them easily to the size I have been reduced by nature and bones. Besides, O horror! Suppose, instead, they should let in a piece of another color? That would annihilate me! Pshaw! I do not care for the dresses, if they had only left me those little articles of father's and Harry's. But that is hard to forgive. If I cry at the thought of Hal's shirt and cap, what would I do if I saw them worn?

* * *

AUGUST 28, 1862

I am satisfied. I have seen my home again. Tuesday I was up at sunrise, and my few preparations were soon completed, and before any one was awake, I walked over to Mr. Elder's through mud and dew to meet Charlie. Fortunate was it for me that I started so early; for I found him hastily eating his breakfast and ready to leave. He was very much opposed to my going; and for some time I was afraid he would force me to remain; but at last he consented—perhaps because I did not insist—and with wet feet, and without a particle of breakfast, I at length found myself in the buggy on the road home. The ride afforded me a series of extraordinary surprises. Half the time I found myself half way out of the little low-necked buggy when I thought I was safely in, and the other half, I was surprised to find myself really in, when I thought I was wholly out. And so on, for mile after mile, over muddy roads, until we came to a most terrific cross road, leading to the plank road, where we were obliged to pass, and which is best undescribed. Four miles from town we stopped at Mrs. Brown's to see mother, and after a few moments' talk, went on our road.

I saw the first Yankee camp that Will Pinckney and Colonel Bird had set fire to the day of the battle. Such a shocking sight of charred wood, burnt clothes, tents, and all imaginable articles strewn around, I had never before seen. I should have been very much excited, entering the town by the route our soldiers took; but I was not. It all seemed tame and familiar. I could hardly fancy I stood on the very spot where the severest struggle had taken place. The next turn of the road brought us to two graves, one on each side of the road, the resting place of two who fell that day. They were merely left in the ditch where they fell, and earth from the side was pulled over them. When Miriam passed, parts of their coats were sticking out of the grave; but some kind hand had scattered fresh earth over them when I saw them.

Beyond, the sight became more common. I was told that their hands and feet were visible from many. And one poor fellow lay unburied, just as he had fallen, with his horse across him, and both skeletons. That sight I was spared, as the road near which he was lying was blocked up by trees, so we were forced to go through the woods, to enter, instead of passing by the Catholic graveyard. In the woods, we passed another camp our men destroyed, while the torn branches above, testified to the number of shells our men had braved to do the work. Next to Mr Barbee's, were the remains of a third camp that was burned; and a few more steps made me suddenly hold my breath, for just before us lay a dead horse with the flesh still hanging, which was hardly endurable. Close by lay a skeleton, whether of man or horse, I did not wait to see.

Not a human being appeared until we reached the penitentiary, which was occupied by our men. After that, I saw crowds of wagons moving furniture out, but not a creature that I knew. Just back of our house was all that remained of a nice brick cottage—namely, four crumbling walls. The offense was that the husband was fighting for the Confederacy; so the wife was made to suffer, and is now homeless, like many thousands besides. It really seems as though God wanted to spare our homes. The frame dwelling adjoining was not touched, even. The town was hardly recognizable; and required some skill to avoid the corners blocked up by trees, so as to get in at all.

Our house could not be reached by the front, so we left the buggy in the back yard, and running through the lot without stopping to examine the store room and servants' rooms that opened wide, I went through the alley, and entered by the front door. Fortunate was it for this record that I undertook to describe the sacking only from Miriam's account. If I had waited until now, it would never have been mentioned; for as I looked around, to attempt such a thing seemed absurd. I stood in the parlor in silent amazement; and in answer to Charlie's "Well?" I could only laugh. It was so hard to realize. As I looked for each well known article, I could hardly believe that Abraham Lincoln's officers had really come so low down as to steal in such a wholesale manner. The *papier-maché* workbox Miriam had given me, was gone. The baby sacque I was crocheting, with all knitting needles and wool, gone also. Of all the beautiful engravings of Annapolis that Will Pinckney had sent me, there remained a single one. Gentlemen, my name is written on each!

Not a book remained in the parlor, except Idyls of the King, that contained my name also, and which, together with the door plate, was the only case in which the name of Morgan was spared. They must have thought we were related to John Morgan, and wreaked their vengeance on us for that reason. Thanks for the honor, but there is not the slightest connection! Where they did not carry off articles bearing our name, they cut it off (as in the visiting-cards) and left only the first name. Every book of any value or interest, except Hume and Gibbon, was "borrowed" permanently. I regretted Macaulay more than all the rest. Brother's splendid French histories went too; all except L'Histoire de la Bastille. However as they spared father's law libraries, (all except one volume they used to support a flour barrel with, while they emptied it near the parlor door) we ought to be thankful.

The dining-room was *very* funny. I looked around for the cut glass celery and preserve dishes that were to be part of my "dot" as mother always said, together with the champagne glasses that had figured on the table the day I was born; but there remained nothing. There was plenty of split up furniture though. I stood in mother's room before the shattered armoir, which I could hardly believe the same that I had smoothed my hair before, as I left home three weeks previously. Father's was split across, and the lock torn off, and in the place of the hundreds of articles it contained, I saw two bonnets at the sight of which I actually sat down to laugh. One was mother's velvet, which looked very much like a foot ball in its present condition. Mine was not to be found, as the officers forgot to return it. Wonder who has my imperial? I know they never saw a handsomer one, with its black velvet, purple silk, and ostrich feathers.

I went to my room. Gone was my small paradise! Had this shocking place ever been habitable? The tall mirror squinted at me from a thousand broken angles. It looked so knowing! I tried to fancy the Yankee officers being dragged from under my bed by the leg, thanks to Charles; but it seemed too absurd; so I let them alone. My desk! What a sight! The central part I had kept as a little curiosity shop with all my little trinkets and keepsakes, of which a large proportion were from my gentlemen friends. I looked, and of all I had left, found only a piece of the McRae, which, as it was labeled in full, I was surprised they had spared. Precious letters, I found under heaps of broken china and rags; all my notes were gone, with many letters. I looked for a letter of poor—, in cipher, with the key attached, and name signed in plain hand. I knew it would hardly be agreeable to him to have it read, and it certainly would be unpleasant to me to have it published; but I could not find it. Miriam thinks she saw something answering the description, somewhere, though.

Bah! What is the use of describing such a scene? Many suffered along with us, though none so severely. Indeed, the Yankees cursed loudly at those who did not leave anything worth stealing. They cannot complain of us, on that score. All our handsome Brussels carpets, together with Lydia's four, were taken too. What did they not take? In the garret, in its darkest corner, a whole gilt edged china set of Lydia's had been overlooked; so I set to work and packed it up, while Charlie packed her furniture in a wagon, to send to her father. It was now three o'clock; and with my light linen dress thrown off, I was standing over a barrel putting in cups and saucers as fast as I could wrap them in the rags that covered the floor, when Mr. Larguier sent me a nice little dinner. I had been so many hours without eating—19, I think, during three of which I had slept, that I had lost all appetite; but nevertheless I eat it, to show my appreciation. If I should here-after think that the quantity of rags was exaggerated, let me here state that after I had packed the barrel and china with them, it made no perceptible diminution of the pile.

As soon as I had finished my task, Charlie was ready to leave again; so I left town without seeing, or hearing, any one, or any thing, except what lay in my path. As we drove out of the gate, I begged Charlie to let me get my bird, as I heard Charles Barker had him. A man was dispatched, and in a few minutes returned with my Jimmy. I have since heard that Tiche deserted him, the day of the battle, as I so much feared she would; and that Charles found him late in the evening and took charge of him. With my pet once more with me, we drove off again. I cast many a longing look at the graveyard; but knowing Charlie did not want to stop, I said nothing, though I had been there but once in three months, and that once, six weeks ago. I could see where the fence had been thrown down by our soldiers as they charged the Federals, but it was now replaced, though many a picket was gone.

Once more I stopped at Mrs. Brown's, while Charlie went on to Clinton, leaving me to drive mother here in the morning. Early yesterday after seeing Miriam's piano and the mattresses packed up and on the road, we started off in the buggy, and after a tedious ride through a melting sun, arrived here about three o'clock, having again missed my dinner, which I kept a profound secret until supper-time. I declare, by next Ash Wednesday, I will have learned how to fast without getting sick! Though very tired, I sat sewing until after sunset, dictating a page and a half to Anna, who was writing to Howell.

* * *

November 9, 1862

I hardly know how these last days have passed. I have an indistinct recollection of rides in cain wagons to the most distant field, coming back perched on the top of the cane singing, "Dye my petticoats" to the great amusement of the General who followed on horseback. Anna and Miriam comfortably reposing in corners were too busy to join in, as their whole time and attention were entirely devoted to the consumption of cane. It was only by singing rough impromptus on Mr Harold and Captain Bradford that I roused them from their task long enough to join in a chorus of "Forty Thousand Chinese." I would not have changed my perch, four mules, and black driver, for queen Victoria's coach and six. And to think old Abe wants to deprive us of all that fun! No more cotton, sugar cane, or rice! No more old black aunties or uncles! No more rides in mule teams, no more songs in the cain field, no more steaming kettles, no more black faces and shining teeth around the furnace fires!

If Lincoln could spend the grinding season on a plantation, he would recall his proclamation. As it is, he has only proved himself a fool, without injuring us. Why last evening I took old Wilson's place at the bagasse shoot, and kept the rollers free from cane until I had thrown down enough to fill several carts, and had my hands as black as his. What cruelty to slaves! And black Frank thinks me cruel too, when he meets me with a patronizing grin, and shows me the nicest vats of candy, and peels cane for me. Oh! very cruel! And so does Jules, when he wipes the handle of his paddle on his apron, to give "Mamselle" a chance to skim the kettles and learn how to work! Yes! and so do all the rest who meet us with a courtesy and "Howd'y, young missus!"

Last night we girls sat on the wood just in front of the furnace—rather Miriam and Anna did, while I sat in their laps—and with some twenty of all ages crowded around, we sang away to their great amusement. Poor oppressed devils! why did you not chunk us with the burning logs instead of looking happy, and laughing like fools? Really, some good old Abolitionist is needed here, to tell them how miserable they are. Cant mass Abe spare a few to enlighten his brethren?

* * *

January 23, 1863

I am particularly happy to day, for we have just heard from Brother for the first time since last July. And he is well, and happy, and wants us to come to him in New Orleans so he can take care of us, and no longer be so anxious for our safety. If we only could—!

To be sure the letter is from a gentleman who is just out of the city, who says he writes at Brother's earnest request; still it is something to hear, even indirectly. One hundred and fifty dollars he encloses, with the request that mother will draw for any amount she wishes. Dear Brother, money is the least thing we need; first of all, we are dying for want of a home. If we could only see ours once more!

During the time we have heard incidentally of Brother; of his having taken the oath of allegiance—which I am confident he did not do until Butler's October decree—of his being a prominent Union man, of his being a candidate for the Federal Congress, and of his withdrawal; and finally of his having gone to New York and Washington, from which places he only returned a few weeks since. That is all we ever heard. A very few people have been insolent enough to say to me, "Your brother is as good a Yankee as any." My blood boils as I answer "Let him be President Lincoln if he will, and I would love him the same." And so I would. Politics cannot come between me and my father's son. What he thinks right, Is right, for him, though not for me. If he is for the Union, it is because he believes it to be in the right, and I honor him for acting from conviction, rather than from dread of public opinion.

If he were to take up the sword against us to-morrow, Miriam and I at least, would say "If he thinks it his duty, he is right; we will not forget he is our father's child." And we will not. From that sad day when the sun was setting for the first time on our father's grave, when the great, strong man sobbed in agony at the thought of what we had lost, and taking us both on his lap put his arms around us and said "Dear little sisters dont cry; I will be father and brother too, now," he has been both. And we love him as such, dont we Miriam? He respects our opinions, we shall respect his.

I confess myself a rebel, body and soul. *Confess?* I glory in it! Am proud of being one; would not forego the title for any other earthly one! Though none could regret the dismemberment of our old Union more than I did at the time, though I acknowledge that there never was a more unnecessary war than this in the beginning, yet once in earnest, from the secession of Louisiana I date my change of sentiment. I have never since then looked back; forward, forward! is the cry; and as the Federal States sink each day in more appalling folly and disgrace, I grow prouder still of my own country and rejoice that we can no longer be confounded with a nation which shows so little fortitude in calamity, so little magnanimity in its hour of triumph.

Yes! I am glad we are two distinct tribes! I am proud of my country; only wish I could fight in the ranks with our brave soldiers, to prove my enthusiasm; would think death, mutilation, glorious in such a cause; cry, "war to all eternity before we submit." But if I cant fight, being unfortunately a woman, which I now regret for the first time in my life, at least I can help in other ways. What fingers can do in knitting and sewing for them, I have done with the most intense delight; what words of encouragement and praise could accomplish, I have tried on more than one bold soldier boy, and not altogether in vain; I have lost my home and all its dear contents for our Southern Rights, have stood on its deserted hearth stone and looked at the ruin of all I loved without a murmur, almost glad of the sacrifice, if it would contribute its mite towards the salvation of the Confederacy.

And so it did, indirectly; for the battle of Baton Rouge, which made the Yankees, drunk with rage, commit outrages in our homes that civilized Indians would blush to perpetrate, forced them to abandon the town as untenable, whereby we were enabled to fortify Port Hudson here, which now defies their strength. True they have reoccupied our town; that Yankees live in our house; but if our generals said burn the whole concern, would I not put the torch to our home readily, though I love its bare skeleton still? Indeed I would, though I know what it is to be without one. Dont Lilly and mother live in a wretched cabin in vile Clinton while strangers rest under our father's roof? Yankees, I owe you one for that!

Well! I boast myself Rebel, sing Dixie, shout Southern Rights, pray for God's blessing on our cause, without ceasing, and would not live in this country if by any possible calamity we should be conquered; I am only a woman, and that is the way I feel. Brother may differ. What then? Shall I respect, love him less? No! God bless him! Union or Secession, he is always my dear, dear Brother, and tortures should not make me change my opinion.

* * *

APRIL 30, 1863

Was not the recollection of this day bitter enough to me already? I did not think it could be more so. Yet behold me crying as I have not cried for many and many a day. Not for Harry; I dare not cry for him. I feel a deathlike quiet when I think of him; a fear that even a deep drawn breath would wake him in his grave. And as dearly as I love you, O Hal, I dont want you in this dreary world again! . . .

Talk of the Revocation of the Edict of Nantes![3] Talk of Louis XIV! Of—Pshaw! my head is in such a whirl that history gets all mixed up, and all parallels seem weak and moderate in comparison to this infamous outrage. To day, thousands of families, from the most respectable down to the least, all who have had the firmness to register themselves enemies to the United States, are ordered to leave the city before the fifteenth of May. Think of the thousands, perfectly destitute, who can hardly afford to buy their daily bread even here, sent to the Confederacy, where it is neither to be earned nor bought, without money, friends, or a home. Hundreds have comfortable homes here, which will be confiscated to enrich those who drive them out. "It is an ill wind that blows no one good."

Such dismal faces as one meets every where! Each looks heart broken. Homeless, friendless, beggars, is written in every eye. Brother's face is too unhappy to make it pleasant to look at him. True, he is safe; but hundreds of his friends are going forth destitute, leaving happy homes behind, not knowing where the crust of bread for famishing children is to come from to-morrow. He went to General Bowen and asked if it were possible that women and children were included in the order. Yes, he said; they should all go, and go in the Confederacy. They should not be allowed to go elsewhere.

Penned up like sheep to starve! That's the idea! With the addition of forty thousand mouths to feed, they think they can invoke famine to their aid, seeing that their negro brothers dont help them much in the task of subjugating us.

* * *

JUNE 21, 1863

How about that oath of allegiance? is what I frequently ask myself, and always an uneasy qualm of conscience troubles me. Guilty, or not guilty of Perjury? According to the law of God in the abstract, and of nations, Yes; according to my conscience, Jeff Davis, and the peculiar position I was placed in, No. Which is it? Had I had any idea that such a pledge would be exacted, would I have been willing to come? Never! The thought would have horrified me. The reality was never placed before me until we reached Bonfouca. There I was terrified at the prospect; but seeing how impossible it would be to go back, I placed all my hopes in some miracle that was to intervene to prevent such a crime, and confidently believed my ill health, or something else would save me, while all the rest of the party declared they would think it nothing, and take forty oaths a day, if necessary.

A forced oath, all men agree, is not binding. The Yankees lay particular stress on this being voluntary, and insist that no one is solicited to take it except of their own free will. Yet look at the scene that followed, when mother showed herself unwilling! Think of being ordered to the Custom house as a prisoner for saying she supposed she would *have* to! *That's* liberty! that is free will! It is entirely optional; you have only to take it quietly or go to jail. That is freedom enough, certainly!

There was not even that choice left to me. I told the officer who took down my name, that I was unwilling to take the oath, and asked if there was no escaping it. "None whatever" was his reply "you have it to do, and there is no getting out of it." His

3. The edict, promulgated by King Henry IV of France in 1598, granted French Protestants equal rights with Catholics. Its revocation in 1685 by King Louis XIV declared Protestantism illegal in France, ushering in a period of religious intolerance, persecution, and Protestant expatriation.

rude tone frightened me into half crying; but for all that, as he said, "I had it to do." If Perjury it is, which will God punish: me, who was unwilling to commit the crime, or the man who forced me to it?

* * *

JULY 15, 1863

It is but too true; both have fallen. All Port Hudson privates have been paroled, and the officers sent here for exchange. Aye! aye! aye! I know some privates I would rather see than the officers! As yet, only ten that we know have arrived. All are confined in the Custom house. Last evening crowds surrounded the place. We did something dreadful, Ada Peirce, Miriam and I. We went down to the Confectionery, and unable to resist the temptation, made a détour by the Custom house in hope of seeing one of our poor dear half starved mule and rat fed defenders. The crowd had passed away then; but what was our horror when we emerged from the river side of the building and turned into Canal, to find the whole front of the pavement lined with Yankees! Our folly struck us so forcibly that we were almost paralyzed with fear. However that did not prevent us from endeavoring to hurry past, though I felt as though walking in a nightmare.

Ada was brave enough to look up at a window where several of our prisoners were standing, and kept urging us to do likewise. "Look! he knows you, Sarah! he has called another to see you! They both recognize you! O look please and tell me who they are! they are watching you still!" she would exclaim. But if my own dear brother stood there, I could not have raised my eyes; we only hurried on faster, with a hundred Yankees eyes fixed on our flying steps.

My friend Colonel Steadman was one of the Commissioners for arranging the terms of the capitulation, I see. He has not yet arrived.

* * *

Dreadful news has come of the defeat of Lee at Gettysburg. Think I believe it all? He may have been defeated; but no one of these reports of total overthrow and rout do I credit. Yankees jubilant, Southerners dismal. Brother, with principles on one side, and brothers on the other, is correspondingly distracted.

* * *

NO. 211 CAMP ST., APRIL 19, 1865

"All things are taken from us, and become portions and parcels of the dreadful pasts." . . .

Thursday the 13th, came the dreadful tidings of the surrender of Lee and his army on the 9th. Every body cried, but I would not, satisfied that God will still save us, even though all should apparently be lost. Followed at intervals of two or three hours by the announcement of the capture of Richmond, Selma, Mobile, and Johnson's army, even the staunchest Southerners were hopeless. Every one proclaimed Peace, and the only matter under consideration was whether Jeff Davis, all politicians, every man above the rank of Captain in the army, and above that of Lieutenant in the navy, should be hanged immediately, or *some* graciously pardoned. Henry Ward Beecher humanely pleaded mercy for us, supported by a small minority. Davis and all leading men *must* be executed; the blood of the others would serve to irrigate the country. Under this lively prospect, Peace! blessed Peace! was the cry. I whispered "Never! let a great earthquake swallow us up first! Let us leave our land and emigrate to any desert spot of the earth, rather than return to the Union, even as it Was!"

Six days this has lasted. Blessed with the silently obstinate disposition, I would not dispute, but felt my heart swell repeating, "God is our refuge and our strength, a very present help in time of trouble," and could not for an instant believe this could end in an overthrow.

This morning when I went down to breakfast at seven, Brother read the announcement of the assassination of Lincoln and Secretary Seward. "Vengeance is mine; I will repay, saith the Lord." This is murder! God have mercy on those who did it!

* * *

Charlotte Corday killed Marat in his bath,[4] and is held up in history as one of Liberty's martyrs, and one of the heroines of her country. To me, it is all Murder. Let historians extol blood shedding; it is woman's place to abhor it. And because I know that they would have apotheosized any man who had crucified Jeff Davis, I abhor this, and call it foul murder, unworthy of our cause—and God grant it was only the temporary insanity of a desperate man that committed this crime! Let not his blood be visited on our nation, Lord!

Across the way, a large building undoubtedly inhabited by officers is being draped in black. Immense streamers of black and white hang from the balcony. Down town, I understand, all shops are closed, and all wrapped in mourning. And I hardly dare pray God to bless us, with the crape hanging over the way. It would have been banners, if our president had been killed, though!

April 22, 1865

To see a whole city draped in mourning is certainly an imposing spectacle, and becomes almost grand when it is considered as an expression of universal affliction. So it is, in one sense. For the more violently "secesh" the inmates, the more thankful they are for Lincoln's death, the more profusely the houses are decked with the emblems of woe. They all look to me like "not sorry for him, but dreadfully grieved to be forced to this demonstration." So all things have indeed assumed a funereal aspect. Men who have hated Lincoln with all their souls, under terror of confiscation and imprisonment which they *understand* is the alternative, tie black crape from every practicable knob and point, to save their homes. Last evening the Bells were all in tears, preparing their mourning. What sensibility! what patriotism! a stranger would have exclaimed. But Bella's first remark was "Is it not horrible? This vile, *vile* old crape! Think of hanging it out when"—tears of rage finished the sentence. One would have thought pity for the murdered man had very little to do with it.

Coming back in the cars, I had a *rencontre* that makes me gnash my teeth yet. It was after dark, and I was the only lady in a car crowded with gentlemen. I placed little Miriam on my lap to make room for some of them when a great, dark man all in black entered, and took the seat and my left hand at the same instant, saying, "Good evening, Miss Sarah." Frightened beyond measure to recognize Captain Todd of the Yankee army in my interlocutor, I however preserved a quiet exterior, and without the slightest demonstration answered as though replying to an internal question, "Mr. Todd." "It is a

4. Revolutionary Jean Paul Marat was murdered in his bathtub by Charlotte Corday on 13 July 1793 during the Reign of Terror that followed the French Revolution.

long while since we met," he ventured. "Four years" I returned mechanically. "You have been well?" "My health has been bad." "I have been ill myself," and determined to break the ice he diverged with "Baton Rouge has changed sadly." "I hope I shall never see it again. We have suffered too much to recall home with any pleasure." "I understand you have suffered severely," he said, glancing at my black dress. "We have yet one left in the army, though," I could not help saying. He too had a brother there, he said.

He pulled the check string as we reached the house, adding unnecessarily "This is it," and absurdly correcting himself with "Where do you live?" "211. I thank you. Good evening" the last with emphasis as he prepared to follow. He returned the salutation, and I hurriedly regained the house. Monsieur stood over the way. A look through the blinds showed him returning to his domicile, several doors below. I returned to my own painful reflections. The Mr. Todd who was my "sweetheart" when I was twelve and he twenty-four, who was my brothers' friend, and daily at our home, was put away from among our acquaintance at the beginning of the war. This one, I should not know. Cords of candy, and mountains of bouquets bestowed in childish days, will not make my country's enemy my friend now that I am a woman.

Questions to Consider

1. Sarah Morgan clearly casts her lot with that of the Confederacy, yet she holds in contempt "patriotic women." How does Morgan distinguish herself from other Confederate women? What does her scorn reveal about class tensions in the Confederate South?
2. In what ways does Morgan accept Antebellum Southern gender and racial conventions? In what ways does she reject those conventions? What does this ambivalence suggest?

PART III
Rebuilding and Repression
1880–1910

While the meeting of Robert E. Lee and Ulysses S. Grant at Appomattox Courthouse signaled the end of slavery and the restoration of the Union, many of the issues that divided the North and South remained unresolved. Matters like the place of African Americans in United States society, the redistribution of wealth, the relative power of state and federal governments, and even the role of women in the redefined Southern family continued to generate tension between the regions. However, once the North had completed its decisive victory of swords and guns, the defeated South began to win the peace, using the weapons with which it had always been highly skilled: language and story.

In capturing the Northern imagination, the South adopted one of the nineteenth-century's most widely read genres: local color. A burgeoning periodical readership was consuming nearly a million pages of articles and fiction by the century's final decade, creating publishing opportunities for many writers. Stimulated by a renewed interest in the nation's diverse territories, the West, New England, and the Midwest all produced substantial bodies of regional fiction, but the South was by far the most popular subject of local color. Practiced by such successful and disparate Southerners as George W. Cable, Joel Chandler Harris, Thomas Nelson Page, Charles Chesnutt, Kate Chopin, and Thomas Dixon, this complex tradition reflects many of the contested issues that shaped both the South and the nation during the final decades of the century.

Formally developed in the frontier tales of Bret Harte and Mark Twain shortly after the Civil War, local color was a version of nineteenth-century realism, characterized by its distinctive regional settings, its portrayal of eccentric characters and unusual cultural practices, and its reliance on dialect. Primarily a post-Reconstruction phenomenon, Southern local color owed important debts to prewar fiction, especially the plantation romances of the 1840s and 1850s, which underscored the aristocratic claims of White Southern society, and the southwest humor fiction of the 1830s, which drew on oral traditions, tall tales, and detailed regional folkways. Local color thrived on the sheer variety of the region, and the diverse landscapes and customs of the South encouraged several variants, from stories set in the blue mountains of Tennessee to those laid out on the brick streets of New Orleans or in the former plantation houses and slave cabins of Georgia and Virginia. The feature that delineated Southern local color most sharply was its intimate connection with what came to be known as the "Lost Cause," an idealized celebration of Old South ideals, the Confederacy, and the glorification of an Antebellum past defined by racial harmony, plantation families, and chivalry.

At times clinging to, at times defined by, and at times reacting against this idealized Old South, Southern local color emerged from the ashes of Reconstruction (1867–1877). This federally mandated and militarily enforced reorganization of a vanquished foe offered a unique opportunity for the nation no less than the region to reimagine itself socially, culturally, and economically. The political and economic gains made by African Americans—including voting and property rights, reformed labor laws, and public education—were swiftly eroded in the 1880s, largely through White resistance to the goals of Reconstruction. Even though Congress, through the Enforcement Acts of 1871, had suppressed the most violent terrorist groups, like Tennessee's Ku Klux Klan or Louisiana's Knights of the White Camellia, political corruption and the economic depression that resulted from the Panic of 1873 disrupted most reform efforts. When Rutherford B. Hayes's Republican victory was bartered for the return of White political control in the South, the aims of Reconstruction were doomed. Its genuine accomplishments, which included voting rights, tax reforms, and improved labor laws, began to be viewed as failures, even in the Northern press. By the election of 1881, the White South was solidly Democratic (see Map III-1) and steadfast in its resolve to reconstruct itself on its own terms.

One literary vehicle of that Reconstruction soon surfaced in New Orleans. In 1879, former Confederate officer and Louisiana native, George W. Cable, published *Old Creole Days* in *Scribner's*, a leading national magazine. The reaction was immediate: "New England is no longer king. Her literary school is dying out," intoned a *Scribner's* editor in 1881; the "North will welcome with no stinted praise . . . [t]he best that the South can do." Cable's success drew a myriad of other Southern writers into print, including Joel Chandler Harris, Thomas Nelson Page, and Mary N. Murfree, as well as many Northern authors who capitalized on Southern settings. Southern local color became a staple of the increasingly lucrative literary and magazine markets.

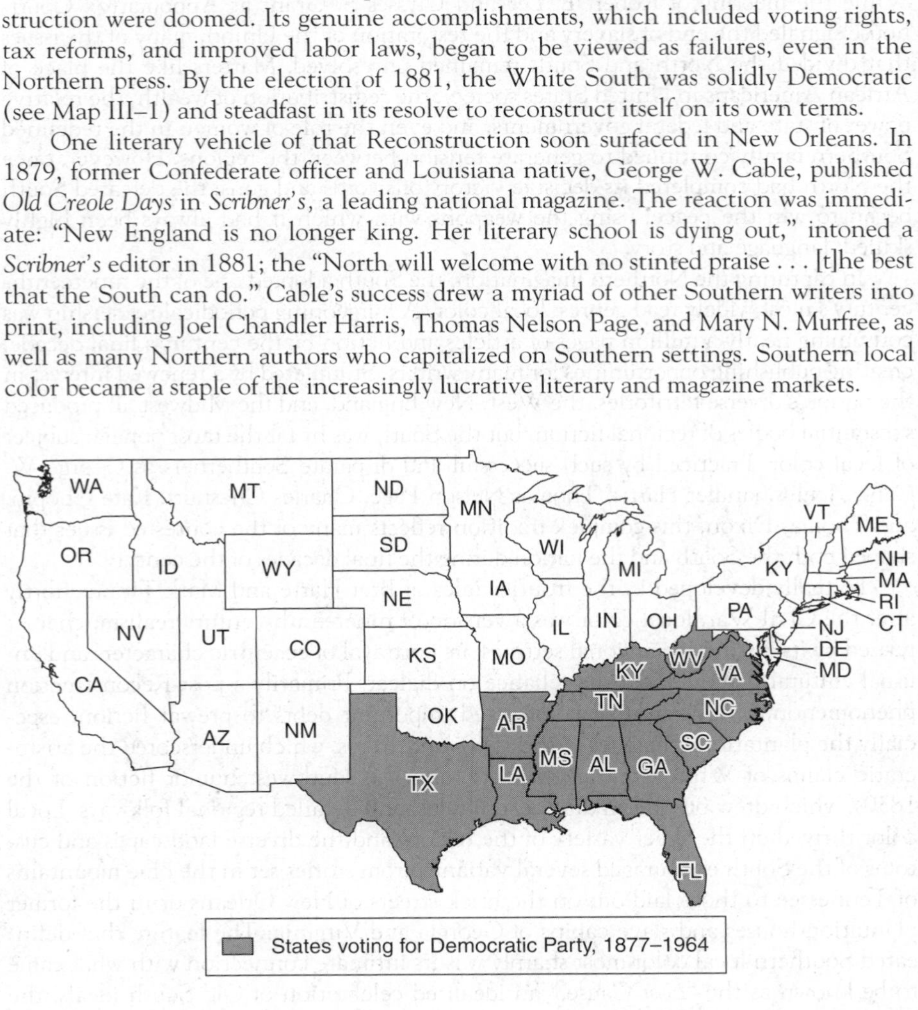

Map III–1: The "Solid South"

In contrast to the local color of other American regions, that of the South was explicitly linked to a distinctive, pre-Emancipation past defined by White paternalism. Writers like Harris and Page became exemplars of the genre, revered for their portrayals of a racial harmony that confirmed the belief that African Americans, however venerable or wily, were well-served by their subservience to White aristocracy. Harris's Uncle Remus entertains and instructs his golden-haired young protégée no less than he does Harris's eager Northern readers. Page's eternally loyal former slaves harken back to the wondrous days "befo' de war," while they continue to serve, admire, and protect their enlightened and courageous young White masters. Even Cable, whose outspoken criticism of racial inequality in *The Grandissimes* (1880) and many essays eventually drove him from the South, achieved national prominence precisely because he celebrated the graceful, eccentric beauty of a doomed Southern past; and though his portraits of African Americans have a unique vigor and realism, Cable still put the "solution" for the "New South" into the hands of enlightened White Southerners and their sympathetic Northern companions. By 1888, Albion W. Tourgée, a highly respected Northern novelist and advocate for racial equality, insisted that all American literature had become "not only Southern in type, but distinctively Confederate in sympathy."

Politically as well as culturally, the Lost Cause was becoming the American cause. White Southerners, who had clung to White supremacy as a vestige of the economic and political power they believed they deserved, now fought strenuously to preserve those racial distinctions that would reinstate their prerogatives. They were also persuading the North to their point of view. As Southern states began to institute legislation requiring racial segregation, known as Jim Crow laws, the Supreme Court obliged in 1883 by overturning the Civil Rights Act of 1875, further disabling the rights of African-American citizens. The "separate but equal" ruling in the *Plessy* v. *Ferguson* case by the 1896 Supreme Court finally ensured a national and legally enforceable system of segregation that relegated African Americans to a decidedly unequal status. Resulting in often underfunded and inferior facilities for education, health, and a wide variety of private and public services, segregation would remain national law until the *Brown* v. *Board of Education* in 1954.

But even if the South had won a questionable victory by transforming its sectional mythology of an Antebellum golden age into a treasured national history, the Lost Cause was not enshrined without protest. Despite the ultimate political failure of Reconstruction, efforts to enfranchise the freedmen lingered in the form of small businesses, educational institutions, and a tenacious sense of political, economic, and social entitlement. Many schools for African-American children, founded by Northern churches, and a few activist groups struggled on after the withdrawal of federal troops. Colleges for African Americans opened all over the South, including Tuskegee Normal and Industrial Institute in Alabama and Straight College (now Dillard University) in New Orleans. Even more important was the opening of 17 new state colleges specifically for African Americans in the South through the 1890 extension of the Morrill Agricultural College Act. Although underfunded and often beleaguered, these institutions were critical centers of hope and opportunity throughout the next half century of racial oppression.

Many writers also responded vigorously to the legislation and reactionary attitudes that were defining the post-Reconstruction South. Most notable was Cable, who denounced racial inequality, slavery, and the pretensions of Southern aristocracy, though he paid a heavy personal price for his perceived disloyalty to the region. His essay, "The Freedman's Case in Equity," which outlined arguments against the post-Reconstruction policies that were returning African Americans to virtual slavery, was fiercely criticized by his fellow Southerners, including Grace King who took Cable to task for his unflattering portrayals of Creole culture. Following his self-imposed exile to Massachusetts in 1885, Cable wrote even more stridently against Southern injustices, exposing the abuses of the convict-lease system and other brutalities practiced in prisons and asylums.

A number of other White writers also used print to resist the tide of racial oppression, including Emory professor and Methodist minister Andrew Sledd, Episcopalian bishop Thomas U. Dudley of Virginia, and perhaps the most famous, John Bassett, a professor of history at Trinity College (now Duke University), who repeatedly urged moderation in dealing with the "Negro problem." In his best-known essay, "Stirring Up the Fires of Racial Antipathy" (1903), Bassett provocatively described Booker T. Washington as second only to General Lee as the greatest Southerner "born in a hundred years." The statement aroused such virulent antagonism that he, like Cable, eventually fled to New England to finish his academic career.

If many White citizens rejected the South's regressive policies and negative images of the freedmen, the most forceful rebuttals came from African Americans themselves. Throughout the region, African Americans resisted efforts to curtail their freedoms in lawsuits, boycotts, and riots, including the 1898 race riots in Wilmington, North Carolina, on which Charles Chesnutt based his 1901 novel, *The Marrow of Tradition*. Chesnutt's fiction was itself a powerful counter to the nostalgic images of slavery promoted in the works of Thomas N. Page, Thomas Dixon, Ruth Stuart, and others. Unlike Uncle Remus, who transfers any dissidence to animal tricksters, Chesnutt's Uncle Julius is subversive, deceiving oblivious Northern Whites with their own effigies of African-American characters. At the same time, in the guise of humor, Chesnutt exposes the brutal truths of slavery in the cruel separation of families, as in "The Wife of His Youth," or the casual abuses of African-American labor in "The Goophered Grapevine." Another writer with Northern roots, Paul Laurence Dunbar, who achieved a national reputation as a writer of dialect poetry, also published fiction debunking the moonlight-and-magnolias version of the prewar South.

Another important vehicle of African-American resistance was the periodical press. Hundreds of African-American newspapers, often associated with churches, appeared throughout the South in the last decades of the century, though most of them encountered violent opposition and were short-lived. Mississippi-born journalist Ida B. Wells, who launched a courageous antilynching campaign in the *Memphis Free Speech*, for example, saw her newspaper office destroyed by a White mob in 1892, after she publicly protested the lynching of three local Black businessmen. Typically based in Northern states where there was less threat of violence and greater capital, scholarly journals, like *The Journal of Negro History* founded in 1915, published a steady stream of conscientious articles, including Alice Dunbar-Nelson's "People of Color in Louisiana," which carefully documents the complexities of racial categories—an implicit feature of her fictional portraits, such as "Little Miss Sophie," as well—and addresses the distinctive presence of African-descent Americans in Southern history. Dunbar-Nelson devoted most of her writing to nonfiction works such as anthologies, essays, diaries, and newspaper columns after 1900. With her second husband, Robert Nelson, she also published the respected and influential newspaper, the *Wilmington Advocate* from 1920 to 1922.

African Americans also protested segregation with their feet. With Jim Crow firmly in place throughout the South, the Great Migration of African Americans to the relative freedom of the North began in earnest in the late 1890s. By 1930, over a million disillusioned African Americans had moved to cities like Chicago, New York, Cincinnati, Detroit, and Cleveland. The improved status that African Americans sought is reflected in Chesnutt's portrayal of the "blue-veined black scion of Cleveland" with a slave past in "The Wife of His Youth." In Northern cities, the resistance to African-American oppression could take more deliberate shape, not only in journals and newspapers, but in activist organizations like the National Association for the Advancement of Colored People (NAACP), founded in 1910, or the National Association of Colored Women, seven years earlier. Perhaps even more important, those transplanted Southern communities provided the basis for the development of imaginative new versions of the African-American experience in music, art, and literature of every type. Half a century later these efforts would evolve into the political and social will to change known as the Civil Rights Movement. As the principal obsession of most White Southerners after Reconstruction, the systematic disempowerment of African Americans profoundly shaped most other events of the period, including woman's struggle for suffrage, workers' efforts to organize, and even the nation's political and economic ambitions abroad.

The association of women's suffrage with abolitionism had ensured a cool public reception in the South following the war, despite the work of early feminists like Angelina and Sarah Grimké of South Carolina. But with the ratification of suffrage for Black men in 1867, Southern women recognized a model for their own enfranchisement. Many of them worked tirelessly in state legislatures on issues like child labor, custody, and inheritance reform before formal organizations for suffrage were developed in the 1890s. Even more encouraging was Oklahoma's inclusion of voting rights for women when it applied for statehood in 1890. However, suffrage efforts were eventually undermined by the racist tactics to which White women resorted. Influential activists tried to court state legislators, for example, by claiming that votes for White women would dilute the voting power of African Americans. But after the Supreme Court upheld Mississippi's new Jim Crow laws in 1898, confirming federal support for segregation, woman's suffrage lost any serious support in Southern legislatures, which turned to more conventional ways to suppress African-American voters. For just as White women had seen in African-American suffrage an opportunity to secure their own voting rights, the Southern hierarchy had accurately perceived an alarming threat to Southern patriarchy in female autonomy. As a result, the Nineteenth Amendment did not become federal law until 1920, when it was ratified, ironically, by one vote in the Tennessee state legislature.

Another element of Southern resistance to women's rights was the image of the Southern belle or the plantation mistress. A central motif of Southern local color, the belle was not simply the object of romance or maternal power (as in "Marse Chan" or "Désirée's Baby"), she was also the motive for Southern chivalry, one of the principal guises of White supremacy. Protecting White women became a paramount expression of White manhood, with African-American men increasingly perceived as the chief threat to both feminine virtue and, by extension, masculine honor. Thomas Dixon's fiction epitomizes this idealization of Southern White womanhood and the concomitant caricatures of African-American bestiality. Unfortunately his work only echoed and enforced the violent strategies of White supremacists throughout the period, who opposed African-American resistance to White rule.

An epidemic of lynchings broke out in the South between 1882 and 1900 (see Map III–2), when over a thousand African-American men, and a number of women, were executed by White mobs, often after barbaric tortures. The most widely held justification for these crimes was the rape of a White woman. Though investigations by Ida B. Wells and others confirmed that only about a third of these executions even mentioned rape, assault on White women became the representative rationale for the suppression of African Americans. Like the politics of the suffrage movement, these pretexts for violence reaffirmed the close links between the status of African Americans, especially African-American men, and the status of White women. Dependent on the subservience of both groups, the Southern patriarchy used the threat of male sexual violence to contain White women, even as the defense of White womanhood justified its brutalization of African-American men. Meanwhile African-American women, like Alice Dunbar-Nelson's Miss Sophie or Ruth Stuart's Lucindy,

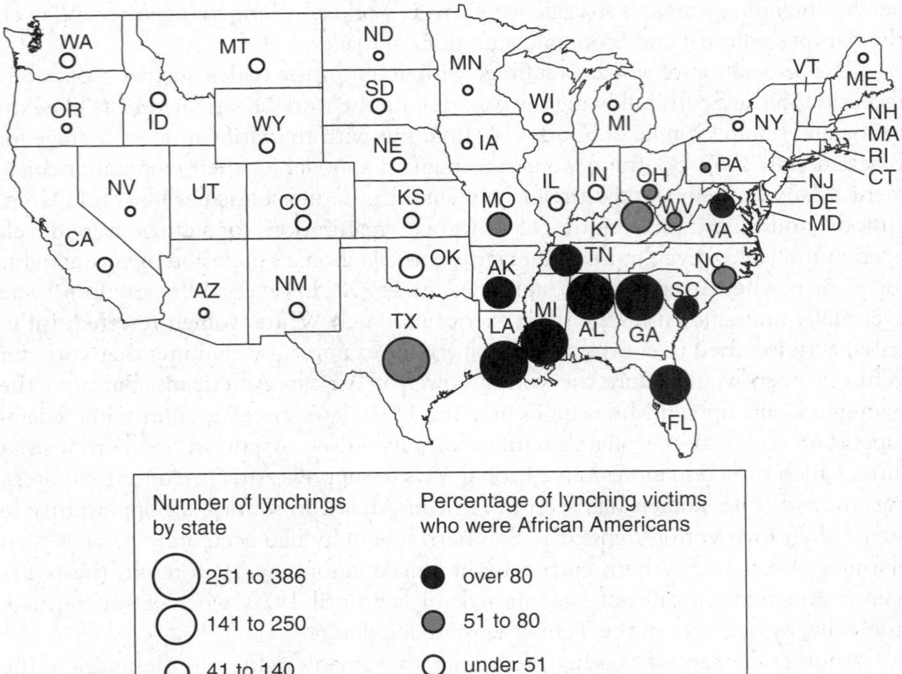

Map III–2: Lynching incidents, 1889–1918

embodied a female sexuality forbidden to White women, thus making women of color susceptible to both rape and retribution.

The Southern belle was often identified in essays and fiction with the South itself. One of the most popular representations of regional reconciliation was the marriage of a Southern belle to a Northern suitor, an image that resonated as both a political and a domestic trope. Changing gender roles, signaled by the emergence of the "new woman" in the 1880s and 1890s, generated a great deal of anxiety among American males. Southern men, with over three hundred thousand of their fellows having been killed or maimed on the battlefields, sought to reestablish their injured manhood by reasserting their authority over the remaining element of their patriarchal households, their loyal women. Northern men, confronted by an increasingly vocal suffragist movement, were likewise comforted by the notion of submissive Southern females, no less than by the prospect of a defeated region newly amenable to economic exploitation.

Southern efforts to redefine White authority in fact occurred in the context of enormous economic, technological, and social changes. The industrialization that had begun before 1880 accelerated during this decade, doubling manufacturing in most Southern states and tripling the number of steel and textile workers. Railroad mileage doubled (see Map III–3), reshaping agriculture and expanding lumbering and cash crops like cotton into new areas. Urban areas also grew, expanding the professional classes and encouraging new amenities like electric lighting, telephones, modern sewer systems, and indoor plumbing.

By the early 1880s, editorials and civic boosters were proclaiming a New South, eager to collaborate with the North in exploiting rich Southern resources. Among

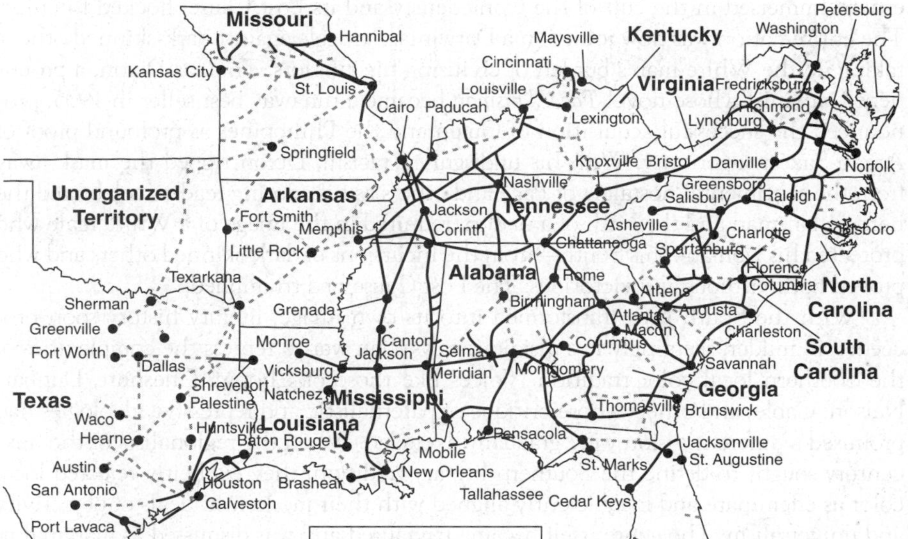

Map III–3: Southern railway route map, circa 1897

these spokesmen was Henry Grady, who with Joel Chandler Harris co-edited the *Atlanta Constitution*. Grady's landmark speech in 1886 projected a potent image of the South, unapologetic for her past and eager to put business above politics. But while such imagery calmed Northern investors and gratified Southern loyalists, widespread misgivings remained about the results of an industrialized regime on ordinary people's lives. An important manifestation of this unrest was the rise of Populism, a movement that reflected the frustration of small farmers and workers who had struggled through depression, sinking crop prices, land devaluation, and a profusion of policies that favored large planters and businesses. Incorporating the Farmers Alliance, an earlier Southern coalition of farmers and mill workers that was remarkably integrated, the Populist or People's Party sought to revise the capitalist principles of the Gilded Age to more egalitarian ends. But like woman's suffrage, Populism in the South was ultimately undermined by race, for while the party had an impact on the national elections of 1892, by the next round of elections, its political base had been eroded by differing views of racial reform.

The event that definitively realigned Southern efforts to affirm White supremacy was another war. Though brief, the War of 1898, popularly known as the Spanish-American War, successfully diverted national attention away from anxieties about the South and its "Negro problem" to an external adversary, onto which many regional and racial concerns were displaced. By the turn of the century, economic depression, the closing of the frontier, the unchecked rise of big business, and widespread corruption all fostered the notion that the country was becoming weak and ineffectual. The outbreak of war generated a welcome opportunity to reassert the manliness of the nation, and popular patriotic rhetoric urged a defense of the nation's honor. Many White Southerners, immersed in the cult of the Confederacy and its Lost Cause, flocked to enlist. The entire nation was now joined in a Darwinian struggle against dark-skinned others, taking up the White man's burden of civilizing his inferiors. Thomas Dixon, a prominent Darwinist whose novel *The Clansman* became a runaway best seller in 1905, pronounced the successful acquisition of Guam and the Philippines as profound proof of Anglo-Saxon superiority. With his undisguised racism, Dixon ripped the mask away from the sentimental nostalgia of Page and others as his adoring readers celebrated the heroic clansman and the birth of a nation, reunited in the image of a White male who protected his woman—his South—from the incursions of dark-skinned others and who proved both virtuous and victorious. The Lost Cause had triumphed.

With the South thus transformed into its own image, literary history soon proceeded in milder, seemingly less insidious ways than war to repress the complexities of the Southern local color tradition. Voices like those of Chopin, Chesnutt, Dunbar-Nelson, Cable, and others whose critique of paternalistic and repressive ideologies had promised a different vision were gradually excluded. When the regionalists of the next century sought to define the Southern literary tradition, they explicitly rejected local color as effeminate and insufficiently aligned with their modernist ideals of objectivity and universalism. The genre itself became trivialized and was dismissed as marginal in the national literary tradition. But even as the next generation of Southern writers decried the sentimentality of local color, the essential elements of the genre persisted in Southern writing: the commitment to place, a fascination with the grotesque, a passion for a past embodying injustices that, even now, will not rest. Though local color soon faded from the national literary landscape and consciousness, the genre had indeed served its purposes: reconstructing the South as central to the national imagination.

Rebuilding and Repression Chronology

1880–1910

1880s • Jim Crow laws instituted across the South.
• Buffalo nearly exterminated by indiscriminate hunting.
• Mass immigration of Europeans, especially to U.S. cities.
1880 • George Washington Cable, *The Grandissimes*.
1883 • Letter postage reduced to two cents.
1885 • Grover Cleveland becomes president.
• Cattle drives largely made obsolete by railroads.
1886 • Geronimo captured.
• Henry Grady's speech coins the term "The New South."
• Linotype composing machine invented.
• Statue of Liberty unveiled in New York.
1887 • Dawes Act reverses U.S. Indian policy, dividing up tribal lands among families.
• President Cleveland signs the Interstate Commerce Act.
1889 • Oklahoma open to settlers.
• North Dakota, South Dakota, Montana, and Washington become states.
1890 • Sherman Anti-Trust Act seeks to protect trade from unlawful restraints.
1891 • International Copyright Treaty.
1892 • Frances Ellen Watkins Harper, *Iola Leroy*, or *Shadows Uplifted*.
• Riots at Carnegie's steel works in Homestead, Pennsylvania.
• Mississippi begins use of literacy tests to curtail voting by African Americans.
1893 • Financial panic, precipitating five-year economic depression.
1896 • *Plessy* v. *Ferguson* establishes doctrine of separate but equal.
• Gold is discovered in Alaska.
1898 • U.S.S. *Maine* destroyed in Havana harbor by mysterious explosion.
• War of 1898 (Spanish-American War); ended by treaty with Spain signed in Paris.
• Annexation of Hawaii.
• Wilmington Race Riots; basis for Charles W. Chesnutt's *Marrow of Tradition*.
1899 • Kate Chopin, *The Awakening*.
• Scott Joplin publishes "Maple Leaf Rag."
1900 • Galveston hurricane kills over 6,000 people, worst natural disaster in U.S. history.
1901 • Booker T. Washington, *Up from Slavery*.
• Frank Norris exposes corruption of railroad industry in *The Octopus*.
• President William McKinley assassinated.
1902 • Great Anthracite strike in Pennsylvania.
1903 • Wright brothers complete first successful flight.
• Panama Canal treaty signed.
• *The Great Train Robbery*, first narrative motion picture.
1904 • Construction of Parchman Farm, Mississippi's infamous state penitentiary.
1905 • Thomas Dixon, *The Clansman*.
1907 • Panic and widespread financial collapse.
1908 • Henry Ford introduces the Model T motorcar.
1909 • National Association for the Advancement of Colored People (NAACP) founded.
1910 • Death of Mark Twain.
• Jane Addams, *Twenty Years at Hull House*.

George Washington Cable

1844–1925

"The true artist," declared George Washington Cable, "must possess the haunted heart." With elegance, talent, and an outspoken commitment to social and racial justice, Cable explored the haunted heart of his beloved New Orleans: a city defined by its exotic Creole, American, and African interdependencies and, like the larger South, by the deeply flawed social and economic structures that perpetuated White privilege, often violently. Cable's authorial career was launched, celebrated, and almost dashed in the process. Although his contemporary Northern critics lauded Cable as among the most distinguished American authors, the condemnation of his fellow Southerners led him to choose exile from his homeland for the last half of his life. Today, knowledgeable twentieth-century critics consider Cable's *The Grandissimes* (1880) a precursor of William Faulkner's fiction and as important as Herman Melville's *Moby Dick* (1851) and Mark Twain's *Huckleberry Finn* (1885); even so, Cable remains virtually unread.

A conservative Protestant and an outspoken champion of African-American civil rights, Cable was fascinated by the steamy decadence of his native New Orleans. He was born on 12 October 1844 in the predominantly Catholic city. His German-descent father came from a slave-holding family in Virginia; his Midwestern mother, who became an ardent Confederate, was of New England Puritan ancestry. His deeply religious parents were very influential, and Cable's lifelong religious convictions prompted Mark Twain to insist that his friend was more upright than the apostles in his oral honesty, limpid innocence, and utterly blameless piety. With the death of Cable's father and the failure of the family's fortunes in 1859, the fourteen-year-old youth left school to support his mother and siblings, fleeing with them when the Union occupied the city in 1862. Though Cable barely weighed a hundred pounds, he joined the Mississippi Cavalry, was twice wounded, and served until the war ended.

Returning to New Orleans, he obtained a position as a cotton warehouse clerk, work he would pursue periodically for 15 years; however, his thirst for adventure and his interest in Louisiana lore led him to join surveyors charting the Atchafalaya basin. Forced to return to New Orleans when he contracted malaria, Cable married New Orleanian Louise Bartlett in 1869, a suitably pious woman of New England heritage, with whom he would eventually have seven children. Cable also became a columnist and reporter for a local newspaper and vigorously pursued a program of self-education, including an avid study of Louisiana culture and history. He also wrote his first story, "Bibi," now lost but based on the Louisiana legend of the proud rebel slave who escaped to the swamps after striking his White master. Eventually recaptured, the African prince was brutally mutilated and executed as mandated by the Antebellum law, the *Code Noir*. For Cable, this "Shadow of the Ethiopian" represented the nightmare that haunted his contemporary South.

In 1873, Cable offered "Bibi" to writer Edward King, who was touring the postwar South for *Scribner's*, a leading Northern magazine. The highly successful reception of Bret Harte's California mining camp story, "The Luck of Roaring Camp" (1868), had signaled a burgeoning market for short, regional stories, a genre that came to be called local color fiction. When King read "Bibi," he immediately recognized Cable's talent. Shocked at the story's brutality and subversive spirit, King's editor rejected the tale, but he later accepted Cable's "Sieur George," a less troubling story of Antebellum indolence and decadence. Cable's next story, "Belle Demoiselles Plantation" (1874), features the romance of Antebellum New Orleans even as it literally embodies the erosion of the aristocratic South: its land, its plantation culture, and its heritage. With these and other stories collected in *Old Creole Days* (1879), Cable unwittingly opened the Southern local color market that would eventually fill millions of magazine pages by the 1890s.

Cable's first and greatest novel, *The Grandissimes* (1880), takes place in 1803 in French-identified New Orleans, just after the American purchase of the Louisiana Territory from France. Cable masks his indictment of contemporary post-Reconstruction White bigotry by choosing an historical setting and by providing a sentimental resolution. However, the thwarted power of Africans and their descendants fills the novel's pages. The enslaved African prince Bras-Coupé dies from the violent reprisals demanded by the *Code Noir.* A wealthy freedman of color (himself a Grandissime family heir) commits suicide, and the wily and articulate seller of sweets, Clemence, a Virginian-born former slave and clandestine voodoo practitioner, is shot in the back. In his novella *Madame Delphine* (1881), Cable returned to the overt romance of *Old Creole Days* to address more subtly the injustice of miscegenation and the prohibitions against interracial marriage.

With the romantic yesterdays of his very saleable fiction muting his call for social and racial justice, Cable became an admired full-time author and a spokesperson for the Creole and African cultures of New Orleans. He wrote nonfiction, including *Creoles of Louisiana* (1884), and published his research on Creole and African dances, songs, and religious ritual in two 1886 *Century Magazine* articles, "The Dance in Place Congo" and "Creole Slave Songs." "The Voodoos," a section in the latter, reflects both Cable's fascination with and his revulsion for the African-American religion he had made a centerpiece in *The Grandissimes*. The selection also reveals the historian Cable, who carefully researched Louisiana culture and transformed that research into detailed, vivid narratives. Similar materials formed the basis of Cable's lucrative national lecture tours with such notables as Mark Twain, who became a lifelong friend.

Also intrigued with the Louisiana Acadian culture, the result of a forced British resettlement in the 1750s, Cable published *Bonaventure* (1888) and established a market that Kate Chopin, who knew his work, would also exploit. Cable became increasingly open as an advocate for social, political, and economic reforms in novels like *Dr. Sevier,* which raised the issue of prison reform (1882), and *John March, Southerner* (1895), which dramatized the region's desperate need for economic revitalization. Removing his literary mask, he aroused Southern furor through his fierce support for freedman's rights and the dissolution of Jim Crow laws in "The Freedman's Case in Equity" (1885), *The Silent South* (1885), and *The Negro Question* (1890). By 1885, Cable had lost the approbation of the South. Longing to be closer to his New England friends, including Twain who was living in Connecticut, he settled in Northampton, Massachusetts, where he lived the remainder of his life.

At the turn of the new century, the nation viewed the Negro question as settled and the Confederacy as noble and romantic. Following the limited success of *John March,* Cable gardened, produced a Biblical commentary, worked to establish integrated reading clubs, and supported the establishment of the League of Nations. Though he continued to write, his biting social criticism abated. He began to paint a nobler, kinder South, including reminiscences of his Confederate youth in *The Cavalier* (1902), which was a runaway best seller and a highly successful Broadway play. Only in his last novel, *Lovers of Louisiana* (1918), does Cable again address Southern isolation and injustice, but his authorial voice, apropos of this fictional coda, is filled with affection. He wrote no other fiction and died on 31 January 1925. His memorial tributes celebrated him as among the greatest of American authors and described *The Grandissimes* as the greatest novel to date.

The Voodoos

The dance and song entered into the Negro worship. That worship was as dark and horrid as bestialized savagery could make the adoration of serpents. So revolting was it, and so morally hideous, that even in the West Indian French possessions a hundred years ago, with the slave trade in full blast and the West Indian planter and slave what they were, the orgies of the Voodoos were forbidden. Yet both there and in Louisiana they were practiced.

The Aradas, St. Méry tells us, introduced them. They brought them from their homes beyond the Slave Coast, one of the most dreadfully benighted regions of all Africa. He makes the word Vaudaux. In Louisiana it is written Voudou and Voodoo, and is often changed on the Negro's lips to Hoodoo. It is the name of an imaginary being of vast supernatural powers residing in the form of a harmless snake. This spiritual influence or potentate is the recognized antagonist and opposite of Obi, the great African manitou or deity, or him whom the Congoes vaguely generalize as Zombi. In Louisiana, as I have been told by that learned Creole scholar the late Alexander Dimitry, Voodoo bore as a title of greater solemnity the additional name of Maignan, and that even in the Calinda dance, which he had witnessed innumerable times, was sometimes heard, at the height of its frenzy, the invocation—

Aïe! Aïe!
Voodoo Magnan!

The worship of Voodoo is paid to a snake kept in a box. The worshipers are not merely a sect, but in some rude, savage way also an order. A man and woman chosen from their own number to be the oracles of the serpent deity are called the king and queen. The queen is the more important of the two, and even in the present dilapidated state of the worship in Louisiana, where the king's office has almost or quite disappeared, the queen is still a person of note.

She reigns as long as she continues to live. She comes to power not by inheritance, but by election or its barbarous equivalent. Chosen for such qualities as would give her a natural supremacy, personal attractions among the rest, and ruling over superstitious fears and desires of every fierce and ignoble sort, she wields no trivial influence. I once saw, in her extreme old age, the famed Marie Laveau. Her dwelling was in the quadroon quarter of New Orleans, but a step or two from Congo Square, a small adobe cabin just off the sidewalk, scarcely higher than its close board fence, whose batten gate yielded to the touch and revealed the crazy doors and windows spread wide to the warm air, and one or two tawny faces within, whose expression was divided between a pretense of contemptuous inattention and a frowning resentment of the intrusion. In the center of a small room whose ancient cypress floor was worn with scrubbing and sprinkled with crumbs of soft brick—a Creole affectation of superior cleanliness—sat, quaking with feebleness in an ill-looking old rocking chair, her body bowed, and her wild, gray witch's tresses hanging about her shriveled, yellow neck, the queen of the Voodoos. Three generations of her children were within the faint beckon of her helpless, waggling wrist and fingers. They said she was over a hundred years old, and there was nothing to cast doubt upon the statement. She had shrunken away from her skin; it was like a turtle's. Yet withal one could hardly help but see that the face, now so withered, had once been handsome and commanding. There was still a faint shadow of departed beauty on the forehead, the spark of an old fire in the sunken, glistening eyes, and a vestige of imperiousness in the fine, slightly aquiline nose, and even about her silent, woebegone mouth. Her grandson stood by, an uninteresting quadroon between forty and fifty years old, looking strong, empty-minded, and trivial enough; but his mother, her daughter, was also present, a woman of some seventy years, and a most striking and majestic figure. In features, stature, and bearing she was regal. One had but to look on her, impute her brilliancies—too untamable and severe to be called charms or graces—to her mother, and remember what New Orleans was long years ago, to understand how the name of Marie Laveau should have driven itself inextricably into the traditions of the town and the times.

Had this visit been postponed a few months it would have been too late. Marie Laveau is dead; Malvina Latour is queen. As she appeared presiding over a Voodoo ceremony on the night of the 23d of June, 1884, she is described as a bright mulattress of about forty-eight, of "extremely handsome figure," dignified bearing, and a face indicative of a comparatively high order of intelligence. She wore a neat blue, white-dotted calico gown, and a "brilliant *tignon* (turban) gracefully tied."

It is pleasant to say that this worship, in Louisiana, at least, and in comparison with what it once was, has grown to be a rather trivial affair. The practice of its midnight forest rites seemed to sink into inanition along with Marie Laveau. It long ago diminished in frequency to once a year, the chosen night always being the Eve of St. John. For several years past even these annual celebrations have been suspended; but in the summer of 1884 they were—let it be hoped, only for the once—resumed.

When the queen decides that such a celebration shall take place, she appoints a night for the gathering, and some remote, secluded spot in the forest for the rendezvous. Thither all the worshipers are summoned. St. Méry, careless of the power of the scene, draws in practical, unimaginative lines the picture of such a gathering in St. Domingo, in the times when the "*véritable Vaudaux*" had lost but little of the primitive African character. The worshipers are met, decked with kerchiefs more or less numerous, red being everywhere the predominating color. The king, abundantly adorned with them, wears one of pure red about his forehead as a diadem. A blue ornamental cord completes his insignia. The queen, in simple dress and wearing a red cord and a heavily decorated belt, is beside him near a rude altar. The silence of midnight is overhead, the gigantic forms and shadows and still, dank airs of the tropical forest close in around, and on the altar, in a small box ornamented with little tinkling bells, lies, unseen, the living serpent. The worshipers have begun their devotions to it by presenting themselves before it in a body, and uttering professions of their fidelity and belief in its power. They cease, and now the royal pair, in tones of parental authority and protection, are extolling the great privilege of being a devotee, and inviting the faithful to consult the oracle. The crowd makes room, and a single petitioner draws near. He is the senior member of the order. His prayer is made. The king becomes deeply agitated by the presence within him of the spirit invoked. Suddenly he takes the box from the altar and sets it on the ground. The queen steps upon it and with convulsive movements utters the answers of the deity beneath her feet. Another and another suppliant, approaching in the order of seniority, present, singly, their petitions, and humbly or exultingly, according to the nature of the responses, which hangs on the fierce caprice of the priestess, accept these utterances and make way for the next, with his prayer of fear or covetousness, love, jealousy, petty spite or deadly malice. At length the last petitioner is answered. Now a circle is formed, the caged snake is restored to the altar, and the humble and multifarious oblations of the worshipers are received, to be devoted not only to the trivial expenses of this worship, but also to the relief of members of the order whose distresses call for such aid. Again, the royal ones are speaking, issuing orders for execution in the future, orders that have not always been in view, mildly says St. Méry, good order and public tranquillity. Presently the ceremonies become more forbidding. They are taking a horrid oath, smearing their lips with the blood of some slaughtered animal, and swearing to suffer death rather than disclose any secret of the order, and to inflict death on any who may commit such treason. Now a new applicant for membership steps into their circle, there are a few trivial formalities, and the Voodoo dance begins. The postulant dances frantically in the middle of the ring, only pausing from time to time to receive heavy alcoholic draughts in great haste and return more wildly to his leapings and writhings until he falls in convulsions. He is lifted, restored, and presently conducted to the altar, takes his oath, and by a ceremonial stroke from one of the sovereigns is admitted a full participant in the privileges and obligations of the devilish freemasonry. But the dance goes on about the snake. The contortions of the upper part of the body, especially of the neck and shoulders, are such as threaten to dislocate them. The queen shakes the box and tinkles its bells, the rum bottle gurgles, the chant alternates between king and chorus—

Eh! eh! Bomba, honc! honc![1]
Canga bafio tay,
Canga moon day lay,
Canga do keelah,
Canga li ———

There are swoonings and ravings, nervous tremblings beyond control, incessant writhings and turnings, tearing of garments, even biting of the flesh—every imaginable invention of the devil.

St. Méry tells us of another dance invented in the West Indies by a Negro, analogous to the Voodoo dance, but more rapid, and in which dancers had been known to fall dead. This was the "Dance of Don Pedro." The best efforts of police had, in his day, only partially suppressed it. Did it ever reach Louisiana? Let us, at a venture, say no.

To what extent the Voodoo worship still obtains here would be difficult to say with certainty. The affair of June 1884 as described by Messrs. Augustin and Whitney, eye-witnesses, was an orgy already grown horrid enough when they turned their backs upon it. It took place at a wild and lonely spot where the dismal cypress swamp behind New Orleans meets the waters of Lake Pontchartrain in a wilderness of cypress stumps and rushes. It would be hard to find in nature a more painfully desolate region. Here in a fisherman's cabin sat the Voodoo worshipers cross-legged on the floor about an Indian basket of herbs and some beans, some bits of bone, some oddly wrought bunches of feathers, and some saucers of small cakes. The queen presided, sitting on the only chair in the room. There was no king, no snake—at least none visible to the onlookers. Two drummers beat with their thumbs on gourds covered with sheepskin, and a white-wooled old man scraped that hideous combination of banjo and violin, whose head is covered with rattlesnake skin, and of which the Chinese are the makers and masters. There was singing—"*M'allé couri dans déser*" (I am going into the wilderness), a chant and refrain not worth the room they would take—and there was frenzy and a circling march, wild shouts, delirious gesticulations and posturings, drinking, and amongst other frightful nonsense the old trick of making fire blaze from the mouth by spraying alcohol from it upon the flame of a candle.

But whatever may be the quantity of the Voodoo *worship* left in Louisiana, its superstitions are many and are everywhere. Its charms are resorted to by the malicious, the jealous, the revengeful, or the avaricious, or held in terror, not by the timorous only, but by the strong, the courageous, the desperate. To find under his mattress an acorn hollowed out, stuffed with the hair of some dead person, pierced with four holes on four sides, and two small chicken feathers drawn through them so as to cross inside the acorn; or to discover on his doorsill at daybreak a little box containing a dough or waxen heart stuck full of pins; or to hear that his avowed foe or rival has

1. "Hen! hen!" is St. Méry's spelling of it for French pronunciation. As he further describes the sound in a footnote, it must have been a horrid grunt.

been pouring cheap champagne in the four corners of Congo Square at midnight, when there was no moon, will strike more abject fear into the heart of many a stalwart Negro or melancholy quadroon than to face a leveled revolver. And it is not only the colored man that holds to these practices and fears. Many a White Creole gives them full credence. What wonder, when African Creoles were the nurses of so nearly all of them? Many shrewd men and women, generally colored persons, drive a trade in these charms and in oracular directions for their use or evasion; many a Creole—white as well as other tints—female, too, as well as male—will pay a Voodoo "*monteure*" to "make a work," i.e., to weave a spell, for the prospering of some scheme or wish too ignoble to be prayed for at any shrine inside the church. These milder incantations are performed within the witch's or wizard's own house, and are made up, for the most part, of a little pound cake, some lighted candle ends, a little syrup of sugar cane, pins, knitting needles, and a trifle of anisette. But fear naught; an Obi charm will enable you to smile defiance against all such mischief; or if you will but consent to be a magician, it is they, the Voodoos, one and all, who will hold you in absolute terror. Or, easier, a frizzly chicken! If you have on your premises a frizzly chicken, you can lie down and laugh—it is a checkmate!

A planter once found a Voodoo charm, or *ouanga* (wongah); this time it was a bit of cotton cloth folded about three cowpeas and some breast feathers of a barnyard fowl, and covered with a tight wrapping of thread. When he proposed to take it to New Orleans his slaves were full of consternation. "Marse Ed, ef ye go on d'boat wid dat-ah, de boat'll sink wi' yer. Fore d'Lord, it will!" For some reason it did not. Here is a genuine Voodoo song, given me by Lafcadio Hearn, though what the words mean none could be more ignorant of than the present writer. They are rendered phonetically in French.

Héron mandé,
Héron mandé,
Tigui li papa,
Héron mandé,
Tigui li papa,
Héron mandé,
Héron mandé,
Héron mandé,
Do sé dan gôdo.

And another phrase: "Ah tingouai yé, Ah tingouai yé, Ah ouai ya, Ah ouai ya, Ah tingouai yé, Do sé dan go-do, Ah tingouai yé," etc.

Belles Demoiselles Plantation

The original grantee was Count ———, assume the name to be De Charleu; the old Creoles never forgive a public mention. He was the French king's commissary. One day, called to France to explain the lucky accident of the commissariat having burned down with his account-books inside, he left his wife, a Choctaw Comptesse, behind.

Arrived at court, his excuses were accepted, and that tract granted him where afterwards stood Belles Demoiselles Plantation. A man cannot remember everything! In a fit of forgetfulness he married a French gentlewoman, rich and beautiful, and "brought her out." However, "All's well that ends well;" a famine had been in the colony, and the Choctaw Comptesse had starved, leaving nought but a half-caste orphan family lurking on the edge of the settlement, bearing our French gentlewoman's own new name, and being mentioned in Monsieur's will.

And the new Comptesse—she tarried but a twelvemonth, left Monsieur a lovely son, and departed, led out of this vain world by the swamp-fever.

From this son sprang the proud Creole family of De Charleu. It rose straight up, up, up, generation after generation, tall, branchless, slender, palm-like; and finally, in the time of which I am to tell, flowered with all the rare beauty of a century-plant, in Artemise, Innocente, Felicité, the twins Marie and Martha, Leontine and little Septima: the seven beautiful daughters for whom their home had been fitly named Belles Demoiselles.

The Count's grant had once been a long Pointe, round which the Mississippi used to whirl, and seethe, and foam, that it was horrid to behold. Big whirlpools would open and wheel about in the savage eddies under the low bank, and close up again, and others open, and spin, and disappear. Great circles of muddy surface would boil up from hundreds of feet below, and gloss over, and seem to float away—sink, come back again under water, and with only a soft hiss surge up again, and again drift off, and vanish. Every few minutes the loamy bank would tip down a great load of earth upon its besieger, and fall back a foot—sometimes a yard—and the writhing river would press after, until at last the Pointe was quite swallowed up, and the great river glided by in a majestic curve, and asked no more; the bank stood fast, the "caving" became a forgotten misfortune, and the diminished grant was a long, sweeping, willowy bend, rustling with miles of sugar-cane.

Coming up the Mississippi in the sailing craft of those early days, about the time one first could descry the white spires of the old St. Louis Cathedral, you would be pretty sure to spy, just over to your right under the levee, Belles Demoiselles Mansion, with its broad veranda and red painted cypress roof, peering over the embankment, like a bird in the nest, half hid by the avenue of willows which one of the departed De Charleus—he that married a Marot—had planted on the levee's crown.

The house stood unusually near the river, facing eastward, and standing four-square, with an immense veranda about its sides, and a flight of steps in front spreading broadly downward, as we open arms to a child. From the veranda nine miles of river were seen; and in their compass, near at hand, the shady garden full of rare and beautiful flowers; farther away broad fields of cane and rice, and the distant quarters of the slaves, and on the horizon everywhere a dark belt of cypress forest.

The master was old Colonel De Charleu—Jean Albert Henri Joseph De Charleu-Marot, and "Colonel" by the grace of the first American governor. Monsieur—he would not speak to any one who called him "Colonel"—was a hoary-headed patriarch. His step was firm, his form erect, his intellect strong and clear, his countenance classic, serene, dignified, commanding, his manners courtly, his voice musical—fascinating. He had had his vices—all his life; but had borne them, as his race do, with a serenity of conscience, and a cleanness of mouth that left no outward blemish on the surface of the gentleman. He had gambled in Royal Street, drank hard in Orleans Street, run his adversary through in the duelling-ground at Slaughter-house Point, and danced and quarreled at the St. Phillippe-street-theater quadroon balls. Even now, with all his courtesy and bounty, and a hospitality which seemed to be entertaining angels, he was bitter-proud and penurious, and deep down in his hard-finished heart loved nothing but himself, his name, and his motherless children. But these!—their ravishing beauty was all but excuse enough for the unbounded idolatry of their father. Against these seven goddesses he never rebelled. Had they even required him to defraud old De Carlos——I can hardly say.

Old De Carlos was his extremely distant relative on the Choctaw side. With this single exception, the narrow thread-like line of descent from the Indian wife, diminished to a mere strand by injudicious alliances, and deaths in the gutters of old New Orleans, was extinct. The name, by Spanish contact, had become De Carlos; but this one surviving bearer of it was known to all, and known only, as Injin Charlie.

One thing I never knew a Creole to do. He will not utterly go back on the ties of blood, no matter what sort of knots those ties may be. For one reason, he is never ashamed of his or his father's sins; and for another—he will tell you—he is "all heart!"

So the different heirs of the De Charleu estate had always strictly regarded the rights and interests of the De Carloses, especially their ownership of a block of dilapidated buildings in a part of the city, which had once been very poor property, but was beginning to be valuable. This block had much more than maintained the last De Carlos through a long and lazy lifetime, and, as his household consisted only of himself, and an aged and crippled negress, the inference was irresistible that he "had money." Old Charlie, though by *alias* an "Injin," was plainly a dark White man, about as old as Colonel De Charleu, sunk in the bliss of deep ignorance, shrewd, deaf, and, by repute at least, unmerciful.

The Colonel and he always conversed in English. This rare accomplishment, which the former had learned from his Scotch wife—the latter from up-river traders—they found an admirable medium of communication, answering, better than French could, a similar purpose to that of the stick which we fasten to the bit of one horse and breast-gear of another, whereby each keeps his distance. Once in a while, too, by way of jest, English found its way among the ladies of Belles Demoiselles, always signifying that their sire was about to have business with old Charlie.

Now a long-standing wish to buy out Charlie troubled the Colonel. He had no desire to oust him unfairly; he was proud of being always fair; yet he did long to engross the whole estate under one title. Out of his luxurious idleness he had conceived this desire, and thought little of so slight an obstacle as being already somewhat in debt to old Charlie for money borrowed, and for which Belles Demoiselles was, of course, good, ten times over. Lots, buildings, rents, all, might as well be his, he thought, to give, keep, or destroy. "Had he but the old man's heritage. Ah! he might bring that into existence which his *belles demoiselles* had been begging for, 'since many years;' a home—and such a home—in the gay city. Here he should tear down this row of cottages, and make his garden wall; there that long rope-walk should give place to vine-covered arbors; the bakery yonder should make way for a costly conservatory; that wine warehouse should come down, and the mansion go up. It should be the finest in the State. Men should never pass it, but they should say—'the palace of the De Charleus; a family of grand descent, a people of elegance and bounty, a line as old as France, a fine old man, and seven daughters as beautiful as happy; whoever dare attempt to marry there must leave his own name behind him!'

"The house should be of stones fitly set, brought down in ships from the land of 'les Yankees,' and it should have an airy belvedere, with a gilded image tip-toeing and shining on its peak, and from it you should see, far across the gleaming folds of the river, the red roof of Belles Demoiselles, the country-seat. At the big stone gate there should be a porter's lodge, and it should be a privilege even to see the ground."

Truly they were a family fine enough, and fancy-free enough to have fine wishes, yet happy enough where they were, to have had no wish but to live there always.

To those, who, by whatever fortune, wandered into the garden of Belles Demoiselles some summer afternoon as the sky was reddening towards evening, it was lovely to see the family gathered out upon the tiled pavement at the foot of the broad front steps, gaily chatting and jesting, with that ripple of laughter that comes so pleasingly from a bevy of girls. The father would be found seated in their midst, the center of attention and compliment, witness, arbiter, umpire, critic, by his beautiful children's unanimous appointment, but the single vassal, too, of seven absolute sovereigns.

Now they would draw their chairs near together in eager discussion of some new step in the dance, or the adjustment of some rich adornment. Now they would start about him with excited comments to see the eldest fix a bunch of violets in his buttonhole. Now the twins would move down a walk after some unusual flower, and be greeted on their return with the high pitched notes of delighted feminine surprise.

As evening came on they would draw more quietly about their paternal center. Often their chairs were forsaken, and they grouped themselves on the lower steps, one above another, and surrendered themselves to the tender influences of the approaching night. At such an hour the passer on the river, already attracted by the dark figures of the broad-roofed mansion, and its woody garden standing against the glowing sunset, would hear the voices of the hidden group rise from the spot in the soft harmonies of an evening song; swelling clearer and clearer as the thrill of music warmed them into feeling, and presently joined by the deeper tones of the father's voice; then, as the daylight passed quite away, all would be still, and he would know that the beautiful home had gathered its nestlings under its wings.

And yet, for mere vagary, it pleased them not to be pleased.

"Arti!" called one sister to another in the broad hall, one morning—mock amazement in her distended eyes—"something is goin' to took place!"

"*Comm-e-n-t?*"—long-drawn perplexity.

"Papa is goin' to town!"

The news passed up stairs.

"Inno!"—one to another meeting in a doorway—"something is goin' to took place!"

"*Qu'est-ce-que c'est!*"—vain attempt at gruffness.

"Papa is goin' to town!"

The unusual tidings were true. It was afternoon of the same day that the Colonel tossed his horse's bridle to his groom, and stepped up to old Charlie, who was sitting on his bench under a China-tree, his head, as was his fashion, bound in a Madras handkerchief. The "old man" was plainly under the effect of spirits, and smiled a deferential salutation without trusting himself to his feet.

"Eh, well Charlie!"—the Colonel raised his voice to suit his kinsman's deafness,—"how is those times with my friend Charlie?"

"Eh?" said Charlie, distractedly.

"Is that goin' well with my friend Charlie?"

"In the house—call her,"—making a pretense of rising.

"*Non, non!* I don't want,"—the speaker paused to breathe—"ow is collection?"

"O!" said Charlie, "every day he make me more poorer!"

"What do you hask for it?" asked the planter indifferently, designating the house by a wave of his whip.

"Ask for w'at?" said Injin Charlie.

"De *house!* What you ask for it?"

"I don't believe," said Charlie.

"What you would *take* for it!" cried the planter.

"Wait for w'at?' "

"What you would *take* for the whole block?"

"I don't want to sell him!"

"I'll give you *ten thousand dollah* for it."

"Ten t'ousand dollah for dis house? O, no, that is no price. He is blame good old house—that old house." (Old Charlie and the Colonel never swore in presence of each other.) "Forty years that old house didn't had to be paint! I easy can get fifty t'ousand dollah for that old house."

"Fifty thousand picayunes; yes," said the colonel.

"She's a good house. Can make plenty money," pursued the deaf man.

"That's what make you so rich, eh, Charlie?"

"*Non,* I don't make nothing. Too blame clever, me, dat's de troub'. She's a good house—make money fast like a steamboat—make a barrel full in a week! Me, I lose money all the days. Too blame clever."

"Charlie!"

"Eh?"

"Tell me what you'll take?"

"Make? I don't make *nothing*. Too blame clever."

"What will you *take?*"

"Oh! I got enough already—half drunk now."

"What you will take for the 'ouse!"

"You want to buy her?"

"I don't know,"—(shrug)—"may*be*—if you sell it cheap."

"She's a bully old house."

There was a long silence. By and by old Charlie commenced—

"Old Injin Charlie is a low-down dog."

"*C'est vrai, oui!*" retorted the Colonel in an undertone.

"He's got Injin blood in him."

The Colonel nodded assent.

"But he's got some blame good blood, too, ain't it?"

The Colonel nodded impatiently.

"*Bien!* Old Charlie's Injin blood says, 'sell the house, Charlie, you blame old fool!' *Mais,* old Charlie's good blood says, 'Charlie! if you sell that old house, Charlie, you low-down old dog, Charlie, what de Compte De Charleu make for you grace-gran'-muzzer, de dev' can eat you, Charlie, I don't care.' "

"But you'll sell it anyhow, won't you, old man?"

"No!" And the *no* rumbled off in muttered oaths like thunder out on the Gulf. The incensed old Colonel wheeled and started off.

"Curl!" [Colonel] said Charlie, standing up unsteadily.

The planter turned with an inquiring frown.

"I'll trade with you!" said Charlie.

The Colonel was tempted. " 'Ow'l you trade?" he asked.

"My house for yours!"

The old Colonel turned pale with anger. He walked very quickly back, and came close up to his kinsman.

"Charlie!" he said.

"Injin Charlie,"—with a tipsy nod.

But by this time self-control was returning. "Sell Belles Demoiselles to you?" he said in a high key, and then laughed "Ho, ho, ho!" and rode away.

A cloud, but not a dark one, overshadowed the spirits of Belles Demoiselles' plantation. The old master, whose beaming presence had always made him a shining Saturn, spinning and sparkling within the bright circle of his daughters, fell into musing fits, started out of frowning reveries, walked often by himself, and heard business from his overseer fretfully.

No wonder. The daughters knew his closeness in trade, and attributed to it his failure to negotiate for the Old Charlie buildings—so to call them. They began to depreciate Belles Demoiselles. If a north wind blew, it was too cold to ride. If a shower had fallen, it was too muddy to drive. In the morning the garden was wet. In the evening the grasshopper was a burden. *Ennui* was turned into capital; every headache was interpreted a premonition of ague; and when the native exuberance of a flock of ladies without a want or a care burst out in laughter in the father's face, they spread their French eyes, rolled up their little hands, and with rigid wrists and mock vehemence vowed and vowed again that they only laughed at their misery, and should pine to death unless they could move to the sweet city. "O! the theater! O! Orleans Street! O! the masquerade! the Place d'Armes! the ball!" and they would call upon Heaven with French irreverence, and fall into each other's arms, whirl down the hall singing a waltz, end with a grand collision and fall, and, their eyes streaming merriment, lay the blame on the slippery floor, that would some day be the death of the whole seven.

Three times more the fond father, thus goaded, managed, by accident—business accident—to see old Charlie and increase his offer; but in vain. He finally went to him formally.

"Eh?" said the deaf and distant relative. "For what you want him, eh? Why you don't stay where you halways be 'appy? This is a blame old rat-hole—good for old Injin Charlie—tha's all. Why you don't stay where you be halways 'appy? Why you don't buy somewheres else?"

"That's none of your business," snapped the planter. Truth was, his reasons were unsatisfactory even to himself.

A sullen silence followed. Then Charlie spoke:

"Well, now, look here; I sell you old Charlie's house."

"*Bien!* and the whole block," said the Colonel.

"Hold on," said Charlie. "I sell you de 'ouse and de block. Den I go and git drunk, and go to sleep; de dev' comes along and says, 'Charlie! old Charlie, you blame low-down old dog, wake up! What you doin' here? Where's de 'ouse what Monsieur le Compte give your grace-gran-muzzer? Don't you see dat fine gentyman, De Charleu, done gone and tore him down and make him over new, you blame old fool, Charlie, you low-down old Injin dog!'"

"I'll give you forty thousand dollars," said the Colonel.

"For de 'ouse?"

"For all."

The deaf man shook his head.

"Forty-five!" said the Colonel.

"What a lie? For what you tell me 'what a lie?' I don't tell you no lie."

"*Non, non!* I give you *forty-five!*" shouted the Colonel.

Charlie shook his head again.

"Fifty!"

He shook it again.

The figures rose and rose to—

"Seventy-five!"

The answer was an invitation to go away and let the owner alone, as he was, in certain specified respects, the vilest of living creatures, and no company for a fine gentyman.

The "fine gentyman" longed to blaspheme—but before old Charlie!—in the name of pride, how could he? He mounted and started away.

"Tell you what I'll make wid you," said Charlie.

The other, guessing aright, turned back without dismounting, smiling.

"How much Belles Demoiselles hoes me now?" asked the deaf one.

"One hundred and eighty thousand dollars," said the Colonel, firmly.

"Yass," said Charlie. "I don't want Belles Demoiselles."

The old Colonel's quiet laugh intimated it made no difference either way.

"But me," continued Charlie, "me—I'm got le Compte De Charleu's blood in me, any 'ow—a litt' bit, any 'ow, ain't it?"

The Colonel nodded that it was.

"*Bien!* If I go out of dis place and don't go to Belles Demoiselles, de peoples will say—day will say, 'Old Charlie he been all doze time tell a blame *lie!* He ain't no kin to his old grace-gran-muzzer, not a blame bit! He don't got nary drop of De Charleu blood to save his blame low-down old Injin soul!' No, sare! What I want wid money, den? No, sare! My place for yours!"

He turned to go into the house, just too soon to see the Colonel make an ugly whisk at him with his riding-whip. Then the Colonel, too, moved off.

Two or three times over, as he ambled homeward, laughter broke through his annoyance, as he recalled old Charlie's family pride and the presumption of his offer. Yet each time he could but think better of—not the offer to swap, but the preposterous ancestral loyalty. It was so much better than he could have expected from his "low-down" relative, and not unlike his own whim withal—the proposition which went with it was forgiven.

This last defeat bore so harshly on the master of Belles Demoiselles, that the daughters, reading chagrin in his face, began to repent. They loved their father as daughters can, and when they saw their pretended dejection harassing him seriously they restrained their complaints, displayed more than ordinary tenderness, and heroically and ostentatiously concluded there was no place like Belles Demoiselles. But the new mood touched him more than the old, and only refined his discontent. Here was a man, rich without the care of riches, free from any real trouble, happiness as native to his house as perfume to his garden, deliberately, as it were with premeditated malice, taking joy by the shoulder and bidding her be gone to town, whither he might easily have followed, only that the very same ancestral nonsense that kept Injin Charlie from selling the old place for twice its value prevented him from choosing any other spot for a city home.

Heaven sometimes pities such rich men and sends them trouble.

By and by the charm of nature and the merry hearts around prevailed; the fit of exalted sulks passed off, and after a while the year flared up at Christmas, flickered, and went out.

New Year came and passed; the beautiful garden of Belles Demoiselles put on its spring attire; the seven fair sisters moved from rose to rose; the cloud of discontent had warmed into invisible vapor in the rich sunlight of family affection, and on the common memory the only scar of last year's wound was old Charlie's sheer impertinence in crossing the caprice of the De Charleus. The cup of gladness seemed to fill with the filling of the river.

How high it was! Its tremendous current rolled and tumbled and spun along, hustling the long funeral flotillas of drift—and how near shore it came! Men were out day and night, watching the levee. Even the old Colonel took part, and grew light-hearted with occupation and excitement, as every minute the river threw a white arm over the levee's top, as though it would vault over. But all held fast, and, as the summer drifted in, the water sunk down into its banks and looked quite incapable of harm.

On a summer afternoon of uncommon mildness, old Colonel Jean Albert Henri Joseph De Charleu-Marot, being in a mood for reverie, slipped the custody of his feminine rulers and sought the crown of the levee, where it was his wont to promenade. Presently he sat upon a stone bench—a favorite seat. Before him lay his broad-spread fields; near by, his lordly mansion; and being still—perhaps by female contact—somewhat sentimental, he fell to musing on his past. It was hardly worthy to be proud of. All its morning was reddened with mad frolic, and far toward the meridian it was marred with elegant rioting. Pride had kept him well nigh-useless, and despised the honors won by valor; gaming had dimmed prosperity; death had taken his heavenly wife; voluptuous ease had mortgaged his lands; and yet his house still stood, his sweet-smelling fields were still fruitful, his name was fame enough; and yonder and yonder, among the trees and flowers, like angels walking in Eden, were the seven goddesses of his only worship.

Just then a slight sound behind him brought him to his feet. He cast his eyes anxiously to the outer edge of the little strip of bank between the levee's base and the river. There was nothing visible. He paused, with his ear toward the water, his face full of frightened expectation. Ha! There came a single plashing sound, like some great beast slipping into the river, and little waves in a wide semi-circle came out from under the bank and spread over the water!

"My God!"

He plunged down the levee and bounded through the low weeds to the edge of the bank. It was sheer, and the water about four feet below. He did not stand quite on the edge, but fell upon his knees a couple of yards away, wringing his hands, moaning and weeping, and staring through his watery eyes at a fine, long crevice just discernible under the matted grass, and curving outward on either hand toward the river.

"My God!" he sobbed aloud—"My God!" and even while he called, his God answered: the tough Bermuda grass stretched and snapped, the crevice slowly became a gape, and softly, gradually, with no sound but the closing of the water at last, a ton or more of earth settled into the boiling eddy and disappeared.

At the same instant a pulse of the breeze brought from the garden behind, the joyous, thoughtless laughter of the fair mistresses of Belles Demoiselles.

The old colonel sprang up and clambered over the levee. Then forcing himself to a more composed movement, he hastened into the house and ordered his horse.

"Tell my children to make merry while I am gone," he left word. "I shall be back to-night," and the big horse's hoofs clattered down a by-road leading to the city.

"Charlie," said the planter, riding up to a window, from which the old man's nightcap was thrust out, "What you say, Charlie—my house for yours, eh, Charlie, what you say?"

"Ello!" said Charlie; "from where you come from dis time of to-night?"

"I come from the Exchange." (A small fraction of the truth.)

"What you want?" said matter-of-fact Charlie.

"I come to trade."

The low-down relative drew the worsted off his ears. "O! yass," he said with an uncertain air.

"Well, old man Charlie, what you say; my house for yours—like you said—eh, Charlie?"

"I dunno;" said Charlie, "it's nearly mine now. Why you don't stay dare you-se'f?"

"*Because I don't want!*" said the Colonel savagely; "is dat reason enough for you? you better take me in de notion, old man, I tell you—yes!"

Charlie never winced; but how his answer delighted the Colonel! quoth Charlie—

"I don't care—I take him!—*mais*, possession give right off."

"Not the whole plantation, Charlie; only—"

"I don't care," said Charlie, "we easy can fix dat. *Mais*, what for you don't want to keep him? I don't want him. You better keep him."

"Don' you try to make no fool of me, old man," cried the planter.

"O, no!" said the other. "O, no! but you make a fool of yourself, ain't it?"

The dumbfounded Colonel stared; Charlie went on.

"Yass! Belles Demoiselles is more wort' dan tree block like dis one. I pass by dare since two weeks. O, pritty Belles Demoiselles! de cane was wave in de wind, de garden smell like a bouquet, de white-cap was jump up and down on de river; seven *belles demoiselles* was ridin' on horses. 'Pritty, pritty, pritty!' say old Charlie; ah! *Monsieur le père*, 'ow 'appy, 'appy, 'appy!"

"Yass!" he continued—the Colonel still staring—"le Compte De Charleu have two familie. One was low-down Choctaw, one was high-up *noblesse*. He give the low-down Choctaw dis old rat-hole; he give Belles Demoiselles to your gran-fozzer; and now you don't be *satisfait*. What I'll do wid Belles Demoiselles? She'll break me in two years, yass. And what you'll do wid old Charlie's house, eh? You'll tear her down and make you'se'f a blame old fool. I rather wouldn't trade!"

The planter caught a big breath-full of anger, but Charlie went straight on.

"I rather wouldn't, *mais* I will do it for you;—just the same, like Monsieur le Compte would say, 'Charlie, you old fool, I want to shange houses wid you.' "

So long as the Colonel suspected irony he was angry, but as Charlie seemed, after all, to be certainly in earnest, he began to feel conscience-stricken. He was by no means a tender man, but his lately-discovered misfortune had unhinged him, and this strange, undeserved, disinterested family fealty on the part of Charlie, touched his heart. And should he still try to lead him into the pitfall he had dug? He hesitated;—no, he would show him the place by broad day-light, and if he chose to overlook the "caving bank," it would be his own fault;—a trade's a trade.

"Come," said the planter, "come at my house to-night; to-morrow we look at the place before breakfast, and finish the trade."

"For what?" said Charlie.

"O, because I got to come in town in the morning."

"I don't want;" said Charlie. "How I'm goin' to come dere?"

"I git you a horse at the liberty stable."

"Well—anyhow—I don't care—I'll go." And they went.

When they had ridden a long time, and were on the road darkened by hedges of Cherokee rose, the Colonel called behind him to the "low-down" scion,

"Keep the road, old man."

"Eh?"

"Keep the road."

"O, yes; all right; I keep my word; we don't goin' to play no tricks, eh?"

But the Colonel seemed not to hear. His ungenerous design was beginning to be hateful to him. Not only old Charlie's unprovoked goodness was prevailing; the eulogy on Belles Demoiselles had stirred the depths of an intense love for his beautiful home. True if he held to it, the caving of the bank, at its present fearful speed, would let the house into the river within three months; but were it not better to lose it so, than sell his birth-right? Again—coming back to the first thought—to betray his own blood! It was only Injin Charlie; but had not the De Charleu blood just spoken out in him? Unconsciously he groaned.

After a time they struck a path approaching the plantation in the rear, and a little after, passing from behind a clump of live-oaks, they came in sight of the villa. It looked so like a gem, shining through its dark grove, so like a great glow-worm in the dense foliage, so significant of luxury and gayety, that the poor master, from an overflowing heart, groaned again.

"What?" asked Charlie.

The Colonel only drew his rein, and, dismounting mechanically, contemplated the sight before him. The high, arched doors and windows were thrown wide to the summer air; from every opening the bright light of numerous candelabra darted out upon the sparkling foliage of magnolia and bay, and here and there in the spacious verandas, a colored lantern swayed in the gentle breeze. A sound of revel fell on the car, the music of harps; and across one window, brighter than the rest, flitted, once or twice, the shadows of dancers. But oh! the shadows flitting across the heart of the fair mansion's master!

"Old Charlie," said he, gazing fondly at his house, "you and me is both old, eh?"

"Yass," said the stolid Charlie.

"And we has both, been bad enough in our time, eh, Charlie?"

Charlie, surprised at the tender tone, repeated, "Yass."

"And you and me is mighty close?"

"Blame close, yass."

"But you never know me to cheat, old man!"

"No,"—impassively.

"And do you think I would cheat you now?"

"I dunno," said Charlie. "I don't believe."

"Well, old man, old man,"—his voice began to quiver—"I shan't cheat you now. My God!—old man, I tell you—you better not make the trade!"

"Because for what?" asked Charlie in plain anger; but both looked quickly toward the house! The Colonel tossed his hands wildly in the air, rushed forward a step or two, and giving one fearful scream of agony and fright, fell forward on his face in the path. Old Charlie stood transfixed with horror. Belles Demoiselles, the realm of maiden beauty, the home of merriment, the house of dancing, all in the tremor and glow of pleasure, suddenly sunk, with one short, wild wail of terror—sunk, sunk, down, down, down, into the merciless, unfathomable flood of the Mississippi.

Twelve long months were midnight to the mind of the childless father; when they were only half gone, he took his bed; and every day, and every night, old Charlie, the "low-down," the "fool," watched him tenderly, tended him lovingly, for the sake of his name, his misfortunes and his broken heart. No woman's step crossed the floor of the sick-chamber, whose western dormer-windows overpeered the dingy architecture of old Charlie's block; Charlie and a skilled physician, the one all interest, the other all gentleness, hope and patience—these only entered by the door; but by the window came in a sweet-scented evergreen vine, transplanted from the caving bank of Belles Demoiselles. It caught the rays of sunset in its flowery net and let them softly in upon the sick man's bed; gathered the glancing beams of the moon at midnight, and often wakened the sleeper to look, with his mindless eyes, upon their pretty silver fragments strewn upon the floor.

By and by there seemed—there was—a twinkling dawn of returning season. Slowly, peacefully, with an increase unseen from day to day, the light of reason came into the eyes, and speech became coherent; but withal there came a failing of the wrecked body, and the doctor said that monsieur was both better and worse.

One evening as Charlie sat by the vine-clad window with his fireless pipe in his hand, the old Colonel's eyes fell full upon his own, and rested there.

"Charl——," he said with an effort, and his delighted nurse hastened to the bedside and bowed his best ear. There was an unsuccessful effort or two, and then he whispered, smiling with sweet sadness ——

"We didn't trade."

The truth, in this case, was a secondary matter to Charlie; the main point was to give a pleasing answer. So he nodded his head decidedly, as who should say—"O yes, we did, it was a bona-fide swap!" but when he saw the smile vanish, he tried the other expedient and shook his head with still more vigor, to signify that they had not so much as approached a bargain; and the smile returned.

Charlie wanted to see the vine recognized. He stepped backward to the window with a broad smile, shook the foliage, nodded and looked smart.

"I know," said the Colonel, with beaming eyes, "—many weeks."

The next day—

"Charl—"

The best ear went down.

"Send for a priest."

The priest came, and was alone with him a whole afternoon. When he left, the patient was very haggard and exhausted, but smiled and would not suffer the crucifix to be removed from his breast.

One more morning came. Just before dawn Charlie, lying on a pallet in the room, thought he was called, and came to the bedside.

"Old man," whispered the failing invalid, "is it caving yet?"

Charlie nodded.

"It won't pay you out."

"O dat makes not'ing," said Charlie. Two big tears rolled down his brown face. "Dat makes not'in."

The Colonel whispered once more—

"*Mes belles demoiselles!*—in paradise;—in the garden—I shall be with them at sunrise;" and so it was.

Questions to Consider

1. In what way does the plantation *Belles Demoiselles* (its name, its status, and its demise) reflect Cable's attraction to and revulsion for the South? Does the story affirm or modify your view(s) of the South before the Civil War? After? Who inherits Cable's postwar South? Why? Who inherits the postwar South in Thomas Nelson Page's "Marse Chan"? Do you see similarities? Differences?
2. What races does Cable mention in his story and in his article? What complexities among racial definitions does he imply? Is White heritage pure in Cable's selections? Is African American? How do blood, race, and heritage interact in Cable's South? And how is cultural knowledge transmitted to subsequent generations or within and across cultures?

Joel Chandler Harris

1848–1908

In 1905, President Theodore Roosevelt praised Joel Chandler Harris as the literary architect of a transformed nation and his writing as "exulting the South in the mind of every man who reads it." Deeply committed to "localism," Harris promoted national healing through an understanding of the "provincial," the particular nuances of cultural place mirrored in his own Georgia folktales, stories, and novels.

Born in the middle Georgia town of Eatonton on 9 December 1848, Harris was raised in a one-room cottage by his industrious, well-educated mother Mary, who was deserted by her Irish lover soon after their child's conception. She and her fatherless son were sustained by the town's generosity. Although young Harris masked his shyness with mischievous pranks, he was troubled by a lifelong speech impediment and was self-conscious about his small stature, red hair, and poverty. Even as an adult, the bashful Harris insisted "obscurity fits me best" and declined to participate in lucrative lecture tours even when urged by his admiring friends George Cable and Mark Twain.

Similarly uneasy with formal schooling, Harris preferred reading and was fascinated by newspapers, particularly the pro-Confederate weekly published by wealthy and influential Joseph Addison Turner at Turnwold, a plantation only nine miles from Eatonton. Hired as Turner's apprentice in 1862, Harris later described his two Turnwold years in *Old Plantation Days* (1892). While his intellectual and journalistic skills grew under Turner's tutelage, his imagination was nurtured by the lives and rituals of the Turnwold slaves and their stories about an African folk world filled with "creetur sense." The arrival of federal troops in 1864 quashed Turner's fortune and his dream to counter Yankee writing with a vibrant Southern literature, but Harris would fulfill Turner's prophecy that the younger man would accomplish the "writing for the South that I shall be unable to do."

Harris's career in journalism flourished. Although he worked briefly in New Orleans, Georgia became the venue for his success. During a productive six-year period in Savannah, he married French Canadian Esther LaRose with whom he fathered eight children, although three died in childhood. Three years later, the family's temporary move to Atlanta to escape a yellow fever epidemic became permanent as Harris joined his friend, fiery reformer Henry W. Grady, at the progressive *Atlanta Constitution* where Harris remained until his retirement in 1900. While Grady ardently argued New South compromise and economic potential, Harris insisted that cross-cultural understanding (particularly through literature) was the only authentic pathway to reconciliation.

In 1876, Harris introduced the political portrait of urban freedman Uncle Remus to challenge Northern opinions. In 1879, he began drawing on his Turnwold memories and transformed Remus into a Southern African-American sage, telling tales to his young master, a little White boy whose parents were a former Union soldier and the daughter of Remus's Antebellum master. This parentage and the White boy's admiration for his African-American mentor modeled the reconciliation Harris and the nation sought. Responding to an enthusiastic readership, Harris published *Uncle Remus: His Songs and Sayings* (1881), a miscellany of proverbs, songs, myths (among them, "Why the Negro Is Black,") and tales (including "How Mr. Rabbit Was Too Sharp for Mr. Fox" and "Tar Baby"). *Nights with Uncle Remus* (1883) soon followed as, eventually, did seven more such collections and a magazine.

Harris's obvious allegiance to plantation harmony tempts modern readers to dismiss Remus as a "happy darky," who is much too loyal to his former mistress and cheerfully complacent with a life of servitude. However, Harris merges African materials and African-American narrative voices in tales that subvert class and racial privilege. The industrious, inventive, and wise Uncle Remus is *teaching* the young boy, and presumably Northern readers, about racial dignity and difference. In the carefully rendered dialect that earned Harris an enduring reputation as a pioneering folklorist, the tales recount again and again the violent desire of the powerful, like the ever-encroaching fox, to claim, even to destroy, the weaker woodland animals, but wariness, persistence, and cunning, like that of the irrepressibly wily rabbit, prevail. "Why the Negro Is Black" identifies Blackness as the common human racial heritage. In this origin story, Remus declares to his listener, a Southern White boy, "We 'uz all niggers tergedder." In subsequent stories like "Free Joe" (*Free Joe and Other Georgian Sketches*, 1887) and "Rosalie" (*Century Magazine*, 1901), Harris reveals that Antebellum African-descent men and women, however free, light-skinned, or educated, remain forever defined and thwarted by White primacy.

Harris's works contain a plethora of dialects, cultural nuances, and issues: poor White "crackers," middle-class villagers, North Georgia mountain folk, African-origin voices (that of Uncle Remus and the South Carolinian Gullah of Daddy Jake), miscegenation ("Where's Duncan," 1891), illegitimacy (*Sister Jane*, 1896), the spirit of reform reflected in Harris's biography of Henry W. Grady (1890), and the reconstructed South (*Gabriel Tolliver*, 1902). Harris's narrative voices and materials have influenced such diverse artists as his contemporary Charles Chesnutt, Walt Disney (*Song of the South*, 1946), Ralph Ellison, and Toni Morrison. Even though he received numerous honors, including election to the American Academy of Arts and Letters in 1905, Harris considered himself no more than a "cornfield journalist."

Harris wrote about those who, like himself, were different: the almost-White slave Rosalie; the prewar outcast Free Joe; the scrappy, seemingly weak Brer Rabbit; and the storytelling Uncle Remus, with whom Harris was most identified during his lifetime and whose humility and carefully crafted tales of subversion and reconciliation voice Harris himself.

The Wonderful Tar Baby Story

"Didn't the fox never catch the rabbit, Uncle Remus?" asked the little boy the next evening.

"He come mighty nigh it, honey, sho's you born—Brer Fox did. One day atter Brer Rabbit fool 'im wid dat calamus root, Brer Fox went ter wuk en got 'im some tar, en mix it wid some turkentime, en fix up a contrapshun w'at he call a Tar-Baby, en he tuck dish yer Tar-Baby en he sot'er in de big road, en den he lay off in de bushes fer to see what de news wuz gwine ter be. En he didn't hatter wait long, nudder, kaze bimeby here come Brer Rabbit pacin' down de road—lippity-clippity, clippity-lippity—dez ez sassy ez a jay-bird. Brer Fox, he lay low. Brer Rabbit come prancin' 'long twel he spy de Tar-Baby, en den he fotch up on his behime legs like he wuz 'stonished. De Tar Baby, she sot dar, she did, en Brer Fox, he lay low.

" 'Mawnin'!' sez Brer Rabbit, sezee—'nice wedder dis mawnin',' sezee.

"Tar-Baby ain't sayin' nuthin', en Brer Fox he lay low.

" 'How duz yo' sym'tums seem ter segashuate?' sez Brer Rabbit, sezee.

"Brer Fox, he wink his eye slow, en lay low, en de Tar-Baby, she ain't sayin' nuthin'.

" 'How you come on, den? Is you deaf?' sez Brer Rabbit, sezee. 'Kaze if you is, I kin holler louder,' sezee.

"Tar-Baby stay still, en Brer Fox, he lay low.

" 'You er stuck up, dat's w'at you is,' says Brer Rabbit, sezee, 'en I'm gwine ter kyore you, dat's w'at I'm a gwine ter do,' sezee.

"Brer Fox, he sorter chuckle in his stummick, he did, but Tar-Baby ain't sayin' nothin'.

" 'I'm gwine ter larn you how ter talk ter 'spectubble folks ef hit's de las' ack,' sez Brer Rabbit, sezee. 'Ef you don't take off dat hat en tell me howdy, I'm gwine ter bus' you wide open,' sezee.

"Tar-Baby stay still, en Brer Fox, he lay low.

"Brer Rabbit keep on axin' 'im, en de Tar-Baby, she keep on sayin' nothin', twel present'y Brer Rabbit draw back wid his fis', he did, en blip he tuck 'er side er de head. Right dar's whar he broke his merlasses jug. His fis' stuck, en he can't pull loose. De tar hilt 'im. But Tar-Baby, she stay still, en Brer Fox, he lay low.

" 'Ef you don't lemme loose, I'll knock you agin,' sez Brer Rabbit, sezee, en wid dat he fotch 'er a wipe wid de udder han', en dat stuck. Tar-Baby, she ain't sayin' nuthin', en Brer Fox, he lay low.

" 'Tu'n me loose, fo' I kick de natal stuffin' outen you,' sez Brer Rabbit, sezee, but de Tar-Baby, she ain't sayin' nuthin'. She des hilt on, en de Brer Rabbit lose de use er his feet in de same way. Brer Fox, he lay low. Den Brer Rabbit squall out dat ef de Tar-Baby don't tu'n 'im loose he butt 'er cranksided. En den he butted, en his head got stuck. Den Brer Fox, he sa'ntered fort', lookin' dez ez innercent ez wunner yo' mammy's mockin'-birds.

" 'Howdy, Brer Rabbit,' sez Brer Fox, sezee. 'You look sorter stuck up dis mawnin',' sezee, en den he rolled on de groun', en laft en laft twel he couldn't laff no mo'. 'I speck you'll take dinner wid me dis time, Brer Rabbit. I done laid in some calamus root, en I ain't gwineter take no skuse,' sez Brer Fox, sezee."

Here Uncle Remus paused, and drew a two-pound yam out of the ashes.

"Did the fox eat the rabbit?" asked the little boy to whom the story had been told.

"Dat's all de fur de tale goes," replied the old man. "He mout, an den agin he moutent. Some say Judge B'ar come 'long en loosed 'im—some say he didn't. I hear Miss Sally callin'. You better run 'long."

How Mr. Rabbit Was Too Sharp for Mr. Fox

"Uncle Remus," said the little boy one evening, when he had found the old man with little or nothing to do, "did the fox kill and eat the rabbit when he caught him with the Tar-Baby?"

"Law, honey, ain't I tell you 'bout dat?" replied the old darkey, chuckling slyly. "I 'clar ter grashus I ought er tole you dat, but ole man Nod wuz ridin' on my eyelids twel a leetle mo'n I'd a dis'member'd my own name, en den on to dat here come yo' mammy hollerin' atter you.

"W'at I tell you w'en I fus' begin? I tole you Brer Rabbit wuz a monstus soon beas'; leas'ways dat's w'at I laid out fer ter tell you. Well, den, honey, don't you go en make no udder kalkalashuns, kaze in dem days Brer Rabbit en his fambly wuz at de head er de gang w'en enny racket wuz en han', en dar dey stayed. 'Fo' you begins fer ter wipe yo' eyes 'bout Brer Rabbit, you wait en see wha'bouts Brer Rabbit gwineter fetch up at. But dat's needer yer ner dar.

"W'en Brer Fox fine Brer Rabbit mixt up wid de Tar-baby, he feel mighty good, en he roll on de groun' en laff. Bimeby he up'n say, sezee:

" 'Well, I speck I got you did time, Brer Rabbit,' sezee; 'maybe I ain't but I speck I is. You been runnin' 'roun' here sassin' atter me a mighty long time, but I speck you done come ter de cen'er de row. You bin currin' up yo' capers en bouncin' 'roun' in dis naberhood ontwel you come ter b'leeve yo'se'f de boss er de whole gang. En der you er allers some'rs whar you got no bixness,' ses Brer Fox, sezee. 'Who ax you fer ter come en strike up a 'quaintence wid dish yer Tar-Baby? En who stuck you up dar whar you iz? Nobody in de 'roun' worril. You des tuck en jam yo'se'f on dat Tar-Baby widout waintin' fer enny invite,' sez Brer Fox, sezee, 'en dar you is, en dar you'll stay twel I fixes up a bresh-pile and fires her up, kaze I'm gwinter bobbycue you dis day, sho,' sez Brer Fox, sezee.

"Den Brer Rabbit talk mighty 'umble,

" 'I don't keer w'at you do wid me, Brer Fox,' sezee, 'so you don't fling me in dat brier-patch. Roas' me, Brer Fox,' sezee, 'but don't fling me in dat brier-patch,' sezee.

" 'I ain't got no string,' sez Brer Fox, sezee, 'en now I speck I'll hatter drown you,' sezee.

" 'Drown me des ez deep ez you please, Brer Fox,' sez Brer Rabbit, sezee, 'but do don't fling me in dat brier-patch,' sezee.

" 'Dey ain't no water nigh,' sez Brer Fox, sezee, 'en now I speck I'll hatter skin you,' sezee.

" 'Skin me, Brer Fox,' sez Brer Rabbit, sezee, 'snatch out my eyeballs, t'ar out my yeras by de roots, en cut off my legs,' sezee, 'but do please, Brer Fox, don't fling me in dat brier-patch,' sezee.

"Co'se Brer Fox wanter hurt Brer Rabbit bad ez he kin, so he cotch 'im by de behime legs en slung 'im right in de middle er de brier-patch. Dar wuz a considerbul flutter whar Brer Rabbit struck de bushes, en Brer Fox sorter hang 'roun' fer ter see w'at wuz gwinter happen. Bimeby he hear somebody call 'im, en way up de hill he see Brer Rabbit settin' crosslegged on a chinkapin log koamin' de pitch outen his har wid a chip. Den Brer Fox know dat he bin swop off mighty bad. Brer Rabbit wuz bleedzed fer ter fling back some er his sass, en he holler out:

" 'Bred en bawn in a brier-patch, Brer Fox—bred en bawn in a brier-patch!' en wid dat he skip out des ez lively ez a cricket in de embers."

Why the Negro Is Black

One night, while the little boy was watching Uncle Remus twisting and waxing some shoe-thread, he made what appeared to him to be a very curious discovery. He discovered that the palms of the old man's hands were as white as his own, and the fact was such a source of wonder that he made it the subject of remark. The response of Uncle Remus led to the earnest recital of a piece of unwritten history that must prove interesting to ethnologists.

"Tooby sho de pa'm er my han's w'ite, honey," he quietly remarked; "en w'en it come ter dat, dey wuz a time we'n all de w'ite folks 'uz black—blacker dan me, kaze I done bin yer so long dat I sorter bleach out."

The little boy laughed. He thought Uncle Remus was making him the victim of one of his practical jokes; but the youngster was never more mistaken. The old man was serious. Nevertheless, he failed to rebuke the ill-timed mouth of the child, appearing to be altogether engrossed in his work. After a while he resumed:

"Yasser. Fokes dunner w'at bin yet, let 'lone w'at gwinter be. Niggers is niggers now, but de time wuz w'en we 'uz all niggers tergedder."

"When was that, Uncle Remus?"

"Way back yander. In dem times we 'uz all un us black; we 'uz all niggers tergedder, en 'cordin' ter all de 'counts w'at I year fokes 'uz gittin' 'long 'bout ez well in dem days ez dey ez now. But atter' w'ile de news come dat dere was a pon' er water some'rs in de naberhood. W'ich if dey'd git inter dey'd be wash off nice en w'te, en den one un um, he fine de place en make er splunge inter de pon', en come out w'ite ez a town gal. En den, bless grashus! w'en de fokes seed it, dey make a break for de pon', en dem w'at wuz de soopless, dey got en fud' en dey come out w'ite: en dem w'at wuz de nex' soopless, dey got in nex', en dey come out merlatters; en dey wuz sech a crowd un um dat dey mighty nigh use de water up, w'ich w'en dem yuthers come 'long, de morest dey could do wuz ter paddle about wid der foots en dabble in it wid der han's. Dem wuz de niggers, en down ter dis day dey ain't no w'ite 'bout a nigger 'ceppin de pa'ms er der han's en de soles er der foot."

The little boy seemed to be very much interested in this new account of the origin of the races, and he made some further inquiries, which elicited from Uncle Remus the following additional particulars:

"De Injun en de Chinee got ter be 'counted 'long er de merlatter. I ain't seed no Chinee dat I knows un, but dey tells me dey er sorter 'twix' a brown en a brindle. Dey er all merlatters."

"But mamma says the Chinese have straight hair," the little boy suggested,

"Co'se, honey," the old man unhesitatingly responded, "dem w'at git ter de pon'time nuff fer ter git der head in de water, de water hit onkink der ha'r. Hit bleedzed ter be dat away."

Free Joe and the Rest of the World

The name of Free Joe strikes humorously upon the ear of memory. It is impossible to say why, for he was the humblest, the simplest, and the most serious of all God's living creatures, sadly lacking in all those elements that suggest the humorous. It is certain, moreover, that in 1850 the sober-minded citizens of the little Georgian village of Hillsborough were not inclined to take a humorous view of Free Joe, and neither his name nor his presence provoked a smile. He was a black atom, drifting hither and thither without an owner, blown about by all the winds of circumstance, and given over to shiftlessness.

The problems of one generation are the paradoxes of a succeeding one, particularly if war, or some such incident, intervenes to clarify the atmosphere and strengthen the understanding. Thus, in 1850, Free Joe represented not only a problem of large concern, but, in the watchful eyes of Hillsborough, he was the embodiment of that vague and mysterious danger that seemed to be forever lurking on the outskirts of slavery, ready to sound a shrill and ghostly signal in the impenetrable swamps, and steal forth under the midnight stars to murder, rapine, and pillage—a danger always threatening, and yet never assuming shape; intangible, and yet real; impossible, and yet not improbable. Across the serene and smiling front of safety, the pale outlines of the awful shadow of insurrection sometimes fell. With this invisible panorama as a background, it was natural that the figure of Free Joe, simple and humble as it was, should assume undue proportions. Go where he would, do what he might, he could not escape the finger of observation and the kindling eye of suspicion. His lightest words were noted, his slightest actions marked.

Under all the circumstances it was natural that his peculiar condition should reflect itself in his habits and manners. The slaves laughed loudly day by day, but Free Joe rarely laughed. The slaves sang at their work and danced at their frolics, but no one ever heard Free Joe sing or saw him dance. There was something painfully plaintive and appealing in his attitude, something touching in his anxiety to please. He was of the friendliest nature, and seemed to be delighted when he could amuse the little children who had made a playground of the public square. At times he would please them by making his little dog Dan perform all sorts of curious tricks, or he would tell them quaint stories of the beasts of the field and birds of the air; and frequently he was coaxed into relating the story of his own freedom. That story was brief, but tragical.

In the year of our Lord 1840, when a negro-speculator of a sportive turn of mind reached the little village of Hillsborough on his way to the Mississippi region, with a caravan of likely negroes of both sexes, he found much to interest him. In that day and at that time there were a number of young men in the village who had not bound themselves over to repentance for the various misdeeds of the flesh. To these young men the negro-speculator (Major Frampton was his name) proceeded to address himself. He was a Virginian, he declared; and, to prove the statement, he referred all the festively inclined young men of Hillsborough to a barrel of peach-brandy in one of his covered wagons. In the minds of these young men there was less doubt in regard to the age and quality of the brandy than there was in regard to the negro-trader's birthplace. Major Frampton might or might not have been born in the Old Dominion—that was a matter for consideration and inquiry—but there could be no question as to the mellow pungency of the peach-brandy.

In his own estimation, Major Frampton was one of the most accomplished of men. He had summered at the Virginia Springs; he had been to Philadelphia, to Washington, to Richmond, to Lynchburg, and to Charleston, and had accumulated a great deal of experience which he found useful. Hillsborough was hid in the woods of Middle Georgia, and its general aspect of innocence impressed him. He looked on the young men who had shown their readiness to test his peach-brandy, as overgrown country boys who needed to be introduced to some of the arts and sciences he had at his command. Thereupon the major pitched his tents, figuratively speaking, and became, for the time being, a part and parcel of the innocence that characterized Hillsborough. A wiser man would doubtless have made the same mistake.

The little village possessed advantages that seemed to be providentially arranged to fit the various enterprises that Major Frampton had in view. There was the auction-block in front of the stuccoed court-house, if he desired to dispose of a few of his negroes; there was a quarter-track, laid out to his hand and in excellent order, if he chose to enjoy the pleasures of horse-racing; there were secluded pine thickets within easy reach, if he desired to indulge in the exciting pastime of cock-fighting; and various lonely and unoccupied rooms in the second story of the tavern, if he cared to challenge the chances of dice or cards.

Major Frampton tried them all with varying luck, until he began his famous game of poker with Judge Alfred Wellington, a stately gentleman with a flowing white beard and mild blue eyes that gave him the appearance of a benevolent patriarch. The history of the game in which Major Frampton and Judge Alfred Wellington took part is something more than a tradition in Hillsborough, for there are still living three or four men who sat around the table and watched its progress. It is said that at various stages of the game Major Frampton would destroy the cards with which they were playing, and send for a new pack, but the result was always the same. The mild blue eyes of Judge Wellington, with few exceptions, continued to overlook "hands" that were invincible—a habit they had acquired during a long and arduous course of training from Saratoga to New Orleans. Major Frampton lost his money, his horses, his wagons, and all his negroes but one, his body-servant. When his misfortune had reached this limit, the major adjourned the game. The sun was shining brightly, and all nature was cheerful. It is said that the major also seemed to be cheerful. However this may be, he visited the court-house, and executed the papers that gave his body-servant his freedom. This being done, Major Frampton sauntered into a convenient pine thicket, and blew out his brains.

The negro thus freed came to be known as Free Joe. Compelled, under the law, to choose a guardian, he chose Judge Wellington, chiefly because his wife Lucinda was among the negroes won from Major Frampton. For several years Free Joe had what may be called a jovial time. His wife Lucinda was well provided for, and he found it a comparatively easy matter to provide for himself; so that, taking all the circumstances into consideration, it is not matter for astonishment that he became somewhat shiftless.

When Judge Wellington died, Free Joe's troubles began. The judge's negroes, including, Lucinda, went to his half-brother, a man named Calderwood, who was a hard master and a rough customer generally—a man of many eccentricities of mind and character. His neighbors had a habit of alluding to him as "Old Spite;" and the name seemed to fit him so completely, that he was known far and near as "Spite" Calderwood. He probably enjoyed the distinction the name gave him, at any rate, he never resented it, and it was not often that he missed an opportunity to show that he deserved it. Calderwood's place was two or three miles from the village of Hillsborough, and Free Joe visited his wife twice a week, Wednesday and Saturday nights.

One Sunday he was sitting in front of Lucinda's cabin, when Calderwood happened to pass that way.

"Howdy, marster?" said Free Joe, taking off his hat.

"Who are you?" exclaimed Calderwood abruptly, halting and staring at the negro.

"I'm name' Joe, marster. I'm Lucindy's ole man."

"Who do you belong to?"

"Marse John Evans is my gyardeen, marster."

"Big name—gyardeen. Show your pass."

Free Joe produced that document, and Calderwood read it aloud slowly, as if he found it difficult to get at the meaning:—

"To whom it may concern: This is to certify that the boy Joe Frampton has my permission to visit his wife Lucinda."

This was dated at Hillsborough, and signed *"John W. Evans."*

Calderwood read it twice, and then looked at Free Joe, elevating his eyebrows, and showing his discolored teeth.

"Some mighty big words in that there. Evans owns this place, I reckon. When's he comin' down to take hold?"

Free Joe fumbled with his hat. He was badly frightened.

"Lucindy say she speck you wouldn't min' my comin', long ez I behave, marster."

Calderwood tore the pass in pieces and flung it away.

"Don't want no free niggers 'round here," he exclaimed. "There's the big road. It'll carry you to town. Don't let me catch you here no more. Now, mind what I tell you."

Free Joe presented a shabby spectacle as he moved off with his little dog Dan slinking at his heels. It should be said in behalf of Dan, however, that his bristles were up, and that he looked back and growled. It may be that the dog had the advantage of insignificance, but it is difficult to conceive how a dog bold enough to raise his bristles under Calderwood's very eyes could be as insignificant as Free Joe. But both the negro and his little dog seemed to give a new and more dismal aspect to forlornness as they turned into the road and went toward Hillsborough.

After this incident Free Joe appeared to have clearer ideas concerning his peculiar condition. He realized the fact that though he was free he was more helpless than any slave. Having no owner, every man was his master. He knew that he was the object of suspicion, and therefore all his slender resources (ah! how pitifully slender they were!) were devoted to winning, not kindness and appreciation, but toleration; all his efforts were in the direction of mitigating the circumstances that tended to make his condition so much worse than that of the negroes around him—negroes who had friends because they had masters.

So far as his own race was concerned, Free Joe was an exile. If the slaves secretly envied him his freedom (which is to be doubted, considering his miserable condition), they openly despised him, and lost no opportunity to treat him with contumely. Perhaps this was in some measure the result of the attitude which Free Joe chose to maintain toward them. No doubt his instinct taught him that to hold himself aloof from the slaves would be to invite from the whites the toleration which he coveted, and without which even his miserable condition would be rendered more miserable still.

His greatest trouble was the fact that he was not allowed to visit his wife; but he soon found a way out of this difficulty. After he had been ordered away from the Calderwood place, he was in the habit of wandering as far in that direction as prudence would permit. Near the Calderwood place, but not on Calderwood's land, lived an old man named Micajah Staley and his sister Becky Staley. These people were old and very poor. Old Micajah had a palsied arm and hand; but, in spite of this, he managed to earn a precarious living with his turning-lathe.

When he was a slave Free Joe would have scorned these representatives of a class known as poor white trash, but now he found them sympathetic and helpful in various ways. From the back door of their cabin he could hear the Calderwood negroes singing at night, and he sometimes fancied he could distinguish Lucinda's shrill treble rising above the other voices. A large poplar grew in the woods some distance from the Staley cabin, and at the foot of this tree Free Joe would sit for hours with his face turned toward Calderwood's. His little dog Dan would curl up in the leaves near by, and the two seemed to be as comfortable as possible.

One Saturday afternoon Free Joe, sitting at the foot of this friendly poplar, fell asleep. How long he slept, he could not tell; but when he awoke little Dan was licking his face, the moon was shining brightly, and Lucinda his wife stood before him laughing. The dog, seeing that Free Joe was asleep, had grown somewhat impatient, and he concluded to make an excursion to the Calderwood place on his own account. Lucinda was inclined to give the incident a twist in the direction of superstition.

"I 'uz settin' down front er de fireplace," she said, "cookin' me some meat, w'en all of a sudden I year sumpin at de do'—scratch, scratch. I tuck'n tu'n de meat over, en make out I aint year it. Bimeby it come dar 'gin—scratch, scratch. I up en open de do', I did, en, bless de Lord! dar wuz little Dan, en it look like ter me dat his ribs done grow tergeer. I gin 'im some bread, en den, w'en he start out, I tuck'n foller 'im, kaze, I say ter myse'f, maybe my nigger man mought be some'rs 'roun'. Dat ar little dog got sense, mon."

Free Joe laughed and dropped his hand lightly on Dan's head. For a long time after that he had no difficulty in seeing his wife. He had only to sit by the poplar-tree until little Dan could run and fetch her. But after a while the other negroes discovered that Lucinda was meeting Free Joe in the woods, and information of the fact soon reached Calderwood's ears. Calderwood was what is called a man of action. He said nothing; but one day he put Lucinda in his buggy, and carried her to Macon, sixty miles away. He carried her to Macon, and came back without her; and nobody in or around Hillsborough, or in that section, ever saw her again.

For many a night after that Free Joe sat in the woods and waited. Little Dan would run merrily off and be gone a long time, but he always came back without Lucinda. This happened over and over again. The "willis-whistlers" would call and call, like phantom huntsmen wandering on a far-off shore; the screech-owl would shake and shiver in the depths of the woods; the night-hawks, sweeping by on noiseless wings, would snap their beaks as though they enjoyed the huge joke of which Free Joe and little Dan were the victims; and the whip-poor-wills would cry to each other through the gloom. Each night seemed to be lonelier than the preceding, but Free Joe's patience was proof against loneliness. There came a time, however, when little Dan refused to go after Lucinda. When Free Joe motioned him in the direction of the Calderwood place, he would simply move about uneasily and whine; then he would curl up in the leaves and make himself comfortable.

One night, instead of going to the poplar-tree to wait for Lucinda, Free Joe went to the Staley cabin, and, in order to make his welcome good, as he expressed it, he carried with him an armful of fat-pine splinters. Miss Becky Staley had a great reputation in those parts as a fortune-teller, and the schoolgirls, as well as older people, often tested her powers in this direction, some in jest and some in earnest. Free Joe placed his humble offering of light-wood in the chimney-corner, and then seated himself on the steps, dropping his hat on the ground outside.

"Miss Becky," he said presently, "whar in de name er gracious you reckon Lucindy is?"

"Well, the Lord he'p the nigger!" exclaimed Miss Becky, in a tone that seemed to reproduce, by some curious agreement of sight with sound, her general aspect of peakedness. "Well, the Lord he'p the nigger! haint you been a-seein' her all this blessed time? She's over at old Spite Calderwood's, if she's anywheres, I reckon."

"No'm, dat I aint, Miss Becky. I aint seen Lucindy in now gwine on mighty nigh a mont'."

"Well, it haint a-gwine to hurt you," said Miss Becky, somewhat sharply. "In my day an' time it wuz allers took to be a bad sign when niggers got to honeyin' 'roun' an' gwine on."

"Yessum," said Free Joe, cheerfully assenting to the proposition—"yessum, dat's so, but me an' my ole 'oman, we 'uz raise tergeer, en dey aint bin many days w'en we 'uz 'way fum one 'n'er like we is now."

"Maybe she's up an' took up wi' some un else," said Micajah Staley from the corner. "You know what the sayin' is, 'New master, new nigger.' "

"Dat's so, dat's de sayin', but tain't wid my ole 'oman like 'tis wid yuther niggers. Me en her wuz des natally raise up tergeer. Dey's lots likelier niggers den w'at I is," said Free Joe, viewing his shabbiness with a critical eye, "but I knows Lucindy mos' good ez I does little Dan dar—dat I does."

There was no reply to this, and Free Joe continued,

"Miss Becky, I wish you please, ma'am, take en run yo' kyards en see sump'n n'er 'bout Lucindy; kaze ef she sick, I'm gwine dar. Dey ken take en take me up en gimme a stroppin', but I'm gwine dar."

Miss Becky got her cards, but first she picked up a cup, in the bottom of which were some coffee-grounds. These she whirled slowly round and round, ending finally by turning the cup upside down on the hearth and allowing it to remain in that position.

"I'll turn the cup first," said Miss Becky, "and then I'll run the cards and see what they say."

As she shuffled the cards the fire on the hearth burned low, and in its fitful light the gray-haired, thin-featured woman seemed to deserve the weird reputation which rumor and gossip had given her. She shuffled the cards for some moments, gazing intently in the dying fire; then, throwing a piece of pine on the coals, she made three divisions of the pack, disposing them about in her lap. Then she took the first pile, ran the cards slowly through her fingers, and studied them carefully. To the first she added the second pile. The study of these was evidently not satisfactory. She said nothing, but frowned heavily; and the frown deepened as she added the rest of the cards until the entire fifty-two had passed in review before her. Though she frowned, she seemed to be deeply interested. Without changing the relative position of the cards, she ran them all over again. Then she threw a larger piece of pine on the fire, shuffled the cards afresh, divided them into three piles, and subjected them to the same careful and critical examination.

"I can't tell the day when I've seed the cards run this a-way," she said after a while. "What is an' what aint, I'll never tell you; but I know what the cards sez."

"W'at does dey say, Miss Becky?" the negro inquired, in a tone the solemnity of which was heightened by its eagerness.

"They er runnin' quare. These here that I'm a-lookin' at," said Miss Becky, "they stan' for the past. Them there, they er the present; and the t'others, they er the future. Here's a bundle,"—tapping the ace of clubs with her thumb,—"an' here's a journey as plain as the nose on a man's face. Here's Lucinda"—

"Whar she, Miss Becky?"

"Here she is—the queen of spades."

Free Joe grinned. The idea seemed to please him immensely.

"Well, well, well!" he exclaimed. "Ef dat don't beat my time! De queen er spades! W'en Lucindy year dat hit'll tickle 'er, sho'!"

Miss Becky continued to run the cards back and forth through her fingers.

"Here's a bundle an' a journey, and here's Lucinda. An' here's ole Spite Calderwood."

She held the cards toward the negro and touched the king of clubs.

"De Lord he'p my soul!" exclaimed Free Joe with a chuckle. "De faver's dar. Yesser, dat's him! W'at de matter 'long wid all un um, Miss Becky?"

The old woman added the second pile of cards to the first, and then the third, still running them through her fingers slowly and critically. By this time the piece of pine in the fireplace had wrapped itself in a mantle of flame, illuminating the cabin and throwing into strange relief the figure of Miss Becky as she sat studying the cards. She frowned ominously at the cards and mumbled a few words to herself. Then she dropped her hands in her lap and gazed once more into the fire. Her shadow danced and capered on the wall and floor behind her, as if, looking over her shoulder into the future, it could behold a rare spectacle. After a while she picked up the cup that had been turned on the hearth. The coffee-grounds, shaken around, presented what seemed to be a most intricate map.

"Here's the journey," said Miss Becky, presently; "here's the big road, here's rivers to cross, here's the bundle to tote." She paused and sighed. "They haint no names writ here, an' what it all means I'll never tell you. Cajy, I wish you'd be so good as to han' me my pipe."

"I haint no hand wi' the kyards," said Cajy, as he handed the pipe, "but I reckon I can patch out your misinformation, Becky, bekaze the other day, whiles I was a-finishin' up Mizzers Perdue's rollin'-pin, I hearn a rattlin' in the road. I looked out, an' Spite Calderwood was a-drivin' by in his buggy, an' thar sot Lucinda by him. It'd in-about drapt out er my min'."

Free Joe sat on the door-sill and fumbled at his hat, flinging it from one hand to the other.

"You aint see um gwine back, is you, Mars Cajy?" he asked after a while.

"Ef they went back by this road," said Mr. Staley, with the air of one who is accustomed to weigh well his words, "it must 'a' bin endurin' of the time whiles I was asleep, bekaze I haint bin no furder from my shop than to yon bed."

"Well, sir!" exclaimed Free Joe in an awed tone, which Mr. Staley seemed to regard as a tribute to his extraordinary powers of statement.

"Ef it's my beliefs you want," continued the old man, "I'll pitch 'em at you fair and free. My beliefs is that Spite Calderwood is gone an' took Lucindy outen the county. Bless your heart and soul! when Spite Calderwood meets the Old Boy in the road they'll be a turrible scuffle. You mark what I tell you."

Free Joe, still fumbling with his hat, rose and leaned against the door-facing. He seemed to be embarrassed. Presently he said,—

"I speck I better be gittin' 'long. Nex' time I see Lucindy, I'm gwine tell 'er w'at Miss Becky say 'bout de queen er spades—dat I is. Ef dat don't tickle 'er, dey ain't no nigger 'oman never bin tickle'."

He paused a moment, as though waiting for some remark or comment, some confirmation of misfortune, or, at the very least, some indorsement of his suggestion that Lucinda would be greatly pleased to know that she had figured as the queen of spades; but neither Miss Becky nor her brother said any thing.

"One minnit ridin' in the buggy 'longside er Mars Spite, en de nex' highfalutin' 'roun' playin' de queen er spades. Mon, deze yer nigger gals gittin' up in de pictur's; dey sholy is."

With a brief "Good-night, Miss Becky, Mars Cajy," Free Joe went out into the darkness, followed by little Dan. He made his way to the poplar, where Lucinda had been in the habit of meeting him, and sat down. He sat there a long time; he sat there until little Dan, growing restless, trotted off in the direction of the Calderwood place. Dozing against the poplar, in the gray dawn of the morning, Free Joe heard Spite Calderwood's foxhounds in full cry a mile away.

"Shoo!" he exclaimed, scratching his head, and laughing to himself, "dem ar dogs is des a-warmin' dat old fox up."

But it was Dan the hounds were after, and the little dog came back no more. Free Joe waited and waited, until he grew tired of waiting. He went back the next night and waited, and for many nights thereafter. His waiting was in vain, and yet he never regarded it as in vain. Careless and shabby as he was, Free Joe was thoughtful enough to have his theory. He was convinced that little Dan had found Lucinda, and that some night when the moon was shining brightly through the trees, the dog would rouse him from his dreams as he sat sleeping at the foot of the poplar-tree, and he would open his eyes and behold Lucinda standing over him, laughing merrily as of old; and then he thought what fun they would have about the queen of spades.

How many long nights Free Joe waited at the foot of the poplar-tree for Lucinda and little Dan, no one can ever know. He kept no account of them, and they were not recorded by Micajah Staley nor by Miss Becky. The season ran into summer and then into fall. One night he went to the Staley cabin, cut the two old people an armful of wood, and seated himself on the door-steps, where he rested. He was always thankful—and proud, as it seemed—when Miss Becky gave him a cup of coffee, which she was sometimes thoughtful enough to do. He was especially thankful on this particular night.

"You er still layin' off for to strike up wi' Lucindy out thar in the woods, I reckon," said Micajah Staley, smiling grimly. The situation was not without its humorous aspects.

"Oh, dey er comin', Mars Cajy, dey er comin', sho," Free Joe replied. "I boun' you dey'll come; en w'en dey does come, I'll des take en fetch um yer, whar you kin see um wid you own eyes, you en Miss Becky."

"No," said Mr. Staley, with a quick and emphatic gesture of disapproval. "Don't! don't fetch 'em anywheres. Stay right wi' 'em as long as may be."

Free Joe chuckled, and slipped away into the night, while the two old people sat gazing in the fire. Finally Micajah spoke.

"Look at that nigger; look at 'im. He's pine-blank as happy now as a killdee by a mill-race. You can't 'faze 'em. I'd in-about give up my t'other hand ef I could stan' flat-footed, an' grin at trouble like that there nigger."

"Niggers is niggers," said Miss Becky, smiling grimly, "an' you can't rub it out; yit I lay I've seed a heap of white people lots meaner'n Free Joe. He grins—an' that's nigger—but I've ketched his under jaw a-trimblin' when Lucindy's name uz brung up. An' I tell you," she went on, bridling up a little, and speaking with almost fierce emphasis, "the Old Boy's done sharpened his claws for Spite Calderwood. You'll see it."

"Me, Rebecca?" said Mr. Staley, hugging his palsied arm; "me? I hope not."

"Well, you'll know it then," said Miss Becky, laughing heartily at her brother's look of alarm.

The next morning Micajah Staley had occasion to go into the woods after a piece of timber. He saw Free Joe sitting at the foot of the poplar, and the sight vexed him somewhat.

"Git up from there," he cried, "an' go an' arn your livin'. A mighty purty pass it's come to, when great big buck niggers can lie a-snorin' in the woods all day, when t'other folks is got to be up an' a-gwine. Git up from there!"

Receiving no response, Mr. Staley went to Free Joe, and shook him by the shoulder; but the negro made no response. He was dead. His hat was off, his head was bent, and a smile was on his face. It was as if he had bowed and smiled when death stood before him, humble to the last. His clothes were ragged; his hands were rough and callous; his shoes were literally tied together with strings; he was shabby in the extreme. A passer-by, glancing at him, could have no idea that such a humble creature had been summoned as a witness before the Lord God of Hosts.

Questions to Consider

1. What is the function of the Remus tales? What is the boy (and the Northern White reader) to learn? How does the use of folklore subvert or enact racial overtones?
2. Charles Chesnutt drew on Harris's popularity, and his Uncle Julius is, in many ways, an African-American writer's response to a White man's Uncle Remus. Compare Harris's Remus and Chesnutt's Julius. How do the listeners of the tales differ? What does Uncle Julius expect to happen as a result of the telling? What does Uncle Remus expect?
3. Is the title of "Free Joe and the Rest of the World" ironic? How would you define "the rest of the world?" Is Harris complicit in plantation sentimentality in this story? How "free" is Joe? Where does his freedom eventually lie? Explore the various classes here: the plantation master, the White "crackers," the townspeople, the field and domestic slaves. Which classes are compassionate? Generous? Greedy? Cruel? Self-serving?

Kate Chopin

1850–1904

Though Kate Chopin is today one of the South's best-known writers, neither her eventual fame nor the beginnings of her career were associated with the region. Aspiring to write fiction that dealt with "human existence in its subtle, complex, true meaning," Chopin produced a novel that was hailed three-quarters of a century after its publication as a feminist classic and one of American literature's most incisive portraits of conventional marriage. While the first several of her nearly one hundred short stories dealt with the dilemmas of contemporary women's lives, it was her fiction about south Louisiana that gained her an enduring reputation as a local color writer.

Chopin's girlhood reflected the privileges of modest wealth and culture. Born Katherine O'Flaherty, she was the only surviving daughter of a prosperous Irish immigrant, who died when she was five, and his young second wife from a prominent French-Creole family of St. Louis. Chopin learned French and music as a child and then studied at a highly respected Catholic school for girls. In 1870, she married Oscar Chopin, the son of a Louisiana planter and French emigré. After a European wedding journey, the young couple settled in Reconstruction New Orleans and began their family. Bearing six children, five sons and a daughter by 1882, makes Chopin exceptional among women writers of her era, few of whom were mothers. Oscar's business as a cotton-broker floundered with the crop failures of 1879 and forced the Chopins to the family plantations in Cloutierville, a tiny village south of Natchitoches in central Louisiana. The rural Acadians (French-speaking immigrants exiled from Nova Scotia in the eighteenth century) fascinated Chopin and later became the subjects of her most successful fiction.

When Oscar succumbed to malaria in 1882, Chopin remained in Louisiana for about a year settling her financial affairs and probably engaging in a romantic liaison with Albert Sampité, a married neighbor with a reputation for womanizing. In 1883, the young widow returned with her children to St. Louis to live with her mother, who died soon after their arrival.

Though left to raise her children alone, Chopin was soon absorbed into the lively literary and publishing community of her native city. Encouraged to try her hand at writing by her freethinking friend and former obstetrician, Frederick Kolbenheyer, she began to publish short fiction and poems in 1888. Though her earliest stories focused on the dilemmas of young women choosing between love and career, Chopin promptly realized that tales with Louisiana settings sold more quickly than others, even to national magazines like *Youth's Companion* and the prestigious *Atlantic Monthly*. By 1894, she had produced her first collection, *Bayou Folk*. Another volume followed in 1897, *A Night in Acadie*, and a third was accepted by a Chicago firm in 1899. That was also the year that Chopin's third and most famous novel was published. Her first, *At Fault* (1890), drew on her experiences in Natchitoches and featured the popular device of marriage as a trope of North-South reconciliation; she destroyed the manuscript of a second novel sometime in the mid-nineties. *The Awakening*, which was recovered in the 1970s as a groundbreaking account of the confinements of marriage for women, was not well-received in 1899. Its descriptions of a young Kentucky woman struggling to achieve selfhood in a stifling marriage to a New Orleans businessman proved unsettling to contemporary audiences, who found Chopin's critique of marriage and female sexuality unseemly if not moral poison. Though somewhat taken aback by her critics, Chopin did not abandon writing as some have suggested, though her failing health did lessen the number of stories she produced in her last years. She died on 22 August 1904, having suffered a stroke while attending the Louisiana Purchase Exposition in St. Louis.

Chopin's fiction reflects high standards of craftsmanship. Her economical descriptions of place and subtle use of imagery suggest how effectively the elements of local color can be employed and also anticipate the modernist techniques of twentieth-century Southern regionalists. Both "Désirée's Baby," a perennial favorite and rarely out of print, and "Nég Créol" exemplify her dexterous handling of two popular tropes of Southern local color, the tragic mulatta and the faithful ex-slave. Nég Créol's loyalty is moderated by his pride and resourcefulness, while Désirée's plight is intensified by Armand's blind arrogance. Though hardly free of racial stereotypes, Chopin's portraits are complicated by a rich irony and subtle humor, as well as by an appreciation for the limitations imposed by gender and social caste. "At the 'Cadian Ball," which foregrounds those issues, also demonstrates Chopin's skillful handling of dialect and the quaint Louisiana customs that made her reputation as a local colorist. "The Story of an Hour," whose setting is only ambiguously Southern, brilliantly illustrates the compression of her art as well as her wry critique of conventional marriage. Evident in all four of these stories is Chopin's abiding interest in the dilemmas of affection and sexual attraction when crossed by class, race, or convention. They also exhibit her adaptation of the ironic twist, made famous by Guy de Maupassant, a French writer whose work was an early inspiration to her. Best-known for her perceptive writing about women's experience, Chopin is increasingly recognized as one of the South's most important writers.

Désirée's Baby

As the day was pleasant, Madame Valmondé drove over to L'Abri to see Désirée and the baby.

It made her laugh to think of Désirée with a baby. Why, it seemed but yesterday that Désirée was little more than a baby herself; when Monsieur in riding through the gateway of Valmondé had found her lying asleep in the shadow of the big stone pillar.

The little one awoke in his arms and began to cry for "Dada." That was as much as she could do or say. Some people thought she might have strayed there of her own accord, for she was of the toddling age. The prevailing belief was that she had been purposely left by a party of Texans, whose canvas-covered wagon, late in the day, had crossed the ferry that Coton Maïs kept, just below the plantation. In time Madame Valmondé abandoned every speculation but the one that Désirée had been sent to her by a beneficent Providence to be the child of her affection, seeing that she was without child of the flesh. For the girl grew to be beautiful and gentle, affectionate and sincere—the idol of Valmondé.

It was no wonder, when she stood one day against the stone pillar in whose shadow she had lain asleep, eighteen years before, that Armand Aubigny riding by and seeing her there, had fallen in love with her. That was the way all the Aubignys fell in love, as if struck by a pistol shot. The wonder was that he had not loved her before; for he had known her since his father brought him home from Paris, a boy of eight, after his mother died there. The passion that awoke in him that day, when he saw her at the gate, swept along like an avalanche, or like a prairie fire, or like anything that drives head-long over all obstacles.

Monsieur Valmondé grew practical and wanted things well considered: that is, the girl's obscure origin. Armand looked into her eyes and did not care. He was reminded that she was nameless. What did it matter about a name when he could give her one of the oldest and proudest in Louisiana? He ordered the *corbeille* from Paris, and contained himself with what patience he could until it arrived; then they were married.

Madame Valmondé had not seen Désirée and the baby for four weeks. When she reached L'Abri she shuddered at the first sight of it, as she always did. It was a sad looking place, which for many years had not known the gentle presence of a mistress, old Monsieur Aubigny having married and buried his wife in France, and she having loved her own land too well ever to leave it. The roof came down steep and black like a cowl, reaching out beyond the wide galleries that encircled the yellow stuccoed house. Big, solemn oaks grew close to it, and their thick-leaved, far-reaching branches shadowed it like a pall. Young Aubigny's rule was a strict one, too, and under it his negroes had forgotten how to be gay, as they had been during the old master's easy-going and indulgent lifetime.

The young mother was recovering slowly, and lay full length, in her soft white muslins and laces, upon a couch. The baby was beside her, upon her arm, where he had fallen asleep, at her breast. The yellow nurse woman sat beside a window fanning herself.

Madame Valmondé bent her portly figure over Désirée and kissed her, holding her an instant tenderly in her arms. Then she turned to the child.

"This is not the baby!" she exclaimed, in startled tones. French was the language spoken at Valmondé in those days.

"I knew you would be astonished," laughed Désirée, "at the way he has grown. The little *cochon de lait!* Look at his legs, mamma, and his hands and fingernails—real fingernails. Zandrine had to cut them this morning. Is n't it true, Zandrine?"

The woman bowed her turbaned head majestically, "Mais si, Madame."

"And the way he cries," went on Désirée, "is deafening. Armand heard him the other day as far away as La Blanche's cabin."

Madame Valmondé had never removed her eyes from the child. She lifted it and walked with it over to the window that was lightest. She scanned the baby narrowly, then looked as searchingly at Zandrine, whose face was turned to gaze across the fields.

"Yes, the child has grown, has changed," said Madame Valmondé, slowly, as she replaced it beside its mother. "What does Armand say?"

Désirée's face became suffused with a glow that was happiness itself.

"Oh, Armand is the proudest father in the parish, I believe, chiefly because it is a boy, to bear his name; though he says not—that he would have loved a girl as well. But I know it is n't true. I know he says that to please me. And mamma," she added, drawing Madame Valmondé's head down to her, and speaking in a whisper, "he has n't punished one of them—not one of them—since baby is born. Even Négrillon, who pretended to have burnt his leg that he might rest from work—he only laughed, and said Négrillon was a great scamp. Oh, mamma, I'm so happy; it frightens me."

What Désirée said was true. Marriage, and later the birth of his son had softened Armand Aubigny's imperious and exacting nature greatly. This was what made the gentle Désirée so happy, for she loved him desperately. When he frowned she trembled, but loved him. When he smiled, she asked no greater blessing of God. But Armand's dark, handsome face had not often been disfigured by frowns since the day he fell in love with her.

When the baby was about three months old, Désirée awoke one day to the conviction that there was something in the air menacing her peace. It was at first too subtle to grasp. It had only been a disquieting suggestion; an air of mystery among the blacks; unexpected visits from far-off neighbors who could hardly account for their coming. Then a strange, an awful change in her husband's manner, which she dared not ask him to explain. When he spoke to her, it was with averted eyes, from which the old love-light seemed to have gone out. He absented himself from home; and when there, avoided her presence and that of her child, without excuse. And the very spirit of Satan seemed suddenly to take hold of him in his dealings with the slaves. Désirée was miserable enough to die.

She sat in her room, one hot afternoon, in her *peignoir,* listlessly drawing through her fingers the strands of her long, silky brown hair that hung about her shoulders.

The baby, half naked, lay asleep upon her own great mahogany bed, that was like a sumptuous throne, with its satin-lined half-canopy. One of La Blanche's little quadroon boys—half naked too—stood fanning the child slowly with a fan of peacock feathers. Désirée's eyes had been fixed absently and sadly upon the baby, while she was striving to penetrate the threatening mist that she felt closing about her. She looked from her child to the boy who stood beside him, and back again; over and over. "Ah!" It was a cry that she could not help; which she was not conscious of having uttered. The blood turned like ice in her veins, and a clammy moisture gathered upon her face.

She tried to speak to the little quadroon boy; but no sound would come, at first. When he heard his name uttered, he looked up, and his mistress was pointing to the door. He laid aside the great, soft fan, and obediently stole away, over the polished floor, on his bare tiptoes.

She stayed motionless, with gaze riveted upon her child, and her face the picture of fright.

Presently her husband entered the room, and without noticing her, went to a table and began to search among some papers which covered it.

"Armand," she called to him, in a voice which must have stabbed him, if he was human. But he did not notice. "Armand," she said again. Then she rose and tottered towards him. "Armand," she panted once more, clutching his arm, "look at our child. What does it mean? tell me."

He coldly but gently loosened her fingers from about his arm and thrust the hand away from him. "Tell me what it means!" she cried despairingly.

"It means," he answered lightly, "that the child is not white; it means that you are not white."

A quick conception of all that this accusation meant for her nerved her with unwonted courage to deny it. "It is a lie; it is not true, I am white! Look at my hair, it is brown; and my eyes are gray, Armand, you know they are gray. And my skin is fair," seizing his wrist. "Look at my hand; whiter than yours, Armand," she laughed hysterically.

"As white as La Blanche's," he returned cruelly; and went away leaving her alone with their child.

When she could hold a pen in her hand, she sent a despairing letter to Madame Valmondé.

"My mother, they tell me I am not white. Armand has told me I am not white. For God's sake tell them it is not true. You must know it is not true. I shall die. I must die. I cannot be so unhappy, and live."

The answer that came was as brief:

"My own Désirée: Come home to Valmondé; back to your mother who loves you. Come with your child."

When the letter reached Désirée she went with it to her husband's study, and laid it open upon the desk before which he sat. She was like a stone image: silent, white, motionless after she placed it there.

In silence he ran his cold eyes over the written words. He said nothing. "Shall I go, Armand?" she asked in tones sharp with agonized suspense.

"Yes, go."

"Do you want me to go?"

"Yes, I want you to go."

He thought Almighty God had dealt cruelly and unjustly with him; and felt, somehow, that he was paying Him back in kind when he stabbed thus into his wife's soul. Moreover he no longer loved her, because of the unconscious injury she had brought upon his home and his name.

She turned away like one stunned by a blow, and walked slowly towards the door, hoping he would call her back.

"Good-by, Armand," she moaned.

He did not answer her. That was his last blow at fate.

Désirée went in search of her child. Zandrine was pacing the sombre gallery with it. She took the little one from the nurse's arms with no word of explanation, and descending the steps, walked away, under the live-oak branches.

It was an October afternoon; the sun was just sinking. Out in the still fields the negroes were picking cotton.

Désirée had not changed the thin white garment nor the slippers which she wore. Her hair was uncovered and the sun's rays brought a golden gleam from its brown meshes. She did not take the broad, beaten road which led to the far-off plantation of Valmondé. She walked across a deserted field, where the stubble bruised her tender feet, so delicately shod, and tore her thin gown to shreds.

She disappeared among the reeds and willows that grew thick along the banks of the deep, sluggish bayou; and she did not come back again.

Some weeks later there was a curious scene enacted at L'Abri. In the centre of the smoothly swept back yard was a great bonfire. Armand Aubigny sat in the wide hallway that commanded a view of the spectacle; and it was he who dealt out to a half dozen negroes the material which kept this fire ablaze.

A graceful cradle of willow, with all its dainty furbishings, was laid upon the pyre, which had already been fed with the richness of a priceless *layette*. Then there were silk gowns, and velvet and satin ones added to these; laces, too, and embroideries; bonnets and gloves; for the *corbeille* had been of rare quality.

The last thing to go was a tiny bundle of letters; innocent little scribblings that Désirée had sent to him during the days of their espousal. There was the remnant of one back in the drawer from which he took them. But it was not Désirée's; it was part of an old letter from his mother to his father. He read it. She was thanking God for the blessing of her husband's love:

"But, above all," she wrote, "night and day, I thank the good God for having so arranged our lives that our dear Armand will never know that his mother, who adores him, belongs to the race that is cursed with the brand of slavery."

At the 'Cadian Ball

Bobinôt, that big, brown, good-natured Bobinôt, had no intention of going to the ball, even though he knew Calixta would be there. For what came of those balls but heartache, and a sickening disinclination for work the whole week through, till Saturday night came again and his tortures began afresh? Why could he not love Ozéina, who would marry him to-morrow; or Fronie, or any one of a dozen others, rather than that little Spanish vixen? Calixta's slender foot had never touched Cuban soil; but her mother's had, and the Spanish was in her blood all the same. For that reason the prairie people forgave her much that they would not have overlooked in their own daughters or sisters.

Her eyes—Bobinôt thought of her eyes, and weakened—the bluest, the drowsiest, most tantalizing that ever looked into a man's; he thought of her flaxen hair that kinked worse than a mulatto's close to her head; that broad, smiling mouth and tip-tilted nose, that full figure; that voice like a rich contralto song, with cadences in it that must have been taught by Satan, for there was no one else to teach her tricks on that 'Cadian prairie. Bobinôt thought of them all as he plowed his rows of cane.

There had even been a breath of scandal whispered about her a year ago, when she went to Assumption—but why talk of it? No one did now. "C'est Espagnol, ça," most of them said with lenient shoulder-shrugs. "Bon chien tient de race," the old men mumbled over their pipes, stirred by recollections. Nothing was made of it, except that Fronie threw it up to Calixta when the two quarreled and fought on the church steps after mass one Sunday, about a lover. Calixta swore roundly in fine 'Cadian French and with true Spanish spirit, and slapped Fronie's face. Fronie had slapped her back; "Tiens, bocotte, va!" "Espèce de lionèse; prends ça, et ça!" till the curé himself was obliged to hasten and make peace between them. Bobinôt thought of it all, and would not go to the ball.

But in the afternoon, over at Friedheimer's store, where he was buying a trace-chain, he heard some one say that Alcée Laballière would be there. Then wild horses could not have kept him away. He knew how it would be—or rather he did not know how it would be—if the handsome young planter came over to the ball as he sometimes did. If Alcée happened to be in a serious mood, he might only go to the card-room and play a round or two; or he might stand out on the galleries talking crops and politics with the old people. But there was no telling. A drink or two could put the devil in his head—that was what Bobinôt said to himself, as he wiped the sweat from his brow with his red bandanna; a gleam from Calixta's eyes, a flash of her ankle, a twirl of her skirts could do the same. Yes, Bobinôt would go to the ball.

* * *

That was the year Alcée Laballière put nine hundred acres in rice. It was putting a good deal of money into the ground, but the returns promised to be glorious. Old Madame Laballière, sailing about the spacious galleries in her white *volante,* figured it all out in her head. Clarisse, her god-daughter, helped her a little, and together they built more air-castles than enough. Alcée worked like a mule that time; and if he did not kill himself, it was because his constitution was an iron one. It was an every-day affair for him to come in from the field well-nigh exhausted, and wet to the waist. He did not mind if there were visitors; he left them to his mother and Clarisse. There were often guests: young men and women who came up from the city, which was but a few hours away, to visit his beautiful kinswoman. She was worth going a good deal farther than that to see. Dainty as a lily; hardy as a sunflower; slim, tall, graceful, like one of the reeds that grew in the marsh. Cold and kind and cruel by turn, and everything that was aggravating to Alcée.

He would have liked to sweep the place of those visitors, often. Of the men, above all, with their ways and their manners; their swaying of fans like women, and dandling about hammocks. He could have pitched them over the levee into the river, if it had n't meant murder. That was Alcée. But he must have been crazy the day he came in from the rice-field, and, toil-stained as he was, clasped Clarisse by the arms and panted a volley of hot, blistering love-words into her face. No man had ever spoken love to her like that.

"Monsieur!" she exclaimed, looking him full in the eyes, without a quiver. Alcée's hands dropped and his glance wavered before the chill of her calm, clear eyes.

"*Par exemple!*" she muttered disdainfully, as she turned from him, deftly adjusting the careful toilet that he had so brutally disarranged.

That happened a day or two before the cyclone came that cut into the rice like fine steel. It was an awful thing, coming so swiftly, without a moment's warning in which to light a holy candle or set a piece of blessed palm burning. Old madame wept openly and said her beads, just as her son Didier, the New Orleans one, would have done. If such a thing had happened to Alphonse, the Laballière planting cotton up in Natchitoches, he would have raved and stormed like a second cyclone, and made his surroundings unbearable for a day or two. But Alcée took the misfortune differently. He looked ill and gray after it, and said nothing. His speechlessness was frightful. Clarisse's heart melted with tenderness; but when she offered her soft, purring words of condolence, he accepted them with mute indifference. Then she and her nénaine wept afresh in each other's arms.

A night or two later, when Clarisse went to her window to kneel there in the moonlight and say her prayers before retiring, she saw that Bruce, Alcée's negro servant, had led his master's saddle-horse noiselessly along the edge of the sward that bordered the gravel-path, and stood holding him near by. Presently, she heard Alcée quit his room, which was beneath her own, and traverse the lower portico. As he emerged from the shadow and crossed the strip of moonlight, she perceived that he carried a pair of well-filled saddle-bags which he at once flung across the animal's back. He then lost no time in mounting, and after a brief exchange of words with Bruce, went cantering away, taking no precaution to avoid the noisy gravel as the negro had done.

Clarisse had never suspected that it might be Alcée's custom to sally forth from the plantation secretly, and at such an hour; for it was nearly midnight. And had it not been for the telltale saddle-bags, she would only have crept to bed, to wonder, to fret and dream unpleasant dreams. But her impatience and anxiety would not be held in check. Hastily unbolting the shutters of her door that opened upon the gallery, she stepped outside and called softly to the old negro.

"Gre't Peter! Miss Clarisse. I was n' sho it was a ghos' o' w'at, stan'in' up dah, plumb in de night, dataway."

He mounted halfway up the long, broad flight of stairs. She was standing at the top.

"Bruce, w'ere has Monsieur Alcée gone?" she asked.

"W'y, he gone 'bout he business, I reckin," replied Bruce, striving to be noncommittal at the outset.

"W'ere has Monsieur Alcée gone?" she reiterated, stamping her bare foot. "I wo n't stan' any nonsense or any lies; mine, Bruce."

"I don' ric'lic ez I eva tole you lie *yit*, Miss Clarisse. Mista Alcée, he all broke up, sho."

"W'ere–has–he gone? Ah, Sainte Vierge! faut de la patience! butor, va!"

"W'en I was in he room, a-breshin' off he clo'es to-day," the darkey began, settling himself against the stair-rail, "he look dat speechless an' down, I say, 'You 'pear tu me like some pussun w'at gwine have a spell o' sickness, Mista Alcée.' He say, 'You reckin?' 'I dat he git up, go look hisse'f stiddy in de glass. Den he go to de chimbly an' jerk up de quinine bottle an po' a gre't hoss-dose on to he han'. An' he swalla dat mess in a wink, an' wash hit down wid a big dram o' w'iskey w'at he keep in he room, aginst he come all soppin' wet outen de fiel'.

"He 'lows, 'No, I ain' gwine be sick, Bruce.' Den he square off. He say, 'I kin mak out to stan' up an' gi' an' take wid any man I knows, lessen hit's John L. Sulvun. But w'en God A'mighty an' a 'oman jines fo'ces agin me, dat's one too many fur me.' I tell 'im, 'Jis so,' whils' I'se makin' out to bresh a spot off w'at ain' dah, on he coat colla. I tell 'im, 'You wants li'le res', suh.' He say, 'No, I wants li'le fling; dat w'at I wants; an I gwine git it. Pitch me a fis'ful o' clo'es in dem 'ar saddle-bags.' Dat w'at he say. Don't you bodda, missy. He jis' gone a-caperin' yonda to de Cajun ball. Uh–uh–de skeeters is fair' a-swarmin' like bees roun' yo' foots!"

The mosquitoes were indeed attacking Clarisse's white feet savagely. She had unconsciously been alternately rubbing one foot over the other during the darkey's recital.

"The 'Cadian ball," she repeated contemptously. "Humph! *Par exemple!* Nice conduc' for a Laballière. An' he needs a saddle-bag, fill' with clothes, to go to the 'Cadian ball!"

"Oh, Miss Clarisse; you go on to bed, chile; git yo' soun' sleep. He 'low he come back in couple weeks o' so. I kiarn be repeatin' lot o' truck w'at young mans say, out heah face o' a young gal."

Clarisse said no more, but turned and abruptly reëntered the house.

"You done talk too much wid yo' mouf a'ready, you ole fool nigga, you," muttered Bruce to himself as he walked away.

* * *

Alcée reached the ball very late, of course—too late for the chicken gumbo which had been served at midnight.

The big, low-ceiled room—they called it a hall—was packed with men and women dancing to the music of three fiddles. There were broad galleries all around it. There was a room at one side where sober-faced men were playing cards. Another, in which babies were sleeping, was called *le parc aux petits*. Any one who is white may go to a 'Cadian ball, but he must pay for his lemonade, his coffee and chicken gumbo. And he must behave himself like a 'Cadian. Grosbœuf was giving this ball. He had been giving them since he was a young man, and he was a middle-aged one, now. In that time he could recall but one disturbance, and that was caused by American railroaders, who were not in touch with their surroundings and had no business there. "Ces maudits gens du raiderode," Grosbœuf called them.

Alcée Laballière's presence at the ball caused a flutter even among the men, who could not but admire his "nerve" after such misfortune befalling him. To be sure, they knew the Laballières were rich—that there were resources East, and more again in the city. But they felt it took a *brave homme* to stand a blow like that philosophically. One old gentleman, who was in the habit of reading a Paris newspaper and knew things, chuckled gleefully to everybody that Alcée's conduct was altogether *chic, mais chic*. That he had more *panache* than Boulanger. Well, perhaps he had.

But what he did not show outwardly was that he was in a mood for ugly things to-night. Poor Bobinôt alone felt it vaguely. He discerned a gleam of it in Alcée's handsome eyes, as the young planter stood in the doorway, looking with rather feverish glance upon the assembly, while he laughed and talked with a 'Cadian farmer who was beside him.

Bobinôt himself was dull-looking and clumsy. Most of the men were. But the young women were very beautiful. The eyes that glanced into Alcée's as they passed him were big, dark, soft as those of the young heifers standing out in the cool prairie grass.

But the belle was Calixta. Her white dress was not nearly so handsome or well made as Fronie's (she and Fronie had quite forgotten the battle on the church steps, and were friends again), nor were her slippers so stylish as those of Ozéina; and she fanned herself with a handkerchief, since she had broken her red fan at the last ball, and her aunts and uncles were not willing to give her another. But all the men agreed she was at her best to-night. Such animation! and abandon! such flashes of wit!

"Hé, Bobinôt! *Mais* w'at's the matta? W'at you standin' *planté là* like ole Ma'ame Tina's cow in the bog, you?"

That was good. That was an excellent thrust at Bobinôt, who had forgotten the figure of the dance with his mind bent on other things, and it started a clamor of laughter at his expense. He joined good-naturedly. It was better to receive even such notice as that from Calixta than none at all. But Madame Suzonne, sitting in a corner, whispered to her neighbor that if Ozéina were to conduct herself in a like manner, she should immediately be taken out to the mule-cart and driven home. The women did not always approve of Calixta.

Now and then were short lulls in the dance, when couples flocked out upon the galleries for a brief respite and fresh air. The moon had gone down pale in the west, and in the east was yet no promise of day. After such an interval, when the dancers again assembled to resume the interrupted quadrille, Calixta was not among them.

She was sitting upon a bench out in the shadow, with Alcée beside her. They were acting like fools. He had attempted to take a little gold ring from her finger; just for the fun of it, for there was nothing he could have done with the ring but replace it again. But she clinched her hand tight. He pretended that it was a very difficult matter to open it. Then he kept the hand in his. They seemed to forget about it. He played with her ear-ring, a thin crescent of gold hanging from her small brown ear. He caught a wisp of the kinky hair that had escaped its fastening, and rubbed the ends of it against his shaven cheek.

"You know, last year in Assumption, Calixta?" They belonged to the younger generation, so preferred to speak English.

"Do n't come say Assumption to me, M'sieur Alcée. I done yeard Assumption till I'm plumb sick."

"Yes, I know. The idiots! Because you were in Assumption, and I happened to go to Assumption, they must have it that we went together. But it was nice—*hein*, Calixta?—in Assumption?"

They saw Bobinôt emerge from the hall and stand a moment outside the lighted doorway, peering uneasily and searchingly into the darkness. He did not see them, and went slowly back.

"There is Bobinôt looking for you. You are going to set poor Bobinôt crazy. You'll marry him some day; *hein*, Calixta?"

"I do n't say no, me," she replied, striving to withdraw her hand, which he held more firmly for the attempt.

"But come, Calixta; you know you said you would go back to Assumption, just to spite them."

"No, I neva said that, me. You mus' dreamt that."

"Oh, I thought you did. You know I'm going down to the city."

"W'en?"

"To-night."

"Betta make has'e, then; it's mos' day."

"Well, to-morrow 'll do."

"W'at you goin' do, yonda?"

"I do n't know. Drown myself in the lake, maybe; unless you go down there to visit your uncle."

Calixta's senses were reeling; and they well-nigh left her when she felt Alcée's lips brush her ear like the touch of a rose.

"Mista Alcée! Is dat Mista Alcée?" the thick voice of a negro was asking; he stood on the ground, holding to the banister-rails near which the couple sat.

"W'at do you want now?" cried Alcée impatiently. "Ca n't I have a moment of peace?"

"I ben huntin' you high an' low, suh," answered the man. "Dey—dey some one in de road, onda de mulbare-tree, want see you a minute."

"I would n't go out to the road to see the Angel Gabriel. And if you come back here with any more talk, I'll have to break your neck." The negro turned mumbling away.

Alcée and Calixta laughed softly about it. Her boisterousness was all gone. They talked low, and laughed softly, as lovers do.

"Alcée! Alcée Laballière!"

It was not the negro's voice this time; but one that went through Alcée's body like an electric shock, bringing him to his feet.

Clarisse was standing there in her riding-habit, where the negro had stood. For an instant confusion reigned in Alcée's thoughts, as with one who awakes suddenly from a dream. But he felt that something of serious import had brought his cousin to the ball in the dead of night.

"W'at does this mean, Clarisse?" he asked.

"It means something has happen' at home. You mus' come."

"Happened to maman?" he questioned, in alarm.

"No; nénaine is well, and asleep. It is something else. Not to frighten you. But you mus' come. Come with me, Alcée."

There was no need for the imploring note. He would have followed the voice anywhere.

She had now recognized the girl sitting back on the bench.

"Ah, c'est vous, Calixta? Comment ça va, mon enfant?"

"Tcha va b'en; et vous, mam'zélle?"

Alcée swung himself over the low rail and started to follow Clarisse, without a word, without a glance back at the girl. He had forgotten he was leaving her there. But Clarisse whispered something to him, and he turned back to say "Good-night, Calixta," and offer his hand to press through the railing. She pretended not to see it.

* * *

"How come that? You settin' yere by yo'se'f, Calixta?" It was Bobinôt who had found her there alone. The dancers had not yet come out. She looked ghastly in the faint, gray light struggling out of the east.

"Yes, that's me. Go yonda in the *parc aux petits* an' ask Aunt Olisse fu' my hat. She knows w'ere 't is. I want to go home, me."

"How you came?"

"I come afoot, with the Cateaus. But I'm goin' now. I ent goin' wait fu' 'em. I'm plumb wo' out, me."

"Kin I go with you, Calixta?"

"I don' care."

They went together across the open prairie and along the edge of the fields, stumbling in the uncertain light. He told her to lift her dress that was getting wet and bedraggled; for she was pulling at the weeds and grasses with her hands.

"I don' care; it's got to go in the tub, anyway. You been sayin' all along you want to marry me, Bobinôt. Well, if you want, yet, I don' care, me."

The glow of a sudden and overwhelming happiness shone out in the brown, rugged face of the young Acadian. He could not speak, for very joy. It choked him.

"Oh well, if you don' want," snapped Calixta, flippantly, pretending to be piqued at his silence.

"*Bon Dieu!* You know that makes me crazy, w'at you sayin'. You mean that, Calixta? You ent goin' turn roun' agin?"

"I neva tole you that much *yet*, Bobinôt. I mean that. *Tiens,*" and she held out her hand in the business-like manner of a man who clinches a bargain with a hand-clasp. Bobinôt grew bold with happiness and asked Calixta to kiss him. She turned her face, that was almost ugly after the night's dissipation, and looked steadily into his.

"I don' want to kiss you, Bobinôt," she said, turning away again, "not to-day. Some other time. *Bonté divine!* ent you satisfy, *yet!*"

"Oh, I'm satisfy, Calixta," he said.

* * *

Riding through a patch of wood, Clarisse's saddle became ungirted, and she and Alcée dismounted to readjust it.

For the twentieth time he asked her what had happened at home.

"But, Clarisse, w'at is it? Is it a misfortune?"

"*Ah Dieu sait!*" It's only something that happen' to me."

"To you!"

"I saw you go away las' night, Alcée, with those saddle-bags," she said, haltingly, striving to arrange something about the saddle, "an' I made Bruce tell me. He said you had gone to the ball, an' wouldn' be home for weeks an' weeks. I thought, Alcée—maybe you were going to—to Assumption. I got wild. An' then I knew if you did n't come back, *now*, to-night, I could n't stan' it—again."

She had her face hidden in her arm that she was resting against the saddle when she said that.

He began to wonder if this meant love. But she had to tell him so, before he believed it. And when she told him, he thought the face of the Universe was changed—just like Bobinôt. Was it last week the cyclone had well-nigh ruined him? The cyclone seemed a huge joke, now. It was he, then, who, an hour ago was kissing little Calixta's ear and whispering nonsense into it. Calixta was like a myth, now. The one, only, great reality in the world was Clarisse standing before him, telling him that she loved him.

In the distance they heard the rapid discharge of pistol-shots; but it did not disturb them. They knew it was only the negro musicians who had gone into the yard to fire their pistols into the air, as the custom is, and to announce "*le bal est fini*."

The Story of an Hour

The Dream of an Hour

Knowing that Mrs. Mallard was afflicted with a heart trouble, great care was taken to break to her as gently as possible the news of her husband's death.

It was her sister Josephine who told her, in broken sentences; veiled hints that revealed in half concealing. Her husband's friend Richards was there, too, near her. It was he who had been in the newspaper office when intelligence of the railroad disaster was received, with Brently Mallard's name leading the list of "killed." He had only taken the time to assure himself of its truth by a second telegram, and had hastened to forestall any less careful, less tender friend in bearing the sad message.

She did not hear the story as many women have heard the same, with a paralyzed inability to accept its significance. She wept at once, with sudden, wild abandonment, in her sister's arms. When the storm of grief had spent itself she went away to her room alone. She would have no one follow her.

There stood, facing the open window, a comfortable, roomy armchair. Into this she sank, pressed down by a physical exhaustion that haunted her body and seemed to reach into her soul.

She could see in the open square before her house the tops of trees that were all aquiver with the new spring life. The delicious breath of rain was in the air. In the street below a peddler was crying his wares. The notes of a distant song which some one was singing reached her faintly, and countless sparrows were twittering in the eaves.

There were patches of blue sky showing here and there through the clouds that had met and piled one above the other in the west facing her window.

She sat with her head thrown back upon the cushion of the chair, quite motionless, except when a sob came up into her throat and shook her, as a child who has cried itself to sleep continues to sob in its dreams.

She was young, with a fair, calm face, whose lines bespoke repression and even a certain strength. But now there was a dull stare in her eyes, whose gaze was fixed away off yonder on one of those patches of blue sky. It was not a glance of reflection, but rather indicated a suspension of intelligent thought.

There was something coming to her and she was waiting for it, fearfully. What was it? She did not know; it was too subtle and elusive to name. But she felt it, creeping out of the sky, reaching toward her through the sounds, the scents, the color that filled the air.

Now her bosom rose and fell tumultuously. She was beginning to recognize this thing that was approaching to possess her, and she was striving to beat it back with her will—as powerless as her two white slender hands would have been.

When she abandoned herself a little whispered word escaped her slightly parted lips. She said it over and over under her breath: "free, free, free!" The vacant stare and the look of terror that had followed it went from her eyes. They stayed keen and bright. Her pulses beat fast, and the coursing blood warmed and relaxed every inch of her body.

She did not stop to ask if it were or were not a monstrous joy that held her. A clear and exalted perception enabled her to dismiss the suggestion as trivial.

She knew that she would weep again when she saw the kind, tender hands folded in death; the face that had never looked save with love upon her, fixed and gray and dead. But she saw beyond that bitter moment a long procession of years to come that would belong to her absolutely. And she opened and spread her arms out to them in welcome.

There would be no one to live for her during those coming years; she would live for herself. There would be no powerful will bending hers in that blind persistence with which men and women believe they have a right to impose a private will upon a fellow-creature. A kind intention or a cruel intention made the act seem no less a crime as she looked upon it in that brief moment of illumination.

And yet she had loved him—sometimes. Often she had not. What did it matter! What could love, the unsolved mystery, count for in face of this possession of self-assertion which she suddenly recognized as the strongest impulse of her being!

"Free! Body and soul free!" she kept whispering.

Josephine was kneeling before the closed door with her lips to the keyhole, imploring for admission. "Louise, open the door! I beg; open the door—you will make yourself ill. What are you doing, Louise? For heaven's sake open the door."

"Go away. I am not making myself ill." No; she was drinking in a very elixir of life through that open window.

Her fancy was running riot along those days ahead of her. Spring days, and summer days, and all sorts of days that would be her own. She breathed a quick prayer that life might be long. It was only yesterday she had thought with a shudder that life might be long.

She arose at length and opened the door to her sister's importunities. There was a feverish triumph in her eyes, and she carried herself unwittingly like a goddess of Victory. She clasped her sister's waist, and together they descended the stairs. Richards stood waiting for them at the bottom.

Some one was opening the front door with a latchkey. It was Brently Mallard who entered, a little travel-stained, composedly carrying his grip-sack and umbrella. He had been far from the scene of accident, and did not even know there had been one. He stood amazed at Josephine's piercing cry; at Richards' quick motion to screen him from the view of his wife.

But Richards was too late.

When the doctors came they said she had died of heart disease—of joy that kills.

Nég Créol

At the remote period of his birth he had been named César François Xavier, but no one ever thought of calling him anything but Chicot, or Nég, or Maringouin. Down at the French market, where he worked among the fishmongers, they called him Chicot, when they were not calling him names that are written less freely than they are spoken. But one felt privileged to call him almost anything, he was so black, lean, lame, and shriveled. He wore a head-kerchief, and whatever other rags the fishermen and their wives chose to bestow upon him. Throughout one whole winter he wore a woman's discarded jacket with puffed sleeves.

Among some startling beliefs entertained by Chicot was one that "Michié St. Pierre et Michié St. Paul" had created him. Of "Michié bon Dieu" he held his own private opinion, and not a too flattering one at that. This fantastic notion concerning the origin of his being he owed to the early teaching of his young master, a lax believer, and a great *farceur* in his day. Chicot had once been thrashed by a robust young Irish priest for expressing his religious views, and at another time knifed by a Sicilian. So he had come to hold his peace upon that subject.

Upon another theme he talked freely and harped continuously. For years he had tried to convince his associates that his master had left a progeny, rich, cultured, powerful, and numerous beyond belief. This prosperous race of beings inhabited the most imposing mansions in the city of New Orleans. Men of note and position, whose names were familiar to the public, he swore were grandchildren, great-grandchildren, or, less frequently, distant relatives of his master, long deceased. Ladies who came to the market in carriages, or whose elegance of attire attracted the attention and admiration of the fishwomen, were all *des 'tites cousines* to his former master, Jean Boisduré. He never looked for recognition from any of these superior beings, delighted to discourse by the hour upon their dignity and pride of birth and wealth.

Chicot always carried an old gunny-sack, and into this went his earnings. He cleaned stalls at the market, scaled fish, and did many odd offices for the itinerant merchants, who usually paid in trade for his service. Occasionally he saw the color of silver and got his clutch upon a coin, but he accepted anything, and seldom made terms. He was glad to get a handkerchief from the Hebrew, and grateful if the

Choctaws would trade him a bottle of *filé* for it. The butcher flung him a soup bone, and the fishmonger a few crabs or a paper bag of shrimps. It was the big *mulatresse, vendeuse de café*, who cared for his inner man.

Once Chicot was accused by a shoe-vender of attempting to steal a pair of ladies' shoes. He declared he was only examining them. The clamor raised in the market was terrific. Young Dagoes assembled and squealed like rats; a couple of Gascon butchers bellowed like bulls. Matteo's wife shook her fist in the accuser's face and called him incomprehensible names. The Choctaw women, where they squatted, turned their slow eyes in the direction of the fray, taking no further notice; while a policeman jerked Chicot around by the puffed sleeve and brandished a club. It was a narrow escape.

Nobody knew where Chicot lived. A man—even a nég créol—who lives among the reeds and willows of Bayou St. John, in a deserted chicken-coop constructed chiefly of tarred paper, is not going to boast of his habitation or to invite attention to his domestic appointments. When, after market hours, he vanished in the direction of St. Philip street, limping, seemingly bent under the weight of his gunny-bag, it was like the disappearance from the stage of some petty actor whom the audience does not follow in imagination beyond the wings, or think of till his return in another scene.

There was one to whom Chicot's coming or going meant more than this. In *la maison grise* they called her La Chouette, for no earthly reason unless that she perched high under the roof of the old rookery and scolded in shrill sudden outbursts. Forty or fifty years before, when for a little while she acted minor parts with a company of French players (an escapade that had brought her grandmother to the grave), she was known as Mademoiselle de Montallaine. Seventy-five years before she had been christened Aglaé Boisduré.

No matter at what hour the old negro appeared at her threshold, Mamzelle Aglaé always kept him waiting till she finished her prayers. She opened the door for him and silently motioned him to a seat, returning to prostrate herself upon her knees before a crucifix, and a shell filled with holy water that stood on a small table; it represented in her imagination an altar. Chicot knew that she did it to aggravate him; he was convinced that she timed her devotions to begin when she heard his footsteps on the stairs. He would sit with sullen eyes contemplating her long, spare, poorly clad figure as she knelt and read from her book or finished her prayers. Bitter was the religious warfare that had raged for years between them, and Mamzelle Aglaé had grown, on her side, as intolerant as Chicot. She had come to hold St. Peter and St. Paul in such utter detestation that she had cut their pictures out of her prayer-book.

Then Mamzelle Aglaé pretended not to care what Chicot had in his bag. He drew forth a small hunk of beef and laid it in her basket that stood on the bare floor. She looked from the corner of her eye, and went on dusting the table. He brought out a handful of potatoes, some pieces of sliced fish, a few herbs, a yard of calico, and a small pat of butter wrapped in lettuce leaves. He was proud of the butter, and wanted her to notice it. He held it out and asked her for something to put it on. She handed him a saucer, and looked indifferent and resigned, with lifted eyebrows.

"Pas d' sucre, Nég?"

Chicot shook his head and scratched it, and looked like a black picture of distress and mortification. No sugar! But tomorrow he would get a pinch here and a pinch there, and would bring as much as a cupful.

Mamzelle Aglaé then sat down, and talked to Chicot uninterruptedly and confidentially. She complained bitterly, and it was all about a pain that lodged in her leg; that crept and acted like a live, stinging serpent, twining about her waist and up her spine, and coiling round the shoulder-blade. And then *les rheumatismes* in her fingers! He could see for himself how they were knotted. She could not bend them; she could hold nothing in her hands, and had let a saucer fall that morning and broken it in pieces. And if she were to tell him that she had slept a wink through the night, she would be a liar, deserving of perdition. She had sat at the window *la nuit blanche*, hearing the hours strike and the market-wagons rumble. Chicot nodded, and kept up a running fire of sympathetic comment and suggestive remedies for rheumatism and insomnia: herbs, or *tisanes*, or *grigris*, or all three. As if he knew! There was Purgatory Mary, a perambulating soul whose office in life was to pray for the shades in purgatory—she had brought Mamzelle Aglaé a bottle of *eau de Lourdes*, but so little of it! She might have kept her water of Lourdes, for all the good it did—a drop! Not so much as would cure a fly or a mosquito! Mamzelle Aglaé was going to show Purgatory Mary the door when she came again, not only because of her avarice with the Lourdes water, but, beside that, she brought in on her feet dirt that could only be removed with a shovel after she left.

And Mamzelle Aglaé wanted to inform Chicot that there would be slaughter and bloodshed in *la maison grise* if the people below stairs did not mend their ways. She was convinced that they lived for no other purpose than to torture and molest her. The woman kept a bucket of dirty water constantly on the landing with the hope of Mamzelle Aglaé falling over or into it. And she knew that the children were instructed to gather in the hall and on the stairway, and scream and make a noise and jump up and down like galloping horses, with the intention of driving her to suicide. Chicot should notify the policeman on the beat, and have them arrested, if possible, and thrust into the parish prison, where they belonged.

Chicot would have been extremely alarmed if he had ever chanced to find Mamzelle Aglaé in an uncomplaining mood. It never occurred to him that she might be otherwise. He felt that she had a right to quarrel with fate, if ever mortal had. Her poverty was a disgrace, and he hung his head before it and felt ashamed.

One day he found Mamzelle Aglaé stretched on the bed, with her head tied up in a handkerchief. Her sole complaint that day was, "Aïe–aïe–aïe! Aïe–aïe–aïe!" uttered with every breath. He had seen her so before, especially when the weather was damp.

"Vous pas bézouin tisane, Mamzelle Aglaé? Vous pas veux mo cri gagni docteur?"

She desired nothing. "Aïe–aïe–aïe!"

He emptied his bag very quietly, so as not to disturb her; and he wanted to stay there with her and lie down on the floor in case she needed him, but the woman from below had come up. She was an Irishwoman with rolled sleeves.

"It's a shtout shtick I'm afther giving her, Nég, and she do but knock on the flure it's me or Janie or wan of us that'll be hearing her."

"You too good, Brigitte. Aïe–aïe–aïe! Une goutte d'eau sucré, Nég! That Purg'-tory Marie—you see hair, ma bonne Brigitte, you tell hair go say li'le prayer là-bas au Cathédral. Aïe–aïe–aïe!"

Nég could hear her lamentation as he descended the stairs. It followed him as he limped his way through the city streets, and seemed part of the city's noise; he could hear it in the rumble of wheels and jangle of carbells, and in the voices of those passing by.

He stopped at Mimotte the Voudou's shanty and bought a *grigri*—a cheap one for fifteen cents. Mimotte held her charms at all prices. This he intended to introduce next day into Mamzelle Aglaé's room—somewhere about the altar—to the confusion and discomfort of "Michié bon Dieu," who persistently declined to concern himself with the welfare of a Boisduré.

At night, among the reeds on the bayou, Chicot could still hear the woman's wail, mingled now with the croaking of the frogs. If he could have been convinced that giving up his life down there in the water would in any way have bettered her condition, he would not have hesitated to sacrifice the remnant of his existence that was wholly devoted to her. He lived but to serve her. He did not know it himself; but Chicot knew so little, and that little in such a distorted way! He could scarcely have been expected, even in his most lucid moments, to give himself over to self-analysis.

Chicot gathered an uncommon amount of dainties at market the following day. He had to work hard, and scheme and whine a little; but he got hold of an orange and a lump of ice and a *chou-fleur*. He did not drink his cup of *café au lait,* but asked Mimi Lambeau to put it in the little new tin pail that the Hebrew notion-vender had just given him in exchange for a mess of shrimps. This time, however, Chicot had his trouble for nothing. When he reached the upper room of *la maison grise,* it was to find that Mamzelle Aglaé had died during the night. He set his bag down in the middle of the floor, and stood shaking, and whined low like a dog in pain.

Everything had been done. The Irish-woman had gone for the doctor, and Purgatory Mary had summoned a priest. Furthermore, the woman had arranged Mamzelle Aglaé decently. She had covered the table with a white cloth, and had placed it at the head of the bed, with the crucifix and two lighted candles in silver candlesticks upon it; the little bit of ornamentation brightened and embellished the poor room. Purgatory Mary, dressed in shabby black, fat and breathing hard, sat reading half audibly from a prayer-book. She was watching the dead and the silver candlesticks, which she had borrowed from a benevolent society, and for which she held herself responsible. A young man was just leaving—a reporter snuffing the air for items, who had scented one up there in the top room of *la maison grise*.

All the morning Janie had been escorting a procession of street Arabs up and down the stairs to view the remains. One of them—a little girl, who had had her face washed and had made a species of toilet for the occasion—refused to be dragged away. She stayed seated as if at an entertainment, fascinated alternately by the long, still figure of Mamzelle Aglaé, the mumbling lips of Purgatory Mary, and the silver candlesticks.

"Will ye get down on yer knees, man, and say a prayer for the dead!" commanded the woman.

But Chicot only shook his head, and refused to obey. He approached the bed, and laid a little black paw for a moment on the stiffened body of Mamzelle Aglaé. There was nothing for him to do here. He picked up his old ragged hat and his bag and went away.

"The black h'athen!" the woman muttered. "Shut the dure, child."

The little girl slid down from her chair, and went on tiptoe to shut the door which Chicot had left open. Having resumed her seat, she fastened her eyes upon Purgatory Mary's heaving chest.

"You, Chicot!" cried Matteo's wife the next morning. "My man, he read in paper 'bout woman name' Boisduré, use' b'long to big-a famny. She die roun' on St. Philip—po', same-a like church rat. It's any them Boisdurés you alla talk 'bout?"

Chicot shook his head in slow but emphatic denial. No, indeed, the woman was not of kin to his Boisdurés. He surely had told Matteo's wife often enough—how many times did he have to repeat it!—of their wealth, their social standing. It was doubtless some Boisduré of *les Attakapas;* it was none of his.

The next day there was a small funeral procession passing a little distance away—a hearse and a carriage or two. There was the priest who had attended Mamzelle Aglaé, and a benevolent Creole gentleman whose father had known the

Boisdurés in his youth. There was a couple of player-folk, who, having got wind of the story, had thrust their hands into their pockets.

"Look, Chicot!" cried Matteo's wife. "Yonda go the fune'al. Mus-a be that-a Boisduré woman we talken 'bout yesaday."

But Chicot paid no heed. What was to him the funeral of a woman who had died in St. Philip street? He did not even turn his head in the direction of the moving procession. He went on scaling his red-snapper.

Questions to Consider

1. How does Chopin shape attitudes toward Blackness in "Désirée's Baby"? To what extent is Désirée confined by contemporary expectations of gender as well as of race? Some have argued that Armand *knew* about his mother; how does that argument change the story? To what extent do these stories resist stereotypes? By what standards are we to judge the biases of nineteenth-century White writers?
2. How do class and racial prejudice shape the characterizations and outcomes of "Nég Créol" or "At the 'Cadian Ball"? What do the characters' motives for marrying in the latter suggest about nineteenth-century relationships? To what extent is Chopin's use of French merely local color or reflective of more systematic purposes?
3. Chopin's authorial distance and modernist refusal to preach in her fiction are among its hallmarks. What do we learn about Chopin's values and concerns from the metaphors and structures of her fiction?

Alcée Fortier

1856–1914

The product of two French families whose roots dated back to the colonial era, Alcée Fortier was born on 5 June 1856 in St. James Parish, Louisiana. Fortier studied law at the University of Virginia and began a career as a banker but soon realized that he wanted to teach. He secured a position as a teacher at the New Orleans Boys' High School, and he went on to become principal of the Preparatory Department of the University of Louisiana (later Tulane University). In 1880, he became the chair of the French Department and eventually was named Dean at Tulane.

Fortier devoted himself to scholarship, conducting research both in the United States and abroad. Despite the breadth of his research in French language and in folklore, his real interest lay in Creole history and customs. Creole, for Fortier, meant people of European heritage, particularly French, who were born in Louisiana. Because of his strong interest in the French language, his work naturally came to revolve around this culture. Fortier extended his research to the examination of the language of the Cajuns, the descendants of immigrants who came to Louisiana after being cast out of Canada in the eighteenth century. He wrote a great deal about the culture, history, and populace of the state, and his history of Louisiana is still well regarded. He served as president of the Modern Language Association (MLA) and was active in several New Orleans organizations. Fortier remained devoted to Tulane and to Louisiana throughout his life, contributing a substantial body of research on the culture and traditions of the state.

Fortier's work, excerpted here, may have provided one of the sources for Kate Chopin's short story "At the 'Cadian Ball," as critic Geraldine Seay convincingly argued. Seay points out that Chopin drew heavily from Fortier's work, which originally appeared in the *Publications of the Modern Language Association* in 1897. This work shows the depth and detail which Fortier developed in his research and the value he placed on oral narrative and folk traditions.

from The Acadians of Louisiana and Their Dialect

. . . On Sunday, September 21st, I went to church where I saw the whole population of the town and after bidding adieu to my newly-made friends, I left St. Martinsville where I had met kind gentlemen and fair ladies, taking with me a good stock of Acadian expressions. A few hours later I was again in St. Mary's Parish. I wished this time to live in the prairie where I thought there would be a better chance of observing the Acadians. The prairie is now entirely cultivated around Jeanerette and is dotted everywhere with the cottages of the small farmers and with the comfortable houses of the large planters. For a week I roamed all over the country with some friends who were kind enough to take me to the places of interest and to the persons who might help me in my work.

Having heard that every Saturday evening there was a ball in the prairie, I requested one of my friends to take me to see one. We arrived at eight o'clock, but already the ball had begun. In the yard were vehicles of all sorts, but three-mule carts were most numerous. The ball room was a large hall with galleries all around it. When we entered it was crowded with persons dancing to the music of three fiddles. I was astonished to see that nothing was asked for entrance, but I was told that any white person decently dressed could come in. The man giving the entertainment derived his profits from the sale of refreshments. My friend, a wealthy young planter, born in the neighborhood, introduced me to many persons and I had a good chance to hear the Acadian dialect, as everybody there belonged to the Acadian race. I asked a pleasant looking man: "Votre fille est-elle ici?" He corrected me by replying: "Oui, ma *demoiselle* est là." However, he did not say *mes messieurs* for his sons but spoke of them as *mes garçons*, although he showed me his *dame*. We went together to the refreshment room where were beer and lemonade, but I observed that the favorite drink was black coffee, which indeed was excellent. At midnight supper was served; it was chicken gombo with rice, the national Creole dish.

Most of the men appeared uncouth and awkward, but the young girls were really charming. They were elegant, well-dressed and exceedingly handsome. They had large and soft black eyes and beautiful black hair. Seeing how well they looked I was astonished and grieved to hear that probably very few of them could read or write. On listening to the conversation I could easily see that they had no education. French was spoken by all, but occasionally English was heard.

After supper my friend asked me if I wanted to see *le parc aux petits*. I followed him without knowing what he meant and he took me to a room adjoining the dancing hall, where I saw a number of little children thrown on a bed and sleeping. The mothers who accompanied their daughters had left the little ones in the *parc aux petits* before passing to the dancing room, where I saw them the whole evening assembled together in one corner of the hall and watching over their daughters. *Le parc aux petits* interested me very much, but I found the gambling room stranger still. There were about a dozen men at a table playing cards. One lamp suspended from the ceiling threw a dim light upon the players who appeared at first sight very wild, with their broad brimmed felt hats on their heads and their long untrimmed sun burnt faces. There was, however, a kindly expression on every face, and everything was so quiet that I saw that the men were not professional gamblers. I saw the latter a little later, in a barn near by where they had taken refuge. About half a dozen men, playing on a rough board by the light of two candles. I understood that these were the black sheep of the crowd and we merely cast a glance at them.

I was desirous to see the end of the ball, but having been told that the break-up would only take place at four or five o'clock in the morning, we went away at one o'clock. I was well-pleased with my evening and I admired the perfect order that reigned, considering that it was a public affair and open to all who wished to come, without any entrance fee. My friend told me that when the dance was over the musicians would rise, and going out in the yard would fire several pistol shots in the air, crying out at the same time: *le bal est fini.*

The names of the children in Acadian families are quite as strange as the old biblical names among the early puritans, but much more harmonious. For instance, in one family the boy was called Duradon, and his five sisters answered to the names of Elfige, Enyoné, Méridié, Ozéina and Fronie. A father who had a musical ear called his sons, Valmir, Valmore, Valsin, Valcour and Valérien, while another, with a tincture of the classics, called his boy Deus, and his daughter Déussa.

All the Acadians are great riders and they and their little ponies never seem to be tired. They often have exciting races. Living is very cheap in the prairie and the small farmers produce on their farms almost everything they use. At the stores they exchange eggs and hens for city goods.

Several farmers in the prairie still have sugar houses with the old-fashioned mill, three perpendicular rollers turned by mules or horses. They have some means, but are so much attached to the old ways that they will not change. It will not be long, however, before the younger generation replaces the antiquated mill with the wonderful modern inventions. The Acadians are an intelligent, peaceful and honest population; they are beginning to improve, indeed many of them, as already stated, have been distinguished, but as yet too many are without education. Let all Louisianians take to heart the cause of education and make a crusade against ignorance in our country parishes.

Before leaving the prairie I took advantage of my proximity to the Gulf to pay a visit to Côte Blanche. The coast of Louisiana is flat, but in the Attakapas country five islands or elevations break the monotony. These are rugged and abrupt and present some beautiful scenes. A few miles from the prairie is a forest called Cypremort: it is being cleared, and the land is admirably adapted to sugar cane. The road leading to Côte Blanche passes for three miles through the forest and along Cypremort Bayou, which is so shallow that large trees grow in it and the water merely trickles around them. On leaving the wood we enter on a trembling prairie over which a road has been built, and we soon reach Côte Blanche. It is called an island, because on one side is the gulf and on the others is the trembling prairie. We ascended a bluff about one hundred feet high and beheld an enchanting scene. In the rear was the wood which we had just left, stretching like a curtain around the prairie, to the right and to the left were a number of hills, one of which was one hundred and fifty-seven feet high, covered with tall cane waving its green lances in the air, while in front of us stood the sugar house with large brick chimneys, the white house of the owner of the place, the small cottages of the negroes on both sides of a wide road, and a little farther the blue waters of the Gulf. I approached the edge of the bluff, and as I looked at the waves dashing against the shore and at the sun slowly setting in a cloudless sky, I exclaimed: "Lawrence, destroyer of the Acadian homes, your cruelty has failed. This beautiful country was awaiting your victims. We have here no Bay of Fundy with its immense tides, no rocks, no snow, but we have a land picturesque and wonderfully fertile, a land where men are free, *our* Louisiana is better than *your* Acadia!"

QUESTIONS TO CONSIDER

1. What characteristics of Fortier's piece may have led critics, such as Geraldine Seay, to see this work as a source for Kate Chopin's "At the 'Cadian Ball"?
2. What groups of people are profiled in this piece? What do Fortier's profiles indicate about race and class structures in the late nineteenth century in Louisiana?

Mary Noailles Murfree (Charles Egbert Craddock)

1850–1922

Enthusiastic reviewers, who had never met acclaimed author Charles Egbert Craddock, praised the masculine vigor of his writing and described him as a strapping six-foot Tennessean. Imagine the astonishment of publishers (including *Atlantic* editors Thomas Bailey Aldrich and Williams Dean Howells) and readers (like thousands of Northerners, including well-respected author Sarah Orne Jewett) when they discovered in 1885 that Craddock was none other than petite, partially paralyzed, golden haired, soft-spoken Mary Murfree.

To secure national publication and to avoid notoriety, Murfree had carefully hidden her identity, using only her initials in professional correspondence and employing the earlier pen name of R. Emmet Dembry in her 1874 and 1875 plantation stories. Her first mountain story, published in the prestigious *Atlantic* in 1878, carried the Craddock signature, as did her subsequent stories, including "The 'Harnt' That Walks Chilhowee" (1883). The publication of her collected stories, *In the Tennessee Mountains*, in 1884 gained Craddock national attention, and the volume remains her most distinctive and effective work. When her serial novel, *The Prophet of the Great Smoky Mountains* (1885), was attributed to her father, Murfree journeyed from St. Louis to Boston with him and Fanny, her sister and lifelong companion. Murfree revealed her identity and became an immediate publishing sensation.

Over the next decade, Murfree produced two novels and seven short story collections that captured the set ways and dignity of mountain folk and that created a poetic canvas of crags, isolated settlements, and mountain tops (Blue Ridge, Bald, Chilhowee, and the Great Smoky). Her readers reveled in the dialect tales of despair, superstition, and courage among these women and men. Murfree thus pioneered a much-traveled literary mountain trail that would prove profitable to numerous authors, including Joel Chandler Harris, Harry Stillwell Edwards, Constance Fenimore Woolson, Sherwood Bonner, John Fox, Jr., and even Thomas Nelson Page.

Born 24 January 1850 into a cotton fortune and a refined, illustrious family, Murfree inherited what she called "the grace of culture." She was raised on Grantland, the family plantation near Murfreesboro, Tennessee, a town named, like its North Carolina counterpart, for her ancestors. Beginning at age five, she spent 15 summers at her family's Beersheba Springs cottage nestled in the Tennessee Cumberland mountains. The spirited Murfree, rendered lame by a childhood illness and unable to run or dance, became an accomplished horsewoman and, with her older sister Fanny, rode, explored, and came to know the landscape and ways of the hospitable, "peculiar" mountain folk.

The girls learned piano and singing from their talented mother, Fanny Priscilla Dickinson. They were tutored in the classics and languages by their well-educated father, who supported his daughters' formal schooling in Nashville, where he relocated to advance his legal career. During the war, she and her sister attended a Philadelphia boarding school. In the evenings, William, an accomplished linguist, would regale his children, including his youngest, William, Jr., with Irish, "Negro," and mountain dialect stories. In 1872, William's successful law practice enabled him to rebuild Grantland, which had been destroyed, together with the family's Mississippi plantation, during the Civil War, as Murfree recounts in *Where the Battle was Fought* (1884). Two years later,

Murfree published her first story based on the "entertainments" she and her father had written together during the hard years of the war. During the decade of the 1880s, the family moved to St. Louis where the younger William had established a lucrative law practice. They returned to Grantland in 1890 because of the elder William's failing health, and he died two years later.

Following another collection of her mountain stories, *The Phantom of Foot-Bridge and Other Stories* (1895), Murfree's career and literary reputation began to wane. After their mother's death in 1902, the sisters moved to Murfreesboro where they remained until Murfree's death. In 1910, Murfree's publisher refused her new short story collection, and in 1912, the sale of publication rights to Murfree's existing 15 works brought little more than one thousand dollars. Even though she remained an active writer throughout her life and produced historical novels, romances, and an urban novella, she never again achieved the acclaim, readership, income, or power of her earlier Tennessee works. A few months after being awarded an honorary degree by the University of the South, a ceremony she was unable to attend due to her blindness and deteriorating health, Murfree died on 31 July 1922. Sadly, in her later years, Murfree was to know the stark emotional hunger of Reuben Crabb, whom she had so vividly portrayed in "The 'Harnt' That Walks Chilowhee" almost forty years before.

Like her best stories, "The 'Harnt' " avoids the local-color staples of the narrative outsider and of the tale within a tale. Instead, Murfree interweaves two vastly different voices: the highly educated, briefly moralistic literary voice and the phonetically reproduced Appalachian dialect, which is often cumbersome to today's readers. Similarly, Murfree links the lyrical beauty of the natural landscape and its simple creatures to a young mountain woman, Clarissa Giles, who in spite of her often impoverished and always uncultured circumstances, demonstrates determination, dignity, and compassion as she reaches out to outsiders, in this instance the purported ghost of an unjustly accused one-armed man, Reuben Crabb. Murfree's undergirding theme reflects her own unwavering kinships: with other humans, however different, and with natural instincts rather than with more civilized, cultural notions of behavior and justice.

The "Harnt" That Walks Chilhowee

June had crossed the borders of Tennessee. Even on the summit of Chilhowee Mountain the apples in Peter Giles's orchard were beginning to redden, and his Indian corn, planted on so steep a declivity that the stalks seemed to have much ado to keep their footing, was crested with tassels and plumed with silk. Among the dense forests, seen by no man's eye, the elder was flying its creamy banners in honor of June's coming, and, heard by no man's ear, the pink and white bells of the azalea rang out melodies of welcome.

"An' it air a toler'ble for'ard season. Yer wheat looks likely; an' yer gyarden truck air thrivin' powerful. Even that cold spell we-uns hed about the full o' the moon in May ain't done sot it back none, it 'pears like ter me. But, 'cording ter my way o' thinkin', ye hev got chickens enough hyar ter eat off every peabloom ez soon ez it opens." And Simon Burney glanced with a gardener's disapproval at the numerous fowls, lifting their red combs and tufted top-knots here and there among the thick clover under the apple-trees.

"Them's Clarsie's chickens—my darter, ye know," drawled Peter Giles, a pale, listless, and lank mountaineer. "An' she hev been gin ter onderstand ez they hev got ter be kep' out 'n the gyarden; 'thout," he added indulgently,— " 'Thout I'm a-plowin', when I lets 'em foller in the furrow ter pick up worms. But law: Clarsie is so spry that she don't ax no better 'n ter be let ter run them chickens off 'n the peas."

Then the two men tilted their chairs against the posts of the little porch in front of Peter Giles's log cabin, and puffed their pipes in silence. The panorama spread out before them showed misty and dreamy among the delicate spiral wreaths of smoke. But was that gossamer-like illusion, lying upon the far horizon, the magic of nicotian, or the vague presence of distant heights? As ridge after ridge came down from the sky in ever-graduating shades of intenser blue, Peter Giles might have told you that this parallel system of enchantment was only "the mountings": that here was Foxy, and there was Big Injun, and still beyond was another, which he had "hearn tell ran spang up into Virginny." The sky that bent to clasp this kindred blue was of varying moods. Floods of sunshine submerged Chilhowee in liquid gold, and revealed that dainty outline limned upon the Northern horizon; but over the Great Smoky mountains clouds had gathered, and a gigantie rainbow bridged the valley.

Peter Giles's listless eyes were fixed upon a bit of red clay road, which was visible through a gap in the foliage far below. Even a tiny object, that ant-like crawled upon it, could be seen from the summit of Chilhowee. "I reckon that's my brother's wagon an' team," he said, as he watched the moving atom pass under the gorgeous triumphal arch. "He 'lowed he war goin' ter the Cross-Roads ter-day."

Simon Burney did not speak for a moment. When he did, his words seemed widely irrelevant. "That's a likely gal o' yourn," he drawled, with an odd constraint in his voice—"a likely gal, that Clarsie."

There was a quick flash of surprise in Peter Giles's dull eyes. He covertly surveyed his guest, with an astounded curiosity rampant in his slow brains. Simon Burney had changed color; an expression of embarrassment lurked in every line of his honest, florid, hard-featured face. An alert imagination might have detected a deprecatory self-consciousness in every gray hair that striped the black beard raggedly fringing his chin.

"Yes," Peter Giles at length replied, "Clarsie air a likely enough gal. But she air mightily sot ter hevin' her own way. An' ef 't ain't give ter her peaceable-like, she jes' takes it, whether or no."

This statement, made by one presumably fully informed on the subject, might have damped the ardor of many a suitor—for the monstrous truth was dawning on Peter Giles's mind that suitor was the position to which this slow, elderly widower aspired. But Simon Burney, with that odd, all-pervading constraint still prominently apparent, mildly observed, "Waal, ez much ez I hev seen of her goin's-on, it 'pears ter me ez her way air a mighty good way. An' it ain't comical that she likes it."

Urgent justice compelled Peter Giles to make some amends to the absent Clarissa. "That's a fac'," he admitted. "An' Clarsie ain't no hand ter jaw. She don't hev no words. But then," he qualified, truth and consistency alike constraining him, "she air a tol-er'ble hard-headed gal. That air a true word. Ye mought ez well try ter hender the sun from shining ez ter make that thar Clarsie Giles do what she don't want ter do."

To be sure, Peter Giles had a right to his opinion as to the hardness of his own daughter's head. The expression of his views, however, provoked Simon Burney to whit: there was something astir within him that in a worthier subject might have been called a chivalric thrill, and it forbade him to hold his peace. He retorted: "Of course ye kin say that, ef so minded; but ennybody ez hev got eyes kin see the change ez hev been made in this hyar place sence that thar gal hev been growed. I ain't a-purtendin' ter know that thar Clarsie ez well ez you-uns knows her hyar at home, but I hev seen enough, an' a deal more 'n enough, of her goin's-on, ter know that what she does ain't done fur *herself*. An' ef she will hev her way, it air fur the good of the whole tribe of ye. It 'pears ter me ez thar ain't many gals like that thar Clarsie. An' she air a merciful critter. She air mighty savin' of the feelin's of every-thing, from the cow an' the mare down ter the dogs, an' pigs, an' chickens; always a-feedin' of 'em jes' ter the time, an' never draggin', an' clawin', an' beatin' of 'em. Why, that thar Clarsie can't put her foot out'n the door, that every dumb beastis on this hyar place ain't a-runnin' ter git nigh her. I hev seen them pigs mos' climb the fence when she shows her face at the door. 'Pears ter me ez that thar Clarsie could tame a b'ar, ef she looked at him a time or two, she 's so savin' o' the critter's feelin's! An' thar's that old yaller dog o' yourn," pointing to an ancient cur that was blinking in the sun, "he 's older in Clarsie, an' no 'count in the worl'. I hev hearn ye say forty times that ye would kill him, 'ceptin' that Clarsie purtected him, an' hed sot her heart on his a-livin' along. An' all the home-folks, an' everybody that kems hyar to sot an' talk awhile, never misses a chance ter kick that thar old dog, or poke him with a stick, or cuss him. But Clarsie!—I hev seen that gal take the bread an' meat off'n her plate, an' give it ter that old dog, ez 'pears ter me ter be the worst dispositionest dog I ever see, an' no thanks lef' in him. He hain't hed the grace ter wag his tail fur twenty year. That thar Clarsie air surely a merciful critter, an' a mighty spry, likely young gal, besides."

Peter Giles sat in stunned astonishment during this speech, which was delivered in a slow, drawling monotone, with frequent meditative pauses, but nevertheless emphatically. He made no reply, and as they were once more silent there rose suddenly the sound of melody upon the air. It came from beyond that tumultuous stream that raced with the wind down the mountain's side; a great log thrown from bank to bank served as bridge. The song grew momentarily more distinct; among the leaves there were fugitive glimpses of blue and white, and at last Clarsie appeared, walking lightly along the log, clad in her checked homespun dress, and with a pail upon her head.

She was a tall, lithe girl, with that delicately transparent complexion often seen among the women of these mountains. Her lustreless black hair lay along her forehead without a ripple or wave; there was something in the expression of her large eyes that suggested those of a deer—something free, untamable, and yet gentle. " 'T ain't no wonder ter me ez Clarsie is all tuk up with the wild things, an' critters ginerally," her mother was wont to say. "She sorter looks like 'em, I 'm a-thinkin'."

As she came in sight there was a renewal of that odd constraint in Simon Burney's face and manner, and he rose abruptly. "Waal," he said, hastily, going to his horse, a raw-boned sorrel, hitched to the fence, "it's about time I war a-startin' home, I reckons."

He nodded to his host, who silently nodded in return, and the old horse jogged off with him down the road, as Clarsie entered the house and placed the pail upon a shelf.

"Who d'ye think hev been hyar a-speakin' of compli*mints* on ye, Clarsie?" exclaimed Mrs. Giles, who had overheard through the open door every word of the loud, drawling voice on the porch.

Clarsie's liquid eyes widened with surprise, and a faint tinge of rose sprang into her pale face, as she looked an expectant inquiry at her mother.

Mrs. Giles was a slovenly, indolent woman, anxious, at the age of forty-five, to assume the prerogatives of advanced years. She had placed all her domestic cares upon the shapely shoulders of her willing daughter, and had betaken herself to the chimney-corner and a pipe.

"Yes, thar hev been somebody hyar a-speakin' of compli*mints* on ye, Clarsie," she reiterated, with chuckling amusement. "He war a mighty peart, likely boy—that he war!"

Clarsie's color deepened.

"Old Simon Burney!" exclaimed her mother, in great glee at the incongruity of the idea.

"*Old Simon Burney!*—jes' a-sittin' out thar, a-wastin' the time, an a-burnin' of daylight—jes' ez perlite an' smilin' ez a basket of chips—a-speakin' of compli*mints* on ye!"

There was a flash of laughter among the sylvan suggestions of Clarsie's eyes—a flash as of sudden sunlight upon water. But despite her mirth she seemed to be unaccountably disappointed. The change in her manner was not noticed by her mother, who continued banteringly—

"Simon Burney air a mighty pore old man. Ye oughter be sorry fur him, Clarsie. Ye must n't think less of folks than ye does of the dumb beastis—that ain't religion. Ye knows ye air sorry fur mos' everything; why not fur this comical old consarn? Ye oughter marry him ter take keer of him. He said ye war a merciful critter; now is yer chance ter show it! Why, air ye a-goin' ter weavin', Clarsie, jes' when I wants ter talk ter ye 'bout 'n old Simon Burney? But law! I knows ye kerry him with ye in yer heart."

The girl summarily closed the conversation by seating herself before a great hand-loom; presently the persistent thump, thump, of the batten and the noisy creak of the treadle filled the room, and through all the long, hot afternoon her deft, practiced hands lightly tossed the shuttle to and fro.

The breeze freshened, after the sun went down, and the hop and gourd vines were all astir as they clung about the little porch where Clarsie was sitting now, idle at last. The rain clouds had disappeared, and there bent over the dark, heavily wooded ridges a pale blue sky, with here and there the crystalline sparkle of a star. A halo was shimmering in the east, where the mists had gathered about the great white moon, hanging high above the mountains. Noiseless wings flitted through the dusk; now and then the bats swept by so close as to wave Clarsie's hair with the wind of their flight. What an airy, glittering, magical thing was that gigantic spider-web suspended between the silver moon and her shining eyes! Ever and anon there came from the woods a strange, weird, long-drawn sigh, unlike the stir of the wind in the trees, unlike the fret of the water on the rocks. Was it the voiceless sorrow of the sad earth? There were stars in the night besides those known to astronomers: the stellular fire-flies gemmed the black shadows with a fluctuating brilliancy; they circled in and out of the porch, and touched the leaves above Clarsie's head with quivering points of light. A steadier and an intenser gleam was advancing along the road, and the sound of languid footsteps came with it; the aroma of tobacco graced the atmosphere, and a tall figure walked up to the gate.

"Come in, come in," said Peter Giles, rising, and tendering the guest a chair. "Ye air Tom Pratt, ez well ez I kin make out by this light. Waal, Tom, we hain't furgot ye sence ye done been hyar."

As Tom had been there on the previous evening, this might be considered a joke, or an equivocal compliment. The young fellow was restless and awkward under it, but Mrs. Giles chuckled with great merriment.

"An' how air ye a-comin' on, Mrs. Giles?" he asked propitiatorily.

"Jes' toler'ble, Tom. Air they all well ter yer house?"

"Yes, they 're toler'ble well, too." He glanced at Clarsie, intending to address to her some polite greeting, but the expression of her shy, half-startled eyes, turned upon the far-away moon, warned him. "Thar never war a gal so skittish," he thought. "She'd run a mile, skeered ter death, ef I said a word ter her."

And he was prudently silent.

"Waal," said Peter Giles, "what's the news out yer way, Tom? Ennything a-goin' on?"

"Thar war a shower yander on the Back-bone; it rained toler'ble hard fur a while, an' sot up the corn wonderful. Did ye git enny hyar?"

"Not a drap."

" 'Pears ter me ez I kin see the clouds a-circlin' round Chilhowee, an' a-rainin' on everybody's corn-field 'ceptin' ourn," said Mrs. Giles. "Some folks is the favored of the Lord, an' t' others hev ter work fur everything an' git nuthin'. Waal, waal; we-uns will see our reward in the nex' worl'. Thar 's a better worl' than this, Tom."

"That's a fac'," said Tom, in orthodox assent.

"An' when we leaves hyar once, we leaves all trouble an' care behind us, Tom; fur we don't come back no more." Mrs. Giles was drifting into one of her pious moods.

"I dunno," said Tom. "Thar hev been them ez hev."

"Hev what?" demanded Peter Giles, startled.

"Hev come back ter this hyar yearth. Thar 's a harnt that walks Chilhowee every night o' the worl'. I know them ez hev seen him."

Clarsie's great dilated eyes were fastened on the speaker's face. There was a dead silence for a moment, more eloquent with these looks of amazement than any words could have been.

"I reckons ye remember a puny, shriveled little man, named Reuben Crabb, ez used ter live yander, eight mile along the ridge ter that thar big sulphur spring," Tom resumed, appealing to Peter Giles. "He war born with only one arm."

"I 'members him," interpolated Mrs. Giles, vivaciously. "He war a mighty porely, sickly little critter, all the days of his life. 'T war a wonder he war ever raised ter be a man—an' a pity, too. An' 't war powerful comical, the way of his takin' off; a stunted, one-armed little critter a-ondertakin' ter fight folks an' shoot pistols. He hed the use o' his one arm, sure."

"Waal," said Tom, "his house ain't thar now, 'kase Sam Grim's brothers burned it ter the ground fur his a-killin' of Sam. That warn't all that war done ter Reuben fur killin' of Sam. The sheriff run Reuben Crabb down this hyar road 'bout a mile from hyar—mebbe less—an' shot him dead in the road, jes' whar it forks. Waal, Reuben war in company with another evil-doer—*he* war from the Cross-Roads, an' I furgits what he hed done, but he war a-tryin' ter hide in the mountings, too; an' the sheriff lef' Reuben a-lying thar in the road, while he tries ter ketch up with the t'other; but his horse got a stone in his hoof, an' he los' time, an' hed ter gin it up. An' when he got back ter the forks o' the road whar he had lef' Reuben a-lyin' dead, thar war nuthin' thar 'ceptin' a pool o' blood. Waal, he went right on ter Reuben's house, an' them Grim boys hed burnt it ter the ground; but he seen Reuben's brother Joel. An' Joel, he tole the sheriff that late that evenin' he hed tuk Reuben's body out'n the road an' buried it, 'kase it hed been lyin' thar in the road ever sence early in the mornin', an' he couldn't leave it thar all night, an' he hed n't no shelter fur it, sence the Grim boys hed burnt down the house. So he war obleeged ter bury it. An' Joel showed the sheriff a new-made grave, an' Reuben's coat whar the sheriff's bullet hed gone in at the back an' kem out'n the breast. The sheriff 'lowed ez they'd fine Joel fifty dollars fur a-buryin' of Reuben afore the cor'ner kem; but they never done it, ez I knows on. The sheriff said that when the cor'ner kem the body would be tuk up fur a 'quest. But thar hed been a powerful big frishet, an' the river 'twixt the cor'ner's house an' Chilhowee could n't be forded fur three weeks. The cor'ner never kem, an' so thar it all stayed. That war four year ago."

"Waal," said Peter Giles, dryly, "I ain't seen no harnt yit. I knowed all that afore."

Clarsie's wondering eyes upon the young man's moonlit face had elicited these facts, familiar to the elders, but strange, he knew, to her.

"I war jes' a-goin' on ter tell," said Tom, abashed. "Waal, ever sence his brother Joel died, this spring, Reuben's harnt walks Chilhowee. He war seen week afore las', 'bout day-break, by Ephraim Blenkins, who hed been a-fishin', an' war a-goin' home. Eph happened ter stop in the laurel ter wind up his line, when all in a minit he seen the harnt go by, his face white, an' his eye-balls like fire, an' puny an' one-armed, jes' like he lived. Eph, he owed me a haffen day's work; I holped him ter plow las' month, an' so he kem ter-day an' hoed along cornsider'ble ter pay fur it. He say he believes the harnt never seen him, 'kase it went right by. He 'lowed ef the harnt hed so much ez cut one o' them blazin' eyes round at him he could n't but hev drapped dead. Waal, this mornin', 'bout sunrise, my brother Bob's little gal, three year old, strayed off from home while her mother was out milkin' the cow. An' we went a-huntin' of her, mightily worked up, 'kase thar hev been a b'ar prowlin' round our corn-field twict this summer. An' I went to the right, an' Bob went to the lef'. An' he say ez he war a-pushin' 'long through the laurel, he seen the bushes ahead of him a-rustlin'. An' he jes' stood still an' watched 'em. An' fur a while the bushes war still too; an' then they moved jes' a little, fust this way an' then that, till all of a suddint the leaves opened, like the mouth of hell mought hev done, an' thar he seen Reuben Crabb's face. He say he never seen sech a face! Its mouth war open, an' its eyes war a-startin' out 'n its head, an' its skin war white till it war blue; an' ef the devil hed hed it a-hangin' over the coals that minit it couldn't hev looked no more skeered. But that war all that Bob seen, 'kase he jes' shet his eyes an' screeched an' screeched like he war *de*stracted. An' when he stopped a second ter ketch his breath he hearn su'thin' a-answerin' him back, sorter weak-like, an' thar war little Peggy a-pullin' through the laurel. Ye know she's too little ter talk good, but the folks down ter our house believes she seen the harnt, too."

"My Lord!" exclaimed Peter Giles. "I 'low I couldn't live a minit ef I war ter see that thar harnt that walks Chilhowee!"

"I know *I* couldn't," said his wife.

"Nor me, nuther," murmured Clarsie.

"Waal," said Tom, resuming the thread of his narrative, "we hev all been a-talkin' down yander ter our house ter make out the reason why Reuben Crabb's harnt hev sot out ter walk *jes' sence his brother Joel died*—'kase it war never seen afore then. An' ez nigh ez we kin make it out, the reason is 'kase thar 's nobody lef' in this hyar worl' what believes he war n't ter blame in that thar killin' o' Sam Grim. Joel always swore ez Reuben never killed him no more'n nuthin'; that Sam's own pistol went off in his own hand, an' shot him through the heart jes' ez he war a-drawin' of it ter shoot Reuben Crabb. An' I hev hearn other men ez war a-standin' by say the same thing, though them Grims tells another tale; but ez Reuben never owned no pistol in his life, nor kerried one, it don't 'pear ter me ez what them Grims say air reasonable. Joel always swore ez Sam Grim war a mighty mean man—a great big feller like him a-rockin' of a deformed little critter, an' a-mockin' of him, an' a hittin' of him. An' the day of the fight Sam jes' knocked him down fur nuthin' at all; an' afore ye could wink Reuben jumped up suddint, an' flew at him like an eagle, an' struck him in the face. An' then Sam drawed his pistol, an' it went off in his own hand, an' shot him through the heart, an' killed him dead. Joel said that ef he could hev kep' that pore little critter Reuben still, an' let the sheriff arrest him peaceable-like, he war sure the jury would hev let him off; 'kase how war Reuben a-goin ter shoot ennybody when Sam Grim never left a-holt of the only pistol between 'em, in life, or in death? They tells me they hed ter bury Sam Grim with that thar pistol in his hand; his grip war too tight fur death to unloose it. But Joel said that Reuben war sartain they 'd hang him. He hed n't never seen no jestice from enny one man, an' he could n't look fur it from twelve men. So he jes' sot out ter run through the woods, like a painter or a wolf, ter be hunted by the sheriff, an' he war run down an' kilt in the road. Joel said *he* kep' up arter the sheriff ez well ez he could on foot—fur the Crabbs never hed no horse—ter try ter beg fur Reuben, ef he war cotched, an' tell how little an' how weakly he war. I never seen a young man's head turn white like Joel's done; he said he reckoned it war his troubles. But ter the las' he stuck ter his rifle faithful. He war a powerful hunter; he war out rain or shine, hot or cold, in sech weather ez other folks would think thar warn't no use in tryin' ter do nuthin' in. I 'm mightily afeard o' seein' Reuben, now, that's a fac'," concluded Tom, frankly; " 'kase I hev hearn tell, an' I believes it, that ef a harnt speaks ter ye, it air sartain ye're bound ter die right then."

" 'Pears ter me," said Mrs. Giles, "ez many mountings ez thar air round hyar, he mought hev tuk ter walkin' some o' them, stiddier Chilhowee."

There was a sudden noise close at hand: a great inverted splint-basket, from which came a sound of flapping wings, began to move slightly back and forth. Mrs. Giles gasped out an ejaculation of terror, the two men sprang to their feet, and the coy Clarsie laughed aloud in an exuberance of delighted mirth, forgetful of her shyness. "I declar' ter goodness, you-uns air all skeered fur true! Did ye think it war the harnt that walks Chilhowee?"

"What 's under that thar basket?" demanded Peter Giles, rather sheepishly, as he sat down again.

"Nuthin' but the duck-legged Dominicky," said Clarsie, "what air bein' broke up from settin'." The moonlight was full upon the dimpling merriment in her face, upon her shining eyes and parted red lips, and her gurgling laughter was pleasant to hear. Tom Pratt edged his chair a trifle nearer, as he, too, sat down.

"Ye oughtn't never ter break up a duck-legged hen, nor a Dominicky, nuther," he volunteered, " 'kase they air sech a good kind o' hen ter kerry chickens; but a hen that is duck-legged an' Dominicky too oughter be let ter set, whether or no."

Had he been warned in a dream, he could have found no more secure road to Clarsie's favor and interest than a discussion of the poultry. "I'm a-thinkin'," she said, "that it air too hot fur hens ter set now, an' 'twill be till the las' of August."

"It don't 'pear ter me ez it air hot much in June up hyar on Chilhowee—thar 's a differ, I know, down in the valley; but till July, on Chilhowee, it don't 'pear ter me ez it air too hot ter set a hen. An' a duck-legged Dominicky air mighty hard ter break up."

"That's a fac'," Clarsie admitted; "but I'll hev ter do it, somehow, 'kase I ain't got no eggs fur her. All my hens air kerryin' of chickens."

"Waal!" exclaimed Tom, seizing his opportunity, "I'll bring ye some ter-morrer night, when I come agin. We-uns hev got eggs ter our house."

"Thanky," said Clarsie, shyly smiling.

This unique method of courtship would have progressed very prosperously but for the interference of the elders, who are an element always more or less adverse to love-making. "Ye oughter turn out yer hen now, Clarsie," said Mrs. Giles, "ez Tom air a-goin' ter bring ye some eggs ter-morrer. I wonder ye don't think it's mean ter keep her up longer 'n ye air obleeged ter. Ye oughter remember ye war called a merciful critter jes' ter-day."

Clarsie rose precipitately, raised the basket, and out flew the "duck-legged Dominicky," with a frantic flutter and hysterical cackling. But Mrs. Giles was not to be diverted from her purpose; her thoughts had recurred to the absurd episode of the afternoon, and with her relish of the incongruity of the joke she opened upon the subject at once.

"Waal, Tom," she said, "we'll be hevin' Clarsie married, afore long, I'm a-thinkin'." The young man sat bewildered. He, too, had entertained views concerning Clarsie's speedy marriage, but with a distinctly personal application; and this frank mention of the matter by Mrs. Giles had a sinister suggestion that perhaps her ideas might be antagonistic. "An' who d'ye think hev been hyar ter-day, a-speakin' of compl*imints* on Clarsie?" He could not answer, but he turned his head with a look of inquiry, and Mrs. Giles continued, "He is a mighty peart, likely boy—*he* is."

There was a growing anger in the dismay on Tom Pratt's face; he leaned forward to hear the name with a fiery eagerness, altogether incongruous with his usual lack-lustre manner.

"Old Simon Burney!" cried Mrs. Giles, with a burst of laughter. "*Old Simon Burney!* Jes' a-speakin' of compl*imints* on Clarsie!"

The young fellow drew back with a look of disgust. "Why, he's a old man; he ain't no fit husband fur Clarsie."

"Don't ye be too sure ter count on that. I war jes' a-layin' off ter tell Clarsie that a gal oughter keep mighty clar o' widowers, 'thout she wants ter marry one. Fur I believes," said Mrs. Giles, with a wild flight of imagination, "ez them men hev got some sort 'n trade with the Evil One, an' he gives 'em the power ter witch the gals, somehow, so 's ter git 'em ter marry; 'kase I don't think that any gal that 's got good sense air a-goin' ter be a man's second ch'ice, an' the mother of a whole pack of step-chil'ren, 'thout she air under some sort 'n spell. But them men carries the day with the gals, ginerally, an' I'm a-thinkin' they 're banded with the devil. Ef I war a gal, an' a smart, peart boy like Simon Burney kem around a-speakin' of compl*imints*, an' sayin' I war a merciful critter, I'd jes' give it up, an' marry him fur second ch'ice. Thar 's one blessin'," she continued, contemplating the possibility in a cold-blooded fashion positively revolting to Tom Pratt: "he ain't got no tribe of chil'ren fur Clarsie ter look arter; nary chick nor child hev old Simon Burney got. He hed two, but they died."

The young man took leave presently, in great depression of spirit—the idea that the widower was banded with the powers of evil was rather overwhelming to a man whose dependence was in merely mortal attractions; and after he had been gone a little while Clarsie ascended the ladder to a nook in the roof, which she called her room.

For the first time in her life her slumber was fitful and restless, long intervals of wakefulness alternating with snatches of fantastic dreams. At last she rose and sat by the rude window, looking out through the chestnut leaves at the great moon, which had begun to dip toward the dark uncertainty of the western ridges, and at the shimmering, translucent, pearly mists that filled the intermediate valleys. All the air was dew and incense; so subtle and penetrating an odor came from that fir-tree beyond the fence that it seemed as if some invigorating infusion were thrilling along her veins; there floated upward, too, the warm fragrance of the clover, and every breath of the gentle wind brought from over the stream a thousand blended, undistinguishable perfumes of the deep forests beyond. The moon's idealizing glamour had left no trace of the uncouthness of the place which the daylight revealed; the little log house, the great overhanging chestnut-oaks, the jagged precipice before the door, the vague outlines of the distant ranges, all suffused with a magic sheen, might have seemed a stupendous alto-rilievo in silver repoussé. Still, there came here and there the sweep of the bat's dusky wings; even they were a part of the night's witchery. A tiny owl perched for a moment or two amid the dew-tipped chestnut-leaves, and gazed with great round eyes at Clarsie as solemnly as she gazed at him.

"I'm thankful enough that ye hed the grace not ter screech while ye war hyar," she said, after the bird had taken his flight. "I ain't ready ter die yit, an' a screech-*owel* air the sure sign."

She felt now and then a great impatience with her wakeful mood. Once she took herself to task: "Jes' a-sittin' up hyar all night, the same ez ef I war a fox, or that thar harnt that walks Chilhowee!"

And then her mind reverted to Tom Pratt, to old Simon Burney, and to her mother's emphatic and oracular declaration that widowers are in league with Satan, and that the girls upon whom they cast the eye of supernatural fascination have no choice in the matter. "I wish I knowed ef that thar sayin' war true," she murmured, her face still turned to the western spurs, and the moon sinking so slowly toward them.

With a sudden resolution she rose to her feet. She knew a way of telling fortunes which was, according to tradition, infallible, and she determined to try it, and ease her mind as to her future. Now was the propitious moment. "I hev always hearn that it won't come true 'thout ye try it jes' before daybreak, an' a-kneelin' down at the forks of the road." She hesitated a moment and listened intently. "They'd never git done a-laffin' at me, ef they fund it out," she thought.

There was no sound in the house, and from the dark woods arose only those monotonous voices of the night, so familiar to her ears that she accounted their murmurous iteration as silence too. She leaned far out of the low window, caught the wide-spreading branches of the tree beside it, and swung herself noiselessly to the ground. The road before her was dark with the shadowy foliage and dank with the dew; but now and then, at long intervals, there lay athwart it a bright bar of light, where the moonshine fell through a gap in the trees. Once, as she went rapidly along her way, she saw speeding across the white radiance, lying just before her feet, the ill-omened shadow of a rabbit. She paused, with a superstitious sinking of the heart, and she heard the animal's quick, leaping rush through the bushes near at hand; but she mustered her courage, and kept steadily on. " 'T ain't no use a-goin' back ter git shet o' bad luck," she argued. "Ef old Simon Burney air my fortune, he 'll come whether or no—ef all they say air true."

The serpentine road curved to the mountain's brink before it forked, and there was again that familiar picture of precipice, and far-away ridges, and shining mist, and sinking moon, which was visibly turning from silver to gold. The changing lustre gilded the feathery ferns that grew in the marshy dip. Just at the angle of the divergent paths there rose into the air a great mass of indistinct white blossoms, which she knew were the exquisite mountain azaleas, and all the dark forest was starred with the blooms of the laurel.

She fixed her eyes upon the mystic sphere dropping down the sky, knelt among the azaleas at the forks of the road, and repeated the time-honored invocation—

"Ef I'm a-goin' ter marry a young man. whistle, Bird, whistle. Ef I'm a-goin' ter marry an old man, low, Cow, low. Ef I ain't a-goin' ter marry nobody, knock, Death, knock."

There was a prolonged silence in the matutinal freshness and perfume of the woods. She raised her head, and listened attentively. No chirp of half-awakened bird, no tapping of wood-pecker, or the mysterious death-watch; but from far along the dewy aisles of the forest, the ungrateful Spot, that Clarsie had fed more faithfully than herself, lifted up her voice, and set the echoes vibrating. Clarsie, however, had hardly time for a pang of disappointment. While she still knelt among the azaleas her large, deer-like eyes were suddenly dilated with terror. From around the curve of the road came the quick beat of hastening footsteps, the sobbing sound of panting breath, and between her and the sinking moon there passed an attenuated, one-armed figure, with a pallid, sharpened face, outlined for a moment on its brilliant disk, and dreadful starting eyes, and quivering open mouth. It disappeared in an instant among the shadows of the laurel, and Clarsie, with a horrible fear clutching at her heart, sprang to her feet.

Her flight was arrested by other sounds. Before her reeling senses could distinguish them, a party of horsemen plunged down the road. They reined in suddenly as their eyes fell upon her, and their leader, an eager, authoritative man, was asking her a question. Why could she not understand him? With her nerveless hands feebly catching at the shrubs for support, she listened vaguely to his impatient, meaningless words, and saw with helpless deprecation the rising anger in his face. But there was no time to be lost. With a curse upon the stupidity of the mountaineer, who could n't speak when she was spoken to, the party sped on in a sweeping gallop, and the rocks and the steeps were hilarious with the sound.

When the last faint echo was hushed, Clarsie tremblingly made her way out into the road; not reassured, however, for she had a frightful conviction that there was now and then a strange stir in the laurel, and that she was stealthily watched. Her eyes were fixed upon the dense growth with a morbid fascination, as she moved away; but she was once more rooted to the spot when the leaves parted and in the golden moonlight the ghost stood before her. She could not nerve herself to run past him, and he was directly in her way homeward. His face was white, and lined, and thin; that pitiful quiver was never still in the parted lips; he looked at her with faltering, beseeching eyes. Clarsie's merciful heart was stirred. "What ails ye, ter come back hyar, an' foller me?" she cried out, abruptly. And then a great horror fell upon her. Was not one to whom a ghost should speak doomed to death, sudden and immediate?

The ghost replied in a broken, shivering voice, like a wail of pain, "I war a-starvin'—I war a-starvin'," with despairing iteration.

It was all over, Clarsie thought. The ghost had spoken, and she was a doomed creature. She wondered that she did not fall dead in the road. But while those beseeching eyes were fastened in piteous appeal on hers, she could not leave him. "I never hearn that 'bout ye," she said, reflectively. "I knows ye hed awful troubles while ye war alive, but I never knowed ez ye war starved."

Surely that was a gleam of sharp surprise in the ghost's prominent eyes, succeeded by a sly intelligence.

"Day is nigh ter breakin'," Clarsie admonished him, as the lower rim of the moon touched the silver mists of the west. "What air ye a-wantin' of me?"

There was a short silence. Mind travels far in such intervals. Clarsie's thoughts had overtaken the scenes when she should have died that sudden terrible death: when there would be no one left to feed the chickens; when no one would care if the pigs cried with the pangs of hunger, unless, indeed, it were time for them to be fattened before killing. The mare—how often would she be taken from the plow, and shut up for the night in her shanty without a drop of water, after her hard day's work! Who would churn, or spin, or weave? Clarsie could not understand how the machinery of the universe could go on without her. And Towse, poor Towse! He was a useless cumberer of the ground, and it was hardly to be supposed that after his protector was gone he would be spared a blow or a bullet, to hasten his lagging death. But Clarsie still stood in the road, and watched the face of the ghost, as he, with his eager, starting eyes, scanned her open, ingenuous countenance.

"Ye do ez ye air bid, or it 'll be the worse for ye," said the "harnt," in the same quivering, shrill tone. "Thar's hunger in the nex' worl' ez well ez in this, an' ye bring me some vittles hyar this time ter-morrer, an' don't ye tell nobody ye hev seen me, nuther, or it'll be the worse for ye."

There was a threat in his eyes as he disappeared in the laurel, and left the girl standing in the last rays of moonlight.

A curious doubt was stirring in Clarsie's mind when she reached home, in the early dawn, and heard her father talking about the sheriff and his posse, who had stopped at the house in the night, and roused its inmates, to know if they had seen a man pass that way.

"Clarsie never hearn none o' the noise, I'll be bound, 'kase she always sleeps like a log," said Mrs. Giles, as her daughter came in with the pail, after milking the cow. "Tell her 'bout 'n it."

"They kem a-bustin' along hyar a while afore day-break, a-runnin' arter the man," drawled Mr. Giles, dramatically. "An' they knocked me up, ter know ef ennybody hed passed. An' one o' them men—I never seen none of 'em afore; they 's all valley folks, I'm a-thinkin'—an' one of 'em bruk his saddle-girt' a good piece down the road, an' he kem back ter borrer mine; an' ez we war a-fixin' of it, he tole me what they war all arter. He said that word war tuk ter the sheriff down yander in the valley—pears ter me them town-folks don't think nobody in the mountings hev got good sense—word war tuk ter the sheriff 'bout this one-armed harnt that walks Chilhowee; an' he sot it down that Reuben Crabb war n't dead at all, an' Joel jes' purtended ter hev buried him, an' it air Reuben hisself that walks Chilhowee. An' thar air two hunderd dollars blood-money reward fur ennybody ez kin ketch him. These hyar valley folks air powerful cur'ous critters—two hunderd dollars blood-money reward fur that thar harnt that walks Chilhowee! I jes' sot myself ter laffin' when that thar cuss tole it so solemn. I jes' 'lowed ter him ez he could n't shoot a harnt nor hang a harnt, an' Reuben Crabb hed about got done with his persecutions in this worl'. An' he said that by the time they hed scoured this mounting, like they hed laid off ter do, they would find that that thar puny little harnt war nuthin' but a mortal man, an' could be kep' in a jail ez handy ez enny other flesh an' blood. He said the sheriff 'lowed ez the reason Reuben hed jes' taken ter walk Chilhowee sence Joel died is 'kase thar air nobody ter feed him, like Joel done, mebbe, in the nights; an' Reuben always war a pore, one-armed, weakly critter, what can't even kerry a gun, an' he air driv by hunger out'n the hole whar he stays, ter prowl round the cornfields an' hen-coops ter steal suthin'—an' that's how he kem ter be seen frequent. The sheriff 'lowed that Reuben can't find enough roots an' yerbs ter keep him up; but law!—a harnt eatin'! It jes' sot me off ter laffin'. Reuben Crabb hev been too busy in torment fur the las' four year ter be a-studyin' 'bout eatin'; an' it air his harnt that walks Chilhowee."

The next morning, before the moon sank, Clarsie, with a tin pail in her hand, went to meet the ghost at the appointed place. She understood now why the terrible doom that falls upon those to whom a spirit may chance to speak had not descended upon her, and that fear was gone; but the secrecy of her errand weighed heavily. She had been scrupulously careful to put into the pail only such things as had fallen to her share at the table, and which she had saved from the meals of yesterday. "A gal that goes a-robbin' fur a hongry harnt," was her moral reflection, "oughter be throwed bodaciously off 'n the bluff."

She found no one at the forks of the road. In the marshy dip were only the myriads of mountain azaleas, only the masses of feathery ferns, only the constellated glories of the laurel blooms. A sea of shining white mist was in the valley, with glinting golden rays striking athwart it from the great cresset of the sinking moon; here and there the long, dark, horizontal line of a distant mountain's summit rose above the vaporous shimmer, like a dreary, sombre island in the midst of enchanted waters. Her large, dreamy eyes, so wild and yet so gentle, gazed out through the laurel leaves upon the floating gilded flakes of light, as in the deep coverts of the mountain, where the fulvous-tinted deer were lying, other eyes, as wild and as gentle, dreamily watched the vanishing moon. Overhead, the filmy, lace-like clouds, fretting the blue heavens, were tinged with a faint rose. Through the trees she caught a glimpse of the red sky of dawn, and the glister of a great lucent, tremulous star. From the ground, misty blue exhalations were rising, alternating with the long lines of golden light yet drifting through the woods. It was all very still, very peaceful, almost holy. One could hardly believe that these consecrated solitudes had once reverberated with the echoes of man's death-dealing ingenuity, and that Reuben Crabb had fallen, shot through and through, amid that wealth of flowers at the forks of the road. She heard suddenly the far-away baying of a hound. Her great eyes dilated, and she lifted her head to listen. Only the solemn silence of the woods, the slow sinking of the noiseless moon, the voiceless splendor of that eloquent day-star.

Morning was close at hand, and she was beginning to wonder that the ghost did not appear, when the leaves fell into abrupt commotion, and he was standing in the road, beside her. He did not speak, but watched her with an eager, questioning intentness, as she placed the contents of the pail upon the moss at the roadside. "I'm a-comin' agin ter-morrer," she said, gently. He made no reply, quickly gathered the food from the ground, and disappeared in the deep shades of the woods.

She had not expected thanks, for she was accustomed only to the gratitude of dumb beasts; but she was vaguely conscious of something wanting, as she stood motionless for a moment, and watched the burnished rim of the moon slip down behind the western mountains. Then she slowly walked along her misty way in the dim light of the coming dawn. There was a footstep in the road behind her; she thought it was the ghost once more. She turned, and met Simon Burney, face to face. His rod was on his shoulder, and a string of fish was in his hand.

"Ye air a-doin' wrongful, Clarsie," he said, sternly. "It air agin the law fur folks ter feed an' shelter them ez is a-runnin' from jestice. An' ye 'll git yerself inter trouble. Other folks will find ye out, besides me, an' then the sheriff 'll be up hyar arter ye."

The tears rose to Clarsie's eyes. This prospect was infinitely more terrifying than the awful doom which follows the horror of a ghost's speech.

"I can't holp it," she said, however, doggedly swinging the pail back and forth. "I can't gin my consent ter starvin' of folks, even ef they air a-hidin' an' a-runnin' from jestice."

"They mought put ye in jail, too—I dunno," suggested Simon Burney.

"I can't holp that, nuther," said Clarsie, the sobs rising, and the tears falling fast. "Ef they comes an' gits me, and puts me in the pen'tiary away down yander, somewhars in the valley, like they done Jane Simpkins, fur a-cuttin' of her step-mother's throat with a butcher-knife, while she war asleep—though some said Jane war crazy—I can't gin my consent ter starvin' of folks."

A recollection came over Simon Burney of the simile of "hendering the sun from shining."

"She hev done sot it down in her mind," he thought, as he walked on beside her and looked at her resolute face. Still he did not relinquish his effort.

"Doin' wrong, Clarsie, ter aid folks what air a-doin' wrong, an' mebbe *hev* done wrong, air powerful hurtful ter everybody, an' henders the law an' jestice."

"I can't holp it," said Clarsie.

"It 'pears toler'ble comical ter me," said Simon Burney, with a sudden perception of a curious fact which has proved a marvel to wiser men, "that no matter how good a woman is, she ain't got no respect fur the laws of the country, an' don't sot no store by jestice." After a momentary silence he appealed to her on another basis. "Somebody will ketch him arter a while, ez sure ez ye air born. The sheriff 's a-sarchin' now, an' by the time that word gits around, all the mounting boys 'll turn out, 'kase thar air two hunderd dollars bloodmoney fur him. An' then he 'll think, when they ketches him—an' everybody'll say so, too—ez ye war constant in feedin' him jes' ter 'tice him ter comin' ter one place, so ez ye could tell somebody whar ter go ter ketch him, an' make them gin ye haffen the blood-money, mebbe. That's what the mounting will say, mos' likely."

"I can't holp it," said Clarsie, once more.

He left her walking on toward the rising sun, and retraced his way to the forks of the road. The jubilant morning was filled with the song of birds; the sunlight flashed on the dew; all the delicate enameled bells of the pink and white azaleas were swinging tremulously in the wind; the aroma of ferns and mint rose on the delicious fresh air. Presently he checked his pace, creeping stealthily on the moss and grass beside the road rather than in the beaten path. He pulled aside the leaves of the laurel with no more stir than the wind might have made, and stole cautiously through its dense growth, till he came suddenly upon the puny little ghost, lying in the sun at the foot of a tree. The frightened creature sprang to his feet with a wild cry of terror, but before he could move a step he was caught and held fast in the strong grip of the stalwart mountaineer beside him. "I hev kem hyar ter tell ye a word, Reuben Crabb," said Simon Burney. "I hev kem hyar ter tell ye that the whole mounting air a-goin' ter turn out ter sarch fur ye; the sheriff air a-ridin' now, an' ef ye don't come along with me they 'll hev ye afore night, 'kase thar air two hunderd dollars reward fur ye."

What a piteous wail went up to the smiling blue sky, seen through the dappling leaves above them! What a horror, and despair, and prescient agony were in the hunted creature's face! The ghost struggled no longer; he slipped from his feet down upon the roots of the tree, and turned that woful face, with its starting eyes and drawn muscles and quivering parted lips, up toward the unseeing sky.

"God A'mighty, man!" exclaimed Simon Burney, moved to pity. "Why n't ye quit this hyar way of livin' in the woods like ye war a wolf? Why n't ye come back an' stand yer trial? From all I 've hearn tell, it 'pears ter me ez the jury air obleeged ter let ye off, an' I 'll take keer of ye agin them Grims."

"I hain't got no place ter live in," cried out the ghost, with a keen despair.

Simon Burney hesitated. Reuben Crabb was possibly a murderer—at the best could but be a burden. The burden, however, had fallen in his way, and he lifted it.

"I tell ye now, Reuben Crabb," he said, "I ain't a-goin' ter holp no man ter break the law an' hender jestice; but ef ye will go an' stand yer trial, I'll take keer of ye agin them Grims ez long ez I kin fire a rifle. An' arter the jury hev done let ye off, ye air welcome ter live along o' me at my house till ye die. Ye air no-'count ter work, I know, but I ain't a-goin' ter grudge ye fur a livin' at my house."

And so it came to pass that the reward set upon the head of the harnt that walked Chilhowee was never claimed.

With his powerful ally, the forlorn little spectre went to stand his trial, and the jury acquitted him without leaving the box. Then he came back to the mountains to live with Simon Burney. The cruel gibes of his burly mockers that had beset his feeble life from his childhood up, the deprivation and loneliness and despair and fear that had filled those days when he walked Chilhowee, had not improved the harnt's temper. He was a helpless creature, not able to carry a gun or hold a plow, and the years that he spent smoking his cob-pipe in Simon Burney's door were idle years and unhappy. But Mrs. Giles said she thought he was "a mighty lucky little critter: fust, he hed Joel ter take keer of him an' feed him, when he tuk ter the woods ter pertend he war a harnt; an' they do say now that Clarsie Pratt, afore she war married, used ter kerry him vittles, too; an' then old Simon Burney tuk him up an' fed him ez plenty ez ef he war a good workin' hand, an' gin him clothes an' house-room, an' put up with his jawin' jes' like he never hearn a word of it. But law! some folks dunno when they air well off."

There was only a sluggish current of peasant blood in Simon Burney's veins, but a prince could not have dispensed hospitality with a more royal hand. Ungrudgingly he gave of his best; valiantly he defended his thankless guest at the risk of his life; with a moral gallantry he struggled with his sloth, and worked early and late, that there might be enough to divide. There was no possibility of a recompense for him, not even in the encomiums of discriminating friends, nor the satisfaction of tutored feelings and a practiced spiritual discernment; for he was an uncouth creature, and densely ignorant.

The grace of culture is, in its way, a fine thing, but the best that art can do—the polish of a gentleman—is hardly equal to the best that Nature can do in her higher moods.

Questions to Consider

1. "The 'Harnt' " portrays an unexpected, if deceptive, growth and resurrection. Consider the interaction of the story plot and its opening burst of summer. How does Nature mirror the rebirth of Reuben? Of Simon? Of Clarissa? Does Nature reflect and/or exist beyond human lives? How does Nature work in terms of speech? For example, what is the effect of the overarching literary voice in the text? What point is Murfree making in her closing comment that distinguishes the "grace of culture/polish of a gentleman" from "Nature" in "her higher moods"? What in the story represents "Nature"? What represents "grace" and "polish"? What might she be saying about the South as opposed to the North?
2. Consider Simon's admonition to Clarissa and his comment: "no matter how good a woman is, she ain't got no respect for the laws of the country, an' don't sot no store by jestice." What is the "law" in this story? Who represents it? Does it provide justice? Why does Clarissa fade away as the story concludes? Why does Simon emerge?

Grace King

1852–1932

Though many Southerners both before and after the Civil War claimed that their writing careers sprang from a need to counter Northern "misreadings" of the region, Grace King's story of how she became a writer was perhaps the most famous account, and it fixed her reputation as an apologist. King was born to a prominent New Orleans lawyer and his energetic wife who lost everything in the war. Despite their reduced circumstances—an injustice King never quite forgave—the three

King daughters were well-educated and remained socially well-connected. As a young woman, King met several important Northern visitors, including Julia Ward Howe and *Century Magazine* editor Richard Watson Gilder. When King complained to Gilder that fellow New Orleanian George Washington Cable had "stabbed the city in the back . . . to please the Northern press" by his unflattering depictions of white Creoles, Gilder challenged her to "write better" of her people. That very night King began "Monsieur Motte," based on her schooldays at the *Institut St. Louis*. The story was published in the *New Princeton Review* (1886), and King was soon introduced to a prominent circle of supportive New England writers, including Sarah Orne Jewett, Mary Wilkins Freeman, and Samuel Clemens, whose wife Olivia became one of King's dearest friends.

King enjoyed immediate literary success, publishing several collections in the following decade, including *Monsieur Motte* (1888), *Tales of a Time and Place* (1892), and her most famous, *Balcony Stories* (1893). King was also a careful researcher and popular historian, writing several volumes on colonial Louisiana, such as the often reprinted *New Orleans, the Place and the People* (1895). She also wrote two short novels, *The Pleasant Ways of St. Medard* (1916), a surprisingly subtle tale of Reconstruction life, and *La Dame de Sainte Hermine* (1924).

King's strengths include her graceful impressionistic prose, her commitment to realism, and her focus on the unjust displacement of women in a world governed by neglectful and indifferent men, qualities that have renewed critical interest in her work. King also reflects a quietly aggrieved attitude that parallels her broader identification as an aristocratic Southerner displaced by Northern ideologies of race and commerce. That her indignation was shared by Northern as well as Southern readers testifies to the broad national sympathy afforded the defeated South after the war. King became a leading interpreter of Southern White experience, particularly of New Orleans, which, as the former center of the slave trade, was pivotal in redefining the meanings of Antebellum society, not only its history but also its social and economic structures.

While "A Crippled Hope" clearly exposes King's conservative notions of race and class, to most White nineteenth-century readers the story was a tender portrait of a slave woman whose service and vicarious motherhood were marks of an unsuspected humanity. Such limited versions of African-American identity were critical to postwar justifications of White sovereignty and contributed to the success of many writers like King.

King's later life personified the Southern lady of letters: gracious hospitality at her home in New Orleans, travel and recognition abroad, a series of tributes from her grateful city. She completed her memoir, *Memories of a Southern Woman of Letters*, just a few months before her death from a stroke on 14 January 1932. Though critics have had difficulty seeing past King's racism, she was a skillful and subtle writer, and her stories, like Chopin's and Stuart's, reflect the complex struggles of Southern women writers to maintain realist standards and feminist sympathies within racist frameworks.

A Crippled Hope

You must picture to yourself the quiet, dim-lighted room of a convalescent; outside, the dreary, bleak days of winter in a sparsely settled, distant country parish; inside, a slow, smoldering log-fire, a curtained bed, the infant sleeping well enough, the mother wakeful, restless, thought-driven, as a mother must be, unfortunately, nowadays, particularly in that parish, where cotton worms and overflows have acquired such a monopoly of one's future.

God is always pretty near a sick woman's couch; but nearer even than God seems the sick-nurse—at least in that part of the country, under those circumstances. It is so good *to look through the dimness and uncertainty*, moral and physical, and to meet those little black, steadfast, all-seeing eyes; to feel those smooth, soft, all-soothing hands; to hear, across one's sleep, that three-footed step—the flat-soled left foot, the tiptoe right, and the padded end of the broomstick; and when one is so wakeful and restless and thought-driven, to have another's story given one. God, depend upon it, grows stories and lives as he does herbs, each with a mission of balm to some woe.

She said she had, and in truth she had, no other name than "little Mammy"; and that was the name of her nature. Pure African, but bronze rather than pure black, and full-sized only in width, her growth having been hampered as to height by an injury to her hip, which had lamed her, pulling her figure awry, and burdening her with a protuberance of the joint. Her mother caused it by dropping her when a baby, and concealing it, for fear of punishment, until the dislocation became irremediable. All the animosity of which little Mammy was capable centered upon this unknown but never-to-be-forgotten mother of hers; out of this hatred had grown her love—that is, her destiny, a woman's love being her destiny. Little Mammy's love was for children.

The birth and infancy (the one as accidental as the other, one would infer) took place in—it sounds like the "Arabian Nights" now!—took place in the great room, caravansary, stable, behind a negro-trader's auction-mart, where human beings underwent literally the daily buying and selling of which the world now complains in a figure of speech—a great, square, dusty chamber where, sitting cross-legged, leaning against the wall, or lying on foul blanket pallets on the floor, the bargains of to-day made their brief sojourn, awaiting transformation into the profits of the morrow.

The place can be pointed out now, is often pointed out; but no emotion arises at sight of it. It is so plain, so matter-of-fact an edifice that emotion only comes afterward in thinking about it, and then in the reflection that such an edifice could be, then as now, plain and matter-of-fact.

For the slave-trader there was no capital so valuable as the physical soundness of his stock; the moral was easily enough forged or counterfeited. Little Mammy's good-for-nothing mother was sold as readily as a vote, in the parlance of to-day; but no one would pay for a crippled baby. The mother herself would not have taken her as a gift, had it been in the nature of a negro-trader to give away anything. Some doctoring was done—so little Mammy heard traditionally—some effort made to get her marketable. There were attempts to pair her off as a twin sister of various correspondencies in age, size, and color, and to palm her off, as a substitute, at migratory, bereaved, overfull breasts. Nothing equaled a negro-trader's will and power for fraud, except the hereditary distrust and watchfulness which it bred and maintained. And so, in the even balance between the two categories, the little cripple remained a fixture in the stream of life that passed through that back room, in the fluxes and refluxes of buying and selling; not valueless, however—rely upon a negro-trader for discovering values as substitutes, as panaceas. She earned her nourishment, and Providence did not let it kill the little animal before the emancipation of weaning arrived.

How much circumstances evoked, how much instinct responded, belongs to the secrets which nature seems to intend keeping. As a baby she had eyes, attention, solely for other babies. One cannot say while she was still crawling, for she could only crawl years after she should have been walking, but, before even precocious walking-time, tradition or the old gray-haired negro janitor relates, she would creep from baby to baby to play with it, put it to sleep, pat it, rub its stomach (a negro baby, you know, is all stomach, and generally aching stomach at that). And before she had a lap, she managed to force one for some ailing nursling. It was then that they began to call her "little Mammy." In the transitory population of the "pen" no one stayed long enough to give her another name; and no one ever stayed short enough to give her another one.

Her first recollection of herself was that she could not walk—she was past crawling; she cradled herself along, as she called sitting down flat, and working herself about with her hands and her one strong leg. Babbling babies walked all around her—many walking before they babbled—and still she did not walk, imitate them as she might and did. She would sit and "study" about it, make another trial, fall; sit and study some more, make another trial, fall again. Negroes, who believe that they must give a reason for everything even if they have to invent one, were convinced that it was all this studying upon her lameness that gave her such a large head.

And now she began secretly turning up the clothes of every negro child that came into that pen, and examining its legs, and still more secretly examining her own, stretched out before her on the ground. How long it took she does not remember; in fact, she could not have known, for she had no way of measuring time except by her thoughts and feelings. But in her own way and time the due process of deliberation was fulfilled, and the quotient made clear that, bowed or not, all children's legs were of equal length except her own, and all were alike, not one full, strong, hard, the other soft, flabby, wrinkled, growing out of a knot at the hip. A whole psychological period apparently lay between that conclusion and—a broom-handle walking-stick; but the broomstick came, as it was bound to come—thank heaven!—from that premise, and what with stretching one limb to make it longer, and doubling up the other to make it shorter, she invented that form of locomotion which is still carrying her through life, and with no more exaggerated leg-crookedness than many careless negroes born with straight limbs display. This must have been when she was about eight or nine. Hobbling on a broomstick, with, no doubt, the same weird, wizened face as now, an innate sense of the fitness of things must have suggested the kerchief tied around her big head, and the burlaps rag of an apron in front of her linsey-woolsey rag of a gown, and the bit of broken pipe-stem in the corner of her mouth, where the pipe should have been, and where it was in after years. That is the way she recollected herself, and that is the way one recalls her now, with a few modifications.

The others came and went, but she was always there. It was n't long before she became "little Mammy" to the grown folks too; and the newest inmates soon learned to cry: "Where 's little Mammy?" "Oh, little Mammy! little Mammy! Such a misery in my head [or my back, or my stomach]! Can't you help me, little Mammy?" It was curious what a quick eye she had for symptoms and ailments, and what a quick ear for suffering, and how apt she was at picking up, remembering, and inventing remedies. It never occurred to her not to crouch at the head or the foot of a sick pallet, day and night through. As for the nights, she said she dared not close her eyes of nights. The room they were in was so vast, and sometimes the negroes lay so thick on the floor, rolled in their blankets (you know, even in the summer they sleep under blankets), all snoring so loudly, she would never have heard a groan or a whimper any more than they did, if she had slept, too. And negro mothers are so careless and such heavy sleepers. All night she would creep at regular intervals to the different pallets, and draw the little babies from under, or away from, the heavy, inert impending mother forms. There is no telling how many she thus saved from being overlaid and smothered, or, what was worse, maimed and crippled.

Whenever a physician came in, as he was sometimes called, to look at a valuable investment or to furbish up some piece of damaged goods, she always managed to get near to hear the directions; and she generally was the one to apply them also, for negroes always would steal medicines most scurvily one from the other. And when death at times would slip into the pen, despite the trader's utmost alertness and precautions—as death often "had to do," little Mammy said—when the time of some of them came to die, and when the rest of the negroes, with African greed of eye for the horrible, would press around the lowly couch where the agonizing form of a slave lay writhing out of life, she would always to the last give medicines, and wipe the cold forehead, and soothe the clutching, fearsome hands, hoping to the end, and trying to inspire the hope that his or her "time" had not come yet; for, as she said, "Our time does n't come just as often as it does come."

And in those sad last offices, which some-how have always been under reproach as a kind of shame, no matter how young she was, she was always too old to have the childish avoidance of them. On the contrary, to her a corpse was only a kind of baby, and she always strove, she said, to make one, like the other, easy and comfortable.

And in other emergencies she divined the mysteries of the flesh, as other precocities divine the mysteries of painting and music, and so become child wonders.

Others came and went. She alone remained there. Babies of her babyhood—the toddlers she, a toddler, had nursed—were having babies themselves now; the middle-aged had had time to grow old and die. Every week new families were coming into the great back chamber; every week they passed out: babies, boys, girls, buxom wenches, stalwart youths, and the middle-aged—the grave, serious ones whom misfortune had driven from their old masters, and the ill-reputed ones, the trickish, thievish, lazy, whom the cunning of the negro-trader alone could keep in circulation. All were marketable, all were bought and sold, all passed in one door and out the other—all except her, little Mammy. As with her lameness, it took time for her to recognize, to understand, the fact. She could study over her lameness, she could in the dull course of time think out the broomstick way of palliation. It would have been almost better, under the circumstances, for God to have kept the truth from her; only—God keeps so little of the truth from us women. It is his system.

Poor little thing! It was not now that her master *could* not sell her, but he *would* not! Out of her own intelligence she had forged her chains; the lameness was a hobble merely in comparison. She had become too valuable to the negro-trader by her services among his crew, and offers only solidified his determination not to sell her. Visiting physicians, after short acquaintance with her capacities, would offer what were called fancy prices for her. Planters who heard of her through their purchases would come to the city purposely to secure, at any cost, so inestimable an adjunct to their plantations. Even ladies—refined, delicate ladies—sometimes came to the pen personally to back money with influence. In vain. Little Mammy was worth more to the negro-trader, simply as a kind of insurance against accidents, than any sum, however glittering the figure, and he was no ignorant expert in human wares. She can tell it; no one else can for her. Remember that at times she had seen the streets outside. Remember that she could hear of the outside world daily from the passing chattels—of the plantations, farms, families; the green fields, Sunday woods, running streams; the camp-meetings, corn-shuckings, cotton-pickings, sugar-grindings; the baptisms, marriages, funerals, prayer-meetings; the holidays and holy days. Remember that, whether for liberty or whether for love, passion effloresces in the human being—no matter when, where, or how—with every spring's return. Remember that she was, even in middle age, young and vigorous. But no; do not remember anything. There is no need to heighten the coloring.

It would be tedious to relate, although it was not tedious to hear her relate it, the desperations and hopes of her life then. Hardly a day passed that she did not see, looking for purchases (rummaging among goods on a counter for bargains), some master whom she could have loved, some mistress whom she could have adored. Always her favorite mistresses were there—tall, delicate matrons, who came themselves, with great fatigue, to select kindly-faced women for nurses; languid-looking ladies with smooth hair standing out in wide *bandeaux* from their heads, and lace shawls dropping from their sloping shoulders, silk dresses carelessly held up in thumb and finger from embroidered petticoats that were spread out like tents over huge hoops which covered whole groups of swarming piccaninnies on the dirty floor; ladies, pale from illnesses that she might have nursed, and over-burdened with children whom she might have reared! And not a lady of that kind saw her face but wanted her, yearned for her, pleaded for her, coming back secretly to slip silver, and sometimes gold, pieces into her hand, patting her turbaned head, calling her "little Mammy" too, instantly, by inspiration, and making the negro-trader give them, with all sorts of assurances, the refusal of her. She had no need for the whispered "Buy me, master!" "Buy me, mistress!" "You 'll see how I can work, master!" "You 'll never be sorry, mistress!" of the others. The negro-trader—like hangmen, negro-traders are fitted by nature for their profession—it came into his head—he had no heart, not even a negro-trader's heart—that it would be more judicious to seclude her during these shopping visits, so to speak. She could not have had any hopes then at all; it must have been all desperations.

That auction-block, that executioner's block, about which so much has been written—Jacob's ladder, in his dream, was nothing to what that block appeared nightly in her dreams to her; and the climbers up and down—well, perhaps Jacob's angels were his hopes, too.

At times she determined to depreciate her usefulness, mar her value, by renouncing her heart, denying her purpose. For days she would tie her kerchief over her ears and eyes, and crouch in a corner, strangling her impulses. She even malingered, refused food, became dumb. And she might have succeeded in making herself salable through incipient lunacy, if through no other way, had she been able to maintain her rôle long enough. But some woman or baby always was falling into some emergency of pain and illness.

How it might have ended one does not like to think. Fortunately, one does not need to think.

There came a night. She sat alone in the vast, dark caravansary—alone for the first time in her life. Empty rags and blankets lay strewn over the floor, no snoring, no tossing in them more. A sacrificial sale that day had cleared the counters. Alarm-bells rang in the streets, but she did not know them for alarm-bells; alarm brooded in the dim space around her, but she did not even recognize that. Her protracted tension of heart had made her fear-blind to all but one peradventure.

Once or twice she forgot herself, and limped over to some heap to relieve an imaginary struggling babe or moaning sleeper. Morning came. She had dozed. She looked to see the rag-heaps stir; they lay as still as corpses. The alarm-bells had ceased. She looked to see a new gang enter the far door. She listened for the gathering buzzing of voices in the next room, around the auction-block. She waited for the trader. She waited for the janitor. At nightfall a file of soldiers entered. They drove her forth, ordering her in the voice, in the tone, of the negro-trader. That was the only familiar thing in the chaos of incomprehensibility about her. She hobbled through the auction-room. Posters, advertisements, papers, lay on the floor, and in the torch-light glared from the wall. Her Jacob's ladder, her stepping-stone to her hopes, lay overturned in a corner.

You divine it. The negro-trader's trade was abolished, and he had vanished in the din and smoke of a war which he had not been entirely guiltless of producing, leaving little Mammy locked up behind him. Had he forgotten her? One cannot even hope so. She hobbled out into the street, leaning on her nine-year-old broomstick (she had grown only slightly beyond it; could still use it by bending over it), her head tied in a rag kerchief, a rag for a gown, a rag for an apron.

Free, she was free! But she had not hoped for freedom. The plantation, the household, the delicate ladies, the teeming children—broomsticks they were in comparison to freedom, but—that was what she had asked, what she had prayed for. God, she said, had let her drop, just as her mother had done. More than ever she grieved, as she crept down the street, that she had never mounted the auctioneer's block. An ownerless free negro! She knew no one whose duty it was to help her; no one knew her to help her. In the whole world (it was all she had asked) there was no white child to call her mammy, no white lady or gentleman (it was the extent of her dreams) beholden to her as to a nurse. And all her innumerable black beneficiaries! Even the janitor, whom she had tended as the others, had deserted her like his white prototype.

She tried to find a place for herself, but she had no indorsers, no recommenders. She dared not mention the name of the negro-trader; it banished her not only from the households of the whites, but from those of the genteel of her own color. And everywhere soldiers sentineled the streets—soldiers whose tone and accent reminded her of the negro-trader.

Her sufferings, whether imaginary or real, were sufficiently acute to drive her into the only form of escape which once had been possible to friendless negroes. She became a runaway. With a bundle tied to the end of a stick over her shoulder, just as the old prints represent it, she fled from her homelessness and loneliness, from her ignoble past; and the heart-disappointing termination of it. Following a railroad track, journeying afoot, sleeping by the roadside, she lived on until she came to the one familiar landmark in life to her—a sick woman, but a white one. And so, progressing from patient to patient (it was a time when sick white women studded the country like mile-posts), she arrived at a little town, a kind of a refuge for soldiers' wives and widows. She never traveled further. She could not. Always, as in the pen, some emergency of pain and illness held her.

That is all. She is still there. The poor, poor women of that stricken region say that little Mammy was the only alleviation God left them after Sheridan passed through; and the richer ones say very much the same thing—

But one should hear her tell it herself, as has been said, on a cold, gloomy winter day in the country, the fire glimmering on the hearth; the overworked husband in the fields; the baby quiet at last; the mother uneasy, restless, thought-driven; the soft black hand rubbing backward and forward, rubbing out aches and frets and nervousness.

The eyelids droop; the firelight plays fantasies on the bed-curtains; the ear drops words, sentences; one gets confused—one sleeps—one dreams.

Questions to Consider

1. How does King invert the meanings of slavery—the auction block, the slave pens, life "outside" on the plantations, emancipation, the potential buyers, the "negro-trader"? What are the effects of these inversions? How are the negative aspects of the slave trade isolated and minimized? How does King redefine the reasons for the privations of the slaves?
2. What do little Mammy's behaviors and hopes reveal about contemporary models of womanhood? To what extent are those models inscribed—or contradicted—by race? What are the sources of Mammy's value in the pen? to King's readers? What are the implications of Mammy's service to sick White women?

Ruth McEnery Stuart

1849–1917

Though Ruth McEnery Stuart is less well known today than other nineteenth-century Louisiana writers—like Cable, King, or Chopin—only Cable achieved greater contemporary fame. Like Cable, Stuart was a popular and adept reader of dialect stories, and, like him, she lived most of her professional life in the North.

The eldest of eight children, Mary Routh McEnery was born in the village of Marksville in central Louisiana. Her parents, politically and economically well-connected, moved to New Orleans when their daughter was three. In 1879, she married Alfred Oden Stuart, a wealthy Arkansas planter 30 years her senior. After he died in 1883, Ruth Stuart returned to New Orleans with their son, Stirling. Her participation in the lively literary and women's club community of the 1880s motivated Stuart to try her hand at writing. In 1888, she published her first two stories, "Uncle Mingo's 'Speculatioms' " and "The Lamentations of Jeremiah Johnson"—both of which drew on the stereotypes of faithful "darkies" made popular by Thomas Nelson Page and Joel Chandler Harris. Their success prompted Stuart's move to New York, where she established herself as a fashionable Southern hostess and author. The accidental death of her son in 1905 led to severe depression, but Stuart eventually recovered and returned to writing. In 1915, she and Grace King were awarded honorary degrees by Tulane University. Two years later on 6 May 1917, Stuart died in White Plains, New York.

Stuart's fiction drew on her plantation experiences in both Louisiana and Arkansas. Her cheerful portraits of African-American life in collections like *A Golden Wedding* (1893)—which included "Christmas Gifts"—and in the skillful monologues of *Sonny: A Christmas Guest* (1896) were appreciated by contemporary White audiences as deeply authentic. Even Joel Chandler Harris asserted that Stuart had "got nearer the heart of the Negro than any of us," thus complimenting the condescending view of African Americans that dialect fiction helped to sustain.

Stuart also published several collections about rural Arkansas, including *The Woman's Exchange of Simpkinsville* (1893), *In Simpkinsville: Character Tales* (1897), and *The Second Wooing of Salina Sue* (1905). Many of these stories treated sensitively women's efforts to cope with the economic realities of the New South and its changed gender relations. Stuart's outspoken village women warrant comparison with the characters of Jewett or Freeman, although Stuart's comic intentions have typically deflected much serious analysis until quite recently. Stuart also wrote many stories depicting ethnic types, including Italians, French, Irish, and Germans. But as in her plantation tales, Stuart's humor is kindly rather than critical, and her urban stories only indirectly reflect contemporary anti-immigrant sentiment.

Many of Stuart's 22 novellas, collections of poetry, and short stories remained in print long after her death. "Christmas Gifts," which recounts a plantation custom cherished by White Southerners as evidence of former masters' benevolence, typifies the mythologies of the Antebellum South prevalent in magazine fiction of the 1880s and 1890s. Although tempered by Stuart's pathos and frank humor, such stories, with their patronizing images of African Americans, beguiled large audiences who sought reassurance that African Americans remained willingly submissive to the benign authority of White Southerners. Stuart's extensive use of dialect, though sometimes distracting, reflects a careful rendition of regional accents.

Christmas Gifts

Christmas on Sucrier plantation, and the gardens are on fire with red flames of salvia, roses, geraniums, verbenas, rockets of Indian shot, brilliant blazes of coreopsis, marigold, and nasturtium, glowing coals of vivid portulaca.

Louisiana acknowledges a social obligation to respond to a Christmas freeze; but when a guest tarries, what is one to do?

She manufactures her ice, it is true. Why not produce an artificial winter? Simply because she does not care for it. If she did —? Such things are easily arranged.

Still, when he comes, *a guest,* she would not forget her manners and say him nay, any sooner than she would shrug her shoulders at a New England cousin or answer his questions in French.

She does the well-bred act to the death, summons her finest, fairest, most brilliant and tender of flower and leaf to await his coming: so to-day all her royal summer family are out in full court dress, ready to prostrate themselves at his feet.

This may be rash, but it is polite.

Her grandfather was both; and so the "Creole State," in touch with her antipodal brother in ancestor-worship, is satisfied.

But winter, the howling swell, forgetful of provincial engagements, does not come. Still, the edge of his promise is in the breeze to-day, and the flaring banana leaves of tender green look cold and half afraid along the garden wall.

The Yule log smoulders lazily and comfortably in the big fireplace, but windows and doors are open, and rocking-chairs and hammocks swing on the broad galleries of the great house.

It is a rich Christmas of the olden time.

Breakfast and the interchange of presents are over.

Cautious approaches of wheels through the outer gates during the night, in the wee short hours when youth sleeps most heavily, have resulted in mysterious appearances: a new piano in the parlor; a carriage, a veritable ante-bellum chariot, and a pair of bays, in the stable; guns, silver-mounted trappings, saddles, books, pictures, jewels, and dainty confections, within and piled about the stockings that hung around the broad dining-room chimney.

For there were sons and daughters on Sucrier plantation.

An easy-going, healthy, hearty, and happy man, of loose purse-strings and lax business habits, old Colonel Slack had grown wealthy simply because he lived on the shore where the tide always came in—the same shore where since '61 the waters move ever to the sea, and those who waited where he stood are stranded.

His highest ambitions in life were realized. His children, the elect by inheritance to luxurious ease, were growing up about him, tall, straight, and handsome, and happily free from disorganizing ambitions, loving the fleece-lined home-nest.

The marriage of an eldest daughter, Louise, to a wealthy next-door planter, five miles away, had seemed but to add a bit of broidery to the borders of his garment.

His pretty, dainty wife, in lieu of wrinkles, had taken on avoirdupois and white hair, and instead of shrivelling like a four-o'clock had bloomed into a regal evening-glory.

So distinctly conscious of all these blessings was the old colonel that his atmosphere seemed always charged with the electric quality which was happiness; but on occasions like to-day, when the depths of his tendernesses were stirred within him by the ecstasy of giving and of receiving thanks and smiles and thanks again from "*my* handsome wife," "*my* fine children," "*my* loyal slaves"—ah, this was the electric *flash!* It was joy! It was delight and exuberance of spirit! It was youth returned! It was Christmas!

In his heart were peace and good-will all the year round, and on Christmas—hallelujahs.

He had often been heard to say that if he ever professed religion it would be on Christmas; and, by the way, so it was, but not *this* Christmas.

A tender-souled, good old man was he, yet thoughtless, withal, as a growing boy.

Down in the quarters, this morning, the negroes, gaudily arrayed in their Sunday best, were congregated in squads about the benches in front of their cabins, awaiting the ringing of the plantation bell which should summon them to "the house" to receive their Christmas packages.

In the grove of China-trees around which the cabins were ranged, a crowd of young men and maidens flirted and chaffed one another on the probable gifts awaiting them.

One picked snatches of tunes on a banjo, another drew a bow across an old fiddle, but the greater number were giddily spending themselves in plantation repartee, a clever answer always provoking a loud, unanimous laugh, usually followed by a reckless duet by the two "musicianers."

Sometimes, when the jokes were too utterly delicious, the young "bucks" would ecstatically hug the China-trees or tumble down upon the grass and bellow aloud.

"What yer reck'n ole marster gwine give you, Unc' Torm?" said one, addressing an old man who had just joined the group and sat sunning his shiny bald head.

" 'Spec' he gwine give Unc' Torm some hair-ile, ur a co'se comb," suggested a pert youth.

"Look like he better give you a wagon-tongue ur a bell-tongue, one, 'caze yo' tongue ai n't long 'nough," replied Uncle Tom quietly, and so the joke was turned.

"I trus' he gwine give Bow-laigged Joe a new pair o' breeches!"

"Ef he do, I hope dey'll be cut out wid a circular saw!" came a quick response, which brought a scream of laughter.

"Wonder what Lucindy an' Dave gwine git?"

Lucinda and Dave were bride and groom of a month.

In a minute two big fellows were screaming and holding their sides over a whispered suggestion, when the word "cradle" escaped and set girls and all to giggling.

"Pity somebody wouldn't drap some o' you smart boys on a *corn-cradle* an' chop you up," protested the bride, with a toss of her head.

"De whole passel ob 'em wouldn't make nothin' but rotten-stone, ef dee was *grine* up," suggested Uncle Tom, with an intolerant sniffle.

"Den you mought use us fur tooth-powder," responded the wit again, and the bald-headed old man, confessing himself vanquished, good-naturedly bared his toothless gums to join in the laughter at his own expense.

A sudden clang of the bell brought all to their feet presently, and, strutting, laughing, prancing, they proceeded up to the house, the musicians tuning up afresh *en route*, for in the regular order of exercises arranged for the day they were to play an important part.

The recipients were to be ranged in the yard in line, about fifty feet from the steps of the back veranda where the master should stand, and, as their names should be called, to dance forward, receive their gifts, courtesy, and dance back to their places.

At the calling of the names music would begin.

The pair who by vote should be declared the most graceful should receive from the master's hand a gift of five dollars each, with the understanding that it should supply the eggnog for the evening's festivities, where the winners should preside as king and queen.

An interested audience of the master's family, seated on the veranda back of him, was a further stimulant to best effort.

The packages, all marked with names, were piled on two tables, those for men on one and the women's on the other, and the couples resulting from a random selection from each caused no little merriment.

All had agreed to the conditions, and when Lame Phœbe was called out with Jake Daniels, a famous dancer, they were greeted with shouts of applause.

Phœbe, enthused by her reception, and in no wise embarrassed by a short leg, made a virtue of necessity, advancing and retreating in a series of graceful bows, manipulating her sinewy body so dextrously that the inclination towards the left foot was more than concealed, and for the first time in his life Jake Daniels came in second best, as, amid deafening applause, Lame Phœbe bowed and wheeled herself back among the people.

Then came Joe Scott, an ebony swell, with Fat Sarey, a portly dame of something like three hundred avoirdupois—a difficult combination again.

That Sarey had not danced for twenty years was not through reluctance of the flesh more than of the spirit, for she was "a chile o' de kingdom," both by her own profession and universal consent.

Laughing good-naturedly, with shaking sides she stepped forward, bowed first to her master and then to her partner, and, raising her right hand, began, in a wavering, soft voice, keeping time to the vibrating melody by easy undulations of her pliable body, to sing:

Dey's a star in de eas' on a Chris'mus morn.
Rise up, shepherd, an' foller!
Hit'll lead ter de place whar de Saviour's born.
Rise up, shepherd, an' foller!
Ef yer take good heed ter de angels' words,
You'll forgit yo' flocks an' forgit yo' herds,
An' rise up, shepherd, an' foller!
Leave yo' sheep an'
Leave yo' lamb an'
Leave yo' ewe an'
Leave yo' ram, an'
Rise up, shepherd, an' foller!

Joe took his cue from the first note, and, accommodating his movements to hers, elaborating them profusely with graceful gestures, he fell in with a rich, high tenor, making a melody so tender and true that the audience were hushed in reverential silence.

The first verse finished, Sarey turned slowly, and by an uplifted finger invited all hands to join in the chorus.

Rich and loud, in all four parts, came the effective refrain:

Foller, foller, foller, foller,
Rise up, shepherd, rise an' foller,
Foller de Star o' Bethlehem!

Still taking the initiative, Sarey now bent easily and deeply forward in a most effusive parlor salutation as she received her gift; while Joe, as ever quick of intuition, also dispensed with the traditional dipping courtesy, while he surrendered himself to a profound bow which involved the entire length of his willowy person.

Turning now, without losing for a moment the rhythmic movement, they proceeded to sing a second verse:

Oh, dat star's still shinin' dis Chris'mus day.
Rise, O sinner, an' foller!
Wid an eye o' faith you c'n see its ray.
Rise, O sinner, an' foller!
Hit'll light yo' way thoo de fiel's o' fros',
While it leads thoo de stable ter de shinin' cross.
Rise, O sinner, an' foller!
Leave yo' father,
Leave yo' mother,
Leave yo' sister,
Leave yo' brother,
An' rise, O sinner, an' foller!

A slightly accelerated movement had now brought the performers back to their places, when the welkin rang with a full all-round chorus:

Foller, foller, foller, foller,
Rise, O sinner, rise an' foller.
Foller de Star o' Bethlehem!

A few fervid high-noted "Amens!" pathetically suggestive of pious senility, were succeeded now by a silence more eloquent than applause.

Other dancers by youthful antics soon restored hilarity, however, and for quite an hour the festivities kept up with unabated interest.

Finally a last parcel was held up—only one—and when the master called, "Judy Collins!" adding, "Judy, you'll have to dance by yourself, my girl!" the excitement was so great that for several minutes nothing could be done.

Judy Collins, by a strange coincidence, was the only "old maid" on the plantation, and, as she was a dashing, handsome woman, she had given the mitten at one time or another to nearly every man present.

That she should have to dance alone was too much for their self-control.

The women, convulsed with laughter, held on to one another, while the men shrieked aloud.

Judy was the only self-possessed person present.

Before any one realized her intention, she had seized a new broom from the kitchen porch near, and stepped out into the arena with it in her hand.

Judy was grace itself. Tall, willowy, and lithe, stately as a pine, supple as a mountain-trout, she glided forward with her broom.

Holding it now at arm's-length, now balancing it on end and now on its wisps, tilting it at hazardous angles, but always catching it ere it fell, poising it on her finger-tips, her chin, her forehead, the back of her neck, keeping perfect time the while with the music, she advanced to receive her parcel, which, with a quick movement, she deftly attached to the broom-handle, and, throwing it over her shoulder, danced back to her place.

The performance entire had proven a brilliant success, and Judy's dance a fitting climax.

Needless to say, Judy insisted on keeping the broom.

The awarding of the prizes by acclamation to Joe Scott and Fat Sarey was the work of a moment, prettily illustrating the religious susceptibility of the voters.

Then followed a "few remarks" from the speaker of the occasion, and a short and playful response from the master, when the crowd dispersed, opening their bundles *en route* as they returned merrily to their cabins.

The parcels had been affectionately prepared. Besides the dresses, wraps, and shoes given to all, there were attractive trinkets, bottles of cologne, ribbons, gilt earrings or pins for the young women, cravats, white collars, shirt-studs, for the beaux, and for the old such luxuries as tobacco, walking-canes, spectacles, and the like, with small coins for pocket-money.

This year, in addition to the extra and expected "gift," each young woman received, to her delight, a flaring hoop-skirt; and such a lot of balloons as were flying about the plantation that morning it would be hard to find again.

Happy and care-free as little children were they, and as easily pleased.

Having retired for the moment necessary for their inflation and adornment, the younger element, balloons and beaux, soon returned to their popular holiday resort under the China-trees.

Though the branches were bare, the benches beneath them commanded a perennial fair-weather patronage; for where a bench and a tree are, there will young men and maidens be gathered together.

Lame Mose was there, with his new cushioned crutch, and Phil Thomas the preacher, looking ultra-clerical and important in a polished beaver; while Lucinda and Dave, triumphant in the cumulative dignity of new bride-and-groomship, hoop-skirt and standing collar, actually strutted about arm in arm in broad daylight, to the intense amusement of the young folk, who nudged one another and giggled as they passed.

Such was the merry spirit of the group when Si, a young mulatto household servant, suddenly appeared upon the scene.

" 'Cindy," said he, "marster say come up ter de house—dat is, ef you an' Dave kin part company fur 'bout ten minutes."

"I don' keer nothin' 'bout no black ogly-lookin' some'h'n-'nother like Dave, nohow!" exclaimed Lucinda flirtatiously, as she playfully grasped Si's arm and proceeded with him to the house, leaving Dave laughing with the rest at her antics.

The truth was that, confidently expecting the descent of some further gift upon her brideship, Lucinda was delighted at the summons, and her face beamed with expectancy as she presented herself before her master.

"Lucindy," said he, as she entered, "I want you to mount Lady Gay and ride down to Beechwood this morning, to take some Christmas things to Louise and her chicks."

Lucinda's smile broadened in a delighted grin.

A visit to Beechwood to-day would be sure to elicit a present from her young mistress, "Miss Louise," besides affording an opportunity to compare presents and indulge in a little harmless gossip with the Beechwood negroes.

Lady Gay stood, ready saddled, waiting at the door. After a little delay in adjusting the assertive springs of her hoop-skirt to the pommel of the saddle, Lucinda started off in a gallop.

When she entered the broad ball at Beechwood, the family, children and all, recognizing her as an ambassador of Santa Claus, gathered eagerly about her, and as boxes and parcels were opened in her presence her eyes fairly shone with pleasure. Nor was she disappointed in her hope of a gift herself.

"I allus did love you de mos' o' all o' ole Miss's chillen, Miss Lou," she exclaimed presently, opening and closing with infantile delight a gay feather-edged fan which Louise gave her.

"I does nachelly love red. Red seem like hit's got mo' color in it 'n any color."

"Dis heah's a reg'lar courtin-fan," she added to herself, as she followed the children out into the nursery to inspect their new toys, fanning, posing, and flirting as she went. "Umph! ef I'd 'a' des had dis fan las' summer I'd 'a' had Dave all but crazy."

After enjoying it for an hour or more, she finally wrapped it carefully in her handkerchief and put it for safe keeping into her pocket. In doing so, her hand came in contact with a letter which she had forgotten to deliver.

"Law, Miss Lou!" she exclaimed, hurrying back, "I mos' done clair forgittin' ter gi' you yo' letter wha' ole marster tol' me ter han' you de fus' thing."

"I wondered that father and mother had sent no message," replied Louise, opening the note. Her face softened into a smile, however, as she proceeded to read it.

"Why, you wretch, Lucindy!" she exclaimed, laughing, "you've kept me out of my two best Christmas gifts for an hour. I always wanted to own Lady Gay, and father writes that you are a fine, capable girl."

Lucinda cast a quick, frightened look at Louise and caught her breath.

"And I am so glad to know that you are pleased. Why didn't you tell me that you were a Christmas gift when you came?"

There was no longer any doubt. Lucinda could not have answered to save her life. The happy-hearted child of a moment ago was transformed into a desperate, grief-stricken woman.

"Why, Lucindy!" Louise was really grieved to discern the tragic look in the girl's face. "I am disappointed. I thought you loved me. I thought you would be delighted to belong to me—to be my maid—and not to work in the field any more—and to have a nice cabin in my yard—and a sewing-machine—and to learn to embroider—and to dress my hair—and to —"

The growing darkness in Lucinda's face warned Louise that this conciliatory policy was futile, and yet, feeling only kindly towards her, she continued,

"Tell me, Lucindy, why you are distressed. Don't you really wish to belong to me? Why did you say that you loved me the best?"

Words were useless. Louise was almost frightened as she looked again into the girl's face. Her eyes shone like a caged lion's, and her bosom rose and fell tumultuously.

After many fruitless efforts to elicit a response, Louise called her husband, and together they tried by kind assurances to pacify her; but it was vain. She stood before them a mute impersonation of despair and rage.

"You'd better go out into the kitchen for a while, Lucindy," said Louise finally, "and when I send for you I shall expect you to have composed yourself." Looking neither to right nor left, Lucinda strode out of the hall, across the gallery, down the steps, through the yard to the kitchen, gazed at by the assembled crowd of children both black and white.

" 'Cindy ain't but des on'y a little while ago married," said Tildy, a black girl who stood in the group as she passed out.

"Married, is she?" exclaimed Louise, eagerly grasping at a solution of the difficulty. "That explains. But why didn't she tell me? There must be some explanation. This is so unlike father. We are to dine at Sucrier this afternoon. Go, Tildy, and tell Lucindy that we will see what can be done."

"Fo' laws-o'-mussy sakes, Miss Lou, please, má'am, don't sen' me ter 'Cindy now. 'Cindy look like she gwine hurt somebody."

If she could have seen Lucinda at this moment, she might indeed have feared to approach her. When she had entered the kitchen a little negro who had followed at her heels had announced to the cook and her retinue,

" 'Cindy mad caze ole marster done sont 'er fur a Chris'mus-gif' ter Miss Lou." Whereupon there were varied exclamations:

"Umph!"

"You is a sorry-lookin' Chris'mus gif', sho!"

"I don't blame 'er!"

"What you frettin' 'bout, chile? You in heab'n here!"

"De gal's married," whispered some one in stage fashion, finally.

"Married!" shrieked old Silvy Ann from her corner where she sat peeling potatoes. "Married! Eh, Lord! Time you ole as I is, you won't fret 'bout no sech. Turn 'im out ter grass, honey, an' start out fur a grass-widder. I got five I done turned out in de pasture now, an' ef dee sell me out ag'in, Ole Abe'll be a-grazin' wid de res'!

"Life is too short ter fret, honey! But ef yer *boun'* ter fret, fret 'bout *some'h'n'!* Don't fret 'bout one o' deze heah long-laigged, good-fur-nothin' sca'crows name' Mister Man! Who you married ter, gal?"

"She married ter cross-eyed Dave," some one answered.

"Cross-eyed! De Lord! Let 'im go fur what he'll fetch, honey! De woods roun' heah is full o' straight-eyed ones, let 'lone game-eyes!" And the vulgar old creature encored her own wit with an outburst of cracked laughter.

"Ain't you 'shame' o' yo'se'f, Aunt Silvy Ann! 'Cindy ain't like you; she *married—wid a preacher*."

"Yas, an' *unmarried 'dout no preacher!* What's de good o' lockin' de do' on de inside wid a key, ef you c'n open it f'om de outside 'dout no key? I done kep' clair o' locks an' keys all my life, an' nobody's feelin's was hurt."

While old Silvy Ann was running on in this fashion, Texas, the cook, had begun to address Lucinda:

"Don't grieve yo' heart, baby. My ole man stay mo' fur 'n ole marster's f'om heah—'way down ter de cross-roads t'other side de bayou. How fur do daddy stay, chillen?" she added, as she broke red pepper into her turkey-stuffing.

"Leb'n mile," answered four voices from as many little black pickaninnies who tumbled over one another on the floor.

"You heah dat! *Leb'n mile,* an' ev'y blessed night he come home ter Texas! Yas, ma'am, an' 'is lone star keep a lookout fur 'im, too—a candle in de winder an' a tin pan o' 'membrance on de hyearth."

Seeing that her words produced no effect, Texas changed her tactics.

Approaching Lucinda, she regarded her with admiration: "Dat's a quality collar you got on, 'Cindy. An', law bless my soul, ef de gal 'ain't got on hoops! You gwine lead de style on dis planta——"

Texas never finished her sentence.

Trembling with fury, Lucinda snatched the collar from her neck and tore it into bits; then, making a dive at her skirts, she ripped them into shreds in her frantic efforts to destroy the hoop-skirt.

Dragging the gilt pendants from her ears, tearing the flesh as she did so, she threw them upon the floor, and, stamping upon them, ground them to atoms.

Attracted next by her new brogans, she kicked them from her feet and hurled them, one after another, into the open fire. No vestige of a gift from the hand that had betrayed her would she spare.

While all this was occurring in the kitchen, a reverse side of the tragedy was enacting in the house.

A few moments after Lucinda's departure, while Louise and her husband were yet discussing the situation, another messenger came from Sucrier, this time a man, and again a gift, the "note" which he promptly delivered proving to be a deed of conveyance of "two adult negroes, by name Lucinda and David." Then followed descriptions of each, which it was unnecessary to read.

The bearer seemed in fine spirits.

"Ole marster des sont me wid de note, missy," said he, courtesying respectfully, "an' ef yer please, ma'am, I'll go right back ef dey ain't no answer. We havin' a big time up our way ter-day."

"Why, don't you know what this is, Dave?"

"Yas, 'm, co'se I knows. Hit's–hit's a letter. Law, Miss Lou, yer reck'n I don' know a letter when I see it?"

"Yes, but this letter says that you are not to go back. Father has sent you as a Christmas gift to us."

"Wh–wh–h–how you say dat, missy?"

"Please don't look so frightened, Dave. From the way you all are acting to-day, I begin to be afraid of myself. Don't you want to belong to me?"

"Y–y–yas, 'm, but yer see, missy, I–I–I's married."

The hat in his hand was trembling as he spoke.

"And where is your wife?" Could it be possible that he did not know?

"She–sh–she–" The boy was actually crying. "She stay wid me. B–b–but marster des sont 'er on a arrant dis mornin'. Gord knows whar he sont 'er. I 'lowed maybe he sont 'er heah, tell 'e sont me."

The situation, which was plain now, had grown so interesting that Louise could not resist the temptation to bring the unconscious actors in the little drama together, that she might witness the happy catastrophe.

She whispered to Tildy to call Lucinda.

That Lucinda should have been summoned just at the crisis of her passion was most inopportune.

Tildy stood at a distance as she timidly delivered the message. Indeed, all the occupants of the kitchen had moved off apace and stood aghast and silent.

As soon as Lucinda heard the command, however, without even looking down at herself, with head still high in air and her fury unabated, she followed Tildy into the presence of her mistress.

Louise was frightened when she looked upon her; indeed it was some moments before she could command herself enough to speak.

The girl's appearance was indeed tragic.

In tearing the ribbon from her hair she had loosened the ends of the short braids, which stood in all directions. Her ears were dripping with blood, and her torn sleeve revealed her black arm, scratched with her nails, also bleeding.

Below her tattered skirt trailed long, detached springs, the dilapidated remains of the glorious structure of the morning.

Her tearless eyes gave no sign of weakening, and the veins about her neck and temples, pulsating with passion, were swollen and knotted like ropes.

She seemed to have grown taller, and the black circles beneath her eyes and about her swelling lips imparted by contrast an ashen hue grimly akin to pallor to the rest of her face.

As her mistress contemplated her, she was moved to pity.

"Lucindy"—she spoke with marked gentleness—"I showed you all our Christmas gifts this morning; but after you went out we received another, and I've sent for you to show you this too."

She hesitated, but not even by a quivering muscle did Lucinda give a sign of hearing.

"Look over there towards the library door, Lucindy, and see the nice carriage-driver father sent me."

Ah! now she looked.

For a moment only young husband and wife regarded each other, and then, oblivious to all eyes, the two Christmas gifts rushed into each other's arms.

The fountains of her wrath were broken up now, and Lucinda's tears came like rain. Crying and sobbing aloud, she threw her long arms around little Dave, and, dragging him out into the floor, began to dance.

Dave, more sensitive than she, abashed after the first surprise, became conscious and ashamed.

"Stop, 'Cindy! I 'clare, gal, stop! Stop, I say!" he cried, trying in vain to wrest himself from her grasp.

"You 'Cindy! You makes me 'shame'! Law, gal! Miss Lou, come here to 'Cindy!"

But the half-savage creature, mad with joy, gave no heed to his resistance as she whirled him round and round up and down the hall.

"Hallelujah! Glory! Amen! Glory be ter Gord, fur givin' me back dis heah little black, cross-eyed, bandy-legged nigger! Glory, I say!"

The scene was not without pathos. And yet—how small a thing will sometimes turn the tide of emotion! By how trifling a by-play does a tragedy become comedy!

In her first whirl, the trailing steels of Lucinda's broken hoop-skirt flew over the head of the cat, who sat in the door, entrapping her securely.

Round and round went poor puss, terror-stricken and wildly glaring, utterly unable to extricate herself, until finally a reversed movement freeing her, she sprang with a desperate plunge and an ear-splitting "*Miaou!*" by a single bound out of the back door.

This served to bring Lucinda to a consciousness of her surroundings.

Screaming with laughter, she threw herself down and rolled on the floor.

In rising, her eyes fell for the first time, with a sense of perception, upon herself.

Suddenly conscience-stricken, she threw herself again before her mistress.

"Fur Gord sake, whup me, Miss Lou!" she began; "whup me, ur put me in de stocks, one! I ain't no mo' fitt'n fur a Chris'mus gif' 'n one o' deze heah tiger-cats in de show-tent. Des look heah how I done ripped up all my purties, an' bus' my ears open, an' broke up all my hoop-granjer, all on 'count o' dat, little black, cross-eyed nigger! I tell yer de trufe, missy, I ain't no bad-hearted nigger! You des try me! I'll hoe fur yer, I'll plough fur yer, I'll split rails fur yer, I'll be yo' hair-dresser, I'll run de sew-machine fur yer, I'll walk on my head fur yer, ef yer des leave me dat one little black scrooched-up some'h'n'-'nother stan'in' over yonner 'g'inst de do', grinnin' like a chessy-cat. He ain't much, but, sech as 'e is an' what dey is of 'im, fur Gord sake, spare 'im ter me! Somehow, de place whar he done settled in my heart is des nachelly my *wil'-cat spot*."

Sitting in her rags at her mistress's feet, in this fashion she approached the formal apology which she felt that her conduct demanded.

Somehow the conventional formula, "I ax yo' pardon," seemed inadequate to the present requirement.

She hardly knew how to proceed.

After hesitating a moment in some embarrassment, she began again, in a lower tone:

"Miss Lou, dis heah's Chris'mus, ain't it?"

"Yes; you know it is."

"An' hit's de day de Lord cas' orf all 'is glory an' come down ter de yearth, des a po' little baby a-layin' in a stable 'longside o' de cows an' calves, ain't it?"

"Yes."

"An' hit's de day de angels come a-singin' 'peace an' good-will,' ain't it?"

"Yes."

"Miss Lou—"

"Well?"

"On de 'count o' all dat, honey, won't yer please, ma'am, pass over my wil'-cat doin's dis time, mistus?"

She waited a moment, and, not understanding how a rising lump in her throat kept her mistress silent, continued to plead:

"Fur Gord sake, mistus, I done said all de scripchur' I knows. What mo' kin I say?"

"What–what–what–what–what's all this?"

It was old Colonel Slack, standing in the front hall door.

At the sound of his voice, the three grandchildren ran to meet him, Louise following.

"You dear old father!" she exclaimed, kissing him. "You've grown impatient and come after us!"

"Certainly I have. What sort of spending the day do you call this? It's two o'clock now. But what's all this?" he repeated, approaching Lucinda, who had risen to her feet.

Dave had gradually backed nearly out of the door.

"Why, Lucindy, my girl! you look as if you'd had a tiff with a panther."

"Tell de trufe, marster, I done been down an' had a han'-ter-han' wrastle wid Satan ter-day, an' he all but whupped me out."

"How did you happen to send these poor children to us separately, father?" said Louise. "They have been almost broken-hearted, each thinking the other was to stay at Sucrier."

"Well, well, well! I am the clumsiest old blunderer! It's from Scylla to Charybdis every time. I didn't want my people to suspect they were going, just because it's Christmas, you know, and saying good-bye will cast a sort of shadow over things. Dave and Lucindy are immensely popular among the darkies. I knew they'd be glad to come; it's promotion, you see. Never thought of a misunderstanding. And so you poor children thought I wanted to divorce you, did you? And you, Lucindy, flew into a tantrum and tore the clothes off your back? I don't blame you. I'd tear mine off too. Rig her up again somehow, daughter, and let her go up to the dance tonight."

Opening his pocket-book, he took out two crisp five-dollar bills.

Handing one of them to Lucinda, he said:

"Here, girl, take this, and—don't you tells 'em I said so, but I thought you beat the whole crowd dancing this morning, anyhow. And Dave, you little cross-eyed rascal you, step up here and get your money. Here's five dollars to pay for spoiling your Christmas. Now, off with you!"

As they passed out, Lucinda seized Dave's arm, and when last seen as they crossed the yard she was dragging the little fellow from side to side, dancing in her rags and flirting high in air the red fan, which by some chance had escaped destruction in her pocket.

Magnificent in a discarded ball-dress of her new mistress, Lucinda was the centre of attraction at the Sucrier festival that evening, and when questioned in regard to her toilet of the morning, she answered, with a playful toss of the head:

"What y'all talkin' 'bout, niggers? I wushes you ter on'erstan' dat I's a house-gal now! Yer reck'n I gwine wear common ornamints, same as you fiel-han's?"

Questions to Consider

1. How do the realistic details of this story such as witty dialect and vivid descriptions of characters and events undercut Stuart's idealizations of plantation life? What economic and social exchanges are echoed in the gift-giving performances, both at the beginning and at the end of the story?
2. Charles Chesnutt once referred approvingly to Stuart as a "fellow craftsman." With what aspects of Stuart's work might an African-American writer identify? How is African-American violence and resistance at once contained and exposed in this story?

Charles W. Chesnutt

1855–1932

Charles Chesnutt, a light-complexioned son of free Black activists, committed his life and his art to addressing the unjust spirit of caste based on White-skin privilege. Chesnutt was born in Cleveland, Ohio, where his parents had relocated from Fayetteville, North Carolina, to escape pre–Civil War oppression. His father joined the Union army, and his mother, who had taught slaves, instilled in her son a passion for learning and for racial justice. Following the war, eight-year-old Charles returned with his family to North Carolina where he attended a Freedman Bureau school. His formal schooling and self-education in languages, history, music, mathematics, and literary classics led to a teaching career, commencing when Chesnutt was 14 and culminating with his appointment in 1880 as principal of the recently established State Normal School for Negroes (now Fayetteville State University). While teaching provided financial subsistence, writing became an increasingly central part of his life. Following his 1878 marriage to fellow teacher Susan Perry and the births of their first two children, Chesnutt decided to realize his dream, to capitalize on his self-preparation as a legal stenographer, and to circumvent the difficult realities of Jim Crow by moving North. After a brief sojourn as a reporter in New York, he resettled his family in his birthplace, Cleveland, where he remained for the rest of his life.

In 1887, Chesnutt traded on the popularity of Joel Chandler Harris's Uncle Remus tales and broke the unacknowledged color line of the prestigious *Atlantic Monthly*, a magazine that generally published only White authors. Chesnutt's Black dialect story is framed by a transplanted, White Ohioan narrator. However, the definitive voice is that of Uncle Julius McAdoo, a crafty former slave. Replete with the superstitions and folkways of North Carolinian African Americans, seven Uncle Julius stories were collected in *The Conjure Woman* (1899). Until this publication, Chesnutt's racial heritage had been kept secret from his readers even though he had made it clear to his publishers years earlier. With its revelation, Chesnutt's nondialect collection, *The Wife of His Youth and Other Stories of the Color Line* (1899) gained national attention, and

Chesnutt, now widely celebrated, gave up his law practice and stenographic firm to become a full-time writer.

Even though he shades cross-racial issues with a sentimental patina in his nine-story collection *The Wife of His Youth*, Chesnutt explores the insidious problems and boundaries besetting those mixed-blood people like himself who must walk the color line. The title story carefully draws on the plight of former plantation slaves known as Cleveland blue veins, who, even though free and upwardly mobile, understand and accept their proper place. At the same time, it addresses complex issues of mixed-blood identity and insists that authenticity and honor reside in the reclamation of African-American slave heritage, not in Northern White mimicry. Such questions resonate with Chesnutt's own torment as evidenced in his 30 January 1881 journal entry: "I am neither . . . 'nigger,' 'white,' nor 'buckrah.' Too 'stuck-up' for colored folks and, of course, not recognized by the whites." Stimulated by the success of his two short-fiction collections, he adopted the more flexible and lucrative genre of the novel as a platform for addressing race problems: racial self-loathing in *The House Behind the Cedars* (1900), racist cruelty and mob violence in *The Marrow of Tradition* (1901), and the failure of Southern Reconstruction in *The Colonel's Dream* (1905). While modern readers have praised these texts, particularly *The Marrow of Tradition*, Chesnutt's contemporary readers and critics found them increasingly disturbing and controversial. His hopes to survive financially as an influential author were dashed, and Chesnutt redirected his energy toward law. He passed the Ohio bar and established a lucrative stenographic firm. Forever the champion and advocate for improved racial relations, Chesnutt became a distinguished and influential citizen.

Chesnutt's pioneering contributions to literature and political activism were recognized by the NAACP, which awarded him the Spingarn Medal in 1928. Although no other novels were published in his lifetime, Chesnutt continued to write and revise and, at his death, left a number of completed and partially finished novels.

The Wife of His Youth

I

Mr. Ryder was going to give a ball. There were several reasons why this was an opportune time for such an event.

Mr. Ryder might aptly be called the dean of the Blue Veins. The original Blue Veins were a little society of colored persons organized in a certain Northern city shortly after the war. Its purpose was to establish and maintain correct social standards among a people whose social condition presented almost unlimited room for improvement. By accident, combined perhaps with some natural affinity, the society consisted of individuals who were, generally speaking, more white than black. Some envious outsider made the suggestion that no one was eligible for membership who was not white enough to show blue veins. The suggestion was readily adopted by those who were not of the favored few, and since that time the society, though possessing a longer and more pretentious name, had been known far and wide as the "Blue Vein Society" and its members as the "Blue Veins."

The Blue Veins did not allow that any such requirement existed for admission to their circle, but, on the contrary, declared that character and culture were the only things considered; and that if most of their members were light-colored, it was because such persons, as a rule, had had better opportunities to qualify themselves for membership. Opinions differed, too, as to the usefulness of the society. There were those who had been known to assail it violently as a glaring example of the very prejudice from which the colored race had suffered most; and later, when such critics had succeeded in getting on the inside, they had been heard to maintain with zeal and earnestness that the society was a lifeboat, an anchor, a bulwark and a shield—a pillar of cloud by day and of fire by night, to guide their people through the social wilderness. Another alleged prerequisite for Blue Vein membership was that of free birth; and while there was really no such requirement, it is doubtless true that very few of the members would have been unable to meet it if there had been. If there were one or two of the older members who had come up from the South and from slavery, their history presented enough romantic circumstances to rob their servile origin of its grosser aspects.

While there were no such tests of eligibility, it is true that the Blue Veins had their notions on these subjects, and that not all of them were equally liberal in regard to the things they collectively disclaimed. Mr. Ryder was one of the most conservative. Though he had not been among the founders of the society, but had come in some years later, his genius for social leadership was such that he had speedily become its recognized adviser and head, the custodian of its standards, and the preserver of its traditions. He shaped its social policy, was active in providing for its entertainment, and when the interest fell off, as it sometimes did, he fanned the embers until they burst again into a cheerful flame.

There were still other reasons for his popularity. While he was not as white as some of the Blue Veins, his appearance was such as to confer distinction upon them. His features were of a refined type, his hair was almost straight; he was always neatly dressed; his manners were irreproachable, and his morals above suspicion. He had come to Groveland a young man, and obtaining employment in the office of a railroad company as messenger had in time worked himself up to the position of stationery clerk, having charge of the distribution of the office supplies for the whole company. Although the lack of early training had hindered the orderly development of a naturally fine mind, it had not prevented him from doing a great deal of reading or from forming decidedly literary tastes. Poetry was his passion. He could repeat whole pages of the great English poets; and if his pronunciation was sometimes faulty, his eye, his voice, his gestures, would respond to the changing sentiment with a precision that revealed a poetic soul and disarmed criticism. He was economical, and had saved money; he owned and occupied a very comfortable house on a respectable street. His residence was handsomely furnished, containing among other things a good library, especially rich in poetry, a piano, and some choice engravings. He generally shared his house with some young couple, who looked after his wants and were company for him; for Mr. Ryder was a single man. In the early days of his connection with the Blue Veins he had been regarded as quite a catch, and young ladies and their mothers had *manoeuvred* with much ingenuity to capture him. Not, however, until Mrs. Molly Dixon visited Groveland had any woman ever made him wish to change his condition to that of a married man.

Mrs. Dixon had come to Groveland from Washington in the spring, and before the summer was over she had won Mr. Ryder's heart. She possessed many attractive qualities. She was much younger than he; in fact, he was old enough to have been her father, though no one knew exactly how old he was. She was whiter than he, and better educated. She had moved in the best colored society of the country, at Washington, and had taught in the schools of that city. Such a superior person had been eagerly welcomed to the Blue Vein Society, and had taken a leading part in its activities. Mr. Ryder had at first been attracted by her charms of person, for she was very good looking and not over twenty-five; then by her refined manners and the vivacity of her wit. Her husband had been a government clerk, and at his death had left a considerable life insurance. She was visiting friends in Groveland, and, finding the town and the people to her liking, had prolonged her stay indefinitely. She had not seemed displeased at Mr. Ryder's attentions, but on the contrary had given him every proper encouragement; indeed, a younger and less cautious man would long since have spoken. But he had made up his mind, and had only to determine the time when he would ask her to be his wife. He decided to give a ball in her honor, and at some time during the evening of the ball to offer her his heart and hand. He had no special fears about the outcome, but, with a little touch of romance, he wanted the surroundings to be in harmony with his own feelings when he should have received the answer he expected.

Mr. Ryder resolved that this ball should mark an epoch in the social history of Groveland. He knew, of course—no one could know better—the entertainments that had taken place in past years, and what must be done to surpass them. His ball must be worthy of the lady in whose honor it was to be given, and must, by the quality of its guests, set an example for the future. He had observed of late a growing liberality, almost a laxity, in social matters, even among members of his own set, and had several times been forced to meet in a social way persons whose complexions and callings in life were hardly up to the standard which he considered proper for the society to maintain. He had a theory of his own.

"I have no race prejudice," he would say, "but we people of mixed blood are ground between the upper and the nether millstone. Our fate lies between absorption by the white race and extinction in the black. The one doesn't want us yet, but may take us in time. The other would welcome us, but it would be for us a backward step. 'With malice towards none, with charity for all,' we must do the best we can for ourselves and those who are to follow us. Self-preservation is the first law of nature."

His ball would serve by its exclusiveness to counteract leveling tendencies, and his marriage with Mrs. Dixon would help to further the upward process of absorption he had been wishing and waiting for.

II

The ball was to take place on Friday night. The house had been put in order, the carpets covered with canvas, the halls and stairs decorated with palms and potted plants; and in the afternoon Mr. Ryder sat on his front porch, which the shade of a vine running up over a wire netting made a cool and pleasant lounging place. He expected to respond to the toast "The Ladies" at the supper, and from a volume of Tennyson—his favorite poet—was fortifying himself with apt quotations. The volume was open at "A Dream of Fair Women." His eyes fell on these lines, and he read them aloud to judge better of their effect:—

At length I saw a lady within call,
Stiller than chisell'd marble, standing there;
A daughter of the gods, divinely tall,
And most divinely fair.

He marked the verse, and turning the page read the stanza beginning—

O sweet pale Margaret,
O rare pale Margaret.

He weighed the passage a moment, and decided that it would not do. Mrs. Dixon was the palest lady he expected at the ball, and she was of a rather ruddy complexion, and of lively disposition and buxom build. So he ran over the leaves until his eye rested on the description of Queen Guinevere—

She seem'd a part of joyous Spring:
A gown of grass-green silk she wore,
Buckled with golden clasps before;
A light-green tuft of plumes she bore
Closed in a golden ring.

* * *

She look'd so lovely, as she sway'd
The rein with dainty finger-tips,
A man had given all other bliss,
And all his worldly worth for this,
To waste his whole heart in one kiss
Upon her perfect lips.

As Mr. Ryder murmured these words audibly, with an appreciative thrill, he heard the latch of his gate click, and a light footfall sounding on the steps. He turned his head, and saw a woman standing before his door.

She was a little woman, not five feet tall, and proportioned to her height. Although she stood erect, and looked around her with very bright and restless eyes, she seemed quite old; for her face was crossed and recrossed with a hundred wrinkles, and around the edges of her bonnet could be seen protruding here and there a tuft of short gray wool. She wore a blue calico gown of ancient cut, a little red shawl fastened around her shoulders with an old-fashioned brass brooch, and a large bonnet profusely ornamented with faded red and yellow artificial flowers. And she was very black—so black that her toothless gums, revealed when she opened her mouth to speak, were not red, but blue. She looked like a bit of the old plantation life, summoned up from the past by the wave of a magician's wand, as the poet's fancy had called into being the gracious shapes of which Mr. Ryder had just been reading.

He rose from his chair and came over to where she stood.

"Good-afternoon, madam," he said.

"Good-evenin', suh" she answered, ducking suddenly with a quaint curtsy. Her voice was shrill and piping, but softened somewhat by age. "Is dis yere whar Mistuh Ryduh lib, suh?" she asked, looking around her doubtfully, and glancing into the open windows, through which some of the preparations for the evening were visible.

"Yes," he replied, with an air of kindly patronage, unconsciously flattered by her manner, "I am Mr. Ryder. Did you want to see me?"

"Yas, suh, ef I ain't 'sturbin' of you too much."

"Not at all. Have a seat over here behind the vine, where it is cool. What can I do for you?"

" 'Scuse me, suh," she continued, when she had sat down on the edge of a chair, " 'scuse me, suh, I's lookin' for my husban'. I heerd you wuz a big man an' had libbed heah a long time, an' I 'lowed you wouldn't min' ef I'd come roun' an' ax you ef you'd ever heerd of a merlatter man by de name er Sam Taylor 'quirin' roun' in de chu'ches ermongs' de people fer his wife 'Liza Jane?"

Mr. Ryder seemed to think for a moment.

"There used to be many such cases right after the war," he said, "but it has been so long that I have forgotten them. There are very few now. But tell me your story, and it may refresh my memory."

She sat back farther in her chair so as to be more comfortable, and folded her withered hands in her lap.

"My name's 'Liza," she began, " 'Liza Jane. W'en I wuz young I us'ter b'long ter Marse Bob Smif, down in ole Missoura. I wuz bawn down dere. W'en I wuz a gal I wuz married ter a man named Jim. But Jim died, an' after dat I married a merlatter man named Sam Taylor. Sam wuz freebawn, but his mammy and daddy died, an' de w'ite folks 'prenticed him ter my marster fer ter work fer 'im 'tel he wuz growed up. Sam worked in de fiel', an' I wuz de cook. One day Ma'y Ann, ole miss's maid, came rushin' out ter de kitchen, an' says she, ' 'Liza Jane, ole marse gwine sell yo' Sam down de ribber.'

" 'Go way f'm yere,' says I; 'my husban' 's free!'

" 'Don' make no diff'ence. I heerd ole marse tell ole miss he wuz gwine take yo' Sam 'way wid 'im ter-morrow, fer he needed money, an' he knowed whar he could git a t'ousan' dollars fer Sam an' no questions axed.'

"W'en Sam come home f'm de fiel' dat night, I tole him 'bout ole marse gwine steal 'im, an' Sam run erway. His time wuz mos up, an' he swo' dat w'en he wuz twenty-one he would come back an' he'p me run erway, er else save up de money ter buy my freedom. An' I know he'd 'a' done it, fer he thought a heap er me, Sam did. But w'en he come back he didn' fin' me, fer I wuzn' dere. Ole marse had heerd dat I warned Sam, so he had me whip' an' sol' down de ribber.

"Den de wah broke out, an' w'en it wuz ober de cullud folks wuz scattered. I went back ter de ole home; but Sam wuzn' dere, an' I couldn' l'arn nuffin' 'bout 'im. But I knowed he'd be'n dere to look fer me an' hadn' foun' me, an' had gone erway ter hunt fer me.

"I's be'n lookin' fer 'im eber sence," she added simply, as though twenty-five years were but a couple of weeks, "an' I knows he's be'n lookin' fer me. Fer he sot a heap er sto' by me, Sam did, an' I know he's be'n huntin' fer me all dese years—'less'n he's be'n sick er sump'n, so he couldn' work, er out'n his head, so he couldn' 'member his promise. I went back down de ribber, fer I 'lowed he'd gone down dere lookin' fer me. I's be'n ter Noo Orleens, an' Atlanty, an' Charleston, an' Richmon'; an' w'en I'd be'n all ober de Souf I come ter de Norf. Fer I knows I'll fin' 'im some er dese days," she added softly, "er he'll fin' me, an' den we'll bofe be as happy in freedom as we wuz in de ole days befo' de wah." A smile stole over her withered countenance as she paused a moment, and her bright eyes softened into a faraway look.

This was the substance of the old woman's story. She had wandered a little here and there. Mr. Ryder was looking at her curiously when she finished.

"How have you lived all these years?" he asked.

"Cookin', suh. I's a good cook. Does you know anybody w'at needs a good cook, suh? I's stoppin' wid a culled fam'ly roun' de corner yonder 'tel I kin git a place."

"Do you really expect to find your husband? He may be dead long ago."

She shook her head emphatically. "Oh no, he ain' dead. De signs an' de tokens tells me. I dremp three nights runnin' on'y dis las' week dat I foun' him."

"He may have married another woman. Your slave marriage would not have prevented him, for you never lived with him after the war, and without that your marriage doesn't count."

"Wouldn' make no diff'ence wid Sam. He wouldn' marry no yuther 'ooman 'tel he foun' out 'bout me. I knows it," she added. "Sump'n's be'n tellin' me all dese years dat I's gwine fin' Sam 'fo' I dies."

"Perhaps he's outgrown you, and climbed up in the world where he wouldn't care to have you find him."

"No, indeed, suh," she replied, "Sam ain' dat kin' er man. He wuz good ter me, Sam wuz, but he wuz n' much good ter nobody e'se, fer he wuz one er de triflin'es' han's on de plantation. I 'spec's ter haf ter suppo't 'im w'en I fin' 'im, fer he nebber would work 'less'n he had ter. But den he wuz free, an' he didn' git no pay fer his work, an' I don' blame 'im much. Mebbe he's done better sence he run erway, but I ain' 'spectin' much."

"You may have passed him on the street a hundred times during the twenty-five years, and not have known him; time works great changes."

She smiled incredulously. "I'd know 'im 'mongs' a hund'ed men. Fer dey wuzn' no yuther merlatter man like my man Sam, an' I couldn' be mistook. I's toted his picture roun' wid me twenty-five years."

"May I see it?" asked Mr. Ryder. "It might help me to remember whether I have seen the original."

As she drew a small parcel from her bosom he saw that it was fastened to a string that went around her neck. Removing several wrappers, she brought to light an old fashioned daguerreotype in a black case. He looked long and intently at the portrait. It was faded with time, but the features were still distinct, and it was easy to see what manner of man it had represented.

He closed the case, and with a slow movement handed it back to her.

"I don't know of any man in town who goes by that name," he said, "nor have I heard of any one making such inquiries. But if you will leave me your address, I will give the matter some attention, and if I find out anything I will let you know."

She gave him the number of a house in the neighborhood, and went away, after thanking him warmly.

He wrote the address on the fly-leaf of the volume of Tennyson, and, when she had gone, rose to his feet and stood looking after her curiously. As she walked down the street with mincing step, he saw several persons whom she passed turn and look back at her with a smile of kindly amusement. When she had turned the corner, he went upstairs to his bedroom, and stood for a long time before the mirror of his dressing-case, gazing thoughtfully at the reflection of his own face.

III

At eight o'clock the ballroom was a blaze of light and the guests had begun to assemble; for there was a literary programme and some routine business of the society to be gone through with before the dancing. A black servant in evening dress waited at the door and directed the guests to the dressing-rooms.

The occasion was long memorable among the colored people of the city; not alone for the dress and display, but for the high average of intelligence and culture that distinguished the gathering as a whole. There were a number of school-teachers, several young doctors, three or four lawyers, some professional singers, an editor, a lieutenant in the United States army spending his furlough in the city, and others in various polite callings; these were colored, though most of them would not have attracted even a casual glance because of any marked difference from white people. Most of the ladies were in evening costume, and dress coats and dancing pumps were the rule among the men. A band of string music, stationed in an alcove behind a row of palms, played popular airs while the guests were gathering.

The dancing began at half past nine. At eleven o'clock supper was served. Mr. Ryder had left the ballroom some little time before the intermission, but reappeared at the supper-table. The spread was worthy of the occasion, and the guests did full justice to it. When the coffee had been served, the toastmaster, Mr. Solomon Sadler, rapped for order. He made a brief introductory speech, complimenting host and guests, and then presented in their order the toasts of the evening. They were responded to with a very fair display of after-dinner wit.

"The last toast," said the toast-master, when he reached the end of the list, "is one which must appeal to us all. There is no one of us of the sterner sex who is not at some time dependent upon woman—in infancy for protection, in manhood for companionship, in old age for care and comforting. Our good host has been trying to live alone, but the fair faces I see around me to-night prove that he too is largely dependent upon the gentler sex for most that makes life worth living—the society and love of friends—and rumor is at fault if he does not soon yield entire subjection to one of them. Mr. Ryder will now respond to the toast—The Ladies."

There was a pensive look in Mr. Ryder's eyes as he took the floor and adjusted his eyeglasses. He began by speaking of woman as the gift of Heaven to man, and after some general observations on the relations of the sexes he said: "But perhaps the quality which most distinguishes woman is her fidelity and devotion to those she loves. History is full of examples, but has recorded none more striking than one which only to-day came under my notice."

He then related, simply but effectively, the story told by his visitor of the afternoon. He gave it in the same soft dialect, which came readily to his lips, while the company listened attentively and sympathetically. For the story had awakened a responsive thrill in many hearts. There were some present who had seen, and others who had heard their fathers and grandfathers tell, the wrongs and sufferings of this past generation, and all of them still felt, in their darker moments, the shadow hanging over them. Mr. Ryder went on—

"Such devotion and confidence are rare even among women. There are many who would have searched a year, some who would have waited five years, a few who might have hoped ten years; but for twenty-five years this woman has retained her affection for and her faith in a man she has not seen or heard of in all that time.

"She came to me to-day in the hope that I might be able to help her find this long-lost husband. And when she was gone I gave my fancy rein, and imagined a case I will put to you.

"Suppose that this husband, soon after his escape, had learned that his wife had been sold away, and that such inquiries as he could make brought no information of her whereabouts. Suppose that he was young, and she much older than he; that he was light, and she was black; that their marriage was a slave marriage, and legally binding only if they chose to make it so after the war. Suppose, too, that he made his way to the North as some of us have done, and there, where he had larger opportunities, had improved them, and had in the course of all these years grown to be as different from the ignorant boy who ran away from fear of slavery as the day is from the night. Suppose, even, that he had qualified himself, by industry, by thrift, and by study, to win the friendship and be considered worthy the society of such people as these I see around me to-night, gracing my board and filling my heart with gladness; for I am old enough to remember the day when such a gathering would not have been possible in this land. Suppose, too, that, as the years went by, this man's memory of the past grew more and more indistinct, until at last it was rarely, except in his dreams, that any image of this bygone period rose before his mind. And then suppose that accident should bring to his knowledge the fact that the wife of his youth, the wife he had left behind him—not one who had walked by his side and kept pace with him in his upward struggle, but one upon whom advancing years and a laborious life had set their mark—was alive and seeking him, but that he was absolutely safe from recognition or discovery, unless he chose to reveal himself. My friends, what would the man do? I will presume that he was one who loved honor, and tried to deal justly with all men. I will even carry the case further, and suppose that perhaps he had set his heart upon another, whom he had hoped to call his own. What would he do, or rather what ought he to do, in such a crisis of a lifetime?

"It seemed to me that he might hesitate, and I imagined that I was an old friend, a near friend, and that he had come to me for advice; and I argued the case with him. I tried to discuss it impartially. After we had looked upon the matter from every point of view, I said to him, in words that we all know—

This above all: to thine own self be true,
And it must follow, as the night the day,
Thou canst not then be false to any man.

"Then, finally, I put the question to him, 'Shall you acknowledge her?'

"And now, ladies and gentlemen, friends and companions, I ask you, what should he have done?"

There was something in Mr. Ryder's voice that stirred the hearts of those who sat around him. It suggested more than mere sympathy with an imaginary situation; it seemed rather in the nature of a personal appeal. It was observed, too, that his look rested more especially upon Mrs. Dixon, with a mingled expression of renunciation and inquiry.

She had listened, with parted lips and streaming eyes. She was the first to speak: "He should have acknowledged her."

"Yes," they all echoed, "he should have acknowledged her."

"My friends and companions," responded Mr. Ryder, "I thank you, one and all. It is the answer I expected, for I knew your hearts."

He turned and walked toward the closed door of an adjoining room, while every eye followed him in wondering curiosity. He came back in a moment, leading by the hand his visitor of the afternoon, who stood startled and trembling at the sudden plunge into this scene of brilliant gayety. She was neatly dressed in gray, and wore the white cap of an elderly woman.

"Ladies and gentlemen," he said, "this is the woman, and I am the man, whose story I have told you. Permit me to introduce to you the wife of my youth."

The Goophered Grapevine

Some years ago my wife was in poor health, and our family doctor, in whose skill and honesty I had implicit confidence, advised a change of climate. I shared, from an unprofessional standpoint, his opinion that the raw winds, the chill rains, and the violent changes of temperature that characterized the winters in the region of the Great Lakes tended to aggravate my wife's difficulty, and would undoubtedly shorten her life if she remained exposed to them. The doctor's advice was that we seek, not a temporary place of sojourn, but a permanent residence, in a warmer and more equable climate. I was engaged at the time in grape-culture in Northern Ohio, and, as I liked the business and had given it much study, I decided to look for some other locality suitable for carrying it on. I thought of sunny France, of sleepy Spain, of Southern California, but there were objections to them all. It occurred to me that I might find what I wanted in some one of our own Southern States. It was a sufficient time after the war for conditions in the South to have become somewhat settled; and I was enough of a pioneer to start a new industry, if I could not find a place where grape-culture had been tried. I wrote to a cousin who had gone into the turpentine business in central North Carolina. He assured me, in response to my inquiries, that no better place could be found in the South than the State and neighborhood where he lived; the climate was perfect for health, land, in conjunction with the soil, ideal for grape-culture; labor was cheap, and land could be bought for a mere song. He gave us a cordial invitation to come and visit him while we looked into the matter. We accepted the invitation, and after several days of leisurely travel, the last hundred miles of which were up a river on a sidewheel steamer, we reached our destination, a quaint old town, which I shall call Patesville, because, for one reason, that is not its name. There was a red brick market-house in the public square, with a tall tower, which held a four-faced clock that struck the hours, and from which there pealed out a curfew at nine o'clock. There were two or three hotels, a court-house, a jail, stores, offices, and all the appurtenances of a county seat and a commercial emporium; for while Patesville numbered only four or five thousand inhabitants, of all shades of complexion, it was one of the principal towns in North Carolina, and had a considerable trade in cotton and naval stores. This business activity was not immediately apparent to my unaccustomed eyes. Indeed, when I first saw the town, there brooded over it a calm that seemed almost sabbatic in its restfulness, though I learned later on that underneath its somnolent exterior the deeper currents of life—love and hatred, joy and despair, ambition and avarice, faith and friendship—flowed not less steadily than in livelier latitudes.

We found the weather delightful at that season, the end of summer, and were hospitably entertained. Our host was a man of means and evidently regarded our visit as a pleasure, and we were therefore correspondingly at our ease, and in a position to act with the coolness of judgment desirable in making so radical a change in our lives. My cousin placed a horse and buggy at our disposal, and himself acted as our guide until I became somewhat familiar with the country.

I found that grape-culture, while it had never been carried on to any great extent, was not entirely unknown in the neighborhood. Several planters thereabouts had attempted it on a commercial scale, in former years, with greater or less success; but like most Southern industries, it had felt the blight of war and had fallen into desuetude.

I went several times to look at a place that I thought might suit me. It was a plantation of considerable extent, that had formerly belonged to a wealthy man by the name of McAdoo. The estate had been for years involved in litigation between disputing heirs, during which period shiftless cultivation had well-nigh exhausted the soil. There had been a vineyard of some extent on the place, but it had not been attended to since the war, and had lapsed into utter neglect.

The vines—here partly supported by decayed and broken-down trellises, there twining themselves among the branches of the slender saplings which had sprung up among them—grew in wild and unpruned luxuriance, and the few scattered grapes they bore were the undisputed prey of the first comer. The site was admirably adapted to grape-raising; the soil, with a little attention, could not have been better; and with the native grape, the luscious scuppernong, as my main reliance in the beginning, I felt sure that I could introduce and cultivate successfully a number of other varieties.

One day I went over with my wife to show her the place. We drove out of the town over a long wooden bridge that spanned a spreading mill-pond, passed the long whitewashed fence surrounding the county fair-ground, and struck into a road so sandy that the horse's feet sank to the fetlocks. Our route lay partly up hill and partly down, for we were in the sand-hill county; we drove past cultivated farms, and then by abandoned fields grown up in scrub-oak and short-leaved pine, and once or twice through the solemn aisles of the virgin forest, where the tall pines, well-nigh meeting over the narrow road, shut out the sun, and wrapped us in cloistral solitude. Once, at a cross-roads, I was in doubt as to the turn to take, and we sat there waiting ten minutes—we had already caught some of the native infection of restfulness—for some human being to come along, who could direct us on our way. At length a little negro girl appeared, walking straight as an arrow, with a piggin full of water on her head. After a little patient investigation, necessary to overcome the child's shyness, we learned what we wished to know, and at the end of about five miles from the town reached our destination.

We drove between a pair of decayed gateposts—the gate itself had long since disappeared—and up a straight sandy lane, between two lines of rotting rail fence, partly concealed by jimson-weeds and briers, to the open space where a dwelling-house had once stood, evidently a spacious mansion, if we might judge from the ruined chimneys that were still standing, and the brick pillars on which the sills rested. The house itself, we had been informed, had fallen a victim to the fortunes of war.

We alighted from the buggy, walked about the yard for a while, and then wandered off into the adjoining vineyard. Upon Annie's complaining of weariness I led the way back to the yard, where a pine log, lying under a spreading elm, afforded a shady though somewhat hard seat. One end of the log was already occupied by a venerable looking colored man. He held on his knees a hat full of grapes, over which he was smacking his lips with great gusto, and a pile of grapeskins near him indicate that the performance was no new thing. We approached him at an angle from the rear, and were close to him before he perceived us. He respectfully rose as we drew near, and was moving away, when I begged him to keep his seat.

"Don't let us disturb you," I said. "There is plenty of room for us all."

He resumed his seat with somewhat of embarrassment. While he had been standing, I had observed that he was a tall man, and, though slightly bowed by the weight of years, apparently quite vigorous. He was not entirely black, and this fact, together with the quality of his hair, which was about six inches long and very bushy, except on the top of his head, where he was quite bald, suggested a slight strain of other than negro blood. There was a shrewdness in his eyes, too, which was not altogether African, and which, as we afterwards learned from experience was indicative of a corresponding shrewdness in his character. He went on eating the grapes, but did not seem to enjoy himself quite so well as he had apparently done before he became aware of our presence.

"Do you live around here?" I asked, anxious to put him at his ease.

"Yas, suh. I lives des ober yander, behine de nex' san'-hill, on de Lumberton plank-road."

"Do you know anything about the time when this vineyard was cultivated?"

"Lawd bless you, suh, I knows all about it. Dey ain' na'er a man in dis settlement w'at won' tell you ole Julius McAdoo 'uz bawn en raise' on dis yer same plantation. Is you de Norv'n gemman w'at's gwine ter buy de ole vimya'd?"

"I am looking at it," I replied; "but I don't know that I shall care to buy unless I can be reasonably sure of making something out of it."

"Well, suh, you is a stranger ter me, en I is a stranger ter you, en we is bofe strangers ter one anudder, but 'f I 'uz in yo' place, I wouldn' buy dis vim ya'd."

"Why not?" I asked.

"Well, I dunno whe'r you believes in cunj'in'er not—some er de w'ite folks don't, er says dey don't—but de truf er de matter is dat dis yer ole vimya'd is goophered."

"Is what?" I asked, not grasping the meaning of this unfamiliar word.

"Is goophered—cunju'd, bewitch'."

He imparted this information with such solemn earnestness, and with such an air of confidential mystery, that I felt somewhat interested, while Annie was evidently much impressed, and drew closer to me.

"How do you know it is bewitched?" I asked.

"I wouldn' spec' fer you ter b'lieve me 'less you know all 'bout de fac's. But ef you en young miss dere doan' min' lis'nin' ter a ole nigger run on a minute er two w'ile you er restin', I kin 'splain to you how it all happen'."

We assured him that we would be glad to hear how it all happened, and he began to tell us. At first the current of his memory—or imagination—seemed somewhat sluggish; but as his embarrassment wore off, his language flowed more freely, and the story acquired perspective and coherence. As he became more and more absorbed in the narrative, his eyes assumed a dreamy expression, and he seemed to lose sight of his auditors, and to be living over again in monologue his life on the old plantation.

"Ole Mars Dugal' McAdoo," he began, "bought dis place long many year befo' de wah, en I 'member well w'en he sot out all dis yer part er de plantation in scuppernon's. De vimes growed monst'us fas', en Mars Dugal' made a thousan' gallon er scuppernon' wine eve'y year.

"Now, ef dey's an'thing a nigger lub, nex' ter 'possum, en chick'n, en watermillyums, it's scuppernon's. Dey ain' nuffin dat kin stan' up side'n de scuppernon' for sweetness; sugar ain't a suckumstance ter scuppernon'. W'en de season is nigh 'bout ober, en de grapes begin ter swivel up des a little wid de wrinkles er ole age—w'en de skin git sot' en brown—den de scuppernon' make you smack yo' lip en roll yo' eye en wush fer mo'; so I reckon it ain' very 'stonishin' dat niggers lub scuppernon'.

"Dey wuz a sight er niggers in de naberhood er de vimya'd. Dere wuz ole Mars Henry Brayboy's niggers, en ol Mars Jeems McLean's niggers, en Mars Dugal's own niggers; den dey wuz a settlement er free niggers en po' buckrahs down by de Wim'l'-ton Road, en Mars Dugal' had de only vimya'd in de naberhood. I reckon it ain' so much so nowadays, but befo' de wah, in slab'ry times, a nigger didn' mine goin' fi' er ten mile in a night, w'en dey wuz sump'n good ter eat at de yuther een'.

"So atter a w'ile Mars Dugal' begin ter miss his scuppernon's. Co'se he 'cuse' de niggers fer it, but dey all 'nied it ter de las'. Mars Dugal' sot spring guns en steel traps, en he en de oberseah sot up nights once't er twice't, tel one night Mars Dugal'—he 'uz a monst'us keerless man—got his leg shot full er cow-peas. But somehow er nudder dey couldn' nebber ketch none er de niggers.

I dunner how it happen, but it happen des like I tell you, en de grapes kep' on a-goin' des de same.

"But bimeby ole Mars Dugal' fix' up a plan ter stop it. Dey wuz a cunjuh 'oman livin' down 'mongs' de free niggers on de Wim'l'ton Road, en all de darkies fum Rockfish ter Beaver Crick wuz feared er her. She could wuk de mos' powerfulles' kin' er goopher—could make people hab fits, er rheumatiz, er make 'em des dwinel away en die; en dey say she went out ridin' de niggers at night, fer she wuz a witch 'sides bein' a cunjuh 'oman. Mars Dugal' hearn 'bout Aun' Peggy's doin's, en begun ter 'flect whe'r er no he couldn' git her ter he'p him keep de niggers off'n de grapevimes. One day in de spring er de year, ole miss pack' up a basket er chick'n en poun'-cake, en a bottle er scuppernon' wine, en Mars Dugal' tuk it in his buggy en driv ober ter Aun' Peggy's cabin.

He tuk de basket in, en had a long talk wid Aun' Peggy.

"De nex' day Aun' Peggy come up ter de vimya'd. De niggers seed her slippin' 'roun', en dey soon foun' out what she 'uz doin' dere. Mars Dugal' had hi'ed her ter goopher de grape vimes. She sa'ntered 'roun' 'mongs' de vimes, en tuk a leaf fum dis one, en a grape-hull fum dat one, en a grape-seed fum anudder one; en den a little twig fum here, en a little pinch er dirt fum dere—en put it all in a big black bottle, wid a snake's toof en a speckle' hen's gall en some ha'rs fum a black cat's tail, en den fill' de bottle wid scuppernon' wine. W'en she got de goopher all ready en fix', she tuk'n went out in de woods en buried it under de root uv a red oak tree, en den come back en tole one er de niggers she done goopher de grapevimes, en a'er a nigger w'at eat dem grapes 'ud be sho ter die inside'n twel' mont's.

"Atter dat de niggers let de scuppernon's 'lone, en Mars Dugal' didn' hab no 'casion ter fine no mo' fault; en de season wuz mos' gone, w'en a strange gemman stop at de plantation one night ter see Mars Dugal' on some business; en his coachman, seein' de scuppernon's growin' so nice en sweet, slip 'roun' behine de smoke-house, en et all de scuppernon's he could hole. Nobody didn' notice it at de time, but dat night, on de way home, de gemman's hoss runned away en kill' de coachman. W'en we hearn de noos, Aun' Lucy, de cook, she up'n say she seed de strange nigger eat'n' er de scuppernon's behine de smoke-house; en den we knowed de goopher had b'en er wukkin'. Den one er de nigger chilluns runned away fum de quarters one day, en got in de scuppernon's, en died de nex' week. W'ite folks say he die' er de fevuh, but de niggers knowed it wuz de goopher. So you k'n be sho de darkies didn' hab much ter do wid dem scuppernon' vimes.

"W'en de scuppernon' season uz ober fer dat year, Mars Dugal' foun' he had made fifteen hund'ed gallon er wine; en one er de niggers hearn him laffin wid de oberseah fit ter kill, en sayin dem fifteen hund'ed gallon er wine wuz monst'us good intrus' on de ten dollars he laid out on de vimya'd. So I 'low ez he paid Aun' Peggy ten dollars fer to goopher de grapevimes.

"De goopher didn' wuk no mo' tel de nex' summer, w'en 'long to'ds de middle er de season one er de fiel' han's died; en ez dat let' Mars Dugal' sho't er han's, he went off ter town fer ter buy anudder. He fotch de noo nigger home wid 'im. He wuz er ole nigger, er de color er a gingy-cake, en ball ez a hoss-apple on de top er his head. He wuz a peart ole nigger, do', en could do a big day's wuk.

"Now it happen dat one er de niggers on de nex' plantation, one er old Mars Henry Brayboy's niggers, had runned away de day befo', en tuk ter de swamp, en ole Mars Dugal' en some er de yuther nabor w'ite folks had gone out wid dere guns en dere dogs fer ter he'p 'em hunt fer de nigger; en de han's on our own plantation wuz all so flusterated dat we fuhgot ter tell de noo han' 'bout de goopher on de scuppernon' vimes. Co'se he smell de grapes en see de vimes, an atter dahk de fus' thing he done wuz ter slip off ter de grapevimes 'dout sayin' nuffin ter nobody. Nex' mawnin' he tole some er de niggers 'bout de fine bait er scuppernon' he et de night befo'.

"W'en dey tole 'im 'bout de goopher on de grapevimes, he 'uz dat tarrified dat he turn pale, en look des like he gwine ter die right in his tracks. De oberseah come up en axed w'at 'uz de matter; en w'en dey tole 'im Henry be'n eatin' er de scuppernon's, en got de goopher on 'im, he gin Henry a big drink er w'iskey, en 'low dat de nex' rainy day he take 'im ober ter Aun' Peggy's, en see ef she wouldn' take de goopher off'n him, seein' ez he didn' know nuffin erbout it tel he done et de grapes.

"Sho nuff, it rain de nex' day, en de oberseah went ober ter Aun' Peggy's wid Henry. En Aun' Peggy say dat bein' ez Henry didn' know 'bout de goopher, en et de grapes in ign'ance er de conseq'ences, she reckon she mought be able fer ter take de goopher off'n him. So she fotch out er bottle wid some cunjuh medicine in it, en po'd some out in a go'd for Henry ter drink. He manage ter git it down; he say it tas'e like whiskey wid sump'n bitter in it. She 'lowed dat 'ud keep de goopher off'n him tel de spring: but w'en de sap begin ter rise in de grapevimes he ha' ter come en see her ag'in, en she tell him w'at e's ter do.

"Nex' spring, w'en de sap commence' ter rise in de scuppernon' vime, Henry tuk a ham one night. Whar'd he git de ham? *I* doan know; dey wa'n't no hams on de plantation 'cep'n' w'at 'uz in de smoke-house, but *I* never see Henry 'bout de smoke-house. But ez I wuz a-sayin', he tuk de ham ober ter Aun' Peggy's; en Aun' Peggy tole 'im dat w'en Mars Dugal' begin ter prune de grapevimes, he mus' go en take 'n scrape off de sap whar it ooze out'n de cut een's er de vimes, en 'n'int his ball head wid it; en ef he do dat once't a year de goopher wouldn' wuk agin 'im long ez he done it. En bein' ez he fotch her de ham, she fix' it so he kin eat all de scuppernon' he want.

"So Henry 'n'int his head wid de sap out'n de big grapevime des ha'f way 'twix' de quarters en de big house, en de goopher nebber wuk agin him dat summer. But de beatenes' thing you eber see happen ter Henry. Up ter dat time he wuz ez ball ez a sweeten' 'tater, but des ez soon ez de young leaves begun ter come out on de grapevimes, de ha'r begun ter grow out on Henry's head, en by de middle er de summer he had de bigges' head er ha'r on de plantation. Befo' dat, Henry had tol'able good ha'r 'roun' de aidges, but soon ez de young grapes begun ter come, Henry's ha'r begun to quirl all up in little balls, de like dis yer reg'lar grapy ha'r, en by de time de grapes got ripe his head look des like a bunch er grapes. Combin' it didn' do no good; he wuk at it ha'f de night wid er Jim Crow,[1] en think he git it straighten' out, but in de mawnin' de grapes 'ud be dere des de same. So he gin it up, en tried ter keep de grapes down by havin' his hair cut sho't.

"But dat wa'n't de quares' thing 'bout de goopher. When Henry come ter de plantation, he wuz gittin' a little ole an stiff in de j'ints. But dat summer he got des ez spry en libely ez any young nigger on de plantation; fac', he got so biggity dat Mars Jackson, de oberseah, ha' ter th'eaten ter whip 'im, ef he didn' stop cuttin' up his didos en behave hisse'f. But de mos' cur'ouses' thing happen' in de fall, when de sap begin ter go down in de grapevimes. Fus', when de grapes 'uz gethered, de knots begun ter straighten out'n Henry's ha'r; en w'en de leaves begin ter fall, Henry's ha'r 'mence' ter drap out; en when de vimes 'uz bar', Henry's head wuz baller'n it wuz in de spring, en he begin ter git ole en stiff in de j'ints ag'in, en paid no mo' 'tention ter de gals dyoin' er de whole winter. En nex' spring, w'en he rub de sap on ag'in, he got young ag'in, en so soopl en libely dat none er de young niggers on de plantation couldn' jump, ner dance, ner hoe ez much cotton ez Henry. But in de fall er de year his grapes 'mence' ter straighten out, en his j'ints ter git stiff, en his ha'r drap off, en de rheumatic begin ter wrestle wid 'im.

"Now, ef you'd 'a' knowed ole Mars Dugal' McAdoo, you'd 'a' knowed dat it ha' ter be a mighty rainy day when he couldn' fine sump'n fer his niggers ter do, en it ha' ter be a mighty little hole he could n' crawl thoo, en ha' ter be a monst'us cloudy night when a dollar git by him in de dahkness; en w'en he see how Henry git young

1. A small card, resembling a currycomb, used by negroes in the rural districts instead of a comb.

in de spring en ole in de fall, he 'lowed ter hisse'f ez how he could make mo' money out'n Henry dan by wukkin' him in de cotton-fiel'. 'Long de nex' spring, atter de sap 'mence' ter rise, en Henry 'n'int 'is head en sta'ted fer ter git young en soopl, Mars Dugal' up 'n tuk Henry ter town, en sole 'im fer fifteen hunder' dollars. Co'se de man w'at bought Henry didn' know nuffin 'bout de goopher, en Mars Dugal' didn' see no 'casion fer ter tell 'im. Long to'ds de fall, w'en de sap went down, Henry begin ter git ole skin same ez yuzhal, en his noo marster begin ter git skeered les'n he gwine ter lose his fifteen-hunder'-dollar nigger. He sent fer a mighty fine doctor, but de med'cine didn' 'pear ter do no good; de goopher had a good holt. Henry tole de doctor 'bout de goopher, but de doctor des laff at 'im.

"One day in de winter Mars Dugal' went ter town, en wuz santerin' 'long de Main Street, when who should he meet but Henry's noo marster. Dey said 'Hoddy,' en Mars Dugal' ax 'im ter hab a seegyar; en atter dey run on awhile 'bout de craps en de weather, Mars Dugal' ax 'im, sorter keerless, like ez ef he des thought of it—

" 'How you like de nigger I sole you las' spring?'

"Henry's marster shuck his head en knock de ashes off'n his seegyar.

" 'Spec' I made a bad bahgin when I bought dat nigger. Henry done good wuk all de summer, but sence de fall set in he 'pears ter be sorter pinin' away. Dey ain' nuffin pertickler de matter wid 'im—leastways de doctor say so—'cep'n' a tech er de rheumatiz; but his ha'r is all fell out, en ef he don't pick up his strenk mighty soon, I spec' I'm gwine ter lose 'im.'

"Dey smoked on awhile, en bimeby ole mars say, 'Well, a bahgin's a bahgin, but you en me is good fren's, en I doan wan' ter see you lose all de money you paid fer dat nigger; en ef w'at you say is so, en I ain't 'sputin' it, he ain't wuf much now. I 'spec's you wukked him too ha'd dis summer, er e'se de swamps down here don't agree wid de san'-hill nigger. So you des lemme know, en ef he gits any wusser I'll be willin' ter gib yer five hund'ed dollars fer 'im, en take my chances on his livin'.'

"Sho 'nuff, when Henry begun ter draw up wid de rheumatiz en it look like he gwine ter die fer sho, his noo marster sen' fer Mars Dugal', en Mars Dugal' gin him what he promus, en brung Henry home ag'in. He tuk good keer uv 'im dyoin' er de winter—give 'im w'iskey ter rub his rheumatiz, en terbacker ter smoke, en all he want ter eat—'caze a nigger w'at he could make a thousan' dollars a year off'n didn' grow on eve'y huckleberry bush.

"Nex' spring, w'en de sap ris en Henry's ha'r commence' ter sprout, Mars Dugal' sole 'im ag'in, down in Robeson County dis time; en he kep' dat sellin' business up fer five year er mo'. Henry nebber say nuffin 'bout de goopher ter his noo marsters, 'caze he know he gwine ter be tuk good keer uv de nex' winter, w'en Mars Dugal' buy him back. En Mars Dugal' made 'nuff money off'n Henry ter buy anudder plantation ober on Beaver Crick.

"But 'long 'bout de een' er dat five year dey come a stranger ter stop at de plantation. De fus' day he 'uz dere he went out wid Mars Dugal' en spent all de mawnin' lookin' ober de vimya'd, en atter dinner dey spent all de evenin' playin' kya'ds. De niggers soon 'skiver' dat he wuz a Yankee, en dat he come down ter Norf C'lina fer ter l'arn de w'ite folks how to raise grapes en make wine. He promus Mars Dugal' he c'd make de grapevimes b'ar twice't ez many grapes, en dat de noo winepress he wuz a-sellin' would make mo' d'n twice't ez many gallons er wine. En ole Mars Dugal' des drunk it all in, des 'peared ter be bewitch' wid dat Yankee. W'en de darkies see dat Yankee runnin' 'roun' de vimya'd en diggin' under de grapevimes, dey shuk dere heads, en 'lowed dat dey feared Mars Dugal' losin' his min'. Mars Dugal' had all de dirt dug away fum under de roots er all de scuppernon' vimes, an' let 'em stan' dat away fer a week er mo'. Den dat Yankee made de niggers fix up a mixtry er lime en ashes en manyo, en po' it 'roun' de roots er de grapevimes. Den he 'vise Mars Dugal' fer ter trim de vimes close't, en Mars Dugal' tuck 'n done eve'ything de Yankee tole him ter do. Dyoin' all er dis time, mind yer, dis yer Yankee wuz libbin' off'n de fat er de lan', at de big house, en playin' kya'ds wid Mars Dugal' eve'y night; en dey say Mars Dugal'los' mo'n a thousan' dollars dyoin' er de week dat Yankee wuz a-ruinin' de grapevimes.

"W'en de sap ris nex' spring, ole Henry 'n'inted his head ez yuzhal, en his ha'r 'mence' ter grow des de same ez it done eve'y year. De scuppernon' vimes growed monst's fas', en de leaves wuz greener en thicker den dey eber be'n dyoin' my rememb'ance; en Henry's ha'r growed out thicker den eber, en he 'peared ter git younger 'n younger, en soopler 'n soopler; en seein' ez he wuz sho't er han's dat spring, havin' tuk in consid'able noo groun', Mars Dugal' 'cluded he wouldn' sell Henry 'tel he git de crap in en de cotton chop'. So he kep' Henry on de plantation.

"But 'long 'bout time fer de grapes ter come on de scuppernon' vimes, dey 'peared ter come a change ober 'em; de leaves withered en swivel' up, en de young grapes turn' yaller, en bimeby eve'ybody on de plantation could see dat de whole vimya'd wuz dyin'. Mars Dugal' tuk'n water de vimes en done all he could, but 't wa'n' no use: dat Yankee had done bus' de watermillyum. One time de vimes picked up a bit, en Mars Dugal' 'lowed dey wuz gwine ter come out ag'in; but dat Yankee done dug too close under de roots, en prune de branches too close ter de vime, en all dat lime en ashes done burn' de life out'n de vimes, en dey des kep' a-with'in' en a-swivelin'.

"All dis time de goopher wuz a-wukkin'. When de vimes sta'ted ter wither, Henry 'mence' ter complain er his rheumatiz; en when de leaves begin ter dry up, his ha'r' 'mence' ter drap out. When de vimes fresh' up a bit, Henry'd git peart ag'in, en when de vimes wither' ag'in, Henry'd git ole ag'in, en des kep' gittin' mo' en mo' fitten fer nuffin; he des pined away, en pined away, en fine'ly tuk ter his cabin; en when de big vime whar he got de sap ter 'n'int his head withered en turned yaller en died, Henry died too—des went out sorter like a cannel. Dey didn't 'pear ter be nuffin de matter wid 'im, 'cep'n' de rheumatiz, but his strenk des dwinel' away 'tel he didn' hab ernuff lef' ter draw his bref. De goopher had got de under bolt, en th'owed Henry dat time fer good en all.

"Mars Dugal' tuk on might'ly 'bout losin' his vimes en his nigger in de same year; en he swo' dat ef he could git holt er dat Yankee he'd wear 'im ter a frazzle, en den chaw up de frazzle; en he'd done it, too, for Mars Dugal' 'uz a monst'us brash man w'en he once git started. He sot de vimya'd out ober ag'in, but it wuz th'ee er fo' year befo' de vimes got ter b'arin' any scuppernon's.

"W'en de wah broke out, Mars Dugal' raise' a comp'ny, en went off ter fight de Yankees. He say he wuz mighty glad dat wah come, en he des want ter kill a Yankee fer eve'y dollar he los' 'long er dat grape-raisin' Yankee.

En I 'spec' he would 'a' done it, too, ef de Yankees hadn' s'picioned sump'n en killed him fus'. Atter de s'render ole miss move' ter town, de niggers all scattered 'way fum de plantation, en de vimya'd ain' be'n cultervated sence."

"Is that story true?" asked Annie doubtfully, but seriously, as the old man concluded his narrative.

"It's des ez true ez I'm a-settin' here, miss. Dey's a easy way ter prove it: I kin lead de way right ter Henry's grave ober yander in de plantation buryin'-groun'. En I tell yer w'at, marster, I wouldn' 'vise you to buy dis yer ole vimya'd, 'caze de goopher's on it yit, en dey ain' no tellin' w'en it's gwine ter crap out."

"But I thought you said all the old; vines died."

"Dey did 'pear ter die, but a few un 'em come out ag'in, en is mixed in 'mongs' de yuthers. I ain' skeered ter eat de grapes, 'caze I knows de old vimes fum de noo ones; but wid strangers dey ain' no tellin' w'at mought happen. I wouldn' 'vise yer ter buy dis vimya'd."

I bought the vineyard, nevertheless, and it has been for a long time in a thriving condition, and is often referred to by the local press as a striking illustration of the opportunities open to Northern capital in the development of Southern industries. The luscious scuppernong holds first rank among our grapes, though we cultivate a great many other varieties, and our income from grapes packed and shipped to the Northern markets is quite considerable. I have not noticed any developments of the goopher in the vineyard, although I have a mild suspicion that our colored assistants do not suffer from want of grapes during the season.

I found, when I bought the vineyard, that Uncle Julius had occupied a cabin on the place for many years, and derived a respectable revenue from the product of the neglected grapevines. This, doubtless, accounted for his advice to me not to buy the vineyard, though whether it inspired the goopher story I am unable to state. I believe, however, that the wages I paid him for his services as coachman, for I gave him employment in that capacity, were more than an equivalent for anything he lost by the sale of the vineyard.

Questions to Consider

1. A contemporary reviewer distinguished "The Wife of His Youth" from Black belt stories because nearly all of the characters are well educated, almost White, and speak singularly elegant English (*The Springfield Sunday Republican*, 17 December 1899). Who speaks in dialect? Why? How do social status and dialect serve as markers in the story?
2. In his December 1901 interview for the *Colored American Magazine*, Chesnutt was questioned about the "hybrid . . . light-black race;" Chesnutt responded that his work lies along the line where the two races come together. Where is there evidence of Whiteness in the story? How is Blackness defined? What is Chesnutt implying about racial categories and racial heritage? What is the color line identified in the collection title? Does Chesnutt cross it, maintain it, and/or reposition it in the story?

Thomas Nelson Page

1853–1922

The Antebellum glories of " 'Dem . . . good ole times" constitute the ideological crucible for the fiction and essays of Thomas Nelson Page, the most influential Old South advocate and most popular Southern author of the 1880s and 1890s. Page's idealized past (ruined by the Civil War) is defined by enlightened aristocrats, who protect and serve their dependents (specifically, slaves, women, and the lower classes); by accepted class, gender, and racial relationships; and by an agrarian economy based on paternalistic family structures. Of course, this Southern past lived primarily in the imagination of those, like Page, who created it. Nonetheless, this seductive vision countered unsettling late nineteenth-century realities like industrialism, immigration, and demands for gender and racial equity. Indeed, Page's contemporaries credited him with singlehandedly revitalizing a profitable market for Southern writing.

Born 23 April 1853 on his family's plantation near Richmond, Virginia, Page inherited an aristocratic tradition of influence and distinguished service that included two Virginia governors and a signer of the Declaration of Independence. As Page recounts in *Two Little Confederates* (1888), this privileged existence was forever changed on his eighth birthday. Standing with his slave playmates, his aunt, and his mother Elizabeth, Tom watched his uncle William Nelson, a newly appointed Confederate officer, doff his plumed hat, bow to the ladies, and ride away to war as his father, an antisecessionist who had rejected officer status, shouldered his gun and marched away as a private. This remembered childhood scene resonates with Page's fictional portrayals of brave, waiting women; of patient, loyal slaves; and of romantic cavaliers, dashing, yet humble, arguing against the war even while accepting their responsibility to serve. Page's dedication to the idealized Old South never waivered. He praised and chronicled Confederate general Robert E. Lee as the emblematic national hero: a man of education, virtue, kindness, and nobility. He detailed chivalric Southern virtues and behaviors in *Social Life in Old Virginia Before the War* (1897) and *The Old Dominion: Her Making and Manners* (1908). His best-selling novels extolled the promise of a New South, indeed a new national society, based on Old South ideals: Confederate valor (*Red Rock*, 1898); rediscovered Virginia riches (*Gordon Keith*, 1903); and, in contrast, Chicago industrial and political corruption (*John Marvel, Assistant*, 1909).

Page's life was one of similarly passionate commitment. Following the war, he attended Washington College, presided over by recently retired Robert E. Lee, and eventually received his law degree from the University of Virginia. He established a successful law practice in Richmond although he continuously wrote, publishing dialect poetry, news stories, obituaries, and, finally, in 1894, "Marse Chan." An immediate success, "Marse Chan" became the centerpiece of his short story collection, *In Ole Virginia*, or *Marse Chan and Other Stories* (1887), which created a huge national demand for similar Old South nostalgia.

"Marse Chan" contains the narrative framework that would become the standard for similar stories: an interested outsider (White and presumably Northern) encounters a former slave (Sam, in this case), who "teaches" his listener about the golden plantation past, implicitly or explicitly, contrasting it with a depressing, diminished postwar present. In the freedman's explanation, no one could be kinder or nobler than his young White master, Tom Channing, and his master's beloved woman, Anne, and no life could be more fulfilling than life before the war: "Dem wuz good ole times . . . De bes' Sam ever see! Niggers didn' hed nothin' 't all to do—jes' . . . Doin' what de marster tell 'em to do." Centuries later, Page's racial and gender stereotyping are disturbing, and even his sentimental, sugar-coated reminiscences cannot mask incidents of cruel and demeaning behavior. However, Page's readers, Northern and Southern, devoured the stories, reveling in the romance of idyllic White paternalism and calling for more.

After the unexpected death in 1888 of his wife of two years, Anne Seddon Bruce, Page used his limited resources to create Richmond's first public library in her name and wrote infrequently, immersing himself in business and travel. As a renowned author, socially adept and welcome in elite circles, he eventually met wealthy Midwestern widow Florence Lathrop Field in Chicago, and they married in 1893.

Financially secure, Page discontinued his law practice and dedicated himself to writing, producing two best-selling novels (*Red Rock* and *Gordon Keith*). With their primary residence in Washington, D.C., the Pages traveled extensively (to London, Paris, Rome, and France, and kept a winter residence on Jekyl's Island, Georgia, and a summer home in York Harbor, Maine). Their dinners, which included politicians, international celebrities, writers, and artists as guests, became as legendary as their generous support of new or struggling writers, particularly those from the South. Although his literary fame was at its zenith at the century's turn, by 1910 the public had tired of Page's themes and approaches. Page turned his energy to conservation, to restoring his Virginia homeplace, Oakland (which had burned), to securing an endowment for the University of Virginia, and to peace efforts. His friendship with Theodore

Roosevelt and active financial and political support for Woodrow Wilson earned him an appointment as ambassador to Italy in 1913. The Pages returned from Rome in 1919, but when his wife died in 1921, Page was devastated; he passed away a year later on 31 October at his beloved Oakland.

from Marse Chan
A Tale of Old Virginia

One afternoon, in the autumn of 1872 I was riding leisurely down the sandy road that winds along the top of the water-shed between two of the smaller rivers of eastern Virginia. The road I was travelling, following "the ridge" for miles, had just struck me as most significant of the character of the race whose only avenue of communication with the outside world it had formerly been. Their once splendid mansions, now fast falling to decay, appeared to view from time to time, set back far from the road, in proud seclusion, among groves of oak and hickory, now scarlet and gold with the early frost. Distance was nothing to this people; time was of no consequence to them. They desired but a level path in life, and that they had, though the way was longer, and the outer world strode by them as they dreamed.

I was aroused from my reflections by hearing some one ahead of me calling, "Heah!—heah—whoo-oop, heah!"

Turning the curve in the road, I saw just before me a negro standing, with a hoe and a watering-pot in his hand. He had evidently just gotten over the "worm-fence" into the road, out of the path which led zigzag across the "old field" and was lost to sight in the dense growth of sassafras. When I rode up, he was looking anxiously back down this path for his dog. So engrossed was he that he did not even hear my horse, and I reined in to wait until he should turn around and satisfy my curiosity as to the handsome old place half a mile off from the road.

The numerous out-buildings and the large barns and stables told that it had once been the seat of wealth, and the wild waste of sassafras that covered the broad fields gave it an air of desolation that greatly excited my interest. Entirely oblivious of my proximity, the negro went on calling "Whoo-oop, heah!" until along the path, walking very slowly and with great dignity, appeared a noble-looking old orange and white setter, gray with age, and corpulent with excessive feeding. As soon as he came in sight, his master began:

"Yes, dat you! You gittin' deaf as well as bline, I s'pose! Kyarnt heah me callin', I reckon? Whyn't yo' come on, dawg?"

The setter sauntered slowly up to the fence and stopped, without even deigning a look at the speaker, who immediately proceeded to take the rails down, talking meanwhile:

"Now, I got to pull down de gap, I s'pose! Yo' so sp'ilt yo' kyahn hardly walk. Jes' ez able to git over it as I is! Jes' like white folks—think 'cuz you's white and I's black, I got to wait on yo' all de time. Ne'm mine, I ain' gwi' do it!"

The fence having been pulled down sufficiently low to suit his dogship, he marched sedately through, and, with a hardly perceptible lateral movement of his tail, walked on down the road. Putting up the rails carefully, the negro turned and saw me.

"Sarvent, marster," he said, taking his hat off. Then, as if apologetically for having permitted a stranger to witness what was merely a family affair, he added: "He know I con' mean nothin' by what I sez. He's Marse Chan's dawg, an' he's so ole he kyahn git long no pearter. He know I'se jes' prodjickin' wid 'im."

"Who is Marse Chan?" I asked; "and whose place is that over there, and the one a mile or two back—the place with the big gate and the carved stone pillars?"

"Marse Chan," said the darky, "he's Marse Channin'—my young marster; an' dem places—dis one's Weall's, an' de one back dyer wid de rock gate-pos's is ole Cun'l Chahmb'lin's. Dey don' nobody live dyer now, 'cep' niggers. Arfter de war some one or nurr bought our place, but his name done kind o' slipped me. I nuver hearn on 'im befo'; I think dey's half-strainers. I don' ax none on 'em no odds. I lives down de road heah, a little piece, an' I jes' steps down of a evenin' and looks arfter de graves."

"Well, where is Marse Chan?" I asked.

"Hi! don' you know? Marse Chan, he went in de army. I was wid 'im. Yo' know he ware' gwine an' lef' Sam."

"Will you tell me all about it?" I said, dismounting.

* * *

"Lawd, marster, hit's so long ago, I'd a'most forgit all about it, ef I hedn' been wid him ever sence he wuz born. Ez 'tis, I remembers it jes' like 'twuz yistiddy. Yo' know Marse Chan an' me-we wuz boys togerr. I wuz older'n he wuz, jes' de same ez he wuz whiter'n me."

* * *

"Well, when Marse Chan wuz born, dey wuz de grettes' doin's at home you ever did see. De folks all hed holiday, jes' like in de Chris'mas. Ole marster (we didn' call 'im ole marster tell arfter Marse Chan wuz born—befo' dat he wuz jes' de marster, so)—well, ole marster, his face fyar shine wid pleasure, an' all de folks wuz mighty glad, too, 'cause dey all loved ole marster, and aldo' dey did step aroun' right peart when ole marster was lookin' at 'em, dyer warn' nyar hen' on de place but what, ef he wanted anythin', would walk up to de back poach, an' say he warn' to see de marster. An' ev'ybody wuz talkin' 'bout de young marster, an' de maids an' de wimmens 'bout de kitchen wuz sayin' how 'twuz de purties' chile dey ever see."

* * *

[*Amid the jubilation, Channing comes to the porch with his son in is arms as the joyful slaves gather around.*]

"An' pres'n'y ole marster, lookin' down at we all chil'en all packed togerr down dyah like a parecel o' sheepburrs, cotch sight o' me (he knowed my name, 'cause I use' to hole he hoss fur 'im sometimes; but he didn' know all de chil'en by name, dey wuz so many on 'em), an' he sez, 'Come up heah.' So up I goes tippin', skeered like, an' old marster sez, 'Ain' you Mymie's son?' 'Yass, seh,' sez I. 'Well,' sez he, 'I'm gwine to give you to yo' young Marse Channin' to be his body-servant,' an' he put de baby right in my arms (it's de truth I'm tellin' yo'!), an' yo' jes' ought to a-heard de folks sayin', 'Lawd! Marster, dat boy'll drap dat chile!' 'Naw, he won't,' sez marster; 'I kin trust 'im.' And den he sez: 'Now, Sam, from dis time you belong to yo' young Marse Channin'; I wan' you to tek keer on 'im ez long ez he lives. You are to be his boy from dis time. An' now,' he sez, 'carry 'im in de house.' . . . An from dat time I was tooken in de house to be Marse Channin's body-servant."

* * *

[*As a schoolboy, Tom meets Miss Anne, the daughter of the neighboring plantation owner, Colonel Chamberlain. Together they attend the plantation schoolhouse.*]

"Well, dey 'peered to tek' a gre't fancy to each urr from dat time. Miss Anne she warn' nuthin' but a baby hardly, en' Marse Chan he wuz a good big boy 'bout mos' thirteen years ole, I reckon. Hows'ever, dey sut'n'y wuz sot on each urr an' (yo' heah me!) ole marster an' Cun'l Chahmb'lin, dey 'peered to like it 'bout well ez de chil'en. Yo' see, Cun'l Chahmb'lin's place j'ined ourn, an' it looked jes' ez natural fur dem two chil'en to marry ant mek it one plantation, ez it did fur de creek to run down de bottom from our place into Cun'l Chahmb'lin's. I don' rightly think de chil'en thought 'bout gittin' married, not den, no mo'n I thought 'bout marryin' Judy when she wuz a little gal at Cun'l Chahmb'lin's, runnin' 'bout de house, huntin' fur Miss Lucy's spectacles; but dey wuz, good frien's from de start."

* * *

[*On the way home from school one summer evening, Tom carries Anne across a flooded creek. His proud father rewards Tom with a pony which Tom promptly gives to Anne.*]

"'Hi! where's yo' pony?' said ole marster. 'I give 'im to Anne,' says Marse Chan. 'She liked 'im, an'—I kin walk.' 'Yes,' sez ole marster, laughin', 'I s'pose you's already done giv' her yo'se'f, an' nex' thing I know you'll be givin' her this plantation and all my niggers.'

"Well, about a fortnight or sich a matter arfter dat, Cun'l Chahmb'lin sont over en' invited all o' we all over to dinner, an' Marse Chan wuz 'spressly named in de note whar Ned brought; an' arfter dinner he made ole Phil, whar wuz his ker'ige-driver, bring roun' Marse Chan's pony wid a little side-saddle on 'im, an' a beautiful little hoss wid a bran-new saddle an' bridle on 'im; an' he gits up an' meks Marse Chan a gre't speech, an' presents 'im de little hoss; an' den he calls Miss Anne, an' she comes out on de poach in a little ridin' frock, an' dey puts her on her pony, an' Marse Chan mounts his hoss, an' dey goes to ride, while de grown folks is a-laughin' an' chattin' an' smokin' dey cigars.

"Dem wuz good ole times, marster—de bes' Sam ever see! Dey wuz, in fac'! Niggers didn' hed nothin' 't all to do—jes' hed to 'ten' to de feedin' an' cleanin' de hosses, en' doin' what de marster tell 'em to do; an' when dey wuz sick, dey had things sont 'em out de house, an' de same doctor come to see 'em whar 'ten' to de white folks when dey wuz po'ly. Dyar warn' no trouble nor nothin'."

* * *

[*Tom and Anne attend separate boarding schools, but when home are constant companions.*]

"Den ole marster he run for Congress, an' ole Cun'l Chahmb'lin he wuz put up to run 'g'inst ole marster by de Dimicrats; but ole marster he beat 'im. Yo' know he wuz gwine do dat! . . . . Den Cun'l Chahmb'lin he sort o' got in debt, an' sell some o' he niggers, an' dat's de way de fuss begun. Dat's whar de lawsuit cum from. Ole marster he didn' like nobody to sell niggers, an' knowin' dat Cun'l Chahmb'lin wuz sellin' o' his, he writ an' offered to buy his M'ria an' all her chil'en, 'cause she hed married our Zeek'yel. An' don' yo' think, Cun'l Chahmb'lin axed ole marster mo' 'n th'ee niggers wuz wuth fur M'ria! Befo' old marster bought her, dough, de sheriff cum an' levelled on M'ria an' a whole parecel o' urr niggers. Ole marster he went to de sale, an' bid for 'em; but Cun'l Chahmb'lin he got some one to bid 'g'inst ole marster. Dey wuz knocked out to ole marster dough, an' den dey hed a big lawsuit, an' ole marster wuz agwine to co't, off an' on, fur some years, till at lars' de bo't decided dat M'ria belonged to ole marster. Ole Cun'l Chahmb'lin den wuz so mad he sued ole marster for a little strip o' lan' down dyah on de line fence, whar he said belonged to 'im. Evy'body knowed hit belonged to ole marster. . . . .

"All dis time, yo' know, Marse Chan wuz agoin' back'ads en' for'ads to college, an' wuz growed up a ve'y fine young man. He wuz a ve'y likely gent'man! Miss Anne she hed done mos' growed up too—wuz puttin' her hyar up like ole missis use' to put hers up, an' 't wuz jes' ez bright ez de sorrel's mane when de sun cotch on it, an' her eyes wuz gre't big dark eyes, like her pa's, on'y bigger an' not so fierce, an' 'twarn' none o' de young ladies ez purty ez she wuz. She an' Marse Chan still set a heap o' sto' by one 'nurr. . . .

"Den ole marster lost he eyes. D' yo' ever heah 'bout dat? Heish! Didn' yo'? Well, one night de big barn cotch fire. De stables, yo' know, wuz under de big barn, an' all de hosses wuz in dyah. . . . Yo' could heah 'em so pitiful, an' pres'n'y old marster said to Ham Fisher (he wuz de ker'ige-driver), 'Go in dyah an' try to save 'em; don' let 'em bu'n to death.' An' Ham he went right in. An' jest arfter he got in, de shed whar it hed fus' cotch fell in, an' de sparks shot 'way up in de air; an' Ham didn' come back, en' de fire begun to lick out under de eaves over whar de ker'ige hosses' stalls wuz, an' all of a sudden ole marster tu'ned an' kissed ole missis, who wuz standin' nigh him, wid her face jes' ez white ez a sperit's, an', befo' anybody knowed what he wuz gwine do, jumped right in de do', an' de smoke come po'in' out behine 'im. Well, she, I nuver 'spects to heah tell Judgment sich a soun ez de folks set up! Ole missis she jes' drapt down on her knees in de mud an' prayed out loud. Hit 'peered like her pra'r wuz heard; for in a minit, right out de same do', kyarin' Ham Fisher in his arms, come ole marster, wid his clo's all blazin'. Dey flung water on 'im, an' put 'im out; an', ef you b'lieve me, yo' wouldn' a-knowed 'twuz ole marster. . . . His beard an' hyar wuz all nyawed off, an' his face an' hen's an' neck wuz scorified terrible. Well, he jes' laid Ham Fisher down, an' then he kind o' staggered for'ad, an' ole missis ketch' 'im in her arms. Ham Fisher, he warn' bu'nt so bad, an' he got out in a month or two; an' arfter a long time, ole marster he got well, too; but he wuz always stone blind arfter that. . . .

"Marse Chan he comed home from college toreckly, an' he sut'n'y did nuss ole marster faithful—jes' like a 'ooman. Den he took charge of de plantation arfter dat; an' I use' to wait on 'im jes' like when we wuz boys togedder; an' sometimes we'd slip off an' have a fox-hunt, an' he'd be jes' like he wuz in ole times, befo' ole marster got bline, an' Miss Anne Chahmb'lin stopt comin' over to our house, an' settin' onder de trees, readin' out de same book. "He sut'n'y wuz good to me. Nothin' nuver made no diffunce 'bout dat. He nuver hit me a lick in his life—an' nuver let nobody else do it, nurr."

* * *

[*Tom's father discovers Tom and Sam playfully sliding down strawstacks—an activity the elder Channing has expressly forbidden. He whips Tom, who stoically endures the whipping, and turns to whip Sam, who is hollering in fear, but young Tom stops him.*]

". . . Marse Chan he hed'n open he mouf long ez ole marster wuz tunin' 'im; but soon ez he commence warmin' me an' I begin to holler, Marse Chan he bu'st out cryin', an' steps right in befo' ole marster, an' ketchin' de whup, sed:

" 'Stop, seh! Yo' sha'n't whup 'im; he b'longs to me, an' ef you hit 'im another lick I'll set 'im free!'

"I wish yo' hed see ole marster. Marse Chan he warn' mo'n eight years ole, an' dyah dey wuz—old marster stan'in' wid he whup raised up, an' Marse Chan red an' cryin', hol'in on to it, an' sayin' I b'longst to 'im.

"Ole marster he raise' de whup, an' den he drapt it, an' broke out in a smile over he face, an' he chuck' Marse Chan onder de chin, an' tu'n right roun' an' went away, laughin' to hisse'f, an' I heah' 'im tellin' ole missis dat evenin', an laughin' 'bout it.

" 'Twan' so mighty long arfter dat when dey fust got to talkin' 'bout de war, Dey wus a-dictatin' back'ads an' for'ds 'bout it fur two or th'ee years 'fo' it come sho' nuff, you know. Ole marster, he wuz a Whig, an' of co'se Marse Chan he tuk after he pa. Cun'l Chahmb'lin, he wus a Dimicrat. He wuz in favor of de war, an' ole marster and Marse Chan dey wuz agin' it. Dey wuz a-talkin' 'bout it all de time, an' purty soon Cun'l Chahmb'lin he went about ev'vywhar speakin' an' noratin' 'bout Ferginia ought to secede; an' Marse Chan he wuz picked up to talk agin' 'im. Dat wuz de way dey come to fight de duil. I sit'n'y wuz skeered fur Mars Chan dat mawnin', an' he was jes' ez cool! Yo' see, it happen so: Marse Chan he wuz a-speakin' down at de Deep Creek Tavern, an' he kind o' got de bes' of ole Cun'l Chahmb'lin. All de white folks laughed an' hoorawed, an' ole Cun'l Chahmb'lin—my Lawd! I t'ought he'd bu'st, he was so mad. . . .

"Ole Cun'l Chahmb'lin he went right on. He said ole marster he taught Marse Chan; dat ole marster wus a wuss ab'litionis dan he son. I looked at Marse Chan, an' sez to myse'f: 'Fo' God! Old Cun'l Chahmb'lin better min', an' I hedn' got de wuds out, when ole Cun'l Chahmb'lin 'cuse' old marster o' cheatin' 'im out 'o he niggers, an' stealin' piece o' he lan'—dat's de lan' I tole you 'bout. Well, seh, nex' thing I knowed, I heahed Marse Chan—hit all happen right 'long togerr, like lightnin' and thunder when they hit right at you—I heah 'im say:

" 'Cun'l Chahmb'lin, what you say is false, an' yo' know it to be so. You have wilfully slandered one of de pures' and nobles' men Gord ever made, an' nothin' but yo' gray hyars protects you.'

"Well, ole Cun'l Chahmb'lin, he ra'ed an' he pitch'd. He said he wan' too ole, an' he'd show 'im so.

" 'Ve'y well,' say Marse Chan."

* * *

[*As a result of this confrontation and to save his honor, Chamberlain challenges Tom to a duel. The arrangements are set, but Tom keeps his silence about the coming event.*]

"Dat night at supper he laugh an' talk, an' he set at de table a long time. Arfter ole marster went to bed, he went in de charmber en' set on de bed by 'im talkin' to 'im en' tellin' 'im 'bout de meetin' an' e'vything; but he nuver mention ole Cun'l Chahmb'lin's name. When he got up to come out to de office in de yard, whar he slept, he stooped down an' kissed 'im jes' like he wuz a baby layin' dyer in de bed, an' he'd hardly let ole missis go at all. I knowed some'n wuz up, an' nex mawnin' I called 'im early befo' light, like he tole me, an' he dressed an' come out pres'n'y jes' like he wuz goin' to church. I had de hosses ready, an' we went out de back way to'ds de river. Ez we rode along, he said:

" 'Sam, you an' I wuz boys togedder, wa'n't we?'

" 'Yes,' sez I, 'Marse Chan, dat we wuz.'

" 'You have been ve'y faithful to me,' sez he, 'an' I have seen to it that you are well provided fur. You want to marry Judy, I know, ant you'll be able to buy her ef you want to.'

"Den he tole me he wuz goin' to fight a duil, an' in case he should git shot, he had set me free an' giv' me nuff to tek keer o' me an' my wife ez long ez we lived. He said he'd like me to stay en' tek keer o' ole marster an' ole missis ez long ez dey lived, an' he said it wouldn' be very long, he reckoned. Dat wuz de on'y time he voice broke—when he said dat; en' I couldn' speak a wud, my th'oat choked me so."

* * *

[*The Duel: As the one offended, Chamberlain has the right to shoot first, but his shot misses Tom. Tom tilts his pistol and shoots straight upward to avoid hitting Chamberlain, saying "I mek you a present to yo' fam'ly, seh!" Chamberlain, denied "satisfaction," is furious and feels disgraced. In dueling, an honorable death would have been preferable. He rides away while Tom and Sam return home.*]

"We come on home to breakfast, I totin' de box wid de pistils befo' me on de roan. Would you b'lieve me, seh, Marse Chan he nuver said a wud 'bout it to ole marster or nobody. Ole missis didn' fin' out 'bout it for mo'n a month, an' den, Lawd! how she did cry and kiss Marse Chan; an' ole marster, aldo' he never say much, he wuz jes' ez please' ez ole missis. He call' me in de room an' made me tole 'im all 'bout it, an' when I got th'oo he gi' me five dollars an' a pyar of breeches.

"But ole Cun'l Chahmb'lin he nuver did furgive Marse Chan, an' Miss Anne she got mad too. Wimmens is mons'us onreasonable nohow. Dey's jes' like a catfish: you can n' tek hole on 'em like udder folks an' when you gits yo' can n' always hole 'em."

* * *

[*On their way to foxhunting, Sam and Tom ride past Miss Anne, who ignores Tom and speaks only to Sam. Tom is devastated by Anne's coldness.*]

"De war come on jes' den, an Marse Chan wuz elected cap'n; but he wouldn' tek it. He said Firginia hadn' seceded, an' he wuz gwine stan' by her. . . . I sut'n'y did wan' Marse Chan to tek de place, cuz I knowed he wuz gwine tek me wid 'im. He wan' gwine widout Sam. An' beside, he look so po' an' thin, I thought he wuz gwine die.

"Of co'se, ole missis she heared 'bout it, an' she met Miss Anne in de road, an' cut her jes' like Miss Anne cut Marse Chan.

"Ole missis, she wuz proud ez anybody! So we wuz mo' strangers den ef we hadn' live' in a hunderd miles of each urr. An' Marse Chan he wuz gittin' thinner en' thinner, an' Firginia she come out, an' den Marse Chan he went to Richmond an' listed, an' come back an' sey he wuz a private, an' he didn' know whe'r he could tek me or not. . . .

"Well, one night Marse Chan come back from de offis wid a telegram dat say, 'Come at once,' so he wuz to start nex' mawnin'. He uniform wuz all ready, gray wid yeller trimmin's, an' mine wuz ready too, an' he had ole marster's sword, whar de State gi' 'im in de Mexikin war; an' he trunks wuz all packed wid ev'rything in 'em, an' my chist was packed too, an' Jim Rasher he druv 'em over to de depo' in de waggin, an' we wuz to start nex mawnin' 'bout light. Dis wuz 'bout de las' o' spring, you know. Dat night ole missis made Marse Chan dress up in he uniform, an' he sut'n'y did look splendid, wid he long mustache en' he wavin' hyar an' he tall figger."

* * *

[*After supper, Tom asks Sam to take a note to Anne. Anne reluctantly honors his request to meet her later that evening. Sam, who has accompanied Tom, describes the meeting.*]

"She spoke fust ('twuz Miss Anne had done come out dyer to meet Marse Chan), an' she sez, jes' ez cold ez a chill, 'Well, seh, I granted your favor. I wished to relieve myse'f of de obligations you placed me under a few months ago, when you made me a present of my father, whom you fust insulted an' then prevented from gittin' satisfaction.'

"Marse Chan he didn' speak fur a minit, an' den he said: 'Who is with you?' (Dat wuz ev'y wud.)

" 'No one,' sez she; 'I came alone.'

" 'My God!' sez he, 'you didn' come all through those woods by yourse'f at this time o' night?'

" 'Yes, I'm not afraid,' sez she. (An' heah dis nigger! I don' b'lieve she wuz.)

"De moon come out, an' I cotch sight o' her stan'in' dyer in her white dress, wid de cloak she had wrapped herse'f up in drapped off on de groun', an' she didn' look like she wuz 'feared o' nuthin'. She wuz mons'us purty ez she stood dyer wid de green bushes behine her, an' she hed jes' a few flowers in her breas'—right hyah—and some leaves in her sorrel hyar; an' de moon come out en' shined down on her hyar an' her frock, an' 'peered like de light wuz jes' stan'in' off it ez she stood dyer lookin' at Marse

Chan wid her head tho'd back, jes' like dat mawnin' when she pahss Marse Chan in de road widout speakin' to 'im, an' sez to me, 'Good mawnin', Sam.'

"Marse Chan, he den tole her he hed come to say good by to her, ez he wuz gwine 'way to de war nex' mawnin'. I wuz watchin' on her, en' I tho't, when Marse Chan tole her dat, she sort o' started an' looked up at 'im like she wuz mighty sorry, an' 'peared like she didn' stan' quite so straight arfter dat. Den Marse Chan he went on talkin' right fars' to her; an' he tole her how he had loved her ever sence she wuz a little bit o' baby mos', an' how he nuver 'membered de time when he hedn' 'spected to marry her. . . .

"Marse Chan he had done been talkin' so serious, he hed done tuk Miss Anne's hen', an' wuz lookin' down in her face like he wuz list'nin' wid his eyes.

"Arfter a minit Miss Anne she said somethin', an' Marse Chan he cotch her urr hen' an' sez:

" 'But if you love me, Anne?'

"When he said dat, she tu'ned her head 'way from 'im, en' wait' a minit, en' den she said—right clear:

" 'But I don' love yo'.' (Jes' dem th'ee wuds!) De wuds fall right slow—like dirt falls out a spade on a coffin when yo's buryin' anybody, an' seys, 'Uth to uth.' Marse Chan he jes' let her hand drap an' he stiddy hisse'f' g'inst de gate-pos', an' he didn' speak torekly. When he did speak, all he sez wuz:

" 'I mus' see you home safe.'

"I 'clar, marster, I didn' know 'twuz Marse Chan's voice tell I look at 'im right good. Well, she wouldn' let 'im go wid her. She jes' wrap' her cloak 'roun' her shoulders, an' wen' 'long back by herse'f, widout doin' more'n jes' look up once at Marse Chan leanin' dyah 'g'inst de gate-pos' in he sodger clo's, wid he eyes on de groun'. She said 'Good by' sort o' sorf, an' Marse Chan, widout lookin' up, shake hen's wid her, en' she wuz done gone down de road. Soon ez she got 'mos' 'roun de curve. . . .

"Nex' mawnin' we all come off to j'ine de army. An' dey wuz a-drillin' an' a-drillin' all 'bout for a while an' dey went 'long wid all de res' o' de army, an' I went wid Marse Chan an' clean he boots, an' look arfter de tent, en' tek keer o' him en' de hosses. An' Marse Chan, he wan' a bit like he use' to be. He wuz so solum an' moanful all de time, at leas' 'cep' when dyah wuz gwine to be a fight. Den he'd peartin' up, en' he alwuz rode at de head o' de company, 'cause he wuz tall; en' hit wan' on'y in battles whar all his company wuz dat he went, but he use' to volunteer whenever de cun'l wanted anybody to fine out anythin', an' 'twuz so dangersome he didn' like to mek one man go no sooner'n anurr, yo' know, an, ax'd who'd volunteer. He 'peered to like to go prowlin' aroun' 'mong dem Yankees, an' he use' to tek me wid 'im whenever he could. Yes, seh, he sut'n'y wuz a good sodger! He didn' mine bullets no more'n he did so many draps o'rain. But I use' to be pow'ful skeered sometimes. It jes' use' to 'pear like fun to 'im. In camp he use' to be so sorrerful he'd hardly open he mouf. . . . "When Cap'n Gordon got he leg shot off, dey mek Marse Chan cap'n on de spot, 'cause one o' de lieutenants got kilt de same day, an' turr one (named Mr. Ronny) wan' no 'count, an' all de company said Marse Chan wuz de man.

"An' Marse Chan he wuz jes' de same. He didn' never mention Miss Anne's name, but I knowed he wuz thinkin' on her constant. . . .

"Well, I got one o' de gent'mens to write Judy a letter for me, an' I tole her all 'bout de fight, an' how Marse Chan knock Mr. Ronny over fur speakin' discontemptuous o' Cun'l Chahmb'lin, an' I tole her how Marse Chan wuz a-dyin' fur love o' Miss Anne. An' Judy she gits Miss Anne to read de letter fur her. Den Miss Anne she tells her pa, an'—you mind, Judy tells me all dis arfterwards, an' she say when Cun'l Chahmb'lin hear 'bout it, he wuz settin' on de poach, an' he set still a good while, an' den he sey to hisse'f:

" 'Well, he carn' he'p bein' a Whig.'

"An' den he gits up an' walks up to Miss Anne an' looks at her right hard; an' Miss Anne she hed done tu'n away her haid en' wuz makin' out she wuz fixin' a rose-bush 'g'inst de poach; an' when her pa kep' lookin' at her, her face got jes' de color o' de roses on de bush, and pres'n'y her pa sez:

" 'Anne!'

"An' she tu'ned roun', an' he sez:

" 'Do yo' want 'im?'

"An' she sez, 'Yes,' an' put her head on he shoulder an' begin to cry; an' he sez:

" 'Well, I won' stan' between yo' no longer. Write to 'im an' say so.'

"We didn' know nuthin' 'bout dis den. We wuz a-fightin' an' a-fightin' all dat time; an' come one day a letter to Marse Chan, an' I see 'im start to read it in his tent, an' he face hit look so cu'ious, an he hen's trembled so I couldn' mek out what wuz de matter wid 'im. An' he fol' de letter up an' wen' out an' wen' way down 'hine de camp, an' stayed dyah 'bout nigh an hour. Well, seh, I wuz on de lookout for 'im when he come back, an', fo' Gord, ef he face didn' shine like a angel's! I say to myse'f, 'Um'm' ef de glory o' Gord ain' done shine on 'im!' An' what yo' 'spose 'twuz?

"He tuk me wid 'im dat evenin', an' he tell me he hed done git a letter from Miss Anne, an' Marse Chan he eyes look like gre't big stars, an' he face wuz jes' like 'twuz dat mawnin' when de sun riz up over de low groun', an' I see 'im stan'in' dyah wid de pistil in he hen', lookin' at it, an' not knowin' but what it mout be de lars' time, an' he done mek up he mine not to shoot ole Cun'l Chahmb'lin fur Miss Anne's sake, what writ 'im de letter."

* * *

"Well, dat night de orders come, an' we all hed to git over to'ds Romney; en' we rid all night till 'bout light; en' we halted right on a little creek, an' we stayed dyah till mos' breakfas' time, an' I see Marse Chan set down on de groun' 'hine a bush an' read dat letter over an' over. I watch 'im, an' de battle wuz a-goin' on, but we had orders to stay 'hine de hill . . . and Marse Chan he calls me, an' I crep' up, en' he sez:

" 'Sam, we'se goin' to win in dis battle, an' den we'll go home an' git married; an' I'se goin' home wid a star on my collar.' An' den he sez, 'Ef I'm wounded, kyar me home, yo' hear?' An' I sez, 'Yes, Marse Chan.'

"Well, jes' den dey blowed boots an' saddles, 'an we mounted; an' de orders come to ride 'roun' de slope, an' Marse Chan's comp'ny wuz de secon', an' when we got 'roun' dyah, we wuz right in it. Hit wuz de wust place ever dis nigger got in. An' dey said, 'Charge 'em!' an' my king! ef ever you see bullets fly, dey did dat day. Hit wuz jes' like hail; an' we wen' down de slope (I long wid de res') an' up de hill right to'ds de cannons, an' de fire wuz so strong dyer (dey hed a whole rigiment o' infintrys layin' down dyer onder de cannons) our lines sort o' broke an' stop; de cun'l was kilt, an' I b'lieve dey wuz jes' 'bout to bre'k all to pieces, when Marse Chan rid up an' cotch hol' de flag an' hollers, 'Foller me!' an' rid strainin' up de hill 'mong de cannons. I seen 'im when he went, de sorrel four good lengths ahead o' ev'y urr hoss, jes' like he use' to be in a fox-hunt, an' de whole rigiment right arfter 'im. Yo' ain' nuver hear thunder! Fust thing I knowed, de roan roll' head over heels an' flung me up 'g'inst de bank, like yo' chuck a nubbin over 'g'inst de foot o' de corn pile. An dat's what kep' me from bein' kilt, I 'spects. Judy she say she think 'twuz Providence, but I think 'twuz de bank. O' co'se, Providence put de bank dyah, but how come Providence nuver saved Marse Chan? When I look' 'roun', de roan wuz layin' dyah by me, stone dead, wid a cannon-ball gone 'mos' th'oo him, an our men hed done swep' dem on t'urr side from de top o' de hill. . . .

"I jumped up an' run over de bank, en' dyer, wid a whole lot o' dead men, an' some not dead yit, onder one o' de guns wid de flag still in he hen', an' a bullet right th'oo he body, lay Marse Chan. I tu'n 'im over an' call 'im, 'Marse Chan!' but 'twan' no use, he wuz done gone home, sho' 'nuff. I pick' 'im up in my arms wid de flag still in he hen's, an' toted 'im back jes' like I did dat day when he wuz a baby, an' ole marster gin 'im to me in my arms, en' sez he could trus' me, en' tell me to tek keer on 'im long ez he lived. I kyar'd 'im 'way off de battilefiel' out de way o' de balls, en' I laid 'im down onder a big tree till I could git somebody to ketch de sorrel for me. He wuz cotched arfter a while, an' I hed some money, so I got some pine plank en' made a coffin dat evenin', en' wraps Marse Chan's body up in de flag, an' put 'im in de coffin; but I didn' nail de top on strong, 'cause I knowed ole missis wan' see 'im; an' I got a' ambulance an' set out for home dat night. We reached dyer de nex' evein', arfter travellin' all dat night an' all nex' day.

"Hit 'peered like somethin' hed tole ole missis we wuz comin' so; for when we got home she wuz waitin' for us—done drest up in her best Sunday-clo'es, an' stan'n' at de head o' de big steps, an' ole marster settin' in his big cheer—ez we druv up de hill to'ds de house, I drivin' de ambulance an' de sorrel leadin' 'long behine wid de stirrups cross over de saddle.

"She come down to de gate to meet us. We took de coffin out de ambulance en' kyar'd it right into de big parlor wid de pictures in it, whar dey use' to dance in ole times when Marse Chan wuz a schoolboy, an' Miss Anne Chahmb'lin use' to come over, an' go wid ole missis into her chamber an' tek her things off. In dyer we laid de coffin on two o'de cheers, an' ole missis nuver said a wud; she jes' looked so ole an' white."

* * *

"When I rid up in de yard, dyer wuz Miss Anne a-stan'in' on de poach watchin' me ez I rid up. I tied my hoss to de fence, an' walked up de parf. She knowed by de way I walked dyer wuz somethin' de motter, an' she wuz mighty pale. I drapt my cap down on de een' o' de steps en' went up. She nuver opened her mouf; jes' stan' right still an' keep her eyes on my face. Fust I couldn' speak; den I cotch my voice, an' I say, 'Marse Chan, he done got he furlough.'

"Her face was mighty ashy, en' she sort o' shook but she didn' fall. She tu'ned roun' an' said, 'Git me de ker'ige!' Dat wuz all."

* * *

"When we got home, she got out, an' walked up de big walk—up to de poach by herse'f. Ole missis hed done fin' de letter in Marse Chan's pocket, wid de love in it, while I wuz 'way, en' she wuz a-waitin' on de poach. Dey sey dat wuz de fust time ole missis cry when she find de letter, an' dat she sut'n'y did cry over it, pintedly.

"Well, seh, Miss Anne she walks right up de steps, mos' up to ole missis stan'in' dyer on de poach, an' jes' falls right down mos' to her, on her knees fuss, an' den flat on her face right on de flo' ketchin' at ole missis' dress wid her two hen's—so.

"Ole missis stood for 'bout a minit lookin' down at her, an' den she drapt down on de flo' by her, an' took her in bofe her arms. "I couldn' see, I wuz cryin' so myself, an' ev'y body wuz cryin'. But dey went in arfter a while in de parlor, an' shet de do'; an' I heahd 'em say, Miss Anne she tuk de coffin in her arms an' kissed it, an' kissed Marse Chan, an' call 'im by his name, en' her darlin', an' ole missis left her cryin' in dyer tell some on 'em went in, an' found her done faint on de flo'.

"Judy (she's my wife) she tell me she heah Miss Anne when she axed ole missis mout she wear mo'nin fur 'im. . . . Well, we buried Marse Chan dyer in de ole grabeyard, wid de flag wrapped roun' 'im, an' he face lookin' like it did dat mawnin' down in de low groun's, wid de new sun shinin' on it so peaceful.

"Miss Anne she nuver went home to stay arfter dat; she stay wid ole marster an' ole missis ez long ez dey lived. Dat warn' so mighty long, 'cause ole marster he died dat fall, when dey wuz fallerin' fur wheat—I had jes' married Judy den—an' ole missis she warn' long behine him. We buried her by him next summer. Miss Anne she went in de hospitals toreckly arfter ole missis died; an' jes' fo' Richmond fell she come home sick wid de fever. Yo' nuver would 'a' knowed her fur de same ole Miss Anne. She wuz light ez a piece o' peth, en' so white, 'cep' her eyes an' her sorrel hyar, an' she kep' on gittin' whiter an' weaker. Judy she sut'n'y did nuss her faithful. But she nuver got no betterment! De fever an' Marse Chan's bein' kilt hed done strain her, an' she died jes' fo' de folks wuz sot free.

"So we buried Miss Anne right by Marse Chan, in a place whar ole missis hed tole us to leave, an' dey's bofe on 'em sleep side by side over in de ole grabeyard at home.

"An' will yo' please tell me, marster? Dey tells me dat de Bible sey dyer won' be marryin' nor givin' in marriage in heaven, but I don' b'lieve it signifies dat—does you?"

I gave him the comfort of my earnest belief in some other interpretation, together with several spare "eighteen-pences," as he called them, for which he seemed humbly grateful. And as I rode away I heard him calling across the fence to his wife, who was standing in the door of a small whitewashed cabin, near which we had been standing for some time:

"Judy, have Marse Chan's dawg got home?"

Questions to Consider

1. Consider the perspective of the story and its effects on the reader. What is the viewpoint of the narrative "I" in the opening passage? How might that narrator create a link with a Northern reader? Why does Page carefully date the narrative as autumn, 1872 (12 years earlier than the story's original publication)? How might the narrator's initial perspective have shifted as the story concludes? Did yours shift?
2. Consider the role of mirroring in this text. What are the sources of power for the men (Tom, Sam, the elder Channing, Chamberlain) and for the women (Anne, Judy, Mistress Channing)? How do Sam and Judy serve as dark mirrors for Tom and Anne and for one another? Does Tom reflect/differ from his father? How do Anne and Mistress Channing reflect/differ? How does Marse Chan's dog (whose presence frames the entire story) mirror the complexities of slave and master? Finally, how are landscapes used to define characters: the men? The women? The slaves? The owners?

Thomas Dixon, Jr.

1864–1946

The novels of Thomas Dixon have been derided by most literary historians as melodramatic, overly didactic and, above all, deeply racist; nonetheless, he remains one of America's most influential figures. But while he was an extremely talented man, excelling in several professions, his lasting legacy depended ironically on his fortuitous collaborations with two other Southerners: a former graduate school friend, Woodrow Wilson, and an aspiring film-maker from Kentucky, David W. Griffith.

The son of an influential Baptist preacher from Shelby, North Carolina, Thomas, Jr., entered Wake Forest College at 15, graduated with its highest honors, and began graduate work in history at Johns Hopkins. Abandoning an academic career, he tried acting, entered law school in Greensboro, married Harriet Bussey, and was elected to the North Carolina state legislature before deciding in 1886 to follow his father into the ministry. A gifted orator, Dixon soon became pastor to New York City's largest Protestant congregation. Anticipating the themes of many twentieth-century evangelists, his message was largely political and social, and it gradually focused on how sectionalism obstructed the unity that would allow America to assume its imperial destiny, manifest in the Spanish-American War in 1898. Made wealthy by his career as a lecturer and eager to reach larger audiences, Dixon turned to novel writing in 1900. After he witnessed a theatrical production of *Uncle Tom's Cabin*, his purposes became sharpened: he determined to tell what he saw as the truth about White Southern society and its relationship with the "Negro."

The Leopard's Spots: A Romance of the White Man's Burden—1865–1900, published in 1902, was an immediate success. Conceived as a sequel to Harriet Beecher Stowe's classic novel, one of dozens written before and after the Civil War, *The Leopard's Spots* articulated the discomfort felt by many Americans over the profound changes affecting the country and named the source: the darker races, whose inherent inferiority and cravings for amalgamation threatened to undermine traditional Anglo-Saxon power. Like many Social Darwinists of the era, Dixon believed that suppression and segregation were the only way to avoid a catastrophic race war and the collapse of civilization, both at home and abroad.

Dixon completed the second volume of his Reconstruction trilogy, *The Clansman*, in 1905, followed by *The Traitor* in 1907. All three novels pursue similar themes: Southerners had fought for liberty, not slavery; African Americans were inferior beings, incapable of democratic self-government or humane behavior; and without firm (White) control, African Americans would rape (White) women or seduce (White) men to achieve the destruction of (White) society. Dixon corroborated these notions with virulent portraits of African Americans as lustful beasts and incompetent buffoons, misusing their new political and economic powers. These racist views were buttressed by Dixon's reactionary conception of White women, whose fragility demanded that their men should violently avenge any transgressions against White supremacy.

Offensive as they are, Dixon's racist fables struck a chord with many Americans, as stereotypes are dangerously wont to do. Indeed, Thomas Nelson Page, Ruth Stuart, Grace King, Mark Twain, Joel Chandler Harris, and many other Southern writers had capitalized on many of these same formulas with similar success. But Dixon's distortions became lasting icons when they caught the imagination of another young Southerner, D. W. Griffith. In 1915, Griffith and Dixon co-produced *The Birth of a Nation*, a feature-length epic, full of stunning innovations that were to mark Griffith as the founder of American movie-making. The film was immediately attacked as racist and incendiary, and its release was accompanied by violent protests. Anxious to avoid a public ban, Dixon asked his old graduate school friend and then president, Woodrow Wilson, to conduct what became the first private film screening at the White House. When it was done, Wilson was quoted as saying, "It is like writing history with lightning; my only regret is that it is all so terribly true." *Birth of a Nation* soon became a huge financial success.

Griffith's film was, of course, no more true than Dixon's novels, but both were terribly effective in shaping popular notions of African Americans as well as of the presumed failure of progressivism and Reconstruction as political policy. With its grotesque images of African-American-dominated legislatures and its glorification of White terrorists, *The Clansman* distorted the history of Reconstruction for over a century. Dixon went on to write another 19 novels, form his own motion-picture company, and lose several fortunes before he died, impoverished, in 1946.

Though Dixon's works were officially marginalized for their lack of artistry, their harmful misrepresentations remained potent. It is still unsettling to encounter shocking caricatures like Gus or the glorification of the Ku Klux Klan's domestic terrorism, many of whose pseudo-Celtic rituals were invented by Dixon and later adopted by a revived Klan. Even the melodrama of Marion and her mother's suicide offers a disturbing image of feminine impotence. Examining and exposing these popular fantasies, however, teaches us a great deal about the fictional forces and personal biases that have, no less than our ideals, shaped our national identity.

from The Clansman

from *Book III—The Reign of Terror*

from THE RIOT IN THE MASTER'S HALL

The day he undertook to present his memorial to the Legislature was one he never forgot. The streets were crowded with negroes who had come to town to hear Lynch, the Lieutenant-Governor, speak in a mass-meeting. Negro policemen swung their clubs in his face as he pressed through the insolent throng up the street to the stately marble Capitol. At the door a black, greasy trooper stopped him to parley. Every decently dressed white man was regarded a spy.

* * *

[T]he introduction of bills began. One after another were sent to the Speaker's desk, a measure to disarm the whites and equip with modern rifles a Negro militia of 80,000 men; to make the uniform of Confederate gray the garb of convicts in South Carolina, with the sign of rank to signify the degree of crime; to prevent any person calling another a "nigger"; to require men to remove their hats in the presence of all officers, civil or military, and all disfranchised men to remove their hats in the presence of voters; to force whites and blacks to attend the same schools and open the State University to negroes; to permit the intermarriage of whites and blacks; and to inforce social equality.

* * *

Dr. Cameron watched the movements of the black judge, already notorious for the sale of his opinions, with a sense of sickening horror. This man was but yesterday a slave, his father a medicine-man in an African jungle who decided the guilt or innocence of the accused by the test of administering poison. If the poison killed the man, he was guilty; if he survived, he was innocent. For four thousand years his land had stood a solid bulwark of unbroken barbarism. Out of its darkness he had been thrust upon the seat of judgment of the laws of the proudest and highest type of man evolved in time. It seemed a hideous dream.

His thoughts were interrupted by a shout. It came spontaneous and tremendous in its genuine feeling. The magnificent figure of Lynch, their idol, appeared walking down the aisle escorted by the little scalawag who was the Governor.

He took his seat on the platform with the easy assurance of conscious power. His broad shoulders, superb head, and gleaming jungle-eyes held every man in the audience before he had spoken a word.

In the first masterful tones of his voice the doctor's keen intelligence caught the ring of his savage metal and felt the shock of his powerful personality—a personality which had thrown to the winds every mask, whose sole aim of life was sensual, whose only fears were of physical pain and death, who could worship a snake and sacrifice a human being.

His playful introduction showed him a child of Mystery, moved by Voices and inspired by a Fetish. His face was full of good humour, and his whole figure rippled with sleek animal vivacity. For the moment, life was a comedy and a masquerade teeming with whims, fancies, ecstasies and superstitions.

He held the surging crowd in the hollow of his hand. They yelled, laughed, howled, or wept as he willed.

Now he painted in burning words the imaginary horrors of slavery until the tears rolled down his cheeks and he wept at the sound of his own voice. Every dusky hearer burst into tears and moans.

* * *

As the doctor emerged from the stifling crowd with his friend, he drew a deep breath of fresh air, took from his pocket his conservative memorial, picked it into little bits, and scattered them along the street as he walked in silence back to his hotel.

from The Beat of a Sparrow's Wing

It was past midnight before [Mrs. LeNoir and her daughter] finished the last touches in restoring their nest to its old homelike appearance and sat down happy and tired in the room in which Marion was born, brooding and dreaming and talking over the future.

The mother was hanging on the words of her daughter, all the baffled love of the dead poet husband, her griefs and poverty consumed in the glowing joy of new hopes. Her love for this child was now a triumphant passion, which had melted her own being into the object of worship, until the soul of the daughter was superimposed on the mother's as the magnetised by the magnetiser.

* * *

"What's that?" whispered the mother, leaping to her feet.

"I heard nothing," Marion answered, listening.

"I thought I heard footsteps on the porch."

"Maybe it's Ben, who decided to come anyhow," said the girl.

"But he'd knock!" whispered the mother.

The door flew open with a crash, and four black brutes leaped into the room, Gus in the lead, with a revolver in his hand, his yellow teeth grinning through his thick lips.

"Scream, now, an' I blow yer brains out," he growled.

Blanched with horror, the mother sprang before Marion with a shivering cry:

"What do you want?"

"Not you," said Gus, closing the blinds and handing a rope to another brute. "Tie de ole one ter de bedpost."

The mother screamed. A blow from a black fist in her mouth, and the rope was tied.

With the strength of despair she tore at the cords, half rising to her feet, while with mortal anguish she gasped:

"For God's sake, spare my baby! Do as you will with me, and kill me—do not touch her!"

Again the huge fist swept her to the floor.

Marion staggered against the wall, her face white, her delicate lips trembling with the chill of a fear colder than death.

"We have no money—the deed has not been delivered," she pleaded, a sudden glimmer of hope flashing in her blue eyes.

Gus stepped closer, with an ugly leer, his flat nose dilated, his sinister bead-eyes wide apart gleaming ape-like, as he laughed:

"We ain't atter money!"

The girl uttered a cry, long, tremulous, heart-rending, piteous.

A single tiger-spring, and the black claws of the beast sank into the soft white throat and she was still.

At the Dawn of Day

It was three o'clock before Marion regained consciousness, crawled to her mother, and crouched in dumb convulsions in her arms.

"What can we do, my darling?" the mother asked at last.

"Die!—thank God, we have the strength left!"

"Yes, my love," was the faint answer.

"No one must ever know. We will hide quickly every trace of crime. They will think we strolled to Lover's Leap and fell over the cliff, and my name will always be sweet and clean—you understand—come, we must hurry—"

With swift hands, her blue eyes shining with a strange light, the girl removed the shreds of torn clothes, bathed, and put on the dress of spotless white she wore the night Ben Cameron kissed her and called her a heroine.

The mother cleaned and swept the room, piled the torn clothes and cord in the fireplace and burned them, dressed herself as if for a walk, softly closed the doors, and hurried with her daughter along the old pathway through the moonlit woods.

At the edge of the forest she stopped and looked back tenderly at the little home shining amid the roses, caught their faint perfume and faltered:

"Let's go back a minute—I want to see his room, and kiss Henry's picture again."

"No, we are going to him now—I hear him calling us in the mists above the cliff," said the girl—"come, we must hurry. We might go mad and fail!"

Down the dim cathedral aisles of the woods, hallowed by tender memories, through which the poet lover and father had taught them to walk with reverent feet and without fear, they fled to the old meeting-place of Love.

On the brink of the precipice, the mother trembled, paused, drew back and gasped:

"Are you not afraid, my dear?"

"No; death is sweet, now," said the girl. "I fear only the pity of those we love."

"Is there no other way? We might go among strangers," pleaded the mother.

"We could not escape ourselves! The thought of life is torture. Only those who hate me could wish that I live. The grave will be soft and cool, the light of day a burning shame."

"Come back to the seat a moment—let me tell you my love again," urged the mother. "Life still is dear while I hold your hand."

As they sat in brooding anguish, floating up from the river valley came the music of a banjo in a negro cabin mingled with vulgar shout and song and dance. A verse of the ribald senseless lay of the player echoed above the banjo's pert refrain:

> "Chicken in de bread tray, pickin' up dough;
> Granny, will your dog bite? No, chile, no!"

The mother shivered and drew Marion closer.

"Oh, dear! oh, dear! has it come to this—all my hopes of your beautiful life!"

The girl lifted her head and kissed the quivering lips.

"With what loving wonder we saw you grow," she sighed, "from a tottering babe on to the hour we watched the mystic light of maidenhood dawn in your blue eyes—and all to end in this hideous, leprous shame!–No!–No! I will not have it! It's only a horrible dream! God is not dead!"

The young mother sank to her knees and buried her face in Marion's lap in a hopeless paroxysm of grief.

The girl bent, kissed the curling hair and smoothed it with her soft hand.

A sparrow chirped in the tree above, a wren twittered in a bush, and down on the river's brink a mocking-bird softly waked his mate with a note of thrilling sweetness.

"The morning is coming, dearest; we must go," said Marion. "This shame I can never forget, nor will the world forget. Death is the only way."

They walked to the brink, and the mother's arms stole round the girl.

"Oh, my baby, my beautiful darling, life of my life, heart of my heart, soul of my soul!"

They stood for a moment, as if listening to the music of the falls, looking out over the valley faintly outlining itself in the dawn. The first far-away streaks of blue light on the mountain ranges, defining distance, slowly appeared. A fresh motionless day brooded over the world as the amorous stir of the spirit of morning rose from the moist earth of the fields below.

A bright star still shone in the sky, and the face of the mother gazed on it intently. Did the Woman-spirit, the burning focus of the fiercest desire to live and will, catch in this supreme moment the star's Divine speech before which all human passions sink into silence? Perhaps, for she smiled. The daughter answered with a smile; and then, hand in hand, they stepped from the cliff into the mists and on through the opal gates of Death.

from *Book IV—The Ku Klux Klan*

from The Hunt for the Animal

. . . They found the bodies close to the water's edge. Marion had been killed instantly. Her fair blonde head lay in a crimson circle sharply defined in the white sand. But the mother was still warm with life. She had scarcely ceased to breathe. In one last desperate throb of love the trembling soul had dragged the dying body to the girl's side, and she had died with her head resting on the fair round neck as though she had kissed her and fallen asleep.

Father and son clasped hands and stood for a moment with uncovered heads. The doctor said at length:

"Go to the coroner at once, and see that he summons the jury you select and hand to him. Bring them immediately. I will examine the bodies before they arrive."

Ben took the negro coroner into his office alone, turned the key, told him of the discovery, and handed him the list of the jury.

"I'll hatter see Mr. Lynch fust, sah," he answered.

Ben placed his hand on his hip-pocket and said coldly:

"Put your cross-mark on those forms I've made out there for you, go with me immediately, and summon these men. If you dare put a negro on this jury, or open your mouth as to what has occurred in this room, I'll kill you."

The negro tremblingly did as he was commanded.

The coroner's jury reported that the mother and daughter had been killed by accidentally falling over the cliff.

In all the throng of grief-stricken friends who came to the little cottage that day, but two men knew the hell-lit secret beneath the tragedy.

When the bodies reached the home, Doctor Cameron placed Mrs. Cameron and Margaret outside to receive visitors and prevent any one from disturbing him. He took Ben into the room and locked the doors.

"My boy, I wish you to witness an experiment."

He drew from its case a powerful microscope of French make.

"What on earth are you going to do, sir?"

The doctor's brilliant eyes flashed with a mystic light as he replied:

"Find the fiend who did this crime—and then we will hang him on a gallows so high that all men from the rivers to ends of the earth shall see and feel and know the might of an unconquerable race of men."

"But there's no trace of him here."

"We shall see," said the doctor, adjusting his instrument.

"I believe that a microscope of sufficient power will reveal on the retina of these dead eyes the image of this devil as if etched there by fire. The experiment has been made successfully in France. No word or deed of man is lost. A German scholar has a memory so wonderful he can repeat whole volumes of Latin, German, and French without an error. A Russian officer has been known to repeat the roll-call of any regiment by reading it twice. Psychologists hold that nothing is lost from the memory of man. Impressions remain in the brain like words written on paper in invisible ink. So I believe of images in the eye if we can trace them early enough. If no impression were made subsequently on the mother's eye by the light of day, I believe the fire-etched record of this crime can yet be traced."

Ben watched him with breathless interest.

He first examined Marion's eyes. But in the cold azure blue of their pure depths he could find nothing.

"It's as I feared with the child," he said. "I can see nothing. It is on the mother I rely. In the splendour of life, at thirty-seven she was the full-blown perfection of womanhood with every vital force at its highest tension —"

He looked long and patiently into the dead mother's eye, rose and wiped the perspiration from his face.

"What is it, sir?" asked Ben.

Without reply, as if in a trance, he returned to the microscope and again rose with the little quick nervous cough he gave only in the greatest excitement, and whispered:

"Look now and tell me what you see."

Ben looked and said:

"I can see nothing."

"Your powers of vision are not trained as mine," replied the doctor, resuming his place at the instrument.

"What do you see?" asked the younger man, bending nervously.

"The bestial figure of a negro—his huge black hand plainly defined—the upper part of the face is dim, as if obscured by a gray mist of dawn—but the massive jaws and lips are clear—merciful God!—yes!—it's Gus!"

The doctor leaped to his feet livid with excitement.

* * *

On the afternoon of the funeral, two days later, Ben received a cypher telegram from the conductor of the train telling him that Gus was on the evening mail due at Piedmont at nine o'clock.

* * *

At the signal of a whistle, the men and horses arrayed in white and scarlet swung into double-file cavalry formation and stood awaiting orders. The moon was now shining brightly, and its light shimmering on the silent horses and men with their tall spiked caps made a picture such as the world had not seen since the Knights of the Middle Ages rode on their Holy Crusades.

As the train neared the flag-station, which was dark and unattended, the conductor approached Gus, leaned over and said: "I've just gotten a message from the sheriff telling me to warn you to get off at this station and slip into town. There's a crowd at the depot there waiting for you and they mean trouble."

Gus trembled, and whispered:

"Den fur Gawd's sake lemme off here."

The two men who got on at the station below stepped out before the negro, and, as he alighted from the car, seized, tripped, and threw him to the ground. The engineer blew a sharp signal, and the train pulled on.

In a minute Gus was bound and gagged.

* * *

from THE FIERY CROSS

Through the narrow crooked entrance they led Gus into the cave which had been the rendezvous of the Piedmont Den of the Klan since its formation. The meeting-place was a grand hall eighty feet deep, fifty feet wide, and more than forty feet in height, which had been carved out of the stone by the swift current of the river in ages past when its waters stood at a higher level.

To-night it was lighted by candles placed on the ledges of the walls. In the centre, on a fallen boulder, sat the Grand Cyclops of the Den, the presiding officer of the township, his rank marked by scarlet stripes on the white-cloth spike of his cap. Around him stood twenty or more clansmen in their uniform, completely disguised. One among them wore a yellow sash, trimmed in gold, about his waist, and on his breast two yellow circles with red crosses interlapping, denoting his rank to be the Grand Dragon of the Realm, or Commander-in-Chief of the State.

The Cyclops rose from his seat:

"Let the Grand Turk remove his prisoner for a moment and place him in charge of the Grand Sentinel at the door, until summoned."

The officer disappeared with Gus, and the Cyclops continued:

"The Chaplain will open our Council with prayer."

Solemnly every white-shrouded figure knelt on the ground, and the voice of the Rev. Hugh McAlpin, trembling with feeling, echoed through the cave:

"Lord God of our Fathers, as in times past thy children, fleeing from the oppressor, found refuge beneath the earth until once more the sun of righteousness rose, so are we met to-night. As we wrestle with the powers of darkness now strangling our life, give to our souls to endure as seeing the invisible, and to our right arms the strength of the martyred dead of our people. Have mercy on the poor, the weak, the innocent and defenseless, and deliver us from the body of the Black Death. In a land of light and beauty and love our women are prisoners of danger and fear. While the heathen walks his native heath unharmed and unafraid, in this fair Christian Southland, our sisters, wives, and daughters dare not stroll at twilight through the streets, or step beyond the highway at noon. The terror of the twilight deepens with the darkness, and the stoutest heart grows sick with fear for the red message the morning bringeth. Forgive our sins—they are many, but hide not thy face from us, O God, for thou art our refuge!"

As the last echoes of the prayer lingered and died in the vaulted roof, the clansmen rose and stood a moment in silence.

* * *

"The Night Hawks will produce their evidence," said the Cyclops, "and the Grand Monk will conduct the case of the people against the negro Augustus Caesar, the former slave of Dr. Richard Cameron."

Dr. Cameron advanced and removed his cap. His snow-white hair and beard, ruddy face and dark-brown brilliant eyes made a strange picture in its weird surroundings, like an ancient alchemist ready to conduct some daring experiment in the problem of life.

"I am here, brethren," he said, "to accuse the black brute about to appear of the crime of assault on a daughter, of the South —"

A murmur of thrilling surprise and horror swept the crowd of white and scarlet figures as with one common impulse they moved closer.

"His feet have been measured and they exactly tally with the negro tracks found under the window of the Lenoir cottage. His flight to Columbia and return on the publication of their deaths as an accident is a confirmation of our case. I will not relate to you the scientific experiment which first fixed my suspicion of this man's guilt. My witness could not confirm it, and it might not be to you credible. But this negro is peculiarly sensitive to hypnotic influence. I propose to put him under this power to-night before you, and, if he is guilty, I can make him tell his confederates, describe and rehearse the crime itself."

The Night Hawks led Gus before Doctor Cameron, untied his hands, removed the gag, and slipped the blindfold from his head.

Under the doctor's rigid gaze the negro's knees struck together, and he collapsed into complete hypnosis, merely lifting his huge paws lamely as if to ward a blow.

They seated him on the boulder from which the Cyclops rose, and Gus stared about the cave and grinned as if in a dream seeing nothing.

The doctor recalled to him the day of the crime, and he began to talk to his three confederates, describing his plot in detail, now and then pausing and breaking into a fiendish laugh.

Old McAllister, who had three lovely daughters at home, threw off his cap, sank to his knees, and buried his face in his hands, while a dozen of the white figures crowded closer, nervously gripping the revolvers which hung from their red belts.

* * *

In spite of Doctor Cameron's warning, the white-robed figures jostled and pressed closer —

Gus rose to his feet and started across the cave as if to spring on the shivering figure of the girl, the clansmen with muttered groans, sobs and curses falling back as he advanced. He still wore his full Captain's uniform, its heavy epaulets flashing their gold in the unearthly light, his beastly jaws half covering the gold braid on the collar. His thick lips were drawn upward in an ugly leer and his sinister bead-eyes gleamed like a gorilla's. A single fierce leap and the black claws clutched the air slowly as if sinking into the soft white throat.

Strong men began to cry like children.

"Stop him! Stop him!" screamed a clansman, springing on the negro and grinding his heel into his big thick neck. A dozen more were on him in a moment, kicking stamping, cursing, and crying like madmen.

Doctor Cameron leaped forward and beat them off:

"Men! Men! You must not kill him in this condition!"

Some of the white figures had fallen prostrate on the ground, sobbing in a frenzy of uncontrollable emotion. Some were leaning against the walls, their faces buried in their arms.

* * *

[Ben Cameron, the Grand Dragon of the Realm] stood for a moment silent, erect, a smouldering fierceness in his eyes, something cruel and yet magnetic in his alert bearing.

He looked on the prostrate negro lying in his uniform at his feet, seized the cross, lighted the three upper ends and held it blazing in his hand, while, in a voice full of the fires of feeling, he said:

"Men of the South, the time for words has passed, the hour for action has struck. The Grand Turk will execute this negro to-night and fling his body on the lawn of the black Lieutenant-Governor of the state."

The Grand Turk bowed.

"I ask for the swiftest messenger of this Den who can ride till dawn."

The man whom Doctor Cameron had already chosen stepped forward:

"Carry my summons to the Grand Titan of the adjoining province in North Carolina whom you will find at Hambright. Tell him the story of this crime and what you have seen and heard. Ask him to report to me here the second night from this, at eleven o'clock, with six Grand Giants from his adjoining counties, each accompanied by two hundred picked men. In olden times when the Chieftain of our people summoned the clan on an errand of life and death, the Fiery Cross, extinguished in sacrificial blood, was sent by swift courier from village to village. This call was never made in vain, nor will it be to-night in the new world. Here, on this spot made holy ground by the blood of those we hold dearer than life, I raise the ancient symbol of an unconquered race of men —"

High above his head in the darkness of the cave he lifted the blazing emblem—

"The Fiery Cross of old Scotland's Hills! I quench its flames in the sweetest blood that ever stained the sands of Time."

He dipped its ends in the silver cup, extinguished the fire, and handed the charred symbol to the courier, who quickly disappeared.

Questions to Consider

1. How does Dixon use the traditional roles of women and the associations of family life to accentuate the audacity of Gus's attack? What elements of the relationship between the women and their reaction to the rape seem credible to you? Isolate the less credible representations and explain why Dixon might have invented them. How are religion and tradition invoked to buttress violence here? What is the relationship between the fear evoked by African Americans and the sanctioned confinement of women in the home?
2. Develop a generic portrait of African Americans, based on Dixon; compare your profile with one or more African-American characters in a story by another Southern writer of this era or that of a later period. What differences in substance or tone do you observe? Do the same with White Southerners. What conclusions can you draw about the nature of stereotypes in Southern fiction?

Alice Ruth Moore Dunbar-Nelson

1875–1935

Although Dunbar-Nelson's biographer and editor, Gloria Hull, suggests that the writer lacked the creative genius to produce a masterpiece, she made up for any such deficit in the sheer breadth of her achievements. Dunbar-Nelson wrote poetry, short fiction, novels, plays, a sassy newspaper column ("Une Femme Dit"), a powerful and revealing diary, and groundbreaking essays; she was a gifted teacher, a stenographer, an editor, a public speaker, a campaign manager, an executive secretary, and a committed activist for both women's rights and racial equity. Moreover, as Hull observes, she performed these extraordinary feats as a divided self, at a cultural moment when authentic self-expression was severely limited for African-American women writers.

A cherished daughter of a former slave and an absent (probably White) father, Alice Ruth Moore grew up in New Orleans, where her light skin gave her access to African-American Creole society. She graduated from Straight College for teachers (now Dillard University) in 1892 and became active in literary and social circles. Her first book, *Violets and Other Tales*, published when she was barely 20, was the first such collection by an African-American woman. Her verse also won a husband. Paul Laurence Dunbar, already a well-known writer of dialect poetry, wrote her a fan letter, and two years later, the couple was married. The relationship was never very stable, however, and they separated in 1902; Dunbar died four years later without reconciliation. Dunbar-Nelson was by that time living in Wilmington, Delaware, where she was briefly married to a fellow teacher in 1910 and then more happily to journalist Robert Nelson in 1916.

Though Dunbar-Nelson was best known for her literary work, after the publication of her second volume, *The Goodness of St. Rocque and Other Stories* (1899), she increasingly turned to nonfiction to express the urgency of the issues reshaping American society. Dunbar-Nelson articulated her views in essays and editorials directed largely to African-American audiences, such as the readers of Harvard-educated Carter G. Woodson's new *Journal of Negro History*, whose first volume in 1916 included "People of Color in Louisiana." Published in two parts, the carefully researched essay describes the contributions of "people of color" to Southern society; but more importantly, just as Jim Crow laws were obsessively drawing racial lines, Dunbar-Nelson lays bare the folly of defining race in a society where intermarriage has made such boundaries indefinable: "it is difficult to enforce laws against a race when you cannot find that race."

Light-skinned enough to "pass" as White when she wanted to attend the opera or a symphony, Dunbar-Nelson was well-acquainted with the painful dilemmas of racial identity, having experienced prejudice from both the African-American and the White communities. Her fiction also reflects that complexity, and the race of her characters is typically coded into the language of the story rather than explicitly named. Race, for example, is clearly a reason for Neale's rejection of Sophie for a more acceptable bride. But Sophie is described only as "dusky-eyed," a "Creole," who first appears to us as a "little, forsaken, black heap at the altar of the Virgin." Her loyalty ultimately restores her lover's fortunes, even though it costs Sophie her life. For Dunbar-Nelson, as for other post–Reconstruction writers, the plight of the "tragic mulatta," a woman caught on the color line, offered a discreet way to examine the complexities of racial identity as well as the limits of gender and social caste.

Though she turned to social activism to resist the hardening lines of race in America, Dunbar-Nelson never quite abandoned literature. Her antiwar and suffragist views are reflected in what is perhaps her most famous work, "I Sit and Sew." Indeed, until the publication of her voluminous diaries in the 1980s, Dunbar-Nelson's critical reputation remained that of a minor poet. The recovery of those remarkable diaries and the ensuing reassessment of her work have redefined her significance. Dunbar-Nelson died in Philadelphia on 18 September 1935, leaving dozens of unpublished manuscripts, a testament to her commitment to the creative spirit.

I Sit and Sew

I sit and sew—a useless task it seems,
My hands grown tired, my head weighed down with dreams—
The panoply of war, the martial tread of men,
Grim-faced, stern-eyed, gazing beyond the ken
Of lesser souls, whose eyes have not seen Death
Nor learned to hold their lives but as a breath—
But—I must sit and sew.

I sit and sew—my heart aches with desire—
This pageant terrible, that fiercely pouring fire
On wasted fields, and writhing grotesque things
Once men. My soul in pity flings
Appealing cries, yearning only to go
There in that holocaust of hell, those fields of woe—
But—I must sit and sew.

The little useless seam, the idle patch;
Why dream I here beneath my homely thatch,
When there they lie in sodden mud and rain,
Pitifully calling me, the quick ones and the slain?
You need me, Christ! It is no roseate dream
That beckons me—this pretty futile seam,
It stifles me—God, must I sit and sew?

Little Miss Sophie

When Miss Sophie knew consciousness again, the long, faint, swelling notes of the organ were dying away in distant echoes through the great arches of the silent church, and she was alone, crouching in a little, forsaken black heap at the altar of the Virgin. The twinkling tapers shone pityingly upon her, the beneficent smile of the white-robed Madonna seemed to whisper comfort. A long gust of chill air swept up the aisles, and Miss Sophie shivered not from cold, but from nervousness.

But darkness was falling, and soon the lights would be lowered, and the great massive doors would be closed; so, gathering her thin little cape about her frail shoulders, Miss Sophie hurried out, and along the brilliant noisy streets home.

It was a wretched, lonely little room, where the cracks let the boisterous wind whistle through, and the smoky, grimy walls looked cheerless and unhomelike. A miserable little room in a miserable little cottage in one of the squalid streets of the Third District that nature and the city fathers seemed to have forgotten.

As bare and comfortless as the room was Miss Sophie's life. She rented these four walls from an unkempt little Creole woman, whose progeny seemed like the promised offspring of Abraham. She scarcely kept the flickering life in her pale little body by the unceasing toil of a pair of bony hands, stitching, stitching, ceaselessly, wearingly, on the bands and pockets of trousers. It was her bread, this monotonous, unending work; and though whole days and nights constant labour brought but the most meagre recompense, it was her only hope of life.

She sat before the little charcoal brazier and warmed her transparent, needle-pricked fingers, thinking meanwhile of the strange events of the day. She had been up town to carry the great, black bundle of coarse pants and vests to the factory and to receive her small pittance, and on the way home stopped in at the Jesuit Church to say her little prayer at the altar of the calm white Virgin. There had been a wondrous burst of music from the great organ as she knelt there, an over-powering perfume of many flowers, the glittering dazzle of many lights, and the dainty frou-frou made by the silken skirts of wedding guests. So Miss Sophie stayed to the wedding; for what feminine heart, be it ever so old and seared, does not de-light in one? And why should not a poor little Creole old maid be interested too?

Then the wedding party had filed in solemnly, to the rolling, swelling tones of the organ. Important-looking groomsmen; dainty, fluffy, white-robed maids; stately, satin-robed, illusion-veiled bride, and happy groom. She leaned forward to catch a better glimpse of their faces. "Ah!" —

Those near the Virgin's altar who heard a faint sigh and rustle on the steps glanced curiously as they saw a slight black-robed figure clutch the railing and lean her head against it. Miss Sophie had fainted.

"I must have been hungry," she mused over the charcoal fire in her little room, "I must have been hungry;" and she smiled a wan smile, and busied herself getting her evening meal of coffee and bread and ham.

If one were given to pity, the first thought that would rush to one's lips at sight of Miss Sophie would have been, "Poor little woman!" She had come among the bareness and sordidness of this neighbourhood five years ago, robed in crape, and crying with great sobs that seemed to shake the vitality out of her. Perfectly silent, too, she was about her former life; but for all that, Michel, the quartee grocer at the corner, and Madame Laurent, who kept the rabbé shop opposite, had fixed it all up between them, of her sad history and past glories. Not that they knew; but then Michel must invent something when the neighbours came to him as their fountain-head of wisdom.

One morning little Miss Sophie opened wide her dingy windows to catch the early freshness of the autumn wind as it whistled through the yellow-leafed trees. It was one of those calm, blue-misted, balmy, November days that New Orleans can have when all the rest of the country is fur-wrapped. Miss Sophie pulled her machine to the window, where the sweet, damp wind could whisk among her black locks.

Whirr, whirr, went the machine, ticking fast and lightly over the belts of the rough jeans pants. Whirr, whirr, yes, and Miss Sophie was actually humming a tune! She felt strangely light to-day.

"Ma foi," muttered Michel, strolling across the street to where Madame Laurent sat sewing behind the counter on blue and brown-checked aprons, "but the little ma'amselle sings. Perhaps she recollects."

"Perhaps," muttered the rabbé woman.

But little Miss Sophie felt restless. A strange impulse seemed drawing her up town, and the machine seemed to run slow, slow, before it would stitch all of the end-less number of jeans belts. Her fingers trembled with nervous haste as she pinned up the unwieldy black bundle of finished work, and her feet fairly tripped over each other in their eagerness to get to Claiborne Street, where she could board the up-town car.

There was a feverish desire to go somewhere, a sense of elation, a foolish happiness that brought a faint echo of colour into her pinched cheeks. She wondered why.

No one noticed her in the car. Passengers on the Claiborne line are too much accustomed to frail little black-robed women with big, black bundles; it is one of the city's most pitiful sights. She leaned her head out of the window to catch a glimpse of the oleanders on Bayou Road, when her attention was caught by a conversation in the car.

"Yes, it's too bad for Neale, and lately married too," said the elder man. "I ca n't see what he is to do."

Neale! She pricked up her ears. That was the name of the groom in the Jesuit Church.

"How did it happen?" languidly inquired the younger. He was a stranger, evidently; a stranger with a high regard for the faultlessness of male attire.

"Well, the firm failed first; he did n't mind that much, he was so sure of his uncle's inheritance repairing his lost fortunes; but suddenly this difficulty of identification springs up, and he is literally on the verge of ruin."

"Wo n't some of you fellows who 've known him all your lives do to identify him?"

"Gracious man, we 've tried; but the absurd old will expressly stipulates that he shall be known only by a certain quaint Roman ring, and unless he has it, no identification, no fortune. He has given the ring away, and that settles it."

"Well, you 're all chumps. Why does n't he get the ring from the owner?"

"Easily said; but—it seems that Neale had some little Creole love-affair some years ago, and gave this ring to his dusky-eyed fiancée. You know how Neale is with his love-affairs, went off and forgot the girl in a month. It seems, however, she took it to heart—so much so that he's ashamed to try to find her or the ring."

Miss Sophie heard no more as she gazed out into the dusty grass. There were tears in her eyes, hot blinding ones that would n't drop for pride, but stayed and scalded. She knew the story, with all its embellishment of heartaches. She knew the ring, too. She remembered the day she had kissed and wept and fondled it, until it seemed her heart must burst under its load of grief before she took it to the pawnbroker's that another might be eased before the end came—that other her father. The little "Creole love affair" of Neale's had not always been poor and old and jaded-looking; but reverses must come, even Neale knew that, so the ring was at the Mont de Piété. Still he must have it, it was his; it would save him from disgrace and suffering and from bringing the white-gowned bride into sorrow. He must have it; but how?

There it was still at the pawn-broker's; no one would have such an odd jewel, and the ticket was home in the bureau drawer. Well, he must have it; she might starve in the attempt. Such a thing as going to him and telling him that he might redeem it was an impossibility. That good, straight-backed, stiff-necked Creole blood would have risen in all its strength and choked her. No; as a present had the quaint Roman circlet been placed upon her finger, as a present should it be returned.

The bumping car rode slowly, and the hot thoughts beat heavily in her poor little head. He must have the ring; but how—the ring—the Roman ring—the white-robed bride starving—she was going mad—ah yes—the church.

There it was, right in the busiest, most bustling part of the town, its fresco and bronze and iron quaintly suggestive of mediæval times. Within, all was cool and dim and restful, with the faintest whiff of lingering incense rising and pervading the gray arches. Yes, the Virgin would know and have pity; the sweet, white-robed Virgin at the pretty flower-decked altar, or the one away up in the niche, far above the golden dome where the Host was.

Titiche, the busybody of the house, noticed that Miss Sophie's bundle was larger than usual that afternoon. "Ah, poor woman!" sighed Titiche's mother, "she would be rich for Christmas."

The bundle grew larger each day, and Miss Sophie grew smaller. The damp, cold rain and mist closed the white-curtained window, but always there behind the sewing-machine drooped and bobbed the little black-robed figure. Whirr, whirr went the wheels, and the coarse jeans pants piled in great heaps at her side. The Claiborne Street car saw her oftener than before, and the sweet white Virgin in the flowered niche above the gold-domed altar smiled at the little supplicant almost every day.

"Ma foi," said the slatternly land-lady to Madame Laurent and Michel one day, "I no see how she live! Eat? Nothin', nothin', almos', and las' night when it was so cold and foggy, eh? I hav' to mek him build fire. She mos' freeze."

Whereupon the rumour spread that Miss Sophie was starving herself to death to get some luckless relative out of jail for Christmas; a rumour which enveloped her scraggy little figure with a kind of halo to the neighbours when she appeared on the streets.

November had merged into December, and the little pile of coins was yet far from the sum needed. Dear God! how the money did have to go! The rent and the groceries and the coal, though, to be sure, she used a precious bit of that. Would all the work and saving and skimping do good? Maybe, yes, maybe by Christmas.

Christmas Eve on Royal Street is no place for a weakling, for the shouts and carousals of the roisterers will strike fear into the bravest ones. Yet amid the cries and yells, the deafening blow of horns and tin whistles, and the really dangerous fusillade of fireworks, a little figure hurried along, one hand clutching tightly the battered hat that the rude merry-makers had torn off, the other grasping under the thin black cape a worn little pocketbook.

Into the Mont de Piété she ran breathless, eager. The ticket? Here, worn, crumpled. The ring? It was not gone? No, thank Heaven! It was a joy well worth her toil, she thought, to have it again.

Had Titiche not been shooting crackers on the banquette instead of peering into the crack, as was his wont, his big, round black eyes would have grown saucer-wide to see little Miss Sophie kiss and fondle a ring, an ugly clumsy band of gold.

"Ah, dear ring," she murmured, "once you were his, and you shall be his again. You shall be on his finger, and perhaps touch his heart. Dear ring, ma chère petite de ma cœur, chérie de ma cœur. Je t'aime, je t'aime, oui, oui. You are his; you were mine once too. To-night, just one night, I'll keep you—then—to-morrow, you shall go where you can save him."

The loud whistles and horns of the little ones rose on the balmy air next morning. No one would doubt it was Christmas Day, even if doors and windows were open wide to let in cool air. Why, there was Christmas even in the very look of the mules on the poky cars; there was Christmas noise in the streets, and Christmas toys and Christmas odours, savoury ones that made the nose wrinkle approvingly, issuing from the kitchen. Michel and Madame Laurent smiled greetings across the street at each other, and the salutation from a passer-by recalled the many-progenied landlady to herself.

"Miss Sophie, well, po' soul, not ver' much Chris'mas for her. Mais, I'll jus' call him in fo' to spen' the day with me. Eet'll cheer her a bit."

It was so clean and orderly within the poor little room. Not a speck of dust or a litter of any kind on the quaint little old-time high bureau, unless you might except a sheet of paper lying loose with something written on it. Titiche had evidently inherited his prying propensities, for the landlady turned it over and read—

Louis—
Here is the ring. I return it to you. I heard you needed it. I hope it comes not too late.
Sophie.

"The ring, where?" muttered the landlady. There it was, clasped between her fingers on her bosom—a bosom white and cold, under a cold happy face. Christmas had indeed dawned for Miss Sophie.

from People of Color in Louisiana[1]

from *Part I*

The title of a possible discussion of the Negro in Louisiana presents difficulties, for there is no such word as Negro permissible in speaking of this State. The history of the State is filled with attempts to define, sometimes at the point of the sword, oftenest in civil or criminal courts, the meaning of the word Negro. By common consent, it came to mean in Louisiana, prior to 1865, slave, and after the war, those whose complexions were noticeably dark. As Grace King so delightfully puts it, "The pure-blooded African was never called colored, but always Negro." The *gens de couleur*, colored people, were always a class apart, separated from and superior to the Negroes, ennobled were it only by one drop of white blood in their veins. The caste seems to have existed from the first introduction of slaves. To the whites, all Africans who were not of pure blood were *gens de couleur*. Among themselves, however, there were jealous and fiercely-guarded distinctions: "griffes, briqués, mulattoes, quadroons, octoroons, each term meaning one degree's further transfiguration toward the Caucasian standard of physical perfection."[2]

Negro slavery in Louisiana seems to have been early influenced by the policy of the Spanish colonies. De las Casas, an apostle to the Indians, exclaimed against the slavery of the Indians and finding his efforts of no avail proposed to Charles V in 1517 the slavery of the Africans as a substitute. The Spaniards refused at first to import slaves from Africa, but later agreed to the proposition and employed other nations to traffic in them. Louisiana learned from the Spanish colonies her lessons of this traffic, took over certain parts of the slave regulations and imported bondmen from the Spanish West Indies. Others brought thither were Congo, Banbara, Yaloff, and Mandingo slaves.

People of color were introduced into Louisiana early in the eighteenth century. . . . When the first came, is not known, but in 1713 twenty of these Negro slaves from Africa are recorded in the census of the little colony on the Mississippi.

* * *

. . . The new colony was not immoral; it may best be described as unmoral. Indolence on the part of the masters was physical, mental and moral. The slave population began to lighten in color, and increase out of all proportion to the importation and natural breeding among themselves. La Harpe comments in 1724 upon the astonishing diminution of the white population and the astounding increase of the colored population. Something was undoubtedly wrong, according to the Caucasian standard, and it has remained wrong to our own day. The person of color was now, in Louisiana, a part of its social system, a creature to be legislated for and against, a person lending his dark shade to temper the inartistic complexion of his white master. Now he

1. Most of Dunbar-Nelson's original scholarly notes have been omitted, but those remaining are the hers.

2. King, "New Orleans, the Place and the People During the Ancien Regime," 333 (author's note).

began to make history, and just as the trail of his color persisted in the complexion of Louisiana, so the trail of his personal influence continued in the history of the colony, the territory and the State.

Bienville, the man of far-reaching vision, saw the danger menacing the colony, and before his recall and disgrace before the French court, he published, in 1724, the famous Black Code. This code followed the order of that of the West Indies but contains some provisions to meet local needs. The legal status of the slave was that of movable property of his master. Children born of Negro parents followed the condition of their mother. Slaves were forbidden to carry weapons. Slaves of different masters could not assemble in crowds by day or night. They were not permitted to sell "commodities, provisions, or produce" without permission from their masters, and had no property which did not belong to their masters. . . .

There were, however, somewhat favorable provisions which made this code seem a little less rigorous. The slaves had to be well fed and the masters could not force them to provide for themselves by working for their own account certain days of the week and slaves could give information against their owners, if not properly fed or clothed. Disabled slaves had to be sent to the hospital. Husbands, wives, and their children under the age of puberty could not be seized and sold separately when belonging to the same master. . . .

. . . The slaves had to be instructed in the Catholic religion. Slaves appointed by their masters as tutors to their children were held set free. Moreover, manumitted slaves enjoyed the same rights, privileges and immunities that were enjoyed by those born free. "It is our pleasure," reads the document, "that their merit in having acquired their freedom shall produce in their favor, not only with regard to their persons, but also to their property, the same effects that our other subjects derive from the happy circumstance of their having been born free."

From the first appearance of the *gens de couleur* in the colony of Louisiana dates the class the *gens de couleur libres*.

* * *

It is in the definition of the word Creole that another great difficulty arises. The native white Louisianian will tell you that a Creole is a white man, whose ancestors contain some French or Spanish blood in their veins. But he will be disputed by others, who will gravely tell you that Creoles are to be found only in the lower Delta lands of the state, that there are no Creoles north of New Orleans; and will raise their hands in horror at the idea of being confused with the "Cajans," the descendants of those Nova Scotians whom Longfellow immortalized in Evangeline. Sifting down the mass of conflicting definitions, it appears that to a Caucasian, a Creole is a native of the lower parishes of Louisiana, in whose veins some traces of Spanish, West Indian or French blood runs. The Caucasian will shudder with horror at the idea of including a person of color in the definition, and the person of color will retort with his definition that a Creole is a native of Louisiana, in whose blood runs mixed strains of everything un-American, with the African strain slightly apparent. The true Creole is like the famous gumbo of the state, a little bit of everything, making a whole, delightfully flavored, quite distinctive, and wholly unique.

From 1724 to the present time, frequent discussions as to the proper name by which to designate this very important portion of the population of Louisiana waged more or less acrimoniously.

from *Part II*

. . . Twenty days after the French tri-color waved in place of the Spanish flag in the old Place d'Armes, the American stars and stripes proclaimed the land American territory. The Creoles, French though they were in spirit, in partisanship, in sympathy, could not but breathe a sigh of relief, for Napoleon had dangerous ideas concerning the freedom of slaves, and already had spoken sharply about the people of color in the province. Were the terrors of San Domingo to be reenacted on the banks of [the] Mississippi? The United States answered with a decided negative.

* * *

The administration of Governor Claiborne from 1803 to 1816 was one long wrestle, not only with the almost superhuman task of adjusting a practically foreign country to American ideals of government but of wrestling with the color problem. Slowly and insidiously it had come to dominate every other problem. The people of color had helped to settle the territory, had helped to make it commercially important, had helped to save it from the Indians and from the English, and they seemed likely to become the most important factors in its history.

* * *

"Americans," says Grace King, "were despised and ridiculed." Men, women and children of color, free and slave, united to insult the American Negro or—"Mericain Coquin," as they called him. The French and the Spaniards, moreover, united in using the people of color to further their own interests, or to annoy the new American government while the intrigues of Spain and France weakened the feeble territory. It was difficult to know how to treat this almost alien people.

* * *

Writers describing the New Orleans of this [antebellum] period agree in presenting a picture of a continental city, most picturesque, most un-American, and as varied in color as a street of Cairo. There they saw French, Spaniards, English, Bohemians, Negroes, mulattoes; varied clothes, picturesque white dresses of the fairer women, brilliant cottons of the darker ones. The streets, banquettes, we should say, were bright with color, the nights filled with song and laughter. Through the scene, the people of color add the spice of color; in the life, they add the zest of romance.

* * *

The minor distinctions of complexion and race so fiercely adhered to by the Creoles of the old regime were at their height at this time. The glory and shame of the city were her quadroons and octoroons, apparently constituting two aristocratic circles of society, the one as elegant as the other, the complexions the same, the men the same, the women different in race, but not in color, nor in dress, nor in jewels. Writers on fire with the romance of this continental city love to speak of the splendors of the French Opera House, the first place in the country where grand opera was heard, and tell of the tiers of beautiful women with their jewels and airs and graces. Above the orchestra circle were four tiers, the first filled with the beautiful dames of the city; the second filled with a second array of beautiful women, attired like those of the first, with no apparent difference; yet these were the octoroons and quadroons, whose beauty and wealth were all the passports needed. The third was for the hoi polloi of the white race, and the fourth for the people of color whose color was more evident. It was a veritable sandwich of races.

With the slaves, especially those outside of New Orleans, the situation was different. The cruelty of the slave owners in the State was proverbial. To be "sent down the Mississippi" became a by-word of horror, a bogie with which slave-holders all over the South threatened their incorrigible slaves. The slave markets, the tortures of the old plantations, even those in the city, which Cable has immortalized, help to fill the pages of romance, which must be cruel as well as beautiful.

* * *

The free people of color, however, kept on amassing wealth and educating their children as ever in spite of opposition, for it is difficult to enforce laws against a race when you cannot find that race. Being well-to-do they could maintain their own institutions of learning, and had access to parochial schools. Some of them like their white neighbors, sent their sons to France and their daughters to the convents to continue their education beyond the first communion. The first free school ever opened for colored children in the United States was the "Ecole Des Orphelins Indigents," a School for Indigent Orphans opened in 1840.

* * *

More about the people of color in Louisiana might be written. It is a theme too large to be treated save by a master hand. It is interwoven with the poetry, the romance, the glamour, the commercial prosperity, the financial ruin, the rise and fall of the State. It is hung about with garlands, like the garlands of the cemeteries on All Saints Day; it may be celebrated in song, or jeered at in the charivaris. Some day, the proper historian will tell the story. There is no State in the Union, hardly any spot of like size on the globe, where the man of color has lived so intensely, made so much progress, been of such historical importance and yet about whom so comparatively little is known. His history is like the Mardi Gras of the city of New Orleans, beautiful and mysterious and wonderful, but with a serious thought underlying it all. May it be better known to the world some day.

Questions to Consider

1. How do the opening scenes establish Miss Sophie's position in the world? What elements of the description link religious authority and belief with racial structures? How do Sophie's descriptions highlight the complexities of her relationship to those structures? Trace the uses of white and various shades of black as an index of racial significance in this story.
2. Dunbar-Nelson's essay appeared in the wake of Dixon's popular novels and Griffith's film. In what ways does her argument refute their slanderous accounts of African Americans? What evidence most tellingly undermines the "plantation myth" promoted by the work of Dixon, Page, Stuart, and others? What details from this essay challenged your own assumptions about color and racial identity? About slavery?

Part IV

The Southern Renascence

INDUSTRIALISM AND THE EMERGING MODERNIST VOICE

1910–1956

As the twentieth century opened, the South continued to suffer the aftereffects of military defeat in the Civil War. The fall of the Confederacy, the imposition of martial law throughout the South, and the suffrage granted to African-American males after 1870 led White Southerners to resent the North and to blame the "damned Yankees" for their troubles. This resentment resulted in a dramatic backlash when Radical Reconstruction ended in 1877, and newly resurgent ex-Confederates legalized White supremacy in the South through the enforcement of Jim Crow laws. Under the rule of Southern planter Democrats, political equality for former slaves deteriorated as African Americans lost voting and property rights, and poor Whites sank deeply into peonage. The disintegration of the old agricultural order based on slavery ushered in a neo-feudal system of tenant farming and sharecropping which provided landowners with cheap labor. At the same time, many advocates of the New South sought to modernize the region, viewing Northern technology and industry—especially railroads and textile manufacturing—as cures for the widespread poverty and cultural isolation of the Postbellum South. Old social divisions left over from the caste system of the plantation South led to abundant abuses by the newly risen industrial class. As a result, the combination of an increased demand for farm products, a growing number of employment opportunities in cities, and the mobility that these positions engendered began to lessen Southern isolation, allowing the region to evolve from its economically marginalized status.

Whether African American or White, wealthy or poor, aristocratic or lower class, most Southerners endured lingering economic consequences for decades following the Civil War. Well into the twentieth century, the South remained a conquered province, in effect, a colonial possession of the victorious North. While the Great Depression of the 1930s staggered all sections of the country, the South was hardest hit. As late as 1938, the continued economic struggles of the South were singled out in one of President Franklin D. Roosevelt's fireside chats, in which he identified the South as "the nation's number-one economic problem." Economic hardship coupled with political inequities and racial intimidation led outsiders to view the South as undemocratic and backward as compared to the rest of the nation. Further, many of those who had been wealthy before the Civil War lived in reduced circumstances. Stripped of their wealth, former slave-owning families clung to totems that symbolized their privileged past: the family tea set, silver service, heirloom jewelry. They maintained an air of supremacy amid altered socioeconomic realities. Poor Whites continued

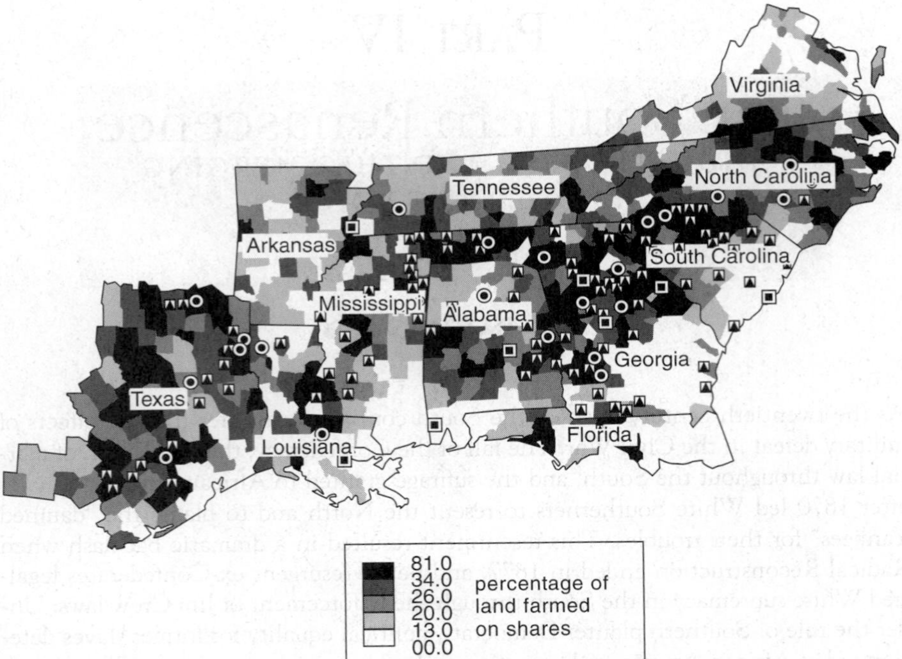

Map IV–1: The crop-lien system, 1880–1915

to struggle, and post-Reconstruction poverty proved harsh and intractable for landless families of both races. Subsistence agriculture became commonplace as families faced starvation in the farmed-out fields of the ruined South (see Map IV–1).

Although life for poor Whites proved harsh, most African Americans fared worse. Poor living conditions, racial oppression, and meager wages led many to seek new opportunities in the North. Given impetus by the homefront industrial expansion of World War I, the Great Migration out of the sharecropper fields of the South into the cities of the North represented a huge population shift (see Map IV–2). Many African-American migrants, however, found the North inhospitable and exploitative. African Americans often were used as pawns in violent labor disputes, hired as scab workers or forced into menial positions. African-American families often found themselves relegated to urban ghettos and tenement housing, as Richard Wright graphically depicts in *Native Son*. Even so, the migration from South to North was reinvigorated by America's entry into World War II (WWII) and by the rise of mechanized agriculture. Fewer agricultural workers were needed as sharecropping gave way to technological advances and corporate farming.

Regional migration also occurred among the upper-class White population. During the 1930s and 1940s, increasing numbers of the Southern intelligentsia left the region in search of better economic opportunities, resulting in what sociologist John Shelton Reed called a regional "brain drain." Artists, literary scholars, scientists, and

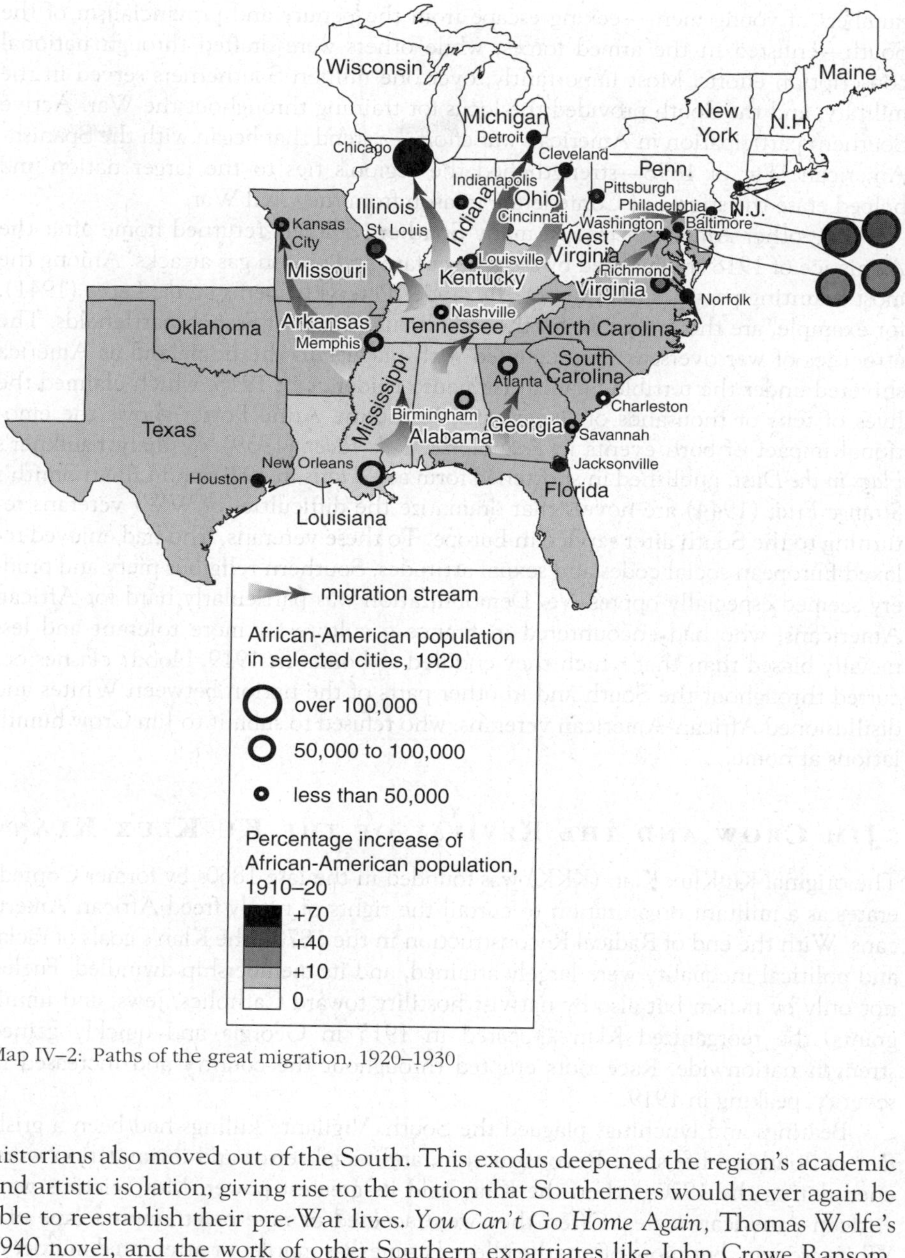

Map IV–2: Paths of the great migration, 1920–1930

historians also moved out of the South. This exodus deepened the region's academic and artistic isolation, giving rise to the notion that Southerners would never again be able to reestablish their pre-War lives. *You Can't Go Home Again*, Thomas Wolfe's 1940 novel, and the work of other Southern expatriates like John Crowe Ransom, Allen Tate, and Robert Penn Warren embody these characteristics.

WORLD WAR I

World War I (WWI) affected the South in subtle yet pervasive ways. This conflict of imperial European powers began in 1914, but the United States entered the War in 1917 after German naval provocations forced an end to American neutrality. Large numbers of young men—seeking escape from the penury and provincialism of the South—enlisted in the armed forces, while others were drafted through national conscription efforts. Most importantly, over one million Southerners served in the military, and the South provided the locus for training throughout the War. Active Southern participation in America's war effort—a trend that began with the Spanish-American War of 1898—strengthened the region's ties to the larger nation and helped erase the stigma of Confederate treason from the Civil War.

Like other American troops, many Southern soldiers returned home after the Armistice of 1918 traumatized by trench warfare and poison gas attacks. Among the most haunting passages in William Alexander Percy's *Lanterns on the Levee* (1941), for example, are those recounting the muddy nightmare of French battlefields. The atrocities of war overseas were coupled with plagues in the homeland as America shivered under the terrible Spanish Influenza epidemic of 1918, which claimed the lives of tens of thousands of Americans. Katherine Anne Porter shows the emotional impact of both events in *Pale Horse, Pale Rider* (1939). William Faulkner's *Flags in the Dust*, published in shortened form as *Sartoris* in 1929, and Lillian Smith's *Strange Fruit* (1944) are novels that dramatize the difficulties of WWI veterans returning to the South after service in Europe. To these veterans, who had enjoyed relaxed European social codes and sexual attitudes, Southern religious piety and prudery seemed especially oppressive. Demobilization was particularly hard for African Americans, who had encountered in France a culture far more tolerant and less racially biased than that which they endured at home. In 1919, bloody clashes occurred throughout the South and in other parts of the nation between Whites and disillusioned African-American veterans, who refused to submit to Jim Crow humiliations at home.

Jim Crow and the Revival of the Ku Klux Klan

The original Ku Klux Klan (KKK) was founded in the late 1860s by former Confederates as a militant organization to curtail the rights of newly freed African Americans. With the end of Radical Reconstruction in the 1870s, the Klan's goals of racial and political inequality were largely attained, and its membership dwindled. Fueled not only by racism but also by nativist hostility toward Catholics, Jews, and immigrants, the reorganized Klan appeared in 1915 in Georgia and quickly gained strength nationwide. Race riots erupted throughout the country and increased in severity, peaking in 1919.

Beatings and lynchings plagued the South. Vigilante killings had been a grisly fact of Southern life since Reconstruction, and racial terror and intimidation worsened during the 1920s, when the Klan held its greatest power. Most victims were African-American males. Often they were accused of rape or attempted rape of a White woman, but more often, the alleged crime was murder or attempted murder of a White man. Victims were hanged, shot, tarred, or burned at the stake. Torture and mutilation were common, as Richard Wright depicts in *Uncle Tom's Children* (1938) when he describes the horrific lynching of a young African-American man. Even though antilynching efforts gained support inside and outside the South, lynchings continued into the 1940s. In 1930, Jessie Daniel Ames, a White progressive from Palestine, Texas, founded Southern Women for the Prevention of Lynching, which grew to 40,000 members by the end of the decade. However, only after WWII did the epidemic of lynchings begin to decline.

Agrarians and Southern Industrialism

World War I also had the effect of accelerating the pace of Southern industrialism as the war effort led to increased national mechanization. Rising industrial cities of the New South included Atlanta, Charlotte, Dallas, Birmingham, and Houston, and urbanization led to an outcry from a circle of poets and scholars at Vanderbilt University in Nashville. Calling themselves the Fugitives, they founded a little magazine in 1922, a date often cited as the beginning of the Southern Renascence. The Fugitive poets gave voice to an almost mystical reverence for the Southern land, as expressed in Ransom's poem, "Antique Harvesters." By degrees, the *aesthetic* regionalism of the Fugitives evolved into the anti-Yankee polemics of the Agrarians, who in 1930 published an outspoken manifesto, *I'll Take My Stand: The South and the Agrarian Tradition.* This essay collection decried the spreading influence of Northern urban, industrial society and defended traditional Southern farm and family values. While liberal critics in both the North and the South ridiculed the Agrarians as ivory tower academics who offered no practical solutions to Southern economic inequality; nevertheless, the controversy drew attention to the social upheavals of the New South.

In fact, the widespread failure of Southern agriculture drove many rural folk into low-paying industrial jobs. After selling their land and relocating to urban areas, these workers came to the realization that they had been misled by false promises of financial prosperity as portrayed by George Sessions Perry in *Hold Autumn in Your Hand* (1940). They found themselves ill-prepared for life away from the farms of the rural South, and with no community support, many floundered and found themselves in greater poverty than when they lived on the farm. Industrial workers in the South struggled with unsafe working conditions, long workdays, starvation wages, and squalid habitation in company cabins, refinery villages, and sawmill towns. Lacking union contracts or federal safeguards, laborers were exploited in Southern industries, which were often financed by Northerners. Led by lintheads—textile mill workers of the Piedmont states—strike efforts sometimes produced violent confrontations with law enforcement, which usually favored the economic interests of owners and operators over the rights of workers. The seasonal cycles of farm life had given way to the boom-and-bust industrial economy of mills, mining, refining, and manufacturing. Periodic economic downturns during the 1920s caused the wartime economy to shrivel, spawning closures, layoffs, unemployment, and worker dislocation.

The Great Depression and Southern Poverty

The Great Depression began in 1929 and worsened over the next decade, yet many Southerners had lived in poverty for years before its onset. Even so, some of the most severe effects were felt in the South and Southwest. Malnutrition and pellagra were commonplace because of reliance on starches to stretch available food. Droughts and crop failures led to widespread hunger, as Bontemps starkly demonstrates in "A Summer Tragedy." From this cauldron of human misery emerged populist leaders, who tapped into the anger felt by the Southern rural poor at their neglect by the elite.

Most memorable of these figures was Louisiana's Huey P. Long, who gained sufficient popularity to lead a national political insurgency called Share Our Wealth (SOW). Long's critics saw in him disturbing dictatorial tendencies, but poor Whites and African Americans hailed him as their champion before his assassination in 1935. For some, the New Deal offered by President Franklin D. Roosevelt and the Democratic Party brought a measure of relief. The Civilian Conservation Corps (CCC) and the Works Progress Administration (WPA) in the late 1930s gave employment to laborers and artists alike; Southern writers like Eudora Welty, Lyle Saxon, and Zora Neale Hurston worked on WPA projects. Large-scale federal projects like the Tennessee Valley Authority (TVA) employed thousands of people and brought electricity and modernization to the remotest corners of Appalachia and the mid-South.

The trans-Mississippi South—the region west of the Mississippi River, including north Louisiana, Arkansas, Missouri, Oklahoma, and Texas—was one of the very hardest hit sections of the nation during the Depression. Dire drought and windstorms caused the area to be known as the Dust Bowl. Dry topsoil blew from the fields and hillsides, darkened the skies, and choked the desperate inhabitants. Perhaps no image of the Depression was as powerful or long-lasting as the Dust Bowl, both a description of ecological disaster and a metaphor for the strangulating effects of poverty and hunger. Many "Okies" and "Arkies" fled to California seeking better opportunities in agriculture, though finding few. Most Oklahomans, however, stayed home and weathered the driving winds as best they could. Woody Guthrie in his *Dust Bowl Ballads* documents the lives of Oklahoma residents and provides biting social critiques of the economy and banking system. An example both of the legacy of ballad music in the South and the radicalizing influence of the Depression appears in the "Ballad of Pretty Boy Floyd," in which Guthrie bitterly compares bankers to armed bandits. The song observes that while robbers steal by using a gun, bankers steal with a pen. This ballad alludes to the record number of home and farm foreclosures during the bleakest period in American history. Bank robbers like Pretty Boy Floyd and Bonnie and Clyde were elevated to cult status. Such tales formed the common lore of Oklahoma, where Pretty Boy Floyd was reared, and Louisiana, where Bonnie and Clyde were gunned down by Texas lawmen in a 1934 ambush. During the 1930s, many storytellers, through both folk songs and oral narratives, glorified the exploits of these bank robbers, finding them less culpable than the bankers they robbed. Edward Anderson drew the inspiration for his hard-bitten novel, *Thieves Like Us*, from the crime spree of Bonnie and Clyde.

Despite the fact that most Southerners did not have much leisure time because of work demands, their oral folk traditions thrived. Telling stories and playing music were inexpensive activities that strengthened the bonds between family and community members. Live music was integral to the lives of many residents, since radios were not yet common in rural areas. Entertainment most often took the form of neighborly visits which included gossiping, yarn-swapping, and sharing news. At some point during the visit, music was likely to be sung or played for entertainment. Such music, derived from the traditions of the Southern past, was gradually transformed after 1925 into stylized string-band music on Nashville's WSM radio station. Its most popular show, the *Grand Ole Opry*, would become the world's longest running radio program. A fictional treatment of the Southern ballad tradition was written in the 1950s by Donald Davidson, one of the Agrarian poet–scholars at Vanderbilt University. Published posthumously in 1996, *The Big Ballad Jamboree* is a novel that honors the traditional social function of authentic Southern folk music while appreciating the artistry of rising country music performers.

World War II and Southern Economic Recovery

World War II began for the United States in 1941 when Japanese bombers attacked the military installation at Pearl Harbor in Hawaii. This raid was part of an all-out onslaught aimed at forcing America and other western colonial powers from Asia. When America declared war on the Axis powers—Japan, Germany, and Italy—almost every Southern community sent soldiers to fight in the Pacific and European theaters of conflict. Wartime service in a variety of capacities engaged many Southern writers—Randall Jarrell, James Dickey, and Mary Lee Settle, to name a few. The war effort ultimately did for the South what the New Deal had not—ended the Depression and restored full employment. Homeland manufacturing and shipbuilding eased poverty by creating many jobs in the military, naval, and civilian sectors. Wartime expansion of the economy created a second wave of migration of poor Southerners to the North. Mobilization for war also led to economic expansion in the South, with the spread of military camps, airbases, naval stations, and shipyards.

Military maneuvers were held in Louisiana, Georgia, and Texas to train American soldiers in a variety of terrains and conditions. North Louisiana became the locus of many of these intricate war training exercises. Sites such as Camp Claiborne, Camp Livingston, Camp Beauregard, and Camp Polk sprang up. These bases provided many local youngsters with an opportunity to earn money shining shoes or selling papers to G.I.s in training. A dollar a day in change could be the equivalent to two to three months' salary in Depression-era Louisiana. Many Northern soldiers trained in Southern states, and they suffered from the South's heat and insects although they often enjoyed the hospitality and food. African-American soldiers from the North came face-to-face with Southern bigotry in the form of harsh Jim Crow laws and social codes. Whites-only hotels, restaurants, and bars were closed to them and their relatives.

Most Southerners felt the need to contribute to the war effort, leading citizens to organize scrap metal drives, collect funds for the Red Cross, and support fuel and food rationing. Citizens were encouraged to deny individual wants for the greater good. Life changed most dramatically for women during the war years. As men went off to war, women were hired to perform war-related jobs. "Rosie the Riveter" became the poster figure for this campaign, and Southern women accepted the call for production on army bases and navy yards and in ammunition plants and steel mills. Women also found positions in journalism, photography, and sales. Southern fiction from this era reflects the change in women's roles, as demonstrated, for instance, in Porter's autobiographical Miranda stories. Professional jobs gave women more money and independence, including more control over their sexual and marital choices. When WWII ended and men returned home, women were displaced from their wartime jobs. Many women, determined to maintain their newfound financial and social independence, took jobs in the postwar business boom, mostly in clerical positions, and the salaries they earned were low compared with the wages that had been available in wartime jobs. The loss of good paying jobs left many women feeling resentful and alienated when they were forced to return to their previous roles as housewives and daughters.

Post–World War II and the Second Red Scare

The end of WWII brought relative prosperity to the region, at least for White families. As soldiers returned, they found abundant employment opportunities and gained access to affordable housing and college training through the G.I. Bill. While social conditions improved in the South, the postwar years also ushered in the Cold War arms race with the Soviet Union, America's former WWII ally. Thus, as the war against fascism ended, Americans were encouraged to prepare for war against a new enemy, Communism. Anti-Communist fervor led to a rightward shift in American politics and brought conservative values to the fore. Business and property rights enjoyed renewed cultural support, and being pro-capitalist was equated with being pro-American. At the same time, economic and social unrest—which had been widespread in the South during the turmoil of the 1930s—were disdained as subversive and un-American.

The fear of Communism rose to a fever pitch in 1947 as the House Un-American Activities Committee (HUAC) began to scour the nation for alleged Communist sympathizers. When the Korean War broke out in 1950, the United States shouldered most of a United Nations effort against troops from North Korea and the People's Republic of China. War fervor turned to hysteria as the HUAC held a second round of hearings from 1951 until 1953. Its efforts to purge America of suspected Communists led to the scapegoating of writers and artists on the Left. Several Southerners were attacked by conservative groups and branded as Communists. John Henry Faulk, a folk humorist from Texas, was blacklisted and unemployable for years until he became a regular on *Hee Haw*, the CBS country music–variety television show, which debuted in 1969. Oklahoma's troubadour Woody Guthrie, a staunch union supporter, lived under the threat of blacklist and was dropped by his record label. Harlem Renaissance writers such as Richard Wright openly espoused the virtues of Communist antioppression ideology.

Developing simultaneously with the distress of the Cold War was unprecedented prosperity as wealth flowed into subdivisions and suburbs, creating a burgeoning Southern urban middle class. The rise of Sun Belt cities like Atlanta and Dallas lifted the South to new prominence in the national economic scene and reversed the "brain drain" of the first half of the century. Technological innovation proved to be one benefit of the South's newfound prosperity, which made lives for rural residents much easier than in the past. The spread of electrical lines and power plants, which began in the 1940s, led to the introduction of electricity into American homes in small cities and rural areas, and the advent of Rural Electric Associations and hydroelectric dams made electrical power inexpensive and plentiful. The Tennessee Valley Authority symbolized the rise of technology and the ways in which it transformed both the environment and the social traditions of a people (see Map IV–3). The damming of the Tennessee River led to many cultural changes as people of the region began to rely on electrical appliances for use in the home and in the workplace. Southerners embraced consumer technology—especially innovations that revolutionized the woman's sphere, such as washing machines, vacuum cleaners, and electric mixers. Domestic labor became less back-breaking and time-consuming. The Southern economy thrived as never before, and the anticapitalist arguments of the Nashville Agrarians now seemed quaint and nostalgic.

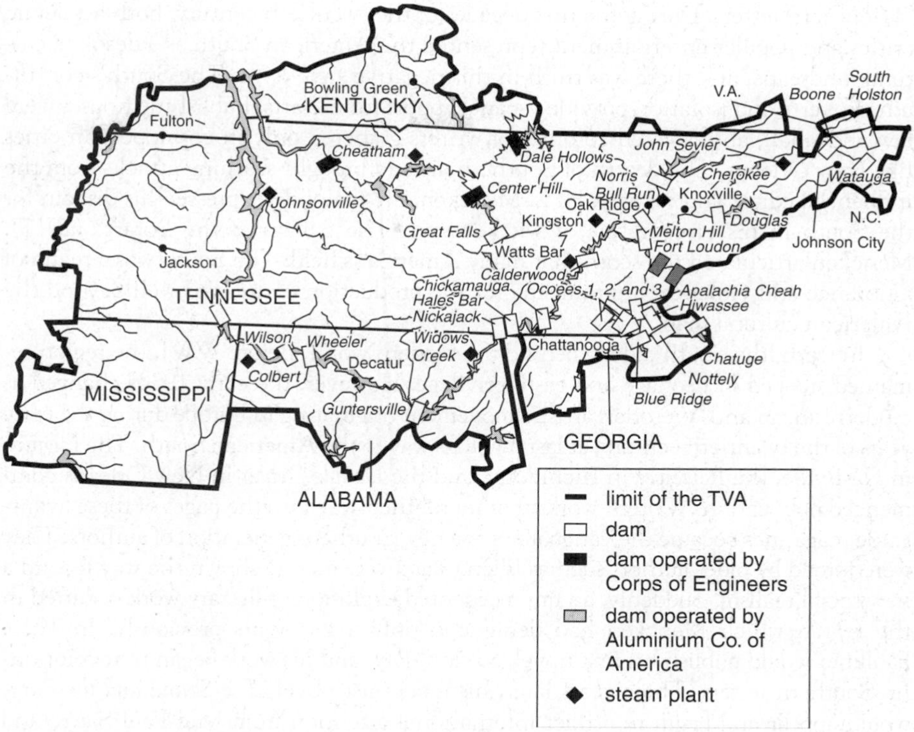

Map IV–3: Region covered by the Tennessee Valley Authority

Indeed, the South was shifting rapidly from an agricultural region to a commercial one. White-collar jobs began to proliferate as WWII veterans completed their college degrees and went on to professional careers in banking, insurance, energy, real estate, and other commercial endeavors. Farm-to-market roads leading to cities were transformed overnight into traffic-clogged highways lined with supermarkets and shopping centers. Workers without college degrees took easily secured jobs in factories and refineries throughout the South, working in industries ranging from garment manufacturing to aluminum mills to offshore drilling. However, because of continuing segregation and employment inequities, minority group members such as Native Americans, Mexican Americans, and African Americans continued to struggle in low-paying agricultural and service jobs. As prosperity finally came to the South in the 1950s and 1960s, the rising Civil Rights movement militantly opposed the region's continuing legacy of economic and political discrimination.

The Dawn of the Southern Literary Renascence

The Southern Renascence is a term coined in hindsight by critics and historians to describe the confluence of Southern literary talent in the first half of the twentieth century. William Faulkner, Robert Penn Warren, Zora Neale Hurston, and Richard Wright were just a few of the new voices that heralded an unprecedented flowering of Southern letters. During the first decades of the twentieth century, both academic critics and popular entertainment represented the American South as a desolate cultural landscape, and there was truth in this negative stereotype. The South's continuing poverty and isolation provided scant support for the arts. Publishing houses were few and small, and isolated colonies of writers gathered only in cosmopolitan cities like New Orleans. The dearth of Southern artistry brought scathing attacks from the influential editor and essayist, H. L. Mencken. He famously expressed his disdain for the South in his vituperative, if witty, essay, "The Sahara of the Bozart" (1917). Mencken articulated the scorn that many Americans held: The South was a realm of ignorance and violence, unpromising for the production of art, and well beyond the American cultural map.

In truth, the South did lag behind the modern world. Before WWI, the region remained steeped in peonage and caste privilege. However, the early 1920s changed as modernism, an anti-Victorian artistic movement originating in Europe during the early years of the twentieth century, at last made its way to the American South. The *Fugitive* in Nashville, the *Reviewer* in Richmond, and the *Double Dealer* in New Orleans commenced publication. Writers' works that found their way into the pages of these avant-garde magazines became the vanguard of the new Southern generation of authors. They were joined by older authors such as Ellen Glasgow, who had shown the way toward a new social realism. Suddenly, an unprecedented explosion of literary work occurred in the region which Mencken had denigrated only a few years previously. In 1926, Faulkner would publish his first novel, *Soldiers' Pay*, and his work began to revolutionize Southern letters. Three years later, his modernist novel, *The Sound and the Fury*, would appear and begin to attract international attention from Jean-Paul Sartre and other European intellectuals, who would hail it as an American masterpiece. Northern critics, however, maintained a bias against the South. They often caricatured Faulkner and other Southern writers as untutored rustics having little artistic insight into or control over their works, which Northern critics belittled as brilliant effusions of style and personality that lacked intellectual content. This regional bias against Southern authors can be dated at least to the critical reception of Edgar Allan Poe in the 1840s.

Agrarianism and New Criticism

The Southern Renascence, however, was scarcely uniform or single-minded. The Vanderbilt Fugitives came together in rejection of the pieties of Southern Lost Cause writing, that is, of popular nineteenth-century novels that falsely glorified the Old South as an illustrious realm of regal lords and ladies. The Fugitives wanted to peel away these layers of artifice and falsehood to reveal the Old South's true worth in their eyes, showing its veneration of land and family. Within a few years, their regional aesthetic had evolved into a political cause. Core members of the now-disbanded Vanderbilt Fugitives—including John Crowe Ransom, Donald Davidson, then-student Allen Tate, and Robert Penn Warren, all of whom enjoyed individual success as poets and critics—became part of the Vanderbilt Agrarians. The Agrarians upheld the rural South as an antidote to Northern industrialism, urban concentration, and mass technology. The Agrarians ardently believed in the virtues of the Old South, where leisure time for the landowning classes allowed for erudition and reflection. The brethren decried the encroachment of industrialization and commercial progress in the New South, arguing that such changes would lead to the loss of

Southern gentility and hospitality, both of which stemmed from an agrarian culture. The Agrarian philosophy upheld the values of the Old South aristocracy and sought to demonstrate that the benefits of its way of life outweighed the drawbacks of its oppressive system of slavery and servitude.

For a time, the Agrarians added their voices to the noisy national chorus of complaint and accusation in the early years of the Great Depression. In 1930, their symposium *I'll Take My Stand* articulated an indictment of twentieth-century American finance and technology. The book stirred a good deal of controversy, leading to debates, follow-up essays, and letters by the score. Even so, the Agrarians were never a majority voice, not even in the South. Progressives from the University of North Carolina quickly countered the Vanderbilt conservatives, and a lively war of words ensued between Chapel Hill and Nashville. Furthermore, Southern radicals joined with Northern leftists in deriding *I'll Take My Stand* as an elitist portrayal of the South as a place of moonlight and magnolias. They accused the Agrarians of turning a blind eye to the worst features of Southern history, including slavery and poverty. Outspoken Southerners on the Left such as Erskine Caldwell and Lillian Smith portrayed the Agrarians as neo-Confederates holding the whip hand over poor Whites and African Americans. The Agrarians shot back with rejoinders that grew increasingly shrill, in some cases nearly pro-fascist, in defense of White supremacy and class privilege. Such outbursts caused the Agrarian movement to dissipate, breathing its last gasp in a second anticollectivist symposium, *Who Owns America? A New Declaration of Independence* (1936), which Tate coedited. By this time, however, the Agrarians were no longer in close proximity to each other, and key members of the brethren soon became Southern expatriates. For all its shortcomings, however, Agrarianism left a lasting effect on American culture. Thirty years after the dispersal of the Nashville group, a younger generation of Americans would begin anew to critique the dehumanizing effects of technological dependency.

Agrarianism soon transformed itself from social theory into literary theory in the academic movement that came to be known as New Criticism. First given its name by Ransom in his book, *The New Critics* (1941), this mode of literary interpretation was taken up and promulgated by other members of the Agrarian group, especially Allen Tate, Robert Penn Warren, and Cleanth Brooks—all former students of Ransom. Brooks and Warren led the way with their classic textbooks: *Understanding Poetry* (1938) and *Understanding Fiction* (1943). Tate and his wife, Caroline Gordon, also published an influential anthology of short stories, *The House of Fiction* (1950). The basic thrust of the movement was antihistoricist, removing the text from its historical, cultural, or social context. Although New Criticism devalued writing that took a social stance or conveyed a political ideology, its tenets did much to professionalize the study and teaching of English. New Criticism reigned as the primary classroom approach to the understanding of literature until well into the 1970s, when new literary theories stressing the social and historical contexts of texts gradually supplanted it.

Gone With the Wind and the Southern Literary Renascence

The Agrarians/New Critics were academics, but authors outside the academy were also part of the foundation of the Southern Literary Renascence. Thus, Southern writers found the success of a then-unknown Margaret Mitchell particularly galling when

Gone With the Wind became the most popular Southern novel ever written. The novel extolled the Old South and endorsed the rise of the urban, commercialized New South from the ashes of the cotton kingdom. The enormous popularity of *Gone With the Wind* outside the South in large measure reflected national escapist yearnings during the Depression as well as a nostalgic longing for a less complicated age. *Gone With the Wind* represents the Antebellum Southern myth in its most essential form. Some of the basic ingredients include dashing cavaliers in waistcoats, glamorous belles in dazzling hoop skirts, columned white mansions approached through lanes of stately oak trees, magnificent ballrooms lit by candles and filled with dancing, and compliant slaves in kitchens and fields. The popularity of *Gone With the Wind* seemed to inspire a new generation of writers to tell about the South in ways that were more authentic.

The book was published in 1936, the same year as two more innovative and realistic Civil War novels—Faulkner's *Absalom, Absalom!* and Caroline Gordon's *None Shall Look Back*—which sold poorly and quickly sank from view. Writers in the South from 1940 to 1965—among them Tennessee Williams, Flannery O'Connor, Truman Capote, Carson McCullers, and William Styron—rejected the platitudes and myths of *Gone With the Wind* and instead explored themes of alienation, cultural decay, and fragmentation of community, themes common to modernist authors outside the South and far beyond the shores of the United States. Williams, especially, developed a new mythology of the South, which he portrayed as a world of longing and anguish. In a string of Broadway hits—among them *A Streetcar Named Desire* (1947) and *Cat on a Hot Tin Roof* (1955)—he delved into explicit themes of sexual exploitation, impotence, and immolation. McCullers also drew from the modernist tradition, using Southern settings for works dealing with isolation and anxiety. In Hollywood's rush to capitalize on these trends, many of Williams's plays and several of McCullers's texts were turned into movies. In addition, novels by older writers like Faulkner were turned into languid, suggestive movies—*The Long, Hot Summer*, *The Sound and the Fury*, and *Sanctuary*.

In her famous 1956 essay, "Place in Fiction," Welty argues that Southern writing by the 1950s had reached a level of diversity and maturity that transcended regional classification. She suggested that Southern writers now might choose or not choose to write about slavery, the Civil War, Reconstruction, sharecropping, and lynching—the major themes of the Southern Literary Renascence. In other words, by 1956, talented writers in the South should no longer be defined by their mailboxes or limited in their subject matter. Focus shifted from the region to the individual author. To paraphrase the literary critic Thomas L. McHaney, by the end of the 1950s, the South had become irrevocably modern.

Regional Difference: The Many Souths of the Renascence

The South is often perceived as a homogeneous region, yet more accurately, it is a construct of many Souths. The region as a whole may share many similarities, but wide variations in geography and material culture complicate its history, resulting in a heterogeneous culture. These subregional differences lead to different literary treatments of such sociological elements as race, class, and gender.

The heterogeneity of these subcultures accounts, in part, for the varied efforts of Southern authors to recreate the Souths of their own experience. Faulkner's achievement towers over twentieth-century Southern literature. His Yoknapatawpha County novels and stories interpret his native region of north Mississippi over a span of almost two centuries. Faulkner's vast tapestry of Scots-Irish pioneers and Native Americans, landowners and sharecroppers, soldiers and slaves, aviators and bootleggers does not come close to exhausting the range and possibilities of Southern writing. A far different world of urbanized and wealthy Richmond aristocrats appears, for example, in Glasgow's novel of manners like *The Sheltered Life* (1938), and the vastly altered world of Depression-era Virginia appears in her *Vein of Iron* (1935).

Similarly, the monoracial African-American town of Eatonville, Florida, which provides the setting for much of Zora Neale Hurston's fiction, bears little resemblance to Thomas Wolfe's North Carolina highlands, or to Flannery O'Connor's Georgia hills and highways. Of course, these differences are partly defined by the race of the author, but even within the African-American community, different Souths emerge. Hurston discloses layers of prejudices within the African-American community and demonstrates ways in which individuals of lighter skin color are privileged over their darker neighbors. Arna Bontemps creates a world of African-American characters more closely aligned with realism than with modernism. Other African-American writers, such as Richard Wright, emphasize the violent prejudice focused upon African Americans as a group. Wright dramatizes lynchings and mistreatment of African Americans, the denial of employment and educational opportunities, and the emotional emasculation of young men. Further, Wright's most important works are set in the North, depicting the migrations of Southern African Americans to Northern cities like Chicago, where new forms of prejudice and violence erupt.

The South is heir to a varied cultural history. During the first half of the twentieth century, writers of the Southern Literary Renascence and the modernist movement drew upon their collective pasts to portray the complexities of a region in change. The rich vein of work they left behind wholly disproved Mencken's charge that the South was an artistic desert. Just the opposite, the South was bursting with innovation and creativity throughout the period from 1910 to 1956, giving rise to vivid new literary portraits of itself.

Southern Renascence Chronology

1910–1956

1910 • Lynchings reported weekly throughout the Southern region.
• Sharecropping and tenant farming replace slave economy throughout the South.

1914 • The blues invade Tin Pan Alley, brought there by W. C. Handy. His "St. Louis Blues" became popular worldwide.

1915 • D. W. Griffith produces a controversial and cinematically important film, *The Birth of a Nation*.

1916 • Francis Scott Key's "The Star Spangled Banner" becomes the national anthem.

1917 • "The Original Dixieland Jazz Band" releases the first jazz record, becoming one of the first records to sell a million copies.

1920 • Louis Armstrong joins King Oliver in Chicago and goes on to a stellar solo career.
• Ratification of the Nineteenth Amendment (Women's Suffrage). Tennessee is the critical thirty-sixth state to ratify and the only Southern state to do so.

1925 • Frances Newman, *New York Herald Tribune*, coins the term "The Southern Renascence" to refer to the new literature of the South.

1929 • The stock market crashes, causing an economic crisis called the Great Depression.
• William Faulkner publishes *The Sound and the Fury*.

1930–1940 • Longest drought of the twentieth century in the United States, resulting in the Dust Bowl.

1933 • President Roosevelt institutes a reform called the New Deal. Emergency relief organizations are formed, such as the Tennessee Valley Authority (TVA).

1935 • Social Security system is established.

1936 • Margaret Mitchell publishes *Gone With the Wind;* wins the Pulitzer Prize.
• William Faulkner publishes *Absalom, Absalom!*

1937 • Zora Neale Hurston publishes *Their Eyes Were Watching God*.

1938 • President Franklin D. Roosevelt declares the South the nation's number-one economic problem.

1939 • John Steinbeck publishes *The Grapes of Wrath;* wins the Pulitzer Prize.

1940 • Richard Wright publishes *Native Son*.

1941 • On 7 December, the naval base at Pearl Harbor is bombed by the Japanese in a surprise attack at dawn.

1946 • Robert Penn Warren publishes *All the King's Men;* wins the Pulitzer Prize.

1948 • Introduction of the long playing vinyl record.

1950 • William Faulkner is awarded the Nobel Prize for Literature.

1954 • *Oliver Brown* v. *Board of Education of Topeka, Kansas* declares segregation unconstitutional.
• The words "under God" added to the Pledge of Allegiance.

1955 • Montgomery Bus Boycott.
• Flannery O'Connor publishes *A Good Man Is Hard to Find*.

are art and industry mutually exclusive?

※ VOICES IN CONTEXT ❦

The Fugitive Poets
and the Southern Agrarians

1930–1956

Writing in response to H. L. Mencken's scathing critique of the aridity of early twentieth-century Southern culture, the Southern Agrarians consisted of a core group of 12 scholars and poets. For the purposes of publishing a symposium articulating their political stance, they identified themselves simply as "Twelve Southerners." Their resulting work, *I'll Take My Stand,* raised the ire of many readers with its controversial analyses of Southern culture and values. Focusing on what they viewed as the valuable attributes of the Antebellum South, as well as specific characteristics of the region such as religion, artistry, economics, and technological progress, the Agrarians decried the simultaneous rush toward industrialization and the resulting disintegration of an agrarian way of life that allowed the luxury of leisure time, reflection, and artistic creativity.

The Agrarians were an eclectic group of intellectuals, including poets and novelists such as John Crowe Ransom, Donald Davidson, Allen Tate, John Gould Fletcher, Andrew Nelson Lytle, and Robert Penn Warren, as well as social scientists and educators such as Henry Blue Kline, Lyle Hicks Lanier, and Herman Clarence Nixon. Despite the diversity of their academic disciplines, these writers—Southern sympathizers all—set out to articulate their views in what Thomas Inge has described as "an anthology attacking industrialism and its basic dogma." Each of the Twelve Southerners was a respected scholar who shared a view of the quality of Antebellum life with the other eleven. The common bond among the group, as John Crowe Ransom stated in the introduction to *I'll Take My Stand,* was their position that "all tend to support a Southern way of life against what may be called the American or prevailing way; and all as much as agree that the best terms in which to represent the distinction are contained in the phrase, Agrarian *versus* Industrial." As Virginia Rock has pointed out, "the achievements of individual members of the group . . . have been honored with an array of awards not to be matched by any other collection of writers grouped in a common cause." Their accomplishments include such accolades as Guggenheim Fellowships, Pulitzer Prizes, National Book Awards, and a sizable number of noteworthy publications.

put on board

Virginia Rock has suggested that the Agrarians saw themselves as answering a metaphorical "call to arms to do battle for the cause of the spirit beleaguered" and serving as "a small band of Agrarian generals." Tagged by some readers as racist holdovers from the Antebellum era, the Agrarians were harshly condemned because of their seeming willingness to revive the slave economy. Critics argued that the Agrarians posited the "peculiar institution" as a necessary expense of ensuring the continuation of a way of life, allowing the landowning classes the privilege of leisure time.

While the Twelve Southerners earnestly yearned for the benefits of the free-labor economy of the prewar South, they did not espouse the ideology of slavery, per se. Rather, they argued that the creative impulse—the fruits of which the likes of Mencken found absent in the early twentieth-century South—would only reemerge in a restful, nurturing environment. In the introduction to *I'll Take My Stand,* John Crowe Ransom argued that the arts could not have a "proper life under industrialism," arguing instead that art required

a right attitude to nature; and in particular . . . a free and disinterested observation of nature that occurs only in leisure. Neither the creation nor the understanding of works of

> art is possible in an industrial age except by some local and unlikely suspension of the industrial drive . . . [the] amenities of life also suffer under the curse of a strictly-business or industrial civilization. They consist in such practices as manners, conversation, hospitality, sympathy, family life, romantic love—in the social exchanges which reveal and develop sensibility in human affairs.

Such an environment would give its *intelligentsia* the liberty to indulge in contemplation, reflection, and discussion as precursors to the creative process.

The Agrarians are frequently conflated with another group of Southerners, the Fugitive Poets, in part because the two groups shared four key members—Ransom, Davidson, Tate, and Warren—and in part because the nucleus of each group was located at Nashville's Vanderbilt University. However, the similarities end with these commonalities in membership and location. The Fugitives were poets who met regularly to discuss each member's work from 1915 until 1928, and who each published their works in the little magazine the *Fugitive*. The magazine survived for slightly over two years, from 1922 to 1925, publishing the works not only of members of the group, but also of writers ranging from Hart Crane to Laura Riding. Aside from predating the beginning of the Agrarian movement by several years, the Fugitives had, as Thomas Inge has pointed out, "only the vaguest sort of manifesto, basically a declaration of artistic freedom, individuality, and unconcern with social commitment." They, in fact, "did not care to be associated with the Southern aristocracy and even [made] the startling suggestion that . . . [they were] bastards . . . and out of the mainstream of Southern culture or without legitimate pedigree." The Fugitives were primarily concerned with the writing and publishing of literature, as opposed to the Agrarians, who were most attentive to the social and political agenda that they attempted to communicate through venues such as *I'll Take My Stand*, and a later volume, *Who Owns America?* (1935), which was edited by Allen Tate and Herbert Agar, a latecomer to the Agrarian cause.

The Agrarian Movement extended into the mid-1950s, when an Agrarian reunion took place at Vanderbilt University. Later in life, some of the contributors to *I'll Take My Stand* softened their positions; most notably Robert Penn Warren, who went so far as to recant his youthful statements in the symposium. Despite the lack of political correctness found in their ideology, the Agrarians made a substantial contribution to Southern literature, as poets and novelists, as scholars and critics, and as heralds announcing the dawn of the Southern Renascence. Their cause, coupled with their prolific production of poetry, fiction, and critical, social, and historical works, celebrated the value of the creative impulse itself, and in so doing, opened the door for writers who would soon emerge from the rural South, such as William Faulkner and Thomas Wolfe.

from I'll Take My Stand: The South and the Agrarian Tradition

Introduction: A Statement of Principles

The authors contributing to this book are Southerners, well acquainted with one another and of similar tastes, though not necessarily living in the same physical community, and perhaps only at this moment aware of themselves as a single group of men. By conversation and exchange of letters over a number of years it had developed that they entertained many convictions in common, and it was decided to make a volume in which each one should furnish his views upon a chosen topic. This was the general background. But background and consultation as to the various topics were enough; there was to be no further collaboration. And so no single author is responsible for any view outside his own article. It was through the good fortune of some deeper agreement that the book was expected to achieve its unity. All the articles bear in the same sense upon the book's title-subject: all tend to support a Southern way of life against what may be called the American or prevailing way; and all as much as agree that the best terms in which to represent the distinction are contained in the phrase, Agrarian *versus* Industrial.

But after the book was under way it seemed a pity if the contributors, limited as they were within their special subjects, should stop short of showing how close their agreements really were. On the contrary, it seemed that they ought to go on and make themselves known as a group already consolidated by a set of principles which could be stated with a good deal of particularity. This might prove useful for the sake of future reference, if they should undertake any further joint publication. It was then decided to prepare a general introduction for the book which would state briefly the common convictions of the group. This is the statement. To it every one of the contributors in this book has subscribed.

Nobody now proposes for the South, or for any other community in this country, an independent political destiny. That idea is thought to have been finished in 1865. But how far shall the South surrender its moral, social, and economic autonomy to the victorious principle of Union? That question remains open. The South is a minority section that has hitherto been jealous of its minority right to live its own kind of life. The South scarcely hopes to determine the other sections, but it does propose to determine itself, within the utmost limits of legal action. Of late, however, there is the melancholy fact that the South itself has wavered a little and shown signs of wanting to join up behind the common or American industrial ideal. It is against that tendency that this book is written. The younger Southerners, who are being converted frequently to the industrial gospel, must come back to the support of the Southern tradition. They must be persuaded to look very critically at the advantages of becoming a "new South" which will be only an undistinguished replica of the usual industrial community.

But there are many other minority communities opposed to industrialism, and wanting a much simpler economy to live by. The communities and private persons sharing the agrarian tastes are to be found widely within the Union. Proper living is a matter of the intelligence and the will, does not depend on the local climate or geography, and is capable of a definition which is general and not Southern at all. Southerners have a filial duty to discharge to their own section. But their cause is precarious and they must seek alliances with sympathetic communities everywhere. The members of the present group would be happy to be counted as members of a national agrarian movement.

Industrialism is the economic organization of the collective American society. It means the decision of society to invest its economic resources in the applied sciences. But the word science has acquired a certain sanctitude. It is out of order to quarrel with science in the abstract, or even with the applied sciences when their applications are made subject to criticism and intelligence. The capitalization of the applied sciences has now become extravagant and uncritical; it has enslaved our human energies to a degree now clearly felt to be burdensome. The apologists of industrialism do not like to meet this charge directly; so they often take refuge in saying that they are devoted simply to science! They are really devoted to the applied sciences and to practical production. Therefore it is necessary to employ a certain skepticism even at the expense of the Cult of Science, and to say, It is an Americanism, which looks innocent and disinterested, but really is not either.

The contribution that science can make to a labor is to render it easier by the help of a tool or a process, and to assure the laborer of his perfect economic security while he is engaged upon it. Then it can be performed with leisure and enjoyment. But the modern laborer has not exactly received this benefit under the industrial regime. His labor is hard, its tempo is fierce, and his employment is insecure. The first principle of a good labor is that it must be effective, but the second principle is that it must be enjoyed. Labor is one of the largest items in the human career; it is a modest demand to ask that it may partake of happiness.

The regular act of applied science is to introduce into labor a labor-saving device or a machine. Whether this is a benefit depends on how far it is advisable to save the labor. The philosophy of applied science is generally quite sure that the saving of labor is a pure gain, and that the more of it the better. This is to assume that labor is an evil, that only the end of labor or the material product is good. On this assumption labor becomes mercenary and servile, and it is no wonder if many forms of modern labor are accepted without resentment though they are evidently brutalizing. The act of labor as one of the happy functions of human life has been in effect abandoned, and is practiced solely for its rewards.

Even the apologists of industrialism have been obliged to admit that some economic evils follow in the wake of the machines. These are such as overproduction, unemployment, and a growing inequality in the distribution of wealth. But the remedies proposed by the apologists are always homeopathic. They expect the evils to disappear when we have bigger and better machines, and more of them. Their remedial programs, therefore, look forward to more industrialism. Sometimes they see the system righting itself spontaneously and without direction: they are Optimists. Sometimes they rely on the benevolence of capital, or the militancy of labor, to bring about a fairer division of the spoils: they are Coöperationists or Socialists. And sometimes they expect to find super-engineers, in the shape of Boards of Control, who will adapt production to consumption and regulate prices and guarantee business against fluctuations: they are Sovietists. With respect to these last it must be insisted that the true Sovietists or Communists—if the term may be used here in the European sense—are the Industrialists themselves. They would have the government set up an economic super-organization, which in turn would become the government. We therefore look upon the Communist menace as a menace indeed, but not as a Red one; because it is simply according to the blind drift of our industrial development to expect in America at last much the same economic system as that imposed by violence upon Russia in 1917.

Turning to consumption, as the grand end which justifies the evil of modern labor, we find that we have been deceived. We have more time in which to consume, and many more products to be consumed. But the tempo of our labors communicates itself to our satisfactions, and these also become brutal and hurried. The constitution of the natural man probably does not permit him to shorten his labor-time and enlarge his consuming-time indefinitely. He has to pay the penalty in satiety and aimlessness. The modern man has lost his sense of vocation.

Religion can hardly expect to flourish in an industrial society. Religion is our submission to the general intention of a nature that is fairly inscrutable; it is the sense of our rôle as creatures within it. But nature industrialized, transformed into cities and artificial habitations, manufactured into commodities, is no longer nature but a highly simplified picture of nature. We receive the illusion of having power over nature, and lose the sense of nature as something mysterious and contingent. The God of nature under these conditions is merely an amiable expression, a superfluity, and the philosophical understanding ordinarily carried in the religious experience is not there for us to have.

Nor do the arts have a proper life under industrialism, with the general decay of sensibility which attends it. Art depends, in general, like religion, on a right attitude to nature; and in particular on a free and disinterested observation of nature that occurs only in leisure. Neither the creation nor the understanding of works of art is possible in an industrial age except by some local and unlikely suspension of the industrial drive.

The amenities of life also suffer under the curse of a strictly-business or industrial civilization. They consist in such practices as manners, conversation, hospitality, sympathy, family life, romantic love—in the social exchanges which reveal and develop sensibility in human affairs. If religion and the arts are founded on right relations of man-to-nature, these are founded on right relations of man-to-man.

Apologists of industrialism are even inclined to admit that its actual processes may have upon its victims the spiritual effects just described. But they think that all can be made right by extraordinary educational efforts, by all sorts of cultural institutions and endowments. They would cure the poverty of the contemporary spirit by hiring experts to instruct it in spite of itself in the historic culture. But salvation is hardly to be encountered on that road. The trouble with the life-pattern is to be located at its economic base, and we cannot rebuild it by pouring in soft materials from the top. The young men and women in colleges, for example, if they are already placed in a false way of life, cannot make more than an inconsequential acquaintance with the arts and humanities transmitted to them. Or else the understanding of these arts and humanities will but make them the more wretched in their own destitution.

The "Humanists" are too abstract. Humanism, properly speaking, is not an abstract system, but a culture, the whole way in which we live, act, think, and feel. It is a kind of imaginatively balanced life lived out in a definite social tradition. And, in the concrete, we believe that this, the genuine humanism, was rooted in the agrarian life of the older South and of other parts of the country that shared in such a tradition. It was not an abstract moral "check" derived from the classics—it was not soft material poured in from the top. It was deeply founded in the way of life itself—in its tables, chairs, portraits, festivals, laws, marriage customs. We cannot recover our native humanism by adopting some standard of taste that is critical enough to question the contemporary arts but not critical enough to question the social and economic life which is their ground.

The tempo of the industrial life is fast, but that is not the worst of it; it is accelerating. The ideal is not merely some set form of industrialism, with so many stable industries, but industrial progress, or an incessant extension of industrialization. It never proposes a specific goal; it initiates the infinite series. We have not merely capitalized certain industries; we have capitalized the laboratories and inventors, and undertaken to employ all the labor-saving devices that come out of them. But a fresh labor-saving device introduced into an industry does not emancipate the laborers in that industry so much as it evicts them. Applied at the expense of agriculture, for example, the new processes have reduced the part of the population supporting itself upon the soil to a smaller and smaller fraction. Of course no single labor-saving process is fatal; it brings on a period of unemployed labor and unemployed capital, but soon a new industry is devised which will put them both to work again, and a new commodity is thrown upon the market. The laborers were sufficiently embarrassed in the meantime, but, according to the theory, they will eventually be taken care of. It is now the public which is embarrassed; it feels obligated to purchase a commodity for which it had expressed no desire, but it is invited to make its budget equal to the strain. All might yet be well, and stability and comfort might again obtain, but for this: partly because of industrial ambitions and partly because the repressed creative impulse must break out somewhere, there will be a stream of further labor-saving devices in all industries, and the cycle will have to be repeated over and over. The result is an increasing disadjustment and instability.

It is an inevitable consequence of industrial progress that production greatly outruns the rate of natural consumption. To overcome the disparity, the producers, disguised as the pure idealists of progress, must coerce and wheedle the public into being loyal and steady consumers, in order to keep the machines running. So the rise of modern advertising—along with its twin, personal salesmanship—is the most significant development of our industrialism. Advertising means to persuade the consumers to want exactly what the applied sciences are able to furnish them. It consults the happiness of the consumer no more than it consulted the happiness of the laborer. It is the great effort of a false economy of life to approve itself. But its task grows more difficult every day.

It is strange, of course, that a majority of men anywhere could ever as with one mind become enamored of industrialism: a system that has so little regard for individual wants. There is evidently a kind of thinking that rejoices in setting up a social objective which has no relation to the individual. Men are prepared to sacrifice their private dignity and happiness to an abstract social ideal, and without asking whether the social ideal produces the welfare of any individual man whatsoever. But this is absurd. The responsibility of men is for their own welfare and that of their neighbors; not for the hypothetical welfare of some fabulous creature called society.

Opposed to the industrial society is the agrarian, which does not stand in particular need of definition. An agrarian society is hardly one that has no use at all for industries, for professional vocations, for scholars and artists, and for the life of cities. Technically, perhaps, an agrarian society is one in which agriculture is the leading vocation, whether for wealth, for pleasure, or for prestige—a form of labor that is pursued with intelligence and leisure, and that becomes the model to which the other forms approach as well as they may. But an agrarian regime will be secured readily enough where the superfluous industries are not allowed to rise against it. The theory of agrarianism is that the culture of the soil is the best and most sensitive of vocations, and that therefore it should have the economic preference and enlist the maximum number of workers.

These principles do not intend to be very specific in proposing any practical measures. How may the little agrarian community resist the Chamber of Commerce of its county seat, which is always trying to import some foreign industry that cannot be assimilated to the life-pattern of the community? Just what must the Southern leaders do to defend the traditional Southern life? How may the Southern and the Western agrarians unite for effective action? Should the agrarian forces try to capture the Democratic party, which historically is so closely affiliated with the defense of individualism, the small community, the state, the South? Or must the agrarians—even the Southern ones—abandon the Democratic party to its fate and try a new one? What legislation could most profitably be championed by the powerful agrarians in the Senate of the United States? What anti-industrial measures might promise to stop the advances of industrialism, or even undo some of them, with the least harm to those concerned? What policy should be pursued by the educators who have a tradition at heart? These and many other questions are of the greatest importance, but they cannot be answered here.

For, in conclusion, this much is clear: If a community, or a section, or a race, or an age, is groaning under industrialism, and well aware that it is an evil dispensation, it must find the way to throw it off. To think that this cannot be done is pusillanimous. And if the whole community, section, race, or age thinks it cannot be done, then it has simply lost its political genius and doomed itself to impotence.

Questions to Consider

1. Given the controversy over the value of the Agrarians' political ideology in the early twenty-first century, why are they important? What insight do they bring to the study of Southern literature?
2. What are the necessary elements that must be in place in order for creativity to occur? Do the Agrarians make a convincing case for the necessity of leisure time as an inherent part of this creative process?

John Crowe Ransom

1888–1974

John Crowe Ransom stood at the forefront of the three major literary movements to emerge from the South during the first half of the twentieth century: the Fugitive Poets, the Agrarians, and the New Critics. In addition to the essays he wrote to promote his theoretical and critical views, he left behind a small but elegant body of poetry and his influence on younger writers including Randall Jarrell, Peter Taylor, and Robert Lowell for whom he served as a teacher and mentor.

Born on 30 April 1888 in Pulaski, Tennessee, Ransom was homeschooled by his parents until the age of ten because of his Methodist minister father's frequent job moves throughout the state. Entering Vanderbilt University at the age of 15, Ransom dropped out after only two years due to financial problems and taught school in Mississippi and Tennessee. Then he resumed his studies at Vanderbilt, graduating first in his class and Phi Beta Kappa in 1907. Following another interlude of teaching, he traveled to Oxford University on a Rhodes Scholarship in 1910 and earned another baccalaureate degree three years later. One more secondary school teaching job, this time at the Hotchkiss School in Connecticut, beckoned before he launched a distinguished college teaching career.

Ransom joined the faculty of Vanderbilt in 1914 but went on military leave from 1917 to 1919 to serve as an artillery officer in Europe during World War I. His first book of poetry, *Poems About God,* was published in 1919, while he was still overseas; the poems have been called amateurish, but they exhibit the preoccupations with love, death, and God that would mark his more mature work.

After the war, Ransom became one of the core group of young intellectuals, including Allen Tate and Donald Davidson, who began meeting in Nashville to discuss poetic modernism and the status of Southern letters. In 1922 they founded a little magazine called the *Fugitive* to publish and promote the work of modern poets. International rather than regional in its scope, the journal derived its title from its mission to "fle[e] from nothing faster than from the high-caste Brahmins of the Old South," as Ransom wrote in his foreword to the first issue. The *Fugitive* would suspend publication only 19 issues later, in 1925, but during that short span of time it presented a new image of the South as a nexus of avant-garde creative and intellectual activity. Robert Penn Warren, Hart Crane, and Laura Riding were among the new writers whose work was introduced in the journal, and Ransom himself published many of his best-known poems in it. Virtually all the poems for which he is remembered were written before his thirty-ninth year, including "Bells for John Whiteside's Daughter," which treats the death of a young girl from an unusually detached and ironic perspective; "Janet Waking," which employs a similar perspective to narrate the death of a child's pet rooster; "Antique Harvesters," which personifies the Old South in the figure of the "Lady" and urges youth to remember Southern history; and "The Equilibrists," which tells the story of two lovers doomed to unconsummated love for all eternity. Two volumes, *Chills and Fever* (1924) and *Two Gentlemen in Bonds* (1927), collected the poems of this period.

Ransom was among those former Fugitives who led the Agrarian movement to promote the values of the traditional South in the face of encroaching industrialization, materialism, and consumerism. He contributed the unsigned "Introduction: A Statement of Principles" and the signed essay titled "Reconstructed but Unregenerate" to the 1930 manifesto of the movement, *I'll Take My Stand*. In "Reconstructed but Unregenerate," Ransom argued that rationalist science and blind faith in progress had eroded the relationships between human beings and nature that were necessary for religion and the arts to flourish. He also claimed that the leisurely life of the Old South planter had been ideal for fostering civility and "the free life of the mind," glossing over the fact that such leisure time had been made possible by the labor of slaves with the line, "Slavery was a feature monstrous enough in theory, but, more often than not, humane in practice." In the late 1930s, however, Ransom distanced himself from his former beliefs, calling his depiction of an idealized agrarian society a "fantasy."

Ransom had always believed in exploring the formal aspects of a poem with his students, rather than teaching its paraphrased "meaning" or its relationship to historical and biographical facts. At Vanderbilt, he was known for devoting an entire, semester-long Shakespeare course to only one play, so as to emphasize its nature as poetry. Following a career move from Vanderbilt to Kenyon College in 1937, Ransom began to promote his pedagogical and critical method in a series of essays and in the pages of the *Kenyon Review*, the new journal that he founded in 1939. Scholars including Tate, Warren, T. S. Eliot, Cleanth Brooks, Lionel Trilling, and Yvor Winters joined Ransom in promulgating "The New Criticism," which became the dominant approach to teaching literature in American universities through the decade of the 1970s. *The World's Body* (1938) and *The New Criticism* (1941) collected Ransom's prose writings from this period. Three editions of his *Selected Poems* were issued prior to his death in 1974, but they contained only a few poems written after 1927.

"The defense of poetry," Mark Malvasi has written, "was not for Ransom, as it was for Davidson, also the defense of the South. For him, poetry flourished only when liberated from the constrictions of politics and patriotism." Particularly in "Equilibrists" and "Antique Harvesters," Ransom demonstrates how his time-bound Southern subject matter can be elevated to a universal and eternal level of meaning.

Bells for John Whiteside's Daughter

There was such speed in her little body,
And such lightness in her footfall,
It is no wonder her brown study[1]
Astonishes us all.

Her wars were bruited[2] in our high window.
We looked among orchard trees and beyond

1. Appearance of being suntanned and in a state of reverie or contemplation.

2. Noised loudly, reported.

Where she took arms against her shadow,
Or harried unto the pond

The lazy geese, like a snow cloud
Dripping their snow on the green grass,
Tricking and stopping, sleepy and proud,
Who cried in goose, Alas,

For the tireless heart within the little
Lady with rod that made them rise
From their noon apple-dreams and scuttle
Goose-fashion under the skies!

But now go the bells, and we are ready,
In one house we are sternly stopped
To say we are vexed at her brown study,
Lying so primly propped.

Janet Waking

Beautifully Janet slept
Till it was deeply morning. She woke then
And thought about her dainty-feathered hen,
To see how it had kept.

One kiss she gave her mother.
Only a small one gave she to her daddy
Who would have kissed each curl of his shining baby;
No kiss at all for her brother.

"Old Chucky, old Chucky!" she cried,
Running across the world upon the grass
To Chucky's house, and listening. But alas,
Her Chucky had died.

It was a transmogrifying[1] bee
Came droning down on Chucky's old bald head
And sat and put the poison. It scarcely bled,
But how exceedingly

And purply did the knot
Swell with the venom and communicate
Its rigor! Now the poor comb stood up straight
But Chucky did not.

So there was Janet
Kneeling on the wet grass, crying her brown hen
(Translated far beyond the daughters of men)
To rise and walk upon it.

1. Changing or altering greatly; the term often carries humorous connotations.

And weeping fast as she had breath
Janet implored us, "Wake her from her sleep!"
And would not be instructed in how deep
Was the forgetful kingdom of death.

The Equilibrists

Full of her long white arms and milky skin
He had a thousand times remembered sin.
Alone in the press of people traveled he,
Minding her jacinth,[1] and myrrh,[2] and ivory.

Mouth he remembered: the quaint orifice
From which came heat that flamed upon the kiss,
Till cold words came down spiral from the head,
Grey doves from the officious tower illsped.

Body: it was a white field ready for love,
On her body's field, with the gaunt tower above,
The lilies grew, beseeching him to take,
If he would pluck and wear them, bruise and break.

Eyes talking: Never mind the cruel words,
Embrace my flowers, but not embrace the swords.
But what they said, the doves came straightway flying
And unsaid: Honor, Honor, they came crying.

Importunate her doves. Too pure, too wise,
Clambering on his shoulder, saying, Arise,
Leave me now, and never let us meet,
Eternal distance now command thy feet.

Predicament indeed, which thus discovers
Honor among thieves, Honor between lovers.
O such a little word is Honor, they feel!
But the grey word is between them cold as steel.

At length I saw these lovers fully were come
Into their torture of equilibrium;
Dreadfully had forsworn each other, and yet
They were bound each to each, and they did not forget.

And rigid as two painful stars, and twirled
About the clustered night their prison world,
They burned with fierce love always to come near,
But Honor beat them back and kept them clear.

Ah, the strict lovers, they are ruined now!
I cried in anger. But with puddled brow
Devising for those gibbeted[3] and brave
Came I descanting:[4] Man, what would you have?

1. An orange-colored precious stone.
2. An aromatic gum resin considered precious in ancient times.
3. Hanging from a gallows.
4. Singing or improvising a part in polyphonic music.

For spin your period out, and draw your breath,
A kinder sæculum[5] begins with Death.
Would you ascend to Heaven and bodiless dwell?
Or take your bodies honorless to Hell?

In Heaven you have heard no marriage is,[6]
No white flesh tinder to your lecheries,
Your male and female tissue sweetly shaped
Sublimed away, and furious blood escaped.

Great lovers lie in Hell, the stubborn ones
Infatuate of the flesh upon the bones;
Stuprate,[7] they rend each other when they kiss,
The pieces kiss again, no end to this.

But still I watched them spinning, orbited nice.
Their flames were not more radiant than their ice.
I dug in the quiet earth and wrought the tomb
And made these lines to memorize their doom:—

EPITAPH

Equilibrists lie here; stranger, tread light;
Close, but untouching in each other's sight;
Mouldered the lips and ashy the tall skull.
Let them lie perilous and beautiful.

Antique Harvesters

(SCENE: Of the Mississippi the bank sinister, and of the Ohio the bank sinister)[1]

Tawny are the leaves turned but they still hold,
And it is harvest; what shall this land produce?
A meager hill of kernels, a runnel of juice;
Declension[2] looks from our land, it is old.
Therefore let us assemble, dry, grey, spare,
And mild as yellow air.

"I hear the croak of a raven's funeral wing."
The young men would be joying in the song
Of passionate birds; their memories are not long.
What is it thus rehearsed in sable?[3] "Nothing."
Trust not but the old endure, and shall be older
Than the scornful beholder.

We pluck the spindling ears and gather the corn.
One spot has special yield? "On this spot stood
Heroes and drenched it with their only blood."
And talk meets talk, as echoes from the horn

5. Lifetime or century.
6. Allusion to Matthew 22:30: "For in the resurrection they neither marry, nor are given in marriage, but are the angels of God in heaven."
7. Disgraced; from the Latin *stuprum*, immorality, rape, disgrace.

1. The sinister bank of the river is on the left side.
2. Deterioration.
3. Clothed in black.

Of the hunter—echoes are the old men's arts,
Ample are the chambers of their hearts.

Here come the hunters, keepers of a rite;
The horn, the hounds, the lank mares coursing by
Straddled with archetypes of chivalry;
And the fox, lovely ritualist, in flight
Offering his unearthly ghost to quarry;
And the fields, themselves to harry.

Resume, harvesters. The treasure is full bronze
Which you will garner for the Lady,[4] and the moon
Could tinge it no yellower than does this noon;
But grey will quench it shortly—the field, men, stones.
Pluck fast, dreamers; prove as you amble slowly
Not less than men, not wholly.

Bare the arm, dainty youths, bend the knees
Under bronze burdens. And by an autumn tone
As by a grey, as by a green, you will have known
Your famous Lady's image; for so have these;
And if one say that easily will your hands
More prosper in other lands,

Angry as wasp-music be your cry then:
"Forsake the Proud Lady, of the heart of fire,
The look of snow, to the praise of a dwindled choir,
Song of degenerate specters that were men?
The sons of the fathers shall keep her, worthy of
What these have done in love."

True, it is said of our Lady, she ageth.
But see, if you peep shrewdly, she hath not stooped;
Take no thought of her servitors that have drooped,
For we are nothing; and if one talk of death—
Why, the ribs of the earth subsist frail as a breath
If but God wearieth.

Questions to Consider

1. In a prose satire of "Janet Waking" entitled "To the Henhouse: In Homage to John Crowe Ransom," critic Clayton Delery has Janet's father ask, upon seeing the dead rooster, "But how could this have happened?" to which Janet replies, "It was a transmogrifying bee came droning down on Chucky's old bald head and sat and put the poison. It scarcely bled, but how exceedingly and purply did the knot swell with the venom and communicate its rigor." What point is Delery trying to make about Ransom's writing style? Do you agree or disagree with Delery?
2. Why do you think Ransom devotes an entire six-line stanza of "Antique Harvesters" to a passing fox hunt that interrupts the work of the scavengers?

4. An idealized feminine symbol of the Old South.

Robert Penn Warren

1905–1989

When Robert Penn Warren died at age 84, Southern literature lost perhaps its most versatile and learned voice. Through seven decades Warren contributed a remarkable outpouring of fiction, nonfiction, poetry, drama, and criticism that bears comparison with the achievement of any American writer of the twentieth century. By most accounts Warren's masterpiece is *All the King's Men* (1946), his Pulitzer Prize-winning novel of government corruption and existential yearning. Warren wrote nine other novels, all set in the South, most of them meditations on history and the clash of competing values. But Warren was first and last a poet. After *A Place to Come To* (1977), his final novel, he abandoned fiction but went on to publish four more collections of powerful new verses as well as a long narrative poem. In 1986 Warren was honored as the first Poet Laureate of the United States. Over his long career, he tried his hand at drama; what became *All the King's Men* began years earlier as a verse play, *Proud Flesh*. He also saw several of his novels turned into films, plays, and even an opera.

Robert Penn Warren was born on 24 April 1905, in Guthrie, a railroad town in south Kentucky's Cumberland Valley, near Clarksville, Tennessee. His grandfather was a captain in the Confederate army; his father was an unsuccessful banker and businessman. Always a good student, Warren was accepted into the U.S. Naval Academy. However, in 1921, his brother accidentally hit him in the left eye with a chunk of coal. This injury resulted in near-total loss of vision in that eye and later a glass replacement. Warren was disqualified from entering the service academy and instead went to Vanderbilt University. Fear of blindness mingled with adolescent despondency led at age 19 to a suicide attempt with a chloroform-soaked towel. He recovered and turned from engineering studies to the circle of young poets and literature students in Nashville who called themselves the Fugitives. The name represented their flight from outworn forms of Southern poetry, either genteel lyrics or sentimental dialect verse. The Fugitives were seeking to start a new Southern literary movement, free from Lost Cause nostalgia and open to new Modernist influences. In 1923 Warren's poetry appeared in their avant-garde "little magazine," and he became lifelong friends with John Crowe Ransom and Allen Tate. Two years later he graduated Phi Beta Kappa. He went on to graduate school in English at the University of California, where he met his first wife, Emma (Cinina) Brescia, and received an M.A. In 1928 he enrolled at Oxford University as a Rhodes Scholar. Two years later he published his first book, a critical biography of John Brown, the radical abolitionist who in 1859 seized the federal arsenal at Harper's Ferry, Virginia, in a failed attempt to foment a slave insurrection. While Warren was in England, the Fugitives back home were branching into politics and some were evolving into the Southern Agrarians. Warren contributed an unwise essay in support of the "separate but equal" doctrine of racial segregation to their manifesto, *I'll Take My Stand: The South and the Agrarian Tradition* (1930), the conservative symposium led by Ransom, Tate, and Donald Davidson. Although at the time, Davidson wanted to reject Warren's essay as too progressive on race relations, by the 1950s, Warren had repudiated his racial paternalism of 1930.

That year Warren began his teaching career at Southwestern at Memphis (now Rhodes College). By 1934, when Huey Long was U.S. Senator, Warren was at Louisiana State University, where he and Brooks founded the *Southern Review,* which quickly became a cutting-edge literary journal. Warren juggled writing projects in numerous genres, publishing his first verse collection in 1935 and his first novel *Night Rider* (1939), a story of the Kentucky tobacco farmers' uprising of 1906. In 1942 he moved to the University of Minnesota and, like other former Fugitives Tate and Ransom, became a Southern expatriate. Nevertheless, his second novel *At Heaven's Gate* (1943) is set in Tennessee and embodies many of the anticorporate themes asserted by the Southern

Agrarians. With the commercial success of his third novel, *All the King's Men*, Warren gained the attention of both the literary establishment and Hollywood; he sold the movie rights to Columbia Pictures for $200,000. The film adaptation was the most honored movie of 1949 and won the Academy Award for Best Picture. But as he attained critical recognition and financial rewards, Warren's marriage was disintegrating. After a mental breakdown his wife was institutionalized in 1950; they were divorced after 22 years (she went on to become an Italian scholar). In 1950 Warren settled at Yale University, his academic home until his retirement in 1973. In 1952 he married Eleanor Clark, a novelist and travel essayist. Two children were born as both parents combined parenting with traveling and pursuing separate literary careers.

When he was in his fifties, Warren's reputation as a novelist dimmed. Critics complained that pressures to produce best-sellers for book clubs and Hollywood had led to haste and melodrama. As critics cooled toward his fiction, Warren gained increasing recognition as a poet. His collection *Promises* (1957) won both the National Book Award and Pulitzer Prize for poetry; Warren became the only writer to win Pulitzer Prizes in fiction and poetry.

In the last two decades of his life Warren's verse emerged as his overriding passion, and appreciative readers compared him to Thomas Hardy and William Butler Yeats, poets whose skills strengthened with age. Warren's style changed as he moved away from the formalist techniques of English Renaissance poetry and the Modernism of T. S. Eliot. These influences had shaped perhaps his finest early poem "Bearded Oaks" (1937), an intense romantic meditation on love and eternity. Twenty years later a poem from his lyric volume *Promises*, "Founding Fathers, Nineteenth-Century Style, Southeast U.S.A.," still is written in rhyming quatrains. But its metrics have loosened and its tone has diversified into idiomatic language, moving easily from coarse to elegiac (much in the style of his best fiction). Its subject matter also extends beyond the personal into the ancestral past and national myth. By degrees Warren was drawing closer to the "New American Poetry" of the fifties and sixties, styles that looked back to Whitman's looping lines and flexible structures. Warren's long narrative poem *Audubon: A Vision* (1969) delved into biography and history through the medium of free verse, including passages of colloquial dialogue and direct address, presented without stanzaic form. Three of Warren's strongest, most exuberant volumes, *Or Else* (1974), *Now and Then* (1978), and *Being Here* (1980), form a loose autobiographical trilogy, perhaps the crowning achievement of a poetic career that had begun more than half a century earlier. In 1979 he won his second Pulitzer Prize in poetry for *Now and Then*.

In old age Warren, diagnosed with prostate cancer, endured the deaths of many literary friends and colleagues. Intensified by declining health and thoughts of mortality, old memories welled into late poems of stark summation. "Last Meeting," from his final volume *Altitudes and Extensions* (1985), recalls his Kentucky hometown, a chance meeting, love and neglect, and a visit to the graveyard. His last published poem, "John's Birches," which appeared when he was 80 years old, begins with a bucolic childhood reminiscence and ends with a benediction for lost youth.

Warren's remaining years brought worsening pain and debilitation. Yet honors and honorary degrees poured in, including election to the American Academy and Institute of Arts and Letters, which gave him its Gold Medal for Poetry in 1985. He died on 15 September 1989.

Bearded Oaks

The oaks, how subtle and marine,
Bearded, and all the layered light
Above them swims; and thus the scene,
Recessed, awaits the positive night.

So, waiting, we in the grass now lie
Beneath the languorous tread of light:

The grasses, kelp-like, satisfy
The nameless motions of the air.

Upon the floor of light, and time,
Unmurmuring, of polyp made,
We rest; we are, as light withdraws,
Twin atolls on a shelf of shade.

Ages to our construction went,
Dim architecture, hour by hour:
And violence, forgot now, lent
The present stillness all its power.

The storm of noon above us rolled,
Of light the fury, furious gold,
The long drag troubling us, the depth:
Dark is unrocking, unrippling, still.

Passion and slaughter, ruth,[1] decay
Descend, minutely whispering down,
Silted down swaying streams, to lay
Foundation for our voicelessness.

All our debate is voiceless here,
As all our rage, the rage of stone;
If hope is hopeless, then fearless is fear,
And history is thus undone.

Our feet once wrought the hollow street
With echo when the lamps were dead
At windows, once our headlight glare
Disturbed the doe that, leaping, fled.

I do not love you less that now
The caged heart makes iron stroke,
Or less that all that light once gave
The graduate dark should now revoke.

We live in time so little time
And we learn all so painfully,
That we may spare this hour's term
To practice for eternity.

Founding Fathers, Early-Nineteenth-Century Style, Southeast USA

They were human, they suffered, wore long black coat and gold watch chain.

They stare from daguerreotype with severe reprehension,
Or from genuine oil, and you'd never guess any pain
In those merciless eyes that now remark our own time's sad declension.

Some composed declarations, remembering Jefferson's language.
Knew pose of the patriot, left hand in crook of the spine or

1. Feel sorry for

With finger to table, while right invokes the Lord's just rage.
There was always a grandpa, or cousin at least, who had been a real Signer.[1]

Some were given to study, read Greek in the forest, and these
Longed for an epic to do their own deeds right honor;
Were Nestor by pigpen, in some tavern brawl played Achilles.[2]
In the ring of Sam Houston[3] they found, when he died, one word engraved: *Honor*.

Their children were broadcast, like millet seed flung in a wind-flare.
Wives died, were dropped like old shirts in some corner of country.
Said, "Mister," in bed, the child-bride; hadn't known what to find there;
Wept all the next morning for shame; took pleasure in silk; wore the keys to the pantry.

"Will die in these ditches if need be," wrote Bowie[4] at the Alamo.
And did, he whose left foot, soft-catting, came forward, and breath hissed:
Head back, gray eyes narrow, thumb flat along knife-blade, blade low.
"Great gentleman," said Henry Clay,[5] "and a patriot." Portrait by Benjamin West.

Or take those, the nameless, of whom no portraits remain,
No locket or seal ring, though somewhere, broken and rusted,
In attic or earth, the long Decherd[6] stock rotten, has lain;
Or the mold-yellow Bible, God's Word, in which, in their strength, they also trusted.

Some wrestled the angel, and took a fall by the corncrib.
Fought the brute, stomp-and-gouge, but knew they were doomed in that glory.
All night, in sweat, groaned; fell at last with spit red and a cracked rib.
How sweet then the tears! Thus gentled, they roved the dark land with the old story.

Some prospered, had black men and acres, and silver on table,
But remembered the owl call, the smell of burnt bear fat on dusk-air.
Loved family and friends, and stood it as long as able—
"But money and women, too much is ruination, am Arkansas-bound." So went there.

One of mine was a land shark, or so the book with scant praise
Denominates him. "A man large and shapeless,
Like a sack of potatoes set on a saddle," it says,
"Little learning but shrewd, not well trusted." Rides thus out of history, neck fat and napeless.

1. One of the 54 signers of the Declaration of Independence on 4 July 1776.
2. Nestor and Achilles are Homeric heroes revered respectively for wisdom and courage.
3. Sam Houston (1793–1863) led Texas to independence by defeating the Mexican army in 1836. After Texas was admitted to statehood in 1845, Houston served first as U.S. senator then governor. A staunch Unionist, he was forced to resign in 1861 for refusing to support secession.
4. Jim Bowie (1796–1836) died when the Alamo, an abandoned mission in San Antonio, Texas, was overrun by the Mexican army during the Texas war of independence. He was famous for his single-edged knife, a foot long and more than an inch wide.
5. Henry Clay (1777–1852), a member of the U.S. House of Representatives from Kentucky, was famous as an orator and statesman.
6. Decherd: a Tennessee rifle.

One fought Shiloh[7] and such, got cranky, would fiddle all night.
The boys nagged for Texas. "God damn it, there's nothing, God damn it,
In Texas"—but took wagons, went, and to prove he was right,
Stayed a year and a day—"hell, nothing in Texas"—had proved it, came back to black vomit,

And died, and they died, and are dead, and now their voices
Come thin, like the last cricket in frost-dark, in grass lost,
With nothing to tell us for our complexity of choices,
But beg us only one word to justify their own old life-cost.

So let us bend ear to them in this hour of lateness,
And what they are trying to say, try to understand,
And try to forgive them their defects, even their greatness,
For we are their children in the light of humanness, and under the shadow of God's closing hand.

Last Meeting

A Saturday night in August when
Farm folks and tenants and black farmhands
Used to crowd the street of a market town
To do their "traden," and chew the rag,

And to hide the likker from women hung out
Behind the poolroom or barbershop—
If you were white. If black, in an alley.
And the odor of whiskey mixed with the sweat

And cheap perfume, and high heels waggled
On worn bricks, and through the crowd
I saw her[1] come. I see her now
As plain as then—some forty years back.

It's like a flash, and still she comes,
Comes peering at me, not sure yet,
For I'm in my city clothes and hat,
But in the same instant we recognize

Each other. I see the shrunken old woman
With bleary eyes and yellow-gray skin,
And walking now with the help of a stick.
We hug and kiss there in the street.

"Ro-Penn, Ro-Penn, my little tadpole,"
She said, and patted my cheek, and said,
"Git off yore hat so I'll see yore haid."
And I did. She ran her hands through thinning hair.

"Not fahr-red, like it used to be."
And ran her fingers some more. "And thinner,

7. Near Shiloh, a rural community in southwest Tennessee, in 1862 a two-day Civil War battle was fought, a Confederate defeat.

1. The elderly woman apparently is Geraldine Carr, hired as a nurse by Bob and Ruth Warren when their first child, Robert Penn, was born.

And sandy color some places too."
Then she rocked her arms like cuddling a child,

And crooned, and said, "Now big and gone
Out in the wide world—but 'member me!"
I tried to say "I couldn't forget,"
But the words wouldn't come, and I felt how frail

Were the vertebrae I clasped. I felt
Tears run down beside her nose,
And a crazy voice, like some half-laugh,
Said, "Chile, yore Ma's dead, yore Pappy ole,

"But I'm hangen on fer what I'm wuth."
So we said goodbye, with eyes staring at us
And laughter in some corner, somewhere.
That was the last time we ever met.

All's changed. The faces on the street
Are changed. I'm rarely back. But once
I tried to find her grave, and failed.
Next time I'll promise adequate time.

And find it. I might take store-bought flowers
(Though not a florist in twenty miles),
But a fruit jar full of local zinnias
Might look even better with jimson weed.

It's nigh half a lifetime I haven't managed,
But there must be enough time left for that.

from All the King's Men

Burden's Landing is one hundred and thirty miles from Mason City, off to the southwest. If you multiply one hundred and thirty by two, it makes two hundred and sixty miles. It was near nine o'clock and the stars were out and the ground mist was beginning to show in the low places. God knew what time it would be when we got back to bed, and up the next morning to face a hearty breakfast and the ride back to the capital.

I lay back in the seat and closed my eyes. The gravel sprayed on the undersides of the fenders, and then it stopped spraying and the tail of the car lurched to one side, and me with it, and I knew we were back on the slab and leveling out for the job.

We would go gusting along the slab, which would be pale in the starlight between the patches of woods and the dark fields where the mist was rising. Way off from the road a barn would stick up out of the mist like a house sticking out of the rising water when the river breaks the levee. Close to the road a cow would stand knee-deep in the mist, with horns damp enough to have a pearly shine in the starlight, and would look at the black blur we were as we went whirling into the blazing corridor of light which we could never quite get into for it would be always splitting the dark just in front of us. The cow would stand there knee-deep in the mist and look at the black blur and the blaze and then, not turning its head, at the place where the black blur and blaze had been, with the remote, massive, unvindictive indifference of God-All-Mighty or Fate or me, if I were standing there knee-deep in the mist, and the blur and the blaze whizzed past and withered on off between the fields and the patches of woods.

But I wasn't standing there in the field, in the dark, with the mist turning slow around my knees and the ticking no-noise of the night inside my head. I was in a car, headed back to Burden's Landing, which was named for the people from whom I got my name, and which was the place where I had been born and raised.

We would go on between the fields until we hit a town. The houses would be lined up along the street, under the trees, with their lights going out now, until we hit the main street, where the lights would be bright around the doorway of the movie house and the bugs would be zooming against the bulbs and would ricochet off to hit the concrete pavement and make a dry crunch when somebody stepped on them. The men standing in front of the pool hall would look up and see the big black crate ghost down the street and one of them would spit on the concrete and say, "The bastard, he reckins he's somebody," and wish that he was in a big black car, as big as a hearse and the springs soft as mamma's breast and the engine breathing without a rustle at seventy-five, going off into the dark somewhere. Well, I was going somewhere. I was going back to Burden's Landing.

We would come into Burden's Landing by the new boulevard by the bay. The air would smell salty, with maybe a taint of the fishy, sad, sweet smell of the tidelands to it, but fresh nevertheless. It would be nearly midnight then, and the lights would be off in the three blocks of down-town then. Beyond the down-town and the little houses, there would be the other houses along the bay, set back in the magnolias and oaks, with the white walls showing glimmeringly beyond the darkness of the trees, and the jalousies,[1] which in the daytime would be green, looking dark against the white walls. Folks would be lying back in the rooms behind the jalousies, with nothing but a sheet over them. Well, I'd put in a good many nights behind those jalousies, from the time I was little enough to wet the bed. I'd been born in one of those rooms behind the jalousies. And behind one set of them my mother would be lying up there tonight, with a little fluting of lace on the straps of her nightgown, and her face smooth like a girl's except for the little lines, which you wouldn't be able to make out in the shadow anyway, at the corners of her mouth and eyes, and one bare arm laid out on the sheet with the sharp, brittle-looking, age-betraying hand showing the painted nails. Theodore Murrell would be lying there, too, breathing with a slightly adenoidal sibilance under his beautiful blonde mustache. Well, it was all legal, for she was married to Theodore Murrell, who was a lot younger than my mother and who had beautiful yellow hair scrolled on top of his round skull like taffy, and who was my stepfather. Well, he wasn't the first stepfather I had had.

Then, on down the row, behind its own live oaks and magnolias, there would be the Stanton house, locked up and nobody behind the jalousies, for Anne and Adam were in town now, and grown up and never went fishing with me any more, and the old man was dead. Then on down the row, where the open country began, would be the house of Judge Irwin. We wouldn't stop before we got there. But we'd make a little call on the Judge.

"Boss," I said.

The Boss turned around, and I saw the chunky black shape of his head against the brightness of our headlights.

"What you gonna say to him?" I asked.

"Boy, you never know till the time comes," he said. "Hell," he amended, "maybe I won't say anything to him a-tall. I don't know as I've got anything to say to him. I just want to look at him good."

1. A window covering that controls the amount of light and air that enter a room.

"The Judge won't scare easy," I said. No, I didn't reckon the Judge would scare easy, thinking of the straight back of the man who used to swing off the saddle and drop the bridle over a paling on the Stanton fence and walk up the shell walk to the veranda with his Panama in his hand and the coarse dark-red hair bristling off his high skull like a mane and the hooked red nose jutting off his face and the yellow irises of his eyes bright and hard-looking as topaz. That was nearly twenty years before, all right, and maybe the back wasn't as straight now as it had been then (a thing like that happens so slowly you don't notice it) and maybe the yellow eyes were a little bleary lately, but I still didn't reckon the Judge would scare easy. That was one thing on which I figured I could bet: he wouldn't scare. If he did, it was going to be a disappointment to me.

"No, I don't count on him scaring easy," the Boss said. "I just want to look at him."

"Well, God damn it," I popped out, and came up off my shoulder blades before I knew it, "you're crazy to think you can scare him!"

"Take it easy," the Boss said, and laughed. I couldn't see his face. It was just a black blob against the glare of the headlights, with the laugh coming out of it.

"I just want to look at him," the Boss said, "like I told you."

"Well, you sure picked a hell of a time and a hell of a long way to go look at him," I said, not feeling anything but peevish now, and falling back on my shoulder blades where I belonged. "Why don't you get him to see you in town sometime?"

"*Sometime* ain't ever *now,*" the Boss said.

"It's a hell of a thing," I said, "for you to be doing."

"So you think it's beneath my dignity, huh?" the Boss asked.

"Well, you're Governor. They tell me."

"Yeah, I'm Governor, Jack, and the trouble with Governors is they think they got to keep their dignity. But listen here, there ain't anything worth doing a man can do and keep his dignity. Can you figure out a single thing you really please-God like to do you can do and keep your dignity? The human frame just ain't built that way."

"All right," I said.

"And when I get to be President, if I want to see somebody I'm gonna go right out and see 'em."

"Sure," I said, "in the middle of the night, but when you do I hope you leave me at home to get a night's sleep maybe."

"The hell I will," he said. "When I'm President I'm gonna take you with me. I'm gonna keep you and Sugar-Boy right in the White House so I can have you all handy. Sugar-Boy can have him a pistol range in the back hall and a brace of Republican Congressmen to be caddy for him and set up the tin cans, and you can bring your girls right in the big front door, and there's gonna be a member of the Cabinet to hold their coats and pick up hair pins after 'em. There's gonna be a special member of the Cabinet to do it. He's gonna be the Secretary of the Bedchamber of Jack Burden, and he will keep the telephone numbers straight and send back any little pink silk articles to the right address when they happen to get left behind. Tiny's got the build, so I'm gonna get him a little operation and put flowing silk pants on him and a turban and give him a tin scimitar like he was a High Grand Shriner or something, and he can sit on a turret outside your door and be the Secretary of the Bedchamber. And how you like that, boy, huh?" And he reached back over the back of the front seat and slapped me on the knee. He had to reach a long way back, for it was a long way from the front seat of the Cadillac to my knee even if I was lying on my shoulder blades.

"You will go down in history," I said.

"Boy, wouldn't I?" And he started to laugh. He turned round to watch the lit-up road, and kept on laughing.

Then we hit a little town and beyond it a filling station and lunch stand. Sugar-Boy got some gas and brought the Boss and me a couple of cokes. Then we went on.

The Boss didn't say another word till we hit Burden's Landing. All he said then was, "Jack, you tell Sugar-Boy how to find the house. It's your pals live down here."

Yes, my pals lived down there. Or had lived down there. Adam and Anne Stanton had lived down there, in the white house where their widowed father, the Governor, lived. They had been my friends, Anne and Adam. Adam and I had fished and sailed all over that end of the Gulf of Mexico, and Anne, who was big-eyed and quiet-faced and thin, had been with us, close and never saying a word. Adam and I had hunted and camped all over the country, and Anne had been there, a thin-legged little girl about four years younger than we were. And we had sat by the fire in the Stanton house—or in my house—and had played with toys or read books while Anne sat there. Then after a long time Anne wasn't a little girl any more. She was a big girl and I was so much in love with her that I lived in a dream. In that dream my heart seemed to be ready to burst, for it seemed that the whole world was inside it swelling to get out and be the world. But that summer came to an end. Time passed and nothing happened that we had felt so certain at one time would happen. So now Anne was an old maid living in the city, and even if she did look pretty good yet and wore clothes that didn't hurt her any, her laugh was getting brittle and there was a drawn look on her face as though she were trying to remember something. What was Anne trying to remember? Well, I didn't have to try to remember. I could remember but I didn't want to remember. If the human race didn't remember anything it would be perfectly happy. I was a student of history once in a university and if I learned anything from studying history that was what I learned. Or to be more exact, that was what I thought I had learned.

We would go down the Row—the line of houses facing the bay—and that was the place where all my pals had been. Anne, who was an old maid, or damned near it. Adam, who was a famous surgeon and who was nice to me but didn't go fishing with me any more. And Judge Irwin, who lived in the last house, and who had been a friend of my family and who used to take me hunting with him and taught me to shoot and taught me to ride and read history to me from leather-bound books in the big study in his house. After Ellis Burden went away he was more of a father to me than those men who had married my mother and come to live in Ellis Burden's house. And the Judge was a man.

So I told Sugar-Boy how to get through town and to the Row where all my pals lived or had lived. We pulled through the town, where the lights were out except for the bulbs hanging from the telephone poles, and on out the Bay Road where the houses were bone-white back among the magnolias and live oaks.

At night you pass through a little town where you once lived, and you expect to see yourself wearing knee pants, standing all alone on the street corner under the hanging bulbs, where the bugs bang on the tin reflectors and splatter to the pavement to lie stunned. You expect to see that boy standing there under the street lamp, out too late, and you feel like telling him he ought to go on home to bed or there will be hell to pay. But maybe you are home in bed and sound asleep and not dreaming and nothing has ever happened that seems to have happened. But, then, who the hell is this in the back seat of the big black Cadillac that comes ghosting through the town? Why, this is Jack

Burden. Don't you remember little Jack Burden? He used to go out in his boat in the afternoon on the bay to fish, and come home and eat his supper and kiss his beautiful mother good night and say his prayers and go to bed at nine-thirty. Oh, you mean old Ellis Burden's boy? Yeah, and that woman he married out of Texas—or was it Arkansas?—that big-eyed thin-faced woman who lives up there in that old Burden place now with that man she got herself. What ever happened to Ellis Burden? Hell, I don't know, nobody around here had any word going on years. He was a queer 'un. Damn if he wasn't queer, going off and leaving a real looker like that woman out of Arkansas. Maybe he couldn't give her what she craved. Well, he give her that boy, that Jack Burden. Yeah.

You come into the town at night and there are the voices.

We had got to the end of the Row, and I saw the house bone-white back among the dark oak boughs.

"Here it is," I said.

"Park out here," the Boss said. And then to me, "There's a light. The bugger ain't in bed. You go on and knock on the door and tell him I want to see him."

"Suppose he won't open up?"

"He will," the Boss said. "But if he won't you make him. What the hell do I pay you for?"

I got out of the car and went in the gate and started up the shell walk under the black trees. Then I heard the Boss coming after me. We went up the walk, with him just behind me, and up the gallery steps.

The Boss stood to one side, and I pulled open the screen and knocked on the door. I knocked again; then looking in through the glass by the door I saw a door open off the hall—where the library was, I remembered—then a side light come on in the hall. He was coming to the door. I could see him through the glass while he fumbled with the lock.

"Yes?" he asked.

"Good evening, Judge," I said.

He stood there blinking into the dark outside, trying to make out my face.

"It's Jack Burden," I said.

"Well, well, Jack—well I'll be jiggered!" And he put out his hand. "Come in." He even looked glad to see me.

I shook hands and stepped inside, where the mirrors in the peeling gold frames glimmered on the walls in the rays of the not bright side light, and the glass of the big hurricane lamps glimmered on the marble-top stands.

"What can I do for you, Jack?" he asked me, and gave me a look out of his yellow eyes. They hadn't changed much, even if the rest of him had.

"Well," I began, and didn't know how I was going to end, "I just wanted to see if you were up and could talk to ———"

"Sure, Jack, come on in. You aren't in any trouble, son? Let me shut the door first, and ———"

He turned to shut the door, and if his ticker hadn't been in good shape for all his near three score and ten he'd have dropped dead. For the Boss was standing there in the door. He hadn't made a sound.

As it was, the Judge didn't drop dead. And his face didn't show a thing. But I felt him stiffen. You turn to shut a door some night and find somebody standing there out of the dark, and you'll take a jump, too.

"No," the Boss said, easy and grinning, taking his hat off his head and stepping inside just as though he'd been invited, which he hadn't been, "no, Jack isn't in any trouble. Not that I know of. Nor me either."

The Judge was looking at me now. "I beg your pardon," he said to me, in a voice he knew how to make cold and rasping like an old phonograph needle scraping on an old record, "I had forgotten for the moment how well your needs are provided for."

"Oh, Jack's making out," the Boss said.

"And you, sir—" the Judge turned on the Boss, and slanted his yellow eyes down on him—for he was a half a head taller—and I could see the jaw muscles twitch and knot under the folds of red-rusty and seamed skin on his long jaw, "do you wish to say something to me?"

"Well, I don't know as I do," the Boss remarked, offhand. "Not at the moment."

"Well," the Judge said, "in that case ———"

"Oh, something might develop," the Boss broke in. "You never can tell. If we get the weight off our arches."

"In that case," the Judge resumed, and it was an old needle and an old record and it was scraping like a file on cold tin and nothing human, "I may say that I was about to retire."

"Oh, it's early yet," the Boss said, and took his time giving Judge Irwin the once-over from head to toe. The Judge was wearing an old-fashioned velvet smoking jacket and tuxedo pants and a boiled shirt, but he had taken off his collar and tie and the gold collar button was shining just under the big old red Adam's apple. "Yeah," the Boss went on, after he'd finished the once-over, "and you'll sleep better if you wait before going to bed and give that fine dinner you had a chance to digest."

And he just began walking down the hall toward the door where the light was, the door to the library.

Judge Irwin looked at the Boss's back as the Boss just walked away, the Palm Beach coat all crumpled up where it had crawled on the Boss's shoulders and the old sweat-stains of the afternoon showing dark at the armpits. The Judge's yellow eyes were near to popping out of his face and the blood was up in his face till it was the color of calf's liver in a butcher shop. Then he began to walk down the hall after the Boss.

I followed the pair of them.

The Boss was already sitting in a big old scuffed leather easy chair when I went in. I stood there against the wall, under the bookshelves that went up to the ceiling, full of old leather books, a lot of them law books, that got lost in the shadows up above and made the room smell musty like old cheese. Well, the room hadn't changed any. I could remember that smell from the long afternoons I had spent in that room, reading by myself or hearing the Judge's voice reading to me, while a log crackled on the hearth and the clock in the corner, a big grandfather's clock, offered us the slow, small, individual pellets of time. It was the same room. There were the big steel engravings on the wall—by Piranesi, in the heavy, scrollwork frames, the Tiber, the Colosseum, some ruined temple. And the riding crops on the mantel and on the desk, and the silver cups the Judge's dogs had won in the field trials and the Judge had won shooting. The gun rack, over in the shadow by the door, was out of the light from the big brass reading lamp on the desk, but I knew every gun in it, and knew the gun's feel.

The Judge didn't sit down. He stood in the middle of the floor and looked down at the Boss, who had his legs stuck out on the red carpet. And the Judge didn't say anything. Something was going on inside his head. You knew that if he had a little glass window in the side of that tall skull, where the one-time thick, dark-red, mane-like hair was thinned out now and faded, you could see inside and see the wheels and springs and cogs and ratchets working away and shining like a beautiful lot of well-kept mechanism.

But maybe somebody had pushed the wrong button. Maybe it was just going to run on and on till something cracked or the spring ran down, and nothing was going to happen.

But the Boss said something. He jerked his head sideways to indicate the silver tray with the bottle and the pitcher of water and a silver bowl and two used glasses and three or four clean ones which sat on the desk, and said, "Judge, I trust you don't mind Jack pouring me a slug? You know, Southern hospitality."

Judge Irwin didn't answer him. He turned to me, and said, "I didn't realize, Jack, that your duties included those of a body servant, but, of course, if I am mistaken ——"

I could have slapped his face. I could have slapped that God-damned handsome, eagle-beaked, strong-boned, rubiginous-hided[2] high old face, in which the eyes weren't old but were hard and bright without any depth to them and were an insult to look into. And the Boss laughed, and I could have slapped his God-damned face. I could have walked right out and left the two of them there, alone in that cheese-smelling room together till hell froze over, and just kept on walking. But I didn't, and perhaps it was just as well, for maybe you cannot ever really walk away from the things you want most to walk away from.

"Oh, nuts," the Boss said, and stopped laughing, and heaved himself up out of the leather chair, and made a pass at the bottle and sloshed out some whisky into a glass and poured in some water. Then he turned round, and grinning up to the Judge, stepped toward me and held out the glass. "Here, Jack," he said, "have a drink."

I can't say that I took the drink. It got shoved into my hand, and I stood there holding it, not drinking it, and watched the Boss look up at Judge Irwin and say, "Sometimes Jack pours me a drink, and sometimes I pour him a drink and—" he stepped toward the desk again—"sometimes I pour myself a drink."

He poured the drink, added water, and looked again at the Judge, leering with a kind of comic cunning. "Whether I'm asked or not," he said. And added, "There's lots of things you never get, Judge, if you wait till you are asked. And I am an impatient man. I am a very impatient man, Judge. That is why I am not a gentleman, Judge."

"Really?" replied the Judge. He stood in the middle of the floor and studied the scene beneath him.

From my spot by the wall, I looked at both of them. *To hell with them*, I thought, *to hell with both of them*. When they talked like that, it was to hell with both of them.

"Yeah," the Boss was saying, "you're a gent, and so you don't ever get impatient. Not even for your likker. You aren't even impatient for your drink right now and it's likker your money paid for. But you'll get a drink, Judge. I'm asking you to have one. Have a drink with me, Judge."

Judge Irwin didn't answer a word. He stood very erect in the middle of the floor.

"Aw, have a drink," the Boss said, and laughed, and sat again in the big chair and stuck out his legs on the red carpet.

The Judge didn't pour himself a drink. And he didn't sit down.

The Boss looked up at him from the chair and said, "Judge, you happen to have an evening paper round here?"

The paper was lying over on another chair by the fireplace, with the Judge's collar and tie on top of it, and his white jacket hung on the back of the chair. I saw the Judge's eyes snap over there to it, and then back at the Boss.

"Yes," the Judge said, "as a matter of fact, I have."

"I haven't had a chance to see one, rushing round the country today. Mind if I take a look?"

2. Rust-colored.

"Not in the slightest," Judge Irwin said, and the sound was the file scraping on that cold tin again, "but perhaps I can relieve your curiosity on one point. The paper publishes my endorsement of Callahan for the Senate nomination. If that is of interest to you."

"Just wanted to hear you say it, Judge. Somebody told me, but you know how rumor hath a thousand tongues, and how the newspaper boys tend to exaggeration, and the truth ain't in 'em."

"There was no exaggeration in this case," the Judge said.

"Just wanted to hear you say it. With your own silver tongue."

"Well, you've heard it," the Judge said, standing straight in the middle of the floor, "and in that case, at your leisure—" the Judge's face was the color of calf's liver again, even if the words did come out cold and spaced—"if you have finished your drink ——"

"Why, thanks, Judge," the Boss said, sweet as chess pie, "I reckon I will take another spot." And he heaved himself in the direction of the bottle.

He did his work, and said, "Thanks."

When he was back in the leather chair with the fresh load in the glass, he said, "Yeah, Judge, I've heard you say it, but I just wanted to hear you say something else. Are you sure you took it to the Lord in prayer? Huh?"

"I have settled the matter in my own mind," the Judge said.

"Well, if I recollect right—" the Boss ruminatively turned the glass in his hands—"back in town, when we had our little talk, you sort of felt my boy Masters was all right."

"I made no commitment," the Judge said sharply. "I didn't make any commitment except to my conscience."

"You been messing in politics a long time, Judge," the Boss said, easy, "and—" he took a drag from the glass—"so has your conscience."

"I beg your pardon," the Judge snapped.

"Nuts," the Boss said, and grinned. "But what got you off Masters?"

"Certain features of his career came to my attention."

"Somebody dug up some dirt for you, huh?"

"If you choose to call it that," the Judge said.

"Dirt's a funny thing," the Boss said. "Come to think of it, there ain't a thing but dirt on this green God's globe except what's under water, and that's dirt too. It's dirt makes the grass grow. A diamond ain't a thing in the world but a piece of dirt that got awful hot. And God-a-Mighty picked up a handful of dirt and blew on it and made you and me and George Washington and mankind blessed in faculty and apprehension. It all depends on what you do with the dirt. That right?"

"That doesn't alter the fact," the Judge said from way up there where his head was, above the rays of the desk lamp, "that Masters doesn't strike me as a responsible man."

"He better be responsible," the Boss said, "or I'll break his God-damned neck!"

"That's the trouble. Masters would be responsible to you."

"It's a fact," the Boss admitted ruefully, lifting his face under the light, and shaking his head in fatalistic sadness. "Masters'd be responsible to me. I can't help it. But Callahan—now take Callahan—it sort of seems to me he's gonna be responsible to you and Alta Power and God knows who else before he's through. And what's the difference? Huh?"

"Well ——"

"Well, hell!" The Boss popped straight up in the chair with that inner explosiveness he had when, all of a sudden, he would snatch a fly out of the air or whip his head at you and his eyes would snap open. He popped up and his heels dug into the red carpet. Some of the liquor sloshed out of his glass onto his Palm Beach pants. "Well, I'll tell you the difference, Judge! I can deliver Masters and you can't deliver Callahan. And that's a big difference."

"I'll have to take my chance," the Judge said from way up there.

"Chance?" And the Boss laughed. "Judge," he said, and quit laughing, "you haven't got but one chance. You been guessing right in this state going on forty years. You been sitting back here in this room and nigger boys been single-footing in here bringing you toddies and you been guessing right. You been sitting back here and grinning to yourself while the rest of 'em were out sweating on the stump and snapping their suspenders, and when you wanted anything you just reached out and took it. Oh, if you had a little time off from duck hunting and corporation law you might do a hitch as Attorney General. So you did. Or play at being a judge. You been a judge a long time. How would it feel not to be a judge any more?"

"No man," Judge Irwin said, and stood up there straight in the middle of the floor, "has ever been able to intimidate me."

"Well, I never tried," the Boss said, "yet. And I'm not trying now. I'm going to give you a chance. You say somebody gave you some dirt on Masters? Well, just suppose I gave you some dirt on Callahan?—Oh, don't interrupt! Keep your shirt on!"—and he held up his hand. "I haven't been doing any digging, but I might, and if I went out in the barn lot and stuck my shovel in and brought you in some of the sweet-smelling and put it under the nose of your conscience, then do you know what your conscience would tell you to do? It would tell you to withdraw your endorsement of Callahan. And the newspaper boys would be over here thicker'n blue-bottle flies on a dead dog, and you could tell 'em all about you and your conscience. You wouldn't even have to back Masters. You and your conscience could just go off arm in arm and have a fine time telling each other how much you think of each other."

"I have endorsed Callahan," the Judge said. He didn't flicker.

"I maybe could give you the dirt," the Boss said speculatively. "Callahan's been playing round for a long time, and he who touches pitch shall be defiled, and little boys just will walk barefoot in the cow pasture." He looked up at Judge Irwin's face, squinting, studying it, cocking his own head to one side.

The grandfather's clock in the corner of the room, I suddenly realized, wasn't getting any younger. It would drop out a *tick*, and the *tick* would land inside my head like a rock dropped in a well, and the ripples would circle out and stop, and the *tick* would sink down the dark. For a piece of time which was not long or short, and might not even be time, there wouldn't be anything. Then the *tock* would drop down the well, and the ripples would circle out and finish.

The Boss quit studying Judge Irwin's face, which didn't show anything. He let himself sink back in the chair, shrugged his shoulders, and lifted the glass up for a drink. Then he said, "Suit yourself, Judge. But you know, there's another way to play it. Maybe somebody might give Callahan a little shovelful on somebody else and Callahan might grow a conscience all of a sudden and repudiate his endorser. You know, when this conscience business starts, ain't no telling where it'll stop, and when you start the digging ——"

"I'll thank you, sir—" Judge Irwin took a step toward the big chair, and his face wasn't the color of calf's liver now—it was long past that and streaked white back from the base of the jutting nose—"I'll thank you, sir, to get out of that chair and get out of this house!"

The Boss didn't lift his head off the leather. He looked up at the Judge, sweet and trusting, and then cocked his eyes over to me. "Jack," he said, "you were sure right. The Judge don't scare easy."

"Get out," the Judge said, not loud this time.

"These old bones don't move fast," the Boss murmured sadly, "but now I have tried to do my bounden duty, let me go." Then he drained his glass, set it on the floor beside the chair, and rose. He stood in front of the Judge, looking up at him, squinting again, cocking his head to one side again, like a farmer getting ready to buy a horse.

I set my glass on the shelf of the bookcase behind me. I discovered that I hadn't touched it, not since the first sip. *Well, to hell with it,* I thought, and let it stand. Some nigger boy would get it in the morning.

Then, as though he had decided against buying the horse, the Boss shook his head and passed around the Judge, as though the Judge weren't a man at all, or even a horse, as though he were the corner of a house or a tree, and headed for the hall door, putting his feet down slow and easy on the red carpet. No hurry.

For a second or two the Judge didn't even move his head; then he swung round and watched the Boss going toward the door, and his eyes glittered up there in the shadow above the lamp.

The Boss laid his hand on the doorknob, opened the door, and then, with his hand still on the knob, he looked back. "Well, Judge," he said, "more in pain than wrath I go. And if your conscience decides it could gag at Callahan, just let me know. In, of course—" and he grinned—"a reasonable time."

Then he looked over at me and said, "Let's haul ass, Jack," and started on down toward the front door, out of sight.

Before I could get into low gear, the Judge swung his face in my direction, and focused his eyes on me, and his upper lip lifted under that nose to form a smile of somewhat massive irony, and he said, "Your employer is calling you, Mr. Burden."

"I don't use any ear trumpet yet," I said, and pulled off toward the door, and thought to myself: *Christ, Jack, you talk like a snot, Christ, you are a smart guy.*

I had just about made the door, when he said, "I'm dining with your mother this week. Shall I tell her you still like your work?"

Why don't he lay off? I thought, but he wouldn't, and that lip lifted up again.

So I said, "Suit yourself, Judge. But if I were you I wouldn't go around advertising this visit to anybody. In case you changed your mind, somebody might figure you had stooped to a low political deal with the Boss. In the dark of night."

And I went out the door and down the hall and out the hall door and left it open but let the screen door slam.

God damn him, why hadn't he laid off me?

But he hadn't scared.

Questions to Consider

1. In your opinion, is "Founding Fathers" sexist in its portrayal of women? Give specific examples to support your argument.
2. The first six stanzas of "Bearded Oaks" draw an analogy between two lovers seated beneath live oak trees draped with Spanish moss and two coral atolls at the bottom of the sea. According to Warren, what specific elements do these very *different* things have in common?

3. In the selection from Chapter 1 of *All the King's Men*, the narrator is Jack Burden, a political fixer for Willie Stark, the governor of an unnamed Deep South state based on Louisiana. The two men are being driven to Jack's hometown to confront a political foe, who was once a father figure to Jack. What shifting feelings does Jack undergo, caught in the tense encounter between the Boss and the Judge?

John Gould Fletcher

1886–1950

John Gould Fletcher was unique among American poets for his involvement in both the European modernist and the Southern Fugitive-Agrarian movements in literature. He was born in Little Rock on 3 January 1886; his wealthy father was a Confederate Army veteran, banker, cotton broker, and three-time losing candidate for state governor, married to a woman 24 years his junior. His father died while Fletcher was an undergraduate at Harvard University, and Fletcher dropped out of college and headed to Europe with his handsome inheritance, where he paid to have five volumes of his poetry published in 1913. This early work was not well received.

After meeting the American expatriate poets Ezra Pound and Amy Lowell in Paris and London, Fletcher became involved with them in promoting Imagism, the precursor to poetic modernism. In contrast to Victorian poetry, much of which was sentimental, rhetorical, abstract in thought, archaic in diction, and written in traditional forms, Imagist poetry was impersonal, objective, concrete, spare in wording, unrhymed, and unmetered. Fletcher's 1915 poetry collection, *Irradiations, Sand and Spray*, was received by reviewers as Imagist, although some critics now argue that Fletcher's work was too symbolic to be exemplary. Returning to the United States upon the outbreak of World War I, Fletcher viewed a Japanese art exhibit in Chicago which exerted a powerful effect upon his poetry and philosophy. Always something of an antimaterialist, despite his family wealth, Fletcher glimpsed in the Japanese prints an underlying spirituality and closeness to nature that found expression in his next two poetry collections, *Goblins and Pagodas* (1916) and *Japanese Prints* (1918). Returning to Europe, Fletcher befriended T. S. Eliot and published poems in the *Criterion*, the modernist organ edited by Eliot, but his Southern roots also drew him to contribute poems to the *Fugitive* from abroad in the early 1920s.

Fletcher traveled throughout the South in 1927, lecturing on the theme of the importance of epic poetry to the future of American letters. In the course of his travels he met Fugitive poets John Crowe Ransom, Donald Davidson, and Allen Tate, and three years later his new friends solicited an essay entitled "Education, Past and Present" from Fletcher for *I'll Take My Stand: The South and the Agrarian Tradition*, the manifesto of the Agrarian movement. Fletcher quoted the Chinese sage Confucius in the epigraph to his essay, and it is easy to see how the qualities Fletcher admired in Asian art and philosophy—classicism, spirituality, closeness to nature—could transfer to support of the Agrarian values of rural life and anti-industrialism.

Returning permanently to the United States in 1933 after the collapse of his marriage and a nervous breakdown, Fletcher settled in Little Rock and became involved in developing regional art, music, and literary resources. His epic poem, "The Story of Arkansas," was published in 1936. Fletcher's *Selected Poems* came out in 1938. Given that the quality of his poetic work had been uneven, selection served him well, and he was awarded a Pulitzer Prize for poetry in 1939. But after being honored at the national level, Fletcher closed out his poetic career with two books of poetry reflecting his identification as an Arkansan and a Southerner: *South Star* (1941) and *The Burning Mountains* (1946). In 1950, battling a recurrence of mental illness, Fletcher committed suicide by drowning himself, leaving behind an unfinished editorial project: an anthology of Southern poetry.

The Evening Clouds

Like long terraces the evening clouds
Prolong themselves to an infinite grey
Of distance, as shadows seen in a dream.

Like old parks full of autumnal branches
Which the winds agitate, slowly, to and fro;
The evening clouds, grey interwoven,
Sway in a stately measure of old.

Like colonnades, like colonnades darkening,
Like colonnades ancient, mouldering, mysterious,
Stand the motionless clouds of evening:
And my old soul goes shivering amid them,
Seeking grey ghosts that resemble me:

Like colonnades along long terraces
Prolonged, the colonnades of temples,
Behind whose bronze gates, never opened,
Crouch the colossal gods of night.

from The Ghosts of an Old House

BEDROOM

The clump of jessamine
Softly beneath the rain
Rocks its golden flowers.

In this room my father died:
His bed is in the corner.
No one has slept in it
Since the morning when he wakened
To meet death's hands at his heart.
I cannot go to this room,
Without feeling something big and angry
Waiting for me
To throw me on the bed,
And press its thumbs in my throat.

The clump of jessamine
Without, beneath the rain,
Rocks its golden flowers.

The Stars

There is a goddess who walks shrouded by day:
At night she throws her blue veil over the earth.
Men only see her naked glory through the little holes in the veil.

Down the Mississippi

I. EMBARKATION

Dull masses of dense green,
The forests range their sombre platforms;

Between them silently, like spirit,
The river finds its own mysterious path.

Loosely the river sways out, backward, forward,
Always fretting the outer side;
Shunning the invisible focus of each crescent,
Seeking to spread into shining loops over fields.

Like an enormous serpent, dilating, uncoiling,
Displaying a broad scaly back of earth-smeared gold;
Swaying out sinuously between the dull motionless forests,
As molten metal might glide down the lip of a vase of dark bronze;

It goes, while the steamboat drifting out upon it,
Seems now to be floating not only outwards but upwards;
In the flight of a petal detached and gradually moving skyward
Above the pink explosion of the calyx of the dawn.

II. Heat

As if the sun had trodden down the sky,
Until no more it holds living air, but only humid vapour,
Heat pressing upon earth with irresistible langour,
Turns all the solid forest into half-liquid smudge.

The heavy clouds like cargo-boats strain slowly against its current;
And the flickering of the haze is like the thunder of ten thousand paddles
Against the heavy wall of the horizon, pale-blue and utterly windless,
Whereon the sun hangs motionless, a brassy disc of flame.

III. Full Moon

Flinging its arc of silver bubbles, quickly shifts the moon
From side to side of us as we go down its path;
I sit on the deck at midnight and watch it slipping and sliding,
Under my tilted chair, like a thin film of spilt water.

It is weaving a river of light to take the place of this river;
A river where we shall drift all night, then come to rest in its shallows;
And then I shall wake from my drowsiness and look down from some dim
 treetop
Over white lakes of cotton, like moonfields on every side.

IV. The Moon's Orchestra

When the moon lights up
Its dull red campfire through the trees;
And floats out, like a white balloon,
Into the blue cup of the night, borne by a casual breeze;
The moon-orchestra then begins to stir.
Jiggle of fiddles commence their crazy dance in the darkness.
Crickets churr
Against the stark reiteration of the rusty flutes which frogs
Puff at from rotted logs

In the swamp.
And then the moon begins her dance of frozen pomp
Over the lightly quivering floor of the flat and mournful river.
Her white feet slightly twist and swirl.
She is a mad girl
In an old unlit ball room
Whose walls, half-guessed at through the gloom,
Are hung with the rusty crape of stark black cypress
Which show, through gaps and tatters, red stains half hidden away.

V. The Stevedores[1]

Frieze[2] of warm bronze that glides with catlike movements
Over the gangplank poised and yet awaiting,
The sinewy thudding rhythm of forty shuffling feet
Falling like muffled drumbeats on the stillness.
O roll the cotton down,
Roll, roll the cotton down,
From the further side of Jordan,[3]
O roll the cotton down!

And the river waits,
The river listens,
Chuckling little banjo-notes that break with a flop on the stillness;
And by the low dark shed that holds the heavy freights,
Two lonely cypress trees stand up and point with stiffened fingers
Far southward where a single chimney stands out aloof in the sky.

VI. Night Landing

After the whistle's roar has bellowed and shuddered,
Shaking the sleeping town and the somnolent river,
The deep toned floating of the pilot's bell
Suddenly warns the engines.

They stop like heart-beats that abruptly stop,
The shore glides to us, in a wide low curve.

And then—supreme revelation of the river—
The tackle is loosed—the long gangplank swings outwards—
And poised at the end of it, half-naked beneath the searchlight,
A blue-black negro with gleaming teeth waits for his chance to leap.

VII. The Silence

There is a silence I carry about with me always;
A silence perpetual, for it is self-created;
A silence of heat, of water, of unchecked fruitfulness
Through which each year the heavy harvests bloom, and burst and fall.

Deep, matted green silence of my South,
Often within the push and scorn of great cities,

1. Workers who load or unload the cargoes of ships.
2. A long, narrow band of material upon which a raised ornamental design has been sculpted.
3. Famous biblical river.

I have seen that mile-wide waste of water swaying out to you,
And on its current glimmering, I am going to the sea.

There is a silence I have achieved: I have walked beyond its threshold;
I know it is without horizons, boundless, fathomless, perfect.
And some day maybe, far away,
I will curl up in it at last and sleep an endless sleep.

August 20–27, 1915

The Unfamiliar House

To an unfamiliar house once more these feet have wandered,
That set forth on the road so many years gone by.
And once again as stranger have I pondered
On the serene blue depths of an unfamiliar sky.
Here where a dead youth passed, unspent yet shattered,
I walk my roads neglected once again;
And whether that strange past or the nearer past much mattered
I do not know. Here I am loosed from pain.

Between me and the boy that held forlornly to his vision
Now stands a lofty shining unsurmountable wall;
I stare at it in vain. Neither sympathy nor derision
Alters its mass at all.
The oak trees stand as they have stood, unchanging;
The dumb stretch of the dusky sunbrowned earth
Still breathes in brooding unison with all my hopes, far ranging,
As on that ever-vanished day when life first brought me birth.

And people come. They may have kept their places
In which they stood a dozen years ago;
But when I grasp their hands and stare into their faces
They seem more strange than once of old. I know
That time and the years sift wrinkles. Now I wonder
What lasts between us, changing day on day.
Once and for all my fate was this, to live though torn asunder
From all I might have shared—there was no other way.

And when I pass, from a dark hearthstone going,
Blue in the rosy dusk the chimney smoke will glide,
But I will be borne from it on the flowing
Drift of a darker tide.
No more than smoke can I blur still these blue skies' changeless splendor,
No more than a faint blue cloud of smoke within these hearts I last.
The mirror fronts me, frozen, cold, untender.
There are no ghosts left now; the past is but the past.

Questions to Consider

1. "Down the Mississippi" presents numerous sensory images of the Mississippi River and the Deep South. Are there any places in the poem where the images selected by the poet seem to be commenting indirectly upon Southern history or society?
2. What images or symbols in the poem "The Evening Clouds" suggest that it was written by a Southerner?

Donald Davidson
1893–1968

Donald Grady Davidson was born on 18 August 1893, in Campbellsville, Tennessee, and he grew up in Lynnville, 65 miles south of Nashville. The oldest of five children born to rural educator parents, Davidson was only 16 when he went off to study at Vanderbilt University, but he had to drop out after a year because of financial problems. He taught school for a few years, returned to Vanderbilt, and left just short of a degree in 1917 to serve as an army officer in France during World War I. He was able to complete his degree by means of correspondence. After the war he taught college in Kentucky for a few years, then returned to Vanderbilt in 1920 with his wife and child to teach English and work toward a master's degree. Davidson stayed at Vanderbilt for the next 44 years, retiring in 1964. Resistance to change would mark his poetic output as well as his career path.

John Crowe Ransom and Allen Tate were also in Nashville in the early 1920s, and by then the story of their lively meetings with Davidson and others to discuss the arts, and the birth of their little magazine called the *Fugitive* in 1922, had become the stuff of legend. Robert Penn Warren joined the group in 1923. Davidson's first book of poetry, *An Outland Piper* (1924), was anachronistically romantic in style and subject matter, but his second collection, *The Tall Men* (1927), fused a more impersonal and image-driven style, influenced by modernism, to the Fugitives' concern with Southern regional subjects and issues. In a series of related poems about important figures in Tennessee history, the narrator moves through time, from colonial days to an apocalyptic future brought about by runaway technology; many critics consider it to be Davidson's best work. Three years after the Fugitive group's short-lived but influential journal had ceased publication, Davidson edited *Fugitives: An Anthology of Verse* (1928), which brought together the best of their poetic output.

When the core membership of the Fugitives evolved into the Agrarians, turning their interests from Southern literature and the future to Southern economics and the past, Davidson was once again among them. He contributed the essay entitled "A Mirror for Artists" to *I'll Take My Stand: The South and the Agrarian Tradition* (1930), the 12-essay "manifesto" of the Agrarian movement. In the essay, Davidson warned that industrialization and the rise of a consumer economy would replace the fine arts with the popular culture of the lower classes, and he urged Southern artists to promote decentralization of the arts and an "agrarian restoration." The title poem of Davidson's next collection, *Lee in the Mountains and Other Poems* (1938), also looked nostalgically to a heavily mythologized Southern past. The poem is a dramatic monologue spoken by the losing general of the Confederacy, Robert E. Lee. Lee looks back upon his surrender at Appomattox and wonders whether it would have been wiser to retreat to the mountains and keep fighting. Modern readers familiar with the offense taken by many citizens at displays of the Confederate flag and other symbols of the Confederate cause may find it shocking that a poem portraying Lee in a heroic light could have been published and praised by critics seven decades after the Civil War had ended. In fact, poems glorifying Lee were quite common during the 1930s, and Davidson's version, as scholar Thomas Daniel Young has pointed out, succeeds in dramatizing Lee's situation without undue didacticism.

Ransom, Warren, and Tate all distanced themselves from their early Agrarian beliefs and came to support civil rights and desegregation later in their lives, but Davidson, who campaigned for Strom Thurmond in 1948, remained a segregationist to the end. What Ransom said of him in 1939 would prove prescient: "Don stopped growing before the rest of us did." While Davidson's literary accomplishments include a two-volume history of the Tennessee River, the libretto for the Charles F. Bryan folk opera *Singin' Billy*, several collections of essays, one of reviews, two books on composition pedagogy, and a posthumously published novel about the clash between authentic folk music and country music in the South, his poetry is read today not for its enduring literary merits, but for its usefulness in illustrating one particular segment of the history of Southern literature.

Lee in the Mountains[1]

1865–1870

Walking into the shadows, walking alone
Where the sun falls through the ruined boughs of locusts
Up to the president's[2] office. . . .
Hearing the voices
Whisper, *Hush, it is General Lee!* And strangely
Hearing my own voice say, *Good morning, boys.*
(Don't get up. You are early. It is long
Before the bell. You will have long to wait
On these cold steps. . . .)
The young have time to wait.
But soldiers' faces under their tossing flags
Lift no more by any road or field,
And I am spent with old wars and new sorrow.
Walking the rocky path, where steps decay
And the paint cracks and grass eats on the stone.
It is not General Lee, young men. . . .
It is Robert Lee in a dark civilian suit who walks,
An outlaw fumbling for the latch, a voice
Commanding in a dream where no flag flies.

My father's house[3] is taken and his hearth
Left to the candle-drippings where the ashes
Whirl at a chimney-breath on the cold stone.
I can hardly remember my father's look, I cannot
Answer his voice as he calls farewell in the misty
Mounting where riders gather at gates.
He was old then—I was a child—his hand
Held out for mine, some daybreak snatched away,
And he rode out, a broken man. Now let
His lone grave keep, surer than cypress roots,
The vow I made beside him. God too late
Unseals to certain eyes the drift
Of time and the hopes of men and a sacred cause.
The fortune of the Lees goes with the land
Whose sons will keep it still. My mother
Told me much. She sat among the candles,
Fingering the *Memoirs*,[4] now so long unread.
And as my pen moves on across the page

1. From 1865 until his death, Robert E. Lee (1807–1870), the defeated general of the Confederate Army, served as president of Washington College (now Washington and Lee University) in Lexington, Virginia.
2. The president of Washington College.
3. Lee's father was Lieutenant Colonel Henry "Light Horse Harry" Lee (1756–1818), an American Revolutionary War hero and United States congressman. Late in his life, Lee's father was jailed for debt as the result of poor investments in land; subsequently, he had to give up living in the ancestral home of his first wife.
4. Lee's father wrote the two-volume *Memoirs of the War in the Southern Department of the United States* (1812).

Her voice comes back, a murmuring distillation
Of old Virginia times now faint and gone,
The hurt of all that was and cannot be.

Why did my father write? I know he saw
History clutched as a wraith out of blowing mist
Where tongues are loud, and a glut of little souls
Laps at the too much blood and the burning house.
He would have his say, but I shall not have mine.
What I do is only a son's devoir[5]
To a lost father. Let him only speak.
The rest must pass to men who never knew
(But on a written page) the strike of armies,
And never heard the long Confederate cry
Charge through the muzzling smoke or saw the bright
Eyes of the beardless boys go up to death.
It is Robert Lee who writes with his father's hand—
The rest must go unsaid and the lips be locked.

If all were told, as it cannot be told—
If all the dread opinion of the heart
Now could speak, now in the shame and torment
Lashing the bound and trampled States—[6]

If a word were said, as it cannot be said—
I see clear waters run in Virginia's Valley
And in the house the weeping of young women
Rises no more. The waves of grain begin.
The Shenandoah[7] is golden with new grain.
The Blue Ridge,[8] crowned with a haze of light,
Thunders no more. The horse is at plough. The rifle
Returns to the chimney crotch and the hunter's hand.
And nothing else than this? Was it for this
That on an April day[9] we stacked our arms
Obedient to a soldier's trust? To lie
Ground by heels of little men,
Forever maimed, defeated, lost, impugned?
And was I then betrayed? Did I betray?

If it were said, as still it might be said—
If it were said, and a word should run like fire,
Like living fire into the roots of grass,
The sunken flag would kindle on wild hills,
The brooding hearts would waken, and the dream
Stir like a crippled phantom under the pines,
And this torn earth would quicken into shouting
Beneath the feet of ragged bands—
The pen
Turns to the waiting page, the sword

5. Duty.
6. The Confederate States.
7. Valley in northern Virginia.
8. Mountain range that borders the Shenandoah Valley.
9. Lee surrendered his forces on 9 April 1865.

Bows to the rust that cankers and the silence.

Among these boys whose eyes lift up to mine
Within gray walls where droning wasps repeat
A hollow reveille, I still must face,
Day after day, the courier with his summons
Once more to surrender, now to surrender all.
Without arms or men I stand, but with knowledge only
I face what long I saw, before others knew,
When Pickett's[10] men streamed back, and I heard the tangled
Cry of the Wilderness[11] wounded, bloody with doom.
The mountains, once I said, in the little room
At Richmond,[12] by the huddled fire, but still
The President[13] shook his head. The mountains wait,
I said, in the long beat and rattle of siege
At cratered Petersburg[14] Too late
We sought the mountains and those people came.
And Lee is in mountains now, beyond Appomattox,[15]
Listening long for voices that never will speak
Again; hearing the hoofbeats come and go and fade
Without a stop, without a brown hand lifting
The tent-flap, or a bugle call at dawn,
Or ever on the long white road the flag
Of Jackson's[16] quick brigades. I am alone,
Trapped, consenting, taken at last in mountains.

It is not the bugle now, or the long roll beating.
The simple stroke of a chapel bell forbids
The hurtling dream, recalls the lonely mind.
Young men, the God of your fathers is a just
And merciful God Who in this blood once shed
On your green altars measures out all days,
And measures out the grace
Whereby alone we live;
And in His might He waits,
Brooding within the certitude of time,
To bring this lost forsaken valor
And the fierce faith undying
And the love quenchless
To flower among the hills to which we cleave,
To fruit upon the mountains whither we flee,
Never forsaking, never denying
His children and His children's children forever
Unto all generations of the faithful heart.

10. General George Pickett (1825–1875), subordinate to Lee, who led an unsuccessful charge against Federal troops at Gettysburg.
11. At the Battle of the Wilderness in May 1864, Lee's outnumbered forces had achieved a victory.
12. Richmond, Virginia, the capital of the Confederacy.
13. Jefferson Davis (1808–1889), the president of the Confederacy.
14. Federal troops laid siege to Petersburg, Virginia, from June 1864 to April 1865.
15. The site of Lee's surrender in 1865.
16. Thomas Jonathan "Stonewall" Jackson (1824–1863), a Confederate Army general under Lee.

Questions to Consider

1. Would you say that the narrator of "Lee in the Mountains" is ashamed of his military defeat? What passages in the poem support your viewpoint?
2. At several points in the poem, Davidson blurs the distinction between Lee's past with his soldiers and Lee's present with his college students. Locate the passages where Davidson seems to be deliberately mixing or confusing the two situations, and explain why you think he does so.

Allen Tate

1899–1979

Allen Tate's parents were born in Illinois but declared themselves Southerners. John Orley Allen Tate, youngest of their four children, was born in Winchester, Kentucky, on 19 November 1899. Like his mother, he claimed to be a Virginian, even though he grew up in Ohio and Indiana. Tate's uncertainty about regional origin and personal identity drew him into an intense preoccupation with Southernness. Emerging during the twenties from a coterie of poets in Nashville, Tennessee, who called themselves the Fugitives, Tate played a leading role in the Agrarian movement. He was deeply involved in publishing the polemical essay collection *I'll Take My Stand: The South and the Agrarian Tradition* (1930) and its sequel, *Who Owns America? A New Declaration of Independence* (1936). Before the thirties were over, however, Tate would loosen his connections to the South and replace Agrarianism with New Criticism. In 1939 he went North to teach at Princeton. Most of his academic career would be spent there and, after 1951, at the University of Minnesota.

Tate's parents' unhappy marriage led to frequent dislocations. A sickly child, Tate often lived with his mother in hotels. Only at college did he emerge from her overprotectiveness. Tate took English classes at Vanderbilt University from John Crowe Ransom and accepted Donald Davidson's invitation to join their circle of poets. When he was a senior in 1922, Tate placed two poems in the first issue of the *Fugitive*, the group's "little magazine." Soon he was publishing poems in other avant-garde journals, writing reviews of Modernist poets like T. S. Eliot and Ezra Pound, and corresponding with Hart Crane. He was drawn particularly to Eliot's insistence on the intellectual detachment and formal complexity of modern poetry. But Tate found himself torn between Modernist literary values and Fugitive regional loyalty, a division of thought and feeling that runs through his best work. In this tension lie the origins of Tate's main contribution to the Agrarian movement. While he rejected sentimental Lost Cause writing as "a decayed magnolia stump," Tate defended the traditional landowning culture of the Old South as a positive alternative to modern mechanized society.

While still in Nashville, Tate befriended Robert Penn Warren and brought him into the Fugitive circle. During a visit to Warren's Kentucky hometown, Tate met Caroline Gordon, whose family lived nearby. Soon they were lovers, and she became pregnant. For months Tate resisted marrying her and did so only weeks before their daughter was born in 1925. Their marriage would be tumultuous, marked by Tate's numerous adulteries and Gordon's furious recriminations. They also proved indifferent parents. Both drank heavily, socialized actively with the literary set, and often lived hand to mouth while scratching a living from writing and teaching. At times Tate belittled Gordon's fiction as narrow and lacking intellectual depth. Yet as much as he resented her, he needed her acceptance. They often helped each other with writing projects, and together they published an influential college textbook, *The House of Fiction* (1950). When she divorced him in 1946, Tate quickly sought a reconciliation; within months they remarried. In 1950 he joined her as a convert to Roman Catholicism. But little changed in their one-sided relationship, and Tate divorced Gordon again in 1959. That year he married Isabella Gardner, a poet. After that marriage ended in divorce, in 1966 Tate married Helen Heinz, a former nun; when he was 67, she had twins. Always frail, Tate suffered for years from liver disease and emphysema. He died on 9 February 1979.

Tate wrote his most famous poem, "Ode to the Confederate Dead," when he was 27 and he and Gordon were enduring an impoverished winter in New York City. The poem solemnly dramatizes the ambivalence toward the Old South that Tate felt as a modern Southerner. He presents the Confederacy as a bygone world cut off from the urban present yet embodying a heroic coherence. Even so, the past poses dangers to the present and can be a fatal lure to pessimism and paralysis. Although criticized as obscure, the "Ode" would become an anthem of Agrarianism and endure as one of the major poems of twentieth-century American literature.

Tate's preoccupation with the Civil War led him to publish biographies of Thomas J. (Stonewall) Jackson (1928) and Jefferson Davis (1929), although Gordon wrote part of the latter book. By 1930 he and Gordon had settled in Clarksville, Tennessee, near her family's farm. Establishing an identity as a public intellectual, Tate took a hand in forming the "brethren," the band of Twelve Agrarian writers who contributed to *I'll Take My Stand.* Its essays railed against Northern industrial society and defended the traditions of the Southern past—the world of the plantation. The book generated wide publicity in the turbulent months after the stock market crash of 1929, when finance capitalism appeared to be collapsing. While American Communist writers attacked the corporate system from the Left, the conservative Agrarians pelted it from the Right. Yet Tate loathed Communism, which he condemned as proindustrial and dehumanizing. Thus, it infuriated him when Left-wing critics derided *I'll Take My Stand* as a neo-Confederate fantasy that ignored the South's historical record of slavery and rural poverty.

Tate's anger toward the Left caused him to become entangled for a time with American fascist sympathizers. He expressed stridently reactionary views, including support for White supremacy—indeed, his first book of literary criticism was titled *Reactionary Essays on Poetry and Ideas* (1936). Tate's belligerence hastened the collapse of the Agrarian movement, and its failure led Tate to withdraw from politics. He rededicated himself to literature and brought out *Selected Poems* (1937). Also, he wrote his only novel, *The Fathers* (1938), a post-Agrarian work that delves into the bloody contradictions in Southern history. It is a novel of divided loyalties that draws on Tate's family history, including miscegenation. By the 1950s, Tate—now a celebrated exponent of New Criticism at leading Northern universities—had greatly moderated his racial views. He endorsed voting rights for African Americans and expressed Southern culpability for racial injustice. His poem "The Swimmers," written in 1951, describes a grisly episode from his Kentucky boyhood—seeing the body of a Black man, murdered by a White lynch mob. This poem was intended to be part of a longer work. But Tate's poetic output dwindled, and he published little thereafter.

Tate was always perceptive about the Southern Literary Renascence, of which he was a catalyst, main participant, and active promoter. He refined his position about the literary South in a series of essays published over a span of decades. He gave perhaps his finest statement in "A Southern Mode of the Imagination," a brilliant survey of Southern literature from William Gilmore Simms to the Southern authors of 1959.

Ode to the Confederate Dead

Row after row with strict impunity
The headstones yield their names to the element,
The wind whirrs without recollection;

In the riven troughs the splayed leaves
Pile up, of nature the casual sacrament
To the seasonal eternity of death;
Then driven by the fierce scrutiny
Of heaven to their election in the vast breath,
They sough the rumour of mortality.

Autumn is desolation in the plot
Of a thousand acres where these memories grow
From the inexhaustible bodies that are not
Dead, but feed the grass row after rich row.
Think of the autumns that have come and gone!—
Ambitious November with the humors of the year,
With a particular zeal for every slab,
Staining the uncomfortable angels that rot
On the slabs, a wing chipped here, an arm there:
The brute curiosity of an angel's stare
Turns you, like them, to stone,
Transforms the heaving air
Till plunged to a heavier world below
You shift your sea-space blindly
Heaving, turning like the blind crab.

Dazed by the wind, only the wind
The leaves flying, plunge

You know who have waited by the wall
The twilight certainty of an animal,
Those midnight restitutions of the blood
You know—the immitigable pines, the smoky frieze
Of the sky, the sudden call: you know the rage,
The cold pool left by the mounting flood,
Of muted Zeno and Parmenides.[1]
You who have waited for the angry resolution
Of those desires that should be yours tomorrow,
You know the unimportant shrift of death
And praise the vision
And praise the arrogant circumstance
Of those who fall
Rank upon rank, hurried beyond decision—
Here by the sagging gate, stopped by the wall.

Seeing, seeing only the leaves
Flying, plunge and expire

Turn your eyes to the immoderate past,
Turn to the inscrutable infantry rising
Demons out of the earth—they will not last.
Stonewall, Stonewall,[2] and the sunken fields of hemp,

1. Parmenides and his pupil Zeno were Greek philosophers of the fifth century BC who held that change cannot occur and is an illusion. Zeno illustrated the principle of changelessness by a series of paradoxes to show that motion (one form of change) is impossible. Reality, therefore, is a static, unchanging whole.

2. Stonewall is Thomas J. Jackson (1825–1863), a celebrated Confederate general of the Civil War. Tate began his biography, *Stonewall Jackson: The Good Soldier*, in 1927, when he was revising "Ode to the Confederate Dead."

Shiloh, Antietam, Malvern Hill, Bull Run.[3]
Lost in that orient of the thick-and-fast
You will curse the setting sun.

Cursing only the leaves crying
Like an old man in a storm

You hear the shout, the crazy hemlocks point
With troubled fingers to the silence which
Smothers you, a mummy, in time.
The hound bitch
Toothless and dying, in a musty cellar
Hears the wind only.
Now that the salt of their blood
Stiffens the saltier oblivion of the sea,
Seals the malignant purity of the flood,
What shall we who count our days and bow
Our heads with a commemorial woe
In the ribboned coats of grim felicity,
What shall we say of the bones, unclean,
Whose verdurous anonymity will grow?
The ragged arms, the ragged heads and eyes
Lost in these acres of the insane green?
The gray lean spiders come, they come and go;
In a tangle of willows without light
The singular screech-owl's tight
Invisible lyric seeds the mind
With the furious murmur of their chivalry.

We shall say only the leaves
Flying, plunge and expire

We shall say only the leaves whispering
In the improbable mist of nightfall
That flies on multiple wing;
Night is the beginning and the end
And in between the ends of distraction
Waits mute speculation, the patient curse
That stones the eyes, or like the jaguar leaps
For his own image in a jungle pool, his victim.
What shall we say who have knowledge
Carried to the heart? Shall we take the act
To the grave? Shall we, more hopeful, set up the grave
In the house? The ravenous grave?
Leave now
The shut gate and the decomposing wall:
The gentle serpent, green in the mulberry bush,
Riots with his tongue through the hush—
Sentinel of the grave who counts us all!

3. Shiloh, Antietam, Malvern Hill, and Bull Run were Civil War battles of 1861–1862. The two battles at Bull Run (Virginia) were Confederate victories. Malvern Hill (Virginia) was a Confederate defeat, as was Shiloh (Tennessee). Antietam (Maryland) was a bloody standoff that ended in Confederate retreat.

The Swimmers

(SCENE: Montgomery County, Kentucky, July 1911)

Kentucky water, clear springs: a boy fleeing
To water under the dry Kentucky sun,
His four little friends in tandem with him, seeing

Long shadows of grapevine wriggle and run
Over the green swirl; mullein under the ear
Soft as Nausicaä's[1] palm; sullen fun

Savage as childhood's thin harmonious tear:
O fountain, bosom source undying-dead
Replenish me the spring of love and fear

And give me back the eye that looked and fled
When a thrush idling in the tulip tree
Unwound the cold dream of the copperhead.

—Along the creek the road was winding; we
Felt the quicksilver sky. I see again
The shrill companions of that odyssey:

Bill Eaton, Charlie Watson, "Nigger" Layne
The doctor's son, Harry Duèsler who played
The flute; and Tate, with water on the brain.

Dog-days: the dusty leaves where rain delayed
Hung low on poison-oak and scuppernong,
And we were following the active shade

Of water, that bells and bickers all night long.
"No more'n a mile," Layne said. All five stood still.
Listening, I heard what seemed at first a song;

Peering, I heard the hooves come down the hill.
The posse passed, twelve horse; the leader's face
Was worn as limestone on an ancient sill.

Then, as sleepwalkers shift from a hard place
In bed, and rising to keep a formal pledge
Descend a ladder into empty space,

We scuttled down the bank below a ledge
And marched stiff-legged in our common fright
Along a hog-track by the riffle's edge:

Into a world where sound shaded the sight
Dropped the dull hooves again; the horsemen came
Again, all but the leader. It was night

Momently and I feared: eleven same
Jesus-Christers unmembered and unmade,
Whose Corpse had died again in dirty shame.

1. In Homer's *Odyssey* Nausicaä is a beautiful princess with lovely white hands and arms who rescues the shipwrecked Odysseus.

The bank then levelling in a speckled glade,
  We stopped to breathe above the swimming-hole;
  I gazed at its reticulated shade

Recoiling in blue fear, and felt it roll
  Over my ears and eyes and lift my hair
  Like seaweed tossing on a sunk atoll.

I rose again. Borne on the copper air
  A distant voice green as a funeral wreath
  Against a grave: "That dead nigger there."

The melancholy sheriff slouched beneath
  A giant sycamore; shaking his head
  He plucked a sassafras twig and picked his teeth:

"We come too late." He spoke to the tired dead
  Whose ragged shirt soaked up the viscous flow
  Of blood in which It lay discomfited.

A butting horse-fly gave one ear a blow
  And glanced off, as the sheriff kicked the rope
  Loose from the neck and hooked it with his toe

Away from the blood.—I looked back down the slope:
  The friends were gone that I had hoped to greet.—
  A single horseman came at a slow lope

And pulled up at the hanged man's horny feet;
  The sheriff noosed the feet, the other end
  The stranger tied to his pommel in a neat

Slip-knot. I saw the Negro's body bend
  And straighten, as a fish-line cast transverse
  Yields to the current that it must subtend.

The sheriff's Goddamn was a murmured curse
  Not for the dead but for the blinding dust
  That boxed the cortège in a cloudy hearse

And dragged it towards our town. I knew I must
  Not stay till twilight in that silent road;
  Sliding my bare feet into the warm crust,

I hopped the stonecrop like a panting toad
  Mouth open, following the heaving cloud
  That floated to the court-house square its load

Of limber corpse that took the sun for shroud.
  There were three figures in the dying sun
  Whose light were company where three was crowd.

My breath crackled the dead air like a shotgun
  As, sheriff and the stranger disappearing,
  The faceless head lay still. I could not run

Or walk, but stood. Alone in the public clearing
This private thing was owned by all the town,
Though never claimed by us within my hearing.

Questions to Consider

1. In "Ode to the Confederate Dead," the visitor standing at the gate to the Confederate cemetery is a man of the twentieth century. It is a dreary autumn evening, and leaves are falling. As he watches them drift, he tries to imagine the troops and battles of the Civil War, but he feels cut off from the romantic Southern past. He cannot see himself in it. What is it about the dead soldiers he envies? What lack does he feel in himself and his own age?
2. "The Swimmers" dramatizes a flashback that Tate had of a violent event from 40 years earlier in his life. The closing lines of the poem present racial terror in a way that made many White Southerners uncomfortable in the 1950s. In what way?

END OF VOICES IN CONTEXT

Anna Julia Cooper

1858–1964

"My mother was a slave and the finest woman I have ever known," remarked Anna Julia Cooper when reflecting on the aspects of her early life that led to her success. Her tour de force, *A Voice from the South by a Black Woman from the South*, is widely acknowledged as the first work of its kind by a Black feminist. During an era when the voices of women of color were suppressed and largely unknown to the American consciousness, Cooper's fluid prose provided insight into the plight of the oppressed in the late nineteenth century, paying special attention to the oppression of women. Cooper published four collections of essays, as well as numerous essays in both English and French that remained uncollected during her lifetime. She also penned a memoir of her life, titled *The Third Step: An Autobiography*, which was privately printed in 1950.

Anna Julia Haywood Cooper was the daughter of George Washington Haywood, a slave owner, and Hannah Stanley, his slave. At the time of Anna's birth on 10 August 1858 in Raleigh, North Carolina, Southern racial laws dictated that, like her mother, Anna would be held in slavery. The status of children followed that of the mother prior to emancipation, which Lincoln proclaimed in 1862. Anna's family also included two elder brothers, Rufus and Andrew, who were well-regarded musicians in the postwar African-American community. Anna Hayward's intelligence led to early opportunities, and she was working as a student-teacher for annual wages of $100 by the time she was eight. She began attending the Episcopalian St. Augustine Normal School and Collegiate Institute, which was founded in Raleigh in 1867 as a training school for African-American teachers and ministers. Upon completing her studies at St. Augustine, Anna accepted a teaching position, and in 1877, she married Episcopal minister George A. Cooper. Her husband died two years after they wed, and the young teacher never remarried.

Anna Cooper returned to school several years after the death of her husband and earned a bachelor's degree from Oberlin College in 1884, and in 1887, she completed a master's degree in mathematics. At the conclusion of her graduate study, Cooper accepted a teaching position in the Preparatory High School for Colored Youth—later Dunbar High School—where she taught for nearly forty years. Cooper argued tirelessly against the restrictions of race and gender in late nineteenth-century America, as Leona Gabel has pointed out: "race should not be a criterion . . . aptitude alone should determine who is admitted to further education. [Cooper] argued as well against the use of sex as a criterion." Cooper's professional and academic success intensified her belief that education provided the key to equality.

Cooper spent several summers in Paris studying French literature and history at the *Guilde Internationale* and received her doctoral degree from the Sorbonne in 1925, at the age of 65. Cooper not only achieved success as an educator, but she was also a highly regarded writer, scholar, and public speaker throughout her career. Following her retirement from teaching, Cooper served as the president of an evening school for working adults and continued to write. She also raised seven children: two foster children and the five offspring of a deceased relative.

Two sources provide much of the inspiration that resulted in Cooper's body of work: her life in Reconstruction-era North Carolina and her personal observations of the struggle for equality and academic success in classes that were dominated by male students. She yearned for an education from the time she was a young child, and as Gabel notes, Cooper "developed a concern for the equality of women in the educational enterprise and their roles in the goals for her race" and she was adamant that "the black woman [is] vital to the regeneration of the race [and] a vital part of the human equation." Cooper's association with other formidable women of color intensified her innate drive to seek equality for all people. "The Status of Woman in America" articulates Cooper's observations of the gender-based expectations that women encountered, examining the ways in which these implicit gender biases were exacerbated for women of color, especially in the pre–Civil Rights era United States. Indeed, much of her writing focused on the need to eradicate the oppressive racial and gender injustices of the postwar South.

The "peculiar institution" of slavery in the South exacted a different price from Anna Cooper than that which many of her formerly enslaved counterparts paid, since North Carolina's geography and farming methods caused slavery to be less profitable and therefore less widespread than in other areas of the South. Further, the state was reputed to be one of the more liberal in terms of the treatment slaves received and was one of the last states to secede from the Union. Despite the relative tolerance found in the state during the Antebellum era, by the late nineteenth century, racial oppression and terrorism had increased markedly, much as they did throughout the rest of the South following the end of Radical Reconstruction. Always a proponent of ending oppression and securing equality for all people, Cooper worked throughout her life to organize other African-American intellectuals in opposition to the Jim Crow atmosphere that developed.

The Status of Woman in America

Just four hundred years ago an obscure dreamer and castle builder,[1] prosaically poor and ridiculously insistent on the reality of his dreams, was enabled through the devotion of a noble woman[2] to give to civilization a magnificent continent.

What the lofty purpose of Spain's pure-minded queen had brought to the birth, the untiring devotion of pioneer women nourished and developed. The dangers of wild beasts and of wilder men, the mysteries of unknown wastes and unexplored forests, the horrors of pestilence and famine, of exposure and loneliness, during all those years of discovery and settlement, were braved without a murmur by women who had been most delicately constituted and most tenderly nurtured.

And when the times of physical hardship and danger were past, when the work of clearing and opening up was over and the struggle for accumulation began, again woman's inspiration and help were needed and still was she loyally at hand. A Mary Lyon,[3] demanding and making possible equal advantages of education for women as for men, and, in the face of discouragement and incredulity, bequeathing to women the opportunities of Holyoke.

A Dorothea Dix, insisting on the humane and rational treatment of the insane and bringing about a reform in the lunatic asylums of the country, making a great step forward in the tender regard for the weak by the strong throughout the world.

A Helen Hunt Jackson, convicting the nation of a century of dishonor in regard to the Indian.

A Lucretia Mott, gentle Quaker spirit, with sweet insistence, preaching the abolition of slavery and the institution, in its stead, of the brotherhood of man; her life and words breathing out in tender melody the injunction

> "Have love. Not love alone for one
> But man as man thy brother call;
> And scatter, like the circling sun,
> Thy charities *on all*."

1. Christopher Columbus.
2. Queen Isabella of Spain.
3. Founder of Mount Holyoke College in Massachusetts, pioneered the struggle to provide higher education for women in the United States.

And at the most trying time of what we have called the Accumulative Period, when internecine war, originated through man's love of gain and his determination to subordinate national interests and black men's rights alike to considerations of personal profit and loss, was drenching our country with its own best blood, who shall recount the name and fame of the women on both sides the senseless strife,—those uncomplaining souls with a great heart ache of their own, rigid features and pallid cheek their ever effective flag of truce, on the battle field, in the camp, in the hospital, binding up wounds, recording dying whispers for absent loved ones, with tearful eyes pointing to man's last refuge, giving the last earthly hand clasp and performing the last friendly office for strangers whom a great common sorrow had made kin, while they knew that somewhere—somewhere a husband, a brother, a father, a son, was being tended by stranger hands—or mayhap those familiar eyes were even then being closed forever by just such another ministering angel of mercy and love.

But why mention names? Time would fail to tell of the noble army of women who shine like beacon lights in the otherwise sordid wilderness of this accumulative period—prison reformers and tenement cleansers, quiet unnoted workers in hospitals and homes, among imbeciles, among outcasts—the sweetening, purifying antidotes for the poisons of man's acquisitiveness,—mollifying and soothing with the tenderness of compassion and love the wounds and bruises caused by his overreaching and avarice.

The desire for quick returns and large profits tempts capital ofttimes into unsanitary, well nigh inhuman investments,—tenement tinder boxes, stifling, stunting, sickening alleys and pestiferous slums; regular rents, no waiting, large percentages,—rich coffers coined out of the life-blood of human bodies and souls. Men and women herded together like cattle, breathing in malaria and typhus from an atmosphere seething with moral as well as physical impurity, revelling in vice as their native habitat and then, to drown the whisperings of their higher consciousness and effectually to hush the yearnings and accusations within, flying to narcotics and opiates—rum, tobacco, opium, binding hand and foot, body and soul, till the proper image of God is transformed into a fit associate for demons,—a besotted, enervated, idiotic wreck, or else a monster of wickedness terrible and destructive.

These are some of the legitimate products of the unmitigated tendencies of the wealth-producing period. But, thank Heaven, side by side with the cold, mathematical, selfishly calculating, so-called practical and unsentimental instinct of the business man, there comes the sympathetic warmth and sunshine of good women, like the sweet and sweetening breezes of spring, cleansing, purifying, soothing, inspiring, lifting the drunkard from the gutter, the outcast from the pit. Who can estimate the influence of these "daughters of the king," these lend-a-hand forces, in counteracting the selfishness of an acquisitive age?

To-day America counts her millionaires by the thousand; questions of tariff and questions of currency are the most vital ones agitating the public mind. In this period, when material prosperity and well earned ease and luxury are assured facts from a national standpoint, woman's work and woman's influence are needed as never before; needed to bring a heart power into this money getting, dollar-worshipping civilization; needed to bring a moral force into the utilitarian motives and interests of the time; needed to stand for God and Home and Native Land *versus gain and greed and grasping selfishness.*

There can be no doubt that this fourth centenary of America's discovery which we celebrate at Chicago, strikes the keynote of another important transition in the history of this nation; and the prominence of woman in the management of its celebration is a fitting tribute to the part she is destined to play among the forces of the future. This is the first congressional recognition of woman in this country, and this Board of Lady Managers constitute the first women legally appointed by any government to act in a national capacity. This of itself marks the dawn of a new day.

Now the periods of discovery, of settlement, of developing resources and accumulating wealth have passed in rapid succession. Wealth in the nation as in the individual brings leisure, repose, reflection. The struggle with nature is over, the struggle with ideas begins. We stand then, it seems to me, in this last decade of the nineteenth century, just in the portals of a new and untried movement on a higher plain and in a grander strain than any the past has called forth. It does not require a prophet's eye to divine its trend and image its possibilities from the forces we see already at work around us; nor is it hard to guess what must be the status of woman's work under the new regime.

In the pioneer days her role was that of a camp-follower, an additional something to fight for and be burdened with, only repaying the anxiety and labor she called forth by her own incomparable gifts of sympathy and appreciative love; unable herself ordinarily to contend with the bear and the Indian, or to take active part in clearing the wilderness and constructing the home.

In the second or wealth producing period her work is abreast of man's, complementing and supplementing, counteracting excessive tendencies, and mollifying over rigorous proclivities.

In the era now about to dawn, her sentiments must strike the keynote and give the dominant tone. And this because of the nature of her contribution to the world.

Her kingdom is not over physical forces. Not by might, nor by power can she prevail. Her position must ever be inferior where strength of muscle creates leadership. If she follows the instincts of her nature, however, she must always stand for the conservation of those deeper moral forces which make for the happiness of homes and the righteousness of the country. In a reign of moral ideas she is easily queen.

There is to my mind no grander and surer prophecy of the new era and of woman's place in it, than the work already begun in the waning years of the nineteenth century by the W. C. T. U.[4] in America, an organization which has even now reached not only national but international importance, and seems destined to permeate and purify the whole civilized world. It is the living embodiment of woman's activities and woman's ideas, and its extent and strength rightly prefigure her increasing power as a moral factor.

The colored woman of to-day occupies, one may say, a unique position in this country. In a period of itself transitional and unsettled, her status seems one of the least ascertainable and definitive of all the forces which make for our civilization. She is confronted by both a woman question and a race problem, and is as yet an unknown or an unacknowledged factor in both. While the women of the white race can with calm assurance enter upon the work they feel by nature appointed to do, while their men give loyal support and appreciative countenance to their efforts, recognizing in most avenues of usefulness the propriety and the need of woman's distinctive co-operation, the colored woman too often finds herself hampered and shamed by a less liberal sentiment and a more conservative attitude on the part of those for whose opinion she cares most. That this is not universally true I am glad to admit. There are to be found both intensely conservative white men and exceedingly liberal colored

4. The Women's Christian Temperance Union was founded in 1874.

men. But as far as my experience goes the average man of our race is less frequently ready to admit the actual need among the sturdier forces of the world for woman's help or influence. That great social and economic questions await her interference, that she could throw any light on problems of national import, that her intermeddling could improve the management of school systems, or elevate the tone of public institutions, or humanize and sanctify the far reaching influence of prisons and reformatories and improve the treatment of lunatics and imbeciles,—that she has a word worth hearing on mooted questions in political economy, that she could contribute a suggestion on the relations of labor and capital, or offer a thought on honest money and honorable trade, I fear the majority of "Americans of the colored variety" are not yet prepared to concede. It may be that they do not yet see these questions in their right perspective, being absorbed in the immediate needs of their own political complications. A good deal depends on where we put the emphasis in this world; and our men are not perhaps to blame if they see everything colored by the light of those agitations in the midst of which they live and move and have their being. The part they have had to play in American history during the last twenty-five or thirty years has tended rather to exaggerate the importance of mere political advantage, as well as to set a fictitious valuation on those able to secure such advantage. It is the astute politician, the manager who can gain preferment for himself and his favorites, the demagogue known to stand in with the powers at the White House and consulted on the bestowal of government plums, whom we set in high places and denominate great. It is they who receive the hosannas of the multitude and are regarded as leaders of the people. The thinker and the doer, the man who solves the problem by enriching his country with an invention worth thousands or by a thought inestimable and precious is given neither bread nor a stone. He is too often left to die in obscurity and neglect even if spared in his life the bitterness of fanatical jealousies and detraction.

And yet politics, and surely American politics, is hardly a school for great minds. Sharpening rather than deepening, it develops the faculty of taking advantage of present emergencies rather than the insight to distinguish between the true and the false, the lasting and the ephemeral advantage. Highly cultivated selfishness rather than consecrated benevolence is its passport to success. Its votaries are never seers. At best they are but manipulators—often only jugglers. It is conducive neither to profound statesmanship nor to the higher type of manhood. Altruism is its *mauvais succes* and naturally enough it is indifferent to any factor which cannot be worked into its own immediate aims and purposes. As woman's influence as a political element is as yet nil in most of the commonwealths of our republic, it is not surprising that with those who place the emphasis on mere political capital she may yet seem almost a nonentity so far as it concerns the solution of great national or even racial perplexities.

There are those, however, who value the calm elevation of the thoughtful spectator who stands aloof from the heated scramble; and, above the turmoil and din of corruption and selfishness, can listen to the teachings of eternal truth and righteousness. There are even those who feel that the black man's unjust and unlawful exclusion temporarily from participation in the elective franchise in certain states is after all but a lesson "in the desert" fitted to develop in him insight and discrimination against the day of his own appointed time. One needs occasionally to stand aside from the hum and rush of human interests and passions to hear the voices of God. And it not unfrequently happens that the All-loving gives a great push to certain souls to thrust them out, as it were, from the distracting current for awhile to promote their discipline and growth, or to enrich them by communion and reflection. And similarly it may be woman's privilege from her peculiar coigne of vantage as a quiet observer, to whisper just the needed suggestion or the almost forgotten truth. The colored woman, then, should not be ignored because her bark is resting in the silent waters of the sheltered cove. She is watching the movements of the contestants none the less and is all the better qualified, perhaps, to weigh and judge and advise because not herself in the excitement of the race. Her voice, too, has always been heard in clear, unfaltering tones, ringing the changes on those deeper interests which make for permanent good. She is always sound and orthodox on questions affecting the well-being of her race. You do not find the colored woman selling her birthright for a mess of pottage. Nay, even after reason has retired from the contest, she has been known to cling blindly with the instinct of a turtle dove to those principles and policies which to her mind promise hope and safety for children yet unborn. It is notorious that ignorant black women in the South have actually left their husbands' homes and repudiated their support for what was understood by the wife to be race disloyalty, or "voting away," as she expresses it, the privileges of herself and little ones.

It is largely our women in the South to-day who keep the black men solid in the Republican party. The latter as they increase in intelligence and power of discrimination would be more apt to divide on local issues at any rate. They begin to see that the Grand Old Party regards the Negro's cause as an outgrown issue, and on Southern soil at least finds a too intimate acquaintanceship with him a somewhat unsavory recommendation. Then, too, their political wits have been sharpened to appreciate the fact that it is good policy to cultivate one's neighbors and not depend too much on a distant friend to fight one's home battles. But the black woman can never forget—however lukewarm the party may to-day appear—that it was a Republican president[5] who struck the manacles from her own wrists and gave the possibilities of manhood to her helpless little ones; and to her mind a Democratic Negro is a traitor and a time-server. Talk as much as you like of venality and manipulation in the South, there are not many men, I can tell you, who would dare face a wife quivering in every fiber with the consciousness that her husband is a coward who could be paid to desert her deepest and dearest interests.

Not unfelt, then, if unproclaimed has been the work and influence of the colored women of America. Our list of chieftains in the service, though not long, is not inferior in strength and excellence, I dare believe, to any similar list which this country can produce.

Among the pioneers, Frances Watkins Harper could sing with prophetic exaltation in the darkest days, when as yet there was not a rift in the clouds overhanging her people:

> "Yes, Ethiopia shall stretch
> Her bleeding hands abroad;
> Her cry of agony shall reach the burning throne of God.
> Redeemed from dust and freed from chains
> Her sons shall lift their eyes,
> From cloud-capt hills and verdant plains
> Shall shouts of triumph rise."

Among preachers of righteousness, an unanswerable silencer of cavilers and objectors, was Sojourner Truth, that unique and rugged genius who seemed carved out

5. Abraham Lincoln.

without hand or chisel from the solid mountain mass; and in pleasing contrast, Amanda Smith, sweetest of natural singers and pleaders in dulcet tones for the things of God and of His Christ.

Sarah Woodson Early and Martha Briggs, planting and watering in the school room, and giving off from their matchless and irresistible personality an impetus and inspiration which can never die so long as there lives and breathes a remote descendant of their disciples and friends.

Charlotte Fortin Grimke, the gentle spirit whose verses and life link her so beautifully with America's great Quaker poet and loving reformer.

Hallie Quinn Brown, charming reader, earnest, effective lecturer and devoted worker of unflagging zeal and unquestioned power.

Fannie Jackson Coppin, the teacher and organizer, pre-eminent among women of whatever country or race in constructive and executive force.

These women represent all shades of belief and as many departments of activity; but they have one thing in common—their sympathy with the oppressed race in America and the consecration of their several talents in whatever line to the work of its deliverance and development.

Fifty years ago woman's activity according to orthodox definitions was on a pretty clearly cut "sphere," including primarily the kitchen and the nursery, and rescued from the barrenness of prison bars by the womanly mania for adorning every discoverable bit of china or canvass with forlorn looking cranes balanced idiotically on one foot. The woman of to-day finds herself in the presence of responsibilities which ramify through the profoundest and most varied interests of her country and race. Not one of the issues of this plodding, toiling, sinning, repenting, falling, aspiring humanity can afford to shut her out, or can deny the reality of her influence. No plan for renovating society, no scheme for purifying politics, no reform in church or in state, no moral, social, or economic question, no movement upward or downward in the human plane is lost on her. A man once said when told his house was afire: "Go tell my wife; I never meddle with household affairs." But no woman can possibly put herself or her sex outside any of the interests that affect humanity. All departments in the new era are to be hers, in the sense that her interests are in all and through all; and it is incumbent on her to keep intelligently and sympathetically *en rapport* with all the great movements of her time, that she may know on which side to throw the weight of her influence. She stands now at the gateway of this new era of American civilization. In her hands must be moulded the strength, the wit, the statesmanship, the morality, all the psychic force, the social and economic intercourse of that era. To be alive at such an epoch is a privilege, to be a woman then is sublime.

In this last decade of our century, changes of such moment are in progress, such new and alluring vistas are opening out before us, such original and radical suggestions for the adjustment of labor and capital, of government and the governed, of the family, the church and the state, that to be a possible factor though an infinitesimal in such a movement is pregnant with hope and weighty with responsibility. To be a woman in such an age carries with it a privilege and an opportunity never implied before. But to be a woman of the Negro race in America, and to be able to grasp the deep significance of the possibilities of the crisis, is to have a heritage, it seems to me, unique in the ages. In the first place, the race is young and full of the elasticity and hopefulness of youth. All its achievements are before it. It does not look on the masterly triumphs of nineteenth century civilization with that *blasé* world-weary look which characterizes the old washed out and worn out races which have already, so to speak, seen their best days.

Said a European writer recently: "Except the Sclavonic, the Negro is the only original and distinctive genius which has yet to come to growth—and the feeling is to cherish and develop it."

Everything to this race is new and strange and inspiring. There is a quickening of its pulses and a glowing of its self-consciousness. Aha, I can rival that! I can aspire to that! I can honor my name and vindicate my race! Something like this, it strikes me, is the enthusiasm which stirs the genius of young Africa in America; and the memory of past oppression and the fact of present attempted repression only serve to gather momentum for its irrepressible powers. Then again, a race in such a stage of growth is peculiarly sensitive to impressions. Not the photographer's sensitized plate is more delicately impressionable to outer influences than is this high strung people here on the threshold of a career.

What a responsibility then to have the sole management of the primal lights and shadows! Such is the colored woman's office. She must stamp weal or woe on the coming history of this people. May she see her opportunity and vindicate her high prerogative.

Questions to Consider

1. Does Cooper seem to privilege the rights and needs of the African-American community or of the larger community of women, regardless of their color? What are the implications of Cooper's stance regarding the needs and potential contributions to society of these two traditionally oppressed groups of people?
2. How would you classify Cooper's attitude(s) toward education? Who is entitled to an education, according to Cooper?

James Weldon Johnson

1871–1938

Multitalented James Weldon Johnson was a poet, novelist, essayist, autobiographer, songwriter, musical performer, lawyer, newspaperman, and diplomat. He also made great contributions to the cause of African-American equality throughout his career as an educator and civil rights leader.

James William Johnson, who later changed his middle name, was born in Jacksonville, Florida, on 17 June 1871. His father had worked his way up to the position of headwaiter in the finest hotel in Jacksonville, and his music teacher mother was the first African-American woman to teach in the Florida public school system. Since Jacksonville had no African-American high school, Johnson's parents sent him to Atlanta University in Georgia for his secondary and collegiate education. An outstanding student, Johnson toured with the university choir and taught school in rural Georgia during one of his summer breaks. The exposure to rural African-American Southern poverty opened Johnson's eyes to the inequalities between the races. Graduating with a B.A. in 1894, he returned to Jacksonville as the reform-minded principal of his former elementary school and founded a newspaper for the African-American community. Access to a White attorney's law office and library helped Johnson prepare to pass the bar exam, and he became the first African American admitted to the Florida bar.

The newspaper failed, and Johnson's early law career was also short-lived. His brother John's interest in musical theater rekindled Johnson's own interest in the arts, and after several short-term visits to New York City, the brothers moved there in 1902, intent upon musical careers. During this early stage in his career, Johnson wrote the words and his brother the music to "Lift Every Voice and Sing," the song that would come to be hailed as the "Negro National Anthem." Along with Bob Cole, the brothers then formed a songwriting and performing trio, Cole and Johnson Brothers, that toured in both the United States and Europe. The three men coauthored nearly two hundred songs, including such hits as "Under the Bamboo Tree" and "Oh, Didn't He Ramble."

In 1904, African-American Republicans in New York sought Johnson's help in reelecting President Theodore Roosevelt. Following the successful campaign, Johnson was awarded diplomatic posts in Venezuela in 1906 and Nicaragua in 1909; the poem "O Black and Unknown Bards," more formal in style than his later dialect poems, dates to this period. During his time in Nicaragua he married a woman from New York and had his first and only novel, *The Autobiography of an Ex-Colored Man*, published anonymously in the United States. The 1912 book told the story of a light-skinned biracial man from Georgia who decides to "pass for White" but later comes to regret his loss of racial heritage. Johnson's diplomatic career ended in 1913 when his nomination as consul to the Azores was blocked by the United States Senate.

Johnson went on to join the staff of the oldest African-American newspaper in New York, the *New York Age*, and in 1916 he was named field secretary of the National Association for the Advancement of Colored People (NAACP). During his 14-year career with the NAACP, he played a large role in increasing membership and publicizing abuses such as lynchings and voter disenfranchisement in the South. During this time period, he also published his two collections of poetry, *Fifty Years and Other Poems* (1917), from which the selection entitled "The White Witch" is taken, and *God's Trombones: Seven Negro Sermons in Verse* (1927), the source of "Go Down Death—A Funeral Sermon." The seven poems of *God's Trombones* were inspired by the great oral tradition of African-American preaching, and Johnson attempted to capture the rhythms, repetitions, and improvisational inventiveness of the verbal genre in his verses. Critic Thadious M. Davis wrote of the volume that it "confirmed the creative possibilities of black southern materials."

The tireless Johnson also edited three major contributions to the canon of African-American literary and cultural studies during the decade of the twenties: *The Book of American Negro Poetry* (1922), *The Book of American Negro Spirituals* (1925), and *The Second Book of American Negro Spirituals* (1926). In the last decade of his life, he held a chair in literature at Fisk University in Tennessee and turned his attention to writing nonfiction. *Black Manhattan* (1930) traced the history of African Americans in New York City, while *Along This Way* (1933) documented Johnson's own life story. His final book, *Negro Americans, What Now?* (1934), argued the need for integration and racial equality in America's future. Johnson's death in an automobile accident in 1938, at the age of 67, silenced the wisdom of his old age, but not the varied voices heard in his impressive body of writing.

O Black and Unknown Bards

O black and unknown bards of long ago,
How came your lips to touch the sacred fire?
How, in your darkness, did you come to know
The power and beauty of the minstrel's lyre?
Who first from midst his bonds lifted his eyes?
Who first from out the still watch, lone and long,
Feeling the ancient faith of prophets rise
Within his dark-kept soul, burst into song?

Heart of what slave poured out such melody
As "Steal Away to Jesus"?[1] On its strains
His spirit must have nightly floated free,
Though still about his hands he felt his chains.
Who heard great "Jordan roll"?[2] Whose starward eye
Saw chariot "swing low"?[3] And who was he
That breathed that comforting, melodic sigh,
"Nobody Knows de Trouble I See"?[4]

What merely living clod, what captive thing,
Could up toward God through all its darkness grope,
And find within its deadened heart to sing
These songs of sorrow, love, and faith, and hope?
How did it catch that subtle undertone,
That note in music heard not with the ears?
How sound the elusive reed so seldom blown,
Which stirs the soul or melts the heart to tears?

Not that great German master[5] in his dream
Of harmonies that thundered amongst the stars
At the creation, ever heard a theme
Nobler than "Go Down, Moses."[6] Mark its bars,
How like a mighty trumpet-call they stir
The blood. Such are the notes that men have sung
Going to valorous deeds; such tones there were
That helped make history when Time was young.

There is a wide, wide wonder in it all,
That from degraded rest and servile toil
The fiery spirit of the seer should call
These simple children of the sun and soil.
O black slave singers, gone, forgot, unfamed,
You—you alone, of all the long, long line
Of those who've sung untaught, unknown, unnamed,
Have stretched out upward, seeking the divine.

You sang not deeds of heroes or of kings;
No chant of bloody war, no exulting pæan[7]
Of arms-won triumphs; but your humble strings
You touched in chord with music empyrean.[8]
You sang far better than you knew; the songs
That for your listeners' hungry hearts sufficed
Still live—but more than this to you belongs:
You sang a race from wood and stone to Christ.

1. Traditional African-American spiritual associated with the Underground Railroad that assisted fugitive slaves.
2. "Roll, Jordan, Roll" was a traditional spiritual which associated the biblical River Jordan with heaven.
3. "Swing Low, Sweet Chariot" was another traditional spiritual expressing a longing for death, symbolized by crossing the River Jordan.
4. Traditional spiritual lamenting personal hardships and praising Jesus.
5. Ludwig van Beethoven (1770–1827), German composer of the Romantic era.
6. Traditional spiritual associating the enslavement of Israelites in ancient Egypt with the enslavement of African Americans.
7. A hymn of praise.
8. Heavenly.

Go Down Death—A Funeral Sermon

Weep not, weep not,
She is not dead;
She's resting in the bosom of Jesus.
Heart-broken husband—weep no more;
Grief-stricken son—weep no more;
Left-lonesome daughter—weep no more;
She's only just gone home.

Day before yesterday morning,
God was looking down from his great, high heaven,
Looking down on all his children,
And his eye fell on Sister Caroline,
Tossing on her bed of pain.
And God's big heart was touched with pity,
With the everlasting pity.

And God sat back on his throne,
And he commanded that tall, bright angel standing at his right hand:
Call me Death!
And that tall, bright angel cried in a voice
That broke like a clap of thunder:
Call Death!—Call Death!
And the echo sounded down the streets of heaven
Till it reached away back to that shadowy place,
Where Death waits with his pale, white horses.

And Death heard the summons,
And he leaped on his fastest horse,
Pale as a sheet in the moonlight.
Up the golden street Death galloped,
And the hoofs of his horse struck fire from the gold,
But they didn't make no sound.
Up Death rode to the Great White Throne,
And waited for God's command.

And God said: Go down, Death, go down,
Go down to Savannah, Georgia,
Down in Yamacraw,[1]
And find Sister Caroline.
She's borne the burden and heat of the day,
She's labored long in my vineyard,
And she's tired—
She's weary—
Go down, Death, and bring her to me.

And Death didn't say a word,
But he loosed the reins on his pale, white horse,
And he clamped the spurs to his bloodless sides,
And out and down he rode,
Through heaven's pearly gates,

1. The city of Savannah was built on Yamacraw Bluff on the Savannah River.

Past suns and moons and stars;
On Death rode,
And the foam from his horse was like a comet in the sky;
On Death rode,
Leaving the lightning's flash behind;
Straight on down he came.

While we were watching round her bed,
She turned her eyes and looked away,
She saw what we couldn't see;
She saw Old Death. She saw Old Death
Coming like a falling star.
But Death didn't frighten Sister Caroline;
He looked to her like a welcome friend.
And she whispered to us: I'm going home,
And she smiled and closed her eyes.

And Death took her up like a baby,
And she lay in his icy arms,
But she didn't feel no chill.
And Death began to ride again—
Up beyond the evening star,
Out beyond the morning star,
Into the glittering light of glory,
On to the Great White Throne.
And there he laid Sister Caroline
On the loving breast of Jesus.

And Jesus took his own hand and wiped away her tears,
And he smoothed the furrows from her face,
And the angels sang a little song,
And Jesus rocked her in his arms,
And kept a-saying: Take your rest,
Take your rest, take your rest.

Weep not—weep not,
She is not dead;
She's resting in the bosom of Jesus.

The White Witch

O brothers mine, take care! Take care!
The great white witch rides out tonight,
Trust not your prowess nor your strength;
Your only safety lies in flight;
For in her glance there is a snare,
And in her smile there is a blight.

The great white witch you have not seen?
Then, younger brothers mine, forsooth,
Like nursery children you have looked
For ancient hag and snaggle-tooth;
But no, not so; the witch appears
In all the glowing charms of youth.

Her lips are like carnations red,
Her face like new-born lilies fair,
Her eyes like ocean waters blue,
She moves with subtle grace and air,
And all about her head there floats
The golden glory of her hair.

But though she always thus appears
In form of youth and mood of mirth,
Unnumbered centuries are hers,
The infant planets saw her birth;
The child of throbbing Life is she,
Twin sister to the greedy earth.

And back behind those smiling lips,
And down within those laughing eyes,
And underneath the soft caress
Of hand and voice and purring sighs,
The shadow of the panther lurks,
The spirit of the vampire lies.

For I have seen the great white witch,
And she has led me to her lair,
And I have kissed her red, red lips
And cruel face so white and fair;
Around me she has twined her arms,
And bound me with her yellow hair.

I felt those red lips burn and sear
My body like a living coal;
Obeyed the power of those eyes
As the needle trembles to the pole;
And did not care although I felt
The strength go ebbing from my soul.

Oh! she has seen your strong young limbs,
And heard your laughter loud and gay,
And in your voices she has caught
The echo of a far-off day,
When man was closer to the earth;
And she has marked you for her prey.

She feels the old Antæan[1] strength
In you, the great dynamic beat
Of primal passions, and she sees
In you the last besieged retreat
Of love relentless, lusty, fierce,
Love pain-ecstatic, cruel-sweet.

O, brothers mine, take care! Take care!
The great white witch rides out tonight.

1. Giant of Greek mythology who wrestled victims to their deaths.

O, younger brothers mine, beware!
Look not upon her beauty bright;
For in her glance there is a snare,
And in her smile there is a blight.

Questions to Consider

1. What do you think Johnson means by in the last line of "O Black and Unknown Bards"?
2. What similarities do you see between Johnson's poem "The White Witch" and Anne Spencer's poem entitled "White Things"? In what ways do these poems differ?

Ellen Glasgow

1873–1945

Ellen Glasgow is a significant Southern feminist voice whose body of work reflects the genres of romance and comedy of manners, providing a record of the social structures of bygone times. Although she places some of her stories and characters in cities and states other than her own, her best novels are set in Virginia, the part of the world most familiar to her. Glasgow's readers identify with the struggles faced by her protagonists, individuals stifled by an unyielding society steeped in tradition.

Ellen Anderson Gholson Glasgow was born on 22 April 1873 in Richmond, Virginia. She was the ninth of ten children born into one of the oldest, most well-established, aristocratic families of the Tidewater Virginia area. Her father, Francis Thomas Glasgow, was a graduate of Washington College (later Washington and Lee University) and a manager at the Tredegar Iron Works in Richmond, which supplied munitions and equipment to the Confederate Army and Navy during the Civil War. Ellen's parents were opposites in temperament. On one hand, her father was formidable and austere; on the other, her mother, Anne Jane Gholson Glasgow, was gracious and genteel, but often suffered from melancholia. Ellen adored her mother, attributing her physical and emotional ailments to bearing ten children, to the difficulties she endured during the Civil War, and to the deprivations of the resulting period of Reconstruction.

Like her mother, Ellen suffered from a variety of health problems. Consequently, she rarely attended school as a child. By the time she was 16 years old, she began to develop a hearing loss. The condition worsened through the years, leaving her completely deaf in her late thirties. Glasgow found solace in her father's library, which contained an extensive collection of literature and history. She was particularly interested in the sciences and read Darwin's *The Origin of Species* as well as books on economics, sociology, and political science. Despite her advanced intellectual abilities, Glasgow could not be admitted into the University of Virginia because she was female. Instead, she successfully passed an examination in political economy privately prepared for her by a professor friend.

Glasgow's early interest in books set her on a literary path. At the age of seven, she decided to become a writer. She began by writing verses, and before her seventeenth year, she had written 400 pages of a novel that she later destroyed, and she destroyed a second manuscript while mourning her mother's death in 1893. Four years later, Glasgow's first novel, *The Descendant,* was published anonymously. Her second, *Phases of an Inferior Planet,* was published in 1898 bearing her name. These novels marked the beginning of a literary career that, in the end, spanned more than four decades. Glasgow wrote 20 novels, including *Barren Ground* (1925), *They Stooped to Folly* (1929), and *In This Our Life* (1941). She was awarded the Pulitzer

Prize in Literature for her last published novel, *In This Our Life* (1942), and she also authored a book of literary criticism titled *A Certain Measure* (1943) and a collection of short stories and poetry. *A Woman Within*, her autobiography, was posthumously published in 1954.

Additional accomplishments and highlights included receiving honorary degrees from four universities, serving as the third vice president of Richmond's Equal Suffrage League, and earning membership in the American Academy of Arts and Letters.

from Dare's Gift

A year has passed, and I am beginning to ask myself if the thing actually happened? The whole episode, seen in clear perspective, is obviously incredible. There are, of course, no haunted houses in this age of science; there are merely hallucinations, neurotic symptoms, and optical illusions. Any one of these practical diagnoses would, no doubt, cover the impossible occurrence, from my first view of that dusky sunset on James River to the erratic behavior of Mildred during the spring we spent in Virginia. There is—I admit it readily!—a perfectly rational explanation of every mystery. Yet, while I assure myself that the supernatural has been banished, in the evil company of devils, black plagues, and witches, from this sanitary century, a vision of Dare's Gift, amid its clustering cedars under the shadowy arch of the sunset, rises before me, and my feeble scepticism surrenders to that invincible spirit of darkness. For once in my life—the ordinary life of a corporation lawyer in Washington—the impossible really happened.

* * *

(*Editor's note: The narrator has rented Dare's Gift, and moved his wife to the home to recuperate from an illness. She becomes emotionally unstable, leading her to betray her husband's confidence in a legal proceeding. The narrator learns, when he consults a doctor about her condition, that the house is haunted by the treachery that took place there during the Civil War. As the story resumes, the doctor begins to hear the story of Dare's Gift.*)

One can never tell how traditions are kept alive. Many things have been whispered about Dare's Gift; some of these whispers may have reached her. Even without her knowledge she may have absorbed the suggestion; and some day, with that suggestion in her mind, she may have gazed too long at the sunshine on these marble urns before she turned back into the haunted rooms where she lived. After all, we know so little, so pitifully little about these things. We have only touched, we physicians, the outer edges of psychology. The rest lies in darkness ———"

I jerked him up sharply. "The house, then, is haunted?"

For a moment he hesitated. "The house is saturated with a thought. It is haunted by treachery."

"You mean something happened here?"

"I mean—" He bent forward, groping for the right word, while his gaze sought the river, where a golden web of mist hung midway between sky and water. "I am an old man, and I have lived long enough to see every act merely as the husk of an idea. The act dies; it decays like the body, but the idea is immortal. The thing that happened at Dare's Gift was over fifty years ago, but the thought of it still lives—still utters its profound and terrible message. The house is a shell, and if one listens long enough one can hear in its heart the low murmur of the past—of that past which is but a single wave of the great sea of human experience ———"

"But the story?" I was becoming impatient of his theories. After all, if Mildred was the victim of some phantasmal hypnosis, I was anxious to meet the ghost who had hypnotized her. Even Drayton, I reflected, keen as he was about the fact of mental suggestion, would never have regarded seriously the suggestion of a phantom. And the house looked so peaceful—so hospitable in the afternoon light.

"The story? Oh, I am coming to that—but of late the story has meant so little to me beside the idea. I like to stop by the way. I am getting old, and an amble suits me better than too brisk a trot—particularly in this weather ———"

Yes, he was getting old. I lit a fresh cigarette and waited impatiently. After all, this ghost that he rambled about was real enough to destroy me, and my nerves were quivering like harp strings.

"Well, I came into the story—I was in the very thick of it, by accident, if there is such a thing as accident in this world of incomprehensible laws. The Incomprehensible! That has always seemed to me the supreme fact of life, the one truth overshadowing all others—the truth that we know nothing. We nibble at the edges of the mystery, and the great Reality—the Incomprehensible—is still untouched, undiscovered. It unfolds hour by hour, day by day, creating, enslaving, killing us, while we painfully gnaw off—what? A crumb or two, a grain from that vastness which envelops us, which remains impenetrable ———"

Again he broke off, and again I jerked him back from his reverie.

"As I have said, I was placed, by an act of Providence, or of chance, in the very heart of the tragedy. I was with Lucy Dare on the day, the unforgettable day, when she made her choice—her heroic or devilish choice, according to the way one has been educated. In Europe a thousand years ago such an act committed for the sake of religion would have made her a saint; in New England, a few centuries past, it would have entitled her to a respectable position in history—the little history of New England. But Lucy Dare was a Virginian, and in Virginia—except in the brief, exalted Virginia of the Confederacy—the personal loyalties have always been esteemed beyond the impersonal. I cannot imagine us as a people canonizing a woman who sacrificed the human ties for the superhuman—even for the divine. I cannot imagine it, I repeat; and so Lucy Dare—though she rose to greatness in that one instant of sacrifice—has not even a name among us today. I doubt if you can find a child in the State who has ever heard of her—or a grown man, outside of this neighborhood, who could give you a single fact of her history. She is as completely forgotten as Sir Roderick, who betrayed Bacon—she is forgotten because the thing she did, though it might have made a Greek tragedy, was alien to the temperament of the people among whom she lived. Her tremendous sacrifice failed to arrest the imagination of her time. After all, the sublime cannot touch us unless it is akin to our ideal; and though Lucy Dare was sublime, according to the moral code of the Romans, she was a stranger to the racial soul of the South. Her memory died because it was the bloom of an hour—because there was nothing in the soil of her age for it to thrive on. She missed her time; she is one of the mute inglorious heroines of history; and yet, born in another century, she might have stood side by side with Antigone—" For an instant he paused. "But she has always seemed to me diabolical," he added.

"What she did, then, was so terrible that it has haunted the house ever since?" I asked again, for, wrapped in memories, he had lost the thread of his story.

"What she did was so terrible that the house has never forgotten. The thought in Lucy Dare's mind during those hours while she made her choice has left an ineffaceable impression on the things that surrounded her. She created in the horror of that hour an unseen environment more real, because more spiritual, than the material fact of the house. You won't believe this, of course—if people believed in the unseen as in the seen, would life be what it is?"

The afternoon light slept on the river; the birds were mute in the elm trees; from the garden of herbs at the end of the terrace an aromatic fragrance rose like invisible incense.

"To understand it all, you must remember that the South was dominated, was possessed by an idea—the idea of the Confederacy. It was an exalted idea—supremely vivid, supremely romantic—but, after all, it was only an idea. It existed nowhere within the bounds of the actual unless the souls of its devoted people may be regarded as actual. But it is the dream, not the actuality, that commands the noblest devotion, the completest self-sacrifice. It is the dream, the ideal, that has ruled mankind from the beginning.

"I saw a great deal of the Dares that year. It was a lonely life I led after I lost my leg at Seven Pines and dropped out of the army, and, as you may imagine, a country doctor's practice in wartimes was far from lucrative. Our one comfort was that we were all poor, that we were all starving together; and the Dares—there were only two of them, father and daughter—were as poor as the rest of us. They had given their last coin to the government—had poured their last bushel of meal into the sacks of the army. I can imagine the superb gesture with which Lucy Dare flung her dearest heirloom—her one remaining brooch or pin—into the bare coffers of the Confederacy. She was a small woman, pretty rather than beautiful—not the least heroic in build—yet I wager that she was heroic enough on that occasion. She was a strange soul, though I never so much as suspected her strangeness while I knew her—while she moved among us with her small oval face, her gentle blue eyes, her smoothly banded hair, which shone like satin in the sunlight. Beauty she must have had in a way, though I confess a natural preference for queenly women; I dare say I should have preferred Octavia to Cleopatra, who, they tell me, was small and slight. But Lucy Dare wasn't the sort to blind your eyes when you first looked at her. Her charm was like a fragrance rather than a color—a subtle fragrance that steals into the senses and is the last thing a man ever forgets. I knew half a dozen men who would have died for her—and yet she gave them nothing, nothing, barely a smile. She appeared cold—she who was destined to flame to life in an act. I can see her distinctly as she looked then, in that last year—grave, still, with the curious, unearthly loveliness that comes to pretty women who are underfed—who are slowly starving for bread and meat, for bodily nourishment. She had the look of one dedicated—as ethereal as a saint, and yet I never saw it at the time; I only remember it now, after fifty years, when I think of her. Starvation, when it is slow, not quick—when it means, not acute hunger, but merely lack of the right food, of the blood-making, nerve-building elements—starvation like this often plays strange pranks with one. The visions of the saints, the glories of martyrdom, come to the underfed, the anemic. Can you recall one of the saints—the genuine sort—whose regular diet was roast beef and ale?

"Well, I have said that Lucy Dare was a strange soul, and she was, though to this day I don't know how much of her strangeness was the result of improper nourishment, of too little blood to the brain. Be that as it may, she seems to me when I look back on her to have been one of those women whose characters are shaped entirely by external events—who are the playthings of circumstance. There are many such women. They move among us in obscurity—reserved, passive, commonplace—and we never suspect the spark of fire in their natures until it flares up at the touch of the unexpected. In ordinary circumstances Lucy Dare would have been ordinary, submissive, feminine, domestic; she adored children. That she possessed a stronger will than the average Southern girl, brought up in the conventional manner, none of us—least of all I, myself—ever imagined. She was, of course, intoxicated, obsessed, with the idea of the Confederacy; but, then, so were all of us. There wasn't anything unusual or abnormal in that exalted illusion. It was the common property of our generation. . . .

"Like most noncombatants, the Dares were extremists, and I, who had got rid of a little of my bad blood when I lost my leg, used to regret sometimes that the Colonel—I never knew where he got his title—was too old to do a share of the actual fighting. There is nothing that takes the fever out of one so quickly as a fight; and in the army I had never met a hint of this concentrated, vitriolic bitterness towards the enemy. Why, I've seen the Colonel, sitting here on this terrace, and crippled to the knees with gout, grow purple in the face if I spoke so much as a good word for the climate of the North. For him, and for the girl, too, the Lord had drawn a divine circle round the Confederacy. Everything inside of that circle was perfection; everything outside of it was evil. Well, that was fifty years ago, and his hate is all dust now; yet I can sit here, where he used to brood on this terrace, sipping his blackberry wine—I can sit here and remember it all as if it were yesterday. The place has changed so little, except for Duncan's grotesque additions to the wings, that one can scarcely believe all these years have passed over it. Many an afternoon just like this I've sat here, while the Colonel nodded and Lucy knitted for the soldiers, and watched these same shadows creep down the terrace and that mist of light—it looks just as it used to—hang there over the James. Even the smell from those herbs hasn't changed. Lucy used to keep her little garden at the end of the terrace, for she was fond of making essences and beauty lotions. I used to give her all the prescriptions I could find in old books I read—and I've heard people say that she owed her wonderful white skin to the concoctions she brewed from shrubs and herbs. I couldn't convince them that lack of meat, not lotions, was responsible for the pallor—pallor was all the fashion then—that they admired and envied."

He stopped a minute, just long enough to refill his pipe, while I glanced with fresh interest at the garden of herbs.

"It was a March day when it happened," he went on presently; "cloudless, mild, with the taste and smell of spring in the air. I had been at Dare's Gift almost every day for a year. We had suffered together, hoped, feared, and wept together, hungered and sacrificed together. We had felt together the divine, invincible sway of an idea.

"Stop for a minute and picture to yourself what it is to be of a war and yet not in it; to live in imagination until the mind becomes inflamed with the vision; to have no outlet for the passion that consumes one except the outlet of thought. Add to this the fact that we really knew nothing. We were as far away from the truth, stranded here on our river, as if we had been anchored in a canal on Mars. Two men—one crippled, one too old to fight—and a girl—and the three living for a country which in a few weeks would be nothing—would be nowhere—not on any map of the world. . . .

"When I look back now it seems to me incredible that at that time any persons in the Confederacy should have been ignorant of its want of resources. Yet remember we lived apart, remote, unvisited, out of touch with realities, thinking the one thought. We believed in the ultimate triumph of the South with that indomitable belief which is rooted not in reason, but in emotion. To believe had become an act of religion; to doubt was rank infidelity. So we sat there in our little world, the world of unrealities, bounded by the river and the garden, and talked from noon till sunset about our illusion—not daring to look a single naked fact in the face—talking of plenty when there were no crops in the ground and no flour in the storeroom, prophesying victory while the Confederacy was in her death struggle. Folly! All folly, and yet I am sure even now that we were sincere, that we believed the nonsense we were uttering. We believed, I have said, because to doubt would have been far too horrible. Hemmed in by the river and the garden, there wasn't anything left for us to do—since we couldn't fight—but believe. Someone has said, or ought to have said, that faith is the last refuge of the inefficient. The twin devils of famine and despair were at work in the country, and we sat there—we three, on this damned terrace—and prophesied about the second president of the Confederacy. We agreed, I remember, that Lee would be the next president. And all the time, a few miles away, the demoralization of defeat was abroad, was around us, was in the air. . . .

"It was a March afternoon when Lucy sent for me, and while I walked up the drive—there was not a horse left among us, and I made all my rounds on foot—I noticed that patches of spring flowers were blooming in the long grass on the lawn. The air was as soft as May, and in the woods at the back of the house buds of maple trees ran like a flame. There were, I remember, leaves—dead leaves, last year's leaves—everywhere, as if, in the demoralization of panic, the place had been forgotten, had been untouched since autumn. I remember rotting leaves that gave like moss underfoot; dried leaves that stirred and murmured as one walked over them; black leaves, brown leaves, wine-colored leaves, and the still glossy leaves of the evergreens. But they were everywhere—in the road, over the grass on the lawn, beside the steps, piled in wind drifts against the walls of the house.

"On the terrace, wrapped in shawls, the old Colonel was sitting; and he called out excitedly, 'Are you bringing news of a victory?' Victory! when the whole country had been scraped with a fine-tooth comb for provisions.

" 'No, I bring no news except that Mrs. Morson has just heard of the death of her youngest son in Petersburg. Gangrene, they say. The truth is the men are so ill-nourished that the smallest scratch turns to gangrene ——'.

" 'Well, it won't be for long—not for long. Let Lee and Johnston get together and things will go our way with a rush. A victory or two, and the enemy will be asking for terms of peace before the summer is over.'

"A lock of his silver-white hair had fallen over his forehead, and pushing it back with his clawlike hand, he peered up at me with his little nearsignted eyes, which were of a peculiar burning blackness, like the eyes of some small enraged animal. I can see him now as vividly as if I had left him only an hour ago, and yet it is fifty years since then—fifty years filled with memories and with forgetfulness. Behind him the warm red of the bricks glowed as the sunshine fell, sprinkled with shadows, through the elm boughs. Even the soft wind was too much for him, for he shivered occasionally in his blanket shawls, and coughed the dry, hacking cough which had troubled him for a year. He was a shell of a man—a shell vitalized and animated by an immense, an indestructible illusion. While he sat there, sipping his blackberry wine, with his little fiery dark eyes searching the river in hope of something that would end his interminable expectancy, there was about him a fitful somber gleam of romance. For him the external world, the actual truth of things, had vanished—all of it, that is, except the shawl that wrapped him and the glass of blackberry wine he sipped. He had died already to the material fact, but he lived intensely, vividly, profoundly, in the idea. It was the idea that nourished him, that gave him his one hold on reality.

" 'It was Lucy who sent for you,' said the old man presently. 'She has been on the upper veranda all day overlooking something—the sunning of winter clothes, I think. She wants to see you about one of the servants—a sick child, Nancy's child, in the quarters.'

" 'Then I'll find her,' I answered readily, for I had, I confess, a mild curiosity to find out why Lucy had sent for me.

"She was alone on the upper veranda, and I noticed that she closed her Bible and laid it aside as I stepped through the long window that opened from the end of the hall. Her face, usually so pale, glowed now with a wan illumination, like ivory before the flame of a lamp. In this illumination her eyes, beneath delicately penciled eyebrows, looked unnaturally large and brilliant, and so deeply, so angelically blue that they made me think of the Biblical heaven of my childhood. Her beauty, which had never struck me sharply before, pierced through me. But it was her fate—her misfortune perhaps—to appear commonplace, to pass unrecognized, until the fire shot from her soul.

" 'No, I want to see you about myself, not about one of the servants.'

"At my first question she had risen and held out her hand—a white, thin hand, small and frail as a child's.

" 'You are not well, then?' I had known from the first that her starved look meant something.

" 'It isn't that; I am quite well.' She paused a moment, and then looked at me with a clear shining gaze. 'I have had a letter,' she said.

" 'A letter?' I have realized since how dull I must have seemed to her in that moment of excitement, of exaltation.

" 'You didn't know. I forgot that you didn't know that I was once engaged—long ago—before the beginning of the war. I cared a great deal—we both cared a great deal, but he was not one of us; he was on the other side—and when the war came, of course there was no question. We broke if off; we had to break it off. How could it have been possible to do otherwise?'

" 'How, indeed!' I murmured; and I had a vision of the old man downstairs on the terrace, of the intrepid and absurd old man.

" 'My first duty is to my country,' she went on after a minute, and the words might have been spoken by her father. 'There has been no thought of anything else in my mind since the beginning of the war. Even if peace comes I can never feel the same again—I can never forget that he has been a part of all we have suffered—of the thing that has made us suffer. I could never forget—I can never forgive.'

"Her words sound strange now, you think, after fifty years; but on that day, in this house surrounded by dead leaves, inhabited by an inextinguishable ideal—in this country, where the spirit had fed on the body until the impoverished brain reacted to transcendent visions—in this place, at that time, they were natural enough. Scarcely a woman of the South but would have uttered them from her soul. In every age one ideal enthralls the imagination of mankind; it is in the air; it subjugates the will; it enchants the emotions. Well, in the South fifty years ago this ideal was patriotism; and the passion of patriotism, which bloomed like some red flower, the flower of carnage, over the land, had grown in Lucy Dare's soul into an exotic blossom.

"Yet even today, after fifty years, I cannot get over the impression she made upon me of a woman who was, in the essence of her nature, thin and colorless. I may have been wrong. Perhaps I never knew her. It is not easy to judge people, especially women, who wear a mask by instinct. What I thought lack of character, of personality, may have been merely reticence; but again and again there comes back to me the thought that she never said or did a thing—except the one terrible thing—that one could remember. There was nothing remarkable that one could point to about her. I cannot recall either her smile or her voice, though both were sweet, no doubt, as the smile and the voice of a Southern woman would be. Until that morning on the upper veranda I had not noticed that her eyes were wonderful. She was like a shadow, a phantom, that attains in one supreme instant, by one immortal gesture, union with reality. Even I remember her only by that one lurid flash.

" 'And you say you have had a letter?'

" 'It was brought by one of the old servants—Jacob, the one who used to wait on him when he stayed here. He was a prisoner. A few days ago he escaped. He asked me to see him—and I told him to come. He wishes to see me once again before he goes North—forever ———' She spoke in gasps in a dry voice. Never once did she mention his name. Long afterwards I remembered that I had never heard his name spoken. Even today I do not know it. He also was a shadow, a phantom—a part of the encompassing unreality.

" 'And he will come here?'

"For a moment she hesitated; then she spoke quite simply, knowing that she could trust me.

" 'He is here. He is in the chamber beyond.' She pointed to one of the long windows that gave on the veranda. 'The blue chamber at the front.'

"I remember that I made a step towards the window when her voice arrested me. 'Don't go in. He is resting. He is very tired and hungry.'

" 'You didn't send for me, then, to see him?'

" 'I sent for you to be with father. I knew you would help me—that you would keep him from suspecting. He must not know, of course. He must be kept quiet.'

" 'I will stay with him,' I answered, and then, 'Is that all you wish to say to me?'

" 'That is all. It is only for a day or two. He will go on in a little while, and I can never see him again. I do not wish to see him again.'

"I turned away, across the veranda, entered the hall, walked the length of it, and descended the staircase. The sun was going down in a ball—just as it will begin to go down in a few minutes—and as I descended the stairs I saw it through the mullioned window over the door—huge and red and round above the black cloud of the cedars.

"The old man was still on the terrace. I wondered vaguely why the servants had not brought him indoors; and then, as I stepped over the threshold, I saw that a company of soldiers—Confederates—had crossed the lawn and were already gathering about the house. The commanding officer—I was shaking hands with him presently—was a Dare, a distant cousin of the Colonel's, one of those excitable, nervous, and slightly theatrical natures who become utterly demoralized under the spell of any violent emotion. He had been wounded at least a dozen times, and his lean, sallow, still handsome features had the greenish look which I had learned to associate with chronic malaria.

"When I look back now I can see it all as a part of the general disorganization—of the fever, the malnutrition, the complete demoralization of panic. I know now that each man of us was facing in his soul defeat and despair; and that we—each one of us—had gone mad with the thought of it. In a little while, after the certainty of failure had come to us, we met it quietly—we braced our souls for the issue; but in those last weeks defeat had all the horror, all the insane terror of a nightmare, and all the vividness. The thought was like a delusion from which we fled, and which no flight could put farther away from us.

"Have you ever lived, I wonder, from day to day in that ever-present and unchanging sense of unreality, as if the moment before you were but an imaginary experience which must dissolve and evaporate before the touch of an actual event? Well, that was the sensation I had felt for days, weeks, months, and it swept over me again while I stood there, shaking hands with the Colonel's cousin, on the terrace. The soldiers, in their ragged uniforms, appeared as visionary as the world in which we had been living. I think now that they were as ignorant as we were of the things that had happened—that were happening day by day to the army. The truth is that it was impossible for a single one of us to believe that our heroic army could be beaten even by unseen powers—even by hunger and death.

" 'And you say he was a prisoner?' It was the old man's quavering voice, and it sounded avid for news, for certainty.

" 'Caught in disguise. Then he slipped through our fingers.' The cousin's tone was querulous, as if he were irritated by loss of sleep or of food. 'Nobody knows how it happened. Nobody ever knows. But he has found out things that will ruin us. He has plans. He has learned things that mean the fall of Richmond if he escapes.'

"Since then I have wondered how much they sincerely believed—how much was simply the hallucination of fever, of desperation? Were they trying to bully themselves by violence into hoping? Or had they honestly convinced themselves that victory was still possible? If one only repeats a phrase often and emphatically enough one comes in time to believe it; and they had talked so long of that coming triumph, of the established Confederacy, that it had ceased to be, for them at least, merely a phrase. It wasn't the first occasion in life when I had seen words bullied—yes, literally bullied into beliefs.

"Well, looking back now after fifty years, you see, of course, the weakness of it all, the futility. At that instant, when all was lost, how could any plans, any plotting have ruined us? It seems irrational enough now—a dream, a shadow, that belief—and yet not one of us but would have given our lives for it. In order to understand you must remember that we were, one and all, victims of an idea—of a divine frenzy.

" 'And we are lost—the Confederacy is lost, you say, if he escapes?'

"It was Lucy's voice; and turning quickly, I saw that she was standing in the doorway. She must have followed me closely. It was possible that she had overheard every word of the conversation.

" 'If Lucy knows anything, she will tell you. There is no need to search the house,' quavered the old man, 'she is my daughter.'

" 'Of course we wouldn't search the house—not Dare's Gift,' said the cousin. He was excited, famished, malarial, but he was a gentleman, every inch of him.

"He talked on rapidly, giving details of the capture, the escape, the pursuit. It was all rather confused. I think he must have frightfully exaggerated the incident. Nothing could have been more unreal than it sounded. And he was just out of a hospital—was suffering still, I could see, from malaria. While he drank his blackberry wine—the best the house had to offer—I remember wishing that I had a good dose of quinine and whiskey to give him.

"The narrative lasted a long time; I think he was glad of a rest and of the blackberry wine and biscuits. Lucy had gone to fetch food for the soldiers; but after she had brought it she sat down in her accustomed chair by the old man's side and bent her head over her knitting. She was a wonderful knitter. During all the years of the war I seldom saw her without her ball of yarn and her needles—the long wooden kind that the women used at the time. Even after the dusk fell in the evenings the click of her needles sounded in the darkness.

" 'And if he escapes it will mean the capture of Richmond?' she asked once again when the story was finished. There was no hint of excitement in her manner. Her voice was perfectly toneless. To this day I have no idea what she felt—what she was thinking.

" 'If he gets away it is the ruin of us—but he won't get away. We'll find him before morning.'

"Rising from his chair, he turned to shake hands with the old man before descending the steps. 'We've got to go on now. I shouldn't have stopped if we hadn't been half starved. You've done us a world of good, Cousin Lucy. I reckon you'd give your last crust to the soldiers?'

" 'She'd give more than that,' quavered the old man. 'You'd give more than that, wouldn't you, Lucy?'

" 'Yes, I'd give more than that,' repeated the girl quietly, so quietly that it came as a shock to me—like a throb of actual pain in the midst of a nightmare—when she rose to her feet and added, without a movement, without a gesture, 'You must not go, Cousin George. He is upstairs in the blue chamber at the front of the house.'

"For an instant surprise held me speechless, transfixed, incredulous; and in that instant I saw a face—a white face of horror and disbelief—look down on us from one of the side windows of the blue chamber. Then, in a rush it seemed to me the soldiers were everywhere, swarming over the terrace, into the hall, surrounding the house. I had never imagined that a small body of men in uniforms, even ragged uniforms, could so posses and obscure one's surroundings. The three of us waited there—Lucy had sat down again and taken up her knitting—for what seemed hours, or an eternity. We were still waiting—though, for once, I noticed, the needles did not click in her fingers—when a single shot, followed by a volley, rang out from the rear of the house, from the veranda that looked down on the grove of oaks and the kitchen.

"Rising, I left them—the old man and the girl—and passed from the terrace down the little walk which led to the back. As I reached the lower veranda one of the soldiers ran into me.

" 'I was coming after you,' he said, and I observed that his excitement had left him. 'We brought him down while he was trying to jump from the veranda. He is there now on the grass.'

"The man on the grass was quite dead, shot through the heart; and while I bent over to wipe the blood from his lips, I saw him for the first time distinctly. A young face, hardly more than a boy—twenty-five at the most. Handsome, too, in a poetic and dreamy way; just the face, I thought, that a woman might have fallen in love with. He had dark hair, I remember, though his features have long ago faded from my memory. What will never fade, what I shall never forget, is the look he wore—the look he was still wearing when we laid him in the old graveyard next day—a look of mingled surprise, disbelief, terror, and indignation.

"I had done all that I could, which was nothing, and rising to my feet, I saw for the first time that Lucy had joined me. She was standing perfectly motionless. Her knitting was still in her hands, but the light had gone from her face, and she looked old—old and gray—beside the glowing youth of her lover. For a moment her eyes held me while she spoke as quietly as she had spoken to the soldiers on the terrace.

" 'I had to do it,' she said. 'I would do it again.' "

Suddenly, like the cessation of running water, or of wind in the treetops, the doctor's voice ceased. For a long pause we stared in silence at the sunset; then, without looking at me, he added slowly:

"Three weeks later Lee surrendered and the Confederacy was over."

The sun had slipped, as if by magic, behind the tops of the cedars, and dusk fell quickly, like a heavy shadow, over the terrace. In the dimness a piercing sweetness floated up from the garden of herbs, and it seemed to me that in a minute the twilight was saturated with fragrance. Then I heard the cry of a solitary whippoorwill in the graveyard, and it sounded so near that I started.

"So she died of the futility, and her unhappy ghost haunts the house?"

"No, she is not dead. It is not her ghost; it is the memory of her act that has haunted the house. Lucy Dare is still living. I saw her a few months ago."

"You saw her? You spoke to her after all these years?"

He had refilled his pipe, and the smell of it gave me a comfortable assurance that I was living here, now, in the present. A moment ago I had shivered as if the hand of the past, reaching from the open door at my back, had touched my shoulder.

"I was in Richmond. My friend Beverly, an old classmate, had asked me up for a weekend, and on Saturday afternoon, before motoring into the country for supper, we started out to make a few calls which had been left over from the morning. For a doctor, a busy doctor, he had always seemed to me to possess unlimited leisure, so I was not surprised when a single visit sometimes stretched over twenty-five minutes. We had stopped several times, and I confess that I was getting a little impatient when he remarked abruptly while he turned his car into a shady street,

" 'There is only one more. If you don't mind, I'd like you to see her. She is a friend of yours, I believe.'

"Before us, as the car stopped, I saw a red-brick house, very large, with green shutters, and over the wide door, which stood open, a sign reading 'St. Luke's Church Home.' Several old ladies sat, half asleep, on the long veranda; a clergyman, with a prayer book in his hand, was just leaving; a few pots of red geraniums stood on little green wicker stands; and from the hall, through which floated the smell of freshly baked bread, there came the music of a Victrola—sacred music, I remember. Not one of these details escaped me. It was as if every trivial impression was stamped indelibly in my memory by the shock of the next instant.

"In the center of the large, smoothly shaven lawn an old woman was sitting on a wooden bench under an ailanthus tree which was in blossom. As we approached her, I saw that her figure was shapeless, and that her eyes, of a faded blue, had the vacant and listless expression of the old who have ceased to think, who have ceased even to wonder or regret. So unlike was she to anything I had ever imagined Lucy Dare could become, that not until my friend called her name and she glanced up from the muffler she was knitting—the omnipresent dun-colored muffler for the war relief associations—not until then did I recognize her.

" 'I have brought an old friend to see you, Miss Lucy.'

"She looked up, smiled slightly, and after greeting me pleasantly, relapsed into silence. I remembered that the Lucy Dare I had known was never much of a talker.

"Dropping on the bench at her side, my friend began asking her about her sciatica, and, to my surprise, she became almost animated. Yes, the pain in her hip was better—far better than it had been for weeks. The new medicine had done her a great deal of good; but her fingers were getting rheumatic. She found trouble holding her needles. She couldn't knit as fast as she used to.

"Unfolding the end of the muffler, she held it out to us. 'I have managed to do twenty of these since Christmas. I've promised fifty to the War Relief Association by autumn, and if my fingers don't get stiff I can easily do them.'

"The sunshine falling through the ailanthus tree powdered with dusty gold her shapeless, relaxed figure and the dun-colored wool of the muffler. While she talked her fingers flew with the click of the needles—older fingers than they had been at Dare's Gift, heavier, stiffer, a little knotted in the joints. As I watched her the old familiar sense of strangeness, of encompassing and hostile mystery, stole over me.

"When we rose to go she looked up, and, without pausing for an instant in her knitting, said, gravely, 'It gives me something to do, this work for the Allies. It helps to pass the time, and in an Old Ladies' Home one has so much time on one's hands.'

"Then, as we parted from her, she dropped her eyes again to her needles. Looking back at the gate, I saw that she still sat there in the faint sunshine—knitting—knitting—"

"And you think she has forgotten?"

He hesitated, as if gathering his thoughts. "I was with her when she came back from the shock—from the illness that followed—and she had forgotten. Yes, she has forgotten, but the house has remembered."

Pushing back his chair, he rose unsteadily on his crutch, and stood staring across the twilight which was spangled with fireflies. While I waited I heard again the loud cry of the whippoorwill.

"Well, what could one expect?" he asked, presently. "She had drained the whole of experience in an instant, and there was left to her only the empty and withered husks of the hours. She had felt too much ever to feel again. After all," he added slowly, "it is the high moments that make a life, and the flat ones that fill the years."

Questions to Consider

1. Why is the doctor so convinced that treachery saturates Dare's Gift? Why is treachery especially heinous when it comes from a woman?
2. How does the Cult of the Lost Cause, a common way of viewing the Civil War and the defeat of the Confederacy, influence your interpretation of Glasgow's story?

William Alexander Percy

1885–1942

Although he published three volumes of verse and was an influential poetry editor, Will Percy is remembered for his last book, the brooding prose memoir *Lanterns on the Levee* (1941). Less than a year after its publication, Percy died at age 56 from a stroke. The book is a nostalgic celebration of the Percy name and ancestry, which his family traced back to Northumberland in feudal England. According to contemporary historians, no conclusive proof of kinship exists, but this putative linkage confirmed for Percy his Mississippi family's claim to gentry status. A childless bachelor, who, in his forties, adopted three orphaned cousins, including Walker Percy, Will Percy saw himself as the last of an Old World ruling-class line that stretched from Medieval Europe to the Mississippi Delta. In *Lanterns on the Levee* he assumed the melancholy role of witness to the global fall of social traditions based on class privilege.

Will Percy was a precocious child of wealth who received private tutoring. Although he was a Roman Catholic, at age 15 he entered the Episcopalian University of the South at Sewanee, where he would later teach. In 1902, when Will was in college, his younger brother, LeRoy, was accidentally shot dead by a playmate. This family tragedy left Will an only child, and led to his decision to go to Harvard Law School and dedicate his life to meeting his parents' career expectations of him instead of pursuing a life in the arts for which he seemed much better suited. After receiving his degree in 1908 he returned to his hometown of Greenville,

Mississippi, to join his father's firm. LeRoy Percy was a wealthy cotton planter and well-connected lawyer-politician who served in the United States Senate. Despite his father's misgivings, Will Percy sought both to practice law and write poetry, and his first volume, *Sappho in Levkas and Other Poems*, appeared in 1915.

Percy traveled widely in Europe as a young man, and he seemed eager to return to the continent during World War I as a relief-agency volunteer. When the United States entered hostilities in 1917, he returned home to enlist in the United States Army at age 32. He served with distinction in France and experienced the horrors of trench warfare, which he described as a nightmare of mud, barbed-wire, gassings, and death. Lieutenant Percy proved brave and capable under fire, received promotion to captain, and returned home a decorated war hero. But the Great War had darkened his sense of life, as expressed in the combat poems of *In April Once* (1919). Always a solitary figure, Percy abandoned Christianity and embraced the austere Stoic philosophy of the classical world, particularly the *Meditations* of Marcus Aurelius. Between traveling abroad and editing the prestigious Young Poets' Series for Yale University Press, almost despite himself he became increasingly involved in civic life in Greenville.

The most controversial phase of Percy's public life was his role as county chairman of the Red Cross relief commission during the devastating Mississippi River flood of 1927. High water in Washington County drove thousands of refugees to the levees. Whites were evacuated downriver to safe ground. But thousands of African Americans, mostly tenant farmers, were detained on the cold, muddy levees. LeRoy Percy and other plantation owners feared that if African Americans were transported out, they would migrate North and never return to sharecropping. Will Percy bowed to his father's wishes and reversed his original order to evacuate the African-American refugees. National Guard soldiers with rifles and fixed bayonets kept them prisoners on the levee for weeks. Guardsmen abused the refugees, and Greenville police fatally shot a man for refusing to be conscripted into a work gang. Soon Greenville attracted national notoriety for its mistreatment of the African-American flood victims. Will Percy condescendingly accused African Americans of bringing the violence on themselves. But perhaps sensing his own failure, he bitterly resigned while the relief effort was still ongoing and left for Japan.

In print for more than 60 years, *Lanterns on the Levee* ranges through public and personal issues, linking them by means of its eloquent prose style. The book's most declamatory chapters offer testy defenses of Southern aristocratic *noblesse oblige* and Jim Crow segregation. But the book also turns inward, giving wry voice to feelings of inadequacy and offering aching testaments to lifelong loneliness, admissions which have led recent scholars to suggest repressed homosexuality. In writing *Lanterns on the Levee*, Percy seems to have had in mind Henry Adams's similarly discouraged memoir, *The Education of Henry Adams* (1907) as well as the pessimistic nineteenth-century essays of Matthew Arnold. Although he fought bravely for his country, Will Percy had lost faith in American democracy, which he feared was disintegrating into mob rule.

However, despite his belief in segregation and antipopulism, Percy was a staunch opponent of the Ku Klux Klan, which reappeared during the postwar social turmoil of the 1920s. The Klan stood for a violent American bigotry that preached hatred of nonWhites and non-Protestants. Will Percy joined his father in 1923 in a political struggle against the Invisible Empire to elect an anti-Klan candidate for sheriff in Greenville. This political victory, however local, is one of the few moments in *Lanterns on the Levee* unshadowed by self-mockery and foreboding of cultural disintegration.

from Lanterns on the Levee

from *The Ku Klux Klan Comes and Goes*

. . . The Klan did not stand for, but against. It stood against Catholics, Jews, Negroes, foreigners, and sin. In our town it chose Catholics as the object of its chief persecution. Catholic employees were fired, Catholic businessmen were boycotted,

Catholic office-holders opposed. At first this seemed strange to me, because our Catholics were a small and obscure minority, but I came to learn with astonishment that of all the things hated in the South, more hated than the Jew or the Negro or sin itself, is Rome. The evangelical sects and Rome—as different and uncomprehending of each other as youth and old age! One seems never to have glimpsed the sorrowful pageant of the race and the other, profoundly disillusioned, profoundly compassionate, sees only the pageant. One has the enthusiasm and ignorance of the pioneer, the other the despair of the sage. One's a cheer-leader, the other an old sad-eyed family doctor from Samaria. We discovered that the Klan had its genesis, as far as our community was involved, in the Masonic Temple. The state head of that fraternal organization, a well-meaning old simpleton, had been preaching anti-Catholicism for years when conferring Masonic degrees. He joined the Klan early and induced other Masonic leaders to follow his example. These composed the Klan leadership in our county, though they were aided by a few politicians who knew better but who craved the Klan vote. It was a pretty leadership—fanatics and scalawag politicians. But not all Masons or all the godly were so misguided. The opposition to the Klan at home was led by a Protestant committee (and every denomination was represented in its ranks), who fought fearlessly, intelligently, and unceasingly this evil which they considered as unchristian as it was un-American. Father was not only head of the Protestant anti-Klan committee but of the anti-Klan forces in the South. He spoke as far north as Chicago and published probably the first article on the Klan in any distinguished magazine. It was reprinted from the *Atlantic Monthly* and distributed over the whole country. He felt the Klan was the sort of public evil good citizens could not ignore. Not to fight it was ineffectual and craven.

It's hard to conceive of the mumbo-jumbo ritual of the Klan and its half-wit principles—only less absurd than the Nazi principles of Aryan superiority and lebensraum—as worthy of an adult mind's attention. But when your living, your self-respect, and your life are threatened, you don't laugh at that which threatens. If you have either sense or courage you fight it. We fought, and it was high time someone did.

The Klan's increasing atrocities culminated in the brutal murders at Mer Rouge,[1] where Skipwith was Cyclops. Mer Rouge is across the river from us, on the Louisiana side. It is very near and the murders were very ghastly. The Klan loathed and feared Father more than any other man in the South. For months I never let him out of my sight and of course we both went armed. Never before nor since have our doors been shut and locked at night.

One Sunday night of torrential rain when Father, Aunt Lady, and I sat in the library and Mother was ill upstairs I answered a knock at the door. It was early and I opened the door without apprehension. A dark, heavy-set man with two days' growth of beard and a soft-brimmed black hat stood there, drenched to the skin. He asked for Father and I, to his obvious surprise, invited him in. He wouldn't put down his hat, but held it in front of him. I didn't like his looks, so while Father talked to him I played the piano softly in the adjoining room and listened. The man's story was that he came from near our plantation, his car had run out of gas a few miles from town,

1. Mer Rouge, a small town in northeast Louisiana, was the site in August 1922, of the kidnapping, torture, sexual mutilation, and murder of two Catholic landowners (both World War I veterans). Although 50 or more Klansmen took part in this brazen crime, no one was indicted by a Morehouse Parish grand jury. An outraged Louisiana Governor John M. Parker attributed the murders to J. K. Skipwith, head of the Klan in nearby Bastrop. The Mer Rouge lynchings caused a national outcry against anti-Catholic Klan terror in the South and led to a war of words between LeRoy Percy and Skipwith, who traveled to nearby Mississippi in 1923 to rouse Klansmen against the Percys. Will believed that Skipwith had targeted LeRoy Percy for assassination.

he'd left his sister in the car and walked to town, he couldn't find a service station open, and would Father help him? Father, all sympathy, started phoning. The stranger seemed neither interested nor appreciative. I watched him with mounting suspicion. Father's effort to find a service station open having failed, he said: "My car is here. We might run out and get your sister—I suppose you can drive my car?" The stranger brightened and observed he could drive any make of car. The two of them were still near the phone when Father's three bridge cronies came stamping in, laughing and shaking out the rain. As they came toward Father, the stranger brushed past them and had reached the door when I overtook him. "Say, what's the matter with you?" I asked. "Wait a minute and some of us will get you fixed up." He mumbled: "Got to take a leak," walked into the rain, and disappeared.

We waited for him, but we did not see him again for two years. Then he was in jail charged with a string of robberies. When he saw I recognized him, he grinned sourly and remarked: "Old Skip nearly put that one over." He refused to enlarge on this statement, which presumably referred to Skipwith, Cyclops of Mer Rouge. We found from the neighbors that the night of his visit to us he had arrived in a car with another man and parked across the street from our house.

It looked too much like an attempt at kidnapping and murder for me to feel easy. I went to the office of the local Cyclops. He was an inoffensive little man, a great Mason, and partial to anti-Catholic tirades. I said: "I want to let you know one thing: if anything happens to my Father or to any of our friends you will be killed. We won't hunt for the guilty party. So far as we are concerned the guilty party will be you."

There were no atrocities, no whippings, no threatening letters, no masked parades in our town. The local Klan bent all of its efforts toward electing one of its members sheriff. If they could have the law-enforcement machinery under their control, they could then flout the law and perpetrate such outrages as appealed to them. Our fight became a political fight to prevent the election of the Klan's choice for sheriff. The whole town was involved and the excitement was at fever heat. What appalled and terrified us most was the mendacity of Klan members. You never knew if the man you were talking to was a Klansman and a spy. Like German parachute jumpers, they appeared disguised as friends. For the Klan advised its members to lie about their affiliation with the order, about anything that concerned another Klansman's welfare, and about anything pertaining to the Klan—and its members took the advice. The most poisonous thing the Klan did to our town was to rob its citizens of their faith and trust in one another. Everyone was under suspicion: from Klansmen you could expect neither frankness nor truth nor honor, and you couldn't tell who was a Klansman. If they were elected judges and law-enforcement officers, we would be cornered into servility or assassination.

Our candidate for sheriff was George B. Alexander, a powerful, square-bearded, Kentucky aristocrat drawn by Holbein. He was one of those people who are always right by no discernible mental process. His fearlessness, warm-heartedness, and sheer character made him a person you liked to be with and for. He was Father's favorite hunting companion and friend.

On election night the town was beside itself with excitement. Crowds filled the streets outside the voting booths to hear the counting of the ballots as it progressed. Everyone realized the race was close and whoever won would win by the narrowest of margins. The whole population was in the street, milling, apprehensive, silent. When the count began, Father went home and started a bridge game. I waited at the polls. About nine o'clock a sweating individual with his collar unbuttoned and his wide red face smeared with tears rushed out on the steps and bellowed: "We've won, we've won! Alexander's elected! God damn the Klan!" Pandemonium broke loose. Men yelled and screamed and hugged one another. Our town was saved, we had whipped the Klan and were safe. I ran home with the news and Father's bridge game broke up in a stillness of thanksgiving that was almost religious.

Mother was away. Being a Frenchwoman, she had been neither hysterical nor sentimental during the months and months of tension and danger. But none of us knew what she went through silently and it was then her health began to fail.

While we were talking about the victory, a tremendous uproar came to us from the street. We rushed out on the gallery. From curb to curb the street was filled with a mad marching crowd carrying torches and singing. They swarmed down the street and into our yard. It was a victory celebration. Father made a speech, everybody made a speech, nobody listened and everybody cheered. Klansmen had taken to cover, but the rest of the town was there, seething over the yard and onto the gallery. They cut Mr. Alexander's necktie to bits for souvenirs. And still they cheered and swarmed.

Father, nonplussed, turned to Adah and me and laughed: "They don't seem to have any idea of going home and I haven't a drop of whisky in the house—at least, I'm not going to waste my *good* liquor on them." Adah and Charlie dashed off in their car and returned with four kegs. Father called to the crowd: "Come on in, boys," and into the house they poured. That was a party never to be forgotten. While Adah was gone, Lucille and her band appeared, unsummoned save by instinct. Lucille, weighing twenty stone, airily pulled the grand piano into her lap, struck one tremendous chord—my Steinway's been swayback ever since—and the dancing began. Adah never touches a drop, but she mixes a mighty punch. Things got under way. There were few inhibitions and no social distinctions. Dancers bumped into knots of heroes who told one another at the same time their harrowing exploits and unforgettable adventures. A banker's wife hobnobbed with the hot-tamale man, a lawyer's careened with a bootlegger. People who hadn't spoken for years swore deathless loyalty on one another's shoulders. The little town had come through, righteousness had prevailed, we had fought the good fight and for once had won. Everybody was affectionate with everybody else, all men were equal, and all were brothers-in-arms.

Hazlewood, the gentlest and most courageous of men, kept on making speeches from the front gallery long after his audience had adjourned to the dining-room and were gyrating like flies around Adah. He was so mortified at this treatment (when it came to his attention) that he joined them and was consoled and liberally refreshed. When at a late hour he started to leave, he couldn't find his hat and became whimpery. After discovering it under the radiator, he couldn't pick it up. When he was hatted at last and started on his way, Fletcher met him on the steps, gasped: "Oh, Hazlewood!" and kissed him. Hazlewood exclaimed: "Fletch, Fletch, you shouldn't have done that," burst into tears, and walked home down the middle of the street, sobbing bitterly.

From down Lake Washington way the swarthy tribe of Steins journeyed in, all seven of them, one behind another, the old man, broad-shouldered, arrogant, and goateed, leading the advance through the side door. You felt certain they'd left a tent and a string of camels under the portecochere. Solemnly they shook hands with everyone down the line, curved into the dining-room around the punch bowl, shook hands again, told everyone good-night, and left through the front door. We had barely recovered from this princely visitation when they again hove into view through the side door, went through the same exchange of courtesies, pausing a bit longer at the punch bowl, and disappeared out the front door. All during the evening, just about time you were getting settled in your mind, this apparition of a Tartar tribe would materialize, unhinge you, and withdraw, always with decorum but with mounting elation. The last time I expected them to produce cymbals and go to it, but instead Mrs. Stein staged a thrilling fandango with Mr. George B.

Old man Finch, bolt upright in a throne-like chair, fell sound asleep in the very center of the revelry. Well-wishers bore him to a car, drove him home, and deposited him with the greatest tact in the swing on his own front gallery. Later he fell off and cut his forehead. Wakened by the bump, his daughters swarmed out, found him unconscious and bathed in blood, summoned half the doctors in town, and went to keening. Next morning Louise telephoned asking if I'd found Papa's teeth. I'm afraid another guest wore them off.

Long after midnight I looked into the pantry and beheld my favorite barber, a plumber acquaintance, an ex-sergeant, and the hot-tamale man seated at the pantry table eating supper. They'd raided the ice-box and found besides a bottle of liquor. They graciously invited me to join them. Instead I routed out my husky soldier friend, Howard Shields, and admonished him to get those people out of the house, one way or another. Howard bowed stiffly and answered: "Certainly, leave it to me." A bit later I again looked into the pantry; Howard was standing with a glass full of straight whisky in his hand making an undisciplined speech about the virtues of his squad. His four listeners beamed foolishly. One of them managed to observe: "Didn't know Howard waised squabs," and went off into giggles, then into hiccups, then into tears. I addressed Howard sternly: "Go to bed," and he disappeared upstairs. On the way to my room I looked in on him: he was sound asleep. Actually, he hadn't taken off a stitch, he was lying under the sheet fully clothed and anticipating my inspection. The coast being clear, he slipped out, found his buddy, George Crittenden, knocked him cold, and lit out in his car for Clarksdale.

It was a memorable evening. On the way home people fell off bicycles and into gutters, ran over street signs and up trees—and all happy (except Hazlewood). The police radiantly gathered them up and located their destinations.

We decided it was just as well, after all, that Mother had been out of town. It wasn't her sort of party. She'd have started clearing the house at the first drink, victory or no victory.

Our Ku Klux neighbors stood on their porch watching—justified and prophesying Judgment Day.

It had been a great fight. It was also a ruthless searchlight on character, of one kind or another. My generation still remembers it, though it all happened eighteen or nineteen years ago, and that's a century of any other time. An old Klansman, one who, being educated, had no excuse for being one, asked me the other day why I'd never forgiven him. I had to answer: "Forgiveness is easy. I really like you. The trouble is I've got your number and people's numbers don't change."

Questions to Consider

1. Outside southern Louisiana, Roman Catholics in the South are a Christian religious minority. Will Percy was raised Catholic by his mother before he rejected Christianity in favor of philosophical stoicism; his father was indifferent to organized religion. Yet both LeRoy and Will Percy risked their lives to condemn Southern anti-Catholicism. What

does he mean when he writes, "I came to learn with astonishment that of all things hated in the South, more hated than the Jew or the Negro or sin itself, is Rome"?

2. Will describes the celebration that breaks out after the sheriff's election, when LeRoy Percy opens his house for a victory party. Class distinctions melt away as the merrymakers drink and dance. What point is Will making about the civic harm done to communities by the bigotry and intimidation of the Klan?

H. L. Mencken

1880–1956

"In 1917, the irreverent Mr. Mencken of Baltimore, in 'The Sahara of the Bozart,' drafted an obituary of the South" proclaimed critic and Southern literary scholar Lewis Lawson, pointing out Mencken's particular disdain for the dearth of Southern artistry during the early decades of the twentieth century. Well known for his caustic wit and incisive social commentary, H. L. Mencken built a career that encompassed journalism, literary and social criticism, and publishing, but as critic Vincent Fitzpatrick has pointed out, he was "above all else a libertarian . . . [who] saw freedom of speech as the most valuable attribute of any society." Mencken frequently exercised this right to freely express his thoughts, and his frank condemnation of the ills of the American South caused him to be viewed in many corners as a misanthropic devil, in spite of characterizations by his friends and colleagues; his long-standing copublisher George Jean Nathan described the journalist as "entirely free of cheapness, toadyism, and hypocrisy." Mencken authored more than thirty volumes of essays, journalistic pieces, and short fiction, as well as a volume of poetry.

Born in Baltimore, Maryland, on 12 September 1880, Henry Louis Mencken was the son of first-generation German Americans, August and Anna Margaret Abhau Mencken. Prior to his marriage to Anna Abhau, August Mencken began a successful cigar factory in partnership with his brother. Mencken remarked in an interview that he "unfortunately, did not come from a log cabin. My misfortune was that my father was relatively well-off. It has been a curse to me all my life. . . . It seems to be the idea in America that no man is worth listening to unless he has some experience in sweat-shops." His father's financial success allowed Mencken to obtain a high-quality education, first at the F. Knapp Institute and later at Baltimore Polytechnic Institute. He graduated first in his high school class at the age of 15, having already begun to write and seek publication for his works. He never attended college and loudly mocked the supposed benefits of higher education. Acquiescing to his father's wishes, Mencken entered the family cigar business, but he hated the work so much that he became depressed and contemplated suicide. He began writing poetry in an effort to curb his depression, and upon his father's death in 1899, he began actively pursuing a position as a journalist. Within six months, Mencken was a salaried employee of the *Baltimore Herald* and had published his first short story in a magazine.

Vincent Fitzpatrick argues that Mencken's career as a journalist consists of three distinct periods: the first, which begins in 1899 and ends in 1908, served as a developmental period for Mencken, during which he "hustled his poetry, short stories, and essays." The second period began in 1908 and concluded at the end of 1933, and accounts for Mencken's years working as a writer and editor of two magazines, *Smart Set* and *Mercury*. The final portion of Mencken's career, from 1934 to 1948, found him working as a freelance writer for a variety of highly regarded publications. Mencken's career as a writer ended abruptly in late 1948, when he suffered a stroke that rendered him unable to read or write.

One of the high points of Mencken's career came in 1924, when he began publishing the *American Mercury* with George Jean Nathan. Only one year later, Mencken assumed editorial control of the magazine, since he and Nathan could not agree on its scope. Mencken wanted

American Mercury to be journalistic, in sharp contrast to the more literary bent of his previous publication, *Smart Set*, which had primarily published the works of "writers and editors. . . . [who] were dedicated to 'liberating' the South," according to critic William Andrews. *American Mercury* published the works of many noteworthy writers, including Theodore Dreiser, F. Scott Fitzgerald, William Faulkner, Sherwood Anderson, and Dorothy Parker. Mencken's predisposition to disparage Southern culture remained prevalent in the pages of *American Mercury*, turning the magazine into a "satiric social commentary," as Williams points out. W. J. Cash, who authored *The Mind of the South* in part because of his association with Mencken, published eight pieces in the magazine.

Mencken ceded control of *American Mercury* to Henry Hazlitt in December 1933, and by this time his interest in debating the cultural value of the South had largely evaporated. As Williams points out, however, Mencken's satiric point of view had "begun as a war on the South [but] had become a war for the South." Ironically, although Mencken reviewed the Agrarian treatise *I'll Take My Stand* in *American Mercury*, dismissing both the volume of essays and the stand itself as "utopian," Williams contends that Mencken never realized "how much of their distaste for the values of industrial America he shared with them." Despite Mencken's disparagement of the "hellawful South," Fred Hobson suggests that the editor "influenced dozens of Southern writers and intellectuals and played a leading role in the first phase of the Southern literary renascence." Mencken's commentary on the aridity of Southern culture unwittingly served as a call to arms for the intellectuals and literary artists of the region.

The Sahara of the Bozart

Alas, for the South! Her books have grown fewer—
She never was much given to literature.

In the lamented J. Gordon Coogler,[1] author of these elegiac lines, there was the insight of a true poet. He was the last bard of Dixie, at least in the legitimate line. Down there a poet is now almost as rare as an oboe-player, a dry-point etcher or a metaphysician. It is, indeed, amazing to contemplate so vast a vacuity. One thinks of the interstellar spaces, of the colossal reaches of the now mythical ether. Nearly the whole of Europe could be lost in that stupendous region of fat farms, shoddy cities and paralyzed cerebrums: one could throw in France, Germany and Italy, and still have room for the British Isles. And yet, for all its size and all its wealth and all the "progress" it babbles of, it is almost as sterile, artistically, intellectually, culturally, as the Sahara Desert. There are single acres in Europe that house more first-rate men than all the states south of the Potomac; there are probably single square miles in America. If the whole of the late Confederacy were to be engulfed by a tidal wave tomorrow, the effect upon the civilized minority of men in the world would be but little greater than that of a flood on the Yang-tse-kiang. It would be impossible in all history to match so complete a drying-up of a civilization.

I say a civilization because that is what, in the old days, the south had, despite the Baptist and Methodist barbarism that reigns down there now. More, it was a civilization of manifold excellences—perhaps the best that the Western Hemisphere has ever seen—undoubtedly the best that These States have ever seen. Down to the middle of the last century, and even beyond, the main hatchery of ideas on this side

1. South Carolina poet best remembered for this line. Otherwise, he is now remembered as one of the worst American poets.

of the water was across the Potomac bridges. The New England shopkeepers and theologians never really developed a civilization; all they ever developed was a government. They were, at their best, tawdry and tacky fellows, oafish in manner and devoid of imagination; one searches the books in vain for mention of a salient Yankee gentleman; as well look for a Welsh gentleman. But in the south there were men of delicate fancy, urbane instinct and aristocratic manner—in brief, superior men—in brief, gentry. To politics, their chief diversion, they brought active and original minds. It was there that nearly all the political theories we still cherish and suffer under came to birth. It was there that the crude dogmatism of New England was refined and humanized. It was there, above all, that some attention was given to the art of living—that life got beyond and above the state of a mere infliction and became an exhilarating experience. A certain noble spaciousness was in the ancient southern scheme of things. The *Ur*-Confederate had leisure. He liked to toy with ideas. He was hospitable and tolerant. He had the vague thing that we call culture.

But consider the condition of his late empire to-day. The picture gives one the creeps. It is as if the Civil War stamped out every last bearer of the torch, and left only a mob of peasants on the field. One thinks of Asia Minor, resigned to Armenians, Greeks and wild swine, of Poland abandoned to the Poles. In all that gargantuan paradise of the fourth-rate there is not a single picture gallery worth going into, or a single orchestra capable of playing the nine symphonies of Beethoven, or a single opera-house, or a single theater devoted to decent plays, or a single public monument (built since the war) that is worth looking at, or a single workshop devoted to the making of beautiful things. Once you have counted Robert Loveman (an Ohioan by birth) and John McClure (an Oklahoman) you will not find a single southern poet above the rank of a neighborhood rhymester. Once you have counted James Branch Cabell (a lingering survivor of the *ancien régime:* a scarlet dragonfly imbedded in opaque amber) you will not find a single southern prose writer who can actually write. And once you have—but when you come to critics, musical composers, painters, sculptors, architects and the like, you will have to give it up, for there is not even a bad one between the Potomac mud-flats and the Gulf. Nor an historian. Nor a sociologist. Nor a philosopher. Nor a theologian. Nor a scientist. In all these fields the south is an awe-inspiring blank—a brother to Portugal, Serbia and Esthonia.

Consider, for example, the present estate and dignity of Virginia—in the great days indubitably the premier American state, the mother of Presidents and statesmen, the home of the first American university worthy of the name, the *arbiter elegantiarum* of the western world. Well, observe Virginia to-day. It is years since a first-rate man, save only Cabell, has come out of it; it is years since an idea has come out of it. The old aristocracy went down the red gullet of war; the poor white trash are now in the saddle. Politics in Virginia are cheap, ignorant, parochial, idiotic; there is scarcely a man in office above the rank of a professional job-seeker; the political doctrine that prevails is made up of hand-me-downs from the bumpkinry of the Middle West—Bryanism, Prohibition, vice crusading, all that sort of filthy claptrap; the administration of the law is turned over to professors of Puritanism and espionage; a Washington or a Jefferson, dumped there by some act of God, would be denounced as a scoundrel and jailed overnight. Elegance, *esprit,* culture? Virginia has no art, no literature, no philosophy, no mind or aspiration of her own. Her education has sunk to the Baptist seminary level; not a single contribution to human knowledge has come out of her colleges in twenty-five years; she spends less than half upon her common schools, *per capita,* than any northern state spends. In brief, an intellectual Gobi or

Lapland. Urbanity, *politesse*, chivalry? Go to! It was in Virginia that they invented the device of searching for contraband whisky in women's underwear. . . . There remains, at the top, a ghost of the old aristocracy, a bit wistful and infinitely charming. But it has lost all its old leadership to fabulous monsters from the lower depths; it is submerged in an industrial plutocracy that is ignorant and ignominious. The mind of the state, as it is revealed to the nation, is pathetically naïve and inconsequential. It no longer reacts with energy and elasticity to great problems. It has fallen to the bombastic trivialities of the camp-meeting and the chautauqua.[2] Its foremost exponent—if so flabby a thing may be said to have an exponent—is a statesman whose name is synonymous with empty words, broken pledges and false pretenses. One could no more imagine a Lee or a Washington in the Virginia of to-day than one could imagine a Huxley in Nicaragua.

I choose the Old Dominion, not because I disdain it, but precisely because I esteem it. It is, by long odds, the most civilized of the southern states, now as always. It has sent a host of creditable sons northward; the stream kept running into our own time. Virginians, even the worst of them, show the effects of a great tradition. They hold themselves above other southerners, and with sound pretension. If one turns to such a commonwealth as Georgia the picture becomes far darker. There the liberated lower orders of whites have borrowed the worst commercial bounderism of the Yankee and superimposed it upon a culture that, at bottom, is but little removed from savagery. Georgia is at once the home of the cotton-mill sweater and of the most noisy and vapid sort of chamber of commerce, of the Methodist parson turned Savonarola and of the lynching bee. A self-respecting European, going there to live, would not only find intellectual stimulation utterly lacking; he would actually feel a certain insecurity, as if the scene were the Balkans or the China Coast. The Leo Frank affair[3] was no isolated phenomenon. It fitted into its frame very snugly. It was a natural expression of Georgian notions of truth and justice. There is a state with more than half the area of Italy and more population than either Denmark or Norway, and yet in thirty years it has not produced a single idea. Once upon a time a Georgian printed a couple of books that attracted notice, but immediately it turned out that he was little more than an amanuensis for the local blacks—that his works were really the products, not of white Georgia, but of black Georgia. Writing afterward *as* a white man, he swiftly subsided into the fifth rank. And he is not only the glory of the literature of Georgia; he is, almost literally, the whole of the literature of Georgia—nay, of the entire art of Georgia.

Virginia is the best of the south to-day, and Georgia is perhaps the worst. The one is simply senile; the other is crass, gross, vulgar and obnoxious. Between lies a vast plain of mediocrity, stupidity, lethargy, almost of dead silence. In the north, of course, there is also grossness, crassness, vulgarity. The north, in its way, is also stupid and obnoxious. But nowhere in the north is there such complete sterility, so depressing a lack of all civilized gesture and aspiration. One would find it difficult to unearth a second-rate city between the Ohio and the Pacific that isn't struggling to establish an orchestra, or setting up a little theater, or going in for an art gallery, or making some other effort to get into touch with civilization. These efforts often fail, and sometimes they succeed rather absurdly,but under them there is at least an impulse

2. Summer school, typically of a religious nature.
3. Georgia man accused of the murder of Mary Phagan in the basement of a pencil factory. His trial was notorious throughout the South, and although he was innocent of the crime, Frank was lynched.

that deserves respect, and that is the impulse to seek beauty and to experiment with ideas, and so to give the life of every day a certain dignity and purpose. You will find no such impulse in the south. There are no committees down there cadging subscriptions for orchestras; if a string quartet is ever heard there, the news of it has never come out; an opera troupe, when it roves the land, is a nine days' wonder. The little theater movement has swept the whole country, enormously augmenting the public interest in sound plays, giving new dramatists their chance, forcing reforms upon the commercial theater. Everywhere else the wave rolls high—but along the line of the Potomac it breaks upon a rock-bound shore. There is no little theater beyond. There is no gallery of pictures. No artist ever gives exhibitions. No one talks of such things. No one seems to be interested in such things.

As for the cause of this unanimous torpor and doltishness, this curious and almost pathological estrangement from everything that makes for a civilized culture, I have hinted at it already, and now state it again. The south has simply been drained of all its best blood. The vast blood-letting of the Civil War half exterminated and wholly paralyzed the old aristocracy, and so left the land to the harsh mercies of the poor white trash, now its masters. The war, of course, was not a complete massacre. It spared a decent number of first-rate southerners—perhaps even some of the very best. Moreover, other countries, notably France and Germany, have survived far more staggering butcheries, and even showed marked progress thereafter. But the war not only cost a great many valuable lives; it also brought bankruptcy, demoralization and despair in its train—and so the majority of the first-rate southerners that were left, broken in spirit and unable to live under the new dispensation, cleared out. A few went to South America, to Egypt, to the Far East. Most came north. They were fecund; their progeny is widely dispersed, to the great benefit of the north. A southerner of good blood almost always does well in the north. He finds, even in the big cities, surroundings fit for a man of condition. His peculiar qualities have a high social value, and are esteemed. He is welcomed by the codfish aristocracy as one palpably superior. But in the south he throws up his hands. It is impossible for him to stoop to the common level. He cannot brawl in politics with the grandsons of his grandfather's tenants. He is unable to share their fierce jealousy of the emerging black—the cornerstone of all their public thinking. He is anæsthetic to their theological and political enthusiasms. He finds himself an alien at their feasts of soul. And so he withdraws into his tower, and is heard of no more. Cabell is almost a perfect example. His eyes, for years, were turned toward the past; he became a professor of the grotesque genealogizing that decaying aristocracies affect; it was only by a sort of accident that he discovered himself to be an artist. The south is unaware of the fact to this day; it regards Woodrow Wilson and Col. John Temple Graves as much finer stylists, and Frank L. Stanton as an infinitely greater poet. If it has heard, which I doubt, that Cabell has been hoofed by the Comstocks, it unquestionably views that assault as a deserved rebuke to a fellow who indulges a lewd passion for fancy writing, and is a covert enemy to the Only True Christianity.

What is needed down there, before the vexatious public problems of the region may be intelligently approached, is a survey of the population by competent ethnologists and anthropologists. The immigrants of the north have been studied at great length, and any one who is interested may now apply to the Bureau of Ethnology for elaborate data as to their racial strains, their stature and cranial indices, their relative capacity for education, and the changes that they undergo under American *Kultur*. But the older stocks of the south, and particularly the emancipated and dominant poor white trash, have never been investigated scientifically, and most of the current generalizations about them are probably wrong. For example, the generalization that they are purely Anglo-Saxon in blood. This I doubt very seriously. The chief strain down there, I believe, is Celtic rather than Saxon, particularly in the hill country. French blood, too, shows itself here and there, and so does Spanish, and so does German. The last-named entered from the northward, by way of the limestone belt just east of the Alleghenies. Again, it is very likely that in some parts of the south a good many of the plebeian whites have more than a trace of negro blood. Interbreeding under concubinage produced some very light half-breeds at an early day, and no doubt appreciable numbers of them went over into the white race by the simple process of changing their abode. Not long ago I read a curious article by an intelligent negro, in which he stated that it is easy for a very light negro to pass as white in the south on account of the fact that large numbers of southerners accepted as white have distinctly negroid features. Thus it becomes a delicate and dangerous matter for a train conductor or a hotel-keeper to challenge a suspect. But the Celtic strain is far more obvious than any of these others. It not only makes itself visible in physical stigmata—*e.g.*, leanness and dark coloring—but also in mental traits. For example, the religious thought of the south is almost precisely identical with the religious thought of Wales. There is the same naïve belief in an anthropomorphic Creator but little removed, in manner and desire, from an evangelical bishop; there is the same submission to an ignorant and impudent sacerdotal tyranny, and there is the same sharp contrast between doctrinal orthodoxy and private ethics. Read Caradoc Evans' ironical picture of the Welsh Wesleyans in his preface to "My Neighbors," and you will be instantly reminded of the Georgia and Carolina Methodists. The most booming sort of piety, in the south, is not incompatible with the theory that lynching is a benign institution. Two generations ago it was not incompatible with an ardent belief in slavery.

religious antecedents

It is highly probable that some of the worst blood of western Europe flows in the veins of the southern poor whites, now poor no longer. The original strains, according to every honest historian, were extremely corrupt. Philip Alexander Bruce (a Virginian of the old gentry) says in his "Industrial History of Virginia in the Seventeenth Century" that the first native-born generation was largely illegitimate. "One of the most common offenses against morality committed in the lower ranks of life in Virginia during the seventeenth century," he says, "was bastardy." The mothers of these bastards, he continues, were chiefly indentured servants, and "had belonged to the lowest class in their native country." Fanny Kemble Butler, writing of the Georgia poor whites of a century later, described them as "the most degraded race of human beings claiming an Anglo-Saxon origin that can be found on the face of the earth—filthy, lazy, ignorant, brutal, proud, penniless savages." The Sunday-school and the chautauqua, of course, have appreciably mellowed the descendants of these "savages," and their economic progress and rise to political power have done perhaps even more, but the marks of their origin are still unpleasantly plentiful. Every now and then they produce a political leader who puts their secret notions of the true, the good and the beautiful into plain words, to the amazement and scandal of the rest of the country. That amazement is turned into downright incredulity when news comes that his platform has got him high office, and that he is trying to execute it.

In the great days of the south the line between the gentry and the poor whites was very sharply drawn. There was absolutely no intermarriage. So far as I know there is not a single instance in history of a southerner of the upper class marrying one of the bondwomen described by Mr. Bruce. In other societies characterized by class distinctions of that sort it is common for the lower class to be improved by extra-legal crosses. That is to say, the men of the upper class take women of the lower class as mistresses, and out of such unions spring the extraordinary plebeians who rise sharply from the common level, and so propagate the delusion that all other plebeians would do the same thing if they had the chance—in brief, the delusion that class distinctions are merely economic and conventional, and not congenital and genuine. But in the south the men of the upper classes sought their mistresses among the blacks, and after a few generations there was so much white blood in the black women that they were considerably more attractive than the unhealthy and bedraggled women of the poor whites. This preference continued into our own time. A southerner of good family once told me in all seriousness that he had reached his majority before it ever occurred to him that a white woman might make quite as agreeable a mistress as the octaroons of his jejune fancy. If the thing has changed of late, it is not the fault of the southern white man, but of the southern mulatto women. The more sightly yellow girls of the region, with improving economic opportunities, have gained self-respect, and so they are no longer as willing to enter into concubinage as their grand-dams were.

As a result of this preference of the southern gentry for mulatto mistresses there was created a series of mixed strains containing the best white blood of the south, and perhaps of the whole country. As another result the poor whites went unfertilized from above, and so missed the improvement that so constantly shows itself in the peasant stocks of other countries. It is a commonplace that nearly all negroes who rise above the general are of mixed blood, usually with the white predominating. I know a great many negroes, and it would be hard for me to think of an exception. What is too often forgotten is that this white blood is not the blood of the poor whites but that of the old gentry. The mulatto girls of the early days despised the poor whites as creatures distinctly inferior to negroes, and it was thus almost unheard of for such a girl to enter into relations with a man of that submerged class. This aversion was based upon a sound instinct. The southern mulatto of to-day is a proof of it. Like all other half-breeds he is an unhappy man, with disquieting tendencies toward anti-social habits of thought, but he is intrinsically a better animal than the pure-blooded descendant of the old poor whites, and he not infrequently demonstrates it. It is not by accident that the negroes of the south are making faster progress, economically and culturally, than the masses of the whites. It is not by accident that the only visible æsthetic activity in the south is wholly in their hands. No southern composer has ever written music so good as that of half a dozen white-black composers who might be named. Even in politics, the negro reveals a curious superiority. Despite the fact that the race question has been the main political concern of the southern whites for two generations, to the practical exclusion of everything else, they have contributed nothing to its discussion that has impressed the rest of the world so deeply and so favorably as three or four books by southern negroes.

Entering upon such themes, of course, one must resign one's self to a vast misunderstanding and abuse. The south has not only lost its old capacity for producing ideas; it has also taken on the worst intolerance of ignorance and stupidity. Its prevailing mental attitude for several decades past has been that of its own hedge ecclesiastics. All who dissent from its orthodox doctrines are scoundrels. All who presume to discuss its ways realistically are damned. I have had, in my day, several experiences in point. Once, after I had published an article on some phase of the eternal race question, a leading southern newspaper replied by printing a column of denunciation of my father, then dead nearly twenty years—a philippic placarding him as an ignorant foreigner of dubious origin, inhabiting "the Baltimore ghetto" and speaking a dialect recalling that of Weber & Fields—two thousand words of incandescent nonsense, utterly false and beside the point, but exactly meeting the latter-day southern notion of effective controversy. Another time, I published a short discourse on lynching, arguing that the sport was popular in the south because the backward culture of the region denied the populace more seemly recreations. Among such recreations I mentioned those afforded by brass bands, symphony orchestras, boxing matches, amateur athletic contests, shoot-the-chutes, roof gardens, horse races, and so on. In reply another great southern journal denounced me as a man "of wineshop temperament, brass-jewelry tastes and pornographic predilections." In other words, brass bands, in the south, are classed with brass jewelry, and both are snares of the devil! To advocate setting up symphony orchestras is pornography! . . . Alas, when the touchy southerner attempts a greater urbanity, the result is often even worse. Some time ago a colleague of mine printed an article deploring the arrested cultural development of Georgia. In reply he received a number of protests from patriotic Georgians, and all of them solemnly listed the glories of the state. I indulge in a few specimens:

> Who has not heard of Asa G. Candler, whose name is synonymous with Coca-Cola, a Georgia product?
>
> The first Sunday-school in the world was opened in Savannah.
>
> Who does not recall with pleasure the writings of . . . Frank L. Stanton, Georgia's brilliant poet?
>
> Georgia was the first state to organize a Boys' Corn Club in the South—Newton county, 1904.
>
> The first to suggest a common United Daughters of the Confederacy badge was Mrs. Raynes, of Georgia.
>
> The first to suggest a state historian of the United Daughters of the Confederacy was Mrs. C. Helen Plane (Macon convention, 1896).
>
> The first to suggest putting to music Heber's "From Greenland's Icy Mountains" was Mrs. F. R. Goulding, of Savannah.

And so on, and so on. These proud boasts came, remember, not from obscure private persons, but from "Leading Georgians"—in one case, the state historian. Curious sidelights upon the ex-Confederate mind! Another comes from a stray copy of a negro paper. It describes an ordinance lately passed by the city council of Douglas, Ga., forbidding any trousers presser, on penalty of forfeiting a $500 bond, to engage in "pressing for both white and colored." This in a town, says the negro paper, where practically all of the white inhabitants have "their food prepared by colored hands," "their babies cared for by colored hands," and "the clothes which they wear right next to their skins washed in houses where negroes live"—houses in which the said clothes "remain for as long as a week at a time." But if you marvel at the absurdity, keep it dark! A casual word, and the united press of the south will be upon your trail, denouncing you bitterly as a scoundrelly Yankee, a Bolshevik Jew, an agent of the Wilhelmstrasse. . . .

Obviously, it is impossible for intelligence to flourish in such an atmosphere. Free inquiry is blocked by the idiotic certainties of ignorant men. The arts, save in the lower reaches of the gospel hymn, the phonograph and the chautauqua harangue, are all held in suspicion. The tone of public opinion is set by an upstart class but lately emerged from industrial slavery into commercial enterprise—the class of "hustling" business men, of "live wires," of commercial club luminaries, of "drive" managers, of forward-lookers and right-thinkers—in brief, of third-rate southerners inoculated with all the worst traits of the Yankee sharper. One observes the curious effects of an old tradition of truculence upon a population now merely pushful and impudent, of an old tradition of chivalry upon a population now quite without imagination. The old repose is gone. The old romanticism is gone. The philistinism of the new type of town-boomer southerner is not only indifferent to the ideals of the old south; it is positively antagonistic to them. That philistinism regards human life, not as an agreeable adventure, but as a mere trial of rectitude and efficiency. It is overwhelmingly utilitarian and moral. It is inconceivably hollow and obnoxious. What remains of the ancient tradition is simply a certain charming civility in private intercourse—often broken down, alas, by the hot rages of Puritanism, but still generally visible. The southerner, at his worst, is never quite the surly cad that the Yankee is. His sensitiveness may betray him into occasional bad manners, but in the main he is a pleasant fellow—hospitable, polite, good-humored, even jovial. . . . But a bit absurd. . . . A bit pathetic.

Questions to Consider

1. Given what you know about the state of the South during the early twentieth century, was Mencken's assessment of the region as a desolate cultural space accurate? Why or why not?
2. What counterevidence exists to refute Mencken's attacks on the South during this era? Did Mencken's criticisms affect literary productivity in the South in the years following his publications? On what do you base your position?

Elizabeth Madox Roberts

1881–1941

Elizabeth Madox Roberts gained critical accolades during her lifetime on the strength of her poetry and her first novel, *The Time of Man* (1926). Her short fiction, however, typifies her lifelong examination of her greatest subject, the Kentucky pioneer, through her adept manipulation of realism, lyrical prose, and literary allusion. Roberts's fiction represents a cultural shift from iconoclasm to a questioning of old Southern ways—questioning that has led to Roberts's identification with the Southern Renascence. Along with William Faulkner and Thomas Wolfe, Roberts and other lesser members of what Donald Davidson once called the Agrarian "men's club" have been credited with the rise of the Southern Renascence, and her novels, most notably *My Heart and My Flesh* (1927), were praised as precursors to Faulkner's *Absalom, Absalom!*

Roberts was born on 30 October 1881 in Perryville, Kentucky, near the site of a pivotal Civil War battle. Her father, Simpson Roberts, was a descendant of the pioneer Abram Roberts, who entered Kentucky from the Southern Piedmont area through Boone's Trace during the eighteenth century. Her mother's family also came from pioneer stock, tracing their roots to David Garvin, a six-month bond slave who served time to repay his passage as a stowaway. Simpson Roberts was a scholar, schoolmaster, surveyor, farmer, and civil engineer, who also served as a Confederate soldier under General Bragg beginning in 1863. In 1878, Simpson Roberts wed Mary Elizabeth Brent, the granddaughter of a Union officer who defected to the Southern cause after being wounded at Shiloh and discharged from the federal army. The second of eight Roberts children, Elizabeth grew up in a family of divided loyalties in a state with similar identity issues. She closely identified with two critical elements in Kentucky's development: the Civil War and Westward Expansion.

Roberts enrolled at the State College of Kentucky (now the University of Kentucky) in 1900, but the ill health she battled for much of her life forced her to withdraw. For the next decade, she taught intermittently but found that teaching taxed her fragile health too greatly, and as a result, in 1910, she moved to Colorado to live with her sister so that she might recover from her respiratory illness. She published her first work while in Colorado, a volume of poetry titled *In the Great Steep's Garden* (1915).

In 1917, Roberts enrolled at the University of Chicago and began to study writing seriously. She became a member, and later president, of the University Poetry Club, where she became acquainted with Harriet Monroe, the editor of *Poetry Magazine*, and this acquaintance led to the publication of several of Roberts's poems. She also met other notable poets whose work was featured in *Poetry*, including Vachel Lindsay, Edgar Lee Masters, and Carl Sandburg. After completing her degree in 1921, Roberts returned to Springfield and began writing full time.

Although Roberts concentrated much of her attention on the novel form, she has largely been remembered as a poet. Her first volume of poetry, *In the Great Steep's Garden*, was intended to attract the attention of tourists, as it described the foliage of Colorado in majestic detail. Two additional volumes of poetry, *Under the Tree* (1922) and *Songs in the Meadow* (1940) are geared to a youthful audience, and these volumes have been compared with works such as Robert Louis Stevenson's *A Child's Garden of Verses*.

Roberts's fiction was simultaneously identified with the emerging Southern and Western literary traditions because of the regional focus of her novels. Her first novel, *The Time of Man*, was also her most successful with both critical and popular audiences. Roberts was continually drawn to Southern themes throughout her career, as can be seen in works such as "The Sacrifice of the Maidens." She subtly probes the female role prescribed by Southern tradition, examining the ways in which the role was challenged by cultural phenomena such as class distinctions, the sacrifices required by faith, and the changes that occurred when traditional groups attempted to pioneer communities outside the established terrain.

Over the course of her career, Roberts produced seven novels, two collections of short fiction, and three volumes of poetry. In 1931, she began suffering from a skin disease that slowed her productivity, although she continued writing until her death. Roberts succumbed to Hodgkin's disease in 1941 at the age of 59.

The Sacrifice of the Maidens

An unnatural dusk lay among the pillars of the little chapel and the candle-glow struggled with the white of the late daylight that came through the windows. Felix Barbour walked along the aisle beside Lester, his brother, and sat in a pew which a nun, who acted as usher, had already pointed out for his sister, Piety. Outside he heard the crying of the crickets and a shrill pulse of frogs that lived about the pond in the field beyond the convent park. Inside were other sounds which were more near and more full of power, the sounds made by a gathering of many people who were hushed to quiet, whose garments whispered softly as limbs were settled, as knees left the prayer stools, as heads were bowed or lifted. The sounds without and those within mingled continually, but the whispers of a throng of bodies worked free of the cries that came from the outer wet and the grass.

The strangeness of the little chapel, a chapel for the worship of nuns, put a strangeness over his sense of himself as being present, as being a part of the praying throng. The seat seemed small and scarcely sufficient for his large strong limbs as he crumpled himself to rest there, and his bulk seemed awkward on the prayer-stool.

That night his sister, Anne, would take the first vows which would make her a nun of the Dominican Order,[1] and he had come now to witness the strange ceremony. He had known in a vague and troubled way that this would be the end of Anne. This knowing dispersed now under the strangeness of the chapel, under the temporary cramping posture of his limbs, as if the old way would be restored when he stretched himself to his stature and walked again into the outer air. Anne had come home from the convent school during the Easter vacation to tell those at home that she would take the vows. Sitting beside the fire, she had risen suddenly, flinging back from the doorway as she stood in the act of going:

"I aim to take the vows, to live the holy life. I aim . . . That's my intention. . . ."

This was followed by a hush that settled over the house broken by their father's awkward protest and then his silent acceptance. Now a warm breath spread over the chapel, the breath of a multitude of men brought together to act as one being. All the congregation had begun to chant the Rosary in recitative,[2] all standing. The priest at the altar would begin, half singing, but on a word, a Word, the congregation would break over him, covering his voice with a rush of acclamation and petition, the whole making a spoken fugue, the many-ply voice of the congregation speaking all together in a rushing chant that ran level with the heads of men and spread laterally beyond, rushing forward. The priest, speaking first then, rapidly intoning:

Hail Mary, full of grace,
Blessed art thou among women
Blessed is the fruit of thy . . .

Over this, over the word, then broke the cries of the people while the priest held the intoned word as a fundamental tone, their words falling swiftly spoken, his word delayed. While he boomed the great thundering word they continued, these words being the whole of their saying:

Holy Mary, Mother of God,
Pray for us now and at the hour of our death . . .

But the priest had begun again, making again the swift words that opened the chant, and the people fell into a stillness that was like dust, a world destroyed. The people were nothing, they had fallen, their cries were lost and they had become the ashes of a burnt-out life, an extinct order. They fell away in a soft patter, not all in one falling, a few surviving one instant beyond the general death, but presently these were lost to the last soul, "hour of our death . . . our death . . ." the last dusty patter, the last expiring utterance. Over this destruction the priest had already begun the onward rush of a new creation.

Hail Mary, full of grace,
Blessed art thou among women
Blessed is the fruit of thy . . .

The great intoned word again, and the people are alive. A great rush of human living and all sprang into life instantly in one act of creation while the immense

1. Catholic religious order founded in 1216.

2. A combination of vocal prayer and mental prayer practiced by the Roman Catholic church. Individuals who pray the Rosary reflect on important events in the life of Jesus Christ and his mother, Mary.

thundering word under them was a power to push them forward and on. Held again as the fundamental and richly intoned, it survived while they ran forward with their lifetime, their creation, their prayers and cries, their falling away at last into the words of departure.

Holy Mary, Mother of God,
Pray for us now and at the hour of our death . . .

Over and over this regeneration and death continued, running around the entire cycle of the Rosary, the Our Father of the large bead partaking of the same pattern, borrowing from the general chant. A mystery stood in a clear pattern, but was not entirely revealed to him, and Felix remembered Anne intently, seeing her from first to last in a sharp sense of her whole being which was made up of pictures and sounds and odors and remembered ways.

He fell into a half dream, his drooping eyes resting on his bent fingers as they lay on his lax thighs. It was a March day three years earlier. The wind was hurling laughter about among the trees and making laughter cry out of the creaking hinge of the barn gate. He walked out to the pasture to salt the young cattle, the yearlings that were feeding there, and as he walked he knew the odors of the salt that came up from the old basket in his hand. The herd came, eager to get what he had brought, and he walked among them, spreading the piles in three places so that all might have a share. The plump calves pushed one another away from the salt, and they bent their greedy muzzles to lick at the stones. While their smooth, sleek coats moved away in the sun and the wind he knew suddenly that there was a loveliness in girls and knew that he had only of late become aware of their prettiness, of their round soft flesh and the shy, veiled laughter that hid under their boldness, even under their profane words when they made as if they were angry, when they enacted distrust and put blame or blight on some matter. They carried a kindness within them that put away any anger that might leap out of their tongues. Walking back toward the house he met Anne in the path.

"What way did the turkey hen go?" she asked him.

He saw that she had grown into a prettiness, that she had put on all that he had been dreaming. A gentleness had come into her body. She had become precious to all men as she stood in the path. His voice was answering her, teasing, "The turkey hens are a woman's work."

"God's own sake, you are a mean boy, Felix Barbour. Won't tell whe'r you saw the old hen or not!"

He heard her calling the turkeys from the distant fence where the pasture gave way to the new field of wheat. Standing on the rail of the fence she was a child again, Annie, scarcely anything at all. She was a thin childish crying that called home the straying fowls.

The great wheel of the Rosary was running forward, rolling over men as they stood in the attitudes of prayer, the priest saying the swift chant:

Hail Mary, full of grace,
Blessed art thou among women
Blessed is the fruit . . .

Summer and winter and Anne, they were running down the channel of the year. The year spread widely then, as if it flowed abroad to fill a wide field with corn. There was sweetness in the high blades of the corn and abundance in the full shucks as he tore each ear from the ripe stem.

"What price will it bring?" Anne was asking. She was standing beside the shock, her basket filled with corn for the turkeys. The half-green corn was hard to break from the ear, and her hands were burnt and sore from the tough husks. "What price will corn bring?" she was asking.

Felix named three other girls quickly, calling three names in his memory while Anne stood beside the shock to ask of the corn. There was a newer prettiness in her laugh and a fresh way of being a woman in her bent cheek when she smiled. He told the value of the corn and the measure of it in bushels to the acre. The four-ply measure of a woman's loveliness passed then down the rows of the cut field and went toward the pen where the turkeys were kept in autumn, and Felix smiled inwardly as he bent to tear apart the shock to get the inner ears. His thought floated on his floating breath where it came and went in his chest, where it beat a rhythm of nothingness against his throat. The picture of the autumn corn faded and the dry odors of the blades of fodder gave way before the crying of frogs in the wet of the grass, but these fell away with the pattering death cries of supplicating men and the greater voice boomed and droned the new creation:

> Hail Mary, full of grace,
> Blessed art thou among women . . .

The thunder broke on the word and the rattle of voices rushed from the sons of men who burst again into being. The first cries of the priest leaped over his thought of Anne and the three girls he had named. He saw Anne playing with the dog in the yard, saw her running after a chicken to drive it into a coop, saw her making herself a dress to wear to the convent school. She was talking to Dominic Brady beside the gate. She was gone from home, she was remembered clearly, remembered, vaguely, forgotten, remembered, she was here, gone, everywhere present. She was saying that she would take the vows, standing beside the door to say this, making a departure to fit her words. A creation had been destroyed; it was falling away now into a clatter of weary death in the hurried leavings of old sayings that dropped from the mouths of weary men. But the priest had opened the earth anew and brought out a new dark vigor of life. There were remembered ways of girls in his leaping words of creation. They were soft to touch, they were given to laughter, easy to come to tears, easy with pity, easy with anger. They easily became women. His thought waked again from its repose on his folded hands. The chant of the Rosary was suddenly finished. The people seated themselves with a broken patter of infinite whispers made by shifting bodies and the ending postures of prayer.

The organ in the loft at the rear of the chapel began to play the Mendelssohn wedding march. It was played, not passionately, as in a human wedding, but softly, legato,[3] as if it were played in a dream. Then Felix knew that the persons of the procession were coming, that they were walking into the chapel. Their coming was like the coming of the doves, was a soft moving of wings. Looking backward quickly he saw that two nuns walked before carrying lighted tapers. The four postulants[4] came then in the procession, walking two and two, and behind them came two novices carrying tapers. The lights from the candles fell on the faces of the women who carried them and lit up the inner surfaces of their white cowls and made more beautiful the life in their cheeks and their brows. The postulants were dressed as brides, each

3. Italian musical term meaning "smoothly."

4. Individuals seeking membership in a religious order or fraternity.

one wearing a white dress and a long white veil that was fastened with a wreath about the hair. They walked, two together, their hands folded as suppliants. A dark-haired girl and a full-breasted girl walked first. Then Anne and her companion, who was a tall slender girl, came. All stepped slowly, their little white shoes making no noise on the smooth boards of the aisle floor.

When their shadows passed him Felix glanced toward Lester, his brother, to see how this passing had touched him. The boy was sitting very still, his hands steady, his thought as if it slept on his folded hands. Their sister, Piety, was married. She had been married out of their home for a number of years and she seemed, therefore, as some one who was related to them, not as one of them. She seemed to be kinsfolk. Felix looked at her intently to see what surrounded her now in this strange moment while Anne mounted the aisle and went toward the altar steps. Three children drifted in the air about Piety, one of them dead now, all hers. She was watching Anne mount the steps in a happy rapture, looking out from behind the fog of the children.

Anne was very small as she stood beside the tall girl whose wreath fitted with a fine grace over her brown hair. The girls were kneeling at the altar now, bowing over their supplicating hands, and as they bowed the tall girl's rounded cheek showed beyond the line of her shoulder. The priest before the altar had a care never to turn his back upon the holies there, but if he had need to cross from one side to the other he turned about and faced whatever was there housed. While he talked of the solemnity of the hour and the sacredness of the rites enacted, his words flattened to a stillness and Felix watched Anne and the girl who wore the wreath with singular grace. She sat or knelt beside Anne, and the two together made a loveliness that surrounded their being and gave a softly shed presence that reached his senses even when he looked away from them, which came home to him with a new pleasure and satisfaction when he returned his look to the place where they waited.

The choir above began to chant a thin hymn to God, a faint, high-pitched, unsonorous singing of nuns and girls, making beautiful Latin vows over the seated multitude. The hour delayed and fell drowsily apart. Felix knew, in the interval that grew into the severed hour, what manner of smile would come to the tall girl's face and how her thin lips would part to speak and how her head would bow over prayers or work. He knew how her eyes would follow printed words over a page or how she would walk out into the sunlight and what her tall lithe flesh would be as it passed over a farm, as it went within doors. He wondered what name he should call her by in his mind and a vapor of fine names poured over his thought. He loved his sister Anne entirely then and was pleased that she knelt near the tall lovely girl whom he named now with these remote pleasures. These two, dressed as brides, in their white lace and thin veils, knelt together a little apart from the other two brides who knelt at the right of the altar, and in his thought he once slipped quietly between the two, Anne and the named one whom he could not name, and took each by the arm to cherish both forever, but this vague wish died slowly in the mind as if some inner hand forbade it, but his eyes clung then to the bent head of the tall girl and saw again the pink of her cheek and the line of her shoulder.

The priest was giving the brides then the garments they were to wear, piece by piece. The tunic was laid first on their outstretched hands. It was folded neatly together and was made of some soft white wool cloth, and the priest called it by its symbolic name, naming it with a speech. When he had given the tunic he turned to the table at his left where other garments were folded. The tall girl took her garments onto her extended hands with an exquisite care. Felix dwelt rather with her bowed head, her faintly tinted cheek, with the fall of her veil and the droop of her wreath, with the line of her throat beneath her veil and the round curve of her shoulder. The priest gave them the girdle or cincture, placing each coiled in a ring upon the folds of the tunic as each girl held it on her flattened hands, and he named its significance with solemn words. The pile of things on the table beside the altar was diminishing and the ceremony rolled along, the hour severed now and lost out of its nearness, touching Felix as a ceremony that went from him remotely as did recurring prayers, while he longed to know the girl's exact name and to be able to say it in his mind, to name his sense of her loveliness with a word.

The priest was giving the scapular,[5] the most essential part of the habit, he said, the gift of the Virgin. All the last burdens were laid now, one by one, upon the outstretched palms of the girls, for he had given the veil, symbol he said of modesty.

"It will cover you," he said.

It would be the symbol of their poverty, chastity, and obedience. The wedding march was played again and the girls came from the altar, led by the two novices with the lighted tapers. Each girl carried her precious burdens on her outstretched palms, as she had taken them, and each looked forward, seeing neither the right nor the left, as she passed. Their small steps were set down softly on the bars of the faintly played march and they went out of the chapel into some hidden part of the convent.

The choir chanted again, another high thin hymn, the singing of girls, and Felix heard girls laughing through the thin outcry of the chant, heard remembered laughter blowing in a wind through the settled bars of the incantation. He heard Anne running down the yard at their farm to drive a hen away from the little turkeys while they had their food under the lilac bush, and he heard her shout in the wind and heard her laugh when the old hen flew wildly over a fence to escape her clamor. Again he wanted the name of the tall fair girl and he felt the touch of soft light hands at his brow and at his throat, the hands of the tall girl fluttering over his face and touching his shoulder, and he felt himself open as if to give out some fine inner essence of himself. He lived upon the laughter that flowed under the hymn and lived swiftly as haunted by an unrealized disaster that threatened to arise from some hidden part and bring the whole earth to a swift consummation. Opened to give all that he had in the brief moments left to life, he thought more minutely of the fair girl's graceful splendors of being and he knew entirely what her laughter would be, longing then for her name, for some word that would signify herself and name his own delight in her.

The steps came back to the tread of the hymn which the voices in the loft had rounded to an amen. The girls wore now the long white robes of young nuns and on their heads were the stiff veils of the women of the holy order. As they passed, Felix looked up into their faces and saw them, recognizing each one with a pleasure in the recognition. The tall girl wore her linen veil as he knew she would and carried her scapular with her own grace, as if she loaned her grace temporarily to it. The priest met them in the sanctuary and again they were kneeling. The priest was giving them their last gifts. He was giving them their rosaries, the long pattern by which, as nuns, they would pray. Then he was giving them their names.

5. According to the *Oxford English Dictionary*: "A short cloak covering the shoulders; . . . adopted by certain religious orders as a part of their ordinary costume."

Felix felt a leaping within his heart to know that he would now hear the name of the lovely girl called and would know it thereafter. The priest was speaking, the large girl at the right of the altar knelt before him:

"You were known in the world as Annette Stevenson."

There was a pause, and Felix flung far across the country to a house on Severn Creek, the home of the Stevensons. His mind was leaping swiftly with recognition and expectations. But the priest was speaking again, taking back all that he had given:

"Your name henceforth will be Sister Mary Agnes."

He had turned from the large girl now to her companion and what passed there went over in a dull dream, a name given and taken away. The priest now turned his back to the congregation and passed the holies, going toward the left of the altar, toward the two small figures that knelt there. A pleasure leaped up within Felix to know that he would now know the name of the lovely girl and he leaped forward in mind to take the name, his thought already caressing it.

The voice leaned above the slender figure that knelt next and said:

"In the world you were known as Aurelia Bannon . . ."

Aurelia, then. He had it. A dim sense of consummation and satisfaction played over him. He stirred in his place and shifted his hands, gratified. Aurelia was the name. He might have known, he reflected, that this lovely creature would carry such a name. It filled his entire mind and flowed over into his sense of all that he had seen of her. But the priest was speaking, continuing, making solemn words over the leaning girl, and Felix caught again at what he had said and held it to try to stay what would follow, but this was useless. The voice moved forward, having spoken the first pronouncement:

"You were known in the world as Aurelia Bannon . . .

"Henceforth your name will be Sister Mary Dolores."

The world broke and disaster followed. The ashes of a burnt-out creation rattled and pattered down endless cliffs of shales and Felix was aware of the rasping breath in his throat, was aware of Anne, of the last of the kneeling postulants, the smallest figure. She knelt bowed, as if to take the pronouncement on her bent shoulders. The priest had soon finished. He moved slightly and settled over the small kneeler, saying softly, as if he were already done:

"In the world you were known as *Anne Barbour* . . .

"Henceforth your name will be Sister Magdalen."

QUESTIONS TO CONSIDER

1. Why does Roberts title this story "Sacrifice of the Maidens"? What is sacrificed in this story?
2. The framework of "Sacrifice of the Maidens" is based on the induction of novices into a Catholic religious order. Would the sacrifice(s) implicit in this story's title remain the same if the characters were not Catholic? Is the sacrifice merely based on the Catholic tradition of allowing women to become cloistered nuns?

Anne Spencer

1882–1975

Although Anne Spencer is recognized today as an important poet of the Harlem Renaissance, fewer than 30 of her poems were published during her lifetime.

Annie Bethel Bannister was born in Henry County, Virginia, on 6 February 1882. Her parents separated when she was 5 years old, and she moved to Bramwell, Virginia, with her mother. While her mother worked as a cook, Spencer was placed into foster care with a prominent family who encouraged the development of her intellectual and creative abilities. Going by her mother's family name of "Scales," Spencer went on to graduate as valedictorian of the Virginia Seminary, an African-American academy in nearby Lynchburg. She married a fellow graduate named Edward Spencer who became a postal worker in Lynchburg, and the couple had three children.

Spencer's lifestyle enabled her to concentrate on writing poetry and on gardening, a frequent subject of her writings. Her poetry first gained the attention of another Southern writer, James Weldon Johnson, after he came to Lynchburg in 1917 to establish a local chapter of the NAACP. Johnson informed essayist H. L. Mencken of Spencer's talent, leading to the publication of approximately twenty of her poems during the 1920s. The Spencer house became a gathering place for contemporary African-American artists and social leaders such as Johnson, Sterling Brown, George Washington Carver, W. E. B. DuBois, Langston Hughes, Georgia Douglas Johnson, Claude McKay, Adam Clayton Powell, and Paul Robeson. Despite her high social standing, Spencer took action to help African Americans less fortunate than herself. Through her civic connections she fought for African-American teachers' rights, and as a school librarian she promoted literacy among African-American students. She also refused to use segregated public transportation.

Many of Spencer's poems employ biblical and mythical themes in combination with images of her beloved garden; others address the oppression of women. Another theme that runs throughout her work is the desire for immortality and beauty in the midst of death and decay, ideas poignantly represented in "At the Carnival." Criticized by contemporaries for not addressing racial issues more directly in her writing, Spencer answered that she preferred to respond to issues from a human, rather than an African-American, perspective. Yet, as poems such as "White Things" demonstrate, Spencer did confront racial issues. In fact, because of the confrontational tone of "White Things," Spencer's editors requested that she revise it upon its publication in 1923. She flatly refused, and the poem was never published again in her lifetime.

Following the death of her husband in 1964, Spencer withdrew from the public spotlight. Her own health began to fail, and she moved in and out of hospitals. She continued to write, however, scribbling on scraps of paper as she had done all her life. Scholars believed for nearly three decades after Spencer's death in 1975 that the bulk of her poetic output had been mistaken for trash and discarded during her last hospitalization; only 50 poems were known to have survived. However, several boxes of poems and papers have recently surfaced in the possession of one of Spencer's surviving relatives. Scholars and poets are now awaiting their compilation and publication.

At the Carnival

Gay little Girl-of-the-Diving-Tank,[1]
I desire a name for you,
Nice, as a right glove fits;
For you—who amid the malodorous
Mechanics of this unlovely thing
Are darling of spirit and form.
I know you—a glance, and what you are
Sits-by-the-fire in my heart.
My Limousine-Lady[2] knows you, or
Why does the slant-envy of her eye mark
Your straight air and radiant inclusive smile?
Guilt pins a fig-leaf; Innocence is its own adorning.
The bull-necked man knows you—this first time
His itching flesh sees form divine and vibrant health,
And thinks not of his avocation.
I came incuriously—
Set on no diversion save that my mind
Might safely nurse its brood of misdeeds
In the presence of a blind crowd.
The color of life was gray.
Everywhere the setting seemed right
For my mood!
Here the sausage and garlic booth
Sent unholy incense skyward;
There a quivering female-thing
Gestured assignations, and lied
To call it dancing;
There, too, were games of chance
With chances for none;
But oh! the Girl-of-the-Tank, at last!
Gleaming Girl, how intimately pure and free
The gaze you send the crowd,
As though you know the dearth of beauty
In its sordid life.
We need you—my Limousine-Lady,
The bull-necked man, and I.
Seeing you here brave and water-clean,
Leaven for the heavy ones of earth,
I am swift to feel that what makes
The plodder glad is good; and
Whatever is good is God.
The wonder is that you are here;
I have seen the queer in queer places,
But never before a heaven-fed

1. In the early twentieth century, a carnival might feature a stunt artist diving from a high platform into a small tank of water.

2. Literally, the woman driving the speaker's limousine; but also the name of a daylily (and Spencer was a veteran gardener).

Naiad[3] of the Carnival-Tank!
Little Diver, Destiny for you,
Like as for me, is shod in silence;
Years may seep into your soul
The bacilli of the usual and the expedient;
I implore Neptune[4] to claim his child to-day!

I Have a Friend

I have a friend
And my heart from hence
Is closed to friendship,
Nor the gods' knees hold but one;
He watches with me thru the long night,
And when I call he comes,
Or when he calls I am there;
He does not ask me how beloved
Are my husband and children,
Nor ever do I require
Details of life and love
In the grave—his home,—
We are such friends.

Innocence

She tripped and fell against a star,
A lady we all have known;
Just what the villagers lusted for
To claim her one of their own;
Fallen but once the lower felt she,
So turned her face and died,—
With never a hounding fool to see
'Twas a star-lance in her side!

Dunbar[1]

Ah, how poets sing and die!
Make one song and Heaven takes it;
Have one heart and Beauty breaks it;
Chatterton, Shelley, Keats[2] and I—
Ah, how poets sing and die!

3. A water nymph (young and beautiful female supernatural creature) from classical mythology.
4. The Roman god of the sea.
1. Paul Laurence Dunbar (1872–1906), the son of former slaves from Kentucky, became a famous African-American dialect poet, but the effects of alcoholism and tuberculosis caused his early death.
2. Thomas Chatterton (1752–1770), Percy Bysshe Shelley (1792–1822), and John Keats (1795–1821) were all English poets who died young: Chatterton by suicide, Shelley by drowning, and Keats of tuberculosis.

White Things

Most things are colorful things—the sky, earth, and sea.
Black men are most men; but the white are free!
White things are rare things; so rare, so rare
They stole from out a silvered world—somewhere.
Finding earth-plains fair plains, save greenly grassed,
They strewed white feathers of cowardice, as they passed;
The golden stars with lances fine
The hills all red and darkened pine,
They blanched with their wand of power;
And turned the blood in a ruby rose
To a poor white poppy-flower.
They pyred a race of black, black men,
And burned them to ashes white; then,
Laughing, a young one claimed a skull,
For the skull of a black is white, not dull,
But a glistening awful thing;
Made, it seems, for this ghoul to swing
In the face of God with all his might,
And swear by the hell that sired him:
"Man-maker, make white!"

Letter to My Sister

It is dangerous for a woman to defy the gods;
To taunt them with the tongue's thin tip,
Or strut in the weakness of mere humanity,
Or draw a line daring them to cross;
The gods own the searing lightning,
The drowning waters, tormenting fears
And anger of red sins.

Oh, but worse still if you mince timidly—
Dodge this way or that, or kneel or pray,
Be kind, or sweat agony drops
Or lay your quick body over your feeble young;
If you have beauty or none, if celibate
Or vowed—the gods are Juggernaut,[1]
Passing over . . . over . . .

This you may do:
Lock your heart, then, quietly,
And lest they peer within,
Light no lamp when dark comes down
Raise no shade for sun;
Breathless must your breath come through
If you'd die and dare deny
The gods their god-like fun.

1. A large chariot pulled as part of a Hindu religious ceremony, which can crush people who get in its way.

Questions to Consider

1. Why do you think Spencer speaks of the "gods" as plural in "Letter to My Sister"?
2. What typical connotations or symbolic associations of the colors "black" and "white" are you used to seeing in literature? How does Spencer reverse or transform those usual associations in her poem "White Things"?

Katherine Anne Porter

1890–1980

Although Katherine Anne Porter concealed her rustic origins in the Lone Star State, she is perhaps Texas's most celebrated author. When fame came to her as a writer, at times she claimed to be from Louisiana plantation gentry and to have been educated at a Roman Catholic boarding school in New Orleans. At others, she cited San Antonio as her hometown and described a fantasy childhood of social prestige, fine houses and books, and class privilege. Always insecure about her rural background and lack of formal education, Porter embellished her early years to claim for herself the aristocratic status of Southern belle. These inventions disguised her hardscrabble Texas experience, which was not fully known until the publication of Joan Givner's biography after Porter's death at age 90.

Born 15 May 1890, at Indian Creek, Porter grew up poor in Kyle, in Texas cotton country. Her father, a widower and Methodist Sunday School superintendent, moved often, taking his four children with him to many towns throughout both Texas and Louisiana. Callie Porter, as she was named at birth, had slaveowning ancestors from Kentucky. Her paternal grandparents had migrated to Texas before the Civil War but over the decades had fallen on hard times. After her mother's death, when Callie was nearly two, she and her three siblings were reared mainly by their father's mother, the model for Sophia Jane Rhea in stories such as "The Old Order." Katherine, the name she adopted as an adult, ran away to Chicago to escape the restrictions of Southern society. In 1916, she fell seriously ill with tuberculosis but recovered and moved to Denver to work as a reporter, where she almost died during the influenza epidemic of 1918. She again recovered and moved to New York City, where she continued doing journalistic work, including an assignment in 1920 to Mexico. She became enmeshed in the political intrigues of the Mexican Revolution, experiences that formed the basis for early great stories like "Flowering Judas" (1930). The enlarged edition, *Flowering Judas and Other Stories* (1935), established her reputation as a literary stylist of the first rank.

During these years Porter, a beautiful and enchanting woman, moved from lover to lover, apparently seeking a stability that always eluded her. Brief affairs, and sometimes briefer marriages (five in all), alternately consumed and repulsed her. One result of her frequent romantic entanglements was long periods of writer's block. Depression, drinking bouts, and financial strains made matters worse. In all Porter published one novel, *Ship of Fools* (1962), and 27 stories and novellas. After 1941, she published only works begun previously in her career. Despite her ambivalence toward her native region, Porter returned to Texas and Louisiana in much of her finest fiction. Her best work is lightly plotted, based on personal experiences, much of it gathered from her early years. Porter was a careful craftsman, renowned for her spare, hard-edged style. She became known as a "writer's writer," who appealed to small but discerning audience of readers and critics.

One of the most fortuitous events of Porter's life was making friends with Allen Tate and Caroline Gordon in New York City in 1927 and through them with other members of the

Fugitive circle. Under their influence, Porter came to reaffirm her Texas roots, which earlier she had rejected. Through her association with key figures in the Agrarian movement, Porter came to view her Southern background more positively and to turn to it as a source for fiction—although with much genteel invention. As the New Criticism emerged from agrarianism during the thirties to become an influential literary theory, Porter continued to benefit from the friendship and editorial support of Allen Tate, Robert Penn Warren, and Cleanth Brooks. These leading New Critics celebrated the literary values of form, style, and concentrated meaning—all hallmarks of Porter's taut, lean stories.

Her conservative Agrarian friends also drew Porter away from radical politics, which she had supported in Mexico and Greenwich Village. Her first story to be set in the South, "He," had been published in 1927 in the *New Masses*, an outspoken New York leftist monthly. But consistent with the credo of New Criticism, by the late 1930s Porter had abandoned her pro-Left sympathies and adopted the position that the true artist must rise above ideological loyalties. Porter also became more elitist in temperament, combining the roles of Southern belle and celebrity author. Fellowships and grants often supported her travels abroad, which included stays in Germany, Switzerland, Italy, France, and Belgium. She struggled for decades to complete *Ship of Fools*, based on a 1931 voyage she took from Mexico to Germany. When it at last appeared more than 30 years later, it soared to best-seller status. A suffragist in her youth, in old age Porter spurned women's and other liberal causes, although her novella "Old Mortality" (1937), written during her most productive decade, contains a strong element of feminist protest. She died on 18 September 1980, two years after suffering a debilitating stroke.

Porter said that her own favorite among her stories was "The Grave" (1934), which like many of her finest works ("Pale Horse, Pale Rider" and "The Jilting of Granny Weatherall") deals with death. One of her "Miranda" stories, "The Grave" features her most autobiographical character, who appears in various texts from early childhood to young womanhood. In this story, Miranda is nine and soon to shed her tomboy identity for a new sense of sexual self-awareness. Miranda's unsettling sight of the dead female rabbit and her fetal young becomes a powerful repressed memory, to be awakened years later by the sight of candy animals in a foreign marketplace. The sudden linking of death and female sexuality strikes horror in the adult Miranda years after the original childhood experience.

from The Old Order

The Grave

The grandfather, dead for more than thirty years, had been twice disturbed in his long repose by the constancy and possessiveness of his widow. She removed his bones first to Louisiana and then to Texas as if she had set out to find her own burial place, knowing well she would never return to the places she had left. In Texas she set up a small cemetery in a corner of her first farm, and as the family connection grew, and oddments of relations came over from Kentucky to settle, it contained at last about twenty graves. After the grandmother's death, part of her land was to be sold for the benefit of certain of her children, and the cemetery happened to lie in the part set aside for sale. It was necessary to take up the bodies and bury them again in the family plot in the big new public cemetery, where the grandmother had been buried. At last her husband was to lie beside her for eternity, as she had planned.

The family cemetery had been a pleasant small neglected garden of tangled rose bushes and ragged cedar trees and cypress, the simple flat stones rising out of uncropped sweet-smelling wild grass. The graves were lying open and empty one burning day when Miranda and her brother Paul, who often went together to hunt rabbits and doves, propped their twenty-two Winchester rifles carefully against the rail fence, climbed over and explored among the graves. She was nine years old and he was twelve.

They peered into the pits all shaped alike with such purposeful accuracy, and looking at each other with pleased adventurous eyes, they said in solemn tones: "These were graves!" trying by words to shape a special, suitable emotion in their minds, but they felt nothing except an agreeable thrill of wonder: they were seeing a new sight, doing something they had not done before. In them both there was also a small disappointment at the entire commonplaceness of the actual spectacle. Even if it had once contained a coffin for years upon years, when the coffin was gone a grave was just a hole in the ground. Miranda leaped into the pit that had held her grandfather's bones. Scratching around aimlessly and pleasurably as any young animal, she scooped up a lump of earth and weighed it in her palm. It had a pleasantly sweet, corrupt smell, being mixed with cedar needles and small leaves, and as the crumbs fell apart, she saw a silver dove no larger than a hazel nut, with spread wings and a neat fan-shaped tail. The breast had a deep round hollow in it. Turning it up to the fierce sunlight, she saw that the inside of the hollow was cut in little whorls. She scrambled out, over the pile of loose earth that had fallen back into one end of the grave, calling to Paul that she had found something, he must guess what . . . . His head appeared smiling over the rim of another grave. He waved a closed hand at her. "I've got something too!" They ran to compare treasures, making a game of it, so many guesses each, all wrong, and a final showdown with opened palms. Paul had found a thin wide gold ring carved with intricate flowers and leaves. Miranda was smitten at sight of the ring and wished to have it. Paul seemed more impressed by the dove. They made a trade, with some little bickering. After he had got the dove in his hand, Paul said, "Don't you know what this is? This is a screw head for a *coffin!* . . . . I'll bet nobody else in the world has one like this!"

Miranda glanced at it without covetousness. She had the gold ring on her thumb; it fitted perfectly. "Maybe we ought to go now," she said, "maybe one of the niggers 'll see us and tell somebody." They knew the land had been sold, the cemetery was no longer theirs, and they felt like trespassers. They climbed back over the fence, slung their rifles loosely under their arms—they had been shooting at targets with various kinds of firearms since they were seven years old—and set out to look for the rabbits and doves or whatever small game might happen along. On these expeditions Miranda always followed at Paul's heels along the path, obeying instructions about handling her gun when going through fences; learning how to stand it up properly so it would not slip and fire unexpectedly; how to wait her time for a shot and not just bang away in the air without looking, spoiling shots for Paul, who really could hit things if given a chance. Now and then, in her excitement at seeing birds whizz up suddenly before her face, or a rabbit leap across her very toes, she lost her head, and almost without sighting she flung her rifle up and pulled the trigger. She hardly ever hit any sort of mark. She had no proper sense of hunting at all. Her brother would be often completely disgusted with her. "You don't care whether you get your bird or not," he said. "That's no way to hunt." Miranda could not understand his indignation. She had seen him smash his hat and yell with fury when he had missed his aim. "What I like about shooting," said Miranda, with exasperating inconsequence, "is pulling the trigger and hearing the noise."

"Then, by golly," said Paul, "whyn't you go back to the range and shoot at bullseyes?"

"I'd just as soon," said Miranda, "only like this, we walk around more."

"Well, you just stay behind and stop spoiling my shots," said Paul, who, when he made a kill, wanted to be certain he had made it. Miranda, who alone brought down a bird once in twenty rounds, always claimed as her own any game they got when they fired at the same moment. It was tiresome and unfair and her brother was sick of it.

"Now, the first dove we see, or the first rabbit, is mine," he told her. "And the next will be yours. Remember that and don't get smarty."

"What about snakes?" asked Miranda idly. "Can I have the first snake?"

Waving her thumb gently and watching her gold ring glitter, Miranda lost interest in shooting. She was wearing her summer roughing outfit: dark blue overalls, a light blue shirt, a hired-man's straw hat, and thick brown sandals. Her brother had the same outfit except his was a sober hickory-nut color. Ordinarily Miranda preferred her overalls to any other dress, though it was making rather a scandal in the countryside, for the year was 1903, and in the back country the law of female decorum had teeth in it. Her father had been criticized for letting his girls dress like boys and go careering around astride barebacked horses. Big sister Maria, the really independent and fearless one, in spite of her rather affected ways, rode at a dead run with only a rope knotted around her horse's nose. It was said the motherless family was running down, with the Grandmother no longer there to hold it together. It was known that she had discriminated against her son Harry in her will, and that he was in straits about money. Some of his old neighbors reflected with vicious satisfaction that now he would probably not be so stiffnecked, nor have any more high-stepping horses either. Miranda knew this, though she could not say how. She had met along the road old women of the kind who smoked corn-cob pipes, who had treated her grandmother with most sincere respect. They slanted their gummy old eyes side-ways at the granddaughter and said, "Ain't you ashamed of yoself, Missy? It's aginst the Scriptures to dress like that. Whut yo Pappy thinkin about?" Miranda, with her powerful social sense, which was like a fine set of antennae radiating from every pore of her skin, would feel ashamed because she knew well it was rude and ill-bred to shock anybody, even bad-tempered old crones, though she had faith in her father's judgment and was perfectly comfortable in the clothes. Her father had said, "They're just what you need, and they'll save your dresses for school. . . ." This sounded quite simple and natural to her. She had been brought up in rigorous economy. Wastefulness was vulgar. It was also a sin. These were truths; she had heard them repeated many times and never once disputed.

Now the ring, shining with the serene purity of fine gold on her rather grubby thumb, turned her feelings against her overalls and sockless feet, toes sticking through the thick brown leather straps. She wanted to go back to the farmhouse, take a good cold bath, dust herself with plenty of Maria's violet talcum powder—provided Maria was not present to object, of course—put on the thinnest, most becoming dress she owned, with a big sash, and sit in a wicker chair under the trees . . . These things were not all she wanted, of course; she had vague stirrings of desire for luxury and a grand way of living which could not take precise form in her imagination but were founded on family legend of past wealth and leisure. These immediate comforts were what she could have, and she wanted them at once. She lagged rather far behind Paul, and once she thought of just turning back without a word and going home. She stopped, thinking that Paul would never do that to her, and so she would have to tell him. When a rabbit leaped, she let Paul have it without dispute. He killed it with one shot.

When she came up with him, he was already kneeling, examining the wound, the rabbit trailing from his hands. "Right through the head," he said complacently, as if he had aimed for it. He took out his sharp, competent bowie[1] knife and started to skin the body. He did it very cleanly and quickly. Uncle Jimbilly knew how to prepare the skins so that Miranda always had fur coats for her dolls, for though she never cared much for her dolls she liked seeing them in fur coats. The children knelt facing each other over the dead animal. Miranda watched admiringly while her brother stripped the skin away as if he were taking off a glove. The flayed flesh emerged dark scarlet, sleek, firm; Miranda with thumb and finger felt the long fine muscles with the silvery flat strips binding them to the joints. Brother lifted the oddly bloated belly. "Look," he said, in a low amazed voice. "It was going to have young ones."

Very carefully he slit the thin flesh from the center ribs to the flanks, and a scarlet bag appeared. He slit again and pulled the bag open, and there lay a bundle of tiny rabbits, each wrapped in a thin scarlet veil. The brother pulled these off and there they were, dark gray, their sleek wet down lying in minute even ripples, like a baby's head just washed, their unbelievably small delicate ears folded close, their little blind faces almost featureless.

Miranda said, "Oh, I want to *see*," under her breath. She looked and looked—excited but not frightened, for she was accustomed to the sight of animals killed in hunting—filled with pity and astonishment and a kind of shocked delight in the wonderful little creatures for their own sakes, they were so pretty. She touched one of them ever so carefully, "Ah, there's blood running over them," she said and began to tremble without knowing why. Yet she wanted most deeply to see and to know. Having seen, she felt at once as if she had known all along. The very memory of her former ignorance faded, she had always known just this. No one had ever told her anything outright, she had been rather unobservant of the animal life around her because she was so accustomed to animals. They seemed simply disorderly and unaccountably rude in their habits, but altogether natural and not very interesting. Her brother had spoken as if he had known about everything all along. He may have seen all this before. He had never said a word to her, but she knew now a part at least of what he knew. She understood a little of the secret, formless intuitions in her own mind and body, which had been clearing up, taking form, so gradually and so steadily she had not realized that she was learning what she had to know. Paul said cautiously, as if he were talking about something forbidden: "They were just about ready to be born." His voice dropped on the last word. "I know," said Miranda, "like kittens. I know, like babies." She was quietly and terribly agitated, standing again with her rifle under her arm, looking down at the bloody heap. "I don't want the skin," she said, "I won't have it." Paul buried the young rabbits again in their mother's body, wrapped the skin around her, carried her to a clump of sage bushes, and hid her away. He came out again at once and said to Miranda, with an eager friendliness, a confidential tone quite unusual in him, as if he were taking her into an important secret on equal terms: "Listen now. Now you listen to me, and don't ever forget. Don't you ever tell a living soul that you saw this. Don't tell a soul. Don't tell Dad because I'll get into trouble. He'll say I'm leading you into things you ought not to do. He's always saying that. So now don't you go and forget and blab out sometime the way you're always doing . . . Now, that's a secret. Don't you tell."

1. Jim Bowie (1796–1836) died when the Alamo, an abandoned mission in San Antonio, Texas, was overrun by the Mexican army during the Texas war of independence. He was famous for his single-edged knife, a foot long and more than an inch wide.

Miranda never told, she did not even wish to tell anybody. She thought about the whole worrisome affair with confused unhappiness for a few days. Then it sank quietly into her mind and was heaped over by accumulated thousands of impressions, for nearly twenty years. One day she was picking her path among the puddles and crushed refuse of a market street in a strange city of a strange country,[2] when without warning, plain and clear in its true colors as if she looked through a frame upon a scene that had not stirred nor changed since the moment it happened, the episode of that far-off day leaped from its burial place before her mind's eye. She was so reasonlessly horrified she halted suddenly staring, the scene before her eyes dimmed by the vision back of them. An Indian vendor had held up before her a tray of dyed sugar sweets, in the shapes of all kinds of small creatures: birds, baby chicks, baby rabbits, lambs, baby pigs. They were in gay colors and smelled of vanilla, maybe. . . . It was a very hot day and the smell in the market, with its piles of raw flesh and wilting flowers, was like the mingled sweetness and corruption she had smelled that other day in the empty cemetery at home: the day she had remembered always until now vaguely as the time she and her brother had found treasure in the opened graves. Instantly upon this thought the dreadful vision faded, and she saw clearly her brother, whose childhood face she had forgotten, standing again in the blazing sunshine, again twelve years old, a pleased sober smile in his eyes, turning the silver dove over and over in his hands.

Questions to Consider

1. When the story opens, Miranda is dressed in overalls and carrying a rifle as she and her older brother go hunting. After they jump into the open graves, the children find and exchange treasures. When Miranda puts on the wedding band, she experiences an abrupt identity change and envisions an entirely new future for herself. What does this sudden vision tell us about Miranda's newly gendered expectations?
2. One adventure gives way to another in the second half of the story, when her brother shoots a rabbit. He draws a hunting knife and slashes the female carcass. On previous hunting trips Miranda had not minded the sight of dead creatures. Now she is repelled and does not want the rabbit's fur to make doll clothes. How does her strong reaction seem linked to her changing self-concept in the first half of the story?

Zora Neale Hurston

1903–1960

"I am not tragically colored. There is no great sorrow damned up in my soul . . . I do not belong to that sobbing school of Negrohood who hold that nature somehow has given them a lowdown dirty deal," proclaimed Zora Neale Hurston in her autobiographical essay, "How It Feels to be Colored Me." Unlike her more radical peers of the Harlem Renaissance, many of whom shared her Southern heritage, Hurston made no secret of her lack of interest in producing the type of protest literature favored by more politically active writers such as Richard Wright. As a trained anthropologist, she spent much of her adult life conducting field work, preserving folk stories and tales from her native African-American community which would have been lost absent her diligent research. Hurston's anthropological work also demonstrates her dedication to celebrating the value

2. The foreign country apparently is Mexico.

of the African-American cultures of the South. Rather than endorsing the ideology of her urban Black contemporaries who argued, often stridently, for complete equality and integration among races and who harshly criticized her for what Sterling Brown called her "evasion of political concerns," Hurston celebrated the value of a uniquely African-American culture, a culture that she feared would be compromised or lost altogether if the races became more fully merged.

While Hurston certainly supported equality among the races, she also strongly believed in what Craig Werner has called "the cultural self-sufficiency of the African-American community," seeing no benefit in "integration into a morally and aesthetically impoverished White middle-class society." Never one to meekly acquiesce to the demands of others, Zora Neale Hurston was an intellectual giant who answered only to herself, and as a result of her political stance, she was frequently at odds with the leaders of the Harlem Renaissance. In many ways, Hurston is, as Werner has pointed out, the literary grandmother of African-American women writers, or, as Alice Walker had engraved on Hurston's headstone, erected some 13 years after the artist's death and interment in an unmarked grave: "A Genius of the South—Novelist, Folklorist, Anthropologist."

Born on 7 January 1903, in Macon County, Alabama, Hurston moved with her family to Eatonville, Florida at an early age. Her father, Reverend John Hurston, rapidly became influential in the community, where he remained following the death of his wife, Lucy Potts Hurston, in 1904. In part because the town was the first incorporated African-American town in the United States, which helped to shield the young Hurston from the virulent racism so common in the Jim Crow South, she grew up with a strong identity that did not arise from her ethnic heritage. In fact, she did not become aware that her color was different from others—or that her color mattered in terms of her perceived value as a person—until she left Eatonville to attend school in Jacksonville. Her departure was necessitated by the remarriage of her father, whose new wife was openly hostile to the child of his prior marriage. In later years, Hurston wrote that she departed Eatonville "as Zora," but by the time she arrived in Jacksonville, she had realized that she "was not Zora of Orange County any more, I was now a little colored girl. I found it out in certain ways. In my heart as well as in the mirror, I became a fast brown—warranted not to rub nor run."

After touring for a year with a theatrical group, Hurston completed her high school education in Baltimore, graduating from Morgan Academy and going on to enroll in courses at Howard University in Washington, D.C. During this time, she began seeking outlets for her creative work, entering her short story, "Spunk," and a dramatic piece, *Drenched in Light*, in a contest sponsored by *Opportunity* magazine; both pieces won prizes. She later transferred to Barnard College in New York, where she earned her bachelor's degree. Hurston also attended Columbia University, where she undertook graduate study with the famed anthropologist, Franz Boas, while simultaneously working as a secretary to Fannie Hurst. Hurston continued to write and publish during this time, rapidly emerging as a leading voice of the Harlem Renaissance, and dubbing herself "Queen of the Niggerati."

Studying with Boas charted the course of Hurston's early career by flaming her interest in folklore. Following the completion of her studies, she contributed works to Alain Locke's *New Negro*, which indirectly led to her introduction to Charlotte Osgood Mason, who became Hurston's literary patron. While Mason's financial support enabled Hurston to conduct much of her anthropological work in her native South, Mason demanded substantial control over all of the work Hurston produced, leading to conflicts between the two over Hurston's desire to use her scientific data in creative works. Under Mason's patronage, Hurston reconnected with her Southern culture, which she had largely left behind as she became more firmly entrenched among other writers of the Harlem Renaissance. Her attempts to reenter Southern communities were met with resistance at first, since as an educated African-American woman, she encountered suspicion and distrust among the people she was trying to interview. Hurston later laughed at her early field experiences, saying in her autobiography, *Dust Tracks on a Road*, that while she was "extremely proud that Papa Franz [Boaz] felt like sending me on that folklore search," she very nearly did not collect the data she needed: "I did not have the right approach . . . I dwelt in marble halls. I knew where the material was all right. But, I went about asking, in carefully accented Barnardese, 'Pardon me, but do you know any folk-tales or folk-songs?' The men and women who had whole treasuries of material just seeping through their pores looked at me and shook their heads. No, they had never heard of anything like that around there." Only after approaching her subjects with the appearance and mannerisms of an insider did Hurston begin eliciting the vast body of folk materials that she had grown up with in the South.

Hurston went on to publish six books—four novels, a collection of folklore, and an autobiography—as well as numerous articles and short stories. Her masterpiece, *Their Eyes Were Watching God,* incorporates many of the themes for which she has become famous and which frame her other works. *Their Eyes* focuses on the coming of age of a young woman of mixed racial heritage, illustrating her growth from a dependent young girl who needs looking after, into a self-sufficient, sensual, and fulfilled middle-aged woman, largely in the context of insular African-American communities. Unlike her counterparts in the Harlem Renaissance, Hurston does not focus her narrative on racial politics. While she characterizes incidents of racial prejudices in the novel, the situations that she creates illustrate the prejudice and the hierarchal class structure within the African-American race, rather than that which was exerted on the African-American community from the outside. The only time in *Their Eyes* that the White community is invoked is during Janie's murder trial. Ironically, the White court system sets her free, realizing that the killing was an act of self-defense, despite the general inclination of the African-American community to hold her accountable for Tea Cake's death.

Despite her prolific writing and extensive research, Hurston often found herself in difficult financial straits. Following her inevitable break from Mason's controlling patronage, Hurston took a variety of jobs to support herself, working, at various times, as a teacher, a librarian, a journalist, a manicurist, and a domestic. She continued to write for most of her life, however, until she suffered a stroke in 1959. She passed her final months in a public nursing home and was buried in a grave that remained unmarked prior to Alice Walker's pilgrimage to reclaim it.

Hurston believed in the inherent value and integrity of African-American institutions and traditions, devoting much of her life to their preservation and taking offense at arguments that segregation should be ended, since she felt that African-American institutions could achieve the same levels of quality as their White counterparts. Her literary works celebrate the African-American communities that she sought to preserve, yet present them truthfully, refusing to shy away from the less flattering aspects of those communities such as the social hierarchy based on skin tone. The revival of interest in Hurston and her works begun by Alice Walker effected nothing less than a redefinition of African-American women's writing of the 1930s and 1940s, challenging the prevailing notion that the Harlem Renaissance represented a united voice speaking for the views and interests of all African Americans.

from Mules and Men

Chapter Two

The very next afternoon, as usual, the gregarious part of the town's population gathered on the store porch. All the Florida-flip players, all the eleven-card layers.[1] But they yelled over to me they'd be over that night in full. And they were.

"Zora," George Thomas informed me, "you come to de right place if lies is what you want. Ah'm gointer lie up a nation."

1. Popular card games in Southern African-American communities.

Charlie Jones said, "Yeah, man. Me and my sworn buddy Gene Brazzle is here. Big Moose done come down from de mountain."[2]

"Now, you gointer hear lies above suspicion," Gene added.

It was a hilarious night with a pinch of everything social mixed with the story-telling. Everybody ate ginger bread; some drank the buttermilk provided and some provided coon dick[3] for themselves. Nobody guzzled it—just took it in social sips.

But they told stories enough for a volume by itself. Some of the stories were the familiar drummer-type of tale about two Irishmen, Pat and Mike, or two Jews as the case might be. Some were the European folk-tales undiluted, like Jack and the Beanstalk. Others had slight local variations, but Negro imagination is so facile that there was little need for outside help. A'nt Hagar's son, like Joseph, put on his many-colored coat an paraded before his brethren and every man there was a Joseph.

Steve Nixon was holding class meeting across the way at St. Lawrence Church and we could hear the testimony[4] and the songs. So we began to talk about church and preachers.

"Aw, Ah don't pay all dese ole preachers no rabbit-foot,"[5] said Ellis Jones. "Some of 'em is all right but everybody dats up in de pulpit whoopin' and hollerin' ain't called to preach."

"They ain't no different from nobody else," added B. Moseley. "They mouth is cut cross ways, ain't it? Well, long as you don't see no man wid they mouth cut up and down, you know they'll all lie jus' like de rest of us."

"Yeah; and hard work in de hot sun done called a many a man to preach," said a woman called Gold, for no evident reason. "Ah heard about one man out clearin' off some new ground. De sun was so hot till a grindstone melted and run off in de shade to cool off. De man was so tired till he went and sit down on a log. 'Work, work, work! Everywhere Ah go de boss say hurry, de cap' say run. Ah got a durn good notion not to do nary one. Wisht Ah was one of dese preachers wid a whole lot of folks makin' my support for me.' He looked back over his shoulder and seen a narrer li'l strip of shade along side of de log, so he got over dere and laid down right close up to de log in de shade and said, 'Now, Lawd, if you don't pick me up and chunk me on de other side of dis log, Ah know you done called me to preach.'

"You know God never picked 'im up, so he went off and tol' everybody dat he was called to preach."

"There's many a one been called just lak dat," Ellis corroborated. "Ah knowed a man dat was called by a mule."

"A mule, Ellis? All dem b'lieve dat, stand on they head," said Little Ida.

"Yeah, a mule did call a man to preach. Ah'll show you how it was done, if you'll stand a straightenin'."

"Now, Ellis, don't mislay de truth. Sense us into dis mule-callin' business."

> *Ellis:* These was two brothers and one of 'em was a big preacher and had good collections every Sunday. He didn't pastor nothin' but big charges. De other brother decided he wanted to preach so he went way down in de swamp behind a big plantation to de place they call de prayin' ground, and got down on his knees.
>
> "O Lawd, Ah wants to preach. Ah feel lak Ah got a message. If you done called me to preach, gimme a sign."

2. Slang phrase meaning "big events are on the horizon."
3. Moonshine or other inexpensive liquor.
4. In some fundamentalist churches, individuals will testify to share their experiences—especially conversion experiences—during services.
5. Slang phrase meaning "I don't pay any attention to those folks."

Just 'bout dat time he heard a voice, "Wanh, uh wanh! Go preach, go preach, go preach!"

He went and tol' everybody, but look lak he never could git no big charge. All he ever got called was on some sawmill, half-pint church or some turpentine still. He knocked around lak dat for ten years and then he seen his brother. De big preacher says, "Brother, you don't look like you gittin' holt of much."

"You tellin' dat right, brother. Groceries is scarce. Ah ain't dirtied a plate today."

"Whut's de matter? Don't you git no support from your church?"

"Yeah, Ah gits it such as it is, but Ah ain't never pastored no big church. Ah don't git called to nothin' but sawmill camps and turpentine stills."

De big preacher reared back and thought a while, then he ast de other one, "Is you sure you was called to preach? Maybe you ain't cut out for no preacher."

"Oh, yeah," he told him. "Ah *know* Ah been called to de ministry. A voice spoke and tol' me so."

"Well, seem lak if God called you He is mighty slow in puttin' yo' foot on de ladder. If Ah was you Ah'd go back and ast 'im agin."

So de po' man went on back to de prayin' ground agin and got down on his knees. But there wasn't no big woods like it used to be. It has been all cleared off. He prayed and said, "Oh, Lawd, right here on dis spot ten years ago Ah ast you if Ah was called to preach and a voice tole me to go preach. Since dat time Ah been strugglin' in Yo' moral vineyard, but Ah ain't gathered no grapes. Now, if you really called me to preach Christ and Him crucified, please gimme another sign."

Sho nuff, jus' as soon as he said dat, de voice said "Wanh-uh! Go preach! Go preach! Go preach!"

De man jumped up and says, "Ah knowed Ah been called. Dat's de same voice. Dis time Ah'm goin ter ast Him where *must* Ah go preach."

By dat time de voice come agin and he looked 'way off and seen a mule in de plantation lot wid his head all stuck out to bray agin, and he said, "Unh hunh, youse de very son of a gun dat called me to preach befo'."

So he went on off and got a job plowin'. Dat's whut he was called to do in de first place.

Armetta said, "A many one been called to de plough and they run off and got up in de pulpit. Ah wish dese mules knowed how to take a pair of plow-lines and go to de church and ketch some of 'em like they go to de lot with a bridle and ketch mules."

Ellis: Ah knowed one preacher dat was called to preach at one of dese split-off churches. De members had done split off from a big church because they was all mean and couldn't git along wid nobody.

Dis preacher was a good man, but de congregation was so tough he couldn't make a convert in a whole year. So he sent and invited another preacher to come and conduct a revival meeting for him. De man he ast to come was a powerful hard preacher wid a good strainin' voice. He was known to get converts.

Well, he come and preached at dis split-off for two whole weeks. De people would all turn out to church and jus' set dere and look at de man up dere strainin' his lungs out and nobody would give de man no encouragement by sayin' "Amen," and not a soul bowed down.

It was a narrer church wid one winder and dat was in de pulpit and de door was in de front end. Dey had a mean ole sexton[6] wid a wooden leg. So de last night of de

6. According to the *Oxford English Dictionary:* "A church officer having the care of the fabric of a church and its contents, and the duties of ringing the bells and digging graves."

protracted meetin' de preacher come to church wid his gripsack in his hand and went on up in de pulpit. When he got up to preach he says, "Brother Sexton, dis bein' de last night of de meetin' Ah wants you to lock de do' and bring me de key. Ah want everybody to stay and hear whut Ah got to say."

De sexton brought him de key and he took his tex and went to preachin'. He preached and he reared and pitched, but nobody said "Amen" and nobody bowed down. So 'way after while he stooped down and opened his suitsatchel and out wid his .44 Special. "Now," he said, "you rounders and brick-bats—yeah, you women, Ah'm talkin' to you. If you ain't a whole brick, den you must be a bat—and gamblers and 'leven-card layers. Ah done preached to you for two whole weeks and not one of you has said 'Amen,' and nobody has bowed down."

He thowed de gun on 'em. "And now Ah say bow down!" And they beginned to bow all over dat church.

De sexton looked at his wooden leg and figgered he couldn't bow because his leg was cut off above de knee. So he ast, "Me too, Elder?"

"Yeah, you too, you peg-leg son of a gun. You bow down too."

Therefo' dat sexton bent dat wooden leg and bowed down. De preacher fired a couple of shots over they heads and stepped out de window and went on 'bout his business. But he skeered dem people so bad till they all rushed to one side of de church tryin' to git out and carried dat church buildin' twenty-eight miles befo' they thought to turn it loose.

"Now Ellis," chided Gold when she was thru her laughter, "You know dat's a lie. Folks over there in St. Lawrence holdin' class meetin' and you over here lyin' like de crossties from Jacksonville to Key West."

"Naw, dat ain't no lie!" Ellis contended, still laughing himself.

"Aw, yes it 'tis," Gold said. "Dat's all you men is good for—settin' 'round and lyin'. Some of you done quit lyin' and gone to flyin'."

Gene Brazzle said, "Get off of us mens now. We *is* some good. Plenty good too if you git de right one. De trouble is you women ain't good for nothin' exceptin' readin' Sears and Roebuck's bible and hollerin' 'bout, 'gimme dis and gimme dat' as soon as we draw our pay."

Shug said, "Well, we don't git it by astin' you mens for it. If we work for it we kin git it. You mens don't draw no pay. You don't do nothin' but stand around and draw lightnin'."

"Ah don't say Ah'm detrimental," Gene said dryly, "but if Gold and Shug don't stop crackin' us, Ah'm gointer get 'em to go."

Gold: "Man, if you want me any, some or none, do whut you gointer do and stop cryin'."

Gene: "You ain't seen me cryin'. See me cryin', it's sign of a funeral. If Ah even look cross somebody gointer bleed."

Gold: "Aw, shut up, Gene, you ain't no big hen's biddy if you do lay gobbler eggs. You tryin' to talk like big wood when you ain't nothin' but brush."

Armetta sensed a hard anger creepin' into the teasing so she laughed to make Gene and Gold laugh and asked, "Did y'all have any words before you fell out?"

"We ain't mad wid one 'nother," Gene defended. "We jus' jokin'."

"Well, stop blowin' it and let de lyin' go on," said Charlie Jones. "Zora's gittin' restless. She think she ain't gointer hear no more."

"Oh, no Ah ain't," I lied. After a short spell of quiet, good humor was restored to the porch. In the pause we could hear Pa Henry over in the church house sending up a prayer:

. . . You have been with me from the earliest rocking of my cradle up until this present moment.
You know our hearts, our Father,
And all de range of our deceitful minds,
And if you find anything like sin lurking
In and around our hearts,
Ah ast you, My Father, and my Wonder-workin' God
To pluck it out
And cast it into de sea of Fuhgitfulness
Where it will never rise to harm us in dis world
Nor condemn us in de judgment.
You heard me when Ah laid at hell's dark door
With no weapon in my hand
And no God in my heart,
And cried for three long days and nights.
You heard me, Lawd,
And stooped so low
And snatched me from the hell
Of eternal death and damnation.
You cut loose my stammerin' tongue;
You established my feet on de rock of Salvation
And yo' voice was heard in rumblin' judgment.
I thank Thee that my last night's sleepin' couch
Was not my coolin' board[7]
And my cover
Was not my windin' sheet.[8]
Speak to de sinner-man and bless 'im.
Touch all those
Who have been down to de doors of degradation.
Ketch de man dat's layin' in danger of consumin' fire;
And Lawd,
When Ah kin pray no mo';
When Ah done drunk down de last cup of sorrow
Look on me, yo' weak servant who feels de least of all;
'Point my soul a restin' place
Where Ah kin set down and praise yo' name forever
Is my prayer for Jesus sake
Amen and thank God.

As the prayer ended the bell of Macedonia, the Baptist church, began to ring.

"Prayer meetin' night at Macedony," George Thomas said.

"It's too bad that it must be two churches in Eatonville," I commented. "De town's too little. Everybody ought to go to one."

"Dey wouldn't do dat, Zora, and you know better. Fack is, de Christian churches nowhere don't stick together," this from Charlie.

Everybody agreed that this was true. So Charlie went on. "Look at all de kind of denominations we got. But de people can't help dat 'cause de church wasn't built on no solid foundation to start wid."

7. The surface on which a dead body was laid out to be prepared for burial.

8. A shroud.

"Oh yes, it 'twas!" Johnnie Mae disputed him. "It was built on solid rock. Didn't Jesus say 'On dis rock Ah build my church?' "

"Yeah," chimed in Antie Hoyt. "And de songs says, 'On Christ de solid rock I stand' and 'Rock of Ages.' "

Charlie was calm and patient. "Yeah, he built it on a rock, but it wasn't solid. It was a pieced-up rock and that's how come de church split up now. Here's de very way it was:

> Christ was walkin' long one day wid all his disciples and he said, "We're goin' for a walk today. Everybody pick up a rock and come along." So everybody got their selves a nice big rock 'ceptin' Peter. He was lazy so he picked up a li'l bit of a pebble and dropped it in his side pocket and come along.
>
> Well, they walked all day long and de other 'leven disciples changed them rocks from one arm to de other but they kept on totin' 'em. Long towards sundown they come 'long by de Sea of Galilee and Jesus tole 'em, "Well, le's fish awhile. Cast in yo' nets right here." They done like he tole 'em and caught a great big mess of fish. Then they cooked 'em and Christ said, "Now, all y'all bring up yo' rocks." So they all brought they rocks and Christ turned 'em into bread and they all had a plenty to eat wid they fish exceptin' Peter. He couldn't hardly make a moufful offa de li'l bread he had and he didn't like dat a bit.
>
> Two or three days after dat Christ went out doors and looked up at de sky and says, "Well, we're goin' for another walk today. Everybody git yo'self a rock and come along."
>
> They all picked up a rock apiece and was ready to go. All but Peter. He went and tore down half a mountain. It was so big he couldn't move it wid his hands. He had to take a pinch-bar to move it. All day long Christ walked and talked to his disciples and Peter sweated and strained wid dat rock of his'n.
>
> Way long in de evenin' Christ went up under a great big ole tree and set down and called all of his disciples around 'im and said, "Now everybody bring up yo' rocks."
>
> So everybody brought theirs but Peter. Peter was about a mile down de road punchin' dat half a mountain he was bringin'. So Christ waited till he got dere. He looked at de rocks dat de other 'leven disciples had, den he seen dis great big mountain dat Peter had and so he got up and walked over to it and put one foot up on it and said, "Why Peter, dis is a fine rock you got here! It's a noble rock! And Peter, on dis rock Ah'm gointer build my church."
>
> Peter says, "Naw you ain't neither. You won't build no church house on *dis* rock. You gointer turn dis rock into bread."
>
> Christ knowed dat Peter meant dat thing so he turnt de hillside into bread and dat mountain is de bread he fed de 5,000 wid. Den he took dem 'leven other rocks and glued 'em together and built his church on it.
>
> And that's how come de Christian churches is split up into so many different kinds—cause it's built on pieced-up rock.

There was a storm of laughter following Charlie's tale. "Zora, you come talkin' bout puttin' de two churches together and not havin' but one in dis town," Armetta said chidingly. "You know better'n dat. Baptis' and Methdis' always got a pick out at one 'nother. One time two preachers—one Methdis' an de other one Baptis' wuz on uh train and de engine blowed up and bein' in de colored coach right back of de engine they got blowed up too. When they saw theyself startin' up in de air de Baptis' preacher hollered, 'Ah bet Ah go higher than you!' "

Then Gold spoke up and said, "Now, lemme tell one. Ah know one about a man as black as Gene."

"Whut you always crackin' me for?" Gene wanted to know. "Ah ain't a bit blacker than you."

"Oh, yes you is, Gene. Youse a whole heap blacker than Ah is."

"Aw, go head on, Gold. Youse blacker than me. You jus' look my color cause youse fat. If you wasn't no fatter than me you'd be so black till lightnin' bugs would follow you at twelve o'clock in de day, thinkin' it's midnight."

"Dat's a lie, youse blacker than Ah ever dared to be. Youse lam' black. Youse so black till they have to throw a sheet over yo' head so de sun kin rise every mornin'. Ah know yo' ma cried when she seen *you*."

"Well, anyhow, Gold, youse blacker than me. If Ah was as fat as you Ah'd be a yaller man."

"Youse a liar. Youse as yaller as you ever gointer git. When a person is poor he look bright and de fatter you git de darker you look."

"Is dat yo' excuse for being so black, Gold?"

Armetta soothed Gold's feelings and stopped the war. When the air cleared Gold asked, "Do y'all know how come we are black?"

"Yeah," said Ellis. "It's because two black niggers got together."

"Aw, naw," Gold disputed petulantly. "Well, since you so smart, tell me where dem two black niggers come from in de first beginnin'."

"They musta come from Zar, and dat's on de other side of far."

"Uh, hunh!" Gold gloated. "Ah knowed you didn't know whut you was talkin' about. Now Ah'm goin' ter tell you how come we so black:

> Long before they got thru makin' de Atlantic Ocean and haulin' de rocks for de mountains, God was makin' up de people. But He didn't finish 'em all at one time. Ah'm compelled to say dat some folks is walkin' round dis town right now ain't finished yet and never will be.
>
> Well, He give out eyes one day. All de nations come up and got they eyes. Then He give out teeth and so on. Then He set a day to give out color. So seven o'clock dat mornin' everybody was due to git they color except de niggers. So God give everybody they color and they went on off. Then He set there for three hours and one-half and no niggers. It was gettin' hot and God wanted to git His work done and go set in de cool. So He sent de angels. Rayfield and Gab'ull[9] to go git 'em so He could 'tend some mo' business.
>
> They hunted all over Heben till dey found de colored folks. All stretched out sleep on de grass under de tree of life. So Rayfield woke 'em up and tole 'em God wanted 'em.
>
> They all jumped up and run on up to de th'one and they was so skeered they might miss sumpin' they begin to push and shove one 'nother, bumpin' against all de angels and turnin' over foot-stools. They even had de th'one all pushed one-sided.
>
> So God hollered "Git back! Git back!" And they misunderstood Him and thought He said, "Git black," and they been black ever since.

Gene rolled his eyeballs into one corner of his head.

"Now Gold call herself gettin' even wid me—tellin' dat lie. 'Tain't no such a story nowhere. She jus' made dat one up herself."

"Naw, she didn't," Armetta defended. "Ah *been* knowin' dat ole tale."

"Me too," said Shoo-pie.

"Don't you know you can't git de best of no woman in de talkin' game? Her tongue is all de weapon a woman got," George Thomas chided Gene. "She could

9. Raphael and Gabriel, from the Christian scriptures.

have had mo' sense, but she told God no, she'd ruther take it out in hips. So God give her her ruthers. She got plenty hips, plenty mouf and no brains."

"Oh, yes, womens is got sense too," Mathilda Moseley jumped in. "But they got too much sense to go 'round braggin' about it like y'all do. De lady people always got de advantage of mens because God fixed it dat way."

"Whut ole black advantage is y'all got?" B. Moseley asked indignantly. "We got all de strength and all de law and all de money and you can't git a thing but whut we jes' take pity on you and give you."

"And dat's jus' de point," said Mathilda triumphantly. "You *do* give it to us, but how come you do it?" And without waiting for an answer Mathilda began to tell why women always take advantage of men.

You see in de very first days, God made a man and a woman and put 'em in a house together to live. 'Way back in them days de woman was just as strong as de man and both of 'em did de same things. They useter get to fussin' 'bout who gointer do this and that and sometime they'd fight, but they was even balanced and neither one could whip de other one.

One day de man said to hisself, "B'lieve Ah'm gointer go see God and ast Him for a li'l mo' strength so Ah kin whip dis 'oman and make her mind. Ah'm tired of de way things is." So he went on up to God.

"Good mawnin', Ole Father."

"Howdy man. Whut you doin' 'round my throne so soon dis mawnin'?"

"Ah'm troubled in mind, and nobody can't ease mah spirit 'ceptin' you."

God said: "Put yo' plea in de right form and Ah'll hear and answer."

"Ole Maker, wid de mawnin' stars glitterin' in yo' shinin' crown, wid de dust from yo' footsteps makin' worlds upon worlds, wid de blazin' bird we call de sun flyin' out of yo' right hand in de mawnin' and consumin' all day de flesh and blood of stump-black darkness, and comes flyin' home every evenin' to rest on yo' left hand, and never once in all yo' eternal years, mistood de left hand for de right, Ah ast you *please* to give me mo' strength than dat woman you give me, so Ah kin make her mind. Ah know you don't want to be always comin' down way past de moon and stars to be straightenin' her out and its got to be done. So give me a li'l mo' strength, Ole Maker and Ah'll do it."

"All right, Man, you got mo' strength than woman."

So de man run all de way down de stairs from Heben till he got home. He was so anxious to try his strength on de woman dat he couldn't take his time. Soon's he got in de house he hollered "Woman! Here's yo' boss. God done tole me to handle you in which ever way Ah please. Ah'm yo' boss."

De woman flew to fightin' 'im right off. She fought 'im frightenin' but he beat her. She got her wind and tried 'im agin but he whipped her agin. She got herself together and made de third try on him vigorous but he beat her every time. He was so proud he could whip 'er at last, dat he just crowed over her and made her do a lot of things she didn't like. He told her, "Long as you obey me, Ah'll be good to yuh, but every time yuh rear up Ah'm gointer put plenty wood on yo' back and plenty water in yo' eyes."

De woman was so mad she went straight up to Heben and stood befo' de Lawd. She didn't waste no words. She said, "Lawd, Ah come befo' you mighty mad t'day. Ah want back my strength and power Ah useter have."

"Woman, you got de same power you had since de beginnin'."

"Why is it then, dat de man kin beat me now and he useter couldn't do it?"

"He got mo' strength than he useter have. He come and ast me for it and Ah give it to 'im. Ah gives to them that ast, and you ain't never ast me for no mo' power."

"Please suh, God, Ah'm astin' you for it now. Jus' gimme de same as you give him."

God shook his head. "It's too late now, woman. Whut Ah give, Ah never take back. Ah give him mo' strength than you and no matter how much Ah give you, he'll have mo'."

De woman was so mad she wheeled around and went on off. She went straight to de devil and told him what had happened.

He said, "Don't be dis-incouraged, woman. You listen to me and you'll come out mo' than conqueror. Take dem frowns out yo' face and turn round and go right on back to Heben and ast God to give you dat bunch of keys hangin' by de mantel-piece. Then you bring 'em to me and Ah'll show you what to do wid 'em."

So de woman climbed back up to Heben agin. She was mighty tired but she was more out-done that she was tired so she climbed all night long and got back up to Heben agin. When she got befo' de throne, butter wouldn't melt in her mouf.

"O Lawd and Master of de rainbow, Ah know yo' power. You never make two mountains without you put a valley in between. Ah know you kin hit a straight lick wid a crooked stick."

"Ast for whut you want, woman."

"God, gimme dat bunch of keys hangin' by yo' mantelpiece."

"Take 'em."

So de woman took de keys and hurried on back to de devil wid 'em. There was three keys on de bunch. Devil say, "See dese three keys? They got mo' power in 'em than all de strength de man kin ever git if you handle 'em right. Now dis first big key is to de do' of de kitchen, and you know a man always favors his stomach. Dis second one is de key to de bedroom and he don't like to be shut out from dat neither and dis last key is de key to de cradle and he don't want to be cut off from his generations at all. So now you take dese keys and go lock up everything and wait till he come to you. Then don't you unlock nothin' until he use his strength for yo' benefit and yo' desires."

De woman thanked 'im and tole 'im, "If it wasn't for you, Lawd knows whut us po' women folks would do."

She started off but de devil halted her. "Jus' one mo' thing: don't go home braggin' 'bout yo' keys. Jus' lock up everything and say nothin' until you git asked. And then don't talk too much."

De woman went on home and did like de devil tole her. When de man come home from work she was settin' on de porch singin' some song 'bout "Peck on de wood make de bed go good."

When de man found de three doors fastened what useter stand wide open he swelled up like pine lumber after a rain. First thing he tried to break in cause he figgered his strength would overcome all obstacles. When he saw he couldn't do it, he ast de woman, "Who locked dis do'?"

She tole 'im, "Me."

"Where did you git de key from?"

"God give it to me."

He run up to God and said, "God, woman got me locked 'way from my vittles, my bed and my generations, and she say you give her the keys."

God said, "I did, Man, Ah give her de keys, but de devil showed her how to use 'em!"

"Well, Ole Maker, please gimme some keys jus' lak 'em so she can't git de full control."

"No, Man, what Ah give Ah give. Woman got de key."

"How kin Ah know 'bout my generations?"

"Ast de woman."

So de man come on back and submitted hisself to de woman and she opened de doors.

He wasn't satisfied but he had to give in. 'Way after while he said to de woman, "Le's us divide up. Ah'll give you half of my strength if you lemme hold de keys in my hands."

De woman thought dat over so de devil popped and tol her, "Tell 'im, naw. Let 'im keep his strength and you keep yo' keys."

So de woman wouldn't trade wid 'im and de man had to mortgage his strength to her to live. And dat's why de man makes and de woman takes. You men is still braggin' 'bout yo' strength and de women is sittin' on de keys and lettin' you blow off till she git ready to put de bridle on you.

B. Moseley looked over at Mathilda and said, "You just like a hen in de barnyard. You cackle so much you give de rooster de blues."

Mathilda looked over at him archly and quoted:

Stepped on a pin, de pin bent
And dat's de way de story went.

"Y'all lady people ain't smarter *than* all men folks. You got plow lines on some of us, but some of us is too smart for you. We go past you jus' like lightnin' thru de trees," Willie Sewell boasted. "And what make it so cool, we close enough to you to have a scronchous time, but never no halter on our necks. Ah know they won't git none on dis last neck of mine."

"Oh, you kin be had," Gold retorted. "Ah mean dat abstifically."

"Yeah? But not wid de trace chains. Never no shack up. Ah want dis tip-in love and tip yo' hat and walk out. Ah don't want nobody to have dis dyin' love for me."

Richard Jones said: "Yeah, man. Love is a funny thing; love is a blossom. If you want yo' finger bit poke it at a possum."

Jack Oscar Jones, who had been quiet for some time, slumped way down in his chair, straightened up and said, "Ah know a speech about love."

Ruth Marshall laughed doubtfully. "Now, Jack, you can't make me b'lieve you know de first thing about no love."

"Yeah he do, too," Clara, Jack's wife defended.

"Whut do he know, then?" Ruth persisted.

"Aw, Lawd," Clara wagged her head knowingly. "You ain't got no business knowing dat. Dat's *us* business. But he know jus' as much about love as de nex' man."

"You don't say!" Johnnie Mae twitted her sister-in-law. "Blow it out, then, Jack, and tell a blind man somethin'."

"Ah'm gointer say it, then me and Zora's goin' out to Montgomery and git up a cool watermelon, ain't we, Zora?"

"If you got de price," I came back. "Ah got de car so all we need is a strong determination and we'll have melon."

"No, Zora ain't goin' nowhere wid my husband," Clara announced. "If he got anything to tell her—it's gointer be right here in front of me."

Jack laughed at Clara's feigned jealousy and recited:

Song Poem

When the clock struck one I had just begun. Begun with Sue, begun with Sal, begun with that pretty Johnson gal.

When the clock struck two, I was through, I was through with Sue, through with Sal, through with that pretty Johnson gal.

When the clock struck three I was free, free with Sue, free with Sal, free with that pretty Johnson gal.

When the clock struck four I was at the door, at the door with Sue, at the door with Sal, at the door with that pretty Johnson gal.

When the clock struck five I was alive, alive with Sue, alive with Sal, alive with that pretty Johnson gal.

When the clock struck six I was fixed, fixed with Sue, fixed with Sal, fixed with that pretty Johnson gal.

When the clock struck seven I was even, even with Sue, even with Sal, even with that pretty Johnson gal.

When the clock struck eight I was at your gate, gate with Sue, gate with Sal, gate with that pretty Johnson gal.

When the clock struck nine I was behind, behind with Sue, behind with Sal, behind with that pretty Johnson gal.

When the clock struck ten I was in the bin, in the bin with Sue, in the bin with Sal, in the bin with that pretty Johnson gal.

When the clock struck eleven, I was in heaven, in heaven with Sue, in heaven with Sal, in heaven with that pretty Johnson gal.

When the clock struck twelve I was in hell, in hell with Sue, in hell with Sal, in hell with that pretty Johnson gal.

"Who was all dis Sue and dis Sal and dat pretty Johnson gal?" Clara demanded of Jack.

"Dat ain't for you to know. My name is West, and Ah'm so different from de rest."

"You sound like one man courtin' three gals, but Ah know a story 'bout three mens courtin' one gal," Shug commented.

"Dat's bogish," cried Bennie Lee thickly.

"Whut's bogish?" Shug demanded. She and Bennie were step-brother and sister and they had had a lawsuit over the property of his late father and her late mother, so a very little of Bennie's sugar would sweeten Shug's tea and vice versa.

"Ah don't want to lissen to no ole talk 'bout three mens after no one 'oman. It's always more'n three womens after every man."

"Well, de way Ah know de story, there was three mens after de same girl," Shug insisted. "You drunk, Bennie Lee. You done drunk so much of dis ole coon dick till you full of monkies."[10]

"Whut you gointer do?" Bennie demanded. "Whut you gointer do?" No answer was expected to this question. It was just Bennie Lee's favorite retort. "De monkies got me, now whut you gointer do?"

"Ah ain't got you to study about, Bennie Lee. If God ain't payin' you no mo' mind than Ah is, youse in hell right now. Ah ain't talkin' to you nohow. Zora, you wanter hear dis story?"

"Sure, Shug. That's what Ah'm here for."

"Somebody's gointer bleed," Bennie Lee threatened. Nobody paid him any mind.

"God knows Ah don't wanter hear Shug tell nothin'," Bennie Lee complained.

"Ah wish yo' monkies would tell you to go hide in de hammock and forgit to tell you de way home." Shug was getting peeved.

"You better shut up befo' Ah whip yo' head to de red. Ah wish Ah was God. Ah'd turn you into a blamed hawg, and then Ah'd concrete de whole world over so you wouldn't have not one nary place to root."

10. Inebriated and possibly seeing things. Similar to seeing "pink elephants" when someone has consumed too much alcohol.

"Dat's dat two-bits in change you got in yo' pocket now dat's talkin' for you. But befo' de summer's over *you'll* be rootin' lak a hawg. You already lookin' over-plus lak one now. Don't you worry 'bout me."

Bennie Lee tried to ask his well-known question but the coon dick was too strong. He mumbled down into his shirt bosom and went to sleep.

QUESTIONS TO CONSIDER

1. What function do folktales—or "lies" as Hurston's narrators often call them—serve in a community? What can later generations learn from folk stories? What elements of this oral narrative tradition differ from what you are accustomed to seeing in writing?
2. What is your reaction to the dialect in these stories? Is it reminiscent of storytelling with which you are familiar? How would these stories differ if they were presented without the dialect? What does Hurston's use of dialect add to these stories?

Lyle Saxon

1891–1946

"There are a few persons who step into legend while yet alive. They possess some unaccountable quality, the mysterious fabric of which legends are made. Lyle Saxon, of Louisiana, is one of these," declared fellow Southerner Caroline Dorman of the colorful scholar who was described by his reviewers as "nine parts poet." Perhaps best known for his work as the program director for the Works Progress Administration (WPA) in Louisiana during the Great Depression, Lyle Saxon was a prolific writer in his own right who wrote and edited five books—*Father Mississippi* (1927), *Fabulous New Orleans* (1928), *Old Louisiana* (1929), *Lafitte the Pirate* (1930), and *Gumbo Ya-Ya* (1945)—before turning his attention to the novel he had always dreamed of writing. He achieved his dream with the publication of *Children of Strangers* (1937), which drew upon his observations of the people and traditions of the Cane River region in central Louisiana.

The son of a plantation owner, Lyle Saxon spent his childhood near Baton Rouge. His early years were seemingly idyllic, filled with horses, puppies, and servants, yet in spite of his privileged background, Saxon's family struggled. Rumors persisted that the author's parents never married, and Saxon's father deserted the family when Lyle was an infant, leaving his mother, Katherine Chambers Saxon, to raise the child with the help of nearby relatives. Saxon attended Louisiana State University (LSU) planning to study agriculture, in part because his family's finances would not allow him to attend an Eastern school as he had hoped. While studying at LSU, he began writing short articles for local newspapers such as the Baton Rouge *State-Times*.

Saxon moved to New Orleans after concluding his studies at LSU, although it is unclear whether he completed a degree. He continued writing newspaper columns and began publishing his fiction in venues such as the *Times-Picayune* Sunday magazine, eventually becoming the highest paid reporter in New Orleans. He gained popularity among the New Orleans literati, becoming enough of a fixture in the French Quarter to warrant a caricature in the whimsical and satirical *Sherwood Anderson and Other Famous Creoles* (1926).

Saxon's first book, *Father Mississippi*, appeared in 1927, the same year he made his first pilgrimage to Melrose Plantation. His ongoing association with Melrose and its owner, Cammie G. Henry, fueled his desire to write a novel. During his extended visits to Cammie Henry's artist colony at Melrose, Saxon observed the members of the Cane River Creole community, which was largely populated by the descendants of Marie Thérèze, known as Coincoin. Coincoin was an emancipated slave formerly owned by early settlers of northern Louisiana. Following her manumission, Coincoin worked diligently to establish a lucrative plantation and to purchase the freedom of each of her enslaved children. Her family prospered, enjoying an elevated, intermediate social status allowed free people of color within the tripartite racial caste system that developed in Louisiana prior to the American purchase. The social and legal freedoms afforded free people of color in Louisiana were unmatched elsewhere in the American South. While not considered equal to their White planter counterparts, *gens de couleur libre*, or free people of color, enjoyed substantially more freedom than the African-American slaves of the region. Saxon's firsthand experiences with the racial tensions of this region are evident in *Children of Strangers*. Recent critics of Saxon's only novel have pointed out that his representation of the three-caste racial hierarchy in Louisiana is too simplistic and that his depictions cast the White community in too favorable of a light. Despite these weaknesses, Saxon's novel is an engaging work that brings to life a rarely seen aspect of Louisiana's cultural heritage. His contemporaries found the novel delightful and fresh, and it received many positive reviews.

By 1935, Saxon had established a reputation as an historian as well as a reporter, and this reputation led to his appointment as the state director of the Federal Writer's Project, a branch of the Depression-era WPA. Charged with the responsibility of assembling Louisiana's contribution to the proposed six-volume, 3,600 page *American Guide*, Saxon was employed to oversee the compilation of this mammoth work, which would give equal attention to each region of the country and would encourage tourism and business travel. As a result of his work with the WPA, *The New Orleans City Guide* appeared in 1938 and was followed by *Louisiana: A Guide to the State* in 1941. When the WPA office in New Orleans officially closed, Saxon was selected to travel to Washington, D.C. to write the summative report on the WPA project prior to the discontinuation of the national program in 1943.

Saxon continued his editorial work until shortly before his death. *Gumbo Ya-Ya*, a collection of oral folk narratives on which he collaborated with Robert Tallant and Edward Dreyer, appeared in 1945. *Gumbo Ya-Ya* represented the culmination of his work with the WPA and the Louisiana State Library Commission, which he had joined following the completion of his WPA duties. Contemporary folklorists question the validity of many of the stories that Saxon and his contemporaries collected, since some evidence exists that they substantially modified some narratives and made up others.

Saxon died in 1946 from complications of bladder cancer, shortly after broadcasting the annual Mardi Gras festivities on national radio. In his obituary, he was described as the "writer without an enemy," and his personal popularity was legendary among his fellow New Orleans authors.

from **Children of Strangers**

Before nine o'clock the ironing was finished and the clothes were folded away into a flat basket of woven oak strips. Famie and her grandmother made ready to go on one of their infrequent trips to the commissary. Usually the small son of a neighbor carried the finer pieces of 'Miss Adelaide's' laundry back and forth, but today old Odalie and Famie were carrying it themselves. They dressed carefully; Famie in a freshly ironed guinea-blue calico dress and sunbonnet, and the woman in a white sacque and sunbonnet, and with the inevitable black skirt of 'half-mourning.' As they stood in their doorway they could see the big-house rising above its trees not more than half a mile away. But the big-house at Yucca was remote, for all that. There are barriers far greater than distance: race and timidity and old, threadbare pride.

Together they walked between the furrows to their gate, the light basket swinging between them and above its swinging shadow on the ground. On one side, the river curved beside the curving road, and on the other side the fields stretched out, freshly turned. Slowly down the long furrows moved straining figures, the plowmen and the mules, coaxing the weary earth into renewed and reluctant fertility. Beyond the fields the far-away woods burned blue in the haze of distance.

The road went to the commissary, then around it in a gentle curve to the gate to the flower garden of the big-house. The commissary was like a large Noah's Ark painted white with green batten doors; its narrow gable projected into the road and a porch beneath the gable-end faced the road and river. The store gallery was the loafing place, the central spot where friends met, and where news was gathered and gossip spread. On the gallery were three rickety chairs, a pair of scales and two rolls of barbed wire. This morning the double doors stood open, but the building was so dark inside that the interior was invisible from the road. "Looks like night in there," Famie said as they approached. Painted in the triangular gable-end was a faded sign: GUY RANDOLPH, and slightly below it, YUCCA PLANTATION STORE, and still lower the two rather mysterious words, GENERAL MERCHANDISE. An old china tree stood at one end of the gallery and to its trunk were tied a horse and a mule. The horse was a beautiful roan animal with a shining saddle—Mr. Guy's own saddle horse—and its presence signified that Mr. Randolph was in the store at the moment and not riding over the fields with the overseer. The mule had neither bridle nor saddle and was tied with a piece of heavy rope; across his back lay a folded gunnysack.

Three brightly dressed negro women loitered on the commissary steps. Their heads with yellow and blue bandanna *tignons* were close together and their attention seemed centered upon a small black girl who approached from the opposite direction, lackadaisically, her rags fluttering about her skinny legs, a coal-oil can swinging in one hand.

"Howdy, Miz Mug!" she piped in a shrill voice to one of the women who watched her approach.

Immediately the three women began to question her, all speaking together:

"What's all dat screamin' down de road?"

"Who was dat a-yellin' at yo'?"

And as the girl stood scraping one bare foot against the other, Mug cried out: "Answer me, gal, don' yo' stan' wid yo' mouth open!"

The girl switched her skirt and answered pertly:

"Dat was Miss Crazy-Susie a-yellin."

"What she yellin' about? What she say?"

"She jus' come a-runnin' out de do' a-yellin' at me, an' she say a hog got in de house an' et up all her cornmeal—an' den she screech some mo' . . ."

"What else she say?" cried the chorus.

"An' she say her daughter Ma'y goin' tuh have a baby an' *nobody* don' know who de pappy is. An' den she go on a-screechin'. . . ."

"Do Jesus!"

"Gawd knows!"

"Hab mussy!"

"An' den she say dat her husban' done slap her down an' lef' her dis very mawnin' . . ."

"Lawd-Gawd!" cried the women in unison.

"An' den she fall down de flo' a-yellin' dat she don' believe in Gawd, no ma'am, nor Jesus neither!"

"Hab mussy!"

"Lissen tuh dat!"

As the girl seemed to have reached her climax, the women inquired: "An' what yo' say to her, gal?"

The child replied in her vacuous, shrill voice, "Ah jus' say: 'Ah don' keer!' "

At this unexpected answer, the three women abandoned their simulated horror and burst into guffaws.

"Lawdy Gawd!"

"Now Jesus!"

"Great Day!"

"Dat's a crazy chile!"

The little girl, greatly pleased with herself, went flouncing into the store, and the women followed, pummeling each other, whooping with laughter.

Famie had lingered, listening, but she felt a sudden tug at the basket. Her grandmother was staring straight ahead, her nostrils distended in scorn: "Niggers!" she said. "That's all they got to do, laughin' at a crazy woman!"

Famie tried to understand her grandmother's distaste, failed, and, watching a red bird's flight across the road, she forgot the incident at once. Together they went on, through the gate and up the path through the flower-garden, to the big-house.

Framed in greenery, the house rose before them. How big it was! The six white columns which supported the roof were enormous, and the galleries were large, too. A negro girl who was sweeping the lower gallery with slow, lazy strokes dropped the broom where she stood and languidly asked their business. Odalie indicated the basket and said that she wanted to talk to Miss Adelaide. Without another word the black girl went up the stairway which rose at one end of the porch. Famie and her grandmother waited, listening to the plop-plop of the girl's feet as she went along the upper gallery. A moment later she called down:

"She say tuh come up heah!"

They began their ascent, Famie stepping warily around the broom to avoid bad luck. The clothes-basket bumped against their legs on the stairway.

The planter's wife lay in a four-post bed in a front room on the upper floor, a bed so large that it occupied nearly one quarter of the big room. Beside her, upon the counterpane, lay the baby fresh from his bath and as naked as the day he was born. In one pudgy fist he grasped the end of his mother's long braid of brown hair.

"Look, Odalie," Miss Adelaide said. "He holds tight to everything he gets his hands on; he'll be rich some day."

She laughed at the familiar superstition, and Odalie smiled, her face falling into many tiny wrinkles. An old black woman with a checkered head-handkerchief smiled grimly and said:

"Ain't yo' shame, Miz Adelaide? Po' li'l man is bucknaked befo' comp'ny," and she lifted the child, swathed him in a pink blanket and carried him from the room.

Miss Adelaide looked at Famie who stood, smiling shyly, just inside the door:

"Who's that you've brought with you, Odalie?"

"That's my gran'chile, Euphémie Vidal. Come speak to Miz Ran'off, Famie."

Miss Adelaide was plantation-raised, and she put the girl at her ease at once by the use of her nickname: "How do you like my baby, Famie?" she asked.

"He's the prettiest li'l baby I ever *did* see," the girl replied, and added, "He's so lovely white."

The white woman understood at once that wistful word. White. Yes, that's what they all wanted, poor things. Mulattoes, neither one thing nor the other.

"Aunt Dicey will bring him back as soon as he's dressed," she said. "Now, Odalie, let's look at his clothes."

While they were examining the laundry, Famie looked about the room. It was beautiful, she thought, as her eyes turned from white wall to white woodwork, to the yellow-and-white flowered curtains, and to the white matting on the floor. The tester of the bed was lined with yellow silk and there were yellow glass bottles on the dressing-table. Even the washbowl and pitcher had a band of yellow, and . . . Famie gasped, startled, for there she was, herself, reflected full length in the mirrored door of the wardrobe. She saw herself as though for the first time, a slim, eager girl with black eyes and parted red lips, her pale face framed in the blue sunbonnet. She stared.

A sharp grunt of disdain brought her to herself, and beyond her shoulder, reflected in the glass, she saw the ironic smile of the old black woman who carried the baby in her arms. Famie flushed and turned away. Luckily, Miss Adelaide had noticed nothing, and as the girl approached the bed again the white woman spoke kindly to her.

"Your grandmother tells me that this is your birthday, and that you've been saving your laundry money for a new dress for Easter. I was wondering if I didn't have something that you would like. I'd like to give you a present, for Odalie tells me that you did all of this lovely fluting. It's beautiful, and nobody on the plantation can do it half so well."

Then she spoke to the old black woman: "Aunt Dicey, give me the baby, and open the *armoire* for me."

The nurse placed the child upon the counterpane again and advanced to the wardrobe and opened its door; the mirror swung out and in its reflection the whole room seemed turning about. A sweet scent of *vertivert* filled the room.

"Look, Famie, you're taller than Aunt Dicey, see if you can reach down that hatbox from the top shelf . . . that's right. Bring it here."

Inside were three hats, piled one on top of the other. One was a big, floppy white leghorn with a bunch of red poppies at one side of the crown and, oddly enough, one poppy sewed under the brim.

Miss Adelaide turned it about in her hands: "Would you like this?" she asked.

Famie caught her breath: "For me?"

"Of course, who else?"

"Yes, *ma'am!*"

Miss Adelaide tossed it toward her: "Here, take it. It's yours. Try it on and let's see how you look."

Famie put aside the sunbonnet and placed the hat on her head.

"No, that's not right . . . Come here and I'll show you," and Miss Adelaide, with a deft touch settled the hat correctly with the single poppy bobbing near the girl's left cheek. Now Famie could look in the mirror unashamed; but she had had her lesson. One glance was enough. The hat was a miracle; she had never dreamed of having one so fine. She took it off again and held it in her hands as though it were a bird about to fly away.

Miss Adelaide appeared to forget all about the hat and began asking questions about Odalie's sister, old Madame Aubert Rocque, the oldest and most revered mulatto woman in the settlement on Isle Brevelle. "Tell her to come and see my new baby. I went to see *her* when she was sick." Miss Adelaide sounded brisk and gay.

A few minutes later the girl and her grandmother were going down the garden walk, the hat swinging in the basket between them.

"Now we got to go to de sto'," the old woman said.

The store was dark and smelled of salt meat and kerosene. Saddles and harness hung from the rafters; there was a pile of bright plow-points just inside the door; glass cases held men's hats and shiny shoes. Shelves on one side held groceries, and there were sacks of flour and cornmeal piled up in the middle of the floor. The clerk, a blond, fat, pimply young man stood playing idly with a pair of scissors and a skinny black woman was fingering a piece of checked material. Behind the clerk the shelves were piled with bolts of gay cotton cloth.

"Yo' wait on dem while I makes up my min'," the woman said; then turning, "Howdy, Miss Odalie, how yo' do?"

It was Lizzie Balize, the granny-doctor. Odalie thanked her for her courtesy, then turned to the clerk. It was hard to decide upon the proper material for Famie's dress—not that there was such a wide choice, but because a new dress is such an event that one must never, never make a mistake. Famie fingered the sprigged muslins and the pink organdy, but they were not quite what she wanted. At last she saw it, there on the shelf, a bolt of white dotted swiss. That was exactly right, and within the price that she could pay. Her enthusiasm was so contagious that the clerk smiled at her and became gracious, and ended by giving her half a yard extra for *lagniappe*.

"I'll give you something pretty if you come here by yourself sometime," the clerk said, too low for Odalie to hear. Then, not waiting for an answer, he turned away and began wrapping up the parcel.

"Law! I clean forgot the cotton and thread," said Odalie. It was true, for she had planned to make petticoats and chemises. The mistake was soon rectified, the money paid, and they made ready to go.

As the clerk handed Famie the fifteen cents in change, she felt his hot fingers pressing into her palm, and she moved away, startled. Odalie had not noticed, but Lizzie had missed nothing of the byplay: "Humph!" she said, looking straight ahead of her.

It could mean anything, or nothing, but the clerk heard and his pasty face flushed. As Famie turned away she heard him say sharply,

"Well, Lizzie, make up your mind. I haven't got all day to fool with niggers."

. . . On Sunday afternoon Famie received a message that old Madame Aubert Rocque wanted to see her. When she arrived at the house she found two horses tied to the garden fence, and John Javilée's dilapidated surrey hitched under the big pecan tree; she knew, by these signs, that a group was gathered inside. As she paused by the gate she felt that eyes were watching her from behind the faded blue-green shutters.

She was thin and bent, in her shabby black dress and sunbonnet, and looked like some frail old woman as she stood hesitating beside tall shrubs of shimmering white bridal-wreath and crimson flowering quince. The house was tight shut, keeping its secrets, but she felt the eyes upon her as she went up the path to the door and rapped with a shaking hand upon the faded panels.

Inside it was so dark that Famie could scarcely see. Madame Aubert sat in an armchair, with other old women gathered around her. In the shadows Famie could see three old men standing. There was a murmur as she entered, but nobody spoke to her.

She went to kiss her great-aunt, but the old woman waved her away. Tersely she told Famie why she had been summoned: her relatives wished to speak to her for the last time.

Standing with her back against the door, Famie heard old John Javilée's voice speaking in a tone that she had never heard him use before.

"Yo' wouldn't let yo' own kin people buy yo' land. No, yo' got to have cash money, an' yo' want it now. We could get together and buy it, maybe if yo' give us time. But yo' can't wait. So yo' goin' to sell it to Mister Guy."

She tried to answer, but he went on speaking: "Land is all we got left. It's all we got to keep us from bein' like the niggers. It's our land, an' it's all a part of what *Grandpère* Augustin lef' to us. Little by little white folks is getting' it all. They're pushin' us out. An' you're helpin' 'em. Yo' sell yo' part of *Grandpère* Augustin's land fo' nothin'. Everybody know it wuth double what yo' getting' fo' it. An' why yo' sell it? Why?"

"Ah always promise Joel. . . ."

"Joel! Yas, yo' son. Yo' think Joel's goin' to take yo' Nawth. Well, wait an' see. He's comin', an' he'll take his money an' go. An' where'll yo' be? Yo' ain't got no kin-people heah no mo' . . . Yo' friends is all niggers . . ."

Famie appealed to her great-aunt: "*Nainaine* . . ."

But the old woman interrupted her. She spoke rapidly in French and the words stung like the flicks of a lash. Famie, she said, had gone down a hill that she could not climb up again. She had been bad in her youth and she had been forgiven for it. Her relatives had rallied around her and had saved her good name. Numa[1] had married her, but she had neglected him for her white bastard child.[2] Her kin-people had forgiven her for that, too, but they did not forget. Since her boy had gone away, she had outraged them all by her association with negroes. John Javilée had seen her eating with them in the kitchen at Yucca. At church people sneered at her behind her back, and pretended not to see her, but Famie was a fool and didn't even notice. Now people said that black Henry Tyler was her lover. Madame Aubert Rocque refused to believe it until proof was brought to her. People had seen him leave her house late at night, and she sewed for him, and even brought coffee to him in the field, like any negro woman waiting on her man. It was too much. This was the end. They had called her today to tell her so. If she sold her land to Mister Guy, it was better that she go away, go with Joel or alone, it didn't matter. They had sent Nita away because she had disgraced them, and now Famie had humbled them all. Her name had become a byword, and men laughed at her when they talked together. She was a traitor to her people, and she made her relatives ashamed that her name was the same as theirs.

Dully, Famie listened, looking from one to another. Numa's mother was crying, her face buried in her hands, but Madame Aubert Rocque sat up stiff and stern. She was very old, very withered, but she had the dignity of a matriarch. The weight of ninety-five years had not broken her spirit.

Famie felt herself trembling. She leaned back against the door and tried to find words with which to answer. This was her own aunt, this was her grandmother's own sister who was speaking to her so bitterly. But today the old woman was the representative of a proud race that had been outraged; family ties were forgotten in the disgrace which she felt Famie had brought upon them.

The old woman rose, her fichu falling to the floor, and, ashen and shaking, she pointed with her cane to the portrait of *Grandpère* Augustin which hung on the wall.

"His own great-great-granddaughter disgracin' him. Yo'! My own sister Odalie's gran'chile! Ah'm through with yo'. If yo' meet me in the road, don't speak to me."

Staggering, she fell back in her chair, and the other old women gathered around her; Numa's mother held a glass of water to her lips. The old men came forward out of the shadows.

1. Famie's deceased husband.

2. Joel, Famie's illegitimate son by a White transient.

Famie heard a confused murmur of voices. Someone took her by the elbow and pushed her outside the door. She heard the door close behind her. She was alone in the sunlit garden. She stood with her hand against her lips, looking about her, seeing nothing. Useless to protest, useless to say anything, it was all finished, done with. She was insulted, shut out, and they had not let her answer.

But, after all, what could she say? How could she explain the purpose to which she had given everything? How could she tell them that her own degradation had come because Joel had risen? Nothing could make them understand that the purpose had become interlaced in the very fabric of her life, a part of every move she made, of every breath she drew. Too late to try to tell them now, there were no words that could explain. They were forcing her out of their group, out of their protection; they were pushing her down into the world of negroes. But Joel had escaped. Her purpose was accomplished. They told her she had failed. No!

She swayed as she went down the path to the gate. The sunlight hurt her eyes. Her sunbonnet was gone; she must have dropped it on the floor in the house. It didn't matter.

As she paused to open the gate, she looked back at the house and again she felt the eyes upon her. She knew that the old people were gathered there, peering through the chinks of the shutters, whispering together, looking at her for the last time.

Suddenly she was proud. She shook the tears from her eyes. Let them look at her now.

She broke a sprig of red quince flowers from the bush beside the gate. Slowly she put it in her hair, adjusted it, squared her shoulders. With steady step, and with her head held high, she walked through the gate and down the road.

Questions to Consider

1. How does Saxon's representation of racial hierarchy in Louisiana differ from the racial system throughout the rest of the Southern region? How is race constructed in the society that Saxon presents?
2. Why does the racial hierarchy that Saxon portrays make it impossible for Famie's family to understand her decision to sell her land to Mr. Guy?

Jean Toomer

1894–1967

Jean Toomer's crowning achievement was *Cane*, a novel of prose and poetry published in 1923. After its release, Toomer was praised by critics for the artistic level he achieved in exploring African-American lives in both the rural South and the urban North. Although Toomer did not continue to write at an equal level of brilliance following the appearance of his masterpiece, *Cane* was a major contribution to American literature and Southern letters.

Born Nelson Eugene Toomer on 26 December 1894 in Washington, D.C., he was the son of Georgia planter Nathan Toomer and his wife, the former Nina Pinchback. Toomer's father abandoned the family in 1895, and mother and son moved in with Nina's parents. Toomer's grandfather, P. B. S. Pinchback, had been the lieutenant governor of Louisiana during the Reconstruction period; he considered himself African American, although the Pinchback family was of mixed racial heritage and its members were light-skinned enough to be considered White. Growing up in his grandparents' affluent White neighborhood, however, Toomer felt ambivalent about his racial identity. When his mother remarried in 1905, Toomer moved with her and his White stepfather to the New York City area, but he returned to Washington for high school following her death in 1909. From 1914 to 1919 he attended several colleges, beginning with the University of Wisconsin and ending with City College of New York, but he did not complete a degree. He did, however, become interested in literature and writing, particularly after meeting contemporary writers such as Hart Crane, Edwin Arlington Robinson, and Waldo Frank in New York City.

In 1921 Toomer met the schoolmaster of a rural African-American school in Sparta, Georgia. Toomer agreed to take over his new acquaintance's job responsibilities for a period of several months, and out of that experience came his masterwork, *Cane*. Modernistic in its collage-like assemblage of passages of poetry and prose, its impressionistic poetic description, its stream-of-consciousness technique in prose sections, and its repetitive patternings of symbols and images, *Cane* also addressed the social contrast between African-American lives that were deeply rooted in a meaningful but racist and decaying Southern culture, and those that had been cast adrift in the urban, industrial North. The selections reprinted herein are all from the first of *Cane*'s three parts, which is set in rural Georgia. The second section moves to the urban North, and the third returns to the Deep South but features a Northern-raised African American as its central figure. Scholars and critics praised the work for its literary beauty; its examination of the theme of African-American identity; its treatment of race, class, gender, religious, and economic issues; and its sensitivity toward Southern folk culture and tradition, among other strengths. To Toomer's dismay, however, many reviewers identified him as an African-American author; disputing their claims about his African ancestry and objecting to being racially categorized, Toomer maintained that identity as an American should negate identification with any one of the races that make up American society. While Toomer never associated himself with the Harlem Renaissance writers, *Cane* continues to stand as a masterpiece of the Harlem Renaissance era.

In 1924 Toomer became a disciple of the mystical philosopher George Gurdjieff, who taught that higher consciousness was attainable to those who embarked upon a secretive program of study. Toomer traveled to France, where Gurdjieff's organization was based, then led local chapters of followers in New York and Chicago until the time of his first marriage, in 1932. Toomer's first wife died in childbirth less than a year later. In 1934 he married for the second time and moved to a rural area of Pennsylvania. Toomer continued to write following the publication of *Cane*, but his Gurdjieff-influenced work did not interest publishers, and he wrote little from the mid-1940s until his death in 1967. Several volumes of Toomer's previously unpublished writings have been published posthumously, enabling readers to examine the ways in which his writing style and attitudes changed after *Cane*.

Reapers

Black reapers with the sound of steel on stones
Are sharpening scythes. I see them place the hones[1]
In their hip-pockets as a thing that's done,
And start their silent swinging, one by one.
Black horses drive a mower through the weeds,
And there, a field rat, startled, squealing bleeds,
His belly close to ground. I see the blade,
Blood-stained, continue cutting weeds and shade.

1. Whetstones.

November Cotton Flower

Boll-weevil's coming, and the winter's cold,
Made cotton-stalks look rusty, seasons old,
And cotton, scarce as any southern snow,
Was vanishing; the branch, so pinched and slow,
Failed in its function as the autumn rake;
Drouth fighting soil had caused the soil to take
All water from the streams; dead birds were found
In wells a hundred feet below the ground—
Such was the season when the flower bloomed.
Old folks were startled, and it soon assumed
Significance. Superstition saw
Something it had never seen before:
Brown eyes that loved without a trace of fear,
Beauty so sudden for that time of year.

Becky

Becky was the white woman who had two Negro sons. She's dead; they've gone away. The pines whisper to Jesus. The Bible flaps its leaves with an aimless rustle on her mound.

Becky had one Negro son. Who gave it to her? Damn buck nigger, said the white folks' mouths. She wouldnt tell. Common, God-forsaken, insane white shameless wench, said the white folks' mouths. Her eyes were sunken, her neck stringy, her breasts fallen, till then. Taking their words, they filled her, like a bubble rising—then she broke. Mouth setting in a twist that held her eyes, harsh, vacant, staring. . . . Who gave it to her? Low-down nigger with no self-respect, said the black folks' mouths. She wouldnt tell. Poor Catholic poor-white crazy woman, said the black folks' mouths. White folks and black folks built her cabin, fed her and her growing baby, prayed secretly to God who'd put His cross upon her and cast her out.

When the first was born, the white folks said they'd have no more to do with her. And black folks, they too joined hands to cast her out. . . . The pines whispered to Jesus. . . . The railroad boss said not to say he said it, but she could live, if she wanted to, on the narrow strip of land between the railroad and the road. John Stone, who owned the lumber and the bricks, would have shot the man who told he gave the stuff to Lonnie Deacon, who stole out there at night and built the cabin. A single room held down to earth. . . . O fly away to Jesus . . . by a leaning chimney. . . .

Six trains each day rumbled past and shook the ground under her cabin. Fords, and horse- and mule-drawn buggies went back and forth along the road. No one ever saw her. Trainmen, and passengers who'd heard about her, threw out papers and food. Threw out little crumpled slips of paper scribbled with prayers, as they passed her eye-shaped piece of sandy ground. Ground islandized between the road and railroad track. Pushed up where a blue-sheen God with listless eyes could look at it. Folks from the town took turns, unknown, of course, to each other, in bringing corn and meat and sweet potatoes. Even sometimes snuff. . . O thank y Jesus. . . . Old David Georgia, grinding cane and boiling syrup, never went her way without some sugar sap. No one ever saw her. The boy grew up and ran around. When he was five years old as folks reckoned it, Hugh Jourdon saw him carrying a baby. "Becky has another son," was what the whole town knew. But nothing was said, for the part of man that says things to the likes of that had told itself that if there was a Becky, that Becky now was dead.

The two boys grew. Sullen and cunning. . . O pines, whisper to Jesus; tell Him to come and press sweet Jesus-lips against their lips and eyes. . . . It seemed as though with those two big fellows there, there could be no room for Becky. The part that prayed wondered if perhaps she'd really died, and they had buried her. No one dared ask. They'd beat and cut a man who meant nothing at all in mentioning that they lived along the road. White or colored? No one knew, and least of all themselves. They drifted around from job to job. We, who had cast out their mother because of them, could we take them in? They answered black and white folks by shooting up two men and leaving town. "Godam the white folks; godam the niggers," they shouted as they left town. Becky? Smoke curled up from her chimney; she must be there. Trains passing shook the ground. The ground shook the leaning chimney. Nobody noticed it. A creepy feeling came over all who saw that thin wraith of smoke and felt the trembling of the ground. Folks began to take her food again. They quit it soon because they had a fear. Becky if dead might be a hant, and if alive—it took some nerve even to mention it. . . O pines, whisper to Jesus. . . .

It was Sunday. Our congregation had been visiting at Pulverton, and were coming home. There was no wind. The autumn sun, the bell from Ebenezer Church, listless and heavy. Even the pines were stale, sticky, like the smell of food that makes you sick. Before we turned the bend of the road that would show us the Becky cabin, the horses stopped stock-still, pushed back their ears, and nervously whinnied. We urged, then whipped them on. Quarter of a mile away thin smoke curled up from the leaning chimney. . . O pines, whisper to Jesus. . . . Goose-flesh came on my skin though there still was neither chill nor wind. Eyes left their sockets for the cabin. Ears burned and throbbed. Uncanny eclipse! fear closed my mind. We were just about to pass. . . . Pines shout to Jesus! . . . the ground trembled as a ghost train rumbled by. The chimney fell into the cabin. Its thud was like a hollow report, ages having passed since it went off. Barlo and I were pulled out of our seats. Dragged to the door that had swung open. Through the dust we saw the bricks in a mound upon the floor. Becky, if she was there, lay under them. I thought I heard a groan. Barlo, mumbling something, threw his Bible on the pile. (No one has ever touched it.) Somehow we got away. My buggy was still on the road. The last thing that I remember was whipping old Dan like fury; I remember nothing after that—that is, until I reached town and folks crowded round to get the true word of it.

> Becky was the white woman who had two Negro sons. She's dead; they've gone away. The pines whisper to Jesus. The Bible flaps its leaves with an aimless rustle on her mound.

Georgia Dusk

The sky, lazily disdaining to pursue
  The setting sun, too indolent to hold
  A lengthened tournament for flashing gold,
Passively darkens for night's barbecue,

A feast of moon and men and barking hounds,
An orgy for some genius of the South
With blood-hot eyes and cane-lipped scented mouth,
Surprised in making folk-songs from soul sounds.

The sawmill blows its whistle, buzz-saws stop,
And silence breaks the bud of knoll and hill,
Soft settling pollen where plowed lands fulfill
Their early promise of a bumper crop.

Smoke from the pyramidal sawdust pile
Curls up, blue ghosts of trees, tarrying low
Where only chips and stumps are left to show
The solid proof of former domicile.

Meanwhile, the men, with vestiges of pomp,
Race memories of king and caravan,
High-priests, an ostrich, and a juju-man,[1]
Go singing through the footpaths of the swamp.

Their voices rise . . the pine trees are guitars,
Strumming, pine-needles fall like sheets of rain . .
Their voices rise . . . the chorus of the cane
Is caroling a vesper to the stars. . .

O singers, resinous and soft your songs
Above the sacred whisper of the pines,
Give virgin lips to cornfield concubines,
Bring dreams of Christ to dusky cane-lipped throngs.

Portrait in Georgia

Hair—braided chestnut,
coiled like a lyncher's rope,
Eyes—fagots,[1]
Lips—old scars, or the first red blisters,
Breath—the last sweet scent of cane,
And her slim body—white as the ash
of black flesh after flame.

Questions to Consider

1. Explain how the reapers in the poem entitled "Reapers" might stand as a metaphor for something larger.
2. How do the characters of Becky and her sons, in the prose piece entitled "Becky," undermine and threaten the racial identities of others in their community?

1. Man who wields the magical powers associated with West African legends.

1. Bundles of sticks.

Caroline Gordon

1895–1981

No women belonged to "the brethren," the 12 writers who contributed to the Southern symposium *I'll Take My Stand: The South and the Agrarian Tradition* (1930). This essay collection became the manifesto of the most conservative wing of the Southern Renascence, the Vanderbilt Agrarians, a group of intellectuals who ascribed an almost mythical power to the land, and Caroline Gordon was a staunch supporter and shared their zealous reverence for the Old South as well as their aesthetic formalism. Over her long career, Gordon published nine novels, numerous short stories, and literary criticism. Highly accomplished in her own right, she married Allen Tate, a founding member of the Agrarians and a celebrated poet, novelist, and New Critic; they coauthored an influential college textbook, *The House of Fiction* (1950). She and Tate were the most prominent Southern literary couple of their time, and they numbered among their friends many important writers of the first half of the twentieth century. In midlife each converted to Roman Catholicism, which was, perhaps, an effort to instill a sense of order into their disintegrating relationship. Always overshadowed by Tate, Gordon felt deepening bitterness over her lack of a substantial reading audience. Even so, she served in her later years as a generous mentor to younger writers, notably Flannery O'Connor and Walker Percy, each of whom, like herself, were Southern Catholics.

Carolyn Gordon (she changed the spelling to Caroline in her thirties) was born 6 October 1895, in southwestern Kentucky at her mother's family home, Merry Mont—the plantation setting that in many respects came to embody the values of the Agrarians. She was the second child of James and Nancy Gordon. Her father had tutored the Meriwether children in Greek and Latin and married his best pupil. Both parents worked as teachers during Gordon's childhood, and in 1905, they founded a preparatory school in nearby Clarksville, Tennessee. When the school faltered in 1908, James Gordon joined the ministry of the Disciples of Christ. In 1912, Carolyn went to Bethany College, near Wheeling, West Virginia, and graduated four years later with a degree in classical studies. Gordon briefly taught school but by 1919 was working for the *Chattanooga News*. She was one of the first reviewers to call attention to the *Fugitive*, the new poetry magazine in Nashville. Back home in Kentucky, in 1924 she met one of the Fugitives, Allen Tate. They became lovers and left for New York City. At 29, Gordon became pregnant, and Tate, who was four years her junior, reluctantly agreed to marry her; their daughter was born in 1925. The couple quickly gave her over to Gordon's mother, who took the baby home to Merry Mont, an event which marked the beginning of a long pattern of negligence in their daughter's upbringing.

Gordon and Tate at times could show mutual professional respect and personal affection, but their relationship was chaotic and abrasive, leading them to marry and divorce one another twice. Frequently on the move to teaching jobs, always attracting a crowd of wild friends, and usually beset by debts, they both drank heavily and verged on alcoholism. Tate was demanding, condescending and repeatedly unfaithful, while Gordon swung erratically from depression to towering rage. She berated editors who turned down her submissions and gave tongue-lashings to critics who did not appreciate her work. For all her bluster, however, Gordon was dedicated to her craft and could be generous to writer friends—as long as they were not critics of the South. These Gordon denounced as communist radicals if they dared question Southern race relations or class barriers.

Never a best-selling novelist, Gordon bashed those who were more successful than she. She dismissed *Gone With the Wind* (1936) as mere "cellophane" when its popularity delayed by a year the release of her own Civil War novel, *None Shall Look Back*, a book which Gordon compared to works by Tolstoy and Henry James. Gordon, however, espoused a neo-

Confederate ideology not greatly different from Margaret Mitchell's. Gordon saw the Old South as a victim of the Civil War, a gracious, slaveholding agricultural civilization destroyed by Yankee might and betrayed by rising urban industrial culture. In old age, Gordon became an arch-conservative, railing against modernity in all its forms, even declaring that women never should have been allowed to vote. She died at age 86 of heart failure in Mexico on 11 April 1981.

Perhaps Gordon's best writings are her tales of Professor Alexander (Aleck) Maury, based on her father, a robust man who was an accomplished outdoorsman and classics teacher. Hunting and fishing are Aleck's passion and means of escape from domesticity. His daughter, Sarah, is Caroline Gordon's self-portrait—small, black-eyed, and feisty. The first of these stories, "Old Red," appeared in 1933. Following this publication, Gordon decided to create a fictional biography of her father. She set up a typewriter and encouraged him to tell hunting and fishing stories of Kentucky and Tennessee while her fingers flew across the keys. This project led to the publication of *Aleck Maury, Sportsman* (1934), her second novel. While the book was in press, she wrote three more Aleck Maury stories, including "The Last Day in the Field" (1935). Here, Aleck is dragging a bad leg and facing the end of his career as a hunter. Gordon did not write her last Aleck Maury story until 1947, an indication of the continuing imaginative hold of this material, perhaps her favorite fictional world.

The Last Day in the Field

That was the fall when the leaves stayed green so long. We had a drought in August and the ponds everywhere were dry and the watercourses shrunken. Then in September heavy rains came. Things greened up. It looked like winter was never coming.

"You aren't going to hunt this year, Aleck?" Molly said. "Remember how you stayed awake nights last fall with that pain in your leg."

In October light frosts came. In the afternoons when I sat on the back porch going over my fishing tackle I marked their progress on the elderberry bushes that were left standing against the stable fence. The lower, spreading branches had turned yellow and were already sinking to the ground but the leaves in the top clusters still stood up stiff and straight.

"Ah-ha, it'll get you yet!" I said, thinking how frost creeps higher and higher out of the ground each night of fall.

The dogs next door felt it and would thrust their noses through the wire fence scenting the wind from the north. When I walked in the back yard they would bound twice their height and whine, for meat scraps Molly said, but it was because they smelled blood on my old hunting coat.

They were almost matched liver-and-white pointers. The big dog had a beautiful, square muzzle and was deep-chested and rangy. The bitch, Judy, had a smaller head and not so good a muzzle but she was springy-loined too and had one of the merriest tails I've ever watched.

When Joe Thomas, the boy that owned them, came home from the hardware store he would change his clothes and then come down the back way and we would stand there watching the dogs and wondering how they would work. They had just been with a trainer up in Kentucky for three months. Joe said they were keen as mustard. He was going to take them out the first good Saturday and he wanted me to come along.

"I can't make it," I said. "My leg's worse this fall than it was last."

The fifteenth of November was clear and so warm that we sat out on the porch till nine o'clock. It was still warm when we went to bed toward eleven. The change must have come in the middle of the night. I woke once, hearing the clock strike two, and felt the air cold on my face and thought before I went back to sleep that the weather had broken at last. When I woke again toward dawn the cold air slapped my face hard. I came wide awake, turned over in bed, and looked out of the window. The sun was just coming up behind a wall of purple clouds streaked with amber. As I watched, it burned through and the light everywhere got bright.

There was a scaly bark hickory tree growing on the east side of the house. You could see its upper branches from the bedroom window. The leaves had turned yellow a week ago. But yesterday evening when I walked out there in the yard they had still been flat, with green streaks showing in them. Now they were curled up tight and a lot of leaves had fallen to the ground.

I got out of bed quietly so as not to wake Molly, dressed, and went down the back way over to the Thomas house. There was no one stirring but I knew which room Joe's was. The window was open and I could hear him snoring. I went up and stuck my head in.

"Hey," I said, "killing frost!"

He opened his eyes and looked at me and then his eyes went shut. I reached my arm through the window and shook him. "Get up," I said. "We got to start right away."

He was awake now and out on the floor stretching. I told him to dress and be over at the house as quick as he could. I'd have breakfast ready for us both.

Aunt Martha had a way of leaving fire in the kitchen stove at night. There were red embers there now. I poked the ashes out and piled kindling on top of them. When the flame came up I put some heavier wood on, filled the coffeepot, and put some grease on in a skillet. By the time Joe got there I had coffee ready and had stirred up some hoecakes to go with our fried eggs. Joe had brought a thermos bottle. We put the rest of the coffee in it and I found a ham in the pantry and made some sandwiches.

While I was fixing the lunch Joe went down to the lot to hitch up. He was just driving the buggy out of the stable when I came down the back steps. The dogs knew what was up, all right. They were whining and surging against the fence and Bob, the big dog, thrust his paw through and into the pocket of my hunting coat as I passed. While Joe was snapping on the leashes I got a few handfuls of straw from the rack and put it in the foot of the buggy. It was twelve miles where we were going; the dogs would need to ride warm coming back.

Joe said he would drive. We got in the buggy and started out, up Seventh Street, on over to College, and out through Scufftown. When we got into the nigger section we could see what a killing frost it had been. A light shimmer over all the ground still and the weeds around all the cabins dark and matted the way they are when the frost hits them hard and twists them.

We drove on over the Red River bridge and out into the open country. At Jim Gill's place the cows had come up and were standing there waiting to be milked but nobody was stirring yet from the house. I looked back from the top of the hill and saw that the frost mists still hung heavy in the bottom and thought it was a good sign. A day like this when the earth is warmer than the air currents is good for the hunter. Scent particles are borne on the warm air; and birds will forage far on such a day.

It took us over an hour to get from Gloversville to Spring Creek. Joe wanted to get out as soon as we hit the big bottom there but I held him down and we drove on through and up Rollow's hill to the top of the ridge. We got out there, unhitched Old Dick and turned him into one of Rob Fayerlee's pastures—I thought how surprised Rob would be when he looked out and saw him grazing there—put our guns together, and started out, with the dogs still on leash.

It was rough, broken ground, scrub oak with a few gum trees and lots of buckberry bushes. One place a patch of corn ran clear up to the top of the ridge. As we passed along between the rows, I could see the frost glistening on the north side of every stalk. I knew it was going to be a good day.

I walked over to the brow of the hill. From there you could see off over the whole valley—I've hunted over every foot of it in my time—tobacco land, mostly. One or two patches of cowpeas there on the side of the ridge. I thought we might start there and then I knew that wouldn't do. Quail will linger on the roost on a cold day and feed in shelter during the morning. It is only in the afternoon that they will work out well into the open.

The dogs' whining made me turn around. Joe had bent down and was about to slip the leashes. "Hey, boy," I said, "wait a minute."

I turned around and looked down the other side of the hill. It looked better that way. The corn land of the bottoms ran high up onto the ridge in several places there and where the corn stopped there were big patches of ironweed and buckberry. I stooped and knocked my pipe out on a stump.

"Let's go that way," I said.

Joe was looking at my old buckhorn whistle that I had slung around my neck. "I forgot to bring mine," he said.

"All right," I said, "I'll handle 'em."

He unfastened their collars and cast off. They broke away, racing for the first hundred yards and barking, then suddenly swerved. The big dog took off to the right along the hillside. The bitch, Judy, skirted a belt of corn along the upper bottomlands. I kept my eye on the big dog. A dog that has bird sense knows cover when he sees it. This big Bob was an independent hunter. I could see him moving fast through the scrub oaks, working his way down toward a patch of ironweed. He caught the first scent traces just on the edge of the weed patch and froze. Judy, meanwhile, had been following the line of the cornfield. A hundred yards away she caught sight of Bob's point and backed him.

We went up and flushed the birds. They got up in two bunches. I heard Joe's shot while I was in the act of raising my gun and I saw his bird fall not thirty paces from where I stood. I had covered a middle bird of the larger bunch—that's the one led by the boss cock—the way I usually do. He fell, whirling head over heels, driven a little forward by the impact. A well-centered shot. I could tell by the way the feathers fluffed as he tumbled.

The dogs were off through the grass. They had retrieved both birds. Joe stuck his in his pocket. He laughed. "I thought there for a minute you were going to let him get away."

I looked at him but I didn't say anything. It's a wonderful thing to be twenty years old.

The majority of the singles had flown straight ahead to settle in the rank grass that jutted out from the bottomland. Judy got down to work at once but the big dog broke off to the left, wanting to get footloose to find another covey. I thought of how Gyges, the best dog I ever had—the best dog any man ever had—used always to want to do the same thing, and I laughed.

"Naw, you won't," I said. "Come back here, you scoundrel, and hunt these singles."

He stopped on the edge of a briar patch, looked at me, and heeled up promptly. I clucked him out again. He gave me another look. I thought we were beginning to understand each other better. We got some nice points among those singles and I found him reasonably steady to both wing and shot, needing only a little control.

We followed that valley along the creek bed through two or three more cornfields without finding another covey. Joe was disappointed but I wasn't worrying yet; you always make your bag in the afternoon.

It was twelve o'clock by this time. We turned up the ravine toward Buck Springs. They had cleared out some of the big trees on the sides of the ravine but the spring itself was just the same: the tall sycamore tree and the water pouring in a thin stream over the slick rocks. I unwrapped the sandwiches and the pieces of cake and laid them on a stump. Joe had got the thermos bottle out of his pocket. Something had gone wrong with it and the coffee was stone cold. We were about to drink it that way when Joe saw a good tin can flung down beside the spring. He made a trash fire and we put the coffee in the can and heated it to boiling.

Joe finished his last sandwich and reached for the cake. "Good ham," he said.

"It's John Ferguson's," I said. I was watching the dogs. They were tired, all right. Judy had scooped out a soft place between the roots of a sycamore but the big dog, Bob, lay there with his fore-paws stretched out before him, never taking his eyes off our faces. I looked at him and thought how different he was from his mate and like some dogs I had known—and men, too—who lived only for hunting and could never get enough no matter how long the day was. There was something about his head and his markings that reminded me of another dog I used to hunt with a long time ago and I asked the boy who had trained him. He said the old fellow he bought the dogs from had been killed last spring, over in Trigg: Charley Morrison.

Charley Morrison. I remembered how he died. Out hunting by himself and the gun had gone off, accidentally, they said. Charley had called the dog to him, got blood all over him, and sent him home. The dog went, all right, but when they got there Charley was dead. Two years ago that was and now I was hunting the last dogs he'd ever trained. . . .

Joe lifted the thermos bottle. "Another cup?"

I held my cup out and he filled it. The coffee was still good and hot. I lit my pipe and ran my eye over the country in front of us. I always enjoy figuring out which way they'll go. This afternoon with the hot coffee in me and the ache gone from my leg I felt like I could do it. It's not as hard as it looks. A well-organized covey has a range, like chickens. I knew what they'd be doing this time of day: in a thicket, dusting—sometimes they'll get up in grapevine swings. Then after they've fed and rested they'll start out again, working always toward the open.

Joe was stamping out his cigarette. "Let's go."

The dogs were already out of sight but I could see the sedge grass ahead moving and I knew they'd be making for the same thing that took my eye: a spearhead of thicket that ran far out into this open field. We came up over a little rise. There they were. Bob on a point and Judy, the staunch little devil, backing him, not fifty feet from the thicket. I saw it was going to be tough shooting. No way to tell whether the birds were between the dog and the thicket or in the thicket itself. Then I saw that the cover was more open along the side of the thicket and I thought that that was the way they'd go if they were in the thicket. But Joe had already broken away to the left. He got too far to the side. The birds flushed to the right and left him standing, flat-footed, without a shot.

He looked sort of foolish and grinned.

I thought I wouldn't say anything and then found myself speaking:

"Trouble with you, you try to outthink the dog."

There was nothing to do about it now, though, and the chances were that the singles had pitched through the trees below. We went down there. It was hard hunting. The woods were open, the ground heavily carpeted everywhere with leaves. Dead leaves make a tremendous rustle when the dogs surge through them; it takes a good nose to cut scent keenly in such dry, noisy cover. I kept my eye on Bob. He never faltered, getting over the ground in big, springy strides but combing every inch of it. We came to an open place in the woods. Nothing but big hickory trees and bramble thickets overhung with trailing vines. Bob passed the first thicket and came to a beautiful point. We went up. He stood perfectly steady but the bird flushed out fifteen or twenty steps ahead of him. I saw it swing to the right, gaining altitude very quickly, and it came to me how it would be.

I called to Joe: "Don't shoot yet."

He nodded and raised his gun, following the bird with the barrel. It was directly over the treetops when I gave the word and he shot, scoring a clean kill.

He laughed excitedly as he stuck the bird in his pocket. "*Man!* I didn't know you could take that much time!"

We went on through the open woods. I was thinking about a day I'd had years ago, in the woods at Grassdale, with my uncle James Morris and his son Julian. Uncle James had given Julian and me hell for missing just such a shot. I can see him now, standing up against a big pine tree, his face red from liquor and his gray hair ruffling in the wind: "*Let him alone. Let him alone!* And establish your lead as he *climbs!*"

Joe was still talking about the shot he'd made. "Lord, I wish I could get another one like that."

"You won't," I said. "We're getting out of the woods now."

We struck a path that led through the woods. My leg was stiff from the hip down and every time I brought it over the pain would start in my knee, zing, and travel up and settle in the small of my back. I walked with my head down, watching the light catch on the ridges of Joe's brown corduroy trousers and then shift and catch again as he moved forward. Sometimes he would get on ahead and then there would be nothing but the black tree trunks coming up out of the dead leaves that were all over the ground.

Joe was talking about that wild land up on the Cumberland. We could get up there some Saturday on an early train. Have a good day. Might even spend the night. When I didn't answer he turned around. "Man, you're sweating!"

I pulled my handkerchief out and wiped my face. "Hot work," I said.

He had stopped and was looking about him. "Used to be a spring somewhere around here."

He had found the path and was off. I sat down on a stump and mopped my face some more. The sun was halfway down through the trees, the whole west woods ablaze with light. I sat there and thought that in another hour it would be good dark and I wished that the day could go on and not end so soon and yet I didn't see how I could make it much farther with my leg the way it was.

Joe was coming up the path with his folding cup full of water. I hadn't thought I was thirsty but the cold water tasted good. We sat there awhile and smoked. It was Joe said we ought to be starting back, that we must be a good piece from the rig by this time.

We set out, working north through the edge of the woods. It was rough going and I was thinking that it would be all I could do to make it back to the rig when we climbed a fence and came out at one end of a long field. It sloped down to a wooded ravine, broken ground badly gullied and covered with sedge everywhere except where sumac thickets had sprung up—as birdy a place as ever I saw. I looked it over and I knew I'd have to hunt it, leg or no leg, but it would be close work, for me and the dogs too.

I blew them in a bit and we stood there watching them cut up the cover. The sun was down now; there was just enough light left to see the dogs work. The big dog circled the far wall of the basin and came upwind just off the drain, then stiffened to a point. We walked down to it. The birds had obviously run a bit, into the scraggly sumac stalks that bordered the ditch. My mind was so much on the dogs that I forgot Joe. He took one step too many and the fullest-blown bevy of the day roared up through the tangle. It had to be fast work. I raised my gun and scored with the only barrel I had time to peg. Joe shouted: I knew he had got one too.

We stood awhile trying to figure out which way the singles had gone. But they had fanned out too quick for us and after beating around the thicket for fifteen minutes or so we gave up and went on.

We came to the rim of the swale, eased over it, crossed the dry creek bed that was drifted thick with leaves, and started up the other side. I had blown in the dogs, thinking there was no use for them to run their heads off now we'd started home, but they didn't come. I walked a little way, then I looked back and saw Bob's white shoulders through a tangle of cinnamon vines.

Joe had turned around too. "Look a yonder! They've pinned a single out of that last covey."

"Your shot," I told him.

He shook his head. "No, you take it."

I went back and flushed the bird. It went skimming along the buckberry bushes that covered that side of the swale. In the fading light I could hardly make it out and I shot too quick. It swerved over the thicket and I let go with the second barrel. It staggered, then zoomed up. Up, up, up, over the rim of the hill and above the tallest hickories. I saw it there for a second, its wings black against the gold light, before, wings still spread, it came whirling down, like an autumn leaf, like the leaves that were everywhere about us, all over the ground.

QUESTIONS TO CONSIDER

1. As he narrates this story, Aleck contrasts himself with Joe Thomas, an eager but inexperienced young man of 20. What complex feelings does Aleck have for his hunting companion? How do these lead to Aleck's wish, as the sinking sun sets, "that the day could go on and not end so soon"?
2. After he takes his last shot at a bird, Aleck watches it soar a final time above the treetops, then come "whirling down, like an autumn leaf, like the leaves that were everywhere about us, all over the ground." As darkness falls on the woods, what unspoken perception does Aleck have about his future?

Katharine Du Pre Lumpkin

1897–1988

At a tender age, Katharine Du Pre Lumpkin acted upon her impulse to grapple with "the burden of Southern history" characterized by historian C. Vann Woodward. Lumpkin came to realize the error of the Southern racial politics into which she had been indoctrinated as a young child and subsequently devoted her efforts to the study and alleviation of human suffering. Biographer Jacquelyn Dowd Hall has suggested that even as early as her college years, Lumpkin was recognized by her peers as a woman whose name would be "remembered for many generations" because of her "love of humanity." This love led Lumpkin to write her memoirs, *The Making of a Southerner*, a work which in many ways meets the burden of Southern history head on. Hall argues that the memoir is a "projection of the self as representative of the group" in which Lumpkin sought to "show how good people could create monstrous systems." Lumpkin's studies led her to analyze Southern history and culture in ways that took into account the experiences of people of color and those who supported the end of oppression. Her sociological studies make her a significant voice in the development of the New South.

Lumpkin was born in 1897 in Macon, Georgia, the daughter of a White elitist who served as a Confederate soldier and later claimed membership in the Ku Klux Klan. She grew up with two sisters, who also became well-educated social critics; the young women were steeped in the rhetoric of what Lumpkin later called the "Old South's disinherited, who had lost so much and regained so little, materially speaking." Elizabeth Lumpkin Glenn became an orator, but focused her attention on extolling the virtues of the Lost Cause, while Grace Lumpkin penned proletarian novels enumerating the plight of industrial workers. Katharine Lumpkin spent much of her adult life committed to a partnership with Dorothy Douglas, a relationship that she vigilantly refused to discuss, and that she went to substantial lengths to excise from her correspondence, notes, and other written documents.

Katharine Lumpkin began her education at Brenau College in Gainesville, Georgia, where she earned a bachelor's degree in history. She later attended Columbia University and the University of Wisconsin, where she completed master's and doctoral degrees in sociology. Lumpkin published five books in addition to *The Making of a Southerner*, and each of her published works draws upon her background in sociology, leading her to settle on the inequities of racial and class-based systems in the United States as a fruitful area of study.

Despite systematic indoctrination into Southern religious values as a child, as an adult Lumpkin rejected the mainstream Judeo-Christian teachings so prevalent in her native region, favoring instead the theories of social Christianity. She later expanded her consideration of social Christianity after coming into contact with the theories of Karl Marx and the Popular Front. Lumpkin was also a long-time supporter of the YWCA, working as the national student secretary of the Southern region while attending Brenau. She served as research director to the Council of Industrial Studies at Smith College and the Institute of Labor Studies in Northampton, Massachusetts.

Despite the high regard with which Lumpkin's sociological studies were received during her lifetime, her most lasting contribution to Southern studies derives from records of her experiences in the Jim Crow South. *The Making of a Southerner* holds a place in a newly emerging genre in Southern letters during the Southern Renascence—what critic Fred Hobson has called the racial conversion narrative. In his 1999 study, *But Now I See: The White Southern Racial Conversion Narrative*, Hobson examines the similarities between racial and religious conversion, noting the presence of the implicit journey from "sinfulness to a recognition of sin and consequently a changed life." Lumpkin's memoir illustrates the overt oppression inherent in the Jim Crow South and the process through which she became aware of the insidious evil that it represented.

from The Making of a Southerner

from Book 3 *A Child Inherits a Lost Cause*

Men like my father spoke of the Lost Cause. It was little more than a manner of speaking. Even of the war they would say, "We were never conquered . . ." and of reconstruction. "I'm an unreconstructed rebel!" They would sing in gayer moods:

I've not been reconstructed,
Nor tuck the oath of allegiance,
I'm the same old red hot rebel,
And that's good enough for me!

Seriously, they would say: "We need not and will not lose those things that made the South glorious." If new features must be permitted the Southern edifice, so be it. At least the fundamentals should be kept intact. It became the preoccupation of their kind to preserve the old foundations at all costs.

In my father's case, as far back as 1874 he had launched upon his career in behalf of Confederate veterans. In that year there met in Union Point, Georgia, then his home, the first regimental reunion of Confederates—this was the claim—ever to be held in the South. This was a gathering of his own, the Third Georgia Regiment. Thenceforth, Father was ever at the beck and call of his comrades' interests.

These were the years when in towns and cities throughout Georgia, South Carolina, and all Southern states, men raised a slender shaft, topped by a tall soldier figure—the Confederate soldier. With solemn ceremony, a "rebel yell" from assembled veterans, a band playing *Dixie,* and oratory of a bygone day, these sacred monuments were unveiled. My father soon became a favorite orator on such occasions: he could be counted on to drop everything for them; also, he spoke such things as his audience wanted to hear, and in the way they wanted—feelingly, eloquently. I should hesitate to guess how many of these shafts in the small towns of South Carolina had the veil lifted from them by his devoted hand.

Besides this there were the Confederate reunions, Southwide, statewide, and even on a smaller scale. Father was an inveterate reunion-goer and planner. So were literally hundreds of his kind, men who were also of the Old South's disinherited, who had lost so much and regained so little, materially speaking. It may well be that these men were a mainspring of this "Lost Cause movement," kept it pulsing, held it to fever pitch while they could, firing it with its peculiar fervor. Where but in the past lay their real glory? Who more than they would have reason to keep lifted up the time of their greatness?

Theirs was certainly a tireless effort in behalf of the Lost Cause, and a labor of love if ever there was one. These men expected to get nothing from it save people's warm approbation, perhaps, and the personal satisfaction that comes with performance of a welcome duty; and of course—indeed above everything—their sense that by this means they were serving the paramount aim of preserving the South's old foundations. Father would say: "The heritage we bear is the noblest on earth; it is for us to say whether . . . we will make the home of the South what the home of the South once was—the center of a nation's life; it is for us to keep bright the deeds of the past, and we will do it." For him it was sufficient reward that people could say, as they did on one occasion of my older sister (nor did anyone mind the fulsome language still so dear to the heart of the South at the turn of the century): "Daughter of an eloquent father, reared in a home where the Confederacy is revered as a cause, holy and imperishable. . . ."

We had lived in South Carolina less than five years when I was dipped deep in the fiery experience of Southern patriotism. This was the Confederate reunion of 1903, held in our home town of Columbia.

It was but one in a long line of reunions. In South Carolina they had a way of placing the first in the year 1876—"the grandest reunion ever held in any State, one of the most sublime spectacles ever witnessed," "thrilling the hearts" of the people of Columbia. They called it the first, but "there were no invitations, no elaborate programme, no committees of reception, no assignment of quarters, no reduced rates of transportation, no bands of music, no streamers flying." Of it they said: "The State was prostrate. The people had with marvelous patience restrained themselves from tearing at the throat of the Radical party. Hampton had been elected governor, and yet the tyrannical party would not yield." (Wade Hampton and his "red shirts" had just overthrown reconstruction.) At that moment, the story goes—"It was the supreme moment of the crisis"—there appeared, coming into Columbia from every direction, by all the highways, "men in apparel which had become the most glorious badge of service since the history of the world—those faded jackets of gray." They came, it is said, ten thousand of them, converging on Columbia, making their way straight to the headquarters of the Democratic party. They were resolved, they said, "to make this State one vast cemetery of free men rather than the home of slaves." Their voices shouted hoarsely, "Hampton!" "Forth came the great captain who stilled the tumult with a wave of his hand." He said: "My countrymen, all is well. Go home and be of good cheer. I have been elected governor of South Carolina, and by the eternal God, I will be governor or there shall be none." Men said, "There will never be another such reunion."

It was not a reunion of course in the later sense. Since 'seventy-six the South had seen an exceedingly complex organization of Confederate sentiment. The United Confederate Veterans covered all the Southern states. Each state had its division of the parent organization, and each division its multitude of "camps" honey-combing the counties, each bearing the name of some hero, living or dead. Not only the veterans, but their wives and widows, sons and daughters, children and grandchildren, were organized. My father was an active veteran; my mother and older sister, "Daughters of the Confederacy"; my brothers, as each grew old enough, "Sons of Confederate Veterans"; we who were the youngest, "Children of the Confederacy." Thousands of families showed such a devotion. While yet the old men lived, on whom centered all the fanfare, it was a lusty movement and fervently zealous. I chanced to know it at the peak of its influence.

I remember nothing of the Lost Cause movement before the Confederate reunion of 1903. I may have been drinking it in since the time of my babyhood, but all before that is indistinct, cloudy. In 1903 I was verily baptized in its sentiments. Sooner or later in those three event-packed days we must surely have run the whole marvelous gamut of exuberant emotions. Not the least of the thrill was the Lumpkin part in it—the sense of our complete belonging to this community cavalcade which paraded before us in so many wonderful guises. I was too young myself to have any direct share in it; school children did, but I was just this side of being an old-enough school child. It meant no deprivation, however, for I felt part of it. So absorbed in its planning and execution was our family that we all felt a part, even I, the youngest. I was permitted to see it all, everything, excepting only the balls and receptions to which children did not go but of which they could hear the glowing accounts.

In the air we felt a sense of urgency, as though the chance might never come again to honor the old men. The oratory stressed it: "Ranks of the men who fought beneath the Stars and Bars—the beautiful Southern Cross[1]—are thinner. . . ." "Pathos . . . there cannot be many more reunions for these oaks of the Confederacy. . . ." "Not far from taps . . . for many the ties that bind will soon be severed . . . the high tribute is but their honor due." Hardly a year before, Wade Hampton, Carolina's foremost citizen, had passed away. We must indeed hasten. "Gone is the peerless chieftain, the bravest of them all, the lordly Hampton, that darling *beau sabreur* of whom Father Ryan,[2] the priest-poet of the dead republic, sang. To his stainless memory the reunion is dedicated . . . for him who sleeps under the great oak in Trinity church-yard." I do not remember seeing him ride at the head of the columns, although I may have. Vaguely I can recall the great funeral, the vast throng; and clearly the many times in ensuing years when our family would troop in reverent pilgrimage to his always flower-strewn grave after Sunday services at Trinity.

The grand reunion was held in the month of May. It was the ideal time for it. Earlier would not do, lest we have April showers; later would not have been good, after the summer's heat had set in, and a torrid, sultry spell might mow the old men down like grain under the sickle. If luck held, May was the perfect time, for refreshing breezes could almost certainly be counted on; trees and shrubs were at their deepest green, the great elms and oaks casting cool shade and not yet filtered over with dust as they would be a little later, when horse-drawn vehicles, rolling along broad unpaved avenues, stirred up the hot dry sediment, sifting it onto everything. And when would flowers ever be so bountiful or varied again as in May, letting us literally strew them on the path of the old men and smother our carriages and floats with them in the parade?

Bustle and business of preparation. What child would not love it, when everywhere was unbounded enthusiasm and her own family in the thick of everything? Twenty thousand veterans and visitors coming—almost more people than in the city itself. Committee meetings every day at the Chamber of Commerce. Indeed, the Chamber was in the heart of it. Its president was a Confederate veteran-businessman; its secretary, son of a veteran. Why would not its every facility be poured into this reunion? Good business, to be sure. But much more than this, it was good Southern patriotism. A true Southern businessman's heart was in it.

Besides businessmen, all the leading people, and some not so leading, were drawn into the effort. No, not drawn; they had poured, all anxious to have a part on this paramount occasion—institutions, organizations, whole families, including parents, young people, and children. Entertainment, housing, parades, decorations, meetings—these were men's tasks. Feeding the veterans, in particular manning two free lunch rooms down town, was the ladies'. Social events fell to the young people, the Sons of Veterans—Maxcy Gragg Camp—and the young ladies; they must plan for balls and receptions, and for the good times of over two hundred sponsors and maids-of-honor, "bevy of the State's most beautiful young ladies." Local bands must serve. Local militia—"wearing uniforms as near like the Confederate butternut as U.S. Arsenals afford"; students of South Carolina College and the two "female" colleges; school children, two hundred of them, to strew flowers, sing in a chorus, execute intricate marches which took hours and days for training; the Cotillon Club, select dancing society; the town's "riding set" for the parade; the Metropolitan Club; the local lodge of Elks; merchants and manufacturers and other businessmen to give

1. Popular names for the several Confederate flags.

2. Poet-cleric Father Abraham Joseph Ryan (1839–1886) published *Poems: Patriotic, Religious, Miscellaneous* in 1880.

their time and money and elaborately decorate their establishments. Everyone must decorate. Stores had stocked their shelves. Everyone must go home loaded down with red and white bunting and Confederate flags.

The day dawned. Tuesday, May 13. A brilliant day. On Monday had come a heavy, prolonged shower, casting us into gloom. But we were quickly comforted. It but laid the dust and sent cool breezes blowing. The paper sang: "Under a sky that was an inverted bowl of sapphire . . . in an air that kissed and caressed them as pleasantly as any zephyr that ever swept across the Southland, the remnants of the thin gray line mustered into Columbia. . . ."

The moment was here. The pageant unfolded. All the way to Main Street, every home festooned in bunting and flags, and Main Street itself, from end to end, red and white bunting, incandescent lights of white and red. By night these lights, in a child's eyes, looked like one's dream of fairyland. Confederate flags. They were everywhere, by the thousands, of every size. People thronging Main Street carried flags. A few might also have South Carolina's banner—a palmetto tree and crescent against a field of blue—but all would have a Confederate flag. Dominating Main Street, at its head, was the State Capitol building, domed and dignified, granite steps mounting to its entrance. From window to window was draped bunting, and spread across its face, a huge Confederate banner. Across from it, both Opera House and City Hall were festooned and flag-draped.

Under the shadow of the State House dome on the Capitol grounds was a huge "bivouac tent"—a circus tent—ninety feet in diameter, they said. Six hundred veterans would be sheltered there, overflow from people's homes. Everyone talked of it; patrolled day and night by militia units; army cots provided from the Armory; only half a block from Convention Hall; information bureau but a stone's throw; General Hampton's grave a hundred yards away. Mr. Gantt, Secretary of State, not being satisfied, had the Negro convicts install a lavatory. General Frost, Adjutant General, pitched some smaller tents like a company street to bring back "old times." They called it Camp Wade Hampton. Hardly a yard, inside and outside the bivouac, but was hung in bunting. On its highest pole floated a grand banner—"of course the emblem of the Lost Cause."

All Tuesday veterans and visitors poured in. Every hour broad Main Street grew more crowded. Committees of men on duty at Union Station from daybreak until midnight. Father's stint was four hours in the afternoon, several men under him, all wearing their conspicuous badges (how proud I was): "Ask Me. Entertainment Committee." Helping the hundreds of old men; assigning them quarters; handing them badges: "Veteran," open sesame to everything, free of charge, nothing excluded, the city theirs. Band music all afternoon on the capitol grounds—martial airs—old Southern songs—and *Dixie!* Ever so often, *Dixie!*

How quaint it seems, but not so then—the veterans' free trolley ride. All over the city on the rumbling, bumping trolleys, for two hours, "to their hearts' content," no nickels called for, special trolleys provided. This to keep them occupied until affairs began.

Parades. Two of them. Best of all the "veterans' parade." The old men marching. Not too long a march; just from post office to State House, half a mile. They were getting so old, more should not be expected. How thronged were the sidewalks—thousands of people—and the windows of buildings—people leaning out to cheer and wave Confederate flags. Men doffing their hats so long as the old men were passing, women fluttering their handkerchiefs. School children ahead of them, spreading the streets with a carpet of flowers, lavishly, excitedly. There in a conspicuous carriage, the surviving signers of the Ordinance of Secession![3] Bands playing march tunes until it seemed one's spine could not stand any more tingles. But then—the Stars and Bars, dipping and floating and—*Dixie!* From end to end along the route, shouting and cheering, always wild shouting and cheering, at the Stars and Bars and *Dixie*. For me too there was the thrill of looking proudly for Father marching with "the Georgians." These were a special contingent, come from Augusta on their own train and given "the place of honor" in the parade, right behind General Carwile, the Commander. "The band of survivors—come from Augusta in their gray jeans . . . with their old muskets . . . to give an exhibition of Hardee's tactics." Everyone was chuckling over the special permission the Georgians asked, to bring the old firearms across the border, telling the Governor, "If fired the old muskets were more dangerous to the shooter than the men aimed at." Wonderful old muskets! Father, particular host to the Georgians—"Col. W. W. Lumpkin, always solicitous for the Georgians, will have charge of their headquarters, and will superintend their arrangements. . . . " And march with them on parade. Also I was looking for my sister. At the end of the long line rode the sponsors and maids-of-honor in carriages. Here also rode the reunion orators.

Hardly less wonderful, on another day, was the "floral parade." "Most beautiful spectacle of the reunion. . . . " One somber note was permitted. Behind the marshals where on other years had ridden a military figure, now there walked an aged Negro, John Johnson, General Hampton's old coachman, " . . . now led by the bridle an unsaddled horse . . . charger of the dead hero." Sponsors and maids-of-honor on splendid floats elaborately decorated as bowers by institutions and businesses. Mounted escort, "ladies and gentlemen of the city's riding set." Carriages of everyone who owned a carriage, swathed in flowers, graced by their owners and by "beautiful young ladies." Even three motor cars, one a "large French one" smothered in white and pink roses. ". . . A series of spectacles . . . parade of flowers with its living buds. . . . "

The meetings. The speeches. Even a child liked to listen, punctuated as they were every few moments with excited handclapping, cheers, stamping of feet, music. And such great men. All were veterans or sons of men in gray: the Chamber of Commerce head; white-haired clergymen pronouncing invocations; Governor Heyward, a veteran; Judge Andrew Crawford, veteran and "silver tongued orator." Most revered of all, Bishop Capers, "warrior-Bishop," by then a pre-eminent religious leader, who at twenty-eight had become a Confederate general, in all eyes saintly, epitome of the South's best. Who there would not feel his Lost Cause blessed when so noble a man could tell them, "We all hold it to be one of the noblest chapters in our history . . ."?

All but one who spoke were veterans or their sons. The one was a daughter. It was the opening night. She was to welcome them—"a daughter of a Confederate." A child would never forget this particular moment. Bands playing a medley of old war tunes. Crowds pushing, for there was not room for all; orchestra and dress circle crammed with old veterans; aisles and entrances packed long before time for opening. The stage—huge to a child's eyes—massed with human figures: great chorus of trained voices waiting their signal; sponsors and maids-of-honor seated tier on tier and trailing from their shoulders broad sashes of office embossed in gold letters. Old soldiers who had been bidden to the stage—generals, colonels, majors, captains, every rank, in spick-and-span gray uniforms. Somewhere among them the slight figure of a young woman.

3. Document that officially proclaimed a state's withdrawal from the United States.

Roll of drums; blare of trumpets; then the first high, clear notes of *Dixie!* All the gathering surging, scrambling to their feet—clapping, stamping, cheering, singing. In time it ended. It must end from sheer exhaustion. Then Bugler Lightfoot coming forward to sound the sharp notes of the "assembly," and with its dying away, the chorus beginning, and every voice swelling and rolling it forth, the Long-Meter Doxology—"Praise God from whom all blessings flow. . . ."

There were speeches, but they were as nothing to me that opening night. The newspaper said: "The veterans were waiting." So was I waiting. "Their enthusiasm . . . seemed to have been kept in check until Miss Elizabeth Lumpkin, who addressed them last year, was presented. . . ."

> *There is nothing stronger or more splendid on this wide earth than to have borne the sorrow you have borne, than to have endured the pain that you have endured. . . . You young men in whose veins beat the blood of heroes, uncover your heads, for the land in which you live is holy, hallowed by the blood of your fathers, purified by the tears of your mothers. . . . If I could write . . . I would tell how the private fought. . . . He came back and fought poverty, ruin, sometimes degradation for his dear ones at the hands of brutal men. . . . Men of the South, the day when the rebel yell could conquer a host is past . . . the day when you fought . . . is past. . . . Think you the day for all action is past as well?*

It was a long speech, but how could I find it so? "Eloquent . . . finished." So said the accounts. It was true, I knew. "Frequently . . . made to pause because of the cheering. . . ." "Time and again interrupted by thunderous applause. . . ." I joined in, beating my hands together and jumping to my feet like the others to stamp them on the floor.

Even the least of our participation was of moment to me. So for Father's every smallest duty; and Mother's assisting at the veterans' free lunch rooms; and my school-age sister's share in the children's chorus; and seeing them march or ride in the parades. It was so when a thirteen-year-old brother spoke before the old men—"In recognition of his gift of oratory and of devotion to the dead Confederacy . . . General Carwile, amid much enthusiasm, pinned the badge of 'honorary member, U.C.V.' upon the child's patriotic breast." It was so, also for the last night of the reunion.

Speeches must be listened to again. Finally, they were ended, and the closing moments came. Lights were extinguished. We waited while the curtain descended and rose again. Gleaming through the darkness was a bright camp fire with a kettle hanging from a tripod. Around the fire one could see men in bedraggled uniforms. One soldier lounged up to the fire—"Quaint reminder of long ago as he stood in the half light, pipe in mouth, pants tucked into his socks, coatless and collarless." He began to tell a tale of war. More men slipped out and settled down by the fire. ". . . A hushed house as the tale proceeded . . . lights gradually brightened . . . the speaker was recognized . . . Col. W. W. Lumpkin, a soldier of the Confederacy again." After that: bright lights, stacked guns seen in the foreground, tents near by, then stories from other veterans, dear to a child's heart, and to adults' too, apparently. A song begun, joined in by the audience, "We are tenting tonight on the old camp ground," rolling up to the very eaves of the Opera House. Then hilarity, the old soldiers frolicking, young soldiers again, gusts of laughter from the audience urging them on. Quiet again, as a soldier thrummed a banjo and began again to sing, and we to sing with him, one after another, the old Southern ballads, plaintive, nostalgic. On the notes of these the reunion of 1903 "passed away into the land of memories."

Questions to Consider

1. What does the narrator mean by the Lost Cause? What impression did the pageantry associated with Confederate reunions leave with the child narrator about the value of the Lost Cause? What moral or social values might a child, by viewing such events on a regular basis, come to associate with the Lost Cause?
2. Given the strength of conviction that Lumpkin's father demonstrated about the validity and righteousness of the Lost Cause, what might have led her to discover the abuse and oppression that allowed the Old South to prosper before the Civil War?

William Faulkner

1897–1962

William Faulkner holds the highest rank of distinction in Southern letters. He emerged with a talented group of writers during the first half of the twentieth century in an artistic flowering now termed the Southern Literary Renascence. Faulkner composed classic fictional chronicles of his time and place. While born and reared in a rural setting, as a young man, he lived in New York and New Orleans. Later, he set stories and novels in places as diverse as France and Italy, New York and Hollywood, Georgia and the Gulf Coast, yet north Mississippi remained the true home of his imagination. For over 50 years Faulkner created a complex artistic world that centered on his fictional Yoknapatawpha County and its county seat, Jefferson. He invested this fictional realm with ideas and themes of such passionate intensity and with such artistic innovation that his works have appealed to readers the world over. Faulkner mined the lore of his region for the great themes of his novels: the incursion of Euro-Americans into the eighteenth-century Mississippi wilderness, the land theft from the southeastern Native American tribes, the African slave trade brought to Southern shores, the ravages of the Civil War, the turmoil of postwar Reconstruction, the brutal reign of racial violence during the Jim Crow period, and the challenges of modernity to rural Southern life. He chronicled the cumulative effects of these experiences on the hearts and minds of Southerners.

Born in the hamlet of New Albany, Mississippi, on 25 September 1897, Faulkner and his family moved to nearby Oxford, where he and his three younger brothers were reared. Faulkner was close to his mother, Maud, who taught him to love literature, including the Bible. She became the prototype for the stalwart, domineering women in his fiction. His father, Murry, a rough "man's man"—a heavy drinker and financial failure but good with horses—seemed unwilling or unable to accept his undersized son with the high-pitched voice and soft features. Young Faulkner became an accomplished horseman, who loved the dress and the chase of the hunt, but not the kill. He showed sufficient athletic ability to become a capable golfer and tennis player. Despite his success in sports during adolescence, he sank into a state of melancholy from which he rarely found relief, even as he matured and aged. When America entered World War I, Faulkner was determined to prove his masculinity by entering the military, but he was rejected as too short. Undeterred, he made his way to Toronto to volunteer for the Canadian Royal Air Force, but while he was still in training the Armistice was signed. He returned to Mississippi, where he styled himself a demobilized aviator, wore his flight uniform, and postured as a wounded veteran of aerial combat. Faulkner affected a British manner, and that combined with his lack of professional prospects caused local skeptics to dub him "Count No 'Count." He told stories of fiery combat, grievous wounds, and a steel plate in his skull. These autobiographical fabrications were not mere youthful rhapsodizing; they carried forward well into his adult years when he continued to embroider the truth.

Faulkner's formal education was sketchy; he did not finish high school and left the University of Mississippi, located in his hometown, after a year. He continued to read widely in the University library, absorbing a wide range of knowledge from contemporary books on history, psychoanalysis, myth study, and comparative religion. A number of Faulkner scholars—Carvel Collins, Richard P. Adams, Thomas L. McHaney, Virginia Hlavsa, and others—have made a thorough case for the depth and influence of Faulkner's reading in the twenties on his later fiction. The first of several literary mentors, Phil Stone, a well-read local attorney, influenced Faulkner at a pivotal moment of his development by introducing him to the avant-garde world of Modernist literature, a movement whose masters—especially T. S. Eliot and James Joyce—Faulkner sought to emulate. Stone also encouraged his young protégé to write verse, which Faulkner doggedly pursued for more than a decade although he lacked true talent as a poet and later sardonically referred to himself as a "failed Kipling." Nevertheless, Stone's loan of books and "little magazines" proved highly influential to Faulkner. Much under the sway of European literature, Faulkner turned during his mid-twenties from poetry and drawing to writing fiction. Joyce, Flaubert, Balzac, and Conrad were early sources of inspiration as he wrote his first novel, *Soldiers' Pay* (1926). While living in New Orleans, Faulkner met the well-established American novelist Sherwood Anderson, who also befriended and encouraged him. Captivated from the outset of his writing career by the ramifications of Freudian theory, Faulkner soon found affinities between his own family history and the structures of psychoanalysis, particularly Freud's Oedipal conflict; anguished parent-child relationships figure prominently from the start in Faulkner's novels and stories.

His apprentice fiction illustrates that Faulkner was an accomplished intellectual before he became a great novelist, a truth that runs counter to the inaccurate and culturally biased image of him as an untutored, backwoods Southern genius, a prejudiced view that prevailed during Faulkner's lifetime and which he encouraged. A far more accurate portrayal acknowledges Faulkner to be a thoughtful, well-informed man who had the talent and drive to write at the highest level of literary accomplishment. His home bases of Oxford and Memphis provided him with the people, places, voices, and issues, as well as the cultural background he needed to succeed.

A series of rejections from girlfriends pursued during his teens and twenties seems to have led Faulkner to see himself as a romantic failure. To compensate, he made up stories about his sexual escapades and bastard children. Faulkner was drawn to wispy, petite women, perhaps incarnations of his mother, Maud, also a woman of small stature with whom Faulkner remained quite close until her death in 1960. At age 31, Faulkner married Estelle Oldham Franklin, his former high school sweetheart, a divorced mother of two children. Marital disappointment came quickly. Estelle apparently attempted to drown herself at the beach at Pascagoula, Mississippi, after a long evening of drinking. Despite this unpromising beginning, the Faulkners remained married until his death.

Back home in Oxford, money problems grew, as did Faulkner's ambivalence toward the woman he had married. He nonetheless pressed on with the duties of husband and stepfather. He settled his family in an unrestored Antebellum house without electricity or running water which he named "Rowan Oak"—a gesture toward James George Frazer's classic of comparative religion, *The Golden Bough*, a major influence on Faulkner's fiction. A skilled carpenter and house painter, Faulkner worked for months to make the house livable, hurried in the renovations by Estelle's pregnancy in 1930. He and Estelle endured the loss of their first daughter, who died in early 1931 after living nine days. A second daughter, Jill, was born in 1933. Despite many domestic setbacks at Rowan Oak, Faulkner was a devoted father to his daughter and two stepchildren, who all called him "Pappy."

Life in Oxford was not easy for the family for other reasons. Because of Faulkner's indifference to organized religion and his perceived aloofness from small-town Mississippi life, he and his family were a continual target of ridicule and even hostility from the Oxford community, a situation with biographical resonance in his first published short story, "A Rose for Emily"

(1930). During difficult times of severe financial and emotional stress, Faulkner was always writing, and he entered the most productive period of his artistic career. His years of great achievement include the masterpieces *The Sound and the Fury* (1929), *Sanctuary* (1931), *Light in August* (1932), and *Absalom, Absalom!* (1936), now revered as among the greatest novels of the twentieth century. His short stories also drew much acclaim. Perhaps as a reflection of his professional and personal frustration, in Faulkner's great novels of the late twenties and early thirties male gender identity is a frequent theme, coupled with the appearance of a disturbing, ambiguous female figure—the haunting Modernist Medusa of the Freudian age—who is both sought and resented, at once incestuously alluring and vengeful. In varying guises, she appears in "Elmer" (published posthumously, written in 1925), *Soldiers' Pay* (1926), *Mosquitoes* (1927), *Flags in the Dust* (published in shortened form as *Sartoris* in 1929), *The Sound and the Fury*, *As I Lay Dying* (1930), *Sanctuary*, *Light in August*, *Absalom, Absalom! The Unvanquished* (1938), and *The Wild Palms* (1939).

Despite his artistic accomplishments during the thirties, Faulkner remained troubled that he had failed to attract a wider reading audience. Self-doubt led to a personal crisis during the early months of World War II. Perhaps trying to make up for having missed the Great War, Faulkner the ex-pilot sought to win a commission as a flight instructor. Rejected again, at 44 he considered himself a failure. Although he won high praise from French intellectuals such as Jean-Paul Sartre, Faulkner had not yet gained high acclaim in the world of American writing. He convinced himself that authorship was a worthless profession, although the homefront movement buoyed him into writing patriotic screenplays. Instead of going to war, in 1942 he went to California to write for Warner Brothers Studios. There Faulkner gave his literary energies to developing original material as story lines for scripts to dramatize themes encouraging patriotism, extolling liberty, and denouncing oppression as part of Hollywood's "war effort." While many of these efforts were rejected by the studio, they served to reinvigorate his enthusiasm for writing.

In collaboration with experienced scenarists, Faulkner gradually learned effective scriptwriting techniques. He also absorbed the Hollywood predisposition for moralizing and preaching the traditional virtues of compassion and equality. By 1944, Warner Brothers regarded him as an accomplished studio hand and charged him with writing the screenplay for *The Big Sleep*, a detective film intended as a star vehicle for Hollywood's hottest romantic couple, Humphrey Bogart and Lauren Bacall. To adapt Raymond Chandler's novel for the screen, Faulkner borrowed from his own novel, *The Sound and the Fury*, and to some extent anticipated the "Appendix/Compson" later composed for the Viking *Portable Faulkner* (1946). This crucial anthology, after the war, would stimulate a revival of interest in Faulkner's fiction.

During the war years, Faulkner shifted from writing intensely private and inwardly directed novels, drawn from family experience, to writing works of public moment, in which he would contribute his voice to the national dialogue and offer his experiences to the younger generation. His first postwar novel, *Intruder in the Dust* (1948), denounces racial injustice with a plot that pushes ahead briskly, like a Raymond Chandler detective thriller. Now Hollywood approached him for the movie rights. At 51, for the first time in his life, Faulkner enjoyed financial security as well as a practical awareness of the literary marketplace. The next year MGM sent a film crew to Oxford to film "Intruder" on location. Two years later, in 1950, Faulkner was awarded the Nobel Prize for Literature, an honor and validation that augmented his popular standing and assured his place in academic circles.

Faulkner undertook the widely publicized role of national emissary and public intellectual. He traveled abroad, gave speeches and took positions on political issues—all of which drew him further away from the solitude he needed to write. He became writer-in-residence at the University of Virginia, put on jodhpurs and took up foxhunting. During the 1950s, now a grandfather as well as a celebrated writer, Faulkner wrote a series of labored sequels to his earlier novels, revisiting some of the most disturbing settings of his early fiction—with mixed results. For example, *The Reivers* (1962) shares some of *Sanctuary*'s Memphis underworld locations, but the once-problematic themes pertaining to erotic urge and family conflict now receive a warm, comic treatment—charming but insubstantial compared to his earlier work. Faulkner transformed psychological issues into cultural matters, which further distanced him from the old anxieties that had been the wellsprings of his imagination. For example, *Intruder in the Dust* advances a far more didactic social agenda concerning civil rights than does *Go Down, Moses* yet lacks the latter's intense concentration on guilt and shame.

Faulkner became depressed by what he considered the inconsequence of art in a mass culture that commodifies everything—including "William Faulkner." Nevertheless, he agreed to appear on network television shows and contribute articles to *Sports Illustrated.* Indeed, despite his eloquent Nobel Prize acceptance speech attesting to the unconquerable capacity of the human spirit to persist and prevail, those ideals did not finally sustain him. Chronic back pain had led to painkillers and tranquilizers, which he downed with whisky. On 6 July 1962, he died of a heart attack in a sanitarium not far from Oxford, where he asked to be taken after a fall from his horse. In retrospect, the last years of Faulkner's life resemble the anguished disorientation of his lost and tragic characters.

The two works in this section demonstrate Faulkner's enduring legacy as a storyteller of prodigious power. An early story, "Red Leaves" (1930), set in Antebellum Mississippi, is an acute examination of the cruelty and moral contradiction of slavery. Local history informs Faulkner's tale: The Chickasaws held Black slaves, acquired by frontier bartering with White men (the Chickasaws also had held enemy Native Americans as slaves). Faulkner develops a series of dramatic ironies in "Red Leaves" by viewing human bondage from a dual perspective. The beginning of the story concentrates on the Native Americans, who continue their ancestral rituals even though their culture has decayed through contact with Whites. Tribal rites require that when Chief Issetibbeha dies, his dog, horse, and bodyservant be buried alive with him. The focus then shifts to the 40-year-old African slave, a runaway who has fled into the swamp to escape this ritual death. His West African culture (he is from Guinea) too, has been debased by Whites, and he now finds himself enslaved by Indians imitating Whites. His flight illustrates above all his desperate will to live.

"Delta Autumn," set during a north Mississippi deer hunt in the early 1940s, is the sixth chapter of *Go Down, Moses*. This novel explores the McCaslin family, whose history is steeped in miscegenation and incest, the two unatoned sexual sins of their slaveholding. Carothers (Roth) Edmonds and his unnamed African-American mistress are direct descendants of the same White progenitor, Lucius Quintus Carothers McCaslin. Roth's life recapitulates in the twentieth century the old wrongs of his slaveowning ancestor, who sexually exploited African-American women a century before. Old Uncle Ike (Isaac) McCaslin, a childless widower, now near death, must confront the enduring frontier legacy of Southern outrages against African Americans, women, and the wilderness.

Red Leaves

I

The two Indians crossed the plantation toward the slave quarters. Neat with whitewash, of baked soft brick, the two rows of houses in which lived the slaves belonging to the clan, faced one another across the mild shade of the lane marked and scored with naked feet and with a few home-made toys mute in the dust. There was no sign of life.

"I know what we will find," the first Indian said.

"What we will not find," the second said. Although it was noon, the lane was vacant, the doors of the cabins empty and quiet; no cooking smoke rose from any of the chinked and plastered chimneys.

"Yes. It happened like this when the father of him who is now the Man, died."

"You mean, of him who was the Man."

"Yao."

The first Indian's name was Three Basket. He was perhaps sixty. They were both squat men, a little solid, burgher-like; paunchy, with big heads, big, broad, dust-colored faces of a certain blurred serenity like carved heads on a ruined wall in Siam or Sumatra, looming out of a mist. The sun had done it, the violent sun, the violent shade. Their hair looked like sedge grass on burnt-over land. Clamped through one ear Three Basket wore an enameled snuffbox.

"I have said all the time that this is not the good way. In the old days there were no quarters, no Negroes. A man's time was his own then. He had time. Now he must spend most of it finding work for them who prefer sweating to do."

"They are like horses and dogs."

"They are like nothing in this sensible world. Nothing contents them save sweat. They are worse than the white people."

"It is not as though the Man himself had to find work for them to do."

"You said it. I do not like slavery. It is not the good way. In the old days, there was the good way. But not now."

"You do not remember the old way either."

"I have listened to them who do. And I have tried this way. Man was not made to sweat."

"That's so. See what it has done to their flesh."

"Yes. Black. It has a bitter taste, too."

"You have eaten of it?"

"Once. I was young then, and more hardy in the appetite than now. Now it is different with me."

"Yes. They are too valuable to eat now."

"There is a bitter taste to the flesh which I do not like."

"They are too valuable to eat, anyway, when the white men will give horses for them."

They entered the lane. The mute, meager toys—the fetish-shaped objects made of wood and rags and feathers—lay in the dust about the patinaed doorsteps, among bones and broken gourd dishes. But there was no sound from any cabin, no face in any door; had not been since yesterday, when Issetibbeha died. But they already knew what they would find.

It was in the central cabin, a house a little larger than the others, where at certain phases of the moon the Negroes would gather to begin their ceremonies before removing after nightfall to the creek bottom, where they kept the drums. In this room they kept the minor accessories, the cryptic ornaments, the ceremonial records which consisted of sticks daubed with red clay in symbols. It had a hearth in the center of the floor, beneath a hole in the roof, with a few cold wood ashes and a suspended iron pot. The window shutters were closed; when the two Indians entered, after the abashless sunlight they could distinguish nothing with the eyes save a movement, shadow, out of which eyeballs rolled, so that the place appeared to be full of Negroes. The two Indians stood in the doorway.

"Yao," Basket said. "I said this is not the good way."

"I don't think I want to be here," the second said.

"That is black man's fear which you smell. It does not smell as ours does."

"I don't think I want to be here."

"Your fear has an odor too."

"Maybe it is Issetibbeha which we smell."

"Yao. He knows. He knows what we will find here. He knew when he died what we should find here today." Out of the rank twilight of the room the eyes, the smell, of Negroes rolled about them. "I am Three Basket, whom you know," Basket said into the room. "We are come from the Man. He whom we seek is gone?" The Negroes said nothing. The smell of them, of their bodies, seemed to ebb and flux in the still hot air. They seemed to be musing as one upon something remote, inscrutable. They were like a single octopus. They were like the roots of a huge tree uncovered, the earth broken momentarily upon the writhen, thick, fetid tangle of its lightless and outraged life. "Come," Basket said. "You know our errand. Is he whom we seek gone?"

"They are thinking something," the second said. "I do not want to be here."

"They are knowing something," Basket said.

"They are hiding him, you think?"

"No. He is gone. He has been gone since last night. It happened like this before, when the grandfather of him who is now the Man died. It took us three days to catch him. For three days Doom lay above the ground, saying 'I see my horse and my dog. But I do not see my slave. What have you done with him that you will not permit me to lie quiet?' "

"They do not like to die."

"Yao. They cling. It makes trouble for us, always. A people without honor and without decorum. Always a trouble."

"I do not like it here."

"Nor do I. But then, they are savages; they cannot be expected to regard usage. That is why I say that this way is a bad way."

"Yao. They cling. They would even rather work in the sun than to enter the earth with a chief. But he is gone."

The Negroes had said nothing, made no sound. The white eyeballs rolled, wild, subdued; the smell was rank, violent. "Yes, they fear," the second said. "What shall we do now?"

"Let us go and talk with the Man."

"Will Moketubbe listen?"

"What can he do? He will not like to. But he is the Man now."

"Yao. He is the Man. He can wear the shoes with the red heels all the time now." They turned and went out. There was no door in the door frame. There were no doors in any of the cabins.

"He did that anyway," Basket said.

"Behind Issetibbeha's back. But now they are his shoes, since he is the Man."

"Yao. Issetibbeha did not like it. I have heard. I know that he said to Moketubbe: 'When you are the Man, the shoes will be yours. But until then, they are my shoes.' But now Moketubbe is the Man; he can wear them."

"Yao," the second said. "He is the Man now. He used to wear the shoes behind Issetibbeha's back, and it was not known if Issetibbeha knew this or not. And then Issetibbeha became dead, who was not old, and the shoes are Moketubbe's, since he is the Man now. What do you think of that?"

"I don't think about it," Basket said. "Do you?"

"No," the second said.

"Good," Basket said. "You are wise."

II

The house sat on a knoll, surrounded by oak trees. The front of it was one story in height, composed of the deck house of a steamboat which had gone ashore and which Doom, Issetibbeha's father, had dismantled with his slaves and hauled on cypress rollers twelve miles home overland. It took them five months. His house consisted at the time of one brick wall. He set the steamboat broadside on to the wall, where now the chipped and flaked gilding of the rococo cornices arched in faint splendor above the gilt lettering of the stateroom names above the jalousied doors.

Doom had been born merely a subchief, a Mingo, one of three children on the mother's side of the family. He made a journey—he was a young man then and New Orleans was a European city—from north Mississippi to New Orleans by keel boat, where he met the Chevalier Sœur Blonde de Vitry, a man whose social position, on its face, was as equivocal as Doom's own. In New Orleans, among the gamblers and cutthroats of the river front, Doom, under the tutelage of his patron, passed as the chief, the Man, the hereditary owner of that land which belonged to the male side of the family; it was the Chevalier de Vitry who called him *du homme,* and hence Doom.

They were seen everywhere together—the Indian, the squat man with a bold, inscrutable, underbred face, and the Parisian, the expatriate, the friend, it was said, of Carondelet and the intimate of General Wilkinson.[1] Then they disappeared, the two of them, vanishing from their old equivocal haunts and leaving behind them the legend of the sums which Doom was believed to have won, and some tale about a young woman, daughter of a fairly well-to-do West Indian family, the son and brother of whom sought Doom with a pistol about his old haunts for some time after his disappearance.

Six months later the young woman herself disappeared, boarding the St. Louis packet, which put in one night at a wood landing on the north Mississippi side, where the woman, accompanied by a Negro maid, got off. Four Indians met her with a horse and wagon, and they traveled for three days, slowly, since she was already big with child, to the plantation, where she found that Doom was now chief. He never told her how he accomplished it, save that his uncle and his cousin had died suddenly. At that time the house consisted of a brick wall built by shiftless slaves, against which was propped a thatched lean-to divided into rooms and littered with bones and refuse, set in the center of ten thousand acres of matchless parklike forest where deer grazed like domestic cattle. Doom and the woman were married there a short time before Issetibbeha was born, by a combination itinerant minister and slave trader who arrived on a mule, to the saddle of which was lashed a cotton umbrella and a three-gallon demijohn of whisky. After that, Doom began to acquire more slaves and to cultivate some of his land, as the white people did. But he never had enough for them to do. In utter idleness the majority of them led lives transplanted whole out of African jungles, save on the occasions when, entertaining guests, Doom coursed them with dogs.

When Doom died, Issetibbeha, his son, was nineteen. He became proprietor of the land and of the quintupled herd of blacks for which he had no use at all. Though the title of Man rested with him, there was a hierarchy of cousins and uncles who ruled the clan and who finally gathered in squatting conclave over the Negro question, squatting profoundly beneath the golden names above the doors of the steamboat.

"We cannot eat them," one said.

"Why not?"

"There are too many of them."

1. Born Hector de Carondelet, he was the Spanish governor of Louisiana from 1791 to 1797. James Wilkinson was a U.S. Army officer who was a secret agent for Spain.

"That's true," a third said. "Once we started, we should have to eat them all. And that much flesh diet is not good for man."

"Perhaps they will be like deer flesh. That cannot hurt you."

"We might kill a few of them and not eat them," Issetibbeha said.

They looked at him for a while. "What for?" one said.

"That is true," a second said. "We cannot do that. They are too valuable; remember all the bother they have caused us, finding things for them to do. We must do as the white men do."

"How is that?" Issetibbeha said.

"Raise more Negroes by clearing more land to make corn to feed them, then sell them. We will clear the land and plant it with food and raise Negroes and sell them to the white men for money."

"But what will we do with this money?" a third said.

They thought for a while.

"We will see," the first said. They squatted, profound, grave.

"It means work," the third said.

"Let the Negroes do it," the first said.

"Yao. Let them. To sweat is bad. It is damp. It opens the pores."

"And then the night air enters."

"Yao. Let the Negroes do it. They appear to like sweating."

So they cleared the land with the Negroes and planted it in grain. Up to that time the slaves had lived in a huge pen with a lean-to roof over one corner, like a pen for pigs. But now they began to build quarters, cabins, putting the young Negroes in the cabins in pairs to mate; five years later Issetibbeha sold forty head to a Memphis trader, and he took the money and went abroad upon it, his maternal uncle from New Orleans conducting the trip. At that time the Chevalier Sœur Blonde de Vitry was an old man in Paris, in a toupee and a corset, with a careful toothless old face fixed in a grimace quizzical and profoundly tragic. He borrowed three hundred dollars from Issetibbeha and in return he introduced him into certain circles; a year later Issetibbeha returned home with a gilt bed, a pair of girandoles by whose light it was said that Pompadour arranged her hair while Louis smirked at his mirrored face across her powdered shoulder, and a pair of slippers with red heels. They were too small for him, since he had not worn shoes at all until he reached New Orleans on his way abroad.

He brought the slippers home in tissue paper and kept them in the remaining pocket of a pair of saddlebags filled with cedar shavings, save when he took them out on occasion for his son, Moketubbe, to play with. At three years of age Moketubbe had a broad, flat, Mongolian face that appeared to exist in a complete and unfathomable lethargy, until confronted by the slippers.

Moketubbe's mother was a comely girl whom Issetibbeha had seen one day working in her shift in a melon patch. He stopped and watched her for a while—the broad, solid thighs, the sound back, the serene face. He was on his way to the creek to fish that day, but he didn't go any farther; perhaps while he stood there watching the unaware girl he may have remembered his own mother, the city woman, the fugitive with her fans and laces and her Negro blood, and all the tawdry shabbiness of that sorry affair. Within the year Moketubbe was born; even at three he could not get his feet into the slippers. Watching him in the still, hot afternoons as he struggled with the slippers with a certain monstrous repudiation of fact, Issetibbeha laughed quietly to himself. He laughed at Moketubbe and the shoes for several years, because Moketubbe did not give up trying to put them on until he was sixteen. Then he quit. Or Issetibbeha thought he had. But he had merely quit trying in Issetibbeha's presence.

Issetibbeha's newest wife told him that Moketubbe had stolen and hidden the shoes. Issetibbeha quit laughing then, and he sent the woman away, so that he was alone. "Yao," he said. "I too like being alive, it seems." He sent for Moketubbe. "I give them to you," he said.

Moketubbe was twenty-five then, unmarried. Issetibbeha was not tall, but he was taller by six inches than his son and almost a hundred pounds lighter. Moketubbe was already diseased with flesh, with a pale, broad, inert face and dropsical hands and feet. "They are yours now," Issetibbeha said, watching him. Moketubbe had looked at him once when he entered, a glance brief, discreet, veiled.

"Thanks," he said.

Issetibbeha looked at him. He could never tell if Moketubbe saw anything, looked at anything. "Why will it not be the same if I give the slippers to you?"

"Thanks," Moketubbe said. Issetibbeha was using snuff at the time; a white man had shown him how to put the powder into his lip and scour it against his teeth with a twig of gum or of alphea.

"Well," he said, "a man cannot live forever." He looked at his son, then his gaze went blank in turn, unseeing, and he mused for an instant. You could not tell what he was thinking, save that he said half aloud: "Yao. But Doom's uncle had no shoes with red heels." He looked at his son again, fat, inert. "Beneath all that, a man might think of doing anything and it not be known until too late." He sat in a splint chair hammocked with deer thongs. "He cannot even get them on; he and I are both frustrated by the same gross meat which he wears. He cannot even get them on. But is that my fault?"

He lived for five years longer, then he died. He was sick one night, and though the doctor came in a skunk-skin vest and burned sticks, he died before noon.

That was yesterday; the grave was dug, and for twelve hours now the People had been coming in wagons and carriages and on horseback and afoot, to eat the baked dog and the succotash and the yams cooked in ashes and to attend the funeral.

III

"It will be three days," Basket said, as he and the other Indian returned to the house. "It will be three days and the food will not be enough; I have seen it before."

The second Indian's name was Louis Berry. "He will smell too, in this weather."

"Yao. They are nothing but a trouble and a care."

"Maybe it will not take three days."

"They run far. Yao. We will smell this Man before he enters the earth. You watch and see if I am not right."

They approached the house.

"He can wear the shoes now," Berry said. "He can wear them now in man's sight."

"He cannot wear them for a while yet," Basket said. Berry looked at him. "He will lead the hunt."

"Moketubbe?" Berry said. "Do you think he will? A man to whom even talking is travail?"

"What else can he do? It is his own father who will soon begin to smell."

"That is true," Berry said. "There is even yet a price he must pay for the shoes. Yao. He has truly bought them. What do you think?"

"What do you think?"

"What do you think?"

"I think nothing."

"Nor do I. Issetibbeha will not need the shoes now. Let Moketubbe have them; Issetibbeha will not care."

"Yao. Man must die."

"Yao. Let him; there is still the Man."

The bark roof of the porch was supported by peeled cypress poles, high above the texas of the steamboat, shading an unfloored banquette where on the trodden earth mules and horses were tethered in bad weather. On the forward end of the steamboat's deck sat an old man and two women. One of the women was dressing a fowl, the other was shelling corn. The old man was talking. He was barefoot, in a long linen frock coat and a beaver hat.

"This world is going to the dogs," he said. "It is being ruined by white men. We got along fine for years and years, before the white men foisted their Negroes upon us. In the old days the old men sat in the shade and ate stewed deer's flesh and corn and smoked tobacco and talked of honor and grave affairs; now what do we do? Even the old wear themselves into the grave taking care of them that like sweating." When Basket and Berry crossed the deck he ceased and looked up at them. His eyes were querulous, bleared; his face was myriad with tiny wrinkles. "He is fled also," he said.

"Yes," Berry said, "he is gone."

"I knew it. I told them so. It will take three weeks, like when Doom died. You watch and see."

"It was three days, not three weeks," Berry said.

"Were you there?"

"No," Berry said. "But I have heard."

"Well, I was there," the old man said. "For three whole weeks, through the swamps and the briers—" They went on and left him talking.

What had been the saloon of the steamboat was now a shell, rotting slowly; the polished mahogany, the carving glinting momentarily and fading through the mold in figures cabalistic and profound; the gutted windows were like cataracted eyes. It contained a few sacks of seed or grain, and the fore part of the running gear of a barouche, to the axle of which two C-springs rusted in graceful curves, supporting nothing. In one corner a fox cub ran steadily and soundlessly up and down a willow cage; three scrawny gamecocks moved in the dust, and the place was pocked and marked with their dried droppings.

They passed through the brick wall and entered a big room of chinked logs. It contained the hinder part of the barouche, and the dismantled body lying on its side, the window slatted over with willow withes, through which protruded the heads, the still, beady, outraged eyes and frayed combs of still more game chickens. It was floored with packed clay; in one corner leaned a crude plow and two hand-hewn boat paddles. From the ceiling, suspended by four deer thongs, hung the gilt bed which Issetibbeha had fetched from Paris. It had neither mattress nor springs, the frame crisscrossed now by a neat hammocking of thongs.

Issetibbeha had tried to have his newest wife, the young one, sleep in the bed. He was congenitally short of breath himself, and he passed the nights half reclining in his splint chair. He would see her to bed and, later, wakeful, sleeping as he did but three or four hours a night, he would sit in the darkness and simulate slumber and listen to her sneak infinitesimally from the gilt and ribboned bed, to lie on a quilt pallet on the floor until just before daylight. Then she would enter the bed quietly again and in turn simulate slumber, while in the darkness beside her Issetibbeha quietly laughed and laughed.

The girandoles were lashed by thongs to two sticks propped in a corner where a ten-gallon whisky keg lay also. There was a clay hearth; facing it, in the splint chair,

Moketubbe sat. He was maybe an inch better than five feet tall, and he weighed two hundred and fifty pounds. He wore a broadcloth coat and no shirt, his round, smooth copper balloon of belly swelling above the bottom piece of a suit of linen underwear. On his feet were the slippers with the red heels. Behind his chair stood a stripling with a punkah-like fan made of fringed paper. Moketubbe sat motionless, with his broad, yellow face with its closed eyes and flat nostrils, his flipperlike arms extended. On his face was an expression profound, tragic, and inert. He did not open his eyes when Basket and Berry came in.

"He has worn them since daylight?" Basket said.

"Since daylight," the stripling said. The fan did not cease. "You can see."

"Yao," Basket said. "We can see." Moketubbe did not move. He looked like an effigy, like a Malay god in frock coat, drawers, naked chest, the trivial scarlet-heeled shoes.

"I wouldn't disturb him, if I were you," the stripling said.

"Not if I were you," Basket said. He and Berry squatted. The stripling moved the fan steadily. "O Man," Basket said, "listen." Moketubbe did not move. "He is gone," Basket said.

"I told you so," the stripling said. "I knew he would flee. I told you."

"Yao," Basket said. "You are not the first to tell us afterward what we should have known before. Why is it that some of you wise men took no steps yesterday to prevent this?"

"He does not wish to die," Berry said.

"Why should he not wish it?" Basket said.

"Because he must die some day is no reason," the stripling said. "That would not convince me either, old man."

"Hold your tongue," Berry said.

"For twenty years," Basket said, "while others of his race sweat in the fields, he served the Man in the shade. Why should he not wish to die, since he did not wish to sweat?"

"And it will be quick," Berry said. "It will not take long."

"Catch him and tell him that," the stripling said.

"Hush," Berry said. They squatted, watching Moketubbe's face. He might have been dead himself. It was as though he were cased so in flesh that even breathing took place too deep within him to show.

"Listen, O Man," Basket said. "Issetibbeha is dead. He waits. His dog and his horse we have. But his slave has fled. The one who held the pot for him, who ate of his food, from his dish, is fled. Issetibbeha waits."

"Yao," Berry said.

"This is not the first time," Basket said. "This happened when Doom, thy grandfather, lay waiting at the door of the earth. He lay waiting three days, saying, 'Where is my Negro?' And Issetibbeha, thy father, answered, 'I will find him. Rest; I will bring him to you so that you may begin the journey.' "

"Yao," Berry said.

Moketubbe had not moved, had not opened his eyes.

"For three days Issetibbeha hunted in the bottom," Basket said. "He did not even return home for food, until the Negro was with him; then he said to Doom, his father, 'Here is thy dog, thy horse, thy Negro; rest.' Issetibbeha, who is dead since yesterday, said it. And now Issetibbeha's Negro is fled. His horse and his dog wait with him, but his Negro is fled."

"Yao," Berry said.

Moketubbe had not moved. His eyes were closed; upon his supine monstrous shape there was a colossal inertia, something profoundly immobile, beyond and impervious to flesh. They watched his face, squatting.

"When thy father was newly the Man, this happened," Basket said. "And it was Issetibbeha who brought back the slave to where his father waited to enter the earth." Moketubbe's face had not moved, his eyes had not moved. After a while Basket said, "Remove the shoes."

The stripling removed the shoes. Moketubbe began to pant, his bare chest moving deep, as though he were rising from beyond his unfathomed flesh back into life, like up from the water, the sea. But his eyes had not opened yet.

Berry said, "He will lead the hunt."

"Yao," Basket said. "He is the Man. He will lead the hunt."

IV

All that day the Negro, Issetibbeha's body servant, hidden in the barn, watched Issetibbeha's dying. He was forty, a Guinea man. He had a flat nose, a close, small head; the inside corners of his eyes showed red a little, and his prominent gums were a pale bluish red above his square, broad teeth. He had been taken at fourteen by a trader off Kamerun, before his teeth had been filed. He had been Issetibbeha's body servant for twenty-three years.

On the day before, the day on which Issetibbeha lay sick, he returned to the quarters at dusk. In that unhurried hour the smoke of the cooking fires blew slowly across the street from door to door, carrying into the opposite one the smell of the identical meat and bread. The women tended them; the men were gathered at the head of the lane, watching him as he came down the slope from the house, putting his naked feet down carefully in a strange dusk. To the waiting men his eyeballs were a little luminous.

"Issetibbeha is not dead yet," the headman said.

"Not dead," the body servant said. "Who not dead?"

In the dusk they had faces like his, the different ages, the thoughts sealed inscrutable behind faces like the death masks of apes. The smell of the fires, the cooking, blew sharp and slow across the strange dusk, as from another world, above the lane and the pickaninnies naked in the dust.

"If he lives past sundown, he will live until daybreak," one said.

"Who says?"

"Talk says."

"Yao. Talk says. We know but one thing." They looked at the body servant as he stood among them, his eyeballs a little luminous. He was breathing slow and deep. His chest was bare; he was sweating a little. "He knows. He knows it."

"Let us let the drums talk."

"Yao. Let the drums tell it."

The drums began after dark. They kept them hidden in the creek bottom. They were made of hollowed cypress knees, and the Negroes kept them hidden; why, none knew. They were buried in the mud on the bank of a slough; a lad of fourteen guarded them. He was undersized, and a mute; he squatted in the mud there all day, clouded over with mosquitoes, naked save for the mud with which he coated himself against the mosquitoes, and about his neck a fiber bag containing a pig's rib to which black shreds of flesh still adhered, and two scaly barks on a wire. He slobbered onto his clutched knees, drooling; now and then Indians came noiselessly out of the bushes behind him and stood there and contemplated him for a while and went away, and he never knew it.

From the loft of the stable where he lay hidden until dark and after, the Negro could hear the drums. They were three miles away, but he could hear them as though they were in the barn itself below him, thudding and thudding. It was as though he could see the fire too, and the black limbs turning into and out of the flames in copper gleams. Only there would be no fire. There would be no more light there than where he lay in the dusty loft, with the whispering arpeggios of rat feet along the warm and immemorial ax-squared rafters. The only fire there would be the smudge against mosquitoes where the women with nursing children crouched, their heavy sluggish breasts nippled full and smooth into the mouths of men children; contemplative, oblivious of the drumming, since a fire would signify life.

There was a fire in the steamboat, where Issetibbeha lay dying among his wives, beneath the lashed girandoles and the suspended bed. He could see the smoke, and just before sunset he saw the doctor come out, in a waistcoat made of skunk skins, and set fire to two clay-daubed sticks at the bows of the boat deck. "So he is not dead yet," the Negro said into the whispering gloom of the loft, answering himself; he could hear the two voices, himself and himself:

"Who not dead?"

"You are dead."

"Yao, I am dead," he said quietly. He wished to be where the drums were. He imagined himself springing out of the bushes, leaping among the drums on his bare, lean, greasy, invisible limbs. But he could not do that, because man leaped past life, into where death was; he dashed into death and did not die, because when death took a man, it took him just this side of the end of living. It was when death overran him from behind, still in life. The thin whisper of rat feet died in fainting gusts along the rafters. Once he had eaten rat. He was a boy then, but just come to America. They had lived ninety days in a three-foot-high 'tween-deck in tropic latitudes, hearing from topside the drunken New England captain intoning aloud from a book which he did not recognize for ten years afterward to be the Bible. Squatting in the stable so, he had watched the rat, civilized, by association with man reft of its inherent cunning of limb and eye; he had caught it without difficulty, with scarce a movement of his hand, and he ate it slowly, wondering how any of the rats had escaped so long. At that time he was still wearing the single white garment which the trader, a deacon in the Unitarian church, had given him, and he spoke then only his native tongue.

He was naked now, save for a pair of dungaree pants bought by Indians from white men, and an amulet slung on a thong about his hips. The amulet consisted of one half of a mother-of-pearl lorgnon[2] which Issetibbeha had brought back from Paris, and the skull of a cottonmouth moccasin. He had killed the snake himself and eaten it, save the poison head. He lay in the loft, watching the house, the steamboat, listening to the drums, thinking of himself among the drums.

He lay there all night. The next morning he saw the doctor come out, in his skunk vest, and get on his mule and ride away, and he became quite still and

2. Spectacles or opera glasses.

watched the final dust from beneath the mule's delicate feet die away, and then he found that he was still breathing and it seemed strange to him that he still breathed air, still needed air. Then he lay and watched quietly, waiting to move, his eyeballs a little luminous, but with a quiet light, and his breathing light and regular, and saw Louis Berry come out and look at the sky. It was good light then, and already five Indians squatted in their Sunday clothes along the steamboat deck; by noon there were twenty-five there. That afternoon they dug the trench in which the meat would be baked, and the yams; by that time there were almost a hundred guests—decorous, quiet, patient in their stiff European finery—and he watched Berry lead Issetibbeha's mare from the stable and tie her to a tree, and then he watched Berry emerge from the house with the old hound which lay beside Issetibbeha's chair. He tied the hound to the tree too, and it sat there, looking gravely about at the faces. Then it began to howl. It was still howling at sundown, when the Negro climbed down the back wall of the barn and entered the spring branch, where it was already dusk. He began to run then. He could hear the hound howling behind him, and near the spring, already running, he passed another Negro. The two men, the one motionless and the other running, looked for an instant at each other as though across an actual boundary between two different worlds. He ran on into full darkness, mouth closed, fists doubled, his broad nostrils bellowing steadily.

He ran on in the darkness. He knew the country well, because he had hunted it often with Issetibbeha, following on his mule the course of the fox or the cat beside Issetibbeha's mare; he knew it as well as did the men who would pursue him. He saw them for the first time shortly before sunset of the second day. He had run thirty miles then, up the creek bottom, before doubling back; lying in a pawpaw thicket he saw the pursuit for the first time. There were two of them, in shirts and straw hats, carrying their neatly rolled trousers under their arms, and they had no weapons. They were middle-aged, paunchy, and they could not have moved very fast anyway; it would be twelve hours before they could return to where he lay watching them. "So I will have until midnight to rest," he said. He was near enough to the plantation to smell the cooking fires, and he thought how he ought to be hungry, since he had not eaten in thirty hours. "But it is more important to rest," he told himself. He continued to tell himself that, lying in the pawpaw thicket, because the effort of resting, the need and the haste to rest, made his heart thud the same as the running had done. It was as though he had forgot how to rest, as though the six hours were not long enough to do it in, to remember again how to do it.

As soon as dark came he moved again. He had thought to keep going steadily and quietly through the night, since there was nowhere for him to go, but as soon as he moved he began to run at top speed, breasting his panting chest, his broad-flaring nostrils through the choked and whipping darkness. He ran for an hour, lost by then, without direction, when suddenly he stopped, and after a time his thudding heart unraveled from the sound of the drums. By the sound they were not two miles away; he followed the sound until he could smell the smudge fire and taste the acrid smoke. When he stood among them the drums did not cease; only the headman came to him where he stood in the drifting smudge, panting, his nostrils flaring and pulsing, the hushed glare of his ceaseless eyeballs in his mud-daubed face as though they were worked from lungs.

"We have expected thee," the headman said. "Go, now."

"Go?"

"Eat, and go. The dead may not consort with the living; thou knowest that."

"Yao. I know that." They did not look at one another. The drums had not ceased.

"Wilt thou eat?" the headman said.

"I am not hungry. I caught a rabbit this afternoon, and ate while I lay hidden."

"Take some cooked meat with thee, then."

He accepted the cooked meat, wrapped in leaves, and entered the creek bottom again; after a while the sound of the drums ceased. He walked steadily until daybreak. "I have twelve hours," he said. "Maybe more, since the trail was followed by night." He squatted and ate the meat and wiped his hands on his thighs. Then he rose and removed the dungaree pants and squatted again beside a slough and coated himself with mud—face, arms, body and legs—and squatted again, clasping his knees, his head bowed. When it was light enough to see, he moved back into the swamp and squatted again and went to sleep so. He did not dream at all. It was well that he moved, for, waking suddenly in broad daylight and the high sun, he saw the two Indians. They still carried their neatly rolled trousers; they stood opposite the place where he lay hidden, paunchy, thick, soft-looking, a little ludicrous in their straw hats and shirt tails.

"This is wearying work," one said.

"I'd rather be at home in the shade myself," the other said. "But there is the Man waiting at the door to the earth."

"Yao." They looked quietly about; stooping, one of them removed from his shirt tail a clot of cockleburs. "Damn that Negro," he said.

"Yao. When have they ever been anything but a trial and a care to us?"

In the early afternoon, from the top of a tree, the Negro looked down into the plantation. He could see Issetibbeha's body in a hammock between the two trees where the horse and the dog were tethered, and the concourse about the steamboat was filled with wagons and horses and mules, with carts and saddle-horses, while in bright clumps the women and the smaller children and the old men squatted about the long trench where the smoke from the barbecuing meat blew slow and thick. The men and the big boys would all be down there in the creek bottom behind him, on the trail, their Sunday clothes rolled carefully up and wedged into tree crotches. There was a clump of men near the door to the house, to the saloon of the steamboat, though, and he watched them, and after a while he saw them bring Moketubbe out in a litter made of buckskin and persimmon poles; high hidden in his leafed nook the Negro, the quarry, looked quietly down upon his irrevocable doom with an expression as profound as Moketubbe's own. "Yao," he said quietly. "He will go then. That man whose body has been dead for fifteen years, he will go also."

In the middle of the afternoon he came face to face with an Indian. They were both on a footlog across a slough—the Negro gaunt, lean, hard, tireless and desperate; the Indian thick, soft-looking, the apparent embodiment of the ultimate and the supreme reluctance and inertia. The Indian made no move, no sound; he stood on the log and watched the Negro plunge into the slough and swim ashore and crash away into the undergrowth.

Just before sunset he lay behind a down log. Up the log in slow procession moved a line of ants. He caught them and ate them slowly, with a kind of detachment, like that of a dinner guest eating salted nuts from a dish. They too had a salt taste, engendering a salivary reaction out of all proportion. He ate them slowly, watching the unbroken line move up the log and into oblivious doom with a steady and terrific undeviation. He had eaten nothing else all day; in his caked mud mask his eyes rolled in reddened rims. At sunset, creeping along the creek bank toward where he had spotted a frog, a cottonmouth moccasin slashed him suddenly across the forearm with a thick, sluggish blow. It struck clumsily, leaving two long slashes across his arm like two razor slashes, and half sprawled with its own momentum and rage, it appeared for the moment utterly helpless with its own awkwardness and choleric anger. "Olé, grandfather," the Negro said. He touched its head and watched it slash him again across his arm, and again, with thick, raking, awkward blows. "It's that I do not wish to die," he said. Then he said it again—"It's that I do not wish to die"—in a quiet tone, of slow and low amaze, as though it were something that, until the words had said themselves, he found that he had not known, or had not known the depth and extent of his desire.

V

Moketubbe took the slippers with him. He could not wear them very long while in motion, not even in the litter where he was slung reclining, so they rested upon a square of fawnskin upon his lap—the cracked, frail slippers a little shapeless now, with their scaled patent-leather surfaces and buckleless tongues and scarlet heels, lying upon the supine obese shape just barely alive, carried through swamp and brier by swinging relays of men who bore steadily all day long the crime and its object, on the business of the slain. To Moketubbe it must have been as though, himself immortal, he were being carried rapidly through hell by doomed spirits which, alive, had contemplated his disaster, and, dead, were oblivious partners to his damnation.

After resting for a while, the litter propped in the center of the squatting circle and Moketubbe motionless in it, with closed eyes and his face at once peaceful for the instant and filled with inescapable foreknowledge, he could wear the slippers for a while. The stripling put them on him, forcing his big, tender, dropsical feet into them; whereupon into his face came again that expression tragic, passive and profoundly attentive, which dyspeptics wear. Then they went on. He made no move, no sound, inert in the rhythmic litter out of some reserve of inertia, or maybe of some kingly virtue such as courage or fortitude. After a time they set the litter down and looked at him, at the yellow face like that of an idol, beaded over with sweat. Then Three Basket or Had-Two-Fathers would say: "Take them off. Honor has been served." They would remove the shoes. Moketubbe's face would not alter, but only then would his breathing become perceptible, going in and out of his pale lips with a faint ah-ah-ah sound, and they would squat again while the couriers and the runners came up.

"Not yet?"

"Not yet. He is going east. By sunset he will reach Mouth of Tippah. Then he will turn back. We may take him tomorrow."

"Let us hope so. It will not be too soon."

"Yao. It has been three days now."

"When Doom died, it took only three days."

"But that was an old man. This one is young."

"Yao. A good race. If he is taken tomorrow, I will win a horse."

"May you win it."

"Yao. This work is not pleasant."

That was the day on which the food gave out at the plantation. The guests returned home and came back the next day with more food, enough for a week longer. On that day Issetibbeha began to smell; they could smell him for a long way up and down the bottom when it got hot toward noon and the wind blew. But they didn't capture the Negro on that day, nor on the next. It was about dusk on the sixth day when the couriers came up to the litter; they had found blood. "He has injured himself."

"Not bad, I hope," Basket said. "We cannot send with Issetibbeha one who will be of no service to him."

"Nor whom Issetibbeha himself will have to nurse and care for," Berry said.

"We do not know," the courier said. "He has hidden himself. He has crept back into the swamp. We have left pickets."

They trotted with the litter now. The place where the Negro had crept into the swamp was an hour away. In the hurry and excitement they had forgotten that Moketubbe still wore the slippers; when they reached the place Moketubbe had fainted. They removed the slippers and brought him to.

With dark, they formed a circle about the swamp. They squatted, clouded over with gnats and mosquitoes; the evening star burned low and close down the west, and the constellations began to wheel overhead. "We will give him time," they said. "Tomorrow is just another name for today."

"Yao. Let him have time." Then they ceased, and gazed as one into the darkness where the swamp lay. After a while the noise ceased, and soon the courier came out of the darkness.

"He tried to break out."

"But you turned him back?"

"He turned back. We feared for a moment, the three of us. We could smell him creeping in the darkness, and we could smell something else, which we did not know. That was why we feared, until he told us. He said to slay him there, since it would be dark and he would not have to see the face when it came. But it was not that which we smelled; he told us what it was. A snake had struck him. That was two days ago. The arm swelled, and it smelled bad. But it was not that which we smelled then, because the swelling had gone down and his arm was no larger than that of a child. He showed us. We felt the arm, all of us did; it was no larger than that of a child. He said to give him a hatchet so he could chop the arm off. But tomorrow is today also."

"Yao. Tomorrow is today."

"We feared for a while. Then he went back into the swamp."

"That is good."

"Yao. We feared. Shall I tell the Man?"

"I will see," Basket said. He went away. The courier squatted, telling again about the Negro. Basket returned. "The Man says that it is good. Return to your post."

The courier crept away. They squatted about the litter; now and then they slept. Sometime after midnight the Negro waked them. He began to shout and talk to himself, his voice coming sharp and sudden out of the darkness, then he fell silent. Dawn came; a white crane flapped slowly across the jonquil sky. Basket was awake. "Let us go now," he said. "It is today."

Two Indians entered the swamp, their movements noisy. Before they reached the Negro they stopped, because he began to sing. They could see him, naked and mud-caked, sitting on a log, singing. They squatted silently a short distance away, until he finished. He was chanting something in his own language, his face lifted to the rising sun. His voice was clear, full, with a quality wild and sad. "Let him have time," the Indians said, squatting, patient, waiting. He ceased and they approached. He looked back and up at them through the cracked mud mask. His eyes were blood-shot, his lips cracked upon his square short teeth. The mask of mud appeared to be loose on his face, as if he might have lost flesh since he put it there; he held his left arm close to his breast. From the elbow down it was caked and shapeless with black mud. They could smell him, a rank smell. He watched them quietly until one touched him on the arm. "Come," the Indian said. "You ran well. Do not be ashamed."

VI

As they neared the plantation in the tainted bright morning, the Negro's eyes began to roll a little, like those of a horse. The smoke from the cooking pit blew low along the earth and upon the squatting and waiting guests about the yard and upon the steamboat deck, in their bright, stiff, harsh finery; the women, the children, the old men. They had sent couriers along the bottom, and another on ahead, and Issetibbeha's body had already been removed to where the grave waited, along with the horse and the dog, though they could still smell him in death about the house where he had lived in life. The guests were beginning to move toward the grave when the bearers of Moketubbe's litter mounted the slope.

The Negro was the tallest there, his high, close, mud-caked head looming above them all. He was breathing hard, as though the desperate effort of the six suspended and desperate days had catapulted upon him at once; although they walked slowly, his naked scarred chest rose and fell above the close-clutched left arm. He looked this way and that continuously, as if he were not seeing, as though sight never quite caught up with the looking. His mouth was open a little upon his big white teeth; he began to pant. The already moving guests halted, pausing, looking back, some with pieces of meat in their hands, as the Negro looked about at their faces with his wild, restrained, unceasing eyes.

"Will you eat first?" Basket said. He had to say it twice.

"Yes," the Negro said. "That's it. I want to eat."

The throng had begun to press back toward the center; the word passed to the outermost: "He will eat first."

They reached the steamboat. "Sit down," Basket said. The Negro sat on the edge of the deck. He was still panting, his chest rising and falling, his head ceaseless with its white eyeballs, turning from side to side. It was as if the inability to see came from within, from hopelessness, not from absence of vision. They brought food and watched quietly as he tried to eat it. He put the food into his mouth and chewed it, but chewing, the half-masticated matter began to emerge from the corners of his mouth and to drool down his chin, onto his chest, and after a while he stopped chewing and sat there, naked, covered with dried mud, the plate on his knees, and his mouth filled with a mass of chewed food, open, his eyes wide and unceasing, panting and panting. They watched him, patient, implacable, waiting.

"Come," Basket said at last.

"It's water I want," the Negro said. "I want water."

The well was a little way down the slope toward the quarters. The slope lay dappled with the shadows of noon, of that peaceful hour when, Issetibbeha napping in his chair and waiting for the noon meal and the long afternoon to sleep in, the Negro, the body servant, would be free. He would sit in the kitchen door then, talking with the women who prepared the food. Beyond the kitchen the lane between the quarters would be quiet, peaceful, with the women talking to one another across the lane and the smoke of the dinner fires blowing upon the pickaninnies like ebony toys in the dust.

"Come," Basket said.

The Negro walked among them, taller than any. The guests were moving on toward where Issetibbeha and the horse and the dog waited. The Negro walked with his high ceaseless head, his panting chest. "Come," Basket said. "You wanted water."

"Yes," the Negro said. "Yes." He looked back at the house, then down to the quarters, where today no fire burned, no face showed in any door, no pickaninny in the dust, panting. "It struck me here, raking me across this arm; once, twice, three times. I said, 'Olé, Grandfather.' "

"Come now," Basket said. The Negro was still going through the motion of walking, his knee action high, his head high, as though he were on a treadmill. His eyeballs had a wild, restrained glare, like those of a horse. "You wanted water," Basket said. "Here it is."

There was a gourd in the well. They dipped it full and gave it to the Negro, and they watched him try to drink. His eyes had not ceased as he tilted the gourd slowly against his caked face. They could watch his throat working and the bright water cascading from either side of the gourd, down his chin and breast. Then the water stopped. "Come," Basket said.

"Wait," the Negro said. He dipped the gourd again and tilted it against his face, beneath his ceaseless eyes. Again they watched his throat working and the unswallowed water sheathing broken and myriad down his chin, channeling his caked chest. They waited, patient, grave, decorous, implacable; clansman and guest and kin. Then the water ceased, though still the empty gourd tilted higher and higher, and still his black throat aped the vain motion of his frustrated swallowing. A piece of water-loosened mud carried away from his chest and broke at his muddy feet, and in the empty gourd they could hear his breath: ah-ah-ah.

"Come," Basket said, taking the gourd from the Negro and hanging it back in the well.

Delta Autumn

Soon now they would enter the Delta. The sensation was familiar to him, renewed like this each last week in November for more than fifty years—the last hill at the foot of which the rich unbroken alluvial flatness began as the sea began at the base of its cliffs, dissolving away beneath the unhurried November rain as the sea itself would dissolve away. At first they had come in wagons—the guns, the bedding, the dogs, the food, the whiskey, the anticipation of hunting—the young men who could drive all night and all the following day in the cold rain and pitch camp in the rain and sleep in the wet blankets and rise at daylight the next morning to hunt. There had been bear then, and a man shot a doe or a fawn as quickly as he did a buck, and in the afternoons they shot wild turkey with pistols to test their stalking skill and marksmanship, feeding all but the breast to the dogs. But that time was gone now and now they went in cars, driving faster and faster each year because the roads were better and they had farther to drive, the territory in which game still existed drawing yearly inward as his life was drawing in, until now he was the last of those who had once made the journey in wagons without feeling it and now those who accompanied him were the sons and even the grandsons of the men who had ridden for twenty-four hours in rain and sleet behind the steaming mules, calling him Uncle Ike now, and he no longer told anyone how near seventy he actually was because he knew as well as they did that he no longer had any business making such expeditions, even by car. In fact, each time now, on that first night in camp, lying aching and sleepless in the harsh blankets, his blood only faintly warmed by the single thin whiskey-and-water which he allowed himself, he would tell himself that this would be his last. But he would stand that trip (he still shot almost as well as he had ever shot, he still killed almost as much of the game he saw as he had ever killed; he no longer knew how many deer had fallen before his gun) and the fierce long heat of the next summer would somehow renew him. Then November would come again and again in the car with two of the sons of his old companions, whom he had taught not only how to distinguish between the prints left by a buck and a doe but between the sound they made in moving, he would look ahead past the jerking arc of the windshield wiper and see the land flatten suddenly, dissolving away beneath the rain as the sea itself would dissolve, and he would say, "Well boys, there it is again."

This time though he didn't have time to speak. The driver of the car stopped it, slamming it to a skidding halt on the greasy pavement without warning, so that old McCaslin, first looking ahead at the empty road, glanced sharply past the man in the middle until he could see the face of the driver, the youngest face of them all, darkly aquiline, handsome and ruthless and saturnine and staring sombrely ahead through the steaming windshield across which the twin arms of the wiper flicked and flicked. "I didn't intend to come in here this time," he said. His name was Boyd. He was just past forty. He owned the car as well as two of the three Walker hounds in the rumble behind them, just as he owned, or at least did the driving of, anything—animal, machine or human—which he happened to be using.

"You said that back in Jefferson last week," McCaslin said. "Then you changed your mind. Have you changed it again?"

"Oh, Don's coming," the third man said. His name was Legate. He seemed to be speaking to no one. "If it was just a buck he was coming all this distance for now. But he's got a doe in here. On two legs—when she's standing up. Pretty light-colored too. The one he was after them nights last fall when he said he was coon-hunting. The one I figured maybe he was still chasing when he was gone all that month last January." He chortled, still in that voice addressed to no one, not quite completely jeering.

"What?" McCaslin said. "What's that?"

"Now, Uncle Ike," Legate said, "that's something a man your age ain't supposed to had no interest in twenty years." But McCaslin had not even glanced at Legate. He was still watching Boyd's face, the eyes behind the spectacles, the blurred eyes of an old man but quite sharp too; eyes which could still see a gun barrel and what ran beyond it as well as any of them could. He was remembering himself now: how last year, during the final stage by motor boat to where they would camp, one of the boxes of food had been lost overboard and how on the second day Boyd had gone back to the nearest town for supplies and had been gone overnight and when he did return, something had happened to him: he would go into the woods each dawn with his gun when the others went, but McCaslin, watching him, knew that he was not hunting.

"All right," he said. "Take Will and me on to shelter where we can wait for the truck, and you can go back."

"I'm going in," Boyd said harshly. "I'm going to get mine too. Because this will be the last of it."

"The last of deer hunting, or of doe hunting?" Legate said. This time McCaslin paid no attention to him even in speech. He still watched Boyd's savage and immobile face.

"Why?" he said.

"After Hitler gets through with it? Or Yokohama or Pelley or Smith or Jones or whatever he will call himself in this country."[1]

"We'll stop him in this country," Legate said. "Even if he calls himself George Washington."

1. The U.S. entered World War II against the Axis powers in December 1941.

"How?" Boyd said. "By singing God Bless America in bars at midnight and wearing dime-store flags in our lapels?"

"So that's what's worrying you," McCaslin said. "I ain't noticed this country being short of defenders yet when it needed them. You did some of it yourself twenty years ago and did it well, if those medals you brought back home mean anything. This country is a little mite stronger and bigger than any one man or even group of men outside or inside of it either. I reckon it can cope with one Austrian paper hanger, no matter what he calls himself. My pappy and some other better men than any of them you named tried once to tear it in two with a war, and they failed."

"And what have you got left?" Boyd said. "Half the people without jobs and half the factories closed by strikes. Too much cotton and corn and hogs, and not enough for all the people to wear and eat. Too much not-butter and not even the guns. . . . "

"We got a deer camp—if we ever get to it," Legate said. "Not to mention does."

"It's a good time to mention does," McCaslin said. "Does and fawns both. The only fighting anywhere that ever had anything of God's blessing on it has been when men fought to protect does and fawns. If it's going to come to fighting, that's a good thing to mention and remember."

"Haven't you discovered in sixty years that women and children are one thing there's never any scarcity of?" Boyd said.

"Maybe that's why all I am worrying about right now is that ten miles of river we still got to run before we can make camp," McCaslin said. "Let's get on."

They went on. Soon they were going fast again—that speed at which Boyd drove, about which he had consulted neither of them just as he had given neither of them any warning when he had slammed the car to a stop. McCaslin relaxed again, watching, as he did each recurrent November while more than fifty of them passed, the land which he had seen change. At first there had been only the old towns along the river and the old towns along the edge of the hills, from each of which the planters with their gangs of slaves and then of hired labor had wrested from the impenetrable jungle of waterstanding cane and cypress, gum and holly and oak and ash, cotton patches which as the years passed became fields and then plantations, the paths made by deer and bear becoming roads and then highways, with towns in turn springing up along them and along the rivers Tallahatchie and Sunflower which joined and became the Yazoo, the River of the Dead of the Choctaws—the thick, slow, black, unsunned streams almost without current, which once each year actually ceased to flow and then moved backward, spreading, drowning the rich land and then subsiding again, leaving it still richer. Most of that was gone now. Now a man drove two hundred miles from Jefferson before he found wilderness to hunt in; now the land lay open from the cradling hills on the east to the rampart of levee on the west, standing horseman-tall with cotton for the world's looms—the rich black land, imponderable and vast, fecund up to the very cabin doorsteps of the Negroes who worked it and the domiciles of the white men who owned it, which exhausted the hunting life of a dog in one year, the working life of a mule in five and of a man in twenty—the land in which neon flashed past them from the little countless towns and constant this-year's cars sped over the broad plumb-ruled highways, yet in which the only permanent mark of man's occupation seemed to be the tremendous gins, constructed in sections of sheet iron and in a week's time though they were, since no man, millionaire though he be, would build more than a roof and walls to live in, with camping equipment to live with, because he knew that once each ten years or so his house would be flooded to the second story and all within it ruined;—the land across which there came now no scream of panther but instead the long hooting of locomotives: trains of incredible length and drawn by a single engine since there was no gradient anywhere and no elevation save those raised by forgotten aboriginal hands as refugees from the yearly water and used by their Indian successors to sepulchure their fathers' bones, and all that remained of that old time were the Indian names on the little towns and usually pertaining to water—Aluschaskuna, Tillatoba, Homachitto, Yazoo.

By early afternoon they were on water. At the last little Indian-named town at the end of the pavement they waited until the other car and the two trucks—the one containing the bedding and tents, the other carrying the horses—overtook them. Then they left the concrete and, after a mile or so, the gravel too, and in caravan they ground on through the ceaselessly dissolving afternoon with chained wheels in the lurching and splashing ruts, until presently it seemed to him that the retrograde of his recollection had gained an inverse velocity from their own slow progress and that the land had retreated not in minutes from the last spread of gravel, but in years, decades, back toward what it had been when he first knew it—the road they now followed once more the ancient pathway of bear and deer, the diminishing fields they now passed once more scooped punily and terrifically by axe and saw and mule drawn plow from the brooding and immemorial tangle instead of ruthless mile-wide parallelograms wrought by ditching and dyking machinery.

They left the cars and trucks at the landing, the horses to go overland down the river to a point opposite the camp and swim the river, themselves and the bedding and food and tents and dogs in the motor launch. Then, his old hammer double gun which was better than half as old as he between his knees, he watched even these last puny marks of man—cabin, clearing, the small and irregular fields which a year ago were jungle and in which the skeleton stalks of this year's cotton stood almost as tall and rank as the old cane had stood, as if man had had to marry his planting to the wilderness in order to conquer it—fall away and vanish until the twin banks marched with wilderness as he remembered it; the tangle of brier and cane impenetrable even to sight twenty feet away, the tall tremendous soaring of oak and gum and ash and hickory which had rung to no axe save the hunter's, had echoed to no machinery save the beat of old-time steamboats traversing it or the snarling of launches like their own of people going into it to dwell for a week or two weeks because it was still wilderness. There was still some of it left, although now it was two hundred miles from Jefferson when once it had been thirty. He had watched it, not being conquered, destroyed, so much as retreating since its purpose was now done and its time an outmoded time, retreating southward through this shaped section of earth between hills and river until what was left of it seemed now to be gathered and for the time arrested in one tremendous density of brooding and inscrutable impenetrability at the ultimate funnelling tip.

They reached the site of their last year's camp with still two hours left of light. "You go on over under that driest tree and set down," Legate told him. "Me and these other young boys will do this." He did neither. In his slicker he directed the unloading of the boat—the tents, the stove, the bedding, the food for themselves and the dogs until there should be meat in camp. He sent two of the Negroes to cut firewood; he had the cook-tent raised and the stove set up and a fire going and a meal cooking while the big tent was still being staked down. Then in the beginning of dusk he crossed in the boat to where the horses waited, backing and snorting at the water. He took the lead-ropes and with no more weight than that and his voice he drew them down into the water and held them beside the boat with only their heads above the surface as though they actually were suspended from his frail and strengthless old man's hands while the boat recrossed and each horse in turn lay prone in the shallows, panting and trembling, its eyes rolling in the dusk until the same weightless hand and the unraised voice gathered surging upward, splashing and thrashing up the bank.

Then the meal was ready. The last of light was gone now save the thin stain of it snared somewhere between the river's surface and the rain. He had the glass of thin whiskey-and-water and they ate standing in the mud beneath the stretched tarpaulin. The oldest Negro, Isham, had already made his bed—the strong, battered iron cot, the stained mattress which was not quite soft enough, the worn, washed blankets which as the years passed were less and less warm enough. Wearing only his bagging woolen underclothes, his spectacles folded away in the worn case beneath the pillow where he could reach them readily and his lean body fitted into the old worn groove of mattress and blankets, he lay on his back, his hands crossed on his breast and his eyes closed while the others went to bed and the last of the talking died into snoring. Then he opened his eyes and lay looking up at the motionless belly of canvas upon which the constant rain murmured, upon which the glow of the sheet-iron heater died slowly away and would fade still further until the youngest Negro, lying on planks before it for that purpose, would sit up and stoke it again and lie back down.

They had had a house once. That was twenty and thirty and forty years ago, when the big bottom was only thirty miles from Jefferson and old Major de Spain, who had been his father's cavalry commander in '61 and -2 and -3 and -4 and who had taken him into the woods his first time, had owned eight or ten sections of it. Old Sam Fathers was alive then, half Chickasaw Indian, grandson of a chief, and half Negro, who had taught him how and when to shoot; such a November dawn as tomorrow would be and the old man had led him straight to the great cypress and he had known the buck would pass exactly there because there was something running in Sam Fathers' veins which ran in the veins of the buck and they stood there against the tremendous trunk, the old man and the boy of twelve, and there was nothing but the dawn and then suddenly the buck was there, smoke-colored out of nothing, magnificent with speed, and Sam Fathers said, "Now. Shoot quick and shoot slow," and the gun leveled without hurry and crashed and he walked to the buck lying still intact and still in the shape of that magnificent speed and he bled it with his own knife and Sam Fathers dipped his hands in the hot blood and marked his face forever while he stood trying not to tremble, humbly and with pride too though the boy of twelve had been unable to phrase it then, "I slew you; my bearing must not shame your quitting life. My conduct forever onward must become your death." They had the house then. That roof, the two weeks of each fall which they spent under it, had become his home; although since that time they had lived during the two fall weeks in tents and not always in the same place two years in succession, and now his companions were the sons and even the grandsons of those with whom he had lived in the house and the house itself no longer existed, the conviction, the sense of home, had been merely transferred into the canvas. He owned a house in Jefferson, where he had had a wife and children once though no more, and it was kept for him by his dead wife's niece and her family and he was comfortable in it, his wants and needs looked after by blood at least related to the blood which he had elected out of all the earth to cherish. But he spent the time between those walls waiting for November, because even this tent with its muddy floor and the bed which was not soft enough nor warm enough was his home and these men, some of whom he only saw during these two weeks, were more his kin. Because this was his land. . . .

The shadow of the youngest Negro loomed, blotting the heater's dying glow from the ceiling, the wood billets thumping into it until the glow, the flame, leaped high and bright across the canvas. But the Negro's shadow still remained, until after a moment McCaslin, rising onto one elbow, saw that it was not the Negro, it was Boyd; when he spoke the other turned his head and he saw in the red firelight the sullen and ruthless profile. "Nothing," Boyd said. "Go on back to sleep."

"Since Will Legate mentioned it," McCaslin said, "I remember you had some trouble sleeping in here last fall too. Only you called it coon-hunting then. Or was it Will Legate that called it that?" Boyd didn't answer. He turned and went back to his bed. McCaslin, propped on his elbow, watched until the other's shadow sank down the wall and vanished. "That's right," he said. "Try to get some sleep. We must have meat in camp tomorrow. You can do all the setting up you want to after that." Then he too lay back down, his hands crossed again on his breast, watching the glow of the heater. It was steady again now, the fresh wood accepted, being assimilated; soon it would begin to fade again, taking with it the last echo of that sudden upflare of a young man's passion and unrest. Let him lie awake for a little while, he thought. He would lie still some day for a long time without even dissatisfaction to disturb him. And lying awake here, in these surroundings, would soothe him if anything could, if anything could soothe a man just forty years old. The tent, the rain-murmured canvas globe, was filled with it once more now. He lay on his back, his eyes closed, his breathing quiet and peaceful as a child's, listening to it—that silence which was never silence but was myriad. He could almost see it, tremendous, primeval, looming, musing downward upon this puny evanescent clutter of human sojourn which after a single brief week would vanish and in another week would be completely healed, traceless in the unmarked solitude. Because it was his land, although he had never owned a foot of it. He had never wanted to, even after he saw its ultimate doom, began to watch it retreating year by year before the onslaught of axe and saw and log-lines and then dynamite and tractor plows, because it belonged to no man. It belonged to all; they had only to use it well, humbly and with pride. Then suddenly he knew why he had never wanted to own any of it, arrest at least that much of what people called progress. It was because there was just exactly enough of it. He seemed to see the two of them—himself and the wilderness—as coevals, his own span as a hunter, a woodsman not contemporary with his first breath but transmitted to him, assumed by him gladly, humbly, with joy and pride, from that old Major de Spain and Sam Fathers who had taught him to hunt, the two spans running out together, not into oblivion, nothingness, but into a scope free of both time and space where once more the untreed land warped and wrung to mathematical squares of rank cotton for the frantic old-world peoples to turn into shells to shoot at one another, would find ample room for both—the shades of the tall unaxed trees and the sightless brakes where the wild strong immortal animals ran forever before the tireless belling immortal hounds, falling and rising phoenix-like before the soundless guns.

Then he had slept. The lantern was lighted, the tent was full of the movement of men getting up and dressing and outside in the darkness the oldest Negro, Isham, was beating with a spoon on the bottom of a tin pan and crying, "Raise up and get yo fo clock coffy. Raise up and get yo fo clock coffy."

He heard Legate too. "Get on out of here now and let Uncle Ike sleep. If you wake him up, he'll want to go on stand. And he aint got any business in the woods this morning." So he didn't move. He heard them leave the tent; he listened to the breakfast sounds from the table beneath the tarpaulin. Then he heard them depart—the horses, the dogs, the last voice dying away; after a while he might possibly even hear the first faint clear cry of the first hound ring through the wet woods from where the buck had bedded, then he would go back to sleep again. Then the tent flap swung in and fell, something jarred against the end of the cot and a hand grasped his knee through the blanket and shook him before he could open his eyes. It was Boyd, carrying a shotgun instead of his rifle. He spoke in a harsh, rapid voice. "Sorry I had to wake you. There will be a. . . ."

"I was awake," McCaslin said. "Are you going to shoot that today?"

"You just told me last night you want meat," Boyd said. "There will be a. . . ."

"Since when did you start having trouble getting meat with your rifle?"

"All right," the other said, with that harsh, restrained, furious impatience. Then McCaslin saw in his other hand a thick oblong, an envelope. "There will be a woman here some time this morning, looking for me. Give her this and tell her I said no."

"What?" McCaslin said. "A what?" He half rose onto his elbow as the other jerked the envelope onto the blanket in front of him, already turning toward the entrance, the envelope striking solid and heavy and soundless and already sliding from the bed until McCaslin caught it, feeling through the paper the thick sheaf of banknotes. "Wait," he said. "Wait." The other stopped, looking back. They stared at one another—the old face, wan, sleep-raddled above the tumbled bed, the dark handsome younger one at once furious and cold. "Will Legate was right," McCaslin said. "This is what you called coon-hunting. And now this." He didn't lift the envelope nor indicate it in any way. "What did you promise her that you haven't the courage to face her and retract?"

"Nothing," Boyd said. "This is all of it. Tell her I said no." He was gone; the tent flap lifted on a waft of faint light and the constant murmur of the rain and fell again while McCaslin still lay half-raised on his elbow, the envelope clutched in his shaking hand. It seemed to him later that he began to hear the approaching boat almost immediately, before Boyd could have got out of sight even. It seemed to him that there had been no interval whatever: the mounting snarl of the engine, increasing, nearer and nearer and then cut short off, ceasing into the lap and plop of water under the bows as the boat slid in to the bank, the youngest Negro, the youth, raising the tent flap beyond which for an instant he saw the boat—a small skiff with a Negro man sitting in the stern beside the upslanted motor—then the woman entering, in a man's hat and a man's slicker and rubber boots, carrying the blanket-and-tarpaulin-wrapped bundle and bringing something else, something intangible, an effluvium which he knew he would recognize in a moment because he knew now that Isham had already told him, warned him, by sending the young Negro to the tent instead of coming himself—a face young and with dark eyes, queerly colorless but not ill and not that of a country woman despite the garments she wore, looking down at him where he sat upright on the cot now, clutching the envelope, the soiled underclothes bagging about him and the twisted blankets huddled about his hips.

"Is that his?" he said. "Don't lie to me!"

"Yes," she said. "He's gone."

"He's gone," he said. "You won't jump him here. He left you this. He said to tell you no." He extended the envelope. It was sealed and it bore no superscription. Nevertheless he watched her take it in one hand and manage to rip it open and tilt the neat sheaf of bound notes onto the blanket without even glancing at them and then look into the empty envelope before she crumpled and dropped it.

"Just money," she said.

"What did you expect?" he said. "You have known him long enough or at least often enough to have got that child, and you don't know him that well?"

"Not very often," she said. "Not very long. Just that week here last fall, and in January he sent for me and we went West, to New Mexico, and lived for six weeks where I could cook for him and look after his clothes. . . ."

"But no marriage," he said. "He didn't promise you that. Don't lie to me. He didn't have to."

"He didn't have to," she said. "I knew what I was doing. I knew that to begin with, before we agreed. Then we agreed again before he left New Mexico that that would be all of it. I believed him. I must have believed him. I don't see how I could have helped but believe him. I wrote him last month to make sure and the letter came back unopened and I was sure. So I didn't even know I was coming back here until last week. I was waiting there by the road yesterday when the car passed and he saw me and I was sure."

"Then what do you want?" he said. "What do you want?"

"Yes," she said. He glared at her, his white hair awry from the pillow, his eyes, lacking the spectacles to focus them, blurred, irisless and apparently pupilless.

"He met you on a street one afternoon just because a box of groceries happened to fall out of a boat. And a month later you went off and lived with him until you got a child from it. Then he took his hat and said good-bye and walked out. Haven't you got any folks at all?"

"Yes. My aunt, in Vicksburg. I came to live with her two years ago when my father died; we lived in Indianapolis until then. But my aunt had a family and she took in washing herself, so I got a job teaching school in Aluschaskuna. . . ."

"Took in what?" he said. "Took in washing?" He sprang, flinging himself backward onto one arm, awry-haired, glaring. Now he understood what it was she had brought in with her, what old Isham had already told him—the lips and skin pallid and colorless yet not ill, the tragic and foreknowing eyes. *Maybe in a thousand or two thousand years it will have blended in America and we will have forgotten it,* he thought. *But God pity these.* He cried, not loud, in a voice of amazement, pity and outrage, "You're a nigger!"

"Yes," she said.

"Then what did you expect here?"

"Nothing."

"Then why did you come here? You said you were waiting in Aluschaskuna yesterday and he saw you."

"I'm going back North," she said. "My cousin brought me up from Vicksburg the day before yesterday in his boat. He's going to take me on to Leland to get the train."

"Then go," he said. Then he cried again in that thin, not loud voice, "Get out of here; I can do nothing for you! Can't nobody do nothing for you!" She moved, turning toward the entrance. "Wait," he said. She paused, turning. He picked up the sheaf of bank notes and laid it on the blanket at the foot of the cot and drew his hand back beneath the blanket. "Here."

"I don't need it," she said. "He gave me money last winter. Provided. That was all arranged when we agreed that would have to be all."

"Take it," he said. His voice began to rise again, but he stopped it. "Take it out of my tent." She came back and took the money. "That's right," he said. "Go back North. Marry, a man in your own race. That's the only salvation for you. Marry a black man. You are young, handsome, almost white; you could find a black man who would see in you whatever it was you saw in him, who would ask nothing from you and expect less and get even still less if it's revenge you want. And then in a year's time you will have forgotten all this; you will forget it even happened, that he ever existed. . . . ." He ceased; for an instant he almost sprang again for it seemed to him that, without moving at all, she had blazed silently at him. But she had not. She had not even moved, looking quietly down at him from beneath the sodden hat.

"Old man," she said, "have you lived so long that you have forgotten all you ever knew or felt or even heard about love?" Then she was gone too; the waft of light and the hushed constant rain flowed into the tent, then the flap fell again. Lying back again, trembling, panting, the blanket huddled to his chin and his hands crossed on his breast, he heard the pop and snarl, the mounting then the descending whine of the motor until it died away and once again the tent held only silence and the sound of the rain. And the cold too: he lay shaking faintly and steadily in it, rigid save for the shaking. 'This Delta,' he thought. 'This Delta.' *This land, which man has deswamped and denuded and derivered in two generations so that white men can own plantations and commute every night to Memphis and black men can own plantations and even towns and keep their town houses in Chicago, where white men rent farms and live like niggers and niggers crop on shares and live like animals, where cotton is planted and grows man-tall in the very cracks in the sidewalks, where usury and mortgage and bankruptcy and measureless wealth. Chinese and African and Aryan and Jew, all breed and spawn together until no man has time to say which is which, or cares. . . .* 'No wonder the ruined woods I used to know don't cry for retribution,' he thought. 'The people who have destroyed it will accomplish its revenge.'

The tent flap swung rapidly in and fell. He did not move save to turn his head and open his eyes. Legate was stooping over Boyd's bed, rummaging hurriedly in it. "What is it?" McCaslin said.

"Looking for Don's skinning knife," Legate said. "We got a deer on the ground. I come in to get the horses." He rose, the knife in his hand and went toward the door.

"Who killed it?" McCaslin said. "It was Don," he said.

"Yes," Legate said, lifting the tent flap.

"Wait," McCaslin said. "What was it?" Legate paused for an instant in the entrance. He did not look back.

"Just a deer, Uncle Ike," he said impatiently. "Nothing extra." He was gone; the flap fell behind him, wafting out of the tent again the faint light, the constant and grieving rain. McCaslin lay back on the cot.

"It was a doe," he said to the empty tent.

QUESTIONS TO CONSIDER

1. Faulkner's Mississippi was infused with violent racism and drew upon a long history of human bondage going back to the culture of the Native Americans. Because he is held in slavery by the Indians, the African bodyservant in "Red Leaves" is condemned to be buried alive with the dead chief. The story dramatizes the tragedy of a human being who runs away in a futile effort to prolong life. What meanings are generated in this story's presentation of early nineteenth-century cultural and racial clash?
2. At the end of "Delta Autumn" Uncle Ike learns that Boyd has killed a deer. Without moving from his cot Ike surmises it is a female, a doe. What leads him to this conclusion? How does this killing link to the preceding scene involving Ike and Boyd's African-American mistress?

Lillian Smith

1897–1966

Looking upon the Southern social cauldron of the 1940s, Lillian Smith had the temerity to articulate the obvious: the South was in trouble. The root cause was White bigotry, she said, but scarcely anyone in a position to address the crisis—politicians, church leaders, public intellectuals—was willing to admit it publicly, much less do anything about it. Born in the same year as William Faulkner, Smith during her long and outspoken career as a novelist and essayist would far surpass him and all other Southern White males of her generation in her activist campaign for equality.

Lillian Smith was born and reared in Jasper, a small town in north Florida, steeped in Jim Crow racial prohibitions and sexual taboos. Her father was a prosperous turpentine processor who was able to afford a second home near Clayton in the mountains of north Georgia. The onset of World War I caused his business to decline sharply following the loss of overseas markets. After losing his mills in 1915, Smith's father permanently moved his family of ten children to their Georgia summer residence on Old Screamer Mountain. Lillian Smith was 17, and rural Georgia would be home for the rest of her life, though Smith briefly attended a nearby college, went off to Baltimore to receive training as a pianist at the Peabody Conservatory, returned to north Georgia for a time as a village schoolteacher, and traveled to China to teach music in a Methodist mission school in *Huchow* (now *Wu-shing*). In 1925 her parents' failing health brought her back to Georgia to take over the Laurel Falls Camp for Girls, which her father had founded in 1920. Smith brought in a young Georgia woman, Paula Snelling, to join the staff. As Smith's letters reveal, they became lovers in a relationship that lasted until Smith's death in 1966, although Smith never openly acknowledged her lesbianism.

In 1936, the two women founded a small magazine that became successively known as *Pseudopodia,* the *North Georgia Review,* and *South Today*. They began writing trenchant social criticism directed at the contemporary South while expressing a commitment to politically engaged literature that sought reform. They rejected all forms of Southern cultural chauvinism such as the work of the Nashville Agrarians and paternalistic romance novels such as *Gone With the Wind* (1936). To put her progressive ideas on race and gender equality into fiction of her own, Smith began work on a protest novel, *Strange Fruit,* one of the most controversial books of the forties. No Southern writer of her time, including Faulkner, would draw a tighter thematic connection between White supremacy and sexual dysfunction.

Strange Fruit was published in 1944. The title derived from a 1939 song written by Abel Meeropal, and made popular by the legendary African-American blues singer Billie Holliday which decried lynching in stark lyrics: "Southern trees bear a strange fruit/ Blood on the leaves, and blood at the root/ Black bodies swinging in the Southern breeze/ Strange fruit hanging from the poplar trees." The novel centers on an interracial love affair during the mid-1920s in a small town, much like Jasper, and portrays the gunshot murder of a White man and the fiery lynching of an innocent Black man. In addition to miscegenation, its sexual subjects include abortion, lesbianism, frigidity, and menopause, as well as language considered risque in the forties. The book met legal resistance in Northern cities such as Boston and Detroit. Such notoriety quickly sent it to the top of the bestseller lists and boosted sales into the millions. Because she liked the book, Eleanor Roosevelt intervened to have a U.S. Post Office ban lifted. A dramatic adaptation of the novel enjoyed a brief run on Broadway in 1945 and 1946. Using her newfound fame, Smith joined the Congress of Racial Equality (CORE) in 1946 and became its most famous White member, heaping scorn on timid White Southern liberals and racial gradualists who would not openly demand an end to segregation.

Smith followed *Strange Fruit* with a powerful memoir, *Killers of the Dream* (1949), a classic of Southern autobiography. The book's intellectual topics include caste, segregation, paternalism, and violence. Smith also offers a psychologically telling analysis of how rigid and paranoid Southern child-rearing practices enforce warped attitudes that define African Americans as inferior to Whites and women as inferior to men—Smith thought of *Killers of the Dream* not just as her memoir but as every White Southerner's story. Unlike *Strange Fruit,* the book sold poorly. It was largely ignored by her conservative literary contemporaries, who dismissed her work as anti-Southern propaganda.

Increasingly in the post–World War II years, Cold War politics reinforced Southern resistance to integration and labeled opponents of segregation as pro-Communist. Perhaps in response, Smith's writings during the fifties took a more global and anticolonial perspective, although she denounced Soviet Communism. In 1953, she had surgery for breast cancer, perhaps a reason for the increased spirituality of her last books, including the nonfiction *The Journey* (1954), *Now Is the Time* (1955), and *Our Faces, Our Words* (1964), and the novel *One Hour* (1959). Smith was an early supporter of the Reverend Martin Luther King, Jr., and the Civil Rights movement. Further, she admired the Civil Rights activism of fellow Southerner, President Lyndon Johnson. Upon her death from cancer in 1966, "Miss Lil" was hailed as the mid-century White South's bravest and most uncompromising opponent of Jim Crow and the twisted legacies of White supremacy.

In the following passage from *Strange Fruit,* Smith targets the hypocrisy of White Southern Christianity. Tracy Deen is an alienated 26-year-old World War I veteran, the privileged son of a medical doctor. He has been having a clandestine affair with Nonnie Anderson, an educated, 21-year-old, African-American woman. Although Nonnie holds a college degree, she can only find work in her segregated Georgia hometown as a domestic worker. Tracy is under pressure from his family to marry Dottie Pusey, the "nice" girl who lives across the street. When Nonnie becomes pregnant with his child, Tracy is trapped by his own weakness. He is too feckless to declare openly his love for an African-American woman, much less to claim responsibility for the child she bears, and too jaded to relish marriage to his starchy White fiancée. As the scene opens, Tracy goes to meet the revivalist preacher, Brother Dunwoodie. Later in Tracy's car, the preacher delivers a racist sermon on African-American female sexuality. During this diatribe, Tracy finds himself driving toward a windy bluff where he and Nonnie have made love.

from Strange Fruit

Tracy turned the switch, started the car. He had eaten breakfast late to avoid his mother. He had eaten just in time to keep his appointment with Brother Dunwoodie at nine o'clock. Even at nine it was hot. What a day it would be! He drove slowly up College Street toward the Harris home, past house after house, each set back in its small or large lawn. Here, there, a colored maid swept a porch or the walk in front of a home, moving slowly along, brushing away moss and sand and small crisp oak leaves, singing low, talking to herself. A child ran across the grass, stopped, pulled a sandspur from his foot, hobbled on, whimpering, suddenly forgot, began to run again. Across the wide street divided so exactly by the railroad was the honeysuckled Pusey home. Someone was in the swing. He would not look. He would not see who was in that swing, or in any swing, this morning.

He was on his way to talk to the preacher. If Gus or any of the boys had bet him, yesterday, that he would be seeing the preacher this morning, he would have laughed and told them he'd see them in hell first. Yet here he was, going to talk to the preacher, like a nice little boy, about his soul. If you thought you had a soul, or anybody had a soul, there'd be a little sense to it!

It'll be damned embarrassing. After all, you don't have to do it. Drive around the block, go on home. Like hell you would—there he is . . . waiting at the gate, lounging against it, a big hard-muscled man, at ease. You wonder why a man like that—

how a man like that ever happened to be a preacher. Didn't seem to fit. A ball player . . . football, maybe, but not preaching. You think of a preacher as soft-fleshed, short-winded except in the pulpit. Grandfather was pudgy, irritable in his old age when he wasn't praying or preaching. You'd always remember him, pink face, blue eyes, heavy snow-white hair brushed back in a high pompadour, looking down at his cereal as if he were going to cry in it. A funny way to remember your grandfather, but that was your memory of him. But people said when Grandfather prayed men's hearts filled with the peace of God. Maybe it was Grandma. Grandma was pretty leathery. Maybe stropping against her day after day put an edge on Grandpa's nerves. You'd never felt that way about her, though everyone else seemed to. With you she had been different. Gentle . . .

The preacher had seen you, was turning slowly. In a moment he'd say something. Lifting his arm now, vaulting the fence, easy, light. Good balance. What you reckon made him waste that body in a pulpit? What you reckon got hold of the man? Once you'd seen him, years ago when he was here, illustrate his text by climbing the pole of the big tent. Yes, he'd done that and you'd laughed at his fanatic craziness and all the other boys sitting on the back pew had laughed too, but you had sort of liked him for it—anybody think it easy to climb a thirty-foot pole had better try it sometime—and five of the boys sitting there with you laughing had joined the church before the meeting was over.

The preacher said, and shook his heavy black hair off his face as he spoke, "Well, you're on the dot."

Tracy smiled, stopped the car.

Brother Dunwoodie got in.

"Be cooler to ride around, don't you think?"

"Suits me all right."

"How about a coke first?"

"Be fine," said the preacher, shifting his wide shoulders to a more comfortable angle against the back of the seat.

Tracy stopped in front of Deen's Drug Store, ordered two Coca-Colas.

"Nothing like a Coca-Cola to cool you off. Old Asa Candler hit on a good thing when he fixed up a soft drink in —"

"In temperance territory?" Tracy grinned, looked at the preacher. Maybe he wouldn't think that funny.

The preacher laughed. "Well, come to think of it, if you take a man's corn away from him, reckon the Lord's right glad to give him some kind of sugar-tit to take the place of it. The Candlers have prospered, must have been God's will." The preacher threw away the straw, lifted his glass.

Tracy. . . Mother's voice had faltered but her eyes had looked steadily into his, *I've arranged for you to have a talk with Brother Dunwoodie at nine o'clock in the morning.* You kept thinking of it.

You've—say that again, will you, Mother?

I think you heard me.

Sure . . . but I want to give you a chance to—take it back. He'd kept his voice low. *Of all the goddam meddling —*

Tracy!

I beg your pardon, Mother. You'd never in your life spoken like that to her or to any woman. What made you lose your head, what made you—You'd stood there staring at your mother, shocked at what you had said —

"They make good cokes here."

"Pretty good."

She'd said, her voice as smooth and deliberate as the judgment of God, *In all your life I have never known you to speak like this before. It seems as if—as if you are deliberately ruining your life, as if you are doing this with a purpose.* Now what on earth could she have meant by that? She had stopped, begun again. *In spite of your*—her eyes traveled across his face slowly as if across his life—*weaknesses . . . I could at least hold to your courtesy to me. And now you've taken that from me.* Her lips suddenly trembled and it seemed as if she could not go on, but quickly her face composed itself, her voice steadied —

The preacher said, "Well, that's a good start for a hot morning. Much obliged."

They'd left the drugstore now and Tracy had turned down College Street toward the south side of town. Preacher talking about Grandfather Mathews. Of course. Everybody knew Grandpa, everybody who was a Methodist—and that meant half of Georgia. It gave the preacher a good opening.

"You remind me of him a little," the preacher was saying, "only you're leaner, harder. You're more like Sister Mathews, but quieter."

"Grandmother," Tracy laughed, "was energetic, all right."

"Energetic's hardly the word—if you remember her rightly. I'd say, more like a piece of shrapnel—if you've ever heard it singing straight at you."

"Were you over?"

"Yes. Y.M.C.A."

Tracy drove slowly through the heavy sand on College Street.

"You asked me, moment ago, how I happened to become a preacher."

Had he? He'd thought it. Didn't know he'd said it aloud.

"Well, it's pretty easy to answer that one. God convicted me of sin. Yeah. Simple as that. And convicting me, called me to preach the Gospel. Laid a burden on me that I couldn't shake off —"

I've given my life to you and Laura—all of it—I've asked little of you in return and you've given me nothing —

"Funny, way I tried. Joined the army—that didn't work. Went into ball playing—got in minor league, looked like I was headed for big league stuff—What? Oh, played shortstop—yeah. Nothing helped. Be on the train, be playing ball and I'd hear the Voice, nagging at me. 'What you going to do about it?' it'd say."

Tracy was driving toward the south of town, now through the glare of hot white sand, now in the cool of oak shade.

"This business of sin . . . strange thing —"

I've asked little of you and you've given me nothing. You couldn't get the words off your mind. *What have you given me? School? You stopped after that half year in college. Job—profession—you knew how I wanted you to be a doctor or a lawyer —*

"Each man has his own way of sinning. I'm not asking you yours. Some folks like to talk about theirs. Shake them out in the air, hoping a big wind will catch them, blow them away. Other folks trample theirs to pieces inside till there's nothing left. Each man has his own way of getting shed of his."

There's Dorothy. You know how I've wanted that. How we all want it. Yet you treat her like a little cheap thing —

"And the way don't matter if you get rid of them to make room for God. I don't know what your way is. But I know a lot about sin. Some folks . . . it's money. Got to have it! You see little children stealing it before they know how to count. It gets folks that way. They just take it."

What I ask now is such a small thing. It is difficult to think of a son making a scene over a small request like this —

"Don't want it for nothing! Just take it. And there's others who want it for something. They go after it wanting it for something. And when they want it bad like that, nothing can stop them. Except Almighty God. And if He don't—death. But when they let Him, God can do it."

When you can't ask a small favor of a son—there's not much left for a mother. And he'd smiled, he remembered that, smiled as he looked straight at her and said, *You have Laura, you know.* By God, he wouldn't give in to her, he'd thought, not this time. He was man enough to hold out.

"I know you're saying, maybe, you don't believe in Him." The preacher looked at Tracy and smiled quickly. "Said it myself once. And what's more, listened to my own words. But I lied. You may not believe there's oxygen in the air. But you can't live more'n a minute or so without it."

And Mother had looked at him quickly. *Yes,* she'd almost whispered, *yes, I have Laura.* And as he had watched, something had happened to her face. Something had ripped the certainty from it, leaving it old and hurt, and unprotected. She who was never hurt —

"It's that way with God," the preacher's words went on. "You can't live in Maxwell without Him. Got to have Him to lean on. Man's a funny critter. Sometimes seems like the minute he lets go his mother's hand, got to have something else to catch hold to."

Yes, something had hurt her. And standing there watching her last night, as she talked to him in the hall, he had felt that he had done something to her. Somehow she who had never needed help, never needed anything, had asked something of him, which had seemed to him a damned piece of meddling but to her was something she needed and he had refused to give it to her. *If it will make you feel any better* he'd heard himself say as he stood there watching her, wishing the hurt look would leave her face, *I'll go talk to Dunwoodie.* Her face had not changed at his words and he had wondered if she could have heard. *Mother,* he called softly.

Yes.

I said I'll go talk to the preacher if it will make you—feel better.

"There're other sins. All kinds. Gambling . . . you know folks who gamble don't want their winnings. Ever thought about it? They want something powerful bad but it's not the winning. When I hear a man's a gambler I know there's a lot of wrestlin with the Lord for somebody to do. Because he's after something else. Kind of like self-abuse. Now those are the ones! *Man, man!* Hard to get em to listen to you, and when they listen, even when they try—sweat with their trying—they turn back after a while to their own bodies. Worship themselves—like they were their own God. I'm going to preach a sermon on that. For men only. Next week. I'm telling you, there's sins most folks never dreamed of! You know, when you're preaching . . . going around from place to place on the Lord's business, you run into a sight of sin! Yes sir! All kinds. Some of em make you tremble to think of. It makes you wonder. Makes you wonder how God in His wisdom could've made a creature who would think up as many ways of doing wrong as man has studied up. You wonder why He couldn't have done a little better while he was thinking up a creature—I say it in all reverence—but it makes you wonder."

Tracy had turned the car, was driving back over the road they had just driven down.

"But God gave us Jesus, His only begotten Son. And I can't forget that. And you can't forget that. To help poor stumbling creatures find the way."

Thank you, Mother had said, and turned, laid her hymnal on the table, for they had just come from the services, and he had come in only to get the car to take Dorothy to ride. And then she had turned back to him, and her face was again as smooth as glass. *I knew you would, dear. I could not believe you would embarrass me by not being a gentleman.* She had stood there, tall, a little heavy now, gray hair brushed up smooth and high above her forehead, heavy brows black against her smooth pale face. *Oh certainly not, he'd whispered to himself, you always win, Mother. Always,* he'd suddenly said aloud, and laughed and walked to the front door.

You're going out—again—tonight?

Yes, I'm going out, he'd said and laughed again, and shut the door, knowing she thought he was going to Colored Town. And it gave him satisfaction to know this. It gave him satisfaction as he crossed the railroad and opened the picket gate which led to the Puseys' small front yard.

"Now there's another sin. Lot of men, when they're young, sneak off to Colored Town. Let their passions run clean away with them. Get to lusting—burning up! And they get to thinking . . . they'd rather have that kind of thing than marriage. A lot rather! Scared of white girls. Scared nice white girls can't satisfy them. And they're right! Of course no decent fine white woman can satisfy you when you let your mind out like you let out a team of wild mules racing straight to —"

Preacher Dunwoodie's voice had risen shrilly. Suddenly he stopped. Spoke more quietly. "Well . . . that's youth," he said and wiped his face with his big handkerchief. "This world's full of young folks wanting—strange things. That's youth and the devil," he added softly, "and sooner or later you have to face it. Funny thing," he said, "once you make up your mind to leave colored women alone and stick to your own kind, you soon get weaned." He laughed shortly. "You don't think you can. But you do. I know . . ." he sighed. "As for the colored women, they manage all right. Always have, haven't they! Most of them sooner or later get a man their color, maybe marry him. Live a fairly decent, respectable life—that is, if a nigger woman can live a decent, respectable life." Voice suddenly bitter.

Someone's been talking to him. He's too smooth—knows too much.

"You see, Deen, you have to keep pushing them back across that nigger line. Keep pushing! That's right. Kind of like it is with a dog. You have a dog, seems right human. More sense than most men. And you a lot rather be around that dog than anybody you ever knew. But he's still a dog. You don't forget that. And you don't forget the other . . . it's the same. God made the white race for a great purpose. Sometimes I've wondered what that purpose is. Between you and I, I've wondered—with all reverence—when God is going to divulge that purpose, for up to now, seems like we been marking time most ways, or making a mess of things. Well," he suddenly smiled, drew his brows close, as quickly relaxed them, threw back his heavy black hair, "I've done all the talking."

"I appreciate your taking time with me. To tell you the truth," Tracy smiled quickly, "I'm—hardly worth it."

"There's people who think you are. The little Pusey girl . . . your own fine mother. A man's lucky to have two such women to love him."

Tracy speeded up the car, as quickly slowed it down.

"You know, Deen," the preacher went on soberly, "most men learn to love God because their women love Him. You know that? Same way they begin to love their own children. Ever thought of that? Or because they're scared . . . . not to. You're not the easy scared kind."

"I don't know. Sometimes I think I am." Tracy spoke gravely. "Trouble with me," he said slowly, "I don't believe all that."

"Most men don't believe when they start. Most of us have to take some things on faith—like our children, for instance." Dunwoodie chuckled. "Yes sir, men have to take a lot on faith! Ever thought of it?"

Tracy suddenly laughed. The preacher wasn't so bad.

"You take things that *matter* on faith. There's no way of proving them! I don't say that in the pulpit, mind you, or to the ladies." He laughed deeply. "Reminds me of a story I heard once. A man had just got married and when he went to get in bed that night he suddenly looked at the girl and—well, never mind that," he frowned, stopped his words, picked them up again. "But I say it now. With all reverence, I say it."

Tracy looked quickly at the preacher. The old boy had almost forgot he was on the Lord's business.

"On this earth there's two worlds," the preacher continued, after a time, "man's and woman's. Now, the woman's has to do with the home and children and love. God's love and man's. The man's world is—different. It has to do with work. Women teach us to love the Lord, and our children, and then *we* build the churches, don't we, and *we* keep them going. Sure. Just as we make the living for those children, we do the farming, we create the cities. We do the work. Sure. That's right. Now, when a man gets over into a woman's world, he gets into bad trouble. He don't belong there. He belongs in a man's world. God wants your soul where it belongs, for then He'll be surer of getting it than if it was on the other side—where some woman'll get it all. May not sound like religion to you. And I'm not saying you can find verse and chapter exactly for it in the Bible. And, as I say, I don't preach it in the pulpit. But it's good preaching, just the same. Too much love makes you soft. No-count! Tying you to a woman's apron strings! That's what too much love'll do. Women wouldn't understand that—and, as I say, I don't preach it in the pulpit.

"Now, some men have a deep feeling for God. It comes to em easy. Others get it slow. The hard way. But a man makes a living and feeds those younguns his wife *says* are his, even if he ain't sure he loves them yet, don't he? And a man gets on the Lord's side and joins the church, supports it and his town's affairs, even when his heart's not in it much, at first.

"But this is what happens after a time. After a time God begins to seem like a real Man to you. Not something your mother loved and told you to love! But your own Kind. I mean that in a holy and sacred way. And what men are doing, their work, their interests, seems more important to you and satisfying than anything in a woman's world. So when I say, get on the Lord's side, I mean one thing when I talk to the ladies and another when I talk to men."

Tracy's teeth flashed again in a quick smile.

"As I say, I don't talk like this in the pulpit." Brother Dunwoodie drew his heavy brows together, and quickly relaxed them. "What you think?" he said softly, and his face eased into a warm smile.

Tracy half smiled. "I think maybe you're right."

"Well," said the preacher, "how about it? How about trying it on the Lord's side—and man's, for a while?"

"I'll think about it." Tracy spoke quickly and turned the car sharply through the deeper ruts in the sand road.

"God bless you," the preacher said and laid his big warm hand on the boy's shoulder. "God bless you," he said, and softly sighed.

Tracy turned the car toward Iron Bridge. You couldn't keep driving up and down through town all morning.

"I'd like for you to see the river," surprised at himself as he said it. "Maybe on the river it'll be cooler."

The preacher looked at his watch. "I'd like to go if we can make it back in an hour."

Tracy took Back Road and cut across the ball diamond.

"Four years ago I got as far as Sulphur Springs. A meeting don't leave much time for sight-seeing."

"We'll make it, all right," Tracy said and speeded up when once they were on the county's eight-mile stretch of pavement. "Most of us around here have been swimming and fishing in the river all our lives." He laughed. "Seems a good sort of place to us." Why did he keep trying to explain?

"Anybody likes a river." The preacher was looking now at the acres of yellowed palmetto brushing by the car like bands of copper in the sun. He half closed his eyes.

"Not much else to see around Maxwell—except sand and prickly pear."

Tracy crossed the Iron Bridge, slowed where the sweeping curve of brown water and white sand banks push sharp against overhanging live oaks, mammoth with age and their heavy burden of gray moss. Took the narrow road to the left, drove through deep sand, around hot-looking scrub-oak thicket and patches of grass and prickly pear, under low-hanging live oaks whose moss snagged at the car as it went under—on up the bluff. There, under a big oak, he stopped the car.

"Now that's fine," the preacher said, "fine! Does you good to see a thing pretty as that, don't it?"

It was cooler here, and the curve of the river was good on the eye, with its dark tree line above the cliffs.

Brother Dunwoodie eased down in the seat, stretched out his legs, sighed softly. "Pretty spot. Pretty as I've ever seen in Georgia." He closed his eyes.

Preaching must be hard on you, Tracy thought, looking at the sagged face. Must be a wearisome business struggling with other folks' sins. The preacher's mouth dropped comfortably open, his tie had pulled to one side, his heavy black hair had slipped down on his forehead. The crease in his neck was filling with sweat and he had begun to breathe deeply. A muscle in his relaxed hand jerked now and then. Might be any drunk sleeping it off.

Tracy turned away, let his eye follow the river, come back, follow the cool shade of the heavy oaks. It was here that they had come that night. Over there on the sand that they had lain, stretched out easy on its deepness. A piece of moss had fallen from the limb above them on her breast, and she had let it rest there. Any other girl would have jumped or exclaimed or thrown it off. But Nonnie let it rest there. Easy. And it had trembled as it lay there, rising and falling with her breathing. Easy and quiet. Everything about Nonnie . . . like that. It was a hot night—two months ago—two hundred years it seemed now! He had driven out to the old Anderson place in the car. She was at the gate waiting. Always there. And he had suddenly thought, It's so damned hot—why not take her in the car somewhere. And he suggested it and she went as casually as if every night of their life they had done the same.

He drove discreetly through the edge of Colored Town, took an old road that cut across to the highway, brought her here. She slipped out of the car, walked to the edge of the bank, stood there looking down at the dark river, at the cliffs white in moonlight. Then she had turned, slowly pushed her hair off her face, and smiled. And he had been profoundly moved. It was a little thing, a quick turn of her body, the slow pushing of hair from her face, her smile. But he knew that she had never seen a river in moonlight before . . . that somehow he had conferred a great favor. And he felt shamed and confused. She took his hand and rubbed it against her lips, then left him and walked a few steps away, and stood with her back to him, looking at the river. The wind was blowing enough to sweep her dress against her body, and to push her hair away from her forehead. And she seemed a sweet lovely thing to him there in the moonlight.

He moved to her quickly and pulled her to him, shamed and deeply touched. He had slipped his hand back of her head as he held her, now kissed her face again and again and again. After a time she turned away, took his hand; held it tightly, suddenly. And when he pulled her around he saw that her chin was shaking and there were tears on her face.

"It's a goddam mess!" he'd said and hushed abruptly.

She shook her head, smiled quickly, wiped her eyes. Then they had sat on the sand and neither had tried to talk. Neither liking to talk much. After a while he had drawn her to him and they were laughing together, for the sand was scratchy as the very devil. And everything seemed right and good, as it had always been.

But later, as they lay there, relaxed, looking up at the sky, she had pulled his hand to her breast. He felt her heart beating under it and suddenly, lying there, she seemed not the Nonnie whom he had a way of taking as for granted as you'd take a piece of cornbread, but a girl off somewhere by herself and sad about something. He drew her to him and ran his hand across her hair, not knowing what to say. Not knowing in this damned upside-down, devilish world what to say to a girl like this. He knew from the trembling through her body that she was crying, but there was no sound. Lying there, looking under the limb of that old tree sagged with moss, he thought about her. He remembered that when her mother died last winter, just after he'd come back from Europe, he'd hardly noticed. After that first night, he'd hardly noticed anything about her. For nothing in Nonnie's life seemed a part of him, except herself. He'd hardly noticed, and it must have meant a hell of a lot to Nonnie. It made him a little sick to remember that now, as he lay on the sand holding the girl in his arms. And a day or two after the old woman had died and the funeral was over, he had gone out there—but to talk to Non about himself, having had another damned row at home. And she had sat under the arbor and listened to him talk, looking peaked and tired as she listened, making him feel good again and comforted by her listening. And the meeting with the Reverend and Roseanna had been almost forgotten as she listened to him.

"Would you like to talk to me, Non, about it?" It made him feel decent to say that to her. It made him feel almost as he had felt the night he danced with her. It was coming back, the feeling he had lost. He was finding it again. And his body and mind were quickening.

After a while she wiped her eyes, pushed back her dark hair. "I can't talk, much," she said low, "about things." She smiled at him, and he knew that, somehow, she was pushing that trouble back from wherever it had come. "I think it's like this—" she said quietly, "I've always known what I wanted. You; and Mummie, when I was little.

I know people are supposed to want other things. I don't seem to. I suppose the way I've always felt about—Mother, goes back to those long days I spent by myself, playing around on the edge of the swamp and fields. All day long . . . saying to myself: when the sun goes down she'll be back. . . Sometimes I was afraid of the woods. I don't quite know how to say it, for I loved them too. But I'd be out playing, whispering to myself, and something would rattle and I'd begin to run . . . not knowing where to run. . ." She laughed and wiped her eyes again. "But when I heard her step at dusk, down on the path by Miss Ada's, things were—all right again. I suppose a lot of children are like that. Colored children," she said, and stopped.

Negro. She'd said it. Now everything would be spoiled. Ruined as it always was!

But it wasn't ruined. Out there on the lime cliff, brown water swirling below you, sky paled out by the moon above you, great oaks with sagging moss draping your nakedness, hiding you from the world, you could think that word without getting sick at your stomach. You could say it, say Nonnie's name after it, and still believe in her and yourself. The world's wrong, you could say. Dead wrong.

She'd turned then, as if she had read his thoughts. "Race is something—made up, to me. Not real. I don't—have to believe in it. Social position—ambition—seem made up too. Games for folks to—forget their troubles with. Bess says I'm crazy, that I live in a dream world." She'd smiled and looked up at the sky and both of them had watched a cloud drop behind the great oaks.

God! You could hear that damned word and not mind it. You didn't give a goddam what the world thought. She was yours, that's all! She's my girl. She's lovely and beautiful, and she's mine. He'd laughed, and pulled her to him again. Holding her there, he knew he loved her—as a man loves the woman who fits all his needs.

And he felt good. He watched a cloud pull across the moon and break in two afterward, he looked at the shadows under the oaks, and felt good inside. He felt he could help Nonnie through her trouble, whatever it now was, as she had helped him . . . all her life long.

She had her arm behind her head now, and the moss was there on her breast, rising and falling in the clear light. "The way things have to be . . . I don't—see much of you. It has to be that way," she said quickly, "I've accepted that. But tonight . . . maybe you shouldn't have brought me," she smiled at him, "it is so beautiful here and I—"

Yeah. The bluff belonged to white folks and every nigger in the county knew it.

"—I suddenly thought if we were—the same—color," she said the words very low, "this separation wouldn't have to be. We could play together—this tonight—drive places in the car—play tennis, maybe . . . I know it sounds funny," she laughed and her breath caught sharply, "but I've never played except by myself. And it suddenly seemed as if it would be—nice—to play with you." She stopped for a moment and they both watched a bird fly slowly from one tree to another. "It's sleep walking," she'd whispered. She went on again, "This evening before you came, I'd been out weeding Mama's grave. It's been hot today too—and Boysie cried so much—maybe all of it together —"

"God . . . I can't let you put up with it!"

"It's all right, Tracy. I want you to know that," she spoke earnestly now. "I like having you come out to me . . . just as you do . . . I like being there—whenever you need me. Those things that mean so much to Eddie and Bess, and meant so much to Mummie, don't mean the same to me. I decided that, when I was a little thing—playing by myself. White boys, people, would try to—bother me . . . and I had to decide things. Maybe that doesn't make sense to you. But one day when I was a little girl, a boy tried to take off my clothes in a gallberry patch, and you stopped him. It sounds funny, saying it out loud, like this, but there you were, and I knew I was—all right. I've felt that way . . . ever since. All those things people think matter, don't matter."

She seemed like a little girl, talking so freely—like this; not the calm, quiet Nonnie who knew somehow always what to give you when you needed something, though she never said much. More the little tike in the gallberry patch. Yes, he remembered it, vaguely. Now Nat Ashley was mayor of some town up in North Carolina, he'd heard, getting ready to run for governor.

They'd gone back to town late. And he had taken her home and driven back to College Street. But the moment he opened the screen door of his house and entered that hall, things changed as if he had found his sense of direction out in the swamp—and lost it again. He had done that when hunting. Many a time. You know you're going right, and suddenly you don't know where you're going. The moment he opened that door, tiptoed through that dark hall and up the steps, past Laura's door, he heard the whole town—*been out all night with a nigger gal . . . wasting your life . . . getting something you can't get here in White Town . . . Well, they've got plenty of that!*

Maxwell talking. All the world talking, maybe.

It's like an obsession. Seems true to you, but everybody else says it isn't. You can't love and respect a colored girl. No, you can't. But you do. If you do—then there must be something bad wrong with you. It's like playing with your body when you were a kid. You had to touch yourself. It felt good. It was good. But everyone told you it wasn't good. Said it would drive you crazy or kill you. Decent people didn't do it. Well . . . you did. You did it and liked it. And felt like hell, afterward. You'd outgrown that. Now the preacher said time to outgrow this other. Past time.

Sitting there under the big oak tree by the preacher, who breathed deep and steadily now, sweat rolling down his neck and forehead, legs spraddled out in comfort—Tracy tried to feel again what he had felt that night two months ago under the same oak tree, on the same old riverbank. But it wouldn't come. He remembered every word they had said, every moment they had been here—as if it had happened to someone else a hundred years ago. Nonnie was only a name today. A name and an obstacle. A colored girl blocking a white path.

I've never asked much of you—you haven't given—anything. There's Dorothy . . . we've all wanted that—and you treat her like a cheap thing.

There's Dorothy. Puseys lived across the street and you'd dated her all your life because she was near, and seemed to like you all right. And now they blame you because she hasn't married—because she is twenty-five years old and has never married!

He touched the preacher's arm. "Reckon we better be going back," he said, and smiled at the startled face.

Reckon we better be going back to White Town. It hadn't worked. He'd come to the river to find her but she wasn't here.

Tracy drove quickly over the eight miles of pavement, slowed down as he once more entered the sand road. "I don't have much of a feeling for God," he said, "and all it seems to stand for in folks' minds. As for the church, it's not important to me. I don't know that I even believe in God."

"I know," the preacher said, and his heavy brows came together. "That's just what I was saying. That's the way it is with men like you. You're going cross-country—sort of cruising by yourself something you don't know what you're cruising . . . or won't do you any good to cruise, for there's no good timber there—climbing through palmettos, over fences and ditches, through the hammock. And along comes somebody and says, Son, you'll wear yourself out, plumb to death, fighting woods like that! Here, come round this thicket. There's the road, right before you. It's a lot easier on you to travel the road men have hewed out and made for themselves. It's a lot more satisfaction. And you might say, But I don't know where it leads. And I say, You don't know where this other leads either. But I know. And other white men know. It leads to death and worse than death. It leads to hell and damnation. And this road leads to life everlasting . . . . and peace. And you can say back, Can you prove it? And I'll say No. I can't prove it. But I've tried it. It works. Thing to do is to git goin. When you once get going, faith comes. How it comes, I don't know. It's a mystery of God. But it comes. There're men all along the way that can tell you the same."

Tracy drove on. The preacher was silent now.

"If I didn't believe in God," he said after a time, "in a personal God, not just some theory—Deen, if I didn't believe in God the Father watching over me day and night, I'd be the meanest man in Georgia. I'd go on such a rampage . . . ." The preacher suddenly sighed and rubbed his hands over his face. "You know, some men have the devil in them from the day they're born. And I'm one of them. Broke my poor mother's heart before I gave in. God help me, I put her in an early grave with my wild ways. Sometimes now when I get to thinking about it, I wonder how God has been so merciful to me, how He's been willing to reach down and save a good-for-nothing scoundrel like me."

Tracy was looking straight down the sand road.

"You haven't got that on your conscience. Don't get it there, boy, it's a hard thing to bear."

"I don't believe—anything," Tracy suddenly laughed, and his hand trembled as he lit a cigarette. "But if you did believe—how does a man get going?"

"For you, seems to me, would be like this: join the church, marry that fine little Pusey girl, set up housekeeping and make her a good living. That would be your way to begin. For other folks it might be different. Some I tell to get down on their knees and stay there until God lays His hand of mercy on their black hearts. Some I call to the altar, so they can prove to men that they mean what they say and in the proving give themselves strength to mean it. There's a way for every man. I've learned that."

Tracy turned the car into Oak Street, suddenly cut into Elm Street, headed toward the Harris home, where Brother Dunwoodie was staying.

"There's a colored girl —" he spoke abruptly, stopped.

Brother Dunwoodie let the car move a hundred yards before he answered. Let Deen drive slowly across the little wooden bridge that spanned the branch which ran through the Harrises' back field.

"Reckon when the merciful Lord listens to sinners down here, He hears that right often."

"She's going to have a baby."

"And what if she is? They all have em! Almost before they have their first sick-time!"

Tracy flushed. "I wouldn't want her to—have trouble."

"As far as I've been able to figure out—they don't." The preacher laughed shortly.

"I wouldn't want her to have trouble," Tracy said again low, and stopped the car at the Harrises' side gate.

"Then fix things! Find some good nigger you can count on to marry her. Give —"

God! If any nigger dared touch her, if any dared —

"—her some money. They all like money—all women like money, no matter what color! Give him some money too. To kindle a fire under him and get him moving fast. Get your Dorothy a ring. Go to her with your hands as clean as that fine little girl deserves, and ask her to marry you and marry you quick."

Tracy half smiled. "That the way you figure things out?"

"That's the way, Deen. And git goin." He said it a little roughly, but turned quickly and smiled and shook hands with the man who had forgotten to start the car. "There's a lot of important folks on your side," he called as he walked up the path under the big oaks in the Harrises' lawn, "and God's among them. Don't forget that."

"I'm much obliged to you, Brother Dunwoodie," Tracy said courteously and, starting the car, drove slowly around the corner to College Street and on to the yellow house where the Deens lived. He left the car in the driveway for his mother, skirted the house, quickly went to Henry's cabin.

Questions to Consider

1. In an earlier passage in *Strange Fruit* Tracy stares at the darkened house where his White virgin fiancée lives. He thinks of her praying before going to bed. He wonders "What would Dottie's sins be? In a life so neat, so orderly, like a folded handkerchief carried around all day and never crumpled—where would there be room for a life-size sin?" What do Tracy's thoughts tell us about his cynical attitude toward Dottie?
2. When Tracy returns home to Maxwell after WWI, he fantasizes that he and Nonnie might leave America and live in France, where an interracial couple could be accepted. But he is quickly demoralized by the rigid racial stereotypes he encounters in his hometown: "All he knew was that thirty minutes ago he had been with the woman he loved. Now there was a colored girl named Nonnie. That was all there was to it." What are the stereotypes that paralyze Tracy?

Thomas Wolfe

1900–1938

"He can do more between 8:25 and 8:30 than the rest of us do all day, and it is no wonder that he is classed as a genius," remarked a colleague of the young Thomas Wolfe. Wolfe demonstrated his eagerness to achieve when, at age five, he followed his sister to school. Although Wolfe was too young to officially enroll, the teacher allowed him to stay. This early drive motivated Wolfe throughout his life.

Wolfe's body of work, which includes *Look Homeward, Angel* (1928), *Of Time and River* (1934), *The Web and the Rock* (1939), and the posthumous *You Can't Go Home Again* (1940), draws heavily upon his childhood and early life experiences in the South, as well as from his travels in Europe. Wolfe made extended trips to the Continent and to England at least seven times in his efforts to perfect his craft. Though he was later championed as a hero by his hometown of Asheville, North Carolina, Wolfe's characters in *Look Homeward, Angel* so closely resembled the townspeople of Asheville that the book was banned by the local public library for over seven years.

Thomas Clayton Wolfe was born in a middle-class resort town in North Carolina, the youngest of six surviving children. His mother, Julia, had been a teacher, but became a successful real estate speculator. Wolfe would later bemoan his mother's ambition, feeling that he and his siblings suffered some neglect during her absence. Wolfe's father, William Oliver

Wolfe, worked as a stone cutter, primarily fashioning tombstones. The elder Wolfe provided a colorful counterinfluence for the family and was more free spirited than his wife. Known for his excessive drinking and his penchant for quoting Shakespeare after he imbibed, he proved a steady provider for his large family. Thomas Wolfe would later describe both parents in a good-natured fashion, albeit satirically. Closest in nature to his brother Benjamin, Wolfe recreated him as Brother Ben in *Look Homeward, Angel*, drawing Ben as a solitary figure who can show love for his brother only through constant impatience and sarcastic remarks.

In 1916, Thomas entered the University of North Carolina at the age of 15. He demonstrated a natural inclination for play writing, and enrolled in Frederick H. Kock's writing course. Additionally, Wolfe worked as editor for the *Tar Heel*, the college newspaper, winning the Worth Prize for Philosophy for an essay titled "The Crisis in Industry." After completing his bachelor's degree, he undertook graduate study at Harvard University in the School of Arts and Sciences. Before Wolfe completed his M.A. and his study of playwriting under George Pierce Baker, his father died, and this event exerted a marked influence on his later fiction.

Wolfe traveled to New York to pursue a career as a playwright, but he became frustrated when most of his efforts were rejected. Producers found that his compositions included too many characters, were too long, and became too unwieldy in production. Struggling with his writing, Wolfe sought a teaching position at Washington Square College in New York. Although he worked as a teacher sporadically over a number of years, he later admitted his disdain for the profession. In 1925, after the first of many visits to Europe, Wolfe met Aline Bernstein, who was working as a scene designer for the Theater Guild. Bernstein was married at the time to a man of wealth and social standing and was the mother of two children. Nevertheless, the two engaged in an affair that lasted several years, and Bernstein proved a great influence on Wolfe's development as a writer, convincing him to turn his attention to novels instead of plays. He later included a dedication to "A.B." in his first novel, *Look Homeward, Angel*, which appeared in 1928.

The impending publication of *Look Homeward, Angel* led Wolfe to return to his hometown of Asheville in an effort to warn his family of the close resemblance between characters in the novel and the residents of Asheville. Even though a note "To the Reader" attempted to dispel comparisons, the citizens of Asheville were horrified at the depiction of the many idiosyncrasies and conflicts recorded in Wolfe's novel, and its publication caused Wolfe to become a virtual outcast from his community for over eight years. Today, Wolfe's transgressions against his hometown have generally been forgiven, and he has been declared one of Asheville's leading citizens.

Although he was beginning to succeed as a writer, Wolfe found it difficult to maintain a working relationship with his editors and publishers. After he ended his relationship with Bernstein, he worked with Maxell Perkins, a famous New York editor who assumed the role of mentor and advisor to the fledgling novelist. Wolfe later felt that he had outgrown this relationship, because he felt that Perkins was exerting undue influence over the editing of his novel, *Of Time and the River* (1935). Wolfe felt pressured to publish this novel before he was satisfied with it, and he would later blame Perkins for forcing its rapid publication. The pressure to write more quickly led to bouts of depression, causing Wolfe to indulge in alcohol abuse. He struggled as a result of the success engendered by *Look Homeward, Angel* and the expectations of greatness that it encouraged among his readers and editors.

Wolfe traveled extensively and made a trip to the West Coast. He planned to visit numerous national parks, but during his trip, he began to suffer from excruciating headaches and fever. Finally, he checked himself into a hospital in Seattle, where he was diagnosed with a possible brain tumor. He was transferred to Johns Hopkins Hospital in Baltimore, where doctors determined that he had a case of tubercular meningitis of the brain, which was far too advanced for doctors to treat successfully. Wolfe died a few days later on 15 September 1938, at the age of 37.

Critics have questioned whether Wolfe's writing itself caused him to be classified as a Southern writer, or whether his Southern upbringing led to his being categorized in this way.

Given the Southern propensity to examine the peculiar traits of family and friends and to relate stories and anecdotes, Wolfe's penchant for sketching characters in vivid detail naturally leads readers to notice his Southern attributes. His storytelling is not malicious, but it instead stems from a certain innate curiosity about the inner workings of others. No doubt Wolfe was intrigued and influenced by the Southern mindset. His interest was further fueled by his experiences growing up in small-town Asheville, where gossip and storytelling were the norm.

After terminating his professional relationship with Maxwell Perkins and the Charles Scribner Publishing Company, Wolfe signed with Harper and Brothers. Edward Ashwell, Harper's editor at the time, undertook the mammoth task of transforming Wolfe's largest manuscript into three new publications: *The Web and the Rock* (1939), *You Can't Go Home Again* (1940), and a series of short stories titled *The Hills Beyond* (1941).

The selection from *You Can't Go Home Again* that is included here demonstrates Wolfe's extraordinary skill at capturing a scene and sketching a character. This vignette relates George Weber's interactions with his downstairs neighbor, a Japanese artist, who repeatedly and humorously reminds George to curtail his habit of "tramp-ling" loudly through the upstairs apartment. After some initial and mutual annoyance and mistrust, the two men become friendly, leading George to witness firsthand the consequences of an artist pouring his whole heart into a single, great masterpiece. "The Microscopic Gentleman from Japan" also shows Wolfe's adeptness at encapsulating everyday events.

from You Can't Go Home Again

from Book 1, Chapter 3 *The Microscopic Gentleman from Japan*

In the old house where George lived that year Mr. Katamoto occupied the ground floor just below him, and in a little while they got to know each other very well. It might be said that their friendship began in mystification and went on to a state of security and staunch understanding.

Not that Mr. Katamoto ever forgave George when he erred. He was always instantly ready to inform him that he had taken a false step again (the word is used advisedly), but he was so infinitely patient, so unflaggingly hopeful of George's improvement, so unfailingly goodnatured and courteous, that no one could possibly have been angry or failed to try to mend his ways. What saved the situation was Katamoto's gleeful, childlike sense of humor. He was one of those microscopic gentlemen from Japan, scarcely five feet tall, thin and very wiry in his build, and George's barrel chest, broad shoulders, long, dangling arms, and large feet seemed to inspire his comic risibilities from the beginning. The first time they met, as they were just passing each other in the hall, Katamoto began to giggle when he saw George coming; and as they came abreast, the little man flashed a great expanse of gleaming teeth, wagged a finger roguishly, and said:

"Tramp-ling! Tramp-ling!"

For several days, whenever they passed each other in the hall, this same performance was repeated. George thought the words were very mysterious, and at first could not fathom their recondite meaning or understand why the sound of them was enough to set Katamoto off in a paroxysm of mirth. And yet when he would utter them and George would look at him in a surprised, inquiring kind of way, Katamoto would bend double with convulsive laughter and would stamp at the floor like a child with a tiny foot, shrieking hysterically: "Yis–yis–yis! You are tramp-ling!"—after which he would flee away.

George inferred that these mysterious references to "tramp-ling" which always set Katamoto off in such a fit of laughter had something to do with the bigness of his feet, for Katamoto would look at them quickly and slyly as he passed, and then giggle. However, a fuller explanation was soon provided. Katamoto came upstairs one afternoon and knocked at George's door. When it was opened, he giggled and flashed his teeth and looked somewhat embarrassed. After a moment, with evident hesitancy, he grinned painfully and said:

"If you ple-e-eze, sir! Will you—have some tea—with me—yis?"

He spoke the words very slowly, with deliberate formality, after which he flashed a quick, eager, and ingratiating smile.

George told him he would be glad to, and got his coat and started downstairs with him. Katamoto padded swiftly on ahead, his little feet shod in felt slippers that made no sound. Halfway down the stairs, as if the noise of George's heavy tread had touched his funnybone again, Katamoto stopped quickly, turned and pointed at George's feet, and giggled coyly: "Tramp-ling! You are tramp-ling!" Then he turned and fairly fled away down the stairs and down the hall, shrieking like a gleeful child. He waited at the door to usher his guest in, introduced him to the slender, agile little Japanese girl who seemed to stay there all the time, and finally brought George back into his studio and served him tea.

It was an amazing place. Katamoto had redecorated the fine old rooms and fitted them up according to the whims of his curious taste. The big back room was very crowded, intricate, and partitioned off into several small compartments with beautiful Japanese screens. He had also constructed a flight of stairs and a balcony that extended around three sides of the room, and on this balcony George could see a couch. The room was crowded with tiny chairs and tables, and there was an opulent-looking sofa and cushions. There were a great many small carved objects and bric-a-brac, and a strong smell of incense.

The center of the room, however, had been left entirely bare save for a big strip of spattered canvas and an enormous plaster figure. George gathered that he did a thriving business turning out sculptures for expensive speakeasies, or immense fifteen-foot statues of native politicians which were to decorate public squares in little towns, or in the state capitals of Arkansas, Nebraska, Iowa, and Wyoming. Where and how he had learned this curious profession George never found out, but he had mastered it with true Japanese fidelity, and so well that his products were apparently in greater demand than those of American sculptors. In spite of his small size and fragile build, the man was a dynamo of energy and could perform the labors of a Titan. God knows how he did it—where he found the strength.

George asked a question about the big plaster cast in the center of the room, and Katamoto took him over and showed it to him, remarking as he pointed to the creature's huge feet:

"He is—like you! . . . He is tramp-ling! . . . Yis! . . . He is tramp-ling!"

Then he took George up the stairs onto the balcony, which George dutifully admired.

"Yis!—You like it?" He smiled at George eagerly, a little doubtfully, then pointed at his couch and said: "I sleep here!" Then he pointed to the ceiling, which was so low that George had to stoop. "You sleep there?" said Katamoto eagerly.

George nodded.

Katamoto went on again with a quick smile, but with embarrassed hesitancy and a painful difficulty in his tone that had not been there before:

"I here," he said pointing, "you there—yis?"

He looked at George almost pleadingly, a little desperately—and suddenly George began to catch on.

"Oh! You mean I am right above you—" Katamoto nodded with instant relief—"and sometimes when I stay up late you hear me?"

"Yis! Yis!" He kept nodding his head vigorously. "Sometimes—" he smiled a little painfully—"sometimes—you will be tramp-ling!" He shook his finger at George with coy reproof and giggled.

"I'm awfully sorry," George said. "Of course, I didn't know you slept so near—so near the ceiling. When I work late I pace the floor. It's a bad habit. I'll do what I can to stop it."

"Oh, no-o!" he cried, genuinely distressed. "I not want—how you say it?—change your life! . . . If you ple-e-ese, sir! Just little thing—not wear shoes at night!" He pointed at his own small felt-shod feet and smiled up at George hopefully. "You like slippers—yis?" And he smiled persuasively again.

After that, of course, George wore slippers. But sometimes he would forget, and the next morning Katamoto would be rapping at his door again. He was never angry, he was always patient and good-humored, he was always beautifully courteous—but he would always call George to account. "You were tramp-ling!" he would cry. "Last night—again—tramp-ling!" And George would tell him he was sorry and would try not to do it again, and Katamoto would go away giggling, pausing to turn and wag his finger roguishly and call out once more, "Tramp-ling!"—after which he would flee downstairs, shrieking with laughter.

They were good friends.

In the months that followed, again and again George would come in the house to find the hall below full of sweating, panting movers, over whom Katamoto, covered from head to foot with clots and lumps of plaster, would hover prayerfully and with a fearful, pleading grin lest they mar his work, twisting his small hands together convulsively, aiding the work along by slight shudders, quick darts of breathless terror, writhing and shrinking movements of the body, and saying all the while with an elaborate, strained, and beseeching courtesy:

"Now, if—*you*—gentleman—a little! . . . *You* . . . yis–yis–yis-s!" with a convulsive grin. "*Oh-h-h!* Yis–yis-s! If you *ple-e-ese,* sir! . . . If you would down—a little—yis-s!–yis-s!–yis-s!" he hissed softly with that prayerful and pleading grin.

And the movers would carry out of the house and stow into their van the enormous piecemeal fragments of some North Dakota Pericles, whose size was so great that one wondered how this dapper, fragile little man could possibly have fashioned such a leviathan.

Then the movers would depart, and for a space Mr. Katamoto would loaf and invite his soul. He would come out in the backyard with his girl, the slender, agile little Japanese—who looked as if she had some Italian blood in her as well—and for hours at a time they would play at handball. Mr. Katamoto would knock the ball up against the projecting brick wall of the house next door, and every time he scored a point he would scream with laughter, clapping his small hands together, bending over weakly and pressing his hand against his stomach, and staggering about with delight and merriment. Choking with laughter, he would cry out in a high, delirious voice as rapidly as he could:

"Yis, yis, yis! Yis, yis, yis! Yis, yis, yis!"

Then he would catch sight of George looking at him from the window, and this would set him off again, for he would wag his finger and fairly scream:

"You were tramp-ling! . . . Yis, yis, yis! . . . Last night—again tramp-ling!"

This would reduce him to such a paroxysm of mirth that he would stagger across the court and lean against the wall, all caved in, holding his narrow stomach and shrieking faintly.

It was now the full height of steaming summer, and one day early in August George came home to find the movers in the house again. This time it was obvious that a work of more than usual magnitude was in transit. Mr. Katamoto, spattered with plaster, was of course hovering about in the hall, grinning nervously and fluttering prayerfully around the husky truckmen. As George came in, two of the men were backing slowly down the hall, carrying between them an immense head, monstrously jowled and set in an expression of farseeing statesmanship. A moment later three more men backed out of the studio, panting and cursing as they grunted painfully around the flowing fragment of a long frock coat and the vested splendor of a bulging belly. The first pair had now gone back in the studio, and when they came out again they were staggering beneath the trousered shank of a mighty leg and a booted Atlantean hoof, and as they passed, one of the other men, now returning for more of the statesman's parts, pressed himself against the wall to let them by and said:

"Jesus! If the son-of-a-bitch stepped on you with that foot, he wouldn't leave a grease spot, would he, Joe?"

The last piece of all was an immense fragment of the Solon's arm and fist, with one huge forefinger pointed upward in an attitude of solemn objurgation and avowal.

That figure was Katamoto's masterpiece; and George felt as he saw it pass that the enormous upraised finger was the summit of his art and the consummation of his life. Certainly it was the apple of his eye. George had never seen him before in such a state of extreme agitation. He fairly prayed above the sweating men. It was obvious that the coarse indelicacy of their touch made him shudder. The grin was frozen on his face in an expression of congealed terror. He writhed, he wriggled, he wrung his little hands, he crooned to them. And if anything had happened to that fat, pointed finger, George felt sure that he would have dropped dead on the spot.

At length, however, they got everything stowed away in their big van without mishap and drove off with their Ozymandias, leaving Mr. Katamoto, frail, haggard, and utterly exhausted, looking at the curb. He came back into the house and saw George standing there and smiled wanly at him.

"Tramp-ling," he said feebly, and shook his finger, and for the first time there was no mirth or energy in him.

George had never seen him tired before. It had never occurred to him that he could get tired. The little man had always been so full of inexhaustible life. And now, somehow, George felt an unaccountable sadness to see him so weary and so strangely grey. Katamoto was silent for a moment, and then he lifted his face and said, almost tonelessly, yet with a shade of wistful eagerness:

"You see statue—yis?"

"Yes, Kato, I saw it."

"And you like?"

"Yes, very much."

"And—" he giggled a little and made a shaking movement with his hands—"you see foot?"

"Yes."

"I sink," he said, "he will be tramp-ling—yis?"—and he made a laughing sound.

"He ought to," George said, "with a hoof like that. It's almost as big as mine," he added, as an afterthought.

Katamoto seemed delighted with this observation, for he laughed shrilly and said: "Yis! Yis!"—nodding his head emphatically. He was silent for another moment, then hesitantly, but with an eagerness that he could not conceal, he said:

"And you see finger?"

"Yes, Kato."

"And you like?"—quickly, earnestly.

"Very much."

"Big finger—yis?"—with a note of rising triumph in his voice.

"Very big, Kato."

"And *pointing*—yis?" he said ecstatically, grinning from ear to ear and pointing his own small finger heavenward.

"Yes, pointing."

He sighed contentedly. "Well, zen," he said, with the appeased air of a child; "I'm glad you like."

For a week or so after that George did not see Katamoto again or even think of him. This was the vacation period at the School for Utility Cultures, and George was devoting every minute of his time, day and night, to a fury of new writing. Then one afternoon, a long passage completed and the almost illegible pages of his swift scrawl tossed in a careless heap upon the floor, he sat relaxed, looking out of his back window, and suddenly he thought of Katamoto again. He remembered that he had not seen him recently, and it seemed strange that he had not even heard the familiar thud of the little ball against the wall outside or the sound of his high, shrill laughter. This realization, with its sense of loss, so troubled him that he went downstairs immediately and pressed Katamoto's bell.

There was no answer. All was silent. He waited, and no one came. Then he went down to the basement and found the janitor and spoke to him. He said that Mr. Katamoto had been ill. No, it was not serious, he thought, but the doctor had advised a rest, a brief period of relaxation from his exhausting labors, and had sent him for care and observation to the near-by hospital.

George meant to go to see him, but he was busy with his writing and kept putting it off. Then one morning, some ten days later, coming back home after breakfast in a restaurant, he found a moving van backed up before the house. Katamoto's door was open, and when he looked inside the moving people had already stripped the apartment almost bare. In the center of the once fantastic room, now empty, where Katamoto had performed his prodigies of work, stood a young Japanese, an acquaintance of the sculptor, whom George had seen there several times before. He was supervising the removal of the last furnishings.

The young Japanese looked up quickly, politely, with a toothy grin of frozen courtesy as George came in. He did not speak until George asked him how Mr. Katamoto was. And then, with the same toothy, frozen grin upon his face, the same impenetrable courtesy, he said that Mr. Katamoto was dead.

George was shocked, and stood there for a moment, knowing there was nothing more to say, and yet feeling somehow, as people always feel on these occasions, that there was something he *ought* to say. He looked at the young Japanese and started to speak, and found himself looking into the inscrutable, polite, untelling eyes of Asia.

So he said nothing more. He just thanked the young man and went out.

Questions to Consider

1. Wolfe uses the device of repetition both to frame the story of *You Can't Go Home Again* and to punctuate sections within the work. What purpose does this repetition serve? What does Wolfe repeat in the section included here?
2. *You Can't Go Home Again* is a book about people and places all over the world; very little of it takes place in the South. Is this really a Southern novel? Why or why not?

George Sessions Perry

1910–1956

Today, few recognize the name of George Sessions Perry, despite his importance as a regional writer during his lifetime. Perry's portrait of rural Texas in *Hold Autumn in Your Hand* (1941) provides one of the best depictions of the struggles inherent in the sharecropper culture of the South. Perry's acclaim as a fiction writer was overshadowed at the time of his death in 1956 by his reputation as a reporter and feature writer, yet *Hold Autumn in Your Hand,* his major fictional work, won the Texas Institute of Letters annual award in 1941 and the National Book Award in 1942.

Born in 1910 in Rockdale, Texas, Perry was orphaned by the age of 14. While his father, a pharmacist, was not directly involved in farming or sharecropping, young Perry was exposed to the sharecropper system throughout his youth, since his father frequently treated the local residents for various ailments, acting as the doctor when none was available. His father generally received little or no fee for his services, much like Dr. White in *Hold Autumn in Your Hand.* The plight of the poor and a dedication to social responsibility were lessons the elder Perry bestowed upon his young son. Perry's father died from Bright's Disease, and his mother, after a painful second marriage, committed suicide. Perry continually felt guilt for his mother's death, and his feisty grandmother, in whose care he was left, did nothing to either build his self-esteem or to temper his feelings of guilt. She was a forceful, if not domineering, woman who was much different from Perry's wife, Claire Hodges.

While attending Southwestern University in Georgetown, Texas, Perry met his future wife. Upon their marriage, Hodges devoted herself to Perry entirely. She was his manager, editor, wife, partner—the stabilizing force in his life. Although Claire was Perry's constant and loyal companion, she was no match for his irascible grandmother, and the tense relationship between the two women took its toll on Perry. The couple traveled a good deal during their early married life; ultimately, however, they decided to return to Rockdale, where Perry settled down to write. He had, in his younger life, traveled as a war correspondent, yet he had no stomach for war. Like many writers of this era, he was haunted by the agonies of the battlefield.

Perry's earlier work, *Walls Rise Up,* a picaresque novel detailing the lives of three characters who live underneath a bridge on the Brazos River, received local acclaim when it was first published during the late 1930s, although it pales in comparison to the finely crafted *Hold Autumn in Your Hand.* Perry's work also includes three nonfiction pieces: *Texas: A World in Itself* (1942), *My Granny Van* (1949), and the *Tale of a Foolish Farmer* (1951). Perry's third novel, *The Hackberry Cavalier* (1934), was based upon a collection of short stories that he had written for various magazines, especially *The Country Gentleman* and *The Saturday Evening Post.* During Perry's relatively short life, he published many articles and serials in well-regarded journals and newspapers.

Perry witnessed the fragility of the agrarian system when the Great Depression hit the small town of Rockdale in the 1930s. Like many writers of the time, he saw the destitution of the lower classes of society, and he raised his voice on their behalf. Because an inheritance made his own financial situation relatively stable, Perry suffered tremendous guilt about having more than others in his community, and ultimately, this guilt defined his writing. Maxine Hairston, Perry's most recent biographer, has stated that "Because of that guilt . . . Perry threw himself into fighting the situation in the only way that he knew—protest through writing. His early works are full of the anguish and misery he saw around him and of anger at a society that simply accepted rural poverty as a way of life." Perry's need to protest led him to write two additional novels between 1933 and 1935, each of which addressed the plight of the impoverished workers in southeast Texas. These novels remained unpublished. Later in his life, Perry found himself in reduced financial circumstances because of ill health, which severely limited his ability to write as he once did. Before his death, he and his wife were forced to sell almost everything they owned to pay hospital and living expenses.

As Perry's health declined, he became caught in an endless cycle of alcoholism, arthritis, and mental illness. After numerous years of toiling to make a living, Perry died tragically. Tormented by his failing health, his lack of resources, his frustration as a writer, and the continued emotional impact of the loss of his parents as a young boy, he walked into a river near his Connecticut home, and his body was not found for nearly two months. The coroner ruled his 1956 death an accidental drowning although his death was no doubt hastened by his sensitive emotions.

Perry continually fought on behalf of the oppressed, and in his writings, his identification with and empathy for the underclasses of society is apparent. His work remains powerful, especially in light of the socioeconomic problems that continue to plague small farmers in contemporary society. While presenting a timeless portrayal of the impoverished, his body of work also provides a vivid depiction of his world, a world he saw passing quickly. Perry was well aware that the way of life he depicted in his Texas fiction was declining, that his state was in transition from rural values and ways of living to a more complex and urban mode of life. He draws upon universal themes of man's struggle against nature, and individual and collective alienation, and uses his works as venue to champion the oppressed—specifically, the tenant farmer. Perry's texts accurately depict the world of the sharecropper and capture the society and culture of the Depression Era underclass.

from Hold Autumn in Your Hand

The Texas January day was all blue and gold and barely crisp. Only the absence of leaves and sap, the presence of straggling bands of awkward crows, the gray-yellow flutter of field larks, and the broad, matter-of-fact hibernation of the earth said it was winter as Sam Tucker walked along the road, his long legs functioning automatically, farmerly. His body had about it the look of country dogs at the end of winter, when they are all ribs and leg muscles and jaw muscles and teeth. His eyes were bright and dark and small, with no more evil or softness in them than a hawk's. His hands were knotty with big knuckles and were gloved with protective calluses.

A cock quail came out of the burdock hedge at the side of the road just ahead and looked at Sam with a strange, casual dignity. Sam knew the quail was examining its surroundings before leading the rest of the covey across the road.

"Hell," Sam said, walking on, "y'all just go on and fly. I ain't got time for no politeness. I got too far to go."

The quail, however, merely withdrew into the burdock thicket and Sam went on.

"Could of charmed the last one of them scamps into walkin acrost the road if I had the time," he told himself. "Only maybe they been shot at."

But he was preoccupied and forgot them. He was on his way to see a man named Ruston about a matter of extreme importance and his mind and imagination were crowded with possibilities: how it would be if Ruston said yes, and what were the best ways to get him to say it.

Ruston was a big landowner who worked paid labor. He was, furthermore, a man who'd as soon say no as yes. He was not, like some of the others, known as an especially bad man to work for. He paid trifling wages because it was customary and because a man working in a cotton field is not doing a very valuable thing. He was not known to be vicious or dishonest with his workers beyond the conventional banditry of the commissary system. Neither he nor any of his foremen had killed any Negroes or even quirted any. Grapevine talk said everything he had was mortgaged to the hilt.

And now as Sam walked along the road toward the commissary, he carefully reviewed the alternatives, carefully thought over what Ruston had to offer. Ruston had one farm of three thousand acres, which meant, of course, that it was a nation, with its own government (Ruston and his overseers), coinage (wages were paid in metal tokens redeemable at the commissary), and civilization. Its citizens lived in a settlement known as a camp. They worked in gangs at the discretion, and under the surveillance, of an overseer on horseback. The workers were separated, the women and girls in one group, the men and boys in another. There was a water cart that followed the gangs, a hoe sharpener, and a mule-drawn privy that ran on skids.

The commissary tokens made you feel bad because you knew they were worth fifteen per cent less than they were supposed to be, since the prices had been jacked up that much. And yet, if you'd really thought the thing through, you knew you were doing as well as when you farmed somewhere on the halves and traded in town on credit. By the time the store got through with you, it had got a little more than fifteen per cent in interest charges; or if you could make arrangements at the bank, the bank got the same fifteen per cent. They got it different ways, made it look cheaper and sound like ten, but they got it. So that canceled out.

There were two things, however, that didn't. One was the overseer. If he were afoot, it would be different. But to have him there all of every day, mounted, looking down at you, shifting in the saddle, was unendurable. No matter how many years you'd known him, you got to hating him, and before long that hating was taking more out of you than the hoe was.

And finally, at the end of the year, whose crop was it? Not legally—you knew the answer to that—but actually. Who had created it? Whose sweat and studying and secret intuition did that crop represent? Why, Ruston's and the gangs'. Which was all right if you happened not to be a farmer, which is to say a man who feels out the darkest of mysteries with the tendrils of his imagination and must watch the result develop and constantly alter his decisions like a commander in the field.

There was no way to cancel out the fact that when autumn came, you had not made a crop, which is a fine thing to have done, but had, instead, only been herded here and there to do the drudgery for another man's plans. Cotton-labor wages were too small to make up to you the emptiness of such a year in which the other man so exclusively got the goody and you got the hull.

Though there was no privacy in the camps, it was pleasant hanging around the blacksmith shop with the others on rainy days or playing dominoes in one of the shacks. Too, there were house dances that formed themselves almost automatically in bad weather. On Sunday there were ball games. And yet there was that hateful son of a bitch on a horse telling you how to hoe corn, or, if not telling you, being there *to* tell you.

But finally, whose crop was it? Not yours.

It was like deciding to have a child and the law said you had to apply to the overseer, which you did, and he happened to be agreeable and said, "O.K., I'll herd the boys right over to your wife and y'all can get busy getting it started."

It is all right to have a road-working or a cemetery-cleaning and all put in together and get the job done, but some things are private, and none of a lot of cooperative people's business. Unless you happen to be interested only in the financial result.

So Sam was sure he wanted no part of the anonymous civilization of Ruston's three thousand acres.

Fifteen miles from the three thousand, Ruston owned sixty-eight acres in the San Pedro bottoms. Forty acres are supposed to be the maximum one-team family crop of cotton and corn, but somehow Sam had never been as sure of anything as that he was a match for those sixty-eight acres of hillside and bottom. Besides, the character and flavor and spirit of the San Pedro were a thing as definitely and distinctly felt by him as the personality of any of the more interesting of his kin people.

Sam was a river man. And while he could have drawn a precise map of this river's course in detail, in his mind, he did not, preferring to go on thinking of the river as something dark and cool and undulant with mystery, a gauzy shirt to be worn instead of a pill to be taken.

The river would be there, and he had been three years away from the river. And those sixty-eight acres, fertile as the sperm of a goat, were re-seeded by the river each winter with Johnson grass which could be removed only by violence from this goat-rich earth in which its ropy roots found ever-greater strength and determination to live stupendously, and to stunt and choke the things a man might plant there.

Yet he'd hit that Johnson grass so hard and fast with plow and harrow that even it must perish, for all its mighty clutching and in-digging.

Ruston would have fine mules, and Sam's mind was bumped by the great brown-black hemispheres of their hawser-muscled rumps before him and the plow handles in his hand, plunging the middle-buster with purposeful emotion into the black earth, which turned into a Negro virgin with black thighs twining, and he had to call back his mind to where he was going, as he would a varmint dog from a rabbit trail.

Six bits was what Ruston paid, every God's day you went to the field. And if Nona went too, say, drove a cultivator or a planter or hoed, that was four bits more.

There would be certainty, for once, at least during the growing season, that the family would not starve, and that the river was near, to wind around you when you wanted and needed it, to baptize you when nothing would do but you enter it physically.

And the land would be there, stinking and gummy with a richness which you would tear away from the weeds and stuff into the corn, the land which you would enter, plow-wise, with the strength of great mules.

It would be there to be made beautiful with fruit, and never mind the money part. Ruston would foot the bills. Your wages would be fixed, and worrying would not raise them. But to have made the substantial beauty of cotton and corn, to have studied the signs, and done things when your experience and your sympathy for crops said do it, that would mean you had made the year big with fulfillment and your insides softly luminous with knowing you were right and that as a creature you made sense, and living did.

But first something had to be taken away from Ruston: his belief that you were of sand caliber, because you had worked there. No one would know better than Ruston that the sand attracts people who have not much to give. Because the sand farms easily, with jack-rabbit mules and a Georgia stock. Yet in the end it crushes your spirit more utterly with its bland refusal to give what it does not possess. For it is the loose, incipient mother of nubbins and stunted cotton, and that is all.

And if you live there long, people know how you are, how you must be after it gets through doing what it does to you, and how you probably were when you went there. So your private despair and surrender are no longer a secret if you stay too long in the sand, where even the weeds have no vitality and are easy to kill. This stigma of having worked lately in the sand was what Sam was going to have to keep small in Ruston's mind.

It was also certain how things would be if Ruston said no. Destitution, not comparative, but utter destitution. No money and no credit. Just none at all. And the problem of trying to keep the family alive till spring, which you would manage somehow to do, and not feel too sorry for yourself in the bargain. After all, you'd done it plenty of times before. Then when spring came, you'd begin working a piece of land somewhere on the halves, sharecropping, which you have been doing for the last three years and your returns on days worked have averaged about forty-six cents. If you had got the breaks on weather and price and bugs, you might have done better, but you didn't, and have enough of farming on the halves. The sterility of the land made it like trying to do a good job of half-soling your shoes with paper, and the river was not there.

Sam came up to the commissary steps and saw Ruston talking to a man who must have lived outside the farming world because his pants were not only wool but had a crease in them.

Sam went inside, where some others like himself were waiting in almost hidden nervousness, and asked them a question he knew was important to them all.

"What kind of humor is he in today?"

"I ain't been able to tell," one of them answered, unconsciously going through the motions of warming his hands and buttocks at the cold stove.

There was blue- and plum-colored gingham on the shelves of the store, and kerosene in a square, red crank tank, and snuff and starch and Irish potatoes. There was also a little, glassed-in bin of mixed candy which you wouldn't get much of for a nickel, and flour and lard and sirup.

When Sam's time came, he went over to Ruston, who was short and whose legs bent fatly backward at the knees, and said, "Mr. Ruston, my name's Sam Tucker. I want to go to work for you."

"I'll have to study about that," Ruston said, looking Sam over.

"You send folks from the big place when you need work done on the little San Pedro place, don't you?"

"Yes."

"Well, I been figgerin out how you could save a lot of truck wear and tear, and worrisomeness for yourself, if you'd just let me move onto the little place and work it."

"House ain't any good and you'd have to borrow water because the well's fell in."

"I've done looked it over and know that. But I still want to, anyhow. Been half-and-halfin for the last three years and you know what kind of years they've been. Most of the time we've been whettin pretty much on the point. Just for a year, anyhow, I'd like to day-labor that little place, and know eatin was took care of for a few months. I'd like to raise a crop on that good land that *was* a crop and have some good big mules to do it with."

"Who'd keep your time?"

"I would, and when you drove by every week or so, you'd know whether a week's work had been done just by lookin."

Ruston was still sizing Sam up, knowing that all farmers are hard workers next summer; that, no matter how lazy or unreliable they are, they are moved to great anxiety in the wintertime to make the dirt fly next summer.

"Where've you been farming?"

"Different places."

"Like exactly what place?"

"Well, four years ago I brought in the first bale to Hackberry and collected the premium. You never saw a sorry farmer bring in the first bale, did you?"

"No, I reckon not."

Ruston thought some more. If this fellow could take over the little farm, which, with its special problems and inconvenient location, was a nuisance, it would be a good thing and would leave him free to concentrate on the big farm.

"You'd be willing to take your money out in trade at the commissary, wouldn't you?" Ruston asked.

"If it was in reach, I would. Don't see how I could hardly walk fifteen miles for groceries and then tote em home."

"I reckon not, either. Look. Here's what I'll do. You don't want to have to walk back over here for an answer, so I'll give you one today. I don't know much about you, but that's a good idea you got for the little place to be run separately. So move on over there and try to stuff up the holes in the house, and I'll take you on a day-to-day basis. By that I mean the first time I come over and don't like the looks of things, I'll fire you and not feel the least bit bad about it. I'll have hands aplenty on the big place and trucks to haul em with and can shoot em over there whenever needed."

Sam grinned. He couldn't help it. All he had to do to hold the little place was what he'd never dreamed of not doing: just farm hell out of it. So easily had he kept the sand years hidden. So easily had the coveted empire of sixty-eight black acres and its ribbon of river fallen into his hands. How firmly and benevolently he would hold it and guide its surging potentialities, its spectacular usefulness! The sixty-eight acres were a wild stallion to be tamed, where the sand had been a spavined old mare that would eat your courage and drink your own vitality and lay back down. He no longer had the impossible task of resurrecting the dead, but of breaking and driving this wild stallion.

"That's a good trade," Sam said. Then, supposing there had better be some official declaration on the matter of payment, he said, "I guess I know what the wages'll be."

"Six bits a day."

"What about my wife?"

"Is she a strong, healthy woman?"

"Yes."

"Four bits. . . . Any kids?"

"None big enough."

"You'll have to hustle, farming that place with just your wife."

"I know . . . I been figgerin: if you let me have about three dollars a month credit against my first money, me and my folks could kinda scratch along till spring."

"No, sir. Our arrangement is day-to-day. The money starts when the plowing starts. I don't want you all to pick up and leave with your bellies full of my unpaid-for groceries."

Sam laughed. He liked a man who talked like that and didn't beat around the bush.

"Well," he said, "it looks like I'm goin to have to make some other rangements bout feedin my bunch till farmin time."

"Go over there," Ruston said, pointing toward the wooden counter, "and get a dollar's worth of what you need. It's a gift. Always give a new family a dollar's worth. Just a habit of mine. It don't make sense, but I do it. Well, our trade's made."

He told the clerk about the dollar's worth and got in his car and left.

And Sam sure liked that man.

Liking and figuring, he went over to the counter.

A box of .22 hulls for the old gun so he and Zoonie could varmint-hunt for pelts for cash and meat to eat.

Seventeen cents.

Wasn't this marvelous? he kept telling himself. Really unbelievable.

The commissary cornmeal was four cents a pound in bulk and Sam knew where he could get fresh-ground yellow for two cents, but this was white and a gift. He got twelve pounds.

Forty-eight cents.

Plus seventeen.

Made sixty-five. All that meal he had, and fifty hunting bullets.

He got two pounds of lard at fifteen cents a pound. Your belly gets lonesome for grease when there isn't any, and you know there's strength in it and satisfaction when it enriches cornpone.

Now there was a nickel left, and a war began between that mixed candy and a nickel's worth of coffee (the man said he would cover the bottom of a little sack with it for a nickel). But the candy won when he thought of the suffocating excitement in the kids' eyes, of everybody nibbling a piece, including Granny and Nona, and all of them impressed by what a good provider Papa was. Before leaving, however, he got the man to take back one pound of meal in exchange for a fifth of a pound of coffee.

Then he started down the road, and stole a piece of candy out of the sack on the way, but only one very small one.

Questions to Consider

1. How does the sharecropper experience depicted in this passage from the novel compare with other stories that you have read about the rural poor?
2. What characteristics makes these characters particularly Southern?

Richard Wright

1908–1960

Richard Wright was born in the small community of Roxie near Natchez, Mississippi on 4 September 1908. His father was a sharecropper, and his mother was a school teacher. Wright's father had little education, and in Jim Crow–era Mississippi, the family struggled for survival. Despite the discrimination that Wright endured throughout much of his life, he became one of America's best-known and most revered writers, for both the power of his ideas and the quality of his prose. Life in Mississippi proved intolerable for Wright, who chafed under the lack of opportunities available to a man of color, and as soon as he was able to leave the state, he moved northward, first to Chicago and later to Harlem, where he would become an integral part of the Harlem Renaissance movement.

Wright grew up in poverty. His parents endured an unsteady relationship which ultimately ended when his father abandoned the family for another woman when Wright was only six years old. His mother was forced into a life of domestic work that threatened her health. Wright and his brother were sent to an orphanage for a time, and finally went to live with their maternal grandmother in Mississippi. An austere woman with strict fundamentalist convictions, Wright's grandmother enforced her religious ideals on anyone living in her household. Because she was a Seventh-day Adventist, she did not believe in working on Saturday, which Adventists view as the Sabbath. Wright clashed with his grandmother frequently over her adherence to this standard, for his inability to work on Saturdays made it nearly impossible for him to secure and keep a job. The family moved many times during Wright's early years, settling for a time in Arkansas, with his mother's sister and her family. Wright grew close to his mother's brother-in-law, Silas Hopkins, a successful saloon-keeper and builder who was murdered by envious poor Whites in 1917. Fearing for their own lives after Hopkins was killed, the family fled to West Helena, Arkansas and later to Mississippi, leaving behind the once-thriving business and financial stability that Hopkins's hard work had supported.

Wright completed ninth grade in 1925 in Jackson, Mississippi as the valedictorian at Smith-Robertson Junior High. His first essay, "The Voodoo of Hell's Half-Acre," was published in *The Southern Register*. Wright left Jackson, Mississippi to seek improved opportunities in Memphis; although after arriving, he felt compelled to move to Chicago with his Aunt Maggie. He secured a temporary position as a postal worker, but lost it because his chronic malnourishment rendered him too weak to pass the required physical examination on the first try. Wright later passed the exam and was reinstated, but was again let go when the Great Depression made jobs scarce throughout the country. He then took a job as a dishwasher, writing only when he found time. During his years in Chicago, Wright met many Communist Party members, and the political ideology of the Party, particularly its emphasis on ending oppression of all kinds, appealed to him. For a time, he worked vigilantly within the Party to attempt to end the systemic racial oppression in the United States.

Wright was largely self-educated, and he read voraciously. His early influences included the writings of Sinclair Lewis, Theodore Dreiser, and Stephen Crane, writers whom he began reading after encountering the works of H. L. Mencken. In June 1937, he moved to New York City where he worked on the short-lived magazine, *New Challenge,* and edited the *Daily Worker*. During this time, Wright wrote three stories which later provided the basis for the collection, *Uncle Tom's Children.* In 1939, despite racial segregation, he was briefly married to a White woman, ballerina Dhima Rose Meadman. Although 1940 was a turbulent year for Wright personally—his marriage had completely deteriorated by this time—his most powerful novel, *Native Son*, appeared and quickly became a best seller. Contemporary reviewers of *Native*

Son such as Joseph H. Jenkins remarked on the novel's condemnation of institutionalized racism:

> Society has its own record of crime—and no mean or scanty one—against its constituent members in the long account of deprivations forced upon the helpless, of fatuous antagonisms created and maintained among men and women who need and want peace and security, and of the exploitation of the consequent maladjustments. The fit punishment for these atrocities is a ruinous waste of the resources of society in not only material goods but human life and spirit as well, together with ultimate confinement in discord, confusion, loss of hope, and final destruction. . . . In *Native Son,* society is the real criminal.

Native Son brought international acclaim to Wright and fueled discussions of the racial discrimination that remained implicit in American society.

By 1941, Wright's growing disenchantment with the Communist movement had festered into a full-blown crisis of conscience that caused him to leave the Party and seek other avenues of racial desegregation. Although he did not publicly announce his break with the Party right away, the publication of two articles, "I Tried to Be a Communist" and "The Man Who Lived Underground," in prominent magazines disassociated Wright from the movement. Despite his self-imposed distance from the Communist Party, his second wife, Ellen Poplar, was a Communist organizer. The distance that he placed between himself and the Party seemed inadequate, however, since nearly ten years after his public rejection of the Communist Party, Wright refused to return to the United States, for fear that he would be required to appear before the congressional committee investigating Communist activities.

The autobiographical *Black Boy*, the story of Wright's pre-Chicago life, was published in 1945 and also became a best seller. *Black Boy* addressed themes similar to those found in *Native Son,* demonstrating the devastating effects of institutionalized racism, and also showing that racism was not just a Southern problem. *Black Boy* drove home the fact that the Jim Crow laws legalized the abuse and oppression of people of color, providing compelling examples of the myriad ways in which this oppression was enacted in daily life. His autobiographical essay, "The Ethics of Living Jim Crow," revisits many of the incidents of racism that he endured as a young man and that he would later examine in greater detail in *Black Boy*.

That same year, Wright traveled to Canada and later to Paris, where he met expatriate writers such as Gertrude Stein and Jean-Paul Sartre. He enjoyed the less restrictive racial mores of Paris, and decided to move to France permanently by 1947 although he continued to work tirelessly to stamp out racism and segregation in the world. Wright traveled to Africa many times and reported the social injustices that he saw in many of his later writings. Although these later writings, which were often philosophical, did not meet with the same critical and popular success of *Native Son* and *Black Boy*, Wright continued to write prolifically throughout his life. Several of his works were made into movies or stage plays, which served to further disseminate his anti-oppression message.

On 28 November 1960, Wright died of a heart attack in Paris and was buried there in Pere Lachaise. Wright dedicated his life and writings to race relations and to ending oppression and discrimination against people of color. Although he lived all over the world, Wright never forgot—nor escaped—his Southern roots, which instilled in him a hatred for institutional racism that motivated him throughout his life.

from Native Son

from Book 1 *Fear*

(Editor's Note: Bigger Thomas, the protagonist of Native Son, *is an angry, poverty-stricken young man who has continually suffered the oppression inherent in the Jim Crow era. He has recently secured a position as a driver for a wealthy family. In the scene that*

follows, he has just spent a very uneasy evening drinking with the White daughter of his employer, Mary, and her male companion, Jan. Because the couple has embraced Communism, they believe in equality and attempt to show their open-mindedness by socializing with their driver. As the scene opens, Mary is extremely intoxicated and Bigger is preparing to take her home.)

He stopped the car. Bigger heard them speak in whispers.

"Good-bye, Jan."

"Good-bye, honey."

"I'll call you tomorrow?"

"Sure."

Jan stood at the front door of the car and held out his palm. Bigger shook timidly.

"It's been great meeting you, Bigger;" Jan said.

"O.K.," Bigger mumbled.

"I'm damn glad I know you. Look. Have another drink."

Bigger took a big swallow.

"You better give me one, too, Jan. It'll make me sleep," Mary said.

"You're sure you haven't had enough?"

"Aw, come on, honey."

She got out of the car and stood on the curb. Jan gave her the bottle and she tilted it.

"Whoa!" Jan said.

"What's the matter?"

"I don't want you to pass out."

"I can hold it."

Jan tilted the bottle and emptied it, then laid it in the gutter. He fumbled clumsily in his pockets for something. He swayed; he was drunk.

"You lose something, honey?" Mary lisped; she, too, was drunk.

"Naw; I got some stuff here I want Bigger to read. Listen, Bigger, I got some pamphlets here. I want you to read 'em, see?"

Bigger held out his hand and received a small batch of booklets.

"O.K."

"I really want you to read 'em, now. We'll have a talk 'bout 'em in a coupla days. . . . " His speech was thick.

"I'll read 'em," Bigger said, stifling a yawn and stuffing the booklets into his pocket.

"I'll see that he reads 'em," Mary said.

Jan kissed her again. Bigger heard the Loop-bound car rumbling forward.

"Well, good-bye," he said.

"Goo'-bye, honey," Mary said. "I'm gonna ride up front with Bigger."

She got into the front seat. The street car clanged to a stop. Jan swung onto it and it started north. Bigger drove toward Drexel Boulevard. Mary slumped down in the seat and sighed. Her legs sprawled wide apart. The car rolled along. Bigger's head was spinning.

"You're very nice, Bigger," she said.

He looked at her. Her face was pasty white. Her eyes were glassy. She was very drunk.

"I don't know," he said.

"My! But you say the *funniest* things," she giggled.

"Maybe," he said.

She leaned her head on his shoulder.

"You don't mind, do you?"

"I don't mind."

"You know, for *three* hours you haven't said *yes* or *no*."

She doubled up with laughter. He tightened with hate. Again she was looking inside of him and he did not like it. She sat up and dabbed at her eyes with a handkerchief. He kept his eyes straight in front of him and swung the car into the driveway and brought it to a stop. He got out and opened the door. She did not move. Her eyes were closed.

"We're here," he said.

She tried to get up and slipped back into the seat.

"Aw, shucks!"

She's drunk, *really* drunk, Bigger thought. She stretched out her hand.

"Here; gimme a lift. I'm wobbly. . . . "

She was resting on the small of her back and her dress was pulled up so far that he could see where her stockings ended on her thighs. He stood looking at her for a moment; she raised her eyes and looked at him. She laughed.

"Help me, Bigger. I'm stuck."

He helped her and his hands felt the softness of her body as she stepped to the ground. Her dark eyes looked at him feverishly from deep sockets. Her hair was in his face, filling him with its scent. He gritted his teeth, feeling a little dizzy.

"Where's my hat? I dropped it shomewhere. . . . "

She swayed as she spoke and he tightened his arms about her, holding her up. He looked around; her hat was lying on the running board.

"Here it is," he said.

As he picked it up he wondered what a white man would think seeing him here with her like this. Suppose old man Dalton saw him now? Apprehensively, he looked up at the big house. It was dark and silent.

"Well," Mary sighed. "I suppose I better go to bed. . . . "

He turned her loose, but had to catch her again to keep her off the pavement. He led her to the steps.

"Can you make it?"

She looked at him as though she had been challenged.

"Sure. Turn me loose. . . . "

He took his arm from her and she mounted the steps firmly and then stumbled loudly on the wooden porch. Bigger made a move toward her, but stopped, his hands outstretched, frozen with fear. Good God, she'll wake up everybody! She was half-bent over, resting on one knee and one hand, looking back at him in amused astonishment. That girl's crazy! She pulled up and walked slowly back down the steps, holding onto the railing. She swayed before him, smiling.

"I sure am drunk. . . . "

He watched her with a mingled feeling of helplessness, admiration, and hate. If her father saw him here with her now, his job would be over. But she was beautiful, slender, with an air that made him feel that she did not hate him with the hate of other white people. But, for all of that, she was white and he hated her. She closed her eyes slowly, then opened them; she was trying desperately to take hold of herself. Since she was not able to get to her room alone, ought he to call Mr. Dalton or Peggy? Naw. . . . That would betray her. And, too, in spite of his hate for her, he was excited standing here watching her like this. Her eyes closed again and she swayed toward him. He caught her.

"I'd better help you," he said.

"Let's go the back way, Bigger. I'll stumble sure as hell . . . and wake up everybody . . . if we go up the front. . . ."

Her feet dragged on the concrete as he led her to the basement. He switched on the light, supporting her with his free hand.

"I didn't know I was sho drunk," she mumbled.

He led her slowly up the narrow stairs to the kitchen door, his hand circling her waist and the tips of his fingers feeling the soft swelling of her breasts. Each second she was leaning more heavily against him.

"Try to stand up," he whispered fiercely as they reached the kitchen door.

He was thinking that perhaps Mrs. Dalton was standing in flowing white and staring with stony blind eyes in the middle of the floor, as she had been when he had come for the glass of water. He eased the door back and looked. The kitchen was empty and dark, save for a faint blue hazy light that seeped through a window from the winter sky.

"Come on."

She pulled heavily on him, her arm about his neck. He pushed the door in and took a step inside and stopped, waiting, listening. He felt her hair brush his lips. His skin glowed warm and his muscles flexed; he looked at her face in the dim light, his senses drunk with the odor of her hair and skin. He stood for a moment, then whispered in excitement and fear:

"Come on; you got to get to your room."

He led her out of the kitchen into the hallway; he had to walk her a step at a time. The hall was empty and dark; slowly he half-walked and half-dragged her to the back stairs. Again he hated her; he shook her.

"Come on; wake up!"

She did not move or open her eyes; finally she mumbled something and swayed limply. His fingers felt the soft curves of her body and he was still, looking at her, enveloped in a sense of physical elation. This little bitch! he thought. Her face was touching his. He turned her round and began to mount the steps, one by one. He heard a slight creaking and stopped. He looked, straining his eyes in the gloom. But there was no one. When he got to the top of the steps she was completely limp and was still trying to mumble something. Goddamn! He could move her only by lifting her bodily. He caught her in his arms and carried her down the hall, then paused. Which was her door? Goddamn!

"Where's your room?" he whispered.

She did not answer. Was she completely out? He could not leave her here; if he took his hands from her she would sink to the floor and lie there all night. He shook her hard, speaking as loudly as he dared.

"Where's your room?"

Momentarily, she roused herself and looked at him with blank eyes.

"Where's your room?" he asked again.

She rolled her eyes toward a door. He got her as far as the door and stopped. Was this really her room? Was she too drunk to know? Suppose he opened the door to Mr. and Mrs. Dalton's room? Well, all they could do was fire him. It wasn't his fault that she was drunk. He felt strange, possessed, or as if he were acting upon a stage in front of a crowd of people. Carefully, he freed one hand and turned the knob of the door. He waited; nothing happened. He pushed the door in quietly; the room was dark and silent. He felt along the wall with his fingers for the electric switch and could not find it. He stood, holding her in his arms, fearful, in doubt. His eyes were growing used to the darkness and a little light seeped into the room from the winter sky through a window. At the far end of the room he made out the shadowy form of a white bed. He lifted her and brought her into the room and closed the door softly.

"Here; wake up, now."

He tried to stand her on her feet and found her weak as jelly. He held her in his arms again, listening in the darkness. His senses reeled from the scent of her hair and skin. She was much smaller than Bessie, his girl, but much softer. Her face was buried in his shoulder; his arms tightened about her. Her face turned slowly and he held his face still, waiting for her face to come round, in front of his. Then her head leaned backward, slowly, gently; it was as though she had given up. Her lips, faintly moist in the hazy blue light, were parted and he saw the furtive glints of her white teeth. Her eyes were closed. He stared at her dim face, the forehead capped with curly black hair. He eased his hand, the fingers spread wide, up the center of her back and her face came toward him and her lips touched his, like something he had imagined. He stood her on her feet and she swayed against him.

He lifted her and laid her on the bed. Something urged him to leave at once, but he leaned over her, excited, looking at her face in the dim light, not wanting to take his hands from her breasts. She tossed and mumbled sleepily. He tightened his fingers on her breasts, kissing her again, feeling her move toward him. He was aware only of her body now; his lips trembled. Then he stiffened. The door behind him had creaked.

He turned and a hysterical terror seized him, as though he were falling from a great height in a dream. A white blur was standing by the door, silent, ghostlike. It filled his eyes and gripped his body. It was Mrs. Dalton. He wanted to knock her out of his way and bolt from the room.

"Mary!" she spoke softly, questioningly.

Bigger held his breath. Mary mumbled again; he bent over her, his fists clenched in fear. He knew that Mrs. Dalton could not see him; but he knew that if Mary spoke she would come to the side of the bed and discover him, touch him. He waited tensely, afraid to move for fear of bumping into something in the dark and betraying his presence.

"Mary!"

He felt Mary trying to rise and quickly he pushed her head back to the pillow.

"She must be asleep," Mrs. Dalton mumbled.

He wanted to move from the bed, but was afraid he would stumble over something and Mrs. Dalton would hear him, would know that someone besides Mary was in the room. Frenzy dominated him. He held his hand over her mouth and his head was cocked at an angle that enabled him to see Mary and Mrs. Dalton by merely shifting his eyes. Mary mumbled and tried to rise again. Frantically, he caught a corner of the pillow and brought it to her lips. He had to stop her from mumbling, or he would be caught. Mrs. Dalton was moving slowly toward him and he grew tight and full, as though about to explode. Mary's fingernails tore at his hands and he caught the pillow and covered her entire face with it, firmly. Mary's body surged upward and he pushed downward upon the pillow with all of his weight, determined that she must not move or make any sound that would betray him. His eyes were filled with the white blur moving toward him in the shadows of the room. Again Mary's body heaved and he held the pillow in a grip that took all of his strength. For a long time he felt the sharp pain of her fingernails biting into his wrists. The white blur was still.

"Mary? Is that you?"

He clenched his teeth and held his breath, intimidated to the core by the awesome white blur floating toward him. His muscles flexed taut as steel and he pressed the pillow, feeling the bed give slowly, evenly, but silently. Then suddenly her fingernails did not bite into his wrists. Mary's fingers loosened. He did not feel her surging and heaving against him. Her body was still.

"Mary! Is that *you?*"

He could see Mrs. Dalton plainly now. As he took his hands from the pillow he heard a long slow sigh go up from the bed into the air of the darkened room, a sigh which afterwards, when he remembered it, seemed final, irrevocable.

"Mary! Are you ill?"

He stood up. With each of her movements toward the bed his body made a movement to match hers, away from her, his feet not lifting themselves from the floor, but sliding softly and silently over the smooth deep rug, his muscles flexed so taut they ached. Mrs. Dalton now stood over the bed. Her hands reached out and touched Mary.

"Mary! Are you asleep? I heard you moving about. . . . "

Mrs. Dalton straightened suddenly and took a quick step back.

"You're dead drunk! You *stink* with whiskey!"

She stood silently in the hazy blue light, then she knelt at the side of the bed. Bigger heard her whispering. She's praying, he thought in amazement and the words echoed in his mind as though someone had spoken them aloud. Finally, Mrs. Dalton stood up and her face tilted to that upward angle at which she always held it. He waited, his teeth clamped, his fists clenched. She moved slowly toward the door; he could scarcely see her now. The door creaked; then silence.

He relaxed and sank to the floor, his breath going in a long gasp. He was weak and wet with sweat. He stayed crouched and bent, hearing the sound of his breathing filling the darkness. Gradually, the intensity of his sensations subsided and he was aware of the room. He felt that he had been in the grip of a weird spell and was now free. The fingertips of his right hand were pressed deeply into the soft fibers of the rug and his whole body vibrated from the wild pounding of his heart. He had to get out of the room, and quickly. Suppose that had been *Mr.* Dalton? His escape had been narrow enough, as it was.

He stood and listened, Mrs. Dalton might be out there in the hallway. How could he get out of the room? He all but shuddered with the intensity of his loathing for this house and all it had made him feel since he had first come into it. He reached his hand behind him and touched the wall; he was glad to have something solid at his back. He looked at the shadowy bed and remembered Mary as some person he had not seen in a long time. She was still there. Had he hurt her? He went to the bed and stood over her; her face lay sideways on the pillow. His hand moved toward her, but stopped in mid-air. He blinked his eyes and stared at Mary's face; it was darker than when he had first bent over her. Her mouth was open and her eyes bulged glassily. Her bosom, her bosom, her—her bosom was not moving! He could not hear her breath coming and going now as he had when he had first brought her into the room! He bent and moved her head with his hand and found that she was relaxed and limp. He snatched his hand away. Thought and feeling were balked in him; there was something he was trying to tell himself desperately, but could not. Then, convulsively, he sucked his breath in and huge words formed slowly, ringing in his ears: *She's dead.* . . .

The reality of the room fell from him; the vast city of white people that sprawled outside took its place. She was dead and he had killed her. He was a murderer, a Negro murderer, a black murderer. He had killed a white woman. He had to get away from here. Mrs. Dalton had been in the room while he was there, but she had not known it. But, *had* she? No! Yes! Maybe she had gone for help? No. If she had known she would have screamed. She didn't know. He had to slip out of the house. Yes. He could go home to bed and tomorrow he could tell them that he had driven Mary home and had left her at the side door.

In the darkness his fear made live in him an element which he reckoned with as "them." He had to construct a case for "them." But, *Jan!* Oh . . . Jan would give him away. When it was found that she was dead Jan would say that he had left them together in the car at Forty-sixth Street and Cottage Grove Avenue. But he would tell them that that was not true. And, after all, was not Jan a *red?* Was not his word as good as Jan's? He would say that Jan had come home with them. No one must know that he was the last person who had been with her.

Fingerprints! He had read about them in magazines. His fingerprints would give him away, surely! They could prove that he had been inside of her room! But suppose he told them that he had come to get the trunk? That was it! The *trunk!* His fingerprints had a right to be there. He looked round and saw her trunk on the other side of the bed, open, the top standing up. He could take the trunk to the basement and put the car into the garage and then go home. *No!* There was a better way. He would not put the car into the garage! He would say that Jan had come to the house and he had left Jan outside in the car. But there was still a *better way!* Make them think that Jan did it. Reds'd do anything. Didn't the papers say so? He would tell them that he had brought Jan and Mary home in the car and Mary had asked him to go with her to her room to get the trunk—and Jan was *with* them!—and he had got the trunk and had taken it to the basement and when he had gone he had left Mary and Jan—who had come back down—sitting in the car, kissing. . . . *That's it!*

He heard a clock ticking and searched for it with his eyes; it was at the head of Mary's bed, its white dial glowing in the blue darkness. It was five minutes past three. Jan had left them at Forty-sixth Street and Cottage Grove. *Jan didn't leave at Forty-Sixth Street; he rode with us.* . . .

He went to the trunk and eased the top down and dragged it over the rug to the middle of the floor. He lifted the top and felt inside; it was half-empty.

Then he was still, barely breathing, filled with another idea. Hadn't Mr. Dalton said that they did not get up early on Sunday mornings? Hadn't Mary said that she was going to Detroit? If Mary were missing when they got up, would they not think that she had already gone to Detroit? He . . . *Yes!* He could, he could put her *in* the trunk! She was small. Yes; put her in the trunk. She had said that she would be gone for three days. For three days, then, maybe no one would know. He would have three days of time. She was a crazy girl anyhow. She was always running around with reds, wasn't she? Anything could happen to her. People would think that she was up to some of her crazy ways when they missed her. Yes, reds'd do anything. Didn't the papers say so?

He went to the bed; he would have to lift her into the trunk. He did not want to touch her, but he knew he had to. He bent over. His hands were outstretched, trembling in mid-air. He had to touch her and lift her and put her in the trunk. He tried to move his hands and could not. It was as though he expected her to scream when he touched her. Goddamn! It all seemed foolish! He wanted to laugh. It was unreal. Like a nightmare. He had to lift a dead woman and was afraid. He felt that he had been dreaming of something like this for a long time, and then, suddenly, it was true. He heard the clock ticking. Time was passing. It would soon be morning. He had to act. He could not stand here all night like this; he might go to the electric chair. He shuddered and something cold crawled over his skin. Goddamn!

He pushed his hand gently under her body and lifted it. He stood with her in his arms; she was limp. He took her to the trunk and involuntarily jerked his head round and saw a white blur standing at the door and his body was instantly wrapped in a sheet of blazing terror and a hard ache seized his head and then the white blur went away. *I thought that was her. . . .* His heart pounded.

He stood with her body in his arms in the silent room and cold facts battered him like waves sweeping in from the sea: she was dead; she was white; she was a woman; he had killed her; he was black; he might be caught; he did not want to be caught; if he were they would kill him.

He stooped to put her in the trunk. Could he get her in? He looked again toward the door, expecting to see the white blur; but nothing was there. He turned her on her side in his arms; he was breathing hard and his body trembled. He eased her down, listening to the soft rustle of her clothes. He pushed her head into a corner, but her legs were too long and would not go in.

He thought he heard a noise and straightened; it seemed to him that his breathing was as loud as wind in a storm. He listened and heard nothing. He had to get her legs in! Bend her legs at the knees, he thought. Yes, almost. A little more . . . . He bent them some more. Sweat dripped from his chin onto his hands. He doubled her knees and pushed her completely into the trunk. That much was done. He eased the top down and fumbled in the darkness for the latch and heard it click loudly.

He stood up and caught hold of one of the handles of the trunk and pulled. The trunk would not move. He was weak and his hands were slippery with sweat. He gritted his teeth and caught the trunk with both hands and pulled it to the door. He opened the door and looked into the hall: it was empty and silent. He stood the trunk on end and carried his right hand over his left shoulder and stooped and caught the strap and lifted the trunk to his back. Now, he would have to stand up. He strained; the muscles of his shoulders and legs quivered with effort. He rose, swaying, biting his lips.

Putting one foot carefully before the other, he went down the hall, down the stairs, then through another hall to the kitchen and paused. His back ached and the strap cut into his palm like fire. The trunk seemed to weigh a ton. He expected the white blur to step before him at any moment and hold out its hand and touch the trunk and demand to know what was in it. He wanted to put the trunk down and rest; but he was afraid that he would not be able to lift it again. He walked across the kitchen floor, down the steps, leaving the kitchen door open behind him. He stood in the darkened basement with the trunk upon his back and listened to the roaring draft of the furnace and saw the coals burning red through the cracks. He stooped, waiting to hear the bottom of the trunk touch the concrete floor. He bent more and rested on one knee. Goddamn! His hand, seared with fire, slipped from the strap and the trunk hit the floor with a loud clatter. He bent forward and squeezed his right hand in his left to still the fiery pain.

He stared at the furnace. He trembled with another idea. He—he could, he—he could put her, he could put her *in* the furnace. He would *burn* her! That was the safest thing of all to do. He went to the furnace and opened the door. A huge red bed of coals blazed and quivered with molten fury.

He opened the trunk. She was as he had put her: her head buried in one corner and her knees bent and doubled toward her stomach. He would have to lift her again.

He stooped and caught her shoulders and lifted her in his arms. He went to the door of the furnace and paused. The fire seethed. Ought he to put her in head or feet first? Because he was tired and scared, and because her feet were nearer, he pushed her in, feet first. The heat blasted his hands.

He had all but her shoulders in. He looked into the furnace; her clothes were ablaze and smoke was filling the interior so that he could scarcely see. The draft roared upward, droning in his ears. He gripped her shoulders and pushed hard, but the body would not go any farther. He tried again, but her head still remained out. Now. . . . Goddamn! He wanted to strike something with his fist. What could he do? He stepped back and looked.

A noise made him whirl; two green burning pools—pools of accusation and guilt—stared at him from a white blur that sat perched upon the edge of the trunk. His mouth opened in a silent scream and his body became hotly paralyzed. It was the white cat and its round green eyes gazed past him at the white face hanging limply from the fiery furnace door. *God!* He closed his mouth and swallowed. Should he catch the cat and kill it and put it in the furnace, too? He made a move. The cat stood up; its white fur bristled; its back arched. He tried to grab it and it bounded past him with a long wail of fear and scampered up the steps and through the door and out of sight. Oh! He had left the kitchen door open. *That* was it. He closed the door and stood again before the furnace, thinking, *Cats can't talk*. . . .

He got his knife from his pocket and opened it and stood by the furnace, looking at Mary's white throat. Could he do it? He had to. Would there be blood? Oh, Lord! He looked round with a haunted and pleading look in his eyes. He saw a pile of old newspapers stacked carefully in a corner. He got a thick wad of them and held them under the head. He touched the sharp blade to the throat, just touched it, as if expecting the knife to cut the white flesh of itself, as if he did not have to put pressure behind it. Wistfully, he gazed at the edge of the blade resting on the white skin; the gleaming metal reflected the tremulous fury of the coals. Yes; he *had* to. Gently, he sawed the blade into the flesh and struck a bone. He gritted his teeth and cut harder. As yet there was no blood anywhere but on the knife. But the bone made it difficult. Sweat crawled down his back. Then blood crept outward in widening circles of pink on the newspapers, spreading quickly now. He whacked at the bone with the knife. The head hung limply on the newspapers, the curly black hair dragging about in blood. He whacked harder, but the head would not come off.

He paused, hysterical. He wanted to run from the basement and go as far as possible from the sight of this bloody throat. But he could not. He must not. He *had* to burn this girl. With eyes glazed, with nerves tingling with excitement, he looked about the basement. He saw a hatchet. *Yes!* That would do it. He spread a neat layer of newspapers beneath the head, so that the blood would not drip on the floor. He got the hatchet, held the head at a slanting angle with his left hand and, after pausing in an attitude of prayer, sent the blade of the hatchet into the bone of the throat with all the strength of his body. The head rolled off.

He was not crying but his lips were trembling and his chest was heaving. He wanted to lie down upon the floor and sleep off the horror of this thing. But he had to get out of here. Quickly, he wrapped the head in the newspapers and used the wad to push the bloody trunk of the body deeper into the furnace. Then he shoved the head in. The hatchet went next.

Would there be coal enough to burn the body? No one would come down here before ten o'clock in the morning, maybe. He looked at his watch. It was four o'clock.

He got another piece of paper and wiped his knife with it. He put the paper into the furnace and the knife into his pocket. He pulled the lever and coal rattled against the sides of the tin chute and he saw the whole furnace blaze and the draft roared still louder. When the body was covered with coal, he pushed the lever back. Now!

Then, abruptly, he stepped back from the furnace and looked at it, his mouth open. Hell! Folks'd *smell* it! There would be an odor and someone would look in the furnace. Aimlessly, his eyes searched the basement. There! That ought to do it! He saw the smutty blades of an electric exhaust fan high up in the wall of the basement, back of the furnace. He found the switch and threw it. There was a quick whir, then a hum. Things would be all right now; the exhaust fan would suck the air out of the basement and there would be no scent.

He shut the trunk and pushed it into a corner. In the morning he would take it to the station. He looked around to see if he had left anything that would betray him; he saw nothing.

He went out of the back door; a few fine flakes of snow were floating down. It had grown colder. The car was still in the driveway. Yes; he would leave it there.

Jan and Mary were sitting in the car, kissing. They said, Good night, Bigger. . . . And he said, Good night. . . . And he touched his hand to his cap. . . .

As he passed the car he saw the door was still open. Mary's purse was on the floor. He took it and closed the door. Naw! Leave it open; he opened it and went on down the driveway.

The streets were empty and silent. The wind chilled his wet body. He tucked the purse under his arm and walked. What would happen now? Ought he to run away? He stopped at a street corner and looked into the purse. There was a thick roll of bills; tens and twenties. . . . Good! He would wait until morning to decide what to do. He was tired and sleepy.

He hurried home and ran up the steps and went on tiptoe into the room. His mother and brother and sister breathed regularly in sleep. He began to undress, thinking, *I'll tell 'em I left her with Jan in the car after I took the trunk down in the basement. In the morning I'll take the trunk to the station, like she told me. . . .*

He felt something heavy sagging in his shirt; it was the gun. He took it out; it was warm and wet. He shoved it under the pillow. *They can't say I did it. If they do, they can't prove it.*

He eased the covers of the bed back and slipped beneath them and stretched out beside Buddy; in five minutes he was sound asleep.

QUESTIONS TO CONSIDER

1. Did Bigger intend to kill Mary upon entering her room? What evidence can you offer for his intentions?
2. Why does Wright use such graphic imagery to portray Mary's murder and placement in the furnace?

James Agee

1909–1955

When he died in a New York City taxi of a heart attack at age 45, James Agee was considered by many to be a spectacular case of wasted talent. He had been a professional writer for 20 years, yet most of his work was considered ephemeral—magazine articles, book reviews, and film criticism. He had published a volume of poetry, a novella, a few short stories, and a sprawling nonfiction book about Southern tenant farmers, *Let Us Now Praise Famous Men* (1941). Now considered a masterpiece, it appeared shortly before the bombing of Pearl Harbor and quickly sank from view as America turned its attention away from the Great Depression to wartime mobilization.

As a young man Agee believed the formative event of his life had occurred when he was six years old and living in his hometown of Knoxville, Tennessee. His father was killed instantly at age 36 in an inexplicable one-car crash. This domestic tragedy forms the central plot of Agee's posthumously published novel, *A Death in the Family* (1957), which received the Pulitzer Prize for fiction. In his youth Agee received years of private schooling, first at St. Andrew's School near Sewanee, and later at Phillips Exeter Academy in New Hampshire. He graduated from Harvard University in 1932 and seemed poised for success in the world of New York journalism. But although talented, articulate, and handsome, Agee was haunted by insecurity and self-doubt. These feelings drew him into self-destructive behaviors, including binge drinking, chain-smoking, and reckless hyperactivity.

The most important assignment of his journalistic career came in the summer of 1936, when he was only 26. *Fortune* magazine sent him along with a photographer, Walker Evans, on loan from the USDA Farm Security Administration staff, to Alabama to report on the plight of Southern sharecroppers in the depths of the Depression. Although Agee had grown up in privileged circumstances, his literary politics were leftist and anticapitalist. He wanted to portray the predicament of landless farm workers trapped in a vicious cycle of work and debt, burned under "the cruel radiance of what is" in the downtrodden South. Seeking an extreme realism that delved beneath magazine veneer, he lived for three weeks in the cotton belt below Tuscaloosa with a White tenant family. Their lice-infested shack had no electricity or plumbing. The whole family picked cotton by hand, back-breaking labor under the blazing summer sun. But when the landowner deducted expenses, the family had little money to show for their crop. As the days wore on, Agee was increasingly outraged by the endless and profitless drudgery, which left the family in an exhausted stupor. Agee worked with them in the fields by day; at night he wrote by the light of a coal-oil lamp, surrounded by the smells of sour clothes, rancid food, and excrement. He returned to New York determined to write the tragedy of "an undefended and appallingly damaged group of human beings," forgotten and helpless in the rural South.

Agee struggled with the manuscript for years, fitfully experimenting and revising. When John Steinbeck's *The Grapes of Wrath* was published (1939), it seemed to lay definitive claim to the story of wretched Southern farmers. So Agee deliberately elevated his characters, portraying them as dignified, even noble, in their poverty. He changed the title from "Three Tenant Families" to *Let Us Now Praise Famous Men* (taken from the apocryphal Hebrew book of Ecclesiasticus) to proclaim their essential worth and heroism. Agee was 31 years old when the book finally appeared in 1941. Reviews were unfavorable and sales few; even Agee thought it a failure. But 20 years later the book was rediscovered and hailed as a precursor to the New Journalism of the sixties. As Linda Wagner-Martin has written, *Let Us Now Praise Famous Men* stands as one of "those inexplicable and unrepeatable American masterpieces," like Thoreau's *Walden* or Melville's *Moby Dick*. The surface narrative as well as undercurrents of thought and feeling appear along with satiric asides, cynical footnotes, questionnaires, inventories, verses, sermonettes, extravagant prose poems, and of course Walker Evans's unforgettable black-and-white photographs taken in and around Hale County, Alabama.

By the time he reached 36, the age of his father at death, Agee was in weakening health. In 1951, he suffered two heart attacks while writing scripts in Hollywood but refused to listen to his doctors. Still living hard until the end, Agee achieved brief fame as a Hollywood screenwriter, receiving an Academy Award nomination for *The African Queen* (1952). This and other film scripts would be published posthumously in 1960. *A Death in the Family*, under the title *All the Way Home*, would become a Pulitzer Prize-winning Broadway play (1960) and a Hollywood movie (1963).

The selection that follows from *Let Us Now Praise Famous Men* presents the George Gudger family (his real name was Floyd Burroughs) in its laborious routine of cotton-picking. Neighbors engaged in the same dull ritual are the Woods and Ricketts families. Agee's dual roles as narrator and actor intertwine most intricately in his treatment of George's wife Annie Mae (Allie Mae), who serves as Agee's central symbol for the family's hardship. Married at 16, she is now 27. Once beautiful, her face and body have been ravaged by malnutrition, childbearing, and heavy farm labor. She represents the hard, hopeless life of any tenant farmer's wife.

from Let Us Now Praise Famous Men

from *Work*

To come devotedly into the depths of a subject, your respect for it increasing in every step and your whole heart weakening apart with shame upon yourself in your dealing with it: To know at length better and better and at length into the bottom of your soul your unworthiness of it: Let me hope in any case that it is something to have begun to learn. Let this all stand however it may: since I cannot make it the image it should be, let it stand as the image it is: I am speaking of my verbal part of this book as a whole. By what kind of foreword I can make clear some essential coherence in it, which I know is there, balanced of its chaos, I do not yet know. But the time is come when it is necessary for me to say at least this much: and now, having said it, to go on, and to try to make an entrance into this chapter, which should be an image of the very essence of their lives: that is, of the work they do.

It is for the clothing, and for the food, and for the shelter, by these to sustain their lives, that they work. Into this work and need, their minds, their spirits, and their strength are so steadily and intensely drawn that during such time as they are not at work, life exists for them scarcely more clearly or in more variance and seizure and appetite than it does for the more simply organized among the animals, and for the plants. This arduous physical work, to which a consciousness beyond that of the simplest child would be only a useless and painful encumbrance, is undertaken without choice or the thought of chance of choice, taught forward from father to son and from mother to daughter; and its essential and few returns you have seen: the houses they live in; the clothes they wear: and have still to see, and for the present to imagine, what it brings them to eat; what it has done to their bodies, and to their consciousness; and what it makes of their leisure, the pleasures which are made available to them. I say here only: work as a means to other ends might have some favor in it, even which was of itself dull and heartless work, in which one's strength was used for another man's benefit: but the ends of this work are absorbed all but entirely into the work itself, and in what little remains, nearly all is obliterated; nearly nothing is obtainable; nearly all is cruelly stained, in the tensions of physical need, and in the desperate tensions of the need of work which is not available.

I have said this now three times. If I were capable, as I wish I were, I could say it once in such a way that it would be there in its complete awfulness. Yet knowing, too, how it is repeated upon each of them, in every day of their lives, so powerfully, so entirely, that it is simply the natural air they breathe, I wonder whether it could ever be said enough times.

The plainness and iterativeness of work must be one of the things which make it so extraordinarily difficult to write of. The plain details of a task once represented, a stern enough effort in itself, how is it possibly to be made clear enough that this same set of leverages has been undertaken by this woman in nearly every day of the eleven or the twenty-five years since her marriage, and will be persisted in in nearly every day to come in all the rest of her life; and that it is only one among the many processes of wearying effort which make the shape of each one of her living days; how is it to be calculated, the number of times she has done these things, the number of times she is still to do them; how conceivably in words is it to be given as it is in actuality, the accumulated weight of these actions upon her; and what this cumulation has made of her body; and what it has made of her mind and of her heart and of her being. And how is this to be made so real to you who read of it, that it will stand and stay in you as the deepest and most iron anguish and guilt of your existence that you are what you are, and that she is what she is, and that you cannot for one moment exchange places with her, not by any such hope make expiation for what she has suffered at your hands, and for what you have gained at hers: but only by consuming all that is in you into the never relaxed determination that this shall be made different and shall be made right, and that of what is 'right' some, enough to die for, is clear already, and the vast darkness of the rest has still, and far more passionately and more skeptically than ever before, to be questioned into, defended, and learned toward. There is no way of taking the heart and the intelligence by the hair and of wresting it to its feet, and of making it look this terrific thing in the eyes: which are such gentle eyes: you may meet them, with all the summoning of heart you have, in the photograph in this volume of the young woman with black hair: and they are to be multiplied, not losing the knowledge that each is a single, unrepeatable, holy individual, by the two billion human creatures who are alive upon the planet today; of whom a few hundred thousands are drawn into complications of specialized anguish, but of whom the huge swarm and majority are made and acted upon as she is: and of all these individuals, contemplate, try to encompass, the one annihilating chord.

But I must make a new beginning:

from PART I

The family exists for work. It exists to keep itself alive. It is a cooperative economic unit. The father does one set of tasks; the mother another; the children still a third, with the sons and daughters serving apprenticeship to their father and mother respectively. A family is called a force, without irony; and children come into the world chiefly that they may help with the work and that through their help the family may increase itself. Their early years are leisurely; a child's life work begins as play. Among his first imitative gestures are gestures of work; and the whole imitative course of his maturing and biologic envy is a stepladder of the learning of physical tasks and skills.

This work solidifies, and becomes steadily more and more, in greater and greater quantity and variety, an integral part of his life.

Besides imitation, he works if he is a man under three compulsions, in three stages. First for his parents. Next for himself, single and wandering in the independence of his early manhood: 'for himself,' in the sense that he wants to stay alive, or better, and has no one dependent on him. Third, for himself and his wife and his family, under an employer. A woman works just for her parents; next, without a transition phase, for her husband and family.

Work for your parents is one thing: work 'for yourself' is another. They are both hard enough, yet light, relative to what is to come. On the day you are married, at about sixteen if you are a girl, at about twenty if you are a man, a key is turned, with a sound not easily audible, and you are locked between the stale earth and the sky; the key turns in the lock behind you, and your full life's work begins, and there is nothing conceivable for which it can afford to stop short of your death, which is a long way off. It is perhaps at its best during the first few years or so, when you are young and perhaps are still enjoying one another or have not yet lost all hope, and when there are not yet so many children as to weigh on you. It is perhaps at its worst during the next ten to twelve years, when there are more and more children, but none of them old enough, yet, to be much help. One could hardly describe it as slackening off after that, for in proportion with the size of the family, it has been necessary to take on more land and more work, and, too, a son or daughter gets just old enough to be any full good to you, and marries or strikes out for himself: yet it is true, anyhow, that from then on there are a number of strong and fairly responsible people in the household besides the man and his wife. In really old age, with one of the two dead, and the children all married, and the widowed one making his home among them in the slow rotations of a floated twig, waiting to die, it does ease off some, depending more then on the individual: one may choose to try to work hard and seem still capable, out of duty and the wish to help, or out of 'egoism,' or out of the dread of dropping out of life; or one may relax, and live unnoticed, never spoken to, dead already; or again, life may have acted on you in such a way that you have no choice in it: or still again, with a wife dead, and children gone, and a long hard lifetime behind you, you may choose to marry again and begin the whole cycle over, lifting onto your back the great weight a young man carries, as Woods has done.

That is the general pattern, its motions within itself lithe-unfolded, slow, gradual, grand, tremendously and quietly weighted, as a heroic dance: and the bodies in this dance, and the spirits, undergoing their slow, miraculous, and dreadful changes; such a thing indeed should be constructed of just these persons: the great, somber, blood-droned, beansprout helmed fetus unfurling within Woods' wife; the infants of three families, staggering happily, their hats held full of freshly picked cotton; the Ricketts children like delirious fawns and panthers; and secret Pearl with her wicked skin; Louise, lifting herself to rest her back, the heavy sack trailing, her eyes on you; Junior, jealous and lazy, malingering, his fingers sore; the Ricketts daughters, the younger stepping beautifully as a young mare, the elder at the stove with her mouth twisted; Annie Mae at twenty-seven, in her angular sweeping, every motion a wonder to watch; George, in his sunday clothes with his cuffs short on his blocked wrists, looking at you, his head slightly to one side, his earnest eyes a little squinted as if he were looking into a light; Mrs. Ricketts, in that time of morning when from the corn she reels into the green roaring glooms of her home, falls into a chair with gaspings which are almost groaning sobs, and dries in her lifted skirt her delicate and reeking head; Miss-Molly, chopping wood as if in each blow of the axe she held captured in focus the vengeance of all time; Woods, slowed in his picking, forced to stop and rest much too often, whose death is hastened against a doctor's warnings in that he is picking at all: I see these among others on the clay in the grave mutations of a dance whose business is the genius of a moving camera, and which it is not my hope ever to record: yet here, perhaps, if not of these archaic circulations of the rude clay altar, yet of their shapes of work, I can make a few crude sketches:

A man: George Gudger, Thomas Woods, Fred Ricketts: his work is with the land, in the seasons of the year, in the sustainment and ordering of his family, the training of his sons:

A woman: Annie Mae Gudger, Ivy Woods, Sadie Ricketts: her work is in the keeping of the home, the preparation of food against each day and against the dead season, the bearing and care of her children, the training of her daughters:

Children: all these children: their work is as it is told to them and taught to them until such time as they shall strengthen and escape, and, escaped of one imprisonment, are submitted into another.

There are times of year when all these three are overlapped and collaborated, all in the field in the demand, chiefly, of cotton; but more largely, the woman is the servant of the day, and of immediate life, and the man is the servant of the year, and of the basis and boundaries of life, and is their ruler; and the children are the servants of their parents: and the center of all their existence, the central work, that by which they have their land, their shelter, their living, that which they must work for no reward more than this, because they do not own themselves, and without hope or interests, that which they cannot eat and get no money of but which is at the center of their duty and greatest expense of strength and spirit, the cultivation and harvesting of cotton: and all this effort takes place between a sterile earth and an uncontrollable sky in whose propitiation is centered their chief reverence and fear, and the deepest earnestness of their prayers, who read in these machinations of their heaven all signs of a fate which the hardest work cannot much help, and, not otherwise than as the most ancient peoples of the earth, make their plantations in the unpitying pieties of the moon.

Work 2: Cotton

Cotton is only one among several crops and among many labors: and all these other crops and labors mean life itself. Cotton means nothing of the sort. It demands more work of a tenant family and yields less reward than all the rest. It is the reason the tenant has the means to do the rest, and to have the rest, and to live, as a tenant, at all. Aside from a few negligiblities of minor sale and barter and of out-of-season work, it is his one possible source of money, and through this fact, though his living depends far less on money than on the manipulations of immediate nature, it has a certain royalty. It is also that by which he has all else besides money. But it is also his chief contracted obligation, for which he must neglect all else as need be; and is the central leverage and symbol of his privation and of his wasted life. It is the one crop and labor which is in no possible way useful as it stands to the tenant's living; it is among all these the one which must and can be turned into money; it is among all these the one in which the landowner is most interested; and it is among all these the one of which the tenant can hope for least, and can be surest that he is being cheated, and is always to be cheated. All other tasks are incidental to it; and it is constantly on everyone's mind; yet of all of them it is the work in which the tenant has least hope and least interest, and to which he must devote the most energy. Any less involved and self-contradictory attempt to understand what cotton and cotton work 'means' to a tenant would, it seems to me, be false to it. It has the doubleness that all jobs have by which one stays alive and in which one's life is made a cheated ruin, and the same sprained and twilight effect on those who must work at it: but because it is only one among the many jobs by which a tenant family must stay alive, and deflects all these others, and receives still other light from their more personal need, reward, and value, its meanings are much more complex than those of most jobs: it is a strong stale magnet among many others more weak and more yielding of life and hope. In the mind of one in whom all these magnetisms are daily and habituated from his birth, these meanings are one somber mull: yet all their several forces are pulling at once, and by them the brain is quietly drawn and quartered. It seems to me it is only through such a complex of meanings that a tenant can feel, toward that crop, toward each plant in it, toward all that work, what he and all grown women too appear to feel, a particular automatism, a quiet, apathetic, and inarticulate yet deeply vindictive hatred, and at the same time utter hopelessness, and the deepest of their anxieties and of their hopes: as if the plant stood enormous in the unsteady sky fastened above them in all they do like the eyes of an overseer. To do all of the hardest work of your life in service of these drawings-apart of ambiguities; and to have all other tasks and all one's consciousness stained and drawn apart in it: I can conceive of little else which could be so inevitably destructive of the appetite for living, of the spirit, of the being, or by whatever name the centers of individuals are to be called: and this very literally: for just as there are deep chemical or electric changes in all the body under anger, or love, or fear, so there must certainly be at the center of these meanings and their directed emotions; perhaps most essentially, an incalculably somber and heavy weight and dark knotted iron of subnausea at the peak of the diaphragm, darkening and weakening the whole body and being, the literal feeling by which the words a broken heart are no longer poetic, but are merely the most accurate possible description.

Yet these things as themselves are withdrawn almost beyond visibility, and the true focus and right telling of it would be in the exact textures of each immediate task.

Of cotton farming I know almost nothing with my own eyes; the rest I have of Bud Woods. I asked enough of other people to realize that every tenant differs a little in his methods, so nothing of this can be set down as 'standard' or 'correct'; but the dissonances are of small detail rather than of the frame and series in the year. I respect dialects too deeply, when they are used by those who have a right to them, not to be hesitant in using them, but I have decided to use some of Woods' language here. I have decided, too, to try to use my imagination a little, as carefully as I can. I must warn you that the result is sure to be somewhat inaccurate: but it is accurate anyhow to my ignorance, which I would not wish to disguise. . . .

It is only in a very unusual year that you do well with both of the most important crops, the two life mainly depends on, because they need rain and sun in such different amounts. Cotton needs a great deal less rain than corn; it is really a sun flower. If it is going to get a superflux of rain, that will best come before it is blooming; and if it has got to rain during that part of the summer when a fairsized field is blooming a bale a day, it had best rain late in the evening when the blooms are shutting or at night, not in the morning or the mid day: for then the bloom is blared out flat; rain gets in it easy and hangs on it; it shuts wet, sours, and sticks to the boll; next morning it turns red and falls. Often the boll comes off with it. But the boll that stays on is sour and rotted and good for nothing. Or to put it the other way around, it can take just one rain at the wrong time of day at the wrong time of summer to wreck you out of a whole bale.

It is therefore not surprising that they are constant readers of the sky; that it holds not an ounce of 'beauty' to them (though I know of no more magnificent skies than those of Alabama); that it is the lodestone of their deepest pieties; and that they have, also, the deep stormfear which is apparently common to all primitive peoples. Wind is as terrifying to them as cloud and lightning and thunder: and I remember how, sitting with the Woods, in an afternoon when George was away at work, and a storm was building, Mrs. Gudger and her children came hurrying three quarters of a mile beneath the blackening air to shelter among company. Gudger says: 'You never can tell what's in a cloud.'

Picking Season

Late in August the fields begin to whiten more rarely with late bloom and more frequently with cotton and then still thicker with cotton, a sparkling ground starlight of it, steadily bursting into more and more millions of points, all the leaves seeming shrunken smaller; quite as at night the whole frontage of the universe is more and more thoroughly printed in the increasing darkness; and the wide cloudless and tremendous light holds the earth clamped and trained as beneath a vacuum bell and burningglass; in such a brilliance that half and two thirds of the sky is painful to look into; and in this white maturing oven the enlarged bolls are streaked a rusty green, then bronze, and are split and splayed open each in a loose vomit of cotton. These split bolls are now *burrs*, hard and edged as chiseled wood, pointed nearly as thorns, spread open in three and four and five gores or cells. It is slow at first, just a few dozen scattered here and there and then a few tens of dozens, and then there is a space of two or three days in which a whole field seems to be crackling open at once, and at this time it seems natural that it must be gone into and picked, but all the more temperate and experienced tenants wait a few days longer until it will be fully worth the effort: and during this bursting of bolls and this waiting, there is a kind of quickening, as if deep under the ground, of all existence, toward a climax which cannot be delayed much longer, but which is held in the tensions of this reluctance, tightening, and delay: and this can be seen equally in long, sweeping drivings of a car between these spangling fields, and in any one of the small towns or the county seats, and in the changed eyes of any one family, a kind of tightening as of an undertow, the whole world and year lifted nearly upon its crest, and soon beginning the long chute down to winter: children, and once in a while a very young or a very old woman or man, whose work is scarcely entered upon or whose last task and climax this may be, are deeply taken with an excitement and a restlessness to begin picking, and in the towns, where it is going to mean money, the towns whose existence is for it and depends on it, and which in most times of year are sunken in sleep as at the bottom of a sea: these towns are sharpening awake; even the white hot streets of a large city are subtly changed in this season: but Gudger and his wife and Ricketts and Woods, and most of the heads of the million and a quarter families who have made this and are to do the working of taking it for their own harm and another's use, they are only a little more quiet than usual, as they might be if they were waiting for a train to come in, and keep looking at the fields, and judging them; and at length one morning (the Ricketts women are already three days advanced in ragged work), Gudger says, Well:

Well; I reckin tomorrow we'd better start to picking:

And the next morning very early, with their broad hats and great sacks and the hickory baskets, they are out, silent, their bodies all slanted, on the hill: and in every field in hundreds of miles, black and white, it is the same: and such as it is, it is a joy which scarcely touches any tenant; and is worn thin and through in half a morning, and is gone for a year.

It is simple and terrible work. Skill will help you; all the endurance you can draw up against it from the roots of your existence will be thoroughly used as fuel to it: but neither skill nor endurance can make it any easier.

Over the right shoulder you have slung a long white sack whose half length trails the ground behind. You work with both hands as fast and steadily as you can. The trick is to get the cotton between your fingertips at its very roots in the burr in all three or four or five gores at once so that it is brought out clean in one pluck. It is easy enough with one burr in perhaps ten, where the cotton is ready to fall; with the rest, the fibers are more tight and tricky. So another trick is, to learn these several different shapes of burr and resistance as nearly as possible by instinct, so there will be no second trying and delay, and none left wasted in the burr; and, too, as quickly to judge what may be too rotted and dirtied to use, and what is not yet quite ready to take: there are a lot suspended between these small uncertainties, and there should be no delay, no need to use the mind's judgement, and few mistakes. Still another trick is, between these strong pulls of efficiency, proper judgement, and maximum speed, not to hurt your fingers on the burrs any worse than you can help. You would have to try hard, to break your flesh on any one burr, whether on its sharp points or its edges; and a single raindrop is only scarcely instrumental in ironing a mountain flat; but in each plucking of the hand the fingers are searched deep in along these several sharp, hard edges. In two hours' picking the hands are just well limbered up. At the end of a week you are favoring your fingers, still in the obligation of speed. The later of the three to five times over the field, the last long weeks of the season, you might be happy if it were possible to exchange them for boils. With each of these hundreds of thousands of insertions of the hands, moreover, the fingers are brought to a small point, in an action upon every joint and tendon in the hand. I suggest that if you will try, three hundred times in succession, the following exercise: touch all five fingertips as closely as possible into one point, trying meanwhile to hold loose cotton in the palm of the hand: you will see that this can very quickly tire, cramp and deteriorate the whole instrument, and will understand how easily rheumatism can take up its strictures in just this place.

Meanwhile, too, you are working in a land of sunlight and heat which are special to just such country at just that time of year: sunlight that stands and stacks itself upon you with the serene weight of deep sea water, and heat that makes the jointed and muscled and fine-structured body glow like one indiscriminate oil; and this brilliant weight of heat is piled upon you more and more heavily in hour after hour so that it can seem you are a diving bell whose strained seams must at any moment burst, and the eyes are marked in stinging sweat, and the head, if your health is a little unstable, is gently roaring, like a private blow-torch, and less gently beating with aching blood: also the bag, which can hold a hundred pounds, is filling as it is dragged from plant to plant, four to nine burrs to a plant to be rifled swiftly, and the load shrugged along another foot or two and the white row stretched ahead to a blur and innumerably manifolded in other white rows which have not yet been touched, and younger bolls in the cleaned row behind already breaking like slow popcorn in the heat, and the sack still heavier and heavier, so that it pulls you back as a beast might rather than a mere dead weight: but it is not only this: cotton plants are low, so that in this heat and burden of the immanent sun and of the heavying sack you are dragging, you are continuously somewhat stooped over even if you are a child, and are bent very deep if you are a man or a woman. A strong back is a godsend, but not even the strongest back was built for that treatment, and there combine at the kidneys, and rill down the thighs and up the spine and athwart the shoulders the ticklish weakness of gruel or water, and an aching that is increased in geometric progressions, and at length, in the small of the spine, a literal and persistent sensation of yielding, buckling, splintering, and breakage: and all of this, even though the mercy of nature has hardened your flesh and has anesthetized your nerves and your powers of reflection and of imagination, yet reaches in time the brain and the more mirror-like nerves, and thereby is redoubled upon itself much more powerfully than before: and this is all compounded upon you during each successive hour of the day and during each successive day in a force which rest and food and sleep only partly and superficially refresh: and though, later in the season, you are relieved of the worst of the heat, it is in exchange at the last for a coolness which many pickers like even less well, since it so slows and chills the lubricant garment of sweat they work in, and seriously slows and stiffens the fingers which by then at best afford an excruciation in every touch.

The tenants' idiom has been used ad nauseam by the more unspeakable of the northern journalists but it happens to be accurate: that picking goes on each day from can to can't: sometimes, if there is a feeling of rush, the Ricketts continue it by moonlight. In the blasting heat of the first of the season, unless there is a rush to beat a rain or to make up an almost completed wagonload, it is customary to quit work an hour and a half or even two hours in the worst part of the day and to sit or lie in the shade and possible draft of the hallway or porch asleep or dozing after dinner. This time narrows off as the weeks go by and a sense of rush and of the wish to be done with it grows on the pickers and is tightened through from the landlord. I have heard of tenants and pickers who have no rest-period and no midday meal,[1] but those I am acquainted with have it. It is of course no parallel in heartiness and variety to the proud and enormous meals which farm wives of the wheat country prepare for harvest hands, and which are so very zestfully regarded by some belated virgilians as common to what they like to call the American Scene. It is in fact the ordinary every day food, with perhaps a little less variety than in the earlier summer, hastily thrown together and heated by a woman who has hurried in exhausted from the field as few jumps as possible ahead of her family, and served in the dishes she hurriedly rinsed before she hurried out on the early morning as few jumps as possible behind them. When they are all done, she hurries through the dish washing and puts on her straw hat or her sun-bonnet and goes on back into the field, and they are all at it in a strung-out little bunch, the sun a bitter white on their deeply bent backs, and the sacks trailing, a slow breeze idling in the tops of the pines and hickories along the far side but the leaves of the low cotton scarcely touched in it, and the whole land, under hours of heat still to go, yet listed subtly forward toward the late end of the day. They seem very small in the field and very lonely, and the motions of their industry are so small, in range, their bodies so slowly moving, that it seems less that they are so hard at work than that they are bowed over so deeply into some fascination or grief, or are as those pilgrims of Quebec who take the great flights of stairs upon their knees, slowly, a prayer spoken in each step. Ellen lies in the white load of the cotton-basket in the shade asleep. Squinchy picks the front of his dress full and takes

1. On the big plantations, where a good deal of the picking is done by day labor and is watched over by riding bosses, all the equations of speed and unresting steadiness are of course intensified; the whole nature of the work, in the men and women and their children, is somewhat altered. Yet not so much as might at first seem. A man and his family working alone are drawn narrowly together in these weeds even within themselves, and know they are being watched: From the very first, in town, their landlords are observant of which tenants bring their cotton first to gin and of who is slow and late; also, there is nearly always, in the tenant's family, the exceedingly sharp need of cottonseed money.(Author's note.)

it to his mother; Clair Bell fills a hat time after time in great speed and with an expression of delight rushes up behind her mother and dumps the cotton on all of her she can reach and goes crazy with laughter, and her mother and the girls stop a minute and she is hugged, but they talk more among themselves than the other families, they are much more quiet than is usual to them, and Mrs. Ricketts only pauses a minute, cleaning the cotton from her skirts and her hair and putting it in her sack, and then she is bowed over deeply at work again. Woods is badly slowed by weakness and by the pain in his shoulder; he welcomes any possible excuse to stop and sometimes has to pause whether there is any excuse or not, but his wife and her mother are both strong and good pickers, so he is able to get by without a hired hand. Thomas is not old enough yet to be any use. Burt too is very young for it and works only by fits and starts; little is expected of children so small, but it is no harm what little they do; you can't learn them too young. Junior is not very quick with it at best. He will work for a while furiously hard, in jealousy of Louise, and then slacken up with sore hands and begin to bully Burt. Katy is very quick. Last summer, when she was only eight, she picked a hundred and ten pounds in a day in a race with Flora Merry Lee. This summer she has had runarounds and is losing two fingernails but she is picking steadily. Pearl Woods is big for her age and is very steadily useful. Louise is an extraordinarily steady and quick worker for her age; she can pick a hundred and fifty pounds in a day. The two Ricketts boys are all right when their papa is on hand to keep them at their work; as it is, with Ricketts at the sawmills they clown a good deal, and tease their sisters. Mrs. Gudger picks about the average for a woman, a hundred and fifty to two hundred pounds a day. She is fast with her fingers until the work exhausts her; 'last half of the day I just don't see how I can keep on with it.' George Gudger is a very poor picker. When he was a child he fell in the fireplace and burnt the flesh off the flat of both hands to the bone, so that his fingers are stiff and slow and the best he has ever done in a day is a hundred and fifty pounds. The average for a man is nearer two hundred and fifty. His back hurts him badly too, so he usually picks on his knees, the way the others pick only when they are resting. Mrs. Ricketts used to pick three hundred and three hundred and fifty pounds in a day but sickness has slowed her to less than two hundred now. Mrs. Ricketts is more often than not a fantast, quite without realizing, and in all these figures they gave me there may be inaccuracy—according to general talk surrounding the Rust machine a hundred pounds a day is good picking—but these are their own estimates of their own abilities, on a matter in which tenants have some pride, and that seems to me more to the point than their accuracy. There are sometimes shifts into gayety in the picking, or a brief excitement, a race between two of the children, or a snake killed; or two who sit a few moments in their sweat in the shaded clay when they have taken some water, but they say very little to each other, for there is little to say, and are soon back to it, and mainly, in hour upon hour, it is speechless, silent, serious, ceaseless and lonely work along the great silence of the unshaded land, ending each day in a vast blaze of dust on the west, every leaf sharpened in long knives of shadow, the day drawn down through red to purple, and the leaves losing color, and the wild blind eyes of the cotton staring in twilight, in those odors of work done and of nature lost once more to night whose sweetness is a torture, and in the slow, loaded walking home, whose stiff and gentle motions are those of creatures just awakened. . . .

That is repeated as many times as you have picked a bale. Your field is combed over three, four or five times. The height of the ginning season in that part of the country is early October, and in that time the loaded wagons are on the road before the least crack of daylight, the waiting is endless hours, and the gin is still pulsing and beating after dark. After that comes hog-killing, and the gristing of the corn and milling of the sorghum that were planted late to come ready late; and more urgent and specific meditation of whether or not to move to another man, and of whether you are to be kept; and settlement time; and the sky descends, the air becomes like dark glass, the ground stiffens, the clay honeycombs with frost, the corn and the cotton stand stripped to the naked bone and the trees are black, the odors of pork and woodsmoke sharpen all over the country, the long dark silent sleeping rains stream down in such grieving as nothing shall ever stop, and the houses are cold, fragile drums, and the animals tremble, and the clay is one shapeless sea, and winter has shut.

Questions to Consider

1. Agee reserves some of his sharpest invective in *Let Us Now Praise Famous Men* for journalists, whom he dismisses as parasites, living off the misery of others. Of course, he and Walker Evans were journalists when they traveled on assignment to Alabama in 1936. Can you find other instances where Agee's uneasy awareness of his dual role as observer/participant expresses itself in the narrative?
2. "Work" makes plain the abject poverty and hardship of sharecropping. But Agee strenuously argues against seeing the three tenant families in his book as symbols of the Depression, as the Joad family in Steinbeck's *The Grapes of Wrath* was perceived. Instead, Agee wants these Alabama farmers to be viewed much like Old Testament patriarchs and matriarchs, distinguished and righteous. Does he succeed in this intention?

W. J. Cash

1900–1941

When journalist turned social historian W. J. Cash published *The Mind of the South,* it represented the compilation of his research into what he termed the "basis and structure of Southern values." His examination of the Southern world view, however, met with hostility from the Fugitives, a group of academics and poets at Vanderbilt University. Rather than reaffirming traditionally Southern values, as Mary Ellen Snodgrass has pointed out, Cash "spoke harsh truths about the shift in values and outlook that permeated Southern fiction." Despite the outrage of the Fugitive group, *The Mind of the South* made its mark on Southern history and culture, leading noted historian C. Vann Woodward to remark that "no other book on Southern history rivals Cash's in influence among laymen and few among professional historians." In fact, Joseph L. Morrison, Cash's first biographer, suggests that it is appropriate to "confer upon Cash the title of prophet," acknowledging the "nature of his role, that of analytical interpreter." Sadly, Cash would not live to see the sustained influence that his only book would exert on the understanding and discussion of Southern history and culture. Despondent and ill, he hung himself in a hotel room before the book saw print. To date, Cash's book has not passed out of print, and the volume remains an integral part of contemporary discussions of Southern history, culture, and literature.

Joseph Wilbur Cash was born on 1 July 1900, in Gaffney, South Carolina, in the heart of the textile mill region. He was the son of devout Baptists Nannie Lutitia Hamrick and John William Cash, a store manager. He soon decided to reverse his given names and generally identified himself by his initials, W. J. An introverted and intelligent child, Cash was also nicknamed "Sleepy" because of his disinterest in sports and other boyish activities. He attended a Baptist academy in Boiling Springs, North Carolina, graduating in 1917. Following his graduation he briefly attended Wofford College and Valparaiso University, but it was at Wake Forest College that he earned his bachelor's degree in 1922. Although he was initially reluctant to attend what he derisively called a "preacher's school," he soon found the intellectual atmosphere of the school invigorating. Cash encountered the works of writers such as William Conrad and James Branch Cabell, but the style and directness of H. L. Mencken struck a chord deep within the fledgling author. He soon began "throwing Menckenian brickbats at Baptist pieties" through the scathing editorials that he published in the school newspaper during his tenure as its editor.

The end of his college career found Cash at loose ends. He attended law school for a year, taught school, and worked as the editor of a small country paper, the *Cleveland Press*, for a brief period of time. He also began writing articles for Mencken's *American Mercury*, in which an abbreviated, early version of *The Mind of the South* first appeared. Mencken was quite impressed with Cash's ideas on the South and showed the young journalist's work to the publisher Alfred A. Knopf, who immediately asked Cash to write a book. Cash continued to write for Mencken's magazine while working on his book, battling financial woes, illness, and depression. He finally secured a position as an associate editor and book reviewer for the *Charlotte News* in 1935. In this position, he reviewed books by many of the best Southern authors of his day, including William Faulkner, Thomas Wolfe, and Erskine Caldwell.

Cash found a forum for his political views in his journalistic work, most especially for his diatribes against Hitler and fascism. C. Vann Woodward has pointed out that Cash wrote as "virtually a lifelong resident of the Carolina Piedmont, and that distorted his view" of life outside the South. Cash also aspired to become a great writer—a great Southern writer—and to be considered one of the Southern elite, despite the fact that he came from the lower middle class. Cash enjoyed popularity during this time, however, spending time among the members of the Charlotte literary community, where he met Mary Ross Northrop. Northrop quickly fell in love with Cash, and the two decided to marry as soon as Cash completed his book.

Cash finished the manuscript for *The Mind of the South* in 1940, struggling with substantial pressure from a publisher frustrated by his repeated delays. *The Mind of the South* pointedly attacked the racial philosophies and social hierarchies of the South, documenting the pervasive prejudice, widespread fundamentalism, and marked hostility toward modernity that had historically characterized the region—the very hostility exalted by the Agrarians. Cash articulated a rationale for the virulent racism that typified Southern attitudes for decades following Reconstruction, offering insight into the depth and duration of White supremacy and the sustaining influence of honor among residents of the region.

Despite its brutal assault on Southern culture and values, *The Mind of the South* was highly regarded, even within the region itself, leading biographer Bruce Clayton to praise Cash's "brilliant style, bold overarching thesis about the unity and continuity of the 'mind' of the South, his psychological insights, tragic tone, and subtle probing of paradox and irony made his book a classic in historical interpretation." John Shelton Reed concurs, noting that Cash's "great organizing concepts . . . . shape our thought about the South, whether we like it or not. Indeed, whether we *know* it or not." Critics such as Bertram Wyatt-Brown have harshly, and aptly, criticized Cash, however, for his inability to speak credibly about the plight of women and African Americans in the South, as Cash only views each of these groups through the "prism of Southern White males." Yet even criticism such as Wyatt-Brown's amounts, on some level, to backhanded praise, insofar as the criticism suggests that the significance of Cash's work demands a response.

In 1940, Cash and Northrop married and made plans to move to Mexico, supported by a Guggenheim fellowship that Cash had recently received. He planned to write a novel, but soon became ill, suffering from a newly developed intolerance to alcohol, a severe digestive disorder, and anxiety. He found himself unable to write, and his frustration was exacerbated by hallucinations during which he heard the voices of Nazis who he believed were plotting to kill him. Cash disappeared without explanation on 1 July 1941, and when he was found, he had hanged himself in his hotel room.

Although some scholars challenge Cash's arguments, citing his lack of specificity in defining his overarching terms—terms critical to his discussion, such as mind, culture, and temperament—many historians and literary scholars continue to find his work invaluable to the study of Southern culture. Cash's insights into the post-Reconstruction era continue to enhance both scholarly and popular discussion of the South.

from The Mind of the South

With all these characteristics established, we are in a position to turn to the examination of the South's claim to a superior culture. Or, more correctly, since everything we have seen falls within the meaning of culture in the wide sense, to that claim in so far as it relates to culture in the narrow sense—to intellectual and æsthetic attainments.

And in this respect, it may be said without ceremony that it was perhaps the least well founded of the many poorly founded claims which the Southerners so earnestly asserted to the world and to themselves and in which they so warmly believed.

I know the proofs commonly advanced by apologists—that at the outbreak of the war the section had more colleges and students in those colleges, in proportion to population, than the North; that many planters were ready and eager to quote you *Cicero or Sallust;*[1] that Charleston had a public library before Boston, and its famous St. Cecilia Society[2] from the earliest days; that these Charlestonians, and with them the older and wealthier residents of Richmond and Norfolk and New Orleans, regularly imported the latest books from London, and brought back from the grand tour the paintings and even the statuary of this or that fashionable artist of Europe; that, in the latest days, the richest among the new planters of the deep South began to imitate these practices; that in communities like those of the Scotch Highlanders in the Cape Fear country[3] there were Shakespeare libraries and clubs; that Langdon Cheves of South Carolina is reported by Joseph LeConte[4] to have discussed the idea of evolution in private conversation long before *The Origin of Species;* and so on *ad infinitum.*

But such proofs come to little. Often, as they are stated, they are calculated to give a false picture of the facts. Thus, the majority of the colleges were no more than academies. And of the whole number of them perhaps the University of Virginia alone was worthy to be named in the same breath with half a dozen Yankee universities and colleges, and as time went on, even it tended to sink into a hotbed of obscurantism and a sort of fashionable club, propagating dueling, drinking, and gambling.

Thus again, the general quoting of Latin, the flourish of "Shakespeare says," so far from indicating that there was some profound and esoteric sympathy with the humanities in the South, a deliberate preference for the Great Tradition coming down from the ancients, a wide and deep acquaintance with and understanding of

1. Cicero was a Roman philosopher and politician who lived in the era of Julius Caesar, Octavian, and Marc Antony. He is best known for the *Phillipics*, a series of speeches to the Roman Senate that he delivered after Caesar's death. Sallust was a Roman historian and politician. A friend of Julius Caesar, Sallust served as governor to Numidia in North Africa. His works include *The Jugurthine War* and *The Cataline Conspiracy*.
2. The St. Cecelia Society was founded in Charleston, South Carolina in 1762 to provide an outlet for the musical talents of White, upper-class women.
3. Scotch Highlanders fled their home country in 1745 following a thwarted rebellion during which they supported the wrong faction. Many settled near Cape Fear, North Carolina.
4. Langdon Cheves (1776–1857) was a member of the U.S. House of Representatives during the early 1800s. He succeeded notable Congressman Henry Clay. One of the first American geologists, Joseph LeConte (1823–1901) was also one of the founders of the Sierra Club (1892). LeConte spent time teaching at the University of Georgia and South Carolina College, which is likely where he encountered Cheves.

the authors quoted, really means only this, it seems to me: that the great body of men in the land remained continuously under the influence of the simple man's almost superstitious awe for the classics, as representing an arcanum beyond the reach of the ordinary.

And over and behind these considerations lies the fact that the South far overran the American average for (white) illiteracy—that not only the great part of masses but a considerable number of planters never learned to read and write, and that a very great segment of the latter class kept no book in their houses save only the Bible.

But put this aside. Say that the South is entitled to be judged wholly by its highest and its best. The ultimate test of every culture is its productivity. What ideas did it generate? Who were its philosophers and artists? And—perhaps the most searching test of all—what was its attitude toward these philosophers and artists? Did it recognize and nurture them when they were still struggling and unknown? Did it salute them before the world generally learned to salute them?

One almost blushes to set down the score of the Old South here. If Charleston had its St. Cecilia and its public library, there is no record that it ever added a single idea of any notable importance to the sum total of man's stock. If it imported Mrs. Radcliffe, Scott, Byron,[5] wet from the press, it left its only novelist, William Gilmore Simms,[6] to find his reputation in England, and all his life snubbed him because he had no proper pedigree. If it fetched in the sleek trumpery of the schools of Van Dyck and Reynolds, of Ingres and Houdon and Flaxman, it drove its one able painter, Washington Allston (though he was born an aristocrat), to achieve his first recognition abroad and at last to settle in New England.[7]

And Charleston is the peak. Leaving Mr. Jefferson aside, the whole South produced, not only no original philosopher but no derivative one to set beside Emerson and Thoreau; no novelist but poor Simms to measure against the Northern galaxy headed by Hawthorne and Melville and Cooper; no painter but Allston to stand in the company of Ryder and a dozen Yankees; no poet deserving the name save Poe—only half a Southerner. And Poe, for all his zeal for slavery, it despised in life as an inconsequential nobody; left him, and with him the *Southern Literary Messenger*,[8] to starve, and claimed him at last only when his bones were whitening in Westminster churchyard.[9]

5. Ann Radcliffe (1764–1823) was a popular English gothic novelist who penned such works as *The Mysteries of Udolpho: A Romance* (1794). Scottish-born Sir Walter Scott (1771–1832) wrote 27 novels, many of which were set in his native country. His best-known works include *Marmion* (1808) and *The Lady of the Lake* (1810). George Gordon, Lord Byron was a Romantic poet (1788–1824) and a contemporary of John Keats and Percy Bysse Shelley.

6. William Gilmore Simms (1806–1870) is considered one of the first Southern writers. A contemporary of Edgar Allan Poe, he is the author of 30 works of fiction, 18 volumes of poetry, and numerous nonfiction works.

7. Baroque painters Anthony Van Dyck of Belgium (1599–1641) and Sir Joshua Reynolds (1723–1792) of England used complex styles to convey dramatic emotion. Van Dyck often painted for the members of the Stuart royal family in England. Reynolds became the first president of the Royal Academy of Arts and believed that artists had a responsibility to celebrate history through their works. Jean Auguste Dominique Ingres (1780–1867) was a French painter of middling reputation. Jean-Antoine Houdon (1741–1828) was a French Neoclassical sculptor and John Flaxman (1755–1826) built his reputation in England, also as a Neoclassical sculptor. The only American in this group that Cash mentions is Washington Allston (1779–1843), the American Romantic painter.

8. The *Southern Literary Messenger* was published from 1834 to 1864. The magazine was briefly revived in 1939, but ceased publication once again by 1945. *Southern Literary Messenger* described itself as being "devoted to every department of literature and the fine arts" during the nineteenth century, and on many occasions served as a venue for pro-Southern ideologies.

9. Edgar Allan Poe is buried in the cemetery of the Westminster church in Baltimore, Maryland.

Certainly there were men in the Old South of wide and sound learning, and with a genuine concern for ideas and, sometimes, even the arts. There were the old Jeffersons and Madisons, the Pinckneys and the Rutledges and the Henry Laurenses,[10] and their somewhat shrunken but not always negligible descendants. Among both the scions of colonial aristocracy and the best of the newcomers, there were men for whom Langdon Cheves might stand as the archetype and Matterhorn—though we must be careful not to assume, what the apologists are continually assuming, that Cheves might just as well have written *The Origin of Species* himself, if only he had got around to it. For Darwin, of course, did not launch the idea of evolution, nor yet of the struggle for existence and the survival of the fittest. What he did was laboriously to clarify and organize, to gather and present the first concrete and convincing proof for notions that, in more or less definite form, had been the common stock of men of superior education for fifty years and more. There is no evidence that Cheves had anything original to offer; there is only evidence that he was a man of first-rate education and considerable intellectual curiosity, who knew what was being thought and said by the first minds of Europe.

To be sure, there were such men in the South: men on the plantation, in politics, in the professions, in and about the better schools, who, in one degree or another, in one way or another, were of the same general stamp as Cheves. There were even men who made original and important contributions in their fields, like Joseph LeConte himself, one of the first of American geologists; like Matthew Fontaine Maury, author of *Physical Geography of the Sea*, and hailed by Humboldt as the founder of a new science; like Audubon, the naturalist. And beneath these were others: occasional planters, lawyers, doctors, country schoolmasters, parsons, who, on a more humble scale, sincerely cared for intellectual and æsthetic values and served them as well as they might.

But in the aggregate these were hardly more than the exceptions which prove the rule—too few, too unrepresentative, and, above all, as a body themselves too sterile of results very much to alter the verdict.

In general, the intellectual and æsthetic culture of the Old South was a superficial and jejune thing, borrowed from without and worn as a political armor and a badge of rank; and hence (I call the authority of old Matthew Arnold to bear me witness)[11] not a true culture at all.

This is the fact. The reason for it is not too far to seek.

If we were dealing with the cotton South alone, one might be tempted to think, indeed, that it resides wholly in the question of time, in the consideration I have emphasized, that there were but seventy years between the invention of the cotton gin and the out-break of the Civil War. But even here the answer is hardly adequate; in view of the wealth and leisure ultimately afforded the master class, in view of the fact that the second generation had largely grown up in this wealth and leisure, one might have expected, even though this cotton South had stood quite alone, to find a greater advance, something more than the blank in production we actually find.

10. Charles Cotesworth Pinckney (1746–1825) became one of the leaders at the Constitutional Convention and lobbied effectively for its adoption in South Carolina. John Rutledge (1739–1800) served as governor of South Carolina during the Revolutionary War. Henry Laurens (1724–1792) headed the effort to overthrow British tyranny during the American Revolution. His efforts began in his native South Carolina and he later served as president of the Continental Congress (1777–1778).

11. Matthew Arnold (1822–1888) was an English poet and literary critic.

But we are not dealing with the cotton South alone, of course. As we have sufficiently seen, it was the Virginians, too. Here was the completed South, the South in flower—a South that, rising out of the same fundamental conditions as the great South, exhibiting, with the obvious changes, the same basic pattern, and played upon in the first half of the nineteenth century by the same forces, had enjoyed riches, rank, and a leisure perhaps unmatched elsewhere in the world, for more than a hundred years at least; a South, therefore, which, by every normal rule, ought to have progressed to a complex and important intellectual culture, to have equaled certainly, probably to have outstripped, New England in production, and to have served as a beacon to draw the newer South rapidly along the same road. And if it did none of these things, why, then, we shall have to look beyond the factor of time for a satisfactory explanation, not only of its barrenness but, to a considerable extent, of that of the great South also.

In reality, the reason is immanent, I think, in the whole of Southern life and psychology. Complexity in man is invariably the child of complexity in environment. The desire for knowledge when it passes beyond the stage of being satisfied with the most obvious answer, thought properly so called, and, above all, æsthetic concern, arise only when the surrounding world becomes sufficiently complicated to make it difficult or impossible for human energies to escape on a purely physical plane, or, at any rate, on a plane of direct activity. Always they represent, among other things, a reaching out vicariously for satisfaction of the primitive urge to exercise of muscle and nerve, and achievement of the universal will to mastery. And always, too, they feed only upon variety and change. Whence it is, no doubt, that they have never reached any notable development save in towns, and usually in great towns.

But the Southern world, you will remember, was basically an extremely uncomplex, unvaried, and unchanging one. Here economic and political organization was reduced to its simplest elements. Here were no towns to rank as more than trading posts save New Orleans, Charleston, Richmond, and Norfolk; here, perhaps, were no true towns at all, for even these four (three of which were scarcely more than overgrown villages) were rather mere depots on the road to the markets of the world, mere adjuncts to the plantation, than living entities in their own right, after the fashion of Boston and New York and Philadelphia. Here was lacking even that tremendous ferment of immigration which was so important in lending variety to the rest of the American scene. And here everywhere were wide fields and blue woods and flooding yellow sunlight. A world, in fine, in which not a single factor operated to break up the old pattern of outdoor activity laid down on the frontier, in which, on the contrary, everything conspired to perpetuate it; a world in which even the Virginian could and inevitably did discharge his energies on the purely physical plane as fully as his earliest ancestor in the land; a world in which horses, dogs, guns, not books, and ideas and art, were his normal and absorbing interests.

And if this was not enough? If his energies and his ambition demanded a wider field of action? He went, in this world at battle, inescapably into politics. To be a captain in the struggle against the Yankee, to be a Calhoun or a Brooks in Congress, or, better still, to be a Yancey or a Rhett ramping through the land with a demand for the sword—this was to be at the very heart of one's time and place, was, for the plantation youth, full of hot blood, the only desirable career. Beside it the pursuit of knowledge, the writing of books, the painting of pictures, the life of the mind, seemed an anemic and despicable business, fit only for eunuchs. "Why," growled a friend of Philip Pendleton Cooke, Virginia aristocrat and author of the well-known lyric, *Florence Vane*, "Why do you waste your time on a damned thing like poetry? A man of your position could be a useful man"—and summed it up exactly.

But it was not only the consumption of available energy in direct action. The development of a considerable intellectual culture requires, in addition to complexity of environment, certain predisposing habits of mind on the part of a people. One of these is analysis. *"L'état de dissociation des lieux communs de la morale semble en corrélation assez étroite avec le degré de la civilization intellectuelle."*[12] says Remy de Gourmont—and says truly. Another is hospitality to new ideas. Still another is a firm grip on reality; and in this connection I am not forgetting the kind of art which is called romantic and the more fanciful varieties of poetry; in so far as they are good, in so far as they are truly art, they also must rise ultimately from the solid earth. And, finally, there is the capacity, at least, for detachment, without which no thinker, no artist, and no scholar can do his work.

But turn back now and examine the South in the light of this. Analysis is largely the outcome of two things: the need to understand a complex environment (a consideration already disposed of) and social dissatisfaction. But, as we are aware, satisfaction was the hallmark of Southern society; masters and masses alike were sunk in the deepest complacency; nowhere was there any palpable irritation, any discontent and conflict, and so nowhere was there any tendency to question. Again, being static and unchanging, the South was, of course, an inherently conservative society—one which, under any circumstances, would have naturally been cold to new ideas as something for which it had no need or use. As for the grip on reality, we know that story fully already. Imagination there was in plenty in this land with so much of the blood of the dreamy Celt and its warm sun, but it spent itself on puerilities, on cant and twisted logic, in rodomontade and the feckless vaporings of sentimentality. And as for detachment, the South, you will recall, was, before all else, personal, an attitude which is obviously the negation of detachment. Even its love of rhetoric required the immediate and directly observable satisfactions of speech rather than the more remote ones of writing.

There is still more here. As well as having nothing to give rise to a developed intellectual culture, as well as having much that was implicitly hostile, much that served as a negative barrier, the Old South also had much that was explicitly hostile and served as a quite positive barrier. The religious pattern will come to mind at once. Theologians have everywhere been the enemies of analysis and new ideas, and in whatever field they have appeared—feeling, quite correctly, that, once admitted, there is no setting limits to them. And in this country in which the evangelical ministers had already won to unusual sway, in which they had almost complete control of the schools, in which they had virtually no opposition, they established their iron will with an effectiveness which went well beyond even its American average.

But the greatest force of all was the result of conflict with the Yankee. In Southern unity before the foe lay the final bulwark of every established commonplace. And the defense of slavery not only eventuated, as we have seen, in a taboo on criticism; in the same process it set up a ban on all analysis and inquiry, a terrified truculence toward every new idea, a disposition to reject every innovation out of hand and hug to the whole of the *status quo* with fanatical resolution. Detachment? In a world in which patriotism to the South was increasingly the first duty of men, in which coolness about slavery was accounted treason, it was next to impossible.

12. "The state of the common morality correlates rather narrowly the degree of the intellectual civilization."

In sum, it was the total effect of Southern conditions, primary and secondary, to preserve—but let Henry Adams tell it, in the pages of the *Education,* from direct observation of Roony Lee, the son of Robert E. Lee, and other young Southerners he knew at Harvard between 1854 and 1858, who had behind them two hundred years of shaping in the pattern, and who are to be taken, as Adams infers, as the typical flower of the Old South at its highest and best:

"Tall, largely built, handsome, genial, with liberal Virginia openness toward all he liked, he [Lee] had also the Virginian habit of command. . . . For a year, at least . . . was the most popular and prominent man in his class, but then seemed slowly to drop into the background. The habit of command was not enough, and the Virginian had little else. He was simple beyond analysis; so simple that even the simple New England student could not realize him. No one knew enough to know how ignorant he was; how childlike; how helpless before the relative complexity of a school. As an animal the Southerner seemed to have every advantage, but even as an animal he steadily lost ground.

" . . . Strictly, the Southerner had no mind; he had temperament. He was not a scholar; he had no intellectual training; he could not analyze an idea, and he could not even conceive of admitting two. . . ."

There it is, then. We return to the point with which we began. It was the total effect of Southern conditions, primary and secondary, to preserve the Southerner's original simplicity of character as it were in perpetual suspension. From first to last, and whether he was a Virginian or a *nouveau,* he did not (typically speaking) think; he felt; and discharging his feelings immediately, he developed no need or desire for intellectual culture in its own right—none, at least, powerful enough to drive him past his taboos to its actual achievement.

Questions to Consider

1. How accurate is Cash's depiction of the state of Southern letters in 1940?
2. In what ways does Cash's work reflect the influence of H. L. Mencken?

Margaret Mitchell

1900–1949

Margaret Mitchell's captivating novel, *Gone With the Wind,* enjoys a popularity that transcends time and gender, having been published in 37 countries and translated into 27 languages. From its first appearance, the novel broke records: 50,000 copies were sold in one day and over a million in the first six months. By its twenty-fifth anniversary in 1961, *Gone With the Wind* had sold over 10 million copies. The novel was awarded the Pulitzer Prize in 1936 and adapted to film in 1939; its characters have become cultural stereotypes of Southerners. *Gone With the Wind*'s success remains a phenomenon, ranking ninth among best-selling fiction titles and holding the title of the best-selling book of all time, with the exception of the Bible.

Margaret Munnerlyn Mitchell was born in Atlanta, Georgia, on 8 November 1900. She was the second child of Eugene Muse, an attorney, and Maybelle Stephens Mitchell. Her father's family had lived in Atlanta since the American Revolution, and her mother's Irish Catholic family settled in Georgia during the early nineteenth century. Mitchell attended both public and private schools and grew up hearing legends about the Civil War and the defeated South. She was surrounded by the city's history, specifically, the stories deriving from the 1864 fall as a result of General Sherman's relentless attacks on the city.

In 1918, Mitchell entered Smith College with the intention of becoming a psychiatrist. However, it was in English composition that she excelled. Her time at Smith was cut short by the death of her mother in 1919, at which time she returned home to help her father and older brother manage the household in Atlanta. On 2 September 1922, Mitchell married Berrien Kinnard Upshaw, but following a turbulent two years, their marriage ended in an annulment. Three years later, she married the best man from her first wedding, John R. Marsh, with whom she enjoyed a successful and happy marriage. The couple had no children.

Mitchell joined the staff at the *Atlanta Journal* in 1922 as a feature writer for the Sunday *Journal Magazine*, using the names Peggy Mitchell and Margaret Mitchell Upshaw. In 1926, an ankle injury forced Mitchell to give up her position at the *Journal*. Encouraged by her husband, Margaret began writing the now-famous novel, an effort that became a ten-year endeavor. She began by writing the last chapter, then drafted various other sections. When the manuscript reached the publisher, Macmillan Company, the completed pile of disorganized chapters, consisting of both hand-written and typed pages, measured five feet high.

Mitchell considered herself an amateur writer. To avoid historical errors, she went to great lengths to ensure accuracy in the dates and places that she used in her novel. Mitchell spent hours at the Atlanta public library researching every detail and as a result, she was less concerned with the plot. Uncomfortable and amazed by all of the fame accompanying her novel, Mitchell made few other attempts at writing fiction. She destroyed an earlier work and devoted much of her time to writing letters and participating in wartime charities. However, her letters have been published in two collections: *Margaret Mitchell's "Gone With the Wind" Letters* and *A Dynamo Going to Waste: Letters to Allen Edee, 1919–1921*.

On 11 August 1949, Mitchell was struck down by a drunk driver while crossing a street with her husband. She never regained consciousness and died five days later. Interest in Mitchell and her novel continues today.

Gone With the Wind earned a variety of awards for its author, including the National Book Award for most distinguished novel, the American Booksellers Association Award, and the Carl M. Bohnenberger Memorial Medal. Mitchell herself was featured on a one-cent U.S. postage stamp in 1986, and in 1989, the film version of *Gone With the Wind* was featured as part of a stamp series honoring the films of 1939. Mitchell was inducted into Georgia Women of Achievement in 1994.

from Gone With the Wind

Scarlett stood on the landing and peered cautiously over the banisters into the hall below. It was empty. From the bedrooms on the floor above came an unending hum of low voices, rising and falling, punctuated with squeaks of laughter and, "Now, you didn't, really!" and "What did he say then?" On the beds and couches of the six great bedrooms, the girls were resting, their dresses off, their stays loosed, their hair flowing down their backs. Afternoon naps were a custom of the country and never were they so necessary as on the all-day parties, beginning early in the morning and culminating in a ball. For half an hour, the girls would chatter and laugh, and then servants would pull in the shutters and in the warm half-gloom the talk would die to whispers and finally expire in silence broken only by soft regular breathing.

Scarlett had made certain that Melanie was lying down on the bed with Honey and Hetty Tarleton before she slipped into the hall and started down the stairs. From the window on the landing, she could see the group of men sitting under the arbor, drinking from tall glasses, and she knew they would remain there until late afternoon. Her eyes searched the group but Ashley was not among them. Then she listened and she heard his voice. As she had hoped, he was still in the front driveway bidding goodby to departing matrons and children.

Her heart in her throat, she went swiftly down the stairs. What if she should meet Mr. Wilkes? What excuse could she give for prowling about the house when all the other girls were getting their beauty naps? Well, that had to be risked.

As she reached the bottom step, she heard the servants moving about in the dining room under the butler's orders, lifting out the table and the chairs in preparation for the dancing. Across the wide hall was the open door of the library and she sped into it noiselessly. She could wait there until Ashley finished his adieux and then call to him when he came into the house.

The library was in semidarkness, for the blinds had been drawn against the sun. The dim room with towering walls completely filled with dark books depressed her. It was not the place which she would have chosen for a tryst such as she hoped this one would be. Large numbers of books always depressed her, as did people who liked to read large numbers of books. That is—all people except Ashley. The heavy furniture rose up at her in the half-light, high-backed chairs with deep seats and wide arms, made for the tall Wilkes men, squatty soft chairs of velvet with velvet hassocks before them for the girls. Far across the long room before the hearth, the seven-foot sofa, Ashley's favorite seat, reared its high back, like some huge sleeping animal.

She closed the door except for a crack and tried to make her heart beat more slowly. She tried to remember just exactly what she had planned last night to say to Ashley, but she couldn't recall anything. Had she thought up something and forgotten it—or had she only planned that Ashley should say something to her? She couldn't remember, and a sudden cold fright fell upon her. If her heart would only stop pounding in her ears, perhaps she could think of what to say. But the quick thudding only increased as she heard him call a final farewell and walk into the front hall.

All she could think of was that she loved him—everything about him, from the proud lift of his gold head to his slender dark boots, loved his laughter even when it mystified her, loved his bewildering silences. Oh, if only he would walk in on her now and take her in his arms, so she would be spared the need of saying anything. He must love her—"Perhaps if I prayed—" She squeezed her eyes tightly and began gabbling to herself "Hail Mary, fullofgrace ———"

"Why, Scarlett!" said Ashley's voice, breaking in through the roaring in her ears and throwing her into utter confusion. He stood in the hall peering at her through the partly opened door, a quizzical smile on his face.

"Who are you hiding from—Charles or the Tarletons?"

She gulped. So he had noticed how the men had swarmed about her! How unutterably dear he was standing there with his eyes twinkling, all unaware of her excitement. She could not speak, but she put out a hand and drew him into the room. He entered, puzzled but interested. There was a tenseness about her, a glow in her eyes that he had never seen before, and even in the dim light he could see the rosy flush on her cheeks. Automatically he closed the door behind him and took her hand.

"What is it?" he said, almost in a whisper.

At the touch of his hand, she began to tremble. It was going to happen now, just as she had dreamed it. A thousand incoherent thoughts shot through her mind, and she could not catch a single one to mold into a word. She could only shake and look up into his face. Why didn't he speak?

"What is it?" he repeated. "A secret to tell me?"

Suddenly she found her tongue and just as suddenly all the years of Ellen's teachings fell away, and the forthright Irish blood of Gerald spoke from his daughter's lips.

"Yes—a secret. I love you."

For an instant there was a silence so acute it seemed that neither of them even breathed. Then the trembling fell away from her, as happiness and pride surged through her. Why hadn't she done this before? How much simpler than all the ladylike maneuverings she had been taught. And then her eyes sought his.

There was a look of consternation in them, of incredulity and something more—what was it? Yes, Gerald had looked that way the day his pet hunter had broken his leg and he had had to shoot him. Why did she have to think of that now? Such a silly thought. And why did Ashley look so oddly and say nothing? Then something like a well-trained mask came down over his face and he smiled gallantly.

"Isn't it enough that you've collected every other man's heart here today?" he said, with the old, teasing, caressing note in his voice. "Do you want to make it unanimous? Well, you've always had my heart, you know. You cut your teeth on it."

Something was wrong—all wrong! This was not the way she had planned it. Through the mad tearing of ideas round and round in her brain, one was beginning to take form. Somehow—for some reason—Ashley was acting as if he thought she was just flirting with him. But he knew differently. She knew he did.

"Ashley—Ashley—tell me—you must—oh, don't tease me now! Have I your heart? Oh, my dear, I lo——"

His hand went across her lips, swiftly. The mask was gone.

"You must not say these things, Scarlett! You mustn't. You don't mean them. You'll hate yourself for saying them and you'll hate me for hearing them!"

She jerked her head away. A hot swift current was running through her.

"I couldn't ever hate you. I tell you I love you and I know you must care about me because—" She stopped. Never before had she seen so much misery in anyone's face. "Ashley, do you care—you do, don't you?"

"Yes," he said dully. "I care."

If he had said he loathed her, she could not have been more frightened. She plucked at his sleeve, speechless.

"Scarlett," he said, "can't we go away and forget that we have ever said these things?"

"No," she whispered. "I can't. What do you mean? Don't you want to—to marry me?"

He replied, "I'm going to marry Melanie."

Somehow she found that she was sitting on the low velvet chair and Ashley, on the hassock at her feet, was holding both her hands in his, in a hard grip. He was saying things—things that made no sense. Her mind was quite blank, quite empty of all the thoughts that had surged through it only a moment before, and his words made no more impression than rain on glass. They fell on unhearing ears, words that were swift and tender and full of pity, like a father speaking to a hurt child.

The sound of Melanie's name caught in her consciousness and she looked into his crystal-gray eyes. She saw in them the old remoteness that had always baffled her—and a look of self-hatred.

"Father is to announce the engagement tonight. We are to be married soon. I should have told you, but I thought you knew. I thought everyone knew—had known for years. I never dreamed that you—You've so many beaux. I thought Stuart ——"

Life and feeling and comprehension were beginning to flow back into her.

"But you just said you cared for me."

His warm hands hurt hers.

"My dear, must you make me say things that will hurt you?"

Her silence pressed him on.

"How can I make you see these things, my dear? You who are so young and unthinking that you do not know what marriage means."

"I know I love you."

"Love isn't enough to make a successful marriage when two people are as different as we are. You would want all of a man, Scarlett, his body, his heart, his soul, his thoughts. And if you did not have them, you would be miserable. And I couldn't give you all of me. I couldn't give all of me to anyone. And I would not want all of your mind and your soul. And you would be hurt, and then you would come to hate me—how bitterly! You would hate the books I read and the music I loved, because they took me away from you even for a moment. And I—perhaps I ———"

"Do you love her?"

"She is like me, part of my blood, and we understand each other. Scarlett! Scarlett! Can't I make you see that a marriage can't go on in any sort of peace unless the two people are alike?"

Some one else had said that: "Like must marry like or there'll be no happiness." Who was it? It seemed a million years since she had heard that, but it still did not make sense.

"But you said you cared."

"I shouldn't have said it."

Somewhere in her brain, a slow fire rose and rage began to blot out everything else.

"Well, having been cad enough to say it ———"

His face went white.

"I was a cad to say it, as I'm going to marry Melanie. I did you a wrong and Melanie a greater one. I should not have said it, for I knew you wouldn't understand. How could I help caring for you—you who have all the passion for life that I have not? You who can love and hate with a violence impossible to me? Why you are as elemental as fire and wind and wild things and I ———"

She thought of Melanie and saw suddenly her quiet brown eyes with their far-off look, her placid little hands in their black lace mitts, her gentle silences. And then her rage broke, the same rage that drove Gerald to murder and other Irish ancestors to misdeeds that cost them their necks. There was nothing in her now of the well-bred Robillards who could bear with white silence anything the world might cast.

"Why don't you say it, you coward! You're afraid to marry me! You'd rather live with that stupid little fool who can't open her mouth except to say 'Yes' or 'No' and raise a passel of mealy-mouthed brats just like her! Why ———"

"You must not say these things about Melanie!"

"'I mustn't' be damned to you! Who are you to tell me I mustn't? You coward, you cad, you—You made me believe you were going to marry me ———"

"Be fair," his voice pleaded. "Did I ever ———"

She did not want to be fair, although she knew what he said was true. He had never once crossed the borders of friendliness with her and, when she thought of this fresh anger rose, the anger of hurt pride and feminine vanity. She had run after him and he would have none of her. He preferred a whey-faced little fool like Melanie to her. Oh, far better that she had followed Ellen and Mammy's precepts and never, never revealed that she even liked him—better anything than to be faced with this scorching shame!

She sprang to her feet, her hands clenched and he rose towering over her, his face full of the mute misery of one forced to face realities when realities are agonies.

"I shall hate you till I die, you cad—you lowdown—lowdown ———" What was the word she wanted? She could not think of any word bad enough.

"Scarlett—please ———"

He put out his hand toward her and, as he did, she slapped him across the face with all the strength she had. The noise cracked like a whip in the still room and suddenly her rage was gone, and there was desolation in her heart.

The red mark of her hand showed plainly on his white tired face. He said nothing, but lifted her limp hand to his lips and kissed it. Then he was gone before she could speak again, closing the door softly behind him.

She sat down again very suddenly, the reaction from her rage making her knees feel weak. He was gone and the memory of his stricken face would haunt her till she died.

She heard the soft muffled sound of his footsteps dying away down the long hall, and the complete enormity of her actions came over her. She had lost him forever. Now he would hate her and every time he looked at her he would remember how she threw herself at him when he had given her no encouragement at all.

"I'm as bad as Honey Wilkes," she thought suddenly, and remembered how everyone, and she more than anyone else, had laughed contemptuously at Honey's forward conduct. She saw Honey's awkward wigglings and heard her silly titters as she hung onto boys' arms, and the thought stung her to new rage, rage at herself, at Ashley, at the world. Because she hated herself, she hated them all with the fury of the thwarted and humiliated love of sixteen. Only a little true tenderness had been mixed into her love. Mostly it had been compounded out of vanity and complacent confidence in her own charms. Now she had lost and, greater than her sense of loss, was the fear that she had made a public spectacle of herself. Had she been as obvious as Honey? Was everyone laughing at her? She began to shake at the thought.

Her hand dropped to a little table beside her, fingering a tiny china rosebowl on which two china cherubs smirked. The room was so still she almost screamed to break the silence. She must do something or go mad. She picked up the bowl and hurled it viciously across the room toward the fireplace. It barely cleared the tall back of the sofa and splintered with a little crash against the marble mantelpiece.

"This," said a voice from the depths of the sofa, "is too much."

Nothing had ever startled or frightened her so much, and her mouth went too dry for her to utter a sound. She caught hold of the back of the chair, her knees going weak under her, as Rhett Butler rose from the sofa where he had been lying and made her a bow of exaggerated politeness.

"It is bad enough to have an afternoon nap disturbed by such a passage as I've been forced to hear, but why should my life be endangered?"

He was real. He wasn't a ghost. But, saints preserve us, he had heard everything! She rallied her forces into a semblance of dignity.

"Sir, you should have made known your presence."

"Indeed?" His white teeth gleamed and his bold dark eyes laughed at her. "But you were the intruder. I was forced to wait for Mr. Kennedy, and feeling that I was perhaps persona non grata in the back yard, I was thoughtful enough to remove my unwelcome presence here where I thought I would be undisturbed. But, alas!" he shrugged and laughed softly.

Her temper was beginning to rise again at the thought that this rude and impertinent man had heard everything—heard things she now wished she had died before she ever uttered.

"Eavesdroppers ———" she began furiously.

"Eavesdroppers often hear highly entertaining and instructive things," he grinned. "From a long experience in eavesdropping, I ———"

"Sir," she said, "you are no gentleman!"

"An apt observation," he answered airily. "And, you, Miss, are no lady." He seemed to find her very amusing, for he laughed softly again. "No one can remain a lady after saying and doing what I have just overheard. However, ladies have seldom held any charms for me. I know what they are thinking, but they never have the courage or lack of breeding to say what they think. And that, in time, becomes a bore. But you, my dear Miss O'Hara, are a girl of rare spirit, very admirable spirit, and I take off my hat to you. I fail to understand what charms the elegant Mr. Wilkes can hold for a girl of your tempestuous nature. He should thank God on bended knee for a girl with your—how did he put it?—'passion for living,' but being a poor-spirited wretch ———"

"You aren't fit to wipe his boots!" she shouted in rage.

"And you were going to hate him all your life!" He sank down on the sofa and she heard him laughing.

If she could have killed him, she would have done it. Instead, she walked out of the room with such dignity as she could summon and banged the heavy door behind her.

Questions to Consider

1. What are the characteristics of the stereotypical Southern belle? How do these characteristics influence your interpretation of Southern texts? What characteristics does Scarlett possess that cause readers to view her as the prototypical Southern belle?
2. Has the image of the Southern belle proven a positive one for women? Why or why not?

Sterling Brown

1901–1989

In his poetry as well as his literary criticism, Sterling Allen Brown replaced the stereotypical African-American characters that had been populating Southern literature prior to the early twentieth century with honest and complex portrayals of real and imagined individuals set against the background of a vibrant folk culture. Born on 1 May 1901 in Washington, D.C., Brown was the son of Sterling Nelson Brown, a former slave from Tennessee who had risen through higher education to become a professor of religion at Howard University. Brown's mother, Adelaide Allen Brown, was also a college graduate, and she transmitted her love of poetry to her son. Graduating in 1918 from Washington's segregated but academically outstanding Dunbar High School, Brown won a scholarship to Williams College in Massachusetts, where he studied literature, served on the debate team, and graduated Phi Beta Kappa in 1922. Earning a master's degree from Howard University the following year, Brown taught English at colleges in Virginia, Missouri, and Tennessee before accepting an appointment to the faculty of Howard in 1929. He was to teach at Howard for the next 40 years, turning down even a job offer from prestigious Vassar College; among his many students at Howard were poet Amiri Baraka (the former LeRoi Jones), novelist Toni Morrison, and actor Ossie Davis.

Brown began to publish poems in African-American periodicals such as *Crisis*, *Opportunity*, and *Ebony* in the mid-1920s, coinciding with the emergence of Harlem Renaissance poets such as Langston Hughes, Claude McKay, and Countee Cullen. Although Brown read and admired their work, he himself would never be considered a core member of the group because of his geographic distance from Harlem and his thematic preference for traditional folk materials over contemporary urban intellectual issues. In 1932, a major New York publishing house brought out Brown's first collection of poetry, *Southern Road*, with an introduction by James Weldon Johnson. The book was recognized almost at once as a landmark in the history of African-American literature. Not only did Brown draw upon the musical sources of blues lyrics, work songs, spirituals, ballads, and jazz rhythms for the forms of his poems, but also he crafted them in freshly rendered diction that reflected attentive listening to the ways African Americans really talked, rather than adherence to the stale conventions of literary dialect. Among the featured selections, "Ma Rainey" derives both its celebrity subject and its form from the blues tradition, while "Memphis Blues" mixes both the earthy language of blues and the fervent, worshipful, apocalyptic language of spirituals. "Slim in Atlanta" stems from a non-musical African-American oral tradition: the tall tale about a folk hero. The real "Slim" was reputedly a storytelling waiter whom Brown had met while living in Missouri.

Despite the critical success of his first book, Brown failed in his efforts to get his second poetry collection, *No Hiding Place*, published a few years later; it would not see print until his *Collected Poems* appeared in 1980. "Remembering Nat Turner" is one of the poems from that manuscript; many of the selections in *Collected Poems* deal with the Southern history and personal memories of African Americans. The 1930s were, of course, the decade of the Great Depression in the United States, and in 1936 Brown joined the Works Project Administration (WPA), the massive government-funded initiative to put Americans back to work. As Editor of Negro Affairs for the Federal Writers Project, Brown oversaw projects including studies of African-American history and folk traditions and the compilation of slave narratives. The year after Brown's WPA appointment, he published *The Negro in American Fiction* and *Negro Poetry and Drama*, two book-length critical works that attacked the stereotypical portrayals of African Americans in American literature from the Colonial era through the early twentieth century. Brown's work with the WPA ended in 1940. In 1941 he added to his scholarly reputation by coediting *The Negro Caravan*, the most comprehensive anthology of African-American writing of the first half-century.

In 1975, Brown succeeded in publishing a second poetry collection, *The Last Ride of Wild Bill*, with Dudley Randall's small, African-American Broadside Press in Detroit. Five years later, the publication of Brown's *Collected Poems*, with an introduction by the then-rising young jazz poet Michael S. Harper, reawakened public interest in Brown's poetry, which had become eclipsed over the years by his critical work. At the time of his death in 1989, this son of a freed Tennessee slave had been awarded a Guggenheim Fellowship, a Julius Rosenwald Fellowship, and more than a dozen honorary doctorates. Bringing his considerable genius to bear upon the lives of common people influenced by folk culture, Brown bequeathed lasting legacies in his roles as creative artist, scholar, teacher, editor, and cultural administrator.

Memphis Blues

I

Nineveh, Tyre,
Babylon,[1]
Not much lef'
Of either one.

1. Three cities destroyed by God in the Old Testament.

All dese cities
Ashes and rust,
De win' sing sperrichals
Through deir dus' . . .
Was another Memphis[2]
Mongst de olden days,
Done been destroyed
In many ways. . . .
Dis here Memphis
It may go;
Floods may drown it;
Tornado blow;
Mississippi wash it
Down to sea—
Like de other Memphis in
History.[3]

II

Watcha gonna do when Memphis on fire,
Memphis on fire, Mistah Preachin' Man?
Gonna pray to Jesus and nebber tire,
Gonna pray to Jesus, loud as I can,
Gonna pray to my Jesus, oh, my Lawd!

Watcha gonna do when de tall flames roar,
Tall flames roar, Mistah Lovin' Man?
Gonna love my brownskin better'n before—
Gonna love my baby lak a do right man,
Gonna love my brown baby, oh, my Lawd!

Watcha gonna do when Memphis falls down,
Memphis falls down, Mistah Music Man?
Gonna plunk on dat box as long as it soun',
Gonna plunk dat box fo' to beat de ban',
Gonna tickle dem ivories, oh, my Lawd!

Watcha gonna do in de hurricane,
In de hurricane, Mistah Workin' Man?
Gonna put dem buildings up again,
Gonna put em up dis time to stan',
Gonna push a wicked wheelbarrow, oh, my Lawd!

Watcha gonna do when Memphis near gone,
Memphis near gone, Mistah Drinkin' Man?
Gonna grab a pint bottle of Mountain Corn,
Gonna keep de stopper in my han',
Gonna get a mean jag on, oh, my Lawd!

2. The ancient city of Memphis, Egypt (as distinguished from Memphis, Tennessee).

3. The Old Testament (Jeremiah 46:19) predicts that the thriving ancient city of Memphis will become "a waste, a ruin, without inhabitant"—a prophecy that was fulfilled by the time of the Muslim conquest.

Watcha gonna do when de flood roll fas',
Flood roll fas', Mistah Gamblin' Man?
Gonna pick up my dice fo' one las' pass—
Gonna fade my way to de lucky lan',
Gonna throw my las' seven—oh, my Lawd!

III

Memphis go
By Flood or Flame;
Nigger won't worry
All de same—
Memphis go
Memphis come back,
Ain' no skin
Off de nigger's back.
All dese cities
Ashes, rust. . . .
De win' sing sperrichals
Through deir dus'.

Slim in Atlanta

Down in Atlanta,
  De whitefolks got laws
For to keep all de niggers
  From laughin' outdoors.

Hope to Gawd I may die
  If I ain't speakin' truth
Make de niggers do deir laughin
  In a telefoam booth.

Slim Greer hit de town
  An' de rebs[1] got him told—
"Dontcha laugh on de street,
  If you want to die old."

Den dey showed him de booth,
  An' a hundred shines[2]
In front of it, waitin'
  In double lines.

Slim thought his sides
  Would bust in two,
Yelled, "Lookout, everybody,
  I'm coming through!"

Pulled de other man out,
  An' bust in de box,

1. Short for "rebels," a slang term for Confederate Army troops and sympathizers.

2. A derogatory term for African Americans.

An' laughed four hours
By de Georgia clocks.

Den he peeked through de door,
An' what did he see?
Three hundred niggers there
In misery.—

Some holdin' deir sides,
Some holdin' deir jaws,
To keep from breakin'
De Georgia laws.

An' Slim gave a holler,
An' started again;
An' from three hundred throats
Come a moan of pain.

An' everytime Slim
Saw what was outside,
Got to whoopin' again
Till he nearly died.

An' while de poor critters
Was waitin' deir chance,
Slim laughed till dey sent
Fo' de ambulance.

De state paid de railroad
To take him away;
Den, things was as usural
In Atlanta, Gee A.

Remembering Nat Turner[1]

(For R. C. L.)[2]

We saw a bloody sunset over Courtland, once Jerusalem,[3]
As we followed the trail that old Nat took
When he came out of Cross Keys[4] down upon Jerusalem,
In his angry stab for freedom a hundred years ago.
The land was quiet, and the mist was rising,
Out of the woods and the Nottaway swamp,[5]
Over Southampton[6] the still night fell,
As we rode down to Cross Keys where the march began.

When we got to Cross Keys, they could tell us little of him,
The Negroes had only the faintest recollections:

1. Nathaniel Turner (1800–1831), Virginia slave who was hanged for leading an 1831 slave rebellion during which many Whites were killed.
2. Believed to be a research associate of Brown's named Roscoe Lewis.
3. Courtland, Virginia, the seat of Southampton County, was named Jerusalem until the late nineteenth century.
4. Community west of Jerusalem where Turner's master's plantation was located; site of the rebellion.
5. Swamp located in Southampton County, Virginia, as was the Nottaway River.
6. Southampton County, Virginia.

"I ain't been here so long, I come from up roun' Newsome;[7]
Yassah, a town a few miles up de road,
The old folks who coulda told you is all dead an' gone.
I heard something, sometime; I doan jis remember what.
'Pears lak I heard that name somewheres or other.
So he fought to be free. Well. You doan say."

An old white woman recalled exactly
How Nat crept down the steps, axe in his hand,
After murdering a woman and child in bed,
"Right in this here house at the head of these stairs"
(In a house built long after Nat was dead).
She pointed to a brick store where Nat was captured,
(Nat was taken in the swamp, three miles away)
With his men around him, shooting from the windows
(She was thinking of Harpers Ferry and old John Brown).[8]
She cackled as she told how they riddled Nat with bullets
(Nat was tried and hanged at Courtland, ten miles away).
She wanted to know why folks would comes miles
Just to ask about an old nigger fool.
"Ain't no slavery no more, things is going all right.
Pervided thar's a good goober[9] market this year.
We had a sign post here with printing on it,
But it rotted in the hole, and thar it lays,
And the nigger tenants split the marker for kindling.
Things is all right, now, ain't no trouble with the niggers
Why they make this big to-do over Nat?"

As we drove from Cross Keys back to Courtland,
Along the way that Nat came down upon Jerusalem,
A watery moon was high in the cloud-filled heavens,
The same moon he dreaded a hundred years ago.
The tree they hanged Nat on is long gone to ashes,
The trees he dodged behind have rotted in the swamps.

The bus for Miami and the trucks boomed by,
And touring cars, their heavy tires snarling on the pavement.
Frogs piped in the marshes, and a hound bayed long,
And yellow lights glowed from the cabin windows.

As we came back the way that Nat led his army,
Down from Cross Keys, down to Jerusalem,
We wondered if his troubled spirit still roamed the Nottaway,
Or if it fled with the cock-crow at daylight,
Or lay at peace with the bones in Jerusalem,
Its restlessness stifled by Southampton clay.

We remembered the poster rotted through and falling,
The marker split for kindling a kitchen fire.

7. Newsoms [*sic*], Virginia, is a few miles southwest of Courtland.
8. John Brown (1800–1859), an abolitionist from Connecticut, led an unsuccessful raid against a federal arsenal at Harpers Ferry, Virginia, in the hopes of inciting a slave rebellion.
9. Peanut.

Ma Rainey[1]

I

When Ma Rainey
Comes to town,
Folks from anyplace
Miles aroun',
From Cape Girardeau,
Poplar Bluff,[2]
Flocks in to hear
Ma do her stuff;
Comes flivverin'[3] in,
Or ridin' mules,
Or packed in trains,
Picknickin' fools. . . .
That's what it's like,
Fo' miles on down,
To New Orleans delta
An' Mobile town,
When Ma hits
Anywheres aroun'.

II

Dey comes to hear Ma Rainey from de little river settlements,
From blackbottom cornrows and from lumber camps;
Dey stumble in de hall, jes a-laughin' an' a-cacklin',
Cheerin' lak roarin' water, lak wind in river swamps.

An' some jokers keeps deir laughs a-goin' in de crowded aisles,
An' some folks sits dere waitin' wid deir aches an' miseries,
Till Ma comes out before dem, a-smilin' gold-toofed smiles
An' Long Boy ripples minors[4] on de black an' yellow keys.

III

O Ma Rainey,
Sing yo' song;
Now you's back
Whah you belong,
Git way inside us,
Keep us strong. . . .

O Ma Rainey,
Li'l an' low;
Sing us 'bout de hard luck
Roun' our do';
Sing us 'bout de lonesome road
We mus' go. . . .

1. Gertrude "Ma" Rainey (1886–1939), American blues singer who helped launch Bessie Smith's career.
2. Towns located in Missouri.
3. Driving a small and inexpensive automobile.
4. Minor musical intervals.

IV

I talked to a fellow, an' the fellow say,
"She jes' catch hold of us, somekindaway.
She sang Backwater Blues one day:
It rained fo' days an' de skies was dark as night,
Trouble taken place in de lowlands at night.

Thundered an' lightened an' the storm begin to roll
Thousan's of people ain't got no place to go.

Den I went an' stood upon some high ol' lonesome hill,
An' looked down on the place where I used to live.

An' den de folks, dey natchally bowed dey heads an' cried,
Bowed dey heavy heads, shet dey moufs up tight an' cried,
An' Ma lef' de stage, an' followed some de folks outside."

Dere wasn't much more de fellow say:
She jes' gits hold of us dataway.

Questions to Consider

1. How does the wildly unbelievable tale of "Slim in Atlanta" relate to the realism of the lives of African Americans in the Deep South during the early twentieth century?
2. In the poem "Remembering Nat Turner," a printed sign that once marked a historic spot has deteriorated, and only factually inaccurate oral legend remains to record Nat Turner's story in the region where it actually happened. Does the narrator of the poem seem to be more sympathetic to written history or to the oral tradition of storytelling?

Arnaud (Arna) Wendell Bontemps

1902–1973

The multi-faceted Arna Bontemps—literary critic, poet, fiction writer, and librarian—once wrote of his decision to write children's literature: "I began to suspect that it was fruitless for a Negro in the United States to address serious writing to my generation, and I began to consider the alternative of trying to reach young readers not yet hardened or grown insensitive to man's inhumanity to man, as it is called." During his life, Bontemps may have felt that his literature made little difference in the lives of his readers although he was a well-respected writer of the Harlem Renaissance who devoted his life to creating literary works and to preserving the works of other African-American writers. His short fiction appears in many text books, and his novel, *God Sends Sunday*, presents one of the most vivid depictions of life in the early half of the twentieth century in American literature.

Bontemps was born on 13 October 1902 in Alexandria, Louisiana. His family lived in Alexandria for only a short time before joining a westward migration to California. Such cross-country moves became commonplace among Creole families, especially those from the Cane River area of Louisiana. These families left seeking new opportunities in California, and Bontemps's family was likely familiar with the California journeys of many of their relatives. The lure of better financial opportunities, coupled with Bontemps's father's brush with some racist Whites on his way home from work one evening, spurred the elder Bontemps to leave Louisiana.

The family settled in Los Angeles and lived well, as Bontemps's father was a talented brick mason. Bontemps's mother died when Arna was 12 years old, but from her influence, he gained a love of reading and an appreciation of the importance of education. After his mother's death, the younger Bontemps spent an increasing amount of time with his grandmother and his uncle, Buddy, on whom Augie of *God Sends Sunday* was modeled. Although Buddy did not have a great deal of formal education, he was well read for a person of limited resources, and he encouraged Bontemps to write. Buddy worked as a chef and lived a life of drinking and carousing that horrified Arna's conservative father, Paul. However, because of the elder Bontemps's work schedule, Arna was often left in the care of Buddy and Arna's grandmother who shared with him many tales of Louisiana life. During this period, Paul Bontemps hoped that Arna would become the fourth generation of Bontemps family brick masons and arranged for him to become an apprentice in the trade; Arna rebelled, for he wanted to pursue his education, and with the hard-won blessing of his father, he was able to continue in school. In 1917, his father agreed to send Arna to a White, Seventh-day Adventist boarding school, San Fernando Academy. He then enrolled at another Adventist institution, Pacific Union College, graduating in 1923.

In 1924, Bontemps moved to New York to teach at Harlem Academy. In 1926, he married Alberta Johnson with whom he had six children. During this time, Bontemps wrote many award-winning poems and published literary works in a variety of genres. While in Harlem, he worked with and encountered all the major cultural and literary figures of the Harlem Renaissance, including Carl Van Vechten, Langston Hughes, Jean Toomer, Claude McKay, James Weldon Johnson, Countee Cullen, and James Baldwin. In 1931, Bontemps left the Harlem Academy and published *God Sends Sunday*. From 1931 until 1934, he taught at Oakwood Junior College in Huntsville, Alabama. His Alabama life was characterized by a continual lack of money and insufferable climate changes from high heat to freezing cold. Because of limited space in his house, Bontemps wrote his works outside under the shade of the house's eaves. Ultimately, his persistence brought about results, and he successfully published books for both adults and children. Bontemps increasingly turned his attention to juvenile literature, for he felt that young people would be a better audience for his work, and his efforts yielded many significant children's books.

In 1943, Bontemps completed a Master of Library Science degree from the University of Chicago and became librarian at Fisk University in Nashville, Tennessee, until 1965. He continued to write poetry, literary criticism, and prose fiction throughout his career until he died at age 71 in 1973. His work as a librarian was crucial to scholars of his day and to contemporary scholars since he gathered one of the most complete collections of Harlem Renaissance and other African-American writing in the world while at Fisk.

Throughout his life, Bontemps's talents as a writer and his interest in African-American literature were sustained as he produced a significant body of work which is still revered by scholars and general readers. Though he left Louisiana at a young age, Bontemps developed an extensive knowledge of the region and its culture through his family's stories. His writings realistically depict African-American life and frequently draw upon cultural and folk traditions. In "A Summer Tragedy," he includes a flashback of a Mardi Gras celebration and folk adages about the "frizzly chickens." Throughout his work, Bontemps weaves elements of modernism, realism, and folk traditions to convey interesting plots and well-developed characters.

A Summer Tragedy

Old Jeff Patton, the black share farmer,[1] fumbled with his bow tie. His fingers trembled and the high, stiff collar pinched his throat. A fellow loses his hand for such vanities after thirty or forty years of simple life. Once a year, or maybe twice if there's a wedding

1. A person who works for a landowner and receives payment in the form of a share of the crop rather than in cash. Generally, a small house was also included during the growing season for the sharecropper and his family.

among his kinfolks, he may spruce up, but generally fancy clothes do nothing but adorn the wall of the big room and feed the moths. That had been Jeff Patton's experience. He had not worn his stiff-bosomed shirt more than a dozen times in all his married life. His swallow-tailed coat lay on the bed beside him, freshly brushed and pressed, but it was as full of holes as the overalls in which he worked on weekdays. The moths had used it badly. Jeff twisted his mouth into a hideous toothless grimace as he contended with the obstinate bow. He stamped his good foot and decided to give up the struggle.

"Jennie," he called.

"What's that, Jeff?" His wife's shrunken voice came out of the adjoining room like an echo. It was hardly bigger than a whisper.

"I reckon you'll have to he'p me wid this heah bow tie, baby," he said meekly. "Dog if I can hitch it up."

Her answer was not strong enough to reach him, but presently the old woman came to the door, feeling her way with a stick. She had a wasted, dead-leaf appearance. Her body, as scrawny and gnarled as a string bean, seemed less than nothing in the ocean of frayed and faded petticoats that surrounded her. These hung an inch or two above the tops of her heavy unlaced shoes and showed little grotesque piles where the stockings had fallen down from her negligible legs.

"You oughta could do a heap mo' wid a thing like that'n me—beingst as you got yo' good sight."

"Looks like I oughta could," he admitted. "But my fingers is gone democrat on me. I get all mixed up in the looking glass an' can't tell wicha way to twist the devilish thing."

Jennie sat on the side of the bed, and old Jeff Patton got down on one knee while she tied the bow knot. It was a slow and painful ordeal for each of them in this position. Jeff's bones cracked, his knee ached, and it was only after a half dozen attempts that Jennie worked a semblance of a bow into the tie.

"I got to dress maself now," the old woman whispered. "These is ma old shoes an' stockings, and I ain't so much as unwrapped ma dress."

"Well, don't worry 'bout me no mo', baby," Jeff said. "That 'bout finishes me. All I gotta do now is slip on that old coat 'n ves' an' I'll be fixed to leave."

Jennie disappeared again through the dim passage into the shed room. Being blind was no handicap to her in that black hole. Jeff heard the cane placed against the wall beside the door and knew that his wife was on easy ground. He put on his coat, took a battered top hat from the bed post, and hobbled to the front door. He was ready to travel. As soon as Jennie could get on her Sunday shoes and her old black silk dress, they would start.

Outside the tiny log house, the day was warm and mellow with sunshine. A host of wasps were humming with busy excitement in the trunk of a dead sycamore. Gray squirrels were searching through the grass for hickory nuts, and blue jays were in the trees, hopping from branch to branch. Pine woods stretched away to the left like a black sea. Among them were scattered scores of log houses like Jeff's, houses of black share farmers. Cows and pigs wandered freely among the trees. There was no danger of loss. Each farmer knew his own stock and knew his neighbor's as well as he knew his neighbor's children.

Down the slope to the right were the cultivated acres on which the colored folks worked. They extended to the river, more than two miles away, and they were today green with the unmade cotton crop. A tiny thread of a road, which passed directly in front of Jeff's place, ran through these green fields like a pencil mark.

Jeff, standing outside the door, with his absurd hat in his left hand, surveyed the wide scene tenderly. He had been forty-five years on these acres. He loved them with the unexplained affection that others have for the countries to which they belong.

The sun was hot on his head, his collar still pinched his throat, and the Sunday clothes were intolerably hot. Jeff transferred the hat to his right hand and began fanning with it. Suddenly the whisper that was Jennie's voice came out of the shed room.

"You can bring the car round front whilst you's waitin'," it said feebly. There was a tired pause; then it added, "I'll soon be fixed to go."

"A'right, baby," Jeff answered. "I'll get it in a minute."

But he didn't move. A thought struck him that made his mouth fall open. The mention of the car brought to his mind, with new intensity, the trip he and Jennie were about to take. Fear came into his eyes; excitement took his breath. Lord, Jesus!

"Jeff . . . O Jeff," the old woman's whisper called.

He awakened with a jolt. "Hunh, baby?"

"What you doin'?"

"Nuthin. Jes studyin'.[2] I jes been turnin' things round 'n round in ma mind."

"You could be gettin' the car," she said.

"Oh yes, right away, baby."

He started round to the shed, limping heavily on his bad leg. There were three frizzly chickens in the yard. All his other chickens had been killed or stolen recently. But the frizzly chickens had been saved somehow. That was fortunate indeed, for these curious creatures had a way of devouring "poison" from the yard and in that way protecting against conjure[3] and black luck and spells. But even the frizzly chickens seemed now to be in a stupor. Jeff thought they had some ailment; he expected all three of them to die shortly.

The shed in which the old T-model Ford stood was only a grass roof held up by four corner poles. It had been built by tremulous hands at a time when the little rattletrap car had been regarded as a peculiar treasure. And, miraculously, despite wind and downpour, it still stood.

Jeff adjusted the crank and put his weight upon it. The engine came to life with a sputter and bang that rattled the old car from radiator to tail light. Jeff hopped into the seat and put his foot on the accelerator. The sputtering and banging increased. The rattling became more violent. That was good. It was good banging, good sputtering and rattling, and it meant that the aged car was still in running condition. She could be depended on for this trip.

Again, Jeff's thought halted as if paralyzed. The suggestion of the trip fell into the machinery of his mind like a wrench. He felt dazed and weak. He swung the car out into the yard, made a half turn, and drove around to the front door. When he took his hands off the wheel, he noticed that he was trembling violently. He cut off the motor and climbed to the ground to wait for Jennie.

A few minutes later she was at the window, her voice rattling against the pane like a broken shutter.

"I'm ready, Jeff."

He did not answer, but limped into the house and took her by the arm. He led her slowly through the big room, down the step, and across the yard.

"You reckon I'd oughta lock the do'?" he asked softly.

They stopped and Jennie weighed the question. Finally she shook her head.

2. Considering, pondering, or thinking.

3. Magic, usually of a sympathetic and harmless sort.

"Ne' mind the do'," she said. "I don't see no cause to lock up things."

"You right," Jeff agreed. "No cause to lock up."

Jeff opened the door and helped his wife into the car. A quick shudder passed over him. Jesus! Again he trembled.

"How come you shaking so?" Jennie whispered.

"I don't know," he said.

"You mus' be scairt, Jeff."

"No, baby, I ain't scairt."

He slammed the door after her and went around to crank up again. The motor started easily. Jeff wished that it had not been so responsive. He would have liked a few more minutes in which to turn things around in his head. As it was, with Jennie chiding him about being afraid, he had to keep going. He swung the car into the little pencil-mark road and started off toward the river, driving very slowly, very cautiously.

Chugging across the green countryside, the small battered Ford seemed tiny indeed. Jeff felt a familiar excitement, a thrill, as they came down the first slope to the immense levels on which the cotton was growing. He could not help reflecting that the crops were good. He knew what that meant, too; he had made forty-five of them with his own hands. It was true that he had worn out nearly a dozen mules, but that was the fault of old man Stevenson, the owner of the land. Major Stevenson had the notion that one mule was all a share farmer needed to work a thirty-acre plot. It was an expensive notion, the way it killed mules from overwork, but the old man held to it. Jeff thought it killed a good many share farmers as well as mules, but he had no sympathy for them. He had always been strong, and he had been taught to have no patience with weakness in men. Women or children might be tolerated if they were puny, but a weak man was a curse. Of course, his own children ——

Jeff's thought halted there. He and Jennie never mentioned their dead children any more. And naturally, he did not wish to dwell upon them in his mind. Before he knew it, some remark would slip out of his mouth and that would make Jennie feel blue. Perhaps she would cry. A woman like Jennie could not easily throw off the grief that comes from losing five grown children within two years. Even Jeff was still staggered by the blow. His memory had not been much good recently. He frequently talked to himself. And, although he had kept it a secret, he knew that his courage had left him. He was terrified by the least unfamiliar sound at night. He was reluctant to venture far from home in the daytime. And that habit of trembling when he felt fearful was now far beyond his control. Sometimes he became afraid and trembled without knowing what had frightened him. The feeling would just come over him like a chill.

The car rattled slowly over the dusty road. Jennie sat erect and silent with a little absurd hat pinned to her hair. Her useless eyes seemed very large and very white in their deep sockets. Suddenly Jeff heard her voice, and he inclined his head to catch the words.

"Is we passed Delia Moore's house yet?" she asked.

"Not yet," he said.

"You must be drivin' mighty slow, Jeff."

"We just as well take our time, baby."

There was a pause. A little puff of steam was coming out of the radiator of the car. Heat wavered above the hood. Delia Moore's house was nearly half a mile away. After a moment Jennie spoke again.

"You ain't really scairt, is you, Jeff?"

"Nah, baby, I ain't scairt."

"You know how we agreed—we gotta keep on goin'."

Jewels of perspiration appeared on Jeff's forehead. His eyes rounded, blinked, became fixed on the road.

"I don't know," he said with a shiver. "I reckon it's the only thing to do."

"Hm."

A flock of guinea fowls, pecking in the road, were scattered by the passing car. Some of them took to their wings; others hid under bushes. A blue jay, swaying on a leafy twig, was annoying a roadside squirrel. Jeff held an even speed till he came near Delia's place. Then he slowed down noticeably.

Delia's house was really no house at all, but an abandoned store building converted into a dwelling. It sat near a crossroads, beneath a single black cedar tree. There Delia, a cattish old creature of Jennie's age, lived alone. She had been there more years than anybody could remember, and long ago had won the disfavor of such women as Jennie. For in her young days Delia had been gayer, yellower, and saucier than seemed proper in those parts. Her ways with menfolks had been dark and suspicious. And the fact that she had had as many husbands as children did not help her reputation.

"Yonder's old Delia," Jeff said as they passed.

"What she doin'?"

"Jes settin' in the do'," he said.

"She see us?"

"Hm," Jeff said. "Musta did."

That relieved Jennie. It strengthened her to know that her old enemy had seen her pass in her best clothes. That would give the old she-devil something to chew her gums and fret about, Jennie thought. Wouldn't she have a fit if she didn't find out? Old evil Delia! This would be just the thing for her. It would pay her back for being so evil. It would also pay her, Jennie thought, for the way she used to grin at Jeff—long ago, when her teeth were good.

The road became smooth and red, and Jeff could tell by the smell of the air that they were nearing the river. He could see the rise where the road turned and ran along parallel to the stream. The car chugged on monotonously. After a long silent spell, Jennie leaned against Jeff and spoke.

"How many bale o' cotton you think we got standin'?" she said.

Jeff wrinkled his forehead as he calculated.

" 'Bout twenty-five, I reckon."

"How many you make las' year?"

"Twenty-eight," he said. "How come you ask that?"

"I's jes thinkin'," Jennie said quietly.

"It don't make a speck o' difference though," Jeff reflected. "If we get much or if we get little, we still gonna be in debt to old man Stevenson when he gets through counting up agin us. It's took us a long time to learn that."

Jennie was not listening to these words. She had fallen into a trancelike meditation. Her lips twitched. She chewed her gums and rubbed her gnarled hands nervously. Suddenly, she leaned forward, buried her face in the nervous hands, and burst into tears. She cried aloud in a dry, cracked voice that suggested the rattle of fodder on dead stalks. She cried aloud like a child, for she had never learned to suppress a genuine sob. Her slight old frame shook heavily and seemed hardly able to sustain such violent grief.

"What's the matter, baby?" Jeff asked awkwardly. "Why you cryin' like all that?"

"I's jes thinkin'," she said.

"So you the one what's scairt now, hunh?"

"I ain't scairt, Jeff. I's jes thinkin' 'bout leavin' eve'thing like this—eve'thing we been used to. It's right sad-like."

Jeff did not answer, and presently Jennie buried her face again and cried.

The sun was almost overhead. It beat down furiously on the dusty wagon-path road, on the parched roadside grass and the tiny battered car. Jeff's hands, gripping the wheel, became wet with perspiration; his forehead sparkled. Jeff's lips parted and his mouth shaped a hideous grimace. His face suggested the face of a man being burned. But the torture passed and his expression softened again.

"You mustn't cry, baby," he said to his wife. "We gotta be strong. We can't break down."

Jennie waited a few seconds, then said, "You reckon we oughta do it, Jeff? You reckon we oughta go 'head an' do it, really?"

Jeff's voice choked; his eyes blurred. He was terrified to hear Jennie say the thing that had been in his mind all morning. She had egged him on when he had wanted more than anything in the world to wait, to reconsider, to think things over a little longer. Now *she* was getting cold feet. Actually, there was no need of thinking the question through again. It would only end in making the same painful decision once more. Jeff knew that. There was no need of fooling around longer.

"We jes as well to do like we planned," he said. "They ain't nothin' else for us now—it's the bes' thing."

Jeff thought of the handicaps, the near impossibility, of making another crop with his leg bothering him more and more each week. Then there was always the chance that he would have another stroke, like the one that had made him lame. Another one might kill him. The least it could do would be to leave him helpless. Jeff gasped—Lord Jesus! He could not bear to think of being helpless, like a baby, on Jennie's hands. Frail, blind Jennie.

The little pounding motor of the car worked harder and harder. The puff of steam from the cracked radiator became larger. Jeff realized that they were climbing a little rise. A moment later the road turned abruptly, and he looked down upon the face of the river.

"Jeff."

"Hunh?"

"Is that the water I hear?"

"Hm. Tha's it."

"Well, which way you goin' now?"

"Down this-a way," he said. "The road runs 'longside o' the water a lil piece."

She waited a while calmly. Then she said, "Drive faster."

"A'right, baby," Jeff said.

The water roared in the bed of the river. It was fifty or sixty feet below the level of the road. Between the road and the water there was a long smooth slope, sharply inclined. The slope was dry, the clay hardened by prolonged summer heat. The water below, roaring in a narrow channel, was noisy and wild.

"Jeff."

"Hunh?"

"How far you goin'?"

"Jes a lil piece down the road."

"You ain't scairt, is you, Jeff?"

"Nah, baby," he said trembling. "I ain't scairt."

"Remember how we planned it, Jeff. We gotta do it like we said. Brave-like."

"Hm."

Jeff's brain darkened. Things suddenly seemed unreal, like figures in a dream. Thoughts swam in his mind foolishly, hysterically, like little blind fish in a pool within a dense cave. They rushed, crossed one another, jostled, collided, retreated, and rushed again. Jeff soon became dizzy. He shuddered violently and turned to his wife.

"Jennie, I can't do it. I can't." His voice broke pitifully.

She did not appear to be listening. All the grief had gone from her face. She sat erect, her unseeing eyes wide open, strained and frightful. Her glossy black skin had become dull. She seemed as thin and as sharp and bony as a starved bird. Now, having suffered and endured the sadness of tearing herself away from beloved things, she showed no anguish. She was absorbed with her own thoughts, and she didn't even hear Jeff's voice shouting in her ear.

Jeff said nothing more. For an instant there was light in his cavernous brain. The great chamber was, for less than a second, peopled by characters he knew and loved. They were simple, healthy creatures, and they behaved in a manner that he could understand. They had quality. But since he had already taken leave of them long ago, the remembrance did not break his heart again. Young Jeff Patton was among them, the Jeff Patton of fifty years ago who went down to New Orleans with a crowd of country boys to the Mardi Gras doings. The gay young crowd, boys with candy-striped shirts and rouged brown girls in noisy silks, was like a picture in his head. Yet it did not make him sad. On that very trip Slim Burns had killed Joe Beasley—the crowd had been broken up. Since then Jeff Patton's world had been the Greenbriar Plantation. If there had been other Mardi Gras carnivals, he had not heard of them. Since then there had been no time; the years had fallen on him like waves. Now he was old, worn out. Another paralytic stroke (like the one he had already suffered) would put him on his back for keeps. In that condition, with a frail blind woman to look after him, he would be worse off than if he were dead.

Suddenly Jeff's hands became steady. He actually felt brave. He slowed down the motor of the car and carefully pulled off the road. Below, the water of the stream boomed, a soft thunder in the deep channel. Jeff ran the car onto the clay slope, pointed it directly toward the stream, and put his foot heavily on the accelerator. The little car leaped furiously down the steep incline toward the water. The movement was nearly as swift and direct as a fall. The two old black folks, sitting quietly side by side, showed no excitement. In another instant the car hit the water and dropped immediately out of sight.

A little later it lodged in the mud of a shallow place. One wheel of the crushed and upturned little Ford became visible above the rushing water.

Questions to Consider

1. What does Bontemps's work say about the place of African Americans in the South during the early half of the twentieth century?
2. What types of images are associated with Jeff and Jennie? Why is the imagery that surrounds them significant?

James Aswell

1906–1955

"Banned, burned—and *Beautiful!*" This advertising slogan grew out of the fires of censorship—fires stoked by a prominent, fundamentalist minister in Natchitoches, Louisiana when he burned *The Midsummer Fires*. Such provocative publicity offered the kind of compelling endorsement about which James Aswell, author of the best-selling novel, could have only dreamed. Equally well known for his fundamental role in the downfall of New York's notorious Tammany Hall and for his literary achievements, Aswell nonetheless found himself unpopular in his home state, as a result of both his political and his literary efforts. Author, columnist, politician, and farmer, he wrote three novels, a collection of short stories, and over one hundred pieces of uncollected short fiction, but perhaps his greatest contribution to Southern letters was his crusade to subvert small town morality and hypocrisy.

Born on 27 April 1906 in Baton Rouge, Aswell grew up in a political family where education was valued and community service was expected. The election of his father, James B. Aswell, to Congress in 1913 caused the younger Aswell to receive his education in Washington D.C., where he then began a career as a reporter for the *Washington Times* at the age of 16. He later attended the University of Virginia, where he published a volume of poetry, *We Know Better* (1927). Aswell soon accepted a position with King Syndicate, the largest news syndicate in the world at that time, where he worked as an investigative reporter for ten years. During his tenure at King Syndicate, Aswell covered such events as the trial of the Lindbergh baby kidnappers and the unraveling of the Tammany-Hall political machine at the hands of Herbert Hoover's commission. These experiences with New York politics solidified Aswell's disdain for political cronyism, which would remain with him throughout his life. While in New York, Aswell enjoyed the glamorous life, attending glittering parties, mingling with celebrities, and becoming acquainted with Rosalind Hightower, the former wife of screen actor Melvyn Douglass. The couple soon married, settling in New York for several years prior to relocating to Natchitoches, Louisiana.

Aswell was strongly influenced by literary giants of his era, including F. Scott Fitzgerald, Erskine Caldwell, and Ernest Hemingway. Caldwell was a college friend with whom Aswell formed a literary group while the two were attending the University of Virginia. In 1929, Aswell's short story, "The Belle of Calomega" was purchased by *Collier's*, rapidly placing the young author in a similar position to that experienced by F. Scott Fitzgerald. Caldwell once remarked that Aswell "suffered ever afterward from the perils of too-early success," for like Fitzgerald, Aswell attained significant success rapidly, leaving him little opportunity to become accustomed to the pressures of fame, and as a result, his weakness for fast living and alcohol abuse ultimately led to his early demise.

Aswell's first novel, *The Midsummer Fires* (1948), was praised by critic Burton Rascoe as "the best novel of the past twenty years" and became a sensation, selling 1.45 million copies. The novel earned the Southern Author's Award in 1948 and drew comparisons to the works of Dante and James Joyce. His second novel, *There's One in Every Town* (1951), takes place in a small Southern town reminiscent of Natchitoches and attacks both the small-mindedness that Aswell saw in his hometown and the complicated racial system of the Jim Crow South. Despite Louisiana's racial history, which was unique in the Southern region, the 1940s saw the former French colony fully embracing both the Southern racial hierarchy and the wholesale oppression of the African-American community. Aswell's second novel raised eyebrows in his native South, in part because of its frank portrayal of a shameless, sexually adventurous young woman, and in part because of its matter-of-fact portrayal of racial passing. *There's One in Every Town* was well received by critics, who compared the novel to Edith Wharton's *Ethan*

Frome and F. Scott Fitzgerald's *The Great Gatsby*. The novel was also selected as a Book-of-the-Month Club alternate selection, ensuring its popularity with the reading public.

Aswell published a third novel, *The Birds and the Bees* (1953), and a collection of short stories, *The Young and Hungry Hearted* (1955). His work continued to receive awards, rewarding him for what he termed the "torture and delight" of fiction writing, and he saw his work republished in prestigious collections such as *Best Short Stories of 1950* and *Best Short Stories of the Past 25 Years*. He was described by the New American Library as a writer who was "rapidly . . . coming to the forefront as one of the greatest American storytellers alive today. Especially when he writes of his native South, a whole new community of fascinating and varied people come alive." Aswell frequently decried Southern writers, whom he felt belonged to a "depraved, sickly, decadent school," openly criticizing "Southern writers, particularly in Louisiana, [who] are infested with a disease, a disease of harping on moonlight and magnolias and iron lace until we tend to forget that human beings also live in Louisiana, in addition to historical phantoms." Despite the influence of a variety of famous writers, with whom Aswell corresponded, the author contended that "good writing is done in lonely rooms by lonely people," and that what the reading public needed was a "new crop of Louisiana writers with a little less iron lace—and a little more interest in the comedy and terror and beauty of man's fate."

The racially tense Jim Crow South did not embrace challenges to the prevailing cultural mores or accurate portrayals of the region and its racial struggles, and James Aswell fell victim to this oppressive political climate. Despite his prolific output—including numerous pieces which were positively reviewed by national critics—his work was attacked, banned, and publicly burned in his native South. Aswell's body of work fell into disfavor because he produced novels in which he frankly addressed threatening moral issues. In addition to casting racial passing in a sympathetic light, Aswell's most important work, *The Midsummer Fires*, openly depicted sexuality, ranging from realistic descriptions of the female body and teenage sexual discovery to alternate sexual lifestyles and impotence. Genteel Southern society found Aswell's frankness appalling, his affronts to their delicate sensibilities intolerable, and his none-too-subtle attacks on their firmly entrenched political and economic establishment overtly threatening. While Aswell's literary output did not decline during his later years, he increasingly felt the effects of the alcoholism that he battled throughout his life. He succumbed to a stroke on 20 February 1955, at the age of 48.

from The Midsummer Fires

This was Gael Ring's world. These were his people. This was his group. This was the net after twenty years. No, the gross. He walked briskly along the blue-tiled lip of the pool, balancing the tray of juleps and smiling.

He knew what they expected. He would be the Gael Ring they had devised in his image. It might even be the true Gael Ring, he didn't know; he'd act his part, the part they wanted. He was a jaunty figure, just under medium height, whose thick, curly hair was going white early. He had a suggestion of a paunch, but if he kept it sucked in no one would notice. He had been a very handsome young man; so much so that he had made women uneasy—they stalked commoner game, the lame bucks, the pimpled and the unanointed and the dumb. Now, bloating faintly, growing soft and beginning to smear around the edges, he looked at once younger and shockingly older than he was.

The water of the pool lay still in jagged diminishing light. It was six in April, an hour of intricate balance between day and dark, between hot and cool in the Deep South. Spring was a rickety caboose on the tail of uncertain winter; it was near an instant in a loud singing and then both were gone together. The implacable summer, the main business of the South, was always just coming or just gone; today had been hot and clear, with a hint of August malice. Already the bland-eyed coach dogs were staking out sanctuaries of shade under the disciplined hedges, the official roses, of Gael's dazzling yard. He offered the drinks to Anne and their friends with a fierce disinclination to look anyone in the eye. If he did they would see him clear and, worse, he would see them. But this passed and when he was comfortable on the sponge-rubber chaise he began to feel integrated with all the other evenings with these people and others in this place; only the faintest apprehension of inexplicit disaster—disaster surprisingly distinct from work or money—stayed on.

Anne said: "Oh, Galey, you're *such* an oaf of a butler! Where've you *been* all this time, and won't somebody find us a good servant?"

She was defensive already, of course, against the fact that they had no servants because they could no longer pay them. There was, yes, the huge Negress who cleaned in the morning and with whom they played a sort of game, finding new hiding places for liquor and cigarettes—she blandly admitted that she was powerless against temptation to steal these commodities but proof against any other form of larceny. She'd go, too, soon. Unlike the literary and dramatic characters who were "ruined" but managed to go on spending money, Gael had no money. He was broke literally, mortgaged over his head and penniless.

Anne sat sidewise on her deck chair, holding the goblet delicately with little finger extended. She was self-conscious as all women are sitting down, with half her mind on the arrangement of her skirt hem. His wife, Anne. So familiar and so strange. She was a redhead, freckled, small. Skin that had been alight with youth for layers down like the graduated tints in a movie lobby mural, had staled into a perpetual sallow flush. But she had bucked the years better than most. She'd only had to start rinsing her hair last year; it had been vivid, authentic flame, lashes, body hair and all. Suddenly and uneasily Gael recalled something he hadn't thought about in a dozen years—how at twenty-three he had been fascinated by the idea of pink pubic hair. Where had all those things gone? The wonder, the clean prurience, the quick and unforeseen fervors and gluttonies of life? Why had he married Anne? Sometime soon he would have to think this over and remember; now it was obscure. He tried to remember what she had been like in the line of the Rendezvous Club; the sanguine figure in the brilliant spot was blurred. A hard pang of pity took him. She was beaten, now, too; utterly vulnerable, trapped—with no weapons left for the closing long night of the poor.

Dan Dunn was speaking in his soft, allusive voice.

"Servants! The time is coming when there won't be any more personal servitude. You rich folks may as well get resigned to it."

Gael regarded Dan sleepily. Who was this man, why were they friends, why was he hanging around? Why was there always a Dan Dunn hanging around? This one was tall, stooped, tweedy. He had one cocked eye which he habitually squinted when talking, so that he seemed to be giving you a huge conspiratorial wink. There had been others like him in New York; studious, self-satisfied, prodigal with a special currency of cant words like liberal, social consciousness, neo-Fascist, reactionary—words which Gael had discovered long ago had no particular meaning but which were only countersigns of a cult. Convention badges. Dan had showed up at one of the big parties of five years back and somehow had attached himself to the Rings; once he had been accompanied by a mousy little wife with a red nose, but there had been a divorce and Dan had come back from a teaching job in one of the Navy cram schools with Cynthia, who was spectacular.

He looked at her. She had a masklike, alabaster face; the too-perfect kind of face, which may have been applied from without and may have been extruded from blank, pampered childhood. She was pretty without character, like a model. Her eyes were large, brown, churlish. They lingered a lot on Gael Ring, they had in fact come and cohabited with him in recent weeks but he had scarcely noticed in his mounting apprehension and despair.

She sat now, sedate on a white iron bench, her legs slimly hooked to minimize the fact that she was fractionally too tall. Cynthia Dunn's startling feature was her figure. There was the plunging pout of the neckline toward a ruffly, crinkly-white-off-the-shoulder play dress. There were the breasts, outlined incredibly high and pugnacious—Ring Girl breasts, Gael thought with a sexless start.

Dan Dunn flickered his bad eye at his wife and said to Gael: "You've always been a puzzle to me, Gael. You're intelligent, although you try not to let anybody know. You're an artist, or at some time in childhood you were, yet you're content to turn out cheap nudes, as if women's breasts were important in a dying civilization."

Gael gave Dan a white smile and murmured: "I'm just money-mad." He said it blandly and without malice. He was always bland and without malice. And he focused his eyes on Cynthia's upper torso.

But Tommy Riordan, chunky, freckled, boundlessly loyal, raised up on an arm. He lay along the brink of the pool in a pair of trunks; he was almost the only one who ever swam in the pool. A wildcat oilwell driller and ex-army top-kick, he was as odd as any of Gael's accretions.

"Bull," he said. "Put on another record, Dunn. Who are you to be telling Gael what to do? He's so far above you you're not even in the same league."

There was a pause, as if the scene were drawing its breath, heaving for the sharper tensions of the night.

Father Shiel said, "Don't quarrel. It's so lovely here by the pool." He was a young priest, thirty perhaps, with a scubbed face and clear blue eyes. For five years he had peopled his starved nights with color from the glitter of the Ring house and the Ring parties. Everybody knew that Gael was forever on the point of taking instruction or perhaps even taking it—being Irish he was incomplete without the Church, Catholics said, and naturally after the abandoned, heretical, New York years he would Come Home; but in their hearts they were saddened too by the sempiternal pattern of one Irishman (even a priest) trying to save another—an old trap for new tears. Now Father Shiel stood sedately handsome in his dark habit, smiling, his goblet held in a hand slightly extended, his black hair glistening; the stance was clerical; the goblet seemed a chalice.

"You mustn't quarrel," he repeated. "Truly, there's no profit in it."

"Profit!" Tommy whooped. "Don't mention profit around Dunn. He doesn't believe in the profit motive."

Dan Dunn blinked his defective eye at Tommy Riordan in a grimace of hard scorn.

"I understand Gael better than you do, I think, Riordan. I happen to know that he's going through a crisis now and he's just as fed up with—with the commercial, the easy stuff, as many of his friends are. Let me ask you. Have you seen any Ring Girls lately? I have a hunch he's working toward really fine, socially conscious work and I happen to be one of his friends who want to help him toward it. Neither a sycophant or—or a Fascist dupe."

"Them's hard words for a non-combatant," Tommy snapped, rising.

But Gael did not notice the mounting tempo of the quarrel. He was thinking: Fed up with the Girl? Jesus God, fed up with the Girl! She had gone away. She was skittering now, a faceless wisp, over the horizon of dark trees and pink cloud. If he could rise and follow fast, if he could gallop away from the scurrilous night, toward high day, he might overtake and know her again, wed her and draw her and hum with her at the height of the bees.

Anne's loose, uneasy laughter fluttered.

"Now, now!" she cried helplessly. "Maybe we're tight—all of us. Let's go indoors." Then in stricken lunacy: "Except you, Father. I mean, come indoors too but of course you're not tight."

Tommy Riordan was on his feet, flexing his shoulders to balance the chips, small square chin outthrust.

Dan's face worked; his game eye blinked while the other one remained fixed and malevolent.

"Only a coward would bring up the fact that my bad eye kept me out of the war. You were lucky enough to go but you don't even know what you fought for."

Tommy moved. "You call me a coward? You pansy of a fake professor?"

"Why don't you hit me? Sitting down! That's what a Storm Trooper would do. You could probably beat me up because of my eye. Of course that would settle the argument." But his voice broke a little toward falsetto.

Father Shiel stepped forward and put a hand soothingly on Tommy. "Don't, Tommy. Don't, Tommy."

"Oh, *fight* him!" Cynthia cried suddenly. "I'm so *tired* of that eye. Fight him. He could put a patch over one eye and then you'd be equal, wouldn't you?" She laughed with rasping blitheness. "Somebody get a patch."

Dan Dunn forgot Tommy and with a low feline screech sprang at his wife four feet away. He launched an expansive haymaker, fist doubled, at her face, before he had even regained his feet completely. Cynthia did a surprising thing. She moved her face about four inches, reached with catlike swiftness to grasp his free wrist. She jerked down and out in an expert Judo movement. Dan was whirled grotesquely downward. His shoulder struck the tile and he cartwheeled over neatly into the pool with a dull splash.

Tommy Riordan knelt to fish him out, laughing.

Anne said, "Oh, oh." Father Shiel shook his head. Cynthia hadn't moved. She watched, giggling. Gael felt far off, disinterested. What was all this angry activity about? He was filled with compassion for all of them, chirping and suffering in the collapsing dusk. Now the pool was an ink smear. A killdee landed on the far edge, ran wildly along the sleek tile and took off, dismayed. And the house, the lovely, white, stone-and-glass glory of a house, began to glow and glisten as the moon rose fast—a ghostly house, unreal, plastered with something, not moonlight, a pistache of mortgage notes.

But the main thing is, Gael thought, *the Girl has gone*. He peered abstractedly at Cynthia as the party disintegrated.

Questions to Consider

1. Aswell describes Gael's world in significant detail. How would you characterize that world? What attributes are especially present in this world? What others are notably absent?
2. Why is Gael concerned that the girl has seemingly disappeared? What is the importance of the girl in Gael's life?

Woody Guthrie

1912–1967

Woody Guthrie's songs, estimated to number over one thousand, forever changed the perception and function of popular music. Paralleling the African-American blues tradition in the South, Guthrie wrote about the human burdens of oppression, poverty, and random misfortune. His lyrics, which have influenced legendary songwriters such as Bob Dylan and Bruce Springsteen, continue to stand as a symbol of the common person's quest for acceptance and justice within American society.

Guthrie was born in Okemah, Oklahoma, on 14 July 1912. By the time he was 15 years old, his father had gone bankrupt and abandoned the family for Texas, a sister had died in a fire, and his demented mother had been institutionalized with a degenerative disease called Huntington's chorea. Guthrie survived on his own for a few years, then followed his father to Texas, supporting himself by playing the harmonica. Guthrie was so impressed by the tough Depression-era lives of the region's people that he began composing songs about their experiences. His songwriting was also influenced by the great dust storms of 1935 that occurred in New Mexico, Kansas, Texas, Colorado, and Oklahoma. The disastrous effects of the storms caused large numbers of families to migrate west in search of work. Many farm families from Tennessee, Georgia, and other Southern states who were still suffering economically from the Depression joined the westward migration, as did Guthrie himself.

He arrived in California in 1937 after walking, hitchhiking, and hopping freight trains to get there, developing a preference for the nomadic lifestyle. Witnessing firsthand the experiences of individuals dislocated by the Dust Bowl, many of whom could find work only as migrant farm hands, and focusing on topics of class, unfair employment practices, and wanderlust for the American West, Guthrie produced several classic songs during this period. "Pretty Boy Floyd" is the most popular of Guthrie's many ballads portraying outlaws as Robin Hood-like antiheroes. Guthrie's working-class sympathies led him into an involvement with the American Communist Party during the 1930s and 1940s; however, his hatred of fascism was so strong that he enlisted in the Merchant Marines and the Army during World War II. Following his military service, Guthrie moved to New York in an attempt to settle down. In 1946 he wrote "The Blinding of Isaac Woodward," a ballad based upon an episode of race-related violence in the Deep South. The song tells the tragic story of an African-American veteran who was blinded as the result of a confrontation with police after attempting to use a restroom reserved for Whites. Guthrie's 1943 autobiography, *Bound for Glory*, was well received by critics, and he wrote a series of popular children's songs during his New York years. However, his health began to deteriorate, and his behavior became erratic; he was eventually diagnosed with the same degenerative disorder that had taken the life of his mother.

Guthrie admitted himself to a New Jersey hospital in 1954, and checked in and out of many similar institutions over the remaining years of his life. In 1961 he was visited by a young and worshipful Bob Dylan. Guthrie died in a hospital in Queens, New York, in 1967, as his son Arlo was achieving success as a folk musician opposed to the Vietnam War. An essay in the *New York Times Book Review* eulogized Guthrie as "by far the most gifted of all the earth-poets, people poets"—and the author of that literary judgment was, quite fittingly, the great Southern poet, James Dickey.

Pretty Boy Floyd[1]

If you'll gather 'round me, children,
A story I will tell
'Bout Pretty Boy Floyd, an outlaw,
Oklahoma knew him well.

It was in the town of Shawnee,
A Saturday afternoon,
His wife beside him in his wagon
As into town they rode.

There a deputy sheriff approached him
In a manner rather rude,
Vulgar words of anger,
An' his wife she overheard.

Pretty Boy grabbed a log chain,
And the deputy grabbed his gun;
In the fight that followed
He laid that deputy down.

Then he took to the trees and timber
To live a life of shame;
Every crime in Oklahoma
Was added to his name.

But a many a starving farmer
The same old story told
How the outlaw paid their mortgage
And saved their little homes.

Others tell you 'bout a stranger
That come to beg a meal,
Underneath his napkin
Left a thousand dollar bill.

It was in Oklahoma City,
It was on a Christmas Day,
There was a whole car load of groceries
Come with a note to say:

Well, you say that I'm an outlaw,
You say that I'm a thief.
Here's a Christmas dinner
For the families on relief.

Yes, as through this world I've wandered
I've seen lots of funny men;
Some will rob you with a six-gun,
And some with a fountain pen.

And as through your life you travel,
Yes, as through your life you roam,

1. Charles Arthur "Pretty Boy" Floyd (1904–1934), the Georgia-born, Oklahoma-raised bank robber who reportedly turned to a life of crime in desperation over conditions of rural poverty.

You won't never see an outlaw
Drive a family from their home.

Blinding of Isaac Woodward[1]

My name is Isaac Woodward, my tale I'll tell to you;
I'm sure it'll sound so terrible you might not think it true;
I joined up with the Army and they sent me 'cross the seas
Through the battles of New Guinea and in the Phillipines.[2]

On the Thirteenth Day of February of Nineteen Forty Six
They sent me to Atlanta to get my discharge fixed;
I caught the bus for Winsboro,[3] going to meet my wife,
To bring her to New York City to visit my parents both.

Just an hour out of Atlanta, the sun was going down,
We stopped the bus at a drug store in a little country town;
I walked up to the driver and I looked him in the eye,
"I'd like to go to the washroom if you think we got time."

The driver started cussing and then he hollered, "No!"
So, then I cussed right back at him and really got him told;
He says, "If you will hurry, I guess we'll take the time!"
It was in a few short minutes we was rolling down the line.

We rolled for Thirty more minutes and I watched the shacks and trees,
I thought of my wife in Winsboro waiting there for me;
In Aiken, South Carolina, the driver he jumped out,
He come back with a policeman to take me off the bus.

"Listen, Mister Policeman," I started to explain;
"I did not cause no trouble and I did not raise no cain".
He struck me with his billy[4] and he cussed me up and down,
"Shut up, you black bastard!" And he walked me down in town.

He walked me along the sidewalk, my right arm he did twist;
I knew he wanted me to fight him back, but I never did resist;
"Have you your Army discharge?" And I told him, "Yes, I had",
He pasted me with a loaded stick down across my head.

I grabbed his stick and made a little run, and then we had a wrastle;
Another cop run up with a gun and jumped into the battle;
"If you don't drop that billy, black boy, it's me that's dropping you!"
I figured to drop that lead sap[5] was the best thing I could do.

They beat me over my head and face and we left a bloody trail
Goin along the sidewalk to the iron door of their jail;
He knocked me down upon the ground and he poked me in my eyes;
When I woke up next morning I found my eyes was blind.

They drug me to the courtroom and I could not see the judge;
He fined me Fifty Dollars for raising all the fuss;

1. African-American World War II veteran who was beaten and blinded by police in Aiken, South Carolina, for causing a "disturbance" on a bus after being denied permission to use the rest room.
2. Locations in the South Pacific where Woodward did his World War II service, earning a battle star.
3. City in South Carolina.
4. Billy club, a heavy wooden bludgeon carried by police.
5. Bludgeon.

The Doctor finally got there, but it took him two whole days;
He handed me some drops and salve and told me treat myself.

It's now you've heard my story, there's one thing I can't see;
How you could treat a human like they have treated me;
I thought I fought on the islands to get rid of their kind;
But I can see the fight's not over, now that I am blind.

QUESTIONS TO CONSIDER

1. Suppose that the crime committed by Pretty Boy Floyd in the poem of the same name had been committed today, in the city when you live. Write out the words that you think a TV newscaster would use to report the crime on the evening news. How does your account differ from Guthrie's?
2. Why does Guthrie frame the story of Isaac Woodward's blinding with references to Woodward's military service?

Randall Jarrell

1914–1965

Randall Jarrell belonged to a tragic generation of American poets that included John Berryman, Delmore Schwartz, Weldon Kees, and Robert Lowell, all of whose lives were beset by emotional turmoil. Jarrell himself was struck by a car and killed while walking along a highway near Chapel Hill, North Carolina, at dusk one day in 1965. The coroner's jury ruled the death accidental, but many who knew of Jarrell's recent psychiatric hospitalization and his characteristic melancholy were led to believe his death was a suicide. Despite his bouts with depression, Jarrell managed to accomplish much as a poet, critic, translator, and writer of children's books and one novel.

Jarrell was born in Nashville, Tennessee, and he attended Vanderbilt University there from 1931 to 1936, initially majoring in psychology before switching to English. His teachers at Vanderbilt included Fugitive Agrarians John Crowe Ransom, Robert Penn Warren, and Donald Davidson, and Allen Tate was a frequent visitor to the campus. Jarrell followed Ransom to teach at Kenyon College in Ohio, completing his M.A. from Vanderbilt by correspondence under the direction of Davidson. Lodging in a room in Ransom's attic while at Kenyon, Jarrell shared the space at different times with the poet Robert Lowell and the fiction writer Peter Taylor. Unlike his Fugitive-Agrarian mentors, however, Jarrell had liberal political views, leaning toward Marxism. He never really embraced his mentors' philosophical beliefs, although he published in their journals, the *Kenyon Review* and the *Southern Review*, and used their considerable influence to obtain teaching positions and attention from editors and publishers. And although his teaching base for 18 years was in Greensboro, North Carolina, Jarrell was more concerned with America as a whole, particularly as it participated in World War II, than with regional issues. The writer who exerted the greatest influence on Jarrell's poetry was not a poet but the founder of psychoanalysis, Sigmund Freud, as evidenced by Jarrell's interest in dreams, his symbolism, and his experimentation with female personas.

Many of Jarrell's most powerful poems came out of his experiences with the U.S. Army Air Corps during World War II. However, Sergeant Jarrell never saw action as a foot soldier or a pilot in either the European or the Pacific theaters. Rather, he remained stateside as an instructor in celestial navigation to pilots and navigators in their last leg of training before they entered the fighting abroad. With his full powers of imagination, he wrote about men he knew solely from his basic training and his duty assignment at an airfield in Tucson, Arizona, recreating their experiences in the midst of combat. Of course, Jarrell, too, must have kept abreast of wartime events through his voracious reading. But to give the reader a concise picture of war, mostly via his poetic imagination, was a remarkable achievement.

Jarrell was above all an impassioned teacher. In the waning years of his life he taught inaugural courses in what was later to be known as "creative writing." Also, he taught his "enthusiasms," as his wife called them, to almost everyone he met. Whatever he was enthusiastic about—visual art, music, tennis, literature, sports cars, professional football, or the career of Ernie Pyle, the famous chronicler of World War II—he wanted to make sure others shared those passions with him. Even in his poetry reviews he tried diligently to separate the good from the bad, and in this way he seemed almost prescient. Many writers were quite literally afraid of being reviewed by him.

The Freudian critic Harold Bloom coined the term "anxiety of influence" to describe the uneasy rivalry felt by young writers toward the strong writers who preceded them; Bloom further suggested that literary works should be read as rewritings of, and rebellions against, earlier works by a given writer's predecessors. Given Jarrell's Freudian groundings and his well-known ingratitude toward his Fugitive-Agrarian mentors for their help in launching his career—he went so far as to break off his relationship with Tate in the mid-1940s—Jarrell's poems should be read not for signs of continuity with Fugitive-Agrarian poetry, but for signs of difference. Indeed, Charlotte Beck has located an early student poem by Jarrell, "A Description of Some Confederate Soldiers," in which he rebels against the philosophy expressed in Tate's "Ode to the Confederate Dead," and the selections that follow demonstrate Beck's observation that Jarrell's World War II poetry addresses the realistic present rather than the romanticized past of the Fugitive-Agrarians' Civil War poetry.

The Death of the Ball Turret Gunner[1]

From my mother's sleep I fell into the State,[2]
And I hunched in its belly till my wet fur froze.
Six miles from earth, loosed from its dream of life,
I woke to black flak and the nightmare fighters.
When I died they washed me out of the turret with a hose.

Eighth Air Force[1]

If, in an odd angle of the hutment,[2]
A puppy laps the water from a can
Of flowers, and the drunk sergeant shaving
Whistles *O Paradiso!*[3]—shall I say that man
Is not as men have said: a wolf to man?

The other murderers troop in yawning;
Three of them play Pitch,[4] one sleeps, and one

1. World War II airman who manned the machine guns in the "ball turret," a small enclosed space on the bottom of a B-17 bomber plane.
2. "State" is being used as a metonym for the U.S. Army Air Corps or one of its B-17 bombers.

1. U.S. air combat unit, founded in 1942, which bombed German targets in Europe during World War II.
2. Encampment.
3. Famous aria from the opera *L'Africaine* by Giacomo Meyerbeer.
4. A card game that involves trumps.

Lies counting missions, lies there sweating
Till even his heart beats: One; One; One.
O *murderers!* . . . Still, this is how it's done:

This is a war. . . . But since these play, before they die,
Like puppies with their puppy; since, a man,
I did as these have done, but did not die—
I will content the people as I can
And give up these to them: Behold the man!

I have suffered, in a dream, because of him,
Many things; for this last saviour, man,
I have lied as I lie now. But what is lying?
Men wash their hands, in blood, as best they can:
I find no fault in this just man.

A Camp in the Prussian[1] Forest

I walk beside the prisoners to the road.
Load on puffed load,
Their corpses, stacked like sodden wood,
Lie barred or galled with blood

By the charred warehouse. No one comes today
In the old way
To knock the fillings from their teeth;
The dark, coned, common wreath

Is plaited for their grave—a kind of grief.
The living leaf
Clings to the planted profitable
Pine if it is able;

The boughs sigh, mile on green, calm, breathing mile,
From this dead file
The planners ruled for them. . . . One year
They sent a million here:

Here men were drunk like water, burnt like wood.
The fat of good
And evil, the breast's star of hope[2]
Were rendered into soap.

I paint the star I sawed from yellow pine—
And plant the sign
In soil that does not yet refuse
Its usual Jews

Their first asylum. But the white, dwarfed star—
This dead white star—

1. Formerly a German state whose capital was Berlin, Prussia was divided between Poland and the Soviet Union in 1947. During the 1930s and 1940s it was the site of several concentration camps.

2. A yellow cloth, six-pointed Star of David required to be worn on the breast by Jews in German territories, 1934–1945.

Hides nothing, pays for nothing; smoke
Fouls it, a yellow joke,

The needles of the wreath are chalked with ash,
A filmy trash
Litters the black woods with the death
Of men; and one last breath

Curls from the monstrous chimney. . . . I laugh aloud
Again and again;
The star laughs from its rotting shroud
Of flesh. O star of men!

A Country Life

A bird that I don't know,
Hunched on his light-pole like a scarecrow,
Looks sideways out into the wheat
The wind waves under the waves of heat.
The field is yellow as egg-bread dough
Except where (just as though they'd let
It live for looks) a locust billows
In leaf-green and shade-violet,
A standing mercy.
The bird calls twice, "*Red* clay, *red* clay";
Or else he's saying, "Directly, directly."
If someone came by I could ask,
Around here all of them must know—
And why they live so and die so—
Or why, for once, the lagging heron
Flaps from the little creek's parched cresses
Across the harsh-grassed, gullied meadow
To the black, rowed evergreens below.

They know and they don't know.
To ask, a man must be a stranger—
And asking, much more answering, is dangerous;
Asked about it, who would not repent
Of all he ever did and never meant,
And think a life and its distresses,
Its random, clutched-for, homefelt blisses,
The circumstances of an accident?
The farthest farmer in a field,
A gaunt plant grown, for seed, by farmers,
Has felt a longing, lorn urbanity
Jailed in his breast; and, just as I,
Has grunted, in his old perplexity,
A standing plea.

From the tar of the blazing square
The eyes shift, in their taciturn
And unavowing, unavailing sorrow.

Yet the intonation of a name confesses
Some secrets that they never meant
To let out to a soul; and what words would not dim
The bowed and weathered heads above the denim
Or the once-too-often-washed wash dresses?

They are subdued to their own element.
One day
The red, clay face
Is lowered to the naked clay;
After some words, the body is forsaken. . . .
The shadows lengthen, and a dreaming hope
Breathes, from the vague mound, *Life;*
From the grove under the spire
Stars shine, and a wandering light
Is kindled for the mourner, man.
The angel kneeling with the wreath
Sees, in the moonlight, graves.

Questions to Consider

1. What is the relationship of human beings to nature in the poem "A Country Life," and how does the idea of death, mentioned in the last stanza, contribute to this relationship?
2. Does the poem "Eighth Air Force" imply that it is morally right to kill during war, or morally wrong?

Margaret Walker

1915–1998

One of the few African-American Southern female writers of her generation who chose to live in the South, Margaret Abigail Walker was born on 7 July 1915 in Birmingham, Alabama, to a Jamaica-born minister and his music-teacher wife. The family later moved to New Orleans, where Walker graduated from high school at the age of 14; she then completed two years at New Orleans University (now Dillard University) before transferring to Northwestern University in Illinois. Earning her B.A. from Northwestern in 1935, she went to work for the Works Progress Administration in Chicago. During Walker's four years with the WPA she developed a close friendship with Richard Wright that would nourish both their literary careers.

On the strength of a handful of poems published in literary magazines, Walker entered the graduate English program at the University of Iowa in 1939. Her M.A. thesis was the volume of poetry that would be published as *For My People* in 1942. The volume was ahead of its time in celebrating African-American folk culture, as in the ballad "Kissie Lee;" exploring the paradoxical bond between Black Southerners and the land that had enslaved their ancestors, as in "Southern Song" and "Sorrow Home;" and calling for solidarity among African Americans in the face of racism and oppression, as in "For My People." Stephen Vincent Benet selected the book as the winner of the Yale Younger Poets Award, the most coveted poetry prize in the nation for poets under age forty.

Walker began teaching college after leaving Iowa, first in North Carolina and then in West Virginia, married, and gave birth to four children. In 1949 she accepted a professorship at Jackson State College in Jackson, Mississippi, which she would hold until her retirement 30 years later. In the 1960s, however, she took a three-year leave from teaching to complete a Ph.D. from the University of Iowa. Once again, her Iowa thesis would become a literary sensation.

Walker's maternal great-grandmother had been a slave on a Georgia plantation; growing up, Walker had often heard stories about her ancestor from her mother's mother, who resided with the Walker family. As an undergraduate, Walker had begun work on a historical novel about her great-grandmother, and she worked on the manuscript intermittently for 30 years. In Iowa City, Walker shaped the heavily researched material into the work that would be published as *Jubilee* in 1966. *Jubilee* told the story of the fifteenth child of a slave mother and White plantation master who survives many forms of abuse under slavery, only to endure additional hardships following her emancipation, including an act of violence by the Ku Klux Klan. Particularly because the book was published during the militant phase of the Civil Rights movement, it offended many readers with its theme of Christian forgiveness toward former slave owners. Vyry, the female protagonist of the novel, nurses her former plantation mistress for a time after the mistress has been widowed, orphaned, impoverished, and driven insane by the Civil War. However, many of the same critics who were disappointed by Vyry's "slave psychology" recognized that the novel broke new ground in incorporating a wide range of African-American folk traditions into its narrative. The folk material included proverbs, songs and spirituals, sermons, superstitions, herbal cures, and children's rhymes. Despite the controversy sparked by its seeming perpetuation of myths about the Old South, *Jubilee* won the Houghton Mifflin Literary Award.

In the decades that followed, Walker went on to publish several more collections of poetry, two collections of essays, a biography of Richard Wright, and a nonfiction book about the process of writing *Jubilee*, but the later works would remain overshadowed by her first two publications. Although never quite in step with what was timely in political attitudes or in literary tastes, Walker produced two books that should survive for all time.

For My People

For my people everywhere singing their slave songs
repeatedly: their dirges and their ditties and their blues
and jubilees, praying their prayers nightly to an
unknown god, bending their knees humbly to an
unseen power;

For my people lending their strength to the years, to the
gone years and the now years and the maybe years,
washing ironing cooking scrubbing sewing mending
hoeing plowing digging planting pruning patching
dragging along never reaping never
knowing and never understanding;

For my playmates in the clay and dust and sand of Alabama
backyards playing baptizing and preaching and doctor
and jail and soldier and school and mama and cooking
and playhouse and concert and store and hair and Miss
Choomby and company;

For the cramped bewildered years we went to school to learn
to know the reasons why and the answers to and the
people who and the places where and the days when, in
memory of the bitter hours when we discovered we

were black and poor and small and different and nobody
cared and nobody wondered and nobody understood;

For the boys and girls who grew in spite of these things to
be man and woman, to laugh and dance and sing and
play and drink their wine and religion and success, to
marry their playmates and bear children and then die
of consumption and anemia and lynching;

For my people thronging 47th Street in Chicago and Lenox
Avenue in New York and Rampart Street in New
Orleans, lost disinherited dispossessed and happy
people filling the cabarets and taverns and other
people's pockets needing bread and shoes and milk and
land and money and something—something all our own;

For my people walking blindly spreading joy, losing time
being lazy, sleeping when hungry, shouting when
burdened, drinking when hopeless, tied, and shackled
and tangled among ourselves by the unseen creatures
who tower over us omnisciently and laugh;

For my people blundering and groping and floundering in
the dark of churches and schools and clubs and
societies, associations and councils and committees and
conventions, distressed and disturbed and deceived and
devoured by money-hungry glory-craving leeches,
preyed on by facile force of state and fad and novelty, by
false prophet and holy believer;

For my people standing staring trying to fashion a better way
from confusion, from hypocrisy and misunderstanding,
trying to fashion a world that will hold all the people,
all the faces, all the adams and eves and their countless
generations;

Let a new earth rise. Let another world be born. Let a
bloody peace be written in the sky. Let a second
generation full of courage issue forth; let a people
loving freedom come to growth. Let a beauty full of
healing and a strength of final clenching be the pulsing
in our spirits and our blood. Let the martial songs be
written, let the dirges disappear. Let a race of men now
rise and take control.

Birmingham

I

With the last whippoorwill call of evening
Settling over mountains
Dusk dropping down shoulders of red hills
And red dust of mines
Sifting across somber sky

Setting the sun to rest in a blue blaze of coal fire
And shivering memories of Spring
With raw wind out of woods
And brown straw of last year's needle-shedding-pines
Cushions of quiet underfoot
Violets pushing through early new spring ground
And my winging heart flying across the world
With one bright bird—
Cardinal flashing through thickets—
Memories of my fancy-ridden life
Come home again.

II

I died today.
In a new and cruel way.
I came to breakfast in my night-dying clothes
Ate and talked and nobody knew
They had buried me yesterday.
I slept outside city limits
Under a little hill of butterscotch brown
With a dusting of white sugar
Where a whistling ghost kept making a threnody[1]
Out of a naked wind.

III

Call me home again to my coffin bed of soft warm clay.
I cannot bear to rest in frozen wastes
Of a bitter cold and sleeting northern womb.
My life dies best on a southern cross[2]
Carved out of rock with shooting stars to fire
The forge of bitter hate.

Southern Song

I want my body bathed again by southern suns, my soul reclaimed again from southern land. I want to rest again in southern fields, in grass and hay and clover bloom; to lay my hand again upon the clay baked by a southern sun, to touch the rain-soaked earth and smell the smell of soil.

I want my rest unbroken in the fields of southern earth; freedom to watch the corn wave silver in the sun and mark the splashing of a brook, a pond with ducks and frogs and count the clouds.

1. A song lamenting a death.

2. The actual Southern Cross is a constellation visible in the southern hemisphere. Also a slang term for one of the Confederate flags.

I want no mobs to wrench me from my southern rest; no
forms to take me in the night and burn my shack and
make for me a nightmare full of oil and flame.

I want my careless song to strike no minor key; no fiend to
stand between my body's southern song—the fusion of
the South, my body's song and me.

Sorrow Home

My roots are deep in southern life; deeper than John Brown[1]
or Nat Turner[2] or Robert Lee.[3] I was sired and weaned
in a tropic world. The palm tree and banana leaf,
mango and coconut, breadfruit and rubber trees know me.

Warm skies and gulf blue streams are in my blood. I belong
with the smell of fresh pine, with the trail of coon, and
the spring growth of wild onion.

I am no hothouse bulb to be reared in steam-heated flats
with the music of El[4] and subway in my ears, walled in
by steel and wood and brick far from the sky.

I want the cotton fields, tobacco and the cane. I want to
walk along with sacks of seed to drop in fallow ground.
Restless music is in my heart and I am eager to be gone.

O Southland, sorrow home, melody beating in my bone and
blood! How long will the Klan[5] of hate, the hounds and
the chain gangs keep me from my own?

Kissie Lee

Toughest gal I ever did see
Was a gal by the name of Kissie Lee;
The toughest gal God ever made
And she drew a dirty, wicked blade.

Now this here gal warn't always tough
Nobody dreamed she'd turn out rough
But her Grammaw Mamie had the name
Of being the town's sin and shame.

When Kissie Lee was young and good
Didn't nobody treat her like they should

1. Connecticut-born abolitionist (1800–1859) who led an unsuccessful raid against a federal arsenal at Harpers Ferry, Virginia, in the hopes of inciting a slave rebellion.
2. Nathaniel Turner (1800–1831), Virginia slave who was hanged for leading an 1831 slave rebellion during which many Whites were killed.
3. Robert E. Lee (1807–1870), the general who commanded the Confederate Army forces during the Civil War.
4. An elevated portion of an urban railway system.
5. The Ku Klux Klan, a secret organization formed in the post–Civil War South to promote White supremacy.

Allus gettin' beat by a no-good shine[1]
An' allus quick to cry and whine.

Till her Grammaw said, "Now listen to me,
I'm tiahed of yoah whinin', Kissie Lee.
People don't ever treat you right,
An' you allus scrappin' or in a fight."

"Whin I was a gal wasn't no soul
Could do me wrong an' still stay whole.
Ah got me a razor to talk for me
An' aftah that they let me be."

Well Kissie Lee took her advice
And after that she didn't speak twice
'Cause when she learned to stab and run
She got herself a little gun.

And from that time that gal was mean,
Meanest mama you ever seen.
She could hold her likker and hold her man
And she went thoo life jus' raisin' san'.

One night she walked in Jim's saloon
And seen a guy what spoke too soon;
He done her dirt long time ago
When she was good and feeling low.

Kissie bought her drink and she paid her dime
Watchin' this guy what beat her time
And he was making for the outside door
When Kissie shot him to the floor.

Not a word she spoke but she switched her blade
And flashing that lil ole baby paid:
Evvy livin' guy got out of her way
Because Kissie Lee was drawin' her pay.

She could shoot glass offa the hinges,
She could take herself on the wildest binges.
And she died with her boots on switching blades
On Talladega Mountain[2] in the likker raids.

Lineage

My grandmothers were strong.
They followed plows and bent to toil.
They moved through fields sowing seed.
They touched earth and grain grew.
They were full of sturdiness and singing.
My grandmothers were strong.

1. Derogatory term for an African American.

2. Mountain in east-central Alabama.

My grandmothers are full of memories
Smelling of soap and onions and wet clay
With veins rolling roughly over quick hands
They have many clean words to say.
My grandmothers were strong.
Why am I not as they?

Questions to Consider

1. Explain what you think the narrator means by the line "My life dies best on a southern cross," in the poem "Birmingham."
2. Critic Angela Davis has suggested that the heroines of songs recorded by Bessie Smith and Ma Rainey provided models of "protofeminist," empowered Black women decades in advance of the Civil Rights and Women's Liberation movements. Can you make the same argument for the heroine of Walker's ballad "Kissie Lee"? If so, why do you think that the song form was more hospitable to portrayals of such heroines than other literary forms and genres?

Part V

The Era of Civil Rights

THE SECOND GENERATION

1956–1974

The years from 1956 to 1974 marked a tumultuous period in Southern history and society, as shown in the arts and letters of the era. Southerners witnessed both the tempestuous struggles of the Civil Rights movement and the shimmering rise of prosperous Sun Belt cities. Beginning with the Montgomery bus boycott of 1955–1956 in Alabama—the first mass protest of the Civil Rights movement—the South entered its most painful and productive era of social change during the twentieth century. Televised images of police terrorizing African-American protesters in the streets of Montgomery and federal troops with bayonets guarding African-American high school students in Little Rock showed the South at its worst to the nation and the world. Contrasting media images such as rocket launches from Florida and glinting skyscrapers in Texas presented a high-tech South now in the vanguard of American innovation and progress. Leading cities of the Old South—Savannah, Charleston, Richmond, and others—were eclipsed by the emerging population centers in Atlanta, Dallas, and Houston, heralding a major socioeconomic transformation of the region. While old social problems like poverty and racism continued to lurk in urban shadows and rural corners, sharecroppers gave way to riveters and welders as Southern manufacturing overtook farming as the region's economic generator.

Many of the authors of the Southern Renascence continued to lead the way into the 1960s and 1970s. William Faulkner died in 1962, but writers like Robert Penn Warren and Eudora Welty continued to produce work of unsurpassed quality. A second generation of authors emerged, sustaining the literary upsurge that had begun in the 1920s and 1930s. The characteristics of modernism that provided the literary cornerstone for novelists like Faulkner and poets such as John Crowe Ransom and Allen Tate remained important in Southern writing, but from the mid-1950s onward, the seeds of postmodernism began to germinate and grow in Southern writing. The high modernism of the Southern Renascence was typified by themes like individual alienation, rejection of institutional religion, loss of community, and erosion of family networks and values and was marked by radical experimentation in narrative forms and methods. However, by mid-century a new wave of Southern writers came forward to expand and modify these approaches. The new generation of authors—among them Flannery O'Connor, Ellen Douglas, Walker Percy, Wendell Berry, and James Dickey—reinterpreted and reinvigorated the modernism of the previous generation. Their works differed from the classics of the Southern Renascence in that elements of the grotesque took on new prominence and often shaped highly distorted plots and characters.

During the 1930s and 1940s, Southern writers were immersed in a culture that increasingly drew national and international attention to its pressing social problems, particularly the continued existence of legalized racial segregation. Southern authors like William Faulkner, Richard Wright, and Lillian Smith powerfully called attention to the prevalence of violence and inequity in the Depression-era South. They paved the way for young African-American writers of the 1950s and 1960s, whose work contributed to the rising Civil Rights movement. Writers who articulated the Southern African-American experience to a widening audience included Margaret Walker, Maya Angelou, and Etheridge Knight. Margaret Danner, a Kentucky-born poet, explored African art and culture for clues to her African-American identity in the late 1950s, long before the search for African roots became a cultural phenomenon. At the same time, writers like Eudora Welty, Flannery O'Connor, and Carson McCullers offered fresh examinations of the lives of lower- and middle-class Whites. Walker Percy's novels reflected the struggle of upper-class Southerners to resolve conflicts between Judeo-Christian culture and twentieth-century existentialism, with its emphasis on human freedom and personal responsibility. Tennessee Williams's body of work explored the tangled intersections of gender identity and cultural repression, presenting a newly eroticized South. Overall, these writers refocused attention, drawing it away from the familiar topics of the Southern Renascence—preoccupation with the Old South and its convoluted legacies of pride, guilt, shame, and anger—onto new issues of cultural change and individual identity.

The Civil Rights Movement

Racial issues had plagued the South since the Antebellum period, heightening with the fall of the Confederacy and the passage of the Thirteenth Amendment abolishing slavery in 1865. Although servitude was officially outlawed as a consequence of the North's victory in the Civil War, the failure of Reconstruction led to new forms of legalized White supremacy. Beginning in the 1870s Jim Crow laws legitimized a separate but equal doctrine that allowed states to impose segregation in public facilities and institutions, continuing suppression of African-American civil liberties. These laws were enforced by both official and illegal means, including vigilante violence. The widespread use of lynching to terrorize African Americans and Hispanics in the South continued from Reconstruction well into the twentieth century and did not abate until after World War II. The prejudices that African Americans confronted on a daily basis became increasingly difficult to bear, and the systematic oppression that they endured made it clear that discrimination would not end without sustained intervention of the federal government and courts. Although President Harry Truman ordered the desegregation of the military in 1948, opening the door for integrated fighting units during the Korean conflict of 1950 to 1953, pervasive domestic changes did not occur immediately. The National Association for the Advancement of Colored People (NAACP, 1909) and other organizations seeking reform in the South had long sought the reversal of *Plessy* v. *Ferguson* (1896), for instance, which was the basis for the Jim Crow doctrine. Even after the momentous U.S. Supreme Court decision in *Brown* v. *Board of Education of Topeka* (1954), which overturned *Plessy* v. *Ferguson* and required the integration of public schools, the South continued to resist the forces of racial change.

However, opposition to *Brown* v. *Board of Education* and to full civil liberties for African Americans led to a White backlash in the South. Membership in the rejuvenated Ku Klux Klan (KKK) grew to levels not seen since the 1920s. The Klan proclaimed that racial integration was a Communist plot hatched in Washington, D.C., marking the beginning of the right-wing trend in the South and elsewhere to regard the United States courts and government as the enemy. The Klan's deadly terrorist activities employed church bombings, arson, and assassination attempts as a means of intimidating people of color. From 1954 to 1968, Klan leaders orchestrated unprecedented levels of violence, including religious terror. The Klan's fierce anti-Catholicism of the early twentieth century transformed itself into anti-Semitism, culminating in synagogue burnings. The *Brown* v. *Board of Education* decision also prompted the rise of White Citizens' Councils, the "country club" Klans of the Deep South, which were formed to prevent school desegregation and to preserve White political dominance. Many White politicians allied themselves to Citizens' Councils, which unlike the Klan, often met publicly in courtrooms and other official facilities.

The first large-scale response on the part of African Americans came in Montgomery in 1955. In that year, Rosa Parks, the mother of the civil rights revolution, refused to give up her front seat on an Alabama bus, in an era in which African Americans were relegated to the rear. Under the leadership of Martin Luther King, Jr., a year-long boycott of the city's bus system began. Bus boycotts spread to Baton Rouge, New Orleans, Birmingham, and Tallahassee. In 1956, the United States Supreme Court ruled bus segregation unconstitutional; however, just as important as the legal outcome were the public boycotts, which elicited acts of violence from the city police and the White community against the protesters. From this cradle of African-American protest and White backlash, King emerged as the national leader of the Civil Rights movement.

The next year, the South drew further adverse attention, when public schools in Little Rock, Arkansas, were integrated by force. The Arkansas National Guard was called out to block African-American students from entering the city's schools, leading President Eisenhower to recall the National Guard in 1957 and to send Army paratroopers with fixed bayonets to force back White mobs and to escort African-American students to class. This highly publicized incident marked the first time since Reconstruction that the federal government had used its authority to turn aside state efforts to maintain White supremacy. These Civil Rights-era struggles are reflected in the work of Maya Angelou, whose autobiographical *I Know Why the Caged Bird Sings* (1970) is set partly in Arkansas and presents the life of the author and her family as they struggle to survive Southern oppression during the waning years of White supremacy. Writers such as Sonia Sanchez and Alice Walker memorialized the struggle to obtain equal rights; public addresses by Martin Luther King, Jr. show the passion and commitment of civil rights activists.

In 1957, the Southern Christian Leadership Conference (SCLC) was founded in Atlanta by Rev. Martin Luther King, Sr., who turned to his son for leadership. The SCLC organized major civil rights demonstrations in the 1960s in Atlanta and Birmingham, as well as in Albany, Georgia; St. Augustine, Florida; and Selma, Alabama. Alabama was, in many respects, the climactic site of the Civil Rights movement because of the televised coverage of police horses trampling demonstrators in the march to Montgomery. Sit-ins and boycotts effectively challenged segregation. In 1960, African-American college students in Greensboro, North Carolina, sat down at a segregated lunch counter. Soon sit-ins spread to dozens of other Southern cities, and the Southern-based Student Non-Violent Coordinating Committee (SNCC) formed to increase pressure on Southern businesses to desegregate. An older, Chicago-based organization, the Congress on Racial Equality (CORE), mobilized to send Freedom Riders to the Deep South in 1961, another effective means of dramatizing the Black Freedom movement (see Map V–1). The increasing brutality of official White resistance reached new lows in 1963 in Birmingham, where city authorities assaulted demonstrators with police dogs, fire hoses, and cattle prods. These outrages led Martin Luther King, Jr. to compose his famous "Letter from Birmingham City Jail" while serving eight days in solitary confinement. The letter sharply criticized White Southern ministers for their inaction in the face of police brutality. King soon led the huge March on Washington and gave his famous "I Have a Dream" speech on the mall in front of the Capitol. In 1964, King received the Nobel Peace Prize, which lifted him to international fame and gave major impetus to the passage of the groundbreaking Civil Rights Act of 1964. This law chipped away at institutionalized racism.

The murders of three CORE and SNCC members in 1964 near Philadelphia, Mississippi, caused a national outcry against violent Southern opposition to the freedom movement and increased pressure to adopt additional legislation to establish political equality. President Lyndon Johnson, a Texan, soon won Congressional passage of the Voting Rights Act of 1965, which abolished literacy tests—a long-standing means of barring poor voters, regardless of race, from the polls. This Act strengthened the Twenty-fourth Amendment (1964), which outlawed poll taxes. Together these measures led to huge increases in voter registration, creating an electorate ca-

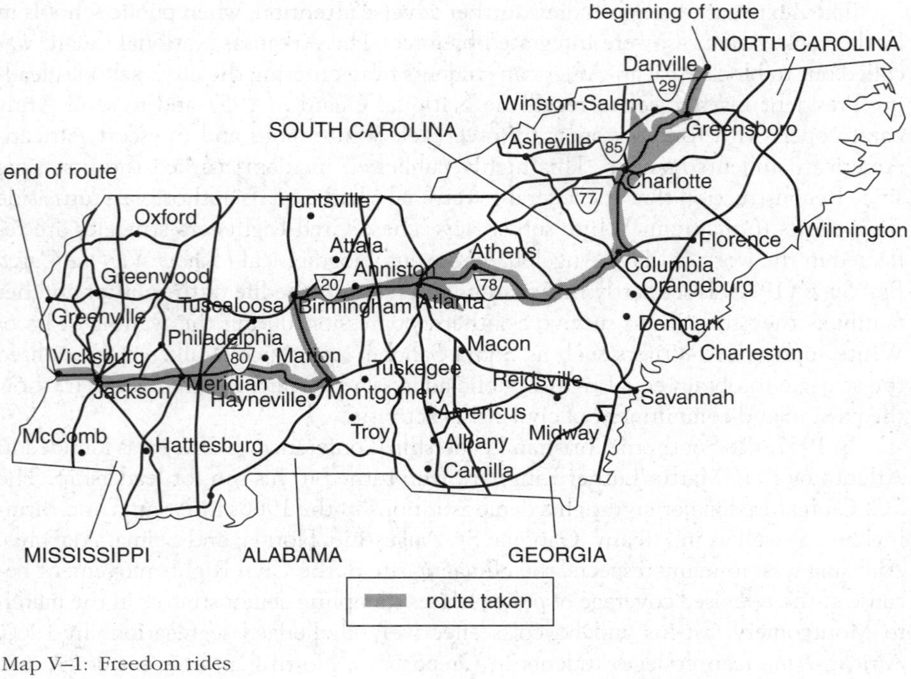

Map V–1: Freedom rides

pable of sending African-American candidates to office for the first time since Reconstruction. With the enactment of these measures, the period of mass demonstrations began to subside. However, King broadened the sweep of his protest movement by joining the rising tide of national opposition to the Vietnam War. He also questioned capitalist business ethics and spoke out against continuing economic injustice in the nation's cities.

The drive towards racial equality was not kindly met in many parts of the United States. Clinging to long-cherished notions that African Americans must be kept in deferential roles—accepting disrespect from Whites humbly, holding only menial jobs, and avoiding even the appearance of desiring a White woman—White supremacist groups such as the KKK often turned to violence. The 1955 Mississippi lynching of Emmett Till, a African-American teenager from Chicago, was a notorious instance of vigilante violence. The media attention attracted by this incident put Southerners on the defensive and swelled national support for the fledgling Civil Rights movement. While public lynching declined as a means of controlling minority populations, individual civil rights workers met violent ends in a number of cases. Medgar Evers, an Army veteran and NAACP official in Mississippi, was assassinated in Jackson in 1963. Malcolm X, a separatist with roots in the Black Muslim organization, was killed in 1965. Martin Luther King, Jr., the internationally celebrated proponent of nonviolence, was assassinated in 1968 in Memphis, where he was leading a sanitation workers' strike.

Both African-American and White literary artists addressed the racial unrest and upheaval that characterized the Civil Rights era in the South. These writers demonstrated the complex range of responses to this chaotic time: from entrenched White resistance to the belief in racial gradualism as a means of ending segregation to the moral defense of integration and pleas for political justice and social change. What became clear were the devastating and lasting consequences of cultural racism on entire generations of individuals and communities. Southern writers helped to move these issues into mainstream consciousness and to call attention to what was, after all, a deeply rooted national disease.

The Rise of the Urban South

The Civil Rights movement dominated Southern culture for decades, but alongside this ongoing struggle, the South was undergoing a rapid transformation, moving from a strictly rural economy to one with burgeoning urban centers (see Table V–1). Poet laureate James Dickey reflects this shift in the most infamous scenes of *Deliverance* (1970), which take place in the wilds of rural Georgia. Dickey's protagonists—middle-class White businessmen from Atlanta—represent not the rural South but the New South of cities and suburbs. Agribusiness was usurping the place of the small farmer, as sociologist John Shelton Reed notes when he points out that the percentage of cotton picked by machine increased from 10 percent to 90 percent between 1950 and 1970. The Southern farm family was becoming an anachronism as corporate farming displaced the small farmer. New fortunes also were being made in petrochemicals and energy markets.

The decline of traditional agriculture was but one of many factors contributing to the rapid growth of Southern cities. For example, the architecture critic Ada Louise Huxtable points out that the widespread availability of air conditioning in

Population By Decades

	1940	1960	1980	2000
Albuquerque	103,534	315,485	485,430	712,738
Atlanta	820,579	1,312,474	2,233,236	4,112,198
Dallas	653,119	1,180,595	2,055,284	3,519,176
Houston	627,311	1,364,569	2,753,155	4,177,646
Los Angeles/ Long Beach	2,785,643	6,038,771	7,477,239	9,519,338
Miami	267,739	935,047	1,625,509	2,253,362
New Orleans	631,869	987,695	1,304,212	1,337,726
Oklahoma City	398,043	584,721	860,969	1,083,346
Phoenix/Mesa	215,034	726,183	1,600,093	3,251,876
San Antonio	393,159	749,279	1,088,881	1,592,383
San Diego	289,348	1,033,011	1,861,846	2,813,833
Tampa/ St. Petersburg	291,622	820,443	1,613,600	2,395,997

Table V–1: The rise of the Sun Belt

the post–World War II commercial building boom made the construction of skyscrapers in the Southern region practical, and with them, the large-scale relocation of Northern business and white-collar workers to Sun Belt cities. Technological change offset the forbidding summer heat, making Southern cities suitable for modern commerce. Other material factors leading to the increasing urbanization of the South include the development of the interstate highway system, which linked the Northeast to the Deep South, allowing the easy transport of goods. The widespread installation of labor-saving kitchen appliances and laundry machines enhanced a new-home building boom. Radio and television stations prospered, providing an instantaneous means of disseminating news, which in turn, increased public awareness of social ills and newsworthy events.

The space race between the United States and the Soviet Union brought positive attention to the South. The National Aeronautics and Space Administration (NASA) mission-control headquarters at the Johnson Space Center in Houston became the focus of America's daring manned space program, and the launch site at Cape Canaveral in Florida became an international symbol for America's technological triumphs. With these highly public advances, many Southerners came to feel that their region at last had reached parity with the rest of the United States. While much remained to be done to improve secondary education and to eradicate poverty and hunger, the South was working to end its long period of social and economic isolation and to become a part of mainstream American culture.

Advances in business and commerce affected Southern men and women equally. Many women had filled the void in the job market while men were overseas in World

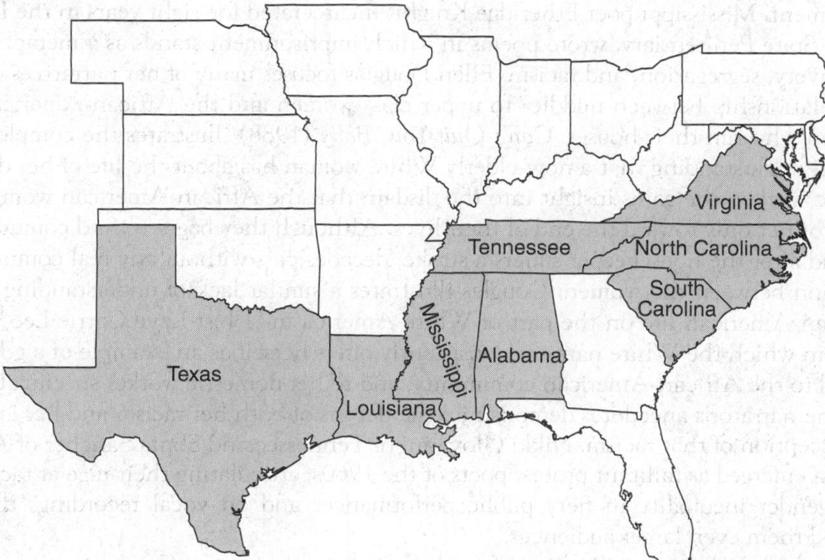

Map V–2: States without legislation outlawing gender discrimination in hiring practices, 1972

War II. When the men returned, women, who had tasted independence and economic freedom, were relegated to low-paying clerical jobs or forced back into the home. However, partly due to the pulsing economy of the postwar era and partly due to their own desire for better lives, women began to enter college in unprecedented numbers. Characters such as Flannery O'Connor's Joy/Hulga, who holds a Ph.D. in philosophy in "Good Country People," illustrate the limitations placed on women by Southern society. Joy/Hulga's mother, Mrs. Hopewell, laments, "You could say, 'My daughter is a nurse,' or 'My daughter is a school teacher,' or even, 'My daughter is a chemical engineer.' You could not say, 'My daughter is a philosopher.'" The story dramatizes a discordant—and culturally symbolic—duel of wits between a female academic and a male con artist posing as a Bible salesman who humiliates her by stealing her prosthetic leg and leaving her stranded in a hay loft. O'Connor's story exemplifies the limited scope of appropriate careers for women during the postwar years. Most colleges offered only a few areas of study to women—education, nursing, home economics, and music—limiting employment opportunities to teaching and nursing.

In spite of the social constraints on women's employment, White women began to realize better job possibilities (see Map V–2). These benefits did not yet extend to people of color—African Americans, Native Americans, and Hispanics—and poverty and political disenfranchisement remained harsh realities. The lives of rural African Americans had changed little in the 100 years between the Emancipation Proclamation and the Cuban Missile Crisis of 1962. Alice Walker's novel *The Third Life of Grange Copeland* (1970) focuses on the cruelties endured and inflicted within an African-American sharecropper and tenant farmer family during the Civil Rights movement. Mississippi poet Etheridge Knight, incarcerated for eight years in the Indiana State Penitentiary, wrote poems in which imprisonment stands as a metaphor for slavery, segregation, and racism. Ellen Douglas focuses many of her narratives on the relationship between middle- to upper-class women and the African-American women who run their houses. *Can't Quit You, Baby* (1988) illustrates the complete lack of understanding that a now-elderly White woman has about the life of her domestic worker; she gains insight into the disdain that the African-American woman feels for her only toward the end of their lives. Although they begin to find common ground after the housekeeper suffers a stroke, decades pass without any real communication between the women. Douglas illustrates a similar lack of understanding of African-American life on the part of White America in "I Just Love Carrie Lee," a story in which the White narrator consistently offers herself as an example of a good friend to the African-American community, and to her domestic worker specifically, but the narrator's anecdotes demonstrate the depths of both her racism and her lack of perception of that racism. Nikki Giovanni of Tennessee and Sonia Sanchez of Alabama emerged as militant protest poets of the 1960s, articulating their rage at racial and gender inequality in fiery public performances and on vocal recordings that earned them even larger audiences.

In earlier times, families lived for generations in the same towns and on family land, yet the Great Depression and subsequent economic developments led people to leave rural areas and migrate to cities to find work and a better life. Thus, the social composition of the South began to change. Children who had once been reared near their grandparents now saw them only during holiday visits or school vacations. The dispersal of family communities forced older Southerners, who typically would have been cared for by family members, into retirement centers and nursing homes. The old ways of life and extended family structures continued to prevail in rural areas, although small town life became less normative as jarring social changes and settlement patterns redefined the region within the span of a generation. For example, in "The Southerner," poet Karl Shapiro describes an old-style Southern gentleman intruding upon a social gathering up North; Shapiro's displaced narrator feels embarrassed by his link to the intruder who represents "The nonsense of the gracious lawn/The fall of hollow columns in the pines." Vassar Miller, a poet disabled by cerebral palsy from birth, lived alone with the aid of housekeepers in the family home she inherited from her wealthy father, writing about loneliness and isolation.

The breakdown of the traditional Southern family was often necessitated by the pursuit of greater material success. High-paying blue-collar jobs opened for Southerners who a generation earlier might have been lashed to a plow behind a rented mule. The Deep South petrochemical industry, for example, while a major environmental polluter from the 1930s to the 1980s, allowed young men who did not possess college educations to earn a solid income for their families. The oil and steel industries, ship and road building, and home and road construction fueled the Southern economy. White-collar jobs also arose in banking, insurance, manufacturing, textiles and furniture, grocery franchises, five-and-dime stores, and small businesses. A new category of employment emerged, and mid- and lower-level managers looked up the corporate ladder and saw a picture of the American dream that was finally coming South. If they worked hard and earned promotions, they could purchase a home in one of the new subdivisions and enjoy the privileges of middle-class life available in more prosperous regions of the nation. Public divisions over race, civil rights, women's rights, abortion rights, the Vietnam War, and relaxed sexual mores caused major changes in the South and across the nation.

Writers After the Renascence: The Second Generation

Following the outpouring of the Southern Renascence, writers from the South continued to create high-quality literature at an astounding rate. They derived inspiration from traditional Southern topics like race, place, and history, but they extended treatments of these and other subjects to include sexuality and gender and to draw out the implications of redefined social codes. Despite a tendency toward homogenization, the South continued to retain a strong measure of cultural difference. Not surprisingly, given the region's history, novelists focused on racial politics. Writers also reflected the effects of Southern religion on social interactions between men and women, Whites and African Americans, and upper and lower classes. Authors grappled with ways in which individuals reared with traditional Southern values and expectations could reconstruct their lives to confront modernity. For example, Georgia's Carson McCullers explores gender ambiguity in works such as *Ballad of the Sad Café* (1951). In this novella, she shows the denigration of a strong, sizable woman—a veiled lesbian character—who is exploited financially and emotionally by a male relative. In numerous plays, Mississippi's Tennessee Williams created characters who experience the alienation of alternative sexual identities and the turmoil associated with divergence from socially accepted behaviors.

Other authors focused on the difficulty of formulating an identity flexible enough to bridge the transition from Old to New South. Traditional Southern values like honor, place, family name, and personal reputation had either fallen into corruption or seemed inaccessible in the modern world. In *The Moviegoer* (1962), Walker Percy illustrates the hollowness of the forms and gestures of the New Orleans patrician class. His protagonist, Binx Bolling, spends his evenings watching movies and dallying with young women; his mentally ill cousin Kate is alternately manic and suicidal. The characters experience difficulties that derive from their edgy rejection of the elitist values in which they were indoctrinated. Shelby Foote, a boyhood friend of Percy's in Greenville, Mississippi, and author of the monumental, three-volume *The Civil War: A Narrative* (1958, 1963, 1974) approaches the shift in Southern values from a different perspective. Foote's dark novel, *Love in a Dry Season* (1951), demonstrates the rigidities of the Old South, drawing attention to the ways in which family name and honor can be used as weapons against the younger generation, when the protagonist loses the man she comes to love because of her father's unreasonable expectations.

Nonfiction forms enjoyed a resurgence during this period with essays and personal narratives finding new audiences as writers sought to articulate their views on the rapidly changing political and social climate in the South. Louisianian Walker Percy mused over the existential implications of being a Roman Catholic and racial liberal in the bigoted South. Kentuckian Wendell Berry argued his concerns for the environment and lamented the diminishing importance of agrarian traditions to the region.

Southern poetry responded to the changes that occurred nationally after the publication of Allen Ginsberg's *Howl* (1956). This defiant Beat-generation work, as well as the intensely emotional and autobiographical works of Confessional poets such as Robert Lowell, Sylvia Plath, and Anne Sexton, challenged the primacy of the "well-made poem," as written and extolled by New Critics such as John Crowe Ransom, Allen Tate, and Robert Penn Warren. The revolution seemed to reinvigorate Warren rather than putting him on the defensive. After a decade of poetic silence, he responded in 1957 with his volume *Promises,* which won the Pulitzer Prize for poetry. Another influential movement in American poetry in the second half of the twentieth century originated in the South, and yet was not "of the South." In the late 1940s and early 1950s at Black Mountain College in North Carolina, non-Southern faculty including Charles Olson, Robert Creeley, and Robert Duncan and students including Edward Dorn and Joel Oppenheimer reacted to then-prevailing New Criticism, not with the personal outbursts of Beat and Confessional poetry, but with a new school of impersonal poetry that envisioned the poem as a free-verse process rather than a polished and completed artifact. Their theories of so-called "Projective" verse would influence the major Southern poet A. R. Ammons, among others.

Eudora Welty and Flannery O'Connor remain two of the most significant voices of this period, populating their fiction with grotesque characters of the rural South. O'Connor's characters, such as the misfit in "A Good Man Is Hard to Find," embody the paradoxical nature of Southern culture as both pious and cruel. O'Connor negotiates the tricky boundaries between secular and religious realms, and her devout Roman Catholic sensibilities inform her understanding of marginalized Southerners, both male and female. She integrates the disparate elements of her fiction through her strong sense of place, making her Georgia settings seem both unique and universal. Mississippian Eudora Welty draws her characterizations from the small-town South, demonstrating the influence of place upon narrative. The narrator in "Why I Live at the P.O." typifies Southern eccentricity, as she moves her primary residence from her family home to the post office of the tiniest place in Mississippi. The narrator embodies the Southern woman's obsession with her looks, the keeping up of physical appearances, and her attractiveness to men, while showing the dark side of an extended family. "The Worn Path" presents a different set of family relationships. Old Phoenix Jackson remains devoted to her weak and sickly grandson, sacrificing her last days to function as his caregiver. As her name implies, she endures many trials to journey to town to obtain medicine for the young boy, but she is reborn as her devotion to family rejuvenates her.

The Civil Rights era in the American South was a time of widespread unrest and hostility, yet writers of exceptional insight arose from the turmoil. Southern authors from this era present the struggles resulting from race relations, redefined gender roles and expectations, and intergenerational conflicts. Although these issues are characteristic of the rapid social change across all levels and regions of American culture, the upheaval was most profound in the South. Rather than being limited by traditional Southern themes and responses, Civil Rights–era writers drew on the work of the previous generation of the Southern Renascence—many of whom remained active through the 1950s and after—to pose new questions and to employ innovative techniques to address their changing region and their place within it.

Civil Rights Era Chronology
1956–1974

1956
- School desegregation at Little Rock, Arkansas.
- U.S. Supreme Court outlaws bus segregation.
- Montgomery bus boycott ends in victory.

1957
- The Southern Christian Leadership Conference is founded to coordinate localized Southern efforts to fight for civil rights.
- Congress passes the Voting Rights Bill of 1957, the first major civil rights legislation in more than 75 years.

1959
- The National Academy of Recording Arts and Sciences presents the first Grammy Award.
- Motown is founded by Berry Gordy and, by the 1960s, features Marvin Gaye, the Supremes, and Stevie Wonder.

1960
- The Student Nonviolent Coordinating Committee is founded at Shaw University, providing African-American students a more organized place in the movement.
- In Greensboro, North Carolina, four African-American college students sit at a lunch counter at Woolworth's until they are served. When the story runs in the *New York Times*, they are joined by more students, both African-American and White.

1961
- Mississippi's NAACP field secretary Medgar Evars is murdered outside his home. His assassin is not convicted until nearly 30 years later.
- Freedom Rides. Bus loads of people wage a cross-country campaign to end segregation.
- South Vietnam signs a military and economic treaty with the United States leading to the arrival of U.S. troops.

1962
- Cuban Missile Crisis.
- President John F. Kennedy orders federal marshalls to escort James Meredith, the first African-American student to enroll at the University of Mississippi, to campus. A riot breaks out, resulting in the death of two students.

1963
- The March on Washington is the largest civil rights demonstration to date.
- Martin Luther King, Jr. delivers his "I Have a Dream" speech.
- President Kennedy is assassinated on 22 November in Dallas.
- Four young girls attending Sunday school are killed when a bomb explodes at the Sixteenth Street Baptist Church in Birmingham, Alabama.

1964
- President Johnson signs the Civil Rights Act of 1964, making segregation in public facilities and discrimination in employment practices illegal.
- Bob Dylan becomes popular with songs objecting to the condition of American society.
- Martin Luther King, Jr. wins the Nobel Peace Prize at Oslo, Norway.
- The Beatles release "I Want to Hold Your Hand," igniting the British Invasion.

1965 • Congress passes the Voting Rights Act of 1965, making it easier for African Americans to register to vote. Literacy tests become illegal.
- Malcolm X is assassinated.
- Bloody Sunday: African Americans begin a march to Montgomery in support of voting rights but are stopped at the Pettus Bridge by a police blockade. Police use gas, whips, and clubs against them.

1966 • 190,000 U.S. troops are sent to Vietnam.

1967 • Thurgood Marshall becomes the first African-American justice appointed to the U.S. Supreme Court.

1968 • Civil Rights Act of 1968 prohibits discrimination in the sale, rental, and financing of housing.
- Martin Luther King, Jr. is shot on the balcony outside his hotel room.
- Robert F. Kennedy is assassinated on 5 June in Los Angeles, after winning California's Democratic presidential primary election.

1969 • The U.S. Supreme Court orders immediate desegregation of the nation's schools.
- 500,000 people attend the Woodstock Music Festival in Bethel, New York.

VOICES IN CONTEXT

Proletarian Writers of the South

In the early decades of the twentieth century, labor remained unorganized in the South while it strengthened in other parts of the nation. Part of the reason for the South's resistance to unionism was its fundamental economic difference as a farming region based on the plantation system of agriculture. This difference was widened by institutionalized White supremacy in the South, which allowed the owning class to keep White and African-American low-income workers divided through racial fear and intimidation. Cultural reinforcement for worker compliance came as well from the region's churches, which often preached acceptance of economic suffering. During the chaos of the late 1920s, as the nation teetered on the brink of the Depression, union organizers in the North began to direct their activities toward workers laboring under unsafe conditions in Southern cotton manufacturing plants.

The first major uprisings of Southern labor occurred in textile and hosiery manufacturing in the region known as the Piedmont, the area between the Southern highlands and lowlands stretching from Virginia to Alabama. The Southern textile industry had grown rapidly in the early twentieth century as New England mill owners moved South for cheap labor. Working and living conditions were abysmal in the Piedmont mills. Employees worked ten-hour shifts six days a week in unsafe weaving rooms for little more than a dollar per day and lived in overcrowded, squalid company towns. Many employees were women and girls. They often died young, work injuries were common, and 40 was considered old. Company paternalism, religious indifference, and class discrimination kept these "lintheads" trapped in a harsh cycle of overwork, malnutrition, and disease.

Gastonia, North Carolina, near Charlotte, was home to the Loray Mill, the largest in the South with more than 2,200 employees. Setting the pattern of out-of-state ownership, Loray had been operated for years by the Manville-Jenckes Company of Rhode Island. The distance of the owners from the factory allowed them to ignore the systematic misuse of their workers. The National Textile Workers Union (NTWU), a radical collective affiliated with the Communist Party USA (CPUSA), led an organizing effort. But Northern organizers were unprepared for the pent-up fury of the Carolina mill hands. On 1 April 1929, nearly all workers walked out, demanding union recognition, a 40-hour/five-day work-week, a minimum wage, and an end to the dangerous "stretch-out" system of forcing one employee to tend several machines at once. Wealthy mill owners, already closely aligned with North Carolina's political elite, received government backing in the form of the National Guard. These soldiers escorted "scabs" (employees hired to replace strikers) to the mill and broke up picket lines with bayonets. Many of the strike organizers and participants were women, and they were abused and terrorized by both the police and the Ku Klux Klan, who were often one and the same. A mob of masked men, for example, was allowed to destroy the Union's headquarters and torch food supplies. The strikers armed themselves, and both sides suffered fatal shootings, but only strikers, not guards, were ever convicted of crimes.

The murder on 14 September of Ella May Wiggins, the tragic heroine of the strike, provoked national outrage more than five months after the strike began. A 29-year-old mother of five, Wiggins was a strike leader, speechmaker, and songwriter. On her way to a union meeting she was ambushed while riding in an open truck and shot dead by Loray gunmen in front of numerous witnesses, but at trial not one of the five defendants was convicted. Her murder presaged the failure of the union. No match for the combined forces of big business and state authority, the strike crumbled. Workers won a few concessions, such as the eventual abolition of night work for women and children. However, the brutal tactics of the mill operators raised indignation among Southern liberals and led several Left-leaning novelists to address the need for social change in the South: notably Erskine Caldwell but also women writers like Olive Tilford Dargan and Myra Page. Caldwell's most ambitious work, *God's Little Acre,* portrays a fictional Southern textile strike that turns violent; his novel stands as one of the lasting works of American protest fiction. In the case of the two women novelists, each author's major work is a specifically Gastonia-based strike novel with a strong female character at the center. Each of these protagonists comes down from the Southern highlands to work in a Piedmont cotton mill modeled on Loray. She eventually rebels against her exploitation and becomes politically conscious and even militant in her resistance to domination.

Olive Tilford Dargan (Fielding Burke)

1869–1968

Born in 1869 in Grayson County, Kentucky, Olive Tilford Dargan lived for nearly a century writing poetry, drama, short fiction, and novels. Dargan witnessed and recorded the industrialization of the American South, and the devastating conditions that resulted for the poor, whose efforts provided the cheap labor source that allowed factory owners to prosper. Her most memorable fiction highlights the life-threatening effects of mechanization on the powerless, poverty-stricken class of factory workers. Dargan is most often remembered as a regional writer whose protest novels, written under the pseudonym Fielding Burke, revealed the plight of the working class and realistically portrayed Southern highlanders.

The daughter of schoolteachers Rebecca Day Tilford and Elisha Francis Tilford, Dargan helped her father in his schoolroom until she reached the age of 14, when she began teaching alone, replacing her mother, who had fallen ill. Dargan stayed on at her father's school until she secured a better position in Missouri, and later entered Peabody College in Nashville on a scholarship. After completing two years at Peabody, Dargan enrolled in courses at Radcliffe College in Cambridge, Massachusetts. While living in Cambridge, she met would-be poet Pegram Dargan. The couple married and moved to New York, intent on launching their respective literary careers. While Olive Dargan was soon publishing in prestigious magazines such as *Scribner's, Century,* and *McClure's,* her husband only succeeded in publishing his poetry at his own expense. The couple later moved to North Carolina, but following the loss of their only child, a daughter who was born prematurely, they rarely lived together. Dargan moved to England, where she continued to write and publish. She became intrigued and horrified by the sufferings of the lower classes and by the idea that violence might be necessary to end their exploitation. Shortly after her return to the United States, her husband drowned in a bizarre accident that was never fully explained.

Dargan's comments on the sad plight of poor industrial workers and the ways in which the capitalist system exploited them became increasingly direct. She used her writing to raise public awareness of the oppression of the underclasses and became acquainted with the ideology of the Communist Party. Dargan may not have actually joined the Party, but she described herself as "vivid Red" on numerous occasions. Her anticapitalist ideals influenced her writings for the remainder of her career, much of which was spent in the seclusion of her rural North Carolina home following the death of her husband. She died quietly in 1968 in a nursing home in Asheville.

Dargan's body of work includes drama, collections of poetry and short stories, and several novels. Her most compelling novel, *Call Home the Heart,* tells the heart-wrenching story of a destitute mountain woman, Ishma, who must choose between a way of life that offers the elusive promise of financial solvency and one of abject poverty shared with the man she loves. Although she leaves the mountains in search of economic success, Ishma ultimately returns to agrarian life with her beloved, rejecting the exploitative grind of the mill towns in an act of love for her homeland and family. Not surprisingly, given her political leanings, Dargan's novel condemns the capitalist system that reduced the quality and financial stability of Ishma's life. *Call Home the Heart* promotes Dargan's belief that commercialism was the source of suffering, deprivation, and premature death for the oppressed members of the underclasses.

from Call Home the Heart

A Wife She Must Carry, Heigh-Ho!

The middle South was again under the spell of April. Ishma Waycaster and Britton Hensley had been married four years. Four years since that night of fragrance and a wan moon, of disaster and aching joy.

Ishma sat on the cabin porch, looking over some scraps of print and gingham which she had taken out of a tow bag. Far to the left sat Laviny, sorting beans, with aunt Cynthy Webb in a chair near her. Against the wall back of them was the big, invalid's chair, piled high with farm miscellany and household clutter. On the house and its surroundings the four years had left no sign of alteration for the better. The cabin roof wore a more mottled and mossy coat, the walls had lost more chinking, and the long porch sagged and rallied on its faithful locust pillars. The only thriving thing in the yard was the blue balsam. It had struggled upward and outward, and now exhibited an almost portly beauty. Everything else in the unkempt place advertised poverty and indifference.

* * *

Ishma was sitting on the rock wall of the spring looking down at the water. It was black in the twilight, but she knew it was crystal clear. Perhaps that was the way with things around her. They looked black, but maybe they weren't.

It was always this way with Ishma. Whenever she got out of the house and sat alone, her mood, after the first few breaths of release, became self-accusing. She had the sky, the woods, the winds, the stars; all so clean and mighty. How could she let anything that happened in a little house bother her? She ought to bring it help—be to the house what the sky and woods were to her. Yes, that was the way she ought to stand in life. Not forget that the winds and the stars were behind her—that she could lean against their clean strength. Youth and health! She and Britt possessed both. How could a few little debts matter? They would soon sweep them aside and forget them. Her anger was gone. She was sorry for Julie. But of course Britt couldn't have that money. That was hers.

Why, she believed she was hungry. She'd forgotten to eat any supper. A tin cup hung on a nail in the spring-house door. She filled it with milk, and as she drank she heard a whistle on the lower trail. Steve was getting in. Big old Steve, like his father, with jolly words for everybody, and never a dollar ahead.

He had come up the trail whistling, but when he saw no light and felt the silence, he advanced cautiously. Here was his opportunity. He crossed the porch to the ladder-like steps nailed to the wall, and climbed to the loft. Up there, under the shattering roof, smelling of rot and moss, he had his sleeping bunk and his few clothes. Hastily he began stuffing his things into an old kit. When Ishma, her feet in sneakers, and stepping lightly as always, entered the kitchen with the jar of cream, he didn't hear her. He was over the big room, absorbed and hurried. Ishma, finding the house silent, supposed that he had passed it and gone on up the hill. Of course he had heard all about the fire. She went back to the big chair and again laid herself down. It was good to have the place to herself. Her mother must have gone with Bainie and Julie up the hill. They had slipped away from her, afraid she might go. That was fine! All she wanted was a chance to get up to the fire by herself. But she'd rest a few minutes before she started. She'd go, and Britt would forgive her when he found it hadn't hurt her at all. And that nonsense about markin' the baby—she knew there was nothing to that.

She had thought she would enjoy the silent house, relieved of its assertive human presences. But too quickly it began to oppress her with its own claims to dirt and disorder. She forgot the crystal water and clean-swept skies, and thought of the bones which she had heard Jim's dog crunching under her bed the night before. She knew the floors had two days' litter on them. All of the quilts needed washing. She wished she could have two sheets on her bed. Bainie quarrelled because she used *one*. Bainie and Jim slept between the quilts. Every pillow case was worn out. She had to put her pillow under the sheet. What would the doctor think? She couldn't be sick in that room again. She couldn't have Bainie bringing her soppy messes, whining at every step. She couldn't. She would never breathe again if she had to stay in that room. Jed said he would bring the money and the wagons in three days. Could she wait three days?

She began to feel sick. It was that sour mud in the yard. She'd get up and go on to the fire. But she was strangely heavy, and lay still. There was a noise in the loft. She listened. Steve must be up there. She wanted to call out, but that would be an effort too. When he came down with a kit-bag in his hand, he started off almost on a run, without seeing her. She knew what it meant. Steve was leaving. He was going away.

"Steve! Steve!" she shouted. Forgetting all heaviness, she was up and running after him. "Steve, you're leavin' out!"

He stopped, and waited until she came up. "What if I am? Whad I stay here for? You reckon my brain's all bug-juice? Whad I stay for?"

Ishma felt stunned. "Nothing," she replied.

"You got it right. Nothin'."

"Where'll you go, Steve?"

"It'll be the navy this time, I reckon."

"Oh, Steve, you'll never come back!"

"You needn't keer. I'm no good here to anybody. A feller kain't git along here at all without a little money to stock up with an' set him right. He'll stand in his tracks till the wind blows him down. If a man's got his land paid for, an' stock to work it, an' machinery, an' the right seed to put in the ground, an' 's able to hire help in a pinch, an' there's market for his stuff without givin' it all to the railroad, or the man at the other end, I reckon he can get along in the mountains. But when he's got nothin' but his two bare hands, he kain't swing it. Not nowadays."

"You're going to leave *us* here."

"Well, I kain't carry you all along with me, can I? An' I tell you, Ish, it's no bed o' roses I'm going to. It's a slave's life, but this is a dog's, an' a slave, after all, is human, an' can look out an' see something. But it ain't no cinch. I want a home same as anybody else. I'd stay here an' marry that darned little Julie, only me an' my kids couldn't eat rocks. 'By, Ish!"

She was clinging to him, and he wouldn't push her off. "Take me with you, Steve," she was crying. "Take me with you!"

"Lord, girl, whad I do with you?"

"I'll work, Steve."

"You ain't able now, Ish."

"I'll work right on. I'll not miss more'n two weeks. You don't know how I'll work. You can get me a place."

"Nobody wants a woman in your fix, Ish. An' I won't have a cent to pay for you when you're down. It'll take me a while to save up something. I'm strapped now. Britt's all right, Ish. You've got a good man. Wish I's half as good. You stand by Britt."

She was still holding to him. Her hands wouldn't loosen. "I'm going with you, Steve. I've got to get off this mountain."

"Now you listen to me, Ish. A woman's a woman. She's bound to carry the baggage in this life. They's no gittin' out of it for her. A man can walk off any time, but a woman kain't. God, or Nature, or something we kain't buck against, has fixed it that way. You make up your mind it's all right. That's all you can do right now. Goodbye, old sis. I've got to beat it 'fore mom comes along. You tell her I'll send her ever' cent I can spare. An' I won't fergit *you* either."

He pushed her from him then, and ran. She watched until she could see his tall figure no longer. Her gallant shoulders were slumped as she turned back to the house. Her head had forgotten utterly its deer-like poise. She was aching from head to foot, as if she had been thrown back from a stone wall against which she had violently flung her whole body. But her mind hurt most. Her thoughts seemed to be like fine stabbing needles that couldn't make their way out anywhere.

She was asking so little of life, she thought. That was her great accusation. So little of life; when, in fact, she was asking for more than life has ever given to anyone; an understanding of itself.

In her early years Ishma had rested sanely on her love of beauty in nature, and her unthinking union with it. She had moved largely and unconfined in that roominess of personal being. A leaf in the dawn, glittering on its twig, belonged to her as much as her shaken, clinging curls. A glance upward at an amiable, drifting cloud could ease a growing irritation within her, and sometimes her sense of grace would not abandon her for a whole day. A storm on Cloudy Knob would leave her feeling that she had taken a breath as deep as her being. Wind, curving about a ridge of silver poplars, could sweep life clean.

With adolescence, beauty was not enough. Nature made her lonely, hungry, impatient. An inquisitive denial of sensuous adequacy became her torture. Then Britt had entered, overwhelming, undeniable, restoring. Being was again complete. For how long? Surely their love had not vanished; it had strangely deepened; but where was its joy, its fullness, its soothing finality? She could still surge and grow dizzy with the thought of those first months together; but memory was not life. Life was again barren. It was a stripped, stark question. It hurt all the more because of Britt and Ned and the little new soul on its way into the barrenness, where its cry would never be answered.

Ishma didn't know that, to the mind born for questing, somewhere on its burning road, love and beauty must become hardly more than little nests for the comfort of the senses. Unaware of her high demands, she mistook the source of her suffering. Clean sheets and a sweet-smelling door might help but would never heal her mind.

She stumbled toward the house, and halted near it, despairingly turning her eyes to the sky. There, in the north, was a quivering, growing light. Thought of the fire seized her. She would go to the ridge. No one would be on Lame Goat Knob. From there she could look down on that burning glory. It could hurt no one. It could only help.

She heard someone opening the back door of the kitchen, and moved softly to the west end of the house. There she waited until her mother passed through to the front, then she started up the hill.

Laviny came out on the porch talking. "Ishmalee, them crazy gals went on to the fire. Where you at anyhow?" She went to the end of the porch and called her daughter, who was fifty yards up the hill, panting and pressing her heart.

"She's cruisin' aroun', I reckon," concluded Laviny, "an' I hope it will do the pore thing a little good. I'll go to bed soon as I've hung the lantern. Steve's shore to git in tonight, an' no moon to hep him." He would need no help, she knew; but the lantern was her way of telling him he was welcome in spite of her bitter tongue. "Bainie can sniff till her nose is hot," she said, as she lit and hung it to the corner post nearest the down trail, "but I've got a right to hang out a light fer the only boy-child I've got that the Lord let live."

It was three hours later when Ishma came around the house from the upper yard, struggled up the steps, and fell down on the porch. Laviny, hearing a noise, came out, her head wrapped in a large handkerchief. She looked about, and by the help of the lantern discovered Ishma.

"I thought I heard ye," she said, crossing to her in a small fury. "Whad you mean, makin' me lose sleep like this? You've 'bout killed yerself, an' t'other one too, I reckon."

"I'm all right," Ishma faintly assured her.

"You look it! Where you been? You ain't been to the fire?"

"No."

"I knowed you had more sense than to go."

"I couldn't get there. My breath kept giving out. I nearly choked more'n once."

"Thank the Lord! I'd laid out to give you a good combin' down, but looks like you've had enough. You git to bed now."

"I'll stay out here awhile. I want all the air I can get. My breath's comin' hard."

"Kain't I git something to hep ye?"

"No, go to bed, mommie."

"Well, I got to have my rest, an' they's no danger you slippin' off agin. You can please yerself 'bout layin' out here. But you'd better git on the chair."

Laviny went back to bed. "She'll lay still," she told herself, as she dropped to sleep. "No need to tie a cow with a broken leg."

Ishma reached the chair, and after lying still a few minutes she was breathing naturally. "My way is down the mountain, not up," she said. And she, too, went to sleep. It was sometime after midnight when she was awakened by footsteps nearing the cabin in the rear. That might be Britt coming down. No, it wasn't his step. Thinking she would ask about the fire, she went to the end of the porch, where she sat down, leaning against the corner post, with the lantern above her head. Beyond its rays the night was black. She had only a moment to wait before a man came into the faint circle of light, and she saw that it was Rad. He stopped when he saw her, and spoke her name. When she didn't answer, he softly repeated it.

"Yes, it's me, Rad."

His feet felt like stone, but he couldn't stand there without saying something. "I'm goin' down. They've got enough up there without me. We got the fire purty well shut off."

"Are the haystacks well out of danger, Rad?"

"They are now. But it looked fer a while like they'd have to go. We all laid ourselves out to save 'em. What you settin' up for?"

"Resting a little, out here by myself, and waiting for Britt. I like to sit in the night by myself sometimes."

"If you like it black you've got what you want tonight."

He came closer to her, and the look on his face made her say, "You go on, Rad."

"Yes, I'm goin'. Goin' furder 'n you think, Ishma. I'm leavin' out."

Oh, men could always go! "Where to, Rad?" Her cool voice had sharpened a little.

"Anywhere is better'n here if I kain't have you, Ish. I've been savin' a long time, to have something to go out on. Ever' since you got married. I made up my mind then I'd leave out. I'll never quit thinkin' about you till I git where I kain't see you."

"You don't see much of me, Rad. Not enough to bother you, I'd say."

"But I know you're over here, only three coves from my place, an' it's all I can do every day o' my life to keep from tearin' across where I can say a word to you."

"You know better than to talk to me like that. I know better than to listen too. You go on, Rad. And I hope you'll like it where you're going."

"I'm all ready to leave at daylight. I'm takin' Bud Wells' car over to him. He's in Waynesville, an' left his car over here at his daddy's. I've got it waitin' for me down at the turnin' place below Si's. My suit-case an' all in it."

"Where you going from Waynesville?"

"Well, the world is big. I'll find some place I like. I'll take the train at Waynesville, an' set out. My God, if you's goin' too, Ishma!" Rad looked as if he were staggering backwards as he said it, but there was a crude glory in his face.

"You hush that, Rad," said Ishma, like a smothered storm.

"I kain't. I've held in for four year. You might let a man bust loose once in that time. It won't hurt you, Ish. There's been days when I've dropped the plough-handles an' turned my horse loose, an' got halfway over here 'fore I come to an' turned back. An' knowin' you's so troubled youself only made it worse."

"You've got nothing to do with my troubles."

"But how can I help it hurtin' me to see you so disappointed-like ——"

"I'm not! Not with Britt, I mean. If that's what *you* meant."

"He don't git for'd at all, an' you're feelin' it. If I could hep you I wouldn't go, but I kain't hep you, an' I'm goin'."

"And leave Lizzie Welch?"

"I wouldn't marry Lizzie noway. If ever I marry I've got to go fur enough to forget you first."

"Well, go."

"You don't mean to be hard, Ish. You're just feelin' bad."

"What do you know about my feelings?"

"I know you're miserable."

Ishma stepped into the yard. "But that mustn't bother you, Rad."

"There's a big, happy world out yonder, Ishma. Don't you ever think about it?"

She was standing with her back to the balsam bush, and her hands were spread out toward the invisible valley.

"Yes, I think about it."

She knew she had to have it—that world. It might not be happy, but she had to go and see. In three days she would have Jed's money, and she could take the first step. Somewhere men must see clearly. Somewhere life held out an answer.

"Anybody can see what you're comin' to here, Ishma. It gets harder ever' year, an' you know it. You're not foolin' yerself. I've sold my horse, an' my yearlin's an' my bees; everything except my land and timber. I'll find work where I'm goin'. There's work out there for any man that wants it. I put four hundred dollars in the Carson bank last Friday. I'll show you my bank-book."

Ishma had never seen a bank-book. Rad held it carefully under the lantern. She looked at it, but didn't touch the wondersome leaves.

"You see the figgers. Four hundred dollars."

"You can go a long way with that, Rad. You can go far."

"It's enough for you too, Ish! I can take you too!" He was frightened again, and the words hurried out tumblingly.

"Don't, Rad! If I want to go away, I've got money of my own. I can leave if I want to. Now you go on from here."

"You've got money? You goin' away, Ish?"

"Maybe I am, and maybe I'm not. Anyway it's nothing to you."

"You kain't have much money, Ishma. Not near enough. A little egg-money maybe. You couldn't get along by yourself. Not now you couldn't. If you'll let me help you, I'll take Ned along with us, an' I'll give him a big chance when he grows up."

"Take Ned? I want you to know that if ever I go away from Britt I'll go without stealing from him. Ned is his as much as mine. I'd be fair."

"Ishma ———"

She began to cry silently. What was the matter with her? Why didn't the man go?

"You leave me by myself. Can't I never be by myself?"

They heard steps on the trail above them. She couldn't let anybody find her with Rad. It would make talk. Bad talk. She stepped into the darkness behind the balsam bush. Rad, knowing what she meant, sat on the porch under the lantern, and was scanning his bank-book when Alec Craig came down.

"Hello, Rad? What you doin'?"

"Thought I'd rest a spell an' figger on something. Are you all through up there?"

"Jest about. But we got into it bad after you left. It's quiet now, an' I told my old woman I'd be back soon as I could leave the fire. They'll all be down d'reckly, lessn it's old Britt."

"What about Britt? He ain't hurt, is he?"

"Not what you'd call hurt. He's settin' up there on the ridge like a stone man."

"What's happened to him?"

"Haystacks all burnt. What's that jumped behind that balsam?"

"A cat run from under the floor. There it goes now."

"I kain't see good at night. Yes, sir, his hay's all burnt. Not a straw left. An' he's jest settin' there. I thought there was a man in Britt, but he acts like a dead un."

"Couldn't you get the fire shet off?"

"I say! A big, dry pine, hangin' with bark, caught afire close to the field, an' when it got to burnin' high it fell lam over the fence. After the stubble an' trash got to blazin' nothin' could a stopped it lessn a rainspout busted on it. You comin' out now?"

"Not down the trail. It's nigher for me across the woods."

"Well, look out for snakes. The fire's got 'em runnin'."

When the dark had disposed of him, Ishma came from behind the balsam. The lantern's light was on her face.

"Lordy, Ish! You're as white as a skinned locust. You ain't feelin' that bad about the hay, are you?"

"Don't talk, Rad. Please don't talk." She stumbled forward and sat down on the steps, her hands covering her face. Rad stood by her, dumb and afraid to move. It was minutes, perhaps ten, before she made sound or motion. When she rose she seemed to stand tall, and reached her arms toward the unseen valley and beyond.

"It's all there," she whispered. There were walls about her. But walls had gates.

Rad, at her shoulder, began talking kindly. "What is there, Ish?" She didn't hear him. Again her arms were flung out.

"All there!"

"What, Ishma?"

"Everything."

"I'll give you everything you want—out yonder—if you'll go."

She turned to him, though she didn't see him. The wall has a gate. Here was a way to open it. At that moment Rad was hardly a human being to her. He was a friendly force who would help her turn the lock and let her pass out. She had forgotten her own body; and if she could have remembered it, she would have held insignificant anything that could be done to it. The side of her face toward the lantern shone as if light were quivering through the skin. Her heart was transparent, winged.

"I'll go, Rad," she said.

"With *me?*"

"Yes."

"You mean it? When?"

"Now, we can't go fast enough."

She was strong and sure. It was the man who was white and trembling.

"I'll be good to you—an' to the baby that's comin'."

She didn't know what he said. She didn't know that Britt was on the ridge, engulfed in woe. She began walking down the road. Her feet were light, her shoulders high.

"Fast, Rad, fast!" she said, walking before him.

Questions to Consider

1. Is Ishma's decision to leave the mountain a good decision at the time that she makes it? What does she give up in order to go to work in the mill? What does she gain by leaving the mountain?
2. How does the relationship between Ishma and her husband influence your perception of her decision to leave the mountain? Could Dargan have made a similar case for the wretchedness of life in the mill towns if Ishma had been accompanied by her husband?

Myra Page (Dorothy Gary Markey)

1897–1993

A doctor's daughter from a Southern industrial city, Newport News, Virginia, Dorothy Gary grew up in solidly middle-class circumstances, the granddaughter of Confederate slaveowners. Her father, although rigid in his expectations for his daughter, was a humane physician who treated poor Whites and African Americans. Gary struggled against her parents' genteel sensibilities and questioned the inflexible attitudes that shaped their world. At age 8, she was crushed when her father told her that she could never become a physician because she was a girl.

Determined to get an education, Gary went to Westhampton College, the women's division of the University of Richmond. There she joined the YWCA and became involved in liberal causes, including prounion and antisegregation efforts. She graduated in 1917, and two years later went to Columbia University, where she earned a master's degree in 1920. Working for the YWCA, Gary returned to Virginia, encouraging women textile workers in Norfolk to unionize. Becoming more militant, she moved to Philadelphia, where she became a garment factory worker in solidarity with the Amalgamated Clothing Workers Union. After recovering from a serious kidney infection in 1924, she returned to graduate school at the University of Minnesota, where she earned a Ph.D. in 1928 and married John Markey, a fellow doctoral candidate.

A crucial point in her intellectual development occurred in 1925 and 1926, when Gary traveled to the Piedmont South to do field work for her dissertation. She lived in a succession of dirty mill towns in the Carolinas, including Gastonia, and experienced firsthand the harsh conditions faced by textile workers. Appalled by what she found, Gary engaged in union organizing in the face of entrenched corporate opposition, and she began writing for such Leftist publications as the *Daily Worker* and the *New Masses*. To protect her family from the consequences of her radical journalism, she took the pen name Myra Page.

By the late twenties, Page had joined the Communist Party USA (CPUSA). Many American intellectuals of the era embraced Marxism as a positive alternative to capitalism, which seemed to be in its death throes after the Wall Street Crash of 1929. Page and other writers on the Left were confident the workers' revolution was not long off and that it would bring an end to the abuses of laissez-faire capitalism in America.

Her first novel, *Gathering Storm: A Story of the Black Belt* (1932), was based on the Gastonia strike and drew from her field research in mill towns. Combining union advocacy with a strong stand against White supremacy, the novel quickly sank from view, ignored by the national press and the conservative Southern literary establishment. Disillusioned with the slow pace of social change in the United States in response to the crisis of the Depression, Page and her husband moved to the Soviet Union. Called home to assist with labor efforts, she held teaching jobs in Mena, Arkansas, and Monteagle, Tennessee, while traveling and organizing through the South.

Page never recanted her Leftist position. After settling in Yonkers, New York, in 1943 she continued promoting social activism. Although she left the Communist Party, Page was blacklisted by publishers during the 1950s, yet she continued publishing nonfiction under the name Dorothy Markey. Page was active in the Civil Rights, antiwar, ecology, and feminist movements of the 1960s and 1970s. In 1980, at the age of 82, she returned to Newport News to support a strike by steelworkers. She died in a New York nursing home at age 95.

In this passage from *Gathering Storm*, the central character, Marge Crenshaw, is a teenager living on Row Hill, a company village outside Greenville, South Carolina, and already working in the mill. In time she will become radicalized, go to "Riverton" (Gastonia), lead women workers out of the "Corey" (Loray) mill, and be arrested on the picket line. But before labor organizing takes over the narrative, much of the early part of the book centers on poor young women's struggles with their bodies—worries about sexual assault, fears of pregnancy, the dangers of childbearing, and crude attempts at contraception and abortion. Marge also learns that African-American women on Back Row are even more vulnerable. In the following chapter Marge tries to imagine being an independent woman. She envies her older brother Tom, who has gone North to find union work and better living conditions. But when Marge meets a new boy on the Hill, her adolescent conflict between fear of pregnancy and longing for intimacy is sharpened.

from Gathering Storm

Young Marge and Bob

The weary winter took its yearly toll from Row Hill and Back Row, then gave way to a rainy spring. But it was still winter in Marge's heart. With Granny gone, and Tom far away, what was there in life for her but spinning, spinning, and moving on with the family in a vain search for a better break on the next hill, while winter turned into spring, year upon year, just to have summer come and be swallowed up by fall? And all the while, old age would be creeping up on her, with nothing between her and the poor house at the end of the road. For there would be no children to give her food and shelter in her old age. She would never marry, she vowed to herself. She'd not be like Ma and the other women. Never! Better be ridiculed as an old maid, than that. Life was bad enough without a string of lil'uns coming along as regular as the seasons, weighing you down and sucking your spirit.

Sex? Marge shuddered. What knowledge she possessed had been picked up from the kids in the street, or gleaned from observing her elders. The crowded household allowed of little privacy in such matters. Marge, as a child, had slept in the same room with her parents. One night she was wakened by the sounds of struggle and Ma crying, "Doan, Pa, doan, I'm a-scairt," and a muffled answer. Ma had gotten out of bed and run into the far corner, and Pa had followed. After awhile they had gone back to bed, and Marge, listening, cringed beneath her covers. Then she hadn't fully understood, but now she did. Sex—a forbidden, evil thing, that got you in the corner, and cursed you with extra mouths to feed.

She was going to keep clear. She knew about the carryins-on in the field beyond the mill in spring and summer nights, the scandals of babies without fathers, of city boys taking mill girls for rides. Marge held aloof. Being pretty and desirable as a "girl," this made her conscious. But disgust and fear made her cold, crushed back the strange feelings that welled up in her at the spring of the year. While others walked arm in arm across the fields or spooned beneath the moonlight, Marge pored over a book, or struck out across the fields, alone. Some called her hoity-toity, though they had to admit she was pleasant enough to talk with, at the mill or after church meetings. Because she was gay and glum by turns, Sal whined over her, and even hinted that she was "worrit if your mind is gittin' touched."

"Aw, Ma, fer Pete's sake, leave me be."

Everything went round and round, like the seasons. A monotonous tread mill, with her, Marge, and the other mill hands tromping out cloth. Where was any meaning in it all? Wearily she turned the matter over in her mind. Fight, Granny had said. But how? Everybody was so poor, so ignorant, and down-trodden. Could they ever learn to stick together? Marge struggled against a feeling of helplessness and despair that threatened to engulf her.

In school the teacher had told them about love of country, dignity of labor, and everyone having an equal opportunity to get ahead. Now these seemed just words. The America of which the books and Miss Sanderson had told was quite unlike the one she knew, on the hill.

On Saturday afternoons, she'd tramp into Greenville and brave the entrance to the austere-looking library, in search for books which would throw some light on her problem. The librarian gave her sentimental love stories of rich girls and boys, or stories about college and the Wild West, an Elsie book, "Three Little Women," Thomas Nelson Page, and "Barriers Burned Away." What did all of this have to do with a cotton mill girl?

Finally Marge took her copy of "The Jungle"[1] with her, and timidly offered it to the librarian. "Ain't you got any books like this hyar one?" she inquired. The librarian voiced her horror in a fifteen minute monologue, then pressed "When Patty Went to Boarding School" into Marge's reluctant hands. After this, Marge went less often to the city's centre of learning.

1. *The Jungle* (1906), a protest novel by Upton Sinclair (1878–1968), is the greatest work of the "muckraking" period in American literature. After spending several weeks in the Chicago stockyards, Sinclair wrote his shocking exposé of the meatpacking industry. The novel offers a stinging socialist critique of laissez-faire capitalism, which in its ruthless pursuit of profits has turned the American economic landscape into a savage "jungle" that butchers people like livestock.

"Dear Tom," she wrote, "please send me another book like the other one. How much it cost? I'll save up an pay you back. When you comin to see us, like you said. No news here. Your lovin sis, Marge."

But there was no reply. What could have happened?

Desperately, Marge turned to religion for peace and understanding. Ma found solace in it, why not she? With summer came the revivals. Every night for a week, meetings were held in the company church and all turned out to hear the visiting preacher, who exhorted old and young to turn away from sin and the ways of this world, and fix their eyes and thoughts on the next. After the singing of many hymns, prayers and collections, he launched into tearful stories of wayward sons, daughters plunged in sin, sorrowing mothers and death-bed repentances, while the audience moaned and wept with him. Then, in contrast he waxed eloquent over the joys of "the land whar all is res' 'n peace" and the dire fate of those whom Saint Peter sent hurtling through space to the lower depths. He pictured Jesus, arms open, waiting to rescue them. His audience was swayed, lifted up to the heights and plunged to the depths, swept completely off their feet. Forgotten for a few hours was the mill drudgery and their devastating poverty and ignorance, as the revivalist's voice rose and fell, sounding on their ears like poetry or a rushing waterfall. By the time he had reached the climax, moaning and cries of "Praise the Lawd," "Oh, Jesus, save this sinner!" accompanied by shuddering and jerking movements had spread throughout the church. Men and women were clasping each other by the hand or leaned, sobbing, against their neighbor's shoulder.

In a voice vibrating with passion, the pastor gave the invitation to come forward, "as we stand 'n sing, 'Why do you wait, dear brother?'" First bent figures left their seats and went up the aisle, followed by two young boys, paled by their conviction of sin. Girls, sniffling into their handkerchiefs or sobbing openly and unashamed, struggled to the front, while "Sisters" and "Brothers" moved in and out among the benches, joining the preacher in pleading with the sinners to "cast all your burdens on Him." One woman, holding her baby high over her head, half-stumbled down the aisles, shouting "Hallelujah, Hallelujah."

"Let us sing," the revivalist shouted above the tumult, "Are you weak'n heavy-laden, burdened with a load o' care?" Marge was caught up in the emotional fervor that was sweeping through the hall. Feeling strange, powerful emotions welling up in her, she struggled blindly against them. This must be the consciousness of sin? With a shuddering thrill, she felt herself give way, as the pious ones urged, "Doan hold out. It's th' devil promptin' you." Now she was swaying and chanting with the rest "Oh, Come to the Lawd Today," and surging forward, to the Sinners' Bench. At last she was saved, saved!

In through the church windows poured the rhythmic growls of the mill, where the night shift was at work, spinning and weaving cotton cloth for Mr. Haines. "Hallelujah, Hallelujah," shouted the revival meeting, as some threw themselves on the floor, twitching and sobbing with joy. "Growl, growl," rumbled the mill, as other repentant sinners reached high into the air, or threw their arms indiscriminately around one another.

The revivalist, approaching Marge, put his arms around her. "Dear Sister, receive the Savin' Grace of our Lawd Jesus." Involuntarily Marge drew back. The next night he again sought her out, and the next. Startled, she noticed he made a practice of bringing comfort to the young girls. A married man, with grown children, too, why did he do it? Frightened at her half-formed thought, Marge kept away from the remaining services, and Ma could not scold her into going or giving a sensible reason for staying away. "It's as I a-feart," Sal muttered to herself, "ever since Granny ceasted, Marge's gittin' quare. Thar's no two ways about that."

"It's been a wonderful week, a record o'soul-savin'," Sal and her neighbor agreed, "ain't so many gone forward at a Row Hill revival in these nine year." "Uh, huh, 'n that collection we took up of eighty-nine dollars 'n fifty cints, fer the visitin' parson, that was an outpourin' of the spirit, lak he said. He said he'll put this to the sum he's savin' up from meetin's like this 'un, to buy him 'n his wife a house 'n lot." When Sal repeated this at the supper table, Marge shifted restlessly in her chair. She couldn't really have been saved, to have such evil thoughts. Yet, why should mill folks, who had so little, deny their little ones to make presents to that huggin' pastor? He and his family were lots better off than anybody on Row Hill ever would be.

"It ain't two month," Sal complained later on, to her neighbor, "since the revival meetin's, 'n you could never tell we had one, from the carryin's on. Ole man Prescott is mistreatin' his ole 'oman agin, 'n sharp tongues 'n back-bitin' is flyin' all over the hill. The Devil 'n His Forces of Darkness is shore powerful, 'n hard to rout. Sech drinkin' 'n gamblin' over to the lodge too, whar the men's hangs out, a-Sadday night—it's a caution."

Tales of this evangelist drifted back to the village. Down in Georgia, so the story ran, he had gotten into trouble with a young girl and had left in a hurry, not even waiting for the baptizing of the converted! Sal was sure these stories were works of the Devil, but Marge wondered if there was not some fire in all this smoke.

It was Holy-ness meetin' time, too, for those in Back Row. The company had not thought it advisable to build a church and hire a pastor for its colored families, so they traveled out to one in the country, where twice a month they attended preaching, along with Negro share croppers. The services and scene were similar to that at Row Hill, except the singing was more their own, and far more beautiful. At the close of the revivals, baptizing would take place on a Saturday afternoon, in a stream up the county.

At the Wednesday evening service, some rich white folks from Greenville came, with two out-of-town visitors, and sat in the balcony. They told the parson they had come to hear the singing and preaching, but then why did they exchange glances and hide their smiles behind their fans? Martha was not the only one who resented these white folks' curiosity and intrusion. "What they think we is, a circus?" But their resentment the Negroes hid behind a polite servility. For one visitor was young Elbert Haines, the mill owner's son, and another was a daughter of the banker, Mister Alexander, who owned the land which more than one share cropper tilled.

Martha caught Elbert Haines' eye on her, and trembled. For nigh a year now she'd kept out of his way, and the incident in the pantry she hoped he had forgotten. But lately she'd noticed his eyes again wandering in her direction. Martha slumped low in her seat, putting Mammy between her and young Haines' vision.

Uncle Mat, hurrying home at noon, noted a crowd around the Kendricks' door. Going over, he saw Miz Kendricks leaning against the door sill, and explaining rapidly in angry, helpless tones. "That thar loan shark come this mornin' while we-uns was at the mill 'n took all the furnishin's, 'cause we coulden pay him the dollar last week. Yes-sur, he dumped my baby 'n my sick husband on the bare boards, 'n even went off with the bed. What're we gona do?"

"The dirty, nasty thing;"

"Them loan sharks is 'bout the ornerest men what ever lived, I reckon!"

"What're we gona do?" Miz Kendricks wailed, twisting her hands.

"Doan you mind. We'll fix it." While Uncle Mat passed around the hat, mill hands dug down into their jeans, overalls, and apron pockets, and as word traveled along the street, enough dimes and quarters were collected to equal the five dollars necessary, as the first payment on another lot of furniture. Beaming, Miz Kendricks rushed off to use the store phone, and by four o'clock another loan shark had "furnished the house complete," with bed, chest of drawers, table and chairs, on the five-dollar-down-one-dollar-a-week plan.

"I doan know how the poor'd ever manage without they helpen each other," Marge remembered Granny had remarked, when, during her illness the "Home Comfort" had been loaned the Crenshaws by the mill workers' Aid Society. The Comfort included a pair of sheets, bed-pan, and a small chest of medicine and bandages, and was passed from family to family, as the need arose.

During the summer months, like now, hill folks shared with one another the beans, corn, and "taters" which they grew in the little garden patches behind their houses or at the edge of the village. Together with berry-hunting and fishing on Saturday afternoons, living was easier in the summer, though the heat in the close rooms at the mills was harder to bear. The bosses had orders not to let the windows open, because a warm, damp atmosphere, although hard on human lungs, was good for the thread.

In ways like these, hill folks had learned, like the poor all over the world, to share and aid one another. It was a necessity, in order to be able to survive at all. Thus petty mean-ness, drunken-ness, selfish pinching and narrow-mindedness—products of a bare, sickly soil—are blended with kindlier traits. So poverty and common toil weaves its bonds and leavens the loaf which in good time rises.

At the very time Row Hill and Back Row were in the ecstactic throes of their annual revivals, some thousands of miles away, the furies of hell were being turned loose on mankind. For this was August, 1914, when the Wall Streets of Europe launched their death struggle for supremacy.[2]

Although the papers blazoned the news, it meant little to Marge and the others. It all seemed vague, far-away, and rather senseless. Just because an arch duke got shot, Uncle Mat asked, did they have to start a war over that? When lurid stories of defenceless Belgium began to appear, arguments among the mill hands, gathered round the store in the evenings after work, sometimes waxed hot. But it was like arguing over the nature of the sun, or salvation, or some other remote question. While thousands in Europe were being rushed to the front, and slaughtering one another, the daily routine in the village went on as usual. By spring, however, the war had touched even Row Hill. Orders poured in, all mills went on double shifts or worked overtime, new cotton and munition plants sprang up over night. For when food and clothing are being destroyed, along with men, on a colossal scale, they have to be replaced. And it takes a whole industry to supply armies with death-dealing weapons.

2. In August 1914, the struggle among European imperial powers that would become World War I broke out weeks after the Austrian Archduke Franz Ferdinand was shot dead in Bosnia. The United States at first proclaimed neutrality but joined the hostilities in 1917. The American Left opposed involvement, denouncing the conflict as a rich man's war to benefit Wall Street financiers and wealthy industrialists.

"It's an ill wind blows nobody good," Uncle Mat reflected, "from what I hears from Slim Williams, who's back from Virginny, this here Mr. Dupont[3] must be making a pile of money outta his gun factories."

"He says thar's bread lines 'n lotta men outta work in Baltimore," Harry put in.

"Is that so? Wal, we can't kick 'bout that. We got more work'n we kin handle, here at the mills. But a lil' mo' silver'd come in handy."

"You said it, Uncle Mat. But try'n get it!"

"Yah, I'spose." The old man spit neatly between the rails.

Marge's pride in her independence was destined for a mighty fall. For the weekly shufflings of families in and out brought in the Gregory household, one of whom was a lad of nineteen, Bob. Coming home from work one Friday afternoon, Marge was startled from her hazy musings by a gay voice directing her, "Lassie, hand me that thar knife, will you, I drapped on the ground." Glancing over her shoulder, she spied a bronze-headed, merry-eyed lad grinning down at her. Bob was sitting astride all the Gregory's wordly belongings, which were stacked in rakish fashion in one of the moving carts which mill hands hire for such purposes.

"I'm needin' it," he explained, "to cut this here rope." Silently Marge reached over and handed him the knife. "Whew, what a day for movin'! But the sight of you makes me think this time it'll be worth it." Marge blushing in spite of herself, tossed her head.

"With that tongue, mebbe you're Irish?"

"Yes 'n no. Scotch-Irish. Got all the failin's of both. Say, is all we hear 'bout this hill true? They're needin' extry hands, ain't that?"

It was a second before Marge answered. "Yah, I reckon they is. That is, I hear they're wantin' them. We're workin' overtime." (What'm I standing here for, talkin' with a stranger?) Marge started off.

"Heh, wait a minute. Where do you live, me pretty one?"

Not answering, Marge quickened her steps.

"Oh doan think you'll be rid of me so easy-lak," Bob's voice trailed after her, "if I warn't a-top this furniture, you'd be payin' fer leavin' me so."

"That ain't so easy as you might think," Marge retorted angrily. The anger stayed by her, but she wasn't sure if she was not more provoked at herself than him. Resolutely she determined to put that impudent fellow out of her mind. But on Sunday morning in church she caught herself looking around for the sight of him. He was not to be seen. Those rovin', care-free kind never were. Maybe he'd only be in town a few weeks and then gone. She hoped, Marge told herself, that he would be.

Monday night, at the close of work, Marge felt a hand on her elbow and a gay voice demanding, "Kin I walk up the street your way?" "Naw," Marge answered shortly, " 'n I'll thank-ya to drap my arm." The boy's low whistle followed her up the dirt street. Before the week was out, he had arranged with his new friend, Allen, who boarded at the Crenshaw's, to bring him around to the house. "Meet my friend, Bob Gregory," Allen announced, introducing him to each in turn. As he shook Marge's hand Bob grinned, putting a special emphasis on the words, "Pleased to meetcha." The girl found herself laughing back, "The same to you." But the troubled look had not left her eyes nor did it in the days that followed, except for rare moments when she reached out eagerly, thought-free, toward the bright unknown which beckoned her on.

3. Pierre S. Du Pont, head of the E. I. Du Pont Company, which manufactured war material in Wilmington, Delaware.

Such a moment was the hay-ride, when twenty young folks from the hill and Farmer Jones' place nearby had packed into the Jones' wagon and gone jogging down the roads behind his two work mules, frolicking in the straw and warbling sentimental songs at the harvest moon which rested low in the sky, like a monstrous orange waiting to be plucked. Bob was pressed close to Marge's side, one arm along the board behind her shoulders, his warm breath fanning her cheek as he joined ardently in the old favorite, "Let Me Call You Sweetheart, I'm in Love With You." With one hand he was teasing her neck and ear with strands he had pulled from their soft couch. Marge sat quietly, drinking in the smells of the new-mown hay and of the grey-blue fields and black woods which slipped past in magic succession, and marveling at the delicious, terrifying sensations of his nearness.

But the routine of the mill and house broke the spell which the night had woven, and Marge, panicky, took to flight, abruptly refusing all the boy's endeavors at further friendliness. Puzzled and chagrined, Bob stopped his visits to the house, transferring his attentions to Becky Smithers who lived up the street. Often in the evenings he would stroll past the Crenshaw's, pulling at his companion's arm while she laughed loudly at the sallies he whispered into her ready ear. Marge gave no outward signs of minding this sudden desertion, even when the girls at the mill tried teasing her about "Easy Come 'n Easy Go," and "that thar Bob Gregory shore has a takin' way with the ladies."

Once more she took to her lone walks along the country roads, and worried Sal with her brooding.

At last there was word from Tom. "Been sick, so coulden write before. Hope to see you soon, will bring some books. How's all at home, I'm alrite now, Tom." As a matter of fact, Tom had been with Fred in the workhouse for three months, on the charge of resisting an officer. At a street meeting he had gone to Fred's aid when two of the blue coats had decided to "learn this nigger some love fer his country."

"Well, boys," Jake greeted them on their release, "get ready. It ain't gonna be long now, till this land of the free is in the fracas too."

Tom coming home! The dull cloud oppressing Marge's spirits lifted, she felt happier, stronger than at any time since Granny had left her. Tom, her old playmate, coming home with books and news. This Bob Gregory could just take his walking papers and clear out—Tom was coming home!

Bob, however, had no intention of leaving Row Hill, or Marge either—except temporarily—"to larn her a lesson." This reserved, flaxen-haired girl with her shadowed eyes drew him strangely. At a Young People's candy pull which occurred late in the fall, he maneuvered to become her partner. As they pulled the sticky molasses their fingers touched and their eyes gripped, and Bob, his own knees trembling, exulted at the unwilling flush that swept over Marge's face and neck and the unsteadiness of her voice and hands. She couldn't hide it, she was glad to have him back!

Once again the hill observed them walking home from work together, bronze head bending close to flaxen one; and Bob hanging around the Crenshaw house in the evenings, making even Sal smile with his gay nonsense. For a few weeks Marge lived each day as it came, happily and to the full; then, startled afresh into a realization of what was happening to her, drew back and took to flight. Bob, perplexed and deeply hurt, this time kept stubbornly on the trail. Now the old game of hunted and hunter was reenacted, although, as the youth sensed, it was not mere coquetry but genuine dread which sped the girl's footsteps.

"What's it Marge?" he asked her once. They were walking across the now barren, hardened fields of early winter. "What makes you act so diff'rent from other girls?" His voice lowered. "You know I'm crazy bout you, 'n," now he spoke banteringly, "thar's no use you denyin' you likes me, for I kin see it in your eye."

"You flatter yourself, Bob Gregory," she jerked her arm free, "You think any girl you want'd eat outta your hand. You're that conceited!" Suddenly he threw his arms around her, pressed his body hard against hers, kissing her desperately, hungrily. For a moment she responded, then gasping, struggled away. "Oh . . . You . . . You!" One hand across her eyes she started blindly across the fields, then, tripping, she slid to her knees and sat crouched, motionless, on the hard earth.

Disconcerted, Bob kicked with one foot against a clod of stubble and waited for her to rise. "Aw, Marge. Say . . . doan take it thisaway." When still she didn't respond, he dropped to the ground beside her, gently touching her shoulder. "Marge," he called softly, "Marge . . . honey . . . I'm sorry. Honest. Woan you speak to me?" There was no answer. "Marge, I'll not do it again, that is" (even now his sense of humor broke through irresistably), "that is, unless you want me to."

At this she sat up, eyes and cheeks ablaze. "I thought that'd get you," he teased, but his bantering tone fell away when he saw the misery looking out of her face. "Listen, honey," his voice now was gentle, awed, "I'd not want to hurt you fer anything. I've run around some, but . . . but I never meant it like this before." He slipped over the turf nearer to where she sat, huddled up like an old woman. "Because, you see," he hesitated, then whispered huskily, "because lil' Marge, I love you."

She could feel his breath on her cheek, like that night on the hay ride; although now it came in quick, breathless irregularity like a child's. Why, he was frightened, too. For some reason, this gave her courage.

Lil' Marge. No one had called her that since Granny had died.

"You like me some . . . doan you Marge?" Her face turned from him, she nodded. Searching, he found her hand. "Mebbe more'n a little?" Again she nodded. "Woan you say it?" he pleaded. There was no answer. Gladness, desire struggled against tormenting fear. Oh, how could she ever make him understand?

"What is it, Marge?" Girls were sure queer. "Was I too rough or sudden-like? Seemed lak a feeling went through me." Her palm felt moist, hot against his. "I woan again like that."

Marge turned toward him. "Please Bob. I can't say why. But just-doan."

"All right," he agreed. Yet, as they walked silently back toward the village, both knew in their hearts it was a futile promise. For the yearning that was in them, growing with each month that passed, was not to be denied.

Very soon all of Row Hill took it that Marge Crenshaw and Bob Gregory were as good as engaged. Sal, disgruntled, tried questioning her daughter, but all the information she was able to obtain was that Marge had no intention of marrying anybody. "Leastways, not fer another year," Sal counseled, "till you're eighteen." "Not next year, nuther," the girl retorted, "Bob knows I ain't aimin' to git married. We're just good friends." Sal slammed the lid down on the kettle, "Wal, of all fool notions, this hyar's the beatin'est yet," but her daughter had already fled beyond earshot.

Questions to Consider

1. What stereotypes and ironies are involved when the librarian in Greenville presses on Marge, "a cotton mill girl," romance novels about going to boarding school and college?
2. When a revivalist comes to Row Hill, he preaches a message of sin, repentance, and acceptance of suffering. Through the church windows Marge hears the sounds of the factory, "where the night shift was at work, spinning and weaving cotton cloth for Mr. Haines." What is Page suggesting about the response of Southern Christianity to economic misery during the Depression?

Erskine Caldwell

1903–1987

More eloquently than any Southern writer of the Depression, Erskine Caldwell used the economic blight of his native region to dramatize the degrading effects of dire poverty on its victims, White and African-American. After the national economy recovered in the 1940s and social conditions slowly improved in the South, the quality (if not quantity) of Caldwell's work declined. By the 1970s, he had been largely forgotten by American academic critics, even as he rose in esteem in France and the Soviet bloc. Over the last decade, however, a scholarly rehabilitation has been under way in the United States. Caldwell at last has gained recognition as a literary figure central to the rise of both American leftist writing and modern Southern literature. Unlike his contemporaries in the Southern Literary Renascence, Caldwell wrote next to nothing about the past; his consuming interest was always in the present. He wrote his best fiction in the cause of social change and believed that what he wrote could make a positive difference in the lives of the deprived. When he was at the top of his form as an author, he made a decisively original contribution to American protest literature.

In his youth, Caldwell learned much about the lives of the downtrodden from his father, an activist Presbyterian minister who preached the Social Gospel in South Carolina, Tennessee, and Georgia. Reverend. I. S. Caldwell was often at odds with the Presbytery because of his outspoken criticism of the church's failure to address social injustice. Georgia Klansmen denounced him as a "nigger lover" and threatened violence. Young Erskine, early on, showed concern for the tenant farmers and mill hands who toiled in the vicinity of his father's church near Augusta, Georgia. In later years he liked to call attention to the nearness of the lush golf course—where the Masters Tournament is played—to dusty Tobacco Road. Always restless, after dropping out of high school, Caldwell studied at the University of Virginia and the University of Pennsylvania. In time, he became a newsman in Atlanta and began writing short stories. Now Caldwell had found his life's mission. In 1931 he wrote, "The masses in the South have always been undernourished, uneducated, and without a spokesman," thereby declaring his intention to speak out on their behalf.

He made good on this vow, publishing *Tobacco Road* in 1932, when he was 28 years old. With its abrasive combination of sexual and economic degradation, the novel shows the influence of William Faulkner's *Sanctuary* (1932). Caldwell, however, gave his novel a political edge—an unmistakable hostility toward capitalism—absent in Faulkner. Caldwell meant his novel to be an exposé of the Southern system of sharecropping, which trapped poor farmers in a hopeless cycle of debt and left them at the mercy of absentee landlords. Book sales were poor, but the critics were enthusiastic, placing Caldwell with Faulkner in the first rank of young Southern novelists. Thrust into the spotlight, Caldwell quarreled with conservative Southern authors like Allen Tate and Caroline Gordon, whom he ridiculed as magnolia worshippers. He allied himself with the Northern-based literary Left and wrote fiery letters and articles describing the misery of the Southern poor.

The lasting furor over alleged degeneracy in *Tobacco Road* and an obscenity trial over *God's Little Acre* (1933) overshadowed the publication of some of Caldwell's best fiction, including his short story collection *Kneel to the Rising Sun* (1935) and his short story cycle *Georgia Boy* (1943), as well as his bitter novel about vigilante violence, *Trouble in July* (1940). The Depression also saw the publication of his photo-essay, *You Have Seen Their Faces* (1937), the best of Caldwell's nonfiction. Caldwell became interested in the camera as a means to document squalor and starvation in the South, especially after Southern chauvinists accused him of falsifying his data. In 1936, he met Margaret Bourke-White, a rising photographer and staunch leftist. They became lovers when they traveled through the rural South, and she took the stark pictures for *You Have Seen Their Faces*. Caldwell and Bourke-White married in 1939, making her the second of his four wives.

With widespread industrialization during the World War II era, poverty abated in the South, at least among working-class Whites. Caldwell turned to mass publishers and placed the sexual exploitation of women at the center of his paperback novels. These changes eroded his critical standing as an author and led to accusations that he had sunk to writing pornography. Furthermore, as the Cold War intensified in the 1950s and 1960s, Caldwell's patriotism was questioned by cultural jingoists who cited his travels with Bourke-White to the Soviet Union during World War II as proof of his anti-Americanism. However, buoyed by his support of the Civil Rights movement in the South, Caldwell produced his last significant books, *In Search of Bisco* (1965) and *Deep South* (1968). *Deep South* infuriated a new generation of Sun Belt Southerners as Caldwell spoke out against the South's new "First Baptist" disease—the flight of evangelical Protestants to big urban churches that were long on commercialism but short on social conscience. In the last decade of his life Caldwell fell into worsening health caused by lung cancer. He died at the age of 83 in Scottsdale, Arizona.

God's Little Acre is Caldwell's most complex novel, combining elements of social criticism, religious satire, and economic protest. Because of its several sex scenes (more stylized than graphic), the book was denounced as obscene by some reviewers. It was put on trial in New York, but a magistrate there acquitted the novel as a realistic depiction of the South. The setting is "Scottsville," a dirty mill town located in the Horse Creek Valley of lower South Carolina. This area lies across the Savannah River from Augusta, the center of Caldwell's East Georgia fictional world in the 1930s. Caldwell was familiar with Southern cotton manufacturing, as Augusta was home to a number of large textile mills, and he knew the surrounding area well from his boyhood travels with his father. Labor strife between mill owners and textile workers in the region dated back to the 1890s and continued into the first decades of the twentieth century. In 1929 alone (the year of the Gastonia strike in North Carolina) dozens of textile strikes in South Carolina cotton mills idled tens of thousands of workers. Although no fatalities were recorded in South Carolina, Caldwell may have had in mind the violent mill strike of 1929 in Marion, North Carolina. In that episode, a striker shut off the power in the factory. In the police action that followed outside the plant, deputies fatally shot 6 strikers in the back and wounded 18 more. The sheriff and 14 other defendants were tried but acquitted.

The narrative centers on Will Thompson, a loomweaver, who along with the rest of Scottsville's textile workers has been idled for a year and a half because management has closed the mill rather than meet worker demands. Will complains bitterly about the causes of the strike, the "stretch-out" system of forcing one employee to do the jobs of several, and the scant $1.10 per day for a 55-hour workweek. He also resents the union, which has done little to help the workers. As it is, the mistreated strikers barely subsist on flour from the Red Cross. Pellagra is widespread because of malnutrition, and lung fibrosis (caused by inhaling cotton lint) disables many strikers.

Along with other male employees, Will plans to tear down the fences surrounding the building, break open the doors, turn on the power, and take over the plant. However, this plan has been leaked to management, which has brought in armed gunmen. Among Will's entourage are his wife, Rosamond, and his sisters-in-law Griselda and Darling Jill Walden (and Jill's lumpish suitor Pluto Swint). Caldwell's lyrical prose celebrates the lusty vitality of the mill workers and the strange beauty of their hard industrial world. His sensual language implies that a mighty potential for human betterment lies just beneath the tattered surface of mill town debasement, disease, and demoralization.

from God's Little Acre

"There they go!" Rosamond said, clutching the arms of her sister and Griselda. "Will is at the door now!"

Women all around them were crying hysterically. After eighteen months of waiting it looked as if there would again be work in the mill. Women and children pushed forward, stronger than the force of the walled-up water in Horse Creek below, pushing close behind the men at the mill door. Some of the older children had climbed up the trees and they were above the crowd now, hanging to the limbs and shouting at their fathers and brothers.

"I can't believe it's true," a woman beside them said. She had stopped crying long enough to speak.

All around them women and girls were crying with joy. When the men had first said they were going to take over the mill and turn on the power, the women had been afraid; but now, now when they were crushed against the mill, it looked as if everything would come true. Here in the mill yard now were the wild-eyed Valley girls with erect breasts; behind the mill windows they would look like morning-glories.

"It's open!" somebody shouted.

There was a sudden surge of closely pressed bodies, and Rosamond and Darling Jill and Griselda were pushed forward with the mass.

"We'll have something beside fat-back and Red Cross flour now," a little woman with clenched fists said in a low voice beside them. "We've been starving on that, but we won't any longer. The men are going to work again."

Already the mass of men were pouring through the opened doors. They fought their way in silently, hammering at the narrow doors with their fists and pushing them with their muscles, angry because the doors were not wide enough to admit them quicker. Windows on the first floor were being tilted open. The crowd of women and children could follow the advance of the men by watching the opening of the mill windows one after the other. Before the first floor windows were all opened, several on the second floor were suddenly tilted wide.

"There they are," Rosamond said. "I wonder where Will is now."

Somebody said that the company had hired fifteen additional guards and placed them in the mill. The new guards had arrived that morning from the Piedmont.

The entire mill was occupied. The third and fourth floor windows were being opened. Already men were running to the windows on all floors, jerking off their shirts and flinging them to the ground. When men in the Valley went back to work after a long lay-off, they took off their shirts and threw them out the windows. Down on the green, where the three company sheep so fat had grazed for eighteen months, the ground was covered with shirts. The men on the last two floors were throwing out their shirts, and down on the ground the piled shirts were knee deep on the green.

"Hush!" the whisper went over the crowd of women and girls and yelling children in the trees.

It was time for the power to be turned on. Everyone wished to hear the first concerted hum of the machinery behind the ivy-walled building.

"I wonder where Will is," Rosamond said.

"I haven't seen him at the window yet," Griselda said. "I've been looking for him."

Darling Jill stood on her toes, straining to see over the heads of the people. She clutched Rosamond, pointing to a window above.

"Look! There's Will! See him at the window?"

"What's he doing?"

"He's tearing his shirt to pieces!" Rosamond cried.

They stood on their toes trying their best to see Will before he left the window.

"It is Will!" Griselda said.

"Will!" Darling Jill cried, urging all the strength of her body into her lungs so he might hear her above the noise. "Will! Will!"

For a moment they thought he had heard her. He stopped and bent far out the window trying to see down into the densely packed mass below. With a final tear he balled the ripped cloth in his hands and threw it out into the crowd. The women nearest the mill reached up and fought for the torn strips of cloth. The ones who caught parts of it quickly took it from the reach of the others who wished to have a part of it.

Rosamond and Darling Jill and Griselda could not get close enough to fight for Will's torn shirt. They had to stand where they were and see the other women and girls struggle over it until there was none left.

"Let's hear the machinery, Will Thompson!" an excited woman cried.

"Turn the power on, Will Thompson!" another girl cried at him.

He turned and ran out of sight. The crowd below was as still as the empty mill yard had been before they came. They waited to hear the first hum of the machinery.

Rosamond's heart beat madly. It was Will whom the crowd begged to turn the power on. It was he whom they had acknowledged by acclamation as their leader. She wished to climb up high above the mass of crying women and shout that Will Thompson was her husband. She wished to have all the people there know that Will Thompson was her Will.

Through the tilted glass windows they could see the men at their places, waiting for the wheels to turn. Their voices were raised in shouts that burst through the windows, and their bare backs gleamed in the rising sun like row after row of company houses in the early morning.

"It's on!" somebody cried. "The power is on!"

"Will has turned on the power," Griselda said, dancing with joy. She was on the verge of bursting into tears again. "Will did it! It was Will! Will turned the power on!"

All of them were too excited to speak coherently. They jumped up and down on their toes, each trying to see over the head of the other. Men ran to the windows shaking their fists into the air. Some of them were laughing, some were cursing, some were standing as though they were in a daze. When the machinery turned, they ran back and stood in their accustomed positions beside the looms.

There was a sound of sudden small explosions in the eastern end of the mill. It sounded like small firecrackers bursting. In the roar of the machinery it had almost been drowned out, but it was loud enough to be heard.

Everyone turned his head to look down at the eastern end of the mill. Down there the power room was located.

"What was that?" Griselda asked, clutching Rosamond.

Rosamond was like a ghost. Her face was drawn and white, and her pale lips were dry like cotton.

The other women began talking excitedly among themselves. They spoke in whispers, in hushed undertones that made no sound.

"Rosamond, what was that!" Griselda cried frantically. "Rosamond, answer me!"

"I don't know," she murmured.

Darling Jill trembled beside her sister. She could feel a convulsive throb surge through her heart and head. She leaned heavily upon Griselda for support.

A man on one of the middle floors ran to a window and shook his fist into the air, cursing and shouting. They could see warm blood trickle from the corners of his lips,[1] dropping to his bare chest. He raised his fists into the air, screaming to the heavens.

Soon others ran to the windows excitedly, staring down into the crowd of wives and sisters below, cursing and shouting while their fists shook into the air.

"What's the matter!" a woman in the crowd cried. "What happened! Dear God, help us!"

The windows were filled with cursing, bare-chested men who looked down into the faces of the women and girls.

Suddenly there was a cessation of noise in the mill. The machinery whirled to a stop, dying. There was not a sound anywhere, not even in the crowd below. Women turned to each other, helplessly.

First one man, his bare chest gleaming in the sun, appeared at the big double-doors below. He came out slowly, his hands holding fists that were too weak to remain doubled any longer. Another man came behind him, then two, then others. The door was filled with men walking slowly, turning at the steps until the glow of the sun covered their pale backs with thin blood.

"What happened?" a woman cried. "Tell us what happened! What's wrong?"

Rosamond and Darling Jill and Griselda were not close enough to hear what the men answered in weak voices. They stood on tiptoes, clutching each other, waiting to see Will and to hear from him what the trouble was.

A woman nearby screamed, sending shudders through Griselda. She cried with the pain of the woman's scream.

They pushed and fought their way towards the men coming from the mill. Griselda clung to Rosamond, Darling Jill clung to Griselda. They went forward slowly, pushing frantically through the crowd to the men coming so slowly from the mill.

"Where's Will?" Griselda cried.

A man turned and looked at them. He came toward them to speak to the three of them.

"You're Will Thompson's wife, aren't you?"

"Where is Will?" Rosamond cried, throwing herself upon the man's bare chest.

"They shot him."

"Who shot him?"

"Will! Will! Will!"

1. The mill workers spit blood because long-term inhalation of lint in the weaving rooms has caused them to develop silicosis, a lung disease.

"Those Piedmont guards shot him."

"Dear God!"

"Is he badly hurt?"

"He's dead."

That was all. There was no more to hear.

The women and girls behind them were silent like people in slumber. They pressed forward, supporting Will Thompson's widow and sisters-in-law.

More men filed out, walking slowly up the hill towards the long rows of yellow company houses, while the muscles on their bare backs hung like cut tendons under the skin. There was a man with blood on his lips. He spat into the yellow dust at his feet. Another man coughed, and blood oozed through the corners of his tightly compressed mouth. He spat into the yellow dust of Carolina.

Women were beginning to leave, running to the sides of the men and walking beside them up the hill towards the long rows of yellow company houses. There were tears in the eyes of the girls so beautiful who walked homeward with their lovers. These were the girls of the Valley whose breasts were erect and whose faces were like morning-glories when they stood in the windows of the ivy-walled mill.

Rosamond was not beside Griselda and Darling Jill when they turned to put their arms around her. She had run towards the mill door. She fell against the side of the building, clutching in her hands the ivy that grew so beautifully.

They ran to be with her.

"Will!" Rosamond cried frantically. "Will! Will!"

They put their arms around her and held her.

Several men stepped out the door and waited. Then several others came out slowly, carrying the body of Will Thompson. They tried to keep his wife and sisters-in-law back, but they ran closer until they could look at him.

"Oh, he's dead!" Rosamond said.

She had not realized that Will was dead until she saw his limp body. She still could not believe that he would not come to life. She could not believe that he would never be alive again.

The men in front took Rosamond and Darling Jill and Griselda up the hill towards the long rows of yellow company houses, holding them and supporting them. The bare backs of the men were strong with their arms around Will Thompson's wife and sisters-in-law.

When they reached the front of the house, the body was kept in the street until a place could be provided for it. The three women were carried to the house. Women from the yellow company houses up the street and down it came running to help.

"I don't know what we're going to do now," a man said. "Will Thompson isn't here any more."

Another man looked down at the ivy-walled mill.

"They were afraid of Will," he said. "They knew he had the guts to fight back. I don't reckon there'll be any use of trying to fight them without Will. They'll try to run now and make us take a dollar-ten. If Will Thompson was here, we wouldn't do it. Will Thompson would fight them."

The body was carried to the porch and placed in the shade of the roof. His back was bare, but the three drying blood-clogged holes were hidden from sight.

"Let's turn him over," somebody said. "Everybody ought to know how Will Thompson was shot in the back by those sons-of-bitches down there."

"We'll bury him tomorrow. And I reckon everybody in Scottsville will be at the funeral. Everybody but those sons-of-bitches down there."

"What's his wife going to do now? She's all alone."

"We'll take care of her, if she'll let us. She's Will Thompson's widow."

An ambulance came up the street and the strong bare-backed men lifted the body from the porch and carried it out to the street. The three women in the house came to the door and stood close together while the bare-backed men carried Will from the porch and put him into the ambulance. He was Will Thompson now. He belonged to those bare-backed men with bloody lips. He belonged to Horse Creek Valley now. He was not theirs any longer. He was Will Thompson.

The three women stood in the door watching the rear end of the ambulance while it went slowly down the street to the undertaker. The body would be prepared for burial, and the next day there would be a funeral in the cemetery on the hill that looked down upon Horse Creek Valley. The men with blood-stained lips who carried him down to his grave would some day go back to the mill to card and spin and weave and dye. Will Thompson would breathe no more lint into his lungs.

Inside the house one of the men was trying to explain to Pluto how Will had been killed. Pluto was more frightened than ever. Until that time he had been scared of only the darkness in Scottsville, but now he was afraid of the day also. Men were killed in broad daylight in the Valley. He wished he could make Darling Jill and Griselda go home right away. If he had to remain in the yellow company house another night, he knew he probably would not sleep. The man with the bare chest and back sat in the room with Pluto, talking to him about the mill, but Pluto was not listening any longer. He had become afraid of the man beside him; he was afraid the man would suddenly turn with a knife in his hand and cut his throat from ear to ear. He knew then that he was out of place in a cotton mill town. The country, back at home in Marion, was the place for him to go as quickly as possible. He promised himself he would never again leave it if only he could get back safely this time.

Late that evening some of the women from the yellow company houses on the street came and prepared the first meal any of them had had that day. Will had eaten breakfast early that morning, but none of the others had. Pluto felt starved after missing two meals. He had never been so hungry in all his life. Back home in Marion he had never been forced to go hungry for the lack of food. He could smell the cooking food and the boiling coffee through the open doors, and he was unable to sit still. He got up and went to the door just as one of the women came to call him to the kitchen. Out in the hall he became frightened again and would have gone back, but the woman took his arm and went with him to the kitchen.

While he was there, Darling Jill came in and sat down beside him. He felt much safer then. Somehow, he felt that she was a protection in a foreign country. She ate a little, and when she had finished, she remained seated beside him.

Later, Pluto ventured to ask Darling Jill when they could go back to Georgia.

"Tomorrow as soon as the funeral is over," she said.

"Can't we go now?"

"Of course not."

"They can bury Will all right without us," he suggested. "They'll do it all right. I wish I could go home right away, Darling Jill. I don't feel safe in Scottsville."

"Hush, Pluto. Don't be such a child."

He remained silent after that. Darling Jill took his hand and led him to one of the dark rooms across the hall. He felt exactly as he once had many years before when he was a small boy holding the hand of his mother in a dark night.

Outside the windows was the sound of the Valley town with all its strange noises and unfamiliar voices. He was glad the street light shone through the leaves of the tree and partly lighted the room. It was safer with a little light, and he was not so afraid as he had been earlier that evening. If somebody should come to the window and crawl inside to slit his throat from ear to ear he would be able to see them before he felt the blade under his chin.

Darling Jill had brought him to the bed and had made him lie down upon it. He was reluctant then to release her hand, and when he saw that she was going to lie down beside him, he was no longer afraid. The Valley was still there, and the strange company town, but he had Darling Jill to lie beside him, her hand in his, and he could close his eyes without fear.

Just before both of them dropped off to sleep, he felt her arms around his neck. He turned to her, holding her tightly. There was nothing to be afraid of then.

Questions to Consider

1. Will's obsession with turning on the electricity at the spinning mill is both a rejection of economic impotence and a fantasy of masculine power—his attack on the mill follows a sexual assault on his sister-in-law, Griselda. Why does Caldwell link Will's suicidal invasion of the mill with his feelings of male aggression?
2. When the mill guards shoot Will in the back, his life seems to end in failure. Yet much of the imagery of the passage suggests religious martyrdom. What does Caldwell imply about the meaning of Will's murder for the other loomweavers?

END OF VOICES IN CONTEXT

Eudora Welty

1909–2001

Eudora Welty once said: "We come to terms as well as we can with our lifelong exposure to the world, and we use whatever devices we may need to survive. . . . One day up in Tishomingo County, I knew . . . that my wish, indeed my continuing passion, would not be to point the finger in judgment but to part a curtain, that invisible shadow that falls between people, the well of indifference to each other's presence, each other's wonder, and each other's human plight." Welty, indeed, lived up to her mission to lift the veil that divides people from one another in her fiction, and she did so with grace, humor, and truth. She created a fictional world that is vivid, honest, and one with which most readers can immediately identify. Although she was clearly influenced by the Southern region where she spent her life, Welty's themes and her depiction of the human condition make her writing universal in its appeal.

Welty's work garners much praise from critics, readers, and fellow writers and has inspired many fledgling authors in their own crafts. Clyde Edgerton, Reynolds Price, and Tony Early openly and frequently praise Welty's prolific work and her personal support of their efforts. Edgerton credits Welty with his decision to become a writer, saying that he underwent a literary conversion of sorts while watching Eudora Welty read one of her short stories on public television. "Why I Live at the P.O." showed Edgerton that the people of his own region and town could become the subjects of literary works. Referring to the same story, Early said: "In 'Why I Live at the P.O.' I found a small salvation and a personal promised land, but that is less than incidental to the story's main message: the human voice crying out, no matter how small or far away, is always worthy of attention." Shannon Ravenel has called Welty "an enormous figure in American literature, not just Southern literature. She's been an enormous influence on the current generation of writers, probably much more of an influence than Faulkner." Few would argue with such glowing assessments of Welty's work, for her writing has, over the past 50 years, presented the South with unvarnished reality. Her depictions of dialect and lifestyles of Southerners continue to delight and to intrigue readers.

Welty generally finds her setting in Mississippi, the state of her birth and residence. Her characters speak in the Mississippi voices that she heard throughout her life, and her depictions of varying social classes reflect her lifelong observations of people in and around the state capital of Jackson. Her themes generally address man's inhumanity to man, alienation, love and the quest for it, the family, and loss of community. While Welty's themes are similar to those depicted by William Faulkner and Flannery O'Connor, she breaks away from the traditions of the literary grotesque, for the most part, and presents average individuals and their families struggling with realistic foibles and reveling in successes.

Welty was an expert on Mississippi life, for she lived it daily. Born on 13 April 1909, the daughter of Christian Welty, who was a native of Ohio, and Chestina Andrews, who had grown up in West Virginia, Welty herself was a first-generation Mississippian. She was the oldest of three children and the only daughter in a family of voracious readers. Her father worked for an insurance company, and though not extravagantly rich, the Weltys were wealthy enough to provide Eudora and her brothers with a stable home and environment. Welty enjoyed a happy childhood, leading her to remark that her only source of childhood suffering was her father's having been a Yankee from Ohio. After high school, she attended the Mississippi State College for Women, where she contributed drawings, prose, and poetry to student publications. She transferred to the University of Wisconsin, from which she graduated two years later with a bachelor's degree in English. Welty had developed an interest in painting and sketching in her youth, and later, she became enthralled by photography. Her background in the visual arts proved useful in her literary pursuits, leading critics to praise her for her description and essay visual imagery.

Welty attended the Columbia School of Business for a year to prepare herself for practical employment. Her attempts to enter the job market in 1931, at the height of the Great Depression, yielded no positive results, and she returned to Jackson. Shortly thereafter, her father died, dealing a hard blow to the Welty clan. From 1931 to 1933, Welty found part-time work with radio and newspapers, and she wrote stories. In 1933, she began work that would put all her talents to use when she became a publicity agent for the Mississippi office of the Works Progress Administration (WPA). In this job, she traveled for three years around the 82 counties of Mississippi, writing feature stories about local projects, meeting and conversing with many different types of people, and gathering and recording impressions of the varied persons, groups, landscapes, and towns she visited. While working for the WPA, Welty began to photograph Mississippi residents and continued writing her short stories. Her breakthrough story came in the form of "Death of a Traveling Salesman." Later, this success was followed by her three popular collections of short stories: *A Curtain of Green*, *The Robber Bridegroom*, and *The Wide Net*. Her "snapshots," as she always called them, became notable when they were published in 1973 and 1989. During the years from the 1940s to the end of her life, she continued to write, publishing many works. She cared for her mother for many years and lived in her family home until her death in 2001. She never married, yet she maintained a wide circle of acquaintances and friends in Jackson.

Acclaim for Welty's writing grew from the 1940s onward. In both 1940 and 1942, she received Guggenheim Fellowships. In 1973, she was awarded the Pulitzer Prize for her semiautobiographical novel, *The Optimist's Daughter*. Over the years, her work earned the O. Henry Short Story Award many times, and she was the recipient of the National Book Award for *Losing Battles* in 1971. In 1980, she received the National Medal for Literature, and she was awarded honorary degrees by Smith University, the University of the South, the University of Wisconsin, Harvard University, Yale University, and Mt. Holyoke College.

Throughout her long life, Welty experienced many turbulent periods of American history. She lived through the Great Depression, World War II, the Korean Conflict, the Civil Rights era, the Vietnam War, and the Persian Gulf War. She endured a particularly difficult period professionally during the Civil Rights era when she was criticized for not writing fiction that was racially sensitive. Upon the publication of *Delta Wedding* (1946), critics Diana Trilling and Isaac Rosenfeld chastised her for her lack of social conscience. Welty felt that her depictions of African Americans had been favorable, as in "A Worn Path," and was stunned and puzzled to receive this kind of criticism. Her eloquent response to her detractors, "Must the Novelist Crusade?" appeared in the *Atlantic Monthly* in October 1965. In it, she stated that fiction is a private endeavor and should not be politicized in the form of a crusade that deals in general concepts rather than in specific moralities and in the human condition.

Welty's success continued through the Civil Rights era, and she maintained her popular and critical reputation until the time of her death; her detractors, for the most part, fell silent. Although Welty writes of the South, she transcends the notion of regional writing through her use of universal themes and the presentation of well-developed characters who appeal to Southerners and non-Southerners alike.

A Worn Path

It was December—a bright frozen day in the early morning. Far out in the country there was an old Negro woman with her head tied in a red rag, coming along a path through the pinewoods. Her name was Phoenix Jackson. She was very old and small and she walked slowly in the dark pine shadows, moving a little from side to side in her steps, with the balanced heaviness and lightness of a pendulum in a grandfather clock. She carried a thin, small cane made from an umbrella, and with this she kept tapping the frozen earth in front of her. This made a grave and persistent noise in the still air, that seemed meditative like the chirping of a solitary little bird.

She wore a dark striped dress reaching down to her shoe tops, and an equally long apron of bleached sugar sacks, with a full pocket: all neat and tidy, but every time she took a step she might have fallen over her shoelaces, which dragged from her unlaced shoes. She looked straight ahead. Her eyes were blue with age. Her skin had a pattern all its own of numberless branching wrinkles and as though a whole little tree stood in the middle of her forehead, but a golden color ran underneath, and the two knobs of her cheeks were illumined by a yellow burning under the dark. Under the red rag her hair came down on her neck in the frailest of ringlets, still black, and with an odor like copper.

Now and then there was a quivering in the thicket. Old Phoenix said, "Out of my way, all you foxes, owls, beetles, jack rabbits, coons and wild animals! . . . Keep out from under these feet, little bobwhites. . . . Keep the big wild hogs out of my path. Don't let none of those come running my direction. I got a long way." Under her small black-freckled hand her cane, limber as a buggy whip, would switch at the brush as if to rouse up any hiding things.

On she went. The woods were deep and still. The sun made the pine needles almost too bright to look at, up where the wind rocked. The cones dropped as light as feathers. Down in the hollow was the mourning dove—it was not too late for him.

The path ran up a hill. "Seem like there is chains about my feet, time I get this far," she said, in the voice of argument old people keep to use with themselves. "Something always take a hold of me on this hill—pleads I should stay."

After she got to the top she turned and gave a full, severe look behind her where she had come. "Up through pines," she said at length. "Now down through oaks."

Her eyes opened their widest, and she started down gently. But before she got to the bottom of the hill a bush caught her dress.

Her fingers were busy and intent, but her skirts were full and long, so that before she could pull them free in one place they were caught in another. It was not possible to allow the dress to tear. "I in the thorny bush," she said. "Thorns, you doing your appointed work. Never want to let folks pass, no sir. Old eyes thought you was a pretty little *green* bush."

Finally, trembling all over, she stood free, and after a moment dared to stoop for her cane.

"Sun so high!" she cried, leaning back and looking, while the thick tears went over her eyes. "The time getting all gone here."

At the foot of this hill was a place where a log was laid across the creek.

"Now comes the trial," said Phoenix.

Putting her right foot out, she mounted the log and shut her eyes. Lifting her skirt, leveling her cane fiercely before her, like a festival figure in some parade, she began to march across. Then she opened her eyes and she was safe on the other side.

"I wasn't as old as I thought," she said.

But she sat down to rest. She spread her skirts on the bank around her and folded her hands over her knees. Up above her was a tree in a pearly cloud of mistletoe. She did not dare to close her eyes, and when a little boy brought her a plate with a slice of marble-cake on it she spoke to him. "That would be acceptable," she said. But when she went to take it there was just her own hand in the air.

So she left that tree, and had to go through a barbed-wire fence. There she had to creep and crawl, spreading her knees and stretching her fingers like a baby trying to climb the steps. But she talked loudly to herself: she could not let her dress be torn now, so late in the day, and she could not pay for having her arm or her leg sawed off if she got caught fast where she was.

At last she was safe through the fence and risen up out in the clearing. Big dead trees, like black men with one arm, were standing in the purple stalks of the withered cotton field. There sat a buzzard.

"Who you watching?"

In the furrow she made her way along.

"Glad this not the season for bulls," she said, looking sideways, "and the good Lord made his snakes to curl up and sleep in the winter. A pleasure I don't see no two-headed snake coming around that tree, where it come once. It took a while to get by him, back in the summer."

She passed through the old cotton and went into a field of dead corn. It whispered and shook and was taller than her head. "Through the maze now," she said, for there was no path.

Then there was something tall, black, and skinny there, moving before her.

At first she took it for a man. It could have been a man dancing in the field. But she stood still and listened, and it did not make a sound. It was as silent as a ghost.

"Ghost," she said sharply, "who be you the ghost of? For I have heard of nary death close by."

But there was no answer—only the ragged dancing in the wind.

She shut her eyes, reached out her hand, and touched a sleeve. She found a coat and inside that an emptiness, cold as ice.

"You scarecrow," she said. Her face lighted. "I ought to be shut up for good," she said with laughter. "My senses is gone. I too old. I the oldest people I ever know. Dance, old scarecrow," she said, "while I dancing with you."

She kicked her foot over the furrow, and with mouth drawn down, shook her head once or twice in a little strutting way. Some husks blew down and whirled in streamers about her skirts.

Then she went on, parting her way from side to side with the cane, through the whispering field. At last she came to the end, to a wagon track where the silver grass blew between the red ruts. The quail were walking around like pullets, seeming all dainty and unseen.

"Walk pretty," she said. "This the easy place. This the easy going."

She followed the track, swaying through the quiet bare fields, through the little strings of trees silver in their dead leaves, past cabins silver from weather, with the doors and windows boarded shut, all like old women under a spell sitting there. "I walking in their sleep," she said, nodding her head vigorously.

In a ravine she went where a spring was silently flowing through a hollow log. Old Phoenix bent and drank. "Sweet-gum makes the water sweet," she said, and drank more. "Nobody know who made this well, for it was here when I was born."

The track crossed a swampy part where the moss hung as white as lace from every limb. "Sleep on, alligators, and blow your bubbles." Then the track went into the road.

Deep, deep the road went down between the high green-colored banks. Overhead the live-oaks met, and it was as dark as a cave.

A black dog with a lolling tongue came up out of the weeds by the ditch. She was meditating, and not ready, and when he came at her she only hit him a little with her cane. Over she went in the ditch, like a little puff of milkweed.

Down there, her senses drifted away. A dream visited her, and she reached her hand up, but nothing reached down and gave her a pull. So she lay there and presently went to talking. "Old woman," she said to herself, "that black dog come up out of the weeds to stall you off, and now there he sitting on his fine tail, smiling at you."

A white man finally came along and found her—a hunter, a young man, with his dog on a chain.

"Well, Granny!" he laughed. "What are you doing there?"

"Lying on my back like a June-bug waiting to be turned over, mister," she said, reaching up her hand.

He lifted her up, gave her a swing in the air, and set her down. "Anything broken, Granny?"

"No sir, them old dead weeds is springy enough," said Phoenix, when she had got her breath. "I thank you for your trouble."

"Where do you live, Granny?" he asked, while the two dogs were growling at each other.

"Away back yonder, sir, behind the ridge. You can't even see it from here."

"On your way home?"

"No sir, I going to town."

"Why, that's too far! That's as far as I walk when I come out myself, and I get something for my trouble." He patted the stuffed bag he carried, and there hung down a little closed claw. It was one of the bob-whites, with its beak hooked bitterly to show it was dead. "Now you go on home, Granny!"

"I bound to go to town, mister," said Phoenix. "The time come around."

He gave another laugh, filling the whole landscape. "I know you old colored people! Wouldn't miss going to town to see Santa Claus!"

But something held old Phoenix very still. The deep lines in her face went into a fierce and different radiation. Without warning, she had seen with her own eyes a flashing nickel fall out of the man's pocket onto the ground.

"How old are you, Granny?" he was saying.

"There is no telling, mister," she said, "no telling."

Then she gave a little cry and clapped her hands and said, "Git on away from here, dog! Look! Look at that dog!" She laughed as if in admiration. "He ain't scared of nobody. He a big black dog." She whispered, "Sic him!"

"Watch me get rid of that cur," said the man. "Sic him, Pete! Sic him!"

Phoenix heard the dogs fighting, and heard the man running and throwing sticks. She even heard a gunshot. But she was slowly bending forward by that time, further and further forward, the lids stretched down over her eyes, as if she were doing this in her sleep. Her chin was lowered almost to her knees. The yellow palm of her hand came out from the fold of her apron. Her fingers slid down and along the ground under the piece of money with the grace and care they would have in lifting an egg from under a setting hen. Then she slowly straightened up, she stood erect, and the nickel was in her apron pocket. A bird flew by. Her lips moved. "God watching me the whole time. I come to stealing."

The man came back, and his own dog panted about them. "Well, I scared him off that time," he said, and then he laughed and lifted his gun and pointed it at Phoenix.

She stood straight and faced him.

"Doesn't the gun scare you?" he said, still pointing it.

"No, sir, I seen plenty go off closer by, in my day, and for less than what I done," she said, holding utterly still.

He smiled, and shouldered the gun. "Well, Granny," he said, "you must be a hundred years old, and scared of nothing. I'd give you a dime if I had any money with me. But you take my advice and stay home, and nothing will happen to you."

"I bound to go on my way, mister," said Phoenix. She inclined her head in the red rag. Then they went in different directions, but she could hear the gun shooting again and again over the hill.

She walked on. The shadows hung from the oak trees to the road like curtains. Then she smelled wood-smoke, and smelled the river, and she saw a steeple and the cabins on their steep steps. Dozens of little black children whirled around her. There ahead was Natchez shining. Bells were ringing. She walked on.

In the paved city it was Christmas time. There were red and green electric lights strung and crisscrossed everywhere, and all turned on in the daytime. Old Phoenix would have been lost if she had not distrusted her eyesight and depended on her feet to know where to take her.

She paused quietly on the sidewalk where people were passing by. A lady came along in the crowd, carrying an armful of red-, green- and silver-wrapped presents; she gave off perfume like the red roses in hot summer, and Phoenix stopped her.

"Please, missy, will you lace up my shoe?" She held up her foot.

"What do you want, Grandma?"

"See my shoe," said Phoenix. "Do all right for out in the country, but wouldn't look right to go in a big building."

"Stand still then, Grandma," said the lady. She put her packages down on the sidewalk beside her and laced and tied both shoes tightly.

"Can't lace 'em with a cane," said Phoenix. "Thank you, missy. I doesn't mind asking a nice lady to tie up my shoe, when I gets out on the street."

Moving slowly and from side to side, she went into the big building, and into a tower of steps, where she walked up and around and around until her feet knew to stop.

She entered a door, and there she saw nailed up on the wall the document that had been stamped with the gold seal and framed in the gold frame, which matched the dream that was hung up in her head.

"Here I be," she said. There was a fixed and ceremonial stiffness over her body.

"A charity case, I suppose," said an attendant who sat at the desk before her.

But Phoenix only looked above her head. There was sweat on her face, the wrinkles in her skin shone like a bright net.

"Speak up, Grandma," the woman said. "What's your name? We must have your history, you know. Have you been here before? What seems to be the trouble with you?"

Old Phoenix only gave a twitch to her face as if a fly were bothering her.

"Are you deaf?" cried the attendant.

But then the nurse came in.

"Oh, that's just old Aunt Phoenix," she said. "She doesn't come for herself—she has a little grandson. She makes these trips just as regular as clockwork. She lives away back off the Old Natchez Trace." She bent down. "Well, Aunt Phoenix, why don't you just take a seat? We won't keep you standing after your long trip." She pointed.

The old woman sat down, bolt upright in the chair.

"Now, how is the boy?" asked the nurse.

Old Phoenix did not speak.

"I said, how is the boy?"

But Phoenix only waited and stared straight ahead, her face very solemn and withdrawn into rigidity.

"Is his throat any better?" asked the nurse. "Aunt Phoenix, don't you hear me? Is your grandson's throat any better since the last time you came for the medicine?"

With her hands on her knees, the old woman waited, silent, erect and motionless, just as if she were in armor.

"You mustn't take up our time this way, Aunt Phoenix," the nurse said. "Tell us quickly about your grandson, and get it over. He isn't dead, is he?"

At last there came a flicker and then a flame of comprehension across her face, and she spoke.

"My grandson. It was my memory had left me. There I sat and forgot why I made my long trip."

"Forgot?" The nurse frowned. "After you came so far?"

Then Phoenix was like an old woman begging a dignified forgiveness for waking up frightened in the night. "I never did go to school, I was too old at the Surrender," she said in a soft voice. "I'm an old woman without an education. It was my memory fail me. My little grandson, he is just the same, and I forgot it in the coming."

"Throat never heals, does it?" said the nurse, speaking in a loud, sure voice to old Phoenix. By now she had a card with something written on it, a little list. "Yes. Swallowed lye. When was it?—January—two, three years ago—"

Phoenix spoke unasked now. "No, missy, he not dead, he just the same. Every little while his throat begin to close up again, and he not able to swallow. He not get his breath. He not able to help himself. So the time come around, and I go on another trip for the soothing medicine."

"All right. The doctor said as long as you came to get it, you could have it," said the nurse. "But it's an obstinate case."

"My little grandson, he sit up there in the house all wrapped up, waiting by himself," Phoenix went on. "We is the only two left in the world. He suffer and it don't seem to put him back at all. He got a sweet look. He going to last. He wear a little patch quilt and peep out holding his mouth open like a little bird. I remembers so plain now. I not going to forget him again, no, the whole enduring time. I could tell him from all the others in creation."

"All right." The nurse was trying to hush her now. She brought her a bottle of medicine. "Charity," she said, making a check mark in a book.

Old Phoenix held the bottle close to her eyes, and then carefully put it into her pocket.

"I thank you," she said.

"It's Christmas time, Grandma," said the attendant. "Could I give you a few pennies out of my purse?"

"Five pennies is a nickel," said Phoenix stiffly.

"Here's a nickel," said the attendant.

Phoenix rose carefully and held out her hand. She received the nickel and then fished the other nickel out of her pocket and laid it beside the new one. She stared at her palm closely, with her head on one side.

Then she gave a tap with her cane on the floor.

"This is what come to me to do," she said. "I going to the store and buy my child a little windmill they sells, made out of paper. He going to find it hard to believe there such a thing in the world. I'll march myself back where he waiting, holding it straight up in this hand."

She lifted her free hand, gave a little nod, turned around, and walked out of the doctor's office. Then her slow step began on the stairs, going down.

Petrified Man

"Reach in my purse and git me a cigarette without no powder in it if you kin, Mrs. Fletcher, honey," said Leota to her ten o'clock shampoo-and-set customer. "I don't like no perfumed cigarettes."

Mrs. Fletcher gladly reached over to the lavender shelf under the lavender-framed mirror, shook a hair net loose from the clasp of the patent-leather bag, and slapped her hand down quickly on a powder puff which burst out when the purse was opened.

"Why, look at the peanuts, Leota!" said Mrs. Fletcher in her marvelling voice.

"Honey, them goobers has been in my purse a week if they's been in it a day. Mrs. Pike bought them peanuts."

"Who's Mrs. Pike?" asked Mrs. Fletcher, settling back. Hidden in this den of curling fluid and henna packs, separated by a lavender swing-door from the other customers, who were being gratified in other booths, she could give her curiosity its freedom. She looked expectantly at the black part in Leota's yellow curls as she bent to light the cigarette.

"Mrs. Pike is this lady from New Orleans," said Leota, puffing, and pressing into Mrs. Fletcher's scalp with strong red-nailed fingers. "A friend, not a customer. You see, like maybe I told you last time, me and Fred and Sal and Joe all had us a fuss, so Sal and Joe up and moved out, so we didn't do a thing but rent out their room. So we rented it to Mrs. Pike. And Mr. Pike." She flicked an ash into the basket of dirty towels. "Mrs. Pike is a very decided blonde. *She* bought me the peanuts."

"She must be cute," said Mrs. Fletcher.

"Honey, 'cute' ain't the word for what she is. I'm tellin' you, Mrs. Pike is attractive. She has her a good time. She's got a sharp eye out, Mrs. Pike has."

She dashed the comb through the air, and paused dramatically as a cloud of Mrs. Fletcher's hennaed hair floated out of the lavender teeth like a small storm-cloud.

"Hair fallin'."

"Aw, Leota."

"Uh-huh, commencin' to fall out," said Leota, combing again, and letting fall another cloud.

"Is it any dandruff in it?" Mrs. Fletcher was frowning, her hair-line eyebrows diving down toward her nose, and her wrinkled, beady-lashed eyelids batting with concentration.

"Nope." She combed again. "Just fallin' out."

"Bet it was that last perm'nent you gave me that did it," Mrs. Fletcher said cruelly. "Remember you cooked me fourteen minutes."

"You had fourteen minutes comin' to you," said Leota with finality.

"Bound to be somethin'," persisted Mrs. Fletcher. "Dandruff, dandruff. I couldn't of caught a thing like that from Mr. Fletcher, could I?"

"Well," Leota answered at last, "you know what I heard in here yestiddy, one of Thelma's ladies was settin' over yonder in Thelma's booth gittin' a machineless, and I don't mean to insist or insinuate or anything, Mrs. Fletcher, but Thelma's lady just happ'med to throw out—I forgotten what she was talkin' about at the time—that you was p-r-e-g., and lots of times that'll make your hair do awful funny, fall out and God knows what all. It just ain't our fault, is the way I look at it."

There was a pause. The women stared at each other in the mirror.

"Who was it?" demanded Mrs. Fletcher.

"Honey, I really couldn't say," said Leota. "Not that you look it."

"Where's Thelma? I'll get it out of her," said Mrs. Fletcher.

"Now, honey, I wouldn't go and git mad over a little thing like that," Leota said, combing hastily, as though to hold Mrs. Fletcher down by the hair. "I'm sure it was somebody didn't mean no harm in the world. How far gone are you?"

"Just wait," said Mrs. Fletcher, and shrieked for Thelma, who came in and took a drag from Leota's cigarette.

"Thelma, honey, throw your mind back to yestiddy if you kin," said Leota, drenching Mrs. Fletcher's hair with a thick fluid and catching the overflow in a cold wet towel at her neck.

"Well, I got my lady half wound for a spiral," said Thelma doubtfully.

"This won't take but a minute," said Leota. "Who is it you got in there, old Horse Face? Just cast your mind back and try to remember who your lady was yestiddy who happ'm to mention that my customer was pregnant, that's all. She's dead to know."

Thelma drooped her blood-red lips and looked over Mrs. Fletcher's head into the mirror. "Why, honey, I ain't got the faintest," she breathed. "I really don't recollect the faintest. But I'm sure she meant no harm. I declare, I forgot my hair finally got combed and thought it was a stranger behind me."

"Was it that Mrs. Hutchinson?" Mrs. Fletcher was tensely polite.

"Mrs. Hutchinson? Oh, Mrs. Hutchinson." Thelma batted her eyes. "Naw, precious, she come on Thursday and didn't ev'm mention your name. I doubt if she ev'm knows you're on the way."

"Thelma!" cried Leota staunchly.

"All I know is, whoever it is 'll be sorry some day. Why, I just barely knew it myself!" cried Mrs. Fletcher. "Just let her wait!"

"Why? What're you gonna do to her?"

It was a child's voice, and the women looked down. A little boy was making tents with aluminum wave pinchers on the floor under the sink.

"Billy Boy, hon, mustn't bother nice ladies," Leota smiled. She slapped him brightly and behind her back waved Thelma out of the booth. "Ain't Billy Boy a sight? Only three years old and already just nuts about the beauty-parlor business."

"I never saw him here before," said Mrs. Fletcher, still unmollified.

"He ain't been here before; that's how come," said Leota. "He belongs to Mrs. Pike. She got her a job but it was Fay's Millinery. He oughtn't to try on those ladies' hats, they come down over his eyes like I don't know what. They just git to look ridiculous, that's what, an' of course he's gonna put 'em on: hats. They tole Mrs. Pike they didn't appreciate him hangin' around there. Here, he couldn't hurt a thing."

"Well! I don't like children that much," said Mrs. Fletcher.

"Well!" said Leota moodily.

"Well! I'm almost tempted not to have this one," said Mrs. Fletcher. "That Mrs. Hutchinson! Just looks straight through you when she sees you on the street and then spits at you behind your back."

"Mr. Fletcher would beat you on the head if you didn't have it now," said Leota reasonably. "After going this far."

Mrs. Fletcher sat up straight. "Mr. Fletcher can't do a thing with me."

"He can't!" Leota winked at herself in the mirror.

"No, siree, he can't. If he so much as raises his voice against me, he knows good and well I'll have one of my sick headaches, and then I'm just not fit to live with. And if I really look that pregnant already ———"

"Well, now, honey, I just want you to know—I habm't told any of my ladies and I ain't goin' to tell 'em—even that you're losin' your hair. You just get you one of those Stork-a-Lure dresses and stop worryin'. What people don't know don't hurt nobody, as Mrs. Pike says."

"Did you tell Mrs. Pike?" asked Mrs. Fletcher sulkily.

"Well, Mrs. Fletcher, look, you ain't ever goin' to lay eyes on Mrs. Pike or her lay eyes on you, so what diffunce does it make in the long run?"

"I knew it!" Mrs. Fletcher deliberately nodded her head so as to destroy a ringlet Leota was working on behind her ear. "Mrs. Pike!"

Leota sighed. "I reckon I might as well tell you. It wasn't any more Thelma's lady tole me you was pregnant than a bat."

"Not Mrs. Hutchinson?"

"Naw, Lord! It was Mrs. Pike."

"Mrs. Pike!" Mrs. Fletcher could only sputter and let curling fluid roll into her ear. "How could Mrs. Pike possibly know I was pregnant or otherwise, when she doesn't even know me? The nerve of some people!"

"Well, here's how it was. Remember Sunday?"

"Yes," said Mrs. Fletcher.

"Sunday, Mrs. Pike an' me was all by ourself. Mr. Pike and Fred had gone over to Eagle Lake, sayin' they was goin' to catch 'em some fish, but they didn't a course. So we was settin' in Mrs. Pike's car, it's a 1939 Dodge——"

"1939, eh," said Mrs. Fletcher.

"—An' we was gettin' us a Jax beer apiece—that's the beer that Mrs. Pike says is made right in N.O., so she won't drink no other kind. So I seen you drive up to the drugstore an' run in for just a secont, leavin' I reckon Mr. Fletcher in the car, an' come runnin' out with looked like a perscription. So I says to Mrs. Pike, just to be makin' talk, 'Right yonder's Mrs. Fletcher, and I reckon that's Mr. Fletcher—she's one of my regular customers,' I says."

"I had on a figured print," said Mrs. Fletcher tentatively.

"You sure did," agreed Leota. "So Mrs. Pike, she give you a good look—she's very observant, a good judge of character, cute as a minute, you know—and she says, 'I bet you another Jax that lady's three months on the way.' "

"What gall!" said Mrs. Fletcher. "Mrs. Pike!"

"Mrs. Pike ain't goin' to bite you," said Leota. "Mrs. Pike is a lovely girl, you'd be crazy about her, Mrs. Fletcher. But she can't sit still a minute. We went to the travellin' freak show yestiddy after work. I got through early—nine o'clock. In the vacant store next door. What, you ain't been?"

"No, I despise freaks," declared Mrs. Fletcher.

"Aw. Well, honey, talkin' about bein' pregnant an' all, you ought to see those twins in a bottle, you really owe it to yourself."

"What twins?" asked Mrs. Fletcher out of the side of her mouth.

"Well, honey, they got these two twins in a bottle, see? Born joined plumb together—dead a course." Leota dropped her voice into a soft lyrical hum. "They was about this long—pardon—must of been full time, all right, wouldn't you say?—an' they had these two heads an' two faces an' four arms an' four legs, all kind of joined *here*. See, this face looked this-a-way, and the other face looked that-a-way, over their shoulder, see. Kinda pathetic."

"Glah!" said Mrs. Fletcher disapprovingly.

"Well, ugly? Honey, I mean to tell you—their parents was first cousins and all like that. Billy Boy, git me a fresh towel from off Teeny's stack—this 'n's wringin' wet—an' quit ticklin' my ankles with that curler. I declare! He don't miss nothin'."

"Me and Mr. Fletcher aren't one speck of kin, or he could never of had me," said Mrs. Fletcher placidly.

"Of course not!" protested Leota. "Neither is me an' Fred, not that we know of. Well, honey, what Mrs. Pike liked was the pygmies. They've got these pygmies down there, too, an' Mrs. Pike was just wild about 'em. You know, the teeniniest men in the universe? Well, honey, they can just rest back on their little bohunkus an' roll around an' you can't hardly tell if they're sittin' or standin'. That'll give you some idea. They're about forty-two years old. Just suppose it was your husband!"

"Well, Mr. Fletcher is five foot nine and one half," said Mrs. Fletcher quickly.

"Fred's five foot ten," said Leota, "but I tell him he's still a shrimp, account of I'm so tall." She made a deep wave over Mrs. Fletcher's other temple with the comb. "Well, these pygmies are a kind of a dark brown, Mrs. Fletcher. Not bad lookin' for what they are, you know."

"I wouldn't care for them," said Mrs. Fletcher. "What does that Mrs. Pike see in them?"

"Aw, I don't know," said Leota. "She's just cute, that's all. But they got this man, this petrified man, that ever'thing ever since he was nine years old, when it goes through his digestion, see, somehow Mrs. Pike says it goes to his joints and has been turning to stone."

"How awful!" said Mrs. Fletcher.

"He's forty-two too. That looks like a bad age."

"Who said so, that Mrs. Pike? I bet she's forty-two," said Mrs. Fletcher.

"Naw," said Leota, "Mrs. Pike's thirty-three, born in January, an Aquarian. He could move his head—like this. A course his head and mind ain't a joint, so to speak, and I guess his stomach ain't, either—not yet, anyways. But see—his food, he eats it, and it goes down, see, and then he digests it"—Leota rose on her toes for an instant—"and it goes out to his joints and before you can say 'Jack Robinson,' it's stone—pure stone. He's turning to stone. How'd you like to be married to a guy like that? All he can do, he can move his head just a quarter of an inch. A course he *looks* just *terrible*."

"I should think he would," said Mrs. Fletcher frostily. "Mr. Fletcher takes bending exercises every night of the world. I make him."

"All Fred does is lay around the house like a rug. I wouldn't be surprised if he woke up some day and couldn't move. The petrified man just sat there moving his quarter of an inch though," said Leota reminiscently.

"Did Mrs. Pike like the petrified man?" asked Mrs. Fletcher.

"Not as much as she did the others," said Leota deprecatingly. "And then she likes a man to be a good dresser, and all that."

"Is Mr. Pike a good dresser?" asked Mrs. Fletcher sceptically.

"Oh, well, yeah," said Leota, "but he's twelve or fourteen years older'n her. She ast Lady Evangeline about him."

"Who's Lady Evangeline?" asked Mrs. Fletcher.

"Well, it's this mind reader they got in the freak show," said Leota. "Was real good. Lady Evangeline is her name, and if I had another dollar I wouldn't do a thing but have my other palm read. She had what Mrs. Pike said was the 'sixth mind' but she had the worst manicure I ever saw on a living person."

"What did she tell Mrs. Pike?" asked Mrs. Fletcher.

"She told her Mr. Pike was as true to her as he could be and besides, would come into some money."

"Humph!" said Mrs. Fletcher. "What does he do?"

"I can't tell," said Leota, "because he don't work. Lady Evangeline didn't tell me enough about my nature or anything. And I would like to go back and find out some more about this boy. Used to go with this boy until he got married to this girl. Oh, shoot, that was about three and a half years ago, when you was still goin' to the Robert E. Lee Beauty Shop in Jackson. He married her for her money. Another fortune-teller tole me that at the time. So I'm not in love with him any more, anyway, besides being married to Fred, but Mrs. Pike thought, just for the hell of it, see, to ask Lady Evangeline was he happy."

"Does Mrs. Pike know everything about you already?" asked Mrs. Fletcher unbelievingly. "Mercy!"

"Oh, yeah, I tole her ever'thing about ever'thing, from now on back to I don't know when—to when I first started goin' out," said Leota. "So I ast Lady Evangeline for one of my questions, was he happily married, and she says, just like she was glad I ask her, 'Honey,' she says, 'naw, he idn't. You write down this day, March 8, 1941,' she says, 'and mock it down: three years from today him and her won't be occupyin' the same bed.' There it is, up on the wall with them other dates—see, Mrs. Fletcher? And she says, 'Child, you ought to be glad you didn't git him, because he's so mercenary.' So I'm glad I married Fred. He sure ain't mercenary, money don't mean a thing to him. But I sure would like to go back and have my other palm read."

"Did Mrs. Pike believe in what the fortune-teller said?" asked Mrs. Fletcher in a superior tone of voice.

"Lord, yes, she's from New Orleans. Ever'body in New Orleans believes ever'thing spooky. One of 'em in New Orleans before it was raided says to Mrs. Pike one summer she was goin' to go from State to State and meet some grey-headed men, and, sure enough, she says she went on a beautician convention up to Chicago. . . ."

"Oh!" said Mrs. Fletcher. "Oh, is Mrs. Pike a beautician too?"

"Sure she is," protested Leota. "She's a beautician. I'm goin' to git her in here if I can. Before she married. But it don't leave you. She says sure enough, there was three men who was a very large part of making her trip what it was, and they all three had grey in their hair and they went in six States. Got Christmas cards from 'em. Billy Boy, go see if Thelma's got any dry cotton. Look how Mrs. Fletcher's a-drippin'."

"Where did Mrs. Pike meet Mr. Pike?" asked Mrs. Fletcher primly.

"On another train," said Leota.

"I met Mr. Fletcher, or rather he met me, in a rental library," said Mrs. Fletcher with dignity, as she watched the net come down over her head.

"Honey, me an' Fred, we met in a rumble seat eight months ago and we was practically on what you might call the way to the altar inside of half an hour," said Leota in a guttural voice, and bit a bobby pin open. "Course it don't last. Mrs. Pike says nothin' like that ever lasts."

"Mr. Fletcher and myself are as much in love as the day we married," said Mrs. Fletcher belligerently as Leota stuffed cotton into her ears.

"Mrs. Pike says it don't last," repeated Leota in a louder voice. "Now go git under the dryer. You can turn yourself on, can't you? I'll be back to comb you out. Durin' lunch I promised to give Mrs. Pike a facial. You know—free. Her bein' in the business, so to speak."

"I bet she needs one," said Mrs. Fletcher, letting the swing-door fly back against Leota. "Oh, pardon me."

A week later, on time for her appointment, Mrs. Fletcher sank heavily into Leota's chair after first removing a drugstore rental book, called *Life Is Like That*, from the seat. She stared in a discouraged way into the mirror.

"You can tell it when I'm sitting down, all right," she said.

Leota seemed preoccupied and stood shaking out a lavender cloth. She began to pin it around Mrs. Fletcher's neck in silence.

"I said you sure can tell it when I'm sitting straight on and coming at you this way," Mrs. Fletcher said.

"Why, honey, naw you can't," said Leota gloomily. "Why, I'd never know. If somebody was to come up to me on the street and say, 'Mrs. Fletcher is pregnant!' I'd say, 'Heck, she don't look it to me.' "

"If a certain party hadn't found it out and spread it around, it wouldn't be too late even now," said Mrs. Fletcher frostily, but Leota was almost choking her with the cloth, pinning it so tight, and she couldn't speak clearly. She paddled her hands in the air until Leota wearily loosened her.

"Listen, honey, you're just a virgin compared to Mrs. Montjoy," Leota was going on, still absent-minded. She bent Mrs. Fletcher back in the chair and, sighing, tossed liquid from a teacup onto her head and dug both hands into her scalp. "You know Mrs. Montjoy—her husband's that premature-grey-headed fella?"

"She's in the Trojan Garden Club, is all I know," said Mrs. Fletcher.

"Well, honey," said Leota, but in a weary voice, "she come in here not the week before and not the day before she had her baby—she come in here the very selfsame day, I mean to tell you. Child, we was all plumb scared to death. There she was! Come for her shampoo an' set. Why, Mrs. Fletcher, in an hour an' twenty minutes she was layin' up there in the Babtist Hospital with a seb'm-pound son. It was that close a shave. I declare, if I hadn't been so tired I would of drank up a bottle of gin that night."

"What gall," said Mrs. Fletcher. "I never knew her at all well."

"See, her husband was waitin' outside in the car, and her bags was all packed an' in the back seat, an' she was all ready, 'cept she wanted her shampoo an' set. An' havin' one pain right after another. Her husband kep' comin' in here, scared-like, but couldn't do nothin' with her a course. She yelled bloody murder, too, but she always yelled her head off when I give her a perm'nent."

"She must of been crazy," said Mrs. Fletcher. "How did she look?"

"Shoot!" said Leota.

"Well, I can guess," said Mrs. Fletcher. "Awful."

"Just wanted to look pretty while she was havin' her baby, is all," said Leota airily. "Course, we was glad to give the lady what she was after—that's our motto—but I bet a hour later she wasn't payin' no mind to them little end curls. I bet she wasn't thinkin' about she ought to have on a net. It wouldn't of done her no good if she had."

"No, I don't suppose it would," said Mrs. Fletcher.

"Yeah man! She was a-yellin'. Just like when I give her perm'nent."

"Her husband ought to make her behave. Don't it seem that way to you?" asked Mrs. Fletcher. "He ought to put his foot down."

"Ha," said Leota. "A lot he could do. Maybe some women is soft."

"Oh, you mistake me, I don't mean for her to get soft—far from it! Women have to stand up for themselves, or there's just no telling. But now you take me—I ask Mr. Fletcher's advice now and then, and he appreciates it, especially on something important, like is it time for a permanent—not that I've told him about the baby. He says, 'Why, dear, go ahead!' Just ask their *advice*."

"Huh! If I ever ast Fred's advice we'd be floatin' down the Yazoo River on a houseboat or somethin' by this time," said Leota. "I'm sick of Fred. I told him to go over to Vicksburg."

"Is he going?" demanded Mrs. Fletcher.

"Sure. See, the fortune-teller—I went back and had my other palm read, since we've got to rent the room agin—said my lover was goin' to work in Vicksburg, so I don't know who she could mean, unless she meant Fred. And Fred ain't workin' here—that much is so."

"Is he going to work in Vicksburg?" asked Mrs. Fletcher. "And ———"

"Sure. Lady Evangeline said so. Said the future is going to be brighter than the present. He don't want to go, but I ain't gonna put up with nothin' like that. Lays around the house an' bulls—did bull—with that good-for-nothin' Mr. Pike. He says if he goes who'll cook, but I says I never get to eat anyway—not meals. Billy Boy, take Mrs. Grover that *Screen Secrets* and leg it."

Mrs. Fletcher heard stamping feet go out the door.

"Is that that Mrs. Pike's little boy here again?" she asked, sitting up gingerly.

"Yeah, that's still him." Leota stuck out her tongue.

Mrs. Fletcher could hardly believe her eyes. "Well! How's Mrs. Pike, your attractive new friend with the sharp eyes who spreads it around town that perfect strangers are pregnant?" she asked in a sweetened tone.

"Oh, Mizriz Pike." Leota combed Mrs. Fletcher's hair with heavy strokes.

"You act like you're tired," said Mrs. Fletcher.

"Tired? Feel like it's four o'clock in the afternoon already," said Leota. "I ain't told you the awful luck we had, me and Fred? It's the worst thing you ever heard of. Maybe *you* think Mrs. Pike's got sharp eyes. Shoot, there's a limit! Well, you know, we rented out our room to this Mr. and Mrs. Pike from New Orleans when Sal an' Joe Fentress got mad at us 'cause they drank up some home-brew we had in the closet—Sal an' Joe did. So, a week ago Sat'day Mr. and Mrs. Pike moved in. Well, I kinda fixed up the room, you know—put a sofa pillow on the couch and picked some ragged robbins and put in a vase, but they never did say they appreciated it. Anyway, then I put some old magazines on the table."

"I think that was lovely," said Mrs. Fletcher.

"Wait. So, come night 'fore last, Fred and this Mr. Pike, who Fred just took up with, was back from they said they was fishin', bein' as neither one of 'em has got a job to his name, and we was all settin' around in their room. So Mrs. Pike was settin' there, readin' a old *Startling G-Man Tales* that was mine, mind you, I'd bought it myself, and all of a sudden she jumps!—into the air—you'd 'a' thought she'd set on a spider—an' says, 'Canfield'—ain't that silly, that's Mr. Pike—'Canfield, my God A'mighty,' she says, 'honey,' she says, 'we're rich, and you won't have to work.' Not that he turned one hand anyway. Well, me and Fred rushes over to her, and Mr. Pike, too, and there she sets, pointin' her finger at a photo in my copy of *Startling G-Man*, 'See that man?' yells Mrs. Pike. 'Remember him, Canfield?' 'Never forget a face,' says Mr. Pike. 'It's Mr. Petrie, that we stayed with him in the apartment next to ours in Toulouse Street in N.O. for six weeks. Mr. Petrie.' 'Well,' says Mrs. Pike, like she can't hold out one secont longer, 'Mr. Petrie is wanted for five hundred dollars cash, for rapin' four women in California, and I know where he is.' "

"Mercy!" said Mrs. Fletcher. "Where was he?"

At some time Leota had washed her hair and now she yanked her up by the back locks and sat her up.

"Know where he was?"

"I certainly don't," Mrs. Fletcher said. Her scalp hurt all over.

Leota flung a towel around the top of her customer's head. "Nowhere else but in that freak show! I saw him just as plain as Mrs. Pike. *He* was the petrified man!"

"Who would ever have thought that!" cried Mrs. Fletcher sympathetically.

"So Mr. Pike says, 'Well whatta you know about that,' an' he looks real hard at the photo and whistles. And she starts dancin' and singin' about their good luck. She meant our bad luck! I made a point of tellin' that fortune-teller the next time I saw her. I said, 'Listen, that magazine was layin' around the house for a month, and there was the freak show runnin' night an' day, not two steps away from my own beauty parlor, with Mr. Petrie just settin' there waitin'. An' it had to be Mr. and Mrs. Pike, almost perfect strangers.' "

"What gall," said Mrs. Fletcher. She was only sitting there, wrapped in a turban, but she did not mind.

"Fortune-tellers don't care. And Mrs. Pike, she goes around actin' like she thinks she was Mrs. God," said Leota. "So they're goin' to leave tomorrow, Mr. and Mrs. Pike. And in the meantime I got to keep that mean, bad little ole kid here, gettin' under my feet ever' minute of the day an' talkin' back too."

"Have they gotten the five hundred dollars' reward already?" asked Mrs. Fletcher.

"Well," said Leota, "at first Mr. Pike didn't want to do anything about it. Can you feature that? Said he kinda liked that ole bird and said he was real nice to 'em, lent 'em money or somethin'. But Mrs. Pike simply tole him he could just go to hell, and I can see her point. She says, 'You ain't worked a lick in six months, and here I make five hundred dollars in two seconts, and what thanks do I get for it? You go to hell, Canfield,' she says. So," Leota went on in a despondent voice, "they called up the cops and they caught the ole bird, all right, right there in the freak show where I saw him with my own eyes, thinkin' he was petrified. He's the one. Did it under his real name—Mr. Petrie. Four women in California, all in the month of August. So Mrs. Pike gits five hundred dollars. And my magazine, and right next door to my beauty parlor. I cried all night, but Fred said it wasn't a bit of use and to go to sleep, because the whole thing was just a sort of coincidence—you know: can't do nothin' about it. He says it put him clean out of the notion of goin' to Vicksburg for a few days till we rent out the room agin—no tellin' who we'll git this time."

"But can you imagine anybody knowing this old man, that's raped four women?" persisted Mrs. Fletcher, and she shuddered audibly. "Did Mrs. Pike *speak* to him when she met him in the freak show?"

Leota had begun to comb Mrs. Fletcher's hair. "I says to her, I says, 'I didn't notice you fallin' on his neck when he was the petrified man—don't tell me you didn't recognize your fine friend?' And she says, 'I didn't recognize him with that white powder all over his face. He just looked familiar,' Mrs. Pike says, 'and lots of people look familiar.' But she says that ole petrified man did put her in mind of somebody. She wondered who it was! Kep' her awake, which man she'd ever knew it reminded her of. So when she seen the photo, it all come to her. Like a flash. Mr. Petrie. The way he'd turn his head and look at her when she took him in his breakfast."

"Took him in his breakfast!" shrieked Mrs. Fletcher. "Listen—don't tell me. I'd 'a' felt something."

"Four women. I guess those women didn't have the faintest notion at the time they'd be worth a hundred an' twenty-five bucks apiece some day to Mrs. Pike. We ast her how old the fella was then, an' she says he musta had one foot in the grave, at least. Can you beat it?"

"Not really petrified at all, of course," said Mrs. Fletcher meditatively. She drew herself up. "I'd 'a' felt something," she said proudly.

"Shoot! I did feel somethin'," said Leota. "I tole Fred when I got home I felt so funny. I said, 'Fred, that ole petrified man sure did leave me with a funny feelin'.' He says, 'Funny-haha or funny-peculiar?' and I says, 'Funny-peculiar.' " She pointed her comb into the air emphatically.

"I'll bet you did," said Mrs. Fletcher.

They both heard a crackling noise.

Leota screamed, "Billy Boy! What you doin' in my purse?"

"Aw, I'm just eatin' these ole stale peanuts up," said Billy Boy.

"You come here to me!" screamed Leota, recklessly flinging down the comb, which scattered a whole ashtray full of bobby pins and knocked down a row of Coca-Cola bottles. "This is the last straw!"

"I caught him! I caught him!" giggled Mrs. Fletcher. "I'll hold him on my lap. You bad, bad boy, you! I guess I better learn how to spank little old bad boys," she said.

Leota's eleven o'clock customer pushed open the swing-door upon Leota paddling him heartily with the brush, while he gave angry but belittling screams which penetrated beyond the booth and filled the whole curious beauty parlor. From everywhere ladies began to gather round to watch the paddling. Billy Boy kicked both Leota and Mrs. Fletcher as hard as he could, Mrs. Fletcher with her new fixed smile.

Billy Boy stomped through the group of wild-haired ladies and went out the door, but flung back the words, "If you're so smart, why ain't you rich?"

Why I Live at the P.O.

I was getting along fine with Mama, Papa-Daddy and Uncle Rondo until my sister Stella-Rondo just separated from her husband and came back home again. Mr. Whitaker! Of course I went with Mr. Whitaker first, when he first appeared here in China Grove, taking "Pose Yourself" photos, and Stella-Rondo broke us up. Told him I was one-sided. Bigger on one side than the other, which is a deliberate, calculated falsehood: I'm the same. Stella-Rondo is exactly twelve months to the day younger than I am and for that reason she's spoiled.

She's always had anything in the world she wanted and then she'd throw it away. Papa-Daddy gave her this gorgeous Add-a-Pearl necklace when she was eight years old and she threw it away playing baseball when she was nine, with only two pearls.

So as soon as she got married and moved away from home the first thing she did was separate! From Mr. Whitaker! This photographer with the popeyes she said she trusted. Came home from one of those towns up in Illinois and to our complete surprise brought this child of two.

Mama said she like to made her drop dead for a second. "Here you had this marvelous blonde child and never so much as wrote your mother a word about it," says Mama. "I'm thoroughly ashamed of you." But of course she wasn't.

Stella-Rondo just calmly takes off this *hat*, I wish you could see it. She says, "Why, Mama, Shirley-T.'s adopted, I can prove it."

"How?" says Mama, but all I says was, "H'm!" There I was over the hot stove, trying to stretch two chickens over five people and a completely unexpected child into the bargain, without one moment's notice.

"What do you mean—'H'm!'?" says Stella-Rondo, and Mama says, "I heard that, Sister."

I said that oh, I didn't mean a thing, only that whoever Shirley-T. was, she was the spit-image of Papa-Daddy if he'd cut off his beard, which of course he'd never do in the world. Papa-Daddy's Mama's papa and sulks.

Stella-Rondo got furious! She said, "Sister, I don't need to tell you you got a lot of nerve and always did have and I'll thank you to make no future reference to my adopted child whatsoever."

"Very well," I said. "Very well, very well. Of course I noticed at once she looks like Mr. Whitaker's side too. That frown. She looks like a cross between Mr. Whitaker and Papa-Daddy."

"Well, all I can say is she isn't."

"She looks exactly like Shirley Temple to me," says Mama, but Shirley-T. just ran away from her.

So the first thing Stella-Rondo did at the table was turn Papa-Daddy against me.

"Papa-Daddy," she says. He was trying to cut up his meat. "Papa-Daddy!" I was taken completely by surprise. Papa-Daddy is about a million years old and's got this long-long beard. "Papa-Daddy, Sister says she fails to understand why you don't cut off your beard."

So Papa-Daddy l-a-y-s down his knife and fork! He's real rich. Mama says he is, he says he isn't. So he says, "Have I heard correctly? You don't understand why I don't cut off my beard?"

"Why," I says, "Papa-Daddy, of course I understand, I did not say any such of a thing, the idea!"

He says, "Hussy!"

I says, "Papa-Daddy, you know I wouldn't any more want you to cut off your beard than the man in the moon. It was the farthest thing from my mind! Stella-Rondo sat there and made that up while she was eating breast of chicken."

But he says, "So the postmistress fails to understand why I don't cut off my beard. Which job I got you through my influence with the government. 'Bird's nest'—is that what you call it?"

Not that it isn't the next to smallest P.O. in the entire state of Mississippi.

I says, "Oh, Papa-Daddy," I says, "I didn't say any such of a thing, I never dreamed it was a bird's nest, I have always been grateful though this is the next to smallest P.O. in the state of Mississippi, and I do not enjoy being referred to as a hussy by my own grandfather."

But Stella-Rondo says, "Yes, you did say it too. Anybody in the world could of heard you, that had ears."

"Stop right there," says Mama, looking at *me*.

So I pulled my napkin straight back through the napkin ring and left the table.

As soon as I was out of the room Mama says, "Call her back, or she'll starve to death," but Papa-Daddy says, "This is the beard I started growing on the Coast when I was fifteen years old." He would of gone on till nightfall if Shirley-T. hadn't lost the Milky Way she ate in Cairo.

So Papa-Daddy says, "I am going out and lie in the hammock, and you can all sit here and remember my words: I'll never cut off my beard as long as I live, even one inch, and I don't appreciate it in you at all." Passed right by me in the hall and went straight out and got in the hammock.

It would be a holiday. It wasn't five minutes before Uncle Rondo suddenly appeared in the hall in one of Stella-Rondo's flesh-colored kimonos, all cut on the bias, like something Mr. Whitaker probably thought was gorgeous.

"Uncle Rondo!" I says. "I didn't know who that was! Where are you going?"

"Sister," he says, "get out of my way, I'm poisoned."

"If you're poisoned stay away from Papa-Daddy," I says. "Keep out of the hammock. Papa-Daddy will certainly beat you on the head if you come within forty miles of him. He thinks I deliberately said he ought to cut off his beard after he got me the P.O., and I've told him and told him and told him, and he acts like he just don't hear me. Papa-Daddy must of gone stone deaf."

"He picked a fine day to do it then," says Uncle Rondo, and before you could say "Jack Robinson" flew out in the yard.

What he'd really done, he'd drunk another bottle of that prescription. He does it every single Fourth of July as sure as shooting, and it's horribly expensive. Then he falls over in the hammock and snores. So he insisted on zigzagging right on out to the hammock, looking like a half-wit.

Papa-Daddy woke up with this horrible yell and right there without moving an inch he tried to turn Uncle Rondo against me. I heard every word he said. Oh, he told Uncle Rondo I didn't learn to read till I was eight years old and he didn't see how in the world I ever got the mail put up at the P.O., much less read it all, and he said if Uncle Rondo could only fathom the lengths he had gone to to get me that job! And he said on the other hand he thought Stella-Rondo had a brilliant mind and deserved credit for getting out of town. All the time he was just lying there swinging as pretty as you please and looping out his beard, and poor Uncle Rondo was *pleading* with him to slow down the hammock, it was making him as dizzy as a witch to watch it. But that's what Papa-Daddy likes about a hammock. So Uncle Rondo was too dizzy to get turned against me for the time being. He's Mama's only brother and is a good case of a one-track mind. Ask anybody. A certified pharmacist.

Just then I heard Stella-Rondo raising the upstairs window. While she was married she got this peculiar idea that it's cooler with the windows shut and locked. So she has to raise the window before she can make a soul hear her outdoors.

So she raises the window and says, "*Oh!*" You would have thought she was mortally wounded.

Uncle Rondo and Papa-Daddy didn't even look up, but kept right on with what they were doing. I had to laugh.

I flew up the stairs and threw the door open! I says, "What in the wide world's the matter, Stella-Rondo? You mortally wounded?"

"No," she says, "I am not mortally wounded but I wish you would do me the favor of looking out that window there and telling me what you see."

So I shade my eyes and look out the window.

"I see the front yard," I says.

"Don't you see any human beings?" she says.

"I see Uncle Rondo trying to run Papa-Daddy out of the hammock," I says. "Nothing more. Naturally, it's so suffocating-hot in the house, with all the windows shut and locked, everybody who cares to stay in their right mind will have to go out and get in the hammock before the Fourth of July is over."

"Don't you notice anything different about Uncle Rondo?" asks Stella-Rondo.

"Why, no, except he's got on some terrible-looking flesh-colored contraption I wouldn't be found dead in, is all I can see," I says.

"Never mind, you won't be found dead in it, because it happens to be part of my trousseau, and Mr. Whitaker took several dozen photographs of me in it," says Stella-Rondo. "What on earth could Uncle Rondo *mean* by wearing part of my trousseau out in the broad open daylight without saying so much as 'Kiss my foot,' *knowing* I only got home this morning after my separation and hung my negligee up on the bathroom door, just as nervous as I could be?"

"I'm sure I don't know, and what do you expect me to do about it?" I says. "Jump out the window?"

"No, I expect nothing of the kind. I simply declare that Uncle Rondo looks like a fool in it, that's all," she says. "It makes me sick to my stomach."

"Well, he looks as good as he can," I says. "As good as anybody in reason could." I stood up for Uncle Rondo, please remember. And I said to Stella-Rondo, "I think I would do well not to criticize so freely if I were you and came home with a two-year-old child I had never said a word about, and no explanation whatever about my separation."

"I asked you the instant I entered this house not to refer one more time to my adopted child, and you gave me your word of honor you would not," was all Stella-Rondo would say, and started pulling out every one of her eyebrows with some cheap Kress tweezers.

So I merely slammed the door behind me and went down and made some green-tomato pickle. Somebody had to do it. Of course Mama had turned both the Negroes loose; she always said no earthly power could hold one anyway on the Fourth of July, so she wouldn't even try. It turned out that Jaypan fell in the lake and came within a very narrow limit of drowning.

So Mama trots in. Lifts up the lid and says, "H'm! Not very good for your Uncle Rondo in his precarious condition, I must say. Or poor little adopted Shirley-T. Shame on you!"

That made me tired. I says, "Well, Stella-Rondo had better thank her lucky stars it was her instead of me came trotting in with that very peculiar-looking child. Now if it had been me that trotted in from Illinois and brought a peculiar-looking child of two, I shudder to think of the reception I'd of got, much less controlled the diet of an entire family."

"But you must remember, Sister, that you were never married to Mr. Whitaker in the first place and didn't go up to Illinois to live," says Mama, shaking a spoon in my face. "If you had I would of been just as overjoyed to see you and your little adopted girl as I was to see Stella-Rondo, when you wound up with your separation and came on back home."

"You would not," I says.

"Don't contradict me, I would," says Mama.

But I said she couldn't convince me though she talked till she was blue in the face. Then I said, "Besides, you know as well as I do that that child is not adopted."

"She most certainly is adopted," says Mama, stiff as a poker.

I says, "Why, Mama, Stella-Rondo had her just as sure as anything in this world, and just too stuck up to admit it."

"Why, Sister," said Mama. "Here I thought we were going to have a pleasant Fourth of July, and you start right out not believing a word your own baby sister tells you!"

"Just like Cousin Annie Flo. Went to her grave denying the facts of life," I remind Mama.

"I told you if you ever mentioned Annie Flo's name I'd slap your face," says Mama, and slaps my face.

"All right, you wait and see," I says.

"I," says Mama, "*I* prefer to take my children's word for anything when it's humanly possible." You ought to see Mama, she weighs two hundred pounds and has real tiny feet.

Just then something perfectly horrible occurred to me.

"Mama," I says, "can that child talk?" I simply had to whisper! "Mama, I wonder if that child can be—you know—in any way? Do you realize," I says, "that she hasn't spoken one single, solitary word to a human being up to this minute? This is the way she looks," I says, and I looked like this.

Well, Mama and I just stood there and stared at each other. It was horrible!

"I remember well that Joe Whitaker frequently drank like a fish," says Mama. "I believed to my soul he drank *chemicals*." And without another word she marches to the foot of the stairs and calls Stella-Rondo.

"Stella-Rondo? O-o-o-o-o! Stella-Rondo!"

"What?" says Stella-Rondo from upstairs. Not even the grace to get up off the bed.

"Can that child of yours talk?" asks Mama.

Stella-Rondo says, "Can she what?"

"Talk! Talk!" says Mama. "Burdyburdyburdyburdy!"

So Stella-Rondo yells back, "Who says she can't talk?"

"Sister says so," says Mama.

"You didn't have to tell me, I know whose word of honor don't mean a thing in this house," says Stella-Rondo.

And in a minute the loudest Yankee voice I ever heard in my life yells out, "OE'm Pop-OE the Sailor-r-r-r Ma-a-an!" and then somebody jumps up and down in the upstairs hall. In another second the house would of fallen down.

"Not only talks, she can tap-dance!" calls Stella-Rondo. "Which is more than some people I won't name can do."

"Why, the little precious darling thing!" Mama says, so surprised. "Just as smart as she can be!" Starts talking baby talk right there. Then she turns on me. "Sister, you ought to be thoroughly ashamed! Run upstairs this instant and apologize to Stella-Rondo and Shirley-T."

"Apologize for what?" I says. "I merely wondered if the child was normal, that's all. Now that she's proved she is, why, I have nothing further to say."

But Mama just turned on her heel and flew out, furious. She ran right upstairs and hugged the baby. She believed it was adopted. Stella-Rondo hadn't done a thing but turn her against me from upstairs while I stood there helpless over the hot stove. So that made Mama, Papa-Daddy and the baby all on Stella-Rondo's side.

Next, Uncle Rondo.

I must say that Uncle Rondo has been marvelous to me at various times in the past and I was completely unprepared to be made to jump out of my skin, the way it turned out. Once Stella-Rondo did something perfectly horrible to him—broke a chain letter from Flanders Field—and he took the radio back he had given her and gave it to me. Stella-Rondo was furious! For six months we all had to call her Stella instead of Stella-Rondo, or she wouldn't answer. I always thought Uncle Rondo had all the brains of the entire family. Another time he sent me to Mammoth Cave, with all expenses paid.

But this would be the day he was drinking that prescription, the Fourth of July.

So at supper Stella-Rondo speaks up and says she thinks Uncle Rondo ought to try to eat a little something. So finally Uncle Rondo said he would try a little cold biscuits and ketchup, but that was all. So *she* brought it to him.

"Do you think it wise to disport with ketchup in Stella-Rondo's flesh-colored kimono?" I says. Trying to be considerate! If Stella-Rondo couldn't watch out for her trousseau, somebody had to.

"Any objections?" asks Uncle Rondo, just about to pour out all the ketchup.

"Don't mind what she says, Uncle Rondo," says Stella-Rondo. "Sister has been devoting this solid afternoon to sneering out my bedroom window at the way you look."

"What's that?" says Uncle Rondo. Uncle Rondo has got the most terrible temper in the world. Anything is liable to make him tear the house down if it comes at the wrong time.

So Stella-Rondo says, "Sister says, 'Uncle Rondo certainly does look like a fool in that pink kimono!' "

Do you remember who it was really said that?

Uncle Rondo spills out all the ketchup and jumps out of his chair and tears off the kimono and throws it down on the dirty floor and puts his foot on it. It had to be sent all the way to Jackson to the cleaners and re-pleated.

"So that's your opinion of your Uncle Rondo, is it?" he says. "I look like a fool, do I? Well, that's the last straw. A whole day in this house with nothing to do, and then to hear you come out with a remark like that behind my back!"

"I didn't say any such of a thing, Uncle Rondo," I says, "and I'm not saying who did, either. Why, I think you look all right. Just try to take care of yourself and not talk and eat at the same time," I says. "I think you better go lie down."

"Lie down my foot," says Uncle Rondo. I ought to of known by that he was fixing to do something perfectly horrible.

So he didn't do anything that night in the precarious state he was in—just played Casino with Mama and Stella-Rondo and Shirley-T. and gave Shirley-T. a nickel with a head on both sides. It tickled her nearly to death, and she called him "Papa." But at 6:30 A.M. the next morning, he threw a whole five-cent package of some unsold one-inch firecrackers from the store as hard as he could into my bedroom and they every one went off. Not one bad one in the string. Anybody else, there'd be one that wouldn't go off.

Well, I'm just terribly susceptible to noise of any kind, the doctor has always told me I was the most sensitive person he had ever seen in his whole life, and I was simply prostrated. I couldn't eat! People tell me they heard it as far as the cemetery, and old Aunt Jep Patterson, that had been holding her own so good, thought it was Judgment Day and she was going to meet her whole family. It's usually so quiet here.

And I'll tell you it didn't take me any longer than a minute to make up my mind what to do. There I was with the whole entire house on Stella-Rondo's side and turned against me. If I have anything at all I have pride.

So I just decided I'd go straight down to the P.O. There's plenty of room there in the back, I says to myself.

Well! I made no bones about letting the family catch on to what I was up to. I didn't try to conceal it.

The first thing they knew, I marched in where they were all playing Old Maid and pulled the electric oscillating fan out by the plug, and everything got real hot. Next I snatched the pillow I'd done the needlepoint on right off the davenport from behind Papa-Daddy. He went "Ugh!" I beat Stella-Rondo up the stairs and finally found my charm bracelet in her bureau drawer under a picture of Nelson Eddy.

"So that's the way the land lies," says Uncle Rondo. There he was, piecing on the ham. "Well, Sister, I'll be glad to donate my army cot if you got any place to set it up, providing you'll leave right this minute and let me get some peace." Uncle Rondo was in France.

"Thank you kindly for the cot and 'peace' is hardly the word I would select if I had to resort to firecrackers at 6:30 A.M. in a young girl's bedroom," I says back to him. "And as to where I intend to go, you seem to forget my position as postmistress of China Grove, Mississippi," I says. "I've always got the P.O."

Well, that made them all sit up and take notice.

I went out front and started digging up some four-o'clocks to plant around the P.O.

"Ah-ah-ah!" says Mama, raising the window. "Those happen to be my four-o'clocks. Everything planted in that star is mine. I've never known you to make anything grow in your life."

"Very well," I says. "But I take the fern. Even you, Mama, can't stand there and deny that I'm the one watered that fern. And I happen to know where I can send in a box top and get a packet of one thousand mixed seeds, no two the same kind, free."

"Oh, where?" Mama wants to know.

But I says, "Too late. You 'tend to your house, and I'll 'tend to mine. You hear things like that all the time if you know how to listen to the radio. Perfectly marvelous offers. Get anything you want free."

So I hope to tell you I marched in and got that radio, and they could of all bit a nail in two, especially Stella-Rondo, that it used to belong to, and she well knew she couldn't get it back, I'd sue for it like a shot. And I very politely took the sewing-machine motor I helped pay the most on to give Mama for Christmas back in 1929, and a good big calendar, with the first-aid remedies on it. The thermometer and the Hawaiian ukulele certainly were rightfully mine, and I stood on the step-ladder and got all my watermelon-rind preserves and every fruit and vegetable I'd put up, every jar. Then I began to pull the tacks out of the bluebird wall vases on the archway to the dining room.

"Who told you you could have those, Miss Priss?" says Mama, fanning as hard as she could.

"I bought 'em and I'll keep track of 'em," I says. "I'll tack 'em up one on each side the post-office window, and you can see 'em when you come to ask me for your mail, if you're so dead to see 'em."

"Not I! I'll never darken the door to that post office again if I live to be a hundred," Mama says. "Ungrateful child! After all the money we spent on you at the Normal."

"Me either," says Stella-Rondo. "You can just let my mail lie there and *rot*, for all I care. I'll never come and relieve you of a single, solitary piece."

"I should worry," I says. "And who you think's going to sit down and write you all those big fat letters and postcards, by the way? Mr. Whitaker? Just because he was the only man ever dropped down in China Grove and you got him—unfairly—is he going to sit down and write you a lengthy correspondence after you come home giving no rhyme nor reason whatsoever for your separation and no explanation for the presence of that child? I may not have your brilliant mind, but I fail to see it."

So Mama says, "Sister, I've told you a thousand times that Stella-Rondo simply got homesick, and this child is far too big to be hers," and she says, "Now, why don't you all just sit down and play Casino?"

Then Shirley-T. sticks out her tongue at me in this perfectly horrible way. She has no more manners than the man in the moon. I told her she was going to cross her eyes like that some day and they'd stick.

"It's too late to stop me now," I says. "You should have tried that yesterday. I'm going to the P.O. and the only way you can possibly see me is to visit me there."

So Papa-Daddy says, "You'll never catch me setting foot in that post office, even if I should take a notion into my head to write a letter some place." He says, "I won't have you reachin' out of that little old window with a pair of shears and cuttin' off any beard of mine. I'm too smart for you!"

"We all are," says Stella-Rondo.

But I said, "If you're so smart, where's Mr. Whitaker?"

So then Uncle Rondo says, "I'll thank you from now on to stop reading all the orders I get on postcards and telling everybody in China Grove what you think is the matter with them," but I says, "I draw my own conclusions and will continue in the future to draw them." I says, "If people want to write their inmost secrets on penny postcards, there's nothing in the wide world you can do about it, Uncle Rondo."

"And if you think we'll ever *write* another postcard you're sadly mistaken," says Mama.

"Cutting off your nose to spite your face then," I says. "But if you're all determined to have no more to do with the U.S. mail, think of this: What will Stella-Rondo do now, if she wants to tell Mr. Whitaker to come after her?"

"Wah!" says Stella-Rondo. I knew she'd cry. She had a conniption fit right there in the kitchen.

"It will be interesting to see how long she holds out," I says. "And now—I am leaving."

"Good-bye," says Uncle Rondo.

"Oh, I declare," says Mama, "to think that a family of mine should quarrel on the Fourth of July, or the day after, over Stella-Rondo leaving old Mr. Whitaker and having the sweetest little adopted child! It looks like we'd all be glad!"

"Wah!" says Stella-Rondo, and has a fresh conniption fit.

"*He* left *her*—you mark my words," I says. "That's Mr. Whitaker. I know Mr. Whitaker. After all, I knew him first. I said from the beginning he'd up and leave her. I foretold every single thing that's happened."

"Where did he go?" asks Mama.

"Probably to the North Pole, if he knows what's good for him," I says.

But Stella-Rondo just bawled and wouldn't say another word. She flew to her room and slammed the door.

"Now look what you've gone and done, Sister," says Mama. "You go apologize."

"I haven't got time, I'm leaving," I says.

"Well, what are you waiting around for?" asks Uncle Rondo.

So I just picked up the kitchen clock and marched off, without saying "Kiss my foot" or anything, and never did tell Stella-Rondo good-bye.

There was a girl going along on a little wagon right in front.

"Girl," I says, "come help me haul these things down the hill, I'm going to live in the post office."

Took her nine trips in her express wagon. Uncle Rondo came out on the porch and threw her a nickel.

And that's the last I've laid eyes on any of my family or my family laid eyes on me for five solid days and nights. Stella-Rondo may be telling the most horrible tales in the world about Mr. Whitaker, but I haven't heard them. As I tell everybody, I draw my own conclusions.

But oh, I like it here. It's ideal, as I've been saying. You see, I've got everything cater-cornered, the way I like it. Hear the radio? All the war news. Radio, sewing machine, book ends, ironing board and that great big piano lamp—peace, that's what I like. Butter-bean vines planted all along the front where the strings are.

Of course, there's not much mail. My family are naturally the main people in China Grove, and if they prefer to vanish from the face of the earth, for all the mail they get or the mail they write, why, I'm not going to open my mouth. Some of the folks here in town are taking up for me and some turned against me. I know which is which. There are always people who will quit buying stamps just to get on the right side of Papa-Daddy.

But here I am, and here I'll stay. I want the world to know I'm happy.

And if Stella-Rondo should come to me this minute, on bended knees, and *attempt* to explain the incidents of her life with Mr. Whitaker, I'd simply put my fingers in both my ears and refuse to listen.

Questions to Consider

1. In many of Welty's stories, several members of the family are presented to the reader. What significance does the family play in Welty's stories? How do these families reflect the traditional Southern focus on family units?
2. Examine the ways in which Welty depicts characters such as Phoenix Jackson and the narrator in "Why I Live at the P.O." How would you describe their characterization? What aspect(s) of the human condition does Welty seem to be examining in this story?
3. How does Welty depict race in "A Worn Path?" How does this story reflect her position that the writer needn't crusade, but should instead portray real human experience?

Tennessee Williams

1911–1983

Considered by many literary critics to be the premier American dramatist of the twentieth century, Tennessee Williams is also an icon of Southern literature. He is compared more frequently to novelist William Faulkner than to other dramatists and emerged as one of the first group of twentieth-century Southern writers to earn an international reputation. The author of such classics as *A Streetcar Named Desire* (1947), *Cat on a Hot Tin Roof* (1956), and *The Glass Menagerie* (1945), Williams enjoyed a career highlighted by accolades, including two Pulitzer Prizes and numerous successful runs on Broadway. The collection of disenfranchised souls who populate his works evoke compassion from his readers, in part because of frequent autobiographical references.

Growing up as the son of a frustrated Southern belle, the brother of a mentally ill sister who could never live up to her mother's expectations of Southern womanhood, and the heir of a drunken father, Williams found that the South of his youth provided fertile ground for his imagination. Thomas Lanier Williams was born in Columbus, Mississippi on 26 March 1911 in the home of his mother's parents. His father, Cornelius Coffin Williams, descended from Tennessee pioneer John Sevier. One of the several legends about Williams's adoption of the name "Tennessee" purports that his family heritage provided its basis. Williams is also reputed to have changed his first name after becoming convinced that his birth name had been compromised by the quality of his early writing efforts. The playwright himself reported, however, that he acquired the name "when I was going to the University of Iowa because the fellows in my class could only remember that I was from a Southern State with a long name. And when they couldn't think of Mississippi, they settled on Tennessee. That was all right with me, so when it stuck I changed to it permanently."

The Williams family lacked economic advantages during the author's youth. When Tennessee was 12 years old, Cornelius Williams, a traveling shoe salesman, moved his family to St. Louis so that he could accept a position as sales manager at the corporate headquarters of the company. The Southern mannerisms of the Williams children, internalized during their early years in Mississippi, brought ridicule from schoolmates, as did Williams's inability to participate in sports. He was afflicted with diphtheria shortly before his family moved to St. Louis, and the illness left his legs partially paralyzed. Home life did not offer a refuge from the unkindness of the school children, as the family's apartment, located in a building that Williams described as "the color of dried blood and mustard," was populated by a mother who resented the loss of the Southern gentility that had marked her youth, and a father who, according to Williams's mother, was a "man's man and liked long poker games and drinking bouts." Even Williams's beloved elder sister, Rose, was a source of sadness and disappointment to the young writer. Her introverted personality disintegrated into schizophrenia; doctors eventually convinced Mrs. Williams that a prefrontal lobotomy might cure her daughter, but the operation was unsuccessful, forcing Rose to remain institutionalized for the remainder of her life. Williams's abiding love for his sister and his sustained guilt over her condition became a recurring theme in his work and form a central concern in *The Glass Menagerie*.

Williams sought escape from his intolerable life through writing. At the age of 16, he received a prize from *Smart Set* for an early essay, titled "Can a Good Wife Be a Good Sport?" and a year later, in 1928, his first story was published in *Weird Tales*. He attended the University of Missouri but was forced to withdraw during his third year when his father refused to continue supporting him because he failed ROTC. Williams returned home and worked for two years in the same shoe factory that employed his father. He tried to write at night, but found the work at the factory so routine and depressing that he suffered a nervous breakdown. As a part of his recovery from the breakdown, he spent some time recuperating with his maternal grandparents in Memphis, traveled a bit, and finally earned his bachelor's degree in English from the University of Iowa in 1938. He then attempted to secure a position with the WPA, and in what would prove to be a life-altering decision, he relocated to New Orleans when these attempts proved fruitless.

The move to New Orleans set the stage for two defining events in Williams's life, his first homosexual experience and his first literary success. He entered several of his short plays in a contest sponsored by the Group Theater in New York and won a small prize from the contest. More importantly, he gained the attention of Audrey Wood, who became Williams's manager and helped him obtain a grant from the Rockefeller Foundation that allowed him to further his study of writing. An instructor at the New School for Social Research encouraged a local theater group to produce one of Williams's plays, but the production was panned by critics and theatergoers alike and quickly closed. Rejected for military service in World War II, Williams worked at a variety of jobs with little success until he was offered a job by MGM studios, where he was to write a script for Lana Turner. He drafted several scripts during his time at MGM, but the studio ultimately did not find any of them acceptable. Ironically, two of the ideas that MGM rejected—a script called "The Gentleman Caller" and an idea for another, which Alice Griffin has described as "a mammoth Southern epic"—later became *The Glass Menagerie* and *A Streetcar Named Desire*, respectively. When Williams was released by MGM, the studio paid him for the term of his contract, and the severance allowed him to complete *The Glass Menagerie*. When the play opened on Broadway in 1945, it shattered previous box-office records for attendance.

Williams's substantial body of work frequently addresses the expectations of womanly propriety in the South, which remained prevalent during his lifetime. Such expectations formed his mother's character and then embittered her when she saw them fail, leading

Williams to cast a critical light on the cultural icon of the Southern belle and the damaging characteristics of the role. Kimball King suggests that Williams's works frequently demonstrate a "patriarchal society, dedicated to worshiping a deceased elite, join[ed] with a more updated money-hungry, pleasure-seeking culture to create a symbolic torture chamber for the sensitive or idealistic individual." His protagonists find themselves caught between their desire to maintain the genteel old ways and the harsh and often degrading demands of modern society.

In true Southern form, Williams attacks racism in such works as *Orpheus Descending* and *Sweet Bird of Youth;* he subtly denounces sexual oppression in many others, including *Streetcar* and *Cat on a Hot Tin Roof.* Williams not only offers sensitive examinations of alternate sexualities in many of his plays, he also demonstrates the self-loathing and loneliness suffered by heterosexuals, especially those who do not conduct themselves in a socially appropriate manner. His characters may turn to sex seeking an escape from loneliness, a source of identity, or a means of enjoying the illusion of love, no matter how temporary. His examination of the nature of sexuality is especially poignant in *Cat on a Hot Tin Roof,* in terms of both Maggie's frustration at Brick's rejection of her and Brick's inability to come to terms with his own sexuality. Rather than condemning characters with alternate sexual identities, King asserts that Williams attributes the "many perversions and distortions of human behavior . . . to the rigid gender stereotypes he uncovers in the Southern landscape. The nearly schizophrenic division between the strong sexual needs and chaste public image that [his characters] try to maintain is not a conflict shared by [straight] male characters, who are free to boast of their sexuality." Williams frequently shows the alpha male in direct competition with feminized men—in *Cat on a Hot Tin Roof,* Brick drinks to avoid conflict, while Big Daddy seeks opportunities to demonstrate his prowess; *Streetcar*'s Stanley terrorizes women, while Mitch passively watches him victimize and vilify the woman he loves because he does not possess the strength of character to stand up for her or to forgive her for her miserable past. Such conflicts frequently lead Williams's characters to choose death or to suffer a mental breakdown rather than submit to a domineering form of sexuality: Brick crawls into a bottle of alcohol rather than face his sexual identity, and even Mitch is weakened by the play's end, crying impotently as Blanche is taken away to the sanitarium. Williams's characterizations suggest his personal animosity for a society that allows its men to brag about their conquests while damning its women for similar urges.

In the two decades that followed the successful debut of *The Glass Menagerie,* Williams wrote and produced the majority of his major works, receiving two Pulitzer prizes, two Donaldson Awards and four Drama Critics' Circle Awards. In 1947, he met Frank Merlo, and the two forged a tempestuous relationship that lasted until Merlo died of cancer in 1963. Later in his life, Williams served as writer-in-residence at several universities, received an honorary doctorate from Harvard University, spent time in a psychiatric hospital, and was baptized as a Roman Catholic. He died in Manhattan on 25 February 1983 after choking on a bottle cap, leaving behind a legacy of dramatic work that is unmatched in the Southern tradition and which is also without equal in the American literary canon.

Cat on a Hot Tin Roof

CHARACTERS OF THE PLAY

MARGARET
BRICK
MAE, sometimes called Sister Woman
BIG MAMA
DIXIE, a little girl
BIG DADDY
REVEREND TOOKER
GOOPER, sometimes called Brother Man

DOCTOR BAUGH, pronounced "Baw"
LACEY, a Negro servant
SOOKEY, another
Another little girl and two small boys
(The playing script of Act III also includes TRIXIE, another little girl, also DAISY, BRIGHTIE and SMALL, servants.)

NOTES FOR THE DESIGNER

The set is the bed-sitting-room of a plantation home in the Mississippi Delta. It is along an upstairs gallery which probably runs around the entire house; it has two pairs of very wide doors opening onto the gallery; showing white balustrades against a fair summer sky that fades into dusk and night during the course of the play, which occupies precisely the time of its performance, excepting, of course, the fifteen minutes of intermission.

Perhaps the style of the room is not what you would expect in the home of the Delta's biggest cotton-planter. It is Victorian with a touch of the Far East. It hasn't changed much since it was occupied by the original owners of the place, Jack Straw and Peter Ochello, a pair of old bachelors who shared this room all their lives together. In other words, the room must evoke some ghosts; it is gently and poetically haunted by a relationship that must have involved a tenderness which was uncommon. This may be irrelevant or unnecessary, but I once saw a reproduction of a faded photograph of the verandah of Robert Louis Stevenson's home on that Samoan Island where he spent his last years, and there was a quality of tender light on weathered wood, such as porch furniture made of bamboo and wicker, exposed to tropical suns and tropical rains, which came to mind when I thought about the set for this play, bringing also to mind the grace and comfort of light, the reassurance it gives, on a late and fair afternoon in summer, the way that no matter what, even dread of death, is gently touched and soothed by it. For the set is the background for a play that deals with human extremities of emotion, and it needs that softness behind it.

The bathroom door, showing only pale-blue tile and silver towel racks, is in one side wall; the hall door in the opposite wall. Two articles of furniture need mention: a big double bed which staging should make a functional part of the set as often as suitable, the surface of which should be slightly raked to make figures on it seen more easily; and against the wall space between the two huge double doors upstage: a monumental monstrosity peculiar to our times, a *huge* console combination or radio-phonograph (Hi-Fi with three speakers) TV set *and* liquor cabinet, bearing and containing many glasses and bottles, all in one piece, which is a composition of muted silver tones, and the opalescent tones of reflecting glass, a chromatic link, this thing, between the sepia (tawny gold) tones of the interior and the cool (white and blue) tones of the gallery and sky. This piece of furniture (?!), this monument, is a very complete and compact little shrine to virtually all the comforts and illusions behind which we hide from such things as the characters in the play are faced with. . . . The set should be far less realistic than I have so far implied in this description of it. I think the walls below the ceiling should dissolve mysteriously into air; the set should be roofed by the sky; stars and moon suggested by traces of milky pallor, as if they were observed through a telescope lens out of focus.

Anything else I can think of? Oh, yes, fanlights (transoms shaped like an open glass fan) above all the doors in the set, with panes of blue and amber, and above all, the designer should take as many pains to give the actors room to move about freely (to show their restlessness, their passion for breaking out) as if it were a set for a ballet.

An evening in summer. The action is continuous, with two intermissions.

ACT ONE

[At the rise of the curtain someone is taking a shower in the bathroom, the door of which is half open. A pretty young woman, with anxious lines in her face, enters the bedroom and crosses to the bathroom door.]

MARGARET *[shouting above roar of water]*: One of those no-neck monsters hit me with a hot buttered biscuit so I have t' change!

[Margaret's voice is both rapid and drawling. In her long speeches she has the vocal tricks of a priest delivering a liturgical chant, the lines are almost sung, always continuing a little beyond her breath so she has to gasp for another. Sometimes she intersperses the lines with a little wordless singing, such as "Da-da-daaaa!" Water turns off and Brick calls out to her, but is still unseen. A tone of politely feigned interest, masking indifference, or worse, is characteristic of his speech with Margaret.]

BRICK: Wha'd you say, Maggie? Water was on s' loud I couldn't hearya. . . .

MARGARET: Well, I!—just remarked that!—one of th' no-neck monsters messed up m' lovely lace dress so I got t'—cha-a-ange. . . .

[She opens and kicks shut drawers of the dresser.]

BRICK: Why d'ya call Gooper's kiddies no-neck monsters?

MARGARET: Because they've got no necks! Isn't that a good enough reason?

BRICK: Don't they have any necks?

MARGARET: None visible. Their fat little heads are set on their fat little bodies without a bit of connection.

BRICK: That's too bad.

MARGARET: Yes, it's too bad because you can't wring their necks if they've got no necks to wring! Isn't that right, honey?

[She steps out of her dress, stands in a slip of ivory satin and lace.]

Yep, they're no-neck monsters, all no-neck people are monsters . . .

[Children shriek downstairs.]

Hear them? Hear them screaming? I don't know where their voice-boxes are located since they don't have necks. I tell you I got so nervous at that table tonight I thought I would throw back my head and utter a scream you could hear across the Arkansas border an' parts of Louisiana an' Tennessee. I said to your charming sister-in-law, Mae, honey, couldn't you feed those precious little things at a separate table with an oilcloth cover? They make such a mess an' the lace cloth looks *so* pretty! She made enormous eyes at me and said, "Ohhh, noooooo! On Big Daddy's birthday? Why, he would never forgive me!" Well, I want you to know, Big Daddy hadn't been at the table two minutes with those five no-neck monsters slobbering and drooling over their food before he threw down his fork an' shouted, "Fo' God's sake, Gooper, why don't you put them pigs at a trough in th' kitchen?"—Well, I swear, I simply could have di-ieed!

Think of it, Brick, they've got five of them and number six is coming. They've brought the whole bunch down here like animals to display at a county fair. Why, they have those children doin' tricks all the time! "Junior, show Big Daddy how you do this, show Big Daddy how you do that, say your little piece fo' Big Daddy,

Sister. Show your dimples, Sugar. Brother, show Big Daddy how you stand on your head!"—It goes on all the time, along with constant little remarks and innuendos about the fact that you and I have not produced any children, are totally childless and therefore totally useless!—Of course it's comical but it's also disgusting since it's so obvious what they're up to!

BRICK *[without interest]*: What are they up to, Maggie?

MARGARET: Why, you know what they're up to!

BRICK *[appearing]*: No, I don't know what they're up to.

[He stands there in the bathroom doorway drying his hair with a towel and hanging onto the towel rack because one ankle is broken, plastered and bound. He is still slim and firm as a boy. His liquor hasn't started tearing him down outside. He has the additional charm of that cool air of detachment that people have who have given up the struggle. But now and then, when disturbed, something flashes behind it, like lightning in a fair sky, which shows that at some deeper level he is far from peaceful. Perhaps in a stronger light he would show some signs of deliquescence, but the fading, still warm, light from the gallery treats him gently.]

MARGARET: I'll tell you what they're up to, boy of mine!—They're up to cutting you out of your father's estate, and—

[She freezes momentarily before her next remark. Her voice drops as if it were somehow a personally embarrassing admission.]

—Now we know that Big Daddy's dyin' of—*cancer*. . . .

[There are voices on the lawn below: long-drawn calls across distance. Margaret raises her lovely bare arms and powders her armpits with a light sigh. She adjusts the angle of a magnifying mirror to straighten an eyelash, then rises fretfully saying:]

There's so much light in the room it ———

BRICK *[softly but sharply]*: Do we?

MARGARET: Do we what?

BRICK: Know Big Daddy's dyin' of cancer?

MARGARET: Got the report today.

BRICK: Oh . . .

MARGARET *[letting down bamboo blinds which cast long, gold-fretted shadows over the room]*: Yep, got th' report just now . . . it didn't surprise me, Baby. . . .

[Her voice has range, and music; sometimes it drops low as a boy's and you have a sudden image of her playing boys' games as a child.]

I recognized the symptoms soon's we got here last spring and I'm willin' to bet you that Brother Man and his wife were pretty sure of it, too. That more than likely explains why their usual summer migration to the coolness of the Great Smokies was passed up this summer in favor of—hustlin' down here ev'ry whipstitch with their whole screamin' tribe! And why so many allusions have been made to Rainbow Hill lately. You know what Rainbow Hill is? Place that's famous for treatin' alcoholics an' dope fiends in the movies!

BRICK: I'm not in the movies.

MARGARET: No, and you don't take dope. Otherwise you're a perfect candidate for Rainbow Hill, Baby, and that's where they aim to ship you—over my dead body! Yep, over my dead body they'll ship you there, but nothing would please them better. Then Brother Man could get a-hold of the purse strings and dole out remittances to us, maybe get power-of-attorney and sign checks for us and cut off our credit wherever, whenever he wanted! Son-of-a-bitch!—How'd you like that, Baby?—Well, you've been doin' just about ev'rything in your power to bring it about, you've just been doin' ev'rything you can think of to aid and abet them in this scheme of theirs! Quittin' work, devoting yourself to the occupation of drinkin'!—Breakin' your ankle last night on the high school athletic field: doin' what? Jumpin' hurdles? At two or three in the morning? Just fantastic! Got in the paper. *Clarksdale Register* carried a nice little item about it, human interest story about a well-known former athlete stagin' a one-man track meet on the Glorious Hill High School athletic field last night, but was slightly out of condition and didn't clear the first hurdle! Brother Man Gooper claims he exercised his influence t' keep it from goin' out over AP or UP or every goddam "P." But, Brick? You still have one big advantage!

[During the above swift flood of words, Brick has reclined with contrapuntal leisure on the snowy surface of the bed and has rolled over carefully on his side or belly.]

BRICK *[wryly]*: Did you *say* something, Maggie?

MARGARET: Big Daddy dotes on you, honey. And he can't stand Brother Man and Brother Man's wife, that monster of fertility, Mae; she's downright odious to him! Know how I know? By little expressions that flicker over his face when that woman is holding fo'th on one of her choice topics such as—how she refused twilight sleep!—when the twins were delivered! Because she feels motherhood's an experience that a woman ought to experience fully!—in order to fully appreciate the wonder and beauty of it! HAH!

[This loud "HAH!" is accompanied by a violent action such as slamming a drawer shut.]

—and how she made Brother Man come in an' stand beside her in the delivery room so he would not miss out on the "wonder and beauty" of it either!—producin' those no-neck monsters. . . .

[A speech of this kind would be antipathetic from almost anybody but Margaret; she makes it oddly funny, because her eyes constantly twinkle and her voice shakes with laughter which is basically indulgent.]

—Big Daddy shares my attitude toward those two! As for me, well—I give him a laugh now and then and he tolerates me. In fact!—I sometimes suspect that Big Daddy harbors a little unconscious "lech" fo' me. . . .

BRICK: What makes you think that Big Daddy has a lech for you, Maggie?

MARGARET: Way he always drops his eyes down my body when I'm talkin' to him, drops his eyes to my boobs an' licks his old chops! Ha ha!

BRICK: That kind of talk is disgusting.

MARGARET: Did anyone ever tell you that you're an ass-aching Puritan, Brick?

I think it's mighty fine that that ole fellow, on the doorstep of death, still takes in my shape with what I think is deserved appreciation!

And you wanta know something else? Big Daddy didn't know how many little Maes and Goopers had been produced! "How many kids have you got?" he asked at the table, just like Brother Man and his wife were new acquaintances to him! Big Mama said he was jokin', but that ole boy wasn't jokin', Lord, no!

And when they infawmed him that they had five already and were turning out number six!—the news seemed to come as a sort of unpleasant surprise . . .

[Children yell below.]

Scream, monsters!

[Turns to Brick with a sudden, gay, charming smile which fades as she notices that he is not looking at her but into fading gold space with a troubled expression. It is constant rejection that makes her humor "bitchy."]

Yes, you should of been at that supper-table, Baby.

[Whenever she calls him "baby" the word is a soft caress.]

Y'know, Big Daddy, bless his ole sweet soul, he's the dearest ole thing in the world, but he does hunch over his food as if he preferred not to notice anything else. Well, Mae an' Gooper were side by side at the table, direckly across from Big Daddy, watchin' his face like hawks while they jawed an' jabbered about the cuteness an' brillance of th' no-neck monsters!

[She giggles with a hand fluttering at her throat and her breast and her long throat arched. She comes downstage and recreates the scene with voice and gesture.]

And the no-neck monsters were ranged around the table, some in high chairs and some on th' *Books of Knowledge,* all in fancy little paper caps in honor of Big Daddy's birthday, and all through dinner, well, I want you to know that Brother Man an' his partner never once, for one moment, stopped exchanging pokes an' pinches an' kicks an' signs an' signals!—Why, they were like a couple of cardsharps fleecing a sucker.—Even Big Mama, bless her ole sweet soul, she isn't th' quickest an' brightest thing in the world, she finally noticed, at last, an' said to Gooper, "Gooper, what are you an' Mae makin' all these signs at each other about?"—I swear t' goodness, I nearly choked on my chicken!

[Margaret, back at the dressing-table, still doesn't see Brick. He is watching her with a look that is not quite definable.—Amused? shocked? contemptuous?—part of those and part of something else.]

Y'know—your brother Gooper still cherishes the illusion he took a giant step up on the social ladder when he married Miss Mae Flynn of the Memphis Flynns.

[Margaret moves about the room as she talks, stops before the mirror, moves on.]

But I have a piece of Spanish news for Gooper. The Flynns never had a thing in this world but money and they lost that, they were nothing at all but fairly successful climbers. Of course, Mae Flynn came out in Memphis eight years before I made my debut in Nashville, but I had friends at Ward-Belmont who came from Memphis and they used to come to see me and I used to go to see them for Christmas and spring vacations, and so I know who rates an' who doesn't rate in Memphis society. Why, y'know ole Papa Flynn, he barely escaped doing time in the Federal pen for shady manipulations on th' stock market when his chain stores crashed, and as for Mae having been a cotton carnival queen, as they remind us so often, lest we forget, well, that's one honor that I don't envy her for!—Sit on a brass throne on a tacky float an' ride down Main Street, smilin', bowin', and blowin' kisses to all the trash on the street ———

[She picks out a pair of jeweled sandals and rushes to the dressing-table.]

Why, year before last, when Susan McPheeters was singled out fo' that honor, y'know what happened to her? Y'know what happened to poor little Susie McPheeters?

BRICK *[absently]:* No. What happened to little Susie McPheeters?

MARGARET: Somebody spit tobacco juice in her face.

BRICK *[dreamily]:* Somebody spit tobacco juice in her face?

MARGARET: That's right, some old drunk leaned out of a window in the Hotel Gayoso and yelled, "Hey, Queen, hey, hey, there, Queenie!" Poor Susie looked up and flashed him a radiant smile and he shot out a squirt of tobacco juice right in poor Susie's face.

BRICK: Well, what d'you know about that.

MARGARET *[gaily]:* What do I know about it? I was there, I saw it!

BRICK *[absently]:* Must have been kind of funny.

MARGARET: Susie didn't think so. Had hysterics. Screamed like a banshee. They had to stop th' parade an' remove her from her throne an' go on with—

[She catches sight of him in the mirror, gasps slightly, wheels about to face him. Count ten.]

—Why are you looking at me like that?

BRICK *[whistling softly, now]*: Like what, Maggie?

MARGARET *[intensely, fearfully]*: The way y' were lookin' at me just now, befo' I caught your eye in the mirror and you started t' whistle! I don't know how t' describe it but it froze my blood!—I've caught you lookin' at me like that so often lately. What are you thinkin' of when you look at me like that?

BRICK: I wasn't conscious of lookin' at you, Maggie.

MARGARET: Well, I was conscious of it! What were you thinkin'?

BRICK: I don't remember thinking of anything, Maggie.

MARGARET: Don't you think I know that—? Don't you—?—Think I know that—?

BRICK *[coolly]*: Know *what*, Maggie?

MARGARET *[struggling for expression]*: That I've gone through this—*hideous!*—*transformation*, become—*hard! Frantic!*

[Then she adds, almost tenderly:]

—*cruel!*

That's what you've been observing in me lately. How could y' help but observe it? That's all right. I'm not—thin-skinned any more, can't afford t' be thin-skinned any more.

[She is now recovering her power.]

—But Brick? Brick?

BRICK: Did you say something?

MARGARET: I was *goin'* t' say something: that I get—lonely. Very!

BRICK: Ev'rybody gets that . . .

MARGARET: Living with someone you love can be lonelier—than living entirely *alone!*—if the one that y' love doesn't love you. . . .

[There is a pause. Brick hobbles downstage and asks, without looking at her:]

BRICK: Would you like to live alone, Maggie?

[Another pause: then—after she has caught a quick, hurt breath:]

MARGARET: *No!—God!—I wouldn't!*

[Another gasping breath. She forcibly controls what must have been an impulse to cry out. We see her deliberately, very forcibly, going all the way back to the world in which you can talk about ordinary matters.]

Did you have a nice shower?

BRICK: Uh-huh.

MARGARET: Was the water cool?

BRICK: No.

MARGARET: But it made y' feel fresh, huh?

BRICK: Fresher. . . .

MARGARET: I know something would make y' feel *much* fresher!

BRICK: What?

MARGARET: An alcohol rub. Or cologne, a rub with cologne!

BRICK: That's good after a workout but I haven't been workin' out, Maggie.

MARGARET: You've kept in good shape, though.

BRICK *[indifferently]*: You think so, Maggie?

MARGARET: I always thought drinkin' men lost their looks, but I was plainly mistaken.

BRICK *[wryly]*: Why, thanks, Maggie.

MARGARET: You're the only drinkin' man I know that it never seems t' put fat on.
BRICK: I'm gettin' softer, Maggie.
MARGARET: Well, sooner or later it's bound to soften you up. It was just beginning to soften up Skipper when—

[She stops short.]

I'm sorry. I never could keep my fingers off a sore—I wish you *would* lose your looks. If you did it would make the martyrdom of Saint Maggie a little more bearable. But no such goddam luck. I actually believe you've gotten better looking since you've gone on the bottle. Yeah, a person who didn't know you would think you'd never had a tense nerve in your body or a strained muscle.

[There are sounds of croquet on the lawn below: the click of mallets, light voices, near and distant.]

Of course, you always had that detached quality as if you were playing a game without much concern over whether you won or lost, and now that you've lost the game, not lost but just quit playing, you have that rare sort of charm that usually only happens in very old or hopelessly sick people, the charm of the defeated.—You look so cool, so cool, so enviably cool.

[Music is heard.]

They're playing croquet. The moon has appeared and it's white, just beginning to turn a little bit yellow. . . .

You were a wonderful lover. . . .

Such a wonderful person to go to bed with, and I think mostly because you were really indifferent to it. Isn't that right? Never had any anxiety about it, did it naturally, easily, slowly, with absolute confidence and perfect calm, more like opening a door for a lady or seating her at a table than giving expression to any longing for her. Your indifference made you wonderful at lovemaking—*strange?*—but true. . . .

You know, if I thought you would never, never, *never* make love to me again—I would go downstairs to the kitchen and pick out the longest and sharpest knife I could find and stick it straight into my heart, I swear that I would!

But one thing I don't have is the charm of the defeated, my hat is still in the ring, and I am determined to win!

[There is the sound of croquet mallets hitting croquet balls.]

—What is the victory of a cat on a hot tin roof?—I wish I knew. . . .

Just staying on it, I guess, as long as she can. . . .

[More croquet sounds.]

Later tonight I'm going to tell you I love you an' maybe by that time you'll be drunk enough to believe me. Yes, they're playing croquet. . . .

Big Daddy is dying of cancer. . . .

What were you thinking of when I caught you looking at me like that? Were you thinking of Skipper?

[Brick takes up his crutch, rises.]

Oh, excuse me, forgive me, but laws of silence don't work! No, laws of silence don't work. . . .

[Brick crosses to the bar, takes a quick drink, and rubs his head with a towel.]

Laws of silence don't work. . . .

When something is festering in your memory or your imagination, laws of silence don't work, it's just like shutting a door and locking it on a house on fire in hope of forgetting that the house is burning. But not facing a fire doesn't put it out. Silence about a thing just magnifies it. It grows and festers in silence, becomes malignant. . . .

Get dressed, Brick.

[He drops his crutch.]

BRICK: I've dropped my crutch.

[He has stopped rubbing his hair dry but still stands hanging onto the towel rack in a white towel-cloth robe.]

MARGARET: Lean on me.

BRICK: No, just give me my crutch.

MARGARET: Lean on my shoulder.

BRICK: *I don't want to lean on your shoulder, I want my crutch!*

[This is spoken like sudden lightning.]

Are you going to give me my crutch or do I have to get down on my knees on the floor and ———

MARGARET: *Here, here, take it, take it!*

[She has thrust the crutch at him.]

BRICK *[hobbling out]*: Thanks . . .

MARGARET: We mustn't scream at each other, the walls in this house have ears. . . .

[He hobbles directly to liquor cabinet to get a new drink.]

—but that's the first time I've heard you raise your voice in a long time, Brick. A crack in the wall?—Of composure?

—I think that's a good sign. . . .

A sign of nerves in a player on the defensive!

[Brick turns and smiles at her coolly over his fresh drink.]

BRICK: It just hasn't happened yet, Maggie.

MARGARET: What?

BRICK: The click I get in my head when I've had enough of this stuff to make me peaceful. . . .

Will you do me a favor?

MARGARET: Maybe I will. What favor?

BRICK: Just, just keep your voice down!

MARGARET *[in a hoarse whisper]*: I'll do you that favor, I'll speak in a whisper, if not shut up completely, if *you* will do *me* a favor and make that drink your last one till after the party.

BRICK: What party?

MARGARET: Big Daddy's birthday party.

BRICK: Is this Big Daddy's birthday?

MARGARET: You know this is Big Daddy's birthday!

BRICK: No, I don't, I forgot it.

MARGARET: Well, I remembered it for you. . . .

[They are both speaking as breathlessly as a pair of kids after a fight, drawing deep exhausted breaths and looking at each other with faraway eyes, shaking and panting together as if they had broken apart from a violent struggle.]

BRICK: Good for you, Maggie.

MARGARET: You just have to scribble a few lines on this card.

BRICK: You scribble something, Maggie.

MARGARET: It's got to be your handwriting; it's your present, I've given him my present; it's got to be your handwriting!

[The tension between them is building again, the voices becoming shrill once more.]

BRICK: I didn't get him a present.

MARGARET: I got one for you.

BRICK: All right. You write the card, then.

MARGARET: And have him know you didn't remember his birthday?

BRICK: I didn't remember his birthday.

MARGARET: You don't have to prove you didn't!

BRICK: I don't want to fool him about it.

MARGARET: Just write "Love, Brick!" for God's—

BRICK: No.

MARGARET: You've *got* to!

BRICK: I don't have to do anything I don't want to do. You keep forgetting the conditions on which I agreed to stay on living with you.

MARGARET *[out before she knows it]*: I'm not living with you. We occupy the same cage.

BRICK: You've got to remember the conditions agreed on.

MARGARET: They're impossible conditions!

BRICK: Then why don't you—?

MARGARET: HUSH! Who is out there? Is somebody at the door?

[There are footsteps in hall.]

MAE *[outside]*: May I enter a moment?

MARGARET: Oh, *you!* Sure. Come in, Mae.

[Mae enters bearing aloft the bow of a young lady's archery set.]

MAE: Brick, is this thing yours?

MARGARET: Why, Sister Woman—that's my Diana Trophy. Won it at the intercollegiate archery contest on the Ole Miss campus.

MAE: It's a mighty dangerous thing to leave exposed round a house full of nawmal rid-blooded children attracted t'weapons.

MARGARET: "Nawmal rid-blooded children attracted t'weapons" ought t'be taught to keep their hands off things that don't belong to them.

MAE: Maggie, honey, if you had children of your own you'd know how funny that is. Will you please lock this up and put the key out of reach?

MARGARET: Sister Woman, nobody is plotting the destruction of your kiddies.—Brick and I still have our special archers' license. We're goin' deer-huntin' on Moon Lake as soon as the season starts. I love to run with dogs through chilly woods, run, run, leap over obstructions—

[She goes into the closet carrying the bow.]

MAE: How's the injured ankle, Brick?

BRICK: Doesn't hurt. Just itches.

MAE: Oh, my! Brick—Brick, you should've been downstairs after supper! Kiddies put on a show. Polly played the piano, Buster an' Sonny drums, an' then they turned out the lights an' Dixie an' Trixie puhfawmed a toe dance in fairy costume with *spahkluhs!* Big Daddy just beamed! He just beamed!

MARGARET *[from the closet with a sharp laugh]*: Oh, I bet. It breaks my heart that we missed it!

[She reenters.]

But Mae? Why did y'give dawgs' names to all your kiddies?

MAE: *Dogs'* names?

[Margaret has made this observation as she goes to raise the bamboo blinds, since the sunset glare has diminished. In crossing she winks at Brick.]

MARGARET *[sweetly]*: Dixie, Trixie, Buster, Sonny, Polly!—Sounds like four dogs and a parrot . . . animal act in a circus!

MAE: Maggie? *[Margaret turns with a smile.]*
Why are you so catty?

MARGARET: Cause I'm a cat! But why can't *you* take a joke, Sister Woman?

MAE: Nothin' pleases me more than a joke that's funny. You know the real names of our kiddies. Buster's real name is Robert. Sonny's real name is Saunders. Trixie's real name is Marlene and Dixie's ———

[Someone downstairs calls for her. "Hey, Mae!"—She rushes to door, saying:]
Intermission is over!

MARGARET *[as Mae closes door]*: I wonder what Dixie's real name is?

BRICK: Maggie, being catty doesn't help things any . . .

MARGARET: I know! *WHY!*—Am I so catty?—Cause I'm consumed with envy an' eaten up with longing?—Brick, I've laid out your beautiful Shantung silk suit from Rome and one of your monogrammed silk shirts. I'll put your cuff-links in it, those lovely star sapphires I get you to wear so rarely. . . .

BRICK: I can't get trousers on over this plaster cast.

MARGARET: Yes, you can, I'll help you.

BRICK: I'm not going to get dressed, Maggie.

MARGARET: Will you just put on a pair of white silk pajamas?

BRICK: Yes, I'll do that, Maggie.

MARGARET: *Thank* you, thank you so *much!*

BRICK: Don't mention it.

MARGARET: *Oh, Brick!* How long does it have t' go on? This punishment? Haven't I done time enough, haven't I served my term, can't I apply for a—pardon?

BRICK: Maggie, you're spoiling my liquor. Lately your voice always sounds like you'd been running upstairs to warn somebody that the house was on fire!

MARGARET: Well, no wonder, no wonder. Y'know what I feel like, Brick?

[Children's and grownups' voices are blended, below, in a loud but uncertain rendition of "My Wild Irish Rose."]
I feel all the time like a cat on a hot tin roof!

BRICK: Then jump off the roof, jump off it, cats can jump off roofs and land on their four feet uninjured!

MARGARET: Oh, yes!

BRICK: Do it!—fo' God's sake, do it . . .

MARGARET: Do what?

BRICK: Take a lover!

MARGARET: I can't see a man but you! Even with my eyes closed, I just see you! Why don't you get ugly, Brick, why don't you please get fat or ugly or something so I could stand it?

[She rushes to hall door, opens it, listens.]
The concert is still going on! Bravo, no-necks, bravo!
[She slams and locks door fiercely.]

BRICK: What did you lock the door for?

MARGARET: To give us a little privacy for a while.

BRICK: You know better, Maggie.

MARGARET: No, I don't know better. . . .

[She rushes to gallery doors, draws the rose-silk drapes across them.]

BRICK: Don't make a fool of yourself.

MARGARET: I don't mind makin' a fool of myself over you!

BRICK: I mind, Maggie. I feel embarrassed for you.

MARGARET: Feel embarrassed! But don't continue my torture. I can't live on and on under these circumstances.

BRICK: You agreed to—

MARGARET: I know but—

BRICK: —Accept that condition!

MARGARET: *I CAN'T! CAN'T! CAN'T!*

[She seizes his shoulder.]

BRICK: Let go!

[He breaks away from her and seizes the small boudoir chair and raises it like a lion-tamer facing a big circus cat. Count five. She stares at him with her fist pressed to her mouth, then bursts into shrill, almost hysterical laughter. He remains grave for a moment, then grins and puts the chair down. Big Mama calls through closed door.]

BIG MAMA: Son? Son? Son?

BRICK: What is it, Big Mama?

BIG MAMA *[outside]*: Oh, son! We got the most wonderful news about Big Daddy. I just had t' run up an' tell you right this—

[She rattles the knob.]

—What's this door doin', locked, faw? You all think there's robbers in the house?

MARGARET: Big Mama, Brick is dressin', he's not dressed yet.

BIG MAMA: That's all right, it won't be the first time I've seen Brick not dressed. Come on, open this door!

[Margaret, with a grimace, goes to unlock and open the hall door, as Brick hobbles rapidly to the bathroom and kicks the door shut. Big Mama has disappeared from the hall.]

MARGARET: Big Mama?

[Big Mama appears through the opposite gallery doors behind Margaret, huffing and puffing like an old bulldog. She is a short, stout woman; her sixty years and 170 pounds have left her somewhat breathless most of the time; she's always tensed like a boxer, or rather, a Japanese wrestler. Her "family" was maybe a little superior to Big Daddy's, but not much. She wears a black or silver lace dress and at least half a million in flashy gems. She is very sincere.]

BIG MAMA *[loudly, startling Margaret]*: Here—I come through Gooper's and Mae's gal-l'ry door. Where's Brick? *Brick*—Hurry on out of there, son, I just have a second and want to give you the news about Big Daddy.—I hate locked doors in a house. . . .

MARGARET *[with affected lightness]*: I've noticed you do, Big Mama, but people have got to have *some* moments of privacy, don't they?

BIG MAMA: No, ma'am, not in *my* house.

[Without pause]

Whacha took off you' dress faw? I thought that little lace dress was so sweet on yuh, honey.

MARGARET: I thought it looked sweet on me, too, but one of m' cute little table-partners used it for a napkin so—!

BIG MAMA *[picking up stockings on floor]*: What?

MARGARET: You know, Big Mama, Mae and Gooper's so touchy about those children—thanks, Big Mama . . .

[Big Mama has thrust the picked-up stockings in Margaret's hand with a grunt.]

—that you just don't dare to suggest there's any room for improvement in their ———

BIG MAMA: Brick, hurry out!—Shoot, Maggie, you just don't like children.

MARGARET: I do SO like children! Adore them!—well brought up!

BIG MAMA *[gentle—loving]*: Well, why don't you have some and bring them up well, then, instead of all the time pickin' on Gooper's an' Mae's?

GOOPER *[shouting up the stairs]*: Hey, hey, Big Mama, Betsy an' Hugh got to go, waitin' t' tell yuh g'by!

BIG MAMA: Tell 'em to hold their hawses, I'll be right down in a jiffy!

[She turns to the bathroom door and calls out.]

Son? Can you hear me in there?

[There is a muffled answer.]

We just got the full report from the laboratory at the Ochsner Clinic, completely negative, son, ev'rything negative, right on down the line! Nothin' a-tall's wrong with him but some little functional thing called a spastic colon. Can you hear me, son?

MARGARET: He can hear you, Big Mama.

BIG MAMA: Then why don't he say something? God Almighty, a piece of news like that should make him shout. It made *me* shout, I can tell you. I shouted and sobbed and fell right down on my knees—Look!

[She pulls up her skirt.]

See the bruises where I hit my kneecaps? Took both doctors to haul me back on my feet!

[She laughs—she always laughs like hell at herself.]

Big Daddy was furious with me! But ain't that wonderful news?

[Facing bathroom again, she continues:]

After all the anxiety we been through to git a report like that on Big Daddy's birthday? Big Daddy tried to hide how much of a load that news took off his mind, but didn't fool *me*. He was mighty close to crying about it *himself!*

[Goodbyes are shouted downstairs, and she rushes to door.]

Hold those people down there, don't let them go!—Now, git dressed, we're all comin' up to this room fo' Big Daddy's birthday party because of your ankle.—How's his ankle, Maggie?

MARGARET: Well, he broke it, Big Mama.

BIG MAMA: I know he broke it.

[A phone is ringing in hall. A Negro voice answers: "Mistuh Polly's res'dence."]

I mean does it hurt him much still.

MARGARET: I'm afraid I can't give you that information, Big Mama. You'll have to ask Brick if it hurts much still or not.

SOOKEY *[in the hall]*: It's Memphis, Mizz Polly, it's Miss Sally in Memphis.

BIG MAMA: Awright, Sookey.

[Big Mama rushes into the hall and is heard shouting on the phone:]

Hello, Miss Sally. How are you, Miss Sally?—Yes, well, I was just gonna call you about it. *Shoot!*—

[She raises her voice to a bellow.]

Miss Sally? Don't ever call me from the Gayoso Lobby, too much talk goes on in that hotel lobby, no wonder you can't hear me! Now listen, Miss Sally. They's nothin' serious wrong with Big Daddy. We got the report just now, they's nothin' wrong but a thing called a—spastic! *SPASTIC!*—colon . . .

[She appears at the hall door and calls to Margaret.]

—Maggie, come out here and talk to that fool on the phone. I'm shouted breathless!

MARGARET *[goes out and is heard sweetly at phone]*: Miss Sally? This is Brick's wife, Maggie. So nice to hear your voice. Can you hear *mine?* Well, *good!*—Big Mama just wanted you to know that they've got the report from the Ochsner Clinic and what Big Daddy has is a spastic colon. Yes. Spastic colon, Miss Sally. That's right, spastic colon. G'*bye, Miss Sally, hope I'll see you real soon!*

[Hangs up a little before Miss Sally was probably ready to terminate the talk. She returns through the hall door.]

She heard me perfectly. I've discovered with deaf people the thing to do is not shout at them but just enunciate clearly. My rich old Aunt Cornelia was deaf as the dead but I could make her hear me just by sayin' each word slowly, distinctly, close to her ear. I read her the *Commercial Appeal* ev'ry night, read her the classified ads in it, even, she never missed a word of it. But was she a mean ole thing! Know what I got when she died? Her unexpired subscriptions to five magazines and the Book-of-the-Month Club and a LIBRARY full of ev'ry dull book ever written! All else went to her hellcat of a sister . . . meaner than she was, even!

[Big Mama has been straightening things up in the room during this speech.]

BIG MAMA *[closing closet door on discarded clothes]*: Miss Sally sure is a case! Big Daddy says she's always got her hand out fo' something. He's not mistaken. That poor ole thing always has her hand out fo' somethin'. I don't think Big Daddy gives her as much as he should.

[Somebody shouts for her downstairs and she shouts:]

I'm comin'!

[She starts out. At the hall door, turns and jerks a forefinger, first toward the bathroom door, then toward the liquor cabinet, meaning: "Has Brick been drinking?" Margaret pretends not to understand, cocks her head and raises her brows as if the pantomimic performance was completely mystifying to her. Big Mama rushes back to Margaret:]

Shoot! Stop playin' so dumb!—I mean has he been drinkin' that stuff much yet?

MARGARET *[with a little laugh]*: Oh! I think he had a highball after supper.

BIG MAMA: Don't laugh about it!—Some single men stop drinkin' when they git married and others start! Brick never touched liquor before he—!

MARGARET *[crying out]*: *THAT'S NOT FAIR!*

BIG MAMA: Fair or not fair I want to ask you a question, one question: D'you make Brick happy in bed?

MARGARET: Why don't you ask if he makes *me* happy in bed?

BIG MAMA: Because I know that ———

MARGARET: It works both ways!

BIG MAMA: Something's not right! You're childless and my son drinks!

[Someone has called her downstairs and she has rushed to the door on the line above. She turns at the door and points at the bed.]

—When a marriage goes on the rocks, the rocks are *there*, right *there!*

MARGARET: *That's—*

[Big Mama has swept out of the room and slammed the door.]

—not—*fair* . . .

[Margaret is alone, completely alone, and she feels it. She draws in, hunches her shoulders, raises her arms with fists clenched, shuts her eyes tight as a child about to be stabbed with a vaccination needle. When she opens her eyes again, what she sees is the long oval mirror and she rushes straight to it, stares into it with a grimace and says: "Who are you?"—Then she crouches a little and answers herself in a different voice which is high, thin, mocking: "I am Maggie the Cat!"—Straightens quickly as bathroom door opens a little and Brick calls out to her.]

BRICK: Has Big Mama gone?

MARGARET: She's gone.

[He opens the bathroom door and hobbles out, with his liquor glass now empty, straight to the liquor cabinet. He is whistling softly. Margaret's head pivots on her long, slender throat to watch him. She raises a hand uncertainly to the base of her throat, as if it was difficult for her to swallow, before she speaks:]

You know, our sex life didn't just peter out in the usual way, it was cut off short, long before the natural time for it to, and it's going to revive again, just as sudden as that. I'm confident of it. That's what I'm keeping myself attractive for. For the time when you'll see me again like other men see me. Yes, like other men see me. They still see me, Brick, and they like what they see. Uh-huh. Some of them would give their—Look, Brick!

[She stands before the long oval mirror, touches her breast and then her hips with her two hands.]

How high my body stays on me!—Nothing has fallen on me—not a fraction. . . .

[Her voice is soft and trembling: a pleading child's. At this moment as he turns to glance at her—a look which is like a player passing a ball to another player, third down and goal to go—she has to capture the audience in a grip so tight that she can hold it till the first intermission without any lapse of attention.]

Other men still want me. My face looks strained, sometimes, but I've kept my figure as well as you've kept yours, and men admire it. I still turn heads on the street. Why, last week in Memphis everywhere that I went men's eyes burned holes in my clothes, at the country club and in restaurants and department stores, there wasn't a man I met or walked by that didn't just eat me up with his eyes and turn around when I passed him and look back at me. Why, at Alice's party for her New York cousins, the best lookin' man in the crowd—followed me upstairs and tried to force his way in the powder room with me, followed me to the door and tried to force his way in!

BRICK: Why didn't you let him, Maggie?

MARGARET: Because I'm not that common, for one thing. Not that I wasn't almost tempted to. You like to know who it was? It was Sonny Boy Maxwell, that's who!

BRICK: Oh, yeah, Sonny Boy Maxwell, he was a good end-runner but had a little injury to his back and had to quit.

MARGARET: He has no injury now and has no wife and still has a lech for me!

BRICK: I see no reason to lock him out of a powder room in that case.

MARGARET: And have someone catch me at it? I'm not that stupid. Oh, I might sometime cheat on you with someone, since you're so insultingly eager to have me do it!—But if I do, you can be damned sure it will be in a place and a time where no one but me and the man could possibly know. Because I'm not going to give you any excuse to divorce me for being unfaithful or anything else. . . .

BRICK: Maggie, I wouldn't divorce you for being unfaithful or anything else. Don't you know that? Hell. I'd be relieved to know that you'd found yourself a lover.

MARGARET: Well, I'm taking no chances. No, I'd rather stay on this hot tin roof.

BRICK: A hot tin roof's 'n uncomfo'table place t' stay on. . . .

[He starts to whistle softly.]

MARGARET: *[through his whistle]:* Yeah, but I can stay on it just as long as I have to.

BRICK: You could leave me, Maggie.

[He resumes whistle. She wheels about to glare at him.]

MARGARET: *Don't want to and will not!* Besides if I did, you don't have a cent to pay for it but what you get from Big Daddy and he's dying of cancer!

[For the first time a realization of Big Daddy's doom seems to penetrate to Brick's consciousness, visibly, and he looks at Margaret.]

BRICK: Big Mama just said he *wasn't*, that the report was okay.

MARGARET: That's what she thinks because she got the same story that they gave Big Daddy. And was just as taken in by it as he was, poor ole things. . . .

But tonight they're going to tell her the truth about it. When Big Daddy goes to bed, they're going to tell her that he is dying of cancer.

[She slams the dresser drawer.]

—It's malignant and it's terminal.

BRICK: Does Big Daddy know it?

MARGARET: Hell, do they *ever* know it? Nobody says, "You're dying." You have to fool them. They have to fool *themselves*.

BRICK: Why?

MARGARET: *Why?* Because human beings dream of life everlasting, that's the reason! But most of them want it on earth and not in heaven.

[He gives a short, hard laugh at her touch of humor.]

Well. . . . *[She touches up her mascara.]* That's how it is, anyhow. . . . *[She looks about.]* Where did I put down my cigarette? Don't want to burn up the home-place, at least not with Mae and Gooper and their five monsters in it!

[She has found it and sucks at it greedily. Blows out smoke and continues:]

So this is Big Daddy's last birthday. And Mae and Gooper, they know it, oh, *they* know it, all right. They got the first information from the Ochsner Clinic. That's why they rushed down here with their no-neck monsters. Because. Do you know something? Big Daddy's made no will? Big Daddy's never made out any will in his life, and so this campaign's afoot to impress him, forcibly as possible, with the fact that you drink and I've borne no children!

[He continues to stare at her a moment, then mutters something sharp but not audible and hobbles rather rapidly out onto the long gallery in the fading, much faded, gold light.]

MARGARET: *[continuing her liturgical chant]:* Y'know, I'm *fond* of Big Daddy, I am genuinely fond of that old man, I really *am*, you know. . . .

BRICK *[faintly, vaguely]:* Yes, I know you are. . . .

MARGARET: I've always sort of admired him in spite of his coarseness, his four-letter words and so forth. Because Big Daddy *is* what he *is*, and he makes no bones about it. He hasn't turned gentleman farmer, he's still a Mississippi red neck, as much of a red neck as he must have been when he was just overseer here on the old Jack Straw and Peter Ochello place. But he got hold of it an' built it into th' biggest an' finest plantation in the Delta.—I've always *liked* Big Daddy. . . .

[She crosses to the proscenium.]

Well, this is Big Daddy's last birthday. I'm sorry about it. But I'm facing the facts. It takes money to take care of a drinker and that's the office that I've been elected to lately.

BRICK: You don't have to take care of me.

MARGARET: Yes, I do. Two people in the same boat have got to take care of each other. At least you want money to buy more Echo Spring when this supply is exhausted, or will you be satisfied with a ten-cent beer?

Mae an' Gooper are plannin' to freeze us out of Big Daddy's estate because you drink and I'm childless. But we can defeat that plan. We're *going* to defeat that plan! *Brick, y'know, I've been so God damn disgustingly poor all my life!*—That's the *truth*, Brick!

BRICK: I'm not sayin' it isn't.

MARGARET: Always had to suck up to people I couldn't stand because they had money and I was poor as Job's turkey. You don't know what that's like. Well, I'll tell you, it's like you would feel a thousand miles away from Echo Spring!—And had to get back to it on that broken ankle . . . without a crutch!

That's how it feels to be as poor as Job's turkey and have to suck up to relatives that you hated because they had money and all you had was a bunch of hand-me-down clothes and a few old moldy three per cent government bonds. My daddy loved his liquor, he fell in love with his liquor the way you've fallen in love with Echo Spring!—And my poor Mama, having to maintain some semblance of social position, to keep appearances up, on an income of one hundred and fifty dollars a month on those old government bonds!

When I came out, the year that I made my debut, I had just two evening dresses! One Mother made me from a pattern in *Vogue*, the other a hand-me-down from a snotty rich cousin I hated!

—The dress that I married you in was my grandmother's weddin' gown. . . .

So that's why I'm like a cat on a hot tin roof!

[Brick is still on the gallery. Someone below calls up to him in a warm Negro voice, "Hiya, Mistuh Brick, how yuh feelin'?" Brick raises his liquor glass as if that answered the question.]

MARGARET: You can be young without money but you can't be old without it. You've got to be old *with* money because to be old without it is just too awful, you've got to be one or the other, either *young* or *with money*, you can't be old and *without* it.—That's the truth, Brick. . . .

[Brick whistles softly, vaguely.]

Well, now I'm dressed, I'm all dressed, there's nothing else for me to do.

[Forlornly, almost fearfully.]

I'm dressed, all dressed, nothing else for me to do. . . .

[She moves about restlessly, aimlessly, and speaks, as if to herself.]

I know when I made my mistake.—What am I—? Oh!—my bracelets. . . .

[She starts working a collection of bracelets over her hands onto her wrists, about six on each, as she talks.]

I've thought a whole lot about it and now I know when I made my mistake. Yes, I made my mistake when I told you the truth about that thing with Skipper. Never should have confessed it, a fatal error, tellin' you about that thing with Skipper.

BRICK: Maggie, shut up about Skipper. I mean it, Maggie; you got to shut up about Skipper.

MARGARET: You ought to understand that Skipper and I ——

BRICK: You don't think I'm serious, Maggie? You're fooled by the fact that I am saying this quiet? Look, Maggie. What you're doing is a dangerous thing to do. You're–you're–you're–foolin' with something that—nobody ought to fool with.

MARGARET: This time I'm going to finish what I have to say to you. Skipper and I made love, if love you could call it, because it made both of us feel a little bit closer to you. You see, you son of a bitch, you asked too much of people, of me, of him, of all the unlucky poor damned sons of bitches that happen to love you, and there was a whole pack of them, yes, there was a pack of them besides me and Skipper, you asked too goddam much of people that loved you, you—superior creature!—you godlike being!—And so we made love to each other to dream it was you, both of us! Yes, yes, yes! Truth, truth! What's so awful about it? I like it, I think the truth is—yeah! I shouldn't have told you. . . .

BRICK *[holding his head unnaturally still and uptilted a bit]*: It was Skipper that told me about it. Not you, Maggie.

MARGARET: I told you!

BRICK: After he told me!

MARGARET: What does it matter who—?

[Brick turns suddenly out upon the gallery and calls:]

BRICK: Little girl! Hey, little girl!

LITTLE GIRL *[at a distance]*: What, Uncle Brick?

BRICK: Tell the folks to come up!—Bring everybody upstairs!

MARGARET: I can't stop myself! I'd go on telling you this in front of them all, if I had to!

BRICK: Little girl! Go on, go on, will you? Do what I told you, call them!

MARGARET: Because it's got to be told and you, you!—you never let me!

[She sobs, then controls herself, and continues almost calmly.]

It was one of those beautiful, ideal things they tell about in the Greek legends, it couldn't be anything else, you being you, and that's what made it so sad, that's what made it so awful, because it was love that never could be carried through to anything satisfying or even talked about plainly. Brick, I tell you, you got to believe me, Brick, I *do* understand all about it! I—I think it was—*noble!* Can't you tell I'm sincere when I say I respect it? My only point, the only point that I'm making, is life has got to be allowed to continue even after the *dream* of life is—all—over. . . .

[Brick is without his crutch. Leaning on furniture, he crosses to pick it up as she continues as if possessed by a will outside herself:]

Why I remember when we double-dated at college, Gladys Fitzgerald and I and you and Skipper, it was more like a date between you and Skipper. Gladys and I were just sort of tagging along as if it was necessary to chaperone you!—to make a good public impression—

BRICK *[turns to face her, half lifting his crutch]*: Maggie, you want me to hit you with this crutch? Don't you know I could kill you with this crutch?

MARGARET: Good Lord, man, d' you think I'd care if you did?

BRICK: One man has one great good true thing in his life. One great good thing which is true!—I had friendship with Skipper.—You are naming it dirty!

MARGARET: I'm not naming it dirty! I am naming it clean.

BRICK: Not love with you, Maggie, but friendship with Skipper was that one great true thing, and you are naming it dirty!

MARGARET: Then you haven't been listenin', not understood what I'm saying! I'm naming it so damn clean that it killed poor Skipper!—You two had something that had to be kept on ice, yes, incorruptible, yes!—and death was the only icebox where you could keep it. . . .

BRICK: I married you, Maggie. Why would I marry you, Maggie, if I was—?

MARGARET: Brick, don't brain me yet, let me finish!—I know, believe me I know, that it was only Skipper that harbored even any *unconscious* desire for anything not perfectly pure between you two!—Now let me skip a little. You married me early that summer we graduated out of Ole Miss, and we were happy, weren't we, we were blissful, yes, hit heaven together ev'ry time that we loved! But that fall you an' Skipper turned down wonderful offers of jobs in order to keep on bein' football heroes—pro-football heroes. You organized the Dixie Stars that fall, so you could keep on bein' team-mates forever! But somethin' was not right with it!—*Me included!*—between you. Skipper began hittin' the bottle . . . you got a spinal injury—couldn't play the Thanksgivin' game in Chicago, watched it on TV from a traction bed in Toledo. I joined Skipper. The Dixie Stars lost because poor Skipper was drunk. We drank together that night all night in the bar of the Blackstone and when cold day was comin' up over the Lake an' we were comin' out drunk to take a dizzy look at it, I said, "SKIPPER! STOP LOVIN' MY HUSBAND OR TELL HIM HE'S GOT TO LET YOU ADMIT IT TO HIM!"—one way or another!

HE SLAPPED ME HARD ON THE MOUTH!—then turned and ran without stopping once, I am sure, all the way back into his room at the Blackstone. . . .

—When I came to his room that night, with a little scratch like a shy little mouse at his door, he made that pitiful, ineffectual little attempt to prove that what I had said wasn't true. . . .

[Brick strikes at her with crutch, a blow that shatters the gemlike lamp on the table.]

—In this way, I destroyed him, by telling him truth that he and his world which he was born and raised in, yours and his world, had told him could not be told?

—From then on Skipper was nothing at all but a receptacle for liquor and drugs. . . .

—*Who shot cock-robin? I with my—*

[She throws back her head with tight shut eyes.]

—*merciful arrow!*

[Brick strikes at her; misses.]

Missed me!—Sorry,—I'm not tryin' to whitewash my behavior, Christ, no! Brick, I'm not good. I don't know why people have to pretend to be good, nobody's good. The rich or the well-to-do can afford to respect moral patterns, conventional moral patterns, but I could never afford to, yeah, but—I'm honest! Give me credit for just that, will you *please?*—Born poor, raised poor, expect to die poor unless I manage to get us something out of what Big Daddy leaves when he dies of cancer! But Brick?!—Skipper is dead! I'm alive! Maggie the cat is—

[Brick hops awkwardly forward and strikes at her again with his crutch.]

—alive! I am alive, alive! I am . . .

[He hurls the crutch at her, across the bed she took refuge behind, and pitches forward on the floor as she completes her speech.]

—alive!

[A little girl, Dixie, bursts into the room, wearing an Indian war bonnet and firing a cap pistol at Margaret and shouting: "Bang, bang, bang!" Laughter downstairs floats through the open hall door. Margaret had crouched gasping to bed at child's entrance. She now rises and says with cool fury:]

Little girl, your mother or someone should teach you—*[Gasping]*—to knock at a door before you come into a room. Otherwise people might think that you—lack—good breeding. . . .

DIXIE: Yanh, yanh, yanh, what is Uncle Brick doin' on th' floor?

BRICK: I tried to kill your Aunt Maggie, but I failed—and I fell. Little girl, give me my crutch so I can get up off th' floor.

MARGARET: Yes, give your uncle his crutch, he's a cripple, honey, he broke his ankle last night jumping hurdles on the high school athletic field!

DIXIE: What were you jumping hurdles for, Uncle Brick?

BRICK: Because I used to jump them, and people like to do what they used to do, even after they've stopped being able to do it. . . .

MARGARET: That's right, that's your answer, now go away, little girl.

[Dixie fires cap pistol at Margaret three times.]

Stop, you stop that, monster! You little no-neck monster!

[She seizes the cap pistol and hurls it through gallery doors.]

DIXIE *[with a precocious instinct for the cruelest thing]*: You're *jealous!*—You're just jealous because you can't have babies!

[She sticks out her tongue at Margaret as she sashays past her with her stomach stuck out, to the gallery, Margaret slams the gallery doors and leans panting against them. There is a pause. Brick has replaced his spilt drink and sits, faraway, on the great four-poster bed.]

MARGARET: You see?—they gloat over us being childless, even in front of their five little no-neck monsters!

[Pause. Voices approach on the stairs.]

Brick?—I've been to a doctor in Memphis, a—a gynecologist. . . .

I've been completely examined, and there is no reason why we can't have a child whenever we want one. And this is my time by the calendar to conceive. Are you listening to me? Are you? Are you *LISTENING TO ME!*

BRICK: Yes. I hear you, Maggie.

[His attention returns to her inflamed face.]

—But how in hell on earth do you imagine—that you're going to have a child by a man that can't stand you?

MARGARET: That's a problem that I will have to work out.

[She wheels about to face the hall door.]

Here they come!

[The lights dim.]

CURTAIN

ACT TWO

[There is no lapse of time. Margaret and Brick are in the same positions they held at the end of Act I.]

MARGARET: *[at door]: Here they come!*

[Big Daddy appears first, a tall man with a fierce, anxious look, moving carefully not to betray his weakness even, or especially, to himself.]

BIG DADDY: Well, Brick.

BRICK: Hello, Big Daddy.—Congratulations!

BIG DADDY: —Crap. . . .

[Some of the people are approaching through the hall, others along the gallery: voices from both directions. Gooper and Reverend Tooker become visible outside gallery doors, and their voices come in clearly. They pause outside as Gooper lights a cigar.]

REVEREND TOOKER *[vivaciously]*: Oh, but St. Paul's in Grenada has three memorial windows, and the latest one is a Tiffany stained-glass window that cost twenty-five hundred dollars, a picture of Christ the Good Shepherd with a Lamb in His arms.

GOOPER: Who give that window, Preach?

REVEREND TOOKER: Clyde Fletcher's widow. Also presented St. Paul's with a baptismal font.

GOOPER: Y'know what somebody ought t' give your church is a *coolin'* system, Preach.

REVEREND TOOKER: Yes, siree, Bob! And y'know what Gus Hamma's family gave in his memory to the church at Two Rivers? A complete new stone parish-house with a basketball court in the basement and a ———

BIG DADDY: *[uttering a loud barking laugh which is far from truly mirthful]:* Hey, Preach! What's all this talk about memorials, Preach? Y' think somebody's about t' kick off around here? 'S that it?

[Startled by this interjection, Reverend Tooker decides to laugh at the question almost as loud as he can. How he would answer the question we'll never know, as he's spared that embarrassment by the voice of Gooper's wife, Mae, rising high and clear as she appears with "Doc" Baugh, the family doctor, through the hall door.]

MAE *[almost religiously]:* —Let's see now, they've had their *tyyy*-phoid shots, and their tetanus shots, their diphtheria shots and their hepatitis shots and their polio shots, they got *those* shots every month from May through September, and—Gooper? Hey! Gooper!—What all have the kiddies been shot faw?

MARGARET *[overlapping a bit]:* Turn on the Hi-Fi, Brick! Let's have some music t' start off th' party with!

[The talk becomes so general that the room sounds like a great aviary of chattering birds. Only Brick remains unengaged, leaning upon the liquor cabinet with his faraway smile, an ice cube in a paper napkin with which he now and then rubs his forehead. He doesn't respond to Margaret's command. She bounds forward and stoops over the instrument panel of the console.]

GOOPER: We gave 'em that thing for a third anniversary present, got three speakers in it.

[The room is suddenly blasted by the climax of a Wagnerian opera or a Beethoven symphony.]

BIG DADDY: *Turn that dam thing off!*

[Almost instant silence, almost instantly broken by the shouting charge of Big Mama, entering through hall door like a charging rhino.]

BIG MAMA: *Wha's my Brick, wha's mah precious baby!!*

BIG DADDY: *Sorry! Turn it back on!*

[Everyone laughs very loud. Big Daddy is famous for his jokes at Big Mama's expense, and nobody laughs louder at these jokes than Big Mama herself, though sometimes they're pretty cruel and Big Mama has to pick up or fuss with something to cover the hurt that the loud laugh doesn't quite cover. On this occasion, a happy occasion because the dread in her heart has also been lifted by the false report on Big Daddy's condition, she giggles, grotesquely, coyly, in Big Daddy's direction and bears down upon Brick, all very quick and alive.]

BIG MAMA: Here he is, here's my precious baby! What's that you've got in your hand? You put that liquor down, son, your hand was made fo' holdin' somethin' better than that!

GOOPER: Look at Brick put it down!

[Brick has obeyed Big Mama by draining the glass and handing it to her. Again everyone laughs, some high, some low.]

BIG MAMA: Oh, you bad boy, you, you're my bad little boy. Give Big Mama a kiss, you bad boy, you!—Look at him shy away, will you? Brick never liked bein' kissed or made a fuss over, I guess because he's always had too much of it!

Son, you turn that thing off!

[Brick has switched on the TV set.]

I can't stand TV, radio was bad enough but TV has gone it one better, I mean—*[Plops wheezing in chair]*—one worse, ha ha! Now what'm I sittin' down here faw? I want t' sit next to my sweetheart on the sofa, hold hands with him and love him up a little!

[Big Mama has on a black and white figured chiffon. The large irregular patterns, like the markings of some massive animal, the luster of her great diamonds and many pearls, the brilliants set in the silver frames of her glasses, her riotous voice, booming

laugh, have dominated the room since she entered. Big Daddy has been regarding her with a steady grimace of chronic annoyance.]

BIG MAMA *[still louder]*: Preacher, Preacher, hey, Preach! Give me you' hand an' help me up from this chair!

REVEREND TOOKER: None of your tricks, Big Mama!

BIG MAMA: What tricks? You give me you' hand so I can get up an' ——

[Reverend Tooker extends her his hand. She grabs it and pulls him into her lap with a shrill laugh that spans an octave in two notes.]

Ever seen a preacher in a fat lady's lap? Hey, hey, folks!

Ever seen a preacher in a fat lady's lap?

[Big Mama is notorious throughout the Delta for this sort of inelegant horseplay. Margaret looks on with indulgent humor, sipping Dubonnet "on the rocks" and watching Brick, but Mae and Gooper exchange signs of humorless anxiety over these antics, the sort of behavior which Mae thinks may account for their failure to quite get in with the smartest young married set in Memphis, despite all. One of the Negroes, Lacey or Sookey, peeks in, cackling. They are waiting for a sign to bring in the cake and champagne. But Big Daddy's not amused. He doesn't understand why, in spite of the infinite mental relief he's received from the doctor's report, he still has these same old fox teeth in his guts. "This spastic thing sure is something," he says to himself, but aloud he roars at Big Mama:]

BIG DADDY: *BIG MAMA, WILL YOU QUIT HORSIN'?*—You're too old an' too fat fo' that sort of crazy kid stuff an' besides a woman with your blood-pressure—she had two hundred last spring!—is riskin' a stroke when you mess around like that. . . .

BIG MAMA: *Here comes Big Daddy's birthday!*

[Negroes in white jackets enter with an enormous birthday cake ablaze with candles and carrying buckets of champagne with satin ribbons about the bottle necks. Mae and Gooper strike up song, and everybody, including the Negroes and Children, joins in. Only Brick remains aloof.]

EVERYONE: Happy birthday to you.
Happy birthday to you.
Happy birthday, Big Daddy—
[Some sing: "Dear, Big Daddy!"]
Happy birthday to you.
[Some sing: "How old are you?"]

[Mae has come down center and is organizing her children like a chorus. She gives them a barely audible: "One, two, three!" and they are off in the new tune.]

CHILDREN: Skinamarinka—dinka—dink
Skinamarinka—do
We love you.
Skinamarinka—dinka—dink
Skinamarinka—do
[All together, they turn to Big Daddy.]
Big Daddy, you!
[They turn back front, like a musical comedy chorus.]
We love you in the morning;
We love you in the night.
We love you when we're with you,
And we love you out of sight.
Skinamarinka—dinka—dink

Skinamarinka—do.

[Mae turns to Big Mama.]

Big Mama, too!

[Big Mama bursts into tears. The Negroes leave.]

BIG DADDY: Now Ida, what the hell is the matter with you?

MAE: She's just so happy.

BIG MAMA: I'm just so happy, Big Daddy, I have to cry or something.

[Sudden and loud in the hush:]

Brick, do you know the wonderful news that Doc Baugh got from the clinic about Big Daddy? Big Daddy's one hundred per cent!

MARGARET: Isn't that wonderful?

BIG MAMA: He's just one hundred per cent. Passed the examination with flying colors. Now that we know there's nothing wrong with Big Daddy but a spastic colon, I can tell you something. I was worried sick, half out of my mind, for fear that Big Daddy might have a thing like ——

[Margaret cuts through this speech, jumping up and exclaiming shrilly:]

MARGARET: Brick, honey, aren't you going to give Big Daddy his birthday present?

[Passing by him, she snatches his liquor glass from him. She picks up a fancily wrapped package.]

Here it is, Big Daddy, this is from Brick!

BIG MAMA: This is the biggest birthday Big Daddy's ever had, a hundred presents and bushels of telegrams from—

MAE: *[at same time]*: What is it, Brick?

GOOPER: I bet 500 to 50 that Brick don't *know* what it is.

BIG MAMA: The fun of presents is not knowing what they are till you open the package. Open your present, Big Daddy.

BIG DADDY: Open it you'self. I want to ask Brick somethin! Come here, Brick.

MARGARET: Big Daddy's callin' you, Brick.

[She is opening the package.]

BRICK: Tell Big Daddy I'm crippled.

BIG DADDY: I see you're crippled. I want to know how you got crippled.

MARGARET: *[making diversionary tactics]: Oh, look, oh, look, why, it's a cashmere robe!*

[She holds the robe up for all to see.]

MAE: You sound surprised, Maggie.

MARGARET: I never saw one before.

MAE: That's funny.—*Hah!*

MARGARET *[turning on her fiercely, with a brilliant smile]*: Why is it funny? All my family ever had was family—and luxuries such as cashmere robes still surprise me!

BIG DADDY *[ominously]*: Quiet!

MAE *[heedless in her fury]*: I don't see how you could be so surprised when you bought it yourself at Loewenstein's in Memphis last Saturday. You know how I know?

BIG DADDY: I said, Quiet!

MAE: —I know because the salesgirl that sold it to you waited on me and said, Oh, Mrs. Pollitt, your sister-in-law just bought a cashmere robe for your husband's father!

MARGARET: Sister Woman! Your talents are wasted as a housewife and mother, you really ought to be with the FBI or ———

BIG DADDY: QUIET!

[Reverend Tooker's reflexes are slower than the others'. He finishes a sentence after the bellow.]

REVEREND TOOKER *[to Doc Baugh]*: —the Stork and the Reaper are running neck and neck!

[He starts to laugh gaily when he notices the silence and Big Daddy's glare. His laugh dies falsely.]

BIG DADDY: Preacher, I hope I'm not butting in on more talk about memorial stained-glass windows, am I, Preacher?

[Reverend Tooker laughs feebly, then coughs dryly in the embarrassed silence.]

Preacher?

BIG MAMA: Now, Big Daddy, don't you pick on Preacher!

BIG DADDY *[raising his voice]*: You ever hear that expression all hawk and no spit? You bring that expression to mind with that little dry cough of yours, all hawk an' no spit. . . .

[The pause is broken only by a short startled laugh from Margaret, the only one there who is conscious of and amused by the grotesque.]

MAE *[raising her arms and jangling her bracelets]*: I wonder if the mosquitoes are active tonight?

BIG DADDY: What's that, Little Mama? Did you make some remark?

MAE: Yes, I said I wondered if the mosquitoes would eat us alive if we went out on the gallery for a while.

BIG DADDY: Well, if they do, I'll have your bones pulverized for fertilizer!

BIG MAMA *[quickly]*: Last week we had an airplane spraying the place and I think it done some good, at least I haven't had a—

BIG DADDY *[cutting her speech]*: Brick, they tell me, if what they tell me is true, that you done some jumping last night on the high school athletic field?

BIG MAMA: Brick, Big Daddy is talking to you, son.

BRICK *[smiling vaguely over his drink]*: What was that, Big Daddy?

BIG DADDY: They said you done some jumping on the high school track field last night.

BRICK: That's what they told me, too.

BIG DADDY: Was it jumping or humping that you were doing out there? What were you doing out there at three A.M., layin' a woman on that cinder track?

BIG MAMA: Big Daddy, you are off the sick-list, now, and I'm not going to excuse you for talkin' so ———

BIG DADDY: Quiet!

BIG MAMA: —*nasty* in front of Preacher and ———

BIG DADDY: *QUIET!*—I ast you, Brick, if you was cuttin' you'self a piece o' poon-tang last night on that cinder track? I thought maybe you were chasin' poon-tang on that track an' tripped over something in the heat of the chase—'sthat it?

[Gooper laughs, loud and false, others nervously following suit. Big Mama stamps her foot, and purses her lips, crossing to Mae and whispering something to her as Brick meets his father's hard, intent, grinning stare with a slow, vague smile that he offers all situations from behind the screen of his liquor.]

BRICK: No, sir, I don't think so. . . .

MAE *[at the same time, sweetly]*: Reverend Tooker, let's you and I take a stroll on the widow's walk.

[She and the preacher go out on the gallery as Big Daddy says:]

BIG DADDY: Then what the hell were you doing out there at three o'clock in the morning?

BRICK: Jumping the hurdles, Big Daddy, runnin' and jumpin' the hurdles, but those high hurdles have gotten too high for me, now.

BIG DADDY: Cause you was drunk?

BRICK *[his vague smile fading a little]:* Sober I wouldn't have tried to jump the *low* ones. . . .

BIG MAMA *[quckly]:* Big Daddy, blow out the candles on your birthday cake!

MARGARET *[at the same time]:* I want to propose a toast to Big Daddy Pollitt on his sixty-fifth birthday, the biggest cotton-planter in —

BIG DADDY *[bellowing with fury and disgust]:* I told you to stop it, now stop it, quit this ——!

BIG MAMA *[coming in front of Big Daddy with the cake]:* Big Daddy, I will not allow you to talk that way, not even on your birthday, I ——

BIG DADDY: I'll talk like I want to on my birthday, Ida, or any other goddam day of the year and anybody here that don't like it knows what they can do!

BIG MAMA: You don't mean that!

BIG DADDY: What makes you think I don't mean it?

[Meanwhile various discreet signals have been exchanged and Gooper has also gone out on the gallery.]

BIG MAMA: I just know you don't mean it.

BIG DADDY: You don't know a goddam thing and you never did!

BIG MAMA: Big Daddy, you don't mean that.

BIG DADDY: Oh, yes, I do, oh, yes, I do, I mean it! I put up with a whole lot of crap around here because I thought I was dying. And you thought I was dying and you started taking over, well, you can stop taking over now, Ida, because I'm not gonna die, you can just stop now this business of taking over because you're not taking over because I'm not dying, I went through the laboratory and the goddam exploratory operation and there's nothing wrong with me but a spastic colon. And I'm not dying of cancer which you thought I was dying of. Ain't that so? Didn't you think that I was dying of cancer, Ida?

[Almost everybody is out on the gallery but the two old people glaring at each other across the blazing cake. Big Mama's chest heaves and she presses a fat fist to her mouth. Big Daddy continues, hoarsely:]

Ain't that so, Ida? Didn't you have an idea I was dying of cancer and now you could take control of this place and everything on it? I got that impression, I seemed to get that impression. Your loud voice everywhere, your fat old body butting in here and there!

BIG MAMA: Hush! The Preacher!

BIG DADDY: Rut the goddam preacher!

[Big Mama gasps loudly and sits down on the sofa which is almost too small for her.]

Did you hear what I said? I said rut the goddam preacher!

[Somebody closes the gallery doors from outside just as there is a burst of fireworks and excited cries from the children.]

BIG MAMA: I never seen you act like this before and I can't think what's got in you!

BIG DADDY: I went through all that laboratory and operation and all just so I would know if you or me was boss here! Well, now it turns out that I am and you ain't—and that's my birthday present—and my cake and champagne!—because for three years now you been gradually taking over. Bossing. Talking. Sashaying your fat old body around the place I made! I made this place! I was overseer on it! I was the overseer on the old Straw and Ochello plantation. I quit school at ten! I quit school at ten years old and went to work like a nigger in the fields. And I rose to be overseer of the Straw and Ochello plantation. And old Straw died and I was Ochello's partner and the place got bigger and bigger and bigger and bigger and bigger! I did all that myself with no goddam help from you, and now you think you're just about to take over. Well, I am just about to tell you that you are not just about to take over, you are not just about to take over a God damn thing. Is that clear to you, Ida? Is that very plain to you, now? Is that understood completely? I been through the laboratory from A to Z. I've had the goddam exploratory operation, and nothing is wrong with me but a spastic colon—made spastic, I guess, by *disgust!* By all the goddam lies and liars that I have had to put up with, and all the goddam hypocrisy that I lived with all these forty years that we been livin' together! Hey! Ida!! Blow out the candles on the birthday cake! Purse up your lips and draw a deep breath and blow out the goddam candles on the cake!

BIG MAMA: Oh, Big Daddy, oh, oh, oh, Big Daddy!

BIG DADDY: What's the matter with you?

BIG MAMA: In all these years you never believed that I loved you??

BIG DADDY: Huh?

BIG MAMA: And I did, I did so much, I did love you!—I even loved your hate and your hardness, Big Daddy!

[She sobs and rushes awkwardly out onto the gallery.]

BIG DADDY *[to himself]*: *Wouldn't it be funny if that was true. . . .*

[A pause is followed by a burst of light in the sky from the fireworks.]

BRICK! HEY, BRICK!

[He stands over his blazing birthday cake. After some moments, Brick hobbles in on his crutch, holding his glass. Margaret follows him with a bright, anxious smile.]

I didn't call you, Maggie. I called Brick.

MARGARET: I'm just delivering him to you.

[She kisses Brick on the mouth which he immediately wipes with the back of his hand. She flies girlishly back out. Brick and his father are alone.]

BIG DADDY: Why did you do that?

BRICK: Do what, Big Daddy?

BIG DADDY: Wipe her kiss off your mouth like she'd spit on you.

BRICK: I don't know. I wasn't conscious of it.

BIG DADDY: That woman of yours has a better shape on her than Gooper's but somehow or other they got the same look about them.

BRICK: What sort of look is that, Big Daddy?

BIG DADDY: I don't know how to describe it but it's the same look.

BRICK: They don't look peaceful, do they?

BIG DADDY: No, they sure in hell don't.

BRICK: They look nervous as cats?

BIG DADDY: That's right, they look nervous as cats.

BRICK: Nervous as a couple of cats on a hot tin roof?

BIG DADDY: That's right, boy, they look like a couple of cats on a hot tin roof. It's funny that you and Gooper being so different would pick out the same type of woman.

BRICK: Both of us married into society, Big Daddy.

BIG DADDY: Crap . . . I wonder what gives them both that look?

BRICK: Well. They're sittin' in the middle of a big piece of land, Big Daddy, twenty-eight thousand acres is a pretty big piece of land and so they're squaring off on it, each determined to knock off a bigger piece of it than the other whenever you let it go.

BIG DADDY: I got a surprise for those women. I'm not gonna let it go for a long time yet if that's what they're waiting for.

BRICK: That's right, Big Daddy. You just sit tight and let them scratch each other's eyes out. . . .

BIG DADDY: You bet your life I'm going to sit tight on it and let those sons of bitches scratch their eyes out, ha ha ha. . . .

But Gooper's wife's a good breeder, you got to admit she's fertile. Hell, at supper tonight she had them all at the table and they had to put a couple of extra leafs in the table to make room for them, she's got five head of them, now, and another one's comin'.

BRICK: Yep, number six is comin'. . . .

BIG DADDY: Brick, you know, I swear to God, I don't know the way it happens?

BRICK: The way what happens, Big Daddy?

BIG DADDY: You git you a piece of land, by hook or crook, an' things start growin' on it, things accumulate on it, and the first thing you know it's completely out of hand, completely out of hand!

BRICK: Well, they say nature hates a vacuum, Big Daddy.

BIG DADDY: That's what they say, but sometimes I think that a vacuum is a hell of a lot better than some of the stuff that nature replaces it with.

Is someone out there by that door?

BRICK: Yep.

BIG DADDY: Who?

[He has lowered his voice.]

BRICK: Someone int'rested in what we say to each other.

BIG DADDY: Gooper?———*GOOPER!*

[After a discreet pause, Mae appears in the gallery door.]

MAE: Did you call Gooper, Big Daddy?

BIG DADDY: Aw, it was you.

MAE: Do you want Gooper, Big Daddy?

BIG DADDY: No, and I don't want you. I want some privacy here, while I'm having a confidential talk with my son Brick. Now it's too hot in here to close them doors, but if I have to close those rutten doors in order to have a private talk with my son Brick, just let me know and I'll close 'em. Because I hate eavesdroppers, I don't like any kind of sneakin' an' spyin'.

MAE: Why, Big Daddy ———

BIG DADDY: You stood on the wrong side of the moon, it threw your shadow!

MAE: I was just ———

BIG DADDY: You was just nothing but *spyin'* an' you *know* it!

MAE *[begins to sniff and sob]:* Oh, Big Daddy, you're so unkind for some reason to those that really love you!

BIG DADDY: Shut up, shut up, shut up! I'm going to move you and Gooper out of that room next to this! It's none of your goddam business what goes on in here at night between Brick an' Maggie. You listen at night like a couple of rutten peek-hole spies and go and give a report on what you hear to Big Mama an' she comes to me and says they say such and such and so and so about what they heard goin' on between Brick an' Maggie, and Jesus, it makes me sick. I'm goin' to move you an' Gooper out of that room, I can't stand sneakin' an' spyin', it makes me sick. . . .

[Mae throws back her head and rolls her eyes heavenward and extends her arms as if invoking God's pity for this unjust martyrdom; then she presses a handkerchief to her nose and flies from the room with a loud swish of skirts.]

BRICK *[now at the liquor cabinet]*: They listen, do they?

BIG DADDY: Yeah. They listen and give reports to Big Mama on what goes on in here between you and Maggie. They say that—

[He stops as if embarrassed.]

—You won't sleep with her, that you sleep on the sofa. Is that true or not true? If you don't like Maggie, get rid of Maggie!—What are you doin' there now?

BRICK: Fresh'nin' up my drink.

BIG DADDY: Son, you know you got a real liquor problem?

BRICK: Yes, sir, yes, I know.

BIG DADDY: Is that why you quit sports-announcing, because of this liquor problem?

BRICK: Yes, sir, yes, sir, I guess so.

[He smiles vaguely and amiably at his father across his replenished drink.]

BIG DADDY: Son, don't guess about it, it's too important.

BRICK *[vaguely]*: Yes, sir.

BIG DADDY: And listen to me, don't look at the damn chandelier. . . .

[Pause. Big Daddy's voice is husky.]

—Somethin' else we picked up at th' big fire sale in Europe.

[Another pause.]

Life is important. There's nothing else to hold onto. A man that drinks is throwing his life away. Don't do it, hold onto your life. There's nothing else to hold onto. . . .

Sit down over here so we don't have to raise our voices, the walls have ears in this place.

BRICK *[hobbling over to sit on the sofa beside him]*: All right, Big Daddy.

BIG DADDY: Quit!—how'd that come about? Some disappointment?

BRICK: I don't know. Do you?

BIG DADDY: I'm askin' you, God damn it! How in hell would I know if you don't?

BRICK: I just got out there and found that I had a mouth full of cotton. I was always two or three beats behind what was goin' on on the field and so I———

BIG DADDY: Quit!

BRICK *[amiably]*: Yes, quit.

BIG DADDY: Son?

BRICK: Huh?

BIG DADDY *[inhales loudly and deeply from his cigar; then bends suddenly a little forward, exhaling loudly and raising a hand to his forehead]*: —Whew!—ha ha!—I took in too much smoke, it made me a little light-headed. . . .

[The mantel clock chimes.]

Why is it so damn hard for people to talk?

BRICK: Yeah. . . .

[The clock goes on sweetly chiming till it has completed the stroke of ten.]

—Nice peaceful-soundin' clock, I like to hear it all night. . . .

[He slides low and comfortable on the sofa; Big Daddy sits up straight and rigid with some unspoken anxiety. All his gestures are tense and jerky as he talks. He wheezes and pants and sniffs through his nervous speech, glancing quickly, shyly, from time to time, at his son.]

BIG DADDY: We got that clock the summer we wint to Europe, me an' Big Mama on that damn Cook's Tour, never had such an awful time in my life, I'm tellin' you, son, those gooks over there, they gouge your eyeballs out in their grand hotels. And

Big Mama bought more stuff than you could haul in a couple of boxcars, that's no crap. Everywhere she wint on this whirlwind tour, she bought, bought, bought. Why, half that stuff she bought is still crated up in the cellar, under water last spring!

[He laughs.]

That Europe is nothin' on earth but a great big auction, that's all it is, that bunch of old worn-out places, it's just a big fire-sale, the whole rutten thing, an' Big Mama wint wild in it, why, you couldn't hold that woman with a mule's harness! Bought, bought, bought!—lucky I'm a rich man, yes siree, Bob, an' half that stuff is mildewin' in th' basement. It's lucky I'm a rich man, it sure is lucky, well, I'm a rich man, Brick, yep, I'm a mighty rich man.

[His eyes light up for a moment.]

Y'know how much I'm worth? Guess, Brick! Guess how much I'm worth!

[Brick smiles vaguely over his drink.]

Close on ten million in cash an' blue chip stocks, outside, mind you, of twenty-eight thousand acres of the richest land this side of the valley Nile!

[A puff and crackle and the night sky blooms with an eerie greenish glow. Children shriek on the gallery.]

But a man can't buy his life with it, he can't buy back his life with it when his life has been spent, that's one thing not offered in the Europe fire-sale or in the American markets or any markets on earth, a man can't buy his life with it, he can't buy back his life when his life is finished. . . .

That's a sobering thought, a very sobering thought, and that's a thought that I was turning over in my head, over and over and over—until today. . . .

I'm wiser and sadder, Brick, for this experience which I just gone through. They's one thing else that I remember in Europe.

BRICK: What is that, Big Daddy?

BIG DADDY: The hills around Barcelona in the country of Spain and the children running over those bare hills in their bare skins beggin' like starvin' dogs with howls and screeches, and how fat the priests are on the streets of Barcelona, so many of them and so fat and so pleasant, ha ha!—Y'know I could feed that country? I got money enough to feed that goddam country, but the human animal is a selfish beast and I don't reckon the money I passed out there to those howling children in the hills around Barcelona would more than upholster one of the chairs in this room, I mean pay to put a new cover on this chair!

Hell, I threw them money like you'd scatter feed corn for chickens, I threw money at them just to get rid of them long enough to climb back into th' car and—drive away. . . .

And then in Morocco, them Arabs, why, prostitution begins at four or five, that's no exaggeration, why, I remember one day in Marrakech, that old walled Arab city, I set on a broken-down wall to have a cigar, it was fearful hot there and this Arab woman stood in the road and looked at me till I was embarrassed, she stood stock still in the dusty hot road and looked at me till I was embarrassed. But listen to this. She had a naked child with her, a little naked girl with her, barely able to toddle, and after a while she set this child on the ground and give her a push and whispered something to her. This child come toward me, barely able t' walk, come toddling up to me and ———

Jesus, it makes you sick t' remember a thing like this!

It stuck out its hand and tried to unbutton my trousers!

That child was not yet five! Can you believe me? Or do you think that I am making this up? I wint back to the hotel and said to Big Mama, Git packed! We're clearing out of this country. . . .

BRICK: Big Daddy, you're on a talkin' jag tonight.

BIG DADDY *[ignoring this remark]*: Yes, sir, that's how it is, the human animal is a beast that dies but the fact that he's dying don't give him pity for others, no, sir, it—

—Did you say something?

BRICK: Yes.

BIG DADDY: What?

BRICK: Hand me over that crutch so I can get up.

BIG DADDY: Where you goin'?

BRICK: I'm takin' a little short trip to Echo Spring.

BIG DADDY: To where?

BRICK: Liquor cabinet. . . .

BIG DADDY: Yes, sir, boy—

[He hands Brick the crutch.]

—the human animal is a beast that dies and if he's got money he buys and buys and buys and I think the reason he buys everything he can buy is that in the back of his mind he has the crazy hope that one of his purchases will be life everlasting!—Which it never can be. . . . The human animal is a beast that—

BRICK *[at the liquor cabinet]*: Big Daddy, you sure are shootin' th' breeze here tonight.

[There is a pause and voices are heard outside.]

BIG DADDY: I been quiet here lately, spoke not a word, just sat and stared into space. I had something heavy weighing on my mind but tonight that load was took off me. That's why I'm talking.—The sky looks diff'rent to me. . . .

BRICK: You know what I like to hear most?

BIG DADDY: What?

BRICK: Solid quiet. Perfect unbroken quiet.

BIG DADDY: Why?

BRICK: Because it's more peaceful.

BIG DADDY: Man, you'll hear a lot of that in the grave.

[He chuckles agreeably.]

BRICK: Are you through talkin' to me?

BIG DADDY: Why are you so anxious to shut me up?

BRICK: Well, sir, ever so often you say to me, Brick, I want to have a talk with you, but when we talk, it never materializes. Nothing is said. You sit in a chair and gas about this and that and I look like I listen. I try to look like I listen, but I don't listen, not much. Communication is—awful hard between people an'—somehow between you and me, it just don't—

BIG DADDY: Have you ever been scared? I mean have you ever felt downright terror of something?

[He gets up.]

Just one moment. I'm going to close these doors. . . .

[He closes doors on gallery as if he were going to tell an important secret.]

BRICK: What?

BIG DADDY: Brick?

BRICK: Huh?

BIG DADDY: Son, I thought I had it!

BRICK: Had what? Had what, Big Daddy?

BIG DADDY: Cancer!

BRICK: Oh . . .

BIG DADDY: I thought the old man made out of bones had laid his cold and heavy hand on my shoulder!

BRICK: Well, Big Daddy, you kept a tight mouth about it.

BIG DADDY: A pig squeals. A man keeps a tight mouth about it, in spite of a man not having a pig's advantage.

BRICK: What advantage is that?

BIG DADDY: Ignorance—of mortality—is a comfort. A man don't have that comfort, he's the only living thing that conceives of death, that knows what it is. The others go without knowing which is the way that anything living should go, go without knowing, without any knowledge of it, and yet a pig squeals, but a man sometimes, he can keep a tight mouth about it. Sometimes he—

[There is a deep, smoldering ferocity in the old man.]

—can keep a tight mouth about it. I wonder if ———

BRICK: What, Big Daddy?

BIG DADDY: A whiskey highball would injure this spastic condition?

BRICK: No, sir, it might do it good.

BIG DADDY: *[grins suddenly, wolfishly]:* Jesus, I can't tell you! The sky is open! Christ, it's open again! It's open, boy, it's open!

[Brick looks down at his drink.]

BRICK: You feel better, Big Daddy?

BIG DADDY: Better? Hell! I can breathe!—All of my life I been like a doubled up fist. . . .

[He pours a drink.]

—Poundin', smashin', drivin'!—now I'm going to loosen these doubled up hands and touch things *easy* with them. . . .

[He spreads his hands as if caressing the air.]

You know what I'm contemplating?

BRICK *[vaguely]:* No, sir, What are you contemplating?

BIG DADDY: Ha ha!—*Pleasure!*—pleasure with *women!*

[Brick's smile fades a little but lingers.]

Brick, this stuff burns me!—

—Yes, boy. I'll tell you something that you might not guess. I still have desire for women and this is my sixty-fifth birthday.

BRICK: I think that's mighty remarkable, Big Daddy.

BIG DADDY: Remarkable?

BRICK: *Admirable*, Big Daddy.

BIG DADDY: You're damn right it is, remarkable and admirable both. I realize now that I never had me enough. I let many chances slip by because of scruples about it, scruples, convention—crap. . . . All that stuff is bull, bull, bull!—It took the shadow of death to make me see it. Now that shadow's lifted, I'm going to cut loose and have, what is it they call it, have me a—ball!

BRICK: A ball, huh?

BIG DADDY: That's right, a ball, a ball! Hell!—I slept with Big Mama till, let's see, five years ago, till I was sixty and she was fifty-eight, and never even liked her, never did!

[The phone has been ringing down the hall. Big Mama enters, exclaiming:]

BIG MAMA: Don't you men hear that phone ring? I heard it way out on the gall'ry.

BIG DADDY: There's five rooms off this front gall'ry that you could go through. Why do you go through this one?

[Big Mama makes a playful face as she bustles out the hall door.]

Hunh!—Why, when Big Mama goes out of a room, I can't remember what that woman looks like, but when Big Mama comes back into the room, boy, then I see what she looks like, and I wish I didn't!

[Bends over laughing at this joke till it hurts his guts and he straightens with a grimace. The laugh subsides to a chuckle as he puts the liquor glass a little distrustfully down on the table. Brick has risen and hobbled to the gallery doors.]

Hey! Where you goin'?

BRICK: Out for a breather.

BIG DADDY: Not yet you ain't. Stay here till this talk is finished, young fellow.

BRICK: I thought it was finished, Big Daddy.

BIG DADDY: It ain't even begun.

BRICK: My mistake. Excuse me. I just wanted to feel that river breeze.

BIG DADDY: Turn on the ceiling fan and set back down in that chair.

[Big Mama's voice rises, carrying down the hall.]

BIG MAMA: Miss Sally, you're a case! You're a caution, Miss Sally. Why didn't you give me a chance to explain it to you?

BIG DADDY: Jesus, she's talking to my old maid sister again.

BIG MAMA: Well, goodbye, now, Miss Sally. You come down real soon, Big Daddy's dying to see you! Yaisss, goodbye, Miss Sally. . . .

[She hangs up and bellows with mirth. Big Daddy groans and covers his ears as she approaches. Bursting in:]

Big Daddy, that was Miss Sally callin' from Memphis again! You know what she done, Big Daddy? She called her doctor in Memphis to git him to tell her what that spastic thing is! Ha-*HAAAA!*—And called back to tell me how relieved she was that—Hey! Let me in!

[Big Daddy has been holding the door half closed against her.]

BIG DADDY: Naw I ain't. I told you not to come and go through this room. You just back out and go through those five other rooms.

BIG MAMA: Big Daddy? Big Daddy? Oh, big Daddy!—You didn't mean those things you said to me, did you?

[He shuts door firmly against her but she still calls.]

Sweetheart? Sweetheart? Big Daddy? You didn't mean those awful things you said to me?—I know you didn't. I know you didn't mean those things in your heart. . . .

[The childlike voice fades with a sob and her heavy footsteps retreat down the hall. Brick has risen once more on his crutches and starts for the gallery again.]

BIG DADDY: All I ask of that woman is that she leave me alone. But she can't admit to herself that she makes me sick. That comes of having slept with her too many years. Should of quit much sooner but that old woman she never got enough of it—and I was good in bed . . . I never should of wasted so much of it on her. . . . They say you got just so many and each one is numbered. Well, I got a few left in me, a few, and I'm going to pick me a good one to spend 'em on! I'm going to pick me a choice one, I don't care how much she costs, I'll smother her in—minks! Ha ha! I'll strip her naked and smother her in minks and choke her with diamonds! Ha ha! I'll strip her naked and choke her with diamonds and smother her with minks and hump her from hell to breakfast. *Ha aha ha ha ha!*

MAE *[gaily at door]*: Who's that laughin' in there?

GOOPER: Is Big Daddy laughin' in there?

BIG DADDY: Crap!—them two—*drips*. . . .

[He goes over and touches Brick's shoulder.]

Yes, son. Brick, boy.—I'm—*happy!* I'm happy, son, I'm happy!

[He chokes a little and bites his under lip, pressing his head quickly, shyly against his son's head and then, coughing with embarrassment, goes uncertainly back to the table where he set down the glass. He drinks and makes a grimace as it burns his guts. Brick sighs and rises with effort.]

What makes you so restless? Have you got ants in your britches?

BRICK: Yes, sir . . .

BIG DADDY: Why?

BRICK: —Something—hasn't—happened. . . .

BIG DADDY: Yeah? What is that!

BRICK *[sadly]*: —the click. . . .

BIG DADDY: Did you say click?

BRICK: Yes, click.

BIG DADDY: What click?

BRICK: A click that I get in my head that makes me peaceful.

BIG DADDY: I sure in hell don't know what you're talking about, but it disturbs me.

BRICK: It's just a mechanical thing.

BIG DADDY: What is a mechanical thing?

BRICK: This click that I get in my head that makes me peaceful. I got to drink till I get it. It's just a mechanical thing, something like a—like a—like a—

BIG DADDY: Like a—

BRICK: Switch clicking off in my head, turning the hot light off and the cool night on and—

[He looks up, smiling sadly.]

—all of a sudden there's—peace!

BIG DADDY: *[whistles long and soft with astonishment; he goes back to Brick and clasps his son's two shoulders]*: Jesus! I didn't know it had gotten that bad with you. Why, boy, you're—*alcoholic!*

BRICK: That's the truth, Big Daddy. I'm alcoholic.

BIG DADDY: This shows how I—let things go!

BRICK: I have to hear that little click in my head that makes me peaceful. Usually I hear it sooner than this, sometimes as early as—noon, but—

—Today it's—dilatory. . . .

—I just haven't got the right level of alcohol in my bloodstream yet!

[This last statement is made with energy as he freshens his drink.]

BIG DADDY: Uh—huh. Expecting death made me blind. I didn't have no idea that a son of mine was turning into a drunkard under my nose.

BRICK *[gently]*: Well, now you do, Big Daddy, the news has penetrated.

BIG DADDY: UH-huh, yes, now I do, the news has—penetrated. . . .

BRICK: And so if you'll excuse me—

BIG DADDY: No, I won't excuse you.

BRICK: —I'd better sit by myself till I hear that click in my head, it's just a mechanical thing but it don't happen except when I'm alone or talking to no one. . . .

BIG DADDY: You got a long, long time to sit still, boy, and talk to no one, but now you're talkin' to me. At least I'm talking to you. And you set there and listen until I tell you the conversation is over!

BRICK: But this talk is like all the others we've ever had together in our lives! It's nowhere, nowhere!—it's—it's *painful*, Big Daddy. . . .

BIG DADDY: All right, then let it be painful, but don't you move from that chair!—I'm going to remove that crutch. . . .

[He seizes the crutch and tosses it across room.]

BRICK: I can hop on one foot, and if I fall, I can crawl!

BIG DADDY: If you ain't careful you're gonna crawl off this plantation and then, by Jesus, you'll have to hustle your drinks along Skid Row!

BRICK: That'll come, Big Daddy.

BIG DADDY: Naw, it won't. You're my son and I'm going to straighten you out; now that *I'm* straightened out, I'm going to straighten out you!

BRICK: Yeah?

BIG DADDY: Today the report come in from Ochsner Clinic. Y'know what they told me?

[His face glows with triumph.]

The only thing that they could detect with all the instruments of science in that great hospital is a little spastic condition of the colon! And nerves torn to pieces by all that worry about it.

[A little girl bursts into room with a sparkler clutched in each fist, hops and shrieks like a monkey gone mad and rushes back out again as Big Daddy strikes at her. Silence. The two men stare at each other. A woman laughs gaily outside.]

I want you to know I breathed a sigh of relief almost as powerful as the Vicksburg tornado!

BRICK: You weren't ready to go?

BIG DADDY: GO WHERE?—crap. . . .

—When you are gone from here, boy, you are long gone and no where! The human machine is not no different from the animal machine or the fish machine or the bird machine or the reptile machine or the insect machine! It's just a whole God damn lot more complicated and consequently more trouble to keep together. Yep. I thought I had it. The earth shook under my foot, the sky come down like the black lid of a kettle and I couldn't breathe!—Today!!—that lid was lifted, I drew my first free breath in—how many years?—*God!—three*. . . .

[There is laughter outside, running footsteps, the soft, plushy sound and light of exploding rockets. Brick stares at him soberly for a long moment; then makes a sort of startled sound in his nostrils and springs up on one foot and hops across the room to grab his crutch, swinging on the furniture for support. He gets the crutch and flees as if in horror for the gallery. His father seizes him by the sleeve of his white silk pajamas.]

Stay here, you son of a bitch!—till I say go!

BRICK: I can't.

BIG DADDY: You sure in hell will, God damn it.

BRICK: No, I can't. We talk, you talk, in—circles! We get nowhere, nowhere! It's always the same, you say you want to talk to me and don't have a ruttin' thing to say to me!

BIG DADDY: Nothin' to say when I'm tellin' you I'm going to live when I thought I was dying?!

BRICK: Oh—*that!*—Is that what you have to say to me?

BIG DADDY: Why, you son of a bitch! Ain't that, ain't that—*important?!*

BRICK: Well, you said that, that's said, and now I—

BIG DADDY: Now you set back down.

BRICK: You're all balled up, you ———

BIG DADDY: I ain't balled up!

BRICK: You are, you're all balled up!

BIG DADDY: Don't tell me what I am, you drunken whelp! I'm going to tear this coat sleeve off if you don't set down!

BRICK: Big Daddy ———

BIG DADDY: Do what I tell you! I'm the boss here, now! I want you to know I'm back in the driver's seat now!

[Big Mama rushes in, clutching her great heaving bosom.]

What in hell do you want in here, Big Mama?

BIG MAMA: Oh, Big Daddy! Why are you shouting like that? I just cain't *stainnnnnnnd*—it. . . .

BIG DADDY *[raising the back of his hand above his head]*: GIT!—outa here.

[She rushes back out, sobbing.]

BRICK *[softly, sadly]*: *Christ*. . . .

BIG DADDY *[fiercely]*: Yeah! Christ!—is right . . .

[Brick breaks loose and hobbles toward the gallery. Big Daddy jerks his crutch from under Brick so he steps with the injured ankle. He utters a hissing cry of anguish, clutches a chair and pulls it over on top of him on the floor.]

Son of a—tub of—hog fat. . . .

BRICK: Big Daddy! Give me my crutch.

[Big Daddy throws the crutch out of reach.]

Give me that crutch, Big Daddy.

BIG DADDY: Why do you drink?

BRICK: Don't know, give me my crutch!

BIG DADDY: You better think why you drink or give up drinking!

BRICK: Will you please give me my crutch so I can get up off this floor?

BIG DADDY: First you answer my question. Why do you drink? Why are you throwing your life away, boy, like somethin' disgusting you picked up on the street?

BRICK *[getting onto his knees]*: Big Daddy, I'm in pain, I stepped on that foot.

BIG DADDY: Good! I'm glad you're not too numb with the liquor in you to feel some pain!

BRICK: You—spilled my—drink . . .

BIG DADDY: I'll make a bargain with you. You tell me why you drink and I'll hand you one. I'll pour you the liquor myself and hand it to you.

BRICK: Why do I drink?

BIG DADDY: Yeah! Why?

BRICK: Give me a drink and I'll tell you.

BIG DADDY: Tell me first!

BRICK: I'll tell you in one word.

BIG DADDY: What word?

BRICK: DISGUST!

[The clock chimes softly, sweetly. Big Daddy gives it a short, outraged glance.]

Now how about that drink?

BIG DADDY: What are you disgusted with? You got to tell me that, first. Otherwise being disgusted don't make no sense!

BRICK: Give me my crutch.

BIG DADDY: You heard me, you got to tell me what I asked you first.

BRICK: I told you, I said to kill my disgust!

BIG DADDY: DISGUST WITH WHAT!

BRICK: You strike a hard bargain.

BIG DADDY: What are you disgusted with?—an' I'll pass you the liquor.

BRICK: I can hop on one foot, and if I fall, I can crawl.

BIG DADDY: You want liquor that bad?

BRICK *[dragging himself up, clinging to bedstead]*: Yeah, I want it that bad.

BIG DADDY: If I give you a drink, will you tell me what it is you're disgusted with, Brick?

BRICK: Yes, sir, I will try to.

[The old man pours him a drink and solemnly passes it to him. There is silence as Brick drinks.]

Have you ever heard the word "mendacity"?

BIG DADDY: Sure. Mendacity is one of them five dollar words that cheap politicians throw back and forth at each other.

BRICK: You know what it means?

BIG DADDY: Don't it mean lying and liars?

BRICK: Yes, sir, lying and liars.

BIG DADDY: Has someone been lying to you?

CHILDREN *[chanting in chorus offstage]*: We want Big Dad-dee!
We want Big Dad-dee!

[Gooper appears in the gallery door.]

GOOPER: Big Daddy, the kiddies are shouting for you out there.

BIG DADDY *[fiercely]*: Keep out, Gooper!

GOOPER: 'Scuse *me!*

[Big Daddy slams the doors after Gooper.]

BIG DADDY: Who's been lying to you, has Margaret been lying to you, has your wife been lying to you about something, Brick?

BRICK: Not her. That wouldn't matter.

BIG DADDY: Then who's been lying to you, and what about?

BRICK: No one single person and no one lie. . . .

BIG DADDY: Then what, what then, for Christ's sake?

BRICK: —The whole, the whole—thing. . . .

BIG DADDY: Why are you rubbing your head? You got a headache?

BRICK: No, I'm tryin' to ——

BIG DADDY: —Concentrate, but you can't because your brain's all soaked with liquor, is that the trouble? Wet brain!

[He snatches the glass from Brick's hand.]

What do you know about this mendacity thing? Hell! I could write a book on it! Don't you know that? I could write a book on it and still not cover the subject? Well, I could, I could write a goddam book on it and still not cover the subject anywhere near enough!!—Think of all the lies I got to put up with!—Pretenses! Ain't that mendacity? Having to pretend stuff you don't think or feel or have any idea of? Having for instance to act like I care for Big Mama!—I haven't been able to stand the sight, sound, or smell of that woman for forty years now!—even when I *laid* her!—regular as a piston. . . . Pretend to love that son of a bitch of a Gooper and his wife Mae and those five same screechers out there like parrots in a jungle? Jesus! Can't stand to look at 'em!

Church!—it bores the Bejesus out of me but I go!—I go an' sit there and listen to the fool preacher!

Clubs!—Elks! Masons! Rotary!—*crap!*

[A spasm of pain makes him clutch his belly. He sinks into a chair and his voice is softer and hoarser.]

You I *do* like for some reason, did always have some kind of real feeling for—affection—respect—yes, always. . . .

You and being a success as a planter is all I ever had any devotion to in my whole life!—and that's the truth. . . .

I don't know why, but it is!

I've lived with mendacity!—Why can't *you* live with it? Hell, you *got* to live with it, there's nothing *else* to *live* with except mendacity, is there?

BRICK: Yes, sir. Yes, sir there is something else that you can live with!

BIG DADDY: What?

BRICK *[lifting his glass]*: This!—Liquor. . . .

BIG DADDY: That's not living, that's dodging away from life.

BRICK: I want to dodge away from it.

BIG DADDY: Then why don't you kill yourself, man?

BRICK: I like to drink. . . .

BIG DADDY: Oh, God, I can't talk to you. . . .

BRICK: I'm sorry, Big Daddy.

BIG DADDY: Not as sorry as I am. I'll tell you something. A little while back when I thought my number was up—

[This speech should have torrential pace and fury.]

—before I found out it was just this—spastic—colon, I thought about you. Should I or should I not, if the jig was up, give you this place when I go—since I hate Gooper an' Mae an' know that they hate me, and since all five same monkeys are little Maes an' Goopers.—And I thought, No!—Then I thought, Yes!—I couldn't make up my mind. I hate Gooper and his five same monkeys and that bitch Mae! Why should I turn over twenty-eight thousand acres of the richest land this side of the valley Nile to not my kind?—But why in hell, on the other hand, Brick—should I subsidize a goddam fool on the bottle?—Liked or not liked, well, maybe even—*loved!*—Why should I do that?—Subsidize worthless behavior? Rot? Corruption?

BRICK *[smiling]*: I understand.

BIG DADDY: Well, if you do, you're smarter than I am, God damn it, because I don't understand. And this I will tell you frankly. I didn't make up my mind at all on that question and still to this day I ain't made out no will!—Well, now I don't *have* to. The pressure is gone. I can just wait and see if you pull yourself together or if you don't.

BRICK: That's right, Big Daddy.

BIG DADDY: You sound like you thought I was kidding.

BRICK *[rising]*: No, sir, I know you're not kidding.

BIG DADDY: But you don't care—?

BRICK *[hobbling toward the gallery door]*: No, sir, I don't care. . . .

Now how about taking a look at your birthday fireworks and getting some of that cool breeze off the river?

[He stands in the gallery doorway as the night sky turns pink and green and gold with successive flashes of light.]

BIG DADDY: *WAIT!*—Brick. . . .

[His voice drops. Suddenly there is something shy, almost tender, in his restraining gesture.]

Don't let's—leave it like this, like them other talks we've had, we've always—talked around things, we've—just talked around things for some rutten reason. I don't know what, it's always like something was left not spoken, something avoided because neither of us was honest enough with the—other. . . .

BRICK: I never lied to you, Big Daddy.

BIG DADDY: Did I ever to *you?*

BRICK: No, sir. . . .

BIG DADDY: Then there is at least two people that never lied to each other.

BRICK: But we've never *talked* to each other.

BIG DADDY: We can *now*.

BRICK: Big Daddy, there don't seem to be anything much to say.

BIG DADDY: You say that you drink to kill your disgust with lying.

BRICK: You said to give you a reason.

BIG DADDY: Is liquor the only thing that'll kill this disgust?

BRICK: Now. Yes.

BIG DADDY: But not once, huh?

BRICK: Not when I was still young an' believing. A drinking man's someone who wants to forget he isn't still young an' believing.

BIG DADDY: Believing what?

BRICK: Believing. . . .

BIG DADDY: Believing *what?*

BRICK *[stubbornly evasive]*: Believing. . . .

BIG DADDY: I don't know what the hell you mean by believing and I don't think you know what you mean by believing, but if you still got sports in your blood, go back to sports announcing and ———

BRICK: Sit in a glass box watching games I can't play? Describing what I can't do while players do it? Sweating out their disgust and confusion in contests I'm not fit for? Drinkin' a coke, half bourbon, so I can stand it? That's no goddam good any more, no help—time just outran me, Big Daddy—got there first . . .

BIG DADDY: I think you're passing the buck.

BRICK: You know many drinkin' men?

BIG DADDY *[with a slight, charming smile]*: I have known a fair number of that species.

BRICK: Could any of them tell you why he drank?

BIG DADDY: Yep, you're passin' the buck to things like time and disgust with "mendacity" and—crap!—if you got to use that kind of language about a thing, it's ninety-proof bull, and I'm not buying any.

BRICK: I had to give you a reason to get a drink!

BIG DADDY: You started drinkin' when your friend Skipper died.

[Silence for five beats. Then Brick makes a startled movement, reaching for his crutch.]

BRICK: What are you suggesting?

BIG DADDY: I'm suggesting nothing.

[The shuffle and clop of Brick's rapid hobble away from his father's steady, grave attention.]

—But Gooper an' Mae suggested that there was something not right exactly in your ———

BRICK *[stopping short downstage as if backed to a wall]*: "Not right"?

BIG DADDY: Not, well, exactly *normal* in your friendship with ———

BRICK: They suggested that, too? I thought that was Maggie's suggestion.

[Brick's detachment is at last broken through. His heart is accelerated; his forehead sweat-beaded; his breath becomes more rapid and his voice hoarse. The thing they're discussing, timidly and painfully on the side of Big Daddy, fiercely, violently on Brick's side, is the inadmissible thing that Skipper died to disavow between them. The fact that if it existed it had to be disavowed to "keep face" in the world they lived in, may be at the heart of the "mendacity" that Brick drinks to kill his disgust with. It may be the root of his collapse. Or maybe it is only a single manifestation of it, not even the most important. The bird that I hope to catch in the net of this play is not the solution of one man's psychological problem. I'm trying to catch the true quality of experience in a group of people, that cloudy, flickering, evanescent—fiercely charged!—interplay of live human beings in the thundercloud of a common crisis. Some mystery should be left in the revelation of character in a play, just as a great deal of mystery is always left in the revelation of character in life, even in one's own character to himself. This does not absolve the playwright of his duty to observe and probe as clearly and deeply as he legitimately can: *but it should steer him away from "pat" conclusions, facile definitions which make a play just a play, not a snare for the truth of human experience.]*

[The following scene should be played with great concentration, with most of the power leashed but palpable in what is left unspoken.]

Who else's suggestion is it, is it *yours?* How many others thought that Skipper and I were—

BIG DADDY *[gently]:* Now, hold on, hold on a minute, son.—I knocked around in my time.

BRICK: What's that got to do with ———

BIG DADDY: I said 'Hold on!'—I bummed, I bummed this country till I was ———

BRICK: Whose suggestion, who else's suggestion is it?

BIG DADDY: Slept in hobo jungles and railroad Y's and flophouses in all cities before I ———

BRICK: Oh, *you* think so, too, you call me your son and a queer. Oh! Maybe that's why you put Maggie and me in this room that was Jack Straw's and Peter Ochello's, in which that pair of old sisters slept in a double bed where both of 'em died!

BIG DADDY: Now just don't go throwing rocks at ———

[Suddenly Reverend Tooker appears in the gallery doors, his head slightly, playfully, fatuously cocked, with a practised clergyman's smile, sincere as a bird-call blown on a hunter's whistle, the living embodiment of the pious, conventional lie. Big Daddy gasps a little at this perfectly timed, but incongruous, apparition.]

—What're you lookin' for, Preacher?

REVEREND TOOKER: The gentleman's lavatory, ha ha!—heh, heh . . .

BIG DADDY *[with strained courtesy]:* —Go back out and walk down to the other end of the gallery, Reverend Tooker, and use the bathroom connected with my bedroom, and if you can't find it, ask them where it is!

REVEREND TOOKER: Ah, thanks.

[He goes out with a deprecatory chuckle.]

BIG DADDY: It's hard to talk in this place . . .

BRICK: Son of a ———!

BIG DADDY *[leaving a lot unspoken]:* —I seen all things and understood a lot of them, till 1910. Christ, the year that—I had worn my shoes through, hocked my—I hopped off a yellow dog freight car half a mile down the road, slept in a wagon of cotton outside the gin—Jack Straw an' Peter Ochello took me in. Hired me to manage this place which grew into this one.—When Jack Straw died—why, old Peter Ochello quit eatin' like a dog does when its master's dead, and died, too!

BRICK: Christ!
BIG DADDY: I'm just saying I understand such ———
BRICK *[violently]*: Skipper is dead. I have not quit eating!
BIG DADDY: No, but you started drinking.

[Brick wheels on his crutch and hurls his glass across the room shouting.]

BRICK: YOU THINK SO, TOO?
BIG DADDY: *Shhh!*

[Footsteps run on the gallery. There are women's calls. Big Daddy goes toward the door.]

Go way!—Just broke a glass. . . .

[Brick is transformed, as if a quiet mountain blew suddenly up in volcanic flame.]

BRICK: You think so, too? You think so, too? You think me an' Skipper did, did, did!—*sodomy!*—together?
BIG DADDY: Hold ——!
BRICK: That what you ———
BIG DADDY: —*ON*—a minute!
BRICK: You think we did dirty things between us, Skipper an' ———
BIG DADDY: Why are you shouting like that? Why are you ———
BRICK: —Me, is that what you think of Skipper, is that ———
BIG DADDY: —so excited? I don't think nothing. I don't know nothing. I'm simply telling you what ———
BRICK: You think that Skipper and me were a pair of dirty old men?
BIG DADDY: Now that's ———
BRICK: Straw? Ochello? A couple of ———
BIG DADDY: Now just ———
BRICK: —ducking sissies? Queers? Is that what you ———
BIG DADDY: Shhh.
BRICK: —think?

[He loses his balance and pitches to his knees without noticing the pain. He grabs the bed and drags himself up.]

BIG DADDY: Jesus!—Whew. . . . Grab my hand!
BRICK: Naw, I don't want your hand. . . .
BIG DADDY: Well, I want yours. Git up!

[He draws him up, keeps an arm about him with concern and affection.]

You broken out in a sweat! You're panting like you'd run a race with ———

BRICK *[freeing himself from his father's hold]*: Big Daddy, you shock me, Big Daddy, you, you—*shock* me! Talkin' so—

[He turns away from his father.]

—casually!—about a—thing like that . . .

—Don't you know how people *feel* about things like that? How, how *disgusted* they are by things like that? Why, at Ole Miss when it was discovered a pledge to our fraternity, Skipper's and mine, did a, *attempted* to do a, unnatural thing with ———

We not only dropped him like a hot rock!—We told him to git off the campus, and he did, he got!—All the way to ———

[He halts, breathless.]

BIG DADDY: —Where?
BRICK: —North Africa, last I heard!

BIG DADDY: Well, I have come back from further away than that. I have just now returned from the other side of the moon, death's country, son, and I'm not easy to shock by anything here.

[He comes downstage and faces out.]

Always, anyhow, lived with too much space around me to be infected by ideas of other people. One thing you can grow on a big place more important than cotton!—is *tolerance!*—I grown it.

[He returns toward Brick.]

BRICK: Why can't exceptional friendship, *real, real, deep, deep friendship!* between two men be respected as something clean and decent without being thought of as—

BIG DADDY: It can, it is, for God's sake.

BRICK: —Fairies. . . .

[In his utterance of this word, we gauge the wide and profound reach of the conventional mores he got from the world that crowned him with early laurel.]

BIG DADDY: I told Mae an' Gooper—

BRICK: Frig Mae and Gooper, frig all dirty lies and liars!—Skipper and me had a clean, true thing between us!—had a clean friendship, practically all our lives, till Maggie got the idea you're talking about. Normal? No!—It was too rare to be normal, any true thing between two people is too rare to be normal. Oh, once in a while he put his hand on my shoulder or I'd put mine on his, oh, maybe even, when we were touring the country in pro-football an' shared hotel-rooms we'd reach across the space between the two beds and shake hands to say goodnight, yeah, one or two times we ———

BIG DADDY: Brick, nobody thinks that that's not normal!

BRICK: Well, they're mistaken, it was! It was a pure an' true thing an' that's not normal.

[They both stare straight at each other for a long moment. The tension breaks and both turn away as if tired.]

BIG DADDY: Yeah, it's—hard t'—talk. . . .

BRICK: All right, then, let's—let it go. . . .

BIG DADDY: Why did Skipper crack up? Why have you?

[Brick looks back at his father again. He has already decided, without knowing that he has made this decision, that he is going to tell his father that he is dying of cancer. Only this could even the score between them: one inadmissible thing in return for another.]

BRICK *[ominously]:* All right. You're asking for it, Big Daddy. We're finally going to have that real true talk you wanted. It's too late to stop it, now, we got to carry it through and cover every subject.

[He hobbles back to the liquor cabinet.]

Uh-huh.

[He opens the ice bucket and picks up the silver tongs with slow admiration of their frosty brightness.]

Maggie declares that Skipper and I went into pro-football after we left "Ole Miss" because we were scared to grow up . . .

[He moves downstage with the shuffle and clop of a cripple on a crutch. As Margaret did when her speech became "recitative," he looks out into the house, commanding its attention by his direct, concentrated gaze—a broken, "tragically elegant" figure telling simply as much as he knows of "the Truth":]

—Wanted to—keep on tossing—those long, long!—high, high!—passes that—couldn't be intercepted except by time, the aerial attack that made us famous! And so we did, we did, we kept it up for one season, that aerial attack, we held it high!—Yeah, but—that summer, Maggie, she laid the law down to me, said, Now or never, and so I married Maggie. . . .

BIG DADDY: How was Maggie in bed?

BRICK *[wryly]*: Great! the greatest!

[Big Daddy nods as if he thought so.]

She went on the road that fall with the Dixie Stars. Oh, she made a great show of being the world's best sport. She wore a—wore a—tall bearskin cap! A shako, they call it, a dyed moleskin coat, a moleskin coat dyed red!—Cut up crazy! Rented hotel ballrooms for victory celebrations, wouldn't cancel them when it—turned out—defeat. . . .

MAGGIE THE CAT! Ha ha!

[Big Daddy nods.]

—But Skipper, he had some fever which came back on him which doctors couldn't explain and I got that injury—turned out to be just a shadow on the X-ray plate—and a touch of bursitis. . . .

I lay in a hospital bed, watched our games on TV, saw Maggie on the bench next to Skipper when he was hauled out of a game for stumbles, fumbles!—Burned me up the way she hung on his arm!—Y'know, I think that Maggie had always felt sort of left out because she and me never got any closer together than two people just get in bed, which is not much closer than two cats on a—fence humping. . . .

So! She took this time to work on poor dumb Skipper. He was a less than average student at Ole Miss, you know that, don't you?!—Poured in his mind the dirty, false idea that what we were, him and me, was a frustrated case of that ole pair of sisters that lived in this room, Jack Straw and Peter Ochello!—He, poor Skipper, went to bed with Maggie to prove it wasn't true, and when it didn't work out, he thought it *was* true!—Skipper broke in two like a rotten stick—nobody ever turned so fast to a lush—or died of it so quick. . . . —Now are you satisfied?

[Big Daddy has listened to this story, dividing the grain from the chaff. Now he looks at his son.]

BIG DADDY: Are *you* satisfied?

BRICK: With what?

BIG DADDY: That half-ass story!

BRICK: What's half-ass about it?

BIG DADDY: Something's left out of that story. What did you leave out?

[The phone has started ringing in the hall. As if it reminded him of something, Brick glances suddenly toward the sound and says:]

BRICK: Yes!—I left out a long-distance call which I had from Skipper, in which he made a drunken confession to me and on which I hung up!—last time we spoke to each other in our lives. . . .

[Muted ring stops as someone answers phone in a soft, indistinct voice in hall.]

BIG DADDY: You hung up?

BRICK: Hung up. Jesus! Well ———

BIG DADDY: Anyhow now!—we have tracked down the lie with which you're disgusted and which you are drinking to kill your disgust with, Brick. You been passing the buck. This disgust with mendacity is disgust with yourself.

You!—dug the grave of your friend and kicked him in it!—before you'd face truth with him!

BRICK: *His* truth, not *mine!*

BIG DADDY: His truth, okay! But you wouldn't face it with him!

BRICK: Who *can* face truth? Can *you?*

BIG DADDY: Now don't start passin' the rotten buck again, boy!

BRICK: How about these birthday congratulations, these many, many happy returns of the day, when ev'rybody but you knows there won't be any!

[Whoever has answered the hall phone lets out a high, shrill laugh; the voice becomes audible saying: "no, no, you got it all wrong! Upside down! Are you crazy?" Brick suddenly catches his breath as he realized that he has made a shocking disclosure. He hobbles a few paces, then freezes, and without looking at his father's shocked face, says:]

Let's, let's—go out, now, and ———

[Big Daddy moves suddenly forward and grabs hold of the boy's crutch like it was a weapon for which they were fighting for possession.]

BIG DADDY: Oh, no, no! No one's going out. What did you start to say?

BRICK: I don't remember.

BIG DADDY: "Many happy returns when they know there won't be any"?

BRICK: Aw, hell, Big Daddy, forget it. Come on out on the gallery and look at the fireworks they're shooting off for your birthday. . . .

BIG DADDY: First you finish that remark you were makin' before you cut off. "Many happy returns when they know there won't be any"?—Ain't that what you just said?

BRICK: Look, now. I can get around without that crutch if I have to but it would be a lot easier on the furniture an' glassware if I didn' have to go swinging along like Tarzan of th' ———

BIG DADDY: FINISH! WHAT YOU WAS SAYIN'!

[An eerie green glow shows in sky behind him.]

BRICK *[sucking the ice in his glass, speech becoming thick]:* Leave th' place to Gooper and Mae an' their five little same little monkeys. All I want is ———

BIG DADDY: "LEAVE TH' PLACE," did you say?

BRICK *[vaguely]:* All twenty-eight thousand acres of the richest land this side of the valley Nile.

BIG DADDY: Who said I was "leaving the place" to Gooper or anybody? This is my sixty-fifth birthday! I got fifteen years or twenty years left in me! I'll outlive *you!* I'll bury you an' have to pay for your coffin!

BRICK: Sure. Many happy returns. Now let's go watch the fireworks, come on, let's ———

BIG DADDY: Lying, have they been lying? About the report from th'—clinic? Did they, did they—find something?—*Cancer*. Maybe?

BRICK: Mendacity is a system that we live in. Liquor is one way out an' death's the other. . . .

[He takes the crutch from Big Daddy's loose grip and swings out on the gallery leaving the doors open. A song, "Pick a Bale of Cotton," is heard.]

MAE *[appearing in door]: Oh, Big Daddy, the field-hands are singin' fo' you!*

BIG DADDY *[shouting hoarsely]:* BRICK! BRICK!

MAE: He's outside drinkin', Big Daddy.

BIG DADDY: *BRICK!*

[Mae retreats, awed by the passion of his voice. Children call Brick in tones mocking Big Daddy. His face crumbles like broken yellow plaster about to fall into dust. There is a glow in the sky. Brick swings back through the doors, slowly, gravely, quite soberly.]

BRICK: I'm sorry, Big Daddy. My head don't work any more and it's hard for me to understand how anybody could care if he lived or died or was dying or cared about anything but whether or not there was liquor left in the bottle and so I said what I said without thinking. In some ways I'm no better than the others, in some ways worse because I'm less alive. Maybe it's being alive that makes them lie, and being almost *not* alive makes me sort of accidentally truthful—I don't know but—anyway—we've been friends . . .

—And being friends is telling each other the truth. . . .

[There is a pause.]

You told *me!* I told *you!*

[A child rushes into the room and grabs a fistful of firecrackers and runs out again.]

CHILD *[screaming]*: Bang, bang, bang, bang bang, bang, bang, bang, bang!

BIG DADDY *[slowly and passionately]*: CHRIST—DAMN—ALL—LYING SONS OF—LYING BITCHES!

[He straightens at last and crosses to the inside door. At the door he turns and looks back as if he had some desperate question he couldn't put into words. Then he nods reflectively and says in a hoarse voice:]

Yes, all liars, all liars, all lying dying liars!

[This is said slowly, slowly, with a fierce revulsion. He goes on out.]

—Lying! Dying! Liars!

[His voice dies out. There is the sound of a child being slapped. It rushes, hideously bawling, through room and out the hall door. Brick remains motionless as the lights dim out and the curtain falls.]

CURTAIN

ACT THREE

[There is no lapse of time. Mae enters with Reverend Tooker.]

MAE: Where is Big Daddy! Big Daddy?

BIG MAMA *[entering]*: Too much smell of burnt fireworks makes me feel a little bit sick at my stomach.—Where is Big Daddy?

MAE: That's what I want to know, where has Big Daddy gone?

BIG MAMA: He must have turned in, I reckon he went to baid. . . .

[Gooper enters.]

GOOPER: Where is Big Daddy?

MAE: We don't know where he is!

BIG MAMA: I reckon he's gone to baid.

GOOPER: Well, then, now we can talk.

BIG MAMA: What *is* this talk, *what* talk?

[Margaret appears on gallery, talking to Dr. Baugh.]

MARGARET *[musically]*: My family freed their slaves ten years before abolition, great-great-grandfather gave his slaves their freedom years before the war between the States started!

MAE: Oh, for God's sake! Maggie's climbed back up in her family tree!

MARGARET *[sweetly]*: What, Mae?—Oh, where's Big Daddy?!

[The pace must be very quick. Great Southern animation.]

BIG MAMA *[addressing them all]*: I think Big Daddy was just worn out. He loves his family, he loves to have them around him, but it's a strain on his nerves. He wasn't himself tonight, Big Daddy wasn't himself, I could tell he was all worked up.

REVEREND TOOKER: I think he's remarkable.

BIG MAMA: Yaisss! Just remarkable. Did you all notice the food he ate at that table? Did you all notice the supper he put away? Why, he ate like a hawss!

GOOPER: I hope he doesn't regret it.

BIG MAMA: Why, that man—ate a huge piece of cawn-bread with molasses on it! Helped himself twice to hoppin' john.

MARGARET: Big Daddy loves hoppin' john.—We had a real country dinner.

BIG MAMA *[overlapping Margaret]:* Yais, he simply adores it! An' candied yams? That man put away enough food at that table to stuff a nigger *field*-hand!

GOOPER *[with grim relish]:* I hope he don't have to pay for it later on. . . .

BIG MAMA *[fiercely]:* What's *that*, Gooper?

MAE: Gooper says he hopes Big Daddy doesn't suffer tonight.

BIG MAMA: Oh, shoot, Gooper says, Gooper says! Why should Big Daddy suffer for satisfying a normal appetite? There's nothin' wrong with that man but nerves, he's sound as a dollar! And now he knows he is an' that's why he ate such a supper. He had a big load off his mind, knowin' he wasn't doomed t'—what he thought he was doomed to. . . .

MARGARET *[sadly and sweetly]:* Bless his old sweet soul. . . .

BIG MAMA *[vaguely]:* Yais, bless his heart, wher's Brick?

MAE: Outside.

GOOPER: —Drinkin' . .

BIG MAMA: I know he's drinkin'. You all don't have to keep tellin' *me* Brick is drinkin'. Cain't I see he's drinkin' without you continually tellin' me that boy's drinkin'?

MARGARET: Good for you, Big Mama!

[She applauds.]

BIG MAMA: Other people *drink* and *have* drunk an' will *drink*, as long as they make that stuff an' put it in bottles.

MARGARET: That's the truth. I never trusted a man that didn't drink.

MAE: Gooper never drinks. Don't you trust Gooper?

MARGARET: Why, Gooper don't you drink? If I'd known you didn't drink, I wouldn't of made that remark—

BIG MAMA: *Brick?*

MARGARET: —at least not in your presence.

[She laughs sweetly.]

BIG MAMA: *Brick!*

MARGARET: He's still on the gall'ry. I'll go bring him in so we can talk.

BIG MAMA *[worriedly]:* I don't know what this mysterious family conference is about.

[Awkward silence. Big Mama looks from face to face, then belches slightly and mutters, "Excuse me. . . ." She opens an ornamental fan suspended about her throat, a black lace fan to go with her black lace gown, and fans her wilting corsage, sniffing nervously and looking from face to face in the uncomfortable silence as Margaret calls "Brick?" and Brick sings to the moon on the gallery.]

I don't know what's wrong here, you all have such long faces! Open that door on the hall and let some air circulate through here, will you please, Gooper?

MAE: I think we'd better leave that door closed, Big Mama, till after the talk.

BIG MAMA: Reveren' Tooker, will *you* please open that door?!

REVEREND TOOKER: I sure will, Big Mama.

MAE: I just didn't think we ought t' take any chance of Big Daddy hearin' a word of this discussion.

BIG MAMA: *I swan!* Nothing's going to be said in Big Daddy's house that he cain't hear if he wants to!

GOOPER: Well, Big Mama, it's ———

[Mae gives him a quick, hard poke to shut him up. He glares at her fiercely as she circles before him like a burlesque ballerina, raising her skinny bare arms over her head, jangling her bracelets, exclaiming:]

MAE: *A breeze! A breeze!*

REVEREND TOOKER: I think this house is the coolest house in the Delta.—Did you all know that Halsey Banks' widow put air-conditioning units in the church and rectory at Friar's Point in memory of Halsey?

[General conversation has resumed; everybody is chatting so that the stage sounds like a big bird-cage.]

GOOPER: Too bad nobody cools your church off for you. I bet you sweat in that pulpit these hot Sundays, Reverend Tooker.

REVEREND TOOKER: Yes, my vestments are drenched.

MAE *[at the same time to Dr. Baugh]*: You reckon those vitamin B_{12} injections are what they're cracked up t' be, Doc Baugh?

DOCTOR BAUGH: Well, if you want to be stuck with something I guess they're as good to be stuck with as anything else.

BIG MAMA *[at gallery door]*: Maggie, Maggie, aren't you comin' with Brick?

MAE *[suddenly and loudly, creating a silence]*: I have a strange feeling, I have a peculiar feeling!

BIG MAMA *[turning from gallery]*: What feeling?

MAE: That Brick said somethin' he shouldn't of said t' Big Daddy.

BIG MAMA: Now what on earth could Brick of said t' Big Daddy that he shouldn't say?

GOOPER: Big Mama, there's somethin' ———

MAE: NOW, WAIT!

[She rushes up to Big Mama and gives her a quick hug and kiss. Big Mama pushes her impatiently off as the Reverend Tooker's voice rises serenely in a little pocket of silence:]

REVEREND TOOKER: Yes, last Sunday the gold in my chasuble faded into th' purple. . . .

GOOPER: Reveren', you must have been preachin' hell's fire last Sunday!

[He guffaws at this witticism but the Reverend is not sincerely amused. At the same time Big Mama has crossed over to Dr. Baugh and is saying to him:]

BIG MAMA *[her breathless voice rising high-pitched above the others]*: In my day they had what they call the Keeley cure for heavy drinkers. But now I understand they just take some kind of tablets, they call them "Annie Bust" tablets. But *Brick* don't need to take *nothin'*.

[Brick appears in gallery doors with Margaret behind him.]

BIG MAMA *[unaware of his presence behind her]*: That boy is just broken up over Skipper's death. You know how poor Skipper died. They gave him a big, big dose of that sodium amytal stuff at his home and then they called the ambulance and give him another big, big dose of it at the hospital and that and all of the alcohol in his system fo' months an' months an' months just proved too much for his heart. . . . I'm scared of needles! I'm more scared of a needle than the knife. . . . I think more people have been needled out of this world than ———

[She stops short and wheels about.]

OH!—here's Brick! My precious baby ———

[She turns upon Brick with short, fat arms extended, at the same time uttering a loud, short sob, which is both comic and touching. Brick smiles and bows slightly, making a burlesque gesture of gallantry for Maggie to pass before him into the room. Then he hobbles on his crutch directly to the liquor cabinet and there is absolute silence, with everybody looking at Brick as everybody has always looked at Brick when he spoke or moved or appeared. One by one he drops ice cubes in his glass, then suddenly, but not quickly, looks back over his shoulder with a wry, charming smile, and says:]

BRICK: I'm sorry! Anyone else?

BIG MAMA *[sadly]:* No, son. I *wish* you wouldn't!

BRICK: I wish I didn't have to, Big Mama, but I'm still waiting for that click in my head which makes it all smooth out!

BIG MAMA: Aw, Brick, you—BREAK MY HEART!

MARGARET *[at the same time]: Brick, go sit with Big Mama!*

BIG MAMA: I just cain't *staiiiiiiii-nnnnnd*—it. . . . *[She sobs.]*

MAE: Now that we're all assembled—

GOOPER: We kin talk. . . .

BIG MAMA: Breaks my heart. . . .

MARGARET: Sit with Big Mama, Brick, and hold her hand.

[Big Mama sniffs very loudly three times, almost like three drum beats in the pocket of silence.]

BRICK: You do that, Maggie. I'm a restless cripple. I got to stay on my crutch.

[Brick hobbles to the gallery door; leans there as if waiting. Mae sits beside Big Mama, while Gooper moves in front and sits on the end of the couch, facing her. Reverend Tooker moves nervously into the space between them; on the other side, Dr. Baugh stands looking at nothing in particular and lights a cigar. Margaret turns away.]

BIG MAMA: Why're you all *surroundin'* me—like this? Why're you all starin' at me like this an' makin' signs at each other?

[Reverend Tooker steps back startled.]

MAE: Calm yourself, Big Mama.

BIG MAMA: Calm you'self, *you'self*, Sister Woman. How could I calm myself with everyone starin' at me as if big drops of blood had broken out on m' face? What's this all about, Annh! What?

[Gooper coughs and takes a center position.]

GOOPER: Now, Doc Baugh.

MAE: Doc Baugh?

BRICK *[suddenly]:* SHHH!—

[Then he grins and chuckles and shakes his head regretfully.]

—Naw!—that wasn't th' click.

GOOPER: Brick, shut up or stay out there on the gallery with your liquor! We got to talk about a serious matter. Big Mama wants to know the complete truth about the report we got today from the Ochsner Clinic.

MAE *[eagerly]:* —on Big Daddy's condition!

GOOPER: Yais, on Big Daddy's condition, we got to face it.

DOCTOR BAUGH: Well. . . .

BIG MAMA *[terrified, rising]:* Is there? Something? Something that I? Don't—Know?

[In these few words, this startled, very soft, question, Big Mama reviews the history of her forty-five years with Big Daddy, her great, almost embarrassingly true-hearted and simple-minded devotion to Big Daddy, who must have had something Brick has, who made himself loved so much by the "simple expedient" of not loving enough to disturb

his charming detachment, also once coupled, like Brick's, with virile beauty. Big Mama has a dignity at this moment: she almost stops being fat.]

DOCTOR BAUGH *[after a pause, uncomfortably]*: Yes?—Well—

BIG MAMA: *I!!!*—want to—*knowwwwwww*. . . .

[Immediately she thrusts her fist to her mouth as if to deny that statement. Then, for some curious reason, she snatches the withered corsage from her breast and hurls it on the floor and steps on it with her short, fat feet.]

—Somebody must be lyin'!—I want to know!

MAE: Sit down, Big Mama, sit down on this sofa.

MARGARET *[quickly]*: Brick, go sit with Big Mama.

BIG MAMA: What is it, what is it?

DOCTOR BAUGH: I never have seen a more thorough examination than Big Daddy Pollitt was given in all my experience with the Ochsner Clinic.

GOOPER: It's one of the best in the country.

MAE: It's *THE* best in the country—bar *none!*

[For some reason she gives Gooper a violent poke as she goes past him. He slaps at her hand without removing his eyes from his mother's face.]

DOCTOR BAUGH: Of course they were ninety-nine and nine-tenths percent sure before they even started.

BIG MAMA: Sure of what, sure of what, sure of—*what?*—*what!*

[She catches her breath in a startled sob. Mae kisses her quickly. She thrusts Mae fiercely away from her, staring at the doctor.]

MAE: Mommy, be a brave girl!

BRICK *[in the doorway, softly]*: *"By the light, by the light,*
Of the sil-ve-ry mo-ooo-n . . ."

GOOPER: Shut up!—Brick.

BRICK: —Sorry. . . .

[He wanders out on the gallery.]

DOCTOR BAUGH: But now, you see, Big Mama, they cut a piece off this growth, a specimen of the tissue and—

BIG MAMA: Growth? You told Big Daddy—

DOCTOR BAUGH: Now wait.

BIG MAMA *[fiercely]*: You told me and Big Daddy there wasn't a thing wrong with him but—

MAE: Big Mama, they always—

GOOPER: Let Doc Baugh talk, will yuh?

BIG MAMA: —little spastic condition of—

[Her breath gives out in a sob.]

DOCTOR BAUGH: Yes, that's what we told Big Daddy. But we had this bit of tissue run through the laboratory and I'm sorry to say the test was positive on it. It's—well—malignant. . . .

[Pause.]

BIG MAMA: —Cancer?! Cancer?!

[Dr. Baugh nods gravely. Big Mama gives a long gasping cry.]

MAE AND GOOPER: Now, now, now, Big Mama, you had to know. . . .

BIG MAMA: *WHY DIDN'T THEY CUT IT OUT OF HIM? HANH? HANH?*

DOCTOR BAUGH: Involved too much, Big Mama, too many organs affected.

MAE: Big Mama, the liver's affected and so's the kidneys, both! It's gone way past what they call a ———

GOOPER: A surgical risk.
MAE: —Uh-huh. . . .
[Big Mama draws a breath like a dying gasp.]
REVEREND TOOKER: Tch, tch, tch, tch, tch!
DOCTOR BAUGH: Yes, it's gone past the knife.
MAE: *That's why he's turned yellow, Mommy!*
BIG MAMA: Git away from me, git away from me, Mae!
[She rises abruptly.]
I want Brick! Where's Brick? Where is my only son?
MAE: Mama! Did she say "*only* son"?
GOOPER: What does that make *me?*
MAE: A sober responsible man with five precious children!—*Six!*
BIG MAMA: I want Brick to tell me! Brick! Brick!
MARGARET *[rising from her reflections in a corner]:* Brick was so upset he went back out.
BIG MAMA: *Brick!*
MARGARET: Mama, let *me* tell you!
BIG MAMA: No, no, leave me alone, you're not my blood!
GOOPER: *Mama, I'm your son!* Listen to *me!*
MAE: Gooper's your son, he's your first-born!
BIG MAMA: Gooper never liked Daddy.
MAE *[as if terribly shocked]:* That's not TRUE!
[There is a pause. The minister coughs and rises.]
REVEREND TOOKER *[to Mae]:* I think I'd better slip away at this point.
MAE *[sweetly and sadly]:* Yes, Doctor Tooker, you go.
REVEREND TOOKER *[discreetly]:* Goodnight, goodnight, everybody, and God bless you all . . . on this place. . . .
[He slips out.]
DOCTOR BAUGH: That man is a good man but lacking in tact. Talking about people giving memorial windows—if he mentioned one memorial window, he must have spoke of a dozen, and saying how awful it was when somebody died intestate, the legal wrangles, and so forth.
[Mae coughs, and points at Big Mama.]
DOCTOR BAUGH: Well, Big Mama. . . .
[He sighs.]
BIG MAMA: It's all a mistake, I know it's just a bad dream.
DOCTOR BAUGH: We're gonna keep Big Daddy as comfortable as we can.
BIG MAMA: Yes, it's just a bad dream, that's all it is, it's just an awful dream.
GOOPER: In my opinion Big Daddy is having some pain but won't admit that he has it.
BIG MAMA: Just a dream, a bad dream.
DOCTOR BAUGH: That's what lots of them do, they think if they don't admit they're having the pain they can sort of escape the fact of it.
GOOPER *[with relish]:* Yes, they get sly about it, they get real sly about it.
MAE: Gooper and I think ———
GOOPER: Shut up, Mae!—Big Daddy ought to be started on morphine.
BIG MAMA: Nobody's going to give Big Daddy morphine.
DOCTOR BAUGH: Now, Big Mama, when that pain strikes it's going to strike mighty hard and Big Daddy's going to need the needle to bear it.
BIG MAMA: I tell you, nobody's going to give him morphine.
MAE: Big Mama, you don't want to see Big Daddy suffer, you know you ———

[Gooper standing beside her give her a savage poke.]

DOCTOR BAUGH *[placing a package on the table]*: I'm leaving this stuff here, so if there's a sudden attack you all won't have to send out for it.

MAE: I know how to give a hypo.

GOOPER: Mae took a course in nursing during the war.

MARGARET: Somehow I don't think Big Daddy would want Mae to give him a hypo.

MAE: You think he'd want *you* to do it?

[Dr. Baugh rises.]

GOOPER: Doctor Baugh is goin'.

DOCTOR BAUGH: Yes, I got to be goin'. Well, keep your chin up, Big Mama.

GOOPER *[with jocularity]*: She's gonna keep *both* chins up, aren't you Big Mama?

[Big Mama sobs.]

Now stop that, Big Mama.

MAE: Sit down with me, Big Mama.

GOOPER *[at door with Dr. Baugh]*: Well, Doc, we sure do appreciate all you done. I'm telling you, we're surely obligated to you for ———

[Dr. Baugh has gone out without a glance at him.]

GOOPER: —I guess that doctor has got a lot on his mind but it wouldn't hurt him to act a little more human. . . .

[Big Mama sobs.]

Now be a brave girl, Mommy.

BIG MAMA: It's not true, I know that it's just not true!

GOOPER: Mama, those tests are infallible!

BIG MAMA: Why are you so determined to see your father daid?

MAE: Big Mama!

MARGARET *[gently]*: I know what Big Mama means.

MAE *[fiercely]*: Oh, do you?

MARGARET *[quietly and very sadly]*: Yes, I think I do.

MAE: For a newcomer in the family you sure do show a lot of understanding.

MARGARET: Understanding is needed on this place.

MAE: I guess you must have needed a lot of it in your family, Maggie, with your father's liquor problem and now you've got Brick with his!

MARGARET: Brick does not have a liquor problem at all. Brick is devoted to Big Daddy. This thing is a terrible strain on him.

BIG MAMA: Brick is Big Daddy's boy, but he drinks too much and it worries me and Big Daddy, and, Margaret, you've got to cooperate with us, you've got to cooperate with Big Daddy and me in getting Brick straightened out. Because it will break Big Daddy's heart if Brick don't pull himself together and take hold of things.

MAE: Take hold of *what* things, Big Mama?

BIG MAMA: The place.

[There is a quick violent look between Mae and Gooper.]

GOOPER: Big Mama, you've had a shock.

MAE: Yais, we've all had a shock, but. . . .

GOOPER: Let's be realistic ———

MAE: —Big Daddy would never, would *never*, be foolish enough to ———

GOOPER: —put this place in irresponsible hands!

BIG MAMA: Big Daddy ain't going to leave the place in anybody's hands; Big Daddy is *not* going to die. I want you to get that in your heads, all of you!

MAE: Mommy, Mommy, Big Mama, we're just as hopeful an' optimistic as you are about Big Daddy's prospects, we have faith in *prayer*—but nevertheless there are certain matters that have to be discussed an' dealt with, because otherwise ——

GOOPER: Eventualities have to be considered and now's the time. . . . Mae, will you please get my briefcase out of our room?

MAE: Yes, honey.

[She rises and goes out through the hall door.]

GOOPER *[standing over Big Mama]*: Now Big Mom. What you said just now was not at all true and you know it. I've always loved Big Daddy in my own quiet way. I never made a show of it, and I know that Big Daddy has always been fond of me in a quiet way, too, and he never made a show of it neither.

[Mae returns with Gooper's briefcase.]

MAE: Here's your briefcase, Gooper, honey.

GOOPER *[handing the briefcase back to her]*: Thank you. . . . Of cou'se, my relationship with Big Daddy is different from Brick's.

MAE: You're eight years older'n Brick an' always had t'carry a bigger load of th' responsibilities than Brick ever had t'carry. He never carried a thing in his life but a football or a highball.

GOOPER: Mae, will y' let me talk, please?

MAE: Yes, honey.

GOOPER: Now, a twenty-eight thousand acre plantation's a mighty big thing t'run.

MAE: Almost singlehanded.

[Margaret has gone out onto the gallery, and can be heard calling softly to Brick.]

BIG MAMA: You never had to run this place! What are you talking about? As if Big Daddy was dead and in his grave, you had to run it? Why, you just helped him out with a few business details and had your law practice at the same time in Memphis!

MAE: Oh, Mommy, Mommy, Big Mommy! Let's be fair! Why, Gooper has given himself body and soul to keeping this place up for the past five years since Big Daddy's health started failing. Gooper won't say it, Gooper never thought of it as a duty, he just did it. And what did Brick do? Brick kept living in his past glory at college! Still a football player at twenty-seven!

MARGARET *[returning alone]*: Who are you talking about, now? Brick? A football player? He isn't a football player and you know it. Brick is a sports announcer on TV and one of the best-known ones in the country!

MAE: I'm talking about what he was.

MARGARET: Well, I wish you would just stop talking about my husband.

GOOPER: I've got a right to discuss my brother with other members of MY OWN family which don't include *you*. Why don't you go out there and drink with Brick?

MARGARET: I've never seen such malice toward a brother.

GOOPER: How about his for me? Why, he can't stand to be in the same room with me!

MARGARET: This is a deliberate campaign of vilification for the most disgusting and sordid reason on earth, and I know what it is! It's *avarice, avarice, greed, greed!*

BIG MAMA: Oh, I'll scream! I will scream in a moment unless this stops!

[Gooper has stalked up to Margaret with clenched fists at his sides as if he would strike her. Mae distorts her face again into a hideous grimace behind Margaret's back.]

MARGARET: We only remain on the place because of Big Mom and Big Daddy. If it is true what they say about Big Daddy we are going to leave here just as soon as it's over. Not a moment later.

BIG MAMA *[sobs]:* Margaret. Child. Come here. Sit next to Big Mama.

MARGARET: Precious Mommy. I'm sorry, I'm sorry, I ——!

[She bends her long graceful neck to press her forehead to Big Mama's bulging shoulder under its black chiffon.]

GOOPER: How beautiful, how touching, this display of devotion!

MAE: Do you know why she's childless? She's childless because that big beautiful athlete husband of hers won't go to bed with her!

GOOPER: You jest won't let me do this in a nice way, will yah? Aw right—Mae and I have five kids with another one coming! I don't give a goddam if Big Daddy likes me or don't like me or did or never did or will or will never! I'm just appealing to a sense of common decency and fair play. I'll tell you the truth. I've resented Big Daddy's partiality to Brick ever since Brick was born, and the way I've been treated like I was just barely good enough to spit on and sometimes not even good enough for that. Big Daddy is dying of cancer, and it's spread all through him and it's attacked all his vital organs including the kidneys and right now he is sinking into uremia, and you all know what uremia is, it's poisoning of the whole system due to the failure of the body to eliminate its poisons.

MARGARET *[to herself, downstage, hissingly]: Poisons, poisons! Venomous thoughts and words! In hearts and minds!—That's poisons!*

GOOPER *[overlapping her]:* I am asking for a square deal, and I expect to get one. But if I don't get one, if there's any peculiar shenanigans going on around here behind my back, or before me, well, I'm not a corporation lawyer for nothing, I know how to protect my own interests.—*OH! A late arrival!*

[Brick enters from the gallery with a tranquil, blurred smile, carrying an empty glass with him.]

MAE: Behold the conquering hero comes!

GOOPER: The fabulous Brick Pollitt! Remember him?—Who could forget him!

MAE: He looks like he's been injured in a game!

GOOPER: Yep, I'm afraid you'll have to warm the bench at the Sugar Bowl this year, Brick!

[Mae laughs shrilly.]

Or was it the Rose Bowl that he made that famous run in?

MAE: The punch bowl, honey. It was in the punch bowl, the cut-glass punch bowl!

GOOPER: Oh, that's right, I'm getting the bowls mixed up!

MARGARET: Why don't you stop venting your malice and envy on a sick boy?

BIG MAMA: *Now you two hush, I mean it, hush, all of you, hush!*

GOOPER: All right, Big Mama. A family crisis brings out the best and the worst in every member of it.

MAE: *That*'s the truth.

MARGARET: *Amen!*

BIG MAMA: *I said, hush!* I won't tolerate any more catty talk in my house.

[Mae gives Gooper a sign indicating briefcase. Brick's smile has grown both brighter and vaguer. As he prepares a drink, he sings softly:]

BRICK: *Show me the way to go home,*
I'm tired and I wanta go to bed,
I had a little drink about an hour ago—

GOOPER *[at the same time]:* Big Mama, you know it's necessary for me t'go back to Memphis in th' mornin' t'represent the Parker estate in a lawsuit.

[Mae sits on the bed and arranges papers she has taken from the briefcase.]

BRICK *[continuing the song]: Wherever I may roam,*
On land or sea or foam.

BIG MAMA: Is it, Gooper?

MAE: Yaiss.

GOOPER: That's why I'm forced to—to bring up a problem that—

MAE: Somethin' that's too important t' be put off!

GOOPER: If Brick was sober, he ought to be in on this.

MARGARET: Brick is present; we're here.

GOOPER: Well, good. I will now give you this outline my partner, Tom Bullitt, an' me have drawn up—a sort of dummy—trusteeship.

MARGARET: Oh, that's it! You'll be in charge an' dole out remittances, will you?

GOOPER: This we did as soon as we got the report on Big Daddy from th' Ochsner Laboratories. We did this thing, I mean we drew up this dummy outline with the advice and assistance of the Chairman of the Boa'd of Directors of th' Southern Plantahs Bank and Trust Company in Memphis, C. C. Bellowes, a man who handles estates for all th' prominent fam'lies in West Tennessee and th' Delta.

BIG MAMA: Gooper?

GOOPER *[crouching in front of Big Mama]:* Now this is not—not final, or anything like it. This is just a preliminary outline. But it does provide a basis—a design—a—possible, feasible—*plan!*

MARGARET: Yes, I'll bet.

MAE: It's a plan to protect the biggest estate in the Delta from irresponsibility an'—

BIG MAMA: Now you listen to me, all of you, you listen here! They's not goin' to be any more catty talk in my house! And Gooper, you put that away before I grab it out of your hand and tear it right up! I don't know what the hell's in it, and I don't want to know what the hell's in it. I'm talkin' in Big Daddy's language now; I'm his *wife,* not his *widow,* I'm still his *wife!* And I'm talkin' to you in his language an' ———

GOOPER: Big Mama, what I have here is ———

MAE: Gooper explained that it's just a plan. . . .

BIG MAMA: I don't care what you got there. Just put it back where it came from, an' don't let me see it again, not even the outside of the envelope of it! Is that understood? Basis! Plan! Preliminary! Design! I say—what is it Big Daddy always says when he's disgusted?

BRICK *[from the bar]:* Big Daddy says "crap" when he's disgusted.

BIG MAMA *[rising]:* That's right—*CRAP!* I say *CRAP* too, like Big Daddy!

MAE: Coarse language doesn't seem called for in this ———

GOOPER: Somethin' in me is *deeply outraged* by hearin' you talk like this.

BIG MAMA: *Nobody's goin' to take nothin'!*—till Big Daddy lets go if it, and maybe, just possibly, not—not even then! No, not even then!

BRICK: *You can always hear me singin' this song,*
Show me the way to go home.

BIG MAMA: Tonight Brick looks like he used to look when he was a little boy, just like he did when he played wild games and used to come home all sweaty and pink-cheeked and sleepy, with his—red curls shining. . . .

[She comes over to him and runs her fat shaky hand through his hair. He draws aside as he does from all physical contact and continues the song in a whisper, opening the ice

bucket and dropping in the ice cubes one by one as if he were mixing some important chemical formula.]

BIG MAMA *[continuing]:* Time goes by so fast. Nothin' can outrun it. Death commences too early—almost before you're half-acquainted with life—you meet with the other. . . .

Oh, you know we just got to love each other an' stay together, all of us, just as close as we can, especially now that such a *black* thing has come and moved into this place without invitation.

[Awkwardly embracing Brick, she presses her head to his shoulder. Gooper has been returning papers to Mae who has restored them to briefcase with an air of severely tried patience.]

GOOPER: Big Mama? Big Mama?

[He stands behind her, tense with sibling envy.]

BIG MAMA *[oblivious of Gooper]:* Brick, you hear me, don't you?

MARGARET: Brick hears you, Big Mama, he understands what you're saying.

BIG MAMA: Oh, Brick, son of Big Daddy! Big Daddy does so love you! Y'know what would be his fondest dream come true? If before he passed on, if Big Daddy has to pass on, you gave him a child of yours, a grandson as much like his son as his son is like Big Daddy!

MAE *[zipping briefcase shut: an incongruous sound]:* Such a pity that Maggie an' Brick can't oblige!

MARGARET *[suddenly and quietly but forcefully]:* Everybody listen.

[She crosses to the center of the room, holding her hands rigidly together.]

MAE: Listen to what, Maggie?

MARGARET: I have an announcement to make.

GOOPER: A sports announcement, Maggie?

MARGARET: Brick and I are going to—*have a child!*

[Big Mama catches her breath in a loud gasp. Pause. Big Mama rises.]

BIG MAMA: Maggie! Brick! This is too good to believe!

MAE: That's right, too good to believe.

BIG MAMA: Oh, my, my! This is Big Daddy's dream, his dream come true! I'm going to tell him right now before he ——

MARGARET: We'll tell him in the morning. Don't disturb him now.

BIG MAMA: I want to tell him before he goes to sleep, I'm going to tell him his dream's come true this minute! And Brick! A child will make you pull yourself together and quit this drinking!

[She seizes the glass from his hand.]

The responsibilities of a father will ——

[Her face contorts and she makes an excited gesture; bursting into sobs, she rushes out, crying.]

I'm going to tell Big Daddy right this minute!

[Her voice fades out down the hall. Brick shrugs slightly and drops an ice cube into another glass. Margaret crosses quickly to his side, saying something under her breath, and she pours the liquor for him, staring up almost fiercely into his face.]

BRICK *[Coolly]:* Thank you, Maggie, that's a nice big shot.

[Mae has joined Gooper and she gives him a fierce poke, making a low hissing sound and a grimace of fury.]

GOOPER *[pushing her aside]*: Brick, could you possibly spare me one small shot of that liquor?

BRICK: Why, help yourself, Gooper boy.

GOOPER: I will.

MAE *[shrilly]*: Of course we know that this is ———

GOOPER: *Be still, Mae!*

MAE: I won't be still! I know she's made this up!

GOOPER: God damn it, I said to shut up!

MARGARET: Gracious! I didn't know that my little announcement was going to provoke such a storm!

MAE: *That* woman isn't *pregnant!*

GOOPER: Who said she was?

MAE: *She* did.

GOOPER: The doctor didn't. Doc Baugh didn't.

MARGARET: I haven't gone to Doc Baugh.

GOOPER: Then who'd you go to, Maggie?

MARGARET: One of the best gynecologists in the South.

GOOPER: Uh huh, uh huh!—I see. . . .

[He takes out pencil and notebook.]

—May we have his name, please?

MARGARET: No, you may not, Mister Prosecuting Attorney!

MAE: He doesn't have any name, he doesn't exist!

MARGARET: Oh, he exists all right, and so does my child, Brick's baby!

MAE: You can't conceive a child by a man that won't sleep with you unless you think you're—

[Brick has turned on the phonograph. A scat song cuts Mae's speech.]

GOOPER: Turn that off!

MAE: We know it's a lie because we hear you in here; he won't sleep with you, we hear you! So don't imagine you're going to put a trick over on us, to fool a dying man with a ———

[A long drawn cry of agony and rage fills the house. Margaret turns phonograph down to a whisper. The cry is repeated.]

MAE *[awed]*: Did you hear that, Gooper, did you hear that?

GOOPER: Sounds like the pain has struck.

MAE: Go see, Gooper!

GOOPER: Come along and leave these love birds together in their nest!

[He goes out first. Mae follows but turns at the door, contorting her face and hissing at Margaret.]

MAE: *Liar!*

[She slams the door. Margaret exhales with relief and moves a little unsteadily to catch hold of Brick's arm.]

MARGARET: Thank you for—keeping still . . .

BRICK: OK, Maggie.

MARGARET: It was gallant of you to save my face!

BRICK: —It hasn't happened yet.

MARGARET: What?

BRICK: The click. . . .

MARGARET: —the click in your head that makes you peaceful, honey?

BRICK: Uh-huh. It hasn't happened. . . . I've got to make it happen before I can sleep. . . .

MARGARET: —I—know what you—mean. . . .

BRICK: Give me that pillow in the big chair, Maggie.

MARGARET: I'll put it on the bed for you.

BRICK: No, put it on the sofa, where I sleep.

MARGARET: Not tonight, Brick.

BRICK: I want it on the sofa. That's where I sleep.

[He has hobbled to the liquor cabinet. He now pours down three shots in quick succession and stands waiting, silent. All at once he turns with a smile and says:]

There!

MARGARET: What?

BRICK: The *click*. . . .

[His gratitude seems almost infinite as he hobbles out on the gallery with a drink. We hear his crutch as he swings out of sight. Then, at some distance, he begins singing to himself a peaceful song. Margaret holds the big pillow forlornly as if it were her only companion, for a few moments, then throws it on the bed. She rushes to the liquor cabinet, gathers all the bottles in her arms, turns about undecidedly, then runs out of the room with them, leaving the door ajar on the dim yellow hall. Brick is heard hobbling back along the gallery, singing his peaceful song. He comes back in, sees the pillow on the bed, laughs lightly, sadly, picks it up. He has it under his arm as Margaret returns to the room. Margaret softly shuts the door and leans against it, smiling softly at Brick.]

MARGARET: Brick, I used to think that you were stronger than me and I didn't want to be overpowered by you. But now, since you've taken to liquor—you know what?—I guess it's bad, but now I'm stronger than you and I can love you more truly!

Don't move that pillow. I'll move it right back if you do!—Brick?

[She turns out all the lamps but a single rose-silk-shaded one by the bed.]

I really have been to a doctor and I know what to do and—Brick?—this is my time by the calendar to conceive!

BRICK: Yes, I understand, Maggie. But how are you going to conceive a child by a man in love with his liquor?

MARGARET: By locking his liquor up and making him satisfy my desire before I unlock it!

BRICK: Is that what you've done, Maggie?

MARGARET: Look and see. That cabinet's mighty empty compared to before!

BRICK: Well, I'll be a son of a—

[He reaches for his crutch but she beats him to it and rushes out on the gallery, hurls the crutch over the rail and comes back in, panting. There are running footsteps. Big Mama bursts into the room, her face all awry, gasping, stammering.]

BIG MAMA: Oh, my God, oh, my God, oh, my God, where is it?

MARGARET: Is this what you want, Big Mama?

[Margaret hands her the package left by the doctor.]

BIG MAMA: I can't bear it, oh, God! Oh, Brick! Brick, baby!

[She rushes at him. He averts his face from her sobbing kisses. Margaret watches with a tight smile.]

My son, Big Daddy's boy! Little Father!

[The groaning cry is heard again. She runs out, sobbing.]

MARGARET: And so tonight we're going to make the lie true, and when that's done, I'll bring the liquor back here and we'll get drunk together, here, tonight, in this place that death has come into. . . .

—What do you say?

BRICK: I don't say anything. I guess there's nothing to say.

MARGARET: Oh, you weak people, you weak, beautiful people!—who give up.— What you want is someone to—

[She turns out the rose-silk lamp.]

—take hold of you.—Gently, gently, with love! And—

[The curtain begins to fall slowly.]

I *do* love you, Brick, I *do!*

BRICK *[smiling with charming sadness]*: Wouldn't it be funny if that was true?

THE CURTAIN COMES DOWN

THE END

NOTE OF EXPLANATION

Some day when time permits I would like to write a piece about the influence, its dangers and its values, of a powerful and highly imaginative director upon the development of a play, before and during production. It does have dangers, but it has them only if the playwright is excessively malleable or submissive, or the director is excessively insistent on ideas or interpretations of his own. Elia Kazan and I have enjoyed the advantages and avoided the dangers of this highly explosive relationship because of the deepest mutual respect for each other's creative function: we have worked together three times with a phenomenal absence of friction between us and each occasion has increased the trust.

If you don't want a director's influence on your play, there are two ways to avoid it, and neither is good. One way is to arrive at an absolutely final draft of your play before you let your director see it, then hand it to him saying, Here it is, take it or leave it! The other way is to select a director who is content to put your play on the stage precisely as you conceived it with no ideas of his own. I said neither is a good way, and I meant it. No living playwright, that I can think of, hasn't something valuable to learn about his own work from a director so keenly perceptive as Elia Kazan. It so happened that in the case of *Streetcar,* Kazan was given a script that was completely finished. In the case of *Cat,* he was shown the first typed version of the play, and he was excited by it, but he had definite reservations about it which were concentrated in the third act. The gist of his reservations can be listed as three points: one, he felt that Big Daddy was too vivid and important a character to disappear from the play except as an offstage cry after the second act curtain; two, he felt that the character of Brick should undergo some apparent mutation as a result of the virtual vivisection that he undergoes in his interview with his father in Act Two. Three, he felt that the character of Margaret, while he understood that I sympathized with her and liked her myself, should be, if possible, more clearly sympathetic to an audience.

It was only the third of these suggestions that I embraced wholeheartedly from the outset, because it so happened that Maggie the Cat had become steadily more charming to me as I worked on her characterization. I didn't want Big Daddy to reappear in Act Three and I felt that the moral paralysis of Brick was a root thing in his tragedy, and to show a dramatic progression would obscure the meaning of that tragedy in him and because I don't believe that a conversation, however revelatory, ever effects so immediate a change in the heart or even conduct of a person in Brick's state of spiritual disrepair.

However, I wanted Kazan to direct the play, and though these suggestions were not made in the form of an ultimatum, I was fearful that I would lose his interest if I didn't re-examine the script from his point of view. I did. And you will find included in this published script the new third act that resulted from his creative influence on the play. The reception of the playing-script has more than justified, in my opinion, the adjustments made to that influence. A failure reaches fewer people, and touches fewer, than does a play that succeeds.

It may be that *Cat* number one would have done just as well, or nearly, as *Cat* number two; it's an interesting question. At any rate, with the publication of both third acts in this volume, the reader can, if he wishes, make up his own mind about it.

Tennessee Williams

Act Three

As Played in New York Production

[Big Daddy is seen leaving as at the end of Act II.]

BIG DADDY *[shouts, as he goes out DR on gallery]:* ALL—LYIN'—DYIN'—LIARS! LIARS! LIARS!

[After Big Daddy has gone, Margaret enters from DR on gallery, into room through DS door. She X to Brick at LC.]

MARGARET: Brick, what in the name of God was goin' on in this room?

[Dixie and Trixie rush through the room from the hall, L to gallery R, brandishing cap pistols, which they fire repeatedly, as they shout: "Bang! Bang! Bang!" Mae appears from DR gallery entrance, and turns the children back UL, along gallery. At the same moment, Gooper, Reverend Tooker and Dr. Baugh enter from L in the hall.]

MAE: Dixie! You quit that! Gooper, will y'please git these kiddies t'baid? Right now?

[Gooper and Reverend Tooker X along upper gallery. Dr. Baugh holds, UC, near hall door. Reverend Tooker X to Mae near section of gallery just outside doors, R.]

GOOPER *[urging the children along]:* Mae—you seen Big Mama?

MAE: Not yet.

[Dixie and Trixie vanish through hall, L.]

REVEREND TOOKER *[to Mae]:* Those kiddies are so full of vitality. I think I'll have to be startin' back to town.

[Margaret turns to watch and listen.]

MAE: Not yet, Preacher. You know we regard you as a member of this fam'ly, one of our closest an' dearest, so you just got t'be with us when Doc Baugh gives Big Mama th' actual truth about th' report from th' clinic.

[Calls through door:]

Has Big Daddy gone to bed, Brick?

[Gooper has gone out DR at the beginning of the exchange between Mae and Reverend Tooker.]

MARGARET *[replying to Mae]:* Yes, he's gone to bed.

[To Brick:]
Why'd Big Daddy shout "liars"?

GOOPER *[off DR]:* Mae!
[Mae exits DR. Reverend Tooker drifts along upper gallery.]

BRICK: I didn't lie to Big Daddy. I've lied to nobody, nobody but myself, just lied to myself. The time has come to put me in Rainbow Hill, put me in Rainbow Hill, Maggie, I ought to go there.

MARGARET: Over my dead body!
[Brick starts R. She holds him.]
Where do you think you're goin'?
[Mae enters from DR on gallery, X to Reverend Tooker, who comes to meet her.]

BRICK *[X below to C]:* Out for some air, I want air—

GOOPER *[entering from DR to Mae, on gallery]:* Now, where is that old lady?

MAE: Cantcha find her, Gooper?
[Reverend Tooker goes out DR.]

GOOPER *[X to Doc above hall door]:* She's avoidin' this talk.

MAE: I think she senses somethin'.

GOOPER *[calls off L]:* Sookey! Go find Big Mama an' tell her Doc Baugh an' the Preacher've got to go soon.

MAE: Don't let Big Daddy hear yuh!
[Brings Dr. Baugh to R on gallery.]

REVEREND TOOKER *[off DR, calls]:* Big Mama.

SOOKEY AND DAISY *[running from L to R on lawn, calling]:* Miss Ida! Miss Ida!
[They go out UR.]

GOOPER *[calling off upper gallery]:* Lacey, you look downstairs for Big Mama!

MARGARET: Brick, they're going to tell Big Mama the truth now, an' she needs you!
[Reverend Tooker appears in lawn area, UR, X C.]

DOCTOR BAUGH *[to Mae, on R gallery]:* This is going to be painful.

MAE: Painful things can't always be avoided.

DOCTOR BAUGH: That's what I've noticed about 'em, Sister Woman.

REVEREND TOOKER *[on lawn, points off R]:* I see Big Mama!
[Hurries off L and reappears shortly in hall.]

GOOPER *[hurrying into hall]:* She's gone round the gall'ry to Big Daddy's room. Hey, Mama!
[Off:] Hey, Big Mama! Come here!

MAE *[calls]:* Hush, Gooper! Don't holler, go to her!
[Gooper and Reverend Tooker now appear together in hall. Big Mama runs in from DR, carrying a glass of milk. She X past Dr. Baugh to Mae, on R gallery. Dr. Baugh turns away.]

BIG MAMA: Here I am! What d'you all want with me?

GOOPER *[steps toward Big Mama]:* Big Mama, I told you we got to have this talk.

BIG MAMA: What talk you talkin' about? I saw the light go on in Big Daddy's bedroom an' took him his glass of milk, an' he just shut the shutters right in my face.
[Steps into room through R door.]
When old couples have been together as long as me an' Big Daddy, they, they get irritable with each other just from too much—devotion! Isn't that so?
[X below wicker seat to RC area.]

MARGARET *[X to Big Mama, embracing her]*: Yes, of course it's so.

[Brick starts out UC through hall, but sees Gooper and Reverend Tooker entering, so he hobbles through C out DS door and onto gallery.]

BIG MAMA: I think Big Daddy was just worn out. He loves his fam'ly. He loves to have 'em around him, but it's a strain on his nerves. He wasn't himself tonight, Brick—

[XC toward Brick. Brick passes her on his way out, DS.]

Big Daddy wasn't himself, I could tell he was all worked up.

REVEREND TOOKER *[USC]*: I think he's remarkable.

BIG MAMA: Yaiss! Just remarkable.

[Faces US, turns, X to bar, puts down glass of milk.]

Did you notice all the food he ate at that table?

[XR a bit.]

Why he ate like a hawss!

GOOPER *[USC]*: I hope he don't regret it.

BIG MAMA *[turns US toward Gooper]*: What! Why that man ate a huge piece of cawn bread with molassess on it! Helped himself twice to hoppin' john!

MARGARET *[X to Big Mama]*: Big Daddy loves hoppin' john. We had a real country dinner.

BIG MAMA: Yais, he simply adores it! An' candied yams. Son—

[X to DS door, looking out at Brick. Margaret X above Big Mama to her L.]

That man put away enough food at that table to stuff a field-hand.

GOOPER: I hope he don't have to pay for it later on.

BIG MAMA *[turns US]*: What's that, Gooper?

MAE: Gooper says he hopes Big Daddy doesn't suffer tonight.

BIG MAMA *[turns to Margaret, DC]*: Oh, shoot, Gooper says, Gooper says! Why should Big Daddy suffer for satisfyin' a nawmal appetite? There's nothin' wrong with that man but nerves; he's sound as a dollar! An' now he knows he is, an' that's why he ate such a supper. He had a big load off his mind, knowin' he wasn't doomed to—what—he thought he was—doomed t'—

[She wavers. Margaret puts her arms around Big Mama.]

GOOPER *[urging Mae forward]*: MAE!

[Mae runs forward below wicker seat. She stands below Big Mama, Margaret above Big Mama. They help her to the wicker seat. Big Mama sits. Margaret sits above her. Mae stands behind her.]

MARGARET: Bless his ole sweet soul.

BIG MAMA: Yes—bless his heart.

BRICK *[DS on gallery, looking out front]*: Hello, moon, I envy you, you cool son of a bitch.

BIG MAMA: I want Brick!

MARGARET: He just stepped out for some fresh air.

BIG MAMA: Honey! I want Brick!

MAE: Bring li'l Brother in here so we kin talk.

[Margaret rises, X through DS door to Brick on gallery.]

BRICK *[to the moon]*: I envy you—you cool son of a bitch.

MARGARET: Brick, what're you doin' out here on the gall'ry, baby?

BRICK: Admirin' an' complimentin' th' man in the moon.

[Mae X to Dr. Baugh on R gallery. Reverend Tooker and Gooper move R UC, looking at Big Mama.]

MARGARET *[to Brick]*: Come in, Baby. They're gettin' ready to tell Big Mama the truth.

BRICK: I can't witness that thing in there.

MAE: Doc Baugh, d'you think those vitamin B_{12} injections are all they're cracked up t'be?

[Enters room to upper side, behind wicker seat.]

DOCTOR BAUGH *[X to below wicker seat]:* Well, I guess they're as good t'be stuck with as anything else.

[Looks at watch; X through to LC.]

MARGARET *[to Brick]:* Big Mama needs you!

BRICK: I can't witness that thing in there!

BIG MAMA: What's wrong here? You all have such long faces, you sit here waitin' for somethin' like a bomb—to go off.

GOOPER: We're waitin' for Brick an' Maggie to come in for this talk.

MARGARET *[X above Brick, to his R]:* Brother Man an' Mae have got a trick up their sleeves, an' if you don't go in there t'help Big Mama, y'know what I'm goin' to do—?

BIG MAMA: Talk. Whispers! Whispers!

[Looks out DR.]

Brick! . . .

MARGARET *[answering Big Mama's call]:* Comin', Big Mama!

[To Brick.]

I'm goin' to take every dam' bottle on this place an' pitch it off th' levee into th' river!

BIG MAMA: Never had this sort of atmosphere here before.

MAE *[sits above Big Mama on wicker seat]:* Before what, Big Mama?

BIG MAMA: This occasion. What's Brick an' Maggie doin' out there now?

GOOPER *[X DC, looks out]:* They seem to be havin' some little altercation.

[Brick X toward DS step. Maggie moves R above him to portal DR. Reverend Tooker joins Dr. Baugh, LC.]

BIG MAMA *[taking a pill from pill box on chain at her wrist]:* Give me a little somethin' to wash this tablet down with. Smell of burnt fireworks always makes me sick.

[Mae X to bar to pour glass of water. Dr. Baugh joins her. Gooper X to Reverend Tooker, LC.]

BRICK *[to Maggie]:* You're a live cat, aren't you?

MARGARET: You're dam' right I am!

BIG MAMA: Gooper, will y'please open that hall door—an' let some air circulate in this stiflin' room?

[Gooper starts US, but is restrained by Mae who X through C with glass of water. Gooper turns to men DLC.]

MAE *[X to Big Mama with water, sits above her]:* Big Mama, I think we ought to keep that door closed till after we talk.

BIG MAMA: I swan!

[Drinks water. Washes down pill.]

MAE: I just don't think we ought to take any chance of Big Daddy hearin' a word of this discussion.

BIG MAMA *[hands glass to Mae]:* What discussion of what? Maggie! Brick! Nothin' is goin' to be said in th' house of Big Daddy Pollitt that he can't hear if he wants to!

[Mae rises, X to bar, puts down glass, joins Gooper and the two men, LC.]

BRICK: How long are you goin' to stand behind me, Maggie?

MARGARET: Forever, if necessary.

[Brick X US to R gallery door.]

BIG MAMA: Brick!

[Mae rises, looks out DS, sits.]

GOOPER: That boy's gone t' pieces—he's just gone t' pieces.

DOCTOR BAUGH: Y'know, in my day they used to have somethin' they called the Keeley cure for drinkers.

BIG MAMA: Shoot!

DOCTOR BAUGH: But nowadays, I understand they take some kind of tablets that kill their taste for the stuff.

GOOPER *[turns to Dr. Baugh]:* Call 'em anti-bust tablets.

BIG MAMA: Brick don't need to take nothin'. That boy is just broken up over Skipper's death. You know how poor Skipper died. They gave him a big, big dose of that sodium amytal stuff at his home an' then they called the ambulance an' give him another big, big dose of it at th' hospital an' that an' all the alcohol in his system fo' months an' months just proved too much for his heart an' his heart quit beatin'. I'm scared of needles! I'm more scared of a needle than th' knife ———

[Brick has entered the room to behind the wicker seat. He rests his hand on Big Mama's head. Gooper has moved a bit URC, facing Big Mama.]

BIG MAMA: Oh! Here's Brick! My precious baby!

[Dr. Baugh X to bar, puts down drink. Brick X below Big Mama through C to bar.]

BRICK: Take it, Gooper!

MAE *[rising]:* What?

BRICK: Gooper knows what. Take it, Gooper!

[Mae turns to Gooper URC. Dr. Baugh X to Reverend Tooker. Margaret, who has followed Brick US on R gallery before he entered the room, now enters room, to behind wicker seat.]

BIG MAMA *[to Brick]:* You just break my heart.

BRICK *[at bar]:* Sorry—anyone else?

MARGARET: Brick, sit with Big Mama an' hold her hand while we talk.

BRICK: You do that, Maggie. I'm a restless cripple. I got to stay on my crutch.

[Mae sits above Big Mama. Gooper moves in front, below, and sits on couch, facing Big Mama. Reverend Tooker closes in to RC. Dr. Baugh X DC, faces upstage, smoking cigar. Margaret turns away to R doors.]

BIG MAMA: Why're you all *surroundin'* me?—like this? Why're you all starin' at me like this an' makin' signs at each other?

[Brick hobbles out hall door and X along R gallery.]

I don't need nobody to hold my hand. Are you all crazy? Since when did Big Daddy or me need anybody—?

[Reverend Tooker moves behind wicker seat.]

MAE: Calm yourself, Big Mama.

BIG MAMA: Calm you'self *you'self,* Sister Woman! How could I calm myself with everyone starin' at me as if big drops of blood had broken out on m'face? What's this all about, Annh! What?

GOOPER: Doc Baugh—

[Mae rises.]

Sit down, Mae—

[Mae sits.]

—Big Mama wants to know the complete truth about th' report we got today from the Ochsner Clinic!

[Dr. Baugh buttons his coat, faces group at RC.]

BIG MAMA: Is there somethin'—somethin' that I don't know?

DOCTOR BAUGH: Yes—well . . .

BIG MAMA *[rises]:* I—want to—*knowwwww!*

[X to Dr. Baugh.]

Somebody must be lyin'! *I want to know!*

[Mae, Gooper, Reverend Tooker surround Big Mama.]

MAE: Sit down, Big Mama, sit down on this sofa!

[Brick has passed Margaret Xing DR on gallery.]

MARGARET: Brick! Brick!

BIG MAMA: *What is it, what is it?*

[Big Mama drives Dr. Baugh a bit DLC. Others follow, surrounding Big Mama.]

DOCTOR BAUGH: I never have seen a more thorough examination than Big Daddy Pollit was given in all my experience at the Ochsner Clinic.

GOOPER: It's one of th' best in th' country.

MAE: It's *THE* best in th' country—bar none!

DOCTOR BAUGH: Of course they were ninety-nine and nine-tenths per cent certain before they even started.

BIG MAMA: Sure of what, sure of what, sure of what—*what!?*

MAE: Now, Mommy, be a brave girl!

BRICK *[on DR gallery, covers his ears, sings]: "By the light, by the light, of the silvery moon!"*

GOOPER *[breaks DR. Calls out to Brick]:* Shut up, Brick!

[Returns to group LC.]

BRICK: Sorry . . .

[Continues singing.]

DOCTOR BAUGH: But now, you see, Big Mama, they cut a piece off this growth, a specimen of the tissue, an'—

BIG MAMA: Growth? You told Big Daddy—

DOCTOR BAUGH: Now, wait—

BIG MAMA: You told me an' Big Daddy there wasn't a thing wrong with him but—

MAE: Big Mama, they always—

GOOPER: Let Doc Baugh talk, will yuh?

BIG MAMA: —little spastic condition of—

REVEREND TOOKER *[throughout all this]: Shh! Shh! Shh!*

[Big Mama breaks UC, they all follow.]

DOCTOR BAUGH: Yes, that's what we told Big Daddy. But we had this bit of tissue run through the laboratory an' I'm sorry t'say the test was positive on it. It's malignant.

[Pause.]

BIG MAMA: Cancer! Cancer!

MAE: Now now, Mommy—

GOOPER *[at the same time]:* You had to know, Big Mama.

BIG MAMA: *Why didn't they cut it out of him? Hanh? Hannh?*

DOCTOR BAUGH: Involved too much, Big Mama, too many organs affected.

MAE: Big Mama, the liver's affected, an' so's the kidneys, both. It's gone way past what they call a—

GOOPER: —a surgical risk.

[Big Mama gasps.]

REVEREND TOOKER: Tch, tch, tch.

DOCTOR BAUGH: Yes, it's gone past the knife.

MAE: That's why he's turned yellow!

[Brick stops singing, turns away UR on gallery.]

BIG MAMA *[pushes Mae DS]:* Git away from me, git away from me, Mae!

[X DSR]

I want Brick! Where's Brick! *Where's my only son?*

MAE *[a step after Big Mama]:* Mama! Did she say "only" son?
GOOPER *[following Big Mama]:* What does that make me?
MAE *[above Gooper]:* A sober responsible man with five precious children—*six!*
BIG MAMA: I want Brick! Brick! Brick!
MARGARET *[a step to Big Mama above couch]:* Mama, let *me* tell you.
BIG MAMA *[pushing her aside]:* No, no, leave me alone, you're not my blood!
[She rushes onto the DS gallery.]
GOOPER *[X to Big Mama on gallery]:* Mama! I'm your son! Listen to me!
MAE: Gooper's your son, Mama, he's your first-born!
BIG MAMA: Gooper never liked Daddy!
MAE: That's not true!
REVEREND TOOKER *[UC]:* I think I'd better slip away at this point. Goodnight, goodnight everybody, and God bless you all—on this place.
[Goes out through hall.]
DOCTOR BAUGH *[X DR to above DS door]:* Well, Big Mama ———
BIG MAMA *[leaning against Gooper, on lower gallery]:* It's all a mistake, I know it's just a bad dream.
DOCTOR BAUGH: We're gonna keep Big Daddy as comfortable as we can.
BIG MAMA: Yes, it's just a bad dream, that's all it is, it's just an awful dream.
GOOPER: In my opinion Big Daddy is havin' some pain but won't admit that he has it.
BIG MAMA: Just a dream, a bad dream.
DOCTOR BAUGH: That's what lots of 'em do, they think if they don't admit they're havin' the pain they can sort of escape th' fact of it.
[Brick X US on R gallery. Margaret watches him from R door.]
GOOPER: Yes, they get sly about it, get real sly about it.
MAE *[X to R of Dr. Baugh]:* Gooper an' I think ———
GOOPER: Shut up, Mae!—Big Mama, I really do think Big Daddy should be started on morphine.
BIG MAMA *[pulling away from Gooper]:* Nobody's goin' to give Big Daddy morphine!
DOCTOR BAUGH: Now, Big Mama, when that pain strikes it's goin' to strike mighty hard an' Big Daddy's goin' t'need the needle to bear it.
BIG MAMA *[X to Dr. Baugh]:* I tell you, nobody's goin' to give him morphine!
MAE: Big Mama, you don't want to see Big Daddy suffer, y'know y' ———
DOCTOR BAUGH *[X to bar]:* Well, I'm leavin' this stuff here
[Puts packet of morphine, etc., on bar.]
so if there's a sudden attack you won't have to send out for it.
[Big Mama hurries to L side bar.]
MAE *[X C, below Dr. Baugh]:* I know how to give a hypo.
BIG MAMA: Nobody's goin' to give Big Daddy morphine!
GOOPER *[X C]:* Mae took a course in nursin' durin' th' war.
MARGARET: Somehow I don't think Big Daddy would want Mae t'give him a hypo.
MAE *[to Margaret]:* You think he'd want *you* to do it?
DOCTOR BAUGH: Well—
GOOPER: Well, Doc Baugh is goin'—
DOCTOR BAUGH: Yes, I got to be goin'. Well, keep your chin up, Big Mama.
[X to hall.]
GOOPER *[as he and Mae follow Dr. Baugh into the hall]:* She's goin' to keep her ole chin up, aren't you, Big Mama?
[They go out L.]

Well, Doc, we sure do appreciate all you've done. I'm telling you, we're obligated ———

BIG MAMA: Margaret!

[XRC.]

MARGARET *[meeting Big Mama in front of wicker seat]*: I'm right here, Big Mama.

BIG MAMA: Margaret, you've got to cooperate with me an' Big Daddy to straighten Brick out now ———

GOOPER *[off L, returning with Mae]*: I guess that Doctor has got a lot on his mind, but it wouldn't hurt him to act a little more human ———

BIG MAMA: —because it'll break Big Daddy's heart if Brick don't pull himself together an' take hold of things here.

[Brick X DSR on gallery.]

MAE *[UC, overhearing]*: Take hold of what things, Big Mama?

BIG MAMA *[sits in wicker chair, Margaret standing behind chair]*: The place.

GOOPER *[UC]*: Big Mama, you've had a shock.

MAE *[X with Gooper to Big Mama]*: Yais, we've all had a shock, but ———

GOOPER: Let's be realistic ———

MAE: Big Daddy would not, would *never*, be foolish enough to ———

GOOPER: —put this place in irresponsible hands!

BIG MAMA: Big Daddy ain't goin' t'put th' place in anybody's hands, Big Daddy is *not* goin' t'die! I want you to git that into your haids, all of you!

[Mae sits above Big Mama, Margaret turns R to door, Gooper X LC a bit.]

MAE: Mommy, Mommy, Big Mama, we're just as hopeful an' optimistic as you are about Big Daddy's prospects, we have faith in prayer—but nevertheless there are certain matters that have to be discussed an' dealt with, because otherwise ———

GOOPER: Mae, will y'please get my briefcase out of our room?

MAE: Yes, honey.

[Rises, goes out through hall L.]

MARGARET *[X to Brick on DS gallery]*: Hear them in there?

[X back to R gallery door.]

GOOPER *[stands above Big Mama. Leaning over her]*: Big Mama, what you said just now was not at all true, an' you know it. I've always loved Big Daddy in my own quiet way. I never made a show of it. I know that Big Daddy has always been fond of me in a quiet way, too.

[Margaret drifts UR on gallery. Mae returns, X to Gooper's L with briefcase.]

MAE: Here's your briefcase, Gooper, honey.

[Hands it to him.]

GOOPER *[hands briefcase back to Mae]*: Thank you. Of cou'se, my relationship with Big Daddy is different from Brick's.

MAE: You're eight years older'n Brick an' always had t'carry a bigger load of th' responsibilities than Brick ever had t'carry; he never carried a thing in his life but a football or a highball.

GOOPER: Mae, will y'let me talk, please?

MAE: Yes, honey.

GOOPER: Now, a twenty-eight thousand acre plantation's a mighty big thing t'run.

MAE: Almost single-handed!

BIG MAMA: You never had t'run this place, Brother Man, what're you talkin' about, as if Big Daddy was dead an' in his grave, you had to run it? Why, you just had t'help him out with a few business details an' had your law practice at the same time in Memphis.

MAE: Oh, Mommy, Mommy, Mommy! Let's be fair! Why, Gooper has given himself body an' soul t'keepin' this place up fo' the past five years since Big Daddy's health started failin'. Gooper won't say it, Gooper never thought of it as a duty, he just did it. An' what did Brick do? Brick kep' livin' in his past glory at college!

[Gooper places a restraining hand on Mae's leg; Margaret drifts DS in gallery.]

GOOPER: Still a football player at twenty-seven!

MARGARET *[bursts into UR door]*: Who are you talkin' about now? Brick? A football player? He isn't a football player an' you know it! Brick is a sports announcer on TV an' one of the best-known ones in the country!

MAE *[breaks UC]*: I'm talkin' about what he was!

MARGARET *[X to above lower gallery door]*: Well, I wish you would just stop talkin' about my husband!

GOOPER *[X to above Margaret]*: Listen, Margaret, I've got a right to discuss my own brother with other members of my own fam'ly, which don't include *you!*

[Pokes finger at her; she slaps his finger away.]

Now, why don't you go on out there an' drink with Brick?

MARGARET: I've never seen such malice toward a brother.

GOOPER: How about his for me? Why he can't stand to be in the same room with me!

BRICK *[on lower gallery]*: That's the truth!

MARGARET: This is a deliberate campaign of vilification for the most disgusting and sordid reason on earth, and I know what it is! *It's avarice, avarice, greed, greed!*

BIG MAMA: Oh, I'll scream, I will scream in a moment unless this stops! Margaret, child, come here, sit next to Big Mama.

MARGARET *[X to Big Mama, sits above her]*: Precious Mommy.

[Gooper X to bar.]

MAE: How beautiful, how touchin' this display of devotion! Do you know why she's childless? She's childless because that big, beautiful athlete husband of hers won't go to bed with her, that's why!

[X to L of bed, looks at Gooper.]

GOOPER: You jest won't let me do this the nice way, will yuh? Aw right—

[X to above wicker seat.]

I don't give a goddam if Big Daddy likes me or don't like me or did or never did or will or will never! I'm just appealin' to a sense of common decency an' fair play! I'm tellin' you th' truth—

[X DS through lower door to Brick on DR gallery.]

I've resented Big Daddy's partiality to Brick ever since th' goddam day you were born, son, an' th' way I've been treated, like I was just barely good enough to spit on, an' sometimes not even good enough for that.

[X back through room to above wicker seat.]

Big Daddy is dyin' of cancer an' it's spread all through him an' it's attacked all his vital organs includin' the kidneys an' right now he is sinkin' into uremia, an' you all know what uremia is, it's poisonin' of the whole system due to th' failure of th' body to eliminate its poisons.

MARGARET: Poisons, poisons, venomous thoughts and words! In hearts and minds! That's poisons!

GOOPER: I'm askin' for a square deal an' by God I expect to get one. But if I don't get one, if there's any peculiar shenanigans goin' on around here behind my back, well I'm not a corporation lawyer for nothin'!

[X DS toward lower gallery door, on apex.]

I know how to protect my own interests.

[Rumble of distant thunder.]

BRICK *[entering the room through DS door]:* Storm comin' up.

GOOPER: Oh, a late arrival!

MAE *[X through C to below bar, LCO]:* Behold, the conquerin' hero comes!

GOOPER *[X through C to bar, following Brick, imitating his limp]:* The fabulous Brick Pollitt! Remember him? Who could forget him?

MAE: He looks like he's been injured in a game!

GOOPER: Yep, I'm afraid you'll have to warm th' bench at the Sugar Bowl this year, Brick! Or was it the Rose Bowl that he made his famous run in.

[Another rumble of thunder, sound of wind rising.]

MAE *[X to L of Brick, who has reached the bar]:* The punch bowl, honey, it was the punch bowl, the cut-glass punch bowl!

GOOPER: That's right! I'm always gettin' the boy's *bowls* mixed up!

[Pats Brick on the butt.]

MARGARET *[rushes at Gooper, striking him]:* Stop that! You stop that!

[Thunder. Mae X toward Margaret from L of Gooper, flails at Margaret; Gooper keeps the women apart. Lacey runs through the US lawn area in a raincoat.]

DAISY AND SOOKEY *[off UL]:* Storm! Storm comin'! Storm! Storm!

LACEY *[running out UR]:* Brightie, close them shutters!

GOOPER *[X onto R gallery, calls after Lacey]:* Lacey, put the top up on my Cadillac, will yuh?

LACEY *[off R]:* Yes, suh, Mistah Pollit!

GOOPER *[X to above Big Mama]:* Big Mama, you know it's goin' to be necessary for me t'go back to Memphis in th' mornin' t'represent the Parker estate in a lawsuit.

[Mae sits on L side bed, arranges papers she removes from briefcase.]

BIG MAMA: Is it, Gooper?

MAE: Yaiss.

GOOPER: That's why I'm forced to—to bring up a problem that ———

MAE: Somethin' that's too important t' be put off!

GOOPER: If Brick was sober, he ought to be in on this. I think he ought to be present when I present this plan.

MARGARET *[UC]:* Brick is present, we're present!

GOOPER: Well, good. I will now give you this outline my partner, Tom Bullit, an' me have drawn up—a sort of dummy—trusteeship!

MARGARET: Oh, that's it! You'll be in charge an' dole out remittances, will you?

GOOPER: This we did as soon as we got the report on Big Daddy from th' Ochsner Laboratories. We did this thing, I mean we drew up this dummy outline with the advice and assistance of the Chairman of the Boa'd of Directors of th' Southern Plantuhs Bank and Trust Company in Memphis, C. C. Bellowes, a man who handles estates for all th' prominent fam'lies in West Tennessee and th' Delta!

BIG MAMA: Gooper?

GOOPER *[X behind seat to below Big Mama]:* Now this is not—not final, or anything like it, this is just a preliminary outline. But it does provide a—basis—a design—a—possible, feasible—*plan!*

[He waves papers Mae has thrust into his hand, US.]

MARGARET *[X DL]:* Yes, I'll bet it's a plan!

[Thunder rolls. Interior lighting dims.]

MAE: It's a plan to protect the biggest estate in the Delta from irresponsibility an' ———

BIG MAMA: Now you listen to me, all of you, you listen here! They's not goin' to be no more catty talk in my house! And Gooper, you put that away before I grab it out of your hand and tear it right up! I don't know what the hell's in it, and I don't want to know what the hell's in it. I'm talkin' in Big Daddy's language now, I'm his *wife*, not his *widow*, I'm still his *wife!* And I'm talkin' to you in his language an' ———

GOOPER: Big Mama, what I have here is ———

MAE: Gooper explained that it's just a plan . . .

BIG MAMA: I don't care what you got there, just put it back where it come from an' don't let me see it again, not even the outside of the envelope of it! Is that understood? Basis! Plan! Preliminary! Design!—I say—what is it that Big Daddy always says when he's disgusted?

[Storm clouds race across sky.]

BRICK *[from bar]*: Big Daddy says "crap" when he is disgusted.

BIG MAMA *[rising]*: That's right—*CRAPPPP!* I say *CRAP* too, like Big Daddy!

[Thunder rolls.]

MAE: Coarse language don't seem called for in this ———

GOOPER: Somethin' in me is *deeply outraged* by this.

BIG MAMA: *Nobody's goin' to do nothin'!* till Big Daddy lets go of it, and maybe just possibly not—not even then! No, not even then!

[Thunder clap. Glass crash, off L. Off UR, children commence crying. Many storm sounds, L and R: barnyard animals in terror, papers crackling, shutters rattling. Sookey and Daisy hurry from L to R in lawn area. Inexplicably, Daisy hits together two leather pillows. They cry, "Storm! Storm!" Sookey waves a piece of wrapping paper to cover lawn furniture. Mae exits to hall and upper gallery. Strange man runs across lawn, R to L. Thunder rolls repeatedly.]

MAE: Sookey, hurry up an' git that po'ch fu'niture covahed; want th' paint to come off?

[Starts DR on gallery. Gooper runs through hall to R gallery.]

GOOPER *[yells to Lacey, who appears from R]*: Lacey, put mah car away!

LACEY: Cain't, Mistah Pollit, you got the keys!

[Exit US.]

GOOPER: Naw, you got 'em, man.

[Exit DR. Reappears UR, calls to Mae:]

Where th' keys to th' car, honey?

[Runs C.]

MAE *[DR on gallery]*: You got 'em in your pocket!

[Exit DR. Gooper exits UR. Dog howls. Daisy and Sookey sing off UR to comfort children. Mae is heard placating the children. Storm fades away. During the storm, Margaret X and sits on couch, DR. Big Mama X DC.]

BIG MAMA: BRICK! Come here, Brick, I need you.

[Thunder distantly. Children whimper, off L Mae consoles them. Brick X to R of Big Mama.]

BIG MAMA: Tonight Brick looks like he used to look when he was a little boy just like he did when he played wild games in the orchard back of the house and used to come home when I hollered myself hoarse for him! all—sweaty—and pink-cheeked—an' sleepy with his curls shinin' ———

[Thunder distantly. Children whimper, off L. Mae consoles them. Dog howls, off.]

Time goes by so fast. Nothin' can outrun it. Death commences too early—almost before you're half-acquainted with life—you meet with the other. Oh, you know we just got to love each other, an' stay together all of us just as close as we can, specially now that such a *black* thing has come and moved into this place without invitation. *[Dog howls, off.]*

Oh, Brick, son of Big Daddy, Big Daddy does so love you. Y'know what would be his fondest dream come true? If before he passed on, if Big Daddy has to pass on . . . *[Dog howls, off.]*

You give him a child of yours, a grandson as much like his son as his son is like Big Daddy. . . .

MARGARET: I know that's Big Daddy's dream.

BIG MAMA: That's his dream.

BIG DADDY *[off DR on gallery]:* Looks like the wind was takin' liberties with this place. *[Lacey appears UL, X to UC in lawn area; Brightie and Small appear UR on lawn. Big Daddy X onto the UR gallery.]*

LACEY: Evenin', Mr. Pollitt.

BRIGHTIE AND SMALL: Evenin', Cap'n. Hello, Cap'n.

MARGARET *[X to R door]:* Big Daddy's on the gall'ry.

BIG DADDY: Stawm crossed th' river, Lacey?

LACEY: Gone to Arkansas, Cap'n.

[Big Mama has turned toward the hall door at the sound of Big Daddy's voice on the gallery. Now she X's DSR and out the DS door onto the gallery.]

BIG MAMA: I can't stay here. He'll see somethin' in my eyes.

BIG DADDY *[on upper gallery, to the boys]:* Stawm done any damage around here?

BRIGHTIE: Took the po'ch off ole Aunt Crawley's house.

BIG DADDY: Ole Aunt Crawley should of been settin' on it. It's time fo' th' wind to blow that ole girl away!

[Field-hands laugh, exit, UR. Big Daddy enters room, UC, hall door.]

Can I come in?

[Puts his cigar in ash tray on bar. Mae and Gooper hurry along the upper gallery and stand behind Big Daddy in hall door.]

MARGARET: Did the storm wake you up, Big Daddy?

BIG DADDY: Which stawm are you talkin' about—th' one outside or th' hullaballoo in here?

[Gooper squeezes past Big Daddy.]

GOOPER *[X toward bed, where legal papers are strewn]:* 'Scuse me, sir . . .

[Mae tries to squeeze past Big Daddy to join Gooper, but Big Daddy puts his arm firmly around her.]

BIG DADDY: I heard some mighty loud talk. Sounded like somethin' important was bein' discussed. What was the powwow about?

MAE *[flustered]:* Why—nothin', Big Daddy . . .

BIG DADDY *[X DLC, taking Mae with him]:* What is that pregnant-lookin' envelope you're puttin' back in your briefcase, Gooper?

GOOPER *[at foot of bed, caught, as he stuffs papers into envelope]:* That? Nothin', suh—nothin' much of anythin' at all . . .

BIG DADDY: Nothin'? It looks like a whole lot of nothing!

[Turns US to group:]

You all know th' story about th' young married couple ———

GOOPER: Yes, sir!

BIG DADDY: Hello, Brick ———

BRICK: Hello, Big Daddy.

[The group is arranged in a semi-circle above Big Daddy, Margaret at the extreme R, then Mae and Gooper, then Big Mama, with Brick at L.]

BIG DADDY: Young married couple took Junior out to th' zoo one Sunday, inspected all of God's creatures in their cages, with satisfaction.

GOOPER: Satisfaction.

BIG DADDY *[X USC, face front]*: This afternoon was a warm afternoon in spring an' that ole elephant had somethin' else on his mind which was bigger'n peanuts. You know this story, Brick?

[Gooper nods.]

BRICK: No, sir, I don't know it.

BIG DADDY: Y'see, in th' cage adjoinin' they was a young female elephant in heat!

BIG MAMA *[at Big Daddy's shoulder]*: Oh, Big Daddy!

BIG DADDY: What's the matter, preacher's gone, ain't he? All right. That female elephant in the next cage was permeatin' the atmosphere about her with a powerful and excitin' odor of female fertility! Huh! Ain't that a nice way to put it, Brick?

BRICK: Yes, sir, nothin' wrong with it.

BIG DADDY: Brick says the's nothin' wrong with it!

BIG MAMA: Oh, Big Daddy!

BIG DADDY *[X DSC]*: So this ole bull elephant still had a couple of fornications left in him. He reared back his trunk an' got a whiff of that elephant lady next door!—began to paw at the dirt in his cage an' butt his head against the separatin' partition and, first thing y'know, there was a conspicuous change in his *profile*—very *conspicuous!* Ain't I tellin' this story in decent language, Brick?

BRICK: Yes, sir, too ruttin' decent!

BIG DADDY: So, the little boy pointed at it and said, "What's that?" His Mam said, "Oh, that's—nothin'!"—His Papa said, "She's spoiled!"

[Field-hands sing off R, featuring Sookey: "I Just Can't Stay Here by Myself," through following scene. Big Daddy X to Brick at L.]

BIG DADDY: You didn't laugh at that story, Brick.

[Big Mama X DRC crying. Margaret goes to her. Mae and Gooper hold URC.]

BRICK: No, sir, I didn't laugh at that story.

[On the lower gallery, Big Mama sobs. Big Daddy looks toward her.]

BIG DADDY: What's wrong with that long, thin woman over there, loaded with diamonds? Hey, what's-your-name, what's the matter with you?

MARGARET *[X toward Big Daddy]*: She had a slight dizzy spell, Big Daddy.

BIG DADDY *[ULC]*: You better watch that, Big Mama. A stroke is a bad way to go.

MARGARET *[X to Big Daddy at C]*: Oh, Brick, Big Daddy has on your birthday present to him, Brick, he has on your cashmere robe, the softest material I have ever felt.

BIG DADDY: Yeah, this is my soft birthday, Maggie. . . .

Not my gold or my silver birthday, but my soft birthday, everything's got to be soft for Big Daddy on this soft birthday.

[Maggie kneels before Big Daddy C. As Gooper and Mae speak, Big Mama X USRC in front of them, hushing them with a gesture.]

GOOPER: Maggie, I hate to make such a crude observation, but there is somethin' a little indecent about your—

MAE: Like a slow-motion football tackle—

MARGARET: Big Daddy's got on his Chinese slippers that I gave him, Brick. Big Daddy, I haven't given you my big present yet, but now I will, now's the time for me to present it to you! I have an announcement to make!

MAE: What? What kind of announcement?

GOOPER: A sports announcement, Maggie?

MARGARET: Announcement of life beginning! A child is coming, sired by Brick, and out of Maggie the Cat! I have Brick's child in my body, an' that's my birthday present to Big Daddy on this birthday!

[Big Daddy looks at Brick who X behind Big Daddy to DS portal, L]

BIG DADDY: Get up, girl, get up off your knees, girl.

[Big Daddy helps Margaret rise. He X above her, to her R, bites off the end of a fresh cigar, taken from his bathrobe pocket, as he studies Margaret.]

Uh-huh, this girl has life in her body, that's no lie!

BIG MAMA: BIG DADDY'S DREAM COME TRUE!

BRICK: *JESUS!*

BIG DADDY *[X R below wicker seat]*: Gooper, I want my lawyer in the mornin'.

BRICK: Where are you goin', Big Daddy?

BIG DADDY: Son, I'm goin' up on the roof to the belvedere on th' roof to look over my kingdom before I give up my kingdom—twenty-eight thousand acres of th' richest land this side of the Valley Nile!

[Exit through R doors, and DR on gallery.]

BIG MAMA *[following]*: Sweetheart, sweetheart, sweetheart—can I come with you?

[Exits DR. Margaret is DSC in mirror area.]

GOOPER *[X to bar]*: Brick, could you possibly spare me one small shot of that liquor?

BRICK *[DLC]*: Why, help yourself, Gooper boy.

GOOPER: I will.

MAE *[X forward]*: Of course we know that this is a lie!

GOOPER *[drinks]*: Be still, Mae!

MAE *[X to Gooper at bar]*: I won't be still! I know she's made this up!

GOOPER: God damn it, I said to shut up!

MAE: That woman isn't pregnant!

GOOPER: Who said she was?

MAE: She did.

GOOPER: The doctor didn't. Doc Baugh didn't.

MARGARET *[X R to above couch]*: I haven't gone to Doc Baugh.

GOOPER *[X through to L of Margaret]*: Then who'd you go to, Maggie?

[Offstage song finishes.]

MARGARET: One of the best gynecologists in the South.

GOOPER: Uh-huh, I see ———

[Foot on end of couch, trapping Margaret:]

May we have his name please?

MARGARET: No, you may not, Mister—Prosecutin' Attorney!

MAE *[X to R of Margaret, above]*: He doesn't have any name, he doesn't exist!

MARGARET: He does so exist, and so does my baby, Brick's baby!

MAE: You can't conceive a child by a man that won't sleep with you unless you think you're ———

[Forces Margaret onto couch, turns away C. Brick starts C for Mae.]

He drinks all the time to be able to tolerate you! Sleeps on the sofa to keep out of contact with you!

GOOPER *[X above Margaret, who lies face down on couch]*: Don't try to kid us, Margaret—

MAE *[X to bed, L side, rumpling pillows]*: How can you conceive a child by a man that won't sleep with you? How can you conceive? How can you? How can you!

GOOPER *[sharply]*: MAE!

BRICK *[X below Mae to her R, takes hold of her]:* Mae, Sister Woman, how d'you know that I don't sleep with Maggie?

MAE: We occupy the next room an' th' wall between isn't soundproof.

BRICK: Oh . . .

MAE: We hear the nightly pleadin' and the nightly refusal. So don't imagine you're goin' t'put a trick over on us, to fool a dyin' man with—a ———

BRICK: Mae, Sister Woman, not everybody makes much noise about love. Oh, I know some people are huffers an' puffers, but others are silent lovers.

GOOPER *[behind seat, R]:* This talk is pointless, completely.

BRICK: How d'y'know that we're not silent lovers?

Even if y'got a peep-hole drilled in the wall, how can y'tell if sometime when Gooper's got business in Memphis an' you're playin' scrabble at the country club with other ex-queens of cotton, Maggie and I don't come to some temporary agreement? How do you know that ———?

[He X above wicker seat to above R and couch.]

MAE: Brick, I never thought that you would stoop to her level, I just never dreamed that you would stoop to her level.

GOOPER: I don't think Brick will stoop to her level.

BRICK *[sits R of Margaret on couch]:* What is your level? Tell me your level so I can sink or rise to it.

[Rises.]

You heard what Big Daddy said. This girl has life in her body.

MAE: That is a lie!

BRICK: No, truth is something desperate, an' she's got it. Believe me, it's somethin' desperate, an' she's got it.

[X below seat to below bar.]

An' now if you will stop actin' as if Brick Pollitt was dead an' buried, invisible, not heard, an go on back to your peep-hole in the wall—I'm drunk, and sleepy—not as alive as Maggie, but still alive. . . .

[Pours drink, drinks.]

GOOPER *[picks up briefcase from R foot of bed]:* Come on, Mae. We'll leave these love birds together in their nest.

MAE: Yeah, nest of lice! Liars!

GOOPER: Mae—Mae, you jes' go on back to our room—

MAE: Liars!

[Exits through hall.]

GOOPER *[DR above Margaret]:* We're jest goin' to wait an' see. Time will tell.

[X to R of bar.]

Yes, sir, little brother, we're just goin' to wait an' see!

[Exit, hall. The clock strikes twelve. Maggie and Brick exchange a look. He drinks deeply, puts his glass on the bar. Gradually, his expression changes. He utters a sharp exhalation. The exhalation is echoed by the singers, off UR, who commence vocalizing with "Gimme a Cool Drink of Water Fo' I Die," and continue till end of act.]

MARGARET *[as she hears Brick's exhalation]:* The click?

[Brick looks toward the singers, happily, almost gratefully. He XR to bed, picks up his pillow, and starts toward head of couch, DR, Xing above wicker seat. Margaret seizes the pillow from his grasp, rises, stands facing C, holding the pillow close. Brick watches her with growing admiration. She moves quickly USC, throwing pillow onto bed. She X to bar. Brick counters below wicker seat, watching her. Margaret grabs all

the bottles from the bar. She goes into hall, pitches the bottles, one after the other, off the platform into the UL lawn area. Bottles break, off L. Margaret re-enters the room, stands UC, facing Brick.]

Echo Spring has gone dry, and no one but me could drive you to town for more.

BRICK: Lacey will get me ——

MARGARET: Lacey's been told not to!

BRICK: I could drive ——

MARGARET: And you lost your driver's license! I'd phone ahead and have you stopped on the highway before you got halfway to Ruby Lightfoot's gin mill. I told a lie to Big Daddy, but we can make that lie come true. And then I'll bring you liquor, and we'll get drunk together, here, tonight, in this place that death has come into! What do you say? What do you say, Baby?

BRICK *[X to L side bed]*: I admire you, Maggie.

[Brick sits on edge of bed. He looks up at the overhead light, then at Margaret. She reaches for the light, turns it out; then she kneels quickly beside Brick at foot of bed.]

MARGARET: Oh, you weak, beautiful people who give up with such grace. What you need is someone to take hold of you—gently, with love, and hand your life back to you, like something gold you let go of—and I can! I'm determined to do it—and nothing's more determined than a cat on a tin roof—is there? Is there, Baby?

[She touches his cheek, gently.]

CURTAIN

QUESTIONS TO CONSIDER

1. Why is *Cat on a Hot Tin Roof* an appropriate title for this play? What themes in the play does its title highlight? Why does Maggie repeatedly describe herself in this way?
2. Williams includes a quotation as a part of the play that states "We're all of us sentenced to solitary confinement inside our own skins." How is this isolation exhibited in *Cat on a Hot Tin Roof?*
3. What is the root cause of Brick's ambivalence toward Maggie, as opposed to its proximate cause?

Karl Shapiro

1913–2000

On 10 November 1913, a future poet was born in Washington Hospital in Baltimore, Maryland—the same hospital where Edgar Allan Poe had breathed his last in 1849. Carl Jay Shapiro (who would later change the spelling of his first name to "Karl") was the son of traveling salesman Joseph Shapiro and his wife, Sarah Omansky Shapiro. Shapiro's grandparents were Jewish immigrants from Russia who had gravitated to Baltimore, and although Shapiro went on to claim an ethnic identity as a Jewish-American writer, his roots as a Southerner proved to be significant to his body of poetry.

Shapiro's older brother dabbled in poetry, and his father kept an edition of Oscar Wilde's verse on display in the family's living room. Shapiro himself began to write poetry in high school and got an uncle to pay for the private printing of his first collection of poetry, *Poems*, in 1935. By then, he was 21 years old and had dropped out of the University of Virginia after only a year of study. The poem "University," which begins, "To hurt the Negro and avoid the

Jew/ Is the curriculum," reveals how ostracized Shapiro felt while a student there. As Ross Labrie explains in his essay on Shapiro, even the German-Jewish students looked down upon the Russian-Jewish students. "University" also gives an indication of the lifelong empathy that Shapiro felt for African Americans as fellow victims of prejudice. As the editor of *Poetry* magazine during the 1950s, Shapiro promoted the career of poet Margaret Danner (then "Margaret Cunningham") as well as other minority writers, and in a 1963 address to four historically African-American colleges in the Deep South (collected in Madden), he spoke thoughtfully and prophetically about the need for African-American poetry to break with the Anglo-American formal tradition and find a voice of its own.

In 1937, however, Shapiro was still trying to find himself as a college student, first at Johns Hopkins University in Baltimore and then at Baltimore's Enoch Pratt Library School. World War II interrupted his third try at higher education but, drafted into the army in 1941, he began to write with increasing skill about love, dehumanizing technology, and war. In rapid succession, he published four books of poetry while in the service: *The Place of Love* (1942), *Person, Place and Thing* (1942), *V-Letter and Other Poems* (1944), and *Essay on Rime* (1945). *Person, Place and Thing* contained a group of poems that won the Levinson Prize from *Poetry* magazine, and Fugitive-Agrarian poet Allen Tate, among other critics, praised the book in writing. But it was *V-Letter* that truly stunned critics, winning the Pulitzer Prize for Poetry the year after it came out. The title of the book referred to the edited, microfilmed, reduced-size format into which letters to and from American soldiers overseas were transformed by government censors. The poems in *V-Letter* were acknowledged to be among the best written about the war that was then still in progress.

Returning to civilian life, Shapiro embarked upon a distinguished career as a poet, critic, college professor, editor, and consultant in poetry to the Library of Congress, although he never did complete his own college studies. *Poems of a Jew,* published in 1958, was very unusual for its times in proudly embracing Jewish ethnic identity and criticizing Christianity; a decade earlier, Shapiro had raised conformists' eyebrows by voting against the nomination of Ezra Pound for the Bollingen Prize in poetry, declaring that he could not vote for an anti-Semite. Following *Poems of a Jew,* Shapiro surprised his public once again by abandoning traditional poetic form for free-verse prose poems. He continued to write capably even in his old age and died in New York City in 2000 at the age of 86.

In each of the following poems, Shapiro wrestles with the burden of Southern history upon the present-day Southern intellectual. Like the orthodox Jewish grandfather he describes as "keeping his beard/ In difficult Virginia, yet endeared/ Of blacks and farmers," Shapiro is both alienated from the South and of the South: a paradox whose tensions can be briefly contained in the language of poetry.

University[1]

To hurt the Negro and avoid the Jew
Is the curriculum. In mid-September
The entering boys, identified by hats,
Wander in a maze of mannered brick
    Where boxwood and magnolia brood
    And columns with imperious stance
    Like rows of ante-bellum girls
        Eye them, outlanders.

1. The University of Virginia in Charlottesville.

In whited cells, on lawns equipped for peace,
Under the arch, and lofty banister,
Equals shake hands, unequals blankly pass;
The exemplary weather whispers, "Quiet, quiet"
And visitors on tiptoe leave
For the raw North, the unfinished West,
As the young, detecting an advantage,
Practice a face.

Where, on their separate hill, the colleges,
Like manor houses of an older law,
Gaze down embankments on a land in fee,
The Deans, dry spinsters over family plate,
Ring out the English name like coin,
Humor the snob and lure the lout.
Within the precincts of this world
Poise is a club.

But on the neighboring range, misty and high,
The past is absolute: some luckless race
Dull with inbreeding and conformity
Wears out its heart, and comes barefoot and bad
For charity or jail. The scholar
Sanctions their obsolete disease;
The gentleman revolts with shame
At his ancestor.

And the true nobleman,[2] once a democrat,
Sleeps on his private mountain. He was one
Whose thought was shapely and whose dream was broad;
This school he held his art and epitaph.
But now it takes from him his name,
Falls open like a dishonest look,
And shows us, rotted and endowed,
Its senile pleasure.

Conscription Camp

Your landscape sickens with a dry disease
Even in May, Virginia, and your sweet pines
Like Frenchmen runted in a hundred wars
Are of a child's height in these battlefields.

For Wilson[1] sowed his teeth where generals prayed
—High-sounding Lafayette[2] and sick-eyed Lee—[3]

2. Thomas Jefferson (1743–1826), third president of the United States, who founded the University of Virginia in 1819.

1. Woodrow Wilson (1856–1924), the twenty-eighth president of the United States, was born in Staunton, Virginia, and lived there until the age of two; he later led the United States into World War I.

2. France's Marquis de Lafayette (1757–1834) fought on the American side during the Revolutionary War and wintered at Valley Forge, Virginia, with General George Washington.

3. Robert E. Lee (1807–1870), the Commander of the Confederate Army during the American Civil War.

The loud Elizabethan[4] crashed your swamps
Like elephants and the subtle Indian fell.

Is it for love, you ancient-minded towns,
That on the tidy grass of your great graves
And on your roads and riverways serene
Between the corn with green flags in a row,

Wheat amorous as hair and hills like breasts
Each generation, ignorant of the last,
Mumbling in sheds, embarrassed to salute,
Comes back to choke on etiquette of hate?

You manufacture history like jute—
Labor is cheap, Virginia, for high deeds,
But in your British dream of reputation
The black man is your conscience and your cost.

Here on the plains perfect for civil war
The clapboard city like a weak mirage
Of order rises from the sand to house
These thousands and the paranoid Monroe;[5]

The sunrise gun rasps in the throat of heaven;
The lungs of dawn are heavy and corrupt;
We hawk and spit; our flag walks through the air
Breathing hysteria thickly in each face.

Through the long school of day, absent in heart,
Distant in every thought but self we tread,
Wheeling in blocks like large expensive toys
That never understand except through fun.

To steal aside as aimlessly as curs
Is our desire; to stare at corporals
As sceptically as boys; not to believe
The misty-eyed letter and the cheap snapshot.

To cross the unnatural frontier of your name
Is our free dream, Virginia, and beyond,
White and unpatriotic in our beds,
To rise from sleep like driftwood out of surf.

But stricter than parole is this same wall
And these green clothes, a secret on the fields,
In towns betray us to the arresting touch
Of lady-wardens, good and evil wives.

4. A metonymical figure intended to stand for all European settlers.

5. James Monroe (1758–1831), the fifth president of the United States, was from Westmoreland County, Virginia; his 1820 "Missouri Compromise" prolonged the status quo of legalized slavery in the South.

And far and fabulous is the word "Outside"
Like "Europe" when the midnight liners sailed,
Leaving a wake of ermine on the tide
Where rubies drowned and eyes were softly drunk.

Still we abhor your news and every voice
Except the Personal Enemy's,[6] and songs
That pumped by the great central heart of love
On tides of energy at evening come.

Instinctively to break your compact law
Box within box, Virginia, and throw down
The dangerous bright habits of pure form
We struggle hideously and cry for fear.

And like a very tired whore who stands
Wrapped in the sensual crimson of her art
High in the tired doorway of a street
And beckons half-concealed the passerby,

The sun, Virginia, on your Western stairs
Pauses and smiles away between the trees,
Motioning the soldier overhill to town
To his determined hungry burst of joy.

The Southerner

He entered with the authority of politeness
And the jokes died in the air. A well-made blaze
Grew round the main log in the fireplace
Spontaneously. I watched its brightness
Spread to the altered faces of my guests.
They did not like the Southerner. I did.
A liberal felt that someone should forbid
That soft voice making its soft arrests.

As when a Negro or a prince extends
His hand to an average man, and the mind
Speeds up a minute and then drops behind,
So did the conversation of my friends.
I was amused by this respectful awe
Which those hotly deny who have no prince.
I watched the frown, the stare, and the wince
Recede into attention, the arms thaw.

I saw my southern evil memories
Raped from my mind before my eyes, my youth
Practicing caste, perfecting the untruth
Of staking honor on the wish to please.
I saw my honor's paradox:
Grandpa, the saintly Jew, keeping his beard

6. Thomas Jefferson wrote in a letter to James Maury in April 1812 that "The English newspapers suppose me the personal enemy of their nation."

In difficult Virginia, yet endeared
Of blacks and farmers, although orthodox.

The nonsense of the gracious lawn,
The fall of hollow columns in the pines,
Do these deceive more than the rusted signs
Of Jesus on the road? Can they go on
In the timeless manner of all gentlefolk
There in a culture rotted and unweeded
Where the black yoni[1] of the South is seeded
By crooked men in denims thin as silk?

They do go on, denying still the fall
Of Richmond[2] and man, who gently live
On the street above the violence, fugitive,
Graceful, and darling, who recall
The heartbroken country once about to flower,
Full of black poison, beautiful to smell,
Who know how to conform, how to compel,
And how from the best bush to receive a flower.

Questions to Consider

1. In the poem "Conscription Camp," the state of Virginia is addressed as if it were a person. Does this rhetorical technique seem false or believable to you? Why?
2. Does the narrator of "The Southerner" love or hate the South, and why?

Margaret Danner

1915–1986

Pryorsburg, Kentucky, was the birthplace of Margaret Esse Danner. She was born on 12 January 1915 to Caleb and Naomi Esse Danner, Christian Scientists who moved the family to Chicago while Danner was still a child. Danner began to write poetry in grade school, and an eighth-grade poem titled "The Violin" won first prize in a contest. Graduating from Chicago's Englewood High School, Danner remained in the city to attend Loyola University, married, and gave birth to a daughter. When poet Paul Engle led a creative writing workshop in Chicago in the late 1930s, Danner was among his students, as was the equally gifted African-American poet Gwendolyn Brooks. At the 1945 Midwestern Writers Conference held at Northwestern University, Danner captured second prize in a poetry contest and began to solidify her regional reputation as a rising young poet.

Karl Shapiro, who had won the Pulitzer Prize for Poetry in 1945, took over the reins of the Chicago-based journal *Poetry* in 1950. The following year, Danner was hired as an editorial assistant and had "Far from Africa," a series of four poems about the land of her ancestry, accepted for publication. "Danner's Africa, the predominant subject of her poems," critic Erlene Stetson has written, "is both real and symbolic, for she writes of a living, vibrant, and dynamic

1. A symbol of the female genitalia.

2. Richmond, Virginia, the capital of the Confederacy, fell to the Union Army in 1865.

African culture. She explores private and public myths to arrive at an authenticated African past." So impressed with the poems were the trustees of the John Hay Whitney Foundation that they awarded Danner a 1951 fellowship to travel to Africa. However, she would postpone taking the trip for 15 years. In 1956, she was promoted to assistant editor of *Poetry*, which was then the highest rank ever held by an African American on the historic publication, but she stayed at *Poetry* only one year after Shapiro's 1956 departure.

In 1960, Danner published her first collection of poetry, *Impressions of African Art Forms*, with Broadside Press, one of the first independent African-American publishing houses in the United States. She began teaching at Wayne State University in 1961 and, during her years in Detroit, founded a community arts center named "Boone House" that has been described by D. H. Melhem as a forerunner to similar, government-assisted projects that would arise later. After publishing another single volume of poems in 1963, Danner collaborated on an interesting project with Dudley Randall, the founder of Broadside Press: each wrote 10 poems on the same 10 subjects. The collaborative effort was published by Broadside Press as *Poem Counterpoem* in 1966. *Iron Lace*, Danner's third book, came out in 1968, by which time she was poet-in-residence at Virginia Union University, an historically African-American college. She also edited anthologies of African-American poets in 1968 and 1969. But, as a new generation of militant, outspoken African-American women poets came to prominence in the late 1960s, Danner's quiet, nonconfrontational poetic voice became unfashionable. Having returned to the South, she remained after the Virginia Union job ended, taking a position as poet-in-residence at LeMoyne-Owen College in Tennessee from 1970 to 1975. Her only remaining publication would be *The Down of a Thistle: Selected Poems, Prose Poems, and Songs*, in 1976. Danner died in 1986 at the age of 71.

Danner lived in the South only in early childhood and old age, but her fascination with her African ancestry, as mediated through the Southern institution of slavery, furnished most of the material for her poems. A "painterly," visually oriented poet who focused on describing colors, forms, and materials, Danner succeeded in joining both "disparate cultures (Africa and America) and disciplines (the plastic arts and poetry)," as Stetson has written.

The Convert

When in nineteen-thirty-seven, Etta Moten, sweetheart
of our Art Study group, kept her promise, as if clocked,
to honor my house at our first annual tea, my pride

tipped sky, but when she, Parisian-poised and as smart
as a chrome-toned page from *Harper's Bazaar*,[1] gave my shocked
guests this hideous African nude, I could have cried.

And for many subsequent suns, we, who had placed apart
this hour to proclaim our plunge into modern art, mocked
her "Isn't he lovely?" whenever we eyed this thing,

for by every rule we'd learned, we'd been led to discern
this rankling figure as ugly. It hunched in a squat
as if someone with maliciously disfiguring intent

had flattened it with a press, bashing its head,
bloating its features, making huge bulging blots
of its lips and nose, and as my eyes in dread anticipation

pulled downward, there was its navel, without a thread
of covering, ruptured, exposed, protruding from a pot
stomach as huge as a mother-to-be's, on short, bent legs,

1. Women's fashion magazine founded in 1867.

extending as far on each side as swollen back limbs
of a turtle. I could look no farther and nearly dispensed
with being polite while pretending to welcome her gift.

But afterwards, to the turn of calendar pages, my eyes would skim
the figure, appraising this fantastic sight,
until, finally, I saw on its stern

ebony face, not a furniture polished, shellacked shine,
but a radiance, gleaming as though a small light
had flashed internally; and I could discern

through the sheen that the bulging eyes
were identical twins to the bulging nose.
The same symmetrical form was dispersed again

and again through all the bulges, the thighs
and the hands and the lips, in reverse, even the toes
of this fast turning beautiful form were a selfsame chain,

matching the navel. This little figure stretched high
in grace, in its with-the-grain form and from-within-glow,
in its curves in concord. I became a hurricane

of elation, a convert undaunted, who wanted to flaunt
her discovery, parade her fair-contoured find.

Art clubs, like leaves in autumn fall,
scrabble against concrete and scatter.
And Etta Moten, I read, is at tea with the Queen.

But I find myself still framing word structures
of how much these blazing forms ascending the centuries
in their muted sheens, matter to me.

This Is an African Worm

This is an African worm
but then a worm in any land
is still a worm.

It will not stride, run, stand up
before the butterflies, who
have passed their worm-like state.

It must keep low, not lift its head.
I've had the dread experience, I know.
A worm can do no thing but crawl.

Crawl, and wait.

The Painted Lady

The Painted Lady is a small African
butterfly, gayly toned orchid or peach
that seems as tremulous and delicately sheer

as the objects I treasure, yet, this cosmopolitan
can cross the sea at the icy time of the year
in the trail of the big boats, to France.

Mischance is as wide and somber grey as the lake here
in Chicago. Is there strength enough in my huge
peach paper rose, or lavender sea-laced fan?

The Slave and the Iron Lace

The craving of Samuel Rouse for clearance to create
was surely as hot as the iron that buffeted him. His passion
for freedom so strong that it molded the smouldering fashions
he laced, for how also could a slave plot
or counterplot such incomparable shapes,

form or reform, for house after house,
the intricate Patio pattern, the delicate
Rose and Lyre, the Debutante Settee,
the complex but famous Grape; frame the classic vein
in an iron bench?

How could he turn an iron Venetian urn, wind the Grape Vine, chain
the trunk of a pine with a Round-the-Tree-settee,
mold a Floating Flower tray, a French chair—create all this
in such exquisite fairyland taste, that he'd be freed
and his skill would still resound a hundred years after?

And I wonder if I, with this thick asbestos glove of an
attitude could lace, forge and blend this ton of lead-chained
spleen surrounding me?
Could I manifest and sustain it into a new free-form screen
of, not necessarily love, but (at the very least, for all concerned) grace.

Questions to Consider

1. What does the poem "This Is an African Worm" suggest about the narrator's racial politics?
2. "Iron Lace," in the title of the poem "The Slave and the Iron Lace," is an oxymoron, which is a juxtaposition of two contradictory terms. Why is the oxymoron appropriate for Danner's treatment of the theme of slavery?

Walker Percy

1916–1990

Called by Alfred Kazin "the satiric Dostoyevsky of the bayou," Walker Percy produced a body of work strongly influenced by his interest in existentialism and his conversion to Roman Catholicism as an adult. Frequently focusing his attention on what the *New York Times* called the "dislocation of man in the modern age," Percy is best known for his novel *The Moviegoer* and for helping to secure a publisher for the Pulitzer Prize-winning novel, *A Confederacy of Dunces*, by John Kennedy Toole.

Percy was born in Birmingham, Alabama on 28 May 1916, to parents Martha Susan Phinizy and Leroy Pratt Percy, an attorney. His father committed suicide when Percy was 11, and he lost his mother in a car accident only two years later. Percy and his two brothers were adopted by William Alexander Percy, their paternal uncle and author of *Lanterns on the Levee*. The brothers spent several years with the elder Percy in Greenville, Mississippi, where they were indoctrinated into a traditionally Southern lifestyle based in White paternalism and exposed to their uncle's disgust for "the race-baiting populists" who had run William Percy's father out of the Senate years earlier. William Percy also entertained literary notables with some regularity, and as a result, Walker was introduced early in his life to a wide range of poets, folk singers, and politicians. Walker read widely as a youth, digesting the works of the British Romantics and Shakespeare and developing an appreciation for classical music. He admired his uncle greatly, an admiration made tangible when he contributed the introduction to a reissued version of *Lanterns on the Levee*.

Percy began trying to publish his work when he was in elementary school, selling his sonnets to classmates to fulfill assignments in their English classes. In spite of his love for poetry and the classics, he studied chemistry at the University of North Carolina, Chapel Hill, completing his bachelor's degree in 1937 as a premedical student, after which he continued his studies at the Columbia University College of Physicians and Surgeons. He earned his medical degree in 1941 and began working as a pathologist at Bellevue Hospital, a position he was forced to relinquish when he contracted tuberculosis. Two years recovering in a sanitarium gave Percy ample time to consider the direction of his life. He found himself drawn to the works of existentialists such as Sartre, Heidegger, and Camus, which led him to reflect on his spiritual convictions. Upon his release from the sanitarium, supported by an inheritance left him by his uncle, Percy settled in Covington, a small city on the outskirts of New Orleans, joined the Catholic Church, and set out to "think about the curiousness of man's condition and perhaps even to write about it." Percy spent the remainder of his life living in and around New Orleans.

Because of the years spent preparing for a career in the medical profession, Percy did not begin writing seriously until later in his life, and his first novel, *The Moviegoer*, was published when he was 45. The novel won the National Book Award in 1961, to the great pleasure and surprise of his publishers at Knopf. Prior to its appearance, Percy had published several essays on philosophical subjects, and he later collected many of his essays in the volume *The Message in the Bottle* (1975). *Signposts in a Strange Land* (1991), published posthumously, collected many of Percy's remaining and revised essays.

Percy published six novels, which are generally satiric and are often described by critics as "social observation[s] of contemporary America, particularly the New South." Percy once remarked that *The Moviegoer* is about a man who "feels himself quite alienated from both worlds, the old South and the new America." *The Moviegoer* establishes the themes of alienation, despair, and religious angst to which the author would return throughout his career, and which play a major role in his later novels, *The Last Gentleman* (1966) and *Love in the Ruins* (1971).

Much of Percy's fiction, as well as his many essays, address issues of religious faith and the ways in which a Southern identity is negotiated in the post–Reconstruction-era South. In spite of his penchant for examining the Southern experience, critics have consistently noted that Percy appears to be more strongly influenced by European existential philosophers than by William Faulkner.

Percy was married to Mary Bernice Townsend in 1946, and the couple had two daughters. Percy passed away on 10 May 1990 in Covington, Louisiana.

The selection from *The Moviegoer* presented here demonstrates the level of alienation implicit in the lives of Binx and Kate, alienation that their long-standing family lineage cannot assuage. Their actions, which are largely incomprehensible to Binx's aunt, place them at odds with the types of societal and familial expectations typically placed on upper-class Southerners and highlight the extent to which respectable people would go to keep their secrets "in the family."

from The Moviegoer

It is impossible to find a seat on a flight to New Orleans the night before Mardi Gras. No trains are scheduled until Tuesday morning. But buses leave every hour or so. I send my aunt a telegram and call Stanley Kinchen and excuse myself from the talk on Selling Aids—it is all-right: the original speaker had recovered. Stanley and I part even more cordially than we met. It is a stratospheric cordiality such as can only make further meetings uneasy. But I do not mind. At midnight we are bound for New Orleans on a Scenicruiser which takes a more easterly course than the Illinois Central, down along the Wabash to Memphis by way of Evansville and Cairo.

It is good to be leaving; Chicago is fit for no more than a short rotation. Kate is well. The summons from her stepmother has left her neither glum nor fearful. She speaks at length to her stepmother and, with her sure instinct for such matters, gets her talking about canceling reservations and return tickets, wins her way, decides we'll stay, then changes her mind and insists on coming home to ease their minds. Now she gazes curiously about the bus station, giving way every few seconds to tremendous face-splitting yawns. Once on the bus she collapses into a slack-jawed oblivion and sleeps all the way to the Ohio River. I doze fitfully and wake for good when the dawn breaks on the outskirts of Terre Haute. When it is light enough, I take out my paper-back *Arabia Deserta* and read until we stop for breakfast in Evansville. Kate eats heartily, creeps back to the bus, takes one look at the black water of the Ohio River and the naked woods of the bottom lands where winter still clings like a violet mist, and falls heavily to sleep, mouth mashed open against my shoulder.

Today is Mardi Gras, fat Tuesday, but our bus has left Chicago much too late to accommodate Carnival visitors. The passengers are an everyday assortment of mothers-in-law visiting sons-in-law in Memphis, school teachers and telephone operators bound for vacations in quaint old Vieux Carré. Our upper deck is a green bubble where, it turns out, people feel themselves dispensed from the conventional silence below as if, in mounting with others to see the wide world and the green sky, they had already established a kind of freemasonry and spoken the first word among themselves. I surrender my seat to Kate's stretchings out against me and double up her legs for her and for the rest of the long day's journey down through Indiana and Illinois and Kentucky and Tennessee and Mississippi hold converse with two passengers—the first, a romantic from Wisconsin; the second, a salesman from a small manufacturing firm in Murfreesboro, Tennessee who wrecked his car in Gary.

Now in the fore seat of the bubble and down we go plunging along the Illinois bank of the Mississippi through a region of sooty glens falling steeply away to the west and against the slope of which are propped tall frame houses with colored windows and the spires of Polish churches. I read:

> We mounted in the morrow twilight; but long after daybreak the heavens seemed shut over us, as a tomb, with gloomy clouds. We were engaged in horrid lava beds.

The romantic sits across the aisle, slumped gracefully, one foot propped on the metal ledge. He is reading *The Charterhouse of Parma.* His face is extraordinarily well-modeled and handsome but his head is too small and, arising as it does from the great collar of his car coat, it makes him look a bit dandy and dudish. Two things I am curious about. How does he sit? Immediately graceful and not aware of it or mediately graceful and aware of it? How does he read *The Charterhouse of Parma?* Immediately as a man who is in the world and who has an appetite for the book as he might have an appetite for peaches, or mediately as one who finds himself under the necessity of sticking himself into the world in a certain fashion, of slumping in an acceptable slump, of reading an acceptable book on an acceptable bus? Is he a romantic?

He is a romantic. His posture is the first clue: it is too good to be true, this distillation of all graceful slumps. To clinch matters, he catches sight of me and my book and goes into a spasm of recognition and shyness. To put him out of his misery, I go over and ask him how he likes his book. For a tenth of a second he eyes me to make sure I am not a homosexual; but he has already seen Kate with me and sees her now, lying asleep and marvelously high in the hip. (I have observed that it is no longer possible for one young man to speak unwarily to another not known to him, except in certain sections of the South and West, and certainly not with a book in his hand.) As for me, I have already identified him through his shyness. It is pure heterosexual shyness. He is no homosexual, but merely a romantic. Now he closes his book and stares hard at it as if he would, by dint of staring alone, tear from it its soul in a word. "It's—very good," he says at last and blushes. The poor fellow. He has just begun to suffer from it, this miserable trick the romantic plays upon himself: of setting just beyond his reach the very thing he prizes. For he prizes just such a meeting, the chance meeting with a chance friend on a chance bus, a friend he can talk to, unburden himself of some of his terrible longings. Now having encountered such a one, me, the rare bus friend, of course he strikes himself dumb. It is a case for direct questioning.

He is a senior at a small college in northern Wisconsin where his father is bursar. His family is extremely proud of the educational progress of their children. Three sisters have assorted PhDs and MAs, piling up degrees on into the middle of life (he speaks in a rapid rehearsed way, a way he deems appropriate for our rare encounter, and when he is forced to use an ordinary word like "bus"—having no other way of conferring upon it a vintage flavor, he says it in quotes and with a wry expression). Upon completion of his second trimester and having enough credits to graduate, he has lit out for New Orleans to load bananas for a while and perhaps join the merchant marine. Smiling tensely, he strains forward and strikes himself dumb. For a while, he says. He means that he hopes to find himself a girl, the rarest of rare pieces, and live the life of Rudolfo on the balcony, sitting around on the floor and experiencing soul-communions. I have my doubts. In the first place, he will defeat himself, jump ten miles ahead of himself, scare the wits out of some girl with his great choking silences, want her so desperately that by his own peculiar logic he can't have her; or having her, jump another ten miles beyond both of them and end by fleeing to the islands where, propped at the rail of his ship in some rancid port, he will ponder his own loneliness.

In fact, there is nothing more to say to him. The best one can do is deflate the pressure a bit, the terrible romantic pressure, and leave him alone. He is a moviegoer, though of course he does not go to movies.

The salesman has no such trouble. Like many businessmen, he is a better metaphysician than the romantic. For example, he gives me a sample of his product, a simple ell of tempered and blued steel honed to a two-edged blade. Balancing it in his hand, he tests its heft and temper. The hand knows the blade, practices its own metaphysic of the goodness of the steel.

"Thank you very much," I say, accepting the warm blade.

"You know all in the world you have to do?"

"No."

"Walk into the office—" (He sells this attachment to farm implement stores) "—and ask the man how much is his bush hog blade. He'll tell you about nine and a half a pair. Then all you do is drop this on his desk and say thirty five cents and you can't break it."

"What does it do?"

"Anything. Clears, mulches, peas, beans, saplings so big, anything. That little sombitch will go now." He strikes one hand straight out past the other, and I have a sense of the storied and even legendary properties of the blade, attested in the peculiar Southern esteem of the excellence of machinery: the hot-damn beat-all risible accolade conferred when some new engine sallies forth in its outlandish scissoring side-winding foray.

We sit on the rear seat, the salesman with his knee cocked up, heel under him, arm levered out over his knee. He wears black shoes and white socks for his athlete's foot and now and then sends down a finger to appease the itching. It pleases him to speak of his cutter and of his family down in Murfreesboro and speak all the way to Union City and not once to inquire of me and this pleases me since I would not know what to say. Businessmen are our only metaphysicians, but the trouble is, they are one-track metaphysicians. By the time the salesman gets off in Union City, my head is spinning with facts about the thirty five cent cutter. It is as if I had lived in Murfreesboro all my life.

Canal Street is dark and almost empty. The last parade, the Krewe of Comus, has long since disappeared down Royal Street with its shuddering floats and its blazing flambeau. Street cleaners sweep confetti and finery into soggy heaps in the gutters. The cold mizzling rain smells of sour paper pulp. Only a few maskers remain abroad, tottering apes clad in Spanish moss, Frankenstein monsters with bolts through their necks, and a neighborhood gang or two making their way arm in arm, wheeling and whip-popping, back to their trucks.

Kate is dry-eyed and abstracted. She stands gazing about as if she had landed in a strange city. We decide to walk up Loyola Avenue to get our cars. The romantic is ahead of us, at the window of a lingerie shop, the gay sort where black net panties invest legless torsos. Becoming aware of us before we pass and thinking to avoid the embarrassment of a greeting (what are we to say, after all, and suppose the right word fails us?), he hurries away, hands thrust deep in his pockets, his small well-modeled head tricking to and fro above the great collar of his car coat.

* * *

"I am not saying that I pretend to understand you. What I am saying is that after two days of complete mystification it has at last dawned on me what it is I fail to understand. That is at least a step in the right direction. It was the novelty of it that put me off, you see. I do believe that you have discovered something new under the sun."

It is with a rare and ominous objectivity that my aunt addresses me Wednesday morning. In the very violence of her emotion she has discovered the energy to master it, so that now, in the flush of her victory, she permits herself to use the old forms of civility and even of humor. The only telltale sign of menace is the smile through her eyes, which is a bit too narrow and finely drawn.

"Would you verify my hypothesis? Is not that your discovery? First, is it not true that in all of past history people who found themselves in difficult situations behaved in certain familiar ways, well or badly, courageously or cowardly, with distinction or mediocrity, with honor or dishonor. They are recognizable. They display courage, pity, fear, embarrassment, joy, sorrow, and so on. Such anyhow has been the funded experience of the race for two or three thousand years, has it not? Your discovery, as best as I can determine, is that there is an alternative which no one has hit upon. It is that one finding oneself in one of life's critical situations need not after all respond in one of the traditional ways. No. One may simply default. Pass. Do as one pleases, shrug, turn on one's heel and leave. Exit. Why after all need one act humanly? Like all great discoveries, it is breathtakingly simple." She smiles a quizzical-legal sort of smile which reminds me of Judge Anse.

The house was no different this morning. The same chorus of motors, vacuum cleaners, dishwasher, laundromat, hum and throb against each other. From an upper region, reverberating down the back stairwell, comes the muted hollering of Bessie Coe, as familiar and querulous a sound as the sparrows under the eaves. Nor was Uncle Jules different, except only in his slight embarrassment, giving me wide berth as I passed him on the porch and saying his good morning briefly and sorrowfully as if the farthest limit of his disapproval lay in the brevity of his greeting. Kate was nowhere to be seen. Until ten o'clock my aunt, I know, is to be found at her roll-top desk where she keeps her "accounts." There is nothing to do but go directly in to her and stand at ease until she takes notice of me. Now she looks over, as erect and handsome as the Black Prince.

"Yes?"

"I am sorry that through a misunderstanding or thoughtlessness on my part you were not told of Kate's plans to go with me to Chicago. No doubt it was my thoughtlessness. In any case I am sorry and I hope that your anger ——"

"Anger? You are mistaken. It was not anger. It was discovery."

"Discovery of what?"

"Discovery that someone in whom you had placed great hopes was suddenly not there. It is like leaning on what seems to be a good stalwart shoulder and feeling it go all mushy and queer."

We both gaze down at the letter opener, the soft iron sword she has withdrawn from the grasp of the helmeted figure on the inkstand.

"I am sorry for that."

"The fact that you are a stranger to me is perhaps my fault. It was stupid of me not to believe it earlier. For now I do believe that you are not capable of caring for anyone, Kate, Jules, or myself—no more than that Negro man walking down the street—less so, in fact, since I have a hunch he and I would discover some slight tradition in common." She seems to notice for the first time that the tip of the blade is bent. "I honestly don't believe it occurred to you to let us know that you and Kate were leaving, even though you knew how desperately sick she was. I truly do not think it ever occurred to you that you were abusing a sacred trust in carrying that poor child off on a fantastic trip like that or that you were betraying the great trust and affection she has for you. Well?" she asks when I do not reply.

I try as best I can to appear as she would have me, as being, if not right, then wrong in a recognizable, a right form of wrongness. But I can think of nothing to say.

"Do you have any notion of how I felt when, not twelve hours after Kate attempted suicide, she vanishes without a trace?"

We watch the sword as she lets it fall over the fulcrum of her forefinger; it goes *tat't't* on the brass hinge of the desk. Then, so suddenly that I almost start, my aunt sheathes the sword and places her hand flat on the desk. Turning it over, she flexes her fingers and studies the nails, which are deeply scored by longitudinal ridges.

"Were you intimate with Kate?"

"Intimate?"

"Yes."

"Not very."

"I ask you again. Were you intimate with her?"

"I suppose so. Though intimate is not quite the word."

"You suppose so. Intimate is not quite the word. I wonder what is the word. You see—" she says with a sort of humor, "—there is another of my hidden assumptions. All these years I have been assuming that between us words mean roughly the same thing, that among certain people, gentlefolk I don't mind calling them, there exists a set of meanings held in common, that a certain manner and a certain grace come as naturally as breathing. At the great moments of life—success, failure, marriage, death—our kind of folks have always possessed a native instinct for behavior, a natural piety or grace, I don't mind calling it. Whatever else we did or failed to do, we always had that. I'll make you a little confession. I am not ashamed to use the word class. I will also plead guilty to another charge. The charge is that people belonging to my class think they're better than other people. You're damn right we're better. We're better because we do not shirk our obligations either to ourselves or to others. We do not whine. We do not organize a minority group and blackmail the government. We do not prize mediocrity for mediocrity's sake. Oh I am aware that we hear a great many flattering things nowadays about your great common man—you know, it has always been revealing to me that he is perfectly content so to be called, because that is exactly what he is: the common man and when I say common I mean common as hell. Our civilization has achieved a distinction of sorts. It will be remembered not for its technology nor even its wars but for its novel ethos. Ours is the only civilization in history which has enshrined mediocrity as its national ideal. Others have been corrupt, but leave it to us to invent the most undistinguished of corruptions. No orgies, no blood running in the street, no babies thrown off cliffs. No, we're sentimental people and we horrify easily. True, our moral fiber is rotten. Our national character stinks to high heaven. But we are kinder than ever. No prostitute ever responded with a quicker spasm of sentiment when our hearts are touched. Nor is there anything new about thievery, lewdness, lying, adultery. What is new is that in our time liars and thieves and whores and adulterers wish also to be congratulated and are congratulated by the great public, if their confession is sufficiently psychological or strikes a sufficiently heartfelt and authentic note of sincerity. Oh, we are sincere. I do not deny it. I don't know anybody nowadays who is not sincere. Didi Lovell is the most sincere person I know: every time she crawls in bed with somebody else, she does so with the utmost sincerity. We are the most sincere Laodiceans who ever got flushed down the sinkhole of history. No, my young friend, I am not ashamed to use the word class. They say out there we think we're better. You're damn right we're better. And don't think they don't know it—" She raises the sword to Prytania Street. "Let me tell you something. If he out yonder is your prize exhibit for the progress of the human race in the past three thousand years, then all I can say is that I am content to be fading out of the picture. Perhaps we are a biological sport. I am not sure. But one thing I am sure of: we live by our lights, we die by our lights, and whoever the high gods may be, we'll look them in the eye without apology." Now my aunt swivels around to face me and not so bad-humoredly. "I did my best for you, son. I gave you all I had. More than anything I wanted to pass on to you the one heritage of the men of our family, a certain quality of spirit, a gaiety, a sense of duty, a nobility worn lightly, a sweetness, a gentleness with women—the only good things the South ever had and the only things that really matter in this life. Ah well. Still you can tell me one thing. I know you're not a bad boy—I wish you were. But how did it happen that none of this ever meant anything to you? Clearly it did not. Would you please tell me? I am genuinely curious."

I cannot tear my eyes from the sword. Years ago I bent the tip trying to open a drawer. My aunt looks too. Does she suspect?

"That would be difficult for me to say. You say that none of what you said ever meant anything to me. That is not true. On the contrary, I have never forgotten anything you ever said. In fact I have pondered over it all my life. My objections, though they are not exactly objections, cannot be expressed in the usual way. To tell the truth, I can't express them at all."

"I see. Do you condone your behavior with Kate?"

"Condone?" Condone. I screw up an eye. "I don't suppose so."

"You don't suppose so." My aunt nods gravely, almost agreeably, in her wry legal manner. "You knew that Kate was suicidal?"

"No."

"Would you have cared if Kate had killed herself?"

"Yes."

After a long silence she asks: "You have nothing more to say?"

I shake my head.

Mercer opens the door and sticks his head in, takes one whiff of the air inside, and withdraws immediately.

"Then tell me this. Yes, tell me this!" my aunt says, brightening as, groping, she comes at last to the nub of the matter. "Tell me this and this is all I shall ever want to know. I am assuming that we both recognize that you had a trust toward Kate. Perhaps my assumption was mistaken. But I know that you knew she was taking drugs. Is that not correct?"

"Yes."

"Did you know that she was taking drugs during this recent trip?"

"Yes."

"And you did what you did?"

"Yes."

"That is all you have to say?"

I am silent. Mercer starts the waxer. It was permission for this he sought. I think of nothing in particular. A cry goes up in the street outside, and there comes into my sight the Negro my aunt spoke of. He is Cothard, the last of the chimney sweeps, an outlandish blueblack Negro dressed in a frock coat and bashed-in top hat and carrying over his shoulder a bundle of palmetto leaves and broom straw. The cry comes again. "*R-r-r-ramonez la chiminée du haut en bas!*"

"One last question to satisfy my idle curiosity. What has been going on in your mind during all the years when we listened to music together, read the *Crito*, and spoke together—or was it only I who spoke—good Lord, I can't remember—of goodness and truth and beauty and nobility?"

Another cry and the *ramoneur* is gone. There is nothing for me to say.

"Don't you love these things? Don't you live by them?"

"No."

"What do you love? What do you live by?"

I am silent.

"Tell me where I have failed you."

"You haven't."

"What do you think is the purpose of life—to go to the movies and dally with every girl that comes along?"

"No."

A ledger lies open on her desk, one of the old-fashioned kind with a marbled cover, in which she has always kept account of her properties, sundry service stations, Canadian mines, patents—the peculiar business accumulation of a doctor—left to her by old Dr Wills. "Well." She closes it briskly and smiles up at me, a smile which, more than anything which has gone before, marks an ending. Smiling, she gives me her hand, head to one side, in her old party style. But it is her withholding my name that assigns me my new status. So she might have spoken to any one of a number of remotely connected persons, such as a Spring Fiesta tourist encountered by accident in her own hall.

We pass Mercer who stands respectfully against the wall. He murmurs a greeting which through an exquisite calculation expresses his affection for me and at the same time declares his allegiance to my aunt. Out of the corner of my eye, I see him hop nimbly into the dining room, full of fizzing good spirits. We find ourselves on the porch.

"I do thank you so much for coming by," says my aunt, fingering her necklace and looking past me at the Vaudrieul house.

Kate hails me at the corner. She leans into my MG, tucking her blouse, as brisk as a stewardess.

"You're stupid stupid stupid," she says with a malevolent look.

"What?"

"I heard it all, you poor stupid bastard." Then, appearing to forget herself, she drums her nails rapidly upon the windshield. "Are you going home now?"

"Yes."

"Wait for me there."

Questions to Consider

1. In the selection from *The Moviegoer,* the protagonist, Binx Bolling, remarks that the South will be remembered not for technology or wars, but for its "novel ethos" because the South, as he sees it is "the only civilization in history which has enshrined mediocrity

as its national ideal." What does he mean by this statement, and what leads him to make it? Is this an accurate representation of the New South?

2. Percy comments at length on the characteristics of Southern literature. What attributes does he identify as being especially Southern? Why do you think that these attributes have come to be identified with literature from the South?

Carson McCullers
1917–1967

Carson McCullers is recognized as a member of the community of Southern women writers that included Flannery O'Connor, Katherine Anne Porter, Caroline Gordon, and Eudora Welty. As critic Louise Westling has pointed out, "nowhere else in American literature is there a group of accomplished women writers so closely bound together by regional qualities of setting, character, and time." A precise and deliberate writer, McCullers published five novels, a volume of children's poetry, a drama, and a few dozen short stories, poems, sketches, and essays. McCullers's gothic tales and grotesque characters offer keen insights into the human condition, especially as it pertains to love and loneliness.

Lula Carson Smith, the oldest child of Lamar and Marguerite Waters Smith was born 17 February 1917 in the small Southern town of Columbus, Georgia. Encouraged by her mother, McCullers developed her musical talent, often practicing piano for as much as eight hours each day. Her fate as a concert pianist was decided early; however, it was shortened by a case of rheumatic fever that left her too weak for the sustained periods of practice and travel that such a career would require. McCullers left Georgia for New York in 1934, ostensibly to attend Juilliard School of Music. McCullers had other plans and instead began to study creative writing at Columbia University and New York University. Another protracted illness forced her to return home to recover, and while she was convalescing, McCullers began writing *The Heart Is a Lonely Hunter* (1940).

McCullers's literary career began with the publication of the stories "Wunderkind" and "Like That" (1936), each of which was published in *Story* magazine. At the age of 23, McCullers secured her position as a notable writer with *The Heart Is a Lonely Hunter,* which introduced the themes to which she would return throughout her career—loneliness and isolation. Critic Carlos Dews recalls the remarks of a *New York Times* reviewer Rose Feld, who found the novel "akin to the vocation of pain to which a great poet is born." McCullers published many more novels and pieces of short fiction during her career, the most notable of which include *The Ballad of the Sad Café* (1943) and *The Member of the Wedding* (1946). Her productivity declined later in her life, in large part because of a series of debilitating strokes that were the result of her early bout with rheumatic fever.

Reading widely throughout her life, McCullers became familiar with works by authors as diverse as F. Scott Fitzgerald, Katherine Mansfield, and Ernest Hemingway, whom she described as providing the "heritage to the American prose writer," despite the fact that she "deplore[d] his sentimentality, and fake toughness." She mentions in her autobiography feeling the influence of a wide variety of authors, including Thomas Wolfe—"partly because of his wonderful gusto in describing food"—as well as Dostoevsky, Tolstoy, James Joyce, and E. M. Forster. As an artist, McCullers often considered the sources of illumination—inspiration that led to creative works—leading her to title her incomplete, posthumously published autobiography *Illumination and Night Glare*. In this autobiography, McCullers remarks that her use of the word illumination might be "misleading, because there were so many frightful times when I was totally 'un-illuminated,' and feared that I could never write again. This fear is one of the horrors of an author's life."

McCullers's personal life was marked by struggles with depression, illness, and alcoholism. Her tumultuous marriages to James Reeves McCullers contributed to her depression, as the relationship was "simultaneously the most supportive and destructive relationship in her life," as Dews has suggested. Over the next 16 years, the couple separated and reconciled on numerous occasions, although the letters that they exchanged during Reeves's World War II military service—service that occurred during the interlude between their two marriages—indicate that they continued to care deeply for each other. In 1947, a stroke paralyzed McCullers's left side, leading her to attempt suicide. In 1953, Reeves committed suicide in a Paris hotel, which Carson had recently fled in fear for her life, since Reeves had tried to convince her to die with him.

Although McCullers is classed among the most well-respected of Southern writers, she was ambivalent about her Southern heritage and the region itself. Dews argues that her disgust with Southern attributes such as the "economic inequities . . . the South's racism, and her own personal experience of the South's intolerance," as well as her "gender ambiguity (most significantly the negative reaction by those around her to her androgynous nature and masculine dress" influenced her decision to leave the South. Despite her distaste for living in the region herself, all of her major works are set in the South.

McCullers's abilities as a writer earned her a variety of awards, including the Houghton Mifflin Fiction Fellowship, two Guggenheim Fellowships, a National Institute of Arts and Letters Grant in Literature, two Donaldson Awards, and the Theatre Club Gold Medal. She also received a New York Drama Critics' Circle Award for the dramatization of her fiction, and was inducted as a fellow of the American Academy of Arts and Letters in 1952.

During the last years of her life McCullers battled constant pain and a heavy drinking problem, which she described to Reeves in a 1944 letter as leading her to feel "completely crushed" physically; she also remarked that she suffered from "guilty and hopeless penitence." In August 1967, Carson McCullers suffered a fatal stroke and died at Nyack Hospital in New York after lingering for six weeks in a coma.

Like That

Even if Sis is five years older than me and eighteen we used always to be closer and have more fun together than most sisters. It was about the same with us and our brother Dan, too. In the summer we'd all go swimming together. At nights in the wintertime maybe we'd sit around the fire in the living room and play three-handed bridge or Michigan, with everybody putting up a nickel or a dime to the winner. The three of us could have more fun by ourselves than any family I know. That's the way it always was before this.

Not that Sis was playing down to me, either. She's smart as she can be and has read more books than anybody I ever knew—even school teachers. But in High School she never did like to priss up flirty and ride around in cars with girls and pick up the boys and park at the drugstore and all that sort of thing. When she wasn't reading she'd just like to play around with me and Dan. She wasn't too grown up to fuss over a chocolate bar in the refrigerator or to stay awake most of Christmas Eve night either, say, with excitement. In some ways it was like I was heaps older than her. Even when Tuck started coming around last summer I'd sometimes have to tell her she shouldn't wear ankle socks because they might go down town or she ought to pluck out her eyebrows above her nose like the other girls do.

In one more year, next June, Tuck'll be graduated from college. He's a lanky boy with an eager look to his face. At college he's so smart he has a free scholarship. He started coming to see Sis the last summer before this one, riding in his family's car when he could get it, wearing crispy white linen suits. He came a lot last year but this summer he came even more often—before he left he was coming around for Sis every night. Tuck's O.K.

It began getting different between Sis and me a while back, I guess, although I didn't notice it at the time. It was only after a certain night this summer that I had the idea that things maybe were bound to end like they are now.

It was late when I woke up that night. When I opened my eyes I thought for a minute it must be about dawn and I was scared when I saw Sis wasn't on her side of the bed. But it was only the moonlight that shone cool looking and white outside the window and made the oak leaves hanging down over the front yard pitch black and separate seeming. It was around the first of September, but I didn't feel hot looking at the moonlight. I pulled the sheet over me and let my eyes roam around the black shapes of the furniture in our room.

I'd waked up lots of times in the night this summer. You see Sis and I have always had this room together and when she would come in and turn on the light to find her nightgown or something it woke me. I liked it. In the summer when school was out I didn't have to get up early in the morning. We would lie and talk sometimes for a good while. I'd like to hear about the places she and Tuck had been or to laugh over different things. Lots of times before that night she had talked to me privately about Tuck just like I was her age—asking me if I thought she should have said this or that when he called and giving me a hug, maybe, after. Sis was really crazy about Tuck. Once she said to me: "He's so lovely—I never in the world thought I'd know anyone like him —"

We would talk about our brother too. Dan's seventeen years old and was planning to take the co-op course at Tech in the fall. Dan had gotten older by this summer. One night he came in at four o'clock and he'd been drinking. Dad sure had it in for him the next week. So he hiked out to the country and camped with some boys for a few days. He used to talk to me and Sis about diesel motors and going away to South America and all that, but by this summer he was quiet and not saying much to anybody in the family. Dan's real tall and thin as a rail. He has bumps on his face now and is clumsy and not very good looking. At nights sometimes I know he wanders all around by himself, maybe going out beyond the city limits sign into the pine woods.

Thinking about such things I lay in bed wondering what time it was and when Sis would be in. That night after Sis and Dan had left I had gone down to the corner with some of the kids in the neighborhood to chunk rocks at the street light and try to kill a bat up there. At first I had the shivers and imagined it was a smallish bat like the kind in Dracula. When I saw it looked just like a moth I didn't care if they killed it or not. I was just sitting there on the curb drawing with a stick on the dusty street when Sis and Tuck rode by slowly in his car. She was sitting over very close to him. They weren't talking or smiling—just riding slowly down the street, sitting close, looking ahead. When they passed and I saw who it was I hollered to them. "Hey, Sis!" I yelled.

The car just went on slowly and nobody hollered back. I just stood there in the middle of the street feeling sort of silly with all the other kids standing around.

That hateful little old Bubber from down on the other block came up to me. "That your sister?" he asked.

I said yes.

"She sure was sitting up close to her beau," he said.

I was mad all over like I get sometimes. I hauled off and chunked all the rocks in my hand right at him. He's three years younger than me and it wasn't nice, but I couldn't stand him in the first place and he thought he was being so cute about Sis.

He started holding his neck and bellering and I walked off and left them and went home and got ready to go to bed.

When I woke up I finally began to think of that too and old Bubber Davis was still in my mind when I heard the sound of a car coming up the block. Our room faces the street with only a short front yard between. You can see and hear everything from the sidewalk and the street. The car was creeping down in front of our walk and the light went slow and white along the walls of the room. It stopped on Sis's writing desk, showed up the books there plainly and half a pack of chewing gum. Then the room was dark and there was only the moonlight outside.

The door of the car didn't open but I could hear them talking. Him, that is. His voice was low and I couldn't catch any words but it was like he was explaining something over and over again. I never heard Sis say a word.

I was still awake when I heard the car door open. I heard her say, "Don't come out." And then the door slammed and there was the sound of her heels clopping up the walk, fast and light like she was running.

Mama met Sis in the hall outside our room. She had heard the front door close. She always listens out for Sis and Dan and never goes to sleep when they're still out. I sometimes wonder how she can just lie there in the dark for hours without going to sleep.

"It's one-thirty, Marian," she said. "You ought to get in before this."

Sis didn't say anything.

"Did you have a nice time?"

That's the way Mama is. I could imagine her standing there with her nightgown blowing out fat around her and her dead white legs and the blue veins showing, looking all messed up. Mama's nicer when she's dressed to go out.

"Yes, we had a grand time," Sis said. Her voice was funny—sort of like a piano in the gym at school, high and sharp on your ear. Funny.

Mama was asking more questions. Where did they go? Did they see anybody they knew? All that sort of stuff. That's the way she is.

"Goodnight," said Sis in that out of tune voice.

She opened the door of our room real quick and closed it. I started to let her know I was awake but changed my mind. Her breathing was quick and loud in the dark and she did not move at all. After a few minutes she felt in the closet for her nightgown and got in the bed. I could hear her crying.

"Did you and Tuck have a fuss?" I asked.

"No," she answered. Then she seemed to change her mind. "Yeah, it was a fuss."

There's one thing that gives me the creeps sure enough—and that's to hear somebody cry. "I wouldn't let it bother me. You'll be making up tomorrow."

The moon was coming in the window and I could see her moving her jaw from one side to the other and staring up at the ceiling. I watched her for a long time. The moonlight was cool looking and there was a wettish wind coming cool from the window. I moved over like I sometimes do to snug up with her, thinking maybe that would stop her from moving her jaw like that and crying.

She was trembling all over. When I got close to her she jumped like I'd pinched her and pushed me over quick and kicked my legs over. "Don't," she said. "Don't."

Maybe Sis had suddenly gone batty, I was thinking. She was crying in a slower and sharper way. I was a little scared and I got up to go to the bathroom a minute. While I was in there I looked out the window, down toward the corner where the street light is. I saw something then that I knew Sis would want to know about.

"You know what?" I asked when I was back in the bed.

She was lying over close to the edge as she could get, stiff. She didn't answer.

"Tuck's car is parked down by the street light. Just drawn up to the curb. I could tell because of the box and the two tires on the back. I could see it from the bathroom window."

She didn't even move.

"He must be just sitting out there. What ails you and him?"

She didn't say anything at all.

"I couldn't see him but he's probably just sitting there in the car under the street light. Just sitting there."

It was like she didn't care or had known it all along. She was as far over the edge of the bed as she could get, her legs stretched out stiff and her hands holding tight to the edge and her face on one arm.

She used always to sleep all sprawled over on my side so I'd have to push at her when it was hot and sometimes turn on the light and draw the line down the middle and show her how she really was on my side. I wouldn't have to draw any line that night, I was thinking. I felt bad. I looked out at the moonlight a long time before I could get to sleep again.

The next day was Sunday and Mama and Dad went in the morning to church because it was the anniversary of the day my aunt died. Sis said she didn't feel well and stayed in bed. Dan was out and I was there by myself so naturally I went into our room where Sis was. Her face was white as the pillow and there were circles under her eyes. There was a muscle jumping on one side of her jaw like she was chewing. She hadn't combed her hair and it flopped over the pillow, glinty red and messy and pretty. She was reading with a book held up close to her face. Her eyes didn't move when I came in. I don't think they even moved across the page.

It was roasting hot that morning. The sun made everything blazing outside so that it hurt your eyes to look. Our room was so hot that you could almost touch the air with your finger. But Sis had the sheet pulled up clear to her shoulders.

"Is Tuck coming today?" I asked. I was trying to say something that would make her look more cheerful.

"Gosh! Can't a person have *any* peace in this house?"

She never did used to say mean things like that out of a clear sky. Mean things, maybe, but not grouchy ones.

"Sure," I said. "Nobody's going to notice you."

I sat down and pretended to read. When footsteps passed on the street Sis would hold onto the book tighter and I knew she was listening hard as she could. I can tell between footsteps easy. I can even tell without looking if the person who passes is colored or not. Colored people mostly make a slurry sound between the steps. When the steps would pass Sis would loosen the hold on the book and bite at her mouth. It was the same way with passing cars.

I felt sorry for Sis. I decided then and there that I never would let any fuss with any boy make me feel or look like that. But I wanted Sis and me to get back like we'd always been. Sunday mornings are bad enough without having any other trouble.

"We fuss lots less than most sisters do," I said. "And when we do it's all over quick, isn't it?"

She mumbled and kept staring at the same spot on the book.

"That's one good thing," I said.

She was moving her head slightly from side to side—over and over again, with her face not changing. "We never do have any real long fusses like Bubber Davis's two sisters have —"

"No." She answered like she wasn't thinking about what I'd said.

"Not one real one like that since I can remember."

In a minute she looked up the first time. "I remember one," she said suddenly.

"When?"

Her eyes looked green in the blackness under them and like they were nailing themselves into what they saw. "You had to stay in every afternoon for a week. It was a long time ago."

All of a sudden I remembered. I'd forgotten it for a long time. I hadn't wanted to remember. When she said that it came back to me all complete.

It was really a long time ago—when Sis was about thirteen. If I remember right I was mean and even more hardboiled than I am now. My aunt who I'd liked better than all my other aunts put together had had a dead baby and she had died. After the funeral Mama had told Sis and me about it. Always the things I've learned new and didn't like have made me mad—mad clean through and scared.

That wasn't what Sis was talking about, though. It was a few mornings after that when Sis started with what every big girl has each month, and of course I found out and was scared to death. Mama then explained to me about it and what she had to wear. I felt then like I'd felt about my aunt, only ten times worse. I felt different toward Sis, too, and was so mad I wanted to pitch into people and hit.

I never will forget it. Sis was standing in our room before the dresser mirror. When I remembered her face it was white like Sis's there on the pillow and with the circles under her eyes and the glinty hair to her shoulders—it was only younger.

I was sitting on the bed, biting hard at my knee. "It shows," I said. "It does too!"

She had on a sweater and a blue pleated skirt and she was so skinny all over that it did show a little.

"Anybody can tell. Right off the bat. Just to look at you anybody can tell."

Her face was white in the mirror and did not move.

"It looks terrible. I wouldn't ever ever be like that. It shows and everything."

She started crying then and told Mother and said she wasn't going back to school and such. She cried a long time. That's how ugly and hardboiled I used to be and am still sometimes. That's why I had to stay in the house every afternoon for a week a long time ago . . .

Tuck came by in his car that Sunday morning before dinner time. Sis got up and dressed in a hurry and didn't even put on any lipstick. She said they were going out to dinner. Nearly every Sunday all of us in the family stay together all day, so that was a little funny. They didn't get home until almost dark. The rest of us were sitting on the front porch drinking ice tea because of the heat when the car drove up again. After they got out of the car Dad, who had been in a very good mood all day, insisted Tuck stay for a glass of tea.

Tuck sat on the swing with Sis and he didn't lean back and his heels didn't rest on the floor—as though he was all ready to get up again. He kept changing the glass from one hand to the other and starting new conversations. He and Sis didn't look at each other except on the sly, and then it wasn't at all like they were crazy about each other. It was a funny look. Almost like they were afraid of something. Tuck left soon.

"Come sit by your Dad a minute, Puss," Dad said. Puss is a nickname he calls Sis when he feels in a specially good mood. He still likes to pet us.

She went and sat on the arm of his chair. She sat stiff like Tuck had, holding herself off a little so Dad's arm hardly went around her waist. Dad smoked his cigar and looked out on the front yard and the trees that were beginning to melt into the early dark.

"How's my big girl getting along these days?" Dad still likes to hug us up when he feels good and treat us, even Sis, like kids.

"O.K.," she said. She twisted a little bit like she wanted to get up and didn't know how to without hurting his feelings.

"You and Tuck have had a nice time together this summer, haven't you, Puss?"

"Yeah," she said. She had begun to see-saw her lower jaw again. I wanted to say something but couldn't think of anything.

Dad said: "He ought to be getting back to Tech about now, oughtn't he? When's he leaving?"

"Less than a week," she said. She got up so quick that she knocked Dad's cigar out of his fingers. She didn't even pick it up but flounced on through the front door. I could hear her half running to our room and the sound the door made when she shut it. I knew she was going to cry.

It was hotter than ever. The lawn was beginning to grow dark and the locusts were droning out so shrill and steady that you wouldn't notice them unless you thought to. The sky was bluish grey and the trees in the vacant lot across the street were dark. I kept on sitting on the front porch with Mama and Papa and hearing their low talk without listening to the words. I wanted to go in our room with Sis but I was afraid to. I wanted to ask her what was really the matter. Was hers and Tuck's fuss so bad as that or was it that she was so crazy about him that she was sad because he was leaving? For a minute I didn't think it was either one of those things. I wanted to know but I was scared to ask. I just sat there with the grown people. I never have been so lonesome as I was that night. If ever I think about being sad I just remember how it was then—sitting there looking at the long bluish shadows across the lawn and feeling like I was the only child left in the family and that Sis and Dan were dead or gone for good.

It's October now and the sun shines bright and a little cool and the sky is the color of my turquoise ring. Dan's gone to Tech. So has Tuck gone. It's not at all like it was last fall, though. I come in from High School (I go there now) and Sis maybe is just sitting by the window reading or writing to Tuck or just looking out. Sis is thinner and sometimes to me she looks in the face like a grown person. Or like, in a way, something has suddenly hurt her hard. We don't do any of the things we used to. It's good weather for fudge or for doing so many things. But no she just sits around or goes for long walks in the chilly late afternoon by herself. Sometimes she'll smile in a way that really gripes—like I was such a kid and all. Sometimes I want to cry or to hit her.

But I'm hardboiled as the next person. I can get along by myself if Sis or anybody else wants to. I'm glad I'm thirteen and still wear socks and can do what I please. I don't want to be any older if I'd get like Sis has. But I wouldn't. I wouldn't like any boy in the world as much as she does Tuck. I'd never let any boy or any thing make me act like she does. I'm not going to waste my time and try to make Sis be like she used to be. I get lonesome—sure—but I don't care. I know there's no way I can make myself stay thirteen all my life, but I know I'd never let anything really change me at all—no matter what it is.

I skate and ride my bike and go to the school football games every Friday. But when one afternoon the kids all got quiet in the gym basement and then started telling certain things—about being married and all—I got up quick so I wouldn't hear and went up and played basketball. And when some of the kids said they were going to start wearing lipstick and stockings I said I wouldn't for a hundred dollars.

You see I'd never be like Sis is now. I wouldn't. Anybody could know that if they knew me. I just wouldn't, that's all. I don't want to grow up—if it's like that.

Questions to Consider

1. What causes the narrator to conclude that growing up has disadvantages that she had not thought of? What are the drawbacks to growing up for the narrator?
2. How does McCullers represent the expectations generally placed on young women in traditional Southern families? Does Sis abide by these expectations? What are the results of her choices? How do Sis's choices effect the narrator?

Peter Taylor

1917–1994

Peter Taylor honed his writing craft under the direction of such respected Southern writers and scholars as Allen Tate, John Crowe Ransom, and Robert Penn Warren, but paradoxically, he suffered from an anxiety of influence at seeing their talents up close. Charlotte Beck has pointed out that the success of each of his mentors led Taylor to avoid writing poetry and literary criticism for many years, choosing instead to focus his efforts on the areas in which they were less prolific, the genres of fiction and drama. Despite his reluctance to compete with the giants of the Southern Renascence, Taylor nonetheless credits Allen Tate with leading him to "identify myself as to who I was, as a southerner." He later called Tate the "best teacher I ever had;" Tate helped the aspiring writer publish his earliest works, gain admission to Vanderbilt University where he continued his studies with Ransom, and strategize the advancement of his literary career.

Peter Hillsman Taylor was born on 8 January 1917 in Trenton, Tennessee, a ninth anniversary present to his parents, attorney Matthew Hillsman Taylor and Katherine Baird Taylor. His grandfather, Robert L. Taylor, once served as the governor of Tennessee. After graduating from Memphis Central High School in 1935, Peter Taylor was accepted at Columbia University, but he departed for England when his father refused to supplement the partial scholarship he received. After returning from England, Taylor spent his first semester of undergraduate study at Southwestern University in Memphis, where he studied with Allen Tate. Soon afterward, Taylor reached a compromise with his father in which he would attend his father's alma mater, Vanderbilt University, to study law. He left Vanderbilt without completing his degree shortly after Ransom left the University, following him to Kenyon College. Here Taylor joined what he called his "newly adopted literary family," including Robert Lowell, Randall Jarrell, and David McDowell, once again against his father's wishes. This time, however, the scholarship awarded to Taylor allowed him to continue his studies without his father's financial support, and he "joined a faction of literary students who were 'disciples' of Randall Jarrell," whom Taylor viewed as the "god of literary undergraduate students," according to Beck.

Taylor was strongly influenced by the legacy of the Fugitives throughout his career. He held Jarrell's opinion in especially high esteem, despite the fact that Jarrell underestimated the value of Taylor's talent, and that he was at times needlessly disparaging of Taylor's work behind his back. In fact, critics have argued that in many ways, Taylor did not begin to come of age as a writer until after Jarrell's death. Robert Penn Warren, the editor of the prestigious

Southern Review, accepted several of Taylor's stories for publication early in his career, and these publications helped to establish him as a writer; Warren also wrote the introduction to Taylor's first volume of fiction. Taylor maintained a friendly relationship with Robert Lowell throughout his life. The two young men attended Kenyon College together and later enrolled in the graduate program at Louisiana State University, where they were roommates and colleagues studying with Robert Penn Warren. On at least one occasion, Taylor wrote a story—"The Fancy Woman"—in response to Lowell's remarks on Taylor's earlier story—"The Spinster's Tale." The anxiety of influence that Taylor suffered because of his relationships with many of the Fugitive poets served to both limit and challenge him as a writer.

After completing only part of one semester, Taylor left LSU to concentrate on his writing. In addition to publishing in the *Southern Review*, he placed stories in the *Partisan Review*, the *Kenyon Review*, and the *Sewanee Review*, and his story, "The Fancy Woman," was included in the 1942 edition of *The Best American Short Stories*. He began publishing in the *New Yorker* around this time, and many of Taylor's best works originally appeared in this magazine.

In 1941, Taylor was drafted into the Army, when the United States abruptly entered World War II, and he served first in Georgia and later in England. He married poet Eleanor Ross while in the military. After his discharge from the service in 1945 and a brief stint with a New York publisher, the couple settled in North Carolina. While in North Carolina, Taylor taught at the Women's College of the University of North Carolina at Greensboro. During his Army years, he had continued to publish, and both he and his wife enjoyed growing literary reputations. His first book, *A Long Fourth*, appeared in 1948, the same year as the first of their two children. Taylor held a variety of teaching positions at prestigious universities over the course of his long career, including the University of Chicago, Harvard University, the University of Virginia, and the University of Georgia. He was also a founding member of the elite Fellowship of Southern Writers.

As a fiction writer, Taylor frequently returned to Tennessee, the home of his youth, as the source of his works, feeling as if he "knew that the South was what I was interested in, the only thing I knew about." In a 1987 interview, Taylor explained his attraction to the South as his primary subject: "The reason the South interests me primarily is that I think of it in terms of the family. I think this is the great loss to civilization, the death of the family. . . . The South was the place where the family still operated more than any other place in the country." Although his fiction seemingly romanticizes the South of bygone days, Taylor does not placate his readers with images of an inviolate South immune to the ravages of societal change, seeking instead to reassess the Southern experience. Yet at times, he exhibits the Southern tendency to revere the old ways and the inclination to define the boundaries of relationships and hierarchies, both geographically and socially. His examinations of the Old South revisit the complexities of racial and social caste and their implicit barriers.

The quality and quantity of Taylor's body of work unwittingly influenced the generation of writers that followed him—the third wave to evolve out of the Southern Renascence. Anne Tyler, the author of numerous novels including the award-winning *The Accidental Tourist*, commented in a review for *USA Today* that she was one of a number of then-fledgling writers who had "practically memorized all [Taylor] has produced," proclaiming him the "undisputed master of the short story form." Critic Jonathan Yardley offered similarly high praise when he compared Taylor to Eudora Welty, saying that the two authors stood alone among living writers in their production of "rich, durable and accessible" fiction. Not surprisingly, Taylor's substantial body of work led to a variety of prestigious awards, including the PEN/Faulkner award, the Ritz Hemingway Prize for fiction, and the O. Henry Memorial award. His novel, *A Summons to Memphis*, won the Pulitzer Prize and was also considered for the American Book Award in 1986, but Taylor withdrew the novel from consideration. Taylor succumbed to pneumonia in 1994 while living in Charlottesville, Virginia.

In the selection that follows, Taylor depicts the life of a politician who has sold out after proudly basing his career on honesty and integrity. Taylor shows the man alternately suffering the mental and physical symptoms of distress and reveling in his power in a sexualized way. As the story opens, he has checked into a motel, where he waits for his wife to join him so that they can attend an important political event. Their relationship is also irrevocably colored by the actions of the politician.

First Heat

He turned up the air conditioning and lay across the bed, wearing only his jockey shorts. But it didn't stop. Two showers already since he came in from the afternoon session! Showers had done no good. Still, he might take another presently if it continued. The flow of perspiration was quite extraordinary. Perhaps it was the extra sleeping pill he took last night. He had never been one to sweat so. It was rather alarming. It really was. And with the air conditioner going full blast he was apt to give himself pneumonia.

What he needed of course was a drink, and that was impossible. He was not going to have a single drink before she arrived. He was determined to be cold sober. She would telephone up from the desk—or from one of the house phones nearby. He always thought of her as telephoning directly from the desk. Somehow that made the warning more official. But she did always telephone, did so out of fear he might not have his regular room. So she said. He knew better, of course. Married for nearly fifteen years, and at home she still knocked on doors—on the door to his study, on the door to the bathroom, even on the door to their bedroom. She even had the children trained to knock on doors, even each other's doors. Couldn't she assume that since he knew she was on the way, knew she was by now wheeling along the Interstate—doing seventy-five and more in her old station wagon—couldn't she assume that whatever kind of fool, whatever kind of philanderer she might suspect him of being, he would have the sense to have set matters right by the time she got there? But what rot! As if he didn't *have* a problem, as if he needed to make one up!

He could hear his own voice in the Senate Chamber that afternoon. Not his words, just his guilty voice. Suddenly he got up off the bed, pulled back the spread, the blanket, the top sheet. He threw himself down on his back, stuck his legs in the air, and pulled off his shorts. They were wringing wet with his damnable perspiration! He wadded them into a ball and, still lying on his back, still holding his legs in the air, he hurled the underwear at the ceiling, where it made a faintly damp spot before falling to the carpeted floor. And she—she would already know what his voice in the Senate Chamber had said. (His legs still in the air.) And knowing how the voting went, know who betrayed whom, who let whom down, who let what bill that was supposed to go through intact be amended. It would all have been reported on the local six o'clock state news, perhaps even with his taped voice uttering the words of betrayal. She would have picked it up on the radio in the station wagon just after she set out, with her evening dress in a suitbox beside her. Maybe she would even have turned back, feeling she just couldn't face certain people at the mansion reception tonight . . . or couldn't face him.

Now—only now—he let his legs drop to the bed, his feet coming down wide apart on the firm, first-rate-hotel mattress. And he threw out his arms, one hand palm upward landing on each pillow of the double bed. He *would* relax, *would* catch a quick nap. But a new charge of sweat pressed out through every pore of his skin, on his forehead, on his neck, in the soft area just above his collarbone, from the exposed inner sides of his thighs and his ankles, from the exposed armpits and upper arms and forearms, from the palms of his hands and the soles of his feet. He felt he was aware of every infinitesimal modicum of sweat that was passing through every pore of every area of his body. Somehow it made him feel more utterly, thoroughly naked than he had ever before felt in his entire life. Yes, and this time the sweat came before the thought—just a little before the thought this time. The thought of what he had done and left undone concerning the amendment, said and left unsaid concerning the amendment, the thought of the discrepancy between his previously announced position and the position he finally took on the floor, all thought of *that* seemed something secondary and consequential to the sweat. Perhaps he was ill, really ill! Perhaps it was only a coincidence that this sickening sweat had come over his body. But no, he was not that sort—to claim illness. One thing for certain, though, the sweat was already like ice water on his skin.

Now he would have to get up and dry himself off again. There was a scratching sensation in his throat. He even coughed once. He would have to turn *down* the air conditioner. And he would have to find something else to focus his mind on. After all, he had not betrayed his country or his family. And not, God knew, his constituents. Was it only old man Nat Haley he was worrying about? He had agreed to support Nat Haley's waterways bill, had been quite outspoken in favor of it. The newspapers all over the state had quoted him. And then, yesterday, he had received promises from other sources, promises so much to the interest of his constituents that he could not resist. By God, it was the sort of thing he—*and* she—had known he would have to do if he stood for the legislature and got elected, the sort of thing he would have to face up to if he went into politics, where everybody had said *he* ought not to go. He and she had looked each other in the eye one day—before he ever announced—and said as much . . . Well, at the last minute he had agreed to support the very amendment which Nat Haley had said would be ruinous, would take all the bite out of his bill. But Nat Haley was, himself, the damnedest kind of double-dealer. Even *he* had observed that. Ah, he was beginning to know politics. And he was beginning to understand what "everybody" had meant. Old Nat Haley was well known for the deals he arranged and didn't live up to. Everyone knew about Nat Haley. Nat Haley wouldn't have hesitated to fight this bill itself if he had discovered, even at the last minute, that that was to his advantage.

Who, then, was he betraying? And it wasn't a bill of any great import, either.

He sat up and swung his feet over the side of the bed. His hand came down briefly on the moisture his body had left on the otherwise starchy hotel sheet. He glanced backward and saw the wet shadow of himself that his perspiration had left there, and he turned away from it. But as he turned away from his silhouette on the sheet, there he was, in all his nakedness, in the large rectangular mirror above the dresser. And there he was in the mirror on the open bathroom door. He reached to the floor and took up a bath towel he had dropped there earlier and began drying himself—and hiding himself. He stood up and went over his body roughly with the towel; then, his eyes lighting on the mirror on the bathroom door, he wadded up the towel, just as he had the jockey shorts, and hurled it at the door. It came right up against his face there! And when it had fallen, he realized that this time it wasn't—as so often—his face in the mirror that offended him. He didn't care about the face. He knew it too well and what its every line and look meant. The body interested him as never before, or as it had not in years. For a moment, it was like meeting someone from the past, someone he had almost forgotten—an old friend, and old enemy. It was—almost—a young man's body still; he was not forty yet and he exercised as much as he ever had and ate and drank with moderation. The body in the door mirror and in the large mirror over the dresser had good tone, was only a little heavier about the hips than it had once been, and the arm muscles were really better developed than when he was twenty. Taking in the different views he had of the body in the two mirrors he recalled that as late as his college days he had sometimes shadow-boxed before mirrors, usually wearing his ordinary boxer shorts and imagining they were made of silk, with his name, or some title, like *The Killer*, embroidered on them in purple or orange letters. He didn't smile over the recollection. But neither did he take any such stance before the mirrors now. The body in the mirrors was tense, as if prepared to receive a blow; and he looked at it objectively as a painter or a sculptor might, as a physician might. He observed features that particularized it: the modest island of dark hair on the chest, which narrowed into a peninsula pointing down below the navel and over the slightly rounded belly, almost joining the pubic hair above the too-innocent-looking penis; the elongated thighs; the muscular calves; the almost hairless arms; the shoulders, heavy and slightly stooped. Presently, his interest in himself seemed entirely anatomical. And all at once it was as though his eyes were equipped with X-rays. He could see beneath the skin and under the flesh to the veins and tendons and the ropelike muscles, the heart and lungs, the liver, the intestines, the testicles, as well as every bone and joint of the skeleton. And now it was as though a klieg light—no, a supernatural light—shone from behind him and through him. Only when at last he moved one foot, shifting his weight from one leg to the other, did the flesh and the covering skin return. Had it been a dream? A vision? It seemed to him now that he was not naked at all, or that this was not the nakedness he had sought when he removed his clothes. At any rate, his body had ceased to sweat.

He stepped back to the bed and lay down on his side, his back to the mirrors. He experienced momentary relief. It was as though he had seen beyond mere nakedness of body and spirit, had looked beyond all that which particularized him and made his body and his life meaningful, human. Was that the ultimate nakedness? Why, it could just as well have been old Nat Haley's insides he had seen. And he did relax now. He closed his eyes . . . But then it came on again. Only this time there was no sweat. There was just the explicit dread of that moment—soon now, soon—when he would open the door to her. And he thought of how other, older politicians would laugh at his agonizing over so small a matter. *They* would know what a mistake politics was for him. Or perhaps they would know that, like them, he was *made* for politics. Wasn't this merely his baptism—in betrayal? In politics the ends were what mattered, had to matter. In politics that was the only absolute. If you were loyal to other men, you were apt to betray your constituency. Or did he have it all backward? No, he had it right, he was quite sure. And for that very reason, wasn't the state Senate as far as he would go and farther than he should have gone? Friends had warned him against state politics especially. His father had said to him: "You are the unlikeliest-looking political candidate I have ever seen." But it was a decision she and he had made together, and together they had agreed that one's political morality could not always coincide with one's private morality. They had read that somewhere, hadn't they? At any rate, one had to be prepared to face up to that morality. . . . And now, though he felt chilled to the bone, the sweat came on again. He rolled over and reached for the towel on the floor, forgetting he had thrown it at the mirror. As he got off the bed, the same hand that had reached for the towel reached out to the wall and turned down the air conditioner. He went into the bathroom and got a dry towel and came back drying himself—or those two hands were drying him. He stopped before the long mirror on the bathroom door, the hands still drying him. He remembered something else his father had said to him once when they were on a fishing trip at Tellico Plains. He had gone for a swim in the river and stood on a rocky slab beside the water afterward, first rubbing his chest and his head with a towel and then fanning his body with it before and aft. His father, watching the way he was fanning himself with the towel, said, "You do cherish that body of yours, don't y'?" But what mistaken notions his father had always had about him. Or perhaps it was only wishful thinking on his father's part. Perhaps he had only *wished* that kind of concern for him. Ah, if only his body *had* been his great care and concern in life—his problem! And no doubt that's what his sweating meant! He *wished* it were only a bodily ill!

He wasn't, as a matter of fact, a man who was given to lolling about this way with no clothes on—either at home or in a hotel room. And it occurred to him now that it wasn't the sweat alone that had made him do so today. As soon as he had walked into the room and closed the door after him he had begun pulling off his clothes. It seemed to him almost that the sweat began *after* he had stripped off his clothes. But he couldn't definitely recall now whether it had begun before or after he got to the room. At any rate, he wasn't *sure* it had begun before. Had it? Else, why had he undressed at once? . . . He lay down on the bed again and his eye lit on the black telephone beside the bed. The first thing some men did when alone in a hotel room, he knew, was to take up the telephone and try to arrange for a woman to come up. Or that was what he always understood they did. The point was, he should have *known*. But he—he would hardly know nowadays how to behave with such a woman. He would hardly know what to say or do if one of those hotel creatures came into the room. Or would he know very well, indeed! Yes, how simple it all would be. What a great satisfaction, and how shameful it would seem afterward. How sinful—how clearly sinful—he would know himself to be. There the two of them are, in bed. But suddenly there comes a knock on the door! He will have to hide her. His wife is out there in the passage. The baby-sitter came a little early. And the traffic was not as bad as she had anticipated. With the new Interstate, a forty-mile drive is nothing. He has no choice. There isn't anything else he can do: he will have to hide the creature. She will have to stand naked, her clothes clutched in her arms, behind the drapery or in the closet, while he and his wife dress for the reception at the governor's mansion. If only—But the telephone, the real, black telephone was ringing now, there on the real bedside table.

He let it ring for thirty seconds or so. Finally, he took up the instrument. He said nothing, only lay on his side breathing into the mouthpiece.

"Hello," she said on the house phone. He could hear other voices laughing and talking in the lobby.

"Hello," he managed.

"I'm downstairs," she said, as she always said, waiting for him to invite her to come up. He invited her now, and she replied, "Is everything all right? You sound funny."

"Everything's fine. Come on up," he said. "You've heard the news?"

"I listened in the car, on the way over."

"I changed my mind about the bill," he said.

"Is Mr. Haley pretty angry?"

"He cut me cold on the Capitol steps afterward."

"I thought so," she said. "He was icy to me when I passed him in the lobby just now. Or I imagined he was."

"Do you still want to go to the reception?"

She laughed. "Of course I do. I'm sure you had good reasons."

"Oh, yes, I had good reasons."

"Then, shall I come on up?"

"Do," he said. But then he caught her before she hung up. "Wait," he said. He sat on the bed, pulling the sheet up about his hips. "Why don't you wait down there? Why don't we go somewhere and have a drink and something to eat before we dress for the reception? I'm starved."

"I'm starved, too," she said. "I had only a very small snack with the children at four-thirty."

"I'll be right down," he said.

"Well—" She hesitated and then said, "No, I have my dress with me in a box—my dress for tonight. I want to put it on a hanger. I'll be right up—that is, if you don't mind."

"Good," he said.

"And why don't we have our drink up there? It might be easier."

"Good," he said.

As soon as he had put down the telephone, he sprang from the bed, ran to pick up his sweaty shorts and the sweaty hotel towels. He began straightening the room and pulling on his clothes at the same time, with desperate speed. She must not find him undressed, this way. It would seem too odd. And if he should begin the sweating again, he was lost, he told himself. He would have to try to ignore it, but she would notice, and she would know . . . She would be on the elevator now, riding up with other members of the legislature and their wives, wives who had also come to town for the reception at the mansion. He felt utterly empty, as though not even those veins and tendons and bones and organs were inside him. Wearing only his shirt and fresh shorts and his black socks and supporters, he stopped dressing long enough to give the bed a haphazard making up. He yanked the sheet and blanket and spread about. Fluffed the pillows. But if only there were something besides his body, something else tangible to hide. Catching a glimpse of himself in the mirror, he blushed bashfully and began pulling on his trousers to cover his naked legs. While slipping his tie under his collar, he was also pushing his feet into his shoes. As he tied the necktie and then tied the shoe strings, he was listening for her footsteps in the passage. Oh, if only, if only—if only there were a woman, herself covered with sweat, and still—still panting, for him to hide. What an innocent, simple thing it would be. But there was only himself . . . When the knock came at the door, he was pulling on his jacket. "Just a second," he called. And for no reason at all, before opening the door he went to the glass-topped desk on which lay his open briefcase and closed the lid to the case, giving a quick snap to the lock. Then he threw open the door.

It was as though only a pair of blue eyes—bodiless, even lidless—hung there in the open doorway, suspended by invisible wires from the lintel. He read the eyes as he had not been able to read the voice on the telephone. They were not accusing. They had done their accusing in the car, no doubt, while listening to the radio. Now they were understanding and forgiving . . . He bent forward and kissed the inevitable mouth beneath the eyes. It too was understanding and forgiving. But if only the mouth and eyes would not forgive, not yet. He wanted their censure, first. She entered the room, with the suitbox under her arm, and went straight over to the closet. He held his breath, his eyes fixed on the closet door. She paused with her hand on the doorknob and looked back at him. Suddenly he understood the kind of sympathy she felt for him. Is it the lady or the tiger? her hesitation seemed to say. If only, she seemed to say with him, if only it *were* the lady, naked and clutching her bundle of clothing to her bosom. But he knew of course, as did she, it would be the tiger, the tiger whose teeth they had drawn beforehand, whose claws they had filed with their talk about the difference between things private and things political. The tiger was that very difference, that very discrepancy, and the worst of it was that they could never admit to each other again that the discrepancy existed. They stood facing each other well and fully clothed. When, finally, she would open the closet door, they would see only his formal evening clothes hanging there, waiting to be worn to the governor's mansion tonight. And while he looked over her shoulder, she would open the cardboard box and hang her full-length white evening gown beside his tuxedo. And after a while the tuxedo and the evening gown would leave the hotel room together and go down the elevator to the lobby and ride in a cab across town to the governor's mansion. And there was no denying that when the tuxedo and the evening gown got out of the taxi and went up the steps to the mansion and then moved slowly along in the receiving line, he and she, for better or for worse, would be inside them. But when the reception was over and the gown and the tuxedo came down the steps from the mansion, got into another taxi, and rode back across town to their empty hotel room, who was it that would be in them then? Who?

Questions to Consider

1. What causes the senator to break into a cold sweat? Why does this experience lead him to feel disembodied, yet more aware of his physicality at the same time? What does he find when he examines the inside of his body, underneath his skin?
2. What point does Taylor seem to be making about the difference between political and private morality? Why does this event in the senator's life make it impossible for him and his wife to discuss this difference ever again?

Ellen Douglas

1921–

Novelist Ellen Douglas frequently objects to the contemporary inclination to classify her as a Southern writer: "I think there are a great many things about the South that are still exceedingly individual," she says, "and that there is a world here to be seen by the individual writer as very specific, and crochety and idiosyncratic, and comical and tragic in its own way. And I think that's true in every part of the world, not just the South." Although Douglas rejects the moniker of Southern writer, she concedes that "that's where I come from. I can't but be influenced by small-town Southern life. That's what I know." Douglas recreates the small-town South in the fictional community of Homochitto, where the sensibilities of place, family, and propriety provide a foundation upon which stories of the troubled racial inheritance of the region, the ways in which family members relate among themselves and with outsiders, and the sexual roles foisted upon middle-class, White women may be examined. Although critics have described her fiction in terms ranging from "old-fashioned" to "postmodern" and "avante-garde," Charline McCord suggests that one of the significant strengths of Douglas's body of work is that "the voice is incredibly consistent throughout [her] work."

Born as Josephine Ayers on 12 July 1921 in Natchez, Mississippi, while her parents were visiting their families, she is the second daughter of Richardson Ayers, an MIT-educated engineer, and homemaker Laura Davis Ayers. Josephine grew up with two sisters, Anna and Archer, and a brother, John Richardson and spent the early years of her childhood in Hope, Arkansas, living on the same street where former president Bill Clinton would later live. The family moved to Alexandria, Louisiana, when the writer was ten and lived there until after she graduated from high school. Ayers earned a bachelor's degree in English literature and sociology from the University of Mississippi in 1942. She then married Kenneth Haxton in 1945 and bore three sons before they divorced.

Douglas taught for many years at the University of Mississippi but later moved to Jackson, Mississippi, where she presently resides. She also served for several years as writer-in-residence at Northeastern Louisiana University (now the University of Louisiana at Monroe), and filled a similar position at the University of Virginia for a semester. Most recently, she was awarded an honorary doctorate by the University of the South and spent a semester teaching in the prestigious Iowa Writer's Workshop.

Douglas's fiction frequently examines extended familial relationships as well as the family's collective identity, which defines the public face that each member presents to the community. Drawing heavily on the traditional family values of honor, integrity, and family name, Douglas's semiautobiographical first novel, *A Family's Affairs,* traces the lives of a multigenerational family focusing on important events in the life of its matriarch, Kate Anderson. The relationships between siblings, married couples, and in-laws are scrutinized in this novel, but the primary focus falls on the women of the family, which, by the novel's end, include three generations. Douglas refrains from intruding into the narrative to comment on the quality of the interactions between her characters, yet she infuses her women with common sense, emotional fortitude, and physical strength that match their good breeding. Such characterizations reflect the author's perception of women's roles in general: "I have tended always to think of women as being realists and less likely to delude themselves," she once remarked in an interview. "It is essential for them not to delude themselves in order to survive. That's a quality that's possibly truer in the South than in other parts of the country because there are so many illusions and delusions here that women have to skirt their way around. Survival is essential in order to deal with the sort of ideas that are being promulgated by the Southern man." For these characters, survival, not surprisingly, often comes at the cost of self-sacrifice and self-denial.

Douglas also examines the implicit racial and class hierarchies of the South, showing the pervasiveness of racism, especially among those who believe they have overcome it. "I Just Love Carrie Lee" is narrated from the perspective of a privileged White woman. The narrator believes herself to be enlightened about racial issues, but her entire narrative, in fact, demonstrates just the opposite. For example, she boasts that she pays her gardener even in the winter, shaming a "Yankee" neighbor for not considering the well-being of their workers. She repeatedly proclaims that Carrie Lee is just like one of the family, yet her comments belie the unconscious paternalism that motivates her. Douglas addresses the incipient racism of the region in much of her fiction, looking closely at those who believe that they have transcended the racist heritage of the region and frequently disclosing that they are, in fact, guilty of an equally insidious and destructive form of the social disease.

Under the pen name Ellen Douglas, the author has published two collections of short stories and six novels. She decided to assume the pseudonym at the request of two of her aunts. *A Family's Affairs* was loosely based on their experiences, and while they gave their blessing to publish the novel, they did so with two requests: that the family name not be used and that they never be asked to read the book. *A Family's Affairs* won critical notice from the *New York*

Times, whose editors named the novel one of the ten best fiction titles of the year; *Black Cloud, White Cloud* won the same accolades when it appeared in 1963. Douglas's novel, *Apostles of Light* (1973), was nominated for the National Book Award, and she was honored with the Hillsdale Award for Fiction by the Fellowship of Southern Writers. She is also a two-time recipient of the Literature Award from the Mississippi Institute of Arts and Letters and has received fellowship support from the National Endowment for the Humanities.

I Just Love Carrie Lee

All the time we were away from here, living in Atlanta, I paid Carrie Lee's wages—seven dollars a week for eight years. Of course, part of the time, after Billy married and came back to Homochitto, she was working for him in the country. She rides the bus to Wildwood, seven miles over the river, every day. I don't know why she doesn't move back over there, but she likes to live in town. She owns her own house and she likes to visit around. The truth of the matter is, she thinks she might miss something if she moved over the river; and besides, she never has had any use for "field niggers." (That's Carrie Lee talking, not me.) Anyway, as I was saying, I did pay her wages all those years we were away from here. I knew Mama would have wanted me to, and besides, I feel the same responsibility toward her that Mama did. You understand that, don't you? She was our responsibility. So few people think that way nowadays. Nobody has the feeling for Negroes they used to have. People look at me as if they think I'm crazy when I say I paid Carrie Lee all that time.

I remember when I first had an inkling how things were changing. It was during the Depression when the Edwardses moved next door to us. They were Chicago people, and they'd never had any dealings with Negroes. Old Mrs. Edwards expected the baseboards to be scrubbed every week. I suppose she scrubbed them herself in Chicago. Oh, I don't mean there was anything wrong with her. She was a good, hard-working Christian soul; and *he* was a cut above *her*. I've heard he came from an old St. Louis family. But a woman sets the tone of a household, and her tone was middle-western to the marrow. All her children said "come" for "came," and "I want in," and I had a time keeping mine from picking it up.

To make a long story short, she came to me one day in the late fall and asked me what the yardmen in Homochitto did in the winter.

"What do you mean?" I said.

"I mean where do they work?"

"Well," I said, "mine sits around the kitchen and shells pecans and polishes silver all winter."

"You mean you keep him on when there's actually nothing for him to do?" she said.

"He *works* for us," I said. "He's been working for us for years."

"I haven't got that kind of money," she said. "I had to let mine go yesterday, and I was wondering where he would get a job."

I tried to explain to her how things were down here, how you couldn't let a man go in the winter, but she didn't understand. She got huffy as could be.

"I suppose that's what you call *noblesse oblige*," she said.

"You could, if you wanted to be fancy," I said.

And do you know what she said to me? She said, "They're not going to catch me in that trap, the *Nee*-grows. I can do all my own work and like it, if it comes to that. I'm going to stand on my rights."

They didn't stay in Homochitto long.

Wasn't that odd? Everyone is like that nowadays. Maybe not for such a queer reason, but no one feels any responsibility any more. No one cares, white or black.

That's the reason Carrie Lee is so precious to us. She cares about us. She knows from experience what kind of people we are. It's a boon in this day and age just to be recognized.

The truth of the matter is I couldn't tell you what Carrie Lee has meant to us. She's been like a member of the family for almost fifty years. She raised me and she's raised my children. Ask Sarah and Billy, Carrie Lee was more of a mother to them than I was. I was too young when I first married to be saddled with children, and too full of life to stay at home with them. Bill was always on the go, and I wouldn't have let him go without me for anything. It was fortunate I could leave the children with Carrie Lee and never have a moment's worry. She loved them like they were her own, and she could control them without ever laying a hand on them. She has her own philosophy, and while *I* don't always understand it, children do.

Carrie Lee is a bright Negro—both ways, I mean, and both for the same reason, I reckon. I don't know exactly where the white blood came from (it's not the kind of thing they told young ladies in my day), but I can guess. Probably an overseer. Her mama was lighter than she, and married a dark man. The old mammy, Carrie Lee's grandmother, was black as the ace of spades, so Mama said. I judge some overseer on Grandfather's place must have been Carrie Lee's grandfather. She has always said she has Indian blood, too, said her mama told her so. But how much truth there is in that I don't know. The hawk nose and high cheekbones look Indian, all right, and there is something about her—maybe that she won't make a fool of herself to entertain you. You know she's different. And she could put the fear of God into the children, like a Cherokee chief out after their scalps.

Billy says Carrie Lee taught him his first lesson in getting along with people. He was the youngest boy in the neighborhood, and of course the other children made him run all their errands; they teased and bullied him unmercifully until he was big enough to stand up for himself. This is the kind of thing they'd do. One day in the middle of my mah-jongg club meeting, he came running in the house crying. Some of the children had mixed up a mess of coffee grounds and blackberry jam and tried to make him eat it. It was an initiation. They formed a new club every week or two and Billy was the one they always initiated.

"Mama's busy, honey," I said. "Tell it to Carrie Lee. She'll tend to 'em for you."

Carrie Lee took him on her lap like a baby and rocked him and loved him until he stopped crying, and then he sat up and said. "But Carrie Lee, who am I going to play with? Everybody's in the club but me."

And she said, "Honey, they bigger than you. If you wants to play, you gits on out there and eats they pudding. If you don't like it, you holds it in your mouth and spits it out when they ain't looking."

"But s'pose they feed me more than I can hold in my mouth?" he said.

"Honey, if they does, you got to make your mouth stretch," she said.

Billy has never forgotten that.

Carrie Lee came to work for Mama when she was fourteen years old. She was only a child, it's true, but even then she had more sense than most grown Negroes. Mama had seen her on their place outside Atlanta and taken a fancy to her. *Her* mother (Carrie Lee's, I mean) cooked for the manager's family there, and Carrie Lee was already taking care of five or six younger brothers and sisters while the mother was at work. You can imagine what it meant to her to come to town. Mama clothed her and fed her and made a finished servant of her. Why, she even saw to it that Carrie Lee went to school through the fifth grade; she'd never been able to go more than a couple of terms in the country. Fifty years ago, practically none of the Negroes went more than a year or two, if that long. When they were seven or eight, they either went to the field or stayed at home to nurse the younger ones.

By the time we moved to Homochitto, Mama couldn't have gotten along without Carrie Lee, and so she came with us. At first Mama was miserable here—homesick for Georgia and her own family and the social life of Atlanta. Compared to Atlanta, Homochitto then was nothing but a village. And the weather! We had never been through a Mississippi summer before, or, for that matter, a Georgia summer; we'd always gone to the mountains—Monteagle, or White Sulphur Springs, or some place like that. But that first year in Homochitto Papa couldn't leave, and Mama got in one of her stubborn spells and wouldn't go without him. To tell you the truth, I think she wanted him to see her suffer, so he'd take her back to Atlanta. She used to say then that no one understood how she felt except Carrie Lee. And I suppose it's true that Carrie Lee missed her family too, in spite of the hard life she'd had with them. In the mornings she and Mama would sit in the kitchen peeling figs or pears or peaches, or washing berries, preserving together, and Carrie Lee would tell stories to entertain Mama. I'd hang around and listen. I remember one day Carrie Lee had said something 'specially outrageous, and Mama said, "Carrie Lee, I don't believe half you say. Why do you make up those awful tales?"

Carrie Lee stopped peeling pears and began to eat the peelings. She always did eat the peelings when they were preserving, everything except figs—a hangover from hungry days, I reckon. She hushed talking a minute, eating and thinking, and then she looked at Mama and said:

> To keep us from the lonely hours,
> And being sad so far from home.

It was just like a poem. I had to get up and run out of the house to keep them from seeing me cry. Do you suppose she understood what she'd said and how beautifully she'd said it? Or is it something about language that comes to them as naturally as sleeping—and music?

When Mama died, I felt as if she had more or less left Carrie Lee to me, and I've been taking care of her ever since. Oh, she's no burden. There's no telling *how* much money she has in the bank. There she is, drawing wages from Billy and from me, owns her own house and rents out a room, nobody to spend it on but herself and one step-daughter, and she never has to spend a dime on herself. Between us, Sarah and I give her everything she wears; and as for her house, every stick she has came out of our old house.

When we sold the house, after Mama died, Carrie Lee took her pick of what was left. Of course, I had gotten all the good pieces—the things that were bought before the war—but she wouldn't have wanted them anyway; nothing I chose would have suited her taste. She has a genius for the hideous. She took the wicker porch chairs—

you know, the kind with fan backs and magazine racks in the arms and trays hooked onto the sides for glasses—and painted them blue and put them in her living room; and she took a set of crocheted table mats that Mama made years ago. (They were beautiful things, but if you've ever had a set, you know what a nuisance they are. Not a washwoman in Homochitto does fine laundering any more, and *I* certainly wouldn't wash and starch and stretch them *myself*. And besides, where would anyone in a small apartment like this keep those devilish boards with nails in them, that you have to stretch them on?) Anyway, Carrie Lee took those place mats and put them on the wicker chairs like antimacassars, if you can believe it. But that's just the beginning. All the junk collected by a houseful of pack rats like Bill's family—the monstrosities they acquired between 1890 and 1930 would be something to read about. And Bill and Mama had stored everything in Mama's attic when Bill sold his father's house in 1933. Why, I couldn't say, except that Bill always hated to throw anything away. That's a trait that runs in his family: they hang on to what they have. And if his father hadn't hung on to Wildwood during hard times and good, where would we be now?

Fortunately, he did hang on to it, and to everything else *his* father left him. You know, Bill's family didn't have the hard time most people had after the Civil War. His grandfather started the little railroad line from Homochitto to Jackson that was eventually bought by the Southern. He was a practical businessman and he didn't sit back like so many people, after we were defeated, and let his property get away from him out of sheer outrage. And so, the family was able to travel and to buy whatever was stylish at the time. Carrie Lee loved everything they bought, and she has as much of it as she can squeeze into her house: heavy golden oak sideboard and table, a fine brass bed polished up fit to blind you, a player piano that doesn't work, with a Spanish shawl draped over it, and on the walls souvenir plates from Niagara Falls and the St. Louis Exposition, and pictures of Mama and me and the children, sandwiched in between pictures of all her sisters and brothers and their families. It's too fine.

Actually, there are some people around here who disapprove of Carrie Lee and me; but as far as I'm concerned they can say what they like. I just love Carrie Lee and that's all there is to it. When she comes to call, she sits in the parlor with the white folks. She has good sense about it. If she's in the house on Sunday afternoon visiting with me, and guests come, she goes to the door and lets them in as if she were working that day, and then she goes back to the kitchen and fixes coffee and finds an apron and serves us. Everything goes smoothly. She knows how to make things comfortable for everybody. But half the time, whoever it is, I wish they hadn't come. I'd rather visit with Carrie Lee.

And people who talk about it don't know what they're saying. They don't know how I feel. When Bill died (that was only a year after Mama died, and there I was, left alone with a houseful of *babies* to raise and all that property to manage), who do you think walked down the aisle with me and sat with me at the funeral? Carrie Lee. If I hadn't been half crazy with grief, I suppose I might have thought twice before I did a thing like that. But I did it, and I wouldn't have let anyone prevent me.

Weddings are a different matter, of course. If you have them at home, it's no problem; the colored folks are all in the kitchen anyhow, and it's easy enough for them to slip in and see the ceremony. I know Winston and Jimmy and the ones we've known for years who turn up at weddings and big parties would *rather* stay in the kitchen. Jimmy takes charge of the punch bowl and sees that all the help stay sober enough to serve, at least until the rector goes home.

But it's not customary in Homochitto to include the servants at a church wedding. There's no balcony in the Episcopal church like the slave gallery in the Presbyterian church, and so there's no place to seat them. I couldn't do anything about that at Sarah's wedding; I just had to leave the rest of the servants out, but we did take Carrie Lee to the church.

I'll never forget how she behaved; if she'd been the mama, she couldn't have been more upset.

Sarah was only nineteen, too young, way too young to marry. To tell you the truth I was crushed at the time. I never, *never* thought any good would come of it. Oh, I realize I was even younger when I married. But in my day young ladies were brought up for marriage, and marriages were made on other terms, terms I understood. Bill was nearly thirty when we married, and he had exactly the same ideas Papa had. He simply finished my education. Which proves my contention—that a woman is old enough to marry when she has sense enough to pick the right man. If she doesn't, she isn't ready. That's the way it was with Sarah.

Wesley was just a boy—a selfish, unpredictable boy. He never understood how sheltered Sarah had been, how little she knew of the world, how indulgent we had been with her as a child, how totally unprepared she was for—for him. And afterwards she said it was all my fault. That's children for you. But I hadn't meant to prepare her for *Wesley*. I wouldn't have had him!

To go back to the wedding, Carrie Lee rode to the church with Sarah, and put the finishing touches on her hair and arranged her train. I didn't see this because of course I was sitting in the front of the church, but the people in the back said when Sarah and Brother George started down the aisle, Carrie Lee ran after them, straightening Sarah's train, the tears streaming down her face. I believe she would have followed them to the altar, but Edwin Ware slipped out of his pew and got her to go back. She was crying like a child, saying, "My baby. She's *my baby*."

You'd never have known she had children of her own the way she worshiped mine—still does.

But she had a married interlude. She was too old to carry a child; she had two miscarriages and lost one shortly after it was born. But she raised two or three of her husband's children. Negroes are so funny. Even Carrie Lee, as well as I know her, surprises me sometimes. She turned up at work one morning just as usual. (She never came until ten-thirty, and then stayed to serve supper and wash the dishes at night.) Bertie, who was cooking for me then, had been muttering and snickering to herself in the kitchen all morning, and, when I came in to plan dinner, she acted like she had a cricket down her bosom.

"What in the world are you giggling and wiggling about, Bertie?" I said.

Bertie *fell* out.

Carrie Lee, forty if she was a day, stood there glowering. "You know Bertie, Miss Emma," she said. "Bertie's crazy as a road lizard."

Bertie pointed her finger at Carrie Lee and then she sort of hollered out, "She *ma'ied*, Miss Emma! She ma'ied."

You could have knocked me over with a feather. I didn't even know she was thinking about it. "Are you really, Carrie Lee?" I said.

"Yes'm."

"Well, Carrie Lee!" I said. "My feelings are hurt. Why didn't you tell us ahead of time. We could have had a fine wedding—something special."

I *was* disappointed, too. I've always wanted to put on a colored wedding, and *there*, I'd missed my chance.

Carrie Lee didn't say a word. I never *have* been able to figure out why she didn't tell us beforehand.

And then that nitwit, Bertie, began to laugh and holler again. "She don't need no special wedding, Miss Emma," Bertie said. "Ain't nothing special about getting ma'ied to Carrie Lee."

I was tickled at that, but I was surprised, too. Oh, I'm not so stupid that I don't understand how different Negro morals are from ours. Most of them simply don't have any. And I understand that it all comes from the way things were in slavery times. But our family was different. Grandmother told me many a time that they always went to a lot of trouble with the slave weddings and, after the war, with the tenants'. She kept a wedding dress and veil for the girls to wear, and she made sure everything was done right—license, preacher, reception, and all the trimmings. There was no jumping the broomstick in our family. And Carrie Lee's people had been on our place for generations. I never would have thought she'd carry on with a man.

She seemed devoted to her husband. If she had carried on with one, she must have carried on with others, but I reckon she'd had her fling and was ready to retire. The husband, Henry, was a "settled man," as they say, fifteen years older than Carrie Lee, and had a half-grown son and daughter and two or three younger children. He farmed about thirty acres of Wildwood. I had known the family ever since we moved to Homochitto. (Can you imangine that—my own place, and I didn't know about him and Carrie Lee!)

Later on, shortly before he died, he managed with Carrie Lee's help to buy a little place of his own.

I always let Carrie Lee off at noon on Saturday and gave her all day Sunday, although I hated running after the children. When they got old enough to amuse themselves, it wasn't so bad, but when they were little . . . ! Usually I got Bertie to take over for me. But I never believed in working a servant seven days a week, even when everybody did it, when they were lucky to get Emancipation Day and the Fourth of July. I never treated a servant like that. Bertie had her day off, too.

Henry would be waiting for Carrie Lee in his buggy when she got off on Saturday, and they'd catch the ferry across the river and drive out to Wildwood; and early Monday morning he'd send his son to drive her in to town—it was a couple of hours ride in the buggy. She didn't want to sell her house and move to the country (thank God!) and Henry wouldn't move to town. As Carrie Lee said, he didn't know nothing but farming, and he wasn't fixing to change his ways.

Once in a while she'd take the children to the country with her on Saturday afternoon, and I'd drive over after supper to get them. Every Saturday they begged to go; it was the greatest treat in the world to them to ride to Wildwood in the buggy, and they were crazy about the old man. For a while I kept their horses there, and when Billy was older he used to go over there to hunt. Henry taught him everything he knows about hunting. That was before cotton-dusting killed all the quail in this part of the country.

Well, Carrie Lee lived like that until we moved back to Atlanta, riding to the country every Saturday afternoon and coming in at daybreak on Monday morning. It's hard to understand how anyone could be satisfied with such a life, but Carrie Lee has a happy nature, and of course the fact that she was so much better off financially than most Negroes made a difference. Besides, I wouldn't be surprised if she wasn't glad to have the peace and quiet of a single life during the week. You might say she had her cake and ate it too.

Then I left Homochitto for several years. It's the only time Carrie Lee and I have ever been separated for more than a month or two.

I'd always heard Mama talk about Atlanta; she kept after Papa to go back, right up to his dying day. I'd been too young when we moved to care, but later, after Mama and Bill died, I got the notion that someday I'd go back. So finally, I went. The children were away at school, Billy at Episcopal High and Sarah at Ardsley Hall, and there was no reason for me to stay in Homochitto.

I thought of course Carrie Lee would go with me, but she didn't. For all her talk in Mama's day about how she missed Georgia, she didn't go back. She stayed with Henry. And, as I told you, I paid her wages all the time I was gone. We wrote to each other, and we saw each other when I brought the children to Homochitto for a visit. They never got used to Atlanta and never wanted to stay there in the summer. Then Billy settled in Homochitto and began to farm Wildwood himself, and I came home.

I wish I had kept some of Carrie Lee's letters. She has a beautiful hand. She used to practice copying Mama's script, and finally got so you could hardly tell them apart. It always gives me a turn to get a letter from her, addressed in Mama's hand, and then, inside, what a difference! When she writes something she thinks will amuse me, she puts "smile" after it in parentheses. Did you know that practically all Negroes do that, even the educated ones? I sometimes see pictures of all the ones that are so much in the news nowadays—diplomats and martyrs and so forth, and I wonder if they put (smile) in their letters.

Carrie Lee used to advise me in her letters, where she would never do such a thing face to face. Like one time, I remember, she wrote me, "All the babies is gone, yours and mine. I writes Miss Sarah and Mr. Billy and they don't answer me. True, I got the old man's kids, but you haven't got none. When will you get married again, Miss Emma? Find you a good man to warm your bed." And then she wrote (smile)—to make sure I understood she wasn't being impudent, I reckon.

It was while I was living in Atlanta that Carrie Lee got her picture in the magazine. I never quite understood how it happened, unless through ignorance on all sides—ignorance on the part of the photographer about Carrie Lee's real circumstances, and ignorance on her part about what the photographer wanted. We all laughed about it afterwards, although, of course, I never mentioned it to Carrie Lee.

When we left Homochitto, she had moved over to Wildwood and rented her house in town. That's how they saved enough money for the old man to buy a place of his own. I think she gave him every cent she made. But they had their pictures taken the winter before they bought the place, the last winter they were on Wildwood.

I'll never forget how shocked I was. I had gone out for dinner and bridge one night, and was quietly enjoying a drink when one of the men at the party picked up a copy of *Life* or *Fortune* or one of those magazines.

"By the way," he said to me, "I was reading about your old stamping ground today."

I might have known he was teasing me. None of those magazines ever has anything good to say about Mississippi. But I was interested in news of Homochitto, and never thought of that; and of course *he* didn't know it was Carrie Lee. I sat there while he found the article, and there she was—there they all were, Carrie Lee, Henry, and all the children, staring at me practically life-sized from a full-page picture.

The article was on sharecropping, and *they* were the examples of the downtrodden sharecropper. I must admit they looked seedy. I recognized my dress on Carrie

Lee and one of Sarah's on the little girl. They were standing in a row outside the old man's house, grinning as if they knew what it was all about. At least, all of them except Carrie Lee were grinning. She's not much of a grinner.

A November day in the South—the trees bare and black, the stubble still standing in the cotton fields, an unpainted Negro cabin with the porch roof sagging, half a dozen dirty, ragged Negro children, and a bedraggled hound. What more could a Northern editor have asked?

What will these children get for Christmas?

I could have told him what they'd get for Christmas, and who had bought the presents and sent them off just the day before. And I could have told him whose money was accumulating in the teapot on the mantelpiece.

To do them justice, I'll say I don't believe Carrie Lee or Henry had the faintest idea why he'd taken their pictures. They just liked to have their pictures taken. But the very idea of them as poverty-stricken, downtrodden tenants! I couldn't have run them off Wildwood with a posse and a pack of bloodhounds.

We got a big kick out of it. I cut the picture out and sent it to Sarah.

The old man died the year after they began to buy their farm, and then Carrie Lee moved to town, and shortly after that I came back to Homochitto for good. Henry, Jr., took over the payments on the farm and lives on it. He's a sullen Negro—not like his father—but he's good to Carrie Lee. In the summer he keeps her supplied with fresh vegetables; he comes in and makes repairs on her house to save her the price of a carpenter; things like that. But he's sullen. I never have liked these Negroes who're always kowtowing and grinning like idiots—"white folks' niggers," some people down here call them—but it wouldn't hurt that boy to learn some manners. I told Carrie Lee as much one time.

I had gone into the kitchen to see about dinner, and he was sitting at the table with his hat on—this was after we moved back here, and old Henry was dead—eating his breakfast—*my* food, need I add. He didn't even look at me, much less get up.

"Good morning, Henry," I said.

He mumbled something and still didn't get up.

"*Good morning, Henry*," I said again.

"Morning," he said, just as sullen as he could be.

I went to Carrie Lee later and told her that any man, black, white, blue, or green, could get up and take off his hat when a lady came into the room. That's not prejudice. That's good manners.

"He ain't *bad*, Miss Emma," she said. "Just seems like he always got one misery or another. Born to trouble, as the sparks fly upward, like the Good Book says."

"Well, he'd feel a lot better, if he'd get a smile on that sullen face of his," I said. "Sometimes people bring trouble on themselves just by their dispositions."

"Ah, Miss Emma," she said, "ever since he married, it's been *root, hog, or die* for Henry, Jr. He ain't settled into it yet."

Of course, I didn't know then about the boy's sister, Carrie Lee's stepdaughter. Didn't know she had left Homochitto, much less that she had come back. She apparently married and moved to "*Dee*-troit" while we were living in Atlanta. I didn't see her until some time after she came to live in town with Carrie Lee, just a few years ago. Henry, Jr., finally had to turn her over to Carrie Lee. I can't blame him for *that*, I don't suppose. By then he had five children of his own, and there was scarcely room for them in the house, much less the sister.

I found out about the sister because Sarah left Wesley. That was a hard year. Sarah packed up the children and everything she owned and came home from Cleveland, inconsolable. I suppose I could have said, "I told you so," but I didn't have the heart. She'd married too young, there's no getting around it, and by the time she was old enough to know her own mind, there she was with two children. I tell you, people say to me: "You don't know how lucky you are that Bill left you so well-fixed. Never any money problems." They don't know how wrong they are. Money's a preoccupying worry. It keeps your mind off worse things. If you don't have to work or to worry about money, you're free to worry more about yourself and your children. Believe me, *nobody's* exempt from disappointment. I'm *proud* of the way I've raised my children. I've taught them everything I know about good manners and responsibility and honor, and I've kept their property safe for them. I've tried to give them everything that my family and Bill gave me. But when love fails you, none of it is any use. Your bed is soft and warm, but one dark night you find that sleep won't come.

I was half crazy over Sarah. She slept until noon every day and moped around the house all afternoon. Then she'd start drinking and keep me up till all hours crying and carrying on. "What am I going to do? What am I going to do?"

She still loved that good-for-nothing man.

I borrowed Carrie Lee from Billy to take care of Sarah's babies while she was here. I'm too old to chase a two-year-old child, and Sarah hardly looked at the children. She was too busy grieving over Wesley. So Carrie Lee was a boon; she took over, and we never had a minute's concern for them. Like all children, they adored her.

Billy's wife was furious with me for taking her, but I simply had to. And Carrie Lee was in seventh heaven, back with Sarah and me; she never has gotten along too well with Billy's wife. Oh, she goes out there faithfully, on account of Billy and the children. But Billy's wife is different from us—a different breed of cat, altogether, there's no getting around it. I get along fine with her because I mind my own business, but Carrie Lee considers our business her business. And then too, as I said, Carrie Lee is a *finished* servant. She has run my house for months at a time without a word of direction from me. She can plan and put on a formal dinner for twelve without batting an eye. Billy's wife doesn't know anything about good servants. She tells Carrie Lee every day what she wants done that day; and she insulted her, the first time she had a party, by showing her how to set the table.

No doubt there are two sides to the story. I'm sure Billy's wife gets sick of hearing Carrie Lee say, "But Miss Emma don't do it that way." It must be like having an extra mother-in-law. I won't go into that. I know it's the style nowadays not to get along with your mother-in-law, although I don't see why. I never had a breath of trouble with mine.

But I'm wandering again. I want to tell you the wonderful thing Carrie Lee said when she was telling us about her step-daughter.

The children were taking their naps one afternoon, and Sarah and I were lying down in my room and Carrie Lee was sitting in there talking to us. Sarah was still thrashing around about Wesley. The truth is she wanted to go back to him. She was hollering to Carrie Lee about how he'd betrayed her and how she could never forgive him—just asking somebody please to find her a good reason why she should forgive him, if the truth be known. But I wasn't going to help her; I knew it would never work.

Carrie Lee listened a while and thought about it a while and then she said, "Miss Sarah, honey, you know I got a crazy child?"

That took the wind out of Sarah's sails, and she sat up and stopped crying and said, "What?"

I was surprised, too. I didn't know a thing about that crazy girl. When I thought about it, I remembered that Carrie Lee had mentioned her to me once or twice, but at the time I hadn't paid any attention.

"I got a crazy child," Carrie Lee says. "Least, she ain't exactly my child, she old Henry's. But she *sho* crazy."

"I didn't know that, Carrie Lee," I said. "Where does she stay?"

"She stay with me," Carrie Lee says. "Right there in the house with me. Neighbors tend to her in the daytime. I ain't had her with me long—no more than a year or two."

"Well, what do I care? What's it got to do with me?" Sarah said, and she began to cry again. She wasn't herself, or she wouldn't have been so mean.

"This what," Carrie Lee says. "You know why she crazy? A man driv her crazy, that's why. You don't watch out, a man gonna drive you crazy."

Sarah lay back on the bed and kicked her feet like a baby.

"Honey, you want me to tell you how to keep a man from driving you crazy? And not only a man. Howsomever it happens, the day comes when one of God's creatures, young or old, is bound to break your heart. I'll tell you how to bear it."

Sarah shook her head.

"I'm gonna tell you anyhow. Look at me. I'm sixty years old. I looks forty-five. No man never driv me crazy, nor nobody else. I tell you how I keep him from it."

Sarah couldn't help it. She sat up and listened.

"See everything, see nothing," says Carrie Lee. "Hear everything, hear nothing. Know everything, know nothing. Trust in the Lord and love little children. That's how to ease your heart."

Did you ever? Well sir, maybe Sarah would have gone anyway, or maybe she heeded Carrie Lee's advice. Anyway, she took the two children soon afterwards and went back to Wesley, and it wasn't until three years later that they got a divorce.

So here we are, Carrie Lee and I, getting old. You might say we've spent our lives together. I reckon I know her better than I would have known my own sister, if I had had one. As Carrie Lee would say, "We've seen some wonderful distressing times."

On Sundays, when she's off, lots of times she bakes me a cake and brings it around and we sit and talk of the old days when Mama and Bill were alive and when the children were little. We talk about the days of the flood, about this year's crop, about the rains in April, and in August the dry weather, about Billy's wife, and Sarah and Billy's grown-up troubles, about the grandchildren, and "all the days we've seen."

If she comes to see me on Sunday, Carrie Lee will tell me something that amuses me the whole week long. Like a couple of weeks ago we were talking about the crop. I'd been worrying all summer about the drought. It looked for a while as if Billy wouldn't make a bale to the acre. And every time I mentioned it to Carrie Lee, she'd say, "Trust in the Lord, Miss Emma." She's still a great one for leaving things to the Almighty.

Then, bless John, the cotton popped open, and, in spite of everything, it's a good year.

"Well, Carrie Lee," I said, "it looks like you were right and I was wrong. Billy's got a fine crop."

And Carrie Lee says (just listen to this), she says, "Miss Emma, if I say a chicken dips snuff, you look under his bill."

Isn't that killing? When I got by myself, I just hollered.

Looking at it another way, though, it isn't so funny. Billy's a man, and a son is never the companion to his mother that a daughter is. You know the old saying, "A son is a son till he gets him a wife, but a daughter's a daughter all of her life." I think if his father had lived, if there were a man in the house, Billy would come to see me more often. If Sarah were here, we would enjoy each other, I know; but she's married again and lives so far away, they seldom come home, and when they do, it's only for a few days.

I've never been a reader, either. I like to visit, to *talk*. I'm an articulate person. And nowadays, instead of visiting, people sit and stare at a television set. Oh, I still play cards and mah-jongg. I have friends here, but we drifted apart during the years I was in Atlanta, and things have never been quite the same since I came back.

So I'm often alone on Sunday afternoon when Carrie Lee comes to see me. That's how it happens we sit so long together, drinking coffee and talking. Late in the afternoon, Billy sometimes comes and brings the children to call, but they never stay for long. They go home to Wildwood because Billy's wife doesn't like to be there alone after dark. Carrie Lee stays on, and we go in the kitchen and she fixes my supper. As I've told you, I'd rather visit with her than with most white folks. She understands me. When I think about it, it sometimes seems to me, with Bill and Mama dead and the children grown and gone, that Carrie Lee is all I have left of my own.

Questions to Consider

1. In what ways do the narrator's protestations about how well she treats Carrie Lee demonstrate her latent, yet virulent, racism?
2. Why do you think Douglas chooses to relate this story from the point of view of the privileged White woman? How might this story have differed if the narrator had been Carrie Lee herself?

James Dickey
1923–1997

The facts about James Lafayette Dickey's birth can be trusted. Once Dickey began to speak and to provide others with "information" about himself, however, facts became more difficult to separate from fiction. He was born on 2 February 1923 in Buckhead, Georgia, to a wealthy attorney named Eugene Dickey and his wife, Maibelle Swift Dickey. James Dickey would later claim that an older brother named Eugene, Jr., had died of meningitis in early childhood, and that he himself had been conceived as a "replacement child" for the boy, despite the risk to his invalid mother's health. The "lost brother" would be a significant theme of Dickey's later poetry.

Dickey enrolled at Clemson A & M College (now Clemson University) in the fall of 1942 but left after one semester to join the United States Air Force in the midst of World War II. According to Dickey and various critical sources that relied on his word, he flew more than one hundred combat missions in the South Pacific with the 418th Night Fighter Squadron between 1943 and 1945. According to Dickey's latest biographer, Henry Hart, however, Dickey never flew a plane in combat. Likewise, Dickey portrayed himself as having been a freshman football star at Clemson and a track star at Vanderbilt University, which he attended after the war, whereas Hart describes Dickey as an indifferent athlete. No one disputes that Dickey was a notorious truth-bender, nor that he was also an immensely talented and influential poet.

Having married and received a B.A. in English from Vanderbilt, Dickey went on to pursue an M.A. from the same institution, writing his thesis on symbolism in Herman Melville's poetry. Dickey himself had begun to write poetry not long before: Vanderbilt was an inspirational place for it, having been the locus of the Fugitive movement in Southern poetry in the 1920s. Following receipt of his master's degree, Dickey taught college English, was recalled to active military duty during the Korean War, and then resumed teaching. After having to defend his poetry from obscenity allegations at the University of Florida in 1956, he left teaching for a successful career in advertising, first in New York City and then in Atlanta. But he continued to write poetry and began to win prizes for it. In 1960, when *Into the Stone and Other Poems* was accepted by Scribners for inclusion in its "Poets of Today" series, Dickey quit his advertising job. Following a year in Italy on a Guggenheim Foundation grant, he began teaching at various universities, finally settling at the University of South Carolina at Columbia in 1969.

Dickey's sixth poetry collection, *Buckdancer's Choice*, propelled him to fame as a poet. It won the 1966 National Book Award for Poetry, the Poetry Society of America's Melville Cane Award, and an award from the National Institute of Arts and Letters. For the next two years, Dickey served as the poetry consultant to the Library of Congress, a position that has since been retitled "U.S. Poet Laureate." When his first novel, *Deliverance*, about a white-water canoe trip by four male friends that results in disaster, became a bestseller in 1970, Dickey's fame in poetic circles was transformed to celebrity status within American popular culture. He went on to write the screenplay for a film version of *Deliverance*, and he himself played the role of an overweight, small-town Southern sheriff. Dickey's name recognition with the American public was further increased when he read a poem at the nationally televised 1977 inauguration of President Jimmy Carter, a fellow Georgian.

Dickey died of lung disease in 1997 at the age of 73, having published over twenty-five collections of poetry plus three novels, numerous volumes of criticism and essays, and four screenplays. Since his death, a revealing memoir published by his son Christopher, the Hart biography, and other reassessments of his life and career have punctured the myth of his swaggering, "macho" persona, but not the worth of his body of poetry. In his poetry as in his life, Dickey sought to portray a sort of "heightened reality" where events and emotions were more vivid, intense, and compressed than they would be in normal day-to-day existence. Love–hate relationships with family members and with his Southern heritage, war and combat, hunting and other confrontations with wild animals, visionary dreams and nightmares, and the Southern grotesque panoply of accidents, diseases, and deformities are his most frequent themes and subjects, evidenced in the three selections in this anthology. Ernest Suarez has compared Dickey's achievements in Southern poetry to those of Robert Penn Warren, concluding that "Many aspects of their poetry—the belief in humans' destructive potential, the mystical emphasis, the expressionistic use of sex and violence, the rhetorical cadences—are common to Southern literature. But unlike the poets of the Renascence, they were able to see beyond the South. . . . " Suarez cites Dickey's early support of the Civil Rights movement, his rejection of the values extolled by the Fugitive and Agrarian poets, and the universality of his appeal to the imagination rather than the history-bound intellect as evidence of his ability to "see beyond the South."

Cherrylog Road

Off Highway 106
At Cherrylog Road I entered
The '34 Ford without wheels,
Smothered in kudzu,
With a seat pulled out to run
Corn whiskey down from the hills,

And then from the other side
Crept into an Essex[1]
With a rumble seat of red leather
And then out again, aboard

1. Essex automobiles were manufactured in Detroit, Michigan, from 1919 to 1933.

A blue Chevrolet, releasing
The rust from its other color,

Reared up on three building blocks.
None had the same body heat;
I changed with them inward, toward
The weedy heart of the junkyard,
For I knew that Doris Holbrook
Would escape from her father at noon

And would come from the farm
To seek parts owned by the sun
Among the abandoned chassis,
Sitting in each in turn
As I did, leaning forward
As in a wild stock-car race

In the parking lot of the dead.
Time after time, I climbed in
And out the other side, like
An envoy or movie star
Met at the station by crickets.
A radiator cap raised its head,

Become a real toad or a kingsnake
As I neared the hub of the yard,
Passing through many states,
Many lives, to reach
Some grandmother's long Pierce-Arrow[2]
Sending platters of blindness forth

From its nickel hubcaps
And spilling its tender upholstery
On sleepy roaches,
The glass panel in between
Lady and colored driver
Not all the way broken out,

The back-seat phone
Still on its hook.
I got in as though to exclaim,
"Let us go to the orphan asylum,
John; I have some old toys
For children who say their prayers."

I popped with sweat as I thought
I heard Doris Holbrook scrape
Like a mouse in the southern-state sun
That was eating the paint in blisters
From a hundred car tops and hoods.
She was tapping like code,

2. In 1929, the Pierce-Arrow Motor Car Company introduced a new "long and low" design that set new sales records.

Loosening the screws,
Carrying off headlights,
Sparkplugs, bumpers,
Cracked mirrors and gear-knobs,
Getting ready, already,
To go back with something to show

Other than her lips' new trembling
I would hold to me soon, soon,
Where I sat in the ripped back seat
Talking over the interphone,
Praying for Doris Holbrook
To come from her father's farm

And to get back there
With no trace of me on her face
To be seen by her red-haired father
Who would change, in the squalling barn,
Her back's pale skin with a strop,
Then lay for me

In a bootlegger's roasting car
With a string-triggered 12-gauge shotgun
To blast the breath from the air.
Not cut by the jagged windshields,
Through the acres of wrecks she came
With a wrench in her hand,

Through dust where the blacksnake dies
Of boredom, and the beetle knows
The compost has no more life.
Someone outside would have seen
The oldest car's door inexplicably
Close from within:

I held her and held her and held her,
Convoyed at terrific speed
By the stalled, dreaming traffic around us,
So the blacksnake, stiff
With inaction, curved back
Into life, and hunted the mouse

With deadly overexcitement,
The beetles reclaimed their field
As we clung, glued together,
With the hooks of the seat springs
Working through to catch us red-handed
Amidst the gray breathless batting

That burst from the seat at our backs.
We left by separate doors
Into the changed, other bodies
Of cars, she down Cherrylog Road
And I to my motorcycle
Parked like the soul of the junkyard

Restored, a bicycle fleshed
With power, and tore off
Up Highway 106, continually
Drunk on the wind in my mouth,
Wringing the handlebar for speed,
Wild to be wreckage forever.

Hunting Civil War Relics at Nimblewill Creek[1]

As he moves the mine detector
A few inches over the ground,
Making it vitally float
Among the ferns and weeds,
I come into this war
Slowly, with my one brother,
Watching his face grow deep
Between the earphones,
For I can tell
If we enter the buried battle
Of Nimblewill
Only by his expression.

Softly he wanders, parting
The grass with a dreaming hand.
No dead cry yet takes root
In his clapped ears
Or can be seen in his smile.
But underfoot I feel
The dead regroup,
The burst metals all in place,
The battle lines be drawn
Anew to include us
In Nimblewill,
And I carry the shovel and pick

More as if they were
Bright weapons that I bore.
A bird's cry breaks
In two, and into three parts.
We cross the creek; the cry
Shifts into another,
Nearer, bird, and is
Like the shout of a shadow—
Lived-with, appallingly close—
Or the soul, pronouncing
"Nimblewill":
Three tones; your being changes.

1. Nimblewill Creek is near Dahlonega, Georgia, a mustering ground for Confederate Army troops from north Georgia; there was no actual "Battle of Nimblewill."

We climb the bank;
A faint light glows
On my brother's mouth.
I listen, as two birds fight
For a single voice, but he
Must be hearing the grave,
In pieces, all singing
To his clamped head,
For he smiles as if
He rose from the dead within
Green Nimblewill
And stood in his grandson's shape.

No shot from the buried war
Shall kill me now,
For the dead have waited here
A hundred years to create
Only the look on the face
Of my one brother,
Who stands among them, offering
A metal dish
Afloat in the trembling weeds,
With a long-buried light on his lips
At Nimblewill
And the dead outsinging two birds.

I choke the handle
Of the pick, and fall to my knees
To dig wherever he points,
To bring up mess tin or bullet,
To go underground
Still singing, myself,
Without a sound,
Like a man who renounces war,
Or one who shall lift up the past,
Not breathing "Father,"
At Nimblewill,
But saying, "Fathers! Fathers!"

Sled Burial, Dream Ceremony

While the south rains, the north
Is snowing, and the dead southerner
Is taken there. He lies with the top of his casket
Open, his hair combed, the particles in the air
Changing to other things. The train stops

In a small furry village, and men in flap-eared caps
And others with women's scarves tied around their heads
And business hats over those, unload him,
And one of them reaches inside the coffin and places
The southerner's hand at the center
Of his dead breast. They load him onto a sled,
An old-fashioned sled with high-curled runners,

Drawn by horses with bells, and begin
To walk out of town, past dull red barns
Inching closer to the road as it snows

Harder, past an army of gunny-sacked bushes,
Past horses with flakes in the hollows of their sway-backs,
Past round faces drawn by children
On kitchen windows, all shedding basic-shaped tears.
The coffin top still is wide open;

His dead eyes stare through his lids,
Not fooled that the snow is cotton. The woods fall
Slowly off all of them, until they are walking
Between rigid little houses of ice-fishers
On a plain which is a great plain of water

Until the last rabbit track fails, and they are
At the center. They take axes, shovels, mattocks,
Dig the snow away, and saw the ice in the form
Of his coffin, lifting the slab like a door
Without hinges. The snow creaks under the sled

As they unload him like hay, holding his weight by ropes.
Sensing an unwanted freedom, a fish
Slides by, under the hole leading up through the snow
To nothing, and is gone. The coffin's shadow
Is white, and they stand there, gunny-sacked bushes,

Summoned from village sleep into someone else's dream
Of death, and let him down, still seeing the flakes in the air
At the place they are born of pure shadow
Like his dead eyelids, rocking for a moment like a boat
On utter foreignness, before he fills and sails down.

Questions to Consider

1. Describe the relationships that the narrator of "Hunting Civil War Relics at Nimblewill Creek" seems to have with the dead and with the living.
2. What is the relationship between nature and technology in the poem "Cherrylog Road"? Does the ending of the poem alter that relationship or reinforce it?

Vassar Miller

1924–1998

Vassar Morrison Miller was born on 19 July 1924 to Jessie Gustavson Miller, a wealthy Houston real estate developer, and his wife, also named Vassar Morrison Miller. But the little rich girl did not "have everything," as one might expect: She was born afflicted with cerebral palsy, and her mother died when she was only a year old. Because she spoke with a speech impediment, her grieving father assumed that she was mentally as well as physically handicapped. A family maid took the neglected child to evangelistic prayer meetings in a tent. When Miller's father remarried, her new stepmother, who was scarcely 20 years old, began to realize that the little girl was actually quite intelligent. She persuaded her husband to bring an electric typewriter home from work to see whether young Vassar could communicate better by typing than by speaking. As Miller has recorded in the poem "Subterfuge," the typewriter unlocked the torrent of words and thoughts that had been dammed up inside her, and she began to "pec[k] at the keys/ with a sparrow's preoccupation." Miller's stepmother educated her at home until she was 12 years old, then "mainstreamed" her in the public school system for junior and senior high school.

Miller went on to earn a bachelor's degree from the University of Houston in 1947 and a master's degree from the same institution in 1952. She studied creative writing under poet Cynthia McDonald in graduate school and wrote her master's thesis on mysticism in the poetry of Edwin Arlington Robinson. Four years later she published her first collection of poetry, *Adam's Footprint,* with Maxine Cassin's New Orleans Poetry Journal Press. Cassin, a New Orleans poet of Miller's generation, would become a lifelong friend. Miller's second collection, *Wage War on Silence* (Wesleyan UP, 1960) was nominated for a Pulitzer Prize. Eight more volumes of poetry followed. Miller's lifetime accomplishments included editing an anthology of stories and poems about the disabled (*Despite This Flesh,* 1984), teaching for a year at St. John's School in Houston, visiting Europe in 1965, and giving poetry readings. She was a three-time winner of the Texas Institute of Letters Award and was inducted into the Texas Women's Hall of Fame in 1998. She died in a nursing home in Texas in 1998, at the age of 74.

Texas poet Leon Stokesbury called Miller "Texas's greatest poet," while Texas novelist Larry McMurtry called her "perhaps the greatest author" from Texas. McMurtry wrote the introduction to a posthumous collection of critical essays on Miller, edited by Steven Ford Brown. Despite such extraordinary praise, however, Miller's work has not been widely read. Her frequent themes of spiritual longing and the difficulty of maintaining faith in the face of God's silence have long been out of fashion in American poetry, even though her humor and erotic imagery make the poems quite timely. She is often compared to Emily Dickinson for her insistent probing of the mysteries of the great unknowns, God and death, as much as for her loneliness, eccentricity, and love of nature.

As critic James Tanner explains, Miller's readership has also been constrained by her reputation as a "Texas poet": national readers and critics tend to bypass her work for that reason, while regionalists find it to be lacking in Southern or Texan flavor. But, as Tanner points out, Miller is quite Southern in her religious preoccupation, her love of nature and of rural life, and her sense of place—although "place" for Miller is the immobile body in which her fierce consciousness is always trapped, more often than it is the external Texas landscape of "cicadas, hurricanes, long hot summers, drab unexciting Januarys" (in Miller's words, as told to Hammond) that she also paints from time to time. The poem "Affinity" shows Miller was a great admirer of the short story writer Flannery O'Connor, whose strong Christian beliefs, personal disability, and empathy for the disabled do, indeed, suggest "affinities" with Miller's poetry.

On Approaching My Birthday

My mother bore me in the heat of summer[1]
when the grass blanched under sun's hammer stroke
and the birds sang off key, panting between notes,
and the pear trees once all winged with whiteness
sagged, breaking with fruit, and only the zinnias,
like harlots, bloomed out vulgar and audacious,
and when the cicadas played all day long
their hidden harpsichords accompanying
her grief, my mother bore me, as I say,
then died shortly thereafter, no doubt
of her disgust and left me her disease[2]
when I grew up to wither into truth.

1. Miller was born on 19 July.

2. Cerebral palsy.

Memento Mori

(In Memory of Anne Sexton[1])

You think that I am smiling,
but I'm practicing my death-grin.
I must wear it for a rather long time.

You think that I am sleeping,
but I'm developing my grave skills
for when I must do death's motionless ballet.

You think that I am breathing,
but I'm toning up my death-gasp.
I owe it to my friends to do one thing right.

You think that I am resting,
but I'm hunched over my decay,
which makes do for the pretty baby I wasn't.

Since No One Will Sing Me a Lullaby . . .

Wind, mad granny,
rocking on darkness,
the tree branches your knitting needles,

knit me a blanket
from sleep's wool
made to snag on the corner of waking.

Raison d'Etre

I grow from my poems
in a green world.

Outside them I suck my breath,
grow pale and poor.

For I am the toad
in my imagined garden.[1]

Affinity

(For Flannery O'Connor[1])

Fearing the city whose knife-narrow buildings
crowd sun and stars, mocking at hill and tree
fit only for the birds, and making geldings
of country heads stuffed full of piety,

1. American confessional poet (1928–1974) who died by suicide; in her youth, the glamorous Sexton was a model in Boston.

1. Miller is alluding to modernist poet Marianne Moore's famous dictum that poets should create "imaginary gardens with real toads in them."

1. Georgia-born fiction writer (1925–1964) who, like Miller, was disabled by disease.

you went home sick as well one might when still
the too long summers of a childhood rage
too long, faith turned a digit of the will.
Yet had Grace struck, like mumps in middle age
to shake you loose and tell law where to go,
or had disease and early death not shut
your door, you might have left the family pew,
thumbing your nose at every holy "Tut!"
matching strict steps to those that weave and falter,
danced David's crazy rock[2] before God's altar.

Reassurance

When you shake hands with my pains,
you know each crease of their palms,
the angle at which they hold
a teacup, read their slightest
tremor precisely for what
it is, follow them upstairs
and lie down among them, less
like Daniel among lions[1]
than a mother with children.
Worry is only a glove
you've tried on and thrown away.
We won't need it any more.

Questions to Consider

1. What images and associations do poets usually employ when writing about the summer? How does the poem "On Approaching My Birthday" differ from the usual portrayal of summer?
2. Do you find any humor in the poem "Memento Mori"? Why or why not?

Donald Justice

1925–

Miami, Florida, was a much more Southern city in the years of Donald Rodney Justice's childhood than it is now: "freshly urban but still very Southern," Justice explained in an interview with Dana Gioia. Justice was born in Miami on 12 August 1925 to Vascoe J. and Mary Ethel Cook Justice. His parents were Southern Baptists who had moved from south Georgia just a few years before. Vascoe, a carpenter, was originally from south Alabama, and every summer the Justice family would visit their relatives in Alabama and Georgia ("poor farmers and store clerks and so on," in Justice's words to Gioia), for an extended stay. Justice, who lost his belief in the family religion at an early age, suffered through the family visits, feeling like an outsider.

2. In the Old Testament (2 Samuel 6:14, 16), David performed a whirling dance in front of the Ark.

1. In the Old Testament (Daniel 6:16), Daniel is thrown to the lions on false charges of corruption but is spared by God.

What he enjoyed most was music. A gifted piano student as a child, he began studying music at the University of Miami under composer Carl Ruggles. Another of Justice's teachers there was the poet George Marion O'Donnell, who had been a fringe member of the "second-generation" Fugitive-Agrarians. O'Donnell encouraged Justice to pursue poetry, and his interests began to shift from music to writing. He proceeded to the University of North Carolina at Chapel Hill, receiving an M.A. in English with a thesis on John Crowe Ransom, Allen Tate, and Robert Penn Warren. Following a year of graduate study at Stanford University, Justice returned to Miami and taught English at his alma mater for two years, then moved to Iowa City to pursue a Ph.D. at the University of Iowa, which he received in 1954. Justice's teachers at Iowa included Karl Shapiro, Robert Lowell, and John Berryman, and among his fellow students were W. D. Snodgrass, Philip Levine, and Jane Cooper—all significant figures in twentieth-century American poetry. Joining the faculty of Iowa himself in 1957 and remaining there for the next nine years, then for eleven more years in the 1970s and early 1980s, Justice taught up-coming poets including Mark Strand, Charles Wright, and Jorie Graham. He also taught at the University of Florida at Gainesville from 1982 to 1992, after which he retired from teaching.

Justice did not publish his first collection of poetry until he was 34 years old, and he has never been a prolific poet, but his books have captured virtually every major award in American poetry. Like many Southern poets, Justice employs rhyme, meter, and traditional poetic forms at a time when they have fallen out of favor with the poetic avant-garde; he has even drawn upon his musical knowledge to experiment with writing poems in sonatina form. The South is significant to Justice's content as well as to his form. As Gioia writes in his essay "Three Poets in Mid Career," Justice "is specially concerned with the loss of his childhood world, and many of his best poems present the Miami of his boyhood and are filled with a brooding nostalgia for its lost people and places." The Fugitive-Agrarian poets were certainly an important influence on Justice, given that his first poetry teacher and the subject figures of his master's thesis came from their ranks. As Justice confessed in an *Iowa Review* interview, "they certainly were a formative influence. I wrote my master's thesis on them, and in a way I've always known their work. Ransom is a favorite." When asked by Gioia if he considered himself to be a Southern writer, Justice explained that being Southern was not a matter of choice, but a matter of fate, and that there was really no escaping that identity for a writer who had been born and raised in the South.

Anonymous Drawing

A delicate young Negro stands
With the reins of a horse clutched loosely in his hands;
So delicate, indeed, that we wonder if he can hold the spirited creature
 beside him
Until the master shall arrive to ride him.
Already the animal's nostrils widen with rage or fear.
But if we imagine him snorting, about to rear,
This boy, who should know about such things better than we,
Only stands smiling, passive and ornamental, in a fantastic livery
Of ruffles and puffed breeches,
Watching the artist, apparently, as he sketches.
Meanwhile the petty lord who must have paid
For the artist's trip up from Perugia,[1] for the horse, for the boy,
 for everything here, in fact, has been delayed,
Kept too long by his steward, perhaps, discussing

1. City in the Umbria region of Italy.

Some business concerning the estate, or fussing
Over the details of his impeccable toilet
With a manservant whose opinion is that any alteration at all would spoil it.
However fast he should come hurrying now
Over this vast greensward, mopping his brow
Clear of the sweat of the fine Renaissance morning, it would be too late:
The artist will have had his revenge for being made to wait,
A revenge not only necessary but right and clever—
Simply to leave him out of the scene forever.

My South

I dont! I dont hate it! I dont hate it! **Q. Compson**[1]

But why do I write of the all unutterable and the all abysmal? Why does my pen not drop from my hand on approaching the infinite pity and tragedy of all the past? It does, poor helpless pen, with what it meets of the ineffable, what it meets of the cold Medusa-face[2] ***of life, of all the life lived, on every side. Basta, basta!***[3] **H. James**[4]

1 On the Porch

There used to be a way the sunlight caught
The cocoons of caterpillars in the pecans.
A boy's shadow would lengthen to a man's
Across the yard then, slowly. And if you thought
Some sleepy god had dreamed it all up—well,
There stood my grandfather, Lincoln-tall and solemn,
Tapping his pipe out on a white-flaked column,
Carefully, carefully, as though it were his job.
(And we would watch the pipe-stars as they fell.)
As for the quiet, the same train always broke it.
Then the great silver watch rose from his pocket
For us to check the hour, the dark fob
Dangling the watch between us like a moon.
It would be evening soon then, very soon.

2 At the Cemetery

Above the fence-flowers, like a bloody thumb,
A hummingbird is throbbing. . . . And some
Petals take motion from the beaten wings
In hardly observable obscure quiverings.
My mother stands there, but so still her clothing
Seems to have settled into stone, nothing
To animate her face, nothing to read there—
O plastic rose O clouds O still cedar!
She stands this way for a long time while the sky
Ponders her with its great Medusa-eye;
Or in my memory she does. And then a

1. Quotation from Quentin Compson, a character in William Faulkner's novel *Absalom, Absalom!*
2. Medusa was the snake-headed Greek goddess whose gaze turned mortals to stone.
3. "Enough, enough!" in Italian.
4. The passage is from the *Notebooks* of Henry James.

Slow blacksnake, lazy with long sunning, slides
Down from its slab, and through the thick grass, and hides
Somewhere among the purpling wild verbena.

3 On The Farm

And I, missing the city intensely at that moment,
Moped and sulked at the window. I heard the first owl, quite near,
But the sound hardly registered. And the kerosene lamp
Went on sputtering, giving off vague medicinal fumes
That made me think of sickrooms. I had been memorizing
"The Ballad of Reading Gaol,"[5] but the lamplight hurt my eyes;
And I was too bored to sleep, restless and bored.
Years later,
Perhaps, I will recall the evenings, empty and vast, when
Under the first stars, there by the back gate, secretly, I
Would relieve myself on the shamed and drooping hollyhocks.
Now I yawned; the old dream of being a changeling returned.
The owl cried, and I felt myself like the owl—alone, proud,
Almost invisible—or like some hero in Homer[6]
Protected by a cloud let down by the gods to save him.

4 On the Train, Heading North
Through Florida, Late at Night and Long Ago, and
Ending with a Line from Thomas Wolfe

Midnight or after, and the little lights
Glitter like lost beads from a broken necklace
Beyond smudged windows, lost and irretrievable—
Some promise of romance these Southern nights
Never entirely keep—unless, sleepless,
We should pass down dim corridors again
To stand, braced in a swaying vestibule,
Alone with the darkness and the wind—out there
Nothing but pines and one new road perhaps,
Straight and white, aimed at the distant gulf—
And hear, from the smoking room, the sudden high-pitched
Whinny of laughter pass from throat to throat;
And the great wheels smash and pound beneath our feet.[7]

Questions to Consider

1. How do the two epigraphs relate to the theme(s) of "My South"?
2. Sections 1 and 4 of "My South" contain the image of a train. What does the train connote or symbolize in each section? Does the meaning of the train change between the beginning of the poem and the end?

5. Poem written by Irish writer Oscar Wilde (1854–1900) after his trial and imprisonment for homosexuality.
6. Greek epic poet of the ninth to eighth centuries B.C.
7. The line is from Thomas Wolfe's novel *Look Homeward, Angel: A Story of the Buried Life*.

Flannery O'Connor

1925–1964

"I think it is safe to say that while the South is hardly Christ-centered, it is most certainly Christ-haunted. The Southerner, who isn't convinced of it, is very much afraid that he may have been formed in the image and likeness of God," mused Flannery O'Connor, contemplating the eroding spiritual values of her native region. A lifelong, devout Catholic, O'Connor created fictions imbued with her religious values. Yet, as Leslie Winfield Williams has pointed out, because the "base of American cultural assumption and a shared understanding of the Christian faith had disappeared," O'Connor was forced to seek striking ways to draw attention to issues of faith. Her efforts led her to incorporate violence and grotesque characters to shock her readers into readiness for the message she set out to deliver. As Williams suggests, despite O'Connor's clear intention to show the reader "how far sin carries human beings," to simply categorize her as a Catholic writer would inappropriately minimize her contributions to Southern literature and to limit the scope of her influence on the American literary canon.

Born in Savannah, Georgia on 25 March 1925, Mary Flannery O'Connor was the only daughter of Edward and Regina Cline O'Connor. She was educated in Catholic schools, yet spent much of her life in a matriarchal family unit. Savannah was an unusually tolerant environment for a young Catholic in a region that was otherwise suspicious of and often hostile toward difference. Georgia's original charter forbade the practice of Catholicism, but it had been tolerated since the 1790s, when Haitian-Catholic refugees settled in the territory. Settlers from the Catholic colony of Maryland lived undisturbed in Georgia at an early date, as well. Despite the prejudice against Catholics in many areas of the South during the pre–Civil Rights era, the O'Connor family found Savannah a comfortable environment in which to raise their daughter.

Following the untimely death of Edward O'Connor, who died of disseminated lupus in 1941, Regina O'Connor governed her family with a combination of strong-mindedness, competence, and quintessentially Southern values. Mother and daughter soon left Savannah, moving first to Atlanta, and then to Andalusia, Regina's family estate in Milledgeville, Georgia. O'Connor enrolled in Georgia State College for Women in 1942, where she spent time as editor of the college literary magazine and as the art editor and cartoonist for the college paper. Because she felt that her originality was unappreciated by the faculty of the English department, however, she completed a bachelor's degree in sociology and applied for a Rinehart Fellowship to the University of Iowa Writers' Workshop in 1945. When she began her studies in Iowa, O'Connor dropped her first name, commenting that Mary O'Connor was far too common a name for the famous author she planned to become. As Flannery O'Connor, she soon began publishing her work. Her first published story, "The Geranium," appeared in *Accent* magazine in 1946 and later became part of her master's thesis. O'Connor's earliest work suggests the themes she developed throughout her writing career, especially the grotesque characterizations of rural Southern residents that would become one of her stylistic trademarks. O'Connor received the Rinehart Iowa Prize for a first novel during this period and spent part of 1948 at the Yaddo writers' colony in Saratoga Springs, New York. Yaddo provided financial support for its resident writers, in return for their adherence to a highly structured work schedule, and the young writer eagerly responded to the regimen.

While at Yaddo, O'Connor engaged Elizabeth McKee as her agent, and due in part to McKee's diligent representation, her works shortly began to appear in publications such as the *Partisan Review* and *Mademoiselle*. Also during this time, O'Connor met Robert Giroux, who became her lifelong friend and was instrumental in her moves, first from Holt Rinehart Publishers—which had contracted for her first novel—to Harcourt Brace, and later to his own publishing house, which published the bulk of her work. O'Connor studied and worked with a number of other notable Southern writers and scholars during this period, including Robert Penn Warren and Andrew Lytle. Lytle and O'Connor were kindred spirits in many ways: they shared concerns for "the techniques of fiction." Each writer placed strong "emphasis on flawed characters obviously in need of salvation" and held a "firm belief in the doctrine of original sin," according to O'Connor's most recent biographer, Jean Wampler Cash. O'Connor also developed an enduring friendship with fellow Catholic writer Caroline Gordon, as well as with Gordon's husband, Allen Tate. The two women remained close until O'Connor's untimely death, and Gordon was ever after an avid proponent of O'Connor's work.

After leaving Yaddo, O'Connor moved briefly to New York, intent on finishing the manuscript for her first novel, *Wise Blood*. She soon decided to join her close friends Robert and Sally Fitzgerald in Connecticut. A life-threatening illness, which was later determined to be lupus, necessitated her permanent return to Milledgeville. O'Connor spent the remainder of her life under the watchful care of her mother and undertook only brief excursions from home, as her health permitted.

In the earliest stages of her career, O'Connor had felt that she could not write about the South if she was immersed in it, a frame of mind that she was forced to overcome at the onset of her illness. Only after leaving her homeland, first to study in Iowa and later to work in New York and Connecticut, did she come to view the South as a creative fount from which she could draw. In leaving the region, she discovered that it was the "true country" that provided the foundation for her best fiction, giving it the inescapable sense of place—both geographic and mystical—so often associated with twentieth-century Southern writing. This intrinsic sense of place became the creative arena for O'Connor to examine the ways in which grace could be achieved in a modern society populated by nonbelievers.

In part, O'Connor's reluctance to return to her native South derived from Regina O'Connor's high expectations for her only daughter, expectations that, at their core, required the writer to uphold the traditional Southern conventions that accompanied wealth and a long-standing family name. As critic Patricia Yaeger demonstrates, even when her daughter's health was failing, Regina expected her to "adhere to the traditional prejudices and etiquette of the white southern elite." Yaeger further argues that, as a lifelong resident of the South, O'Connor had frequently observed that White Southerners "struggled to enforce sharp demarcations between genders, between classes, and most brutally, between races." O'Connor articulated the awkwardness of balancing the expectations of a good Southern daughter and the needs of a literary artist: "I observe the traditions of the society I feed on—it's only fair." Despite her tacit agreement to "abide by southern customs in life," Yaeger suggests that O'Connor refused "to make the reader feel at home in its southern world . . . [or to] share her region's dream of a glamorous southern past." In O'Connor's view, the South did not deserve romanticizing, but instead exemplified the sins of the modern world—sins that could be all too easily scrutinized, thereby providing much-needed spiritual instruction.

O'Connor's body of work includes two novels and two collections of short stories, as well as her master's thesis, which was not published during her lifetime. Her first novel, *Wise Blood* (1952), was followed by her first collection of short stories, *A Good Man is Hard to Find* (1955). She then published her second novel, *The Violent Bear It Away*, in 1960. O'Connor's final collection of short stories, *Everything That Rises Must Converge* (1965), was published posthumously, as were two collections of letters and occasional writing, *Mystery and Manners* (1969) and *The Habit of Being* (1979), which were edited by Robert and Sally Fitzgerald.

O'Connor is praised for her mastery of the short story genre although critics have remarked that her skill with the novel form was still developing at the time of her death. Yaeger argues that O'Connor's best fiction is marked by examinations of the Southern preoccupation with the control and separation of people on the basis of gender, class, and, most stridently, race; by representations of people as "quaint monstrosities" that highlight the depths of depravity into which sin can push them; and by violence as a "precursor of spiritual grace." O'Connor actively resisted the tendency, articulated by Allen Tate, to be "always respectfully conscious of the past's endurance into the present," eschewing the tendency of her literary contemporaries to genuflect at the altar of the South's storied past. Instead, she made use of satire, focusing her artistic gaze on the expectations of class and gender—often showing angry children in rebellion against their mothers, who were white, proper, and clueless—and reserving the most heinous fates for such controlling, matriarchal figures.

At the time of her death on 3 August 1964 of disseminated lupus, the same disease that had claimed the life of her father, O'Connor enjoyed a devoted national audience and had earned numerous prestigious awards. *The Complete Stories* (1971), published posthumously and edited by her old friend Robert Giroux, won the coveted National Book Award. O'Connor remains one of the most respected of writers, in both the Southern and the larger American traditions. Critics consistently rank her with the likes of William Faulkner, Eudora Welty, and Thomas Wolfe. O'Connor's use of the grotesque aspects of the human experience—which she viewed as drastic artistic measures necessary to show her readers the unnaturalness of acts that had come to seem ordinary—and her strong grounding in Southern culture, history, and values makes her a writer without parallel.

Everything That Rises Must Converge

Her doctor had told Julian's mother that she must lose twenty pounds on account of her blood pressure, so on Wednesday nights Julian had to take her downtown on the bus for a reducing class at the Y. The reducing class was designed for working girls over fifty, who weighed from 165 to 200 pounds. His mother was one of the slimmer ones, but she said ladies did not tell their age or weight. She would not ride the buses by herself at night since they had been integrated, and because the reducing class was one of her few pleasures, necessary for her health, and *free,* she said Julian could at least put himself out to take her, considering all she did for him. Julian did not like to consider all she did for him, but every Wednesday night he braced himself and took her.

She was almost ready to go, standing before the hall mirror, putting on her hat, while he, his hands behind him, appeared pinned to the door frame, waiting like Saint Sebastian for the arrows to begin piercing him. The hat was new and had cost her seven dollars and a half. She kept saying, "Maybe I shouldn't have paid that for it. No, I shouldn't have. I'll take it off and return it tomorrow. I shouldn't have bought it."

Julian raised his eyes to heaven. "Yes, you should have bought it," he said. "Put it on and let's go." It was a hideous hat. A purple velvet flap came down on one side of it and stood up on the other; the rest of it was green and looked like a cushion with the stuffing out. He decided it was less comical than jaunty and pathetic. Everything that gave her pleasure was small and depressed him.

She lifted the hat one more time and set it down slowly on top of her head. Two wings of gray hair protruded on either side of her florid face, but her eyes, sky-blue, were as innocent and untouched by experience as they must have been when she was ten. Were it not that she was a widow who had struggled fiercely to feed and clothe and put him through school and who was supporting him still, "until he got on his feet," she might have been a little girl that he had to take to town.

"It's all right, it's all right," he said. "Let's go." He opened the door himself and started down the walk to get her going. The sky was a dying violet and the houses stood out darkly against it, bulbous liver-colored monstrosities of a uniform ugliness though no two were alike. Since this had been a fashionable neighborhood forty years ago, his mother persisted in thinking they did well to have an apartment in it. Each house had a narrow collar of dirt around it in which sat, usually, a grubby child. Julian walked with his hands in his pockets, his head down and thrust forward and his eyes glazed with the determination to make himself completely numb during the time he would be sacrificed to her pleasure.

The door closed and he turned to find the dumpy figure, surmounted by the atrocious hat, coming toward him. "Well," she said, "you only live once and paying a little more for it, I at least won't meet myself coming and going."

"Some day I'll start making money," Julian said gloomily—he knew he never would—"and you can have one of those jokes whenever you take the fit." But first they would move. He visualized a place where the nearest neighbors would be three miles away on either side.

"I think you're doing fine," she said, drawing on her gloves. "You've only been out of school a year. Rome wasn't built in a day."

She was one of the few members of the Y reducing class who arrived in hat and gloves and who had a son who had been to college. "It takes time," she said, "and the world is in such a mess. This hat looked better on me than any of the others, though when she brought it out I said, 'Take that thing back. I wouldn't have it on my head,' and she said, 'Now wait till you see it on,' and when she put it on me, I said, 'We-ull,' and she said, 'If you ask me, that hat does something for you and you do something for the hat, and besides,' she said, 'with that hat, you won't meet yourself coming and going.' "

Julian thought he could have stood his lot better if she had been selfish, if she had been an old hag who drank and screamed at him. He walked along, saturated in depression, as if in the midst of his martyrdom he had lost his faith. Catching sight of his long, hopeless, irritated face, she stopped suddenly with a grief-stricken look, and pulled back on his arm. "Wait on me," she said. "I'm going back to the house and take this thing off and tomorrow I'm going to return it. I was out of my head. I can pay the gas bill with that seven-fifty."

He caught her arm in a vicious grip. "You are not going to take it back," he said. "I like it."

"Well," she said, "I don't think I ought . . ."

"Shut up and enjoy it," he muttered, more depressed than ever.

"With the world in the mess it's in," she said, "it's a wonder we can enjoy anything. I tell you, the bottom rail is on the top."

Julian sighed.

"Of course," she said, "if you know who you are, you can go anywhere." She said this every time he took her to the reducing class. "Most of them in it are not our kind of people," she said, "but I can be gracious to anybody. I know who I am."

"They don't give a damn for your graciousness," Julian said savagely. "Knowing who you are is good for one generation only. You haven't the foggiest idea where you stand now or who you are."

She stopped and allowed her eyes to flash at him. "I most certainly do know who I am," she said, "and if you don't know who you are, I'm ashamed of you."

"Oh hell," Julian said.

"Your great-grandfather was a former governor of this state," she said. "Your grandfather was a prosperous landowner. Your grandmother was a Godhigh."

"Will you look around you," he said tensely, "and see where you are now?" and he swept his arm jerkily out to indicate the neighborhood, which the growing darkness at least made less dingy.

"You remain what you are," she said. "Your great-grandfather had a plantation and two hundred slaves."

"There are no more slaves," he said irritably.

"They were better off when they were," she said. He groaned to see that she was off on that topic. She rolled onto it every few days like a train on an open track. He knew every stop, every junction, every swamp along the way, and knew the exact point at which her conclusion would roll majestically into the station: "It's ridiculous. It's simply not realistic. They should rise, yes, but on their own side of the fence."

"Let's skip it," Julian said.

"The ones I feel sorry for," she said, "are the ones that are half white. They're tragic."

"Will you skip it?"

"Suppose we were half white. We would certainly have mixed feelings."

"I have mixed feelings now," he groaned.

"Well let's talk about something pleasant," she said. "I remember going to Grandpa's when I was a little girl. Then the house had double stairways that went up to what was really the second floor—all the cooking was done on the first. I used to like to stay down in the kitchen on account of the way the walls smelled. I would sit with my nose pressed against the plaster and take deep breaths. Actually the place belonged to the Godhighs but your grandfather Chestny paid the mortgage and saved it for them. They were in reduced circumstances," she said, "but reduced or not, they never forgot who they were."

"Doubtless that decayed mansion reminded them," Julian muttered. He never spoke of it without contempt or thought of it without longing. He had seen it once when he was a child before it had been sold. The double stairways had rotted and been torn down. Negroes were living in it. But it remained in his mind as his mother had known it. It appeared in his dreams regularly. He would stand on the wide porch, listening to the rustle of oak leaves, then wander through the high-ceilinged hall into the parlor that opened onto it and gaze at the worn rugs and faded draperies. It occurred to him that it was he, not she, who could have appreciated it. He preferred its threadbare elegance to anything he could name and it was because of it that all the neighborhoods they had lived in had been a torment to him—whereas she had hardly known the difference. She called her insensitivity "being adjustable."

"And I remember the old darky who was my nurse, Caroline. There was no better person in the world. I've always had a great respect for my colored friends," she said. "I'd do anything in the world for them and they'd . . ."

"Will you for God's sake get off that subject?" Julian said. When he got on a bus by himself, he made it a point to sit down beside a Negro, in reparation as it were for his mother's sins.

"You're mighty touchy tonight," she said. "Do you feel all right?"

"Yes I feel all right," he said. "Now lay off."

She pursed her lips. "Well, you certainly are in a vile humor," she observed. "I just won't speak to you at all."

They had reached the bus stop. There was no bus in sight and Julian, his hands still jammed in his pockets and his head thrust forward, scowled down the empty street. The frustration of having to wait on the bus as well as ride on it began to creep up his neck like a hot hand. The presence of his mother was borne in upon him as she gave a pained sigh. He looked at her bleakly. She was holding herself very erect under the preposterous hat, wearing it like a banner of her imaginary dignity. There was in him an evil urge to break her spirit. He suddenly unloosened his tie and pulled it off and put it in his pocket.

She stiffened. "Why must you look like *that* when you take me to town?" she said. "Why must you deliberately embarrass me?"

"If you'll never learn where you are," he said, "you can at least learn where I am."

"You look like a—thug," she said.

"Then I must be one," he murmured.

"I'll just go home," she said. "I will not bother you. If you can't do a little thing like that for me . . ."

Rolling his eyes upward, he put his tie back on. "Restored to my class," he muttered. He thrust his face toward her and hissed, "True culture is in the mind, the *mind*," he said, and tapped his head, "the mind."

"It's in the heart," she said, "and in how you do things and how you do things is because of who you *are*."

"Nobody in the damn bus cares who you are."

"I care who I am," she said icily.

The lighted bus appeared on top of the next hill and as it approached, they moved out into the street to meet it. He put his hand under her elbow and hoisted her up on the creaking step. She entered with a little smile, as if she were going into a drawing room where everyone had been waiting for her. While he put in the tokens, she sat down on one of the broad front seats for three which faced the aisle. A thin woman with protruding teeth and long yellow hair was sitting on the end of it. His mother moved up beside her and left room for Julian beside herself. He sat down and looked at the floor across the aisle where a pair of thin feet in red and white canvas sandals were planted.

His mother immediately began a general conversation meant to attract anyone who felt like talking. "Can it get any hotter?" she said and removed from her purse a folding fan, black with a Japanese scene on it, which she began to flutter before her.

"I reckon it might could," the woman with the protruding teeth said, "but I know for a fact my apartment couldn't get no hotter."

"It must get the afternoon sun," his mother said. She sat forward and looked up and down the bus. It was half filled. Everybody was white. "I see we have the bus to ourselves," she said. Julian cringed.

"For a change," said the woman across the aisle, the owner of the red and white canvas sandals. "I come on one the other day and they were thick as fleas—up front and all through."

"The world is in a mess everywhere," his mother said. "I don't know how we've let it get in this fix."

"What gets my goat is all those boys from good families stealing automobile tires," the woman with the protruding teeth said. "I told my boy, I said you may not be rich but you been raised right and if I ever catch you in any such mess, they can send you on to the reformatory. Be exactly where you belong."

"Training tells," his mother said. "Is your boy in high school?"

"Ninth grade," the woman said.

"My son just finished college last year. He wants to write but he's selling typewriters until he gets started," his mother said.

The woman leaned forward and peered at Julian. He threw her such a malevolent look that she subsided against the seat. On the floor across the aisle there was an abandoned newspaper. He got up and got it and opened it out in front of him. His mother discreetly continued the conversation in a lower tone but the woman across the aisle said in a loud voice, "Well that's nice. Selling typewriters is close to writing. He can go right from one to the other."

"I tell him," his mother said, "that Rome wasn't built in a day."

Behind the newspaper Julian was withdrawing into the inner compartment of his mind where he spent most of his time. This was a kind of mental bubble in which he established himself when he could not bear to be a part of what was going on around him. From it he could see out and judge but in it he was safe from any kind of penetration from without. It was the only place where he felt free of the general idiocy of his fellows. His mother had never entered it but from it he could see her with absolute clarity.

The old lady was clever enough and he thought that if she had started from any of the right premises, more might have been expected of her. She lived according to the laws of her own fantasy world, outside of which he had never seen her set foot. The law of it was to sacrifice herself for him after she had first created the necessity to do so by making a mess of things. If he had permitted her sacrifices, it was only because her lack of foresight had made them necessary. All of her life had been a struggle to act like a Chestny without the Chestny goods, and to give him everything she thought a Chestny ought to have; but since, said she, it was fun to struggle, why complain? And when you had won, as she had won, what fun to look back on the hard times! He could not forgive her that she had enjoyed the struggle and that she thought *she* had won.

What she meant when she said she had won was that she had brought him up successfully and had sent him to college and that he had turned out so well—good looking (her teeth had gone unfilled so that his could be straightened), intelligent (he realized he was too intelligent to be a success), and with a future ahead of him (there was of course no future ahead of him). She excused his gloominess on the grounds that he was still growing up and his radical ideas on his lack of practical experience. She said he didn't yet know a thing about "life," that he hadn't even entered the real world—when already he was as disenchanted with it as a man of fifty.

The further irony of all this was that in spite of her, he had turned out so well. In spite of going to only a third-rate college, he had, on his own initiative, come out with a first-rate education; in spite of growing up dominated by a small mind, he had ended up with a large one; in spite of all her foolish views, he was free of prejudice and unafraid to face facts. Most miraculous of all, instead of being blinded by love for her as she was for him, he had cut himself emotionally free of her and could see her with complete objectivity. He was not dominated by his mother.

The bus stopped with a sudden jerk and shook him from his meditation. A woman from the back lurched forward with little steps and barely escaped falling in his newspaper as she righted herself. She got off and a large Negro got on. Julian kept his paper lowered to watch. It gave him a certain satisfaction to see injustice in daily operation. It confirmed his view that with a few exceptions there was no one worth knowing within a radius of three hundred miles. The Negro was well dressed and carried a briefcase. He looked around and then sat down on the other end of the seat where the woman with the red and white canvas sandals was sitting. He immediately unfolded a newspaper and obscured himself behind it. Julian's mother's elbow at once prodded insistently into his ribs. "Now you see why I won't ride on these buses by myself," she whispered.

The woman with the red and white canvas sandals had risen at the same time the Negro sat down and had gone further back in the bus and taken the seat of the woman who had got off. His mother leaned forward and cast her an approving look.

Julian rose, crossed the aisle, and sat down in the place of the woman with the canvas sandals. From this position, he looked serenely across at his mother. Her face had turned an angry red. He stared at her, making his eyes the eyes of a stranger. He felt his tension suddenly lift as if he had openly declared war on her.

He would have liked to get in conversation with the Negro and to talk with him about art or politics or any subject that would be above the comprehension of those around them, but the man remained entrenched behind his paper. He was either ignoring the change of seating or had never noticed it. There was no way for Julian to convey his sympathy.

His mother kept her eyes fixed reproachfully on his face. The woman with the protruding teeth was looking at him avidly as if he were a type of monster new to her.

"Do you have a light?" he asked the Negro.

Without looking away from his paper, the man reached in his pocket and handed him a packet of matches.

"Thanks," Julian said. For a moment he held the matches foolishly. A NO SMOKING sign looked down upon him from over the door. This alone would not have deterred him; he had no cigarettes. He had quit smoking some months before because he could not afford it. "Sorry," he muttered and handed back the matches. The Negro lowered the paper and gave him an annoyed look. He took the matches and raised the paper again.

His mother continued to gaze at him but she did not take advantage of his momentary discomfort. Her eyes retained their battered look. Her face seemed to be unnaturally red, as if her blood pressure had risen. Julian allowed no glimmer of sympathy to show on his face. Having got the advantage, he wanted desperately to keep it and carry it through. He would have liked to teach her a lesson that would last her a while, but there seemed no way to continue the point. The Negro refused to come out from behind his paper.

Julian folded his arms and looked stolidly before him, facing her but as if he did not see her, as if he had ceased to recognize her existence. He visualized a scene in which, the bus having reached their stop, he would remain in his seat and when she said, "Aren't you going to get off?" he would look at her as at a stranger who had rashly addressed him. The corner they got off on was usually deserted, but it was well lighted and it would not hurt her to walk by herself the four blocks to the Y. He decided to wait until the time came and then decide whether or not he would let her get off by herself. He would have to be at the Y at ten to bring her back, but he could leave her wondering if he was going to show up. There was no reason for her to think she could always depend on him.

He retired again into the high-ceilinged room sparsely settled with large pieces of antique furniture. His soul expanded momentarily but then he became aware of his mother across from him and the vision shriveled. He studied her coldly. Her feet in little pumps dangled like a child's and did not quite reach the floor. She was training on him an exaggerated look of reproach. He felt completely detached from her. At that moment he could with pleasure have slapped her as he would have slapped a particularly obnoxious child in his charge.

He began to imagine various unlikely ways by which he could teach her a lesson. He might make friends with some distinguished Negro professor or lawyer and bring him home to spend the evening. He would be entirely justified but her blood pressure would rise to 300. He could not push her to the extent of making her have a stroke, and moreover, he had never been successful at making any Negro friends. He had tried to strike up an acquaintance on the bus with some of the better types, with ones that looked like professors or ministers or lawyers. One morning he had sat down next to a distinguished-looking dark brown man who had answered his questions with a sonorous solemnity but who had turned out to be an undertaker. Another day he had sat down beside a cigar-smoking Negro with a diamond ring on his finger, but after a few stilted pleasantries, the Negro had rung the buzzer and risen, slipping two lottery tickets into Julian's hand as he climbed over him to leave.

He imagined his mother lying desperately ill and his being able to secure only a Negro doctor for her. He toyed with that idea for a few minutes and then dropped it for a momentary vision of himself participating as a sympathizer in a sit-in demonstration. This was possible but he did not linger with it. Instead, he approached the ultimate horror. He brought home a beautiful suspiciously Negroid woman. Prepare yourself, he said. There is nothing you can do about it. This is the woman I've chosen. She's intelligent, dignified, even good, and she's suffered and she hasn't thought it *fun*. Now persecute us, go ahead and persecute us. Drive her out of here, but remember, you're driving me too. His eyes were narrowed and through the indignation he had generated, he saw his mother across the aisle, purple-faced, shrunken to the dwarf-like proportions of her moral nature, sitting like a mummy beneath the ridiculous banner of her hat.

He was tilted out of his fantasy again as the bus stopped. The door opened with a sucking hiss and out of the dark a large, gaily dressed, sullen-looking colored woman got on with a little boy. The child, who might have been four, had on a short plaid suit and a Tyrolean hat with a blue feather in it. Julian hoped that he would sit down beside him and that the woman would push in beside his mother. He could think of no better arrangement.

As she waited for her tokens, the woman was surveying the seating possibilities—he hoped with the idea of sitting where she was least wanted. There was something familiar-looking about her but Julian could not place what it was. She was a giant of a woman. Her face was set not only to meet opposition but to seek it out. The downward tilt of her large lower lip was like a warning sign: DON'T TAMPER WITH ME. Her bulging figure was encased in a green crepe dress and her feet overflowed in red shoes. She had on a hideous hat. A purple velvet flap came down on one side of it and stood up on the other; the rest of it was green and looked like a cushion with the stuffing out. She carried a mammoth red pocketbook that bulged throughout as if it were stuffed with rocks.

To Julian's disappointment, the little boy climbed up on the empty seat beside his mother. His mother lumped all children, black and white, into the common category, "cute," and she thought little Negroes were on the whole cuter than little white children. She smiled at the little boy as he climbed on the seat.

Meanwhile the woman was bearing down upon the empty seat beside Julian. To his annoyance, she squeezed herself into it. He saw his mother's face change as the woman settled herself next to him and he realized with satisfaction that this was more objectionable to her than it was to him. Her face seemed almost gray and there was a look of dull recognition in her eyes, as if suddenly she had sickened at some awful confrontation. Julian saw that it was because she and the woman had, in a sense, swapped sons. Though his mother would not realize the symbolic significance of this, she would feel it. His amusement showed plainly on his face.

The woman next to him muttered something unintelligible to herself. He was conscious of a kind of bristling next to him, a muted growling like that of an angry cat. He could not see anything but the red pocketbook upright on the bulging green thighs. He visualized the woman as she had stood waiting for her tokens—the ponderous figure, rising from the red shoes upward over the solid hips, the mammoth bosom, the haughty face, to the green and purple hat.

His eyes widened.

The vision of the two hats, identical, broke upon him with the radiance of a brilliant sunrise. His face was suddenly lit with joy. He could not believe that Fate had thrust upon his mother such a lesson. He gave a loud chuckle so that she would look at him and see that he saw. She turned her eyes on him slowly. The blue in them seemed to have turned a bruised purple. For a moment he had an uncomfortable sense of her innocence, but it lasted only a second before principle rescued him. Justice entitled him to laugh. His grin hardened until it said to her as plainly as if he were saying aloud: Your punishment exactly fits your pettiness. This should teach you a permanent lesson.

Her eyes shifted to the woman. She seemed unable to bear looking at him and to find the woman preferable. He became conscious again of the bristling presence at his side. The woman was rumbling like a volcano about to become active. His mother's mouth began to twitch slightly at one corner. With a sinking heart, he saw incipient signs of recovery on her face and realized that this was going to strike her suddenly as funny and was going to be no lesson at all. She kept her eyes on the woman and an amused smile came over her face as if the woman were a monkey that had stolen her hat. The little Negro was looking up at her with large fascinated eyes. He had been trying to attract her attention for some time.

"Carver!" the woman said suddenly. "Come heah!"

When he saw that the spotlight was on him at last, Carver drew his feet up and turned himself toward Julian's mother and giggled.

"Carver!" the woman said. "You heah me? Come heah!"

Carver slid down from the seat but remained squatting with his back against the base of it, his head turned slyly around toward Julian's mother, who was smiling at him. The woman reached a hand across the aisle and snatched him to her. He righted himself and hung backwards on her knees, grinning at Julian's mother. "Isn't he cute?" Julian's mother said to the woman with the protruding teeth.

"I reckon he is," the woman said without conviction.

The Negress yanked him upright but he eased out of her grip and shot across the aisle and scrambled, giggling wildly, onto the seat beside his love.

"I think he likes me," Julian's mother said, and smiled at the woman. It was the smile she used when she was being particularly gracious to an inferior. Julian saw everything lost. The lesson had rolled off her like rain on a roof.

The woman stood up and yanked the little boy off the seat as if she were snatching him from contagion. Julian could feel the rage in her at having no weapon like his mother's smile. She gave the child a sharp slap across his leg. He howled once and then thrust his head into her stomach and kicked his feet against her shins. "Behave," she said vehemently.

The bus stopped and the Negro who had been reading the newspaper got off. The woman moved over and set the little boy down with a thump between herself and Julian. She held him firmly by the knee. In a moment he put his hands in front of his face and peeped at Julian's mother through his fingers.

"I see yoooooooo!" she said and put her hand in front of her face and peeped at him.

The woman slapped his hand down. "Quit yo' foolishness," she said, "before I knock the living Jesus out of you!"

Julian was thankful that the next stop was theirs. He reached up and pulled the cord. The woman reached up and pulled it at the same time. Oh my God, he thought. He had the terrible intuition that when they got off the bus together, his mother would open her purse and give the little boy a nickel. The gesture would be as natural to her as breathing. The bus stopped and the woman got up and lunged to the front, dragging the child, who wished to stay on, after her. Julian and his mother got up and followed. As they neared the door, Julian tried to relieve her of her pocketbook.

"No," she murmured, "I want to give the little boy a nickel."

"No!" Julian hissed. "No!"

She smiled down at the child and opened her bag. The bus door opened and the woman picked him up by the arm and descended with him, hanging at her hip. Once in the street she set him down and shook him.

Julian's mother had to close her purse while she got down the bus step but as soon as her feet were on the ground, she opened it again and began to rummage inside. "I can't find but a penny," she whispered, "but it looks like a new one."

"Don't do it!" Julian said fiercely between his teeth. There was a streetlight on the corner and she hurried to get under it so that she could better see into her pocketbook. The woman was heading off rapidly down the street with the child still hanging backward on her hand.

"Oh little boy!" Julian's mother called and took a few quick steps and caught up with them just beyond the lamppost. "Here's a bright new penny for you," and she held out the coin, which shone bronze in the dim light.

The huge woman turned and for a moment stood, her shoulders lifted and her face frozen with frustrated rage, and stared at Julian's mother. Then all at once she seemed to explode like a piece of machinery that had been given one ounce of pressure too much. Julian saw the black fist swing out with the red pocketbook. He shut his eyes and cringed as he heard the woman shout, "He don't take nobody's pennies!" When he opened his eyes, the woman was disappearing down the street with the little boy staring wide-eyed over her shoulder. Julian's mother was sitting on the sidewalk.

"I told you not to do that," Julian said angrily. "I told you not to do that!"

He stood over her for a minute, gritting his teeth. Her legs were stretched out in front of her and her hat was on her lap. He squatted down and looked her in the face. It was totally expressionless. "You got exactly what you deserved," he said. "Now get up."

He picked up her pocketbook and put what had fallen out back in it. He picked the hat up off her lap. The penny caught his eye on the sidewalk and he picked that up and let it drop before her eyes into the purse. Then he stood up and leaned over and held his hands out to pull her up. She remained immobile. He sighed. Rising above them on either side were black apartment buildings, marked with irregular rectangles of light. At the end of the block a man came out of a door and walked off in the opposite direction. "All right," he said, "suppose somebody happens by and wants to know why you're sitting on the sidewalk?"

She took the hand and, breathing hard, pulled heavily up on it and then stood for a moment, swaying slightly as if the spots of light in the darkness were circling around her. Her eyes, shadowed and confused, finally settled on his face. He did not try to conceal his irritation. "I hope this teaches you a lesson," he said. She leaned forward and her eyes raked his face. She seemed trying to determine his identity. Then, as if she found nothing familiar about him, she started off with a headlong movement in the wrong direction.

"Aren't you going on to the Y?" he asked.

"Home," she muttered.

"Well, are we walking?"

For answer she kept going. Julian followed along, his hands behind him. He saw no reason to let the lesson she had had go without backing it up with an explanation of its meaning. She might as well be made to understand what had happened to her. "Don't think that was just an uppity Negro woman," he said. "That was the whole colored race which will no longer take your condescending pennies. That was your black double. She can wear the same hat as you, and to be sure," he added gratuitously (because he thought it was funny), "it looked better on her than it did on you. What all this means," he said, "is that the old world is gone. The old manners are obsolete and your graciousness is not worth a damn." He thought bitterly of the house that had been lost for him. "You aren't who you think you are," he said.

She continued to plow ahead, paying no attention to him. Her hair had come undone on one side. She dropped her pocketbook and took no notice. He stooped and picked it up and handed it to her but she did not take it.

"You needn't act as if the world had come to an end," he said, "because it hasn't. From now on you've got to live in a new world and face a few realities for a change. Buck up," he said, "it won't kill you."

She was breathing fast.

"Let's wait on the bus," he said.

"Home," she said thickly.

"I hate to see you behave like this," he said. "Just like a child. I should be able to expect more of you." He decided to stop where he was and make her stop and wait for a bus. "I'm not going any farther," he said, stopping. "We're going on the bus."

She continued to go on as if she had not heard him. He took a few steps and caught her arm and stopped her. He looked into her face and caught his breath. He was looking into a face he had never seen before. "Tell Grandpa to come get me," she said.

He stared, stricken.

"Tell Caroline to come get me," she said.

Stunned, he let her go and she lurched forward again, walking as if one leg were shorter than the other. A tide of darkness seemed to be sweeping her from him. "Mother!" he cried. "Darling, sweetheart, wait!" Crumpling, she fell to the pavement. He dashed forward and fell at her side, crying, "Mamma, Mamma!" He turned her over. Her face was fiercely distorted. One eye, large and staring, moved slightly to the left as if it had become unmoored. The other remained fixed on him, raked his face again, found nothing and closed.

"Wait here, wait here!" he cried and jumped up and began to run for help toward a cluster of lights he saw in the distance ahead of him. "Help, help!" he shouted, but his voice was thin, scarcely a thread of sound. The lights drifted farther away the faster he ran and his feet moved numbly as if they carried him nowhere. The tide of darkness seemed to sweep him back to her, postponing from moment to moment his entry into the world of guilt and sorrow.

Good Country People

Besides the neutral expression that she wore when she was alone, Mrs. Freeman had two others, forward and reverse, that she used for all her human dealings. Her forward expression was steady and driving like the advance of a heavy truck. Her eyes never swerved to left or right but turned as the story turned as if they followed a yellow line down the center of it. She seldom used the other expression because it was not often necessary for her to retract a statement, but when she did, her face came to a complete stop, there was an almost imperceptible movement of her black eyes, during which they seemed to be receding, and then the observer would see that Mrs. Freeman, though she might stand there as real as several grain sacks thrown on top of each other, was no longer there in spirit. As for getting anything across to her when this was the case, Mrs. Hopewell had given it up. She might talk her head off. Mrs. Freeman could never be brought to admit herself wrong on any point. She would stand there and if she could be brought to say anything, it was something like, "Well, I wouldn't of said it was and I wouldn't of said it wasn't," or letting her gaze range over the top kitchen shelf where there was an assortment of dusty bottles, she might remark, "I see you ain't ate many of them figs you put up last summer."

They carried on their most important business in the kitchen at breakfast. Every morning Mrs. Hopewell got up at seven o'clock and lit her gas heater and Joy's. Joy was her daughter, a large blonde girl who had an artificial leg. Mrs. Hopewell thought of her as a child though she was thirty-two years old and highly educated. Joy would get up while her mother was eating and lumber into the bathroom and slam the door, and before long, Mrs. Freeman would arrive at the back door. Joy would hear her mother call, "Come on in," and then they would talk for a while in low voices that were indistinguishable in the bathroom. By the time Joy came in, they had usually finished the weather report and were on one or the other of Mrs. Freeman's daughters, Glynese or Carramae. Joy called them Glycerin and Caramel. Glynese, a redhead, was eighteen and had many admirers; Carramae, a blonde, was only fifteen but already married and pregnant. She could not keep anything on her stomach. Every morning Mrs. Freeman told Mrs. Hopewell how many times she had vomited since the last report.

Mrs. Hopewell liked to tell people that Glynese and Carramae were two of the finest girls she knew and that Mrs. Freeman was a *lady* and that she was never ashamed to take her anywhere or introduce her to anybody they might meet. Then she would tell how she had happened to hire the Freemans in the first place and how they were a godsend to her and how she had had them four years. The reason for her keeping them so long was that they were not trash. They were good country people. She had telephoned the man whose name they had given as a reference and he had told her that Mr. Freeman was a good farmer but that his wife was the nosiest woman ever to walk the earth. "She's got to be into everything," the man said. "If she don't get there before the dust settles, you can bet she's dead, that's all. She'll want to know all your business. I can stand him real good," he had said, "but me nor my wife neither could have stood that woman one more minute on this place." That had put Mrs. Hopewell off for a few days.

She had hired them in the end because there were no other applicants but she had made up her mind beforehand exactly how she would handle the woman. Since she was the type who had to be into everything, then, Mrs. Hopewell had decided, she would not only let her be into everything, she would *see to it* that she was into everything—she would give her the responsibility of everything, she would put her in charge. Mrs. Hopewell had no bad qualities of her own but she was able to use other people's in such a constructive way that she never felt the lack. She had hired the Freemans and she had kept them four years.

Nothing is perfect. This was one of Mrs. Hopewell's favorite sayings. Another was: that is life! And still another, the most important, was: well, other people have their opinions too. She would make these statements, usually at the table, in a tone of gentle insistence as if no one held them but her, and the large hulking Joy, whose constant outrage had obliterated every expression from her face, would stare just a little to the side of her, her eyes icy blue, with the look of someone who has achieved blindness by an act of will and means to keep it.

When Mrs. Hopewell said to Mrs. Freeman that life was like that, Mrs. Freeman would say, "I always said so myself." Nothing had been arrived at by anyone that had not first been arrived at by her. She was quicker than Mr. Freeman. When Mrs. Hopewell said to her after they had been on the place a while, "You know, you're the wheel behind the wheel," and winked, Mrs. Freeman had said, "I know it. I've always been quick. It's some that are quicker than others."

"Everybody is different," Mrs. Hopewell said.

"Yes, most people is," Mrs. Freeman said.

"It takes all kinds to make the world."

"I always said it did myself."

The girl was used to this kind of dialogue for breakfast and more of it for dinner; sometimes they had it for supper too. When they had no guest they ate in the kitchen because that was easier. Mrs. Freeman always managed to arrive at some point during the meal and to watch them finish it. She would stand in the doorway if it were summer but in the winter she would stand with one elbow on top of the refrigerator and look down on them, or she would stand by the gas heater, lifting the back of her skirt slightly. Occasionally she would stand against the wall and roll her head from side to side. At no time was she in any hurry to leave. All this was very trying on Mrs. Hopewell but she was a woman of great patience. She realized that nothing is perfect and that in the Freemans she had good country people and that if, in this day and age, you get good country people, you had better hang onto them.

She had had plenty of experience with trash. Before the Freemans she had averaged one tenant family a year. The wives of these farmers were not the kind you would want to be around you for very long. Mrs. Hopewell, who had divorced her husband long ago, needed someone to walk over the fields with her; and when Joy had to be impressed for these services, her remarks were usually so ugly and her face so glum that Mrs. Hopewell would say, "If you can't come pleasantly, I don't want you at all," to which the girl, standing square and rigid-shouldered with her neck thrust slightly forward, would reply, "If you want me, here I am—LIKE I AM."

Mrs. Hopewell excused this attitude because of the leg (which had been shot off in a hunting accident when Joy was ten). It was hard for Mrs. Hopewell to realize that her child was thirty-two now and that for more than twenty years she had had only one leg. She thought of her still as a child because it tore her heart to think instead of the poor stout girl in her thirties who had never danced a step or had any *normal* good times. Her name was really Joy but as soon as she was twenty-one and away from home, she had had it legally changed. Mrs. Hopewell was certain that she had thought and thought until she had hit upon the ugliest name in any language. Then she had gone and had the beautiful name, Joy, changed without telling her mother until after she had done it. Her legal name was Hulga.

When Mrs. Hopewell thought the name, Hulga, she thought of the broad blank hull of a battleship. She would not use it. She continued to call her Joy to which the girl responded but in a purely mechanical way.

Hulga had learned to tolerate Mrs. Freeman who saved her from taking walks with her mother. Even Glynese and Carramae were useful when they occupied attention that might otherwise have been directed at her. At first she had thought she could not stand Mrs. Freeman for she had found that it was not possible to be rude to her. Mrs. Freeman would take on strange resentments and for days together she would be sullen but the source of her displeasure was always obscure; a direct attack, a positive leer, blatant ugliness to her face—these never touched her. And without warning one day, she began calling her Hulga.

She did not call her that in front of Mrs. Hopewell who would have been incensed but when she and the girl happened to be out of the house together, she would say something and add the name Hulga to the end of it, and the big spectacled Joy-Hulga would scowl and redden as if her privacy had been intruded upon. She considered the name her personal affair. She had arrived at it first purely on the basis of its ugly sound and then the full genius of its fitness had struck her. She had a vision of the name working like the ugly sweating Vulcan who stayed in the furnace and to whom, presumably, the goddess had to come when called. She saw it as the name of her highest creative act. One of her major triumphs was that her mother had not been able to turn her dust into Joy, but the greater one was that she had been able to turn it herself into Hulga. However, Mrs. Freeman's relish for using the name only irritated her. It was as if Mrs. Freeman's beady steel-pointed eyes had penetrated far enough behind her face to reach some secret fact. Something about her seemed to fascinate Mrs. Freeman and then one day Hulga realized that it was the artificial leg. Mrs. Freeman had a special fondness for the details of secret infections, hidden deformities, assaults upon children. Of diseases, she preferred the lingering or incurable. Hulga had heard Mrs. Hopewell give her the details of the hunting accident, how the leg had been literally blasted off, how she had never lost consciousness. Mrs. Freeman could listen to it any time as if it had happened an hour ago.

When Hulga stumped into the kitchen in the morning (she could walk without making the awful noise but she made it—Mrs. Hopewell was certain—because it was ugly-sounding), she glanced at them and did not speak. Mrs. Hopewell would be in her red kimono with her hair tied around her head in rags. She would be sitting at the table, finishing her breakfast and Mrs. Freeman would be hanging by her elbow outward from the refrigerator, looking down at the table. Hulga always put her eggs on the stove to boil and then stood over them with her arms folded, and Mrs. Hopewell would look at her—a kind of indirect gaze divided between her and Mrs. Freeman—and would think that if she would only keep herself up a little, she wouldn't be so bad looking. There was nothing wrong with her face that a pleasant expression wouldn't help. Mrs. Hopewell said that people who looked on the bright side of things would be beautiful even if they were not.

Whenever she looked at Joy this way, she could not help but feel that it would have been better if the child had not taken the Ph.D. It had certainly not brought her out any and now that she had it, there was no more excuse for her to go to school again. Mrs. Hopewell thought it was nice for girls to go to school to have a good time but Joy had "gone through." Anyhow, she would not have been strong enough to go again. The doctors had told Mrs. Hopewell that with the best of care, Joy might see forty-five. She had a weak heart. Joy had made it plain that if it had not been for this condition, she would be far from these red hills and good country people. She would be in a university lecturing to people who knew what she was talking about. And Mrs. Hopewell could very well picture her there, looking like a scarecrow and lecturing to more of the same. Here she went about all day in a six-year-old skirt and a yellow sweat shirt with a faded cowboy on a horse embossed on it. She thought this was funny; Mrs. Hopewell thought it was idiotic and showed simply that she was still a child. She was brilliant but she didn't have a grain of sense. It seemed to Mrs. Hopewell that every year she grew less like other people and more like herself—bloated, rude, and squint-eyed. And she said such strange things! To her own mother she had said—without warning, without excuse, standing up in the middle of a meal with her face purple and her mouth half full—"Woman! do you ever look inside? Do you ever look inside and see what you are *not?* God!" she had cried sinking down again and staring at her plate, "Malebranche was right: we are not our own light. We are not our own light!" Mrs. Hopewell had no idea to this day what brought that on. She had only made the remark, hoping Joy would take it in, that a smile never hurt anyone.

The girl had taken the Ph.D. in philosophy and this left Mrs. Hopewell at a complete loss. You could say, "My daughter is a nurse," or "My daughter is a school teacher," or even, "My daughter is a chemical engineer." You could not say, "My daughter is a philosopher." That was something that had ended with the Greeks and Romans. All day Joy sat on her neck in a deep chair, reading. Sometimes she went for walks but she didn't like dogs or cats or birds or flowers or nature or nice young men. She looked at nice young men as if she could smell their stupidity.

One day Mrs. Hopewell had picked up one of the books the girl had just put down and opening it at random, she read, "Science, on the other hand, has to assert its soberness and seriousness afresh and declare that it is concerned solely with what-is. Nothing—how can it be for science anything but a horror and a phantasm? If science is right, then one thing stands firm: science wishes to know nothing of nothing. Such is after all the strictly scientific approach to Nothing. We know it by wishing to know nothing of Nothing." These words had been underlined with a blue pencil and they worked on Mrs. Hopewell like some evil incantation in gibberish. She shut the book quickly and went out of the room as if she were having a chill.

This morning when the girl came in, Mrs. Freeman was on Carramae. "She thrown up four times after supper," she said, "and was up twict in the night after three o'clock. Yesterday she didn't do nothing but ramble in the bureau drawer. All she did. Stand up there and see what she could run up on."

"She's got to eat," Mrs. Hopewell muttered, sipping her coffee, while she watched Joy's back at the stove. She was wondering what the child had said to the Bible salesman. She could not imagine what kind of a conversation she could possibly have had with him.

He was a tall gaunt hatless youth who had called yesterday to sell them a Bible. He had appeared at the door, carrying a large black suitcase that weighted him so heavily on one side that he had to brace himself against the door facing. He seemed on the point of collapse but he said in a cheerful voice, "Good morning, Mrs. Cedars!" and set the suitcase down on the mat. He was not a bad-looking young man though he had on a bright blue suit and yellow socks that were not pulled up far enough. He had prominent face bones and a streak of sticky-looking brown hair falling across his forehead.

"I'm Mrs. Hopewell," she said.

"Oh!" he said, pretending to look puzzled but with his eyes sparkling, "I saw it said 'The Cedars,' on the mailbox so I thought you was Mrs. Cedars!" and he burst out in a pleasant laugh. He picked up the satchel and under cover of a pant, he fell forward into her hall. It was rather as if the suitcase had moved first, jerking him after it. "Mrs. Hopewell!" he said and grabbed her hand. "I hope you are well!" and he laughed again and then all at once his face sobered completely. He paused and gave her a straight earnest look and said, "Lady, I've come to speak of serious things."

"Well, come in," she muttered, none too pleased because her dinner was almost ready. He came into the parlor and sat down on the edge of a straight chair and put the suitcase between his feet and glanced around the room as if he were sizing her up by it. Her silver gleamed on the two sideboards; she decided he had never been in a room as elegant as this.

"Mrs. Hopewell," he began, using her name in a way that sounded almost intimate, "I know you believe in Chrustian service."

"Well, yes," she murmured.

"I know," he said and paused, looking very wise with his head cocked on one side, "that you're a good woman. Friends have told me."

Mrs. Hopewell never liked to be taken for a fool. "What are you selling?" she asked.

"Bibles," the young man said and his eye raced around the room before he added, "I see you have no family Bible in your parlor, I see that is the one lack you got!"

Mrs. Hopewell could not say, "My daughter is an atheist and won't let me keep the Bible in the parlor." She said, stiffening slightly, "I keep my Bible by my bedside." This was not the truth. It was in the attic somewhere.

"Lady," he said, "the word of God ought to be in the parlor."

"Well, I think that's a matter of taste," she began. "I think . . ."

"Lady," he said, "for a Chrustian, the word of God ought to be in every room in the house besides in his heart. I know you're a Chrustian because I can see it in every line of your face."

She stood up and said, "Well, young man, I don't want to buy a Bible and I smell my dinner burning."

He didn't get up. He began to twist his hands and looking down at them, he said softly, "Well lady, I'll tell you the truth—not many people want to buy one nowadays and besides, I know I'm real simple. I don't know how to say a thing but to say it. I'm just a country boy." He glanced up into her unfriendly face. "People like you don't like to fool with country people like me!"

"Why!" she cried, "good country people are the salt of the earth! Besides, we all have different ways of doing, it takes all kinds to make the world go 'round. That's life!"

"You said a mouthful," he said.

"Why, I think there aren't enough good country people in the world!" she said, stirred. "I think that's what's wrong with it!"

His face had brightened. "I didn't inraduce myself," he said. "I'm Manley Pointer from out in the country around Willohobie, not even from a place, just from near a place."

"You wait a minute," she said. "I have to see about my dinner." She went out to the kitchen and found Joy standing near the door where she had been listening.

"Get rid of the salt of the earth," she said, "and let's eat."

Mrs. Hopewell gave her a pained look and turned the heat down under the vegetables. "*I* can't be rude to anybody," she murmured and went back into the parlor.

He had opened the suitcase and was sitting with a Bible on each knee.

"You might as well put those up," she told him. "I don't want one."

"I appreciate your honesty," he said. "You don't see any more real honest people unless you go way out in the country."

"I know," she said, "real genuine folks!" Through the crack in the door she heard a groan.

"I guess a lot of boys come telling you they're working their way through college," he said, "but I'm not going to tell you that. Somehow," he said, "I don't want to go to college. I want to devote my life to Chrustian service. See," he said, lowering his voice, "I got this heart condition. I may not live long. When you know it's something wrong with you and you may not live long, well then, lady . . ." He paused, with his mouth open, and stared at her.

He and Joy had the same condition! She knew that her eyes were filling with tears but she collected herself quickly and murmured, "Won't you stay for dinner? We'd love to have you!" and was sorry the instant she heard herself say it.

"Yes mam," he said in an abashed voice, "I would sher love to do that!"

Joy had given him one look on being introduced to him and then throughout the meal had not glanced at him again. He had addressed several remarks to her, which she had pretended not to hear. Mrs. Hopewell could not understand deliberate rudeness, although she lived with it, and she felt she had always to overflow with hospitality to make up for Joy's lack of courtesy. She urged him to talk about himself and he did. He said he was the seventh child of twelve and that his father had been crushed under a tree when he himself was eight year old. He had been crushed very badly, in fact, almost cut in two and was practically not recognizable. His mother had got along the best she could by hard working and she had always seen that her children went to Sunday School and that they read the Bible every evening. He was now nineteen year old and he had been selling Bibles for four months. In that time he had sold seventy-seven Bibles and had the promise of two more sales. He wanted to become a missionary because he thought that was the way you could do most for people. "He who losest his life shall find it," he said simply and he was so sincere, so genuine and earnest that Mrs. Hopewell would not for the world have smiled. He prevented his peas from sliding onto the table by blocking them with a piece of bread which he later cleaned his plate with. She could see Joy observing sidewise how he handled his knife and fork and she saw too that every few minutes, the boy would dart a keen appraising glance at the girl as if he were trying to attract her attention.

After dinner Joy cleared the dishes off the table and disappeared and Mrs. Hopewell was left to talk with him. He told her again about his childhood and his father's accident and about various things that had happened to him. Every five minutes or so she would stifle a yawn. He sat for two hours until finally she told him she must go because she had an appointment in town. He packed his Bibles and thanked her and prepared to leave, but in the doorway he stopped and wrung her hand and said that not on any of his trips had he met a lady as nice as her and he asked if he could come again. She had said she would always be happy to see him.

Joy had been standing in the road, apparently looking at something in the distance, when he came down the steps toward her, bent to the side with his heavy valise. He stopped where she was standing and confronted her directly. Mrs. Hopewell could not hear what he said but she trembled to think what Joy would say to him. She could see that after a minute Joy said something and that then the boy began to speak again, making an excited gesture with his free hand. After a minute Joy said something else at which the boy began to speak once more. Then to her amazement, Mrs. Hopewell saw the two of them walk off together, toward the gate. Joy had walked all the way to the gate with him and Mrs. Hopewell could not imagine what they had said to each other, and she had not yet dared to ask.

Mrs. Freeman was insisting upon her attention. She had moved from the refrigerator to the heater so that Mrs. Hopewell had to turn and face her in order to seem to be listening. "Glynese gone out with Harvey Hill again last night," she said. "She had this sty."

"Hill," Mrs. Hopewell said absently, "is that the one who works in the garage?"

"Nome, he's the one that goes to chiropracter school," Mrs. Freeman said. "She had this sty. Been had it two days. So she says when he brought her in the other night he says, 'Lemme get rid of that sty for you,' and she says, 'How?' and he says, 'You just lay yourself down acrost the seat of that car and I'll show you.' So she done it and he popped her neck. Kept on a-popping it several times until she made him quit. This morning," Mrs. Freeman said, "she ain't got no sty. She ain't got no traces of a sty."

"I never heard of that before," Mrs. Hopewell said.

"He ast her to marry him before the Ordinary," Mrs. Freeman went on, "and she told him she wasn't going to be married in no *office*."

"Well, Glynese is a fine girl," Mrs. Hopewell said. "Glynese and Carramae are both fine girls."

"Carramae said when her and Lyman was married Lyman said it sure felt sacred to him. She said he said he wouldn't take five hundred dollars for being married by a preacher."

"How much would he take?" the girl asked from the stove.

"He said he wouldn't take five hundred dollars," Mrs. Freeman repeated.

"Well we all have work to do," Mrs. Hopewell said.

"Lyman said it just felt more sacred to him," Mrs. Freeman said. "The doctor wants Carramae to eat prunes. Says instead of medicine. Says them cramps is coming from pressure. You know where I think it is?"

"She'll be better in a few weeks," Mrs. Hopewell said.

"In the tube," Mrs. Freeman said. "Else she wouldn't be as sick as she is."

Hulga had cracked her two eggs into a saucer and was bringing them to the table along with a cup of coffee that she had filled too full. She sat down carefully and began to eat, meaning to keep Mrs. Freeman there by questions if for any reason she showed an inclination to leave. She could perceive her mother's eye on her. The first roundabout question would be about the Bible salesman and she did not wish to bring it on. "How did he pop her neck?" she asked.

Mrs. Freeman went into a description of how he had popped her neck. She said he owned a '55 Mercury but that Glynese said she would rather marry a man with only a '36 Plymouth who would be married by a preacher. The girl asked what if he had a '32 Plymouth and Mrs. Freeman said what Glynese had said was a '36 Plymouth.

Mrs. Hopewell said there were not many girls with Glynese's common sense. She said what she admired in those girls was their common sense. She said that reminded her that they had had a nice visitor yesterday, a young man selling Bibles. "Lord," she said, "he bored me to death but he was so sincere and genuine I couldn't be rude to him. He was just good country people, you know," she said, "—just the salt of the earth."

"I seen him walk up," Mrs. Freeman said, "and then later—I seen him walk off," and Hulga could feel the slight shift in her voice, the slight insinuation, that he had not walked off alone, had he? Her face remained expressionless but the color rose into her neck and she seemed to swallow it down with the next spoonful of egg. Mrs. Freeman was looking at her as if they had a secret together.

"Well, it takes all kinds of people to make the world go 'round," Mrs. Hopewell said. "It's very good we aren't all alike."

"Some people are more alike than others," Mrs. Freeman said.

Hulga got up and stumped, with about twice the noise that was necessary, into her room and locked the door. She was to meet the Bible salesman at ten o'clock at the gate. She had thought about it half the night. She had started thinking of it as a great joke and then she had begun to see profound implications in it. She had lain in bed imagining dialogues for them that were insane on the surface but that reached below to depths that no Bible salesman would be aware of. Their conversation yesterday had been of this kind.

He had stopped in front of her and had simply stood there. His face was bony and sweaty and bright, with a little pointed nose in the center of it, and his look was different from what it had been at the dinner table. He was gazing at her with open curiosity, with fascination, like a child watching a new fantastic animal at the zoo, and he was breathing as if he had run a great distance to reach her. His gaze seemed somehow familiar but she could not think where she had been regarded with it before. For almost a minute he didn't say anything. Then on what seemed an insuck of breath, he whispered, "You ever ate a chicken that was two days old?"

The girl looked at him stonily. He might have just put this question up for consideration at the meeting of a philosophical association. "Yes," she presently replied as if she had considered it from all angles.

"It must have been mighty small!" he said triumphantly and shook all over with little nervous giggles, getting very red in the face, and subsiding finally into his gaze of complete admiration, while the girl's expression remained exactly the same.

"How old are you?" he asked softly.

She waited some time before she answered. Then in a flat voice she said, "Seventeen."

His smiles came in succession like waves breaking on the surface of a little lake. "I see you got a wooden leg," he said. "I think you're real brave. I think you're real sweet."

The girl stood blank and solid and silent.

"Walk to the gate with me," he said. "You're a brave sweet little thing and I liked you the minute I seen you walk in the door."

Hulga began to move forward.

"What's your name?" he asked, smiling down on the top of her head.

"Hulga," she said.

"Hulga," he murmured, "Hulga. Hulga. I never heard of anybody name Hulga before. You're shy, aren't you, Hulga?" he asked.

She nodded, watching his large red hand on the handle of the giant valise.

"I like girls that wear glasses," he said. "I think a lot. I'm not like these people that a serious thought don't ever enter their heads. It's because I may die."

"I may die too," she said suddenly and looked up at him. His eyes were very small and brown, glittering feverishly.

"Listen," he said, "don't you think some people was meant to meet on account of what all they got in common and all? Like they both think serious thoughts and all?" He shifted the valise to his other hand so that the hand nearest her was free. He caught hold of her elbow and shook it a little. "I don't work on Saturday," he said. "I like to walk in the woods and see what Mother Nature is wearing. O'er the hills and far away. Pic-nics and things. Couldn't we go on a pic-nic tomorrow? Say yes, Hulga," he said and gave her a dying look as if he felt his insides about to drop out of him. He had even seemed to sway slightly toward her.

During the night she had imagined that she seduced him. She imagined that the two of them walked on the place until they came to the storage barn beyond the two back fields and there, she imagined, that things came to such a pass that she very easily seduced him and that then, of course, she had to reckon with his remorse. True genius can get an idea across even to an inferior mind. She imagined that she took his remorse in hand and changed it into a deeper understanding of life. She took all his shame away and turned it into something useful.

She set off for the gate at exactly ten o'clock, escaping without drawing Mrs. Hopewell's attention. She didn't take anything to eat, forgetting that food is usually taken on a picnic. She wore a pair of slacks and a dirty white shirt, and as an afterthought, she had put some Vapex on the collar of it since she did not own any perfume. When she reached the gate no one was there.

She looked up and down the empty highway and had the furious feeling that she had been tricked, that he had only meant to make her walk to the gate after the idea of him. Then suddenly he stood up, very tall, from behind a bush on the opposite embankment. Smiling, he lifted his hat which was new and wide-brimmed. He had not worn it yesterday and she wondered if he had bought it for the occasion. It was toast-colored with a red and white band around it and was slightly too large for him. He stepped from behind the bush still carrying the black valise. He had on the same suit and the same yellow socks sucked down in his shoes from walking. He crossed the highway and said, "I knew you'd come!"

The girl wondered acidly how he had known this. She pointed to the valise and asked, "Why did you bring your Bibles?"

He took her elbow, smiling down on her as if he could not stop. "You can never tell when you'll need the word of God, Hulga," he said. She had a moment in which she doubted that this was actually happening and then they began to climb the embankment. They went down into the pasture toward the woods. The boy walked lightly by her side, bouncing on his toes. The valise did not seem to be heavy today; he even swung it. They crossed half the pasture without saying anything and then, putting his hand easily on the small of her back, he asked softly, "Where does your wooden leg join on?"

She turned an ugly red and glared at him and for an instant the boy looked abashed. "I didn't mean you no harm," he said. "I only meant you're so brave and all. I guess God takes care of you."

"No," she said, looking forward and walking fast, "I don't even believe in God."

At this he stopped and whistled. "No!" he exclaimed as if he were too astonished to say anything else.

She walked on and in a second he was bouncing at her side, fanning with his hat. "That's very unusual for a girl," he remarked, watching her out of the corner of his eye. When they reached the edge of the wood, he put his hand on her back again and drew her against him without a word and kissed her heavily.

The kiss, which had more pressure than feeling behind it, produced that extra surge of adrenalin in the girl that enables one to carry a packed trunk out of a burning house, but in her, the power went at once to the brain. Even before he released her, her mind, clear and detached and ironic anyway, was regarding him from a great distance, with amusement but with pity. She had never been kissed before and she was pleased to discover that it was an unexceptional experience and all a matter of the mind's control. Some people might enjoy drain water if they were told it was vodka. When the boy, looking expectant but uncertain, pushed her gently away, she turned and walked on, saying nothing as if such business, for her, were common enough.

He came along panting at her side, trying to help her when he saw a root that she might trip over. He caught and held back the long swaying blades of thorn vine until she had passed beyond them. She led the way and he came breathing heavily behind her. Then they came out on a sunlit hillside, sloping softly into another one a little smaller. Beyond, they could see the rusted top of the old barn where the extra hay was stored.

The hill was sprinkled with small pink weeds. "Then you ain't saved?" he asked suddenly, stopping.

The girl smiled. It was the first time she had smiled at him at all. "In my economy," she said, "I'm saved and you are damned but I told you I didn't believe in God."

Nothing seemed to destroy the boy's look of admiration. He gazed at her now as if the fantastic animal at the zoo had put its paw through the bars and given him a loving poke. She thought he looked as if he wanted to kiss her again and she walked on before he had the chance.

"Ain't there somewheres we can sit down sometime?" he murmured, his voice softening toward the end of the sentence.

"In that barn," she said.

They made for it rapidly as if it might slide away like a train. It was a large two-story barn, cool and dark inside. The boy pointed up the ladder that led into the loft and said, "It's too bad we can't go up there."

"Why can't we?" she asked.

"Yer leg," he said reverently.

The girl gave him a contemptuous look and putting both hands on the ladder, she climbed it while he stood below, apparently awestruck. She pulled herself expertly through the opening and then looked down at him and said, "Well, come on if you're coming," and he began to climb the ladder, awkwardly bringing the suitcase with him.

"We won't need the Bible," she observed.

"You never can tell," he said, panting. After he had got into the loft, he was a few seconds catching his breath. She had sat down in a pile of straw. A wide sheath of sunlight, filled with dust particles, slanted over her. She lay back against a bale, her face turned away, looking out the front opening of the barn where hay was thrown from a wagon into the loft. The two pink-speckled hillsides lay back against a dark ridge of woods. The sky was cloudless and cold blue. The boy dropped down by her side and put one arm under her and the other over her and began methodically kissing her face, making little noises like a fish. He did not remove his hat but it was pushed far enough back not to interfere. When her glasses got in his way, he took them off of her and slipped them into his pocket.

The girl at first did not return any of the kisses but presently she began to and after she had put several on his cheek, she reached his lips and remained there, kissing him again and again as if she were trying to draw all the breath out of him. His breath was clear and sweet like a child's and the kisses were sticky like a child's. He mumbled about loving her and about knowing when he first seen her that he loved her, but the mumbling was like the sleepy fretting of a child being put to sleep by his mother. Her mind, throughout this, never stopped or lost itself for a second to her feelings. "You ain't said you loved me none," he whispered finally, pulling back from her. "You got to say that."

She looked away from him off into the hollow sky and then down at a black ridge and then down farther into what appeared to be two green swelling lakes. She didn't realize he had taken her glasses but this landscape could not seem exceptional to her for she seldom paid any close attention to her surroundings.

"You got to say it," he repeated. "You got to say you love me."

She was always careful how she committed herself. "In a sense," she began, "if you use the word loosely, you might say that. But it's not a word I use. I don't have illusions. I'm one of those people who see *through* to nothing."

The boy was frowning. "You got to say it. I said it and you got to say it," he said.

The girl looked at him almost tenderly. "You poor baby," she murmured. "It's just as well you don't understand," and she pulled him by the neck, face-down, against her. "We are all damned," she said, "but some of us have taken off our blindfolds and see that there's nothing to see. It's a kind of salvation."

The boy's astonished eyes looked blankly through the ends of her hair. "Okay," he almost whined, "but do you love me or don'tcher?"

"Yes," she said and added, "in a sense. But I must tell you something. There mustn't be anything dishonest between us." She lifted his head and looked him in the eye. "I am thirty years old," she said. "I have a number of degrees."

The boy's look was irritated but dogged. "I don't care," he said. "I don't care a thing about what all you done. I just want to know if you love me or don'tcher?" and he caught her to him and wildly planted her face with kisses until she said, "Yes, yes."

"Okay then," he said, letting her go. "Prove it."

She smiled, looking dreamily out on the shifty landscape. She had seduced him without even making up her mind to try. "How?" she asked, feeling that he should be delayed a little.

He leaned over and put his lips to her ear. "Show me where your wooden leg joins on," he whispered.

The girl uttered a sharp little cry and her face instantly drained of color. The obscenity of the suggestion was not what shocked her. As a child she had sometimes been subject to feelings of shame but education had removed the last traces of that as a good surgeon scrapes for cancer; she would no more have felt it over what he was asking than she would have believed in his Bible. But she was as sensitive about the artificial leg as a peacock about his tail. No one ever touched it but her. She took care of it as someone else would his soul, in private and almost with her own eyes turned away. "No," she said.

"I known it," he muttered, sitting up. "You're just playing me for a sucker."

"Oh no no!" she cried. "It joins on at the knee. Only at the knee. Why do you want to see it?"

The boy gave her a long penetrating look. "Because," he said, "it's what makes you different. You ain't like anybody else."

She sat staring at him. There was nothing about her face or her round freezing-blue eyes to indicate that this had moved her; but she felt as if her heart had stopped and left her mind to pump her blood. She decided that for the first time in her life she was face to face with real innocence. This boy, with an instinct that came from beyond wisdom, had touched the truth about her. When after a minute, she said in a hoarse high voice, "All right," it was like surrendering to him completely. It was like losing her own life and finding it again, miraculously, in his.

Very gently he began to roll the slack leg up. The artificial limb, in a white sock and brown flat shoe, was bound in a heavy material like canvas and ended in an ugly jointure where it was attached to the stump. The boy's face and his voice were entirely reverent as he uncovered it and said, "Now show me how to take it off and on."

She took it off for him and put it back on again and then he took it off himself, handling it as tenderly as if it were a real one. "See!" he said with a delighted child's face. "Now I can do it myself!"

"Put it back on," she said. She was thinking that she would run away with him and that every night he would take the leg off and every morning put it back on again. "Put it back on," she said.

"Not yet," he murmured, setting it on its foot out of her reach. "Leave it off for a while. You got me instead."

She gave a little cry of alarm but he pushed her down and began to kiss her again. Without the leg she felt entirely dependent on him. Her brain seemed to have stopped thinking altogether and to be about some other function that it was not very good at. Different expressions raced back and forth over her face. Every now and then the boy, his eyes like two steel spikes, would glance behind him where the leg stood. Finally she pushed him off and said, "Put it back on me now."

"Wait," he said. He leaned the other way and pulled the valise toward him and opened it. It had a pale blue spotted lining and there were only two Bibles in it. He took one of these out and opened the cover of it. It was hollow and contained a pocket flask of whiskey, a pack of cards, and a small blue box with printing on it. He laid these out in front of her one at a time in an evenly-spaced row, like one presenting offerings at the shrine of a goddess. He put the blue box in her hand. THIS PRODUCT TO BE USED ONLY FOR THE PREVENTION OF DISEASE, she read, and dropped it. The boy was unscrewing the top of the flask. He stopped and pointed, with a smile, to the deck of cards. It was not an ordinary deck but one with an obscene picture on the back of each card. "Take a swig," he said, offering her the bottle first. He held it in front of her, but like one mesmerized, she did not move.

Her voice when she spoke had an almost pleading sound. "Aren't you," she murmured, "aren't you just good country people?"

The boy cocked his head. He looked as if he were just beginning to understand that she might be trying to insult him. "Yeah," he said, curling his lip slightly, "but it ain't held me back none. I'm as good as you any day in the week."

"Give me my leg," she said.

He pushed it farther away with his foot. "Come on now, let's begin to have us a good time," he said coaxingly. "We ain't got to know one another good yet."

"Give me my leg!" she screamed and tried to lunge for it but he pushed her down easily.

"What's the matter with you all of a sudden?" he asked, frowning as he screwed the top on the flask and put it quickly back inside the Bible. "You just a while ago said you didn't believe in nothing. I thought you was some girl!"

Her face was almost purple. "You're a Christian!" she hissed. "You're a fine Christian! You're just like them all—say one thing and do another. You're a perfect Christian, you're . . ."

The boy's mouth was set angrily. "I hope you don't think," he said in a lofty indignant tone, "that I believe in that crap! I may sell Bibles but I know which end is up and I wasn't born yesterday and I know where I'm going!"

"Give me my leg!" she screeched. He jumped up so quickly that she barely saw him sweep the cards and the blue box back into the Bible and throw the Bible into the valise. She saw him grab the leg and then she saw it for an instant slanted forlornly across the inside of the suitcase with a Bible at either side of its opposite ends. He slammed the lid shut and snatched up the valise and swung it down the hole and then stepped through himself.

When all of him had passed but his head, he turned and regarded her with a look that no longer had any admiration in it. "I've gotten a lot of interesting things," he said. "One time I got a woman's glass eye this way. And you needn't to think you'll catch me because Pointer ain't really my name. I use a different name at every house I call at and don't stay nowhere long. And I'll tell you another thing, Hulga," he said, using the name as if he didn't think much of it, "you ain't so smart. I been believing in nothing ever since I was born!" and then the toast-colored hat disappeared down the hole and the girl was left, sitting on the straw in the dusty sunlight. When she turned her churning face toward the opening, she saw his blue figure struggling successfully over the green speckled lake.

Mrs. Hopewell and Mrs. Freeman, who were in the back pasture, digging up onions, saw him emerge a little later from the woods and head across the meadow toward the highway. "Why, that looks like that nice dull young man that tried to sell me a Bible yesterday," Mrs. Hopewell said, squinting. "He must have been selling them to the Negroes back in there. He was so simple," she said, "but I guess the world would be better off if we were all that simple."

Mrs. Freeman's gaze drove forward and just touched him before he disappeared under the hill. Then she returned her attention to the evil-smelling onion shoot she was lifting from the ground. "Some can't be that simple," she said. "I know I never could."

The Life You Save May Be Your Own

The old woman and her daughter were sitting on their porch when Mr. Shiftlet came up their road for the first time. The old woman slid to the edge of her chair and leaned forward, shading her eyes from the piercing sunset with her hand. The daughter could not see far in front of her and continued to play with her fingers. Although the old woman lived in this desolate spot with only her daughter and she had never seen Mr. Shiftlet before, she could tell, even from a distance, that he was a tramp and no one to be afraid of. His left coat sleeve was folded up to show there was only half an arm in it and his gaunt figure listed slightly to the side as if the breeze were pushing him. He had on a black town suit and a brown felt hat that was turned up in the front and down in the back and he carried a tin tool box by a handle. He came on, at an amble, up her road, his face turned toward the sun which appeared to be balancing itself on the peak of a small mountain.

The old woman didn't change her position until he was almost into her yard; then she rose with one hand fisted on her hip. The daughter, a large girl in a short blue organdy dress, saw him all at once and jumped up and began to stamp and point and make excited speechless sounds.

Mr. Shiftlet stopped just inside the yard and set his box on the ground and tipped his hat at her as if she were not in the least afflicted; then he turned toward the old woman and swung the hat all the way off. He had long black slick hair that hung flat from a part in the middle to beyond the tips of his ears on either side. His face descended in forehead for more than half its length and ended suddenly with his features just balanced over a jutting steel-trap jaw. He seemed to be a young man but he had a look of composed dissatisfaction as if he understood life thoroughly.

"Good evening," the old woman said. She was about the size of a cedar fence post and she had a man's gray hat pulled down low over her head.

The tramp stood looking at her and didn't answer. He turned his back and faced the sunset. He swung both his whole and his short arm up slowly so that they indicated an expanse of sky and his figure formed a crooked cross. The old woman watched him with her arms folded across her chest as if she were the owner of the sun, and the daughter watched, her head thrust forward and her fat helpless hands hanging at the wrists. She had long pink-gold hair and eyes as blue as a peacock's neck.

He held the pose for almost fifty seconds and then he picked up his box and came on to the porch and dropped down on the bottom step. "Lady," he said in a firm nasal voice, "I'd give a fortune to live where I could see me a sun do that every evening."

"Does it every evening," the old woman said and sat back down. The daughter sat down too and watched him with a cautious sly look as if he were a bird that had come up very close. He leaned to one side, rooting in his pants pocket, and in a second he brought out a package of chewing gum and offered her a piece. She took it and unpeeled it and began to chew without taking her eyes off him. He offered the old woman a piece but she only raised her upper lip to indicate she had no teeth.

Mr. Shiftlet's pale sharp glance had already passed over everything in the yard—the pump near the corner of the house and the big fig tree that three or four chickens were preparing to roost in—and had moved to a shed where he saw the square rusted back of an automobile. "You ladies drive?" he asked.

"That car ain't run in fifteen year," the old woman said. "The day my husband died, it quit running."

"Nothing is like it used to be, lady," he said. "The world is almost rotten."

"That's right," the old woman said. "You from around here?"

"Name Tom T. Shiftlet," he murmured, looking at the tires.

"I'm pleased to meet you," the old woman said. "Name Lucynell Crater and daughter Lucynell Crater. What you doing around here, Mr. Shiftlet?"

He judged the car to be about a 1928 or '29 Ford. "Lady," he said, and turned and gave her his full attention, "lemme tell you something. There's one of these doctors in Atlanta that's taken a knife and cut the human heart—the human heart," he repeated, leaning forward, "out of a man's chest and held it in his hand," and he held his hand out, palm up, as if it were slightly weighted with the human heart, "and studied it like it was a day-old chicken, and lady," he said, allowing a long significant pause in which his head slid forward and his clay-colored eyes brightened, "he don't know no more about it than you or me."

"That's right," the old woman said.

"Why, if he was to take that knife and cut into every corner of it, he still wouldn't know no more than you or me. What you want to bet?"

"Nothing," the old woman said wisely. "Where you from, Mr. Shiftlet?"

He didn't answer. He reached into his pocket and brought out a sack of tobacco and a package of cigarette papers and rolled himself a cigarette, expertly with one hand, and attached it in a hanging position to his upper lip. Then he took a box of wooden matches from his pocket and struck one on his shoe. He held the burning match as if he were studying the mystery of flame while it traveled dangerously toward his skin. The daughter began to make loud noises and to point to his hand and shake her finger at him, but when the flame was just before touching him, he leaned down with his hand cupped over it as if he were going to set fire to his nose and lit the cigarette.

He flipped away the dead match and blew a stream of gray into the evening. A sly look came over his face. "Lady," he said, "nowadays, people'll do anything anyways. I can tell you my name is Tom T. Shiftlet and I came from Tarwater, Tennessee, but you never have seen me before: how you know I ain't lying? How you know my name ain't Aaron Sparks, lady, and I come from Singleberry, Georgia, or how you know it's not George Speeds and I come from Lucy, Alabama, or you know I ain't Thompson Bright from Toolafalls, Mississippi?"

"I don't know nothing about you," the old woman muttered, irked.

"Lady," he said, "people don't care how they lie. Maybe the best I can tell you is, I'm a man; but listen lady," he said and paused and made his tone more ominous still, "what is a man?"

The old woman began to gum a seed, "What you carry in that tin box, Mr. Shiftlet?" she asked.

"Tools," he said, put back, "I'm a carpenter."

"Well, if you come out here to work, I'll be able to feed you and give you a place to sleep but I can't pay. I'll tell you that before you begin," she said.

There was no answer at once and no particular expression on his face. He leaned back against the two-by-four that helped support the porch roof. "Lady," he said slowly, "there's some men that some things mean more to them then money." The old woman rocked without comment and the daughter watched the trigger that moved up and down in his neck. He told the old woman then that all most people were interested in was money, but he asked what a man was made for. He asked her if a man was made for money, or what. He asked her what she thought she was made for but she didn't answer, she only sat rocking and wondered if a one-armed man could put a new roof on her garden house. He asked a lot of questions that she didn't answer. He told her that he was twenty-eight years old and had lived a varied life. He had been a gospel singer, a foreman on the railroad, an assistant in an undertaking parlor, and he had come over the radio for three months with Uncle Roy and his Red Creek Wranglers. He said he had fought and bled in the Arm Service of his country and visited every foreign land and that everywhere he had seen people that didn't care if they did a thing one way or another. He said he hadn't been raised thataway.

A fat yellow moon appeared in the branches of the fig tree as if it were going to roost there with the chickens. He said that a man had to escape to the country to see the world whole and that he wished he lived in a desolate place like this where he could see the sun go down every evening like God made it to do.

"Are you married or are you single?" the old woman asked.

There was a long silence. "Lady," he asked finally, "where would you find you an innocent woman today? I wouldn't have any of this trash I could just pick up."

The daughter was leaning very far down, hanging her head almost between her knees, watching him through a triangular door she had made in her overturned hair; and she suddenly fell in a heap on the floor and began to whimper. Mr. Shiftlet straightened her out and helped her get back in the chair.

"Is she your baby girl?" he asked.

"My only," the old woman said, "and she's the sweetest girl in the world. I wouldn't give her up for nothing on earth. She's smart too. She can sweep the floor, cook, wash, feed the chickens, and hoe. I wouldn't give her up for a casket of jewels."

"No," he said kindly, "don't ever let any man take her away from you."

"Any man come after her," the old woman said, " 'll have to stay around the place."

Mr. Shiftlet's eye in the darkness was focused on a part of the automobile bumper that glittered in the distance. "Lady," he said, jerking his short arm up as if he could point with it to her house and yard and pump, "there ain't a broken thing on this plantation that I couldn't fix for you, one-arm jackleg or not. I'm a man," he said with a sullen dignity, "even if I ain't a whole one. I got," he said, tapping his knuckles on the floor to emphasize the immensity of what he was going to say, "a moral intelligence!" and his face pierced out of the darkness into a shaft of doorlight and he stared at her as if he were astonished himself at this impossible truth.

The old woman was not impressed with the phrase. "I told you you could hang around and work for food," she said, "if you don't mind sleeping in that car yonder."

"Why listen, Lady," he said with a grin of delight, "the monks of old slept in their coffins!"

"They wasn't as advanced as we are," the old woman said.

The next morning he began on the roof of the garden house while Lucynell, the daughter, sat on a rock and watched him work. He had not been around a week before the change he had made in the place was apparent. He had patched the front and back steps, built a new hog pen, restored a fence, and taught Lucynell, who was completely deaf and had never said a word in her life, to say the word "bird." The big rosy-faced girl followed him everywhere, saying "Burrttddt ddbirrrttdt," and clapping her hands. The old woman watched from a distance, secretly pleased. She was ravenous for a son-in-law.

Mr. Shiftlet slept on the hard narrow back seat of the car with his feet out the side window. He had his razor and a can of water on a crate that served him as a bedside table and he put up a piece of mirror against the back glass and kept his coat neatly on a hanger that he hung over one of the windows.

In the evenings he sat on the steps and talked while the old woman and Lucynell rocked violently in their chairs on either side of him. The old woman's three mountains were black against the dark blue sky and were visited off and on by various planets and by the moon after it had left the chickens. Mr. Shiftlet pointed out that the reason he had improved this plantation was because he had taken a personal interest in it. He said he was even going to make the automobile run.

He had raised the hood and studied the mechanism and he said he could tell that the car had been built in the days when cars were really built. You take now, he said, one man puts in one bolt and another man puts in another bolt and another man puts in another bolt so that it's a man for a bolt. That's why you have to pay so much for a car: you're paying all those men. Now if you didn't have to pay but one man, you could get you a cheaper car and one that had had a personal interest taken in it, and it would be a better car. The old woman agreed with him that this was so.

Mr. Shiftlet said that the trouble with the world was that nobody cared, or stopped and took any trouble. He said he never would have been able to teach Lucynell to say a word if he hadn't cared and stopped long enough.

"Teach her to say something else," the old woman said.

"What you want her to say next?" Mr. Shiftlet asked.

The old woman's smile was broad and toothless and suggestive. "Teach her to say 'sugarpie,' " she said.

Mr. Shiftlet already knew what was on her mind.

The next day he began to tinker with the automobile and that evening he told her that if she would buy a fan belt, he would be able to make the car run.

The old woman said she would give him the money. "You see that girl yonder?" she asked, pointing to Lucynell who was sitting on the floor a foot away, watching him, her eyes blue even in the dark. "If it was ever a man wanted to take her away, I would say, 'No man on earth is going to take that sweet girl of mine away from me!' but if he was to say, 'Lady, I don't want to take her away, I want her right here,' I would say, 'Mister, I don't blame you none. I wouldn't pass up a chance to live in a permanent place and get the sweetest girl in the world myself. You ain't no fool,' I would say."

"How old is she?" Mr. Shiftlet asked casually.

"Fifteen, sixteen," the old woman said. The girl was nearly thirty but because of her innocence it was impossible to guess.

"It would be a good idea to paint it too," Mr. Shiftlet remarked. "You don't want it to rust out."

"We'll see about that later," the old woman said.

The next day he walked into town and returned with the parts he needed and a can of gasoline. Late in the afternoon, terrible noises issued from the shed and the old woman rushed out of the house, thinking Lucynell was somewhere having a fit. Lucynell was sitting on a chicken crate, stamping her feet and screaming, "Burrddttt! bddurrddtttt!" but her fuss was drowned out by the car. With a volley of blasts it emerged from the shed, moving in a fierce and stately way. Mr. Shiftlet was in the driver's seat, sitting very erect. He had an expression of serious modesty on his face as if he had just raised the dead.

That night, rocking on the porch, the old woman began her business at once. "You want you an innocent woman, don't you?" she asked sympathetically. "You don't want none of this trash."

"No'm, I don't," Mr. Shiftlet said.

"One that can't talk," she continued, "can't sass you back or use foul language. That's the kind for you to have. Right there," and she pointed to Lucynell sitting cross-legged in her chair, holding both feet in her hands.

"That's right," he admitted. "She wouldn't give me any trouble."

"Saturday," the old woman said, "you and her and me can drive into town and get married."

Mr. Shiftlet eased his position on the steps.

"I can't get married right now," he said. "Everything you want to do takes money and I ain't got any."

"What you need with money?" she asked.

"It takes money," he said. "Some people'll do anything anyhow these days, but the way I think, I wouldn't marry no woman that I couldn't take on a trip like she was somebody. I mean take her to a hotel and treat her. I wouldn't marry the Duchesser Windsor," he said firmly, "unless I could take her to a hotel and give her something good to eat.

"I was raised thataway and there ain't a thing I can do about it. My old mother taught me how to do."

"Lucynell don't even know what a hotel is," the old woman muttered. "Listen here, Mr. Shiftlet," she said, sliding forward in her chair, "you'd be getting a permanent house and a deep well and the most innocent girl in the world. You don't need no money. Lemme tell you something: there ain't any place in the world for a poor disabled friendless drifting man."

The ugly words settled in Mr. Shiftlet's head like a group of buzzards in the top of a tree. He didn't answer at once. He rolled himself a cigarette and lit it and then he said in an even voice, "Lady, a man is divided into two parts, body and spirit."

The old woman clamped her gums together.

"A body and a spirit," he repeated. "The body, lady, is like a house: it don't go anywhere; but the spirit, lady, is like a automobile: always on the move, always . . ."

"Listen, Mr. Shiftlet," she said, "my well never goes dry and my house is always warm in the winter and there's no mortgage on a thing about this place. You can go to the courthouse and see for yourself. And yonder under that shed is a fine automobile." She laid the bait carefully. "You can have it painted by Saturday. I'll pay for the paint."

In the darkness, Mr. Shiftlet's smile stretched like a weary snake waking up by a fire. After a second he recalled himself and said, "I'm only saying a man's spirit means more to him than anything else. I would have to take my wife off for the week end without no regards at all for cost. I got to follow where my spirit says to go."

"I'll give you fifteen dollars for a week-end trip," the old woman said in a crabbed voice. "That's the best I can do."

"That wouldn't hardly pay for more than the gas and the hotel," he said. "It wouldn't feed her."

"Seventeen-fifty," the old woman said. "That's all I got so it isn't any use you trying to milk me. You can take a lunch."

Mr. Shiftlet was deeply hurt by the word "milk." He didn't doubt that she had more money sewed up in her mattress but he had already told her he was not interested in her money. "I'll make that do," he said and rose and walked off without treating with her further.

On Saturday the three of them drove into town in the car that the paint had barely dried on and Mr. Shiftlet and Lucynell were married in the Ordinary's office while the old woman witnessed. As they came out of the courthouse, Mr. Shiftlet began twisting his neck in his collar. He looked morose and bitter as if he had been insulted while someone held him. "That didn't satisfy me none," he said. "That was just something a woman in an office did, nothing but paper work and blood tests. What do they know about my blood? If they was to take my heart and cut it out," he said, "they wouldn't know a thing about me. It didn't satisfy me at all."

"It satisfied the law," the old woman said sharply.

"The law," Mr. Shiftlet said and spit. "It's the law that don't satisfy me."

He had painted the car dark green with a yellow band around it just under the windows. The three of them climbed in the front seat and the old woman said, "Don't Lucynell look pretty? Looks like a baby doll." Lucynell was dressed up in a white dress that her mother had uprooted from a trunk and there was a Panama hat on her head with a bunch of red wooden cherries on the brim. Every now and then her placid expression was changed by a sly isolated little thought like a shoot of green in the desert. "You got a prize!" the old woman said.

Mr. Shiftlet didn't even look at her.

They drove back to the house to let the old woman off and pick up the lunch. When they were ready to leave, she stood staring in the window of the car, with her fingers clenched around the glass. Tears began to seep sideways out of her eyes and run along the dirty creases in her face. "I ain't ever been parted with her for two days before," she said.

Mr. Shiftlet started the motor.

"And I wouldn't let no man have her but you because I seen you would do right. Good-by, Sugarbaby," she said, clutching at the sleeve of the white dress. Lucynell looked straight at her and didn't seem to see her there at all. Mr. Shiftlet eased the car forward so that she had to move her hands.

The early afternoon was clear and open and surrounded by pale blue sky. Although the car would go only thirty miles an hour, Mr. Shiftlet imagined a terrific climb and dip and swerve that went entirely to his head so that he forgot his morning bitterness. He had always wanted an automobile but he had never been able to afford one before. He drove very fast because he wanted to make Mobile by nightfall.

Occasionally he stopped his thoughts long enough to look at Lucynell in the seat beside him. She had eaten the lunch as soon as they were out of the yard and now she was pulling the cherries off the hat one by one and throwing them out the window. He became depressed in spite of the car. He had driven about a hundred miles when he decided that she must be hungry again and at the next small town they came to, he stopped in front of an aluminum-painted eating place called The Hot Spot and took her in and ordered her a plate of ham and grits. The ride had made her sleepy and as soon as she got up on the stool, she rested her head on the counter and shut her eyes. There was no one in The Hot Spot but Mr. Shiftlet and the boy behind the counter, a pale youth with a greasy rag hung over his shoulder. Before he could dish up the food, she was snoring gently.

"Give it to her when she wakes up," Mr. Shiftlet said. "I'll pay for it now."

The boy bent over her and stared at the long pink-gold hair and the half-shut sleeping eyes. Then he looked up and stared at Mr. Shiftlet. "She looks like an angel of Gawd," he murmured.

"Hitch-hiker," Mr. Shiftlet explained. "I can't wait. I got to make Tuscaloosa."

The boy bent over again and very carefully touched his finger to a strand of the golden hair and Mr. Shiftlet left.

He was more depressed than ever as he drove on by himself. The late afternoon had grown hot and sultry and the country had flattened out. Deep in the sky a storm was preparing very slowly and without thunder as if it meant to drain every drop of air from the earth before it broke. There were times when Mr. Shiftlet preferred not to be alone. He felt too that a man with a car had a responsibility to others and he kept his eye out for a hitch-hiker. Occasionally he saw a sign that warned: "Drive carefully. The life you save may be your own."

The narrow road dropped off on either side into dry fields and here and there a shack or a filling station stood in a clearing. The sun began to set directly in front of the automobile. It was a reddening ball that through his windshield was slightly flat on the bottom and top. He saw a boy in overalls and a gray hat standing on the edge of the road and he slowed the car down and stopped in front of him. The boy didn't have his hand raised to thumb the ride, he was only standing there, but he had a small cardboard suitcase and his hat was set on his head in a way to indicate that he had left somewhere for good. "Son," Mr. Shiftlet said, "I see you want a ride."

The boy didn't say he did or he didn't but he opened the door of the car and got in, and Mr. Shiftlet started driving again. The child held the suitcase on his lap and folded his arms on top of it. He turned his head and looked out the window away from Mr. Shiftlet. Mr. Shiftlet felt oppressed. "Son," he said after a minute, "I got the best old mother in the world so I reckon you only got the second best."

The boy gave him a quick dark glance and then turned his face back out the window.

"It's nothing so sweet," Mr. Shiftlet continued, "as a boy's mother. She taught him his first prayers at her knee, she give him love when no other would, she told him what was right and what wasn't, and she seen that he done the right thing. Son," he said, "I never rued a day in my life like the one I rued when I left that old mother of mine."

The boy shifted in his seat but he didn't look at Mr. Shiftlet. He unfolded his arms and put one hand on the door handle.

"My mother was a angel of Gawd," Mr. Shiftlet said in a very strained voice. "He took her from heaven and giver to me and I left her." His eyes were instantly clouded over with a mist of tears. The car was barely moving.

The boy turned angrily in the seat. "You go to the devil!" he cried. "My old woman is a flea bag and yours is a stinking pole cat!" and with that he flung the door open and jumped out with his suitcase into the ditch.

Mr. Shiftlet was so shocked that for about a hundred feet he drove along slowly with the door still open. A cloud, the exact color of the boy's hat and shaped like a turnip, had descended over the sun, and another, worse looking, crouched behind the car. Mr. Shiftlet felt that the rottenness of the world was about to engulf him. He raised his arm and let it fall again to his breast. "Oh Lord!" he prayed. "Break forth and wash the slime from this earth!"

The turnip continued slowly to descend. After a few minutes there was a guffawing peal of thunder from behind and fantastic raindrops, like tin-can tops, crashed over the rear of Mr. Shiftlet's car. Very quickly he stepped on the gas and with his stump sticking out the window he raced the galloping shower into Mobile.

Questions to Consider

1. What facets of Southern life does O'Connor satirize in "Good Country People"? In "Everything That Rises Must Converge?" In what ways are O'Connor's satire and the bitterness of a child toward a parent connected?
2. O'Connor considered herself a Catholic writer who could use her writing to share her spiritual concerns, but she also realized that modern readers were difficult to reach. Based on these selections, what are O'Connor's spiritual concerns? What strategies does she use to relate her concerns to her readers?

Maya Angelou

1928–

Maya Angelou has held a variety of jobs, many of which, on the surface, have little connection to her best known occupation, that of a writer. Since her high school graduation in 1945, an event documented in one of her best-known works, *I Know Why the Caged Bird Sings* (1970), Angelou has worked as a cook, a streetcar conductor, and a madam. In 1954, she began performing on stage, singing and dancing with a troupe of touring actors performing *Porgy and Bess* in 22 nations. This tour, sponsored by the Department of State, boosted her career in the arts and led her to perform both on and off Broadway during the late 1950s and early 1960s. After the publication of *I Know Why the Caged Bird Sings* and several collections of poetry, Angelou began teaching, holding appointments at the University of Kansas, Wichita State University, and Wake Forest University. In 1982, she earned a lifetime appointment to the position of Reynolds Professor of American Studies at Wake Forest University, and she currently teaches creative writing courses at the University. Angelou became a household name in 1993 when she was asked to read "On the Pulse of the Morning" at President William J. Clinton's inauguration.

Few could have predicted the success that Angelou would achieve, given her humble beginnings. She was born Marguerite Johnson (though her brother, Bailey, renamed her Maya because he was unable to pronounce Marguerite) in St. Louis, Missouri, but shortly after her birth on 4 April 1928, Angelou's mother sent her to live with relatives in the small town of Stamps, Arkansas. By local standards, her grandmother and her uncle had accumulated a small margin of wealth, since they owned a store, but money was far from free-flowing. Under the eye of their strict, yet devoted grandmother, who encouraged them to be ambitious and taught them the value of hard work, Angelou and her brother flourished. Angelou graduated from the

Lafayette County Training School, and later, in 1945, she graduated from Mission High School in San Francisco. She lived through Jim Crow segregation and fought to succeed despite the many obstacles she encountered. She has worked tirelessly for civil rights advances and was asked by Dr. Martin Luther King, Jr. to serve as the Northern Coordinator for the Southern Christian Leadership Conference. After completing her work with Dr. King's organization, she reported for newspapers in Cairo and Ghana, which led her to write and produce a television series about African traditions in American life.

Angelou began her writing life as a poet, yet most readers know her best for her autobiography, *I Know Why the Caged Bird Sings*, which chronicles her early life. Her later works, such as *Wouldn't Take Nothing for My Journey Now*, continue this tradition by presenting vignettes, recollections, and stories of the ways in which she has struggled, and of the joys she has experienced in her life. Angelou has continued to write in several genres with equal skill and grace, occasionally turning her attention to movie scripts and stage plays.

Angelou's writing addresses many issues that arose in the South of her youth—social class, race, the role of women, relationships, education, religion, violence, and death. Angelou was sexually assaulted as a child, exposing her early to the violence of the world. Because of her experiences, she has remained deeply committed to making the world around her a better place. The work excerpted in this passage focuses upon these early experiences and the ways in which Angelou overcame the many disadvantages she faced in her youth. In an interview with Dannye Romine Powell, Angelou states that: "once I started writing, I realized that I had to be writing for black girls, all black girls . . . and then I thought 'I'd better be writing for black boys, too.' And it was so difficult, I thought, 'Oh, wait. I'd better be writing for white girls, too. And white boys, too.' . . . I realized that I had something to say, and I had to make a decision that I would tell a truth which might liberate me, and might liberate others." Angelou's writing conveys her strong truth without regard to its harshness. Angelou continues to write at her home in Winston-Salem, North Carolina and to offer her wisdom to readers in a readable and lyrical form. In this selection, readers can share in Angelou's struggle as she graduates from high school.

from I Know Why the Caged Bird Sings

Chapter 23 *Graduation Day*

The children in Stamps trembled visibly with anticipation. Some adults were excited too, but to be certain the whole young population had come down with graduation epidemic. Large classes were graduating from both the grammar school and the high school. Even those who were years removed from their own day of glorious release were anxious to help with preparations as a kind of dry run. The junior students who were moving into the vacating classes' chairs were tradition-bound to show their talents for leadership and management. They strutted through the school and around the campus exerting pressure on the lower grades. Their authority was so new that occasionally if they pressed a little too hard it had to be overlooked. After all, next term was coming, and it never hurt a sixth grader to have a play sister in the eighth grade, or a tenth-year student to be able to call a twelfth grader Bubba. So all was endured in a spirit of shared understanding. But the graduating classes themselves were the nobility. Like travelers with exotic destinations on their minds, the graduates were remarkably forgetful. They came to school without their books, or tablets or even pencils. Volunteers fell over themselves to secure replacements for the missing equipment. When accepted, the willing workers might or might not be thanked, and it was of no importance to the pregraduation rites. Even teachers were respectful of the now quiet and aging seniors, and tended to speak to them, if not as equals, as beings only slightly lower than themselves. After tests were returned and grades given, the student body, which acted like an extended family, knew who did well, who excelled, and what piteous ones had failed.

Unlike the white high school, Lafayette County Training School distinguished itself by having neither lawn, nor hedges, nor tennis court, nor climbing ivy. Its two buildings (main classrooms, the grade school and home economics) were set on a dirt hill with no fence to limit either its boundaries or those of bordering farms. There was a large expanse to the left of the school which was used alternately as a baseball diamond or a basketball court. Rusty hoops on the swaying poles represented the permanent recreational equipment, although bats and balls could be borrowed from the P.E. teacher if the borrower was qualified and if the diamond wasn't occupied.

Over this rocky area relieved by a few shady tall persimmon trees the graduating class walked. The girls often held hands and no longer bothered to speak to the lower students. There was a sadness about them, as if this old world was not their home and they were bound for higher ground. The boys, on the other hand, had become more friendly, more outgoing. A decided change from the closed attitude they projected while studying for finals. Now they seemed not ready to give up the old school, the familiar paths and classrooms. Only a small percentage would be continuing on to college—one of the South's A & M (agricultural and mechanical) schools, which trained Negro youths to be carpenters, farmers, handymen, masons, maids, cooks and baby nurses. Their future rode heavily on their shoulders, and blinded them to the collective joy that had pervaded the lives of the boys and girls in the grammar school graduating class.

Parents who could afford it had ordered new shoes and ready-made clothes for themselves from Sears and Roebuck or Montgomery Ward. They also engaged the best seamstresses to make the floating graduating dresses and to cut down second-hand pants which would be pressed to a military slickness for the important event.

Oh, it was important, all right. Whitefolks would attend the ceremony, and two or three would speak of God and home, and the Southern way of life, and Mrs. Parsons, the principal's wife, would play the graduation march while the lower-grade graduates paraded down the aisles and took their seats below the platform. The high school seniors would wait in empty classrooms to make their dramatic entrance.

In the Store I was the person of the moment. The birthday girl. The center. Bailey had graduated the year before, although to do so he had had to forfeit all pleasures to make up for his time lost in Baton Rouge.

My class was wearing butter-yellow piqué dresses, and Momma launched out on mine. She smocked the yoke into tiny crisscrossing puckers, then shirred the rest of the bodice. Her dark fingers ducked in and out of the lemony cloth as she embroidered raised daisies around the hem. Before she considered herself finished she had added a crocheted cuff on the puff sleeves, and a pointy crocheted collar.

I was going to be lovely. A walking model of all the various styles of fine hand sewing and it didn't worry me that I was only twelve years old and merely graduating from the eighth grade. Besides, many teachers in Arkansas Negro schools had only that diploma and were licensed to impart wisdom.

The days had become longer and more noticeable. The faded beige of former times had been replaced with strong and sure colors. I began to see my classmates' clothes, their skin tones, and the dust that waved off pussy willows. Clouds that lazed across the sky were objects of great concern to me. Their shiftier shapes might have held a message that in my new happiness and with a little bit of time I'd soon decipher. During that period I looked at the arch of heaven so religiously my neck kept a steady ache. I had taken to smiling more often, and my jaws hurt from the unaccustomed activity. Between the two physical sore spots, I suppose I could have been uncomfortable, but that was not the case. As a member of the winning team (the graduating class of 1940) I had outdistanced unpleasant sensations by miles. I was headed for the freedom of open fields.

Youth and social approval allied themselves with me and we trammeled memories of slights and insults. The wind of our swift passage remodeled my features. Lost tears were pounded to mud and then to dust. Years of withdrawal were brushed aside and left behind, as hanging ropes of parasitic moss.

My work alone had awarded me a top place and I was going to be one of the first called in the graduating ceremonies. On the classroom blackboard, as well as on the bulletin board in the auditorium, there were blue stars and white stars and red stars. No absences, no tardinesses, and my academic work was among the best of the year. I could say the preamble to the Constitution even faster than Bailey. We timed ourselves often: "WethepeopleoftheUnitedStatesinordertoformamoreperfectunion . . ." I had memorized the Presidents of the United States from Washington to Roosevelt in chronological as well as alphabetical order.

My hair pleased me too. Gradually the black mass had lengthened and thickened, so that it kept at last to its braided pattern, and I didn't have to yank my scalp off when I tried to comb it.

Louise and I had rehearsed the exercises until we tired out ourselves. Henry Reed was class valedictorian. He was a small, very black boy with hooded eyes, a long, broad nose and an oddly shaped head. I had admired him for years because each term he and I vied for the best grades in our class. Most often he bested me, but instead of being disappointed I was pleased that we shared top places between us. Like many Southern Black children, he lived with his grandmother, who was as strict as Momma and as kind as she knew how to be. He was courteous, respectful and soft-spoken to elders, but on the playground he chose to play the roughest games. I admired him. Anyone, I reckoned, sufficiently afraid or sufficiently dull could be polite. But to be able to operate at a top level with both adults and children was admirable.

His valedictory speech was entitled "To Be or Not to Be." The rigid tenth-grade teacher had helped him write it. He'd been working on the dramatic stresses for months.

The weeks until graduation were filled with heady activities. A group of small children were to be presented in a play about buttercups and daisies and bunny rabbits. They could be heard throughout the building practicing their hops and their little songs that sounded like silver bells. The older girls (non-graduates, of course) were assigned the task of making refreshments for the night's festivities. A tangy scent of ginger, cinnamon, nutmeg and chocolate wafted around the home economics building as the budding cooks made samples for themselves and their teachers.

In every corner of the workshop, axes and saws split fresh timber as the woodshop boys made sets and stage scenery. Only the graduates were left out of the general bustle. We were free to sit in the library at the back of the building or look in quite detachedly, naturally, on the measures being taken for our event.

Even the minister preached on graduation the Sunday before. His subject was "Let your light so shine that men will see your good works and praise your Father, Who is in Heaven." Although the sermon was purported to be addressed to us, he used the occasion to speak to backsliders, gamblers and general ne'er-do-wells. But since he had called our names at the beginning of the service we were mollified.

Among Negroes the tradition was to give presents to children going only from one grade to another. How much more important this was when the person was graduating at the top of the class. Uncle Willie and Momma had sent away for a Mickey Mouse watch like Bailey's. Louise gave me four embroidered handkerchiefs. (I gave her three crocheted doilies.) Mrs. Sneed, the minister's wife, made me an underskirt to wear for graduation, and nearly every customer gave me a nickel or maybe even a dime with the instruction "Keep on moving to higher ground," or some such encouragement.

Amazingly the great day finally dawned and I was out of bed before I knew it. I threw open the back door to see it more clearly, but Momma said, "Sister, come away from that door and put your robe on."

I hoped the memory of that morning would never leave me. Sunlight was itself still young, and the day had none of the insistence maturity would bring it in a few hours. In my robe and barefoot in the backyard, under cover of going to see about my new beans, I gave myself up to the gentle warmth and thanked God that no matter what evil I had done in my life He had allowed me to live to see this day. Somewhere in my fatalism I had expected to die, accidentally, and never have the chance to walk up the stairs in the auditorium and gracefully receive my hard-earned diploma. Out of God's merciful bosom I had won reprieve.

Bailey came out in his robe and gave me a box wrapped in Christmas paper. He said he had saved his money for months to pay for it. It felt like a box of chocolates, but I knew Bailey wouldn't save money to buy candy when we had all we could want under our noses.

He was as proud of the gift as I. It was a soft-leather-bound copy of a collection of poems by Edgar Allan Poe, or, as Bailey and I called him, "Eap." I turned to "Annabel Lee" and we walked up and down the garden rows, the cool dirt between our toes, reciting the beautifully sad lines.

Momma made a Sunday breakfast although it was only Friday. After we finished the blessing, I opened my eyes to find the watch on my plate. It was a dream of a day. Everything went smoothly and to my credit. I didn't have to be reminded or scolded for anything. Near evening I was too jittery to attend to chores, so Bailey volunteered to do all before his bath.

Days before, we had made a sign for the Store, and as we turned out the lights Momma hung the cardboard over the doorknob. It read clearly: CLOSED. GRADUATION.

My dress fitted perfectly and everyone said that I looked like a sunbeam in it. On the hill, going toward the school, Bailey walked behind with Uncle Willie, who muttered, "Go on, Ju." He wanted him to walk ahead with us because it embarrassed him to have to walk so slowly. Bailey said he'd let the ladies walk together, and the men would bring up the rear. We all laughed, nicely.

Little children dashed by out of the dark like fireflies. Their crepe-paper dresses and butterfly wings were not made for running and we heard more than one rip, dryly, and the regretful "uh uh" that followed.

The school blazed without gaiety. The windows seemed cold and unfriendly from the lower hill. A sense of ill-fated timing crept over me, and if Momma hadn't reached for my hand I would have drifted back to Bailey and Uncle Willie, and possibly beyond. She made a few slow jokes about my feet getting cold, and tugged me along to the now-strange building.

Around the front steps, assurance came back. There were my fellow "greats," the graduating class. Hair brushed back, legs oiled, new dresses and pressed pleats, fresh pocket handkerchiefs and little handbags, all homesewn. Oh, we were up to snuff, all right. I joined my comrades and didn't even see my family go in to find seats in the crowded auditorium.

The school band struck up a march and all classes filed in as had been rehearsed. We stood in front of our seats, as assigned, and on a signal from the choir director, we sat. No sooner had this been accomplished than the band started to play the national anthem.

We rose again and sang the song, after which we recited the pledge of allegiance. We remained standing for a brief minute before the choir director and the principal signaled to us, rather desperately I thought, to take our seats. The command was so unusual that our carefully rehearsed and smooth-running machine was thrown off. For a full minute we fumbled for our chairs and bumped into each other awkwardly. Habits change or solidify under pressure, so in our state of nervous tension we had been ready to follow our usual assembly pattern: the American national anthem, then the pledge of allegiance, then the song every Black person I knew called the Negro National Anthem. All done in the same key, with the same passion and most often standing on the same foot.

Finding my seat at last, I was overcome with a presentiment of worse things to come. Something unrehearsed, unplanned, was going to happen, and we were going to be made to look bad. I distinctly remember being explicit in the choice of pronoun. It was "we," the graduating class, the unit, that concerned me then.

The principal welcomed "parents and friends" and asked the Baptist minister to lead us in prayer. His invocation was brief and punchy, and for a second I thought we were getting back on the high road to right action. When the principal came back to the dais, however, his voice had changed. Sounds always affected me profoundly and the principal's voice was one of my favorites. During assembly it melted and lowed weakly into the audience. It had not been in my plan to listen to him, but my curiosity was piqued and I straightened up to give him my attention.

He was talking about Booker T. Washington, our "late great leader," who said we can be as close as the fingers on the hand, etc. . . . Then he said a few vague things about friendship and the friendship of kindly people to those less fortunate than themselves. With that his voice nearly faded, thin, away. Like a river diminishing to a stream and then to a trickle. But he cleared his throat and said, "Our speaker tonight, who is also our friend, came from Texarkana to deliver the commencement address, but due to the irregularity of the train schedule, he's going to, as they say, 'speak and run.' " He said that we understood and wanted the man to know that we were most grateful for the time he was able to give us and then something about how we were willing always to adjust to another's program, and without more ado—"I give you Mr. Edward Donleavy."

Not one but two white men came through the door offstage. The shorter one walked to the speaker's platform, and the tall one moved over to the center seat and sat down. But that was our principal's seat, and already occupied. The dislodged gentleman bounced around for a long breath or two before the Baptist minister gave him his chair, then with more dignity than the situation deserved, the minister walked off the stage.

Donleavy looked at the audience once (on reflection, I'm sure that he wanted only to reassure himself that we were really there), adjusted his glasses and began to read from a sheaf of papers.

He was glad "to be here and to see the work going on just as it was in the other schools."

At the first "Amen" from the audience I willed the offender to immediate death by choking on the word. But Amens and Yes, sir's began to fall around the room like rain through a ragged umbrella.

He told us of the wonderful changes we children in Stamps had in store. The Central School (naturally, the white school was Central) had already been granted improvements that would be in use in the fall. A well-known artist was coming from Little Rock to teach art to them. They were going to have the newest microscopes and chemistry equipment for their laboratory. Mr. Donleavy didn't leave us long in the dark over who made these improvements available to Central High. Nor were we to be ignored in the general betterment scheme he had in mind.

He said that he had pointed out to people at a very high level that one of the first-line football tacklers at Arkansas Agricultural and Mechanical College had graduated from good old Lafayette County Training School. Here fewer Amens were heard. Those few that did break through lay dully in the air with the heaviness of habit.

He went on to praise us. He went on to say how he had bragged that "one of the best basketball players at Fisk sank his first ball right here at Lafayette County Training School."

The white kids were going to have a chance to become Galileos and Madame Curies and Edisons and Gauguins, and our boys (the girls weren't even in on it) would try to be Jesse Owenses and Joe Louises.

Owens and the Brown Bomber were great heroes in our world, but what school official in the white-goddom of Little Rock had the right to decide that those two men must be our only heroes? Who decided that for Henry Reed to become a scientist he had to work like George Washington Carver, as a bootblack, to buy a lousy microscope? Bailey was obviously always going to be too small to be an athlete, so which concrete angel glued to what country seat had decided that if my brother wanted to become a lawyer he had to first pay penance for his skin by picking cotton and hoeing corn and studying correspondence books at night for twenty years?

The man's dead words fell like bricks around the auditorium and too many settled in my belly. Constrained by hard-learned manners I couldn't look behind me, but to my left and right the proud graduating class of 1940 had dropped their heads. Every girl in my row had found something new to do with her handkerchief. Some folded the tiny squares into love knots, some into triangles, but most were wadding them, then pressing them flat on their yellow laps.

On the dais, the ancient tragedy was being replayed. Professor Parsons sat, a sculptor's reject, rigid. His large, heavy body seemed devoid of will or willingness, and his eyes said he was no longer with us. The other teachers examined the flag (which was draped stage right) or their notes, or the windows which opened on our now-famous playing diamond.

Graduation, the hush-hush magic time of frills and gifts and congratulations and diplomas, was finished for me before my name was called. The accomplishment was nothing. The meticulous maps, drawn in three colors of ink, learning and spelling decasyllabic words, memorizing the whole of *The Rape of Lucrece*—it was for nothing. Donleavy had exposed us.

We were maids and farmers, handymen and washerwomen, and anything higher that we aspired to was farcical and presumptuous.

Then I wished that Gabriel Prosser and Nat Turner had killed all whitefolks in their beds and that Abraham Lincoln had been assassinated before the signing of the Emancipation Proclamation, and that Harriet Tubman had been killed by that blow on her head and Christopher Columbus had drowned in the *Santa María*.

It was awful to be Negro and have no control over my life. It was brutal to be young and already trained to sit quietly and listen to charges brought against my color with no chance of defense. We should all be dead. I thought I should like to see us all dead, one on top of the other. A pyramid of flesh with the whitefolks on the bottom, as the broad base, then the Indians with their silly tomahawks and teepees and wigwams and treaties, the Negroes with their mops and recipes and cotton sacks and spirituals sticking out of their mouths. The Dutch children should all stumble in their wooden shoes and break their necks. The French should choke to death on the

Louisiana Purchase (1803) while silkworms ate all the Chinese with their stupid pigtails. As a species, we were an abomination. All of us.

Donleavy was running for election, and assured our parents that if he won we could count on having the only colored paved playing field in that part of Arkansas. Also—he never looked up to acknowledge the grunts of acceptance—also, we were bound to get some new equipment for the home economics building and the workshop.

He finished, and since there was no need to give any more than the most perfunctory thank-you's, he nodded to the men on the stage, and the tall white man who was never introduced joined him at the door. They left with the attitude that now they were off to something really important. (The graduation ceremonies at Lafayette County Training School had been a mere preliminary.)

The ugliness they left was palpable. An uninvited guest who wouldn't leave. The choir was summoned and sang a modern arrangement of "Onward, Christian Soldiers," with new words pertaining to graduates seeking their place in the world. But it didn't work. Elouise, the daughter of the Baptist minister, recited "Invictus," and I could have cried at the impertinence of "I am the master of my fate, I am the captain of my soul."

My name had lost its ring of familiarity and I had to be nudged to go and receive my diploma. All my preparations had fled. I neither marched up to the stage like a conquering Amazon, nor did I look in the audience for Bailey's nod of approval. Marguerite Johnson, I heard the name again, my honors were read, there were noises in the audience of appreciation, and I took my place on the stage as rehearsed.

I thought about colors I hated: ecru, puce, lavender, beige and black.

There was shuffling and rustling around me, then Henry Reed was giving his valedictory address, "To Be or Not to Be." Hadn't he heard the whitefolks? We couldn't *be,* so the question was a waste of time. Henry's voice came out clear and strong. I feared to look at him. Hadn't he got the message? There was no "nobler in the mind" for Negroes because the world didn't think we had minds, and they let us know it. "Outrageous fortune?" Now, that was a joke. When the ceremony was over I had to tell Henry Reed some things. That is, if I still cared. Not "rub," Henry, "erase." "Ah, there's the erase." Us.

Henry had been a good student in elocution. His voice rose on tides of promise and fell on waves of warnings. The English teacher had helped him to create a sermon winging through Hamlet's soliloquy. To be a man, a doer, a builder, a leader, or to be a tool, an unfunny joke, a crusher of funky toadstools. I marveled that Henry could go through with the speech as if we had a choice.

I had been listening and silently rebutting each sentence with my eyes closed; then there was a hush, which in an audience warns that something unplanned is happening. I looked up and saw Henry Reed, the conservative, the proper, the A student, turn his back to the audience and turn to us (the proud graduating class of 1940) and sing, nearly speaking,

> Lift ev'ry voice and sing
> Till earth and heaven ring
> Ring with the harmonies of Liberty . . .

It was the poem written by James Weldon Johnson. It was the music composed by J. Rosamond Johnson. It was the Negro national anthem. Out of habit we were singing it.

Our mothers and fathers stood in the dark hall and joined the hymn of encouragement. A kindergarten teacher led the small children onto the stage and the buttercups and daisies and bunny rabbits marked time and tried to follow:

Stony the road we trod
Bitter the chastening rod
Felt in the days when hope, unborn, had died.
Yet with a steady beat
Have not our weary feet
Come to the place for which our fathers sighed?

Every child I knew had learned that song with his ABC's and along with "Jesus Loves Me This I Know." But I personally had never heard it before. Never heard the words, despite the thousands of times I had sung them. Never thought they had anything to do with me.

On the other hand, the words of Patrick Henry had made such an impression on me that I had been able to stretch myself tall and trembling and say, "I know not what course others may take, but as for me, give me liberty or give me death."

And now I heard, really for the first time:

We have come over a way that with tears
has been watered,
We have come, treading our path through
the blood of the slaughtered.

While echoes of the song shivered in the air, Henry Reed bowed his head, said "Thank you," and returned to his place in the line. The tears that slipped down many faces were not wiped away in shame.

We were on top again. As always, again. We survived. The depths had been icy and dark, but now a bright sun spoke to our souls. I was no longer simply a member of the proud graduating class of 1940; I was a proud member of the wonderful, beautiful Negro race.

Oh, Black known and unknown poets, how often have your auctioned pains sustained us? Who will compute the lonely nights made less lonely by your songs, or by the empty pots made less tragic by your tales?

If we were a people much given to revealing secrets, we might raise monuments and sacrifice to the memories of our poets, but slavery cured us of that weakness. It may be enough, however, to have it said that we survive in exact relationship to the dedication of our poets (include preachers, musicians and blues singers).

QUESTIONS TO CONSIDER

1. How authentic does Angelou's voice appear in this selection? Does she actually sound as though she is giving an address?
2. How does Angelou portray the status of people of color in this selection?

Martin Luther King, Jr.

1929–1968

Martin Luther King, Jr. was an effective leader and inspirational speaker during the African-American civil rights struggle of the twentieth century. His face, voice, and nonviolent philosophy have become cultural icons for racial justice and unity, not only in the South where he was born and reared, but also throughout the United States and the world. "Rarely has one individual espousing so difficult a philosophy, served as a catalyst for so much significant social change," remark Filp Schulke and Penelope McPhee in *King Remembered*. "There are few men of whom it can be said their lives changed the world."

Born in Atlanta on 15 January 1929, Michael, who later changed his name to Martin, was the son of Martin Luther King, Sr., a Baptist minister, and Alberta Williams King. Martin King attended segregated public schools during his early years, and later enrolled in Morehouse College, an elite, all-Black school, where he earned a bachelor's degree in sociology in 1948. King then attended Crozer and Chicago Theological Seminaries and took classes at the University of Pennsylvania and Harvard University. He earned doctoral degrees from Boston University in 1955 and 1959, as well as from the Chicago Theological Seminary in 1957.

At the age of 26, King became the pastor of the Dexter Avenue Baptist Church in Montgomery, Alabama. He was active in the Civil Rights movement and successfully led the Montgomery bus boycott under the auspices of the Montgomery Improvement Association. He also formed the Southern Christian Leadership Conference (SCLC), which provided the means for organizing African Americans in protests against discrimination, segregation, and social injustice.

On 17 May 1957, King delivered his first national address, "Give Us the Ballot, We Will Transform the South," to thousands gathered at the Lincoln Memorial in Washington, D.C., during a Prayer Pilgrimage for Freedom. King's first book, entitled *Stride Toward Freedom: The Montgomery Story* chronicled the bus boycott in Montgomery.

During the early 1960s, King led a series of protests that gained national attention for him and for the ongoing Civil Rights movement. One of these protests led to his arrest in Birmingham, one of the South's most racially segregated cities. During his week in jail he wrote a "Letter from Birmingham Jail" (1968), an eloquent response to the critics who accused him of being an outsider: "I am in Birmingham because injustice is here . . . I cannot sit idly by in Atlanta and not be concerned about what happens in Birmingham. Injustice anywhere is a threat to justice everywhere. We are caught in an escapable network of mutuality, tied in a single garment of destiny."

King's concern over racial inequities in the South continued to grow, pushing him to become increasingly active in the cause. On 28 August 1963, approximately 250,000 people gathered in front of the Lincoln Memorial to hear King's now-famous "I Have A Dream" speech, in which he elaborated his vision of freedom for all Americans, regardless of their ethnicity. Following this address, King's popularity soared among Blacks and many Whites. In January of 1964, he became the first African American to be honored with *Time* magazine's "Man of the Year" award. During the same year, he received the Nobel Peace Prize for his commitment to nonviolent social change. He was only the twelfth American, and the third African American, to receive the award; he was also the youngest person on whom it had been conferred.

On 3 April 1968, King delivered what turned out to be a prophetic final speech, entitled "I've Been to the Mountaintop." He was assassinated on 4 April 1968 at the Lorraine Motel in Memphis. As the news of his death reached the public, violence erupted throughout the country. A conservative estimate suggests that at least thirty people were killed; hundreds more were injured. Millions of dollars of property damage also occurred. Federal troops and National Guardsmen were mobilized in an effort to help restore peace to a heartbroken and angry country.

King's works include *The Autobiography of Martin Luther King, Jr.* (1998) and *A Knock at Midnight: Inspiration from the Great Sermons of Reverend Martin Luther King, Jr.* (1998). Today, King's profound and visionary rhetoric continues to echo in the hearts and memories of people around the globe. His life and work are memorialized at the Martin Luther King, Jr. Center for Nonviolent Social Change in Atlanta.

I Have a Dream

(This is perhaps the most well-known and most quoted address Dr. King delivered. He delivered this speech before the Lincoln Memorial on 28 August 1963 as the keynote address of the March on Washington, D.C., for Civil Rights. The television cameras allowed the entire nation to hear and see him plead for justice and freedom. Mrs. Coretta King once commented, "At that moment it seemed as if the Kingdom of God appeared. But it only lasted for a moment.")

I am happy to join with you today in what will go down in history as the greatest demonstration for freedom in the history of our nation.

Fivescore years ago, a great American, in whose symbolic shadow we stand today, signed the Emancipation Proclamation. This momentous decree came as a great beacon light of hope to millions of Negro slaves who had been seared in the flames of withering injustice. It came as a joyous daybreak to end the long night of their captivity.

But one hundred years later, the Negro still is not free; one hundred years later, the life of the Negro is still sadly crippled by the manacles of segregation and the chains of discrimination; one hundred years later, the Negro lives on a lonely island of poverty in the midst of a vast ocean of material prosperity; one hundred years later, the Negro is still languished in the corners of American society and finds himself in exile in his own land.

So we've come here today to dramatize a shameful condition. In a sense we've come to our nation's capital to cash a check. When the architects of our republic wrote the magnificent words of the Constitution and the Declaration of Independence, they were signing a promissory note to which every American was to fall heir. This note was the promise that all men, yes, black men as well as white men, would be guaranteed the unalienable rights of life, liberty, and the pursuit of happiness.

It is obvious today that America has defaulted on this promissory note in so far as her citizens of color are concerned. Instead of honoring this sacred obligation, America has given the Negro people a bad check; a check which has come back marked "insufficient funds." We refuse to believe that there are insufficient funds in the great vaults of opportunity of this nation. And so we've come to cash this check, a check that will give us upon demand the riches of freedom and the security of justice.

We have also come to this hallowed spot to remind America of the fierce urgency of now. This is no time to engage in the luxury of cooling off or to take the tranquilizing drug of gradualism. Now is the time to make real the promises of democracy; now is the time to rise from the dark and desolate valley of segregation to the sunlit path of racial justice; now is the time to lift our nation from the quicksands of racial injustice to the solid rock of brotherhood; now is the time to make justice a reality for all God's children. It would be fatal for the nation to overlook the urgency of the moment. This sweltering summer of the Negro's legitimate discontent will not pass until there is an invigorating autumn of freedom and equality.

Nineteen sixty-three is not an end, but a beginning. And those who hope that the Negro needed to blow off steam and will now be content, will have a rude awakening if the nation returns to business as usual.

There will be neither rest nor tranquility in America until the Negro is granted his citizenship rights. The whirlwinds of revolt will continue to shake the foundations of our nation until the bright day of justice emerges.

But there is something that I must say to my people who stand on the warm threshold which leads into the palace of justice. In the process of gaining our rightful place we must not be guilty of wrongful deeds.

Let us not seek to satisfy our thirst for freedom by drinking from the cup of bitterness and hatred. We must forever conduct our struggle on the high plane of dignity and discipline. We must not allow our creative protest to degenerate into physical violence. Again and again we must rise to the majestic heights of meeting physical force with soul force.

The marvelous new militancy which has engulfed the Negro community must not lead us to a distrust of all white people, for many of our white brothers, as evidenced by their presence here today, have come to realize that their destiny is tied up with our destiny and they have come to realize that their freedom is inextricably bound to our freedom. This offense we share mounted to storm the battlements of injustice must be carried forth by a biracial army. We cannot walk alone.

And as we walk, we must make the pledge that we shall always march ahead. We cannot turn back. There are those who are asking the devotees of civil rights, "When will you be satisfied?" We can never be satisfied as long as the Negro is the victim of the unspeakable horrors of police brutality.

We can never be satisfied as long as our bodies, heavy with fatigue of travel, cannot gain lodging in the motels of the highways and the hotels of the cities. We cannot be satisfied as long as the Negro's basic mobility is from a smaller ghetto to a larger one.

We can never be satisfied as long as our children are stripped of their selfhood and robbed of their dignity by signs stating "for whites only." We cannot be satisfied as long as a Negro in Mississippi cannot vote and a Negro in New York believes he has nothing for which to vote. No, we are not satisfied, and we will not be satisfied until justice rolls down like waters and righteousness like a mighty stream.

I am not unmindful that some of you have come here out of excessive trials and tribulation. Some of you have come fresh from narrow jail cells. Some of you have come from areas where your quest for freedom left you battered by the storms of persecution and staggered by the winds of police brutality. You have been the veterans of creative suffering. Continue to work with the faith that unearned suffering is redemptive.

Go back to Mississippi; go back to Alabama; go back to South Carolina; go back to Georgia; go back to Louisiana; go back to the slums and ghettos of the northern cities, knowing that somehow this situation can, and will be changed. Let us not wallow in the valley of despair.

So I say to you, my friends, that even though we must face the difficulties of today and tomorrow, I still have a dream. It is a dream deeply rooted in the American dream that one day this nation will rise up and live out the true meaning of its creed—we hold these truths to be self-evident, that all men are created equal.

I have a dream that one day on the red hills of Georgia, sons of former slaves and sons of former slave-owners will be able to sit down together at the table of brotherhood.

I have a dream that one day, even the state of Mississippi, a state sweltering with the heat of injustice, sweltering with the heat of oppression, will be transformed into an oasis of freedom and justice.

I have a dream my four little children will one day live in a nation where they will not be judged by the color of their skin but by content of their character. I have a dream today!

I have a dream that one day, down in Alabama, with its vicious racists, with its governor having his lips dripping with the words of interposition and nullification, that one day, right there in Alabama, little black boys and black girls will be able to join hands with little white boys and white girls as sisters and brothers. I have a dream today!

I have a dream that one day every valley shall be exalted, every hill and mountain shall be made low, the rough places shall be made plain, and the crooked places shall be made straight and the glory of the Lord will be revealed and all flesh shall see it together.

This is our hope. This is the faith that I go back to the South with.

With this faith we will be able to hear out of the mountain of despair a stone of hope. With this faith we will be able to transform the jangling discords of our nation into a beautiful symphony of brotherhood.

With this faith we will be able to work together, to pray together, to struggle together, to go to jail together, to stand up for freedom together, knowing that we will be free one day. This will be the day when all of God's children will be able to sing with new meaning—"my country 'tis of thee; sweet land of liberty; of thee I sing; land where my fathers died, land of the pilgrim's pride; from every mountain side, let freedom ring"—and if America is to be a great nation, this must become true.

So let freedom ring from the prodigious hilltops of New Hampshire.

Let freedom ring from the mighty mountains of New York.

Let freedom ring from the heightening Alleghenies of Pennsylvania.

Let freedom ring from the snow-capped Rockies of Colorado.

Let freedom ring from the curvaceous slopes of California.

But not only that.

Let freedom ring from Stone Mountain of Georgia.

Let freedom ring from Lookout Mountain of Tennessee.

Let freedom ring from every hill and molehill of Mississippi, from every mountainside, let freedom ring.

And when we allow freedom to ring, when we let it ring from every village and hamlet, from every state and city, we will be able to speed up that day when all of God's children—black men and white men, Jews and Gentiles, Catholics and Protestants—will be able to join hands and to sing in the words of the old Negro spiritual, "Free at last, free at last; thank God Almighty, we are free at last."

Eulogy for the Martyred Children

(The Reverend Dr. King delivered this sermon at the funeral of the little girls who were killed on 15 September 1963 by a bomb as they attended the Sunday school of the 16th Street Baptist Church in Birmingham, Alabama.)

This afternoon we gather in the quiet of this sanctuary to pay our last tribute of respect to these beautiful children of God. They entered the stage of history just a few years ago, and in the brief years that they were privileged to act on this mortal stage, they played their parts exceedingly well. Now the curtain falls; they move through the exit; the drama of their earthly life comes to a close. They are now committed back to that eternity from which they came.

These children—unoffending; innocent and beautiful—were the victims of one of the most vicious, heinous crimes ever perpetrated against humanity.

Yet they died nobly. They are the martyred heroines of a holy crusade for freedom and human dignity. So they have something to say to us in their death. They have something to say to every minister of the gospel who has remained silent behind the safe security of stained-glass windows. They have something to say to every politician who has fed his constituents the stale bread of hatred and the spoiled meat of racism. They have something to say to a federal government that has compromised with the undemocratic practices of southern dixiecrats and the blatant hypocrisy of right-wing northern Republicans. They have something to say to every Negro who passively accepts the evil system of segregation, and stands on the sidelines in the midst of a mighty struggle for justice. They say to each of us, black and white alike, that we must substitute courage for caution. They say to us that we must be concerned not merely about *WHO* murdered them, but about the system, the way of life and the philosophy which *PRODUCED* the murderers. Their death says to us that we must work passionately and unrelentingly to make the American dream a reality.

So they did not die in vain. God still has a way of wringing good out of evil. History has proven over and over again that unmerited suffering is redemptive. The innocent blood of these little girls may well serve as the redemptive force that will bring new light to this dark city. The holy Scripture says, "A little child shall lead them." The death of these little children may lead our whole Southland from the low road of man's inhumanity to man to the high road of peace and brotherhood. These tragic deaths may lead our nation to substitute an aristocracy of character for an aristocracy of color. The spilt blood of these innocent girls may cause the whole citizenry of Birmingham to transform the negative extremes of a dark past into the positive extremes of a bright future. Indeed, this tragic event may cause the white South to come to terms with its conscience.

So in spite of the darkness of this hour we must not despair. We must not become bitter; nor must we harbor the desire to retaliate with violence. We must not lose faith in our white brothers. Somehow we must believe that the most misguided among them can learn to respect the dignity and worth of all human personality.

May I now say a word to you, the members of the bereaved families. It is almost impossible to say anything that can console you at this difficult hour and remove the deep clouds of disappointment which are floating in your mental skies. But I hope you can find a little consolation from the universality of this experience. Death comes to every individual. There is an amazing democracy about death. It is not aristocracy for some of the people, but a democracy for all of the people. Kings die and beggars die; rich men die and poor men die; old people die and young people die; death comes to the innocent and it comes to the guilty. Death is the irreducible common denominator of all men.

I hope you can find some consolation from Christianity's affirmation that death is not the end. Death is not a period that ends the great sentence of life, but a comma that punctuates it to more lofty significance. Death is not a blind alley that leads the human race into a state of nothingness, but an open door which leads man into life eternal. Let this daring faith, this great invincible surmise, be your sustaining power during these trying days.

At times, life is hard, as hard as crucible steel. It has its bleak and painful moments. Like the ever-flowing waters of a river, life has its moments of drought and its moments of flood. Like the ever-changing cycle of the seasons, life has the soothing warmth of the summers and the piercing chill of its winters. But through it all, God walks with us. Never forget that God is able to lift you from fatigue of despair to the buoyancy of hope, and transform dark and desolate valleys into sunlit paths of inner peace.

Your children did not live long, but they lived well. The quantity of their lives was disturbingly small, but the quality of their lives was magnificently big. Where they died and what they were doing when death came will remain a marvelous tribute to each of you and an eternal epitaph to each of them. They died not in a den or dive nor were they hearing and telling filthy jokes at the time of their death. They died within the sacred walls of the church after discussing a principle as eternal as love.

Shakespeare had Horatio utter some beautiful words over the dead body of Hamlet. I paraphrase these words today as I stand over the last remains of these lovely girls. "Good-night sweet princesses; may the flight of angels take thee to thy eternal rest."

(Epilogue: The doors of the 16th Street Baptist Church reopened on Sunday, June 7, 1964. The "reentry" sermon was preached by a White clergyman, the Reverend H. O. Hester, secretary of the Department of Missions, Alabama Baptist Convention.)

Questions to Consider

1. What rhetorical strategies does King use to make his message memorable and convincing?
2. Why do contemporary readers continue to find King's ideology compelling?

Etheridge Knight

1931–1991

Mississippi, said Etheridge Knight in an interview with Steven C. Tracy, is "where I learned the American language. The stories and the music." Knight was born in the town of Corinth on 19 April 1931 to Etheridge (nicknamed "Bushie") and Belzora Cozart Knight. Some time later, the family moved to Paducah, Kentucky. Growing up in a rough environment of drinking, drugs, and crime—but also blues, country and western music, storytelling, and street poetry—Knight found out early that "[t]he ability to talk is a power . . . . the people who could rap and write, you didn't have to fight as much," as he told Tracy. While still in his early teens, Knight became a master at "toasting": reciting boastful or insulting rhymed couplets, laced with curse words and slang, about sex, drugs, violence, daredevil deeds, and getting the best of one's enemies. Despite Knight's obvious gift for language, however, he dropped out of school in the eighth grade, got hooked on drugs, and joined the army at the age of 17. Wounded in action in the Korean War, Knight took more drugs to escape the pain and became a full-fledged narcotics addict. In 1960, arrested for a drug-related robbery in Indianapolis, Knight found himself sentenced to 10 to 25 years in the Indiana State Penitentiary.

In prison, Knight entertained his fellow prisoners by reciting toasts and began to write and publish poetry. Critic Shirley Lumpkin quotes a prophetic entry from Knight's 1965 prison diary: "I will write well. I will be a famous writer. I will work hard and my work will be good. I will be a famous writer. My voice will be heard and I will help my people." Famous African-American writers including Gwendolyn Brooks, Dudley Randall, and Sonia Sanchez visited and corresponded with Knight in prison. Randall's Broadside Press published Knight's first book, *Poems from Prison*, in 1968, the year he was paroled and released. Knight married

Sanchez the same year, but the marriage failed despite the birth of twin sons and their mutual regard for each other's poetry. Although Knight never conquered his drinking and drug problems, he taught at the college level in the early 1970s and received a Guggenheim Foundation fellowship and two National Endowment for the Arts grants. In the late 1970s, he moved to Memphis, Tennessee. The bulk of his great creative work was behind him, although he continued to give poetry readings until his death in 1991.

Following the publication of *Poems from Prison,* which contains many of the lyrics for which he is famous, Knight contributed new prose and previously published poems to a 1970 anthology of prison writing. Knight's second Broadside Press book, *Belly Song and Other Poems* (1973), was nominated for a Pulitzer Prize in Poetry and the National Book Award. His third collection, *Born of a Woman: New and Selected Poems* (1980), marked Knight's change from Broadside Press to a major New York publisher. *The Essential Etheridge Knight* (1986), a compilation of the best work written by Knight during the 1960s and 1970s, won an American Book Award.

As he himself has observed, Knight's Southern heritage shows up most strongly in the influence of the oral tradition upon his work. Criticized by some academics for looking to the blues for inspiration and using rhyme in his work, Knight never lost his belief that poetry should be an oral, communal art: "I think a good poet understands the direct relationship between the poet, the poem, and the people. I see the art of poetry as this Trinity," Knight told Tracy. Sense of place is also important to Knight's literary aesthetic: In the interview with Tracy, he praised White Mississippi writer William Faulkner for having it but criticized Black Mississippi writer Richard Wright for lacking it. Knight's poem "The Idea of Ancestry," with its emphasis on family ties and family ancestry, could only have been written by a Southerner. And while Knight often writes about prison, the theme of imprisonment functions as a metaphor within his work for slavery, racism, and all other forms of oppression that hold body and soul in chains.

Hard Rock Returns to Prison from the Hospital for the Criminal Insane

Hard Rock / was / "known not to take no shit
From nobody," and he had the scars to prove it:
Split purple lips, lumped ears, welts above
His yellow eyes, and one long scar that cut
Across his temple and plowed through a thick
Canopy of kinky hair.

The WORD / was / that Hard Rock wasn't a mean nigger
Anymore, that the doctors had bored a hole in his head,
Cut out part of his brain, and shot electricity
Through the rest.[1] When they brought Hard Rock back,
Handcuffed and chained, he was turned loose,
Like a freshly gelded stallion, to try his new status.
And we all waited and watched, like a herd of sheep,
To see if the WORD was true.

As we waited we wrapped ourselves in the cloak
Of his exploits: "Man, the last time, it took eight
Screws[2] to put him in the Hole." "Yeah, remember when he

1. In the middle decades of the twentieth century, prefrontal lobotomies and electroshock treatments were performed on some U.S. prison inmates to control their behavior.

2. Slang term for prison officers.

Smacked the captain with his dinner tray?" "He set
The record for time in the Hole—67 straight days!"
"Ol Hard Rock! man, that's one crazy nigger."
And then the jewel of a myth that Hard Rock had once bit
A screw on the thumb and poisoned him with syphilitic spit.

The testing came, to see if Hard Rock was really tame.
A hillbilly called him a black son of a bitch
And didn't lose his teeth, a screw who knew Hard Rock
From before shook him down and barked in his face.
And Hard Rock did *nothing*. Just grinned and looked silly,
His eyes empty like knot holes in a fence.

And even after we discovered that it took Hard Rock
Exactly 3 minutes to tell you his first name,
We told ourselves that he had just wised up,
Was being cool; but we could not fool ourselves for long,
And we turned away, our eyes on the ground. Crushed.
He had been our Destroyer, the doer of things
We dreamed of doing but could not bring ourselves to do,
The fears of years, like a biting whip,
Had cut deep bloody grooves
Across our backs.

Haiku

1

Eastern guard tower
glints in sunset; convicts rest
like lizards on rocks.

2

The piano man
is stingy at 3 A.M.
his songs drop like plum.

3

Morning sun slants cell.
Drunks stagger like cripple flies
On jailhouse floor.

4

To write a blues song
is to regiment riots
and pluck gems from graves.

5

A bare pecan tree
slips a pencil shadow down
a moonlit snow slope.

6

The falling snow flakes
Cannot blunt the hard aches nor
Match the steel stillness.

7

Under moon shadows
A tall boy flashes knife and
Slices star bright ice.

8

In the August grass
Struck by the last rays of sun
The cracked teacup screams.

9

Making jazz swing in
Seventeen syllables AIN'T
No square poet's job.

For Freckle-Faced Gerald

Now you take ol Rufus. He beat drums,
was free and funky under the arms,
fucked white girls, jumped off a bridge
(and thought nothing of the sacrilege),
he copped out—and he was over twenty-one.

Take Gerald. Sixteen years hadn't even done
a good job on his voice. He didn't even know
how to talk tough, or how to hide the glow
of life before he was thrown in as "pigmeat"
for the buzzards to eat.

Gerald, who had no memory or hope of copper hot lips—
of firm upthrusting thighs
to reinforce his flow,
let tall walls and buzzards change the course
of his river from south to north.

(No safety in numbers, like back on the block:
two's aplenty. three? definitely not.
four? "you're all muslims."
five? "you were planning a race riot."
plus, Gerald could never quite win
with his precise speech and innocent grin
the trust and fists of the young black cats.)

Gerald, sun-kissed ten thousand times on the nose
and cheeks, didn't stand a chance,
didn't even know that the loss of his balls
had been plotted years in advance

by wiser and bigger buzzards than those
who now hover above his track
and at night light upon his back.

He Sees Through Stone

He sees through stone
he has the secret eyes
this old black one
who under prison skies
sits pressed by the sun
against the western wall
his pipe between purple gums

the years fall
like overripe plums
bursting red flesh
on the dark earth

his time is not my time
but I have known him
in a time gone

he led me trembling cold
into the dark forest
taught me the secret rites
to make it with a woman
to be true to my brothers
to make my spear drink
the blood of my enemies

now black cats circle him
flash white teeth
snarl at the air
mashing green grass beneath
shining muscles

ears peeling his words
he smiles
he knows
the hunt the enemy
he has the secret eyes
he sees through stone

The Idea of Ancestry

1

Taped to the wall of my cell are 47 pictures: 47 black
faces: my father, mother, grandmothers (1 dead), grandfathers (both dead), brothers, sisters, uncles, aunts,
cousins (1st & 2nd), nieces, and nephews. They stare
across the space at me sprawling on my bunk. I know

their dark eyes, they know mine. I know their style,
they know mine. I am all of them, they are all of me;
they are farmers, I am a thief, I am me, they are thee.

I have at one time or another been in love with my mother,
1 grandmother, 2 sisters, 2 aunts (1 went to the asylum),
and 5 cousins. I am now in love with a 7-yr-old niece
(she sends me letters written in large block print, and
her picture is the only one that smiles at me).

I have the same name as 1 grandfather, 3 cousins, 3 nephews,
and 1 uncle. The uncle disappeared when he was 15, just took
off and caught a freight (they say). He's discussed each year
when the family has a reunion, he causes uneasiness in
the clan, he is an empty space. My father's mother, who is 93
and who keeps the Family Bible with everybody's birth dates
(and death dates) in it, always mentions him. There is no
place in her Bible for "whereabouts unknown."

2

Each fall the graves of my grandfathers call me, the brown
hills and red gullies of mississippi send out their electric
messages, galvanizing my genes. Last yr / like a salmon quitting
the cold ocean-leaping and bucking up his birthstream / I
hitchhiked my way from LA with 16 caps[1] in my pocket and a
monkey on my back.[2] And I almost kicked it with the kinfolks.
I walked barefooted in my grandmother's backyard / I smelled the old
land and the woods / I sipped cornwhiskey from fruit jars with the men /
I flirted with the women / I had a ball till the caps ran out
and my habit came down. That night I looked at my grandmother
and split / my guts were screaming for junk[3] / but I was almost
contented / I had almost caught up with me.
(The next day in Memphis I cracked a croaker's crib[4] for a fix.)

This yr there is a gray stone wall damming my stream, and when
the falling leaves stir my genes, I pace my cell or flop on my bunk
and stare at 47 black faces across the space. I am all of them,
they are all of me, I am me, they are thee, and I have no children
to float in the space between.

For Black Poets Who Think of Suicide

Black Poets should live—not leap
From steel bridges (like the white boys do).
Black Poets should live—not lay
Their necks on railroad tracks (like the white boys do).
Black Poets should seek—but not search too much
In sweet dark caves, nor hunt for snipe
Down psychic trails (like the white boys do).

1. At the time the poem was written, a slang term for LSD, a hallucinogenic drug.
2. Figurative term for an addiction.
3. Slang term for heroin.
4. Slang for "broke into a doctor's apartment."

For Black Poets belong to Black People. Are
The Flutes of Black Lovers. Are
The Organs of Black Sorrows. Are
The Trumpets of Black Warriors.
Let All Black Poets die as Trumpets,
And be buried in the dust of marching feet.

Questions to Consider

1. Why is it significant that "Hard Rock Returns to Prison from the Hospital for the Criminal Insane" is written in the first-person plural (we/us) rather than the first-person singular (I/me)?
2. Who is the "he" of the poem "He Sees Through Stone," and how can he see through stone?

Sonia Sanchez

1934–

Sonia Sanchez lived only nine years in the South, but that heritage exerted an influence on her later writing. She was born on 9 September 1934 in Birmingham, Alabama, to Wilson L. and Lena Jones Driver. Her name then was Wilsonia Benita Driver; the surname "Sanchez" would come later upon her first marriage. When Sanchez was only a year old her mother died, and her paternal grandmother, Elizabeth "Mama" Driver, became her primary caregiver. Mama held the position of head deaconness in Birmingham's African Methodist Episcopal Church, so Sanchez and her sister were immersed in its oral traditions of preaching and singing gospel songs. Mama "gave the children a sense of community," as critic Joanne Veal Gabbin has observed, introducing them to their extended family members and showing them the importance of the community to a needy individual. Sanchez was only 5 years old when Mama died, and the second loss of a mother figure was such a blow to the young child that she began to stutter and became painfully shy. Sanchez and her sister moved in with their remote schoolteacher father and uncaring stepmother. Four years later, the family moved to a tiny apartment in New York City's Harlem district. Sanchez has lived on the East or West coasts ever since, with the exception of two short-term writer-in-residencies in the South.

Sanchez majored in political science at Hunter College in New York City and received her B.A. in 1955. While doing postgraduate work at New York University, she took a poetry writing course with Louise Bogan, who emphasized that a poem should be read out loud, not silently on the page. As she continued to write, Sanchez, who had lost her stutter in her teens, became a masterful performer of her own poetry, confidently incorporating the speech rhythms, grammar, slang, and obscenities of African-American English into her work. On the printed page, she used unconventional spellings, punctuation, and line breaks to show how the poems should sound when read aloud. Initially a supporter of racial integration, Sanchez became inspired by Malcolm X and other militant African-American leaders in the early 1960s, and her poetry became a vehicle for her beliefs in revolutionary change. Following her brief marriage to Albert Sanchez, she married poet Etheridge Knight upon his release from prison in 1968, but the marriage failed a year later, despite the birth of twin sons. Her first book, *Homecoming*, a celebration of African-American pride and condemnation of American racism, was brought out by Dudley Randall's Broadside Press in 1969.

Since that first publication, Sanchez has published many more volumes of poetry, children's books, and plays and has recorded her distinctive oral performances on a half-dozen CDs, records, and tapes. Awards for her poetry have included a PEN prize and fellowship, a National Institute of Arts and Letters award, a National Endowment for the Arts grant, and an American Book Award. As a scholar and professor, Sanchez is recognized as a founder of the scholarly discipline of African-American studies. She has taught at more than ten colleges and universities.

In her article on the Southern imagination of Sanchez, Gabbin summarized the themes that can be traced to Sanchez's origins in the Deep South: "[t]he importance of the family and love relationships, her fascination with the past and her ancestry, her search for identity amid the chaos and deracination of the North, her communion with nature, her exploration of the folk culture, her response to an evangelical religious experience, and her embracing of a militancy nurtured in fear and rage. . . ." To that detailed list might be added Sanchez's approach to poetry as an oral, communal art, and her delight in teaching and employing traditional poetic forms—particularly the haiku form—despite the revolutionary nature of her content.

We a badddDDD people

(for gwendolyn brooks[1]
a fo real bad one)

i mean.
we bees real
bad.
we gots bad songs
sung on every station
we gots some bad NATURALS[2]
on our heads
and brothers gots
some bad loud (fo real)
dashiki threads[3]
on them.
i mean when
we dance u know we be doooen it
when we walk
we be doooen it
when we rap
we be doooen it
and
when we love. well. yeh. u be knowen
bout that too. (uh - huh!)
we got some BAADDD
thots and actions
like off those white mothafuckers
and rip it off if it ain't nailed
down and surround those wite/
knee / grow / pigs & don't let them
live to come back again into
our neighborhoods (we ain't
no museum for wite

1. African-American poet from Chicago (1917–2000).
2. Nonstraightened hairstyle adopted by many African Americans during the 1960s as a sign of cultural identity.
3. A loose pullover garment of colorful, African-inspired design, worn as a sign of cultural identity.

queer/minds/dicks/to
fuck us up)
and we be gitten into a
SPIRITUAL thing.
like discipline
of the mind.
soul. body. no drinken cept to celebrate
our victories / births.
no smoken. no shooten
needles into our blk / veins
full of potential blk/
gold cuz our
high must come from
thinking working
planning fighting loving
our blk / selves
into nationhood.
i mean.
when we spread ourselves thin over our
land and see our young / warriors /
sistuhs moven / runnen on blk /
hills of freedom.
we'll boo ga loo
in love.
aaa-ee-ooo-wah / wah
aaa-ee-ooo-wah / wah
aaa-ee-ooo-wah / wah
aaa-ee-ooo-wah / wah
git em with yo bad self. don. rat now.
go on & do it. dudley.[4] rat now. yeah.
run it on down. gwen.[5] rat now. yeah. yeah.
aaa-e-ooooooo. wah / wah.
aaa-e-ooooooo. wah / wah.
we a BAAAADDD people
& every day
we be gitting
BAAAADDER

right on: white america

this country might have
been a pio
neer land
once.
but. there ain't
no mo
indians blowing
custer's[1] mind
with a different

4. Dudley Randall (b. 1914), whose Broadside Press published Sanchez's first book.
5. Gwendolyn Brooks.

1. General George Custer (1839–1876), who spent a decade fighting Native American tribes.

image of america.
this country
might have
needed shoot/
outs/ daily/
once.
but. there ain't
no mo real/ white/ allamerican
bad/guys.
just.
u & me.
blk/ and un/ armed.

this country might have
been a pion
eer land. once.
and it still is.
check out
the falling
gun/shells on our blk/tomorrows.

poem

(for dc's 8th graders—1966–1967)

look at me 8th
grade
i am black
beautiful. i have a
man who looks at
my face and smiles.
on my face
are black warriors
riding in ships
of slavery;
on my face
is malcolm[1]
spitting his metal seeds
on a country of sheep;
on my face
are young eyes
breathing in black crusts.
look at us
8th grade
we are black
beautiful and our black
ness sings out
while america wanders
dumb with her wet bowels.

1. Malcolm X (Malcolm Little) (1925–1965), militant African-American leader who was assassinated.

now poem. for us.

don't let them die out
all these old / blk / people
don't let them cop out
with their memories
of slavery / survival.
it is our
heritage.
u know. part / african.
part / negro.
part / slave
sit down with em brothas & sistuhs.
talk to em. listen to their
tales of victories / woes / sorrows.
listen to their blk /
myths.
record them talken their ago talk
for our tomorrows.
ask them bout the songs of
births. the herbs
that cured
their aches. the crazy /
niggers blowen
some cracker's cool.
the laughter
comen out of tears.
let them tell us of their juju[1] years
so ours will be that much stronger.

Questions to Consider

1. Do you find the attitudes expressed toward White people in the poem "we a badddDDD people" to be offensive? Why or why not?
2. What is the meaning of the title of the poem "right on: white america"?

Wendell Berry

1934–

Wendell Berry has spent the better part of his life on or near the land which has been in his family for generations. With the exception of the time he has spent away from Henry County, Kentucky studying or traveling, he has been faithful to his family legacy. Berry is best known for his dedication to the rural way of life and to independent, small-scale farming. His literary works frequently draw upon this personal heritage, creating a fictional community that bolsters awareness of his nouveau-agrarian cause.

The devoted attention to place, community, and family that characterizes Berry's novels, short fiction, and poetry derives, not surprisingly, from his own life. Wendell Erdman Berry was born to John M. and Virginia Berry on 5 August 1934, and he was the eldest of four chil-

1. A type of magic attributed to certain persons of West African heritage.

dren. His family has lived in Henry County, Kentucky for at least four generations and has owned land continuously in the region. In addition to building a reputation as one of the county's most prominent attorneys, John Berry was one of the founding members of the Kentucky Burley Tobacco Growers Cooperative Association, and Berry passed along his dedication to the needs of individual farmers to his son. The Berrys had long been activists for small farmers who seemed to struggle more each year after the Great Depression. Wendell Berry's strong familial ties, his devotion to a specific—and Southern—place, his ties to his community, and his passion for rural life reflect the author's dedication to the presentation of the traditional stories of his native environment.

Many of Berry's works take place in the fictional community of Port William, Kentucky. The identity of Port William is well developed, sharing a communal mythology and heritage that lead critics to compare Berry with William Faulkner. His most popular novels, *The Memory of Old Jack* (1974), *Nathan Coulter* (1960), *A World Lost* (1996), and *Remembering* (1988), establish his rural motif and render Berry's community authentic and credible. The voices of his intricate characters and their experiences reinforce the verisimilitude of his novels. The source of this authenticity perhaps derives from the reality of its model, for Port William is a fictional version of Berry's tightly knit community, Port Royal. His characters clash over the differences between old ways and new ones, as families puzzle over the changes in agriculture and the rise of commercial industry.

Berry's body of work reflects his desire to curtail commercial agriculture, which he views as destructive to both families and communities. In fact, Berry was one of the first twentieth-century writers after the generation of the Agrarians to focus attention upon the changing face of agriculture in the United States, and particularly in the South. The selection included here deals with Berry's perception of the role of the writer in society, incorporating his passion for the untarnished landscape and his aversion to large scale, commercial agriculture.

The Work of Local Culture

For many years, my walks have taken me down an old fencerow in a wooded hollow on what was once my grandfather's farm. A battered galvanized bucket is hanging on a fence post near the head of the hollow, and I never go by it without stopping to look inside. For what is going on in that bucket is the most momentous thing I know, the greatest miracle that I have ever heard of: it is making earth. The old bucket has hung there through many autumns, and the leaves have fallen around it and some have fallen into it. Rain and snow have fallen into it, and the fallen leaves have held the moisture and so have rotted. Nuts have fallen into it, or been carried into it by squirrels; mice and squirrels have eaten the meat of the nuts and left the shells; they and other animals have left their droppings; insects have flown into the bucket and died and decayed; birds have scratched in it and left their droppings or perhaps a feather or two. This slow work of growth and death, gravity and decay, which is the chief work of the world, has by now produced in the bottom of the bucket several inches of black humus. I look into that bucket with fascination because I am a farmer of sorts and an artist of sorts, and I recognize there an artistry and a farming far superior to mine, or to that of any human. I have seen the same process at work on the tops of boulders in a forest, and it has been at work immemorially over most of the land-surface of the world. All creatures die into it, and they live by it.

The old bucket started out a far better one than you can buy now. I think it has been hanging on that post for something like fifty years. I think so because I remember hearing, when I was just a small boy, a story about a bucket that must have been this one. Several of my grandfather's black hired hands went out on an early spring day to burn a tobacco plantbed, and they took along some eggs to boil to eat with their dinner. When dinner time came and they looked around for something to boil the eggs in, they could find only an old bucket that at one time had been filled with tar. The boiling water softened the residue of tar, and one of the eggs came out of the water black. The hands made much sport of seeing who would have to eat the black egg, welcoming their laughter in the midst of their day's work. The man who had to eat the black egg was Floyd Scott, whom I remember well. Dry scales of tar still adhere to the inside of the bucket.

However small a landmark the old bucket is, it is not trivial. It is one of the signs by which I know my country and myself. And to me it is irresistibly suggestive in the way it collects leaves and other woodland sheddings as they fall through time. It collects stories too as they fall through time. It is irresistibly metaphorical. It is doing in a passive way what a human community must do actively and thoughtfully. A human community too must collect leaves and stories, and turn them to account. It must build soil, and build that memory of itself—in lore and story and song—which will be its culture. And these two kinds of accumulation, of local soil and local culture, are intimately related.

In the woods, the bucket is no metaphor; it simply reveals what is always happening in the woods, if the woods is let alone. Of course, in most places in my part of the country, the human community did not leave the woods alone. It felled the trees, and replaced them with pastures and crops. But this did not revoke the law of the woods, which is that the ground must be protected by a cover of vegetation, and that the growth of the years must return—or be returned—to the ground to rot and build soil. A good local culture, in one of its most important functions, is a collection of the memories, ways, and skills necessary for the observance, within the bounds of domesticity, of this natural law. If the local culture cannot preserve and improve the local soil, then, as both reason and history inform us, the local community will decay and perish, and the work of soil-building will be resumed by nature.

A human community, then, if it is to last long, must exert a sort of centripetal force, holding local soil and local memory in place. Practically speaking, human society has no work more important than this. Once we have acknowledged this principle, we can only be alarmed at the extent to which it has been ignored. For though our present society does generate a cetripetal force of great power, this is not a local force, but one centered almost exclusively in our great commercial and industrial cities, which have drawn irresistibly into themselves both the products of the countryside and the people and talents of the country communities.

There is, as one assumes there must be, a countervailing or centrifugal force that also operates in our society, but this returns to the countryside, not the residue of the land's growth to refertilize the fields, not the learning and experience of the greater world ready to go to work locally, and not, or not often, even a just monetary compensation. What are returned, instead, are overpriced manufactured goods, pollution in various forms, and garbage. A landfill on the edge of my own rural county in Kentucky, for example, daily receives about eighty truckloads of garbage. About fifty of these loads come from cities in New York, New Jersey, and Pennsylvania. Thus, the end result of the phenomenal modern productivity of the countryside is a debased countryside, which becomes daily less pleasant, and which will inevitably become less productive.

The cities, which have imposed this inversion of forces upon the country, have been unable to preserve themselves from it. The typical modern city is surrounded by a circle of affluent suburbs, eating its way outward, like ringworm, leaving the so-called "inner city" desolate, filthy, ugly, and dangerous.

My walks in the hills and hollows around my home have inevitably produced in my mind the awareness that I live in a diminished country. The country has been and is being reduced by the great centralizing process that is our national economy. As I walk, I am always reminded of the slow, patient building of soil in the woods. And I am reminded of the events and companions of my life—for my walks, after so long, are cultural events. But under the trees and in the fields I see also the gullies and scars, healed or healing or fresh, left by careless logging and bad farming. I see the crumbling stone walls, and the wire fences that have been rusting out ever since the 1930's. In the returning woods growth out of the hollows, I see the sagging and the fallen barns, the empty and ruining houses, the houseless chimneys and foundations. As I look at this evidence of human life poorly founded, played out, and gone, I try to recover some understanding, some vision, of what this country was at the beginning: the great oaks and beeches and hickories, walnuts and maples, lindens and ashes, tulip poplars, standing in beauty and dignity now unimaginable, the black soil of their making, also no longer imaginable, lying deep at their feet—an incalculable birthright sold for money, most of which we did not receive. Most of the money made on the products of this place has gone to fill the pockets of people in distant cities who did not produce the products.

If my walks take me along the roads and streams, I see also the trash and the junk, carelessly manufactured and carelessly thrown away, the glass and the broken glass and the plastic and the aluminum that will lie here longer than the lifetime of trees—longer than the lifetime of our species, perhaps. And I know that this also is what we have to show for our participation in the American economy, for most of the money made on these things too has been made elsewhere.

It would be somewhat more pleasant for country people if they could blame all this on city people. But the old opposition of country versus city—though still true, and truer than ever economically, for the country is more than ever the colony of the city—is far too simple to explain our problem. For country people more and more live like city people, and so connive in their own ruin. More and more country people, like city people, allow their economic and social standards to be set by television and salesmen and outside experts. Our garbage mingles with New Jersey garbage in our local landfill, and it would be hard to tell which is which.

As local community decays along with local economy, a vast amnesia settles over the countryside. As the exposed and disregarded soil departs with the rains, so local knowledge and local memory move away to the cities, or are forgotten under the influence of homogenized salestalk, entertainment, and education. This loss of local knowledge and local memory—that is, of local culture—has been ignored, or written off as one of the cheaper "prices of progress," or made the business of folklorists. Nevertheless, local culture has a value, and part of its value is economic. This can be demonstrated readily enough.

For example, when a community loses its memory, its members no longer know each other. How can they know each other if they have forgotten or have never learned each other's stories? If they do not know each other's stories, how can they know whether or not to trust each other? People who do not trust each other do not help each other, and moreover they fear each other. And this is our predicament now. Because of a general distrust and suspicion, we not only lose one another's help and companionship, but we are all now living in jeopardy of being sued.

We don't trust our "public servants" because we know that they don't respect us. They don't respect us, as we understand, because they don't know us; they don't know our stories. They expect us to sue them if they make mistakes, and so they must insure themselves, at great expense to them and to us. Doctors in a country community must send their patients to specialists in the city, not necessarily because they believe that they are wrong in their diagnoses, but because they know that they are not infallible, and they must protect themselves against lawsuits, at great expense to us.

The government of my home county, which has a population of about 10,000 people, pays an annual liability insurance premium of about $34,000. Add to this the liability premiums that are paid by every professional person who is "at risk" in the county, and you get some idea of the load we are carrying. Many decent family livelihoods are annually paid out of the county to insurance companies for a service that is only negative and provisional.

All of this money is lost to us by the failure of community. A good community, as we know, insures itself by trust, by good faith and good will, by mutual help. A good community, in other words, is a good local economy. It depends upon itself for many of its essential needs and is thus shaped, so to speak, from the inside—unlike most modern populations that depend upon distant purchases for almost everything, and are thus shaped from the outside by the purposes and the influence of salesmen.

I was walking one Sunday afternoon several years ago with an older friend. We went by the ruining log house that had belonged to his grandparents and great-grandparents. The house stirred my friend's memory, and he told how the oldtime people used to visit each other in the evenings, especially in the long evenings of winter. There used to be a sort of institution in our part of the country known as "sitting till bedtime." After supper, when they weren't too tired, neighbors would walk across the fields to visit each other. They popped corn, my friend said, and ate apples and talked. They told each other stories. They told each other stories, as I knew myself, that they had all heard before. Sometimes they told stories about each other, about themselves, living again in their own memories, and thus keeping their memories alive. Among the hearers of these stories were always the children. When bedtime came, the visitors lit their lanterns and went home. My friend talked about this, and thought about it, and then he said, "They had everything but money."

They were poor, as country people have often been, but they had each other, they had their local economy in which they helped each other, they had each other's comfort when they needed it, and they had their stories, their history together in that place. To have everything but money is to have much. And most people of the present can only marvel to think of neighbors entertaining themselves for a whole evening without a single imported pleasure and without listening to a single minute of salestalk.

Most of the descendents of those people have now moved away, partly because of the cultural and economic failures that I mentioned earlier, and most of them no longer sit in the evenings and talk to anyone. Most of them now sit until bedtime, watching TV, submitting every few minutes to a salestalk. The message of both the TV programs and the salestalks is that the watchers should spend whatever is necessary to be like everybody else.

By television and other public means, we are encouraged to imagine that we are far advanced beyond sitting till bedtime with the neighbors on a Kentucky ridgetop, and indeed beyond anything we ever were before. But if, for example, there should occur a forty-eight hour power failure, we would find ourselves in much more backward circumstances than our ancestors. What, for starters, would we do for entertainment? Tell each other stories? But most of us no longer talk with each other, much less tell each other stories. We tell our stories now mostly to doctors or lawyers or psychiatrists or insurance adjusters or the police, not to our neighbors for their (and our) entertainment. The stories that now entertain us are made up for us in New York or Los Angeles or other centers of such commerce.

But a forty-eight hour power failure would involve almost unimaginable deprivations. It would be difficult to travel, especially in cities. Most of the essential work could not be done. Our windowless modern schools and other such buildings that depend on air conditioning could not be used. Refrigeration would be impossible; food would spoil. It would be difficult or impossible to prepare meals. If it was winter, heating systems would fail. At the end of forty-eight hours many of us would be hungry.

Such a calamity—and it is a modest one among those that our time has made possible—would thus reveal how far most of us are now living from our cultural and economic sources, and how extensively we have destroyed the foundations of local life. It would show us how far we have strayed from the locally centered life of such neighborhoods as the one my friend described—a life based to a considerable extent upon what we now call solar energy, which is decentralized, democratic, clean, and free. If we note that much of the difference we are talking about can be accounted for as an increasing dependence upon energy sources that are centralized, undemocratic, filthy, and expensive, we will have completed a sort of historical parable.

How has this happened? There are many reasons for it. One of the chief reasons is that everywhere in our country the local succession of the generations has been broken. We can trace this change through a series of stories that we may think of as cultural landmarks.

Throughout most of our literature the normal thing was for the generations to succeed one another in place. The memorable stories occurred when this succession became difficult or was threatened in one way or another. The norm is given in Psalm 128, in which this succession is seen as one of the rewards of righteousness: "thou shalt see thy children's children, and peace upon Israel."

The longing for this result seems to have been universal. It presides also over the *Odyssey*, in which Odysseus' desire to return home is certainly regarded as normal. And this story is much concerned with the psychology of family succession. Telemachus, Odysseus' son, comes of age in preparing for the return of his long-absent father. And it seems almost that Odysseus is enabled to return home by his son's achievement of enough manhood to go in search of him. Long after the return of both father and son, Odysseus' life will complete itself, as we know from Teiresias' prophecy in Book XI, much in the spirit of Psalm 128:

> *a seaborne death*
> *soft as this hand of mist will come upon you*
> *when you are wearied out with sick old age,*
> *your country folk in blessed peace around you.*

The Bible makes much of what it sees as the normal succession—in such stories as those of Abraham, Isaac, and Jacob, David and Solomon—in which the son completes the work or the destiny of the father. The parable of the Prodigal Son is prepared for by such Old Testament stories as that of Jacob, who errs, wanders, returns, is forgiven, and takes his place in the family lineage.

Shakespeare was concerned throughout his working life with the theme of the separation and rejoining of parents and children. It is there at the beginning in *The Comedy of Errors*, and he is still thinking about it when he gets to *King Lear* and

Pericles and *The Tempest*. When Lear walks onstage with Cordelia dead in his arms, the theme of return is fulfilled, only this time in the way of tragedy.

Wordsworth's poem, "Michael," written in 1800, is in the same line of descent. It is the story of a prodigal son, and return is still understood as the norm; before the boy's departure, he and his father make a "covenant" that he will return home and carry on his father's life as a shepherd on their ancestral pastures. But the ancient theme here has two significant differences: the son leaves home for an economic reason, and he does not return. Old Michael, the father, was long ago "bound / In surety for his brother's son." This nephew has failed in his business, and Michael is "summoned to discharge the forfeiture." Rather than do this by selling a portion of their patrimony, the aged parents decide that they must send their son to work for another kinsman in the city in order to earn the necessary money. The country people all are poor; there is no money to be earned at home. When the son has cleared the debt from the land, he will return to it to "possess it, free as the wind / That passes over it." But the son goes to the city, is corrupted by it, eventually commits a crime, and is forced "To seek a hiding place beyond the seas."

"Michael" is a sort of cultural watershed. It carries on the theme of return that goes back to the beginnings of Western culture, but that return now is only a desire and a memory; in the poem it fails to happen. Because of that failure, we see in "Michael," not just a local story of the Lake District of England, which it is, but the story of rural families in the industrial nations from Wordsworth's time until today. The children go to the cities, for reasons imposed by the external economy, and they do not return; eventually the parents die and the family land, like Michael's, is sold to a stranger. By now it has happened millions of times.

And by now the transformation of the ancient story is nearly complete. Our society, on the whole, has forgot or repudiated the theme of return. Young people still grow up in rural families, and go off to the cities, not to return. But now it is felt that this is what they *should* do. Now the norm is to leave and not return. And this applies as much to urban families as to rural ones. In the present urban economy the parent-child succession is possible only among the economically privileged. The children of industrial underlings are not likely to succeed their parents or work, and there is not reason for them to wish to do so. We are not going to have an industrial "Michael" in which it is perceived as tragic that a son fails to succeed his father on an assembly line. According to the new norm, the child's destiny is not to succeed the parents, but to outmode them; succession has given way to supersession. And this norm is institutionalized, not in great communal stories, but in the education system. The schools are no longer oriented to a cultural inheritance which it is their duty to pass on unimpaired, but to the career, which is to say the future, of the child. The orientation is thus necessarily theoretical, speculative, and central. The child is not educated to return home and be of use to the place and community; he or she is educated to *leave* home and earn money in a provisional future that has nothing to do with place or community. And parents with children in school are likely to find themselves immediately separated from their children, and made useless to them, by the intervention of new educational techniques, technologies, methods, and languages. School systems innovate as compulsively and as eagerly as factories. It is no wonder that, under these circumstances, "educators" tend to look upon the parents as a bad influence, and wish to take the children away from home as early as possible. And many parents, in truth, are now finding their children an encumbrance at home—where there is no useful work for them to do—and are glad enough to turn them over to the state for the use of the future. The extent to which this order of things is now dominant is suggested by a recent magazine article on the discovery of what purports to be a new idea:

> The idea that a parent can be a teacher at home has caught the attention of educators. . . . Parents don't have to be graduates of Harvard or Yale to help their kids learn and achieve. . . .

Thus the home as a place where a child can learn becomes an *idea* of the professional "educator," who retains control of the idea. The home, as the article makes clear, is not to be a place where children may learn on their own, but a place where they are taught by parents according to the instructions of professional "educators." In fact, "The Home and School Institute, Inc., of Washington, D.C." (known, of course, as "The HSI") has been "founded to show . . . how to involve families in their kids' educations."

In such ways as this, the nuclei of home and community have been invaded by the organizations, just as have the nuclei of cells and atoms. And we must be careful to see that the old cultural centers of home and community were made vulnerable to this invasion by their failure as economies. If there is no household or community economy, then family members and neighbors are no longer useful to each other. When people are no longer useful to each other, then the centripetal force of family and community fails, and people fall into dependence upon exterior economies and organizations. The hegemony of professionals and professionalism erects itself upon local failure. And from then on the locality exists merely as a market for consumer goods and as a source of "raw material," human and natural. The local schools no longer serve the local community; they serve the government's economy and the economy's government. Unlike the local community, the government and the economy cannot be served with affection, but only with professional zeal or professional boredom. Professionalism means more interest in salary and less interest in what used to be known as disciplines. And so we arrive at the idea, endlessly reiterated in the news media, that education can be improved by bigger salaries for teachers—which may be true, but not, as the proponents too often imply, by bigger salaries alone. There must also be love of learning and of the cultural tradition and of excellence. And this love cannot exist, because it makes no sense, apart from the love of a place and a community. Without this love, education is only the importation into a local community of centrally prescribed "career preparation" designed to facilitate the export of young careerists.

Our children are educated, then, to leave home, not to stay home, and the costs of this have been far too little acknowledged. One of the costs is psychological, and the other is at once cultural and ecological.

The natural or normal course of human growing-up must begin with some sort of rebellion against one's parents, for it is clearly impossible to grow up if one remains a child. But the child, in the process of rebellion and of achieving the emotional and economic independence that rebellion ought to lead to, finally comes to understand the parents as fellow humans and fellow sufferers, and in some manner returns to them as their friend, forgiven and forgiving the inevitable wrongs of family life. That is the old norm, of which the story of the Prodigal Son is an example.

The new norm, according to which the child leaves home as a student and never lives at home again, interrupts the old course of coming of age at the point of rebellion, so that the child is apt to remain stalled in adolescence, never achieving any kind of reconciliation or friendship with the parents. Of course, such a return and reconciliation cannot be achieved without the recognition of mutual practical need. However, in the present economy where individual dependences are so much exterior to both household and community, family members often have no practical need or use for one another. Hence, the frequent futility of attempts at a purely psychological or emotional reconciliation.

And this interposition of rebellion and then of geographical and occupational distance between parents and children may account for the peculiar emotional intensity that our society attaches to innovation. We appear to hate whatever went before, very much as an adolescent hates parental rule, and to look upon its obsolescence as a kind of vengeance. Thus we may explain industry's obsessive emphasis upon "this year's model," or the preoccupation of the professional "educators" with theoretical and methodological innovation. And thus, in modern literature we have had for many years an emphasis upon "originality" and "the anxiety of influence" (an adolescent critical theory), as opposed, say, to Spenser's filial admiration for Chaucer, or Dante's for Virgil.

But if the new norm interrupts the development of the relation between children and parents, that same interruption, ramifying through a community, destroys the continuity and so the integrity of local life. As the children depart, generation after generation, the place loses its memory of itself, which is its history and its culture. And the local history, if it survives at all, loses its place. It does no good for historians, folklorists, and anthropologists to collect the songs and the stories and the lore that comprise local culture and store them in books and archives. They cannot collect and store, because they cannot know, the pattern of reminding that can survive only in the living human community in its place. It is this pattern that is the life of local culture, and that brings it usefully or pleasurably to mind. Apart from its local landmarks and occasions, the local culture may be the subject of curiosity or of study, but it is also dead.

The loss of local culture is, in part, a practical loss and an economic one. For one thing, such a culture contains, and conveys to succeeding generations, the history of the use of the place and the knowledge of how the place may be lived in and used. For another, the pattern of reminding implies affection for the place and respect for it, and so, finally, the local culture will carry the knowledge of how the place may be well and lovingly used, and moreover the implicit command to use it *only* well and lovingly. The only true and effective "operator's manual for spaceship earth" is not a book that any human will ever write; it is hundreds of thousands of local cultures.

Lacking an authentic local culture, a place is open to exploitation, and ultimately destruction, from the center. Recently, for example, I heard the dean of a prominent college of agriculture interviewed on the radio. What have we learned, he was asked, from last summer's drouth? And he replied that "we" need to breed more drouth resistance into plants, and that "we" need a government "safety net" for farmers. He might have said that farmers need to reexamine their farms and their circumstances in light of the drouth, and to think again on such subjects as diversification, scale, and the mutual helpfulness of neighbors. But he did not say that. To him, the drouth was merely an opportunity for agribusiness corporations and the government, by which the farmers and rural communities could only become more dependent on the economy that is destroying them. This is as good an example as any of the centralized thinking of a centralized economy—to which the only effective answer that I know is a strong local community with a strong local economy and a strong local culture.

For a long time now, the prevailing assumption has been that if the nation is all right, then all the localities within it will be all right also. I see little reason to believe that this is true. At present, in fact, both the nation and the national economy are living at the expense of localities and local communities—as all small town and country people have reason to know. In rural America, which is in many ways a colony of what the government and the corporations think of as the nation, most of us have experienced the losses that I have been talking about: the departure of young people, of soil and other so-called natural resources, and of local memory. We feel ourselves crowded more and more into a dimensionless present, in which the past is forgotten, and the future, even in our most optimistic "projections," is forbidding and fearful. Who can desire a future that is determined entirely by the purposes of the most wealthy and the most powerful, and by the capacities of machines?

Two questions, then, remain: Is a change for the better possible? And who has the power to make such a change? I still believe that a change for the better is possible, but I confess that my belief is partly hope and partly faith. No one who hopes for improvement should fail to see and respect the signs that we may be approaching some sort of historical waterfall, past which we will not, by changing our minds, be able to change anything else. We know that at any time an ecological or a technological or a political event that we will have allowed may remove from us the power to make change and leave us with the mere necessity to submit to it. Beyond that, the two questions are one: the possibility of change depends upon the existence of people who have the power to change.

Does this power reside at present in the national government? That seems to me extremely doubtful. To anyone who has read the papers during the recent presidential campaign, it must be clear that at the highest level of government there is, properly speaking, no political discussion. Are the corporations likely to help us? We know, from long experience, that the corporations will assume no responsibility that is not forcibly imposed upon them by government. The record of the corporations is written too plainly in verifiable damage to permit us to expect much from them. May we look for help to the universities? Well, the universities are more and more the servants of government and the corporations.

Most urban people evidently assume that all is well. They live too far from the exploited and endangered sources of their economy to need to assume otherwise. Some urban people are becoming disturbed about the contamination of air, water, and food, and that is promising, but there are not enough of them yet to make much difference. There is enough trouble in the "inner cities" to make them likely places of change, and evidently change is in them, but it is desperate and destructive change. As if to perfect their exploitation by other people, the people of the "inner cities" are destroying both themselves and their places.

My feeling is that, if improvement is going to begin anywhere, it will have to begin out in the country and in the country towns. This is not because of any intrinsic virtue that can be ascribed to rural people, but because of their circumstances. Rural people are living, and have lived for a long time, at the site of the trouble. They see all around them, every day, the marks and scars of an exploitive national economy. They have much reason, by now, to know how little real help is to be expected from somewhere else. They still have, moreover, the remnants of local memory and local community. And in rural communities there are still farms and small businesses that can be changed according to the will and the desire of individual people.

In this difficult time of failed public expectations, when thoughtul people wonder where to look for hope, I keep returning in my own mind to the thought of the renewal of the rural communities. I know that one resurrected rural community would be more convincing and more encouraging than all the government and university programs of the last fifty years, and I think that it could be the beginning of the renewal of our country, for the renewal of rural communities ultimately implies the renewal of urban ones. But to be authentic, a true encouragement and a true beginning, this would have to be a resurrection accomplished mainly by the community itself. It would have to be done, not from the outside by the instruction of visiting experts, but from the inside by the ancient rule of neighborliness, by the love of precious things, and by the wish to be at home.

Questions to Consider

1. What do you think the role of the writer should be? Should a writer have a political, ecological, moral agenda, or can writers create pieces that are set outside of these biases? When does literature stop being literature and become propaganda? How would you evaluate Berry's piece in terms of this question?
2. How has the role of the American farmer changed? Has the practice of farming increased or decreased within your lifetime? Can you think of how it might have changed, even during your life?

Nikki Giovanni

1943–

Gus Jones Giovanni, who was from Ohio, met and married Yolande Cornelia Watson, from Tennessee, while both were students at Knoxville College in Tennessee. Their second child, Yolande Cornelia "Nikki" Giovanni, would grow up to be a rare phenomenon in American popular culture: a celebrity as well as a poet. Two months after her birth in Knoxville on 7 June 1943, her parents moved the family to Cincinnati, but Giovanni would later spend her sophomore and junior years of high school living with her grandmother in Knoxville, then skip her senior year of high school to attend Fisk University in Nashville.

Like the poet Edna St. Vincent Millay fifty years earlier, Giovanni was expelled from college for flaunting the social rules for women by leaving the campus without permission. She returned to college a year later, however, to study creative writing under John O. Killens with fellow student LeRoi Jones (later to be known as Imanu Amiri Baraka) and to edit the college literary magazine. During her college years she also metamorphosed from a conservative "Goldwater Republican" into a supporter of the militant Black power movement that had supplanted the nonviolent, integrationist philosophy of Martin Luther King, Jr. Graduating magna cum laude with a B.A. in history in 1967, Giovanni returned to Cincinnati and organized the first Black Arts Festival there later that year. Although she secured a Ford Foundation fellowship for graduate study in social work at the University of Pennsylvania, then switched to studying creative writing at Columbia University, political activism and African-American nation-building were becoming more important than academics to her as she met and associated with movement leaders such as H. Rap Brown, and she dropped out. Despite her lack of a graduate degree, her later achievements in poetry would make her sought after as a professor by many American universities.

Using her poetry as a vehicle to express her pride in her Blackness, her anger at racism, and her desire for revolutionary change, Giovanni self-published her first volume of poetry, *Black Feeling, Black Talk,* in 1968. The political poems in her early books, which advocate killing White people and express anti-Semitic sentiments, can be very difficult to read in the changed world following 11 September 2001. However, like Donald Davidson's poem "Lee in the Mountains," they are expressive of viewpoints that are significant to an accurate portrayal of Southern history, culture, and literature. Even so, Giovanni's political poems, such as "For Saundra," shared space in her early collections with gentle reminiscences about her girlhood such as "Nikki-Rosa" and "Knoxville, Tennessee," and in later years her poetry would take a much more humanistic direction. Giovanni proved to be a master at promoting *Black Feeling, Black Talk,* organizing a huge publication party at Birdland in Harlem that was covered by *The New York Times.* Distributed by Dudley Randall's Broadside press, the book sold more than ten thousand copies in eight months. That same year, Giovanni published a follow-up volume, *Black Judgement.*

By the time she was 28 years old, Giovanni would publish three more books of poetry and an autobiography, edit an anthology of poems by African-American women, and become a media celebrity thanks to her frequent appearances on television and in magazine articles. She would also become a legendary stage performer of her own poetry: as Virginia C. Fowler points out in her introduction to *Selected Poems,* many of Giovanni's fans would attend a live poetry reading and then read her books, rather than the other way around. In middle age, having published 17 books of poetry and received a National Book Award nomination, a National Endowment for the Arts grant, and many organizational awards and honorary doctorates, Giovanni remains a best-selling author and a popular lecturer on college campuses throughout the country.

Knoxville, Tennessee

I always like summer
best
you can eat fresh corn
from daddy's garden
and okra
and greens
and cabbage
and lots of
barbecue
and buttermilk
and homemade ice-cream
at the church picnic
and listen to
gospel music
outside
at the church
homecoming
and go to the mountains with
your grandmother
and go barefooted
and be warm
all the time
not only when you go to bed
and sleep

For Saundra

i wanted to write
a poem
that rhymes
but revolution doesn't lend
itself to be-bopping[1]

1. Dancing to a complex form of jazz.

then my neighbor
who thinks i hate
asked—do you ever write
tree poems—i like trees
so i thought
i'll write a beautiful green tree poem
peeked from my window
to check the image
noticed the school yard was covered
with asphalt
no green—no trees grow
in manhattan

then, well, i thought the sky
i'll do a big blue sky poem
but all the clouds have winged
low since no-Dick[2] was elected

so i thought again
and it occurred to me
maybe i shouldn't write
at all
but clean my gun
and check my kerosene supply

perhaps these are not poetic
times
at all

Questions to Consider

1. Compare and contrast the food imagery in Giovanni's poem "Knoxville, Tennessee," with Martha McFerren's "The Bad Southern Cooking Poem in Part VI, page 1283."
2. Do you find "For Saundra" to be a humorous poem, or not? Explain why.

Alice Walker

1944–

Over the course of a highly productive career, Alice Walker has played many roles—activist, spiritualist, speaker, mother, daughter, novelist, and poet. She has become one of America's foremost writers, despite the potential disadvantages posed by her humble origins. Walker was born in Eatonton, Georgia, on 9 February 1944 to Minnie Tallulah Grant Walker and Willie Lee Walker. Sharecropping was her father's primary occupation causing the family to struggle under grinding poverty. Walker was raised with seven siblings—five boys and two girls; she was the youngest. When she was eight years of age, Walker was accidentally shot in the eye with a BB gun by one of her brothers. She lost the use of her right eye, and this event drastically changed her life. The eye injury was a source of embarrassment and shame for her, and she has come to terms with this visual impairment only as an adult.

2. Richard Nixon (1913–1994), the 37th president of the United States.

Walker attended Spellman College from 1961 to 1963, and after a trip to Africa and a period of involvement in the Civil Rights movement, she earned her bachelor's degree from Sarah Lawrence College in 1965. While at Sarah Lawrence, she found a mentor in writer Muriel Rukeyser. Rukeyser showed a sample of Walker's writing to her editor, and this editor later became Walker's editor, as well. Walker continued to write, and during the period from 1965 to 1968, she worked actively in the Civil Rights movement in both Georgia and New York. During this time, she met and married attorney Melvyn Roseman Levanthal; they have one daughter, but her marriage to Levanthal was short lived. From 1967 to 1970, Walker taught at several universities in Mississippi; she also held teaching positions at Wellesley College, the University of Massachusetts at Amherst, the University of California at Berkley, and Brandeis University. Walker published her first novel, *The Third Life of Grange Copeland,* in 1970, and her second novel, *Meridian*, appeared in 1976.

In 1974, Walker left academia to take a position as an editor at *Ms.* magazine, but she returned to teaching a few years later. By 1978, Walker had moved to San Francisco, along with a friend and fellow writer, Robert Allen. She and Allen lived comfortably on her Guggenheim Fellowship funds and a retainer from *Ms.*; after a short time, the pair moved to Mendocino County, where Walker concentrated exclusively on her writing. She continues to live in northern California and has produced many of her works while living in the region.

Like her character, Meridian Hill, Walker describes her life as a journey. She has questioned organized religion, politics, sexual preference, and her purpose in life. Walker has lived through some of the most turbulent times in American history, experiencing the rise of suburbia, the Red Scare, the tumultuous Civil Rights and antiwar movements, the Vietnam War, the legalization of abortion, the emergence of conservative politics in the United States during the 1980s, and the death of apartheid. She has also endured a variety of personal tragedies, including the death of her parents and a serious illness of her own. Today, Walker works for a variety of social and political causes.

Walker's body of work requires little introduction, particularly her best-known novel, *The Color Purple* (1982). Her novels, poetry, short stories, and essays have made her a household name. Walker's other novels, *The Third Life of Grange Copeland, Meridian, The Temple of My Familiar* (1989), and *Possessing the Secret of Joy* (1992) have drawn positive reviews but have not captured the public's interest to the same extent as *The Color Purple*. Although Walker's works are widely disparate in terms of characterization, plot, and setting, her writing consistently addresses themes of oppression, love, healing, survival, the consequences of choices, and the disparity of power in American society. Although her fiction has attracted more critical attention than her work in other genres, Walker's career as a poet and essayist has also been prolific. Her collections of essays, such as *In Search of Our Mothers' Gardens* (1983), *The Same River Twice* (1996), and *Anything We Love Can Be Saved* (1997), contain thought-provoking and challenging selections. Topics include politics, sexism, female genital mutilation, the place of woman in society, and the need for people to find practical ways to survive intact in the fast-paced, often out-of-control, twentieth century. Walker's works have been well received by both popular and scholarly audiences, though her later works have been criticized for their overtly strident political messages. In the piece presented in this volume, Walker addresses many of these themes. Her body of fiction, essays, and poetry reflects these issues.

The Black Writer and the Southern Experience

My mother tells of an incident that happened to her in the thirties during the Depression. She and my father lived in a small Georgia town and had half a dozen children. They were sharecroppers, and food, especially flour, was almost impossible to obtain. To get flour, which was distributed by the Red Cross, one had to submit vouchers signed by a local official. On the day my mother was to go into town for flour she received a large box of clothes from one of my aunts who was living in the North. The clothes were in good condition, though well worn, and my mother needed a dress, so she immediately put on one of those from the box and wore it into town. When she reached the distribution center and presented her voucher she was confronted by a white woman who looked her up and down with marked anger and envy.

"What'd you come up here for?" the woman asked.

"For some flour," said my mother, presenting her voucher.

"Humph," said the woman, looking at her more closely and with unconcealed fury. "Anybody dressed up as good as you don't need to come here *begging* for food."

"I ain't begging," said my mother; "the government is giving away flour to those that need it, and I need it. I wouldn't be here if I didn't. And these clothes I'm wearing was given to me." But the woman had already turned to the next person in line, saying over her shoulder to the white man who was behind the counter with her, "The *gall* of niggers coming in here dressed better than me!" This thought seemed to make her angrier still, and my mother, pulling three of her small children behind her and crying from humiliation, walked sadly back into the street.

"What did you and Daddy do for flour that winter?" I asked my mother.

"Well," she said, "Aunt Mandy Aikens lived down the road from us and she got plenty of flour. We had a good stand of corn so we had plenty of meal. Aunt Mandy would swap me a bucket of flour for a bucket of meal. We got by all right."

Then she added thoughtfully, "And that old woman that turned me off so short got down so bad in the end that she was walking on *two* sticks." And I knew she was thinking, though she never said it: Here I am today, my eight children healthy and grown and three of them in college and me with hardly a sick day for years. Ain't Jesus wonderful?

In this small story is revealed the condition and strength of a people. Outcasts to be used and humiliated by the larger society, the Southern black sharecropper and poor farmer clung to his own kind and to a religion that had been given to pacify him as a slave but which he soon transformed into an antidote against bitterness. Depending on one another, because they had nothing and no one else, the sharecroppers often managed to come through "all right." And when I listen to my mother tell and retell this story I find that the white woman's vindictiveness is less important than Aunt Mandy's resourceful generosity or my mother's ready stand of corn. For their lives were not about that pitiful example of Southern womanhood, but about themselves.

What the black Southern writer inherits as a natural right is a sense of *community*. Something simple but surprisingly hard, especially these days, to come by. My mother, who is a walking history of our community, tells me that when each of her children was born the midwife accepted as payment such home-grown or homemade items as a pig, a quilt, jars of canned fruits and vegetables. But there was never any question that the midwife would come when she was needed, whatever the eventual payment for her services. I consider this each time I hear of a hospital that refuses to admit a woman in labor unless she can hand over a substantial sum of money, cash.

Nor am I nostalgic, as a French philosopher once wrote, for lost poverty. I am nostalgic for the solidarity and sharing a modest existence can sometimes bring. We knew, I suppose, that we were poor. Somebody knew; perhaps the landowner who grudgingly paid my father three hundred dollars a year for twelve months' labor. But we never considered ourselves to be poor, unless, of course, we were deliberately humiliated. And because we never believed we were poor, and therefore worthless, we could depend on one another without shame. And always there were the Burial Societies, the Sick-and-Shut-in Societies, that sprang up out of spontaneous need. And no one seemed terribly upset that black sharecroppers were ignored by white insurance companies. It went without saying, in my mother's day, that birth and death required assistance from the community, and that the magnitude of these events was lost on outsiders.

As a college student I came to reject the Christianity of my parents, and it took me years to realize that though they had been force-fed a white man's palliative, in the form of religion, they had made it into something at once simple and noble. True, even today, they can never successfully picture a God who is not white, and that is a major cruelty, but their lives testify to a greater comprehension of the teachings of Jesus than the lives of people who sincerely believe a God *must* have a color and that there can be such a phenomenon as a "white" church.

The richness of the black writer's experience in the South can be remarkable, though some people might not think so. Once, while in college, I told a white middle-aged Northerner that I hoped to be a poet. In the nicest possible language, which still made me as mad as I've ever been, he suggested that a "farmer's daughter" might not be the stuff of which poets are made. On one level, of course, he had a point. A shack with only a dozen or so books is an unlikely place to discover a young Keats. But it is narrow thinking, indeed, to believe that a Keats is the only kind of poet one would want to grow up to be. One wants to write poetry that is understood by one's people, not by the Queen of England. Of course, should she be able to profit by it too, so much the better, but since that is not likely, catering to her tastes would be a waste of time.

For the black Southern writer, coming straight out of the country, as Wright did—Natchez and Jackson are still not as citified as they like to think they are—there is the world of comparisons; between town and country, between the ugly crowding and griminess of the cities and the spacious cleanliness (which actually seems impossible to dirty) of the country. A country person finds the city confining, like a too tight dress. And always, in one's memory, there remain all the rituals of one's growing up: the warmth and vividness of Sunday worship (never mind that you never quite believed) in a little church hidden from the road, and houses set so far back into the woods that at night it is impossible for strangers to find them. The daily dramas that evolve in such a private world are pure gold. But this view of a strictly private and hidden existence, with its triumphs, failures, grotesqueries, is not nearly as valuable to the socially conscious black Southern writer as his double vision is. For not only is he in a position to see his own world, and its close community ("Homecomings" on First Sundays, barbecues to raise money to send to Africa—one of the smaller ironies—the simplicity and eerie calm of a black funeral, where the beloved one is buried way in the middle of a wood with nothing to mark the spot but perhaps a wooden cross already coming apart), but also he is capable of knowing, with remarkably silent accuracy, the people who make up the larger world that surrounds and suppresses his own.

It is a credit to a writer like Ernest J. Gaines, a black writer who writes mainly about the people he grew up with in rural Louisiana, that he can write about whites and blacks exactly as he sees them and *knows* them, instead of writing of one group as a vast malignant lump and of the other as a conglomerate of perfect virtues.

In large measure, black Southern writers owe their clarity of vision to parents who refused to diminish themselves as human beings by succumbing to racism. Our parents seemed to know that an extreme negative emotion held against other human beings for reasons they do not control can be blinding. Blindness about other human beings, especially for a writer, is equivalent to death. Because of this blindness, which is, above all, racial, the works of many Southern writers have died. Much that we read today is fast expiring.

My own slight attachment to William Faulkner was rudely broken by realizing, after reading statements he made in *Faulkner in the University*, that he believed whites superior morally to blacks; that whites had a duty (which at their convenience they would assume) to "bring blacks along" politically, since blacks, in Faulkner's opinion, were "not ready" yet to function properly in a democratic society. He also thought that a black man's intelligence is directly related to the amount of white blood he has.

For the black person coming of age in the sixties, where Martin Luther King stands against the murderers of Goodman, Chaney, and Schwerner, there appears no basis for such assumptions. Nor was there any in Garvey's day, or in Du Bois's or in Douglass's or in Nat Turner's. Nor at any other period in our history, from the very founding of the country; for it was hardly incumbent upon slaves to be slaves and saints too. Unlike Tolstoy, Faulkner was not prepared to struggle to change the structure of the society he was born in. One might concede that in his fiction he did seek to examine the reasons for its decay, but unfortunately, as I have learned while trying to teach Faulkner to black students, it is not possible, from so short a range, to separate the man from his works.

One reads Faulkner knowing that his "colored" people had to come through "Mr. William's" back door, and one feels uneasy, and finally enraged that Faulkner did not burn the whole house down. When the provincial mind starts out *and continues* on a narrow and unprotesting course, "genius" itself must run on a track.

Flannery O'Connor at least had the conviction that "reality" is at best superficial and that the puzzle of humanity is less easy to solve than that of race. But Miss O'Connor was not so much of Georgia, as in it. The majority of Southern writers have been too confined by prevailing social customs to probe deeply into mysteries that the Citizens Councils insist must never be revealed.

Perhaps my Northern brothers will not believe me when I say there is a great deal of positive material I can draw from my "underprivileged" background. But they have never lived, as I have, at the end of a long road in a house that was faced by the edge of the world on one side and nobody for miles on the other. They have never experienced the magnificent quiet of a summer day when the heat is intense and one is so very thirsty, as one moves across the dusty cotton fields, that one learns forever that water is the essence of all life. In the cities it cannot be so clear to one that he is a creature of the earth, feeling the soil between the toes, smelling the dust thrown up by the rain, loving the earth so much that one longs to taste it and sometimes does.

Nor do I intend to romanticize the Southern black country life. I can recall that I hated it, generally. The hard work in the fields, the shabby houses, the evil greedy men who worked my father to death and almost broke the courage of that strong woman, my mother. No, I am simply saying that Southern black writers, like most writers, have a heritage of love and hate, but that they also have enormous richness and beauty to draw from. And, having been placed, as Camus says, "halfway between misery and the sun," they, too, know that "though all is not well under the sun, history is not everything."

No one could wish for a more advantageous heritage than that bequeathed to the black writer in the South: a compassion for the earth, a trust in humanity beyond our knowledge of evil, and an abiding love of justice. We inherit a great responsibility as well, for we must give voice to centuries not only of silent bitterness and hate but also of neighborly kindness and sustaining love.

Questions To Consider

1. What does Walker suggest about the nature of being a writer who is a woman of color?
2. How does living in the South complicate her experience as a woman of color? As a writer?

PART VI

Writers of the Contemporary South

THE THIRD GENERATION 1974–PRESENT

The Civil Rights movement, not surprisingly, exerted a more sustained influence on the development of Southern culture and effected a more systematic attack upon racial prejudices and presumptions than any event since the Civil War and Reconstruction. Political and historical landmarks of the contemporary period include the end of the much-reviled Vietnam War, the movement toward equal rights for women and minorities, and the increasingly frequent election of Southerners to the White House. Called postmodern by critics and historians, the era beginning in 1974 provides a study in social contradictions. Although critics rarely agree on a definition of the postmodern era, in part because it continued to evolve until the end of the century, critic David Caudle has articulated four general attributes that characterize the period: a focus on the surreal or bizarre; a self-referential style that creates distance between characters and readers, diminishing any sense of identification with the experiences of the characters; a decentered narrative voice; and a philosophical preoccupation with ethical dilemmas. Postmodernism held center stage nationally, but Southern letters did not as readily embrace the abstract nature of postmodern discourse. Instead, throughout the South, the social climate and the literature that evolved from it demonstrated the growing sense of American nationalism, and conversely, an increased interest in regional, ethnic, and sexual identities. Readers and writers alike struggle with the seemingly conflicting ideology of family values on one hand and the value of difference—especially sexually, socially, and gender-based difference—on the other.

As the Civil Rights era drew to a close, a third generation of Southern writers emerged. Growing out of the second, or post-Renascence, generation of writers that included Eudora Welty, Flannery O'Connor, Walker Percy, and Tennessee Williams, the contemporary Southern canon expanded to include an ever-increasing number of women and minority writers. These diverse new voices—exemplified by authors like Lee Smith, Dorothy Allison, Randall Kenan, Larry Brown, and Harry Crews—describe Southern experiences outside the realm of the upper classes. Many contemporary writers portray the lives of those Southerners who do not live in upscale homes and whose lives have not been enhanced by the privileges of relative wealth or of long-standing family name, moving them to the forefront of the Southern, and by extension, the American literary landscape. The issues examined by contemporary Southern authors derive from their experiences—from the historical, economic, and cultural events that have shaped the outlook of the American South, and indeed, the American reading public as a whole, in the last decades of the twentieth century and the early years of the new millennium.

The Growth of Commercial Culture in the Contemporary South

In the closing decades of the twentieth century, the South underwent rapid commercial development. Major corporations such as Wal-Mart, Fed-Ex, and Coca-Cola established corporate offices and built production plants throughout the South. As Southern streets and highways filled up with nationally franchised fast food outlets, gas stations, and video rental stores, they began to look just like other regions of the country, contributing to a loss of geographical identity. Poet Rodney Jones writes about the experience of geographical homogenization in the poem "Simulated Woodgrain Vinyl," describing the dreary architectural sameness of housing projects and "identical two-bedroom brick or clapboard bungalows." From small towns like Bentonville, Arkansas, to metropolitan areas such as Atlanta, commercial enterprises flourished, providing workers with improved employment opportunities. African Americans, women, and poor White males began to find jobs with salaries that supported middle-class lifestyles although many Southern residents continued to falter in terms of sociological and economic development. Those who were left behind often were single mothers who had not benefited from the strong support systems envisioned by the "Great Society" and "War on Poverty" initiatives of the Johnson and Kennedy administrations.

These Democratic party agendas had been advanced during Johnson's presidency, yet their development and progress took a backseat to the Vietnam War, and a dramatic shift in moral values shook the country to its foundation. Although the United States pulled its troops out of Vietnam in 1972, it was not until the late 1970s and early 1980s that novels and poems about the war began to assimilate the reality of the nightmarish conflict that had killed more than 50,000 U.S. troops and split the country into two opposing camps. In the South, Yusef Komunyakaa's poetry collection *Dien Cai Dau* (1988) explored the complex relationships among Black and White U.S. soldiers and Vietnamese women.

While Vietnam War protests were held in the South, so too, were free-love rallies. Premarital sex and drug use challenged the strict mores of the 1950s. Many younger Southerners rejected the "square" attitudes of their parents' generations, but by the 1980s, conservative groups such as Jerry Falwell's Moral Majority had reemerged and fought to reduce abortion rights and to reinstate prayer in schools, which had been outlawed in 1963 by *Murray* v. *Curlett*. The seeds of conflict were sown during the late 1960s and early 1970s, a conflict that erupted into the frequently heated discussions of family values that bombarded the media in the closing decade of the century.

Southerners rode a political roller coaster during the contemporary era, finding themselves jostled between right-wing conservative religious ideologies and the political posturings of the liberal media. This political whiplash resulted from economic difficulties, elections that swayed the government from conservative to liberal and back to ultra-conservative, scandals that brought disgrace and decreasing credibility to politicians, and attacks from foreign sources that even a few decades before had seemed impossible. The 1970s brought the Watergate break-in, revealing criminal activity that plunged the nation into an unprecedented political scandal reaching all the way to the Oval Office. Almost simultaneously, the national celebration of the bicentennial of the Declaration of Independence took place, shifting popular focus to America's roots, the positive qualities of American life, and the founding fathers' goals for the nation.

Following the leadership of President Jimmy Carter of Georgia, a man of principles whom many political analysts described as too honest to be a good president, Ronald Reagan was elected to office. Reagan's election was especially significant for the Southern region, as it marked a partisan shift that continued to affect Southern politics at the turn of the twenty-first century. Many Southern Democrats increasingly found the Democratic party becoming too liberal for their tastes and ultimately changed their party allegiance to Republican (see Map VI–1). Prior to Reagan's first run for the White House, such a shift would have been unthinkable, for the Republicans had long been the party of the hated Reconstruction. The reemergence of conservatism transformed the South, and on present-day political–demographic maps, the "Solid South" is home to far more Republicans than Democrats. Southern states were key players in subsequent elections when voters became important pieces in the electoral puzzle, as demonstrated by the narrow margin by which Florida's election returns decided the 2000 election. The confusion about how to mark ballots, the mishandling of those ballots, and the resulting finger-pointing among well-known political figures, when combined with the recent and bitter memory of the sexual exploits and perjury allegations leveled against then-sitting president, William Jefferson

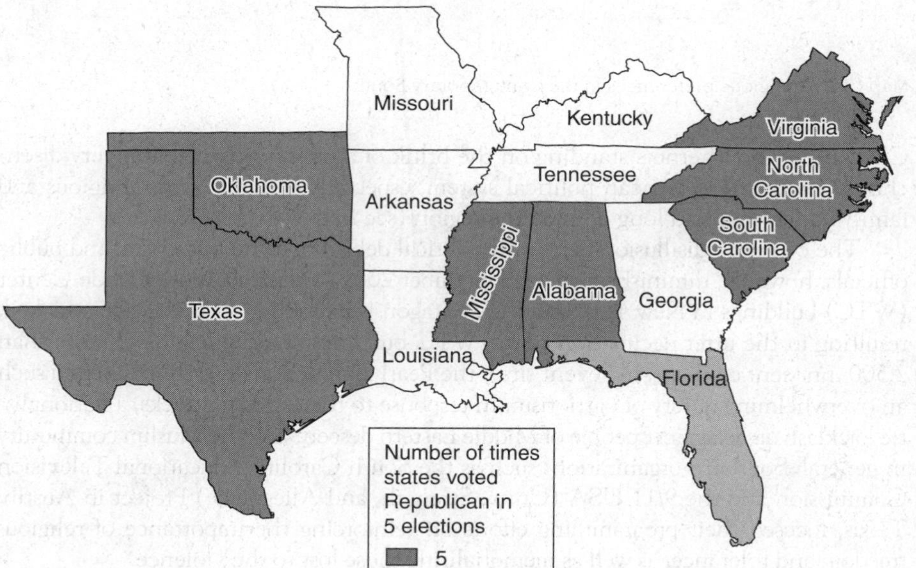

Map VI–1: Southern voting patterns in recent elections

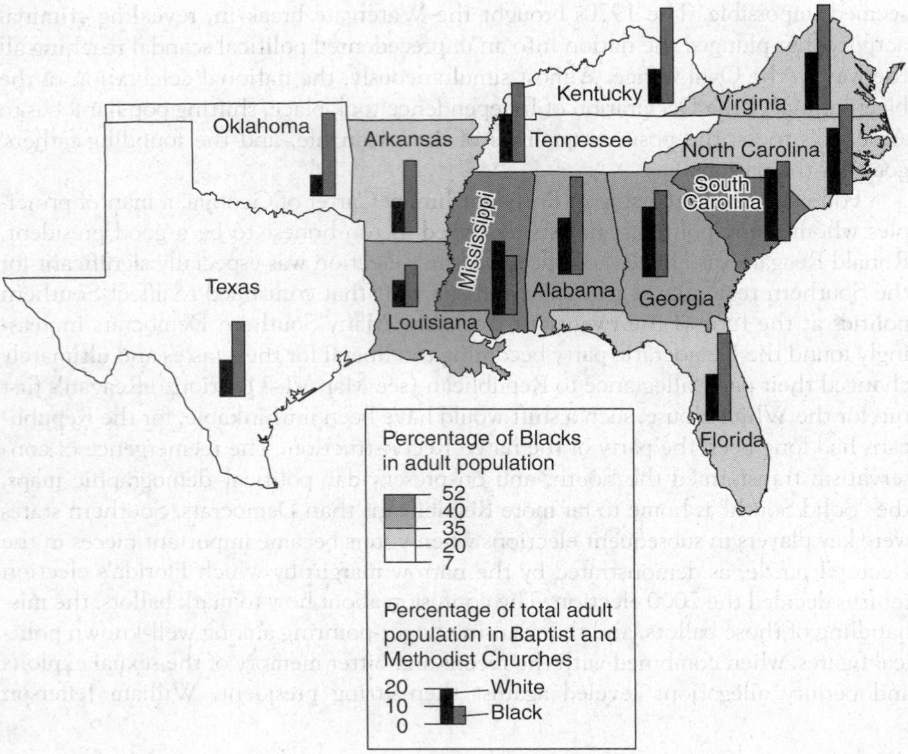

Map VI–2: Religious preferences in the Contemporary South

Clinton, left Southerners standing on the brink of a new century feeling very disenchanted with the American political system, especially in light of the religious and family values that had long defined the region (see Map VI–2).

The country's disillusionment with political debacles, economic crises, and public officials, however, diminished on 11 September 2001, when the World Trade Center (WTC) buildings in New York and the Pentagon in Washington D.C. were attacked, resulting in the utter decimation of the WTC buildings and the deaths of more than 2,500 innocent civilians. No event since the Pearl Harbor attacks of 1941 elicited such an overwhelming outcry of patriotism. In response to the terrorist attacks, a nationalistic backlash arose against people of Middle Eastern descent and the Muslim community in general. Southern organizations such as the South Carolina Educational Television Commission and the 9/11 USA (Unity, Strength, and Allegiance) Project in Austin, Texas, focused their programming efforts on reinforcing the importance of religious freedom and tolerance, as well as memorializing those lost to the violence.

The leadership role of Southern institutions in the wake of the events of 11 September are indicative of the increasing importance of Southern commerce, science, arts, and politics in the contemporary world. Although the region has continued to struggle against economic hardships and negative stereotypes over the last forty years, Southerners have played increasingly significant roles in U.S. and world leadership, as evidenced by the number of U.S. presidents who hailed from Southern states during the last half of the twentieth century. Recent historical events have provided ample fodder for Southern writers who have continued to produce literary works of the highest quality in quantities that have not diminished since the dawn of the Southern Renascence.

The writers of the Southern Renascence and their influence on the second generation continue to be felt in contemporary Southern letters, leading to a third generation of Southern authors, which is in many ways dominated by women and people of color. Yet to suggest that Southern writers have continued to produce works limited to the same themes and topics as their predecessors is to minimize the accomplishments of each of the three generations of writers. Contemporary Southern writers create their works in a turbulent social and cultural context, a context in which even literary texts themselves have existed in a state of transition. The effects of literary theory—what many critics have termed the "postmodern condition"—as well as the transformation of the publishing industry itself have dramatically altered the face of Southern literature.

Generation Next: Postmodernism and Literary Trends in the Contemporary South

Contemporary Southern literature has departed from traditional Southern topics. Although contemporary Southern writers continue to examine issues of race, gender, place, class, family, religion, and honor, they do so from different perspectives and from previously marginalized voices. This departure raises questions about the void created by the absence of a prototypical Southern literary text, especially in light of the sustained and extensive productivity of Southern writers throughout the twentieth century. Does a Southern literary tradition exist at all in the twenty-first century? Certainly, the sheer scope of the body of literature emerging from the region suggests a literary tradition is alive and well and living in the South.

As the modernist period drew to a close, writers sought new ways of self-expression, and nowhere was this impulse stronger than among Southern writers. By the late 1960s, postmodern narrative forms had moved to the forefront of American letters. Postmodern forms exhibited elements such as a decentered point of view, rapidly shifting narrators, and nonlinear plots. These narratives diverged from traditional storytelling methods in ways that were not always well-received by popular readers, despite their seeming acceptance by publishers and critics. The popularity of the works of contemporary Southern writers, who revived and built upon the realist tradition, in many ways reflects the widespread dissatisfaction readers have consistently expressed with postmodern literature. Postmodernists created what Robert Scholes calls "self-reflexive fiction," suggesting that because of the nature of postmodern narrative, its forms would be short-lived. As critic Robert Rebein has pointed out, readers of postmodern narratives find "little joy in reading," experiencing instead a powerful "feeling of ambivalence" as their primary response to postmodern texts.

The ambivalence of contemporary readers derives from the nonlinear narrative techniques that typify postmodern works. Contemporary Southern literature offers viable alternatives to postmodern narratives, relying on storytelling techniques to which readers can easily relate. Southern fiction, in particular, has revitalized a realist tradition in which writers portray everyday life, common hardships, and familial and romantic relationships. As the twentieth century unfolded, and the literary establishment moved further away from the modernist techniques of writers such as Walker Percy and Flannery O'Connor, the South produced what critic Matthew Guinn has called a "new class of writers who approach literary convention with either indifference or hostility." Poet Martha McFerren tells funny, catty, gossipy stories like a good Southerner, but she is also a postmodern iconoclast, deconstructing Southern images such as the belle, the historical landmark sign, and Southern cooking in her poems. The third generation of Southern writers to arise since the Renascence has sought alternative means of identifying and interpreting the Southern experience, methods which, as Guinn argues, depart from the critical approach of the "Rubin generation" in which "one looks for the stock motifs of history, place and community (as established by Louis D. Rubin and others) in new works." Despite the continued influence of the ideology of place—a sense of rootedness that comes from a communal identity based in the characteristics of a geographic region—Guinn points out that defining writers as Southern simply because they write about the region is no longer viable, because it "ignores the large number of authors who do not fit the pattern." Poet Marilyn Nelson, for example, grew up as an "Air Force brat," moving from one military base to another, yet she imaginatively returns, in her poems, to the Kentucky, Alabama, and Oklahoma towns where her parents and grandparents once lived. James Lee Burke illustrates a similar diversity of place in two series of novels placing one set in Texas and the other in Louisiana. Similarly, Jayne Anne Phillips sets her stories in distinctly Southern places. In her critically acclaimed novel, *Shelter* (1994), she tells the story of a religious zealot whose convictions lead to death and destruction. Rather than telling more traditional Southern stories of religious conversion or of the difficulties that befall a backslider, she uses the grotesque to demonstrate the extremism that is too often the result of religious fervor and the damage it can inflict on those who come into contact with it. Guinn contends that contemporary Southern writers seek "not continuity but discontinuity," defying the traditional view of one South as opposed to many Souths, stressing the heterogeneity of the region in the process. This heterogeneity is seen not only in subregional differences, but also in variants deriving from race, gender, and class distinctions.

Contemporary Southern poetry was not immune to the influence of postmodernism. The United States as a whole saw two major trends in poetry beginning with the decade of the eighties. New Formalists returned to the rhymed and metered poetic forms that had been out of fashion since the advent of poetic modernism and free verse early in the twentieth century, while L*A*N*G*U*A*G*E poets were influenced by postmodern critical theories of words as arbitrary signifiers and the individual self as a false social construction. The South, with its fondness for order and tradition, produced more than its share of New Formalist poets. Fred Chappell, Robert Morgan, Everette Maddox, Marilyn Nelson, Yusef Komunyakaa, Julie Kane, and Ellen Bryant Voigt have all worked in rhymed and metered forms as well as in free verse; in fact, Chappell's epic poem *Midquest* (1981) contains an example of virtually every conceivable poetic form from the sonnet, sestina, and villanelle through rhymed couplets. The South, with its love of language and the eccentricities of individuality, shunned L*A*N*G*U*A*G*E poetry altogether.

In a league by himself stands A. R. Ammons of North Carolina, classed among the greatest of American poets by most contemporary critics. His long, rambling, conversational poems reveal his fondness for Southern oral narrative traditions, yet his poems are aggressively postmodern and regionless in their mixing of high and low syntax, incorporation of elements from popular culture, fascination with science and technology, exploration of the nature of consciousness, and resistance to closure. Having won the National Book Award for his *Collected Poems* in 1973, Ammons went on to win a second award for *Garbage* in 1994. A book-length poem exhibiting these postmodern tendencies, *Garbage* is a meditation on a Florida garbage dump that incorporates everything from the decay of disposable diapers, corpses, and radioactive waste to the decay of language and of stars in outer space.

Dirty Realism and the Rejection of Postmodernism

Contemporary Southern writers share common narrative strategies, including dirty realism; assimilation narratives that reflect the experiences of non-Southerners living in the region; the development and characterization of subcultural communal identities and the ways in which they inform individual identities; and a renewed emphasis on folk traditions and the ways in which they reflect universal as well as regional concerns. Perhaps most importantly, Southern writers share a common interest in the stories of those whose voices have long been silenced, whose stories may heretofore have been told only in small, disenfranchised, and often oppressed communities: people of color, members of lower socioeconomic classes, or individuals from subregions whose populations have traditionally been stereotyped by their heritage or the area in which they live, such as the Cajuns in South Louisiana or the poor Whites in the Appalachian Mountains (see Map VI–3).

Critics and historians continue to debate the ways in which the Southern literary tradition is evolving, and a part of the ongoing conversation is demonstrated by the ways in which the region itself is named. Concern over the name of the Southern region itself speaks to the ideologies of postcolonialism and globalization that many critics bring to bear on Southern texts. As Fred Hobson has noted in his introduction to *South to the Future* (2002), the region originally called "The South," later came to be known as the "American South," and more recently has been termed the "U.S. South," acknowledging the "Southernness" of Central and South America. Hobson further points out that while the first and second generations of twentieth-century Southern writers have focused on the ways in which the region diverges from American culture, contemporary Southern writers have focused on the region's similarities to other regions, both within the United States and outside of it, examining shared experiences such as defeat, poverty, and ideological failure. Presumptions about the South as a region—and by extension, about its literary heritage—are "changing radically because concepts of religion, place, race, culture, and community are being reevaluated." Hobson acknowledges that another example of this shift in presumptions is found in the closing gap between high culture and folk culture. Despite the critical debate over the underpinnings of contemporary Southern literature, the fact remains that the works of Southern writers represent a substantial force in contemporary American literature. Regardless of their quarrels with or intentional disregard for

Map VI–3: The Contemporary South

traditional Southern themes and subject matters, contemporary writers continue to labor under the influence of the now-longstanding Southern literary tradition.

Although they clearly demonstrate the influence of realism, contemporary Southern writers have expanded the scope of the realist tradition, rather than replicating nineteenth-century techniques. Recent Southern writers account for the majority of Americans who have created "a curious, dirty realism about the belly-side of contemporary life" according to Bill Buford, the expatriate editor of *Granta*, who has been credited with first identifying this literary trend. Buford argues that dirty realism incorporates the

> unadorned, unfurnished, low-rent tragedies about people who watch daytime television, read cheap romances, or listen to country and western music. They are waitresses in roadside cafes, cashiers in supermarkets, construction workers, secretaries and unemployed cowboys. They play bingo, eat cheeseburgers, hunt deer and stay in cheap hotels. They drink a lot and are often in trouble: for stealing a car, breaking a window, and pickpocketing. They are from Kentucky or Alabama or Oregon, but, mainly, they could just about be from anywhere: drifters in a world cluttered with junk food and the oppressive details of modern consumerism.

Buford's working definition of dirty realism, which critics have dubbed "grit lit" when referring to the South, not only incorporates many attributes of contemporary Southern writing, but also draws many of its most pointed examples from the Southern region.

Contemporary grit lit writers—a diverse group which includes Lee Smith, Dorothy Allison, Lewis Nordan, Larry Brown, Jayne Anne Phillips, Harry Crews, and Bobbie Anne Mason—record the experiences of the lower echelons of Southern society. Members of the working classes have been most directly influenced by the demands and expectations of the burgeoning industrial and commercial concerns throughout the South, yet they have reaped the fewest benefits for their efforts. Writers such as Lee Smith and Bobbie Ann Mason bring their readers inside working-class and lower-class families, showing the ways in which family dynamics and secrets inform their lives. Class struggles emerge in contemporary works, demonstrating the financial struggles of the perennially poor, working-class residents of the South. Such characters are often plagued by problems with substance abuse, troubled relationships with friends, peers, and family, and un- or underemployment that ranges from intermittent to perennial. Smith illustrates the importance of women's relationships and communities in her works, themes that are also integral to works of writers such as Kaye Gibbons, Jill McCorkle, and Michael Lee West. Dorothy Allison shows her readers what it feels like to be a part of a large extended family, subtly stressing the point that no matter how heinous the behavior of blood relatives might be, they remain family, while also demonstrating the ways in which the actions of one person may serve to stigmatize an entire family. She does not flinch from describing, in brutal detail, such atrocities as the incestuous rape of a child or the callous and self-absorbed choices of a mother who chooses an abusive mate over the welfare of her child. Far from shying away from the emotionally charged topics favored by many of their female counterparts, writers such as Lewis Nordan and Harry Crews address the devastation inherent in the death of a child, and the particular hell endured by those who hold themselves culpable in these deaths. Nordan writes of a young boy who inadvertently allows his baby brother to drink kerosene, an act that results in his death. Harry Crews relates the autobiographical tale of his young son's drowning in a neighbor's pool and the resulting dissolution of his marriage. These writers tell their stories as they happened, and do not whitewash the truth, instead relating their graphic stories in all their horror and grit. They provide an eyeful of blood and death; hatred, abuse, and disillusionment; and the strength and determination of people who overcome the horrific events that they describe in their fiction.

The dirty realism that Buford describes equally informs the narratives of African-American writers. Writers such as Randall Kenan picture life in poor communities with deadly clarity. Ernest Gaines's approach to realism differs, leading him to tell stories such as *A Lesson Before Dying*. Unlike the condemned characters in many death row novels, although Gaines's protagonist is sentenced to death within the first twenty pages, the narrative does not center on efforts to secure a pardon for an innocent man. Because of the racial bias implicit in Southern culture, the presumption of every character—from the sheriff to the attorneys, from the accused to his family members—is that the accused will be convicted and put to death. Gaines focuses his attention instead on the struggle for dignity and the ways in which an individual may fashion a sense of self-worth while in the grip of flagrant injustice. Gaines's works are equally compelling in their depictions of the efforts to define masculinity and responsibility in a society that continues to denigrate and disempower men of color. He vividly portrays the frustration, the hopelessness, and sometimes even the violence that erupts in the face of an oppression that will not allow individuals to realize their potential—or even to approach it.

Gothicism, Class Struggles, and Assimilation Narratives

Along with their frequent use of techniques of dirty realism, Southern writers often return to gothicism, a mode of storytelling that dates to the Antebellum period in the works of Edgar Allan Poe and that regained popularity with writers of the Southern Renascence such as William Faulkner. Implicit in the gothic mode is a heavy reliance on grotesque characters who are alienated from their communities, as well as the tendency to examine long-standing Southern myths and their psychological effects. Writers such as James Lee Burke, in his detective tales of the Louisiana bayou, evoke the darkness, mystery, other-worldliness, and danger inherent in the gothic tradition. In works such as *Louisiana Power and Light* (1994) and *Deep in the Shade of Paradise* (2002), John Dufresne adeptly fashions narratives which join humorous depictions of poor, Southern life with the darker side of religious fanaticism and dogmatic acceptance of predetermined fate. Jayne Anne Phillips, in novels such as the award-winning *Shelter*, demonstrates the ways in which the stigma of poverty, crime, and overzealous religious practices may irrevocably limit life choices. Additionally, popular Southern fiction, such as *Midnight in the Garden of Good and Evil* (1994), *Daughters of the Dust* (1997), or *The Oldest Living Confederate Widow Tells All* (1984), draws on the well-established gothic tradition, adding a Southern flavor to narratives by evoking voodoo, conjuring, and incantations into the same contemporary narratives that are populated by cross-dressing drag queens and nosy Yankee reporters.

Literary examinations of the Southern class system illustrate the conflicts that arise when *nouveau riche*, "white trash," or people of mixed racial heritage attempt to climb the social ladder. White trash rarely ascends to acceptable society, as they are generally a little too loud, too flashily dressed, too lazy and slovenly, or too eager to remove their clothes as a means of advancing their social position. DeeDee Robichaux in Michael Lee West's *She Flew the Coop*, Cindy in Jill McCorkle's *Tending to Virginia*, or the pot-smoking husband in Bobbie Anne Mason's "Shiloh" demonstrate thwarted attempts at assimilating successfully into the Southern social hierarchy, returning to a traditional Southern theme, albeit with a contemporary twist.

Religion frequently provides the foundation for Southern texts and continues to motivate the storytelling of many Southern writers. For example, Lee Smith writes, in her autobiographical story "Tongues of Fire," of the emotional pull she felt toward charismatic religion, recounting the events of a time when she became enamored of a snake-handling church, an interest that horrified her mother since such religious practices were considered low class. Dorothy Allison relates similar religious leanings, telling of the ways in which gospel music influenced the protagonist in *Bastard Out of Carolina* (1992). Robert Morgan illustrates the close relationship of religion to rural Appalachian daily life in "Sunday Toilet," a poem about his father dusting their hog pen with lime powder, or quick lime, before going to church on Sundays. The whiteness and disinfecting qualities of the lime when applied to hog slop foreshadow the purifying effects of the church service upon the sinful human being. Other contemporary Southerners, including John Dufresne, Randall Kenan, Doris Betts, Reynolds Price, and Clyde Edgerton examine the effects of religion on Southern culture and the world view of its citizens.

Racial struggles are a staple of Southern literature, and contemporary writers continue to consider the issues raised by this perennial problem. Rather than relating stories of lynchings and outright intimidation, however, contemporary writers deal with the insidious nature of racism, demonstrating its effects on both African Americans and Whites. Ernest Gaines shows overt racial conflict in many of his novels. Character growth occurs only in the context of all-Black communities, whose members must also find ways to coexist with racist Whites while developing or maintaining their sense of dignity and self-worth. African-American characters are often forced to assume responsibility for keeping the White family functioning but are denied the power that should accompany this responsibility. In "Shadrach," William Styron provides a seemingly stereotypical depiction of a former slave who returns to his former owner's plantation to die, so that he may be buried there. However, Styron subverts the reader's expectations, for the poor family who now resides on the former plantation takes great care to fulfill the old man's wishes, not because of his ties to the plantation-era South, but because of an inherent respect for the aged that is culturally encoded in them from their youth.

Family relationships continue to inspire Southern writers. The depiction of familial relationships, however, exhibits a more distinct connection to traditional, multigenerational European families than to the American nuclear family. Southern writers examine the extended family, showing both the solidarity and support that it can provide, along with the profound sense of embarrassment and alienation from the larger community it can engender. The dichotomy of always belonging to a group, of a birthright, is coupled with the inescapable grip of extended family relationships. In this same vein, the short, autobiographical lyric influenced by the Beat and Confessional poetry movements continued to dominate poetry in both the United States as a whole and in the South. To a greater extent than poets from other regions, however, contemporary Southern poets tended to explore their personal experiences not in isolation from but in relationship to the experiences of preceding generations of family members. Standing in a muddy field with sinkholes that seem to be pulling him toward the dead, Fred Chappell's autobiographical narrator muses, "A man could live down here forever, Where his blood is." Marilyn Nelson writes a poem about the New Year's party where her mother met her father.

Southern writers often depict fractured nuclear families, placing these damaged characters within extended family groups. Jill McCorkle creates a group of interrelated women—grandmothers who are also sisters, their daughters, and granddaughters—in *Tending to Virginia* (1987), and follows the experiences of a group of high school girls throughout much of *The Cheerleader* (1984) in her effort to demonstrate the depths of her protagonist's emotional breakdown. Similarly, Kaye Gibbons places her narratives in the context of extended families, showing relationships between grandmother, mother, sister, and daughter in novels such as *Charms for the Easy Life* (1993), *On the Occasion of My Last Afternoon* (1998), and *A Cure for Dreams* (1991).

This emphasis on extended families offers a natural means for authors to draw upon the rich heritage of Southern folk traditions. Folk traditions permeate the lives of most Americans, but in the rural South particularly, they are practiced and glorified in ways that they are not in urban areas. Many Southern writers—Ron Rash, Lee Smith, and Robert Morgan, to name only a handful—attest to the influence of the oral folk stories that they grew up hearing in the South. Oral folk narrative is far from the only folk practice apparent in Southern fiction. Clyde Edgerton, Randall Kenan, and Michael Lee West write of Southern funeral and burial traditions in their work, and the characteristics and practices of hunting, fishing, and regional foodways appear in many Southern writers' works.

The Southern literary tradition continues to evolve in dynamic ways in the contemporary era and shows no signs of decreasing its momentum. Despite disagreement among critics and literary historians as to the ways in which contemporary Southern literature should be interpreted, readers clamor for the next Southern offering, and new voices continue to emerge at a rate with which even the most dedicated reader cannot keep pace. The third wave of Southern literature has fulfilled the promise of the Southern Renascence and, by all indications, will continue to make significant contributions to the American literary canon.

Contemporary South Chronology

1974–Present

1974 • Henry Aaron slams his 715th home run to become the all-time major league leader and hits a total of 755 homers by the end of his career.

1977 • Elvis Presley dies at Graceland at age 42.

1980 • John Lennon is shot dead in New York City.

1981 • Iranian terrorists release 52 American hostages in January after holding them in captivity for 14 months.
- Assassination attempt on Ronald Reagan on 30 March by John Hinckley, Jr.
- Sandra Day O'Connor becomes the first female Supreme Court justice.
- First launch of Columbia space shuttle.

1982 • Vietnam War memorial is erected in Washington, D.C.

1983 • Compact disks are introduced, causing record sales to decline sharply.
- Sally Ride, crew member of the Challenger, becomes the first American woman in space.
- HIV discovered.

1985 • RMS *Titanic* wreckage found and filmed by robotic camera in July.

1986 • The space shuttle Challenger explodes 73 seconds after liftoff. Teacher Christa McAuliffe is a civilian passenger on the shuttle. NASA suspends shuttle flights until 1988, when they announce that civilians will no longer be allowed on shuttle flights.
- Halley's Comet returns.

1987 • Black Monday. On 19 October, the stock market drops 22%, a fall that far surpasses the 1929 crash, when stock prices dropped 12.9%, signaling the beginning of the Great Depression.

1988 • Pan Am Flight 103 explodes over Lockerbie, Scotland. Terrorists are suspected of planting the bomb.

1989 • Students protest government oppression in Tiananmen Square, Beijing, China. The army intervenes, killing between 3,000 and 7,000.
- Colin Powell is appointed chairman of the Joint Chiefs of Staff, the highest Army post ever to be held by an African-American officer.
- Berlin wall falls.

1995 • American terrorists bomb the Murrah Federal Building in Oklahoma City, killing 168 people, including 19 children.

1996 • Bombing at Olympic Games in Atlanta, Georgia.
- Jazz great Ella Fitzgerald dies.

1998 • Legendary crooner Frank Sinatra dies of a heart attack at age 82.

1999 • Two students go on a shooting rampage in Columbine High School in Littleton, Colorado, killing twelve students, one teacher, and themselves.
- Y2K Scare. Billions of dollars are spent worldwide on Y2K software upgrades. As the new year passes in Fiji, the supposed Y2K bug does not throw the world back to the nineteenth century.
- U.S. Senate impeaches President William Jefferson Clinton on two counts, although he is ultimately acquitted of all charges.

2001 • 11 September: Simultaneous terrorist attacks on the World Trade Center in New York and the Pentagon in Washington, D.C., leave thousands dead. President George W. Bush declares war on international terror and those who harbor or assist terrorists.

2003 • The United States declares war on Iraq, launching an air assault and sending in ground forces in an effort to remove Saddam Hussein from power. Hussein is ultimately captured ten months later while hiding in a hole in the ground.

2004 • City of San Francisco grants marriage licenses to gay and lesbian couples, in defiance of state law. More than 3,700 ceremonies are performed before the California Supreme Court issues an injunction barring additional ceremonies.

VOICES IN CONTEXT

Death and Burial Traditions

Throughout Southern culture, death and death-related practices receive careful attention. From the Deep South to the border states, people practice many kinds of burial and memorial traditions, and not surprisingly, the literature of the South reflects this tradition. Works from all periods of Southern literature depict funerals, burials, and death practices, demonstrating folk traditions that are illustrative of their local communities. In this particular section, a group of death-related stories have emerged, and these works so eloquently complement one another that they have been grouped together.

Of all the observable Southern cultural practices, death, burial, and memorial traditions are perhaps the best indicators of the nature of these communities and of the ways in which they mourn and honor their dead. Death practices include many folklife elements, such as foodways, material culture, and oral narrative. Whether the death occurs in an urban or rural community, death still draws its fair share of attention from the South as can be seen in the many pieces of Southern literature that portray death practices.

In many Southern states, church members or relatives continue the tradition of "sitting up" with the dead. Some churches have elaborately encoded ways of scheduling who will sit with whom and the amount of hours that these people will stay and sit near the deceased. In some families, an adult child will sit with a parent or vice versa, while in others, a more distant relative will stay to receive relatives and friends so that immediate family can have private time to grieve and to prepare for the funeral. In some Southern subcultures, elaborate wakes may take place at funeral homes, in the deceased person's home, or at the church. Generally, those of European heritage—specifically, German, Anglo-Scots-Irish origins—bury their dead within two or three days, while some African-American families may wait as long as five to six days before burial. In almost all cases, however, friends of the family or more distant relatives bring food and perform small daily tasks to assist the deceased person's family. In the urban South, death rituals differ from the ways in which they are practiced in the rural South, but a pared-down version of these rural activities generally occurs.

Once a person has been buried, many Southern families devote a weekend or two each year to cemetery care. Grave cleaning in the South has become ubiquitous in many communities and is sometimes viewed as a miniature family reunion, or grave cleanings may even be held in conjunction with church homecomings. For those families whose loved ones are buried in perpetual care cemeteries, grave decoration activities occur. In many eastern and central Oklahoma communities and parts of east Texas, for example, Memorial Day has become a day to honor and remember all those who have passed away; the day is not confined to the remembrance of those who died in military service. On Memorial Day, families decorate graves and pause to reflect upon the lives of the departed. These grave cleaning and decorating days are firmly grounded in many communities, and multiple generations within families share in the activities. Clyde Edgerton's novel, *The Floatplane Notebooks*, depicts one such grave cleaning through the eyes of a family outsider. Edgerton is not alone in his portrayal of grave cleaning and memorial traditions, for as this section illustrates, many Southern writers elect to present such scenes in their works.

Along with grave cleanings, another Southern burial tradition occurs in some small Louisiana communities, where the hand digging of graves is still practiced. Though this tradition is decreasing as many Louisiana residents move away from their communities in search of work, some churches and small cemeteries maintain the practice. When a person within a community passes away, either a committee within the church or friends or distant relatives of the deceased decide which members and friends will dig the grave. Generally, only two men can fit in the grave to dig, but the graveside becomes the site where many of the older male community members gather and advise the younger grave diggers about the best ways to dig the grave. These older gentlemen also share stories of the deceased or of other graves they helped to dig in their younger days. While women are not expressly forbidden to participate in this ritual, they do not. Grave digging, in these communities, is men's work. Women may bring biscuits and coffee or other refreshments, but they do not remain in the cemetery while the digging occurs. Most diggers state that they dig the grave as a way of paying the last respects to a departed friend, but some dig because a family may not be able to afford the services of a backhoe operator. No matter what the reason, the smaller communities of Louisiana continue to hand dig many of their graves—a surprise to many urban Southerners.

The stories of this section have been selected for their depictions of death, burial, and memorial traditions. Some of these focus on the emotional aspects of loss such as Harry Crews's and Andre Dubus's works while others like Randall Kenan and Michael Lee West focus upon the cultural aspects of death. Within this section the funereal practices of the Anglo-Scots-Irish and African-American cultures are depicted and provide readers with a view into these specific cultures' practices.

Doris Betts

1932–

In a 1972 interview, Doris Betts remarked on the prevalence of death in her work: "I write about the lower and lower-middle class, because the mortality is much closer to the edge of the veil there . . . one is conscious every time you sing old down-home, thumping hymns that death is always present, and that one is talking about it in terms of blood, flesh, and perishing." Betts sees "time and mortality" as defining themes of her work, the bulk of which is set in her native South, despite the fact that she does not self-identify as a Southern writer. In fact, Betts eschews such descriptions: "the only adjective a writer wants before that designation is 'good,'" she once remarked to critic Dorothy Scura. Place is a significant force in Betts's fiction, though, and her characters are inextricably intertwined with their Southern roots.

Doris Waugh Betts was born on 4 June 1932 in Statesville, North Carolina, to William Elmore Waugh and Mary Ellen Freeze Waugh. Betts's father was the adopted son of a poor, sharecropping family. Following their marriage, the Waughs settled in an industrial mill town. Despite the squalid conditions that often existed in newly industrialized areas during the early twentieth century, Betts does not recall lacking material goods. She did not realize her family was poor, except in retrospect, since all the families in the mill town experienced similar financial circumstances. Her family subscribed to a fundamentalist religious faith, the influence of which has caused her, in later years, to refer to herself as a "recovering Calvinist." Nonetheless, she acknowledges the benefits of her early and thorough training in scripture, which instilled a "wonder at the power of words." Betts's faith often frames her fiction, despite the fact that she is "distrustful of 'Christian' as a term that 'spoils to a rancid adjective,' and she objects to stereotypical images of both Southern and women writers. She does not, however, diminish the significance of religious themes in her work, nor the importance of her religious Southern background," as critic Deborah E. Barker has observed.

The Waugh family created a loving and supportive environment that nurtured their daughter's talents. Doris's mother encouraged her early interest in storytelling by serving as a scribe when the child was still too young to write. Betts began writing poetry and novels in junior high school and always assumed that she would be a writer. She attended the Women's College at the University of North Carolina and there received the first objective evaluation of her work when a professor praised her fiction, but discouraged her poetic efforts. She met

Lowry Matthew Betts and married him in 1952, and the couple has three children. Following her marriage, Betts enrolled at the University of North Carolina–Chapel Hill, at the same time that her husband was enrolled in law school, but she never took a degree. In an interview with Scura, Betts states that she "wanted to be a writer, to have a family, and to have a career, and she didn't want those things in any order"; she has been fortunate enough to enjoy all three. Early in her professional career, Betts worked as a reporter and as a newspaper editor, and by 1966, she had begun teaching part-time at UNC–Chapel Hill. She quickly became a respected member of the University community, serving at times as the dean of the honors program and the chair of the faculty, in addition to her teaching responsibilities.

Religion is a strong undercurrent in Betts's fiction, and her interest in examining faith and religious practices perhaps derives from her personal belief system. Southern writer Lee Smith once commented in an interview with Susan Ketchin that "Doris Betts describes herself as someone who consciously deals with Christian themes and images in her fiction. She says she tries not to hit you over the head with her beliefs, but instead to speak in a whisper, as one does in trying to get the attention of small children." Her delicate approach to matters of faith and forgiveness is inviting, avoiding the often-seen trap of preaching to the reader or condemning characters for the frailties of their faith. "Three Ghosts" questions the nature of faith, and the things that we have faith in, when a woman is confronted with the ghost of a long-deceased relative just as her own mother is facing death.

Betts has published three critically acclaimed collections of short fiction, *Gentle Insurrection and Other Stories* (1954), *The Astronomer and Other Stories* (1965) and *Beasts of the Southern Wild* (1973). One of her most popular short stories, "The Ugliest Pilgrim," has also been made into both an award-winning Broadway play and a film, entitled *Violet*, which earned an Academy Award in 1982. Betts has successfully published six novels, although she contends that she has written novels only so that she can get her short fiction published, since novels tend to be more lucrative than collections of short fiction. Her novels have received numerous awards, including the Sir Walter Raleigh award, and *Women's Review of Books* listed her novel, *Heading West*, as one of the top hundred best books by women. Most recently, Betts published a memoir, *My Love Affair with Carolina* (1998).

Three Ghosts

I hurried from bed thinking Mama had called; she often does. But instead my Aunt Jean was standing in the hall, still wearing very black hair in a coil wrapped on what they called a "ratt"[1] in the '40s—still tall and slender, having no face wrinkles, with a jaw line that had not sagged.

I didn't blink. I don't believe in ghosts.

She was wearing a pale blue dress with gold buttons and a brooch at the neckline. I hadn't thought the word "brooch" in so long that it sounded mispronounced in my mind. "Hello! Hello, Hallucination!" I called to her, using all I've learned about false cheer.

She didn't move—her silence was a bit unnerving—but only fixed on me those overly big blue eyes I had almost forgotten. Aunt Jean had that combination of bright blue eyes with black hair years before entertainers created this striking effect using contact lenses. From puberty on, though, her eyeballs had always bulged. Perhaps in life she'd had a thyroid problem.

But tonight I knew Jean had not been "in life" since the late '70s, after three minor husbands and one major car wreck. When her body lay reassembled and sculpted

1. A small wad of hair that would be pinned underneath the hair to increase the hair's thickness or fullness. Also a device around which hair could be wrapped to create a bun or other style.

together in her coffin, thinner and faded hair had hung beside those rebuilt cheekbones like a pair of shingles. This younger face she showed now I only knew from photograph albums: the pretty girl entering nurse's training, the pretty woman posed beside various young men under flat straw boaters like bottle caps, the pretty nurse in her dark cape swirling off to World War II and the bedsides of wounded soldiers.

(All they taught Mama was how to cook and to half-sole a shoe.)

But like Jean and Mama, I'm Scots-Presbyterian and hard to fool. I stepped smartly down that hall carpet runner I got overcharged for, demanding, "Aunt Jean? What are you doing here?"

She spoke in the old way—that twangy edge-of-the-Blue Ridge way. "How's my sister?"

I said, "She's 92, how do you think she is?"

Jean would be, if alive, 97. If she hadn't died when she did, I'd be looking after them both.

"Does she hurt?"

That stopped me. Was she sick, old, failing—I could have answered those. Did she limp, fall, suffer from nightmares, wet the bed—I knew these answers as well.

"Probably so," I said. But then I took a deep breath, shook all confusion out of my head, and slotted this very vivid, multicolored Jean into the figment category. I declared her to be no more than a figment of my imagination, perhaps my resentment, certainly my fatigue. She'd had husbands to spare while I never married. In the South, marrying is what determines which old invalids women will care for—male or female.

Immediately I knew I'd robbed power from this image of Jean by reducing her to size, cramping her inside my head where she was no bigger than a brain cell. I took a firm step or two closer down the hall, confident. In fact, my real self was probably two doors back, in bed and sound asleep, merely exaggerating her dream until it swelled to the size of Mama's nightmares in which she killed hogs and wrung chicken necks.

But Aunt Jean, still looking solid, kept backing ahead of me down the hall, at last resting her firm white fingers with too many rings against Mama's door. It's an unnatural gait, to go backward for more than a step or two, and her easy movements made my stiff knee hurt.

"Let Mama alone; she's had her medicine, let her sleep!" I said, springing forward.

As if Jean had turned into Mama's figment instead of mine, she half-opened that door and half-melted into its edge and corners, then disappeared into the dark.

I dreaded to follow! Mama would be lying on her back, her mouth empty and open. Dentures were soaking nearby. Ears empty, too—her hearing aids now in their moisture-absorbent jar. If it was much after midnight, her diaper would be wet and the rubber sheet below would only have trapped the wide stain. Unless recent, it would smell. A wen[2] growing by one eye looked like old chewing gum. If startled awake, Mama would scream. Long minutes of soothing would be required.

I whispered, "Oh, please!" but Aunt Jean was already at the bedside, drawing off the sheet Mama always wrapped around her face because breathing downward warmed the bed.

I slumped in the doorway.

In a shocked voice, Aunt Jean exclaimed, "But this isn't Lucille!"

And her words answered, perhaps, my questions about whether we die by degrees or all at once, whether the soul seeps across by drips and spiritual leakage or only de-

2. A knot or wart on the skin, usually appearing on the head.

parts with a single thump when the bottom drops out of the heart. Jean, of course, stabbed by a steering column, fled in the second way.

I managed to answer her, pointing. "It's what's left." My hand wavered.

But Jean's revelation that Mama's best, true, and barely remembered self had not already left this room to squeeze by stages into the hereafter was harder to endure than all the surgeries and bandages and bedpans combined.

I wanted to kill Aunt Jean a second time.

"You go back!" I ordered her, feeling my teeth sharpen themselves on my lower lip. "Who do you think you are to come back here making trouble after all these years?" I moved past the bed where Mama lay like a white apparition herself.

Now I could accuse Jean by shaking my finger hard in midair. "Lucille has forgot you, forgot you were the prettiest, forgot Jerry boy, forgot your mother and your papa, forgot my daddy, forgot me most of the time! So you've got no business here, get away! go on!" An ancient word rose in my mouth. "Begone!"

Aunt Jean, again backing away in an effortless slide I doubted, a gait so artificially smooth I might have invented it, touched the back bedroom window.

She said in some wonderment, "You love your mother!" and half raised the frame, became half transparent against the glass. Now I could not separate her gold buttons from gold stars beyond.

I hurried quickly after her to slam down the sash against cold air. She was gone. I worked the lock shut against dried paint.

What do they know about love—the dead? Who have escaped it?

I checked my watch, its stretch-band too loose on a wrist growing rapidly thin itself. Soon Mama would wake and need her pill.

Questions to Consider

1. How is impending death presented in this selection? The narrator perceives that the ghost of her deceased Aunt Jean visits the house as her mother nears death. How does Aunt Jean's visitation affect the narrator's reaction to her mother's impending death?
2. Who are the three ghosts in this story? What purpose do they serve?

Harry Crews

1935–

Reading Harry Crews's work "is a bit like undergoing major surgery with laughing gas," an assertion based on the vividness of Crews's work that oftentimes mirrors reality a little more closely than some readers might prefer. Crews is a guru of the craft of Southern gothic storytelling but is not without humor in the tragic, abnormal world of freakish characters that he creates. One of the "grit lit" writers of the contemporary period, he is frequently praised for extracting Southern language, products, and mannerisms, and then using them to infuse the story with the very essence of the region's vitality.

Crews makes use of the Southern sensibility of place in his works: "Place is very important to me. What I was writing about [in *Childhood*] was about my part of the country, the land I was raised on, the house I was raised in, and [what it was like to] come back and see it as a grown man." Although Crews does not appreciate the restrictions that regional labels place on writers, he admits that his most important criteria when considering a new story is the locus of character and place: "I write about the South because I'm stuck with it," he has remarked, explaining that although an author must have firsthand knowledge of a place or circumstance to write about it successfully, readers from other locales can infer meaning if the themes are universal.

Harry Eugene Crews was born on 7 June 1935 in Alma, Georgia during the depths of the Great Depression. His parents, Ray and Myrtice Crews, were tenant farmers who toiled over the rural south Georgia land, eking out a living for their family. When Harry was only 21 months old, Ray died of a heart attack at the age of 35 after a short, harsh life of manual labor. Harry's mother quickly remarried, as she was unable to sustain the family on her own. Harry and his older brother grew up thinking of his stepfather, Pascal, as Daddy, in spite of his often hostile and domineering presence.

One of Crews's first memories of his childhood is of a debilitating episode he suffered at the age of 5. A painful muscle contraction caused his heels to draw up under his legs, leaving young Crews bedridden for six weeks. Of this experience, he has remarked that, "Maybe I just retreated to the bed because I couldn't deal with what was outside of the bed." Doctors did not believe that infantile paralysis or polio caused this enfeebling symptom, but suggested that the cause was more likely a psychosomatic illness. Some of Crews's happier childhood moments were spent sitting around the fireplace telling stories. On cold nights, after working long hours in the field, the Crews family would wash their feet in a tub warmed by the fire and tell stories. Tobacco-selling and hog-killing time were also greatly anticipated by the Crews boys, as the temporary prosperity that resulted brought strange store-bought things into their impoverished home—items such as new overalls, shoes, hot dogs, and sliced bread.

Crews joined the Marine Corps at the age of 17 to escape his miserable home life. After serving three years, he was discharged in 1956 and enrolled in the University of Florida under the G.I. Bill. Crews quickly became infamous for his barroom brawls, hard drinking, and self-destructive behavior. He admits in the introduction of his 1994 compilation of memoirs, novellas, and essays, *Classic Crews,* that he went to the University, "not because anyone there might teach me to write fiction, but because I thought someone there might teach me how to make a living while I taught myself how to write fiction." Two years later, Crews quit school and traveled the country on his Triumph motorcycle, working odd jobs as a short-order cook, a bartender, and a caller at a carnival sideshow. Eighteen months, several barroom skirmishes, and a night in jail later, Harry Crews returned to the University. This time, he enrolled in his first creative writing class with Andrew Lytle, twice-editor of the *Sewanee Review* and member of the Southern Agrarian movement. Lytle's demanding teaching techniques forced Crews to learn perseverance and purpose while discovering his writing style.

Before leaving Gainesville for a teaching position in Jacksonville, Harry met Sally Ellis, a sophomore at the University, and they quickly found themselves expecting a child. Harry Crews and Sally Ellis married on 24 January 1960. The pair had two sons, and Crews and his family returned to Gainesville, where he entered the master's program in English Education. He admits that his family suffered due to his fixation on becoming a writer. The couple soon divorced, and Sally and the boys left Florida. Harry graduated, began teaching English at Broward Community College in Fort Lauderdale, and persuaded Sally to remarry him. Soon after their reconciliation in July, 1961, their oldest son, then three and a half years old, drowned in a neighbor's swimming pool, a tragedy that Crews recounts in "Fathers, Sons, Blood." Devastated and burdened with guilt, Harry and Sally divorced a second time. Regretfully, Crews realized that his preoccupation with becoming a writer had cost him his family. Later, he slowly began to make peace with himself; he told an interviewer that, "I tell stories. That's what I do." Crews cites Graham Greene as a major influence on his story telling techniques, and the strong narrative line found in Greene's work can also be traced in Crews's writing.

Crews has published more than 20 books during his 20-year career, including a 1996 collection of Southern plays entitled *Blood Issue*. When Crews is not writing fiction, he hunts, lifts weights, and travels in search of new material for his fiction. Harry Crews taught at the University of Florida in the English department from 1968 until he retired in 1997 to devote himself to writing full time.

Fathers, Sons, Blood

On July 31, 1961, in Fort Lauderdale, Florida, I was sleeping late after writing all night when I heard my wife, Sally, scream above the yammering of children's voices. I didn't know what was wrong, but whatever it was, I knew instantly that it was bad. I sprinted down the hallway, and before I ever reached the front door, I had made out what the children, all talking at once, were trying to say.

"Patrick . . ."

". . . can't . . ."

". . . in the pool . . ."

". . . get him out."

The only house in the neighborhood with a pool was two doors away. I didn't break stride going through the front door and over the hedge onto the sidewalk.

As I went through the open gate of the high fence surrounding the pool, I saw my son face down in the water at the deep end, his blond hair wafting about his head the only movement. I got him out, pinched his nose and put my mouth on his mouth. But from the first breath, it didn't work. I thought he had swallowed his tongue. I checked it and he had not.

I struggled to breathe for him on the way to the emergency room. But the pulse in his carotid artery had stopped under my fingers long before we got there, and he was dead. That morning, at breakfast with his mother, he'd had cereal. The doctor told me that in the panic of drowning, he had thrown up and then sucked it back again. My effort to breathe for him had not worked, nor could it have. His air passages were blocked. In a little more than a month, September fourth, he would have been four years old.

A man does not expect to be the orphan of his son. Standing by the open grave, returning to his room, taking his clothes out of the closet and folding them into boxes, sorting through the stuff that was his, taking it up from the place he last left it—all of this is the obligation of the son, not of the father. Not of the father, that is, unless some unnatural and unthinkable collaboration of circumstances and events takes the life of the son before that of the father.

Patrick had never gotten out of the yard before, but that morning, some neighborhood children, most not much older than he, had come by and helped him out, and he had gone with them. The family that owned the pool always kept the gate locked, but that day the gate was open. There, two doors away, somebody was always at home on Saturday, and certainly somebody was *always* at home when the gate was unlocked, but nobody was at home when Patrick sat down on the cement lip of the pool, took off his shoes and socks and slipped into the water, thinking, probably, that he was going wading.

As I worked through Patrick's things after the funeral, I could hear Byron, my other son, bubbling and gurgling across the hall. I quit with the Slinkys and the Dr. Seuss books and the stacks of wild crayon drawings and walked into Byron's room, where he lay on his back watching a mobile of butterflies dancing over his head in the mild breeze from the open window. He would be one year old in less than a month, on August 24, and he was a happy baby even when he had befouled himself, which he had managed to do only moments before I walked in. I unpinned his diaper and a ripe fog of baby shit floated up and hung about my face. I looked at his pristine little cock, standing at half-mast about as big as a peanut, and I thought of my own cock and of the vasectomy I'd had a month after his birth.

"It's just you and I now, Buckshot," I said, "just the two of us."

I thought then and I think now that two children make up my fair share. Sally and I had reproduced ourselves and, in a world drowning in a population problem, that was all we were entitled to. If I had it to do all over again, I'd do it the same way. It is not something I ever argue about with anybody. It's only what I believe; whatever other people believe is their own business. Fair share or not, though, I had lost half of the children I would ever have. And behind that fact came the inevitable questions. Who needs this kind of grief? Who needs the trouble that will surely come with the commitment to fatherhood? Isn't a son at times disappointing and frustrating to the father? And isn't he at all times an emotional and financial responsibility that could just as easily have been avoided? And the ultimate question: Is it worth it?

I've had that final question answered time and again over the past 20 years, and the answer has always been yes, it is worth it.

The answer has come in many forms, out of many circumstances. One of the answers was given to me a short time ago when I came in on a plane and Byron was there to meet me. I was dead tired from days of airports and motel rooms and taxi-cabs.

When I walked up to him, I said, "I'd kiss you, son, but I don't think I can reach you."

He smiled, put his hand on my shoulder and said, "Hell, I'll bend down for an old man."

And the baby, who was now in the first flower of manhood and 6'3" tall to boot, bent and kissed me.

What affected me so much was not what he said or that he kissed me. Rather, it was the tone of his voice, a tone that can be used only between men who are equals in each other's eyes, who admire and respect each other. It was the voice of men who have been around a lot of blocks together, who have seen the good times and bad and, consequently, know the worst as well as the best about each other. Finally, it was the voice of love, the sort of love that asks nothing and gives everything, that will go to the wall *with* you or *for* you. In my experience, it is the voice hardest to find in the world, and when it is found at all, it is the voice of blood speaking to blood.

Blood, begetting it and spilling it. In those nightmare days following Patrick's death, I inevitably thought long and hard, usually against my will, about the circumstances of his brief life and his death. Much of it came as incriminations against myself. It is part of the price of parenthood. And anybody who would keep you from the knowledge of that hard price is only lying, first to himself and then to you.

The boy had developed a hideous stutter by the time he drowned. The great pain it had given me while he was alive was only compounded when he was dead. Somehow I must have caused it. I must have been too strict or too unresponsive or too unloving or. . . . The list went on—just the sort of low-rent guilt that we heap upon ourselves where blood is concerned. Being low-rent, though, doesn't keep guilt from being as real as an open wound. But in my case, it got worse, much worse. Part of me insisted that I had brought him to the place of his death.

Sally and I had been married when I was 25 and a senior at the University of Florida. She was 18 and a sophomore. A year and a half later, when I was in graduate school, she divorced me and took the baby to live in Dayton, Ohio. I'm not interested in assigning blame about who was at fault in the collapse of our marriage, but I do know that I was obsessed to the point of desperation with becoming a writer and, further, I lived with the conviction that I had gotten a late start toward that difficult goal. Nobody knew better than I how ignorant, ill read and unaccomplished I was, or how very long the road ahead of me was to the place I wanted most to be in the world. Consequently, perhaps I was impatient, irritable and inattentive toward Sally as a young woman and mother. But none of that kept me from missing my son when he was gone, longing for him in much the same way I had longed for my father, who had died before I could ever know him. So out of love and longing for my son (selfishness?), I persuaded her to marry me again, come back to Florida and join her life with mine.

And my efforts to have Sally come back to Florida haunted me in those first hard days following the death of my son. If I had not remarried her, if she had stayed in Dayton, Patrick could not have found his death in that swimming pool in Fort Lauderdale, could he? But the other side of that question was yet another. If I had not remarried Sally, I could never have known and loved my second son, Byron, could I? The crazed interrogation with myself went on. Was there somehow a way to balance things there? Was there a way to trade off in my head and heart the life of one son for the life of another? Patently not. That was madness. But . . . . ? Always another but.

Enter my uncle Alton, who was as much a father to me as any man could ever have asked for. When he heard that my son had drowned, he walked out of his tobacco field in south Georgia and drove the 500 miles to be with me. While neighbors and friends stood about in my house eating funeral food, Uncle Alton and I hunkered on our heels under a tree in the back yard, smoking. We'd walked out there together and, as I'd seen him do all my life, Uncle Alton dropped onto his heels and started making random markings in the dirt with a stick. And just as naturally as breathing, I talked to him about the questions that were about to take me around the bend of madness, questions that I had not talked about to anybody else before and have not told anybody since. It was a long telling, and he never once interrupted.

I finished by saying, "It feels like I'm going crazy."

His gray eyes watched me from under the brim of his black-felt hat. He had only two hats, one for the fields and one for funerals. He was hunkered there in the only suit of clothes he owned. He couldn't afford this trip any more than he could afford to walk out of the field during the harvest of the only money crop he had on the farmed-out piece of south Georgia dirt he'd scratched a living out of for 40 years, any more than he could have afforded to give me a home when I was eight years old and had nowhere else to go. He needed another mouth to feed like he needed screwworms in his mules or cutworms in his tobacco. But he had taken me in and treated me the same way he treated Theron and Don and Roger and Ed and Robert, his other boys.

"You ain't gone go crazy, son," he said.

He had not responded until he had taken out a Camel cigarette and turned it in his hands, studying it, and then examining a long kitchen match the same way before firing it against his thumbnail. He was nothing if not the most reticent and considered of men.

"That's what it feels like," I said. "Crazy."

"Well, crazy," he said, acknowledging it and dismissing it at the same time. "What you gone do is the next thing."

"That's what the next thing feels like."

"I reckon it might. But it's some of us that cain't afford to go crazy. The next thing is lying in yonder in a crib. You ain't gone give up on blood, are you, boy?"

It was not a rhetorical question. He wanted an answer, and his steady eyes, webbed with veins from crying himself, held mine until I gave him one.

"No, sir, I'm not."

He put his hand on my shoulder. "Then let's you and me go on back in the house and git something to eat."

"You feel like a drink of whiskey?" I said.

"We can do that, too," he said. "I'd be proud to have a drink with you."

"Good," I said.

The two of us went into the back room where I worked and sat down with two whiskeys. As we drank, both of us heard the sudden furious crying of Byron from somewhere in the house. Funerals and death be damned; the baby was hungry. Uncle Alton lifted his glass toward the sound of the angry, healthy squalling, a brief smile touching his face, and said, "There it is. There it is right there."

And so it is. Part of the way I am bonded to my son is made up of the way I will always be bonded to Uncle Alton, dead now these many years, dead before Byron could ever know him. But no great matter. Blood is our only permanent history, and blood history does not admit of revision. Or so some of us believe.

I picked up a magazine not long ago in which a man was writing about his children. In the very beginning of the piece, he said, "The storms of childhood and adolescence had faded into the past." He would be the poorer for it if that were true. But it is not true, not for him or for any father. The storms don't fade into the past, nor do all the moments that are beautiful and full of happiness, the moments that quicken our hearts with pride. In early July of the summer Byron would turn 12, we were sitting on the top of Springer Mountain in Georgia. It was raining and we were soaked and exhausted to the bone, having made the long steep climb of the approach to the Appalachian Trail, which winds its way across the Eastern United States and finally ends on Mount Katahdin in Maine. Between us, embedded in the boulder on which we were sitting, was the metal image of a young hiker.

Byron put his hand on the stone and said, "Well, we made it to the beginning."

And so we had, but a hell of a beginning it had been. It hadn't stopped raining all day as we'd climbed steadily over broken rock. He was carrying a 20-pound pack and mine weighed 45, both probably too heavy, but we'd decided to pack enough with us so that we could hike for as long as we wanted to without getting out of the mountains to restock our supplies. I had put him in the lead to set the pace.

"Remember, we're not in a hurry," I called after we'd been going awhile. "This is not a goddamn contest."

I was forced to say it because he'd taken off over the brutally uneven trail like a young goat. He'd looked back at me for only an instant and kept climbing.

Then, as the mud and rock made the footing more and more unsure, I said, "You think we ought to find a place to wait out this rain?"

He stopped and turned for just an instant to look at me. "Did we come to by God hike or did we come to hike?"

He was smiling, but he'd said it with just the finest edge of contempt, which is the way you are supposed to say it, and I scrambled to follow him, my heart lifting. Byron had heard me ask him much the same thing many times before, because if you change a couple of words, the question will serve in any number of circumstances. And now, in great high spirits, he was giving it back to me. I would not be surprised if someday he gave it to his own son.

The question had come down to him through my own mouth from Uncle Alton. When he would be in the woods with me and his other sons hunting on a freezing November morning and one of us said something about being cold or otherwise uncomfortable, he'd say, "Did we come to by God hunt or did we come to hunt?" And the other boys and I would feel immediately better, because that was something men said to other men. It was a way a man had of reminding other men who they were. We had been spoken to as equals.

All of that is what I was thinking while we sat there in a misting rain on a boulder with the metal image of a hiker in it signaling the official beginning of the Appalachian Trail atop Springer Mountain. But it was not what he was thinking.

"Dad, you remember about the time with the rain?"

"The time about the rain? Hell, son, we been in the rain a lot together." I was wet and my feet hurt. I wanted to get the tent up and start a fire.

He cut his eyes toward me. Drops of rain hung on the ends of his fine lashes. He was suddenly very serious. What in the hell was coming down here? What was coming down was the past that is never past and, in this case, the past against which I had no defense except my own failed heart.

"We weren't in it together," he said. "You made me stand in it. Stand in it for a long time."

Yes, I had done that, but I had not thought about it in years. It's just not the sort of thing a man would want to think about. Byron's mother had gone North for a while and left me to take care of him. He was then seven years old and just starting in the second grade. I had told him that day to be home at six o'clock and we would go out to dinner. Truthfully, we'd been out to eat every night since Sally had been gone, because washing dishes is right up at the top of the list of things I won't do. It had started misting rain at midday and had not stopped. Byron had not appeared at six, nor was he there at 6:45. That was back when I was bad to go to the bottle, and while I wasn't drunk, I wasn't sober, either. Lay it on the whiskey. A man will snatch at any straw to save himself from the responsibility of an ignoble action. When he did come home at 7:15, I asked him where he'd been.

"At Joe's," he said. But I had known that. I reminded him of when we had said we were going to dinner. But he had known that.

"It was raining," he said.

I said, "Let's go out and look at it."

We went out into the carport and watched the warm spring rain.

"And you thought the rain would hurt you if you walked home in it?"

"It's *raining*, Dad," he said, exasperated now.

"I'll tell you what," I said. "You go out there and stand in it and we'll see how bad it hurts you."

He walked out into the rain and stood looking at me. "How long do I have to stand here?"

"Only until we see if it hurts you. Don't worry, I'll tell you when you are about to get hurt."

I went back inside. So far, pretty shitty, but it gets worse. When I went back inside, I sat down in a recliner, meaning to stay there only a minute. But I hadn't reckoned with the liquor and the rain on the roof. I woke with a start and looked at my watch. It was a quarter of nine. I went outside and there the boy stood, his blond hair plastered and every thread on him soaked. He didn't look at all sad or forlorn; what he did look was severely pissed.

"Come on in," I said. And then: "Where do you want to eat?"

"I don't want to eat."

"How do you feel?" I asked.

He glared at me. "Well, I'm not *hurt*."

We sat there on the top of Springer Mountain and looked at each other with the rain falling around us. I'd forgotten entirely about my feet and the tent and the fire. My throat felt like it was closing up and I had to speak to keep breathing.

"I wanted to apologize, but I had done such a sorry-assed thing that I couldn't bring myself to do it. But at the time, it didn't seem like it'd do any good."

"It probably wouldn't have," he said. "Then."

"Well, I'm sorry. I was wrong. I should have said so, but. . . ." I'd run out of words.

He said, "I know. And I was only down the block. I've thought about it. I could have called. But, shit, I was only a *little* kid."

I loved that. I loved how he said he was only a little kid. "What were you thinking while you were out there? I mean, you had plenty of time to think."

He shook his head and laughed as though he couldn't believe the memory of his thinking himself. "I never thought but one thing."

"What was that?"

"I thought, That drunk fucker thinks I'm going to call and ask him to come in out of the rain . . . but I'm *not*." Then he laughed like it was the funniest thing in the world, and I laughed, too.

That was the first time I knew he was the kind of guy who could be put out on the street naked and he'd survive. The kid had grit in his craw. I thought it then and I think it now. But more than that, there on the mountain, the boy and I had been privileged to share a moment of grace that we could never have shared if I had not fucked up so badly all those years ago and if he had not had the kind of heart he has. But that moment is the privilege of blood.

Sons grow up, though. God knows they do in a New York heartbeat. Byron grew up running with me. By the time he was a teenager, we had a four-mile course full of hills laid out. But the very worst of the hills was the last one. On the four miles, we jogged and talked, nothing serious; but at the bottom of that last, long hill, we'd always turn to shout at each other, "*Balls!* Who's got 'em?" And then we'd sprint and I always won. Somehow, I thought I always would. But the day came at the beginning of his 14th year when he beat me by 20 yards. I shook his hand, but I was pissed. I don't like to lose at anything. But then, neither does he. And we always had the understanding between us—never, to my knowledge, spoken—that neither of us, whether playing handball or whatever, gave the other anything. If you wanted the point, you had to win it. As we cooled out walking, I began to feel better and then proud of him. But the only thing I said was, "There's always tomorrow."

He patted my back, a little too kindly, a little too softly, I thought, and said, "Sure, Dad, there's always tomorrow."

I never beat him on the hill again. But I still had the gymnasium. Lungs and speed may go, but strength stays. Well, it stays for a while. And I don't even have to tell you, do I?, that the day came when he was stronger on the bench and at the rack than I was. Strange feeling for a father. No, not strange; sad. Part of me wanted him to grow into manhood, but another part of me had a hard time accepting it. Maybe, in my private heart, I'll never be entirely able to accept it. If I live to be 70, he'll still be my boy at 40. I know; mushy, isn't it? I don't even like it myself. But I don't have to like it; all I have to do is live with it.

And out of the feeling of the father for the son comes the desire to save him from pain, knowing full well that it is impossible. But that in no way diminishes the desire. You want to save him from the obvious things, like broken legs or lacerated flesh; but more than that, you are at some trouble to see that he is not hurt by life. I am talking here about education. Maybe I'm particularly sensitive about that because nobody in the history of my family ever went to college except me, and I had to join the Marine Corps during the Korean War so I could get the GI Bill to do that. So imagine how I felt six months ago when I walked by Byron's apartment and, as we were talking, he told me that he was quitting the university after being there two years.

"What are you going to do, son?"

"Play guitar," he said.

The guitar has been his passion for years. It is not unusual for him to practice six hours a day for weeks running. And to give him his due, he is a righteous picker. But if he just continued in the university, he would. . . . But you probably know the kinds of things I tried to tell him. Father things. But he wasn't having any of it.

Finally, in exasperation, I said a dumb fatherly thing: "Byron, do you know how many boys there are in this country with guitars who think they're going to make a living picking?"

He only smiled and asked, "Dad, when you were my age, how many boys do you think there were in this country who owned typewriters who thought they were going to make a living writing?"

There it is. The father has his dream. The son has his. And a dream is unanswerable. All you can do for a man with a dream is wish him well.

"Do well, son," I said.

"I'll try," he said.

Questions to Consider

1. What funeral traditions do you see in Crews's story? How does Crews's discussion of these traditions add to—or take away from—the pathos of this story?
2. How does Crews lead the reader to believe that blood and family legacy are significant?

Clyde Edgerton

1944–

When the administrators at Southern Baptist-affiliated Campbell University called Clyde Edgerton into their office after the publication of his first novel, *Raney* (1985), he thought he was going to hear praise for his hard work; instead the University notified him that his contract as a college professor would not be renewed for the following year. The administration claimed that the novel was sacrilegious and failed to depict wholesome family values. After a protracted struggle and difficult legal maneuvering, Edgerton decided to leave Campbell. Fortunately for his readers, he remained faithful to his art, took a position at another university, and has since produced nine novels.

Clyde (Carlyle) Edgerton was born on 20 May 1944 and grew up in a middle-class home in rural North Carolina. Edgerton's early life provided him with ample fodder for his imagination. His family enjoyed the prosperity that followed World War II, and during the 1960s, he attended the University of North Carolina and joined the Air Force upon completing his degree. Edgerton served as a reconnaissance pilot flying missions in Southeast Asia for a year and remained in the Air Force from 1966 to 1971. Though his missions generally kept him high above the combat raging on the ground, his wartime experiences were traumatic enough to effect a permanent change in the young man, who would be haunted by concerns that took years to express. His writing, however, unlike that of many veterans of the same period, focuses less upon the trauma and difficulties associated with war, and more upon the everyday worlds of average Americans as they go through their lives.

While in the service, Edgerton pursued a Master of Arts in Teaching from the University of North Carolina. Upon completion of his degree, he accepted a teaching position at Southern High School in Durham, North Carolina. In 1973, he began work on a doctoral degree in English Education at the University of North Carolina where he met Susan Ketchin, now a well-known literary scholar, who would eventually become his wife.

Edgerton's first novel, *Raney*, chronicles the life of a young, naive, "good girl," Raney Shepherd as she marries and adjusts to her new life. Raney hails from an upper middle-class home where keeping up appearances is fundamental to survival. Her parents are prosperous Baptists, and this upbringing becomes a point of conflict between the character and her new husband, an Episcopalian who was raised in a much more liberal manner than was she. *Raney* illustrates the complexities of Southern life, and in particular, the work focuses upon religion and hypocrisy—two themes that appear in most of Edgerton's work.

Edgerton's importance in the contemporary Southern canon cannot be overlooked, for he realistically depicts the lives of many kinds of Southerners from halfway-house residents to upstanding church members. His careful attention to detail in the creation of his characters leads readers to recognize the similarities between Edgerton's characters and people they know. He takes great care in presenting the folkways of the characters, a strategy which reinforces their realism. While Edgerton's works exhibit a thematic universality, they would function far differently if not set in the South. Works such as *In Memory of Junior* (1992) almost beg to be set in the South, for Edgerton's characters are products of the landscape, culture, and traditions of North Carolina. Like *In Memory of Junior*, *The Floatplane Notebooks* is a difficult novel to envision with anything other than a Southern setting, for the dedication to Southern ways is apparent from its grave cleaning scenes to its foodways, as can be seen in the first chapter entitled "Bliss," which is excerpted here.

In 1989, Edgerton received a Guggenheim Fellowship, which allowed him to finish his fourth novel, *Killer Diller*, one of his most popular works. Edgerton currently lives with his wife and their daughter in North Carolina where he continues to write.

Edgerton's trademark is his skill in recreating the world he knows best—rural, small-town North Carolina. His work returns to the universal themes of hypocrisy, religion, and the quest for love, yet it also presents a sampling of the many social classes and voices of the South from the poorest of poor to the very wealthy.

from The Floatplane Notebooks

Bliss

My first association with Thatcher's entire family was at their annual gravecleaning last summer. What an event! Cousins, aunts, uncles, and such got together, complete with picnic lunch, and when their work was finished that graveyard was as clean and neat as a whistle.

There is a path—wide enough for a car—which goes down into the woods behind their house, and if you walk or drive on it for a little ways you come to another car path which leads to their family graveyard. There beside the graveyard is a little open grassy area, and beside that is a raging wisteria vine, beyond which is a pond. The graveyard itself is very serene, with shafts of light coming down through tall pines onto the gravestones, which go back into the 1800s. So, one day each summer this wonderful event happens: cousins and such roll up their sleeves, and then cut, mow, trim and rake up a storm.

That was association number one.

Association number two was a trip to Florida, occurring this past Christmas, before our marriage.

I, of course, had no idea that I would ever be going to Florida this early in my life, but Thatcher and I got more and more serious up until November third, when he, at nineteen, asked me to marry him, and I, at eighteen, said I would. My words were, "I will, Thatcher. I will." The words I like to say about Thatcher are these: "Thatcher stands tall." He is slightly over six feet and I think he stands tall not only in stature but in spirit. He has a firmament about him. A steadiness.

They are a wonderful family, full of wonderful family members and names. Isn't Thatcher a fun, but somehow masculine, name? And Meredith, his brother? Doesn't that name have a rolling ring to it? And Noralee, his little sister? Soft and sweet?

The trip to Florida, an annual event for the Copelands, to visit Thatcher's Uncle Hawk and Aunt Sybil, started out on an even-enough keel at four A.M., having to do with lighter traffic in the early morning hours. My parents weren't too happy with the whole idea—they are less enthralled with the Copeland family than I am—but they finally said yes when they found out that Thatcher's aunt, Miss Esther, was going along. Miss Esther is a wellknown upholding block of the community.

Speaking of Meredith, Thatcher's thirteen-year-old brother, he is the has-a-sparkle-in-his-eye type, as cute as a button, and always having something up his sleeve. He runs up to me, holds out his hands for me to pop his knuckles, then pretends it hurts terribly. His hair, dark brown, is naturally curly—the only one in the family that way. Along with him on the trip was Mark, a cousin his age, Miss Esther's son. Mark is a very polite young man and spends a good deal of time with Meredith. Mark's father was lost in World War II.

Before we left, Thatcher, Meredith, and Mark told me all about Silver Springs, which is near Locklear, Florida, where Uncle Hawk lives. I, having never been beyond North Carolina, was amazed at their talk of this "Silver Springs"—which was: glass-bottom boats, monkeys in the trees, and catfish playing football with a wad of loafbread underneath said glass-bottom boats. And it all did turn out to be true.

Florida definitely has an excitement in the air.

One of the things my parents had a hard time understanding was: anybody taking four bird dogs to Florida.

They were necessary because the men needed to hunt. Two dogs were carried in the trunk of each car, and could get air because the trunks were not completely closed. Old blankets were available for them to lie on. The places we stopped for the dogs to get out—going down and coming back—were little dirt side roads that seemed to be made for the occasion.

Miss Esther drove her car and Mr. Copeland, his.

I loved being on the road, traveling before light, with the one I love.

* * *

We arrived in the fairly late afternoon.

Yes, there we were in Florida—a very warm state with a sense of exhilaration which hangs in the air like the very fog.

Uncle Hawk walked out of the front of his store to greet us. He is the oldest and the largest, and Miss Esther, his sister, is, I think, a little older than Mr. Copeland, who is the youngest—Thatcher's daddy, Mr. Albert Copeland. They all look alike too. Uncle Hawk immediately hit Meredith on the shoulder and then grabbed him around the head and spoke loudly, "Boy, you done gone up like a okra stalk." Then he grabbed Thatcher and Mark around their heads and pulled them to his chest with them laughing and enjoying it and then hugged Miss Esther and Mildred and shook hands with Mr. Copeland, pulling on Mr. Copeland's hand and grabbing him by the shoulder and laughing. Then he reached out his hand to me and was exceedingly nice, saying nice things about me, Mildred having written that I'd be coming along on the trip. Then he picked up little Noralee and carried her as we all went inside.

The store is quite an establishment—it's a cafe-grocery-hardware store combination with gas pumps and a large fruit stand out front. Their home is next to the store, across a little side road, surrounded by a rock wall, and with palms and Spanish moss hanging from big oak trees. Very pleasant.

Inside the store we were greeted by my aunt-to-be Sybil. She was carrying a tiny, short-haired dog named Dixie B., which Mr. Copeland had talked about on the way down—saying he hoped she had died.

"Come on in," said Aunt Sybil. She hugged everybody with one arm. She wore frilly lace around her neck and had a pleasant round face. "I'm going to hug you too," she said to me. And did. "Anyone like something to eat?"

"Oh, no," said Miss Esther. "We still got chicken in the car."

Thatcher's mother, a beautiful, thick-brown-haired woman who keeps up her fingernails—and who asked me to call her Mildred—said, "What you got today?"

"The usual," said Aunt Sybil. "Tuna, chicken, ham, hamburger, hot dogs."

"I could use a hot dog—without onions," said Mildred.

"What's tuna?" said Meredith. Bless his heart.

"You know what tuna is."

"No, I don't."

"Fish. It's a kind of fish. Comes in a can."

"Ain't you going to school up there, boy?" said Uncle Hawk.

"No sir—I mean yes sir, but we don't study tuna."

Meredith is a regular spark plug.

Sleeping arrangements were available for all. Miss Esther and I settled into the bedroom of Uncle Hawk and Aunt Sybil's daughter, Lee, who lives and works in Kentucky, and had left to go back on the morning of the day we arrived—the day after Christmas. Lee's a social worker and Christmas is one of her busiest times, Aunt Sybil said. I was to sleep on a rollaway bed, Miss Esther on the single bed, Mildred and little Noralee in the living room on a foldout couch.

Mr. Copeland, Thatcher, Meredith, and Mark were to sleep in the guest room built onto the garage, out behind the house. From there they would get up early and go to the fields to hunt. I, of course, did not visit Thatcher in those quarters, nor did I wish to.

The first night, we watched television for a while in the living room, then Aunt Sybil said maybe we ought to turn off the television and talk a little bit, catch up, which Miss Esther agreed with.

One of the first things Uncle Hawk wanted to talk about was the floatplane kit which Mr. Copeland bought from Mr. Hoover, who is going to teach Mr. Copeland to fly—in exchange for hickory shavings that Mr. Copeland gets from the sawmill he runs. The Anderson Sawmill. Mr. Hoover has a restaurant and cooks barbecue with the hickory shavings.

"How big is the thing, Albert?" asked Uncle Hawk.

"Twenty feet—the fuselage—the middle part is called the fuselage, and the wing span is thirty-four feet. She can sit one or two. I'm using the two option. It's called a floatplane. Fly it off the water."

"Mr. Hoover said all the pages to the plans weren't there," said Mildred.

"It's mostly aluminum tubing," said Mr. Copeland. "I'll fly it off the lake."

"What kind of engines?" asked Uncle Hawk.

"All the plans aren't there?" said Aunt Sybil.

"I'll find them. I just got me a notebook to keep up with all I'm doing right now, what I do to it, and the test runs. That's required by law—the FAA. It's an experimental aircraft."

"He don't write it accurate about what happened though," said Thatcher.

"I do too."

"Not on that first test run."

"Well I sure did."

Thatcher said one thing happened at the lake, but when Mr. Copeland wrote it down it sounded quite different.

Questions to Consider

1. In this excerpt, how does Edgerton depict family in his work?
2. What does Edgerton's work suggest about memorial practices in the South? Do these practices reflect the class and/or race of the people who make use of them?

Michael Lee West

1953–

Michael Lee West says that her love of reading blossomed when she was confined to bed for an extended period after contracting histoplasmosis on a Girl Scout trip to Mammoth Cave. During her confinement, she received a set of Louisa May Alcott's *Little Women* and *Little Men*, which quickly became her favorite reading.

Michael Lee West's upbringing was in many ways typical for the time; her family was upper middle class, and she grew up in an era of post–World War II prosperity. She was born in Lake Providence, Louisiana on 15 October 1953 where the Helton family resided until their daughter was about 8 years old. They then moved to Cookeville, Tennessee. Her father was the manager of a department store, and her mother, Ary Jean, a homemaker, encouraged and supported Michael Lee's love of reading. The Heltons were fanatical readers who rarely bought books, but instead frequented their local library with alacrity. In an unpublished interview, West says that her mother still "loves and supports her public library." Growing up, West's reading habit continued, and she was a serious student. She says of her high school years, "I wasn't a cheerleader or anything like that. I worked in my father's dime store and had a tidy little babysitting 'career' on the side." West graduated from Cookeville High School and shortly thereafter began college course work in nursing.

West credits the works of Eudora Welty and Flannery O'Connor for piquing her interest in Southern literature, yet she asserts that the greatest influence upon her writing was that of Lee Smith. In the late 1970s and early 1980s, Smith's work drew much acclaim, and West devoured Smith's novels. A few years later, the two met at a writers' workshop in Nashville where Smith read the fledgling writer's work in class. West recounts the story: "She read my short story in class and made me believe that it was possible for a little nurse (and soccer mom) who had *not* read the classics to become a writer. And it happened!" Smith's confidence in West encouraged the aspiring writer, and by 1990, West had published her first novel, *Crazy Ladies*.

West continues to live in Tennessee with her husband, family, and a vast array of dogs and cats. Her life, by all accounts, is like that of any mother with a husband and high school-aged children. She attends football games, supports her son's high school programs, and takes care of her family. The notable difference between West and everyone else's mother is that she has, over the last 20 years, managed to balance her writing career and her family's needs—no small feat.

The characters that West depicts in her work are drawn from a variety of people she has known over the years and others that she imagines, and for this reason, her work displays a wide array of Southern voices. Her characters, many of whom are flawed or who struggle to search for their identities, endure common troubles—divorce, death, and family tragedy—yet within these tragic circumstances humor appears. West's devotion to realism appears throughout her body of work. In her memoir/cookbook, *Consuming Passions*, she embodies the life of a Southern woman in both tragedy and success. This chapter, taken from West's memoir, discusses funeral food and burial traditions in the South.

from Consuming Passions

Funeral Food

Live and learn. Die and get food. That's the Southern way.

—Anonymous casserole enthusiast, on her way to the mayor's funeral, Cookeville, Tennessee, 1995

In small towns, after a death, it is traditional to bring covered dishes to the family. When words fail us, we offer food. A platter of fried chicken says, *I'm sorry for your loss*. A chocolate layer cake whispers, *I know you feel that life has soured, so here is something sweet*.

In church lingo it is called "food for the bereaved." Southern churches have traditionally provided the meal after the funeral; it can be grand or pathetic. And you can't go by a church's size, either—even though church kitchens are built to feed the multitudes. Nowadays they are professionally outfitted with six-burner stoves (electric, most likely), convection ovens, and walk-in pantries. When it comes to good funeral food, it all depends on how many good cooks are in the congregation.

Even the funeral home anticipates the culinary hodgepodge. The undertakers thoughtfully provide the family with a little booklet, a food log to jot down the donor's name, offering, and description of the plate. They even provide gummed stickers to affix to the bottom of dishes, so each one can be returned to its proper owner. All funeral food is acknowledged with a thank-you note. The dishes are washed and promptly returned to the donor (although I know a family in Texas who received so much food it took them eight months to return all the bowls). My mama says the returning of dishes forces widows and orphans to get dressed and crawl out of their shells; after a spell of grieving, it is therapeutic to visit with friends.

Taking food to the bereaved always throws me into a panic—what to prepare? Food lore suggests that eggplant helps the grieving soul come to terms with endings. Zucchini is also a comfort food, and poppy seeds are said to induce sleep. Other cultures literally bring food to the dead. In Mexico, the deceased's favorite foods are brought to the cemetery and left on the grave. A burning candle sheds light on the feast, leading the recently departed to his earthly delights.

Funeral food has a few unwritten rules. It must transport with ease, and be reheatable. Spicy foods should be avoided. Choose dishes that comfort the brokenhearted, entice blunted appetites, and satisfy the nongrieving relatives—distant kin who, for various reasons, always seem to gather at funerals. They come in four types: the curious, the dutiful, the greedy, and the reluctant. This last group consists of children and preteenagers who have been dragged to the event. One thing never changes: They all want food, and plenty of it.

After a death, fried chicken is usually the first dish to appear on the bereaved's table. I've often thought it would be interesting to do a comparative study of funeral chicken. Some crusts are flaky and crisp, the color of mahogany; others are pale brown and damp, with the consistency of wet toilet paper. Still others clearly come from KFC. My friend John Myers recently lamented the passing of good church food. At a family funeral, his mother's church brought fried chicken from Hardee's. John was aghast, especially since this was the Deep South, and for decades, his mother had been supplying the church with jugs of sun tea, baked hams, and potato salad. In her basement was a whole set of funeral dishes, with her name scrawled in laundry ink on the bottom of each pan.

In addition to fried chicken, typical funeral fare ranges from baked ham to rump roast to pit barbecue. Other dishes include deviled eggs, potato salad, coleslaw, cheese grits, macaroni and cheese. Large quantities of sweet tea are usually available. Crock-Pots always show up at a funeral, usually filled with green beans or a roast. A dozen Jell-O salads will materialize, spread out on the table like quivering jewels. Some are sweet, with marshmallows, nuts, and canned fruit; others are savory, with mayonnaise, chopped celery, and olives.

The casserole will make an appearance at every funeral dinner. Hot chicken salad topped with crushed potato chips is a perpetual favorite, along with a broccoli-and-chicken concoction. Chicken and dumplings fall under the category of old-fashioned funeral food, but it takes time and effort to prepare. Chicken pot pie is another funeral dish that's fallen out of favor, probably because it's best eaten the same day it's cooked, otherwise the crust suffers.

If the death occurs in the summer, when gardens are producing, someone is bound to bring a platter of sliced tomatoes. Squash casserole is a favorite dish, along with simple bowls of peas, snap beans, and fried corn. Any time of year, a platter of sandwiches is appealing: egg salad, tuna, ham, chicken, roast beef. For breakfast, a pan of sweet rolls, with a sprinkling of pecans, can soothe an anguished heart. Every church usually has a home baker who supplies yeast rolls, sausage and biscuits, and corn bread (although I have begun to see an influx of store-bought rolls).

At the home of any bereaved soul, you will find extravagant desserts, mostly pies and layer cakes. This is a time when home cooks bring their specialties. The pies are typical Southern holiday fare: lemon icebox, chocolate, coconut, pecan. In the South, chess pie is also known as funeral pie:

Lemon Chess Pie
Yield: One 9-inch pie

PREPARATION

1 1/2 cups sugar
1 stick unsalted butter, melted
4 eggs, beaten
2 teaspoons fresh lemon juice
1 teaspoon vanilla

Preheat the oven to 325 degrees. Cream together the sugar and the butter. Add the eggs and blend well. Add the other ingredients. Pour into a 9-inch unbaked pie shell. Bake 40 to 50 minutes, until set. Test by inserting a knife toward the pie's center; if it emerges clean, the pie is ready. This basic recipe cries out for tinkering. If you want to make a chess coconut pie, add 3 1/2 ounces flaked coconut. If you dislike lemony pies, substitute 1 1/2 teaspoons vinegar. For buttermilk pie, omit the lemon juice and add 1 teaspoon all-purpose flour and 1 1/2 cups buttermilk. If anyone asks why it's called chess pie, explain that old Southern cooks used to keep their pies in a chest, or safe. The doors of the chest were made of perforated tin to allow air circulation.

Pound cakes and sheet cakes are also popular offerings. They are quick to bake and easy to transport. Sometimes the simplest desserts are the most pleasing: a yellow Bundt cake with a plain confectioners' glaze is a soothing thing to feed a child. Banana pudding, usually made in a round Pyrex[1] bowl and topped with two inches of meringue, is an eternal favorite. Lemon squares, piled up on a cut-glass plate, will make you smile—they are cheerful and soul-lifting, the culinary equivalent of spending time on a sunporch. My mother used to say that a lemon square, served with a cup of hot tea, revives the spirit. It's a recipe that requires a little effort, but it pays you back tenfold.

Lemon Squares
Yield: 16 bars

TO MAKE THE CRUST

1 cup all-purpose flour
1 cup confectioners' sugar
⅛ teaspoon salt
1 stick unsalted butter, cut up

Preheat the oven to 350 degrees. In a large bowl, sift together the flour, sugar, and salt. Using a pastry blender (or two knives), cut the butter into the mixture until it is crumbly. Press the dough into a greased 9-inch square pan. Bake 15 to 20 minutes. The crust should be lightly browned.

TO MAKE THE FILLING

3 large eggs
1 cup granulated sugar
1 tablespoon lemon zest, finely chopped
4 tablespoons fresh lemon juice
2 tablespoons all-purpose flour
½ teaspoon baking powder
⅛ teaspoon salt

In a large bowl, beat the eggs until blended. Add the sugar and blend. Add the zest. Gradually stir in the lemon juice. Sift the flour, baking powder, and salt into the egg mixture and blend until smooth. Pour the mixture over the crust. Bake 25 minutes. Cool on a rack—do not remove from the pan.

1. Pyrex is a glass manufacturer that produces measuring cups, bowls, casserole pans, and other kitchen implements.

To Make the Topping

1 1/2 cups confectioners' sugar
3 tablespoons lemon juice

Mix sugar and lemon juice. Spread over cooled filling. When the icing sets, cut into squares.

Some food is inappropriate for the bereaved. This is not the time to bring Better Than Sex Cake or Death by Chocolate. And it's never a good idea to use uncooked eggs in funeral food. For instance, butter-cream frosting is easy to make and outrageously delicious, but it calls for raw egg yolk. This can be dangerous for the very young and the elderly, or anyone suffering from immunosuppression. If your famous chicken salad recipe calls for homemade mayonnaise, you might want to substitute a commercial brand.

It is wise to consider the effects of grief on the gastrointestinal system. During times of stress, the body is delicate. Also, depending on the geographical region, it's probably not wise to bring a platter of stuffed jalapeños or *anacuchos*. Even something as ubiquitous as chili might throw the digestive system into a tizzy. Personally, I think a tongue-burning salsa would be a welcome distraction from mourning, but in sensitive souls, the jalapeños might produce reflux, better known as indigestion, which feels like a powerful heartache. A stressed-out person might confuse the pain with angina, resulting in an unnecessary trip to the emergency room.

Another improper funeral dish is baked beans. At first glance, this classic food seems to fulfill the criteria of bereavement cuisine: It's easy to make, easy to transport, and feeds a throng of guests. But this dish is traditionally hard on the gut. Unless you lay in a supply of Beano, flatulence will most certainly result, and this condition is not welcome in closed-up houses and funeral parlors. The results have been known to incite bitter family quarrels.

I myself have never seen appetizers at a funeral. And I have yet to see chicken soup. You'd think it would be just the thing to take the edge off grief: It serves a crowd, it's a snap to reheat, and it possesses amazing powers to console and cure. However, it sloshes while being transported. Unless you bring it in a huge Tupperware bowl, the poor widow, who is already distracted by grief and guests, will have to find a great big pot to reheat the soup. Unless a kind neighbor is pulling kitchen duty, the widow has two pans to wash—yours and hers.

Mashed potatoes is the ultimate comfort food, but no one ever shows up with it at wakes. For all its virtues, meat loaf hits the wrong notes; but I'm sure it has been offered—and devoured. I have never seen beef stew, liver and onions, or hamburgers brought to the bereaved—but I'm sure it's been done. Many years ago, I brought a piña colada cake to grieving teetotalers, with my name carefully taped to the bottom of the pan, and my cousin Lula once brought bourbon balls to a deacon's widow.

For those of us who can't think of anything appropriate to say or cook, my mother suggests bringing paper plates. After a funeral, or in the days preceding one, someone is always eating, and the last thing a widow needs is dishpan hands. It is also a good idea to provide plastic forks, knives, and cups. Napkins are thoughtful. A pound of freshly ground coffee beans will be put to good use, along with Styrofoam cups, sugar cubes, packets of Sweet'n Low, and a jar of Coffee-mate. My mother once said that coffee seems to be the beverage of choice after a death. I have never seen wine or beer brought to the bereaved's house, although on some occasions a tiny nip of something stout, like Jack Daniel's or Wild Turkey, might be just the thing.

When you bring food to a neighbor or a friend, you are wisely letting the food fill in the gaps. Sometimes we say all the wrong things, but food knows all languages. It says, I know you are inconsolable. I know you are fragile right now. And I am so sorry for your loss. I am here if you need me. The bringing of food has no denomination and no race. It is concern and sympathy in a Pyrex bowl. In the kindest sort of way, it reminds us that life continues, that we must sustain and nourish it. Funeral cuisine may be an old custom, but it is the ultimate joining of community and food—it is humanity at its finest.

Questions to Consider

1. What role does food play in Southern traditions? How do these traditions differ based on the occasion—baptisms, funerals, weddings?
2. Can you think of other pieces of literature that contain food as a significant motif? What functions does food serve in these narratives?

Randall Kenan

1963–

On 12 March 1962, Randall Kenan was born out of wedlock. At six weeks of age, he was taken by his paternal grandfather to live in Wallace, North Carolina. Shortly thereafter, he settled with his great-aunt, who raised him in nearby Chinquapin. The world of the Kenans was one of prosperous farmers who held a staunchly conservative religious faith. Kenan lived under the influence of many older female relatives, and he grew up hearing their stories and living in a traditional Southern manner.

Though he came from an established and well-respected family, throughout his youth Kenan felt like an outsider, in part because he attended integrated schools and as a result had far more contact with White people than did his family. He fought his homosexual desires for many years in his effort to fit into the life that his family expected. A good student, Kenan graduated and began attending the University of North Carolina at Chapel Hill when he was only 17. He loved science and planned to be a physicist, but he also took classes in African-American studies. In his sophomore year, he signed up for a creative writing class with H. Maxwell Steele just for fun and began reading the works of Toni Morrison. This combination of influences seduced him away from physics and into an English major. The summer after his junior year, he went to Oxford University to study British literature. He graduated from the University of North Carolina with a B.A. in English and a minor in physics in December 1985.

During his course of undergraduate study, Kenan corresponded with novelist Toni Morrison, and through his connection with her, he was offered a job at Random House after his graduation. At Random House, Kenan quickly advanced from receptionist to assistant editor. All the while he worked on his first novel, *A Visitation of Spirits*, which was published by Grove Press in 1989. Kenan's renowned *Let the Dead Bury Their Dead* was published in 1992, and he has continued to work on other projects as well as his fiction writing. Kenan published a biography of James Baldwin in 1992 and another nonfiction work in 1999 about African Americans in America, *Walking on Water: Black American Lives at the Turn of the Twenty-First Century*. His work continues to earn the respect of literary scholars and enjoys a substantial popular readership as well.

Kenan's two fiction works, *A Visitation of Spirits* and *Let the Dead Bury Their Dead*, illustrate life in the African-American community without relying upon timeworn stereotypes to depict characters and develop plots. In the Southern storytelling tradition, Kenan's humor is well placed. He develops fantastic, tall-tale characters such as Francis, the talking pig, as well as a host of demons and ghosts. He interweaves examinations of race relations and homosexuality in his stories, despite the controversial nature of these issues, even in turn-of-the-century America. Kenan's work entertains while conveying many significant themes in Southern writing.

The story, "Clarence and the Dead," is one of Kenan's most entertaining and thought-provoking. In it he tells the story of Clarence, a clairvoyant, who lives a very short, but significant life. Kenan integrates folklore through the use of the caul and the many references to ghosts which often appear in tall tales in the South.

Clarence and the Dead

On the day Clarence Pickett died, Wilma Jones's hog Francis stopped talking. Now of course no one else had ever heard the swine utter word the first, but Wilma swore up and down that the creature had first said to her "Jesus wept" on a sunny day in June. But the peculiar thing was that Wilma had not known of Clarence's death when she declared the hog's final hushing up; and oddly enough it was on the exact day of Clarence's birth, five years before, that Wilma had commenced preaching that the hog could talk.

They say that day the sun shone while the rain poured—the old folk say that's when the devil beats his wife—the day Estelle Pickett died giving birth to Clarence. Her mama was out in the cucumber patch when Estelle went into labor and we came to get her—Miss Eunice, not being an excitable woman, asked if the midwife had been sent for and when we said yeah, she insisted on topping off her bushel before heading home. Estelle's papa, Mr. George Edward, was away in Wilmington that day looking for a new tractor since he was sick and tired of his old Farmall[1] breaking down every other row and needing more oil than gasoline.

We never knew if Miss Eunice blamed herself, cause she never admitted to it, one, and two we never saw much sign that she did. We all arrived at the Pickett place at the same time as the midwife. We walked in on one of the most hideous sights we can remember seeing or hearing tell of: there lay Estelle on the bed, her legs apart, her eyes rolled back in her head, her body kind of twisted to the side in a pool so deep red it could have been a maroon sheet she was sitting on instead of white; and on the floor squalling like a stuck pig was Clarence, a twitching, pitiful little thing, in a soup of blood and purple mess and shit. There wont no caul[2] to worry about being over his face as people came to gossip. Just not so. The caul seemed to be everywhere else though, on his head, on his hands, on his belly like a raw liver, quivery and oozy, him coated in a mucky white paste like snot. A nasty enough mess to make you lose your breakfast. Miss Eunice went to fix him up straightaway and the midwife looked to Estelle.

"She's gone, child. Poor thing," she said.

"Well . . ." Miss Eunice didn't say anything else, but that "Well . . ." seemed to say everything and nothing. She handed the baby to the midwife to cut and tuck

1. A brand of tractor commonly used throughout the South.

2. A covering of white membrane which sometimes covers babies when they are born. If the caul covers the face, the child is said to possess the ability to be clairvoyant and lucky. This motif is a common one in American folklore of the South.

his stem. (Folk who said he didn't have a belly button just don't know what they're talking about, cause we saw it knotted.)

That summer turned out to be a mild one—only a few days over a hundred. And ever since that day back in June folk had been wondering if we should take it upon ourselves to have Wilma committed and her talking hog butchered proper, seeing as she didn't have any children to see after her. But we left her alone, saying that all that meanness she had had all her life and all that insurance money she'd collected from two husbands and all that land they left her had come back to visit her in the form of a hallucination about a talking hog which she'd collar folk to come hear, only to be met by an occasional grunt or squeal, them scratching their noggins[3] and casting sideways glances at Wilma, feeling a little sorry for her but not daring to say a word since she may well of kicked them out of their houses or called in mortgages they owed her. So when she took the damn thing into her house, making it a canopy bed with frills and ruffles, feeding it topshelf Purina Hog Chow, along with Spanish omelettes and tuna casserole (she forbore to give it pork cause that would be cannibalism, of course), we didn't say a thing other than "Oh that's nice, Wilma," and rolled our eyes.

Nothing much happened to point out that Clarence was different, not until that summer three years later when he began to talk, the day Ed Phelps found him out in his cow pasture surrounded by buzzards and talking in complete sentences. Of course folk said they knew of strange thises and thats to have occurred in hindsight, but we didn't believe none of it cause we hadn't heard tell of any of it at the time; we didn't believe anything except what happened after he turned three and commenced to talk, which we did believe cause we were witness to most of it—unlikely though it seems.

But Ed Phelps found him that day—some claim it was the exact same day of Clarence's third birthday, but we couldn't seem to come to an agreement after the fact, seeing as nobody had thought to note it down—after Miss Eunice and Mr. George Edward had like to gone crazy looking for the boy. They were already perturbed, understandably, over the child since, at near on three years, he hadn't yet said a blessed word, and neither Miss Eunice, nor Mr. George Edward for that matter, was too keen on having a retarded heir, seeing as Estelle had been their last living child—Henry, the oldest, died in Korea, and Frederick, who called himself Long John, had died in a shoot-out in Detroit. So when the child disappeared, its leave-taking allowed them to give vent to a whole slew of emotions these normally buttoned-down folk kept under their hats. About six hours after they'd searched and called and hollered, having the whole town in a fit to find the child, Ed drove up into Miss Eunice and Mr. George Edward's yard with Clarence in his arms. The toddler ran to Miss Eunice and hollered, "Miss Eunice, Miss Eunice." She just looked at the boy, her eyes big as Mr. George Edward's, who asked Ed where he found the boy. Ed said he'd come out on his porch after his after-dinner catnap and heard this awful fuss coming from the side of the house. He went to investigate, he said, and came to see seven or eight buzzards playing—that was the word he used—playing with little Clarence Pickett. All the cows were at the other end of the pasture avoiding the birds. Said he went and got his shotgun and fired but the scavengers didn't pay him no notice, so he shot one of them through the neck—had to shoot the damn thing again to kill it—and the others took off hopping and tripping and stumbling into the air.

When they asked Clarence what he was doing in the cow pasture and how he got there and a whole other passel of questions, he just smiled and grinned possum-

3. Slang term for head.

like. And just as Ed Phelps was about to leave, Clarence turned to Miss Eunice with all the innocence and seriousness you're apt to see on the face of a three-year-old and asked: "Why'd he kill it, Miss Eunice?" Of course she didn't answer him; of course she didn't know how to answer him. The look on her face seemed only to ask for peace.

Yet it seemed the end of peace in that house. Even though Clarence still sucked on his bottle he could and would talk to Miss Eunice and Mr. George Edward like an adult. We had to admire the two of them cause where it would of spooked some into their graves they took it all in stride. But people will accept some pretty outrageous behavior from their own blood, and after all it was just talking. But it wont the talking itself that caused the problem: it was what he said.

One time Emma Chaney stopped by to say hey to Miss Eunice and Mr. George Edward and just before she left Clarence walked into the room and said: "Your mama says Joe Hattan is stepping out on you with that strumpet Viola Stokes." Well, everybody was shocked and embarrassed and Mr. George Edward took a switch to Clarence telling him he shouldn't say such things to grownfolks, and all the while Clarence yelled through his tears: "But Miss Ruella told me to tell her." "Boy, quit your lying," Mr. George Edward said through his teeth. "Miss Ruella been dead." Mr. George Edward gave Clarence a few extra licks for lying, all the while wondering how on earth the boy'd come to know about a woman long dead before Clarence was even thought about.

Well, come to find out—seems Emma's curiosity was piqued and she followed Hattan on the sly—that her husband *was* cheating on her with that low-down Viola Stokes. Emma had a bullwhip of her daddy's and went into the house right on the spot and lashed the both of them good-fashioned. Viola got out her pistol and—not being a good shot—got Hattan in the hind parts.

Emma went straight back to Mr. George Edward and Miss Eunice wanting to know how the boy knew, and when he said Miss Ruella told him Mr. George Edward took the switch to him again.

Of course it didn't stop there. Clarence would tell people who happened by the Pickett place that this or that person was out to get them; that this woman was going to have twins; that that man had prostate cancer; that that woman's husband intended to give her a cruise for their wedding anniversary. He was good for getting up in the morning and announcing: "Such and such a person's going to die today," or "Such and such a person died last night." He told one person where they put an old insurance policy they'd lost, another where they mislaid their keys. Most folk came to avoid going by Miss Eunice and Mr. George Edward's house if they could, and prayed they wouldn't bring along Clarence when they came a-calling.

One green May day Mabel Pearsall stopped by to give Miss Eunice a mess of mustard greens. As they sat gossiping over a glass of lemonade in the kitchen, Clarence walked in clutching his soldier-doll. "Mr. Joe Allen wants a apple pie tonight," he said to Mabel the way an old woman coaches a new bride. "He been wanting one for months. You ought to make it for him."

Mabel laughed nervous-like and looked to Miss Eunice for help, who shooed Clarence away with a broom, presently turning to admit to Mabel: "I just don't know what to do with that boy." Mabel left not long after that.

On the way home Mabel stopped by McTarr's Grocery Store and got fixings for a pie—she said she wont paying any mind to that crazy boy, just had a craving for one, she said; but who could believe her? She baked the pie and her husband Joe Allen ate it without a word; and Mabel *harrumphed* and washed the dishes and went to bed laughing at herself and that strange boy, thinking she should tell Miss Eunice to be harder on him in the future. But that night, she said, she had a dream, and in the dream she dreamt that Joe Allen had come home and she hadn't baked the pie and in the middle of supper they had an argument and Joe Allen up and left her that very night. Mabel said she woke up from that dream in the wee hours of the morning powerfully afeared since the dream had the taste and feel of real life. She went back to sleep, to be waked up not by the rooster but by Joe Allen rocking on top of her, singing in her ear. (She admitted to some of us that he hadn't touched her in a year; though we suspect it had been closer to five, considering Mabel.)

Soon the boy seemed to get more outlandish in his testaments—as if what he'd said before wont outlandish enough. He told Sarah Phillips to stop fretting, that her husband forgave her for the time she tried to stab him with that hunting knife; he told Cleavon Simpson his mama despised him for tricking her to sign all of her property over to him and for putting her in a nursing home; he told Sealey Richards her daddy apologized for the times he tried to have his way with her. Clarence told people things a four-year-old boy ain't had no business knowing the language for, let alone the circumstances around them. All from people dead five, six, ten, twenty, and more years. Secrets people had shared with no living person, much less a boy who could do well to stand and walk at the same time and who refused to give up his bottle. Miss Eunice and Mr. George Edward tried as hard as they could to ignore the boy, to shrug off his testimonials from the grave, but you could see that it preyed on their minds heavily, and it's a wonder they could get to sleep at night in the same house with him. God only knows what all went on in the dark in that old house.

Wilma soon started throwing parties for the Holy Hog Francis (as she'd taken to calling him in mixed company "My Holy Hog"). She'd invite all the little children (except Clarence) and they had ice cream and cake and orange and grape and strawberry soda and little hats, and Francis sat at the head of the table with a hat on, making a mess of his German chocolate cake, and the parties were a great success, and one boy, Perry Mitchell, came away and somebody asked if he heard the pig talk, and everybody was amazed cause he said yes, kind of offhanded-like and unimpressed, and they asked what did the pig say, and the boy said: "Oink, oink."

When Clarence was four and a half, folk started seeing things. Ben Stokes was driving down the road and saw a white shepherd come up to Clarence in Miss Eunice and Mr. George Edward's yard—and he said he didn't think much of it at first but he backed up and looked again and he said he could swear it was Rickie Jones's ole dog Sweetpea that got hit by a truck a year back, and he said the dog had the same ole red collar on. Ab Batts said he drove by one day and saw Clarence sitting up in a walnut tree with crows all on the limbs like black fruit, caw-cawing to beat the band. Hettie Mae Carr said she saw him swinging in a porch swing with a woman she swore had to be Mr. George Edward's mother, Miss Maybelle, dead now on twenty-seven years. G. W. Gillespie said he came to visit one day and as he knocked at the door he heard a whole bunch of menfolk talking. He knocked again and Mr. George Edward came from the side of the house. "You having a party inside, Mr. George Edward?" "No," said Mr. George Edward. "Ain't nobody in there but Clarence." When they opened the door, he said, they both could hear men's voices in the kitchen. Mr. George Edward called out and the voices stopped. They went into the kitchen and saw six hands of cards set in midgame of poker, with Clarence sitting at the head of the table holding a hand. A flush. Mr. George Edward didn't ask for explanation, just fussed about

Clarence knowing better than to mess with his playing cards and collected them and put them on a high shelf out of the boy's reach. G. W. left right soon after that.

But it was around the time Wilma decided Francis needed to attend regular church services, and argued down the Reverend Barden that the hog should and could attend First Baptist. That's when all hell—or whatever you've a mind to call it—really broke loose.

Seems one day things just didn't want to go right at the Pickett place: Miss Eunice couldn't seem to find her car keys; the refrigerator broke down; the hens didn't lay egg one; the water pump lost pressure; the fuse box blew; plates fell out of the cabinet and broke. But the most curious thing had to do with Clarence. He acted like he was scared to death, Miss Eunice said. He'd cling to Mr. George Edward's leg like he might to be gobbled up any minute. Mr. George Edward and Miss Eunice were so distracted and annoyed by all those other fixes that they were just more bothered by the boy and just didn't think to put two and two together.

Mr. George Edward took Clarence with him to disk the old field over the branch, and riding on the dusty tractor Clarence kept looking back like they were being followed; but when Mr. George Edward would ask what the matter was the boy'd just look at him, not saying a word.

Now after Mr. George Edward had disked up one piece of land—he recollected later that the five-year-new tractor was suddenly giving him the devil with stalling and the hydraulic lifts just wouldn't lift without coaxing—he got tired of Clarence sitting in his lap and put him down at the end of a row and told him to sit out a couple of turns.

The boy pitched a fit, but Mr. George Edward had no intention of giving in, and as he headed back to the tractor Clarence started talking.

"He says he's gone get you, Granddaddy. He says you's a dead man!"

Mr. George Edward turned around, a little spooked. "Who, boy? Who you talking bout?"

"Fitzhugh Oxendine. Fitzhugh Oxendine! He say he gone fix you good, Granddaddy!"

Mr. George Edward was doubly spooked now. Specially seeing as how the five-year-old boy had no way heard tell of ole Fitzhugh Oxendine. Seems when he was a young turk, Mr. George Edward worked laying new track for the railroad all along the southeast of the state. Now among the boys he worked with there was a fellow by the name of Fitzhugh Oxendine from Lumberton, who was just plain bad news. Well, the long and the short of it is that one payday while enjoying the end of the week them boys got themselves into a piece of trouble with a bunch of white sailors in Wilmington. A white boy got bad-off hurt, and Fitzhugh went on the lam. The law was giving them colored boys hell to find Fitzhugh and finally Mr. George Edward broke down and told them where they'd find him. Fitzhugh went to jail and from then on went in and out of the state penitentiary like it had a revolving door. Mr. George Edward said he always did regret doing what he done.

But that day Mr. George Edward just shook his head and tried to put that hollering boy and his queer knowledge out of his mind and looked onto the lower back field, which he wanted to finish before dinnertime. He climbed up on the tractor and put it in gear.

Now a ole John Deere tractor—which is the kind Mr. George Edward had—if you play the clutch and the gas and the brake just right, will rear up its front part just like a horse. Boys round Tims Creek use to do it all the time to impress folk, pretending they were in the wild wild west. It's not too likely it'll rear up like that with a cultivator attached to the back; but it happens. Well, that's what Mr. George Edward's tractor done that day, he said, and it went higher than he could ever recollect one going without flipping over—which happens too—and he fell slam off his seat, onto the ground, and the tractor kept going and the cultivator went right over his hand. It didn't slice clean off, but seeing how he'd just got the cultivator new it was sharp as the devil and cut into the bone deep. What done the true damage was the dragging since he couldn't well get aloose.

The most curious thing happened next. Mr. George Edward said amidst his agony and yelling for help he saw through all the tears and dust in his eyes a woman hop up on the tractor and jerk it to a stop. Wilma Jones leapt down and pulled Mr. George Edward free. He said he could hear the bone crack as she got him loose. He said he couldn't verify for true as he was so overcome by the pain and the sight of his blood-muddy mangled hand, but he heard what he thought was Clarence screaming, and as Wilma got him to his feet and begun walking him to her station wagon he could tell it wasn't Clarence at all: it was Francis, caterwauling and squealing and rolling about and biting in the dirt, like it was fighting with something or somebody. Mr. George Edward said this brought to his mind the scene from the Good Book when our Lord cast the demon from the man and sent it into the swine. Soon the dust was so thick you couldn't see the hog, only hear it; and after a while the thing came trotting out with a look like contentment about its face.

"How . . . ?" was about all Mr. George Edward could utter. Wilma had tied off the hand with her apron to keep him from bleeding to death.

"Just rest easy now, Mr. George Edward. You gone be all right. You'll be at York General before you know it. I can drive this ole Bessie when I got to. Francis took care of everything else."

Mr. George Edward said he passed out then with the hog staring at him with them beady eyes, its great big head stuck over the front seat staring at him, its frothy slobber drooling on his overalls. When he come to he found Miss Eunice humming "At the Cross" and saw that them know-nothing doctors had left him with a stump instead of a left hand. But all he could think about was them gray eyes. "Eunice, that hog got eyes like a human person's."

"Go on back to sleep, George Edward. All hogs do."

We found out a few weeks later that the day before all this happened Fitzhugh Oxendine had died in Central Prison.

Well, after that episode if you think folk avoided Miss Eunice and Mr. George Edward and their grandbaby before, you should of seen how they stayed away now. From Wilma too, for that matter. And her sacred hog. When she told them the pig had told her Fitzhugh Oxendine was after Mr. George Edward and up to evil business, people whispered a little louder about calling the folks at Dorothea Dix. But after all, she did save Mr. George Edward from his tractor. How did she know? Probably just happened by, we said. Paying no mind to the fact that you didn't "just happen by" a field a mile off a secondary road.

Of course we all hear and all have heard tell about children born with a sixth sense or clairvoyance or ESP or some such, out of the mouths of babes and all that, but, we being good, commonsensical, level-headed, churchgoing folk, we didn't have no truck with such nonsense and third-hand tales. But the evidence kept accumulating and accumulating till you'd have to be deaf, dumb, blind, and stupid to whistle, nod your head, and turn away. But that's exactly what most of us did anyhow. Ain't it strange how people behave?

Some folk didn't ignore it though. Those full of the Holy Ghost preached against the boy, and at a Pentecostal revival meeting one preacher, after a round of prayers for the souls of Mr. George Edward and Miss Eunice, said the boy ought to be bound to a stake and burnt or left on a dry riverbed for the devil to claim his own. (Oddly, he didn't mention the hog Francis, who was at that moment attending prayer meeting at First Baptist.) Dead chickens and blood on the doorpost became regular morning greetings at the Pickett place.

Now there were a few who saw opportunity in the boy; just as there'll always be scheming rascals who see opportunity in other folks' misery. But they soon learned their lesson. One woman came to see if she had a prosperous future. Clarence told her she'd die at forty-nine of heartbreak and sugar diabetes. One man came to get in touch with his dead grandmother—we later found out rumor had it that she'd buried gold somewhere on her property. Clarence just told him: "Wont no gold, Jimmy, you damn fool. Why don't you quit looking for get-rich-quick and learn to work for what you want in life?" The man stormed out after cussing Mr. George Edward good-fashioned. In two weeks the man and his family just went, left everything, without a word. Finally come back that the man had moved to Oregon to get as far away from Tims Creek as he could. Said, according to what we heard, strange things commenced to happening in the house, which was his grandma's in the first place: doors slamming, lights coming on and going off, footsteps, you know, the usual. We just laughed and said, some people . . .

Nobody looking for profit much bothered Clarence after that.

The summer before Clarence was about to begin school—Wilma had set out to start a church for Francis, seems the Deacon Board and the Board of Trustees at First Baptist finally put their foot down about cleaning up hog droppings after service—well, Clarence met Ellsworth Batts. Miss Eunice had taken Clarence with her to do the Saturday shopping at McTarr's, and Ellsworth had just been dropped off there after helping Ab Batts clean out his turkey house. Ellsworth didn't show his face much in Tims Creek but he was a good and hard worker who did an odd job now and again for beer money. Miss Eunice said they passed Ellsworth on the way to the car, him not smelling or looking too pretty after a hot morning of shoveling turkey manure. She gave her most courteous hey, not being one to discourage hard and decent work, and kept going, but Clarence stopped and went back to Ellsworth.

"Clarence, come back here."

She said Clarence reached out for the man's hand but didn't touch it and said: "She says she grieves for your pain, but you were wrong to give it all up for her. . . ."

"What? Who?" Miss Eunice said Ellsworth's eyes looked madder than she'd ever seen them look and he commenced to quake and tremble.

"Mildred. She says she wants you to return to the living folk. She says you have eternity to be dead. You love too much, she says. There's more to life than love."

"Mildred? Mildred. Mildred!"

Well, Miss Eunice said she grabbed Clarence by the hand and ran to the car cause Ellsworth put the fear of God in her and after she had thrown the groceries in the backseat and rolled the windows up and locked the door, Ellsworth kept calling: "Mildred, Mildred," crying and pounding on the door. She said he had the look of a wild bear on his face with all his beard and hair. Fearing for herself and the boy, Miss Eunice slowly pulled the car out and started down the road, leaving Ellsworth running behind in the dust hollering: "Mildred, Mildred, Mildred."

Mildred had been his childhood sweetheart, a fresh cocoa-brown gal with the biggest, brightest eyes and the prettiest smile. Even before they were married Ellsworth was crazy with love for her, once almost beating a boy to death who he claimed looked too long at her. Sweethearts since childhood, they'd agreed to marry after he got out of the army. He'd see Mildred as often as he could, writing her once a day, sometimes more, and dreaming of that little house and children and nice supper after a hard day's work and all the foolishness young boys have in their heads that marriage is all about and ain't.

Well, when he got out they got married at First Baptist Church and set up a home so nice and pretty it'd make you sick—in a house owned by Wilma Jones's first husband, by the way. Nobody's sure exactly what caused the fire; Ellsworth always blamed Wilma's husband for faulty wiring—but three months after their honeymoon at Myrtle Beach, the house caught afire. They couldn't even show Mildred's body at her funeral.

They say Ellsworth cried every day for a month and after that just seemed to give up. Seems he didn't have any other dreams than that one with Mildred and didn't see the use in conjuring up any more to replace it the way folk have to do sometime. When his mama died and the house started to fall apart from plain ole neglect, Ellsworth took to living in a broken-down bus shell one of his brothers bought for him at a junkyard.

He let his hair grow wild, his teeth go bad, his clothes get ragged and tattered. His brothers tried to help, but he refused more than an occasional meal and pocket change now and again, and made it clear he wanted to be left alone. We just shrugged and accepted his crazy behavior as one of those things that happen. And the memory of why he'd come to live like he did just faded in our minds the way colors in a hand-me-down quilt wash out after time.

Clarence had set off something deep in Ellsworth. The next day, first thing in the morning, he presented himself at the Pickett place and asked Mr. George Edward if he could talk to the boy.

"I don't want no trouble now, Ellsworth. You hear me? You like to scared Miss Eunice clear to death. You shoulda heard —"

"I beg you and Miss Eunice's pardon, Mr. George Edward. But if I. . . . "

Clarence came out and he and Ellsworth talked for about half an hour, sitting in the swing on the front porch. Mr. George Edward said he couldn't remember what all was said, but he could testify to a change coming over Ellsworth. First he cried and the boy admonished him stern-like, Mr. George Edward said, saying the time for tears had long passed. They talked and talked and directly Ellsworth and the boy laughed and giggled and after a while Mr. George Edward, who said he was coming to feel a touch uneasy, said he figured it was time for Ellsworth to be on his way. Ellsworth stood to go, Mr. George Edward said, and the look on his face made Mr. George Edward worried. Tweren't the sort of look a grown man shows to a five-year-old boy.

The next day Ellsworth came at dusk dark, and lo and behold, said Miss Eunice, he'd fixed himself up, washed and trimmed his hair, and had on a nice clean set of clothes—God knows where he got them from—looking in a spirit she hadn't seen him in since he went off to the army. Not knowing what to do, after a spell she invited Ellsworth in to supper and they all ate listening to the boy talk to Ellsworth about what Mildred had said. At one point, forgetting himself, Ellsworth grasped the boy's hand. Mr. George Edward had to clear his throat to reacquaint Ellsworth with the impropriety of doing what he was doing. Right then and there, Miss Eunice said, she knew this was going to be nothing but trouble but could see no way to put a peaceable end to it.

Every day for a week Ellsworth showed up to see Clarence and every day Miss Eunice and Mr. George Edward would exchange weary glances and shrugs, while one would stand guard over what begun to look more and more like courting and sparking. Ellsworth brought candy and then flowers, which Miss Eunice took from Clarence straightaway and finally said to Mr. George Edward: "This has just got to stop." And Mr. George Edward said: "I know. I know. I'll talk to him."

Nothing like talk of crimes against nature[4] gets people all riled up and speculating and conjecturing and postulating the way they did when word got out about Ellsworth Batts's "unnatural affection" for Clarence Pickett. The likelihood of him conversing with his dead Mildred through the boy paled next to the idea of him fermenting depraved intentions for young and tender boys. Imaginations sparked like lightning in a dry August wood, and folk took to shunning poor Ellsworth and keeping an extra eye on their womenfolk and children and locking doors after dark.

Thrice Ellsworth tried to get to Clarence, who seemed about as indifferent to his grandparents' commands as he was to Ellsworth's advances. Once Ellsworth motioned to him from under a sweetgum tree and embraced and kissed him in the shade; Clarence didn't say a mumbling word. When Mr. George Edward saw it he hollered and ran to get his gun but lost Ellsworth after chasing him and missing him—Mr. George Edward had been a good shot but the lack of a hand hindered him something awful—after missing him four times in the thick of the woods.

The second time, Ellsworth snuck into the house after twelve midnight and had the nerve to slip under the covers with the boy. Miss Eunice heard noises and woke Mr. George Edward. He had the gun this time when he found him, but he missed again and Ellsworth was covered by the night. He left his shoes.

By this time folk were on the lookout for Ellsworth Batts, figuring he was a true menace. They staked out his bus and had his brothers come to town to take charge of him but they found no Ellsworth.

About a week later—and we still can't believe that he did—Ellsworth snuck into the house again and tried to take the boy away. It was soon in the morning and everybody had just got out of bed. Mr. George Edward had only his long drawers on and Miss Eunice was out in the chicken coop collecting eggs. Ellsworth had the boy up in his arms when Mr. George Edward came out of the bathroom.

"You can't keep us apart. We were meant to be together."

"You one crazy son of a bitch is what you is, Ellsworth Batts."

Miss Eunice saw him running out the back door and tackled him, breaking all her eggs. Mr. George Edward had his gun by now, and having learned how to aim the gun with his stump finally shot Ellsworth in the foot. Running as best he could Ellsworth got a lead in the woods, but by now Mr. George Edward was joined by seven men who'd heard the shotgun and were ready.

They chased Ellsworth Batts for a good hour, figuring this time they had him. Cleavon Simpson and G. W. Gillespie had their bloodhounds on the trail now. They finally spotted him on the Chinquapin River bridge and he tried to double back but they had him trapped on both sides. Ellsworth Batts didn't look, they said,

4. A euphemism for homosexuality.

he just jumped. The Chinquapin was at its lowest, so it was pretty easy to find the body with the broken neck.

We were all mostly relieved seeing what we considered a threat to our peace and loved ones done away with; a few of us—the ones who dared put one iota of stock in believing in Clarence and his talking dead folk—figured it to be a kind of happy ending, seeing as Ellsworth would now be reunited with his beloved beyond the pale. But the most of us thought such talk a load of horse hockey, reckoning if that was the answer why didn't he just kill himself in the first place and leave us off from the trouble?

Some of us entertained fancies about the type of stories we'd begin hearing when Clarence got to school. But we never got to hear any such tales. Just before he was to start kindergarten, he took sick and died. Doctors say it was a bad case of the flu on top of a weak heart we'd never heard tell of. We figured there was more to it than that, something our imaginations were too timid to draw up, something to do with living and dying that we, so wound up in harvesting corn, cleaning house, minding chickenpox, building houses, getting our hair done, getting our cars fixed, getting good loving, fishing, drinking, sleeping, and minding other people's business, really didn't care about or have time or space to know. Why mess in such matters?—matters we didn't really believe in in the first place, and of which the memory grows dimmer and dimmer every time the sun sets.

At his funeral Miss Eunice and Mr. George Edward looked neither relieved nor sad. Just worn out; like two old people who did what their Lord had asked of them, and who, like Job, bore the tiresome effort unhappily but faithfully. Robins and sparrows perched on the tombstones near the grave as the dust-to-dust was said and the dirt began to rain down on the too-short coffin, and as we walked away from the Pickett cemetery we noted a herd of deer congregating at the edge of the wood. Of course we put this all out of our minds, eager to forget. And life in Tims Creek went on as normal after he died: folk went on propagating, copulating, and castigating, folk loved, folk hated, folk debauched, got lonely and died. No one talks about Clarence, and God only knows what lies they'd tell if they did.

As for Francis, oddly enough Wilma Jones stopped proclaiming the hog's oracular powers and eventually butchered him. But at the last minute, with the poor thing roasting over a pit, Wilma had a crisis of conscience and couldn't eat it; so she gave it a semi-Christian burial with a graveside choir and a minister and pall-bearers, all made hungry by the scent of barbecue. Finally Wilma stopped raising hogs altogether. She opened a shoe store with her cousin Joceline in Crosstown.

Questions to Consider

1. How does this depiction of funeral traditions compare with others presented in Southern texts? Why is the Southern funeral tradition important in the text and in Southern culture?
2. Who is Kenan's narrator in this piece and why is the narrative voice important to the reader? Is this voice authentic?

END OF VOICES IN CONTEXT

George Garrett

1929–

George Garrett is extolled by his long-time colleague and friend R. H. W. Dillard as a man who has "thoroughly fulfilled the traditional definition of *man of letters*" and by protégée Richard Bausch as possessing a talent that is "enormously versatile and eclectic." Arguably a Renaissance man of the twentieth century, Garrett initially emerged as a member of the second generation of Southern writers following the Southern Renascence, an auspicious group that includes writers such as Walker Percy, James Dickey, and Shelby Foote. Garrett is the author of nearly thirty books covering the genres of poetry, short fiction, drama, and the novel, as well as numerous essays, both personal and scholarly. In addition to his creative work, Garrett has edited more than twenty books, all while serving as a professor of English and as a mentor to hundreds of aspiring writers. Perhaps Garrett's most impressive achievement, however, is his systematic effort to redefine the historical novel, a feat that he has ably accomplished with his Elizabethan trilogy.

George Palmer Garrett was born on 11 June 1929 in Orlando, Florida. His father, George P. Garrett, was an attorney who successfully fought opponents such as the Ku Klux Klan and the powerful Florida railroads, actions that supported his belief in the need to improve the plight of the poor. The younger Garrett attended Princeton University, where he graduated Phi Beta Kappa with a bachelor's degree. He then joined the army, spending two years on active duty in Austria and returned to Princeton after his discharge from the military to complete both a master's degree and a doctorate. Garrett married Susan Parrish Jackson in 1952, and the couple has three children. Garret has served as a professor at institutions including Hollins College, the University of South Carolina, Princeton, Columbia, Virginia Military Institute, and the University of Virginia. In addition to his professorial work, Garrett also spent some time as a writer for CBS.

Garrett published his first poems in 1957, and by 1962, three poetry collections had appeared. During this time, he also authored two story collections and two novels. His literary output was so prodigious that three of his books—*Which Ones are the Enemy?* (a novel), *Abraham's Knife* (a poetry collection), and *In the Briar Patch* (a story collection)—were published on the same day in 1961. The major novels that followed—the Elizabethan trilogy consisting of *Death of the Fox* (1971), *The Succession* (1983), and *Entered from the Sun* (1990)—are considered by many critics to be his most significant works, in part because they serve to revitalize a genre. Garrett is also well known as a mentor to young, up-and-coming writers. The list of writers who have benefitted from his instruction and support is extensive, including Richard Bausch, Fred Chappell, Jill McCorkle, Mary Lee Settle, and Madison Smartt Bell.

J. William Berry has remarked that the tone of Garrett's diverse works is that of personal conversations that are "often heated, within the self, between the self and the community, between the South and the country, and with those outsiders within, the other race. Literary southerners, called by American opportunities for self-making, have left the South often enough. The South, nonetheless, abides in them." The intimate tone to which Berry refers evokes the long-standing oral narrative tradition in the South, as does Garrett's ability to find humor in everyday occurrences. Garrett appears most at home in the realm of Southern realism, a genre that allows him to present the unvarnished truth, albeit with a large enough dose of humor to make the truth not merely palatable, but at times wickedly delicious. His talent for creating realism shines through "Feeling Good, Feeling Fine," a story that rapidly moves from a young boy's irritation at being compelled to play baseball with his odd uncle to the heart-wrenching revelation of the source of the uncle's idiosyncracies. The uncle makes a selfless decision that ends life as he knows it so that he will not continue to be a burden to his family.

Although many of his colleagues in the literary community feel that Garrett has not received the critical and popular attention he deserves, he has been the recipient of numerous prestigious awards, most recently, the Aiken-Taylor Award in Poetry. He has also received the PEN/Malamud Award for Short Story, the T. S. Eliot Award, and on two occasions, awards from the American Academy of Arts and Letters. He is also a founding member of the Fellowship of Southern Writers. Garret currently holds the Henry Hoyns Professorship in creative writing at the University of Virginia.

Feeling Good, Feeling Fine

A boy and a man in the park. Between them an old wooden bat, a battered and dirty baseball and one leather glove, well tended and cared for, oiled and supple, but old, too, its pocket as thin as paper.

The boy and the man are sweating in the late afternoon light. Lazy end of a long summer day. The park (no more than a rough grass field, really) is empty now except for the two of them. Somewhere not far away a car horn toots, a dog barks, a woman calls her children in for supper.

"Come on," the man shouts. "Knock it to me!"

The boy carefully, all concentration, tosses the ball up and swings the bat to loft it high above the man. Who, skinny and raggedy as a scarecrow, moves gracefully back and away and underneath the high fly ball. Spears it deftly with the glove. Then throws it high and easy back toward the boy. The ball rolls dead an easy reach from his feet. "Let's quit and go home," the boy calls.

The tall thin man shakes his head and moves back deeper.

"One more," he hollers. "Just one more."

Crack of the bat on the ball and this is the best one yet. A homerun ball high in the fading light, almost lost in the last blue of the sky. The man shading his eyes as he runs smoothly and swiftly back and back until he's there where he has to be to snag it. Snags it.

Then comes running in toward the boy, hugely grinning, a loping fielder who has made the final catch of an inning.

You might think the boy would be pleased to have swung his bat (the glove and the bat and the ball are his) that well and knocked the ball so high and far. But truth is the boy hates baseball. "It's my least favorite sport," he will tell anyone who asks. Anyone except the man running toward him, his uncle, his mother's brother, who has recently come to live with them after several years at the state hospital.

Uncle Jack, he's had a hard time of it. First time he went crazy, his wife ran off with their two daughters, the boy's cousins, to California or some place like that and disappeared for keeps. Boy doesn't know it, can't comprehend it even if he could imagine it, but he won't ever see that woman and his two cousins again. Uncle Jack is living with them for the time being, "until he has a chance to get things straightened out," the boy's father explains. When the boy complains about the hours spent—wasted as far as he's concerned—knocking fungoes[1] and chasing flys and grounders with Uncle Jack, his father simply says: "Humor him, boy. He's good at it. Let him be."

He ain't that good, the boy sometimes thinks but doesn't say. Said it once, though, and his father corrected him.

1. Fly balls hit especially for practice fielding by a player who tosses a ball in the air and hits them as they come down.

"Listen, boy, he's rusty and he hasn't been well. But believe me, I'm here to tell you, he was some kind of a baseball player. A real pleasure to watch."

"Minor league," the boy said scornfully. Who can't imagine anyone settling for anything less than the top of the heap. If he liked baseball enough to want to play at it, he would be in the majors or nothing. He sure enough wouldn't be happy with some old photographs in an album and some frail, yellowing newspaper clippings.

And if he was a crazy old man back from the state hospital and had a nephew who was required to humor him, the boy would never pretend, let alone believe for one minute that he was getting himself back in shape so he could join the New York Yankees or the Washington Senators or somebody like that. Shit, Uncle Jack couldn't even play for the Brooklyn Dodgers.[2]

Uncle Jack now has the bat in one hand and the other arm around the boy's shoulders (the boy carries the glove and the ball) as the two of them slowly head for home in the twilight.

"You hit that last one just a helluva good lick," Uncle Jack says. "You could be a real hitter if you put your mind to it. It's all in the coordination and you have got that, all you could ever need."

Why, if he hates baseball, does the boy relish and rejoice in the man's words? Why, if his Uncle Jack is some kind of crazy person and is fooling himself and everybody else, too, about what a great ballplayer he was and thinks he still is, why does the boy automatically accept and enjoy his uncle's judgment? Why, if his uncle is mostly embarrassment and trouble, someone to be ashamed of, does the boy at this very instant, altogether in spite of himself, wish more than anything that the tall, thin, raggedy, graceful man was and is everything he ought to be or could have been?

(Years and years later, when this boy is a grandfather himself, for reasons he won't understand then any more than he does now, he will tell his grandchildren, and anyone else who will bother to listen to him, all about his Uncle Jack who was, briefly briefly—but is not all beauty and great achievement as brief as the flare of a struck match?—a wonderful athlete, a baseball player much admired and envied by his peers, someone who, except for a piece or two of bad luck, would have been named and honored among the very best of them. Someone to be proud of. Someone who once tried to teach him how to play the game.)

They are close to home now. They have left the raw wide field behind and are coming under a dark canopy of shade. Houses with green crisp lawns, dark earth and, here and there, a sprinkler pulsing bright water. Can see the lights of the boy's house being switched on downstairs. Can hear briefly, before his father's voice calls out a crisp command, music playing loudly on the radio. That will be his sister or his little brother fooling around. Upstairs probably. They are almost close enough to see through the lighted windows of the dining room his mother and Hattie, the maid, who works late and long for them in this Great Depression, setting the supper table with flat silver, napkins and water glasses. For a little time, the short walk, more of a stroll into the gradual dark, he has been almost perfectly content. Weary, sweated out, but feeling good, feeling fine, soothed by his uncle's complimentary words. Suddenly confident that whatever he does from here and now to the end of his life will

2. Formerly the major league baseball team of Washington, D.C., the Senators became the Texas Rangers when they moved to Arlington, Texas in 1972. Similarly, the Brooklyn Dodgers moved to Los Angeles in 1958. Each team continues to play in the cities to which they moved.

go well. Even more: that he will be able not only to enjoy this feeling of satisfaction, of joy, really, but will be able to share it with others less fortunate than himself.

What he cannot know, even as he and his uncle come across the lawn and into the house and shut the front door behind him, what he can't know and will not choose even to remember years and years later when he bitterly rakes the ashes of his life searching for even one remaining glowing coal, is what happens next.

At the table his father (who includes the whole family, even Hattie, in almost everything) will tell them about the long distance telephone call he received at his office this same afternoon from a doctor at the state hospital in Chattahoochie. The doctor has told him that there is a new kind of an operation on the brain that might, just might, cure Uncle Jack for good and all. No more coming and going, no more breakdowns and slow recoveries. It is a new thing. There can be no promises or guarantees, of course. And, as in any operation, there is always danger, there are always risks. But . . .

Everybody listens intently. (Except Hattie who elects to go back into the kitchen quietly.) Everybody listens. And then before Jack or anyone can say anything, his mother bursts into tears. Sobs at the table, trying to hide her face with her hands, her shoulders shaking.

Later that evening the boy will see his father, for the first and probably the only time, slap his mother full across her soft face, making her sob again and more as they quarrel about what may be the best thing for her brother to do. His uncle will settle the quarrel by freely and cheerfully choosing to return to the hospital to undergo this operation. And—the boy and man would warn them then and now, if there were some way, any way, if only he could—it went badly, as badly as can be, leaving his uncle no more than half alive, a vegetable, really, in that hospital for the rest of his life. The boy will live to be an old man, will go to war and live through it, will learn all the lessons—of love and death, of gain and loss, of pride and of regret—a long life can teach.

But none of this has happened yet. Man and boy have spent a long afternoon in the park together and, at the end of it, have come home. They come in the front door. Jack grabs his sister, the boy's mother, and gives her a bear hug, lifts her in the air. The boy goes to put the bat and the ball and the glove in the hall closet. Over his shoulder he hears his sister and brother coming down the stairs like a pair of wild ponies. Looking up, turning, he sees his father, smiling in shirtsleeves, coming out of the living room with the evening paper in his hands.

"Here they are," he says. "Here come our baseball players just in time for supper."

Questions to Consider

1. What does Garrett's story demonstrate about the nature of Southern families? Why does the brother consent to a dangerous brain operation that may turn him into a vegetable?
2. Why does the narrator relate the story of his uncle so frequently in his old age, especially since he held the uncle in such low esteem when he was a child?

Reynolds Price

1933–

Reynolds Price has outlived the predictions of many prominent physicians. Diagnosed with spinal cancer in 1984, he underwent many painful treatments that left him a paraplegic and was then released from the hospital, ostensibly to live out his last few weeks at home. In spite of the harsh side effects of his treatments, he has surpassed the doctors' predictions by nearly twenty years. During this time, he has produced some of his most interesting and profound work.

Price was born on 1 February 1933 to Elizabeth Rodwell Price and William Solomon Price in his mother's family home in Macon, North Carolina. Price's birth was difficult because he was a breech baby, but this tumultuous experience ultimately cemented a strong bond between Price and his parents. Three years later, the Prices prepared to welcome another child into the family, but unfortunately, this sister was stillborn. Eight years after Price's birth, a brother, William Solomon Price, Jr. was born. The Prices, though financially devastated by the Great Depression, formed a closely knit family, living in many of the small towns surrounding Macon throughout Price's early years, for his father was an appliance salesman for the Carolina Power and Light Company. Even though the family moved often, they sustained contact with the extended Rodwell and Price families. Through these experiences in the South, Price developed an ear for storytelling and sharing, and his works abound with traditional stories and motifs.

Price was a sickly child, yet he desired to do well in school. His first literary endeavor was a play, *The Wise Men,* which he wrote when he was in eighth grade. Throughout his life, his parents were supportive and loving, and both he and his brother marvel at the sense of humor, love, and grace that their parents expressed throughout their lives together. During his high school years, Price felt drawn to religion, becoming active in the Episcopal church although Price's mother was Methodist, and his father was Baptist. His works reflect a well-rooted allegiance to the Protestant traditions of the South.

Price earned his bachelor's degree in English from Duke University in 1955, and shortly after graduation, was awarded a Rhodes Scholarship. From 1955 to 1958, he attended Merton College at Oxford University in England. He returned home from Oxford and settled down to teach and write. While attending Duke University, he went to a talk that Eudora Welty delivered at the women's college. He finagled a way to escort Welty to her hotel and around campus, and during her time at Duke, the pair became fast friends. She forwarded his story, "Michael Egerton," to her agent and helped the developing writer launch his career. Like many Southern writers, Price credits Welty with much of his success.

Price's works illustrate tremendous universality through their themes and characters. His first novel, *A Long and Happy Life* (1961), earned critical praise, and his subsequent works were equally well received. Price's novels reflect many aspects of Southern life: religion, relationships that are not always viable, race relations, familial and community duties, and death. His novels have also become well known for the author's adeptness at expressing Southern Christianity. Although Price has set much of his fiction in the South, he avoids the label of Southern writer because of the limitations it sometimes imposes.

In Price's story, "Summer Games," the author creates a protagonist who learns a valuable lesson about his power as a human. Guilt and the notion of free will underlie the child's learning experience.

Summer Games

Outside, in our childhood summers—the war.[1] The summers of 1939 to '45. I was six and finally twelve; and the war was three thousand miles to the right where London, Warsaw, Cologne crouched huge, immortal under nights of bombs or, farther, to the left where our men (among them three cousins of mine) crawled over dead friends from foxhole to foxhole towards Tokyo or, terribly, where there were children (our age, our size) starving, fleeing, trapped, stripped, abandoned.

Far off as it was, still we dreaded each waking hour that the war might arrive on us. A shot would ring in the midst of our play, freezing us in the knowledge that here at last were the first Storm Troopers till we thought and looked—Mrs. Hightower's Ford. And any plane passing overhead after dark seemed pregnant with black chutes ready to blossom. There were hints that war was nearer than it seemed—swastikaed subs off Hatteras or the German sailor's tattered corpse washed up at Virginia Beach with a Norfolk movie ticket in his pocket.

But of course we were safe. Our elders said that daily. Our deadly threats were polio, being hit by a car, drowning in pure chlorine if we swam after eating. No shot was fired for a hundred miles. (Fort Bragg—a hundred miles.) We had excess food to shame us at every meal, excess clothes to fling about us in the heat of play. So, secure, guilty, savage, we invoked war to us by games which were rites.

All our games ended desperately. Hiding, Prisoner's Base, Sling-Statue, Snake in Gutter, Giant Step, Kick the Can. We would start them all as friends, cool, gentle enough; but as we flung on under monstrous heat, sealed in sweat and dirt, hearts thudding, there would come a moment of pitch when someone would shout "Now *war!*" and it would be war—we separating, fleeing for cover, advancing in stealth on one another in terror, inflicting terror, mock death, surrender, till evening came and the hand of the day relaxed above us and cool rose from the grass and we sank drained into calm again, a last game of Hide in the dusk among bitter-smelling lightning bugs, ghost stories on the dark porch steps; then bath, bed, prayers for forgiveness and long life, sleep.

Only once did we draw real blood in our games; and I was the cause, the instrument at least. One August afternoon we had gone from, say, Tag into War. It was me, my cousins Marcia and Pat, and a Negro boy named Walter (who played with us for a quarter a week) against older, rougher boys. They massed on the opposite side of the creek that split the field behind our house. We had gathered magnolia seed pods for hand grenades; but as the charge began and swept toward us, as Madison Cranford leapt the creek and came screaming at me, he ceased being Madison (a preacher's son), the game ceased, the day rose in me, I dropped my fake grenade, stooped, blindly found a stone (pointed flint) and before retreating, flung it. My flight was halted by sudden silence behind me. I turned and by the creek on the ground in a huddle of boys was Madison, flat, still, eyes shut, blood streaming from the part in his sweaty hair, from a perfect circle in the skin which I had made. Walter, black and dry and powdered with dust, knelt by the head and the blood and looking through the day and the distance, said to me, "What ails you, boy? You have killed *this* child."

I had not, of course. He lived, never went to bed though a doctor did see him and pass on to us the warning that, young as we were, we were already deadly. My

1. World War II is the war to which the protagonist refers.

rock an inch farther down in Madison's temple would have done the work of a bullet—death. Death was ours to give, mine.

The warning was passed through my mother that night when she came from the Cranfords', having begged their pardon, and climbed to my room where I feigned sleep in a walnut bed under photographs of stars. I "woke" with a struggle, oaring myself from fake drowned depths, lay flat as she spread covers round me and heard her question launched, tense but gentle. "Why on earth did you throw a rock when everyone else was playing harmless?" What I suddenly knew I held back from her—that the others were not playing harmless, were as bent on ruin as I but were cowards, had only not yet been touched hard enough by hate. So I blamed the summer. "It was so hot I didn't know I *had* a rock. I was wild, for a minute. I will try not to do it again next summer." She said "*Ever* again" and left me to sleep which, tired as I was, did not come at once.

I lay in half dark (my sacred familiar objects crouched in horror from me against my walls) and thought through the lie I had told to save my mother—that summer was to blame. Then I said aloud as a promise (to my room, to myself), "I will tame *myself*. When the war is over and I am a man, it will all be peace, be cool. And when it is not, when summer comes, we will go to the water—my children and I—and play quiet games in the cool of the day. In the heat we will rest, separate on cots, not touching but smiling, watching the hair grow back on our legs."

Then sleep came unsought, untroubled to seal that further lie I had told to hide from myself what I knew even then—that I was not wrong to blame the summer, not wholly wrong; that wherever summer strikes (its scalding color), even in years of relative peace, something thrusts from the earth, presses from the air, compresses that in us which sets us wild against ourselves, in work, in games, in worst of all our love. Summer is the time wars live, thrive, on.

Questions to Consider

1. Why does the protagonist of Price's story throw the rock rather than a magnolia pod? Why does he blame his action on the summer season?
2. How does war function as a motif in this story?

William Styron

1925–

Despite his sometimes vehement exclamations to the contrary, William Styron's writing is fraught with what Georgann Eubanks, in a 1984 interview, correctly identifies as a "Southern sensibility." Although Styron has lived in Connecticut for several decades, his choice of residence has not kept him from revisiting his Southern Tidewater roots in his best fiction, leading Robert Penn Warren to argue that Styron is "one of the last among a handful of living writers . . . who can justifiably be classified as 'Southern writers' in the tradition of Wolfe and Faulkner."

William Clark Styron, Jr., was born in Newport News, Virginia on 11 June 1925, the only son of Pauline Abraham Styron, a music teacher, and William Clark Styron, Sr., a shipyard engineer. Styron enjoyed an idyllic childhood, crabbing and sailing on the James River, until his mother's untimely death from cancer when her son was only 13. Styron demonstrated an affinity for literature from an early age, but his misbehavior in school following his mother's death led his father to enroll him in boarding school at the Episcopal Christchurch School; he later attended Duke University, graduating Phi Beta Kappa with a bachelor's degree after World War II. Styron served in the Marine Corps during World War II, which interrupted his college years, achieving the rank of First Lieutenant in spite of his distaste for military discipline. He left the Marines at the end of the war, but returned to service in 1951 as the Korean conflict flared. Styron's second stint in the military was brief, ending with a medical discharge because of an eye problem. Between tours of duty in the military, Styron accepted a position with a subsidiary of McGraw-Hill Publishing, but the job lasted only six months, with Styron citing his "general inattention" as the reason for his dismissal.

Styron had not allowed military service to interfere with his writing, and he began publishing essays and fiction pieces that he had written during his time in the Marines; some appeared before he was discharged from military service. He briefly lived in Durham, North Carolina, where he enjoyed the benefits of Duke's extensive library, but soon settled in Brooklyn and set about the business of writing his first novel. During these transient years, Styron took a course at the New School for Social Research in New York (now New School University), and wrote his first novel, *Lie Down in Darkness* (1951), for which he won the *Prix de Rome* of the American Academy of Arts and Letters. He used the proceeds of the award to travel in Italy following his discharge, and upon his return to the United States in 1953, he married Rose Burgunder. The couple soon settled in Roxbury, Connecticut, where they continue to reside.

Although Styron had already published three novels—*Lie Down in Darkness* (1951), *The Long March* (1953), and *Set This House on Fire* (1960)—the 1967 publication of *The Confessions of Nat Turner* placed Styron on the literary map and firmly established him as a Southern writer. The story of a pre–Civil War-era slave insurrection and escape gone awry, the novel portrays the anger, hatred, and ensuing violence commonly glossed over by earlier generations of White Southern writers. The novel concludes with the execution of the men who planned the escape, and Styron adeptly manipulates the physicality of the swampy Southern landscape to represent Turner's dark mental state. Styron did not set out to write an historical novel, but rather, as he revealed in a 1968 interview for the *Yale Review,* a novel that is a "reflection of an historical incident" and simultaneously a "work of metaphorical and allegorical significance." Styron has described *Confessions* as the "story of man's quest for faith and certitude in a pandemonious world, symbolized by bondage." As such, the novel transcends the limitations of historical reporting.

Despite an initially chilly reception from critics, *Sophie's Choice* (1979) won popular attention and was later made into an Oscar-winning film featuring Meryl Streep. Life after the Nazi death camps frequently left the survivors permanently damaged, and in *Sophie's Choice*, the efforts of Stingo, the native Southerner, are inadequate to save Sophie from a destructive relationship with the mentally unstable Nathan. Styron's Southern sensibility infuses his narrative, drawing on a tradition in the South that dates back to Antebellum times—that of remembering the fallen but relying on the strength of those who remain. Styron's short story, "Shadrach," demonstrates the depths of Southern tradition from the perspective of a former slave. Aged and near death, Shadrach returns to the dilapidated plantation where he was once enslaved because he wishes to die there. He locates remnant descendants of the family who had once owned him. Despite the family's dire financial circumstances and their reluctance to take on the old man, especially when it becomes apparent that burying him will be expensive and will potentially involve a protracted legal struggle, they acquiesce to Shadrach's wishes. Styron inverts the master–slave relationship, placing Shadrach in the position of making demands on his former owners and expecting that he will be cared for because of his former status with the family.

Styron himself came late to the acceptance of his position in Southern letters. In a 1954 interview with Peter Matthiessen and George Plimpton, he forcefully stated that he did not "consider myself in the Southern school, whatever that is. *Lie Down in Darkness*, or most of it was set in the South, but I don't care if I never write about the South again, really." By 1984, Styron softened this stance, musing in an interview with Georgann Eubanks that "I've always had a sense of the uniqueness of my Southern roots. I identify strongly with my father's side of the family, which is ancient. The family goes back in Virginia and North Carolina as far back as you can go in this country . . . I have a very strong attachment to the South as an idea." He elaborates on his sense of detachment from the Southern Renascence-era writers when he continues: "I wouldn't go so far as to say that the South is dead as a source, but I don't think you can say there will be a continuum of Southern literature as we have known it. . . . I don't know if it makes much difference any longer, whether the voice is so distinctive as to make it peculiarly Southern anymore." Styron is not immune to the influence of his literary ancestors of the Southern Renascence, however. Mary Ellen Snodgrass notes that Styron was pleased to find his first three novels in Faulkner's library when he covered the author's funeral in 1962, enjoying the revelation that Faulkner was an admirer of his work.

Styron's literary career has been highlighted by a variety of awards, yet it has taken place in the shadow of his struggle with alcohol and depression, an illness for which he was hospitalized at one time. He reported in his interview with Matthiessen and Plimpton that he prefers to write in the afternoon, when he may be recovering from the previous day's hangover and preparing to imbibe again in the evening. In spite of his personal struggles, Styron's literary productivity has been substantial, earning the Pulitzer Prize in 1967 for *Confessions of Nat Turner*. The controversial *Sophie's Choice* won the coveted American and National Book Awards in 1980. Styron was a founding editor of the *Paris Review* and a founding member of the Fellowship of Southern Writers. He is also a member of the American Academy of Arts and Sciences and the American Academy of Arts and Letters.

Shadrach

My tenth summer on earth, in the year 1935, will never leave my mind because of Shadrach[1] and the way he brightened and darkened my life then and thereafter. He turned up as if from nowhere, arriving at high noon in the village where I grew up in Tidewater Virginia. He was a black apparition of unbelievable antiquity, palsied and feeble, blue-gummed and grinning, a caricature of a caricature at a time when every creaky, superannuated Negro grandsire was (in the eyes of society, not alone the eyes of a small southern white boy) a combination of Stepin Fetchit[2] and Uncle Remus.[3] On that day when he seemed to materialize before us, almost out of the ether, we were playing marbles. Little boys rarely play marbles nowadays but marbles were an obsession in 1935, somewhat predating the yo-yo as a kids' craze. One could admire these elegant many-colored spheres as potentates admire rubies and emeralds; they had a sound yet slippery substantiality, evoking the tactile delight—the same aesthetic yet opulent pleasure—of small precious globes of jade. Thus, among other things, my memory of Shadrach is bound up with the lapidary feel of marbles in my fingers and the odor of cool bare earth on a smoldering hot day beneath a sycamore tree, and still another odor (ineffably a part of the moment): a basic fetor which that squeamish decade christened B.O., and which radiated from a child named Little

1. In the Hebrew Scriptures, one of the three young Hebrew children in the Book of Daniel who were cast into a fiery furnace for their refusal to abandon their religious beliefs. Because of their faith, they were unharmed by the flames.

2. African-American character actor (1902–1985).

3. African-American storyteller created by Joel Chandler Harris. Derided by some contemporary critics as a stereotype of the contented ex-slave, Uncle Remus's stories often drew attention to social and racial inequities.

Mole Dabney, my opponent at marbles. He was ten years old, too, and had never been known to use Lifebuoy soap, or any other cleansing agent.

Which brings me soon enough to the Dabneys. For I realize I must deal with the Dabneys in order to try to explain the encompassing mystery of Shadrach—who after a fashion was a Dabney himself. The Dabneys were not close neighbors; they lived nearby down the road in a rambling weatherworn house that lacked a lawn. On the grassless, graceless terrain of the front yard was a random litter of eviscerated Frigidaires, electric generators, stoves, and the remains of two or three ancient automobiles, whose scavenged carcasses lay abandoned beneath the sycamores like huge rusted insects. Poking up through these husks were masses of weeds and hollyhocks, dandelions gone to seed, sunflowers. Junk and auto parts were a sideline of Mr. Dabney's. He also did odd jobs, but his primary pursuit was bootlegging.

Like such noble Virginia family names as Randolph and Peyton and Tucker and Harrison and Lee and Fitzhugh[4] and a score of others, the patronym Dabney is an illustrious one, but with the present Dabney, christened Vernon, the name had lost almost all of its luster. He should have gone to the University of Virginia; instead, he dropped out of school in the fifth grade. It was not his fault; nor was it his fault that the family had so declined in status. It was said that his father (a true scion of the distinguished old tree but a man with a character defect and a weakness for the bottle) had long ago slid down the social ladder, forfeiting his F.F.V.[5] status by marrying a half-breed Mattaponi or Pamunkey Indian girl from the York River, which accounted perhaps for the black hair and sallowish muddy complexion of the son.

Mr. Dabney—at this time, I imagine he was in his forties—was a runty, hyperactive entrepreneur with a sourly intense, purse-lipped, preoccupied air and a sometimes rampaging temper. He also had a ridiculously foul mouth, from which I learned my first dirty words. It was with delectation, with the same sickishly delighted apprehension of evil that beset me about eight years later when I was accosted by my first prostitute, that I heard Mr. Dabney in his frequent transports of rage use those words forbidden to me in my own home. His blasphemies and obscenities, far from scaring me, caused me to shiver with their splendor. I practiced his words in secret, deriving from their amalgamated filth what, in a dim pediatric way, I could perceive was erotic inflammation. "Son of a bitch whorehouse bat shit Jesus Christ pisspot asshole!" I would screech into an empty closet, and feel my little ten-year-old pecker rise. Yet as ugly and threatening as Mr. Dabney might sometimes appear, I was never really daunted by him, for he had a humane and gentle side. Although he might curse like a stevedore[6] at his wife and children, at the assorted mutts and cats that thronged the place, at the pet billy goat, which he once caught in the act of devouring his new three-dollar Thom McAn shoes, I soon saw that even his most murderous fits were largely bluster. This would include his loud and eccentric dislike of Franklin D. Roosevelt. Most down-and-out people of the Tidewater revered F.D.R.,[7] like poor people everywhere; not Mr. Dabney. Much later I surmised that his tantrums probably derived from a pining to return to his aristocratic origins.

Oh, how I loved the Dabneys! I actually wanted to *be* a Dabney—wanted to change my name from Paul Whitehurst to Paul Dabney. I visited the Dabney home-

4. Each of these names belonged to "First Families of Virginia" (FFV); many had illustrious careers as military officers, politicians, and attorneys.
5. First Families of Virginia.
6. Worker who either unloads cargo from merchant ships or oversees others doing this work.
7. Franklin Delano Roosevelt, thirty-second president of the United States who established the New Deal that pulled America out of the Great Depression.

stead as often as I could, basking in its casual squalor. I must avoid giving the impression of Tobacco Road;[8] the Dabneys were of better quality. Yet there were similarities. The mother, named Trixie, was a huge sweaty generous sugarloaf of a woman, often drunk. It was she, I am sure, who propagated the domestic sloppiness. But I loved her passionately, just as I loved and envied the whole Dabney tribe and that total absence in them of the bourgeois aspirations and gentility which were my own inheritance. I envied the sheer teeming multitude of the Dabneys—there were seven children—which made my status as an only child seem so effete, spoiled, and lonesome. Only illicit whiskey kept the family from complete destitution, and I envied their near poverty. Also their religion. They were Baptists: as a Presbyterian I envied that. To be totally immersed—how wet and natural! They lived in a house devoid of books or any reading matter except funny papers—more envy. I envied their abandoned slovenliness, their sour unmade beds, their roaches, the cracked linoleum on the floor, the homely cur dogs leprous with mange that foraged at will through house and yard. My perverse longings were—to turn around a phrase unknown at the time—downwardly mobile. Afflicted at the age of ten by *nostalgie de la boue*,[9] I felt deprived of a certain depravity. I was too young to know, of course, that one of the countless things of which the Dabneys were victims was the Great Depression.

Yet beneath this scruffy façade, the Dabneys were a family of some property. Although their ramshackle house was rented, as were most of the dwellings in our village, they owned a place elsewhere, and there was occasionally chatter in the household about "the Farm," far upriver in King and Queen County. Mr. Dabney had inherited the place from his dissolute father and it had been in the family for generations. It could not have been much of a holding, or else it would have been sold years before, and when, long afterward, I came to absorb the history of the Virginia Tidewater—that primordial American demesne[10] where the land was sucked dry by tobacco, laid waste and destroyed a whole century before golden California became an idea, much less a hope or a westward dream—I realized that the Dabney farm must have been as nondescript and as pathetic a relic as any of the scores of shrunken, abandoned "plantations" scattered for a hundred miles across the tidelands between the Potomac and the James. The chrysalis, unpainted, of a dinky, thrice-rebuilt farmhouse with a few mean acres in corn and second-growth timber—that was all. Nonetheless it was to this ancestral dwelling that the nine Dabneys, packed like squirming eels into a fifteen-year-old Model T Ford pockmarked with the ulcers of terminal decay, would go forth for a month's sojourn each August, as seemingly bland and blasé about their customary estivation as Rockefellers decamping to Pocantico Hills. But they were not entirely vacationing. I did not know then but discovered later that the woodland glens and lost glades of the depopulated land of King and Queen were every moonshiner's dream for hideaways in which to decoct white lightning, and the exodus to "the Farm" served a purpose beyond the purely recreative: each Dabney, of whatever age and sex, had at least a hand in the operation of the still, even if it was simply shucking corn.

All of the three Dabney boys bore the nickname Mole, being differentiated from each other by a logical nomenclature—Little, Middle, and Big Mole; I don't think I ever knew their real names. It was the youngest of the three Moles I was playing marbles with when Shadrach made his appearance. Little Mole was a child

8. Erskine Caldwell's novel of this title is a literary depiction of abject and hopeless poverty.
9. Literally, nostalgia of mud.
10. According to the *Oxford English Dictionary*: to hold in one's own hands as possessor by free tenure.

of stunning ugliness, sharing with his brothers an inherited mixture of bulging thyroid eyes, mashed-in spoonlike nose, and jutting jaw that (I say in retrospect) might have nicely corresponded to Cesare Lombroso's[11] description of the criminal physiognomy. Something more remarkable—accounting surely for their collective nickname—was the fact that save for their graduated sizes they were nearly exact replicas of each other, appearing related less as brothers than as monotonous clones, as if Big Mole had reproduced Middle, who in turn had created Little, my evil-smelling playmate. None of the Moles ever wished or was ever required to bathe, and this accounted for another phenomenon. At the vast and dismal consolidated rural school we attended, one could mark the presence of any of the three Dabney brothers in a classroom by the ring of empty desks isolating each Mole from his classmates, who, edging away without apology from the effluvium, would leave the poor Mole abandoned in his aloneness, like some species of bacterium on a microscope slide whose noxious discharge has destroyed all life in a circle around it.

By contrast—the absurdity of genetics!—the four Dabney girls were fair, fragrant in their Woolworth perfumes, buxom, lusciously ripe of hindquarter, at least two of them knocked up and wed before attaining full growth. Oh, those lost beauties. . . .

That day Little Mole took aim with a glittering taw of surreal chalcedony; he had warts on his fingers, his odor in my nostrils was quintessential Mole. He sent my agate spinning into the weeds.

Shadrach appeared then. We somehow sensed his presence, looked up, and found him there. We had not heard him approach; he had come as silently and portentously as if he had been lowered on some celestial apparatus operated by unseen hands. He was astoundingly black. I had never seen a Negro of that impenetrable hue: it was blackness of such intensity that it reflected no light at all, achieving a virtual obliteration of facial features and taking on a mysterious undertone that had the blue-gray of ashes. Perched on a fender, he was grinning at us from the rusted frame of a demolished Pierce-Arrow. It was a blissful grin, which revealed deathly purple gums, the yellowish stumps of two teeth, and a wet mobile tongue. For a long while he said nothing but, continuing to grin, contentedly rooted at his crotch with a hand warped and wrinkled with age: the bones moved beneath the black skin in clear skeletal outline. With his other hand he firmly grasped a walking stick.

It was then that I felt myself draw a breath in wonder at his age, which was surely unfathomable. He looked older than all the patriarchs of Genesis whose names flooded my mind in a Sunday school litany: Lamech, Noah, Enoch, and that perdurable old Jewish fossil Methuselah.[12] Little Mole and I drew closer, and I saw then that the old man had to be at least partially blind; cataracts clouded his eyes like milky cauls,[13] the corneas swam with rheum. Yet he was not entirely without sight. I sensed the way he observed our approach; above the implacable sweet grin there were flickers of wise recognition. His presence remained worrisomely biblical; I felt myself drawn to him with an almost devout

11. Italian physician, psychiatrist, and pioneer criminologist whose 1876 book, *Criminal Man*, drew upon Charles Darwin's theories of evolution to explain human criminal behavior.

12. In the Hebrew Scriptures, Lamech was a descendent of Cain, which caused him to be cursed. He was also the father of Noah, whom God charged with building an ark to save himself and his family from the impending flood that would destroy the world. Enoch was the father of Methuselah, and because he walked with God, was translated directly to heaven without experiencing death. Methuselah lived to be nearly 1,000 years old.

13. In folklore, a caul is often a sign of other-worldly insight and perception and may also signal good luck. A caul was believed to give its possessor the power to see and communicate with the spirits of the dead.

compulsion, as if he were the prophet Elijah[14] sent to bring truth, light, the Word. The shiny black mohair mail-order suit he wore was baggy and frayed, streaked with dust; the cuffs hung loose, and from one of the ripped ankle-high clodhoppers protruded a naked black toe. Even so, the presence was thrillingly ecclesiastical and fed my piety.

It was midsummer. The very trees seemed to hover on the edge of combustion; a mockingbird began to chant nearby in notes rippling and clear. I walked closer to the granddaddy through a swarm of fat green flies supping hungrily on the assorted offal carpeting the Dabney yard. Streams of sweat were pouring off the ancient black face. Finally I heard him speak, in a senescent voice so faint and garbled that it took moments for it to penetrate my understanding. But I understood: "Praise de Lawd. Praise his sweet name! Ise arrived in Ole Virginny!"

He beckoned to me with one of his elongated, bony, bituminous fingers; at first it alarmed me but then the finger seemed to move appealingly, like a small harmless snake. "Climb up on ole Shad's knee," he said. I was beginning to get the hang of his gluey diction, realized that it was a matter of listening to certain internal rhythms; even so, with the throaty gulping sound of Africa in it, it was nigger talk I had never heard before. "Jes climb up," he commanded. I obeyed. I obeyed with love and eagerness; it was like creeping up against the bosom of Abraham. In the collapsed old lap I sat happily, fingering a brass chain which wound across the grease-shiny vest; at the end of the chain, dangling, was a nickel-plated watch upon the face of which the black mitts of Mickey Mouse marked the noontime hour. Giggling now, snuggled against the ministerial breast, I inhaled the odor of great age—indefinable, not exactly unpleasant but stale, like a long-unopened cupboard—mingled with the smell of unlaundered fabric and dust. Only inches away the tongue quivered like a pink clapper in the dark gorge of a cavernous bell. "You jes a sweetie," he crooned. "Is you a Dabney?" I replied with regret, "No," and pointed to Little Mole. "That's a Dabney," I said.

"You a sweetie, too," he said, summoning Little Mole with the outstretched forefinger, black, palsied, wiggling. "Oh, you jes de sweetest thing!" The voice rose joyfully. Little Mole looked perplexed. I felt Shadrach's entire body quiver; to my mystification he was overcome with emotion at beholding a flesh-and-blood Dabney, and as he reached toward the boy I heard him breathe again: "Praise de Lawd! Ise arrived in Ole Virginny!"

Then at that instant Shadrach suffered a cataclysmic crisis—one that plainly had to do with the fearful heat. He could not, of course, grow pallid, but something enormous and vital did dissolve within the black eternity of his face; the wrinkled old skin of his cheeks sagged, his milky eyes rolled blindly upward, and uttering a soft moan, he fell back across the car's ruptured seat with its naked springs and its holes disgorging horsehair.

"Watah!" I heard him cry feebly, "*Watah!*" I slid out of his lap, watched the scrawny black legs no bigger around than pine saplings begin to shake and twitch. "Watah, please!" I heard the voice implore, but Little Mole and I needed no further urging; we were gone—racing headlong to the kitchen and the cluttered, reeking sink. "That old cullud man's dying!" Little Mole wailed. We got a cracked jelly glass, ran water from the faucet in a panic, speculating as we did: Little Mole ventured the notion of a heat stroke; I theorized a heart attack. We screamed and babbled; we debated whether the water should be at body temperature or iced. Little Mole added

14. According to the Hebrew Scriptures, Elijah was a prophet in the era before Christ. Like Enoch, he was translated directly to heaven.

half a cupful of salt, then decided that the water should be hot. Our long delay was fortunate, for several moments later, as we hurried with the terrible potion to Shadrach's side, we found that the elder Dabney had appeared from a far corner of the yard and, taking command of the emergency, had pried Shadrach away from the seat of the Pierce-Arrow, dragged or carried him across the plot of bare earth, propped him up against a tree trunk, and now stood sluicing water from a garden hose into Shadrach's gaping mouth. The old man gulped his fill. Then Mr. Dabney, small and fiercely intent in his baggy overalls, hunched down over the stricken patriarch, whipped out a pint bottle from his pocket, and poured a stream of crystalline whiskey down Shadrach's gorge. While he did this he muttered to himself in tones of incredulity and inwardly tickled amazement: "Well, kiss my ass! Who are you, old uncle? Just who in the goddamned hell *are* you?"

We heard Shadrach give a strangled cough; then he began to try out something resembling speech. But the word he was almost able to produce was swallowed and lost in the hollow of his throat.

"What did he say? What did he say?" Mr. Dabney demanded impatiently.

"He said his name is Shadrach!" I shouted, proud that I alone seemed able to fathom this obscure Negro dialect, further muddied by the crippled cadences of senility.

"What's he want, Paul?" Mr. Dabney said to me.

I bent my face toward Shadrach's, which looked contented again. His voice in my ear was at once whispery and sweet, a gargle of beatitude: "Die on Dabney ground."

"I think he said," I told Mr. Dabney at last, "that he wants to die on Dabney ground."

"Well, I'll be goddamned," said Mr. Dabney.

"Praise de Lawd!" Shadrach cried suddenly, in a voice that even Mr. Dabney could understand. "Ise arrived in Ole Virginny!"

Mr. Dabney roared at me: "Ask him where he came from!"

Again I inclined my face to that black shrunken visage upturned to the blazing sun; I whispered the question and the reply came back after a long silence, in fitful stammerings. At last I said to Mr. Dabney: "He says he's from Clay County down in Alabama."

"*Alabama!* Well, kiss my ass!"

I felt Shadrach pluck at my sleeve and once more I bent down to listen. Many seconds passed before I could discover the outlines of the words struggling for meaning on the flailing, ungovernable tongue. But finally I captured their shapes, arranged them in order.

"What did he say now, Paul?" Mr. Dabney said.

"He said he wants you to bury him."

"*Bury him!*" Mr. Dabney shouted. "How can I bury him? He ain't even dead yet!"

From Shadrach's breast there now came a gentle keening sound which, commencing on a note of the purest grief, startled me by the way it resolved itself suddenly into a mild faraway chuckle; the moonshine was taking hold. The pink clapper of a tongue lolled in the cave of the jagged old mouth. Shadrach grinned.

"Ask him how old he is, Paul," came the command. I asked him. "Nimenime" was the glutinous reply.

"He says he's ninety-nine years old," I reported, glancing up from the ageless abyss.

"*Ninety-nine!* Well, I'll be goddamned!"

Now other Dabneys began to arrive, including the mother, Trixie, and the two larger Moles, along with one of the older teenage daughters, whalelike but meltingly beautiful as she floated on the crest of her pregnancy, and accompanied by her hulking, acne-cratered teenage spouse. There also came a murmuring clutch of neighbors—sun-reddened shipyard workers in cheap sport shirts, scampering towhead children, a quartet of scrawny housewives in sacklike dresses, bluish crescents of sweat beneath their arms. In my memory they make an aching tableau of those exhausted years. They jabbered and clucked in wonder at Shadrach, who, immobilized by alcohol, heat, infirmity, and his ninety-nine Augusts, beamed and raised his rheumy eyes to the sun. "Praise de Lawd!" he quavered.

We hoisted him to his feet and supported the frail, almost weightless old frame as he limped on dancing tiptoe to the house, where we settled him down upon a rump-sprung glider that squatted on the back porch in an ambient fragrance of dog urine, tobacco smoke, and mildew. "You hungry, Shad?" Mr. Dabney bellowed. "Mama, get Shadrach something to eat!" Slumped in the glider, the ancient visitor gorged himself like one plucked from the edge of critical starvation: he devoured three cantaloupes, slurped down bowl after bowl of Rice Krispies, and gummed his way through a panful of hot cornbread smeared with lard. We watched silently, in wonderment. Before our solemnly attentive eyes he gently and carefully eased himself back on the malodorous pillows and with a soft sigh went to sleep.

Some time after this—during the waning hours of the afternoon, when Shadrach woke up, and then on into the evening—the mystery of the old man's appearance became gradually unlocked. One of the Dabney daughters was a fawn-faced creature of twelve named Edmonia; her fragile beauty (especially when contrasted with ill-favored brothers) and her precocious breasts and bottom had caused me—young as I was—a troubling, unresolved itch. I was awed by the ease and nonchalance with which she wiped the drool from Shadrach's lips. Like me, she possessed some inborn gift of interpretation, and through our joint efforts there was pieced together over several hours an explanation for this old man—for his identity and his bizarre and inescapable coming.

He stayed on the glider; we put another pillow under his head. Nourishing his dragon's appetite with Hershey bars and, later on, with nips from Mr. Dabney's bottle, we were able to coax from those aged lips a fragmented, abbreviated, but reasonably coherent biography. After a while it became an anxious business for, as one of the adults noticed, old Shad seemed to be running a fever; his half-blind eyes swam about from time to time, and the clotted phlegm that rose in his throat made it all the more difficult to understand anything. But somehow we began to divine the truth. One phrase, repeated over and over, I particularly remember: "Ise a Dabney." And indeed those words provided the chief clue to his story.

Born a slave on the Dabney plantation in King and Queen County, he had been sold down to Alabama in the decades before the Civil War. Shadrach's memory was imperfect regarding the date of his sale. Once he said "fifty," meaning 1850, and another time he said "fifty-five," but it was an item of little importance; he was probably somewhere between fifteen and twenty-five years old when his master—Vernon Dabney's great-grandfather—disposed of him, selling him to one of the many traders prowling the worn-out Virginia soil of that stricken bygone era; and since in his confessional to us, garbled as it was, he used the word "coffle"[15] (a word beyond my ten-year-old knowledge but one whose meaning I later understood), he must have journeyed those six hundred miles to Alabama on foot and in the company of God knows how many other black slaves, linked together by chains.

15. A gang of slaves chained together for the purposes of working or driving them from one place to another.

So now, as we began slowly to discover, this was Shadrach's return trip home to Ole Virginny—three quarters of a century or thereabouts after his departure from the land out of which he had sprung, which had nurtured him, and where he had lived his happy years. Happy? Who knows? But we had to assume they were his happy years—else why this incredible pilgrimage at the end of his life? As he had announced with such abrupt fervor earlier, he wanted only to die and be buried on "Dabney ground."

We learned that after the war he had become a sharecropper, that he had married three times and had had many children (once he said twelve, another time fifteen; no matter, they were legion); he had outlived them all, wives and offspring. Even the grandchildren had died off, or had somehow vanished. "Ah was dibested of all mah plenty" was another statement I can still record verbatim. Thus divested and (as he cheerfully made plain to all who gathered around him to listen) sensing mortality in his own shriveled flesh and bones, he had departed Alabama on foot—just as he had come there—to find the Virginia of his youth.

Six hundred miles! The trip, we were able to gather, took over four months, since he said he set out from Clay County in the early spring. He walked nearly the entire way, although now and then he would accept a ride—almost always, one can be sure, from the few Negroes who owned cars in the rural South of those years. He had saved up a few dollars, which allowed him to provide for his stomach. He slept on the side of the road or in barns; sometimes a friendly Negro family would give him shelter. The trek took him across Georgia and the Carolinas and through Southside Virginia. His itinerary is still anyone's conjecture. Because he could not read either road sign or road map, he obviously followed his own northward-questing nose, a profoundly imperfect method of finding one's way (he allowed to Edmonia with a faint cackle), since he once got so far astray that he ended up not only miles away from the proper highway but in a city and state completely off his route—Chattanooga, Tennessee. But he circled back and moved on. And how, once arrived in Virginia with its teeming Dabneys, did he discover the only Dabney who would matter, the single Dabney who was not merely the proprietor of his birthplace but the one whom he also unquestioningly expected to oversee his swiftly approaching departure, laying him to rest in the earth of their mutual ancestors? How did he find *Vernon Dabney*? Mr. Dabney was by no means an ill-spirited or ungenerous man (despite his runaway temper), but was a soul nonetheless beset by many woes in the dingy threadbare year 1935, being hard pressed not merely for dollars but for dimes and quarters, crushed beneath an elephantine and inebriate wife, along with three generally shiftless sons and two knocked-up daughters, plus two more likely to be so, and living with the abiding threat of revenue agents swooping down to terminate his livelihood and, perhaps, get him sent to the Atlanta penitentiary for five or six years. He needed no more cares or burdens, and now in the hot katydid-shrill hours of summer night I saw him gaze down at the leathery old dying black face with an expression that mingled compassion and bewilderment and stoppered-up rage and desperation, and then whisper to himself: "He wants to die on Dabney ground! Well, kiss my ass, just kiss my ass!" Plainly he wondered how, among all his horde of Virginia kinfolk, Shadrach found *him*, for he squatted low and murmured: "Shad! Shad, how come you knew who to look for?" But in his fever Shadrach had drifted off to sleep, and so far as I ever knew there was never any answer to that.

* * *

The next day it was plain that Shadrach was badly off. During the night he had somehow fallen from the glider, and in the early morning hours he was discovered on the floor, leaking blood. We bandaged him up. The wound just above his ear was superficial, as it turned out, but it had done him no good; and when he was replaced on the swing he appeared to be confused and at the edge of delirium, plucking at his shirt, whispering, and rolling his gentle opaque eyes at the ceiling. Whenever he spoke now, his words were beyond the power of Edmonia or me to comprehend, faint highpitched mumbo jumbo in a drowned dialect. He seemed to recognize no one. Trixie, leaning over the old man as she sucked at her first Pabst Blue Ribbon[16] of the morning, decided firmly that there was no time to waste. "Shoog," she said to Mr. Dabney, using her habitual pet name (diminutive form of Sugar), "you better get out the car if we're goin' to the Farm. I think he ain't gone last much longer." And so, given unusual parental leave to go along on the trip, I squeezed myself into the backseat of the Model T, privileged to hold in my lap a huge greasy paper bag full of fried chicken which Trixie had prepared for noontime dinner at the Farm.

Not all of the Dabneys made the journey—the two older daughters and the largest Mole were left behind—but we still composed a multitude. We children were packed sweatily skin to skin and atop each other's laps in the rear seat, which reproduced in miniature the messiness of the house with this new litter of empty RC Cola and Nehi bottles, funny papers, watermelon rinds, banana peels, greasy jack handles, oil-smeared gears of assorted sizes, and wads of old Kleenex. On the floor beneath my feet I even discerned (to my intense discomfort, for I had just learned to recognize such an object) a crumpled, yellowish used condom, left there haphazardly, I was certain, by one of the older daughters' boyfriends who had been able to borrow the heap for carnal sport. It was a bright summer day, scorchingly hot like the day preceding it, but the car had no workable windows and we were pleasantly ventilated. Shadrach sat in the middle of the front seat. Mr. Dabney was hunched over the wheel, chewing at a wad of tobacco and driving with black absorption; he had stripped to his undershirt, and I thought I could almost see the rage and frustration in the tight bunched muscles of his neck. He muttered curses at the balky gearshift but otherwise said little, rapt in his guardian misery. So voluminous that the flesh of her shoulders fell in a freckled cascade over the back of her seat, Trixie loomed on the other side of Shadrach; the corpulence of her body seemed in some way to both enfold and support the old man, who nodded and dozed. The encircling hair around the shiny black head was, I thought, like a delicate halo of the purest frost or foam. Curiously, for the first time since Shadrach's coming, I felt a stab of grief and achingly wanted him not to die.

"Shoog," said Trixie, standing by the rail of the dumpy little ferry that crossed the York River, "what kind of big birds do you reckon those are behind that boat there?" The Model T had been the first car aboard, and all of us had flocked out to look at the river, leaving Shadrach to sit there and sleep during the fifteen-minute ride. The water was blue, sparkling with whitecaps, lovely. A huge gray naval tug with white markings chugged along to the mine depot at Yorktown,[17] trailing eddies of garbage and a swooping flock of frantic gulls. Their squeals echoed across the peaceful channel.

"Seagulls," said Mr. Dabney. "Ain't you never recognized seagulls before? I can't believe such a question. Seagulls. Dumb greedy bastards."

"Beautiful things," she replied softly, "all big and white. Can you eat one?"

"So tough you'd like to choke to death."

16. An inexpensive brand of beer.

17. In Virginia, the site of the British surrender to the colonists at the conclusion of the American Revolution.

We were halfway across the river when Edmonia went to the car to get a ginger ale. When she came back she said hesitantly: "Mama, Shadrach has made a fantastic mess in his pants."

"Oh, Lord," said Trixie.

Mr. Dabney clutched the rail and raised his small, pinched, tormented face to heaven. "Ninety-nine years old! Christ almighty! He ain't nothin' but a ninety-nine-years-old *baby!*"

"It smells just awful," said Edmonia.

"Why in the goddamned hell didn't he go to the bathroom before we left?" Mr. Dabney said. "Ain't it bad enough we got to drive three hours to the Farm without—"

"*Shoosh!*" Trixie interrupted, moving ponderously to the car. "Poor ol' thing, he can't help it. Vernon, you see how you manage your bowels fifty years from now."

Once off the ferry we children giggled and squirmed in the backseat, pointedly squeezed our noses, and scuffled amid the oily rubbish of the floorboards. It *was* an awful smell. But a few miles up the road in the hamlet of Gloucester Court House, drowsing in eighteenth-century brick and ivy, Trixie brought relief to the situation by bidding Mr. Dabney to stop at an Amoco station. Shadrach had partly awakened from his slumbrous trance. He stirred restlessly in his pool of discomfort, and began to make little fretful sounds, so softly restrained as to barely give voice to what must have been his real and terrible distress. "There now, Shad," Trixie said gently, "Trixie'll look after you." And this she did, half-coaxing, half-hoisting the old man from the car and into a standing position, then with the help of Mr. Dabney propelling his skinny scarecrow frame in a suspended tiptoe dance to the rest room marked COLORED, where to the muffled sound of rushing water she performed some careful rite of cleansing and diapering. Then they brought him back to the car. For the first time that morning Shadrach seemed really aroused from that stupor into which he had plunged so swiftly hours before. "Praise de Lawd!" we heard him say, feebly but with spirit, as the elder Dabneys maneuvered him back onto the seat, purified. He gazed about him with glints of recognition, responding with soft chuckles to our little pats of attention. Even Mr. Dabney seemed in sudden good humor. "You comin' along all right now, Shad?" he howled over the rackety clattering sound of the motor. Shadrach nodded and grinned but remained silent. There was a mood in the car of joy and revival. "Slow down, Shoog," Trixie murmured indolently, gulping at a beer, "there might be a speed cop." I was filled with elation, and hope tugged at my heart as the flowering landscape rushed by, green and lush with summer and smelling of hay and honeysuckle.

The Dabney country retreat, as I have said, was dilapidated and rudimentary, a true downfall from bygone majesty. Where there once stood a plantation house of the Palladian stateliness required of its kind during the Tidewater dominion in its heyday, there now roosted a dwelling considerably grander than a shack yet modest by any reckoning. Boxlike, paintless, supported by naked concrete blocks, and crowned by a roof of glistening sheet metal, it would have been an eyesore almost anywhere except in King and Queen County, a bailiwick so distant and underpopulated that the house was scarcely ever viewed by human eyes. A tilted privy out back lent another homely note; junk littered the yard here too. But the soft green acres that surrounded the place were Elysian; the ancient fields and the wild woods rampant with sweet gum and oak and redbud had reverted to the primeval glory of the time of Pocahontas and Powhatan. Grapevines crowded the emerald-green thickets that bordered the house on every side, a delicious winey smell of cedar filled the air, and the forest at night echoed with the sound of whippoorwills. The house itself was relatively clean, thanks not to any effort on the part of the Dabneys but to the fact that it remained unlived in by Dabneys for most of the year.

That day after our fried chicken meal we placed Shadrach between clean sheets on a bed in one of the sparsely furnished rooms, then turned to our various recreations. Little Mole and I played marbles all afternoon just outside the house, seeking the shade of a majestic old beech tree; after an hour of crawling in the dirt our faces were streaked and filthy. Later we took a plunge in the millpond, which, among other things, purged Little Mole of his B.O. The other children went fishing for perch and bream in the brackish creek that ran through the woods. Mr. Dabney drove off to get provisions at the crossroads store, then vanished into the underbrush to tinker around his well-hidden still. Meanwhile Trixie tramped about with heavy footfalls in the kitchen and downed half a dozen Blue Ribbons, pausing occasionally to look in on Shadrach. Little Mole and I peered in, too, from time to time. Shadrach lay in a deep sleep and seemed to be at peace, even though now and then his breath came in a ragged gasp and his long black fingers plucked convulsively at the hem of the sheet, which covered him to his breast like a white shroud. Then the afternoon was over. After a dinner of fried perch and bream we all went to bed with the setting of the sun. Little Mole and I lay sprawled naked in the heat on the same mattress, separated by a paper-thin wall from Shadrach's breathing, which rose and fell in my ears against the other night sounds of this faraway and time-haunted place: katydids and crickets and hoot owls and the reassuring cheer—now near, now almost lost—of a whippoorwill.

Late the next morning the county sheriff paid a visit on Mr. Dabney. We were not at the house when he arrived, and so he had to wait for us; we were at the graveyard. Shadrach still slept, with the children standing watch by turns. After our watch Little Mole and I had spent an hour exploring the woods and swinging on the grapevines, and when we emerged from a grove of pine trees a quarter of a mile or so behind the house, we came upon Mr. Dabney and Trixie. They were poking about in a bramble-filled plot of land which was the old Dabney family burial ground. It was a sunny, peaceful place, where grasshoppers skittered in the tall grass. Choked with briars and nettles and weeds and littered with tumbledown stone markers, unfenced and untended for countless decades, it had been abandoned to the encroachments of summer after summer like this one, when even granite and marble had to give way against the stranglehold of spreading roots and voracious green growing things.

All of Mr. Dabney's remote ancestors lay buried here, together with their slaves, who slept in a plot several feet off to the side—inseparable from their masters and mistresses, but steadfastly apart in death as in life. Mr. Dabney stood amid the tombstones of the slaves, glaring gloomily down at the tangle of vegetation and at the crumbling lopsided little markers. He held a shovel in his hand but had not begun to dig. I peered at the headstones, read the given names, which were as matter-of-fact in their lack of patronymic as the names of spaniels or cats: *Fauntleroy, Wakefield, Sweet Betty, Mary, Jupiter, Lulu. Requiescat in Pace. Anno Domini 1790 . . . 1814 . . . 1831*. All of these Dabneys, I thought, like Shadrach.

"I'll be goddamned if I believe there's a square inch of space left," Mr. Dabney observed to Trixie, and spat a russet gob of tobacco juice into the weeds. "They just crowded all the old dead uncles and mammies they could into this piece of land here. They must be shoulder to shoulder down there." He paused and made his characteristic sound of anguish—a choked dirgelike groan. "Christ Almighty! I hate to think of diggin' about half a ton of dirt!"

"Shoog, why don't you leave off diggin' until this evenin'?" Trixie said. She was trying to fan herself with a soggy handkerchief, and her face—which I had witnessed before in this state of drastic summer discomfort—wore the washed-out bluish shade of skim milk. It usually preceded a fainting spell. "This sun would kill a mule."

Mr. Dabney agreed, saying that he looked forward to a cool glass of iced tea, and we made our way back to the house along a little path of bare earth that wound through a field glistening with goldenrod. Then, just as we arrived at the back of the house we saw the sheriff waiting. He was standing with a foot on the running board of his Plymouth sedan; perched on its front fender was a hulkingly round, intimidating silver siren (in those days pronounced si-*reen*). He was a potbellied middle-aged man with a sun-scorched face fissured with delicate seams, and he wore steel-rimmed spectacles. A gold-plated star was pinned to his civilian shirt, which was soaked with sweat. He appeared hearty, made an informal salute and said: "Mornin', Trixie, Mornin', Vern."

"Mornin', Tazewell," Mr. Dabney replied solemnly, though with an edge of suspicion. Without pause he continued to trudge toward the house. "You want some ice tea?"

"No, thank you," he said. "Vern, hold on a minute. I'd like a word with you."

I was knowledgeable enough to fear in a vague way some involvement with the distillery in the woods, and I held my breath, but then Mr. Dabney halted, turned, and said evenly: "What's wrong?"

"Vern," the sheriff said, "I hear you're fixin' to bury an elderly colored man on your property here. Joe Thornton down at the store said you told him that yesterday. Is that right?"

Mr. Dabney put his hands on his hips and glowered at the sheriff. Then he said: "Joe Thornton is a goddamned incurable blabbermouth. But that's right. What's wrong with that?"

"You can't," said the sheriff.

There was a pause. "Why not?" said Mr. Dabney.

"Because it's against the law."

I had seen rage, especially in matters involving the law, build up within Mr. Dabney in the past. A pulsing vein always appeared near his temple, along with a rising flush in cheeks and brow; both came now, the little vein began to wiggle and squirm like a worm. "What do you mean, it's against the law?"

"Just that. It's against the law to bury anybody on private property."

"*Why* is it against the law?" Mr. Dabney demanded.

"I don't *know* why, Vern," said the sheriff, with a touch of exasperation. "It just *is*, that's all."

Mr. Dabney flung his arm out—up and then down in a stiff, adamant, unrelenting gesture, like a railroad semaphore.

"Down in that field, Tazewell, there have been people buried for nearabout two hundred years. I got an old senile man on my hands. He was a slave and he was born on this place. Now he's dyin' and I've got to bury him here. And I am."

"Vern, let me tell you something," the sheriff said with an attempt at patience. "You will not be permitted to do any such a thing, so please don't try to give me this argument. He will have to be buried in a place where it's legally permitted, like any of the colored churchyards around here, and he will have to be attended to by a licensed colored undertaker. That's the *law,* Commonwealth of Virginia, and there ain't any which, whys, or wherefores about it."

Trixie began to anticipate Mr. Dabney's fury and resentment even before he erupted. "Shoog, keep yourself calm —"

"*Bat shit!* It is an *outrage!*" he roared. "Since when did a taxpaying citizen have to answer to the gov'ment in order to bury a harmless sick old colored man on his own property! It goes against every bill of rights I ever heard of —"

"Shoog!" Trixie put in. "*Please*—" She began to wail.

The sheriff put out placating hands and loudly commanded: "*Quiet!*" Then when Mr. Dabney and Trixie fell silent he went on: "Vern, me an' you have been acquainted for a long time, so please don't give me no trouble. I'm tellin' you for the last time, this. Namely, you have *got* to arrange to get that old man buried at one of the colored churches around here, and you will also have to have him taken care of by a licensed undertaker. You can have your choice. There's a well-known colored undertaker in Tappahannock and also I heard of one over in Middlesex, somewhere near Urbanna or Saluda. If you want, I'll give them a telephone call from the courthouse."

I watched as the red rage in Mr. Dabney's face was overtaken by a paler, softer hue of resignation. After a brooding long silence, he said: "All right then. *All right!* How much you reckon it'll cost?"

"I don't know exactly, Vern, but there was an old washerwoman worked for me and Ruby died not long ago, and I heard they buried her for thirty-five dollars."

"*Thirty-five dollars!*" I heard Mr. Dabney breathe. "Christ have mercy!"

Perhaps it was only his rage that caused him to flee, but all afternoon Mr. Dabney was gone and we did not see him again until that evening. Meanwhile, Shadrach rallied for a time from his deep slumber, so taking us by surprise that we thought he might revive completely. Trixie was shelling peas and sipping beer while she watched Little Mole and me at our marbles game. Suddenly Edmonia, who had been assigned to tend to Shadrach for an hour, came running from the house. "Come here, you all, real quick!" she said in a voice out of breath. "Shadrach's wide awake and talking!" And he was: when we rushed to his side we saw that he had hiked himself up in bed, and his face for the first time in many hours wore an alert and knowing expression, as if he were at least partially aware of his surroundings. He had even regained his appetite. Edmonia had put a daisy in the buttonhole of his shirt, and at some point during his amazing resurrection, she said, he had eaten part of it.

"You should have heard him just now," Edmonia said, leaning over the bed. "He kept talking about going to the millpond. What do you think he meant?"

"Well, could be he just wants to go see the millpond," Trixie replied. She had brought Shadrach a bottle of RC Cola from the kitchen and now she sat beside him, helping him to drink it through a paper straw. "Shad," she asked in a soft voice, "is that what you want? You want to go see the millpond?"

A look of anticipation and pleasure spread over the black face and possessed those old rheumy eyes. And his voice was high-pitched but strong when he turned his head to Trixie and said: "Yes, ma'am, I does. I wants to see de millpond."

"How come you want to see the millpond?" Trixie said gently.

Shadrach offered no explanation, merely said again: "I wants to see de millpond."

And so, in obedience to a wish whose reason we were unable to plumb but could not help honoring, we took Shadrach to see the millpond. It lay in the woods several hundred yards to the east of the house—an ageless murky dammed-up pool bordered on one side by a glade of moss and fern, spectacularly green, and surrounded on all its other sides by towering oaks and elms. Fed by springs and by the same swiftly rushing stream in which the other children had gone fishing, its water mirrored the overhanging trees and the changing sky and was a pleasurable ordeal to swim in, possessing the icy cold that shocks a body to its bones. For a while we could not figure out how to transport Shadrach down to the place; it plainly would not do to let him try to hobble that long distance, propelled, with our clumsy help, on his nearly strengthless legs in their dangling gait. Finally someone thought of the wheelbarrow, which Mr. Dabney used to haul corn to the still. It was fetched from its shed, and we quickly made of it a not unhandsome and passably comfortable sort of a wheeled litter, filling it with hay and placing a blanket on top.

On this mound Shadrach rested easily, with a look of composure, as we moved him gently rocking down the path. I watched him on the way: in my memory he still appears to be a half-blind but self-possessed and serene African potentate being borne in the fullness of his many years to some longed-for, inevitable reward.

We set the wheelbarrow down on the mossy bank, and there for a long time Shadrach gazed at the millpond, alive with its skating waterbugs and trembling beneath a copper-colored haze of sunlight where small dragonflies swooped in nervous filmy iridescence. Standing next to the wheelbarrow, out of which the shanks of Shadrach's skinny legs protruded like fragile black reeds, I turned and stared into the ancient face, trying to determine what it was he beheld now that created such a look of wistfulness and repose. His eyes began to follow the Dabney children, who had stripped to their underdrawers and had plunged into the water. That seemed to be an answer, and in a bright gleam I was certain that Shadrach had once swum here too, during some unimaginable August nearly a hundred years before.

I had no way of knowing that if his long and solitary journey from the Deep South had been a quest to find this millpond and for a recaptured glimpse of childhood, it might just as readily have been a final turning of his back on a life of suffering. Even now I cannot say for certain, but I have always had to assume that the still-young Shadrach who was emancipated in Alabama those many years ago was set loose, like most of his brothers and sisters, into another slavery perhaps more excruciating than the sanctioned bondage. The chronicle has already been a thousand times told of those people liberated into their new and incomprehensible nightmare: of their poverty and hunger and humiliation, of the crosses burning in the night, the random butchery, and, above all, the unending dread. None of that madness and mayhem belongs in this story, but without at least a reminder of these things I would not be faithful to Shadrach. Despite the immense cheerfulness with which he had spoken to us of being "dibested of mah plenty," he must have endured unutterable adversity. Yet his return to Virginia, I can now see, was out of no longing for the former bondage, but to find an earlier innocence. And as a small boy at the edge of the millpond I saw Shadrach not as one who had fled darkness, but as one who had searched for light refracted within a flashing moment of remembered childhood. As Shadrach's old clouded eyes gazed at the millpond with its plunging and calling children, his face was suffused with an immeasurable calm and sweetness, and I sensed that he had recaptured perhaps the one pure, untroubled moment in his life. "Shad, did you go swimming here too?" I said. But there was no answer. And it was not long before he was drowsing again; his head fell to the side and we rolled him back to the house in the wheelbarrow.

On Saturday nights in the country the Dabneys usually went to bed as late as ten o'clock. That evening Mr. Dabney returned at suppertime, still sullen and fretful but saying little, still plainly distraught and sick over the sheriff's mandate. He did not himself even pick up a fork. But the supper was one of those ample and blessed meals of Trixie's I recall so well. Only the bounty of a place like the Tidewater backcountry could provide such a feast for poor people in those hard-pressed years: ham with red-eye gravy, grits, collard greens, okra, sweet corn, huge red tomatoes oozing juice in a salad with onions and herbs and vinegar. For dessert there was a delectable bread pudding drowned in fresh cream. Afterward, a farmer and bootlegging colleague from down the road named Mr. Seddon R. Washington arrived in a broken-down pickup truck to join with Mr. Dabney at the only pastime I ever saw him engage in—a game of dominoes. Twilight fell and the oil lanterns were lit. Little Mole and I went back like dull slugs to our obsessive sport, scratching a large circle in the dust beside the porch and crouching down with our crystals and agates in a moth-crazed oblong of lantern light, tiger-yellow and flickering. A full moon rose slowly out of the edge of the woods like an immense, bright, faintly smudged balloon. The clicking of our marbles alternated with the click-click of the dominoes on the porch bench.

"If you wish to know the plain and simple truth about whose fault it is," I heard Mr. Dabney explain to Mr. Washington, "you can say it is the fault of your Franklin D-for-Disaster Roosevelt. The Dutchman millionaire. And his so-called New Deal ain't worth diddley squat. You know how much I made last year—legal, that is?"

"How much?" said Mr. Washington.

"I can't even tell you. It would shame me. They are colored people sellin' deviled crabs for five cents apiece on the streets in Newport News made more than me. There is an injustice somewhere with this system." He paused. "Eleanor's near about as bad as he is." Another pause. "They say she fools around with colored men and Jews. Preachers mainly."

"Things bound to get better," Mr. Washington said.

"They can't get no worse," said Mr. Dabney. "I can't get a job anywhere. I'm unqualified. I'm only qualified for making whiskey."

Footsteps made a soft slow padding sound across the porch and I looked up and saw Edmonia draw near her father. She parted her lips, hesitated for a moment, then said: "Daddy, I think Shadrach has passed away."

Mr. Dabney said nothing, attending to the dominoes with his expression of pinched, absorbed desperation and muffled wrath. Edmonia put her hand lightly on his shoulder. "Daddy, did you hear what I said?"

"I heard."

"I was sitting next to him, holding his hand, and then all of a sudden his head—it just sort of rolled over and he was still and not breathing. And his hand—it just got limp and—well, what I mean, cold." She paused again. "He never made a sound."

Mr. Washington rose with a cough and walked to the far edge of the porch, where he lit a pipe and gazed up at the blazing moon. When again Mr. Dabney made no response, Edmonia lightly stroked the edge of his shoulder and said gently: "Daddy, I'm afraid."

"What're you afraid about?" he replied.

"I don't know," she said with a tremor. "Dying. It scares me. I don't know what it means—death. I never saw anyone—like that before."

"Death ain't nothin' to be afraid about," he blurted in a quick, choked voice. "It's life that's fearsome! *Life!*" Suddenly he arose from the bench, scattering dominoes to the floor, and when he roared "*Life!*" again, I saw Trixie emerge from the black hollow of the front door and approach with footfalls that sent a shudder through the porch timbers. "Now, *Shoog*—" she began.

"*Life* is where you've got to be terrified!" he cried as the unplugged rage spilled forth. "Sometimes I understand why men commit suicide! Where in the goddamned hell am I goin' to get the money to put him in the ground? Niggers have always been the biggest problem! Goddamnit, I was brought up to have a certain respect and say 'colored' instead of 'niggers' but they are always a problem. They will always just drag you down! I ain't got thirty-five-dollars! I ain't got *twenty-five* dollars! I ain't got *five* dollars!"

"*Vernon!*" Trixie's voice rose, and she entreatingly spread out her great creamy arms. "Someday you're goin' to get a *stroke!*"

"And one other thing!" He stopped.

Then suddenly his fury—or the harsher, wilder part of it—seemed to evaporate, sucked up into the moonlit night with its soft summery cricketing sounds and its scent of warm loam and honeysuckle. For an instant he looked shrunken, runtier than ever, so light and frail that he might blow away like a leaf, and he ran a nervous, trembling hand through his shock of tangled black hair. "I know, I know," he said in a faint, unsteady voice edged with grief. "Poor old man, he couldn't help it. He was a decent, pitiful old thing, probably never done anybody the slightest harm. I ain't got a thing in the world against Shadrach. Poor old man."

Crouching below the porch I felt an abrupt, smothering misery. The tenderest gust of wind blew from the woods and I shivered at its touch on my cheek, mourning for Shadrach and Mr. Dabney, and slavery and destitution, and all the human discord swirling around me in a time and place I could not understand. As if to banish my fierce unease, I began to try—in a seizure of concentration—to count the fireflies sparkling in the night air. Eighteen, nineteen, twenty . . .

"And anyway," Trixie said, touching her husband's hand, "he died on Dabney ground like he wanted to. Even if he's got to be put away in a strange graveyard."

"Well, he won't know the difference," said Mr. Dabney. "When you're dead nobody knows the difference. Death ain't much."

Questions to Consider

1. Why do you think Shadrach wanted to return to Virginia, and why was seeing the millpond important to him? What did he find when he arrived? Does Shadrach appear to have found what he was seeking?
2. Why does Mr. Dabney become so angry at the end of the story? What does his anger reveal about the nature of the post–Civil War South, especially for those living in poverty?

A. R. Ammons

1926–2001

Whiteville, North Carolina, was not an auspicious home town for a great American poet. As William Harmon has explained, the landscape there is parched, flat, and sparsely populated, and though it is not very far from the Atlantic Ocean, it is not very close, either. The Bible was the only book in the modest house where Archie Randolph Ammons was born on 18 February 1926 to subsistence farmers Willie M. and Lucy Della McKee Ammons, and it was opened far too frequently to record deaths during the Great Depression years of Ammons's youth. A younger brother died when Ammons was three, and another brother was stillborn the following year; a baby sister had died not long before Ammons was born.

Although Willie was a Baptist and Lucy a Methodist, the area had no Methodist church, and the New Hope Baptist Church was too far away to attend except for major holidays and funerals. As a result, the Ammons family sent their children to Sunday school at the nearby Spring Branch Fire-Baptized Pentecostal Church and attended occasional services there. As Ammons explained in a 1994 interview with David Lehman (collected in *Set in Motion*), "I identify coldly with the family religion. I take my religious spirit, whatever that is, from the Fire-Baptized Pentecostal."

At the age of 18, with World War II underway, Ammons enlisted in the U.S. Naval Reserve and spent 12 months of his service on board a destroyer escort ship in the South Pacific. A poetry anthology in the ship's library caught his interest, and he began to write poems of his own. When his tour of duty ended in 1946, Ammons used the G.I. Bill to enroll at Wake Forest College (now University) in North Carolina, where he majored in general science but minored in English. There he began courting his Spanish instructor, Phyllis Plumbo, a New Jersey native. They married and Ammons served for a year as principal of the three-teacher elementary school in Hatteras, North Carolina. Then literary studies beckoned again, and Ammons began studying at the University of California at Berkeley, where his poetic talent came to the attention of poet and critic Josephine Miles. But Ammons left Berkeley after only a year and began working for a glass manufacturing company in Millville, New Jersey—which might seem an inexplicable career leap if one did not know that the company was owned by Phyllis's father. Living at the Jersey shore and commuting to work, Ammons rose to the position of executive vice president in the course of his nine-year industrial career.

Ammons had not given up writing poetry, however. He published his first book of poetry, *Ommateum*, with a vanity press in 1955, and he made the acquaintance of the great New Jersey poet William Carlos Williams. Offered a one-year position teaching creative writing at Cornell University, Ammons retired 34 years later as the Goldwin Smith Professor of English, having earned two National Book Awards, Yale's Bollingen prize, and a MacArthur "genius grant" along the way. At Cornell, Ammons was renowned as a great one-on-one conversationalist, sitting in campus coffeehouses for hours every day with a close friend or fortunate student; his poetry reflects that same rhetorical situation of an "I" chatting intimately and expansively with a "you."

Critics like to maintain that Ammons is American rather than Southern, that he aligned himself with the tradition of New England transcendentalists Ralph Waldo Emerson and Henry David Thoreau when he moved from South to North. His worldview is modern and scientific, not traditional and religious, and his poetry has been called "cold" and "abstract." His open poetic form, punctuated by his trademark colons, also seems, on its surface, to be a sharp break from the characteristic Southern reverence for inherited forms. Harmon has observed that Ammons rarely uses the Southern vernacular in his poetry and argues that, while

Ammons has the sense of place that is characteristic of most Southern writers, the places he writes about are usually in New York or New Jersey, not the South. But Ammons himself claimed, in a 1989 interview with William Walsh (collected in *Set in Motion*), that "I feel my verbal and spiritual home is still the South. When I sit down and play hymns on the piano my belly tells me I'm home no matter where I am." Ammons's deep-rooted Southern identity is most apparent not in his usual choice of subject matter or theme, but in his poetic voice. That voice is informal, conversational, often funny, and given to flights of storytelling or exaggeration; it delights in playing with words and playing tricks on the "listener." Even Harmon admits that "one can say that Ammons is both peculiarly Southern (plain, modest, humble, country-courtly, reverent, eloquent, stubborn, humorous, somatic, idiosyncratic) and not particularly of any region or period." The following selections highlight some of the poems on Southern themes and subjects that critics frequently overlook, although they rank among Ammons's finest lyric work.

Mule Song

Silver will lie where she lies
sun-out, whatever turning the world does,
longeared in her ashen, earless,
floating world:
indifferent to sores and greenage colic,
where oats need not
come to,
bleached by crystals of her trembling time:
beyond all brunt of seasons, blind
forever to all blinds,
inhabited by
brooks still she may wraith over broken
fields after winter
or roll in the rye-green fields:
old mule, no defense but a mule's against
disease, large-ribbed,
flat-toothed, sold to a stranger, shot by a
stranger's hand,
not my hand she nuzzled the seasoning-salt from.

Nelly Myers

I think of her
while having a bowl of wheatflakes
(why? we never had wheatflakes
or any cereal then
except breakfast grits)
and tears come to my eyes
and I think that I will die
because
the bright, clear days when she was with me
and when we were together
(without caring that we were together)

can never be restored:
my love wide-ranging
I mused with clucking hens
and brought in from summer storms
at midnight the thrilled cold chicks
and dried them out
at the fireplace
and got up before morning
unbundled them from the piles of rags and
turned them into the sun:

I cannot go back
I cannot be with her again

and my love included the bronze
sheaves of broomstraw
she would be coming across the fields with
before the household was more than stirring out to pee

and there she would be coming
as mysteriously from a new world
and she was already old when I was born but I love
the thought of her hand
wringing the tall tuft of dried grass

and I cannot see her beat out the fuzzy bloom
again
readying the straw for our brooms at home,
I can never see again the calm sentence of her mind
as she
measured out brooms for the neighbors and charged
a nickel a broom:

I think of her
but cannot remember how I thought of her
as I grew up: she was not a member of the family:
I knew she was not my mother,
not an aunt, there was nothing
visiting about her: she had her room,
she kept her bag of money
(on lonely Saturday afternoons
you could sometimes hear the coins
spilling and spilling into her apron):
she never went away, she was Nelly Myers, we
called her Nel,
small, thin, her legs wrapped from knees to ankles
in homespun bandages: she always had the soreleg
and sometimes
red would show at the knee, or the ankle would swell
and look hot
(and sometimes the cloths would
dwindle,
the bandages grow thin, the bowed legs look

pale and dry—I would feel good then,
maybe for weeks
there would seem reason of promise,
though she rarely mentioned her legs
and was rarely asked about them): she always went,

legs red or white, went, went
through the mornings before sunrise
covering the fields and
woods
looking for huckleberries
or quieting some wild call to move and go
roaming the woods and acres of daybreak
and there was always a fire in the stove
when my mother rose (which was not late):

my grandmother, they say, took her in
when she was a stripling run away from home
(her mind was not perfect
which is no bar to this love song
for her smile was sweet,
her outrage honest and violent)
and they say that after she worked all day her relatives
would throw a handful of dried peas into her lap
for her supper
and she came to live in the house I was born in the
northwest room of:

oh I will not end my grief
that she is gone, I will not end my singing;
my songs like blueberries
felt-out and black to her searching fingers before light
welcome her
wherever her thoughts ride with mine, now or in any time
that may come
when I am gone; I will not end visions of her naked feet
in the sandpaths: I will hear her words
"Applecandy"[1] which meant Christmas,
"Lambesdamn" which meant Goddamn (she was forthright
and didn't go to church
and nobody wondered if she should

and I agree with her the Holcomb pinegrove bordering our
field was
more hushed and lovelier than cathedrals
not to mention country churches with unpainted boards
and so much innocence as she carried in her face
has entered few churches in one person)

and her exclamation "Founshy-day!"[2] I know no meaning for
but knew she was using it right:

1. Fruit-flavored candy manufactured and distributed in the South beginning in 1927.

2. Possibly a corruption of "St. Fanchea's Day," January 1.

and I will not forget how though nearly deaf
she heard the tender blood in lips of children
and knew the hurt
    and knew what to do:

and I will not forget how I saw her last, tied in a chair
lest she rise to go
and fall
            for how innocently indomitable
    was her lust
and how her legs were turgid with still blood as she sat
and how real her tears were as I left
    to go back to college (damn all colleges):
      oh where her partial soul, as others thought,
roams roams my love,
mother, not my mother, grandmother, not my grandmother,
slave to our farm's work, no slave I would not stoop to:
I will not end my grief, earth will not end my grief,
I move on, we move on, some scraps of us together,
    my broken soul leaning toward her to be touched,
listening to be healed.

The Foot-Washing

Now you have come,
the roads
humbling your feet with dust:

I ask you to
sit by this
spring:

I will wash your feet
with springwater
and silver care:

I lift leaking handbowls
to your ankles:
O ablutions!

Who are you
sir
who are my brother?

I dry your feet
with sweetgum
and mint leaves:

the odor of your feet
is newly earthen,
honeysuckled:

bloodwork in blue
raisures over the white
skinny anklebone:

if I have wronged you
cleanse me with the falling
water of forgiveness.

And woman, your flat feet
yellow, gray with dust,
your orphaned udders flat,

lift your dress
up to your knees
and I will wash your feet:

feel the serenity
cool as cool springwater
and hard to find:

if I have failed to know
the grief in your gone time,
forgive me wakened now.

Hippie Hop

I have no program for
saving this world or scuttling
the next: I know no political,
sexual, racial cures: I make
analogies, my bucketful of
flowers: I give flowers to people
of all policies, sexes, and races
including the vicious, the
uncertain, and the white.

Questions to Consider

1. Are the thoughts expressed in "Mule Song" typical of a Southern farm worker's response to the death of a mule? Why or why not?
2. Explain why the poem "Nelly Myers" can be read as an elegy (poem expressing sorrow over a death or other great loss) for a lost world, as well as for a person.

Ernest Gaines

1933–

The eldest of twelve children of Adrienne Gaines Colar, Ernest J. Gaines was born on 15 January 1933 in Point Coupée Parish, near New Roads, Louisiana. His father, Manuel, deserted his wife and seven children when Ernest was a young child, forcing Adrienne to seek employment in New Orleans, and to leave her children in the care of a disabled aunt, Augusteen Jefferson. Aunt Augusteen's sustained influence on Gaines's development as a writer and as a man is apparent in his dedication to *The Autobiography of Miss Jane Pittman*. Gaines embraces the strength that he learned from his aunt, proclaiming that she "did not walk a day in her life, but [she] taught me the importance of standing." Gaines was working in the fields on the plantation by the age of eight, but before he reached his twelfth birthday, the only work he could find was in the swamps, as Cajun farmers had largely replaced the African-American sharecroppers in the region. By this time, Ernest's mother had remarried and moved to Vallejo, California, with her husband, Ralph Norbert Colar. Gaines joined his parents in Vallejo in 1948 and enrolled in school, as Point Coupée offered severely limited opportunities for African-American students during the era of legalized segregation. Before he graduated from high school, Gaines submitted an early version of *Catherine Carmier* to a New York publisher. When the work was rejected, he destroyed the manuscript but did not abandon his goal of becoming a writer.

Gaines continued his education, reading extensively from local libraries, attending junior college for two years prior to serving in the Armed Forces, and completing his bachelor's degree from San Francisco State College in 1957. He then entered Stanford University's creative writing program, supported by the Wallace Stegner Creative Writing Fellowship. During this period, he successfully published his first work, a short story titled "A Long Day in November." He followed this success with the publication of "Just Like a Tree" (1962) and "The Sky is Gray" (1963). By 1964, Gaines had published the first of his six novels, *Catherine Carmier,* and followed it with *Of Love and Dust* (1967). He has since published four additional novels to substantial critical acclaim, including *The Autobiography of Miss Jane Pittman* (1971), *In My Father's House* (1978), *A Gathering of Old Men* (1983), and *A Lesson Before Dying* (1993)—many of which have been made into feature-length films.

Perhaps the greatest strength of Gaines's fiction is the authenticity of his characters' voices, which derive from his native South Louisiana, the setting of his fictional communities. Growing up in a highly oral society honed his natural ear for capturing voices, voices that he describes as "the sound of my people talking." Gaines once told an interviewer that "I came up in a place that was oral . . . we *talked* stories." He articulates stories of racism, both virulent and subtle; of strong women who hold together fragmented and tormented families; and of socially encoded limitations placed on African-American men coming of age in the era of Jim Crow and its aftermath. He frequently questions the ways in which masculinity is constructed in light of the long-term destructive influence of slavery and its aftermath on family units, extending his examinations of manhood to the south Louisiana Creole community as well. The settlement patterns of South Louisiana caused a sizeable Creole population to grow alongside the Acadians who immigrated to the region after their repeated expulsion and exile, first from France and later from Canada. The relationship between these groups has traditionally been an uneasy one, with people of color in the region suffering the brunt of the frustration of exiles whose ancestors had suffered similar forms of oppression themselves. *A Lesson Before Dying* demonstrates the importance of becoming a man, even in the face of an unjustified death, and of resisting the efforts of a White establishment that would break the spirits of African-American males. Gaines's characters triumph over the oppression controlling their lives—as in the award-winning *A Gathering of Old Men*—even when the triumph is punctuated with violence or injustice. While oppressors may not be overthrown in Gaines's novels, they are frequently held at bay and rarely do they defeat the human spirit.

Over the course of his career, Gaines has been awarded an honorary doctoral degree by Denison University. He has also received numerous awards, including the Louisiana Library Association Award, the Black Academy of Arts and Letters Award, a Guggenheim Fellowship, and a MacArthur Foundation Award. In 1998, he was elected to the American Academy of Arts and Letters, and he received the National Book Critics Circle Award for *A Lesson Before Dying*.

from A Lesson Before Dying

I was not there, yet I was there. No, I did not go to the trial, I did not hear the verdict, because I knew all the time what it would be. Still, I was there. I was there as much as anyone else was there. Either I sat behind my aunt and his godmother or I sat beside them. Both are large women, but his godmother is larger. She is of average height, five four, five five, but weighs nearly two hundred pounds. Once she and my aunt had found their places—two rows behind the table where he sat with his court-appointed attorney—his godmother became as immobile as a great stone or as one of our oak or cypress stumps. She never got up once to get water or go to the bathroom down in the basement. She just sat there staring at the boy's clean-cropped head where he sat at the front table with his lawyer. Even after he had gone to await the jurors' verdict, her eyes remained in that one direction. She heard nothing said in the courtroom. Not by the prosecutor, not by the defense attorney, not by my aunt. (Oh, yes, she did hear one word—one word, for sure: "hog.") It was my aunt whose eyes followed the prosecutor as he moved from one side of the courtroom to the other, pounding his fist into the palm of his hand, pounding the table where his papers lay, pounding the rail that separated the jurors from the rest of the courtroom. It was my aunt who followed his every move, not his godmother. She was not even listening. She had gotten tired of listening. She knew, as we all knew, what the outcome would be. A white man had been killed during a robbery, and though two of the robbers had been killed on the spot, one had been captured, and he, too, would have to die. Though he told them no, he had nothing to do with it, that he was on his way to the White Rabbit Bar and Lounge when Brother and Bear drove up beside him and offered him a ride. After he got into the car, they asked him if he had any money. When he told them he didn't have a solitary dime, it was then that Brother and Bear started talking credit, saying that old Gropé should not mind crediting them a pint since he knew them well, and he knew that the grinding season was coming soon, and they would be able to pay him back then.

The store was empty, except for the old storekeeper, Alcee Gropé, who sat on a stool behind the counter. He spoke first. He asked Jefferson about his godmother. Jefferson told him his nannan was all right. Old Gropé nodded his head. "You tell her for me I say hello," he told Jefferson. He looked at Brother and Bear. But he didn't like them. He didn't trust them. Jefferson could see that in his face. "Do for you boys?" he asked. "A bottle of that Apple White, there, Mr. Gropé," Bear said. Old Gropé got the bottle off the shelf, but he did not set it on the counter. He could see that the boys had already been drinking, and he became suspicious. "You boys got money?" he asked. Brother and Bear spread out all the money they had in their pockets on top of the counter. Old Gropé counted it with his eyes. "That's not enough," he said. "Come on, now, Mr. Gropé," they pleaded with him. "You know you go'n get your money soon as grinding start." "No," he said. "Money is slack everywhere. You bring the money, you get your wine." He turned to put the bottle back on the shelf. One of the boys, the one called Bear, started around the counter. "You, stop there," Gropé told him. "Go back." Bear had been drinking, and his eyes were glossy, he walked unsteadily, grinning all the time as he continued around the counter. "Go back," Gropé told him. "I mean, the last time now—go back." Bear continued. Gropé moved quickly toward the cash register, where he withdrew a revolver and started shooting. Soon there was shooting from another direction. When it was quiet again, Bear, Gropé, and Brother were all down on the floor, and only Jefferson was standing.

He wanted to run, but he couldn't run. He couldn't even think. He didn't know where he was. He didn't know how he had gotten there. He couldn't remember ever getting into the car. He couldn't remember a thing he had done all day.

He heard a voice calling. He thought the voice was coming from the liquor shelves. Then he realized that old Gropé was not dead, and that it was he who was calling. He made himself go to the end of the counter. He had to look across Bear to see the storekeeper. Both lay between the counter and the shelves of alcohol. Several bottles had been broken, and alcohol and blood covered their bodies as well as the floor. He stood there gaping at the old man slumped against the bottom shelf of gallons and half gallons of wine. He didn't know whether he should go to him or whether he should run out of there. The old man continued to call: "Boy? Boy? Boy?" Jefferson became frightened. The old man was still alive. He had seen him. He would tell on him. Now he started babbling. "It wasn't me. It wasn't me, Mr. Gropé. It was Brother and Bear. Brother shot you. It wasn't me. They made me come with them. You got to tell the law that, Mr. Gropé. You hear me, Mr. Gropé?"

But he was talking to a dead man.

Still he did not run. He didn't know what to do. He didn't believe that this had happened. Again he couldn't remember how he had gotten there. He didn't know whether he had come there with Brother and Bear, or whether he had walked in and seen all this after it happened.

He looked from one dead body to the other. He didn't know whether he should call someone on the telephone or run. He had never dialed a telephone in his life, but he had seen other people use them. He didn't know what to do. He was standing by the liquor shelf, and suddenly he realized he needed a drink and needed it badly. He snatched a bottle off the shelf, wrung off the cap, and turned up the bottle, all in one continuous motion. The whiskey burned him like fire—his chest, his belly, even his nostrils. His eyes watered; he shook his head to clear his mind. Now he began to realize where he was. Now he began to realize fully what had happened. Now he knew he had to get out of there. He turned. He saw the money in the cash register, under the little wire clamps. He knew taking money was wrong. His nannan had told him never to steal. He didn't want to steal. But he didn't have a solitary dime in his pocket. And nobody was around, so who could say he stole it? Surely not one of the dead men.

He was halfway across the room, the money stuffed inside his jacket pocket, the half bottle of whiskey clutched in his hand, when two white men walked into the store.

That was his story.

The prosecutor's story was different. The prosecutor argued that Jefferson and the other two had gone there with the full intention of robbing the old man and then killing him so that he could not identify them. When the old man and the other two robbers were all dead, this one—it proved the kind of animal he really was—stuffed the money into his pockets and celebrated the event by drinking over their still-bleeding bodies.

The defense argued that Jefferson was innocent of all charges except being at the wrong place at the wrong time. There was absolutely no proof that there had been a conspiracy between himself and the other two. The fact that Mr. Gropé shot only Brother and Bear was proof of Jefferson's innocence. Why did Mr. Gropé shoot one boy twice and never shoot at Jefferson once? Because Jefferson was merely an innocent bystander. He took the whiskey to calm his nerves, not to celebrate. He took the money out of hunger and plain stupidity.

"Gentlemen of the jury, look at this—this—this boy. I almost said man, but I can't say man. Oh, sure, he has reached the age of twenty-one, when we, civilized men, consider the male species has reached manhood, but would you call this—this—this a man? No, not I. I would call it a boy and a fool. A fool is not aware of right and wrong. A fool does what others tell him to do. A fool got into that automobile. A man with a modicum of intelligence would have seen that those racketeers meant no good. But not a fool. A fool got into that automobile. A fool rode to the grocery store. A fool stood by and watched this happen, not having the sense to run.

"Gentlemen of the jury, look at him—look at him—look at this. Do you see a man sitting here? Do you see a man sitting here? I ask you, I implore, look carefully—do you see a man sitting here? Look at the shape of this skull, this face as flat as the palm of my hand—look deeply into those eyes. Do you see a modicum of intelligence? Do you see anyone here who could plan a murder, a robbery, can plan—can plan—can plan anything? A cornered animal to strike quickly out of fear, a trait inherited from his ancestors in the deepest jungle of blackest Africa—yes, yes, that he can do—but to plan? To plan, gentlemen of the jury? No, gentlemen, this skull here holds no plans. What you see here is a thing that acts on command. A thing to hold the handle of a plow, a thing to load your bales of cotton, a thing to dig your ditches, to chop your wood, to pull your corn. That is what you see here, but you do not see anything capable of planning a robbery or a murder. He does not even know the size of his clothes or his shoes. Ask him to name the months of the year. Ask him does Christmas come before or after the Fourth of July? Mention the names of Keats, Byron, Scott, and see whether the eyes will show one moment of recognition. Ask him to describe a rose, to quote one passage from the Constitution or the Bill of Rights. Gentlemen of the jury, this man planned a robbery? Oh, pardon me, pardon me, I surely did not mean to insult your intelligence by saying 'man'—would you please forgive me for committing such an error?

"Gentlemen of the jury, who would be hurt if you took this life? Look back to that second row. Please look. I want all twelve of you honorable men to turn your heads and look back to that second row. What you see there has been everything to him—mama, grandmother, godmother—everything. Look at her, gentlemen of the jury, look at her well. Take this away from her, and she has no reason to go on living. We may see him as not much, but he's her reason for existence. Think on that, gentlemen, think on it.

"Gentlemen of the jury, be merciful. For God's sake, be merciful. He is innocent of all charges brought against him.

"But let us say he was not. Let us for a moment say he was not. What justice would there be to take this life? Justice, gentlemen? Why, I would just as soon put a hog in the electric chair as this.

"I thank you, gentlemen, from the bottom of my heart, for your kind patience. I have no more to say, except this: We must live with our own conscience. Each and every one of us must live with his own conscience."

The jury retired, and it returned a verdict after lunch: guilty of robbery and murder in the first degree. The judge commended the twelve white men for reaching a quick and just verdict. This was Friday. He would pass sentence on Monday.

Ten o'clock on Monday, Miss Emma and my aunt sat in the same seats they had occupied on Friday. Reverend Mose Ambrose, the pastor of their church, was with them. He and my aunt sat on either side of Miss Emma. The judge, a short, red-faced man with snow-white hair and thick black eyebrows, asked Jefferson if he had anything to say before the sentencing. My aunt said that Jefferson was looking down at the floor and shook his head. The judge told Jefferson that he had been found guilty of the charges brought against him, and that the judge saw no reason that he should not pay for the part he played in this horrible crime.

Death by electrocution. The governor would set the date.

Questions to Consider

1. What does it mean to die like a man? Why is it critical that Jefferson die like a man? What events call his manhood into question?
2. Why is Grant reluctant to become involved in Jefferson's case? Why do you think Jefferson's relatives see a teacher and a minister as equally important to his redemption? Why is redemption of an intellectual or emotional sort important for Jefferson?

Ellen Gilchrist

1935–

The author of short stories, novels, poetry, and plays, Ellen Gilchrist invites her readers into a social milieu of extended family and friends. The vivacious, free-spirited young women who populate Gilchrist's works struggle to transcend the boundaries of Southern social restrictions as they seek to balance domestic expectations and creative freedom. Gilchrist began her career in 1979 with a collection of poetry entitled *The Land Surveyor's Daughter*, which she soon followed with a collection of short stories, *In the Land of Dreamy Dreams*. Although enjoying her success as a new author, Gilchrist soon felt stifled by the genre of short fiction, as it did not allow her to connect her characters to the larger world of cousins, friends, and lovers, all of whom play an important role in the author's own life.

Ellen Louise Gilchrist was born on 20 February 1935 in Vicksburg, Mississippi to Aurora Alford and William Garth Gilchrist, Jr. Ellen and her older brother, Dooley, spent their early years at Hopedale Plantation, the home of their paternal grandfather. In Gilchrist's 1987 journal, *Falling Through Space*, she recounts an idyllic childhood, where "the black people and white people worked together . . . and only sickness or death or rain in September could make us sad." In the eyes of the young Gilchrist, a wealthy White girl, Hopedale was "the richest land in the world." At the beginning of World War II, her father, an engineer, began moving the family in and out of small towns across the Midwest. Gilchrist missed the South of her youth and wrote many letters to relatives and friends still living at Hopedale. She continued to spend summers there fishing, swimming, and reading voraciously. Gilchrist graduated from Southern Seminary in Buena Vista, Virginia and then spent her first year of college at Vanderbilt University, her sophomore year at the University of Alabama, and a summer session at Emory University.

In 1955, Gilchrist dropped out of college and eloped, bearing three children before she began to write seriously. Between the births of her middle and youngest sons, Gilchrist divorced, entered into a second marriage that lasted six months, then remarried her first husband. Soon after the birth of her third son, the couple divorced for a second time. Gilchrist enrolled at Millsaps College, where she studied with Eudora Welty and earned a bachelor's degree in philosophy.

Gilchrist attempted a new beginning in 1968, when she married for a fourth time and moved to New Orleans. Although the city provided the backdrop for some of her best fiction, and her new marriage offered the advantages of a live-in father for her sons and an uptown New Orleans social life for Gilchrist, her life left her creativity unfulfilled. In 1976, she enrolled in the Creative Writing Program at the University of Arkansas in Fayetteville, commuting between Fayetteville and New Orleans for several years. She divorced once again, set up permanent residence in Fayetteville, and published her first novel, *The Annunciation*, in 1983.

Gilchrist's personal friendships with painters, writers, potters, and poets sustained her through this important journey of self-discovery. In 1984, she won the National Book Award for a collection of short stories, *Victory Over Japan*, and began syndicated broadcasts for Morning Edition on National Public Radio. Gilchrist finally emerged as a public figure, and her friends affectionately dubbed her "The Writer."

Gilchrist's journey did not end in Arkansas. She presently lives in Jackson, Mississippi, Manhattan, and Fayetteville. She identifies herself as a Southern writer, and although she is best known for her fiction, she has also found success as a poet and playwright. In a 1992 interview, Gilchrist describes the language of her South, "I was taught to speak by people who take a long time to say things, and it's heavily voweled and full of adjectives, it's Faulkner's language." Her use of the Southern vernacular, as well as her surprise endings and frustrated protagonists, have earned Gilchrist a readership that transcends regional boundaries. "In the Land of Dreamy Dreams" demonstrates the extent to which a woman will go to maintain the social standards that she believes should be inviolate. LaGrande's frustration with the presumptuous posturings of a new woman in her club cause the socialite to stoop to surprising lows in order to maintain what she perceives to be her rightful place—a place guaranteed to her by birth and breeding. Gilchrist none too subtly critiques the Southern sensibility of entitlement that often accompanies belonging to an important family.

In the Land of Dreamy Dreams

On the third of May, 1977, LaGrande McGruder drove out onto the Huey P. Long Bridge, dropped two Davis Classics and a gut-strung PDP tournament racket[1] into the Mississippi River, and quit playing tennis forever.

"That was it," she said. "That was the last goddamn straw." She heaved a sigh, thinking this must be what it feels like to die, to be through with something that was more trouble than it was worth.

As long as she could remember LaGrande had been playing tennis four or five hours a day whenever it wasn't raining or she didn't have a funeral to attend. In her father's law office was a whole cabinet full of her trophies.

After the rackets sank LaGrande dumped a can of brand-new Slazenger tennis balls into the river and stood for a long time watching the cheerful, little, yellow constellation form and re-form in the muddy current.

"Jesus Fucking A Christ," she said to herself. "Oh, well," she added, "maybe now I can get my arms to be the same size for the first time in my life."

LaGrande leaned into the bridge railing, staring past the white circles on her wrists, souvenirs of twenty years of wearing sweatbands in the fierce New Orleans sunlight, and on down to the river where the little yellow constellation was overtaking a barge.

"That goddamn little new-rich Yankee bitch," she said, kicking the bridge with her leather Tretorns.[2]

There was no denying it. There was no undoing it. At ten o'clock that morning LaGrande McGruder, whose grandfather had been president of the United States Lawn Tennis Association, had cheated a crippled girl out of a tennis match, had deliberately and without hesitation made a bad call in the last point of a crucial game, had defended the call against loud protests, taken a big drink of her Gatorade, and proceeded to win the next twelve games while her opponent reeled with disbelief at being done out of her victory.

At exactly three minutes after ten that morning she had looked across the net at the impassive face of the interloper who was about to humiliate her at her own tennis club and she had changed her mind about honor quicker than the speed of light. "Out," she had said, not giving a damn whether the serve was in or out. "Nice try."

"It couldn't be out," the crippled girl said. "Are you sure?"

"Of course I'm sure," LaGrande said. "I wouldn't have called it unless I was sure."

"Are you positive?" the crippled girl said.

"For God's sake," LaGrande said, "look, if you don't mind, let's hurry up and get this over with. I have to be at the country club for lunch." That ought to get her, LaGrande thought. At least they don't let Jews into the country club yet. At least that's still sacred.

1. Two wooden tennis racquets and one competition quality racquet, which La Grande throws into the Mississippi River.

2. Tennis shoes.

"Serving," the crippled girl said, trying to control her rage.

LaGrande took her position at the back of the court, reached up to adjust her visor, and caught the eye of old Claiborne Redding, who was sitting on the second-floor balcony watching the match. He smiled and waved. How long has he been standing there, LaGrande wondered. How long has that old fart been watching me? But she was too busy to worry about Claiborne now. She had a tennis match to save, and she was going to save it if it was the last thing she ever did in her life.

The crippled girl set her mouth into a tight line and prepared to serve into the forehand court. Her name was Roxanne Miller, and she had traveled a long way to this morning's fury. She had spent thousands of dollars on private tennis lessons, hundreds of dollars on equipment, and untold time and energy giving cocktail parties and dinner parties for the entrenched players who one by one she had courted and blackmailed and finagled into giving her matches and return matches until finally one day she would catch them at a weak moment and defeat them. She kept a mental list of such victories. Sometimes when she went to bed at night she would pull the pillows over her head and lie there imagining herself as a sort of Greek figure of justice, sitting on a marble chair in the clouds, holding a scroll, a little parable of conquest and revenge.

It had taken Roxanne five years to fight and claw and worm her way into the ranks of respected Lawn Tennis Club Ladies. For five years she had dragged her bad foot around the carefully manicured courts of the oldest and snottiest tennis club in the United States of America.

For months now her ambitions had centered around LaGrande. A victory over LaGrande would mean she had arrived in the top echelons of the Lawn Tennis Club Ladies.

A victory over LaGrande would surely be followed by invitations to play in the top doubles games, perhaps even in the famous Thursday foursome that played on Rena Clark's private tennis court. Who knows, Roxanne dreamed, LaGrande might even ask her to be her doubles partner. LaGrande's old doubles partners were always retiring to have babies. At any moment she might need a new one. Roxanne would be there waiting, the indefatigable handicapped wonder of the New Orleans tennis world.

She had envisioned this morning's victory a thousand times, had seen herself walking up to the net to shake LaGrande's hand, had planned her little speech of condolence, after which the two of them would go into the snack bar for lunch and have a heart-to-heart talk about rackets and balls and backhands and forehands and volleys and lobs.

Roxanne basked in her dreams. It did not bother her that LaGrande never returned her phone calls, avoided her at the club, made vacant replies to her requests for matches. Roxanne had plenty of time. She could wait. Sooner or later she would catch LaGrande in a weak moment.

That moment came at the club's 100th Anniversary Celebration. Everyone was drunk and full of camaraderie. The old members were all on their best behavior, trying to be extra nice to the new members and pretend like the new members were just as good as they were even if they didn't belong to the Boston Club or the Southern Yacht Club or Comus or Momus or Proteus.

Roxanne cornered LaGrande while she was talking to a famous psychiatrist-player from Washington, a bachelor who was much adored in tennis circles for his wit and political connections.

LaGrande was trying to impress him with how sane she was and hated to let him see her irritation when Roxanne moved in on them.

"When are you going to give me that match you promised me?" Roxanne asked, looking wistful, as if this were something the two of them had been discussing for years.

"I don't know," LaGrande said. "I guess I just stay so busy. This is Semmes Talbot, from Washington. This is Roxanne, Semmes. I'm sorry. I can't remember your last name. You'll have to help me."

"Miller," Roxanne said. "My name is Miller. Really now, when will you play with me?"

"Well, how about Monday?" LaGrande heard herself saying. "I guess I could do it Monday. My doubles game was canceled." She looked up at the doctor to see if he appreciated how charming she was to everyone, no matter who they were.

"Fine," Roxanne said. "Monday's fine. I'll be here at nine. I'll be counting on it so don't let me down." She laughed. "I thought you'd never say yes. I was beginning to think you were afraid I'd beat you."

"Oh, my goodness," LaGrande said, "anyone can beat me, I don't take tennis very seriously anymore, you know. I just play enough to keep my hand in."

"Who was that?" Semmes asked when Roxanne left them. "She certainly has her nerve!"

"She's one of the new members," LaGrande said. "I really try so hard not to be snotty about them. I really do believe that every human being is just as valuable as everyone else, don't you? And it doesn't matter a bit to me what anyone's background is, but some of the new people are sort of hard to take. They're so, oh, well, so *eager*."

Semmes looked down the front of her silk blouse and laughed happily into her aristocratic eyes. "Well, watch out for that one," he said. "There's no reason for anyone as pretty as you to let people make you uncomfortable."

Across the room Roxanne collected Willie and got ready to leave the party. She was on her way home to begin training for the match.

Willie was glad to leave. He didn't like hanging around places where he wasn't wanted. He couldn't imagine why Roxanne wanted to spend all her time playing tennis with a bunch of snotty people.

Roxanne and Willie were new members. Willie's brand-new 15 million dollars and the New Orleans Lawn Tennis Club's brand-new $700,000 dollar mortgage had met at a point in history, and Willie's application for membership had been approved by the board and railroaded past the watchful noses of old Claiborne Redding and his buddies. Until then the only Jewish member of the club had been a globe-trotting Jewish bachelor who knew his wines, entertained lavishly at Antoine's, and had the courtesy to stay in Europe most of the time.

Willie and Roxanne were something else again. "What in the hell are we going to do with a guy who sells ties and a crippled woman who runs around Audubon Park all day in a pair of tennis shorts," Claiborne said, pulling on a pair of the thick white Australian wool socks he wore to play in. The committee had cornered him in the locker room.

"The membership's not for him," they said. "He doesn't even play. You'll never see him. And she really isn't a cripple. One leg is a little bit shorter than the other one, that's all."

"I don't know," Claiborne said. "Not just Jews, for God's sake, but Yankee Jews to boot."

"The company's listed on the American Stock Exchange, Claiborne. It was selling at 16 1/2 this morning, up from 5. And he buys his insurance from me. Come on, you'll never see them. All she's going to do is play a little tennis with the ladies."

Old Claiborne rued the day he had let himself be talked into Roxanne and Willie. The club had been forced to take in thirty new families to pay for its new building and some of them were Jews, but, as Claiborne was fond of saying, at least the rest of them tried to act like white people.

Roxanne was something else. It seemed to him that she lived at the club. The only person who hung around the club more than Roxanne was old Claiborne himself. Pretty soon she was running the place. She wrote *The Lawn Tennis Newsletter*. She circulated petitions to change the all-white dress rule. She campaigned for more court privileges for women. She dashed in and out of the bar and the dining room making plans with the waiters and chefs for Mixed Doubles Nights, Round Robin Galas, Benefit Children's Jamborees, Saturday Night Luaus.

Claiborne felt like his club was being turned into a cruise ship.

On top of everything else Roxanne was always trying to get in good with Claiborne. Every time he settled down on the balcony to watch a match she came around trying to talk to him, talking while the match was going on, remembering the names of his grandchildren, complimenting him on their serves and backhands and footwork, taking every conceivable liberty, as if at any moment she might start showing up at their weddings and debuts.

Claiborne thought about Roxanne a lot. He was thinking about her this morning when he arrived at the club and saw her cream-colored Rolls-Royce blocking his view of the Garth Humphries Memorial Plaque. He was thinking about her as he got a cup of coffee from a stand the ladies had taken to setting up by the sign-in board. This was some more of her meddling, he thought, percolated coffee in Styrofoam cups with plastic spoons and some kind of powder instead of cream.

At the old clubhouse waiters had brought steaming cups of thick chicory-flavored café au lait out onto the balcony with cream and sugar in silver servers.

Claiborne heaved a sigh, pulled his pants out of his crotch, and went up to the balcony to see what the morning would bring.

He had hardly reached the top of the stairs when he saw Roxanne leading LaGrande to a deserted court at the end of the property. My God in Heaven, he thought, how did she pull that off? How in the name of God did she get hold of Leland's daughter.

Leland McGruder had been Claiborne's doubles partner in their youth. Together they had known victory and defeat in New Orleans and Jackson and Monroe and Shreveport and Mobile and Atlanta and as far away as Forest Hills during one never to be forgotten year when they had thrown their rackets into a red Ford and gone off together on the tour.

Down on the court LaGrande was so aggravated she could barely be civil. How did I end up here, she thought, playing second-class tennis against anyone who corners me at a party.

LaGrande was in a bad mood all around. The psychiatrist had squired her around all weekend, fucked her dispassionately in someone's *garçonnière*,[3] and gone back to Washington without making further plans to see her.

She bounced a ball up and down a few times with her racket, thinking about a line of poetry that kept occurring to her lately whenever she played tennis. "Their only monument the asphalt road, and a thousand lost golf balls."

"Are you coming to Ladies Day on Wednesday?" Roxanne was saying, "we're going to have a great time. You really ought to come. We've got a real clown coming to

3. Bachelor's quarters.

give out helium balloons, and we're going to photograph the winners sitting on his lap for the newsletter. Isn't that a cute idea?"

"I'm afraid I'm busy Wednesday," LaGrande said, imagining balloons flying all over the courts when the serious players arrived for their noon games. "Look," she said, "let's go on and get started. I can't stay too long."

They set down their pitchers of Gatorade, put on their visors and sweatbands, sprayed a little powdered resin on their hands, and walked out to their respective sides of the court.

Before they hit the ball four times LaGrande knew something was wrong. The woman wasn't going to warm her up! LaGrande had hit her three nice long smooth balls and each time Roxanne moved up to the net and put the ball away on the sidelines.

"How about hitting me some forehands," LaGrande said. "I haven't played in a week. I need to warm up."

"I'll try," Roxanne said, "I have to play most of my game at the net, you know, because of my leg."

"Well, stay back there and hit me some to warm up with," LaGrande said, but Roxanne went right on putting her shots away with an assortment of tricks that looked more like a circus act than a tennis game.

"Are you ready to play yet?" she asked. "I'd like to get started before I get too tired."

"Sure," LaGrande said. "Go ahead, you serve first. There's no reason to spin a racket over a fun match." Oh, well, she thought, I'll just go ahead and slaughter her. Of course, I won't lob over her head, I don't suppose anyone does that to her.

Roxanne pulled the first ball out of her pants. She had a disconcerting habit of sticking the extra ball up the leg of her tights instead of keeping it in a pocket. She pulled the ball out of her pants, tossed it expertly up into the air, and served an ace to LaGrande's extreme backhand service corner.

"Nice serve," LaGrande said. Oh, well, she thought, everyone gets one off occasionally. Let her go on and get overconfident. Then I can get this over in a hurry.

They changed courts for the second serve. Roxanne hit short into the backhand court. LaGrande raced up and hit a forehand right into Roxanne's waiting racket. The ball dropped neatly into a corner and the score was 30-love.

How in the shit did she get to the net so fast, LaGrande thought. Well, I'll have to watch out for that. I thought she was supposed to be crippled.

Roxanne served again, winning the point with a short spinning forehand. Before LaGrande could gather her wits about her she had lost the first game.

Things went badly with her serve and she lost the second game. While she was still recovering from that she lost the third game. Calm down, she told herself. Get hold of yourself. Keep your eye on the ball. Anticipate her moves. It's only because I didn't have a chance to warm up. I'll get going in a minute.

Old Claiborne stood watching the match from a secluded spot near the door to the dining room, watching it with his heart in his throat, not daring to move any farther out onto the balcony for fear he might distract LaGrande and make things worse.

Why doesn't she lob, Claiborne thought. Why in the name of God doesn't she lob? Maybe she thinks she shouldn't do it just because one of that woman's legs is a little bit shorter than the other.

He stood squeezing the Styrofoam cup in his hand. A small hole had developed in the side, and drops of coffee were making a little track down the side of his Fred Perry flannels, but he was oblivious to everything but the action on the court.

He didn't even notice when Nailor came up behind him. Nailor was a haughty old black man who had been with the club since he was a young boy and now was the chief groundskeeper and arbiter of manners among the hired help.

Nailor had spent his life tending Rubico tennis courts without once having the desire to pick up a racket. But he had watched thousands of tennis matches and he knew more about tennis than most players did.

He knew how the little fields of energy that surround men and women move and coalesce and strike and fend off and retreat and attack and conquer. That was what he looked for when he watched tennis. He wasn't interested in the details.

If it was up to Nailor no one but a few select players would ever be allowed to set foot on his Rubico courts. The only time of day when he was really at peace was the half hour from when he finished the courts around 7:15 each morning until they opened the iron gates at 7:45 and the members started arriving.

Nailor had known LaGrande since she came to her father's matches in a perambulator. He had lusted after her ass ever since she got her first white tennis skirt and her first Wilson autograph racket. He had been the first black man to wax her first baby-blue convertible, and he had been taking care of her cars ever since.

Nailor moonlighted at the club polishing cars with a special wax he had invented.

Nailor hated the new members worse than Claiborne did. Ever since the club had moved to its new quarters and they had come crowding in bringing their children and leaving their paper cups all over the courts he had been thinking of retiring.

Now he was watching one of them taking his favorite little missy to the cleaners. She's getting her little booty whipped for sure this morning, he thought. She can't find a place to turn and make a stand. She don't know where to start to stop it. She's got hind teat today whether she likes it or not and I'm glad her daddy's not here to watch it.

Claiborne was oblivious to Nailor. He was trying to decide who would benefit most if he made a show of walking out to the balcony and taking a seat.

He took a chance. He waited until LaGrande's back was to him, then walked out just as Roxanne was receiving serve.

LaGrande made a small rally and won her service, but Roxanne took the next three games for the set. "I don't need to rest between sets unless you do," she said, walking up to the net. "We really haven't been playing that long. I really don't know why I'm playing so well. I guess I'm just lucky today."

"I just guess you are," LaGrande said. "Sure, let's go right on. I've got a date for lunch." Now I'll take her, she thought. Now I'm tired of being polite. Now I'm going to beat the shit out of her.

Roxanne picked up a ball, tossed it into the air, and served another ace into the backhand corner of the forehand court.

Jesus Fucking A Christ, LaGrande thought. She did it again. Where in the name of God did that little Jewish housewife learn that shot.

LaGrande returned the next serve with a lob. Roxanne ran back, caught it on the edge of her racket and dribbled it over the net.

Now LaGrande lost all powers of reason. She began trying to kill the ball on every shot. Before she could get hold of herself she had lost three games, then four, then five, then she was only one game away from losing the match, then only one point.

This is it, LaGrande thought. Armageddon.

Roxanne picked up the balls and served the first one out. She slowed herself down, took a deep breath, tossed up the second ball and shot a clean forehand into the service box.

"Out," LaGrande said. "Nice try."

"It couldn't be out," Roxanne said, "are you sure?"

"Of course I'm sure," LaGrande said. "*I wouldn't have called it unless I was sure.*"

Up on the balcony Old Claiborne's heart was opening and closing like a geisha's fan. He caught LaGrande's eye, smiled and waved, and, turning around, realized that Nailor was standing behind him.

"Morning, Mr. Claiborne," Nailor said, leaning politely across him to pick up the cup. "Looks like Mr. Leland's baby's having herself a hard time this morning. Let me bring you something nice to drink while you watch."

Claiborne sent him for coffee and settled back in the chair to watch LaGrande finish her off, thinking, as he often did lately, that he had outlived his time and his place. "I'm not suited for a holding action," he told himself, imagining the entire culture of the white Christian world to be stretched out on some sort of endless Maginot Line besieged by the children of the poor carrying portable radios and boxes of fried chicken.

Here Claiborne sat, on a beautiful spring morning, in good spirits, still breathing normally, his blood coursing through his veins on its admirable and accustomed journeys, and only a few minutes before he had been party to a violation of a code he had lived by all his life.

He sat there, sipping his tasteless coffee, listening to the Saturday lawn mowers starting up on the lawn of the Poydras Retirement Home, which took up the other half of the square block of prime New Orleans real estate on which the new clubhouse was built. It was a very exclusive old folks' home, with real antiques and Persian rugs and a board of directors made up of members of the New Orleans Junior League. Some of the nicest old people in New Orleans went there to die.

Claiborne had suffered through a series of terrible luncheons at the Poydras Home in an effort to get them to allow the tennis club to unlock one of the gates that separated the two properties. But no matter how the board of directors of the Lawn Tennis Club pleaded and bargained and implored, the board of directors of the Poydras Home stoutly refused to allow the tennis-club members to set foot on their lawn to retrieve the balls that flew over the fence. A ball lost to the Poydras Home was a ball gone forever.

The old-fashioned steel girders of the Huey P. Long Bridge hung languidly in the moist air. The sun beat down on the river. The low-hanging clouds pushed against each other in fat cosmic orgasms.

LaGrande stood on the bridge until the constellation of yellow balls was out of sight around a bend in the river. Then she drove to her house on Philip Street, changed clothes, got in the car, and began to drive aimlessly up and down Saint Charles Avenue, thinking of things to do with the rest of her life.

She decided to cheer herself up. She turned onto Carrollton Avenue and drove down to Gus Mayer.

She went in, found a saleslady, took up a large dressing room, and bought some cocktail dresses and some sun dresses and some summer skirts and blouses and some pink linen pants and a beige silk Calvin Klein evening jacket.

Then she went downstairs and bought some hose and some makeup and some perfume and some brassieres and some panties and a blue satin Christian Dior gown and robe.

She went into the shoe department and bought some Capezio sandals and some Bass loafers and some handmade espadrilles. She bought a red umbrella and a navy blue canvas handbag.

When she had bought one each of every single thing she could possibly imagine needing she felt better and went on out to the Country Club to see if anyone she liked to fuck was hanging around the pool.

Questions to Consider

1. How does Gilchrist convey the ways in which her characters search for identity? From what sources does LaGrande's identity derive? What sacrifices is she willing to make in order to maintain her identity, at least outwardly?
2. What folk elements, such as foodways and vernacular language usage, can be found in Gilchrist's fiction? How do these elements affect your reading of her work?

James Lee Burke

1936–

James Lee Burke has remarked that the best job he ever had was as a land surveyor for pipelines in Texas and Colorado: "You don't use your mind in the sense that you don't use up creative energy. It's a real good life. You're outdoors. You're rolling all the time. You're never in the same place two days in a row. The pay's good and there are great guys to work with. Pipeliners were the most unusual, interesting people I ever knew. They've been everywhere. They have no last names and they don't have first names–W. J., R. C., L. T. And if the guy's name isn't W. J., it's J. W." Burke's work experience has provided fodder for his literary endeavors, as many of his characters come from this working world.

First cousin to noted writer Andre Dubus, Burke was born on 5 December 1936 in Houston, Texas, where he lived until he graduated from Lamar High School. Burke proudly states that his great-great-grandfather fought with Sam Houston before settling in New Iberia to become a sugar farmer and that his family has lived in New Iberia, Louisiana since 1836. His father worked as an engineer for a natural gas company, and his mother was a secretary. While the Burkes lived and worked in Houston, they maintained close ties to their Louisiana roots, frequently returning to New Iberia for visits with family. When Burke was only eighteen, his father was killed in an automobile accident in Anahuac, Texas. In addition to this tragedy, during high school, Burke became an alcoholic when he attempted to use alcohol as a weapon in his battle against low self-esteem. He enrolled in college at Southwestern Louisiana Institute (now the University of Louisiana at Lafayette), and his life began to change when he discovered writing. Burke credits his success to his first-year composition teacher, Lyle Williams, who was firm, but encouraging of Burke's early efforts. During his third year in college, Burke transferred to the University of Missouri in Columbia, intending to study journalism. He began studying creative writing instead, and he completed his B.A. in 1960. He stayed on in Columbia to earn an M.A. in English. During his time in Missouri, he met his wife, Pearl Chu-Pai, a native of China. The pair were soon inseparable, and they have four children. In 1977, Burke began the arduous task of becoming sober and remains so today.

Best known for two series of detective novels—the Dave Robicheaux series, set in south Louisiana, and the Billy Bob Holland stories set in Texas—Burke has written nearly thirty novels. He credits part of his success in writing to the influences of William Faulkner, Robert Penn Warren, and to his cousin, Andre Dubus. His experiences in Louisiana and Texas lead him to recognize and celebrate the subtle differences among the cultures of places as diverse as New Orleans, New Iberia, or the piney woods of Texas, and the Robicheaux and Holland novels depict the cultural heritage of the regions. Dave Robicheaux, the Cajun detective, embodies South Louisiana culture; he works hard, relishes Cajun delicacies, dances to Zydeco music, drinks heavily, and maintains a healthy respect for the otherworldly. The worldview that Burke instills in his characters suggests the value of south Louisiana culture and the necessity of preserving it. As critic Thomas Easterling has pointed out, "Burke's Robicheaux series is anything but a eulogy for a lost way of life. Because he is an officer of the law, Robicheaux can literally arrest the developments he finds threatening to the culture he loves. We come to see him as a protector not only of those citizens who live within the law but also of a way of life." Burke has also written numerous short stories which, like his novels, frequently focus upon life in South Louisiana. The short story featured here, "Losses" illustrates the life of a young Catholic boy as he learns an object lesson about his faith and life, in general.

In the context of a firmly established regional identity, Burke's fiction presents a wide array of characters who struggle with class and race inequities, love, morality and crime, and religion. His works have been heartily received by critics and general readers alike, and his intricately woven plots leave his readers eagerly anticipating the next twist of the tale.

Throughout his career, Burke worked at a variety of jobs to support his writing habit. In 1986, a Guggenheim Fellowship allowed him to devote all his time to writing. He currently splits his time between New Iberia, Louisiana, and Missoula, Montana.

Losses

Strange things happened to me in the fifth grade at St. Peter's Catholic School in 1944. One morning I woke up and felt guilty because I had thoughts about the breasts of the Negro women who worked in the lunchroom. Then I started to feel guilty about everything, an idle or innocent activity of only a few days ago now became a dark burden on my soul. I had looked at a picture of a nude statue in a book, repeated profane words I'd heard older boys use down at the filling station, noticed for the first time the single woman next door hanging her undergarments on the clothesline.

I confessed my bad thoughts and desires to Father Melancon but it did no good. I felt the light going out of the world and I didn't know why. My sins throbbed in my chest like welts raised by a whip. When I lay in my bed at night, with the winter rain hitting against the window glass, my fists clenched under the sheets, my mind would fill with fearful images of the war[1] and eternal perdition, which somehow melded together in an apocalyptical vision of the world's fiery end.

Out on the Gulf southeast of New Iberia,[2] Nazi submarines had torpedoed oil tankers that sailed unescorted out of the mouth of the Mississippi. Shrimpers[3] told stories about the fires that burned on the horizon late at night and the horribly charred sailor that one skipper had pulled up in his shrimp net. I knew that the Nazis and the Japanese had killed people from New Iberia, too. When the war broke out, families hung a small flag with a blue star on a white field in the window to show they had a boy in service. As the war progressed, many of those blue stars were replaced by gold ones; sometimes the lawns of those small wood-frame houses remained uncut, the rolled newspapers moldered in the flower beds, the shades were drawn and never raised again.[4]

I believed that a great evil was at work in the world.

1. The war to which Burke refers is World War II.
2. A small town in southwestern Louisiana that contains a very high Cajun—and hence, Catholic—population.
3. People who fish commercially for shrimp in the Gulf of Mexico.
4. During World War II, families who had sons, husbands, or grandsons at war often hung rectangular shaped pennants with a blue star for each man in service in their windows to illustrate that they had a relative at war. If the soldier was killed, his blue star would be replaced with a gold one.

My mother, who was a Baptist from Texas and who did not go to church, said my thoughts were foolish. She said the real devil in the world lived in a bottle of whiskey. She meant the whiskey that made my father drunk, that kept him at Broussard's Bar down on Railroad Avenue after he got fired from the oil rig.

I heard them late on a Saturday night. It was raining hard, lightning jumped outside the window, and our pecan tree thrashed wildly on the roof.

"You not only fall down in your own yard, you've spent our money on those women. I can smell them on you," she said.

"I stopped at Provost's and shot pool. I put some beers on the tab. I didn't spend anything."

"Empty your pockets, then. Show me the money I'm going to use for his lunches next week."

"I'll take care of it. I always have. Father Melancon knows we've had some bad luck."

"Jack, I won't abide this. I'll take him with me back to Beaumont."

"No ma'am, you won't."

"Don't you come at me, Jack. I'll have you put in the parish jail."

"You're an evil-mouthed woman. You're a nag and you degrade a man in front of his son."

"I'm picking up the phone. So help me . . . I won't tolerate it."

I don't think he hit her, he just slammed out the door into the rain and backed his truck over the wood stakes and chicken wire that bordered our Victory garden.[5] My arms were pinched on my ears, but I could hear my mother crying while the water kettle screamed on the stove.

My fifth-grade teacher was Sister Uberta, who had come to us from the North that year. Her face was pretty and round inside her nun's wimple, but it glowed as bright as paper when she was angry, and sometimes she shouted at us for no reason. Her hands were white and quick whenever she wrote on the blackboard or helped us make color-paper posters for the lunchroom walls. She seemed to have an energy that was about to burst out of her black habit. Her stories in catechism class made me swallow and grip the bottoms of my thighs.

"If you wonder what eternity means, imagine an iron ball as big as the earth out in the middle of space," she said. "Then once every thousand years a sparrow flies from the moon to that iron ball and brushes one wing against its surface. And by the time that bird's feathery wing has worn away the iron ball to a burnt cinder, eternity is just beginning."

I couldn't breathe. The oaks outside the window were gray and trembling in the rain. I wanted to resist her words, what they did to me, but I wasn't strong enough. In my childish desperation I looked across the aisle at Arthur Boudreau, who was folding a paper airplane and never worried about anything.

Arthur's head was shaped like a lightbulb. His burr haircut was mowed so close into the scalp that it glistened like a peeled onion. He poured inkwells into fishbowls, thumbtacked girls' dresses to the desks, put formaldehyde frogs from the science lab in people's lunch sandwiches.

"Claude, are you talking to Arthur?" Sister Uberta said.

5. During World War II, Americans were encouraged to plant small gardens to feed themselves so that commercially manufactured food could be sent to the troops.

"No, Sister."

"You were, weren't you?"

"No, Sister."

"I want you to stay after school today."

At three o'clock the other children sprinted through the rain for home, and Sister Uberta made me wash the blackboards. She put away her books and papers in her desk, then sat down behind it with her hands folded in front of her. Her hands looked small and white against the black folds of her habit.

"That's enough," she said. "Come up here and sit down."

I walked to the front of the room and did as she said. My footsteps seemed loud on the wooden floor.

"Do you know why Arthur misbehaves, Claude?" she said.

"I don't think he's that bad."

"He does bad things and then people pay attention to him. Do you want to be like that?"

"No, Sister."

She paused and her large brown eyes examined my face from behind her big, steel-rimmed glasses. She made me feel funny inside. I was afraid of her, afraid of what her words about sin could do to me, but I felt a peculiar kinship with her, as though she and I understood something about loss and unhappiness that others didn't know about.

"You didn't buy a scapula for Sodality Sunday," she said.

"My father isn't working now."

"I see." She opened the bottom drawer to her desk, where she kept her paint set, and took out a small medal on a chain. "You take this one, then. If your father buys you one later, you can give mine to someone else. That way, you pass on the favor."

She smiled and her face was truly beautiful. Then her mouth turned downward in a melancholy way and she said, "But, Claude, remember this: there are people we shouldn't get close to; they'll cause us great trouble. Arthur is one of them. He'll hurt you."

A week later I was back at the confessional with another problem. The inside of the church was cool and smelled of stone and water and burning candles. I looked at Father Melancon's silhouette through the confessional screen. He had played bush-league baseball before he became a priest, and he was still thin and athletic and wore his graying hair in a crewcut.

"Bless me, Father, for I have sinned," I began.

He waited, the side of his face immobile.

"Tell me what it is, Claude." His voice was soft but I thought I heard him take a tired breath.

"Sister Uberta says it's a sin to use bad words."

"Well, that all depends on . . . ."

"She said if you heard somebody else use them, you have to tell on them or you're committing a sin, too."

Father Melancon pinched the bridge of his nose between his eyes. I felt my face burn with my own shame and weakness.

"Who did you hear using bad words?" he said.

"I don't want to tell, Father."

"Do you think it's going out of this confessional?"

"No . . . I don't know."

"You've got to have some trust in me, Claude."

"It was Arthur Boudreau."

"Now you listen to me. There's nothing wrong with Arthur Boudreau. The Lord put people like Arthur here to keep the rest of us honest. Look, you're worrying about all kinds of things that aren't important. Sister Uberta means well but sometimes . . . . well, she works too hard at it. This might be hard for you to understand now, but sometimes when people are having trouble with one part of their lives, the trouble pops up someplace else that's perfectly innocent."

I only became more confused, more convinced that I was caught forever inside my unexplained and unforgivable guilt.

"Claude, spring and baseball season are going to be here soon, and I want you to think about that and try to forget all this other stuff. How is your daddy?"

"He's gone away."

I saw his lips crimp inward, and he touched his forehead with his fingertips. It was a moment before he spoke again.

"Don't be too hard on him," he said. "He'll come back one day. You'll see. In the meantime you tell Arthur to get his fast ball in shape."

"Father, I can't explain what I feel inside me."

I heard him sigh deeply on the other side of the screen.

That night I sat by the big wood radio with the tiny yellow dial in our living room and listened to the "Louisiana Hayride"[6] and oiled my fielder's glove. My mother was ironing in the kitchen. She had started taking in laundry, which was something done only by Negro women at that time in New Iberia. I worked the Neetsfoot[7] oil into my glove, then fitted a ball deep into the pocket and tied down the fingers with twine to give it shape. The voices of the country musicians on the radio and the applause of their audience seemed beamed to me from a distant place that was secure from war and the sins that pervaded the world. I fell asleep sitting in the big chair with my hand inside my fielder's glove.

I awoke to an electric storm, a huge vortex of air swirling around our house, and a static-filled news report about waves of airplanes that were carpet-bombing the earth.

Spring didn't come with baseball season; it arrived one day with the transfer of Rene LeBlanc from boarding school to my fifth-grade class. Her hair was auburn and curly and seemed transfused with light when she sat in her desk by the window. Her almond eyes were always full of light, too, and they looked at you in a curious, open way that made something drop inside you. Her cream-colored pleated skirt swung on her hips when she walked to the blackboard, and while she worked an arithmetic problem with the chalk, her face thoughtful under Sister Uberta's gaze, I'd look at the smooth, white curve of her neck, the redness of her mouth, the way her curls moved with the air from the fan, the outline of her slip strap against her blouse, and in my fantasies I'd find ways to sit next to her at morning mass or in the lunchroom or maybe to touch her moist hand during the recess softball game.

But even though she was French and Catholic, she didn't belong to the Cajun world I came from. She lived in a huge, pillared home on Spanish Lake. It had a deep, green lawn, with water sprinklers turning on it in the sunlight, a pea-gravel drive shaded by rows of mossy oaks, and a clay tennis court and riding ring in back

6. The Louisiana Hayride was an immensely popular radio show that featured country and later, rockabilly, musicians. The weekly radio show was broadcast from Shreveport, and even today, the Louisiana Hayride occasionally holds shows in Shreveport.

7. A leather conditioner used to soften baseball gloves, saddles, and other leather items.

beyond which the blue lake winked through the cypress trees. Some of the other kids said she was a snob. But I knew better. Silently I gave her my heart.

I never thought a time would come when I could offer it to her openly, but one fine spring afternoon, when the air was heavy with the bloom of azalea and jasmine and myrtle and the wind blew through the bamboo and clumps of oaks along East Main, Arthur Boudreau and I walked home from school together and saw Rene, alone and under siege, at the bus stop.

A gang of boys who lived down by Railroad Avenue were on the opposite side of the street, flinging pecans at her. The pecans were still in their wet, moldy husks, and they thudded against her back and rump or exploded against the brick wall behind her. But her flushed, angry face had the solitary determination of a soldier's, and she wouldn't give an inch of ground. Her little fists were crossed in front of her like a knight-errant's.

Arthur Boudreau was not only a terror in any kind of fight, he had a pitching arm that could make batters wince when they saw a mean glint in his eye. In fact, years later, when he pitched Class-C ball in the Evangeline League, people would say he could throw a baseball through a car wash without getting it wet.

We scooped up handfuls of pecans, Arthur mounted a garbage-can lid on his arm, and we charged the enemy across the street, slamming one pecan after another into their bodies. They tried to resist but Arthur had no mercy and they knew it. He nailed one boy in the back of the neck, another flush on the ear, and drove the garbage-can lid into the leader's face. They turned and ran down a side street toward the south side of town, one of them impotently shooting a finger and still shouting at us.

"Come around again and I'll kick this can up your hole," Arthur yelled after them.

Rene brushed at the green stains on her blouse. There were still circles of color in her cheeks.

"We'll walk with you tomorrow in case those guys come back," I said.

"I wasn't afraid," she said.

"Those are bad guys. One of them beat up Arthur's little brother with a stick."

But she wasn't buying it. She'd let those guys throw pecans at her every afternoon before she'd ask for help. She was that kind, a real soldier.

"I have a nickel," I said. "We can get a twin Popsicle at Veazey's."

Her face hesitated a moment, then her eyes smiled at me.

"There's three of us," she said.

"I don't want one. My mother always fixes something for me when I come home," I said.

"I have some money," she said. "It's my treat today. Look at the scratch on your arm. You can get lockjaw from that. It's terrible. Your jaws turn to stone and they have to feed you through a tube in your nose."

She wet her handkerchief with her tongue and wiped at the red welt on my forearm.

"I'm going to get some bandages at Veazey's and some iodine and alcohol, and then you should go to the hospital later for shots," she said. "Here, I'll tie the handkerchief on it to keep out infection till we can wash it off. The air is full of germs."

The three of us walked down to the ice-cream parlor next to the drawbridge that spanned Bayou Teche. Cypress trees grew along the banks of the bayou, and on the other side of the bridge the small gray-stone hospital run by the sisters was set back deep in the shade of the oaks. Purple wisteria grew on the trellises by the adjacent convent, and I could see some of the sisters in their white habits working in their Victory garden. Rene, Arthur, and I sat on the bridge and ate ice-cream cones, with our feet hanging over the water, and watched a shrimp boat move slowly down the bayou between the corridor of trees and bamboo. I knew that long, cypress-framed ribbon of brown water eventually flowed into the salt, where I believed Nazi submariners still waited to burn and drown the good people of the world, but on that spring afternoon, with the wind blowing through the trees and ruffling the water under our feet, the red and yellow hibiscus blazing on the convent lawn, the war had ended for me like heat thunder dying emptily over the Gulf.[8]

Small drops of water started to dent the dust on the school playground. Through the bamboo that grew along the bayou's banks I could see the brown current being dimpled, too. We were a group of five boys by the corner of the school building, and Arthur Boudreau had a thin, cellophane-wrapped cardboard box enclosed in his palm.

"Hold out your hand," he said. The other boys were grinning.

"What for?" I said.

"Put out your hand. What's the matter, you afraid?" he said.

"You put chewing gum in a guy's hand one time."

"Well, you better not chew on these," he said, grabbing my wrist and pressing into my hand the thin white box with the image of a black Trojan horse on it.

I stared at it numbly. Both my hand and face felt dead. The boys were all laughing now.

"This is crazy. I don't want something like this," I said, my voice rising, then catching in my throat like a nail.

"Sorry, they're yours now," Arthur said.

I tried to push the box at Arthur. I felt wooden all over, my skin tainted with something loathsome and obscene.

"I found them behind Provost's pool hall. They got a machine there in the men's room," Arthur said.

I was swallowing hard and my heart was clicking in my chest. My face rang with the kind of deadness you feel after you've been slapped.

"You're my friend, Arthur, but I don't want in on this kind of joke," I said. I knew my voice was weak and childlike, and now I felt doubly ashamed.

"I don't want in on this joke because I'll piss my little diapers and my mommie will be mad at me," one of the other boys said.

Then a second boy glanced sideways and whispered, "Sister's looking!"

Thirty yards away Sister Uberta watched us with a curious, even gaze, her body and the wings of her habit absolutely motionless.

"Oh, shit," Arthur said, and shoved the bunch of us around the corner of the building. I tripped on my shoes and revolved in a foolish circle, my hand still trying to give him back the box.

"Gimmie that," he said, and slipped it into the back pocket of his jeans and walked hurriedly toward the opposite end of the building in the soft rain. His tennis shoes made stenciled impressions in the fine dust under the trees.

"Fling it in the coulee," one of the boys called after him.

"Like hell I will. You haven't seen the last of these babies," he answered. He grinned at us like a spider.

8. Short for the Gulf of Mexico.

It was raining hard when we came back into the classroom from the playground. The raindrops tinked against the ginning blades of the window fan while Sister Uberta diagramed a compound sentence on the blackboard. Then we realized we were listening to another sound, too—a rhythmic thumping like a soft fist on the window glass.

Sister Uberta paused uncertainly with the chalk in her hand and looked at the window. Then her eyes sharpened, the blood drained from her face, and her jaws became ridged with bone.

Arthur Boudreau had filled the condom with water, knotted a string around one end, and suspended it from the third story so that it hung even with the window and swung back and forth against the glass in the wind. It looked like an obscene, bulbous nose pressed against the rain-streaked pane.

Some of the kids didn't know what it was; others giggled, scraped their feet under the desks in delight, tried to hide their gleeful faces on the desktops. I watched Sister Uberta fearfully. Her face was bright and hard, her angry eyes tangled in thought, then she opened her desk drawer, removed a pair of scissors, lifted the window with more strength than I thought she could have, and in a quick motion snipped the string and sent the condom plummeting into the rain.

She brought the window down with one hand and the room became absolutely still. There was not a sound for a full minute. I could not bear to look at her. I studied my hands, my untied shoelaces, Arthur Boudreau's leg extended casually out into the aisle. A solitary drop of perspiration ran out of my hair and splashed on the desktop. I swallowed, raised my head, and saw that she was looking directly at me.

"That's what you had out on the playground, wasn't it?" she said.

"No, Sister," I said desperately.

"Don't you compound what you've done by lying."

"It was just a box. It wasn't mine." I felt naked before her words. Everyone in the class was looking at me. My face was hot, and through my shimmering eyes I could see Rene LeBlanc watching me.

"Somebody else put you up to it, but you did it, didn't you?" she said.

"I didn't. I swear it, Sister."

"Don't you swear, Claude. I saw you on the playground."

"You didn't see it right, Sister. It wasn't me. I promise."

"You took the box from Arthur, and then you made everybody laugh by bragging about what you were going to do."

"I didn't know what was in it. I gave it —"

"You ran around the corner with it when you saw me watching."

I looked over at Rene LeBlanc. Her face was stunned and confused. I felt as though I were drowning while other people watched, that I was hideous and perverse in her eyes and in the eyes of every decent person on the earth.

"Look at me," Sister Uberta said. "You weren't in this by yourself. Arthur put you up to it, and he's going to wait for me in Father Melancon's office at three o'clock, but you're going to stay here in this room and tell me the truth."

"I have to help my daddy at the filling station," Arthur said.

"Not today you don't," Sister Uberta said.

Until the bell rang I kept my eyes fixed on the desktop and listened to the beating of my own heart and felt the sweat run down my sides. I couldn't look up again at Rene LeBlanc. My moment to exonerate myself had passed in failure, the class was listening to Sister talk about the Norman Conquest, and I was left alone with my bitter cup of gall, my fear-ridden, heart-thudding wait in Gethsemane. The three o'clock bell made my whole body jerk in the desk.

The other kids got their raincoats and umbrellas from the cloakroom and bolted for home. Then Sister sent Arthur to Father Melancon's office to wait for her. I looked once at his face, praying against my own want of courage that he would admit his guilt and extricate me from my ordeal. But Arthur, even though he was ethical in his mischievous way, was not one to do anything in a predictable fashion. Sister Uberta and I were alone in the humid stillness of the classroom.

"You've committed a serious act, Claude," she said. "Do you still refuse to own up to it?"

"I didn't do anything."

"All right, fine," she said. "Then you write that on this piece of paper. You write down that I didn't see you with something on the playground, that you don't know anything about what happened this afternoon."

"I hate you." The words were like the snap of a rubber band in my head. I couldn't believe I had said them.

"What did you say?"

My face was burning, and my head was spinning so badly that I had to grip the desktop as though I were falling.

"Stand up, Claude," she said.

I rose to my feet. The backs of my legs were quivering. Her face was white and her eyeballs were clicking back and forth furiously.

"Hold out your hand," she said.

I extended my hand and she brought the tricorner ruler down across my palm. My fingers curled back involuntarily and the pain shot up my forearm.

"I hate you," I said.

She stared hard, incredulously, straight into my eyes, then gripped my wrist tightly in her hand and slashed the ruler down again. I could hear her breathing, see the pinpoints of sweat breaking out on her forehead under her wimple. She hit me again and examined my face for pain or tears or shock and saw none there and whipped the ruler down twice more. My palm shook like a dead, disembodied thing in her grip. Her face was trembling, as white and shining now as polished bone. Then suddenly I saw her eyes break, her expression crumple, her mouth drop open in a moan, and she flung her arms around me and pulled my head against her breast. Her face was pressed down on top of my head, and she was crying uncontrollably, her tears hot against my cheek.

"There, there, it's all right now," Father Melancon was saying. He had walked quietly into the room and had put his big hands on each side of her shoulders. "Hop on down to my office now and wait for me. It's all right now."

"I've done a terrible thing, Father," she said.

"It's not so bad. Go on and wait for me now. It's all right."

"Yes, Father."

"You're going to be all right."

"Yes, yes, I promise."

"That's a good girl," he said.

She touched her tears away with her hand, widened her eyes stiffly, and walked from the room with her face stretched tight and empty. Father Melancon closed the door and sat down in the desk next to me. He looked tall and strange and funny sitting in the small desk.

"Arthur told me he's responsible for all this," he said. "I just wish he'd done it a little sooner. She was pretty rough on you, huh?"

"Not so much. I can take it."

"That's because you're a stand-up guy. But I need to tell you something about Sister Uberta. It's between us men and it doesn't go any farther. Understand?"

"Sure."

"You know, sometimes we look at a person and only see the outside, in other words the role that person plays in our own lives, and we forget that maybe this person has another life that we don't know anything about. You see, Claude, there was a boy up in Michigan that Sister Uberta almost married, then for one reason or another she decided on the convent instead. That was probably a mistake. It's not an easy life; they get locked up and bossed around a lot and those black habits are probably like portable ovens." He stopped and clicked his fingernails on the desk, then focused his eyes on my face. "Last week she got a heavy load to carry. She heard his ship was torpedoed out on the North Atlantic, and well, I guess her sailor boy went down with it."

"I'm sorry," I said.

"So let's show her we think she's a good sister. She'll come around all right if we handle things right."

We sat silently for a moment, side by side, like Mutt and Jeff in the two desks.

"Father, I told her I hated her. That was a sin, wasn't it?"

"But you didn't mean it, did you?"

"No."

"Claude, think of it this way . . ." His face became concentrated, then he glanced out the window and the seriousness faded from his eyes. "Look, the sun's out. We're going to have ball practice after all," he said.

He rose from the desk, opened the window wide, and the rain-flecked breeze blew into the room. His eyes crinkled as he looked down on the playground.

"Come here a minute," he said. "Isn't that Rene LeBlanc standing down there by the oak trees? I wonder who she might be waiting for."

Two minutes later I was bounding down the steps, jumping over the dimpled puddles under the trees, and waving my hand like a liberated prisoner at Rene, who stood in the sunlight just outside the dripping oak branches, her yellow pinafore brilliant against the wisteria and myrtle behind her, her face an unfolding flower in the rain-washed, shining air.

Sister Uberta went back North that year and we never saw her again. But sometimes I would dream of an infinite, roiling green ocean, its black horizon trembling with lightning, and I'd be afraid to see what dark shapes lay below its turbulent surface, and I'd awake, sweating, with an unspoken name on my lips—Sister Uberta's, her drowned sailor's, my own—and I would sit quietly on the side of the bed, awaiting the gray dawn and the first singing of birds, and mourn God's people for just a moment lest our innocence cause us to slip down the sides of the world beyond the tender, painful touch of humanity.

Questions to Consider

1. What is lost in "Losses"?
2. How does Burke's depiction of Catholicism compare with other stories that you have read that present a Protestant view of Southern religion? How might this story be different if it were told from a Protestant point of view?

Andre Dubus

1936–1999

Although Andre Dubus lived much of his life in the Northeast, where he taught for many years at Bradford College in Massachusetts, he is considered a Southern writer. Dubus was born in Lake Charles, Louisiana and educated in nearby Lafayette. He earned a bachelor's degree in English and journalism from McNeese State College (now McNeese State University) in Lake Charles. In 1958, he graduated from college, married Patricia Lowe, and entered the United States Marine Corps as a lieutenant. During the next few years, the couple had four children, one of whom has become a noted writer in his own right, Andre Dubus III. In 1963, after the death of his father, Andre Dubus decided to change the direction of his life by resigning his commission as Captain in the United States Marine Corps and entering the University of Iowa Creative Writing Program.

His decision was not an easy one, since leaving a solid, relatively high-paying job in the military seemed foolish in light of the fact that the University of Iowa paid only $2,400.00 annually to graduate assistants. With children in tow, the Dubus family moved to Iowa City. Luckily, success came relatively quickly for Dubus; his first story, "The Intruder," was published in the *Sewanee Review* within a year of his move to Iowa, and he began to publish extensively, producing both short fiction and novels. In 1965, he accepted a position as a lecturer at Nicholls State College in Thibodeaux, Louisiana. One year later, he was offered a position at Bradford and accepted. Hence, his life as a Northern resident began.

As Dubus's writing career gained momentum, his personal life underwent many changes. He divorced in 1970 and married two more times over the course of his life; he had two daughters by his third marriage. In 1986, Dubus was assisting an accident victim along a highway when he was hit by another car, and the injuries resulting from this accident caused him to lose one of his legs. Crises in his personal life, both physical and emotional, are reflected in his fiction through the examination of themes such as love, disappointment, fear, sexuality, and religion. Death becomes a pivotal theme of his work, especially in the story included in this anthology.

Though Dubus's work is not always set in the South, his oral narrative style and the development of characters from a wide variety of social classes always carry some of the South in them. For example, Louise, in the short story "The Fat Girl" illustrates the importance of appearance and strict adherence to class mores as guides through life. While social class appears as an element in his work, the pervasiveness of family relationships is notable as well, especially in stories such as "At Night." The specter of death hangs in the air of this story, in which an elderly woman contemplates life as a widow. She has always assumed that she would be a widow, and she and her husband have planned so that managing their dying and their deaths will be as painless as possible. "At Night," which is narrated from the third person point of view, poignantly shows that we can never be truly prepared for the suddenness—and stealth—of death. Critics find Dubus's work thought provoking because of his unadorned style and character development. Throughout his career, his body of work has repeatedly drawn praise from literary critics, fellow writers, and the reading public for its intriguing and original representations of human nature.

At Night

She always knew she would be a widow; why, even before she was a bride, when she was engaged, she knew, in moments when she imagined herself very old, saw herself slow and lined and gray in a house alone, with photographs of children and grandchildren on a mantel over the fire. It was what women did, and she glimpsed it, over the years, as she glimpsed her own death. She had the children and the grandchildren, and some of the grandchildren moved to other states, but most of them stayed, and all her children did, close enough to visit by car, and they came to her, too, and filled her little house. The photographs hung in the bedroom and in the hall, and were on the mantel above the fireplace.

She was seventy-seven and her husband was, too, and by now she had buried her parents and his, and a sister, and two of his brothers, and so many friends; and that had begun in her thirties, burying friends who were taken young. So she knew death was inside of her, inside him, too; something in her body would change—would stumble and fall, or stop, or let go; and something in his would. She did not want to lie helpless in bed for a long time, in pain, and she did not want him to, but she knew it was the way: you went to a doctor because of some trouble your body couldn't leave behind; then you were in the hospital; then you came home and took medicine and died.

Her life ending worried her very little, for here she was each morning, with him; he was long retired from the post office, and they ate breakfast and went for a walk in good weather, sometimes even in the cold when one of their sons shoveled the driveway and the sidewalk and poured rock salt so they wouldn't slip and fall and break a bone; and they went to the children and grandchildren, and the children and grandchildren came to them, and there was the house to keep, and the cooking, and their garden, and friends for a visit. They had plots in the cemetery and she knew everything that had to be done. She had four children, and when she called them with news, she started with the firstborn, then the next, and so on to the last; and this is how she planned to phone them, after she called the doctor, when whatever was coming to her husband came. Then she would watch as in the hospital bed and then in their bed he shrank and died, and near the end the family would all gather to see him alive. Then he would not be, and she would be alone in the house, with the telephone and the car and the children coming to see her.

But on the summer night when he died while she slept, probably while he slept, too, she woke in the cool dark, the windows open and a pale light in the sky, and the birds singing, and she knew before she turned to him, and she did not think of her children, or of being alone. She rolled toward him and touched his face, and her love went out of her, into his cooling skin, and she wept for what it had done to him, crept up and taken him while he slept and dreamed. Maybe it came out of a dream and the dream became it. Wept, lying on her side, with her hand on his cheek, because he had been alone with it, surprised, maybe confused now as he wandered while the birds sang, seeing the birds, seeing her lying beside his flesh, touching his cheek, saying: "Oh hon—"

Questions to Consider

1. What role does death play in the female protagonist's life? What happens to her when she realizes that her husband is dead?
2. Does the widow's reaction to the death surprise you? How does her reaction compare with that of other widows with whom you might have had contact?

Fred Chappell

1936–

Fred Davis Chappell was born on 28 May 1936 in the Appalachian Mountain town of Canton, North Carolina. Twenty years earlier, the Champion Paper and Fiber Company had opened a paper mill in Canton, transforming the town's economy from a rural to an industrial base and making it a perfect symbol of the forces and changes affecting the rest of the South at that time. Chappell's father, James, managed to keep a small farm going but had to turn to teaching, then furniture sales, to support his family. Still, the traditional past of mountain legends and agrarian practices lived on in the skilled storytelling of Canton residents such as Chappell's grandparents and his mother, Anne Davis Chappell, and their oral narratives competed with written, published words for the bookish child's imagination.

While still in high school, Chappell began publishing science fiction in little magazines, but it was at Duke University, under the influence of fiction writing teacher William Blackburn and fellow student Reynolds Price, that he began to study writing as a literary craft. Chappell went on to complete his M.A. in English at Duke in 1964, submitting an 1100-page concordance to the poetry of Samuel Johnson as his thesis. Married and with a child, Chappell managed a small-town supply company, then the credit department of a furniture store during his college years. Reversing his father's trajectory, he then switched from the furniture business to teaching, joining the faculty of the University of North Carolina at Greensboro in 1964. Randall Jarrell, Greensboro's star faculty poet at the time, died shortly after Chappell began teaching there, but Allen Tate remained a frequent guest lecturer during the mid-1960s, and he and Chappell often enjoyed watching football games on TV together. Except for a year in Italy on a Rockefeller Foundation grant (1967–1968), Chappell has taught at UNC-Greensboro ever since.

Chappell's first three books were dark, Faulknerian character studies; the third one, *Dagon*, won a prestigious foreign book prize in France in 1971. The same year that he was honored by the French Academy, Chappell published his first collection of poems, *The World Between the Eyes*. The move from prose to poetry was not as much of a departure as it might have seemed: Chappell's poems have been called "novelistic" or "narrative" and his fiction "lyrical" or "poetic," and Chappell himself has explained that works begun as stories or poems have sometimes metamorphosed into the opposite form. In *Understanding Fred Chappell*, John Lang identifies some of the characteristics that unify Chappell's fiction and poetry, which are also "traits commonly associated with Southern literature": sense of place, sense of history and of the past's influence upon the present, concern with ties to family and community, narrative style and the influence of the oral tradition, and preoccupation with religious issues.

Although Chappell has admitted, in *Plow Naked*, that his favorite poem is the *Iliad*, he claims to have had no conscious intention of creating a postmodern epic when he began writing the book-long poem that would be published as *River* in 1975. After he finished it, however, he says he realized that it was an "overture or prelude, I'm not quite sure which." Over the course of the next four years, Chappell published three more interconnected, book-length poems, each centering around one of the four elements of water, fire, air, and earth: *Bloodfire* in 1978, *Wind Mountain* in 1979, and *Earthsleep* in 1979. Each poem in the tetralogy traces the thirty-fifth birthday of a North Carolina poet named "Old Fred" who, like Chappell, was born on 28 May 1936, was raised in a rural Appalachian community now losing its character and traditions in the wake of industrialization, and is married to a woman named Susan. As in Dante's *Divine Comedy*, Chappell's protagonist, adrift in the middle of his life, is guided by a wise old man named Virgil—in Chappell's version, a hard-drinking Appalachian country storekeeper named Virgil Campbell. The four separate volumes were collected and republished as one unified work under the title *Midquest* in 1981. In *Plow Naked,* Chappell reveals that his aesthetic model for *Midquest* was a very nonliterary genre of rural American folk art: the sampler. Not only did Chappell strive to incorporate "folk-like material," in the form of stories, legends, proverbs, and traditions, but also, his epic was meant to be "a kind of showpiece like an early American sampler of different kinds of verse forms for stitches." Chappell goes on to describe how he made a list of poetic forms and then tried them all.

Chappell published a story collection and a verse-drama after finishing his tetralogy, but he then returned to the territory he had mined in *Midquest*. This time, he reworked his material in a series of four novels known as the "Kirkman Quartet": *I Am One of You Forever,* 1985; *Brighten the Corner Where You Are,* 1989; *Farewell, I'm Bound to Leave You,* 1996; and *Look Back All the Green Valley,* 1999. In the novels, the middle-aged, North Carolina writer-protagonist is named "Jess Kirkman" but publishes poetry under the pseudonym "Fred Chappell." A prolific writer, Chappell continues to publish both poetry and fiction, but *Midquest* and the Kirkman Quartet (collectively known as the "octave") are almost certain to stand as his masterwork.

from Wind Mountain

Second Wind

The day they laid your Grandfather away
Was as hot and still as any I recall.
Not the least little breath of air in hall
Or parlor. A glossy shimmering July day,
And I was tired, so tired I wanted to say,
"Move over, Frank-my-husband, don't hog all
The space there where you are that looks so cool";
But it's a sin to want yourself to die.

And anyhow there was plenty enough to do
To help me fend off thoughts I'd be ashamed
Of later. (Not that ever I'd be blamed.)
The house was full of people who all knew
Us from way back when. Lord knows how
They'd even heard he died. And so it seemed
I owed them to stand firm. I hadn't dreamed
There'd be so terrible many with me now.

I'd fancied, don't you see, we'd be alone.
A couple growing old, until at last
There's one of them who has to go on first,
And then the other's not entirely *one*.
Somehow I'd got it in my mind that none
Of the rest of the world would know. Whichever passed
Away would have the other to keep fast
By, and the final hours would be our own.

It wasn't like that. I suppose it never is.
Dying's just as public as signing a deed.
They've got to testify you're really dead
And haven't merely changed an old address;
And maybe someone marks it down: *One less*.
Because it doesn't matter what you did
Or didn't do, just so they put the lid
On top of someone they think they recognize.

All those people . . . So many faces strained
With the proper strain of trying to look sad.
What did they feel truly? I thought, what could
They feel, wearing their Sunday clothes and fresh-shined
Prayer-meeting shoes? . . . Completely drained,
For thoughts like that to come into my head,
And knowing I'd thought them made me feel twice bad . . .
Ninety degrees. And three weeks since it rained.

I went into the kitchen where your mother
And your aunts were frying chicken for the crowd.
I guess I had in mind to help them out,
But then I couldn't. The disheartening weather
Had got into my heart; and not another
Thing on earth seemed worth the doing. The cloud
Of greasy steam in there all sticky glued
My clothes flat to my skin. I feared I'd smother.

I wandered through the house to the bedroom
And sat down on the bed. And then lay back
And closed my eyes. And then sat up. A black
And burning thing shaped like a tomb
Rose up in my mind and spoke in flame
And told me I would never find the pluck
To go on with my life, would come down weak
And crazed and sickly, waiting for my time.

I couldn't bear that . . . Would I ever close
My eyes again? I heard the out-of-tune
Piano in the parlor and knew that soon
Aunt Tildy would crank up singing "Lo, How a Rose
E'er Blooming."[1]—Now I'll admit Aunt Tildy tries,
But hadn't I been tried enough for one
Heartbreaking day? And then the Reverend Dunn
Would speak . . . *A Baptist preacher in my house!*

That was the final straw. I washed my face
And took off all my mourning clothes and dressed
Up in my everyday's, then tiptoed past
The parlor, sneaking like a scaredey mouse
From my own home that seemed no more a place
I'd ever feel at home in. I turned east
And walked out toward the barns. I put my trust
In common things to be more serious.

Barely got out in time. Aunt Tildy's voice
("Rough as a turkey's leg," Frank used to say)
Ran through the walls and through the oily day
Light and followed me. Lord, what a noise!
I walked a little faster toward where the rose
Vine climbed the cowlot fence and looked away

1. Hymn originating from a fifteenth-century German Christmas carol that was translated into English by Theodore Boler in 1894.

Toward Chambers Cove, out over the corn and hay,
All as still as in a picture pose.

What was I thinking? Nothing nothing nothing.
Nothing I could nicely put a name to.
There's a point in feeling bad that we come to
Where everything is hard as flint: breathing,
Walking, crying even. It's a heathen
Sorrow over us. Whatever we do,
It's nothing nothing nothing. We want to die,
And that's the bitter end of all our loving.

But then I thought I saw at the far end
Of the far cornfield a tiny stir of blade.
I held my breath; then, sure enough, a wade
Of breeze came row to row. One stalk would bend
A little, then another. It was the wind
Came tipping there, swaying the green sad
Leaves so fragile-easy it hardly made
A dimpling I could see in the bottom land.

I waited it seemed like hours. Already I
Felt better, just knowing the wind was free once more,
That something fresh rose out of those fields where
We'd worn off half our lives under the sky
That pressed us to the furrows day by day.
And I knew too the wind was headed here
Where I was standing, a cooling wind as clear
As anything that I might ever know.

It was the breath of life to me, it was
Renewal of spirit such as I could never
Deny and still name myself a believer.
The way a thing is is the way it is
Because it gets reborn; because, *because*
A breath gets in its veins strong as a river
And inches up toward light forever and ever.
As long as wind is, there's no such thing as *Was*.

The wind that turned the fields had reached the rose
Vine now and crossed the lot and brushed my face.
So fresh I couldn't hear Aunt Tildy's voice.
So strong it poured on me the weight of grace.

Here

Burdened with diadem, the
Queen Anne's lace overhangs the ditch.
The lace is full of eyes, cold eyes
That draw a cold sky into their spheres.
The ditch twinkles now the rain has stopped.
And the ground begins to puff and suck
With little holes. A man could live down here forever,
Where his blood is.

from Earthsleep

My Mother's Hard Row to Hoe

Hard, I say. Mostly I can't think how
To make it clear, the times have changed so much.
Maybe it's not possible to know
Now how we lived back then, it was such
A different life.
"Did you like it?"
I
Felt that I had to get away or die
Trying. I felt it wasn't *me* from dawn
To dawn, "slaving my fingers to the bone,"
As Mother used to say; and yet so bored
It was a numbing torture to carry on.
Because that world was just plain hard.

Mother was always up at five o'clock,
Winter and summer, and jarred us out of bed
With her clanging milkcans and the knock
Of water in the pipes. Out to the shed
I went, and milked five cows and poured the milk
Into the cans—so rich it looked like silk
And smelled like fresh-cut grass. Then after that
The proper work-day started. I did what
She told me to, no never-mind how tired
I was, and never once did she run out,
Because that world was just plain hard.

Because from May through August we put up hay
And worked tobacco and, sure as you were born,
We'd find the hottest stillest July day
To start off in the bottom hoeing corn.
From the pear orchard to the creek's big bend,
Corn rows so long you couldn't see the end;
And never a breeze sprang up, never a breath
Of fresh, but all as still and close as death.
We hoed till dark. I was hoeing toward
A plan that would preserve my mental health,
Because that world was so almighty hard.

I'd get myself more schooling, and I'd quit
These fields forever where the hoe clanged stone
Wherever you struck, and the smell of chickenshit
Stayed always with you just like it was your own.
I felt I wasn't *me,* but some hired hand
Who was being underpaid to work the land,
Or maybe just a fancy farm machine
That had no soul and barely a jot of brain
And no more feelings than any cat in the yard
And not good sense to come out of the rain.
That world, I say, was just too grinding hard.

But I'd learn Latin and Spanish and French and math
And English literature. Geography.
I wouldn't care if I learned myself to death
At the University in Tennessee
So long as I could tell those fields goodbye
Forever, for good and all and finally.
—"You really hated it then?"
No, that's not true.
. . . Well, maybe I did. It's hard to know
Just how you feel about a place; a blurred
Mist-memory comes over it all blue,
No matter if that place was flintrock hard.

There were some things I liked, of course there were:
I walked out in the morning with the air
All sweet and clean and promiseful and heard
A mourning dove— . . . *No! I couldn't care.*
You've got to understand how it was *hard*.

Bee

The house is changed where death has come,
as the rose is changed
by the visit of the bee and his freight of pollen.
The house is opened to the mercies
of strangers to whom the dead father
is presented like a delectable veal,
for whom the linens are unearthed
and spread to air, the whiskies decanted.

Survivors gossip their last respects:
a bumble of voices in the living room
like the drowse of music
around the white hive busy in the sunny field.

In the breathless upstairs bedroom,
one lost bee
crawls the pane behind the glass curtain,
searching to enter that field and all its clovers.

The Encyclopedia Daniel

Yesterday *cows* and the day before that *clouds*, but today he had skipped all the way to *fish*.

"What about *dreams?*" his mother asked. "What about *dandelions* and *dodo* and *Everest* and *Ethiopia?*"

Danny's reply was guarded. "I'll come back to them. *Fish* is what I've got to write about today. Today is fish day."

"Do you think that's the best way to compose an encyclopedia? You're twelve years old now. That's old enough to be methodical. You were taking your subjects in alphabetical order before. When you were in the *b*'s you didn't go from *baseball* to *xylophone*. Why do you want to jump over to *fish?*"

"I don't know," Danny said, "but today is fish day."

"Well," she said, "you're the encyclopedia-maker. You must know best."

"That's right," he said and his tone was as grave as that of an archbishop settling a point of theology. He rose from his chair at the yellow dinette table. "I have to go think now," he announced.

"All right," his mother said. "Just don't hurt yourself."

Her customary remark irritated Danny. He didn't reply as he tucked two blue spiral notebooks under his arm and headed toward his tiny upstairs bedroom. Going up the steps, he found his answer but it came too late: "It doesn't hurt me to think, not like some people I know."

He closed his door tight, dropped his notebooks on the rickety card table serving for a desk, and flung himself down on the narrow bed. Then he rolled over, cradled his hands behind his head, and watched the ceiling. It was an early May dusk and the headlights of cars played slow shadows above him.

He tried to think about fish but the task was boring. Fish lived dim lives in secret waters and there were many different kinds and he knew only a few of their names. People ate them. People ate a lot of the things Danny wrote about in his Encyclopedia: apples, bananas, beans, coconuts. Cows too—Danny had written about eating cows in a way that distressed his mother. "Slaughterhouses!" she exclaimed. "Why write about that? You don't have to put that in." He had explained, with a patient sigh, that everything had to go in. An encyclopedia was about everything in the world. If he left something out, it would be like telling a lie. He wrote what was given him to write.

Yet today he had skipped from cows to fish, leaping over lots of interesting things. He would come back to *daredevil* and *Excalibur*, *eclipse* and *dentists*, but it wouldn't be the same. His mother was right. It was sloppy, zipping on to *fish*; it was unscientific. He said aloud: "This method is unscientific."

Then another sentence came into his mind. He could not keep it out. It was like trying to hold a door closed against someone bigger and stronger and crazier than you. You pushed hard but he pushed harder, swept you aside and came on in, sweaty and purplefaced and too loud for the little bedroom. This sentence was as audible in his mind as if it had been spoken to him in the dark and lonely midnight: "He tore the living room curtains down and tried to set them on fire."

He sat up on the edge of the bed and gazed out the window above his table. The dusk had thickened and the lights made the houses on Orchard Street look warm and inviting. But that was only illusion. They were not inviting, all full of people who whispered and said ugly things. They lived happy lives, these people, you could tell from the lights in their windows, but you were not to be any part of that. Those lives were as remote and secret as the lives of fish in the depths of the ocean.

He turned on the dinky little lamp with the green shade and sat down in the creaky wooden chair. Dully he opened a notebook and began to read what he had written in his encyclopedia about cars:

> The best kind of car is a Corvette. It is really flash. Lots of kids say they will buy Corvettes when they grow up but I dont' think so. You have to be rich. Billy Joe Armistead is not going to be rich, just look at him. Anyway by the time we grow up Corvettes wont' be the hot car. The hot car will be something we dont' know about yet, maybe it has like an atomic motor.

Danny flipped the page. He had written a great deal about cars; that was his favorite subject. He had learned all about them by looking at magazine photos and articles and talking to the guys in the neighborhood. Corvette, they all said.

He turned through the scribbled pages until he came to a blank one to fill up with the facts about fish. Except that he didn't know any facts. Well, a few maybe—not enough to help. And then while he was looking at the page with its forbiddingly empty lines another sentence sounded in his head so strongly that he reached for the green ballpoint: "Then he vomits a lot of red stuff, yucky smelly red stuff." But he couldn't write and dropped the pen.

The house began to tang with kitchen smells and Danny understood they would have spaghetti for supper, he and his mother chatting at the dinette table. He understood too that he had better write at least a paragraph about fish because it would soon be time to go down. With a heartfelt groan, he began:

> Fish have gills so they can breathe water. They are hard to see but fisher men find them anyhow with radar they have. Some fish are real big like whales but most are not as big as people. When the police men come he tries to hit them all and then they put hand cuffs on him and drive off.

Three times he read the last sentence and then slowly and with close deliberate strokes marked out the words one at a time. Then he used his red ballpoint to make black rectangles of the canceled words. Red on green makes black.

He had interpreted the smells correctly. Supper was spaghetti and meatballs with his mother's pungent tomato sauce. She offered him a spoonful of her red wine in water but he preferred his Pepsi. There was a green salad too, with the pasty raw mushrooms he would avoid.

His mother raised her glass in his direction. "So—what is your schedule tomorrow? After school, I mean."

"Baseball practice," Danny said. "I'll be home about five."

"Homework?"

"I don't know. Math, probably. Maybe history."

"How about tonight?"

"None tonight."

"So you can go back to writing The Encyclopedia Daniel. How is *fish* coming along?"

"Not so hot."

"That's because you skipped," she said. "You were going like a house afire when you wrote the entries in order. Now you've lost your rhythm."

"I'll come back," he said. "I'll pick up *doors* and the *Dodgers* and *elephants* and *engines* and *farming* and *falcons*. I'll do *fathers*."

Her eyes went wet and she set her glass down as gently as a snowflake. "*Fathers*," she said. "That's what you skipped over, isn't it? You didn't want to do that part."

"I don't know. I guess not."

"Maybe you'll be a writer when you grow up," she said. "Then you'll have to write about sad things whether you want to or not."

"No. I'm not going to be a writer. Just my Encyclopedia. When I get it finished I won't need to write any more."

"Maybe I could be a writer." His mother spoke in a murmur—as if she was listening instead of talking. "When I think about your poor father I believe I could write a book."

"No," he said. His tone was imperious. "Everybody says they could write a book but they couldn't. It's real hard, it's real real hard. Harder than anybody thinks."

"Are you going to finish your Encyclopedia?"

"I don't know. If I can get past this part. But it's hard."

"Maybe it will be good for you to write it out."

"It makes me scared," he said. "Stuff comes in my mind and I'm scared to write it down."

"Like what? What are you scared to write?"

New sentences came to him then and Danny couldn't look into her face. He stared at his cold spaghetti and recited, "He said he would kill her no matter what and she said he never would, she would kill him first. If that was the only way, she would kill him first."

"Oh Danny," his mother said. "I didn't know you heard us that time. I didn't realize you knew."

"I know everything," he said. "I know everything that has already happened and everything that is going to happen. When you write an encyclopedia you have to know everything."

"But that night was a time when we were both pretty crazy. I wouldn't hurt your father. You understand that. And he's never coming back. They won't let him. You understand that too, don't you?"

"Maybe. Maybe if I write it down I'll understand better."

"Yes," she said. "Why don't you write it all down?"

But it was coming too fast to write down. Already there were new words in his head, words that spoke as sharply as a fire engine siren:

"Then in August the father got away and came back to the house. It was late at night and real dark. He didn't come to the front door. He went around back. He was carrying something red in his hand."

Questions to Consider

1. What famous poetic meter is being used in "Second Wind," and what is the rhyme scheme of each stanza? Given that the poets Chappell, Morgan, Voigt, Maddox, Nelson, Komunyakaa, McFerren, and Kane from the Contemporary section of this anthology have all worked in "traditional" poetic forms, why do you think that a Southern-identified poet might be more likely than a poet from another region of the country to employ such forms?
2. Trace the symbolism of the element air in "Second Wind," and then the symbolism of the elements earth and air in "My Mother's Hard Row to Hoe."

Lewis Nordan

1939–

"I was a storyteller a long time before I became a writer," Lewis Nordan says of his conversational writing style. In the South, a region where stories are traditions that are passed down from one generation to the next and prized like antique family heirlooms, the ability to tell an engaging story is a large measure of the success of a writer. Nordan is a thriving Southern writer who draws upon the storytelling tradition to enlighten and entertain his readers by relating stories of life on the Mississippi Delta and recounting his early experiences in the rural South. He represents a new breed of Southern writer who has changed the perceptions of the

South—those held by both native Southerners and outsiders—by describing the culture realistically. Nordan focuses unrelentingly on the South and the memories that are tied to the culture. In his works, he has dealt with such pivotal issues as race, violence, sex, insanity, and the hierarchy implicit within the Southern culture. His works present these themes that have appeared many times in Southern literature, yet he treats the topics in a manner that is at times very graphic.

Lewis Nordan was born into a family of storytellers on 23 August 1939. His father, Lemuel Alonzo, died when Nordan was quite young, and his mother, Sara Hightower Bayles remarried when he was a boy. His step-father, while sometimes fatherly and attentive, was an alcoholic whose binges deeply influenced the writer. In 1962, Nordan married Mary Mitman; they had three children but later divorced; after which, Nordan married Alicia Blessing in 1986.

Following his first marriage, Nordan enrolled at Millsaps College where he earned his Bachelor of Arts degree in 1963. He then embarked on a teaching career with a job in the public schools in Titusville, Florida. He continued his education at Mississippi State University, where he completed his Master of Arts degree in 1966. After earning his Master's degree, Nordan worked as an instructor in English at Auburn University while pursuing his doctoral degree, which he completed in 1973. He secured a teaching position at the University of Georgia, but he left the University in 1975, and for six years he worked at odd jobs as an orderly, night watchman, and clerk, while beginning to write seriously. In 1981, he returned to teaching, securing a position at the University of Arkansas. In 1983, he began his long-standing employment at the University of Pittsburgh, but during his time at the University of Arkansas, he had come under the influence of prominent Southern writers Ellen Gilchrist, William Harrison, and Lee K. Abbott. His work flowered as he realized that he, too, wanted to chronicle the South he knew.

After three years of teaching at the University of Arkansas, Nordan published his first book, a collection of stories titled *Welcome to the Arrow-Catcher Fair* (1983). Since 1983, he has published three collections of short stories and four novels: *The All-Girl Football Team: Stories* (1986), *Music of the Swamp* (1991), *Wolf Whistle: A Novel* (1993), *The Sharpshooter Blues: A Novel* (1995), *Sugar Among the Freaks: Selected Stories* (1996), *Lightning Song* (1997), and *Boy with Loaded Gun: A Memoir* (2000). Nordan has created a vast body of work containing characters who are both realistic and gritty, however, humor also plays an important role in his work. Nordan introduces his readers to a world in which the past is an integral part of the present. Memories and events of childhood and adulthood often intermingle, and past conflicts are reconfigured, reenvisioned, and reevaluated. This use of time has become an important element in much of his writing.

Nordan has received many prestigious awards, including the John Gould Fletcher Award for fiction, a National Endowment for the Arts grant, a Notable Book Award, and a Best Fiction Award for the Mississippi Institute of Arts and Letters. Nordan's work has garnered widespread critical acclaim.

Nordan's "Sears and Roebuck Catalog Game," provides readers with an insider's view of the sad disintegration of a Southern family. His protagonist presents the compelling story of his parents' struggles and failure to survive life intact.

The Sears and Roebuck Catalog Game

I had known for a long time that my mother was not a happy woman. When I was a young child in Mississippi, the stories she read to me at bedtime were always tales of Wonderland—of little worlds into which one might escape through rabbit holes or looking glasses or magic wardrobes. The same was true of the games she and I played together.

My favorite game was to open a Sears and Roebuck[1] catalog and to sit with my mother on the floor or in her lap in a chair and to point to each model on the page and to say, What does this one do?—where does this one live?—which one is her boyfriend?

My mother was wonderful at this game. She made up elaborate dossiers on each of the characters I asked her to invent. She found names and occupations and addresses and proper mates for each. Sears and Roebuck was a real world to me, with lakes and cities and operas and noisy streets and farmlands and neighborhoods.

There was even death. Mother shocked me when I was ten by reporting a suicide among the inhabitants of Sporting Goods. I loved and was terrified by the unpredictable drama and pain.

My father had no imagination. He disapproved of the game. It is more fair to say that he was baffled by it, as he was by all forms of imaginative invention. He did not forbid games or movies or books or Bible stories; he simply did not understand what use they could be to anyone. At night when my mother had finished saying my bedtime nursery rhymes to me, he would sometimes say to her, "Why do you do that?"

The summer I was fourteen I had occasion to think of the catalog game again.

I had taken a job working for my father on a painting site at the county high school. The local swimming pool was directly behind one wing of the schoolhouse, so while I should have been carrying ladders or washing brushes or wiping up paint drippings, I was usually hanging out the window watching the swimmers in the pool.

That's what I was doing one Friday afternoon, when I happened to see a child drowning. I don't know how I happened to see her. Even the lifeguard had not noticed yet. It was a gangly retarded girl with long arms and stringy hair plastered to her face.

I watched her rise up out of the water, far up, so that half her body showed above the surface, then she sank out of sight. Once more she came back up, and then she sank again.

By now the lifeguard was in the water and the other swimmers were boiling up onto the sides of the pool to get out of his way.

After a while the child's body was retrieved, slick and terrible.

We stopped work for the day. Nobody said anything, we just stopped and loaded the van and drove away.

That evening Father sat in his room in his overstuffed chair and drank glass after glass of whiskey until he slept. He was not grieving the death of the child. Death sparked no tragic thoughts for him, no memories, he drew no tragic conclusions. He felt the shock of its initial impact, and then he forgot about it.

The reason he was drinking had to do with my mother. He was preparing himself for whatever drama was certain to develop now that she knew of the death. Drama was the thing for my mother. When there was none she invented it. When one came along she milked it for its every effect.

My mother went into the guest bedroom—the room she called the guest bedroom, because she loved the sound of the phrase, which suggested to her the possibility of unexpected visitors, long-term guests, though actually it was her own room. It

1. Sears and Roebuck was the original company from which the current department store, Sears, has emerged. Originally, Sears and Roebuck was a catalog-order store, and the arrival of the "wish book" was a major event in many households. Some people welcomed the catalog for a more practical reason; past catalogs were often times used for toilet paper in the days of outhouses.

had her bobbypins on the dresser, her facial creams, a hairbrush, her underwear in a drawer. She closed the door.

Down the hall my father was drunk and snoring in his chair.

I went into my father's room and watched him snore. I opened the drawer of his bedside table, as I had many times when I was alone in the house. I took his pistol from the drawer and found the clip. I shoved the clip into the handle and shucked a cartridge into the chamber. I flicked the safety on and off, clickety-click. I unloaded the pistol again and put everything back where it belonged.

My mother was standing in the doorway of the bedroom. My insides leaped when I saw her there in her nightgown. She said, "You are your mother's child."

We walked together to her room, her arm around me, my arms stiff at my sides. We sat on the edge of her bed together. She told me she understood why I wanted to kill my father. She said, "It's natural. Every son wants his father to die."

I wanted to say, "I don't want him to die," but I knew this would disappoint her, would spoil the drama of her pronouncement.

She said, "Death is a beautiful thing. Death is the mother of beauty."

I said, "I guess so."

She said, "Do you love me?"

I said, "Yes."

She said, "I love you, too."

She said, "How much do you love me?"

I wished I was in my father's room watching him snore.

She smiled when I didn't answer. It was a very cute smile. She seemed younger than she was. Younger than me, even. She said, "If I asked you to—oh, let me see now, what could I ask my young man to do for me?—if I asked you to, well, to *kill me*"—here she laughed a silvery little-girl laugh with silvery bright eyes—"if I asked you to do that, honey, would you do it?"

I was terrified and sick. I thought I might vomit. And yet in a way I thought she might be joking with me, that there was a grown-up joke here that I didn't understand. I said nothing, I couldn't speak.

She looked at me and suddenly her face changed. Her voice changed.

She said, "I just want you to know, there is no reason to be ashamed of discussing the subject of death. Death is a natural part of the whole life process."

She propped two pillows against the headboard and leaned against them. She motioned for me to sit beside her, but I stayed where I was, on the edge of the bed.

She said, "Do you want to talk about the drowning?"

I couldn't answer.

She said, "After an incident of this kind, the healthiest thing in the world is to talk about it. I'm interested in your feelings about death."

I said, "I saw her drowning before anybody else. Before the lifeguard."

She told me the strangest story. It was exactly like a story she might make up about the Sears and Roebuck people, except that it was about herself; there was no catalog. She told me she was born in Saskatchewan. (Remember that not a word of this is true. She was born in Mississippi and had lived nowhere else in her life.) She said that her family had lived in a four-room fifth-floor walk-up with cold Canadian winds whistling through the chinks in the thin walls. "Cold Canadian winds," she actually said. "The thin walls."

I wanted to call out to my father, but I knew he was too drunk to wake up. I knew I could not call out anyway, because it would say the truth to her, it would say, "You are insane, you are ruining my life." I wanted to protect her from that embarrassment.

She said that her mother had earned a pitiful living for their entire family by beading bags for rich women. (Where on earth did she come up with occupations for her characters? One of her catalog people was a crowd estimator. Another was a pigeon trainer.) "My mother," she went on, tearful, "sat huddled over her georgette-stretched beading frame, her fingers feeding beads and thread to her crochet needle like lightning." I was torn between the wonderful melodrama of the story and the dangerous madness of it. "My cruel Canadian father," she said (her father was a man from Tennessee with a white mustache and stooped shoulders and a brace on one leg), "my cruel father spent every penny of my mother's hard-earned money on a mahogany gold-handled walking cane and sunglasses and pointy-toed shoes made of kangaroo skin."

She stopped suddenly and swung her legs off the bed and stood up. She sent me from the room and closed the door hard behind me, as if she were annoyed.

I was relieved to be set free. I got undressed in my room upstairs and slipped into bed and lay still. I thought of the things she said: the beaded bags, the kangaroo-skin shoes.

I never mentioned this incident to my father. I was afraid he would find out I had been playing with his pistol.

In many ways, despite my mother's lapse into madness, I remember this as the happiest summer of my life. There were quiet times and funny times. Mother sewed in the dining room on the portable Kenmore. Father went to work and came home smelling of paint and turpentine and whiskey. He fed the chickens in the backyard.

Mother redecorated the living room. It was not a big project, but not small either. The sofa was reupholstered, there were new pictures for the walls (one, I remember, was a bright poster with parrots). A white-painted wicker chair was brought in, the old rug was replaced. There was a tropical theme, I would say, with a couple of large ferns and hanging baskets.

Who knows what the decoration of this room meant to my mother. Something from a Bogart movie, a Graham Greene novel.

I continued to work (to loaf!) at the schoolhouse. I fetched and toted, I cleaned up paint drippings. I collected my weekly paycheck.

Though I worked six days a week, my time seemed my own. I swam in Roebuck Lake—a lake that, according to one of my mother's stories, was created by an earthquake and was "bottomless." I dived into it and brought up its stinking mud in my hand. I tasted whiskey for the first time, with two other boys at a dance. A girl named Alice Blessing let me take off her bra. The summer was golden and filled with new joys.

The schoolhouse job was nearly completed. Summer was almost over. One day late in August, my father sent me home from work early. Later he said he sent me to check on my mother, though I didn't know this at the time.

I walked into the living room and found Mother sitting naked in a wicker chair. I had not seen her naked since I was a small child.

She was holding a razor blade in the air above the veins of her left arm. She did not press the blade to her flesh, only held it and pretended to draw it along her arm. A pantomime of suicide. The skin was untouched.

When she was done, she placed the blade on the glass-topped table in front of her and slipped into a silk robe that lay across the arm of her chair.

She sat back and looked at me. It was a brazen look, without apology.

And then—this sounds as if it is a dream, but it is not—my mother picked up the razor blade again and put it to her left arm and opened an artery.

I couldn't move. The blood soaked her robe to the armpit. It spilled through the wicker. I watched my mother's face become the face of a child and then of an old woman and then a hag-witch, unrecognizable.

I saw all her life in her shattered face—the hidden tyranny of her father, her frightened acquiescent mother, a drunken husband she never loved, a child she never wanted—and at the same time a sad dream of dances with the governor's son on someone's cypress-shaded veranda, the wisteria and jonquils and lanterns and laughter and music.

I moved toward my mother, one step, another, until I had crossed the room. I stood in her slick blood and clamped her arm in my hands.

I pressed hard, with such a fierceness of anger and love that the near-lifeless arm rose up at the elbow as if it had life of its own.

I let go with one hand and stripped a shoelace from my shoe and brought it up as a tourniquet. I picked up a brass letter opener from the table beside her and slipped it into the tourniquet and twisted it like an airplane propeller. The shoestring bit into my mother's arm. I twisted and twisted until I thought the shoestring would break.

I held the tourniquet tight and did not faint.

My father came home and found us there, statue that we made together, pale as marble.

My mother lived longer than my father, it turned out. She is alive today, in Mississippi, where she is friend to a woman I once loved and was married to. My mother is an attentive grandmother to my children—two sons, whom I no longer see. She plays charades and board games with them on her porch and offers them Coca-Colas from her refrigerator. She makes shadow-shows for them on her bedroom wall at night. She is gray-haired and serene and funny.

She calls me on the phone occasionally and laughs that she is not much of a letter-writer.

The scars on my mother's forearm are pale and scarcely noticeable. Nobody seems to care what happened so long ago.

But the afternoon my mother opened her arm and was taken to the hospital, I believed my father would live forever and that the world would always be as manageable as it seemed then. I had saved my mother's life—there was a practical fact that could not be changed. It was the kind of simple, necessary thing that my father could understand and appreciate, and now I could appreciate it too. I could do it and then go on living, with no replays of the event in dreams, no additions or corrections, no added details, no conclusions about life. I was my father's son.

While Mother was still sick, we spent our days alone together doing man's work—the paint and the ladders. Afternoons, we spent beside Mother's hospital bed. We adjusted the IV bottles, we saw the stitches, we heard the doctor's suggestion that Mother go into therapy.

Nights we spent in the kitchen of our home. We boiled potatoes, we floured and fried cubed steaks, we made milk-gravy in the grease. It was a simple, manageable life. It required no imagination.

Many years later, when I was grown and my mother had learned to live her life, I would travel back to Mississippi to wait out my father's last days. His liver was large and hard and showed through his clothing. His eyes were as yellow as gold, his face was swollen.

One afternoon of the visit, I took my eyes off him for a few minutes and, sick as he was, he escaped from the house and, with the last of his strength, crawled far back under the house and died there in a corner, beneath the low water pipes. I crawled on my belly, back where his body lay, and tied a length of rope around his feet and pulled out the jaundiced corpse dressed in pajamas. A retarded woman named Mavis Mitchum, who lived next door, watched the whole operation while sucking on the hem of her skirt.

At my father's funeral the minister said, "He brightened many a corner." It was hard to know whether to laugh or cry.

But at our kitchen table those late nights when my mother's life was so recently out of danger, we were alive and beautiful together, two men in the fullness of our need and love. Each night my father was fragrant with whiskey, and each night I relinquished more of my heart to his care.

I joked with him, knowing how he would respond. "So Roebuck Lake has no bottom—is that the story?"

He said, "You'll never get me to believe it."

We laughed, without guilt, at my mother's expense.

I said, "I can dive down and bring up mud."

He said, "Well, there you are. No two ways about it."

He poured Aunt Jemima syrup over the last of his cornbread. He was ripe and wonderful with alcohol.

I don't remember now, these many years later, who suggested that we play the Sears and Roebuck catalog game. I must have suggested it. I must have wanted to tease him in some way, by suggesting a thing so antithetical to his nature. I must have thought it would make him laugh. Or maybe I thought to dispel more of the influence of my mother's bad magic, the strength of imagination that had brought her to madness and near death. The game must have been my idea.

And yet I think I remember that it was my father who wanted to play. I think I remember that he pushed back from the table, contented and tired from the day's work, happy with a stomachful of cornbread, and that when he had wiped his mouth on his napkin, he said to me, "You know what we ought to do? You know what might be fun, now that Mama's all better and coming home soon? We ought to play us a little game of Sears and Roebuck."

Anyway, I got the catalog and brought it to the kitchen table. We opened it at random and sat and stared into its pages and waited for the game to happen. It was not easy to do this without Mother.

We were awkward at first, embarrassed. We looked up at each other and laughed. We looked at the catalog again.

Nothing.

We were in Women's Clothing. There were models: one woman stood alone and looked off into the distance, as if she were expecting someone. The wind seemed to be blowing. I said, "Who is she waiting for?"

My father stared at her for a long time. He was serious. I could see the strain in his face. He was trying to read the mind of the model in the picture, trying to imagine what on earth she might be doing there.

My father had no experience in this. It was painful for him. Despite his efforts, he was drawing a blank. He began to breathe hard and to perspire.

I said, "We don't have to play."

He said, "She's . . ." But it would not come to him. Finally he said, "I don't know." There was defeat in his voice. He had lost the early confidence he had had when the game first began.

I said, "Let's try somebody else."

We turned a page or two. We found two women laughing, with their arms hooked together. One of them seemed to be inspecting the heel of her shoe. I said, "Are they sisters, maybe?"

Father was working hard. He wiped sweat off his upper lip and stared. At last he shook his head, very slow, side to side. He said, "I just don't know."

We tried other models, in other sections of the catalog. One man with a thumb hooked in his jacket pocket—he was looking back over one shoulder. There were men in hunting clothes and camouflage and raingear. Women in winter coats or in their underwear.

They seemed false. Nobody seemed alive. There was no geography to read from their faces, which were poses for a camera.

At one point my father said, "Your mom would look nice in a coat like this."

My father and I were incapable of inventing a world together. We were too much at peace in the one we already shared. The best we could do was to shop for clothes for the woman we loved.

My father seemed resigned but disappointed that the game was over. We sat back in our chairs. The kitchen was warm from the oven, where we had made cornbread. The dishes were still on the table, the food was beginning to congeal on the plates. Father closed the catalog.

And then, as an afterthought, he opened it again. He turned to Women's Clothing and found the picture of the woman standing in the wind and looking into the distance.

He said, "I think I'm beginning to see."

What might a man see, sitting at a table with his son? I wonder what I might say to my own sons if they were near me. I might say, "She is looking into the past to see what went wrong." Or maybe, "She sees pitfalls to avoid, opportunities to embrace."

At the time I only felt a vague fear, a tearing loose of something I had imagined to be permanent.

My father said, "She sees me."

It was in this moment that my father's imagination was born.

The rest of his days he spent in misery. He remembered the war. Though he had never spoken of it before, now he told funny stories about it, touching stories. Over time he changed the stories, embellished them, emphasized their comedy, their pathos, he added characters and details. He remembered a woman he had met in Florida at the circus. Later he said she worked in the circus as a sword swallower and fire-eater. Another time he claimed to have been in love with her and to have asked her to marry him. He could weep real tears over this loss.

He became secretive. He hid peppermint candy in his sock drawer. He carried his pistol in his car. He bought a black suit of clothes with the words *Rock 'n' Roll Music* spelled out in sequins on the back. He kept it hidden in the back of his closet and never wore it in public. He learned to dance at the American Legion Building and I am almost certain he had an affair with a woman who worked there. He watched television day and night. He thought about his childhood. The Sears and Roebuck catalog had ruined my father's life.

Even at the kitchen table I knew it was ruined.

I said, "This game is not true. This is Mother's game."

It didn't matter. The damage was already done. I looked at my father through the eyes of the model in the picture and saw what she saw: the face of a yellow corpse beneath our house and in that face an emptiness too vast ever to be filled up or given meaning. I looked away, in fear of what else I might see.

Questions to Consider

1. How does setting influence the story in this instance?
2. Explore the ways in which Nordan presents the lives of his characters—what makes this depiction appear realistic or not? Could this story be set anywhere else and still maintain the same qualities?

Bobbie Ann Mason

1940–

"I don't think I write fiction that's for a select group," declares Bobbie Ann Mason, who has been called a Dirty Realist, a member of a generation of late-twentieth century writers whose fiction deals with the gritty ruthlessness of life in contemporary society. Telling tales of the Southern populace—members of the working and middle classes whose lives bear no resemblance to the economic and social elite often featured by Southern writers of earlier generations—Mason is a part of the third wave of Southern literature to emerge since the outpouring of creativity of the Southern Renascence. Contemporary writers such as Mason diverge from the topics and literary styles of revered authors such as Tennessee Williams and William Faulkner, moving their narratives away from traditional Southern topics such as race, religion, or hierarchy, and favoring instead straightforward, compelling storytelling. While her stories sometimes engage Southern topics, Mason does not place such subjects at the center of her narratives. Her realistic style, engagement with contemporary issues, and ability to capture the essence of Southern culture and place it in a larger American context has led Mason to play a significant role in the late-twentieth century alteration of the character of Southern literature.

Bobbie Ann Mason was born 1 May 1940 to Wilbur Arnett and Christianna Lee Mason in Mayfield, Kentucky, a town that provided the inspiration for many of her stories. Mason is the eldest of four children—three girls and one boy—born to the dairy farmer and his wife. Her early years were spent in rural schools in and around Mayfield, and by 1960, Mason was pursuing a bachelor's degree in journalism at the University of Kentucky and supporting herself by writing for the local newspaper, the *Mayfield Messenger*. After obtaining her degree, she moved to New York City and began to work as a writer for Ideal Publishing Company. She earned a Master of Arts degree from the State University of New York at Binghamton in 1966 and a Ph.D. in English from the University of Connecticut in 1972. While completing her doctoral work, Mason married Roger B. Rawlings, and at the conclusion of her studies, the couple moved to Pennsylvania, where Mason began teaching at Mansfield State College.

Mason's first publications were nonfiction pieces. The first was her doctoral dissertation, entitled *Nabokov's Garden: A Guide to Ada*, which was published in 1974. She then undertook a systematic examination of beloved characters from her childhood reading experiences, entitled *The Girl Sleuth: A Feminist Guide to the Bobbsey Twins, Nancy Drew, and Their Sisters* (1975). Mason also began publishing fiction during this time; her first short story, "Offerings," was published in 1980 in the *New Yorker*, which has since published many of her other stories. In 1982, Mason collected her previously published stories into a volume titled *Shiloh and Other Stories*, which garnered numerous accolades, including nominations for the National Book Critics Circle Award, the American Book Award, and the PEN/Faulkner Award for Fiction. In 1983, she received the Ernest Hemingway Foundation Award for best first fiction for the volume.

Since the publication of *Shiloh and Other Stories*, Mason has published three novels, *In Country* (1985) which was made into a feature-length film, *Spence + Lila* (1988), and *Feather*

Crowns (1993). She has written three additional collections of short stories—*Love Life* (1989), *Midnight Magic* (1998), and *Zigzagging Down a Wild Trail* (2001)—as well as, *Clear Springs: A Memoir* (1999). Most recently, she completed a biography of Elvis Presley, which combines her interests in Southern and popular culture. Throughout her career, Mason has continued to receive both popular and critical acclaim, receiving prestigious honors such as a National Endowment for the Arts Fellowship (1983), a Guggenheim Fellowship (1984), an American Academy and Institute of Arts and Letters Award (1984), and a Southern Book Award and National Book Critics Circle Award (1994).

Mason's work examines small-town life and the ways in which these communities are affected by change, especially the change inherent in modernization and technological innovations. In "Shiloh," arguably Mason's most famous short story to date, she demonstrates the ways that such changes can affect relationships. The protagonist and his wife find their marriage irreparably damaged when, in the course of pursuing her own interests, she realizes that her husband has not grown along with her. Mason often depicts marriage critically, highlighting the ever-evolving social role of such relationships, as well as the ways in which partners may change within a relationship. Her work also scrutinizes cultural and familial traditions, raising questions about the roles of individuals in communal situations. "Drawing Names" subtly shows family roles evolving: grandparents become more child-like; parents are relegated from positions of authority and respect to those in which their values are tolerated or disregarded as old-fashioned or restrictive; children either become sources of support and stability within the family or resentfully reject such expectations. Such generational changes occur over time, transforming essential values and the familial traditions they represent and resulting in a delicate but inescapable redefinition of the position of each family member.

"Drawing Names" shows the lives of an ordinary Southern family as they prepare for Christmas. Mason vividly creates a family that, like all families, possesses its own idiosyncrasies that become apparent as the elders of the family must embrace the various daughters' partners.

Drawing Names

On Christmas Day, Carolyn Sisson went early to her parents' house to help her mother with the dinner. Carolyn had been divorced two years before, and last Christmas, coming alone, she felt uncomfortable. This year she had invited her lover, Kent Ballard, to join the family gathering. She had even brought him a present to put under the tree, so he wouldn't feel left out. Kent was planning to drive over from Kentucky Lake by noon. He had gone there to inspect his boat because of an ice storm earlier in the week. He felt compelled to visit his boat on the holiday, Carolyn thought, as if it were a sad old relative in a retirement home.

"We're having baked ham instead of turkey," Mom said. "Your daddy never did like ham baked, but whoever heard of fried ham on Christmas? We have that all year round and I'm burnt out on it."

"I love baked ham," said Carolyn.

"Does Kent like it baked?"

"I'm sure he does." Carolyn placed her gifts under the tree. The number of packages seemed unusually small.

"It don't seem like Christmas with drawed names," said Mom.

"Your star's about to fall off." Carolyn straightened the silver ornament at the tip of the tree.

"I didn't decorate as much as I wanted to. I'm slowing down. Getting old, I guess." Mom had not combed her hair and she was wearing a workshirt and tennis shoes.

"You always try to do too much on Christmas, Mom."

Carolyn knew the agreement to draw names had bothered her mother. But the four daughters were grown, and two had children. Sixteen people were expected today. Carolyn herself could not afford to buy fifteen presents on her salary as a clerk at J. C. Penney's, and her parents' small farm had not been profitable in years.

Carolyn's father appeared in the kitchen and he hugged her so tightly she squealed in protest.

"That's all I can afford this year," he said, laughing.

As he took a piece of candy from a dish on the counter, Carolyn teased him. "You'd better watch your calories today."

"Oh, not on Christmas!"

It made Carolyn sad to see her handsome father getting older. He was a shy man, awkward with his daughters, and Carolyn knew he had been deeply disappointed over her failed marriage, although he had never said so. Now he asked, "Who bought these 'toes'?"

He would no longer say "nigger toes," the old name for the chocolate-covered creams.[1]

"Hattie Smoot brought those over," said Mom. "I made a pants suit for her last week," she said to Carolyn. "The one that had stomach bypass?"

"When PeeWee McClain had that, it didn't work and they had to fix him back like he was," said Dad. He offered Carolyn a piece of candy, but she shook her head no.

Mom said, "I made Hattie a dress back last spring for her boy's graduation, and she couldn't even find a pattern big enough. I had to 'low a foot. But after that bypass, she's down to a size twenty."

"I think we'll all need a stomach bypass after we eat this feast you're fixing," said Carolyn.

"Where's Kent?" Dad asked abruptly.

"He went to see about his boat. He said he'd be here."

Carolyn looked at the clock. She felt uneasy about inviting Kent. Everyone would be scrutinizing him, as if he were some new character on a soap opera. Kent, who drove a truck for the Kentucky Loose-Leaf Floor, was a part-time student at Murray State. He was majoring in accounting. When Carolyn started going with him early in the summer, they went sailing on his boat, which had "Joyce" painted on it. Later he painted over the name, insisting he didn't love Joyce anymore—she was a dietician who was always criticizing what he ate—but he had never said he loved Carolyn. She did not know if she loved him. Each seemed to be waiting for the other to say it first.

While Carolyn helped her mother in the kitchen, Dad went to get her grandfather, her mother's father. Pappy, who had been disabled by a stroke, was cared for by a live-in housekeeper who had gone home to her own family for the day. Carolyn diced apples and pears for fruit salad while her mother shaped sweet potato balls with marshmallow centers and rolled them in crushed cornflakes. On TV in the living

1. Use of the pejorative term describing African Americans. While Mason uses it here to describe chocolate candies, in other parts of the South, the term describes the Brazil nut.

room, *Days of Our Lives* was beginning, but the Christmas tree blocked their view of the television set.

"Whose name did you draw, Mom?" Carolyn asked, as she began seeding the grapes.

"Jim's."

"You put Jim's name in the hat?"

Mom nodded. Jim Walsh was the man Carolyn's youngest sister, Laura Jean, was living with in St. Louis. Laura Jean was going to an interior decorating school, and Jim was a textiles salesman she had met in class. "I made him a shirt," Mom said.

"I'm surprised at you."

"Well, what was I to do?"

"I'm just surprised." Carolyn ate a grape and spit out the seeds. "Emily Post says the couple should be offered the same room when they visit."

"You know we'd never stand for that. I don't think your dad's ever got over her stacking up with that guy."

"You mean shacking up."

"Same thing." Mom dropped the potato masher, and the metal rattled on the floor. "Oh, I'm in such a tizzy," she said.

As the family began to arrive, the noise of the TV played against the greetings, the slam of the storm door, the outside wind rushing in. Carolyn's older sisters, Peggy and Iris, with their husbands and children, were arriving all at once, and suddenly the house seemed small. Peggy's children Stevie and Cheryl, without even removing their jackets, became involved in a basketball game on TV. In his lap, Stevie had a Merlin electronic toy, which beeped randomly. Iris and Ray's children, Deedee and Jonathan, went outside to look for cats.

In the living room, Peggy jiggled her baby, Lisa, on her hip and said, "You need you one of these, Carolyn."

"Where can I get one?" said Carolyn, rather sharply.

Peggy grinned. "At the gittin' place, I reckon."

Peggy's critical tone was familiar. She was the only sister who had had a real wedding. Her husband, Cecil, had a Gulf franchise,[2] and they owned a motor cruiser,[3] a pickup truck, a camper, a station wagon, and a new brick colonial home. Whenever Carolyn went to visit Peggy, she felt apologetic for not having a man who would buy her all these things, but she never seemed to be attracted to anyone steady or ambitious. She had been wondering how Kent would get along with the men of the family. Cecil and Ray were standing in a corner talking about gas mileage. Cecil, who was shorter than Peggy and was going bald, always worked on Dad's truck for free, and Ray usually agreed with Dad on politics to avoid an argument. Ray had an impressive government job in Frankfort. He had coordinated a ribbon-cutting ceremony when the toll road opened. What would Kent have to say to them? She could imagine him insisting that everyone go outside later to watch the sunset. Her father would think that was ridiculous. No one ever did that on a farm, but it was the sort of thing Kent would think of. Yet she knew that spontaneity was what she liked in him.

2. Gulf was an oil company that sold many franchises throughout the United States during the 1940s through the 1980s. Gulf Oil Company was purchased by Chevron Oil in the late 1980s.

3. A motor cruiser is an expensive boat sometimes containing living quarters.

Deedee and Jonathan, who were ten and six, came inside then and immediately began shaking the presents under the tree. All the children were wearing new jeans and cowboy shirts, Carolyn noticed.

"Why are y'all so quiet?" she asked. "I thought kids whooped and hollered on Christmas."

"They've been up since *four,*" said Iris. She took a cigarette from her purse and accepted a light from Cecil. Exhaling smoke, she said to Carolyn, "We heard Kent was coming." Before Carolyn could reply, Iris scolded the children for shaking the packages. She seemed nervous.

"He's supposed to be here by noon," said Carolyn.

"There's somebody now. I hear a car."

"It might be Dad, with Pappy."

It was Laura Jean, showing off Jim Walsh as though he were a splendid Christmas gift she had just received.

"Let me kiss everybody!" she cried, as the women rushed toward her. Laura Jean had not been home in four months.

"Merry Christmas!" Jim said in a booming, official-sounding voice, something like a TV announcer, Carolyn thought. He embraced all the women and then, with a theatrical gesture, he handed Mom a bottle of Rebel Yell bourbon and a carton of boiled custard which he took from a shopping bag. The bourbon was in a decorative Christmas box.

Mom threw up her hands. "Oh, no, I'm afraid I'll be a alky-holic."

"Oh, that's ridiculous, Mom," said Laura Jean, taking Jim's coat. "A couple of drinks a day are good for your heart."

Jim insisted on getting coffee cups from a kitchen cabinet and mixing some boiled custard and bourbon. When he handed a cup to Mom, she puckered up her face.

"Law, don't let the preacher in," she said, taking a sip. "Boy, that sends my blood pressure up."

Carolyn waved away the drink Jim offered her. "I don't start this early in the day," she said, feeling confused.

Jim was a large, dark-haired man with a neat little beard, like a bird's nest cupped on his chin. He had a Northern accent. When he hugged her, Carolyn caught a whiff of cologne, something sweet, like chocolate syrup. Last summer, when Laura Jean brought him home for the first time, she had made a point of kissing and hugging him in front of everyone. Dad had virtually ignored him. Now Carolyn saw that Jim was telling Cecil that he always bought Gulf gas. Red-faced, Ray accepted a cup of boiled custard. Carolyn fled to the kitchen and began grating cheese for potatoes au gratin. She dreaded Kent's arrival.

When Dad arrived with Pappy, Cecil and Jim helped set up the wheelchair in a corner. Afterward, Dad and Jim shook hands, and Dad refused Jim's offer of bourbon. From the kitchen, Carolyn could see Dad hugging Laura Jean, not letting go. She went into the living room to greet her grandfather.

"They roll me in this buggy too fast," he said when she kissed his forehead.

Carolyn hoped he wouldn't notice the bottle of bourbon, but she knew he never missed anything. He was so deaf people had given up talking to him. Now the children tiptoed around him, looking at him with awe. Somehow, Carolyn expected the children to notice that she was alone, like Pappy.

At ten minutes of one, the telephone rang. Peggy answered and handed the receiver to Carolyn. "It's Kent," she said.

Kent had not left the lake yet. "I just got here an hour ago," he told Carolyn. "I had to take my sister over to my mother's."

"Is the boat O.K.?"

"Yeah. Just a little scraped paint. I'll be ready to go in a little while." He hesitated, as though waiting for assurance that the invitation was real.

"This whole gang's ready to eat," Carolyn said. "Can't you hurry?" She should have remembered the way he tended to get sidetracked. Once it took them three hours to get to Paducah, because he kept stopping at antique shops.

After she hung up the telephone, her mother asked, "Should I put the rolls in to brown yet?"

"Wait just a little. He's just now leaving the lake."

"When's this Kent feller coming?" asked Dad impatiently, as he peered into the kitchen. "It's time to eat."

"He's on his way," said Carolyn.

"Did you tell him we don't wait for stragglers?"

"No."

"When the plate rattles, we eat."

"I know."

"Did you tell him that?"

"No, I didn't!" cried Carolyn, irritated.

When they were alone in the kitchen, Carolyn's mother said to her, "Your dad's not his self today. He's fit to be tied about Laura Jean bringing that guy down here again. And him bringing that whiskey."

"That was uncalled for," Carolyn agreed. She had noticed that Mom had set her cup of boiled custard in the refrigerator.

"Besides, he's not too happy about that Kent Ballard you're running around with."

"What's it to him?"

"You know how he always was. He don't think anybody's good enough for one of his little girls, and he's afraid you'll get mistreated again. He don't think Kent's very dependable."

"I guess Kent's proving Dad's point."

Carolyn's sister Iris had dark brown eyes, unique in the family. When Carolyn was small, she tried to say "Iris's eyes" once and called them "Irish eyes," confusing them with a song their mother sometimes sang, "When Irish Eyes Are Smiling." Thereafter, they always teased Iris about her smiling Irish eyes. Today Iris was not smiling. Carolyn found her in a bedroom smoking, holding an ashtray in her hand.

"I drew your name," Carolyn told her. "I got you something I wanted myself."

"Well, if I don't want it, I guess I'll have to give it to you."

"What's wrong with you today?"

"Ray and me's getting a separation," said Iris.

"Really?" Carolyn was startled by the note of glee in her response. Actually, she told herself later, it was because she was glad her sister, whom she saw infrequently, had confided in her.

"The thing of it is, I had to beg him to come today, for Mom and Dad's sake. It'll kill them. Don't let on, will you?"

"I won't. What are you going to do?"

"I don't know. He's already moved out."

"Are you going to stay in Frankfort?"

"I don't know. I have to work things out."

Mom stuck her head in the door. "Well, is Kent coming or not?"

"He *said* he'd be here," said Carolyn.

"Your dad's about to have a duck with a rubber tail. He can't stand to wait on a meal."

"Well, let's go ahead, then. Kent can eat when he gets here."

When Mom left, Iris said, "Aren't you and Kent getting along?"

"I don't know. He said he'd come today, but I have a feeling he doesn't really want to."

"To hell with men." Iris laughed and stubbed out her cigarette. "Just look at us—didn't we turn out awful? First your divorce. Now me. And Laura Jean bringing that guy down. Daddy can't stand him. Did you see the look he gave him?"

"Laura Jean's got a lot more nerve than I've got," said Carolyn, nodding. "I could wring Kent's neck for being late. Well, none of us can do anything right—except Peggy."

"Daddy's precious little angel," said Iris mockingly. "Come on, we'd better get in there and help."

While Mom went to change her blouse and put on lipstick, the sisters brought the food into the dining room. Two tables had been put together. Peggy cut the ham with an electric knife, and Carolyn filled the iced tea glasses.

"Pappy gets buttermilk and Stevie gets Coke," Peggy directed her.

"I know," said Carolyn, almost snapping.

As the family sat down, Carolyn realized that no one ever asked Pappy to "turn thanks" anymore at holiday dinners. He was sitting there expectantly, as if waiting to be asked. Mom cut up his ham into small bits. Carolyn waited for a car to drive up, the phone to ring. The TV was still on.

"Y'all dig in," said Mom. "Jim? Make sure you try some of these dressed eggs like I fix."

"I thought your new boyfriend was coming," said Cecil to Carolyn.

"So did I!" said Laura Jean. "That's what you wrote me."

Everyone looked at Carolyn as she explained. She looked away.

"You're looking at that pitiful tree," Mom said to her. "I just know it don't show up good from the road."

"No, it looks fine." No one had really noticed the tree. Carolyn seemed to be seeing it for the first time in years—broken red plastic reindeer, Styrofoam snowmen with crumbling top hats, silver walnuts which she remembered painting when she was about twelve.

Dad began telling a joke about some monks who had taken a vow of silence. At each Christmas dinner, he said, one monk was allowed to speak.

"Looks like your vocal cords would rust out," said Cheryl.

"Shut up, Cheryl, Granddaddy's trying to tell something," said Cecil.

"So the first year it was the first monk's turn to talk, and you know what he said? He said, 'These taters is lumpy'. "

When several people laughed, Stevie asked, "Is that the joke?"

Carolyn was baffled. Her father had never told a joke at the table in his life. He sat at the head of the table, looking out past the family at the cornfield through the picture window.

"Pay attention now," he said. "The second year Christmas rolled around again and it was the second monk's turn to say something. He said, 'You know, I think you're right. The taters *is* lumpy'."

Laura Jean and Jim laughed loudly.

"Reach me some light-bread,"[4] said Pappy. Mom passed the dish around the table to him.

"And so the third year," Dad continued, "the third monk got to say something. What he said"—Dad was suddenly overcome with mirth—"what he said was, 'If y'all don't shut up arguing about them taters, I'm going to leave this place!' "

After the laughter died, Mom said, "Can you imagine anybody not a-talking all year long?"

"That's the way monks are, Mom," said Laura Jean. "Monks are economical with everything. They're not wasteful, not even with words."

"The Trappist Monks are really an outstanding group," said Jim. "And they make excellent bread. No preservatives."

Cecil and Peggy stared at Jim.

"You're not eating, Dad," said Carolyn. She was sitting between him and the place set for Kent. The effort at telling the joke seemed to have taken her father's appetite.

"He ruined his dinner on nigger toes," said Mom.

"Dottie Barlow got a Barbie doll for Christmas and it's black," Cheryl said.

"Dottie Barlow ain't black, is she?" asked Cecil.

"No."

"That's funny," said Peggy. "Why would they give her a black Barbie doll?"

"She just wanted it."

Abruptly, Dad left the table, pushing back his plate. He sat down in the recliner chair in front of the TV. The Blue-Gray game was beginning, and Cecil and Ray were hurriedly finishing in order to join him. Carolyn took out second helpings of ham and jello salad, feeling as though she were eating for Kent in his absence. Jim was taking seconds of everything, complimenting Mom. Mom apologized for not having fancy napkins. Then Laura Jean described a photography course she had taken. She had been photographing close-ups of car parts—fenders, headlights, mud flaps.

"That sounds goofy," said one of the children, Deedee.

Suddenly Pappy spoke. "Use to, the menfolks would eat first, and the children separate. The womenfolks would eat last, in the kitchen."

"You know what I could do with you all, don't you?" said Mom, shaking her fist at him. "I could set up a plank out in the field for y'all to eat on." She laughed.

"Times are different now, Pappy," said Iris loudly. "We're just as good as the men."

"She gets that from television," said Ray, with an apologetic laugh.

Carolyn noticed Ray's glance at Iris. Just then Iris matter-of-factly plucked an eyelash from Ray's cheek. It was as though she had momentarily forgotten about the separation.

Later, after the gifts were opened, Jim helped clear the tables. Kent still had not come. The baby slept, and Laura Jean, Jim, Peggy, and Mom played a Star Trek board game at the dining room table, while Carolyn and Iris played Battlestar Galactica with Cheryl and Deedee. The other men were quietly engrossed in the football game,

4. A term sometimes used in the South to describe store-bought bread rather than homemade bread.

a blur of sounds. No one had mentioned Kent's absence, but after the children had distributed the gifts, Carolyn refused to tell them what was in the lone package left under the tree. It was the most extravagantly wrapped of all the presents, with an immense ribbon, not a stick-on bow. An icicle had dropped on it, and it reminded Carolyn of an abandoned float, like something from a parade.

At a quarter to three, Kent telephoned. He was still at the lake. "The gas stations are all closed," he said. "I couldn't get any gas."

"We already ate and opened the presents," said Carolyn.

"Here I am, stranded. Not a thing I can do about it."

Kent's voice was shaky and muffled, and Carolyn suspected he had been drinking. She did not know what to say, in front of the family. She chattered idly, while she played with a ribbon from a package. The baby was awake, turning dials and knobs on a Busy Box. On TV, the Blues picked up six yards on an end sweep. Carolyn fixed her eyes on the tilted star at the top of the tree. Kent was saying something about Santa Claus.

"They wanted me to play Santy at Mama's house for the littluns. I said—you know what I said? 'Bah, humbug!' Did I ever tell you what I've got against Christmas?"

"Maybe not." Carolyn's back stiffened against the wall.

"When I was little bitty, Santa Claus came to town. I was about five. I was all fired up to go see Santy, and Mama took me, but we were late, and he was about to leave. I had to run across the courthouse square to get to him. He was giving away suckers, so I ran as hard as I could. He was climbing up on the fire engine—are you listening?"

"Unh-huh." Carolyn was watching her mother, who was folding Christmas paper to save for next year.

Kent said, "I reached up and pulled at his old red pants leg, and he looked down at me, and you know what he said?"

"No—what?"

"He said, 'Piss off, kid'."

"Really?"

"Would I lie to you?"

"I don't know."

"Do you want to hear the rest of my hard-luck story?"

"Not now."

"Oh, I forgot this was long distance. I'll call you tomorrow. Maybe I'll go paint the boat. That's what I'll do! I'll go paint it right this minute."

After Carolyn hung up the telephone, her mother said, "I think my Oriental casserole was a failure. I used the wrong kind of mushroom soup. It called for cream of mushroom and I used golden mushroom."

"Won't you *ever* learn, Mom?" cried Carolyn. "You always cook too much. You make *such* a big deal—"

Mom said, "What happened with Kent this time?"

"He couldn't get gas. He forgot the gas stations were closed."

"Jim and Laura Jean didn't have any trouble getting gas," said Peggy, looking up from the game.

"We tanked up yesterday," said Laura Jean.

"Of course you did," said Carolyn distractedly. "You always think ahead."

"It's your time," Cheryl said, handing Carolyn the Battlestar Galactica toy. "I did lousy."

"Not as lousy as I did," said Iris.

Carolyn tried to concentrate on shooting enemy missiles, raining through space. Her sisters seemed far away, like the spaceships. She was aware of the men watching football, their hands in action as they followed an exciting play. Even though Pappy had fallen asleep, with his blanket in his lap he looked like a king on a throne. Carolyn thought of the quiet accommodation her father had made to his father-in-law, just as Cecil and Ray had done with Dad, and her ex-husband had tried to do once. But Cecil had bought his way in, and now Ray was getting out. Kent had stayed away. Jim, the newcomer, was with the women, playing Star Trek as if his life depended upon it. Carolyn was glad now that Kent had not come. The story he told made her angry, and his pity for his childhood made her think of something Pappy had often said: "Christmas is for children." Earlier, she had listened in amazement while Cheryl listed on her fingers the gifts she had received that morning: a watch, a stereo, a nightgown, hot curls,[5] perfume, candles, a sweater, a calculator, a jewelry box, a ring. Now Carolyn saw Kent's boat as his toy, more important than the family obligations of the holiday.

Mom was saying, "I wanted to make a Christmas tablecloth out of red checks and green fringe. You wouldn't think knit would do for a tablecloth, but Hattie Smoot has the prettiest one."

"You can do incredible things with knit," said Jim with sudden enthusiasm. The shirt Mom had made him was bonded knit.

"Who's Hattie Smoot?" asked Laura Jean. She was caressing the back of Jim's neck, as though soothing his nerves.

Carolyn laughed when her mother began telling Jim and Laura Jean about Hattie Smoot's operation. Jim listened attentively, leaning forward with his elbows on the table, and asked eager questions, his eyes as alert as Pappy's.

"Is she telling a joke?" Cheryl asked Carolyn.

"No. I'm not laughing at you, Mom," Carolyn said, touching her mother's hand. She felt relieved that the anticipation of Christmas had ended. Still laughing, she said, "Pour me some of that Rebel Yell, Jim. It's about time."

"I'm with you," Jim said, jumping up.

In the kitchen, Carolyn located a clean spoon while Jim washed some cups. Carolyn couldn't find the cup Mom had left in the refrigerator. As she took out the carton of boiled custard, Jim said, "It must be a very difficult day for you."

Carolyn was startled. His tone was unexpectedly kind, genuine. She was struck suddenly by what he must know about her, because of his intimacy with her sister. She knew nothing about him. When he smiled, she saw a gold cap on a molar, shining like a Christmas ornament. She managed to say, "It can't be any picnic for you either. Kent didn't want to put up with us."

"Too bad he couldn't get gas."

"I don't think he wanted to get gas."

"Then you're better off without him." When Jim looked at her, Carolyn felt that he must be examining her resemblances to Laura Jean. He said, "I think your family's great."

Carolyn laughed nervously. "We're hard on you. God, you're brave to come down here like this."

"Well, Laura Jean's worth it."

5. Heated curlers for hair styling.

They took the boiled custard and cups into the dining room. As Carolyn sat down, her nephew Jonathan begged her to tell what was in the gift left under the tree.

"I can't tell," she said.

"Why not?"

"I'm saving it till next year, in case I draw some man's name."

"I hope it's mine," said Jonathan.

Jim stirred bourbon into three cups of boiled custard, then gave one to Carolyn and one to Laura Jean. The others had declined. Then he leaned back in his chair—more relaxed now—and squeezed Laura Jean's hand. Carolyn wondered what they said to each other when they were alone in St. Louis. She knew with certainty that they would not be economical with words, like the monks in the story. She longed to be with them, to hear what they would say. She noticed her mother picking at a hangnail, quietly ignoring the bourbon. Looking at the bottle's gift box, which showed an old-fashioned scene, children on sleds in the snow, Carolyn thought of Kent's boat again. She felt she was in that snowy scene now with Laura Jean and Jim, sailing in Kent's boat into the winter breeze, into falling snow. She thought of how silent it was out on the lake, as though the whiteness of the snow were the absence of sound.

"Cheers!" she said to Jim, lifting her cup.

Questions to Consider

1. Is "Drawing Names" an example of dirty realism? What characteristics of this story support your position?
2. In "Drawing Names," the family redefines the ways in which holiday gifts are exchanged, and this change is representative of the ways in which the family structure has changed in the contemporary South. What does Mason's story suggest about the changes that have occurred in Southern families, and how does the minimized gift-giving strategy demonstrate these changes?

Frederick Barthelme

1943–

Frederick Barthelme has said of his approach to fiction writing: "I try to write about people who show what they think and feel through actions and reactions, through choices, through oblique bits of dialogue." Like many contemporary Southern authors, Barthelme places the focus of his works on his characters, and not surprisingly, he has been praised for his use of language and dialogue. He is also well known for his diverse artistic talents, which have allowed him to create works as a painter, musician, architect, sculptor, writer, and teacher. Barthelme often places his literary characters in or around the Gulf States and shows them dealing with everyday problems and learning to overcome or adjust to new situations.

Barthelme was born on 10 October 1943 in Houston, to Donald, an architect, and Helen Bechtold Barthelme, a teacher. Frederick was one of five children, all of whom became writers. His brother, Donald, before his untimely death from cancer, was one of the most noted postmodern writers of the later twentieth century, and his other brothers, Peter and Steven also write.

Fredrick's college career began at Tulane University in 1961, but he transferred to the University of Houston, which he attended intermittently until he completed his bachelor's degree in 1966. During this time, he also spent a year working at the Houston Museum of Fine Arts. Barthelme received a teaching fellowship to Johns Hopkins University to support his work toward his master's degree, and he earned the University's Coleman Prose Award for his short story entitled "Storyteller" in 1977, the same year that he completed his M.A. He has received grants from the National Endowment for the Arts and the University of Southern Mississippi to pursue his creative endeavors.

From 1965 to 1966, Barthelme served as a corporate architect, but his artistic bent drew him toward museum work. He then secured a position as an exhibition organizer at St. Thomas University. He soon advanced to the Kornblee Gallery in New York City, where he worked as the assistant to the gallery director. Barthelme has also worked as a creative director and senior writer for an advertising firm. In 1977, he accepted a position as a Professor of English at the University of Southern Mississippi in Hattiesburg and has remained in this position for many years. While at the University of Southern Mississippi, Barthelme has served as a professor of English, director of the Center for Writers, and editor of the *Mississippi Review*.

Barthleme's work, over his long career, has included both minimalism and the experimentalism of the postmodern era inspired by his study of John Barth and Thomas Pynchon. His latest collection, *The Law of Averages: New and Selected Stories* (2000) focuses on characters and their development rather than plot and story line and illustrates the importance of life here and now without glorifying the past. Absent from his writing is a tribute to the "good old days."

Barthelme's work has been called moralistic, but not in the didactic sense; in it, he attempts to address the ways that people live in postmodern America. His characters face shifting ideas about right and wrong, changing views of sexuality, and subsequently, the need to find their own code of ethics to survive rather than grasping at generalities that might work for society as a whole. His use of second person narration further illustrates his innovation in writing.

Domestic

Marie watches her husband from the porch of their bungalow, leaning against the open screen door as he digs in their backyard. The sun is out and warm, although it is fall, and late afternoon. They have been married eight years.

"Albert," she asks, "why are you doing that?" She is not entirely sure what it is that he is doing, but has asked that question already with unsatisfactory result, so she has opted for the question of motive.

"Why?" Albert says. He always repeats her questions.

He has been digging in the yard since eleven that morning, without a break, and his wife has come out of the house to ask him if he would like an early dinner. He straightens and pushes the long-handled spade into the dirt. "Marie, I am doing this because this is what I like, this is something I like, digging this hole. There are too few things in this life that are in and of themselves likable, and for me this is one of them. This is valuable to me and from this I derive pleasure. You might say I enjoy working with my hands, although that isn't the whole thing, not by a long shot." Albert stops to wipe his brow with a dime-store neckerchief, then turns to look at the hole he has dug, to gauge his progress. "Did you have something in mind?" he asks, turning back to his wife.

"Why don't you come have dinner now," Marie says, waving a fly away from her face.

He points to the sky and reaches for his shovel. "Got some light yet," he says. "Best use it."

Marie suddenly feels stupid for having suggested dinner at four o'clock in the afternoon, and feels angry that her husband has made a fool of her again, in another one of the small ways that he often makes a fool of her, and she snaps, "Well, I don't like it, frankly," and goes back inside.

After watching him from the kitchen window for a few minutes, Marie climbs the hardwood stairs and flops on the king-size bed in the bedroom, on her back, her arms outstretched. Even with her arms and legs spread, she is swallowed up in the huge mattress, enveloped by it, unable to touch the edges. She looks straight up at the ceiling and tries to imagine a great battle from the Middle Ages pictured there—horses, and cannon, and armor—but sees instead a lone knight in black mail astride an equally black horse, riding backward, bent over inspecting the rump of the animal. "Oh Lord," she says, and she rolls off the bed and reaches for the telephone. She calls her mother.

"What're you doing, Mama? How are you? I haven't talked to you in such a long time."

"I talked to you Thursday, Peaches. Is something wrong between you and Albert?"

"Mama! You always think that. And don't call me Peaches, please."

"Marie," her mother says, "you didn't call me two thousand miles across this great continent to ask me the time of day in the middle of the afternoon on the long-distance telephone, I know that don't I?"

"Albert is digging in the backyard is why I called," Marie says. "I don't know why—it isn't even Saturday."

"Your father dug, Peaches."

"This is different, Mama. And don't call me Peaches."

"So you called me now when the rates are high to tell me that your husband and the father of your eventual child is in the backyard digging a hole? Is that all you have to say to me? And you want me to believe that nothing is wrong in your marriage?"

Marie looks out the upstairs window at the bent white shoulders of her husband, watches as he hoists a small mound of dirt, gazes at the shovel's attenuated arc. "It's a serious problem, Mama, or I wouldn't have called. You know what happened to Papa."

"That was different, Peaches. Your papa went a little crazy, that's all. I suspect it ran in his family. When he bought the P-38 for the neighborhood kids, when he cut the hole in the roof of the den, remember? There were reasons, there were explanations—Papa was always up to some good. And, by the way, have you asked about me yet? How I am and what I'm doing out here all alone on this barren coast? No you have not. Maybe if you had brought that Albert out here last summer like I asked you to, I could have straightened him out, and you wouldn't have this terrible problem you have right now, which, if I may say, doesn't sound all that terrible from this distance."

"Thank you, Mama," Marie says.

"Don't start with me, young lady," her mother says. "I'm just trying to help. A mother has an investment in a daughter, as you might well learn one day if that Albert ever gets his head out of the clouds and gets down to business like a real man."

"I have to go now, Mama," Marie says.

"Of course you do, Peaches. You should've gone before you called, if you get my meaning. And, by the way, thank you very much, I'm getting along fine. Mr. Carleton is coming over this evening, and we're going to walk down by the water and maybe take in a show at the Showcase, if you want to know, just by way of information."

"Mr. Carleton?"

"Yes. And if you want my advice you'll stop your whimpering and get out there with a shovel of your own, if you see what I mean."

Albert and Marie live in a small suburb near Conroe, Texas. All of their neighbors own powerboats which, during the week, clutter the driveways and front lawns. Albert and Marie do not own a powerboat, although Albert does subscribe to *Boats & Motors,* a monthly magazine devoted to powerboating. Marie is small, freckled, delicate, blond. Albert is overweight.

That evening, when he finishes digging and comes inside for dinner, Marie presses the question of the hole. "I can't stand it anymore, Albert," she says. "You took a day off from work and you spent the whole day outside digging a hole. If you don't explain this minute, I will leave you."

He looks at her across the dinner table, fatigue and discomfort on his face in equal measures, then pushes an open hand back over his head, leaving some strands of hair standing straight up in a curious peak. Finally he looks at the pork chop on his dinner plate and says, "I love the work, Marie. I love the product. For many years I have been interested in holes—how many times have I pointed out a hole to you when we drive to the store? A hole for telephone equipment, or for a gas line, or for the foundation of a great building? And, of course, I need the exercise, don't I? Marie, there are many wonderful holes in life—dogs dig holes, as do other animals. Pretty women dig small holes on weekend afternoons—can't you understand?"

"I think you're being foolish, Albert," she says, twisting a silver chain around her fingers until the tips of the digits turn purple. Then she unwinds the chain and twists it again, on new fingers. "You may even be silly. Still, you are my husband, and even though you have not provided me with any children, I love you. What are you going to do with this hole when you get it dug?"

Albert's eyes go suddenly very dark, flashing. "Ha!" he says, thrusting himself out of his chair, his arm at full extension, his fork teetering between the tips of his fingers. "You see? *You* are the foolish one! *You* ask stupid questions!" With that he slaps the fork flat onto the table and rushes upstairs to the bedroom, slamming the door behind him.

Marie sighs deeply and continues the meal alone, chewing and thinking of Albert's fingernails, which looked to her like tiny slivers of black moon.

In the morning, after Albert has gone to work at the airline, Marie takes her coffee to the hall table where she sits staring at the telephone for a long time. The hands of the electric clock on the table fly around the clock's face, making a barely audible whir.

An airplane passes overhead, through the clouds.

In the distance, there is a siren.

Marie begins to cry, falling forward on the table, her arms folded there and cradling her head. Between sobs she whispers, "I don't want my husband to dig this hole, I don't want my husband to dig this hole . . ."

The telephone rings. It is her friend Sissy, now a secondary school teacher in Vermont. Marie begins to tell Sissy the story of Albert and the hole, but is unable to make her objection clear, and Sissy responds unsympathetically. Marie is surprised that she isn't clearer about why she is upset by Albert's behavior, and instead of listening to Sissy, she gazes at Albert's university diploma which is framed and mounted above the hall table and wonders why she can't explain herself more clearly.

Finally she says, "I don't know why this upsets me so much, it's silly really." But she has interrupted Sissy's explanation of Albert's behavior, and Sissy insists on finishing the explanation.

"A metaphor," Sissy says, "works in a lot of ways to release the feelings of an individual, opening that individual to expressions which are, for some reason, closed to him. Albert may simply be depressed, and the physical digging is for him a model of the emotional digging that's going on, see what I'm saying? Reflects his disaffection, or something. Maybe he's bored?"

"I see what you mean," Marie says, and she marks another minute gone on the pink pad in front of her, a horizontal stroke crossing four vertical strokes.

"Why don't you dig some, too?" Sissy asks. "Seems like that'd be more to the point."

"I've been thinking about that," Marie says.

"Don't think," Sissy says. "*Do.*" Then, her voice rising with relief and new interest, she says, "We're on strike up here, that's why I'm home today. I know it's terrible for the kids, but business is business, right? Besides, they're probably grateful."

"Strike?"

"Yeah," Sissy says. "We're going to bury the bastards if they don't pay up. There've been promises—it's real complicated, but we're up against the school board and an old jerk named Watkins who'd just as soon see us work for room and board. Anyway, we've been out three weeks and no end in sight. I've got a little money tucked away, so it's all right. Maybe you ought to get a job yourself, give you something to take your mind off Albert. I mean, you never worked at all after we finished school, did you?"

"I worked in that hospital," Marie says.

"Oh that. That wasn't work, darling, that was recreation. Try getting an office job these days. Maybe you should take a graduate course? Or pottery, pottery's always good."

When Albert returns from work he goes directly into the yard to work on the hole. Marie watches him from the porch for a few minutes, then goes outside and sits in the passenger seat of their Plymouth station wagon, with the door closed, watching her husband. When, after twenty minutes of sustained digging, he stops to rest, she leans out the car window and says, "You're making this to hurt me, aren't you? I know. I know you, Albert."

"Maybe you're right," he says, looking at the hole. "About knowing me, I mean."

He climbs out of the hole, and Marie gets out of the car. They walk to the house together, side by side, their arms bumping into each other as they walk. He is thirty-nine years old. She is younger.

"I want to watch television tonight," he says. "And then make love. What do you say?"

"You're not trying to hurt me?"

"No, I'm not," he says, and he links arms with her and together they turn to survey the yard.

"But," she says.

"It'll be beautiful," he says. "Just wait."

Marie glances at the neighbor's crisp green bushes, then nods tentatively. "It's hard to understand."

They stand for a moment together on the concrete steps of the porch, then go into the house. Albert washes his hands in the kitchen sink while Marie burns the hairs off the chicken they will have for dinner.

"Why can't we refurbish an old house like everybody else?" she asks. "Or refinish furniture together?"

Albert looks at her and grins. "I lied about the television," he says, and he reaches for her with his hands still soapy, staggering across the kitchen, Frankenstein fashion.

She glares at Albert as hard as she can, then giggles and runs up the stairs very fast. At the landing she stops and leans over the rail and shouts, "I'm not having a baby, Albert!"

She slams the bedroom door, and Albert, who has followed her from the kitchen still acting out his monster role, allows his shoulders to slump, and sighs, and moves on up the stairs. He taps on the bedroom door with a knuckle. "Marie?" he calls through the door.

"What if it rains, Albert?"

"What?"

"My mother doesn't like you," Marie shouts. Then, a little less loudly, "Sissy likes you, but Sissy's ugly."

"What? Who's Sissy?"

"But you can't dig that hole anymore, or I will not do anything you want me to do," she says, still shouting as he enters the room.

"What are you talking about?" he asks.

"Promise me that you won't," she says. "Promise it's over."

"Oh Jesus," Albert says. "Forget the hole for shit's sake. It's just a hole. Jesus."

"Maybe it's just a hole to you, but it's more to me—it's something I don't want you to do—promise, Albert, please."

Marie is on the bed, her knees held tight by her arms up under her chin. She isn't smiling. Albert stands in the doorway with one hand still on the knob. "I just want to see what's under there," he says.

"You don't mean that," Marie says.

"I'm going downstairs to watch television," Albert says.

Much later, Marie tiptoes down the stairs to see what Albert is doing. He is asleep on the couch in front of the television set, and, seeing him asleep, Marie squats on the stairs and weeps.

The following morning Marie eats a late breakfast alone on the porch, staring at the hole through the screen door. It is a cool day, cooler than yesterday, and she feels the closeness of winter, sees it in the graying sky, smells it in the scent of the morning air. The leaves on the trees seem darker to her, as if mustered for a final battle with the season. Taking a fresh cup of coffee in her striped mug, she goes down the steps into the yard. She walks in circles around the hole there, sipping her coffee and surveying the perimeter of their property—the fragment of an old stone fence, a willow, some low bushes with unremarkable fat leaves. The lot is a little more than half an acre—large, Albert has said, for this particular development.

At first she gives the hole a wide berth, almost ignoring it, but as she completes her third circle, she bears in toward it, stopping a few feet from its edge at a point on its perimeter farthest from the house. The hole, she observes, is about five feet in diameter and four feet deep. The sides are cut at ninety degrees to the horizontal, and the bottom of the hole is very flat. Albert's spade is jammed into the spreading pile of dirt that borders the hole on the side away from the driveway. She drops to her knees in the still-damp grass of the lawn and then leans forward over the edge of the hole, looking to see what's inside. "Nothing," she says, "just nothing." She tosses the dregs of her coffee into the hole and watches the coal-colored earth turn instantly darker as it absorbs the liquid. "I don't know what Albert is so smug about," she says. "Just a damn hole in the ground, for Christ's sake." Marie walks forward on her knees and then pivots her legs over the edge and into the hole. Now she realizes that the hole is a little deeper than she had thought, that it is very nearly five feet deep. Standing in the hole she can barely see over its edge and her coffee mug, which is now only inches from her nose, looms very large. She bends to inspect the wall of the hole and finds there only ordinary dirt and a few small brown worms, working their ways across what is for them a suddenly brighter terrain. Above her the sky is going very dark, and the rain is no longer a suggestion, it is a promise. This makes her excited and nervous at once—like a child, she is seduced by the prospect of passing the rainstorm outside, in the splashing mud of the hole, in the cold of the water on her skin. Like an adult, she is apprehensive about getting out of the hole, about tracking the mud into the house, about the scrubbing that now seems inevitable. She looks at her hands, then her arms, then her feet and knees—all muddied—and her pink dressing gown, which is marked and smudged in a dozen places. "Oh my," she mutters. "I suppose I'd better not." But she doesn't make an effort to climb out of the hole, and instead sits down abruptly on the bottom, leaning her back against the dirt wall.

The rain comes. Fitfully at first, the few surprisingly large drops slap into the hole with what is to Marie a charming music. Then the storm is upon her and suddenly her gown is soaked through, showing darker brown where the cloth is stuck to her skin. Under her legs she feels a puddle beginning to form, then sees it, its surface constantly agitated by the rain. She pops the shallow water with the flat of her hand, and the dark splashes stain her gown, and she laughs, and she wipes thick strands of hair away from her face with a wet palm, laughing and splashing the water all about her, and then she begins to sing, in a very wonderful voice, "The Battle Hymn of the Republic," because she has always been a soldier in her heart.

Questions to Consider

1. What is the turning point in the story between Marie and Albert?
2. What role does dialogue play in this story? How does it advance the plot?

John Shelton Reed

1942–

John Shelton Reed has spent his entire career examining what he has termed "either the existence or the implication of Southern cultural distinctiveness." Since the publication of his first book, *The Enduring South* (1972) he has created a unique approach to and understanding of Southern regionalism. Although there has long been interest in the cultural peculiarity of Southerners, Reed has contributed substantially to the ways in which scholary and popular perceptions of this dynamic region have been reconfigured.

Reed's interest in the defining characteristics of Southerners and his theories surrounding regional identity are rooted in his childhood. Growing up in Kingsport, Tennessee with his parents, J. Shelton Reed, a surgeon, and Alice Greene Reed, he had little reason to contemplate the idiosyncrasies of Southernism. East Tennessee familiarized Reed with the industrial and technological realities of Southern life, which fueled his later interest in economics, politics, and science. He attended the Massachusetts Institute of Technology, where he graduated in 1964 with a bachelor's degree in political science and mathematics. During his years at MIT, he internalized the distinctiveness of his Southern heritage, remarking that: "when a young man or woman from the South goes to school in the North, you are reminded where you came from. You are called on to defend it . . . or apologize for it." Reed found himself struggling to negotiate his identity in the midst of a larger culture.

On 11 July 1964, John Shelton Reed married musician Dale Volberg and continued his examination of Southern identity at Columbia University. He earned his Ph.D. in sociology, with distinction, in 1971. John and Dale Reed have two children.

Well known among scholars and popular readers alike for his essays and lectures about the South, Reed has written over a dozen books on the subject, largely aimed at academic readers. However, in 1996, he and his wife coauthored *1001 Things Everyone Should Know About the South*, which found substantial success with mainstream readers. Some of Reed's other books of nonfiction essays include *Southern Folk, Plain and Fancy* (1986); *Whistling Dixie* (1990); and *Kicking Back* (1995).

Reed's collections of often humorous, yet invariably accurate demographic maps of the South establish defining boundaries, using illustrations to demonstrate everything from the prime locations of rampant kudzu growth and rural areas that lack indoor plumbing, to the birthplaces of country music notables. Further, he suggests that the dual emphasis on the "regional fascination with words" and "the verbal emphasis of the Southern religious tradition may help to explain the remarkable Southern contribution to American literature." In the selection that follows, "New South or No South," Reed examines the ways in which the contemporary South is evolving, leading to the question of how the South should be characterized as we move into the twenty-first century.

Reed served in the sociology department at the University of North Carolina–Chapel Hill from 1969 until his retirement in 2000. He has been a visiting professor at Millsaps College, Auburn University, and the University of Cambridge, and a visiting scholar at the University of London in the Institute of United States Studies. He has also consulted on projects such as International Elvis Conferences, publications such as *Southern Living* magazine, and products such as Quaker Grits. Reed is also a contributor to the now defunct *Oxford American* and a founding coeditor of *Southern Cultures*.

New South or No South? Southern Culture in 2036

The year 1986 marked several significant Southern anniversaries. It had been 50 years since the founding of the Southern Sociological Society; 50 years since the publication of *Gone With the Wind*; 50 years since Howard W. Odum's classic *Southern Regions of the United States*; and, not least, an even century since Henry Grady, editor of the *Atlanta Constitution*, gave a speech in Boston that popularized the phrase *New South*.

There is a sort of numerological magic about the round numbers, these half-centuries and centuries (not to mention millennia, as we will have occasion to observe soon enough), and we probably ought to remind ourselves that these divisions are social conventions, reflecting only the evolutionary accident or divine whim that gave us ten fingers. Still, it has been a hundred years since Grady's speech, which does mean that very few who were living then are still with us; certainly nobody remembers the speech firsthand.

But, since 1886, many of us have heard a great deal about its subject. As Edwin Yoder put it, different versions of the New South have come and gone "like French constitutions and theories of the decline of Rome." Talk of a New South probably reached its high point in 1976, when Americans elected the first undeniably Southern president since Andrew Johnson. So much was said about it then that Walker Percy was driven to complain:

> Of all the things I'm fed up with, I think I'm fed up most with hearing about the New South. . . . One of the first things I can remember in my life was hearing about the New South. I was three years old, in Alabama. Not a year has passed since that I haven't heard about a new South. I would dearly love never to hear the New South mentioned again. In fact my definition of a new South would be a South in which it never occurred to anybody to mention the New South.

Percy is right, of course. But the phrase is convenient shorthand for whatever the South is becoming. And I want to ask a question about the next "New South": how much and in what respects will its culture be assimilated to national patterns?

Continuing Southern Distinctiveness

There was a time when few even thought to ask that question about Southern culture. Nearly everyone just assumed that the South would remain culturally distinctive. Certainly Henry Grady did. In his "New South" speech, Grady made some concession to the fact that the North had won the Civil War; he was willing, even eager, to adopt Northeastern economic ways, to build an urban, industrial economy like the one that had defeated his own. But scholars like Paul Gaston have pointed out quite rightly that Grady and his many admirers intended to pour the old cultural wine of planter rule and white supremacy into those new economic and demographic bottles. It apparently never crossed their minds to wonder whether traditional Southern ways were consistent with life in a radically altered society.

Later, though, particularly as Grady's economic prescriptions actually began to take effect, others began to wonder. As Broadus Mitchell put it in 1928, will "these great industrial developments . . . banish the personality of the South," or will industrialism "submit to be modified by a persistent Southern temperament?" Scholars from many disciplines—historians and anthropologists, folklorists and students of literature, geographers and political scientists—all have applied their disciplines' characteristic modes of inquiry to this question. Many brilliant and sensitive journalists have asked that question, too, and it is foolishness, mere academic snobbery, to ignore what they have written. Their work can be called "impressionistic" by those who wish to dismiss it, but at its best it is brilliant and sensitive ethnography.

One of the greatest of those journalists, W. J. Cash, put the case for cultural persistence as strongly as it has ever been put, in his masterpiece, *The Mind of the South.* Cash thought even Southern skyscrapers were expressions of continuity, reflecting an old tradition of civic pride and the search for glory. "Softly," he asked, "do you not hear behind that the gallop of Jeb Stuart's cavalrymen?" Not everyone has agreed, of course—C. Vann Woodward replied to Cash's rhetorical question: "The answer is 'no'! Not one ghostly echo of a gallop"—and that argument itself is on the way to becoming a persistent feature of our region's culture.

Few these days deny that the South has always been changing, and will continue to change as it moves into the next century. The disagreement today is about the extent and nature of the changes. The question has become: Does "New South" mean no South?

The Sociological Contribution

Oddly enough, it is only recently that sociologists have really had anything to say about this, despite the fact that it would seem on the face of it to be a sociological question. (The "regional sociologists" of the thirties and forties had other concerns, pressing ones related to the South's painfully evident social problems.) But the past quarter-century has seen the emergence of what is now a fairly large body of sociological literature, most of it based on survey research into attitudes and values. Lewis Killian, Andrew Greeley, Norval Glenn and his colleagues, Harry Holloway and Ted Robinson, Jeanne Hurlbert, myself—all of us have addressed one or more articles or books to the question. For the most part, these studies have adopted the rough-and-ready expedient of defining "Southerners" as residents of the Southern states (themselves variously defined) and comparing these respondents to other Americans on selected measures of attitudes, values, and behavior. Some studies have examined trends in regional difference over time; others have compared regional differences among younger Americans to those found among older ones; most have introduced controls for such confounding factors as education, occupation, and size of place. The methodological shortcomings of these studies are obvious enough, I should think, but they may be offset by the fact that the question of convergence is by its nature quantitative; survey methods can address it with a precision no other approach offers, a precision that may be misleading but one that at least establishes which side of the argument must bear the burden of proof.

In any case, this accumulating literature demonstrates that some important regional differences in the United States are getting smaller: many of them because the South is coming to resemble the rest of the United States; a few because the rest of the United States is starting to look like the South. But, at the same time, it shows that a great many large regional differences still exist. Some of these differences are not going away, and some, indeed, are increasing. In other words, nearly all the logical possibilities of what could be happening *are* happening, in one respect or another.

Can anything sensible be said about which differences are doing what? I think we can begin to make sense of this mass of data by distinguishing between two different sorts of attitudes and values that have, until recently, been "Southern" ones—by which I mean only that they have been found more often among Southerners than among other Americans.

Disappearing Traditional Values

In the first place, Southerners in the aggregate, black and white, have been characterized by a constellation of values that are common to folk, village, and peasant cultures everywhere in the world—not surprisingly, since that is what the whole South was as recently as fifty years ago, and what parts of it still are today. Any student of modernization could list these attributes; it seems perfectly clear that they are linked to economic development, and we do not have to take sides here in the quarrel about whether they are cause or effect. Among these attributes would be such things as fatalism and suspicion of innovation. Other traditional values seem to involve emphasizing firm and fixed boundaries between categories: between family members and others, for instance; between local people and strangers, or between ethnic brethren and aliens; between men and women, leaders and followers, and so forth. Indeed, cultural modernization seems to consist largely of learning to live with fuzzy and ambiguous boundaries.

Harold Grasmick, whose literature review and research on this subject I have leaned on heavily, calls this cluster of values "the" traditional value orientation, and he shows that, among Southerners, it is eroded by urban life, by education, by travel and residence outside the South, by exposure to the mass media. Since all these experiences are more common in each new generation of Southerners, it is not surprising to find that the traditional value orientation is less common among young Southerners than old ones, and less common now than a generation ago.

One consequence of the continuing economic and demographic convergence between the South and the rest of the United States will surely be regional convergence with respect to these traditional values as well. Indeed, the process has been going on slowly but steadily for some time now, and there is no reason to suppose that convergence will not soon be complete. Already regional differences in religious prejudice have virtually vanished, and differences in racial prejudice are so much smaller now than twenty years ago that they can almost be ignored. (Some of the demographic differences, however, have disappeared only to reemerge as differences in the opposite direction, as Ronald Rindfuss has shown, and there is always the possibility that the same may happen with some of the decreasing cultural differences.)

Another factor to consider, of course, is migration to the South. If it continues at anything like its present level, it will also nudge regional convergence along, because migrants to the South are conspicuously "untraditional": they are, that is, much less likely to display these characteristics than native Southerners, white or (especially) black. (By most of these measures, incidentally, blacks are the most "Southern" of all Southerners.)

Enduring Differences

But there have been other regional differences. Some Southern characteristics are not linked in any obvious way to rural residence, agricultural pursuits, poor education and not much of it, limited exposure to the "wider world." In *The Enduring South,* I examined some of them and ventured to predict that regional differences in some of these characteristics are going to be with us for a while.

Although it is presumptuous for me to mention my book in the same breath as Cash's *Mind of the South,* there is at least a genetic connection between the two books that I would like to put on the record. When I first read *The Mind of the South,* for recreation, in graduate school, I found it methodologically exasperating. I kept asking (as I was being trained to ask), "How does he know that?" When it came time to write a dissertation, I set out to study the mind of the South the way my teacher Paul Lazarsfeld had studied "the academic mind"—that is, with survey data. The result became *The Enduring South.* And I must say I emerged from the experience with a new respect for the achievement, and the "methodology," of W. J. Cash.

The differences my book documented would not have surprised Cash at all. Most of them can be seen as manifestations of the individualism that Cash saw as central to Southern culture. They reflect an anti-institutional ethic that says: In the last analysis, you are on your own—and should be. Southerners in 1900, Cash wrote, "would see the world in much the same terms in which their fathers had seen it in 1830; as, in its last aspect, a simple solution, an aggregation of self-contained and self-sufficient monads, each of whom was ultimately and completely responsible for himself."

Well, Walter Hines Page said once that "next to fried foods, the South has suffered most from oratory," and maybe Cash got carried away. But certainly an individualistic, anti-institutional note is evident in many aspects of Southern life. It is obvious, for example, in the Evangelical Protestantism to which most Southerners subscribe, a form of religion that sees salvation as something to be worked out by the individual, in a direct, unmediated relationship with Jesus. As Tom T. Hall sings it, in a classic country song, he and Jesus have their own thing going, and don't need anybody to tell them what it's all about.

The same pattern is evident, I think, in a disposition to redress grievances privately, which sometimes means violently—a disposition that gives black and white Southerners homicide rates at which the rest of the civilized world marvels. Anti-institutionalism can also be seen in a sort of localism and familism that reflects, not ignorance of the alternatives (as in the traditional value orientation), but simple preference for the palpable and close at hand, as opposed to the distant and formal. And, finally, individualism may be reflected in a sort of economic libertarianism that was apparently suppressed during the hard times of the past 120 years, but that seems to be coming back strong in our own times, at least among Southern whites.

All of these are "Southern" attributes, more common in the South than elsewhere. And in these respects, the South is not becoming more like the rest of the country: indeed, in some of them, regional differences are increasing. Unlike the traditional value orientation, these attributes are by no means universal among "folk societies," nor are they limited to such societies. And their statistical behavior is different, too: some of these traits are more common among educated Southerners than uneducated ones, or among urban Southerners than rural ones. Economic conservatism, as Robert Freymeyer has shown, is even more common among migrants to the South than among natives, so one cannot expect migration to reduce that difference.

Origins of Southern Anti-Institutionalism

Where these traits came from in the first place is an interesting question, but it is obviously a historical one, and it is tempting to leave it to the historians, especially since they disagree among themselves. Some point to the ethnic origins of Southerners and argue a Celtic influence, or an African one, or some catalytic interaction of the two—each an explanation that at least moves the problem back across the Atlantic and out of the hair of American historians. Others point to the legacy of the plantation, or the persistence of the frontier, or one of a half-dozen other "central themes" of Southern history. A sociologist would be foolhardy indeed to step into that fracas, but I will venture to suspect that the explanation for continuing Southern distinctiveness does repose somehow in the fact that black and white Southerners are *groups to which things have happened*, groups whose members have learned lessons from their collective histories.

In one well-known version of this argument, C. Vann Woodward has suggested that the un-American experiences of defeat, military occupation, poverty, frustration, and moral guilt have given white Southerners an outlook qualitatively different from that of other Americans. Obviously, a similar argument could easily be made for black Southerners (leave aside the moral guilt). This has been a very appealing line of thought, and there may be something to it, although it leaves a number of questions unanswered. This is not the place for a critique of Woodward's argument, much less a test of his hypothesis, but let me just observe that he does not spell out how events and experiences of a century or more ago are supposed to affect values and attitudes today. My own research suggests that it is seldom a matter of lessons continuing to be learned from reflections on that history: indeed, artists and historians aside, few Southerners of either race seem to know or to care much about their groups' histories. Rather, it appears that lessons drawn from group experience may have been passed on to succeeding generations without knowledge of the facts from which the conclusions were drawn.

It is not clear either exactly what lessons Southern history is supposed to have taught. Returning to our pattern of individualism and anti-institutionalism, however, it seems to me that long experience with an environment seemingly uncaring or even hostile could produce or reinforce traits like those to be explained. And both black and white Southerners, in their different ways, have had good reason in the past to view their environments as unresponsive if not actually malevolent.

The Future of Regional Differences

What difference does it make where this pattern of individualism comes from? Well, it has some implications for what we can expect as we move into the next century. Regional differences brought about by different historical experiences will not go away simply because Southerners come to have economic and demographic circumstances like those of other Americans. This sort of "Southern characteristic" could prove much more durable—apparently is proving much more durable—than traits that reflect simply economic underdevelopment. Some might want to argue that group differences tend to decrease in the absence of forces operating to maintain them—sort of a cultural version of the Second Law of Thermodynamics—but that is not at all a self-evident proposition; at least its validity needs to be demonstrated.

All this is speculation, of course, but if this view is correct, regional differences of this sort will decrease if history teaches its lessons more indiscriminately. Some course of events might cause Southerners to forget the lessons of their past, or teach other Americans what have heretofore been "Southern" lessons. Either way, regional differences would decrease.

In 1986, the revised edition of *The Enduring South* brought many of the data in the book forward another twenty years, from about the mid-1960s to the 1980s. For the most part, the book's original analysis held up pretty well. The regional differences that should have become smaller did so. Some cultural differences were largely due to Southerners' lower incomes and educational levels, to their predominantly rural and small-town residence, to their concentration in agricultural and low-level industrial occupations. Those differences were smaller in the 1960s than they had been in the past, and they are smaller still today. A few, indeed, have vanished altogether. There are important respects in which Southerners look more like other Americans, culturally, than they have at any time for decades, if ever.

On the other hand, differences that were persisting in the 1960s—in localism (as *The Enduring South* measured it), in attitudes toward some sorts of violence, in a number of religious and quasi-religious beliefs and behaviors—are mostly still with us, usually as large as they were then, and occasionally larger. This, I believe, supports the book's conclusion that those are differences of a quasi-ethnic sort, with their origins in the different histories of American regional groups, not merely epiphenomena of different levels of current economic and demographic "modernization."

There were, however, a few—only a very few—instances where these differences, too, were smaller than a generation before. And where that happened it was not because the South became less Southern, but because the non-South changed to resemble the South.

This pattern is evident in survey items of several different sorts, but my favorite example involves responses to the question, "What man that you have heard or read about, living today in any part of the world, do you admire the most?" When the Gallup Poll asks this question, as it often does, it is obviously fishing for the name of a public figure. Nevertheless, many Southerners perversely insist on naming people the interviewer never heard of: relatives, friends, miscellaneous local figures. In 1965, nearly a third of white Southern respondents did that, and they were almost twice as likely as non-Southerners to do so.

If this response indicates a species of localism, by this measure the regional difference in localism had decreased by 1980: from 14 percentage points to 5. But not because Southerners had become less localistic. The percentage of Southerners who refused to name a public figure had actually risen, from 32 percent to 38 percent, but the percentage of non-Southerners who gave this kind of response had risen, too, even faster: from 18 percent to 33 percent. (The same pattern can be observed, by the way, with a similar question about most-admired women.)

This is not the model of regional convergence that most observers have had in mind. But the 1960s and 1970s gave all Americans some un-American experiences: Vietnam, Watergate, Iran, assassinations, urban riots, economic stagnation, double-digit inflation, rising crime rates, urban decay, and a host of other distressing, frustrating, alienating developments. Is it stretching a point to speculate that many non-Southerners have begun to believe, as many Southerners already did, that they cannot always get what they want or even keep what they have, that hard work and good intentions are not always enough, that politicians and bureaucracies are not to be trusted, that people out there don't like them? And if non-Southerners come to believe that, would it be surprising if they took up the values of a nearby subculture that came to those conclusions some time ago—for example, the value that says your family, friends, and neighbors are more reliably admirable than people you have only "heard or read about"?

Let me close with a general point. It is fairly easy to predict the future of regional cultural differences that are merely reflections of economic and demographic differences. All it takes are economic and demographic projections (and the willingness to trust them, which is the hard part). But if we allow that group culture can also be shaped by history, by events, prediction becomes much more difficult. It becomes nothing less than a matter of predicting events. If sociologists could do that any better than anyone else, we could put a lot of stockbrokers and fortune-tellers out of work.

Questions to Consider

1. Who are contemporary Southerners? What characteristics do they share? How do Southerners identify with the South today?
2. What are the ways in which the South is changing and evolving?

Dave Smith

1942–

David Jeddie Smith's identity as a poet is intimately bound up with the landscape and seascape of his native region. "Smith wrote initially about tidewater Virginia as if it were Troy, a place of elemental struggles and defeats," critic Michael True has observed. Smith was born in Portsmouth, Virginia, on 19 December 1942 to Ralph Gerald and Catherine Cornwell Smith, but grew up in and around Poquoson, a tiny coastal village at the mouth of the Poquoson River on the Chesapeake Bay. Although Smith's father was a naval engineer, Smith would come to identify with the working-class shell fishermen of the region, celebrating their strength and stoicism in his work, and the search for a father figure would remain a persistent theme in his poetry.

Smith proved himself to be a brilliant student at the University of Virginia, graduating with highest distinction—unlike his literary idol, Edgar Allan Poe, who had to withdraw from the same institution after only one semester because of gambling debts. Smith told interviewer Ernest Suarez that he used to walk by Poe's dorm room every morning on his way to class: "Poe was always part of my consciousness and, I think, part of the American consciousness." In the long, six-part poem "Homage to Edgar Allan Poe" in his book of the same title, Smith acknowledged Poe's literary influence and the extent to which he had conflated Poe's identity with his own as a teenager. Smith also edited and wrote the introduction to the Ecco Press critical work *The Essential Poe*.

While teaching high school in Poquoson, coaching the football team, and marrying, Smith began studying toward a master's in English at the College of William and Mary in Williamsburg, but he transferred to Southern Illinois University to complete his degree in 1969. Enlisting in the Air Force with the Vietnam War raging in Southeast Asia, Smith had the good fortune not to be sent there during his three-year tour of duty. He then taught college English for a year each in Michigan and Missouri and completed a Ph.D. from Ohio State University in 1976. Smith's relationship with one of his poetry professors there, Hollis Summers, is the subject of one of the poems in this selection.

While still a student, Smith had published two small-press poetry collections. A third collection, from a university press (*The Fisherman's Whore*, 1974) captured the attention and esteem of critic Helen Vendler. From that point on, Smith was recognized as a major voice in

American poetry, as well as a distinctively Southern one. His poetic language is not the language of everyday speech, but an elevated rhetoric that is capable of taking on both tragic and celebratory themes. Influenced by the ancient Anglo-Saxon poets who wrote about seafaring people and their heavily fated lives in strong-stressed, alliterative verse, Smith writes a "thick" line that is dense with consonants and stresses. Like an Anglo-Saxon "scop" (bard) of the oral tradition, Smith also likes to tell stories in his poems, although narrative poetry has fallen out of favor in regions other than the American South. Traditional Southern themes of sex, violence, grotesque characters, and male rite-of-passage rituals figure heavily in Smith's work, but it is his sense of place and of the history associated with each place that marks his work as being of the South. In an interview with Suarez, he described himself as a regionalist with an "historical imagination," going on to explain that "it isn't difficult for me to see a stand of trees outside Cold Harbor, and see in them the Battle of Cold Harbor, and men dying uselessly and violently and painfully. It isn't difficult for me to see slaves standing before the auction block in Shocko Bottom in Richmond, nor to imagine the horror in a man's breast as he sees his wife sold one way, his children another way, and to know there's nothing he can do; he'll never see them again." Smith further explained to Suarez that his sense of place had been with him since the time he started to write.

In the course of three decades, Smith has published 21 collections of poetry, including three "new and selected" volumes and one reprint of three of his early books. Besides poetry, he has written a novel and a collection of essays on contemporary poetry. Smith is also one of the most important poetry editors of the contemporary period. Among other editorial achievements, he founded the journal *Back Door* and edited it for most of a decade, coedited *The Southern Review* from 1990 to 2002, and coedited the 1985 *Morrow Anthology of Younger Poets*. The recipient of National Endowment for the Arts and Guggenheim Foundation fellowships, he has also received an Award of Excellence from the American Academy and Institute for Arts and Letters. In 2002 he moved from Louisiana State University in Baton Rouge, where he had been a professor since 1990, to a chair in poetry at Johns Hopkins University, returning to the Chesapeake Bay region that has inspired so many of his poems.

Smithfield Ham[1]

Aged, bittersweet, in salt crusted, the pink meat
lined with the sun's flare, fissured.
I see far back the flesh fall
as the honed knife goes
through the plate, the lost
voice saying ". . . it cuts easy as butter. . . ."

Brown sugar and grease tries to hold itself
still beneath the sawed knee's white.
Around the table the clatter of china
kept in the highboy echoes,
children squeal in a near room.

The hand sawing is grandfather's, knuckled,
steadily starting each naked plate
heaped when it ends. Mine
waits shyly to receive
under the tall ceiling
all the aunts, uncles have gathered to hold.

My shirt white as the creased linen, I shine
before the wedge of cherry pie, coffee

1. A type of country ham made only in Smithfield, Virginia, that is dry-cured, not cooked, after being rubbed with salt.

black as the sugarless future.
My mother, proud in his glance,
whispers he has called for me and for ham.

Tonight I come back to eat in that house the sliced
muscle that fills me with an old thirst.
With each swallow, unslaked, I feel
his hand fall more upon mine,
that odd endless blessing
I cannot say the name of . . .
the dead recalled, the jobless
with low sobs, sickness, the Depression.

Chewing, I ask how he is. Close your mouth, she says.
This time, if he saw me, maybe he'd remember
himself, who thanklessly carved us
the cured meat. The Home holds
him in darkness like coffee
we poured those days. I gnaw
a roll left too long, dried hard.

When my knife drags across the plate,
my mother shakes her head, whining like a child.
Nothing's sharp anymore, I can't help it, she says.
Almost alone, I lift the scalded coffee.
My mouth, as if incontinent,
dribbles and surprises us.

Her face is streaked with summer
dusk where katydids drill and die out.
Wanting to tell her there's always tomorrow,
I say "You're sunburned. Beautiful as ever."
Gardening puts the smell of dirt on her.
Like a blade, her hand touches mine.

"More?" Then, "You'll never get
enough, you think, so sweet,
until the swelling starts,
the ache, the thirst that wants
to bust a person open late at night."
I fill my cup again, drink, nod, and listen.

Wedding Song

(for Dee)

Camden, North Carolina, is not picturesque
though it is the place we remember
where many men and women have gone
in good luck and bad to repair
aching hearts: for five dollars
no one asks your age or looks for the curve

swelling under the skirt of the cheerleader.
Our justice of the peace pumped gas

and spoke the words through gums
long toothless and tobacco black.
A tourist honked for help.

He gave each of us a sample box of Cheer.[1]
Y'all come on back anytime!

The first time down Route 17, by George Washington's
ditch, he of the chopped cherries,
we turned back in the Dismal Swamp.
Who could make up a truer thing than that?

You weren't fooling. Neither was I.
The second time we made it.
A wheezing clerk above an X-rated movie house
slowly printed our names.
He chewed an onion's golden rings.
He said *Are you now or have you ever been crazy?*

Weren't we? Isn't love something that breaks,
drooling and dangling inside
like a car's hot-water hose
that leaves you helpless,
godforsaken in the middle of nowhere?

Y'all come on back anytime.
Fifty bucks and two economy boxes of Cheer—
how far could we get on that?

I was certain you'd end up croaking home
to mother after those early months.

Our first house had more holes
than we could cover, mice,
snakes, spiders, our dinner guests.

In that place you woke to the screams of a mare
who dropped half of her foal, dragging
half around the rented house until
with tractor and chain
the landlord delivered us.

The chain still dangles in your dreams,
and his *Y'all come on back anytime!*

Sometimes when I think we have learned
to live in the world, the faces
of children lining our walls,
the darkness waiting ahead
like a swamp that's no joke,

I turn and find you coiled in a corner of light.
I think of the five green dollars unfurled
for that clerk of hunger and fools,
the blue acrid soap

1. A brand of laundry detergent.

that scoured us cherry red,
and the screams of our years.

Are we now or were we ever crazy?
Sign here, the man said, and we did,
the voices of men and women
making love, cracking up
through that black movie floor.

I hear them still.

Cumberland Station

Gray brick, ash, hand-bent railings, steps so big
it takes hours to mount them, polished oak
pews holding slim hafts of sun, and one
splash of the *Pittsburgh Post-Gazette*. The man
who left Cumberland gone, come back, no job
anywhere. I come here alone, shaken
the way I came years ago to ride down
mountains in Big Daddy's cab. He was
the first set cold in the black meadow.

Six rows of track, photographed, gleam, rippling
like water on walls where famous engineers steam, half
submerged in frothing crowds with something
to celebrate and plenty to eat. One's mine,
taking children for a free ride, a frolic
like an earthquake. Ash cakes his hair.
I am one of those who walked uphill
through flowers of soot to zing
scared to death into the world.

Now whole families afoot cruise South Cumberland
for something to do, no jobs, no money for bars,
the old stories cracked like wallets.

This time there's no fun in coming back. The second
death. My roundhouse uncle coughed his youth
into a gutter. His son slid on the ice,
losing his need to drink himself
stupidly dead. In this vaulted hall
I think of all the dirt poured down
from shovels and trains and empty pockets.
I stare into the huge malignant headlamps
circling the gray walls and catch a stuttered
glimpse of faces stunned like deer on a track.

Churning through the inner space of this godforsaken
wayside, I feel the ground try to upchuck and I dig
my fingers in my temples to bury a child
diced on a cowcatcher, a woman smelling
alkaline from washing out the soot.
Where I stood in that hopeless, hateful room

will not leave me. The scarf of smoke I saw
over a man's shoulder runs through me
like the sored Potomac River.

Grandfather, you ask why I don't visit you
now you have escaped the ticket-seller's cage
to fumble hooks and clean the Shakespeare reels.
What could we catch? I've been sitting in the pews
thinking about us a long time, long enough to see
a man can't live in jobless, friendless Cumberland
anymore. The soot owns even the fish.

I keep promising I'll come back, we'll get out,
you and me, like brothers, and I mean it.
A while ago a man with the look of a demented cousin
shuffled across this skittery floor and snatched up
the *Post-Gazette* and stuffed it in his coat
and nobody gave a damn because nobody cares
who comes or goes here or even who steals
what nobody wants: old news, photographs
of dead diesels behind chipped glass.

I'm the man who stole it and I wish you were here
to beat the hell out of me because what you said
a long time ago welts my face and won't go away.
I admit it isn't mine, even if it's nobody's.
Anyway, that's all I catch today—bad news.
I can't catch my nephew's life, my uncle's,
Big Daddy's, yours, or the ash-haired kids'
who fell down to sleep here after the war.

Outside new families pick their way along tracks
you and I have walked home on many nights.
Every face on the walls goes on smiling,
and, Grandfather, I wish I had the guts
to tell you this is a place I hope
I never have to go through again.

In Memory of Hollis Summers[1]

Christmas Eve. Wild Turkey[2] in my glass,
my country's finest drink, I sit remembering
the poet, plump, tall, bald, wisps of
smoke coiled from a cigarette holder.
I offer my poetry thesis. He laughs, says
"I'm a prissy man." He might have said
exact, or strict, as Allen Tate[3] often did.
Later, as if bruised, he'd scowl, "Must you
say *beautiful eyes?*" And years later,

1. Kentucky-born writer and professor (1916–1987) who taught at Ohio University when Smith was a student there.
2. A type of bourbon whiskey manufactured in Kentucky.
3. Kentucky-born poet and professor (1899–1979) who was a member of the Fugitive and Agrarian movements in Southern literature.

as if by accident, after my graduation,
he meets me in the hall, his hand out,
so I accept his almost-last manuscript
of poems, many speckled and moled
as his forehead, veined by hours
of burning tobacco, ash-dark as coffee,
each with scars of excisions, connections
looping word to word like metastacized
disease, but his steady strong heart
still visible, and what he wanted heard.
"Mr. Summers," I'd begin, despite quick
sputters of protest, refusing still to give
the *Hollis* he asked me many times to say
against the decades between us, being
in his view countrymen, Virginia
and Kentucky joined in that Ohio room
always bare, bright as the northern snow
we'd met in that first day. Like pioneers
with dangers in common. Now this one
came, I handed him his manuscript, not
wanting the grim words I had to give also,
circling like a scout back and forth at
the obvious, his love for her, the boys,
an old dog, a man's ways. But I knew
I'd been taught his truths, and now
fumbling to address what shadowed
what he was I made my clumsy cuts
and watched him stiffen bit by bit, who
every Christmas had a poem to send
I don't know how many students in the end.
Handwritten, the same long fingers
sharp as an aunt's needling memory as he
pointed and rasped. "Say the poem
as if it matters, David," he once groaned,
so I feel that distant hurt close in again,
being alone with those cold walls,
the chill that's in my hand as I try to find
today a heat that summered in his words,
beginning with *Hollis*, then reading from
the posthumous backward to the start
where I must shake his hand and say *Sir*.

Canary Weather in Virginia

It comes in sharp, salt smell above James River's foam.
It clatters past azalea, willow, the exhumed sway
Of laurel, camellia's pink-smoked buds dawning open,
Oiling a woman's hands to spill moonlight in woe's rooms.
It flings unseen to anywhere he lives bands of wind
Unfolding so many gold birds dawn sings with god-breath.
Yellow-red streaks pass like her hair over his pillow.

What mission has it in droughty fields, uncoiling faith
That remembers to bring also cardinals, owls, gulls?
Swamp-sheen, a dew-gilt mast, mullet's leap, cold horse-eye
Lift, hold him up, though he stiffens, alone in his yard.
When tides wash distance in, he floats, fate's kite, back
To silhouettes of pine, boats, that whirling yellow bird.

Questions to Consider

1. How does food, in the poem "Smithfield Ham," function as a symbol that unites the narrator's family? How does it function as a symbol of the family's dysfunction and possible dissolution?
2. Does the poem "Cumberland Station" contain a positive adult male role model for a boy or young man? Evaluate each of the male figures in the poem from that perspective.

James Alan McPherson

1943–

James McPherson's two collections of short stories, *Hue and Cry* (1969) and *Elbow Room* (1977), examine the theme of humanity's transcendence of race, focusing upon the ways in which American identity has developed because of the many different cultures which are a part of it. Racial tensions are well known to McPherson, who came of age during the era when the Civil Rights movement was evolving into the Black Power movement, which embraced a pride in its separateness from White culture, allowing for a celebration of African-American achievement and identity. In the midst of this highly politicized antiintegrationist agenda, McPherson "eschews the impulse to depict life as a series of victimizations, but rather opts to create what his mentor [Ralph] Ellison would appreciate as an 'open-ended' notion of American life," argues critic Herman Beavers, yet he "must be thought of as a Southern writer who came of age as Jim Crow segregation was being put to a slow death." McPherson's articulation of the sensibilities of African-American culture in the twentieth-century South has enjoyed a consistent and appreciative readership.

James Alan McPherson was born on 16 September 1943 in Savannah, Georgia, to Mabel Smalls McPherson, a domestic worker, and James Allen McPherson, an electrician. Describing his childhood in a "lower-class black community," he sensed the underlying fear of the White community that pervaded the era, but as a result of his father's work, which brought him into daily contact with White people, the young McPherson did not internalize this fear. By 1965, he had completed a bachelor's degree in English and history at Morris Brown College in Atlanta, and he went on to earn a law degree at Harvard University in 1968. He published his first collection of short fiction, *Hue and Cry* (1969), soon after. He later pursued an M.F.A. from the influential Writer's Workshop at the University of Iowa in 1972, and in later years returned to the Workshop as a professor.

McPherson, who had friends of many races and political leanings, reports feeling conflicted about some of these friendships during his youth because of the diversity of world views they represented. Since his identity as a writer was still developing, he found himself grappling with feelings of fragmentation resulting from the shift in the racial climate in the United States. *Hue and Cry* demonstrates McPherson's burgeoning conviction that "universal human traits run deeper than race." He rejected the singular Black aesthetic that grew out of the African-American community during this time, remarking that instead, he sought to tell stories about "all kinds of people . . . certain of these people happen to be black, and certain of them happen to be white; but I have tried to keep the color part of most of them far in the background, where these things should rightly be kept." As Beavers points out, McPherson chooses, instead, to examine the "contradictions of personality, values, and fortune [that] exist on both sides of the color line."

McPherson continued to examine human nature in his second collection, *Elbow Room* (1977), which won the Pulitzer Prize for fiction; he was the first African American to win the award in this category and only the second ever to win a Pulitzer. Critics praised McPherson for his adeptness in depicting speech patterns of Southern African Americans, and for his examinations of displaced Southerners. The *New York Times Book Review* noted the diversity of voices—the "extraordinarily various group of Black Americans"—that McPherson gathered between the covers of one book.

McPherson's career has included stints as a contributing editor for *Atlantic Monthly*, as well as several prestigious teaching appointments at institutions such as the University of California, Morgan State University in Baltimore, Maryland, the University of Virginia, and the University of Iowa. His stories have been included in volumes such as *The Best American Short Stories* and *The O. Henry Prize Stories*. Since the 1980s, McPherson has turned his attention to the personal essay form, which has led to the publication of two additional volumes, *Crabcakes* (1998) and *A Region Not Home: Reflections from Exile* (2000).

McPherson has been the recipient of numerous awards, including a Guggenheim Fellowship, a MacArthur Prize Fellowship, and a fellowship at the Stanford University Center for Advanced Study. In 1995, he was elected to the American Academy of Arts and Sciences. He has also served on awards panels for the National Book Award and the Pulitzer Prize.

I Am an American

It was not the kind of service one would expect, considering the quality of the hotel. At eight o'clock both Eunice and I were awakened by a heavy pounding on the door of our room that sounded once, loud and authoritatively, then decreased into what seemed a series of pulsing echoes. I staggered across the dirty rug, feeling loose grit underfoot, and opened the door. Halfway down the hall a rotund little man, seeming no more than a blur of blue suit and red tie, was pounding steadily on another door and shouting, "American girlies, wake up! Breakfast!"

"Telephone?" I called to him.

"Breakfast!" he shouted cheerily, turning his face only slightly in my direction. I could not see the details of his face, although it seemed to me his nose was large and red, and his hair was close-cropped and iron gray. For some reason, perhaps because of the way his suit was cut, I nursed the intuition that he was a Bulgarian; although there are many other eastern Europeans who wear the same loose style of suit. Just then the door before him opened. "Breakfast, American girlies!" he called into the room. From where I stood in my own doorway, stalled by sleepiness as much as by lingering curiosity, I glimpsed a mass of disarranged blond hair leaning out the door toward the man. "We'll be right down," a tired voice said. But the man was already moving down the hall toward the next door.

"Who was it?" Eunice asked from the bed.

"Time for breakfast," I said, and slammed the door. I had been expecting something more than a call for breakfast. We had come over from Paris to London in hopes of making a connection. All during the hot train ride the previous afternoon, from Gare du Nord to Calais, from Dover to Paddington Station, we had built up in our imaginations X, our only local connection, into a personage of major importance and influence in matters of London tourism. But so far he had not called.

While Eunice unpacked fresh clothes, I sat on the bed smoking a cigarette and assessed our situation. We could wander about the city on our own, call X again, or wait politely for him to call on us. But the thought of waiting in the room through the morning was distasteful. Looking around, I saw again what I had been too reluctant to perceive when we checked in the evening before. The room was drab. Its high ceiling, watermarked and cracked in places, seemed a mocking reminder of the elegance that might have once characterized the entire building. The rug was dusty and footworn from tramping tourists and the sheer weight of time. The thin mattress, during the night, had pressed into my back the history of the many bodies it had borne. This was not Dick Whittington's magic London.

"Hurry up!" Eunice ordered. "They stop serving breakfast at nine o'clock." She opened the door, pulling her robe close about her neck. "I'll use that john down the hall, and then you get out until after I wash up in the face bowl." As she went out, I glanced over at the yellowing face bowl. The sight of it provided another reason for giving up the room. After digging out my toothbrush from my suitcase, I stood over the bowl brushing my teeth and trying to remember just why we had come to London.

One reason might have been our having grown tired of being mere tourists. In the Louvre two mornings before, among a crowd of American tourists standing transfixed before the Old Masters of Renaissance painting, I had suddenly found myself pointing a finger and exclaiming to Eunice, "Hey, didn't they name a cheese after that guy?"

"Leroy, they did no such a-thing!" Eunice had hissed.

The other tourists had laughed nervously.

Eunice had pulled me out of the Louvre, though not by the ear.

That same morning I had decided to wire one of a list of London people suggested to us by friends back home in Atlanta. Their advice had been the usual in such matters: "Be sure to look up X. We're good friends. He showed us a good time when we were in London, and we showed him a good time when he came to Atlanta. Be sure to tell him all the news about us." My wire to X had been humble: "We are Leroy and Eunice Foster from Atlanta, friends of Y and Z. Will be in London on weekend. Would like to see you." X's reply, which arrived the next morning, was efficient: "Call at home on arrival. X." And so we had raced from Paris to London. Upon arrival, as instructed, I called up X.

"Y and Z who?" he asked, after I introduced myself.

I gave their full names. "They send warm regards from Atlanta," I added smoothly.

"Yes," X said. "They're fine people. I always regretted I never got to know them well."

"They're fine people," I said.

"Yes," X allowed. "I've got a bit of a flu right now, you know."

So we were in London. We located a room a few blocks from the train station and were content to let be. The room was in a neat, white Georgian house that, at some point during that time when American tourists first began arriving en masse, had been converted into a hotel. Such places abound in London; many of them are quite pleasant. But the interior of this one was bleak, as was the room we secured on the fourth floor. To compound our displeasure, the landlady had insisted that we declare exactly how long we planned to stay, and then pay for that period in advance. This was one of those periodic lapses of faith in the American dollar. American tourists suffered with it. But watchful landlords from Lyons to Wales refused to show the slightest mercy. "These are class rooms, love," the landlady had declared, inspecting our faces over the tops of her glasses. She was a plump woman who fidgeted impatiently inside a loose gray smock. "There's lots of people callin' for rooms," she reminded us. "All the time," she added.

We had been in no position to haggle. Having entered London on the eve of a bank holiday weekend, we had no choice but to cash more traveler's checks and pay rent through the following Monday morning. Only then did the landlady issue us a single set of keys: one for the street door, which was always locked, and one for our room. To further frustrate us, I found that the lobby pay telephone did not work. This required me to walk back to the station to ring up X and supply him with our address. He did not seem enthusiastic about getting it, but said he might call on us the next day, if his flu showed signs of abating. Discovering, finally, that the toilet on our floor barely flushed, and that the bathtub was unhealthily dirty, we went to bed with curses rumbling in us and the dust of the road still clinging to our skins.

Considering the many little frustrations that marred our arrival in London, we were very pleased to have been awakened for breakfast by the house porter. After Eunice returned to the room, I went out into the hall and waited in line for my turn in the john. I was not even perturbed that the two Orientals, occupying the room next to ours, took long chances at the toilet. While one occupied the stall, the other stood outside the door as if on guard. Standing behind him, I noted that he was tall and slim and conservatively dressed in a white shirt and black trousers. He seemed aloof, even reserved, though not inscrutable. This I could tell from the way his brows lifted and his ears perked, like mine, each time his companion made a vain attempt to flush the slowly gurgling toilet. Indeed, the two of us outside the door tried with the companion: we strained to apply our own pressures to the loose handle, to join in his anticipation of a solid and satisfying flush. But, unlike me, the Oriental did not shift from foot to foot each time his companion's failure was announced by strained gurgles and hisses from behind the closed door. Standing straight as a Samurai, he seemed more intent on studying my movements, without seeming to, than on commandeering the john. I wanted to communicate with him, but did not want to presume that he spoke English. To further compound the problem, I could not tell if he was Japanese or Chinese. In Paris I had seen Chinese tourists, but they had been uniformed in the colors of Chairman Mao. This fellow wore western clothes. The problem became academic, however, when I recalled that the only Oriental phrases I knew were derived from a few sessions in a class in Mandarin I had once attended. I could never hope to master the very intricate and delicate degrees of inflection required, but I had managed to bring away from the class a few phrases lodged in memory, one of which was a greeting and the other introducing me as an American.

"Ni hau ma?" I inquired with a broad smile.

At first the Oriental stared at me in silence. Then he pointed a finger at his chest. "I next," he said. Then he pointed a finger at my chest. "You next."

He was right. I shifted from one foot to the other until finally there came the welcome sound of his companion's mastery of English hydraulics. As the companion stepped out of the stall and my acquaintance went in, I wanted to caution him that he need not be as concerned with a matter as ephemeral as decorum. But the desire died aborning. I did not have the language, and could only continue to shift from foot to foot. And sadly, very shortly afterward, while the second Oriental waited by the stairs, there came the same dry, strained sound of the very same difficulty. The situation was hopeless. I brushed past the companion and raced down the stairs to the third floor. But that stall too was in use. The one on the second floor offered even less hope: an elderly couple and a young man stood shifting in front of it.

On the ground floor, off the lobby, I ran into the same little man, still seeming to me like nothing if not a Bulgarian, still knocking on doors and shouting, "Americans! Americans! Get up for breakfast!" When he saw me he turned, again ever so slightly, and said, "That way," pointing toward the door to the street. "Hurry! Hurry! Only served from eight to nine." I nodded my thanks and, seeing no stall on that floor, raced back up the stairs. Just below the third floor the two Orientals passed me on their way down. "Ni hau ma?" I called to them. They stopped and looked at each other, then at me. The taller man spoke in a high, hurried tone to the other. Then his companion nodded enthusiastically and said, "Oh!" He looked at me, pointed a finger up the stairs and said, "Open now."

He was right.

Going down for breakfast, finally, Eunice and I passed the little blue-suited man in the lobby. He seemed about to go out the door, but as we approached he stepped aside and held the portal open for us. "Breakfast that way," he said, smiling. "In the basement." We thanked him and walked out the door, along a few feet of pavement, and down into the basement of the adjoining house. The little room was dank and smelled of rancid bacon. About a score of people, mostly Americans, were seated at the cloth-covered tables. We could tell they were Americans by the way they avoided eye contact. One girl was speaking halting French with a West Texas accent to two male companions who only listened. Over against the wall a middle-aged couple was poring over a *Herald-Tribune* stretched out beside their plates of bacon and eggs. "You just wait till we get back," the man was saying in a loud voice. "I'll *get* the sonsofbitches for doin' this to me!" His wife kept looking up from her reading and saying, "Now Bob . . . now Bob . . . " Eunice and I went to a table at the far side of the room. At the table next to ours a rather attractive girl was eating rapidly and saying to the young man with her, "Cadiz was an utter bore. Madrid was an utter bore. . . . There's too many kids in Copenhagen. . . . Italian men are the *nastiest* men on earth! . . ."

"Aw, shut up and eat," her friend said.

Across the room, seemingly at a distance, the two Orientals ate their meal in silence, looking only at each other.

The landlady's assistant brought our plates out from the kitchen. She was pale and dumpy, with dull auburn hair done up in a ragged bun. She seemed immune to all of us in the room. She slid two plates onto our table, plunked down a dish of jam, and sashayed back into the kitchen.

"You know," Eunice said, inspecting the food, "it's kind of funny."

"What?" I asked.

"That a place as sloppy as this can afford to have somebody wake you up for breakfast. This kind of place, the more people miss breakfast, the more food they save."

"You know," I said, after reflecting a moment, "it *is* kind of funny that that little Bulgarian was heading *out* the door when we came down, but stepped back *inside* the second we went out."

Eunice laid down her fork. "It's more than funny," she said. "It's pure-dee suspicious."

"It's more than suspicious," I added. "It could be downright slick."

Both of us looked round the room. Everyone was eating.

"I been telling you, Leroy," Eunice said. "It's good sense to riff in a place where you don't know the score." She fished the keys from her purse. "Which one of us go'n go up?"

But I had already eased out of my seat and was on my way. In a few seconds I had unlocked the front door and stepped quickly into the hall. Although I ran up the three flights of stairs on tiptoe, the aged boards betrayed my presence. And just as I reached the fourth floor landing, I saw the little blue-suited man backing quickly out the door of the room next to ours. I paused. He turned and smiled at me, shutting the door and giving a theatrical turn to the doorknob. Then he walked calmly over to the linen closet, opened it, and peered inside. At first he frowned in exasperation, then he patted a stack of folded sheets and smiled reassuringly at me. Turning, he waltzed slowly to the stairs and went down. By this time I had opened my own door. Nothing in the room seemed to have been disturbed. I checked our suitcases. Eunice's camera was still there, as were the gifts she had purchased in Paris. But my suspicions were not eased. After locking the door, I rushed down to the breakfast room and directly to the table where the two Orientals were eating their meals. "Ni hau mau?" I said hurriedly. Again they stared at each other, then at me. "Not open?" the one who had the better command of English, the shorter of the two, said to me. He was dressed like his companion, except that his short-sleeved shirt was light green. And he carried a row of pens on a plastic clip in the breast pocket of his shirt.

"I think you had better check your room," I said as slowly as my excitement would allow. "I-think-you-had-better-check-your-room," I repeated even more slowly. "I-just-saw-a-man-com-ing-out-of-it."

He screwed up his face. "English is not good to us," he said. "Please to speak more slow."

I pointed to my keys and then raised a finger in the direction of the other building. "I-think-your-room-may-have-been-*robbed!*" I said.

"*Rob?*" he said.

"I saw a man come out of there."

"Rob," he repeated slowly to his companion.

To avoid seeming to caricature a fine and extremely proud people, I will not attempt to relate the development of their conversation after that point. They consulted extensively across the table in their own language. From their gestures and eye movements I could tell that the discussion included references to me, Eunice, the landlady, the quality of the meal, and the lazy toilet way up on the fourth floor. Then one word of their own language, sounding like "New Sunday," seemed to come suddenly into focus. It bounded back and forth between them across the table. The word excited them, made them anxious, perhaps even angry. The spokesman repeated "New Sunday" to me with sufficient force to make me know that my suspicion had been absorbed, and then run through their own language until it settled around a corresponding thought. "New Sunday—*robbed,*" I said in answer, nodding my head.

Both of them leaped up from the table and rushed toward the door. Most people in the room turned to look after them. Only after the two had vanished did the tourists turn their eyes on me. I slipped back to where Eunice waited at our table. By this time my eggs had hardened into a thin layer of yellow mush encrusted in bacon fat. I sipped the cup of cold tea and waited.

"Leroy, maybe it was a false alarm," Eunice said.

"Those Chinese don't think so," I told her.

Eunice frowned. "Those aren't Chinese."

"Well, they ain't Koreans," I observed.

"They're Japanese," Eunice said, "How could you be so dumb?"

"How can *you* be so sure?"

"All you have to do is *look* at them," Eunice told me. "Japanese are like upper-class people down home. They don't look around much because they *know* who *they* are in relation to everybody else."

"Bullshit," I said. "They're Chinese. Whoever saw Japanese without cameras?"

"Leroy, you're a black bigot," Eunice told me. "And a *dumb* one at that," she added.

"But not in *public!*" I whispered through my teeth. Over at the next table the young man was watching us intently. But soon he turned back to his companion and her complaints—this time against Etruscan art.

We waited.

In a few minutes the two Orientals came rushing back into the room. The taller one pointed at me and spoke hurriedly to his companion. Then the two of them came over to our table. "Please to say Japanese students are . . . rob in hotel."

"New Sundayed?" I asked.

The young man nodded.

I said I was sorry to hear it.

"You see doorrobber?" He breathed excitedly.

I admitted that both of us had seen the man, although I was careful not to say that to me he seemed to be a Bulgarian.

The taller student spoke to his companion.

"He complains for police," the spokesman translated.

I agreed that should be done. Leaving Eunice at the table gloating pridefully over the sharpness of her insight, I led the two students back into the kitchen. The landlady was scraping bacon fat off the top of her black range. She glanced up at the three of us over her glasses and said, "What you want, love?"

The man in the green shirt, the shorter of the two, attempted to explain; but he seemed unable to muster sufficient English, or sufficient interest on the landlady's part, to make her appreciate how seriously he viewed the situation. While he was speaking, the service lady came in from the breakfast room with a stack of plates. She squeezed past the three of us, further upsetting the student in his recital. "Pity what these blokes does to the language," she muttered.

At this point I interrupted the student with a bow intended to be polite. I explained to the landlady the ploy used in the robbery and a description of the man whom I suspected of the deed. But I did not volunteer my suspicion that he looked to me to be a Bulgarian.

"What was took off you?" the landlady asked the two, and I thought I detected suspicion in her voice. They did not understand, so I translated as best I could, using sign language and the smallest part of pig Latin. Between the three of us it was finally determined that the thief had taken two Eurail passes, two Japanese passports, and about one hundred dollars in traveler's checks drawn on the bank of Tokyo.

"Shssss!" whispered the landlady. "Don't talk so *loud,* love! You want the other guests to hear?" Then she turned to the service lady, who leaned against a cupboard with her thick arms folded, and said, "Think they'd know enough to lock up their valuables." Then she faced the three of us again and said, "We can't be *responsible* for all that, duckies. There's signs on all the doors tellin' you to keep valuables under padlock. Regulations, you know."

Even without understanding fully what had been said, both students seemed to sense they could make more progress into the theft on their own. "Go search door-robber," the short man said.

The electricity of their excitement sparked into me. As they left the basement I stepped quickly behind them, recalling all the scenes dealing with personal honor I had viewed in Japanese movies. I had the feeling of being part of a posse. As one of the students was unlocking the door, his companion suddenly gave out a shrill cry and jumped several feet in the air. He kept repeating, "*Aa! Aa! Aa!*" and pointed down the street with a quick movement of his arm. I looked immediately where he pointed, but did not see the man whom I suspected of being the thief. But the other student looked in the same direction, and what he saw made him shout back to his comrade. Looking again, I saw the cause of their excitement: a rather chubby Oriental man was walking up the street toward us. The two students rushed toward the man. After greeting him, and after a few gestures, the three of them, shouting something that sounded like "Waa! Waa! Waa!" swept past me and into the building. The spokesman paused beside me long enough to say, "Please to watch door."

Waiting excitedly on the bottom step, I imagined them searching the building from attic to basement, peering into keyholes, dark stairwells, the johns on each floor, trying doors, linen closets, open windows. I pictured the little Bulgarian cornered in the hall, trying to understand what they could possibly mean when they said in cultured Japanese, "You have dishonored the hospitality of this house. You will please commit hara-kiri." And the little fellow, sneak thief that he was, would echo the countercode: "*Why?* I want to *live!*" I expected to see at any moment the little blue-suited fellow come pumping out the door, his red tie trailing in the wind he made, with the three Japanese in hot pursuit. When Eunice came up from the basement, I urged her to take a long walk around the block. I advised that I anticipated horrors from which her modesty should be protected. But Eunice refused to budge from where she stood on the sidewalk.

"Leroy, you're overreacting," she said.

Eunice was right as usual.

Instead of three samurai bearing the head of the thief, only the two Japanese students and their newfound tourist ally emerged from the building. They sighed and looked up and down the street, perhaps looking for additional Samurai, perhaps looking for bobbies. I sighed, and looked with them. But there was nothing else on the street we could add to our resources. The three conversed among themselves in Japanese, and then the stranger turned to me. "This Japanese salaryman from Osaka," the English-speaking student announced.

"Ni hau ma?" I said, offering my hand as the man bowed smartly.

"You are African?" the man asked, smiling pleasantly as we shook. "Nigerian, yes?"

"Woo sh Meei-gworen," I said.

He looked perplexed. "I do not know this tribe," he confessed finally. "But now I must go. They should get the officials to help them," he told me. He turned and made a short statement to the students in Japanese. Then he shook my hand again, bowed smartly to the students, and went on his way up the block.

"What was that foolishness you were talking?" Eunice asked.

The English-speaking student strolled closer to me. He looked deep into my face and said, "All *open* upstair."

"You ought to be horsewhipped for carryin' on such foolishness at a serious time like this," Eunice said.

Of course Eunice was right.

For the second time we crowded into the kitchen to register our complaint with the landlady. "Pipe *down,* love!" she muttered. "We don't want the others to hear, now do we?"

"Why not?" I asked.

She stood with her back against the black gas range. "What can *I* do?"

"Call up the bobbies."

She mumbled some more to herself, gave us a cold stare, then fished around in the pocket of her gray smock and produced a shilling and a few pence for the telephone. As we passed again through the breakfast room, the other tourists stared at us as though we were entertainers employed by the landlady to make the breakfast hour less monotonous. I wondered how many of them had been robbed while they sat leisurely over their bacon and eggs. And I wondered whether the little Bulgarian had anticipated they would have this blind spot.

I glanced at the table Eunice and I had occupied. It had been cleared and another couple, who looked German, now occupied it. They ate in silence and looked only at each other. But at the next table the little brunette was still preaching over cold tea to her companion: "Spain was *so* depressing. The French ignore you in August. Zurich looks like a big computer. Greek men . . ."

We were inside the lobby before I remembered the telephone did not work.

After getting directions from a passerby and advising Eunice to wait outside, lest the Bulgarian should be lurking in our room, the two Japanese and I walked toward a bobby station, said to be about a mile from the hotel. During the walk they managed to communicate to me their names and the outline of their dilemma. The spokesman's name was Toyohiko Kageyama. His tall companion, who apparently knew little English, was Yoshitsune Hashima. I told them to call me Lee. Toyohiko explained that without the traveler's checks, passports and rail passes they could not get to Amsterdam, where their flight back to Japan would depart in a few days. And with the bank holiday in effect, they would not be able to obtain more traveler's checks until Monday, when the banks reopened. Unfortunately, Monday was also the day their flight was to leave Amsterdam.

They talked between themselves in Japanese, working through the problem. They decided that with help from the Japanese embassy they might be able to obtain money for a flight to Amsterdam. But there was still the matter of the missing passports. I did not learn this by listening to their conversation, but through the pains taken by Toyohiko Kageyama to explain the problem to me in English. So far as I could tell, neither of them made any unkind remarks about the thief. Instead, they seemed to have accepted the loss and were working toward solution of the problem it caused. As we talked, Yoshitsune Hashima looked at the two of us, nodding occasional, though hesitant, agreement with whatever Kageyama said to me. But neither one of them smiled.

When we arrived at the bobby station, a bleak little building containing almost no activity, I excused myself and sat in the waiting room while the two Japanese stood at the reception desk and reported the robbery to the desk officer. He was a pale, elderly man with a gray-speckled pencil-line mustache. He listened carefully, occasionally drumming his pen on a report form, while suggesting words to Toyohiko Kageyama. The student had difficulty making the bobby recognize the name of the hotel and the street on which it was located, as well as the items that had been stolen. After many trials and errors by the bobby, Kageyama came over to me. "Please tell," he said.

I went to the desk and reported to the bobby as much as I knew about the robbery. I gave him a description of the man whom I suspected of being the thief, but I did not volunteer my suspicion that to me he seemed to be a Bulgarian. The bobby wrote it all down on a report form, then questioned us again for corroboration. Afterward, he wrote something of his own at the bottom of the form, perhaps a private comment, perhaps his own name. Then the students and I sat in the waiting room, while a pair of bobbies was summoned to accompany us back to the hotel. These were somewhat younger men, although one of them sported the same kind of thin mustache as the bobby at the desk. The other was plump, with tufts of bright red hair showing beneath his tall hat. He had a cold manner that became evident when he motioned us out of the building and into the back seat of their patrol car. The gesture was one of professional annoyance.

During the drive back to the hotel, the students and I were silent, but the two bobbies in the front seat discussed a recent rally of homosexuals in Trafalgar Square.[1]

"What a hellish sight that one was," the redhead observed.

"No doubt," the other said. "No doubt."

"At least five hundred of them parading round like the Queens of Elfin."

"No doubt," said the other. "Any trouble?"

The redhead laughed. "No," he said grimly.

The two Japanese students sat next to each other, their eyes looking past the bobbies and through the windshield of the car. Only I concentrated on the conversation. And after a while, I found myself wondering about how I had come to be driving through the streets of London in the back seat of a bobby car listening to commentary on a rally of homosexuals, when my major purpose in coming over from Paris had been to contact X, that elusive knower of London nightlife, and give him the warm regards of Y and Z, friends of his who lived in Atlanta.

The two bobbies searched the hotel from top to bottom, but they did not find the man. No one else had reported anything missing. The landlady flitted around with a great show of sympathy, explaining to the bobbies that this sort of thing had not happened in her place since the boom in American tourists back in '65. Both bobbies were cool and efficient, asking questions in a manner that suggested their suspicion of everyone and of no one in particular. But the redhead, it seemed to me, was more than probing in his questions concerning the part Eunice and I had played in the drama. He said finally, "There's little else we can do now except get a notice out. You'll have to go over to the station for the Paddington district and make a report there. This isn't our district, you know; so they'll need a bit of a report over there."

"People should be careful of these things," the landlady said, wiping her hands on her apron.

"It's ten-thirty," Eunice cried. "We want to go sightseeing."

The redhead smiled cryptically. "He'll have to go along to make a proper description," he advised Eunice. "It would be quite helpful to these two chaps here."

"I'm sick and tired of all this running around," Eunice said.

1. London's most famous public square was completed in 1841 and commemorates the British victory in the Battle of Trafalgar in 1805.

The bobby smiled.

The two Orientals stood watching all of us.

The drive to the other district station was short. The bobbies did not talk more about the rally of homosexuals. They let us out in front of the station and wished us luck. I wished them a happy bank holiday. Inside the station the routine was the same as before: while the students explained their predicament as best they could, I stayed in the waiting room until I was needed. Waiting, I amused myself by studying the wanted posters on the bulletin board hanging between the windows. Walking close to the board for a closer inspection, I saw that four of the seven wanted men were black. Moreover, one of them, a hardcase named Wimberly Lane, priced at fifty pounds and wanted for extortion, looked somewhat familiar. I studied his face. Lane had high cheekbones, prominent eyes, and a dissolute look about him. I looked closer and saw that he resembled, especially in profile, my cousin Freddy Tifton back home in Atlanta. But Lane was a desperado, probably hiding out in the London underworld, and my cousin was a world away in Atlanta, probably at that moment eating fried chicken on Hunter Street.

"Please tell about . . . doorrobber," someone said. Toyohiko Kageyama was standing behind me.

I turned and followed him back to the desk. This bobby's pale blue eyes flickered over my face. He and another man, a clerk who had obviously been helping him piece together the story told by the students, glanced quickly at each other and then back at me. "You saw the alleged robber?" the bobby asked.

"I did."

"Can you describe him?"

I gave what I thought was an accurate description. But this time I was sure not to venture my suspicion that he seemed to me to be a Bulgarian. The bobby wrote with his left hand. He wrote beautiful script with his pen turned inward toward his wrist. I watched his hands.

The two students stood behind me, one on each side.

"Just what is your relation to the complainants?" the bobby asked.

"I am an American," I said. "My room is next to theirs."

The bobby stopped writing and frowned. "You are the only person who actually *saw* this man, you know?" His eyes narrowed.

"What about it?" I said.

"A friend indeed, what?" the clerk said. He looked at the bobby and winked.

The two students stood behind me, conversing between themselves.

"Now let's go through this *once* more," the bobby said.

Suddenly Yoshitsune Hashima stepped from behind me and up to the desk. "Lee . . . good . . . de*tail*," he said, pointing firmly at me. "Japanese students . . . take *Lee* detail . . . *doorrobber*."

The bobby stopped smiling and began writing again. He wrote a beautiful script.

Yoshitsune Hashima did not speak again.

The bobby advised them to go quickly to the Japanese embassy.

I wanted to go quickly and see the rest of London.

We saw the two students again in the late afternoon at Madame Tussaud's. Eunice and I had wandered down into one of the lower chambers with exhibits commemorating the French Revolution. When I saw them I was standing beside a rusty guillotine that had been used to behead Marie Antoinette. The Japanese were standing together, peering into a lighted showcase containing wax replicas of famous murderers who had once plagued London. I motioned to Eunice, then walked over and touched Kageyama on the shoulder. He started, as if intruded upon too much by the mood of the place. But when they saw who we were, both of them smiled nervously and bowed. Toyohiko Kageyama reported that the Japanese embassy had secured temporary passports for them, had ordered the checks cancelled, and had lent them enough money for living expenses and a flight to Amsterdam. Now that business had been taken care of, they were seeing the sights of London. Both of them thanked us for our help, Kageyama in English and Hashima in Japanese. Both of them bowed politely. Then Yoshitsune Hashima pulled a notebook from the pocket of his trousers, leafed through it to a certain page, and read in a slow voice, "Please-to-give-Japanese-students-name-and-house-number."

I wrote them for him.

Yoshitsune Hashima accepted back the notebook, leafed through several more pages, and read in an uncertain voice: "I thank you kindness at New Sunday to help Japanese students. . . . I hope Lee visit Nihon one day. . . . Please visit home of Yoshitsune Hashima in suburb of Tokyo."

Then he handed me a packet of Japanese stamps.

The two of them bowed again.

"You see?" Eunice said, as we walked away. "The Japanese ain't nothing but part-time Southerners."

I had to concede that once again Eunice was right.

But it was too dark inside the wax museum. The colored lights shining on the exhibits did not improve the mood of the place. "Let's get out," I said to Eunice.

Toward dusk we stood in a crowd of tourists on a green outside the Tower of London. We had spent about ten minutes inside the tower. Before us on the green was an old man, encased in a white sack crisscrossed with chains and padlocks. He wriggled and moaned inside the sack while the crowd laughed. Standing beside him was a muscular, bald-headed man who beat himself on the naked chest with a sledgehammer. In certain respects this man resembled the thief, but he not at all resembled a Bulgarian. From time to time this strong man marched with a tin cup around the inside of the circle, holding it out to onlookers. He collected pence and shillings from some of those standing closest to the recreation. He said things like, "Me old daddy left near a thousand pound when he died; but I ain't yet found out where he left it." When the crowd laughed, he laughed with them. But he cursed those who put slugs and very small change in his cup. He seemed to be a foreigner, but he spoke with the accents of the British lower class. "A man 'as got to live!" he shouted at us while rattling the cup. "The old man there can't get out the sack till you pay up."

"Leroy," Eunice said beside me. "I don't think X will ever call. Now that we've seen London, let's please go home."

As usual, Eunice was right.

Questions to Consider

1. Why do you think that McPherson titled this story "I Am an American"? How does the title influence your interpretation of the story?
2. Why does Lee place such emphasis on not mentioning that he thought the robber was Bulgarian? What does Eunice mean when she remarks that the Japanese students "ain't nothing but part-time Southerners"?

Ellen Bryant Voigt
1943–

Ellen Bryant Voigt was born on 9 May 1943 in Danville, Virginia, and she grew up on a farm in nearby Chattam. Her family moved only once during that time, to a house just down the road. Voigt later told Ernest Suarez that she thought being raised in just one place was an experience common to many Southern writers, giving rise to their characteristic sense of place: "that spot becomes the metaphor, provides the imagery of the childhood." Lloyd Gilmore Bryant and Missouri Yeatts Bryant encouraged their daughter to take piano lessons and to practice, and at the age of 17 she entered Converse College in Spartanburg, South Carolina, intending to major in piano performance. But a friend introduced Voigt to poems by Rilke, cummings, and Yeats. Realizing that poetry, like music, was a sonic art, but that it possessed a dimension of sense and meaning that music lacked, Voigt began to take as many poetry and literature courses as she could, graduating with a B.A. in 1964.

Because Vanderbilt University was associated with the Fugitive-Agrarian poets and James Dickey, Voigt planned to seek a master's degree in literature there. While visiting the campus in 1964, she dropped in on a poetry course being taught by Donald Davidson, then met with the graduate dean about the possibilities of financial aid. According to Voigt, the dean told her that Vanderbilt did not give financial assistance to female graduate students because they were just going to find husbands and get married. A stunned Voigt applied to the University of Iowa instead. Her teachers in the M.F.A. program there included Donald Justice, another Southern poet and pianist whose work had been influenced by music. Voigt received her graduate degree in 1968. Newly married (but still, despite the predictions of the Vanderbilt dean, working and honing her craft as a writer), Voigt taught at Iowa Wesleyan University while her husband was finishing graduate school. Then, deliberately avoiding a return to the South because of shame over its civil rights struggles, Voigt and her husband moved to rural Vermont in 1970. She taught at Goddard College until 1978, then at the Massachusetts Institute of Technology. Since 1981 she has taught in the low-residency M.F.A. program at Warren Wilson College, a curriculum that combines distance learning courses with brief campus visits.

After finishing her graduate studies, Voigt spent a decade writing and polishing the poems in her first collection, *Claiming Kin* (1976). Its portrayal of the unsentimental bond between human beings and nature, as well as the drama at the heart of family relations, drew praise from reviewers including poets Stanley Kunitz and Edward Hirsch. Many of the poems were obviously drawn from Voigt's Southern childhood memories. While her second book, *The Forces of Plenty* (1983), was set in Vermont, her third collection, *The Lotus Flowers* (1987), returned to the rural Virginia of her childhood; Voigt has called it her "most Southern book." *The Two Trees* (1992) probed questions of fate and free will. *Kyrie* (1995), nominated for the National Book Critics Circle Award, presented a narrative sequence of blank verse sonnets about the great influenza epidemic of 1918–1919. *Shadow of Heaven* (2002) was a finalist for the National Book Award in poetry. Voigt has also been honored with a Discovery/*The Nation* Award, a National Endowment for the Arts grant, a Guggenheim Foundation grant, two Pushcart Prizes, the Emily Clark Balch Award, and a citation from the American Academy of Arts and Letters.

Voigt is skilled at both the narrative and lyric modes of poetry, which she is able to fuse together into a hybrid mode, as in a poem aptly titled "Song and Story." She can write objectively or emotionally, in spare or florid language, in traditional forms or in free verse. Her wide range of poetic styles is always unified by the musicality of her lines and by her thematic concerns with the duality and ambiguity of human experience: humans and nature, children and adults, fate and free will, innocence and experience, individuals and communities, mortality and immortality, order and chaos. Speaking of the genesis of *The Lotus Flowers*, Voigt told Suarez that the deaths of her parents had severed her last remaining tie to the South, forcing her to imaginatively revisit her relationship to it. Several collections later, Voigt does not seem to be finished with the process of revisiting her Southern childhood. "The dead should just shut up," she wails in *Shadow of Heaven;* but, because they do not, many of the best poems in that most recent collection return to the fertile poetic ground of Chattam, Virginia.

Lesson

Whenever my mother, who taught
small children forty years,
asked a question, she
already knew the answer.
"Would you like to" meant
you would. "Shall we" was
another, and "Don't you think."
As in, "Don't you think
it's time you cut your hair."

So when, in the bare room,
in the strict bed, she said
"You want to see?" her hands
were busy at her neckline,
untying the robe, not looking
down at it, stitches
bristling where the breast
had been, but straight at me.

I did what I always did:
not weep—she never wept—
and made my face a kindly
white-washed wall, so she
could write, again, whatever
she wanted there.

"This is the double bed where she'd been born"

This is the double bed where she'd been born,
bed of her mother's marriage and decline,
bed her sisters also ripened in,
bed that drew her husband to her side,
bed of her one child lost and five delivered,
bed indifferent to the many bodies,
bed around which all of them were gathered,
watery shapes in the shadows of the room,
and the bed frail abroad the violent ocean,
the frightened beasts so clumsy and pathetic,
heaving their wet breath against her neck,
she threw off the pile of quilts—white face like a moon—
and then entered straightway into heaven.[1]

1. Compare to Matthew 3:16: "And Jesus, when he was baptized, went up straightway out of the water and, lo, the heavens were opened unto him. . . ."

Short Story

My grandfather killed a mule with a hammer,
or maybe with a plank, or a stick, maybe
it was a horse—the story varied
in the telling. If he was planting corn
when it happened, it was a mule, and he was plowing
the upper slope, west of the house, his overalls
stiff to the knees with red dirt, the lines
draped behind his neck.
He must have been glad to rest
when the mule first stopped mid-furrow;
looked back at where he'd come, then down
to the brush along the creek he meant to clear.
No doubt he noticed the hawk's great leisure
over the field, the crows lumped
in the biggest elm on the opposite hill.
After he'd wiped his hatbrim with his sleeve,
he called to the mule as he slapped the line
along its rump, clicked and whistled.

My grandfather was a slight, quiet man,
smaller than most women, smaller
than his wife. Had she been in the yard,
seen him heading toward the pump now,
she'd pump for him a dipper of cold water.
Walking back to the field, past the corncrib,
he took an ear of corn to start the mule,
but the mule was planted. He never cursed
or shouted, only whipped it, the mule
rippling its backside each time
the switch fell, and when that didn't work
whipped it low on its side, where it's tender,
then cross-hatched the welts he'd made already.
The mule went down on one knee,
and that was when he reached for the blown limb,
or walked to the pile of seasoning lumber; or else,
unhooked the plow and took his own time to the shed
to get the hammer.
By the time I was born,
he couldn't even lift a stick. He lived
another fifteen years in a chair,
but now he's dead, and so is his son,
who never meant to speak a word against him,
and whom I never asked what his father
was planting and in which field,
and whether it happened before he married,
before his children came in quick succession,
before his wife died of the last one.
And only a few of us are left
who ever heard that story.

Questions to Consider

1. English teachers usually tell students to avoid using the same word twice in one sentence. Why do you think that Voigt uses the word "bed" eight times in the sentence that makes up the poem "This is the double bed where she'd been born"?
2. How do you think the grandfather in the poem "Short Story" would tell the story of the mule's death? Write out his version of events and then compare it to his granddaughter's version.

Robert Morgan

1944–

Named after a B-17 fighter-pilot uncle who was killed in World War II, Robert Ray Morgan was born on 3 October 1944 in Hendersonville, North Carolina. Morgan's father, Clyde, an eloquent talker who sometimes spoke in tongues during Pentecostal Holiness Church services, eked out a living on a small Blue Ridge Valley farm that had been purchased by Morgan's Welsh great-great-grandfather in 1840. His mother, Fannie Levi Morgan, a Southern Baptist, worked in cotton mills and beauty shops but loved to read fiction and knew the names of every bird, flower, and plant in the region. The reticence and detailed observation of the natural world that are so evident in Morgan's poetry can thus be traced to the example of his mother rather than to his flamboyant father and uncle.

A gifted student, Morgan entered college at the age of 16, studying science at Emory University. But the Cold War was in progress in the early 1960s, and young Morgan, caught up in the fervor to beat the Russians in the space race, soon transferred to the University of North Carolina at Chapel Hill to study applied mathematics. Signing up for a creative writing course because it was the only one that fit an empty slot in his schedule, he began writing poetry with the encouragement of professors Guy Owen and Jessie Rehder and ultimately changed his major to English. He went on to earn an M.F.A. in creative writing from the University of North Carolina at Greensboro, where he studied with Fred Chappell, then painted houses and farmed for two years before being hired in 1971 by Cornell University. He has taught creative writing there ever since.

Morgan's early books of poetry exhibited a detailed, objective, "scientific" perspective toward the phenomena of the natural world. "Science is in a way the theology of the twentieth century; it's important to us in the way that mystic philosophy and theology were to Dante," he said in an interview with Stan Rubin and William Heyen (collected in *Good Measures*). With the publication of *Land Diving* in 1976, however, Morgan began to write poetry about his proud, poor, hard-working relatives, their Welsh-Appalachian legends and traditions, and the mine-scarred, rural mountain landscape of his childhood. In an essay on Morgan written a few years later, William Harmon joked that twenty-first-century folklorists would have to depend upon Morgan's writing for information about vanishing Appalachian tales and practices. Morgan's latest collection of poetry, *Topsoil Road*, explores the historical past of his Green River Valley region of North Carolina from the perspective of Cherokee history, then the personal history of his Welsh immigrant ancestors. From incorporating storytelling and narrative into his poetry, it was a natural progression for Morgan to begin publishing short stories (*The Blue Valleys*, 1989; *The Mountains Won't Remember Us*, 1992; and *The Balm of Gilead Tree*, 1999) and novels (*The Hinterland*, 1994; *The Truest Pleasure*, 1995; *Gap Creek*, 1999; and *This Rock*, 2001). Although Morgan's writing was recognized with three National Endowment for the Arts grants, the *Southern Poetry Review* Prize, *Poetry* magazine's Eunice Tietjiens Prize for Poetry, and a Guggenheim Fellowship, among other honors, it was not until TV personality Oprah Winfrey picked *Gap Creek* as the twenty-ninth selection for her popular book club, in January 2000, that Morgan broke through to a wide public readership.

Hayfield

It is the syrup in the grass
that must be caught, the sweet juice drawn
up from the roots and brewed in leaves
until the stalks are full from joint
to joint like little pipes of ale
mellowing in late midsummer.
And quick, before the last leaf dries
or roots withdraw, it is the sap
in grass that must be cut and left
to crystallize in fibers, preserving
like honey in a mummy's chest
the blade and vein intact, storing
the high sugars of the sun in
aromatic teas, tobaccos,
and little corn of timothy
and slender sorghum's golden flutes,
to scent the barn and sweeten milk
far into the bleaching winter.

Sunday Toilet

On the hottest Sundays of the year,
in the morning shift of bird hymn
and dew song, before the church bell
split the poised whole, Daddy raked
a waterbucket full of lime
from the pile beside the toolshed
and flung comets and smoking hands
on the walls of the hogpen.
The young shoat's feet sucked mud as he
ran to corners from the fog that
flurried over sty and ripening
puddles and drifted on the spillage
of cobs rotting on the downhill side.
The dusting finished, the pen looked
white as confectioner's sugar
in the cooling talc, the whiteness
somehow medicinal if not
opiate, and the air was
sweeter floating up to the house
where the preacher would come to dinner.
After the hogpen Daddy sprinkled
the chicken yard and floor of the

brooder house, dropped what was left
down the holes of the two-seat
toilet. When the make-up was hit
by early sun the mire looked
pristine and cool as the tops of
cumulus reaching to heaven
while women powdered their faces
for church and flies got chalk on their
feet to write on the back screen door.

Firecrackers at Christmas

In the Southern mountains, our big
serenade was not the Fourth but
always Christmas Eve and Christmas.
Starting at midnight the valleys
and branch coves fairly shook with barks
of crackers, boom of shotguns, jolt
even of sticks of dynamite.
You would have thought a new hunting
season had begun in the big-star
night, or that a war had broken
out in the scattered hollows: all
the feuds and land disputes come to
a magnum finale. The sparks
everywhere of match and fuse
and burst were like giant lightning bugs.
Thunder doomed the ridges though
the sky shone clear and frost sugared
the meadows. Yankees were astonished
at the violence and racket
on the sacred day, they said, as
cherrybombs were hurled into yards
and placed expanding mailboxes
same as Halloween. Perhaps the custom
had its origins in peasant-pagan
times of honoring the solstice
around a burning tree, or in
the mystery centuries of
saluting the miraculous
with loudest brag and syllable.
Certainly the pioneer had
no more valuable gift to bring
than lead and powder to offer
in the hush of hills, the long rifles
their best tongues for saying the peace
they claimed to carry to the still
unchapeled wilderness, just as
cannon had been lit in the Old
World to announce the birth of kings.
They fired into the virgin skies

a ceremony we repeated
ignorantly. But what delight
I felt listening in the unheated
bedroom dark, not believing in
Santa Claus or expensive gifts,
to the terrible cracks along
the creek road and up on Olivet,
as though great rivers of ice were
breaking on the horizon and
trees were bursting at the heart
and new elements were being born
in whip-stings and distant booms
and the toy chatter of the littlest
powder grace notes. That was our
roughest and best caroling.

Overalls

Even the biggest man will look
babylike in overalls, bib
up to his neck holding the trousers
high on his belly, with no chafing
at the waist, no bulging over
the belt. But it's the pockets on
the chest that are most interesting,
buttons and snaps like medals, badges,
flaps open in careless ease, thin
sheath for the pencil, little pockets
and pouches and the main zipper
compartment like a wallet over
the heart and the slit where the watch
goes, an eye where the chain is caught.
Every bit of surface is taken
up with patches, denim mesas
and envelopes, a many-level
cloth topography. And below,
the loops for hammers and pliers
like holsters for going armed
and armored yet free-handed
into the field another day
for labor's playful war with time.

Uranium

Red-faced and sweating in autumn
heat, Grandpa and his khaki friend
from town unloaded picks and hammers
off the truck, and took out a case
with dials that seemed a radio
or recording machine with spiral
cord and microphone and needles.

All afternoon they circled fields
and pasture gullies, climbed the ledge
above the road, knocked on spoil of
the old zircon digs, chipped at
the cliff face, and shoveled mud from
the branch bed. Each time they found
a specimen they put the mike
to its gritty form and listened,
and checked the needles' sway. The crops
were in and Grandpa looked for a new
harvest in the soil. I watched them
lug the equipment and armloads
of rocks like apples to the truck,
and knew the Russians might blow us
up any day, they said, and what
they looked for bombs were made of. At
the barn they let me listen to
the counter's faint static. And while
the old men talked of wealth and sure
Armageddon[1] and the Bible's
plans for our annihilation
I heard the white chatter of rock,
a noise that seemed to go back in
time inside the bright machine, and
inside the hammered flakes in hand,
to the crackle of creation's
distant fires still whispering in us.

Bare Yard

My grandma swept her yard
often as the floor
and wore out willow switches
and swatches of broomsedge[1]
sewn in bundles
to whisk away the twigs
and pebbles, leaves and chicken piles.
She washed down the soiled places
with buckets from the spring
and sprinkled branch sand
over any chicken tracks or stains
that might show through,
and brushed it clean as snow.
How fresh the yard looked then.
You didn't want to track
the virgin cover so white,
so perfect a sheet sparkling
with quartz and mica, and kept

1. The apocalyptic battle between the forces of good and evil foretold in the New Testament's Book of Revelations.

1. A type of wild grass that grows in the southeastern United States.

to the edges of the boxwoods.
The yard was isled with tufts
of grass near its borders.
Grandma placed her geraniums out there
in their brick-clay pots.
The ground looked plain and hard
as her expression while she worked.
Cropped grass was for the pasture
and graveyard and meadow.
She set a few gourds and unusual
rocks by the steps and flowerbeds.
Otherwise the space was bare and bright
in the sun as her conscience.

Questions to Consider

1. "Everything is language," said Morgan in the Rubin/Heyen interview in *Good Measures*. How many instances of nonhuman "language," or of "writing" appearing in unusual places, can you find in the poems, and how do they illustrate the meaning of Morgan's remark?
2. What details suggest to you that Morgan's poem "Uranium" is set during the Cold War between the United States and the Soviet Union?

Richard Ford

1944–

Mississippi native Richard Ford renounces his ties to the South regularly, in spite of a heritage that includes literary giants William Faulkner, Walker Percy, Shelby Foote, and Eudora Welty. The author of numerous short stories and essays, as well as the five novels for which he is most famous, Ford is recognized as one of an emergent group of "dirty realists" who unflinchingly represent the gritty aspects of modern life. Critic Elinor Ann Walker dismisses the significance of Ford's Southern heritage, saying that he "likes places, but does not call one place home," and arguing that the author's "self-imposed itinerancy, combined with his resistance against Southern literary prescriptions" invalidates attempts to categorize him as a Southern writer.

Ford is a Southern writer not merely because of the geography of his birthplace, but because his work reflects the influence of Southern literary techniques, particularly the concern with place. Much of Ford's fiction is undeniably Southern in its characterizations, its settings, and its attention to Southern pastimes such as hunting, sports, and rural life. His body of work exhibits a minimalist social and psychological realism, a defining characteristic of "grit lit," a genre that merges attributes of popular and high culture. Grit lit has become an increasingly influential movement among contemporary Southern writers such as Dorothy Allison, Lee Smith, Larry Brown, and Harry Crews.

Born on 16 February 1944 in Jackson, Mississippi, Richard Ford is the only child of Parker Carrol Ford and Edna Akin Ford. When Ford was 16, his father suffered a fatal heart attack. His mother explained to her teenaged son that he needed to assume additional responsibility and that they would henceforth be "partners in life," according to Walker. At 17, Ford began working to supplement the family income, first as a fireman and later as a switch operator for the Missouri Pacific Railroad. In 1962, he enrolled at Michigan State University, eventually turning his attention to literature. After completing his bachelor's degree, Ford spent a year teaching school and another in law school, but he soon made two decisions that he credits with changing his life: he asked Kristina Hensley, his college sweetheart, to marry him, and he decided to become a writer.

Ford completed a Master of Fine Arts degree at the University of California in Irvine in 1970. His early creative works were short stories, which he had little luck in publishing. Around this time, he also received a fellowship at the University of Michigan, where he taught writing and worked on his first novel, *A Piece of My Heart,* (1976) which was a runner-up for the Ernest Hemingway Award for a best first novel. Ford followed this success with two additional novels, *The Ultimate Good Luck* (1981) and *The Sportswriter* (1986), as well as *Rock Springs* (1987), a collection of short stories.

Ford's work enjoyed largely positive reviews during this period of his career. He acquired a loyal popular readership with the publication of *The Sportswriter*, a novel that some reviewers compared favorably with Walker Percy's *The Moviegoer*. Praised by *The New York Times* as a "devastating chronicle of contemporary alienation," *The Sportswriter* won a PEN/Faulkner award in 1986 and was chosen as one of the year's best books by *Time* magazine. Ford's fourth novel, *Wildlife* (1990), was not as well received by critics, who suggested that the author might have "bitten off more than he could chew." He regained the critical acclaim of his earlier novels with the publication of *Independence Day* (1995), a sequel to *The Sportswriter*. *Independence Day* earned both the Pulitzer Prize and the PEN/Faulkner Award for fiction.

Ford's success has "hinged on his abdication of the South as subject and setting," suggests Matthew Guinn, arguing that he has created a "new voice for his fiction—that of the ambivalent southerner in exile." Some of his best fiction draws on traditionally Southern settings, themes and activities. "Going to the Dogs" is not only set in a rural area but focuses on a favored sport of the region: hunting. For a variety of reasons, readers and critics alike find themselves inclined to read Ford as a Southerner.

Ford has served as a creative writing instructor in a variety of postsecondary institutions, including Princeton University, Williams College, and Harvard University, but in recent years he has given up teaching in order to devote his full attention to his writing. Ford shares his self-described itinerant lifestyle with his wife, an urban and regional planner. The Fords presently reside in New Orleans.

Going to the Dogs

My wife had just gone out West with a groom from the local dog track, and I was waiting around the house for things to clear up, thinking about catching the train to Florida to change my luck. I already had my ticket in my wallet.

It was the day before Thanksgiving, and all week long there had been hunters parked down at the gate: pickups and a couple of old Chevys sitting empty all day—mostly with out-of-state tags—occasionally, two men standing beside their car doors drinking coffee and talking. I hadn't given them any thought. Gainsborough—who I was thinking at that time of stiffing for the rent—had said not to antagonize them, and let them hunt unless they shot near the house, and then to call the state police and let them handle it. No one had shot near the house, though I had heard shooting back in the woods and had seen one of the Chevys drive off fast with a deer on top, but I didn't think there would be any trouble.

I wanted to get out before it began to snow and before the electricity bills started coming. Since my wife had sold our car before she left, getting my business settled wasn't easy, and I hadn't had time to pay much attention.

Just after ten o'clock in the morning there was a knock on the front door. Standing out in the frozen grass were two fat women with a dead deer.

"Where's Gainsborough?" the one fat woman said. They were both dressed like hunters. One had on a red plaid lumberjack's jacket and the other a green camouflage suit. Both of them had the little orange cushions that hang from your back belt loops and get hot when you sit on them. Both of them had guns.

"He's not here," I said. "He's gone back to England. Some trouble with the government. I don't know about it."

Both women were staring at me as if they were trying to get me in better focus. They had green-and-black camouflage paste on their faces and looked like they had something on their minds. I still had on my bathrobe.

"We wanted to give Gainsborough a deer steak," said the one who was wearing the red lumberjack's jacket and who had spoken first. She turned and looked at the dead deer, whose tongue was out the side of his mouth and whose eyes looked like a stuffed deer's eyes. "He lets us hunt, and we wanted to thank him in that way," she said.

"You could give *me* a deer steak," I said. "I could keep it for him."

"I suppose we could do that," the one who was doing the talking said. But the other one, who was wearing the camouflage suit, gave her a look that said she knew Gainsborough would never see the steak if it got in my hands.

"Why don't you come in," I said. "I'll make some coffee and you can warm up."

"We *are* pretty cold," the one in the plaid jacket said and patted her hands together. "If Phyllis wouldn't mind."

Phyllis said she didn't mind at all, though it was clear that accepting an invitation to have coffee had nothing to do with giving away a deer steak.

"Phyllis is the one who actually brought him down," the pleasant fat woman said when they had their coffee and were holding their mugs cupped between their fat hands, sitting on the davenport. She said her name was Bonnie and that they were from across the state line. They were big women, in their forties with fat faces, and their clothes made them look like all their parts were sized too big. Both of them were jolly, though—even Phyllis, when she forgot about the deer steaks and got some color back in her cheeks. They seemed to fill up the house and make *it* feel jolly. "He ran sixty yards after she hit him, and went down when he jumped the fence," Bonnie said authoritatively. "It was a heart shot, and sometimes those take time to take effect."

"He ran like a scalded dog," Phyllis said, "and dropped like a load of shit." Phyllis had short blond hair and a hard mouth that seemed to want to say hard things.

"We saw a wounded doe, too," Bonnie said and looked aggravated about it. "That really makes you mad."

"The man may have tracked it, though," I said. "It may have been a mistake. You can't tell about those things."

"That's true enough," Bonnie said and looked at Phyllis hopefully, but Phyllis didn't look up. I tried to imagine the two of them dragging a dead deer out of the woods, and it was easy.

I went out to the kitchen to get a coffee cake I had put in the oven, and they were whispering to each other when I came back in. The whispering, though, seemed good-natured, and I gave them the coffee cake without mentioning it. I was happy they were here. My wife is a slender, petite woman who bought all her clothes in the children's sections of department stores and said they were the best clothes you could buy because they were made for hard wearing. But she didn't have much presence in the house; there just wasn't enough of her to occupy the space—not that the house was so big. In fact it was very small—a prefab Gainsborough had had pulled in on a trailer. But these women seemed to fill everything and to make it seem like Thanksgiving was already here. Being that big never seemed to have a good side before, but now it did.

"Do you ever go to the dogs?" Phyllis asked with part of her coffee cake in her mouth and part floating in her mug.

"I do," I said. "How did you know that?"

"Phyllis says she thinks she's seen you at the dogs a few times," Bonnie said and smiled.

"I just bet the quinellas," Phyllis said. "But Bon will bet anything, won't you, Bon? Trifectas, daily doubles, anything at all. She doesn't care."

"I sure will." Bon smiled again and moved her orange hot-seat cushion from under her seat so that it was on top of the davenport arm. "Phyllis said she thought she saw you with a woman there once, a little, tiny woman who was pretty."

"Could be," I said.

"Who was *she?*" Phyllis said gruffly.

"My wife," I said.

"Is she here now?" Bon asked, looking pleasantly around the room as if someone was hiding behind a chair.

"No," I said. "She's on a trip. She's gone out West."

"What happened?" said Phyllis in an unfriendly way. "Did you blow all your money on the dogs and have her bolt?"

"No." I didn't like Phyllis nearly as well as Bon, though in a way Phyllis seemed more reliable if it ever came to that, and I didn't think it ever could. But I didn't like it that Phyllis knew so much, even if the particulars were not right on the money. We had, my wife and I, moved up from the city. I had some ideas about selling advertising for the dog track in the local restaurants and gas stations, and arranging coupon discounts for evenings out at the dogs that would make everybody some money. I had spent a lot of time, used up my capital. And now I had a basement full of coupon boxes that nobody wanted, and they weren't paid for. My wife came in laughing one day and said my ideas wouldn't make a Coke fizz in Denver, and the next day she left in the car and didn't come back. Later, a fellow had called to ask if I had the service records on the car—which I didn't—and that's how I knew it was sold, and who she'd left with.

Phyllis took a little plastic flask out from under her camouflage coat, unscrewed the top, and handed it across the coffee table to me. It was early in the day but, I thought, what the hell. Thanksgiving was tomorrow. I was alone and about to jump the lease on Gainsborough. It wouldn't make any difference.

"This place is a mess." Phyllis took back the flask and looked at how much I'd had of it. "It looks like an animal starved in here."

"It needs a woman's touch," Bon said and winked at me. She was not really bad looking, even though she was a little heavy. The camouflage paste on her face made her look a little like a clown, but you could tell she had a nice face.

"I'm just about to leave," I said and reached for the flask, but Phyllis put it back in her hunting jacket. "I'm just getting things organized back in the back."

"Do you have a car?" Phyllis said.

"I'm getting antifreeze put in it," I said. "It's down at the BP. It's a blue Camaro. You probably passed it. Are you girls married?" I was happy to steer away from my own troubles.

Bon and Phyllis exchanged a look of annoyance, and it disappointed me. I was disappointed to see any kind of displeasure cloud up on Bon's nice round features.

"We're married to a couple of rubber-band salesmen down in Petersburg. That's across the state line," Phyllis said. "A real pair of monkeys, if you know what I mean."

I tried to imagine Bonnie's and Phyllis's husbands. I pictured two skinny men wearing nylon jackets, shaking hands in the dark parking lot of a shopping mall in front of a bowling alley bar. I couldn't imagine anything else. "What do you think about Gainsborough?" Phyllis said. Bon was just smiling at me now.

"I don't know him very well," I said. "He told me he was a direct descendant of the English painter.[1] But I don't believe it."

"Neither do I," said Bonnie and gave me another wink.

"He's farting through silk," Phyllis said.

"He has two children who come snooping around here sometimes," I said. "One's a dancer in the city. And one's a computer repairman. I think they want to get in the house and live in it. But I've got the lease."

"Are you going to stiff him?" Phyllis said.

"No. I wouldn't do that. He's been fair to me, even if he lies sometimes."

"He's farting through silk," Phyllis said.

Phyllis and Bonnie looked at each other knowingly. Out the little picture window I saw it had begun to snow, just a mist, but unmistakable.

"You act to me like you could use a good snuggle," Bon said, and she broke a big smile at me so I could see her teeth. They were all there and white and small. Phyllis looked at Bonnie without any expression, as if she'd heard the words before. "What do you think about that?" Bonnie said and sat forward over her big knees.

At first I didn't know what to think about it. And then I thought it sounded pretty good, even if Bonnie was a little heavy. I told her it sounded all right with me.

"I don't even know your name," Bonnie said, and stood up and looked around the sad little room for the door to the back.

"Henderson," I lied. "Lloyd Henderson is my name. I've lived here six months." I stood up.

"I don't like *Lloyd*," Bonnie said and looked at me up and down now that I was up, in my bathrobe. "I think I'll call you Curly, because you've got curly hair. As curly as a Negro's," she said and laughed so that she shook under her clothes.

"You can call me anything you want," I said and felt good.

"If you two're going into the other room, I think I'm going to clean some things up around here," Phyllis said. She let her big hand fall on the davenport arm as if she thought dust would puff out. "You don't care if I do that, do you, Lloyd?"

"Curly," said Bonnie, "say Curly."

"No, I certainly don't," I said, and looked out the window at the snow as it began to sift over the field down the hill. It looked like a Christmas card.

"Then don't mind a little noise," she said and began collecting the cups and plates on the coffee table.

Without her clothes on Bonnie wasn't all that bad looking. It was just as though there were a lot of heavy layers of her, but at the middle of all those layers you knew she was generous and loving and as nice as anybody you'd ever meet. She was just fat, though probably not as fat as Phyllis if you'd put them side by side.

1. Thomas Gainsborough (1727–1788) painted portraits and landscapes and was considered a genius of British art.

A lot of clothes were heaped on my bed and I put them all on the floor. But when Bon sat on the cover she sat on a metal tie tack and some pieces of loose change and she yelled and laughed, and we both laughed. I felt good.

"This is what we always hope we'll find in the woods," Bonnie said and giggled. "Somebody like you."

"Same here," I said. It wasn't at all bad to touch her, just soft everywhere. I've often thought that fat women might be better because they don't get to do it so much and have more time to sit around and think about it and get ready to do it right.

"Do you know a lot of funny stories about fatties," Bonnie asked.

"A few," I said. "I used to know a lot more, though." I could hear Phyllis out in the kitchen, running water and shuffling dishes around in the sink.

"My favorite is the one about driving the truck," Bonnie said.

I didn't know that one. "I don't know that one," I said.

"You don't know the one about driving the truck?" she said, surprised and astonished.

"I'm sorry," I said.

"Maybe I'll tell you sometime, Curly," she said. "You'd get a big kick out of it."

I thought about the two men in the nylon jackets shaking hands in the dark parking lot, and I decided they wouldn't care if I was doing it to Bonnie or to Phyllis, or if they did they wouldn't find out until I was in Florida and had a car. And then Gainsborough could explain it to them, along with why he hadn't gotten his rent or his utilities. And maybe they'd rough him up before they went home.

"You're a nice-looking man," Bonnie said. "A lot of men are fat, but you're not. You've got arms like a wheelchair athlete."

I liked that. It made me feel good. It made me feel reckless, as if I had killed a deer myself and had a lot of ideas to show to the world.

"I broke one dish," Phyllis said when Bonnie and I were back in the living room. "You probably heard me break it. I found some Magic Glue in the drawer, though, and it's better now than ever. Gainsborough'll never know."

While we were gone, Phyllis had cleaned up almost everything and put away all the dishes. But now she had on her camouflage coat and looked like she was ready to leave. We were all standing in the little living room, filling it, it seemed to me, right up to the walls. I had on my bathrobe and felt like asking them to stay over. I felt like I could grow to like Phyllis better in a matter of time, and maybe we would eat some of the deer for Thanksgiving. Outside, snow was all over everything. It was too early for snow. It felt like the beginning of a bad winter.

"Can't I get you girls to stay over tonight?" I said and smiled hopefully.

"No can do, Curly," Phyllis said. They were at the door. Through the three glass portals I could see the buck lying outside in the grass with snow melting in its insides. Bonnie and Phyllis had their guns back over their shoulders. Bonnie seemed genuinely sorry to be leaving.

"You should see his arms," she was saying and winked at me a last time. She had on her lumberjack's jacket and her orange cushion fastened to her belt loops. "He doesn't look strong. But he is strong. Oh my God! You should see his arms," she said.

I stood in the door and watched them. They had the deer by the horns and were pulling him off down the road toward their car.

"You be careful, Lloyd," Phyllis said. Bonnie smiled over her shoulder.

"I certainly will," I said. "You can count on me."

I closed the door, then went and stood in the little picture window watching them walk down the road to the fence, sledding the deer through the snow, making a swath behind them. I watched them drag the deer under Gainsborough's fence, and laugh when they stood by the car, then haul it up into the trunk and tie down the lid with string. The deer's head stuck out the crack to pass inspection. They stood up then and looked at me in the window and waved, each of them, big wide waves. Phyllis in her camouflage and Bonnie in her lumberjack's jacket. And I waved back from inside. Then they got in their car, a new red Pontiac, and drove away.

I stayed around in the living room most of the afternoon, wishing I had a television, watching it snow, and being glad that Phyllis had cleaned up everything so that when I cleared out I wouldn't have to do that myself. I thought about how much I would've liked one of those deer steaks.

It began to seem after a while like a wonderful idea to leave, just call a town cab, take it all the way in to the train station, get on for Florida and forget about everything, about Tina on her way to Phoenix with a guy who only knew about greyhounds and nothing else.

But when I went to the dinette to have a look at my ticket in my wallet, there was nothing but some change and some matchbooks, and I realized it was only the beginning of bad luck.

Questions to Consider

1. Based on the selection included here, would you consider Ford a Southern writer? Why or why not? Is it useful to characterize writers based on their regional flavor? How does such categorization enhance your understanding of a text?
2. How do hunting metaphors provide structure in "Going to the Dogs"? The narrator begins the story by telling the reader that he is planning to go to Florida to change his luck; by the end of the story, he realizes that not being able to go to Florida marks the beginning of his bad luck. Does a relationship exist between the hunting metaphors and the narrator's feeling that his luck has changed twice in a small space of time?

Everette Maddox

1944–1989

"It was a one-horse town and the horse died," Everette Maddox said of his home town of Prattville, Alabama. Maddox was born on 9 October 1944 to Everette Maddox, a sign painter and factory worker, and Dorothy Stuckey Maddox, a homemaker who read Rupert Brooke's poetry and danced to big-band records to enliven her barren environment. An imaginative child, young Maddox read Keats and Shelley with his brother William (later to become a novelist) and was all too happy to leave the red clay hills and pine woods of Prattville for the University of Alabama at Tuscaloosa. There he studied poetry writing with August Mason and struck up an enduring friendship with fellow student and poet Rodney Jones, who wrote of Maddox that "he was, at that time, by consensus, the most talented graduate student that anyone in the English department at the University of Alabama had ever seen." While still a student, Maddox had a poem accepted by the *New Yorker*. He earned a B.A. and M.A. in English, then received a one-year poet-in-residence appointment at Xavier University in New Orleans.

But both of Maddox's alcoholic parents had died of cancer by his twenty-fifth birthday, and his own worsening drinking problem caused him to lose his Xavier University job, then his wife and stepdaughter, by 1978. He slid from part-time teaching at the University of New Orleans, to occasional poet-in-the-schools appearances, to a menial attendant's job at the New Orleans Maritime Museum, and eventually to homelessness. Always a brilliant and witty literary talker who made friends easily, Maddox "held court" nightly at the Maple Leaf Bar in New Orleans, the site of the Sunday afternoon literary reading series, now the longest-running in the South, that he founded in 1979 and emceed for a decade. Literary friends helped him to edit and publish his first two collections of poetry, in 1982 and 1988, and produced his posthumous collection in 1993. The latter book, *American Waste,* was compiled from a year's worth of late-flowering poems scribbled by Maddox on beer coasters, bar napkins, and band fliers, then preserved for posterity (in a purple plastic shopping bag that Maddox fondly called "the archives") by Maple Leaf bartender and part-owner Henry Lee "Hank" Staples III. Staples and William Roberts, a Louisiana natural gas industry executive from Long Island who wrote fiction, were the founders of Pirogue Publishing, which published books by both Maddox and Julie Kane. Maddox died of esophageal cancer in Charity Hospital, New Orleans, on 13 February 1989. His jazz funeral drew a crowd of five hundred people and made the national news. His sorrowing friends had him cremated and scattered his ashes in the Mississippi River and on the back patio of the Maple Leaf Bar.

"Granted I'm the prize jackass of the Post-Modern period," Maddox wrote in a 1981 letter to his friend Robert Woolf. Indeed, what is most postmodern about Maddox's poetry is the way he deconstructs the Southern romantic poetic tradition while perpetuating it better than anyone else. Poet William Matthews, writing for the *New Orleans Review*, observed that Maddox's usual rhetorical situation is unrequited love, but that Maddox always pokes fun at himself while pining for an idealized female muse. "I have always been a sort of poor man's Gatsby," Maddox once wrote to Woolf. His transports of the imagination can be triggered by the lingering stench of hot sauce spilled on a bar room floor. He names and celebrates the bars, all-night diners, and dime stores of the Carrollton district of New Orleans as if Woolworth's and the Steak & Egg were as sublime as an Alp and an ocean. And he reveals the absurdity of the moonlight-and-magnolia-dripping, romanticized Southern "past" that never existed at the same time that he clings to it to blot out the sordidness of the present. "When the present storm is on, isn't the violent past the safest place to be?" Maddox asks in the poem "Cleaning the Cruiser." Given that the epigraph to his first book is the line from F. Scott Fitzgerald in which Gatsby insists that it *is* possible to repeat the past, it is clear that Maddox is not just being ironic. Maddox's legend lives on in New Orleans, where a memorial plaque can be found on the Maple Leaf Bar patio and a papier-maché likeness of him adorns a Mardi Gras parade float.

Cleaning the Cruiser

The model of the cruiser *New Orleans*[1]
is smaller than life
but larger than me. The glass case
with table stands six feet
seven inches high (I'm 5'8"
sober) and about fifteen
feet long. How I clean it,
once a month, on a small aluminum
stepladder, is, first, to brasso[2]

1. U.S. cruiser that served with distinction in the Pacific theater during World War II, including the 1944 Battle of the Philippine Sea against the Japanese fleet.

2. A brand of commercial brass polish.

the dim brass frame all over
with a rag—a pain in the aft,
as well as futile. Next, as to
the glass: one squirt of windex[3]
under a paper towel becomes
a sort of filthy halo, a swirl
of drunkard's breath, which I rub
and rub, until at some point suddenly
everything disappears except
what appears to be nothing
but the reality of the fake
ship itself, its gray guns and planes
as plain as rain beneath my raised
hand . . . Dangerous point!
at which I imagine that I may fall,
or crash, through that drab
clarity, and hit the deck,
bound for the Philippines. Mean draft
indeed! into World War II,
which I only remember in sepia . . .
On the other hand,
talk about your escapes!
When the present storm is on, isn't
the violent past the safest place to be?
Oh I would do it—run away
and fight my father's war
all over again, to wear
the black gold-buttoned coat
that hung in some dream-closet
of my childhood, and find, at armistice,
you. Kiss me once,
I'd say, and kiss me twice,
and kiss me once again,
it's been a long, long time.

New Orleans

(for Ralph Adamo)

From the air it's all puddles:
a blue-green frog town
on lily pads. More canals
than Amsterdam.[1] You don't
land—you sink. When
we met, you, the Native, shook
your head. Sweat dropped
on the bar. You said:
"You're sunk. You won't

3. A brand of commercial window cleaner.

1. Capital city of The Netherlands, famous for its maze of canals.

write a line. You won't make
a nickel. You won't hit
a lick at a snake in this
antebellum sauna-bath. You
won't shit in the morning if
you don't wake up with
your pants down." And you
were right: Three years later
I'm in it up to my eyebrows,
stalled like a streetcar.
My life is under the bed
with the beer bottles.
I'll never write another line
for anything but love
in this city where steam
rises off the street after
a rain like bosoms heaving.

Questions to Consider

1. Where (in time and space) does the poem "Cleaning the Cruiser" begin, and where (in time and space) does it end? At what point does the tone of the poem change from humorous to serious?
2. In the poem "New Orleans," what is the speaker's attitude toward the city?

Lee Smith

1944–

Lee Smith learned early on that her mother placed great stock in propriety, for she frequently sent her daughter to Birmingham to witness ladylike behavior firsthand. Smith describes her early encounters with learning to be a lady: "Aunt Gay Gay used to say, 'Let's have a drink. It's already dark underneath the house.' " Women as lively and sassy as her Aunt Gay Gay populate Smith's fiction, leading critics such as Fred Brown and Jeanne McDonald to praise her as the "foremost voice in Appalachian fiction today," and motivating contemporaries such as Tony Earley to remark that "Lee Smith is the fairy godmother to all of us [North Carolina writers]." She loves to tell stories of what friend and one-time fellow student Anne Goodwyn Jones describes as the "gross world," refusing to let her characters exist on an abstract plain, instead placing them in gritty emotional situations. Her works draw deeply from her Appalachian heritage, illustrating the importance of a sense of place, the deep-rooted influence of family and community, and the sliding continuum between religion and superstition. Her fiction reflects her Southern roots, not only in its themes, but in the authenticity of her characters' voices, which derive from the strong oral tradition in Southern culture. Smith once remarked to Brown and McDonald that "The way southerners tell a story is really specific to the South. . . . It's a whole narrative strategy. It's an approach. Every kind of information is imparted in the form of a story."

Born on 1 November 1944 in Grundy, Virginia, Lee Smith naturally began telling stories at a very young age. She is the only daughter of Ernest Lee and Virginia Marshall Smith, and her father's family traces its lineage back four generations in the small Virginia town; her mother hails from Chincoteague on the eastern shore of Virginia. Smith graduated from St. Catherine's School in Richmond, and then enrolled in Hollins College, where she earned her bachelor's degree. While at Hollins, Smith attended classes with noted fiction writer Annie Dilliard and literary critics Anne Goodwyn Jones and Lucinda MacKethan. She wrote her first novel, *The Last Day the Dogbushes Bloomed* (1968), while a senior at Hollins. Shortly after graduating from college, Smith married James Seay and took a position as a reporter for the *Tuscaloosa News*. She has held teaching positions at Duke University, the University of North Carolina at Chapel Hill, and North Carolina State University. Smith has two children with Seay, from whom she was divorced in 1982. She has since remarried noted Southern columnist Harold B. Crowther and resides with him in North Carolina.

Jones argues that the "metaphor for art in [Smith's] stories comes out of women's culture; not only does it shape life, but it is useful as well, like cakes or quilts or hairstyles. Her tendency to prefer traditionally female immanent art to traditionally male transcendent art parallels her preference for the spoken to the written word." Not surprisingly, given her penchant for traditional women's tools and interests, Smith's characterizations of women are insightful, those of an inside member of a community. Jones points out that Smith's women are "usually married, caught in a cycle of guilt, self-deprecation, entrapment, rebellion, and again guilt that screens them from themselves." Brown and McDonald point out that while early criticism of Smith's works argued that her women were stronger than her men, Smith imbues her women with strength because "Women were closed in by the mountains and by their families. It was difficult for them, being bound biologically and geographically, to free themselves from the constrictions of male society." The lives of Smith's women are not idealized—far from it—but they frequently possess poignant voices that gloss over their difficulties by the very nature of their matter-of-fact retelling of them.

Smith draws heavily from the oral narrative tradition, and elements of Southern folk culture give her fiction a distinctly regional flavor. Her interest in regional culture does not limit her; instead, readers and critics alike find her work well grounded in the human conflicts and emotions that transcend region. This realism leads Smith to examine the class conflicts that remain at issue in the South. While she sympathizes with the lower classes, suggesting that "the further the class from Southern gentility, the more likely it will offer some hope . . . for genuine feeling," she "consistently distinguishes the deracination of 'lowlife' from the rootedness of mountain folk culture," intimating that a sense of place—of where you come from and the family to which you belong—is perhaps the best defense against slothfulness and trashiness. In an interview with Jeanne McDonald, Smith explained that in Southern culture, "sense of place implies who you are and what your *family* did. It's not just literally the physical surroundings, what stuff looks like. It's a whole sense of the past." A strong sense of place provides a defense against the vicious cycle of guilt and self-destruction in which people, particularly women, tend to become trapped. By focusing on the cohesive elements of family, place, and belonging, Smith articulates a viable alternative to these cycles.

Similarly, Smith portrays not only the strength of religion in the South, but the ways in which it motivates those who ascribe to religious faith—and those who do not. Agreeing with Flannery O'Connor's assertion that the region is more "Christ-haunted" than "Christ-centered," Smith has talked at length about her personal struggles with religion, with her somewhat obsessive attraction to it in her youth, and her fears, later in life, that she would be consumed by it if she allowed it to become a part of her life again. Her fiction reflects the effects of patriarchally constructed religious ideologies, however, and demonstrates that traditional religious values are not always constructive for women because of their implicit paternalism.

Smith's celebrated career, spanning three decades thus far, has been highlighted by many prestigious awards, including the PEN-Faulkner Award, a Lyndhurst Fellowship, the John Dos Passos Award for Literature, and the Sir Walter Raleigh Award for Fiction. She is a member of the Fellowship of Southern Writers and frequently delivers lectures and public readings of her work.

In "Me and My Baby View the Eclipse," Smith subtly illustrates the consequences that may befall women who take the socially prescribed path by marrying young, starting families, and supporting hard-working husbands. Quite by accident, the narrator becomes embroiled in an emotionally satisfying affair, only to decide to end it abruptly when her lover comes face-to-face with her young child. The carefree nature of the affair quickly loses its luster when the narrator faces the possibility of replacing her husband with her lover, who, in a somewhat ironic twist, is judged to be a homosexual by some members of the local community. Rather than positing her narrator's decision as a moral one, she suggests that ending the affair is more a matter of expediency or responsibility. In "Me and My Baby View the Eclipse," Smith examines women's reactions to the modes of behavior that have traditionally been expected of them and the types of men with whom they should become involved.

Me and My Baby View the Eclipse

Sharon Shaw first met her lover, Raymond Stewart, in an incident that took place in broad daylight at the Xerox machine in Stewart's Pharmacy three years ago—it *can't* be that long! Sharon just can't believe it. Every time she thinks about him now, no matter what she's doing, she stops right in the middle of it while a hot crazy ripple runs over her entire body. This makes her feel like she's going to die or throw up. Of course she never does either one. She pats her hair and goes right on with her busy life the way she did *before* she met him, but everything is different now, all altered, all new. Three years! Her children were little then: Leonard Lee was eleven, Alister was ten, and Margaret, the baby, was only three. Sharon was thirty-four. Now she's over the hill, but who cares? Since the children are all in school, she and Raymond can meet more easily.

"Is the *coast clear?*" Raymond will ask with his high nervous giggle, at her back door. Raymond speaks dramatically, emphasizing certain words. He flings his arms around. He wears huge silky handkerchiefs and gold neckchains and drives all the way to Roanoke to get his hair cut in what he calls a modified punk look. In fact Raymond is a figure of fun in Roxboro, which Sharon knows, and this knowledge just about kills her. She wants to grab him up and soothe him, smooth down his bristling blond hair and press his fast-beating little heart against her deep soft bosom and wrap him around and around in her big strong arms. Often, she does this. "Hush now, honey," she says.

For Raymond is misunderstood. Roxboro is divided into two camps about him, the ones who call him Raymond, which is his name, and the ones who call him Ramón, with the accent on the last syllable, which is what he *wants* to be called. "Putting on airs just like his daddy did," sniffs Sharon's mama, who works at the courthouse and knows everything. Raymond's daddy was a pharmacist who, according to Sharon's mama, never got over not being a doctor. She says this is common among pharmacists. She says he was a dope fiend too. Sharon doesn't know if this part is true or not, and she won't ask; the subject of his father—who killed himself—gives Raymond nervous palpitations of the heart. Anyway this is how Raymond came to be working at Stewart's Pharmacy, where he mostly runs the Xerox machine and helps ladies order stationery and wedding invitations from huge bound books which he keeps on a round coffee table in his conversation area—Raymond likes for things to be nice. A tall, sour-faced man named Mr. Gardiner is the actual manager—everybody knows that Raymond could never run a store. Raymond stays busy, though. He does brochures and fliers and handouts, whatever you want, on his big humming Xerox machine, and he'll give you a cup of coffee to drink while you make up your mind. This coffee is strong, sweet stuff. Sharon had never tasted anything quite like it before the day she went in there to discuss how much it would cost to print up a little cookbook of everybody's favorite recipes from the Shady Mountain Elementary School PTA to make extra money for art.

It was late August, hot as blazes outside, so it took Sharon just a minute to recover from the heat. She's a large, slow-moving woman anyway, with dark brown eyes and dark brown hair and bright deep color in her cheeks. She has what her mother always called a "peaches-'n'-cream complexion." She used to hear her mother saying that on the phone to her Aunt Marge, talking about Sharon's "peaches-'n'-cream complexion" and about how she was so "slow," and wouldn't "stand up for herself." This meant going out for cheerleader. Later, these conversations were all about how Sharon would never "live up to her potential," which meant marrying a doctor, a potential that went up in smoke the day Sharon announced that she was going to marry Leonard Shaw, her high school sweetheart, after all.

Now Sharon talks to her mother every day on the telephone, unless of course she sees her, and her mother still talks every day to Sharon's Aunt Marge. Sharon has worn her pretty hair in the same low ponytail ever since high school, which doesn't seem so long ago to her either. It seems like yesterday, in fact, and all the friends she has now are the same ones she had then, or pretty much, and her husband Leonard is the same, only older, heavier, and the years between high school and now have passed swiftly, in a strong unbroken line. They've been good years, but Sharon can't figure out where in the world they went, or tell much difference between them.

Until she met Raymond, that is. Now she has some high points in her life. But "met" is the wrong word. Until she saw Raymond with "new eyes" is how Sharon thinks of it now.

She went into Stewart's that day in August and showed Raymond her typed recipes and told him what she wanted. He said he thought he could do that. What kind of paper? he wanted to know. What about the cover? Sharon hadn't considered the cover. Raymond Stewart bobbed up and down before her like a jack-in-the-box, asking questions. It made her feel faint, or it might have been the sudden chill of the air-conditioning, she'd just come from standing out in her hot backyard with the hose, watering her garden. "What?" she said. Sharon has a low, pretty voice, and a way of patting her hair. "Sit right down here, honey," Raymond said, "and let me get you a cup of coffee." Which he did, and it was *so strong*, tasting faintly of almonds.

They decided to use pale blue paper, since blue and gold were the school colors. Sharon looked at Raymond Stewart while he snipped and pasted on the coffee table. "Aha!" he shrieked, and "Aha!" Little bits of paper went flying everywhere. Sharon looked around, but nobody seemed to notice: people in Stewart's were used to Raymond. She found herself smiling.

"Hmmm," Raymond said critically, laying out the pages, and "This sounds *yummy*," about Barbara Sutcliff's Strawberries Romanoff. Sharon had never heard a grown man say "yummy" out loud before. She began to pay more attention. That day Raymond was wearing baggy, pleated tan pants—an old man's pants, Sharon thought—a Hawaiian shirt with blue parrots on it, and red rubber flip-flops. "Oh, this sounds *dreadful*," Raymond said as he laid out Louise Dart's famous chicken recipe where you spread drumsticks with apricot preserves and mustard.

"Actually it's pretty good," Sharon said. "*Everybody* makes that." But she was giggling. The strong coffee was making her definitely high, so high that he talked her into naming the cookbook *Home on the Range* (which everybody thought was just darling, as it turned out), and then he drew a cover for it, a woman in a cowboy hat and an apron tending to a whole stovetop full of wildly bubbling pans. The woman had a funny look on her face; puffs of steam came out of some of the pots.

"I used to draw," Sharon said dreamily, watching him. Raymond has small, white hands with tufts of gold hair on them.

"What did you draw?" He didn't look up.

"Trees," Sharon said. "Pages and pages and pages of trees." As soon as she said it, she remembered it—sitting out on the porch after supper with the pad on her lap, drawing tree after tree with huge flowing branches that reached for God. She didn't tell him the part about God. But suddenly she knew she *could,* if she wanted to. You could say anything to Raymond Stewart, just the way you could say anything to somebody you sat next to on a bus: *anything.*

He grinned at her. His hair stood up in wild blond clumps and behind the thick glasses his magnified eyes were enormous, the pale, flat blue of robins' eggs. "How's that?" He held up the drawing and Sharon said it was fine. Then he signed his name in tiny peaked letters across the bottom of it, like an electrocardiogram, which she didn't expect. Something about him doing this tugged at her heart.

Sharon drank more coffee while he ran off four copies of the recipe booklet; he'd do five hundred more later, if her committee approved. Raymond put these copies into a large flat manila envelope and handed it to her with a flourish and a strange little half-bow. Then somehow, in the midst of standing up and thanking him and taking the envelope—she was all in a flurry—Sharon cut her hand on the flap of the envelope. It was a long, bright cut—a half-moon curve in the soft part of her hand between thumb and index finger. "Oh!" she said.

"*Oh my God!*" Raymond said dramatically. Together they watched while the blood came up slowly, like little red beads on a string. Then Raymond seized her hand and brought it to his mouth and kissed it!—kissed the cut. When Sharon jerked her hand away, it left a red smear, a bloodstain, on his cheek.

"Oh, I'm sorry! I'm so sorry!" Raymond cried, following Sharon out as she fled through the makeup section of the pharmacy where Missy Harrington was looking at lipstick and that older, redheaded lady was working the cash register, and where nobody, apparently, had noticed *anything.*

"I'll call you about the recipe book," Sharon tossed back over her shoulder. It was only from years of doing everything right that she was able to be so polite . . . or was it? Because what *had* happened, anyway? Nothing, really . . . just not a thing. But Sharon sat in her car for a long time before she started back toward home, not minding how the hot seat burned the backs of her legs. Then, on the way, she tried to remember everything she had ever known about Raymond Stewart.

He was younger—he'd been three or four years behind Sharon in school. Everybody used to call him Highwater because he wore his pants so short that you could always see his little white socks, his little white ankles. He'd been a slight, awkward boy, known for forgetting his books and losing his papers and saying things in class that were totally beside the point. Supposedly, though, he was "bright"; Sharon had had one class with him because he had advanced placement in something, she couldn't remember what now—some kind of English class. How odd that he'd never gone on to college. . . . What Sharon *did* remember, vividly, was Raymond's famous two-year stint as drum major for the high school, after her graduation. Sharon, then a young married woman sitting in the bleachers with her husband, had seen him in this role again and again. Before Leonard Lee was born, Sharon went to all the games with Leonard, who used to be the quarterback.

So she was right there the first time Raymond Stewart—wearing a top hat, white gloves, white boots, and an electric-blue sequined suit which, it was rumored, he had designed himself—came strutting and dancing across the field, leading the band like a professional. Nobody ever saw anything like it! He'd strut, spin, toss his baton so high it seemed lost in the stars, then leap up to catch it and land in a split. Sharon remembered remarking to Leonard once, at a game, that she could hardly connect this Raymond Stewart, the drum major—wheeling like a dervish across the field below them—with that funny little guy who had been, she thought, in her English class. That little guy who wore such high pants. "Well," Leonard had said then, after some deliberation—and Leonard was no dummy—"well, maybe it just took him a while to find the right clothes."

Raymond had a special routine he did while the band played "Blue Suede Shoes" and formed itself into a giant shoe on the field. Everybody in the band had showed more spunk and rhythm then, Sharon thought, than any of them had ever shown before—or since, for that matter. Under Raymond's leadership, the band won two AAA number-one championships, an all-time record for Roxboro High. They even went to play at the Apple Blossom Festival the year the governor's daughter was crowned queen, all because of Raymond Stewart.

And just what had Raymond done since? After his father's suicide, which must have happened around the end of his senior year, he had turned "nervous" for a while. He had gone to work at Stewart's Pharmacy and had continued to live with his mother in their big old nubby green concrete house on Sunset Street. Everybody said something should be done about the house, the shameful way Raymond Stewart had let it run down. Since the leaves had not been raked for years and years, all the grass had died—that carefully tended long sloping lawn which used to be Paul Stewart's pride and joy back in the days when he walked to work every morning in his gleaming white pharmacist's jacket with a flower in his buttonhole, speaking to everybody. Paint was peeling from the dark green shutters now, and some of them hung at crazy angles. The hedge had grown halfway up the windows. The side porch was completely engulfed in wisteria, with vines as thick as your arm. It was just a shame. Of course Raymond Stewart wouldn't notice anything like that, or think about raking leaves . . . and his mother!

Miss Suetta was as crazy as a coot. Raymond hired somebody to stay with her all the time. The Stewarts had plenty of money, of course, but Miss Suetta thought she was dirt poor. She'd sneak off from her companion, and hitchhike to town and go into stores and pick out things, and then cry and say she didn't have any money. So the salespeople would charge whatever it was to Raymond, and then they'd call him to come and get her and drive her home. Sharon had been hearing stories about Miss Suetta Stewart for years and years.

But about Raymond—what else? Every Sunday, he played the organ at the First Methodist Church, in a stirring and dramatic way. The whole choir, including Sharon's Aunt Marge, was completely devoted to him. They all called him Ramón. And he had had his picture in the paper last year for helping to organize the Shady Mountain Players, an amateur theatrical group which so far had put on only one show, about a big rabbit. Sharon saw that, but she couldn't remember if Raymond had had a part in it or not. Mainly you thought of Raymond in connection with weddings—everybody consulted Raymond about wedding plans—or interior decoration.

Several of Sharon's friends had hired him, in fact. What he did was help you pick your colors through your astral sign. He didn't *order* anything for you, he just advised. In fact, come to think of it, Sharon herself had ordered some new business cards from Raymond Stewart several years ago, for Leonard when he got his promotion. Gray stock with maroon lettering, which Leonard hadn't liked. Leonard said they looked gay. When he found out where she got them, he said it figured, because Raymond Stewart was probably gay too. Sharon smiled at this memory now, driving home. How funny to find that she knew so much about him, after all! How funny that he'd been right here all along—that you could live in the same town with somebody all these years and just simply never notice them, never think of them once as a person. This idea made Sharon feel so weird she wished she'd never thought it up in the first place.

Then she pulled into her driveway and there was Margaret playing with the hose, pointing it down to drill holes in the soft black dirt of the flower bed. "Stop it! You stop it right now!" Sharon jerked her daughter's little shoulder much harder than she meant to, grabbing the hose.

Later, after Margaret had run in the house yelling and Sharon had turned off the water, she stood out in the heat with the dripping hose and stared, just stared, at the row of little pines that Leonard had planted all along the back of their property, noticing for the first time how much they had grown since he set them out there six years before, when they'd built the house. The pines were big now, as symmetrical as Christmas trees, their green needles glistening in the sun. Sharon thought she might try to draw them. Then she burst into tears, and when Raymond Stewart came by her house in early September to deliver the PTA's five hundred recipe booklets, she went to bed with him.

Raymond was an ardent, imaginative lover. Sometimes he brought her some candy from the pharmacy. Sometimes he brought flowers. Once he brought her a butterfly, still alive, and kissed her on the mouth when she let it go. Sometimes he dressed up for her: he'd wear one of his father's pin-striped suits, or a Panama hat and army-green Bermuda shorts with eight pockets, or a dashiki and sandals, or mechanic's coveralls with "Mike" stitched on the pocket, or jeans and a Jack Daniel's cap. "Honestly!" Sharon would say. Because Raymond thought she was beautiful, she came to *like* her large soft body. She loved the way he made everything seem so special, she loved the way he made everything seem so special, she loved the way he talked—his high-pitched zany laugh—and how he stroked her tumbling hair. He was endlessly fascinated by how she spent her day, by all the dumb details of her life.

Oh, but there was no time, it seemed, at first, and no place to go—two hours once a week at Sharon's, once Margaret had been deposited at Mother's Morning Out—or late afternoon in the creepy old Sutton house, after the boys came home from school to watch Margaret, while Miss Suetta went to group therapy at the Senior Citizens' Center, with her companion. Miss Suetta hated both group therapy and her companion. Sharon lay giggling in Raymond's four-poster bed on these occasions, aware that if she'd ever acted so silly in her own house, Leonard would have sent her packing years ago. But Raymond gave her scuppernong wine in little green-stemmed crystal glasses. The strong autumn sun came slanting across his bed. The wine was sweet. Raymond was blind as a bat without his glasses. Oh, she could have stayed there forever, covering his whole little face, his whole body with kisses.

Raymond had a way of framing things with words that made them special. He gave events a title. For their affair, he had adopted a kind of wise-guy voice and a way of talking out of the side of his mouth, like somebody in *The Godfather*. "Me and my baby sip *scuppernong wine*," he'd say—to nobody—rolling his eyes. Or, "Me and my baby *take in a show*," when once they actually did this, the following summer when Sharon's kids spent the night with her mother and Leonard went to the National Guard. Raymond picked an arty movie for them to see, named *The Night of the Shooting Stars*, and they drove over to Greenville together to see it after meeting in a 7-Eleven at the city limits, where Sharon left her car. *The Night of the Shooting Stars* turned out to be very weird in Sharon's opinion and not anything you would really want to make a movie about. But Raymond thought it was great. Later, on the way back, he drove down a dirt road off the highway and parked in the warm rustling woods.

"Me and my baby *make out!*" Raymond crowed, pulling her into his arms. Oh, it was crazy!

And it got worse. They grew greedier and greedier. Several times, Raymond had just left by the back door when Leonard came in at the front. Several times, going or coming, Sharon encountered Raymond's mother, who never seemed to notice until the day Sharon picked her up hitchhiking downtown and drove her back to the house on Sunset Street. Just before Miss Suetta went in the front door, she stopped dead in her tracks and turned to point a long skinny finger back at Sharon. "Just who *is* this woman?" she asked loudly. And then her companion came and thanked Sharon and guided Miss Suetta inside.

By this time, of course, Sharon called him Ramón.

After two years, he finally talked her into going to a motel, the new Ramada Inn in Greenville. Built on a grander scale than anything else in the county, this Ramada Inn was really more like a hotel, he told her, promising saunas and a sunken bar and an indoor pool and Nautilus equipment. "You know I wouldn't do any of that," said Sharon. Leonard had to go out of town on a selling trip anyway—Leonard can sell or trade anything, which is what he does for the coal company he works for. For instance, he will trade a piece of land for a warehouse, or a rear-end loader for a computer. Sharon doesn't know exactly what Leonard does. But he was out of town, so she let Alister and Leonard Lee spend the night with their friends and asked her mother to keep Margaret. "Why?" her mother had asked. "Well, I've been spotting between my periods," Sharon said smoothly, "and Dr. King wants me to go over to Greenville for some tests." She could lie like a rug! But before Sharon saw Raymond with new eyes, she had never lied in her whole life. Sharon felt wonderful and terrible, checking into the Ramada Inn with Raymond as Mr. and Mrs. John Deere. The clerk didn't bat an eye.

This Ramada was as fancy, as imposing as advertised. Their room was actually a suite, with a color TV and the promised sunken tub, and a king-size bed under a tufted velvet spread and a big brass lamp as large as Margaret. Sharon stifled a sob. She was feeling edgy and kind of blue. It was one thing to find an hour here and an hour there, but another thing to do this. "All I want for Christmas is to sleep with you *all night long*," Raymond had said. Sharon wanted this too. But she hadn't thought it would be so hard. She looked around the room. "How much did this cost?" she asked. "Oh, not much. Anyway, I've got plenty of *money*," Raymond said airily, and Sharon stared at him. This was true, but she always forgot it.

Raymond went out for ice and came back and made two big blue drinks out of rum and a bottled mix. The drinks looked like Windex. "Me and my baby go Hawaiian," Raymond said gravely, clicking his glass against hers. Then they got drunk and had a wonderful time. The next morning Sharon was terrified of seeing somebody she knew, but it turned out that nobody at all was around. Nobody. Raymond joked about this as they walked down the long pale corridor. He made his voice into a Rod Serling *Twilight Zone* voice. "They think they're checking out of . . . the *ghost motel,*" he said.

Then Sharon imagined that they had really died in a wreck on the way to the motel, only they didn't know it. When they turned a corner and saw themselves reflected in a mirror in the lobby, she screamed.

"She screams, but no one can hear her in . . . the *ghost motel,*" said Raymond. He carried his clothes in a laundry bag.

"No, hush, I mean it," Sharon said.

She looked in the mirror while Raymond paid the bill, and it seemed to her then that she was wavy and insubstantial, and that Raymond, when he came up behind her, was nothing but air. They held hands tightly and didn't talk, all the way back to the 7-Eleven where Sharon had parked her car.

And now, Raymond is all excited about the eclipse. He's been talking about it for weeks. He's just like a kid. Sharon's real kids, Leonard Lee and Alister and Margaret, have been studying eclipses at school, but they couldn't care less.

"I want to be with you, baby, to view the eclipse." Raymond has said this to Sharon again and again. He has made them both little contraptions out of cardboard, with peepholes, so they won't burn their retinas. Luckily, the eclipse is set for one-thirty on a Tuesday afternoon, so the children are at school. Leonard is at work.

Raymond arrives promptly at one, dressed in his father's white pharmacist's jacket. "I thought I ought to look scientific," he says, twirling around in Sharon's kitchen to give her the full effect. His high giggle ricochets off the kitchen cabinets. He has brought a bottle of pink champagne. He pops the cork with a flourish and offers her a glass. Which Sharon accepts gladly because in truth she's not feeling so good—it's funny how that lie she told her mother a couple of months ago seems to be coming true. Probably her uterus is just falling apart. The truth is, she's getting *old*—sometimes she feels just ancient, a hundred years older than Raymond.

Sharon sips the champagne slowly while Raymond opens all of her kitchen cabinets and pokes around inside them.

"What are you looking for?" she finally asks.

"Why—nothing!" When Raymond smiles, his face breaks into crinkles all over. He clasps her forcefully. "I like to see where you keep things," he says. "You're an endless mystery to me, baby." He kisses her, then pulls out a pocket watch she's never seen before. Perhaps he bought it just for the eclipse. "One-twelve," he says. "Come on, you *heavenly body* you. It's time to go outside."

In spite of herself, Sharon has gotten excited too. They take plastic lawn chairs and sit down right in the middle of the backyard, near the basketball goal but well away from the pines, where they can get the most open view. It's a cloudless day in early March. Sharon's daffodils are blooming. She has thought this all through ahead of time: the only neighbor with a view of her backyard, Mrs. Hodges, is gone all day. Raymond refills his glass with champagne. Sharon's lettuce is coming up, she notices, in crinkly green waves at the end of the garden. But Raymond is telling her what will happen next, lecturing her in a deep scientific voice which makes him sound exactly like the guy on *Wild Kingdom:* "When the moon passes directly between the earth and the sun so that its shadow falls upon the earth, there's a solar eclipse, visible from the part of the earth's surface on which the shadow lies. So it's the shadow of the moon which will pass across us."

I don't care! Sharon nearly screams it. *All I want,* she thinks, *honey, all I ever want is you.* Raymond sits stiffly upright in her plastic lawn chair, his head leaning to the side in a practiced, casual manner, lecturing about the umbra and penumbra. He has smoothed his spiky blond hair down for this occasion and it gleams in the early spring sun.

"A total solar eclipse occurs only once in every four hundred years in any one place. Actually this won't be a total eclipse, not where we are. If we'd driven over to Greensboro, we would have been right in the center of it." For a minute, his face falls. "Maybe we should have done that."

"Oh, no," Sharon assures him. "I think this is just fine." She sips her champagne while Raymond shows her how to look through the little box in order to see the eclipse. Raymond consults his watch—one-fifteen. Mrs. Hodges's golden retriever, Ralph, starts barking.

"Dogs will bark," Raymond intones. "Animals will go to bed. Pregnant women will have their babies. Birds will cease to twitter."

"*Twitter?*" Sharon says. "Well, they sure are twittering now." Sharon has a lot of birds because of the bird feeder Alister made in Shop II.

"*Trust me.* It's coming," says Raymond.

While Sharon and Raymond sit in her backyard with their boxes on their knees, waiting, Sharon has a sudden awful view of them from somewhere else, a view of how they must look, doing this, drinking champagne. It's so wild! Ralph barks and the birds twitter, and then, just as Raymond promised, they cease. Ralph ceases too. Raymond squeezes Sharon's hand. A hush falls, a shadow falls, the very air seems to thicken suddenly, to darken around them, but still it's not *dark.* It's the weirdest thing Sharon has ever seen. It's like it's getting colder too, all of a sudden. She bets the temperature has dropped at least ten degrees. "Oh, baby! Oh, honey!" Raymond says. Through the peephole in her cardboard box, Sharon sees the moon, a dark object moving across the sun's face and shutting more and more of its bright surface from view, and then it's really twilight.

"Me and my baby view the eclipse," says Raymond.

Sharon starts crying.

The sun is nothing now but a crazy shining crescent, a ghost sun. Funny shadows run all over everything—all over Sharon's garden, her house, her pine trees, the basketball goal, all over Raymond. His white jacket seems alive, dimly rippling. Sharon feels exactly like somebody big is walking on her grave. Then the shadows are gone, and it's nearly dark. Sharon can see stars. Raymond kisses her, and then the eclipse is over.

"It was just like they said it would be!" he says. "Just exactly!" He's very excited. Then they go to bed, and when Margaret comes home from school he's still there, in the hall bathroom.

"Hi, honey," says Sharon, who ran quickly into the kitchen when she first heard Margaret, so as to appear busy. Sharon moves things around in the refrigerator.

"Who's *that?*" Margaret drops her knapsack and points straight at Raymond, who has chosen just this moment to come out of the bathroom waving Sharon's new Dustbuster. Margaret is a skinny, freckled little girl who's mostly serious. Now she's in first grade.

"What's *this?*" Raymond waves the Dustbuster. He's delighted by gadgets, but whenever he buys one, it breaks.

"I'll show you," Margaret says. She demonstrates the Dustbuster while Raymond buttons his daddy's white pharmacy jacket.

"See?" Margaret says gravely.

"That's *amazing*," Raymond says.

Sharon, watching them, thinks she will die. But Raymond leaves before the boys get home, and Margaret doesn't mention him until the next afternoon. "He was nice," Margaret says then.

"Who, honey?" Sharon is frying chicken.

"That man who was here. Who was he?" Margaret asks again.

"Oh, just nobody," Sharon says. Because it's true. Her affair with Raymond Stewart is over now as suddenly and as mysteriously as it began. Sharon aches with loss. When she tells Raymond, he'll be upset, as she is upset, but he'll live, as she will. He'll find things to do. He has just been given the part of Ben in the Shady Mountain Players production of *The Glass Menagerie*, for instance, a part he's always wanted. He'll be okay. Sharon plans to say, "Raymond, I will never love anyone in the world as much as I love you." This is absolutely true. She loves him, she will love him forever with a fierce sweet love that will never die. For Raymond Stewart will never change. He'll grow older, more eccentric. People will point him out. Although their mothers will tell them not to, children will follow him in the street, begging him to talk funny and make faces. Maybe he'll have girlfriends. But nobody will ever love him as much as Sharon—he's shown her things. She knows this. And oh, she'll be around, she'll run into Raymond from time to time—choosing Leonard's new business cards, for instance, when Leonard gets another promotion, or making up the Art Guild flier, or—years and years from now—ordering Margaret's wedding invitations.

Questions to Consider

1. What does Smith's characterization of Sharon suggest about the roles that Southern women are expected to fulfill? Do these roles have the potential to be satisfying?
2. Why does Raymond become so engrossed in viewing the eclipse? What does the eclipse come to represent in their relationship? Does the collision of the two facets of Sharon's life serve a symbolic function?

Josephine Humphreys

1945–

In the essay "A Disappearing Subject Called the South" (1988), Josephine Humphreys warns that the region is destroying its towns and landscapes in the name of progress, expressing her fears that "the concert of human lives"—long a focus of Southern writers—will be threatened as a result. Humphreys contrasts the individualism of New England literature with the South's more communal spirit, a spirit embodied in her four novels. Whether her setting is contemporary Charleston, South Carolina, or the North Carolina wilderness of the late nineteenth century, Humphreys emphasizes the links between generations and the ties between races that her protagonists come to recognize and cultivate.

Humphreys was born in Charleston on 2 February 1945, the oldest daughter of businessman William Wirt Humphreys and Martha Lynch Humphreys. Her mother and her grandmother, two artistically talented women, encouraged her to write when she was a young girl; as an undergraduate at Duke University, she found an important mentor in the author Reynolds Price. Humphreys received a master's degree at Yale University and pursued doctoral studies at the University of Texas at Austin but did not complete her dissertation on William Cowper, the eccentric English religious poet. She married Thomas A. Hutcheson, a lawyer, and the couple raised their two sons in Charleston. Humphreys taught English at the city's Baptist College and was almost 40 when she published *Dreams of Sleep* (1984).

With allusions to myths and legends, this first book introduced the themes of family, innocence and betrayal, racial tension, and loss and restoration that mark all of Humphreys's fiction. Lucille Odom, the resilient narrator of *Rich in Love* (1987) is among several teenaged girls who bring hope to Humphreys's troubled households by coping with drastic changes in traditional domestic patterns. A movie adaptation of *Rich in Love,* with screenplay by Alfred Uhry (best known for *Driving Miss Daisy*), widened Humphreys's audience a year after she published *The Fireman's Fair* (1991). Rob Wyatt, the main character of this third novel, has been compared to the philosophical protagonists of Walker Percy, one of Humphreys's favorite writers. In the wake of Hurricane Hugo, Rob retreats from his busy law office to a beach bungalow during a major period of readjustment. She revisits the idea of withdrawal when Rhoda Strong retreats into the deep Carolina forest in Humphreys's most recent book, *Nowhere Else on Earth* (2000). The author says that the Native American Rhoda, based on a legendary Lumbee woman, forced her to revise her notions of Southern community; moreover, the novel increased her interest in Southerners who have been neglected by the standard histories. Humphreys's detailed evocation of nature relates *Nowhere Else on Earth* to the environmentally sensitive works of Wendell Berry, Barbara Kingsolver, and Janisse Ray.

Elected to the Fellowship of Southern Writers, Humphreys has received a Guggenheim grant, a Lyndhurst Foundation award, and other prizes for her fiction. She has reviewed the works of many well-known authors, including Southerners Reynolds Price, Bobbie Ann Mason, and Allan Gurganus, in the *New York Times* and other national media. Her descriptive style, her plots of transience and endurance, and her sympathetic depiction of the region's ethnic diversity all contribute to her reputation as one of the contemporary South's leading novelists.

from Rich in Love

On an afternoon two years ago my life veered from its day-in day-out course and became for a short while the kind of life that can be told as a story—that is, one in which events appear to have meaning. Before, there had been nothing worth telling the world. We had our irregularities; but every family has something or other out of whack. We had my mother's absent-mindedness, my sister's abnormal beauty, my father's innocence; and I was not without oddities of my own. We were characters, my friend Wayne said. But nothing about us was story material.

Until the day, May 10, when one of us betrayed the rest and set off a series of events worth telling.

I rode my bicycle home from school. All looked normal. I sniffed: high spring, Carolina, health and prosperity. People were shopping like crazy in stores along the highway. Plants were growing in the median, big sturdy weeds that looked a lot like carrots and celery, with thick stalks and ferny leaves dense enough to hide the underlying road trash. Traffic was a carefree stream of cars. The afternoon was average and happy, to the eye of a casual observer.

Supposedly your hair stands on end in the instant before you get struck by lightning. I had a similar sensation that afternoon on the highway. I recognized the tingle as a premonition but a useless one: no specific details, only the feeling. Feelings were a problem to me at the time. I was prey to them, and yet I could never tell exactly what they meant. They seemed uselessly vague. For example, what good is a premonition (*advance warning*, by the Latin root) if it doesn't say what you are being warned against? I looked around me. I rubbed my upper lip, a habit of nervousness.

Seventeen years old and in possession of a valid driver's license, I could have been driving my mother's VW camper—she didn't drive it much—or my father's Buick—his license had been temporarily suspended for speeding. But I preferred the open air and the way the afternoon spread out around me with its sounds and smells. I could form a good idea of where I was, whereas in a car I couldn't quite get the feel of a place except as a sort of television show sliding flat past the window, dull as advertising. My sister Rae felt like I did on the subject, only she didn't ride a bike anymore. She had a twenty-year-old Impala convertible, a car as huge and smooth as a parade float. Because it opened up, you could ride in it and still feel the scenery. She had driven herself to Sweet Briar College in that car four years in a row, and then to Washington, D.C., where she worked for a U.S. senator. When the car malfunctioned, she cussed it up and down. "The salesman said this car runs like a dream, Lucille," she said in her joke Southern voice, easygoing and high. "But I swear he must have been thinking of those dreams adolescent boys have. The engine overheats and the thing revs up and then sputters and spits and cuts off." But she loved the car. She had never had a pet or a doll in her life, and when the Impala came along, I guess it filled a void.

I liked Rae's car fine, but the bicycle was better for me because it was quiet. I liked to travel silently.

Where I rode, the old zones of country, town, and city had run together. Originally we had the city of Charleston, the town of Mount Pleasant, and then the country, but now they were jumbled, haphazard as a frontier settlement. This new section of highway had been laid out with no regard to preexisting roads, and some of the old roads came up to the highway and dead-ended in striped barricades. Wild animals, to judge by the carcasses, had not yet adjusted to the new system. Out in the developments, some of the new roads curved back upon themselves, and I sometimes lost my sense of direction trying to get somewhere; or I might be riding along and all of a sudden the smooth asphalt turns to soft dirt and I'm in the country, with wooden houses balanced on concrete blocks, and the tragic crowing of roosters, and the black people on porches, innocent as natives.

It was as if new places had been slapped down over the old ones, but some of the old was still showing through. I tried not to lose myself in those pockets. It could sometimes be too much for me, a house at the edge of a field, the rim of pines, the smoke. It wrenched my heart. There was too much emotion for me in the country.

Every so often I'd run across what I called a dream house, one that somebody had started but never finished. They were scattered through the woods like ruins of a defunct civilization, but they were only the ruins of defunct families. Somebody had wanted a house, and had gotten as far as slab and walls; but then the money had run out, or the wife had run out, and all that was left was a cinderblock shell, the house a dream of itself, square-eyed and black-mouthed. Soon weeds would hide it, snakes and raccoons find shelter in it. Whenever I saw one, I stopped by the side of the road and stood leaning on my bicycle to look.

Sometimes out there I would get the hollow feeling. I called it loneliness, though I knew it wasn't exactly loneliness because I was the type of person that likes solitude. But maybe it was pre-loneliness, or loneliness anticipated. Whatever it was, it was hollow and sad. Had I known someone who had died? I couldn't think of anybody. My grandparents had died before I knew them well enough to grieve their loss.

Rae was never lonely.

In high school she had been friends with all the boys and more than friends with more than a few, but she had never paired up with one. She had never acted in love like most girls do, and thank goodness. Rae was on her own. She was well-known as wild, although she was actually conservative when it came to drinking, drugs, and sex. But she had an unpredictability of the sort that distinguishes an untamed creature from a domestic one. People were in awe of her because she was so brave. She sang with a black band and had a black best friend. She laughed whenever she wanted to. She was Miss Wando High and had left a trail of stammering boys behind her. Her looks were unnerving, brown eyes and blond hair.

But I knew her better than anyone did, and I knew the little shiver that now and then came across her mouth. Recently her postcards from Washington had worried me; the handwriting had changed, loosened, and risen off the horizontal like a child's. I was pretty good at analyzing handwriting, and I could discern three things in Rae's: kindness, strength, and future disappointment. Women like Rae sooner or later run into disappointment because beauty has given them a heightened awareness of themselves. It isn't vanity. It is high hopes and optimism. Think of starlets, how they begin and how they end.

From Wando High to Mount Pleasant was straight uninterrupted shopping with no letup, a hive of purchasing activity that was reassuring. I was a poor shopper myself, too easily baffled by the array of goods. In malls I became overstimulated and wound up taking a seat in the community service area watching cloggers or the kids' poster contest. So if I really wanted something I tried to buy it out of a catalog or at a yard sale, and once I even stole a lipstick rather than go through the process of legitimate purchase. Kleptomania did not strike me as a weird disorder: I could imagine ethics outweighed by desire. But methodical shopping as a daily activity was beyond me, and I was always impressed on this highway by the hordes of people stocking up on new shoes, blue jeans, groceries, hamsters, mini-vans, tomato plants, sheets of plywood, ice-cream cones. The level of shopping was an indicator, in my opinion, of human trust in the future. I myself sometimes woke up in the middle of the night scared to death. When I tried to pinpoint the fear, nothing logical came to mind. All I could come up with was the end of the world, but nobody else feared that. Look at them swarming into the Garden Centre, coming out with flats of two-tone petunias and soaker-hoses!

But I had that tingling. Maybe ordinary life can continue only so long before the extraordinary will pop into it. I didn't know where it might come from, but I was prepared. I admired the Boy Scouts (though I didn't know one personally) for their "Be Prepared" motto. Good advice. I kept my head down. The most immediate danger I could think of was from trash. If I hit a bottle or a shoe I might swerve into traffic, most of which was people my age heading for the beach.

People my age were murder. Sometimes they tossed stuff out of cars. I could tell when something was coming at me, even though I never gave them the satisfaction of a glance over my shoulder. Their car would slow down and let out a puff of music as the window opened. Then the beer can or whatever would hit my arm, and the car was already so far past I couldn't see who it was. Possibly the people in the car did not know what harm they could do me. Possibly they did know.

But if I had one personality trait it was vigilance. My personality *in toto* was a mystery to me; for some time now I had been trying to figure it out but could not seem to get a good look at it. I kept a diary by my bed so that if I thought of an attribute I had, I could write it down. But the list was short. One I was sure of was "vigilance." Let the world do its worst, Lucille Odom was ready.

I sensed that I was on a verge. A large block of time was due to crack open in front of me, the future that up till then had been impenetrable.

I stuck to the highway. Even though I had traveled it that morning, I saw new things. I noticed for the first time a new TV tower in the distance, making a string of six now in the long stretch of marsh up the Intracoastal Waterway.[1] And then I saw that the small swamp between Seagull Shores and Oakview had turned into dry land, and a sign had gone up saying, "Gator Pond Estates." I noticed that the names chosen for these places were memorials to what had been bulldozed into oblivion.

A car went by. Something pinged against my helmet. A jelly bean could do me in, I realized.

I wore a safety helmet and did not care how it looked. When other seniors were screeching out of the Wando parking lot in their Cherokees and Broncos, I strapped on my helmet and backpack in plain sight and let them have a laugh if they needed one so desperately. If I had been a normal teenage girl I might have cared, but I wasn't and didn't.

When I say I was not normal, I don't just mean I had the usual adolescent delusions of being different from everyone else. My upper lip had failed to fuse during a critical embryonic stage, and I had been born with a split there. Not a full-fledged harelip, but a small, neat slice not quite all the way through. When I was three, the lip had been repaired, and now, they said, it was hardly noticeable.

Well: Does "hardly noticeable" mean "noticeable" or "not noticeable"?

But I wasn't one to set store by looks. In fact, my scar had taught me a thing or two. It had put me into a different sphere. I sometimes felt as if I were a member of a third gender or secret species. On occasion, I saw people in the street who for one reason or another struck a chord in me—a man with a rocking limp, a boy with one side of his face stained red—and I would say to myself, "There's one."

Of course, I never spoke this thought.

For a long time I felt guilty about my lip, and I had an urge to apologize to my mother for it. Imagine, expecting another wonder baby and getting one with a flapping lip. However, I later found out that I had no need to apologize. It was more likely that she needed to apologize to me. I accepted the seam, ran my finger over its shiny ridge whenever I was in deep thought, and went on with my life. I had no time for guilt or resentment; I had interests that required all my attention, interests unlike those of most teenagers. I was studying certain things.

Not that I counted myself superior. Gladly I'd have given up my pursuits in exchange for an afternoon in the hair stylist's chair getting my hair flipped over one eye, or lying on the beach slathered in Bain de Soleil, or trying on lingerie at Sweet

1. A long, partly natural, partly artificial waterway with sheltered passage for commercial and leisure boats along the U.S. Atlantic coast. The Intracoastal Waterway extends from Boston to Key West and along the Gulf of Mexico from Florida to the Rio Grande in Texas.

Nothings in the shopping plaza. I'd have enjoyed those things as much as the next girl. But I wasn't free.

Something had come over me. Recently, like within the past few weeks. I could not tell at first whether it was an affliction or a gift. It was primarily a feeling, but different from the others in that it was constant, it didn't ebb and flow. I called it "invision" because it was almost as if I could see into things. I could not take my eyes off physical objects—plants, dogs, faces, birds, all the world of nature—but also manufactured items such as cars, mailboxes, chain-link fencing. Things glittered at me as I rode past. They had started glittering after I read in the paper about a study done by Clemson University scientists concerning the greenhouse effect.[2] The level of the ocean, they had learned, was on the rise. Their computer had generated a map of the coastline of South Carolina as it would appear fifty years from now. I studied this map carefully. *We were not on it*. Our house, town, most of the city of Charleston, were shown in blue, i.e., covered by water.

Inundation would be gradual, inches per year, but inevitable, unless everyone in the world immediately stopped burning coal, using fertilizer, and spraying aerosol deodorant. Fat chance, I said to myself. So every time I looked at my own yard, every time I rode the bicycle, I saw not the good old world I had known forever, but a world it was nearly time to say good-bye to. Beauty doubled and tripled around me. The place was doomed.

"Invision," I decided, was a gift, and I received it the way a child receives something that may very well not have been meant for him. I hid it.

One time I mentioned it to Wayne, who was just nuts enough himself to sometimes know what I was talking about. We were at a Dixie Youth League[3] baseball game; Wayne was coaching a team of twelve-year-olds. He sat on the bench with the team, and I sat behind the fence in the bleachers. Our team, which was quasi-integrated (a pale brown right-fielder whose parents were lawyers) was up against a black team. We didn't have a chance, even though some of the opponents had no gloves and caught with their caps.

I saw the red infield, the parched yellow outfield, the white lime baseline. The playground was a new one in the middle of nowhere: you could still smell pine resin from leaking stumps. I saw the little boys, ours tough and foul-mouthed out of fear, theirs wiry and friendly out of fear. I saw an aluminum bat flash in the sun, which was heading down behind a stand of long-leaf pine. Seagulls passed over with their disjointed flappy style of flying, and I heard thin radio music. Radio music out-of-doors has always been hard on me. I experienced a sort of heart flutter and called out to Wayne.

He motioned time out to the umpire and came up to the fence. "Yeah?" he said.

"Um," I said. "Is there something funny here?"

"We're getting our butts knocked in the dirt. I can't get another pitcher in there until the next inning, goddammit."

"No, I mean here." I waved to include the world. "Is there something about this whole design?"

"Design?"

"Well, the scene. I thought . . . the trees looked like they turned black. Our uniforms turned pink. I heard this song."

2. The gradual increase of the temperature of the earth's lower atmosphere resulting from the increase in gaseous emissions since the Industrial Revolution.

3. Southern baseball league for children, similar to Little League.

"Lucille?" he said, cocking his head at me. "Did you smoke something before you got here?"

"Of course not."

"Where'd you get it?"

"I didn't. I don't."

"That's what I thought, but now you're making me wonder."

So I said, "It must be the sun going down."

If Wayne didn't see what I meant, who would? I gave up. I don't recall the score of that game, but I know how the slow sun moved and the pines loomed and everything—*everything out there*—sank through a million changes before night fell onto it.

Questions to Consider

1. How does the narrator of *Rich in Love* reflect Josephine Humphreys's concern that urban development is drastically modifying the South?
2. In what other ways do the opening pages of this novel introduce Humphreys's central theme of vulnerability and loss?

Mary Hood

1946–

Mary Hood once said: "I cannot think of a single more important influence on my writing, and certainly upon my life, than my parentage." Hood's mother hailed from Georgia, while her father grew up in New York, and she asserts that, as an author, she "made the decision to try to sound like the Southern talkers I had heard tell such wonderful things" and to tweak the "Northern conscience . . . . that stands ready, tapping its foot, jingling the car keys, rustling the map, wanting me to *get on with it,* asking with every turn and delay of plot, 'so?' " Hood aptly describes the different ways that Northerners and Southerners perceive detail and seeks to bring those differences to life in her fiction.

Hood was born on 16 September 1946 and raised in northern Georgia. As a result of her long-time residence in the area, coupled with her mother's regional heritage and dialect, she developed an ear for the voices that surrounded her. She earned an A.B. in Spanish at Georgia State University in 1967 and began writing fiction. Hood was one of the first writers to be a part of the third wave of the Southern Renascence, and her work has played a significant role in the return to a more vivid, detailed variety of fiction which other Southern writers of the 1980s eschewed in order to avoid the title of regional writers. Hood embraces the details that make characters and stories believable. The quality and success of her work encouraged other Southern writers to believe that detail and traditional, linear narrative in a fiction piece need not limit their work's appeal. Hood credits the lush, Southern voices created by Eudora Welty, Lee Smith, and Flannery O'Connor as influences upon her work. While other writers have influenced Hood, her intimate knowledge of the flora and fauna of the South and her love for the Southern voice distinguish her fiction from that of her peers. Her stories often focus on love relationships and the struggles between men and women, yet her treatments differ subtly because of her focus on the connection between the environment and her characters.

Hood has won great acclaim throughout her career. She has been the recipient of the Flannery O'Connor Award for Short Fiction, as well as the *Southern Review* and the Louisiana State University Short Fiction Awards. Her work is often praised for its accurate depiction of narrative voices and for the realism of her characters. The foothills of the Appalachians serve as her inspiration for writing and clearly are reflected in her stories. Hood currently lives in Woodstock, Georgia where she takes care of a large garden and many pets.

In this story, "Inexorable Progress," Hood depicts a woman of the 1970s as she attempts to find her place in society. Issues such as the Equal Rights Amendment and progressive social mores become important elements of this story; the character, Angelina, like many women of her time, feels displaced from her world due to the societal changes of the era.

Inexorable Progress

There's not much difference between a bare tree and a dead tree in winter. Only when the others begin to leaf out the next spring and one is left behind in the general green onrush can the eye tell. By then it is too late for remedy. That's how it was with Angelina: a tree stripped to the natural bone, soul-naked in the emptying wind. She was good at pretending; she hung color and approximations of seasonal splendor on every limb, and swayed like a bower in the autumn gales around her, but her heart was hollow, and her nests empty. You could tell a little something by her eyes, with their devious candor (like a drunk's), but her troubles, whatever they were, didn't start with the bottle, and after a while the bottle wasn't what stopped them.

Glory be to the Father she sang the Sunday before Labor Day. She wore her neckline low, her hem and heels and spirits as high as fashion and propriety would allow.

and to the Son and to the Holy Ghost

When she warbled in the sanctuary, her freckled bosom rippled in vibrato. She left no fingerprints on the salver as she dropped in her tithe.

as it was in the beginning

She kept herself retouched, forever presenting the same bright portrait to the saints.

is now and ever shall be

Her cordial eyes, fixed in bravado, were shining windows, bolted against bad weather.

world without end, amen

Behind them, fear, that restless housecat, paced.

amen.

She hated many things, but Sundays most of all.

The congregation settled in for the sermon now that it was paid for. To her daughter beside her Angelina whispered, "Listen, Bon"—as though she were still a fidgety child, impervious as stone, around whose innocence the words and water of life would pour unproved; as though Bonnie were still six, to be cajoled into rectitude (or at least silence) with carefully doled bribes of Lifesavers tasting of the scented depths of her purse.

Part of what Angelina hated about Sundays was sitting alone in church while her husband went fishing or hunting. The way he saw it, he always made it up to her afterward, but from black-powder season to doe[1] days she might as well have been a widow. Of course, Bonnie was growing up there beside her, but it wasn't the same. To

1. This reference pertains to hunting seasons. Certain times of the hunting season are designated for hunting with particular equipment—bow and arrow and black powder rifles are two such specialized subseasons within the larger seasons for deer, squirrel, duck, and geese.

make sure nobody thought she was getting resigned to it, or ever would, Angelina always reserved a space beside her in the pew, so the world would know at a glance that Chick was expected back.

Sometimes she thought more than was reasonable about who was missing. Sometimes she dreamed about her stillborn son; every month just before her period she dreamed about him. Perhaps he was just born and they laid him wailing, wriggling, on her belly. Or perhaps he was a little older, running to her with a pinecone pipe, calling, "See what I found? Come see!" She always recognized him, who he would have been. Once she dreamed they were camping in hunting season and he came fretting up, arms out in a "Love me, love me, mama" pose, and she gave him a bloody fox foot to teethe on, to hush him. She never told Chick about the dreams, nor what it was she had been suffering in her sleep when she cried, "Help!" and woke them both.

Here lately she had been dreaming about her mother; always the same thing: just before they sealed the coffin (her mother had died in April) she saw her mama's eyelids flicker; no one believed her (suddenly everybody was a stranger; dark-suited, efficient, looming, they closed ranks against her, and she cried "Stop!" but they did not stop), and the inexorable progress toward the dark, the sealing, the lowering, the losing sight of, the closing went on until she woke herself dry-mouthed, heart-pounding, telling herself it was only a dream. Its persistence shamed her, haunted her; she could not tell anyone how she felt, that she had got off too light, that she deserved worse than heartbreak. She had felt that way from the beginning; indeed, had tried to comfort the comforters at the funeral. The feeling of guilt, of some punishment deserved, haunted her through the summer until one night she dreamed she had a pain in her left breast, and the sensation of pain woke her like a noise, like a light. She lay panting in fright, unable to disbelieve, or perhaps unwilling. Waking fully, she investigated and found a lump: a dream come true. It somehow satisfied her; it was her secret. She would not see a doctor; she knew how it went. Her mother had died of such a lump. Sometimes Angelina imagined herself wasted like that; when she raised her own hand before her eyes she saw her mother's skeleton instead.

Angelina lost her appetite. She began cleaning out closets. During a rainy spell she got out the carton of snapshots and began putting them in an album for Bonnie, labeling who and what and when. She smoked heavily (Bonnie always after her to quit, saying, "Mama, I want you around") and the fruitcake brandy (a bottle had lasted five years) vanished in one afternoon. When Elsie Bland and her boy Jude came in the afternoon to pick windfall apples on shares, Angelina crouched close against the kitchen cabinet, out of sight, while they knocked and knocked. After a while they went away. When Bonnie got home from school, she found her mama rubber-legged, penitent, incapacitated. Bonnie cleaned her up, mopped, ran the laundry through, and had the place aired out and sweet-smelling when Chick got home. They called it the flu that time; there were other times . . . .

Lost in reverie, Angelina did not realize the service was over; Bonnie was touching her arm and saying, "Mama? Mama!" and it made her start. She stood perhaps too quickly, for she had to stop a moment, resting her hand on the rubbed pew-end till the stained glass on her periphery swung and settled. Then she walked down (it seemed uphill) the burgundy carpet in which her sharp heels picked little dimples, and out into the dazzling sunlight, her left hand holding up the bulletin to fend off the noon. Reverend Martin made his small remarks at the door, gentle pleasantries served with a handshake to each departing member. He was speaking to Angelina, but she couldn't make out the words. All around her thrummed an expectant, dimming silence like the instant between lightning and thunder. She turned away, troubled, from the lips soundlessly moving, and shut her eyes against the intolerable glare off the whited church front. Very suddenly the porch tilted up and she pitched down the steps, unconscious before she relinquished the Reverend's hand, which is why (the doctor said later) there were no bones broken.

She told the doctor some of what she had been going through: not the dreams, not the brandy. He gave her something for her nerves and arranged for a biopsy on the lump. Overnight in the hospital, and she would know for sure (but she *was* sure!). Chick gave up a bow-and-arrow weekend to be with her; he was what she saw when she opened her eyes after the surgery; he was the one who exulted, "Benign." But she didn't believe him. Hadn't they lied to her mother? Finally, finally they persuaded her.

Relieved, yet oddly disappointed, she went home determined to make the most of her spared life. At Sunday-night services she laid her cigarettes on the altar rail and asked for prayer to help her kick the habit. Dust gathered on the unopened conscience bottle of brandy. She built up to four miles of brisk walking every morning and was able to sleep without medication. She took up crafts, and began hooking a rug for Bonnie's room. ("Do something for yourself," Bonnie said, when her mama finished that and began a matching pillow, but Angelina said, "Doing for others, that's the reason we're here.")

The doctors advised her to cut out caffeine too and she was able to break a fourteen-cup-a-day habit. ("Jesus can fix anything," she told her neighbor as they jogged in the fine fall weather.) For her forty-third birthday Chick bought her a hair-fine chain with a gold charm: PERFECT it announced. She fastened it on and wore it along with the little silver cross her mother left her. She was on a streak of pure happiness.

But, of course, there is no such thing unalloyed. Cakes fall. Cars break down. A roofing staple manages to penetrate the week-old radial. The eggs on the top shelf of the refrigerator freeze. Dogs, even the most kindly treated, chase cats, wander, bark well off cue. Bills get lost in the mails. Angelina's streak ended with vapor lock. She had been shopping for groceries for the week; they and milk and frozen foods were in the trunk when the car cut out. She had an appointment in an hour, so she took a shortcut in repairs; rather than wait for the car to cool, she ran in the bait shop and bought a bag of ice and held it to the hot engine, and the engine block cracked. Still, she expected sympathy, not a scolding, and could hardly believe it when Chick roared up behind the wrecker and jumped out and began yelling, "How can you be so goddam stupid!" before God and the gathering crowd. And while he was on the subject, why didn't she wash her car once in a while? A little soap in a bucket of water wouldn't kill her . . .

She pointed out (while the wrecker hooked up) that she might have more motivation if the car were in her name. (Nothing was—not the house, not the lot at Hammermill, nor the pontoon, nothing. "I bet if I polished the Revereware I'd find his Social Security number engraved on the bottom," she fumed later.) She rode in the wrecker, wouldn't ride with Chick.

"A thousand bucks for a new engine," he told her as she climbed into the wrecker. "You want it fixed, *you* earn it." As though what she did, what she was, wasn't worth anything to him! To say it like that before the wide world! If he meant it, about her paying for the repairs, he only meant it when he said it, not a moment later, but it pleased Angelina to prolong the quarrel. Nothing he thought to do could stop it now. It must run its course, like a disease.

Tuesday was election day. Angelina had been on her way to the courthouse to be sworn in as poll chief for Deerfield when the car tore up and she and Chick boiled over. Grace Arnold had had to be the one to run up to Hammermill for the materials. She offered Angelina a ride election day, too, and came by before six-thirty that morning with her car loaded with supplies (extension cord, flag, posterboard, hampers of lunch and magazines, folding chairs). Angelina was waiting at the foot of the drive with a look of righteous malice on her face; she got in bragging what she had done (looking a little scared too): she had locked Chick's truck in the garage, along with the ladder, and had thrown both sets of keys up on the roof, as high as indignation would allow.

How he solved the problem Grace never knew, but he came in to vote around noon. They had the precinct set up in the Fish and Game Clubhouse, the old schoolhouse on the pine hill, high enough so you could see the traffic passing by on the road; the magnolia blocked the north view, but you could see the cars a half-mile off looking south, and Grace, with her bright eye, spotted the blue truck and said, "Isn't that Chick?" Instantly, Angelina fled. They could hear her in back, dropping incorrect change through the Coke machine, over and over. Grace signed Chick up and he voted; it didn't take very long. When the curtains swept open and he emerged, cheerful with done duty, he glanced all around, encountering nowhere his wife. He didn't inquire.

"All right then," he said, pocketing his hands and staring out the window toward the reservoir where a yellow boat sped along. It looked like Chick might be going to announce something, but he didn't, just mentioned the weather, and went on out jingling his keys loudly enough so that if you were listening and interested in the back of the building, you could hear them. He cast another proud look at the sky as he got into his truck, as though it were all his doing, as though he had invented blue.

"He said, 'Have a nice day,' " Grace told Angelina when she came back to her chair.

"A *good* day," Angelina corrected. "He didn't mean me." She gave a little laugh, a single bark of desperation.

At the end of the day they closed the door, took down the notices of penalties and warnings, counted and recapped, signed the quadruplicate forms, sorted the papers into the proper envelopes, posted the results, and loaded the stuff (chairs, cushions, crochet, magazines, thermoses, flag, and extension cord) into Grace's car and headed for the courthouse at Hammermill. The key to the Fish and Game Clubhouse stayed between times in the cash register at Bully's store, so they stopped by there and Angelina ran in with it. When she came back out, she had a shock: it felt like terror; it felt like triumph. There was Chick, his truck parked alongside Grace's car on the far side of the gas pumps. Without a pause or hitch Angelina got back into Grace's Monte Carlo as though she hadn't *seen*, but Grace knew better.

"Aw, honey, can't you budge just a little?" Grace cried. "Please! I'll take care of this." She patted the official boxes with the state seals on the side. Angelina hesitated. Almost too long.

They heard Chick's truck crank, final offer.

At the last possible instant Angelina jumped out and ran across, leaning a little forward on her wedgies[2] as though battling head winds. Chick offered her a hand up, but she ignored it. When they drove out, Angelina was stiff-backed, eyes shut. Chick

2. A low-heeled, rubber-soled wedge style shoe popular in the 1970s.

hung a vehement right onto the road home, tipping her over against his shoulder. "Thanky ma'am," he said. He had that energized look he always wore when he had a secret; Angelina suspected some grand gesture; perhaps he had bought her another car . . .

But when they got home (and they rode, after his 'thanky,' without speaking, in an uneasy truce) it wasn't a new car at all. They had cooked supper and done the laundry, that was the surprise. They had helped out. Bonnie stood with the sheets in her arms and Chick went over to help her fold them. Were they waiting for praise? Angelina looked at the table with its little bouquet of persimmon leaves and oak and sourwood. Candles, too, and Sunday dishes. Everything in its proper place. They didn't need her, that's what they were saying! They could get along without her! (She mentioned that.)

Bonnie's stricken face in the candlelight was more than Angelina could bear.

"Don't 'Mama, please,' me! I've had enough of your whining about how things ought to be! It's not going to be 'Mommy and Daddy' on their wedding cake, and Santa, and the Easter Bunny like a roof over you, and happily ever after all your life! The roof leaks. It blows off in chunks. It rots. It stinks! You have to save yourself, don't you 'Mama, Mama' me, don't you 'Now Angelina, honey,' me!" She jerked her shoulder from Chick's grasp and sent herself to bed without supper. To punish herself or them? She lay wondering as the codeine in her migraine medication took effect.

Later she woke in terror and loneliness. The house was so silent all around her. She put out her hand and Chick was there; he hadn't left her; he hadn't given up on her. He wanted her. A real treaty, mouth to mouth, was signed. In the morning she made a last-minute call to the Avon lady (order was going in that day) for that chain and charm necklace Bonnie had admired, a peace offering. And she gave in about music camp. She told Bonnie that afternoon, said they'd just have to learn to get along without Bonnie this once, even if it was Thanksgiving, since it meant so much to the girl. She helped her fill out the forms (a church-run retreat): *Who is the most influential person in your life?* Bonnie paused at that blank and considered. Angelina had absolutely no doubt.

"Jesus Christ," she told her. "Write it in."

Bonnie, who had been about to write *parents*, blushed, ashamed she had not even thought of it.

"Write it in," Angelina said again. Bonnie wrote.

After Christmas Angelina canvassed door to door, handing out pamphlets ("ERA—The Trojan Horse"),[3] saying till she was numb, "I'm Mrs. Chester Cole, I'd like to speak with you a few moments on a subject vital to the survival of the American home and leave you some literature to study." Mixed results.

"You Jehovah's Witness?"[4] The woman peered out through the rusty screen, reaching for the pamphlet, holding it to the sun, studying the illustrated cover. "Are you for or against?"

3. The reference is to the Equal Rights Amendment. While many women in the United States favored the ratification of the Equal Rights Amendment which would guarantee equal wages for equal work, some women were distrustful of the amendment fearing that it would force them to work and would further lead to societal changes which conservative women of the time did not welcome. Many women worked against the passage of the Equal Rights Amendment, and ultimately, the amendment, because of many reasons aside from those espoused by conservatives, did not gain enough votes to be ratified.

4. This reference is to the religious sect that sends missionaries door to door to proselytize for the religion. Mormons send young missionaries to share their faith in the same fashion.

And Angelina said, "I hope you'll read and then pass it on to your friends; write your congressmen and legislators —"

"Them Jehovah's Witness stay and stay. I tell her, 'Lady, please, my carrots is scorching,' but she just sits like she never smelled smoke."

"If you or your friends have any questions —"

"Mormon fellers the same. Nice-looking boys prayed and prayed on me. Left me a whole book to read. Say they coming back."

"I thank you for your time," Angelina said.

At another house she tried to interest the woman in joining the bus rally to the capitol.

"Shoot, I got me a job, ma'am. You let someone else have my seat." She handed the pamphlet back. "I'm only home today because of the flu. Head's aching so bad I can't read."

"And thank you for your time," Angelina said.

When she stopped by Grace's for more brochures, Grace reminded her about printing costs.

"So you think I'm throwing them out of an airplane over the reservoir?" Angelina pried off her boots and rested her legs on the coffee table. "Although I might as well . . . ." She rubbed her ankles. "Just look. Mama's feet did the same, swelled so they nearly burst. Be so much easier to *phone*."

Grace kept on counting out pamphlets. She had something new, a Xeroxed page from the *Congressional Record*. "A copy for each field worker," she said, handing Angelina hers.

"You ever get the idea what's the use?" Angelina wondered.

"Tomorrow we're going to run off another thousand 'Things You Can Do' fact sheets . . ."

"Nobody listens," Angelina said. "You ever notice?"

"—getting some of those bumper stickers and litter bags (did I show you those? around here somewhere) and maybe get some of those—"

"I guess you never did notice," Angelina decided. "I bet I could tell you I was going home and pipe a bottle of Valium and sleep till the daisies sprung and you'd say—"

"—like stop signs, real cute; they're red and say STOP; we could pass them out at the bank on Saturday."

Angelina zipped her boots back on and stood up. "May I quote you? And you'd say . . ."

"Why anything you can use," Grace said, flattered, smiling, puzzling it out. (Something like that, if you remember it later, is the only hint you get, the kind of joke the whole world makes one down day or another.)

But Angelina didn't have her mind made up; she was still trying. She made lists of things to get done, lists for the day, the week, the month; goals for the coming year. She drove over to the house and went through her mother's clothes, one closet at a time, and made all these decisions without crying for help, or receiving any. She had the trunk and the backseat of her Maverick (Chick got the engine rebuilt before Christmas) crammed with sacks and boxes for Goodwill and was on her way there, Ash Wednesday, when she had more car trouble. This wasn't like the old trouble; this time the car stalled and she couldn't get it to restart. She coasted down to the stop sign at the corner and set the brake, resting her head on the wheel and considering her luck. She rolled her window down and wished she had a cigarette. It was unsettling to be sitting there stalled, with the faint scent of her mother's household all around her. Was it a sign she wasn't supposed to get rid of all the stuff? She decided to walk home. It wasn't half a mile.

As she got out, a voice said, "I thought it was you. I've been watching you. What were you doing, praying?"

Angelina whirled around and there stood Ginnie Daniels, in pristine Adidas,[5] with a dry sweatband holding back her hair. She pressed her hand on the stitch in her side.

"That Roy. I told him I couldn't keep up. Maybe I lied when I said I was doing three miles a day, but he promised to go slow, then he said never mind. Said he'd go on without me. And he did!"

"I'd offer you a lift," Angelina said, "but my car's conked out."

"Maybe it's flooded," Ginnie said. "Maybe you flooded it." She walked over and reached in and gave the hood latch a yank. "Let's see."

They stood there listening to the oil drip back into the pan.

"You know something about cars?" Angelina hoped.

"Me?" Ginnie blew a pink bubble. "Nah." She spelled F-O-X-Y in the dust on the air cleaner, careful of her nails. She noticed the gold charm at Angelina's throat and pointed at it. "Going to get me one of those. Maybe the one that says '10'."[6]

Reminded, Angelina raised her hand to her throat and touched the little cross. "Do you believe in prayer?" she asked, with that incandescent look people had about gotten used to.

Ginnie blinked and formed another bubble, enlarging it slowly to cosmic proportions. It burst. "Couldn't hurt."

Angelina laid her hands on certain blue objects under the hood. Then she got in and turned the key. The car cranked instantly.

Ginnie slammed the hood. "Praise the Lord anyway," she drawled, settling herself on the seat, propping her feet on the dash. "You can drop me off at the light in town."

"I can remember when you were born," Angelina said as Ginnie lit a cigarette. "I went to your mama's shower."

"Yeah?"

"It goes so fast."

"The faster the better . . . I'm getting me a T-roof Z[7] for graduation," Ginnie said. She made a gesture of running through gears. "We're already planning what to do. Not going to spray SENIORS on the bridges or LEGALIZE POT on the water tower . . . Kid stuff . . . They'll remember us a while . . . Raise us a little hell . . . Going down to Daytona, Lauderdale maybe . . ."

Angelina frowned, remembering. "Our class went to Panama City."

"Bet you had a ball," Ginnie said indulgently.

"One of the boys hit a cow in the rain. Wiped out his brand-new T-bird. The girl with him went right through the windshield. It blinded her. Broke Danny's neck, they said instantly."

"Yeah?" Ginnie shook her head. "Wow." She pointed up ahead. "This is my corner." When they stopped, Ginnie got out and stretched. "Beats jogging. Thanks a bunch for the lift." She hipped the door shut.

5. A popular brand of athletic clothing and shoes during the 1970s.

6. This number refers to the eponymous movie that starred Bo Derek and was immensely popular in the early 1980s. Ten was deemed the number of perfection.

7. This phrase describes a car which became very popular in the early 1980s—a Z-28 Chevy Camaro. These often sported T-tops which were glass panels held in place by a steel strip in the middle of the roof of the car.

"Something always happens," Angelina realized.

"Ma'am?" Ginnie peered back in at her.

"Death," Angelina said.

When she got home from the trip to Goodwill, JoJo was missing. The dog didn't come in for supper, and in the night when Angelina got up and walked around the yard, calling, there was no sign of him. He had never stayed out all night before.

"If only I had locked him in the garage when I left!" Angelina, pacing, making coffee, calling, and the lights on managed to rouse the household. Bonnie stood in the glare of the kitchen and pled for her mama not to get upset.

"Why do you think it's you? Why do you have to be the one?" Bonnie asked.

"Because I'm guilty," Angelina said simply. "Who else is to blame?"

Chick stood in the door, backlit, haloed by moths, and called to Angelina out wandering in the yard to come to bed, to be sensible. But she had to take the lantern and search along the roadside for his body, if he had been hit by a car . . . She didn't find him.

From the first they ruled out stealth; he wasn't the sort of dog you'd kidnap for ransom. He was a stray mutt puppy who required so much medical attention when he took up with them that it kept Angelina's mind off the stillbirth of their son. She sometimes bragged that JoJo's vet bills ran as much as a pediatrician's, and early on, when Chick, holding up the silly little green sweater she had crocheted for the dog, teased, "Without JoJo, Bonnie would be an only child," Angelina's sudden tears washed the remarks completely away. Now she couldn't shake the feeling that her prayer to get the Maverick going (but hadn't she said *Thy* will?) had cost her the dog.

"Christ's sake, it's nobody's fault!" Chick said. He pretended not to worry, but she heard him in the woods whistling the come-here-boy note that JoJo had always run to. They searched for a week, night and day, patrolling the near roads and calling, calling. When Chick said, "Face it," and Bonnie said, "He was getting old," Angelina said, "Was? Was!" and went on looking, after Bonnie went to school, after Chick drove away to work. She walked early. Later, she and her jogging partner made the rounds; no clues, no telltale ravens, nothing.

The Friday before Palm Sunday was frosty. Angelina was jogging alone and she smelled something. She tried to kid herself, but she cut the run short and with growing dread followed the old wagon road to the hilltop. There was a springhouse, fallen in for years, smothered in vinca and lilies in season. The pool was dark and leaf-clotted. That's where he lay; that's where JoJo had died. It might have been his heart; it might have been poison. What difference now?

He lay with his head a little way over the lip of the pool. After considering, she decided to take only his collar; his collar and tags only would she salvage for burial. When she touched him, it surprised her; he was warm. A little steam rose from his body, the work of worms. She caught the leather of the collar in her hands and began to unfasten it. The unforeseen: as she tried to slip the collar off, the dog's head detached itself and fell ripely into her hands. Angelina caught it. She tried to put it back. Tried beyond reason to put it back. She cried out and stood and stomped and shook herself free of the maggots which had climbed past her elbows. She scooped the collar out of the water and ran, ran without looking back.

Chick took care of it that night. When he asked if she wanted the collar buried in the little grove of dogwoods, Angelina didn't care.

Sometime during the week of Easter, Angelina made up her mind. On Wednesday after Easter she took Chick's good dark suit to the cleaners and on the way home she stopped in the Van Shop to buy a replacement windbreaker for Bonnie, who had left hers on the school bus again—the third one the girl had lost. Chick had said, "Let her do without," the only way to teach her. "But here I am again," Angelina told the clerk.

"Same with my kids," the clerk agreed. "What would they do without us?"

Angelina considered that a moment, her pen poised above the check. "I don't know," she admitted. She signed her name gravely, as to a warrant, as though lives and honor were at stake. The sound the check made as she tore it from the book, that papery final complaint made her sad. Tears stung her eyes.

"Going to be pretty today. Even prettier tomorrow. Not a cloud in the—Oops, spoke too soon," the clerk said, pointing. Shoulder to shoulder they examined the sky through the amber sun film.

"That cloud's looking for me," Angelina laughed. "I washed my car." She laughed, as though she recognized it of old. The heavy door with its COME ON IN decal and cowbell swung shut behind her. The clerk called, "See you," and Angelina raised her hand.

She drove home and got there in time to answer the phone: Grace reminding her about the Tupperware party. "Two-thirty," Grace said. "A little early so we can talk. Been missing you lately."

"Two-thirty," Angelina lied.

She wrote a note and with the TODAY IS THE FIRST DAY magnet pinned it to Thursday: *Blue suit ready at noon*. She wrote it in red to catch Chick's eye. He would be needing that suit.

She wasn't hungry, hadn't eaten all day. She felt light-headed and breezy, the way she had felt when she was about to be married, when she knew the tremendous doom and peace of being sure, of knowing her fate, of being espoused, and trusting her choice. She sat in Chick's chair, with its shape martyred to his. She could faintly smell his hairdressing. She reached toward the little table and turned on the reading lamp. The Bible fell open to the place she had marked with a rose from her mother's funeral blanket. She read, then in the center of a clean page of paper she made a note, folded it, sealed it in an envelope. She wasn't going to mail it; she didn't need a stamp. She left it on the table.

After that, she filled the bird feeder which the squirrels had raided again. She walked down to the mailbox and read the weekly news on her way back up the drive. There was a pine cone on the steps; she picked it up and dropped it in the kindling bin. There were handprints on the refrigerator; she buffed them away and put up the rag. It was time to be on her way. Angelina glanced around the house; everything was tidy. She picked up her pocketbook and went out. In a moment she unlocked and went back in, to check if she had unplugged the coffee maker (she had), and after that she got away.

She drove slowly down the road, her window open, breathing in the sweet scent of crab apples. She kept to the old familiar routes, heading out west as far as Tubby's Lake, then circling back toward town. She drove past Grace's street, but didn't turn in. Every landmark she passed seemed to lurch up at her, dragging her back. She drove on, determined. Everything caught her eye.

VidALiA ONiON a new sign announced, paint still wet. It was propped against the front wheel of a car backed up to the railroad tracks on the dead side of the depot. A man and his children were busy, were happy, arranging cabbages on the fenders. There were trays of tomatoes and (she craned to be sure) the year's first peaches. A baby sat in the driver's seat tooting the horn. As Angelina went by, the baby leaned from the window and waved a tattered little rebel flag.

At the next corner Angelina stopped (YIELD TO PEDESTRIANS was painted man-sized in the road both ways) to let Mrs. Nesby in her fresh print dress cross the street on her way to the library to return a Janice Holt Giles. She blew Angelina a God-bless-you kiss. A quarter of a mile farther north the Highway Department was surveying. The yellow Travelall was parked with its door open, and a flagman was stopping traffic in both directions.

"Left . . . left . . . left . . . right . . . WHOA! Whoa!"

Tap-tap-tap. They were using an ax for a hammer to drive the pins in. It was warm enough for the chain-pullers and target men to go shirtless. Their visibility vests were stark against their winter-pale skin. Each man (there were six, Angelina noticed: six strong men, like pallbearers) had hold of the tape or chain or stick or rod. The ledger man stared through the transit and shouted. "Left . . . left . . . left . . . good . . . WHOA!" and then again, the tap-tap-tap.

The flagman noticed Angelina checking her watch. "Won't be long now," he estimated. The crew was already snaking its way down the street toward the next mark. Then the flagman swung his STOP sign out of service to SLOW and waved her past. "Sorry for the delay," he called.

Angelina drove north till she came to the scar where the new road was being graded. She turned down the diminishing old farm track toward the reservoir and rode till the young weeds and brambles scratched and clawed her to a stop. She could feel the earth rumbling from the prime movers a mile away chewing up the red hills into four lanes. She set the brake and rolled up the window against the dust. She left her pocketbook and keys. She took only the little pistol.

She had not been here before. She looked around her for a place. There were birdfoot violets in the dry clay. She had always loved them, yet none she had ever transplanted survived to bloom the next year. She bent to pick one, then changed her mind. A C-130 on a training flight made a slow turn and headed out over the lake toward the mountains. She watched it till it was only a noise on the horizon, then she sought out the tender-green shade beneath a broken willow. She aimed the gun approximately at her heart and pulled the trigger.

The noise as much as the charge toppled her. She thought, I should have been lying down! Too late. She had planned to cease instantly, and this delay caused her chagrin; she failed, as she had all her life, by degrees. She stared up into the ferny, fretted crown of the willow. "Oh, soon, oh soon oh soon," she panted, laboring to deliver herself of this final burden, life. She lay watching the sky go white as a shell over her. All the color bled from the day. A jay spotted her, flew over to investigate, hopped lower in the branches, and cried THIEF! THIEF! as he flew away west to shrill the news. Soon that sound was lost in the surf-roar of her inner ear, and Angelina lost contact . . .

No one had the least notion. They called around when she failed to show up at the Tupperware party, and Grace finally called Chick at work. But he didn't begin worrying until Bonnie called too; she was due at the orthodontist's and Angelina had not come by school to pick her up as she had promised. Chick guessed then it was car trouble. No one guessed it would turn out as it did.

The reservoir manager noticed her car on toward sundown, went to check on it, and found her, so she didn't have to lie out there all night.

She was in surgery till nearly midnight, and in the waiting room the little crowd of shocked well-wishers gradually thinned to Angelina's husband, her father, her daughter, and a few silent comforters. Bonnie, from the first, felt indicted, never mind who pulled the trigger. She was her mother's child all right, and the tenderest victim. She kept to herself, and spent hours in the rest room; Chick could hear her congested crying but didn't know how to help her. He couldn't even help himself. When the surgeon came out and told them Angelina would live, Bonnie had her mama's note, tear-stained now and folded, folded into triviality, as though it were some everyday something that could be forgotten, left behind in an ashtray, lost in a pocket, unimportant. (All the note said was *Job 7*—that's all she wrote, addressed *To Whom It May Concern*, not to Chick and Bonnie, not even *Sorry*, not even *Love*, as though in forgetting everything she lived for she forgot them first. Bonnie had looked up the quote in the little white calf-bound King James Angelina had given her for Christmas. She read and reread that whole early chapter from "Is there not an appointed time?" to the last exulting despair of "For now I shall sleep in the dust; and thou shalt seek me in the morning but I shall not be.") Bonnie, in a wizened whisper in the general echoing ignorance, asked the surgeon, asked anyone, "Why?" She turned on them all, on herself in the dark glass of the midnight windows and shouted it this time, "Why didn't she want to read to the end of the book?"

Which is, of course, the question. Her father, her grandfather, Reverend Martin, Dr. Spence, the neighbors—all met her harrowing, wild gaze for a moment only, then looked away.

In the morning they let Chick go in and see her for five minutes. Angelina was awake, but she lay with her eyes shut against him, her chin aimed at God. She knew as well as if she were floating in a corner of the ceiling looking down at him exactly what Chick was doing, heard him lift the one chair and turn it around and straddle it and sit, knew he was resting his chin on his fists, watching her. Four of his minutes, then thirty seconds more, elapsed. Finally she had to open her eyes and let him in.

"Oh, babe," he said when she looked his way. "You very nearly broke my heart."

She beat at the bed with her pale hands, clawing at the IV's in her wrists that tethered her to life. The nurse came, then another, and they restrained her. Chick turned at the door for a last look.

Septic with regret, he didn't have time to arrange his face before Bonnie saw him. Terrified, she cried, "She didn't die, did she? She'll have another chance?"

He thought of Angelina lying there small and sharp-eyed and at bay somehow, vulnerable but valiant, like a little beast who would gnaw off its own foot to escape the trap.

"Another chance," he said.

Questions to Consider

1. Why does Hood call her story "Inexorable Progress"? Can you see a connection between the main character and the title?
2. What motivates Angelina to finally attempt suicide?

Marilyn Nelson

1946–

The great-great-granddaughter of a Kentucky slave, Marilyn Nelson is not really from anywhere. Her father was a career Air Force officer, and her childhood was spent moving from one military base to another, "falling home down the highway," as she writes in the poem "I Imagine Driving Across Country." She earned her B.A. on the West coast and her Ph.D. in the Midwest, and she has taught for over twenty years on the East coast after short assignments teaching abroad in Denmark and Germany. But Nelson carries a strong sense of the South as her ancestral and spiritual "home," and that deep-rootedness resonates throughout her poetry. She was born in Cleveland, Ohio, on 26 April 1946 to Melvin M. and Johnnie Mitchell Nelson. As she explains in a note to the poem "The Fortunate Spill," her parents met when her serviceman father spilled black-eyed peas in her mother's lap at a New Year's Eve party in Oklahoma. Black-eyed peas are a traditional New Year's food in the South, believed to bring good luck, and Nelson clearly appreciates the irony that the "down-home" Southern food not only brought her parents good luck in love but brought her into the world.

Melvin Nelson was a navigator on B-52 bombers and a member of the famous "Tuskegee Airmen" in the early 1940s. Nearly one thousand African-American men were trained to be Air Force pilots at Tuskegee Institute in Alabama, founded by Booker T. Washington in 1881, and 450 of the graduates saw combat in World War II. Of that number, 150 were killed in action. In her 1990 book titled *The Homeplace* (published under her former married name of Marilyn Nelson Waniek), Nelson writes movingly about the racial prejudice that the Tuskegee Airmen encountered, despite their proven abilities as pilots. *The Homeplace* also traces three generations of family history on Nelson's mother's side, beginning with Diverne, the Kentucky slave who had a liaison with her white master that produced two children. One of those children became a successful and respected storekeeper in the segregated Kentucky town of Hickman, and one of the storekeeper's five cultured daughters moved to Boley, Oklahoma, with her farmer husband, where she gave birth to two children including Nelson's mother. Many of the poems in *The Homeplace* are in traditional forms such as the sonnet, villanelle, rhymed quatrains, or ballad stanzas, as if to rein in and contain their thematic undercurrents of racism, miscegenation, and violence.

With her latest book of poetry, *Carver: A Life in Poems*, Nelson has returned to the grounds of the Tuskegee Institute to trace the career of the great African-American scientist, George Washington Carver, in verse. Although the volume was recognized as a Newbery Honor Book in children's literature, Nelson explained in her acceptance speech for the *Boston Globe*-Horn Book Award that she had envisioned an "audience of grown-ups" when she wrote the book, and that "Professor Carver's message was—is—a message we need to hear again: a message of conservation, simplicity, humility, reverence, and nonviolence." *Carver* was also a finalist for the 2001 National Book Award in poetry, Nelson's third nomination for that award. Among her many other honors are two Pushcart Prizes, two National Endowment for the Arts grants, a Guggenheim Foundation grant, and a Fulbright Scholarship. In 2002, the poet without a region to call home was named Poet Laureate of Connecticut.

Diverne's Waltz

Diverne stands in the kitchen as they dance,
laughing and flirting, on the bare parlor floor.
She's taken up the rug, glad for the chance,
at last, to beat it free of sins outdoors.

Her fancy cakes are popular, her punch
has earned light giggles from Miss Atwood's friends.
She'd struggled at Miss Atwood's back to cinch
that tiny waist. *Miss Atwood look right grand.*

Mister Tyler asks for a water-glass of rye:
he's just enlisted, a drop-out from law school.
She notices something dangerous in his eye:
Crazy damn white man, acting like a fool.

Taking her hands, Henry Tyler gives her a twirl
and off they waltz. He swirls Diverne so fast
her head kerchief unknots itself. He smiles
down at Diverne's embarrassment, and gasps:

They blush! Hearing the whispers from the walls,
he sees men grin. His father shakes his head.
But (*That dark rose . . .*) he dances. *What the hell,
who knows? next week, next month, I could be dead.*

Chopin[1]

It's Sunday evening. Pomp[2] holds the receipts
of all the colored families on the Hill
in his wide lap, and shows which white store cheats
these patrons, who can't read a weekly bill.
His parlor's full of men holding their hats
and women who admire his girls' good hair.
Pomp warns them not to vote for Democrats,
controlling half of Hickman[3] from his chair.
The varying degrees of cheating seen,
he nods toward the piano. Slender, tall,
a Fisk[4] girl passing-white, almost nineteen,
his Blanche[5] folds the piano's paisley shawl
and plays Chopin. And blessed are the meek
who have to buy in white men's stores next week.

Alderman

One year the town Republicans[1]
asked Pomp if he would mind
if they put him up for office.
Pomp told them they were kind,
but he had seven children
and a wife he cared about:
He was too young to die—

1. Polish pianist and composer (1810–1849) of the Romantic era.
2. Rufus "Pomp" Atwood (1862–1933), Nelson's great-grandfather on her mother's side.
3. A small town in western Kentucky where the Atwoods lived.
4. A Nashville, Tennessee, university founded in 1866 to educate newly freed slaves.
5. The second of Pomp's seven children; the name Blanche is French for "White."

1. Northern White members of the pro–Civil Rights "Radical Republicans" who held positions of power in the South during Reconstruction.

which he sure would, without a doubt,
if his name stood on that ballot.
Two white men came to call
a few days later at his store,
younger than he, but tall
like he was. They told Pomp he was their brother:
It ain't your fault you had a nigra mother.
They said they'd stand behind him if he ran.

After they left, the local Ku Klux Klan[2]
sent Pomp a message: *Boy, we understand*
you need to learn your place. And Pomp withdrew
because the Klan was wrong: By God, he knew.

Tuskegee Airfield

(For the Tuskegee Airmen[1])

These men,
these proud black men:
our first to touch
their fingers to the sky.

The Germans learned to call them
Die Schwarzen Vogelmenschen,[2]
They called themselves
The Spookwaffe.[3]

Laughing.
And marching to class under officers
whose thin-lipped ambition
was to *wash the niggers out.*

Sitting at attention
for lectures about ailerons, airspeed, altimeters
from boring lieutenants who believed
you monkeys ain't meant to fly.

Oh, there were parties,
cadet-dances, guest appearances
by the Count
and the lovely Lena.[4]

There was the embarrassing
adulation of Negro civilians.
A woman approached my father in a bar
where he was drinking with his buddies.
Hello, Airman. She held out her palm.
Will you tell me my future?

2. A secret society of White supremacists founded in opposition to Reconstruction policies and particularly active in the South following World War I.

1. A group of nearly 1,000 African-American men who were trained as World War II pilots and navigators at the Tuskegee Institute airbase in Alabama.

2. German for "the Black menfolk."

3. Term combined from an American racial slur plus the German word "waffe," meaning "weapon."

4. Count Basie and Lena Horne, big band leader and jazz singer who performed in Tuskegee during the 1940s.

There was that,
like a breath of pure oxygen.
But first
they had to earn wings.

There was this one instructor
who was pretty nice.
I mean, we just sat around
and *talked* when a flight had gone well.

But he was from Minnesota,
and he made us sing
the Minnesota Fight Song
before we took off.

If you didn't sing it,
your days were numbered.
"Minnesota, hats off to thee. . . ."
That bastard!

One time I had a check-flight
with an instructor from Louisiana.
As we were about to head for base,
he chopped the power.

Force-landing, nigger.
There were trees everywhere I looked.
Except on that little island . . .
I began my approach.

The instructor said, *Pull Up.*
That was an excellent approach.
Real surprised.
But where would you have taken off, wise guy?

I said, *Sir,*
I was ordered
to land the plane.
Not take off.

The instructor grinned.
Boy, if your ass
is as hard as your head,
you'll go far in this world.

Questions to Consider

1. The poem "Alderman," about Nelson's great-grandfather Pomp Atwood, is set during the Reconstruction years after the Civil War. Who are the two groups of Whites pulling Pomp in different directions, and what is it that he "knows" in the poem's last line?
2. At the ending of "Tuskegee Airfield," has the White flight instructor from Louisiana changed his mind about the Black student pilot, or not?

Martha McFerren

1947–

In the poem "For My First Biographer," Martha McFerren offers a biographical note about herself that parodies the usual dry, academic effort: "Martha McFerren, poet of the/ caftan-and-heavy-earring school,/ was greatly influenced by cheap/ novels, the Baptists, and a second-rate Villon she finally/ got rid of. . . . " To that lively introduction, one need add only the bare facts that Martha Dean McFerren was born on 25 April 1947 in Henderson, Texas, to Manley Edward and Emma Louise Turner McFerren, and raised in the nearby town of Gladewater. From that region of east Texas, she ventured less than two hundred miles to earn her B.S. in library science from North Texas State University (now the University of North Texas) in Denton. From there she moved to Pasadena, outside Houston, to work as a reference librarian at San Jacinto College for the next five years.

Moving to New Orleans in 1976, she married a fellow librarian and became involved in the activities of the New Orleans Poetry Forum, a weekly writing workshop and reading series newly founded by local poet Lee Grue. Maxine Cassin, another member of the Forum and the publisher of the New Orleans Poetry Journal Press, brought out McFerren's first book, *Delusions of a Popular Mind,* in 1983. *Get Me Out of Here!* was published by a small press in Massachusetts the following year. It contained McFerren's masterpiece, "Mountain Soprano," a formal verse narrative of almost 400 lines about a refined nineteenth-century woman who must endure life in the Appalachian wilderness. "Mountain Soprano" had earlier been the longest poem ever published by the *Georgia Review.* Encouraged by good reviews of her first two collections, McFerren quit her library job and began studying toward an M.F.A. in creative writing from Warren Wilson College, which she earned in 1988. From that point forward, McFerren's writing began to attract a larger audience. Louisiana State University published her third book, *Contours for Ritual,* in 1988. Two years later, in 1991, she received a National Endowment for the Arts fellowship, and, the following year, she won the Marianne Moore Poetry Prize for her fourth book, *Women in Cars.* Plagued by poor health, McFerren has written little in the past decade, but she has seen her work become widely anthologized.

Like most Southern writers, McFerren shows a strong sense of place (in her case, suburbanized east Texas) and a long memory for regional history. She is a born storyteller, but one given to female modes of storytelling that are not often validated by high culture. As William Matthews observed, "[s]he knows how much durable wisdom there is in gossip and chatter and anecdote—I'm reminded now and again of Eudora Welty—and how much emotional survival information there is in what men think of as 'merely women's talk.' " Like Welty, Flannery O'Connor, and Carson McCullers, McFerren is often drawn to Southern grotesque characters and situations. Yet her voice is postmodern in its ironic humor, its frequent allusions to popular culture, and its persistent deconstruction of the myth of Southern femininity and, particularly, the Southern belle. McFerren's steely Texan women must use all their wits to survive in a violent, patriarchal society where sex roles are destiny and "women's own dangerous fascination with the brooding and dangerous in men," as Charles Taylor has put it, is more of a threat than a loaded gun.

The Princess and the Goblins

(for Leda Bartlett)

Leda I don't keep
bunnies puppies kittens
I have no plants except

an aloe vera and
I don't trust it

also I don't breed children
or like them very much
but you of course are
cute as bisque
therefore
as a marginal auntie
I must warn you about
dissuading violence

folklore or Shirley Temple[1]
would let you think
little girls save empires
by merely being lovable
during the riot

in sash and golden dimple
they curtsey
and the Visigoth[2]
the Hun[3] the Martian
turn away shedding a tear
worthy of Rev. Dodgson[4]
nevertheless I must remark
two exceptions

in the first monster movie
Boris Karloff[5] not being
socialized threw a kid
into the river because
he thought pretty little things
bouyant as daisy petals
she however did not surface

also when Tamburlaine the Great[6]
was beseiging Damascus
a herd of virgins was sent out
with garlands pink earlobes
flowing hair et al.
to dissuade him

virgins
he said
addressing them en masse
in vain you labor to prevent

1. Dimpled, ringleted Hollywood child movie star of the 1930s.
2. Member of a Germanic tribe that invaded the Roman Empire.
3. Member of a Mongol tribe that waged war on the Roman Empire.
4. Real name of Lewis Carroll (1832–1898), the author of *Alice in Wonderland* who had an excessive interest in the company of young girls.
5. Actor who played the monster in the 1931 screen version of Mary Shelley's *Frankenstein*.
6. Mongol warlord who sacked Damascus in the year 1400.

that which mine honor swears
shall be perform'd

and being too
downright mean to socialize
he killed them in advance
and proceeded with Damascus

again I warn you Leda
in case some Yankee major
plans on burning
your granddaddy's cotton

no matter how kitty innocent
you become
when you get into the
childlike business you
takes
your
chances

The Famous Picnic of 1906

(The town of Post, Texas, has placed a historic marker commemorating "The Famous Picnic of 1906." Why? I don't know.)

Don't ask *me* what went on.
I thought it marked the site where
good old Fatty Arbuckle[1]
smacked Pancho Villa[2] with a pie,
but that was near El Paso[3]
and anyway, Pancho caught the pie
and ate it, which diminishes the impact.
Maybe it celebrates the day
Colonel Vance Mobley[4] refused
a free bourbon and branch water
with a manly flourish
or the equally notorious time
Mrs. Potter Meese[5] of the WCTU[6]
drank herself silly on syllabubs.[7]
Or possibly it was where
Miss Lucy Jean Porterhouse[8] screamed,
"Mercy sakes, how I hate armadillos!"
and plugged six of them
smack through the eyeballs
with a single shot, though
that story may be apocryphal

1. Silent film star who played in slapstick comedies, including the first film to contain a pie-in-the-face routine.
2. Assumed name of Doroteo Arango (1878–1923), Mexican bandit and revolutionary leader.
3. According to a legend recorded by at least one Arbuckle biographer, Villa rode up on horseback one day while Arbuckle was picnicking along the Rio Grande, and Arbuckle tossed a pie that Villa caught.
4. Fictitious character.
5. Fictitious character.
6. The Women's Christian Temperance Union, a group organized in 1874 to promote abstinence from alcohol.
7. A mildly alcoholic milk punch popular in the South.
8. Fictitious character.

because armadillos don't line up.
Or maybe, just for once,
nobody had a pistol, snakes or no snakes.
Who knows what folks in those parts
consider a hot date.
Maybe Ethel simply made
one HECK of a potato salad.

Seven Petticoats

(Starrville Academy*[1]*)

Reputable: that's the word. Reputable. And the only decent curriculum
between Shreveport[2] and Dallas. Out
stepped the young ladies, down into

pinestraw, burrs, pinworms, the vast
hot sun of the uncultivated. Dowered
with Papa's beef, fresh on the hoof,
and Mama's virgin china cups. Sent

to be finished with rhetoric, music,
a dozen cherry pies.
Good women are
forts with buttresses of whalebone.
Men leave and go forward to a better

wilderness, free again until cooking
grows dull. Invariably it grows dull.

The sun in Baltimore is a teacake,
the sun in Boston a thin dime. You

asphyxiate at home in seven petticoats
and those cool Yankees dictate veils,
gloves, camisoles, corsets as tight as
birth canals. If you unlace, dust and

copperheads slide into you.
Nothing
is completely satisfactory, my girl.
You must make do. Your pathfinder is
on his way. He will burn like the wide

sun, certify your piecrust and
French and release you to a room with
wallpaper. His silences, his eyes
flat as two pine boxes, are no great

concern. See he has his meals on
time: he is your blood, your energy.
Your frontier.

1. Starrville, Texas, had two private secondary schools and a college for women in the late nineteenth century.

2. A city in northwest Louisiana.

The Bad Southern Cooking Poem

Where I was raised, salt is an exotic spice.

—George Cleveland[1]

I learned to cook bad because that's the way he liked it.

—A wife on television

We cook it like he wants it.
He wants it like she fixed it—
Mama, who was not much
but who sat peeling things
when he was four and empty.
Mama back to Mama
to the first hot Mama
who ever scorched a cow,
because what's love but
Mama and her meat
and the pie with flies?

And the man who
caught the cow says,
"I love good plain cooking."
Meaning his own good Mama:
good woman cooking bad
in his unspiced memory.
Mama shoveling grub, saying,
"Eat it, it's good for you,"
and, by butterbeans, it's not,
though boiled to hush up
small bugs in the collards
and absolutely expurgated
of pimento.

He is eating hot
because we are not trashy;
six vegetables and cake
because somebody might stop by;
six used-to-be vegetables
he doesn't even like
reduced to butterflood and sludge
and salt—the resurrection.

And the man who bought the bacon
hates that simmering green
but he wants it there
like Mama's massacres,
because what's love but Mama
and her heat in heat
and all that tongue sweat?
And the man with the mouth says,

1. Pseudonym for Steve Schwartz, a New Orleans writer who was raised in Cleveland.

"I love good plain cooking
if you give it plenty of salt."

Daddy back to Daddy back to
umpteenth old Daddy,
laid back in their chairs
dreaming jubilations
of okra and blackeyed pea,
forgetting all that boil
and the turnips with syrup,
and cauliflower redeemed
of any fatal crisp.
They poke the pink
with their Sunday forks and
holler, "Hey, Evangeline,
this cow's not dead yet!"
Mama, they always whisper.
And Mama, still cooking,

comes in to dish the salt:
"Eat it! I'm good for you!"

Questions to Consider

1. In "Seven Petticoats," what relationship does McFerren portray between young Southern women and the American frontier? How does it differ from the relationship between young men and the frontier?
2. What particular social class and ethnic group does McFerren seem to be satirizing in "The Bad Southern Cooking Poem"? Does the poem have "universal" appeal to all readers, or is it more meaningful to those who share the same social and ethnic background as the narrator?

Yusef Komunyakaa

1947–

Yusef Komunyakaa was born in the segregated mill town of Bogalusa, Louisiana, on 29 April 1947 and given the name James Willie Brown, Jr. His father, James, Sr., was an illiterate but hard-working carpenter; his mother, Mildred, loved listening to blues and jazz on the radio and singing gospel songs while doing housework for her family of six children. The cadences and images of the Bible were also an important artistic influence on the future poet; he read it through twice as a teenager. Growing up, he also heard oral legends about his daring great-grandparents, surnamed Komunyakaa, who had sneaked into the country as stowaways on board a ship from the West Indies; but when James, Jr., changed his name to Yusef Komunyakaa at a time when many other young African Americans were changing their "slave names" to names more reflective of their African ethnic origins, his father was crushed.

Certain parallels can be seen between Komunyakaa's upbringing and that of other contemporary Southern poets in this volume. Like Fred Chappell, he lived in a mill town; like Jones and Maddox, he came from working-class origins; and, like the majority, he grew up in a small, rural community and was immersed in a vital oral tradition of language and an omnipresent religious faith quite unlike those in other regions of the country. But there the parallels cease, for White poets were not forbidden to enter the one and only public library in their towns, nor did they have reason to fear the "Night Riders" of the Ku Klux Klan who roamed the countryside at night. Even the experience of reading the Fugitive and Agrarian poets was different for Komunyakaa: "For the most part, 'the Fugitives,' those Southern Agrarians, attempted to erase people like me from their idea of history," he told interviewer Ernest Suarez. Despite such obstacles, Komunyakaa managed to read widely as a child and teenager. Susan Conley cites the Bible, Poe, Tennyson, Shakespeare, the Harlem Renaissance writers, Gwendolyn Brooks, and James Baldwin as Komunyakaa's early influences and notes that he wrote the graduation poem for his high school senior class.

Komunyakaa did some traveling throughout the United States and Puerto Rico after graduating from high school. Then, enlisting in the U.S. Army during the Vietnam War, he was shipped to Chu Lai, Vietnam, in 1969. Recognizing Komunyakaa's English language skills, his army superiors assigned him to be a battlefield reporter for the *Southern Cross*, a military newspaper. Although Komunyakaa received a Bronze Star during his time in Vietnam, he preferred not to speak or write about his experiences there for more than a decade afterward. Upon his return to the United States, Komunyakaa enrolled in the University of Colorado and took a creative writing class from Alex Blackburn, receiving high praise and encouragement to pursue the craft of poetry. He pursued an M.A. in creative writing from Colorado State University in 1979, then an M.F.A. in creative writing from the University of California at Irvine in 1980. While at Irvine, Komunyakaa studied with Charles Wright, a distinguished poet from Tennessee and North Carolina whose work does not normally reflect his Southern origins; like his pupil Komunyakaa, Wright uses imagery rather than narrative to drive the movement of his poems forward.

Komunyakaa had published two small-press collections of poetry while still a student, but it was his third collection, *Copacetic*, that brought him national attention. In jazz- and blues-flavored poems about his childhood and young adulthood, he exhibited a compressed, laconic, imagistic style that was uniquely his own. While paying homage to the great jazz and blues musicians of the past in his work, Komunyakaa also aligned himself with postmodernist theory in viewing his reader as "a cocreator of meaning," as he phrased the concept to Suarez. "I would like to create images with an urgency that inspires the willing reader to go the distance and become emotionally or psychologically involved in the possibilities. Everyone brings something different to a poem," he went on to explain. Prior to the 1984 publication of *Copacetic*, Komunyakaa had been teaching in New Orleans, 70 miles south of his home town of Bogalusa: first as an instructor at the University of New Orleans, and then as a poet-in-the-schools. The year after *Copacetic* came out, however, he was offered a visiting assistant professorship at the University of Indiana. Except for sabbaticals, he remained in Bloomington for the next 12 years, rising to full professor. In 1997, he moved to a professorship at Princeton University.

Continuing to publish a well-received volume of poetry every two years or so, Komunyakaa next stunned critics with his sixth collection of poems, *Dien Cai Dau*, in 1988. Nearly two decades after returning home from the war, Komunyakaa had issued a sequence of 43 poems that captured the surrealist nightmare of the Vietnam War experience, as well as the stark realities of race relations between Black and White American soldiers and Vietnamese women. For a long time after the war, Komunyakaa admitted to interviewer William Baer, he had been "resisting those memories, yet also moving on to other things that I thought were a more appropriate subject matter for poetry." One poem in particular from the collection—"Facing It," about an African-American veteran's pilgrimage to the Vietnam War Memorial in search of closure—has become widely anthologized.

Neon Vernacular, Komunyakaa's ninth publication, combined a selection of poems from his first seven books, including *Dien Cai Dau*, with 12 new poems about growing up in the Deep South. The book won both the Pulitzer Prize for Poetry and the $50,000 Kingsley Tuft Poetry Award. In the decade of the nineties, Komunyakaa further expanded his range as a literary figure by coediting two anthologies of jazz poetry, publishing a collection of essays and interviews, cotranslating a book by the Vietnamese poet Nguyen Quang Thieu, recording a CD of jazz poetry, and trying his hand at jazz song lyrics and short plays. *Talking Dirty to the Gods* (2000), his eleventh book of poetry, received a 2001 National Book Critics Circle nomination. His twelfth and latest book, *Pleasure Dome* (2001), is a volume of new and collected poems.

Untitled Blues

(after a photograph by Yevgeni Yevtushenko[1])

I catch myself trying
to look into the eyes
of the photo, at a black boy
behind a laughing white mask
he's painted on. I
could've been that boy
years ago.
Sure, I could say
everything's copacetic,[2]
listen to a Buddy Bolden[3] cornet
cry from one of those coffin-
shaped houses called
shotgun.[4] We could
meet in Storyville,[5]
famous for quadroons,
with drunks discussing God
around a honky-tonk piano.
We could pretend we can't
see the kitchen help
under a cloud of steam.
Other lurid snow jobs:
night & day, the city
clothed in her see-through
French lace, as pigeons
coo like a beggar chorus
among makeshift studios
on wheels—Vieux Carré[6]
belles having portraits painted
twenty years younger.
We could hand jive
down on Bourbon & Conti[7]
where tap dancers hold
to their last steps,

1. Russian poet (b. 1933) who, like Komunyakaa, is a friend of the New Orleans poet Lee Meitzen Grue (b. 1934).

2. Slang term meaning "very satisfactory," in vogue among members of the U.S. military during the late 1960s and early 1970s.

3. Jazz bandleader and cornet player from New Orleans (1868–1931).

4. A house that is one story tall and one room wide with no central hall; each room opens to the next by means of a door. Theoretically, one could stand at the front door and fire a shotgun straight through all of the open doors and out the back door.

5. Famous New Orleans red-light district of the early twentieth century.

6. "Old Square" in French; the French Quarter of New Orleans.

7. Intersection of two streets in the French Quarter of New Orleans.

mammy dolls frozen
in glass cages. The boy
locked inside your camera,
perhaps he's lucky—
he knows how to steal
laughs in a place
where your skin
is your passport.

Boy Wearing a Dead Man's Clothes

1

I must say I never liked
gabardine's wornout shine.

Cold weather fills this coat,
& the shoulders have drooped anyhow!

Jesus, his yellow silk handkerchief;
I'm keeping this next to my heart.

The police chief's daughter's smile
has started to peel off

the curled photo I found
here in his breast pocket.

2

Blue denim cap, no other
crown for a poor man's head.

I wear it the same angle
he did, hipper than thou.

If I tilt it over my eyes,
a bit to the left this way,

cut the sky in half,
can I see the world

through his eyes? Cloud-cap
washed till there's hardly any blue left.

3

Uncle Jimmy's flowered shirt
keeps its shape. Body's character—

enamored of sweat, touch
gone out of the cloth,

no dark red map widening
across my chest to recall

that night.
Sleeves filled with silence.

The lipstick won't
come off.

4

I don't belong here. I
can't help but say

to Uncle's cordovan boots,
Get me outta East Texas, back to L.A.,

but please don't take me
by their place: Four weeks ago, that time

I saw him & Mrs. Overstreet
kissing in the doorway,

& Mr. Overstreet drunk
with his head on the table.

Night Muse & Mortar Round

She shows up in every war.
Basically the same, maybe
her flowing white gown's a little less
erotic & she's more desperate.
She's always near a bridge.
This time the Perfume River.[1]
You trace the curve in the road
& there she is

trying to flag down your jeep,
but you're a quarter-mile away
when you slam on the brakes.
Sgt. Jackson says, "What the hell
you think you're doing, Jim?"
& Lt. Adonis riding shotgun
yells, "Court-martial."

When you finally drive back
she's gone, just a feeling
left in the night air.
Then you hear the blast
rock the trees & stars
where you would've been that moment.

Tu Do Street

Music divides the evening.
I close my eyes & can see
men drawing lines in the dust.
America pushes through the membrane
of mist & smoke, & I'm a small boy
again in Bogalusa.[1] *White Only*
signs & Hank Snow.[2] But tonight
I walk into a place where bar girls
fade like tropical birds. When

1. A river in central Vietnam.

1. Komunyakaa's hometown in northeast Louisiana.

2. A Canadian-born country music singer (1914–1999).

I order a beer, the mama-san[3]
behind the counter acts as if she
can't understand, while her eyes
skirt each white face, as Hank Williams[4]
calls from the psychedelic jukebox.
We have played Judas[5] where
only machine-gun fire brings us
together. Down the street
black GIs hold to their turf also.
An off-limits sign pulls me
deeper into alleys, as I look
for a softness behind these voices
wounded by their beauty & war.
Back in the bush at Dak To[6]
& Khe Sanh,[7] we fought
the brothers of these women
we now run to hold in our arms.
There's more than a nation
inside us, as black & white
soldiers touch the same lovers
minutes apart, tasting
each other's breath,
without knowing these rooms
run into each other like tunnels
leading to the underworld.

Facing It

My black face fades,
hiding inside the black granite.
I said I wouldn't,
dammit: No tears.
I'm stone. I'm flesh.
My clouded reflection eyes me
like a bird of prey, the profile of night
slanted against morning. I turn
this way—the stone lets me go.
I turn that way—I'm inside
the Vietnam Veterans Memorial[1]
again, depending on the light
to make a difference.
I go down the 58,022 names,
half-expecting to find
my own in letters like smoke.
I touch the name Andrew Johnson;
I see the booby trap's white flash.
Names shimmer on a woman's blouse

3. Pidgin term for an older Vietnamese woman.

4. An American country music star from Alabama (1923–1953).

5. The apostle who betrayed Christ.

6. Jungle region in the western Central Highlands of Vietnam, the site of a 1967 battle between U.S. and North Vietnamese Army (NVA) forces.

7. Marine corps base in northwestern South Vietnam that came under siege by NVA forces during the 1968 Tet Offensive of the Vietnam War.

1. Memorial to the Americans who died in the Vietnam War, located on the mall in Washington, D.C.

but when she walks away
the names stay on the wall.
Brushstrokes flash, a red bird's
wings cutting across my stare.
The sky. A plane in the sky.
A white vet's image floats
closer to me, then his pale eyes
look through mine. I'm a window.
He's lost his right arm
inside the stone. In the black mirror
a woman's trying to erase names:
No, she's brushing a boy's hair.

Questions to Consider

1. Explain how Komunyakaa tells a story using images instead of conventional linear narrative in "Boy Wearing a Dead Man's Clothes."
2. What is the "it" that the narrator is facing in the poem "Facing It"?

Tim Gautreaux

1948–

Although he does not like to be considered a regional writer, believing that his themes are universal, Tim Gautreaux writes movingly about blue-collar workers in southern Louisiana. Often his characters, like his own family members, are the Cajun descendants of the French Acadian settlers who were driven out of Canada by the British in 1755. Gautreaux, whose full first name is Timothy, was born on 19 October 1947 in Morgan City, Louisiana, an oil industry town on the edge of Cajun country. While his elderly relatives spoke Cajun French and his father, a tugboat captain, spoke French to communicate with them, Gautreaux and other members of his generation were discouraged from learning the language, as his parents' generation felt ashamed of the linguistic markers that branded their ethnic group as different from other Americans. Gautreaux grew up in a family of skilled oral storytellers: His male relatives, who worked in the oil, railroad, and shipping industries, would try to top each other with outrageous tales about their jobs and other adventures. Unlike many postmodern writers, Gautreaux continues to write fiction with action-driven plots and memorable characters, hearkening back to the stories he heard as a child.

While an undergraduate at Nicholls State University in Thibodaux, Louisiana, Gautreaux won a poetry contest judged by James Dickey. Dickey went on to offer Gautreaux a teaching assistantship at the University of South Carolina at Greensboro, where he was then teaching, and Gautreaux earned his Ph.D. in English there in 1972. Gautreaux and his wife, Winborne, then accepted teaching positions at Southeastern Louisiana University in Hammond. But it was not until Gautreaux took a Loyola University fiction writing course with novelist Walker Percy in 1977 that he began to think of himself as a fiction writer rather than a poet. During the 1980s he published short stories in respected little magazines while working on several unfinished novels. His period of craft apprenticeship came to a close in the 1990s, when his short stories began appearing in magazines such as *Story*, the *New Yorker*, *Gentleman's Quarterly*, and the *Atlantic Monthly*. Gautreaux captured a National Magazine Award for fiction and saw his stories included in collections such as *Best American Short Stories*, *New Sto-*

ries from the South: The Year's Best, and *Prize Stories: The O. Henry Awards*. Two volumes of his stories were issued by Picador/St. Martin's Press: *Same Place, Same Things* in 1996 and *Welding with Children* in 1999. Picador/St. Martin's also published Gautreaux's first novel, *The Next Step in the Dance* (1998), which traced the fortunes of a young Cajun French machinist and his restless wife in small-town Louisiana during the oil bust years of the 1980s. His second novel, *The Clearing*, is about a shell-shocked World War I veteran who flees from his family responsibilities to a south-Louisiana cypress logging camp.

Many reviewers have compared Gautreaux's fiction to that of Flannery O'Connor because of its regionalism, strongly drawn characters, concern with moral issues, use of Roman Catholic symbolism, flashes of violence, and ironic humor. In addition to O'Connor, other major influences upon Gautreaux have been Walker Percy, another Louisiana writer who wrestles with moral issues from a Roman Catholic theological perspective, and Mark Twain, whose regionalism, humor, and obvious affection for his blue-collar characters and their technologies find their counterparts in Gautreaux's narratives.

Rodeo Parole

Four inmates walked out into the hot, powdery dirt of the corral to sit in folding chairs at a neon-orange card table. Where they dragged their boots, the soil smoked. Jimmy, the burglar, was the youngest, a tall, bent rail of a man with scrambled-egg hair and a barbecued, narrow face. He didn't want to sit at the table under the blowtorch sun with his palms down on the flimsy surface, waiting for the pain, but the others had told him that if he stayed with them longest, if they all could just sit there with their hands on the table while it happened, they could win, and the reporters would put their pictures in the statewide paper, where the parole board would see what good Joes they were, brave competitors, winners. Two members of last year's winning team were free already.

Minutes before, Jimmy had leaned over the rough-cut fence and watched what had happened to the other teams. The first foursome to compete had tried not to look. They were veterans. He had watched Rex Ted and Black Diamond and Mollyfish and Ray-Ray sit like statues in a tornado, as though no kind of movement could save them. He'd looked and willed to be like them, draining himself of feeling as he heard the knock of the wood latch, the explosion of breath from the animal, and the ground-trembling plants of the hooves as the bull came on, but he'd turned his head from the arena at the first yell, which was followed by a sympathetic "*Awwww*" from the crowd. Three men had scattered, Rex Ted was rolling on the ground, gored, and the card table had not come down yet. Two trusties came out with a stretcher and carried Rex Ted away, passing by the fence where Jimmy stood looking into the bloody man's face, which bore an expression saying, It finally happened and I'm not surprised one damned bit.

Now Jimmy was in the arena, waiting for the bull to arrive like a decision come out of thin air. Nookey, a hairless older man, who was in for dynamiting a toxic-waste dump, sat across the table. "Okay," he said. "Look at it like this. It's like a judge saying something and you can't stop it or change it."

Little Claude, an accordionist who had burned down his wife's lover's house, nodded agreement. "Don't look at that judge; don't look at that bull," he said, spreading his palms out on the plywood. The fourth was a new man, a murderer who would never get out, not even after death, for no family would claim him, and someday he would be buried in the prison graveyard by the swamp. He was big, with a head of thick black hair combed back and eyes wild as a bear's, a man whom any stupid woman would notice and love at once.

Jimmy spat, and his spit sat on top of the dust like quicksilver. "Rex Ted's group has the best time. Ray-Ray picked up his hands right before the bull hooked."

"Let's don't talk about it," Little Claude said. "If you talk about it, you gonna try to get out the way. You gonna pick up your hands."

Nookey closed his eyes just for a moment. "We got to be still and hope he goes for the table."

"This is something," the murderer said, and the other men looked at his eyes, which were open too wide for the strobe-hot sun, as though they were unaffected by light. He had the worst position. His back was to the gate, and behind him a prison guard gave a Brahma repeated shocks with a cattle prod, the animal shrieking and trying to climb the boards.

Jimmy turned to the murderer. "Why you doing this? We can get out."

"I can get out," said the murderer.

"You doing over three hundred years, man," Nookey said, tilting the white dome of his head so sweat could roll off sideways, missing his eyes. "They welded the door on you."

"I can get out," he said again, looking at nobody.

A little cloud passed over, and the table turned dark. The men looked at their hands on the dusty surface. Jimmy heard the gate latch knock open, and then the cloud uncovered the sun. The wood under his hands glowed with fire.

The bull spun out of the pen like a tornado of angry meat, a gray animal with shadowed black eyes, a lurching hump on his back and, under him, his tortured, swinging bag loaded with electricity from the shock sticks of the howling guards. His hooves kicked up the floury dust, and it seemed for a moment that he had camouflaged the men and their bright table, that the onion eyeballs would not turn on them and the animal would not bolt into their quiet pocket of territory. Jimmy felt the dirt under his boot soles jump each time the animal planted a hoof, but he looked at nothing and willed his mind empty, waiting for whatever fact was about to be proved on him. He saw Nookey's face go blank, Little Claude's lids close. The murderer's eyes got even wider, and he looked over at the bull. "Easy," Jimmy said in his direction.

"Easy," the murderer repeated, with no inflection. Jimmy saw the man's black hair gleam, every strand in place in soft oiled lines like the hair on holy statues, and then the bull whirled and jumped for them, its haunches digging in, its sea of angry muscles directed at something it sought without knowing why, choosing the table and the men as a target with the logic a thunderbolt uses to select a tree or a house or a man walking along with a rake hoisted on his shoulder.

The animal could choose, if they sat still enough, to go for the table, to come in beside one of them and put a horn on the underneath, or even its whole head, and give it a murderous heave out of their hands. If they all kept their palms down, they would do better than Rex Ted's team. Or the Brahma could choose to lay his skull against the table's edge, and then it would go hard for the man on the other side. Or he might lay the barrel of a horn against a man and push them all down like bowling pins. None of the men thought any of this; they were not there, as far as Jimmy could tell. They had drained themselves of feeling and were white and empty.

What the bull did do was lower his head and hit Nookey from the rear, the animal's flat skull battering the chair and the man's backbone together, shoving his chest against the table, which shocked into Jimmy's ribs, the plywood top breaking in two and heaving up in the middle. Little Claude raised his hands right before a horn tip went through his cheek and into his mouth. Jimmy's long arms cracked like a whip over his head when the table hit him, and then he was in the dust, watching a hoof come down next to his face. Two rodeo clowns fell off the fence and distracted the animal as Little Claude dragged Jimmy clear into an opened gate, and a trusty hustled a white-faced Nookey over the fence, where he was put down in fresh manure, his legs kicking as a man with a cross on his shirt-sleeve knelt down to blow breath into his flattened lungs. The clowns got to the pen where Jimmy lay, jumping in ahead of the bull, and then Jimmy looked under the bottom board to see the murderer, whom everyone had seemed to forget, sitting untouched in front of nothing, his hands still out flat, palms down, in the center of the ring, his hair flawless, his eyes open. Jimmy wanted to yell, but there was no air in him. The rodeo announcer said something incomprehensible and awful, a squawk of speech, and before the clowns could get back over the fence, the bull ran into the murderer like a train, hitting him so hard that rivets flew out of the folding chair.

Jimmy lay back and robbed his share of the atmosphere in little sips until he could breathe again. He saw arms come under a board and drag out the murderer's body. After a minute or two, a guard holding a shock stick climbed into the pen with Jimmy and told him that Rex Ted's group had won the competition.

"That right?" Jimmy rasped.

"They gonna get their pictures in the paper," the guard told him. He looked at Jimmy as though he almost felt sorry about something. "We can only have one winner."

"Well," Jimmy said, looking under the bottom board to where the bull was trying to kill a clown trapped in a barrel, "maybe so."

Questions to Consider

1. Why do you suppose that "the murderer" is never mentioned by name in the story?
2. At Angola Prison in Louisiana, Gautreaux's native state, the inmates traditionally put on an annual rodeo that draws many outside spectators. Does the fact that visitors will pay to watch inmates of a maximum-security prison risk their lives performing rodeo stunts affect your interpretation of the story?

Dorothy Allison

1949–

Dorothy Allison may not be "The Meanest Woman Ever Left Tennessee," but many lesbian, feminist activists might characterize her as such because of her beliefs in sexual freedom among consenting adult women, freedom that includes the possibility of violence. Allison is active in promoting this belief. While lesbian activists protested the appropriateness of values such as promiscuous sexuality, sadomasochism, and butch/femme role playing at a conference on female sexuality in 1982, Allison helped organize a counterconference, which defended the rights of women to explore these very ideas. She has been sharply criticized by the lesbian community for her stance on women's sexuality, and conversely for confronting sexual violence—especially violence against children—in her writing, which includes fiction, poetry, and creative nonfiction.

Allison was born on 11 April 1949, in Greenville, South Carolina, to Ruth Gibson Allison, who was fifteen and unmarried, a significant social faux pas in the small-town South. Her mother later married and gave birth to additional children. When Allison was five, her stepfather began sexually abusing her. This abuse continued for many years until Allison told a relative, who reported the situation to Allison's mother. Allison's mother stopped the abuse, but unlike Bone, the young protagonist of Allison's widely acclaimed debut novel, *Bastard Out of Carolina (1992)*, Allison did not get away from her abuser. The family stayed together.

Allison attended college in Florida, receiving her bachelor's degree in anthropology from Florida Presbyterian College, and later earned a graduate degree, also in anthropology, at the New York School for Social Research. She began writing seriously in the early 1980s, following graduate school. Her first book of poetry, *The Women Who Hate Me: Poetry 1980–1990*, was initially published in 1983, and then reissued in an expanded and revised edition in 1991. Between these two editions, Allison published *Trash* (1988), a collection of short stories directly addressing the struggles of poverty-stricken Southern families, which provides a view contrary to the picturesque portrait of Southerners who are poor but happy generally seen by mainstream America. Many reviewers have noted that while Allison portrays poor Whites in all their ugliness, she also treats them with "understanding and love."

Allison's body of work depicts the types of sordid Southern characters that other authors hide or disparage, while embracing many of the characteristics common to Southern literature such as family and communal identities. Her depictions of poor "white trash," which she claims are modeled on her own dysfunctional family, are invariably characterized by critics as uncomfortably accurate. These proud Southerners are the ones that many people would rather not acknowledge, safe in the perception that they have somehow brought their low standard of living on themselves by slovenliness or low moral standards. *Trash* portrays these kinds of people, loosely linking them to Allison's own life in the South and her personal experiences with family violence. "The Meanest Woman Ever Left Tennessee," which was published in *Trash*, exemplifies the anxiety of members of the lower socioeconomic classes and their struggles to escape poverty and the implicit disregard it brings from others.

Critic Lisa Moore argues that the stories in *Trash* clearly present the dichotomy in Allison's life and in her activism—her condemnation of child abuse and male-on-female violence, and her arguments for a woman's right to "artistic and sexual expressions, including violent ones." The stories included in *Trash* provide the basis for *Bastard*. Allison has said that writing *Trash* allowed her to work out her rage at being sexually abused, which in turn allowed her to create a credible, yet loving, treatment of Bone as a victim.

The publication of *Bastard* garnered widespread notice and acclaim for Allison from critics and readers alike. The book was too conventional, however, for many of her fellow lesbian activists who argued that it was not "lesbian" enough. While *Bastard* was nominated for a National Book Award, it was not nominated for a Lambda Literary Award. At one time, such awards from lesbian activist groups were important to Allison because she claims that she thought they would add validity to her life. She now finds that her writing—not the awards—save her, because she uses her writing as a way to understand her life, and more particularly, her anger.

Allison followed the success of *Bastard* with a book of essays, *Skin: Talking About Sex, Class, and Literature* (1994) in which she focuses on her personal style of feminist and lesbian activism. Her second novel, *Cavedweller (1998)*, is similarly populated with the poor Whites associated with her writing, but the narrative is more subdued than that of *Bastard*, a difference that reviewers are quick to point out. While *Cavedweller* has not received the critical acclaim of *Bastard*, it was awarded the Lambda Literary Award. Allison continues to write and grant interviews but has curtailed her public appearances due to health problems. She lives in San Francisco with her companion, Alix, and their son Wolf.

The Meanest Woman Ever Left Tennessee

My Grandmother Mattie always said my Great-Grandmother Shirley lived too long.

Shirley Wilmer, of the Knoxville County Wilmers, married Tucker Boatwood when she was past nineteen and he was just barely sixteen. Her family had a peanut farm off to the north of Knoxville, a piece of property they split between the five sons. Shirley was the only daughter. Her inheritance was a cedar chest full of embroidered linen and baby clothes that she and her mama had gotten together over the years, that and sixty dollars in silver that her daddy gave her—a fortune in those days. Granny Mattie swore that when Grandma Shirley died those silver coins were still tied in the same cloth in which she'd gotten them.

Two of her children died of the flu after gathering melons on a frosty fall day. People swore you could cure the flu with a bath of hot oil and comfrey, but Shirley wasn't the kind to gather herbs and certainly not the kind to spend her silver on someone who would. She'd never wanted children anyway and hated the way her own body continuously swelled and delivered. She called the children devils and worms and trash, and swore that, like worms, their natural substance was dirt and weeds.

Shirley Boatwood believed herself to be one of the "quality." "The better people," she told her daughters, "know their own. You watch how it goes, you watch how people treat me down at the mill. They can see who I am. It's in the eyes if nothing else." Mattie, the oldest girl, watched the way her mama's lips thinned and tightened, the way her sisters and brothers held their own mouths pinched together so their lips stuck out. Shirley Boatwood was very proud of getting on at the mill and how much she was earning there, as proud of that as she was ashamed that Tucker still worked in the mine.

"A tight mouth," Tucker Boatwood was heard to say, "a tight mouth betrays a tight heart, and a shallow soul." His wife said nothing, but pulled her lips in tighter still, and the next day he found the doors locked against him when he came home from the mine.

"Woman, what do you think you're doing?" He beat on the front door with a swollen dirty right fist. "Woman! Open this door." He spit and shouted and began to kick the base of the door jam. "Kids, do you hear me? Shirley! Woman!"

Inside, Shirley Boatwood sat at her kitchen table sipping hot tea and staring straight ahead. Mattie stood at the sink with her hands flat to the nozzle of the pump. She stood still, unsure of how she could get past her mama to let her father in the door, and absolutely sure that if she tried it, she'd find herself locked out with him before either of them could get inside.

"Put on another kettle," Shirley told her, staring straight ahead and using her right hand to smooth her hair back behind her pristine white collar. "Make me up another cup of tea." Outside, Tucker went on screaming and kicking. Mattie made the tea while the other children sat quietly on the stairs to the second floor. After a while, the shouting let off and Tucker stomped off the porch. Shirley fed the kids sidemeat and grits, then put them all to bed.

When they got up the next morning, Tucker was sitting at the kitchen table drinking cold water and looking like someone had tried to pull out all his hair. He said nothing, but at the end of the week quit his job in the mine and took a position at the JCPenney textile mill.

"A machinist is a higher class of man," Shirley told the children.

Tucker never got the hang of fixing the big bobbin gears. He'd had a fine talent for the winches and pumps at the mine, but the cables and wheels of the spinning machines confused him. After a few weeks he found himself standing in front of a wheeled cart, pulling off full bobbins and popping on empty ones. His ears rang with the noise and his eyes watered from the dust, but Shirley just shrugged. "Mill workers are a better class of people than miners. I never planned to live my life as a miner's wife." Tucker Boatwood took to slipping whiskey into his cold tea, while his blue eyes faded to a pale grey.

The Boatwood children had bad dreams. After supper they were all required to wash again while their mama watched. "That neck don't look clean to me, Bo. You trying to grow mold in those armpits, Mattie? Why are you all so dirty and stupid?" The children scrubbed and scrubbed, while Shirley rubbed her neck with one hand and her bulging belly with another. "I'd kill this thing if I could," she muttered. Her five sons and three daughters dreamed often of their mother, dreamed she came in to wash their faces with lye, to cut off the places where their ears stuck out, to tie down their wagging tongues and plane down their purplish genitals.

"You won't need this," they dreamed she told them, as she pulled off one piece or another of their flesh. They dreamed and screamed and woke each other in terror. Sometimes, Shirley beat on the stairs with a broom handle to remind them how much she and Tucker needed their sleep. She hated the way they cringed away from her. After all, she never hit them. A pinch was enough if you knew how it should be done. But more than their shameful fear of her, she hated the way Mattie would stare back at her and refuse to drop her eyes.

"You think you're something, don't you?" Shirley would push her face right up to her daughter's flushed and sweating cheekbones. "You think God's got his eye on you?" Shirley would pinch the inside of Mattie's arm and twist her mouth at the girl's stubborn expression. "Wouldn't nobody take an interest in you if you were to birth puppy dogs and turtles—which you might. You might any day now." She beat the foot of each bed with her broomstick until the children squeezed up near the top. "Boatwoods, you're all purelybred Boatwoods. My side of the family don't even want to know you're alive, I'd swear you an't no kin to me at all."

It was true that Shirley's family took no interest in her children. Once a year Shirley would go alone to visit her mother, but neither her parents nor her brothers ever visited them. The only thing the children knew about their grandparents was Shirley's stories about their house, how big and clean it was, how the porch shone with soapstoned wood and baskets of sweet herbs that Grandma Wilmer used in her cooking, how the neighbors admired her mother and looked up to her daddy. By contrast, their father's father, a widower, was nothing but a drunk.

"Vegetables . . . Hell! The man sells whiskey out of that roadside stand, whiskey I tell you, not tomatoes and squash. He just has those runty old tomatoes there to keep the law off."

"Now Shirley, you know that an't true," Tucker always protested.

"I know what's true, Tucker Boatwood, and I won't have these children spared the truth. You want them to grow up like their grandfather? Like those lazy sisters of yours in their dirt-floor cabins? I surely don't. They grow up to live in dirt and I'll renounce them."

"That woman hates her children," the neighbors all said. They did not say that the children hated her back. It was not possible to know what those children thought, so quiet and still they were. They all had the same face, the same pinched features, colorless hair, and nervous hands. Only their eyes varied in shade, from Bo's seawater blue to Mattie's grapeskin hazel. In the warmer weather, they all took on the same shade of deep red-brown tan acquired from staying away from the house as much as they could, and from long hours spent weeding and picking at their mama's direction in a half-dozen farmers' fields.

"Money is hard come by," Shirley told them, pocketing eight cents a week on the boys and three on the girls. "Dreams are all that come free, dreams and talk. And that's all lazy people know about. You should see those bent-necks down at the mill, trying to pretend they're working when they're dreaming or talking. Talk about how badly they're used. Trash don't know the meaning of use. Just like you kids." She tucked the pennies in her kerchief and that in her apron. "The way you eat, you'd think you didn't know the cost of boiled rice."

"Two cents a pound."

When Mattie spoke all the other kids dropped their heads, though Bo and Tucker Junior always turned their faces so they could look up from the side. They knew Mattie was crazy, but they worshipped her craziness and suspected that without her they might have all curled up and died.

"You little whore." Shirley gripped the fabric of her apron in twisted fingers. Her voice was an outraged hiss. "You an't worth two cents a night yourself." Mattie's tanned features paled but she kept her mouth closed and her eyes level with her mother's. They stared each other down, while Tucker wiped his forehead and licked dry cracked lips.

"It's got to be supper time," he pleaded, and Shirley nodded slowly into Mattie's face.

"Let the whore cook it."

"Whores and thieves and bastards," she cursed them when she went into labor that last time. She cursed steadily for hours till Tucker sent all the kids off to one of his sister's. "I never wanted no man to touch me. I sure never wanted *you* to touch me. You put death and dirt in me every time. Death, you hear me. All I've got out of you is death and mud and worms."

"It's just the pain," the midwife told Tucker, but neither of them really believed that. Tucker believed that this was the time when Shirley told him the whole truth. The midwife did squeeze Tucker's arm once and say, "Do you notice how she don't really scream?"

The baby finally came in two pieces covered in a stinking bloody scum. Tucker borrowed a car and wrapped Shirley in three blankets to take her into the county hospital. The midwife wrapped up the baby in flour sacks to carry in, too, but Shirley became hysterical when they tried to put it in the car. They had to put it in the trunk before she would calm down.

"Don't you think I knew it was dead?" Shirley curled her fist around Tucker's wrist so tight he thought the little bones would crack. "I told you. You put death in me."

"No telling what causes this kind of thing," the doctor told Tucker. "But she's had her last child, that's for sure."

"You've had your last poke at me," Shirley whispered to Tucker when she could finally talk again. "I never wanted it, and if you ever come to me for it again, I'll cut your thing off and feed it to those damn brats you pulled out of me." Tucker said nothing. The doctor had told him he'd have to be very gentle with Shirley for a while, that she was gonna be weak for a good long while.

"You don't know Shirley," Tucker said, "She might be sick, but she an't never gonna be weak."

It was October when the baby was born dead, and Shirley Boatwood didn't go back to work until May. The pennies saved up over the summer were gone by then, as were the canned goods Tucker's sisters had sent over in the fall. By February, half the Boatwood children were wearing strips of sacking tied around their broken shoes. Every morning they'd stand still while Shirley directed Mattie in tying the sacking correctly. It was Bo's birthday, the eleventh of that month, when she caught hold of Mattie's sleeve as she headed for the door with the other children.

"No," she said. "You're thirteen now, no need to waste your time in school. You either, Bo." All the children stood still for a moment, and then Mattie and Bo stepped back and let the others go. It took Shirley half an hour to get herself dressed, shaking off Mattie's hand when she came to help. It took them all another hour to walk the eight blocks together to the mill. Neither Bo nor Mattie spoke. Both of them just kept looking up to their mother with swollen frightened eyes.

Mattie had small quick hands and a terror of the speeding shuttles. She kept her lower lip clenched in her teeth while she worked to untangle bunched and knotted threads. Bo was clumsy and spent most of his time crawling underneath frames to grease the wheels that turned the bobbin belts. Sometimes he crawled right under Mattie's hands and would hiss up at her to get her attention. Both of them avoided their father. When their mother came back to work in May, they avoided her too, but that was easier. Shirley had been transferred from the carding room to finishing. Safely separated from the rest of the mill by a wire and glass wall, Shirley and twenty other women ran up towels, aprons, and simple skirts from the end runs of sample fabric bolts.

"You see what I mean?" Shirley's mouth had grown so tight she seemed to have no lips at all. "Quality always shows, always finds its place. That foreman knows who I am."

Mattie sucked her gums and thought of the women at the mill who stepped aside when her mama passed. Everybody said Shirley Boatwood believed her piss was wine. Everybody said she repeated things she heard to the foreman on the second shift. And if Shirley Boatwood pissed wine, then there was no doubt that nasty son of a bitch pissed store-bought whiskey.

"When we grow up . . ." Bo started whispering every night, and each child would finish the line in turn.

"I'm gonna move to Texas."

"I an't never gonna eat tripe no more."

"I'm gonna have six little babies and buy them anything they want."

"Gonna treat them good."

"Gonna tell them how pretty they are."

"Gonna love them, love them."

Sometimes Mattie would let the youngest, Billy, climb up into her lap. She'd hug and stroke him and quietly sing some gospel songs for him, making up the words she couldn't remember. "When we grow up," Bo kept whispering. "When we grow up. . . ."

None of them knew what they might not do. Only Mattie had an idea that it was possible to do anything at all. Walking to work every morning, she passed the freight siding where James Gibson pulled barrels off his father's wagon. The Gibsons ran a lumber business, and most of the cane syrup shipped out of Greenville went out in their barrels. If he was there, James stopped and watched her walk by. Every time he saw her pass, he smiled.

"I've got nine brothers," he told her one time, "and not one sister. Lord, I love to look at pretty girls!"

It was the first time anyone had ever suggested Mattie might be pretty. She started leaving home earlier so she could walk slower past the railway siding. On the mornings when one of the other Gibson boys was there, she felt disappointed. They tended to giggle when they saw her, which always made her wonder what James said about her to them.

"I told them to keep an eye on you," James told her when she asked. "I told them to keep their hands off and their eyes open. What you think about that?"

"I think you talking a lot for nothing having been said between us."

"What do we need to say?"

But Mattie couldn't answer that. She didn't know what she wanted to say to anybody. She only knew she wanted to start finding out. She felt as if her eyes were opening, as if light were coming into a dark place inside her. At the dinner table Mattie watched her mama spoon rice out of the bowl, all the while talking about how only trash served food out of a cooking pot.

"Quality people use serving dishes." She slapped Bo's hand. "Quality people don't come to the table with grease under their nails."

"I washed!"

Mattie watched rice grains fall off her fork. She hated butter beans with rice. White on white didn't suit her. Black-eyed peas with pork was better. Best was deep-brown pinto beans cooked soft and thick.

"If you'd really washed, you'd be clean. Nobody in my family even came to the table with dirt under their nails. You go wash again."

Bo's face creased and uncreased, as if the words he wasn't saying were pushing up inside him. But he kept quiet and went out to the porch to wash again. His father slapped his behind lightly as he went past. Mattie put her fork between her teeth, realizing how bad their father was looking. He wasn't eating nothing either, didn't seem as if he ever ate much anymore, though he drank lots of tea out of his special jar from under the pump.

He's a drunk, Mattie thought, examining the broken veins in her father's nose. He really is a drunk.

"What are you thinking about, Miss High and Mighty?" Shirley spooned butter beans onto another plate and pursed her lips at Mattie.

"Nothing." Mattie filled her mouth with rice so she wouldn't have to talk.

"You got a lot in that face for nothing to say. Mabel Moseley told me she saw you out behind the mill talking to that Gibson boy day before yesterday. She said you were shaking your ass and swinging your hair like some kind of harlot."

Mattie scooped up more rice so that her cheeks bulged out. She looked back at her mother steadily, seeing for the first time not only the thin lips but the corded neck muscles and high red spots on the cheeks. She's pretty ugly, Mattie thought. She let her eyes wander up to her mother's, to the hazel color that reflected her own. You're ugly and old, she thought to herself, but went on chewing steadily.

"Now woman," Tucker pushed his plate forward out of his way. "You know Mabel Moseley an't quite right in her head. Mattie Lee's a good girl. . . ."

"She's trash. She's nothing but trash, and you know it." Calmly, Shirley Boatwood set the plate down in front of her youngest and started to fill another plate for herself. "Don't matter what I do, I can't make nothing out of these kids. Seems like they're all bound to grow up to be trash."

Tucker closed his eyes and sighed. "I'm tired," he whispered. "I'm gonna lay me down for a while."

"An't no food gonna be kept warm for you."

"Don't want it no way."

Mattie spooned more rice into her mouth. She watched her mother watching her father as he walked away, shuffling his feet on the floorboards. There were gaps between most of the floorboards, and Shirley was always stuffing them with one thing or the other. What would it be like, Mattie wondered, to live in a house with dirt floors?

"You hear about that union man?" she heard herself say, and her heart seemed to pause briefly in shock.

Her mama was looking at her again. Her mama's mouth was hanging open. Past her shoulder, Bo had stopped in the doorway, wiping his hands on his overalls. "Union?"

"Trade union." Mattie filled her fork again and then looked past her mama to Bo. "You think we ought to sign up, Bo?"

Bo's mouth fell open. "Uh." He stopped and looked from his mama to Mattie to the curtain swaying at the door to the back bedroom where his father had just gone.

"You've gone crazy." Shirley dropped the spoon into the beans. "You've gone absolutely crazy. There an't no union in the mill. There an't gonna be no union in the mill. And I wouldn't let you join one if some fool was to try to bring one in."

"You couldn't stop me."

It felt to Mattie as if the rice was swelling inside her. There was a kind of heat in her belly that was spreading down her legs and tingling. Once she had sipped at her Daddy's tea glass and felt the same thing. "You're drunk, little girl," he'd told her, and she'd kind of liked the feeling. She liked it even more now. She watched her mama's hands flatten on the table. She watched the little red spots in her mama's face get bigger. She watched Bo's eyes widen and a little gleam of light come on in them. There was a kind of laugh in her belly that wanted to roll out her mouth, but she held it in. She imagined Bo's chorus of *when we grow up* and found herself thinking that when she had kids, she'd sit 'em all down on the dirt floor and tell 'em all to sign with the union. Her mother's chair made a hollow sound on the bare wood floor.

Now, she thought. Now she will get up and come over here and slap me. What will I do then? She took another bite of rice and smiled.

What will I do then?

Granny Mattie always said my Great-Grandmother Shirley lived too long. "One hundred and fourteen when she died, and didn't nobody want to wash her body for the burying. Had to hire an undertaker's assistant to pick out something to bury her in. She'd left instructions but didn't nobody want to read 'em. Bo had always swore that when she died, he'd throw a party, but shit, he didn't live to see it and his sons didn't have the guts to do it for him. Only thing he ever managed to do was piss on her porch steps the year before he died, while she sat up there staring over his head, pretending she didn't see his dick or nothing. Anybody ever tells you I'm mean, you tell 'em about your Great-Grandma Shirley, the meanest woman that ever left Tennessee."

Questions to Consider

1. What causes Shirley to feel so strongly about her own inherent quality while she views her children as trash? Where does Shirley fall in the class hierarchy?
2. What causes Shirley to be such a mean person?

Rodney Jones

1950–

Rodney Jones was born to a struggling north Alabama family on 11 February 1950. His father, E. Lavon Jones, had to give up cotton farming to work in a factory that made metal tubes; his mother, Wilda Owen Jones, was a homemaker. The family did not own a functional TV set until Jones was almost 12 years old. Spoken and written language, not visual images, stirred Jones's youthful imagination—particularly, the Southern oral traditions of sermons, stories, jokes, and songs. His family belonged to the Protestant Church of God, and one of his grandfathers composed gospel songs. From that rural, working-class background where he himself picked cotton to support the family in his teens, Jones would grow up to become "perhaps the supreme example we have in American poetry of the Southern human person speaking," as poet Kate Daniels has phrased it.

Two poets in particular influenced Jones's work while he was an undergraduate at the University of Alabama at Tuscaloosa: creative writing instructor Jim Seay and fellow student Everette Maddox, six years older and vastly more well read. Before he was 20 years old, Jones had published poems in *Shenandoah*, *Kansas Quarterly*, and *Back Door*. He went on to earn an M.F.A. in creative writing from the University of North Carolina at Greensboro in 1973. There he took classes from Allen Tate but learned from faculty poets Fred Chappell and Louise Gluck on an informal basis, in conversations held outside the classroom. After four years of teaching in public schools in three different Southern states (Tennessee, Alabama, and Virginia), Jones began his career as a college teacher of creative writing at Virginia Intermont College. Since 1984 he has taught at Southern Illinois University at Carbondale.

Ironically, Jones has written his best work about the South since leaving it. "Our good fortune," writes Daniels, "is that his compulsion to remember makes him write. Jones's exile from the language of his birth and boyhood has yielded some wonderful verse." Although Jones writes in a rhetorical and narrative style and his subjects are often "flamboyantly doomed characters from America's South," as Peter Harris has called them, his allusions to popular culture, mixing of high and low speech registers in the same poem, and tendency to subvert the normal linear progression of narrative mark him as distinctly postmodern. Awards for his writing have included the National Book Critics Circle Award (for *Transparent Gestures*), the Lavan Younger Poets Award from the Academy of American Poets, and grants from the Guggenheim Foundation and the National Endowment for the Arts.

Mule

Here is this horse from a bad family, hating his burden and snaffle,
 not patient
So much as resigned to his towpath around the sorghum mill,
 but pawing the grist,
Laying back his missile ears to balk, so the single spoke of his wheel
 freezes, the gears lock.
Not sad, but stubborn, his temperament is tolerance,
 though his voice,

Old door aching on a rusty hinge, blasts the martins from their gourds,[1]
    and he would let
Nothing go behind him: the speckled hen, the green world
    his blinders magnify.
With the heel of one ecclesiastical hoof, he would stun goats or gods.
Half-ass, garrulous priest, his religion's a hybrid appetite that feasts
    on contradictions.
In him Jefferson[2] dreamed the end of slavery and endless fields,
    but the labor goes on
In prefabricated barns, by stalled regiments of canopied tractors,
    in offices
Where the harvest is computed to the least decimal point,
    to the last brown bowl of wheat.
Not with him, the soil yields and futures swell into the radio.
His place, finally, is to be loved as a curiosity, as an art
    almost dead, like this sulfurous creek
Of molasses he brings oozing down from the bundles of cane.

Sometimes in the library I pause suddenly and think of the mule,
    desiring, perhaps, some lost sweetness,
Some fitful husk or buttercup that blooms wildly beyond the margins.
Such a peace comes over the even rows, the bound volumes
    where the unicorn
Bows his unearthly head, where the horned gods of fecundity rear
    in the pages of the sun.
All afternoon I will think of the mule's dignity, of his shrunken lot—
While the statistics slip the tattered net of my attention,
While the lullabies erect their precise nests in the footnotes.

I like to think of the silver one of my childhood, and the dark red one,
    Red.
Avuncular, puritanical, he stands on hooves as blue as quarries,
And I think his is the bray I have held back all of my life,
    in churches
Where the offering passed discreetly from one laborer to the next,
    in the factories of sleep,
Plunging a greased hand into the vat of mineral spirits.
And I think I have understood nothing better than the mule's cruelty
    and petty meanness:
How, subjugated, he will honk his incomparable impudence;
    stop for no reason;
Or, pastured with inferiors, stomp a newborn calf on a whim.

This is the mule's privilege: not to be governed badly by lashes,
    nor to be turned
Easily by praise; but, sovereign of his own spirit, to take his own time,
To meditate in the hardening compost under the rotting collars.
To sleep in wet straw. To stand for nothing but himself.

1. The purple martin, a migratory bird that spends part of the year in the American South, will nest in hollowed-out gourds.

2. Thomas Jefferson (1743–1826), the third president of the United States.

In August he will stand up to his withers in the reeking pond.
In the paradise of mules,
He will stand with the old cows, contemplative, but brooding a little over the sores in his shoulders,
Remembering the dull shoes of the cultivator and the jet heads of the mowing machine.
Being impotent and beautiful, he will dream of his useless romances.

Alma

Sometimes in late summer I come to
the husks of cicadas. In death
they are rooted in the scaly bark
of the pine,
become their own coffins,
these hard and glossy shells
that had contained
the secrets of flight.

That's why I like it in the South.
The afterlife is with you
all the time. It holds you
like that shack you pass
on the interstate,
so colorless and shapeless,
like all the rest of the world
you will never recognize
until it falls on you.

If I had learned in a better school
that offered more
than the lilyish English of Jesus,
I might have known, when I went to look up the word
that meant soul in my love's language,[1]
that it would be Alma,
who cursed her picksack up the row ahead of me,
her black hair tied up with a red handkerchief,
her painted mouth opening,
and the black words loosening like crows.

In the fields, in the fifties, in Alabama,
there were women who loved to cha-cha,
bending all day to ruin their fingernails,
dragging behind them
the dead weight of cotton.
Full of work, their bodies were shaking
to the tinny beat of portable radios,
and their husbands were thinking
of joining the Church of God.[2]

She died absurdly
at one of the sideshows

1. The language is Spanish.

2. A fundamentalist Protestant religious denomination.

at the Limestone County Fair.[3] Her heart
is no secret now, fabric
of a dimestore purse.

While most of the wives cowered
around booths of otherworldly vegetables,
while most of the husbands
were creeping down the midway to the girlie shows,
pausing to become the shadows of tents,
she listened to the trick-rider
gun the engine of his chrome Harley,[4]
watched him spin up the impossible wall
of a giant barrel. Against
that din and blur, death must have seemed
a precipitate absentmindedness,
a freakish loss of balance.

I have always believed in the soul
that is lighter than the body's shadow
and the shadow
that drags a heavy sack
or pushes a plow oiled with dew.
I stand in my father's field
where Alma sang with the rich women
on the radio
of cheating hearts and ricochet romances.
Then I hear again the slow
engines starting in the pines,
the sharp and persistent voices
of cicadas.

Simulated Woodgrain Vinyl

I was not there long, between the housing project and the
seediest of developments, the identical two-bedroom
brick or clapboard bungalows, advertised for newlyweds,
occupied by the very old.
The house where I lived (mildewed and leaky, crosshatched
with ancient wiring, its plaster and lath walls
still spindling and spider-cracking under the landlord's creamy
K-mart[1] paneling) I shared
with a teenage mother who beat her child, and two fiftyish
spinster sisters who every afternoon
walked their primped poodle past my front window down the
street to the park.
Most days were artless, innocuous—rife with bad salesmen
and fake catastrophes.
Nights the potboilers I took to bed revealed their feeble plots
like pretty girls feigning bashfulness,

3. A county in northern Alabama.
4. A Harley Davidson motorcycle, known for power and ruggedness and the "outlaw" image of its riders.

1. A chain of discount stores prevalent in the South in the late twentieth century.

while the crescendo of Black Sabbath[2] ravaged the Mormon
Tabernacle Choir.[3]

Nothing else!
No ora, no acs, no smee, no Eris,[4] no eider from the smalltown
crossword puzzle!
I did not imagine my fate as the common one—infinitely
distributable, statistical—stroking itself, clumsily, in the
dark.
Neither did I conjure a forest from the unconvincing grain of
those walls: trees with plastic leaves,
like the leaves that hem in coffins but do not diminish the
immaculate corpse; and noble savages,
Tennessee Watusis[5] popping their clutches in the parking lots of
burger palaces.
But my thoughts were like those walls, like the side panels of
stationwagons, like the basements of churches
where Little League[6] coaches bully aphorisms from the chubby
sons of realtors.

There still must be some trinket, in a box I no longer unpack,
and obsolete keys, O necklace of lost addresses.
I've lived since then in twenty places, better and worse, that
run together now in the glaze
of abstract memory, totem of the vacant gaze, so all I have for
touchstone is one infantile, sugary tune,
one of the hits of that year, that still clings in what remote
precinct of the brain.
So the sauce the sisters stewed all day comes back with its
sickening garlic,
and the child who would not stop crying turns to me his
white, lopsided face, the way
a wave plants in darkened sand the treble hooks of a single
phosphorescent lure.

And what can I expect now? The whole boring ambience
swelling until I die of too much past,
die of the unassuaged guilts, the cumulative sighs, grunts, and
titters of disgust?
It's time to rearrange the stories, to milk permanence from the
walls.
These nights the moon's slow plow still opens its gash in the
sterile heavens above the Second Methodist Church.
Down the street, if my old house crumbles, most things
weren't meant to last, but do.
In memory, which admonishes loss and shines most repeating
the commonplace, even the paneling

2. A British heavy metal rock band led by singer Ozzy Osbourne that was popular in the late 1970s.
3. A Mormon musical choir founded in Salt Lake City in 1847 and still in existence.
4. Deliberately obscure words meant to stump a crossword puzzle enthusiast; "Eris" is the Greek goddess of discord, sister of Mars, the god of war.
5. Members of an African tribe of Rwanda and Burundi.
6. An organized baseball league for American children.

takes on the shabby character of small airports and out-of-the-
way diners,
and I remember the older sister, how fiercely she held the
jeweled leash as she walked
toward her frog pond and magnolias, towing her twelve
pounds of affection.

Questions to Consider

1. Trace the images of "soul" and "flight" as opposed to the images of "body" and "weight" in the poem "Alma." How are the two contradictory themes resolved in the last stanza of the poem?
2. How does the poem "Simulated Woodgrain Vinyl" relate to the theme of the industrialization and commercialization of the contemporary South?

Larry Brown

1951–

Larry Brown, one of Mississippi's best known writers, began his career as a fire fighter and performed a wide variety of jobs in order to make ends meet. Struggle has been a lifelong motif.

Brown was born on 9 July 1951 in Oxford, Mississippi to a sharecropper father and a mother who was a postmaster and store owner. He lived part of his life in Memphis, Tennessee, but the family moved back to Oxford when he was about 14 years of age. Brown's early life would not necessarily indicate writing as a career choice. He failed twelfth-grade English and did not graduate from high school with his class, choosing instead to spend hours hunting and fishing near his rural hometown of Oxford, Mississippi. He finally graduated from high school in the summer of 1969 and went to work at Chamber's stove factory until he enlisted in the Marines in 1970. Since his number had been the first pulled in the draft, his decision to join the Marines stemmed from his desire not to be drafted into the army. Brown served his time in the military at the Marine Barracks in Philadelphia. After his discharge, he returned home to Lafayette County, where he courted and eventually married Mary Annie Coleman, a local girl some three years his junior. The Browns soon became parents to four children, one of whom died in infancy.

Brown's family provides a strong foundation for him. By 1973, the Browns were living on a tight budget; even with his regular salary as a fireman for the town of Oxford, Brown worked a wide variety of odd jobs to augment the family's income, but at age 29, he decided to change his life. He dedicated himself to writing, and he quickly produced over one hundred stories and a draft of a novel. Unfortunately, he had little luck with his initial publishing efforts and received a thick stack of rejections from periodicals and small presses alike.

Always a voracious reader, Brown threw himself into reading the works of successful writers, and after drafting two additional novels, he decided to enter a writing program. In the early 1980s, he learned that Ellen Douglas was teaching creative writing at the University of Mississippi. Brown received special permission to attend Douglas's class since he had never attended college, and under her guidance, he honed his skills and began to publish some of his work. In 1988, Brown's first collection of short stories, *Facing the Music,* was published, and since that time, his works have drawn a tremendous amount of critical attention. His contemporaries praise his work for its grit and truthfulness.

Brown's work, like that of fellow Southerners Dorothy Allison, Lee Smith, and Harry Crews, focuses upon the lives of the working-class world of the South. His novels and short stories frequently include explicitly sexual characters, yet these characters are not defined strictly by their sexual needs and foibles. They exhibit many flaws and reflect the complex society of the South. Brown eloquently depicts both African-American and White characters with intensity and tragedy as is seen in *Dirty Work* (1989), and he creates poignant female characters in *Facing the Music*.

Brown's success came fairly quickly, yet he still maintains a private life near Oxford on a farm of 60 acres where he writes for five to ten hours each day. In 2000, Brown finally switched from a typewriter to a computer which he says has, in some ways, made his life easier. Brown has written nine book-length works including his best known *Facing the Music*, *Dirty Work*, *Big Bad Love* (1990), *Joe* (1991), *On Fire* (1994), *Father and Son* (1996), and *Fay* (2000). "The End of Romance," included here illustrates Brown's "grit lit" characteristics. The characters are volatile and difficult. In them, Brown depicts the seedier side of Southern life.

The End of Romance

Miss Sheila and I were riding around, as we often did in those days. But I was pretty sure it was going to be the last afternoon of our relationship. Things hadn't been good lately.

It was hot. We'd been drinking all day, and we'd drunk almost enough. We lacked just a little getting to a certain point. I'd already come to a point. I'd come down to the point where I could still get an erection over her, but my heart wouldn't be going crazy and jumping up in my throat like a snake-bit frog. I wouldn't be fearing for my life when I mounted her. I knew it was time for me to book for a fat man's ass. She bitched about how much time I spent locked in my room, how my mother was bossy, when would I ever learn some couth? And you get them started nagging at you, you might as well be married. Well. I'd been out of women when I found her and I'd be out of women again until I found another one. But there were hundreds of other women, thousands, millions. They'd been making new ones every day for years.

"I ain't drunk," she said.

"Well, I'm not drunk, either."

"You look like you are."

"So do you."

"You got enough money to get some more? You can take all that Nobel Prize money and get us a coupla sixers, can't you?"

She was bad about chagrinning me like that.

"I magine I can manage it," I said.

So she whipped it into one of those little quick-joints that are so popular around here, one of those chicken-scarfing places, whipped it up in front of the door and stopped. She stared straight ahead through the windshield. Nothing worse than a drunken woman. Empty beer cans were all piled up around our feet. The end of romance is never easy.

"What matter?" I said.

"Nuttin matter. Everything just hunkin funkin dunky."

"You mean hunky dory?"

She had some bloodshot eyes and a ninety-yard stare. I'd known it would come down to this. The beginning of romance is wonderful. I don't know why I do it over and over. Starting with a new one, I can just about eat her damn legs off. Then, later, some shit like this. Women. Spend your whole life after the right one and what do they do? Shit on you. I always heard the theory of slapping them around to make them respect you, that that's what they want. But I couldn't. I couldn't stand to hit that opposite flesh. That slap would ring in my head for the rest of my life. This is what I do: take what they give and give what I can and when it's over find another one. Another one. That's what's so wonderful about the beginning of romance. She's different. She's new. Unique. Everything's fresh. Crappola. You go in there to shave after the first night and what does she do while you've got lather all over your face? Comes in and hikes her nightgown and then the honeymoon's over.

I'm not trying to get away from the story. I mean, just a few minutes later, some stuff actually happened. But sitting in that car at that moment, I was a little bitter. I had all sorts of thoughts going through my head, like: *Slapper. Slapper ass off.* I held that down.

She looked at me with those bloodshot eyes. "You really somethin, you know that? You really really really."

I knew it was coming. We'd had a bad afternoon out at the lake. Her old boyfriend had been out there, and he'd tried to put the make on her. I and seven of my friends had ripped his swim trunks off of him, lashed him to the front of her car, and driven him around blindfolded but with his name written on a large piece of beer carton taped to his chest for thirty-seven minutes, in front of domestic couples, moms and dads, family reunions, and church groups. She hadn't thought it was funny. We, we laughed our asses off.

I got out of the car. She didn't want to have any fun, that was fine with me. I bent over and gathered up an armload of beer cans and carried them to the trash can. They clattered all over the place when I dropped them in. I was a little woozy but I didn't think anybody could see it. Through the window of the store this old dyed woman with great big breasts and pink sunglasses looked out at me with a disapproving frown. I waved. Then I went back for more cans.

"Don't worry about the damn cans, all right?"

"I can't move my feet for them," I said.

"I'll worry about the damn cans," she said.

It sort of crumpled me. We were in her convertible, and once it was fun to just throw them straight up while we were going down the road. The wind, or I guess just running out from under them was fun. It was a game. Now it didn't seem to matter. I think we both had the creep of something bad coming up on us. She could have beat the shit out of me, I could have beat the shit out of her. It's no way to live. You don't want to go to sleep nervous, fearing the butcher knife, the revolver, the garrote.

"Just go in and get some beer," she said. "We got to talk."

Then she started crying. She wasn't pretty when she was crying. Her whole face turned red and wrinkled up. I knew it was me. It's always me.

"You're just so damn great, ain't you?" she said. "Don't even want nobody overt the house, cept a bunch of old drunks and freaks and whores."

My friends. Poets, artists, actors, English professors out at Ole Miss. She called them drunks and freaks. *Slapper. Slap shit out of her.*

"Just go on git the damn beer," she said. "I got something to tell you."

It's awful to find pussy so good that treats you so bad. It's like you've got to *pay* for it being good. But you've got to be either a man or a pussy. You can't just lay around and pine. I thought at that point that maybe I'd gotten out of that particular car for the last time.

I went on in. I was even starting to feel better. If she left, I could go home, open all the doors, crank up the stereo, get free. I could start sleeping in the daytime and writing at night again, nonstop if I wanted to, for eight or ten hours. I could have a party without somebody sullen in one corner. Everything would be different and the same again.

Well, hell, I wasn't perfect though, was I? I'd probably been a shitass a few times. Who's not? Even your best friend will turn asshole on you from time to time. He's only human.

I knew somebody else would come along. I just didn't know how long it would be. So I did a little quick rationalizing inside the store.

Whatever I was going back outside to wasn't going to be good. She was bracing herself up to be nasty to me, I could see that. And there wasn't any need in a bit of it. I could do without all the nastiness. I could take an amicable breakup. All I had to do was hang around inside the store for a while, and she'd probably get tired of waiting for me, and run off and leave me. So I went back toward the rear. The old bag was watching me. She probably thought I was a criminal. All I was doing was sitting back there gnawing my fingernails. But it was no good. I couldn't stand to know she was out there waiting on me.

So I got back up and went up the beer aisle. I figured I might as well go on and face it. Maybe we'd have a goodbye roll. I got her a sixpack of Schlitz malt liquor and got myself a sixer of Stroh's in bottles. The old bag was eyeing me with distaste. I still had my trunks on, and flip-flops, and my FireBusters T-shirt. I was red from passing out under the sun.

I could see Miss Sheila out there. I set the beer on the counter just as a black guy pulled up beside her car and got out. I started pulling my money out and another car pulled up beside the first one. It had a black guy in it, too, only this one had a shotgun. The first black guy was up against the door, just coming in, and the second black guy suddenly blew the top of the first black guy's head off. The first black guy flopped inside.

"*AAAAAAAAAAAAHHHHHHHHHHHH!*" he said. "*HHHHHHWWWWWW WAAAAAAAAAAAAAAAHHH!*" Blood and meat and black hair had flown inside everywhere with him, glass. It stuck to the walls, to the cigarettes in the rack over the counter, to the warming oven where they had the fried chicken. I'd eaten a lot of that fried chicken. The guy flopped down the detergent aisle. "*WAAAAAA AAAAAAAAH!*" he said.

I just stood there holding my money. I'd been wrong. The top of his head hadn't been blown off after all. He just didn't have any hair up there.

"*HAAAAAAAAAAAAAAAAAAH!*" he said. He was flopping around like a fish. He flopped down to the end of the aisle, then flopped over a couple of tables where people ate their barbecue at lunchtime, (where I'd been sitting just a few minutes before) and then he flopped over in the floor. I looked outside. The second black guy had gotten back into his car with his shotgun and was backing out of the parking lot. I couldn't see Miss Sheila.

"Let me pay for my beer and get out of here," I said, to the woman who had ducked down behind the counter. "The cops'll be here in a minute."

The black guy got off the floor back there and flopped over the meat market. "*AAAAAAAAAAAAAH!*" he said. He flopped up against the coolers, leaving big bloody handprints all over the glass. He started flopping up the beer aisle, coming back toward us.

"Come on, lady," I said. "Shitfire."

He flopped over a bunch of Vienna sausage and Moon Pies, and then he flopped over the crackers and cookies. Blood was pouring out of his head. I looked down at one of the coolers and saw a big piece of black wool sliding down the glass in some blood. He was tracking it all over the store, getting it everywhere.

I knew what the beer cost. It was about six dollars. I didn't wait for a sack. But I watched him for a moment longer. I couldn't take my eyes off him. He flopped over the candy and the little bags of potato chips, and across the front, and flopped across the chicken warmer and the ice cream box and the magazine racks. "*HAAAAAAAAAAAH!*" he said. I put some money up on the counter. Then I went outside.

The guy had shot the whole place up. All the glass in the windows was shattered, and he'd even shot the bricks. He'd even shot the newspaper machines. He'd murdered the hell out of *The Oxford Eagle*.

When I looked back inside, the guy had flopped up against the counter where the woman was hiding, flopping all over the cash register. Sheila wasn't dead or murdered either one.

I asked her, "You all right?" She was down in the floorboard. She looked up at me. She didn't look good.

"I thought you's dead," she screamed. "*OH, GOD, HOW COULD I HAVE BEEN SO FOOLISH?*"

I set the beer on the back seat and got in. "You better git this sumbitch outa here," I said. I reached over and got me a beer. I could hear the sirens coming. They were wailing way off in the distance. She latched onto me.

"*I WOULDN'T LEAVE YOU NOW FOR NOTHIN*," she screamed. "*COULDN'T RUN ME OFF*," she hollered.

"I'm telling you we better get our ass out of here," I said.

"Look out," she screamed. I looked. The wounded black guy was flopping through the door where there wasn't any door anymore. He flopped up beside the car. "*WAAAAAAAAAAAH!*" he said. He was slinging blood all over us. But other than that he seemed harmless.

"What I wanted to say was maybe we should watch more TV together," she said. "If you just didn't write so much. . . ."

The cops screamed into the parking lot. They had their shotguns poking out the windows before they even stopped. Five or six cruisers. Blue uniforms and neat ties and shiny brass. They'd taken their hats off. They had shiny sunglasses. You could tell that they were itching to shoot somebody, now that they'd locked and loaded. The black guy was leaning against the car, heaving. I knew I wouldn't get to finish my beer. I heard them shuck their pumps. I raised my hands and my beer. I pointed to Miss Sheila.

"She did it," I said.

Questions to Consider

1. How would you describe the protagonist of Brown's work?
2. What role does violence play in the story? Why does Brown depict this violence in this manner?

Jayne Anne Phillips

1952–

Jayne Anne Phillips's body of work reflects the ways in which the postmodern Southern family is being redefined. Her fictional examinations of familial relationships; alienation and the self-centered narcissism that may result from it; death, the ways in which families prepare for it, and its aftermath; and the exploration of sexuality and religious ideologies draw upon many of the pervasive themes that influenced writers dating back to the Southern Renascence. Unlike her literary predecessors, Phillips's examination of these issues extends beyond traditional constructions of extended families to include blended and single-parent families. Influenced by the impact of late twentieth-century American culture on long-standing Southern values, Phillips creates scenes that are believable and characters who are humanized by their imperfections.

Phillips hails from Buckhanon, West Virginia, where she was born in 1952. She earned her B.A. from West Virginia University in 1974, experiencing success as a writer and publishing her work prior to completing her degree. Phillips completed an M.F.A. from the University of Iowa in 1978 and has held teaching positions at the University of Iowa, Radcliffe College, Boston University, and Harvard University. In 1996, she was named writer-in-residence at Brandeis University, where she currently teaches.

Phillips's fiction frequently focuses on domestic issues, examining the ways families establish, accept, or reject a collective identity, as well as the ways in which individual family members come to terms with experiences outside of the family. "Because we move around so much," Phillips has said, "families are forced to be immediate; they must stand on their relationships rather than on stereotypes or assumptions or a common history." Phillips's work suggests that the realities of contemporary society require individuals to build lives independent of the types of communities exemplified in the fiction of earlier Southern writers. Despite the pervasive emphasis on family in Southern culture, the postmodern era has witnessed the weakening of the traditional family unit, even in the South. Writers can no longer assume the existence of a familial unit; instead, families are created in unconventional ways. Further, the emphasis on developing a strong sense of self—an individual identity—frequently takes precedence over family obligations in the postmodern era. This reversal, in which the importance of the family becomes secondary to the importance of the self, is an issue that Phillips repeatedly examines in her fiction.

Families in Phillips's fiction tend to be alienated both from each other and from the larger community. This alienation is poignantly demonstrated by the numerous women populating Phillips's fiction who never recover from an early disappointment, and who become "supremely confident, unfulfilled [women who are] vigilant and damaged." These characters function effectively in their day-to-day activities—they nurture children, support them financially, guilt them onto the right path—but they eschew romantic relationships because of unhealed wounds inflicted by early relationships. Phillips's women exemplify the long-standing Southern stereotype of the strong matron who cares for others while keeping nothing for herself. Her works peer beneath the veneer of strength, however, often revealing an irreparably damaged soul. Despite their flaws, Phillips's dysfunctional families band together when external threats loom, intervening to protect children, whether from unworthy interlopers or the perils of war. Even when the effort to avert the impending disaster ultimately fails, support may be found in the bosom of the family, though it may not take the most desirable of forms.

The author of several collections of short stories and three novels, Phillips began winning awards with her earliest work of short fiction, *Sweethearts* (1976), which received the Pushcart Prize and the Fels Award for Fiction. Also to her credit are the short story collections *Black*

Tickets (1979) and *Fast Lanes* (1984). Her novels include the critically acclaimed *Machine Dreams* (1984), which was honored by a *New York Times* best book citation, a National Book Critics Circle Award nomination, and a citation as a Notable Book by the American Library Association. Her second novel, *Shelter* (1994), received high praise for its lush use of language and its adept shifting of narrative perspectives. Most recently, Phillips published her third novel, *MotherKind* (2000), which examines the strength of the bond between mother and daughter, a theme which she returns to often, as in "Home." *MotherKind* demonstrates the ways in which the mother-daughter bond "evolves and transforms as the parent approaches the end of her life." Phillips has been the recipient of two National Endowment for the Arts fellowships, a Guggenheim Fellowship, the Sue Kaufman Prize for First Fiction in 1980, and the Academy Award in Literature in 1997.

Home

I'm afraid Walter Cronkite has had it, says Mom. Roger Mudd always does the news now—how would you like to have a name like that? Walter used to do the conventions and a football game now and then. I mean he would sort of appear, on the sidelines. Didn't he? But you never see him anymore. Lord. Something is going on.

Mom, I say. Maybe he's just resting. He must have made a lot of money by now. Maybe he's tired of talking about elections and mine disasters and the collapse of the franc. Maybe he's in love with a young girl.

He's not the type, says my mother. You can tell *that* much. No, she says, I'm afraid it's cancer.

My mother has her suspicions. She ponders. I have been home with her for two months. I ran out of money and I wasn't in love, so I have come home to my mother. She is an educational administrator. All winter long after work she watches television and knits afghans.

Come home, she said. Save money.

I can't possibly do it, I said. Jesus, I'm twenty-three years old.

Don't be silly, she said. And don't use profanity.

She arranged a job for me in the school system. All day, I tutor children in remedial reading. Sometimes I am so discouraged that I lie on the couch all evening and watch television with her. The shows are all alike. Their laugh tracks are conspicuously similar; I think I recognize a repetition of certain professional laughters. This laughter marks off the half hours.

Finally, I make a rule: I won't watch television at night. I will watch only the news, which ends at 7:30. Then I will go to my room and do God knows what. But I feel sad that she sits there alone, knitting by the lamp. She seldom looks up.

Why don't you ever read anything? I ask.

I do, she says. I read books in my field. I read all day at work, writing those damn proposals. When I come home I want to relax.

Then let's go to the movies.

I don't want to go to the movies. Why should I pay money to be upset or frightened?

But feeling something can teach you. Don't you want to learn anything?

I'm learning all the time, she says.

She keeps knitting. She folds yarn the color of cream, the color of snow. She works it with her long blue needles, piercing, returning, winding. Yarn cascades from her hands in long panels. A pattern appears and disappears. She stops and counts; so many stitches across, so many down. Yes, she is on the right track.

Occasionally I offer to buy my mother a subscription to something mildly informative: *Ms., Rolling Stone, Scientific American*.

I don't want to read that stuff, she says. Just save your money. Did you hear Cronkite last night? Everyone's going to need all they can get.

Often, I need to look at my mother's old photographs. I see her sitting in knee-high grass with a white gardenia in her hair. I see her dressed up as the groom in a mock wedding at a sorority party, her black hair pulled back tight. I see her formally posed in her cadet nurse's uniform. The photographer has painted her lashes too lushly, too long; but her deep red mouth is correct.

The war ended too soon. She didn't finish her training. She came home to nurse only her mother and to meet my father at a dance. She married him in two weeks. It took twenty years to divorce him.

When we traveled to a neighboring town to buy my high school clothes, my mother and I would pass a certain road that turned off the highway and wound to a place I never saw.

There it is, my mother would say. The road to Wonder Bar. That's where I met my Waterloo. I walked in and he said, 'There she is. I'm going to marry that girl.' Ha. He sure saw me coming.

Well, I asked, Why did you marry him?

He was older, she said. He had a job and a car. And Mother was so sick.

My mother doesn't forget her mother.

Never one bedsore, she says. I turned her every fifteen minutes. I kept her skin soft and kept her clean, even to the end.

I imagine my mother at twenty-three; her black hair, her dark eyes, her olive skin and that red lipstick. She is growing lines of tension in her mouth. Her teeth press into her lower lip as she lifts the woman in the bed. The woman weighs no more than a child. She has a smell. My mother fights it continually; bathing her, changing her sheets, carrying her to the bathroom so the smell can be contained and flushed away. My mother will try to protect them both. At night she sleeps in the room on a cot. She struggles awake feeling something press down on her and suck her breath: the smell. When my grandmother can no longer move, my mother fights it alone.

I did all I could, she sighs. And I was glad to do it. I'm glad I don't have to feel guilty.

No one has to feel guilty, I tell her.

And why not? says my mother. There's nothing wrong with guilt. If you are guilty, you should feel guilty.

My mother has often told me that I will be sorry when she is gone.

I think. And read alone at night in my room. I read those books I never read, the old classics, and detective stories. I can get them in the library here. There is only one bookstore; it sells mostly newspapers and *True Confessions* oracles. At Kroger's by the checkout counter I buy a few paperbacks, best sellers, but they are usually bad.

The television drones on downstairs.

I wonder about Walter Cronkite.

When was the last time I saw him? It's true his face was pouchy, his hair thinning. Perhaps he is only cutting it shorter. But he had that look about the eyes—

He was there when they stepped on the moon. He forgot he was on the air and he shouted, 'There . . . there . . . now—We have Contact!' Contact. For those who tuned in late, for the periodic watchers, he repeated: 'One small step . . .'

I was in high school and he was there with the body count. But he said it in such a way that you knew he wanted the war to end. He looked directly at you and said the numbers quietly. Shame, yes, but sorrowful patience, as if all things had passed before his eyes. And he understood that here at home, as well as in starving India, we would pass our next lives as meager cows.

My mother gets *Reader's Digest*. I come home from work, have a cup of coffee, and read it. I keep it beside my bed. I read it when I am too tired to read anything else. I read about Joe's kidney and Humor in Uniform. Always, there are human interest stories in which someone survives an ordeal of primal terror. Tonight it is Grizzly! Two teen-agers camping in the mountains are attacked by a bear. Sharon is dragged over a mile, unconscious. She is a good student loved by her parents, an honest girl loved by her boyfriend. Perhaps she is not a virgin; but in her heart, she is virginal. And she lies now in the furred arms of a beast. The grizzly drags her quietly, quietly. He will care for her all the days of his life . . . Sharon, his rose.

But alas. Already, rescuers have organized. Mercifully, her boyfriend is not among them. He is sleeping en route to the nearest hospital; his broken legs have excused him. In a few days, Sharon will bring him his food on a tray. She is spared. She is not demure. He gazes on her face, untouched but for a long thin scar near her mouth. Sharon says she remembers nothing of the bear. She only knows the tent was ripped open; that its heavy canvas fell across her face.

I turn out my light when I know my mother is sleeping. By then my eyes hurt and the streets of the town are deserted.

My father comes to me in a dream. He kneels beside me, touches my mouth. He turns my face gently toward him.

Let me see, he says. Let me see it.

He is looking for a scar, a sign. He wears only a towel around his waist. He presses himself against my thigh, pretending solicitude. But I know what he is doing; I turn my head in repulsion and stiffen. He smells of a sour musk and his forearms are black with hair. I think to myself, It's been years since he's had an erection—

Finally he stands. Cover yourself, I tell him.

I can't, he says, I'm hard.

On Saturdays I go to the Veterans of Foreign Wars rummage sales. They are held in the drafty basement of a church, rows of collapsible tables piled with objects. Sometimes I think I recognize the possessions of old friends: a class ring, yearbooks, football sweaters with our high school insignia. Would this one have fit Jason?

He used to spread it on the seat of the car on winter nights when we parked by country churches and graveyards. There seemed to be no ground, just water, a rolling, turning, building to a dull pain between my legs.

What's wrong? he said, What is it?

Jason, I can't . . . This pain —

It's only because you're afraid. If you'd let me go ahead —

I'm not afraid of you, I'd do anything for you. But Jason, why does it hurt like this?

We would try. But I couldn't. We made love with our hands. Our bodies were white. Out the window of the car, snow rose up in mounds across the fields. Afterward, he looked at me peacefully, sadly.

I held him and whispered, Soon, soon . . . we'll go away to school.

His sweater. He wore it that night we drove back from the football awards banquet. Jason made All-State but he hated football.

I hate it, he said. So what? he said, that I'm out there puking in the heat? Screaming 'Kill' at a sandbag?

I held his award in my lap, a gold man frozen in midleap. Don't play in college, I said. Refuse the money.

He was driving very slowly.

I can't see, he said, I can't see the edges of the road . . . Tell me if I start to fall off.

Jason, what do you mean?

He insisted I roll down the window and watch the edge. The banks of the road were gradual, sloping off into brush and trees on either side. White lines at the edge glowed up in dips and turns.

We're going to crash, he said.

No, Jason. You've driven this road before. We won't crash.

We're crashing, I know it, he said. Tell me, tell me I'm OK —

Here on the rummage sale table, there are three football sweaters. I see they are all too small to have belonged to Jason. So I buy an old soundtrack, *The Sound of Music*. Air, Austrian mountains. And an old robe to wear in the mornings. It upsets my mother to see me naked; she looks at me so curiously, as though she didn't recognize my body.

I pay for my purchases at the cash register. Behind the desk I glimpse stacks of *Reader's Digests*. The Ladies Auxiliary turns them inside out, stiffens and shellacs them. They make wastebaskets out of them.

I give my mother the record. She is pleased. She hugs me.

Oh, she says, I used to love the musicals. They made me happy. Then she stops and looks at me.

Didn't you do this? she says. Didn't you do this in high school?

Do what?

Your class, she says. You did *The Sound of Music*.

Yes, I guess we did.

What a joke. I was the beautiful countess meant to marry Captain von Trapp before innocent Maria stole his heart. Jason was a threatening Nazi colonel with a bit part. He should have sung the lead but sports practices interfered with rehearsals. Tall, blond, aged in makeup under the lights, he encouraged sympathy for the bad guys and overshadowed the star. He appeared just often enough to make the play ridiculous.

My mother sits in the blue chair my father used for years.

Come quick, she says. Look —

She points to the television. Flickerings of Senate chambers, men in conservative suits. A commentator drones on about tax rebates.

There, says my mother. Hubert Humphrey. Look at him.

It's true. Humphrey is different, changed from his former toady self to a desiccated old man, not unlike the discarded shell of a locust. Now he rasps into the microphone about the people of these great states.

Old Hubert's had it, says my mother. He's a death mask.

That's what he gets for sucking blood for thirty years.

No, she says. No, he's got it too. Look at him! Cancer. Oh.

For God's sake, will you think of something else for once?

I don't know what you mean, she says. She goes on knitting.

All Hubert needs, I tell her, is a good roll in the hay.

You think that's what everyone needs.

Everyone does need it.

They do not. People aren't dogs. I seem to manage perfectly well without it, don't I?

No, I wouldn't say that you do.

Well, I do. I know your mumbo jumbo about sexuality. Sex is for those who are married, and I wouldn't marry again if it was the Lord himself.

Now she is silent. I know what's coming.

Your attitude will make you miserable, she says. One man after another. I just want you to be happy.

I do my best.

That's right, she says. Be sarcastic.

I refuse to answer. I think about my growing bank account. Graduate school, maybe in California. Hawaii. Somewhere beautiful and warm. I will wear few clothes and my skin will feel the air.

What about Jason, says my mother. I was thinking of him the other day.

Our telepathy always frightens me. Telepathy and beyond. Before her hysterectomy, our periods often came on the same day.

If he hadn't had that nervous breakdown, she says softly, do you suppose —

No, I don't suppose.

I wasn't surprised that it happened. When his brother was killed, that was hard. But Jason was so self-centered. You're lucky the two of you split up. He thought everyone was out to get him. Still, poor thing.

Silence. Then she refers in low tones to the few months Jason and I lived together before he was hospitalized.

You shouldn't have done what you did when you went off to college. He lost respect for you.

It wasn't respect for me he lost—He lost his fucking mind if you remember —

I realize I'm shouting. And shaking. What is happening to me?

My mother stares.

We'll not discuss it, she says.

She gets up. I hear her in the bathroom. Water running into the tub. Hydrotherapy. I close my eyes and listen. Soon, this weekend. I'll get a ride to the university a few hours away and look up an old lover. I'm lucky. They always want to sleep with me. For old time's sake.

I turn down the sound of the television and watch its silent pictures. Jason's brother was a musician; he taught Jason to play the pedal steel. A sergeant in uniform delivered the message two weeks before the State Play-Off games. Jason appeared at my mother's kitchen door with the telegram. He looked at me, opened his mouth, backed off wordless in the dark. I pretend I hear his pedal steel; its sweet country whine might make me cry. And I recognize this silent movie—I've seen it four times. Gregory Peck and his submarine crew escape fallout in Australia, but not for long. The cloud is coming. And so they run rampant in auto races and love affairs. But in the end, they close the hatch and put out to sea. They want to go home to die.

Sweetheart? my mother calls from the bathroom. Could you bring me a towel?

Her voice is quavering slightly. She is sorry. But I never know what part of it she is sorry about. I get a towel from the linen closet and open the door of the steamy bathroom. My mother stands in the tub, dripping, shivering a little. She is so small and thin; she is smaller than I. She has two long scars on her belly, operations of the womb, and one breast is misshapen, sunken, indented near the nipple.

I put the towel around her shoulders and my eyes smart. She looks at her breast.

Not too pretty is it, she says. He took out too much when he removed that lump —

Mom, it doesn't look so bad.

I dry her back, her beautiful back which is firm and unblemished. Beautiful, her skin. Again, I feel the pain in my eyes.

But you should have sued the bastard, I tell her. He didn't give a shit about your body.

We have an awkward moment with the towel when I realize I can't touch her any longer. The towel slips down and she catches it as one end dips into the water.

Sweetheart, she says. I know your beliefs are different than mine. But have patience with me. You'll just be here a few more months. And I'll always stand behind you. We'll get along.

She has clutched the towel to her chest. She is so fragile, standing there, naked, with her small shoulders. Suddenly I am horribly frightened.

Sure, I say, I know we will.

I let myself out of the room.

Sunday my mother goes to church alone. Daniel calls me from D.C. He's been living with a lover in Oregon. Now he is back East; she will join him in a few weeks. He is happy, he says. I tell him I'm glad he's found someone who appreciates him.

Come on now, he says. You weren't that bad.

I love Daniel, his white and feminine hands, his thick chestnut hair, his intelligence. And he loves me, though I don't know why. The last few weeks we were together I lay beside him like a piece of wood. I couldn't bear his touch; the moisture his penis left on my hips as he rolled against me. I was cold, cold. I huddled in blankets away from him.

I'm sorry, I said. Daniel, I'm sorry please—what's wrong with me? Tell me you love me anyway . . .

Yes, he said, Of course I do. I always will. I do.

Daniel says he has no car, but he will come by bus. Is there a place for him to stay?

Oh yes, I say. There's a guest room. Bring some Trojans. I'm a hermit with no use for birth control. Daniel, you don't know what it's like here.

I don't care what it's like. I want to see you.

Yes, I say. Daniel, hurry.

When he arrives the next weekend, we sit around the table with my mother and discuss medicine. Daniel was a medic in Vietnam. He smiles at my mother. She is charmed though she has reservations; I see them in her face. But she enjoys having someone else in the house, a presence; a male. Daniel's laughter is low and modulated. He talks softly, smoothly: a dignified radio announcer, an accomplished anchorman.

But when I lived with him, he threw dishes against the wall. And jerked in his sleep, mumbling. And ran out of the house with his hands across his eyes.

After we first made love, he smiled and pulled gently away from me. He put on his shirt and went to the bathroom. I followed and stepped into the shower with him. He faced me, composed, friendly, and frozen. He stood as though guarding something behind him.

Daniel, turn around. I'll soap your back.

I already did.

Then move, I'll stand in the water with you.

He stepped carefully around me.

Daniel, what's wrong? Why won't you turn around?

Why should I?

I'd never seen him with his shirt off. He'd never gone swimming with us, only wading, alone, down Point Reyes Beach. He wore long-sleeved shirts all summer in the California heat.

Daniel, I said, You've been my best friend for months. We could have talked about it.

He stepped backwards, awkwardly, out of the tub and put his shirt on.

I was loading them on copters, he told me. The last one was dead anyway; he was already dead. But I went after him, dragged him in the wind of the blades. Shrapnel and napalm caught my arms, my back. Until I fell, I thought it was the other man's blood in my hands.

They removed most of the shrapnel, did skin grafts for the burns. In three years since, Daniel made love five times; always in the dark. In San Francisco he must take off his shirt for a doctor; tumors have grown in his scars. They bleed through his shirt, round rust-colored spots.

Face-to-face in bed, I tell him I can feel the scars with my fingers. They are small knots on his skin. Not large, not ugly. But he can't let me, he can't let anyone, look: he says he feels wild, like raging, and then he vomits. But maybe, after they remove the tumors—Each time they operate, they reduce the scars.

We spend hours at the veterans' hospital waiting for appointments. Finally they schedule the operation. I watch the black-ringed wall clock, the amputees gliding by in chairs that tick on the linoleum floor. Daniel's doctors curse about lack of supplies; they bandage him with gauze and layers of Band-Aids. But it is all right. I buy some real bandages. Every night I cleanse his back with a sponge and change them.

In my mother's house, Daniel seems different. He has shaved his beard and his face is too young for him. I can only grip his hands.

I show him the house, the antiques, the photographs on the walls. I tell him none of the objects move; they are all cemented in place. Now the bedrooms, my room.

This is it, I say. This is where I kept my Villager sweaters when I was seventeen, and my dried corsages. My cups from the Tastee Freeze labeled with dates and boy's names.

The room is large, blue. Baseboards and wood trim are painted a spotless white. Ruffled curtains, ruffled bedspread. The bed itself is so high one must climb into it. Daniel looks at the walls, their perfect blue and white.

It's a piece of candy, he says.

Yes, I say, hugging him, wanting him.

What about your mother?

She's gone to meet friends for dinner. I don't think she believes what she says, she's only being my mother. It's all right.

We take off our clothes and press close together. But something is wrong. We keep trying. Daniel stays soft in my hands. His mouth is nervous; he seems to gasp at my lips.

He says his lover's name. He says they aren't seeing other people.

But I'm not other people. And I want you to be happy with her.

I know. She knew . . . I'd want to see you.

Then what?

This room, he says. This house. I can't breathe in here.

I tell him we have tomorrow. He'll relax. And it is so good just to see him, a person from my life.

So we only hold each other, rocking.

Later, Daniel asks about my father.

I don't see him, I say. He told me to choose.

Choose what?

Between them.

My father. When he lived in this house, he stayed in the dark with his cigarette. He sat in his blue chair with the lights and television off, smoking. He made little money; he said he was self-employed. He was sick. He grew dizzy when he looked up suddenly. He slept in the basement. All night he sat reading in the bathroom. I'd hear him walking up and down the dark steps at night. I lay in the dark and listened. I believed he would strangle my mother, then walk upstairs and strangle me. I believed we were guilty; we had done something terrible to him.

Daniel wants me to talk.

How could she live with him, I ask. She came home from work and got supper. He ate it, got up and left to sit in his chair. He watched the news. We were always sitting there, looking at his dirty plates. And I wouldn't help her. She should wash them, not me. She should make the money we lived on. I didn't want her house and his ghost with its cigarette burning in the dark like a sore. I didn't want to be guilty. So she did it. She sent me to college; she paid for my safe escape.

Daniel and I go to the Rainbow, a bar and grill on Main Street. We hold hands, play country songs on the jukebox, drink a lot of salted beer. We talk to the barmaid and kiss in the overstuffed booth. Twinkle lights blink on and off above us. I wore my burgundy stretch pants in here when I was twelve. A senior pinched me, then moved his hand slowly across my thigh, mystified, as though erasing the pain.

What about tonight? Daniel asks. Would your mother go out with us? A movie? A bar? He sees me in her, he likes her. He wants to know her.

Then we will have to watch television.

We pop popcorn and watch the late movies. My mother stays up with us, mixing whiskey sours and laughing. She gets a high color in her cheeks and the light in her eyes glimmers up; she is slipping, slipping back and she is beautiful, oh, in her ankle socks, her red mouth and her armor of young girl's common sense. She has a beautiful laughter. She and Daniel end by mock arm wrestling; he pretends defeat and goes upstairs to bed.

My mother hears his door close. He's nice, she says. You've known some nice people, haven't you?

I want to make her back down.

Yes, he's nice, I say. And don't you think he respects me? Don't you think he truly cares for me, even though we've slept together?

He seems to, I don't know. But if you give them that, it costs them nothing to be friends with you.

Why should it cost? The only cost is what you give, and you can tell if someone is giving it back.

How? How can you tell? By going to bed with every man you take a fancy to?

I wish I took a fancy oftener, I tell her. I wish I wanted more. I can be good to a man, but I'm afraid—I can't be physical, not really . . .

You shouldn't.

I should. I want to, for myself as well. I don't think—I've ever had an orgasm.

What? she says, Never? Haven't you felt a sort of building up, and then a dropping off . . . a conclusion? like something's over?

No, I don't think so.

You probably have, she assures me. It's not necessarily an explosion. You were just thinking too hard, you think too much.

But she pauses.

Maybe I don't remember right, she says. It's been years, and in the last years of the marriage I would have died if your father had touched me. But before, I know I felt something. That's partly why I haven't . . . since . . . what if I started wanting it again? Then it would be hell.

But you have to try to get what you want —

No, she says. Not if what you want would ruin everything. And now, anyway. Who would want me?

I stand at Daniel's door. The fear is back; it has followed me upstairs from the dead dark bottom of the house. My hands are shaking. I'm whispering . . . Daniel, don't leave me here.

I go to my room to wait. I must wait all night, or something will come in my sleep. I feel its hands on me now, dragging, pulling. I watch the lit face of the clock: three, four, five. At seven I go to Daniel. He sleeps with his pillow in his arms. The high bed creaks as I get in. Please now, yes . . . he is hard. He always woke with erections . . . inside me he feels good, real, and I tell him no, stop, wait . . . I hold the rubber, stretch its rim away from skin so it smooths on without hurting and fills with him . . . now again, here, yes but quiet, be quiet . . . oh Daniel . . . the bed is making noise . . . yes, no, but be careful, she. . . . We move and turn and I forget about the sounds. We push against each other hard, he is almost there and I am almost with him and just when it is over I think I hear my mother in the room directly under us—But I am half dreaming. I move to get out of bed and Daniel holds me. No, he says, stay.

We sleep and wake to hear the front door slam.

Daniel looks at me.

There's nothing to be done, I say. She's gone to church.

He looks at the clock. I'm going to miss that bus, he says. We put our clothes on fast and Daniel moves to dispose of the rubber—how? the toilet, no, the wastebasket—He drops it in, bends over, retrieves it. Finally he wraps it in a Kleenex and puts it in his pocket. Jesus, he swears. He looks at me and grins. When I start laughing, my eyes are wet.

I take Daniel to the bus station and watch him out of sight. I come back and strip the bed, bundle the sheets in my arms. This pressure in my chest . . . I have to clutch the sheets tight, tighter —

A door clicks shut. I go downstairs to my mother. She refuses to speak or let me near her. She stands by the sink and holds her small square purse with both hands. The fear comes. I hug myself, press my hands against my arms to stop shaking. My mother runs hot water, soap, takes dishes from the drainer. She immerses them, pushes them down, rubbing with a rag in a circular motion.

Those dishes are clean, I tell her. I washed them last night.

She keeps washing. Hot water clouds her glasses, the window in front of us, our faces. We all disappear in steam. I watch the dishes bob and sink. My mother begins to sob. I move close to her and hold her. She smells as she used to smell when I was a child and slept with her.

I heard you, I heard it, she says. Here, in my own house. Please, how much can you expect me to take? I don't know what to do about anything . . .

She looks into the water, keeps looking. And we stand here just like this.

QUESTIONS TO CONSIDER

1. Describe the relationship between the narrator and her mother in "Home." Do these characters communicate effectively? How does their "telepathy," as the narrator calls it, affect their efforts to communicate? Does the absence of a father husband figure in their family unit influence the way they relate to each other?
2. Why is the narrator intrigued by the stories of her mother's past? What does the narrator's seeming ignorance about portions of her mother's past suggest about their relationship? Given what the narrator knows of her mother's values, why does she decide to violate those values at the end of the story?

Julie Kane

1952–

Is it possible for a Yankee to become a Southerner? Julie Ellen Kane was born on 20 July 1952 in Boston, Massachusetts, to Edwin Julian and Nanette Spillane Kane. Although the family's roots were Boston Irish Catholic, Ed Kane's career as a radio and TV newscaster caused the family to move frequently from state to state. Kane's mother was a grade school teacher who published a few short stories in little magazines. From high school in Montclair, New Jersey, Kane went on to study for a B.A. in English at Cornell University in Ithaca, New York. There she took creative writing courses from Southern poets A. R. Ammons and Robert Morgan, as well as from the poet William Matthews. After winning first prize in the 1973 *Mademoiselle* Magazine College Poetry Competition that was judged by her idol, Anne Sexton, and James Merrill, Kane won a scholarship to Boston University to study toward an M.A. in creative writing under Sexton. Sexton's suicide in the fall of 1974, only a few weeks after classes had begun, left Kane deeply shaken. After graduation she went to Exeter, New Hampshire, as the first woman named to the George Bennett Fellowship in Writing at Phillips Exeter Academy. Marrying a Louisiana native, Kane moved to Baton Rouge in 1976 so that her husband could attend law school. Louisiana has been her home ever since, despite the breakup of her marriage.

Working as a grant writer and administrator in a Baton Rouge antipoverty agency, then as a technical writer in New Orleans, Kane continued to write and publish poetry. In 1982 she had a two-woman poetry collection, *Two Into One*, published by a small press in England. Her first full-length book, *Body and Soul*, came out in 1987 from a New Orleans small press, Pirogue. When Harold Pinter's Greville Press published Kane's chapbook, *The Bartender Poems*, in 1991, Pinter introduced Kane at the publication reading held in London's South Bank Centre. That same year, Kane entered the Ph.D. program in literature at Louisiana State University in Baton Rouge. Her dissertation on the villanelle was directed by Southern poet Dave Smith. Since 1999, Kane has taught at Northwestern State University in Natchitoches, Louisiana, and in the spring of 2002 she taught in Vilnius, Lithuania, under a Fulbright Scholarship. Upon her return from Lithuania, she was selected by poet Maxine Kumin as a winner in the 2002 National Poetry Series competition. Two of Kane's poems have been set to music by composer Libby Larsen and recorded on CDs by The American Boychoir and mezzo-soprano Susanne Mentzer, and the literary nonfiction Vietnam memoir that she coauthored with Kiem Do was selected as a History Book Club Featured Alternate.

Much like Southern poet Ellen Voigt, Kane writes about the conflict between fate and free will and the effects of the past upon the present: critic Norman German has suggested that the "mark of Cain" resonates behind her symbolic obsession with scars and tattoos. Also, like many native Southern poets, Kane displays a powerful sense of place in her work, but her vision is always doubled by her status as an outsider. German calls her "Louisiana's petite de Tocqueville, for she surely allows us natives 'to see ourselves as others see us';" and reviewer Glenn Swetman agrees with German that "Kane, with her New England background, is able somehow to look at Louisiana in a way that picks out details a native might miss." Whereas many native Southern poets write of the lost, pastoral South of their childhoods, Kane writes in real time about her adopted homeplace.

Reasons for Loving the Harmonica

Because it isn't harmonious;

Because it gleams like the chrome
on a '57 Chevy's[1] front grille;

Because it fits in a hobo's bandanna;

Because it tolerates spit;
a little spit means the music is fervent;

Because it's easily rigged
to a contraption that frees the human
hands;

Because it's cynical, yet sings;

Because it sings breathing in.

Dead Armadillo Song

I've never seen a live
armadillo, but I drive

Route 90,[1] where the shoulder's
littered with the colder,

deader little critters,
getting stiffer and stiffer.

They seem to have weights
like living room drapes

in their bottoms, for they lie
with their feet to the sky.

By God, there's a lot of 'em,
fat as stuffed ottomans,

World War I tanks snared
in terrorist warfare,

or small coats of armor
whose knights became farmers.

1. Chevrolet automobiles of this time period were lavish in their decorative use of chrome.

1. Vintage highway that runs east-west from Louisiana to Texas.

Kissing the Bartender

The summer we kissed across the bar,
I felt sixteen at thirty-six:
as if you were a movie star

I had a crush on from afar.
My chest was flat, my legs were sticks
the summer we kissed across the bar.

Balancing on the rail was hard.
Spilled beer made my elbows stick.
You could have been a movie star,

backlit, golden, lofting a jar
of juice or Bloody Mary[1] mix
the summer we kissed across the bar.

Over the sink, the limes, as far
as you could lean, you leaned. I kissed
the movie screen, a movie star.

Drinks stayed empty. Ashtrays tarred.
The customers got mighty pissed
the summer we kissed across the bar.
Summer went by like a shooting star.

Ode to the Big Muddy

1

Because I grew up a half hour's drive
from the North Atlantic, always within reach
of the dried-blood-colored cranberry bogs,
the ice bucket water, the desolate beach
with its circular rhythms, I looked down
on linear things, so like an erection
straining against a blue-jeans zipper,
always pushing in the same direction,
spine for brains. But I have learned to mimic,
quick for a girl, the river's predilection.

2

The first time I saw the Mississippi,
under the curving wing of a jet plane,
it lay there listless as a garden slug:
glistening, oozing, brown. Surely Mark Twain's[1]
paddlewheel visions, Hart Crane's[2] hosannas
to the Gulf,[3] Muddy Waters's[4] delta blues
hadn't sprung forth from a drainage canal?

1. A cocktail made from vodka and tomato juice.

1. Pseudonym of Samuel Langhorne Clemens (1835–1910), American novelist who worked as an apprentice riverboat pilot on the Mississippi River.

2. Modernist American poet (1899–1932) who committed suicide by leaping from a ship into the Gulf of Mexico.

3. The Gulf of Mexico, into which the Mississippi River flows.

4. Stage name of McKinley Morganfield (1915–1983), American blues singer from the delta region of Mississippi.

"Fasten your seatbelts for descent into
New Orleans. Looking to the left, you'll see
the Mississippi River"—so it was true.

3

Unlike the ocean, the river's life is
right on the surface, bobbing there like turds:
a load of tourists on the Delta Queen[5]
drunkenly singing half-remembered words
to showtunes played on steam calliope;
the push-boats nudging at oil tankers;
and nothing underneath but chicken necks
in crawfish nets, and our own dropped anchors.
The sea is our collective unconscious;
the river our blank slate, growing blanker.

4

And yet the river gathers memories:
the ugliest things grow numinous
over time—the trail of a garden slug
crystalline, opaline, luminous
when the garden slug itself has gone
as the river itself will one day go,
already trying to change its course—
an afternoon we watched the ferryboat
go back and forth until the sun went down,
skimming the water like a skipping stone.

5

Or the morning we gave back Everette's[6] ashes:
homeless alcoholic poet-prince.
A cold March wind was ruffling the water.
Wouldn't you know, the ashes wouldn't sink;
so someone jumped in to wrestle them under.
It hit me then: I didn't want to die.
And so I made a choice, against my nature,
to throw my lot in with that moving line:
abstract, rational, conscious, sober—
cutting a path through human time.

Questions to Consider

1. What features or associations of the harmonica (both those named in "Reasons for Loving the Harmonica" and those you can think of) make it a "Southern" rather than a "Northern" instrument?
2. Contrast Kane's use of sea imagery with her use of river imagery in the poem "Ode to the Big Muddy."

5. The last original Mississippi River steamboat still operating, built in 1926.

6. New Orleans poet Everette Hawthorne Maddox (1944–1989).

Jill McCorkle

1958–

Considered one of the finest young writers of the contemporary era, Jill McCorkle made American publishing history when her first two novels were published simultaneously. *The Cheerleader* and *July 7th* were each published by Algonquin Press of Chapel Hill in 1992. Such a bold move by an American publisher was unprecedented, and especially impressive given McCorkle's status as a thoroughly unknown writer. Her obvious talent, however, made the founder of the fledgling Algonquin Press, which was established in part to provide a venue for the works of new Southern voices, willing to kick-start her career with what critic S. Keith Graham called the "literary equivalent of a rebel yell."

The author of five novels and three collections of short stories to date, Jill McCorkle has remained close to her North Carolina roots. A native of Lumberton, North Carolina, she is the daughter of John Wesley McCorkle, a postal worker, and Melba Collins McCorkle, a medical secretary. McCorkle attended the local high school, where she was a cheerleader, an honor student, and the homecoming queen, yet she found time to be the son her father always wanted, going fishing with him and listening to his stories.

McCorkle earned her undergraduate degree from the University of North Carolina at Chapel Hill, but at first, she was overwhelmed by the university environment. She tells critic Barbara Bennett of feeling "somewhat invisible in huge undergraduate classes," a feeling that was doubtlessly intensified by comparison to her experiences in a small-town high school. She began enrolling in creative writing courses during her second year at UNC, quickly becoming a member of a community of writers and winning the first of many literary awards that she would receive during her career.

McCorkle's parents grew up together in Lumberton, and similarly, McCorkle's first marriage was to a hometown boy, Steven Alexander, whom she married after earning her master's degree from Hollins College in Roanoke, Virginia. The couple moved to Florida, where McCorkle taught junior high school and worked as a librarian. During this period, she finished her first novel, *The Cheerleader*, and sent it to graduate school friend and fellow writer Lee Smith. Smith suggested that McCorkle place the manuscript with her own agent, who shortly secured a contract to publish the novel. Before *The Cheerleader* appeared, however, McCorkle finished *July 7th*, and Louis D. Rubin, the founder of Algonquin, was so impressed with her newest effort that he agreed to publish it simultaneously with *The Cheerleader*.

Following the dissolution of her marriage to Alexander, McCorkle moved back to Chapel Hill, eventually securing teaching positions at UNC and Duke University. She continued to write, and her third novel, *Tending to Virginia*, appeared in 1987. Two additional novels, *Ferris Beach* (1990) and *Carolina Moon* (1996), as well as three collections of short stories, *Crash Diet* (1992), from which the selection in this volume is taken, *Final Vinyl Days* (1998), and *Creatures of Habit* (2001) have continued to appear at regular intervals. In addition to writing, she has held lectureships at institutions including Tufts, Harvard, and Bennington College. She is presently married to physician Daniel Shapiro; they have two children.

McCorkle cites a variety of influences on her writing style that range from Mark Twain, Zora Neale Hurston, Flannery O'Connor, and Eudora Welty to biographical writings such as *The Diary of Anne Frank* and *The Story of Helen Keller*. Her development as a writer was shaped by the oral narratives that she heard from her father and grandmother, and she has enjoyed the guidance of other writers, as well. McCorkle was a student in the first creative writing class taught by fellow Southerner Lee Smith, who enjoys a well-earned literary reputation in her own right.

McCorkle is representative of what contemporary critics identify as the third generation of Southern writers. Rather than drawing from a "collective southern consciousness," writers of this third generation tend to be influenced by the fact that their history "may go no further back than to the Civil Rights era, to the Vietnam War, or to the memories of a southern childhood" rather than to the influences of earlier generations of Southern writers who suffered under the burden of resolving, or at least explaining, the rise and demise of an overromanticized way of life. McCorkle's storytelling engages personal history more than regional history, and accordingly, Barbara Bennett points out that her characters "tell stories of a region no longer burdened by the past, but rather one that is grappling with the problems found in average homes within ordinary families."

McCorkle frequently makes use of the *bildungsroman* (coming of age) novel form, focusing on the complexities of finding fulfillment in light of the expectations placed on Southern women. McCorkle's fiction probes issues that affect women of all ages, often revealing the search for what Bennett has termed "love in its true form." While her female characters seek—and sometimes believe that they have found—ideal love, they learn the nature and value of real love: love for self, platonic love for other women, and the romantic love that many of her characters seek, grapple with, and, as often as not, lose. "Crash Diet" aptly illustrates these struggles from the perspective of a newly separated woman who fluctuates between despair because her husband has left her and excitement over the new possibilities that are open to her as a single woman. The multifaceted nature of contemporary femininity has intrigued McCorkle throughout her literary career.

Childhood experiences with natural storytellers such as her grandmother have contributed to McCorkle's "keen sense of language," which has been repeatedly praised by critics. The voices of generations of Southern storytellers, and the strong oral traditions that they represent, echo through her works. The resulting voice, suggests Bennett, "marks McCorkle's stories as strongly southern." McCorkle does not stray far from the region that has shaped both her storytelling and her voice—a voice with a distinctly Southern accent.

Crash Diet

Kenneth left me on a Monday morning before I'd even had the chance to mousse my hair, and I just stood there at the picture window with the drapes swung back and watched him get into that flashy red Mazda, which I didn't want him to get anyway, and drive away down Marnier Street, and make a right onto Seagrams. That's another thing I didn't want, to live in a subdivision where all the streets are named after some kind of liquor. But Kenneth thought that was cute because he runs a bartending school, which is where he met Lydia to begin with.

"I'll come back for the rest of my things," he said, and I wondered just what he meant by that. What was his and what was mine?

"Where are you going to live, in a pup tent?" I asked and took the towel off of my head. I have the kind of hair that will dry right into big clumps of frosted-looking thread if I don't comb it out fast. Once, well before I met Kenneth at the Holiday Inn lounge where he was giving drink-mixing lessons to the staff, I wrote a personal ad and described myself as having angel hair, knowing full well that whoever read it would picture flowing blond curls, when what I really meant was the stuff that you put on a Christmas tree or use to insulate your house. I also said I was average size, which at the time I was.

"I'm moving in with Lydia," he said in his snappy, matter-of-fact way, like I had just trespassed on his farmland. Lydia. It had been going on for a year and a half though I had only known of it for six weeks. *LYDIA*, a name so old-sounding even my grandmother wouldn't have touched it.

"Well, give her my best," I said like you might say to a child who is threatening to run away from home. "Send me a postcard," I said and laughed, though I already felt myself nearing a crack, like I might fall right into it, a big dark crack, me and five years of Kenneth and liquor streets and the microwave oven that I'd just bought to celebrate our five years of marriage and the fact that I had finally started losing some of the weight that I had put on during the first two years.

"Why did you do this?" he asked when he came home that day smelling of coconut because he had been teaching pina coladas, and approached that microwave oven that I had tied up in red ribbon.

"It's our anniversary," I said and told him that he was making me so hungry for macaroons or those Hostess Snoballs with all that pink coconut. I'd lost thirty pounds by that time and needed to lose only ten more and they were going to take my "after" picture and put me on the wall of the Diet Center along with all the other warriors (that's what they called us) who had conquered fat.

"But this is a big investment," Kenneth said and picked up the warranty. Five years, and he stared at that like it had struck some chord in his brain that was high-pitched and off-key. Five years, that's how long it had been since we honeymooned down at Sea Island, Georgia, and drank daiquiris that Kenneth said didn't have enough rum and ate all kinds of wonderful food that Kenneth didn't monitor going down my throat like he came to do later.

"Well, sure it's an investment," I told him. "Like a marriage."

"Guaranteed for five years," he said and then got all choked up, tried to talk but cried instead, and I knew something wasn't right. I sat up half the night waiting for him to say something. *Happy anniversary*, *You sure do look good these days*, anything. It must have been about two A.M. when I got out of him the name Lydia, and I didn't do a thing but get up and out of that bed and start working on the mold that wedges in between those tiles in the shower stall. That's what I do when I get upset because it's hard to eat while scrubbing and because there's always mold to be found if you look for it.

"You'll have to cross that bridge when you come to it," my mama always said, and when I saw Kenneth make that right turn onto Seagrams, I knew I was crossing it right then. I had two choices: I could go back to bed or I could do something. I have never been one to climb back into the bed after it's been made, so I got busy. I moussed my hair and got dressed, and I went to my pocketbook and got out the title to that Mazda that had both our names on it. I poured a glass of wine, since it was summer vacation from teaching sixth grade, painted my toenails, and then, in the most careful way, I wrote in Kenneth's handwriting that I (Kenneth I. Barkley) gave full ownership of the Mazda to Sandra White Barkley, and then I signed his name. Even Kenneth couldn't have told that it wasn't his signature; that's just how well I forged. I finished my wine, got dressed, and went over to my friend Paula's house to get it notarized.

"Why are you doing this?" Paula asked me. She was standing there in her bathrobe, and I could hear some movement in the back where her bedroom was. I didn't know if she meant why was I stopping by her house unannounced or why I was changing the title on the car. I know it's rude to stop by a person's house unannounced and hated to admit I had done it, so I just focused on the title. Sometimes I can focus so well on things and other times I can't at all.

"Kenneth and I are separating and I get the Mazda," I told her.

"When did this happen?" Paula asked, and glanced over her shoulder to that cracked bedroom door.

"About two hours ago," I told her and sat down on the sofa. Paula just kept standing there like she didn't know what to do, like she could have killed me for just coming in and having a seat in the middle of her activities, but I didn't focus on that. "Just put your stamp on it and I'll be going." I held that title and piece of paper out to her, and she stared down at it and shook her head back and forth. "Did Kenneth write this?" she asked me, like my reputation might not be the best.

"Haven't I been through enough this morning?" I asked her and worked some tears into my eyes. "What kind of friend questions such a thing?"

"I'm sorry, Sandra," she said, her face as pink as her bathrobe. "I have to ask this sort of thing. I'll be right back." She went down the hall to her bedroom, and I got some candy corn out of her little dish shaped like a duck or something in that family. I wedged the large ends up and over my front teeth so I had fangs like little kids always do at Halloween.

"Who was that?" I heard a man say, frustrated. I could hear frustration in every syllable that carried out there to the living room, and then Paula said, "Shhh." When she came back with her little embosser, I had both front teeth covered in candy corn and grinned at her. She didn't laugh so I took them off my teeth and laid them on her coffee table. I don't eat sweets.

"I'm sorry I can't talk right now," Paula said. "You see . . ."

"What big eyes you have," I said and took my notarized paper right out of her hand. "Honey, go for it," I told her and pointed down the hall. "I'm doing just fine."

"I feel so guilty, though," Paula said, her hair all flat on one side from sleeping that way. "I feel like maybe you need to talk to somebody." That's what people always say when they feel like they should do something but have no intention of doing it, *I feel so bad,* or *If only*. I just laughed and told Paula I had to go to Motor Vehicles and take care of a piece of business and then I had to go to the police station and report a stolen car.

"What?" Paula asked, and her mouth fell open and she didn't even look over her shoulder when there were several frustrated and impatient knocks on her bedroom wall. "That's illegal."

"And you're my accomplice," I told her and walked on down the sidewalk and got into that old Ford Galaxy, which still smelled like the apples that Kenneth's granddaddy used to keep in it to combat his cigar smoke. If there'd been a twenty-year-old apple to be found rolling around there under the front seat, I would've eaten it.

I didn't report the car, though. By the time I had driven by Lydia's house fourteen times—the first four of which the Mazda was out front and the other ten parked two blocks away behind the fish market (hidden, they thought)—I was too tired to talk to anybody so I just went home to bed. By ten o'clock, I'd had a full night's sleep so I got up, thawed some hamburger in the microwave, and made three pans of lasagna, which I then froze because mozzarella is not on my diet.

The next day, I was thinking about going to the grocery store because I didn't have a carrot in the house, but it was as if my blood was so slow I couldn't even put on a pair of socks. I felt like I had taken a handful of Valium but I hadn't. I checked the bottle there at the back of the medicine cabinet that was prescribed for Kenneth when he pulled his back lifting a case of Kahlúa about a year ago. The bottle was there with not a pill touched, so I didn't have an excuse to be found for this heaviness. "When you feel heavy, exercise!" we warriors say, so before my head could be turned toward something like cinnamon toast, I got dressed and did my Jane Fonda routine twice, scrubbed the gasoline spots from the driveway, and then drove to the

Piggly Wiggly for some carrots. It felt good being in the car with the radio going, so I didn't get out at the Piggly Wiggly but kept driving. I had never seen that rotating bar that is in a motel over in Clemmonsville, so I went there. It was not nearly as nice as Kenneth had made it sound; I couldn't even tell that I was moving at all, so I rode the glass elevator twice, and then checked into the motel across the street. It was a motel like I'd never seen, electric finger massages for a quarter and piped-in reggae. I liked it so much I stayed a week and ate coleslaw from Kentucky Fried Chicken. When I got home, I bought some carrots at the Piggly Wiggly.

"I was so worried about you!" my buddy Martha from the Diet Center said, and ran into my house. Martha is having a long hard time getting rid of her excess. "I was afraid you were binging."

"No, just took a little trip for my nerves," I told her, and she stood with her mouth wide open like she had seen Frankenstein. "Kenneth and I have split." Martha's mouth was still hanging open, which is part of her problem: oral, she's an oral person.

"Look at you," Martha said, and put her hands on my hips, squeezed on my bones there, love handles they're sometimes called if you've got somebody who loves them. "You've lost, Sandra."

"Well, Kenneth and I weren't right for each other, I guess."

"The hell with Kenneth," Martha said, her eyes filling with tears. "You've lost more weight." Martha shook my hips until my teeth rattled. She is one of those people who her whole life has been told she has a pretty face. And she does, but it makes her mad for people to say it because she knows what they mean is that she's fat, and to ignore that fact they say what a pretty face she has. Anybody who's ever been overweight has had this happen. "I'm going to miss you at the meetings," Martha said, and looked like she was going to cry again. Martha is only thirty, just five years younger than me, but she looks older; the word is *matronly*, and it has a lot to do with the kind of clothes you have to wear if you're overweight. The mall here doesn't have an oversize shop.

I went to the beauty parlor and told them I wanted the works—treatments, facials, haircut, new shampoo, mousse, spray, curling wand. I spent a hundred and fifty dollars there, and then I went to Revco and bought every color of nail polish that they had, four different new colognes because they each represented a different mood, five boxes of Calgon in case I didn't get back to Revco for a while, all the Hawaiian Tropic products, including a sun visor and beach towel. I bought a hibachi and three bags of charcoal, a hammock, some barbecue tongs, an apron that says KISS THE COOK, and one of those inflatable pools so I could stretch out in the backyard in some water. I bought one of those rafts that will hold a canned drink in a little pocket, in case I should decide to walk down to the pool in our subdivision over on Tequila Circle. Summer was well under way, and I had to catch up on things. I bought a garden hose and a hoe and a rake, thinking I might relandscape my yard even though the subdivision doesn't really like you to take nature into your own hands. I had my mind on weeping willows and crepe myrtle. I went ahead and bought fifteen azaleas while I was there, some gardening gloves, and some rubber shoes for working in the yard. Comet was on sale so I went ahead and got twenty cans. I bought a set of dishes (four place settings) because Kenneth had come and taken mine while I was in Clemmonsville; I guess Lydia didn't have any dishes. Then I thought that wouldn't be enough if I should have company, so I got two more sets so that I'd have twelve place settings. I figured if I was to have more than twelve people for dinner then I'd need not only a new dining-room set but also a new dining room. I didn't have any place mats that matched those dishes so I picked up some and some glasses that matched the blue border on my new plates and some stainless because I had always loved that pattern with the pistol handle on the knife.

They had everything in this Revco. I thought if I couldn't sleep at night I'd make an afghan, so I picked out some pretty yarn, and then I thought, well, if I was going to start making afghans at night, I could get ahead on my Christmas shopping, and so I'd make an afghan for my mama and one for Paula, who had been calling me on the phone non-stop to make sure I hadn't reported the stolen car, and one for Martha that I'd make a little bigger than normal, which made me think that I hadn't been to the Diet Center in so long I didn't even know my weight, so I went and found the digital scales and put one right on top of my seventy-nine skeins of yarn. I bought ten each of Candy Pink, Watermelon, Cocoa, Almond, Wine, Cinnamon, Lime, and only nine of the Cherry because the dye lot ran out. It made me hungry, so I got some dietetic bonbons. By the time I got to the checkout I had five carts full and when that young girl looked at me and handed me the tape that was over a yard long, I handed her Kenneth I. Barkley's MasterCard and said, "Charge it."

It was too hot to work in the yard, and I was too tired to crochet or unpack the car and felt kind of sick to my stomach. Thinking it was from the bonbon I ate on the way home, I went to the bathroom to get an Alka-Seltzer, but Kenneth had taken those too, so I just took two Valiums and went to bed.

"I feel like a yo-yo," I told the shrink when Paula suggested that I go. All of my clothes were way too big, so I had given them to Martha as an incentive for her to lose some weight and had ordered myself a whole new wardrobe from Neiman-Marcus on Kenneth I. Barkley's MasterCard number. That's why I had to wear my KISS THE COOK apron and my leotard and tights to the shrink's. "My clothes should be here any day now," I told him, and he smiled.

"No, I feel like a yo-yo, not a regular yo-yo either," I said. "I feel like one of those advanced yo-yos, the butterfly model, you know where the halves are turned facing outward and you can do all those tricks like 'walk the dog,' 'around the world,' and 'eat spaghetti.' " He laughed, just threw back his head and laughed, so tickled over "eat spaghetti"; laughing at the expense of another human being, laughing when he was going to charge me close to a hundred dollars for that visit that I was going to pay for with a check from my dual checkbook, which was what was left of Kenneth I. Barkley's account over at Carolina Trust. I had already taken most of the money out of that account and moved it over to State Employee's Credit Union. That man tried to be serious, but every time I opened my mouth, it seemed he laughed.

But I didn't care because I hadn't had so much fun since Kenneth and I ate a half-gallon of rocky-road ice cream in our room there in Sea Island, Georgia.

"Have you done anything unusual lately?" he asked. "You know, like going for long rides, spending lots of money?"

"No," I said and noticed that I had a run in my tights. After that, I couldn't think of a thing but runs and running. I wanted to train for the Boston Marathon. I knew I'd win if I entered.

* * *

Lydia was ten years younger than Kenneth, I had found that out during the six weeks when he fluctuated between snappy and choked up. That's what I knew of her, ten years younger than Kenneth and studying to be a barmaid, and that's why I rolled the trees in the yard of that pitiful-looking house she rented with eleven rolls of decorator toilet paper. My new clothes had come by then so I wore my black silk dress with the ruffled off-the-shoulder look. Lydia is thirteen years younger than me and, from what I could tell of her shadow in the window, about twenty pounds heavier. I was a twig by then. "I'd rather be an old man's darlin' than a young man's slave," my mama told me just before I got married, and I said, "You mind your own damn business." Lydia's mama had probably told her the same thing, and you can't trust a person who listens to her mama.

I stood there under a tree and hoisted roll after roll of the decorator toilet paper into the air and let it drape over branches. I wrapped it in and out of that wrought-iron rail along her steps and tied a great big bow. I was behind the shrubs, there where it was dark, when the front door opened and I heard her say, "I could have sworn I heard something," and then she said, "Just look at this mess!" She was turning to get Kenneth so I got on my stomach and slid along the edge of the house and hid by the corner. I got my dress covered with mud and pine straw, but I didn't really care because I liked the dress so much when I saw it there in the book that I ordered two. The porch light came on, and then she was out in that front yard with her hands on her hips and the ugliest head of hair I'd ever seen, red algae hair that looked like it hadn't been brushed in four years. "When is *she* going to leave us alone?" Lydia asked, and looked at Kenneth, who was standing there with what looked like a tequila sunrise in his hand. He looked terrible. "You've got to do something!" Lydia said, and started crying. "You better call your lawyer right now. She's already spent all your money."

"I'll call Sandra tomorrow," Kenneth said, and put his arm around Lydia, but she wasn't having any part of that. She twisted away and slapped his drink to the dirt.

"Call *her?*" Lydia screamed, and I wished I had my camera to catch her expression right when she was beginning to say "her"; that new camera of mine could catch anything. "What good is that going to do?"

"Maybe I can settle it all," he said. "I'm the one who left her. If it goes to court, she'll get everything."

"She already has," Lydia said, sat down in the yard, and blew her nose on some of that decorator toilet paper. "The house, the money. She has taken everything except the Mazda."

"I got the dishes," he said. "I got the TV and the stereo."

"I don't know why you didn't take your share when you had the chance," Lydia said. "I mean, you could've taken the microwave and the silver or something."

"It's going to be fine, honey," Kenneth said, and pulled her up from the dirt. "We've got each other."

"Yes," Lydia nodded, but I couldn't help but feel sorry for her, being about ten pounds too heavy for her own good. I waited until they were back inside before I finished the yard, and then walked over behind the fish market where I had parked the car. There wasn't much room in the car because I had six loads of laundry that I'd been meaning to take to the subdivision Laundromat to dry. Kenneth had bought me a washer but not a dryer, and I should have bought one myself but I hadn't; the clothes had mildewed something awful.

Not long after that all my friends at the Diet Center took my picture to use as an example of what not to let happen to yourself. They said I had gone overboard and needed to gain a little weight for my own health. I was too tired to argue with Martha, aside from the fact that she was five times bigger than me, and I just let her drive me to the hospital. I checked in as Lydia Barkley, and since I didn't know how Lydia's handwriting looked, I used my best Kenneth imitation. "Her name is Sandra," Martha told the woman, but nobody yelled at me. They just put me in a bed and gave me some dinner in my vein and knocked me out. As overweight as I had been, I had never eaten in my sleep. It was a first, and when I woke up, the shrink was there asking me what I was, on a scale of one to ten. "Oh, four," I told him. It seemed like I was there a long time. Paula came and did my nails and hair, and Martha came and confessed that she had eaten three boxes of chocolate-covered cherries over the last week. She brought me a fourth. She said that if she had a husband, she'd get a divorce, that's how desperate she was to lose some weight, but that she'd stop before she got as thin as me. I told her I'd rather eat a case of chocolate-covered cherries than go through it again.

My mama came, and she said, "I always knew this would happen." She shook her head like she couldn't stand to look at me. "A man whose business in life depends on others taking to the bottle is no kind of man to choose for a mate." I told her to mind her own damn business, and when she left, she took my box of chocolate-covered cherries and told me that sweets were not good for a person.

By the time I got out of the hospital, I was feeling much better. Kenneth stopped by for me to sign the divorce papers right before it was time for my dinner party. His timing had never been good. There I was in my black silk dress with the table set for twelve, the lasagna getting ready to be thawed and cooked in the microwave.

"Looks like you're having a party," he said, and stared at me with that same look he always had before he got choked up. I just nodded and filled my candy dish with almonds. "I'm sorry for all the trouble I caused you," he said. "I didn't know how sick you were." And I noticed he was taking me in from head to toe. "You sure look great now."

"Well, I'm feeling good, Kenneth," I told him and took the papers from his hand.

"I'm not with Lydia anymore," he said, but I focused instead on signing my name, my real name, in my own handwriting, which if it was analyzed would be the script of a fat person. Some things you just can't shake; part of me will always be a fat person and part of Kenneth will always be gutter slime. He had forgotten that when he *had* me he hadn't wanted me, and I had just about forgotten how much fun we'd had eating that half-gallon of ice cream in bed on our honeymoon.

"Well, send me a postcard," I told him when I opened the front door to see Martha coming down the walk in one of my old dresses that she was finally able to wear. And then came Paula and the man she kept in her bedroom, and my mama, who I had sternly instructed not to open her mouth if she couldn't be pleasant, my beautician, the manager of Revco, my shrink, who, after I had stopped seeing him on a professional basis, had called and asked me out to lunch. They were all in the living room, mingling and mixing drinks; I stood there with the curtains pulled back and watched Kenneth get in that Mazda that was in my name and drive down Marnier and take a left onto Seagrams. Summer was almost over, and I couldn't wait for the weather to turn cool so that I could stop working in the yard.

"I want to see you do 'eat spaghetti,'" my shrink, who by then had told me to call him Alan, said and pulled a butterfly yo-yo like I hadn't seen in years from his pocket. I did it; I did it just as well as if I were still in the seventh grade, and my mama hid her face in embarrassment while everybody else got a good laugh. Of course, I'm not one to overreact or to carry a situation on and on, and so when they begged for more tricks, I declined. I had plenty of salad on hand for my friends who were dieting so they wouldn't have seconds on lasagna, and while I was fixing the coffee, Alan came up behind me, grabbed my love handles, and said, "On a scale of one to ten, you're a two thousand and one." I laughed and patted his hand because I guess I was still focused on Kenneth and where was he going to stay, in a pup tent? Some things never change, and while everybody was getting ready to go and still chatting, I went to my bedroom and turned my alarm clock upside down, which would remind me when it went off the next day to return the title to Kenneth's name and to maybe write him a little check to help with that MasterCard bill.

I could tell that Alan wanted to linger, but so did my mama and so I had to make a choice. I told Alan it was getting a little late and that I hoped to see him real soon, *socially*, I stressed. He kissed me on the cheek and squeezed my hip in a way that made me get gooseflesh and also made me feel sorry for both Kenneth and Lydia all at the same time. "A divorce can do strange things to a person," Alan had told me on my last visit; the man knew his business. He was cute, too.

"It was a nice party, Sandra," my mama said after everybody left. "Maybe a little too much oregano in the lasagna. You're a tad too thin still, and I just wonder what that man who calls himself a psychiatrist has on his mind."

"Look before you leap," I told her, and gave her seventy-nine skeins of yarn in the most hideous colors that I no longer had room for in my closet. "A bird in the hand is worth two in the bush."

"That's no way to talk to your mother," she said. "It's not my fault that you were overweight your whole life. It's not my fault your husband left you for a redheaded bar tramp."

"Well, send me a postcard," I said and closed the door, letting out every bit of breath that I'd held inside my whole life. I washed those dishes in a flash, and when I got in my bed, I was feeling so sorry for Kenneth, who had no birds in his hand, and sorry for Mama, who would never use up all that yarn. I hurried through those thoughts because my eyelids were getting so heavy and I wanted my last thought of the night to be of Alan, first with the yo-yo and then grabbing my hipbone. When you think about it, if your hipbones have been hidden for years and years, it's a real pleasure to have someone find them, grab hold, and hang on. You can do okay in this world if you can just find something worth holding on to.

QUESTIONS TO CONSIDER

1. In what ways does the narrator of "Crash Diet" cope with the pain of losing her husband to another woman? How do her strategies reflect contemporary relationships? How do the narrator's coping strategies differ from those of her mama, who always said, "You'll have to cross that bridge when you come to it"?
2. The narrator frequently tells people in her life to send her a postcard. Is it significant that she returns to this catch phrase with some regularity? Why or why not?

Kaye Gibbons
1960–

Kaye Gibbons hails from inauspicious literary origins, having spent much of her youth in the clutches of "various bizarre, kleptomaniac, hypochondriac, pathological-liar, sociopath relatives." From her struggles with familial difficulties and mental illness emerged a prolific Southern writer whose fiction has garnered extensive praise from critics and gained national recognition through lengthy stints on the best-seller list. Much of Gibbons's fiction derives from her experience growing up in rural North Carolina, which provides the setting of her novels. She writes of women's efforts to become self-reliant despite the restrictive nature of Southern culture—of their efforts to make order from emotional chaos, efforts made somewhat ironic by the inherent order of traditional Southern society—and this theme illustrates the importance of communal support in the development of female voices and independence. Gibbons's fiction also demonstrates the strength that women draw from their familial histories and from passing their oral histories on to the generations that follow them. Her stories are strongly influenced by Southern folk traditions, demonstrating the significance of folk healing methods and foodways, as well as the communal nature of oral narrative traditions.

Bertha Kaye Batts Gibbons was born on 5 May 1960 in the small rural community of Bend of the River in Nash County, North Carolina. Her father, Charles Batts, was a tobacco farmer, and her mother, Alice, was a homemaker. Gibbons and her siblings, a brother 13 years her senior, and a sister 9 years older, are descendants of the first permanent White settler in North Carolina, Nathaniel Batts. Gibbons grew up in a poor family, residing in a frame farmhouse. According to journalist Julian Mason, Alice Batts provided "order and stability through perseverance and hard work," serving as a role model to her young daughter. Gibbons's childhood came to an abrupt end, however, with her mother's suicide in March, 1970, when Kaye was not quite 10 years old. After staying on with her abusive, alcoholic father for a brief period, Gibbons went to live with her mother's sister, but quickly found this arrangement untenable, as well. After bouncing among relatives for several years, she finally found a stable home with her older sibling. Gibbons learned at a young age that her family's lack of financial means placed her at a social disadvantage in the hierarchical South, and many of her protagonists suffer from the prejudice and disdain inherent in this system.

Gibbons attended the University of North Carolina, where she studied creative writing. During her time at UNC, her first novel, *Ellen Foster*, was conceived, based in large part on her adolescent experiences. The novel was later published by Algonquin Press in 1987. Gibbons has continued to produce high-quality, award-winning fiction since that time, despite her ongoing struggle with manic-depressive disorder. In interviews, she has credited many of her creative bursts to her illness, describing writing sessions which have lasted 40 to 60 hours at a stretch. After divorcing her first husband and spending some time in New York City, Gibbons returned to Raleigh, North Carolina, where she presently lives with her husband, attorney Frank Ward, her three daughters, and her two step-children.

Gibbons's novels examine the conflicts that women face in their marital relationships, as well as the strong bonds that develop between mothers and daughters, especially when male–female relationships are unsatisfying. She relates these stories from a variety of perspectives and voices, demonstrating the consequences that befall women who enter into marriages with the wrong men. Sadly, many of her women do choose the wrong men—those who come from the lower social classes or who are emotionally closed, and accordingly, fail to engage in the fulfilling relationships that their wives crave. Gibbons explodes the myths of the Southern belle and the tireless matron, while retaining characteristics of those myths that continue to hold sway in the region.

Gibbons's novels do not degenerate into pitiful examinations of the state of women's lives, however, but instead, they demonstrate the ways in which they find contentment after they have "privately withdrawn their affections" from their husbands. Gibbons's women find their purposes through their relationships with other women and by building fulfilling lives with the tools at hand. They do not bemoan the results of their poor choices, but instead learn to live with them and to take happiness wherever they find it.

Gibbons's body of work includes six novels, which have been afforded extensive critical and popular acclaim. *Ellen Foster* won the coveted Sue Kaufman Prize for First Fiction, and she has also been the recipient of a National Endowment for the Arts fellowship. Gibbons is a significant voice in Southern letters because of ways in which she represents Southern womanhood and the expectations implicit in its construction. Her characters are realistically drawn, demonstrating the inconsistencies inherent in the cultural mores that to a large extent continue to govern women's behavior. The tightly knit groups of women that Gibbons creates in her novels, whether familial or community-based, illustrate the ways in which women may learn to control their own destinies and to overcome the confines of the Southern social code. The excerpt from *Charms for the Easy Life* included here introduces a family of women who support each other despite their differences. Gibbons's body of work celebrates what Julian Mason has termed "the perseverance of the human spirit" as it redefines the shape of women's lives.

from Charms for the Easy Life

Mr. Baines was glory in my mother's life. He came to our house almost every night for dinner, always showing up in one of his beautiful suits, his straight white teeth gleaming, giddy as a forty-year-old man could be without appearing drunk, retarded, or foolish. After dinner he would sit on the sofa with his arm around my mother's shoulders and talk about places he wanted to take her. He compiled such a long list that after a while I worried that the plans would never materialize. My grandmother noticed this as well, and asked my mother several times, "Well, where'd he take you tonight?" They were never grand places, and his attitude was not that of a self-satisfied traveler who wanted to impress this homebound woman with how much he'd seen of the world. He wanted to take her to Middleton Plantation in Charleston to show her the ancient live oak tree because she'd look so pretty standing next to it in a picture. He wanted to take her to Cypress Gardens because she'd look radiant in the light. He wanted to take her to the Homestead resort because she deserved to be pampered.

The first place they went together was Charlotte. Mr. Baines closed up his family's home there and brought his elderly mother back to Raleigh to live with him. She suffered from a form of dementia that would later be called Alzheimer's. She brought all her ferns with her on the train. They had lined her porch in Charlotte. My mother told us how she arranged the ferns around her feet, in her lap, in my mother's lap, stroked them as if they were lapdogs, and repeated all the way to Raleigh, "Maidenhair fern, very pretty. Lady fern, very pretty. Angel's hair, very pretty. Boston fern, also very pretty." My mother helped settle Mrs. Baines into her bedroom, and she wrapped the planters in green tissue and tied large red bows around them, winning the old woman's heart, as she suspected she would.

Although my grandmother was not yet too fond of Mr. Baines, she stepped in to help with his mother. She wanted to make sure the woman's needs were well met. She called all the hospitals in the county and located a private duty nurse for her. She interviewed several women before finally hiring one who did not appear to be lying when she said she would not allow Mrs. Baines to wander out into traffic or sit around in soiled underthings while she lazed off in front of the radio.

If Mr. Baines had never taken my mother anywhere but Charlotte, she would've been content to sit by him three hours a night in that one spot, with my grandmother sitting across from them, pretending to read. When they did leave the house, it was on foot. They'd take our old railroad lantern and walk the trail by Crabtree Creek for hours. My grandmother would decide when it was past time for them to be home, and would start watching the back door, saying things like, "I hate to think what they could be doing out there. Those woods are owned by the city. If they got caught doing something, the newspaper would have a big time with the story. They're old enough to do it at home. That's where they should do it." Several times I caught my mother coming back in and whispered for her to check her clothing, particularly her skirts, which would be twisted around her hips. Mr. Baines always stopped and combed his hair and straightened his tie in the cloudy mirror that hung over the utility sink.

One evening, deep into that exceptionally cold January of 1940, they ignored my grandmother's frostbite warnings and went out anyway. I helped bundle them up as if they were my children, and sent them out with the lantern, making them promise as I turned up the wick that they wouldn't be gone for too long. I fell asleep listening for the door to creak. After midnight, I woke up feeling a coldness next to me, not a sharp chill, but a spready, cloudlike sensation of the sort one would notice with a ghost beside the bed. It was my mother, stooped over with her face inches from mine. She looked so tender in the dim light. She asked if she could sleep with me and borrow my heat. I said she could, and she crawled over me to get to the other side of the bed, saying as she nestled underneath the covers, "I have never felt such wind." The night had been still, and so I asked her where the wind had come from. She explained that during the walk she had mentioned her unfulfilled desire to ice skate, and how the fear of broken bones had been the only thing that ever stopped her. Mr. Baines then walked her back to the house, crept inside and got a dining room chair, put it in the trunk of his car, and drove her to Lassiter Mill Pond. He pushed her about on the frozen pond while she sat in the chair, head back and legs out, as if she were riding a swing. As my mother lay there with her dress on and her stockings, I could feel the cold night air still about her. She turned on her side with her back to me. She was asleep before I could take all the pins out of her hair, warm now, melting in love.

In the next months, Mr. Baines took her everywhere he said he would. She stayed in a swivet, packing and unpacking, rushing film to the drugstore, pasting snapshots in a new album. She would write underneath them in white ink, her head down almost touching the page, concentrating on neatness and style as if she were copying penmanship lessons. It seemed that every other page had a snapshot captioned: "Sophia having the time of her life."

She became so attached to him that after he had spent a day with her, particularly a Sunday, she would cry when he left. As his car disappeared down the highway, she would press her cheek to the windowpane and whimper like a lonesome pet. She generally had terrible monthlies, and during especially rough ones her reaction to his leaving was highly dramatic. She would lie across her bed and sob, threatening to present herself at the door of the state asylum. She would say, "Maybe I need to be locked up. I don't feel so good." When she was cried out, she would wash her face, dose herself up with evening primrose oil and False Unicorn, and pretend to pay attention to the radio, and after enough hours had passed for her to have forgiven him for leaving, she would start to smile again. And after more time had gone by, she would be reeling in love, showing me whatever trinket he had most recently brought her, things like marcasite earrings, pearl hatpins, and leather-bound editions of her favorite books.

But if my grandmother was around, she'd force herself to tolerate his departure, no matter how furiously her hormones were warring inside her. If my grandmother had seen such an excess of emotion, she would've warned her of an even sadder day to come, the day Mr. Baines would drive off and keep on driving. Then would come the fight. Charles Nutter would be flagged about, as well as my father and his yellow wedding shoes, his girlfriends, and if things really escalated, my mother would ask her mother why, exactly, her own husband had left. And so, if it took my mother's biting herself to hide these departure miseries from my grandmother, she would do it. The alternative bruised her spirit, as well as my grandmother's, and mine.

I realized fairly early into my mother's courtship that in order to live in the same house with these two women, I would need to decide whom I would defend over what issue and when. Usually I chose my grandmother, as I believed she possessed the wisdom of the ages, and when I saw my mother buck and kick against her authority, I would gently say, "Don't you think Grandmother's probably been through this, and so she might sort of know what to do?" If my mother responded to me at all, it was to say something like, "She's been through twenty more years than I have. That's it."

In a very bold mood, my mother announced she was not going out on any more house calls that might cause her to miss a date with Mr. Baines. My grandmother went haywire-flooey. She shouted, "Suppose Sophia Snow had had a date when you were born? We'd both be in the ground!" My mother backed down, and out the three of us would go whenever a call came. My mother would tie tourniquets, set broken fingers, wrap sprained ankles, build bronchitis tents, doing everything perfectly, but with one eye on the clock. She almost always managed to make it home on time, even though more than once she met Mr. Baines at the door with dried blood still underneath her fingernails and plaster of Paris flecking the soft hair around her face.

My grandmother made her miss only one date, but at least I was able to leave the patient's house and speed through half the county to stop Mr. Baines just as he was turning out onto the highway, looking confused and forlorn, driving slumped over the wheel, as if he had been shot in the back. I took him to our house and sat inside with him until my mother and grandmother came home, or rather, until my grandmother came in and told Mr. Baines to go lift my mother out of the backseat of their ride's car. He looked so alarmed that I regretted having avoided telling him what had happened to my mother on the house call.

She had fainted and awakened vomiting at the home of an old man known as the Hermit Willoughby, and as she was to say later, "Yes, I did it, and with good reason." My grandmother had been called to his house early that afternoon, and she insisted that both my mother and I go with her, as she didn't know what she'd find when she got there. The Hermit Willoughby had lived alone since the death of his mother twenty years before, subsisting on handouts that Sunday-school classes left by his door and on whatever he could shoot or trap or cause to grow in the swampy wetlands around his cabin. The news that he needed medical help came to us by way of a rural relay of sorts that involved no fewer than three tenant farmers, a housewife or two, the postman, and a stranger who was pumping gas at a store. He showed up at our door and said, "I was asked to come here to tell you that the hermit has cut his throat." My grandmother knew whom he meant. She rounded us up and we left hurriedly, my mother huffing because she was given no time either to call Mr. Baines or to leave him a note.

My automatic reaction upon entering the man's house was to put my hand to my mouth and pinch my nostrils with my fingers. The place called to mind Miss Havisham's scrambled and filthy dining room in *Great Expectations,* only a thousand times worse. My mother's reaction was to stick by the door, which she kept propped open with one foot to give herself some fresh air. What did my grandmother do? She plowed forward, edging kittens and baby rabbits and chewed ears of corn out of her path, until she reached the Hermit Willoughby. He was sitting at a rough wooden table with his head in his hands. She said, "You smell like Satan. They're saying you cut your throat." And then, looking about the cabin, she added, "So why didn't you?" He lifted his head, and when he did I saw why we were there. His throat was covered by a massive boil that seemed to have crawled up from his chest through the neck of his greasy undershirt, and if this thing had had a voice, it would've screamed its rage and vengeance. He didn't say anything to my grandmother. He just blinked at her, very slowly, like a turtle. On the table beside him lay an open pocketknife, which my grandmother picked up and shook at him, saying, "Did you use this? Did you go after that boil with this?" He blinked again.

My grandmother shouted, "Come on, you two! Let's start on him!" My mother and I dragged ourselves over to her. I resigned myself to doing anything but touching his neck. My mother glanced around the kitchen, sighed, and said, "Well, I guess rubber gloves are out of the question." I pumped water at the sink, and my grandmother washed her hands and arms. Then I laid her sterile cloth on the table and displayed the instruments I knew she would need. As she circled the man's chair, contemplating exactly how to proceed, she asked him to tell her how he had gotten his neck into this hideous condition.

He told her he had started going after the boil the day before, and could not stop, driven as he was by that lurid curiosity and involuntary compulsion that makes some people incapable of leaving their bodies alone. He had used the fish-scaling, can-opening, pedicuring pocketknife that now lay beside him, and he had resorted to this only after a week's worth of magical cures had failed him. My grandmother asked if he had learned the cures from his parents. He said he had.

According to local legend, his mother had been a true witch and his father a warlock. In order to find all the charms for his incantations, he had left his house for the first time in twenty years, and had gotten as far as the crossroads when he discovered that the world had changed so much that he didn't know which road to choose. He remembered the old signposts—the stone well, the big stump, the owl tree—but now all these things were gone. So he stood there in the middle of the crossroads, with this boil throbbing a purple spasm on his throat, scaring the smittens out of women and children as he flagged down cars and asked after his charms: "Where is a faithful wife? Where is a blind dog? Where is a black cat, and does it belong to an old hag? Where is a white nigger with pink rabbit eyes?" He collected everything. It took him all day. He sponged his boil with the urine of the faithful wife. He caused a blind dog to lick his neck by lathering the spot with hog grease. He held the black cat's tail and made the sign of the cross over the boil. He used the dirty handkerchief of an accommodating albino to tie a slice of raw onion around his neck. None of these things worked. When he felt worse, and when the red streak started its course toward his heart, he put a toad under a pot and walked around it three times. He swallowed lead shot to absorb the poison. He pricked the boil with a gooseberry thorn until his blood ran black to red, and then he tossed the thorn over his left shoulder. None of these things worked either. When he developed a spiking fever, he walked back down to the crossroads and sent for my grandmother, whom he had met right before his mother died, when she appeared at the door to ask permission to take herb cuttings from her yard. Upon looking at his mother, my grandmother diagnosed her with Bell's palsy, a condition the woman attributed to the evil eye someone had cast upon her. My grandmother held forth on neurological disorders, making such an impression on the son that he remembered her for years as somebody who sounded like she knew what she was talking about. That was almost exactly what he told my grandmother: "I thought you might know what to do about me. Ma being dead and all." She assured him that she did. He was near tears as he continued: "I did not care to die. I like being by myself too much. I'm not ready to go be around everybody that's ever died. That's a lot of people."

My grandmother agreed that it was indeed, and then she told my mother to stand ready by his neck with a basin. She said, "Don't be particular. Just grab anything you can find that'll hold all this matter. It doesn't have to be clean. This stuff certainly isn't." My mother poked around the kitchen counter and finally produced a ceramic bowl that looked as if it hadn't been washed in years. She stood beside my grandmother, holding the bowl out as far from her body as she could. She was staring at the man's neck sideways. She looked woozy. My job was to hand over instruments, starting first with a benzocaine swab, which my grandmother took from me and held before the hermit's yellow eyes, saying, "You see this? This won't hurt. Everything else will, but this won't." She swabbed his neck, humming as she did. Then she stood behind his chair and said, "Now lean back. Ease your neck."

She put both her hands on his head as if it were a cabbage she was about to wash and cut up for slaw, and after much turning it this way and that, she rested it on her stomach. She seemed satisfied that it was settled in at the best angle. I asked whether she was ready to proceed, and she nodded and reached her hand flat out to me. And then, with the scalpel in her hand and so far up in the air, she looked as if she could easily and without a dash of emotion cut his throat from ear to ear. Before she brought her hand down she told him not to yell, or it would make her nervous. She said, "My hand will slip and you will surely die." Then she told my mother to get ready. She made two rapid crossed incisions oh so close to his jugular, and then shouted, "God-dammit, Sophia! Where's the basin?" It was clattering on the floor, where my mother had just dropped.

I didn't know what to do, and I looked for my grandmother to tell me. She told me to pick up the basin, catch the drainage, and swab the wound so she could have a clearer view of things. "Let's hurry this along," she said. "Just straddle Sophia while we finish." So I stood with one foot on either side of my mother's chest and swallowed back what I felt to be a gallon of saliva while I cleaned the hermit's wound with iodine and hydrogen peroxide. My grandmother then began hurriedly coating his neck with ichthammol salve, glancing down at my mother every few seconds, getting more salve in his hair than on the wound. She was very distracted. It was the first time I had seen her rush through a routine procedure. I offered to take over. She nodded and told the man to sit still while she tended to my mother, cold as death as she was, still unconscious among pet rabbit droppings, dog hair, and the other decayed or decaying matter of a hermit's life. She awakened when my grandmother passed ammonia under her nostrils, and then she turned her head to the side and vomited. When she was through, she looked up at me and said, "Go tell Richard I'm dead. I can't go to the movies." Once again, I looked to my grandmother for instruction. She said, "Go ahead. Drive home and tell him she'll be late. I'll drag her home before long. I'll go to the crossroads and flag a ride."

So that would account for why Mr. Baines blanched when he opened the car door and saw my mother in a heap on the backseat. The man who had given them the ride looked as though he expected to be paid, and Mr. Baines opened his wallet and gave the man more money than he probably made in three months. Mr. Baines carried my mother inside, slung across his shoulder as if he were taking her off a battlefield, and in a way I guess he was. When he laid her across her bed, she started to whimper that she never wanted to go through that again. When he asked how she had gotten in this shape, my grandmother said, "Sophia's always been weak about running infection. Plus she didn't eat breakfast this morning." Then she excused herself to the kitchen, saying, "I think I'm going to fix a little glass of whiskey. I think that would be in order." I heard ice hit the glass, and then I heard her shout out loud, "Mr. Baines! Would you care to take a drink? Sophia's already made you too late for the movies. Might as well have one." My mother and I were shocked at this miraculous offer. She motioned for Mr. Baines to go on to the kitchen, saying groggily, "My mother has lost touch with her reason. Take advantage of it." He left the room, and as I helped my mother out of her dress and into a sandalwood-flake bath, we heard more miracles, my grandmother laughing with him, telling funny stories about delivering backwoods babies.

My mother and I never asked my grandmother why she so suddenly changed her attitude about Mr. Baines. If we had asked her, either she would've told us it was none of our business—a response we could've tolerated because we always had—or she would've started ignoring him again out of some childlike mixture of defiance and embarrassment over having flashed a light into such a rarely seen corner of herself. We didn't want this to happen. Days later, when my mother's curiosity had eaten a nearly visible place in her, I volunteered an answer. I told her she had looked dead there on the floor, as dead as a person could appear and still be breathing. Her face was pale from having the blood rush downward so quickly. Her lips were blue. It would've been disturbing for any mother to see her child crumpled on the floor like that, but in this case it was much worse, because my grandmother was so familiar with death, and there it seemed to lie by her feet. And while I hesitate to romanticize the event by saying that my grandmother realized how suddenly she could lose her daughter, and thus made some sort of silent promise to try to let her have the life she wanted, I'm convinced this is what happened.

Questions to Consider

1. Why is Charlie Kate suspicious of Mr. Baines initially? What causes Charlie Kate to accept Mr. Baines, despite this early suspicion?
2. What is the nature of the relationship between the three women in this selection? How do their familial relationships to one another influence their interpersonal relationships?

❧ VOICES IN CONTEXT ❧
Religion and the Southern Experience

Self-identified Catholic author Flannery O'Connor described her native South as "Christ-haunted," and this ideology results in religious characters and ideologies populating the works of contemporary Southern writers, with results that range from the spiritually uplifting to the profane. A region populated by what H. L. Mencken described as a "cesspool of Baptists, a miasma of Methodists, snake charmers, phony real estate operators, and syphilitic evangelists," the contemporary South provides its writers with a seemingly endless stream of real-life models: Protestants, Catholics, fundamentalists, and "recovering" fundamentalists. Critic Susan Ketchin points out that in the South, spiritual concerns are "a pervasive cultural force acting upon the individual in paradoxical ways . . . religion sometimes brings the human spirit closer to the Divine, and conversely, it reinforces human depravity and enables suffering and evil in its name."

The influence of religion in the American South, most especially the Protestant and Catholic faiths, cannot be underestimated, given its long-standing presence, with roots that reach back to the pre-Revolutionary era. Religion provided the basis for condoning slavery, for oppressing women in general and their sexuality specifically. This "Christ-haunted" region, as O'Connor so insightfully described it, is "haunted because it has long been under the virtually hegemonic religious control of Protestant denominations—both Black and White—that stress the need for personal salvation," argues Timothy P. Caron. The journey toward personal salvation becomes oppressive to some and a means of manipulating behavior, albeit often with the best of intentions. In short, Caron suggests, "the South is a battlefield, a site of struggle" that continues into the present era.

Strains of fundamentalism and evangelism are deeply encoded into the region's history, and religious beliefs underlie nearly every aspect of Southern culture, rivaling racial strife as one of the most enduring and sweeping influences in the region. Willard Gatewood argues that for decades following the close of the Civil War and the Reconstruction era

> southerners had long been accustomed to describing their region as a Garden of Eden. Whatever the characteristics this biblical metaphor was used to project, it almost invariably included the notion of God-fearing, Bible-reading people allied in "common defense of the truth and common warfare upon iniquity." In no other respect was the region so deserving of the label "Solid South" as in its commitment to a Bible-centered, individualistic, low church Protestantism which provided a religion of certitude.

Perhaps because of its inherent certainty of both purpose and correctness, Southern religion is often a hands-on experience, a "save the sinners from themselves" proposition. Journalist Hal Crowther quips that "the Bible Belt likes its religion the same as its whiskey—strong, homemade, and none too subtle. The Lord works in strange ways," he acknowledges, but Southerners rarely need to be reminded "that the Lord works in *stranger* ways down South." Late-night radio preachers warn recalcitrant backsliders against the evils of "computers, debit cards, and ATM machines, [which are a] part of the Antichrist's plan to take over the world by eliminating money and locking up everything we own in the devil's database." Bible stories, revivals, baptisms, camp meetings, dinners on the ground, choir practice, and a host of similar religious events are a part of the social fabric of the region and are as familiar to most Southerners as the late summer heat. Religious events provide both a communal identity for believers and a method for evaluating and categorizing the morality of others, of determining whether their values are acceptable or suspect.

Religion in the South often defines social class as well as social ritual, governing the ways in which people meet, court, mourn, and conduct their daily lives. A Catholic community in

South Louisiana would be less likely to support a series of summer tent meetings, while a Pentecostal congregation might find it worrisome to be denied the opportunity for spiritual rejuvenation. Congregations of all but the largest churches in small Southern towns tend to remain segregated in their attendance patterns, and rejecting any spiritual affiliation remains a sure indicator of being an outsider—a "not from here" who is deserving of suspicion at best and at times, outright social rejection. Lee Smith has pointed out that families in the South are frequently identified by their religion and by which church they attend. She suggests that individual Southerners are forced to confront religion:

> if you grew up in a southern community . . . you can't evade it . . . in Grundy where I grew up, when some family was mentioned, somebody'd say, well, they're Methodist, or they're Presbyterian, or they go to So-and-So's church, or whatever. In the South, if you grew up at the time when we did in a small community, you were exposed to it intensely as a part of daily life. It is still true in small towns; it's only not true in university towns and in towns as big as Atlanta and Charlotte.

The common bond among the South's diverse groups of believers is the strength of conviction that they demonstrate, and the security and communal identity that stems from them. Religious ideologies have traditionally exerted a significant influence on the development of Southern literature. This influence is not limited to activities stemming directly from church attendance: death and burial rituals, weekly prayer meetings, tent revivals or camp meetings, or the mandatory attendance days such as Christmas and Easter. Literary artists show religion as a palpable force in secular social gatherings, as well—at cake walks and ladies' luncheons, in the blessings offered before business meetings. All of these activities highlight the difference between socially acceptable behaviors and those actions which will be deemed immoral. Religious practices inform social choices: Can I dance, drink alcohol, wear short skirts, or smoke cigarettes? What will the consequences be if I choose to engage in these activities, despite the spiritual peril? Further, religious convictions determine the ways in which marriages are contracted and carried out, the age at which young people may begin to date, whether an adulterer will be forgiven or shunned by a congregation.

In many ways, O'Connor's observation that the South is not Christ-centered, but Christ-haunted remains apt in the contemporary period, despite the increasing emphasis on the secular at the expense of the spiritual. As Smith suggests, the influence of religion has raised tensions in the region against which its writers continue to struggle. Not surprisingly, the stories that Southerners tell frequently derive from religious beliefs or events, with stories ranging from everyday gossip ("the neighbor thought she saw Jesus's face in her freezer!") to more emotional stories concerning snake handling, speaking in tongues, or healing services. These tensions derive from numerous sources: Calvinism and its sustained influence on fundamentalist Christianity; the residual guilt from the "Lost Cause" which caused Southerners to wonder why, since they were decent, God-fearing people, God had allowed the Confederacy to fall; the conviction that, in the final analysis, salvation was the result of a personal relationship with God. The religious tensions inherent in the South have provided its writers with what Susan Ketchin has described as "a sustaining sense of kinship, identity, community, and continuity" on one hand, while simultaneously assailing them with "the region's legacies of violence, slavery, poverty, and defeat engendered [which] engendered an undeniable sense of tragedy and alienation."

A multitude of Southern authors could reasonably be as part of a segment on religion—some would argue that most Southern writers have at least the occasional religious theme in their works—yet the four represented here offer especially poignant examples of religion in the South in all its diversity and intensity. Religion is a fundamental aspect of Southern culture, yet Southerners frequently depict their religious views without undue seriousness, despite the profundity that accompanies these beliefs. Elizabeth Spencer's "The Everlasting Light" is moving in its simplicity, depicting a crisis of faith and personal isolation against the communal background of the local choir practicing its Christmas program. John Dufresne's "Freezer Jesus" reflects on the nature of iconography and the ways in which fervent religious faith may escalate into an emotional state that tricks the senses. Ron Rash's story, "The Night New Jesus Fell to Earth" offers a tongue-in-cheek glimpse at small-town hypocrisy while providing much-needed comic relief when an arrogant ex-husband receives his comeuppance. Despite the variety present in these selections, they share a common concern with spiritual matters that is historically reflective of the Southern experience.

Elizabeth Spencer

1921–

Mississippian Elizabeth Spencer's birth coincided with the birth of the Southern literary Renascence and her first three novels bring to life the gradual shift from traditional agrarian culture to the increasingly urbanized lifestyles of the twentieth-century South. Having grown up in the culture that spawned great writers such as William Faulkner, Katherine Anne Porter, and Robert Penn Warren, Spencer implicitly understood the implications of coming of age during this tumultuous era in Southern history. She re-creates the landscape of her youth, examining images of community which are familiar to her rather than adapting earlier writer's interpretations of her world.

Born in Carrollton, Mississippi on 19 July 1921, Elizabeth Spencer spent her childhood among family members who firmly instilled the love of books, family, and place. Her mother's family maintained a working plantation, and her parents, James Luther and Mary James McCain Spencer, were staunch Presbyterians who believed a good education was invaluable to their daughter. In 1942, Spencer earned her bachelor's degree in English from Belhaven College in Jackson, Mississippi. She went on to pursue her master's degree at Vanderbilt University, where she studied with poet Donald Davidson, a member of the Fugitive Poets and the Agrarian movement that spawned the treatise *I'll Take My Stand*. After completing her schooling, Spencer worked as a journalist for a brief period, reporting for the Nashville *Tennessean*, but left this position to finish her first novel, *Fire in the Morning* (1948). She married Englishman John Rusher, and the couple lived briefly in Europe before relocating to Montreal, Canada, where they resided for many years. Spencer finally returned to her native South and settled in Chapel Hill, North Carolina in 1986.

Spencer is the author of nine novels, four short story collections, and a memoir, each of which has been praised for what Peggy Whitman Prenshaw calls their "unusual versatility and subtlety," as well as the strength of the communities populating them. Terry Roberts argues that Spencer focuses on the "confining social web of small southern towns" in her early novels, and while her interest in communal power expanded in her later novels to address communities that are both more complex and more urban, she also began to examine the ways in which an individual's inner life may be effected by the local community. Even in her later novels, which are set outside of the South, Spencer returns to this characteristically Southern theme that defines her body of work.

While themes of community and place are integral to Spencer's fiction, examinations of religion and its multifaceted cultural and personal influences recur frequently in her fiction. Spencer has spoken of the importance of religion in her writing, saying: " 'community' is a kind of ancient theme. . . . The whole sort of mystical issue of just who your brothers and sisters really are. It occurs over and over again in religious writing. All the central characters in my stories do seem to have that problem—finding out where they belong . . . and who they belong with." Spencer's fiction engages traditional Southern themes, melding them into compelling stories of interpersonal struggles within often-restrictive communities. In "The Everlasting Light," Spencer explores the effects on an individual who feels excluded from the community, demonstrating the internal struggle that may occur when the need to belong is at odds with a more private nature.

Lauded for her short stories and novels alike, Spencer has, in recent years, enjoyed supportive reviews from writers such as James Dickey, Reynolds Price, and Eudora Welty. She spent a year in Italy on a Guggenheim Fellowship and has received five O. Henry Awards, as well as the Award of Merit Medal for the Short Story from the American Academy and Institute of Arts and Letters. Her works have appeared in publications such as the *Southern Review*, the *Atlantic*, and the *New Yorker*. She is a member of the American Institute of Arts and Letters and a charter member of the Fellowship of Southern Writers, and she continues to reside in Chapel Hill.

The Everlasting Light

Kemp Donahue was standing at the window one December afternoon, watching his daughter Jessie come up the walk. Without reason or warning, his eyes filled with tears.

What on earth?

She came closer, books in her old frayed satchel, one sock slipped into the heel of her shoe, looking off and thinking and smiling a little. Kemp scrubbed the back of his hand across his eyes.

Why had he cried? Something to do with Jessie?

Jessie was not at all pretty (long face, uneven teeth, thin brown hair) and though Sheila, Kemp's trim and lovely looking wife, never mentioned it, they both knew how she felt about it. But what did pretty mean?

Jessie, now in the kitchen rummaging in the fridge, was into everything at school. She sold tickets to raffles, she tried out for basketball. Once rejected for the team, she circulated announcements for the games, and lobbied for door prizes.

Kemp came to the kitchen door. "What's new, honey?"

"Oh, nothing. Choir practice."

Mentioning it, she turned and grinned, ear to ear. ("Smile," her mother admonished. "Don't grin.")

Jessie loved choir practice. Non-churchgoers, the parents had decided a few years back it would be in order to send Jessie to Sunday School a few times. To their surprise, she liked it. She went back and back. She colored pictures, she came home and told Bible stories, she loved King David, she loved Joshua, she loved Jesus, she loved Peter and Paul. Sheila and Kemp listened to some things they didn't even know. ("Good Lord," said Sheila, hearing about the walls of Jericho.)

"Choir practice," Kemp repeated.

Sheila was out for the evening at one of her meetings. She was a secretary at the history department at the university. Twilight was coming on. "Are you eating enough?" asked Kemp. He wanted to talk to his daughter, just him and her. What did he want to say? It was all in his throat, but he couldn't get it out. "Honey . . . ," he began. Jessie looked up at him, munching a tuna sandwich in the side of one jaw. ("Don't chew like that," Sheila said.) "Honey . . . ," Kemp said again. He did not go on.

After a lonely dinner at the cafeteria Kemp drove up to the church and wandered around. The churchyard was dark, but light was coming from the windows, and the sound of singing as well was coming out. It was very sweet and clear, the sound of young voices. At the church, there were two morning services. At the early, nine o'clock service, the young choir sang. At the 11:15 service, the grown-up choir took over, the best in town, so people said.

Kemp did not go in the church, but stood outside. He crept closer to the church wall to listen. They were singing Christmas carols. He knew "Silent Night" and "Jingle Bells" and that silly one about Rudolph. But as for the others, they had a familiar ring, sure enough, and he found himself listening for Jessie's voice and thinking he heard it.

> O little town of Bethlehem,
> How still we see thee lie
> Above thy deep and dreamless sleep
> The silent stars go by.
> Still in thy dark streets shineth
> The everlasting light. . . .

"Everlasting light. . . ." That stuck in Kemp's mind. He kept repeating it. He strained to hear the rest. What came after little town, and dreamless sleep and silent stars? He was leaning against the wall, puzzling out the words until the song faded, and he could even hear the rap of the choir director's wand, and his voice too. Another song?

Kemp looked up. A strange woman was approaching the church and was looking at him. She was stooped over and white-haired and every bit of her said he'd no business leaning up against the church wall on a December night. He straightened, smiled and spoke to her and hastened away, pursued by strains of

> Away in a manger, no crib for a bed,
> The little Lord Jesus. . . .

At breakfast the next morning, Kemp said, "Tell me, Jessie, what's that Christmas carol that says something about 'the everlasting light' . . . ?"

Jessie told him. She knew the whole thing. She was about to start on "Joy to the World," but her mother stopped her. "Your eggs are getting cold as ice," she pointed out firmly.

"Why don't we all go to church tomorrow," Kemp proposed. "We can hear them all sing."

Sheila valued her Sunday sleep more than average, but she finally agreed and the Donahues, arriving in good time, listened to all sorts of prayers and Bible readings and music and a sermon too. Everyone was glad to see them. Jessie wore her little white robe.

"Well, now," said Kemp when they reached home. "Maybe that's how Sunday ought to be."

Sheila looked at him in something like alarm.

Sheila was from New England, graduate of one of those schools people spoke of with awe. Kemp was Virginia born and though it seemed odd for a Southern family, he had never been encouraged to attend church. Kemp did audits for a Piedmont chain of stores selling auto parts; he drove a good bit to various locations. Driving alone, he found himself repeating, "dark streets . . . the everlasting light. . . ." He especially liked that last. Didn't it just *sound* everlasting? Then, because they didn't have one, he had sneaked and borrowed Jessie's Bible. It took him a long time, but he found the story and relished the phrases: ". . . the glory of the Lord shone round about them. . . ." That's great! thought Kemp.

One week more and it would be the weekend of Christmas. Sheila said at breakfast, "Now, Jessie, you're certainly going to the Christmas party at school?"

"I have to go to choir practice," said Jessie.

"No, you do not," said Sheila. "It won't matter to miss one time. Miss Fagles rang up and said she especially wanted you. There's some skit you wrote for the class."

"They did that last year," said Jessie. "Anyway, I told Mr. Jameson I'd come."

"Then tell him you can't."

"I don't want to," said Jessie.

Sheila put down her napkin. She appealed to Kemp. "I am not going to have this," she said.

Kemp realized he was crucial, but he said it anyway. "Let her go where she wants to."

Sheila went upstairs in a fury. She had always wanted a pretty daughter who had lots of boyfriends begging for her time. "She's impossible," she had once muttered to Kemp.

Church on Christmas and Easter was what even the Donahues usually attended, and this year was no exception. The church was packed and fragrant with boughs of cedar. They heard carols and once more the stories of shepherds and angels read from the pulpit. They heard the choir and told Jessie later how proud they were of the way she sang. "But you couldn't hear me for everybody else," said Jessie.

It was at dinner a day or so later that she said: "The funniest thing happened the last night we practiced right before Christmas. This man came in the back of the church and sat down, way on the back row in the dark. We were singing carols. But then somebody noticed him and he was bent way over. He kept blowing his nose. Somebody said, 'He's crying.' Mr. Jameson said maybe he ought to go and ask him to leave, because he was probably drunk, but then he said, 'Maybe he just feels that way.' I guess he was drunk, though, don't you?"

* * *

Through years to come, Kemp would wonder if Jessie didn't know all the time that was her dad, sitting in the back, hearing about the 'everlasting light,' welling up with tears, for her, for Christmas, for Sheila, for everything beautiful. Someday I'll ask her, he thought. Someday when she's forty or more, with a wonderful job or a wonderful husband and wonderful children, I'll say, Didn't you know it was me? And she won't have to be told what I mean, she'll just say, Yes, sure I did.

Questions to Consider

1. Why does Spencer return to the refrain of "Everlasting Light" in this story? What is the significance of this refrain to the narrator of the story?
2. Organized religion has traditionally been an important element in Southern culture and society, yet this story demonstrates a good deal of ambivalence toward religion. How does the ambivalence of the parents affect their daughter's interest in church activities? What is the nature of the daughter's religious affiliation?

Richard Bausch
1945–

"My vital subjects are family, fear, love, and anything that is irrecoverable and missed; but I'll dispense with all of that for a good story," Richard Bausch's stories of life in the contemporary South present realistic, if not sometimes bleak, depictions of families and their struggles. A favorite professor once told Bausch that his interest in family made him a Southerner, but although his writing illustrates family life, like many contemporary Southern writers, he does not fill a customary role. The works of earlier generations of Southern authors often conveyed messages about race, religion, the Civil War, or long-deceased families. Bausch deals with traditionally Southern themes only as they relate to his stories and characters. Like his contemporaries Bobbie Anne Mason, Lewis Nordan, and Larry Brown, he has been associated with Dirty Realism, despite his tendency to focus more on middle class families than on the poor families that populate the fiction of the Dirty Realists.

On 18 April 1945, Richard Bausch and his twin brother, Robert, who is also a novelist, were born to Robert Carl and Helen Simmons Bausch in Fort Bennings, Georgia. Bausch was one of six children in the family of established storytellers—his parents and relatives had always been able to tell a good story. When he was three, his family moved to Washington, D.C., where the author has spent most of his life. Bausch attended Wheaton High School, and as a young man, he entertained the idea of becoming either a poet or a priest in the Roman Catholic Church; the priesthood was a vocation that his contemporary, John Dufresne, also considered. After deciding against the priesthood, Bausch entered the Air Force in 1965, serving as a survival school instructor at Chanute Base in Illinois. While in the Air Force, he became interested in singing and songwriting, forming a group, "The City Sounds," with fellow serviceman David Garmorstein. After the group broke up, Bausch managed a band called "The Luv'd Ones." In 1969, he married photographer Karen Miller, with whom he has five children. By 1974, Bausch had completed a Bachelor of Arts from George Mason University, then enrolled at the University of Iowa in the famed Writers' Workshop. In 1980, he began teaching at George Mason University where he presently serves as a professor of English.

Bausch's career has been highlighted by numerous awards. Among them are his two nominations for the PEN/Faulkner Award for *Take Me Back* in 1982 and *Spirits and Other Stories* in 1988. He won a National Endowment for the Arts Fellowship in 1982, a Guggenheim Fellowship in 1984, as well as the Lila Wallace Reader's Digest Best Writers Award and the American Academy of Arts and Letters Award in Literature in 1993. His stories have been selected for prestigious publications such as *Prize Stories: O. Henry Awards*, *The Best American Short Stories*, and *The Pushcart Prize Stories*, and he is a two-time National Magazine Award for Fiction recipient.

Bausch's work focuses upon universal literary themes: death, illness, struggles with family or job, and quest for identity, yet his stories and novels provide interesting twists and realistic characters, as well. In fact, his work, which has been praised for its realism, presents a snapshot of the world of American families as they struggle to survive. The story that follows, "1951," deals with the themes of love, religion, racial tension, and family struggle. In this piece, Bausch gives voice to the motherless child, Missy, as she strives to adjust to her father's distant nature and the loss of her mother.

1951

One catastrophe after another, her father said, meaning her. She knew she wasn't supposed to hear it. But she was alone in that big drafty church house, with just him and Iris, the maid. He was an Episcopal minister, a widower. Other women came in, one after another, all on approval, though no one ever said anything—Missy was seven, and he expected judgments from her about who he would settle on to be her mother. Terrifying. She lay in the dark at night, dreading the next visit, women looking her over, until she understood that they were nervous around her, and she saw what she could do. Something hardened inside her, under the skin. It was beautiful because it made the fear go away. Ladies with a smell of fake flowers about them came to the house. She threw fits, was horrid to them all.

One April evening, Iris was standing on the back stoop, smoking a cigarette. Missy looked at her through the screen door. "What you gawkin' at, girl?" Iris said. She laughed as if it wasn't much fun to laugh. She was dark as the spaces between the stars, and in the late light there was almost a blue cast to her brow and hair. "You know what kind of place you livin' in?"

"Yes."

Iris blew smoke. "You don't know *yet*." She smoked the cigarette and didn't talk for a time, staring at Missy. "Girl, if he settles on somebody, you gonna be sorry to see me go?"

Missy didn't answer. It was secret. People had a way of saying things to her that she thought she understood, but couldn't be sure of. She was quite precocious. Her mother had been dead since the day she was born. It was Missy's fault. She didn't remember that anyone had said this to her, but she knew it anyway, in her bones.

Iris smiled her white smile, but now Missy saw tears in her eyes. This fascinated her. It was the same feeling as knowing that her daddy was a minister, but walked back and forth sleepless in the sweltering nights. If your heart was peaceful, you didn't have trouble going to sleep. Iris had said something like that very thing to a friend of hers who stopped by on her way to the Baptist Church. Missy hid behind doors, listening. She did this kind of thing a lot. She watched everything, everyone. She saw when her father pushed Iris up against the wall near the front door and put his face on hers. She saw how disturbed they got, pushing against each other. And later she heard Iris talking to her Baptist friend. "He ain't always thinkin' about the Savior." The Baptist friend gasped, then whispered low and fast, sounding upset.

Now Iris tossed the cigarette and shook her head, the tears still running. Missy curtsied without meaning it. "Child," said Iris, "what you gonna grow up to be and do? You gonna be just like all the rest of them?"

"No," Missy said. She was not really sure who the rest of them were.

"Well, you'll miss me until you *forget* me," said Iris, wiping her eyes.

Missy pushed open the screen door and said, "Hugs." It was just to say it.

When Iris went away and swallowed poison and got taken to the hospital, Missy's father didn't sleep for five nights. Peeking from her bedroom door, with the chilly, guilty dark looming behind her, she saw him standing crooked under the hallway light, running his hands through his thick hair. His face was twisted; the shadows made him look like someone else. He was crying.

She didn't cry. And she did not feel afraid. She felt very gigantic and strong. She had caused everything.

QUESTIONS TO CONSIDER

1. Does Bausch exemplify the ideals of traditional Southern culture in this story? What type of Southern culture is he describing?
2. Is this story the work of a Dirty Realist? What characteristics of this genre do you see in this story? How do these characteristics influence your reading of the story?

John Dufresne

1948–

Southerners have traditionally been drawn to examine religious faith, and not infrequently to the most extreme versions of faith. Novelist John Dufresne aptly characterizes Southern fundamentalist religion in a fiction piece that he contributed to the *Miami Herald*, in which he describes a late-night evangelist's show in images familiar to Southerners: "The Reverend Blaine Mattox of the Vidalia True Vine Powerhouse Church of the Saved but Struggling is talking about how Jesus may not be the florist's son, but He is the Rose of Sharon; not the baker's son, but the Bread of Life; may not be the geologist's son, but He's the Rock of Ages! Am I right this evening? the reverend shouts." Dufresne captures the emotional intensity that coexists alongside the mixed metaphors encapsulating the fundamentalism of many branches of Southern Protestantism. His ability to simultaneously satirize and respect this cultural taproot is indicative of his deep understanding of the Southern mind and character and accounts for his success in bringing members of the working classes to life in his fiction. His best work is set in the Deep South and examines the ways in which Southern culture—most especially the deeply held Southern religious ideologies—influences the actions of those native to the region.

John Dufresne may not be a native Southerner, but his fiction suggests that he wishes he were one. He lives in Florida, spent a number of years residing in Louisiana, and returns to the Bayou State frequently. Born in Worcester, Massachusetts on 30 January 1948, John Dufresne spent his early life intending to become a "cowboy/priest," as he told the *Washington Post*, and "wast[ing] his youth playing baseball and going to movies." He remained committed to entering the priesthood for many years, since the vocation provided a venue that would allow him to serve his community. Dufresne's plans for the priesthood were derailed when he encountered a crisis of faith and discovered that even after seeking counsel from his church, he was unable to resolve his questions. He then refocused his aspirations, still determined to enter a field in which he could serve others.

Dufresne received his bachelor's degree from Worcester State College in 1970 and went on to complete a master's degree at the University of Arkansas in 1984. Before devoting his attention to graduate school and later to writing and teaching, however, he spent more than a decade as a social worker, providing crisis intervention assistance. In 1984, he accepted a position as an English instructor at Northeast Louisiana University (now the University of Louisiana at Monroe). Monroe provides the setting for his first novel, *Louisiana Power and Light* (1994), and for his most recent effort, *Deep in the Shade of Paradise* (2002). Perhaps, the most noteworthy aspect of the novel's regional quality is found in the depiction of the Fontanas, the family on which the novel focuses. Dufresne describes the Fontanas as "the most executed white family in the history of Louisiana . . . [who] came from the primordial ooze," providing a rollicking introduction to a deeply trashy and perennially unlucky Southern family. The Fontana's collective identity comes complete with profound religious conflicts, an extensive family tree, and a lineage that has carried a curse—which may or may not be real—for generations.

Dufresne's fiction has been described by critics as postmodern depictions of the types of stories told by Faulkner, Caldwell, Welty, and O'Connor. Building on the work of these literary predecessors, Dufresne has been credited with deconstructing stereotypes of working and lower-middle class Southerners that readers have heretofore taken for granted. His novels work at an allegorical level as well, drawing upon his early religious training to examine such Christian narratives as the life of Christ and the crucifixion story. "The Freezer Jesus" depicts fervent religious faith in a tongue-in-cheek manner, questioning the ways in which faith becomes emotion that manipulates the senses and perceptions. Dufresne describes his experiences as a writer who has arrived at this creative pass, saying in the *Washington Post* that "I write novels, make up stories that did not happen, but could have. I pretend, and I remember. As I become someone new, someone like my father, I cling to what I was."

The author of three novels and a collection of short stories, Dufresne has been the recipient of the *Transatlantic Review* Award, and the *Yankee* magazine fiction award, as well as a PEN Syndicated Fiction Award. His first two novels, *Louisiana Power and Light* and *Love Warps the Mind a Little* (1997), were named Notable Books of the Year by *The New York Times*. Dufresne presently serves as a professor of creative writing at Florida International University and lives in Dania Beach, Florida with his wife and son.

The Freezer Jesus

Two days after we learned we had Jesus on our freezer, my sister Elvie had this dream where all the mystery was explained to her. Freezer's this ordinary, yellow Amana.[1] Sets out there on the porch on account of we got no room for it inside the house. What Jesus explained to Elvie in the dream was that He supernaturally connected the porch light to the freezer and turned the freezer into a TV and on that TV was Jesus Himself. Elvie, He says to her, I've chosen you and your brother Arlis this time because you all been so alone and so good these fifty, sixty years and because your bean crop's going to fail again this spring. And tell Arlis, He said, to call the Monroe newspaper and tell them Jesus has come again and everyone should know what that means.

Now, I've never been a strictly religious person like most of my neighbors. Naturally, I believe in the Lord and salvation and Satan and all of that. I just never reckoned what all that had to do with planting beans or chopping cotton, you see. And then comes that Friday and I'm walking Elvie up the path from the bean field at dusk and I notice the porch light on and I tell Elvie we must have had a visitor stop by. As we get closer, I notice a blemish on the freezer door that wasn't there before. Then suddenly the blemish erupts like a volcano and commences to changing shape, and what were clouds at first become a beard and hair, and I recognize immediately and for certain that the image is the very face of Jesus right down to the mole near his left eye.

What is it, Arlis? Elvie says to me. Why you shaking? Of course Elvie can't see what I see because she's blind as a snout beetle. So I tell her about this Jesus, and somehow she knows it's true and falls to her knees and sobs. Praise God, Arlis, she says.

We're not accustomed to much excitement in Holly Ridge, Louisiana. Only time we made the news was seven years ago when a twelve-point buck jumped

1. A brand of household appliances.

through Leamon Dozier's bathroom window while he was shaving and thrashed itself to unconsciousness. Still, the Dream Jesus had told Elvie we were to let the world know, so I called the paper. The boy they sent along didn't mind telling me he was mighty skeptical before he witnessed the freezer with his own eyes. Said, though, it looked more like Willie Nelson than Jesus unless you squinted your eyes, and then it looked like the Ayatollah of Iran. Of course, any way you look at it, he said, it's a miracle. He took out his little notebook and asked Elvie what she thought this means. She said, well, this here's Jesus, and evidently He has chosen Richland Parish for His Second Coming. My advice, she told the boy, is that people should get ready.

First off, just a few people came at twilight to watch the freezer erupt with Jesus. Then they brought friends. Then the gospel radio station in Rayville hired a bus and drove folks out here. Pretty soon, the Faulkner Road was crowded all the way to 138 with dusty pilgrims. I spent my afternoons and evenings trying to regulate the toilet line through the house. Either that or I'd be fetching water from the well for the thirsty or faint or trying to keep the cars off my melon patch. Anyway, I got little work done in the fields and soon the Johnson grass had choked the life from my beans. Elvie reminded me how the Lord had prophesied the crop failure, and she reassured me that He would provide.

Every night at nine-thirty, the Amana TV would begin to fade slowly and within minutes the divine image would be gone. Then I'd spend an hour or so picking up soda cans and candy wrappers all over the yard. Once in a while I'd find a pilgrim still lingering by the coop, up to something, I don't know what, and I'd have to ask him to leave. One time this Italian lady from Vicksburg says to me could she have a morsel of food that I kept in the freezer. She was sure if she could just eat something out of that holy freezer, she would be cured of her stomach cancer. I gave her a channel cat I'd caught in Bayou Macon and said I hoped it worked.

Then this TV evangelist drove up from Baton Rouge in a long, white limousine, walked up on the porch, looked the freezer up and down without a word, followed the arc of the extension cord plugged into the porch light, gazed out at the gape-mouthed crowd, turned to me, smiled sort of, said Praise Jesus in a whispery voice, combed his fingers through his long hair, nodded to his chauffeur, got back into the limousine, and drove away.

The TV minister wasn't the only preacher who came calling. The Reverend Danny Wink from the True Vine Powerhouse Pentecostal Church came every day and took to sitting beside Elvie in a seat of honor, I suppose he thought, up on the porch by the screen door. It was the Reverend Wink's idea to transfer the freezer to his church, where it could be worshiped properly before a splendid congregation and all, which was sure okay with me so long as the Reverend furnished us with another freezer. I had a shelf full of crawfish tails to think about. Elvie, though, told him she was waiting on a sign from Jesus. One evening, the Reverend Wink presented Elvie with a brass plaque that read: "This Freezer Donated by Elvie and Arlis Elrod," and pointed to where he'd screw it onto the freezer.

About a month after Jesus first appeared to us, I'm sleeping when I hear this racket out on the porch and I get up quietly, figuring it's one of the idolaters come back in the middle of the night to fool with the freezer. What I see, though, is Elvie kneeling in a pool of light from the open freezer door, holding handfuls of ice cubes over her eyelids, weeping, asking Jesus to scrub the cataracts from her milky old eyes. I watched Elvie for three nights running. On that last night, Elvie started jabbering in tongues the way the Reverend Wink does, and she's so like a lunatic there in her nightgown screaming at this big, cold machine that I can't watch no more.

In the morning, I found Elvie slumped on the kitchen floor. She said, Arlis, I'm as blind as dirt and always will be. She called the Reverend Wink and had him haul off the freezer that morning. And then what happened was this:

Jesus never did reappear on that freezer, which made the believers at the True Vine Powerhouse Church angry and vengeful. Right from his pulpit, the Reverend Wink called me and Elvie schemers, charlatans, and tools of the Devil. Elvie, herself, grew bitter and remote, asked me did I do something clever with that Amana maybe. I said no I didn't, and she said it surely wasn't kind of the Lord to give her hope and then snatch it away like He done. Our bean crop's ruined, cotton's all leggy and feeble, and I don't know what we'll do.

Can't even say the Lord will provide, but I do know that He's still here with us. I see Him everywhere I look, only this time I'm keeping the news to myself. I saw Him in that cloud that dropped a lightning bolt this afternoon. I see His face in the knot on the trunk of that live oak out back. What I notice this time is those peculiar wine-dark eyes, drunk with the sadness of rutted fields and empty rooms. I can squint my eyes and see Jesus smiling back at me from the dots on the linoleum floor, and I think He must be comforted by my attention. I hear His voice in the wind calling to me, and I feel calm. I hear Him whisper, Arlis, get ready. In her room, Elvie sits at the edge of the bed, coughs once in a while, and fingers the hem of her housedress.

Questions to Consider

1. Early in his narrative, Arlis describes himself as not "strictly religious," and he later refers to the visitors to the Freezer Jesus as "idolaters." Near the end of his story, Arlis sees Jesus "everywhere." How do Arlis's religious beliefs and attitudes evolve over the course of the story?
2. How does Dufresne use irony to illuminate the motivations and actions of the characters in this piece? For example, how does Elvie's blindness effect the narrative and the development of her character? What other examples of irony do you find in this piece?

Ron Rash

1953–

The grandson of a man who could neither read nor write, Ron Rash has become one of North Carolina's most entertaining writers. An introvert as a young boy because of a speech impediment, Ron Rash grew up listening to people talk, and his writing is all the better for the hours spent listening. Rash eventually outgrew his speech difficulty, but the stories that he heard growing up had a profound influence upon his work.

Born 25 September 1953 to Sue Holder Rash and James Rash—North Carolinians who met while employed in Chester, South Carolina at the Eureka Cotton Mill. Rash's father worked during the day and took GED courses at night; he pursued his studies and ultimately became an art professor at Gardner-Webb University. Rash's mother went to college when she was in her forties and also became an educator, teaching for 20 years after she earned her degree. Ron Rash grew up in Boiling Springs, North Carolina, a small town located in the western half of the state. He earned his bachelor's degree at Gardner-Webb University and completed his graduate degree at Clemson University. He now lives in Clemson, South Carolina, with his wife and two children. He teaches English at Tri-County Technical College, and he teaches poetry in the M.F.A. program at Queens College in Charlotte, North Carolina.

Rash's poetry and fiction have appeared in many prestigious journals, including *Poetry*, *The Oxford American*, *The Southern Review*, *Shenandoah*, and *The Sewanee Review*. He is the author of four previous books: *The Night the New Jesus Fell to Earth* (1994) and *Casualties* (2000), both collections of stories, and *Eureka Mill* (1998) and *Among the Believers* (2000), collections of poetry. In 1987, Rash's fiction won a General Electric Younger Writers Award, and in 1994 he was awarded an NEA Poetry Fellowship. He has also been the recipient of the Sherwood Anderson Prize in 1996, and his first novel, *One Foot in Eden* (2002), won the Novello Prize and was nominated for a Pulitzer Prize.

Rash sets his poetry and prose in the Appalachian Mountains and foothills near where he was reared, and the culture and the traditions of the region influence his fiction, giving his works a strong sense of the region from which it comes. The fundamentalist religion of the area plays a great role in his work, as well. "A lot of my imagery is religious," Rash once told a reviewer, yet he does not limit himself to traditional Judeo-Christian images. He often melds Pagan and Christian images, because he is intrigued by the coexistence of formal Christianity and folk religious practices. A good example comes from Rash's grandfather, a devout Christian who nonetheless believed that killing black snakes during a drought could bring on rain. Rash gives equal voice to Christian and Pagan practices, demonstrating their parallel existence in the region. These folk elements give Rash's work humor and realism, elements that are both common to Southern storytellers and integral to the ways in which their stories are delivered.

Along with the influence of place upon his writing, Rash credits the works of writers such as Gerard Manley Hopkins, John Donne, and Henry Vaughn as significant influences upon his poetry. Rash maintains that the greatest influences upon his prose have been the works of Flannery O'Connor and James Joyce. "The Night the New Jesus Fell to Earth" demonstrates Rash's interest in religion and his ability to create compelling characters.

The Night the New Jesus Fell to Earth

The day after it happened, and Cliffside's new Jesus and my old husband was in the county hospital in fair but stable condition, Preacher Thompson, claiming it was all his fault, offered his resignation to the board of deacons. But he wasn't to blame. He'd only been here a couple of months, fresh out of preacher's college, and had probably never had to deal with a snake like Larry Rudisell before. A man or a woman, as I've found out the hard way, usually has to get bit by a snake before they start watching out for them.

What I mean is, Preacher Thompson's intentions were good. At his very first interview the pulpit committee had told him what a sorry turn our church had taken in the last few years, and they hadn't left out much either. They told him about Len Deaton, our former choir director, who left his choir, wife, and eight children to run off to Florida with a singer at Harley's Lounge who wasn't even a Baptist. And they told about Preacher Crowe, who had gotten so senile he had preached the same sermon four weeks in a row, though they didn't mention that a lot of the congregation hadn't even noticed. The committee told him about how membership had been slipping for several years, how the church was in a rut, and how when Preacher Crowe had finally retired in November, it had been clear that some major changes had to be made if the church was going to survive. And this was exactly why they wanted him to be the new minister, they told him. He was young and energetic and could bring some fresh blood into the church and help get it going in the right direction. Which was exactly what he tried to do, and exactly why Larry was able to talk his way onto that cross.

It did take a few weeks, though. At first Preacher Thompson was so nervous when he preached that I expected him to bolt for the sanctuary door at any moment. He wouldn't even look up from his notes, and when he performed his first baptism he almost drowned poor little Eddie Gregory by holding him under the water too long. Still, each week you could see him get a little more comfortable and confident, and by the last Sunday in February, about two months ago, he gave the sermon everybody had been waiting for. It was all about commitment and the need for new ideas, about how a church was like a car, and our church was in reverse and we had to get it back in forward. You could tell he was really working himself up because he wasn't looking at his notes or his watch. It was 12:15, the first time he'd ever kept us up after twelve, when he closed, telling us that Easter, a month away, was a time of rebirth, and he wanted us all to go home and think of some way our church could be reborn too, something that would get Cliffside Baptist Church back in the right gear.

Later I wondered if maybe all the car talk had something to do with what happened, because the next Sunday Preacher Thompson announced he'd gotten many good suggestions, but there was one in particular that was truly inspired, one that could truly put the church back on the right road, and he wanted the man who had come up with the idea, Larry Rudisell, to stand up and tell the rest of the congregation about it.

Like I said earlier, once you've been bitten by a snake you start looking out for them, but there's something else too. You start to know their ways. So I knew right off that whatever Larry was about to unfold, he was expecting to get something out of it, because having been married to this snake for almost three years, I knew him better than he knew himself. Larry's a hustler. Always has been. He came out of his momma talking out of both sides of his mouth, trying to hustle her, the nurse, the doctor, whichever one he saw first. He hasn't stopped talking or hustling since.

Larry stood up, wearing a sport coat he couldn't button because of his beer gut, no tie, and enough gold around his neck to fill every tooth in Cleveland County. He was also wearing his sincere "I'd swear on my dead momma's grave I didn't know that odometer had been turned back" look, which was as phony as the curls in his brillo-pad hairdo, which he'd done that way to cover up his bald spot.

Then Larry started telling about what he was calling his "vision," claiming that late Friday night he'd woke up, half blinded by bright flashing lights and hearing a voice coming out of the ceiling, telling him to recreate the crucifixion on the front lawn of Cliffside Baptist Church, at night, with lights shining on the three men on the crosses. The whole thing sounded more like one of those U.F.O. stories in *The National Examiner*[1] than a religious experience, and about as believable.

Larry looked around and started telling how he just knew people would come from miles away to see it, just like they went to McAdenville every December to see the Christmas lights, and then he said he believed in his vision enough to pay for it himself.

Then Larry stopped to see if his sales pitch was working. He was selling his crucifixion idea the same way he would sell a '84 Buick in his car lot. And it was working. Larry

1. A reference to tabloid newspapers that recount scandalous and sometimes untrue stories.

has always been a smooth talker. He talked me into the back seat of his daddy's car when I was seventeen, talked me into marrying him when I was eighteen, and talked me out of divorcing him on the grounds of adultery a half dozen times. I finally got smart and plugged up my ears with cotton so I couldn't hear him while I packed my belongings.

Larry started talking again, telling the congregation he didn't want to take any credit for the idea, that he was just a messenger and that the last thing God had told him was that he wanted Larry to play Jesus, and his mechanic, Terry Wooten, to play one of the thieves, a role, as far as I was concerned, Terry had been playing as long as he'd worked for Larry. When I looked over at Terry, the expression on his face made it quite clear that God hadn't bothered to contact him about all of this. Then I looked up at the ceiling to see if it was about to collapse and bury us all. Everybody was quiet for about five seconds. Then the whole congregation started talking at once, and it sounded more like a tobacco auction than a church service.

After a couple of minutes people remembered where they were, and it got a little more civilized. At least they were raising their hands and getting acknowledged before they started shouting. The first to speak was Jimmy Wells, who had once bought an Olds 88 from Larry and had the transmission fall out not a half mile from where he had driven it off Larry's lot. Jimmy was still bitter about that, so I wasn't too surprised when he nominated his brother-in-law Harry Bayne to play Jesus.

As soon as Jimmy sat down, Larry popped up like a jack-in-the-box, claiming Harry's hair was too straight for him to be Jesus, that Jesus was a Jew and Jews had curly hair. When Larry said that, people started arguing about whether Jesus was really a Jew or not, and it was fifteen minutes before they got back to who should play Jesus, and it was past one o'clock before Harry got up and said if it meant that much to Larry to let him do it, that he was too hungry to care anymore.

Preacher Thompson had pretty much stayed out of all this till Harry said that, but then he suggested that Harry play the thief who gets saved, leaving Terry as the other one. The Splawn brothers, Donnie and Robbie, were nominated to be the Roman soldiers. To the credit of the church, when Preacher Thompson asked for a show of hands as to whether we should let this be our Easter project, it was close. My hand wasn't the only one that went up against it, and I still believe it was empty stomachs as much as a belief in Larry and his scheme that got it passed.

But it did pass, and a few days later Preacher Thompson called me up and asked, since I was on the church's building and grounds committee, if I would help build the crosses. You see, I'm a carpenter, the only full-time one, male or female, in the church, so whenever the church's softball field needs a new backstop or the parsonage needs some repair work, I'm the one who usually does it. And I do it right. Carpentry is in my blood. People around here say my father was the best carpenter to ever drive a nail in western North Carolina, and after my mother died when I was nine, he would take me with him every day I wasn't in school. By the time I was fourteen, I was working fulltime with him in the summers. I quit school when I was sixteen. I knew how I wanted to make my living. I've been a carpenter for the last fifteen years.

It was hard at first. Since I was a woman, a lot of men didn't think I could do as good a job as they could. But one good thing about being a carpenter is someone can look at your work and know right away if you know what you're doing. Nowadays, my reputation as a carpenter is as good as any man's in the county.

Still, I was a little surprised that Preacher Thompson asked me to work on a project my ex-husband was so involved in. But, being new, he might not have known we had once been married. I do go by my family's name now. Or maybe he did know, figuring since the divorce was over five years ago we had forgiven each other like Christians should. Despite its being Larry's idea, I did feel obligated since I was on the building and grounds committee, so I said I would help. Preacher Thompson thanked me and said we would meet in front of the church at ten on Saturday morning.

On Saturday, me, Preacher Thompson, Larry, and Ed Watt, who's an electrician, met on the front lawn. From the very start, it was obvious Larry was going to run the show, telling us the way everything should be, pointing and waving his arms like he was a Hollywood director. He had on a white, ruffled shirt that was open to his gut, his half-ton of gold necklaces, and a pair of sunglasses. Larry was not just trying to act like but look like he was from California, which meant, as far as I was concerned, that, unlike Jesus, he actually deserved to be nailed to a cross.

Larry showed me where he wanted the three crosses, and he gave me the length he wanted them. His was supposed to be three feet taller than the other two. Preacher Thompson was close by, so we acted civil to one another till I walked over to my truck to go get the wood I'd need. Larry followed me, and as soon as I got in the truck and cranked it, he asked me how it felt to have only a pillow to hold every night. "Lot of advantages to it," I said as I drove off. "A pillow don't snore and it don't have inch-long toenails and it don't smell like a brewery." I was already out of shouting distance before he could think of anything to say to that.

I was back an hour later with three eight-inch-thick poles, just like the ones I used to build the backstop for the softball field, and a railroad crosstie I'd sawed into three lengthwise pieces for the part the arms would be stretched out on. I'd also gotten three blocks of wood I was going to put where their feet would be to take the strain off their arms.

As I turned into the church parking lot, I saw that Wanda Wilson's LTD[2] was parked in the back of the church. She was out by the car with Larry, wearing a pink sweatshirt and a pair of blue running shorts, even though it was barely 60 degrees, just to show off her legs. When they saw me they started kissing and putting their hands all over each other. They kept that up for a good five minutes, in clear view of not just me but Ed Watt and Preacher Thompson, and I thought we were going to have to get a water hose and spray them, the same way you would two dogs, to get them apart.

Finally, Wanda got into her LTD and left, maybe to get a cold shower, and Larry came over to the truck. As soon as he saw the poles in the back of the truck he got all worked up, saying they were too big around, that they looked like telephone poles that he was supposed to be Jesus, not the Wichita Lineman.[3] That was enough for me. I put my toolbox back in the cab and told Preacher Thompson Benny Brown was coming over with his post-hole digger around noon. I pointed at Larry. "I forgot all about Jesus being a carpenter," I said. "I'm taking all of this back over to Hamrick's Lumberyard." Then I drove off and didn't look back.

Why is it that some men always have to act like they know more than another human being just because that other human being happens to be a woman? Larry's never driven a nail in his life, but he couldn't admit that I would know what would make the best and safest cross. I guess some people never change. Ever since the divorce was made final, Larry has gone out of his way to be as ugly as possible to me.

2. A Ford sedan-style automobile popular in the 1970s.

3. A country music song by the same name, made popular by singer Glen Campbell in the late 1960s. In the love song, a lineman for an electric company longed for his lover.

The worst thing about being divorced in a small town is that you're always running into your ex. Sometimes it seems I see him more now than I did when I was married to him. I can live with that. But it's been a lot harder to live with the lies he's been spreading around town, lies about me being an unnatural woman.[4]

What goes on between a man and a woman behind closed doors is nobody else's business, but I will say I proved to Larry four times a week that I was a woman with a capital W, and the whole time I was married to him, even when I knew he was being unfaithful to me, I never even looked at another man, much less a woman. But just like the Bible says, it's a fallen world. A lot of people want to believe the worst, so a lot of them believed Larry when he started spreading his lies. I couldn't get a date for almost two years, and I lost several girlfriends too. Like the song says, "Her hands are callused but her heart is tender." That rumor caused me more heartache than you could believe.

I have no idea what they did after I drove off that Saturday, but the Sunday before Easter the crosses were up, so after church let out just about everybody in the congregation went out on the front lawn to get a better look.

I've always said you can tell a lot about a person by how carefully they build something or put something together, but looking at Larry's crosses didn't tell me a thing I didn't already know. Instead of using a pole for the main section, he had gotten four-by-eight boards made out of cedar, which anybody who knows anything about wood can tell you is the weakest wood you can buy. The crossties and footrests were the same. I'm not even going to mention how sorry the nailing was.

I walked over to the middle cross, gave it a push, and felt it give like a popsicle stick in sand. I kneeled beside it and dug up enough dirt to see they hadn't put any cement in the hole Benny Brown had dug for them but had just packed dirt in it. I got up and walked over to the nearest spigot and washed the red dirt off my hands while everybody watched me, waiting for me to pass judgment on Larry's crosses.

"All I'm going to say is this," I said as I finished drying my hands. "Anybody who gets up on one of those things had better have a whole lot of faith." Of course Larry wasn't going to let me have the last word. He started saying I was just jealous that he'd done such a good job, that I didn't know the difference between a telephone pole and a cross. I didn't say another word, but as I was walking to my truck I heard Harry Bayne tell Larry he was going to have to find somebody else to play his role, that he'd rather find a safer way to prove his faith, like maybe handling a rattlesnake or drinking strychnine.

I went back that night to look at the crosses some more. I left convinced more than ever that the crosses, especially the taller middle one, wouldn't support the weight of a full-grown man.

On Good Friday I went on over to the church about an hour before they were scheduled to start, mainly because I didn't believe they would be able to get up there without at least one of the crosses snapping like a piece of dry kindling. There were already a good number of people there, including Larry's cousin Kevin, who wasn't a member of our church or anybody else's, but who worked part-time for Larry and was enough like Larry to be a good salesman and a pitiful excuse for a human being. Kevin was spitting tobacco juice into a paper cup while Mrs. Murrel, who used to teach drama over at the high school, dabbed red paint on his face and hands and feet, trying to make him look like the crucified thief Larry had talked, paid, or threatened

4. Euphemism for lesbianism.

him into playing. Besides the paint, the only thing he was wearing was a sweatshirt with a picture of Elvis on it and what looked like a giant diaper, though I'd already heard the preacher explain to several people it was supposed to be what the Bible called a loincloth. Terry Wooten was standing over by the crosses, dressed up the same way, looking like he was about to vomit as he stared up at where he would be hanging in only a few more minutes.

Then I saw the sign and suddenly everything that had been going on for the last month made sense. It was one of those portable electric ones with about a hundred colored lightbulbs bordering it. "The Crucifixion of JESUS CHRIST Is Paid for and Presented by LARRY RUDISELL'S Used Cars of Cliffside, North Carolina" was spelled out in red plastic letters at the top of the message board. Near the bottom in green letters it said, "If JESUS Had Driven a Car, He Would Have Bought It at LARRY'S." It was the tackiest, most sacrilegious thing I'd ever seen in my life.

Finally, the new Jesus himself appeared, coming out of the church with what looked like a brown, rotting halo on his head—it was his crown of thorns—fifty yards of extension cord covering his shoulder, and a cigarette hanging out of his mouth. He unrolled the cord as he came across the lawn, dressed like Kevin and Terry except he didn't have any red paint on his face. Larry didn't have a fake beard either. He wanted everyone to know it was Larry Rudisell up on that cross. He walked over to the sign and plugged the extension cord into it.

You know what it's like when the flashbulb goes off when you're getting a picture taken and you stagger around half blind for a while? Well, that's about the effect Larry's sign had when it came on. The colored lights were flashing on and off, and you could have seen it from a mile away. Larry watched for a minute to make sure it was working right and then announced it was twenty minutes to showtime so they needed to go ahead and get up on the crosses. Preacher Thompson and the Splawn brothers went and got the stepladders and brought them over to where the crosses were. Terry and Kevin slinked over behind the sign, trying to hide. It was obvious Larry was going to have to get up there first.

Larry took off his sweatshirt, and I realized for the first time they were going to go up there with nothing except the bedsheets wrapped around them. It wasn't that cold right then, but like it always is in March, it was windy. I knew that in a few minutes, when the sun went down, the temperature would really fall fast.

While Donnie and Robbie Splawn steadied the cross, Larry crawled up the ladder. With only the "loincloth" wrapped around him, he looked more like a Japanese Sumo wrestler on "Wide World of Sports"[5] than Jesus. When he got far enough up, Larry reached over, grabbed the crosstie, and put his feet on the board he was going to stand on. He turned himself around until he faced us. I'll never know how the cross held, but it did.

Larry cleared his throat and then looked right at me as he spoke his first words from the cross. "Oh ye of little faith," he said.

It was completely dark, except of course for Larry's sign, by the time Terry and Kevin had been placed on their crosses. As I watched I couldn't help thinking that if they ever did want to bring back crucifixion, the three hanging up there in the dark

5. Wide World of Sports debuted on 29 April 1961 on the ABC network.

would be as good a bunch to start with as any. I looked over my shoulder and saw the traffic was already piled up, and the whole front lawn was filled with people. There was even a TV crew from WSOC in Charlotte.

At 6:30 the music began, and the spotlights Ed Watt had rigged up came on. I had to admit it was impressive, especially if you were far enough away so you didn't see Larry's stomach or Terry's chattering teeth. The WSOC cameras were rolling, and more and more people were crowding onto the lawn and even spilling out into the road, making the first traffic jam in Cliffside's history even worse.

The crucifixion was supposed to last an hour, but after twenty minutes the wind started to pick up, and the crosses began making creaking noises, moving back and forth a little more with each gust of wind. It wasn't long before Terry began to make some noises too, screaming over the music for someone to get a ladder and get him down. I didn't blame him. The crosses were really starting to sway, and Terry, Kevin, and Larry looked like acrobats in some circus high-wire act. But there wasn't a net for them to land in if they fell.

Preacher Thompson and Ed Watt were running to get the ladders, but at least for Larry, it was too late. His cross swung forward one last time, and then I heard the sound of wood cracking. Donnie Splawn heard it too, and he tripped on his Roman Soldier's robe as he ran to get out of the way. Larry screamed out "God help me," probably the sincerest prayer of his life. But it went unanswered. The cross began to fall forward, and Larry, with his arms outstretched, looked like a man doing a swan dive. I closed my eyes at the last second but heard him hit.

Then everything was chaos. People were screaming and shouting and running around in all directions. Janice Hamrick, who's a registered nurse, came out of the crowd to tend to Larry till the rescue squad could get there and take him to the county hospital. Several other people ran over to stabilize the other two crosses. When Terry saw what had happened to his boss, he stained his loincloth. His eyes were closed, and he was praying so fast only God could understand what he was saying. Kevin wasn't saying or doing anything because he had fainted dead away the second his cousin hit the ground.

It's been three weeks now since all this happened. Larry got to leave the county hospital, miraculously, alive, on Easter morning, but his jaw is still wired shut, and it's going to stay that way for at least another month. But despite the broken jaw and broken nose, he still goes out to his car lot every day. Since people over half the state saw him hit the ground, in slow motion, on WSOC's six o'clock news, Larry's become western North Carolina's leading tourist attraction. They come from more miles away than you would believe just to see him, and then he gets his pad and pencil out and tries to sell them a car. Quite a few times he does. As a matter of fact, I hear he's sold more cars in the last two weeks than any two-week period in his life, which is further proof that, as the Bible tells us, we live in a fallen world.

Still, some good things have happened. When Preacher Thompson offered to resign, the congregation made it clear they wanted him to stay, and he has. But he's toned down his sermons a good bit, and last Sunday, when Larry handed him a proposal for an outdoor manger scene with you know who playing Joseph, Preacher Thompson just crumpled it up and threw it in the trashcan.

As for me, a lot of people remember that I was the one who said the crosses were unsafe in the first place, especially one person, Harry Bayne. Two weeks ago Harry took me out to eat as a way of saying thank you. We hit it off and have spent a lot of time together lately. We're going dancing over at Harley's Lounge tonight. I'm still a little scared, almost afraid to hope for too much, but I'm beginning to believe that even in a fallen world things can sometimes look up.

QUESTIONS TO CONSIDER

1. What role does humor play in this story? Why are Rash's descriptions humorous, despite the seriousness of the topic?
2. How would you characterize religion as it appears in this piece? How does the writer represent religion and the individuals who identify with it?

BIBLIOGRAPHY

James Agee

Agee, James. *A Death in the Family*. 1957. New York: Bantam Books, 1969.
———. *Let Us Now Praise Famous Men*. 1941. Boston: Houghton Mifflin, 1988.
Lofaro, Michael A., ed. *James Agee: Reconsiderations*. Knoxville: U of Tennessee P, 1992.
Spiegel, Alan. *James Agee and the Legend of Himself*. Columbia: U of Missouri P, 1998.

Dorothy Allison

Allison, Dorothy. *Bastard Out of Carolina*. New York: Dutton, 1992.
———. *Cavedweller*. New York: Dutton, 1998.
———. *Trash*. Ithaca, NY: Firebrand, 1988.
Bronski, Michael. "Dorothy Allison." *Gay and Lesbian Literature*. Vol.1. Ed. Sharon Malinowski. Detroit: St. James P, 1994. 8–9.
Megan, Carolyn E. "Moving Toward Truth: An Interview with Dorothy Allison." *Kenyon Review* 16 (1994): 71–83.
Moore, Lisa. "Dorothy Allison." *Contemporary Lesbian Writers of the United States: A Bio-Bibliographical Critical Sourcebook*. Ed. Sandra Pollack and Denise D. Knight. Westport, CT: Greenwood P, 1993. 13–18.

A. R. Ammons

Ammons, A.R. *Collected Poems, 1951–1971*. New York: Norton, 1972.
———. *Garbage*. New York: Norton, 1993.
———. *Selected Poems: Expanded Edition*. New York: Norton, 1986.
———. *Set in Motion: Essays, Interviews, and Dialogues*. Ed. Zofia Burr. Ann Arbor: U of Michigan P, 1996.
Bloom, Harold. *A. R. Ammons*. New York: Chelsea House, 1986.
Harmon, William. "Archie Randolph Ammons." *The History of Southern Literature*. Ed. Louis D. Rubin et al. Baton Rouge: Louisiana State UP, 1985. 563–65.
Holder, Alan. *A. R. Ammons*. Boston: Twayne, 1978.
Kirschten, Robert. *Critical Essays on A. R. Ammons*. New York: G. K. Hall, 1997.

Maya Angelou

Angelou, Maya. *And Still I Rise*. New York: Random House, 1978.
———. *I Know Why the Caged Bird Sings*. New York: Random House, 1970.
———. *Wouldn't Take Nothing for My Journey Now*. New York: Random House, 1993.
Bloom, Harold, ed. *Maya Angelou*. Philadelphia: Chelsea House, 2002.
Bloom, Lynne Z. "Maya Angelou." *Dictionary of Literary Biography, Volume 38: Afro-American Writers After 1955: Dramatists and Prose Writers*. Ed. Thadious M. Davis and Trudier Harris. Detroit: Gale, 1985. 3–12.
Powell, Dannye Romine. *Parting the Curtain: Interviews with Southern Writers*. Winston-Salem, NC: John F. Blair, 1994.

James Aswell

Aswell, James. *The Midsummer Fires*. New York: Morrow, 1948.
———. *There's One in Every Town*. Indianapolis: Bobbs-Merrill, 1951.
———. *The Young and Hungry Hearted*. New York: New American Library, 1955.

Aswell, Rosalind Hightower. "James Aswell." Unpublished manuscript. March, 1958. Northwestern State University of Louisiana, Watson Memorial Library, Cammie G. Henry Research Center. James Aswell Collection, Folder 10.

Green, Suzanne Disheroon and David J. Caudle. "Southern Gentility Meets Modern Morality: The Case of James Aswell." *Southern Studies* 7 (1996): 79–87.

FREDERICK BARTHELME

Barthelme, Frederick. *The Brothers*. New York: Viking, 1993.

———. *The Law of Averages: New & Selected Stories*. Washington, DC: Counterpoint, 2002.

———. *Natural Selection*. New York: Viking, 1990.

Blacles, John. "Frederick Barthelme: The Writer as Highroller." *Publishers Weekly* 6 October 1997: 60–62.

Cobb, Emma. "Frederick Barthelme." *Contemporary Southern Writers*. Ed. Roger Matuz. Detroit: St. James, 1999. 218–19.

RICHARD BAUSCH

Bausch, Richard. *Mr. Field's Daughter*. New York: Linden Press-Simon & Schuster, 1989.

———. *Someone to Watch Over Me: Stories*. New York: HarperFlamingo, 1999.

Elie, Paul. "The Way Things Are: Richard Bausch's Unadorned Work" *Commonwealth* 9 November 1990: 242–47.

Lilly, Paul R., Jr. "Richard Bausch." *Dictionary of Literary Biography, Volume 130: American Short-Story Writers Since World War II*. Ed. Patrick Meanor. Detroit: Gale, 1993. 28–34.

WENDELL BERRY

Angyal, Andrew J. *Wendell Berry*. New York: Twayne, 1995.

Berry, Wendell. *The Memory of Old Jack*. New York: Harcourt Brace, 1974.

———. *Nathan Coulter*. Boston: Houghton Mifflin, 1960.

———. *A World Lost*. Washington, D.C.: Publisher's Group West, 1996.

Mortan, Speer. "Wendell Berry: A Fatal Singing." *Southern Review* 10 (1974): 865–77.

Slovic, Scott. *Seeking Awareness in American Nature Writing: Henry Thoreau, Annie Dillard, Edward Abbey, Wendell Berry, Barry Lopez*. Salt Lake City: U of Utah P, 1992.

DORIS BETTS

Betts, Doris. *Astronomer and Other Stories*. New York: Harper and Row, 1965.

———. *Beasts of the Southern Wild*. New York: Harper and Row, 1973.

———. *Sharp Teeth of Love*. New York: Knopf-Random House, 1997.

Ferguson, Mary Anne Heyward. "Doris Betts." *The History of Southern Women's Literature*. Ed. Carolyn Perry and Mary Louise Weaks. Baton Rouge: Louisiana State UP, 2002. 530–34.

Scura, Dorothy M. "Doris Betts at Mid-Career: Her Voice and Her Art." *Southern Women Writers: The New Generation*. Ed. Tonette Bond Inge. Tuscaloosa: U of Alabama P, 1990. 161–79.

ARNA WENDELL BONTEMPS

Abney, Lisa. "Cakewalks, Cauls, and Conjure: Folk Practices in Arna Bontemps's *God Sends Sunday* and "A Summer Tragedy." *Songs of the Reconstructing South: Building Literary Louisiana 1865–1945*. Ed. Suzanne Disheroon-Green and Lisa Abney. Westport, CT: Greenwood P, 2002. 137–48.

Bontemps, Arna Wendell. *Black Thunder*. New York: MacMillan, 1936.

———. *God Sends Sunday*. New York: Harcourt, 1931.

Jones, Kirkland C. *Renaissance Man From Louisiana: A Biography of Arna Wendell Bontemps*. Westport, CT: Greenwood P, 1992.

Larry Brown

Bledsoe, Erik. "The Rise of the Southern Redneck and White Trash Writers." *Southern Cultures* 6.1 (2000): 68–90.

Bonetti, Kay. "An Interview with Larry Brown." *Missouri Review* 18 (1995): 79–107.

Brown, Larry. *Dirty Work*. Chapel Hill, NC: Algonquin, 1989.

———. *Facing the Music*. Chapel Hill, NC: Algonquin, 1988.

———. *Fay*. Chapel Hill, NC: Algonquin, 2000.

Ketchin, Susan. "An Interview with Larry Brown." *Southern Quarterly* 32 (1994): 94–109.

Sterling Brown

Sterling Brown. *The Collected Poems of Sterling Brown*. Ed. Michael S. Harper. New York: Harper, 1980.

———. *A Son's Return: Selected Essays of Sterling A. Brown*. Ed. Mark A. Sanders. Boston: Northeastern UP, 1996.

Gabbin, Joanne V. *Sterling Brown: Building the Black Aesthetic Tradition*. Westport, CT: Greenwood P, 1985.

Sanders, Mark A. *Afro-Modernist Aesthetics & the Poetry of Sterling A. Brown*. Athens: U of Georgia P, 1999.

"Sterling A. Brown: A Special Issue." *Callalloo* 21.4 (1998): 725–1079.

James Lee Burke

Burke, James Lee. *The Convict and Other Stories*. Boston: Little, Brown, 1990.

———. *The Lost Get-Back Boogie*. Baton Rouge: Louisiana State UP, 1986.

———. *Purple Cane Road*. New York: Doubleday, 2000.

Coale, Samuel. "The Dark Domain of James Lee Burke: Mysteries." *Clues: A Journal of Detective Fiction* 18 (1997): 113–35.

Easterling, Thomas. "'All Our Stories Begin Here': Heroism and Sense of Place in James Lee Burke's Dave Robicheaux Mystery Series." *Songs of the New South: Writing Contemporary Louisiana*. Ed. Suzanne Disheroon-Green and Lisa Abney. Westport, CT: Greenwood P, 2001. 57–65.

Hall, Dean G. "James Lee Burke." *Dictionary of Literary Biography, Volume 226: American Hard-Boiled Crime Writers*. Ed. George Parker Anderson and Julie B. Anderson. Detroit: Gale, 2002. 19–30.

William Byrd

Byrd, William. *The Correspondence of the Three William Byrds of Westover, Virginia*. Ed. Marion Tinling. Charlottesville: UP of Virginia, 1977.

———. *The Prose Works of William Byrd: Narratives of a Colonial Gentleman*. Ed. Louis B. Wright. Cambridge: Harvard UP, 1966.

Hatch, Alden. *The Byrds of Virginia*. New York: Holt, Rinehart & Winston, 1969.

Marambaud, Pierre. *William Byrd of Westover, 1674–1744*. Charlottesville: UP of Virginia, 1971.

Siebert, Jr., Donald T. "William Byrd's Histories of the Line." *American Literature* 47 (1976): 535–51.

George Washington Cable

Cable, George Washington. *Old Creole Days*. New York: Scribner's 1879. 1883.

———. *The Creoles of Louisiana*. New York: Scribner's, 1884.

———. *The Silent South*. New York: Scribner's, 1885; expanded 1889. Ed. Arlin Turner. Montclair, NJ: Patterson Smith, 1969.

Cleman, John. *George Washington Cable Revisited*. New York: Twayne P, 1996.

Petry, Alice Hall. *A Genius in His Way: The Art of Cable Old Creole Days*. Rutherford: Fairleigh Dickinson UP, 1988.

Rubin, Louis D., Jr. *George W. Cable, The Life and Times of a Southern Heretic*. New York: Pegasus, 1969.

Erskine Caldwell

Caldwell, Erskine. *God's Little Acre*. 1933. Athens: U of Georgia P, 1995.

———. *Tobacco Road*. 1932. Athens: U of Georgia P, 1995.

Klevar, Harvey L. *Erskine Caldwell: A Biography*. Knoxville: U of Tennessee P, 1993.

Miller, Dan B. *Erskine Caldwell: The Journey from Tobacco Road*. New York: Knopf, 1995.

John C. Calhoun

Calhoun, John C. *Union and Liberty: The Political Philosophy of John C. Calhoun*. Indianapolis: Liberty Fund, 1992.

Ericson, David F. "The Nullification Crisis, American Republicanism, and the Force Bill Debate." *Journal of Southern History* 61.2 (1995): 249–70.

Ford, Lacy K. *Origins of Southern Radicalism: The South Carolina Upcountry, 1800–1860*. New York: Oxford UP, 1988.

Sinha, Manisha. *The Counterrevolution of Slavery; Politics and Ideology in South Carolina*. Chapel Hill: U of North Carolina P, 2000.

W. J. Cash

Cash, W. J. *The Mind of the South*. New York: Knopf, 1940.

Clayton, Bruce. "Cash, W. J." *American National Biography*. Vol. 4. New York: Oxford UP, 1999.

———. *W. J. Cash: A Life*. Baton Rouge: Louisiana State UP, 1991.

Eagles, Charles W. *The Mind of the South: Fifty Years Later*. Jackson: UP of Mississippi, 1992.

Morrison, Joseph L. *W. J. Cash: Southern Prophet. A Biography and Reader*. New York: Knopf, 1967.

Fred Chappell

Bizzarro, Patrick. *Dream Garden: The Poetic Vision of Fred Chappell*. Baton Rouge: Louisiana State UP, 1997.

Chappell, Fred. *The Fred Chappell Reader*. New York: St. Martin's P, 1987.

———. *Midquest: A Poem*. 1981. Baton Rouge: Louisiana State UP, 1989.

———. *Plow Naked: Selected Writings on Poetry*. Ann Arbor: U of Michigan P, 1993.

———. *Spring Garden: New and Selected Poems*. Baton Rouge: Louisiana State UP, 1995.

Lang, John. *Understanding Fred Chappell*. Columbia: U of South Carolina P, 2000.

Mary Boykin Miller Chesnut

Chesnut, Mary Boykin. *A Diary from Dixie, as written by Mary Boykin Chesnut*. Ed. Isabella D. Martin and Myrta Avary Lockett. New York: D. Appleton, 1905.

Fox-Genovese, Elizabeth. *Within the Plantation Household: Black and White Women of the Old South*. Chapel Hill: U of North Carolina P, 1988.

Muhlenfeld, Elisabeth. *Mary Boykin Chesnut: A Biography*. Baton Rouge: Louisiana State UP, 1981.

Woodward, C. Vann, ed. *Mary Chesnut's Civil War*. New Haven: Yale UP, 1981.

Woodward, C. Vann and Elisabeth Muhlenfeld, eds. *The Private Mary Chesnut: The Unpublished Civil War Diaries*. New York: Oxford UP, 1984.

Charles W. Chesnutt

Andrews, William L. *The Literary Career of Charles W. Chesnutt*. Baton Rouge: Louisiana State UP, 1980.

Chesnutt, Charles W. *To Be an Author: Letters of Charles W. Chesnutt, 1885–1905*. Ed. Joseph R. McElrath, Jr. and Robert C. Leitz, III. Princeton: Princeton UP, 1997.

———. *Charles W. Chesnutt: Selected Writings*. Ed. Sally Ann H. Ferguson. Boston: Houghton Mifflin, 2001.

Duncan, Charles. *The Absent Man: The Narrative Craft of Charles W. Chesnutt*. Athens: Ohio UP, 1998.

McElrath, Joseph R., Robert C. Leitz, III, and Jesse S. Crisler, eds. *Charles W. Chesnutt: Essays and Speeches*. Stanford, CA: Stanford UP, 1999.

Wonham, Henry B. *Charles W. Chesnutt: A Study of the Short Fiction*. New York: Twayne, 1998.

Kate Chopin

Chopin, Kate. *At Fault*. 1890. Ed. Suzanne Disheroon-Green and David J. Caudle. Knoxville: U of Tennessee P, 1999.

———. *The Complete Works of Kate Chopin*. Ed. Per Seyersted. Baton Rouge: Louisiana State UP, 1969.

———. *Kate Chopin's Private Papers*. Ed. Emily Toth and Per Seyersted. Bloomington: Indiana UP, 1998.

Ewell, Barbara C. *Kate Chopin*. New York: Ungar, 1986.

Koloski, Bernard. *Kate Chopin: A Study of the Short Fiction*. New York: Twayne, 1996.

Petry, Alice Hall, ed. *Critical Essays on Kate Chopin*. New York: G. K. Hall, 1996.

Toth, Emily. 1990. *Kate Chopin*. Austin: U of Texas P, 1993.

Ebenezer Cook

Cohen, Edward H. *Ebenezer Cooke: The Sot-Weed Canon*. Athens: U of Georgia P, 1975.

Cook, Ebenezer. *Early American Poetry: The Works of Ebenezer Cook*. Ed. Bernard C. Steiner. Baltimore: John Murphy, 1900.

———. *The Maryland Muse*. Annapolis: W. Parks, 1731.

Diser, Philip E. "The Historical Ebenezer Cooke." *Critique: Studies in Modern Fiction* (1968): 48–59.

John Esten Cooke

Aaron, Daniel. *The Unwritten War: American Writers and the Civil War*. New York: Oxford UP, 1973.

Bratton, Mary Jo. "John Esten Cooke and His 'Confederate Lies.'" *Southern Literary Journal* 13 (1981): 72–91.

Cooke, John Esten. *Mohun, or, the Last Days of Lee and His Paladins*. 1869. Ridgewood, NJ: Gregg P, 1968.

———. *Surry of Eagle's Nest, or, The Memoirs of a Staff Officer Serving in Virginia*. 1866. Ridgewood, NJ: Gregg P, 1968.

Solomon, Eric. "The Novelist as Soldier: Cooke and De Forest." *American Literary Realism* 19 (1987): 80–88.

Anna Julia Cooper

Cooper, Anna Julia. *Equality for Races and the Democratic Movement*. Washington, DC: np, 1942 (privately published).
———. *The Third Step: An Autobiography*. np, 1950 (privately published).
———. *A Voice from the South by a Black Woman of the South*. New York: Oxford UP, 1988.
Gabel, Leona C. *From Slavery to the Sorbonne and Beyond: The Life and Writings of Anna Julia Cooper*. Northhampton, MA: Smith College, 1982.
Hutchinson, Louise Daniel. *Anna J. Cooper: A Voice from the South*. Washington, DC: Smithsonian Institution P, 1981.

Harry Crews

Crews, Harry. *Celebration*. New York: Simon and Schuster, 1998.
———. *A Childhood: The Biography of a Place*. Boston: G. K. Hall, 1978.
———. *Classic Crews: A Harry Crews Reader*. New York: Poseidon, 1993.
Guinn, Matthew. *After Southern Modernism: Fiction of the Contemporary South*. Jackson: UP of Mississippi, 2000.
Walsh, William J. *Speak So I Shall Know Thee: Interviews with Southern Writers*. Jefferson NC: McFarland, 1990.

Kate Cumming

Cumming, Kate. *Gleanings from the Southland: Sketches of Life and Manners of the People of the South Before, During, and After the War of Secession, with Extracts from the Author's Journal and Epitome of the New South*. Birmingham: Roberts and Son, 1892.
———. *A Journal of Hospital Life in the Confederate Army of Tennessee, from the Battle of Shiloh to the End of the War; with Sketches of Life and Character, and Brief Notices of Current Events During That Period*. Louisville: John P. Morgan, 1866.
Faust, Drew Gilpin. *Mothers of Invention: Women of the Slaveholding South in the American Civil War*. Chapel Hill: U of North Carolina P, 1996.
Linderman, George F. *Embattled Courage: The Experience of Combat in the American Civil War*. New York: Free P, 1987.
Rable, George C. *Civil Wars: Women and the Crisis of Southern Nationalism*. Urbana: U of Illinois P, 1989.

Margaret Danner

Aldridge, June M. "Benin to Beale Street: African Art in the Poetry of Margaret Danner." *College Language Association Journal* 31.2 (1987): 201–9.
Danner, Margaret. *The Down of a Thistle: Selected Poems, Prose Poems, and Songs*. Waukesha, WI: Country Beautiful, 1976.
———. *Iron Lace*. Millbrook, NY: Kriya P, 1968.
Danner, Margaret and Dudley Randall. *Poem Counterpoem*. Detroit: Broadside P, 1966.
Stetson, Erlene. "Dialectic Voices in the Poetry of Margaret Esse Danner." *Black American Poets Between Worlds, 1940–1960*. Ed. Miller R. Baxter. Knoxville: U of Tennessee P, 1986.

Taft, Claire. "'Her Blood Sings': Margaret Danner's Impressions of African Art Forms." *Langston Hughes Review* 12.2 (1993): 45–49.

Olive Tilford Dargan (Fielding Burke)

Alaimo, Stacy. "'Skin Dreaming': The Bodily Transgressions of Fielding Burke, Octavia Butler, and Linda Hogan." *Ecofeminist Literary Criticism: Theory, Interpretation, Pedagogy*. Ed. Greta Gaard and Patrick D. Murphy. Urbana: U of Illinois P, 1998. 123–38.

Dargan, Olive Tilford. *Call Home the Heart*. Old Westbury, NY: Feminist, 1983.

———. *From My Highest Hill*. Philadelphia: J.B. Lippincott, 1941.

———. *Innocent Bigamy and Other Stories*. Winston-Salem, NC: J. F. Blair, 1962.

Elfenbein, Anna Shannon. "A Forgotten Revolutionary Voice: 'Woman's Place' and Race in Olive Dargan's *Call Home the Heart*." *The Female Tradition in Southern Literature*. Ed. Carol S. Manning. Urbana: U of Illinois P, 1993. 193–208.

Schreibersdorf, Lisa. "Radical Mothers: Maternal Testimony and Metaphor in Four Novels of the Gastonia Strike." *Journal of Narrative Theory* 29.3 (1999): 303–22.

Donald Davidson

Conkin, Paul K. *The Southern Agrarians*. Knoxville: U of Tennessee P, 1988.

Davidson, Donald. "A Mirror for Artists." *I'll Take My Stand: The South and the Agrarian Tradition*. 1930. Baton Rouge: Louisiana State UP, 1977. 28–60.

———. *Poems: 1922–1961*. Minneapolis: U of Minnesota P, 1966.

Young, Thomas Daniel. "The Fugitives: Ransom, Davidson, Tate." *The History of Southern Literature*. Ed. Louis D. Rubin, Jr., et al. Baton Rouge: Louisiana State UP, 1985. 319–32.

Young, Thomas Daniel and M. Thomas Inge. *Donald Davidson: An Essay and a Bibliography*. Nashville: Vanderbilt UP, 1965.

Jefferson Davis

Davis, Jefferson. *The Papers of Jefferson Davis*. Ed. Linda Lasswell Crist. Baton Rouge: Louisiana State UP, 1983–1989.

Davis, Jefferson. *Rise and Fall of the Confederate Government*. 2 vols. New York: D. Appleton, 1881.

Davis, William C. *Jefferson Davis: The Man and His Hour*. New York: HarperCollins, 1991.

Faust, Drew Gilpin. *The Creation of Confederate Nationalism: Ideology and Identity in the Civil War South*. Baton Rouge: Louisiana State UP, 1988.

Gallagher, Gary W. *The Confederate War: How Popular Will, Nationalism, and Military Strategy Could Not Stave Off Defeat*. Cambridge: Harvard UP, 1997.

James Dickey

Baughman, Ronald. *Understanding James Dickey*. Columbia: U of South Carolina P, 1985.

Bloom, Harold, ed. *James Dickey: Modern Critical Views*. New York: Chelsea House, 1987.

Dickey, James. *The James Dickey Reader*. Ed. Henry Hart. New York: Simon & Schuster, 1999.

———. *James Dickey: The Selected Poems*. Ed. Robert Kirschten. Hanover, NH: UP of New England, 1998.

———. *Self-Interviews*. Ed. Barbara Reiss and James Reiss. Garden City, NY: Doubleday, 1970.

———. *The Whole Motion: Collected Poems, 1945–1992*. Middletown, CT: Wesleyan UP, 1992.

Hart, Henry. *James Dickey: The World as a Lie*. New York: Picador, 2000.

Suarez, Ernest. "Toward a New Southern Poetry: Southern Poetry in Contemporary American Literary History." *The Southern Review* 33 (1997): 181–96.

Thomas Dixon, Jr.

Cooke, Raymond. *Thomas Dixon*. New York: Twayne, 1974.

Dixon, Thomas, Jr. *The Clansman: An Historical Romance of the Ku Klux Klan*. 1905. Intro. Thomas D. Clark. Lexington: UP of Kentucky, 1970.

———. *The Leopard's Spots: A Romance of the White Man's Burden—1865–1900*. 1902. Ridgewood, NJ: Gregg P, 1967.

———. *Southern Horizons: The Autobiography of Thomas Dixon*. Ed. Karen Crowe. Alexandria, VA: IWV P, 1984.

Gunning, Sandra. *Race, Rape, and Lynching: The Red Record of American Literature 1890–1912*. New York: Oxford UP, 1996.

Ellen Douglas

Douglas, Ellen. *Apostles of Light*. New York: Houghton, 1973.

———. *Black Cloud, White Cloud*. New York: Houghton, 1963.

———. *Can't Quit You, Baby*. New York: Atheneum, 1988.

McHaney, Thomas L. and Noel Polk, eds. *Southern Quarterly* 33.4 (1995).

Reid, Panthea, ed. *Conversations with Ellen Douglas*. Jackson: UP of Mississippi, 2000.

Weaks, Mary Louise. "Ellen Douglas." *The History of Southern Women Writers*. Ed. Mary Louise Weaks and Carolyn Perry. Baton Rouge: Louisiana State UP, 2002. 512–16.

Frederick Douglass

Blight, David W. "The Private Worlds of Frederick Douglass." *Transition: An International Review* 61 (1993): 161–68.

Bontemps, Arna. *Free at Last: The Life of Frederick Douglass*. New York: Dodd, Mead, 1971.

Douglass, Frederick. *Life and Times of Frederick Douglass, Written by Himself*. New York: Bonanza Books, 1962.

———. *My Bondage and My Freedom*. Urbana: U of Illinois P, 1987.

———. *Narrative of the Life of Frederick Douglass, an American Slave, Written by Himself*. New York: Penguin, 1982.

Martin, Waldo, Jr. *The Mind of Frederick Douglass*. Chapel Hill: U of North Carolina P, 1984.

Andre Dubus

Anderson, Donald and Thomas J. Bonner, eds. *Andre Dubus: Tributes*. New Orleans: Xavier Review P, 2001.

Dubus, Andre. *Adultery and Other Choices*. Boston: Godine, 1977.

———. *Dancing After Hours: Stories*. New York: Knopf, 1996.

———. *We Don't Live Here Anymore: The Novellas of Andre Dubus*. New York: Crown, 1984.

Kennedy, Thomas E. *Andre Dubus: A Study of His Short Fiction*. Boston: Twayne, 1988.

Rowe, Anne E. "Andre Dubus." *Contemporary Fiction Writers of the South: A Bio-Bibliographical Sourcebook*. Ed. Joseph Flora and Robert Bain. Westport, CT: Greenwood P, 1993. 101–11.

John Dufresne

Bell, Kevin Blaine and David J. Caudle. "Fiction is My Religion: Conversations with John Dufresne." *Songs of the New South: Writing Contemporary Louisiana*. Ed. Suzanne Disheroon-Green and Lisa Abney. Westport, CT: Greenwood P, 2001. 87–98.

Caudle, David J. "Postmodernism Goes South: John Dufresne's *Louisiana Power and Light*." *Songs of the New South: Writing Contemporary Louisiana*. Ed. Suzanne Disheroon-Green and Lisa Abney. Westport, CT: Greenwood P, 2001. 77–86.

Dufresne, John. *Deep in the Shade of Paradise*. New York: Norton, 2002.

———. "John Dufresne." 25 July 2002. **www.johndufresne.com**. 5 August 2002.

———. *Louisiana Power and Light*. New York: Norton, 1994.

———. *The Way That Water Enters Stone*. New York: Norton, 1991.

Alice Ruth Moore Dunbar-Nelson

Alexander, Eleanor. *Lyrics of Sunshine and Shadow: The Tragic Courtship and Marriage of Paul Laurence Dunbar and Alice Ruth Moore*. New York: New York UP, 2002.

Bryan, Violet Harrington. "Race and Gender in the Early Works of Alice Dunbar-Nelson." *Louisiana Women Writers: New Essays and a Comprehensive Bibliography*. Ed. Dorothy H. Brown and Barbara C. Ewell. Baton Rouge: Louisiana State UP, 1992. 122–38.

Dunbar-Nelson, Alice Ruth Moore. *Violets and Other Tales*. Boston: Monthly Review P, 1895.

———. *Give Us Each Day: The Diary of Alice Dunbar-Nelson*. Ed. Gloria T. Hull. New York: Norton, 1984.

———. *The Works of Alice Dunbar-Nelson*. 3 vols. Ed. Gloria T. Hull. New York: Oxford UP, 1988.

Hull, Gloria T. *Color, Sex, and Poetry: Three Women Writers of the Harlem Renaissance*. Bloomington: Indiana UP, 1987.

Clyde Edgerton

Abney, Lisa. "Clyde Edgerton." *Contemporary Novelists*. Ed. Neil Schlager and Josh Lauer. Detroit: St. James P, 2001. 283–84.

Edgerton, Clyde. *The Floatplane Notebooks*. Chapel Hill, NC: Algonquin Books, 1988.

———. *Killer Diller*. Chapel Hill, NC: Algonquin Books, 1991.

———. *Raney*. Chapel Hill, NC: Algonquin Books, 1985.

Hennis, R. Sterling. "Clyde Edgerton." *Contemporary Fiction Writers of the South: A Bio-Bibliographical Sourcebook*. Ed. Joseph M. Flora and Robert Bain. Westport, CT: Greenwood P, 1993. 112–22.

Huggins, Cynthia. "Witnessing by Example: Southern Baptists in Clyde Edgerton's *Walking Across Egypt* and *Killer Diller*." *Southern Quarterly* 35.3 (1997): 91–96.

William Faulkner

Blotner, Joseph. *William Faulkner: A Biography*. New York: Random House, 1984.

Faulkner, William. *Collected Stories of William Faulkner.* 1950. New York: Vintage, 1977.

———. *Go Down, Moses*. 1942. New York: Vintage International, 1990.

Davis, Thadious M. *Faulkner's "Negro": Art in a Southern Context*. Baton Rouge: Louisiana State UP, 1983.

Polk, Noel. *Children of the Dark House: Text and Context in Faulkner*. Jackson: UP of Mississippi, 1996.

Roberts, Diane. *Faulkner and Southern Womanhood*. Athens: U of Georgia P, 1994.

Williamson, Joel. *William Faulkner and Southern History*. New York: Oxford UP, 1993.

John Gould Fletcher

Carpenter, Lucas. *John Gould Fletcher and Southern Modernism*. Fayetteville: U of Arkansas P, 1994.

Fletcher, John Gould. "Education, Past and Present." *I'll Take My Stand: The South and the Agrarian Tradition*. 1930. Baton Rouge: Louisiana State UP, 1977. 92–121.

———. *Life Is My Song: The Autobiography of John Gould Fletcher*. New York: Farrar, 1937.

———. *Selected Poems*. New York: Farrar, 1938.

Stephens, Edna B. *John Gould Fletcher*. New York: Twayne, 1967.

Richard Ford

Ford, Richard. *Independence Day*. New York: Knopf, 1995.

———. *Rock Springs*. New York: Atlantic Monthly P, 1987.

———. *The Sportswriter*. New York: Knopf, 1986.

Guinn, Matthew. *After Southern Modernism: Fiction of the Contemporary South*. Jackson: UP of Mississippi, 2000.

Hobson, Fred. "Richard Ford and Josephine Humphreys: Walker Percy in New Jersey and Charleston." *The Southern Writer in the Postmodern World*. Athens: U of Georgia P, 1991. 41–72.

Walker, Elinor Ann. *Richard Ford*. New York: Twayne, 2000.

Alcée Fortier

Fortier, Alcée. *A History of Louisiana*. 2nd ed. Baton Rouge: Claitor's Book Store, 1966.

———. *History of Louisiana*. New York: Goupil, 1904.

———. *Louisiana Folk-Tales, in French Dialect and English Translation*. Ed. Alcée Fortier. New York: Publications of the American Folklore Society—Houghton Mifflin, 1895.

King, Grace. *New Orleans: The Place and the People*. New York: Macmillan, 1937.

Seay, Geraldine. "Kate Chopin's Source for 'At the 'Cadian Ball.' " *Southern Studies* 8.1 (1997): 37–42.

Ernest Gaines

Champion, Laurie. "Equality for African-American (Wo)Men: Quests for Masculinity in Ernest Gaines's *Bloodline*." *Songs of the New South: Writing Contemporary Louisiana*. Ed. Suzanne Disheroon-Green and Lisa Abney. Westport, CT: Greenwood P, 2001. 143–52.

Doyle, Mary Ellen. *Voices from the Quarters: The Fiction of Ernest J. Gaines*. Baton Rouge: Louisiana State UP, 2002.

Gaines, Ernest. *Bloodline*. New York: Dial P, 1968.

———. *A Gathering of Old Men*. New York: Knopf, 1983.

———. *A Lesson Before Dying*. New York: Knopf, 1993.
Lowe, John, ed. *Conversations with Ernest Gaines*. Jackson: UP of Mississippi, 1995.

George Garrett

Dillard, R. H. W. "George Garrett: An Appreciation." *Virginia Quarterly Review* 75 (1999): 459–72.
Garrett, George. *Bad Man Blues: A Portable George Garrett*. Dallas: Southern Methodist UP, 1998.
———. *Poison Pen; or, Live Now and Pay Later*. Winston-Salem, NC: Wright, 1986.
———. *The Succession: A Novel of Elizabeth and James*. Garden City, NY: Doubleday, 1983.
———. *Understanding George Garrett*. Columbia: U of South Carolina P, 1988.
Ruffin, Paul and Stuart Wright, eds. *To Come Up Grinning: A Tribute to George Garrett*. Huntsville, Texas Review P, 1989.

Tim Gautreaux

Gautreaux, Tim. *The Clearing*. New York: Knopf, 2003.
———. *The Next Step in the Dance*. New York: Picador–St. Martin's P, 1998.
———. *Same Place, Same Things*. New York: Picador–St. Martin's, 1996.
———. *Welding with Children*. New York: Picador–St. Martin's P, 1999.
Kane, Julie. "Tim Gautreaux." *Dictionary of Literary Biography: Twenty-First Century American Novelists*. Ed. Lisa Abney and Suzanne Disheroon-Green. Detroit: Bruccoli Clark Layman-Gale, 2004. 119–25.
Levasseur, Jennifer and Kevin Rabelais. "Tim Gautreaux." *Mississippi Review* 27.3 (1999): 19–40.

Kaye Gibbons

Branan, Tonita. "Women and 'the Gift for Gab': Revisionary Strategies in *A Cure for Dreams*." *Southern Literary Journal* 26 (1994): 91–101.
Gibbons, Kaye. *Charms for the Easy Life*. New York: Putnam, 1993.
———. *Ellen Foster*. Chapel Hill, NC: Algonquin, 1988.
———. *On the Occasion of My Last Afternoon*. New York: Putnam, 1998.
Disheroon-Green, Suzanne. "Kaye Gibbons." *Dictionary of Literary Biography: Twenty-First Century American Novelists*. Ed. Lisa Abney and Suzanne Disheroon-Green. Columbia, SC: Bruccoli, Clark, Layman-Gale, 2004. 126–34.
Guinn, Matthew. *After Southern Modernism: Fiction of the Contemporary South*. Jackson: UP of Mississippi, 2000. 57–90.
McKee, Kathryn. "Simply Talking: Women and Language in Kaye Gibbons's *A Cure for Dreams*." *Southern Quarterly* 35.4 (1997): 97–106.

Ellen Gilchrist

Bauer, Margaret Donovan. *The Fiction of Ellen Gilchrist*. Gainesville: UP of Florida, 1999.
Gilchrist, Ellen. *The Annunciation*. Boston: Brown, 1983.
———. *Ellen Gilchrist: Collected Stories*. New York: Bay Back Books, 2001.
———. *In the Land of Dreamy Dreams*. Fayetteville: U of Arkansas P, 1981.
Johnson, Tonya Stremlau. "Ellen Gilchrist's Rhoda: Managing the Fiction." *Southern Quarterly* 35.4 (1997): 87–96.
McCay, Mary A. *Ellen Gilchrist*. New York: Twayne, 1997.

Caroline Howard Gilman

Gilman, Caroline. *Recollections of a Housekeeper*. New York: Harper and Row, 1834.

———. *Recollections of a Southern Matron*. New York: Harper and Row, 1838.

Macdonald, Christine. "Judging Jurisdictions: Geography and Race in Slave Law and Literature of the 1830s." *American Literature* 71 (1999): 625–55.

McCandless, Amy Thompson. "Concepts of Patriarchy in the Popular Novels of Antebellum Southern Women." *Studies in Popular Culture* 10.2 (1987): 1–15.

Moss, Elizabeth. *Domestic Novelists of the Old South: Defenders of the Old South*. Baton Rouge: Louisiana State UP, 1992.

Nikki Giovanni

Fowler, Virginia, ed. *Conversations with Nikki Giovanni*. Jackson: UP of Mississippi, 1992.

Giovanni, Nikki. *Black Feeling, Black Talk/Black Judgement*. New York: Morrow, 1970.

———. *Blues: For All the Changes: New Poems*. New York: Morrow, 1999.

———. *Gemini: An Extended Autobiographical Statement on My First Twenty-Five Years of Being a Black Poet*. Indianapolis: Bobbs-Merrill, 1971.

———. *Nikki Giovanni*. Boston: Twayne, 1992.

———. *The Selected Poems of Nikki Giovanni (1968–1995)*. Intro. Virginia C. Fowler. New York: Morrow, 1996.

Mitchell, Mozella G. "Nikki Giovanni." *Dictionary of Literary Biography, Vol. 41: Afro-American Poets Since 1955*. Ed. Trudier Harris and Thadious M. Davis. Detroit: Gale, 1985. 135–51.

Ellen Glasgow

Glasgow, Ellen. *Barren Ground*. New York: Doubleday-Page, 1925.

———. *They Stooped to Folly*. New York: Doubleday-Page, 1929.

———. *The Woman Within*. New York: Harcourt Brace, 1954.

Godbold, E. Stanly, Jr., *Ellen Glasgow and the Woman Within*. Baton Rouge: Louisiana State UP, 1972.

Thiebaux, Marcelle. *Ellen Glasgow*. New York: Frederick Ungar, 1982.

Wagner, Linda W. *Ellen Glasgow: Beyond Convention*. Austin: U of Texas P, 1982.

Caroline Gordon

Gordon, Caroline. *Aleck Maury, Sportsman*. 1934. Carbondale: Southern Illinois UP, 1980.

———. *Collected Stories of Caroline Gordon*. New York: Farrar, Straus, & Giroux, 1981.

———. *None Shall Look Back*. 1937. Nashville: J. S. Sanders, 1992.

Jonza, Nancylee Novell. *The Underground Stream: The Life and Art of Caroline Gordon*. Athens: U of Georgia P, 1995.

Makowski, Veronica A. *Caroline Gordon: A Biography*. New York: Oxford UP, 1989.

William J. Grayson

Calhoun, Richard J. "The Anti-Secessionist Satires of William J. Grayson." *South Carolina Review* 22 (1990): 50–57.

Grayson, William. *The Hireling and the Slave, Chicora, and Other Poems*. Manchester, NH: Ayer, 1977.

———. *Witness to Sorrow: The Antebellum Autobiography of William J. Grayson*. Ed. Richard James Calhoun. Columbia: U of South Carolina P, 1990.

Hubbell, Jay B. "William J. Grayson." *The South in American Literature, 1607–1900*. Ed. Jay B. Hubbell. Durham, NC: Duke UP, 1954. 438–46.

Parks, Edd Winfield. "William J. Grayson: Neo-Classicist." *Ante-Bellum Southern Literary Critics*. Ed. Winfield Parks. Athens: U of Georgia P, 1962: 185–92.

Angelina Emily Grimké

Browne, Stephen Howard. *Angelina Grimké: Rhetoric, Identity, and the Radical Imagination*. East Lansing: Michigan State UP, 1999.

Degler, Carl N. *The Other South: Southern Dissenters in the Nineteenth Century*. Gainesville: UP of Florida, 2000.

Grimké, Angelina Emily. *An Appeal to the Women of the Nominally Free States; Issued by an Anti-Slavery Convention of American Women & Held by Adjournment from the 9th to the 12th of May, 1837*. 1st ed. New York: W.S. Dorr, 1837.

———. *Appeal to the Christian Women of the Southern States*. New York: n.p., 1836.

———. *Letters to Catherine E. Beecher, in Reply to an Essay on Slavery and Abolitionism, Addressed to A. E. Grimké*. Revised by the Author. Boston: Isaac Knapp, 1838.

Lerner, Gerda. *The Grimké Sisters from South Carolina: Pioneers for Woman's Rights and Abolition*. New York: Schocken Books, 1967.

Woody Guthrie

Guthrie, Woody. *Bound for Glory*. 1943. New York: New American Library, 1995.

———. *Seeds of Man: An Experience Lived and Dreamed*. 1976. Lincoln: U of Nebraska P, 1995.

Klein, Joe. *Woody Guthrie: A Life*. New York: Knopf, 1980.

Yates, Janelle. *Woody Guthrie: American Balladeer*. Staten Island: Ward Hill P, 1995.

George Washington Harris

Caron, James E. and M. Thomas Inge. *Sut Lovingood's Nat'ral Born Yarnspinner: Essays on George Washington Harris*. Tuscaloosa: U of Alabama P, 1996.

Day, Donald. "The Life of George Washington Harris." *Tennessee Historical Quarterly* 4 (1945): 320–38.

Harris, George Washington. *High Times and Hard Times: Sketches and Tales by George Washington Harris*. Ed. M. Thomas Inge. Nashville. Vanderbilt UP, 1967.

———. *Sut Lovingood*. Ed. Brom Weber. New York: Grove, 1954.

———. *Sut Lovingood's Yarns: Edited for the Modern Reader*. Ed. M. Thomas Inge. New Haven, CT: College and University P, 1966.

Plater, Ormand. "Before Art: Folklore in the Early Works of George Washington Harris." *Southern Folklore Quarterly* 34 (1970): 104–14.

Joel Chandler Harris

Bickley, R. Bruce, Jr., *Joel Chandler Harris*. Athens: U of Georgia P, 1987.

Brasch, Walter. *Brer Rabbit, Uncle Remus, and the "Cornfield-Journalist": The Tales of Joel Chandler Harris*. Macon, GA: Mercer UP, 2000.

Brookes, Stella Brewer. *Joel Chandler Harris—Folklorist*. Athens: U of Georgia P, 1950.

Harris, Joel Chandler. *The Complete Tales of Uncle Remus*. Ed. Richard Chase. Boston: Houghton Mifflin, 1955.

———. *Joel Chandler Harris: Editor and Essayist: Miscellaneous Literary, Political, and Social Writings*. Ed. Julia Collier Harris. Chapel Hill: U of North Carolina P, 1931.

———. *On The Plantation: A Story of a Georgia Boy Adventures During the War*. New York: Appleton, 1892.

Caroline Lee Whiting Hentz

Cuenca, Carme Manuel. "An Angel in the Plantation: The Economics of Slavery and the Politics of Literary Domesticity in Caroline Lee Hentz's *The Planter's Northern Bride*." *Mississippi Quarterly* 51 (1997–1998): 86–104.

Hentz, Caroline Lee. *The Planter's Daughter: A Tale of Louisiana*. Philadelphia: Hart, 1858.

———. *The Planter's Northern Bride*. Philadelphia: T. B. Peterson, 1854.

Stanesa, Jamie. "Caroline Hentz's Rereading of Southern Paternalism: Or, Pastoral Naturalism in *The Planter's Northern Bride*." *Southern Studies* 3 (1992): 221–52.

Wimsat, Mary Ann. "Caroline Hentz's Balancing Act." *The Female Tradition in Southern Literature*. Ed. Carol S. Manning. Urbana: U of Illinois P, 1993. 161–75.

Mary Hood

Hood, Mary. *And Venus Is Blue: Stories*. New York: Ticknor & Fields, 1986.

———. *Familiar Heat*. New York: Knopf, 1995.

———. *How Far She Went: Stories*. Athens: U of Georgia P, 1984.

Yow, Dede. "Mary Hood." *Dictionary of Literary Biography, Volume 234: American Short-Story Writers Since World War II, Third Series*. Ed. Patrick Meanor and Richard E. Lee. Detroit: Gale Group, 2001. 135–41.

Johnson Jones Hooper

Hoole, W. Stanley. *Alias Simon Suggs: The Life and Times of Johnson Jones Hooper*. Tuscaloosa: U of Alabama P, 1952.

Hooper, Johnson Jones. *Adventures of Captain Simon Suggs, Late of the Tallapoosa Volunteers*. Ed. Manly W. Wellman. Chapel Hill: U of North Carolina P, 1969.

Smith, Howard Winston. *Johnson Jones Hooper: A Critical Study*. Lexington: U of Kentucky P, 1963.

Yates, Norris W. *William T. Porter and the Spirit of the Times: A Study of the Big Bear School of Humor*. Baton Rouge: Louisiana State UP, 1957. 44–56.

George Moses Horton

Blyde, Jackson. "George Moses Horton, North Carolinian." *North Carolina Historical Review* 53 (1976): 140–47.

Farris, W. Edward. "George Moses Horton: Poet for Freedom." *College Language Association Journal* 14 (1971): 227–41.

Horton, George Moses. *The Black Bard of North Carolina: George Moses Horton and His Poetry*. Ed. Joan R. Sherman. Chapel Hill: U of North Carolina P, 1997.

———. *The Poetical Works of George Moses Horton, the Colored Bard of North-Carolina*. Hillsborough, NC: Heartt, 1845.

Richmond, M. A. *Bid the Vassal Soar: Interpretive Essays on the Life and Poetry of Phyllis Wheatley (ca. 1753–1784) and George Moses Horton (ca. 1797–1883)*. Washington: Howard UP, 1974.

Josephine Humphreys

Bennett, Barbara. "Making Peace with the (M)other." *The World Is Our Home: Society and Culture in Contemporary Southern Writing*. Ed. Jeffrey J. Folks and Nancy Summers Folks. Lexington: UP of Kentucky, 2000. 186–200.

Humphreys, Josephine. "A Disappearing Subject Called the South." *The Prevailing South: Life & Politics in a Changing Culture*. Ed. Dudley Clendinen. Atlanta: Longstreet, 1988. 212–20.
———. *Nowhere Else on Earth*. New York: Viking, 2000.
———. *Rich in Love*. New York: Viking, 1987.
Powell, Dannye Romine. "Josephine Humphreys." *Parting the Curtains: Interviews with Southern Writers*. Winston-Salem, NC: John F. Blair, 1994. 182–95.
Walker, Elinor Ann. "Josephine Humphreys' *Rich in Love*: Redefining Southern Fiction." *Mississippi Quarterly* 47 (1994): 301–15.

ZORA NEALE HURSTON

Harris, Trudier. *The Power of the Porch: The Storyteller's Craft in Zora Neale Hurston, Gloria Naylor, and Randall Kenan*. Athens: U of Georgia P, 1996.
Hemenway, Robert. *Zora Neale Hurston: A Literary Biography*. Urbana: U of Illinois P, 1977.
Hurston, Zora Neale. *The Complete Stories*. New York: HarperCollins, 1995.
———. *Seraph on the Suwanee*. New York: HarperCollins, 1948.
———. *Their Eyes Were Watching God*. New York: HarperPerennial, 1937.
Meisenhelder, Susan Edwards. *Hitting a Straight Lick with a Crooked Stick: Race and Gender in the Work of Zora Neale Hurston*. Tuscaloosa: U of Alabama P, 1999.

HARRIET JACOBS

Andrews, William. *To Tell a Free Story: The First Century of Afro-American Autobiography, 1760–1865*. Urbana: U of Illinois P, 1989.
Foster, Frances Smith. *Written By Herself: Literary Production by African American Women, 1746–1892*. Bloomington: Indiana UP, 1993.
Garfield, Deborah M. and Rafia Zafar, eds. *Harriet Jacobs and Incidents in the Life of a Slave Girl*. Cambridge: Cambridge UP, 1996.
Jacobs, Harriet. *Incidents in the Life of a Slave Girl, Written by Herself*. New York: Signet Classics, 2000.

RANDALL JARRELL

Beck, Charlotte H. "Randall Jarrell: The Precocious Pupil." *The Fugitive Legacy: A Critical History*. Baton Rouge: Louisiana State UP, 2001. 73–88.
Bryant, J. A. *Understanding Randall Jarrell*. Columbia, South Carolina: U of South Carolina P, 1986.
Jarrell, Randall. *The Complete Poems*. New York: Farrar, Straus, & Giroux, 1969.
———. *The Lost World*. New York: Macmillan, 1965.
———. *Selected Poems*. New York: Farrar, Straus, & Giroux, 1990.
Jarrell, Mary von Schrader. *Remembering Randall*. New York: HarperCollins, 1999.
Pritchard, William H. *Randall Jarrell: A Literary Life*. New York: Farrar, Straus, & Giroux, 1990.

THOMAS JEFFERSON

Brodie, Fawn. *Thomas Jefferson: An Intimate History*. New York: Norton, 1974.
Dabney, Virginius. *The Jefferson Scandals: A Rebuttal*. New York: Dodd, Mead, 1981.
Jefferson, Thomas. *Notes on the State of Virginia*. Ed. William Peden. Chapel Hill: U of North Carolina P, 1954.
———. *Thomas Jefferson: Writings*. Ed. Merrill D. Peterson. New York: Library of America, 1984.
Koch, Andrienne. *The Philosophy of Thomas Jefferson*. New York: Columbia UP, 1943.
Peterson, Merrill D. *Thomas Jefferson and the New Nation: A Biography*. New York: Oxford UP, 1970.

James Weldon Johnson

Fleming, Robert E. *James Weldon Johnson*. Boston: Twayne, 1987.

Johnson, James Weldon. *Along This Way: The Autobiography of James Weldon Johnson*. 1933. Ed. Sondra Kathryn Wilson. New York: DaCapo, 2000.

———. *The Autobiography of an Ex-Colored Man*. 1912. Ed. William L. Andrews. New York: Penguin, 1990.

———. *The Selected Writings of James Weldon Johnson*. Ed. Sondra Kathryn Wilson. 2 vols. New York: Oxford UP, 1995.

———. *Complete Poems*. Ed. Sondra Kathryn Wilson. New York: Penguin, 2000.

Levy, Eugene. *James Weldon Johnson: Black Leader, Black Voice*. Chicago: U of Chicago P, 1973.

Price, Kenneth M. and Lawrence J. Oliver. *Critical Essays on James Weldon Johnson*. London: G. K. Hall, 1997.

Rodney Jones

Daniels, Kate. "Human Voices." Rev. of *Elegy for the Southern Drawl*, by Rodney Jones, and *The Dead Alive and Busy*, by Alan Shapiro. *The Southern Review* 36.1 (2000): 165–78.

Harris, Peter. "Varieties of Religious Experience: New Work by Galway Kinnell, Jane Hirshfield, and Rodney Jones." *The Virginia Quarterly Review* 71 (1995): 656–73.

Jones, Rodney. *Apocalyptic Narrative and Other Poems*. Boston: Houghton Mifflin, 1993.

———. *Elegy for the Southern Drawl*. Boston: Houghton Mifflin, 2000.

———. *Transparent Gestures*. Boston: Houghton Mifflin, 1989.

———. *The Unborn*. Boston: Houghton Mifflin, 1985.

Summerlin, Tim. "Rodney Jones." *Dictionary of Literary Biography, Vol. 120: American Poets Since World War II*, Third Series. Ed. R. S. Gwynn. Detroit: Bruccoli Clark Layman—Gale, 1992. 169–72.

Donald Justice

Bawer, Bruce. " 'Avec une Elegance Grave et Lente': The Poetry of Donald Justice." *Verse* 8.3 and 9.1 combined (1992): 44–49.

Gioia, Dana. "Donald Justice: An Interview." *The American Poetry Review* 25 (1996): 37–46.

———. "Three Poets in Mid Career." *The Southern Review* 17.3 (1981): 667–674.

Gioia, Dana and William Logan, eds. *Certain Solitudes: Essays on the Poetry of Donald Justice*. Fayetteville: University of Arkansas P, 1997.

Justice, Donald. *A Donald Justice Reader: Selected Poetry and Prose*. Middlebury, VT: Middlebury College P, 1991.

———. *New and Selected Poems*. New York: Knopf, 1995.

———. *Orpheus Hesitated Beside the Black River: Poems, 1952–1997*. Vancouver, B.C.: Anvil P Poetry, 1998.

———. *The Sunset Maker: Poems/Stories/A Memoir*. New York: Atheneum, 1987.

Julie Kane

Brown, Dorothy H. and Barbara C. Ewell. "Julie Kane." *Louisiana Women Writers: New Essays and a Comprehensive Bibliography*. Baton Rouge: Louisiana State UP, 1992. 308–9.

Do, Kiem and Julie Kane. *Counterpart: A South Vietnamese Naval Officer's War*. Annapolis: Naval Institute P, 1998.

German, Norman. Rev. of *Body and Soul*, by Julie Kane. *The Chiron Review* 9.1 (1990): 18–19.

Kane, Julie. *Body and Soul*. New Orleans: Pirogue Publishing, 1987.

———. *Rhythm & Booze*. Urbana and Chicago: U of Illinois P, 2003.
Swetman, Glenn. Rev. of *Body and Soul*, by Julie Kane. *Louisiana Literature* 6.1 (1989): 81–82.

Elizabeth Keckley

Andrews, William L. "The Changing Moral Discourse of Nineteenth-Century African American Women's Autobiography: Harriet Jacobs and Elizabeth Keckley." *De/Colonizing the Subject: The Politics of Gender in Women's Autobiography*. Ed. Sidonie Smith and Julie Watson. Minneapolis: U of Minnesota P, 1991. 225–41.
Foster, Francis Smith. *Written By Herself: Literary Production by African American Women, 1746–1892*. Bloomington: Indiana UP, 1993.
Hoffert, Sylvia D. "Jane Gray Swisshelm, Elizabeth Keckley, and the Significance of Race Consciousness in American Women's History." *Journal of Women's History* 13 (2001): 8–33.
Keckley, Elizabeth. *Behind the Scenes: Thirty Years a Slave, and Four Years in the White House*. New York: G. W. Carleton, 1868.

Randall Kenan

Harris, Trudier. *The Power of the Porch: The Storyteller's Craft in Zora Neale Hurston, Gloria Naylor, and Randall Kenan*. Athens: U of Georgia P, 1996.
Keith Byerman. "Randall Kenan." *Dictionary of Literary Biography: Twenty-first Century American Novelists*. Vol. 292. Ed. Lisa Abney and Suzanne Disheroon-Green. Detroit: BCL-Gale, 2004. 194–98.
Kenan, Randall. *James Baldwin*. New York: Chelsea House, 1994.
———. *Let the Dead Bury Their Dead*. New York: Harcourt Brace, 1992.
———. *A Visitation of Spirits*. New York: Grove Press, 1989.
McRoer, Robert. "Randall Kenan." *Contemporary Gay American Novelists: A Bio-Bibibliographical Critical Sourcebook*. Westport, CT: Greenwood P, 1993. 232–36.

John Pendleton Kennedy

Kennedy, John Pendleton. *Horse-Shoe Robinson: A Tale of the Tory Ascendency*. New York: Putnam, 1852.
———. *Swallow Barn; or, a Sojourn in the Old Dominion*. Baton Rouge: Louisiana State UP, 1986.
MacKethan, Lucinda. *The Dream of Arcady: Place and Time in Southern Literature*. Baton Rouge: Louisiana State UP, 1980.
Rubin, Louis D. *The Edge of the Swamp: A Study in the Literature and Society of the Old South*. Baton Rouge: Louisiana State UP, 1989.
Simpson, Lewis P. *The Dispossessed Garden: Pastoral and History in Southern Literature*. Baton Rouge: Louisiana State UP, 1983.

Grace King

Bush, Robert. *Grace King: A Southern Destiny*. Baton Rouge: Louisiana State UP, 1983.
Elfenbein, Anna Shannon. *Women on the Color Line: Evolving Stereotypes and the Writings of George Washington Cable, Grace King, Kate Chopin*. Charlottesville: UP of Virginia, 1994.
Jones, Anne Goodwyn. *Tomorrow Is Another Day: The Woman Writer in the South, 1859–1936*. Baton Rouge: Louisiana State UP, 1981.

King, Grace. *Balcony Stories*. New York: Century, 1893.
———. *Grace King of New Orleans: A Selection of Her Writings*. Ed. Robert Bush. Baton Rouge: Louisiana State UP, 1973.
———. *Memories of a Southern Woman of Letters*. 1932. Freeport, NY: Books for Libraries P, 1971.

Martin Luther King, Jr.

Collins, David R., *Not Only Dreamers: The Story of Martin Luther King, Sr. and Martin Luther King, Jr.* Elgin, IL: Brethren P., 1986.
King, Coretta Scott. *My Life with Martin Luther King, Jr.* New York: Holt, 1969.
King, Martin Luther, Jr. *The Autobiography of Martin Luther King, Jr*. Ed. Clayborne Carson. New York: Warner Books, 1998.
———. *A Knock at Midnight: Inspiration from the Great Sermons of Reverend Martin Luther King, Jr*. Ed. Clayborne Carson and Peter Holloran. New York: Warner Books, 1998.
———. *Where Do We Go from Here: Chaos or Community?* Boston: Beacon P, 1968.
Schulke, Flip and Penelope O. McPhee. *King Remembered*. New York: Norton, 1986.

Etheridge Knight

Knight, Etheridge. *Belly Song and Other Poems*. Detroit: Broadside P, 1973.
———. *Born of a Woman: New and Selected Poems*. New York: Houghton Mifflin, 1980.
———. *The Essential Etheridge Knight*. Pittsburgh: U of Pittsburgh P, 1986.
———. *Poems from Prison*. Detroit: Broadside P, 1968.
Lumpkin, Shirley. "Etheridge Knight." *Dictionary of Literary Biography, Vol. 41: Afro-American Poets Since 1955*. Ed. Trudier Harris and Thadious M. Davis. Detroit: Gale, 1985. 202–11.
Nelson, Howard. "Belly Songs: The Poetry of Etheridge Knight." *The Hollins Critic* 18.5 (1981): 1–11.
Tracy, Steven C. "An Interview with Etheridge Knight." MELUS 12.2 (1985): 7–23.

Yusef Komunyakaa

Baer, William. "Still Negotiating with the Images: An Interview with Yusef Komunyakaa." *The Kenyon Review* 20.3–4 (1998): 5–20.
Conley, Susan. "About Yusef Komunyakaa." *Ploughshares* 23 (1997): 202–7.
Komunyakaa, Yusef. *Blue Notes: Essays, Interviews, and Commentaries*. Ed. Radiciani Clytus. Ann Arbor: U of Michigan P, 2000.
———. *Dien Cai Dau*. Middletown, CT: Wesleyan UP, 1988.
———. *Neon Vernacular: New and Selected Poems*. Middletown, CT: Wesleyan UP, 2001.
———. *Pleasure Dome: New and Collected Poems*. Middletown, CT: Wesleyan UP, 2001.
———. *Talking Dirty to the Gods*. New York: Farrar, Straus, 2000.
Stein, Kevin. "Vietnam and the 'Voice Within': Public and Private History in Yusef Komunyakaa's *Dien Cai Dau*." *The Massachusetts Review* 36 (1995–1996): 541–61.
Suarez, Ernest. "Yusef Komunyakaa." *Southbound: Interviews with Southern Poets*. Columbia: U of Missouri P, 1999.130–43.

Robert E. Lee

Eicher, David J. *Robert E. Lee: A Life Portrait*. Lanham, MD: Taylor Publishing, 2002.
Fellman, Michael. *The Making of Robert E. Lee*. Baltimore: Johns Hopkins UP, 2003.

Lee, Robert E. *Personal Remembrances of General Robert E. Lee*. Ed. J. William Jones. New York: Forge, 2003.
———. *The Recollections and Letters of General Robert E. Lee*. Ed. Robert E. Lee, Jr. Collingdale, PA: Diane Publishing, 2000.
Thomas, Emory M. *Robert E. Lee: A Biography*. New York: Norton, 1997.

Henry Clay Lewis

Anderson, John Q. *Louisiana Swamp Doctor: The Life and Writings of Henry Clay Lewis, Alias "Madison Tensas, M.D."* Baton Rouge: Louisiana State UP, 1962.
Keller, Mark A. " 'Aesculapius in Buckskin': The Swamp Doctor as Satirist in Henry Clay Lewis' *Odd Leaves*." *Southern Studies* 18 (1979): 425–48.
Lewis, Henry Clay. *Odd Leaves from the Life of a Louisiana Swamp Doctor*. Baton Rouge: Louisiana State UP, 1997.
Watts, Edward. "In the Midst of a Noisome Swamp: The Landscape of Henry Clay Lewis." *Southern Literary Journal* 22 (1990): 119–28.

Abraham Lincoln

Donald, David Herbert. *Lincoln*. New York: Simon and Schuster, 1995.
Lincoln, Abraham. *Abraham Lincoln, Slavery, and the Civil War: Selected Writings and Speeches*. Ed. Michael P. Johnson. Boston: Bedford Books, 2001.
Miller, William Lee. *Lincoln's Virtues: An Ethical Biography*. New York: Knopf, 2002.
White, Ronald C., Jr. *Lincoln's Greatest Speech: The Second Inaugural Address*. New York: Simon and Schuster, 2002.

Augustus Baldwin Longstreet

Longstreet, Augustus Baldwin. *Augustus Baldwin Longstreet's Georgia Scenes Completed: A Scholarly Text*. Ed. David Rachels. Athens: U of Georgia P, 1998.
Pearson, Michael. "Rude Beginnings of the Comic Tradition in Georgia Literature." *Journal of American Culture* 11 (1988): 51–54.
Rachels, David. "A Biographical Reading of A. B. Longstreet's *Georgia Scenes*." *The Humor of the Old South*. Ed. M. Thomas Inge and Edward J. Piacentino. Lexington: UP of Kentucky, 2001. 113–29.
Wade, John D., et al. *Augustus Baldwin Longstreet: A Study of the Development of Culture in the South*. Athens: U of Georgia P, 1969.

Katharine Du Pre Lumpkin

Hall, Jacquelyn Dowd. " 'To Widen the Reach of Our Love': Autobiography, History, and Desire." *Feminist Studies* 26.1 (2000): 231–47.
———. " 'You must remember this': Autobiography as Social Critique." *Journal of American History* 85 (1998): 439–65.
Hobson, Fred. "The Sins of the Fathers: Lillian Smith and Katharine Du Pre Lumpkin." *Southern Review* 34.4 (1998): 755–79.
Lumpkin, Katharine Du Pre. *The Emancipation of Angelina Grimké*. Chapel Hill: U of North Carolina P, 1974.
———. *The Making of a Southerner*. New York: Knopf, 1947.
———. *The South in Progress*. New York: International P, 1940.

Everette Maddox

Harris, Nancy. Intro. *The Maple Leaf Rag 15th Anniversary Anthology*. New Orleans: Portals P, 1994.

Kunian, David, writer and producer. *He Was a Mess: The Short Life of New Orleans Poet Everette Maddox*. Radio documentary, premiered on WWOZ-FM, New Orleans, April 2002. CD recording.

Maddox, Everette. *American Waste*. New Orleans: Portals P, 1993.

———. *Bar Scotch*. New Orleans: Pirogue Publishing, 1988.

———. "Everette Maddox, 1945 [sic]–1989: Umpteen! or A Preliminary Report on the Poet's Life and Work." Special issue. *The New Orleans Review* 20.3–4 (1994).

———. *The Everette Maddox Song Book*. New Orleans: New Orleans Poetry Journal P, 1982.

Bobbie Ann Mason

Mason, Bobbie Ann. *Clear Springs: A Memoir*. New York: Random House, 1999.

———. *In Country*. New York: Harper & Row, 1985.

———. *Shiloh and Other Stories*. New York: Modern Library, 2001.

Price, Joanna. *Understanding Bobbie Ann Mason*. Columbia: U of South Carolina P, 2000.

Schomburg, Connie R. "Southern Women Writers in a Changing Landscape." *A History of Southern Women Writers*. Ed. Mary Louise Weaks and Carolyn Perry. Baton Rouge: Louisiana State UP, 2002. 478–90.

Wilhelm, Albert. *Bobbie Ann Mason: A Study of the Short Fiction*. New York: Twayne, 1998.

Louisa Susanna Cheves McCord

Fox-Genovese, Elizabeth. *Within the Plantation Household: Black and White Women of the Old South*. Chapel Hill: U of North Carolina P, 1988.

Genovese, Eugene D. and Elizabeth Fox-Genovese. "Slavery, Economic Development, and the Law: The Dilemma of Southern Political Economists, 1800–1860." *Washington and Lee Law Review* 41.1 (1984): 1–29.

McCord, Louisa. *Louisa McCord: Political and Social Essays*. Ed. Richard C. Lounsbury. Charlottesville: UP of Virginia, 1995.

———. *Louisa McCord: Poems, Drama, Biography, Letters*. Ed. Richard C. Lounsbury. Charlottesville: UP of Virginia, 1996.

McCurry, Stephanie. "The Two Faces of Republicanism: Gender and Proslavery Politics in Antebellum South Carolina." *Journal of American History* 78 (1992): 1245–64.

Jill McCorkle

Bennett, Barbara. *Understanding Jill McCorkle*. Columbia: U of South Carolina P, 2000.

McCord, Charline. " 'I Still See with a Southern Eye': An Interview with Jill McCorkle." *Southern Quarterly* 36.3 (1998): 103–12.

McCorkle, Jill. *The Cheerleader*. Chapel Hill, NC: Algonquin Books, 1984.

———. *Creatures of Habit*. Chapel Hill, NC: Algonquin Books, 2001.

———. *Tending to Virginia*. Chapel Hill, NC: Algonquin Books, 1987.

Pierce, Todd. "Jill McCorkle: The Emergence of the New South." *Southern Studies* 5.3–4 (1994): 19–30.

Carson McCullers

Carr, Virginia Spencer. *The Lonely Hunter: A Biography of Carson McCullers*. Athens: U of Georgia P, 2003.

Dews, Carlos L. *Illumination and Night Glare: The Unfinished Autobiography of Carson McCullers*. Madison: U of Wisconsin P, 1999.

Gleeson–White, Sarah. *Strange Bodies: Gender and Identity in the Novels of Carson McCullers*. Tuscaloosa: U of Alabama P, 2003.

McCullers, Carson. *The Ballad of the Sad Café and Other Stories*. Boston: Houghton Mifflin, 1951.

———. *The Heart is a Lonely Hunter*. Boston: Houghton Mifflin, 1940.

———. *The Mortgaged Heart: Stories*. New York: Penguin, 1975.

Martha McFerren

Brown, Dorothy H. and Barbara C. Ewell. "Martha McFerren." *Louisiana Women Writers: New Essays and a Comprehensive Bibliography*. Baton Rouge: Louisiana State UP, 1992. 314.

McFerren, Martha. *Contours for Ritual*. Baton Rouge: Louisiana State UP, 1988.

———. *Delusions of a Popular Mind*. New Orleans: New Orleans Poetry Journal P, 1983.

———. *Get Me Out of Here!* Green Harbor, MA: Wampeter Press, 1984.

———. *Women in Cars*. Kansas City, MO: Helicon Nine Editions, 1992.

Matthews, William. "Terrors." Rev. of *Women in Cars*, by Martha McFerren. *Shenandoah* 43.4 (1993): 94–102.

Taylor, Charles. Rev. of *Delusions of a Popular Mind*, by Martha McFerren. *Pawn Review* 8.1 (1984): 152–53.

James Alan McPherson

Beavers, Herman. *Wrestling Angels into Song: The Fictions of Ernest J. Gaines and James Alan McPherson*. Philadelphia: U of Pennsylvania P, 1995.

Lubiana, Wahneema. "Shuckin' Off the African-American Native Other: What's 'Po-Mo' Got to Do with It?" *Dangerous Liaisons: Gender, Nation, and Postcolonial Perspectives*. Ed. Anne McClintock, Aamir Mufti, and Ella Shohat. Minneapolis: U of Minnesota P, 1997. 204–29.

McPherson, James Alan. *Crabcakes*. New York: Simon and Schuster, 1998.

———. *Elbow Room*. Boston: Little, Brown, 1977.

———. *Hue and Cry*. Boston: Little, Brown, 1969.

Wallace, Jon. "The Story Behind the Story in James Alan McPherson's *Elbow Room*." *Studies in Short Fiction* 25 (1988): 447–52.

H. L. Mencken

Hobson, Fred. " 'This Hellawful South': Mencken and the Late Confederacy." *Critical Essays on H. L. Mencken*. Ed. Douglas C. Stenerson. Boston: G. K. Hall, 1987.

Lawson, Lewis A. *Another Generation: Southern Fiction Since World War II*. Jackson: UP of Mississippi, 1984.

Mencken, H. L. *Damn! A Book of Calumny*. New York: Philip Goodman, 1918.

———. *In Defense of Women*. New York: Philip Goodman, 1918.

———. *Prejudices: First Series*. New York: Knopf, 1919.

(*Note:* Mencken went on to publish a total of six volumes in his *Prejudices* series, with the final one appearing in 1927).

Vassar Miller

Banks, Joanne Trautmann. "Vassar Miller: A Retrospective." *Literature and Medicine* 19.2 (2000): 137–164.

Brown, Steven Ford, ed. *Heart's Invention: On the Poetry of Vassar Miller*. Houston: Ford-Brown, 1988.

Griffin, Shaun. "A Genius Obscured: Vassar Miller Is the Emily Dickinson of the 20th Century. Who Knew?" *Sojourners* 29.3 (2000): 50–51.

Miller, Vassar, ed. *Despite This Flesh: The Disabled in Stories and Poems*. Austin: U of Texas P, 1985.

———. *If I Had Wheels or Love: Collected Poems of Vassar Miller*. Dallas: Southern Methodist UP, 1991.

———. *Selected and New Poems*. Austin, TX: Latitudes P, 1982.

Margaret Mitchell

Allen, Patrick, ed. *Margaret Mitchell: Reporter*. Athens, GA: Hill Street P, 2000.

Edwards, Anne, *Road to Tara: The Life of Margaret Mitchell*. New Haven, CT: Ticknor & Fields, 1983.

Harwell, Richard, ed. *Gone with the Wind as Book and Film*. Columbia: U of South Carolina P, 1983.

Mitchell, Margaret. *Before Scarlett: Girlhood Writings of Margaret Mitchell*. Ed. Jane Eskridge. Athens, GA: Hill Street P, 2000.

———. *Gone With the Wind*. New York: Macmillan, 1936.

———. *Lost Laysen*. Ed. Debra Freer. New York: Scribner's, 1996.

Robert Morgan

Chappell, Fred. "Double Language: Three Appalachian Poets." *Appalachian Journal: A Regional Studies Review* 8 (1980): 55–59.

Harmon, William. "Robert Morgan's Pelagian Georgics: Twelve Essays." *Parnassus: Poetry in Review* 9.2 (1981): 5–30.

Lang, John. " 'Coming Out from under Calvinism': Religious Motifs in Robert Morgan's Poetry." *Shenandoah* 42.2 (1992): 46–60.

Morgan, Robert. *Green River: New and Selected Poems*. Hanover, NH: Wesleyan UP, 1991.

———. *Good Measure: Essays, Interviews, and Notes on Poetry*. Baton Rouge: Louisiana State UP, 1993.

———. *Topsoil Road*. Baton Rouge: Louisiana State UP, 2000.

Sarah Morgan

Dawson, Sarah Morgan. *The Civil War Diary of Sarah Morgan*. Ed. Charles East. Athens: U of Georgia P, 1991.

———. *A Confederate Girl's Diary*. Boston: Houghton Mifflin, 1913.

Faust, Drew Gilpin. *Mothers of Invention: Women of the Slaveholding South in the Civil War*. Chapel Hill: U of North Carolina P, 1996.

Rable, George. *Civil Wars: Women and the Crisis of Southern Nationalism*. Urbana: U of Illinois P, 1991.

Wilson, Edmund. *Patriotic Gore: Studies in the Literature of the American Civil War*. New York: Oxford UP, 1962.

Mary Noailles Murfree (Charles Egbert Craddock)

Cary, Richard. *Mary Noailles Murfree*. New Haven: Twayne, 1967.

Murfree, Mary Noailles. *In the Tennessee Mountains*. 1884. Ed. Nathalia Wright. Knoxville: U of Tennessee P, 1970.

———. *The Phantoms of the Foot-Bridge, and Other Stories*. New York: Harper, 1895.

———. *The Story of Duciehurst: A Tale of the Mississippi*. New York: Macmillan, 1914.

Parks, Edd Winfield. *Charles Egbert Craddock (Mary Noailles Murfree)*. Chapel Hill: U of North Carolina P, 1941.

Pryse, Marjorie. "Exploring Contact: Regionalism and the 'Outsider' Standpoint in Mary Noailles Murfree's Appalachia." *Legacy* 17 (2000): 199–212.

Marilyn Nelson

Jones, Kirkland C. "Marilyn Nelson Waniek." *Dictionary of Literary Biography, Vol. 120: American Poets Since World War II*. Ed. R. S. Gwynn. Detroit: Bruccoli Clark Layman-Gale, 1992. 311–15.

Martin, Herbert Woodward. Review of *Carver: A Life in Poems*, by Marilyn Nelson. *African-American Review* 36.2 (2002): 345–50.

Nelson, Marilyn. *Carver: A Life in Poems*. Asheville, NC: Front Street, 2001.

———. *The Fields of Praise: New and Selected Poems*. Baton Rouge: Louisiana State UP, 1997.

———. *The Homeplace*. Baton Rouge: Louisiana State UP, 1990.

Williams, Miller. Rev. of *The Fields of Praise: New and Selected Poems*, by Marilyn Nelson. *African-American Review* 33.1 (1999): 179–82.

Lewis Nordan

Baker, Barbara A. *The Blues Aesthetic and the Making of American Identity in the Literature of the South*. New York: Peter Lang, 2003.

Bjerre, Thomas Aervold. "Interview with Lewis Nordan, at His Home in Pittsburgh, May 19, 2001." *Mississippi Quarterly* 54 (2001): 367–81.

Dupuy, Edward J. "Memory, Death, and Delta, and St. Augustine: Autobiography in Lewis Nordan's *The Music of the Swamp*." *Southern Literary Journal* 30 (1998): 96–108.

Nordan, Lewis. *Boy with Loaded Gun: A Memoir*. Chapel Hill, NC: Algonquin, 2000.

———. *Music of the Swamp*. Chapel Hill, NC: Algonquin, 1991.

———. *Sugar Among the Freaks: Selected Stories*. Chapel Hill, NC: Algonquin, 1996.

Flannery O'Connor

Cash, Jean Wampler. *Flannery O'Connor: A Life*. Knoxville: U of Tennessee P, 2002.

O'Connor, Flannery. *A Good Man Is Hard to Find*. New York: Harcourt Brace, 1955.

———. *Everything That Rises Must Converge*. New York: Farrar, Straus, & Giroux, 1965.

———. *The Violent Bear It Away*. New York: Farrar, Straus, & Giroux, 1960.

Westling, Louise. *Sacred Groves and Ravaged Gardens: The Fiction of Eudora Welty, Carson McCullers, and Flannery O'Connor*. Athens: U of Georgia P, 1985.

Yaeger, Patricia S. "Flannery O'Connor." *Modern American Women Writers*. Ed. Elaine Showalter, Lea Baechler, and A. Walton Litz. New York: Collier-Macmillan, 1993. 247–57.

Myra Page

Baker, Christina L. *In a Generous Spirit: A First-Person Biography of Myra Page*. Urbana: U of Illinois P, 1996.

Page, Myra. *Daughter of the Hills: A Woman's Part in the Coal Miners' Struggle*. 1950. Old Westbury, NY: Feminist P, 1986.

———. *Gathering Storm: A Story of the Black Belt*. New York: International, 1932.

Thomas Nelson Page

Gross, Theodore L. *Thomas Nelson Page*. New York: Twayne P, 1967.

MacKethan, Lucinda Hardwick. *The Dream of Arcady: Time and Place in Southern Literature*. Baton Rouge: Louisiana State UP, 1980.

Page, Rosewell. *Thomas Nelson Page: A Memoir of a Virginia Gentleman by His Brother*. New York: Charles Scribner's Sons, 1923.

Page, Thomas Nelson. *In Ole Virginia or Marse Chan and Other Stories*. 1887. Ed. Kimball King. Chapel Hill: U of North Carolina P, 1969.

———. *Red Rock: A Chronicle of Reconstruction*. New York: Charles Scribner's Sons, 1898.

———. *Social Life in Old Virginia Before the War*. New York: Charles Scribner's Sons, 1897.

Walker Percy

O'Gorman, Farrell. "Walker Percy, the Catholic Church, and Southern Race Relations." *Mississippi Quarterly* 53.1 (1999): 443–52.

Percy, Walker. *The Message in the Bottle*. New York: Picador USA—Farrar, Straus, & Giroux, 1975.

———. *The Moveigoer*. New York: Vintage—Random House, 1960.

———. *Signposts in a Strange Land*. New York: Picador USA—Farrar, Straus, & Giroux, 1991.

Rudnicki, Robert W. *Percyscapes: The Fugue State in Twentieth–Century Southern Fiction*. Baton Rouge: Louisiana State UP, 1999.

Wyatt-Brown, Bertram. *The Literary Percys: Family History, Gender, and the Southern Imagination*. Athens: U of Georgia P, 1994.

William Alexander Percy

Barry, John M. *Rising Tide: The Great Mississippi Flood of 1927 and How It Changed America*. New York: Simon & Schuster, 1997.

Percy, William Alexander. *Lanterns on the Levee: Recollections of a Planter's Son*. 1941. Baton Rouge: Louisiana State UP, 1973.

Wyatt-Brown, Bertram. *The House of Percy: Honor, Melancholy, and Imagination in a Southern Family*. New York: Oxford UP, 1994.

George Sessions Perry

Abney, Lisa. "Textual Suppression in George Sessions Perry's *Hold Autumn in Your Hand* and Alice Walker's *The Third Life of Grange Copeland*." *Humanities in the South* 81 (1998): 17–34.

Hairston, Maxine. *George Sessions Perry: His Life and Works*. Austin: Pemberton P, 1973.
Perry, George Sessions. *Hackberry Cavalier*. New York: Viking, 1944.
———. *Hold Autumn in Your Hand*. New York: Viking, 1941.
———. *Walls Rise Up*. New York: Doubleday Doran, 1939.

Jayne Anne Phillips

Disheroon-Green, Suzanne. "Jayne Anne Phillips." *The History of Southern Women's Literature*. Ed. Carolyn Perry and Mary Louise Weaks. Baton Rouge: Louisiana State UP, 2002. 594–98.
Grove, James. " 'Because God's Eye Never Closes': The Problem of Evil in Jayne Anne Phillips's *Shelter*." *The World Is Our Home: Society and Culture in Contemporary Southern Writing*. Ed. Jeffrey J. Folks and Nancy Summers Folks. Lexington: UP of Kentucky, 2000. 73–92.
Lyons, Bonnie. "The Mystery of Language." *Passion and Craft: Conversations with Notable Writers*. Ed. Bonnie Lyons and Bill Oliver. Urbana: U of Illinois P, 1998. 159–70.
Phillips, Jayne Anne. *Fast Lanes*. New York: Vintage Contemporaries, 2000.
———. *Machine Dreams*. New York: Dutton/S. Lawrence, 1984.
———. *Shelter*. Boston: Seymour Lawrence-Houghton Mifflin, 1994.

Edgar Allan Poe

Carlson, Eric W., ed. *A Companion to Poe Studies*. Westport, CT: Greenwood P, 1996.
Kennedy, J. Gerald., ed. *A Historical Guide to Edgar Allan Poe*. New York: Oxford UP, 2001.
Poe, Edgar Allan. *Poetry and Tales of Edgar Allan Poe*. Ed. Patrick Quinn. New York: Library of America, 1984.
Quinn, Arthur Hobson. *Edgar Allan Poe: A Critical Biography*. Baltimore: Johns Hopkins UP, 1998.
Silverman, Kenneth. *Edgar A. Poe: Mournful and Never-Ending Remembrance*. New York: HarperCollins, 1991.

Katherine Anne Porter

Busby, Mark, Dick Heaberlin, and Betsy Colquitt, eds. *From Texas to the World and Back: Essays on the Journeys of Katherine Anne Porter*. Fort Worth: Texas Christian UP, 2001.
Givner, Joan. *Katherine Anne Porter: A Life*. Rev. ed. Athens: U of Georgia P, 1991.
Porter, Katherine Anne. *Collected Essays and Occasional Writings of Katherine Anne Porter*. Boston: Houghton Mifflin, 1970.
———. *Collected Stories of Katherine Anne Porter*. New York: Harcourt Brace Jovanovich, 1979.
———. *Uncollected Early Prose of Katherine Anne Porter*. Ed. Ruth M. Alvarez and Thomas F. Walsh. Austin: U of Texas P, 1993.
Stout, Janis P. *Katherine Anne Porter: A Sense of the Times*. Charlottesville: UP of Virginia, 1995.

Reynolds Price

Humphries, Jefferson. *Conversations with Reynolds Price*. Jackson: UP of Mississippi, 1991.
Price, Reynolds. *Good Hearts*. New York: Antheneum, 1988.
———. *A Long and Happy Life*. New York: Antheneum, 1962.
———. *Permanent Errors*. New York: Antheneum, 1970.
Rooke, Constance. *Reynolds Price*. Boston: Twayne, 1983.

John Crowe Ransom

Malvasi, Mark G. *The Unregenerate South: The Agrarian Thought of John Crowe Ransom, Allen Tate, and Donald Davidson*. Baton Rouge: Louisiana State UP, 1997.

Parsons, Thornton H. *John Crowe Ransom*. New York: Twayne, 1969.

Ransom, John Crowe. *Beating the Bushes: Selected Essays, 1941–1970*. Norfolk, CT: New Directions, 1972.

———. "Introduction: A Statement of Principles" and "Reconstructed but Unregenerate." *I'll Take My Stand: The South and the Agrarian Tradition*. 1930. Baton Rouge: Louisiana State UP, 1977. xxxvii–xlviii.

———. *Selected Poems*. 3rd ed. New York: Knopf, 1969.

Young, Thomas Daniel. *Gentleman in a Dustcoat: A Biography of John Crowe Ransom*. Baton Rouge: Louisiana State UP, 1976.

Ron Rash

Brown, Joyce Compton. "The Dark and Clear Vision of Ron Rash." *Appalachian Heritage* 30.4 (2000): 15–24.

House, Silas. "Making Himself Heard." *Appalachian Heritage* 30.4 (2000): 11–14.

Rash, Ron. *Casualties*. Beaufort, SC: Bench P, 2000.

———. *The Night New Jesus Fell to Earth*. Columbia, SC: Bench P, 1994.

———. *One Foot in Eden*. Charlotte, NC: Novello Festival P, 2002.

John Shelton Reed

Reed, John Shelton. *The Enduring South: Subcultural Persistence in Mass Society*. Lexington, MA: Lexington Books, 1972.

———. "The South According to Reed." Special Issue of *Southern Cultures* 7.1 (2001).

———. *1001 Things Everyone Should Know About the South*. New York: Doubleday, 1996.

———. *Whistling Dixie: Dispatches from the South*. Columbia: U of Missouri P, 1990.

Elizabeth Madox Roberts

Hall, Wade. "Place in the Short Fiction of Elizabeth Madox Roberts." *Kentucky Review* 6.3 (1986): 3–16.

Harrison, Elizabeth Jane. *Female Pastoral: Women Writers Re-Visioning the American South*. Knoxville: U of Tennessee P, 1991.

Mellard, James. "The Fiction of Social Commitment." *The History of Southern Literature*. Ed. Louis D. Rubin, Blyden Jackson, Rayburn S. Moore, Lewis P. Simpson, and Thomas Daniel Young. Baton Rouge: Louisiana State UP, 1985. 351–62.

Roberts, Elizabeth Madox. *The Haunted Mirror: Stories*. New York: Viking P, 1932.

———. *Not By Strange Gods*. New York: Viking P, 1941.

———. *The Time of Man*. New York: Viking P, 1926.

Sonia Sanchez

Gabbin, Joanne Veal. "The Southern Imagination of Sonia Sanchez." *Southern Women Writers: The New Generation*. Ed. Tonette Bond Inge. Birmingham: U of Alabama P, 1990. 180–202.

Joyce, Joyce A. *Ijala: Sonia Sanchez and the African Poetic Tradition*. Chicago: Third World P, 1996.

Leibowitz, Herbert. "Exploding Myths: An Interview with Sonia Sanchez." *Parnassus* 12.2 and 13.1 (1985): 357–68.

Sanchez, Sonia. *Homegirls & Handgrenades*. New York: Thunder's Mouth P, 1984.

———. *I've Been a Woman: New and Selected Poems*. Sausalito, CA: Black Liberation P, 1983.
———. *Shake Loose My Skin: New and Selected Poems*. Boston: Beacon P, 1999.

Lyle Saxon

Disheroon-Green, Suzanne. "Bleaching the Color Line: Caste Structures in Lyle Saxon's *Children of Strangers* and Zora Neale Hurston's *Their Eyes Were Watching God*." *Songs of the Reconstructing South: Building Literary Louisiana, 1865–1945*. Westport, CT: Greenwood P, 2002. 109–21.
Dorman, Caroline. "Southern Personalities: Lyle Saxon." *Hollands: The Magazine of the South*. Jan. 1931: 66–67.
Saxon, Lyle. *Children of Strangers*. 1937. Gretna, LA: Pelican, 1989.
———. *Father Mississippi*. New York: Century, 1927.
———. *Lafitte the Pirate*. New York: Century, 1930.
Thomas, James W. *Lyle Saxon: A Critical Biography*. Birmingham: Summa P, 1991.

Karl Shapiro

Madden, Charles F. "Karl Shapiro." *Talks with Authors*. Carbondale: Southern Illinois UP, 1968.
Mills, Ralph J., Jr. "Karl Shapiro." *Contemporary American Poetry*. New York: Random House, 1965. 101–21.
Reino, Joseph. *Karl Shapiro*. Boston: Twayne, 1981.
Shapiro, Karl. *Collected Poems: 1948–1978*. New York: Random House, 1978.
———. *New and Selected Poems, 1940–1986*. Chicago: U of Chicago P, 1987.
———. *The Poetry Wreck: Selected Essays, 1950–1970*. New York: Random House, 1975.
———. *The Wild Card: Selected Poems, Early and Late*. Ed. Stanley Kunitz and David Ignatow. Champaign: U of Illinois P, 1998.

William Gilmore Simms

Guilds, John Caldwell. *Simms: A Literary Life*. Fayetteville: U of Arkansas P, 1992.
Simms, William Gilmore. *Selected Poems of William Gilmore Simms*. Ed. James Everett Kibler. Athens: U of Georgia P, 1990.
———. *The Simms Reader: Selections from the Writings of William Gilmore Simms*. Ed. John Caldwell Guilds. Charlottesville: UP of Virginia, 2001.
———. *Tales of the South by William Gilmore Simms*. Ed. Mary Ann Wimsatt. Columbia: U of South Carolina P, 1996.
Wakelyn, Jon L. *The Politics of a Literary Man: William Gilmore Simms*. Westport, CT: Greenwood P, 1973.
Wimsatt, Mary Ann. *The Major Fiction of William Gilmore Simms: Cultural Traditions and Literary Forms*. Baton Rouge: Louisiana State UP, 1989.

Dave Smith

DeMott, Robert. "Dave Smith." *Dictionary of Literary Biography, Vol. 5: American Poets Since World War II*. Ed. Donald J. Greiner. Detroit: Gale, 1980. 253–62.
Smith, Dave. *Floating on Solitude: Three Volumes of Poetry*. Urbana: U of Illinois P, 1996.
———. *Local Assays: On Contemporary American Poetry*. Urbana: U of Illinois P, 1985.
———. *The Roundhouse Voices: Selected and New Poems*. New York: Harper & Row, 1985.
———. *The Wick of Memory: New and Selected Poems, 1974–2000*. Baton Rouge: Louisiana State UP, 2000.

Suarez, Ernest. "Dave Smith." *Southbound: Interviews with Southern Poets*. Columbia: U of Missouri P, 1999. 20–38.

Weigl, Bruce, ed. *The Giver of Morning: On the Poetry of Dave Smith*. Birmingham, AL: Thunder City P, 1982.

John Smith

Barbour, P. L. *The Three Worlds of Captain John Smith*. Boston: Houghton Mifflin, 1964.

Smith, Bradford. *Captain John Smith, His Life and Legend*. NY: Lippincott, 1953.

Smith, John. *Captain John Smith: A Selection of His Writings*. Ed. Karen Ordahl Kupperman. Chapel Hill: U of North Carolina P, 1988.

———. *The Complete Works of Captain John Smith*. Ed. Philip L. Barbour. Chapel Hill: U of North Carolina P, 1986.

Vaughan, Alden T. *American Genesis: Captain John Smith and the Founding of Virginia*. Boston: Little, Brown, 1975.

Lee Smith

Hill, Dorothy Combs. *Lee Smith*. New York: Twayne, 1992.

Jones, Anne Goodwyn. "The World of Lee Smith." *Southern Quarterly* 22 (1983): 115–39.

Smith, Lee. *Me and My Baby View the Eclipse*. New York: Putnam, 1990.

———. *News of the Spirit*. New York: Putnam, 1997.

———. *Oral History*. New York: Putnam, 1983.

Tate, Linda, ed. *Conversations with Lee Smith*. Jackson: UP of Mississippi, 2001.

Lillian Smith

Gladney, Margaret Rose, ed. *How Am I To Be Heard? Letters of Lillian Smith*. Chapel Hill: U of North Carolina P, 1993.

Hobson, Fred. *The White Southern Racial Conversion Narrative*. Baton Rouge: Louisiana State UP, 1999.

Jenkins, McKay. *The South in Black and White: Race, Sex, and Literature in the 1940s*. Chapel Hill: U of North Carolina P, 1999.

Smith, Lillian. *Killers of the Dream*. 1949; New York: Norton, 1994.

———. *Strange Fruit*. 1944: New York: Harvest, 1992.

Southern Agrarians

Conkin, Paul. K. *The Southern Agrarians*. Knoxville: U of Tennessee P, 1988.

I'll Take My Stand: The South and the Agrarian Tradition. 1930. New Introduction by Louis D. Rubin, Jr. Baton Rouge: Louisiana State UP, 1977.

Inge, M. Thomas. "The Fugitives and the Agrarians: A Clarification." *American Literature* 62.3 (1990): 486–93.

Malvasi, Mark G. *The Unregenerate South: The Agrarian Thought of John Crowe Ransom, Allen Tate, and Donald Davidson*. Baton Rouge: Louisiana State UP, 1997.

Rock, Virginia. "Twelve Southerners: Biographical Essays." *I'll Take My Stand: The South and the Agrarian Tradition*. Baton Rouge: Louisiana State UP, 1977. 361–410.

Anne Spencer

Greene, J. Lee. *Time's Unfading Garden: Anne Spencer's Life and Poetry*. Baton Rouge: Louisiana State UP, 1977.

Johnson, James Weldon, ed. *The Book of American Negro Poetry*. New York: Harcourt, 1922.

Johnston, Sara Andrews. "Anne Spencer." *American Women Writers, 1900–1945: A Bio-Bibliographical Sourcebook*. Ed. Laurie Champion. Westport, CT: Greenwood, 2000. 312–17.

Stetson, Erlen "Anne Spencer." *College Language Association Journal* 21 (1978): 400–9.

Elizabeth Spencer

Prenshaw, Peggy Whitman. *Elizabeth Spencer*. Boston: Twayne, 1985.

———. *Self and Community in the Fiction of Elizabeth Spencer*. Baton Rouge: Louisiana State UP, 1994.

Spencer, Elizabeth. *Jack of Diamonds and Other Stories*. New York: Viking, 1988.

———. *The Stories of Elizabeth Spencer*. Garden City, NY: Doubleday, 1981.

———. *Voice at the Back Door*. New York: McGraw-Hill, 1956.

Ruth McEnery Stuart

Hall, Joan Wylie. "'White Mamma . . . Black Mammy': Replacing the Absent Mother in the Works of Ruth McEnery Stuart." *Southern Mothers: Fact and Fictions in Southern Women's Writing*. Ed. Nagueyalti Warren and Sally Wolff. Baton Rouge: Louisiana State UP, 1999. 64–80.

Johanningsmeier, Charles. "Ruth McEnery Stuart (1849–1917)." *Nineteenth-Century American Women Writers: A Bio-Bibliographical Critical Sourcebook*. Ed. Denise D. Knight and Emmanuel S. Nelson. Westport, CT: Greenwood, 1997. 414–19.

Stuart, Ruth McEnery. *A Golden Wedding and Other Tales*. New York: Harper & Brothers, 1893.

———. *Simpkinsville and Vicinity: Arkansas Stories of Ruth McEnery Stuart*. Ed. Ethel C. Simpson. 1983. Fayetteville: U of Arkansas P, 1999.

———. *Sonny: A Christmas Guest*. New York: Century, 1896.

Taylor, Helen. *Gender, Race, and Region in the Writings of Grace King, Ruth McEnery Stuart, and Kate Chopin*. Baton Rouge: Louisiana State UP, 1989.

William Styron

Casciato, Arthur D. and James L. W. West, III, eds. *Critical Essays on William Styron*. Boston: G. K. Hall, 1982.

Crane, John Kenny. *The Root of All Evil: The Thematic Unity of William Styron's Fiction*. Columbia: U of South Carolina P, 1984.

Styron, William. *The Confessions of Nat Turner*. New York: Random House, 1967.

———. *Lie Down in Darkness*. Indianapolis: Bobbs-Merrill, 1951.

———. *Sophie's Choice*. New York: Random House, 1979.

West, James L. W., III, ed. *Conversations with William Styron*. Jackson: UP of Mississippi, 1985.

Allen Tate

Murphy, Paul V. *The Rebuke of History: The Southern Agrarians and American Conservative Thought*. Chapel Hill: U of North Carolina P, 2001.

Tate, Allen. *Collected Poems, 1919–1976*. 1977; Baton Rouge: Louisiana State UP, 1989.

———. *Essays of Four Decades*. Chicago: Swallow P, 1968.

———. *The Fathers*. Rev. ed. Baton Rouge: Louisiana State UP, 1977.

Underwood, Thomas A. *Allen Tate: Orphan of the South*. Princeton: Princeton UP, 2000.

Peter Taylor

Beck, Charlotte H. *The Fugitive Legacy: A Critical History*. Baton Rouge: Louisiana State UP, 2001.

McAlexander, Hubert H., ed. *Critical Essays on Peter Taylor*. New York: G. K. Hall, 1993.

Robison, James Curry, ed. *Peter Taylor: A Study of the Short Fiction*. Boston: Twayne, 1988.

Taylor, Peter. *A Long Fourth and Other Stories*. New York: Harcourt, 1948.

———. *A Summons to Memphis*. New York: Knopf, 1986.

———. *In the Miro District and Other Stories*. New York: Knopf, 1977.

The Tennessee Civil War Veterans' Questionnaires

Dyer, Gustavus W. and John Trotwood Moore, eds. *The Tennessee Civil War Veterans' Questionnaires*. Easley, SC: Southern Historical P., 1985.

Thomas Bangs Thorpe

Rickels, Milton. *Thomas Bangs Thorpe: Humorist of the Old Southwest*. Baton Rouge: Louisiana State UP, 1962.

Stanton, Garner. "Thomas Bangs Thorpe in the Gilded Age: Shifty in a New Country." *Mississippi Quarterly* 36 (1982–1983): 35–52.

Thorpe, Thomas Bangs. *A New Collection of Thomas Bangs Thorpe's Sketches of the Old Southwest: A Critical Edition*. Ed. David C. Estes. Baton Rouge: Louisiana State UP, 1989.

Henry Timrod

Budd, John. "Henry Timrod: Poetic Voice of Southern Nationalism." *Southern Studies* 20 (1981): 437–46.

Murphy, Christina. "The Artistic Design of Societal Commitment: Shakespeare and the Poetry of Henry Timrod." *Shakespeare and Southern Writers: A Study in Influence*. Ed. Philip C. Kolin. Jackson: UP of Mississippi, 1985: 29–47.

Parks, Edd W. *Henry Timrod*. NY: Twayne, 1964.

Timrod, Henry. *Collected Poems: A Variorum Edition*. Ed. Edd Winfield Parks and Aileen Wells Parks. Athens: U of Georgia P, 1965.

———. *Essays of Henry Timrod*. Ed. Edd Winfield Parks. Athens: U of Georgia P, 1942.

———. *The Uncollected Poems of Henry Timrod*. Ed. Guy A. Cardwell, Jr. Athens: U of Georgia P, 1942.

Jean Toomer

Byrd, Rudolph P. *Jean Toomer's Years with Gurdjieff: Portrait of an Artist, 1923–1936*. Athens: U of Georgia P, 1990.

Toomer, Jean. *Cane*. 1923. New York: Boni & Liveright, 1975.

———. *The Collected Poems of Jean Toomer*. Ed. Robert B. Jones and Margery Toomer Lalimer. Chapel Hill: U of North Carolina P, 1988.

———. *A Jean Toomer Reader: Selected Unpublished Writings*. Ed. Frederik L. Rusch. New York: Oxford UP, 1993.

McKay, Nellie Y. *Jean Toomer, Artist: A Study of His Literary Life and Work, 1894–1936*. Chapel Hill: U of North Carolina P, 1984.

Mark Twain (Samuel Langhorne Clemens)

Anderson, Frederick. *Mark Twain: The Critical Heritage*. Boston: Routledge & Kegan Paul, 1971.
Howells, William Dean. *My Mark Twain*. Mineola, NY: Dover, 1997.
Lynn, Kenneth S. *Mark Twain and the Southwestern Humorists*. Boston: Little, Brown, 1959.
Twain, Mark. *Collected Tales, Sketches, Speeches, and Essays*. NY: Library of America, 1992.
———. *The Outrageous Mark Twain: Some Lesser-Known But Extraordinary Works*. Ed. Charles Neider. Garden City, NY: Doubleday, 1987.
———. *The Unabridged Mark Twain*. Ed. Lawrence Teacher. Birmingham, AL: Sweetwater P, 1997.

Ellen Bryant Voigt

Hoagland, Tony. "About Ellen Bryant Voigt." *Ploughshares* 22 (1996–1997): 222–25.
Suarez, Ernest. "Ellen Bryant Voigt." *Southbound: Interviews with Southern Poets*. Columbia: U of Missouri P, 1999.
Voigt, Ellen Bryant. *Claiming Kin*. Middletown, CT: Wesleyan UP, 1976.
———. *Kyrie*. New York: Norton, 1995.
———. *The Lotus Flowers*. New York: Norton, 1987.
———. *Shadow of Heaven*. New York: Norton, 2002.

Alice Walker

Bloom, Harold, ed. *Alice Walker*. New York: Chelsea, 1989.
Christian, Barbara. "Alice Walker: The Black Woman Artist as Wayward." *Black Women Writers 1950–80: A Critical Evaluation*. Ed. Mari Evans. New York: Anchor—Doubleday, 1984. 457–77.
———. "The Contrary Women of Alice Walker: A Study of Female Protagonists in *In Love and Trouble*." *Black Feminist Criticism: Perspectives on Black Women Writers*. New York: Pergamon, 1985. 31–46.
Walker, Alice. *The Color Purple*. New York: Harcourt, 1982.
———. *In Search of Our Mothers' Gardens*. New York: Harcourt, 1983.
———. *The Third Life of Grange Copeland*. New York: Harcourt, 1970.

Margaret Walker

Berke, Nancy. *Women Poets on the Left: Lola Ridge, Genevieve Taggart, Margaret Walker*. Gainesville: UP of Florida, 2001.
Campbell, Jane. "Margaret Walker." *African American Writers*. Ed. Valerie Smith, Lee Baechler, and A. Walton Litz. New York: Scribners, 1991. 459–71.
Pettis, Joyce. "Margaret Walker: Black Woman Writer of the South." *Southern Women Writers: The Next Generation*. Ed. Tonette Bond Inge. Tuscaloosa: U of Alabama P, 1990. 9–19.
Walker, Margaret. *Jubilee*. Boston: Houghton, 1966.
———. *This is My Century: New and Collected Poems*. Athens: U of Georgia P, 1989.
Walker, Margaret and Nikki Giovanni. *A Poetic Equation: Conversations Between Nikki Giovanni and Margaret Walker*. Washington, DC: Howard UP, 1974.

Robert Penn Warren

Blotner, Joseph, *Robert Penn Warren: A Biography*. New York: Random House, 1997.
Cullick, Jonathan S. *Making History: The Biographical Narratives of Robert Penn Warren*. Baton Rouge: Louisiana State UP, 2000.

Grimshaw, James A., Jr. *Understanding Robert Penn Warren*. Columbia: U of South Carolina P, 2001.

Warren, Robert Penn. *All The King's Men: Restored Edition*. Ed. Noel Polk. New York: Harcourt, 2001.

———. *Collected Poems of Robert Penn Warren*. Ed. John Burt. Baton Rouge: Louisiana State UP, 1998.

———. *New and Selected Essays*. New York: Random House, 1989.

EUDORA WELTY

Champion, Laurie, ed. *The Critical Response to Eudora Welty's Fiction*. Westport, CT: Greenwood P, 1994.

Jones, John Griffin, ed. *Mississippi Writers Talking*. Jackson: UP of Mississippi, 1982–1983.

Prenshaw, Peggy Whitman. *Conversations with Eudora Welty*. Jackson: UP of Mississippi, 1984.

———. *More Conversations with Eudora Welty*. Jackson: UP of Mississippi, 1996.

Welty, Eudora. *The Collected Stories of Eudora Welty*. New York: Harcourt Brace Jovanovich, 1980.

———. *Delta Wedding*. New York: Harcourt Brace, 1946.

———. *One Writer's Beginnings*. Cambridge: Harvard UP, 1984.

———. *The Optimist's Daughter*. New York: Random House, 1972.

Westling, Louise. *Sacred Groves and Ravaged Gardens: The Fiction of Eudora Welty, Carson McCullers, and Flannery O'Connor*. Athens: U of Georgia P, 1985.

MICHAEL LEE WEST

Abney, Lisa. "Food and Foodways in Michael Lee West's *She Flew the Coop: A Novel Concerning Life, Death, Sex, and Recipes in Limoges, Louisiana*." *Songs of the New South: Writing Contemporary Louisiana*. Ed. Suzanne Disheroon-Green and Lisa Abney. Westport, CT: Greenwood P, 2001. 11–18.

West, Michael Lee. *Consuming Passions: A Food Obsessed Life*. New York: HarperCollins, 1999.

———. *Crazy Ladies*. Atlanta: Longstreet P, 1990.

———. *She Flew the Coop: A Novel Concerning Life, Death, Sex, and Recipes in Limoges, Louisiana*. New York: HarperCollins, 1994.

TENNESSEE WILLIAMS

Devlin, Albert J. *Conversations with Tennessee Williams*. Jackson: UP of Mississippi, 1986.

Griffin, Alice. *Understanding Tennessee Williams*. Columbia: U of South Carolina P, 1995.

Roudané, Matthew C. *The Cambridge Companion to Tennessee Williams*. Cambridge: Cambridge UP, 1997.

Williams, Tennessee. *Cat on a Hot Tin Roof*. New York: New Directions, 1955.

———. *The Glass Menagerie*. New York: New Directions, 1945.

———. *A Streetcar Named Desire*. New York: New Directions, 1947.

AUGUSTA JANE EVANS WILSON

Bakker, Jan. "Overlooked Progenitors: Independent Women and Southern Renaissance in Augusta Jane Evans Wilson's *Macaria; or Altars of Sacrifice*." *Southern Quarterly* 25 (1987): 131–42.

Faust, Drew Gilpin. "Altars of Sacrifice: Confederate Women and Narratives of War." *Journal of American History* 76 (1990): 1200–28.
Fidler, William Perry. *Augusta Jane Evans Wilson, 1835–1909, a Biography*. University, AL: U of Alabama P, 1951.
Saxton, Rebecca Grant, ed. *A Southern Women of Letters: The Correspondence of Augusta Jane Evans Wilson*. Columbia: U of South Carolina P, 2002.
Wilson, Augusta Jane Evans. *Macaria; or Altars of Sacrifice*. 1864. Ed. Drew Gilpin Faust. Baton Rouge: Louisiana State, 1992.

Thomas Wolfe

Holliday, Shawn. *Thomas Wolfe and the Politics of Modernism*. New York: Peter Lang, 2001.
Roberts, Terry. "O Lost: A Family History." *Mississippi Quarterly* 55 (2001–02): 63–73.
Sparrow, W. Keats. "The Concept of Home in the South in Thomas Wolfe's *You Can't Go Home Again*." *Mount Olive Review* 1.1 (1987): 51–60.
Wolfe, Thomas. *Look Homeward, Angel*. New York: Charles Scribner's Sons, 1929.
———. *The Web and the Rock*. New York: Harper & Brothers, 1939.
———. *You Can't Go Home Again*. New York: Harper & Brothers, 1940.

Richard Wright

Ray, David and Robert M. Farnsworth, eds. *The Life and Works of Richard Wright*. Kansas City: U Missouri P, 1979.
Rowley, Hazel. *Richard Wright: The Life and Times*. New York: Holt, 2001.
Walker, Margaret. *Richard Wright: Daemonic Genius*. New York: Warner Books/Armistead P, 1988.
Wright, Richard. *Black Boy*. New York: Perrenial Classics, 2002.
———. *Native Son*. New York: HarperCollins, 1993.
———. *Uncle Tom's Children*. New York: HarperCollins, 1993.

CREDITS

Mary Boykin Miller Chesnut. From *Mary Chesnut's Civil War*, ed. C. Vann Woodward. © 1981. Yale University Press. Reprinted by permission of Yale University Press.

Sarah Morgan. From *The Civil War Diary of Sarah Morgan*, ed. Charles East. © 1991 by The University of Georgia Press. Reprinted by permission of The University of Georgia Press. All rights reserved.

Sarah E. Gardner. From *Blood and Irony: Southern White Women's Narratives of the Civil War, 1861–1937*. © 2004 by the University of North Carolina Press. Used by permission of the publisher.

Louisa Susanna Cheves McCord. Excerpted from *Louisa S. McCord: Political and Social Essays*, ed. Richard C. Lounsbury. Charlottesville, Virginia, 1995. Reprinted with permission of the University of Virginia Press.

Twelve Southerners. "Introduction: A Statement of Principles," from *I'll Take My Stand: The South and the Agrarian Tradition*. © 1930 by Harper & Brothers. © renewed 1958 by Donald Davidson. Introduction © 1962, 1977 by Louis D. Rubin, Jr. Biographical essays © 1962, 1977 by Virginia Rock.

John Crowe Ransom. "Bells for John Whiteside's Daughter," "Janet Waking," "The Equilibrists," and "Antique Harvesters," from *Selected Poems, Third Edition, Revised and Enlarged*. © 1924, 1927 by Alfred A. Knopf, Inc. © renewed 1952, 1955 by John Crowe Ransom. Used by permission of Alfred A. Knopf, a division of Random House, Inc.

Robert Penn Warren. "Bearded Oaks," "Founding Fathers," and "Last Meeting," from *New and Selected Poems*. © 1985 by Robert Penn Warren. Reprinted by permission of William Morris Agency, Inc. on behalf of the author.

Robert Penn Warren. Excerpt from *All the King's Men*. © 1946, 1974 by Robert Penn Warren. Reprinted by permission of Harcourt, Inc.

John Gould Fletcher. "The Evening Clouds," "Bedroom," "The Stars," "Down the Mississippi," and "The Unfamiliar House," from *Selected Poems*. © 1988 by John Gould Fletcher. Reprinted by permission of University of Arkansas Press. All rights reserved.

Donald Davidson. "Lee in the Mountains," from *Poems 1922–1961*. University of Minnesota Press, 1966. © 1934, 1938 by Donald Davidson.

Allen Tate. "Ode to the Confederate Dead" and "The Swimmers," from *Collected Poems: 1919–1976*. © 1977 by Allen Tate. Reprinted by permission of Farrar, Straus, and Giroux, LLC.

James Weldon Johnson. "O Black and Unknown Bards," "Go Down Death—A Funeral Sermon," and "The White Witch," from *James Weldon Johnson: Complete Poems*, ed. Sondra Kathryn Wilson. © 2000 Sondra Kathryn Wilson, literary executor of the estate of James Weldon Johnson. Used by permission of Penguin, a division of Penguin Group (USA), Inc.

Ellen Glasgow. "Dare's Gift" as it appeared in *Harper's Magazine*, February and March of 1917.

William Alexander Percy. "The Ku Klux Klan Comes and Goes," from *Lanterns on the Levee*, by William Alexander Percy, copyright 1941 by Alfred A. Knopf, a division of Random House, Inc. and renewed 1969 by LeRoy Pratt Percy. Used by permission of Alfred A. Knopf.

H. L. Mencken. "Sahara of the Bozart," from *Prejudices: A Selection*. © 1958 by Alfred A. Knopf, a division of Random House, Inc. Used by permission of Alfred A. Knopf, a division of Random House, Inc.

Elizabeth Madox Roberts. "The Sacrifice of the Maidens," from *The Haunted*. © 1932 by Elizabeth Madox Roberts. © renewed 1960 by Ivor S. Roberts. Used by permission of Viking Penguin, a division of Penguin Putnam, Inc.

Anne Spencer. "At the Carnival," "I Have a Friend," "Innocence," "Dunbar," "White Things," and "Letter to My Sister," from *Time's Unfading Garden: Anne Spencer's Life and Poetry*. © 1977 by Anne Spencer. Reprinted by permission of Louisiana State University Press. All rights reserved.

Katherine Anne Porter. "The Grave," from *The Leaning Tower and Other Stories*. © 1944, 1972 by Katherine Anne Porter, reprinted by permission of Harcourt, Inc.

Zora Neale Hurston. From *Mules and Men*. © 1935 by Zora Neale Hurston; © renewed 1963 by John C. Hurston and Joel Hurston. Reprinted by permisson of HarperCollins Publishers, Inc.

Lyle Saxon. From *Children of Strangers*. © 1989. Used by permission of the publisher, Pelican Publishing Company, Inc.

Jean Toomer. "Reapers," "November Cotton Flower," "Becky," and "Portrait in Georgia," from *Cane*. © 1923 by Boni & Liveright. © renewed 1951 by Jean Toomer. Used by permission of Liveright Publishing Corporation.

Caroline Gordon. "The Last Day in the Field," from *The Collected Stories*. © 1981 by Caroline Gordon. Reprinted by permission of Farrar, Straus & Giroux, LLC.

Katharine Du Pre Lumpkin. From "A Child Inherits a Lost Cause," from *The Making of a Southerner*. © 1946 by Alfred A. Knopf, a division of Random House, Inc. Used by permission of Alfred A. Knopf, a division of Random House, Inc.

William Faulkner. "Red Leaves," from *Collected Stories of William Faulkner*. © 1950 by Random House, Inc. © renewed 1978 by Jill Faulkner Summers. Used by permission of Random House, Inc.

William Faulkner. "Delta Autumn," from *Uncollected Stories of William Faulkner*. © 1942 by William Faulkner. Used by permission of Random House, Inc.

Lillian Smith. Excerpt from *Strange Fruit*. © 1944 by Lillian Smith. © renewed 1971 by Paula Snelling. Reprinted by permission of Harcourt, Inc.

Thomas Wolfe. From *You Can't Go Home Again*. © 1934, 1937, 1938, 1939, 1940 by Maxwell Perkins as executor of the estate of Thomas Wolfe. © renewed 1968 by Paul Gitlin. Reprinted by permission of HarperCollins Publishers, Inc.

George Sessions Perry. Chapter 1, from *Hold Autumn in Your Hand*. © 1950 by George Sessions Perry. Reprinted by permission of Curtis Brown, Ltd.

Richard Wright. From *Native Son*. © 1940 by Richard Wright. © renewed 1968 by Ellen Wright. Reprinted by permission of HarperCollins Publisher, Inc.

James Agee. "Work," from *Let Us Now Praise Famous Men*, by James Agee and Walker Evans. © 1941 by James Agee and Walker Evans. © renewed 1969 by Mia Fritsch Agee and Walker Evans. Reprinted by permission of Houghton Mifflin Company. All rights reserved.

W. J. Cash. From *The Mind of the South*. © 1941 by Alfred A. Knopf, Inc. © renewed 1969 by Mary R. Maury. Used by permission of Alfred A. Knopf, a division of Random House, Inc.

Sterling Brown. "Memphis Blues," from *The Collected Poems of Sterling A. Brown*, ed. Michael S. Harper. © 1980 by Sterling A. Brown. Reprinted by permission of HarperCollins Publishers, Inc.

Sterling Brown. "Slim in Atlanta" and "Remembering Nat Turner," from *The Collected Poems of Sterling A. Brown*, ed. by Michael S. Harper. © 1939 by Sterling A. Brown. © renewed 1960. Reprinted by permission of HarperCollins Publishers, Inc.

Sterling Brown. "Ma Rainey," from *The Collected Poems of Sterling A. Brown*, ed. Michael S. Harper. © 1932 by Harcourt Brace & Co. © renewed 1960 by Sterling A. Brown. Reprinted by permission of HarperCollins Publishers, Inc.

Arna Wendell Bontemps. " A Summer Tragedy," from *Opportunity, A Journal of Negro Life*. © 1933 by Arna Bontemps. Reprinted by permission of Harold Ober Associates, Incorporated.

Woody (Woodrow Wilson) Guthrie. "Pretty Boy Floyd," by Woody Guthrie © 1961 (renewed) by Sanga Music, Inc. All rights reserved. Used by permission.

Woody (Woodrow Wilson) Guthrie. "The Blinding of Isaac Woodard," by Woody Guthrie © 1965 (renewed) by Woody Guthrie Publications, Inc. All rights reserved. Used by permission.

Randall Jarrell. "The Death of the Ball Turret Gunner," "Eighth Air Force," "A Camp in the Prussian Forest," and "A Country Life," from *The Complete Poems*. © 1969, 1997 by Mary von S. Jarrell.

Margaret Walker. "Lineage," "For My People," "Birmingham," "Southern Song," "Sorrow Home," and "Kissie Lee," from *This Is My Country: New and Collected Poems*. © 1989 by Margaret Walker. Reprinted by permission of University of Georgia Press. All rights reserved.

Olive Tilford Dargan (Fielding Burke). "A Wife She Must Carry, Heigh-Ho!" from *Call Home the Heart*. New York: Longmans, Green and Co., 1932.

Myra Page. From *Gathering Storm*. 1932. Reprinted by permission of International Publishers Co., Inc.

Erskine Caldwell. "Kneel to the Rising Sun." © 1933 by Erskine Caldwell. Reprinted with the permission of McIntosh and Otis, Inc.

Eudora Welty. "The Petrified Man," *from A Curtain of Green and Other Stories*. © 1939, 1967 by Eudora Welty. Reprinted by permission of Harcourt, Inc.

Eudora Welty. "Why I Live at the P. O." and "The Worn Path," from *A Curtain of Green and Other Stories*. © 1941, © 1969 by Eudora Welty. Reprinted by permission of Harcourt, Inc.

Tennessee Williams. *Cat on a Hot Tin Roof*. © 1954, 1955, 1971, 1975 by The University of the South. Reprinted by permission of New Directions Publishing Corporation.

Karl Shapiro. "University," "Conscription Camp," and "The Southerner," from *Collected Poems*. © 1978 by Karl Shapiro. Reprinted by permission of Wieser & Wieser. All rights reserved.

Margaret Danner. "The Convert," from *Impressions of African Art*. By permission of Broadside Press. © 1964.

Margaret Danner. "This Is an African Worm," "The Painted Lady," and "The Slave and the Iron Lace," from *The Black Poets*. © 1972. Bantam.

Walker Percy. From *The Moviegoer*. © 1960, 1961 by Walker Percy. Used by permission of Alfred A. Knopf, a division of Random House, Inc.

Carson McCullers. "Like That," from *Collected Stories of Carson McCullers*. © 1987 by Flora V. Lasky, executrix of the estate of Carson McCullers. Reprinted by permission of Houghton Mifflin Company. All rights reserved.

Peter Taylor. "First Heat," from *The Collected Stories of Peter Taylor*. © 1968 by Peter Taylor. Reprinted by permission of Farrar, Straus, and Giroux, LLC.

Ellen Douglas. "I Just Love Carrie Lee," from *Black Cloud, White Cloud*. © 1963 by Houghton Mifflin Company. © renewed 1991 by Josephine A. Haxton. Reprinted by permission of Houghton Mifflin Company. All rights reserved.

James Dickey. "Cherrylog Road," "Hunting Civil War Relics at Nimblewill Creek," and "Sled Burial, Dream Ceremony," from *Poems 1957–1967*. © 1968 by James Dickey. Reprinted by permission of Wesleyan University Press. All rights reserved.

Vassar Miller. "On Approaching My Birthday," "Memento Mori," "Since No One Will Sing Me a Lullaby," "Raison D'Etre," "Affinity," and "Reassurance," from *If I Had Wheels or Love: Collected Poems of Vassar Miller*. © 1990. Southern Methodist University Press.

Donald Justice. "Anonymous Drawing" and "My South," from *New and Selected Poems*. © 1995 by Donald Justice. Used by permission of Alfred A. Knopf, a division of Random House, Inc.

Flannery O'Connor. "Everything That Rises Must Converge," from *Everything That Rises Must Converge*. © 1965 by the Estate of Mary Flannery O'Connor. © renewed 1993 by Regina O'Connor.

Flannery O'Connor. "Good Country People" and "The Life You Save May Be Your Own," from *A Good Man Is Hard to Find and Other Stories*. © 1955 by Flannery O'Connor. © renewed 1983 by Regina O'Connor. Reprinted by permission of Harcourt, Inc.

Maya Angelou. "Graduation Day," from *I Know Why the Caged Bird Sings*. © 1969, 1997 by Maya Angelou. Used by permission of Random House, Inc.

Martin Luther King, Jr. "I Have a Dream" and "Eulogy for the Martyred Children." © 1963 Dr. Martin Luther King, Jr. © renewed 1991 Coretta Scott King. © 1968 Dr. Martin Luther King, Jr. © renewed 1996 Coretta Scott King. Reprinted by arrangement with the estate of Martin Luther King Jr., c/o Writers House as agent for the proprietor New York, New York.

Etheridge Knight. "Hard Rock Returns to Prison from the Hospital for the Criminal Insane," "Haiku," "For Freckle-Faced Gerald," "He Sees Through Stone," "The Idea of Ancestry," and "For Black Poets Who Think of Suicide," from *The Essential Etheridge Knight*. © 1986. Reprinted by permission of the University of Pittsburgh Press.

Sonia Sanchez. "we a badddDDD people," "right on: white america," "poem for dc's 8th graders—1966–67," and "now poem. for us." © 1973, 1995 by Sonia Sanchez. Reprinted by permission of the author. All rights reserved.

Wendell Berry. "The Work of Local Culture," from *What Are People For?* © 1990 by Wendell Berry. Reprinted by permission of North Point Press, a division of Farrar, Straus, and Giroux, LLC.

Nikki Giovanni. "Knoxville, Tennessee" and "For Saundra," from *The Selected Poems of Nikki Giovanni*. © 1996 by Nikki Giovanni. Reprinted by permission of HarperCollins Publishers, Inc. William Morrow.

Alice Walker. "The Black Writer and the Southern Experience," from *In Search of Our Mothers' Gardens: Womanist Prose*. © 1983 by Alice Walker. Reprinted by permission of Harcourt, Inc.

Doris Betts. "Three Ghosts." © by Doris Betts. Reprinted by permission of Doris Betts. All rights reserved.

Harry Crews. "Fathers, Sons, Blood." © 1982 by Harry Crews. Reprinted by permission of John Hawkins & Associates, Inc.

Clyde Edgerton. "Bliss," from *the Floatplane Notebooks*. © 1988 by the author. Reprinted by permission of Algonquin Books of Chapel Hill, a division of Workman Publishing.

Michael Lee West. "Funeral Food," from *Consuming Passions*. Reprinted with the permission of the author. © 1999 by the author.

Randall Kenan. "Clarence and the Dead," from *Let the Dead Bury Their Dead and Other Stories*. © 1992 by Randall Kenan. Reprinted by permission of Harcourt, Inc.

George Garrett. "Feeling Good, Feeling Fine," from *The Cry of an Occasion*. © 2001 by George Garrett. Reprinted by permission of George Garrett. All rights reserved.

Reynolds Price. "Summer Games," from *Permanent Errors*.© 1970 by Reynolds Price. Reprinted with permission of Scribner, an imprint of Simon & Schuster Adult Publishing Group.

William Styron. "Shadrach," from *A Tidewater Morning*. © 1993 by William Styron. Reprinted by permission of Vintage New York—Random House. All rights reserved.

A. R. Ammons. "Mule Song," "Nelly Myers," "Foot-Washing," and "Hippie Hop," from *Collected Poems 1951–1971*. © 1972 by A. R. Ammons. Used by permission of W. W. Norton & Company, Inc.

Ernest Gaines. From *A Lesson Before Dying*. © 1993 by Ernest J. Gaines. Used by permission of Alfred A. Knopf, a division of Random House, Inc.

Ellen Gilchrist. "In the Land of Dreamy Dreams," from *In the Land of Dreamy Dreams* © 1981 by Ellen Gilchrist. Published by University of Arkansas Press, Little, Brown and Co. and Louisiana State University Press. Reprinted by permission of Don Congdon Associates, Inc.

James Lee Burke. "Losses," from *The Convict and Other Stories*. © 1995 James Lee Burke. Reprinted by permission of Hyperion.

Andre Dubus. "At Night," from *Dancing After Hours*. © 1995 by Andre Dubus. Used by permission of Alfred A. Knopf, a division of Random House, Inc.

Fred Chappell. "Second Wind," from *Wind Mountain*. © 1979. Louisiana State University Press.

Fred Chappell. "Here," from *Source*. © 1985 by Fred Chappell. Permission by Louisiana State University.

Fred Chappell. "My Mother's Hard Row to Hoe" and "Bee," from *Earthsleep*. © 1980 by Fred Chappell. Permission by Louisiana State University.

Fred Chappell. "The Encyclopedia Daniel," from *The Cry of an Occasion: Fiction from the Fellowship of Southern Writers*," ed. Richard Bausch. © 2001 by Louisiana State University Press.

Lewis Nordan. "The Sears and Roebuck Catalog Game," from *Sugar Among the Freaks*. © 1996 by the author. Reprinted by permission of Algonquin Books of Chapel Hill, a division of Workman Publishing.

Bobbie Ann Mason. "Drawing Names," from *Midnight Magic*. Reprinted by permission of International Creative Management, Inc.

Frederick Barthelme. "Domestic," from *The Law of Averages*. © 2001 by Frederick Barthelme. Reprinted by permission of Counterpoint Press, a member of Perseus Books, L.L.C.

John Shelton Reed. "New South or No South? Southern Culture in 2036," from *The South Moves Into Its Future*, ed. Joseph Himes. Tuscaloosa: The University of Alabama Press, 1991.

Dave Smith. "Smithfield Ham," "Wedding Song," "Cumberland Station," "In Memory of Hollis Summers," and "Canary Weather in Virginia," from *The Wick of Memory: New and Selected Poems 1970–2000*. © 2000 by Dave Smith. Reprinted with the permission of Louisiana State University Press.

James A. McPherson. "I Am an American," from *Elbow Room*. © 1972 by James A. McPherson. Reprinted by permission of the author. All rights reserved.

Ellen Bryant Voigt. "Lesson," from *Shadow of Heaven*. © 2002 by Ellen Bryant Voigt. Used by permission of W. W. Norton & Company, Inc.

Ellen Bryant Voigt. "This is the double bed where she'd been born," from *Kyrie*. © 1995 by Ellen Bryant Voigt. Used by permission of W. W. Norton & Company, Inc.

Ellen Bryant Voigt. "Short Story," from *The Lotus Flowers*. © 1987 by Ellen Bryant Voigt. Used by permission of W. W. Norton & Company, Inc.

Robert Morgan. "Bare Yard," "Sunday Toilet," and "Firecrackers at Christmas," from *At the Edge of the Orchard Country*. © 1987 by Robert Morgan. Reprinted by permission of Wesleyan University Press. All rights reserved.

Robert Morgan. "Hayfield," "Uranium," and "Overalls," from *Sigodlin*. © 1990 by Robert Morgan. Reprinted by permission of Wesleyan University Press. All rights reserved.

Richard Ford. "Going to the Dogs," from *Rock Springs*. © 1987 by Richard Ford. Used by permission of Grove/Atlantic, Inc.

Everette Maddox. "Cleaning the Cruiser" and "New Orleans," from *Bar Scotch*. © 1988 by Everette Maddox. Reprinted by permission of Pirogue Press. All rights reserved.

Lee Smith. "Me and My Baby View the Eclipse," from *Me and My Baby View the Eclipse*. © 1988, 1990 by Lee Smith. Used by permission of G. P. Putnam's Sons, a division of Penguin Group (USA), Inc.

Josephine Humphreys. From *Rich in Love* © 1987 by Josephine Humphreys. Used by permission of Viking Penguin, a division of Penguin Putnam, Inc.

Mary Hood. "Inexorable Progress," from *How Far She Went*. © 1984 by Mary Hood. Reprinted by permission of The University of Georgia Press. All rights reserved.

Marilyn Nelson. "Diverne's Waltz," "Chopin," "Alderman," and "Tuskegee Airfield," from *The Homeplace: Poems*. © 1990 by Marilyn Nelson.

Martha McFerren. "The Princess and the Goblins," from *Delusions of a Popular Mind*. © 1983 by Martha McFerren. Reprinted by permission of New Orleans Poetry Journal Press. All rights reserved.

Martha McFerren. "The Famous Picnic of 1906" and "Seven Petticoats," from *Get Me Out of Here*. © 1984. Reprinted by permission of Martha McFerren.

Martha McFerren. "The Bad Southern Cooking Poem," from *Women in Cans*. © 1992 by Martha McFerren. Reprinted by permission of Helicon Nine. All rights reserved.

Yusef Komunyakaa. "Untitled Blues," from *Copacetic*. © 1984 by Yusef Komunyakaa. Reprinted by permission of Wesleyan University Press. All rights reserved.

Yusef Komunyakaa. "Boy Wearing a Dead Man's Clothes," from *I Apologize for the Eyes in My Head*. © 1986 by Yusef Komunyakaa. Reprinted by permission of Wesleyan University Press. All rights reserved.

Yusef Komunyakaa. "Night Muse and Mortar Round," "Tu Do Street," and "Facing It," from *Dien Cai Dau*. © 1988 by Yusef Komunyakaa. Reprinted by permission of Wesleyan University Press. All rights reserved.

Tim Gautreaux. "Rodeo Parole," from *Welding with Children*. © 1999 by Tim Gautreaux. Reprinted by permission of Picador USA.

Dorothy Allison. "The Meanest Woman Ever Left Tennessee," from *Trash*. © 1988. Used by permission of Frances Goldin Literary Agency, Inc.

Rodney Jones. "Mule," from *Transparent Gestures*. © 1989 by Rodney Jones. Reprinted by permission of Houghton Mifflin Company. All rights reserved.

Rodney Jones. "Alma" and "Simulated Woodgrain Vinyl," from *The Unborn*. © 1985 by Rodney Jones. Used by permission of Grove/Atlantic, Inc.

Larry Brown. "End of Romance," from *Facing the Music*. © 1996 by the author. Reprinted by permission of Algonquin Books of Chapel Hill, a division of Workman Publishing.

Jayne Anne Phillips. "Home," from *Black Tickets*. © 1975 by Jayne Anne Phillips. Reprinted by permission of the author.

Julie Kane. "Reasons for Loving the Harmonica" and "Dead Armadillo Song," from *Body and Soul*. © 1987 by Julie Kane. Reprinted by permission of Pirogue. All rights reserved.

Julie Kane. "Ode to the Big Muddy." Reprinted by permission of author.

Julie Kane. "Kissing the Bartender," from *The Bartender Poems*. © 1991 by Julie Kane. Reprinted by permission of Greville Press. All rights reserved.

Jill McCorkle. "Crash Diet," from *Crash Diet*. © 1992 by Algonquin Books of Chapel Hill. Reprinted by permission.

Kaye Gibbons. From *Charms for the Easy Life*. © 1993 by Kaye Gibbons. Used by permission of G. P. Putnam's Sons, a division of Penguin Putnam, Inc.

Elizabeth Spencer. "The Everlasting Light," from *The Cry of an Occasion: Fiction from the Fellowship of Southern Writers*, ed. Richard Bausch. © 2001 by Louisiana State University Press.

Richard Bausch. "1951," from *Someone to Watch Over Me*. © 1999 by Richard Bausch. Reprinted by permission of HarperCollins Publishers, Inc.

John Dufresne. "The Freezer Jesus," from *The Way That Water Enters Stone*. © 1991 by John Dufresne. Used by permission of W. W. Norton & Company, Inc.

Ron Rash. "The Night the New Jesus Fell to Earth," from *The Night the New Jesus Fell to Earth and Other Stories from Cliffside, North Carolina*. © 1994 by Ron Rash. Reprinted by permission of Ron Rash. All rights reserved.

INDEX